S0-BJB-756

# THE BEST BOOKS

# THE BEST BOOKS

## A READER'S GUIDE AND LITERARY REFERENCE BOOK

BEING A CONTRIBUTION TOWARDS SYSTEMATIC BIBLIOGRAPHY

By

WILLIAM SWAN SONNENSCHEIN

(WILLIAM SWAN STALLYBRASS)

*THIRD EDITION*
*Entirely Rewritten*



PART II

## D: SOCIETY

## E: GEOGRAPHY

LONDON
GEORGE ROUTLEDGE AND SONS, LIMITED
1912

REPUBLISHED BY GALE RESEARCH COMPANY, BOOK TOWER, DETROIT, 1969

NOTE

This, the final edition of the late Mr. William Swan Sonnenschein's *The Best Books*, the fi edition of which appeared in 1887, records some 150,000 works, with dates of the first a last editions, and price, size and publishers' names, English and American. It contains a Index, Synopsis of Classification, Table of Abbreviations, etc., and List of British Publishe Learned Societies, etc.

Library of Congress Catalog Card Number 68–58760

# PUBLISHERS' NOTE.

The present issue (PART II) of **THE BEST BOOKS** contains Classes D and E, and deals with the following Subjects:

## CLASS D: Society.

SECTION
- I. INTRODUCTION TO THE SCIENCE OF LAW.
- II. STATUTES, CODES, REPORTS AND DIGESTS.
- III. GENERAL TREATISES ON LAW.
- IV. HISTORY AND ANTIQUITIES OF LAW.
- V. SPECIAL DEPARTMENTS OF LAW.
- VI. PROCEDURE AND PRACTICE OF THE COURTS.

SECTION
- VII. ROMAN AND ORIENTAL LAW.
- VIII. HINDU AND MOHAMMEDAN LAW.
- IX. INTERNATIONAL LAW.
- X. POLITICAL (NATIONAL) ECONOMY.
- XI. SOCIAL ECONOMY.
- XII. SCIENCE OF POLITICS.
- XIII. COMMERCE AND TRADE.
- XIV. EDUCATION.

## CLASS E: Geography, Ethnology, Travel and Topography

- I. UNIVERSAL GEOGRAPHY.
- II. HISTORICAL GEOGRAPHY.
- III. EUROPE.
- IV. ASIA MINOR.
- V. ASIA.
- VI. AFRICA.
- VII. AMERICA.
- VIII. AUSTRALASIA.
- IX. THE POLAR REGIONS.

**PART III (Classes F—K):** dealing with HISTORY AND HISTORICAL BIOGRAPHY (in 9 Sections), ANTIQUITIES AND HISTORICAL COLLATERALS (in 4 Sections), SCIENCE (in 12 Sections), MEDICINE (in 16 Sections), ARTS AND TRADES (in 13 Sections, including SPORTS, in 30 Chapters), LITERATURE (in 13 Sections), and PHILOLOGY (in 31 Sections) and including the PREFACES, INDEX OF AUTHORS AND OF SUBJECTS (in one alphabet), etc., will be ready shortly, when the whole work will be issued also in a single volume, with an edition interleaved with thin but very opaque writing-paper for the purpose of additions.

# CLASS D: SOCIETY

## I: Introduction to the Science of Law in General

### 1: BIBLIOGRAPHY OF LAW. JURISPRUDENCE; etc.

*Bibliography of Bibliography*

Dramard, E. Bibliogr. d. l. Bibl. Générale d. Droit frç. et étranger Larose, *Paris* 93.
Extract from *Répertoire Générale et Alphabétique du Droit frç.* 120 pp. Very useful. Public and Private Law.

ABBOTT, Nathan Brief Making and the Use of Law Books $2 *n.* 8° West Pb. Co., *St Paul, Mann.* 06.
Shows proper way of using decisns. and stats., expls. relative value of diff. classes of law-bks., etc.

Bibliographie Générale des Livres d. Droit et d. Jurisprudence 8° Marchal, *Paris* 06.

CASPAR, C. N. Practical Catalogue of Law Books $4 12° Caspar, *Milwaukee* [ ] 94
Arranged acc. to subjects, with an index of authors and a key to publishers.

DUCKERS, J. S. Guide to Students' Law Books [for exam. purposes] 3/6 *n.* c 8° Sweet 06.

ELLIS (Geoff.) + ROBERTSON (M. A.) Lawyer's Manual of Reference 10/ *n.* 8° Green, *Edin.* 07
Points of law alphabetically arranged. A useful compendium.

Incorporated Law Soc.: Catal. of Printed Bks. in Lib. of. By F. Boase r 8° *priv. prin.* (Spottiswoode) 91
Chiefly collected since 1832, when the stock of books was ab. 1000. Authors and titles in one alphabet: nearly all are English bks.

,, Supplement to the Catalogue. By W. M. Sinclair r 8° *priv. prin.* (Spottiswoode) 06.
Contains additions to Library to July 1906. Total no. of vols. in Library is now 47,000.

JELF, E. A. Where to Find your Law 10/6 8° Cox [97] 07
A useful bibliogr. for practitioners, wr. in narrative style, w. refs. to statutes, repts., and text-bks. Appendices of abbrevns.

JONES, Leon. A. Index to Legal Periodical Literature, 2 vols. ea. $10 *n.* 4° Boston Bk. Co. 88–10

MARVIN, J. G. Legal Bibliography [Amer. & Brit. bks.] *o.p.* [*rare*; *w.* £3] r 8° *Boston* 47

MÜHLBRECHT, O. Wegweiser durch die Litter. der Rechts-u. Staatswissenschaften 15 *m.* 8° Puttkammer, *Berlin* [86] 93.
Modern bks. Incl. all countries, and is very full; but gives no Christian names to authors.

STEVENS (H. G.) + HAYNES (R. W.) Bibliotheca Legum [incl. Repts.; w. Supp. to 1908] 2/ *n.* 12° Stevens & H.

WALLACE, J. W. Reporters Chronologically Arranged, ed. F. F. Heard $5·50 *n.* 8° Soule, *Boston* [43] 82

Where to Look for your Law [full list of titles] 1/ *n.* 8° Stevens 07

***Belgium***

PICARD (E.) + LARCIER (F.) Bibliogr. Génér. et Raisonnée du Droit Belge 8° Larcier, *Brussels* 82 *sqq.*

***Netherlands***

Bibliotheca Juridica: Catalogus v. alle Boeken sedert 1837 in Nederl. verschenen 4/ 8° Nijhoff, *Hague* 74
Books on statesmanship, legislation, and jurisprudence; w. Subjects Index.

**Introduction** —*v. also* Bentham, Hastie, Heron, *inf.*

AUSTIN, Prf. J. —*ut inf.*

BLACKSTONE, Sir W. Commentaries on Law of England, Sect. i [*ut* **D** § 4] [on study of law]
Refers specially to the uses and history of the study of the law of England.

CLARKE, R. Floyd The Science of Law and Law-making 17/ *n.* ($4) 8° Macmillan 98
An introd. to law somewhat similar to ILBERT; but devotes more space to codificn.

COHEN, Herm. The Spirit of our Laws 5/ *n.* c 8° Sweet 07
Describes Engl. legal institns. without use of techn. terms, for use of J.P.'s, general readers, etc.

HASTIE, W. —*in his* Outlines of Science of Jurisprudence, *ut inf.*

ILBERT, Sir C. P. Legislative Methods and Forms 16/ ($4) Clar. Press 01
Shows in brief histor. outl. the reln. betw. Common Law and Statute Law, and the way to find what enactmts. have been made on given subjs.

MENZIES, Prf. A. —Introd. *to his* Conveyancing acc. to Law of Scotland, *ut* **D** § 30

**Jurisprudence**

AMOS, Prf. Sheldon Systematic View of Science of Jurisprudence *o.p.* [*pb.* 18/] 8° Longman 72

" The Science of Law [Internat. Scientific Ser.] 5/ 8° Paul [74]

AUSTIN, Prf. J. Lects. on General Jurisprudence [1832], ed. R. Campbell, 2 v. 32/8° Murray [69] 85

" The same: Students' Edition, ed. R. Campbell 12/12° Murray [75] 04

Brown, Prf. W. J. [ed.] The Autinian Theory of Law 10/6 *n.* 8° Murray 06
Preserves all that is still valuable of AUSTIN, w. good Introd., notes, and excursus. A valuable wk.

Campbell, Gordon Analysis of Austin's Lectures 6/12° Murray [77] 05

Clark, Prf. E. C. Pract. Jurisprudence: comm. on Austin [$2·50 *n.* Putnam, *N.Y.*] 9/c 8° Camb. Pr. 83

" Analysis of Criminal Liability [based on Austin] *o.p.* [*pb.* 7/6] c 8° Camb. Press 80

BENTHAM, Jer. Introduction to Principles of Morals & Legislation 6/6 ($1·75) c 8° Clar. Press [1789] 76

" Theory of Legislation [1802], tr. fr. Fch. R. Hildreth 3/6 8° Paul [40] 04
This, BENTHAM's most import. work, was first pub. in French [*Paris*, 1802], 'traduit par M. Dumont d'après les MSS. confiés par l'auteur'.

BRYCE, Dr Jas. Studies in History and Jurisprudence, 2 vols.—*ut* **F** § 1
Jurisprudence is here used in a wide sense, but the work conts. several essays on Roman Law, and comparisons betw. it and English Law.

CAMPBELL, E. L. Science of Law acc. to Am. Theory of Govt. $3 8° Linn, *Jersey City* 87

CARTER, Dr J. Coolidge Law: its origin, growth, and function—*ut* **F** § 2

DILLON, Prf. J. F. Laws & Jurisprudence of England & America $4 *n.* 8° Little & Brown, *Boston* 94
16/ *n.* Macmillan. A series of non-technical Yale Univ. lects., the princ. purpose of wh.—apart fr. enlightening Amer. readers on origins of their laws—is to protest agst. the 'continentalization' of Amer. law by free infusions of Roman jurisprudce., and to show that the law of Engl. and Amer. is superior to the Rom. or any other alien system.

HASTIE, W. [ed. & tr.] Outlines of the Science of Jurisprudence 6/c 8° Clark, *Edin.* 88
An edited tr. fr. the Juristic Encyclopædia of PUCHTA + FRIEDLÄNDER + FALCK + AHRENS.

HEARN, Hon. W. E. Theory of Legal Duties and Rights 14/8° *Melbourne* 83

HERKLESS, W. R. Jurisprudence: princs. of Polit. Right, ed. A. Williamson 5/*n.* 8° Green, *Edin.* 01

HERON, D. C. Introduction to the History of Jurisprudence *o.p.* [*pb.* 10/6] 8° Longman [60] 68

HOLLAND, Prf. T. E. Elements of Jurisprudence 10/6 ($2·50) 8° Clar. Press [80] 10
An excellent work, practically superseding AUSTIN, *ut sup.*

KORKUNOV, Prf. N. M. General Theory of Law, tr. Prf. W. G. Hastings $3·50 8° Boston Bk. Co., *Bost.* 09
Tr. fr. Russian. A vigorous and lucid, tho' condensed, statemt. of views wh. have prevailed.

LINDLEY, Sir Nath. Introduction to Study of Jurisprudence r 8° Higginbotham, *Madras* [ ] 91
A tr. of the General Part of THIBAUT's *Sytem des Pandekten-Rechts*, w. notes and illustrations.

LORIMER, Prf. J. Institutes of Law: princs. of jurispr. as determ. by nature *o.p.* [*pb.* 18/] 8° Blackwood [72] 80

MARKBY, Sir Wm. Elements of Law w. ref. to Princs. of Gen. Jurispr. 12/6 ($3) 8° Clar. Press [85] 05

MERRILL, G. Comparative Jurisprudence & the Conflict of Laws $2 *n.* c 8° Little & Brown, *Boston* 86

MILLER, W. G. The Data of Jurisprudence 10/*n.* 8° Green, *Edin.* 03

POLLOCK, Sir Fredk. Essays in Jurisprudence and Ethics *o.p.* [*pb.* 10/6] 8° Macmillan 82

" Oxford Lectures and other Discourses 9/($2·50) 8° Macmillan 90
*Methods of Jurispr., English Manor, Oxford Law Studies, Sir H. Maine and his Work, etc.*, w. papers on *Relig. Equality, Home Rule* [*ut* **D** § 142], *Examinations and Educ.* [*ut* **D** § 170], *Hist. of the Sword* [*ut* **I** § 164], *Library of Alpine Club* [*ut* **E** § 28], *etc.*

" First Bk. of Jurispr. f. Studts. of Common Law 6/($1·75) c 8° Macmillan [96] 04
Concise, lucid, and well-wr. Pt. i conts. just what every intelligent Englishman ought to know; Pt. ii is more practical and more exclusively addr. to studts., contg., amg. other things, a connected acc. of sources and authorities of Engl. law and of mod. practice.

PULSKY, Prf. A. Theory of Law and Civil Society [tr.] 18/8° Unwin 88

RATTIGAN, W. H. Science of Jurisprudence [chfly. for Indian studts.] 16/6 *n.* 8° Wildy [ ] 99

SALMOND, Prf. J. W. Jurisprudence, or the Theory of the Law 12/6 *n.* 8° Stevens [02] 07
On the scientific foundn. of law, and conn. of law and ethical or polit. science. Incorporates a former wk., *First Princs. of Jurisprudence.*

" Essays in Jurisprudence and Legal History 6/c 8° Stevens 91

TAYLOR, Hannis The Science of Jurisprudence $3·50 (15/*n.*) 8° Macmillan 08

WILSON, R. W. Rankine Inquiry into Meaning of Law and Responsibility 5/*n.* 8° Butterworth 08

## Philosophy of Right and of Law

FICHTE, J. G. Science of Rights [tr.]; w. Introd. Dr. W. T. Harris [Eng. & For. Philos. Lib.; $5 *n.* Scribner, *N.Y.*] 12/8° Paul [70] 89

HEGEL, G. W. F. Philosophy of Right, tr. S. W. Dyde [$1·90 *n.* Macmillan, *N.Y.*] 7/6 8° Bell 96

HOBBES, Thos. [1588–1679] Elements of Law, Natural and Politic [1684], ed. F. Tönnies 8/6 8° Thornton, *Oxon.* 89
With Pref. and notes. Subjoined are some selected pieces of hitherto unprtd. MSS. of HOBBES.

KANT, Immanuel Philosophy of Law, tr. Prf. W. Hastie 5/c 8° Clarke, *Edin.* 87
$1·50 *n.* Scribner, *N.Y.* From the *Metaphysik der Sitten* [*ut* **C** § 70]. Conts. a bibliography.

LIOY, Prf. Diodato Philosophy of Right, tr. Prf. W. Hastie, 2 vols. 21/p 8° Paul 91
[Eng. & For. Phil. Lib.] With spec. refer. to the principles and developmt. of law. Written fr. pt.-of-view of the philosopher rather than of the jurist—the bk. in fact forms a very good summary of the history of philosophy fr. the earliest period to the present time.

MAINE, Sir Hy. Ancient Law—*ut* **F** § 5
Of a philosoph. character, tracing many of the principles and rules of positive legislation back to their first beginnings. *V.* also his other wks. in **F** § 5.

MILLER, W. G. Lectures on the Philosophy of Law 12/8° Griffin 84
Designed as an introd. to the study of International Law fr. the metaphysical standpoint.

de MONTESQUIEU, C. de S. Spirit of the Laws [tr.]—*ut* **F** § 2

RODBERTUS, K. J. [1805–75]—*v.* **D** § 126

SIDGWICK, Prf. H. —*in his* The Elements of Politics, *ut* **D** § 134

STIRLING, J. H. Lectures on the Philosophy of Law *o.p.* [*pb.* 5/] 8° Oliver & Boyd, *Edin.* 73

WATT, Dr W. A. Outline of Legal Philosophy [Hegelian] 5/ c 8° Clark, *Edin.* 93

,, A Study of Social Morality—*ut* **A** § 113 ,,

An academic statemt. of pts. in conn. w. social virtues and social organizn. No very definite philos. expounded.

,, Theory of Contract in its Social Light 3/ 8° Clark, *Edin.* 97

$1·25 *n.* Scribner, *N.Y.* A protest, by a Hegelian, agst. the attempt to extend the limits of contract beyond its legitimate scope. Labour, marrge., the State, property, agency.

**Natural Rights :** HOBBES (Thos.)—*in his* Elements of Law, Natural and Politic (1684], *ut* **C** § 36

HUXLEY, Prf. T. H. Natural Rights and Political Rights—*in his* Coll. Essays, vol. i, *ut* **K** § 83

PAINE, Thos. Rights of Man—*in his* Writings, ed. Moncure Conway—*ut* **D** § 139

RITCHIE, Prf. D. G. Natural Rights [Library of Philosophy] 10/6 *n.* 8° Sonnenschein 95

$2·75 *n.* Macmillan, *N.Y.* A comprehensive and searching criticism of politico-ethical conceptions ; in 2 Pts. i (1) *Princs. of '89.* (2) *Hist. of Idea of 'Nature' in Law and Politics,* (3) *Rousseau and Rousseauism,* (4) *De Divisione Naturae,* (5) *What determines Rights ? ;* Pt. ii (6) *Right of Life,* (7) *Right of Liberty : Liberty of Thought,* (8) *Toleration,* (9) *Public Mectg. and Assocn.,* (10) *Freedom of Contract, National Freedom, etc.,* (11) *Resistance to Oppression,* (12) *Equality,* (13) *Property,* (14) *Happiness.* Appendices : *Virginian Declarn. of Rts.* (1776), Extr. fr. *Decl. of Indepce.* (1776), *Fch. Declar. of Rts.* (1789), w. PAINE's tr. (1793), *Preamble to Fch. Constitn.* (1848). Index.

ROUSSEAU, Jean-Jacques [1712–78] The Social Contract [tr.]—*ut* **F** § 49

SPENCER, Herb. —*in his* Social Statics, *ut* **D** § 134

**Construction of Statutes, and Statute Law**

BEAL, E. Cardinal Rules of Legal Interpretation [$5·25 Boston Bk. Co.] 20/ r 8° Stevens 08

BLACK, H. Campbell Treat. on Constrn. & Interpretn. of Laws $3·75 8° West Pb. Co., St Paul, *Minn.* 96

CRAIES, W. F. Statute Law 28/ r 8° Stevens & Haynes [79] 07

Being the 4th edn. of HARDCASTLE'S *Treat. on Constr. and Effect of Statute Law.*

ENDLICH, G. A. Commentaries on the Interpretn. of Statutes $6 8° Linn, *Jersey City* 88

LIEBER, F. Legal and Political Hermeneutics $3 *n.* 8° Thomas, *St Louis* [39] 85

On the principles of interpretation in law and politics.

MAXWELL, Sir P. B. Interpretation of Statutes, ed. J. A. Theobald 25/ 8° Sweet [75] 05

SEDGWICK, T. Constructn. of Statutory & Constit. Law, ed. J. N. Pomeroy $6·50 8° Baker, *N.Y.* [57] 74

STIMSON, Prf. F. J. Popular Law-Making [10/6 *n.* Chapman] 8° 11

A study of origin, history, and pres. tendencies of law-making by Statute.

SUTHERLAND, J. G. Statutes and Statutory Construction $6 8° Callaghan, *Chicago* 91

Discussn. of legisl. powers, constit. regulns. rel. to forms of legisln. and to procedure ; w. exposn. at length of princs. of interp., etc.

THRING, Lord Practical Legislation [comp. & lang. of Acts of Par.] 7/6 *n.* 8° Murray [78] 02

WILBERFORCE, E. Principles wh. Govern Constrn. & Operation of Statutes 18/ 8° Stevens & H. 81

# II: Statutes, Codes, Reports, Digests

## 2 : STATUTES AND CODES : COLLECTIVELY

For Codes of Procedure *v.* **D** §§ 101–8

**England**

Revised Edition of the Statutes : 1235–1886 ; prep. by Statute Law Committee, vols. i–xvi ea. 7/6 *n.* i 8° Stevens [70–84] 88–00

The first compl. edn. of Eng. Acts of Parl. pub. by State authority appeared 1810–24. It incl. the early charters and ends w. rn. of Anne. The Acts were first prtd. in rn. of Rich. III ; wr. in Latin till *Statutum de Scaccario* (Hy. III ; 1266), which is in Fch. The Acts of Edw. I are in Lat. or Fch. indiscriminately, but fr. 4th yr. of Hy. VII onwards are exclusively in English.

Rev. Edn. of the Statutes, New [=2nd], ed. G. A. R. Fitzgerald, 13 vols. ea. 7/6 i 8° Eyre & Spottisw. 90–7

Public General Acts [w. indexes. tables, etc.] ea. 3/ r 8° Eyre & Spottiswoode *ann.*

CHITTY, Jos. [ed.] Collection of Statutes of Practical Utility [to 1907], ed. J. M. Lely + W. H. Aggs, 15 vols. *red. to* £12 r 8° Sweet 94–07

Aggs, W. H. Supplements about 15/ r 8° Sweet *ann.*

Index to the Statutes in Force : 15th edn. [to end of Sessn. 62 & 63 Vict.] 10/ 8° Eyre & Spottisw. [ ] 99

PATERSON (W.) [ed.] Pract. Statutes of the Session, ed. J. S. Cotton *ann. vol.* 10/6 12° H. Cox [49] *ann.*

Conts. Lists of Local, Personal, and Private Acts. Vols. fr. 1858–1907 may be had at 5/ a vol. if complete sets are bought.

Index to Statutes public and private : 1801–1865, 2 vols. f° Eyre & Spottisw. 67

Vol. ii. conts. Local and Personal Acts, Local Acts and Private Acts.

Index to Local and Private Acts : 1866–1877 ; 1878–1887, 2 vols. f° Eyre & Spottisw. 78 ; 90

Lawyer's Manual of Reference 21/ *n.* 8° Green, *Edin.* 09

A compendium of useful Stats., grouped into subject-sectns., w. costs, fees, stamps, etc.

Standing Orders of the Lords and Commons rel. to Private Bills *ea. session* 5 / 12° *ann.*

*Statutes for Students*

GIBSON (A.) + WELDON (A.) [eds.] Students' Statute Law 30 /; Suppl. 3 / r 8° *Law Notes* Off. [ ] 05–7

HARRISON, J. C. [ed.] Selection of Statutes for Students: notes and cases 12/6 r 8° Reeves 85

**Scotland**

Public General Statutes affecting Scotland: 1707–1847, w. chron. table & index, 3 v. r 8° *Edinburgh* 76

Scots Statutes Revised, 1424–1907: ed. Jas. A. Fleming, 12 vols. £8 16/ *n.* r 8° Green, *Edin.*
All the Public General Statutes affectg. Scotld. still in force, w. notes on repealed Sections and Acts, and index. Annual Suppl. 1/6 to 2/6.

**Wales**

BOWEN, Ivor [ed.] Statutes of Wales; w. Introd. (105 pp.) and gloss. 21 / *n.* 8° Unwin 08
Brings together for first time all the Acts of Parliament and pts. thereof since Magna Charta rel. to Wales, w. chronol. table.

**BRITISH COLONIES**

**Africa** —*for* Roman-Dutch Law (*still in force in S.-A. Colonies*), *v.* **D** § 110

*Bechuanaland*

WARD, D. [ed.] Orders in Council and H. Comr's. Proclams., 1891–8 10 / 8° 99

*Cape Colony*

Statutes of Cape of Good Hope: 1652–1886, ed. J. Foster + H. Tennant + E. M. Jackson, v. i–iii 8° *Cape Town* 88

TENNANT, H. [ed.] Chron. Table and Indexes of Stat. Law of Cape Colony 10/6 8° *Cape Town* 88

TODD, S. B. Handy Guide to Laws and Regulns. at C. of G. Hope 7/6 8° *London* 88

*Gambia*

RUSSELL, A. D. [ed.] Ordinances of the Colony of Gambia, 2 vols. £3 *n.* f° 00

*Gold Coast*

GRIFFITH [ed.] Ordinances of Gold Coast Colony & Rules & Orders, 2 v. 70 / r 8° Stevens & H. 03

*Lagos*

Ordinances and Rules in force in Lagos on Apl. 30, 1901 30 / *n.* r 8° 02

*Natal*

HITCHENS, R. L. [ed.] Statutes of Natal: 1900–6 67/6 *n.* r 8° Stevens & H. 07

*Nigeria*

Northern Nigeria Laws, Orders in Council, and Proclamations 42 / r 8° 05

SPEED, E. A. Laws of Colony of Southern Nigeria, 2 vols. 30 / *n.* r 8° 08

*Orange River Colony*

Statute Law of Orange River Colony: translated 42 / r 8° 01

*Sierra Leone*

Ordinances of Colony of Sierra Leone, vols. i–iv [1811–1909] 2/6 *n.*, 3/6 *n.*, 4/6 *n.*, 4/6 *n.* r 8° 00–9

*Transvaal*

BARBER (S. H.) + MACFADYEN (W. A.) + FINDLAY (J. H. L.) [trs.] Statute Law of Transvaal 42 / r 8° 01

Transvaal Colony Proclamations: 1900–2 25 / r 8° 04

**Australasia**

*New South Wales*

OLIVER, A. [ed.] Coll. of Statutes of Pract. Utility in force in N.S.W., 3 v. 105 / r 8° Stevens & H. 79–81

*New Zealand* —*v. also* **D** § 107

BADGER, W. [ed.] Statutes of New Zealand, 2 vols. 25 / r 8° *Wellington, N.Z.*

BARTON, G. B. [ed.] Practical Stats. of N.Z., w. notes & index, 2 vols. 105 / s 4° *Wellington, N.Z.* 76–7

WILSON, W. M. [ed.] Practical Statutes of New Zealand, 3 vols. 67 *sqq.*

WORSFOLD, W. B. Abridgment of Statute Law of New Zealand 10/6 8° *Wellington, N.Z.* 88

*Victoria*

Public General Statutes of Victoria, vols. i–iv 84 / 4° *Melbourne* 75–87

WEBB, T. P. [ed.] Compend. of Imperial Law & Stats. in force in Vict. 12/6 8° *Melbourne* 74

**Canada** —*v. also* **D** § 107

DUBREUILL, J. T. [ed.] Reference Book to Statutes of Canada 12/6 79

EWART, J. S. [ed.] Index to Statutes of Canada: 1859–78, Ontario '67–77, Quebec '67–77 10 / 8°

Ontario Statutes, 13 vols. 50 / 8°

Revised Statutes of Canada : 2 vols. 22/6 8° *Ottawa* 82

WEIR, W. A. [ed.] The Civil Code of Canada 9/ *n.* 12° 90

**Bermudas** Acts of Legisl. of Bermudas in force 1860, ed. J. H. Darrell r 8° 62

„ Acts of Legislature of Bermuda Islands f° 75–6

**India** —*v. also* **D** § 107; *for* Penal Code *v.* **D** § 32; *for* Roman-Dutch Law (*still in force in Ceylon*), *v.* **D** § 110

General Rules and Orders in force in Brit. India, vols. i–iii ea. 7/6 8° Govt. Prg. Off., *Calcutta* 06–7

Index to Enactments relating to India, ed. Stephen Jacob 15/ 8° Govt. Prg. Off. *Calcutta* 80

MACPHERSON, J. M. [ed.] List of Brit. Enactmts. in force in Native States, 5 v. Govt. Prg. Off., *Calc.* 88–95
A valuable, though unofficial, colln. of enactments conc. Madras, Mysore, N. India, Hyderabad, Central India, Rajputana and W. India.

SARASWATI, P. P. N. [ed.] Student's Indian Law Code 18/ 8° *Calcutta*

STOKES, Whitley [ed.] Anglo-Indian Codes, 2 vols.
65/ ($16·25) ; 2 Suppls. in 1 v. 6/6 ($1·60) 8° Clar. Press 87–8 ; 91
Vol. i : *Substantive Law*, 30/ ($7·50) ; ii : *Adjective Law*, 35/ ($8·75). Each code preceded by a valuable introd.. giving general view of its objects and contents, its princ. divergencies fr. Eng. law, and suggestns. for amendment—a sort of Anglo-Indian CHITTY'S *Statutes*.

Unrepealed General Acts of Governor-General in Council, vols. i–vi ea. 10/ 8° Govt. Prg. Off., *Calc.* 07–9

WIGLEY, F. G. Annotated Tables of the Indian Statutes 6/ 4° Govt. Prg. Off., *Calcutta* 10

*Separate Provinces* —*Acts and Codes of most are pubd. separately*

**South America** : *British Guiana*

BELMONTE (B. E. J. C.) [ed.] Alphab. Digest of Cases in Br. Guiana :
1856–1906, 42/ *n.*; Suppl., 12/6 *n.* 8°. 07–8

**West Indies**

*Antigua* Laws of : Acts of Leeward Islands 1696–1798, and of Antigua 1668–1854, 4 v. 4° 54

*Bahamas* Statute Law of : all Acts of General Assembly, 2 v. 8° 62–8

„ The Laws of Bahamas f° 68–70

*Barbadoes* The Laws of Barbadoes 21/ r 8° 55

**United States** —*the several States publish edns. of their Statutes, etc.*

Compiled Statutes, 1901 : ed. J. A. Mallory, 3 vols. ; w. notes $18 8° West Pb. Co., *St Paul, Minn.* 03

„ „ Supplement, 1907 $6 8° West Pb. Co., *St. Paul, Minn.* 07

Federal Statutes, annotated : ed. W. M. McKinney + P. Kemper, jr., vols. i–x, and Suppl.
ea. $6 8° Thompson, *Newport, L.I.* 03–8

General Statutes for the Year : all laws of public or general nature $2·50 8° *New York* 91 *sqq.*, *in prg.*

GOULD (J. M.) + TUCKER (G. F.) Notes on Revised Stats. of U.S. $10 *n.* 8° Little & Brown, *Boston* 88

STIMSON, F. J. [ed.] American Statute Law ; w. Supplement $7·50 8° Boston Bk. Co., *Bost.* 86–9
An analytic and compared digest of Constitns. and Civil Public Statutes of all States and Territs. in force 1 Jan. 1886 ; w. Suppl. to 1888.

**Belgium** —*for* Maritime Code *v.* **D** § 58

TODD, E. Treat. on Belgian Law, contg. complete tr. of Code of Commerce
and Code of Procedure 25/ *n.* 8° Butterworth 05

**France** —*for* Commercial Code *v.* **D** § 63

CACHARD, Hy. [tr.] French Civil Code 20/ 8° 95

WRIGHT, E. B. [tr.] French Civil Code [w. notes & comparative refs.] 25/ r 8° Stevens 08

**Germany** —*v. also* **D** § 4 ; *for* Commerc. Code *v.* **D** § 63 ; Criminal Code *v.* **D** § 32

LOEWY, W. [tr.] German Civil Code : tr. [21/ *n.* Sweet] $5 8° Boston Bk. Co., *Boston* 10

MAITLAND, Prf. F. W. —*in his* Coll. Papers, 3 v., *ut* **F** § 1 [regards the Germ. code as 'the best the world has ever seen']

WANG, Chung Hui [tr.] German Civil Code : tr. & annotated : w. hist. intr. 21/ r 8° Stevens 07

**Oriental** —*v.* **D** § 112*; *for* Criminal Codes *v.* **D** § 32

## 3 : DIGESTS AND REPORTS : COLLECTIVELY

**Great Britain** —*v. also* **D** § 103
A Chronolog. List of Reports in the Eng., Scot. and Irish Courts, w. prices, may be obtd. of Stevens & Sons ; *v.* also JELF [*ut* **D** § 1].

CAMPBELL, Rob. [ed.] Ruling Cases : arranged and annotated ; w. Amer. notes
by Irving Browne + L. A. Jones, 27 vols. £26 r 8° Stevens 94–08
Collects in alphab. order of subjects the more useful authorities of Engl. case-law on points of general applicn.. more important cases bg. set forth at length. Ea. vol. conts. alphab. table of cases ref. to. Complete Table of Cases by E. MANSON.

BUTTERWORTH [pub.] Ten Years' Digest of Reported Cases, 4 vols. 60/ *n.* r 8° Butterworth 08

„ The same : First Annual Suppl., ed. G. R. Hill + H. Clover 10/ *n.* r 8° Butterworth 09 *ann.*

„ Yearly Digest : 1899–1902, ed. E. Beal ; 1903 *sqq.*, ed. G. R. Hill
ea. 15/ r 8° Butterworth 00 *sqq.*, *in prg.*

EMDEN (A.) + THOMPSON (H.) Annual Digest of Rep. Cases in All Courts, 11 v. ea. 15/ r 8° Clowes 83–93

,, Digest of Cases not cont. in 'Law Reports': 1881–83, 3 v. r 8° Clowes 81–3 *not cont.*

English Reports (The) r 8° Stevens *v.y.*

*House of Lords* (1694–1866), 11 vols. £22 *n.* | *Rolls Court* (1829–1866), 8 vols. £12
*Privy Council* (1809–1872), 9 vols. £13 10*s. n.* | *Vice-Chancellors* (1815–1865), 16 vols. £24
*Chancery* (1557–1866), 27 vols. £40 10*s. n.* | *K.B. and Q.B.* (1378–1865), vols. i–xxviii [in 40 vols.] ea. 30/ *n.*
A complete verbatim reissue of all decisns. prior to 1866, w. refs. to later decisns.

English Ruling Cases with American Notes, 26 vols. in 13 $78 8° Boston Bk. Co., *Boston* 05
The most important and useful Engl. cases in full, grouped under subj.-hgs., w. notes and references.

Incorp. Council of Law Reptg. for Engl. and Wales

Law Reports; *and* Weekly Notes; 1866–84. ea. 105/; 1885–90, New Ser. 1891 *sqq.*
ea. 84/ Clowes 66–10 *in prg.*
Reports of Decisions in Ho. of Lords, Privy Co., Supr. Ct. & H. C. of Just. *Statutes* of the year supplied gratis. Have an authority wh. no other *Reports* can have.

Current Index of all Cases reptd. in 'Law Reports' and 'Wkly. Notes [quarterly] Clowes
Each quarterly pt. incorporates (and thus supersedes) all previous pts. of same yr. Gratis w. *Law Repts.* and *Wkly. Notes.*

Law Journal Quinquennial Digest, 1901–5, ed. J. S. Henderson 30/ 4° *Law Jl.* Off. 06
Digest of cases in *Law Journal Reports*, and *Law Reports*, w. refs. to contemp. Statutes.

Law Journ. Reports & Authorized Edn. of Statutes [monthly] *ann.* 64/ 4° [22 *sqq.*] *in prg. Law Jl.* Off.

Law Reports Digest: ed. A. P. Stone, 1865–90, 3 vols. 42/ *n.*; 1891–5 r 8° Clowes 92–6

'Law Times' Reports: Ser. i, vols. i–xxxiv; New Ser., vol. i *sqq.*
[*iss. w.* 'Law Times Jl.'] f° *Law Times* Off. 43–59; 60–10 *in prg.*
A *General Index* to the New Series is pubd. every 10 yrs.: particularly valuable because cases are indexed under dft's. as well as plff's. names.

MANSON, Edw. Digest of English Case Law, 1898–1907, 2 vols. 63/ r 8° Sweet 08
Forms a supplement to MEWS, *ut inf.*

*MEWS, J. [ed.] Digest of English Case Law, 16 vols. [to 1897] £20 r 8° Sweet 98
$96 Boston Bk. Co. Supersedes all previous digests down to 1897, consolidatg. Fisher's *Comm. Law Digest* and Chitty's *Equity Index.*

,, [ed.] Annual Digest of All Reptd. Cases of Super. Cts., includg. a selection fr. Irish Cases 15/ r 8° Sweet *ann.*

NEALE, J. A. English Law by English Judges 12/6 r 8° Butterworth 92
An exposn., for layman and for lawyer, from decisions 1886–91.

PETERS, A. P. Analysis and Digest of Decisions of Sir G. Jessel 16/ 8° Stevens & H. 83

POLLOCK, (Sir F.) + CAMPBELL (R.) + SAUNDERS (O. A.) [eds.] Revised Reports in English Courts of Common Law and Equity from 1785, v. i–cvii ea. 25/ *n.* r 8° Sweet 91–09 *in prg.*
Index to vols. i-xc 45/ *n.* 08.

'Times' Index and Digest for 1884–95 50/ f° *Times* Office 96
*The Times Law Reports* are pubd. weekly. Annual subscrn. 25/.

Year Books of the Reign of Edward i [our earliest Law Reports]—*ut* **D** § 5

*Over-ruled, etc., Cases*

KANT, A. N. Index of Cases Judicially Noticed [Law Repts. '65–04] 30/ r 8° Butterworth 05

TALBOT (G. J.) + FORT (H.) Index of Cases Judicially Noticed, ed. M. R. Mehta ['65–07] 38/ r 8° Sweet 08

WOODS (W. A. G.) + RITCHIE (J.) Digest of Cases Over-ruled, Approved or Otherwise Considered, 3 vols. 105/ r 8° Sweet 07
Based on DALE + LEHMANN'S *Digest of Cases Over-ruled.* It deals with over 30,000 cases, incl. some Scottish and Irish.

*Chambers*

BITTLESTON, A. H. [ed.] Reports in Chambers, Q.B.D., 1883–4 12/6 r 8° Butterworth 84

*Commercial Court*

MATHEW, T. [ed.] Repts. of Commerc. Cases in Commerc. Ct., vols. i–xv
[6 Pts. ann.] *subscr.* 15/ 8° Butterworth 95 *sqq., in prg.*

*Consistory Courts* (London, Hereford, Ripon, Wakefield, *etc.*)

TRISTRAM, Chanc. [ed.] Principal Judgments deliv. in Consistory Courts 18/ 8° Butterworth 93

*Justice of the Peace*

ALLAN, C. E. [ed.] Magist. Cases as reptd. in 'Justice of Peace' ea. 4/ 8° Butterworth 96 *sqq. qtly.*

Digest of Justice of the Peace Cases: 1883–1908 30/ *n.* 8° Butterworth 09

*Irish Reports*

Digest of Irish Reports, 1894–1903 30/ *n.* r 8° 05

*Scottish Reports*

Annual Digest of all Cases in Supr. Ct. of Scotld., ed. J. C. S. Sandeman, vols. i–v
15/ *n.* r 8° Green, *Edin.* 04–9 *ann.*

Private Legislation (Scotl.) Reports, ed. A. H. B. Constable + H. P. Macmillan, etc., vols. i–ix
ea. 15/ *n.* r 8° Green, *Edin.* 01–9 *in prg.*

Scots Digest 1800–1873, vols. i–ii ea. 30/ *n.* r 8° Green, *Edin.*

,, 1873–1904, ed. J. C. S. Sandeman, etc., 2 vols. 60/ *n.* r 8° Green, *Edin.*

Scots Revised Reports : 45 vols. r 8° Green, *Edin.* [1728 *sqq.*]

A re-issue of the offic. Scots Decisions prior to 1873 in follg. series : (1) *House of Lords*, 1707–1865, 10 vols., £15 *n.* ; (2) SHAW's *Reports* (Session Cases, Ser. i), 1821–38, 6 v., £9 *n.* ; (3) DUNLOP's *Repts.* (Sess. Cases, Ser. ii), 1838–62, 13 v., £19 10/ *n.*; (4) MACPHERSON's *Repts.* (Sess. Cases, Ser. iii), 1862–73, 11 v., £16 10/ *n.* ; (5) *Faculty Decisns.*, 1807–25, 2 v., £3 *n.* ; (6) *Scottish Jurist Cases not reptd. elsewhere*, 1829–65, £2 ; (7) MORISON's *Dict. of Decisns.*, 2 v., £3 *n.* Cases repr. verbatim, w. addns. to or corrns. of rubrics and new notes, where necessary, all within sq. brackets.

## BRITISH COLONIES

### Africa

*Cape Colony*

BUCHANAN, J. Repts. of Cases dec. in Supr. Ct., C. of G. H. 1868–74, 3 v. Ann. Suppl. r 8° *Cape Town ann.*

" Index and Digest of Cases dec. in Supr. Ct. of C. of G. H. r 8° *Cape Town*

JUTA, H. H. [ed.] Seln. of Leadg. Cases on Law of Cape Colony, Pts. i–ii 8° *Cape Town* 96

Pt. i : *Law of Purchase and Lease* ; ii : *Law of Wills.* With notes.

SEARLE, M. W. Digest of Reptd. Cases in Cts. of C. of G. H., fr. 1850 10/6 8° *Cape Town* 88

*Gold Coast : Fanti Law*

HAYFORD, C. Gold Coast Native Institutions 15/ 8° Stevens & Haynes 03

SARBAH, J. M. Fanti Customary Laws : native laws & customs—*ut* **B** § 34

" Fanti Law Report of the Gold Coast—*ut* **B** § 34

" Fanti National Constitution 15/ *n.* 8° Clowes 04

*South African Republic*

HERTZOG [tr.] Reports of the High Ct. of S.A. Republic, 1893 : tr. 50/ *n.* r 8° 94

Reports of the High Ct., S.A. Repub., tr. W. S. Webber, vols. i–iv. [1894–7] ea. 50/ *n.* r 8° 95 *sqq.*

### Australasia

*New South Wales*

WATKINS, J. L. Digest of Cases dec. in Supr. Ct. of N.S.W. : 1861–85 105/ r 8° *Sydney* 88

*New Zealand*

SMITH, T. S. Digest of Reptd. Cases in Ct. of App. & Supr. Ct., N.Z., 1885–7, 2 v. ea. 25/ 8° *Sydney* 87–8

*Victoria*

DAVIS, A. S. Analyt. Index of Cases in Supr. Ct., Ct. of Mines, and Vice-Admir. Ct. of Victoria, 1871–83 34/ r 8°

Digest of Law Reports : 1861–85, 105/ *n.* ; 1885–1905, 4 vols. 100/ *n.* r 8° *Melbourne* 88–07

Victorian Statutes of Practical Utility : 1902–7, 3 vols. 60/ *n.* 4° *Melbourne* 08

### Canada

BLIGH, H. H. The Ontario Law Index 8° *Ottawa* 96

SMITH, Jas. F. [ed.] The Ontario Reports, vols. i– $4 r 8° Rowsell, *Toronto* 89 *in prg.*

STEPHENS, C. H. Digest of all Reptd. Decisns. in Prov. of Quebec to 1877 65/ r 8°

STEVENS, Judge Digest of Cases decided in Supr. Ct. of N. Brunsw., 2 v. 63/ 8° [ ] 80

STOCKTON, A. A. Reports of Cases in Vice-Adm. Ct. of N. Brunsw. 1879–91 36/ *n.* r 8° 96

### India

—*v. also* **D** § 107

AIYAR, S. S. Digest of Indian Cases, 1903–4 12/ *n.* r 8° 05

COWELL, H. Compl. Index to Reptd. Cases of H. Cts. in India 28/ r 8° *Calcutta* [ ] 73

ILBERT, Sir Courtenay P. The Governmt. of India : digest of Stat. Law 10/6 *n.* ($3·40) 8° Clar. Pr. [98] 07

Indian Law Reports : Calcutta Series, vols. i– *subscr.* 25/ r 8° *Calcutta* 90 *sqq.*, *in prg.*

Similar *Reports* are pub. annually for Allahabad, Bombay and Madras.

NORMANBY, F. Digest of Cases rep. in Beng. Law Reps., vols. i–xv, in Suppl. Vol., in Madras H. C. Reps. i–viii, Bomb. H. C. Reps. i–xii, N. W. Prov. H. C. Reps. i–vii 40/ 8° *Madras* 81

SINGH, Bává Naráin Digest of Indian Law Cts. : Allahabad Series, v. i–x [1876–88] 10/ 8° *Lahore* 89

STRANGE, Sir T. Manual of Hindu Law, ed. J. D. Mayne 12/ 8° Higginbotham, *Madras* 64

A new edn. of his *Notes of Cases in Ct. of Recorder's Supr. Ct. at Madras*, 2 vols. 1827.

SUNDERLAND, D. Digest of Indian Law Reports 63/ r 8° Thacker, *Calcutta* 77

WOODMAN, J. V. Digest of Cases rep. in Bengal Law Repts., 1868–75 24/ r 8° Thacker, *Calc.* 78

**Jamaica** Digest of Laws. By J. Minot, 48/ ; Contin. to 1872 by J. Minot + W. R. Lee 65 ; 73

**United States** —*Digests and Repts. of the several States are also pubd.*

Amer. & Engl. Annotated Cases, v. i–xiv [4 vols. ann.] ea. $5 8° Thompson, *Northport, L.I.* 06 *sqq.*, *in prg.*

American Decisions: cases of general value decid. in Cts. of several States, vols. i–c
ea. $5 8° Bancroft, *San Francisco* 68 *sqq., in prg.*

„ Digest & Index to above, vols. xxxi–lx, by A. C. Freeman $4·50 8° Bancroft, *San Francisco* 85

„ The same, vols. lxi–c, by A. J. Brunner $4·50 8° Bancroft, *San Francisco* 88

American Digest of all Reported Cases: 1658–1896: Century Edn. vols. i– ; ea. $6 *n.*; cont. ann.
ea. $6 *n.* 8° West Pb. Co., *St Paul, Minn.* 97 *sqq.*

American Reports: decisns. of general interest decid. in Courts of Last Resort, vol. i–lx
ea. $6 8° Parsons, *Albany, N.Y.* 70 *sqq.*

American State Reports: cases of general value and authority, vols. i–cxxx
ed. A. C. Freeman, w. notes [1760–1907] ea. $4 8° Bancroft, *San Francisco* 86–07, *in prg.*
A continuation of the cases contained in *American Decisions* and the *Amer. Reports.*

DESTY, R. [ed.] Lawyers' Reports Annotated: all current cases in U.S. and territories,
bks. i– ea. $5 8° Lawyers' Co-op. Pb. Co., *Rochester, N.Y. in prg.*

Digest of Decisns. of Cts. of Last Resort of the several States fr. Earliest Period to 1888,
ed. S. Rapalje, 3 vols. $15 8° Bancroft, *San Francisco* [91] 10

„ The same, fr. 1887–92, cont. in ' Am. St. Rep. ' i–xxiv $4 8° Bancroft, *San Francisco* 92

„ The same, cont. in ' Am. St. Rep. ' xxv–xlviii $6 8° Bancroft, *San Francisco* 85

National Reporter System, vols. i–
[several hundred vols. pb.] ea. $5 8° West Pb. Co., *St Paul, Minn.* 94 *sqq., in prg.*

Digest of Decisions of U.S. Courts, 4 vols. $25 West Pub. Co., *St. Paul, Minn.* 00

SMITH, J. W. Selection of Leadg. Cases on var. Branches of Law, 4 v. $22 8° Johnson, *Phila.* [ ] 85

*Circuit Courts of Appeal*

Circuit Courts of Appeals: Reports, w. annotns., vols. i–lix
ea. $3·35 8° Lawyers' Co-op. Pb. Co., *Rochester, N.Y. in prg.*

„ Index Digest of same, vols. i–xl and i–lxiii of U.S. Appeals
$5 8° Lawyers' Co-op. Pb. Co., *Rochester, N.Y.* 00

*Federal Courts*

Federal Reporter: Permanent Edn., vols. i–clxii ea. $3·50 8° West Pb. Co., *St Paul, Minn.* –08 *in prg.*

*Supreme Court*

CLARKE, H. de F. Handbk. of all Decisns. of Supr. Ct. to 1891, 2 Pts., $7·50; 1891–8, 2 Pts.
$7·50 Lawyers' Co-op. Pb. Co., *Rochester, N.Y.* 92–9

Digest of Supreme Court Cases, vols. i–ccvi Lawyers' Co-op. Pb. Co., *Rochester, N.Y.* –08 *in prg.*

Encyclopædia of Reports to vol. ccvi, ed. T. J. Michie, vol. i Michie, *Charlottesville, Va.* 08 *in prg.*

Index Digest of Decs. fr. 1 Dallas to 202 U.S., ed. W. H. Russell + W. B. Winslow, 4 vols.
30 *n.* 8° Banks Law Pb. Co., *N.Y.* 07–9

Obiter Digest of U.S. Supreme Court Reports, 2 vols. $12 8° Thompson, *Northport, L.I.*

ROSE, W. M. Digest of U.S. Reports, v. i–clxxxvi, 3 v. ea. $6·50 Bancroft, *San Francisco* 03

„ Notes on U.S. Supr. Ct. Reports to July 1901, 12 v. $85 8° Bancroft, *San Francisco*

Thompson, C. L. Notes Suppl. to Rose's Notes, 1901–9, 5 v. $32·50 Bancroft, *San Francisco* 05

Supreme Court Cases argued and decided on, Bks. i–xliii, $2·20; xliv–li
ea. $5 8° Lawyers' Co-op. Pb. Co., *Rochester, N.Y.* 01–7 *in prg.*

„ Indexed Digest of Opins. & Cases, 1894–1901 $3·50 8° Lawyers' Co-op. Pb. Co., *Rochester, N.Y.* 03

Supreme Court Reporter, vols. i–xxviii ea. $4 8° West Pb. Co., *St Paul, Minn.* –08 *in prg.*

Supreme Court Reports, vols. i–ccvi ea. $2·30 8° Banks Law Pb. Co., *N.Y. in prg.*

# III: Comprehensive General Treatises on Law

## 4: TREATISES; COMMENTARIES; DICTIONARIES

### TREATISES AND COMMENTARIES

**England**

BACON Abridgment, ed. J. Bouvier, 10 vols. $35 *n.* 8° Johnson, *Phila.* [ ]

BLACKSTONE, Sir Wm. Commentaries on the Laws of England [1765–9], ed. Broom + Hadley, 4 vols. *o.p.* [*pb.* 21/] 8° Maxwell 69

* „ The same, ed. R. M. N. Kerr, 4 vols. 60/ r 8° Murray 76

„ The same: abridged, *s.t.* Student's Blackstone, ed. Kerr 7/6 8° Clowes [65] 96

„ The same, ed. G. Sharswood, 2 vols. $6 *n.* 8° Lippincott, *Phila.* 99

Blickenscherfer, M. [ed.] Blackstone's Elements of Law; w. anal. charts, etc. 20/ 8° Stevens 89
Browne, W. H. [ed.] Blackstone's Commentaries [w. gloss. of terms] $4 *n.* 8° West Pb. Co., *St Paul, Minn.* 92
Chase, G. [ed.] Blackstone's Comms. on Law of Engl., for Am. students $6·50 8° Banks, *N.Y.* [76] 96
Hammond, W. G. [ed.] Blackstone's Comms. for Am. Lawyers, 4 vols. $10 8° Bancroft-Whitney Co., *San Francisco* 90
Stephen, H. St J. New Commentaries—*ut inf.*
*Blackstone's Commentaries* still remains the best survey, at once concise and comprehensive, of English law.

BRETT, Thos. Commentaries on Present Laws of England, 2 v. *o.p.* [*pb.* 38/] 8° Clowes [90] 91
Brings into spec. prominence pres. and living law, dealg. w. past or pract. obsolete law only so far as enables reader to understand present. It supplies an excellent bird's-eye view of mod. Engl. law: clear, accurate, and well arranged.

BROOM, H. Commentaries on the Common Law—*ut* **D** § 25
CAMPBELL, R. Principles of English Law [based on Blackstone] 20/ 8° Stevens 07
EWELL, M. D. Essentials of the Law, 3 vols. ea. $2·50 8° Boston Bk. Co., *Boston* 82–8
FOLKARD, H. C. A Concise Abridgment of the Law 21/ r 8° E. Wilson [ ] 08
HALSBURY, Earl of, *etc.* The Laws of England, vols. i–xii ea. 25/ *n.* r 8° Butterworth 07 *in prg.*
A complete and uniform statemt., in alphab. order, of the law of England by the late Lord Chancellor in co-oper. w. the most eminent lawyers of the day. Supplies in convenient and easily accessible form the whole body of Engl. law, w. refs. to decisns., authorities, and statutes. Historical and theoret. discussns. are avoided exc. where necess. for purposes of elucidn. of text. To be complete in about 20 vols. Suppl. No. i [to vols. i-xii] '11

JENKS, Edw. Digest of English Civil Law, 7 vols. ea. 5/ *n.* r 8° Butterworth 05 *sqq.*, *in prg.*
Bk. I: *General*; Bk. II, Pt. i: *Contract*, General; Pt. ii: *Particular Contracts*; Pt. iii: *Quasi-Contract and Tort.*

NEALE, J. A. [ed.] Exposition of English Law by English Judges 12/6 8° Clowes 92
A convenient compilation, for use of layman and lawyer, fr. decisions of 1886–91.

STEPHEN, H. St J. New Comments. on Laws of Engl., ed. E. Jenks, 4 vols. [based on Blackstone; $22 Boston Pk. Co.] 84/ 8° Butterworth [41–5] 03
Gibson, A. Guide to Stephen's Commentaries 12/ 8° Reeves & Turner [79–81] 08
TYSSEN, Amherst D. Elementary Law for the General Public 2/6 8° Butterworth 98

**Scotland**

BARCLAY, H. Digest of Law of Scotland [esp. of Justices] 31/6 8° *Edinburgh* [53] 80
BELL, G. J. Principles of Law of Scotl., ed. W. Guthrie, 2 v. 52/6 r 8° *Edinburgh* [04] 99
" Commentaries on Laws of Scotl., ed. J. Maclaren, 2 v. 105/ 4° *Edinb.* [5th ed. 26] 70
" Synopsis of Princs. of Law of Scotl., ed. F. H. Morrison 5/ *n.* 8° Clark, *Edin.* 03
ERSKINE, Prf. J. Institutes of Law of Scotl., ed. J. B. Nicolson, 2 v. 20/ 4° Green, *Ed.* [1773] 71
" Principles of Law of Scotland, ed. J. Rankine 21/ 8° Green, *Edin.* [1754–64] 03
LORIMER, Prf. J. Handbook of Law of Scotland, ed. R. Bell 10/ 12° Blackwood [ ] 94
MORE, Prf. Jno. S. Lectures on Law of Scotland, ed. J. McLaren, 2 v. 5/ *n.* r 8° Green, *Edin.* 64
MORTON, W. K. Manual of Scots Law [student's-bk.] 8/ *n.* 8° Green, *Edin.* 96
STAIR, Vis. Institutions of Law of Scotl., ed. J. S. More, 2 v. 15/ *n.* 4° Green, *Edin.* [ ]

**BRITISH COLONIES** *v. also* **D** § 107

**Africa:** *South Africa* *v. also* **D** § 25

BELL (W. H. S.) + NATHAN (M.) Legal Handbk. of Brit. South Africa 25/ *n.* 8° Sweet 05

**Canada**

KINGSFORD, R. E. Commentaries on Law of Ontario 8° Carswell, *Toronto* 96
An attempt to adapt BLACKSTONE to the current law of Ontario.

**India** *v.* **D** § 111

**United States**

ANDREWS, J. de W. Amer. Law: jurispr., const., & laws of U.S. $6·50 8° Callagham, *Chicago* 00
BLACKSTONE, Sir Wm. —*ut supra* (ed. CHASE, ed. HAMMOND)
BOUVIER, J. Institutes of Law of Amer., ed. D. A. Gleason, 2 v. $10 8° Lippincott, *Phila.* [51] 75
HILLIARD, Fcs. Compreh. Summary of Am. Law in var. Depts, $7·50 8° Baker, *N.Y.* 77
KENT, J. Commentaries on American Law, ed. W. H. Browne $4 *n.* 8° West Pb. Co., *St Paul, Minn.* [26–30] 94
" Comments. on Amer. Law, ed. C. M. Barnes, 4 vols. ea. $3·50 *n.* r 8° Little & Brown, *Boston* [26–30] 84
" The Student's Kent [abgmt. of above] $2·50 *n.* 8° Houghton, *Boston* 86
Dickson, F. S. Analysis of Kent's Commentaries $5 8° Welsh, *Phila.* [72] 75
Powell, T. W. Analysis of American Law $4·50 8° Lippincott, *Phila.* [70] 78
Thompson, E. F. Abridgment of Kent's Commentaries $2·50 8° *Boston* 86

SMITH, T. L. Elements of Laws: outl. of civil & crim. laws in U.S. $1·50 12° Lippincott, *Phila.* [53] 82
STIMSON, F. J. Amer. Statute Law: anal. & comp. digest, 2 v. $14 4° Boston Bk. Co., *Boston* 86–93
TERRY, H. T. Some Leading Principles of Anglo-American Law $5·50 8° Johnson, *Phila.* 84
WALKER, A. American Law $6 8° Little & Brown, *Boston* [4–] 78
WALKER, T. Introd. to Amer. Law, ed. C. Bates [studt.'s bk.] $6 8° Little & Brown, *Bost.* [37] 87
WHARTON, F. Commentaries on Law $6 8° Kay, *Phila.* 84

**Burma**

FORCHAMMER, Dr E. Essay on Sources & Developmt. of Burmese Law *o.p.* [*pb.* 10/6] i 8° Trübner 85

**France**

BROWNE, A. S. French Law and Customs for the Anglo-Saxon 2/6 *n.* 07
COXE, H. C. Manual of French Law and Commercial Information 6/ *n.* c 8° Simpkin 02
SEWELL, J. I. B. French Law affecting British Subjects 10/6 8° 97

**Germany**

SCHUSTER, E. J. Principles of German Civil Law 12/6 *n.* ($4·15) 8° Clar. Press 07

**Hebrew Law: Ancient** —*v.* **A** § 12

**Holland** —*for* Roman-Dutch Law, *v.* **D** § 110

van der KEESSEL, D. G. Select Theses on Laws of Holland & Zeeland [tr.] 15/ 12° *Cape Town* [6–] 88
van der LINDEN, J. Institutes of Holland, tr. H. Juta 31/6 8° *Cape Town* 88

**Mexico**

HAMILTON, L. Mexican Law 18/ 8° Stevens 84

**DICTIONARIES**

ABBOTT, B. V. Law Dictionary, 2 vols. [Am. & Engl. terms & phrases] $12 8° Little & Brown, *Bost.* 79
Amer. & Engl. Encyclo. of Law, ed. D. S. Garland + C. Porterfield, 32 vols. & Suppl. 4 vols. ea. $7·50 8° Thompson, *Northport, L.I.* [87–92] 96–07
ANDERSON, W. C. Dictionary of Law $7·50 8° Flood, *Chicago* 90
HALSBURY, Earl of, *etc.* The Laws of England—*ut* **D** § 3
MOZLEY (H. N.) + WHITELEY (G. C.) Concise Law Dictionary, ed. Drs L. H. West + F. G. Neave 10/6 *n.* 8° Butterworth [76] 08
RAWSON (H. G.) + REMNANT (J. F.) Pocket Law Lexicon, ed. J. E. Morris [pop.] 6/6 12° Stevens [82] 05
STROUD, F. The Judicial Dictionary, 3 vols. & Suppl. 84/ 8° Sweet [90] 01; 08
A monumental wk., quoting *ipsissimis verbis* the definitions wh. have been given by judicial authority to words and phrases of all sorts from Domesday Book to statutes and cases of Vict. Supplement only, 21/.
SWEET, Chas. Dictionary of English Law [technical terms, rules, etc.] 40/ i 8° Sweet 82
THORNTON, W. W. Universal Cyclopædia of Law $5 8° Thompson, *Boston* 83
WHARTON, J. J. S. Law Lexicon, ed. J. M. Lely 38/ i 8° Stevens [47] 11
Epitome of law of Engl., contg. full explan. of techn. terms—anc., mod., and commercial—together w. a tr. of Latin maxims, and selected titles fr. Civil, Scotch and Indian law.
WOOD-RENTON (A.) + ROBERTSON (M. A.) [eds.] Encyclopædia of Laws of England, 15 vols. £15 15*s.*; Ann. Suppl ts. i-ii, 8° Green, *Edin.* 06–11

*Scotland*

BELL, G. J. Dict. & Digest of Law of Scotl., ed. G. Watson 25/ *n.* r 8° Green, *Edin.* [82] 90
Contains most of the Scottish archaic terms in SKENE'S *De Verborum Significatione* [1599].
CHISHOLM, J. [ed.] Encyclo. of Laws of Scotl. By leading authorities, vols. i–iii [in 12 vols.] ea. 20/ *n.* r 8° Green, *Edin.* [96–04]
Most comprehensive; alphabetically arranged. Contributed to by leading Scottish jurists.

*United States*

BOUVIER, J. Law Dictionary, ed. F. Rawle, 2 vols. [adapted to constitn. of U.S.] $12 *n.* r 8° Boston Bk. Co., *Boston* [39] 99
Cyclop. of Law & Procedure, ed. W. Mack, etc., v. i–xxx ea. $6 *n.* 8° Am. Law Bk. Co., *N.Y.* 01–8 *in prg.*
„ Annual Cyclop. Annotations to same, ea. $4·60 *n.* 8° Am. Law Bk. Co., *N.Y.* 02 *sqq.*
KINNEY, J. K. Law Dictionary and Glossary $5 *n.* 8° Callaghan, *Chicago* 94

*Terms, Phrases, Quotations*

BETTS, Arth. Glossary of Ancient Words, Pt. i [A] 10/6 *n.* 4° 07
BLACK, H. Dict. of Law [Am. & Eng. terms, anc. & mod.] $6*n.* 8° West Pb. Co., *St Paul, Minn.* 91
COCHRANE, W. C. Student's Law Lexicon [terms, phrases, abbrevns., etc.] $2·50 12° Clarke, *Cincin.* [89] 92

COTTERELL, J. N. Latin Maxims and Phrases 4/ [ ] 04

ELPHINSTONE, H. W., etc. Rules f. Interpretn. of Deeds, w. Gloss. of Terms 25/ 8° Maxwell 85

ENGLISH, A. Dict. of Words & Phrases in Anc. & Mod. Law $6·50 *n.* Law Bk. Co., *Washn.* 99

NORTON-KYSHE, J. W. Dictionary of Legal Quotations 10/6 8° Sweet 04

A coll. of selected *dicta* of Engl. judges upon various legal subjects; mainly of historical interest.

---

# IV: History and Antiquities of Law

## 5: HISTORY OF LAW AND EARLY LEGAL WORKS

**Primitive** —*v.* **F** § 5

**Greek:** *Rhodian* —*v.* **F** § 10 (Ashburner)

### Early Celtic; Brehon Laws

Ancient Laws and Institutes of Ireland, ed. Dr Atkinson, vols. i–vi ea. 10/1 8° Rolls Series 65–02

A very important edn. of the Brehon Laws. Contains *Senchus Mor*, *Book of Aiide* [a sort of code of criminal law] and texts, with trs., rel. to Old-Irish custom of law and procedure.

Ancient Laws & Institutes of Wales, ed. Aneurin Owen, 1 v. f° 44/ and 2 v. r 8° 36/ Scot. Rolls Series 41

The Laws of HOWEL THE GOOD, in 3 provincial variants, w. tr. and a mass of legal *dicta*, triads, and Lat. versns. of the laws.

GRINNELL, L. The Brehon Laws: a legal handbook 6/ c 8° Unwin 94

A useful monograph on the celebrated Irish laws, which, dating fr. *c.* B.C. 750, were codified orally *c.* A.D. 250, and reduced to writing *c.* 441 by a commission of 9, of whom St. Patrick was one. Wr. fr. pt. of view of jurisprudent, politician and sociologist.

MAINE, Sir H. S. —*in his* Early History of Institutions, *ut* **F** § 5

Contains an admirable account of the Brehon law and the tribal system.

WADE-EVANS, A. W. [ed.] Welsh Medieval Law: text of laws of Howel the Good 8/6 *n.* ($2·90) Clar. Pr. 09

The Brit. Mus. Harleian MS. 4353 of 13 cent., w. tr. (based on OWEN's), Introd., appendix, glossary, index, and map. An original and scholarly survey, forming a valuable contribn. to hist. of earliest stages in the polit. evoln. of Wales.

### Mediæval: *Generally*

GAUDENTIUS, Dr Aug. [ed.] Bibliotheca Juridica Medii Aevi, vol. ii 48*m.* f° Treves, *Bonn* 92

*Scripta Anecdota Antiquissimorum Glossatorum* [RANIERII DE PERUSIO *Ars Notaria*; ROFREDI BENEVENTANI *Summula de Pugna*; ANSELMI DE ORTO *Juris Civilis Instrumentum*; HUGOLINI *Summa super Usibus Feudorum*; JOHANNIS BASSIANI *De Ordine Judiciorum*; *etc.*, with HINCMARI REMENSIS [HINCMAR, Abp. of Rheims] *Collectio de Eccles. et Cappellis*, and BONCOMPAGNI *Rhetorica Novissima*], ed. GAUDENTIUS, Joh. Bapt. PALMERIUS, Fr. PATETTA, Joh. TAMASSIA, Vict. SCIALOJA.

### History of English Law —*v. also* **F** § 17

BRUNNER, H. Sources of Law of England [tr.] [w. bibliogr. appendices] 2/6 c 8° Clark, *Edin.*

CARTER, A. T. Hist. of English Legal Institutions 14/ 8° Butterworth [99] 06

A lucid but inconsequent manual for students.

DUGDALE, Sir Wm. [1605–86] Origines Juridicales: historical memorials f° *London* [2nd ed. 1671] 1680

The source of most subsequent informn. on hist. of English law, Courts, antiqs., biography.

HOLDSWORTH, Dr W. S. History of English Law, vols. i–iii ea. 10/6 *n.* 8° Methuen 03–09

To occupy 4 vols. Chfly. for Univ. teachers and students. Vol. i deals w. the various Cts. wh. have admin. Eng. law, and the beginning of the various branches—Equity, Admiralty, Commercial, Ecclesiastical—which make up the Common Law of pres. day; vols. ii–iii w. Ang.-Sax. and medieval periods, and the later history of some pts. of common law doctr. wh. attained in substance their final form in medieval period.

INDERWICK, F. A. The King's Peace: hist. of Engl. law-courts 4/6 c 8° Sonnenschein 95

$1.50 Macmillan, *N.Y.* [Social Engl. Ser.] A lucid sk. of the growth and pres. condn. of the law-courts.

JENKS, Edw. Law and Politics in the Middle Ages 12/ 8° Murray 98

LEE, Dr G. C. Historical Jurisprudence $3 *n.* (12/6 *n.*) 8° Macmillan 00

A good sketch of legal systems from earliest to present times.

MAITLAND, Prf. F. W. English Law and the Renaissance 2/6 c 8° Camb. Press [01] 07

40 c. Putnam, *N.Y.* [Rede Lect.] *Vide* also his *Collected Papers*, 3 vols. [*ut* **F** § 1], and in *Social England*, *ut* **F** § 16.

POLLOCK (Sir F.) —*in his* Equity, etc., *ut* **D** § 42

* ,, + MAITLAND (F. W.) History of English Law before Edward I, 2 v. 40/ r 8° Camb. Pr. [95] 98

A very learned, scholarly, and luminous wk. setting forth the law as it stood at period betw. 1154 and 1272 (the age of GLANVILL and of BRACTON), in non-techn. lang., ill. by a wealth of first-hand knowledge and abundance of suggestion. 'Of all the centuries the twelfth is the most legal' and the middle of that cent. (the authors assert) was the most critical point in the developmt. of Eng. law. They are of opinion that the law wh. prevailed bef. coming of Normans was, in the main, pure Germanic, and are unable to assign any definite share to anc. Brit. law and custom.

REEVES, J. Hist. of Eng. Law, ed. W. F. Finlason, 3 vols. [Romans to end of Eliz.] 42/ 8° Reeves & Turner [1784–5] 69

ROSCOE, E. S. The Growth of English Law 7/6 8° Stevens 11

THAYER, Dr J. B. Legal Essays $3·50 8° Boston Bk. Co., *Boston* 09

*Internat. Usages*; DICEY'S *Engl. Const.*; *Bedingfield's Case*; *Trial by Jury of Things Supernatl.*: *Bracton's Note-Bk.*; etc.

WHITE, Archer M. Outlines of Legal History [student's-bk.] 7/6 c 8° Sonnenschein 95

WILSON, Sir R. K. History of Modern English Law *o.p.* [*pb.* 3/6] c 8° Longman [75]

*Gray's Inn; Staple Inn v.* **E** § 17; *Temple —for* Records of the Temple *v.* **E** § 17

*Anglo-Saxon and Anglo-Norman*

ADAM, H. [ed.] Essays in Anglo-Saxon Law *o.p.* [*pb.* 18/] *m* 8° Macmillan 76

Law courts, land and family law, procedure.

ALFRED the GREAT [9 cent.] Legal Code of: ed. Dr M. H. Turk $1 12° Ginn, *Boston* 93

LIEBERMANN, Dr F. [ed.] Quadripartitus: ein englisches Rechtsbuch d. 1114 4*m*.40 8° Niemeyer, *Halle* 91
A learned and elaborate wk. on MS. origins and date of Anglo-Norm. laws and charters (*i.e.* Latinized versn. of laws of A.-S. kings, w. texts of constit. ordinances and charters of their Norm. successors). Excellent notes and index.

,, [ed.] Die Gesetze der Angelsachsen, Pt. i 8*m*. 8° Niemeyer, *Halle* 98

,, [ed.] Consiliatio Cnuti: Uebertragung A.-S. Gesetze a. d. 12 Jahrh. 1*m*.20 8° Niemeyer, *Halle* 93

,, [ed.] Institutio Cnuti aliorumque Regum—*in* Transns. of Roy. Hist. Soc., 1893

,, [ed.] Ueber Pseudo-Cnuts Constitutiones de Foresta 1*m*.60 8° Niemeyer, *Halle* 94

,, [ed.] Ungedruckte anglo-normanische Geschichtsquellen 7*m*. 8° Trübner, *Strassbg.* 79

,, Ueber d. Leges Anglorum saec. xiii ineunte Londiniis collectae 3*m*. 8° Niemeyer, *Halle* 94
Traces the interpolatns. in so-called *Laws of Edw. Confessr. and Wm. i* to a lost archetype, wr. in rn. of John, whose chief object was to magnify the histor. importce. of City of London.

,, Ueber die Leges Edwardi Confessoris 3*m*.60 8° Niemeyer, *Halle* 96
Assigns the date of the MS. to the last five years of Henry i.

BIGELOW, M. M. [Am.] Hist. of Procedure in Engl. [Angl.-Norm.; 1066–1204] *o.p.* [*pb.* 16/] 8° Macmillan 80

,, Placita Anglo-Normannica [cases fr. monastic records] 18/ 8° Low 81

COOK, Prf. A. S. Extracts fr. Anglo-Saxon Laws [in orig. A.-S.] 50 c. 12° Heath, *N.Y.* 80

SCHMID, Reinh. [ed. & tr.] Die Gesetze der Angelsachsen, Pt. i [text and Germ. tr.] 19*m*.50 8° Brockhaus, *Leipzig* [32] 58

THORPE, Benj. [ed.] Ancient Laws & Institutions of Engl. 1 v. f° 40/ and 2 v. r 8° 30/ Rolls Series 40
Laws of the A.-S. Kings, w. tr.; of Edw. Confess.; of Wm. i, Henry i; *Monum. Ecclcs. Anglic.* fr. 7-10 cent.; and anc. Lat. versn. of A.-S. Laws.

*Twelfth to Fourteenth Centuries*

Azo —*v.* Bracton, *inf.*

BAILDON, W. P. [ed.] Select Civil Pleas, vol. i [1200–3] 28/ 4° Selden Soc. 90
Taken fr. same early plea-rolls as MAITLAND'S *Select Pleas of Crown*, now assigned to rn. of Hy. ii: mostly concerned w. real property.

,, [ed.] Select Cases in Chancery: 1364–1471 28/ 4° Selden Soc. 96
Throw light on connexion of Chanc. w. the Council, and their gradual separation.

BATESON, Mary. Borough Customs, 2 vols. ea. 28/ 4° Selden Soc. 04–6
A masterly analysis and digest of customary law of the boroughs and ports extendg. over whole of Middle Ages, largely based on unpubd. sources. Introd. on primitive laws embodied in the Local Custumals.

de BRACTON, H. [13 cent.] De Legibus Angliæ [1569]: ed. Sir T. Twiss, 6 v. ea. 10/ r 8° Rolls Ser. 78–83

,, Note Book, ed. Prf. F. W. Maitland, 3 vols. 63/ *n*. 8° Camb. Press 87
$25·20 Putnam, *N.Y.* A colln. of cases decided in King's Courts dur. rn. of Henry iii, annot. by (?) BRACTON.

,, Select Passages fr. Bracton & Azo, ed. F. W. Maitland 28/ 4° Selden Soc. 95
Those portions of BRACTON'S Note-Book wh. follow Azo's *Summa*, prtd. in parall. cols., the texts cited fr. *Code* and *Digest* in footnotes. Azo's *Summa* was at one time (as the proverb *Chi non ha Azzo non vada a Palazzo* still attests) a necessary possession of every Italian judge, and from it BRACTON is supposed to have drawn most of his knowledge of the Civil Law.

Güterbock, C. Bracton, and his Relation to Roman Law [tr.] $2 8° *Phila.* 66

FORTESCUE, Sir Jno. De Laudibus Legum Angliae; tr. F. Gregor; w. notes A. Amos $3 8° Clarke, *Cincin.* 74
A famous treatise. The 1st edn. was probably wr. dur. FORTESCUE'S exile in France, for guidance of young Prince Edward; w. notes.

GROSS, Prf. Chas. [ed.] Select Cases from Coroners Rolls: 1265–1413 28/ 4° Selden Soc. 96
With a valuable Introd. on office of Coroner (in wh. he differs fr. MAITLAND as to origin of the office, tracing it to an earlier date than the eyre of 1194,) appendices and Index. The Oxford rolls narrate some tragic consequences of the Town and Gown feud.

HALL, Hubert [ed.] Red Book of the Exchequer, Parts i–iii ea. 10/ r 8° Rolls Series 96

HUDSON, Rev. W. [ed.] Leet Jurisd. in City of Norwich, 13–14 cents. 28/ 4° Selden Soc. 92
Its chief value consists in early character of its evidence of workg. of frank-pledge syst. and on subj. of municip. devel. in a chartered borough, the orig. of munic. divisns., and on social, commerc., and judic. arrangemts. of 13 cent. in one of the largest cities in the kingdom.

MAITLAND, Prf. F. W. [ed.] Select Pleas of the Crown, vol. i [1220–5] 28/ 4° Selden Soc. 88
Seln. fr. earliest records of Engl. criminal justice, mostly felony: throws much light on manners and customs, and ill. the working of the ordeals of fire and water, showing how this was gradually replaced by trial by jury.

,, [ed.] Select Pleas in Manorial & other Signorial Cts., v. i Hy. iii & Edw. i] 28/ 4° Selden Soc. 89
Embraces whole legal life and much of social life of a medieval village.

,, [ed.] Pleas of the Crown for County of Gloucester: 1221 7/6 ($2·50) 8° Macmillan 84

,, + BAILDON, W. P. [eds.] The Court Baron; w. elab. pref. 28/ 4° Selden Soc. 91
Four bks. of preceds. and forms in manor. and other Cts. fr. MS. tracts on court-keeping, 'at least as old as Edw. ii's rn.'

Mirror of Justices: ed. W. J. Whittaker + Prf. F. W. Maitland 28/ 4° Selden Soc. 95
An excellent edn. of an early legal wk.: of legal curiosity rather than genuinely ill. developmt. of Engl. law. Ed. fr. unique MS. w. sparkling Introd. (55 pp.) by MAITLAND, dealg. w. (1) *date of comp.* [prob. betw. 1285 and 1290], (2) *object of its comp.* [partly to agitate for legal reform, partly 'a squib, a skit, a "topical" medley, a "variety entertainment" blended of truth and falsehood'], (3) *authorship*, [discussn. of evidence for (and agst.) Andr. HORN, a chamberlain of City of Lond. in or bef. 1328, a rather learned archivist and very imaginative historian],

Trench, W. F. Mirr. f. Magistrates: its orig. & influence [146 pp.] c 8° *priv. prin. Edin.* 98

Pleas for the Hundred of Swineshead and Bristol: 1221 8° *Bristol* 02

RIGG, J. M. [ed.] Select Pleas, Starrs, etc., of Jewish Exchequer: 1218–86 28/ c 4° Sweden Soc. 01
A valuable contribn. to hist. of the Engl. Jewry for 70 yrs. bef. their expulsion under Edw. i. Fr. the registry of deeds ('starrs') [in H.M. Record Off.] used by the *Justiciarii Judæorum*, who exerc. jurisdn. betw. Jews and Crown, and Jews and Christians.

Select Essays in Anglo-Amer. Legal History. By various Authors, 3 v. $12 *n*. r 8° Little & Brown, *Bost.* 08–9
Ea. 12/ *n*. Camb. Press. Repr. essays of perm. value fr. periodicals, etc. i: *Gen. Surveys*; ii–iii: *Hist. of Partic. Topics.*

TURNER, G. J. [ed.] Select Pleas of the Forests 28/ 4° Selden Soc. 99
Selns. fr. the little-known *Placita Forestae*, wh. begin w. rn. of JOHN. This vol. deals w. 13th cent. admin. of the Forests, their judges, officers, Courts-procedure, etc.; the beasts. chase, warren; hounds and implemts. of hunting, etc.

Year-Books of the Reign of Edw. i, yrs. 20–2, 30–5; Edw. iii, 11–9, ed. & tr. A. J. Horwood pts. i–ii ea. 10/ r 8° Rolls Series 63–06
Repts. in Norm.-Fch. of Common Law cases, forming to a great extent the 'lex non scripta' of England.

Year Books Series, vols. i–iv ea. 28/ 4° Selden Soc. 03–7 *in prg.*
i: 1 *and* 2 *Edw. II* (1307–9), ed. F. W. MAITLAND: text of these early Law Repts., tr., notes, Introd. on orig. of Law Repts. and anal. of Ang.-Fch. lang. in wh. the earliest Repts. were wr.; ii: 2 *and* 3 *Edw. II* (1308–10), ed. MAITLAND; iii: *Edw. II* (1309–10), ed. MAITLAND; w. dissertn. on the MSS., discussn. of the hist., paternity, trustworthiness, etc.; iv: *Edw. II* (1310), ed. MAITLAND + TURNER (G. J.), w. Introd. on the Cts. and judges of the period.

*Fifteenth and Sixteenth Centuries*

DASENT, J. R. [ed.] Acts of Privy Council of Engl., New Ser., v. i–xxxii ea. 10/ r 8° Rolls Ser. 90–07 *in prg*
Vol. i begins where NICOLAS [*ut inf.*] leaves off, in 1542; vol. xxxii ends w. 1604.

HAMILTON, A. H. A. Quarter Sessions from Queen Eliz. to Queen Anne 10/6 c 8° Low 78

LEACH, A. F. [ed.] Beverley Town Documents 28/ 4° Selden Soc. 00
Ill. the developmt. of munic. govt. in 14–15 cents., communal ownersh. of land, guilds, etc.

LEADHAM, I. S. [ed.] Select Cases in Court of Requests: 1497–1569 28/ 4° Selden Soc. 98
The Ct. of Requests (or 'Court of Conscience') was estab. by Hy. vii as a Ct. of Poor Men's Causes, but later took cognizance of all Equity suits or supplicns. to the Prince.

,, [ed.] Select Pleas of Court of Star Chamber, vol. i 28/ 4° Selden Soc. 02
Bills, Answers, Depositions, *etc.* Vol. i covers rn. of HENRY vii.

NICOLAS, Sir Harris [ed.] Proceedgs & Ordinces. of Privy Co. of Engl., 7 v. ea. 14/ r 8° Record Commrs. 34–7
Commences w. the year 1386 [10 RICHARD ii] and continues to 1542 [33 HENRY viii].

TURNER, G. J. [ed.] Select Pleas of the Forests 28/ c 4° Selden Soc. 01

*Seventeenth Century*

AXON, E. [ed.] Proceedings before Oswald Morley: 1616–23 Lanc. & Chesh. Rec. Soc. 02

RAINE, [Can.] J. [ed.] Seln. fr. Depositions in Crim. Cases bef. North. Magistrates 8° Surtees Soc. 61

SAUNDERS, Sir E. Reports of Pleadings and Cases in Kg's. Bench in rn. of Chas. II; w. notes Sir E. V. Williams, 3 vols. *o.p.* [*pb.* 84/] r 8° Benning [ ] 45

Williams, Sir E. V. Notes to Saunders' Reports, 2 vols. *o.p.* [*pb.* 50/] r 8° Stevens 71

*Nineteenth Century*

A Century of Law Reform 5/ *n.* c 8° Macmillan 01
12 lect. on the changes in law of Engl. dur. 19th cent., del. at Lincoln's Inn.

DICEY, Prf. A. V. Law and Public Opinion in Engld. in Nineteenth Century—*ut* **D** § 126

**Scottish** —*v. also* Yeatman, *supra*; *and in* Burton's *Hist. of Scotland*, *ut* **F** § 35

INNES, Cosmo Lectures on Scotch Legal Antiquities *o.p.* [*pb.* 10/6] 8° *Edinburgh* 72

**Indian**

MALABARI, Phiroze B. M. Bombay in the Making 12/6 *n.* 8° Unwin 10
A hist. of orig. and growth of judicial institns. in the Western Presidency from 1661 to 1726.

**American Colonies**

REINSCH, Prf. P. S. Engl. Common Law in Early American Colonies 50 c. 8° Univ. of Wisconsin 99

**United States:** *Supreme Court*

CARSON, H. L. History of Supreme Court of U.S. $10 r 8° Huber, *Phila.* 91

WILLOUGHBY, W. W. The Supreme Ct.: hist. & influence $1·25 8° Johns Hopk. Pr., *Baltimore* 90

**French**

MORIARTY, G. P. [tr.] Paris Law Courts: sk. of men and manners; 140 ill. 16/ 8° Seeley 93
Conts. pop. acc. of Fch. judic. syst., w. graphic and humor. sketches of scenes in Paris Cts.

**Russian**

KOVALESKY, Maxime Modern Customs and Ancient Laws of Russia—*ut* **F** § 5

**Slavonic**

SIGEL, Prf. F. Lectures on Slavonic Law [Ilchester Lects.] 5/ *n.* ($2) 8° Clar. Press 02

**Admiralty**

Monumenta Juridica: Black Book of Admiralty; ed. Sir T. Twiss, 4 vols. ea. 10/ i 8° Rolls Series 71–6
Contains the ancient ordinances and laws relating to the Navy.

MARSDEN, R. G. [ed.] Select Pleas in Ct. of Admiralty, 2 vols. 28/ 4° Selden Soc. 94–7
Vol. i is a colln. of cases, fr. 1525 onw. Edr. traces orig. of Adm. Ct. to period 1340–57, and describes and discusses that 'memorable record' the *Fasciculus de Superioritatis Maris* [A.D. 1339], on wh. the question largely turns. Vol. ii covers rns. of Edw. vi, Mary, and Elizab., illg. the for. policy of the last, the Armada, etc.

**Bar, The**

KELLY, B. W. Short History of English Bar 2/6 c 8° Sonnenschein 08
Orig. and growth of legal professn., esp. Inns of Ct., fr. days of 'Serjeant-Counters' to pres. time.

*Order of the Coif*

PULLING, A. The Order of the Coif; ill. 10/ 8° Clowes [84] 97
Conts. not merely a hist. of the Order of the Coif [a white silk cap wh. Sergs.-at-Law are supposed to wear in Ct.], but also much infonnn. on constitl. hist. of Engld., w. list of over 1,000 Judges and Sergs. of the Coif who made their mark in hist. of bench or bar.

**Common Law**

BRITTON, Bp Jno. Treat. on Common Law, compiled by ord. Edw. i: Fch. text, w. tr. & notes F. M. Nichols, 2 vols. *o.p.* 8° Clar. Press 65
An ancient treatise on the law, written in French, and attributed to John de Breton, Bp. of Hereford.

HALE, Sir Mat. [1609-76] History of the Common Law of England; w. notes C. Runnington [notes spec. valuable] *o.p.* 8° *London* [ ] 20

POLLOCK, Sir Fredk. The Expansion of the Common Law 6/ 8° Stevens 04

YEATMAN, J. P. History of Common Law of Gt. Britain & Gaul *o.p.* [*pb.* 6/] p 8° Longman 74

**Constitutional History** —*v.* **D** § 140

**Court of Chancery**

GILBERT, L'd Chf. Bar. Jeff. Forum Romanum, ed. S. Tylor [Am.] $4 8° Morrison, *Washington* [1758] 74
Engl. edn. *o.p.* The history and practice of the High Court of Chancery.

KERLY, D. M. Hist. Sketch of Equit. Jurisd. of Ct. of Chancery 12/6 8° Camb. Press 90
$3 *n.* Putnam, *N.Y.* [Yorke Prize E.] Its main object is to show how the King's Chancellor came in time to be a great judge, and what were the forces wh. compelled, or enabled, him to create the great system of equity as distinguished fr. ordinary or 'common' law.

ROBINSON, Conway Hist. of Ct. of Chancery & other Instits. of Engl., vol. i $7·50 *n.* r 12° Randolph, *Richmond, Va.* 82
36/ Stevens. Commences w. time of Cæsar and ends w. d. of Hy. viii; vol. ii to continue the wk. to accession of Wm. and Mary.

**Law Merchant**

GROSS, Prf. C. [ed.] Select Cases conc. the Law Merchant: 1270-1638, vol. i Selden Soc. 08
Cases tried in fair, staple, and tolsey Cts., the 3 kinds of local tribunals in which the law merchant was chiefly admin. Introd. devoted mainly to origin, developmt., and decline of the fair-courts. Glossary and indices.

MITCHELL, W. Essay on the Early Hist. of the Law Merchant 4/ *n.* c 8° Camb. Press 04
$1·25 *n.* Putnam, *N.Y.* [Yorke Prize Essay.]

**Law Reports**

DANIELL, W. T. S. History of Origin of the Law Reports 10/ r 8° Clowes 84

**Law Society [solicitors]**

FRESHFIELD, Edwin Records of the Law Society 8° Incorp. Law Soc. 99

MACDONELL, Dr Jno. Judicial Statistics, England & Wales, 2 Pts. 8° Eyre & Spottiswoode -97

**Trial by Combat**

COCKBURN, Dr Jno. —*in his* History of Duels, *ut* **F** § 14

NEILSON, Geo. Trial by Combat 7/6 *n.* c 8° Hodge, *Glasgow* 90
A good popular histor. sketch of the duel as a legal instit.—a mode of trial—in Gt. Brit., full of interesting cases; the first Engl. monograph on subj.

**Trial by Jury** —*v. also* **D** § 135

FORSYTH, Wm. Hist. of Trial by Jury, ed. J. A. Morgan [Engl. edn. *o.p.*] $3·50 8° Cockcroft, *N.Y.* [52] 75

LESSER, M. A. Histor. Developmt. of Jury System $2·50 8° Lawyers' Co-op. Pb. Co., *Rochester, N.Y.* 94

**Commons**—*v.* **D** § 78
**Consideration**—*v.* **D** § 29
**Contract**—*v.* **D** § 110
**Lord High Steward**—*v.* **D** § 27
**Peerage Law**—*v.* **D** § 27
**Property, Real and Personal** —*v.* **D** § 78, 119
**Roman Law**—*v.* **D** § 110
**Tithes**—*v.* **A** § 111
**Title to Realty**—*v.* **D** § 78

## 6: TRIALS

**Collectively**

ATLAY, J. B. Famous Trials of the Century; ports. 6/ c 8° Richards 99
$1·75 Stone, *Chicago.* The Tichborne case occupies half the book: it also includes the Burke and Hare case; Weare *v.* Thurtell; The King against Courvoisier; Barber's case; The Queen against Dr Pritchard, etc.

BURNABY, Evelyn Memories of Celebrated Trials 7/6 *n.* 8° Sisley 07

CLINTON, H. L. Celebrated Trials $2·50 c 8° Harper 97

DEANS, R. S. Notable Trials: romances of law courts; ill. 6/ c 8° Cassell 06
Short narratives of 19 cases fr. last 3 cents., as diverse as Rex *v.* Hampden and trial of Chas. Peace.

DUFFY (T.) + CUMMINGS (T. J.) Remarkable Trials of All Countries: fr. offic. sources $3·50 8° Ward & Peloubet, *N.Y.* 73

MORSE, J. T., jun. [ed.] Famous Trials $2·25 12° Little & Brown, *Boston* 74

*Divorce Court*

FENN, H. E. Thirty-five Years in the Divorce Court [cases; practice] 10/6 *n.* 8° Laurie 10

*Jury Trials*

DONOVAN, Judge J. W. Modern Jury Trials $4·50 8° Banks, *N.Y.* [83] 08

*Naval and Military*

BURKE, P. [ed.] Celebrated Naval and Military Trials 10/6 p 8° W. H. Allen [65]

*Poison, Murders by*

BROWNE (G. L.) + STEWART (C. G.) [eds.] Reports of Trials for Murder by Poison 12/6 8° Stevens 83

*State Trials*

BROWNE, G. L. [ed.] Narrative of State Trials in 19 Cent., Ser. i [1801–30], 2 v. 26/ c 8° Low 82

BUND, Prf. J. Willis [ed.] Seln. of State Trials [for treason], 3 v. [1327–1681] 30/ c 8° Camb. Press 80–2

DEANS, R. S. The Trials of Five Queens 10/6 *n.* 8° Methuen 09
A study of the trials of KATH. OF ARAGON, ANNE BOLEYN, MARY OF SCOTS, MARIE ANTOINETTE, CAROLINE OF BRUNSWICK.

HOWELL, T. B. [ed.] State Trials; ed. Jardine, 34 v. [earliest per. to 1826] *o.p.* [*w.* £15] r 8° *Lond.* 09–28

MACDONELL (J.) + WALLIS (J. E. P.) [eds.] Repts. of State Trials, New Ser., vols. i–viii
ea. 10/ *n.* 8° Eyre & Spottiswoode 88–98, *in prg.*
Well ed., w. very numerous references and short notes.

STEPHEN, H. L. [ed.] State Trials, Political and Social, 4 vols. 10/ *n.* f 8° Duckworth 99–02
Raleigh; Charles I; Regicides; Col. Turner, etc.; Suffolk Witches; Alice Lisle; Lord Russell: Earl of Warwick; Spencer Cowper, etc.; Samuel Goodere, etc.; Earl of Essex; Capt. Lee; John Perry; Green, etc.; Ct. Coningsmark; Beau Fielding; Annesley; Carter, Macdaniell; Barnard; Byron.

TOUT (T. F.) + JOHNSTONE (H.) [eds.] State Trials [1289–93] 06

TOWNSEND, W. C. [ed.] Modern State Trials, revised & ill., 2 v. [1814–48] *o.p.* [*pb.* 30/] 8° Longman 50

*Witchcraft* —*v.* **B** § 5

**Scotland**

COCKBURN, Lord [ed.] Exam. of Trials for Sedition in Scotl. [1793–1849] 28/ 8° Douglas, *Edin.* 88

Notable English Trials: vol. i: Fritz Müller. By H. B. Irving 5/ *n.* 8° Hodges, *Glasgow* 11

Notable Scottish Trials: w. Introds., etc. ea. 5/ *n.* 8° Hodge, *Glasgow in prg.*
*Brodie (Deacon)* ed. Wm. ROUGHEAD | *Chantrelle (Eugene M.)* ed. A. Duncan SMITH | *City of Glasgow Bank Directors* ed. Wm. WALLACE | *Douglas Case (The)* ed. A. F. STEUART | *Lovat (Lord)* ed. D. N. MACKAY, *in prep.* | *Monson (A. J.)* ed. Jno. W. MORE | *Porteous (Capt.)* ed. ROUGHEAD | *Pritchard (Dr E.)* ed. ROUGHEAD | *Slater (Oscar)* ed. ROUGHEAD | *Smith (Madeleine)* ed. SMITH | *Stewart (Jas.)* [The Appin murder] ed. MACKAY
The trial on wh. STEVENSON based *Kidnapped* and which he used for *Catriona.*

PITCAIRN, Rob. [ed.] Ancient Criminal Trials in Scotland, 7 vols. 4° Bannatyne Cb. 29–33
The best edn., w. Suppl. and Index. Only 100 printed. Undertaken at suggestn. of Sir W. SCOTT, several of whose plots and scenes are drawn fr. them. Covers period–1488–1624, *i.e.*, rns. of Jas. iv–v, Mary Q. of Scots, and Jas. vi. Also in Maitland Club pubns.

**India**

GHOSAL (J.) Celebrated Trials in India, vol. i 4/6 *n.* r 8° Luzac

**France and Germany**

FULLER, H. W. [ed.] Noted French Trials [impostors and adventurers] $1 8° Soule, *Boston* 82

FEUERBACH, A. R. [ed.] Germ. Criminal Trials, tr. L'y Duff Gordon [Eng. edn. *o.p.*] $1 12° Harper, *N.Y.*

**United States**

WHARTON, F. [ed.] State Trials of U.S. dur. Admins. of Washington & Adams $7·50 8° W. C. Little, *Albany* 49

*Baroda Case:* The Great Baroda Case 6/ r 8° Luzac
A full Rept. of procgs. of the trial and depositn. of H. H. MULHAR RAO GAEKWAR of Baroda for instigtg. attempt to poison Brit. Resid. at his Ct.

*City of Glasgow Bank:* COUPER, C. T. [ed.] Rep. of Trial agnst. Directors 10/6 8° *Edinburgh* 79

*Dreyfus:* —*v.* **A** § 12, *s.v.* Anti-Semitism

*Overend & Gurney:* FINLASON, W. F. [ed.] Report of Case 10/6 8° Stevens 70

*Parnell Commission:* [Parnell *v.* 'Times' Opening Speech, del. by Sir Chas. Russell 6*d.* 8° Macmillan [89] 89

*Tichborne Case:* COCKBURN's Charge [*in re* Castro], 2 vols. *o.p.* [*pb.* 63/] r 8° Sweet 75

" Report of the Case, 9 vols. [*v. also* Kenealy, *inf.*] *o.p.* r 8° 75

## 7: LEGAL BIOGRAPHY, incl. LETTERS, SPEECHES, REMINISCENCES, etc.

**Collectively**

ANDREWS, W. [ed.] The Lawyer in History, Literature and Humour 7/6 8° Andrews, *Hull* 96
A medley of instruction and amusement, of legal archæology and legal anecdote, by var. writers.

BROWNE, Irving [ed.] Law and Lawyers in Literature [extrs. fr. liter.] $1·50 12° Soule, *Boston* 83

" Short Studies of Great Lawyers $2 c 8° Law Jl., *Albany* 78

FORSYTH, Wm. History of Lawyers [Engl. edn. *o.p.*] $3·50 8° Cockcroft, *N.Y.* 75

SNYDER, W. L. Great Opinions by Great Judges $4·50 r 8° Baker, *N.Y.* 83

" [ed.] Great Speeches by Great Lawyers $4·50 8° Baker, *N.Y.* 81

*England*

ATLAY, J. B. Victorian Chancellors, vols. i–ii [ea. $4 *n.* Little & B., *Bost.*] ea. 14/ *n.* 8° Smith & Elder 06–8

CAMPBELL, L'd J. Lives of Lord Chancellors & Keepers of Gt. Seal, 10 v. ea. 6/ p 8° Murray [45–8] 81
From Saxon times to the death of Lord ELDON, in 1838. Incl. LYNDHURST and BROUGHAM.

,, Lives of Chief Justices of England, 4 vols. ea. 6/ p 8° Murray [49–57] 81
5 vols. $25 Thompson, *Northport, L.I.* From the Norman Conquest to the death of Lord TENTERDEN.

CHRISTIAN, E. B. V. A Short History of Solicitors 6/ c 8° Reeves & Turner 96

,, Leaves of the Lower Branch ; ill. 6/ *n.* c 8° Smith & Elder 09
A modest apology for attorneys (since 1875 solicitors), with passages from novels, etc., dealing with them.

FOSS, E. Lives of the Judges of England, 9 vols. [1068–1853] *o.p.* 8° Murray 48–64

,, Biographia Juridica *o.p.* [*pb.* 21/] r 8° Murray 70
An abridgment of above, in alphabetical dictionary form, carried on to 1870.

FOSTER, Jos. Men at the Bar: biogr. h'dlist of Inns of Court 31/6 i 8° Reeves & Turner 85

HARDY, Sir T. D. Catal. of L'ds Chanc., K'pers of Gt. Seal, M'rs of Rolls, etc. 20/ r 8° Butterworth 43

HOLLAMS, Sir J. Jottings of an Old Solicitor 8/ *n.* 8° Macmillan 06

HUTCHINSON, J. Catalogue of Notable Middle Templars: 1501–1901 10/6 *n.* r 8° Butterworth 02

JAMES, Croake Curiosities of Law and Lawyers 7/6 8° Low [82] 91

JEAFFRESON, J. C. A Book about Lawyers, 2 vols. [chatty] *o.p.* [*pb.* 24/] 8° Hurst 67

MANSON, Edw. Builders of Law dur. rn. of Victoria [35 Judges] 10/6 8° Cox [96] 04

ROBINSON, Serj. Bench and Bar: reminiscences 6/ c 8° Hurst [89] 91

TOWNSEND, W. C. Lives of Twelve Emin. Judges of Last Cent., 2 v. *o.p.* [*pb.* 28/] 8° Longman 46

WATT, F. Terrors of the Law ; ports. 4/6 *n.* c 8° Lane 02
Repr. articles on Judge JEFFREYS, MACKENZIE, and BRANFIELD.

WELSBY, W. S. Lives of Emin. Engl. Judges of 18 and 19 Cents., 2 v. *o.p.* [*pb.* 14/] 8° Sweet 46

WOOLRYCH M. W. Lives of Eminent Serjeants-at Law, 2 vols. *o.p.* [*pb.* 30/ 8° W. H. Allen 69

*Scotland:* COWAN (S.) The Lord Chancellors of Scotl. ; 2 v. [to the Union] 21/ *n.* 8° Johnston, *Edin.* 11

OMOND, G. W. T. The Lord Advocates of Scotland, 2 v. [1600–1832] 28/ 8° Douglas, *Edin.* 83
From close of 15 cent. to passing of Reform Bill. Enlivened by accs. of trials in wh. the Advocates played a part, and glimpses of the ways of Scotsmen at various periods. A good contrib. to Scottish history.

STEWART, Chas. Legal Life in Edinburgh and London, 1850–1900 7/6 Blackwood 01
Sketches of eminent members of the Scottish Bar.

*Ireland*

BURKE, O. J. Lives of the Chancellors of Ireland [1186–1874] 12/6 8° Hodges, *Dublin* 75

O'FLANAGAN, J. R. Lives of L'd Chancs. & Kprs. of Gt. Seal of Irel., 2 v. [to Vict.] *o.p.* [*pb.* 36/] 8° Longman 70

SHEIL, R. L. Sketches of the Irish Bar, 2 vols. ; w. notes R. S. Mackenzie $3 12° Widdleton, *N.Y.* [ ]

*United States*

BAY, W. V. N. Reminiscences of Bench and Bar of Missouri $3 8° Soule, *St Louis* 78

BELL, C. H. Bench and Bar of New Hampshire $6 8° Houghton, *Boston* 93

BIGELOW, L. J. Bench and Bar [wit and humour] $2 c 8° Harper, *N.Y* [71] 7–

BINNEY, H. Leaders of the Old Bar of Philadelphia *o.p.* [*pb.* $5] 8° Campbell, *Phila.* 66

DONOVAN, J. W. Tact in Court: cases won by skill, wit, courage, *etc.* $1 12° Williamson, *Rochester, N.Y.* [85] 90

FLANDERS, H. Lives of Chief Justices of U.S. Supr. Ct., 2 vols. $7 8° Cockcroft, *N.Y.* [55] 57

FOOTE, H. S. Bench and Bar of the South and South West $2 8° Soule, *St Louis* 76

LEWIS, W. D. [ed.] Great Amer. Lawyers, v. i ; ports. [to occupy 8 v.] ea. $7·50 *n.* 8° Winston, *Phila.* 07

LYNCH, J. D. Bench and Bar of Mississippi $5 8° Hale, *N.Y.* 81

PROCTOR, L. B. Bench and Bar of New York *o.p.* [*pb.* $5·50 8° Ward & Peloubet, *N.Y.* 70

van SANTVOORD, G. Lives & Services of Chf. Justices of U.S. *o.p.* [*pb.* $3·50] 8° Scribner, *N.Y.* 54

SHUCK, Oscar T. Bench and Bar in California $5 Occidental Pb. Co., *San Franc.* 89

## Individually

ABINGER, L'd [1769–1844] Memoir of. By P. C. Scarlett [son] 15/ 8° Murray 77

ACLAND, Sir Henry Memoir of. By J. B. Atlay 14/ *n.* 8° Smith & Elder 03

ANDERSON, J. H. An Inverness Lawyer & his sons: 1796–1878 5/ c 8° Univ. Press, *Aberdeen* 00

BALLANTYNE, Serj. [1812–87] Some Experiences of a Barrister's Career [autobiogr.] *o. p.* [*pb.* 2/6] c 8° Bentley [82] 89

,, The Old World and the New [continuation of above] *o.p.* [*pb.* 14/] 8° Bentley 85

BELLASIS, Serj. [1800–73] Memorials of. By Edw. Bellasis—*ut* **A** § 98
The first chapter only is devoted to his early life and legal career.

BINNEY, Hor. [1780–1875] Life of. By C. C. Binney [g'son] $3 *n.* 8° Lippincott, *Phila.* 03
BINNEY was prob. the leading lawyer in U.S. for several years before 1850, and regarded as the first citizen of Philadelphia for nearly the latter half of his long life. He sat in the 23rd Congress on the Anti-Jackson ticket.

BLACKBURNE, F. [1782–1867] Life of. By Edw. Blackburne [son] *o.p.* [*pb.* 12/] 8° Macmillan 75

BOWEN, L'd [1835–94] Biographical Sketch of. By Sir H. S. Cunningham 10/6 f 4° Murray 97
Previously pubd. in a smaller form for private circulation.

BRAMWELL, L'd [1808–92]
Fairfield, C. Some Account of Baron Bramwell 10/ *n.* 8° Macmillan 98
Manson, Edw. [ed.] Bramwelliana: wit and wisdom of Lord Bramwell 2/ *n.* c 8° Clowes 92

BRAMPTON, Lord —*v.* Hawkins, Sir Hy.

BROUGHAM, L'd [1779–1869] Lives of Brougham & Lyndhurst. By L'd Campbell *o.p.* [*pb.* 16/] 8° Murray 69

BURKE, Edm. [1729–97] —*v.* **F** § 25

BUTLER, Gen. B. F. Autobiography and Personal Reminiscences—*ut* **F** § 75

CAMPBELL, L'd [1779–1861] Life & Letters, ed. Hon. Mrs Hardcastle [dau.], 2 v. 30/ 8° Murray [81] 81

COCKBURN, L'd [1779–1854] Memorials of his Time, ed. H. A. Cockburn [g'son]; col. ports. 6/ *n.* 8° Foulis, *Edin.* [56] 09
Cockburn, the Scottish Judge and Solicitor-General under the Grey Ministry in 1830, belonged to the coterie of SCOTT, Sydney SMITH, BROUGHAM, etc.
,, Circuit Journeys 6/ c 8° Douglas, *Edin.* [88] 89
Impressns. of Scottish life and scenery 1837–54, interspersed w. records of vile or insane deeds and the curious idiosyncrasies of their perpetrators.

COKE, Sir Edw. [1552–1634] Life of. By C. W. Johnson, 2 vols. *o.p.* [*pb.* 28/] 8° Colburn 37

COLERIDGE, L'd [1820–94] Life & Correspondence, ed. E. H. Coleridge, 2 vols. 30/ *n.* 8° Heinemann 04
A life of the Lord Chief Justice, of great importance for the hist. of the latter half of 19 cent.
Fishback, W. P. Recollections of Lord Coleridge $1·25 12° Bowen, *Indianapolis* 95

CRISPE, T. E. Reminiscences of a K.C.; 2 ports. 10/6 *n.* 8° Methuen 09
Begins w. London life in the 'fifties. Full of racy anecdotes.

CURRAN, J. P. [1750–1817] Speeches while at Bar, ed. J. A. L. Whittier $3·50 8° Callaghan, *Chicago* [44] 73
Curran, W. H. [son] Life of J. P. Curran; w. notes R. S. Mackenzie $1·75 c 8° Widdleton, *N.Y.* [19] 55
Davis, Thos. Life of the Rt. Hon. J. P. Curran *o.p.* 8° *Dublin* 46
Phillipps, C. Memoir of Curran & his Contemporaries *o.p.* [*pb.* 7/6] c 8° Blackwood [18] 57
,, Life and Speeches of Curran *o.p.* 8° *London* [05] 57

CUTLER, Judge Ephr. [1767–1853] Life & Times of: ed. Julia P. Cutler [dau.] $2·50 8° Clarke, *Cinc.* 90

DALRYMPLE, Sir J. [*d.* 1810] Memoir of. By A. J. G. Mackay *o.p.* [*pb.* 12/] 8° Douglas, *Edin.* 73

DANA, R. H., jun. [1815–82] R. H. Dana: a biography. By C. F. Adams, 2 v. c $4 8° Houghton, *Bost.* 90
Mr DANA, a prominent member of the Boston bar, was also author of the well-known bk. *Two Yrs. before the Mast*, a record of a voyage he made before the mast as a seaman on the brig *Pilgrim* round Cape Horn to W. coast of N. Amer. (an excellent personal narr. of a sailor's life at sea).

DENMAN, L'd [1779–1815] Memoir of. By Sir J. Arnould, 2 vols. *o.p.* [*pb.* 32/] 8° Longman 73

ELDON, L'd-Chc. [1751–1838] Public & Private Life of. By [Sir] H. Twiss, 2 v. *o.p.* [*pb.* 21/] p 8° Murray [44] 44

ERSKINE, L'd [1750–1823] Speeches at Bar & in Parl.; mem. by L'd Brougham, 4 v. *o.p.* [*pb.* 42/] 8° Ridgway 47

FIELD, Dav. Dudley Life of. By Rev. H. M. Field $3 8° Scribner, *N.Y.* 98
FIELD was a great codifier of the N.Y. State Laws.

HARDWICKE, L'd [1690–1764] Life of. By G. Harris, 3 vols. *o.p.* 8° Moxon 47

HATHERLEY, L'd [1801–81] Memoir of. By Rev. W. R. W. Stephens *o.p.* [*pb.* 21/] c 8° Bentley 83

HAWKINS, Sir Hy. [Bar. BRAMPTON; 1817–1907] Reminiscences, ed. R. Harris [Cheap Ed. 1/ *n.* Nelson] 6/ c 8° Arnold [04] 05

HOLLAMS, Sir Jno. Jottings of an Old Solicitor 8/ *n.* 8° Murray 06

INGLIS, Jno. [Lord-Justice General of Scotl.; 1810–91]
Watt, J. Crabb John Inglis: a memoir 15/ *n.* r 8° Green, *Edin.* 93
A somewhat inadequate biogr. of the greatest of Scottish judges, whose fame as an advocate was chiefly made by his famous and successful defence (1857) of Madeleine SMITH, charged w. poisoning her paramour (the address to the jury is given in one of the Appendices).

JAY, Jno. [1745–1829; 1st Chf.-Just. of U.S.]—*v.* **F** § 74

JEFFREY, L'd [1773–1850] Life of. By Lord Cockburn, w. sel. of corresp. 5/ c 8° Black [52] 74

JEFFREYS, Judge [1648–86] Life. By H. B. Irving 12/6 *n.* 8° Heinemann 98

KENEALY, Dr E. V. [1819–80] Life of. By Arabella Kenealy [dau.] 16/ *n.* 8° Long 08

KENT, Jas. Memoir and Letters, ed. W. Kent $2·50 12° Little & Brown, *Boston* 98

KENYON, L'd [1732–1802] Life of *o.p.* [*pb.* 14/] 8° Longman 73

KERR, Commr. Commr. Kerr, an Individuality. By G. Pitt-Lewis 10/6 *n.* 8° Unwin 03

LOCKWOOD, Sir Fk. [1846–97] Biographical Sketch of. By A. Birrell; ill. 10/6 8° Smith & Elder 98

LYNDHURST, L'd [1772–1863] Life of. By Sir Theodore Martin *o.p.* [*pb.* 16/] 8° Murray 84
,, Lives of Brougham & Lyndhurst. By Lord. Campbell *o.p.* [*pb.* 16/] 8° Murray 69
MAULE, Sir Wm. Early Life of. By Emma Leathley [niece] *o.p.* [*pb.* 7/6] c 8° Bentley 72
NORTHS, The [1640–83] Lives of. By Roger North—*ut* **F** § 24
PLOWDEN, A. C. Grain or Chaff: the autobiography of a police magistrate 16/ *n.* 8° Unwin 03
POLLOCK, Sir W. F. Personal Reminiscences, 2 vols. 16/ c 8° Macmillan 88
RUSSELL, L'd [1832–1900] Life of. By R. B. O'Brien [Cheap Ed. 1/ *n.* Nelson] 10/6 *n.* r 8° Smith & E. 01
SCOTT, Jas. Hope Memoirs of. By Prf. R. Ornsby, 2 vols. *o.p.* [*pb.* 24/] 8° Murray [82] 84
SELBORNE, Roundell Palmer, Earl of [1812–95] Memorials, Pt. i: Family and Personal [1766–1865], 2 vols.; ill. 25/ *n.* 8° Macmillan 96
SETON, Alex. [Chanc. of Scotl., 1555–1622] Memoir of. By G. Seton 21/ s 4° Blackwood 82
STEPHEN, Sir J. Fitzjames [1829–94] Life of. By Leslie Stephen [bro.] 16/ 8° Smith & Elder 95
$4·50 Putnam, *N.Y.* Throws light on characteristics and movemts. of intellectual life in 2nd half of 19 cent.
WESTBURY, L'd Life of. Ed. T. A. Nash; 2 vols. *o.p.* [*pb.* 30/] 8° Bentley 88
WETMORE, William His Story and His Friends. By Hy. James 24/ *n.* 8° Blackwood 03
WILLIAMS, Montagu S. [1835–92] Leaves of a Life [reminiscences] 2/6 c 8° Macmillan [90] 90
,, Round London—*ut* **D** § 127

---

# V: Special Departments of Law

## 8: ADMINISTRATIVE LAW

**Comparative** —*v.* **D** § 139 (GOODNOW) and **D** § 134 (WILSON)

**Great Britain** —*for* Constitutional Law *v.* **D** § 27

*ROBERTSON, G. S. Law and Practice of Civil Proceedings by and against the Crown and Depts. of Govt. 38/ r 8° Stevens 08
Bk. i deals w. law affectg. partic. Govt. depts., ii w. proceedgs. on Revenue side of K.B. Div., iii w. Petition of Right, iv w. escheat, v w. 'other civil procgs. in wh. Crown participates', vi is 'Points of Practice and Procedure', vii covers actns. agst. executive officers of the govt.

*Military Forces: Relation to the Crown*—*v.* **D** § 64 (CLODE)

*Peerage Law* —*v.* **D** § 27

*Petition of Right* —*v.* **D** § 109 (CLODE)

**India**

KINNEY, A. Handbook of Administrative Law of India 12/ *n.* 8° Thacker 10
GOODNOW, Prf. F. J. Principles of Administrative Law of U.S. $3 *n.* (12/6 *n.*) 8° Putnam 05

## 8*: ADVERTISEMENTS

JONES, T. A. The Law relating to Advertisements 5/ *n.* c 8° Butterworth 06

**United States**

CHAPMAN, Clowry Law of Advertising and Sales, 2 vols. $10 8° Chapman, *Denver* 00

## 9: AFFILIATION

BOTT, W. H. Law and Pract. of Affiliation Proceed.; w, statutes, etc. 6/ c 8° Stevens 94
LUSHINGTON, G. Law of Affiliation and Bastardy [useful] 6/6 c 8° Butterworth [97] 04
,, S. G. + G. [eds.] Summary Jurisdiction (Married Women) Act, 1895 5/ *n.* c 8° Butterworth [96] 04
MARTIN, T. C. + G. T. Law of Maintenance & Desertn. & Orders in Bastardy 9/ 8° Stevens [86] 10
SAUNDERS, T. W. + W. E. Law and Practice of Orders of Affiliation and Proceedings in Bastardy [a full treatise] 6/6 c 8° H. Cox [6–] 99

## 10: AGENCY—*v. also* D § 29, D § 40

BOWSTEAD, W. Digest of the Law of Agency 18/ 8° Sweet [96] 09
CAMPBELL, R. Laws rel. to Sale of Goods, and Commerc. Agency 32/ r 8° Stevens [81] 91
*EVANS, W. Law of Principal & Agent in Contract & Tort *o.p.* [*pb.* 30/] 8° Sweet [78] 87
PORTER, J. B. Law of Principal and Agent 10/6 8° Stevens & Haynes 05
WOODYATT, R. G. The Law of Agency 8/6 8° Stevens 00
WRIGHT, E. B. Law of Principal and Agent [a handy text-bk.] 18/ 8° Stevens [94] 01

**United States**

CLARK (W. L.) + SYKES (H. H.) The Law of Agency, 2 vols. $12 8° Keefe, *St Paul, Minn.* 05
HUFFCUT, E. W. Law of Agency [incl. Master & Servt.] $3 8° Little & Brown, *Boston* [95] 01
,, [ed.] Cases in the Law of Agency $3 *n.* 8° Little & Brown, *Boston* 96
MECHEM, Floyd R. Treatise on the Law of Agency $6 8° Callaghan, *Chicago* 89
,, Outlines of the Law of Agency $2 8° Callaghan, *Chicago* [01] 03
,, [ed.] Cases on the Law of Agency $4 8° Callaghan, *Chicago* 93
PAIGE, J. [ed.] Illustrative Cases in Agency [w. anal. & citatns.] $2 8° Johnson, *Phila.* 95
*STORY, J. Commentaries on Law of Agency, ed. C. P. Greenough $6 8° Little & Brown, *Boston* [39] 82
TIFFANY, F. B. Handbook of Law of Principal & Agent $3·75 8° West Pb. Co., *St Paul, Minn.* 03
WAMBAUGH, E. [ed.] Selection of Cases on Agency $6 *n.* 8° *Harvard Law Rev.* Pb. Ass., *Camb.* 96
WHARTON, Fcs. Commentary on Law of Agency and Agents $6·50 8° Kay, *Phila.* 76

**Commission Agent**

DANIELS, G. St L. [ed.] Compendium of Commission Cases 8° E. P. Wilson [ ] 00
EVANS, W. Law rel. to Remuneration of Commiss. Agents, ed. W. de B. Herbert 7/6 c 8° Cox [91] 00
GIVEEN, H. M. Law relating to Commission Agents 2/6 12° Clement Wilson 98
Espec. auctioneers, estate- and house-agents, and public-house brokers.

**Election Agents** —*v.* **D** § 40

**Power of Attorney ; Proxy**

MACKENZIE, V. St C. Law rel. to Powers of Attorney and Proxies 3/6 c 8° E. Wilson 03

**AGREEMENTS**—*v.* **D** § 29 **ALIENS**—*v.* **D** § 68 **ALIMONY**—*v.* **D** § 59 **ANCIENT LIGHTS**—*v.* **D** § 78

## 11 : ANIMALS—*v. also* D § 87

INGHAM, J. H. Treatise on Property in Animals, Wild and Domestic, and Rts. and Responsibs. arising therefrom [25/ *n.* Stevens] $6 *n.* r 8° Johnson *Phila.* 00

**Prevention of Cruelty to Animals**

BURTON (P. M.) + SCOTT (G. H. G.) Law rel. to Preventn. of Cruelty to Animals 3/6 *n.* c 8° Murray 06

**APPRENTICES**—*v.* **D** § 61

## 12 : ARBITRATION AND AWARD ; REFERENCES

CREWE, W. O. Law of Arbitration 8/6 p 8° Clowes [ ] 98
FLETCHER, Prf. B. F. + H. P. Law of Arbitrations : text-bk. for surveyors 5/6 c 8° Batsford [75] 04
GREGORY, C. C. Engineer or Architect as Arbitrator betw. Employer and Contractor [and his other functions] 12/6 8° Clowes 01
LYNCH, H. F. Redress by Arbitration [a digest] 5/ *n.* 8° E. Wilson [88] 92
REDMAN, J. H. Law of Arbitrns. & Awards [w. preceds. & stats.] 18/ 8° Butterworth [72] 03
RUDALL, A. R. Duties and Powers of an Arbitrator 4/ *n.* c 8° E. Wilson 07
*RUSSELL, F. + H. Power and Duty of Arbitrator and of Submissions and Awards, ed. E. + H. W. Pollock 30/ 8° Sweet [52] 06
SLATER, J. Law of Arbitration and Awards 6/6 8° Stevens & Haynes 05

**Scotland**

BELL, J. M. Treatise on the Law of Arbitration in Scotland 21/ r 8° *Edinburgh* [61] 77
INNES (J. C.) + MELVILLE (R. D.) Law of Arbitration in Scotland 25/ *n.* r 8° Green, *Edin.* 03
WOOD (J. P.) + MACPHAIL The Law of Arbitration in Scotland 10/ r 8° Green, *Edin.* 00

**India**

BANERJEE, D. C. The Law of Arbitration in India 14/ *n.* 8° (*India*) 08

**United States**

FISHER, R. W. Principles of Law of Arbitration and Award $1 c 8° West Pb. Co., *St Paul, Minn.* 96
HOFFMAN, M. The Law and Practice as to References $6·50 8° Ward & Peloubet, *N.Y.* 75
MORSE, J. T. On Arbitration and Award $6 8° Little & Brown, *Boston* 72

**Chamber of Arbitration**

SALAMAN, J. S. Arbitrator's Manual under Chamber of Arbitration 3/6 f 8° Heinemann 92
SHEARMAN (M.) + HAYCRAFT (T. W.) London Chamber of Arbitratn. : law & practice 2/6 *n.* 8° E. Wilson 93

**Industrial Conciliation and Arbitration**—*v.* **D** § 118

## ASSIGNMENTS, VOLUNTARY—*v.* D § 17; ARCHITECTS—*v.* D § 20

## 13 : AUCTIONS AND AUCTIONEERS

BATEMAN, J. Law of Auctions, ed. Graham Mould [$5 Soule, *Phila.*] 12/6 8° *Estate Gaz.* Off. [46] 08
,, Auctioneer's Guide, ed. Graham Mould 15/ 8° Sweet [46] 09
HART, Heber Law rel. to Auctioneers, House-Agents, Valuers & Commission 15/ 8° Stevens [ ] 03
SQUIBBS, R. Auctioneers, their Duties and Liabilities 12/6 8° Lockwood [79] 91

## 14 : AUDITORS

PIXLEY, F. W. Auditors, their Duties and Responsibilities, 2 Pts. ea. 20/ *n.* 8° Good [81] 06–06
Pt. i : *Under Companies Acts and other Acts of Parliament* ; Pt. ii : *Under Local Govt. Acts.*

## 15 : BAILMENTS

BEAL, Edw. Law of Bailments and Carriers 27/6 r 8° Butterworth 00
PAINE, W. On Bailment 25/ 8° Sweet 01
A comment. on law of custody of and possessn. in chattels. Inc. Indian and Australian law.

**United States**

BROWNE, I. Elements of Law of Bailments. and Carriers $3 *n.* 8° Banks, *N.Y.* 96
EDWARDS, Is. On the Law of Bailments $4 8° Banks, *N.Y.* [55] 93
HALE, W. B. Handbk. on Law of Bailments & Carriers $3·75 8° West Pb. Co., *St Paul, Minn.* 96
LAWSON, Dr J. D. Principles of American Law of Bailments $5 8° Thomas, *St Louis* 95
SCHOULER, J. Treat. on Bailmts. : pledge, inn keepers, carriers $3 *n.* 8° Little & Brown, *Boston* [80] 05
STORY, Jos. Comms. on Law of Bailments, ed. E. H. Bennett $6 8° Little & Brown, *Boston* [56] 78
VAN ZILE, P. T. Elements of Law of Bailments & Carriers $5 *n.* 8° Callaghan, *Chicago* [02] 07

## 16 : BANKING

AGAR, W. T. Questns. on Bankg. Practice Classified and Indexed *o.p.* 8° E. Wilson [ ] 98
BROWN, A. T. Lectures on Banking Law 3/ 8° Tutorial Institute 09
BUTTERWORTH, A. R. Bankers' Advances—*ut* **D** § 18
EDDIS, A. C. Rule of *Ex pte Waring* *o.p.* 12° Stevens 76
GRANT, J. Law of Bankers and Banking Companies ; ed. C. C. M. Plumptre + I. K. Mackay 29/6 8° Butterworth [56] 97
HART, Heber Law of Banking 30/ 8° Stevens [ ] 06
HOLLAND (R. W.) + NIXON (A.) Banking Law [elementary] 5/ ($1·75) c 8° Longman 08
HUTCHISON, J. Practice of Banking: cases at law and in equity, 2 vols. 36/ 8° E. Wilson 81–83
PAGET, Sir J. R. The Law of Banking 12/6 *n.* 8° Butterworth [04] 08
,, [ed.] Legal Decisions affecting Bankers 6/ *n.* 8° Blades 01
SMITH, J. W. Law of Banker and Customer [popular] 2/6 *n.* 8° E. Wilson [ ] 07
SYKES, E. Banking and Currency 5/ *n.* c 8° Butterworth [04] 05
TILLYARD, E. Banking & Negot. Instrumts. [semi-pop. ; $2 *n.* Macmillan, *N.Y.*] 5/ *n.* c 8° Black [91] 08
WALKER, J. D. Treatise on Banking Law 15/ 8° Stevens [77] 85

**Scotland**

ROBERTSON, Hy. Handbook of Bankers' Law, ed. J. G. Johnston 5/ *n.* 8° Green, *Edin.* [7–] 01
WALLACE (W.) + McNEIL (A.) Banking Law, with Forms (Scotland) 15/ *n.* 8° Green, *Edin.* [94] 06

**Australia and New Zealand**

HAMILTON, E. B. Law and Practice of Banking in Austr. and N. Zeald. 25/ *n.* 8° *Melbourne* [80] 00

**Canada**

CORNWELL, W. C. Currency and Banking Law of Canada 75 c. c 8° Putnam, *N.Y.* 95
DAVIDSON, C. P. [ed.] Acts relating to Banks and Banking 8/6 r 8° *Toronto* 76

**United States**

BOLLES, A. S. Law rel. to Banks and their Depositors $4·50 8° Homans, *N.Y.* 87
,, [ed.] The National Bank Act, and its Judicial Meaning $3 8° Homans, *N.Y.* 88
,, Treat. on Modern Law of Banking, 2 vols. $10 8° Bisel, *Phila.* 07
BROWNE, I. [ed.] National Bank Cases $6 8° Bancroft, *San Francisco* 89
CARROLL, Edw. Principles & Practice of Finance [banking laws & pract.] $1·75 8° Putnam, *N.Y.* 95
DUNBAR, Prf. C. F. [ed.] Laws of United States relating to Currency, Finance, and Banking: 1789–1891 $2·50 8° Ginn, *Boston* 91
ELLIS, How. [ed.] Banking Decisions of U.S. and Canada $10 8° Case Law Co., *N.Y.* 05
MAGEE, H. W. Treatise on Law of National & State Banks $6·50 8° Lyon, *Albany, N.Y.* 06
MORSE, J. T., jun. Treat. on Law of Banks and Banking, ed. W. F. Parsons, 2 v. $12 8° Little & Brown, *Boston* [70] 07
NEWMARK, N. Law relating to Bank Deposits $3 8° Stevenson, *St Louis* 88
ROLLINS, Montg. [ed.] Laws regulating Investment of Bank Funds $2·50 8° Author, *N.Y.* [99] 05
SMITH, H. H. [ed.] Digest of all Decisns. of all Cts. rel. to Natl. Banks ['64–'98] $4 8° Flood, *Meadville* 99
WERNSE, W. F. American Bankers' Manual $5 8° Wernse, *St Louis* 89
ZANE, J. M. Law of Banks and Banking $6 8° Flood, *Meadville* 00

**Bank Notes and Cheques**—*v.* **D** § 18 **Savings Banks**—*v.* **D** § 84 **Practice of Banking**—*v.* **D** § 116

## 17: BANKRUPTCY AND INSOLVENCY—*v. also* D § 35

BALDWIN, E. T. Treat. upon Law of Bankruptcy and Bills of Sale 30/– c 8° Stevens [79] 10
BALL, W. Valentine Bankruptcy and Bills of Sale [popular] 5/ *n.* c 8° Pitman 08
Bankruptcy Law and its Administration [a Blue-Book] 3/9 f° Wyman 08
Report of the Committee; with evidence.
CHALMERS (M. D.) + HOUGH (E.) [eds.] Bankruptcy Acts 1883 to 1890, ed. Muir Mackenzie 25/ *n.* 8° Waterlow [84] 06
EDDIS, A. S. Principles of Administr. of Assets in Paymt. of Debts 6/ 8° Stevens 80
JOEL, J. E. Manual of Bankruptcy and Bills of Sale Law 25/ 8° Stevens 84
MANSON, E. Short View of Bankruptcy Law [good student's bk.] 7/6 8° Sweet [04] 10
,, [ed.] Reports of Bankruptcy & Company Cases: 1894 *sqq.* ea. 25/ 8° Sweet *ann.*
Cook W. Ivimey Digest-Index of Cases in above, 1884–1901 7/6 *n.* 8° Sweet 02
MORRELL, C. F. [ed.] Reports of Cases in Bankruptcy 1884–94, 10 vols. 180/ *n.* 8° Sweet 84–94
Continued by Manson, *ut sup.*
RIBTON, T. Law and Practice in Bankruptcy 22/6 8° Clowes 84
RIGG, J. McM. [ed.] Bankruptcy Act 1883, Debtor's Act '69, and Bill of Sales Acts '69–78 10/6 r 12° Stevens 84
RINGWOOD, R. Principles of Bankruptcy: w. scale of costs [useful introd.] 10/6 8° Stevens & Haynes [79] 08
ROBSON, G. Y. Treatise on the Law of Bankruptcy 38/ r 8° Clowes [70] 94
,, Treatise of Law of Priv. Arrangements w. Creditors—*ut* **D** § 35
ROCHE (H. P.) + HAZLITT (W.) Law and Practice in Bkptcy.: Bkptcy. Act '69, Debtor's Act '69 *o.p.* [pb. 30/] 8° Stevens & Haynes [70] 73
Learned authority on the old law.
SAMSON, C. L. Law and Practice under Bankruptcy Act 1883 25/ r 8° Clowes 84
WACE, Hy. Law and Practice of Bankruptcy 27/6 *n.* r 8° Sweet [71] 01
*WILLIAMS, Sir R. L. Vaughan Law & Practice in Bankruptcy, ed. E. W. Hansell 30/ r 8° Stevens [70] 08

**Scotland**

KINNEAR, J. B. Law of Bankruptcy in Scotland 15/ 8° *Edinburgh* [58] 69
MURDOCK, J. Manual of Law of Insolvency & Bankruptcy in Scotl. 20/ 8° Blackwood [63] 86
WALLACE, Wm. Law of Bankruptcy in Scotland [w. forms] 25/ *n.* r 8° Green, *Edin.* 07

**South Africa**

BUCHANAN, D. M. [ed.] Decisions in Insolvency (South Africa) 43/ *n.* 8° *Capetown* [ ] 06

**United States and Canada**—*v. also* **D** § 46

BISHOP, J. L. Law and Practice of Insolvency and Assignments $5 8° Baker, *N.Y.* 79

BRANDENBURG, E. C. Law of Bankruptcy $5 8° Callaghan, *Chicago* 98
,, [ed.] Index Digest of Bankruptcy Decisions, 1800–99 $6·50 8° Callaghan, *Chicago* 99
BUMP, O. F. Law and Practice of Bankruptcy $6·50 r 8° Lowdermilk, *Washington* [69] 98
BURRILL, A. M. Law and Pract. of Voluntary Assignmt., ed. J. L. Bishop $6·50 r 8° Baker, *N.Y.* [53]
LOWELL, J. The Law of Bankruptcy $6 8° Little & Brown, *Boston* 99
LOWELL, J. + A. Treatise on Bankruptcy $6 *n.* 8° Little & Brown, *Boston* 99

**France**

PELLERIN, P. French Law of Bkptcy. & Winding-up & Conflict of Laws arising 2/6 *n.* c 8° Stevens 07

**Insolvent Corporations:** *United States*

HAWES, G. P. Law of Voluntary Assignments for Benefit of Creditors $2 8° Baker, *N.Y.* 76
KEILEY, W. S. Law and Practice rel. to Voluntary Assignments $2 8° Banks, *N.Y.* 76
MOSES, R. Insolvency Laws of United States and Canada $4 *n.* 8° Baker, *N.Y.* 76
WAIT, F. S. Practical Treatise on Insolvent Corporations $6 8° Baker, *N.Y.* 88

**Receiver and Manager; Liquidor; Trustee-in-Bankruptcy**

BINNIE, A. The Receiver and Manager in Possession 2/6 *n.* 8° Gee 09
WILLSON, W. R. Law of Trustees, Liquidators and Receivers 10/6 *n.* 8° Gee [05] 10

## 18: BILLS OF EXCHANGE; I.O.U.'S; BANK NOTES; NEGOCIABLE INSTRUMENTS

AGABEG (Aviet) + BARRY (W. F.) [eds.] Bills of Exchange Act, 1882; w. notes 12/6 r 8° Butterworth 84
BUTTERWORTH, A. R. Banker's Advances on Mercantile Advances other than B. o. E. and Promissory Notes 7/6 8° Sweet 02
*BYLES, Sir J. B. Law of B. of Ex., Prom. No., Bk. No. and Cheques, ed. M. B. + W. J. B. Byles [$6·50 Johnson, *Phila.*] 25/ 8° Sweet [29] 99
CAVANAGH, C. Law of Money Securities 30/ 8° Clowes [79] 85
*CHALMERS, Sir M. D. Digest of Law of B. of Ex., Prom. Notes & Cheques 20/ 8° Stevens [79] 09
CHITTY, J., jun. Treat. on B. of Ex., Prom. No., Cheqs., etc., ed. J. A. Russell 28/ r 8° Sweet [40] 78
HAMILTON, A. M. [ed.] The Bills of Exchange Act, 1882 12/ *n.* 8° Green, *Edin.* 04
McNEIL (A.) Law of Bills of Exch., Chqs., Pro. Notes [w. Act of '82] 2/6 *n.* c 8° Green, *Edin.* [ ] 10
RINGWOOD, R. Outlines of Banking Law 5/ 12° Stevens & Haynes 06
SMITH, J. W. Handy Book on Law of Bills, Cheques, Notes & I.O.U.'s [popular] 1/6 f 8° E. Wilson [59]
TILLYARD, F. Banking and Negotiable Instruments—*ut* § **D** 16
WATSON, E. R. On Cheques 2/6 *n.* 8° Sweet [ ] 04
WILLIS, Judge W. Law of Negotiable Securities [6 lectures] 7/6 8° Stevens & Haynes [96] 01

**Scotland**

THOMSON, R. Law of Bills of Exch., Prom. Notes, etc., ed. J. D. Wilson 28/ r 8° Stevens [37] 65

**Canada**

CLARKE, S. R. Bills, Notes, Cheques and I.O.U.'s 10/ 8° *Toronto* 75

**South Africa:** *Transvaal*

EVANS, M. O. Bills of Exchange in the Transvaal 10/6 *n.* p 8° 02

**United States**

AMES, J. B. [ed.] Seln. of Cases on Laws of Bills, Notes & Neg. Papers, 2 v. $12 r 8° Soule, *Boston* 81
BIGELOW, M. M. [ed.] Leading Cases on Bills, Notes, and Checks $3 *n.* r 8° Little & Brown, *Boston* [71] 05
,, Elements of Law of Bills, Notes, and Cheques $2·50 *n.* 8° Little & Brown, *Boston* [93] 00
DANIEL, J. W. Law of Negotiable Instruments, 2 vols. $12·60 r 8° Baker, *N.Y.* [76] 91
EDWARDS, Is. Treat. on Bills of Exch., Prom. Notes, etc., 2 vols. $10 *n.* r 8° Banks, *N.Y.* [57] 91
HUFFCUT, E. W. Law of Negotiable Instruments $4·50 8° Baker, *N.Y.* 98
NORTON, C. P. Handbook of the Law of Bills & Notes $3·75 8° West Pb. Co., *St Paul, Minn.* [93] 00
RANDOLPH, J. F. Treat. on Law of Commercial Paper, 3 vols. $18 8° West Pb. Co., *St Paul, Minn.* [86–8] 99
Contains the text of the Commercial Codes of Gt. Britain, France, Germany, and Spain.
SIMONTON, T. C. Law of Cheques, Notes, and Banks $4 8° Van Horen, *N.Y.* [06] 07
,, Law of Commercial Paper and Banking $4 8° Author, *N.Y.* 07
STORY, Jos. Commentaries on Law of B. of E., Prom. Notes, etc. $6 r 8° Little & Brown, *Boston* [43] 78
VAN SCHAACK, H. C. Law of Bank Cheques in U.S. $3·50 8° Chain, *Denver* 92

**France**

ARGLES, N. Handbook on French Law of Bills of Exchange 1/ 12° E. Wilson 78

**Notary** —*v.* **D** § 53

## 19 : BILLS OF SALE ; MONEYLENDERS—*v. also* D § 52

ALABASTER, C. G. Law of Money-Lenders and Borrowers 6/ 8° Stevens 08
BELLOT, H. H. L. Legal Princ. & Pract. of Bargains w. Money-Lenders 21/r 8° Stevens & Haynes [97] 06
FITHIAN, E. W. [ed.] Bills of Sale Acts, '78 and '82 : w. Introd. and notes 6/ 12° Stevens [82] 84
Mr FITHIAN was the draftsman of the 1882 Bill.
HASTINGS, P. Law of Moneylenders 3/6 *n.* 8° Butterworth 05
JOEL, J. E. Manual of Bankruptcy and Bills of Sale Law—*ut* **D** § 17
LYON (G. E.) + REDMAN (J. H.) Law of Bills of Sale 7/6 8° Reeves & Turner [2nd edn. 77] 96
MACALPIN, D. R. Law relating to Money Lenders and Borrowers 9/ r 8° Reeves & Turner 80
MACASKIE, S. Law rel. to Bills of Sale, and on Fraud. Assignmt. 8/ p 8° Stevens 82
MACHUGH, A. Bills of Sale 15/ *n.* 8° Sweet 95
MATTHEWS, J. B. Law of Money-Lending, Past and Present 5/ c 8° Sweet 06
„ + SPEAR (G. F.) [eds.] Money-Lenders Act : 1900 [new ed. of Pt. ii of above] 7/6 8° Sweet [06] 08
REED, Haythorne [ed.] Money-Lenders Act, 1900 3/6 *n.* 12° Waterlow 00
*REED, Herb. Bills of Sale Acts : w. epitome of law 7/6 12° Waterlow [79] 03
WEIR, J. Law of Bills of Sale : w. introd. 20/ *n.* 8° Jordan 96
Pt. i (two-fifths of bk.) is a valuable *General Introd.* ; Pt. ii comprises the Statutes repealed ; Pt. iii those now in force (Acts '78, '78, '82, '90 '91,), fully annotated. Appendix gives forms.

**Canada**

BARRON, J. A. Handy Bk. of Law of Bills of Sale & Chattel Mortgages 16/6 8° *Toronto* 80

**Assignment** —*v.* **D** § 17 ; *for* Fraudulent Conveyances, *v.* **D** § 46

**Hire-purchase Agreements**

RUSSELL, W. H. Law relating to Hire-purchase Agreements 4/ *n.* c 8° Waterlow [95] 07

## 20 : BUILDING ; ENGINEERS

BALL, W. Valentine The Law affecting Engineers 10/6 *n.* 8° Constable 09
CONNELL, Is. Law affecting Building Operations and Contracts 7/6 *n.* 8° Green, *Edin.* 03
EMDEN, A. Building Contracts, Loans, and Statutes, ed. T. B. Matthews + W. V. Ball 27/6 8° Butterworth [82] 07
*HUDSON, A. A. Law of Building, Engineering, & Shipbuilding Contracts, 2 v. 52/6 8° Sweet [91] 07
Deals also w. duties and liabilities of engineers, architects, surveyors, and valuers. Suppl., 3/6 *n.* '10.
JENKINS (E.) + RAYMOND (J.) Architect's Legal Handbook [on building contracts] 6/ c 8° Paul [ ] 89
MACASSEY (L. L.) + STRAHAN (J. A.) Law rel. to Civil Engineers, Architects, and Contractors 12/6 8° Stevens [90] 97
MACEY, F. W. Conditions of Contract rel. to Building Works, ed. B. J. Leverson 15/ *n.* 8° Sweet 02
MORROW, F. St J. Digest of Building Cases 15/ *n.* r 8° Butterworth 06
ROSCOE, E. S. [ed.] Digest of Building Cases 6/ 12° Reeves & Turner [79] 00
TODD, Ern. Law of Building and Dilapidation 15/ 8° Eyre & Spottiswoode 07

**United States**

CLARK, T. M. Architect, Owner, and Builder before the Law $3 *n.* 8° Macmillan 05
WAIT, J. C. Operations prelim. to Construction in Engineerg. and Archit., Boundaries, Easemts., etc. $5 8° Wiley, *N.Y.* 00

**Engineer or Architect as Arbitrator**—*v.* **D** § 12 (GREGORY)

**Metropolitan Building Acts** —*v.* **D** § 67

## 21 : BUILDING AND FRIENDLY SOCIETIES ; LOAN ASSOCIATIONS

**Building Societies** —*for* Management, etc., *v.* **D** § 120

DAVIS, H. F. A. Law of Building and Land Societies, ed. J. E. Walker 21/ 8° Sweet [70] 96
FOWKE, V. de S. [ed.] The Industrial and Provident Societies Acts 6/ *n.* 12° Jordan 94
SCRATCHLEY (A.) + BRABROOK (E. W.) The Law of Building Societies 7/6 p 8° Shaw [75] 96

*WURTZBURG, E. A. Law relating to Building Societies 16/ 8° Stevens [87] 02
Appendices cont. Statutes, Treasury Regulations, Acts of Sederunt, and Precedents of Rules and Assces.

**United States**

BACON, F. H. Law of Benefit Societies & Life Insurance, 2 v. $12 8° Thomas, *St Louis* [88] 05

ENDLICH, G. A. Law of Building Associations, etc., in U.S. $6 8° Linn, *Jersey City* [82] 95

ROSENTHAL, H. S. Manual for Building & Loan Associations $1·50 8° Clarke, *Cincinnati* [88] 91

THOMPSON, C. N. Treatise on Building Associations [f. lawyrs. & officers] $3 8° Callaghan, *Chicago* [92] 99

THORNTON (W. W.) + BLACKLEDGE (F. H.) Law rel. to Building and Loan Associations $6 *n.* 8° Bender, *Albany* 98

**Friendly Societies** —*for* Management, etc., *v.* **D** § 120

DIPROSE (J.) + GAMMON (J.) [eds.] Reports of Cases affecting Friendly Societies 21/ 8° Reeves & Turner 97

FULLER, F. H. The Law relating to Friendly Societies 15/– 8° Stevens [ ] 10

PRATT, W. T. The Law of Friendly Societies, ed. E. W. Brabrook 10/6 12° Shaw [50] 09

**BY-LAWS**—*v.* **D** § 26 **CANALS**—*v.* **D** § 81

## 22 : CARRIERS—*v. also* D § 81 *and* D § 15

BROWNE, J. H. B. Treatise on Law of Carriers by Land and Water 18/ 8° Stevens 72

CARVER, T. G. Treat. on Law of Carriage of Goods by Sea, ed. R. A. Wright 38/ r 8° Stevens [86] 09

MACNAMARA, W. H. Digest of Law of Carriers of Merchandise and Passengers by Land, ed. W. A. Robertson 30/ r 8° Stevens [88] 08

STEPHENS, J. E. R. The Law of Carriage [popular] 5/ *n.* c 8° Pitman 09

**United States**

BROWNE, Is. Elements of Law of Bailmts. & Common Carriers $3 *n.* 8° Banks, *N.Y.* 96

FETTER, N. Treatise on the Law of Carriers, 2 vols. $12 8° West Pb. Co., *St Paul, Minn.* 97

HALE, W. B. Handbook on Law of Bailments and Carriers $3·75 8° West Pb. Co., *St Paul, Minn.* 96

HUTCHINSON, R. Treat. on Law of Carriers as admin. in Cts. of U.S., Canada., & Engl., ed. J. S. Mathews + W. F. Dickinson, 3 vols. $18 *n.* 8° Callaghan, *Chicago* [80] 07

MCCLAIN, E. [ed.] Seln. of Cases on Law of Carriers $4·50 *n.* 8° Little & Brown, *Boston* [93] 96

MOORE, De Witt C. Treat. on Law of Carriers as admin. in Cts. of U.S., Canada, and England $6 8° Bender, *Albany, N.Y.* 06

RAY, C. A. Negligence of Imposed Duties, Carriers of Freight $6·50 8° Lawyers' Co-op. Pb. Co., *Rochester* 95

VAN ZILE, P. T. Elements of Law of Bailments and Carriers—*ut* **D** § 15

WHEELER, E. P. Modern Law of Carriers $5 *n.* 8° Baker, *N.Y.* 90

**India**

KNOX, G. E. [ed.] The Indian Contract and Common Carriers' Acts 37/ 8° (*India*) 78

## 23 : CHARITIES

BOURCHIER-CHILCOTT, T. Administration of Charities under Char. Trusts Acts '53–'94 and L.G.A. '94 21/ 8° Stevens [ ] 02

,, Law of Mortmain 12/6 8° Stevens 05

COOKE (H.) + HARWOOD (R. G.) [eds.] Charitable Trusts Acts, 1853, '55, '60; w. notes 16/ 8° Stevens [61] 67

KENNY, C. S. True Principles of Legislation with regard to Property given for Charitable Uses 7/6 8° Reeves & Turner 79

MADDISON, A. J. S. Law rel. to Child-saving & Reformatory Efforts 2/6 8° Reformatory Union [ ] 09

MITCHESON, R. E. Charitable Trusts 18/ 8° Stevens 87

*TUDOR, O. D. Law of Charities and Mortmain, ed. L. S. Bristowe + C. A. Hunt + H. G. Burdett 45/ *n.* 8° Sweet [54] 06

TYSSEN, Amherst D. The Law of Charitable Bequests 21/ 8° Clowes 89
With an account of the Mortmain and Charitable Uses Act 1888.

,, New Law of Charit. Bequests [Act of 1891] 1/6 *n.* 8° Clowes 91

WHITEFORD, F. M. Law relating to Charities, especially Bequests 6/8° Stevens & Haynes 78

**United States**

FOWLER, R. L. Law of Charitable Uses, Trusts, & Donations in N.Y. $3 8° Diossy, *N.Y.* 96

**Old-Age Pensions** —*for* Treatises *v.* **D** § 127*

BARLOWE, Dr C. A. M. [ed.] Old-Age Pensions Act, 1908; w. notes 2/6 c 8° Eyre & Spottiswoode 08

**Hospitals** —*v.* **D** § 67 **Parochial Charities**—*v.* **D** § 67, *s.v.* Parochial

## 24 : CLUBS

BALL (W. V.) + THOMAS (S. J.) Law relating to Registration of Clubs 1/6 8° J. Davy 03

DALY, D. Handbk. of Rts. and Liabilities of Officers and Members of Clubs and other Unregistered Societies 3/6 *n.* 8° Butterworth [ ] 89

WERTHEIMER, J. Law relating to Clubs, ed. A. W. Chaster 7/6 c 8° Stevens & Haynes [85] 03

## CHILDREN—*v.* D §§ 48, 38

## COMMERCIAL LAW—*v.* D § 63

## 25 : COMMON LAW

BROOM, H. Commentaries on the Common Law—*v.* ODGERS, *inf.*

„ Philosophy of Common Law, ed. J. C. H. Flood, *sub tit.* Primer of Legal Principles 6/ 8° Sweet [76] 83

INDERMAUR, J. Princ. of Com. Law, ed. Chas. Thwaites ['cram' bk.] 20/ 8° Stevens & Haynes [76] 09

„ [ed.] Epitome of Leading Common Law Cases 6/ 8° Stevens & Haynes [74] 03

ODGERS, W. Blake + Walter B. On the Common Law [based on Broom] Sweet *in prep.*

SAUNDERS (Sir E.) Pleadings, *and* Williams (Sir E. V.) Notes to same—*v.* **D** § 5

SHIRLEY, W. S. [ed.] Selection of Leading Cases in Common Law 16/ 8° Stevens [80] 08
An excellent bk., based on SMITH, wr. in a racy, humorous style: orig. intended for students, but of considerable value for practitioners.

*SMITH, Jno. W. [ed.] Selection of Leading Cases, ed. T. W. Chitty + J. H. Williams + H. Chitty, 2 vols. [w. Am. notes, 3 v. $12 *n.* Johnson, *Phila.*] 70/ r 8° Sweet [ ] 03

SMITH, Josiah W. Manual of the Common Law, ed. C. Spurling 15/ 8° Stevens [62] 05

STREET, T. A. The Foundations of Legal Liability, 3 vols. $15 r 8° Thompson, *Northport, L.I.* 06
63/ *n.* Butterworth. i: *Theory and Princs. of Tort*; ii: *Hist. and Theory of Engl. Contract Law*; iii: *Common Law Actions.*

WALPOLE, C. G. Rubric of the Common Law: illustrated by cases, ed. S. Hastings 14/ 8° Shaw [80] 91

*History* —*v.* **D** § 5

**Canada**

HARRISON, R. A. [ed.] The Common Law Procedure Act 21/ 8° *Toronto* [ ] 70

**South Africa** —*v. also* **D** § 4

NATHAN, M. The Common Law of South Africa, 4 vols. £9 13/ *n.* r 8° Butterworth 04-7

**United States**

BARTON, R. T. Practice in the Courts of Law in Civil Cases $6 8° Randolph, *Richmond, Va.* 78

COX, W. S. Common Law Practice in Civil Actions $4 8° Morrison, *Washington* 77

HENDRICK, F. Power to Regulate Corporations and Commerce $4 *n.* 8° Putnam, *N.Y.* 06

HOLMES, O. W., jun. The Common Law [lects.; 12/ Macm.] $4 8° Little & Brown, *Boston* 81

LAWSON, J. D. [ed.] Leading Cases Simplified [a collection of cases] $3 8° Thomas, *St Louis* 82

„ Rights, Remedies, & Practice at Law, 7 vols. $6 8° Bancroft, *San Francisco* 89-91
A treatise on American law in civil cases—in Equity and under the Codes.

„ Index Digest of Rights, Remedies, & Practice $3 8° Bancroft, *San Francisco* 91

MINOR, J. B. Institutes of Common and Statute Law, 4 vols. in 5 $40 8° Randolph, *Richmond, Va.* [73-83] 77-83

PUTERBAUGH, S. D. Common Law Pleading and Practice $7·50 8° Callaghan, *Chicago* [63] 76

**Maxims**

BROOM, H. [ed.] Selection of Legal Maxims: classified and illustrated, ed. H. F. Manisty + Herb. Chitty 28/ 8° Maxwell [45] 00

HUGHES, W. T. [ed.] Technology of Law [coll. of maxims, leading cases, *etc.*] 28/ *n.* r 8° Stevens 93

JONES [tr.] Translations $1·50 *n.* c 8° Johnson, *Phila.*
Trs. of the Gk., Lat., Ital., and French quotns. and maxims in BLACKSTONE'S *Commentaries* [ut **D** § 4].

MORGAN, J. A. [ed.] English Version of Legal Maxims: w. orig. forms $2 12° Clarke, *Cincinnati* [78] 78

TRAYNER, J. [ed.] Latin Maxims and Phrases on Law of Scotl. [w. trs.] 21/ 8° Green, *Edin.* [ ] 94

WHARTON, G. F. [ed.] Legal Maxims: w. observations and cases 5/ c 8° Cox [65] 03

**Popular Treatises** —*v.* **D** § 74

**Fraudulent Conveyances**—*v.* **D** § 46 **Real Property**—*v.* **D** § 78 **Title**—*v.* **D** § 78 **Vendor and Purchaser**—*v.* **D** § 96

## 26 : COMPANIES, JOINT-STOCK

ASTBURY, C. J. Guide to Companies (Consolidation) Act, 1908 7/6 *n.* r 8° Stevens [08] 09

*BUCKLEY, L'd Just. H. B. Law and Practice under Companies Acts and Limited Partnership Acts 36/ r 8° Stevens & Haynes [73] 09

CHADWYCK-HEALEY (C. C. H.) + WHEELER (P. F.) + BURNEY (C.) Treatise on the Law and Practice relating to Joint-Stock Companies 40/ r 8° Sweet 94

CONNELL, A. C. Companies & Company Law [for the 'business-man'] 5/ *n.* 8° Pitman 09

EMERY, G. F. Treatises on Company Law 21/ 8° E. Wilson 01

EVANS (L. W.) + COOPER (F. S.) Notes on the Companies (Consolidation) Act 12/ *n.* 8° Knight 09

,, + KING Companies (Consolidation) Act, 1908 5/ *n.* r 12° Butterworth 09

FOWKES, V. De S. Companies Acts 1862–90, and other Statut. Enactmts. *o.p.* 8° Jordan [93] 99

GODDEN (W.) + HUTTON (S.) [eds.] Companies Acts, 1862–1907; w. cross-refs. & index 5/ *n.* c 8° E. Wilson 08

GOIRAND, L. French Law rel. to English Companies in France 2/6 *n.* c 8° Stevens 02

HAMILTON, W. F. Manual of Company Law, ed. P. Tindal-Robertson 21/ 8° Butterworth [91] 10

HEMMANT, D. G. [ed.] The Companies Act, 1907 2/6 *n.* 8° Jordan [ ] 08

,, The Companies (Consolidation) Act, 1908 6/ *n.* 8° Jordan [09] 09

,, Table A 1/6 *n.* 8° Jordan 06

,, The Law of Limited Partnerships, 1907 2/6 *n.* 8° Jordan 08

HURRELL (H.) + HYDE (C. G.) Joint-Stock Companies Practical Guide 6/ *n.* 8° Waterlow [89] 09

JORDAN, H. W. A B C Guide to the Companies Acts, 1862–1907 2/6 *n.* 4° Jordan 09

,, A B C Guide to Companies (Consolidation) Act, 1908 2/6 *n.* 4° Jordan [08] 09

,, + GORE-BROWN (F.) Handbk. on Formatn., Managemt. and Winding-up of Jt.-Stock Cos. 7/6 *n.* 12° Jordan [ ] 09

KELKE, W. H. H. Epitome of Company Law [student's-bk.] 6/ 8° Sweet [04] 09

*LINDLEY, Sir N. + W. B. Treatise on the Law of Joint-Stock and other Companies, 2 vols. 70/ r 8° Sweet [63] 02

MCILRAITH, J. R. Law rel. to Companies and Limited Partnerships [popular] 1/ 8° Routledge 08

MACKENZIE (M. M.) + GEARE (E. A.) + HAMILTON (G. B.) Company Law: abgmt. of law cont. in stat. and decisions 21/ r 8° Stevens 93

MANSON, Edw. Law of Trading and other Companies *red. to* 25/ r 8° Clowes [92] 93
A digest of company law of easy reference. Index of cases cited occupies 84 pp.

NICOLAS, Vale Law and Pract. rel. to Formatn. of Companies 17/6 *n.* r 8° Butterworth [ ] 08

*PALMER, Sir Fcs. B. [ed.] Company Precedents 95/ r 8° Stevens [77] 07–9
Pt. i: *General Forms*, 38/ '09; Pt. ii: *Winding-up Forms and Practice, in prep.* (last edn. 32/ '04); Pt. iii: *Debentures and Debenture Stock*, 25/ '07.

,, Shareholder's, Director's, and Volunt. Liquidator's Legal Companion 2/6 *n.* 12° Stevens [78] 09

,, Private Companies and Syndicates [popular] 1/ *n.* 8° Stevens [77] 09

,, Companies Act and Limited Partnerships Act, 1907 7/6 r 8° Stevens [07] 08

,, Company Law [practical handbk; based. on lects.] 12/6 r 8° Stevens [05] 09

,, Revised Table A 1/6 *n.* r 8° Stevens 06

PULBROOK, A. [ed.] Companies Acts [1862–86], Stannaries Act ['69], Life Assur. Co.'s Act ['70] 6/ c 8° E. Wilson [67] 89

,, [ed.] Common Company Forms 7/6 *n.* c 8° E. Wilson 02

,, Law and Practice of Joint-Stock Companies 4/ *n.* c 8° E. Wilson 08

*RAWLINS (W. D.) + MACNAGHTON (M. M.) Law and Practice in rel. to Companies 35/ r 8° Butterworth 01
Unlike other similar wks., it includes the Companies Clauses Acts.

REID, J. W. [ed.] Companies Acts, 1900–07 [popular statemt. of changes] 2/6 *n.* c 8° E. Wilson 08

SIMONSON, P. F. [ed.] Companies Acts, 1900 and 1907; w. comments. 5/ *n.* r 8° E. Wilson 08

,, The Revised Table A [1906]; w. notes 3/6 *n.* r 8° E. Wilson 07

SMITH, J. W. Law of Joint-Stock Companies under Acts '62–'07 2/6 *n.* f 8° E. Wilson [ ] 08

SMITH (T. E.) + WILLIAMS (E. R. V.) Short Practical Company Forms 8/ 8° Stevens & Haynes 96

,, [ed.] Summary of Companies (Consolidation) Act, 1908 7/6 8° Stevens & Haynes [78] 09

THRING, Lord Law & Pract. of Jt.-Stk. & other Cos.; ed. J. Rendel 30/ 8° Stevens [57] 90

TOPHAM, A. F. Principles of Companies Law 6/ c 8° Butterworth [ ] 10
An admirable student's-bk., useful also to others concerned w. Cos.—a lucid statemt. of the principles.

**Scotland**

McNeil, Allan — Manual of Company Law in Scotland — 8° Green, *Edin.* [01] *in prep.*
With the text of all the Statutes.

**Africa : *Transvaal***

Nathan, M. — Company and Commercial Law of Transvaal — 25/ 8° Butterworth 05

**Australia and New Zealand**

De Lissa — Companies' Work & Mining Law in N.S.W. & Victoria — 10/6 c 8° Clowes 94
Morison, C. B. — Law rel. to Lim. Liab. Cos. in New Zealand — 42/ *n.* r 8° 04

**Canada**

Parker (W. R. P.) + Clark (G. M.) Canadian Company Law — $6·50 8° Cromarty, *Phila.* 08
Stephens, C. H. — Law and Practice of Joint Stock Companies — 21/ 8° *Toronto* 81

**British Companies in France**

Barclay, Thos. — Law rel. to British Companies and Securities in France and Formation of French Cos. — 7/6 8° Green, *Edin.* [ ] 99

**United States**

Abbott, B. V. + A. — Digest of Law of Corpns., Publ. and Priv., 2 v. — $8·50 r 8° *New York* 69–79
American Corporation Legal Manual, vols. i–xiii — ea. $4·50–$5 8° Corp. Legal Manl. Co., *N.Y.* 93–05
Beach, C. F., jun. — Company Law : comms. on law of priv. corps., 2 v. — $12 8° Bowen-Merrill, *Indianapolis* [91] 93
Carr, C. T. — General Principles of Law Corporations — $2·25 *n.* 8° Macmillan, *N.Y.* 05
Clark (W. L., jun.) — Handbk. of Law of Private Corpns. $3·75 8° West Pb. Co., *St Paul, Minn.* [97] 07
,, + Marshall (W. L.) Treatise on Law of Private Corporations, 3 vols. — ea. $6 8° Keefe, *St Paul, Minn.* 01–2
,, The same, Supplement [vol. iv], by A. L. Helliwell $6·50 8° Keefe, *St Paul, Minn.* 08
Clephane, W. C. — Organizn. & Managemt. of Business Corpns. $2·50 8° West Pb. Co., *St Paul, Minn.* 05
Conyngton, T. — Manual of Corporate Management — $3·50 8° Ronald Press, *N.Y.* [03] 09
,, — Manual of Corporate Organization — $3 8° Ronald Press, *N.Y.* [00] 08
,, Modern Corporation : mechanism, meths., formn., managemt. $2 8° Ronald Press, *N.Y.* [04] 08
Cook, W. W. — Treatise on Law of Corporations, 4 vols. $26 *n.* 8° Callaghan, *Chicago* [87] 08
Cumming, R. C., *etc.* [eds.] Annotated Corpn. Laws of All the States, 3 vols. $18 ; Suppl. i, $6 ; ii, $4·50 — 8° Lyon, *Albany* 99–03
Dean, M. B. [ed.] — Digest of Corporation Cases — $5 8° Banks, *N.Y.* 06
Elliott, C. B. — Principles of Laws of Public Corporns. $6 8° Callaghan, *Chicago* [2 edn. 95] 98
Frost, T. G. — Treatise on Incorpn. & Organizn. of Corpns. $5 *n.* 8° Little & Brown, *Boston* [05] 08
Harvey, R. S. — Handbk. of Corporn. Law of Priv. Business Corpns. $6 8° Bleyer Law Pb. Co., *N.Y.* 06
Keener, W. A. [ed.] — Seln. of Cases on Law of Private Corpns., 2 vols. — $11 8° Baker, *N.Y.* 99
Machen, A. W., jun. — Treatise on Modern Law of Corporations, 2 v. $12 *n.* 8° Little & Brown, *Boston* 08
Overland, Martha U. — Manual of Statutory Corporation Law — $4 8° Ronald Press, *N.Y.* 08–9
Purdy, J. H. — Treatise on Law of Private Corporations & Jt.-St. Cos., and other unincorpated Assocns. — $18 8° Flood, *Chicago* 05
Smith, Jerem. [ed.] Selectn. of Cases on Private Corpns., 2 v. $6 *n.* 8° *Harvard Law Rev.* Ass., *Camb.* [98] 02
Sullivan, J. J. — American Corporations [law and practical wk.] $2 *n.* (7/6 *n.*) c 8° Appleton 11
Taylor, H. O. — Treatise on Law of Private Corporations — $6 8° Kay, *Phila.* [84] 94
Thompson, S. D. + J. — Commentaries on Law of Private Corporations, vol. i [6 vols.] — 8° Bobbs *Indianapolis* [ –99] 08 *in prg.*
Tompkins, L. J. [ed.] — Seln. of Cases on Law of Private Corporations — $6 8° Baker, *N.Y.* 08
Tucker, G. F. — Formatn. & Managemt. of Mercantile Corpns. $3 *n.* 8° Little & Brown, *Boston* [ ] 05
Waterman, T. W. — Treatise on Law of Corporatns. other than Munic., 2 v. $12·50 8° Baker, *N.Y.* 88
White, F. — Manual f. Business Corporns. in State of N.Y. $1·50 8° White Law Bk. Co., *Phila.* [95] 05
Wilgus, H. L. [ed.] — Cases on General Principles of the Law of Private Corporations, 2 vols. — $9 8° Bobbs, *Indianapolis* 01–2
Withrow, T. F. [ed.] — Corporatn. Cases of Supr. & Circuit Cts. of U.S., 5 v. ea. $5 8° Myers, *Chicago* 76–82
Wood, W. A. — Modern Business Corpns. [forms of procedure] $2·50 *n.* 8° Bobbs, *Indianapolis* 07
*Foreign Corporations :* Mann, (J. H.) Treatise on the Law of Foreign Business Corporations doing Business in State of New York — $3·50 8° Banks, *N.Y.* 06

MURFREE, W. L., jun. Law of Foreign Corporations $4 8° *Cent. Law Jl.* Co., *St Louis* 93

**Japan**

de BECKER, J. E. Japanese Law of Tradg. Partnerships and Companies 5/ *n.* 8° 07

**Accounts and Finance :** *United States*

BENTLEY (H. C.) + CONYNGTON (T.) Corporate Finance and Accounting $4 8° Ronald Press, *N.Y.* 08
KEISTER, D. A. Corporation Accounting and Auditing $4 8° Burrows, *Cleveland* [5 edn. 97] 05
MEADE, E. S. Corporation Finance $2 *n.* (7/6 *n.*) c 8° Appleton 10
MULHALL, J. F. J. Quasi-public Corporation Accounting & Managemt. $5 *n.* 8° Corp. Pb. Co., *N.Y.* 07
RAHILL, J. J. Corporation Accounting and Corporation Law $3 8° Rahill, *Fresno* [99] 06
REID, W. A. Treat. on Law pertg. to Corporate Finance, 2 v. $12 8° Parsons, *Albany* 96

*Finance of Early British and Irish Cos.*

SCOTT, Dr. W. R. Constitn. of Finance of Eng., Sc., & Ir. Jt.-St. Cos. to 1720, vol. ii 15/ *n.* r 8° Camb. Press 10
Putnam, *N.Y.* Companies for foreign trade, colonizn., fishg., and mining. Vol. i to appear later.

**Bonds :** *United States*

JONES, L. A. Treatise on the Law of Corporate Bonds & Mortgages $6 *n.* 8° Houghton, *Boston* [79] 90
A 2nd edn. of the author's *Railroad Securities.*

**By-laws**

BOISOT, L., jun. By-laws of Private Corporations $3 8° Keefe, *St Paul, Minn.* [92] 02
LUMLEY, W. G. Essay on Bye-Laws : w. appendix on model bye-laws 10/ 8° Knight 77

**Clauses Consolidation Acts, 1845–77**

BIGG, J. [ed.] The Clauses Consolidation Acts 16/ 12° Waterlow [66] 77
RAWLINS (W. D.) + MACNAGHTEN (Hon. M. M.)—*ut sup.*

**Compulsory Purchase (Sale)** —*v.* **D** § 51

**Companies (Incorp.) operating under Municipal Franchises**—*v.* **D** § 67

**Contributories**

COLLIER, Rob. Treatise on Law of Contributories in the Winding-up 9/ c 8° Butterworth 75

**Conversion**

TURNER, C. W. Treat. on Conversn. of a Business into Priv. Lim. Co. 6/ 8° Solrs.' Law Stat. Soc. [ ] 09

**Debentures and Debenture Stock**

MANSON, Edw. Debentures and Debenture Stock of Trading and other Cos. 17/6 8° Butterworth [94] 10
PALMER, Sir F. B. [ed.] Debentures and Debenture Stock [precedents]—*ut supra*
SIMONSON, P. F. Law rel. to Debentures and Debenture Stock 21 / r 8° E. Wilson [98] 02

**Directors**

BOWER, G. S. [ed.] The Directors' Liability Act, 1890 ; w. notes 9/ c 8° Butterworth 90
HAYCRAFT, T. W. Handy Book of Liabilities of Directors [popular] 1/6 f 8° E. Wilson 91
HURRELL (H.) + HYDE (G. C.) Law of Directors & Officers of Jt.-Stock Cos. 6/ *n.* 8° Waterlow [84] 05
PULBROOK, A. Responsibilities of Directors under Cos. Acts, 1862–1907, ed. G. F. Emery 3/6 *n.* c 8° E. Wilson 08
THOMPSON, S. D. Liability of Directors, Officers, & Agents of Corpns. $6 8° Stevenson, *St Louis* 81

**Formation and Registration**

PAINE, Tyrrell J. Formation and Registration of Cos. 3/6 8° Sol. Law Stat. Soc. [ ] 01
PICKEN, C. H. Pract. Hints on Prep. & Registrn. of J.-St. Cos.' Forms 3/6 *n.* 8° Waterlow [ ] 09

**Insolvency :** *United States* —*v. also* **D** § 17

JONES, S. W. Treatise on Law of Insolvent Corpns. $6·50 8° Vernon Law Bk. Co., *Kansas* 08

**Liabilities of Stockholders :** *United States*

THOMPSON, S. D. Treatise on Liability of Stockholders in Corporations $5 8° Thomas, *St Louis* 79

**Limited Partnership** —*v.* **D** § 71

**Liquidators, Trustees, Receivers**

LYNCH, H. F. Rights & Duties of Liquidators, Trustees, & Receivers 11/ *n.* 8° Gee [ ] 08

**Precedents**

GORE-BROWN, F. Concise Precedents under the Companies Acts 1862–1890 25/ *n.* c 8° Jordan [92] 02
PALMER, Sir F. B. —*ut sup.*

**Railway Companies** —*v.* **D** § 81

**Rating** —*ut* **D** § 67

**Reconstruction**

SIMONSON, P. F. Law rel. to Reconstrn. and Amalgam. of Jt.-St. Cos. 10/6 8° E. Wilson [01] 10

**Secretary**

BLAIN, H. E. [ed.] Pitman's Secretary's Manual 5/ *n.* 8° Pitman 08
In 5 Pts. by 5 wrs.: Sec. to M.P., to Country Gentleman, to Charitable Institn., to Jt.-St. Co., etc.
EMERY, H. C. Company Management [for directors and secretaries] 5/ *n.* 8° E. Wilson 09
FITZPATRICK (J.) + HAYDON (T. E.) Secy.'s Manl. of Law & Pract. of Jt.-St. Cos. 7/6 *n.* c 8° Jordan [91] 08
FOX, W. H. The Company Secretary [w. 149 forms and precdts.] 25/ *n.* s f° Gee
FRY (T. H.) + DEIGHTON (T. H.) Everyday Guide for the Secretary 2/6 *n.* c 8° E. Wilson 08
NIXON (A.) + RICHARDSON (G. H.) Secretarial Work and Practice 5/ c 8° Longman 06

**Shareholders** —*v. also* **D** § 71

PALMER, F. B. Shareholders', Directors', Liquidators' Legal Companion—*ut sup.*
PIXLEY, F. W. The Shareholder's Handbook 2/6 p 8° E. Wilson 83

**Transfers:** *United States*

LOWELL, A. L. + F. C. Transfer of Stock in Private Corpns. $3 *n.* 8° Little & Brown, *Boston* 84

**Ultra Vires:** *England* and *United States*

BRICE, Dr. S. Law of Corporations and Companies: treat. on Doctrine of Ultra Vires 38/ r 8° Stevens & Haynes [74] 93
FIERO, J. N. Treatise on Ultra Vires $5 81
REESE, R. A. True Doctrine of *Ultra Vires* in Law of Corpns. $4 8° Flood, *Chicago* 97

**Winding-up**

EMDEN, Alf. Pract. & Forms in Winding-up Cos., ed. H. Johnston 22/6 8° Butterworth [83] 09
GORE-BROWN, F. Winding-up of Companies 15/ *n.* 8° Jordan [04] 07
MACKENZIE (M. M.) + STEWART (C. J.) [eds.] Cos.' Winding Practice [Act '90 & Cos.' Act '62, pt. 4] 10/ c 8° Shaw 90
PALMER, F. B. [ed.] Winding-up Forms and Practice—*in his* Company Precedents—*v. supra*
PITT-LEWIS, G. [ed.] Practice as to Winding-up [Wdg.-up Act '90] 7/6 8° Stevens 91

## COMPENSATION UNDER AGRICULTURAL HOLDINGS ACT—*v.* D § 51

## 27: CONSTITUTIONAL AND PARLIAMENTARY LAW

### CONSTITUTIONAL LAW

**Comparative** —*v. also* **D** § 134 (BURGESS), **D** § 139 (GOODNOW), **D** § 144 (ROBINSON)

BOUTMY, E. Studies in Constitutional Law [tr.] *o.p.* [*pb.* 6/] c 8° Macmillan 91
England, France, and United States. Introd. by Prf. A. V. DICEY.

**Great Britain** —*v. also* **D** § 140, **F** § 17

*ANSON, Sir W. R. Law and Custom of the Constitution, 2 vols. 8° Clar Press [86–08] 09–8
The most authoritative wk. on Brit. Constit., invaluable to student of politics or history. Orderly statement, constant and accurate refer. to orig. authorities. It conts. much histor. matter of value. Vol. i: *Parliament*, 12/6 *n.* ($3·90); v. ii: *The Crown*, Pt. i 10/6 *n.* ($3·40), Pt. ii 8/6 *n.* ($2·90)
BOWYER, Sir Geo. Commentaries on the Constit. Law of England *o.p.* [*pb.* 22/] r 8° Stevens [41] 46
BROOM, H. Constitut. Law viewed in rel. to Common Law *o.p.* [*pb.* 31/6] 8° Maxwell [66] 85
,, [ed.] Leading Cases on Constitutional Law, ed. G. L. Denman *o.p.* [*pb.* 25/6] 8° Sweet [66] 85
*DICEY, Prf. A. V. Introd. to Study of Law of Constitution 10/6 *n.* 8° Macmillan [85] 10
For notes on this bk. and on its companion, *Relation betw. Law and Publ. Opin.*, *v.* D § 140 and F § 2.
FORSYTH, W. [ed.] Cases and Opinions on Constitutional Law *o.p.* [*pb.* 30/] r 8° Stevens 69
MAITLAND, Prf. F. W. Constitutional History of England—*ut* **F** § 17
RIDGES, E. W. Constitutional Law of England 12/6 8° Stevens 05
THOMAS, E. C. [ed.] Leading Cases in Constit. Law, ed. C. L. Attenborough 6/ 8° Stevens & Haynes [76] 08

**British Colonies, etc.:** *Collectively*—*v.* **D** §§ 136, 143

**Canada**

BOURINOT, Sir J. G. Parliamentary Procedure and Practice $8 l 8° (*Montreal*)
LEFROY Law of Legislative Power in Canada 8° Law Bk. & Pb. Co., *Toronto*

**India**

RAY, P. C. Separation of Judic. & Exec. Functns. in Brit. India 8° *Calcutta* 02

**United States** —*v. also* **D** § 145

BATEMAN, W. O. Political and Constitutional Law of the U.S. $3 8° Thomas, *St Louis* 76
BLACK, H. C. Handbook of American Constitutional Law $3·75 8° West Pb. Co., *St Paul, Minn.* [95] 97
BOYD, C. E. [ed.] Cases on American Constitutional Law $3 *n.* 8° Callaghan, *Chicago* [98] 07
CHADMAN, C. E. Constitutional Law $3 8° Am. Sch. of Law, *Chicago* 07
COOLEY, T. M. General Principles of Constitut. Law in U.S. $2·50 *n.* 8° Little & Brown, *Boston* [80] 98
DAVIS, G. B. Elements of Law : constit. & milit. laws of U.S. [10/6 *n.* Chapman] $2·50 8° Wiley, *N.Y.* 97
,, Treat. on Milit. Law and Court Martial $7 8° Wiley, *N.Y.* 98
HARE, Dr J. I. C. American Constitutional Law, 2 v. [63/ Low] $12 8° Little & Brown, *Boston* 89
v. HOLST, Prf. H. Constitutional Law of U.S. [tr.] $2 8° Callaghan, *Chicago* 87
A concise epitome, tr. from a part of H. MARQUARDSEN'S *Handbuch des Oeffentlichen Rechts.*
McCLAIN, E. Constitutional Law in U.S., ed. A. B. Hart [Am. Citiz. Ser.] $2 (7/6 *n.*) c 8° Longman 05
MARSHALL, J. [ed.] Constitutional Decisions, ed. J. P. Cotton, 2 v. $10 *n.* 8° Putnam, *N.Y.* 05
ORDRONAUX, J. Constitutional Legislation in United States $6 *n.* 8° Johnson, *Phila.* 91
POMEROY, J. N. Introd. to Constit. Law of U.S., ed. E. H. Bennett $5 8° Houghton, *Boston* [68] 86
POORE, B. P. Federal and State Constitutions, Colonial Charters, etc., of U.S., 2 vols. $13 r 8° Houghton, *Boston* 78
SMITH, J. D. [ed.] Illustrative Cases on Constitutional Law $2 8° West Pb. Co., *St Paul, Minn.* 96
STIMSON, Prf. F. J. Law of Federal & State Constitns. of U.S. $3·50 *n.* 8° Boston Bk. Co., *Boston* 08
Brings together and analyses the provisns. of the Federal and State Constitns., elucidatg. by comparison the features of interest in considern. of the problems of to-day—an enlargemt. of pt. of his *American Statute Law* [*ut* **D** § 2].
THAYER, J. B. [ed.] Cases on Constitutional Law, 2 vols. $12 *n.* 8° Siever, *N.Y.* 95
TIEDEMAN, Prf. C. G. The Unwritten Constitn. of U.S. : philosoph. inquiry $1 (4/) c 8° Putnam 90

## PARLIAMENTARY LAW AND PRACTICE

**Great Britain** —*v. also* **D** § 38

*ANSON, Sir W. R. —*ut sup.*
BRADLAUGH, Chas. Rules, Custom, & Proced. of House of Commons 2/6 f 8° Sonnenschein 89
FREEMAN, W. M. A B C Guide to Parliamentary Procedure 2/6 *n.* c 8° Butterworth 06
GRAY, G. G. Handbook of Procedure of House of Commons 2/6 *n.* f 8° Cox 96
MACKENZIE (M. M.) + LUSHINGTON (S. G.) Parliament. & Local Govt. Registration Manual 17/6 8° Shaw [88] 97
MAY, Sir T. Erskine Practical Treatise on the Law, etc., of Parliament., ed. T. L. Webster + W. Grey 45/ r 8° Clowes [44] 06
Bk. i : *Constitution, Powers, and Privileges of Parl.* ; bk. ii : *Practice and Proceedings* ; bk. iii : *Private Bills, etc.*
PEEL, Rt. Hon. A. W. Decisions on Pts. of Order, Rules of Debate & Gen. Pract. in H. of C., ed. E. G. Blackmore [1884–95] 10/6 *n.* 8° 00
REDLICH, Prf. J. Procedure of Ho. of Commons : hist. & pres. form [tr.], 3 v. 31/6 *n.* r 8° Constable 08
TODD, Dr Alpheus On Parliamentary Government in England—*vide* **D** § 140

**United States :** *Congress* —*v.* **D** § 146

**Costs**—*v.* **D** § 109, *s.v.* Costs **Elections**—*v.* **D** § 41

**Peerage Law**

HARCOURT, L. W. Vernon His Grace the Steward and Trial of Peers 16/ *n.* ($5 *n.*) 8° Longman 07
Claims to prove that the High Steward's connectn. w. the trial of peers (as Presidt. of the Ct. bef. wh. the trial is conducted) has no histor. basis, and that his reputed succession to the office of the Justiciar is due to a careless readg. of a 13th-cent. law-bk. Long histor. acc. of the office of Steward is given.
PALMER, Sir F. B. Peerage Law in England 12/6 r 8° Stevens 07
With an Appendix of Peerage Charters and Letters Patent. The previous bk. on subj. was by CRUISE on *Dignities* [ ] 23.
ROUND, J. Hor. Peerage and Pedigree, 2 vols.—*ut* **G** § 22

**Private Bills** —*v. also* **D** § 67

ALLAN, C. E. Rights of Local Authorities as reg. Private Bills 2/6 *n.* p 8° Shaw 00
CLIFFORD, Fred. Hist. of Private Bill Legisl., vol. i, 20/ ; vol. ii, 35/ 8° Butterworth 85–7
,, + STEPHENS (C. S.) Pract. of Ct. of Referees on Priv. Bills in Parl.—*ut* **D** § 105

DODD (C.) + WILBERFORCE (H. W. W.) Private Bill Procedure [w. forms] 7/6 8° Eyre & Spottiswoode 98
MACASSEY, L. L. Private-Bill Legisl. and Provis. Orders : a hdbk. 25/ 8° Lockwood 87
SMETHURST, J. M. Locus Standi of Petitions agst. Priv. Bills in Parl. *o.p.* [*pb.* 12/] p 8° Stevens [66] 76
WHEELER, G. J. Practice of Private Bills 25/ r 8° Shaw 00

**Reform, etc.**—*v.* **D** § 141 **Registration**—*v.* **D** § 40

## 28 : CONSULS

INGLIS, A. P. Consular Formulary [coll. of forms and preceds.] 12/6 8° Harrison 79
JOEL, L. Consul's Manual and Shipowner's Guide 12/ 8° Paul 79
PIGGOTT, Sir F. T. Exterritoriality 21/ r 8° Butterworth [92] 07
Law rel. to cons. jurisd. and resid. in Orient. countries; w. spec. chs. on effect of 'foreign jurisdn.' on Domicil, Naturalizn., Marriage, Divorce, Bankruptcy, Companies, Contracts, *etc.*
TARRING, C. J. Brit. Consular Jurisdn. in East [w. cases & stats.] 7/6 8° Stevens & Haynes 87

**Nigeria**

HODGES, F. E. Consular Jurisdiction in Protectorate of Niger Coast 15/ r 8° Stevens 95
An analytical Index to Africa Orders in Council 1889, '92 and '93.

**United States**

HINCKLEY, F. E. American Consular Jurisdiction in the Orient $3·50 *n.* 8° Lowdermilk, *Washington* 06
SCHUYLER, Eng. —*in his* American Diplomacy, *ut* **D** § 113

## 29 : CONTRACTS—*v. also* D § 7

ADDISON, C. G. Treat. on Law of Contracts, ed. A. P. Keep + W. E. Gordon 42/ 8° Stevens [47] 11
Amer. edn., ed. B. V. ABBOTT + H. G. WOOD, 3 vols. $12 *n.* r 8° Johnson, *Phila.*
*ANSON, Sir W. R. Principles of the English Law of Contract and Agency in rel. to Contract [excell. studt.'s-bk.] 10/ *n.* ($3) 8° Clar. Press [79] 10
CARTER, A. T. Elements of the Law of Contracts 7/6 c 8° Sweet [02] 07
CHITTY, J., jun. Treatise on Law of Contracts, ed. Wyatt Paine 30/ r 8° Sweet [3–] 09
EMANUEL, M. R. The Law of Contract 10/ *n.* 8° Jordan [ ] 06
FINCH, G. B. [ed.] Seln. of Cases on the English Law of Contract, ed. R. T. Wright + W. W. Buckland [$7 *n.* Putnam, *N.Y.*] 28/ r 8° Camb. Press [86] 96
*LEAKE, S. M. Digest of Principles of the Law of Contracts, ed. A. E. Randall [excellent practitioner's bk.] 32/ 8° Stevens [67] 11
McKEAG, E. C. Mistakes in Contract : study in compar. jurisprudence [Columbia Univ. Studies] $1 *n.* 8° Macmillan, *N.Y.* 05
MAUDE (W. C.) + LEACH (C. H.) Contracts of Local Authorities 12/6 *n.* 8° Poor Law Pbns. Co. 07
PEASE (J. G.) + LATTER (A. M.) Student's Summary of the Law of Contracts 10/6 8° Butterworth 09
*POLLOCK, Prf. E. Treatise on Principles of Contract [rather theoretical] 28/ 8° Stevens [75] 02
SMITH, Jno. W. Law of Contracts, ed. V. T. Thompson 21/ 8° Sweet [3/] 85
Amer. edn., ed. J. D. BROWN, jun., $5 8° Johnson, *Phila.*

**India**

*CUNNINGHAM (Sir H) + SHEPHARD (Sir H.) Indian Contract Act ; w. Introd. & notes 24/ 8° *Madras* [73] 08
POLLOCK (Sir F.) + MULLA (D. F.) [eds.] The Indian Contract Act 25/ *n.* r 8° Stevens [05] 09

**United States**

BEACH, C. F. Modern Law of Contracts, 2 vols. 65/ r 8° Clowes 97
BISHOP, J. P. Comments. on Law of Contracts on a New Method $6 8° Flood, *Chicago* 87
BRANTLY, W. T. The Law of Contract $3 8° Scrimger, *Baltimore* 93
CLARK, W. L., jun. Treatise on the Law of Contracts $3·75 8° West Pb. Co., *St Paul, Minn.* 04
HARE, J. I. Clark The Law of Contracts $5 8° Little & Brown, *Boston* 87
LANGDELL, C. C. [ed.] Leading Cases on Law of Contracts, w. refs., 2 v. $10 8° Little & Brown, *Bost.* [71] 79
PARSONS, T., jun. Treatise on the Law of Contracts, 3 v. $18 8° Little & Brown, *Boston* [53] 83
STORY, W. W. Treat. on Law of Contracts, ed. M. M. Bigelow, 2 v. $12 8° Little & Brown, *Boston* [44] 74

**Roman Law** —*v.* **D** § 110

**Agreements**

MOORE, H. Practical Forms of Agreements, ed. E. Manson 20/ 8° Clowes [84] 05
*Hire-purchase Agreements* —*v.* **D** § 19
*Verbal Agreements : United States*

THROOP, H. M. Treatise on Validity of Verbal Agreements *o.p.* [*pb.* $7·50] 8° Parsons, *Albany, N.Y.* 70

**Carriers** —*v.* **D** § 22

**Choses in Action**

WARREN, W. R. Law rel. to Choses in Action 16/ 8° Sweet 99

**Consideration**

JENKS, Edw. Hist. of Doctr. of Considern. in Engl. Law [Yorke Prize Ess.] *o.p.* [*pb.* 3/6] 8° Camb. Press 92

**Married Women's Contracts**

EMANUEL, M. R. The Law of Married Women's Contracts 7/6 r 8° Butterworth 07

**Quasi-Contracts :** *United States*

KEENER, W. A. Treatise on the Law of Quasi-Contracts $5 8° Baker, *N.Y.* 93

**Specific Performance :** *England* and *United States*

BOWEN, H. S. Outlines of Specific Performance 3/6 p 8° Butterworth 86

FRY, Sir E. Treat. on Specific Performance of Contracts, ed. W. D. Rawlins 36/ r 8° Stevens [58] 03

POMEROY, J. N. Treat. on Specific Performance of Contracts $5·50 8° Bancroft, *San Franc.* 79

RAWLINS, W. D. On Specific Performance 5/ *n.* 8° Sweet 99

WATERMAN, T. W. On the Specific Performance of Contracts $6·50 8° Baker, *N.Y.* 81

## 30 : CONVEYANCING

BROUGHTON, H. M. Reminders for Conveyancers [w. refs. to precedts.] 3/6 *n.* c 8° Cox [92] 03

BURNS, Jno. Handbook of Conveyancing 12/ *n.* 8° Green, *Edin.* [ ] 01

*BYTHEWOOD (W. M.) + JARMAN (T.) Precedents in Conveyancing, ed. L. G. G. Robbins + A. T. Murray, 8 vols. *red. to* 100/ r 8° Sweet [39–49] 84–93

Alphab. arrgd. Vol. i : *General ;* ii : *Agreemts. and Sales, Mortgages ;* iii : *Settlemts. ;* iv : *Wills and Trustees ;* v : *Leases, Deeds, Bonds,* etc. ; vi : *Settlemts., Misc. Deeds ;* vii : *Stamp Duties, Wills ;* viii : *Supplementary.*

CLARK, J. W. [ed.] Student's Precedents in Conveyancing 6/ r 12° Sweet [93] 05

CLERKE (A. St J.) + BRETT (T.) [eds.] Conveyancing Acts, Vend. and Purch. Acts, etc. 10/6 c 8° Butterworth [81] 97

COPINGER, W. A. Index to Precedents in Conveyancing *o.p.* 8° Stevens & Haynes 72

An invaluable alphabetical index to precedents contained in works published prior to 1872.

DAVIDSON, C., *etc.* [eds.] Precedents and Forms in Conveyancing, ed. T. C. Wright + J. K. Darley, etc., 5 vols. in 8 *o.p.* r 8° Maxwell [*v.y.*] 73–81

,, Concise Preceds. in Conveycg., ed. M. G. Davidson + S. Wadsworth 25/ c 8° Sweet [44] 04

ELPHINSTONE, Sir H. + L. H. Practical Introduction to Conveyancing 15/ 8° Sweet [71] 06

*Encyclopædia of Forms and Precedents other than Court Forms, ed. A. Underhill, 17 v. & vol. xviii (Index) 467/6 r 8° Butterworth 02–09

GREENWOOD, G. W. Practice of Conveyancing [w. concise preceds.] 20/ 8° Stevens [7–] 97

HALLILAY, R. Concise Treat. on Law and Pract. of Conveycg. 18/ p 8° Cox [83] 00

*HOOD (H. J.) + CHALLIS (H. W.) [eds.] Conveycg., Settl. Ld. & Trustee Acts 20/ 8° Stevens [82] 09

INDERMAUR, J. [ed.] Epitome of Leading Conveyancing and Equity Cases, ed. C. Thwaites 6/ 8° Stevens & Haynes [73] 03

,, Princs. and Practice of Conveycg., ed. C. Thwaites 20/ 8° Stevens & Haynes [ ] 04

JACKSON (W. H.) + GOSSET (T.) Precedents of Purchase and Mortgage Deeds 7/6 8° Stevens 99

KELLY, J. H. The Draftsman : colln. of concise precs. and orms, ed. L. H. West + S. B. Scott 15/ c 8° Butterworth [73] 06

*KEY (T.) + ELPHINSTONE (Sir H. W.) [eds.] Compend. of Preceds. in Conveycg., ed. F. T. Maw + E. M. Bonus, 2 vols. 84/ 8° Sweet [78] 04

MOORE, H. [ed.] Handbk. of Practical Forms of Agreements, ed. E. Manson 20/ 8° Stevens [84] 05

*PRIDEAUX, F. [ed.] Precedents in Conveyancing, ed. J. Whitcombe + B. L. Cherry, 2 vols. 70/ r 8° Stevens [53] 04

Indermaur, J. Student's Guide to Prideaux's Conveyancing *o.p.* 12° Stevens & Haynes [83] 99

SMITH (Jos. W.) + TRUSTRAM (J.) Compendium of Law of Real and Personal Property, as conn. w. Conveyancing, 2 vols. 42/ 8° Stevens [55] 84

STRACHAN, Walt. Practical Conveyancing 8/6 r 12° 01

STRAHAN, J. A. Concise Introduction to Conveyancing [good studt.'s-bk.] 10/6 8° Butterworth 00

*WOLSTENHOLME (E. P.) + BRINTON (W.) + CHERRY (B. L.) [eds.] Conveyancing and Settled Land Acts 25/ r 8° Clowes [81] 05

WOLSTENHOLME, E. P. [ed.] Forms & Precedents for use under C.A. & S.L.A. 21/ r 8° Clowes [ ] 05

**Scotland**

BEGG, J. H. [ed.] The Conveyancing Code 20/ 8° Green, *Edin.* 79

BELL, Prf. A. M. Lectures on Conveyancing, 2 vols. 20/ *n.* r 8° Green, *Edin.* [67] 82

BURNS, Jno. Conveyancing Practice acc. to Law of Scotland 30/ *n.* r 8° Green, *Edin.* [ ] 04

CRAIGIE, Jno. Digest of Scottish Law of Conveyancg. : moveable rights 18/ ; heritable rights 30/ 8° Green, *Edin.* [87] 94 ; [88] 99

,, Elements of Conveyancing : heritable rights 12/ *n.* 8° Green, *Edin.* 08

,, [ed.] Conveyancing Statutes (Scotland) 1214–1894 25/ *n.* r 8° Green, *Edin* 95

HENDRY, Jno. Manual of Conveyancing in Scotland, ed. J. P. Wood 16/ 8° Green, *Edin.* [26] 88

*Juridical Soc. of Edinb. : Juridical Styles. By var. contributors, 3 vols. r 8° Green, *Edin.* [1790] 08 ; 86
Vols. i–ii : *Heritable and Moveable Rights*, 60/ *n.* ; iii. *Forms of Process* [*ut* D § 106], 36/.

MENZIES, Prf Allan Lects. on Conveycg. acc. to Law of Scotl. 31/6 r 8° Green *Edin.* [58] 01

*Scots Style Book, ed. Prfs. J. Rankine + J. Mounsey + Dr D. Murray, 7 vols. [very comprehensive] ea. 20/ *n.* 8° Green, *Edin.*

WILLIAMSON, A. M. Digest of Scotch Conveyancing Acts, 1874–92 15/ 8° Green, *Edin.* 92

WOOD, Jno. P. Lectures on Conveyancing in Univ. of Edinb. 42/ r 8° Green, *Edin.* 03

**New South Wales**

HOGG, J. E. Conveyancing & Property Law in New South Wales 30/ Law Bk. Co., *Sydney* [ ] 09

**New Zealand**

MARTIN, T. F. Concise & Pract. View of Conveyancing in N. Zeal. 30/ *n.* 8° *Christchurch, N.Z.* 02

**United States**

JONES, Leon. A. [ed.] Forms in Conveyancing, and General Legal Forms $6 *n.* 8° Houghton, *Boston* [86] 94

OLIVER, B. L. Conveyancing $4·50 8° Dresser, *Portland, U.S.* [4 edn. 45] 81

**Leases**

ANDREWS, J. Precedents of Leases, ed. C. de C. Hamilton 7/6 p 8° Reeves & Turner [71] 97

**Registered Land** —*v.* **D** § 51

**Title**

WITHERS, A. H. Investigation of Title to and Completion of Purchases and Mortgages of Life and Reversy. Interests 10/6 8° Butterworth 09
Personality, trust-funds, and life-insurance policies.

## COPYRIGHTS—*v.* D § 72

## 31 : CORPORATIONS

ADLER, H. M. Summary of Law relating to Corporations 7/6 c 8° Butterworth 03

ALLEN, E. K. Law of Corporate Executors and Trustees—*v.* **D** § 100

Amer. & Engl. Corporation Cases, v. i–xvii [priv. & municipal] ea. $4·50 8° Michie, *Charlottesville* 81–03

BRICE, Dr S. Law of Corporns. and Companies on Ultra Vires—*v.* **D** § 26

CARR, C. T. Gen. Princs. of Law of Corpns. [Yorke Prize Ess. ; $3 *n.* Putnam, *N.Y.*] 7/6 8° Camb. Pr. 05

DAVIS, Jno. P. Corporations $4·50 *n.* (21/ *n.*) 8° Putnam 05
A study of origin and developmt. of great business combinations, and their relation to authority of State.

GRANT, J. Practical Treatise on the Law of Corporations *o.p.* [*pb.* 26/] 8° Butterworth 50
Still of the utmost importance.

HEWITT, T. Treatise on Law rel. to Corporation Duty [w. cases] 6/ c 8° Butterworth 92

**Municipal** —*v.* **D** § 67

**United States** —*v.* **D** § 26

## COVERTURE—*v.* D § 19

## 32 : CRIMINAL LAW

ALLEN, W. Baugh [ed.] Crim. Evidence Act 1898 [w. hist. of act by Sir H B. Poland] 5/ 8° Butterworth 98

ANDERSON, R. [ed.] Prisons Acts of 1877 and 1865 [w. notes & rules] *o.p.* [*pb.* 7/6] 12° Shaw 78

*ARCHBOLD, J. F. Pleading, Evidence, and Practice in Criminal Cases, ed. Sir Jno. Jervis + W. F. Craies + H. D. Roome 35/ 8° Sweet [ ] 10

BOULTON, A. C. F. Criminal Appeals under Act of 1907 5/ *n.* 8° Butterworth 08

BOWEN-ROWLANDS, E. Criminal Proceedings on Indictment and Information 12/6 8° Stevens 04
BRIDGEWATER, T. R. [ed.] Poor Prisoners' Defence Act, 1903 1/ *n.* 8° Butterworth 04
CLARK, E. C. Analysis of Criminal Liability 7/6 c 8° Camb. Press 80
COHEN, Herman [ed.] Criminal Appeal Act, 1907; w. notes 5/ *n.* 8° Jordan 08
,, [ed.] Criminal Appeal Reports, vol. i 27/6 *n.* 8° Stevens & Haynes 09
COX, E. W. Principles of Punishmt. as appl. by Judges & Magistrates 7/6 8° Cox 78
*Cox's Criminal Law Cases, 1843–1910, 2 vols. 5/6 ea. pt. 8° *Law Times* Off., *quarterly*
DISNEY (H. W.) + GUNDRY (H.) The Criminal Law: its princs. & pract. [student's-bk.] 7/6 8° Stevens 95
HARRIS, S. F. Principles of Criminal Law, ed. C. L. Attenborough 20/ 8° Stevens [77] 08
*KENNY, Prf. C. S. Outlines of Criminal Law [an admirable introd.] 10/ 8° Camb. Press 07
,, [ed.] Cases on Criminal Law [numerous but abbreviated] 12/6 8° Camb. Press 07
Former $2·50 *n.*, latter $3 *n.* Putnam, *N.Y.*
MEWS, J., *etc.* [eds.] Digest of Cases rel. to Criminal Law; 1756–1897 25/ r 8° Sweet [84] 98
RUSSELL, Sir W. O. On Crimes and Misdemeanours, ed. W. F. Craies + L. W. Kershaw, 3 vols. 90/ r 8° Sweet [19] 09
,, The same: Amer. edn., ed. G. Sharswood, 3 vols. $15 *n.* 8° Johnson, *Phila.*
A digest of criminal law, w. a wealth of illustrn., but fitted by reason of its bulk rather to the library than as a circuit companion.
SHIRLEY, W. S. Sketch of the Criminal Law, ed. C. S. Hunter 7/6 8° Stevens [80] 89
,, [ed.] A Selection of Leading Cases in Criminal Law 6/ 8° Stevens 88
STEPHEN, Sir J. F. Digest of Crim. Law [learned; but weak in authorits.] 16/ 8° Macmillan [77] 04
,, General View of Crim. Law of Engl. [studt.'s-bk.] 14/($3·50) 8° Macmillan [63] 90
,, + STEPHEN (Sir Herb.) Digest of Law of Crim. Procedure f. Indict. Offences 12/6 8° Macmillan 83
THWAITES, Chas. Guide to Criminal Law & Procedure [student's-bk.] 10/ *n.* 8° Barber [ ] 10
WARBURTON, H. [ed.] Leading Cases in the Criminal Law 12/6 8° Stevens [88] 08
An excellent bk. for students, founded on Shirley, with good notes unlike KENNY, wh. has none.
WILSHERE, A. M. Elements of Criminal Law [effective 'cram' bk.] 7/6 c 8° Sweet 06

**Comparative; International**

McCROSSAN, G. E., *etc.* International Digest of Criminal Law, 3 vols. ea. $6 8° Poole, *Toronto* 06
PHILLIPS, H. A. D. Comparative Criminal Jurisprudence, 2 vols. 24/ 8° Thacker, *Calcutta* 89

**Scotland**

ANDERSON, A. M. The Criminal Law of Scotland 12/ *n.* 8° Green, *Edin.* [92] 04
ANGUS, J. W. Dict. of Crimes & Offences acc. to Law of Scotl. 12/ *n.* 8° Green, *Edin.* 95
MACDONALD, J. H. A. [L'd KINGSBURGH] Pract. Treat. on Criminal Law of Scotland [standard] 31/6 8° Green, *Edin.* [ ] 94
MONCREIFF, L'd Review in Criminal Cases 15/ 8° Green, *Edin.* 77
RENTON (R. W.) + BROWN (H. H.) Criminal Procedure acc. to Law of Scotld. 16/ *n.* 8° Green, *Edin.* 09

**Australia**

GURNER, H. F. Criminal Law 16/ 8° *Melbourne* 71

*New South Wales*

ADDISON, C. G. Digest of Crim. & Magist. Cases in N.S.W.: 1840–94 42/ r 8° Sweet 95
WATKINS (I. L.) + O'CONOR (R. E.) Digest of Crim. & Mag. Cases in N.S.W.: 1840–81 31/6 *n.* r 8° 81

**Canada**

CLARKE, S. R. The Criminal Law of Canada 25/ 8° *Toronto* 72
,, Magistrate's Manual [a digest of criminal law] 21/ r 8° *Toronto* [78] 88
McCROSSAN (G. E.) + SCHULTZ (J. D.) + HARPER (A. M.) Digest of Canadian Criminal Case Law $8 8° Poole, *Toronto* 08
TASCHERAU, H. E. Criminal Law Acts of Canada, 2 vols. 40/ 8° *Toronto* 74–5

**China**

ALABASTER, Sir C. Notes and Commentaries on Chinese Criminal Law 18/ *n.* r 8° Luzac
Posth. ed. Ezn. ALABASTER. A full and trustworthy acc. of Chinese criminal practice.

**India**, *incl.* Penal Code —*for* Crim. Procedure *v.* **D** § 107

BAMPADA MUKHARJI + HEM CHANDRA MITRA [eds.] Ind. Penal Code; w. notes & gloss. 9/ c 8° *Calcutta* 96
CRANENBURGH, D. E. [ed.] The New Criminal Court Manual 24/ 8° *Calcutta* [2nd edn. 84]
CUTLER (J.) + GRIFFIN (E. F.) Analysis of Indian Penal Code; w. notes 6/ 8° Butterworth [69] 71

GOUR, Dr H. S. — The Penal Law of India, vol. i [in 2 vols.] 15/ 8° Spink, *Calcutta* 09
KNOX, G. E. — Criminal Law of Bengal Presidency, 2 vols. 25/ 8° *Calcutta* 83
*MAYNE, J. Dawson — Commentaries on Indian Penal Code [Act xlv of 1860] 30/ 8° Higginbotham, *Madras* (Bain) [61] 91
,, — The Criminal Law of India 32/ *n.* 8° Clowes [96] 04
NELSON, R. A. [ed.] — Indian Penal Code 16/ *n.* 8° Sweet [ ] 99
PHILLIPS, H. A. D. — Manual of Indian Criminal Law 8° *Madras* 85
STARLING (M. H.) + CONSTABLE (F. B.) Indian Criminal Law and Procedure 42/ 8° W. H. Allen [ ] 77
WATSON, Eric R. — Principles of Indian Criminal Law 7/6 *n.* 8° Sweet 07

**United States** —*v. also* **D** § 108

American Criminal Reports, vols. i–xv ea. $5 *n.* 8° Callaghan, *Chicago* 78–09 *in prg.*
BEALE, J. H., jun. [ed.] Sel. of Cases & Auths. in Crim. Law $5 8° *Harv. Law Rev.* Pb. Ass., *Cambr.* [00–2] 07
BISHOP, J. P. — Commentaries on Criminal Law, 2 v. $12 8° Little & Brown, *Boston* [56–8] 92
,, — Commentaries on Law of Statutory Crimes $6 8° Little & Brown, *Boston* [73] 83
CHAPLIN, H. W. [ed.] — Cases on Criminal Law $3 *n.* 8° Little & Brown, *Boston* [ ] 96
CLARK, W. L. jun. Hdbk., of Crim. Law, ed. F. B. Tiffany $3·75 8° West Pb. Co., *St Paul, Minn.* [94] 02
,, [ed.] Selected Cases on Criminal Law [compn. to above] $5 8° West Pb. Co., *St Paul, Minn.* 95
,, + MARSHALL (W. L.) Treatise on the Law of Crimes, 3 v. $18 8° Keefe, *St Paul, Minn.* [00] 05
DESTY, Rob. — Compendium of American Criminal Law $3 8° Whitney, *San Francisco* 82
GROSS, H. — Criminal Investigation, tr. J. Adam $10 8° Lawyers' Co-op. Pb. Co., *Rochester* 07
HEARD, F. F. — Law and Pract. in Criminal Law [w. forms, etc.] $6 8° Little & Brown, *Boston* [79] 82
HUGHES, C. — Criminal Law $6 8° Bowen-Merrill, *Indianapolis* 01
MCCLAIN, E. — Treat. on Crim. Law admin. in U.S., 2 vols. $12 8° Callaghan, *Chicago* 97
MAY, J. W. — Law of Crimes, ed. H. A. Bigelow $3·50 8° Little & Brown, *Boston* [81] 08
MIKELL, W. E. [ed.] — Cases on Criminal Law [Am. & Engl.] $4 8° West Pb. Co., *St Paul, Minn.* 08
ROOD, J. R. [ed.] — Digest on Important Cases on Law of Crimes $3·75 *n.* 8° Wahr, *Ann Arbor, Mich.* 07
TRAIN, Arth. — The Prisoner at the Bar $1·50 8° Scribner, *N.Y.* 07
8/6 Laurie. An acc. of the actual administration of criminal law in New York by an Assistant-District-Attorney.
WASHBURN, E. Manual of Criminal Law [for studts.; incl. proced.] $2·50 12° Callaghan, *Chicago* [78] 89
WHARTON, F. — Treatise on Criminal Law, 2 vols. $12 8° Kay, *Phila.* [46] 96

**Germany**

DRAGE, G. [ed.] — Criminal Code of the German Empire [tr.] 8/ c 8° Chapman 85

**Japan**

BECKER, J. E. [tr.] — Criminal Code of Japan 3/ *n.* 8° 07

**Jews**

BENNY, P. B. — Criminal Code of Jews [acc. to Talmud; 3rd cent.] 4/6 c 8° Smith & Elder 80

**Turkey**

WALPOLE, C. G. [tr.] — Ottoman Penal Code [tr. fr. French text] 7/6 c 8° Clowes 89

**Consent**

CHAND, Hukm — The Law of Consent 21/ 4° Butterworth 97
Chfly. w. refer. to Criminal law, inclg. doctrs. of Mistake, Duress, and Waiver.

**Criminal Appeal Act**

SIBLEY, N. W. — Criminal Appeal and Evidence 15/ *n.* 8° Unwin 08
Expounds synthetically and analytically the Criminal Appeal Act. Gives some remarkable cases of circumstantial evidence, a histor. sketch of the Royal Prerogative of Mercy; and deals w. questn. of compensation on wrongful conviction (e.g. Geo. EDALJI).
WROTTESLEY (F. J.) + JACOBS (B.) Law and Practice of Criminal Appeals 20/ 8° Sweet 10

**Criminal Law Amendment Act**

MEAD (F.) + BODKIN (A. H.) Criminal Law Amendment Act, 1885 3/6 12° Shaw [86] 90

**Defences**

LAWSON, J. D. — Defenses [*sic*] to Crime, 6 vols. $18 8° Bancroft, *San Francisco* 87–92
The adjudged cases in the Amer. and Engl. Repts. in wh. the different defences to crime are contained.

**Evidence** —*v.* **D** § 43*

**History**

CHERRY, R. R. Growth of Criminal Law in Ancient Communities *o.p.* [*pb.* 5/] 8° Macmillan 90

*STEPHEN, Sir J. F. History of Criminal Law of England, 3 v. 48/ ($12·50 *n.*) 8° Macmillan [83] 83

**Larceny**

ATTENBOROUGH, C. L. Recovery of Stolen Goods & Goods obtained by Fraud 7/6 8° Stevens & Haynes 06

**Theft** —*v.* **D** § 75 [POLLOCK + WRIGHT—deals fully w. law of Theft]

**History of Criminal Law**—*v.* **F** § 5 **Homicide**—*v.* **D** § 47** **Magisterial Law**—*v.* **D** § 105 **Navy, Criminal Law of**—*v.* **D.** § 61 **Police Law**—*v.* **D** § 67

## CURRENCY LAWS—*v.* D § 115

## 33 : CUSTOMS AND USAGES—*v. also* D § 56

ASKE, R. W. Law rel. to Custom and Usages of Trade 16/ 8° Stevens 09

BROWNE, J. H. B. Law of Usages and Customs [practical] *o.p.* [*pb.* 7/6] 8° Stevens 75

**India**

NELSON, J. H. Indian Usage and Judge-made Law in Madras 12/ 8° Paul 87

**United States**

LAWSON, J. D. The Law of Usages and Customs $5·50 8° Thomas, *St Louis* 80

## 34 : DAMAGES

*MAYNE, J. D. Treatise on Law of Damages, ed. Lumley Smith 28/ 8° Stevens & Haynes [72] 09
A very learned work, dealing with the subject in all its aspects.

*SEDGWICK, H. D. [ed.] Leading Cases American and English in Damages $7·50 8° Baker, *N.Y.* 78
Arranged according to subjects. A mine of learning on the law of damage.

**India**

COLLETT, C. Manual of Law of Torts, and Measure of Damages 16/ 8° *Madras* [ ] 77

**United States**

HALE, W. B. Treatise on the Law of Damages $3·75 *n.* 8° West Pb. Co., *St Paul, Minn.* 96

JOYCE (J. A.) + HOWARD (C. F.) Treatise on Damages $18 8° Banks, *N.Y* 03

MECHEM, F. R. [ed.] Cases on the Law of Damages $4 8° West Pb. Co., *St Paul, Minn.* [95] 02

SEDGWICK, A. G. Elements of Law of Damages $2·50 *n.* 8° Little & Brown, *Boston* 96

*SEDGWICK, T. Treatise on Measure of Damages, ed. A. G. Sedgwick + J. H. Beale $15 *n.* 8° Baker, *N.Y.* [47] 91
A very exhaustive work, useful to English lawyers as well as to American.

SUTHERLAND, J. G. Treatise on Law of Damages, ed. J. R. Berryman, 3 vols. ea. $6 8° Callaghan, *Chicago* [82-3] 03

VOORHEIS, G. P. Treat. on Law of Measure of Damages for Pers. Injuries $6 8° Laning, *Norwalk, O.* 07

WATSON, A. R. Treat. on Law of Damages for Pers. Injuries $6 8° Michie, *Charlottesville* 01

## 35 : DEBTOR AND CREDITOR—*v. also* D § 17

ARCHER, J. A. Tables for the Repayment of Loans 17/6 *n.* 8° Shaw [ ] 06

HURRY, A. A. Small Debt Procedure 4/ *n.* 8° Green, *Edin.* 08

PYE, H. J. Notes on Conflicting Claims to Property of Debtor 3/6 *n.* c 8° Butterworth 80

**United States** *and* **Canada**

BUMP, O. F. Treat. on Conveyances made by Drs. to Defraud Crs. $6·25 8° Lowdermilk, *Washgtn.* [72] 95

MUNGER, G. G. Application of Payments by Debtor to Creditor 12/ 8° *Toronto* 79

WAPLES, R. Law of Debt. & Cred. rel. to Situs of Debt $3·50 8° Flood, *Chicago* 98

**Money-lenders** —*v.* **D** § 19

**Private Arrangements**

LAWRANCE, A. [ed.] Preced. of Deeds of Arrangemt. betw. Debt. & Cred. 7/6 8° Stevens [84] 00

ROBSON, G. Y. Treatise on Law of Private Arrangemts. w. Creditors *o.p.* [*pb.* 9/] 8° Clowes 88

*WINSLOW, Reg. Law of Private Arrangemts. betw. Debtors and Creditors *o.p.* 8° Clowes 85

* „ [ed.] Deeds of Arrangemt. Act, 1887, w. Rules 1888 3/6 *n.* 8° Clowes 88

## 36: DEEDS

BETTS, A. — Glossary of Ancient Words, Pt. i [to Azenaria] 10/6 *n.* 8° Stevens 07 *in prg.*
For the antiquary and lawyer: concerned chfly. w. fines and mulcts, punishmts, services, etc., due to the King, Church, lords of manors. Refs. in each case, and quotns.

DEVLIN, R. T. — Treatise on the Law of Deeds, 2 vols. ea. $12 8° Bancroft, *San Francisco* 85–7

NORTON (R. F.) + DUN (R. H.) + KOE (D. L. F.) Treat. on Deeds [based on Elphinstone (1885)] 30/ 8° Maxwell 06

**Deciphering of Deeds** —*v. also* **D** § 4, *s.v.* Terms, etc.

EARLE, Prf. J. — Hdbk. to Land Charters & other Saxon Documts. 16/ ($4) c 8° Clar. Press 88
Intended to facilitate study of legal documts. in KEMBLE'S *Codex Diplomaticus*, repub. by BIRCH in his *Cartularium Saxonicum* [*ut* **F** § 18].

ELPHINSTONE, H. W., etc. — Rules for Interpretn. of Deeds, w. Gloss. of Terms—*ut* **D** § 4

MARTIN, C. Trice — The Record Interpreter 12/6 8° Reeves & Turner 92
A colln. of abbrevns., Lat. words, and names used in Engl. histor. MSS. and records.

THOYTS, E. E. — How to Decipher and Study Old Documents 5/ *n.* 8° [93] Stock 10
Chiefly documts. rel. to family and local history, genealogy, and antiquarian matters. Introd. by C. Trice MARTIN.

WRIGHT, Andr. — Court Hand Restored, or Assistant in Reading Deeds, Charters, etc., ed. C. T. Martin 21/ 4° Chatto [1776] 79
23 copper plates, describg. the Old Law Lands, w. their contractns. and abbrevns. Appendix conts. Anc. Names of Gt. Brit. and Ireland, List of Anc. Surnames, and Glossary of Latin words of early lawyers and wrgs. omitted fr. the ordinary dictionaries.

**Registration** —*v.* **D** § 82

## 37: DELIBERATIVE ASSEMBLIES, PUBLIC MEETINGS, ETC.

BLACKWELL, G. — Law of Meetings 2/6 *n.* p 8° Stevens [ ] 07

CREWS, A. — Conduct and Procedure at Public and Company Meetings 2/6 *n.* c 8° Jordan 10

CHAMBERS, G. F. — Handbook for Public Meetings 2/6 r 12° Stevens [78] 07

MUIRHEAD, J. — The Law of Meetings 3/ *n.* c 8° 07

PALGRAVE, Sir R. F. D. — The Chairman's Handbook 2/ 12° Low [77] 03

RANSOM, D. M. — The Chairman's Hand Debater's Hdbk. 1/ *n.* 64° Routledge [09] 09
50 c. Dutton, *N.Y.* [Miniature Reference Lib.] A convenient and trustworthy little bk.

TAYLER, J. — Guide to the Business of Public Meetings 2/6 *n.* c 8° E. Wilson [93] 02

**United States**

CROCKER, Geo. G. — Principles of Procedure in Deliberative Bodies 75 c. (3/) 32° Putnam 89

CUSHING, L. S. — Law and Practice of Legisl. Assemblies in U.S. $6 8° Little & Brown, *Boston* [56] 66

,, — Manl. of Parliam. Practice, Rules, etc., ed. E. C. Cushing 75 c. 18° Thompson, *Boston* [53] 77

ROBERT, Lt.-Col. H. M. — Rules of Order for Delib. Assemblies [standard authority] 75 c. 12° Griggs, *Chicago* [76] 89

## DIVORCE—*v.* D § 59

## 38: DOMESTIC RELATIONS—*v. also* D § 48, D § 49, D § 59, D § 61

*EVERSLEY, W. P. — The Law of Domestic Relations 38/ 8° Stevens & Haynes [85] 06
Deals w. 'Husband and Wife', 'Parent and Child', 'Guardian and Ward', etc.

SLATER, J. A. — Household Law 5/ *n.* 8° Pitman 07

**United States**

REEVE, Tapping — Law of Baron and Feme, Domestic Relations, etc.—*ut* **D** § 48

RODGERS, W. C. — Treatise on Law of Domestic Relations $6 8° Flood, *Chicago* 99

SCHOULER, J. — Treatise on Law of Domestic Relations $6 8° Little & Brown, *Boston* [70] 95

TIFFANY, W. C. — Handbk. on Law of Persons & Dom. Relns. $3·75 8° West Pb. Co., *St Paul, Minn.* 96

WOODRUFF, E. H. [ed.] — Seln. of Cases on Dom. Relns. & Law of Persons $4 8° Baker, *N.Y.* 97

## DOMICILE—*v.* D § 113

## 38*: DOWER; GIFT

SCRIBNER — The Law of Dower, ed. A. I. Phillips, 2 vols. $13 8° Johnson, *Phila.* [ ]

THORNTON, W. W. — Treatise on Law rel. to Gifts and Advancements $6 *n.* 8° Johnson, *Phila.*

## 39: DRUNKENNESS

BARNETT, H. N. — Legal Responsibility of the Drunkard 2/6 *n.* c 8° Baillière 08

BLACKWELL, G. — Habitual Inebriates Acts, 1879–'98 3/6 *n.* c 8° Butterworth 99

FREEMAN, S. — Guide to Stat. Law agst. Drunkenness in Engl. 6/ *n.* 8° Butterworth 06

PAINE, Wyatt — Law of Inebriate Reformatories and Retreats [w. Acts '79–'98] 6/ c 8° Sweet 99

## EASEMENTS—*v.* D § 78

## 39* : ECCLESIASTICAL LAW—*v.* A § 111

## 40 : ELECTIONS, PETITIONS, REGISTRATION (PARLIAMENTARY AND MUNICIPAL

ANDERSON (Y.) + ELLIS (C. E.) Election Law, and Pract. of Election Petitions 17/6 8° Clowes 85
COLTMAN, F. J. [ed.] Registr. Cases : appeals fr. Revis. Barristers, 1879–'85 48/*n.* r 8° Stevens 79–85
In continuation of LUTWYCHE, KEANE and GRANT, HOPWOOD and PHILBRICK, and HOPWOOD and COLTMAN.
DAVIS, J. E. Manual of Law of Registration [parliam. & munic.] 15/ 12° Butterworth [68] 80
DAY, S. H. [ed.] Election Cases in 1892 and 1893 7/6 r 12° Stevens 94
ELLIS, A. J. Handbook for Electors and Election Agents 2/6 c 8° Sonnenschein 92
ELLIS, R. G. Practical Notes on Parliamentary Elections [mainly Scottish] 2/6 *n.* 8° Green, *Edin.* [05] 10
FLETCHER, C. G. E. Registration of Electors 5/*n.* c 8° Butterworth 08
FOX + SMITH [eds.] Registration Cases, 1886–'95 [contin. of Coltman] 50/*n.*
FRASER, Dr. Hugh Law of Parliam. Elections and Election Petitions 15/*n.* 8° Butterworth [06] 10
HEDDERWICK, T. C. H. The Parliamentary Election Manual 10/6 12° Stevens [91] 00
LAWSON, W. Notes of Decisions in Registration Cases, 1885–1908, 16 vols. 94/6 94–09
1885–1893, 24/; 1894–1897 ea. 4/6 *n.*; 1898, 7/6; 1899–1908, ea. 4/6 *n.*
LELY (J. M.) + FOULKES (W. D.) [eds.] Parliamt. Elect. Acts ; w. notes & Supp. 17/6 8° Butterworth 85
MACKENZIE (M. M.) + LUSHINGTON (S. G.) Parliam. & Loc. Gov. Registr. Manl. 22/6 *n.* 8° Shaw [ ] 09
MOLONEY, M. Registration of Voters 7/6 r 12° Sweet [ ] 07
O'MALLEY (E. L.) + HARDCASTLE (H.) Election Petitions, 5 vols. [reports 1869–1906] 117/ r 8° *in prg.*
POWELL, Ellis T. Pract. Notes on the Management of Elections 1/6 *n.* c 8° P. S. King & Son 10
*ROGERS, F. N. On Elections and Petitions, 3 vols. ea. 21/ 8° Stevens [3–] 09–6
Vol. i : *Registration*, ed. Maur. POWELL '09 ; ii : *Parl. Elections and Petitions*, ed. C. W. WILLIAMS '06 ; iii : *Municipal and other Elections and Petitions*, ed. C. W. WILLIAMS + G. H. B. KENRICK '06.
SAINT, J. J. H. [ed.] Digest of Parl. and Munic. Registr. Cases, ed. T. Mathew [1843–1906] 15/ c 8° Butterworth [79] 06
SEAGER, J. R. Notes on Registration 3/6 *n.* c 8° Bemrose [ ] 08
SMITH, C. L. [ed.] Registration Cases, 1895–'09 [contin. of Fox + Smith] r 8° 05–9
Vol. i, '95–'05, 54/ *n.*; ii, Pt. i, '06–'07, 5/ *n.*; Pt. ii, '07–'08, 5/ *n.*; Pt. iii, '08–'09, 6/ *n.*
WARD, D. Practice at Parliamentary Elections and Law 9/ r 12° Butterworth [ ] 06

### Scotland

BLAIR, P. J. Manual for Parliam., County Council and Municipal Elections and Election Petitions 15/*n.* 8° Green, *Edin.* 93
Borough and County Council Elections, excl. Metrop. Borough Councils 2/6 *n.* 8° Green, *Edin.* 07
ELLIS, R. G. Practical Notes—*ut sup.*
GRAHAM, J. E. Manl. of Electns. (Scotl.) Corr. Pract. Act, 1890 4/6 8° Blackwood 91
NICOLSON, J. Law of Parl. Elections in Scotland *o.p.* [*w.* 18/] 8° Green, *Edin.* [ ] 79
,, Analysis of Recent Statutes affectg. Parl. Electns. in Scotl. [suppl. to above] 7/6 8° Bell & Bradfute, *Edin.* 85
WHITELAW, J. W. Qualification and Registration of Voters 6/*n.* 8° Green, *Edin.* 04
,, [ed.] Statutes rel. to Qualificn. & Registrn. of Voters 6/*n.* 8° Green, *Edin.* 08
,, Treat. on Law of Parliam. Elections in Scotl. 18/ 8° Bell & Bradfute, *Edin.* 7)

### United States

JEWETT, F. G. Manual for Election Officers and Voters in N.Y. $2 8° Bender, *Albany* [93] 08
McCRARY, G. W. Treatise on the American Law of Elections $6 8° Callaghan, *Chicago* [80] 97

### Ballot Act

FITZGERALD, G. A. [ed.] Ballot Act ; w. Introd. : guide to proc. at electns. 5/6 f 8° Stevens [72] 76

### Corrupt Practices

JELF, E. A. [ed.] Corrupt and Illegal Practices Prev. Act, 1893 7/6 8° Sweet [94] 05
RICHARDS, H. C. [ed.] Corr. & Illeg. Pract. Prev. Acts, 1883–5, ed. M. R. Emanuel 3/6 *n.* c 8° Jordan 06

### Election Agent

PARKER, F. R. Powers, Duties & Liabilities of an Elect. Agent & Return. Officer 31/6 8° Knight [85] 91

**Local Boards**

DILL, T. R. C. Poor Law Guardn's & Dist. C'r's Electn. Manl. 15/ r 12° Shaw 94
HUNT, Jno. Metropolitan Borough Councils Elections 3/6 8° Stevens 00
LUMLEY, W. G. Poor Law Election Manual; ed. Glen 6/ 12° Shaw [45] 86
LUSHINGTON, S. G. County Council and Municipal Election Manual 7/6 12° Butterworth [88] 92
PARKER, F. R. Electn. of Co. Councils und. Loc. Govt. Act, 1888 20/ 8° Knight [89] 92
,, Electn. of Guardns. and Distr. Counclrs., etc., under L.G. Act 21/ 8° Knight [ ] 99
,, Election of Parish Councils under Loc. Govt. Act 1894 6/ 8° Knight 94
RYDE, W. C. Election Manual for Parish Councillors, District Councillors, and Guardians outside London 7/6 8° Butterworth 94

## 41 : EMPLOYERS' LIABILITY—*v. also* D § 45, D § 69

ARONSON, V. R. [ed.] The Workman's Compensation Act, 1906 15/ *n.* 8° Unwin 09
BARNETT, H. N. [F.R.C.S.] Accidental Injuries to Workmen w. ref. to Wm. Comp. Act, '06 7/6 *n.* 8° Rebman 09
*BEVEN, T. Law of Employer's Liability and Workmen's Compensation 21/ 8° Stevens & Haynes [ ] 09
BIRRELL, A. Four Lectures on Employers' Liability at Home and Abroad 2/6 c 8° Macmillan 97
BUTTERWORTH'S [pub.] Workmen's Compensation Cases, vol. i [1907–8] 7/6 *n.* 8° Butterworth 09
CLEGG, A. T. Commentary on Workmen's Compensation Act, 1897 7/6 *n.* 8° Green, *Edin.* [98] 99
,, + ROBERTSON (M. A.) Digest of Workmen's Compensation Acts, 1897–1902 10/ *n.* 8° Green, *Edin.* 02
DAWBARN, C. Y. C. Employers' Liability to their Servants 25/ *n.* 8° Sweet [ ] 11
EAGLESON, J. G. The Liability of Employers: statutes, forms 15/ *n.* 8° Sweet 95
ELLIOTT, A. [ed.] Workm. Comp. Acts, 1897, 1900, 10/6 *n.*; Act, 1906 15/ *n.* 8° Stevens [97] 03; 07
HILL, W. E. [ed.] Workmen's Compensation Act, 1906 3/6 *n.* 8° Waterlow 07
,, Law of Workmen's Compensation & Employers' Liability 10/ *n.* 8° Waterlow [98] 07
KNOWLES, C. M. Law rel. to Compensation for Injuries to Workmen 8/ *n.* 8° Stevens 07
MINTON-SENHOUSE, R. M. [ed.] Workmen's Compensation Cases, vols. i–ix [1898–1906] [for contin. *v.* Ruegg, *inf.*] ea. 6/ 8° Butterworth 99–08 *in prg.*
NEAVE, Dr F. G. Law rel. to Injuries to Workmen 1/6 *n.* c 8° E. Wilson [03] 10
PARSONS (A.) + ALLEN (R.) [eds.] Workmen's Compens. Acts, 1897 & 1906 10/ *n.* 8° Butterworth [98] 07
ROBERTS (W. H.) + WALLACE (G. H.) + GRAHAM (A. H.) Duty and Liability of Employers 35/ r 8° Butterworth [83] 08
ROBINSON, A. Employer's Liability under Acts of 1897 and 1880 *o.p.* [*pb.* 7/6] r 12° Stevens [98] 81
RUEGG, Judge A. H. [ed.] Emp. Liab. Act, 1880, & Workmen's Comp. Act, 1897 8° Butterworth [ ] *in prep.*
,, Laws regul. Relatn. of Empl. & Wkman. in Eng. [6 lects.] 7/6 c 8° Clowes 05
,, [ed.] Workmen's Compens. Cases, vols. i-iv. 8° Butterworth 09–11
UMPHERSTON, F. A. [ed.] Workmen's Compensation Act, 1906 12/ *n.* 8° Green, *Edin.* 07
WILLIS, W. A. [ed.] Workmen's Compensation Acts, 1897, 1900, 1906 5/ *n.* c 8° Butterworth [98] 11

**Scotland**

SYM, J. D. Analysis of the Employers' Liability Act, 1880 5/ 8° Bell & Bradfute, *Edin.* [80]

**United States**

ALGER (G. W.) + SLATER (S. S.) Treatise on N.Y. Employers' Liability Act $3 8° Bender, *Albany* [03] 07
BAILEY, W. F. Law of Pers. Injury rel. to Master & Servant, 2 v. $12 8° Callaghan, *Chicago* 97
DRESSER, F. F. [ed.] Empl. Liab. Acts in N.Y., Mass, Ind., Ala., Colo., & Eng. ea. $6 8° Keefe, *St Paul, Minn.* [02] 03
RENO, C. Treatise on Law of Employers' Liability Acts $5 *n.* 8° Houghton, *Boston* 96

*Mining Injuries*

WHITE, E. J. Law of Personal Injuries in Mines $6·75 8° Thomas, *St Louis* [03] 05

**Continent of Europe**

HIGGINS, A. P. Employers' Liab. & Compens. on the Continent 5/ *n.* 8° Green, *Edin.* 98

**Industrial Diseases Compensation**

LAWES, E. T. H. Compensation for Industrial Diseases 7/6 8° Stevens 09
LUSON (Dr T.) + HYDE (R.) Diseases of Workmen [Workm. Comp. Act 1906, Sched. 3] 4/ *n.* p 8° Butterworth 08

## 42 : EQUITY

ASHBURNER, W. Principles of Equity [student's-bk.] 21 / 8° Butterworth 02
BRETT, Thos. [ed.] Leading Cases in Modern Equity, ed. J. A. Strahan 15/ 8° Butterworth [87] 08
HAYNES, F. O. Outlines of Equity, ed. C. J. W. Farwell p 8° Sweet [60] *in prep.*
INDERMAUR, J. Manual of Principles of Equity [excell. studt's.-bk.] 20/ Barber [86] 06
,, [ed.] Epitome of Leading Conveyancing and Equity Cases—*ut* **D** § 30
MAITLAND, Prf. F. W. Equity ; also Forms of Action at Comm. Law 12/6 8° Camb. Press 09
$4 *n.* Putnam, *N.Y.* Posthum. ed. A. H. CHAYTOR + W. J. WHITTAKER. Two courses of lects., providing a scholarly and valuable acc. of that system of wh., acc. to an old saying, the parents were 'fraud and fear, and a Court of conscience was the nurse'.
RANDALL, A. E. [ed.] Selection of Leading Cases in Equity Stevens *in prep.*
*SMITH, H. Arth. Principles of Equity : pract. exposn. [*Analysis* 5 / '09] 21 / 8° Stevens [4–] 08
SMITH, Jos. W. Manual of Equity Jurisprudence 12/6 12° Stevens [80] 00
*SNELL, E. H. T. Principles of Equity, ed. Arch. Brown [student's-book] 21 / 8° Stevens [74] 08
Blyth, E. Analysis of Snell 6/ 8° Stevens [85] 08
Gibson, A. Aids to Equity, as a help to Snell 10/ 8° Reeves & Turner [82] 08
STORY, J. —*ut infra, s.v.* United States
STRAHAN (J. A.) + KENRICK (G. H. B.) A Digest of Equity 17/6 8° Butterworth [05] 09
Equity reduced to a series of propositions, for the use of students—lucid, but not entirely trustworthy or accurate.
,, [ed.] Leading Cases in Equity—*v.* BRETT, *sup.*
THOMSON, Dr Andr. Princs. of Equity and Equity Pract. of County Ct. 32/6 8° Clowes 96
,, Compendium of Modern Equity 30/ 8° Clowes 99
WATSON, W. W. Practical Compendium of Equity, ed. B. P. Newman, 2 vols. 60/ r 8° Sweet 86
*WHITE (F. T.) + TUDOR (O. D.) [eds.] Seln. of Leading Cases in Equity, ed. W. J. Whittaker, 2 vols. 75/ r 8° Maxwell [49] 11
Holds a position in Equity as high as, if not higher than, SMITH in Common Law. An indispensable classic—the fount fr. wh. all other wks. on Equity derive their inspiration and learning. Amer. edn., ed. F. S. DICKSON, 4 vols. $14 8° Banks, *N.Y.* 89.
Kelke, W. H. H. Epitome of Leading Cases in Equity [bas. on above] 6/ c 8° Sweet [01] 10

### Australia

WALKER, W. G. [ed.] Practice in Equity [Equity Act of 1880, and rules] 18/ 8° *Sydney* 88

### United States

ADAMS, Jno. Doctrine of Equity, ed. R. Railston $6·50 8° Johnson, *Phila.*
American and English Decisions in Equity, vols. i–x ea. $4·75–$6·50 8° Murphy, *Phila.* 95–07
BATES, C. S. Federal Equity Procedure, 2 vols. $12 8° Flood, *Chicago* 01
BEACH, C. F., jun. Mod. Equity as determ. by Cts. & Stats. of Engl. & U.S., 2 v. $12 *n.* 8° Baker, *N.Y.* 92
,, Modern Practice in Equity in States & Fed. Cts. of U.S., 2 v. $12 *n.* 8° Anderson, *Cincinnati* 94
,, Modern Equity : comms. on law of injunctions, 2 vols. $12 8° Parsons, *Albany* 95
BISPHAM, G. T. The Principles of Equity, ed. Sharswood Brinton $6 n. 8° Banks, *N.Y.* [ ] 09
EATON, J. W. Equity Jurisprudence $3·75 *n.* 8° West Pb. Co., *St Paul, Minn.* 01
FETTER, N. [ed.] Illustrative Cases upon Equity Jurisprudence $3·50 8° West Pb. Co., *St Paul, Minn.* 95
HOGG, C. E. Equity Principles $7·50 8° Clarke, *Cincinnati* 00
,, Equity Procedure, 2 vols. $15 8° Anderson, *Cincinnati* 03
KEENER, W. A. [ed.] Selection of Cases on Equity Jurisdiction, 3 vols. $17 *n.* 8° Baker, *N.Y.* 94–7
KINLEY, J. M. [ed.] American and English Precedents $6 8° Crocker, *San Francisco* 99
LAWSON, J. D. [ed.] Leading Cases Simplified: equity & constit. law $2·50 8° Thomas, *St Louis* 83
,, Rights, Remedies, and Practice at Law *and* Index Digest—*ut* **D** § 25
MARTIN, A. [ed.] Selection of Cases on Equity Jurisdiction $4·50 8° Stephens, *Columbia* 02
MAXWELL, S. Treat. on Pleading, Pract., Procedure, and Precedents in Actns. at Law & Suits in Equity $6 8° *State Jl.* Co., *Lincoln, Neb.* [ ] 96
MERWIN, E. Principles of Equity and Equity Pleading $6 8° Houghton, *Boston* 95
POMEROY, J. N. Treatise on Equity Jurisprudence, 4 vols., ea. $6 ; Student's Edn., 1 vol. $6 8° Bancroft, *San Francisco* [81–3] 05 ; 07
Pomeroy, J. N., jun. Treatise on Equitable Remedies, 2 vols., ea. $6 ; [suppl. to above] 8° Bancroft, *San. Franc.* 05
SCOTT, J. B. [ed.] Cases on Equity Jurisdiction, 2 vols. ea. $4·50 8° Baker, *N.Y.* 06–7

*STORY, J. Commentaries on Equity Jurisprudence as admin. in Eng. & Amer., ed. W. E. Grigsby 45 / r 8° Stevens [35–6] 92

* ,, Commentaries on orig. text restored [fr. 4th ed. (1846)], ed. M. M. Bigelow, 2 vols. $12 8° Little & Brown, *Boston* [35–6] 86

* ,, Commentaries on Equity Pleading, ed. J. M. Gould—*ut* **D** § 109

THOMPSON, B. M. [ed.] Cases on Equity Pleading and Practice $3 *n.* 8° Callaghan, *Chicago* 03

## 43 : ESTOPPEL

CABABE, M. Essay on the Principles of Estoppel 3/6 c 8° Sweet 88

EVEREST (L. F.) + STRODE (E.) The Law of Estoppel 25 / 8° Stevens [84] 07

EWART, J. S. Exposition of Principles of Estoppel by Misrepresentation [$5 *n.* Callaghan, *Chicago*] 25 / 8° Stevens 00

### India

BROUGHTON, L. Estoppel by Matters of Record in Civil Suits in India *o.p.* [*pb.* 7/6] 8° Clar. Press 93

### United States

BIGELOW, M. M. Treatise on the Law of Estoppel $6 r 8° Little & Brown, *Boston* [ ] 82

HERMAN, H. M. Comments. on Law of Estoppel & Res Judicata, 2 v.—*ut* **D** § 109

## 43* : EVIDENCE

BEST, W. M. Principles of Law of Evidence, ed. J. M. Lely [$3·50 Boston Bk. Co.] 25 / r 8° Sweet [49] 06

COCKLE, E. [ed.] Leading Cases on Law of Evidence [excell. small bk.] 7/6 8° Sweet 07

GULSON, J. R. Philosophy of Proof in rel. to Engl. Law of Judicial Evid. 10/6 8° Routledge 05

JELF, E. A. Princs. of Law of Evidence peculiar to Crim. Cases 3/6 8° Cox [ ] 99

PHIPSON, S. L. Law of Evidence [good bk. of moderate compass] 15 / c 8° Stevens & Haynes [92] 07

,, Manual of the Law of Evidence 7/6 c 8° Stevens & Haynes 08

POWELL, E. Principles and Practice of Law of Evidence, Dr. W. Blake Odgers 20 / c 8° Butterworth [56] 10

*ROSCOE, E. S. Digest of Law of Evid. & Pract. in Crim. Cases, ed. Herm. Cohen 31/6 r 12° Sweet [35] 08

,, The same : Amer. edn., ed. F. L. Wayland, 2 vols. $11 *n.* 8° Johnson, *Phila.*

*ROSCOE, H. Digest of Law of Evid. in Nisi Prius, ed. M. Powell, 2 v. 42 / 8° Sweet [2nd ed. 31] 07

STARKIE, Thos. On Evidence, ed. Geo. Sharswood $6·50 8° Johnson, *Phila.* [ ]

*STEPHEN, Sir J. F. Digest of Law of Evid., ed. Sir H. Stephen + H. L. Steven 6 / c 8° Macmillan [76] 07
$2·50 Callaghan, *Chicago.* A marvellously compressed statemt. *New South Wales Edn.*, ed. H. G. Shaw, 10/ 8° Macmillan '09.

TAYLOR, J. Pitt Treat. on Law of Evid., ed. W. E. Hume-Williams, 2 vols. 63 / r 8° Sweet [48] 06

WILLS, W. Essay on Principles of Circumst. Evid., ed. Sir Alf. Wills 12/6 8° Butterworth [38] 02
Amer. edn., ed. G. E. BEERS + A. L. CORBIN, $5 *n.* Boston Bk. Co., *Boston*, '05.

,, Theory & Practice of Law of Evidence, ed. Thornton Lawes 15 / 8° Stevens [94] 07
A useful book for the student and young practitioner in the ordinary run of *nisi prius* and criminal work. The subjects are arranged alphabetically in 1st col.; 2nd enumerates 'facts to be proved'; and 3rd states what is sufficient proof.

### Scotland

KIRKPATRICK, Prf. J. Digest of the Scottish Law of Evidence 8 / 8° Green, *Edin.* [82] 86

### India

CRANENBURGH, D. E. [ed.] Indian Evidence Act ; w. notes [Act no. 1, 1872] 4/6 8° *Calcutta* 88

CUNNINGHAM, Sir H. S. [ed.] Indian Evidence Act, 1872 18 / 8° *n. Madras* [73] 08

FIELD, C. D. [ed.] Law of Evidence in British India 35 / 8° (*India*) [ ] 94

GRIFFITH, Wm. [ed.] Indian Evidence Acts [Nos. 1 and 18, 1872] 15 / 8° W. H. Allen 90

MARKBY, Sir W. The Indian Evidence Act ; w. notes 3/6 *n.* ($1·10) 8° Clar. Press 97

NORTON, J. B. Law of Evidence applicable to India 30 / r 8° (*India*) [ ] 77

STEPHEN, Sir J. F. [ed.] Indian Evidence Act 1872 [w. introd.] 12/6 8° (*India*) 72

### United States

ABBOTT, Austin Treatise on Evidence at Nisi Prius $6·50 8° Baker, *N.Y.* 81

,, Trial Evidence, ed. J. J. Crawford $6·50 *n.* 8° Baker, *N.Y.* [80] 00

ELLIOTT, B. K. + W. F. Treat. on Law of Evidence, 4 v. ea. $6 8° Bobbs-Merrill, *Indianapolis* 04–5

Encyclopædia of Evidence, vols. i–xii ; 1st. Biennial Suppl. ea. $6 8° Powell, *Los Angeles in prg.*

GILLETT, J. H. Treat. on Law of Indirect & Collateral Evidence $4 *n.* 8° Bowen-Merrill, *Indianapolis* 97

GREENLEAF, S. Treatise on Law of Evidence, 3 vols. ea. $5 *n.* 8° Little & Brown, *Boston* [42–53] 99
HAMMON, L. L. On Evidence covering Burden of Prf., Presumptions, Judic. Notice, Judic. Admissions, and Estoppel $6 8° Keefe, *St Paul, Minn.* 08
HUGHES, T. W. Illustrated Treatise on Law of Evidence $5 *n.* 8° Callaghan, *Chicago* 06
JONES, B. W. Law of Evidence in Civil Cases $6·50 8° Bancroft, *San Francisco* [97] 08
MCKELVEY, J. J. Handbook on Law of Evidence $3·75 8° West Pb. Co., *St Paul, Minn.* [98] 07
MOORE, C. C. Treat. on Facts, or Weight & Bal. of Evid., 2 v. $12 8° Thompson, *Northport, L.I.* 08
REYNOLDS, W. Digest of Law of Evidence as establ. in U.S. $2·50 8° Callaghan, *Chicago* [ ] 96
,, Theory of Law of Evid., as est. in U.S. $2 8° Callaghan, *Chicago* [83] 05
THAYER, J. B. Prelim. Treat. on Law of Evid. at Com. Law, 2 v. $3 *n.* 8° Little & Brown, *Boston* 96–8
,, [ed.] Select Cases on Evidence at Common Law; w. notes $6 8° Sever, *Cambridge, Mass.* [92] 00
UNDERHILL, H. C. Treatise on Law of Criminal Evidence $6 8° Bowen-Merrill, *Indianapolis* [94] 98
WHARTON, F. Commentary on Law of Evidence in Civil Issues, 2 v. $12 8° Kay, *Phila.* [5–] 88
,, Treat. on Law of Evidence in Criminal Issues $6·50 8° Kay, *Phila.* [ ] 84
WIGMORE, J. H. Treatise on the System of Evidence in Trials at Common Law, 4 vols. $26 *n.*; Suppl. $6 *n.* 8° Little & Brown, *Boston* 05–07
WILGUS, H. L. [ed.] Cases on the Law of Evidence $3 8° West Pb. Co., *St Paul, Minn.* 96
WILL, A. P. Treatise on Law of Circumstantial Evidence $5 8° Johnston, *Phila.* 96

**France**

BODINGTON, O. E. Outline of French Law of Evidence 5/ 8° Stevens 04

**Detection of Crime** —*v.* **D** § 123
**Estoppel** —*v.* **D** § 43
**Evidence in Criminal Cases** —*v. also* **D** § 123
**Presumption of Life:** *Scotland*

STEVENSON, J. H. Law of Scotl. in rel. to Presumption of Life of Absent Persons 6/ 8° Green, *Edin.* 93

## 44 : EXECUTIVE OFFICERS

CHASTER, A. W. Public Officers having Executive Authority in U.K. 15/ 8° Stevens & Haynes [ ] 09

## EXECUTORS—*v.* D § 100

## 44* : EXPLOSIVES

MAJENDIE, Sir V. D. Guide Book to Explosives Acts, 1875 & 1883 2/6 12° Eyre & Spottiswoode [97] 02

## 45 : FACTORY AND LABOUR LAWS ; TRADE UNIONS

ABRAHAM (M. E.) + DAVIES (A. L.) Law rel. to Facts. & Workshops 6/ 8° Eyre & Spottiswoode [96] 08
ASSINDER, G. F. The Legal Position of Trade Unions 2/6 *n.* 12° 05
AUSTIN, E. Law relating to Factories and Workshops 7/6 8° Knight [95] 02
,, Law rel. to Laundries, Charitable, Reformatory, and Public Institns. under Factory Act, 1901 4/6 *n.* 8° Wyma 07
BOWSTEAD, W. Law of Factories and Workshops 9/ 8° Sweet 01
CHALMERS-HUNT, D. R. Law relating to Trade Unions 12/6 8° Butterworth 02
COHEN, Herm. Trade Union Law and Cases 6/ *n.* c 8° Sweet 07
DAVIS, J. E. [ed.] Labour Laws of 1875, w. Introd. and notes 12/ 8° Butterworth 75
HOWELL, Geo. [ed.] Handy Bk. of Labour Laws; w. Introds. & notes 3/6 *n.* ($1·50) c 8° Macmillan [76] 95
,, Labour Legislation, Labour Movements, and Labour Leaders 10/6 8° Unwin 02
HUTCHINS (Miss B. L.) + HARRISON (Miss A.) History of Factory Legislation 6/ *n.* 8° P. S. King [03] 11
International Labour Office: Bulletin, 3 vols. 8/ *n.* 8° 3, *New Rd., Woolwich, Lond.* 07
The labour-legislation of all countries. Germ. and Fch. edns. were pubd. in 1902.
JEANS, Victorine Factory Act Legislation—*ut* **D** § 118
A careful and well-reasoned piece of wk. w. good remarks on (and rather large inferences from) Act of 1850.
JEVONS, Prf. W. Stanley The State in relation to Labour—*ut* **D** § 126
MARKHAM, Violet R. Factory & Shop Acts of Brit. Dominions 2/6 n. c 8° Eyre & Spottiswoode 08
MINTON-SENHOUSE, R. M. Work and Labour 16/ r 8° Sweet 04
A compendium of the law affecting conditions under wh. manual labour of working-classes is performed in England.

PENNANT, D. F. Trade Unions and the Law 5/ 8° Stevens 05
REDGRAVE, Alex. [ed.] Factory and Truck Acts, ed. C. F. Lloyd 10/6 8° Shaw [78] 09
RUEGG, Judge A. H. Employer and Workman in England [six lectures] 7/6 c 8° Stevens 05
,, + MOSSOP (L.) Law of Factories and Workshops 12/6 8° Stevens 02
SPENS (W. C.) + YOUNGER (R. F.) Employers and Employed 14/ c 8° Macmillan 87
(1) Exposn. of law of reparation f. phys. injury, (2) E. L. Act, 1880, w. spec. ref. to decisns. in Engl. and Scotl., (3) suggested amendmts. of law.
WEBB, Mrs S. [ed.] Case for the Factory Acts 1/- c 8° Richards [01] 02
Papers by the ed. and four other ladies giving good survey of Acts at home and in Colonies.
WILLIAMS (C. W.) + MUSGRAVE (C. E.) [eds.] Factory and Workshop Act, 1901 3/6 *n.* 8° E. Wilson 02
General effect and parliamentary hist. of the Act, with its text, notes, etc., for laymen.

**Factory Laws: Economic Effect**—*v.* **D** § 118

**Labour Contracts**

GIBBONS, D. Labour Contracts, ed. T. F. Uttley [popular] 3/6 f 8° Lockwood 92

**Laundries**

BOWSTEAD, W. Law relating to Laundries 2/6 *n.* c 8° Sweet 02

**Shop Hours Acts**

BARRINGTON, C. V. [ed]. The Shop Hours Acts, 1892–1904 2/6 *n.* c 8° Butterworth 05

**Strikes, Lock-outs, etc.**

COGLEY, T. S. Law of Strikes, Lock-outs, Labour Organizns., etc. 8° *Washington* 94
NEVILLE, R. J. N. The Law of Strikes 1/ *n.* c 8° Clowes 90
STIMSON, F. J. Handbook to Labour Law of United States $1·50 12° Scribner, *N.Y.* 96
An admirable little manual, arrgd. topically, stating the existing laws in a direct, straightforward way.
,, Labour in its Relations to Law [4 lectures] 75c. 16° Scribner, *N.Y.* 95

## 46: FRAUD AND FRAUDULENT CONVEYANCES

HASTINGS, Syd. Short Treat. on Law of Fraud and Misrepresentation 9/ 8° Clowes [88] 93
HUNT, A. J. Law of Fraudulent Conveyances 9/ r 12° Butterworth [72] 97
*KERR, W. Law of Fraud and Mistake, ed. S. E. Williams 25/ r 8° Sweet [68] 02
MAY, H. W. Fraudul. & Volunt. Dispositns. of Prop., ed. W. D. Edwards 20/ *n.* r 8° Stevens [71] 08
MONCRIEFF, F. Treatise on Law of Fraud and Misrepresentation 21/ 8° Stevens 91

**India**

POLLOCK, Sir Fredk. Law of Fraud & Misrepresentation in Brit. India 12/ r 8° Thacker 94

**United States**

BIGELOW, M. M. Treat. on Law of Fraud on its Civil Side, 2 v. ea. $6 8° Little & Brown, *Boston* [88] 90
,, Law of Fraud, and Procedure for Redress $6 8° Little & Brown, *Boston* 77–9
BROWN, C. Treatise on Construction of Statute of Frauds $6 8° Little & Brown, *Boston* [70] 95
BUMP, O. F. Treatise on Fraudulent Conveyancing $5 8° *New York* [72] 76
SMITH, J. W. Treatise on the Law of Frauds $6 8° Bobbs-Merrill, *Indianapolis* 07

## 46*: GAMBLING; BETTING

COLDRIDGE (W.) + HAWKSFORD (C. V.) Law of Gambling, Civil & Criminal [w. forms] 8/6 8° 95
JONES (T. A.) + PREEDY (K. L.) [eds.] Street Betting Act, 1906 3/6 *n.* Jessel Pb. Co. 06
STUTFIELD (G. H.) + CANTLEY Law rel. to Betting, Time-Bargains, & Gaming *o.p.* 8° Waterlow [ ] 92

**Stock Exchange** —*v.* **D** § 88

## 47: GUARANTEES AND SURETIES

de COLYAR, H. A. Law of Guarantees, and Principal and Surety 17/6 8° Butterworth [74] 97
*ROWLATT, S. A. T. Law of Principal and Surety 16/ 8° Stevens & Haynes 99
One of the very best new books added to the lawyer's library of recent years.

**United States**

BRANDT, G. W. Law of Suretyship and Guarantee, 2 vols. $12 r 8° Callaghan, *Chicago* [78] 05
CHILDS, F. H. Handbk. of Law of Suretyship & Guarantee $3·75 *n.* 8° West Pb. Co., *St Paul, Minn.* 07
PINGREY, D. H. Treatise on Law of Suretyship and Guaranty $4 *n.* 8° Bender, *Albany* 01
STEARNS, A. A. Law of Suretyship $6 8° Anderson, *Cincinnati* 03
.. [ed.] Annot. Cases on Law of Suretyship $6 8° Anderson, *Cincinnati* 07

WILSON, H. H. [ed.] Cases: Suretyship and Guaranty $4 *n.* 8° Callaghan, *Chicago* 07

## 47*: GUARDIANSHIP—*v. also* D § 49

*EVERSLEY, W. P. —*in his* Law of Domestic Relations, *ut* **D** § 38

**Scotland**

FRASER, Pat., L'd. Law of Parent and Child, and Guardian and Ward—*ut* **D** § 49

**United States**

TIEDEMAN, C. G. Treat. on State & Federal Control of Persons and Property in the United States, 2 vols. $12 8° Thomas, *St Louis* 00

WOERNER, J. G. Treatise on Amer. Law of Guardianship of Minors and Persons of Unsound Mind $6 *n.* 8° Little & Brown, *Boston* 97

## 47**: HOMICIDE

**United States**

KERR, J. M. Treatise on the Law of Homicide $6 8° Banks, *N.Y.* 91

TIFFANY, Fcs. B. Law of Death by Wrongful Act $4·50 8° West Pb. Co., *St Paul, Minn.* 93

WHARTON, Fcs. Law of Homicide, ed. F. H. Bowlby $7·50 8° Lawyers' Co-op. Pb. Co., *Rochester* [ ] 07

## 48: HUSBAND AND WIFE—*v. also* D § 38, *and* D § 49

CRAWLEY, Chas. The Law of Husband and Wife 20/ 8° Clowes 92

GEARY, Nevill Marriage and Family Relations—*ut* **D** § 59

JENKS, Edw. Husband and Wife in the Law [popular] 2/6 *n.* c 8° Dent 09

LUSH, Montague Law of Husband and Wife, ed. W. H. Griffith 25/ 8° Stevens [84] 10

*MACQUEEN, J. F. Rights and Liabilities of Husband and Wife, ed. W. Paine 25/ r 8° Sweet [72] 05

SMITH, J. W. Law of Husband and Wife [Legal Handy Bks.] 2/6 f 8° E. Wilson [ ]

THICKNESSE, R. Digest of Law of Husband & Wife as to Property *o.p.* [*pb.* 20/] 8° Maxwell 84

**Scotland**

FRASER, Pat., L'd Treat. on Husband & Wife acc. to Law of Scotl., 2 v. [standard] 80/ r 8° *Edin.* [46] 78

WALTON, F. P. The Law of Husband and Wife in Scotland 20/ *n.* 8° Green, *Edin.* 93

**United States**

BULLOCK, W. E. Law of Husband and Wife in State of N.Y. $4·50 8° Parsons, *Albany* 97

LOELE, I. Legal Property Relns. of Married Parties [Col. Univ. Studs.] $1·50 *n.* 8° Macmillan, *N.Y.* 01

REEVE, Tapping Law of Baron & Feme, Domestic Relns., etc. [standard] $6 8° Gould, *Albany* [16] 74

SCHOULER, J. Treatise on Law of Husband and Wife $6 r 8° Little & Brown, *Boston* 82

**Married Women**—*v.* **D** § 60; *Disabilities*—*v.* **D** § 48

## 49: INFANTS, INFANCY, COVERTURE; CHILDREN; PARENT AND CHILD

ATHERLEY-JONES (L. L.) + BELLOT (H. H. L.) Law of Child. & Young Persons 10/6 *n.* 8° Butterworth 09
In relation to penal offences, incl. Children Act, 1908.

CLARK, J. The Law of Parent and Child 45/ *n.* r 8° Green, *Edin.* 06

DEANS, R. Storry Law of Parent and Child, Guardian and Ward, and Rights, Duties, and Liabilities of Infants 6/ c 8° 95

DEWAR, Dav. [ed.] The Children Act, 1908, & other Acts affg. Children 7/6 *n.* 8° Green, *Edin.* 09

HALL (W. Clarke) + PRETTY (A. H. F.) The Children Act, 1908; w. notes & forms 6/ 8° Stevens [94] 09

,, The Queens Reign. for Children 3/6 c 8° Unwin 97
Deals w. the Statutes of the rn. rel. to children, esp. the 1889 Act. Advocates other reforms.

LEWIS (G. C.) + BARROWS [eds.] Prevent. of Cruelty to Childr. Act, 1894; w. notes 5/ p 8° Butterworth 94

MATTHEWS, J. B. Law as to Children and Young Persons 10/6 8° Sweet 95

SIMPSON, A. H. Law and Practice rel. to Infants, ed. E. J. Elgood 22/ 8° Stevens & Haynes [75] 09

**Scotland**

FRASER, Pat., L'd Law of Parent & Child, & Guard. & Ward, ed. J. Clark 45/ *n.* r 8° Green, *Edin.* [ ] 06

**United States**

EWELL, M. D. [ed.] Leadg. Cases on Disabs. of Inf'cy, Coverture, & Idiocy $6 8° Little & Brown, *Bost.* 76

HOCHHEIMER, L. Treatise on Law rel. to Custody of Infants $3·50 8° Murphy, *Baltimore* 87

TYLER, R. H. On the Law of Infancy and Coverture $6·25 8° Gould, *Albany* [73] 82

## 50 : INSURANCE : FIRE, LIFE, MARINE, ACCIDENT

**Generally ; Life ; Fire ; Accidents**

BUCKLEY, H. B. —*in his* Law and Practice under Comp. Acts, Life Assurance Acts, etc., *ut* **D** § 26

BUNYON, C. J. Law of Fire Insurance, ed. R. J. Quin + F. E. Colenso 30 / *n.* r 8° Layton [66] 05

,, Law of Life Insurance, ed. J. V. V. Fitzgerald 31 /6 *n.* Layton [6–] 04

CRAWLEY, Chas. Law of Life Insurance [w. ch. on Accid. Ins.] 12 /6 8° Clowes 82

FITZGERALD (J. V. V.) + QUIN (R. J.) [eds.] The New Law reg. Assur. Cos. [Act '09 ; w. notes] 10/ *n.* 8° C. & E. Layton 10

FOOT, Alf. Pract. of Ins. agst. Accidts. & Em. Liab. [lects.] 5 / *n.* 8° Smith & Ebbs [08] 09

PORTER (J. B.) + CRAIES (W. F.) Laws of Insur. : Fire, Life, Accident, Guarantee 21 / 8° Stevens [84] 08
A learned wk., the value of wh. is, however, greatly reduced by difficulty in ascertaining authority for ea. proposn., cases bg. cited equally fr. Eng., Irish, Scotch, Amer., and Canad. Courts, and it is difficult to discover wh. is the law in any particular Court.

SCRATCHLEY, A. Law of Life Assurance, and Valuation of Reversions 12 /6 8° Layton [ ] 82

,, [ed.] Decisions in Life Assurance Law [w. Statutes] 21 / 8° Shaw 87

TRUELOVE, M. H. [ed.] The Assurance Companies Act, 1909 ; w. notes 5/ *n.* 8° P. S. King & Son 10

WELFORD (A. W.) + OTTER-BARRY (W. W.) Law rel. to Fire Insurance 35/ r 8° Butterworth 11

**Canada**

CLARKE, S. R. The Law of Insurance [w. decisns. to 1877] 25 / 8° *Toronto* 73–7

**United States**

BEACH, C. F. Commentaries on the Law of Insurance, 2 v. $12 *n.* 8° Houghton, *Boston* 95

BERRYMAN, J. R. Digest of Law of Ins., 4 v. [fire, mar., life, accid.] $25 8° Callaghan, *Chicago* [88] 00–1

BIDDLE, A. Treatise on Law of Insurance, 2 vols. $10 8° Kay, *Phila.* 93
Fire, life, accid., guarantee, etc., risks, w. ref. to U.S., Brit., and Colonial decisions.

BIGELOW, M. M. [ed.] Life and Accident Insurance Reports, 5 v. ea. $7·50 8° Hurd, *Boston* 71–7

CLEMENT, G. A. [ed.] Digest of Fire Insurance Decisions $5·50 *n.* 8° *New York* 93
U.S., Great Britain, and Canada ; fr. earliest period to present time, w. refs. to statutory provisions, *etc.*

COOLEY, R. W. Briefs on Law of Insurance, 5 vols. $27 8° West Pb. Co., *St Paul, Minn.* 05–6

Digest of Insurance Cases, vols. i–xx ea. $2–$3 8° *Rough Notes* Co., *Indianapolis* 90–08 *in prg.*
Fire, Life Marine, Accident, and Assessment Cases in U.S. and other countries.

ELLIOTT, C. B. Outline on the Law of Insurance $3·50 8° West Pb. Co., *St Paul, Minn.* [95] 96

,, Law of Insurance : a treatise $4 *n.* 8° Bobbs-Merrill, *Indianapolis* [02] 07

FLANDERS The Law of Fire Insurance $5 8° Johnson, *Phila.*

JOYCE, Jos. A. Marine, Fire, Life, Accident & all other Insurances, 4 v. $24 8° Bancroft, *San Franc.* 97

MAY, J. W. Law of Insurance, ed. F. Parsons, 2 vols. $12 r 8° Little & Brown, *Boston* [ ] 00

OSTRANDER, D. The Law of Fire Insurance $6 *n.* 8° West Pb. Co., *St Paul, Minn.* 97

RICHARDS, Geo. Insurance Law in all its Branches $6·75 *n.* 8° Banks, *N.Y.* [92] 09

VANCE, Prf. W. R. Handybook of Law of Insurance $3·75 *n.* 8° West Pb. Co., *St Paul, Minn.* 04

WOODRUFF, E. H. [ed.] Seln. of Cases on Law of Insurance $4 8° Baker, *N.Y.* 00

**Average**

GOURLIE, J. H. General Average Laws of U.S. [and other countries] $10 r 8° Sherrerd, *Phila.* 81

*HOPKINS, M. Handbook of Average, w. chapter on Arbitration 21 / 8° Stevens [5–] 84

LOWNDES, R. Law of General Average, English and Foreign 30 / r 8° Stevens [51] *in prep.*

**Friendly Societies** —*v.* **D** § 21, **D** § 120

**Guaranty Insurance**

FROST, T. G. Treatise on Guaranty Insurance [$5 Little & Brown, *Boston*] 22 /6 *n.* 8° Sweet 02

**Insurable Interest**

LOWNDES, R. Insurable Interest and Valuations 5 / 8° Stevens 84

**Marine** —*v. also* **D** § 58

*ARNOULD, J. Law of Marine Insurance, ed. E. L. De Hart + R. I. Simey, 2 v. [$15 Boston Bk. Co.] [a classic] 63 / r 8° Stevens [48] 09

BRUCE (J. R. B.) + BROOMFIELD (R. C.) Shipping and Marine Insurance 10/6 8° 98

CHALMERS (M. D.) + OWEN (D.) Digest of Law of Marine Insurance 10 /6 8° Clowes [01] 03

,, ,, [eds.] Marine Insurance Act, 1906 10 /6 8° Clowes [06] 07

CRUMP, F. O. Principles of Marine Insurance 21/ r 8° Butterworth 75

DE HART (E. L.) + SIMEY (R. I.) [eds.] Marine Insurance Act, 1906 6 / r 8° Sweet 07

DUCKWORTH, L. Epitome of Law affectg. Marine Insurance 3 /6 *n.* c 8° E. Wilson [ ] 07

ELDRIDGE, W. H. Marine Policies 20 / 8° Butterworth 07

McArthur, Chas. The Contract of Marine Insurance 16/ 8° Stevens [85] 90
Newson, H. Law of Shipping and Marine Insurance 15/ 8° Reeves & Turner [79] 83
Tyser, C. R. Law relating to Losses under Marine Insurance 10/6 8° Stevens 94
*During War* —*v.* **D** § 113, *s.v.* War (Douglas, Owen)

**Salvage (Civil)** —*for* Maritime Salvage *v.* **D** § 58
*Kennedy, Sir W. R. Treatise on Law of Civil Salvage, ed. A. R. Kennedy 15/ r 8° Stevens [91] 07

## LABOUR LAWS—*v.* D § 45

## 51 : LAND LAWS—*v. also* D § 78

**Generally** —*v.* **D** § 78 : Real Property ; *also* **D** § 119

**Scotland**

Rankine, Prf. Jno. Rights & Burdens of Ownership of Land in Scotl. 45/ r 8° Bell & Bradfute, *Ed.* [79]
" The Law of Land Ownership in Scotland 38/ *n.* r 8° Green, *Edin.* [ ] 09
Ross, Geo. [ed.] Leadg. Cases in Law of Scotl. : Land Rights, 3 v. 30/ 8° Green, *Edin.*

**New Zealand**

Martin, T. F. Practical Handbk. on Land Laws of N. Zealand 8° Whitcombe, *Christchurch* 08

**India**

Markby, W. Lects. on Ind. Law conn. w. Law of Landed Prop. in Bengal 7/ c 8°
Phillips, A. Law rel. to Land Tenures of Lower Bengal [Tagore Lects. '74-5] 8° *Calcutta* 76

**United States**

Copp, H. N. [ed.] Public Land Laws 1875-82, 2 v., 1882-90, 2 v. $26 8° Copp, *Washington* 83-91
" [ed.] Land Laws of U.S. : local & temporary, gen. & permanent, & the public domain, 4 vols. $6 8° Copp, *Washington* 84
Lester, W. W. [ed.] Decisns. of Interior Dept. in Pub. Ld. Cases, & Laws, 2 v. $12·50 8° Kay, *Phila.* 60-70
Contains also the regulatns. of General Land Office. Contin. 1882-87, 5 vols. $16 8° *Washington* '82-7.
Zabriskie, J. C. On Public Land Laws of the United States $6·50 8° Bancroft, *San Francisco* 70-8

**History of Land Tenures** —*v.* **F** § 5, **D** § 117*

**Agricultural Holdings**

Cripps-Day, F. H. Adulteration (Agricultural Fertilisers & Feeding Stuffs) 5/ r 12° Stevens 94
*Dixon, H. H. Law of the Farm, ed. A. J. Spencer [cases, Stats., etc.] 26/ 8° Stevens [58] 04
Higgins, A. Pearce The Elements of Agricultural Law 3/6 c 8° Vinton 96
Johnston, G. A. [ed.] Agricultural Holdings Act, 1906 3/6 *n.* 8° E. Wilson [07] 08
" [ed.] The Agricultural Holdings Act, 1908 10/6 *n.* r 8° E. Wilson 09
" Small Holdings and Allotments—*ut inf.*
Lely (J. M.) + Aggs (W. H.) [eds.] Agricult. Holdgs. Acts '83 & '00 ; & other Stats. 27/6 8° Clowes [6-] 01
Mayer, Sylvian [ed.] Law of Agricultural Holdings [=Act 1908] 7/6 *n.* 8° Waterlow 08
Spencer, A. J. [ed.] Agricultural Holdings Act, 1908 ; w. notes, etc. 6/ 8° Stevens 09

*Scotland*

Connell, Is. [ed.] Agricultural Holdings (Scotland) Acts, 1883-1908 10/ *n.* 8° Green, *Edin.* [ ] 09
Johnston, C. N. [ed.] Agr. Holdgs. (Scot.) Act, '08, & Grd. Game Acts '80 & '06 6/ *n.* 8° Blackwood 09
Rankine, Prf. Jno. Lectures on Agric. Holdings Act (Scotland), 1883 2/ *n.* 12° Green, *Edin.* 94

**Allotments ; Small Holdings**

Clarke, S. W. Small Holdings in England and Wales 5/ *n.* 8° Butterworth 08
Dumsday, W. H. Law of Allotments and Small Holdings 5/ 8° Hadden 09
Hall, T. Hall Law of Allotments [w. Stats., forms & precs.] 7/6 c 8° Longman 86
Johnston, G. A. [ed.] Small Holdings & Allotments [Acts '92, '07 ; '87-'07] 16/ *n.* r 8° E. Wilson [08] 09
Little, J. B. Law of Allotments ; w. Acts, cases and Statutes 10/6 p 8° Shaw [88] 95
Spencer, A. J. [ed.] Small Holdings and Allotments Act, 1908 7/6 8° Stevens 09

**Compulsory Purchase (Sale) ; Compensation**

Bond + Stephens Agricultural Improvements 8° Butterworth [ ] 04
Boyle (Sir E.) + Waghorn (T.) [eds.] Law of Compensation, Lands Clauses Acts 37/6 8° Clowes 03

BROWNE, J. H. B. Compuls. Purch. of Undertakgs. of Cos. by Corpns. 7/6 8° Stevens & Haynes 76
,, + ALLAN (C. E.) [eds.] Public General Acts rel. to Compulsory Purchase of Land 37/6 r 8° Butterworth [96] 04
BUND, J. W. Law of Compens. f. Unexhausted Agr. Improvemts. 12/6 p 8° Butterworth [76] 04
*CRIPPS (C. A.) + LAURENCE (A. T.) Treatise on Principles of Law of Compensation 26/ r 8° Stevens [81] 05
DANIEL, A. Compendium of Compensation Cases 8° *Estates Gazette* Off. 03
FLETCHER, B. Valuations and Compensation 6/6 p 8° Batsford [93] 05
FREEMAN, G. M. Law and Practice of Compensation 25/ 8° 99
*HUDSON, A. A. The Law of Compensation, 2 vols. 37/6 r 8° Sweet 06
LAWRENCE, N. T. Sale under the Partition Act, 1868 8/ 8° Butterworth 77
LLOYD, E. Law of Compensation, ed. W. J. Brooks 21/ 8° Stevens [67] 95
MAYER, Dr S. Code of Law of Compens. und. Land Clauses Acts, etc. 18/ 8° Sweet 03
RICHARDS (H. C.) + SOPER (J. P. H.) The Law of Compensation 12/6 c 8° Sweet 98
WOOLF (S.) + MIDDLETON (J. W.) The Law and Practice of Compensation 32/ 8° Clowes 84

**Consolidation Acts**

JEPSON, A. [ed.] Land Clauses Acts, ed. Lightwood [w. decisns., etc.] 21/ 8° Stevens [80] 00

**Forest Law : Dean Forest**

BADEN-POWELL, B. H. Forest Law 7/6 8° 94

**Dean Forest**

WOOD, J. G. The Laws of the Dean Forest 25/ 8° Sweet 78

**Land Charges Acts**

EATON (E. W.) + PURCELL (J. P.) [eds.] Land Charges Acts, 1888 & 1900 2/6 *n.* r 12° Stevens 01

**Leases :** *Scotland*

RANKINE, Prf. Jno. The Law of Leases in Scotland 32/ r 8° Green, *Edin.* 93

**Rent (Chief)** —*v.* **D** § 83

**Restrictive Covenants**

JOLLY, W. A. Restrictive Covenants affecting Land 5/ 8° Stevens 09

**Transfer and Registration of Land and Title**—*v. also* **D** § 82

*BRICKDALE (C. F.) + SHELDON (W. R.) [eds.] Land Transfer Acts, 1875 & 1897 [w. comment.] 25/ r 8° Stevens [ ] 05
CHERRY, B. L. + H. W. M. [eds.] Land Transfer Acts, 1875 & 1897 [w. annots., rules, etc.] 18/ 8° Sweet 99
HARVEY, E. J. Land Law and Registration of Title 7/6 *n.* ($2·60 *n.*) 8° Longman 10
HOGG, J. E. Law rel. to Ownership and Incumbr. of Reg. Land 20/ *n.* r 8° Butterworth 06
An interesting introduction, showing analogies with the law of other countries.
,, [ed.] Precedents of Conveyancing Documents for use in Transactions under Land Transfer Acts '75 & '97 12/6 r 8° Stevens 07
,, Deeds Registrn. in Australia und. Regn. of Deeds Acts 12/6 8° Stevens 08
With references to analogous Statutes and cases on them in Engl., Ireland, and other Colonies.
JENNINGS (A. R. G.) + KINDERSLEY (G. M.) Principles & Practice of Land Registrn. 12/6 r 8° Stevens 04
NOTTAGE, W. G. Registration of Title to Land 3/6 *n.* 8° Sweet 02
RUDALL (A. H.) + GREIG (J. W.) Law of Land Transfer by Registration of Title 5/ *n.* 8° Stevens 99
*Yorkshire:* Haworth, C. J. [ed.] Yorkshire Registries Acts 1884, 1885 5/ *n.* r 12° Stevens 07
*Canada :* TIFFANY, E. H. Registration of Titles [annotns. of Stats. of Ontario] 16/6 8° *Toronto* 80

*Australia* and *New Zealand*

A'BECKET, T. T. [ed.] Transfer of Land Statutes 15/ 8° *Melbourne* 67
HOGG, J. E. The Australian Torrens System 75/ r 8° Butterworth 05
Treat. on law of Land Transfer and Reg. of Title throughout Austral., New Zeald., Fiji, and Brit. Columbia.
NIBLACK, W. C. The Torrens System 10/ *n.* r 8° 03

**Tithes** —*v.* **A** § 111

**Trees and Woods**

CRAIG, R. D. Legal & Equit. Rts. & Liabs. as to Trees & Woods *o.p* [*pb.* 7/6] 8° Maxwell 66

**Uses and Profits**

LEAKE, S. M. Digest of the Law of Uses and Profits of Land *o.p.* [*pb.* 22/] 8° Stevens 89
Being Pt. iii of *Digest of Law of Property in Land*, ed. A. E. RANDALL [*ut* **D** § 78].

## 52 : LANDLORD AND TENANT

EMANUEL, M. R. Landlord and Tenant 3/6 *n.* 8° Jordan 04
FAWCETT, W. M. Law of Landlord and Tenant, ed. W. D. Rawlins 25/r 8° Butterworth [71] 05
*FOÀ, E. The Relationship of Landlord and Tenant 30/r 8° Stevens [91] 07
,, Outlines of Law of Landlord and Tenant [six lects.] 6/c 8° Stevens 06
HOLDSWORTH, W. A. Landlord & Tenant, ed. J. F. Waley [good popular bk.] 1/f 8° Routledge [5–] 08
REDMAN, J. H. Law of Landlord and Tenant, with Ejectment 25/ 8° Stevens [76] 01
SMITH, Jno. W. Law of Landlord & Tenant, ed. W. T. Thompson [learned lects.] 18/ 8° Maxwell [4–] 82
SWAN, E. A. Law of Quiet Enjoyment and Title 7/6 c 8° Sweet 08
*WOODFALL, W. Law of Landlord & Tenant, ed. J. M. Lely + H. A. Aggs 38/r 8° Stevens [3–] 07
WRIGHT, S. Law of Landlord and Tenant 12/6 12° Sweet 00

**Scotland**

GUTHRIE, W. Law of Landlord and Tenant in Scotland, 2 vols. 60/ 8° *Edinburgh* [ ] 80
HUNTER, R. The Law of Landlord and Tenant, 2 v. 60/, *red. to* 16/ 8° Green, *Edin.* [ ] 76

**Africa, South**

BAYNE, G. C. Landlord and Tenant in South Africa 3/6 *n.* c 8° Juta, *Cape Town* [9–] 02

**India**

BELL, H. Law of Landlord and Tenant as admin. in Bengal 17/ 8° *Calcutta* [ ] 74

**United States**

CHAPLIN, S. Treat. on Law of Landlord and Tenant in N.Y. $6·50 8° Baker, *N.Y.* 99
JONES, L. A. Treatise on Law of Landlord & Tenant $6 8° Bobbs-Merrill, *Indianapolis* 06
MCADAM, D. Rights, Remedies, and Liabs. of Landlord & Tenant, 3 v. $16·75 8° Remick, *N.Y.* [75] 00–1

**Distress**

BULLEN, E. Law of Distress, ed. C. Dodd + T. J. Bullen 20/ 8° Butterworth [41] 99
DANIELS, G. St L. Handbook of the Law of Distress 3/6 *n.* c 8° *Estates Gazette* Off. [94] 99
HUNTER, R. T. Guide to Law of Distress for Rent [incl. Stats.] 5/ *n.* c 8° Waterlow [88] 05
OLDHAM (A.) + FOSTER (A. L.) Law of Distress [w. forms, table of Stats., etc.] 18/ 8° Stevens [86] 89
WARD (H. G.) + GRANTHAM (F. W.) [eds.] Law of Distress Amendmt. Acts, '88 & '95 8° Law Stat. Soc. 97

**Ejectment**

WILLIAMS (J. H.) + YATES (W. B.) Law of Ejectmt. or Recovery of Possession of Land 16/ 8° Sweet 94

**Fixtures; Dilapidations:** *England* and *United States*

AMOS (A.) + FERARD (J.) Treatise on Law of Fixtures, ed. W. H. Roberts 18/ 8° Stevens [4–] 83
BROWN, A. Law of Fixtures [incl. Agr. Hldgs. Act '75] *o.p.* [*pb.* 12/] 8° Stevens [71] 81
EWELL, M. D. Treatise on the Law of Fixtures $7·50 r 8° *Chicago* 76
FLETCHER, Banister The Law of Dilapidations 6/6 c 8° Batsford [72] 06
GRADY, S. G. Law of Fixtures and Dilapidations 15/6 12° Wildy [66] 76
MACER, A. T. The Law of Dilapidations 6/ c 8° F. P. Wilson [96] 07
TYLER, R. H. Treat. on Law of Fixtures [w. Engl. & Am. decisns.] $7·50 8° *Albany* 77
WRIGHT, S. Handbook of the Law of Fixtures 5/ *n.* c 8° Sweet 96

**Leases and Leaseholds** —*v.* **D** § 30

**Repairs and Improvements**

CAHILL, M. F. Householder's Duty respecting Repairs 3/6 *n.* c 8° E. Wilson 09
JACKSON, J. H. Law of Repairs and Improvements 15/ 8° Butterworth 05

**Tenement Houses and Flats**

CLODE, W. Law rel. to Tenemt. Houses & Flats [incl. Taxatn. & Rating] 10/6 8° Butterworth 89
DANIELS, G. St L. Flats 8° *Estates Gazette* Off. [ ] 05

## 53 : LEGAL PROFESSION

COPE (E. A.) + ROBINS (H. W. H.) Solicitor's Office Management 5/ *n.* 8° Pitman 10

CORDERY, A. Law rel. to Solicitors of Supr. Ct. of Jud. [w. Stats., rules, etc.] 21 / 8° Stevens [75] 99
DONOVAN, Judge J. W. Tact in Court $1 *n.* 8° Williamson, *Rochester, N.Y.* [85] 98
,, Speeches and Speech-making $1·50 8° Williamson, *Rochester, N.Y.* 95
,, Skill in Trials $1 *n.* 8° Williamson, *Rochester, N.Y.* [91] 99
,, Trial Practice and Trial Lawyers $3 8° Stevenson, *St Louis* [83]
EUSTACE, A. A. Practical Hints on Pleading 5 / 8° Stevens 07
FORSYTH, W. Hortensius: office & duties of advocate [histor. essay] 7/6 r 8° Murray [49] 79
FOWKE (V. de S.) + HENDERSON (E. B.) Partnership betw. Solicitors [preceds. w. notes] 6 / 8° Jordan 94
FREEMAN, Sam. Complete Guide to County Ct. Costs—*ut* **D** § 109
HARDWICKE, H. The Art of Winning Cases $5 *n.* 8° Banks, *N.Y.* [94] 03
HARRIS, Rich. Hints on Advocacy [conduct of cases, witnesses, etc.] 7/6 r 12° Stevens [ ] 06
,, Illustrations in Advocacy [Tichborne case, etc.] 7/6 12° Stevens & Haynes [84] 04
MARCHANT, J. R. V. Barrister-at-Law: essay upon legal positn. of counsel 9 / 8° Clowes 05
MOORE, H. Practical Instructions and Suggestions to Young Solicitors and Articled Clerks 7/6 c 8° Clowes [85] 88
POLEY, A. P. Law affecting Solicitors of Supreme Court 21 / 8° Clowes 97
PULLING, A. Law and Pract. rel. to Attorneys, Solrs., Notaries, Proctors, etc. *o.p.* 8° Stevens [49] 62
ROUSE, R. The Practical Man, ed. Rolla Rouse + E. E. H. Birch [legal forms, etc.] 10/6 16° Sweet [40] 00
TURNER, E. F. Dutes of Solicitor to Client as to Sale, Purchases & Mortgages of Land, ed. W. L. Hacon 10/6 8° Stevens [83] 93
,, Duties of Solicitor to Client as to Partnership Agreemts., etc. 10/6 8° Stevens 84
WELLMAN, F. L. The Art of Cross-Examination $2·50 *n.* (10/6 *n.*) 8° Macmillan 04
WHITEWAY, A. R. Hints to Solicitors: law rel. to duties in H. Ct. 6 / 12° Stevens 83
WROTTESLEY, F. J. The Examination of Witnesses in Court 5/ *n.* 8° Sweet 10
Based on HARDWICKE, and on Serj. E. W. Cox, *The Advocate*, vol. i [all pb.], 1852, adapted for modern readers and brot. down to date.

**Scotland**

BEGG, J. H. Treat. on Law of Scotl. rel. to Law Agents 21 / r 8° Green, *Edin.* [73] 83
IRONS, J. C. Judicial Factors: law and practice in Scotland 30 / *n.* 8° Green, *Edin.* 08
THOMS, G. H. Treatise on Judicial Factors, Curators Bonis, & Managers of Burghs, ed. H. J. E. Fraser 21 / 8° Bell & Bradfute, *Edin.* [59] 81

**United States**

WEEKS, E. P. Treatise on Attorneys and Councillors at Law $6 r 8° Bancroft, *San Franc.* 78

**Articled Clerks**

JONES, C. The Solicitor's Clerk, 2 Pts. ea. 2/6 *n.* c 8° E. Wilson [91] 11
Pt. i on ordinary pract. wk. of a solicitor's office, and on conveyancing and pract. of Courts. Pt. ii. Magist. and Crim. Law, Licensing, Bkptcy., etc.
,, Practical Forms for use in a Solicitor's Office, 2 vols. ea. 5 / *n.* r 12° [ ] 03; 08
STIFF, Hor. W. New Guide for Articled Clerks 6 / c 8° Sweet 95
UTTLEY, T. F. How to become a Solicitor: hints for Art. Clerks 5 / c 8° Stevens 94

**Bills of Costs** —*v.* **D** § 109

**Book-Keeping for Solicitors**

HALE, Matth. System of Book-Keeping for Solicitors 5/6 8° Stevens 84
HAWKINS, L. W. Book-Keeping: princ. & pract. of Double Entry 5 / *n.* 8° Good 04
KAIN, G. J. Solicitors' Book-Keeping by Double Entry [3-col. system] 3 / *n.* c 8° Waterlow [74] 02
ONSLOW, H. H. Lawyer's Manual of Book-Keeping 10 / *n.* 8° Butterworth [06] 08
SPICER (E. E.) + PEGLER (E. C.) Book-Keeping and Accounts 15/6 *n.* 4° Lynch 08
WOODMAN, J. M. Manual of Solicitors' Book-Keeping 6 / *n.* p 8° Butterworth [ ] 06

**Briefs and Counsel's Fees**

FORD Briefs and Counsel's Fees 8° King & Sell [ ] 01

**Forensic Oratory** —*v.* **K** § 86 **Legal Education**—*v.* **D** § 169

**Ethics of Legal Profession**

SHARSWOOD, G., jun. Profes ional Ethics $1·50 *n.* 12° Johnson, *Phila.* [7–] 84

**Notary Public**

BROOKE, R. Office and Pract. of Notary, ed. J. Cranstoun 25 / 8° Stevens [47] 01

*Scotland*

MURRAY, J. C. The Law rel. to Notaries Public [Scotland] 12 / 8° Green, *Edin.* 90

*S. African Colonies*

TENNANT, H. The Notary's Manual 21 / 8° *Cape Town* [5–] 02

VAN ZYL, C. H. Notarial Practice of South Africa 42/ *n.* 8° Sweet 09

*United States*

GIAUQE, Florien Manl. for Notaries Public, General Convyers., etc. $2·50 8° Clarke, *Cincinnati* [88] 07

PROFFATT, J. Law of Notaries Public in U.S. [w. forms, etc.] $5 8° Bancroft, *San Francisco* [77] 92

SNYDER, W. L. Notaries' and Commissioners' Manual $1·50 8° Baker, *N.Y.* [84] 06

WHITE, H. H. [ed.] Notarial Guide and Book of Forms $10 8° Hansell, *New Orleans* [97] 08

## 54 : LIBEL AND SLANDER ; DEFAMATION

*BOWER, G. S. Code of Law of Actionable Defamation 30 / r 8° Sweet 08
Reduces the law of libel and slander into form of a Code. Tho' professedly dealing only w. the Civil law, the Code consists of 16 Pts. and 64 articles, ea. w. subdivns., provisoes, cross-refs., etc. Copious notes.

COOPER, F. T. Defamation and Verbal Injury, ed. D. O. Dykes 16 / *n.* 8° Green, *Edin.* 06

FOLKARD, H. C. Law of Slander & Libel [based on Starkie] 31 /6 *n.* r 8° Butterworth [69] 08

FRASER, Dr Hugh Princs. & Practice of Law of Libel & Slander 15 / 8° Butterworth [93] 08
In same form as his wk. *inf.*, coverg. much the same ground, the law bg. stated in form of propositns. followed by notes.

*ODGERS, Dr W. Blake Digest of Law of Libel and Slander, ed. J. B. Eames 32 / 8° Stevens [81] 05

" Outline of the Law of Libel 3 /6 Macmillan 97
Six lectures deliv. in Middle Temple Hall, 1896 ; semi-popular, and thoroughly practical.

STARKIE, T. Treat. on Law of Slander and Libel, ed. H. C. Folkard 31/6 *n.* r 8° [5–] 08

**United States**

MERRILL, S. Newspaper Libel : handbk. for press [w. cases] $2 12° *Boston* 88

NEWELL, M. L. Law of Libel and Slander as admin. in U.S. $6 8° Callaghan, *Chicago* [ ] 98

TOWNSHEND, J. Treat. on Wrongs called Slander & Libel, & on the Remedy $6·50 8° *New York* [69] 90

**Newspaper Libel**

ELLIOTT, G. Newspaper Libel and Registration Act, 1881 4 /6 8° Stevens & Haynes 84

FISHER + STRAHAN —*in their* The Law of the Press, *ut* **D** § 75*

FRASER, Dr Hugh Law of Libel in its relation to the Press 6 / 8° Reeves & Turner 89

KELLY, R. J. Law of Newspaper Libel [w. spec. ref. to Libel Amend. Act '88] 7 /6 c 8° Butterworth 89

SHORTT, J. Law rel. to Works of Literature and Art 30 / 8° Reeves & Turner 84

**Trade Libel** —*v.* **D** § 72, *s.v.* Trade Marks

## 55 : LIBERTY, CIVIL AND RELIGIOUS

PATERSON, J. Commentaries on Liberty of Subject and Laws of England rel. to Security of the Person, 2 vols. *o.p.* [*pb.* 21 /] c 8° Macmillan [77] 78

" Liberty of the Press, Speech, and Public Worship *o.p* [*pb.* 12 /] c 7° Macmillan 80

**United States**

HURD, J. C. Law of Freedom and Bondage in U.S., 2 vols. *o.p.* [*pb.* $10] 8° Baker, *N.Y.* 58–62

WEBSTER, Prentiss Treatise on the Law of Citizenship—*v.* **D** § 135

**LIENS**—*v.* **D** § 60 **LIGHTS, ANCIENT**—*v.* **D** § 78, *s.v.* Easements

## 56 : LIMITATIONS ; PERPETUITIES ; PRESCRIPTION

BROWN, W. Law of Limitation as to Real Property 28 / 8° Sweet 69

CARSON, T. H. Prescription and Custom 6/ c 8° Sweet 07

*DARBY (J. G. N.) + BOSANQUET (F. A.) Treatise on Statutes of Limitations, ed. Marchant ; 27 /6 ; Suppl. 2 /6 8° Butterworth [67] 99 ; 99

HEWITT, E. P. Treatise on the Statutes of Limitations 16 / 8° Sweet 93

LIGHTWOOD, J. M. The Time Limit of Actions 25 / r 8° Butterworth 09
A painstaking treatise on the Statute of Limitations and the equitable doctrine of laches.

**Scotland**

MILLAR, J. H. Handbook of Prescription acc. to Law of Scotland 12 / 8° Green, *Edin.* 93

**India**

BROUGHTON, L. P. D. [ed.] Limitation of Suits in India [Act of 1877] 63 / 8° *Calcutta*

GRIFFITH, W. Commentaries on Indian Limitation Act, No. xv of 1897 as modified from 1877–1893 17/6 Author 94

**United States**

ANGELL, J. K. Treat. on Limitation of Actions & Suits $6 r 8° Little & Brown, *Boston* [2 edn. 46] 76
BUSWELL, H. F. The Statute of Limitations & Adverse Possession $6 8° Little & Brown, *Boston* 89
GRAY, J. C. Rule against Perpetuities [26/ Sweet] $6 8° Little & Brown, *Boston* [86] 06
GRAY, J. M. Limitations of the Taxing Power $6 8° Bancroft, *San Francisco* 06
PATTERSON, Prf. C. S. Federal Restraints on State Action $3·50 *n.* 8° Johnson, *Phila.* 88
WOOD, H. G. Treat. on Limitns. of Actions at Law and in Equity, ed. J. Gould $6·50 8° Boston Bk. Co., *Boston* [83] 01

**Actions and Suits**

BANNING, H. T. Law of Limitations of Actions, ed. Arch. Brown 16/ 8° Stevens & Haynes [77] 06
With observations on the equitable doctrines of laches.

**Prescription : History of**

HERBERT, T. A. Hist. of Law of Prescription in Engl. *o.p.* [*pb.* 10/] 8° Camb. Press 91
[Yorke Prize Essay.] A good contribution to a much neglected department of English legal historical research.

## LOCAL GOVERNMENT—*v.* D § 67

## 57 : LUNACY—*v. also* D § 62

ARCHBOLD, J. F. Lunacy, ed. S. G. Lushington [w. Acts, etc.] 42 / 8° Stevens [54] 95
ELMER, Jos. Practice in Lunacy under Commissions and Inquisitions 21/ 8° Stevens [71] 92
FRY, D. P. Lunacy Laws, ed. G. F. Chambers [priv., pauper, crim.] 15 / 8° Knight [64] 90
GOWERS, Sir W. R. Lunacy and Law 1 / 8° Churchill 03
HEYWOOD (N. A.) + MASSEY (A. S.) Lunacy Practice, ed. R. C. Romer 25/ r 8° Stevens [ ] 07
HUME-WILLIAMS, J. W. Unsoundness of Mind in leg. and med. considns. 7/6 8° Butterworth 90
OPPENHEIMER, Dr H. Criminal Responsibility of Lunatics : study in compar. law 10 /6 *n.* 8° Sweet 09
PITT-LEWIS (G.) + SMITH (Dr R. P.) + HAWKE (J. A.) The Insane and the Law 14 / 8° Churchill 90
*POPE, H. M. R. Law and Practice of Lunacy, ed. J. H. Boome + V. de S. Fowke 21 / 8° Sweet [77] 92
*RENTON, A. Wood Law & Pract. in Lunacy [w. forms & preceds.] 50/ *n.* r 8° Green, *Edin.* 97
WILLIAMS, S. E. Law and Pract. rel. to Petitns. in Chanc. and Lunacy 18 / 8° Stevens 80
WILSON, R. W. R. Responsibility in Law 5 / *n.* c 8° Butterworth 08

**United States**

HARRISON, G. L. [ed.] Colln. of all Lunacy Laws in U.S.A. to 1883 r 8° *priv. print.* 84

## 57* : MALICIOUS PROSECUTION

*STEPHEN, Sir Herb. Law of Malicious Prosecutions 6/ r 12° Stevens 88

**United States**

NEWELL, M. L. Treat. on Law of Malic. Pros., False Imprisonmt., *etc.* $5·50 8° Callaghan, *Chicago* 92

## 58 : MARITIME LAW—*v. also* D § 50

ABBOTT, C. [Ld. TENTERDEN] Law of Merchant Ships and Seamen, ed. J. P. + B. Aspinall + H. S. Moore 60/ Butterworth [1802] 01
DOUGLAS, R. R. [ed.] Alphabet. Ref. Index to Recent Marit. Law Decisns. 7/6 8° Stevens 88
DUCKWORTH, Lawr. Encyclopaedia of Marine Law [popular] 5/ *n.* c 8° Pitman [07] 10
GINSBURG, B. W. Hints on Legal Duties of Shipmasters 4 /6 c 8° Griffin [ ] 03
*KAY, J. Law rel. to Ship-Masters & Seamen, ed. Hon. J. W. Mansfield, 2 v. 46/ r 8° Stevens [75] 95
LEES, J. [ed.] Laws of Brit. Shippg. & Mar. Insur., ed. J. A. Hamilton 15 / *n.* 8° Philip [55] 03
„ [ed.] Digest of Merch. Shppg. Acts '54–92, ed. J. C. Bigham + J. A. Hamilton 3 /6 *n.* c 8° Philip [55] 93
MACLACHLAN, D. Treatise on the Law of Merchant Shipping 50/ r 8° Sweet [60] 11
MANSFIELD (G. W.) + DUNCAN (G. W.) [eds.] Mercht. Shipping Consolidatn. Act, 1894 10/6 r 8° Stevens 95
A Supplement to KAY [*ut sup.*], w. references throughout to it. *Regns. for Preventg. Collisions* are added.
MARSDEN, R. G. [ed.] Digest of Cases rel. to Shppg., Admlty., & Marine Insur. to end of '97 30/ r 8° Sweet 99
MAUDE (F. P.) + POLLOCK (C. E.) Law of Merchant Shipping, ed. Bar. Pollock + G. Bruce, 2 v. 70/ r 8° Sweet [53] 81

NEWSON, H. Digest of Law of Shipping and Marine Insurance—*ut* **D** § 50
OMOND, G. W. T. [ed.] The Merchant Shipping Acts, 1854–76; w. notes 18/ 8° *Edinburgh* 77
PRITCHARD, R. A. + W. T. Digest of Admiralty and Maritime Law—*ut* **D** § 103
PULLING, A. [ed.] The Shipping Code [Merchant Shipping Act 1894] 7/6 *n.* r 8° Butterworth 94
SAUNDERS, Alb. Master Mariner's Legal Guide 10/6 *n.* 12° E. Wilson [ ] 08
,, Maritime Law 21/ r 8° E. Wilson [01] 03
In narrat. form; ill. by hist. of a ship fr. agreemt. to build her till she becomes a total loss.
*SCRUTTON, T. E. [ed.] Merchant Shipping Act 1894 [w. notes, etc.] 30/ 8° Clowes [ ] 95
*TEMPERLEY (R.) + MOORE (H. S.) [eds.] Merchant Shipping Acts 1894–1906, ed. A. Bucknill 30/ r 8° Stevens [95] 07
TUDOR, O. D. [ed.] Leading Cases on Merc. & Marit. Law; w. notes 21/ *n.* r 8° Sweet [6–] 84
URQUHART, G. D. Dues and Charges on Shipping in Foreign Ports 25/ 8° Philip [69] 83
WENDT, Dr E. E. Papers on Maritime Legislation 31/6 r 8° Longman [ ] 88
WHITE, J. D. [ed.] Merchant Shipping Acts, w. notes & appendices 10/ 8° Eyre & Spottiswoode [95] 08

**Scotland**

BLACK, W. G. Digest & Review of Decisns. in Scott. Shippg. Cases, 1865–90 10/6 8° Green, *Edin.* 91

**United States**

DESTY, R. Law. rel. to Shipping of Engl. and U.S. $3 8° Whitney, *San Francisco* 80
PARSONS, T. Treatise on Law of Shipping & Admiralty, 2 v. $12 8° Little & Brown, *Boston* 69

*Collisions*

SPENCER, H. R. Treatise on Law of Marine Collisions $7·50 8° Callaghan, *Chicago* 95

**Germany**

SIEVEKING, Dr Alf. German Law rel. to Carriage of Goods by Sea 15/ 8° Stevens 07

**Admiralty Court** —*v.* **D** § 103, *s.v.* Admiralty

**Bills of Lading and Charter-Parties**

*CARVER, T. G. —*in his* Treat. on Law of Carriage of Goods by Sea, *ut* **D** § 22
DUCKWORTH, L. Epitome of Law of Charter-parties & Bills of Lading 2/6 *n.* c 8° E. Wilson [ ] 04
LEGGETT, E. Treatise on the Law of Bills of Lading *o.p.* [*pb.* 30/] 8° Stevens [80] 93
,, Treatise on the Law of Charter-parties 25/ 8° Clowes 94
POLLOCK, H. E. Bill of Lading Exceptions 10/6 8° [ ] 95
*SCRUTTON, Prf. T. E. Contract of Affreightmt. in Ch.-Parties & Bills of Ladg. 18/ 8° Clowes [86] 04
STEPHENS, J. E. R. The Law rel. to Bills of Lading 7/6 *n.* 8° *Syren & Shipping* 08
,, The Law rel. to Charter Parties 7/6 *n.* 8° *Syren & Shipping* 08

**Carriers, Law of** —*v.* **D** § 22: Carriers, and **D** § 15: Bailments

**Collisions at Sea and Rule of the Road**

HOLT, W. [ed.] Admiralty Court Cases on the Rule of the Road at Sea 10/6 8° Maxwell 67
LOWNDES, R. Admiralty Law of Collisions at Sea 7/6 8° Stevens 67
*MARSDEN, R. G. Treatise on the Law of Collisions at Sea 30/ 8° Stevens [80] 10
MATSUNAMI, Dr N. Collisions between Warships and Merchant Vessels 21/ 8° Butterworth 00
MOORE, H. S. New Rules of the Road at Sea 7/6 *n.* c 8° J. D. Potter [97] 00
ROSCOE, E. S. Measure of Damages arising from Collisions at Sea 10/6 *n* 8° Butterworth 09
With descrns. of law of France by L. DOR, and of law of Germy by Dr SCHROEDER.
SMITH, D. W. [ed.] Leadg. Cases on Regulns. f. Preventg. Collisns. at Sea 5/ *n.* 8° Simpkin 07
,, Law rel. to Rule of the Road at Sea 8/6 *n.* 8° Brown 10

**Freight; Demurrage**

STEPHENS, J. E. R. Law rel. to Freight; Law rel. to Demurrage ea. 7/6 *n.* 8° *Syren & Shipping* 07; 07

**Insurance, Maritime**—*v.* **D** § 50 **Navigation Rights**—*v.* **D** § 98

**Salvage**

NEWSON, H. Law of Salvage, Towage, and Pilotage 15/ 8° Butterworth 89

**Stowage and Cargoes**

STEVENS, R. W. On the Stowage of Ships and their Cargoes 21/ 8° Longman [58] 94

**Foreign Maritime Codes**

*Germany:* ARNOLD, W. [tr.] Marine Code of Germ. Emp.: tr. 6/ *n.* 8° E. Wilson 00

*Holland and Belgium :* Raikes, Judge F. W. [tr.] Marit. Codes of Holl. and Belg. : tr. 10/6 *n.* 8° E. Wilson 98
*Italy :* ,, [tr.] Maritime Code of Italy : tr. 12/6 *n.* 8° E. Wilson 00
*Spain and Portugal :* ,, [tr.] Marit. Codes of Spain and Portug. : tr. 7/6 *n.* 8° E. Wilson 96

## 59 : MARRIAGE AND DIVORCE—*v. also* D § 48, D § 49

Browne (G.) + Powles (L. D.) Law & Pract. in Div. & Matrim. Causes 25/ 8° Stevens 05
Dixon, W. J. Law in Divorce and other Matrimonial Causes 22/6 8° Butterworth [ ] 08
Geary, N. Law of Marriage & Family Relns. [popular ; $3 Macmillan, *N.Y.*] 12/6 c 8° Black 92
Hall, G. J. Law and Pract. of Divorce and Matrim. Causes 15/ *n.* 8° Butterworth 05
With chronological digest [1730–1905] and Index to Marriage and Divorce Acts.
Hammick, J. T. Marriage Law : legal incidents connect. w. constitution of matrim. contract *o.p.* 12° Shaw [ ] 87
Hardy, G. L. Law and Practice of Divorce [succinct] 5/ *n.* 8° E. Wilson 07

**British Empire :** Eversley (W. P.) + Craies (W. F.) Marriage Laws of British Empire 22/6 8° Stevens & Haynes 11

**India**

Rattigan, H. A. B. Law of Divorce Applicable to Christians in India 18/ *n.* 8° Wildy 97

**Africa :** Ward (D.) Handbook to Marrge. Laws of Cape Colony, etc. 6/ *n.* c 8° *Cape Town* 02

**Australia**

McKean, J. Treatise on the Law of Divorce 12/6 8° *Melbourne* 61

**United States**

Bishop, J. P. Commentaries on Law of Marriage & Divorce, 2 v. $12 8° Little & Brown, *Boston* [53] 81
,, New Commentaries on Marr., Div., & Separation on a New System of Legal Exposition, 2 vols. $12·60 8° Flood, *Chicago* 91
Geary, W. M. N. Law of Marriage and Family Relations $3 8° Macmillan, *N.Y.* 93
Keezer, F. Law of Marriage and Divorce in U.S. $4 8° Nagel, *Boston* 06
Lloyd, A. P. Treat. on Law of Divorce [w. causes f. div. in ea. State] $2 8° Houghton, *Boston* 87
Woolsey, T. D. Essay on Divorce & Divorce Legislation [chfly. U.S.] $1·75 c 8° Scribner, *N.Y.* [69] 82

**France**

Kelly, E. French Law of Marriage and Divorce and Conflict of Laws Arising, ed. O. E. Bodington 21/ r 8° Stevens [85] 95

**Foreign Marriages** —*v.* D § 113
**Divorce Court** —*v.* D § 103

## 60 : MARRIAGE SETTLEMENTS, MARRIED WOMEN'S PROPERTY—*v. also* D § 49

Banning, H. T. Concise Treatise on Law of Marriage Settlements 15/ 8° Stevens 84
Griffith, J. R. [ed.] Marr. Women's Prop. Acts 1870, '74, '82, '84, ed. G. Brown 9/ 8° Stevens & Haynes [71] 91
Matthews, J. B. Manual of Law rel. to Married Women 10/6 c 8° Sweet 92
Vaizey, J. S. Law of Settlemt. of Prop. on Marr. [& other occas.], 2 v. 63/ r 8° Sweet 87
,, Precedents of Settlements [= vol. iii of above] 15/ r 8° Sweet 88
Williams, Josh. On the Settlement of Real Estates [24 lectures] 14/ 8° Sweet 79

**Scotland**

Birnie, J. B. L. [ed.] Married Women's Property (Scotland) Act, 1881 [w. notes] 4/ 8° Green, *Edin.* 83
Murray, Dav. Law rel. to Property of Married Person [w. stats. & notes] 9/ m 8° MacLehose, *Glasgow* 91

**Canada**

Walkem, R. T. [ed.] The Married Women's Property Acts of Ontario 8/6 8° *Toronto* 74

**United States**

Snyder, W. L. The Geography of Marriage $1·50 8° Putnam, *N.Y.* 89
A consideration of the legal complexities connected w. marriage in the United States.
Wells, J. C. Treatise on Separate Property of Married Women $6 8° Clarke, *Cincinnati* [78] 79

## 61 : MASTER AND SERVANT

Baylis, T. H. Rights and Duties of Domestic Servants, ed. Monckton 1/ *n.* f 8° Butterworth [ ] 97

*MACDONELL, Sir Jno. Law of Master and Servant, ed. E. A. M. Innes 25/ 8° Stevens [83] 08
PARKYN, E. A. Law rel. to Masters and Servants [w. ch. on apprentices] 7/6 p 8° Butterworth 97
*SMITH, C. M. Law of Master and Servant, ed. E. M. Smith 30/ 8° Sweet [6-] 06
UMPHERSTON, F. A. The Law of Master and Servant 18/ *n.* r 8° Green, *Edin.* 04

**Scotland**

FRASER, Pat. Treatise on Law of Scotl. rel. to Master and Servant and Master and Apprentice 36/ r 8° *Edinburgh* [4-] 82

**United States**

HUFCUT, E. W. —*in his* Law of Agency, *ut* **D** § 10
WOOD, H. G. On the Law of Master and Servant $7·50 8° *Albany* 77

**Apprentices** —*v. also* Parkyn, *sup.*

AUSTIN, E. Law relating to Apprentices 12/ 8° Knight 90

**Employers' Liability**—*v.* **D** § 41 **Factory and Labour Laws**—*v.* **D** § 45 **Shipmasters and Seamen**—*v.* **D** § 58
**Workmen's Compensation**—*v.* **D** § 41

## 62 : MEDICAL JURISPRUDENCE—*v. also* H* § 54

BROWNE (G. L.) + STEWART (C. G.) [eds.] Reports of Trials for Murder by Poison—*ut* **D** § 6 [w. chemical introds.]
CASPER, J. L. Handbook of Practice of Forensic Medicine [tr.], 4 v. 8° New Sydenh. Soc. 61-5
CRAVEN, J. Law relating to Medical Practitioners 7/6 p 8° Butterworth 90
GLENN, R. G. Manual of Laws affecting Medical Men 14/ 8° Churchill 71
SELLERS, W. Handbook of Legal Medicine; ill. 7/6 *n.* c 8° Sherratt, *Mancs.* 06
TAYLOR, Dr A. S. Manual of Medical Jurisprudence 14/ c 8° Churchill [43] 01
" Principles and Practice of Medical Jurisprudence, 2 v. 36/ *n.* r 8° Churchill [65] 05
" On Poisons in rel. to Medical Jurisprudence and Medicine 16/ c 8° Churchill [47] 95
*TIDY, Dr C. M. Legal Medicine, 2 vols. 46/ r 8° Smith & Elder 82-3
i: *Evidence, Signs and Causes of Death, Post-Mortems, Explosions, etc.*, 25/; ii: *Legitimacy, Pregnancy, Rape, Drowning, Suffocation, etc.*, 21/.

**India**

CHEEVER, N. Medical Jurisprudence for India 8° (*India*) 70

**United States**

CHAPMAN, H. C. Manl. of Med. Jurisprudence & Toxicology $1·75 *n.* 8° Saunders, *Phila.* [92] 03
DRAPER, F. W. Text-book of Legal Medicine $4 *n.* 8° Saunders, *Phila.* 05
ELWELL, J. J. Treatise on Malpractice, Medical Evidence and Insanity $6 8° *New York* [71] 81
EWELL, M. D. Manual of Medical Jurisprudence $3 12° *Boston* 88
POORE, G. V. Treatise on Medical Jurisprudence $4 8° Longman, *N.Y.* 01
REESE, J. J. Text-bk. of Med. Jurispr. & Toxicology $3 *n.* 8° Blakiston, *N.Y.* [ ] 06
WHARTON (F.) + STILLÉ (M.) Medical Jurispr., 3 v. ea. $7·50 Lawyers' Co-op. Pb. Co., *Rochester* [55] 05
WITTHAUS (R. A.) + BECKER (T. C.) Medical Jurisprudence, Forensic Medicine, and Toxicology, vols. i-ii [in 4 cols.] ea. $6 *n.* 8° Wood, *N.Y.* [94-6] 07

**Hospitals** —*v.* **D** § 67

**Blood-Stains**

SUTHERLAND, Maj. W. D. Blood Stains: detectn. and determin. of source 10/6 *n.* 8° Baillière 07

**Medical Partnerships**

BARNARD (W.) + STOCKER (G. B.) Medical Partnerships, Transfers, & Assistantships 10/6 8° 95

**Lunacy**—*v.* **D** § 57 **Toxicology**—*v. also* **H*** § 54

## 63 : MERCANTILE LAW, GENERALLY—*v. also* Special Headings (esp. § 58 : Maritime)

**Universal and International** —*v. also* **D** § 113

HOPKINS, J. L. Law of Unfair Trade, incl. Tr. Mks., Tr. Secrets, etc. $6 8° Callaghan, *Chicago* 00
LEVI, Prf. Leone Commercial Law of the World, 2 vols. *o.p.* [*pb.* 120/] 4° Smith & Elder 54
" International Commercial Law, 2 v. *o.p.* [*pb.* 35/] r 8° Smith & Elder [50] 63

**England**

BLACKWELL, P. T. Law relating to Factors 5 / *n.* 8° E. Wilson 97
BURDICK, F. M. Essentials of Business Law [popular] $1·25 (5 / *n.*) c 8° Appleton [03] 04
CREW Synopsis of Mercantile Law 3/6 *n.* p 8° Butterworth 09
EDWARDS, W. D. Commercial Law [Comm. Ser.; an outline] 2 / *n.* c 8° Methuen [00] 05
FARLEIGH, E. A. Manual of Commercial Law 9 / 8° Stevens 09
HURST (Jos.) + CECIL (Ld. Rob.) Principles of Commercial Law 10 /6 8° Stevens & Haynes [91] 06
MUNRO, Prf. J. E. C. Commercial Law [Elementary Commercial Ser.] 3 /6 (90 c. *n.*) gl 8° Macmillan 93
NIXON (A.) + HOLLAND (R. T.) Commercial Law [Commercial Series] 5 / ($1·50) c 8° Longman 07
PEARCE, J. Merchant's Clerk [laws regulg. operns. of ctg.-house] 2/ c 8° E. Wilson [ ] 87
SCRUTTON, Prf. T. E. The Elements of Mercantile Law *o.p.* [*pb.* 7 /6] c 8° Clowes 91
SLATER, J. A. Principles of Mercantile Law 6/6 c 8° Stevens & Haynes [ ] 07
,, Pitman's Mercantile Law 5 / *n.* c 8° Pitman [05] 09
SMITH, Jno. W. Compendium of Mercantile Law, ed. E. L. de Hart + R. I. Simey, 2 vols. 42 / Stevens [34] 05
STEVENS, T. M. Elements of Mercantile Law, ed. H. Jacobs 10 /6 8° Butterworth [90] 03
TUDOR, O. D. [ed] Leading cases on Mercantile and Maritime Laws—*ut* **D** § 58
WILSON, H. A. Law in Business [popular] 2 /6 *n.* c 8° Methuen 04

**Scotland**

BELL, G. J. Commentaries on Law of Scotl., and on Princs. of Mercantile Jurisprud., 2 vols. *o.p.* [*pb.* 105 /] 4° *Edin.* [5th edn. 26] 70
CAMPBELL, R. V. Principles of Mercantile Law, ed. A. McNeil 12 / *n.* 8° Green, *Edin.* [81] 04
ROSS, Geo. [ed.] Leadg. Cases in Law of Scotl.: Commercial Law, 3 v. 20/ 8° Green, *Edin.*

**United States**

CALVERT, T. H. The Regulation of Commerce $3 8° Thompson, *Northport, L.I.* 07
DOS PASSOS, J. R. Inter-state Commerce Act [anal. & hist.: Questns. of Day] $1·25 12° Putnam, *N.Y.* 87
HAMILTON, A. [ed.] The Inter-state Commerce Law; w. annotns. $2·50 8° Thompson, *Northport, L.I.* 87
HARPER, J. C. [ed.] The Inter-state Commerce Law; w. notes $2 8° Clarke, *Cincinnati* 87
JUDSON, F. N. Law of Interstate Commerce $5 8° Flood *Chicago* 07
NELSON, J. H. [ed.] The Inter-state Commerce Commission, 1908 $5 *n.* 8° Banks, *N.Y.* 08
The Interstate Commerce Comm., the Sherman Anti-Trust Act, the Bureau of Corporns., etc.
PARSONS, Dr Theoph. Laws of Business for all States and Territories of the Union and of Canada $3·50 8° Scranton, *Hartford* [57] 07
SPALDING, H. M. Encyclopædia of Business Law and Forms $3 8° Ziegler, *Phila.* 03

**America (Central); Mexico**

HAMILTON, L. Mexican Legislation affecting Foreigners *o.p.* [*pb.* 18 /] 8° Stevens 82
WALTON, C. S. Leyes Commerciales y Maritimas dela América Latina, 5 v. 105 / *n.* 8° Hirschfeld 08

**Argentine Republic**

Code of Commerce: tr. G. Wilson-Rae + B. de Speluzzi 20 / *n.* 8° 04

**France**

ARGLES, N. Treat. upon French Merc. Law and Pract. of Cts. 16 / 8° 82
COXE, H. C. Manual of French Law and Commerc. Informn. 6/ *n.* c 8° Simpkin 02
GOIRAND, L. Treatise upon French Commercial Law and Pract. of the Courts 20 / 8° Stevens [80] 98
Text of laws, w. tr. of Code of Commerce and Commentary, and Dict. of French judicial terms.
MAYER, Sylvain [tr.] French Code of Commerce; w. notes and index 9 / p 8° Butterworth 87

**Germany**

PLATT, B. A. [tr.] Commercial Code of German Empire: tr. 10/6 8° 00

**Goodwill** —*v.* **D** § 96

**Merchandize Marks**

FINCH, H. M. [ed.] Merchandise Marks Acts '87–94 7/6 c 8° Clowes 04
KERLY, D. M. Law of Merchandize Marks, etc., ed. F. G. Underhay 10 / r 8° Sweet [94] 09
SAFFORD, F The Law of Merchandize Marks 7/6 8° Waterlow 93

**Unfair Competition**

NIMS On Unfair Business Competition 27/6 *n.* r 8° 09
Chapters on Trade Secrets and Confidential Business Relations, Unfair Interference with Contracts, etc.

## 64 : MILITARY AND NAVAL LAW

**MILITARY LAW**

BANNING, Lt.-Col. S. T. Military Law Made Easy 4/6 *n.* c 8° Gale & Polden [ ] 07
BIRKHIMER, W. E. Military Government and Martial Law 15/ 8° Paul [ ] 05
BURN, W. A. Claims against the Military 10/6 *n.* c 8° 03
BUXTON, J. W. Elements of Military Administration and Law 7/6 c 8° Paul 83
CLODE, C. M. Administration of Justice under Military and Martial Law 12/ 8° Murray 72
COCHRAN, Maj. F. Handy Text Book on Military Law 7/6 p 8° Blackwood 84
Manual of Military Law [excellent wk.; official text-bk.] H.M. Stationery Off. [84] 87
MORGAN, Cpt. H. F. Summary of the Military Law 5/ c 8° Marcus Ward 83
PRATT, Maj. S. C. Military Law : procedure and practice [a good précis] 4/6 12° Paul [83] 08
TOVEY, Lt.-Col. Martial Law and Custom of War in Troublous Times 6/ c 8° Chapman 86
,, Military Law; w. military law of foreign states 5/ c 8° Simpkin 87

**India**

POYNDER, Maj. C. E. [ed.] The Indian Articles of War 9/ 12° *Calcutta* 96
With illns. of charges, rules and forms of Courts Martial, and a comparison betw. Engl. and Indian Evidence and Military Law.

**United States**

DAVIS, G. B. Treat. on Mil. Law and Cts. Martial of U.S. $7 8° Wiley, *N.Y.* 98
DUDLEY, E. S. Military Law and Procedure of Courts Martial $2·50 *n.* 8° Wiley, *N.Y.* 07
IVES, Lt. R. A. Treat. on Military Law & Jurisdiction of Military Cts. $4 8° *New York* 79
WINTHROP, W. W. Military Law and Precedents, 2 vols. $12 8° Little & Brown, *Boston* [86] 96
,, Abridgment of Military Law $2·50 12° Wiley, *N.Y.* [87] 93

**Courts Martial**

O'DOWD, T. C. Hints to Court Martial Command. Officers 4/6 c 8° Clowes [ ] 83
SIMMONS, Cpt. T. F. Constitution and Practice of Courts Martial 15/ 8° Murray [30] 73

**International Law of War** —*v.* **D** § 113

**Trials** —*v.* **D** § 6, *s.v.* Trials

**Volunteers**

BURN (W. A.) + RAYMOND (W. T.) Manual of Law regulatg. Volunteer Forces 2/ 12° Stevens 82

**NAVAL LAW**

STEPHENS (J. E. R.) + GIFFORD (C. E.) + SMITH (F. H.) Manual of Naval Law and Court Martial Procedure 15/ 8° Stevens 01
Embodies L'd T. THRING's *Criminal Law of the Navy* [*o.p* (*pb.* 8/6) p 8° Stevens 61; ed. C. E. GIFFORD, 12/6 8°].

**Naval Prize Law**

LUSHINGTON, G. Manual of Naval Prize Law 10/6 i 8° Butterworth 66

## 65 : MINES, MINERALS, AND COLLIERIES

**Collieries**

FOWLER, J. C. Hdbk. of Law of Collieries, ed. J. Bell White [w. leadg. cases] 7/6 p 8° Sweet [61] *in prep.*
HAMILTON (H. B. H.) + FORBES (U. A.) Digest of Statutory Laws of Collieries 17/6 *n.* 8° Walter Scott 02

*Coal Mines Regulation Acts*

CHISHOLM, J. C. [ed.] Manl. of Coal Mines Reguln. Act, ed. Sheldon + Craigie 7/6 8° Stevens 88
PEACE, M. W. [ed.] Coal Mines Reg. Act 1887, & Truck Acts '31, '87; w. notes 10/6 8° Reeves & Turner 88
WILLIAMS (B. F.) + PITT-LEWIS (G.) Coal Mines Reg. Acts, 1887-96; w. introd., notes, and forms 10/6 8° Butterworth 97

**Mines and Minerals**

ALFORD, C. J. [ed.] Mining Laws of Brit. Empire [$3 *n.* Lippincott, *Phila.*] 8/6 *n.* 8° Griffin 06
BAINBRIDGE, W. Law of Mines and Minerals, ed. Arch. Brown 42/ r 8° Butterworth [41] 00
COCKBURN, J. H. Law of Coal, Coal Mining . . . and Trading w. Minerals generally 36/ r 8° Stevens 02

*MacSwinney, R. F. Law of Mines, Quarries, and Minerals 42 / r 8° Sweet [84] 07
Walmesley, C. Guide to the Mining Laws of the World 5 / r 8° Eyre & Spottiswoode 94

**Scotland**

Stewart, D. Ross Law rel. to Mines, etc., in Scotland 30 / *n.* r 8° Green, *Edin.* 94

**Africa:** *Egypt*

Alford, C. J. [ed.] Egyptian Mining Laws 6 / 8° *Mining Jl.* Off. 07

**Africa:** *South*

Barber, S. H. Gold Laws of the Transvaal 30 / *n.* r 8° *Capetown* 05
Bell, W. H. S. Mineral Laws of Orange River Colony 12/6 *n.* 8° Sweet 04

**Australia; New Zealand**

Armstrong, H. J. Law of Gold Mining in Austral. and N. Zealand 40/ *n.* r 8° Sweet [ ] 01
De Lissa, A. Companies Work & Mining Law in N.S.W. and Vict. 10/6 c 8° Clowes 94
Eagleson (J. G.) + Sanderson (W. A.) + O'Dowd (B. P.) Digest of Australian Mining Cases 40/ r 8° Sweet 97
Macfarlane, J. [ed.] Digest of Mining Cases: 1858–73 10/6 8° *Melbourne* 73

**United States**

Barringer (D. M.) + Adams (J. S.) Law of Mines & Mining in U.S. $7·50 8° Little & Brown, *Boston* 97
Emery, G. D. Miner's Manual: laws of mines and mining $2·50 8° Herald Pb., *Washgtn.* 06
Lindley, C. H. Amer. Law rel. to Mines & Mineral Lands, 2 v. $15 8° Bancroft, *San Francisco* [97] 03
Martin, T. Mining Law and Land Office Procedure $7·50 r 8° Bender, *Albany* 08
Morrison, R. S. Digest of Law of Mines and Minerals $6 8° Callaghan, *Chicago* 78
,, + Munroe (C. E.) [eds.] Mining Reports, vols. i–xxii [Eng. & Amer. cases] ea. $5 8° Callaghan, *Chicago* 83–07 *in prg.*
Shamel, C. H. Mining, Mineral, and Geological Law $5 8° Hill Pb. Co., *N.Y.* 07
Snyder, W. I. Mines and Mining, 2 vols. $12 8° Flood, *Chicago* 02

**Royalties** —*v.* **I** § 79

**MISREPRESENTATION**—*v.* **D** § 46 **MONEY LENDERS**—*v.* **D** § 19

## 66: MORTGAGES AND LIENS

Andrews, J. [ed.] Precedents of Mortgages 7/6 12° Reeves & Turner 79
Ashburner, W. Treatise on Mortgages, Pledges and Liens 25 / r 8° Butterworth 97
Atkinson, F. W. Law and Pract. rel. to Solicitors' Liens and Charging Orders 7/6 *n.* 8° Sweet 05
Beddoes, W. F. Concise Treatise on the Law of Mortgage 12/6 8° Stevens [93] 08
*Coote, R. H. Treat. on Law of Mortgage, ed. S. E. Williams, 2 v. 63 / r 8° Sweet [22] 04
*Fisher, W. R. Law of Mortg. & other Securs. on Prop., ed. A. Underhill 52/6 r 8° Butterworth [6–] 11
Gloag (W. M.) + Irvine (J. M.) Law of Rights in Security, Heritable and Moveable, incl. Cautionary Obligations 40 / *n.* r 8° Green, *Edin.* 98
Harnett, E. St C. Mortgages: a Handbk. on the Law 6/ r 12° Stevens 09
Stephenson, C. H. S. Mortgages: a Study of the Law 7/6 *n.* 8° E. Wilson 09

**Canada**

Barron, J. A. Handy Bk. of Law of Bills of Sale and Chattel Mortgages 16/6 8° *Toronto* 80

**India**

Bihari Ghose, Ras Law of Mortgage in India [Tagore Law Lects., '75–6] 32/6 8° *Calcutta* [77] 89
Macpherson, A. G. Law of Mortgage in Bengal and North-West Provinces 21 / 8° *Calcutta* [ ]

**United States**

Boisot, A. B., jun. Treatise on Mechanics' Liens $6 *n.* 8° West Pb. Co., *St Paul, Minn.* 97
Cobbey, J. E. Law of Chattel Mortgages, 2 v. $10 8° West Pb. Co., *St Paul, Minn.* 93
Herman, H. M. Commentaries on Mortgages and Liens, 2 vols. $12 8° Cockcroft, *N.Y.* 77
,, Treatise on Chattel Mortgages $7·50 8° Cockcroft, *N.Y.* 79
Jones, L. A. Law of Mortgage of Personal Property $6 *n.* 8° Houghton, *Boston* [81] 08
,, Law of Mortgage on Real Property, 2 v. $12 *n.* 8° Houghton, *Boston* [82] 94

JONES, L. A. Treatise on Liens, 2 vols. [comprehensive] $13 8° Houghton, *Boston* 88
OVERTON, D. Y. Law of Liens at Common Law, Equity, Statut., Marit. $6 r 8° Banks, *N.Y.* 84
PHILLIPS, S. L. Treat. on Law of Mechanics' Liens on Real & Pers. Prop. $6 8° Little & Brown, *Bost.* [73] 83
PINGREY, D H. Law of Chattel Mortgages $6 8° Linn, *Jersey City* 91
,, Law of Mortgages on Real Property, 2 vols. $12 8° Parsons, *Albany* [93] 95
WILTSIE, C. H. Law & Pract. of Foreclosg. Mortgs. on Real Prop., 2 v. $12·75 8° Williamson, *Rochester* 97

**Bills of Sale**—*v.* **D** § 19 **Pawnbrokers**—*v.* **D** § 73

## MOTOR CARS—*v.* D § 67

## 67 : MUNICIPAL AND LOCAL LAW—*v. also* D § 124

### Municipal Corporations

ARNOLD, T. J. Law rel. to Mun. Corpns., ed. W. Mackenzie + G. R. Hill 42/ 18° Butterworth [3–] 10
ATKINSON, C. J. F. Concise Hdbk. of Provincial Loc. Govt. Law 3/6 c 8° E. Wilson 02
BAZALGETTE (C. N.) + HUMPHREYS (G.) [eds.] Local and Municipal Government 60/, *red.* to 20/ *n.* r 8° Stevens [85] 88
Statutes of Pub. Health, Municip. Corps., Highways, Burial, Gas and Water, Pub. Loans, Tramways, Elect. Lightg., Artisans' Dwellings, etc.
County Council Cases: Memorials & Bye-Laws, 1890–1909, Pts. i–xv. ea. 6/ *n.* 8° Green, *Ed.* 95–09 *in prg.*
LELY, J. M. [ed.] Law of Municipal Corporations [ = Act of 1882, etc.] 15/ 8° Sweet 82
Local Government Manuals: ed. Bertram Jacobs Sweet 10 *in prg.*
i: *County, District, and Parish Councils*, by J. H. MENZIES. To be followed by *Munic. Corporatns.*, and *Public Health.*
RAWLINSON, Sir C. [ed.] Municipal Corporation Acts, ed. J. F. P. Rawlinson + J. A. Johnston 42/ 8° Maxwell [4–] 10
SCHOLEFIELD, J. [ed.] Encyclo. of Loc. Gov. Law excl. Metropolis, 7 vols. 175/ r 8° Butterworth 05–8
THATCHER, J. W. Pitman's Handbook of Local Government Law 3/6 *n.* c 8° Pitman 09
WRIGHT (R. S.) + HOBHOUSE (H.) Local Govt. & Loc. Taxatn. in Engl. & Wales 7/6 r 8° Sweet [84–8] 06
The best general survey of the whole subject. Excludes London.

#### Scotland

HOWMAN, M. L. [ed.] The Town Councils (Scotland) Act, 1900 [w. notes] 3/6 *n.* 8° Green, *Edin.* 00
HUNTER, Thos. [ed.] Edinburgh Municipal and Police Acts [w. Introd.] 40/ *n.* r 8° Green, *Edin.* 09
IRONS (J. C.) + MELVILLE (R. D.) + MITCHELL (W.) Burgh Government [Suppl. to ' Burgh Police Act ' *inf.*] 20/ *n.* 8° Green, *Edin.* 05
MURRAY, A. Councillor's Manual: guide to Scottish local govt. 7/6 *n.* 8° Green, *Edin.* [ ] 10
All Acts, Reguln., etc., dealg. w. the subj. (Police, Poor Law, Pub. Health, Lunacy, Valuatn., Electns., Roads, Bridges, Boundaries, Educn., etc.) in one vol. 1,600 pp.

#### United States

ABBOTT, H. S. Treatise on Law of Municipal Corporations, 3 vols. $18 8° Keefe, *St Paul, Minn.* 06
DILLON, J. F. Commentaries on Law of Municipal Corpns., 2 vols. $11 r 8° Little & Brown, *Boston* [72] 81
GOODNOW, Prf. Fk. Municipal Home Rule: study in administration $1·50 *n.* (6/6 *n.*) 8° Macmillan 95
Chiefly concerned w. technical Amer. law, espec. judge-made law, in the various States, bearg. on constitutl. positn. of municipalities in Amer. Urges that the lack of civic patriotism is due to the small amt. of local autonomy assigned to the cities, and that reform should be attempted. A careful and accurate book.
MICHIE, T. J. Municipal Corporation Cases Annotated, vols. i–x ea. $5 8° Michie, *Charlottesville* 89–03

### Adulteration of Foods

BARTLEY, D. C. [ed.] Adulteration of Food [statutes and cases] 10/ 8° Stevens [ ] 07

### Artisans' and Labourers' Dwellings—*v. also* D § 127

ALLAN, C. E. + F. J. [eds.] Housing of Working Classes Acts annot. & expl. 12/6 8° Butterworth [91] 11
LLOYD, E. —*in his* Law of Compensation for Land, Houses, etc., *ut* **D** § 51
HOWKINS, F. [ed.] Housing Acts 1890–1909, & Town Planning 7/6 *n.* 8° *Lond. Estates Gaz.* 10

### Borough Funds Acts

WILLIAMS, W. L. [ed.] Borough Funds Acts 12/6 *n.* 8° Butterworth 04

### Burials

AUSTIN, E. Burial Grounds and Cemeteries 5/ *n.* 8° Butterworth 06
BAKER, T. Law rel. to Burials, ed. E. L. Thomas 25/; Suppl. 2/ *n.* 8° Sweet [55] 98; 01
LITTLE, J. B. Law of Burial [w. Acts, Reguln., notes, cases] 22/6 8° Butterworth [88] 02
,, [ed.] The Burial Act, 1900; w. notes and appendix 3/6 *n.* c 8° Butterworth 01

**By-Laws** —*v.* **D** § 26

**Citizenship :** *United States*
WEBSTER, Prentiss Treat. on Law of Citizenship in U.S. [historical] $4 8° Bender, *Albany* 91

**Companies (Incorp.) operating under Municipal Franchises**
FOOTE (A. R.) + EVERETT (C. E.) Law of Incorp. Cos. Operating under Munic. Franchises, 3 v. $15 *n.* 8° Clarke, *Cincinn.* [92] 93
Illuminatg. Gas, Fuel Gas, Electric Central Station, Telephone, Street Ry., Water and other Cos., w. prelim. [economic] discussn.

**Compulsory Purchase by Corporations**—*v.* **D** § 26

**Contracts** —*v.* **D** § 29 (MAUDE + LEACH)

**Coroners**
HERBERT The Payment of Coroners 2/6 8° Butterworth 91
JERVIS, Sir Jno. Office and Duties of Coroners, ed. R. E. Melsheimer 10/6 c 8° Sweet [29] 98
WELLINGTON, R. H. The King's Coroner, 2 vols. 18/ c 8° Clowes 05–6
Vol. i contains a complete collection of statutes, w. short history, 10/6 ; ii deals w. pract. and procedure, 7/6 *n.*

**Drainage**
*MACMORRAN (A.) + WILLIS (W. A). Law of Sewers and Drains 25/ *n.* 8° Shaw 04
POLEY, A. P. Treat. on Law affectg. Sewers and Drains : w. plans 5/ r 8° 05

**Education**—*v.* **D** § 159 **Elections**—*v.* **D** § 40

**Electric Lighting, etc.** —*v. also inf., s.v.* Gas
JOYCE (J. A.) + HOWARD (C.) Treatise on Electric Law, 2 vols. $12 *n.* 8° Banks, *N.Y.* [00] 07
KNOWLES, C. M. Law rel. to Electricity, incl. El. Traction, 2 Pts. 42/ r 8° Stevens 11
WILL, J. S. Law rel. to Electric Lighting, Traction, & Power 25/ r 8° Butterworth [ ] 03

**Gas and Water**
DUCKWORTH, L. Consumer's Handbk. of Law rel. to Gas, Water, and Electr. Lightg. 1/6 *n.* 12° E. Wilson [ ] 05
GRIFFITH, P. Waterworks Law as applied to Small Undertakings 5/ 8° Biggs 02
MICHAEL (W. H.) + WILL (J. S.) Law rel. to Gas, Water, and El. Lightg., ed. M. J. Michael 35/ r 8° Butterworth [72] 01
REESON, J. [ed.] Acts rel. to Supply of Gas & Water, 1817–1905 ; w. notes 21/ *n.* 8° Butterworth [02] 05
RICKARDS (A. G.) + PEMBER (F. W.) The Metropolis Water Act, 1902 7/6 *n.* 8° Butterworth 03

**Highways ; Surveyors of Highways ; Private Streets**
BAKER, T. Law of Highways in England and Wales 15/ 12° Stevens 80
BARLOW (C. A. M.) + HICKS (W. J.) Mechan. Traction on Highways in U.K. 8/6 *n.* 8° Pitman 06
COPNALL, H. H. Pract. Guide to Administration of Highway Law 15/ *n.* 8° Knight 05
GLEN, A. Powers & Duties of Surveyors of H'ways, ed. R. C. Glen 5/ c 8° Knight [ ] 88
GLEN, W. C. + A. [eds.] Law rel. to Highways, Bridges, Interference of Railways, w. Highways, Tramways, etc. 52/6 8° Butterworth [83] 97
PRATT (W. T.) + MACKENZIE (W.) Law of Highways, Main Roads & Bridges 52/6 r 8° Butterworth [81] 11
SCHOLEFIELD (J.) + HILL (G. R.) [eds.] Private Street Works Act, 1892 7/6 8° Butterworth 02
SPEARMAN, R. H. Common & Statute Law rel. to Highways in Engl. & N. Wales *o.p.* [*pb.* 9/] 8° Sweet 80
SPINKS, Wm. Law and Pract. as to Paving and Makg. good Priv. Streets 8/6 8° Spon [87] 92
STEPHENS, J. E. R. Digest of Highway Cases 21/ *n.* 8° Sanitary Pb. Co. 03
THATCHER (J. W.) + HARTLEY (D. H. J.) Law of the Road [sel. of leadg. cases] 7/6 8° Stevens 09

*Scotland*
DYKES (J. E.) + STUART (D.) [eds.] County Council Guide to Roads and Bridges Acts 7/6 8° Green *Edin.* 90
FERGUSON, Jas. Law of Roads, Streets, Rights-of-Way, Bridges, & Ferries 30/ *n.* r 8° Green, *Edin.* 04

*United States*
ANGELL (J. K.) + DURFEE (T.) Treat. on Law of H'ways, ed. G. F. Choate $5 8° Little & Brown, *Bost.* [68] 86
ELLIOTT, B. K. + W. F. Treat. on Law of Roads & Streets $6 *n.* 8° Bowen-Merrill, *Indianapolis* [90] 00
THOMPSON, Is. G. Treatise on Law of Highways, ed. C. H. Mills $5 8° Little, *Albany* [ ] 90

*Cyclists*
CHALMERS, D. Law as it affects Cyclists 2/ *n.* c 8° Butterworth 99

*Motor Cars ; Cabs*

BONNER (G. A.) + FARRANT (H. G.) Law of Motor Cars, Hackney & other Carriages 12/6 8° 04
COHEN, M. The Law of Cabs [incl. motor cars] 2/6 *n.* c 8° 99
LEWIS (H. L.) + PATER (W. H.) Law relating to Motor Cars 2/6 *n.* c 8° Butterworth [04] 04
LUCAS (W.) + CRANE (A. C.) Law affecting Motor Cars 5/ *n.* 05
MAHAFFY (R. P.) + DODSON (G.) Law relating to Motor Cars 12/6 8° Butterworth 10
PETTITT, D. H. Lives of Motor-cars and Motor-cycles 3/6 *n.* c 8° 05
,, Law of Heavy Motor-cars 3/6 *n.* c 8° 05
SANDBACK, J. B. Law of Motor Cars 2/6 *n.* c 8° J. E. Cornish, *Mancs.* 07

**Hospitals, Infirmaries, etc.**

BRISTOWE, L. S. Legal Handbk. for Use of Hospital Authorities 3/6 c 8° Reeves & Turner 94
MURRAY, A. T. Law of Hospitals, Infirmaries and Kindred Institns. 10/6 *n.* 8° Murray 08

**Libraries and Museums** (**Public**)

CHAMBERS (G. F.) + FOVARGUE (H. W.) Digest of Law rel. to Public Libraries and Museums 10/6 8° Knight [74] 99
FOVARGUE (H. W.) + OGLE (J. J.) Public Library Legislation 2/6 *n.* 8° Library Assoc. [91] 93
The former edn. was pub. *sub. tit. A Digest of Public Library Law: 1855–1890.*

**Licensing, Innkeepers** —*v. also* **D** § 15, **D** § 131

CURLEWIS (H. R.) + EDWARD (D. S.) Law of Prohibition 35/ *n.* r 8° Sweet 11
DAVIES, A. T. Handbk. on Licensing Acts and their Admin. 2/6 *n.* 8° Macmillan [ ] 98
FORTESCUE, C. [ed.] Digest of Licensing Cases 3/6 p 8° Stevens 81
GRAYSON (J.) + WOODS (W. J.) Dictionary of Licensing Law 10/6 c 8° Premier Pb. Co. 08
HIME (G.) + LAMB (W. R.) Licensing Act, 1902; w. explan. treatise 3/ 8° Simpkin 02
HYNES (T.) + JAMESON (T.) Law rel. to County Council Licenses 10/6 *n.* 8° Butterworth 09
JELF (E. A.) + HURST (C. J. B.) The Law of Innkeepers 5/ 8° Cox 04
LELY (J. M.) + FOULKES (W. D.) [eds.] Licensing Acts, 1828–69, & '72–'74; w. notes, etc. 10/6 r 12° Sweet [72] 87
LIVESEY, D. Manual of Licensing Applications 3/6 *n.* c 8° Butterworth 06
MACKENZIE, W. W. [ed.] Licensing Act, 1904 3/6 *n.* c 8° Butterworth 04
,, + WOODCOCK (H. D.) Digest of Licensing Cases 12/6 p 8° Butterworth [99] 09
MONTGOMERY, R. M. Licensing Laws 12/6 8° Sweet [ ] 05
,, + WOODCOCK (H. D.) [eds.] Annual Licensing Practice 12/6 8° Sweet *ann.*
PATERSON, Jas. [ed.] Licensing Acts, 1828–1906, ed. W. W. Mackenzie 15/ *n.* p 8° Butterworth [70] 11
Gives also laws rel. to clubs, dancing, racecourses, etc.
TALBOT, G. J. Law and Practice of Licensing 10/6 12° Butterworth [96] 05
WHITELEY, G. C. Licensing Laws 8/6 c 8° Knight [75] 01
,, [ed.] The Licensing Acts 12/6 *n.* 8° Stevens & Haynes 11
WILLIAMSON, J. B. Law of Licensing in England 20/ 8° Stevens [98] 11
,, Law and Pract. of Licensing Sessions and Appeals 12/6 8° Clowes 01

*Scotland*

BARCLAY, H. [ed.] Public House Statutes [w. notes, cases, etc.] 4/ 12° *Edinburgh* [ ] 76
DEWAR, Dav. The Liquor Laws of Scotland 7/6 *n.* 8° Green, *Edin.* [ ] 03
PURVES, Jas. [ed.] Scottish Licensing Laws [Scot. Lic. Act, 1903] 10/ *n.* c 8° Green, *Edin.* [03] 03

*Ireland*

SARGENT, W. A. Liquor Licensing Laws of Ireland 12/ c 8° McGee, *Dublin* 90
Conts. all the statutes fr. 1660 to 1890, w. notes of all Irish and Eng. cases rel. to Licensed Houses.

*United States and Canada* —*v. also* **D** § 131 (FANSHAWE), *and sup.* (WINES)

BEALE (J. H., jun.) + WYMAN (B.) Treatise on Hotels and Innkeepers $6 *n.* 8° Nagel, *Boston* 06
BLACK, H. C. Law reg. Manuf. & Sale of Intox. Liquors $6 *n.* 8° West Pb. Co., *St Paul, Minn.* 92
WINES (F. H.) + KOREN (J.) Liquor Probl. in its Legislative Aspects $1·25 12° Houghton, *Boston* 96
Results of careful investign. into working of prohib. and license laws in Maine, Iowa, S. Carol., Mass., Ohio, Indiana, Pennsyl., Missouri.

**Local Government Act, 1888** (*County Councils*)

BAZALGETTE (C. N.) + HUMPHREYS (G.) The Law relating to County Councils 7/6 r 8° Stevens [88] 89
FIRTH (J. F. B.) + SIMPSON (E. R.) [eds.] London Government under Act of 1888 20/ r 8° Knight 88
GLEN, A. Law rel. to County Govt. under Act 1888, ed. W. E. Gordon 42/ 8° Knight 90
,, + CUNNINGHAM (A. R.) + JENKIN (A. F.) District Councillor's Guide 8/6 *n.* r 8° Knight [88] 08

MACMORRAN (A.) + DILL (T. R. C.) [eds.] Local Government Act 1888, w. Introd. and notes 40/ r 8° Butterworth [88] 98
PARKER, F. R. Election of County Councils under Act of 1888—*ut* **D** § 40
RYDE (W. C.) + THOMAS (E. L.) [eds.] Loc. Govt. Act, Co. Electors' Act, 1888, etc. 24/ 8° Butterworth 88
STEPHEN (H.) + MILLER (H. E.) [eds.] County Council Compendium [digest of Acts 1880, '88 ; w. notes] 21/ 8° Waterlow 88

*History*

SAUNDERS, Wm. History of the First London County Council 10/6 8° National Press Agency 92

*Scotland*

BLACK, W. G. Law relating to Scottish County Councils 6/ 8° Bell & Bradfute, *Edin.* [89] 90
NICOLSON (J. R.) + MURE (W. J.) [eds.] County Council Guide for Scotland 5/ 8° Blackwood 90
SHENNAN, Hay [ed.] Parish Councillor's Hdbk. [= Loc. Govt. (Sc.) Act '94] 3/6 *n.* c 8° Green, *Edin.* [ ] 08

**Local Government Act, 1894** (*Parish Councils*)

CORNISH, H. D. District Councils : concise guide to powers and duties 7/6 8° Stevens 08
DILL, T. R. C. Parish Councils Election Manual 4/6 c 8° Shaw [94] 96
,, Parish Councillor's Manual 5/ p 8° Butterworth 96
DUMSDAY, W. H. [ed.] Local Government Acts, 1894–7 9/ *n.* 8° Hadden & Best 97
HUMPHREYS, Geo. [ed.] Law rel. to Parish Councils : Local Govt. Act 1894 10/ r 8° Stevens [94] 95
HUNT, J. Lond. Loc. Govt. : law rel. to L.C.C., etc., 2 vols. 63/ r 8° Stevens 97
,, [ed.] London Government Act, 1899 7/6 r 8° Stevens 99
JENKIN, A. F. [ed.] The London Government Act, 1899 7/6 8° Knight 99
LITHIBY, J. [ed.] Law of Distr. & Par. Councils : Local Govt. Act '94 15/ 8° E. Wilson [94] 97
MACHUGH (A.) + O'DOWD (B. P.) [eds.] Local Government Acts 31/6 8°
MACKENZIE, W. W. The Overseers' Handbook 5/ *n.* c 8° [ ] 06
*MACMORRAN (A.) + DILL (T. R. C.) Loc. Govt. Act '94, and Later Stats. affg. Par. Cls. 22/6 *n.* r 8° Butterworth [ ] 07
,, + LUSHINGTON (S. G.) + NALDRETT (E. J.) [eds.] Lond. Govt. Act, 1899 12/6 r 8° Butterworth 99
OWEN, H. Manual f. Overseers and Paroch. Officers, ed. A. F. Jenkin 5/ *n* 12° Knight [71] 06
RICHARDS (H. C.) + PAYNE (W. H. C.) + SOPER (J. P. H.) Parish Councillor's Guide to L.G.A. '94 7/6 *n.* c 8° Jordan [94] 95
TERRY (G. P. W.) + MORLE (P. B.) [eds.] London Government Act, 1899 7/6 8° Butterworth 99

*Elections* —*v.* **D** § 40

*Scotland*

MACDOUGALL (J. P.) + DODDS (J. M.) [eds.] Parish Council Guide for Scotland 2/6 *n.* 12° Blackwood 94

**Local Government Board**

CASSON, W. A. Decisions of the Local Government Board 10/6 *n.* 8° Knight 04
KNIGHT'S [pub.] Annot. Model Bye-laws of L.G.B, ed. W. A. Casson 16/ *n.* r 8° Knight [ ] 05
MACKENZIE (W.) + HANDFORD (P.) Model Bye-Laws, 2 vols. ; pl. 25/ r 8° Butterworth 99
Rules and Regulations under Public Health and other Acts.
,, Model Bye-laws as to Nuisances & New Streets & Bldgs. 12/6 r 8° Butterworth 04
WOOD (A. E.) + JOHNSON (T. R.) Encycl. of Loc. Gov. Bd. Requiremts. & Pract., 2 v. 50/ *n.* r 8° 08

**Markets, Fairs, etc.**

GACHES, L. Markets and Fairs 2/6 12° Eyre & Spottiswoode 98
KEEN, F. N. Markets, Fairs, and Slaughterhouses 3/6 *n.* 8° P. S. King & Co. 04
PEASE (J. G.) + CHITTY (H.) Treat. on Law of Markets and Fairs [w. Statutes] 8/6 8° 99

**Metropolitan Building and Management Acts, etc.**

BARTLEY, D. C. [ed.] Metropolis Water Act 6/ 8° Stevens 03
*COHEN, E. A. London Building Acts, 1894–1905 25/ r 8° Stevens 06
CRAIES, W. F. [ed.] London Building Act, 1894 : w. notes and indices 5/ 8° Sweet 94
DAVID, A. J. [ed.] London Building Act, 1894 3/6 c 8° Crosby Lockwood 94
DICKSEE, B. [ed.] The London Building Acts, 1894–1908 10/ *n.* c 8° Stanford [95] 08
EMDEN, A. Law rel. to Building Leases and Contracts—*ut* **D** § 20
FLETCHER, B. [ed.] The London Building Acts, 1894–1905 6/6 c 8° Batsford [94] 07
GLEN (R. C.) + BETHUNE (A. A.) Law reg. Streets & Bldgs. und. Lond. Bdg. Act '94 25/ 8° Knight 95

GLEN, W. C. + R. C. [eds.] Metropolitan Building Acts [1855–1882] 10/6 c 8° Stevens 83
GRIFFITH (W. R.) + PEMBER (F. W.) [eds.] London Building Act, 189 12/6 r 12° Butterworth 95
HUNT, J. London Local Government, 2 vols. 63/r 8° Stevens 97
„ Guide to Electn. of Mayor, Aldermen, & Councillors of Metr. Boroughs 3/6 8° Stevens 06
MACMORRAN (A.) + LUSHINGTON (S. G.) + NALDRETT (E. J.) Lond. Govt. Act, '99 12/6 r 8° Butterworth 99
MOLLOY, B. C. [ed.] London Buildg. Acts (Amendmt.) Act 5/ n. 8° 05
TAGG, C. W. [ed.] London Laws and Bye-Laws 7/6 8° Tarrant 08
The Acts of Parl., Orders, and Bye-laws under wh. London is governed for local purposes. Pref. G. L. GOMME.

**Nuisances** —v. **D** § 70

**Parochial**

DILL, T. R. Colquhoun Parish Councillor's Manual 5/ p 8° Butterworth 96
„ Parochial Valuer's Assistant, ed. J. Dolby 10/6 8° Butterworth [ ]
„ Law of Parochial Charities 2/6 c 8° Butterworth 94
HOLDSWORTH, W. A. Handy-Book of Parish Law [Legal Handbooks] 1/ n. f 8° Routledge [81] 07
SHAW, J. Parish Law, ed. J. T. Dodd 15/ c 8° Stevens [ ] 95
*STEER, J. Digest of Law rel. to Parishes & Relief of Poor, ed. W. H. Macnamara 20/ 8° Stevens [3–] 99

*Scotland*

BLACK, W. G. Handbook of Parochial Ecclesiastical Law of Scotld. 12/ n. 8° Green, *Edin.* [88] 01
„ Parochial Law of Scotland other than Ecclesiastical 8/ c 8° Green, *Edin.* 93

*Overseers*

MACKENZIE, W. W. The Overseer's Handbook 5/ n. p 8° Butterworth [9–] 06
For use of overseers, churchwardens, collectors of poor-rate, vestry-clerks and other parish-officers.

**Police** —*v. also* **D** § 105

ARCHIBALD + GREENHALGH + ROBERTS Metropolitan Police Guide r 8° H.M. Station. Off. [ ] 01
CARMICHAEL, E. G. M. County and Borough Police Acts, 1831–1900 18/ 8° Butterworth 00
GREENWOOD (H. C.) + MARTIN (T. C.) Magisterial and Police Guide 32/ 8° Stevens & Haynes [74] 90
HAYCRAFT, T. W. Powers of Police in England 6/ 8° Butterworth 97
KEEN, F. N. Urban Police and Sanitary Legislation—*ut inf.*
MARRIOTT, Thos. A Constable's Duty, and How to Do it 3/6 n. c 8° E. Wilson [02] 04
SNOWDEN, R. L. Magistrates' Assistant and Police Officers' Guide, ed. H. Lees + R. Shield 10/6 8° Shaw [46] 05
VINCENT, Col. Sir H. Police Code and Manual of the Law 2/6 n. 12° Simpkin [81] 07

*Scotland*

ANGUS, J. W. Powers and Duties of Police Consts. in Scotland 5/ n. 8° Green, *Edin.* 04
IRONS, J. C. [ed.] Burgh Police (Scotland) Act 22/ n. 8° Green, *Edin.* 93
For Supplement *v. sup., s.n.* IRONS + MELVILLE + MITCHELL.

*Canada*

CLARKE, S. R. The Constable's Manual [summary of the law] 7/6 8° *Toronto* 78
WILSON, A. Constables' Duties 4/ 8° *Toronto* 61
HARLOW, W. S. Duties of Sheriffs and Constables under Practice in California and Pacific States and Territories $6 8° Bancroft, *San Francisco* [ ] 07

**Poor Law** —*v. also* Parochial, *sup.* For bks. on effect, etc., of Poor Laws, *v.* **D** § 127

ARCHBOLD, J. F. Poor Law, Poor Rate, etc., ed. J. B. Little 45/ 8° Butterworth [42] 98
DAVEY, H. [ed.] Poor Law Acts, 1894 to 1908; w. notes 12/6 n. 8° Hadden 09
„ Poor Law Settlement and Removal [a text-bk.] 9/ 8° Stevens 08
GLEN, W. C. [ed.] Poor Law Orders: w. notes, cases, and index 42/ 8° Shaw [47] 98
„ [ed.] Statutes in Force rel. to Poor Laws, 4 vols. 88/ 8° Shaw 73–90
JENNER-FUST, H. [ed.] Poor Law Orders: arranged and annotated 42/ n. r 8° P. S. King & Co. 07
LITTLE, J. B. [ed.] Poor Law Statutes fr. Eliz. to Victoria, 3 vols. 90/ n. 8° Butterworth 01–2
MACKENZIE, M. M. The Poor Law Guardian 7/6 c 8° Shaw [72] 95
MACMORRAN (A.) + LUSHINGTON (S. G.) + NALDRETT (E. J.) [eds.] Poor Law General Orders, 2 vols. 52/6 n. 8° Butterworth [ ] 05
MAXWELL (R. C.) + SMITH (T.) Points for Guardians and their Officers 5/ n. c 8° Shaw 07
Summary of Poor Law syst., the points bg. given concisely in alphab. order. Appendices of statistics, forms, bibliogr., etc.
'OFFICIAL, AN' The Guardian's Guide 5/ n. c 8° Knight 01

SYMONDS, J. F. Law of Settlement and Removal of Union Poor 10/6 8° Shaw [ ] 03
VULLIAMY, A. F. Law of Settlement and Removal of Paupers 12/6 *n.* 8° Knight 95
*Pauper Children* —*v. also* **D** § 127; *for* Pauper Lunatics *v.* **D** § 127
LEACH, R. A. Pauper Children: their educn. and training [hdbk. of the law] 5/ c 8° Haddon 90
*Relieving Officer* —*v.* **D** § 127
*Scotland*
GRAHAM, J. E. Poor Law and Law rel. to Parish Councils 36/ *n.* r 8° Green, *Edin.* 05
MACKAY, G. A. Practice of Poor Law of Scotland 5/ *n.* 8° Green, *Edin.* 07
REID, J. A. Digest of Decisions rel. to Poor Law of Scotland 21/ 8° *Edinburgh* 80
SMITH, J. G. Digest of Law of Scotland relating to the Poor 18/ 8° *Edinburgh* [ ] 80
*United States*
COWEN, P. H. Poor Laws of State of N.Y. [w. law of drunkards], etc. $4 8° W. C. Little, *Albany* 87

**Public Health**

AMOS, Prf. Sheldon [ed.] Laws for Prohibition, Regulation, and Licensing of Vice 18/ 8° Stevens 77
BARTLEY, D. C. Adulteration of Food [statutes and cases] 10/ r 12° Stevens 07
BELL (Sir W. J.) + SCRIVENER (H. S.) Sale of Food and Drugs Acts, '75 & '99 7/6 *n.* 12° Shaw [94] 03
BLYTH, A. Wynter Lectures on Sanitary Law 8/6 *n.* ($2·50 *n.*) 8° Macmillan 93
CHAMBERS, G. F. Digest of Law of Distr. Councils rel. to Pub. Hlth. & Loc. Govt. 10/ i 8° Stevens 95
,, [ed.] Digest of 2,750 Cases rel. to Pub. Hlth. & Loc. Govt. 12/6 8° Knight 93
DAVEY, H. [ed.] Public Health Act, 1875 8/6 *n.* 8° Knight [90] 08
ELDER, B. S. [ed.] Appeal Cases und. Food & Drugs Acts & Margarine Act 3/6 *n.* c 8° Butterworth 05
FITZGERALD, V. [ed.] Public Health and Local Gov. Acts 1875–94; w. notes 17/6 8° Longman [75] 95
GLEN, W. C. + A. + R. A. [eds.] Law rel. to Public Health & Loc. Govt., ed. A. F. Jenkin, 2 v. 70/ *n.* 8° Knight [95] 09
HALL (W. E.) + PICKERING (G. N.) Law of Food Condemnation 2/6 *n.* 8° 07
HEDDERWICK, T. C. H. [ed.] Sale of Foods and Drugs [Acts '75 and '79, w. notes] 7/6 8° Eyre & Spottiswoode [94] 00
HOWMAN, M. L. [ed.] The Sale of Food & Drugs Acts, 1875–99 5/ *n.* 8° Green, *Edin.* 01
KEEN, F. N. Urban Police and Sanitary Legislation 10/6 *n.* 8° P. S. King & Son 05
LEE, A. C. Local Government Formulist 21/ *n.* r 8° Stevens 03
Precedents for use of Sanitary Authorities.
LEMMOIN-CANNON, H. The Sanitary Inspector's Guide 3/6 *n.* c 8° P. S. King & Son
LEWIS + BALFOUR Public Health and Preventive Medicine 25/ *n.* 8° Green, *Edin.* 02
*LUMLEY, W. G. E. [ed.] Public Health Acts, 2 vols. 77/6 *n.* r 8° Butterworth [76] 08
Ed. A. Macmorran + J. Scholefield + S. G. Lushington. Vol. i: *The Public Health Acts*; ii; *Appendices.*
MACMORRAN, A. [ed.] Public Health Acts, 1888–1890 18/ 8° Shaw 91
,, [ed.] Public Health (London) Act, 1891 10/6 c 8° Butterworth [91] 08
ROBERTSON (W.) + PORTER (C.) Sanitary Law and Practice 10/6 *n.* 8° Sanit. Pb. Co. [09] 09
STEPHENS, J. E. R. [ed.] Digest of Public Health Cases 21/ *n.* 8° Sanit. Pubn. Co. 02
STEVENSON (Dr T.) + MURPHY (S. F.) Treatise on Hygiene & Public Health, v. iii: Sanitary Law—*ut* **H*** § 55
STOCKMAN, F. C. Sanitary Inspector's Guide 5/ *n.* c 8° Butterworth [ ] 04
*Scotland*
BROCK, W. J. Sanitary Laws of Scotland 7/6 12° Gurney 05
DYKES (J. E.) + STUART (D.) [eds.] Law rel. to Pub. Health [= Acts '67, '71, '75, '82] 7/6 8° Bell & Bradfute, *Edin.* 90
SKELTON, J. Handbook of Public Health for Scotland 7/6 8° Blackwood 90
*Cremation* —*for* Hygienic treatises *v.* **H*** § 56
RICHARDSON, Aubr. [ed.] Law of Cremation [w. rules of Brit. & for. societies] 5/ c 8° Reeves & Turner 93
*Vaccination* —*v.* **D** § 95

**Rating** —*for* economic aspect *v.* **D** § 152, *s. v.* Rates

BELL, W. L. L. Rating Forms and Grounds of Notices of Objection 6/ 8° Sweet 03
BOYLE (E.) + DAVIES (G. H.) Princs. of Rating pract. consid. [w. cases, stats., etc.] r 8° Clowes [90] *in prep.*
Conts. an admirable acc. of the complicated legal provisions wh. have grown ab. the orig. simple law for imposition of poor-rate.
BROWN, Arch. Rating of Mines and Quarries 5/ 8° Butterworth 98
A short treatise on rating generally, in its spec. applicn. to mines, iron wks., and quarries.

BROWNE, J. H. B. Rating of Hereditamts. in occup. of Cos., ed. D. N. Macnaughton 25/ 8° Stevens [75] 86
CASTLE, E. J. Law and Practice of Rating 25/r 8° Stevens [79] 03
CHORLTON, J. D. Rating of Land Values [Mancs. Univ. Econ. Ser.] 3/6 *n.* 8° Sherratt, *Mancs.* 07
CLODE (W.) + CRIPPS-DAY (F. H.) Rating of Railways 10/6 r 8° Eyre & Spottiswoode 99
FARADAY, P. M. Rating: princs., pract., proced., ed. A. J. Vulliamy 21/ 8° Sweet [03] 07
FRY, D. P. [ed.] Union Assessment Acts; with notes 17/6 p 8° Stevens [63] 97
GACHES, L. Rates and Assessments 3/6 *n.* c 8° Eyre & Spottiswoode 98
HIGHMORE, Sir N. J. Local Taxation Licenses 6/ 8° Stevens 09
KONSTAM, E. M. History of Rates and Taxes [pract. handbk.] 5/ *n.* 8° Butterworth 06
,, [ed.] Reports of Rating Appeals, 1904–1908, 2 vols. ea. 12/6 *n.* 8° Butterworth 09
A continuation of RYDE's work, *infra.*
LAWRIE, A. D. How to Appeal agst. your Rates, 2 Pts. [Legal Handy-Bks.] ea. 1/ f 8° E. Wilson [87]
i: *In the Metropolis;* ii: *Outside London.*
LUMLEY, W. G. [ed.] Union Assessment Committee Acts, ed. W. C. Ryde 6/ p 8° Knight [6–] *in prep.*
MAYER, Dr S. [ed.] Code of Law of Rating and Procedure on Appeal 25/r 8° Stevens [97] 05
PEARCE, A. J. Municipal Rating and the Collection of Rates 5/ *n.* c 8° Gee 07
PENFOLD, C. Rating of Ry., Gas, Water, & other Cos., ed. A. Glen + A. F. Jenkin 21/ 8° Knight [47] 93
RYDE, W. C. Law and Practice of Rating 35/r 8° Butterworth [ ] 04
,, [ed.] Repts. of Rat. Appeals 1871–85, 16/; '86–90, 18/; '91–3, 16/; '94–1904 16/ 8° Butterworth 91; 93; 04
SARGANT, C. H. Urban Rating—*v.* **D** § 117, *v.* also Konstam, *ut supra*
WESTALL Rateable Machinery 8° Aston 05

*Scotland*

ARMOUR, S. B. Valuatn. of Prop. f. Ratg. in Scotl. [digest of decisns.] 18/ 8° Bell & Bradfute, *Edin.* 92

**Registration** —*v.* **D** § 40

**Riots**

HASTINGS, S. The Law relating to Riots 2/6 *n.* c 8° Sweet 86
WISE, E. Riots and Unlawful Assemblies, ed. A. H. Bodkin + L. W. Kershaw 5/ *n.* 8° Butterworth [48] 07

**Rivers Pollution Prevention** —*v. also* **D** § 98

FITZGERALD, G. V. [ed.] Pollution of Rivers and Water Generally 7/6 *n.* 8° Stevens [96] 02
HAWORTH, C. J. Statute Law rel. to Rivers Pollution 10/6 *n.* r 12° Stevens [ ] 06

**Securities (Municipal)** —*v.* **D** § 85

**Sheriff**

MATHER, P. E. Sheriff and Execution Law 30/r 8° Stevens [94] 03

**Shop Hours; Early Closing**

BARRINGTON, C. V. Law rel. to Shops and Early Closing 2/6 *n.* p 8° Butterworth 05

**Tramways and Light Railways**—*v. also* Highways, *sup.*

AUSTIN, E. Light Railways Act of 1896 5/ *n.* 8° Knight [ ] 99
BRICE, Dr S. Law rel. to Tramways and Light Railways 18/ *n.* 8° Stevens [98] 02
DODD (Cyril) + ALLAN (C. E.) Law of Light Railways 12/6 8° Butterworth 96
KEEN, F. N. Tramways Companies and Local Authorities 10/ *n.* 8° Merritt & Hatcher 02
OXLEY, J. S. Light Railways: proced., repts., & precedents, 2 v. 38/6 *n.* 8° P. S. King 01–4
ROBERTSON, G. S. Law of Tramways and Light Railways in Gt. Brit. 25/r 8° Stevens [74] 03
This is the third edn. of SUTTON's *Tramway Acts of United Kingdom.*
STEWARD [ed.] Light Railways Act, 1896 8° Eyre & Spottiswoode 97
SUTTON [ed.] Tramways and Light Railways, ed. G. S. Robertson 25/r 8° Stevens [ ] 03

*United States*

BOOTH, H. J. Street Railway Law: Surf., Undergr., Elevated $6 *n.* 8° Johnson, *Phila.* 92

**Ultra Vires** —*v.* **D** § 26

**Water** —*v.* Gas, *sup.*

## 68: NATURALIZATION; ALIENS

CUTLER, J. Law of Naturalization [as amended by Acts of 1870] 3/6 *n.* 12° Butterworth 70
HENRIQUES, H. S. Q. Law as to Aliens and Naturalization 7/6 *n.* 8° Butterworth 06

PIGGOTT, Sir F. —*in his* Nationality, *ut* **D** § 113
SIBLEY (N. W.) + ELLIS (A.) [eds.] Aliens Act, 1905 4/6 c 8° Butterworth 06

**United States**

GIAUQUE, Florien Election and Naturalization Laws of United States $1 8° *Cincinnati* 81
JACOBS, M. W. Treatise on Law of Domicile [Brit. and Amer.] $5 8° *Boston* 87
WEBSTER, Prentiss Law of Naturalizn. in U.S. & other Countries $4 8° Little & Brown, *Boston* 96

## 69 : NEGLIGENCE—*v. also* D § 41

*BEVEN, Thos. Negligence in Law, 2 vols. 70/ r 8° Stevens & Haynes [90] 08
The third edn. of the author's *Principles of the Law of Negligence.*
SAUNDERS, T. W. Treatise on Law of Negligence, ed. E. B. Wright 9/ p 8° Butterworth [71] 98
SINGTON, A. Consideration of the Law of Negligence 16/ 8° Butterworth 03
SMITH, Hor. Treat. on Law of Negligence [$6 Thomas, *St Louis*] 12/6 8° Stevens [80] 84

**United States**

BARROWS, M. Treatise on the Law of Negligence $3·75 8° West Pb. Co., *St Paul, Minn.* 99
BUSWELL, H. F. Civil Liability f. Pers. Injuries aris. fr. Negligence $6 *n.* 8° Little & Brown, *Boston* [93] 99
EAGLE, W. J. [ed.] Amer. Negligence Cases, v. i–xvi ea. $5·50–$6·50 8° Remick, *N.Y.* 95–05 *in prg.*
GARDNER, J. M. [ed.] Amer. Negligence Reports, v. i–xx ea. $5·50–$6·50 8° Remick, *N.Y* 97–05 *in prg.*
HOOK, A. J. American Negligence Digest fr. Earliest Times to 1902 $6·50 8° Remick, *N.Y.* 02
JONES, Dwight, A. Treatise on Negligence of Municipal Corporations $8 8° Baker, *N.Y.* 92
LEAVITT, J. B. Code of Negligence: law of New York $6·50 8° Beader, *Albany* 03
SHEARMAN (T. G.) + REDFIELD (A. A.) Law of Negligence and Remedies f. Priv. Wrongs, 2 v. $12·50 r 8° Baker, *N.Y.* [ ] 98
THOMPSON, S. D. Law of Negligence in all Rel., 6 v. & Suppl. ea. $6 r 8° Bobbs, *Indianapolis* [80] 01–7
WHARTON, Fcs. Treatise on Law of Negligence [Engl. & Am.] $6·50 8° Kay, *Phila.* [74] 78
A learned work, occasionally supplementing the English books.

**Employers' Liability** —*v.* **D** § 41

## 70 : NUISANCES

BEWES, W. A. Law of Waste 18/ 8° Sweet 94
GARRETT, E. W. The Law of Nuisances [w. statutory appendix] 21/ *n.* 8° Butterworth [91] 08
KEANE, D. D. [ed.] The Nuisances Removal Acts, etc., ed. W. C. Glen *o.p.* [*pb.* 5/] 12° Shaw [56] 70

**Scotland**

BROWN, J. C. The Law of Nuisance in Scotland 8/ 8° Green, *Edin.* 91

**United States**

JOYCE, J.A. + H. C. Treatise on Law governing Nuisance $6 8° Bender, *Albany* 07
WOOD, H. G. Practical Treatise on the Law of Nuisances, 2 vols. $12 8° *Albany* [75] 93

**PARENT AND CHILD**—*v.* **D** § 49 **PARLIAMENTARY LAW**—*v.* **D** § 27 **PARTITION** —*v.* **D** § 78

## 71 : PARTNERSHIP

*LINDLEY, Lord Law of Partnership, ed. W. B. Lindley + J. C. Tomlin 42/ r 8° Sweet [62] 05–9
Ed. A. B. WENTWORTH, $6 *n.* Johnson, *Phila.* '88. Supplement, cont. Limited Partnerships Act '07, w. Introd., notes, etc., is incl., and may be had separ. 7/6, *id.* '09. Conts. Appendix on Law of Scotland, by J. C. LORIMER. The work is a model of legal text-bk. writing.
POLLOCK, Sir Fredk. Digest of the Law of Partnership 10/ *n.* 8° Stevens [78] 09
With Appendix on the Limited Partnership Act, 1907.
UNDERHILL, A. Law of Partnership [six lectures] 5/ *n.* 12° Butterworth [ ] 06

**Scotland**

CLARK, F. W. Law of Partnership & Jt.-St. Cos. in Scotl., 2 vols. *o.p.* [*pb.* 45/] r 8° Stevens 66
LORIMER, J. C. —Appendix *to* Lindley's Law of Partnership, *sup.*

**United States**

BATES, Clement The Law of Partnership, 2 vols. $11 *n.* 8° Flood, *Chicago* 88
BURDICK, F. M. The Law of Partnership $3 *n.* 8° Little & Brown, *Boston* [99] 06
„ [ed.] Selected Cases on Law of Partnership $4·50 8° Little & Brown, *Boston* 98

CONYNGTON, T. Manual of Partnership Relations $2 8° Ronald Press, *N.Y.* 06
GILMORE, E. A. [ed.] Cases on Law of Partnership, ed. J. Brown Scott [Engl. & Amer. cases] $3·75 8° West Pb. Co., *St Paul, Minn.* [ ] 08
MECHEM, F. R. Elements of the Law of Partnership $2·50 8° Callaghan, *Chicago* 96
[ed.] Cases on the Law of Partnership $4·50 8° Callaghan, *Chicago* [96] 05
PARSONS, T. Treatise on Law of Partnership, ed. J. H. Beale $6 r 8° Little & Brown, *Boston* [67] 93
SHUMAKER, T. Treatise on the Law of Partnership $3 8° Keefe, *St Paul, Minn.* [01] 05
STORY, Jos. Commentaries on the Law of Partnership $6 8° Little & Brown, *Boston* [41] 81

**Limited Partnerships**

BATES Limited Partnership $3 *n.* 8° 86
HEMMANT, D. G. Law of Limited Partnerships under Act of 1907 2/6 *n.* 8° Stevens 08
LINDLEY, Lord Supp. to his Law of Partnership, *ut sup.*
SMITH, J. W. Law of Priv. P'ships, incl. Ld. P'ship Act '07 1/6 *n* c 8° E. Wilson 08

**Joint Ownership**—*v.* **D** § 78 **Joint Stock Companies**—*v.* **D** § 26

## 72 : PATENTS, COPYRIGHT, TRADE-MARKS

### COPYRIGHT

**International ; British Empire**

BIRRELL, A. Seven Lectures on the Law and History of Copyright in Books [$1·25 *n.* Putnam, *N.Y.*] 3/6 *n.* c 8° Cassell 99
BRIGGS, W. M. Law of International Copyright 16/ 8 Stevens & Haynes 09
With special sections on the Colonies and the United States.
CHAMIER, Dan. Law rel. to Literary Copyright & Authorship & Prodn. of Bks. 5/ *n.* 8° E. Wilson 95
A concise little bk., spec. useful for its chaprs. on legal relns. betw. authors and pubrs. Good chap. on *Property in Titles*.
COHEN, B. A. Law of Copyright [w. Appendix of Stats.] 3/6 *n.* c 8° Jordan 96
COLLES (W. M.) + HARDY (H.) Playright & Copyright in All Countries 7/6 *n.* ($2·50 *n.*) 8° Macmillan 06
The means of protecting a play or book throughout the world.
COPINGER, W. A. Law of Copyright in Wks. of Literature & Art, ed. J. M. Easton 36/ r 8° Stevens & Haynes [70] 04
DRONE, E. A. Law of Property in Intellectual Productions—*ut inf.*
FISHER (J. R.) + STRAHAN (J. A.) —*in their* Law of the Press, *ut* **D** § 75*
HINKSON, H. A. Copyright Law 6/ c 8° Bullen 03
MACGILLIVRAY, E. J. Digest of the Law of Copyright 7/6 *n.* 8° Butterworth 06
" Law of Copyright in U.K. & Dominions, & U.S. 25/ *n.* r 8° Murray 02
$8 *n.* Dutton, *N.Y.* W. App. of all Acts of Parl., Intern. Convns., Orders in Council, Treasury Mins., and Acts of Congress now in force.
*SCRUTTON, T. E. [Judge] The Law of Copyright 15/ 8° Clowes [83] 03
The 1st edn. was an enlargemt. of the author's Yorke Prize Essay [1882]. The version is again improved and conts. an annot. text of the Copyrt. Statutes; following the example of celebrated piratical abridger of *Rasselas*, the author has 'left out all the moral reflections', but w. a different result.
SHORTT, J. Law of Literature and Art [copyright, libel, etc.] 30/ 8° Reeves [71] 84
STRAHAN, J. A. Notes and Comments on some Copyright Cases 1/ *n.* 8° Butterworth 07

*Artistic*

WINSLOW, Reginald The Law of Artistic Copyright [w. append. of stat. and coll. of precedts.] 10/ 8° Butterworth 89

*Designs*

EDMUNDS (L.) + BENTWICK (H.) Law of Copyright in Designs 25/ 8° Sweet [95] 09
KNOX (H.) + HIND (S. W.) Law of Copyright in Designs 12/6 r 8° Reeves 98

*Musical and Dramatic*

COLLES (W. M.) + HARDY (H.) Playwright and Copyright in all Countries—*ut sup.*
CUTLER, E. Manual of Musical Copyright Law 3/6 *n.* 8° Simpkin 05
STRONG, A. A. Dramatic and Musical Law ; w. copyright 3/6 *n.* 8° Stevens 01

*Newspapers* —*v. also* **D** § 75*

**Canada, et**

DAWSON, S. E. Copyright in Books [orig. and then state of Canad. law] 5/ 8° *Montreal* 82
LANCEFIELD, R. T. Notes on Copyright, Domestic and International 2/ 12° *Hamilton* 97
With synopsis of Canadian, Imperial, and U.S. Copyright Acts.

**United States**

BOWKER, R. R. Copyright, its Law & Literature [Pt. ii = bibliogr., by T. Solberg] $3·50 8° *N.Y.* [86] 92

DRONE, E. A. Law of Prop. in Intellectual Productns. in Gt. Brit. & U.S. $6 8° Little & Brown, *Bost.* 79

HAMLIN, A. S. [ed.] Copyright Cases and Decisions 8° Am. Pubs.' Copyrt. League 04
8/6 *n.* Putnam. A summary of lead. Amer. decisns. on copyrt. and on liter. property fr. 1891–1903, w. some Engl. and Canadian decisns., and text of U.S. Copyrt. Statutes.

MACGILLIVRAY, E. J. —*in his* Law of Copyright, *ut sup.*

PUTNAM, Geo. Haven [ed.] Question of Copyright [Questions of Day] $1·75 (7/6) c 8° Putnam [91] 96
A series of papers by several wrs. dealg. w. origin and devel. of law of copyrt. and its positn. in present day. Mr PUTNAM's paper on *The Contest for Internat. Copyrt.* supplies a useful history of the attempts made to secure internat. copyrt. betw. Amer. and for. countries fr. Hy. Clay's Report to Congress in 1837 in favour of the petition for copyrt. of Brit. authors down to Act of 1891. His *Internat. Copyrt. and the Prices of Books* and Mr Brander MATTHEWS' *Cheap Books and Good Books* (covering much the same ground) and *Evolution of Copyrt.* are other good articles.

SANDERS, L. M. [ed.] Supreme Court Decisions—*ut inf.*

**Continent of Europe**

Law of Copyright in Austria: tr. of Austrian Act, Order of '95 and Conventn. 1/ *n.* 8° Longman 02

Law of Copyright in Germany: tr. of two German Acts of '01 1/ *n.* 8° Longman 02

## PATENTS AND TRADE-MARKS

ABBOTT, B. V. [ed.] Decisns. [Engl.] on Law of Patents fr. 17 Cent., 3 vols. [1662–1843] ea. $6·50 8° Brodix, *Washington* 87

,, [ed.] The Patent Laws of all Nations $13 8° Brodix, *Washington* 86

BOULT, A. J. [ed.] Digest of British and Foreign Patent Laws 7/6 8° Boult & Wade [95] 99

BRICE, S. Law, Practice, & Procedure rel. to Patents, etc. 18/ 8° Butterworth 85

CAMPBELL [ed.] Patent Cases = Engl. Ruling Cases, vol. xx [1890]—*ut* **D** § 30

CARPMAEL, A. + E. [eds.] Patent Laws of the World, 25/; Supplement, 10/ 8° Butterworth [85] 89; 89

CUNYNGHAME, Hy. English Patent Practice [w. rules, forms, preceds, etc.] 25/ 8° Clowes 94

EDMUNDS, L. Law and Practice of Letters Patent, ed. T. M. Stevens 32/ r 8° Stevens [90] 97

EMERY, G. F. Patent Law and Practice [forms & precedents] 15/ *n.* 8° E. Wilson [ ] 04

,, The Solicitors Patent Practice 3/6 *n.* c 8° E. Wilson 09

FREEMAN, W. M. [ed.] The Patents and Designs Act, 1907 3/6 *n.* 8° Cox 08

*FROST, Rob. Treatise on Law and Practice rel. to Letters Patent 36/ r 8° Stevens & Haynes [91] 06
Has appendix of statutes, internat. conventions, rules, forms and precedents and orders.

,, [ed.] Patents and Designs Acts, 1907 10/ r 8° Stevens & Haynes 08

FULTON, D. Law & Practice rel. to Patents, Trademarks, & Designs 12/6 *n.* 8° Jordan [95] 05
With a Digest of colonial and foreign patent laws. Excellently arranged, and well indexed.

GOODEVE, T. M. [ed.] Abstract of Reported Cases rel. to Letters Patent [to 1883] 30/ r 8° Sweet 84
For continuation *v.* GRIFFIN, *inf.*

,, Patent Practice before the Comptroller, *etc.* 6/ 8° Sweet 93

GORDON, J. W. Monopolies by Patents & Statutable Remedies available to Public 18/ 8° Stevens 98
A theoretical work, with discussion of the policy of the subject.

,, Compulsory Licenses under Patent Acts 15/ 8° Stevens 99

,, Statute Law rel. to Patents of Inventions and Registrn. of Designs 5/ *n.* 8° Jordan 08

GREELEY, A. P. [ed.] Foreign Patent & Trade Mark Law: compar. study $5 8° Byrne, *Washington* 99

GRIFFIN, R. [ed.] Abstract of Patent Cases, 1884–6 [Supp. 1887 8° Waterlow '88] 25/ 8° Sweet 87

HADDEN, R. Inventor's Adviser: every man his own patent agent 5/ c 8° Harrison [ ] 00

HEMMING, H. B. Practical Guide to Law of Patents 6/ *n.* 8° Waterlow 05

HIGGINS (C.) + JONES (G. E.) [eds.] Digest of the Law of Patents 25/ 8° Clowes [75–80] 90
Alphabetically arranged, with an excellent Table of Cases.

JOHNSON, J. + J. H. Patentees' Manual [treatise on law and practice] 10/6 8° Longman [6–] 90

LAWSON, W. N. Law rel. to Patents, Designs and Trade Marks 27/6 8° Butterworth [89] 98

MARKS, G. C. Inventions, Patents & Designs; w. text of 1907 Act 3/6 *n.* c 8° Technical Pb. Co. 07

MORRIS, Rob. [ed.] Patents Conveyancing: collection of precedents 25/ r 8° Stevens 87

NICOLAS, V. Law and Pract. rel. to Letters Patent 15/ *n.* r 8° Butterworth 04

PIRANI, S. G. Index of Patent, Design, & Tr. Mark Cases, 1884–1909 21/ *n.* r 8° Sweet 10

RAVENSHEAR, A. F. Industr. and Commerc. Influence of Engl. Patent System 5/ *n.* 8° Unwin 09

ROBERTS, J. The Grant and Validity of British Patents; ill. 25/ *n.* r 8° Murray 03

,, Inventors' Guide to Patent Law 2/6 *n.* 8° Murray 05

,, + MOULTON (H. F.) [eds.] Patents and Designs Act, 1907 4/ *n.* r 8° Butterworth 07

RUSHEN, P. C. Critical Study of Form of Letters Patent 3/6 *n.* 12° 08

TERRELL, T. + C.  Law and Practice rel. to Letters Patent  30 / 8° Sweet [84] *in prep.*
THOMPSON, W. P.  Hdbk. of Patent Law of all Countries [Brit. portion 6*d.* *n.*] 2 /6 *n.* 18° Stevens [78] 08
WALLACE (R. W.) + WILLIAMSON (J. B.) Law and Pract. rel. to Letters Patent 40 / r 8° Butterworth 00
WEBSTER (Thos.) + MACRORY [eds.] Patent Cases, 3 vols.  50 / *n.* r 8° Blenkarn (Stevens) 44

*Trade Marks*

CARTMELL, J. A. [ed.]  Abstract of Reported Cases rel. to Trade Marks: 1876–92  25 / r 8° Sweet 93
*KERLY (D. M.) + UNDERHAY (F. G.) Law of Trade Marks and Trade Name  35 / r 8° Sweet [95] 08
With chapters on Trade Secret and Trade Libel.
,, [eds.]  Trade Marks Act, 1905  6 / *n.* 8° Sweet 07
SEBASTIAN, L. B.  Law of Trade Marks and their Registration, ed. H. B. Hemming  30 / r 8° Stevens [78] *in prep.*
,, [ed.]  Digest of Cases of Trade Mark, Name, Secret, etc.  21 / 8° Stevens 79
,,  Law of Trade Mark Registration under Trade Marks Act, 1905  7/6 r 8° Stevens 06

**United States**

BROWNE, W. H.  Treatise on Law of Trade Marks, etc. \$7·50 *n.* 8° Little & Brown, *Boston* [73] 98
BUMP, O. F.  Law of Patents, Trade Marks & Copyright  \$6·50 8° Baker, *N.Y.* [77] 84
FENTON, Hector T.  Law of Patents for Designs  \$5 8° Campbell, *Phila.* 90
FOSTER, R.  Treat. on Federal Practice . . . esp. Patent Cases, 2 v. \$12 8° Boston Bk. Co., *Boston* [ ] 92
HALL, T. B.  Infringement of Patents, \$5 *n.*; Infringement Outline \$1 *n.* 8° Clarke, *Cincinnati* 93; 95
LOWERY, W. [ed.]  Decisions on Law of Patents by U.S. Supreme Ct.  \$6·50 8° Brodrix, *Washington* 91
,,  Index-Digest of Patent Cases; 1800–97  \$5 8° 97
MERWIN, H. C.  The Patentability of Inventions  \$6 r 8° Little & Brown, *Boston* 83
NEWTON, J. T.  Digest of Pat. Off. Trade Mark Decisions  \$5 *n.* 8° Callaghan, *Chicago* 96
PRICE (A.) + STEUART (B.) [eds.] American Trade Mark Cases, 1879–87  \$7·50 8° Cushings, *Baltimore* 87
RICE (L. H.) + BEACH  Digest of Patent Office Decisions, 3 v.  [1869–1900] \$11 8° Reed, *Boston* 00
ROBINSON, W. C.  Law of Patents for Useful Inventions, 3 v. \$19·50 *n.* 8° Little & Brown, *Boston* 90
SANDERS, L. M. [ed.]  Annual Digest of Supreme Court Decisions rel. to Patents, Trade Marks, Copyrights, etc.  ea. \$3·50 8° Byrne, *Washington* 98 *sqq. ann.*
SIMONDS, W. E. [ed.]  Digest of Pat. Cases in Feder. & State Cts. [1789–1888] \$8 6° Strouse, *N.Y.* 88
SWAN, K. R.  Law and Commerc. Usage of Patents, Tr. Mks., etc.  [6 / *n.* Constable] \$2 *n.* 8° Van Nostrand, *N.Y.* 08
WALKER, A. H.  Text-book of Patent Laws of United States  \$6·50 8° Baker, *N.Y.* [8–] 96

**France**

BARCLAY, Thos.  Law of France relating to Industrial Property  6 / c 8° Sweet 89
Patents, trade marks, merchant marks, patterns, designs, prospectuses, *etc.*

**Germany**

REITZENBAUM, S.  Important Decisions reg. Germ. Patents [w. trs. of the laws] 3 / *n.* 8° Asher 08

**Japan**

BRINDLEY, H. S. B.  Japanese Patents: hdbk. to Japanese laws  5 / *n.* 8° British Press 09
HALL, W. S.  Japanese Laws and Rules as to Patents, Trade Marks, Designs 2 / *n.* 8° Low 01
,,  Review of Japanese Patent Law  1 / 16° *Engineer* Office 00

**Prolongation of Term of Patents**

WAGGETT, J. F.  Law and Practice rel. to Prolongation of Letters Patent 7 / 8° Butterworth 87
WHEELER, J. G.  Prolongation of Letters Patent  5 / *n.* 8° Eyre & Spottiswoode 98

## 73: PAWNBROKERS—*v. also* D § 15, D § 66

ATTENBOROUGH, C. L.  Law of Pawnbroking  [w. Acts of 1878, 1889] 3 / *n.* p 8° Stevens 97
TURNER, Fcs.  The Contract of Pawn  *o.p.* [*pb.* 12 /] 8° Stevens [81] 83

**United States**

JONES, L. A.  Treat. on Law of Pledges & Collat. Securities \$6 8° Bowen-Merrill, *Indianapolis* [83] 01

## 73*: PENSIONS, incl. OLD-AGE PENSIONS

BARLOW, C. A. M. [ed.]  The Old Age Pensions Act, 1908  2/6 8° Eyre & Spottiswoode 06
EVANS, D. Owen [ed.]  The Old Age Pensions Act, 1908  6 / c 8° Sweet 08

**United States**

BROWNING, Arth. Handbook of Pension Laws $1 *n.* 8° Browning, *Washington* 94

ECKSTEIN On Pensions $1 *n.* 8° Johnson, *Phila.*

Incl. a hist. of Pension Laws of the world and a summary of those of the U.S.

Pension Lawyer's Digest (The) [copy of all laws of U.S. rel. to pensions] $2 8° Lowell, *Washn.* 90

## PERPETUITIES—*v.* D § 56 : Limitations

## 74 : POPULAR BOOKS ON LAW GENERALLY

'Banker's Daughter (A)' Guide in Every-Day Matters [property & income] 3/6 c 8° Macmillan [67] 00

'Barrister (A)' Every Man's Own Lawyer 6/8 *n.* c 8° Lockwood [5–] 09

'Barrister-at-Law (A)' Family Lawyer, 10/6 r 8°; Home Lawyer 1/6 *n.* c 8° Cassell 98; 05

" My Lawyer 6/ *n.* c 8 E. Wilson [91] 05

v. IHERING, R. Law in Daily Life [tr.]; w. notes by H. Goudy 3/6 *n.* ($1·15) c 8° Clar. Pr. 04

KING (J.) + BIGHAM (F. T. R.) + GWYER (M. L.) *etc.* Management of Private Affairs 2/6 *n.* c 8° Clar. Pr. 08

A useful bk. for young people setting up in life: comprehensive and clear.

'Two Barristers-at-Law' Law without Lawyers 6/ 8° Murray [00] 05

**Dictionary:** *English*

RENTON, A. Wood The People's Dictionary of English Law 5/ c 8° Hodder 89

*United States*

GASTON, H. A. People's Encyclopædia of Law $5 8° Merchants' Speciality Co., *Chicago* 89

KOONES, J. A. Everybody's Law-book: legal rights and remedies $2·50 8° *New York* 93

**Curiosities of the Law; Legal Facetiae**

A'BECKETT, Gilbert The Comic Blackstone; ill. Geo. Cruikshank 5/ 12° Bradbury [46] 78

ANDREWS, Wm. [ed.] Legal Lore: curiosities of the law 7/6 8° Andrews 97

BIGELOW, L. J. Bench and Bar: wit, humour, etc., of law $2 12° *New York* [67] 71

DARLING, Justice Scintillæ Juris, etc. 3/6 12° Stevens [79] 03

" On the Oxford Circuit, and other Verses; ill. 5/ *n.* 16° Smith & Elder 09

HEARD, F. F. Curiosities of the Law Reporters $1·25 12° *Boston* 71

" Oddities of the Law $1 12° *Boston* 81

HEYWOOD, N. A. Oddities of the Law 2/6 *n.* 8° Ouseley 07

17 papers on treason, villeins, wager of battle, bribery, benefit of clergy, forest-law, pillory, press-gang, etc.

JAMES, Croake Curiosities of Law and Lawyers 7/6 c 8° Low 82

OUTRAM, G. Legal and other Lyrics: w. notes and glossary 5/ c 8° Blackwood [74] 89

WATT, Fcs. The Law's Lumber Room 3/6 *n.* f 8° Lane 95

WILCOX, H. S. Fallacies of the Law $1·50 8° Legal Lit. Co., *Chicago* 07

Last vol. of a series, of wh. others are *Foibles of Bench, Foibles of Bar, Frailties of Jury.* All exhibit weaknesses in the laws and suggest remedies

## 75 : POSSESSION

POLLOCK (Sir F.) + WRIGHT (R. S.) Essay on Possession in the Common Law 8/6 ($2·25) 8° Clar. Press 88

v. SAVIGNY, F. C. Possession in the Civil Law tr. [abgd.] J. Kelleher 16/ 8° Thacker, *Calcutta* 88

Previously tr. Sir Edw. PERRY, 6th Edn. 8° Sweet '48.

**United States**

BUSWELL, H. F. Limitations and Adverse Possession—*ut* D § 56

## PRESCRIPTION—*v.* D § 56

## 75* : PRESS

FISHER (J. R.) + STRAHAN (J. A.) The Law of the Press 15/ 8° Clowes [91] 98

Registn., Advs., Copyrt., Libel, foreign Press Codes, *etc.*; much useful informatn. not readily obtainable elsewhere. App. gives text of leadg. Stats.

## PRIMOGENITURE—*v.* D § 89

## 76 : PRISONS

ANDERSON, R. [ed.] Prisons Acts of 1877 and 1865; w. notes *o.p.* [*pb.* 7/6] 12° Shaw 78

WILKINSON, R. [ed.] Law of Prisons in England and Wales; w. notes 6/ 12° Knight 78

## 77 : PROPERTY : GENERALLY, AND PERSONAL

GOODEVE, L. A. Modern Law of Pers. Prop., ed. J. H. Williams + W. M. Crowdy 18/ r 8° Sweet [87] 04

KELKE, W. H. H. Epitome of Personal Property Law [student's-bk.] 6/ c 8° Sweet [01] 05
RALEIGH, Thos. Outline of the Law of Property 7/6 ($1·90) 8° Clar. Press 90
A brief and lucid exposition of the leading principles which govern all property law.
SMITH (Josiah W.) + TRUSTRAM (J.) Compendium of Law of Real & Pers. Prop., 2 v. 42/ 8° Stevens [55] 84
STRAHAN (J. A.) + BAXTER (J. S.) General View of the Law of Property 12/6 8° Stevens [95] 08
A first bk. for studts., treatg. both real and pers. prop. together: 'Recent legislation has so greatly approximated the law of realty to the law of personality that they may now be profitably considered together'.
WILLIAMS, Joshua Princs. of Law of Pers. Prop.; ed. T. C. Williams [son] 21/ 8° Sweet [49] 06
Wilshere, A. M. Analysis of Williams on Personal Property 5/ 8° Sweet 11

**United States**

BRANTLEY, W. T. Principles of Law of Personal Property $3 8° Bancroft, *San Francisco* 90
DARLINGTON, Prf. J. J. On Personal Property [founded on Williams] $4 *n.* 8° Johnson, *Phila.* 91
DWIGHT, T. W. Commentaries on Law of Persons & Property $6 *n.* 8° Little & Brown, *Bost.* 94
GRIFFIN (L. T.) + SMITH (W. D.) [eds.] Cases on Pers. Prop. $2 8° West Pb. Co., *St Paul, Minn.* 95
RICE, F. S. Treatise on Modern Law of Property $6·50 8° Diossy, *N.Y.* 97
SCHOULER, J. Treatise on Law of Personal Property, 2 v. $12 8° Little & Brown *Boston* [73-6] 96
SMITH, H. E. Treatise on Law of Personal Property $4 *n.* 8° Flood, *Chicago* 93
VAN ZILE, P. T. [ed.] Illustrative Cases on Personality $2 8° West Pb. Co., *St Paul, Minn.* 96

**Conveyancing** —*v.* **D** § 30

**Leases:** *Scotland*

RANKINE, Prf. Jno. Treatise on the Law of Leases in Scotland 32/ r 8° Bell & Bradfute, *Edin.* [87] 93

**Sale** —*v.* **D** § 96

## 78: PROPERTY: REAL (COPYHOLDS AND FREEHOLDS)—*v. also* D § 51, D § 77

ADKIN, B. W. Copyhold and other Land Tenures 10/ 8° Sweet 07
BROWN, A. [ed.] Enfranchisements and Commutations 16/ c 8° Butterworth [88] 03
CARSON, T. H. [ed.] Real Property Statutes, ed. T. H. Carson + H. B. Bompas 38/ r 8° Sweet [02] 10
CHALLIS, H. W. Law of Real Property [chfly. conveycg.; $3 Blackstone, *Phila.*] 20/ 8° Reeves & Turner [85] 92
EDWARDS, W. D. Compendium of Law of Property in Land & Conveycg. 20/ 8° Stevens & Haynes [88] 04
ELTON, C. I. Law of Copyholds & Cust. Tenures 28/; Suppl. 5/6 *n.* 8° Wildy 74 [93]; 98
,, Custom and Tenant Right 4/ 8° Wildy 82
*GOODEVE, L. A. Mod. Law of Real Prop., ed. Sir H. Elphinstone + F. T. Maw 21/ r 8° Sweet [83] 06
*JENKS, Prf. Edw. Modern Land Law 15/ ($3·75) 8° Clar. Press 99
KELKE (W. H. H.) + PARTINGTON (A.) Epitome of Real Property Law 6/ c 8° Sweet [92] 07
LEAKE, S. M. Elem. Digest of Law of Prop. in Land, ed. A. E. Randall 20/ r 8° Stevens [74] 09
LIGHTWOOD, M. The Possession of Land 15/ 8° Stevens 94
Elab. statemt. of pres. positn. of Engl. law reg. possessn. of land, theoret., histor., and pract. discussed and ill. by many cases.
POLLOCK, Sir Fredk. The Land Laws [Engl. Citizen; admirable introd.] 2/6 ($1) c 8° Macmillan [83] 96
ROBINSON, T. On Gavelkind, ed. C. I. Elton + H. J. H. Mackay 15/ 8° Butterworth [c. 1750] 97
The Common Law of Kent. With additions relating to Borough English and other customs.
RUDALL (A.R.) + GREIG (J. R.) Copyhold Enfranchisement und. Copyhold Act, 1894 10/ *n.* 12° Jordan 95
SCRIVEN, J. Law of Copyhold, and other Tenures, ed. A. Brown 32/6 r 8° Butterworth [67] 96
SHELFORD, L. [ed.] Real Property Statutes, ed. T. H. Carson + H. B. Bompas 35/ r 8° Sweet [35] 02
SMITH (Jos. W.) + TRUSTRAM (J.) Compendium of Law of Real and Personal Property—*ut* **D** § 77
THEOBALD, H. S. Law of Land [a useful book] *red. to* 6/ *n.* 8° Clowes 02
TOPHAM, A. F. Real Property: introd. explan. of law rel. to land 12/6 8° Butterworth 08
TUDOR, O. D. [ed.] Leadg. Cases on Real Prop., Convcg., etc., ed. T. H. Carson + H. B. Bompas 50/ r 8° Butterworth [56] 98
*WILLIAMS, Josh. Princs. of Law of Real Prop., ed. T. C. Williams [son] 21/ 8° Sweet [44] 10
Ed. Prf. E. C. MITCHELL, $4 Johnson, *Phila.* Cf. WILSHERE (A. M.) *Analysis of Williams on Law of Real Property*, 5/ 8° Sweet '08.
,, Seisin of the Freehold [12 lectures] 8/ 8° Sweet 78

*History*

DE VILLIERS, J. E. R. Hist. of Legisl. concern. Real & Pers. Prop. in Eng. dur. rn. of Victoria [Yorke Prize Ess. 1900; $1 *n.* Putnam, *N.Y.*] 3/6 c 8° Camb. Press 01
DIGBY, Kenelm E. Introd. to Hist. of Law of Real Prop. [w. authorits.] 12/6 ($3) c 8° Clar. Press [76] 97
FOWLER, Rob. History of Law of Real Property in N.Y. $3 8° Baker, *N.Y.* 95

MACLAURIN, R. C. On the Nature and Evidence of Title to Reality
[Yorke Prize Essay, '98; $4·20 *n.* Putnam, *N.Y.*] 10/6 8° Camb. Press 01

SCRUTTON, Prf. P. E. Land in Fetters 7/6 8° Camb. Press 86
$2 *n.* Putnam, *N.Y.* [Yorke Prize Ess. 1885.] Hist. and policy of laws restraing. alienatn. and settlemt. of land in Engl.

**Scotland**

COWAN, H. [ed.] Land Rights of Scotland [colln. of stats., w. notes] 12/ 8° *Edinburgh* 76

**Ireland**

FOTTRELL, G. Law and Pract. in Sales fr. Landld. to Tenant in Irel. 5/ c 8° Gill, *Dublin*

" [ed.] Land Purchase Acts (Ireland) 1870–91 18/ 8° Gill, *Dublin* 92

**United States**

BALLARD, T. E. + E. E. [eds.] The Law of Real Prop., v. i–xi ea. $6·50 8° Flood, *Chicago* 92–07 *ann.*

BOONE, C. T. The Law of Real Property, 3 vols. $9 8° Bancroft, *San Francisco* [82] 01

FINCH, W. A. [ed.] Selected Cases on Law of Property in Land $6 *n.* 8° Baker, *N.Y.* 98

FOWLER, Rob. Real Property Law of New York $6 8° Baker, *N.Y.* 99

GOODWIN, F. Treatise on the Law of Real Property $4 *n.* 8° Little & Brown, *Boston* 05

GRAY, J. C. [ed.] Select Cases & other Authors. on Law of Prop., vols. i–vi
ea. $3·50 *n.* 8° Kent, *Cambr., Mass.* [88–90] 05–8

HAWLEY (J. G.) + MCGREGOR (M.) Treat. on Law of Real Property $4·50 8° Collector Pb. Co., *Detroit* 00

HILLIARD, F. On the American Law of Real Property, 3 vols. $10 8° Houghton, *Boston* [46] 69

HOPKINS, E. P. Handbook on the Law of Real Property $3·75 *n.* 8° West Pb. Co., *St Paul, Minn.* 96

JONES, L. A. Law of Real Prop. as appl. betw. Vendor & Purchaser, 2 v. $12 8° Houghton, *Boston* 96

KERR, J. M. Treatise on the Law of Real Property, 3 vols. $16 *n.* 8° Banks, *N.Y.* 95

MINER, R. C. The Law of Real Property, vol. i 8° Anderson, *Charlottesville* 08

NEWELL, G. Elements of Law of Real Property $4 8° Flood, *Chicago* 02

RICE, F. S. Real Property, 2 vols. $12 8° Diossy, *N.Y.* 96

SHARSWOOD (G.) + BUDD (H.) [ed.] Leadg. Cases in Law of Real Prop., 4 v. ea. $6 8° Murphy, *Phila.* 83–9

TIEDEMAN, C. G. Amer. Law of Real Property, ed. E. J. White $6 *n.* r 8° Thomas, *St Louis* [83] 06

" [ed.] Selected Cases on Real Property $3·50 8° Thomas, *St Louis* 97

WALSH, W. F. [ed.] Select Cases on the Law of Real Property $6 8° Tompkins, *N.Y.* 07

WARVELLE, G. W. Principles of Law of Real Property $4 *n.* 8° Callaghan, *Chicago* [96] 00

WASHBURN, E. Amer. Law of Real Prop., ed. J. Wurts, 3 v. $18 *n.* 8° Little & Brown, *Boston* [60–2] 02

**Boundaries and Fences** —*v. also* **D** § 98

HUNT, A. J. Law of Boundaries and Fences, ed. H. Stephen 14/ p 8° Butterworth [6–] 04

RUDALL, A. R. Party-Walls 7/6 *n.* 8° Jordan 06

*United States* —*v. also* **D** § 20 (WAIT)

THORNTON, W. W. Law of Railroad Fences and Crossings—*ut* **D** § 81

TYLER, R. H. Law of Boundaries & Fences, & . . . Sea Shore $6·50 8° Gould, *Albany* 74

**Capital and Income**

GOVER, W. H. Law of Capital & Income as betw. Life-tenant & Remainderman 7/6 8° Sweet [01] 10

**Commons and Inclosures** —*v. also* **D** § 119

ELTON, C. I. Treat. on Common & Waste Lands [learned, but antiquated] *op.* [*pb.* 10/] 12° 67

HALL, J. E. Law rel. to Profits à prendre and Rights of Common 16/ 8° Sweet 71

HUNTER, Sir Rob. —*ut* **D** § 119

SCRUTTON, Prf. T. E. Commons and Common Fields: hist. and policy of Engl. laws
[Yorke Prize Essay 1886; $2·50 *n.* Putnam, *N.Y.*] 10/6 8° Camb. Press 87

WILLIAMS, Josh. On Rights of Common and other Prescriptive Rights 14/ 8° Sweet 80

**Contingent Remainders**

*FEARNE, C. Contingent Remainders and Executory Devises, 2 vols.
*o.p.* [*pb.* 6/6] 8° Saunders & Benning [1772] 45

Post, W. M. C. Epitome of Fearne on Contingent Remainders 6/6 p 8° Stevens 78

**Conveyancing** —*v.* **D** § 30

**Covenants**

BROWN, R. C. Covenants running with the Land 10/6 8° Sweet 07

HAMILTON, G. B. Concise Treatise on the Law of Covenants 10/6 8° Stevens [88] 04
JOLLY, W. A. Restrictive Covenants affecting Land 5/ 8° Stevens 09
RAWLE, W. H. Pract. Treat. on Covenants for Title $6 8° Little & Brown, *Boston* [52] 87

**Easements, and Ancient Lights**

BANKS, G. The Law of Support 12/r 8° 94
BLYTH, T. T. Epitome of Law of Easements 6/ 8° Sweet 05
COX, H. Law and Science of Ancient Lights 6/ 8° Sweet [ ] 71
FLETCHER, B. Light and Air: text-bk. for Architects & Surveyors 6/6 12° Batsford [95] 08
*GALE, C. J. Treatise on Law of Easements, ed. R. R. Reeve 25/r 8° Sweet [46] 08
GODDARD, J. L. Treatise on the Law of Easements 25/ 8° Stevens [71] 10
HUDSON, A. A. Law of Light and Air 7/6 c 8° Stevens & Haynes [98] 05
INNES, L. C. Digest of the English Law of Easements 7/6 r 12° Stevens [80] 03
ROSCOE, E. S. Digest of Law of Light [w. stats. & forms] 7/6 8° Stevens [81] 04
STEPHEN, H. L. Law of Support and Subsidence 5/r 12° Butterworth 90

*India*

GRIFFITH, Wm. Commentaries on Indian Easement Act No. 5 of 1882 7/6 8° Higginbotham, *Madras* 90
MICHELL, R. B. Law of Easements and Licenses in India 5/6 8° Higginbotham, *Madras* [91] 98

*United States* —*v. also* **D** § 20 (WAIT)

JONES, L. A. Treatise on the Law of Easements $6 8° Baker, *N.Y.* 98
WASHBURN, E. Treatise on Am. Law of Easements & Servitudes $6 8° Little & Brown, *Boston* [63] 85

**Foreshore and Seashore** —*v.* **D** § 98

**Joint Ownership and Partition**

FOSTER, E. J. Law of Joint Ownership and Partition of Real Estate 10/6 8° Stevens 78
GRIFFITH, W. H. Treatise on Joint Rights and Liabilities 5/ 8° Butterworth 97
WALKER, W. G. [ed.] Partition Acts 1868 and '76 8/ 8° Stevens [76] 82

*United States*

FREEMAN, A. C. Co-tenancy and Partition $6 8° Whitney, *San Francisco* [ ] 86
KNAPP, C. D. Law of Partition of Real & Pers. Property $6 8° Peloubet, *N.Y.* 87

**Mortmain Acts**

BOURCHIER-CHILCOTT, T. Law of Mortmain 12/6 8° Sweet 05

**Perpetuities**—*v.* **D** § 56 **Sale of Real Property**—*v.* **D** § 96

**Settled Estates and Land**

CLERKE, A. St J. Law and Practice und. Settled Ld. Acts 1882–90 9/ 8° Sweet [90] 91
UNDERHILL, A. [ed.] Settled Land Acts [1882 & '84] [w. introd., etc.] 8/ p 8° Butterworth [82] 84
WOLSTENHOLME (E. P.) + TURNER (R. O.) [eds.] Settled Land Act, '82 [w. notes, forms, preceds.] 15/ r 8° Clowes [83] 05

**Title; Title Deeds**

COMYNS, W. H. [ed.] Series of Abstracts of Title to Freeholds [for studts.] 10/6 8° Reeves [7–] 95
COPINGER, W. A. Title Deeds: their custody, inspection, production 14/ 8° Stevens 75
DICKINS, H. A. Precedents of General Requisitions on Title 5/r 12° Stevens [ ] 97
EMMET, L. E. Notes on Perusing Titles 12/6 *n.* 8° Jordan [95] 03
GOVER, W. H. Hints as to Advising on Title 8/ 8° Sweet [92] 05
An excellent bk., contg. practical suggestions for perusing and analysing abstracts.
JACKSON (W. H.) + GOSSET (T.) Investigation of Title 15/ 8° Stevens 07
An alphabetical digest of the law connected with title to land.
MOORE, H. Instructions for Preparing Abstracts of Titles 10/6 12° Wildy [5–] 86
SCOTT, C. E. Abstract Drawing 4/6 c 8° Stevens & Haynes 92
STEAD, Fcs. R. Title Deeds, and Rudimts. of Real Prop. Law 5/ *n.* 8° Blades 08

*United States*

CURWEN, M. E. Searching of Records & Prep. of Abstrs. of Title $2 *n.* 8° Clarke, *Phila.* 83
DEMBITZ, L. N. Treatise on Land Titles in the U.S., 2 v. $12 *n.* 8° West Pb. Co., *St Paul, Minn.* 95
DEVLIN, R. T. Law of Deeds covrg. Alienation of Title to Real Prop., 2 v. $12 8° Bancroft, *San Francisco* 87

MARTINDALE, W. B. Examination of Titles of Real Estate $2·50 8° *Central Law Jl.* Co., *St Louis* 90
" Abstracts of Title $2·50 *n.* 8° [ ] 90
MAUPIN, C. W. Marketable Title to Real Estate $6 8° Baker, *N.Y.* 97
SEDGWICK + WAIT Trial of Title to Land $6 8° 86
WARVELLE, G. W. Pract. Treat. on Abstracts & Exam. of Title $6 *n.* 8° Callaghan, *Chicago* [ ] 92
WEBB, B. R. Law of Record of Title of Real & Pers. Prop. $6 8° Gilbert, *St Louis* 90

**Valuation** —*v.* also **D** § 150
WEBB, C. A. Valuation of Real Property 7/6 *n.* 8° Lockwood 09

**Vendor and Purchaser** —*v.* **D** § 96

## 79 : PUBLIC MEETING

BLAGG, J. W. The Law as to Public Meeting 3/ c 8° Butterworth 88

## 80 : QUARANTINE

BAKER, Sir G. S. Laws relating to Quarantine 12/6 c 8° Paul 79

## 81 : RAILWAYS AND CANALS

**Canals** —*v. also* **D** § 98
HUTCHINS, J. B. [ed.] Law as to Canal Boats used as Dwellings [Canal Bts. Act '77, *etc.*] 2/6 12° Knight 77
WEBSTER, R. G. Law relating to Navigable Rivers and Canals 21/ 8° Stevens 85

**Railways**
Amer. & Engl. Railroad Cases, v. i–lxi, & New Ser. i–xxx ea. $4·50 8° Michie, *Charlottesville* 95 *sqq., in prg.*
BIGG, J. [ed.] Coll. of Acts reln. to Railways, 1830–98 25/ *n.* 12° Waterlow [75–83] 98
BOYLE (E.) + WAGHORN (T.) Law rel. to Traffic on Railways and Canals, 3 vols. 50/ 8° Clowes 01
BROWNE, J. H. B. Practice bef. Railway Commissrs. under Acts 1873–4 18/ 8° Stevens 76
" + THEOBALD (H. S.) [eds.] Law of Railways [colln. of Acts & Orders] 42/ r 8° Stevens [81] 99
DARLINGTON, H. K. [ed.] Railway and Canal Traffic Acts 16/ 8° Reeves 89
DISNEY, H. W. Law of Carriage by Railway 7/6 8° Stevens [05] 09
Hdbk. for railw.-men and lawyers, based on lects. at London School of Economics.
EDALJI, G. E. T. Railway Law for the 'Man in the Train' 2/ *n.* c 8° E. Wilson 01
FREND (H. T.) + WARE (T. H.) [eds.] Precedents rel. to Transfer of Land to Railway Companies, ed. D. Sturges + T. L. Browne 20/ 8° Stevens [46] 66
HAINES, H. S. Restrictive Railway Legislation 5/ *n.* ($1·25 *n.*) c 8° Macmillan 05
HODGES, Sir W. Law of Ry. Cos. & Ry. Investment, ed. J. M. Lely, 2 v. 52/ r 8° Sweet [47] 90
MACNAMARA, W. H. Digest of Law of Carriers of Goods and Passsengers—*ut* **D** § 22
NEVILLE (R.) + BROWNE (J. H. B.) + MACNAMARA (W. H.) [eds.] Ry. and Canal Traffic Cases, vols. i–xii £19 *os.* 6*d.* r 8° Sweet 74–06
REDMAN, J. H. Law of Railway Companies as Carriers 5/ 12° Reeves & Turner [70] 80
WAGHORN, Thos. Law relating to Railway Traffic 2/ *n.* c 8° E. Wilson 06
" Traders and Railways (The Trader's Case) 4/ *n.* c 8° E. Wilson 07

**Scotland**
DEAS, Fcs. The Law of Railways applicable to Scotland 45/ *n.* r 8° Green, *Edin.* [73] 97
FERGUSON, Jas. [ed.] The Public Statutes rel. to Railways in Scotland 25/ *n.* r 8° Green, *Edin.* 98

**Canada**
MACMURCHY (A.) + DENISON (S.) [eds.] Canadian Rly. Act, 1903 $7·50 8° Canada Law Bk. Co., *Toronto* 06

**India**
RUSSELL (L. P.) + BAYLEY (V. B. F.) [eds.] Indian Railways Act ix of 1890 20/ *n.* 8° (*India*) [ ] 03

**United States**
American Railroad and Corporation Repts., ed. J. Lewis, vols. i–xii ea. $5 8° Myers, *Chicago* 90–7
BEACH, C. F. Mod. Law of Rys. as determ. in Engl. & U.S. 2 *v.* $6 8° Bancroft, *San Francisco* 90
ELLIOTT, B. K. + W. F. Treat. on the Law of Railroads, 4 v. $24 *n.* 8° Bowen-Merrill, *Indianapolis* 97
LACEY, J. F. Digest of Railway Decisions, 2 vols. $15 8° Callaghan, *Chicago* 75–84
American cases since 1875, w. selns. fr. Engl., Scottish, Irish, Canadian, and Australian cases.

PATTERSON, C. S. Railway Accident Law $6 *n.* 8° Johnson, *Phila.* 86

RAPALJE (S.) + MACK (W.) Digest of Ry. Decisns. fr. Earliest Period in U.S., Engl., & Canada, vols. i–viii ea. $7·50 8° Thompson, *Northport, L.I.* 95–8

REDFIELD, I. F. Law of Railways, ed. J. K. Kinney, 2 v. $12 8° Little & Brown, *Boston* [56] 88

RORER, D. Treatise on the Law of Railways, 2 vols. $12 8° Callaghan, *Chicago* 84

SWINGLE, C. F., *etc.* Modern American Railroad Practice, 10 vols. $60 8° Drake, *Detroit* 08

WOOD, H. G. Treat. of the Law of Railroads, ed. H. D. Minor, 3 v. $18 8° Boston Bk. Co., *Boston* [ ] 94

**Accidents (Railway)**

HAMILTON, A. M. Railway & other Accidents w. rel. to Injury & Disease of the Nervous System 15/ *n.* r 8° 04

**Fences and Crossings**

THORNTON, W. W. Law of Railroad Fences & Private Crossings $6 8° Bowen-Merrill, *Indianapolis* 92

**Liability for Negligence**

PARSONS, A. Liability of Railway Cos. for Negligence to Passengers 5/ 8° Cox 93

**Private Railways**

COCKBURN, J. H. Law of Priv. Ry. Sidings and Priv. Traders' Traffic 7/6 8° Stevens 09

**Rates:** —*v. also* **D** § 152

BUTTERWORTH, A. K. Law rel. to Maximum Rates and Charges on Rys. 12/6 r 8° Butterworth 97

,, Law rel. to Rates & Traffic on Rys. & Canals *o.p.* m 8° Butterworth [89] 90

DARLINGTON, H. K. Railway Rates and Carriage of Merchandize by Railway—*ut* **D** § 152

RUSSELL, Har. Railway Rates and Charging Orders 10/6 r 8° Stevens 07

*United States*

BEALE (J. H., jun.) + WYMAN (B.) Law of Railroad Rate Regulation $6 *n.* 8° Nagel, *Boston* 06

**Carriers**—*v.* **D** § 22 **Light Railways**—*v.* **D** § 67 **Railway Economics and History**—*v.* **D** § 152 **Securities**—*v.* **D** § 85 **Street Railways**—*v.* **D** § 67

## 81*: RECEIVERS

KERR, W. W. Law and Practice of Receivers appointed by High Court of Justice, ed. W. D. Rawlins 10/ 8° Sweet [69] 05

LYNCH, H. F. —*ut* **D** § 26, *s.v.* Liquidators

WILLIAMS, S. E. Law of Account and Accountant's Charges 10/ 8° Stevens 99

**United States**

ALDERSON, W. A. Practical Treatise on the Law of Receivers $6 8° Baker, *N.Y.* 05

BEACH, C. F., jun. Practical Treatise on Law of Receivers $6·30 8° Baker, *N.Y.* [ ] 97

GLUCK (J. F.) + BECKER (A.) Law of Receivers of Corporns., incl. Nat. Banks $6 8° Banks, *N.Y.* [91] 96

HIGH, J. L. Treatise on the Law of Receivers $6 8° Callaghan, *Chicago* [76] 94

SMITH, J. W. Law of Receiverships in U.S., Grit. Brit. & Colonies $6 *n.*; Suppl. $1·50 8° Lawyers' Co-op. Pb. Co., *Rochester* 97; 00

## 82: REGISTRATION

**Births and Deaths**

FLAXMAN, A. J. Registrn. of Births & Deaths in Engl., Wales, & at Sea *o.p.* [*pb.* 6/] 8° Stevens 75

GLEN, W. C. + A. [eds.] Law of Registrn. of Births, Deaths, & Marriages *o.p.* [*pb.* 5/6] 12° Knight [59] 75

HAMMICK, J. T. [ed.] Acts rel. to Registrn. of Births, Deaths, & Marrs. 6/ c 8° Butterworth 75

SMITH, G. T. Bisset Vital Registration [births, marriages, deaths] 10/ *n.* 8° Green, *Edin.* [ ] 07

**Deeds**

MADDEN, D. H. Pract. Treat. on Regn. of Deeds, etc. 15/ *n.* c 8° McGee, *Dubl.* [ ] 01

*Africa: Cape Colony*

FOSTER, J. Pract. of Deeds Registry Office of Cape Colony 10/6 *n.* 8° *Cape Town* [ ] 03

*Australasia*

HOGG, J. E. Deeds Registration . . of Land und. Reg. of Deeds Acts of Austr. 12/6 8° Stevens 08

**Land**—*v.* **D** § 51 **Parliamentary and Municipal**—*v.* **D** § 40

## 83 : RENT (CHIEF)

COPINGER (W. A.) + MONRO (J. E.) Law of Rents 31/6 8° Clowes 86
With special reference to sale of land for chief rent.
HARRISON, W. Law rel. to Chief Rents and other Rent Charges 6/ 12° Stevens 84

## 83* : RESTRAINT OF TRADE

JOLLY, W. A. Contracts in Restraint of Trade 4/ *n.* 8° E. Wilson [95] 00
MATTHEWS, J. B. Law rel. to Covents. in Restrt. of Trade, ed. H. M. Adler 7/6 *n.* 8° Sweet [93] 07
**Trusts and Monopolies** —*v.* **D** § 93*

## REVENUE : Customs, Income Tax, Stamps—*v.* D § 91

## 83** REVERSIONS

WITHERS On Reversions 15/ *n.* 8° Butterworth 09

## 84 : SAVINGS AND NATIONAL BANKS

FORBES, U. A. Statutory Law rel. to Trustee Savings Banks: 1863-91 5/ 12° Stevens & Haynes [78] 92
Law rel. to Trustees & P.O Savings Banks, 2 v. 10/6 12° Stevens & Haynes 78-84
WATT, J. Y. Law of Savings Banks 20/ 8° Butterworth 05

**United States**

BALL, F. Q. National Banks $3·50 8° 81
BROWNE, J. [ed.] National Bank Cases, 1878-80 $5 8° 80
THOMPSON, I. G. [ed.] National Bank Cases; w. notes and references $7·50 8° *Albany* 78

## 85 : SECURITIES

CAVANAGH, C. Law of Money Securities 30/ 8° Clowes [79] 85

**United States**

BURROUGHS, W. H. Public Securities $5 8° Baker, *N.Y.* 81
CLEMENS, G. C. Law of Corporate Securities as decided in Federal Cts. $3 8° Gilbert, *St Louis* 77
COLEBROOKE, W. Treat. on Law of Collateral Securities $6 8° Callaghan, *Chicago* [83] 98
HAINER, B. T. Treat. on Modern Law of Municipal Securities $6 8° Bowen-Merrill, *Indianapolis* 98
JONES, L. A. Treatise on Railroad & other Corporate Securities $6·50 8° Houghton, *Boston* 77
SHORT, E. L. The Law of Railway Securities $6·50 *n.* 8° Little & Brown, *Boston* 91

**Bills of Sale**—*v.* **D** § 19 **Corporate**—*v. also* **D** § 31 **Mortgages and Liens**—*v.* **D** § 66 **Municipal Securities**—*v.* **D** § 67 **Pawnbrokers**—*v.* **D** § 73 **Stock Exchange**—*v.* **D** § 88

## 86 : SETTLEMENTS

VAIZEY (J. S.) *and* WILLIAMS (Jos.) —*ut* **D** § 60, *incl. also Settlements on other occasions*

**SLANDER**—*v.* **D** § 54 **SLAVERY**—*v.* **D** § 55 **SOLICITORS**—*v.* **D** § 53 **SPECIFIC PERFORMANCE**—*v.* **D** § 29

## 87 : SPORTS

**Dogs**

EMANUEL, M. R. The Law relating to Dogs 3/6 12° Stevens 08
FREEMAN, W. M. The Law affecting Dogs and their Owners 5/ *n.* 8° Jordan 09
MANSON, E. The Law relating to Dogs 3/6 c 8° Clowes 93

**Fisheries**

BUND, J. Willis Law of Salmon Fisheries of Engl. & Wales, w. Suppl. 16/ p 8° Butterworth 73; 76
MOORE, S. A. + H. A. History and Law of Fisheries 21/ 8° Stevens & Haynes 03
OKE, G. C. Handbk. of Fishery Laws, ed. J. W. Bund + A. C. McBarnet 15/ c 8° Butterworth [5-] 03
PATERSON, J. [ed.] Fishery Laws [Salm. & Sea Fish. Acts, w. notes] *o.p.* [*pb.* 7/6] 12° Macmillan [63] 73

**Game**

CAMERON, P. H. Summary of the Game Laws of Scotland 3/6 c 8° Bell & Bradfute, *Edin.* 86
EVERITT, Nich. Shots from a Lawyer's Gun; ill. 7/6 *n.* 8° Everett [01]
Combines amusing anecdotes w. a lucid expositn. of the game-laws.

INGHAM, J. H. —*in his* The Law of Animals, *ut* **D** § 11
On property in animals, wild and domestic, and the rts. and responsibilities arising from it.

MARCHANT (J. K. V.) + WATKINS (W.) [eds.] Wild Birds Protection Acts, 1880–96 Porter [ ] 98

OKE, G. C. [ed.] Game Laws, w. Wild Birds & Grd. Game Acts, ed. J. W. Bund 14/ p 8° Butterworth [62] 97

PORTER, A. [ed.] Gamekeeper's Manual [game-laws, gun-licenses, Wild Birds Acts] 3/ *n.* c 8° Douglas, *Edin.* [81] 07

ROW, C. Practical Guide to Game Laws 5/ *n.* c 8° Longman 07
For use of preservers, sportsmen, gamekeepers, and police.

'Solicitor (A)' Handy Guide to the Game Laws 2/6 *n.* c 8° Cox 05

WARRY, G. T. Game Laws of England, w. Statutes 10/6 r 12° Stevens 96

*Scotland*

TAIT, J. H. Law of Scotl. appl. to Game Laws, Trout & Salmon Fishing 15/ *n.* 8° Green, *Edin.* 02

*United States*

KENT, G. E. Fish and Game Laws of State of New York 75 c. 8° *Troy* 88

REYNOLDS, C. B. [ed.] Game Laws in Brief: laws of U.S. & Canada 25 c. 8° *Forest and Stream* Pb. Co. *N.Y.* [91] 92

**Horses**

LASCELLES, F. H. Horse Warranty: w. hints as to procedure 5/ 8° Stevens [ ] 80

OLIPHANT, G. H. Law of Horses, ed. C. E. Lloyd + F. T. Barton 20/ 8° Sweet [47] 08
Incl. law of Inn-keepers, Veter. Surgeons, and of Hunting, Racing, Wagers, and Gaming. With Canadian notes by C. MORSE.

STEWART, D. Ross The Law of Horses 10/6 8° Green, *Edin.* 92

*United States*

HANOVER, M. D. Law of Horses, Livery Stable-keepers, Racing, *etc.* $4 8° Clarke, *Cincinnati* [ ] 75

**Theatrical**

HAMLYN, C. Manual of Theatrical Law 5/ 12° 91

**Yachting**

JEMMETT (C. H.) + PRESTON (R. A. B.) Treatise on Law rel. to Pleasure Yachts 10/6 *n.* r 8° [ ] 03

*United States*

PATTERSON, How. Yachting under Am. Statute [U.S. laws & Treasy. instructions] $1·50 8° Bliss, *N.Y.* 90

## 88 : STOCKS, STOCK-EXCHANGES, STOCKBROKERS

**London Stock-Exchange** —*v. also* **D** § 153

BRODHURST, B. E. S. Law and Practice of the Stock Exchange 12/6 8° Clowes 97

CHISWELL, Fcs. Key to the Rules of the Stock Exchange 7/6 8° E. Wilson 02

HEAD, F. D. Transfer of Stocks, etc. [law and practice] 5/ *n.* 8° Good 10

MELSHEIMER (R. E.) + GARDNER (S.) Law & Custs. of Stk. Exch., ed. W. Bowstead 7/6 c 8° Sweet [79] 05

SCHWABE (W. S.) + BRANSON (G. A. H.) Treatise on Law of the Stock Exchange 12/6 8° Stevens 04

STALLARD, C. F. Law of Sales of Stocks and Shares [popular] 2/6 f 8° E. Wilson 97

STUTFIELD (G. H.) + CAUTLEY (H. S.) Rules and Usages of the Stock Exchange 6/ *n.* 8° E. Wilson [91] 01
Conts. the text of the Rules, w. explan. of general course of business, notes and comments, and exposition of legal cases

**United States**

COOK, W. W. Treatise on Law of Stock & Stockholders, 2 v. $12·50 8° Callaghan, *Chicago* [87] 94

DOS PASSOS, J. R. Treat. on Law of Stockbrokers & Stock Exchanges, 2 v. $12 8° Banks, *N.Y.* [82] 05

**Capital and Income** —*v.* **D** § 78

## 89 : SUCCESSION

HENDERSON, R. C. Principles of Vesting in the Law of Succession 16/ *n.* 8° Green, *Edin.* 05

HOLDSWORTH (W. S.) + VICKERS (C. W.) Law of Succession, Testamentary, and Intestate 10/6 8° Blackwell, *Oxon.* 99

KEITH, A. B. Theory of State Succession [w. ref. to Eng. & Colon. Law] 6/ *n.* r 8° Stevens 09

POTTS, T. R. Principles of Law of Succession to Deceased Persons 7/6 8° Stevens 88

**Primogeniture**

CECIL, E. Law of Primogeniture 10/6 8° Murray 95

KENNY (C. S.) + LAURENCE (P. M.) Two Essays on the Law of Primogeniture 7/6 8° Reeves & Turner 78

LAURENCE, P. M. The Law and Custom of Primogeniture 5/ 8° Reeves & Turner 78
LLOYD, E. Succession Laws of Christian Countries 7/ 8° Stevens & Haynes 77

**Scotland**

CAMERON, P. H. Summary of Law of Intestate Succession in Scotl. 16/ 8° Bell & Bradfute *Edin.* [70]

**India**

HENDERSON, G. S. Law of Intestate & Testamentary Succession in India 36/ 8° *Calcutta* 82

**Chili**

GRAIN, W. On the Succession Laws of Chili *o.p.* [*pb.* 10/6] 12° 80

**France**

COLIN, B. H. Essay on Intestate Successions acc. to French Code *o p.* [*pb.* 6/] 12° Stevens 76

**Inheritance** —*v.* **D** § 111 : Hindu Law ; **D** § 112 Mohammedan Law

**Succession Duties** —*v.* **D** § 110

## SUICIDE—*v.* C § 70 SURETIES—*v.* D § 47

## 91 : TAXATION—*v. also* D § 117

Reports of Tax Cases : 3 vols. r 8° *Board of Inland Revenue* 84 *in prg.*

**United States**

BLACK, H. C. Treatise on Law of Tax Titles $6 *n.* 8° West Pb. Co., *St Paul, Minn.* [ ] 93
BROWNE Assessments and Taxation $5·50 8° 87
BURROUGHS, W. H. Law of Taxation as imposed by States and Municipalities $6·50 ; Suppl. $2·50 8° Baker, *N.Y.* 78 ; 83
COOLEY, T. H. Law of Taxation, incl. Local Assessments, 2 v. $12 8° Callaghan, *Chicago* [76] 03
DESTY, R. Compendium of the Law of Taxation, 2 v. $11 8° West Pb. Co., *St Paul, Minn.* 84
GOODNOW, F. J. [ed.] Selected Cases on Law of Taxation $4·50 8° Callaghan, *Chicago* 06
GRAY, J. M. Limitations of the Taxing Power in U.S.—*ut* **D** § 56
HAMILTON, C. H. Law of Taxation by Special Assessments $7·50 8° Lawyers' Co-op. Bk. Co., *Rochester* 07
JUDSON Treat. on Power of Taxation, State & Federal $6 8° Thomas, *St Louis* 02

**Customs and Excise**

BELL (J.) + DWELLY (J. H.) [eds.] The Laws of Excise [colln. of statutes] 9/ 8° Stevens 73
HAMEL, F. J. [ed.] Laws of Customs and Tariff Act, 1876 ; w. notes 4/6 c 8° Butterworth [76] 81
HIGHMORE, N. J. Customs Laws, inclg. Customs Consolidation Act 6/ 8° Stevens [ ] 07
" Excise Laws, 2 vols. 30/ r 8° Stevens [ ] 99

*United States*

ADAMS, G. H. Handbk. of Tariff on Imports into U.S., etc. $3 8° Baker, *N.Y.* [90] 91
CARR, W. W. Judic. Interpretn. by U.S. Cts. of Acts rel. to Tariffs $5·50 *n.* 8° Johnson, *Phila.*
ELMES, W. The Law of the United States Customs $4·50 8° Little & Brown, *Boston* 87
HEYL, L. Digest of Statutes of U.S. prescribg. Rates of Duties on Imports $3 8° *Washington* [ ] 75

**Death Duties ; Estate Duties ; Finance Acts**

AGGS, W. H. [ed.] The Finance (1909–10) Act 1910 ; w. notes 3/ 8° Sweet [10] 10
AUSTEN-CARTMELL, J. [ed.] The Finance Acts, 1894–1907 18/ r 8° Wildy [94] 08
BEATTY, C. Pract. Guide to Dth. Duties and to Prep. D. D. Accs. 4/ *n.* c 8° E. Wilson [05] 07
BRAMLEY, L. Death Duties 3/6 *n.* 8° Jordan 04
BUXTON (S.) + BARNES (G. S.) Handbook to the Death Duties 3/6 c 8° Murray 90
A detailed descr. of the complicated Engl. methods of taxation : probate, account, legacy, succession and estate duties.
DOBSON, W. G. Death Duties ; partic. Finance Acts, 1894–1907 9/ 8° Sweet 09
FREETH (Sir E.) + ELLIOTT (C. R.) [eds.] Acts rel. to Estate Duty and other Death Duties 12/6 8° Stevens [95] 08
HANSON, A. Death Duties, ed. L. T. Dibdin + F. H. L. Errington 30/ 8° Stevens & Haynes [83] 04
HARMAN, J. E. [ed.] Finance Act, 1894, and Acts amending same 6/ 12° Stevens [95] 03
NORMAN, A. W. [ed.] Digest of Death Duties ; w. exx. ill. their incidence 25/ r 8° Clowes [93] 99
" Death Duty Tables 7/6 r 8° Clowes 96
SOWARD, A. W. Law and Practice of Estate Duty 8/ *n.* 8° [ ] 00

WEBSTER-BROWN, J. [ed.] Finance Acts, 1894, 6, 8, 00, 07 and Reven. Act, 1903 8/ *n.* 8° Cox [08] 10

**Income Tax**

BERRY, J. Index to Income Tax Acts [1842–1910; in index-form] 10/6 *n.* 8° Butterworth 10
BUCHAN, Jno. Law rel. to Taxation of Foreign Income 10/6 8° Stevens 05
CARTER, R. N. Simplex Guide to the Income Tax [popular] 2/6 *n.* c 8° Gee 09
CHAPMAN, Alf. Income Tax: how to get it refunded 1/6 c 8° E. Wilson [86]
DOWELL, S. [ed.] Income Tax Laws in force in U.K., ed. J. E. Piper 21/ *n.* 8° Butterworth [74] 07
FLINT, S. W. Schedule D and How to Deal with it 1/ c 8° E. Wilson [04] 10
FRY, F. H. Income Tax: its return, assessment, and recovery 6/ *n.* 8° Jordan [05] 09
,, [ed.] Finance Act, 1907, in relation to Income Tax 6/ r 12° Stevens 07
HARRISON, E. R. Index to Official Repts. of Income Tax Cases 10/6 *n.* 8° Butterworth 08
Income-Tax Accounts and How to Prepare them [popular] 2/ *n.* c 8° Pitman 05
MURRAY (A) + CARTER (R. N.) Guide to Income Tax Practice 12/6 *n.* c 8° Gee [ ] 01
PEACOCK, H. St G. [ed.] Income Tax Acts, ed. R. S. G. Campbell 15/ r 8° Sweet 04
PRATT, W. T. [ed.] The Income Tax Acts, ed. J. H. Redman 8/ *n.* 12° Shaw [82] 08
ROBINSON, Arth. Law rel. to Income Tax; w. Stats., forms, & cases 25/ r 8° Stevens [95] 08
SPICER (E. E.) + PEGLER (E. C.) Income-Tax in relation to Accounts 6/ *n.* 8° Foulks 07
WHYBROW, G. H. Income Tax Tables for use of Companies, etc. 5/ 8° Stevens 05

**Inhabited House Duty**

DOWELL, S. [ed.] Acts rel. to Tax on Inhabited Dwelling Houses 5/ 8° Butterworth 93
ELLIS, A. M. Guide to the House Tax Acts 6/ r 12° Stevens 85
PIPER, J. E. [ed.] Acts rel. to House Tax [incorps. Dowell's House Tax Laws] 10/6 8° Butterworth 03

**Land Taxes** *v. also* **D** § 117

BOURDIN, M. A. Exposition of the Land Tax, ed. C. C. Atchison 7/6 r 12° Stevens [6–] 94
Atchison, C. C. Changes affected by Finance Act, 1896 [supp. to above] 2/6 *n.* 12° Stevens 97
CHANDLER, P. W. The Land Tax; w. practical instructions 3/6 *n.* 8° Reeves & Turner 99
COX-SINCLAIR (E. S.) + HYNES (T.) Taxn. of Ld. Values und. Finance ('09–10) Act '10 10/ *n.* 8° Knight 10
DEVONSHIRE (G. H.) + SAMUEL (F.) Duties on Land Values 20/ r 8° Stevens & Haynes 10
MOFFET, Thos. Land Taxes and Mineral Rights Duties 5/ *n.* 8° Murray 10
An exposn. of var. Sectns. of Finance (1909–10) Act, 1910, fr. surveyor's and valuer's standpt.
NAPIER, T. P. The New Land Taxes and their Pract. Applicn. 12/6 8° Stevens 10
WYLIE, J. [ed.] The Duties on Land Values and Mineral Rights 3/6 c 8° Jordan 10

*India*

BRIGGS, Lt.-Col. J. Land Tax in India [standard text-bk. of legislators] *o.p.* 8° *London* 30

**Municipal and Local** —*v.* **D** § 67

**Probate, Legacy, and Succession Duties:** *United States*

DOS PASSOS, B. F. Law of Collat. Inherit., Legacy and Success. Taxes [w. Am. & Engl. decisns. and N.Y. forms] $6 8° West Pb. Co., *St. Paul, Minn.* [90] 95
WEST, Max The Inheritance Tax [Columb. Univ. Studies] $2·50 *n.* 8° Macmillan, *N.Y.* 08

**Rating** —*v.* **D** § 67

**Revenue, Inland**

HIGHMORE, N. J. Summary Procgs. in Inl. Rev. Cases in Engl. & Wales 7/6 r 12° Stevens [82] 01
,, [ed.] Inland Revenue Regulation Act, 1890 7/6 8° Stevens 90
,, [ed.] Inland Revenue Cases: England and Wales 7/6 8° Stevens [ ] 87
PITHIE, M. Summary Proceedgs. in Inland Revenue Cases 7/6 *n.* 8° Green, *Edin.* 99

*United States*

ELDRIDGE, C. W. The United States Internal Revenue Tax System $5 8° Houghton, *Boston* 95
Conts. all Internal Revenue Laws in force, as amended by Act of 1894, incl. Income Tax; w. a History of developmt. of Internal Revenue Tax System

**Stamp Acts and Laws**

ALLEN, E. K. Stamps on Sea Insurance 8° 04
ALPE, E. N. Law of Stamp Duties on Deeds, etc., ed. A. B. Cane 10/ *n.* 8° Jordan [91] 07
BOND, H. S. Handbook to Stamp Duties, ed. C. H. Picken 2/6 *n.* 8° Waterlow [88] 07
COPINGER, W. A. Tables of Stamp Duties, 1815–78 2/6 *n.* 8° Stevens 78

DOWELL, S. History and Explanation of the Stamp Duties 12/6 8° Longman 73
GRIERSON, J. P. H. Law of Stamp Duties on Written Instruments 15/ n. 8° Green, *Edin.* [ ] 07
GRIFFITH, G. W. C. Digest of Stamp Duties and Judicial Decisions 8/ f 8° Vacher [71] 94
HIGHMORE, N. J. [ed.] Stamp Laws 10/ 8° Stevens [91] 11
KING, H. H. The Alphabetical Stamp Guide 3/6 n. 8° Butterworth 10
Stamp Laws as charged by Stamp Act '91 ; w. amendmts. 2/6 n. 12° Waterlow [ ] 10

*United States*

BUMP, O. F. [ed.] The United States Stamp Laws $5 8° *New York* 70

*India*

GHOSH, J. K. [ed.] The Indian Stamp Act, 1879 6/ 8° *Bhawanipore* 88

## 91* : TELEGRAPHS

CARMICHAEL, E. G. M. Telegraph, Telephone and Submarine Cable Law 10/6 n. 8° Knight 04

## 92 : TENDER (LEGAL)—*for* Economical books, *v.* D § 115

CERNUSCHI, H. Nomisma, or Legal Tender $1·25 12° Appleton, *N.Y.* 78
HARRIS, G. L. B. The Law of Tender 21/ n. r 8° Routledge 09
LINDERMANN, H. R. Money and Legal Tender in the United States $1·25 12° Putnam, *N.Y.* 77

## 93 : TORTS—*v. also* D § 10

*ADDISON, C. G. Treat. on Law of Torts, ed. A. P. P. Keep + W. E. Gordon 42/ r 8° Stevens [57] 03
" The same, ed. H. Smith ; w. Am. notes E. Baylies, 2 v. $10 8° Banks, *N.Y.* [57] 91
BALL, Dr W. E. [ed.] Leading cases on Law of Torts [founded on Bigelow] 21/ 8° Stevens 84
*CLERK (J. F.) + LINDSELL (W. H. B.) Treatise on Law of Torts, ed. Wyatt Paine 30/ r 8° Sweet [89] 09
Perhaps the most useful practical book on the subject.
FRASER, H. Compendium of Law of Torts [student's-bk.] 8/ c 8° Sweet [98] 10
HASTINGS, S. Treatise on Torts 28/ r 8° Sweet 85
KENNY, C. S. [ed.] Select. of Cases illustrative of Engl. Law of Torts [$4 n. Putnam, *N.Y.*] 12/6 n. 8° Camb. Press 04
PIGGOTT, F. T. Principles of the Law of Torts 20/ 8° Clowes 85
" Two Chapters on Law of Torts 1/6 n. r 8° Clowes 98
POLLOCK, Sir. Fredk. Law of Torts [learned but over-theoretical] 25/ 8° Stevens [87] 08
Amer. edn., fr. 3rd Engl. edn., ed. J. A. WEBB, w. notes and refs. to Amer. cases, $5 8° Thomas, *St Louis* '94.
RADCLIFFE (F. R. Y.) + MILES (J. C.) [eds.] Cases ill. Princs. of Law of Torts 12/6 n. ($4·15) 8° Clar. Pr. 04
Whilst KENNY gives numerous cases greatly curtailed, RADCLIFFE + MILES give fewer cases, but at considerable length. Both good books.
RINGWOOD, Rich. Outlines of the Law of Torts 10/6 8° Stevens & Haynes [87] 06
The substance of a series of lectures to the students at the Law Institution : merely an outline.
SALMOND, J. W. Law of Torts : Eng. law of liab. f. civil injuries 18/ n. 8° Stevens & Haynes 07
UNDERHILL, A. Summary of Law of Torts, ed. J. G. Pease 10/6 p 8° Butterworth [78] 05
Amer. edn., fr. 2nd Engl. edn. (by C. C. M. PLUMPTRE), ed. N. C. MOAK, w. refs. to Amer. cases, $4·25 8° Gould, *Albany* 81.

**United States**

BIGELOW, M. M. Elements of Law of Torts [12/6 Camb. Press] $4 n. c 8° Putnam, *N.Y.* [89] 08
Simpson, F. L. [ed.] Cases on Torts [to accompany above] $4·50 8° Little & Brown, *Boston* 08
BURDICK, F. M. The Law of Torts $3 8° Banks, *N.Y.* [05] 08
" [ed.] Cases on Torts [to accompany above] $4 8° Banks, *N.Y.* [91] 05
CHASE, G. [ed.] Leading Cases on Torts $3·50 n. 8° West Pb. Co., *St Paul, Minn.* 91
COOLEY, T. M. Treat. on Law of Torts, 2 v. $12 ; Studt's. Edn. $5·25 r 8° Callaghan, *Chicago* [79] 07 ; 07
ERWIN, F. A. [ed.] Cases on Torts $3·50 n. 8° Banks, *N.Y.* 00
HALE, W. B. Handbk. on Law of Torts [Handbk. Ser.] $3·75 8° West Pb. Co., *St Paul, Minn.* 96
JAGGARD, E. A. Handbook on Law of Torts, 2 vols. [Handbk. Ser.] ea. $3·75 n. 8° West Pb. Co., *St Paul, Minn.* 95
KINKEAD, E. B. Commentary on the Law of Torts, 2 v. $12 8° Bancroft, *San Francisco* 03
PAIGE, J. [ed.] Illustrative Cases in Torts [w. anal. and citns.] $6 8° Johnston, *Phila.* 96
POMEROY, J. N. Remedies and Remedial Rights by Civil Action, ed. J. N. Pomeroy, jun. $6 n. 8° Little & Brown, *Boston* [76] 94
WEEKS, E. P. Treatise on Doctrine of *Damnum absque Injuria* $4 8° Bancroft, *San Francisco* 79

**Negligence** —*v.* D § 69

## 93* : TRUSTS AND MONOPOLIES—*v. also* D §§ 81*, 120

BEACH, C. F. Treat. on Law of Monops. & Industr. Trusts in Engl. & U.S. $6 8° *Centr. Law Jl.* Co., *St Louis* 98

SPELLING, T. C. Treatise on Trusts and Monopolies [$3·50 *n.* Little & B., *Bost.*] 16/ r 8° Sweet 93
An exposition of the rule of public policy agst. contracts and combinations in restraint of trade, w. review of anc. and mod. cases.

**United States**

SNYDER, W. L. Interstate Commerce Act & Federal Anti Trust Laws, 2 v. $6 8° Baker, *N.Y.* 07

## 94 : TRUSTS AND TRUSTEES

BEACH, C. F., jun. Commentaries on the Law of Trusts and Trustees in England and the U.S., 2 vols. $13 8° *Centr. Law Jl.* Co., *St Louis* 97

BIRRELL, Augustine The Duties and Liabilities of Trustees 3/6 c 6° Macmillan 96
Six lects. del. in Inner Temple, 1896: popular in character and contg. many anecdotes, epigrams, *mots*, etc., with illns. fr. literature.

CHAMPERNOWNE (F. G.) + JOHNSTON (H.) [eds.] Trustee Act, 1893 12/ r 8° Butterworth 04

ELLIS, A. L. [ed.] Trustee Acts, incl. Guide to Investments, ed. L. W. Byrne 6/ c 8° Stevens [94] 03

FLINT, J. H. Law of Trusts and Trustees, as determ. by Eng. and Am. Cts. $3 c 8° Bancroft, *San Francisco* 90

GODEFROI, H. Digest of Principles of Law of Trusts and Trustees, ed. W. L. Richards + J. J. Stirling 28/ 8° Stevens [79] 07

HART, W. Gray Digest rel. to Private Trusts and Trustees 15/ r 8° *Law Notes* Off. 09

*LEWIN, T. + F. A. Pract. Treat. on Law of Trusts, ed. C. C. M. Dale 42/ r 8° Sweet [61] 04
Amer. edn., after 8th Engl. edn., ed. W. C. SCOTT, w. Amer. notes, 3 vols., ea. $1·25 Blackstone, *N.Y.* '88.

RICHARDS (W. L.) + STIRLING (J. I.) Law rel. to Trusts and Trustees 38/ r 8° Stevens [94] 07

RUDALL (A. R.) + GREIG (J. W.) [eds.] Law of Trusts and Trustees 12/6 *n.* c 8° Jordan [93] 04

,, Public Trustee Act, 1906 [supp. to above] 3/6 *n.* c 8° Jordan 07

SANDERS, F. W. Essay on Uses and Trusts, ed. G. W. Sanders + J. Warner, 2 v. r 8° Maxwell [44] 84
Still useful though rather antiquated.

UNDERHILL, A. Manl. of Law rel. to Priv. Trusts & Trustees 17/6 c 8° Butterworth [78] 04
Amer. edn., after 4th Engl. edn., ed. F. A. + A. WISLIZENUS, $5 8° Thomas, *St Louis* '96.

**Scotland**

MENZIES, A. J. P. Law of Scotland affecting Trustees, 2 vols. 34/ *n.* 8° Green, *Edin.* 93–7

WOOD, P. F. [ed.] The Trusts (Scotland) Acts, 1861–84 3/6 8° Green, *Edin.* 86

**United States**

LEWIN, Thos. The Law of Trusts and Trustees, 2 vols. $11 *n.* 8° Johnson, *Phila.* 88

LORING, A. P. Trustee's Handbook $1·50 *n.* c 8° Little & Brown, *Boston* [98] 07

PERRY, J. W. Law of Trusts & Trustees, ed. F. Parsons, 2 v. $12 *n.* 8° Little & Brown, *Bost.* [72] 99

**India**

AGNEW, W. F. Law of Trusts of British India [Tagore Law Lect.] 25/ 8° *Calcutta* 82

GRIFFITH, Wm. [ed.] Indian Trusts Act, No. 11 of 1882; w. comments. 10/6 8° Higginbotham, *Madras* 90

**Appointment of New Trustees**

EASTON, J. M. Law as to apptmt. of New Trustees 7/6 8° Stevens & Haynes 00

**Deeds of Arrangement**

DAVIES, D. P. Deeds of Arrangement: pract. manl. f. use of trustees 8/ *n.* 8° Gee 08

**Investment of Trust Funds**

ELLIS, A. L. —*in his* Trustee Acts, *ut sup.*

ELLISSEN, H. Trust Investmts. [annot. & classif. list of securities] 6/ r 8° Butterworth 04

GEARE, E. A. The Investment of Trust Funds 7/6 12° Stevens [86] 89

URLIN, R. D. Handybook on Investment of Trust Funds 1/ 12° E. Wilson [93] 02

VAIZEY, J. S. [ed.] The Trust Investment Act, 1889 9/ 8° Sweet 90

**Judicial Trustees**

ROMER, T. A. Judicial Trustee's Guide 8/ 8° Sweet 98

WHEELER, G. J. [ed.] Judicial Trustees Act, 1896 10/ 8° Butterworth 98

**Public Trustee** —*v. also sup.* (RUDALL + GREIG)

CHAMPERNOWNE (F. G.) + JOHNSTON (H.) + BRIDGE (J. S. L.) [eds.] Public Trustee Act, 1906 6/ *n.* r 8° Butterworth 08

FULTON, L. J. Law rel. to Pub. Trustee & Pract. in the Dept. 6/ *n.* 8° Butterworth 08
MORGAN, T. W. Practical Analysis of Publ. Trustee Act, 1906 1/6 *n.* c 8° Stevens & Haynes 07

**Trust Accounts**

CHANDLER, F. W. A Guide to Trust Accounts 7/6 *n.* 8° Butterworth 07
,, Accounts of Executors and Trustees, 2 vols.—*ut* **D** § 100

**Trustee-in-Bankruptcy** —*v.* **D** § 18

## 95 : VACCINATION—*for* Medical and Social Aspects, *v.* H* § 22

Barrister-at-Law, (A) ' Manual of the Vaccination Law 7/6 *n.* p 8° Shaw [88] 08
FRY, D. P. [ed.] Law rel. to Vaccination, ed. A. F. Vulliamy [the Acts, w. notes] 7/6 8° Knight [6–] 99
SHAW [ed.] Vaccination Law [the Acts, w. notes] 7/6 c 8° Butterworth [ ] 08

## 96 : VENDOR AND PURCHASER—*v. also* D § 10

*BENJAMIN, J. P. Law of Sale of Pers. Prop., ed. W. C. A. Ker + A. R. Butterworth 42/ r 8° Sweet [68] 06
With references to American decisions, and to French Code and Civil Law.
BLACKBURN, L'd Effect of Contract of Sale on Rts. of Property, ed. W. N. Raeburn + L. C. Thomas 21/ r 8° Stevens [45] 09
*CHALMERS, Judge [ed.] Sale of Goods Act, incl. Factors Acts, 1889 and 1890 10/6 8° Clowes [90] 05
*DART, J. H. Law and Pract. of Vendors & Purchasers of Real Estate, ed. B. L. Cherry + G. E. Tyrrell + A. Dickson + I. Marshall + L. H. Elphinstone, 2 v. 75/ r 8° Stevens [4–] 05
FARRER (F. E.) + LAW (T. P.) Precedts. of Conditns. of Sale of Real Estates, etc. 16/ r 8° Stevens [02] 09
KER, C. A. Digest of Law rel. to Sale of Goods 6/ 8° Reeves & Turner 88
NEWBOLT, F. Sale of Goods Act, 1893 [w. notes fr. Benjamin] 3/ 8° Sweet 97
*SEABORNE, H. Law of Vends. & Purchrs., ed. W. A. Jolly [studt's.-bk.] 10/6 p 8° Butterworth [71] 08
SUGDEN, E. B. [L'd ST LEONARDS] Law of Vendors & Purchasers of Estates *o.p.* [*pb.* 38/] Sweet [ ] 62
Amer. edn., ed. J. C. PERKINS, 2 vols. $12 8° Kay, *Phila.* '73.
TURNER, E. F. Duties of Solicitor to Client as to Sales, Purchases & Mortgages of Land, ed. W. L. Hacon 10/6 8° Stevens [ ] 93
WEBSTER, W. F. Law rel. to Partics. & Condn. of Sale on Sale of Land 25/ r 8° Stevens [90] 07
WILLIAMS (T. C.) + ISELIN (J. F.) Law of Vendor and Purchaser, 2 vols. 45/ r 8° Sweet 03–06
WILLIS, Wm. Law of Contract of Sale [6 valuable lects.] 7/6 8° Stevens & Haynes 02

**Scotland**

BROWN, Rich. Comment. on Sale of Gds. Act, '93, w. spec. ref. to Scotl. 16/ *n.* 8° Green, *Edin.* 95

**United States**

BROWNE, Irving Elements of Law of Sales of Personal Property $3 8° *Boston* 94
BURDICK, F. M. Sales of Personal Property $3 *n.* 8° Little & Brown, *Boston* [ ] 01
,, [ed.] Cases on Sales of Personal Property $4·50 *n.* 8° Little & Brown, *Boston* 01
TIEDEMAN, C. G. Treatise on Law of Sales of Personal Property $6 8° Thomas, *St Louis* 91
TIFFANY, F. B. Treatise on the Law of Sales $3·75 8° West Pb. Co., *St Paul, Minn.* [ ] 08
WARVELLE, G. W. Amer. Law of Vend. & Purchr. of Real Prop., 2 v. $12 *n.* 8° Callaghan, *Chicago* [90] 02

**Goodwill**

ALLAN, C. E. The Law relating to Goodwill 7/6 8° Stevens 90
DICKSEE (L. R.) + TILLYARD (F.) Goodwill 5/6 8° Gee [ ]

**Hire-purchase System**

DUNSTAN, R. Law rel. to the Hire-Purchase System [w. forms] 6/ c 8° Sweet 10
RUSSELL, W. H. The Hire-Purchase System 3/ *n.* 8° Waterlow [ ] 98

## 97 : WARRANTIES

SAUNDERS, T. W. Law of Warranties, etc., on Sale of Personal Chattels *o.p.* [*pb.* 6/] 12° Stevens 74

**United States**

BIDDLE, A. Law of Warranties in Sale of Personal Chattels $3 8° Kay, *Philadelphia* 84

## 98 : WATERS—*v. also* D § 78, *s.v.* Boundaries

COULSON (H. J. W.) + FORBES (U. A.) Law rel. to Waters: sea, tidal, and inland 35/ 8° Sweet [80] 10

MOORE, S. A. History and Law of Foreshore and Seashore 38/m 8° Stevens 88
Contains also *De Jure Maris*, by Lord HALE (hitherto unpub.), and a repr. of HALL's *Essay on Rights of Crown in Seashore.*

WOOLRYCH, H. W. Treatise on Law of Waters *o.p.* 8° Benning [49] 81

**Scotland**

FERGUSON, Jas. Law of Water and Water Rights in Scotland 45/*n.* r 8° Green, *Edin.* 07

**United States**

ANGELL, J. K. Treat. on Law of Watercourses, ed. J. C. Perkins $6 8° Little & Brown, *Boston* [3-] 77

CRAIG, Prf. G. W. [ed.] Sel. Cases on Water Rts. & Irrig. Law in Calif. $3 8° Bancroft, *San Francisco* 10

GOULD, J. M. Treatise on the Law of Waters $5 8° Callaghan, *Chicago* 00

POMEROY, J. N. Treatise on Water Rights, ed. H. C. Black $5 *n.* 8° West Pb. Co., *St Paul, Minn.* 93

TYLER, R. H. Treatise on Boundaries & Fences, and Rights of Seashore—*ut* **D** § 78

*Mining Water Rights* —*v.* **D** § 65 (BLANCHARD + WEEKS)

*Rivers Pollution* —*v.* **D** § 67

*Thames River Law*

PITT-LEWIS, G. [ed.] Handbook of Thames River-Law [Acts & Orders] 15/*n.* 8° E. Wilson 00

*Port of London:* BARLOW (Dr C. A. M.) [ed.] Port of London Act: 1908 20/*n.* 8° E. Wilson 08

## 99 : WEIGHTS AND MEASURES

ALLWOOD, G. F. [ed.] Appeal Cases under Weights and Measures Acts, Bread Act, Licensing Act 1872, and Merchandize Marks Act 1887 6/*n.* c 8° Butterworth 06

BOUSFIELD, W. E. [ed.] Weights and Measures Acts, 1878-1904 6/ 8° Stevens 07

FLETCHER, J. D. [ed.] Weights and Measures Acts, 1878-1904 5/ *n.* 8° Sherratt, *Mancs.* 08

ROBERTS, J. Handbook of Weights and Measures 8/*n.* 8° Knight [99] 09

## 100 : WILLS, EXECUTORS, PROBATE, AND SUCCESSION DUTIES

**Executors and Administrators**—*v. also* **D** § 150, *s.v.* Book-Keeping

ALLEN, E. K. Law of Corporate Executors and Trustees 6/8° 96

BENNETT (J. C. F.) + EADES (E. J.) Guide to Duties of Exors. & Administr 15/*n.* r 8° [ ] 06

CHANDLER, F. W. Accounts of Executors and Trustees, 2 vols. 10/*n.* r 8° Butterworth 06

DENDY, F. W. The Duties of Executors 2/*n.* 8° Waterlow [8-] 08

GOFFIN, R. J. R. The Testamentary Executor in England and Elsewhere [Yorke Prize Ess. 1899; $2 *n.* Putnam, *N.Y.*] 5/ 8° Camb. Press 01

INGPEN, A. R. Law rel. to Executors and Administrators 25/r 8° Stevens 08

MCLAREN, L'd The Laws of Wills and Succession, 2 vols. 63/r 8° Green, *Edin.* [ ] 94

RANKING + SPICER + PEGLER Executorship Law and Accounts 12/6 *n.* 4° Foulks & Lynch [ ] 08

ROBBINS (L. G. G.) + MAW (F. T.) Devolution of Real Estate on Death 15/*n.* 8° Butterworth [ ] 08
A complete working textbook on the law of exors. and admins.

WALKER (W. G.) + ELGOOD (E. J.) Compendium of Law rel. to Exors. and Admins. 21/8° Stevens [80] 05

" " Law and Pract. rel. to Admin. of Estates of Deceased 15/8° Stevens 83

WILLIAMS, Sir E. V. Treat. on Law of Exors. and Admrs., ed. Sir R. V. Williams + A. R. Ingpen, 2 vols. 80/r 8° Stevens [32] 05

WILLIAMS, S. E. Law rel. to Legal Representatives 9/8° Stevens [ ] 08

WOOD, F. Digest of Princs. & Pract. in Administrns., Executorships & Trusteeships 15/*n.* 8° Cox 95

*Scotland*

CURRIE, J. G. The Confirmation of Executors in Scotland 16/*n.* 8° Green, *Edin.* [ ] 02

*Australia*

WOOD, J. D. Laws of Austral. Colonies as to Admin. of Estates 6/12° Stevens 84

*South Africa*

FOSTER, J. The Executor's Reference for South Africa 3/*n.* 8° 03

*United States*

CROSWELL, S. G. Hdbk. on Law of Exors. & Administrs. $3·75 8° West Pb. Co., *St Paul, Minn.* [89] 97

MCCLELLAN, R. H. Manual for Executors, Admins., & Guardians $2 8° Banks, *N.Y.* [7-] 93

SCHOULER, J. Treat. on Law of Executors & Administrators $5·50 *n.* 8° Boston Bk. Co., *Boston* [83] 01

WOERNER, Judge J. G. Treat. on Amer. Law of Administrn., 2 v. $12 *n.* 8° Little & Brown, *Boston* [89] 99

**Wills**

DAVIDSON, C. [ed.] Precedents in Wills & App. of Trustees [=Conveyancing, vol. iv]—*ut* **D** § 30
FLOOD, J. C. H. Law of Wills relating to Personal Property 30/ 8° Maxwell 77
,, Pitfalls of Testators 5/ p 8° Butterworth 84
HAYES (W.) + JARMAN (T.) [eds.] Concise Forms of Wills, ed. J. B. Matthews ; w. notes 21/ 8° Sweet [38] 10
HOLDSWORTH, W. A. Law of Wills, Exors., Adminrs., ed. J. F. Waley 1/ 12° Routledge [59] 05
HUDSON, J. C. Guide to Makg. & Provg. Wills, ed. H. W. Hart + A. T. Layton 10/6 *n.* 8° Longman [5–] 92
*JARMAN, T. Treatise on Wills, ed. C. Sweet, 2 vols. 70/ r 8° Sweet [41–44] 10
MATHEWS, A. G. Short Treatise on the Law of Wills 7/6 c 8° Stevens & Haynes 08
STRAHAN, J. A. The Law of Wills 7/6 8° Sweet 08
*THEOBALD, H. S. Concise Treatise on Law of Wills [w. Statutes] 35/ 8° Stevens [76] 08
TUDOR, O. D. [ed.] Seln. of Leadg. Cases on Law rel. to Real Prop., Conveycg., Constrn. of Wills, etc. 50/ r 8° Stevens [ ] 98
UNDERHILL (A.) + STRAHAN (J. A.) Princs. of Interpretn. of Wills & Settlemts 15/ p 8° Butterworth [ ] 06
WEAVER, C. [ed.] Colln. of Concise Precedents of Wills ; w. notes 5/ c 8° Stevens [82] 04

*Scotland*

MCLAREN, J. Law of Scotl. in rel. to Wills & Succession, 2 v. 63/ r 8° *Edinb.* [68] 94

*United States* —*v. also* **D** § 108, *s.v.* Surrogate's Courts

CHATTERTON, M. D. Probate Law, 2 vols. $12 *n.* 8° Smith, *Lansing* 01
GARDNER, G. E. Handbook of the Law of Wills $3·75 8° West Pb. Co., *St Paul, Minn.* 03
HAWKINS, F. V. Treat. on Construction of Wills, ed. F. M. Leonard $5 8° Johnson, *Phila.* 85
PAGE, W. H. Concise Treatise on the Law of Wills $6 8° Anderson, *Cincinnati* 01
REDFIELD, I. F. Treatise on the Law of Wills, 3 v. $18 8° Little & Brown, *Boston* [64–6] 76–7
,, [ed.] Leadg. Amer. Cases & Notes on Law of Wills $6 8° Little & Brown, *Boston* 74
REMSEN, D. S. On the Preparation and Contest of Wills $6 *n.* 8° Baker, *N.Y.* 07
ROSS, P. V. Probate Law & Practice, 2 v. [wills, admin., etc.] $13 8° Bancroft, *San Franc.* 08
SCHOULER, J. Treatise on the Law of Wills $5·50 8° Boston Bk. Co., *Boston* [78] 00
THORNTON, W. W. The Law of Lost Wills $3 8° Callaghan, *Chicago* [90] 98
UNDERHILL, H. C. Treatise on the Law of Wills, 2 vols. $12 8° Flood, *Chicago* 00

*France*

PELLERIN, P. French Law of Wills, Prob., Admin., D'th Duties of Ests. of Deceased Englishmen leavg. prop. in France 2/ *n.* c 8° Stevens 09

*Hindu* —*v.* **D** § 111

**Powers**

FARWELL, L'd Justice Concise Treatise on Powers, ed. W. R. Sheldon 25/ r 8° Stevens [74] 93

**Probate Practice**—*v.* **D** § 103 **Succession Duty**—*v.* **D** § 91

# VI : Procedure and Practice of the Courts

## 101 : ENGLAND (*a*) : HOUSE OF LORDS—*v. also* D § 27

DENISON (C. M.) + SCOTT (C. H.) Proced. & Pract. rel. to Engl., Sc., & Ir. Appeals 16/ 8° Butterworth 79
GORDON, J. W. Appellate Jurisdiction of House of Lords 2/6 *n.* 8° Murray 05
Evolves the somewhat whimsical theory that a right of appeal lies to both Houses of Parliament.
KINNEAR, J. B. Digest of Ho. of Lds., Cases dec. on Appeal fr. Scotl. : 1709–1864 15/ 8° Green, *Edin.* 65
MACQUEEN, J. F. Practical Treatise on Appellate Jurisdiction of House of Lords and Privy Council *o.p.* [*pb.* 31/6] r 8° Maxwell 42
PATERSON, Jas. [ed.] Rept. of Scotch Appeals in Ho. of L'ds, 1851–93 ; 2 v. 8°
Incl. all Repts. in 4 vols. of MACQUEEN's *Repts.* [*o.p.*] and vols. i and ii of the *Law Repts.*, as well as many omitted fr. former bk. Notes and index.
WEBB, L. Practice of Supr. Court and on Appeal to Ho. of Lords 30/ 8° Butterworth 77

## 102 : ENGLAND (*b*) : PRIVY COUNCIL

Acts of the Privy Council of England : New Series, ed. J. R. Dasent—*ut* **D** § 5
BEAUCHAMP, J. J. Jurisprudence of the Privy Council 60/ *n.* r 8° 92
Digest of jurispr., sketch of hist., notes on constitn. of Judicial Committee, summary of procedure.

BLACKMORE [ed.] Decisions of Rt. Hon. Arth. Wellesley: 1884-94, '95 8° Govt. Press, *Adelaide* 00
BRODRICK (G. C.) + FREMANTLE (W. H.) [eds.] Judgments of Privy Council *o.p.* [*pb.* 10/6] 8° Murray 65
DICEY, Prf. A. V. The Privy Council [Arnold Prize Essay, 1860] *o.p.* [*pb.* 3/6] c 8° Macmillan [60] 87
MACPHERSON, W. Pract. of Judic. Comm. of Privy Co. 16/; Suppl. 1/ *n.* r 12° Sweet [60] 73; 00
MACQUEEN, J. F. —*ut* **D** § 101
MICHELL, E. B. + R. B. Pract. and Procedure in Appeals fr. India to Privy Council 12/ 8° Stevens 76
MITRA, A. C. Rulings of the Privy Council: 1825-97 15/ *n.* r 8° 97
PRESTON, T. Privy Council Appeals: manual of practice 10/ c 8° Eyre & Spottiswoode 00
Register of the Privy Council of Scotland, Ser. i-ii, 21 vols. [1545-1643]—*ut* **F** §§ 38-9
SAFFORD (F.) + WHEELER (G.) Practice of Privy Council in Judicial Matters 50/ r 8° Sweet 01
SELBORNE, L'd Judicial Procedure in the Privy Council 1/ *n.* 8° Macmillan 91
WHEELER, G. Privy Council Law [synopsis of appeals decid. 1876-91] 31/6 r 8° Stevens 93
Conts. much otherwise inaccessible informatn., incl. précis of import. Canadian cases. *Vide* also **D** § 107, *s.n.* WHEELER.
,, Confederation Law of Canada—*ut* **D** § 107
Privy Council Cases on Brit. North Amer. Act, 1867, and The Practice on Special Leave to Appeal.

## 103: ENGLAND (*c*): SUPREME COURT OF JUDICATURE, AND HIGH COURT OF JUSTICE

GIBSON, A. Students' Practice of the Courts [Supr. Ct. and County Cts.] 16/ 8° Stevens [81] 09
MACKENZIE (M. M.) + WHITE (C. A.) Supr. Court Funds & Rules; w. Introd. & notes 8/6 8° Stevens 84
PARKER, F. R. Analyt. Index & Guide to Judic. Acts & Rules 12/6 8° Butterworth [83] 83
PEMBERTON, L. L. Treatise on Judgment and Orders of High Court of Justice and Court of Appeal 40/ r 8° Stevens & Haynes [76] 89
QUICK (Sir J.) + GROOM (L. E.) Judicial Power of the Commonwealth with the Practice and Procedure of the High Court 30/ *n.* r 8° 05
*SETON, H. W. Forms of Judgmts. & Orders in H. Cts. & Ct. of App., esp. Chanc. Div., ed. C. C. M. Dale + W. T. King + W. O. Goldschmidt, 3 v. 126/ r 8° Stevens [62-63] 01
STRINGER, F. R. P. A B C Guide to Practice of Supreme Court 5/ *n.* r 12° Sweet *ann.*
WALKER, W. H. Practice on Signing Judgment in High Ct. of Justice 4/6 c 8° Stevens 79
WHITEWAY, A. R. Pract. Notes on Judic. Acts, Orders, etc., of Supr. Ct. 14/ 12° Stevens 83
WILSON, A. Practice of Supreme Court of Judicature, ed. C. Burney + M. M. Mackenzie + C. A. White 20/ r 8° Stevens [75] 88

**King's Bench, Common Pleas, Exchequer, Chancery Divisions**—*v. also* **D** § 42
*Annual Practice (The): ed. B. F. Lock + C. Burney + F. A. Stringer 25/ *n.* 8° Stevens *ann.*
Conts. all the Orders of Supr. Ct., Judicature Acts, etc., elab. annotated. This (or *The Yearly Practice*) forms the one really indispensable bk. to every practitioner. It is known as 'The White Book.'
*ARCHBOLD, J. F. Pract. in Q.B., C.P. & Exch., & on App., ed. T. W. Chitty + J. St L. Leslie, 2 vols. 73/6 8° Sweet [8th edn. 40] 85
AYCKBOURN, H. Chancery Pract., Pt. i, 12/; Chancery Forms & Orders 14/ r 12° Wildy [49] 80; [5-] 73
BULLEN (E.) + LEAKE (S. M.) [eds.] Preced. of Plead., adapt. to K.B. D., ed. C. Dodd + T. W. Chitty 38/ r 12° Stevens [4-] 05
The 3rd edn. (1868), pubd. bef. passing of Judic. Acts, is still extremely valuable—more so than more recent edns. [*w.* 60/].
CHITTY, T. [ed.] Forms of Civil Proceedings in K.B. Division, ed. H. + T. W. Chitty + P. E. Vizard [w. Statutes & Rules] 36/ 8° Stevens [32] 02
*DANIELL, E. R. Pract. of Chanc. Div. & on Appeal, ed. C. C. M. Dale, etc., 2 vols. 105/ 8° Stevens [2nd edn. 45] 01
Amer. edn., 3 vols. $18, 8° Little & Brown, *Boston*, '94.
,, [ed.] Forms & Preceds. of Proceedgs. in Chanc. & on Appeal, ed. C. Burney 50/ r 8° Stevens [ ] 01
INDERMAUR, J. Student's Manl. of Practice of Supr. Court [Q.B. and Chanc.] 15/ 8° Stevens [78] 05
*ROBERTSON, G. S. Law and Pract. of Civil Procgs. by & agst. Crown 38/ r 8° Stevens 08
SHORT, F. H. [ed.] Crown Office Rules and Forms. 1886 12/ 8° Stevens & Haynes 86
,, Taxation of Costs in Crown Office 10/ 8° Stevens & Haynes 79
,, + MELLOR (F. H.) Practice on Crown Side of K.B.D. 30/ r 8° Stevens & Haynes [90] 08
Founded on Rich. CORNER'S *Crown Office Practice* (1844).
UNDERHILL, A. Pract. and Concise Manl. of Procedure of Chanc. Div. 10/6 p 8° Butterworth 81
WILD (E. E.) + COOPER (F. S.) Common Form Draftsman [Q.B. forms] 7/6 *n.* c 8° Stevens 99
WILLIAMS, S. E. Law and Pract. of Petitns. rel. to Chancery and Lunacy 18/ 8° Stevens 80

*Yearly Supreme Court Practice (The), ed. M. M. Mackenzie + S. G. Lushington + J. C. Fox 25 / *n.* 8° Butterworth *ann.*
The great rival to *The Annual Practice*—known as *The Red Book.*

*History of Equitable Jurisdiction*—*v.* **D** § 5, *s.v.* Court of Chancery

**Commercial Court**

MATHEW, T. Practice of the Commercial Court 5 / *n.* c 8° Butterworth 02

**Admiralty, Divorce, and Probate Division**

**Admiralty** —*v. also* **D** § 58 ; *for* History, *v.* **D** § 5

BURRELL, Sir W. [ed.] Admiralty Cases, 1648–1840, ed. R. G. Marsden 31/6 *n.* r 8° Butterworth 85

PRITCHARD, R. A. + W. T. Digest of Admiralty and Maritime Law, ed. J. C. Hannen + W. T. Pritchard, 2 vols. £5 r 8° Butterworth [47] 87

ROSCOE, E. S. Treat. on Jurisd. & Pract. of Admir. Div., ed. T. L. Mears 25 / 8° Stevens [78] 03

,, [ed.] Admiralty Forms and Precedents [w. notes on practice] 9/ c 8° Butterworth 84

SMITH, T. E. Summary of Law & Pract. in Admiralty [for students] 10 / 8° Stevens & Haynes [80] 92

WILLIAMS (R. G.) + BRUCE (Sir G.) Jurisdiction and Practice in Admiralty Actions and Appeals, ed. C. F. Jemmett + G. G. Phillimore 32 / 8° Sweet [69] 02

*Admiralty Jurisdiction and Practice of County Courts*—*v.* **D** § 105

**Divorce** —*v. also* **D** § 59

BROWNE (G.) + POWLES (L. D.) Law and Practice in Divorce & Matrimonial Causes 25 / 8° Sweet [64] 05

DIXON, W. J. Law, Pract., and Procgs. in Divorce & Matrim. Causes 15 / 8° Reeves & Turner 83

OAKLEY, T. W. H. Divorce Practice, ed. W. M. F. Waterton 21 / *n.* 8° Griffith [ ] 05

RAYDEN, W. Practice and Law in the Divorce Division 15 / 8° Butterworth 10

**Probate** —*v. also* **D** § 100

DIXON, W. J. Law & Practice of Probate & Administration 15 / 8° Reeves & Turner [80] 85

HARRISON, J. C. Epitome of Laws of Probate and Divorce 7/6 8° Stevens & Haynes [80] 91

MORTIMER, H. C. Law and Practice of Probate Division 42/ *n.* r 8° Sweet 11

NAPIER (T. B.) + STEPHENSON (R. M.) Digest of Probate, Divorce, etc. [for students] 12 / 8° Maxwell 88

NELSON, How. A. Handbook on Probate Practice (Non-contentions) 12/6 8° 01

PICKEN, C. H. The Practitioner's Probate Manual [w. Rules, etc.] 6/ *n.* 8° Waterlow [ ] 08

POWLES (L. D.) + OAKLEY (T. W. H.) Probate Practice, ed. W. M. F. Waterton + E. L. Mansbridge 30 / 8° Stevens [73] 06

TRISTRAM (Dr T. H.) + COOTE (H. C.) Probate Practice, ed. W. F. L. de Quetteville & B. H. Thomson 32/6 8° Butterworth [70–81] 06

*Costs*

FREEMAN, Saml. Handy Guide to Probate and Admin. Costs 2/6 *n.* 8° Butterworth 03

## 104 : ENGLAND (*d*) : COURT OF CHANCERY OF CO. PALATINE OF LANCASTER

[Equity only]

SNOW (T.) + WINSTANLEY (H.) [eds.] Chanc. Pract. of Co. Palatine of Lancaster 15 / r 8° Stevens [80] 85

## 105 : ENGLAND (*e*) : INFERIOR COURTS

**County Courts**

de COLYAR, H. A. [ed.] Reports of Cases in County Cts., 1867–83 [circuits 45 & 46] 10 / r 8° Stevens 83

DALE The County Court Formalist 21 / r 8° Butterworth 87

JONES, Chas. The Business Man's County Court Guide 3/6 *n.* c 8° Wilson [93] 09

LLOYD, C. E. [ed.] County Courts Act, 1888 10/6 8° Knight 88

McCULLAGH, J. G. Procedure and Practice in County Courts 8° Waterlow [ ] 90

SHUTTLEWORTH, E. [ed.] County Courts Acts, 1888 ; w. notes, etc. 5 / 8° J. Smith 97

SMYLY (Judge) + BROOKS (W. J.) Annual County Courts Practice, 2 vols. 25 / 8° Stevens *ann.*
The County Court *White Book.*

TEBBS, H. L. A.B.C. County Court Practice 10/6 *n.* 8° Butterworth 07

WICKHAM, G. E. Guide to an Ordinary County Court Action 5 / c 8° [ ] 04

Yearly County Court Practice (The), ed. Judge Woodfall + E. H. T. Atkinson, 2 v. 25 / 8° Butterworth *ann.*
The County Court *White Book.*

*Admiralty Jurisdiction and Practice*

RAIKES (F. W.) + KILBURN (B. D.) Treat. on Admir. Jurisd. & Pract. in Co. Cts. 12/6 8° Butterworth 96

*Appeals*
CHAMIER, D. Law and Pract. rel. to County Court Appeals 10 / 8° Stevens 96
*Costs* —*v.* **D** § 109

**Mayor's Court**

*GLYN (L. E.) + PROBYN (L.) + JACKSON (F. S.) Jurisdiction and Practice of Mayor's Court 17 / 8° Butterworth [88] 96
RAILTON (E. H.) + GILL (R.) Practice and Pleading in the Mayor's Court 8 / 8° Sweet 88

**Quarter Sessions and Magisterial Law**

ALLAN, C. E. [ed.] Questions and Answers fr. ' Justice of the Peace,' 1877–96 4° Butterworth 02
Conts. 8,000 opinions of Council on subjects dealt w. in courts of summary jurisdiction.
ARCHBOLD, J. F. Quarter Sessions Practice, ed. F. R. Y. Radcliffe 25 / *n.* 8° Shaw [36] 08
ATKINSON, C. M. Magistrate's General Practice 20 / 8° Stevens *ann.*
ATKINSON, Serjt. Offices of High Sheriff, Under-Sheriff, etc., ed. R. E. Melsheimer 14 / p 8° Sweet [39] 78
BEARD, C. A. Office of J.P. in England [Col. Univ. Studs.] $1·50 *n.* 8° Macmillan, *N.Y.* 04
BRIDGES, A. Handbook for Justices of the Peace 6 / p 8° Stevens [ ] 79
CHURCHILL, C. Law of Office and Duties of the Sheriff 24 / 8° Stevens [79] 82
DOUGLAS, C. G. [ed.] Summary Jurisdiction Procedure 15 / *n.* 8° Butterworth [ ] 07
The Summary Jurisd. Acts 1848–99 regulatg. the duties of J.P.'s w. resp. to summ. convictns. and orders, etc.
GREENWOOD (H. C.) + MARTIN (T. C.) Magist. & Police Guide [Stat. law ; w. notes] 32 / 8° Stevens [74] 90
JELF, E. A. [ed.] Treatise on Order xiv and Rules and Practs. thereunder 5 / 4° Cox 06
LEEMING (H.) + CROSS (R.) General and Qr. Sessns. of Peace : jurisd. and pract. in other than criminal Matters, ed. H. Lloyd + H. F. Thurlow 21 / r 12° Sweet [58] 76
LITTLER (R. D. M.) + HUTTON (A.) The Rights and Duties of Justices 5 / c 8° Butterworth 00
' MIDDLESEX MAGISTRATE (A) ' The Justice of the Peace [functions ; popular] 2/6 *n.* c 8° Dent 11
OKE, G. C. Magisterial Synopsis : guide for magistrates, solicitors, constables, etc., ed. H. L. Stephen, 2 vols. 58 / 8° Butterworth [49] 93
,, [ed.] Magisterial Formulist, ed. C. G. Douglas [forms and preceds.] 40 / Butterworth [50] 10
PALEY Law and Pract. of Summ. Convns., ed. W. H. Macnamara + R. Neville 25 / 8° Stevens [ ] 04
PRITCHARD, T. S. Jurisd., Pract., & Proced. of Qr. Sessns. in Crim., Civ., & Appell. Matters, ed. V. G. Milward + J. C. Matthews 31 /6 8° Sweet [75] 04
SAUNDERS, T. W. Pract. of Magistr. Courts, ed. R. M. Stephenson + J. H. Lindsay 12 / *n.* 12° Crockford [55] 02
SCHOLEFIELD (J.) + HILL (G. R.) Appeals from Justices 15 / *n.* 8° Butterworth 02
SHIRLEY, W. S. Elem. Treat. on Magist. Law & Pract., ed. L. H. West 7/6 12° Stevens [81] 96
SMITH, F. J. Quarter Sessions Practice [Appellate & Civil cases] 20 / 12° Stevens 82
SNOWDEN, R. L. Magistrate's Assistant and Police Officer's Guide—*ut* **D** § 67, *s.v.* Police
STONE, S. Practice for Justices of Peace, ed. W. H. Macnamara 25 / 8° Sweet [3–] 82
* ,, Justices' Manual, ed. J. R. Roberts 25 / c 8° Shaw [42] *ann.*
TROTTER, J. G. Appeals from Convictions and Orders of Justices 18/ 8° Butterworth [84] 91
WIGRAM, W. Knox Justices' Note Book, ed. C.M. Atkinson 7 /6 12° Stevens [79] 10
WRIGHT, Har. The Office of Magistrate 5 / p 8° Butterworth [89] 98
Yearly Justices' Practice —*v.* Stone's Justices' Manual, *supra*
*Criminal Law* —*v.* **D** § 33 *Police* —*v.* **D** § 67

**Referees Court**

CLIFFORD (F.) + STEPHENS (P. S.) Practice of Court of Referees on Private Bills in Parliament, 1867–72, 2 vols. 70 / *n.* r 8° Butterworth
Continuation : 1873–84 (CLIFFORD + RICKARDS), 3 vols., 163/6 *n.* ; 1885–9 (RICKARDS + MICHAEL), 1 v., 48/6 *n.* ; 1890–4 (RICKARDS + SAUNDERS) 50/ *n.* ; 1895–1902 (SAUNDERS + AUSTIN), ea. yr. 10/6 *n.* ; 1903–4 (SAUNDERS), ea. yr. 10/6 *n.* ; 1905–6 (SAUNDERS + BIDDER), ea. yr. 10/6 *n.*
SAUNDERS, R. C. [ed.] Consolid. Index of Cases decid. by Ct. of Referees [1867–90] 12 /6 r 8° Butterworth 91

## 105* : ECCLESIASTICAL COURTS—*v. also* A § 111

SMITH, T. E. Summary of Law and Pract. of Eccles. Cts. 8 / 8° Stevens & Haynes [80] 02

## 106 : COURTS OF SCOTLAND, AND OF IRELAND

**Burgh Court**

WATSON, Chas. Burgh Court Procedure [w. forms] 12 / *n.* 8° Green, *Edin.* 04

**Court of Session**

BALFOUR, Dav. Handbook of Court of Session Practice, ed. R. Berry 12/ *n.* 8° Green, *Edin.* [ ] 04

COLDSTREAM, J. P. Procedure in the Court of Session 12/ c 8° *Edinburgh* 81

GRIERSON, P. J. H. Index of all Cases Commented upon in Judgmts. in Ct. of Sessn. & in Sc. Appeals to H. of Lds., 1862–93 [*v.* Welsh, *inf.*] 25/ *n.* r 8° Green, *Edin.* 94

*MACKAY, Æ. J. G. Manual of Practice in the Court of Session 30/ *n.* r 8° Green, *Edin.* [77–9] 90

WELSH, Jno. A. Index of Cases Commented on, etc. [contin. of Grierson, *sup.*] 15/ *n.* r 8° Green, *Edin.* 06

**Dean of Guild Court**

IRONS, J. C. Law and Practice of the Dean of Guild Court 25/ *n.* 8° Green, *Edin.* 95

**Private Legislation**

CONSTABLE + BEVERIDGE + MACMILLAN Treatise on Provisional Orders applic. to Scotl. und. Priv. Legisln. Proced. (Scotl.) Act 1899 and other Statutes 25/ *n.* r 8° Green, *Edin.* 00

CONSTABLE + MACMILLIAN + BEVERIDGE [eds.] Private Legislation Reports, 9 vols. ea. 15/ *n.* r 8° Green, *Edin.* 01–9 *in prg.*

GREIG, J. W. + W. G. [eds.] Private Legislation Procedure (Scotl.) Act, 1899 7/6 8° Green, *Edin.* 00

**Sheriff Courts**

FORREST + SHEARER [eds.] Styles of Writs in Sheriff-Courts 12/ 8° *n.* Green, *Edin.* 83

GUTHRIE, W. [ed.] Select Cases decided in Sheriff Courts of Scotland 20/ 8° *Edinburgh* 79

LEES, J. M. [ed.] Sheriff Court Styles; w. notes & authorits. [in dict. form] 26/ 8° Green, *Edin.* [83] 92

LEWIS, W. J. Handbook of Sheriff-Court Practice, Civil and Criminal 16/ *n.* 8° Green, *Edin.* [87] 10

MCKECHNIE + LYELL [eds.] Styles of Writs in Court of Session 16/ 8° Green, *Edin.* 86

SMITH, W. P. [ed.] Acts of Parliament rel. to Sheriff Ct. Pract., Scotl. 7/6 8° Bell & Bradfute, *Edin.* 76

WALLACE, Wm. Sheriff Court Practice 30/ *n.* r 8° Green, *Edin.* 09

WILSON, Jno. Dove Pract. of Sheriff Cts. in Civil Causes, ed. J. C. D. Wilson 30/ 8° Bell & Bradfute, *Edin.* [75]
With a historical Introduction, and an appendix of Statutes and Acts of Parliament.

,, [ed.] Law of Process under Sheriff Cts. (Scotl.) Act, 1876; w. notes 6/6 8° Bell & Bradfute, *Ed.* 76

**Supreme Courts**

Juridical Soc. of Edinb.: Forms of Process in the Supr. Cts. of Scotland 36/ r 8° Green, *Edin.* [1790] 88
Forms the 3rd vol. of *Juridical Styles* [for vols. i–ii, *v.* D § 30].

**Magisterial Law**

IRONS, J. C. The Scottish Justice's Manual 7/6 *n.* 8° Green, *Edin.* 00

**IRELAND**

DILLON, W. [ed.] Supreme Ct. of Judicature (Irel.) Act, 1877; w. notes, etc. 12/ 8° *Dublin* 79

EIFFE, L. S. [ed.] Judic. Acts (Irel.), 1877 and '78, w. Orders, Rules, etc. 31/6 8° *Dublin* 81

MADDEN, D. H. Law and Practice of H. Ct. of Just.; w. forms and preceds. 20/ 8° *Dublin* [ ] 80

**Probate Court**

MILLER, W. R. Practice of Ct. of Prob. and of Quartersessns. in Ireld. resp. Testamentary and Intestate Business 30/ 8° [ ] 00

SMITH, G. H. Guide to Pract. of Ct. of Probate and District Registries 10/6 8° *Dublin* [ ]

## 107: COLONIAL AND INDIAN COURTS AND LAW

BEDWELL, C. E. A. The Legislation of the Empire, 4 vols. ea. 12/6 r 8° Soc. of Compar. Legisln. 09
Gives the substance of the principal legisln. of all the Colonies and Depends. of the Empire dur. decade 1898–1907—over 18,000 enactmts.

BURGE, Wm. [1786–1849] Commentaries on Colonial & Foreign Laws & Courts, ed. A. Wood-Renton + G. G. Phillimore, vol. i [in 7 vols.] *the set* 168/ *n.* r 8° Sweet [37] 07
The only legal work wh. attempts to deal compar. w. main divisns. of law of persons and property in systs. of Brit. domins. and those of foreign countries.

PIGGOTT, F. T. [ed.] Imperial Statutes applicable to the Colonies, 2 vols. 105/ *n.* i 8° Butterworth 02–4
Vol. i: *Statutes of General Application*; vol. ii: *Statutes of Special Application*.

TARRING, C. J. Chapters on Law rel. to the Colonies 21/ 8° Stevens & Haynes [82] 06
Deals mainly w. the principles of constitutions, and less fully (and systematically) w. that pt. of the law of Gt. Brit. wh. applies to the Colonies, particular local laws, and how far they can be enforced in the parent State, *etc.*

**AUSTRALIA AND NEW ZEALAND**

**Victoria:** *Magisterial Law*

CASEY, J. J. Justice's Manual: incl. Statutes, w. explan. and pract. notes 30/ 8° *Melbourne* [72] 79

MCKEAN, J. The Law and Practice of the County Courts 15/ 8° *Melbourne* 69

WALLIS, W. J. Guide to the County Courts 10/6 8° *Melbourne* [ ] 72

**New Zealand :** *Supreme Court*

FOSTER — Principles and Practice of Supr. Ct. Code, N.Z. — 90 / 4° *Christchurch* 88

*Code of Civil Procedure*

PENNEFATHER + BROWN [eds.] Code of Civil Procedure, New Zealand — 30 / 8° *Wellington* 88

*Magisterial Law*

BROAD, L. — New Zealand Magistrates' Court Guide — 10 / 8° *Wellington* 88

JOHNSTON, A. J. — N.Z. Justice of Peace, Magistrates, Coroner, etc., 2 vols. — 35 / 8° *Wellington* [70] 88

" — Powers, Duties, and Liabs. of Magistr., Coroners, etc., in N.Z. — 42 / 8° *Wellington* 64

**CANADA**

WHEELER, G. [ed.] — Confederation Law of Canada — 42 / r 8° Eyre & Spottiswoode 96

A colln. of all Privy Council cases on confederatn. policy and constitn. of the Dominion, giving under ea. section of Brit. North Amer. Act, 1867, notes of all leading appeals and petitns. It further incls. many Imperial Acts affectg. the Confedern., and Appendix contg. a statemt. of the Courts fr. wh. appeals lie to the Judicial Committee, the *minimum* appealable amounts and the conditns. of appeal. *Vide* also **D** § 102, *s.n.* WHEELER.

*Supreme and Exchequer Courts*

CAMERON, E. R. — Practice of Supreme Court of Canada — $9 8° Canada Law Bk. Co., *Toronto* 06

CASSELS, Rob. — Manual of Supreme and Exchequer Courts Procedure — 21 / 12° *Toronto* [77] 89

*Chancery Court*

BOTSFORD, G. — Rules and Statutes regulating the Court of Chancery — 8/6 8° *Toronto* 65

LEGGO, W. — Chancery Practice of Ontario, 2 vols. — 8° *Toronto* 76

" — Forms & Preceds. of Pleadgs. & Procgs. in H. C. of Chanc. — 8° *Toronto* [ ] 76

*Civil Procedure*

de BELLEFEUILLE [ed.] — Civil Code of Procedure of Lower Canada — 25 / 8° *Toronto* [ ] 79

FORAN, T. P. [ed.] — Code of Civil Procedure in Prov. of Quebec; w. notes — 31/6 8° *Toronto* 79

*Magisterial Law*

CLARKE, S. R. — The Magistrates' Manual [a digest of criminal law] — 21 / r 8° *Toronto* [78] 88

*Parliamentary Procedure and Practice—v.* **D** § 27

*Probate Court*

HOWELL, A. — Probate Practice — 25 / 8° *Toronto* 08

**WEST INDIES : Leeward Islands**

WALPOLE, C. G. — The Leeward Islands; w. appendix of forms — 25 / 8° Butterworth 92

**AFRICA : Cape of Good Hope**—*for* Roman-Dutch Law (*still in force in S.-A. Colonies*), *v.* **D** § 110

TENNANT, H. [ed.] — Rules, Orders, etc., in Civ. & Crim. Cases in C. of G. H. — 31/6 8° *Cape Town* [ ] 82

VAN ZYL, C. H. — Judicial Practice of Cape of Good Hope — 36 / 8° *Cape Town* [ ] 02

*Magisterial Law*

BAYNE, G. C. — Manual for Magistrates at C. of G. H. [crim. jurispr.] — 21 / 8° *Cape Town* 88

TENNANT, H. — Manual for Guidance of Justice of the Peace — 10/6 8° *Cape Town* [ ] 88

**British South Africa**

BELL, W. H. S. — Legal Hdbk. of Pract. Laws and Proc. in Br. S. Afr. — 26 / *n.* c 8° Sweet 05

**GOLD COAST : Fanti** —*v.* **D** § 3 (SARBAH, 3 books)

**Mauritius**

PIGGOTT (Sir C. T.) + THIBEAUD + HERCHENRODER — Mauritius, 3 vols. — 42 / *n.* i 8° Butterworth 97

**Sierra Leone**

Rules of Supreme Court of Colony of Sierra Leone — 3/6 *n.* r 8° 08

**Transvaal**

BUCKLE, H. O. — Civil Practice in Magistrates' Cts. in Transvaal — 25 / *n.* Butterworth 05

**SOUTH AMERICA (British)**

**British Guiana :** *Magisterial Law*

POUND, A. J. — Magisterial Law of British Guiana — 50 / *n.* 8° Stevens 88

**INDIA AND CEYLON** —*for* Roman-Dutch Law (*still in force in Ceylon*), *v.* **D** § 110; *v. also* **D** § 111

COWELL, H. — History & Constitution of the Courts & Legislative Assemblies in India [Tagore Lects. 1872] — 21 / r 8° *Calcutta* 72

LEE-WARNER, Sir Wm. — The Native States of India — 10 / *n.* 8° Macmillan [94] 10

A new edn. of his *The Protected Princes of India* ('94): a treat. on the rel. betw. the States and the Brit. govt., on the legal and diplomatic side. There are in all some 680 Native States enjoyg. a kind of independence.

*Civil Procedure*

BROUGHTON, L. P. D. [ed.] Indian Civil Procedure, ed. C. J. Wilkinson 42 / r 8° *Calcutta* [ ] 78–82
CHAND, Hukm Comments. on Proced. of Civil Cts. in Br. India, v. i 32 / r 8° Butterworth 99
CRANENBURGH, D. E. [ed.] New Code of Civ. Proced. [w. rulings of H.C. to '87] 9 / r 8° *Calcutta* 88
GRIFFITH, W. [ed.] Code of Civ. Pro., Act xiv of '82 as modif. to '88 ; w. comms. 21 / 8° W. H. Allen 90
KNOX, G. E. Digest of Civil Proceedings in British India, 2 vols. 60 / r 8° *Allahabad* 77
NELSON, J. H. [ed.] Code of Civil Procedure ; w. notes 42 / 8° *Madras* [77] 78

*Criminal Procedure* —*v. also* **D** § 32

AGNEW (D. H.) + HENDERSON (G. S.) [eds.] Code of Crim. Procedure : Act x of 1882 42 / r 8° *Calcutta* 82
CURRIE, F. [ed.] Indian Code of Criminal Procedure 24 / r 8° *Calcutta* [ ] 74
NELSON, J. H. [ed.] Code of Criminal Procedure ; w. notes
PRINSEP, H. T. [ed.] Code of Criminal Procedure in British India 36 / r 8° *Calcutta* [*c.* 40] 88
SOHINI [ed.] Code of Crim. Proc. (Act x of 1892) ; w. notes 28 / r 8° *Bombay* [ ] 92

*Magisterial Law*

BROUGHTON, L. P. D. The Indian Magistrate's Guide 26 / r 8° *Calcutta*

*Pleading*

NAICK Pleader's Text Book, 2 vols. 22 /6 8° *Madras* 90

*Provincial Small Courts*

AIER, C. Rámachandra [ed.] Provincial Small Courts Act ix of 1887 ; w. notes 8 / 8° *Madras* 90

*Transfer of Property*

GRIFFITH, W. Commentaries on the Indian Transfer of Property Act *o.p.* [*pb.* 18 /] 8° Griffith 92
With statements of Hindu and Mohammedan laws.
SHEPHARD (Sir H. H.) + BROWN (J. C. K.) Commentaries on Ind. Trsf. Prop. Act r 8° Sonnenschein *in prep.*

**CHINA : Hong Kong**

NORTON-KYSHE, W. J. History of Laws and Courts of Hong Kong, 2 vols. 60 / *n.* 8° Unwin 99

## 108 : COURTS OF THE UNITED STATES

**The Courts Generally** —*v. also* **D** § 109, *s.v.* Pleading

ABBOTT, Austin Princs. & Forms of Practice in Civil Actions in Cts. of Record under the Codes of Procedure, 2 v. $13 8° Baker, *N.Y.* [88] 07
ANDREWS, J. D. Princs. of Pleading in Civil Actions $5 8° Callaghan, *Chicago* [ ] 01
ARMES, C. H. [ed.] Cases on Motion in U.S. Courts $3 *n.* 8° Johnson, *Phila.* 86
BATES, C. L. Federal Procedure at Law, 2 vols. $12 8° Flood, *Chicago* 08
BATES, Clement Pleadg., Practice, Parties, & Forms und. the Code, 3 v. $18 8° Anderson, *Cincinnati* 08
BAYLIES, Edm. Questions and Answers on Law and Practice $4·50 8° Banks, *N.Y.* [ ] 92
BISHOP, J. L. Code Practice in Personal Actions $4·50 *n.* 8° Baker, *N.Y.* 93
BLACK, H. C. Treat. on Laws and Practice governg. Removal of Causes fr. State Courts to Federal Courts $4 8° West Pb. Co., *St Paul, Minn.* 98
BLATCHFORD, S. Rules and Statistics of U.S. Courts $7·50 8° Baker, *N.Y.* 84
BRADBURY, H. B. Forms of Pleadg. in Legal & Equitable Actions, 2 v. $13 8° Banks, *N.Y.* 08
BUMP, O. F. Federal Procedure $6·50 *n.* 8° Cushings, *Baltimore* 81
CARTER, H. M. Jurisdiction of Federal Courts as Limited by the Citizenship and Residence of the Parties $3·50 *n.* 8° Little & Brown, *Boston* 99
CURTIS, B. R. Jurisd., Pract., and Jurispr. of Cts. of U.S., ed. H. C. Merwin $2·50 *n.* 8° Little & Brown, *Boston* [80] 96
DABNEY, W. D. Outlines of Federal Jurisdiction & Procedure $3 8° Olivier, *Univ. of Virginia* 97
DESTY, R. Federal Procedure : a manual of practice $3 8° Bancroft, *San Francisco* [ ] 89
,, Manual of Practice in Courts of U.S., 4 vols. $12 8° Bancroft, *San Francisco* [ ] 99
DEWHURST, W. W. Annotated Rules of the Federal Courts $5·50 8° Banks, *N.Y.* 1
Gives the practice of the U.S. Courts as announced by justices of Supr. Ct. and judges of these Cts.
DONOVAN, Judge J. W. —*ut* **D** § 53 (3 books)
ELLIOTT, B. K. + W. F. Treatise on General Practice, 2 v. $12 *n.* 8° Bowen-Merrill, *Indianapolis* 94
Encyclopaedia of Forms and Precedents for Pleading & Practice, ed. W. A. Michael + W. Mack + H. P. Nash, vols. i–xxvii ea. $6 *n.* 8° Thompson, *Northport, L.I.* 96–09
At Common Law, in Equity, and under the various Codes and Practice Acts.
FIELD, G. W. Treatise on Constitution and Practice of U.S. Courts $6·50 8° Johnson, *Phila.* 83

FIELD (G. W.) + MILLER (W. E.) Federal Practice $6 8° *Phila.* 81
FIERO, J. N. Practice in Special Proceedings in Cts. of Record of N.Y., 2 vols. $12·50 8° Bender, *Albany* [ ] 99
FITNAM, J. C. Treat. on Procedure in Civil Actions & Proceedgs. in Trial Cts. of Record under Civil Codes $6 *n.* 8° West Pb. Co., *St Paul, Minn.* 94
FOSTER, Roger Treatise on Federal Practice, 3 vols. ea. $3·50 8° Callaghan, *Chicago* [8–] 09
FOSTER, S. H. First Book of Practice [w. forms] $4 8° Collector Pb. Co., *Detroit* [97] 00
GARLAND, A. H., *etc.* Treatise on Constitution and Jurisdiction of U.S. Courts on Pleading, Practice, and Procedure therein, 2 vols. $12 8° Johnson, *Phila.* 98
,, + RALSTON Federal Practice : constitn. & jurisd. of U.S. Cts., 2 v. $12 *n.* 8° Johnson, *Phila.* 98
HEPBURN, C. M. [ed.] Cases & Statutes on Principles of Code Pleading $5 8° Anderson, *Cincinnati* [99] 01
HINTON, E. W. [ed.] Seln. of Cases on Law of Pleadg. und. Mod. Codes $5 8° Callaghan, *Chicago* 06
HOLT, G. C. Concurrent Jurisd. of Feder. and State Cts. $3 8° Baker, *N.Y.* 88
HUGHES, R. M. Treatise on Federal Jurisdiction & Procedure $3·75 8° West Pb. Co., *St Paul, Minn.* 04
HUGHES, W. T. Procedure : its theory and practice, 2 vols. $12 *n.* 8° Callaghan, *Chicago* 05
JOHNSTON, W. Forensic Arguments to Courts & Juries : 1846–74 $3 *n.* 8° Clarke, *Cincinnati* 87
KEEN, J. T. [ed.] Cases on Pleading $4 8° Boston Bk. Co., *Boston* 05
KINKEAD, E. B. Treatise on Law of Court Practice and Procedure $6 8° Anderson, *Cincinnati* 00
LANSING, W. [ed.] Forms of Civil Procedure of N.Y. State, 3 v. $13·50 *n.* 8° Banks, *N.Y.* [ ] 96–8
LOVELAND, F. O. [ed.] Forms of Federal Procedure $6 8° Anderson, *Richmond, Va.* 94
MCKINNEY, W. M. [ed.] Encyclop. of Pleading and Practice, 23 vols. & Suppl. i–iii ea. $6 8° Thompson, *Northport, L.I.* 95–05
MARTIN, A. Civil Procedure at Common Law $3·50 8° Boston Bk. Co., *Boston* [99] 02
MAXWELL, S. Pleadg., Pract., Procedure, & Precedents in Actions at Law and Suits in Equity, etc. $6 8° *State Jl.* Co., *Lincoln, Neb.* [92] 96
MUNSON, C. La Rue Manual of Elementary Practice $3 *n.* 8° Bowen-Merrill, *Indianapolis* 97
PAGIN, O. E. [ed.] Precedents and Forms of Indictmts., Pleas, etc. $6 8° Callaghan, *Chicago* 94
PHELPS, W. W. Chronology of Amer. Case Law to 1897 $6 8° West Pb. Co., *St Paul, Minn.* 97
REED, J. C. Conduct of Law Suits $3 *n.* 8° Little & Brown, *Boston* [75] 85
ROSE, W. M. Code of Federal Procedure, 3 vols. $18 8° Bancroft, *San Francisco* 07
RUMSEY, W. New York Practice, 3 vols. $18 8° Banks, *N.Y.* 88–97
SIMONTON, C. H. Federal Courts : organizn., jurisd., procedure $2 8° Johnson, *Richmond, Va.* [96] 98
WAIT, W. Law and Practice in Civil Actions, 3 v. $19 8° Bender, *Albany* [3rd edn. 74] 02–3
WHITTAKER, W. H. Forms of Pleading und. Codes of Civil Procedure, 2 v. ea. $6 8° Anderson, *Cincinnati* 00–2
WILLEY, W. P. Procedure in Com. Law Actns., in Equity, etc. $2·50 8° Flood, *Chicago* [94] 96

**Admiralty**

AMES, J. B. [ed.] Seln. of Cases on Law of Admlty., 3 Pts. $2·50 *n.* 8° *Harvard Law Rev.* Ass., *Cambr.* 01
BENEDICT, E. C. Admiralty Jurisdiction and Practice $6 8° Banks, *N.Y.* [50] 94
Cases on the Law of Admiralty $3 8° West Pb. Co., *St Paul, Minn.* 96
COHEN, M. M. Admiralty Jurisdiction : law and practice $5 r 8° Soule, *Boston* 83
CONKLING, A. Jurisd., Law, and Pract. of Admiralty Cts., 2 vols. $6 8° Little, *Albany* [ ] 57
DESTY, R. Shipping and Admiralty [Engl. and U.S.] $3 8° Bancroft, *San Francisco* 79
HENRY, M. P. Jurisd. and Procre. of Adm. Cts. of U.S. in Civil Cases $6 8° *Phila.* 85
,, Jurisd. and Proced. of Admir. Cts. of U.S. $5 8° Kay, *Phila.* 85
HUGHES, R. M. Admiralty Law $3·75 8° West Pb. Co., *St Paul, Minn.* 01
PARSONS, Theoph. Law of Shipping and Admiralty—*ut* **D** § 58
PUGH, E. F. Forms of Procedure in Courts of Admiralty of U.S. $5 *n.* 8° Johnston, *Phila.* [90] 03

**Appellate Procedure**

BAYLIES, Edm. New Trials and Appeals $6 8° Williamson, *Rochester* [86] 00
CURTIS, R. H. Federal Appellate Courts $2 *n.* 8° Callaghan, *Chicago* 91
ELLIOTT, R. L. Appellate Procedure and Trial Practice $6 8° 92
POWELL Appellate Proceedings $5 8° Johnson, *Phila.*

**Chancery ; Equity**

BARBOUR, O. L. Treatise on Practice of Ct. of Chancery, 3 vols. $12 8° Banks, *N.Y.* [43] 74–5
BARTON, C. History of a Suit in Equity $2·50 8° Clarke, *Cincinnati* 84
BEACH, C. F., jun. Modern Equity Practice, 2 vols. $12 8° Parsons, *Albany* 94
BISPHAM, G. T. Treat. on System of Justice admin. in Cts. of Chanc. $6·50 8° Kay, *Phila.* [ ] 82
GIBSON, H. R. Treatise in Suits in Chancery $10 r 8° Gaut-Ogden Co., *Tennessee* [74] 07
MITFORD (J.) + TYLER (S.) Pleadings and Practice in Equity $4·50 8° Baker, *N.Y.* 76
PUTERBAUGH, S. D. Chanc. Pleadg. & Practice, ed. L. D. Puterbaugh $6 *n.* 8° Callaghan, *Chicago* [82] 02
SANDS, A. H. History of a Suit in Equity $6 8° Randolph, *Richmond, Va.* [7–] 82
SHIRAS, O. P. Equity Practice in U.S. Circuit Courts $2·50 *n.* 8° Callaghan, *Chicago* [89] 98
STREET, T. A. Federal Equity Practice, 3 vols. $19·50 8° Thompson, *Northport, L.I.* 09
VAN HEYTHUYSEN, F. [ed.] The Equity Draftsman $6 8° Kay, *Phila.* [ ] 61
VAN SANTVOORD Equity Practice under New York Code, 2 vols. $6 8° Little, *Albany* [ ] 74

**Courts of Record**

NICHOLS, C. A. Pleadg. and Pract. in Cts. of Record in N.Y., 5 vols. ea. $6 8° Bender, *Albany* 04–6

**Criminal**

BISHOP, J. P. New Criminal Procedure, 2 vols. [commentaries] $12 *n.* 8° Flood, *Chicago* [80] 95
CLARK, W. L., jun. Treatise on Criminal Procedure $3·75 8° West Pb. Co., *St Paul, Minn.* 95
MAXWELL, S. Practical Treatise on Criminal Procedure $6 8° Callaghan, *Chicago* [87] 96
ROE, E. T. Criminal Procedure in United States Courts $3·50 *n.* 8° Callaghan, *Chicago* 87

**Divorce**

BISHOP, J. P. Commentaries on Law of Marriage & Divorce, 2 v. $12 8° Little & Brown, *Boston* [53] 81
WOOLSEY, T. D. Divorce and Divorce Legislation in United States $1·75 8° Scribner, *N.Y.* [69] 82

**Justices' Courts**

BRYANT, E. E. Civil & Crim. Jurisdictn. of Justices of Peace $6·50 *n.* 8° Callaghan, *Chicago* [84] 08
COWDERY, J. F. Treat. on Law & Pract. in Justices' Courts, 2 v. $13 8° Bancroft, *San Francisco* 89–92
As determ. by Statutes of Cal., Col., Nev., Oreg., Ariz., Ida., Mont., Utah, Wash.

DUGAN, P. C. Law and Pract. f. J.P.'s in State of N.Y., 2 v. $6·50 8° Bender, *Albany* 07
HAINES, E. M. Practical Treatise on Justices of the Peace $7 8° *Chicago* [ ] 93
THOMAS, Armstrong Procedure in Justice Cases [w. forms] $4·50 8° Baltimore Bk. Co., *Baltimore* 06
WAIT, W. Law & Pract. in Civil Actns. in Justices' Cts., N.Y., 3 v. ea. $6·35 8° Bender, *Albany* [65] 02–3

**Probate**

American Probate Reports, 8 vols. $40 8° Baker, *N.Y.* 81–96
GARY, G. Probate Practice $5·50 8° Callaghan, *Chicago* 79
MCCLELLAN, R. H. Probate Practice $3 8° Gould, *Albany* 75
RICE, F. S. American Probate Law and Practice $6·50 8° Bender, *N.Y.* 94
SMITH, W. L. Practice in Proceedings in Probate Court $3·50 8° *Boston* [63] 85
WOERNER, J. G. Treat. on Amer. Law of Administration, 2 v. $12 *n.* 8° Little & Brown, *Boston* [ ] 99

**Supreme Court**

ARMES, C. H. Practice of Supreme Court as to Cases Summarily Disposed of on Motion $3 *n.* 8° Johnson, *Phila.* 86
CARSON, H. L. History of Supreme Court of U.S. ; w. *c.* 50 ports. $10 8° Huber, *Phila.* 91
MAY, H. J. Treat. on Pract. and Procedure of U.S. Supr. Ct. $6 8° Byrne, *Washington* 99
PHILLIPS, P. Statutory Jurisdiction and Practice of Supr. Ct. of U.S. $5 8° [ ] 87
TAYLOR, Hannis Jurisd. & Proced. of U.S. Supr. Court $6 8° Lawyers' Co-op. Pb. Co., *Rochester, N.Y.* 05
WILLOUGHBY, W. W. The Supreme Court of the United States $1·25 8° Johns Hopk. Pr., *Baltimore* 91
[Johns Hopkins Univ. Studies : Extra vol. (vii).] Its history and influence on Amer. constitutional system.

**Surrogate's Courts** —*v. also* **D** § 100

JESSUP, H. W. Practice in Surrogate's Courts of N.Y. $8·50 8° Banks, *N.Y.* 99
MCCLELLAN, R. H. Jurisdiction of Surrogate's Courts ; w. forms $6·50 8° *Albany* [75] 80
REDFIELD, A. A. Law and Practice of Surrogate's Courts $7·50 8° Baker, *N.Y.* [77] 81

## 109 : SPECIAL WORKS ON PROCEDURE AND PRACTICE OF ALL THE COURTS

**Actions at Law**

BOYLE, H. E. Précis of an Action at Common Law 5/ 8° Butterworth 81
DICEY, Prf. A. V. Rules for Selectn. of Parties to Action 6/ 8° Maxwell 70
Amer. edn., ed. W. ALDRICH, $4 8° Linn, *Jersey City* [76] 86.
FOULKES, W. D. I. Elementary View of Proceedg. in Action [Supreme Court] 7/6 8° Sweet [75] 84
PRENTICE, S. Procedure and Evidence rel. to Indictable Offences 12/ 12° Stevens 82
" Proceedgs. in Action in Q.B., C.P., and Exch. Divs. 12/ r 12° Stevens [77] 80

*United States*

ABBOTT, B. V. + A. [eds.] Forms of Practice & Proceedings in Actions, 3 v. $15 8° Baker, *N.Y.* [73–81]
BARBOUR, O. L. Summary of Law of Parties to Actions $5 8° Little, *Albany* [7–] 84
FIERO, J. N. Practice in Special Actions in Cts. of Record of N.Y., 2 vols. $12·50 8° Bender, *N.Y.* 97
HAWES, H. Law respecting Parties to Action, Legal and Equitable $3 8° Bancroft, *San Francisco* 84
WAIT, W. [ed.] Actions and Defences, 9 vols. $40 8° Gould, *N.Y.* 77–95
WAPLES, Rufus Treatise on Proceedings in Rem $6 8° Callaghan, *Chicago* 82

*Limitations of Actions* —*v.* **D** § 56

**Affidavits** —*v.* Oaths, *inf.*

**Arbitration** —*v.* **D** § 12

**Arrest**

HAWLEY, J. G. Law of Arrest on Criminal Charges 75 c. 8° Backus, *Richmond, Va.* 86
VOORHEES, H. C. Law of Arrest in Civ. and Crim. Actions $2 8° Boston Bk. Co., *Boston* 04

**Attachment and Garnishment :** *United States—for* Attachment of Debts, *v. inf., s.v.* Debts

CABABE, M. Attachment of Debts and Equitable Execution 6/ c 8° Maxwell [81] 00
DRAKE, C. D. Treatise on Law of Suits by Attachment in U.S. $6 8° Little & Brown, *Boston* [55] 91
ROOD, J. R. Treatise on the Law of Garnishment $5 *n.* 8° West Pb. Co., *St Paul, Minn.* 96
SHINN, R. Amer. Law of Attachmt. & Garnishmt., 2 v. $12 8° Bowen-Merrill, *Indianapolis* 96
WAPLES, Rufus Attachment and Garnishment $6 *n.* 8° Flood, *Chicago* [85] 95

**Bankruptcy**

'Solicitor (A.)' Bankruptcy Procedure, Motions, and Appeals 4/ *n.* c 8° Butterworth 08

**Case Stated**

BOULTON, A. C. P. Law & Pract. of Case Stated by Ct. of Summ. Jurisd. 6/ p 8° Butterworth 02

**Certiorari :** *United States*

HARRIS, G. E. Treat. on Law of Certiorari : its use in pract. $5 8° Lawyers' Co-op. Pb. Co., *Rochester* 93

**Chambers Practice**

ARCHIBALD (W. F. A.) + VIZARD (P. E.) Practice at Judges, Chambers and in District Registries 15/ r 12° Stevens 86

**Citations**

CONNOLY (Th.) + BENJAMIN + HAVILAND + GREENE [eds.] New York Citations, 3 vols. : 1794–1898 $15 8° Little, *Albany* 87
GREENE [ed.] Analyzed Citations of N.Y. Ct. of Appeals Repts., vols. i–clix $5 8° Little, *Albany*
SILVERNAIL, W. H. [ed.] Table of New York Citations, 2 vols. $15 8° Little, *Albany* 98

**Contempt of Court**

OSWALD, J. F. Contempt of Court, Committal, and Attachment 12/6 8° Butterworth [92] 10
The first separate book on the subject. A lucid and exhaustive treatise.

*United States :* RAPALJE, S. Treatise on Contempt : civil and criminal $3·50 8° Strouse, *N.Y.* 84

**Costs** —*for* Conveyancing Acts, *v.* **D** § 30

BENNETT, J. F. C. Models of Bills of Costs [based on Layton, 1882] 21/ r 8° Stevens [82] 97
DAYES, A. C. Handybook to Solicitors' Costs 5/ *n.* 8° Sweet [ ] 06
FREEMAN, S. Guide to County Court Costs 21/ *n.* r 8° Butterworth 09
GORDON, W. E. Treat. on Law of Costs in Q.B. Div. and Ct. of Appeal *o.p.* [*pb.* 15/] 8° Knight 84
HOUGH, A. P. Handy Guide to County Court Costs 12/6 8° W. Scott [ ] 03
HUNTER, R. T. Costs in the County Courts 6/ 4° Waterlow & Layton 92
HYDE, Louis County Court Costs 12/ 8° Butterworth 04
*JOHNSON, H. M. Bills of Costs [exhaustive, dealing w. all courts] 35/ r 8° Stevens [97] 01

KING, G. A. — Costs on the High Court Scale — 20 / r 8° Stevens 10
MORGAN (G. O.) + WURTZBURG (E. A.) Treat. on Law of Costs in Chanc. *o.p.* [*pb.* 30 /] 8° Stevens [ ] 82
POCOCK, W. A. — Principles of Law of Costs under Judic. Acts — 5 / 8° Stevens 81
SCOTT, C. W. — A.B.C. Guide to Costs in Conveyancing, etc. — 5 / *n.* r 8° Waterlow 05
„ + PORTER (A. W.) — Guide to Preparation of Bills of Costs, 2 vols. — 42 / r 8° Waterlow [ ] 07
SCOTT, J. — Costs in High Court of Justice and other Courts — 26 / 8° Stevens [56] 80
SHORT, F. H. — Taxation of Costs in the Crown Office — 10 / 8° Stevens 79
SUMMERHAYS (W. F.) + TOOGOOD (T.) [eds.] Precedents of Bills of Costs, ed. T. C. Summerhays + C. G. Barber — 30 / r 8° Butterworth [77] 05
WEBSTER, E. — Parliamentary Costs, ed. C. Cavanagh — 20 / p 8° Stevens [3 edn. 67] 81

*United States*

BAIN, Donald — Costs, Fees, and Taxes (New York) — $3 8° Banks, *N.Y.* [ ] 97
BRADNER — Costs and Fees (New York) — $4·50 8° Banks, *N.Y.* 94

**Counter-claim :** *United States*

DERBY, J. S. — Counter-Claim und. Code of Civ. Proced. — $1·50 8° Williams, *Rochester* 88

**Debts, Attachment of** — —*v.* Attachment, *sup.*

**Deligence.**

STEWART, J. Graham — The Law of Diligence — 40 / *n.* r 8° Green, *Edin.* 99

**Discovery and Interrogatories**

BRAY, Judge E. — The Principles and Practice of Discovery — 12 /6 8° Stevens 85
„ — Digest of Law of Discovery, w. Pract. notes — 3 / *n.* 8° Sweet 04
PEILE, C. J. — Law and Practice of Discovery in Supr. Ct. of Justice — 12 / 8° Stevens 83
SICHEL (W. S.) + CHANCE (W.) The Law of Interrogatories and Discovery — 12 / 8° Stevens 83

**Estoppel** — —*v.* **D** § 43

**Evidence** — —*v.* **D** § 43*

**Executions**

ANDERSON, T. K. — Law of Execution in High Cts. and Inferior Cts. — 32 / 8° Butterworth 89
EDWARDS, C. J. — Law of Execution upon Judgmts. & Orders of Chanc. & Q.B. Divs. — 16 / 8° Stevens 88

*United States*

FREEMAN, A. C. — Law of Executions in Civil Cases, 3 vols. — $18 *n.* 8° Bancroft, *San Francisco* [76] 00
HERMAN, H. M. — Treatise on the Law of Executions — $4·50 r 8° Cockcroft, *N.Y.* 75
KLEBER, J. C. — Void Judicial and Execution Sales — $4·50 *n.* 8° Banks, *N.Y.* 99

**Exhibits :** *United States*

DIDIER, C. Peale — The Exhibits in an Attachment Suit — 7/6 *n.* 4° Williams Co., *Baltimore* 96

**Expert Evidence :** *United States*

BELL, J. S. — The Use and Abuse of Expert Testimony — 8° *New York* 79
ROGERS, H. W. — The Law of Expert Testimony — $3·50 8° Stevenson, *St. Louis* 83

**Extraordinary Relief**

HIGH, J. L. — Treat. on Law of Extraord. Legal Remedies — $6 *n.* 8° Callaghan, *Chicago* [74] 96
SHORTT — Extraordinary Legal Remedies, ed. F. F. Heard — $5·50 *n.* 8° Johnson, *Phila.*
SPELLING, T. C. — Treat. on Extraord. Relief in Equity and at Law, 2 vols. — $11 *n.* 8° Little & Brown, *Boston* [93] 01

Injunction, Habeas Corpus, Mandamus, Prohibition, Quo Warranto, Certiorari : an exposition of principles, w. citations of authorities.

**Habeas Corpus :** *United States*

CHURCH, W. S. — Treatise on Writ of Habeas Corpus — $7·50 r 8° Bancroft, *San Francisco* [ ] 93
HURD, R. C. — Treat on Writ. of H.C. and its Pract., ed. F. H. Hurd — $7·50 8° Little, *Albany* [ ] 76
WOOD, H. G. — On Mandamus, Prohibn., Hab. Corp., Certior., etc. — $3·50 8° Little, *Albany* [80] 91

**In Banco**

VIZARD, P. E. — Practice of the Court in Banco — 5 / 12° Sweet 80

**Indictments**

SAUNDERS, T. W. [ed.] — Precedents of Indictments — 7/6 12° Cox [72] 01
WHARTON, Fcs. [ed.] — Precedents of Indictments, 2 v. [Engl. & Amer.] — $12 8° Kay, *Phila.* [49] 84

*United States*

PAGIN, O. E. [ed.] Preceds. & Forms of Indictmts., Informatns. Complts., Declarns., Pleas, Bills in Chanc., Ansrs., etc., adapted to U.S. crim. & civ. cases, etc. $6 8° Callaghan, *Chicago* 94

**Informations ; Mandamus ; Prohibition ; Quo Warranto**

SHORTT, Jno. Informations [crim. and Quo Warranto], Mandamus, & Prohibition 42 / r 8° Butterworth 87

*United States*

BLACK, H. C. Essay on Constitutional Prohibitions $3·50 *n.* 8° Little & Brown, *Boston* 87

HIGH, J. L. —*in his* Extraordinary Remedies, *ut sup.*

MERRILL, S. S. The Law of Mandamus $5 *n.* 8° Flood, *Chicago* 92

MOSES, H. H. The Law of Mandamus $3·50 8° Gould, *Albany* 66

SPELLING, T. C. —*in his* Injunctions, *ut inf.*

WOOD, H. G. On Mandamus—*ut sup.*, *s.v.* Habeas Corpus

**Injunctions**

JOYCE, W. Law and Practice of Injunctions, 2 v. [comprehensive] 70 / r 8° Stevens 72

,, Doctrine and Principle of Law of Injunctions 30 / r 8° Stevens 77

KERR, W. W. Treatise on Law and Pract. of Injunctions, ed. E. P. Hewitt 35 / r 8° Sweet [67] 03
Amer. edn., ed. DICKSON, $4 8° '89.

*United States*

BEACH, C. F., Jun. Modern Equity: Law of Injunctions, 2 vols $12 8° Parsons. *Albany, N.Y.* 95

HIGH, J. L. Treatise on the Law of Injunctions, 2 v. $11 *n.* r 8° Callaghan, *Chicago* [73] 90

HILLIARD, F. The Law of Injunctions $6 8° Kay, *Phila.* [2 edn. 69] 74

SPELLING, T. C. The Law of Injunctions, 2 vols. $12 *n.* 8° Little & Brown, *Boston* [ ] 01

**Interpleaders**

CABABE, M. Interpleader in High Ct. of Justice and County Courts 6 / 8° Sweet [81] 00

MACLENNAN, R. J. Law of Interpleader [Eng., Ir., Am., Can., Austr.] 25 / 8° Stevens 02

MERLIN, S. P. Law and Pract. of Interpleader in High Ct. and Cty. Cts. 6 / *n.* 8° Butterworth 07

WARDE, D. Pract. of Interpleader by Sheriff and High Bailiff 5 /6 p 8° [ ] 04

**Interrogatories** —*v.* Discovery, *sup.*

**Judgments** —*v. also* Executions, *sup.*, and **D** § 103

*PIGGOTT, Sir Fcs. T. Foreign Judgmts. and Parties out of Jurisd., Pt. i 40 / *n.*, ii 35 / *n.*, iii r 8° Butterworth [79–81] 08–9

,, Service out of the Jurisdiction 15 / r 8° Butterworth 92

*United States*

BLACK, H. C. Treatise on the Law of Judgments, 2 v. $12 8° Bancroft, *San Francisco* [97] 02

FREEMAN, A. C. Treatise on the Law of Judgments $10 *n.* r 8° Bancroft, *San Francisco* [2nd ed. 74] 92

**Jurisdiction :** *United States*

BAILEY, W. F. Law of Jurisdiction, 2 vols. $12 8° Flood, *Chicago* 99

BROWN, Tim. Commentaries on the Jurisdiction of Courts $6 *n.* 8° Callaghan, *Chicago* [91] 01

CURTIS, B. R. Jurisdiction of the United States Cts. $2·50 *n.* 8° Little & Brown, *Boston* [ ] 96

HAWES, Hor. Law rel. to Jurisdiction of Courts $3 8° Whitney, *San Francisco* 86

HOLT, G. Concurrent Jurisdiction of Federal and State Courts $3 8° Baker, *N.Y.* 88

KEENER, W. A. [ed.] Cases on Equity Jurisdiction, 3 vols. ea. $6 *n.* 8° Baker, *N.Y.* 95

MURFREE, W. L., jun. Jurisdiction of the Justice Courts $5 8° Thomas, *St Louis* 87

Works' Courts and their Jurisdiction $6 8° [ ] 97

**Jury** —*v. also* **D** § 135

ERLE, J. W. Jury Laws and their Amendment 5 / 8° 8:

HOLLAND, S. L. The Juryman's Handbook [Legal Handybooks] 1 / f 8° E. Wilson 91

*History of Trial by Jury* —*v.* **D** § 5

*Ireland*

FOOT, C. H. [ed.] Grand Jury Laws of Ireland *o.p.* [*pb.* 12 /6] 8° **Dublin 61**

HUBAND, W. G. Practical Treatise on the Law rel. to Grand Jury, Coroner's Jury, and Petty Jury in Ireland 25 / *n.* r 8° **96**

*United States*

CLEMENTSON, G. B. Treatise on Special Verdicts & Special Findings by Jury $3·75 8° West Pb. Co., *St Paul, Minn.* 05

DONOVAN, Judge J. W. Modern Jury Trials [*v. also* **D** § 53] $4·50 *n.* 8° Banks, *N.Y.* [ ] 85

HIRSH, H. On Juries: treatise on powers, duties, and uses $4 8° 79

PROFFATT, J. Treatise on Trial by Jury; w. questns. of law & fact $7·50 8° Whitney, *Phila.* 76

SACKETT, F. Instructions to Juries $6 8° Callaghan, *Chicago* [ ] 88

THOMPSON, S. D. Charging the Jury $2 8° Stevenson, *St Louis* 80

,, + MERRIAM (E. G.) Treatise on Juries, including Grand Juries $6·50 8° Stevenson, *St Louis* 82

**Mandamus** —*v.* Informations, *sup.*

**Notice:** *United States*

WADE, W. P. Notice as affectg. Civil Rights and Remedies $6 8° Callaghan, *Chicago* [ ] 86

**Oaths**

BRAITHWAITE, T. W. Manual for Administration of Oaths in Supr. Ct. of Judic. 2/6 12° Stevens [54] 84

FORD, C. Oaths in Supr. Ct. of Judicature, ed. F. H. Short 3/6 *n.* 12° Stevens [ ] 03

HUME-WILLIAMS (W. E.) + MACKLIN (A. R.) Taking of Evidence on Commission 12/6 8° Stevens [ ] 02

STRINGER, F. A. Oaths and Affirmations in Great Britain and Ireland 4/ c 8° Stevens [90] 93

*Colonial*

SOLOMON, G. E. New Manual for Colonial Commissioners for Oaths 3/ *n.* 8° 03

*United States*

ENDLICH, G. A. Law of Affidavits of Defence in Pennsylvania $5 8° Linn, *Jersey City* 84

**Onus Probandi**

BAILEY, W. H. Onus Probandi, Prep. for Trial, etc. $6 8° Banks, *N.Y.* 86

**Parties to Actions** —*v.* Actions, *sup.*

**Petition of Right**

CLODE, Walt. [ed.] Law and Prac. of Petit. of Right [=Act of 1860] 10/6 8° Butterworth 87

**Petitions** —*v.* **D** § 103, *s.v.* Chancery; **D** § 26; **D** § 41

**Pleading** —*for* Art of Pleading *v.* **D** § 53

*Civil*

ALLAN, G. B. + W. B. [eds.] Forms of Indorsements of Writs of Summons, Pleadings and other Proceedings in Q.B.D. prior to Trial 18/ 12° Stevens 83

ARCHBOLD, J. F. Civil Pleading & Evidence [$3 *n.* Banks, *N.Y.*] *o.p.* [*pb.* 16/] 8° Benning [ ] 38

BULLEN (E.) + LEAKE (S. M.) Precedents of Pleading—*ut* **D** § 103, *s.v.* King's Bench

CUNNINGHAM (J.) + MATTINSON (M. W.) Precdts. of Plg., ed. M. W. Mattinson + S. C. Macaskie 28/ 8° Stevens [78] 84

ODGERS, Dr W. B. Princs. of Pleading in Civil Actns. und. Judic. Acts 12/6 8° Stevens [91] 06

*South African Colonies*

BUCHANAN, J. [ed.] Precedents of Pleading in Supr. Ct., Cape of Good Hope 21/ 8° *Cape Town* 78

*United States* —*v. also* **D** § 108

*Code*

ABBOTT, Austin [ed.] Select Cases on Code Pleading [w. notes] $6 8° Diossy, *N.Y.* [ ] 95

,, [ed.] Forms of Pleading, 2 vols. $13 *n.* 8° Baker, *N.Y.* [77] 99

BAYLIES, Edm. Code Pleading and Forms $6 8° Williamson, *Rochester* 90

BLISS, Philemon Law of Code Pleading, ed. Prf. E. F. Johnson $6 *n.* 8° West Pb. Co., *St Paul, Minn.* [79] 94

BOONE, C. T. Pleading under the Codes $3 8° Whitney, *San Francisco* 85

BRYANT, E. E. Law of Pleading under the Codes $2·50 *n.* 8° Little & Brown, *Boston* 99

ESTEE, M. M. [ed.] Pleadgs., Pract., & Forms, ed. C. T. Boone, 3 v. $18 8° Bancroft, *San Francisco* [70] 98

EVANS, H. D. Pleading in Civil Actions, ed. W. Miller $2·50 8° [ ] 86

HEARD, F. Principles of Pleading in Civil Actions $2·50 *n.* 8° Little & Brown, *Boston* 80

HEPBURN, C. McG. Development of Code Pleading [Am. & Engl.] $2·50 *n.* 8° Anderson, *Cincinnati* 97

MAXWELL, S. Treat. on Law of Pleading under the Code $6 *n.* 8° Callaghan, *Chicago* 92

PHILLIPS, G. L. Princs. of Pleading und. Codes of Civ. Proc. $5 *n.* 8° Callaghan, *Chicago* 96

SUTHERLAND, W. A. Treatise on Code Pleading and Practice, 4 v. $26 *n.* 8° Bancroft, *San Francisco* 10
VAN SANTVOORD, G. [ed.] Pleadings and Precedents under the Code, 2 vols. $8 8° Little, *Albany* 73

*Common Law*

GOULD, Jas. Princs. of Pleading in Civ. Actns., ed. F. F. Heard $2·50 8° Gould, *Albany* [4th edn. 73] 87
,, The same, ed. A. Hamilton $4 *n.* 8° Lawyers' Co-op. Pb. Co., *Rochester* [4th edn. 73] 99
MCKELVEY, J. J. Principles of Common Law Pleading $2 *n.* 8° Baker, *N.Y.* 94
PERRY, R. R. Common Law Pleading: hist. and principles $3·50 *n.* 8° Little & Brown, *Boston* 97
SHIPMAN, B. J. Handbook of Common-Law Pleading $3·75 *n.* 8° West Pb. Co., *St Paul, Minn.* [94] 95
STEPHEN, H. J. Princs. of Pleading in Civil Actions, ed. Andrews $5 *n.* 8° Callaghan, *Chicago* [ ] 01
Other Amer. edns. (1) ed. TYLER, $2·50 *n.* Morrison, *Washgtn.* 71; (2) ed. F. F. HEARD, $2·50 *n.* 8° Kay, *Phila.* [ ] 67; (3) ed. S. WILLISTON, $4 8° *Harvard Law Rev.*, Pb. Ass., *Camb.* 96.

*Criminal*

BASSETT, Jas. Criminal Pleading and Practice, ed. H. Binmore $5 8° Myers, *Chicago* [69] 85
BEALE, J. H., jun. Law of Criminal Pleading $2·50 *n.* 8° Little & Brown, *Boston* 99
HEARD, F. F. Criminal Pleading $2·50 *n.* 8° Little & Brown, *Boston* 79
WHARTON, Fcs. Criminal Pleading and Practice $6 8° Kay, *Phila.* [ ] 89

*Equity*

HEARD, F. Concise Treat. on Princs. of Equity Pleading $2 *n.* 8° Soule, *Boston* 82
,, [ed.] Precedents of Equity Pleadings $3 8° Little & Brown, *Boston* 84
LANGDELL, C. C. [ed.] Cases in Equity Pleading $5 *n.* 8° 78
,, Summary of Equity Pleading $3 *n.* 8° Sever, *Cambr., Mass.* [ ] 83
MERWIN, Elias Princs. of Equity & Eq. Pleading, ed. H. C. Merwin $6 8° Houghton, *Boston* 95
MITFORD (J.) + TYLER (S.) Pleadings and Practice in Equity—*ut* **D** § 108
SHIPMAN, B. J. Treatise in Equity Pleading $3·75 *n.* 8° West Pb. Co., *St Paul, Minn.* 97
STORY, Jos. Commentaries on Equity Pleadings, ed. J. M. Gould [Engl. and Amer.] $6 8° Little & Brown, *Boston* [38] 92

**Power of Attorney; Proxy**

MACKENZIE, V. St C. Law rel. to Powers of Attorney and Proxies 3/6 *n.* c 8° E. Wilson 03

**Quo Warranto**—*v.* Informations, *sup.* **Receivers**—*v.* **D** § 17

**Removal of Causes**

BLACK, H. C. Treat. on Removal of Causes [based on Dillon] $4 *n.* 8° West Pb. Co., *St Paul, Minn.* 98
DILLON, Judge J. F. Removal of Causes fr. State to Federal Cts. $3 8° *Cent. Law Jl.* Co., *St Louis* [77] 89

**Replevin** —*v. also* **D** § 15; **D** § 105 (PITT-LEWIS)

MORRIS, P. P. Practical Treatise on Law of Replevin in U.S. $5 r 8° Kay, *Phila.* [49] 78
WELLS, H. W. Treatise on the Law of Replevin $6·50 8° Callaghan, *Chicago* 79

**Res Judicata; Stare Decisis**

CHAMBERLAIN Stare Decisis 75 c. *n.* 8° 85
CHAND, Hukm Treatise on the Law of Res Judicata 42/ r 8° Butterworth 94
Incl. Doctrines of Jurispr., Bar by Suit, and Lis Pendens: intended for legal profession in India, but generally useful.

*United States*

HERMAN, H. M. Comments. on Law of Estoppel and Res Judicata—*ut* **D** § 43
WELLS, J. C. Treatise on Doctrines of Res Adjudicata & Stare Decisis $6 *n.* 8° Miles, *Des Moines* 78

**Service out of the Jurisdiction**

PIGGOTT, F. T. Service out of the Jurisdiction 15/ r 8° Clowes 92

**Subrogation**

HARRIS, G. E. Treatise on the Law of Subrogation $6 8° Banks, *N.Y.* 89
SHELDON, H. N. The Law of Subrogation $5 8° Boston Bk. Co., *Boston* [82] 93

**Summary Jurisdiction** —*v.* **D** § 105

**Summons for Directions**

STRINGER, F. A. Practice on the Summons for Directions 5/ 8° Sweet 99

**Summons (Originating)**

MARCY (G. N.) + SIMPKIN (O. R. A.) [eds.] Forms of Orig. Summons and Procgs. conn. therewith 6/ 8° Cox [95] 09

**Witnesses**

SICHEL, Walt. S. Practice rel. to Witnesses [Superior & Inferior Cts.] 7/6 c 8° Butterworth 87

*United States*

HEADLEY, R. Competency and Rights of Witnesses and Parties $3·50 8° Bender, *Albany* 97

RAPALJIE, S. Treatise on the Law of Witnesses $6 8° Banks, *N.Y.* 87

**Writs of Summons**

CLAY, W. G. Law and Pract. rel. to Writs of Summ.: issue & service 5/ c 8° Butterworth 94

*United States*

ALDERSON, Wm. A. Law of Judic. Writs & Process in Civ. & Crim. Cases $6 *n.* 8° Baker, *N.Y.* 95

---

# VII: Roman, and Oriental, Law

## 110: ROMAN LAW

**Bibliography** —*in* MACKENZIE, *and* MUIRHEAD, *ut inf.*, *s.v.* History

**Sources, and Latin Jurists**

BRUNS, C. G. [ed.] Fontes Juris Romani Antiqui, ed. Th. Mommsen 8*m.* 50 8° *Freiburg* [79] 86–7

Corpus Juris Civilis: edd. Fratres Kriegelii, 3 Pts. 15*m.* 8° Kohlhammer, *Stuttgart* [ ] 87

The cheapest edn. Pt. i: *Institutiones Digesta* (KREIGEL); ii: *Codex* (Aem. HERMANN); iii: *Novellae* (OSENBRÜGGEN).

,, rec. P. Krüger + Th. Mommsen, 3 vols. 21*m.* 4° *Berlin* [77] 95

i: *Institutiones*, (KRÜGER), *Digesta* (MOMMSEN), 10 *m.*; ii: *Codex Justin.* (KRÜGER), 6*m.*; iii: *Novellae* [R. SCHÖLL], 5*m.*

Novellae extra Codicem, rec. C. E. Zacharias a Lingenthal, 2 v., 10*m.* 50; Appendix 1*m.* s 8° *Leipzig* 81–4

Codex Justinianus: rec. P. Krüger, 2 vols.; plates 42*m.* 4° Weidmann, *Berlin* 73–7

Jurisprud. Antejustin. quae supersunt, ed. P. Krüger + Th. Mommsen + W. Studemund, 2 Pts.
6*m.* p 8° Weidmann, *Berlin* [77–8] 91

i: Gaius, 3*m.*; ii: Ulpian, 3*m.*

**Gaius**

TEXTS: Instit. Codiciis Veron. collati, ed. W. Studemund 36*m.* 4° *Leipzig* 74

,, w. JUSTIN. & ULPIAN: rec. R. Gneist, *s.t.* Instit. Juris Rom. Syntagma
[in parallel cols.] 5*m.* 50 p 8° *Leipzig* [58] 81

ANNOTATED TEXTS AND TRANSLATIONS

Institutes, and Rules of Ulpian: tr. J. T. Abdy + B. Walker; w. notes
[$4 Putnam, *N.Y.*] 16/ c 8° Camb. Press [70]

,, and Rules of Ulpian: ed. Jas. Muirhead; w. tr. and notes 21/ 8° Clark, *Edin.* [80] 04

Former ed. fr. STUDEMUND'S Apograph of the Verona Codex. Crit. and explan. notes, and alphab. digest.

* ,, ed. E. Poste, w. tr. and comm.; rev. A. Whittuck 16/ ($5·25) 8° Clar. Press [71] 04

,, Digest xiv, Digest xlv: tr. J. G. Trapnell
[New Classical Lib.] 1/6 *n.*; 3/6 *n.* c 8° Sonnenschein 09–09

**Justinian**

TEXTS —*v.* Corpus Juris Civilis, *sup.*

ANNOTATED TEXTS AND TRANSLATIONS

Digest: tr. C. H. Monro, 2 vols. [ea. $4 *n.* Putnam, *N.Y.*] ea. 12/ *n.* r 8° Camb. Press 04–9

vii, 1: *De Usufructu*, ed. H. J. ROBY; w. legal and philolog. comm. [$2·50 *n.* Putnam, *N.Y.*] 9/ 8° Camb. Press 86
ix, 2: *Lex Aquilia*, tr. C. H. MONRO: w. tr. and notes [$1·25 *n.* Putnam, *N.Y.*] 5/ c 8° Camb. Press 98
xvii, 2: *Pro Socio*, tr. C. H. MONRO: w. notes [$1·25 *n.* Putnam, *N.Y.*] 5/ c 8° Camb. Press 02
xviii 1, and xix, 1: *Law of Sale*, tr. J. MACKINTOSH 10/ *n.* 8° Clark. *Edin.* [ ] 07
xix, 2: *Locali Conducti*, tr. C. H. MONRO; w. notes [$1·25 *n.* Putnam, *N.Y.*] 5/ c 8° Camb. Press 94
xx: ed. S. C. JACKSON; w. tr. 7/6 *n.* c 8° Sweet 08

Incl. an Essay on the law of mortgage in Roman law.

xli, 1: *De Adquirendo Rerum Dominio*, tr. C. H. MONRO; w. notes [$1·25 *n.* Putnam, *N.Y.*] 5/ c 8° Camb. Press 00
xlvii, 2: *De Furtis*, tr. C. H. MONRO; w. notes [$1·25 *n.* Putnam, *N.Y.*] 5/ c 8° Camb. Press 93

Selected Titles: ed. Prf. T. E. Holland + C. L. Shadwell 14/ ($3·75) 8° Clar. Press [74–81] 84

Also in parts—i: *Introd. Titles*, 2/6 (60 c.); ii: *Family Law*, 1/ (25 c.); iii: *Property Law*, 2/6 (60 c.); *Obligations* (1), 3/6 (90 c.); (2), 4/6 ($1·10).

,, ed. Bryan Walker [Putnam, *N.Y.*] c 8° Camb. Press 79–81

Pt. i: *Mandati vel Contra* (Dig. xvii, 1), 5/ ($1·50 *n.*); Pt. ii: *Dig. xli*, 1 and 2; *o.p.*; Pt. iii: *De Condictionibus* (Dig. xii, 1 and 4–7; xiii, 1–3), 6/ ($1·75 *n.*); Pt. iv: *De Servitutibus* (Dig. viii) *o.p.*

Institutions: *ed. J. B. Moyle, 2 vols. 22/ ($5·50) 8° Clar. Press [83] 03–6

Vol. i.: Introd., text, and Commentary, 16/ ($4); ii: Translation, 6/ ($1·50).

,, ed. Prf. T. E. Holland [as a recension of Gaius] 5/ ($1·25) f 8° Clar. Press [73] 81

,, ed. T. C. Sandars; w. tr., Introd., and notes 18/ ($6) 8° Longman [59] 05

Institutes: tr. J. T. Abdy + B. Walker; w. notes [$4 Putnam, *N.Y.*] 16/ c 8° Camb. Press 76

AIDS

ORTOLAN, J. L. E. Explication des Institutions de Justinien : vol. i [Introd.], 9/; ii–iii [text & Fch. tr.] 18/ 8° *Paris* [ ] 80

ROBY, Prf. H. J. Introd. to Study of Justinian's Digest [$2·50 *n.* Putnam, *N.Y.*] 9/ 8° Camb. Press 84

VOET, G. Commentary on the Pandects, tr. T. Berwick 21/ 8° Stevens & Haynes [ ] 02
Other edns., by var. trs. : *Bk. xii, Tit.* 1, 5/ *n.* ; xviii, 10/6 *n.* ; xviii–xxi and xiii, *Tit.* 7, 24/6 *n.* ; xxiv, *Titt.* 1–3, 8/6 *n.* ; xxx–xxxii, 8/6 *n.* ; xxxix, *Titt.* 5/6, 10/ *n.* ; xlvi, *Titt.* 1–3, 22/ *n.* ; xlvii, *Tit.* 10, 5/ *n.* ; xlviii, *Titt.* 4 and 6, 8/6 *n.*

" Pandects, Bk. xlvii, tit. 10 : Injuries, tr. M. De Villiers 42/ 8° 99

WILLIAMS, J. Institutes of Justinian illustrated by English Law 7/6 p 8° Butterworth [83] 93

**Legis XII Tabularum Reliquiae :** ed. Schoell 3*m.* 50 8° *Leipzig* 66
Is also contained in BRUNS' *Fontes Juris Romani Antiqui* and GAIUS, rec. Gneist, *ut sup.*

VOIGT, M. Civil- u. Crimin.-Recht. der XII. Tafeln, 2 vols. 30*m.* 8° *Leipzig* 83

" Ueber die Leges Regiae, 2 Pts. 12*m.* i 8° *Leipzig* 76–7

**Lex Salica :** the ten texts, ed. J. H. Hessels + Kern [synopt. arrangemt., w. glosses] 42/ 4° Murray 80

**Ulpian** —*v. sup.*, Jurisp. Antejustin. ; GAIUS

**Salvius Julianus**

WALKER, B. [ed.] Fragments of the Perpetual Edict of Salvius Julianus ; w. notes [$1·50 *n.* Putnam, *N.Y.*] 6/ c 8° Camb. Press 77

**History, Exposition, Introduction**—*for* English Civil Law, *v.* **D** § 25

AMOS, Prf. Sheldon History and Principles of Civil Law of Rome 16/ 8° Paul 83

BERNARD, Fern. First Year of Roman Law, tr. C. P. Sherman $1 16° Clar. Press *N.Y.* 06

BUSS, S. Roman Law and History in the New Testament—*ut* **A** § 46

CAMPBELL, Gordon Compendium of Roman Law [based on Justinian] 12/ 8° Murray [78] 92

CHALMERS (D.) + BARNES (L. H.) Guide to Roman Law : Justinian & Gaius 7/6 *n.* c 8° Butterworth 07

CLARK, Prf. E. C. History of Roman Private Law, Pt. i : Sources and Chronol. Sketch [$1·50 *n.* Putnam, *N.Y.*] 4/6 *n.* c 8° Camb. Press 06

GIBBON, E. —*in his* Decline and Fall of Rom. Emp. [*ut* **F** § 12], *esp.* chap. xliv
A fine chapter on Roman law. *Cf.* also the Roman Histories of NIEBUHR and of MOMMSEN [*ut* F § 12].

GIRARD, P. F. Short Hist. of Roman Law [tr.] [w. bibliogr.] 12/6 *n.* c 8° Canada Law Bk. Co., *Toronto* 07

*GREENIDGE, A. H. J. Legal Procedure in Cicero's Time 25/ *n.* ($7·75) 8° Clar. Press 01
A very complete and valuable study. Full indexes.

" —*in his* Roman Public Life, *ut* **F** § 12

HADLEY, Prf. Jas. Introduction to Roman Law [twelve lectures] $1·25 16° Appleton, *New York* [73] 04
The complete Institutes of Roman Law apart fr. law of actions. Interestingly wr., and clear.

HARRIS, S. F. Elements of Roman Law Summarized 6/ c 8° Stevens & Haynes [ ] 99

HOWE, W. W. Studies in Civil Law and its Relations to the Jurisprudence of England and America $3 *n.* 8° Little & Brown, *Boston* [96] 05

HUNTER, Prf. W. A. Exposn. of Rom. Law in order of a Code, ed. J. A. Cross 32/ 8° Sweet [76] 03
Systematic and historical. Embodies the *Institutes* of GAIUS and of JUSTINIAN translated.

" Introd. to Study of Roman Law [w. gloss. of terms] 7/6 p 8° Sweet [80] 08

LEAGE, R. W. Roman Private Law 10/ *n.* ($3·25 *n.*) 8° Macmillan 06
Gives the subject-matter of the *Institutes* of GAIUS and JUSTINIAN. An excellent introduction for students.

VAN LEEUWEN, S. Censura Forensis r 8° –02
Pt. i, Bk. ii [*Law of Things*], tr. A. J. FOORD, 12/6 ; Bk. iii, 19/6 ; Bk. iv [tr S. H. BARBER + W. A. MACFADYEN], 37/6 *n.*

MACKELDEY Roman Law, ed. Dropsie $6·50 *n.* 8° Johnson, *Phila.* [ ]

MACKENZIE, L'd Studies in Roman Law, ed. J. Kirkpatrick 21/ 8° Blackwood [62] 98
$8·40 Scribner, *N.Y.* With compar. views of laws of France, Engl. and Scotl. One of the best bks. for the non-professional student.

MUIRHEAD, Prf. Jas. Hist. Introd. to the Private Law of Rome, ed. H. Goudy [$5 *n.* Macmillan, *N.Y.*] 21/ 8° Black [86] 99
Orig. wr. for the *Encyclo. Brit.*, but found to be too long and abridged. Here pubd. *in extenso.*

NASMITH, Dav. Outline of Roman History fr. Romulus to Justinian *red. to* 10/ *n.* 8° Butterworth 90
With special reference to Roman jurisprudence, inclg. trs. of *Institutes* of GAIUS and of JUSTINIAN.

ORTOLAN, J. L. E. History of Rom. Law, tr. T. T. Prichard + D. Nasmith, ed. J. Cutler 15/ 8° Butterworth [71] 96

ROBY, H. J. Roman Private Law in the Time of Cicero and the Antonines, 2 v. 30/ *n.* 8° Camb. Pr. 02
$8 *n.* Putnam, *N.Y.* A detailed study of pre-Justinian Roman law.

SALKOWSKI, Dr F. C. Instits. & Hist. of Rom. Private Law, tr. E. E. Whitfield 32/ 8° Stevens 86

v. SAVIGNY, F. C. Roman Law during Middle Ages, 2 vols. 8° Wildy 29–84
Vol. i, tr. CATHCART, *o.p.* ; ii [*Relations*], tr. W. H. RATTIGAN, 16/. Shows influence of Roman law on laws, customs, and institns. of the Germanic nations and races dur. Middle Ages.

SCRUTTON, Prf. T. E. Influence of Roman Law on Law of England [Yorke Prize Ess.] *o.p.* [*pb.* 10/6] 8° Camb. Press 85

*SOHM, Prf. Rud. Institutes of Roman Law, tr. J. C. Leslie 16/ ($5·25) 8° Clar. Press [92] 07
TOMKINS (F. J.) + JENKEN (H. D.) Modern Rom. Law [a compendium] *o.p.* [*pb.* 14/] 8° Butterworth 70
VINOGRADOFF, Prf. P. Rom. Law in Mediaev. Europe [Lib. of Living Thought] 2/6 *n.* (75*c.*) c 8° Harper 09
WALTON, F. P. Historical Introduction to Roman Law 7/6 *n.* 8° Green, *Edin.* 03

**Contracts**

BUCKLER, W. H. Orig. & Hist. of Contract in Rom. Law [Yorke Pr. Ess.] *o.p.* c 8° Camb. Pr. 94
HARVEY, W. F. Brief Digest of Roman Law of Contract 3/6 12° Simpkin 78
MOYLE, J. B. Contract of Sale in Civil Law 10/6 ($2·50) 8° Clar. Press 92
With reference to the laws of England, Scotland, and France.

**Damage to Property**

GRUEBER, Dr E. Roman Law of Damage to Property 10/6 ($2·75) 8° Clar. Press 86
A commentary on the title of the Digest *Ad Legem Aquilam* (ix, 2), w. Introd. to study of *Corpus Juris Civilis*.

**Infamia**

GREENIDGE, A. H. J. Infamia, its Place in Roman Public & Private Law 10/6 ($2·60) 8° Clar. Press 94

**Persons**

RATTIGAN, W. H. De Jure Personarum *o.p.* [*pb.* 15/] 8° Wildy 73
v. SAVIGNY, Dr F. C. Jural Relations, tr. W. H. Rattigan 16/ 8° Wildy 84
The Rom. law of persons as subjs. of jural relations. A tr. of the 2nd Bk. of the author's *System d. heutigen Römischen Rechts*, 2 vols. 8°, 51–3.

**Procedure** *v.* Greenidge, Legal Procedure—*ut sup.*

**Roman-Dutch Law** [still in force in Ceylon, Guiana and all S. Afr. Cols. and States]

BELMONTE, B. E. J. C. The Law of Inheritance ab Intestato 40/ *n.* r 8° Sweet 08
,, Legitimate Portion under Roman-Dutch Law 4/6 *n.* c 8° Sweet 07
GROTIUS, Hugo [1583–1645] Introduction to Dutch Jurisprudence, w. notes S. van G. van der Made, tr. A. F. S. Maasdorp 35/ *n.* c 8° *Cape Town* [86] 03
Van der Kessel, D. G. Select Theses on Laws of Holland and Zeeland [tr.] 15/ *n.* 12° Sweet, [ ] 84
A commentary on GROTIUS *Introduction*.
,, Opinions of, as cont. in 'Hollandsche Consultatien en Advijsen,' tr. D. P. de Bruyn; w. notes 40/ 8° 94
,, De Jure Belli et Pacis—*ut* **D** § 113
MAASDORP, A. F. S. Institutes of Cape Law, 4 vols. ea. 31/ *n.* 8° *Cape Town* [ ] 07–9
i: *Law of Persons*; ii: *Law of Things*; iii: *Obligations and Contracts*; iv: *Delicts, or Torts.*
MORICE, G. T. English and Roman-Dutch Law 28/6 *n.* 8° Butterworth [ ] 05
NATHAN, Dr Manfred The Common Law of South Africa, 4 vols. £9 13/ *n.* 8° Butterworth 04–7
A treatise based on VOET'S *Comms.* [*ut sup.*]. Vols. i–ii £4 *n.*, iii £3 3/ *n.*, iv £2 10/ *n.*
THOMSON, H. Bryerley Institutes of the Laws of Ceylon, 2 vols. *o.p.* [*pb.* 32/] 8° Trübner (Paul) 66
VAN LEEUWEN, S. Commentaries on Roman Dutch Law, ed. C. W. Decker [1820], w. notes; tr. J. G. Kotzé vol. i, 40/; ii, 50/ r 8° *Cape Town* 81–7
VAN DER LINDE Institutes of Laws of Holland, tr. H. Juta 32/6 *n.* 8° [ ] 06
Lee, W. T. Elements of Roman-Dutch Law [digest of above] 10/6 *n.* 8° 03
WESSELS, Hon. J. W. History of Roman Dutch Law 31/ *n.* r 8° Afric. Bk. Co., *Grahamstown* 08

**Slavery**

BUCKLAND, W. W. The Roman Law of Slavery 18/ *n.* 8° Camb. Press 08
$5·75 *n.* Putnam, *N.Y.* A substantial wk., of a standard character—the first comprehensive study of the subj. Pt. i deals w. condition of the slave, divided into sectns. on the slave as *res*, slave as man, *servus vicarius*, *hereditarius*, *fugitivus*, etc.; Pt. ii w. enslavement and manumission. Five Appendices.

**Trichotomy**

GOUDY, Prf. H. Trichotomy in Roman Law 4/ *n.* 8° Clar. Press 10

**Wills**

DROPSIE Roman Law of Testaments $3 *n.* 8° Johnson, *Phila.* 92

**Spain and Spanish-America**

WALTON, C. S. Civil Law in Spain & Spanish-America $6·25 *n.* 8° Lowdermilk, *Washington* 00

---

# VIII: Hindu, and Mohammedan, Law

## 111: HINDU LAW

**Commentaries, Digests, etc.**

COWELL, H. Short Treat. on Hindu Law as admin. in Brit. India 10/ *n.* 8° Thacker 95

CUNNINGHAM, H. S. Digest of Hindu Law as admin. in Cts. of Madras Presid. 15 / 8° *Calcutta* 77
GHOSE, Prf. Jogendra Chunder The Principles of Hindu Law 10rs. 8° Auddy, *Calcutta* 03
MACNAGHTEN, Sir W. H. Princs. of Hindu and Mohamm. Law, ed. Prf. Wilson 6 / 8° Norgate [25–9] 82
,, Principles and Precedents of Hindu Law, 2 v.; w. notes 30 / 8° Norgate [2nd ed. 62] 74
MARKBY, Sir W. Introd. to Hindu & Mahom. Law [Student's bk.] 6 / *n.* ($2) 8° Clar. Press 06
*MAYNE, J. D. Treatise on Hindu Law and Usage 30 / *n.* 8° Stevens [57] 06
NELSON, J. H. View of Hindu Law as admin. by H. C. of Madras 14 / 8° *Madras* 77
,, Scientific Study of the Hindu Law 9 / 8° Paul 81
,, Indian Usage and Judge-made Law in Madras 12 / 8° Paul 87
RATTIGAN, W. H. Digest of Civil Law of the Punjab 11 / *n.* 8° Stevens & Haynes [ ] 01
,, [ed.] Select Cases in Hindu Law decided in Privy Council and Superior Cts. in India, 2 vols.; w. notes 50 / *n.* 8° Wildy 71

**Adoption**: RATTIGAN (W. H.) The Hindu Law of Adoption *o.p.* [*pb.* 8/6] 8° Wildy 73

**Castes** —*v.* **E** § 35, *s.v.* Castes

**Contracts and Successions**

COLEBROOKE, H. T. [tr.] Digest of Hindu Law on Contrs. and Succns., 2 vols [tr. fr. Sanskrit.] 63 / 8° *Madras* [1797] 74

**Customary Law** —*v. also* **E** § 35, *s.v.* Ethnology

ROSE, H. A. Compendium of Punjab Customary Law [pp. 103] 8° *Civ. & Mil. Gaz.* Pr., *Lahore* 09
Punjab Customary Law, vols. i–xix. 8° *Calcutta* 81

**Inheritance, Partition, Stridhan, Wills**

COLEBROOK, H. T. Two Treats. on Hindu Law of Inheritance [' Dáya-Bhága ' & ' Mitácshara '] 42 / 8° *Madras* [10] 67
GRADY, S. G. The Hindu Law of Inheritance 42 / 8° W. H. Allen 68
JOLLY, Dr Jul. Outls. of Hist. of Hindu Law of Partitn., Inherit., Adoptn. 10rs. 8° *Calcutta* 85
[Tagore Law Lects. 1883.] Deals with the law as contained in the original Sanskrit treatises.
MITRA, A. C. Hindu Law of Inheritance, Partition, Stridhan, and Wills 15 / 8° *Calcutta* 88
With leading cases from 1825 to 1888. *Stridhan* is Sansk. term for private property of women.
PHILLIPS (A.) + TREVELYAN (E. J.) Law relating to Hindu Wills 25 / *n.* 8° 01
SHASTRI, G. S. Law of Inheritance as in ' Viramitrodaya ' of Mitra Misra [tr.] 24 / 8° *Calcutta*
SIRONAMI, J. S. Commentary on the Hindu Law of Inheritance 21 / 8° *Calcutta* 86
TREVELYAN, E. T. Hindu Family Law 25 / r 8° *Calcutta* 08
WEST (R.) + BÜHLER (J. G.) Digest of the Hindu Law of Inheritance 36 / 8° Paul [68] 84

**Joint Hindu Family**

BHATTACHARYYA, K. K. Law rel. to Joint Hindu Family [Tagore Law Lects. '84–5] 27/6 8° *Calcutta* 85

**Marriage and Widows**

BANERJEE, Gooroodass Hindu Law of Marriage and Stridhan [Tagore Law Lects. '78] 8° *Calcutta* 79
MITRA, T. Law relating to the Hindu Widow [Tagore Law Lects. '79] 8° *Calcutta* 81

**Ancient Law** —*v.* **K** § 124 viii

## 112: MOHAMMEDAN LAW

**Commentaries, Digests, etc.**

ABDUR RAHMAN Institutes of Mussalman Law 30 / *n.* r 8° *Calcutta* (Paul) 08
A treatise on personal law acc. to Hanafite Schl., w. refs. to Arab. sources and cases 1795–1906.
,, Principles of Muhammedan Jurisprudence 21 / *n.* r 8° *Calcutta* 11
AIER (N. R. N.) + SÁMA RAO (P. C.) The Mahomedan Law 10/6 4° *Madras* [ ] 90
ALI, Syed Amir Student's Handbook of Muhammedan Law 8 / 12° *Calcutta* 92
BAILLIE, Neil B. E. Digest of Moohummudan Law as applied in India 16 / 8° Smith & Elder [65–9] 87
HAMILTON, C. [tr.] Hedaya, or Guide: comm. on Mussulman laws, ed. S. G. Grady 35 / 8° W. H. Allen [1791] 70
MACNAGHTEN, Sir W. H. Principles of Hindu and Mohammedan Law—*ut* **D** § 111
,, Princs. and Preceds. of Mooh. Law, w. notes; ed. W. Sloan 52/6 r 8° Norgate [ ] 70
MULLA, D. F. Principles of Mahomedan Law 6 / *n.* c 8° Paul
WILSON, Sir R. K. Anglo-Muhammadan Law: a digest 21 / *n.* 8° Thacker [94] 03

**Inheritance, Contract, Marriage**

BAILLIE, Neil B. E. Moohummudan Law of Inheritance 6 / *n.* 8° Smith & Elder [ ] 74

SMALL CAPS NAMES:

GRADY, S. G. Mahomedan Law of Inheritance and Contract 14/8° W. H. Allen 69
NELL, L. Mohammedan Laws of Ceylon rel. to Inherit. and Marriage 5/8° *Colombo* 73
RUMSEY, Prof. A. Moohummudan Law of Inheritance and Rights and Relations affecting it [Sunni doctrine] 12/8° W. H. Allen [77] 80

**Personal Law**
ALI, Ameer Personal Law of the Mohammedans 15/8° W. H. Allen 80

## 112* : OTHER ORIENTAL LAW

**Abyssinia**
BACHMANN, Dr J. [ed.] Corpus Juris Abessinorum 4° Schneider, *Berlin* 90
Æthiopic and Arabic texts, w. Latin tr. and diss. Pt. i: Jus connubii, 16*m*.

**Japan**
de BEEKER, J. E. [tr.] Annotated Civil Code of Japan, v. i–iii 8° Kelly & Walsh, *Yokohama* –10 *in prg.*

**Turkey**
GRIGSBY, W. E. [tr.] Medjellé, or Ottoman Civil Law 21/8° 95
ONGLEY, F. [tr.] Ottoman Land Code, ed. Hon. E. Miller; w. notes 10/6 p 8° Butterworth 92
WALPOLE, C. G. [tr.] Ottoman Penal Code: tr. fr. French 7/6 p 8° Butterworth 88
YOUNG, Geo. [ed.] Corps de Droit Ottoman, 7 vols. 94/6 *n.* 8° Clar. Press 05

# IX: International Law

## 113 : GENERAL AND SPECIAL WORKS

AMOS, Prf. Sheldon Lectures on International Law 10/6 r 8° Stevens 74
BAKER, Sir Sherston First Steps in International Law 12/*n.* 8° Paul 99
BARCLAY, Sir T. Problems of International Practice and Diplomacy—*ut inf., s.v.* Hague Conferences
BATY, Dr T. International Law 10/6 *n.* 8° Murray 09
By one of the Hon. Gen. Secs. of the Internat. Law Assoc., pointing out need for revisn. of conceptns. of internat. law and national independence.
" International Law in South Africa 5/*n.* 8° Stevens & Haynes 00
Reprint of a course of Oxford lectures dealing w. problems raised by the South African war.
COBBETT, Dr Pitt [ed.] Cases & Opins. on Internat. Law, Pt. i; w. notes and excursus 15/8° Stevens & Haynes [86] 09
DAVIS, C. K. Treatise on International Law, ed. P. J. Healy $3·50 8° Keefe, *St Paul, Minn.* [ ] 00
DAVIS, Prf. G. B. Elements of International Law $3 (12/6 *n.*) c 8° Harper [87] 08
An excellent exposition of preliminary matter that must be mastered before the student tackles the more ambitious writers, fr. GROTIUS to TAKAHASHI, who may be regarded as having made, and as making, international law.
Seoane, Lt. C. A. Syllabus of Davis' 'Internat. Law' [3/6 *n.* Paul] 75 c. 12° Hudson, *Kansas* 05
FIELD International Code $6·50 8° [ ] 76
GLENN, E. F. Treatise on International Law $3·75 8° West Pb. Co., *St Paul, Minn.* 95
*HALL, W. E. Treatise on International Law, ed. J. B. Atlay 21/*n.* ($6) 8° Clar. Press [80] 09
HALLECK, Maj.-Gen. H. W. International Law, ed. Sir G. S. Baker + M. N. Drucquer, 2 vols. 42/*n.* m 8° Paul [66] 08
HOLLAND, Prf. T. E. Studies in International Law 10/6 ($2·60) 8° Clar. Press 98
KENT, J. Commentaries on International Law, ed. J. T. Abdy 10/6 c 8° Stevens [66] 77
LAWRENCE, Rev. Prf. T. J. Principles of International Law $3 c 8° Heath, *Boston* [96] 10
12/6 *n.* Macmillan. An excellent compendium of the law from the Amer. pt.-of-view, contg. nothing new, but putting the matter in an interesting, yet scholarly, form.
" Handbook of Public International Law 3/p 8° Macmillan [88] 09
LEVI, Prf. Leone International Law; w. materials for a code [Intern. Scient. Ser.] 5/c 8° Paul 88
Commerce, Slavery, Prevention of War by Arbitration, Extradition, *etc.* The chaps. on Treaties are very full.
LORIMER, Prf. J. Institutes of the Law of Nations, 2 vols. 36/8° Blackwood 83–4
LYMAN, Theod. Diplomacy of U.S., ed. Theod. Lyman, jun. [son], 2 v. *o.p.* 8° Wells & Lilly, *Boston* [26] 28
An important standard work. From First Treaty w. France [1778] to 1826.
MAINE, Sir H. S. International Law [Whewell Lects. 1887; learned] 7/6 8° Murray [88] 90
MANNING, W. O. Commentaries on Law of Nations, ed. Prf. Sheldon Amos 16/8° Sweet [39] 75
MAXEY, E. International Law; w. illustrative cases $6 8° Thomas, *St Louis* 06
MEILI, F. Internat., Civil, & Commercial Law, tr. A. K. Kuhn $3 (12/6 *n.*) 8° Macmillan 05
MILLER, W. G. Lectures on Philosophy of Law [as introd. to intern. law]—*ut* D § 1
The Law of Nature and Nations in Scotld. 4/*n.* 8° Green, *Edin.* 96

MOORE, J. B. Digest of International Law, 8 vols. r 8° Superint. of Docums., *Washgtn.* 07

MOORE, W. H. Act of State in Engl. Law [$3 *n.* Dutton, *N.Y.*] 10/6 *n.* 8° Murray 06

OPPENHEIM, Prf. L. Internat. Law, 2 v. [i: Peace; ii: War] ea. 18/ *n.* ($6·50 *n.*) r 8° Longman 05–6
Exhaustive treatment of the law of war and neutrality.

" Internat. Incidents f. Discussn. in Conversation Classes 3/6 c 8° Camb. Press 09

PHILLIMORE, Sir R. Commentaries on International Law, 4 v. 122/ 8° Butterworth [54–7] 79–89

PHILLIPSON, C. Two Studies in International Law 5/ *n.* 8° Stevens & Haynes 08

POMEROY, Prf. J. N. Lects. on Internat. Law in time of Peace, ed. T. D. Woolsey $5 8° Houghton, *Bost.* 86

SCHUYLER, Eug. Amer. Diplomacy & the Furtherance of Commerce $2·50 8° Scribner, *N.Y.* 86
Explains the workings of the Consular and Diplomatic Service.

SCOTT, J. B. [ed.] Cases on Internat. Law [found. on Snow] $3·50 8° West Pb. Co., *St Paul, Minn.* [03] 06

SMITH, F. E. International Law [Temple Primers; 40 c. *n.* Macmillan, *N.Y.*] 1/ *n.* f 8° Dent 00

" International Law, ed. J. Wylie 7/6 *n.* 8° Dent [ ] 11

SNOW, Freeman [ed.] Cases & Opinions on Internat. Law; w. notes $3·50 *n.* 8° Boston Bk. Co., *Bost.* 93
The *Syllabus*, a spec. feature of the bk., sets forth about 200 principles or points of Internat. Law, w. names of bks. (Brit., Amer., and foreign) where information may be found. This is followed by two Pts. dealing w. internat. relns. (i) in time of Peace, (ii) in time of War. Appendix conts. *inter alia* acc. of Behring Sea Arbitrn. of 1893, text of Declarn. of Paris 1856, text of Amelioratn. of Sick and Wounded of Armies in the Field.

STEPHEN, J. K. International Law and International Relations 6/ p 8° Macmillan 85

TWISS, Sir Travers Law of Nations consid. as Indept. Polit. Communities, 2 v. 8° Clar. Press [61–3] 84–75
i: *In Time of Peace*, 15/ ($3·75); ii: *In Time of War*, *o.p.* [*pb.* 21/].

TAYLOR, H. Treatise on Internat. Public Law [$6·50 Callaghan, *Chicago*] 30/ *n.* r 8° Sweet 02

de VATTEL, Emmerich Law of Nations, or Principles of Law of Nature, ed. J. Chitty *o.p.* [*pb.* 21/] r 8° Stevens [1759] 34

" The Law of Nations, ed. E. D. Ingraham $3·50 8° Johnson, *Phila.* [1759] 52

WALKER, T. A. The Science of International Law *o.p.* [*pb.* 18/] 8° Camb. Press 93
A general sketch of historic basis of rules observ. by States in normal and abnorm. relns.—both past and present. From a purely scientific standpt.

" Manual of Public Internat. Law [$2·50 *n.* Putn., *N.Y.*] 9/ 8° Camb. Press [95] 08

WESTLAKE, Prf. Jno. Chapters on Principles of International Law 10/ 8° Camb. Press 94
$2·60 *n.* Putnam, *N.Y.* A thoughtful and independent bk.: doctrs. are not worked out in much detail or supported by adequate refs., but it forms a stimulatg. essay on theory of intern. law as ill. by its hist.

" International Law, 2 vols. ea. 9/ *n.* 8° Camb. Press 04–7
Each $3 *n.* Putnam, *N.Y.* Vol. i: *Peace*; vol. ii: *War*.

*WHEATON, H. [Am.] Elements of International Law, ed. J. B. Atlay 32/ r 8° Stevens [36] 04
An important authority for the advanced student.

WHITTUCK, E. A. [ed.] Internat. Documents, 10/6 *n.* ($3·50 *n.*); Ch. Edn., 2/6 *n.* 8° Longman 08; 09
A colln. of internat. conventions and declarations of a law-making kind; w. Introd. and notes.

*WOOLSEY, Prf. T. D. Introduction to the Study of International Law $2·50 8° Scribner, *N.Y.* [60] 01
The best Introd. book. Contains at end a select Bibliography of works and documents on International Law.

**United States**

DEVLIN, R. T. The Treaty-making Power: commentaries on treaty clauses of constitn. of U.S. $6 8° Bancroft, *San Francisco* 09

WHARTON, Fcs. [ed.] Digest of International Law of U.S., 3 v. 8° U.S. Dept. of State, *Washgtn.* 87–8
A seln. of U.S. documts., decisns., speeches, letters, text-bks., mag.-arts., etc. Distrib. free at discretion of Sec. of State.

**France:** SEWELL (J. I. B.) French Law affecting British Subjects 10/6 8° 97

**Egypt:** SCOTT (J. H.) The Law affecting Foreigners in Egypt 15/ *n.* 8° Green, *Edin.* 08

**Greece and Rome (Ancient)**—*v.* **F** § 11

**History** —*also* in Woolsey, *ut supra*

HOSACK, J. On the Rise and Growth of the Law of Nations *o.p.* [*pb.* 12/] 8° Murray 82
From the earliest times to the Treaty of Utrecht (1713).

WALKER, T. A. History of Law of Nations, vol. i 10/ *n.* 8° Camb. Press 99
$3 *n.* Putnam, *N.Y.* This vol. ends at the Peace of Westphalia.

WHEATON, Dr H. History of Law of Nations in Europe & America *o.p.* [*pb.* $7·50] 8° *New York* 45
The standard history, extending fr. earliest times to Treaty of Washington [1842].

WOOLSEY, Prf. T. D. —*in his* Introduction to the Study of International Law, *ut sup.*

**Anglo-American**

TERRY Anglo-American Law $5·50 *n.* 8° Johnson, *Phila.* 84

**Code (International)**

FIELD, D. Dudley Outlines of an International Code $6·50 8° Baker, *N.Y.* [76] 78
Bk. i: *On Peace*; ii: *On War*. A project of law, giv. at same time summary of exist. princs. Full citatn. of treaties, & notes on legal authorities.

**Commercial** —*v.* **D** § 63

**Consuls** —*v.* **D** § 28

**Copyright** —*v.* **D** § 72

**Declaration of Paris**

BOWLES, T. Gibson — The Declaration of Paris of 1856 — 10/6 8° Low 00
Argues for the repudiation of the Declaration by Great Britain.

**Domicile :** *United States*

JACOBS, M. W. — Law of Domicil. : national, quasi-national & munic. — $5 8° Little & Brown, *Boston* 88

**Extradition**

BIRON (H. C.) + CHALMERS (K. E.) Law and Practice of Extradition — 20/ 8° Stevens 03

CLARKE, Sir Edw. — Treatise upon Law of Extradition, ed. E. P. Clarke 25/ 8° Stevens & Haynes [66] 04

HAWLEY, J. G. — Law & Pract of Intern. Extradn. betw. U.S. & For. Ctries. $3·75 8° Callaghan, *Chic.* 93

KIRCHNER, F. J. — Law and Practice relative to Fugitive Offenders — 2/6 8° Stevens 82

„ [ed.] — Extradition : recueil de tous les Traités conclus au 1 Jan., 1883 42/ r 8° Stevens 83

MOORE, J. Bassett — Treat. on Extradition & Interstate Rendition, 2 v. $12 8° Boston Bk. Co., *Boston* 91
An exhaustive treatise dealing w. law of extrad. in vol. i betw. differ. nations, in vol. ii betw. State and State with the Union.

SPEAR, S. T. — The Law of Extradition — $5 8° Weed, *Albany* 79

**Foreign Powers and Jurisdiction of Great Britain**—*v. also* Nationality, *inf.*

HALL, Prf. W. E. — Treat. on Foreign Powers & Jurisd. of British Crown 10/6 ($2·60) 8° Clar. Press 94
A valuable and unique work, treatg. of the for. powers and jurisd. of Crown as a whole, in places not within dominions of Gt. Brit., whatever the source may be fr. wh. such powers and jurisd. are derived. Pt. i is Introductory; ii deals w. the powers and jurisd. of the Crown in States of Europ. civilizn.; iii in Eastern States, in Protectorates, Spheres of Influence, and in Barbarous Countries. Appendices cont. Naturalizn. Act 1870, Foreign Marrge. Act 1892, For. Marrges. Order in Council 1892, Foreign Jurisdiction Act 1890.

JENKYNS, Sir H. — British Rule and Jurisdiction beyond the Seas — 15/ *n.* ($5) 8° Clar. Press 02

*Service out of the Jurisdiction*—*v.* D § 109

**German-Americans in Germany**

TINGLE, E. W. S. — Germany's Claims upon German-Americans in Germany $1 *n.* c 8° Johnson, *Phila.*

**Maritime**

de BURGH, W. — Elements of Maritime International Law — *o.p.* [*pb.* 10/6] 8° Longman 68

OWEN, Douglas — Maritime Warfare & Merchant Shippg. : rts. of capture at sea 2/ *n.* 8° 98

**Monroe Doctrine** —*v. also* D § 146

KEASBY, Dr L. M. — The Nicaragua Canal and the Monroe Doctrine 25 c. 8° Putnam, *N.Y.* 97
A polit. hist. of various projects of interoceanic transit across Amer. isthmus, w. spec. ref. to attitude of U.S. govt. thereto.

McMASTER, Prf. J. B. — Origin, Meaning, and Applic. of Monroe Doctrine 25 c. 12° Altemus, *Phila.* 96

MONROE, Jas. [1758–1831] — Writings, ed. S. M. Hamilton, 6 vols. ea. $5 (21/ *n.*) 8° Putnam, 99 *sqq.*
Vol. i: *Correspondence* 1778–94; ii: *Corresp.* 1794–6. Many papers here printed for first time.

REDDAWAY, W. F. — The Monroe Doctrine — *o.p.* [*pb.* 3/6] c 8° Camb. Press 98
An excellent historical account, based on the older authorities.

TRAVIS, Ira D. — Hist. of the Clayton-Bulwer Treaty; map — $1 8° Univ. of Michigan 02

**Nationality** —*v. also* D § 68, *and* Foreign Powers, etc., *sup.*

COCKBURN, Sir A. — On Nationality : law rel. to subjects and aliens — 5/ 8° Ridgway 69

PIGGOTT, Sir F. — Nationality, 2 vols. — 60/ *n.* r 8° Butterworth 07
Incl. Naturalization and Engl. law on the high seas and beyond the realm.

*France*

PAVITT, A. — Guide to French Laws of 1889 on Nationality and Military Service as they affect British Subjects — 1/ 8° Stevens & Haynes 93

**North Sea Question**

SMITH (F. E.) + SIBLEY (N. W.) International Law and the North Sea Crisis — 21/ *n.* r 8° Unwin 05

**Patents** —*v.* D § 72

**Private International Law**

v. BAR, Dr L. — Theory and Pract. of Priv. Intern. Law [tr.]
[45/ Green, *Ed.*] $6 r 8° Little & Brown, *Boston* [83] 92

*DICEY, Prf. A. V. — Dig. of Law of Engl. w. ref. to Conflict of Laws — 30/ r 8° Stevens [96] 08

FOOTE, J. A. — Concise Treatise on Private International Jurisprudence 25/ 8° Stevens & Haynes [78] 04

HOSACK, J. — Treatise on the Conflict of Laws of Engl. and Scotl., Pt. i *o.p.* [*pb.* 10/6] 8° Blackwood 47

INNES, J. W. Brodie — Compar. Principles of Laws of Engl. & Scotland 40/ *n.* 8° Green, *Edin.* 03
Relates to Procedure and Practice of all the Courts, Superior and Inferior, of both countries.

MINOR, R. C. — Conflict of Laws; or Private Intern. Law — $3 8° Little & Brown, *Boston* 01

NELSON, Hor. [ed.] — Principles of Private International Law — 21/ r 8° Stevens 89
A collection of cases, statutes and orders, with commentary.

RATTIGAN, W. H. — Private International Law — 10/6 8° Stevens 95

v. SAVIGNY, F. C. — Private International Law, tr. W. Guthrie; w. notes 21/ 8° *Edinburgh* [69]

*STORY, J. Comments. on Conflict of Laws, ed. M. M. Bigelow $6 8° Little & Brown, *Boston* [34] 83
WESTLAKE, Prf. Jno. Treatise on Private International Law, ed. A. F. Topham 16/ r 8° Sweet [58] 05
WHARTON, Fcs. Treatise on Conflict of Laws, ed. G. H. Parmele, 2 vols.
$12 8° Lawyers' Co-op. Pb. Co., *Rochester* [5–] 05
With a comparative view of Anglo-American, Roman, German, and French jurisprudence.

**Prize Law**

LUSHINGTON, Godfrey Manual of Naval Prize Law 10/6 p 8° Butterworth 66
ROSCOE, E. S. [ed.] Reports of Prize Cases: 1745 to 1859, 2 vols. 50/ *n.* r 8° Stevens 05

**State Succession**

KEITH, A. B. The Theory of State Succession 6/ 8° Waterlow 07
An acute and original discussion of the problem: When one State is conquered by another, or when a cession of territory is made, what is the relation of the new Sovereign to the liabilities of the former Sovereign?

**Treaties**

CRANDALL, S. B. Treaties: makg. & enforcemt. [Col. Univ. Studs.] $1·50 *n.* 8° Macmillan, *N.Y.* 04
HERTSLET, Lewis + [Sir] E. [eds.] Colln. of Treaties and Conventions betw. Gt. Brit. and For. Powers, vols. i–xxiii r 8° Butterworth 27–05 *in prg.*
From 1820. Vol. xvi conts. an Index to the 15 previous vols. The whole work is practically an epitome of all existing treaties between Engl. and foreign powers, alphab. arranged and dated. Vols. sold separ. at fr. 12/ to 42/ each.
" [eds.] Treaties and Tariffs regulg. Trade betw. Engl. & Foreign Powers
r 8° Wyman 75–91 *in prg.*
i: *Austria*, 7/6 '75; ii: *Turkey*, 15/ '75; iii: *Italy*, 15/ '76; iv: *China*, 2 vols., 35/ ['77] '08; v: *Spain*, 21/ '78; vi: *Japan*, 15/ '79; vii: *Persia*, 10/ '91.
" [eds.] Map of Africa by Treaty, 2 vols.—*ut* **E** § 41
" [eds.] Map of Europe by Treaty: 1814–1891—*ut* **F** § 15
HOLLAND, Prf. T. E. [ed.] Europ. Concert in Eastern Questn. [colln. of treaties] 12/6 ($3·75) 8° Clar. Press 82
Treaties & Conventns. betw. U.S. & other Powers, 1776–1887; w. notes, chron. list, & index
8° Govt. Prg. Off., *Washgtn.* 89

*India*

AITCHISON, C. [ed.] Collection of Treaties, Engagements, and Sunnuds rel. to India, 7 vols.
[betw. India & native States] 8° *Calcutta* 62–5

*China:* MAYERS (W. F.) [ed.] Treaties between China and Foreign Powers 12/6 *n.* r 8° Paul [77] 06

*Russia*

LE MARTENS, F. [ed.] Recueil des Traités et Conventions conclus par la Russie avec les Puissance. Etrangères, vols. i–x [to 1810] [Govt. pubn.] *St Petersburg* ?–93 *in prgs*
A very important contribution to the diplomatic history of Europe in the 17th and 18th centuries.

**War** —*v. also* **D** § 138, *s.v.* War

AMOS, Prf. Sheldon Political and Legal Remedies for War 6/ 8° Cassell 80
ATHERLEY-JONES (L. A.) + BELLOT (H. H. L.) Commerce in War
[rules of intern. law] 21/ *n.* r 8° Methuen 07
BENTWICH, N. Law of Private Property in War [Yorke Prize Essay] 6/ *n.* 8° Sweet 07
BORDWELL, W. P. Law of War between Belligerents $3·50 8° Callaghan, *Chicago* 08
GENTILIS, Albericus De Jure Belli libri tres, ed. Prf. T. E. Holland 21/ ($5·25) s 4° Clar. Press 77
GROTIUS, Hugo De Jure Belli et Pacis, ed. Dr W. Whewell, w. tr. &. notes, 3 v. 12/ 8° Camb. Pr. [53] 80
$4 *n.* Putnam, *N.Y.* Cf. also article Grotius by MARK PATTISON in *Encyclo. Brit.*, vol. xi [*ut* **K** § 1].
HOLLAND, Prf. T. E. Laws of War on Land, Written and Unwritten 6/ *n.* ($2) 8° Clar. Press 08
An excellent compressed exposition, with appendices of documts. and useful information.
LATIFI, Dr Almá Effects of War on Property 5/ *n.* ($1·50 *n.*) 8° Macmillan 09
Deals w. seizure in certain circumstances of the publ. and priv. property of the enemy.
OWEN, Douglas The Declaration of War 21/ 8° Stevens 89
A treatise on war as affecting the commercial relations of belligerents and neutrals, w. considerations of shipping and marine insurance during war.
PHILLIPSON, C. Effect of War on Contracts 3/6 *n.* 8° Stevens & Haynes 09
RISLEY, J. S. The Law of War: study of legal obligns. and condns. applying to belligs. & neutrals in time of war *o.p.* [*pb.* 12/] 8° Innes 97
Useful, but with few references to authorities. Its historical summary is slight and vague.
SPAIGHT, Dr J. M. War Rights on Land 12/ *n.* 8° Macmillan 11

*Chino-Japanese War; Russo-Japanese War*

HERSHEY, Prf. A. S. Intern. Law & Diplomacy of Russo-Jap War $3 *n.* (12/6 *n.*) 8° Macmillan 07
LAWRENCE, Prf. T. J. War and Neutrality in the Far East $1·25 *n.* (3/6 *n.*) c 8° Macmillan 04
SMITH (F. E.) + SIBLEY (N. W.) Internat. Law as interpr. dur. Russo-Jap. War 25/ *n.* r 8° Unwin [05] 07
$5 *n.* Boston Bk. Co., *Boston.* A valuable and rich storehouse of learning in anc. and mod. history—of interest to laymen as much as to lawyer.
TAKAHASHI, Prf. Sakuyé [ed.] Cases on Internat. Law dur. Chino-Jap. War *o.p.* [pb. 10] 8° Camb. Press 99
Introd. by Prf. WESTLAKE. A valuable discussion of the chief points.
" Internat. Law appl. to Russo-Japanese War 32/ *n.* r 8° Stevens 08
$8 *n.* Banks, *N.Y.* A substantial treatise, with many official documts., letters, and tables.

*Hague Conferences*

BARCLAY, Sir Thos. Problems of International Practice and Diplomacy 21 / *n*. 4° Sweet 07
$6·50 Boston Book Co., *Boston*. With special reference to the Hague Conferences.

HIGGINS, A. P. Hague Conference and other International Conferences conc. Laws and Usages of War 3 / *n*. 8° Stevens 04

HOLLS, G. F. W. The Peace Conference at the Hague $3 (10 / *n*.) 8° Macmillan 10

LAWRENCE, Prf. T. J. International Problems and the Hague Conference 3/6 *n*. c 8° Dent 08

*Neutrality* —*v. also* **D** § 63

BERNARD, M. Hist. Acc. of Neutrality of G.B. dur. Am. Civil War *o.p.* [*pb*. 16/] r 8° Longman 70

HALL, W. E. The Rights and Duties of Neutrals *o.p.* [*pb*. 8/6] 8° Longman 74

HOLLAND, Prf. T. E. Neutral Duties in Marit. War [Brit Acad. Pubns.] 1 / *n*. (40 c.) r 8° Clar. Press 05

„ Letters to 'Times' upon War & Neutrality [1881–1909] 6 / *n*. ($1·75 *n*.) 8° Longman 09

SAUNDERS, A. The Neutral Ship in War Time [Legal Handybks.] 1 / *n*. 12° E. Wilson 98

SCOTT, J. B. The Hague Peace Conference of 1899 & 1907, 2 vols. $5 8° Johns Hopk. Pr., *Baltimore* 10
Vol. i: The *Conferences*; ii: *Documts*. By the Solr. for Dept. of State and technical delegate to the Second Conference.

*United States*

CALLAHAN, J. M. Neutrality of Amer. Lakes [a historical study] $1·50 8° Johns Hopkins Pr., *Baltimore* 98

*Pacific Blocade*

HOGAN, A. E. Pacific Blocade 6 / *n*. ($2) 8° Clar. Press 08
About half the bk. gives histor. accounts of blockades 1827–1908. With classified bibliography.

---

# X: Political (National) Economy

## 114: GENERAL WORKS; HIST. OF ECONOMICS; SYSTEMATIC TREATISES; SERIES

### Bibliography

BLOCK, M. Progrès d. la Science Econom. depuis Adam Smith, 2 vols. 16 *fr*. 8° Guillaumin, *Paris* 90
Of considerable bibliographical value as a Supplement to COSSA, *inf*.

BONAR, Dr J. Catalogue of the Library of Adam Smith—*ut* **C** § 61
About two-fifths of the collection consists of books on political economy, politics, and law.

BOWKER (R. R.) + ILES (A.) [eds.] Reader's Guide in Econ., Social, and Political Science $1 c 8° Soc. f. Pol. Educ. (Putnam, *N.Y.*) [84] 92
Amer., Eng., and foreign bks., w. clear descriptive notes, and author-index. Now somewhat out of date.

COSSA, Prf. Luigi Introd. to Study of Polit. Econ. [tr. fr. Ital.] 8/6 *n*. ($2·60 *n*.) c 8° Macmillan [80] 93
New edn. of his *Guide to the Study of Polit. Econ.* [1880]; pract. rewritten. A compreh. histor. survey of progr. and the then conditn. of econ. science in Eur., Engl. and U.S., w. summaries of views of wrs., and sound judgmts. on them, tog. w. a theoret. Introd. on definitn., methods, and scope of polit. econ., its relns. w. other sciences, etc.

Fabian Society: What to Read: list of bks. for social reformers 1/ c 8° Fabian Soc. [91] 10
An excellent brief classified list of books on Social History and Social Theory (incl. Economics proper).

FISHER, Irving Bibliography of Mathematical Economics—*in* Cournot's Researches [tr.], *ut inf*.

HASSE, A. R. Index of Econ. Material in Documts. in U.S. 4° Carnegie Instit., *Washgtn*. 07 *sqq*., *in prg*
A separ. vol. to ea. State, materl. arrgd. alphab. by subjs. and then chronologically. Covers period fr. adoptn. of Federal Constitn. (1789) to 1904. Confined to prtd. Repts. of admin. officers, legisl. committees, and spec. commissions of States, etc. Already issued: *Maine, New Hampshire, Vermont, Rhode Isl., Massachussetts, California*.

JEVONS, Prf. W. S. —Appendix *to his* Theory of Pol. Econ. [*ut inf*.] *conts. list of mathem. econ. bks*.

KEEBLE, S. E. A B C Annot. Bibliogr. of Social Subjects 1 / *n*. c 8° Kelly 07

KING & SON (P. S.) [pbs.] Catalogue of Parliamentary Papers: 1801–1900 [und. subjs.] 7/6 *n*. 4° P. S. King & Son 04

LAUGHLIN, J. L. Study of Political Economy [hints to studts. & tchrs.] $1 16° Appleton, *N.Y.* 85

MCCULLOCH, J. R. Literature of Political Economy *o.p.* [*pb*. 14/] 8° Longman 45
A classified catalogue of selected books, with historical notes.

National Liberal Club: Catalogue of the Gladstone Library [c. 1000 pp.] r 8° Nat. Lib. Club 08
Mainly historical, polit., social, and econ. bks.—some 25,000, w. 20,000 pamphlets.

RAND, Dr Benj. —*in his* Bibliogr. of Philos., Psychology, and Cognate Subjects, *ut* **C** § 1

ROBERTSON, J. M. —*in his* Courses of Study, *ut* **K** § 10

TOLMAN (W. H.) + HULL (W. J.) Bibliog. of Select. Sociolog. References [chfly. Amer.] c 8° *New York* 93

Where is the Information?, v. i [ed. W. D. P. Bliss] $3 *per ann*. 8° Soc. Sci. Lib. Bureau, *N.Y.* 08 *in prg*.
Issued bi-monthly. Gives chief references on social science, alphab. arrgd.

Brief views of the liter. of polit. econ. are also cont. in LALOR, PALGRAVE, ANDREWS, BOWKER, ELY, MILL (ed. LAUGHLIN), PERRY, and SMITH (ed. MCCULLOCH) *ut inf*.

### Dictionaries

BLISS (W. D. P.) + BINDER (R. M.) [eds.] New Encyclopædia of Social Reform, 2 vols. $7·50 (35 / *n*.) r 8° Funk & Wagnalls [97] 08
Incl. all social reform movemts., and econ. industr., and sociolog. facts and statistics of all countries. Compiled w. co-opern. of many specialists giving short bibliogrs. Assist. edr. for Engl. edn. E. P. GASTON. A new bk. rather than a new edn. *Suppl*. $1·50 (7/6 *n*.) '09c

LALOR, J. J. [ed.] Cyclo. of Pol. Sci., Pol. Econ., & Pol. Hist. of U.S., 3 v. $15 r 8° Cary, *Chicago* 83–4
Foreign pt. mostly tr. fr. BLOCK's *Dict. de la Politique*, COQUELIN + GUILLAUMIN's *Dict. de l'Economie* [2 v. 8° Paris (51–3) 64], or BLUNTSCHLI's *Staatswörterbuch* [3 v. 20*m.* 8° Schulthess, Zürich '69–75], w. orig. arts. by late T. E. CLIFFE-LESLIE: U.S. polit. hist., *etc.*, by Prf. A. JOHNSON. A useful wk. of ref., alphab. arrgd.

MACLEOD, H. D. Dictionary of Political Economy, vol. i *o.p.* [*pb.* 30/] 8° Longman [63] 63
A wk. of great research. Vol. ii, completing the bk., will never be published.

MONTGOMERY (H.) + CAMBRAY (P. G.) Dictionary of Political Phrases & Allusions 7/6 8° Sonnenschein 06
$2 Dutton, *N.Y.* Includes foreign and American terms. Conts. short bibliography.

*PALGRAVE, R. H. Inglis [ed.] Dictionary of Pol. Econ., 3 v. ea. 21/*n.* ($6·50 *n.*) 8° Macmillan 91–00
Non-partizan accs. of the subjs., alphab.arrgd., w. concise statemt. of cognate terms in hist., commerce, and law and biogrs. of deceased writers, Engl. and foreign. Pays spec. attention to recording exact titles and dates of bks. More useful than the Germ. dict. of Prfs. CONRAD + LESTER and the Fch. dict. of SAY + CHAILLEZ, wh. are rather collns. of monogrs., the latter defendg. certain econ. doctrs. Vol. iii was re-issued in 1908 w. an Append. of over 100 pp., in wh. are chronicled changes in econom. condns. since vol. i was issued. Appendix sep. 2/6 *n.* 1908.

*Terms:* BOWER (Fk.) Dictionary of Economic Terms [50 c. Dutton, *N.Y.*] 1/*n.* 32° Routledge *n.d.* (06)

## Series

Amer Acad. of Polit. and Social Science: Pubns.
[a long series of pamphlets] 15 c. to $1 8° Acad. of Pol. Sci., *Phila.* 93 *in prg.*

" " " Series of Constitutions: transl. 8° *Phila.* 93–4
*Belgium* [*ut* D § 114] tr. Dr J. M. VINCENT, 50 c.
*Columbia* [*ut* D § 145*] tr. Prf. MOSES, 50 c.
*France* [*ut* D § 144] tr. C. F. A. CURRIER, 50 c.
*Italy* [*ut* D § 144] tr. Prfs. S. M. LINDSAY + L. Sr ROWE, 50 c.
*Mexico* [*ut* D § 145*] tr. Prf. MOSES, 35 c.
*Prussia* [*ut* D § 144] tr. Prf. J. H. ROBINSON, 50 c.

American Citizen Series: ed. Dr A. B. Hart *v.p.* c 8° Longman 99 *sqq.*, *in prg.*
DEWEY (D. R.), *Financ. Hist. of U.S.* [*ut* D § 117] $2 (7/6 *n.*)
HART (A. B.), *Actual Governmt.* [*ut* D § 145] $2·25
LOWELL (A. L.), *Publ. Opinion and Pop. Govt.* [*ut* D § 135] *in prep.*
MCCLAIN (E.). *Constit. Law in U.S.* [*ut* D § 27] $2 (7/6 *n.*)
MOORE (J. B.), *Internatl. Law* *in prep.*
RIPLEY (W. Z.), *Amer. Transportation Problems* *in prep.*
SELIGMAN (E. R.), *Princs. of Economics* [*ut* D § 114] $2·40 (10/6 *n.*)
WRIGHT (C. D.), *Outline of Pract. Sociology* [*ut* D § 125] $2

American Economic Assoc.: Publications, Ser. i–iii (vols. 1–7) 8° Macmillan, *N.Y.* 86–06 *in prg.*
SER. I (1886–96), vols. i–x ea. $4 *n.*; xi, $2 *n.* SER. II (1896–9), vols. i–iv, ea. in 6 Pts., ea. Pt. 50 c. *n.*; NEW SERIES (1896–9), Pts. i–ii, 2 Pts., $1·50 *n.*, $2 *n.*; SER. III (1909 sqq.), vols. i–vii [monogrs.], ea. $4 *n.* Engl. edns. Sonnenschein (50 c. *n.* to 75 c. *n.* = 2/6; $1 *n.* = 3/6 $1·25 *n.* = 5/; $1·50 *n.* = 6/; $1·75 *n.* = 7/).

SERIES I [monographs].

Vol. i, 1: ELY (R. T.), *Organizn. of Am. Ec. Ass.* 50 c. *n.*
2–3: JAMES (E. J.), *Rel. of Munic. to Gas Supply* [*ut* D § 124] *o.p.*
4: SHAW (Alb.), *Co-oper. in a Western City* 75 c. *n.*
5: BEMIS (E. W.), *Co-oper. in New England* *o.p.*
6: ADAMS (H. C.), *Rel. of State to Industr. Action* *o.p.*
ii, 1: WARNER (A. G.), *Three Phases of Co-oper. in West* 75 c. *n.*
2: WORTHINGTON (T. K.), *Hist. of Finan. in Pennsyl.* 75 c. *n.*
3: JAMES (E. J.), *Railway Question* [*ut* D § 152] 75 c. *n.*
4: ASHLEY (W. J.), *Early Hist. of Engl. Woollen Industry* [*ut* D § 117*] 75 c. *n.*
5: SELIGMAN (E. R. A.), *Mediaeval Guilds of Engl.* [*ut* D § 120] 75 c. *n.*
6: ADAMS, *etc.*, *Rel. of Municipalities to Quasi-Public Wks.* [*ut* D § 124] 75 c. *n.*
iii, 1: WRIGHT (C. D.), *Statistics in Colleges*; GIDDINGS (F. H.), *Sociology and Pol. Econ.*; JAMES, *Legal Tender Decisns.* 75 c. *n.*
2: CLARK (J. B.), *Capital and its Earnings* [*ut* D § 118] 75 c. *n.*
3: WALKER (F. A.), *Manual-laboring Class*; BEMIS (E. W.), *Mine-Labor in Hocking Valley*; ELY, *Rept. of 2nd Ann. Mtg.* 75 c. *n.*
4–5: MAYO-SMITH (Richm.), *Statistics & Economics* *o.p.*
6: PATTEN (S. N.), *Stability of Prices* 75 c. *n.*
iv, 1: WOOD (Stuart), *Theory of Wages*; CLARK (J. B.), *Scient. Law of Wages* 75 c. *n.*
2: WEBB (Sidn.), *Socialism in England*
3: JENKS (J. W.), *Road Legisl. f. Amer.* *o.p.*
4: ELY, *Rept. of 3rd Ann. Mtg.* 75 c. *n.*
5: PATTEN, *Malthus and Ricardo*; DEWEY (D. R.), *Study of Statistics*; FOLWELL (W. W.), *Anal. in Pol. Econ.* 75 c. *n.*
6: ANDREWS (E. B.), *An Honest Dollar* [*ut* D § 115] 75 c. *n.*
v, 1: YEIJIRO ONO, *Indust. Transitn. in Japan* [*ut* D § 117*] $1 *n.*
2: WILLOUGHBY (W. F.) + de GRAFFENREID (Clare), *Child Labor* [*ut* D § 118] 75 c. *n.*
3–4: JAMES, *Canal and Railway*; HAUPT (L. M.), *Canals and Transportn.* $1 *n.*
5: SCHWAB (J. C.), *Hist. of N.Y. Property Tax* $1 *n.*
6: PATTEN, *Educ. Value of Polit. Econ.* [*ut sup.*] 75 c. *n.*
vi, 1–2: ELY, *Rept. of 4th Ann. Mtg.* $1 *n.* (3/)
3: PINCHOT (G.), *Govt. Forestry Abroad*; BOWERS (E. A.), *Forests on Public Lands*; FERNOW (B. E.), *Amer. Forest Admin.* 75 c. *n.*
4–5: BEMIS, *Munic. Ownership of Gas in U.S.* [*ut* D § 124] $1 *n.*
6: CLARK (F. C.), *State Railrd. Commissns.* [*ut* D § 152] 75 c. *n.*
vii, 1: TAUSSIG (F. W.), *Silver Situation in U.S.* [*ut* D § 115] 75 c. *n.*
2–3: SELIGMAN, *Incidences of Taxn.* [*ut* D § 117] $1 *n.*
4–5: ROSS (E. A.), *Sinking Funds* [*ut* D § 117] $1 *n.*
6: HAYNES (F. E.), *Reciprocity Treaty w. Canada*: 1854 75 c. *n.*
viii, 1: ELY, *Rept. of 5th Ann. Mtg.* 75 c. *n.*
2–3: REYNOLDS (M. T.), *Housing of Poor* [*ut* D § 127] $1 *n.*
4–5: BALCH (E. G.), *Assist. of Poor in Frce.* [*ut* D § 128] $1 *n.*
6: HILL (W.), *Tariff Policy of U.S.* [*ut* D § 122] $1 *n.*
ix, 1–2: SELIGMANN, *Progressive Taxn.* [*ut* D § 117] $1 *n.*
3: COOLEY (C. H.), *Theory of Transportatn.* [*ut* D § 149] 75 c. *n.*
4: BEVAN (W. L.), *Sir William Petty* [*ut* D § 114] 55 c. *n.*
5: CLARK (J. B.), *etc.*, *Papers on Labr. Probls.* 75 c. *n*
x, 1–3: BRECKENRIDGE (R. M.), *Canad. Bkg. Syst.* [*ut* D § 116] $1·50 *n.*
4: CUMMINGS (J.), *Poor Laws of Mass. and N.Y.* [*ut* D § 128] 75 c. *n.*
5: RICARDO, *Letters to McCulloch* [*ut* D § 114] $1·25 *n.*
xi, 1–3: HOFFMAN (F. L.), *Race Traits, etc., of Am. Negro* [*ut* D § 130] $1·25 *n.*
4: FISHER (I.), *Apprecn. and Interest* [*ut* D § 118] 75 c. *n.*
5: *General Index to Vols. i–xi* 25 c. *n*

SERIES II [Economic Studies]

4 vols., in 6 Pts., ea. Pt. consistg. of an econ. study, ea. Pt. 50 c. *n.*

NEW SERIES.

Pt. i: HAMMOND (M. B.), *Cotton Industry* [*ut* D § 117*] $1·50 *n.*
Pt. ii: *Scope and Method of the Twelfth Census.* By over 20 experts [*ut* D § 121] $2 *n.*

SERIES III

Vol. i, 1: *Papers on Trusts, Railroad Probl.*, etc. $1 *n.*
2: PAGE (T. W.), *End of Villainage in Engl.* [*ut* F § 14] $1 *n.*
3: *Essays in Colon. Finance.* By var. wrs. [*ut* D § 136] $1·50 *n.*
4: DAVIS (A. Mc F.), *Currency and Banking in Mass. Bay*, Pt. i [*ut* D § 116] $1·75 *n.*
ii, 1: *Papers on Commerc. Educn.*, etc. $1·25 *n.*
2: DAVIS, *Currency, etc., Mass.*, Pt. ii [*ut* D § 116] $1·75 *n.*
3: SEWALL (H. R.), *Theory of Value* [*ut* D § 114] $1 *n.*
4: CLOW (F. R.), *Admin. of City Finances in U.S.* [*ut* D § 124] $1
iii, 1: *Papers on Internat. Trade*, etc. $1·50 *n.*
2: TILLINGHAST (J. A.), *Negro in Africa & Amer.* [*ut* D § 130] $1·25 *n.*
3: ROBINSON (H.), *Taxn. in New Hampshire* [*ut* D § 117] $1·25 *n.*
4: JOHNSON (A. S.), *Rent in Mod. Econ. Theory* [*ut* D § 119] 75 c. *n.*
iv, 1: *Papers on Trade Unions*, etc. $1·25 *n.*
2: BUSHEL (F. A.), *Ethnic Factors in Populn. of Boston* $1 *n.*
3: COMAN (K.), *Hist. of Contract Labor in Hawaii* [*ut* D § 118] 75 c. *n.*
4: KINSMAN (D. O.), *Income Tax in U.S.* [*ut* D § 117] $1 *n.*
v, 1: *Papers on Agric. and Industr. Probls.* $1 *n.*
2: *Papers on Surplus Revenue*, etc. $1 *n.*
3: WALKER (F.), *Germ. Coal Industry* [*ut* D § 118] $1·25 *n.*
4: QUAINTANCE (H. W.), *Influ. of Farm Machy.* [*ut* D § 118] 75 c. *n.*
vi, 1: *Papers on Theory of Money*, etc. $1 *n.*
2: *Papers on Govt. Interference*, etc. $1 *n.*
3: MEEKER (R.), *Shipping Subsidies* [*ut* D § 122] $1 *n.*
4: FAIRCHILD (F. R.), *Labor Legisl. in N.Y.* [*ut* D § 118] $1 *n.*
vii, 1: *Papers on Theory of Distribn.*, etc. $1 *n.*
2: SMALLEY (H. S.), *Railrd. State Control* $1 *n.*
3: GRYZANOVSKI (E. G. F.), *Statistical Data* [*ut* D § 148] 75 c. *n.*
BARNETT (Dr G. E.), *The Printers* $1 *n.*
SELIGMAN (E. R. A.), *Progressive Taxation* [*ut* D § 117] $1·25 *n.*
PRICE (W. H.), *Life Insurce. Reform in N.Y.* 50 c. *n.*
WATKINS (G. P.), *Growth of Large Fortunes* [*ut* D § 118] $1 *n.*

Chicago University: Economic Studies, Pts. i–v *v.p.* r 8° Univ. Press, *Chicago in prg*
i: COHN (G.), *Science of Finance*, tr. T. B. VEBLEN [*ut* D § 117] $3·50 *n.*
ii: WHITE (H. Kirke), *Hist. of Union Pacific Ry.* [*ut* D § 152] $1·50 *n.*
iii: ELLSTAETTER (K.), *Indian Silver Currency* [tr.] [*ut* D § 115] $1·25 *n.*
iv: MILLION (J. W.), *State Aid to Rys. in Missouri* [*ut* D § 152] $1·75 *n*
v: WILLIS (H. P.), *Hist. of Latin Monetary Union* [*ut* D § 115] $2 *n*

" Decennial Pubns. *v.p.* 4° Univ. Press, *Chicago*
BRECKINRIDGE (Sophonisba P.), *Legal Tender* [*ut* D § 115] $3 *n.*
CATTERALL (R. C. H.), *Second Bank of U.S.* [*ut* D § 116] $3 *n.*
LAUGHLIN (J. L.), *Credit* 50 c. *n.*
MITCHELL (W. C.), *Hist. of Greenbacks* [*ut* D § 115] $4 *n.*

Citizens' Lib. of Economics, Politics, & Sociol. : ed. Prf. R. T. Ely ea. $1·25 *n.* (5/ *n.*) c 8° Macmillan *in prg.*

ADDAMS (J.), *Democracy and Social Ethics* [ut D § 135]
,, *Newer Ideals of Peace* [ut D § 133]
BAKER (M. N.), *Munic. Engineering and Sanitation* [ut D § 124]
BLACKMAR (F. W.), *Elements of Sociology* [ut D § 125]
BULLOCK (C. J.), *Monetary Hist. of U.S.* [ut D § 115]
CARLTON (F. T.), *Educn. and Industr. Evoln.*
ELY (R. T.), *Custom and Competition* in prep.
,, *Monopolies and Trusts* [ut D § 118]
,, *Outlines of Economics* [ut D § 114]
,, *Evol. of Industr. Society* [ut D § 125]
,, *Labor Movemt. in Amer.* [ut D § 118]
FISK (G. M.), *Intern. Commercial Policies* [ut D § 138]
HOBSON (J. A.), *Economics of Distribution* [ut D § 114]
JONES (E. D.), *Economic Crises* [ut D § 115]
KELLEY (F.), *Ethical Gains thro' Legisln.* [ut D § 125]
KINLEY (D.), *Money* [ut D § 115]
MACY (J.), *Hist. of Pol. Parties in U.S.* [ut D § 146]
MALTBIE (M. R.), *British Cities and their Problems* [ut D § 124]
MEAD (E.), *Irrigation Institutions* [ut I § 30]
MEYER (B. H.), *Railway Legisln. in U.S.* [ut D § 152]
PARMELEE (M.), *Anthropology and Sociology* [ut D § 123]
REINSCH (P. S.), *Colonial Administration* [ut D § 136]
,, *Colonial Government* [ut D § 136]
,, *World Politics* [ut D § 134]
ROSS (E. A.), *Foundations of Sociology* [ut D § 125]
,, *Social Control* [ut D § 125]
SMITH (J. A.), *Spirit of Amer. Govt.* [ut D § 145]
SPARLING (S. E.), *Introd. to Business Organizn.* [ut D § 150]
TAYLOR (H. C.), *Agricultural Economics* [ut I § 24]
VINCENT (E.), *Survey of Sociology* [ut D § 125] in prep.
,, (J. M.), *Government in Switzerland* [ut D § 144]
WEST (M.), *Principles of Taxation* [ut D § 117] in prep.
WILCOX (D. F.), *The American City* [ut D § 124]
ZUEBLIN (C.), *American Municipal Progress* [ut D § 124]

Columbia Univ. : Studies in Hist., Economics, & Public Law [P. S. King] 8° Macmillan, *N.Y.* 91 *in prg.*

AGGER (E. E.), *Budget in Am. C'wealths* [ut D § 117] $1·50 *n.*
ARNER (G. B. L.), *Consanguineous Marrgs. in Am. Populn.* [ut D § 133] 75 c. *n.*
BANKS (E. M.), *Economics of Land Tenure in Georgia* $1 *n.*
BATES (F. C.), *Rhode Isl. and Formatn. of Union* [ut E § 57] $1·50 *n.*
BEARD (C. A.), *Office of J.P. in Engl.* [ut D § 105] $1·50 *n.*
BEER (G. L.), *Commerc. Policy of Engl. tow. Amer. Colonies* not sep.
BERGLUND (A.), *The U.S. Steel Corporation* [ut D § 118] $1·50 *n.*
BISHOP (C. F.), *Hist. of Elections in Am. Colonies* [ut D § 146] $1·50 *n.*
BLACK (G. A.), *Hist. of Munic. Land Ownership on Manhattan Island* $1 *n.*
BONDY (W.), *Separatn. of Govt. Powers* [ut D § 144] $1 *n.*
BOWMAN (H. M.), *Admin. of Iowa* $1·50 *n.*
BOYD (W. K.), *Eccles. Edicts of Theodosian Code* 75 c. *n.*
BRISCO (N. A.), *Econ. Policy of R. Walpole* [ut F § 24] $1·50 *n.*
BURKE (W. M.), *Central Labor Unions* [ut D § 120] $1 *n.*
CAPEN (E. W.), *Hist. Devel. of Poor Law of Conn.* [ut D § 128] $3 *n.*
CHADDOCK (R. E.), *Ohio before 1850* $1·50 *n.*
CHADSEY (C. E.), *Pres. Johnson and Congress* [ut F § 73] $1 *n.*
CLARK (W. E.), *Jos. Tucker, Economist* [ut D § 114] $1·50 *n.*
COKER (F. W.), *Organismic Theories of the State* [ut D § 134] $1·50 *n.*
CRANDALL (S. B.), *Treaties: making and enforcemt.* [ut D § 138] $1·50 *n.*
CROOK (J. W.), *German Wage Theories* [ut D § 118] $1 *n.*
CUSHING (H. A.), *Transition fr. Provincial to C'wealth Govt. in Mass.* [ut E § 57] $2 *n.*
DAVIS (M. M., jun.), *Psychol. Interpretns. of Society* [ut D § 125] $2 *n.*
DOUGLAS (C. H.), *Financ. Hist. of Mass.* [ut D § 117] $1 *n.*
DUGGAN (S. P. H.), *Eastern Question* $1·50 *n.*
DUNSCOMB (S. W.), *Bankruptcy* $1 *n.*
EMERY (H. C.), *Stock and Produce Exchgs. of U.S.* [ut D § 153] $1·50 *n.*
FAIRLIE (J. A.), *Centralizn. of Admin. in N.Y. State* $1 *n.*
FLICK (A. C.), *Loyalism in N.Y. dur. Revoln.* [ut E § 57] $2 *n.*
FORD (G. S.), *Hanover and Prussia: 1795–1803* [ut F § 51] $2 *n.*
FRIEDMAN (H. G.), *Taxn. of Corpns. in Mass.* $1·50 *n.*
GILBERT (J. H.), *Trade and Currency in Early Oregon* $1 *n.*
GLASSON (W. H.), *Milit. Pension Legisl. in U.S.* [ut D § 127*] $1 *n.*
GOSS (J. D.), *Tariff Administrn. in U.S.* [ut D § 122] $1 *n.*
GROAT (G. G.), *Trade Unions* [ut D § 120] $1 *n.*
HALL (A. C.), *Crime* [ut D § 123] $3 *n.*
HALL (F. S.), *Sympathetic Strikes and Lockouts* [ut D § 120] $1 *n.*
HANKINS (F. H.), *Adolphe Quetlet as Statistician* [ut K § 2] $1·25 *n.*
HILL (R. T.), *Public Domain and Democracy* [ut D § 139] $2 *n.*
HISHIDA (S.), *Intern. Position of Japan* [ut F § 63] $2 *n.*
HOURWICH (I. A.), *Econcs. of a Russn. Village* [ut D § 119] $2 *n.*
JACOBSTEIN (M.), *Tobacco Industry in U.S.* [ut I § 35] $1·50 *n.*
JONES (T. J.), *Sociology of a N.Y. City Block* [ut D § 127] $1 *n.*
KINOSITA (Y.), *Japanese Commerce* [ut D § 148] $1·50 *n.*
KRAMER (S.), *Engl. Craft Gilds* [ut D § 120] $1 *n.*
LICHTENBERGER (J. P.), *Divorce* [ut D § 133] $1·50 *n.*
LOEB (I.), *Property Relns. of Married Parties* [ut D § 133] $1·50 *n.*
MCBAIN (H. L.), *Clinton and Spoils Syst.* $1·50 *n.*
MCKEAG (E. C.), *Mistakes in Contract* [ut D § 29] $1 *n.*
MACLEAR (Anne B.), *Early New Engl. Towns* [ut E § 57] $1·50 *n.*
MALTBIE (M. R.), *Engl. Local Govt.* [ut D § 124] $2 *n.*
MERRIAM (C. E., jun.), *Theory of Sovereignty* [ut D § 134] $1·50 *n.*
MILLER (E. I.), *Legislature of Virginia* $1·50 *n.* (6/
MUSSEY (H. R.), *Combin. in Mining Industry* [ut D § 118] $1 *n.*
ORTH (S. P.), *Administration in Ohio* $3·50 *n.*
PARSONS (P. A.), *Responsibility for Crime* [ut D § 123] $1·50 *n.*
POND (O. L.), *Munic. Control of Publ. Utilities* [ut D § 124] $1 *n.*
PROPER (E. E.), *Colonial Immigr. Laws* [ut D § 121] 75 c. *n.*
PUTNAM (B. H.), *Statutes of Labourers* [ut D § 118] $4 *n.*
RAWLES (W. A.), *Centralizing Tendencies* $2·50 *n.*
RIPLEY (W. Z.), *Financ. Hist. of Virginia* [ut D § 117] $1 *n.*
ROSEWATER (V.), *Special Assessmts.* [ut D § 124] $1 *n.*
SCISCO (L. D.), *Polit. Nativism in N.Y.* $2 *n.*
SHEPHERD (R. P.), *Turgot and Six Edicts* [ut D § 114] $1·50 *n.*
SHEPHERD (W. R.), *Proprietary Govt. in Penn.* $4 *n.*
SITES (C. M. L.), *Liquor Laws* [ut D § 131] $1 *n.*
SMITH (P.), *Luther's Table Talk* $1 *n.*
STANGELAND (C. E.), *Pre-Malthusian Doctrs.* [ut D § 121] $2·50 *n.*
STARK (F. R.), *Aboln. of Privateering and Declar. of Paris* $1 *n.*
TANNER (E. P.), *Province of N. Jersey 1664–1738* $4 *n.*
TENNEY (A. A.), *Social Democracy and Population* [ut D § 121] 75 c. *n.*
THOMAS (D. T.), *Milit. Govt. in Newly Acqd. Territy. of U.S.* $2 *n.*
THORNDIKE (L.), *Place of Magic in Intell. Hist.* [ut B § 5] 75 c. *n.*
UNDERWOOD (J. H.), *Distribution of Ownership* $1·50 *n.*
WALKER (F.), *Double Taxn. in U.S.* [ut D § 117] $1 *n.*
WEBER (A. F.), *Growth of Cities* [ut D § 121] $3·50 *n.*
WEBSTER (W. C.), *State Educatl. Admin.* [ut D § 157] 75 c. *n.*
WELD (L. D. H.), *Freight Cars and Am. Rys.* $1·50 *n.*
WEST (M.), *Inheritance Tax* [ut D § 117] $2 *n.*
WESTON (S. F.), *Justice in Taxation* [ut D § 117] $2 *n.*
WHITAKER (A. C.), *Labor Theory of Value* [ut D § 114] $1·50 *n.*
WHITON, *Factory Legisln. in Maine* [ut D § 118] $1 *n.*
WHITTEN (R. H.), *Publ. Admin. in Mass.* [ut D § 124] $1 *n.*
WILCOX (D. F.), *Munic. Govt. in Mich. and Ohio* [ut D § 124] $1 *n.*
WILLCOX (W. F.), *Divorce Problem* [ut D § 133] 75 c. *n.*
WILLETT (A. H.), *Theory of Risk and Insurce.* [ut D § 151] $1·50 *n.*
WILLETT (M. H.), *Employmt. of Women* [ut D § 132] $1·50 *n.*
WILLIAMSON (C. C.), *Finances of Cleveland* $2 *n.*
WOOD (F. A.), *Taxation in Vermont* [ut D § 117] not sep.
WOOLLEY (E. C.), *Reconstruction of Georgia* [ut E § 57] $1 *n.*
Charged in Engl. as $1 = 4/.

Economic Classics : ed. Prf. W. J. Ashley
[texts, selns., trs.: none annot.] ea. 3/ *n.* (75 c. *n.*) gl 8° Macmillan 95 *sqq.*

COURNOT (A.), *Princs. of Wealth*
JONES (R.), *Peasant Rents*
MALTHUS (T. R.), *Chs. fr. 'Princ. of Populn.'* [ut D § 121]
MUN (T.; *b.* 1571), *Treasure of For. Trade* [ut D § 117*]
RICARDO (D.), *Chs. fr. 'Princ. of Pol. Econ.'* [ut inf.] § 117*
SCHMOLLER (G.), *Mercantile System* [tr.] [ut D § 117*]
SMITH (A.), *Chs. fr. 'Wealth of Natns.'* [ut inf.]
TURGOT (R. R. J.), *Formatn., etc., of Riches* [ut inf.]

Economic Tracts : ed. Prf. Hollander; w. Introds. & notes 8° Johns Hopk. Pr., *Baltimore* *in prg.*

ASGILL, *Several Assertions Proved* [1696] 50 c.
BARBON, *Discourse of Trade* [1690] 50 c.
BERKELEY (Geo.), *The Querist*, 3 Pts. [1735–7]
FAUQUIER (Fcs.), *Ways and Means of Raisg. Money fr. Pres. War* [1756]
FORTREY, *England's Interest Considered* [1663] 50 c.
LONGE, *Refutn. of Wag-Fund Theory* [1866] 75 c.
MALTHUS (T. R.), *Nature and Progress of Wealth* [1815] 75 c.
MASSIE (Jos.), *Natural Rate of Interest* [1750]
NORTH, *Discourses upon Trade* [1691] [ut D § 122] 50 c.
RICARDO (D.), *Three Lettrs. on 'Price of Gold'* [1809] [ut inf.] ! 50 c.
WEST, *Applicn. of Capital to Land* [1815] 75 c.

English Citizen (The) : ed. Sir Hy. Craik ea. 2/6 or 3/6 c 8° Macmillan [81–6] *v.y.*

**Deals with the rights and responsibilities of citizens as they *are*, treating of the machinery of our Constitution and the broad lines upon which it has been constructed.**

CHALMERS (M. D.), *Local Government* [ut D § 124] o.p. [*pb.* 3/6]
COTTON (J. S.) + PAYNE (E. J.), *Colonies* [ut D § 136] o.p. [*pb.* 3/6]
CRAIK (H.), *State in rel. to Education* [ut D § 159] 2/6
DU CANE (Sir C.), *Crime* [ut D § 123] o.p. [*pb.* 3/6]
ELLIOT (A.), *State and Church* [ut A § 112] 2/6
FARRER (L'd), *State in rel. to Trade* [ut D § 122] 3/6
FOWLE (Rev. T. W.), *Poor Law* [ut D § 128] 2/6
JEVONS (W. S.), *State in rel. to Labour* [ut D § 118] 2/6
MACKAY (T.), *State and Charity* [ut D § 128] 2/6
MAITLAND (F. W.), *Justice and Police* [ut D § 123] o.p. [*pb.* 3/6]
MAURICE (Sir J. F.), *National Defences* [ut D § 142] 2/6
ODGERS (Dr W. B.), *Local Govt.* [ut D § 136] 3/6
PAYNE (E. J.), *Colonies and Colonial Federns.* [ut D § 136] 3/6
POLLOCK (Sir F.), *Land Laws* [ut D § 119] 2/6
TRAILL (H. D.), *Central Government* [ut D § 140] 3/6
WALPOLE (Spencer), *Electorate and Legislature* [ut D § 135] 2/6
,, *Foreign Relations* [ut D § 138] o.p. [*pb.* 3/6]
WILSON (A. J.), *National Budget* [ut D § 117] o.p. [*pb.* 3/6]

Imperial Parliament Series —*v.* **D** § 142

Johns Hopkins Univ. : University Studies in Hist. & Polit. Science, ed. H. B. Adams
ea. $3·50 8° Johns Hopk. Univ. Pr., *Baltim.* 83–08 *in prg.*

Ser. i : ***Local Amer. Institutions*** ($4)
ii : ***Institutions and Economics*** ($4)
iii : ***Maryld.; Wshgntn.; Virginia*** ($4)
iv : ***Munic. Govt. and Land Tenure***
v : ***Munic. Govt.; History and Politics***
vi : ***Hist. of Co-operation in U.S.***
[Engl. edn. 12/ 8° Macmillan.]
vii : ***Social Science; Educ.; Govt.***
viii : ***History; Politics; Education***
ix : ***Educ.; Hist.; Politics; Soc. Sci.***
x : ***Church and State; Columbus and America***
xi : ***Labor, Slavery, Self-Govt.***
xii : ***Institutional and Economic History***
xiii : ***South Carolina; Maryld.; Virginia***
xiv : ***Baltimore; Slavery; Constitl. History***
xv : ***American Economic History***
xvi : ***Anglo-Amer. Relns. and Southern Hist.***
xvii : ***Econ. Hist.; Maryland and the South***
xviii : ***Taxation; Church and Popular Educn.***
xix : ***Diplomatic and Constitutl. History***
xx : ***Colonial and Economic History***
xxi : ***Indiana; N. Carolina; Maryld.***
xxii : ***Social and Industrial History***
xxiii : ***Colonies; Revolution; Reconstruction***
xxiv : ***Diplomatic History; Trades Unions***
xxv : ***International and Colonial History***
xxvi : ***Administrative and Political History.***

A set of these 26 vols. $85 *n.* *Notes Supplementary* to several of above, ea. 10 c.

EXTRA VOLS.
ALLISON (E. P.) + PENROSE (B.), *Philad.*: 1681–1887 [*ut* **E** § 57] $3
ANDREWS (Prf. C. M.), *Old Engl. Manor* [*ut* **F** § 5] $1·50
BALLAGH (J. C.), *Hist. of Slavery in Va.* [*ut* **D** § 130] $1·52
BLACKMAR, (F. W.), *Spanish Instits. of South West* $2
BRACKETT (J. R.), *Negro in Maryld.* [*ut* **D** § 130] $2
BROUGH (C. H.), *Irrigation in Utah* *o.p.*
BROWN (G. W.), *Baltimore and 19 Apl.* 1861 [*ut* **F** § 71] *o.p.* [*pb.* $1]
A study of the war; by an Amer. judge.
CALLAHAN (J. M.), *Cuba and Internatl. Relns.*
COHN (M. M.), *Introd. to Study of Constitn.* [*ut* **D** § 145] $1·50
FLACK (H. E.), *Adoptn. of 14th Amendmt.* $2
HAZEN (Dr C. D.), *Contemp. Opin. of Fch. Revoln.* [*ut* **F** § 49] $2
HOLLANDER (Dr J. H.), *Financial Hist. of Baltimore* $2
HOWARD, (Prf. G. E.), *Local Const. Hist. of U.S.*, v. i [*ut* **D** § 124] $3
LEVASSEUR (E.), *The American Workman* [tr.] [*ut* **D** § 118] $3
LEVERMORE (Prf. C. H.), *Repub. of New Haven: munic. evolution* *o.p.* [*pb.* $2]
LORD (Eleanor L.), *Industr. Experimts. in Brit. Col. of N. Amer.* $1·25
NITOBE (I.), *Intercourse betw. Japan and U.S.* [*ut* **D** § 117*] $1·25
SCAIFE (W.B.), *America: its geogr. hist.*: 1492–1892 [*ut* **E** § 52] *o.p.* [*pb.* $1·50]
„ *Florentine Life dur. Renaissce.* [*ut* **F** § 53] *o.p.*
*State Aid to Higher Education* [addresses] $1
STEINER (B. C.), *Slavery in Connecticut* [*ut* **D** § 130] 75 c.
STOKES (H. K.), *Finances and Admin. of Providence*: 1636–1901 $3·50
VINCENT (J. M.), *State and Feder. Govt. in Switerzl.* [*ut* **D** § 144] *o.p.* [*pb.* $1·50]
WEEKS (Dr S. B.), *Southern Quakers and Slavery* [*ut* **D** § 130] $2
WILLOUGHBY (W. W.), *Supreme Court of U.S.* [*ut* **D** § 108] $1·25

Library of Economics and Politics : ed. Prf. R. T. Ely *v.pp.* 12° Crowell, *N.Y.* 93–07 *in prg.*

BASCOM (J.), *Social Theory* [*ut* **D** § 125] $1·75
BEMIS (E. W.), *Municipal Monopolies* [*ut* **D** § 124] $2
COMMONS (J. R.), *Proportional Representation* [*ut* **D** § 135] $1·75
„ *Social Reform and the Church* [*ut* **D** § 113] 75 c.
DIXON (F. H.), *State Railroad Control* [*ut* **D** § 147] $1·75
ELY (R. T.), *Labor Movement in America* [*ut* **D** § 120] $1·50
„ *Problems of To-day* [*ut inf.*] $1·50
„ *Social Aspects of Xty.* [*ut* **A** § 113] 90 c.
„ *Socialism and Social Reform* [*ut* **D** § 126] $1·50
*Equitable Taxation* [*ut* **D** § 117] 75 c.
FERNOW (B. E.), *Economics of Forestry* [*ut* **I** § 45] $1·50 *n.*
HOWE (F. C.), *Taxation and Taxes in U.S.* [*ut* **D** § 117] $1·75
*Hull-House Maps and Papers* [*ut* **D** § 127] $2·50
INGLE (E.), *Southern Side Lights* [*ut* **D** § 130] $1·75
KINLEY (D.), *Indep. Treasury Syst. of U.S.* [*ut* **D** § 117] $1·50
LE ROSSIGNOL (J. E.), *Monopolies Past and Present* [*ut* **D** § 118] $1·25
„ *Orthodox Socialism* [*ut* **D** § 126] $1 *n.*
MACCONACHIE (L. G.), *Congressional Committees* [*ut* **D** § 145] $1·75]
NEWELL (F. H.), *Irrigation* [*ut* **I** § 30] $2 *n.*
PEIXOTTO (Jessica B.), *Fch. Revoln. and Mod. Fch. Socialism* [*ut* **D** § 126] $1·50
*Philanthropy and Social Progress* [*ut* **D** § 123] $1·50
PORRITT (E.), *The Englishman at Home* [*ut* **D** § 135] $1·75
ROBINSON (Harriet H.), *Loom and Spindle* [*ut* **D** § 127] $1·25
RUSSELL (C.) + LEWIS (H. S.), *Jew in London* [*ut* **A** § 12] $1·50
SALTER (W. M.), *Anarchy or Government* [*ut* **D** § 126] 75 c.
SCOTT (W. A.), *Repud. of State Debts in U.S.* [*ut* **D** § 117] $1·50
SPAHR (C. B.), *Distribn. of Wealth in U.S.* [*ut* **D** § 119] $1·50
TRENT (W. P.), *Southern Statesmen of Old Régime* [*ut* **F** § 72] $1·75
WARNER (A. G.), *American Charities* [*ut* **D** § 128] $1·75
WILLOUGHBY (W. F.), *Workingmen's Insurance* [*ut* **D** § 127*] $1·75
WINES (F. H.), *Punishment and Reformation* [*ut* **D** § 123] $1·75

Michigan Academy of Science : Publications, vols. i–vi (Pt. i) 8° Univ. of Michigan 83–05
Ea. vol. made up of several papers, etc., by var. wrs. Inactive since 1905.

Nat. Liberal Club, Pol. Econ. Circle : Transactions, vols. i–v (Pts. 1–20) 8° P. S. King 91 *in prg.*
Vol. i, 3/; ii, *o.p.*; iii, 3/; iv, 1/; v, Pts. 1–20, ea. 6*d.* Conts. some useful papers by good authorities.

University of Pennsylvania : Pubns. in Pol. Economy & Public Law 8° Appleton, *N.Y.* 87 *sqq.*, *in prg.*

BARNARD (J. L.), *Factory Legisln. in Penn.* $1·25
CHEYNEY (E. P.), *Anti-rent Agitn.*, 1839–46 50 c.
DU BOIS (W. E. B.), *Philadelphia Negro* [*ut* **D** § 130] $2
*Feder. Constit. of Germy.*, tr. E. J. JAMES [*ut* **D** § 144] 50 c.
„ *Switzerland*, tr. same [*ut* **D** § 144] 50 c.
JOHNSON (J. F.), *Currency Reform* 25 c.
JONES (Chester L.), *Consular Service of U.S.* $1·50
„ *Anthracite Tide Water Canals* $1·50
LANGSTROTH (C. S.) + STILZ (W.), *Railw. Co-opern.* [*ut* **D** § 152] $1
LEWIS (W. D.), *Sheep and the Tariff* $1·50
PATTEN (S. N.), *Consumptn. of Wealth* 50 c.
„ *Dynamic Economics* [*ut* **D** § 114] $1
ROBINSON (J. H.), *German Bundesrath* [*ut* **D** § 144] 75 c.
SMITH (J. R.), *Ocean Commerce* [*ut* **D** § 149] $1·50
TOWER (W. S.), *Amer. Whale Fishery* [*ut* **I** § 43] $1·25
VOGT (P. L.), *Sugar Refing.* [*ut* **I** § 35] $1·50
WEYL (W. E.), *Passenger Traffic of Rys.* [*ut* **D** § 152] $1·50

Questions of the Day *v.p.* c 8° Putnam 80–93 *in prg.*

ALEXANDER (E. P.), *Railw. Prac.* [*ut* **D** § 152] 75 c.
ALLEN (J. H.), *Tariff and its Evils* [*ut* **D** § 122] $1
ATKINSON (E.), *Margin of Profit* 75 c.
„ *Taxation and Work* [*ut* **D** § 117] $1·25
‡BAGEHOT (W.), *Postulates of Polit. Econ.* [*ut* **D** § 114]
BAKER (C. W.), *Monopolies and People* [*ut* **D** § 118] $1·50
†BLACK (W. N.), *Storage and Transportn. in N.Y.*
BLAIR (L. H.), *Unwise Laws* $1
BONHAM (J. M.), *Railwy. Secrecy and Trusts* [*ut* **D** § 152] $1
BOURNE (E. G.), *Surplus Revenue of* 1837 [*ut* **D** § 117] $1·25
BOWKER (R. R.), *Of Work and Wealth* 75 c.
BRUCE (P. A.), *Plantation Negro* [*ut* **D** § 130] $1·25
CHAMBERLAIN (D. H.), *etc.*, *The Spanish Treaty* 25 c.
CLEVELAND (Pres. G.), *The President's Message* 25 c.
CODMAN (J.), *Mormon Problem* *o.p.* [25 c.]
COWLES (J. L.), *Gen. Freight and Passr. Post* [*ut* **D** § 137] $1·25
COWPERTHWAITE (J. H.), *Money and Finance* [*ut* **D** § 115] $1
†COX (S. S.), *Free Land and Free Trade* [*ut* **D** § 119] 75 c.
CROOKES (Sir Wm.), *The Wheat Problem* $1·25
DABNEY (W. D.), *Pub. Reguln. of Railwys.* [*ut* **D** § 152] $1·25
DONNELL (E. J.), *The True Issue* [tariff quest.] 25 c.
„ *Outlines of a New Science* $1
DOS PASSOS (J. R.), *Inter-State Commerce Act* [*ut* **D** § 63] $1·25
DOUGLAS (Jas.), *Canadian Independence* [*ut* **D** § 143] 75 c.
DUGDALE (R. L.), *The Jukes* [*ut* **D** § 123] $1
EHRICH (L. R.), *Question of Silver* [*ut* **D** § 115] $1
ELLIOTT (J. R.), *American Farms* [*ut* **D** § 119] $1·25
FOOTE (A. R.), *Sound Currency and Bkg. System* [*ut* **D** § 115] 75 c.
FORD (W. C.), *Citizen's Manl.*, 2 Pts. [*ut* **D** § 135] $1·25
†FOSTER (R.), *Taxn. of Elevated Railrds. in N.Y.* *o.p.*
FOULKE (W. D.), *Slav or Saxon* $1
GARDINER (C. A.), *Anglo-American Alliance* 25 c.
„ *Our Right to Foreign Territory* 50 c.
GIBBONS (R.), *Physics and Metaphysics of Money* 25 c.
‡GIFFEN (R.), *Progress of Wkg. Classes* [*ut* **D** § 118] 25 c.
GORDON (A. C.), *Congressional Currency* [*ut* **D** § 115] $1·25
GRINNELL, *Soc. Theories & Soc. Facts* [*ut* **D** § 125] $1
HALL (B.) [ed.], *Who pays your Taxes?* [*ut* **D** § 117] $1
HENDRICK, *Ry. Control by Commissns.* [*ut* **D** § 152] $1
HITCHCOCK (H.), *Amer. State Constits.* [*ut* **D** § 145] 75 c.
ISHAM (C.), *Fishery Question* [*ut* **D** § 142] 75 c.
JACOBI (Mrs), '*Common Sense*' *appl. to Woman Suffrage* [*ut* **D** § 132] $1
†JAQUES (W. H.), *Heavy Ordnance* 25 c.
† „ *Ericsson's Destroyer* 50 c.
† „ *Mod. Armour for Natl. Defence* 50 c.
† „ *Torpedoes for Natl. Defence* *o.p.* [50 c.]
JONES (W. H.), *Federal Taxes, etc.* [*ut* **D** § 117] $1
JUGLAR (C.), *Brief Hist. of Panics* [*ut* **D** § 115] $1
'JUNIUS', *Indep. Movemt. in N.Y.* 50c.
‡KEAY (J. S.), *Spoiling the Egyptns.* [*ut* **D** § 142] 75c.
†KELLEY (W. D.), *Lincoln and Stanton* 50c.
„ *The Old South and the New* $1·25 (5/)
LAWTON (G. W.), *Caucus System* [*ut* **D** § 135] $1
LOWELL (J. S.), *Publ. Relief and Priv. Charity* [*ut* **D** § 128] 75 c.
„ *Arbitration and Conciliation* [*ut* **D** § 118] 75 c.
LUNT (E. C.), *Pres. Condn. of Econ. Science* [*ut* **D** § 114] 75 c. (3/)
MACMILLAN (D. C.), *Elect. Franch. in U.S.* [*ut* **D** § 135] *o.p.*
MOORE (J. S.), *Letters to Amer. Farmers* 25 c.
†NORMAN (H.), *Bodyke* 75 c.
PALM (A. J.), *Death Penalty* [*ut* **D** § 123] $1.05

PETERS (Rev. J. P.) [ed.], *Labor and Capital* [*ut* D § 118] $1·50
PHILPOTT (H. J.), *Tariff Chats* 25 c.
PUTNAM (G. H.), *Quest. of Copyright* [*ut* D § 72] $1·75
‡RATHBONE (W.), *Protection and Communism* o.p. [25 c.]
REMSEN (D. S.), *Primary Elections* [*ut* D § 145] 75 c.
‡ROGERS (J. E. T.), *Social Economy* [*ut* D § 125] 75 c.
ROOSEVELT (Th.), *Practical Politics* 75 c.
SCHOENHOF (J.), *Destruct. Infl. of Tariff* [*ut* D § 122] 75 c.
" *Economy of High Wages* [*ut* D § 118] $1·50
" *Industrial Situation* [*ut* D § 118] $1
" *Money and Prices* [*ut* D § 115] $1·50
SHEARMAN (T. G.), *Natural Taxation* [*ut* D § 117] $1
SHERMAN (P.), *Tariff Primer* 25 c.
SHRIVER (E. J.), *Want and Wealth* 25 c.
SMITH (R. H.), *Science of Business* [*ut* D § 116] $1·25
STERNE (S.), *Defective and Corrupt Legislation* 25 c.
STOKES (A. P.), *Joint Metallism* [*ut* D § 115] $1
STOREY (M.), *Politics as Duty and as Career* 25 c.
STRANGE (D.), *Farmer's Tariff Manl.* [*ut* D § 122] $1·25
SWAN (C. H.), *Monetary Problems and Reforms* [*ut* D § 115] 75 c.
TAUSSIG (F. W.), *Tariff Hist. of U.S.* : 1789–1888 [*ut* D § 122] $1·25
Incl. *Protection to Young Industries* and *Hist. of Pres. Tariff*, both pub. prev. in the series [1884, 85].
" *Silver Situation in U.S.* [*ut* D § 115] 75 c.
†'Taxpayer', *True and False Finance* [issue of 1888] 25 c.
TOURGEE (A. W.), *War of the Standards* 75 c.
TYLER (L. G.), *Parties and Patron. in U.S.* [*ut* D § 146] $1
WELLS (D. A.), *Our Merchant Marine* [*ut* D § 148] $1
" *Rel. of Tariff to Wages* 20 c.
" *Question of Ships* 25 c.
WHEELER (E. P.), *Real Bimetallism* [*ut* D § 115] 75 c.
†WHITON (J. M.), *Evolution of Revelation* 25 c.
WINES (F. H.), *Amer. Prisons in 10th Census* 25 c.
WINN (H.), *Property in Land* 25 c.
‡ = repr. of Engl. bk. and thus not available in Engl.
† = no edn. of this (Amer.) bk. issued by the Lond. house.
20 c. = 1/6 ; 25 c. = 2/ ; 50 c. = 2/6 ; 75 c. = 3/ ; $1 = 4/ ; $1·25 = 5/ ; $1·50 = 6/.

## Reformer's Bookshelf (The)
ea. vol. 3/6 c 8° Unwin 93 *sqq.*, *in prg.*

BAMFORD (S.), *Passages in Life of a Radical*, 2 vols. [*ut* D § 125]
BONNER (Hypatia B.), *Chas. Bradlaw*, 2 vols. [*ut* F § 27]
COBDEN (R.), *Political Writings*, 2 vols. [*ut* D § 122]
COX (Har.) [ed.], *Brit. Industries under Free Trade* [*ut* D § 122]
DUFFY (Sir C. Gavan), *My Life in Two Hemispheres*, 2 vols.
HEATH (R.), *Agricultural Labourer* [*ut* D § 117*]
HOBHOUSE (L. T.), *Labour movement* [*ut* D § 118]
HOGAN (J. F.), *The Gladstone Colony*
HOLYOAKE (G. J.), *Sixty Yrs. of an Agitator's Life* [*ut* D § 120]
" *Bygones worth Remembering* [*ut* D § 120]
HOWELL (G.), *Labour Legislation*, 2 vols. [*ut* D § 118]
LEBON (G.), *The Crowd* [*ut* D § 125]
MASSINGHAM (W.) [ed.], *Labour and Protection* [*ut* D § 122]
MORLEY (Jno. = Lord), *Life of Cobden*, 2 vols. [*ut* F § 27]
MORRISON (W. D.), *Juvenile Offenders* [*ut* D § 123]
ROGERS (J. E. T.), *Econ. Interpretn. of Hist.*, 2 vols. [*ut* F § 2]
ROGERS (T. A.), *Indust. Hist. of Engld.*, 2 vols. [*ut* D § 117*]
SPALDING (T. A.), *House of Lords* [*ut* D § 140] o.p.
'STEPNIAK, S.', *Nihilism as it is* [*ut* D § 126] o.p.
WHITE (Wm.), *House of Commons* [*ut* D § 141]

## Social Problems Series
ea. 1/ *n.* c 8° Jack 07 *in prg.*

ADAM (Edwin), *Land Values and Taxation* [*ut* D § 117]
BELL (R.), *Trades Unionism* [*ut* D § 120]
DARROCH (Prf. Alex.), *The Children* [*ut* D § 127]
KAUFMAN (Rev. M.), *Housing of the Working Classes* [*ut* D § 127]
LOCH (C. S.), *Charity Organization* in prep.
MACDONALD (J. Ramsay), *Socialism* [*ut* D § 126]
MATHEW (A. H.), *Woman Suffrage* [*ut* D § 132]
SHERWELL (A.), *The Liquor Question* in prep.
TROTTER (W. F.), *The Citizen and his Duties* [*ut* D § 135]

## Social Questions
ea. 2/ *n.* c 8° Duckworth 07 *in prg.*

BLACK (Clementina), *Sweated Industry and Minimum Wage* [*ut* D § 118]
SHACKLETON (D. J.), *Women in Industry* [*ut* D § 132]
TUCKWELL (Gertr.), *The Worker's Handbook* [*ut* D § 127]

## Social Questions of To-day : ed. H. B. de Gibbins
ea. 2/6 c 8° Methuen 91–6

BASTABLE (C. F.), *Commerce of Nations* [*ut* D § 122]
BOWMAKER (E.), *Housing of Working Classes* [*ut* D § 127]
BUSHILL (T. W.), *Profit-Sharing* [*ut* D § 120]
COOKE-TAYLOR (R. W.), *Factory System and Acts* [*ut* D § 118]
COX (Har.), *Land Nationalization* [*ut* D § 119]
CUNNINGHAM (W.), *Modern Civilization* [*ut inf.*]
DILKE (Lady), *etc.*, *Woman's Work* [*ut* D § 132]
DOLMAN (F.), *Municipalities at Work* [*ut* D § 124]
EDWARDS (Clem.), *Railway Nationalization* [*ut* D § 142]
de GIBBINS (H.) + HADFIELD (R. A.), *Shorter Working Day* [*ut* D § 118]
GRAHAM (P. A.), *Rural Exodus* [*ut* D § 121]
HOBSON (J. A.), *Problems of Poverty* [*ut* D § 127]
" *Problem of Unemployed* [*ut* D § 118]
HOLYOAKE (G. J.), *Co-oper. Movemt.* [*ut* D § 120]
HOWELL (G.), *Trade Unionism* [*ut* D § 120]
JEANS (J. S.), *Trusts, Pools, and Corners* [*ut* D § 118]
KAUFMANN (Rev. M.), *Socialism and Mod. Thought* [*ut* D § 126]
MOORE (H. E.), *Back to the Land* [*ut* D § 121]
REASON (W.) [ed.], *University and Social Settlements* [*ut* D § 127]
SHERWELL (A.), *Life in West London* [*ut* D § 127]
TUCKWELL (Gert. M.), *State and its Children* [*ut* D § 127]
TWINING (Louisa), *Workhouses and Pauperism* [*ut* D § 127]
WILKINS (W. H.), *Alien Invasion* [*ut* D § 121]
WILKINSON (Rev. J. F.), *Mutual Thrift* [*ut* D § 120]

## Social Science Series
[ea. $1 Scribner, *N.Y.*] ea. 2/6 c 8° Sonnenschein 89 *sqq.*, *in prg.*

AVELING (Dr E.), *The Student's Marx* [*ut* D § 114]
" + Elean. M., *Wkg.-Cl. Movement. in Am.* [*ut* D § 120]
BADEN-POWELL (B. H.), *Village Communities in India* [*ut* F § 5]
BALMFORTH (R.), *New Reformation* [*ut* D § 125]
BAX (E. B.), *Ethics of Socialism* [*ut* D § 126]
" *Outlooks fr. New Standpt.* [*ut* D § 126]
" *Religion of Socialism* [*ut* D § 126]
" *French Revolution* [*ut* D § 126]
BEAULIEU (P. Leroy-), *Modern State* [*ut* D § 134]
BEHRENS (L. H.), *Toward the Light*
BERNSTEIN (E.), *Ferdinand Lassalle* [*ut* D § 126]
BLISSARD (Rev. W.), *Usury and Interest* [*u* D § 118]
BLUNDEN (G.), *Local Taxatn.* [*ut* D § 124]
BORGEAUD (C.), *Rise of Democracy* [tr.] [*ut* D § 139]
BOSANQUET (B.), *Essays and Addresses* [*ut* A § 8]
BOWLEY (A. L.), *Foreign Trade* [*ut* D § 117*]
BRENTANO (L.), *Hours and Wages* [tr.] [*ut* D § 118]
BURGIS (E.), *Perils to Brit. Trade*
CARPENTER (E.), *England's Ideal* [*ut* D § 126]
" *Civilisation* [*ut* D § 126]
CESTRE (C.), *John Thelwall* [*ut inf.*]
CHAPMAN (S. J.), *Local Govt.* [*ut* D § 124]
" *Trade betw. U.K. and U.S.* [*ut* D § 117*]
COIT (S.), *Neighbourhood Guilds* [*ut* D § 120]
de COULANGES (F.), *Prop. in Land* [tr.] [*ut* F § 5]
CREPAZ (A.), *Emancip. of Women* [tr.] [*ut* D § 132]
CUMING (A. N.), *Public House Reform* [*ut* D § 131]
*Daily News* Commissr. *Social Horizon* [*ut* D § 118]
DALY (J. B.), *Dawn of Radicalism* [*ut* F § 25]
DAVIDSON (J.), *Commerc. Federn.* [*ut* D § 136]
DAWSON (W. H.), *Bismarck and Socialism* [*ut* D § 126]
" *Socialism and Lassalle* [*ut* D § 125]
" *Unearned Increment* [*ut* D § 119]
ENGELS (F.), *Socialism* [*ut* D § 126]
EPPS (W.), *Land-Systs. of Austral.* [*ut* D § 119]
FOURIER (C.), *Selns. from* [tr.] [*ut* D § 125]
GALTON (F. W. ; ed.), *Workers on Industries* [*ut* D § 118]
‡GEORGE (H.), *Conditn. of Labour* [*ut* D § 119]
GILES (A. E.), *Moral Pathology*
GODARD (J. G.), *Poverty* [*ut* D § 127]
GODWIN (Wm.), *Political Justice* [*ut* D § 134]
GÖHRE (P.), *Three Months in Workshop* [*ut* D § 118]
GREEN (J. L.), *Allotments* [*ut* D § 119]
GRONLUND (L.), *Co-oper. Commonwealth* [*ut* D § 126]
" *Our Destiny* [*ut* D § 126]
GUYOT (Yves), *Tyranny of Socialism* [tr.] [*ut* D § 126]
HARVEY (C. H.), *Biol. of Brit. Politics* [*ut* F § 17*]
HAYCRAFT (J. B.), *Darwinism and Race-Progress* [*ut* D § 125]
HERVEY (M. H.), *Imper. Federation* [*ut* D § 136]
‡HIGGINSON (T. W.), *Commonsense ab. Women* [*ut* D § 132]
HOBSON (J. A. ; ed.), *Labour upon Land* [*ut* D § 119]
HOLYOAKE (G. J.), *Rochdale Pioneers* [*ut* D § 120]
" *Self-Help 100 Yrs. Ago* [*ut* D § 120]
HYNDMAN (H. M.), *Commercial Crises* [*ut* D § 115]
*Irish Peasant* [*ut* D § 142]
KEBBEL (T. E.), *Agricultural Labourer* [*ut* D § 117*]
LAFARGUE (P.), *Evolutn. of Property* [*ut* F § 5]
de LAVELEYE (E.), *Luxury* [*ut* D § 114]
LEFFINGWELL (A.), *Illegitimacy* [*ut* D § 133]
LINTON (W. J.), *English Republic*
LOCH (C. S.), *Charity Organization* [*ut* D § 128]
MACKENZIE (F. A.), *Sober by Act of Parl.* [*ut* D § 131]
MACMILLAN (M.), *General Happiness* [*ut* D § 125]
MARX (K.), *Revolution* [tr.] [*ut* D § 126]
MASSART + VANDERVELDE, *Parasitism* [*ut* D § 125]
MILLIN (G. F.), *The Village Problem* [*ut* D § 119]
MITCHELL (K.), *Drink Question* [*ut* D § 131]
MORRISON (W. D.), *Crime and Causes* [*ut* D § 123]
NAQUET (A.), *Collectivism and Socialism* [tr.] [*ut* D § 126]
NICHOLSON (J. S.), *Effects of Machinery* [*ut* D § 118]
" *Corn Laws* [*ut* D § 117*]
" *Rents, etc., in Agric.* [*ut* D § 117*]
" *Rates and Taxes* [*ut* D § 119]
NITTI (F. S.), *Populatn. and Social Syst.* [tr.] [*ut* D § 121]
OSTROGORSKI (M.), *Rights of Women* [tr.] [*ut* D § 132]
PIZZAMIGLIO (L.), *Distribg. Co-op. Socs.* [tr.] [*ut* D § 120]
POTTER (B.), *Co-oper. Movemt.* [*ut* D § 120]
*Practical Programme for Wkg.-Men*
PRICE (L. L.), *Money and Prices* [*ut* D § 115]
RITCHIE (D. G.), *Darwinism and Politics* [*ut* D § 134]
" *State Interference.* [*ut* D § 134]
ROBERTSON (J. M.), *Eight Hours Question* [*ut* D § 118]
" *Fallacy of Saving* [*ut* D § 127*]
" *Modern Humanists* [*ut* D § 125]
ROCQUAIN (F.), *Revolut. Spirit precedg. Fch. Revol.* [*ut* D § 126]
RODBERTUS (K.), *Over-Prodn. and Crises* [*ut* D § 115]
ROGERS (J. E. T.), *Work and Wages* [*ut* D § 118]
ROUSSEAU (J. J.), *Social Contract* [tr.] [*ut* F § 49]
SCHÄFFLE (A.), *Labour Protection* [tr.] [*ut* D § 126]
" *Quintessence of Socialism* [tr.] [*ut* D § 126]

SIMONSON (G.), *Plain Exam. of Socialism* [ut **D** § 126]
SKOTTOWE (B. C.) *Short Hist. of Parliamt.* [ut **F** § 17]
SPENDER (J. A.), *Pensions in Old Age* [ut **D** § 127*]
SPYERS (T. G.), *Labour Commission* [ut **D** § 118]
STOPES (Charl. M.), *British Freewomen* [ut **D** § 132]
STUBBS (C. W.), *Land and Labourers* [ut **D** § 120]
THOMPSON (H. M.), *Purse and Conscience* [ut **D** § 115]
‡THOREAU (H. D.), *Anti-slav. and Reform Papers* [ut **D** § 130]
WADIA (P. A.), *Philosophers and Fch. Revoln.* [ut **F** § 49]
WALLACE (A. R.), *Land Nationalisation* [ut **D** § 119]
WEBB (S.), *London Programme* [ut **D** § 124]
,, *Socialism in England* [ut **D** § 125]
WHITE (A.), *Destitute Alien* [ut **D** § 121]
WILSON (G. R.), *Drunkenness* [ut **D** § 131]
WINTER (A.), *Elmira Reformatory* [ut **D** § 123]
WOODWORTH (A. V.), *Chr. Socialism in Engl.*
WORTHINGTON (L.), *Dwellings of the Poor* [ut **D** § 127]

Double Volumes [ea. $1.25 Scribner, *N.Y.*] ea. 3/6 c 8° Sonnenschein 92 *sqq.. in prg.*
BLISS (W. D. P.), *Handbk. of Socialism* [ut **D** § 126]
ENGELS (F.), *Cond. of Wkg. Class* [ut **D** § 118]
GUYOT (Yves), *Princs. of Soc. Econ.* [tr.] [ut **D** § 125]
JONES (Lloyd), *Robert Owen* [ut **D** § 125]
LORIA (A.), *Econ. Foundns. of Society* [tr.]
MORRIS (W.) + BAX (E. B.), *Socialism* [ut **D** § 126]
SCHÄFFLE (A.), *Imposs. of Soc. Democ.* [ut **D** § 126]
SCHULZE-GAEVERNITZ, *Social Peace* [tr.] [ut **D** § 120]
‡ = repr. of Amer. bk. and thus not available in Amer. in this form.

Social Service Handbooks : ed. Percy Alden ea. 1/ *n.* ; *cl.* 1/6 *n.* c 8° Headley *v.y.*
*Child Life and Labour* [ut **D** § 118] MRS P. ALDEN
*Health of the State* G. NEWMAN
*Housing* [ut **D** § 127] P. ALDEN + E. E. HAYWARD
*Land and Landless* [ut **D** § 119] G. CADBURY + T. BRYAN
*Poverty* [ut **D** § 127] WILL REASON
*Service of the State* [ut **D** § 124] NEWMAN
*Sweating* [ut **D** § 118] E. CADBURY + G. SHANN
*Unemployable and Unemployed* [ut **D** § 118] P. ALDEN

**History of Economic Theory**—*v. also* **D** § 134, *s.v.* History

ASHLEY, Prf. W. J. —*in his* Introd. to English Economic History and Theory, *ut* **D** § 117*
,, Surveys, Historic and Economic 9/ *n.* ($3) c 8° Longman 00

BLANQUI, J. A. History of Political Economy in Europe [tr.] *o.p.* [*pb.* 12/] 8° Bell 80
Omits annot. bibliogr. of orig. edn. [1837–8]. Embraces acc. of econ. ideas and systs. fr. times of Gks. and Roms. to 1842, and of causes wh. have produced the successive modificns. in civil, industr., and commerc. ideas, and in gov. policy.

*v. BÖHM-BAWERK, Prf. E. V. Capital and Interest [tr.]—*ut inf.*

BONAR, Dr Jas. Philosophy and Economics in their Historical Relations 10/6 8° Sonnenschein [93] 09
$2·75 *n.* Macmillan, *N.Y.* [Lib. of Philosophy.] A hist. of polit. econ. fr. SOCRATES to Karl MARX, w. view of exhibg. its close conn. w. hist. of philos. in general. Spec. prominence given to influ. of HUME on earlier Engl. economics and of HEGEL on later developmts., both on Continent and in Engl. An encyclopædic wk., condensing a whole library of writers in a lucid and impartial manner.

CANNAN, Dr Edwin Hist. of Theories of Production and Distribution in English Political Economy 10/6 *n.* 8° P. S. King [93] 03
From 1776 to 1848, freely criticizing the weak pts. of the 'classical' economists. Treats ea. subj. in a separ. chap. or sectn., and throws consid. light on conn. betw. politics and economics, showing at same time that the Ricardian system was of a much more practical character than is generally supposed.

COHN, Prf. Herm. History of Political Economy, tr. J. A. Hill $1 8° Acad. of Pol. and Soc. Sci., *Phila.* 94
Tr. of vol. i of his *System der Nationalökonomie*, 12m. 8° Enke, *Stuttg.* '85 [vol. ii : *Finanzwissenschaft*, 16m. 8° *id.*, *ib.* '80].

COSSA, Prf. Luigi Introd. to the Study of Political Economy [tr.]—*ut sup.*

CUNNINGHAM, Dr W. Essay on Western Civilisation in its Econ. Aspects, 2 vols.—*ut* **F** § 4

DEWE, Prf. J. A. History of Economics $1·50 8° Benziger, *N.Y.* 08
A popular bk., of an educational character, tracing, by a close record of fact, the influ. of economics on history thro' the Greek, Roman, medieval, and modern periods. Concise and lucid.

ELY, Prf. R. T. Past & Present of Political Economy 35 c. 8° Johns Hopk. Univ. Pr., *Baltimore* 84

FIGGIS, Dr J. N. Studies of Political Thought from Gerson to Grotius : 1414–1625 [$1·10 *n.* Putnam, *N.Y.*] 3/6 *n.* 8° Camb. Press 07

HANEY, Dr L. H. History of Economic Thought (8/6 *n.*) 8° Macmillan 11

INGRAM, Dr J. K. A History of Political Economy 6/ 8° Black [88] 93
$1·50 *n.* Macmillan, *N.Y.* Ancient, mediaeval, and modern. By a strong adherent of the Historical School. Enlarged fr. his article in *Encyclo. Brit.* (9th edn.).

LESLIE, Prf. T. E. Cliffe- Essays in Polit. and Moral Philosophy—*ut inf.*, *s.v.* Collected Essays

MACLEOD, H. D. History of Economics [$4·50 *n.* Putnam, *N.Y.*] 16/ 8° Bliss 96
About one-tenth of bk. is histor., the rest miscellan. or purely polemical : the whole partial and egotistic, but, owing to the author's wide reading, learning, and common-sense, of considerable value.
,, —*his* Elements of Economics, vol. i [*ut inf.*] *gives a history of pure economics*

MEREDITH, H. O. Outlines of the Economic History of England 5/ *n.* 8° Pitman 08
An instructive, impartial, and well-wr. bk., in 4 Pts. (1) *Mediaev. Engl.* (1066–1272), (2) *The Engl. Nation* (1272–1603), (3) *Antecedts. of the Industr. Revoln.* (1603–1760), (4) *The Industr. Revoln. and its Conseqs.* (1760–1900).

NYS, Prf. Ern. Researches in the History of Economics [tr.] 6/ c 8° Black 99
Essays touching on nearly every side of econ. practice and theory fr. Byzant. Emp. to Mercantile System. Numerous summaries.

PATTEN, Prf. S. N. Development of English Thought—*ut* **F** § 2

PRICE, L. L. Short Hist. of Polit. Econ. in England 2/6 c 8° Methuen 91
[Univ. Extens. Ser.] Readable and useful, but not very valuable. Begins w. Adam SMITH and ends w. Arnold TONYBEE, more than one-half being devoted to recent economists (excludes living economists).

RAND, Dr Benj. [ed.] Selectns. ill. Econ. History since Seven Yrs. War [1756–1763] [12/6 Macm.] $3 *n.* 8° Waterman, *Camb., Mass.* [88] 03

ROGERS, Prf. J. E. Thorold The Economic Interpretation of [Engl.] History—*ut* **F** § 2
,, The Industrial and Commercial History of England—*ut* **D** § 117*

TWISS, Sir Travers View of Progress of Pol. Econ. in Eur. since 16 Cent. *o.p.* [*pb.* 10/6] 8° Black 47

*Recent and Contemporary :* LAWSON (W. R.) British Economics in 1904 6/ *n.* Blackwood [04] 06

LUNT, E. C. Present Conditn. of Econ. Science [brilliant essay] 75 c. 8° Putnam 88

MARSHALL, Prf. Alf. Present Position of Economics [inaug. address] 2/ (60 c.) c 8° Macmillan 85
PRICE, L. L. Position and Prospects of Study of Economic History 1/ *n.* 8° Clar. Press 08
SHERWOOD, S. Tendencies in Amer. Economic Thought [Univ. Studies] 8° Johns Hopk. Pr., *Baltimore* 97
SMART, Prf. Wm. Economic Annals of the Nineteenth Century, Pt. i [1801–20] 8° Macmillan *in prep.*

*Austria*

v. BÖHM-BAWERK, Prf. E. V. The Austrian Economists—*inf., s.v.* Mathematical Economics

*France*

HIGGS, Hy. The Physiocrats: 6 lects. on *Économistes* of 18 Cent. 3/6 *n.* c 8° Macmillan 97
A learned and concise wk. on the School, its rise, doctrs., activities, opponents, and influence.
SARGENT, A. J. The Economic Policy of Colbert 2/6 (75 c.) c 8° Longman 99

*Germany: Cameralists*

SMALL, Prf. A. W. The Cameralists: pioneers of Germ. soc. polity $3 *n.* 8° Univ. Press, *Chicago* 09
A detailed acc. of the series of Germ. wrs. fr. middle 16th to end 18th cent. who approached civics fr. a common pt.-of-view.

*Mercantile System*

SCHMOLLER, Prf. G. The Mercantile Syst. & its Hist. Significance [tr.]—*ut* **D** § 117*
[Economic Classics.] Illustrated chiefly from Prussian history.

*Italy*

LORIA, Achille Economics in Italy [pres. tendencies & past developmt.] 25 c. 8° Acad. of Pol. Sci., *Phila.*

**Biography and Criticism of Economists** —*v. also* **D** § 125

BENTHAM, Jeremy [1748–1832]—*v.* **C** § 18
COLBERT, J. B. [1619–83]
Sargent, A. J. The Economic Policy of Colbert 2/6 *n.* c 8° P. S. King & Son 99
GEORGE, Hy. [1839–97] Life of. By Hy. George, jun. $1·50 *n.* 12° Doubleday, *N.Y.* 00
JEVONS, W. Stanley [1835–82] Letters and Journal, ed. by his Wife 14/ 8° Macmillan 86
LIEBER, Fcs. [1800–72]
Harley, Dr L. R. F. Lieber.: his life & polit. philos. [Col. Un. Sts.] $1·75 *n.* (7/6 *n.*) 8° Macmillan 99
LIST, Friedr. [1789–1846] —*v.* **D** § 122
MALTHUS, T. R. [1766–1834] —*v.* **D** § 121
MILL, Jas. [1773–1836] —*v.* **C** § 48
MILL, Jno. Stuart [1806–73] —*v.* **C** § 49
,, Letters, ed. H. S. R. Elliot, 2 vols.; 6 ports. 21/ *n.* 8° Longman 10
With note on MILL's private life, by MARY TAYLOR. (Too late for inclusion in **C** § 49.)
PETTY, Sir Wm. [1623–87]
Bevan, W. L. Sir William Petty [Am. Econ. Ass.; 2/6 Sonnenschein] 55 c. *n.* 8° Macmillan, *N.Y.* 94
RICARDO, Dav. [1772–1823] Letters to Malthus: 1810–23 7/6 ($1·90) 8° Clar. Press 87
,, Letters to Hutches Trower and others: 1811–23, ed. Dr J. Bonar + J. H. Hollander 7/6 ($1·90) 8° Clar. Press 99
,, Three Letters on Price of Gold [Econ. Tracts] 50 c. 8° J. Hopk. Un. Pr., *Baltim.* [1809]
Hollander, J. H. [ed.] Letters of Ricardo to McCulloch: 1816–23; w. Introd. and notes [Am. Ec. Ass.; 5/- Sonnenschein] $1·25 *n.* 8° Macmillan, *N.Y.* 95
Patten, S. H. Malthus & Ricardo [Am. Ec. Ass.; 2/6 Sonnenschein] 75 c. *n.* 8° Macmillan, *N.Y.*
RODBERTUS, J. Carl [1805–75]—*v.* **D** § 126
SMITH, Adam [1723–90] —*v. also* **C** § 61
Hirst, F. W. Adam Smith [English Men of Letters] 2/ *n.* (75 c. *n.*) c. 8° Macmillan 04
Leslie, Prf. T. E. Cliffe The Pol. Econ. of Adam Smith—*in his* Essays, *ut inf.*
Rae, Jno. Life of Adam Smith [the fullest Life] 12/6 *n.* ($4 *n.*) 8° Macmillan 95
STERNE, Simon [1839–1901]
Foord, J. Life and Public Services of Simon Sterne $2 12° Macmillan, *N.Y.* 03
THELWALL, Jno. [1764–1834]
Cestre, C. John Thelwall [Social Science Ser.; $1 Scribner, *N.Y.*] 2/6 c 8° Sonnenschein 06
TOYNBEE, Arnold [1852–83] —*v.* **D** § 128
TUCKER, Jos.
Clark, W. E. Joseph Tucker, Economist [Col. Univ. Studs.] $1·50 *n.* 8° Macmillan, *N.Y.* 03
TURGOT, A. R. J. [1727–81]
B., J. M. Sketch of Turgot [w. tr. of his l'rs to Dr Price] c 8° *priv. prin. Boston* 99

Morley, Jno., L'd — Turgot—*in his* Critical Miscellanies, vol. ii, *ut* **K** § 89
Say, Léon — Turgot [tr.] [Great French Writers] *o.p.* [*pb.* 2/6] c 8° Routledge 88
Shepherd, R. P. — Turgot and the Six Edicts [Col. Univ. Studs.] $1·50 *n.* 8° Macmillan, *N.Y.* 03
YOUNG, Arth. [1741–1820] — Autobiography, ed. M. Betham-Edwards 12/6 8° Smith & Elder 98

**Systematic Works**

ADAMS, Prf. H. C. — Economics and Jurisprudence 50 c. *n.* 8° Macmillan, *N.Y.*
ANDREWS, Prf. E. B. — Institutes of Economics $1·30 12° Silver, *Boston* 89
7/6 Paul. A succinct and thorough college text-bk., with notes and literary references to each section.
BAGEHOT, Walt. — Postulates of Engl. Pol. Econ., ed. Prf. A. Marshall 2/6 c 8° Longman 85
BAIN, F. W. — On the Principle of Wealth Creation 10/6 m 8° Parker 92
Its nature, origin, and evolution : an attempted critical reconstruction of political economy.
" — Body and Soul : method of economy [cont. of above] 10/6 8° Parker 94
BASTIAT, Fred. — Essays on Political Economy [tr.] [forcible & clear] $1·25 12° Putnam, *N.Y.* [74] 93
" — Harmonies of Polit. Econ., tr. P. J. Stirling 7/6 c 8° *Edinburgh* [60] 70
BENSON, Marg. — Capital, Labour, and Trade, and the Outlook 2/6 f 8° S.P.C.K. 92
An excellent primer, rivalling Harriet MARTINEAU in the art of simple illustrations.
BLACKMAR, F. W. — Economics $1·40 *n.* (6/ *n.*) 12° Macmillan [00] 07
" — Economics for High Schools and Academies $1 *n.* (6/ *n.*) 12° Macmillan
BONAR, Dr Jas. — Elements of Political Economy 4/6 c 8° Murray 03
BOWEN, Prf. Fcs. — Principles of Political Economy *o.p.* [*pb.* $2·50] 8° Boston 54
" — American Political Economy $2·50 8° Scribner, *N.Y.* [70] 85
BOWKER, R. R. — Economics for the People 75c. 12° Harper, *N.Y.* [86] 02
'Plain talks' on economics, by a business man, intended for popular reading, w. sketch of econ. hist. and literature.
CAIRNES, Prf. J. B. — Character & Logical Method of Polit. Economy 6/ c 8° Macmillan [2nd edn. 75] 88
Denies, even more strongly than MILL, that there is any room for Induction at all.
" — Some Leading Princs. of Polit. Econ. newly Expounded 14/ 8° Macmillan [74] 83
Especially valuable on Wages and Internat. Trade. Contains also a re-analysis of Cost, and Supply and Demand.
" — Essays in Political Economy : theoret. and applied 10/6 8° Macmillan 73
*Colonization and Colon. Govt., The Revol. in Amer. Internat. Law, Protectn., Free Trade*, etc. SIDGWICK regards CAIRNES as a dissolving force, whose *Leading Principles* did much to shake the unique prestige wh. MILL's exposn. had enjoyed.
CANNAN, Dr Edwin — Elements of Political Economy 1/ (35 c.) f 8° Clar. Press [88] 03
CARLILE, W. W. — Economic Method and Economic Fallacies 10/6 *n.* r 8° Arnold 04
In Pt. i combats view wh. ignores distinctn. betw. physical and mental sciences, or such quasi-mental sciences as economics. Pt. ii, *Types of Econ. Fallacy*, indicates the errors th. have resulted. Pt. iii deals w. the fiscal probl.
CARVER, T. N. — The Distribution of Wealth $1·50 *n.* (6/6 *n.*) c 8° Macmillan 04
CLAREMONT, A. W. — Pictures in Political Economy 3/6 *n.* c 8° Moring 04
CLARK, Prf. J. B. — Philosophy of Wealth : econ. princs. newly formulated $1·10 (6/) 12° Ginn 87
For general readers ; elementary but thoroughly scientific ; fully recognizes influ. of moral forces in the economic field.
" — The Distribution of Wealth $3 *n.* (12/6 *n.*) c 8° Macmillan 00
A theory of wages, interest, and profits.
" — Essentials of Economic Theory $2 *n.* (8/6 *n.*) c 8° Macmillan 07
An instalmt. of a treatise on *Economic Dynamics ; or Laws of Industr. Progress.* Discusses, technically, and somewhat pedantically, econ. theory as appl. to mod. problems of industry and public policy.
" — Theory of Economic Progress [Amer. Econ. Assoc.] 50 c. *n.* 8° Macmillan, *N.Y.* 96
" + GIDDINGS (F. H.) The Modern Distributive Process 75 c. c 8° Ginn, *Boston* 88
Studies of competition, the nature and amount of profits, and the determination of wages.
COMMONS, Prf. J. R. — The Distribution of Wealth ; diagrs. $1·25 *n.* (7/ *n.*) c 8° Macmillan 93
A carefully reasoned wk. : treating the subj. under heads of *Value, Price, Cost ; Factors in Distribn. ; Diminishg. Returns and Rent ; Dimin. Returns and Distribn.*, etc. Illns. mostly drawn fr. Amer. sources.
CROZIER, Dr J. B. — The Wheel of Wealth 12/6 *n.* ($4·50) 8° Longman 06
A reconstrn. of science and art of polit. econ. on lines of modern evolution, by an industrious worker who has set out to prepare 'A New Organon' to deal w. the *Hist. of Intellectual Developmt.* [*ut* **F** § 4], of wh. this wk. forms pt. Assails orthodox pol. econ. with vigour, and takes nothing in the science for granted.
CUNNINGHAM, Dr Wm. — Politics and Economics as Principles of Pol. Econ. 5/ 8° Paul 85
" — Modern Civilization in some of its Economic Aspects 2/6 c 8° Methuen 96
$1 Scribner, *N.Y.* [Social Questns. of To-day.] Its chief object is to correlate economy, humanity and Christianity : mainly based on wrgs. of Prf. MARSHALL.
DANSON, J. T. — The Wealth of Households 5/ ($1·25) c 8° Clar. Press 86
Based on a series of lects. del. at Liverpool. A good little popular bk., on conserv. lines.
DAVENPORT, H. J. — Outlines of Economic Theory 8/6 *n.* ($2) 8° Macmillan 97
Doctrs. of pol. econ. restated in terms of adaptatn. to environmt. Demand is made the primary power. Least resistance in physical world emerges as least sacrifice in world of motive. Upon these two notions is rested a novel conceptn. of value, and applicatns. thereof are made to theory of money and exchange and to taxatn.
" — Outlines of Elementary Economics 3/6 *n.* (80 c. *n.*) gl 8° Macmillan 97
DENSLOW, Van Buren — Princ. of Econ. Philos. of Society, Govt., & Industry $3·50 8° Cassell, *N.Y.* 88
A systematic treatise on economics fr. Protectionist standpt., w. copious quotations fr. leading writers, and diagrams.

DEVAS, C. S. Manual of Polit. Economy [Stonyhurst Philos. Ser. ; R.-C.] 7/6 ($2) c 8° Longman [92] 01

DEVINE, E. T. Economics $1 *n.* (4/6) c 8° Macmillan 98
A clear, thoughtful, and interesting bk., but not for the beginner. Wr. fr. a standpt. opposite to that usually adopted in Engl., regarding the true starting-pt. in the constrn. of a complete theory of econcs. as lying in consumption rather than in productn. : 'wants precede satisfactions'.

ELY, Prf. R. T. Introd. to Political Economy [4/6 Sonnenschein] $1 c 8° Hunt & Eaton, *N.Y.* 89
From sociological side, by a leader of the 'new school' of national economists. Orig. wr. for Chautauqua Reading Circle, it forms an excellent little manual for pop. reading, w. short bibliogr. and courses of reading. Engl. edn. has pref. by Prf. J. K. INGRAM.

,, Outlines of Economics $1·25 *n.* (5/ *n.*) 12° Macmillan [94] 01
A good College text-bk. : more theoretical than above, givg. a system. sketch of theory, and good deal of space and attention to bibliogr.

,, + WICKER (G. R.) Elem. Princs. of Econ., w. sk. of econ. hist. $1 *n.* (4/6 *n.*) c 8° Macmillan 04

FAWCETT, Prf. Hy. Manual of Political Economy 12/ ($2·60 *n.*) c 8° Macmillan [63] 07
The best brief manual on the lines of MILL. Concise and simple. Notes by Mrs FAWCETT.

Waters, C. A. Explan. Digest of Fawcett's 'Manl. of Polit. Econ.' 2/6 c 8° Macmillan 88

,, + [Mrs] M. G. Political Economy for Beginners 2/6 (90 c. *n.*) 12° Macmillan [70] 04
An abridgment by Mrs FAWCETT of her husband's large work, *supra.*

FLUX, Prf. A. W. Economic Principles 7/6 *n.* 8° Methuen 04
A résumé of the teaching of the classical economists, with results of modern thought.

GEORGE, Hy. The Science of Political Economy $ 8° Doubleday, *N.Y.* 98
7/6 Paul. Views are set forth scientifically, not popularly : of very small value. Introd. by Hy. GEORGE, junr.

GIBSON, A. H. Human Econs., Bks. i–ii : Natural Econ. and Cosmop. Econ. 10/6 *n.* ($3·50 *n.*) 8° Longman 09
An instructive, carefully systematized work, on independent lines.

GIDE, Prf. Chas. Principles of Political Economy [tr.] $2 (7/6) c 8° Heath, *Boston* [92] 09
A good guide-bk. for students who have mastered the alphabet of economics, and are feeling their way to a judgmt. of their own. Written by a Frenchman, tr. by E. P. JACOBSEN, an Englishman, w. Introd. by Dr Jas. BONAR, a Scotsman, and pubd. by an Amer. firm. Suggestive, not dogmatic. Excellent notes.

HADLEY, Prf. A. T. Economics $2·50 (12/6) 8° Putnam 96
Acc. of relns. betw. private property and public welfare. A clear, unpretentious, readable bk. Free Trade.

HAWLEY, F. B. Enterprise and the Productive Process $1·50 *n.* (6/) c 8° Putnam 07
A theory of econ. productivity fr. pt. of view of the *entrepreneur*, and based on definitions.

HEARN, W. E. Plutology [an able treatment of production] 16/ 8° Longman [64] 78

HOBSON, J. A. The Evolution of Modern Capitalism—*ut* **D** § 118

,, Economics of Distribution [Citizens' Lib.] 5/ *n.* ($1·25 *n.*) Macmillan 00
Accepts 'marginal' utility hypothesis, but seeks to prove th. there is a fund of surplus profits as well as rents wh. might be confiscated without injustice.

* ,, The Industrial System 7/6 *n.* $2·50 *n.*) 8° Longman 09
An able inquiry into the main operatns. and conditns. of industry, (presentg. the whole as a interdependent living organism) and the orig. and nature of 'the unproductive surplus'—the 'principal source not merely of waste but of economic malady'.

,, The Science of Wealth [Home Univ. Lib.] 1/ *n.* s 8° Williams 11

HUME, Dav. —*in his* Essays, 2 vols., *ut* **C** § 29
Commerce, Money, Interest, Balance of Trade, etc.

*JEVONS, Prf. W. Stanley The Theory of Polit. Econ. [mathem.] 10/6 ($2·50 *n.*) 8° Macmillan [71] 88

,, Political Economy [Primers series ; lucid] 1/ 18° Macmillan [79]

,, The Principles of Economics 10/ *n.* ($3·25 *n.*) 8° Macmillan 05
A fragment of a treat. on the *Industrial Mechanism of Society*, and other posthumous papers. Pref. Hy. HIGGS.

KENWORTHY, J. C. The Anatomy of Misery 1/ *n.* c 8° *Clarion* Press [93] 00
Simple lectures on economics, in familiar lang., by a disciple of TOLSTOY.

LAUGHLIN, J. L. Elements of Pol. Econ. [popular ; w. questns.] $1·50 12° Appleton, *N.Y.* 87

de LAVELEYE, E. Elements of Political Economy, tr. A. W. Pollard *o.p.* [*pb.* 6/] c 8° Chapman 84
An able presentation of the 'Humanitarian' view of economic science.

LEVASSEUR, P. E. Elements of Polit. Economy, tr. T. Marburg $1·75 *n.* 8° Macmillan, *N.Y.* 05

LIBERATORE, F'r Principles of Political Economy, tr. E. H. Dering 7/6 8° Art & Book Co. 91
A Roman-Catholic treatise, in full accord w. LEO xii's Encyclical *On the Condition of Labour*, *ut* **D** § 119.

LIST, F. Natnl. Syst. of Polit. Econ. [tr.] ; Introd. Prf. J. S. Nicholson 6/ *n.* ($2 *n.*) c 8° Longman [85] 04
For note on this book *v.* **D** § 122, *s.v.* Protectionist.

LORIA, Achille Economic Foundations of Society, tr. L. M. Keasbey 3/6 c 8° Sonnenschein [99] 07
$1·25 Scribner, *N.Y.* [Social Science Series, Double Vol.]

McCULLOCH, J. R. Principles of Political Economy 1/ 8° Ward & Lock [25] 85

MACFARLANE, C. W. Value and Distribution : a study in economic theory 12/ 8° Lippincott [ ] 00

MACLEOD, H. D. Princs. of Econ. Philosophy, v. i, 15/ ; v. ii, Pt. i, 12/ ; Pt. ii 7/6 8° Longman 72–5 ; 86

,, Elements of Economics, vol. i 3/6, vol. ii, Pt. i 3/6 c 8° Longman 81–6

,, Economics for Beginners 2/ 12° Longman [78] 99
A general view of the author's independent and theoretical system, more fully set forth in *The Elements*, wh. reproduce the substance of *The Principles*. His *History* [*ut sup.*] deals w. much the same matter.

MAKATO, Tentearo Japanese Notions of European Political Econ. [tr.] 50 c. 8° Highlands, *Phila.* [99] 00
Single Tax League, *Glasgow*. Summary of a voluminous Report to Japan. Govt. by a commissioner apptd. to make an investign. of the opins. and teachgs. of Europ. wrs. on questns. conn. w. polit. econ.

MALTHUS, T. R. —*v.* **D** § 121

*MARSHALL, Prf. Alf. Principles of Economics, vol. i 12/6 *n.* ($4 *n.*) 8° Macmillan [90] 10
Of capital importance. Regardg. econ. laws and reasongs. as merely pt. of material wh. conscience and 'common-sense' have to turn to acc. in solving pract. probls., it reconstructs whole body of doctrs. on broader grounds, givg. spec. prominence not only to the ethical quality of motives, but also to sagacity, energy, and enterprise. Displays a rare power of lucid exposn. and a profound grasp of econ. theory, alike in its histor. devel. and its pract. applicns. The most important bk. on economics since MILL'S *Principles*.

" Elements of Economics, vol i: Economics of Industry 3/6 ($1 *n.*) c 8° Macmillan [92] 05
An abgmt. by way of omissn. rather than compressn. of above, w. addn. of ch. on Trades Unions. Not an expansion of *Economics of Industry* [*inf.*] tho' it supersedes it.

" + Mary P. The Economics of Industry 2/6 f 8° Macmillan [79] 88
An attempt to construct, on the lines laid down by MILL, in his *Pol. Econ.*, a theory of value, wages, and profits, wh. shd. include the chief results of the work of the present generation of economists. Comprehensive and good; based on an extensive knowledge of the actual business of industrial operations.

*MILL, Jno. Stuart Principles of Polit. Econ., 2 vols.
30/ ($10) 8°; People's Edn., 5/ ($1·25) c 8° Longman [48] 78; 85

" The same, ed. Prf. W. J. Ashley 5/ ($1·50 *n.*) c 8° Longman [48] 09
This edn. indicates, w. their dates, all textual changes that show variation or developmt. in MILL'S views. Introd. deals w. MILL'S positn. in econ. thought, and Appendix treats of his influ. on later wrs. Index (by Miss M. A. ELLIS). The standard work, contg. the doctrs. as elab. and expounded by Adam SMITH, MALTHUS, RICARDO, SENIOR, Jas. MILL (his father), and himself. Cheap edn. of text 3/6. Routledge ($1·50 Dutton, *N.Y.*).

" The same: abridged J. L. Laughlin $3·50 8° Appleton, *N.Y.* 84
A good abridgmt. for Amer. studts. of what COSSA calls 'even now the best English treatise on economics', w. ample notes incorp. in text, a series of exam. questns., maps, and diagrs.

MOFFAT, R. S. Economy of Consumption: omitted chapter in pol. econ.—*ut* **D** § 120

MUMMERY (A. F.) + HOBSON (J. A.) Physiology of Industry: expos. of cert. fallacies in pol. econ.
6/ c 8° Murray 89

NEWCOMB, Simon Principles of Polit. Econ. [elaborate and scientific] $2·50 8° Harper, *N.Y.* 86

NICHOLSON, Prf. J. S. Principles of Polit. Econ., 3 v. [$8·25 *n.* Macmillan, *N.Y.*] 42/6 8° Black 93–01
Designed to cover same ground as MILL. An indept. and sober attempt to recast the subj. in a systematic way in light of older doctrs. and their later modificns. Largely made up of lecture-notes. With the exception of MARSHALL the most complete modern treatment.

" Elements of Political Economy [$2·25 *n.* Macmillan, *N.Y.*] 7/6 *n.* 8° Black 03
Based on above, but omits most histor. matter. Mainly uncontroversial, but indicates pts. in dispute. Bibliogrs.

" A Project of Empire—*ut* **D** § 136

PANTALEONI, M. Pure Economics, tr. T. B. Bruce 10/ *n.* ($3·25 *n.*) r 8° Macmillan 98

PATTEN, Prf. S. N. The Theory of Dynamic Economics $1 12° Univ. of Penn., *Phila.* 92
[Polit. Economy and Public Law Ser.] Presents the classical theory in a new form.

" Theory of Prosperity $1·25 *n.* Macmillan, *N.Y.* 02

PERRY, Prf. A. L. Polit. Economy, $2·50; Introd. to Pol. Econ. $1·50 12° Scribner, *N.Y.* [66] 88; [71] 80
Discards the term 'Wealth' and makes 'Value' the subject of the science. Free Trade.

" Principles of Political Economy $2 c 8° Scribner, *N.Y.* 91
9/ Paul. Illustrations chiefly from American life, history, and law—and the Bible.

PETTY, Sir Wm. [1623–87] Economic Writings, ed. Dr C. H. Hull, 2 vols. 25/ 8° Camb. Press 99
$6 *n.* Putnam, *N.Y.* Co'ln. of miscell. wk. of a voluminous wr.; w. full bibliogr. and crit. material, formg. an interestg. study in the *origines* of econ. science. Incl. observns. on *Bills of Mortality* (prob. by Capt. Jno. GRAUNT).

PIERSON, Dr N. G. Principles of Economics [tr. fr. Dutch], vol. i 10/ *n.* ($3·25 *n.*) 8° Macmillan 02
A full crit. statemt. of older theories in light of recent economic theory.

POST, Louis F. Social Service [4/6 *n.* Bell] $1 *n.* c 8° Wessels, *N.Y.* 10
A lucid popular account of the mechanism of production and distribution.

PRICE, Prf. Bonamy Chapters on Practical Political Economy 15/ p 8° Paul [78] 82
Oxford lectures. A good book for the general reader.

PRICE, L. L. Economic Science and Practice 6/ c 8° Methuen 96

PROTHERO, Prf. M. Political Economy [w. useful histor. surveys] 4/6 c 8° Bell 95

RAPER, Prf. C. C. Principles of Wealth and Progress $1·10 *n.* (4/6 *n.*) c 8° Macmillan 06
Economics for High Schools. A distinctly American book.

RICARDO, Dav. [1772–1823] Political Works, ed. J. R. McCulloch 16/ 8° Murray [17] 88
Contains his *Princ. of Pol. Econ. and Taxation*. For his *Letters to Malthus*, v. **D** § 121, *s.v.* Population (MALTHUS).

" Princs. of Pol. Econ. & Taxation [1846], ed. Prf. C. E. K. Gonner 5/ c 8° Bell [17] 91
$1·50 *n.* Macmillan, *N.Y.* [Bohn's Lib.] After passing thro' periods of undiscrimg. praise and reaction, this wk. of RICARDO (a retired banker) is now in that of reconsideration (*teste* MARSHALL in his *Princ. of Econ.*, *ut sup.*, where pains are taken to show how he has been grievously misunderstood). An excellent edn., w. expos. and crit. Introd., notes, and bibliogr. Tho' dry and ill put together, the bk. has exercised a powerful influence, chiefly owing to its theory of rent and doctr. of 'comparative cost' (wh. is at the basis of internat. trade).

" First Six Chaps. of 'Principles of Polit. Econ.' 3/ *n.* (75 c. *n.*) gl 8° Macmillan 95

ROBERTSON, Wm. B. Foundations of Political Economy 5/ c 8° Walter Scott 05

ROSCHER, W. Principles of Political Economy, 2 vols. [tr.] $7·50 8° Holt, *N.Y.* 78
Represents the historical school of Germany, differing fr. that of MILL. A storehouse of learning.

Cunningham, Prf. Wm. Why had Roscher so little Influence in England?
25 c. 8° Acad. of Pol. Sci., *Phila.* 94

RUSKIN, Jno. Arrows of the Chase, Crown of Wild Olive, Fors Clavigera, Munera Pulveris [anal. of utility], Time and Tide [laws of wk., etc.], Unto this Last, A Joy for Ever [econcs. of wk.]—*ut* **K** § 89

SAY, J. B. Treat. on Polit. Econ. [1821], tr. C. R. Prinsep, ed. C. C. Biddle $2·50 8° Claxton, *Phila.* [32] 69

SCHRIJVERS, Rev. C. Handbk. of Practical Economics [tr.] [Rom. Cath.] 5 / c 8^c Sands 10

SEAGER, Prf. H. R. Introduction to Economics [10/6 *n.* Bell] $2 *n.* 8° Holt, *N.Y.* [04] 09
An advanced and elaborate treatise.

,, Economics: a briefer course [6/6 *n.* Bell] $1·75 8° Holt, *N.Y.* 09

SELIGMAN, Prf. E. R. Princs. of Economics; w. 28 maps & charts 10/6 *n.* ($2·40) c 8° Longman [05] 07
[American Citizen Series]. With special reference to American conditions.

SHADWELL, J. L. A System of Political Economy *o.p.* [*pb.* 18/] 8° Trübner 77

,, Political Economy for the People *o.p.* [*pb.* 1/6] f 8° Trübner 80

SIDGWICK, Prf. Hy. Princs. of Pol. Econ., ed. J. H. Keynes 14/ *n.* ($4·50 *n.*) 8° Macmillan [83] 01

SMART, Prf. Wm. Studies in Economics 8/6 *n.* ($2·75 *n.*) c 8° Macmillan 95
Valuable studies on questns. conn. w. wages, currency, and consumptn., by an adherent of the Austrian School. The pages are full of controv. matter, forcibly stated by author, who throughout regards econ. questns. fr. pt.-of-view of human nature and ethics rather than in more abstract manner of older economists.

SMITH, Adam [1723–90] Wealth of Nations [1776], ed. J. E. T. Rogers, 2 v. 21/ ($6·75) 8° Clar. Pr. [70] 80

,, ,, ed. Prf. J. S. Nicholson [w. very useful notes] 4/ 8° Nelson [ ] 84

,, ,, ed. J. R. McCulloch [w. life of Smith] 9/ 8° Black [28] 89

,, ,, ed. E. Belfort Bax, 2 vols. ea. 3/6 c 8° Bell 87
Each $1 *n.* Macmillan, *N.Y.* [Bohn's Lib.] With historical Introd. and notes.

* ,, ,, ed. Dr E. Cannan, w. Introd. and notes 21/ *n.* 8° Methuen 03
Carefully collated fr. the different edns., with summaries, explanations, and full index.

,, ,, 2 vols. [World's Classics] ea. 1/ *n.* (40 c.) pott 8° Frowde 04

,, ,, 2 vols. [Everyman's Lib.; ea. 35 c. *n.* Dutton, *N.Y.*] ea. 1/ *n.* f 8° Dent 10

,, Select Chaps. & Passages fr. ' Wealth of Nations ' 75 c. *n.* (3/ *n.*) gl 8° Macmillan 95
Affords in brief compass (about a fifth of the orig.) a general view of SMITH'S economic philosophy.
Standard; has been called ' the inner atom of political economy '. It is the only bk. that has ever been honoured by a centenary commemoration. For an exhaustive estimate of it, *v.* INGRAM'S article on SMITH in *Encyclo. Brit.*, *ut* C § 61, where biograph. and crit. bks. on SMITH will be found. To these should be added: HIRST (F. W.), *Adam Smith* [Engl. Men of Letters], 2/ (75 c. *n.*) c 8° Macmillan '04.

,, Lects. on Justice, Police, Revenue., & Arms 10/6 *n.* ($3·25) 8° Clar. Press 96
With Introd. and notes by E. CANNAN. Lects. del. at Glasgow and reported by a student in 1763, the yr. bef. SMITH relinquished his chair. Not prev. pubd., *Justice* being quite new: the rest form the first draft for *Wealth of Nations*, and are of interest as explaining genesis of that wk. and setting at rest many moot pts. as to SMITH'S reln. to the Physiocrats.

SYMES, Prf. J. E. Political Economy [short text-book] 2/6 (90 c.) c 8° Longman 88

TAUSSIG, Prf. F. W. Principles of Economics, 2 vols. 8° Macmillan *in prep.*

TURGOT, A. R. J. [1727–81] Reflections on Formation and Distribution of Riches [tr.]
3/ *n.* (75 c. *n.*) 8° Macmillan [1770] 98
[Economic Classics.] A good edn. of an epoch-making work.

WALKER, A. Science of Wealth: manual of political economy $1·50 Lippincott, *Phila.* [66] 72

WALKER, Prf. F. A. Political Economy: Advanced Course [very good] $2 *n.* c 8° Holt, *N.Y.* [84] 87

,, Political Economy: Briefer Course [abgmt. of above] $1·20 *n.* c 8° Holt, *N.Y.* 84
Former 12/6, latter 6/6 Macmillan, *London.*

Hawkins, E. L. Abstract of Walker's ' Political Economy ' 2/6 c 8° Shrimpton, *Oxford* [ ] 97

,, First Lessons in Political Economy $1·25 12° Holt, *N.Y.* [89] 92
5/ Macmillan. An excellent little bk., intended for use in High Schools and Academies. Orthodox, except on Wages.

WOOD, S. T. Primer of Political Economy [suggestive] 50 c. *n.* (2/6) c 8° Macmillan 01

*Mathematical (Abstract) Economics*

*v. BÖHM-BAWERK, Prf. E. V. Capital and Interest, tr. Prf. Wm. Smart 12/ *n.* ($4) 8° Macmillan 90
Austrian School of economy. A critical history of econ. theory, formg. the Introd. to his *Positive Theory of Capital.* It is a complete register of all the ideas wh. have been promulgated by previous writers on the subj., and conts. a new theory of his own by the learned author. A profound and original work, dealg. not only w. Capital and Interest, but w. other econ. subjects.

,, Recent Literature on Interest [tr.] [1884–9; suppl. to above] 4/6 *n.* ($1 *n.*) 8° Macmillan 04

,, Positive Theory of Capital, tr. Prf. Wm. Smart 12/ *n.* ($4) 8° Macmillan 91
Its princ. contribn. to econ. science is its refutn. of the pet Socialistic dogma wh. reduces the function of capital to the ' exploitation of labour ' by means of an oppressive tax (= interest) on the fruits of industry, and its philosophic analysis of bargains relg. to future goods. Both excellently tr. by SMART, who acts as a sort of junior counsel, not infrequently improving on his instructns.

,, Histor. *v.* Deduct. Pol. Ec. [tr.] [defence of deduct. meth.] 25 c. 8° Acad. of Pol. Sci., *Phila.* 92

,, The Austrian Economists [tr.] [acc. of their wk. & meths.] 25 c. 8° Acad. of Pol. Sci., *Phila.* 92

,, Ultimate Standard of Value [tr.] 50 c. 8° Acad. of Pol. Sci., *Phila.* 94

BONAR, Dr Jas. The Austrian Economists—*in* [Harvard] *Quarterly Journal of Economics*, v. iii (1888)

COURNOT, A. Researches into Mathem. Princs. of Theory of Wealth [tr.] 75 c. *n.* (3/ *n.*) 8° Macmillan [38] 97
[Economic Classics.] Tr. N. T. BACON; w. a *Bibliography of Mathematical Economics* by Irving FISHER.

CUNYNGHAME, H. H. Geometrical Political Economy 2/6 *n.* (85 c.) c 8° Clar. Press 04
An elemen. treat. on the method of explaining some of the theories of pure economic science by means of diagrams.

EDGEWORTH, Prf. F. Y. Mathematical Psychics and Moral Sciences *o.p.* [*pb.* 7/6] c 8° Paul 81

FISHER, Irving Mathemat. Investigns. in Theory of Value & Prices.—*in* Trns. of Connecticut Acad. 1892

JEVONS, H. Stanley [son]. Essays in Economics —*ut inf.*

JEVONS, Prf. W. Stanley —*ut sup.*

SMART, Prf. Wm. Introduction to the Theory of Value 3/ *n.* ($1·25) c 8° Macmillan 91
A sort of appendix to his tr. of BÖHM-BAWERK [*ut sup.*], givg. summary of doctrs. enunc. by MENGER and JEVONS and worked out by WIESER and BÖHM-BAWERK. For a bolder and more indept. exposn. of JEVONS *v.* WICKSTEED'S *Alphabet of Econ. Sci.* [*ut. inf.*].

WICKSTEED, P. H. Alphabet of Economic Science, Pt. i [Theory of Value] 2/6 gl 8° Macmillan 88

,, The Common-Sense of Political Economy 14/ *n.* 8° Macmillan 10
A substantial and thoro' study of human basis of econ. law, basing a constructive syst. on the 'marginal' theory (i.e. the principle of regardg. commodities and services as equivalents or substitutes, and findg. likeness and not unlikeness in the services they render) of JEVONS and the Geneva School.

v. WIESER, Prf. Friedr. Natural Value [tr.], ed. Prf. Wm. Smart 10/ *n.* ($3·25) 8° Macmillan 93
The latest developmt. of JEVONS' marginal utility theory of value, seekg. to show that laws of value in mod. industr. State are, fundamentally, natural laws, wh. would reappear in a perfect or a communistic State, and conseq. that rent and interest are not phenomena induced by an artificial state of Society, but essentially economic.

,, The Theory of Value [tr.] 25 c. 8° Acad. of Pol. and Soc. Sci., *Phila.* 92
A reply to some criticisms made by Prf. MACVANE (Harvard) on the Austrian Economists (of whom WIESER is one), the spec. questn. under discussn. bg. the reln. betw. marginal utility and cost of production.

**Capital and Interest**—*v.* **D** § 118 **Economic Interpretation of History**—*v.* **F** § 2

**Educational Value of Economics,** and **Methods of Teaching**—*v.* **D** § 167

**Political Economy illustrated by Tales**

FAWCETT, [Mrs] M. G. Tales in Political Economy *o.p.* [*pb.* 3/] c 8° Macmillan [74] 83

MARTINEAU, Harriet Illustrns. of Polit. Econ., 9 vols. [series of tales] *o.p.* [*pb.* 2/6 ea.] 18° Routledge [32–4] 40–5

**Relation between Economics and Politics**

CUNNINGHAM, Dr W. Politics and Economics 5/ c 8° Paul 85

HADLEY, Prf. A. T. Relations betw. Economics & Politics [Am. Ec. Ass.] 50 c. *n.* 8° Macmillan, *N.Y.* 99

**Relations of Ethics to Political Economy. Luxury**

BOSANQUET, Dr Bern. Luxury and Refinement—*in his* Civilization of Christendom, *ut* **A** § 8

ELY, Prf. R. T. —*in his* Social Aspects of Christianity, *ut* **A** § 113

DE LAVELEYE, Prf. E. Luxury [tr.] [Social Sci. Ser.; $1 Scribner, *N.Y.*] 2/6 c 8° Sonnenschein [91]

SIDGWICK, Prf. Hy. Luxury—*in his* Practical Ethics, *ut* **C** § 70

THOMPSON, H. M. The Purse and the Conscience 2/6 c 8° Sonnenschein [91]
$1 Scribner, *N.Y.* [Social Science Ser.] Attempts to show the connexion betw. ethics and economics.

URWICK, E. J. Luxury and Waste of Life 4/6 *n.* c 8° Dent 08
A non-pedantic discussn. of what 'luxurious' expenditure means—its econ. and social effects and moral aspect.

WRIGHT, Carroll D. Relation of Political Economy to the Labour Question—*ut* **D** § 118

WYLIE, Alex. Labour, Leisure, and Luxury, 1/ c 8° Longman [84] 87

**Scope and Method of Economics**—*v. also* CARLILE, *sup.*

KEYNES, J. Neville The Scope and Method of Political Economy 7/ *n.* ($2·25 *n.*) 8° Macmillan [91] 04
Impartial; mainly analytical: clear in thought and expression, tho' not distinguished by ideas. In questions betw. different economic methods the attitude is one of compromise.

LESLIE, Prf. T. E. Cliffe- On the Philosophical Method of Polit. Economy—*in his* Essays, *ut inf.*

SIDGWICK, Prf. Hy. Scope and Method of Economic Science *o.p.* [*pb.* 2/] 8° Macmillan 85

**Statistics** —*v.* **D** § 148

**Theory of Value** —*v. also sup., s.v.* Mathematical Economics

DAVENPORT, Prf. H. J. Value and Distribution $3·50 *n.* 8° Univ. Press, *Chicago* 08

JEVONS, Prf. W. Stanley —*in his* Theory of Political Economy, *ut sup.* [best general introd. to subj.]

SEWALL, H. R. The Theory of Value before Adam Smith $1 *n.* 8° Macmillan, *N.Y.* 01
3/6 Sonnenschein. [Pubns. of Amer. Econ. Assoc.]

SPRAGUE, R. F. The True Nature of Value $1 *n.* 12° Univ. Press, *Chicago* 07

WALSH, C. M. Measurement of General Exchange Value 17/ *n.* ($3 *n.*) 8° Macmillan 01

,, The Fundamental Problem in Monetary Science 7/6 *n.* ($1·50 *n.*) c 8° Macmillan 03
An elab. and industriously worked out treatmt., attemptg. to master the econom. problem as to precise meaning of 'value'. Quotes fr. almost every wr. on the subject.

WHITAKER, A. C. History and Criticism of the Labor Theory of Value in Engl. Political Economy [Col. Univ. Studs.] $1·50 *n.* 8° Macmillan, *N.Y.* 04

**Collective Essays:** ASHBY (N. B.) The Riddle of the Sphinx $1·50 8° Industr. Pb. Co., *Des Moines* 91
Discussns. on agric., land, transportatn., money, taxatn., and cost of interchange. Author is Lecturer to Farmers' National Alliance.

BAGEHOT, Walt. Economic Studies, ed. R. H. Hutton 3/6 ($1·25) c 8° Longman [80] 95
Fresh and vigorous studies on the early econ. condns. of nations. *Postulates of Engl. Pol. Econ.:* (1) *Transferability of Labour;* (2) *Transferability of Capital; Preliminaries of Pol. Econ.; Adam Smith and our Modern Econ.; Malthus–Ricardo–Growth of Capital; Cost of Productn.; Appendix*

BALFOUR, A. J. —*in his* Essays and Addresses, *ut* **K** § 83
The econ. essays are: *Cobden and the Mancs. Schl., Politics and Polit. Econ.,* and *A Fragment on Progress.*

CLARK, Wm. William Clarke: colln. of his writings 7/6 8° Sonnenschein 08
Ed. Herb. BURROWS. Political, personal, and philos. papers by a versatile Liberal journalist. D. 1901.

CUNNINGHAM, Dr W. The Path towards Knowledge 4/6 c 8° Methuen 92
Miscellaneous popular addresses, the best being on *The Malthusian Principle.*

DANSON, J. T. Economic and Statistical Studies, 1840–90 21/*n.* r 8° Unwin 06
Introd. by Prf. E. C. K. GONNER; memr. by Mrs NORMAN HILL (dau.). A ser. of pl. show varatns. in prices of 22 commodities betw. 1851 and 1890.

DUNBAR, C. F. Economic Essays, ed. O. M. W. Sprague $2·50 *n.* (10/6 *n.*) 8° Macmillan 05

ELY, Prf. R. T. Problems of To-day [Lib. of Economics] $1·50 12° Crowell, *N.Y.* 88
A discussion of Tariff, Taxation, and Monopolies.

FAWCETT, Prf. Hy. + [Mrs] M. G. Essays & Lects. on Polit. & Social Subjs. *o.p.* [*pb.* 10/6] 8° Macmillan 72

GIFFEN, Sir Rob. Economic Enquiries and Studies, 2 vols. 21/*n.* 8° Bell 04

GOSCHEN, Visc. Essays and Addresses on Economic Questions: 1865–93 15/*n.* 8° Arnold 05
$5 Longman, *N.Y.* Of the speeches not concerned w. currency and bankg. the two most important are: *Prospects of Trade* (1885), *Increase of Moderate Incomes* ('87) [w. 20 pp. bringing it down to date].

HARRISON, Fredc. National and Social Problems 7/6 *n.* ($1·75 *n.*) c 8° Macmillan 08
Vol. iii of his *Studies*, 4 vols. Reprinted papers, dealg. w. Europ. polit. problems, questns. of labour, unionism, and socialism.

JENKIN, Prf. Fleeming —*in his* Papers, ed. S. Colvin + J. A. Ewing, *ut* **K** § 89
The greater pt. of vol. ii is devoted to Trades Unions Incidence of Taxation, Laws of Supply and Demand, *etc.*

JEVONS, H. Stanley Essays on Economics 5/*n.* ($1·60 *n.*) c 8° Macmillan 05
Based on a course of lects. del. in Sydney. Illustrated by a series of ingenious diagrams.

LESLIE, Prf. T. E. Cliffe- Essays in Political and Moral Philosophy 10/6 8° Hodges, *Dubl.* [79] 88
Good essays on Ad. Smith, Cairnes, J. S. Mill, *Taxation, Prices*, etc. Represents in Engl. the histor. schl. and the 'professional socialists' of Germy.

LILLY, W. S. On Shibboleths—*ut* **D** § 125

MALLET, Sir Louis Free Exchange: papers on pol. and econ. subjs., ed. B. Mallet 12/ 8° Paul 91
Pt. i: *Polit. Opins. of Cobden, Policy of Commerc. Treaties, Free Trade and Free Enterprise, State Rys., Egypt, Letter to Laveleye, Reciprocity, Bimetallic Theory, Natl. Income and Taxn.*; ii (posth.): *Law of Value and Theory of Unearned Increment., The Shattered Science, Value, Natural Monopolies, Unearned Incremt.* Throughout Free Trade in broadest sense of the term, givg. the fullest view of the opinions of Mancs. Schl. yet put forth.

MILL, Jno. Stuart Dissertns. & Discussns., 4 vols.; *and* Essays on some Unsettled Questns.—*ut* **C** § 49

MOLESWORTH, Sir Guilford L. Economic and Fiscal Facts and Fallacies 9*d.* c 8° P. S. King [09] 10

NATHAN, Sir Nathaniel Economic Heresies 10/6 *n.* 8° Constable 09
By Attorney-Gen. of Trinidad 1898–1903. Arguing that all econ. phenomena are ephemeral and subj. to ever-changing causes, and that general axioms shd. therefore be received with great caution, he opposes the theoret. economists of 19th cent. and the Utopian Socialists of 20th.

NICHOLSON, Prf. J. S. Strikes and Social Problems—*ut* **D** § 120

NEWMAN, Prf. F. W. Miscellanies, vol. iv: Political Economy 10/6 8° Paul 90
The science of the market, especially as affected by labour law.

PLAYFAIR, Sir Lyon Subjects of Social Welfare 7/6 8° Cassell 93
Repr. papers, grouped under 3 heads, (1) *Public Health*, (2) *Industrial Wealth*, (3) *National Education.*

RITCHIE, Prf. D. G. —*in his* Darwin and Hegel, *ut* **C** § 4; *and* Princs. of State Interference, *ut* **C** § 4

SIDGWICK, Prf. Hy. Miscellaneous Essays and Addresses 10/*n.* ($3·25 *n.*) 8° Macmillan 04

SMITH, J. C. Legal Tender Essays 3/6 *n.* 8° Paul 10
Essays on national economics, proposg. reforms along lines of Progressive class-legislation.

WALKER, Prf. F. A. Discussions in Economics & Statistics, ed. D. R. Dewey, 2 v. $6 *n.* 8° Holt, *N.Y.* 99

WELLS, D. A. Practical Economics $1·50 (6/) 12° Putnam 85
Essays on economic experiences of the U.S. in the seventies and eighties.

**Selections**

BULLOCK, C. J. [ed.] Sel. Readings in Econcs. [Selns. & Docs. in Econcs.] $2·25 (10/6) 8° Ginn 07

## 115: MONEY; CREDIT; CURRENCY; FOREIGN EXCHANGE; BIMETALLISM

**Bibliography**

Lib. of Congress: List of Bks. rel. to Currency and Banking 25 c. 4° Washington 08
Gives refs. to periodicals, and pays special regard to recent conditions.

,, List of Works rel. to 1st and 2nd Banks of U.S. 25 c. 4° Washington 08
Supplements above list, giving chronological list of Reports, etc.

**Money; Currency** —*v. also* **D** § 153

ANDREWS, Prf. E. B. An Honest Dollar [a suggestive essay] $1 8° Student Pb. Co., *Hartford* [89] 94

ATKINSON, Dr E. The Distribution of Products $1·50 8° Putnam, *N.Y.* [86] 92

*BAGEHOT, Walt. Lombard Street: descrn. of money-market 3/6 c 8° Paul [73] 06
$1·25 Scribner, *N.Y.* An admirable pop. acc. of the mechanism of Engl. credit-institns., w. discussns. of several theoretical points, possessg. the supreme merit of making a difficult and abstruse subj. appear quite clear. A little antiquated now, but notes (by E. JOHNSTONE) bring it more or less down to date. New edn., w. Introd. and corrigenda by Hartley WITHERS, 3/6 c 8° Smith & Elder '10.

BOLLES, A. S. Money, Banking, and Finance $1·25 c 8° Am. Bk. Co., *N.Y.* 03

BROUGH, Wm. The Natural Law of Money $1 c 8° Putnam, *N.Y.* 96
Shows th. substitutn. of credit in place of goods marks progress in art of effecting exchange.

CAIRNES, Prf. J. E. —*in his* Essays, *ut* **D** § 114

CARROLL, Edw., jun. Principles and Practice of Finance $1·75 (7/6) 8° Putnam [95] 97
A guide for bankers, merchants, and lawyers, combing. a treatmt. of princs. w. descrn. of cert. business transns. Former Pt. deals mainly w. *Mechanism of Exch.*, latter (*Practice*) conts. a good deal of useful informn. in currency and banking systs. of U.S., operatn. of N.Y. sub-treasury, clearg.-house, and Stock Exch., meths. of corporatns. and commerc. houses, etc. Gloss. of terms.

Columbia Univ.: Currency Probl. & Present Financial Situation [addresses] $1·50 8° Macmillan, *N.Y.* 08

CONANT, C. A. Principles of Money and Banking, 2 vols. $4 *n.* (16/*n.*) 8° Harper 06
Packed w. useful informn. on many branches of the subj. Gives details of banking and the issues of paper-money, forming a monet. hist. of the past generation. Vol. ii. (sep.) $1·75 *n.* '08.

CUNNINGHAM, Dr W. Use and Abuse of Money [$1 *n.* Scribner, *N.Y.*] 3/ c 8° Murray 91

DEL MAR, Alex. The Science of Money [$2·25 Macmillan, *N.Y.*] 6/ *n.* 8° E. Wilson [85] 96

DEUTSCH, H. Arbitrage in Bullion, Coins, Bills, Stocks, Shares, Options 10/6 *n.* 8° E. Wilson 04
Contains summary of relns. betw. London money-market and other money-markets of the world.

DUNBAR, Prf. C. F. [ed.] Laws of U.S. rel. to Currency, Finance, & Bankg.—*ut* **D** § 16
Brings tog. documts. [1789–1890] otherwise to be sought in Statutes at Large w. much labour. Useful for studts. and teachers of polit. econ.

EASTON, H. T. Money, Exchange, and Banking 5/ *n.* ($1·75) 8° Pitman [05] 07
A manual for bank-officials, business men, and studts., dealg. w. the questions in pract., theoret., and legal aspects.

FARRER, L'd Studies in Currency 12/6 *n.* 8° Macmillan 98

FONDA, A. J. Honest Money $1 (3/6 *n.*) c 8° Macmillan 95
Analysis of money, comparison of views of some authorities, statemt. of requiremts. for an honest money-method, crit. of existing syst., and outl. of a suggested new one. By a disciple of JEVONS and Austrian School.

FOOTE, A. R. A Sound Currency and Banking System [Questns. of Day] 75 c. c 8° Putnam 95
Maintains that the *sine qua non* of a sound curry. is that U.S. must cease doing bankg. business, and that a sufficient gold reserve cannot be maintained by sale of bonds to protect credit of govt. under existing laws.

GIBBS, H. H. [*now* L'D ALDENHAM] A Colloquy on Currency 10/ *n.* 8° E. Wilson [ ] 00

GIFFEN, Sir R. —*in his* Economic Inquiries and Studies, 2 vols., *ut* **D** § 114

GORDON, A. Congressional Currency $1·25 c 8° Putnam 95
[Questions of the Day.] An outline of the Federal money system.

GOSCHEN, Visc. G. J. Essays and Addresses on Economic Questions—*ut* **D** § 114

HULL, W. H. Practical Problems in Banking and Currency—*ut* **D** § 116

*JEVONS, Prf. W. Stanley Money and the Mechanism of Exchange [Intern. Sci. Ser.] 5/ c 8° Paul [75]
$1·75 Appleton, *N.Y.* An excellent popular book. Conts. also descrn. of Clearing House. Bibliog. of bks. 1568–1881.

,, Investigations in Currency and Finance, ed. Prf. H. S. Foxwell
10/ *n.* ($3 *n.*) ($7·50 *n.*) 8° Macmillan [84] 09
Abgd. fr. 1st (1884) edn. Conts. several papers still of value, e.g. *A Serious Fall in Value of Gold Ascertained, Variation of Prices, The Frequent Autumnal Pressure in Money Market, Gold Coinage*, and *Bimetallism*.

JOHNSON, J. F. Money and Currency $1·75 12° Ginn, *Boston* 06
In relation to industry, prices, and the rate of interest.

KEMMERER, Prf. E. W. Money & Credit Instrumts. in rel. to General Prices $1·25 *n.* 8° Holt, *N.Y.* 07
5/ *n.* Bell. [Cornell Studies.] Pt. i sets forth and defends Quantity Theory of money as gen. accepted by mod. economists; ii attempts to test statistically validity of doctrs. in questn.

KINLEY, Prf. D. Money: study of theory of medium of exch. $1·25 *n.* (5/ *n.*) c 8° Macmillan 04

KITSON, Arth. A Scientific Solution of the Money Question 3/6 *n.* 8° C. W. Daniel [94] 05
90 c. Arena Pb. Co., *Boston*. Author's panacea for money-questn. is the free coinage by the people of paper-money, everybody to issue as much as he needs; the only requisite bg. that members of the community shall accept them from each other in exchange for products.

LAUGHLIN, Prf. J. L. Principles of Money [16/ *n.* Murray] $3 *n.* 8° Scribner, *N.Y.* 03

DE LAUNAY, Prf. L. The World's Gold, tr. O. C. Williams 6/ c 8° Heinemann 09
An exposition of the civilizing power of gold, and of its economics as well as its geology.

LOCKE, Jno. Considns. of Conseq. of Lowerg. Interest & Raisg. Value of Money
1/ c 8° Ward & Lock [1692] 83

MCCULLOCH, J. R. Metallic and Paper Money, and Banks [a good bk.] *o.p.* [*pb.* 5/] 4° Black 58

MACLEOD, H. D. Theory of Credit—*ut* **D** § 116

MCPHERSON, L. G. The Monetary and Banking Problem $1 12° Appleton 96

MIGNON, F. Every Man his own Financier 6/ *n.* c 8° Laurie 08

MILLER, H. A. Money & Bimetallism: uses & operns. of money & credit $1·25 (5/) c 8° Putnam 99

MUHLEMANN, M. L. Monetary & Banking Systems of the World $2 *n.* 8° Monetary Pb. Co., *N.Y.* [95] 08
A convenient summary of currency and coinage laws of all the more important countries.

NICHOLSON, Prf. J. S. Treatise on Money and Essays on Monet. Problems 7/6 c 8° Black [88] 01
1·25 *n.* Macmillan, *N.Y.* First half forms one of the best elem. expos. of generally accepted doctrines. Second half controversial.

,, Bankers' Money [suppl. to above; $1·10 *n.* Macm., *N.Y.*] 2/6 *n.* c 8° Black 02

NORMAN, J. H. Complete Guide to World's 29 Metal Monet. Systems $2·25 8° Putnam, *N.Y.* 92
Also a guide to foreign and colonial exchgs. of gold, silver, etc., on the 'unit of weight' system.

OVERSTONE, L'd [1796–1883] Tracts on Metallic and Paper Currency *o.p.* [*pb.* 10/] r 8° Longman 57–9

PATTERSON, R. H. New Golden Age, and Influence of Prec. Metals, 2 v. 31/6 8° Blackwood 82
A history of gold and its influence upon the present age.

POOR, H. V. Money and its Laws $5 8° Poor, *N.Y.* 77
21/ Paul. A history of monetary theories and currencies of the United States.

POWELL, Ellis T. Mechanism of the City 3/6 *n.* c 8° P. S. King & Son 10

PRENDERGAST, W. A. Credit and its Uses [Business Series] $1·50 *n.* (6/ *n.*) 8° Appleton 07

PRICE, Prf. Bonamy Principles of Currency [six Oxford lects.] *o.p.* [*pb.* 7/6] 8° Parker 69

,, Currency and Banking *o.p.* [*pb.* 6/] c 8° Paul 76

PRICE, L. L. Money and its relation to Prices 2/6 c 8° Sonnenschein [00] 08
$1 Scribner, *N.Y.* [Social Science Ser.] Inquiry into causes, measuremt., and effects of changes in general prices.

RUSSELL, H. B. International Money Conferences $2·50 (12/6) 8° Harper 98
A clear and interestg. hist. of struggle for restorn. of silver as a money metal, and a valuable acc. of conferces. of 1867, '78, '81 and '92, givg. their purposes, char., and results, w. study of the condns. of currency and finance in Eur. and Am. dur. interveng. periods, and in their relns. to internat. action.

SCOTT, W. A. Money and Banking [10/ *n.* Bell] $2 8° Holt, *N.Y.* 03

SMITH, Rob. H. The Science of Business $1·25 c 8° Putnam 85
[Questions of the Day.] On the principles controlling the laws of exchange.

SPICER, E. E. An Outline of the Money Market 2/ *n.* 8° Gee 10

STRAKER, F. The Money Market [Bks. on Business] 2/6 *n.* c 8° Methuen 04

SWAN, C. H., jun. Monetary Problems & Reforms [Questions of Day] 75 c. (3/) c 8° Putnam 97
Pays special attention to legal tender. Opposed to international currency.

TARDIEU, J. Money, tr. Margaret Watson *o.p.* [*pb.* 7/6] c 8° W. H. Allen 79

TRENHOLM, W. The People's Money [theory of money & curry. of U.S.] $1·50 12° Scribner, *N.Y.* 92

WALKER, Prf. F. A. Money [8/6 Macmillan; non-partizan; very complete] $2 8° Holt, *N.Y.* [78] 91

,, Money in rel. to Trade & Industry [7/6 Macmillan] $1·25 c 8° Holt, *N.Y.* [80] 89

WALSH, Correa M. Fundamental Principle in Monetary Science 7/6 *n.* ($1·50 *n.*) c 8° Macmillan 03

WELLS, D. A. Robinson Crusoe's Money; ill. [sound doctr. in facet. dress] $1 8° Harper, *N.Y.* 76

,, Practical Economics—*ut* **D** § 114

WHITE, H. Money and Banking, ill. by Amer. history $1·80 *n.* (7/6) 12° Ginn [95] 09
A brief summary: very lucid and readable. *Money; Evoln. of Money; Gold Standard; Repres. Money; Fiat Money; Banks;* Appendices. Sch. Edn. $1·50 *n.*

*WITHERS, Hartley The Meaning of Money 7/6 *n.* s 8° Smith & Elder [09] 10
$2 *n.* Dutton, *N.Y.* By City representative of *The Times*, Like BAGEHOT'S *Lombard St.* [*sup.*], an elem. treatise—not a criticism, nor an attempt at constructn. An interestg. and clear bk., providg. the ordinary man w. a means of really understandg. that pt. of a City Article wh. deals w. Money Market.

**History**: *Europe and United States—for* Coins *v.* **G** § 20

AVEBURY, L'd Short History of Coins and Currency; ill. 2/ c 8° Murray 02
60 c. *n.* Dutton, N.Y., Popular, yet full of accurate and well-expressed information.

BISSCHOP, Dr W. R. Rise of the London Money Market [1640–1826] 5/ *n.* c 8° P. S. King & Son 10

BOLLES, A. S. Financial History of the United States: 1774–1885, 3 vols.—*ut* **D** § 117

BROUGH, Wm. Natural Law of Money $1 (5/) 12° Putnam 94
Traces the successive steps in growth of money fr. days of barter to introdn. of mod. clearing-house.

BULLOCK, Prf. C. J. Essays in the Monetary History of U.S. $1·25 *n.* (5/) Macmillan 00
(1) *Three Centuries of Cheap Money*; (2) *Paper Currency of N. Carolina*; (3) *Paper Currency of N. Hampshire.*

CARLILE, W. W. The Evolution of Modern Money 7/6 *n.* ($2·50 *n.*) c 8° Macmillan 01
Origin of money, and nature of the monetary standard, w. its historical transition.

CLEWS, Dr H. Fifty Years in Wall Street [1858–1908] $3 *n.* 8° Irving Pb. Co., *N.Y.* 08

DAVIS, A. M. Currency and Banking in Province of Massachusetts, 2 vols.
[Amer. Econ. Ass.; 14/ Sonnenschein] $4·50 *n.* 8° Macmillan *N.Y.* 01

,, [ed.] Tracts rel. to Currency of Mass. Bay: 1682–1720 $4 *n.* 8° Houghton, *Boston* 02

DEL MAR, Alex. History of Monetary Systems 15/ *n.* 8° E. Wilson 95
$2. Kerr, *Chicago*. An extensive colln. of jottings, coverg. a very wide field, recordg. monet. experimts. of various States, anc. and mod.—the arguments bg. directed to prove that Free Coinage is a pernicious economic heresy, and that all States can settle value of money for themselves by limiting number of tokens they put into circuln. By a London-American banter, a controversialist rather than a historian.

,, History of Money in Ancient Countries [$3·50 Scribner, *N.Y.*] 6/ 8° Bell 85

,, History of Money in America $1·50 8° Camb. Encyc. Co., *Hackensack, N.J.* 00

,, History of Money in England & other States $2 8° Camb. Encyc. Co., *Hackensack, N.J.* 02

,, Hist. of Money in Germany & other Eur. States. $2 *n* 8° Camb. Encyc. Co., *Hackensack, N.J.* 02

,, History of Money in the Netherlands $1 8° Camb. Encyc. Co., *Hackensack, N.J.* 03

,, Hist. of Precious Metals fr. Earliest Times
$3 *n.* 8° Camb. Encyclo. Co., *Hackensack, N.J.* [80] 02

,, Money and Civilization 5/ 8° Bell 86
A hist. of monetary laws and systems, and their influence on civilizn. DEL MAR'S bks. are of no great value, but contain a good deal of useful informn.

DODD, Agnes F. Hist. of Money in Brit. Empire and U.S. 5/ *n.* c 8° Longman 11

HARPER, J. W. Money and Social Problems [historical] 10/6 8° Oliphant 96

HEPBURN, A. B. History of Coinage and Currency in U.S. $2 *n.* (8/6 *n.*) c 8° Macmillan 03
A history of 'the perennial contest for sound money'

LIVERPOOL, 1ST EARL OF [1727–1808] Treatise on Coins of the Realm 5/ 8° E. Wilson [05] 80
The Report on which the English gold-standard was established.

MACLAREN, J. Sketch of the History of Currency *o.p.* [*pb.* 9/] 8° E. Bumpus [58] 79

MILLS, J. Saxon — Landmarks of Brit. Fiscal Hist. [40 c. *n.* Macm., *N.Y.*] 1/ *n.* c 8° Black 07

RIDGEWAY, Prf. W. — *—in his* Origin of Metallic Currency, *ut* **G** § 20

SCHOENHOF, Prf. J. — History of Money and Prices [Questns. of Day] $1·50 (6/) Putnam 96
A clear and readable acc. of relns. betw. money and prices fr. beg. of 13 cent. Devoted to the familiar propositn. that prices reflect the general condns. of prodn. and not the volume of money in circuln. Negative pt. of bk. is given to disprovg. the Quantity Theory of money.

SHAW, W. A. — History of Currency, 1252–1894; maps 15/ 8° E. Wilson [95] 96
$3·75 Putnam, *N.Y.* A hist. of bimetallism fr. 13 cent., by a distinctly hostile critic. In spite of its very controversial tone, it conts. much valuable informn., w. list of authorit., incl. the solid and scholarly wks. of 18 cent. App. B of WHITE'S *Money & Banking* (*ut sup.*) is a review of this bk.

„ [ed.] — Selec. Tracts and Documts. on Engl. Monet. Hist.: 1626–1730 6/ 8° E. Wilson 96
Tracts, *etc.*, by Sir Rob. COTTON, Hy. ROBINSON, Sir Rich. TEMPLE, Sir Is. NEWTON, Jno. CONDUITT, and extrs. fr. the Domestic State Papers at H.M. Record Office.

SHERWOOD, S. S. — History and Theory of Money [12 lects.] $2 (10/6) 8° Lippincott 93

SUMNER, W. G. — History of American Currency $3 8° Holt, *N.Y.* [74] 78

UPTON, J. K. — Money in Politics; Introd. by E. Atkinson $1·25 12° Lothrop, *Boston* [ ] 96
The history of money in the United States from 'sea-shell' currency to date.

WATSON, D. K. — History of American Coinage $1·50 12° Putnam, *N.Y.* 99

WILLIS, H. P. — History of the Latin Monetary Union [Econ. Studs.] $2 8° Univ. Press, *Chicago* 01

*British Colonies*

CHALMERS, Rob. — Hist. of Currency in Brit. Colonies [authoritative] 10/ 8° Eyre & Spottiswoode 93

*India*

ELLSTÄTTER, K. — The Indian Silver Currency, tr. Prf. J. L. Laughlin $1·25 8° Univ. Pr. *Chicago* 95
A painstaking histor. and econ. study of monet. syst. of India, and of influ. of fall in price of silver on its commerce and industry.

MACLEOD H. D. — Indian Currency 2/6 *n.* ($1) 8° Longman 98

PROBYN, L. C. — Indian Coinage and Currency [repr. papers] 4/ *n.* 8° E. Wilson 97

WEBB, M. de P. — The Rupee Problem [plea f. defin. curr. policy] 1/4 8° P. S. King & Son 10

*Japan*

TAKAKI, M. — Hist. of Japanese Paper Currency: 1868–90 [Univ. Studs.] 30 c. 8° Johns Hopk. Univ. Pr., *Baltim.* 03

**Foreign Exchange** — *—for* Exchange Tables, *v.* **D** § 154

CLARE, Geo. — Money-Market Primer, and Key to Exchanges 5/ *n.* 8° E. Wilson [91] 00
In 2 Pts. (1) main heads of transns. of Bk. of Engl. and Bk. Rate, (2) foreign exchs. 18 clever diagrs. show. rel. of Bk. Rate to Market Rate, *etc.*

„ — A B C of Foreign Exchanges: practical guide 3/ *n.* ($1·25) c 8° Macmillan [93] 05
A lucid acc. of mechanism of Money Market. Good intrody. bk. for bankers' and other clerks. Ingenious diagrs.

EASTON, H. T. — Money Exchange and Banking—*ut sup.*

EMERY, Dr H. C. — *—in his* Speculation in Stock and Produce Exchanges of U.S., *ut* **D** § 153

*GOSCHEN, G. J. — Theory of Foreign Exchanges [the standard book] 6/ *n.* 8° E. Wilson [64] 98

*JEVONS, Prf. W. Stanley — Money and the Mechanism of Exchange—*ut sup.*

NORMAN, J. H. — The Universal Cambist $3 *n* 8° Putnam 98
A practical treatise on the theory of exchanges.

SEYD, Ern. — Bullion and Foreign Exchange Considered 20/ 8° E. Wilson 68
By a bullion-broker. A defence of the Double Valuation.

SMITH, R. H. — Science of Business [princs. of laws of exch.; Questns. of Day] $1·25 (5/) Putnam 85

TATE, W. — Modern Cambist, ed. H. T. Easton—*ut* **D** § 148
A standard manual of foreign exchange and bullion.

**Capital and Interest** — *v.* **D** § 118

**Commercial Crises and Panics**

BAXTER, Rob. — The Panic of 1866 *o.p.* [*pb.* 2/6] c 8° Longman 66
With its 'lessons' on the Currency Act. Gives also an account of the crises in 1825, '37, '47, *etc.*

BURTON, T. E. — Financial Crises [w. bibliography] $1·40 *n.* 12° Appleton, *N.Y.* 02
4/6 *n.* E. Wilson. On nature and causes of recurring financial depressns., w. suggestns. f. detectg. approach and f. their preventn. or mitigatn.

CONANT, C. A. — *—in his* History of Modern Banks of Issue, *ut* **D** § 116
Cons. an account of the economic crises of the nineteenth century and that of 1907.

EVANS, D. M. — History of the Commercial Crisis of 1847–8 *o.p.* [*pb.* 8/] 8° Letts [49] 50

„ — History of the Commercial Crisis of 1857–9 *o.p.* [*pb.* 15/] 8° Groombridge 59

GOSCHEN, Visc. G. J. — Essays and Addresses on Economic Questions: 1865–93 15/ *n.* 8° Arnold 05
Valuable reprs. fr. *Edinb. Rev.* 1865, '68, and '76, w. 4 speeches in the eighties and 2 in the early nineties, ea. w. substantial up-to-date note. The *E.R.* arts. describe and analyse the boom of '64, the crisis of '66, and give acc. of the fall of silver wh. began in the seventies; and one speech deals w. the Baring crisis. The whole forms a useful suppl. to BAGEHOT'S *Lombard Street* [*ut sup.*].

HYNDMAN, H. M. — Commercial Crises of the Nineteenth Century 2/6 c 8° Sonnenschein 92
$1 Scribner, *N.Y.* [Social Sci. Ser.] Acc. of crises of 1815, '25, '36–'39, '47, '57, '66, '73, '82, '90, the Introd. and last ch. dealg. w. causes and remedies, fr. Socialist stdpt., regardg. crises as result of 'antagonism betw. social productn. for social purposes and individual appropriatn. and exchange for indiv. profit'.

JEVONS, Prf. W. Stanley — *—in his* Investigations in Currency, etc., *ut sup.*
Attempts a physical explanation of the recurrence of commercial crises.

JONES, Dr E. D. Economic Crises [Citizens' Lib.] $1·25 *n.* (5/ *n.*) c 8° Macmillan 00
Deals w. commercial crises in their relation to capital, wages, speculation, etc. A good book. Bibliography.

JUGLAR, C. Brief Hist. of Panic in U.S. [tr.] [Questns of Day] $1 (4/) c 8° Putnam 93

LAUCK, W. J. Causes of Panic of 1893 [3 prize-essays] $1 *n.* 8° Houghton, *Boston* 07

MACLEOD, H. D. —*in* vol. ii. *of his* Theory of Credit, *ut* **D** § 116 [crises 1764 to 1890]

ROBERTUS, K. J. [1805–75] Over-production and Crises
[$1 Scribn., *N.Y.* ; Soc. Sci. Ser.] 2/6 c 8° Sonnenschein 98

### Mint

ANSELL, G. F. The Royal Mint [working, conduct, operatns.] *o.p.* [*pb.* 12/] i 8° E. Wilson [70] 71

*United States Mint*

EVANS, G. G. Illustrated History of United States Mint ; ill. $1 8° Evans *Phila.* [ ] 92

### Paper Money

COBBETT, Wm. Paper against Money [one of his most famous essays] *o.p.* 8° *London* 17

HARVEY, Jas. Paper Money, the Money of Civilization $2·75 8° Scribner, *N.Y.* 77

KNOX, J. J. U.S. Notes : hist. of var. issues by U.S. govt. $1·50 12° Scribner, *N.Y.* [84] 99

HICKCOX, J. H. History of Bills of Credit [1709–89] $3 8° *Albany* 66

MANN, C. A. Paper Money, the Root of All Evil $2 12° Appleton, *N.Y.* 72

MITCHELL, W. C. History of the Greenbacks $4 *n.* 8° Univ. Press, *Chicago* 03
[Univ. of Chicago Decennial Pubns.] With special refer. to economic consequences of their issue.

,, Gold, Prices, and Wages und. Greenback Standard $5 8° Univ. of California 08

*One Pound Note*

GRAHAM, W. The One Pound Note 7/6 8° Thin, *Edinburgh* [86]
Presents difficulties, trials and triumphs of One Pound Note in Scotld., and urges its adaptability to England.

### Sinking Funds

ROSS, E. A. Sinking Funds [Am. Ec. Ass. ; 3/6 Sonnenschein] $1 *n.* 8° Macmillan, *N.Y.* 92

### Tender, Legal

—*for* Law of Legal Tender, *v.* **D** § 92

BRECKINRIDGE, Sophonisba P. Legal Tender $2 *n.* 8° Univ. Press, *Chicago* 03
[Univ. of Chicago Decennial Pubns.] A study in English and American monetary history.

KINNAIRD, P. The Legal Tender Problem, vol. i $1 12° Ainsworth, *Chicago* 05

SMITH, J. C. Legal Tender Essays—*v.* **D** § 114, *s.v.* Collective Essays

SPAULDING, E. G. Hist. of Legal Tender Paper Money issued dur. Gt. Rebell. $3 8° *Buffalo* 69

WEBSTER, S. The Misuse of Legal Tender $1 12° Appleton, *N.Y.* 93

### Universal Money

BAGEHOT, Walt. International Coinage 2/6 (75 c.) c 8° Longman [69] 89
Plan f. assimilatg. Engl. and Am. money, proposed as a step tow. a Universal Money.

**Interest**—*v.* **D** § 118 **Money, Wts. & Meas. Tables**—*v.* **D** § 154 **Numismatics**—*v.* **G** § 20 **Rent**—*v.* **D** § 119 **Value, Theory of**—*v.* **D** § 114

## Bimetallism and Monometallism

*Bibliography :* N.Y. Public Lib. : List of Bks. rel. to Bimetallism, etc. 10 c. 8° N.Y. Publ. Lib. 07

ATKINSON, Dr E. Bimetallism in Europe [rept. on prec. metals and standards] *o.p.* [*pb.* 8/] 8° Trübner 88

,, —*in his* Taxation and Work, *ut* **D** § 122
Some chs. on silver advance a plan for maintaing. 'silver equal to gold' by means of taxing all silver product, domestic and imported, 'in a sum that would represent exact difference betw. value of silver bullion in its ratio to gold'—prev. advocated by Chauncey SMITH.

BAGEHOT, Walt. Some Articles on the Depreciation of Silver and Connected Topics 5/ 8° Paul. 77

BAIN, F. W. The Corner in Gold : its history and theory [reply to Giffen, *ut inf.*] 2/6 i 8° Parker 93

BARBOUR, D. The Theory of Bi-metallism 6/ c 8° Cassell 85

BARCLAY, R. The Silver Question and the Gold Question 2/6 *n.* c 8° E. Wilson [86] 94

BARKER, W. Bimetallism : evils of gold monometallism [bimetallist] 75 c. 8° Barker, *Phila.* 96

BOISSEVAIN, G. M. The Monetary Question [tr.] 3/ *n.* ($1) 8° Macmillan 91
In support of bi-metallism. The essay obtained Sir H. M. Meysey THOMPSON's prize at Monetary Congress, Paris, 1889.

,, The Monetary Situation in 1897 [tr.] 2/ *n.* (75 c.) 8° Macmillan 97

BROUGH, Wm. Open Mints and Free Banking $1·25 (5/) 12° Putnam 98
Advocates a plan for setting right the Silver Questn. by 'the abolishmt. of a legally fixed ratio of value of gold and silver coin'.

BRYAN, W. J. The First Battle : story of campaign of 1896 $1·50 8° Conkey, *Chicago* 97
10/6 Low. Presentatn. of rise, etc., of bimetallism, in form of a record of silverite campaign in support of BRYAN's candidature for Presidy. of U.S., w. his speeches, a biogr. by his wife, and 50 ports. of Am. bimetallists, etc.

*CARLILE, W. W. —*in his* The Evolution of Modern Money, *ut sup.*

CORNWELL, W. C. Sound Money Monographs $1 12° Putnam, *N.Y.* 97
Colln. of articles arguing agst. greenbacks, and in favour of a single gold-standard.

COWPERTHWAITE, J. H. Money, Silver, and Finance $1·25 (5/) 12° Putnam [92] 93
[Questions of the Day.] Advocates the cessation of silver coinage by U.S.

CRUMP, Arth. Investigation into the Causes of Great Fall in Prices 6/ c 8° Longman 89
Seeks to show that fall in prices is due to causes outside of currency influs., *e.g.*, over-productn., fresh sources of supply, improvemts in productn., etc.

CUTHBERTSON, C. Sketch of the Currency Question 2/ *n.* c 8° E. Wilson 96
An admirable and impartial *résumé* of controversy betw. monometallists and bimetallists, by a monometallist, a Bengal Civil Servant.

DANIELL, C. J. The Industrial Competition of Asia [$2·50 Appleton *N.Y.*] 12/ 8° Paul 89
An inquiry into the influence of currency on Brit. commerce in the East, advocating a gold-standard for India.

DARWIN, Maj. Leon Bimetallism 7/6 c 8° Murray 97
A careful and judicial analysis and discussion of arguments, summing up in fav. of bimetallism (w. reservations).

EDGCUMBE, Sir R. Popular Fallacies regarding Bimetallism 3/6 *n.* c 8° Macmillan 96
A forcible *exposé* of the monometallic theory, on the method of BASTIAT in his *Sophismes Economiques*.

EHRICH, L. R. The Question of Silver $1 (4/) c 8° Putnam 92
[Questions of the Day.] Opposes the free coinage of silver by U.S., and advocates international bimetallism.

FARRER, L'd Studies in Currency, 1898 12/6 *n.* 8° Macmillan 98
Various papers concerned w. bimetallic controversy, or inquiries into certain mod. problems conn. w. standard of value and media of exchange.

FAWCETT, Prf. Hy. Depreciation of Silver—*in his* Manual of Political Economy, *ut* **D** § 114

GIBBS, H. C. A Bimetallic Primer [a pop. exposition; bimetallic] 1/ c 8° E. Wilson [95] 96

*GIBBS (H. H.) + GRENFELL (H. R.) The Bimetallic Controversy 5/ 8° E. Wilson 86
A colln. of pamphlets, speeches, letters, etc., on both sides of the question.

GIFFEN, Sir Rob. —*in his* Essays, *ut* **D** § 117

* „ The Case against Bimetallism [$2 Macmillan, *N.Y.*] 7/6 c 8° Bell 92
Detached essays orig. pub. betw. 1879 and 1890 in *Fortn. Rev.*, *Nineteenth Cent.*, *Times*, and *Statist.* Clear and vigorous. Occupies an extreme monometallist position.

Gold Standard (The): papers iss. by Gold Standard Defence Assoc. 2/6 8° Cassell [95] 98

HALLARD, J. H. Gold and Silver: elementary treatise on bimetallism 2/6 c 8° Longman 97

HAUPT, Ottomar The Monetary Question in 1892 5/ 8° E. Wilson 92
Takes up a position midway between monometallists and bimetallists.

HELM, E. The Joint Standard: a plain exposition 3/6 *n.* ($1·10 *n.*) c 8° Macmillan 94
By a Manchester man of business, who states his reasons for having adopted the bimetallic faith.

HORTON, S. D. The Silver Pound and Engl. Monetary Policy since the Restoration $4 (14/) 8° Macmillan 87
Bi-metallic. Conts. also a hist. of monet. policy of Engl. fr. Jas. ii to pres. day.

„ Silver and Gold: their relation to the problem of resumption $1·50 8° Clarke, *Cincinnati* [77] 95

„ Silver in Europe $1·50 c 8° Macmillan, *N.Y.* 90

*JEVONS, Prf. W. Stanley —*in his* Money, *and in his* Investigations, *ut sup.*
Accepts the view of the 'compensatory action' of a double-standard system.

KITSON, Arth. —*in his* Money Problem, *ut sup.* [anti-bimetallist]

LAUGHLIN, Prf. J. L. Hist. of Bi-metallism in the United States $2·25 8° Appleton, *N.Y.* [85] 97
A comprehensive summary fr. standpt. of a gold monometallist. Appendices, charts, index, and bibliogr.

MACLEOD, H. D. Bimetallism 5/ *n.* ($1·75) 8° Longman 94
By an ardent and very positive monometallist: mainly repr. fr. his *Theory of Credit*, *ut sup.*

MALLET, Sir Louis —*in his* Free Exchange, *ut* **D** § 114

*NICHOLSON, Prf. J. S. —*in his* Treatise on Money, *ut sup.* [pro-bimetallist]

ROTHWELL, R. P. Universal Bimetallism and International Monetary Clearing House 50 c. 8° *Eng. & Ming. Jl.*, *N.Y.* [93] 96

ROTHWELL, W. T. Bimetallism Explained [in favour of bimetallism] 5/ c 8° Chapman 97

SMITH, J. C. Inter-Temporary Values: distribn. of produce of time 7/6 *n.* p 8° Paul 06

„ The Trust and the Gold Trust 1/ *n.* 8° Paul 07

„ Money and Profit-Sharing: double stand. money-syst. 7/6 *n.* 8° Paul 08
Deals w. a criticism on his system of Double Standard Money (wh. is not the same as bimetallism) wh. appeared in *Bankers' Mag.*, Sept. '07

STOKES, A. P. Joint Metallism [Questions of the Day] $1 (4/) c 8° Putnam [94] 96
A plan whereby gold and silver tog. at ratios always based on relative market-values may be made metallic basis of a sound and permanent currency.

TAUSSIG, Prf. F. W. Silver Situation in U.S. [Am. Ec. Ass.; 2/6 Sonnenschein] 75 c. *n.* 8° Macmillan, *N.Y.* 91

„ Silver Situation in U.S. [Questions of Day] 75 c. (2/6) c 8° Putnam [93] 00
Anti-silver and anti-bimetallic, arguing that gold has been an adequate stand. of value, and tamperg. w. currency is a dangerous practice.

TOURGEE, A. W. The War of the Standards 75 c. (3/6) 12° Putnam 96
[Questions of the Day.] Monometallist. Coin *and* credit *v.* coin without credit.

UPTON, J. K. Money in Politics [monometallist] $1·25 12° Lothrop, *Boston* [84] 95

*WALKER, Prf. F. A. International Bimetallism $1·25 12° Holt, *N.Y.* 96
5/ *n.* Macmillan. A reasoned case for Double Standard, fr. pt.-of-view of the New World.

WESTON, G. M. The Silver Question $1·25 8° Homans, *N.Y.* 78

WHEELER, E. P. Real Bi-Metallism [Questions of the Day] 75 c. (3/6) c 8° Putnam 95

WILSON, A. J. Reciprocity, Bi-metallism, and Land Tenure Reform [anti-bimet.] *o.p.* [*pb.* 7/6] 8° Macmillan 8[illegible]

## 116: BANKING AND BANKS

### Principles and Practice

ATTFIELD, J. B. English and Foreign Banks 3/6 *n.* 8° E. Wilson 93
Compar. betw. diff. constitns. of bks. in Gt. Brit. and those in other countries, showg. wherein we excel and where we are susceptible of improvmt.

BAGEHOT, Walt. —*in his* Lombard Street—*ut* **D** § 115

BARRETT, A. R. Modern Banking Methods [incl. book-kpg.] $4 8° Rhodes, *N.Y.* 02

BOLLES, A. S. Pract. Banking and Bankers' Common-place Book $3 8° Homans, *N.Y.* [84] 9–

„ Money, Banking, and Finance—*ut* **D** § 115

CLEVELAND, Prf. F. A. Bank & the Treasury [capitalizn. and elasticity] $2 *n.* (7/6 *n.*) 8° Longman [05] 08

CONANT, C. A. Principles of Banking = Princs. of Money and Banking, Pt. ii—*ut* **D** § 115
Discusses theory of bank-note currency and the evolution of mod. bankg. pract. tow. idea of a Central Bank.

CRUMP, Arth. English Manual of Banking 15/ 8° E. Wilson [77] 86
A compendium of information on banks, methods, phraseology, law, and Continental methods.

DAVIS, Dr J. F. Bank Organization, Management, and Accounts 5/ *n.* 8° Pitman

DUNBAR, Prf. C. F. Chapters on the Theory and History of Banking—*ut inf.*
A convenient statemt., extremely condensed (its chief merit), of ordinary banking operatns., w. histor. chs. added [*v. inf.*].

EASTON, H. T. History and Principles of Banks and Banking—*ut inf.*

„ Work of a Bank [80 c. *n.* Scribner, *N.Y.*] 2/ *n.* c 8° E. Wilson [98] 00

„ Money Exchange, and Banking—*ut* **D** § 115

FISKE, A. K. The Modern Bank $1·50 (6/ *n.*) c 8° Appleton 04
A descrn. of functns. and meths., and a brief acc. of developmt. and pres. systems of banking.

*GILBART, J. W. Hist., Princs. and Pract. of Bankg., ed. E. Sykes, 2 v. ea. 5/ c 8° Bell [34] 07
Ea. $1·50 *n.* Macmillan, *N.Y.* [Bohn's Lib.] A standard bk.: the most exhaustive on the subj. Incl. his *Pract. Treat. on Bkg.* (1871).

HAGUE, G. Banking and Commerce: practical treatise $3 8° Bankers Pb. Co., *N.Y.* 08

HAKE (A. E.) + WESSLAU (O. E.)—*in their* Free Trade in Capital, *ut* **D** § 118

HANKEY, T. Principles of Banking: its unity and economy 2/6 c 8° E. Wilson [67] 88
Organization and working of Bank of England, w. discussns. on disputed points in management.

HULL, W. H. [ed.] Practical Problems in Banking and Currency $3·50 *n.* (15/ *n.*) 8° Macmillan 07

HUSKINSON, T. W. Prosperity of Nations 2/ *n.* 8° Bouverie Press 98
Analysis of pres. methods of banking, and effect of governmt. dealings with Bk. of England.

*HUTCHISON, Jno. Practice of Banking, 4 vols. vol. i 15/; ii 21/; iii 21/; iv 15/ 8° E. Wilson 81–91
A monumental wk., contg. a vast mass of informatn. and learning, really formg. a code detailing whole meth. on wh. bankg. business shd. be conducted. Embraces the cases at law and in equity bearg. on all branches of the subj.

*MACLEOD, H. D. Elements of Banking [standard] 5/ ($1·25) 8° Longman [76] 91

* ,, Lectures on Credit and Banking 5/ 8° Longman [82]

* ,, Theory & Pract. of Bankg., 2 vols. i, 12/ ($4·50); ii, 14/ ($5) 8° Longman [55–6] 92–3
Full of suggestion, and rich in historical materl. Author differs on many important pts. fr. more orthodox economists.

* ,, The Theory of Credit, 2 vols. in 3 Pts. 30/ *n.* ($10·50) 8° Longman [89–91] 93–7
An excellent bk. on practical side of credit. Vol. ii conts. a concise hist. of banking in Engl., Scot., and Irel. to pres. time, incl. commercial crises of 1764, '72, '82, '93, '97, 1825, '38–'39, '47, '57, '63 and '90.

MOXON, T. B. English Practical Banking 4/6 *n.* 8° J. Heywood, *Mancs.* [2nd ed. 86]

NIXON, Alf. Accounting and Banking—*ut* **D** § 150

PATTEN, C. B. Methods and Machinery of Practical Banking $5 *n.* 8° Rhodes, *N.Y.* [ ] 99

PHIPSON, C. B. —*in his* Science of Civilization, *ut* **D** § 125
Incls. a forcible criticism of modern banking and currency systems.

PRICE, Prf. Bonamy Currency and Banking—*ut* **D** § 115

SCOTT, W. A. Money and Banking—*ut* **D** § 115

SYKES, E. Banking and Currency—*ut* **D** § 16

TURNER, B. B. Commerce and Banking—*ut* **D** § 150

WARREN, Hy. Banks and their Customers 1/ c 8° Sutton [99] 08

,, How to Choose your Banker 3/6 c 8° Richards 00

,, How to Deal with your Banker 3/6 c 8° Richards 00

,, Your Banker's Position at a Glance 5/ *n.* c 8° Jordan 01

,, A Bee among the Bankers 3/6 *n.* c 8° Everett 02
Showing how to increase your deposit-rate; and an attack on the honesty of bankers.

,, Customers' Guide to Banking 6/ c 8° Richards 04

**History; Description; Statistics**

COCHRANE, A. D. Banking: orig. and developmt. and lessons fr. its hist. 2/6 *n.* 8° E. Wilson 01

CONANT, C. A. Hist. of Modern Banks of Issue, etc. $3·50 *n.* (12/6 *n.*) 8° Putnam [96] 09
With acc. of econ. crises of the 19th cent. and of 1907. A compilation, not always fr. first-class authorities (all Engl. or Fr.), of facts regarding hist. and character of the great banks of the world—not limited to banks of issue.

DODSWORTH, W. [ed.] History of Banking in the Leading Nations, 4 vols.
[100/ E. Wilson] $24 r 8° *Jl. of Commerce* Off., *N.Y.* 96–7
Vol. i: *Hist. of Bkg. in U.S.* (Prf. W. G. SUMNER) is of the most importce. Vol. ii deals w. *Gt. Brit.* (H. D. MACLEOD), *Russia* (A. E. HORN), *Savings-Bks. in U.S.* (Dr J. P. TOWNSEND); iii: *Latin Nations* (P. DES ESSARS), *Alsace-Lorraine* (A. RAFFALOVITCH), *Canada* (B. E. WALKER); iv: *Germy. and Austr.-Hung.* (Max WIRTH), *Holland* (Prf R. van der BORGHT), *Scand.* (A. JENSEN), *China* (T. R. JERNIGAN), *Japan* (Juichi SOYEDA).

DUNBAR, Prf. C. F. Chaps. on Theory and Hist. of Banking, ed. O. M. W. Sprague
$1·25 (5/) 12° Putnam [91] 01
In addn. to 'theory', it conts. 11 short but full chs., brightly written and easily read, giving hist. of Bk. of Amsterdam (one of the most import. of exchange-bks. wh. flourished 16 and 17 cents.), Bk. of Engl., Bk. of France, Reichsbk. of Germy., and National Bks. of U.S.

EASTON, H. T. History and Principles of Banks and Banking 5/ *n.* 8° E. Wilson [97] 04
$1·40 Scribner, *N.Y.* A historical and descriptive account for students.

GILBART, J. W. —*in his* History, Principles, and Practice of Banking, *ut sup.*

MACLEOD, H. D. —*in* vol. ii *of his* Theory of Credit, *ut sup.*

RHODES, W. E. Italian Bankers in England [1272–1327]—*in* Tout + Tait [eds.] *Histor. Essays*, *ut* **F** § 16

**London**

CRUMP, Arth. Key to Progress dur. 21 yrs. of Lond. Jt.-Stock Banks 21/ f° E. Wilson 83

HOWARTH, Wm. Banks of the Clearing House 3/6 *n.* c 8° E. Wilson 05
A short history of the banks having a seat in the London Bankers' Clearing House.

PRICE, F. G. Hilton Handbook of London Bankers 15/ 8° Leadenhall Press [76] 90–1
Conts. some account of the early goldsmiths, list of bankers since 1670, *etc.*

SKINNER, T. London Banks & Kindred Companies and Firms 10/ *n.* c 8° Skinner [49] 06

*Bank of England* —*v. also* Hankey, *sup.*

ANDRÉADÈS, Prf. A. History of the Bank of England [tr.] 10/6 *n.* 8° P. S. King 09
Wr. by a Greek in Fch., and with foreign readers in view, but described by Prf. FOXWELL (who in a Pref. reviews liter. of subj.) as 'the most comprehensive and most readable acc. yet pubd.' A bk. for the politician and general reader, however, rather than the economist, bg. almost destitute of organized statist. informatn.

FRANCIS, Jno. Hist. of Bk. of Engl.: times and traditns., 2 v.
[1694–1844] *o.p.* [*pb.* 21/] 8° Willoughby [*n.d.* (47)] 48

,, The same, cont. to 1862 by J. S. Homans $4 8° *New York* 62

PATERSON, Wm. [1658–1719; founder of Bk. of Engl.]

Bannister, Saxe William Paterson: his life and trials *o.p.* [*pb.* 5/] c 8° Bryce 58

Pagan, W. Birthplace and Parentage of Wm. Paterson *o.p.* [*pb.* 3/6] 12° *Edinburgh* 65

ROGERS, Prf. J. E. T. First Nine Years of the Bank of England 8/6 ($1·75) 8° Clar. Pres 87
An inquiry into the weekly record of price of Bank stock fr. Aug. 17, 1694, to Sept. 17, 1703.

STEPHENS, T. A. Contribution to Bibliography of the Bank of England 10/6 *n.* 8° E. Wilson 97
Includes pamphlets and books from 1651; with descriptive notes and illns.

TURNER, B. B. Chronicles of the Bank of England; ill. 7/6 c 8° Sonnenschein 97
A good popular account, w. fairly full detail of its history fr. foundation.

WARREN, Hy. Story of the Bank of England [popular] 3/6 *n.* 8° Jordan 02

*Tokens of the Bank of England* —*v* **G** § 20

*Barclay & Co.*

BIDWELL, W. H. Annals of an East Anglian Bank 12/6 *n.* 8° Goose, *Norwich* 00
A history of GURNEY'S (now BARCLAY & Co.), w. much information about the BARCLAY and GURNEY families.

*Child & Co.*

PRICE, C. H. The Marygold by Temple Bar; ill. [250 copies] 36/ *n.* 4° Quaritch 03
Hist. of site occupied by No. 1 Fleet Street, the banking house of CHILD & Co. Ownership of site traced from 1241.

*Coutts & Co.*

RICHARDSON, R. Coutts & Co., Bankers, Edinburgh and London 3/6 8° Stock [00] 02
Concerned more w. the hist. of the COUTTS family than of the Bank.

*Lloyds*

LLOYD, S. —*in his* The Lloyds of Birmingham 7/6 *n.* 8° Cornish, *Birm.* 07

*Martin's Bank*

MARTIN, Jno. B. 'The Grasshopper' in Lombard Street [no. 68]; ill. 21/s 4° Leadenhall Press 92
Full of interesting histor., financial, and personal matter. The 'Grasshopper' was establ. by the GRESHAMS.

**Bristol**

CAVE, C. H. History of Banking in Bristol, 1750–1899 *priv. prin.* 8° Hemmons, *Bristol* 00

**Liverpool**

HUGHES, Jno. Liverpool Banks and Bankers, 1760–1837; ill. 7/6 *n.* 8° Young, *Liverpool* 06
A connected acc. of orig. and progress of the private banks wh. preceded the great jt.-stock concerns in Liverpool.

**Manchester**

GRINDON, L. H. Manchester Banks and Bankers 6/ c 8° *Manchester* [77] 78

**Northumberland, Durham, Yorks**

PHILLIPS, M. History of Banks, Bankers, and Banking in Northumberland, Durham, and N. Yorks; ill. 31/6 r 4° E. Wilson 94
Illustr. commerc. developmt. of N. of Engl. fr. 1755, incl. interestg. matter rel. to Scottish bankg. and Bk. of Engl. Wr. with a good deal of antiquarian knowl. and a relish for anecdote and adventure. Ports., facss. of notes, etc.

**Scotland**

KERR, A. W. History of Banking in Scotl. [$2·50 Macm., *N.Y.*] 7/6 8° Bryce, *Glasgow* 84

" Scottish Banking dur. Period of Publd. Accs. [1865–96] 5/ *n.* 8° E. Wilson 97

**Ireland**

DILLON, M. History and Development of Banking in Ireland 6/ 8° Thom, *Dublin* 90
From the earliest times to the present day.

**Canada**

BRECKENRIDGE, R. M. Canadian Banking System [Am. Ec. Ass.; 6/ Sonnenschein] $1·50 *n.* 8° Macmillan, *N.Y.* 95

**United States**

BOLLES, A. S. —*in his* Financial History of the United States, 3 vols., *ut* **D** § 117

CARROLL, E. —*in his* Principles and Practice of Finance, *ut* **D** § 115

CATTERALL, R. C. H. Second Bank of the United States $3 *n.* 8° Univ. Press, *Chicago* 03
From its foundation in 1816 to the present day.

CONANT, C. A. —*in his* History of Modern Banks, *ut sup.*

DAVIS, A. McF. Currency and Banking in Province of Massachussetts Bay—*ut* **D** § 115

DOMORYETT, H. W. Hist of Bank of New York [1874–84] $3 8° Putnam, *N.Y.* [84] 84

DUNBAR, Prf. C. F. Economical Essays, ed. O. M. W. Sprague—*ut* **D** § 114

KNOX, J. J., etc. History of Banking in the U.S. $5 8° Rhodes, *N.Y.* 00
From 1693; includes National, State, and Savings banks. Standard work.

WHITE, H. Money and Banking—*ut* **D** § 115

*New York County National Bank*

Through Fifty Years: story of a bank's progress [1855–1905] *pr. pr.* 16° R. G. Cooke, *N.Y.* 06

**France**

LAW, Jno., of Lauriston [1671–1729]

Weston-Glynn, A. W. John Law of Lauriston ; 6 ports. 10/6 *n.* 8° Saunders, *Edin.* 07
The first adequate acc. of the romantic career of the founder of the Bank of France, originator of the Mississippi Scheme, and controller of the finances of France. Gives a good idea of the financial state of France after the disastrous wars of Louis xiv.

**Bank Rate**

PALGRAVE, R. H. I. Bank Rate and the Money Market in England, France, Germany, etc. : 1844-1900 10/6 *n.* r 8° Murray [80] 03
Criticism of Engl. bkg. syst. by comparn. betw. bk.-rate fluctns. in Engl. and on Continent.

**Banking Reform**

WILSON, A. J. Banking Reform [banking dangers and remedies] 7/6 c 8° Longman 79

**Clearing System and Houses**

CANNON, J. G. Clearing Houses : hist., methods, and administration ; ill. [10/6 Smith & Elder] $2·50 8° Appleton, *N.Y.* 00

GILMAN, T. Federal Clearing Houses $1 *n.* 12° Houghton, *Boston* 99

HOWARTH, Wm. Our Banking Clearing System & Clearing Houses 3/6 *n.* c 8° E. Wilson [84] 07

" The Banks of the Clearing House—*ut sup., s.v.* London
Short hist. of banks having a seat in London bankers' clearing-house.

JEVONS, Prf. W. Stanley —*his* Money & Mechan. of Exchange [*ut* **D** § 115] *conts.* descrn. of Clearing House

**Co-operative Banking ; Land Banks**—*v.* **D** § 127*

**County Banking**

KIDDY, J. G. The County Banker's Handbook 2/6 c 8° Waterlow 94
A guide to the rules and practice of the Bank of England, the London clearing-house, and the Stock Exchange.

*RAE, G. The County Banker 3/6 *n.* c 8° Murray [85] 02
$1·50 Scribner, *N.Y.* His clients, cares, and work, fr. an experience of 40 years. A good book.

**Foreign Exchange**—*v.* **D** § 115 **Investments**—*v.* **D** § 153 **Law of Banking**—*v.* **D** § 16
**Money and Currency**—*v.* **D** § 115 **Money and Currency Tables**—*v.* **D** § 154 **Note Issue**—*v.* **D** § 115
**Savings Banks**—*v.* **D** § 127*

## 117 : PUBLIC [IMPERIAL] FINANCE AND TAXATION

**Bibliography**

COSSA, Prf. Luigi —*in his* Taxation, *ut inf.* [chiefly foreign books]

Lib. of Congress : List of Wks. rel. to Taxatn. of Inheritces. & Incomes 4° Govt. Prtg. Off., *Washgtn.* 07

ADAMS, Prf. H. C. The Science of Finance [12/6 *n.* Bell] $3·50 *n.* 8° Holt, *N.Y.* [87] 99

" Public Debts : ess. in science of finance $2·50 8° Appleton, *N.Y.* 93

ARMITAGE-SMITH, Prc. G. Principles and Methods of Taxation 2/6 *n.* c 8° Murray [06] 09
A clear and simple acc. of the Brit. system and the princs. on wh. it is based, w. some leadg. histor. facts.

ATKINSON, Dr Edw. Taxation and Work [Questions of Day] $1·25 (5/) c 8° Putnam 92

*BASTABLE, Prf. C. F. Public Finance 12/6 *n.* ($4 *n.*) 8° Macmillan [92] 03
The most important wk. on whole subj. since MCCULLOCH [*ut inf.*]. Defines Pub. Finance (w. the Germans) as the ' supply and applicatn. of State Resources ' (State incl. all bodies that have power to levy contribs. for pub. purposes) not (w. the Engl. and MCCULLOCH) as rel. to money matters in general. Favours taxatn. of ground-rents ; sums up agst. progressive income-tax, agst. infringemt. of Sinkg. Fd., agst. increase of Death-duties : leans to bimetallism.

CLEVELAND, Prf. F. A. Funds and their Uses [modern finance] $1·25 *n.* c 8° Appleton, *N.Y.* [02] 03

*COHN, G. The Science of Finance, tr. Dr T. B. Veblen $3·50 *n.* 8° Univ. Press, *Chicago* 95

COSSA, Prf. Luigi Taxation : principles and methods [tr.], ed. H. White $1 c 8° Putnam, *N.Y.* 88
Appendix gives in brief form the State tax systems of New York and Pennsylvania as they now are.

DANIELS, Prf. W. M. Elements of Public Finance $1·50 *n.* 12° Holt, *N.Y.* 99

Equitable Taxation [Library of Economics] 75 c. 12° Crowell, *N.Y.*

GIFFEN, Sir Rob. Essays in Finance, 2 Ser. Ser. i, 10/6 ; Ser. ii, 14/ 8° Bell [80] 86 ; 87
Ser. i : *Cost of Frco.-Germ. War, Deprecn. of Gold since* 1848, *Liquidns. of* 1873–6, *Depressn. in Trade, Foreign Competitn., Excess of Imports, Accumuln. of Capital in U.K., Deprecn. of Silver, Gladstone's Work in Finance, Taxes on Land, Reductn. of Natl. Debt, Case agst. Bimetallism, Recent Fall of Prices.* Ser. ii : *Trade Depressn., Gold Supply, Rate of Disct. and Prices, Effects on Trade of Supply of Coinage, Bank Reserves, Foreign Trade of U.S., Use of Import and Export Statistics, Foreign Manufs. and Engl. Trade, Utility of Common Statistics, General Uses of Statist. Knowl., Progress of Wrkg. Classes in Last half Century.*

" —*in his* Economic Enquiries and Studies, 2 vols., *ut* **D** § 114

GOSCHEN, Visc. —*in his* Essays and Addresses on Economic Questions : 1865–93, *ut* **D** § 114

GRICE, J. W. National and Local Finance 10/6 *n.* 8° P. S. King & Son 10
Hist. of relns. of local and natl. finance in Engl. fr. 1832 to 1890, w. discussn. of systs. of Frce., Belg., Prussia.

JEVONS, Prf. W. Stanley —*in his* Investigations in Currency and Finance, *ut* **D** § 115

MACADAM, G. Alphabet of Finance [Lib. Polit. Educ. ; v. simple] $1·25 12° Putnam, *N.Y.* 77

McCulloch, J. R. Treat. on Princs. of Taxn. & Fundg. Syst. *o.p.* [*pb.* 14/] 8° Longman [45] 63
„ An Article on Practical and Theoret. Taxation 5/ 4° *Edinburgh* [4–] 86
Nathan, Sir Nathaniel —*in his* Economic Heresies, *ut* **D** § 114
Newcomb, Simon A B C of Finance [good book; quite popular] 25 c. 32° Harper, *N.Y.* 79
Nicholson, Prf. J. S. Rates and Taxes as affecting Agriculture 2/6 c 8° Sonnenschein 05
$1 Scribner, *N.Y.* [Social Science Series.]
Plehn, Prf. C. C. Introduction to Public Finance [w. short bibliogr.] $1·60 *n.* (6/6 *n.*) c 8° Macmillan 96
A lucid summary fr. Amer. stdpt., in 4 Pts. (1) *Public Expenditure,* (2) *Public Revenues,* (3) *Public Indebtedness,* (4) *Financial Administration.* Based largely on Cohn [*ut sup.*], and its classifn. follows Seligman [*ut inf.*].
Raffety (F. W.) + Sharp (W. H. C.) The Nation's Income [nat. and loc. taxn.] 2/ *n.* c 8° Murby 09
Ricardo, Dav. [1772–1823] —*in his* Princ. of Polit. Econ. and Taxation, *ut* **D** § 114
Rogers, Prf. J. E. Thorold —*article* Finance, *in* Encyclo. Brit., 9th edn., vol. ix [*ut* **K** § 1]
Seligman, Prf. E. R. A. Essays in Taxation $3 *n.* (12/6 *n.*) 8° Macmillan [95] 05
Ser. of detached essays, theoret. and technical, on developmt. of taxatn., on the general prop. tax, single land-tax, double taxatn., taxatn. of corporatns., bettermt.-tax, classifn. of pub. revenues, reforms in other countries, review of Europ. liter. and Am. reports on taxatn. Of chief use to Europ. readers for its exposure of the unsatisfacty. condn. of Am. machinery of taxatn.
Smart, Prf. Wm. National Income and its Distribution 5/ *n.* ($1·60 *n.*) c 8° Macmillan 99
Smith, Adam [1723–90] —*in his* Lectures on Justice, Police, Revenue, and Arms, *ut* **D** § 114
West, Max Principles of Taxation [Citizens' Lib.] $1·25 *n.* (5/ *n.*) c 8° Macmilla
Weston, S. F. Princs. of Justice in Taxn. [Col. Univ. Studs.] $2 *n.* 8° Macmillan, *N.Y.* 03

**Great Britain and Ireland**

Cobden, Rich. [1805–65] Speeches on Questns. of Public Policy, ed. J. Bright *o.p* [*pb.* 3/6] c 8° Macmillan [70] 78
Gladstone, W. E. Financial Statements [1853, '60, '63] *o.p.* [*pb.* 12/] 8° Murray [63] 64
Hill, Dr J. A. English Income Tax [Pubs. Am. Econ. Assoc.] $1 *n.* 8° Macmillan, *N.Y.* 00
Levi, Prf. Leone On Taxation: how raised and how expended *o.p.* [*pb.* 7/6] c 8° Parker 60
Mallet, Sir Louis —*in his* Free Exchange, *ut* **D** § 114
Reid, H. L. The British Taxpayer's Rights 12/ 8° Unwin 98
Largely quotatns. fr. standard economic writers, dealg. w. whole science of finance.
Root, J. W. British National Finance 5/ *n.* 8° Eyre & Spottiswoode 09
An enlargement of the author' *Studies in British National Finance* (1901).
Sargant, W. L. Taxation, Past, Present and Future 7/6 8° Williams 74
Tennant, Chas. People's Blue-Book: taxn. as it is & ought to be *o.p.* [*pb.* 7/6] 12° Longman [ ] 72
Very complete in respect of the laws of taxation and their administration: also theory and history.
Williams, W. M. J. The King's Revenue 6/ *n.* 8° P. S. King 09
Acc. of the Revenue and Taxes raised in U.K., w. a short hist. of ea. tax and branch of the revenue.
Wilson, A. J. National Budget [nat. debt, taxes, rates; Eng. Cit. Ser.] *o.p.* [*pb.* 3/6] c 8° Macmillan 82

**India:** Alston (L.) Elements of Indian Taxation [a v. good bk.] 2/ *n.* c 8° Macmillan 11
Fawcett, Prf. Hy. Indian Finance [3 essays, repr. fr. 'Nineteenth Cent.'] 7/6 8° Macmillan 80
Hyndman, H. M. The Bankruptcy of India [repr. fr. 'Contemp. Review'] 7/6 8° Sonnenschein 86
Wilson, A. J. An Empire in Pawn 10/6 8° Unwin 09
Reprs. (mainly fr. *Investor's Rev.*) of econ. and political (old Radical school) essays wr. since 1890: many of historical interest only. Indian, colonial, and domestic finance.

**United States**

Adams, Prf. H. C. Taxatn. in U.S. [1789–1816] [Univ. Stud.] 50 c. 12° Johns Hopk. Univ. Pr., *Baltim.* 84
Agger, E. E. The Budget in Amer. Commonwealths [Col. Univ. Studs.] $1·50 *n.* 8° Macmillan, *N.Y.* 07
Bowen, Fcs. —*in his* American Political Economy, *ut* **D** § 114
Ely, Prf. R. T. —*in his* Problems of To-day, *ut* **D** § 114
„ + Finley (J. H.) Taxation in Amer. States and Cities [popular] $1·75 c 8° Crowell, *N.Y.* 88
Hatfield, Dr H. R. [ed.] American Commerce and Finance [6/ *n.* Unwin] c 8° Univ. Pr., *Chicago* [05] 05
A series of lects., by representative business-men, deliv. at University of Chicago.
Hollander, Prf. J. H. [ed.] Studies in State Taxation $1·25 8° Johns Hopkins Press, *Baltimore* 00
Articles by graduates and students on taxation in Maryland, N. Carolina, Kansas, Mississippi, and Georgia.
Jones, W. H. Federal Taxation and State Expenses [Questions of Day] $1 8° Putnam, *N.Y.* 87
Lane, J. A. [ed.] Equitable Taxation [6 essays by var. wrs.] 75 c. 12° Crowell, *N.Y.* 92
Lawson, W. R. Amer. Finance, Pt. i: Domestic [$2 *n.* Macmillan, *N.Y.*] 6/ *n.* c 8° Blackwood [06] 08
Phillips, Dr J. B. Meths. of Kpg. Publ. Money of U.S. [Mich. Acad. of Sci.] 8° Univ. of Michigan
Seligman, Prf. E. R. A. —*in his* Essays in Taxation, *ut sup.*
Walker, Prf. F. A. Double Taxation in the United States 75 c. 8° Columbia Coll., *N.Y.* 95

WELLS, D. A. Practical Economics [U.S. taxation and finance] $1·50 8° Putnam, *N.Y.* 86

" Theory and Practice of Taxation $2 12° Appleton, *N.Y.* 00

**Incidence and Shifting of Taxation**

LESLIE, T. E. Cliffe- Incidence of Taxation on Working Classes—*in his* Essays, *ut* **D** § 114

MONEY, L. G. Chiozza Riches & Poverty [*ut* **D** § 126] : a study of incidence of taxn. of U.K., w. statistics

SELIGMAN, Prf. E. R. A. Shifting and Incidence of Taxation $3 *n.* (12/6 *n.*) r 8° Macmillan [92] 99
[Pubs. of Am. Econ. Ass.] A compreh. review of this difficult questn. By 'shifting' a tax is meant the act of the person upon whom it is in first instance levied, by wh. he recoups himself at expense of another in course of their business transns. 'Incidence' is the striking of the tax upon the person who, unable to shift it upon any one else, finds himself obliged to pay it himself.

**Income Tax** —*v. also* **D** § 91

KINSMAN, D. O. Income Tax in Commonwealths of U.S. [Am. Econ. Ass.; 3/6 Sonnenschein] $1 *n.* 8° Macmillan, *N.Y.* 03

SELIGMAN, Prf. E. R. A. The Income Tax [history, theory, practice] (12/6 *n.*) 8° Macmillan 11

**Inheritance Tax** —*v.* **D** § 91

**Land Values: Single Tax** —*for* Law, *v.* **D** § 91

ADAM, Edwin Land Values and Taxation [Social Problems Ser.] 1/ *n.* c 8° Jack 07

CHORLTON, J. D. The Rating of Land Values [Mancs. Univ. Pbs.] 3/6 *n.* 8° Sherratt, *Mancs.* 07
A good introd. to the subject. Moderate; reviews foreign experiments.

FOX, A. Wilson The Rating of Land Values 3/6 *n.* 8° P. S. King [06] 08
An impartial epitome of the argumts. *pro.* and *con.* the separate rating of site-values, by Sec. to Roy. Commn. on Local Taxn.

GEORGE, Hy. —*v.* **D** § 119

LAYCOCK, F. U. Economics and Socialism 7/6 8° Sonnenschein 95
Reviews more fundamental princs. of econcs. f. purpose of testg. claims of Socialism on one hand and Single Tax on other, claiming to estab. fallacy of former and beneficence of latter.

MURRAY, Dav. The Land and Finance Bill 1/ *n.* 8° MacLehose, *Glasgow* 09

SHEARMAN, T. G. Natural Taxation $1 c 8° Doubleday, *N.Y.* [95] 98
Natural Taxation is the taxation of economic rent and of monopoly gains, which the author advocates as the sole tax needful; as able an advocacy of the Single Tax on Hy. GEORGE'S, tho' from a practical fiscal side rather than as a scheme of social reform.

SMART, Prf. Wm. Taxation of Land Values and the Single Tax *o.p.* (90 c.) c 8° Macmillan 00

**Law of Taxation** —*v.* **D** § 91

**Progressive Taxation**

SELIGMAN, Prf. E. R. A. Progressive Taxn. in Theory and Practice [Am. Econ. Ass.; 3/6 Sonnenschein] $1·25 *n.* 8° Macmillan, *N.Y.* [94] 09

**Voluntary Taxation**

HERBERT, Auberon The Voluntaryist Creed; and A Plea for Voluntaryism 2/ *n.* (80 c.) 8° Clar. Press 08

**History**

*Great Britain and Ireland*

BUXTON, S. C. Finance and Politics: historical study, 2 vols. [1783–1885] 26/ 8° Murray 88

Calendar of State Papers: Inquisitns. rel. to Feudal Aids: 1284–1431—*ut* **F** § 20

COLLET, C. D. Hist. of Taxes on Knowledge: origin & repeal; 2 vols. 16/ c 8° Unwin 99

DOUBLEDAY, T. Financial History of England [fr. 1688] *o.p.* [*pb.* 12/] 8° E. Wilson [47] 58

*DOWELL, Steph. Hist. of Taxation & Taxes in England, 4 vols. *o.p.* [*pb.* 42/] 8° Longman [84] 88
Vol. i: To Civil War; ii: to present day; iii: Direct taxes and stamp-duties; iv: Taxes on arts. of consumptn.

HEWINS, W. A. S. English Trade and Finance, chiefly in Seventeenth Century—*ut* **D** § 117*

HORNER, Fcs. [1778–1817] —*in his* Memoirs and Correspondence, ed. L. Horner [bro'], 2 vols., *ut* **F** § 27
Throws considerable light on the finance of the period.

NOBLE, Jno. Fiscal Legisln. [1842–65], 3/6; Natl. Finance: last 2 Parlts. [both *o.p.*] 7/6 8° Longm. 67; 75

NORTHCOTE, Sir S. Financial Policy [summary of measures 1843–61] *o.p.* [*pb.* 14/] 8° Saunders 62

WILLIAMS, W. M. J. The King's Revenue 6/ *n.* 8° P. S. King 08
Acc. of existing taxes of U.K., w. brief hist. of ea. tax and statemt. of amt. raised by it in recent years.

*Ireland*

KENNEDY, T. Hist. of Irish Protest agst. Over-Taxation [1853–97] 5/ 8° *Dublin* 97

*Customs; Excise*

ATTON (H.) + HOLLAND (H. H.) The King's Customs, vol. i: to 1800; ii: to 1855 ea. 10/6 *n.* 8° Murray 08-10
A popular acc. of maritime, revenue, and contraband traffic in Engl., Scotl., and Irel.: clear and concise; w. append of documts.

CHESTER, W. D. Chronicles of the Customs Department 6/ p 8° *priv. prin.* 85

HALL, Hubert History of the Custom-Revenue in England 10/6 8° Stock [85] 92
Very useful to students interested in developmt. of country's commerce, forming as it does a hist. fr. earliest times of a subject upon wh. orig. sources of informatn. are not easily available. First Pt. deals w. constitl. hist. of customs, and Second w. their fiscal aspect.

LEFTWICH, B. R. History of the Excise 2/6 *n.* c 8° Simpkin 08

*Smuggling*

GIBBON-SPILSBURY, A. The Tourmaline Expedition 5/*n.* c 8° Dent 06

SHORE, H. N. Smuggling Days and Smuggling Ways; ill. 7/6 8° Cassell 92
A sketchy bk. of some small value. Cornwall and other counties, w. short acc. of rise and devel. of Coast Guard.

WOOD, J. M. Smugglg. in Solway & ar. Galloway Seabd.; ill. 3/*n.* c 8° Maxwell, *Dumfries* 08

*Exchequer* —*for the* Exchequer Rolls (Pipe Rolls) *v.* **F** § 19 [documts. prior to 1200]

FITZ-NIGEL, Bp Rich. [rn. Hy. ii] Dialogus de Scaccario
Contributes a mass of informatn. on every important point in developmt. of constitl. princs. bef. Magna Charta. The text is cont. in STUBBS' *Select Charters* [*ut* **F** § 18], and Engl. tr. is given in HENDERSON'S *Select Documents of Middle Ages* [*ut* **F** § 13].

HALL, Hubert Antiquities and Curiosities of the Exchequer; ill. 3/6 *n.* p 8° Stock [91] 98
$1·75 Armstrong, *N.Y.* [Camden Lib.] A scholarly bk., reconstructg. the anc. Exchequer, its treasury and house, w. its chests and rolls and tallies, its chess-board and game of counters. Most novel portn. of bk. is author's theory on topogr. of Exchequer and its treasuries at Westminster. Incl. a list of MS. and printed authorities. The subj. has also been treated by the author in his *Introd.* to the *Pipe Roll Soc. Pubns* vol. ii [*ut* **F** § 19] and his *Court Life under the Plantagenets* [*ut* **F** § 19].

LIEBERMANN, Dr F. Einleitung in den 'Dialogus de Scaccario' 2*m.* 8° Peppmüller, *Gottgn.* 75

MADOX, Thos. History and Antiquities of the Exchequer, 2 vols. *o.p.* [*w.* 30/] 4° *London* [1711] 1769
From the conquest to 1327. The standard early work on the subject. Incl. the text of the *Dialogus.*

de PARAVINCINI, F. Early History of the Exchequer *priv. prin.* 91

Red Book of the Exchequer [*comp.* 1230]: ed. Hubert Hall, 3 Pts. ea. 10/r 8° Rolls Series 96
With a very exhaustive Introd., dealg. w. the MS. in all its relns. as well as w. hist. of Ct. of Exchequer.

ROUND, J. Hor. Studies on the Red Book of the Exchequer s 8° *priv. prin.* 98

THOMAS, F. S. The Ancient Exchequer of England *o.p.* [*pb.* 10/] 8° Petheram 48

*Lotteries* —*v.* **H** § 7

*Stamp Duties*

DOWELL, Steph. History and Explanation of Stamp Duties *o.p.* [*pb.* 12/6] 8° Longman 73

*United States*

BOLLES, A. S. Financial History of the U.S., 3 vols. $9·50 12° Appleton, *N.Y.* [80–86] 91–4
The standard work. Vol. i: 1774–89 $2·50; ii: 1789–1860 $3·50; iii: 1861–85 $3·50.

BOWEN, Fcs. —*his* Amer. Polit. Economy [*ut* **D** § 114] *conts. remarks on Finance fr.* 1861–70

BULLOCK, C. J. Finances of the U.S. from 1775 to 1789 75 c. 8° Univ. of Wisconsin 95
A scholarly and careful study; w. especial reference to the Budget.

DEWEY, Dr D. R. Financial History of the U.S. [Amer. Citizen Ser.] $2 *n.* (7/6 *n.*) c 8° Longman [03] 08

GALLATIN, Alb. [1761–1849] —*in his* Writings, ed. H. Adams, 3 vols., *ut* **F** § 74
See espec. his *Sketch of Finances of U.S.* [1796], and *Considerns. on Currency and Bankg. Systs. of U.S.* [1831]. For wrgs. of other earlier Am. statesmen, *v.* **F** § 74.

HOWE, Dr F. C. Taxatn. & Taxes in U.S. und. Internal Rev. Syst., 1791–1895 $1·75 c 8° Crowell, *N.Y.* 96
[Lib. of Economics.] A histor. sketch of organizn., developmt., and later modificn. of direct and excise taxatn. under the Constitn.

KEARNEY, J. W. A Sketch of American Finances [1789–1835] $1 12° Putnam, *N.Y.* 87

NOYES, A. D. Forty Years of American Finance $1·50 *n.* (6/*n.*) 8° Putnam [98] 09
A well-wr. financial hist. of U.S. fr. 1865 to 1907. Enlarged fr. his *Thirty Yrs. of Am. Finance* (1898).

SHERMAN, J. Sel. Speeches & Repts. on Finance and Taxatn. [1859–78] $2·50 8° Appleton, *N.Y.* 79

*Property Tax*

SCHWAB, J. C. Hist. of N. Y. Prop. Tax [Am. Ec. Ass.; 2/6 Sonnenschein] $1 8° Macmillan, *N.Y.* 90

*Repudiation of Debts*

SCOTT, Prf. W. A. Repudiation of State Debts in U.S. [Lib. of Economics] $1·50 12° Crowell, *N.Y.* 93
A historical and critical review of repudiation by the States of Union from 1789 to the present day.

*Surplus Revenue*

BOURNE, E. G. History of the Surplus Revenue of 1837 $1·25 (5/) c 8° Putnam 85
[Questns. of Day.] Exhibits disasters wh. resulted fr. distribg. amg. States a surplus of 40 million dollars fr. Federal treasury.

*Tariff* —*v.* **D** § 122

*Treasury*

KINLEY, Dav. Hist., Organiz. & Influ. of Indep. Treasury of U.S. $1·50 c 8° Crowell, *N.Y.* 93
[Lib. of Economics.] Hist. of orig. and results of attempt of U.S. Govt. for last 50 yrs. to 'keep its own money'.

*Baltimore*

HOLLANDER, Prf. J. H. Financial History of Baltimore $2 *n.* c 8° Johns Hopk. Univ. Pr., *Baltim.* 99

*Connecticut*

JONES, F. R. History of Taxation in Connecticut: 1636–1776 50 c. 8° Johns Hopkins Pr., *Baltimore* 96

*Massachusetts*

DOUGLAS, Dr C. H. J. Financial Hist. of Mass. [Columb. Univ. Studs.] $3·50 *n.* 8° Macmillan, *N.Y.* 92

*New Hampshire*

ROBINSON, H. Taxat. in N. Hampshire [Am. Econ. Ass.; 5/Sonnenschein] $1·25 *n.* 8° Macmillan, *N.Y.* 02

*Vermont*

WOOD, F. A. History of Taxation in Vermont [Columb. Univ. Studs.] 75 c. *n.* 8° Macmillan, *N.Y.* 94

*Virginia*

RIPLEY, Dr W. Z. Financial History of Virginia [Columb. Univ. Studs.] $1 *n.* 8° Macmillan, *N.Y.* 93

## 117* : INDUSTRIAL, AGRICULTURAL, AND COMMERCIAL HISTORY

**Generally** —*v. also* **D** § 148

BOWACK, W. M. Another View of Industrialism 6/ *n.* 8° Unwin 03
A description of mod. mechanical progress; full of curious facts conc. pres.-day industry. Popular.

BÜCHER, Prf. C. Industrial Evolution, tr. Dr S. M. Wickett [12/ *n.* Bell] $2·50 *n.* 8° Holt, *N.Y.* 01
Deals ably w. primit. econ. condns. and rise of natl. econ.; w. a good historical survey of industr. systs., etc.

COCHRANE, C. H. Modern Industrial Progress; ill. $3 *n.* (10/6 *n.*) r 8° Lippincott 05

CUNNINGHAM, Dr W. Western Civilization in its Economic Aspects, 2 vols.—*ut* **F** § 4

CURTLER, W. H. R. Short History of English Agriculture 6/6 *n.* c 8° Clar. Press 10
An interesting survey of nearly 15 cents., fr. the arrival of the English to recent times.

DAVIDSON, J. M. Annals of Toil 6/ c 8° W. Reeves 99
Outlines of labour-history, Roman and British.

DAY, Prf. Clive A History of Commerce; maps $2 (7/6 *n.*) 8° Longman 07
[Commercial Text-bks.] Ea. chap. has questions, subjects for essays, and bibliography. Pt. v devoted to U.S.A.

ELY, Prf. R. T. Studies of the Evolution of Industrial Society $1·25 (5/ *n.*) c 8° Macmillan 03

GIBBINS, Dr H. de B. The History of Commerce in Europe; maps 3/6 (90 c.) gl 8° Macmillan 91
Sketch of a few leadg. facts and broad concluns. on progr. of trade fr. Phœnic. times to pres. day, givg. prominence to Engl. trade. Strongly Radical.

,, Economic and Industrial Progress of the Century 5/ *n.* c 8° Chambers 03
[Nineteenth Cent. Ser.] An interesting acc. of the revolutn. caused by machinery wh. has completely changed face of mod. Eur. and New World.

GILBART, J. W. Lectures & Essays on the History & Principles of Ancient Commerce [& other essays] *o.p.* [*pb.* 15/] c 8° Bell 47

HEEREN, Prf. A. H. Historical Researches into Politics, Intercourse and Trade of Principal Nations of Antiquity [tr.], 6 vols. *o.p.* 8° Bohn [29–46] 47–50
Vols. i–iii deal w. Asiatic nations, iv–v w. Africa, vi w. Greece [the weakest vol.]. A sort of polit., internatl., and commerc. hist. of Mediterranean.

LINDSAY, W. S. Hist. of Merchant Shipping & Anc. Commerce, 4 v. [standard] *o.p.* [*pb.* 90/] 8° Low 74–6

LORD, Eleanor L. Industrial Experimts. in Brit. Cols. of N. Amer. $1·25 c 8° Johns Hopkins Pr. *Baltim.* 98
A history of the econ. relations of Britain and the U.S. before the War of Independence.

MCCULLAGH, W. T. Industrial History of Free Nations, 2 vols. *o.p.* [*pb.* 24/] 8° Chapman 46
Vol. i: *The Greeks*; vol. ii (treating of Holland and Flanders) is of especial value.

MCVEY, F. L. Modern Industrialism; ill. 6/ *n.* c 8° Appleton, *London* 06
Outl. of industr. organizn. as seen in hist. and industry of Engl., U.S., and Germany.

MARCHANT, J. R. V. Commercial History; maps [fr. earliest times; school-bk.] 3/ c 8° Pitman 01

SAMUELSON, Jas. [ed.] The Civilization of Our Day 16/ *n.* 8° Low 96
A colln. of essays in the advances in material civilization in the 19th century.

SCHOENHOF, J. A History of Money and Prices—*ut* **D** § 115

*SHADWELL, Arth. Industrial Efficiency 6/ *n.* ($2 *n.*) 8° Longman [06] 09
A very valuable and interestg. comparison betw. phases of mod. industr. life in Engl., Germy., and U.S.A., 'industrial' passing insensibly into 'social', all the factors and forces modifying the econ. energy of the 3 peoples bg. investigated—factory laws, hrs. of labour, rates of wages, condns. of health in factories, habits, betting and gambling, thrift, love of games, relig. educn. Sums up by a note of warning: England is perishing of over-prosperity; 'we are a nation at play'; calling upon her to renounce her Gospel of Ease, and renew her relatively-decaying vitality.

SMART, Prf. Wm. Economic Annals of the Nineteenth Cent.: 1801-20 21/ *n.* 8° Macmillan 10

WARD, Osborne History of the Ancient Working People $2 12° Lowdermilk, *Washgtn.* 89
From the earliest known period to the adoption of Christianity by CONSTANTINE. Of small value.

WEBSTER, W. C. General History of Commerce; maps & ill. $1·40 (6/6) c 8° Ginn 03
Pictures of commerc. growth and decay of several nations, w. the causes wh. have contrib. to expansn. of world's trade.

WELLS, Dr Dav. A. Recent Economic Changes and their Effect $2 c 8° Appleton, *N.Y.* [89] 03
10/6 Longman. A good acc. of econ. changes that have occurred dur. last quarter of 19 cent., due to progr. of inventn. and commerce. Full of facts.

YEATS, Dr J. Manuals of Technical, Indust., & Trade Education, 4 v. ea. 6/ 8° Philip [71–2] 87
i: *Nat. Hist. of Raw Materials of Commerce*; ii: *Technical Hist. of Commerce*; iii: *Growth and Viciss. of Commerce* [fr. 1500–1789]; iv: *Recent and Existing Commerce* [1789–1887].

YOUNG, Dr Edw. —*in his* Labor in Europe and America, *ut* **D** § 118

**England:** *Generally, and Extended Periods*

*ASHLEY, Prf. W. J. Introd. to Engl. Econ. Hist. 2 Pts. [Putnam, *N.Y.*] 15/6 c 8° Longman [88–93] 94–3
Pt. i [Middle Ages] 5/ ($1·50); ii [*End of Mid. Ages*] 10/6 ($3). Pt. i deals w. the manor, and village-community, mercht. and craft guilds, econ. theories and legisln.; Pt. ii w. suprem. of towns, the crafts, woollen industry, agrarian revoln., relief of poor, the Canonist Doctrine, etc. A very useful and careful wk., thoroughly scientific, and embodying a mass of material in shape of quotns. fr. orig. authorities. Bibliogr. to ea. chapter, and notes.

,, Surveys, Historic and Economic—*ut* **D** § 114

,, [ed] British Industries: a series of reviews—*ut inf.*

BURNLEY, Jas. Story of Brit. Trade and Industry [Lib. of Usef. Stories] 1/ 12° Newnes 04

CHEYNEY, E. P. Introduction to Industrial & Social Hist, of England) $1·40 *n.* (6/ *n.*) c 8° Macmillan 01
Elementary, but complete: temperate and well-balanced. Illustrated. Bibliography.

CRAIK, G. L. History of British Commerce fr. Earliest Times, 3 vols. *o.p.* [*pb.* 4/6] 18° Cox 44
Still of some value. A revisn. and condensatn. of MACPHERSON's *Annals of Commerce* [4 v., 4° '05], wh. was itself a revision of ANDERSON's wk. [3 v., 4°, 1787–9].

*CUNNINGHAM, Dr W. Growth of Engl. Industry & Commerce dur. Early & Mid. Ages [$4 *n.* Putnam, *N.Y.*] 12/6 *n.* 8° Camb. Press [82] 05
Covers 16 cents. fr. semi-nomadic condns. of the English in Frisia (as descr. by Cæsar) down to end of Mary's rn. A thoroughly sound piece of wk.—for the student, rather than the general reader.

* ,, Growth of Engl. Industry and Commerce in Modern Times; 2 Pts. 25/ *n.* 8° Camb. Press [92] 07
$5·25 *n.* Putnam, *N.Y.* Pt. i: *The Mercantile System*, 10/ *n.* ($3 *n.*); ii: *Laissez Faire*, 7/6 *n.* ($2·25 *n.*). Deals w. period fr. ELIZABETH to pres. day, i.e. w. the rise and fall of the Mercantile System.

,, + MCARTHUR (Ellen A.) Outlines of Engl. Industrial History 3/ *n.* c 8° Camb. Press [95] 05
$1·50 *n.* Macmillan, *N.Y.* [Cambr. Histor. Ser.] A concise and very readable outl. of the story of the material side of the life of the nation. told as a continuous whole, spec. emphasis bg. laid (as in Dr CUNNINGHAM's other books) on the political—as apart from the econ.—features of material progress. Eminently fair, and characterized by the true historic spirit. Good index.

DYER, Dr Hy. The Evolution of Industry 10/ *n.* ($1·50) c 8° Macmillan 95
Limited to Gt. Brit. Its object is 'to find a social organizn. correspg. to modern condns. of productn., as the social organizn. of the Middle Ages corresponded w. the simple condns. of production then existing both in town and country'—wh. purpose it serves rather than that indicated by the title. Trade-Unions, Positn. of Women, Co-opern., Munic. Control, Mod. State, Control, Industr. Traing., all receive special treatmt.

EDEN, Sir Fredk. M. The State of the Poor, 3 vols.—*ut* **D** § 127

GIBBINS, Dr H. de B. Industrial History of England [Univers. Extens. Ser.] 3/ c 8° Methuen [90] 06
$1·20 *n.* Scribner, *N.Y.* A broad outl. of agric., commerc., and industr. history from Roman period to mod. age of factory syst.

,, British Commerce and Colonies [Commercial Series] 2/ c 8° Methuen 93
From Elizabeth to Victoria. Fairly good. Intended chiefly for commercial schools.

,, Industry in England: historical outlines; maps 10/6 8° Methuen [96] 06
$2·50 *n.* Scribner, *N.Y.* Expansion on above bk., contg. copious well-digested facts presentg. clear view of industr. hist. fr. prehist. times.

HACKWOOD, F. W. The Good Old Times: romance of humble life; ill. 10/6 *n.* 8° Unwin 10

HOBSON, J. A. The Evolution of Modern Capitalism—*ut* **D** § 118

LEVI, Prf. Leone Hist. of Brit. Commerce & Econ. Progress [1763–1878] *o.p.* [*pb.* 18/] 8° Murray [72] 80

MEREDITH, H. O. The Economic History of England 5/ *n.* 8° Pitman 08

MULHALL, M. G. History of Prices since 1850; 8 diagrs. *o.p.* [*pb.* 6/] c 8° Longman 85

NICHOLSON, Prf. J. S. Relation of Rent, Wages, & Profits in Agriculture 2/6 c 8° Sonnenschein 06
$1 Scribner, *N.Y.* [Social Sci. Ser.] Sketch of past and present of agric. on its economic side.

PRICE, L. L. Short History of English Commerce and Industry 3/6 c 8° Arnold 00
A clear summary, intended for use as a text-book.

PUTNAM, Bertha H. Enforcemt. of Statutes of Laborers [Col. Univ. Studs.] $4 *n.* 8° Macmillan, *N.Y.* 09

ROGERS, Prf. J. E. Thorold History of Agriculture and Prices in England, 7 vols. 8° Clar. Press 66–03
Vols. i–ii: 1259–1400, 84/ *n.* ($25·50); iii–iv: 1401–1582, 32/ *n.* ($9·75); v–vi: 1583–1702, 32/ *n.* ($9·75); vii [in 2 Pts., posth. ed. A. G. L. ROGERS (son)]: 1702–93, 32/ *n.* ($9·75).

,, Six Centuries of Work and Wages 10/6 8° Sonnenschein [85]
$3 Putnam, *N.Y.* A very interestg. hist. of the subj. from 14th to 19th cent., condensing above wk., by an economist of the Historical School. Shows that the Golden Age of the English labourer was the 15th century.

,, Work and Wages 2/6 c 8° Sonnenschein [85]
$1 Scribner *N.Y.* [Social Sci. Ser.] Abgmt of above, contg. 8 chaps. only, omitting the historical ones.

,, Industrial and Commercial Hist. of Engl., 2 vols. ea. 3/6 c 8° Unwin [92] 06
$3 Putnam, *N.Y.* Ser. of lects. (1888–9), posthum. ed. A. G. L. ROGERS [son]. Aims rather at expoundg. the lecturer's methods of study than at furnishg. new facts or theories, tho' it gives evid. of much research rel. to prodn. and distribn. of wealth in Engl. dur. Mid. Ages.

,, The Economic Interpretation of History—*ut* **F** § 2
Lects. on Land, Taxation, Currency, Wealth, Distribution, Prices, Protection, etc.

TIPPER, H. England's Attainment of Commercial Supremacy 5/ c 8° Stock 97
A popular hist. of British commerce for the last 300 yrs. By an Associate of Institute of Bankers.

TOOKE (T.) + NEWMARCH (W.) History of Prices, & of the State of Circulation, 6 vols. [1793–1856] *o.p.* 8° Longman 38–57

TRAILL, H. D. [ed.] —*in his* Social England, *ut* **F** § 16

WARNER, G. Townsend Landmarks in English Industrial History 5/ c 8° Blackie [99] 10
$1·60 *n.* Macmillan, *N.Y.* A compreh. surv., dealg. clearly w. Town-life, Agric., Bankg., Machy., etc. Much well-digested informn.

WELSFORD, J. W. The Strength of England 5/ *n.* ($1·75 *n.*) c 8° Longman 10
A politico-economic history of England fr. Saxon times to reign of CHARLES I.

*Fourteenth Century—for* Black Death *v.* **F** § 21, and **H*** 1 *Fifteenth Century—v.* **F** § 21

*Sixteenth and Seventeenth Century—for* Commercial Policy *v.* **D** § 149

HEWINS, W. A. S. English Trade & Finance, chfly. in 17 Cent. 2/6 c 8° Methuen 92
[Univ. Extn. Manls.] Sketch of commercial Engl. 200 yrs. ago. Rather scrappy, but acc. of Russian and other Trading Cos. good.

MACAULAY, L'd Hist. of Engl., ch. iii; w. statist. notes A. L. Bowley 2/6 (50 c.) c 8° Clar. Press [49] 09
A descrn. of state of Engld. at time when the crown passed fr. CHAS. II to his brother.

MUN, Thos. [1571–1641] England's Treasure by Forraign Trade [1664] [Econ. Classics] 3/ *n.* (75 c. *n.*) gl 8° Macmillan 95
MUN, havg. acquired wealth in Levant trade, became (in 1615) member of Committee of recently estab. East India Co. In defence of the Co. he in 1621 pubd. *A Discourse of Trade fr. England into the East Indies.* The present wk., tho' not printed till 1664 (some 23 years after its author's death), was prob. wr. ab. 1630 [2nd edn. 1669, 3rd 1698, *etc.*]. MUN was one of the earliest advocates of a rational view of trade, and one of the earliest opponents of the common superstitn. ab. the precious metal.

NORTH, Sir Dudley  Discourses upon Trade [1691]—*ut* **D** § 122

UNWIN, G.  Industrial Organization in 16th and 17th Cents. 7/6 *n.* ($2·50) 8° Clar. Press 04

*Intercourse with East Indies*—*v.* **E** § 35, *s.v.* East India Company

*Intercourse with Siam*

ANDERSON, Dr J.  English Intercourse w. Siam in 17th Cent.  [Oriental Ser.] 15/ 8° Paul 90

*Eighteenth Century to Present Day*—*v. also* **D** §§ 118, 127

ASHLEY, Prf. W. J. [ed.] British Industries: by various authors 5/6 *n.* ($1·80 *n.*) c 8° Longman [03] 07
A series of general reviews of British industries, for business-men and students of economics.

,, [ed.] British Dominions: pres. commerc. & ind. condn. [by var. wrs.] 6/6 *n.* 8° Longman 11

BEARD, C. A.  The Industrial Revolution  1/ *n.* c 8° Sonnenschein 01

BOWLEY, A. L.  England's Foreign Trade in 19 Cent.
[Soc. Sci. Ser.; $1 Scribner, *N.Y.*] 2/6 c 8° Sonnenschein [93] 05

CASSELL & Co. [pbs.]  Pictorial Descrn. of our Natl. Industries; ill.  12/ f° Cassell 02

COBBETT, Wm.  —*in his* Rural Rides, 2 vols., *ut* **E** § 16 [1821–32]

CUNNINGHAM, Dr Wm.  The Industrial Revolution  5/ *n.* 8° Camb. Press 08
$1·50 *n.* Putnam, *N.Y.* Reprints of *Parliamy. Colbertism* and *Laissez Faire* fr. his *Growth of Engl. Industry* [*ut sup.*], dealg. w. revoln. of 18th and first half of 19th cent.

FUCHS, C. J.  Trade Policy of Gt. Brit. and her Colonies since 1860 [tr.]—*ut* **D** § 122

KALM, P.  —*in his* Account of his Visit to England [in 1748], tr. Jos. Lucas, *ut* **E** § 16
Of great importance for the history of English agriculture in the middle of the 18th century.

MASTERMAN, C. F. G.  The Condition of England  6/ c 8° Methuen 09
A picture, by a Socialist, of a nation bewildered for lack of any 'inner spring of ideals'—of a 'conquering' upper class wh. has lost its old place in the scheme of things without finding a new one, and a middle class unconsciously partg. w. its beliefs, while retaing, some of its prejudices and all its limitatns., followed by a toiling multitude whose content in merely material gain is sadder than bitterness of revolt. Brilliantly written.

MULHALL, M. G.  Hist. of Prices; w. 8 col. diagrs.  [1850–1885] *o.p.* [*pb.* 6/] c 8° Longman 85

SMART, Prf. Wm.  Economic Annals of Nineteenth Century  [1801–20] 21/ *n.* 8° Macmillan 10

TOYNBEE, Arnold  Lects. on Industrial Revolution of the 18th Cent. in Engl.—*ut* **D** § 118

UNWIN, Mrs. Cobden [ed.]  The Hungry Forties: life under the Bread Tax  6/ c 8° Unwin 05
Testimonies of condns. of life of the labourer, esp. in rural Engl., dur. the bitter days of the long peace betw. Waterloo and the Alma.

WEBB, Sidn.  Labour in the Longest Reign: 1837–97  1/ 12° Richards 97
Issued under the auspices of the Fabian Society.

WOOD, Sir Hy. Trueman  Industrial England in Middle of Eighteenth Century  5/ *n.* c 8° Murray 11

*Chartist Movement*  —*v.* **D** § 139

**Scotland**

BREMNER, Dav.  —*in his* Industries of Scotland: rise, progress and pres. condn., *ut* **I** § 52

COCKRAN-PATRICK, Dr R. W. —*in his* Mediæval Scotland, *ut* **F** § 37

DAVIDSON (Prf. Jno.) + GRAY (Alex.) The Scottish Staple at Veere  12/6 *n.* ($4·50 *n.*) 8° Longman 09
The second pt. deals w. the Scottish staple in the Low Countries—almost equivalent to a hist. of Scottish trade.

HALYBURTON, Andr.  Ledger of Andrew Halyburton  r 8° Scot. Record Pub. 67
HALIBURTON was Conservator of Privileges of Scotch Nation in Netherlds. 1492–1503. Conts. also *Bk. of Customs and Valuation of Merchandises* in 1612.

KEITH, Theodora  Commercial Relations of England & Scotland: 1603–1707  2/ *n.* c 8° Camb. Press 10
Form the first volume of a new series to be entitled Girton College Studies.

ROOSEBOHM, Dr M. P.  The Scottish Staple in the Netherlands  15/ *n.* 8° Nijhoff, *Hague* 10
Complements DAVIDSON + GRAY, bg. planned on a more chronolog. and histor. method, and devotg. half its pp. to illustrative documts. (many hitherto unpubd.). Covers period 1292–1676.

ROSS, Provost [ed.]  Scottish Home Industries  Scottish Home Industries Assoc., *Lond.* 94
Papers by heads of var. branches of Scott. Home Ind. Ass.; w Pref. by Ross giving acc. of some of older Scott. industries.

STIRLING, Amel. H.  Sketch of Scott. Industr. and Social Hist. in 18 & 19 Cents. 6/ *n.* 8° Blackie 06
Describes well the developmt. of manufs., shippg., canals, rlwys., etc. Industr. chs. better than social.

WEDDERBURNE, Dav. [16 cent.]  Compt Buik of a Merchant of Dundee [1587–1630] 8° Scot. Hist. Soc. 98
Contains shipping lists of Dundee from 1580 to 1618.

**Ireland**

MURRAY, Dr Alice E.  History of the Commercial and Financial Relations between
England and Ireland [since Restoratn.] 3/6 *n.* 8° P. S. King & Son [03] 07

**France**: YOUNG (Arth.)  —*in his* Travels in France dur. Yrs. 1787–9, *ut* **F** § 49

**Portugal**: SHILLINGTON (Dr Violet M.) + CHAPMAN (Dr A. Beatr. W.) Commercial Relations
of England and Portugal  5/ *n.* c 8° Routledge 07
$2 *n.* Dutton, *N.Y.* Pt. i: *Mediaeval* (SHILLINGTON); pt. ii: *Modern* (CHAPMAN). A useful piece of research. Bibliogr.

**Prussia**

SCHMOLLER, G.  The Mercantile System & its Historical Significance 3/ *n.* (75 c. *n.*) 12° Macmillan [84] 96
Illd. chfly. fr. Prussian hist.: a ch. fr. author's econ. essays on m. of Fredk. the Gt.

**Russia**: CRAWFORD (J. M.) [ed.] The Industries of Russia, 2 vols.—*ut* **E** § 25

**Asia :** DANIELL (C. J.) The Industrial Competition of Asia—*ut* **D** § 115
An inquiry into the influence of currency on the commerce of the empire in the East.

*China*

BRETSCHNEIDER, Dr E. Ess. on Intercourse of Chinese w. Western countries in Mid. Ages p 8° Trübner 89
EAMES, J. B. The English in China ; maps and ill. 20/ *n.* 8° Pitman 09
Acc. of intercourse and relns. betw. Engl. and China fr. 1600 to 1843, w. summary of later developmts.
MORSE, H. B. Internatl. Relns. of Chinese Empire : Period of Conflict [1834–60] 20/ *n* 8° Longman 11

*Japan* —*v. also* NITOBE, *inf.*

DAUTREMER, J. The Japanese Empire and its Economic Conditions 10/6 *n.* 8° Unwin 10
KINOSITA, Y. Past & Pres. of Jap. Commerce [Col. Univ. Studs.] $1·50 *n.* 8° Macmillan, *N.Y.* 02
ONO, Dr Yeijiro Industrial Transition of Japan
[Am. Ec. Ass. ; 2/6 Sonnenschein] 75 c. 8° Macmillan, *N.Y.* 90

*Siam* —*v.* ANDERSON, *sup.*

**United States** —*v. also* **D** § 118, *s.v.* United States

ATKINSON, Edw. The Industrial Progress of the Nation $2·50 (10/6) 8° Putnam 90
Statistics good, theories weak.
BOGART, Dr E. L. Economic History of the United States $1·75 (9/ *n.*) c 8° Longman 07
[Commerc. Text-Bks.] Hist. of developmt. of industry ; mainly for students. Gives refs. ; full bibliogr.
BOLLES, A. S. Industrial History of the United States $3·75 8° Bill, *Norwich, Conn.* 79
From earliest times. Agric., Manufactures, Shippg., Fisheries, Railrds., Mines, Banks, Insurance, Trades Unions, etc.
COMAN, Kath. Industrial History of the United States ; ill. $1·25 *n.* (5/ *n.*) c 8° Macmillan 05
COMMONS, J. R., etc. Documentary Hist. of Amer. Industrial Soc., 10 vols. [to 1880]
$50 8° Clark, *Cleveland* 09–10
GOULD, Dr E. R. L. The Social Condition of Labour 50 c. 8° Johns Hopk. Univ. Press, *Baltimore* 93
[Johns Hopkins Univ. Studies.] Comparison betw. social cond. of wkg.-man in U.S. and other countries.
LAUGHLIN, Prf. J. L. Industrial America [Berlin lects. ; 7/6 Hodder] $1·25 *n.* 8° Scribner, *N.Y.* 06
WEEDEN, W. B. Econ. & Social Hist. of New Engl., 2 v. [1620–1879] $4·50 12° Houghton, *Boston* 90
WRIGHT, Dr C. D. Industrial Evolution of U.S. ; ill. & maps $1 12° Flood, *Meadville* 95
Brief pop. econ. hist. of U.S., fr. Colonial Per. to pres. day : by Feder. Commr. of Labor.

*Intercourse with Japan*

NITOBE, Inazo Intercourse betw. U.S. and Japan [Univ. Studs.] $1·25 Johns Hopk. Univ. Pr., *Baltim.* 91

*Intercourse with Spanish America*

SAVAGE, T. Industr. & Commerc. Interc. betw. U.S. & Sp. Am. : 1890–1 $2·50 Bancroft, *San Franc.* 91

*Virginia*

BRUCE, P. A. Economic Hist. of Virginia in 17th Cent., 2 vols. $6 (25/ *n.*) c 8° Macmillan, *N.Y.* 96
Sources given in a prelim. bibliogr., and w. more detail in foot-notes. Materl. classif. under heads : Econ. Condns., Social Life, Relig. Establishmt., and Moral Influences, Educn., Milit. Regulns., Admin. of Justice, Polit. System—the whole reproducg. w. minute fidelity the life and material condn. of the people of 17th cent.

**Chartered and Trading Companies**

BIGGAR, H. P. Early Trading Companies of New France
[Univ. of Toronto Studies ; 16/ *n.* P. S. King & Son] $4 *n.* r 8° Boston Bk. Co., *Boston* 01
CAWSTON (G.) + KEANE (A. H.) The Early Chartered Companies ; 1296–1858 ; 10/6 8° Arnold 96
Not a continuous hist. of the Engl. Chart. Cos. ; but an acc. of Charters granted and their modificn., 1296–1858.
'Imperialist, An' The Pioneers of Empire [pp. 146] 1/ 8° Methuen 96
In 3 Pts. : (1) *Vindicn. of Principle of Chartered Cos.* ; (2) *Sketch of Engl. Chartered Cos.* ; (3) *Brit. S. Africa Co.*

*East India Co.* —*v.* **E** § 35

*Hon. Company of Merchants-Adventurers* [tradg. into Hudson's Bay]—*v. also* **E** § 55, *s.v.* Hudson Bay

BRYCE, Geo. Remarkable Hist. of the Hudson's Bay Co. [$4 Scribner, *N.Y.*] 14/ *n* 8° Low 00
Covers last 80 yrs. since amalgamatn. of all the fur-interests of Brit. N. Amer. Good complement to WILLSON.
WILLSON, Beckles The Great Company : 1667–1871, 2 vols. ; map
[$5 Dodd, *N.Y.*] 18/ c 8° Smith & Elder 00
A detailed acc. of the Company's commercial and polit. activities, w. Introd. by the pres. Governor, Arth. HEMING.

*Levant Co.* —*v. also* **E** § 29 (BENT)

EPSTEIN, Dr M. Early History of the Levant Company 2/6 *n.* c 8° Routledge 08
$1·25 *n.* Dutton *N.Y.* [Research Lib.] A careful acc. of the third of a series of trading companies estab. 1592, conductg. operatns. till 1821 when it was taken over by the Engl. Govt. Its predecessors were the Turkey Co. (1581) and the Venice Co. (1583).

**Corn Laws** —*v. also* UNWIN, *sup.*, and JEPHSON, in **D** § 139

MARKS, Mary H. M. The Corn Laws : a popular history 2/ *n.* c 8° Fifield 08
NICHOLSON, Prf. J. S. Hist. of Engl. Corn Laws [Soc. Sci. Ser.; $1 Scrib., *N.Y.*] 2/6 c 8° Sonnenschein 05

**Special Industries** —*for history of other* Industries *and* Trades *v.* **I** *passim* ; *also* **D** § 120, *s.v.* Gilds

*Birmingham Fire-arms Trade :* 'ARTIFEX' + 'OPIFEX' Causes of Decay in a British Industry—*ut* **D** § 118

*Coal Trade* —*v. also* Iron and Steel Trades, *inf.* (SORLEY)

WARNE, F. J. Coal-mine Workers: study in labr. organizn. [Amer.] $1 *n.* (3/6) c 8° Longman 06

*Cotton Trade* —*v. also* **I** § 34

BAINES, Thos. —*in his* History of Commerce and Town of Liverpool, *ut* **E** § 17

BESSO, S. L. Cotton Industry in Switzerland, Vorarlberg, and Italy [Mancs. Univ. Pubns.] 3/6 *n.* c 8° Sherratt, *Mancs.* 10

CHAPMAN, Prf. S. J. The Lancashire Cotton Industry [Mancs. Univ. Pbns.] 7/6 *n.* 8° Sherratt, *Mancs.* 04

,, Cotton Industry and Trade [Bks. on Business] 2/6 *n.* c 8° Methuen 05

ELLISON, Thos. Cotton Trade of Gt. Brit.; incl. hist. of L'pl. market 15/ *n.* 8° E. Wilson 86

HAMMOND, M. B. Cotton Industry [Am. Econ. Ass.; 5/ Sonnenschein] $1·50 *n.* 8° Macmillan, *N.Y.* 98

v. SCHULZE-GÄVERNITZ, Dr Cotton Trade in Engl. and on Continent [tr.] 5/ 8° Simpkin 95

WOOD, Geo. Hy. Hist. of Wages in Cotton Tr. dur. past 100 Yrs. 3/ 8° Sherratt, *Mancs.* 10

YOUNG, F. M. Amer. Cotton Industry [study of wk. and wkrs.] 1/6 c 8° Methuen 02

*Engineering Trade*

American Engineering Competition 2/6 ($1) 8° Harper 01

Arts. repr. fr. *The Times.* Give an excellent account of the conditions of the trade.

*Fur Trade*

CHITTENDEN, H. M. Amer. Fur Trade in the Far West, 3 vols. 8° F. P. Harper, *N.Y.* 02

From 1806-43. On importce. and nature of the trade, w. histor. and biograph. matter. *Vide also* **E** § 55, *s.v.* Hudson Bay Co.

*Iron and Steel Trades*

BELL, L'y [Mrs Hugh BELL] At the Works: story of a manufg. town 6/ c 8° Arnold 07

Acc. of daily lives of iron-wkrs. (esp. women and children) in Middlesboro'; based on 30 years' intercourse. By the wife of a great ironmaster.

CASSON, H. N. The Romance of Steel; pl. 10/6 *n.* 8° Richards 08

Since the adoptn. of the Bessemer process: 'the story of a thousand millionaires', incl. Andr. CARNEGIE and his business in great detail.

Iron and Steel Industries of Belgium and Germany 5/ 8° P. S. King & Son 96

Report of Delegn. of Brit. Iron Trade Assn., givg. detailed comparison w. Gt. Brit. (descr. and statist.).

JEANS, J. S. Iron Trade of Gt. Britain [Bks. on Business] 2/6 *n.* c 8° Methuen 06

,, [ed.] American Industrial Conditions & Competition c 8° Brit. Iron Tr. Assoc. 02

Four expert Repts. on Amer. iron and steel industry. Illustrated.

SORLEY, Prf. W. R. Mining Royalties and Effects on Iron & Coal Trades 1/6 8° Clar. Press 89

*Carnegie Steel Co.* —*v.* **D** § 148, *s.nn.* BRIDGE, CARNEGIE

*Mercantile Marine* —*v.* **I** § 23*

*Mining*

DURLAND, Kellogg Among the Fife Miners 2/6 c 8° Sonnenschein 04

*Oil Trade:* 'INVESTIGATOR' The Great Oil Octopus [repr. fr. *Truth*] 5/ *n.* c 8° Unwin 11

LLOYD, H. D. —*in his* Wealth agst. Commonwealth, *ut* **D** § 118, *s.v.* Monopolies and Trusts

MONTAGUE, G. H. Rise and Progress of the Standard Oil Co. $1 *n.* c 8° Harper, *N.Y.* 03

TARBELL, Ida M. [Am.] History of the Standard Oil Company, 2 v.; 80 ill. 24/ *n.* 8° Heinemann 05

A full acc. of the hist. of the 'pre-eminent trust of the world'—one of the few business organ zations the growth of wh. can be traced in trustworthy documents.

*Pottery Trade*

'Old Potter, An' When I was a Child 3/6 c 8° Methuen 03

By a Methodist minister, detailg. his early experces. of social condn. of Staffs potters.

*Tailoring Trade*

GALTON, F. W. [ed.] Tailoring Trade; Introd. S. Webb [docs. illg. hist.] 5/ ($1·50) c 8° Longman 96

*Tin-miners*

LEWIS, G. R. The Stannaries: study of English tin-miners 6/ *n.* c 8° Constable 08

*Woollen & Worsted Trades*

ASHLEY, Prf. W. J. Early History of English Woollen Industry [Am. Ec. Ass.; 2/6 Sonnenschein] 75 c. 8° Macmillan, *N.Y.* 87

CLAPHAM, J. H. The Woollen and Worsted Industries 6/ c 8° Methuen 07

## 118: CAPITAL AND LABOUR; WORK AND WAGES

*Bibliography:* MAROT, Helen Handbook of Labor Literature $1 12° Leach, *Phila.* 09

ABOUT, Edm. Handbook of Social Economy [tr.] $2 12° Appleton, *N.Y.* 73

Deals with the fallacies commonly accepted by wage-earners.

ADAMS (T. S.). + SUMNER (H. L.) Labor Problems: a text-book $1·75 8° Macmillan 05

BANKS, D. C. The Ethics of Work and Wealth 5/ *n.* c 8° Blackwood 04

BOARD OF TRADE: Reports on Cost of Living of Wkg. Classes in Great Towns Wyman 08–10

*United Kingdom*, 6/; *Germany*, 4/11; *France*, 4/1; *Belgium*, 2/2; *Publ. Health and Social Condns.*, 5/.

BOLLES, A. S. The Conflict between Capital and Labour 75 c. 12° Lippincott, *Phila.* [76] 77

BRASSEY, L'd Papers & Addresses: On Work & Wages, ed. G. Howell 5/ ($1·75) 8° Longman [73] 94

" Lectures on the Labour Question *o.p.* [*pb.* 6/] 8° Longman [78] 78

" Foreign Work and English Wages *o.p.* [*pb.* 10/6] 8° Longman [79] 80

By an employer of labour, treatg. rts. of wage-earners in a fair manner, and promulgatg. doctr. of uniform cost of labr. in every pt. of world. *V.* CHAPMAN, *inf.*

BROOKS, J. G. Papal Encyclical on Labour [Am. Econ. Ass.] $1 *n.* c 8° Macmillan

" The Social Unrest—*ut* **D** § 126

CARNEGIE, Andr. Gospel of Wealth; & other essays [8/6 *n.* Warne] $2 8° Century Co., *N.Y.* [01] 03

" Problems of To-day [2/6 *n.* G. Allen] $1·40 c 8° Doubleday, *N.Y.* 08

Deals with wealth, labour, wages, thrift, land, socialism, etc.

CARVER, T. N. The Distribution of Wealth—*ut* **D** § 114

CASSAGNAC, de, A. GRANIER History of the Working and Burgher Classes [tr] $2·50 8° Claxton, *Phila.* 71

CHAPMAN, Prf. S. J. Work & Wages; Introd. by Lord Brassey, 2 Pts. 18/*n.* ($7) 8° Longman 04–8

Pt. i: *Foreign Competition*, 7/6 *n.* ($3); ii: *Wages and Employment*, 10/6 *n.* ($4), bringing down to date BRASSEY'S bks., to be followed by a third vol. dealg. w. factory legisln., co-operatn., and social betterment.

CLARK, C. C. P. Machine Abolished and People restored to Power $1 (4/) c 8° Putnam 00

CLARK, Prf. J. B. The Distribution of Wealth—*ut* **D** § 114 [wages, interest, profits]

COMMONS, Prf. J. B. The Distribution of Wealth—*ut* **D** § 114

DAWBARN, C. Y. C. Liberty and Progress—*ut* **D** § 126

Pt. i: *The Employed*; ii: *Princs. of Employmt.*; iii: *Our Underpaid and Unemployed.* An expositn. and defence of individualism.

GUNTON, G. Wealth and Progress [6/ Macmillan] $1 12° Appleton, *N.Y.* [87] 90

The wages question, and its economic relation to social reform.

GUYOT, Yves Labour, Socialism, and Strikes [tr.] 1/6 c 8° Wilson 96

HUTCHINSON, A. L. The Limit of Wealth $1·25 *n.* (5/*n.*) c 8° Macmillan 07

MALLOCK, W. H. Labour and Popular Welfare—*ut* **D** § 126

PETERS, Rev. J. P. [ed.] Labour and Capital $1·50 (6/) c 8° Putnam 02

[Questions of the Day.] Symposium by prominent Americans on present-day economic questions.

RUSKIN, Jno. Crown of Wild Olive—*ut* **K** § 89

Four essays on work, traffic, war, future of England.

" Time and Tide by Weare and Tyne—*ut* **K** § 89

Letters on the laws of work, co-operation, etc.

ST CLAIR, O. Low Wages and No Wages 2/6 *n.* c 8° Sonnenschein 09

A sensible and thoughtful little bk. on econ. causes of poverty, unemploymt., bad trade.

*SHADWELL, A. Industrial Efficiency—*ut* **D** § 117*

SIMONDS (J. C.) + MCENNIS (J. T.) Story of Manl. Labor in all Lands & Ages $2·75 8° Peale, *Chicago* 87

THORNTON, Wm. T. On Labour: wrongful claims & rightful duties *o.p.* [*pb.* 14/] 8° Macmillan [69] 70

Contains useful information as to trades unions, their organization, laws, purposes, abuses, etc.

TOLSTOI, C't L. The Slavery of Our Times [tr.] 1/ c 8° Free Age Press

WALKER, Prf. F. A. The Manual Laboring Class [Am. Econ. Ass.] 75 c. *n.* 8° Macmillan 88

WRIGHT, Carroll D. Historical Review of Wages and Prices: 1752–1860 $1 8° *Boston* 85

YOUNG, Dr E. Labor in Europe and America [report on wages, etc.] $3·50 r 8° *Washington* 75

Contains a lengthy historical Introduction on ancient labour.

**Great Britain**—*v. also* **D** § 117*, **D** § 127, **D** § 148

*BOOTH, Chas. [ed.] Life & Labour of People in London, 9 v. ea. 7/6 *n.* ($3) c 8° Macmillan [89–97] 93–6

The most important and remarkable inquiry into the problems of life and labour in a great city ever undertaken. Wholly unbiassed, accurate and scientific, and w. the vivid colouring of an ARTHUR YOUNG. The contents are as follows:

Vol. i (Pt. i) *East Lond.*; (ii) *Centr. Lond.*; (iii) *South and Outlying Lond.*

ii: *London Street by Street*; Appendix: *Classifn. and Descrn. by Sch. Bd. Blocks and Divisns.*

iii (i) *Spec. Subjs.* [1. *Model Dwellgs.* (*a*) *Statistics*, (*b*) *Influ. on Character*, (*c*) *Life*; 2. *Influx of Population*; 3. *Jewish Community*]; (ii) *Lond. Children.*

iv: *Trades of E. Lond.* [*Introd.*; *Docks*; *Tailoring*; *Boot-mkg.* (two last include also West End); *Furniture*; *Tobacco*; *Silk*, *Women's Work*, *Sweating*].

v: *Bldg. Trades*, (i) *Introd.*; (ii) *Wood-wkrs.*; (iii) *Metal Wkrs.*

vi: (*Precious Metals*, (i) *Watches and Instruments*; (ii) *Sundry Mnfs.* [1. *Glass and Earthenware*, 2. *Chemicals*, 3. *Soap, Candles, etc.*, 4. *Leather*, 5. *Saddlery*, 6. *Brushes and Combs*; (iii) *Prtg. and Paper* [1. *Printers*, 2. *Bookbdrs.*, 3. *Paper*, 4. *Statrs.*, 5. *Booksellers and Newsagents*]; (iv) *Textiles* 1. *Silk and Wool*, 2. *Dyeing and Cleang.*, 3. *Hemp, Jute, Fibre*, 4. *Floorcloth and Waterproof.*

vii (i) *Dress*, (ii) *Food and Drink*, (iii) *Dealers and Clerks* [1. *Shopkeepers and Gen. Dealers*, 2. *Costers and Street Sellers*, 3. *Merchts. and Clerks*]; (iv) *Locomotn.*, etc. [1. *Cabs and Omnibuses*, 2. *Carmen*, 3. *Rys.*, 4. *Gardeners, etc.*, 5. *Merch. Seamen and Lightermen*]; (*v*) *Labour* [1. *Docks and Wharves*, 2. *Coal Porters and Gas Workers*, 3. *Warehousemen and Messengers*, 4. *Undefined Labour.*

viii (i) *Publ. Service and Profess. Classes* [1. *Civil and Munic. Service*, 2. *Munic. Labr., etc.*, 3. *Soldiers and Police*, 4. *Law and Medicine*, 5. *Art, Amusemts.*, 6. *Literature and Educn.*, 7. *Religion*]; (ii) *Domestic Service*; (iii) *Unoccupied Classes*; (iv) *Inmates of Institns., etc.*; *Summary of Population.*

ix: *Abstract of vols. i–viii*: (i) *Comparisons*; (ii) *Conclusion.*

Valuable *Preliminary Statements* to each of the sections in vols. v–viii, and good Index to each vol.

" The same: New Edn., 17 vols. ea. 5/*n.* c 8° Macmillan [89–97] 02

SER. I: *Poverty*, 4 vols., 15/*n.*, *Maps*, 2/6 *n.*; SER. II: *Industry*, 5 vols., 20/*n.*; SER. III: *Religious Influences*, 7 vols., 30/*n.*; *Final Vol.*: *Notes and Conclns.*, 5/*n.* Ch. Edn. of Ser. III, 7 vols., 15/*n.* (ea. 2/6 *n.*).

Commission on Labour (Royal): vols. i–xl *v.p.* f° Eyre & Spottisw. 93–10 *in prg.*

Spyers, T. G. The Labour Commission [Social Science Series] 2/6 c 8° Sonnenschein 94

$1 Scribner, *N.Y.* Digest and epitome of the evid., and concise acc. of nature and policy of whole movemt. and of legislation demanded.

DRAGE, G. The Labour Problem [$5·60 Scribner, *N.Y.*] 14 / 8° Smith & Elder 96
A laborious compiln., by late Sec. to Labour Commission, on Hrs. of Work, Employers' Liab., Protective Legisln. and Inspectn., Employmt. of Women and Childr., theories of State and of Munic. Employmt., developmt. of Socialism in Engl., Trades Disputes and Housg. of Wkg.-classes. Not well arranged and somewhat biassed, tho' fairly trustworthy as to facts.

EDEN, Sir Fredk. M. —*in his* The State of the Poor, 3 vols. (1797), *ut* **D** § 127

ENGELS, Fredk. Conditn. of Wkg. Class in Engl. in 1844 [Soc. Sci. Ser.] 3 /6 c 8° Sonnenschein [45] 92
$1·25 Scribner, *N.Y.* A survey of the labour problem in Engl. as it presented itself half a century ago to a foreign socialist—very severe on the English 'bourgeoisie', attributg. the misery of the masses to their exploitation by the capitalists.

FAWCETT, Prf. Hy. Economic Position of the British Labourer *o.p.* [*pb.* 5 /] f 8° Macmillan 65

GALTON, F. W. [ed.] Workers on their Industries [Soc. Sci. Ser.] 2 /6 c 8° Sonnenschein 94
$1·25 Scribner, *N.Y.* 14 lects. by pract. workers on orig., developmt., and pres. positn. of several industries.

GIFFEN, [Sir] Rob. Progress of Working Classes in Last half Cent. [Quest. of Day] 25 c. c 8° Putnam 85

HOLE, Dr S. R. Addresses to Working Men from Pulpit and Platform 6 / c 8° Arnold 94
Christianity, Work, Education, Friendly Societies, Home Rule, Bible Temperance, Soldiers, The Gentleman, Gambling, Dissent, *etc.*

HOWARTH (E. G.) + WILSON (M.) West Ham : study in soc. and industr. problems 6 / *n.* 8° Dent 07
The *Report* of the Outer London Committee.

HOWELL, Geo. History of Conflict betw. Capital and Labour *o.p.* [*pb.* 6 /] c 8° Macmillan [78] 90
A hist. and review of the Trades Unions of Gt. Brit., fr. the wrkg.-man's point-of-view.

" Labour Legislation, Labour Movements, and Leaders, 2 v. ea. 3 /6 c 8° Unwin [02] 05
$3·50 Dutton, *N.Y.* [Reformer's Bkshelf.] An exhaust. hist. fr. 1824 to end of cent. Earlier portion more satisfactory than later.

JEVONS, Prf. W. Stanley State in rel. to Labour—*ut* **D** § 126

KAY, Jos. Social Condition & Education of People in Engl., 2 v. [in 1848] *o.p.* [*pb.* 21 /] c 8° Longman 50

Labour Commission [1892–3] : Reports and Minutes of Evidence, Fifth Final Report 2 / 8° Wyman

LEVI, Prf. L. Wages and Earnings of the Working Classes *o.p.* [*pb.* 6 /] 8° Murray 67

" Wages and Earnings of the Working Classes [in 1883–4] *o.p.* [*pb.* 3 /6] 8° Murray 85

LUDLOW (J. M.) + JONES (Lloyd) Progr. of the Wkg. Classes : 1832–1867 *o.p.* [*pb.* 2 /6] f 8° Strahan 67

MALLOCK, W. H. Classes and Masses : wealth, wages, and welfare in U.K. 3 /6 c 8° Black 96
$1·25 *n.* Macmillan, *N.Y.* Seeks to show by figures and arguments that condn. of lower and middle classes has improved in recent yrs. more rapidly than that of the upper and richer classes. Incl. discussn. of 'the living wage', the conclusion bg. that the 'minimum standard of human living' is necessarily determined by the maximum wh. a man who pays no rent can extract fr. his own labour fr. the worst soil under cultivation.'

MALLOCK, W. H. The Nation as a Business Firm 3 /6 *n.* c 8° Black 10
On growth and diffusn. of wealth am. the masses since 1800, and its distribn. amongst all classes to-day.

MASTERMAN, C. F. G., etc. The Heart of the Empire : probls. of mod. city-life 3 /6 *n.* c 8° Unwin 01

PORTER, R. P. Bread-Winners Abroad [England and Europe] $1·50 12° Ogilvie, *N.Y.* 85

de ROUSIERS, Paul The Labour Question in Britain [tr.] 12 / *n.* ($4 *n.*) 8° Macmillan 96
An acc. of condns. of labour of Gt. Brit., and an attempt to ill. by a series of compar. studies of workmen's lives the attitude in wh. these have encountered the vast change that has swept over industr. world dur. past cent. Appreciative and optimistic, looking to individualistic action for the solution of the Labr. Problem. Pt. ii deals w. mines, iii w. condns. of labour under factory syst.

RUSKIN, Jno. Fors Clavigera : letters to workmen of Great Britain—*ut* **K** § 89

SMITH, C. D. Natural Monopolies in rel. to Social Democracy 3 /6 *n.* c 8° Fifield 09
Reply to MALLOCK, whose main argumt. he summarizes in statemt. that 'ownership of capital is only means by wh. directive ability can secure effective directn. of manl. labour'.

STUBBS, Rev. [Bp] C. W. Village Politics [Broad Church ; suggestive] 3 /6 p 8° Macmillan 78

TOYNBEE, Arnold Lects. on the Industrial Revoln. of 18 Cent. in Engl. 2 /6 *n.* ($1) c 8° Longman [84] 08
A colln. of (posth.-pubd.) addresses, notes, etc., inspired by the highest moral feeling. Of considerable permanent value. This cheap edn. omits the lects. on GEORGE'S *Progress & Poverty*.

WEBB, Sid. Labour in the Longest Reign 1 / c 8° De La More Press 97
On the quantity and quality of the progress made by wkg.-class during Victorian era.

**Australia**

CLARK, Dr V. S. The Labour Movement in Australasia 6 / *n.* c 8° Constable 07

**New Zealand**

SCHOLEFIELD, Guy H. New Zealand in Evolution—*ut* **D** § 136

**United States** —*v. also* **D** § 117*, *v.s.* United States

ADAMS, Prf. H. C. Relation of the State to Industrial Action 75 c. 8° *New York* 87

AVELING, Dr + Mrs Edw. The Working-Class Movement in America 2 /6 c 8° Sonnenschein [87] 91
$1 Scribner, *N.Y.* [Social Science Series.] From a Socialistic point-of-view.

Commissioner of Labor [Carroll D. WRIGHT] Annual Report *gratis* 8° Govt. Prtg. Off., *Washgtn.* 86 *sqq*
*First Report* ['85] : *Industr. Depressns.* [*ut* **D** § 115]
*Second Rept.* ['86] : *Convict Labor in U.S.* [*ut* **D** § 123]
*Third Rept.* ['87] : *Strikes and Lock-outs* [*ut* **D** § 120].
*Fourth Rept.* ['88] : *Wkg. Women in Large Cities* [*ut inf.*]
*Fifth Rept.* ['89] : *Railroad Labor.*
*Sixth Rept.* ['90] : *Iron, Steel, etc.*
*Seventh Rept.* ['91] : *Textiles and Glass*, 2 vols.
*Eighth Rept.* ['92] : *Industr. Educatn.* [*ut* **D** § 167].
*Ninth Rept.* ['93] : *Building and Loan Assns.* [*ut* **D** § 120]
*Special Rept.* ['89] : *Marriage and Divorce* [*ut* **D** § 133]
*2nd Spec. Rept.* ['92] : *Labor Laws of Columbia.*
*3rd Spec. Rept.* ['93] : *Anal. and Index of Labo[r] Statistics.*
*4th Spec. Rept.* ['95] : *Compulsory Insurce. in Germy.*
*5th Spec. Rept.* ['93] : *Gothenburg System* [*ut* **D** § 131]
*6th Spec. Rept.* ['93] : *Phosphate Industry of U.S.*
*7th Spec. Rept.* ['94] : *Slums of Baltimore, etc.* [*ut* **D** § 127]

ELY, Prf. R. T. Labor Movement in America $1·25 (5 / *n.*) c 8° Macmillan [86] 05
[Citizen's Lib.] Historical and critical ; the forerunner of a much more extensive work, to be entitled *Hist. of Labor in the New World.*

FAIRCHILD, F. R. Hist. of Labour Legisl. in N.Y. [Am. Ec. Ass.; 3/6 Sonnenschein] $1 *n.* 8° Macmillan, *N.Y.* 05

GHENT, W. J. Our Benevolent Feudalism $1·25 *n.* (5/ *n.*) gl 8° Macmillan 02
A pessimistic view of the preponderating influence of capital in American life and law.

Industrial Conciliation: N.Y. and Chicago Confce. [papers & procgs., 1900–01] $1·25 (6/) c 8° Putnam 02

KELLEY, Flor. Some Ethical Gains through Legislation $1·25 *n.* (5/ *n.*) c 8° Macmillan 05
On the enforcement of proper condns. of labour in U.S., by a lady-member of Illinois bar.

LAWSON, W. R. American Industrial Problems 6/ *n.* c 8° Blackwood 03
A somewhat inadequate exam. of 'the Amer. bogey', for benefit of Brit. competitors; pacifies Brit. fears by anticipg. labr.-troubles there.

LEVASSEUR, E. The American Workman [tr.] [12/6 *n.* Unwin] $3 8° Johns Hopk. Univ. Pr., *Baltimore* 00

SCHOENHOF, J. Industrial Situation and Question of Wages [Questns. of Day] $1 8° Putnam, *N.Y.* 85

SPAHR, C. B. America's Working People $1·25 (5/ *n.*) c 8° Longman 00
Based on personal study of condns. in New Engl. and southern factory-towns, mines, mills, etc.

WILLOUGHBY, W. F. State Activities in rel. to Labour in U.S. 75 c. 8° Johns Hopkins Pr., *Baltimore* 01

WYCKOFF, Prf. W. A. The Workers: an experiment in reality, 2 Pts. ea. $1·50 12° Scribner, *N.Y.* 98–9
Ea. 3/ *n.* Heinemann. Pt. i: *The East*; ii: *The West.* Author's experiences as an unskilled labourer.

**Belgium** —*v.* **D** § 119 (ROWNTREE)

**Germany**

ASHLEY, Prf. W. J. Progress of Germ. Wkg. Classes in last quarter Cent. 1/6 *n.* (60 c. *n.*) c 8° Longman 04

BARKER, J. Ellis —*in his* Modern Germany, *ut* **D** § 144

BASHFORD, J. L. [ed.] Life and Labour in Germany [310 pp.] 2/ *n.* 8° Simpkin 07
Reports of the Gainsborough Commission, a deputn. of wkg.-men organized by C. A. MORRING, of Gainsborough. W. App. on Old-Age Pensions.

CROOK, W. German Wage Theories: hist. of development [Col. Univ. Studs.] $1 *n.* 8° Macmillan, *N.Y.* 98

DAWSON, W. H. The German Workman: study in natl. efficiency 6/ *n.* c 8° P. S. King & Son 06

GÖHRE, Paul Three Months in a Workshop [tr.] [Soc. Sci. Ser.] 2/6 c 8° Sonnenschein 95
$1 Scribner, *N.Y.* Acc. by a Germ. theolog. student (who, disguised as a workman, got himself employed as a common hand at an iron-foundry in Chemnitz, Saxony) of the Germ. working-man's views on politics, relig., family-life, and of his mode of life, *etc.*

HOWARD, Dr E. D. Cause and Extent of Recent Industrial Progress in Germany [4/6 *n.* Constable] $1 8° Houghton, *Boston* 07

Tariff Reform League: Reports on Labour and Social Condns. in Germy., vol. i: Working Men's Tours, nos. 1–3 9*d.* *n.* 8° Tariff Ref. League 10

U.S. Dept. of Commerce: Industr. Educn. & Industr. Condns. in Germy. [Consular Repts.] 8° *Washington* 05

**Hawaii**

COMAN, K. History of Contract Labor in the Hawaiian Islands [Amer. Econ. Ass.; 2/6 Sonnenschein] 75 c. *n.* 8° Macmillan, *N.Y.* 03

**Arbitration; Conciliation** —*v. also* **D** § 120, *s.v.* Strikes

BROADHEAD, H. State Regulatn. of Labour and Labour Disputes in New Zealand 7/6 *n.* 8° Whitcombe, *Christchurch* 08
On workg. of compuls. arbitrn., by Secy. to Canterb. Empl. Ass. The story of an Act wh. failed.

CLEGG, T. B. Trades Disputes Conciliation and Arbitration Act, 1892 c 8° Govt. Prtg. Off., *Sydney* 92

GILMAN, N. P. Methods of Industrial Peace $1·50 c 8° Houghton, *Boston* 04
7/6 *n.* Macmillan. A well-informed bk., marked by moderation and perfect fairness.

JEANS, J. S. Conciliation and Arbitration in Labour Disputes 2/6 c 8° Lockwood 94
A historical sketch and brief statement of the then position of the question in England and abroad.

JOHNSON, Maj. A. G. Leisure for Workmen and National Wealth 3/6 *n.* 8° P. S. King & Son 08
An expositn. of doctr. of R. S. MOFFATT, author of *The Economy of Consumption* [*ut inf.*], reviewg. pres. organizn. of industry, and advocatg. MOFFATT's *Time Policy* [*inf.*].

KNOOP, Dougl. Industrial Conciliation and Arbitration; pref. Prf. J. S. Chapman 3/6 *n* 8° P. S. King & Son [05] 07

LOWELL, Josephine S. Industrial Arbitration & Conciliation [Questns. of Day] 50 c. (2/6) 12° Putnam 93
Account of some of the methods by wh. industrial peace had been attained in Europe and America dur. previous 30 years.

MOFFAT, R. S. Economy of Consumption [comm. crises & trades unions] *o.p.* [*pb.* 18/] 8° Paul 78

" Time Policy *o.p.* [*pb.* 3/6] 8° Paul 78
Proposed settlemt. of labr. disputes without strikes, by barter betw. employrs. and employed on basis of time and wages (the two things wh. ea. party resp. has to dispose of), the point where ordinary time ends and over-time begins bg. continually shifted to suit changes of industr. condns.

PIGOU, Dn A. C. Principles and Methods of Industrial Peace 3/6 *n.* ($1·10 *n.*) c 8° Macmillan 05

PRICE, L. L. Industrial Peace: advantages, methods, difficulties 6/ c 8° Macmillan 87
[Toynbee Trustees' Report.] Preface by Prf. MARSHALL explains the *rationale* of arbitratn. and conciliatn. betw. employers and workmen.

RYAN, D. J. Arbitration between Capital & Labour [hist. & argument] $1 8° Smythe, *Columbus* 87

v. SCHULZE-GAEVERNITZ, Prf. G. Social Peace [tr.]—*ut* **D** § 120

WRIGHT, Carroll D. Industrial Conciliation and Arbitration 50 c. 8° Ellis, *Boston* 81

**Capital; Interest; Income** —*v. also inf.*, *s.vv.* Profit, Wages; *for* Rent *v.* **D** § 119

BÖHM-BAWERK, Prf. E. —*ut* **D** § 114, *s.v.* Mathematical Economics

CASSEL, G. Nature and Necessity of Interest 6/ ($1·90 *n.*) 8° Macmillan 03
An excellent study; interest and its necessity under all conditns. of society.

CLARK, Prf. J. B. —*in his* Distribution of Wealth, *ut* **D** § 114
Makes the distinction between 'capital' and 'capital goods'.

,, Capital & its Earngs. [Am. Ec. Ass.; 2/6 Sonnenschein] 75 c. *n.* 8° Macmillan, *N.Y.* 88

FISHER, Prf. Irving The Nature of Capital and Income $3 *n.* (12/6 *n.*) 8° Macmillan 06
A sort of philos. of econ. acctg., supplying a link betw. ideas and usages underlying pract. business transns. and theories of abstract economics, Defines Capital as 'a stock of wealth existing at a moment of time', thus identifying it w. Wealth generally.

,, The Rate of Interest $3 *n.* (12/6 *n.*) 8° Macmillan 08
A technical treatise of a mathematical character, w. illns. fr. Amer. conditions. Appendices (84 pp.).

,, Appreciation and Interest 75 c. *n.* 8° Macmillan, *N.Y.*

GIBSON, A. H. Fall in Consols and other Investments 5/ *n.* 8° Jackson, *Halifax* 08
An investign. into causes wh. brought about a rise in investment capital-values from 1875–1897 and the fall since—a purely financial wk., for bankers, brokers, and investors.

GIFFEN, [Sir] Rob. The Growth of Capital 7/6 8° Bell 90
$2 Macmillan, *N.Y.* A statistical review of the recent growth of British capital.

GONNER, E. K. Interest and Saving—*ut* **D** § 127*

HAKE (A. E.) + WESSLAU (O. E.) Free Trade in Capital *o.p.* [*pb.* 15/] 8° Remington 90
The views of Free Trade in Capital League on errors in existg. financial arrangemts. Objects strongly to Bimetallism, and to nearly whole of our pres. financ. syst., attribg. nearly all our ills (incl. sweating) to our Bankg. Syst., wh. 'divorces Capital and Labour' and 'destroys Profits and promotes Poverty'.

HOBSON, J. A. The Evolution of Modern Capitalism—*ut inf.*

LESLIE, T. E. Cliffe- History, etc., of Interest—*in his* Essays, *ut* **D** § 114

MARX, Karl Capital [tr.]—*ut* **D** § 126

MINTON, Rev. Fcs. The Evil of the Millionaire 3/6 *n.* c. 8° Sonnenschein 08
By a cleric who was also estate-agent and colliery-proprietor. Maintains pres. unequal distribn. of property is the great impediment to increased productn., and that the property of the rich does not benefit society.

RAE, Jno. The Sociological Theory of Capital 17/ *n.* ($4 *n.*) Macmillan [1834] 05
A complete repr. of the *New Principles of Political Economy*, 1834; ed. w. biog. sketch, by C. W. MIXTER.

SMART, Prf. Wm. The Distribution of Income 5/ *n.* ($1·60 *n.*) 8° Macmillan 99
Defends the existing system.

WATKINS, G. P. Growth of Large Fortunes [Amer. Econ. Assoc.] $1 *n.* 8° Macmillan, *N.Y.* 08

**Child-Labour, etc.** —*v. also* **D** § 127, *s.v.* Children; *for* Law *v.* **D** § 23*

ALDEN, Dr Marg. Child Life and Labour, ed. P. Alden 1/6 *n.* 8° Headley 07
A handbk. on infant mortality, feeding, wage-earng., juvenile offenders, State interferce., etc. Bibliogr.

BRAY, Reg. A. The Town Child 7/6 *n.* c 8° Unwin 07
A thoughtful and illuminatg. treatise, excellently wr. After discussg. the 'problem of the Town' as it affects traing. of childr., as well as pract. questns. of housg., employmt., and other factors wh. affect phys., mental, and moral health of the child, deals w. objects and meth. of educn. Advocates State reguln.

,, Boy Labour and Apprenticeship [w. a remedy] 6/ *n.* c 8° Constable 11

FRERE, Marg. Children's Care Committees 1/ 8° P. S. King & Son 09

GIBBS, Spencer J. The Problem of Boy Work [w. recommendns.] 1/6 c 8° Wells Gardner 07

JOHNSTON, Dr J. Wastage of Child Life . . . in Lancs [Fabian Soc. Ser.] 1/ *n.* c 8° Fifield 09

MACMILLAN, Marg. —*in her* Labour and Childhood, *ut* **D** § 171

MALVERY, G. C. [Mrs MCKIRDY] Baby Toilers [London Children] 2/6 8° Hutchinson 07

SHERARD, R. H. Child Slaves of Britain [journalistic] 1/6 *n.* 12° Fifield [97] 07

URWICK, E. J. Studies of Boy Life in our Cities 3/6 *n.* c 8° Dent 08

VAN VOORST, B. Cry of the Children: study of child labour $1·25 *n.* 8° Moffat, *N.Y.* 08
Personal investigatns. into the pitiable facts associated w. child-labour in Southern States and in Maine and New Hampshire.

WILLOUGHBY (W. F.) + DE GRAFFENRIED (Miss C.) Child Labor 75 c. 8° Macmillan, *N.Y.* 90
Two prize-essays. [Pubns. of Amer. Econ. Assoc.] 2/6 Sonnenschein.

**Depression in Trade** —*v. also* **D** § 115, *s.v.* Commercial Crises & Panics

'ARTIFEX' and 'OPIFEX' Causes of Decay in a Brit. Industry 7/6 *n.* ($2·50 *n.*) 8° Longman 07
Causes of decline in Birmingham fire-arms industry (taxatn., patent-laws, free trade, competitn., etc.).

BRASSEY, Sir T. Foreign Work & English Wages [w. refer. to trade depression] 10/6 8° Longman [79] 80

GIFFEN, [Sir] Rob. —*in his* Essays in Finance, *ut* **D** § 117
*Depression in Trade*, in Ser. i; *Depression and Low Prices*, in Ser. ii.

SMITH, Walt. E. The Recent Depression of Trade [Cobden Prize Essay] *o.p.* [*pb* 3/] c 8° Trübner 80

WALLACE, A. R. Bad Times *o.p.* [*pb* 2/6] c 8° Macmillan 86

**Eight Hours Day** —*v. also inf.* [BRENTANO]

BRADLAUGH, Chas. —*in his* Labour and Law 5/ 8° Bonner 91
A vigorous denunc. of whole princ. of legisl. interference. w. hrs. of adult labour; full of facts. Posthum. ed. Mrs Bradlaugh BONNER (dau.).

GIBBINS (H. de B.) + HADFIELD (R. A.) A Shorter Working Day [Social Questns. of To-day] 2/6 c 8° Methuen 92
Review of effects of 8-hrs. day in Austral., etc., and acc. of experimts. made by HADFIELD and other large employers.

RAE, Jno. Eight Hours for Work *o.p.* [*pb.* 4/6 *n.*] c 8° Macmillan 94
An interesting (almost enthusiastic) wk., carefully sifting evidence as to exact effect of limitg. hrs. of labour, wh. author favours.

SMALLCAPS ROBERTSON, J. M. The Eight Hours Question [Social Science Ser.] 2/6 c 8° Sonnenschein 93
$1 Scribner, *N.Y.* A cogent and sustained argumt. in opposn. to WEBB + COX, insistg. on populn. questn. as dominant factor of the problem.

SCHÄFFLE, Dr A. The Maximum Working Day—*in his* Theory of Labour Protection, *ut* **D** § 126

SHAXBY, W. J. An Eight-Hours Day 2/6 c 8° *Liberty Review* 98
The case against trade-union and legislative interference.

WEBB (S.) + COX (H.) The Eight Hours Day [300 pages] 1/ c 8° Walter Scott 91
Exhaustive histor. acc. (by 2 Fabians) of whole movemt. in Engl., U.S., Austral. and Continent, w. statistics, etc. Bibliogr.

WRIGHT, Carroll D. Uniform Hours of Labor 8° Bur. of Statcs. of Labor, *Bost.* 89
Repr. fr. *Twelfth Annual Report* [1881] of the Bureau. Proves that mills workg. 10 hrs. are as profitable as others workg. 11–12 hrs.

**Factory-System and Legislation**—*v. also inf., s.v.* Working Women ; *for* Law *v.* **D** § 45

CLARKE, Allen The Effects of the Factory System *o.p.* [*pb.* 1/] c 8° Richards [99] 04

COOKE-TAYLOR, R. W. Introd. to History of the Factory System *o.p.* [*pb.* 16/] 8° Bentley 86

,, The Modern Factory System 14/ 8° Paul 91
Sequel to above, contg. hist. of organized labour in Engl. fr. the 'Industrial Revolution' (TOYNBEE), inaug. by Sir Thos. LAMBE's first silk-throwing mill in 1719. down to pres. time and dealg. w. some of its latest developmts. By one of H.M. Inspectors. of Factories. Anticipates extensn. of factory legisl. 'so as to cover most branches of productive labour'.

,, The Factory System & the Factory Acts [Soc. Questns. of To-day] 2/6 c 8° Methuen 94

FOWLES, J. K. Fact. Legisln. in Rhode Isl. [Am. Ec. Ass. ; 3/6 Sonnenschein] $1 *n.* 8° Macmillan, *N.Y.* 09

HOBSON, J. A. The Evolution of Modern Capitalism—*ut inf.*
Incls. a study of the development of the Factory syst., esp. in Textile industries.

JEANS, Victorine Factory Act Legislation [Cobden Club Prize Ess. 1891] 3/6 f 8° Unwin 91
A well-reasoned essay on industr. and commerc. effects of Factory legisln., w. good remarks on effects of 1850 Act.

KROPOTKIN, Pr'ce P. Fields, Factories, and Workshops 1/ *n.* 8° Sonnenschein [99] 04
An argument against the division of labour and the factory-system.

MARKHAM, Violet R. Factory and Workshop Acts of British Dominions [summary]—*ut* **D** § 45

MEAKIN, Budgett Model Factories and Villages 7/6 c 8° Unwin 05
Describes ideal condns. of labour and housing in a great number of business establishmts. in Engl. and abroad.

ROBINSON, Harriet H. Loom and Spindle [Lib. of Economics] $1·25 12° Crowell, *N.Y.*
A description of old-time factory-life. Introd. by Carroll D. WRIGHT.

WHITON Factory Legisln. in Maine [Col. Univ. Studs. ; 4/ P. S. King] $1 *n.* 8° Macmillan, *N.Y.*

**Gilds** —*v.* **D** § 120

**Labour in Relation to Capital**

BARNS, W. E. The Labor Problem ; w. Intro. Prf. R. T. Ely $1 12° Harper, *N.Y.* 86

PHILIP, A. Function of Labour in Production of Wealth 3/6 c 8° Blackwood 90

TRUMBULL, M. M. 'Wheelbarrow's' Articles and Discussns. on Labor Questn.
50 c. 12° Open Ct. Pb. Co., *Chic.* 90
Commonsense and practical papers, written with a COBBETT-like terseness and felicity of illustration. Standpt. purely practical and moral.

WRIGHT, Carroll D. Relatn. of Pol. Econ. to Labor Questn. [ethical stdpt.] 60 c. 12° Williams, *Boston* 82

**Labour in relation to Law** —*v.* **D** § 45 **Labour Movements and Strikes**—*v.* **D** § 120

**Machinery : its effects on Labour and Wages**

HOBSON, J. A. Evolution of Modern Capitalism [Contemp. Science Ser.] 6/ c 8° Walter Scott [94]
$1·25 Scribner, *N.Y.* Inquiry into changes of industr. developmt. dur. 18 and 19 cents. Opening w. exam. of structure of industry ab. 1730 (w. spec. ref. to Engl.), traces forces determining applicn. of machy. and steam-motor to the various departmts. of industry in chief industr. countries, and the changes wh. followed in structure and functional activity of the Business, Trade, and Industr. Organism. Incl. spec. studies of Combination, Trusts, Trade Depression, Influence of Machy. on Labr., Wages, and Employmt. of Women.

,, —*in his* Problems of Poverty, *ut* **D** § 127

NICHOLSON, Prf. J. S. Effects of Machinery on Wages [Social Science Ser.] 2/6 c 8° Sonnenschein [78]
$1 Scribner, *N.Y.* Luminous and impartial : the best general view and criticism of the subject in English.

QUAINTANCE, H. W. Influence of Farm Machinery on Production and Labor
[Am. Econ. Ass. ; 2/6 Sonnenschein] 75 c. *n.* 8° Macmillan, *N.Y.* 04

SAMUELSON, Jas. Labour-Saving Machinery ; ill. 2/6 p 8° Paul 93
A coll. of facts bearing on the effect of mechanical appliances in the displacement of manual labour.

**Monopolies and Trusts** —*v.* **D** § 120

**Profit ; Interest ; Usury** —*for* Law *v.* **D** § 73 ; *for* Rent *v.* **D** § 119

ATKINSON, Dr E. Margin of Profit : how divided, *etc.* [Questns. of Day] 75 c. (3/) 12° Putnam 87

BENTHAM, Jer. [1748–1832] Usury Laws : nature, expediency, influence 25 c. 12° *New York* [1787] 81
Abstr. of his *Defence of Usury*, fr. perus. of wh. Ad. SMITH is said to have bn. led to change views on usury wh. he held at time of wrg. *Wlth. of Natns.*

BLISSARD, Rev. W. Ethic of Usury and Interest [Soc. Sci. Ser.] 2/6 c 8° Sonnenschein 92
$1 Scribner, *N.Y.* A 'study in inorganic socialism', bold, thoro', yet moderate. Assuming that property is a good thing (tho' one of wh. some may have too much and others too little), his chief aim is to show how a man ought to use it.

*BÖHM-BAWERK, Prf. E. Capital & Interest, tr. Prf. W. Smart—*ut* **D** § 114, *s.v.* Mathematical Economics
Contains a statement and criticism of the various theories of interest.

MURRAY, J. B. C. Hist. of Usury from Earliest Period to Pres. Time $2 8° Lippincott, *Phila.* 66

**Relation of Christianity to Conflict betw. Capital and Labour**—*v.* **A** § 113

**Relation of Occupations to Labour**

ARLIDGE, J. T. The Hygiene of Occupations 21 / *n.* 8° Rivington 92
Elucidates and illustrates the truth that occupns. react upon mental and corporal condn. of workers. The instances quoted cover a wide field, all princ. occupns. in Engl. bg. dealt with, and their statistics given. Final ch. devoted to hygienic aspect.

LLOYD, Dr J. H. Diseases of Occupation—*in* vol. iii of Stedman's 'Twentieth-Cent. Practice,' *ut* **H*** § 15

OLIVER, Dr. Thos. Diseases of Occupation [$2·50 *n.* Dutton] 10/6 *n.* 8° Methuen 08
[New Lib. of Medicine.] An excellent textbk. for gen. readrs. and med. men : draws its facts fr. many countries, and covers very wide field.

,, [ed.] Dangerous Trades ; ill. 25 / *n.* 8° Murray 02
$8 *n.* Dutton, *N.Y.* 60 essays by 38 wrs. (of varying merit, and ill-arrgd.) on histor., soc., and legal aspects of industr. occupns. as affg. health.

PARRY, L. A. Risks & Dangers of Various Occupatns., & Prevention 7/6 *n.* 8° Scott & Greenwood 00
For manufacturers, managers, medical men, sanitary inspectors, etc.

**Relation of Wages and Hours to Production**

BRENTANO, Prf. L. Hours and Wages in rel. to Production [tr.] 2/6 c 8° Sonnenschein 93
$1 Scribner, *N.Y.* [Soc. Sci. Ser.] Shows that raisg. wrkr.'s stand. of livg. stimulates to greater and more careful exertn., and that, w. the devel. of his wants, stimulus to prodn. has, from 17 cent., become more and more active, till the seeming paradox is now realized of prodn. bg. cheapest and most efficient precisely in these countries in wh. wages are highest and hours shortest. Characterized by extreme clearness of style and fulness of histor. detail. Ed. W. T. ARNOLD.

**Rich and Poor** —*v.* **D** § 127 **Socialism and Anti-Socialism**—*v.* **D** § 129

**Sweating** —*v. also* Working Women *inf.*

BLACK, Clementina Sweated Industry & the Minimum Wage [Soc. Questns.] 2 / *n.* c 8° Duckworth [07]

CADBURY (E.) + SHANN (G.) Sweating [Social Service Ser.] 1/6 *n.* c 8° Headley 07

Select Committee of House of Lords : Report, 1/6 ; Evidence, 36/5 [Blue-Bks.] 8° Wyman 88–95

MEYER (Mrs C.) + BLACK (Clementina) Makers of our Clothes 5 / *n.* c 8° Duckworth 09

**Unemployment** —*v. also* Working Women, *inf.*

*Bibliography :* TAYLOR, F. I. Bibliogr. of Unemployment & Unemployed 2 / *n.* 8° P. S. King & Son 09

SCHLOSS, D. F. [ed.] Agencies and Methods for Dealing w. Unemployed in Certain Foreign Countries ; w. Introd. [Parly. Rept. of 1893] 1 / Wyman 06

ALDEN, Percy The Unemployed : a national question 2 / *n.* c 8° P. S. King & Son [04] 05

,, + HAYWARD (E.) The Unemployable and Unemployed [Soc. Serv. Hdbks.] 1/6 *n.* c 8° Headley 08

BEVERIDGE, W. H. Unemployment : a problem of industry 7/6 *n.* ($2·40 *n.*) 8° Longman [09] 10
Record of the chief facts, w. continuous argumt. as to causes. Prob. the best bk. on the subject.

CHAPMAN (Prf. J. S.) + HALLSWORTH (H. M.) Unemployment [Mancs. Univ. Pubns.] 2/6 *n.* 8° Sherratt, *Mancs.* 09

DEARLE, N. B. Problems of Unemploymt. in London Buildg. Trade 3/6 *n.* c 8° Dent 08
Causes, nature, consequences. Toynbee Trust Essay. Pref. by L. L. PRICE.

DEWEY, D. R. Irregularity of Employment [Am. Econ. Assoc.] $1 *n.* 8° Macmillan

DRAGE, Geoff. The Unemployed 3/6 *n.* ($1·50) c 8° Macmillan 94
Classifn. of agencies f. dealg. w. Unempld., and acc. of what has been done. Auth. was Sec. to R. Comm. on Labr.

HIGGS, Mary How to Deal w. the Unemployed [Ch. Edn. 6*d.*] 2/ c 8° Brown 04

HOBSON, J. A. Problem of the Unemployed [Social Questions of To-day] 2/6 c 8° Methuen [96] 96
A clear and sincere little book, whose theory is that 'unemploymt. is a natural and necessary result of a maldistribn. of consuming power, vested in economic rent and monopoly elements of profit', resultg. in excessive saving and 'underconsumption', wh. shd. be remedied by taxatn. of unearned incremt. in widest possible sense. Tho' author thinks the nation as a whole is saving too much, he is not (like some of his allies) a professed enemy to thrift.

HUNTER, R. Poverty—*ut* **D** § 127, *s.v.* United States

JACKSON, Cyril Unemployment and Trade Unions 1 / *n.* c 8° Longman 10

KELLOR, Fces. A. Out of Work $1·25 (5 / *n.*) c 8° Putnam 05
A study of employmt. agencies in operatn. in N.Y., Phila., and other places in U.S.

LEIGH, Leighton Brother East and Brother West 3/6 c 8° Heinemann 05

MACKENZIE, F. A. Famishing London : the unemployed & unemployable 1 / c 8° Hodder 03

Massachusetts Board to Investigate Subject of the Unemployed : Report 8° Wright & Potter, *Bost.* 95
A huge mass of experience collected from a variety of fields. 802 pp.

REASON, Will [ed.] Our Industrial Outcasts [by members of Chr. Soc. Brotherhd.] 2 / c 8° Pilgrim Press 05

ROWNTREE (B. S.) + LASKER (B.) Unemployment [mainly in York] 8° Macmillan *in prep.*

SHERARD, R. H. The White Slaves of England ; ill. 1 / c 8° Bowden [97] 98
A journalist's study of the condns. of employmt. and wages in the worst-pd. and most unhealthy Brit. industries.

SPENCER (M. G.) + FALK (H. J.) Employment Pictures from the Census 2/6 *n.* 8° P. S. King & Son 07

SUTHERS, R. B. My Right to Work [Socialist stdpt.] 6*d. n.* c 8° *Clarion* Press

*Insurance against Unemployment*—*v.* **D** § 151

**Wages** —*for* History of Wages, *v.* **D** § 117*

ASHLEY, Prf. W. J. The Adjustment of Wages ; maps 12/6 *n.* ($4 *n.*) 8° Longman 03
A study in the coal and iron industries of Great Britain and America.

BOWLEY, A. L. Wages in United Kingdom in 19th Century 6 / *n.* 8° Camb. Press 00
$2 *n.* Putnam, *N.Y.* Full of statistical infornn., mainly fr. Board of Trade pubns., bg. notes for students of social and econ. questns.

BOWLEY (A. L.) + WOOD (G. H.) Hist. of Wages in U.K. in 19 Cent.—appearg. in Jl. of Statist. Soc. 1898, 1902, 05–6, 09 *in prg.*

BRASSEY, L'd Papers & Addresses—*ut sup.*

CLARK, Prf. J. B. Possibility of a Scientific Law of Wages 75 c. *n.* (3/ *n.*) c 8° Macmillan 89

„ + GIDDINGS (F. H.) The Modern Distributive Process 75 c. 8° Ginn, *Boston* 82
Studies of competition and its limits, of nature and amount of profits, and of determination of wages.

CROOK, Dr J. W. German Wage Theories [Columb. Univ. Studs.] $1 *n.* (4/6) 8° Macmillan 98
A scientific history of developmt. of these theories; w. much informatn. on German socialism.

LAWRENCE, F. W. Local Variations in Wages; maps and diagrs. 7/6 ($2·50) 4° Longman 99
Variations in wages as exemplified by time-work trades in England.

MACDONNELL, W. D. Hist. and Crit. of Various Theories of Wages 2/ 12° Simpkin 87

MORE, Mrs L. B. Wage-earners' Budgets [10/6 *n.* Bell] $2·50 *n.* 8° Holt, *N.Y.* 09
[Greenwich House Ser. of Social Studs.] A study of standards and cost of livg. in N.Y. City (200 cases).

RYAN, J. A. A Living Wage: ethical & economic aspects $1 *n.* (4/6 *n.*) c 8° Macmillan 06

SCHLOSS, Dav. F. Methods of Industrial Remuneration [$1·50 Putnam, *N.Y.*] 3/6 *n.* 8° Williams [92] 07
A storehouse of facts, system. coll., on wage syst. in all its forms and modificns., w. descrns. of 'Sweating', Profit-sharing, Co-operatn.

SCHOENHOF, J. Economy of High Wages [Questns. of Day] $1·50 (6/) c 8° Putnam 92
Inquiry into compar. methds. and cost of prodn. in competg. industries in Am. and Eur., by a staunch Free-trader.

THOMPSON, H. M. The Theory of Wages 3/6 ($1) c 8° Macmillan 92
Applicn. to Eight Hrs. questn. and other probs. Attacks Wage-Fd. theory. Latter pt. of bk. given up to a mathem. treatmt. of cert. labr. probs.

TOWNE, H. R., *etc.* Adjustment of Wages to Efficiency [Am. Ec. Ass.] 50 c. *n.* 8° Macmillan 96

Wages, Earnings, & Condns. of Employmt. of Agric. Labrs. in U.K. [Blue-Bk.] 2/9 f° Wyman 04

WOOD, Stuart Theory of Wages [Am. Ec. Ass.; 2/6 Sonnenschein] 75 c. *n.* 8° Macmillan, *N.Y.* 89

*Wages Fund Theory*

CAIRNES, Prf. J. E. —*in his* Leading Principles [*ut* **D** § 114]: defends Wages Fund theory

DAVIDSON, Prf. J. The Bargain Theory of Wages $1·50 (6/) c 8° Putnam 98
A full discussion of wages and wages-fund theories. A critical development fr. historic theories.

TAUSSIG, Prf. F. W. Wages and Capital [6/ *n.* Macmillan] $1·50 12° Appleton, *N.Y.* 96
Exam. of Wages Fund doctr.; concise and scholarly. First Pt. conts. detailed statemt. of author's views; second is historical.

WALKER, Prf. F. A. Wages Question: treat. on wages and wages class $2 8° Holt, *N.Y.* [77] 91
8/6 *n.* Macmillan. Agst. the Wages Fund theory. Takes sentimental views as to rights of wage-earners.

**Working-women** —*v. also.* Sweating, *sup.*; *for* Domestic Servants, *v.* **D** § 138

BOUCHERETT (J.) + BLACKBURN (Helen), *etc.* Condn. of Wkg. Women & Factory Acts 1/6 c 8° Stock 96
Seeks to show that whilst Factory legisln. is good for yg. people under age of 18, it is fraught w. bad results when applied to adult women.

CADBURY (E.) + MATHESON (M. C.) + SHANN (G.) Women's Work and Wages 6/ c. 8° Unwin 06
$1·50 *n.* Univ. Press, *Chicago.* Positn. of the woman-wrkr. in Birmingham. Full of facts.

CAMPBELL, Helen Women Wage-Earners $1 12° Roberts, *Boston* 93

Comm'r of Labor [C. D. WRIGHT] 4th Rept.: Wkg. Women in Large Cities [pp. 631] *gratis* 8° Govt. Prtg. Off., *Washgtn.* 89

HARRISON, Dr A. Women's Industries in Liverpool 3/ 8° Williams

International Congress of Women: Transactions *ann.*

Labour Commission: Report on the Employment of Women [Blue-Bk.] 2/10 8° Wyman

London County Council: Rept. on Women's Trades [by Mrs G. M. Oakeshott] 9*d.* f° P. S. King & Son 08

LYTTELTON, Mrs Arth. Women and their Work 2/6 c 8° Methuen 01

MACDONALD, J. Ramsay [ed.] Women in the Printing Trades; diagrs. 10/6 *n.* 8° P. S. King & Son 04

PEARSON, Prf. Karl Woman & Labour—*in his* Chances of Death & other Studies in Evolution, *ut* **D** § 125

SCHREINER, Olive Woman and Labour 8/6 *n.* m 8° Unwin 11

SHACKLETON, D. J. [ed.] Woman in Industry fr. 7 Pts. of View [Soc. Questns.] 2/6 c 8° Duckworth 09

SMITH, Constance The Case for Wages Boards 1/ *n.* c 8° Nat. Anti-Sweatg. League 08

VAN VORST, Mrs Jno. + Marie The Woman who Toils; ill. [6/ Richards] $1·50 *n.* c 8° Doubleday, *N.Y.* 03
Expercе. of authors as voluntary factory-girls: a valuable study of condns. of woman-labr. in Southern States.

VYNNE (Nora) + BLACKBURN (Hel.) Women under the Factory Acts 1/ *n.* c 8° Williams 03

WEBB, Sid. + Beatr. —*in their* Problems of Modern Industry, *ut sup.*
*Women's Wages*, by the former; *Women and the Factory Acts*, by the latter.

WILLETT, Mabel H. Employment of Women in the Clothing Trade $1·50 *n.* 8° Macmillan, *N.Y.* 02
[Columbia Univ. Studies.] Chiefly concerned with condns. obtaing. in New York State.

WRIGHT, Carroll D. Working Girls of Boston [fr. 15th Ann. Rept.] 8° Bur. of Statcs. of Labor, *Bost.* 89

*Woman and Man Contrasted* —*v.* **D** § 132, *s.v.* Equality of the Sexes

## 119: LAND AND LAND LAWS

**History of Land Tenures and Land Laws**—*v.* **F** § 5, **D** § 117*

**Primogeniture**

CECIL, Evelyn — Primogeniture: short hist. of its developmt. in var. countries and its practical effect — 10/6 8° Murray 95
A pop. treatise of interest here for the views expressed as to value of great landlords and remarks on subj. of small properties and *morcellements*. The Germ. portn. is exceptionally good, and throughout the economical better than the historical side.

**Early Writers**

JONES, Rich. [1790–1855] — Peasant Rents — [Economic Classics] 3/ *n.* (75 c. *n.*) c 8° Macmillan 95
JONES succeeded MALTHUS as Prf. of Pol. Econ. and Hist. at East India Coll., and was the most systematic and thoroughgoing of the earlier critics of the Ricardian system. *Peasant Rents* is the first half of his *Essay on Distribn. of Wealth and on Sources of Taxatn.*, described by MILL as 'a copious repertory of valuable facts on the landed tenures of different countries'.

S., W. — Discourse of Common Weal of this Realm, ed. Eliz. Lamond — 5/ c 8° Camb. Press [1581] 93
$1·40 *n.* Putnam, *N.Y.* Ed. fr. earliest kn. MS.: that of LAMBARDE, Kentish antiquary (wr. 1565). In 3 *Dialogues* betw. a knight, a 'merchaunte', a doctor, a husbandman and a 'capper' (maker of woollen caps). Full of quaint econ. notions, and of consid. histor. interest. Edr. attribs. authorship to Sir Thos. SMYTHE or Jno. HALES (rns. HY. viii or EDW. vi), favourg. latter. In 1751 edn. publisher ascribed it to W(ILLIAM) S(HAKESPEARE)! It has been previously printed (but not fr. this MS.), *sub tit. Examination of Complaints in* 1751, in *Harleian Misc.* [10 v. 1808–13], *The Pamphleteer* [29 v. 1813–28] and in New Shakesp. Soc. pubns.

TUSSER, Thos. [1515–*c.* 1580] Five Hundred Points of Good Husbandry—*ut* **F** § 22 *(and note)*

WALTER OF HENLEY — Husbandry, w. an [anon.] Husbandry, Seneschaucie, and [Bp] Grosseteste's Rules: transcripts, trss. *en regard* and gloss. by Elizab. Lamond; introd. by Dr W. Cunningham — 15/ 4° Roy. Histor. Soc. (Longman) 91
Of great value for tracg. hist. of Engl. rural econ. back to orig. sources, presentg. a clear and actual view of method of wkg. a manorial estate and keepg. manorial accs. in 13 cent. Treatise on the office of seneschal is really a bk. of instructns. as to estate-managemt. These 4 treats. formed the chief written guidance to husbandry dur. 13 to 16 cent. CUNNINGHAM's Introd. on the econ. of an estate in 13th cent. is a useful sketch.

*United States*

CRÈVECŒUR, J. H. St J. [1735–1813] Letters from an American Farmer — c 8° Duffield, *N.Y.* 09
6/ *n.* Chatto. Ed. Prf. W. P. TRENT, w. Introd. L. LEWISOHN. Letters of a pioneer poet and naturalist—one of the few early Amer. bks. that ranks as a minor classic.

OGILVIE, Prf. W. — Birthright in Land, ed. D. C. Macdonald; w. notes — 7/6 c 8° Paul [1782] 91
Rt. of prop. in land w. resp. to its foundn. in law of nature, munic. laws of Eur., and regulns. by wh. it mt. be rendered more beneficial to lower ranks.

**Economical Works on Land Question and Land Laws**—*for purely Legal Treatises, v.* **D** §§ 51, 78

ARGYLL, Duke of — The Unseen Foundations of Society — 18/ 8° Murray [93] 93
An interesting, but somewhat diffuse and ill-ordered bk., championing the landlords. Incl. acc. of the feudal system and the substitution of rent for pers. services, criticizes the Ricardian theory of rent and that of the Wages Fund, and discourses on the working of econ. laws in our day.

Bain, F. W. — The Unseen Foundation of 'Unseen Foundations of Society' — 6*d.* m 8° Parker 93

ARNOLD, Arth. — Free Land — 6/ c 8° Paul 80
An excellent popular statement of the Land Question in Great Britain in 1880.

ASHLEY, Prf. W. J. — —*in his* Surveys, Historic and Economic — 7/6 ($3) c 8° Longman 00

BEDFORD, Duke of — A Great Agricultural Estate — 6/ c 8° Murray 97
Story of orig. and admin. of the Woburn and Thornley estates. After hg. spent since 1816 £4,250,000 on 51,643 acres (incl. some of the best wheat land in Engld.), estate is now worked at a loss of £7,000 p.a. Many questns. of rural economics wisely discussed.

BRODRICK, G. C. — English Land and Landlords — [w. proposals f. reform] 12/6 8° Cassell 81

CADBURY (G.) + BRYAN (T.) The Land and the Landless — 1/6 *n.* c 8° Headley 08
Descrs. what Parlt. has done f. 'Back to the Land', and surveys hist. of Engl. ld.-tenure, w. remarks on example of Denmark.

CAIRD, Prf. J. — Landed Interest and the Supply of Food — 5/ c 8° Cassell [78] 80

CARPENTER (E.) + DYMOND (T. S.) + PEDDER (D. C.) Socialism and Agriculture — [Fabian Soc.] 1/ *n.* c 8° Fifield 08

CHANNING, Sir F. A. — Truth about Agricultural Depression — 2/6 8° P. S. King & Son 97
An economic study of the evidence of the Royal Commission.

Cobden Club: Systems of Land Tenure in var. Countries, ed. J. W. Probyn [essays] 3/6 8° Cassell [70] 81

COLLINGS, Jesse — Land Reform — 12/6 *n.* ($4·20 *n.*) Ch. Edn. 2/6 *n.* ($1) 8° Longman 06; 08
Occupying Ownership, Peasant Proprietary, and Rural Education.

DOWSETT, C. F. [ed.] — Land, its Attractions and Riches — 27/6 8° Dowsett 92
93 chaps. by 57 wrs., divided into 7 Sectns., on health, pleasure, sports, nat. hist., finance, economics, agric., law—its object bg. to produce a popular interest in land, w. view of attractg. Capital to it and inducg. immigrn. into provinces.

FIELD, C. D. — Landholdg. & Landld. & Tenant in var. Countries — 36/ 8° Thacker 83

GEORGE, Hy. — Progress & Poverty; Social Problems ea. 50 c. 12° Doubleday, *N.Y.* [80–4]
Ea. 1/ Paul. Former attracted a great deal of attention on its appearance, partly owing to its new theories as to land-ownership and advocacy of a single tax (on land to its full value).

" — A Perplexed Philosopher — 50 c. 12° Doubleday, *N.Y.* 93
An exam. of Herb. SPENCER's various utterances on land questn., w. incid. refs. to his synth. philos.—a fierce personal attack, by way of rejoinder to SPENCER's attack on him: claims authority of 1st edn. of *Social Statics* [1850 *ut* **D** § 134—since recanted and re-written]—for his view of landownership ethics.

" — The Condition of Labour — 30 c. c 8° U.S. Bk. Co., *N.Y.* 91
2/6 Sonnenschein. [Soc. Sci. Ser.] Reply to LEO xiii, *ut inf.*, w. tr. of *Encycl. Letter.* Forcible presentatn. of Single Tax argumt. on moral grounds.

Rae, Jno. — Agrarian Socialism of Hy. George—*in his* Contemporary Socialism, *ut* **D** § 126

HAGGARD, H. Rider — Rural England, 2 vols.; 29 ill. — 12/ *n.* ($4 *n.*) 8° Longman 02
Acc. of agricultural and social researches carried out in 1901 and 1902.

HARVEY, E. J. — Land Law and Registration of Title — 7/6 *n.* 8° Longman 10
A comparison of the old and new methods of transferring land.

HIRSCH, M. — Democracy *versus* Socialism—*ut* **D** § 139 [Single Tax]

HOBSON, J. A. [ed.] Labour upon the Land [Soc. Sci. Ser.; $1 c 8° Scrib., *N.Y.*] 2/6 c 8° Sonnenschein 00

KAY, Jos. Free Trade in Land; pref. by Jno. Bright *o.p.* [*pb.* 1/6] c 8° Longman [79] 85
Cobden Club pubn. The position in 1879, with summary of land systems throughout Europe.

KINNEAR, J. B. The Principles of Property in Land *o.p.* [*pb.* 5/] c 8° Smith & Elder 80

KROPOTKIN, Pr'ce P. Fields, Factories, and Workshops—*ut* **D** § 118, *s.v.* Factory System
Advocates reform of ld.-tenures, adoptn. of intensive culture, and estab. of small industries.

LEFEVRE, G. Shaw Agrarian Tenures in Engl., Irel., & Scotl., & Recent Reforms 5/ 8° Cassell [93] 96

" Freedom of Land *o.p.* [*pb.* 2/6] 8° Macmillan 80

" English and Irish Land Questions [coll. essays] *o.p.* [*pb.* 6/] c 8° Cassell 81

LEO xiii, Pope Encyclical Letter on Labour [1891]—tr. *is cont. in* GEORGE, *ut sup.*

Leroy-Beaulieu, P. Papacy, Socialism, and Democracy [tr.] 6/ c 8° Chapman 92
The first of these 3 arts. is a compreh. comm. on Encycl. fr. purely material or polit. std.-pt., by an Anti-Republican and political pessimist.

Stead, W. T. [ed.] The Pope & Labour [=*tr. of* Encycl. Letter] 1/ 4° *Review of Reviews* Off. 91

LESLIE, Prf. T. E. Cliffe- Land Systems and Industrial Economy of Ireland, England, and Continental Countries *o.p.* [*pb.* 12/] 8° Macmillan 73

LEVY, Prf. Hermann Large and Small Holdings [Putnam, *N.Y.*] 10/6 *n.* 8° Camb. Press 11

MARTIN, J. W. The Ruin of Rural England: a warning 3/6 *n.* c 8° Simpkin 02

NICHOLSON, Prf. J. S. Rates and Taxes Affecting Agriculture [$1 Scrib., *N.Y.*] 2/6 c 8° Sonnenschein 05

" Rents, Wages, and Profits in Agriculture—*ut* **D** § 117*

PILLING, W. Land Tenure by Registration [*1st edn. sub tit.* 'Order fr. Chaos'] 18/ c 8° Chapman [86] 90

POLLOCK, Sir F. The Land Laws—*ut* **D** § 78 [favours reform]

PHIPSON, C. B. The Redemption of Labour, 2 vols. 7/6 *n.* 8° Sonnenschein 87–91

PRATT, E. A. Organizn. of Agric., 1/ *n.*; Transition in Agric. 1/ c 8° Murray 05; 06

SCRUTTON, T. E. Land in Fetters —*ut* **D** § 78

TURNOR, Chr. Land Problems and National Welfare 7/6 *n.* 8° Lane 11

**Statistics**

BATEMAN, J. Great Landowners of Great Britain and Ireland *o.p.* [*pb.* 14/] 8° Harrison [76] 79
A list of all owners of 3,000 acres and upwards worth £3,000 per ann., with incomes derived therefrom.

BIRKBECK, W. L. The Distribution of Land in Engl. [historical sketch] *o.p.* [*pb.* 4/6] c 8° Macmillan 85

Financial Reform Almanac 1/ 8° *Liverpool* (Simpkin) *ann.*
Gives very full, but not altogether trustworthy, statistical information on land questions of U.K.

Return of Owners of Land in England and Wales, 2 vols. [Blue-Book] f° Wyman 75

**Scotland**

ARGYLL, Duke of —*his* Scotland as it was and as it is, *ut* **E** § 35: conts. good statemt. of land questn.

BLACKIE, Prf. J. S. Scottish Highlands and the Land Laws *o.p.* [*pb.* 9/] 8° Chapman 85

Return of Owners of Land and Heritages in Scotland [Blue-Book] f° Wyman 74

**Ireland** —*v. also* **F** § 45; *for* Home Rule question, *v.* **D** § 142

BONN, M. J. Modern Ireland and her Agrarian Problem [tr.] 2/6 *n.* 8° Hodges, *Dublin* 06

DAVITT, M. Fall of Feudalism in Ireland 10/6 *n.* ($2·50 *n.*) 8° Harper 04
The story of the Land League revolution.

LESLIE, Prf. T. E. Cliffe- —*in his* Land Systems, *ut sup.*

McCARTHY, M. J. F. Irish Land and Irish Liberty; ill. 7/6 *n.* c 8° Stock 10

MILL, J. Stuart Chapters and Speeches on Irish Land Question *o.p.* [*pb.* 2/6] c 8° Longman 70

MORRIS, W. O'Connor The Land System of Ireland 2/6 c 8° Simpkin 88

" —*in his* Present Irish Questions, *ut* **D** § 142

RICHEY, A. G. The Irish Land Laws [by a Q.C.] *o.p.* [*pb.* 3/6] c 8° Macmillan 80

THORNTON, W. T. Plea for Peasant Proprietors [in Ireland] *o.p.* [*pb.* 7/6] c 8° Longman [48] 74

VINCENT, J. E. The Land Question in North Wales 5/ ($2) 8° Longman 96
A brief survey of the orig., hist., and char. of agrarian agitatn., and of nature and effect of procgs. of Welsh Land Commission.

YOUNG, Arth. —*in his* Tour in Ireland: 1776–1779, 2 vols., *ut* **E** § 20

**Australasia**

EPPS, Wm. Land-Systems of Australia [Social Science Ser.] 2/6 c 8° Sonnenschein 94
$1 Scribner, *N.Y.* A full outline of methods wh. govern the use and alienation of public lands of all Australasian colonies.

**Continent of Europe**

VERNEY, Fces. P. L'y How the Peasant Owner Lives in Parts of France, Germany, Italy, Russia *o.p.* [*pb.* 3/6] c 8° Macmillan 88

" Peasant Properties: and other selected essays, 2 vols. *o.p.* [*pb.* 16/] c 8° Longman 85

**Belgium**

ROWNTREE, B. Seebohm Land and Labour: lessons from Belgium 10/6 ($3·50 *n.*) 8° Macmillan 10
The result of several years' study of the chief aspects of Belgium's social and economic life. Maps and illns.

**France**

EDWARDS, M. Betham —*in her* France of To-day, *ut* **E** § 14 [of some interest here]

YOUNG, Arth. Travels in France dur. yrs. 1787–89, ed. M. Betham Edwards 3/6 c 8° Bell [1792] 89
$1 *n.* Macmillan, *N.Y.* [Bohn's Lib.] With good Introd., biogr. sketch, and notes. A most valuable and delightful bk., carelessly wr. yet clear and forcible, comprising an important contemp. acc. of the land-holdg. classes, agric. condn., etc., and replete. w. econ. object-lessons. Until pres. repr it had not been prtd. since 1794, wh. edn. was formerly worth £5. Cheap edn. [York Lib.] 2/ *n.* f 8° *id* '05.

**Germany**

GOULD, Rev. S. B.- —*his* Germy., Past & Pres. [*ut* **E** § 15] conts. gd. acc. of Germ. peasant proprietors.

OUVRY, H. A. Stein and his Reforms in Prussia [land question] *o.p.* [*pb.* 2/6] c 8° Kerby [74] 75

**Russia**

HOURWICH, Dr I. A. The Economics of a Russian Village $1 8° Columbia Coll., *N.Y.* 92
An elab. acc. of positn. of var. classes, and condn. of agric. in 2 districts within province of Ryazan in Middle Russia.

KENNARD, H. P. The Russian Peasant 6/ *n.* c 8° Laurie 07

ROTH, H. L. The Agriculture and Peasantry of Russia *o.p.* [*pb.* 3/6] 12° Low 78

STEPNIAK' —*in his* The Russian Peasantry, *ut* **E** § 25

**Sweden**

LLOYD, L. Peasant Life in Sweden—*ut* **B** § 20

**India**

BADEN-POWELL, B. H. Land-Systems of British India, 3 v.; 14 maps 63/ ($16) 8° Clar. Press [82] 92
The land-tenures and systs. of land-revenue admin. prevalent in allseveral provinces of Brit. India and Burmah. Holt MACKENZIE, the great authority on land-revenue of N. India dur. first quarter of 19 cent., was asked if he could spare half-an-hour to explain the land system. 'You want me to explain in half-an-hour what I have spent a life-time in trying to understand' was his reply. These 3 massive vols., however, are an important attempt at a solution of an impossible problem.

" Short Acc. of Land Revenue and Admin. in Br. Ind. 5/ *n.* ($1·50) c 8° Clar. Press [93] 07

CONNELL, C. J. Our Land Revenue Policy in Northern India 12/6 8° *Calcutta* 76

HUNTER, Sir W. W. [ed.] —*in his coll. of MS. Letters fr. Bengal Archives*, 4 vols., *ut* **E** § 35
Shows fr. contemp. documts. the status of Bengal land-owners and condn. of landed property in second half of 18 century.

ROGERS, Alex. Land Revenue of Bombay, 2 vols.; 18 maps 30/ 8° W. H. Allen 92
A hist. of its admin., rise, and progress. Prepared und. ausp. of Bombay Govt. by a retired civilian, who searched the records at India Off. and traced var. changes introduced since days when Marathas handed over the task of gatherg. the revenue to the highest bidder. Map of each collectorate.

**United States**

BAILEY, L. H. The State and the Farmer $1·25 *n.* (5/ *n.*) c 8° Macmillan 08

BANKS, E. M. Economics of Ld. Ten. in Georgia [Col. Un. St.] $1 *n.* 8° Macmillan, *N.Y.* 05

BENTLEY, A. F. The Condition of the Western Farmer $1 8° Johns Hopk. Univ. Pr., *Baltim.* 93
[Johns Hopkins Univ. Studs. ser. xi, Pts. 7–8.] As illustrated by the economic history of a Nebraska township.

COX, S. S. Free Land and Free Trade 75 c. 12° Putnam, *N.Y.* 80
An application of the principles of the Corn Law Repeal to the U.S.

ELLIOTT, J. R. Amer. Farms: condn. & future [Questns. of Day] $1·25 (5/) c 8° Putnam 90

GEORGE, Hy. Our Land and Land Policy $2·50 12° Doubleday, *N.Y.* 01
Includes also other speeches, lectures, and miscellaneous writings.

MOODY, W. G. Land and Labour in the United States $1·50 12° Scribner, *N.Y.* 83

SATO, Shosuke History of the Land Question in U.S. $1·25 8° Johns Hopk. Univ. Pr., *Baltim.* 86

SPAHR, Dr C. B. Essay on Present Distribn. of Wealth in U.S. $1·50 c 8° Crowell, *N.Y.* 96
[Lib. of Economics.] The conclusion as regards income is that one per cent. of populn. receives as income an amt. greater than total earnings of poorer half of populn.

**History of the Law of Real Property**—*v.* **D** § 78

**Agricultural Labourer; Peasant**—*v. also* **D** § 117*

ARCH, Jos. Story of his life: told by himself 6/ c 8° Hutchinson 97
Ed. by C'ess of WARWICK. An interesting account of peasant-life by a peasant-agitator.

BOURNE, G. Memoirs of a Surrey Labourer 6/ c 8° Duckworth 07

[BUCKLEY, Jno.] A Village Politician. Ed. J. C. Buckmaster 6/ c 8° Unwin 97
Descrs. hardships of peas.-life in Midlands in mid. 19 cent., givg. first-hand informn. of trying times by a pract. worker in social and educ. effort. Largely autobiogr. of BUCKLEY.

CURTLER, W. H. R. Short History of English Agriculture 6/6 *n.* ($2·15) c 8° Clar. Press 09
A careful and concise history, full of informn. Larger pt. devoted to period after Middle Ages.

GARNIER, R. M. Annals of the British Peasantry [$2·75 Macmillan, *N.Y.*] 10/6 8° Sonnenschein [95] 08

HASBACH, Prf. W. History of the English Agricultural Labourer [tr.] 10/6 *n.* 8° P. S. King & Son 08
Pref. by Sid. WEBB. A thorough piece of research, w. notes, statist. tables, and a useful anal. of best opin. of ea. succeeding epoch.

HEATH, F. G. The English Peasantry [descriptive] *o.p.* [*pb.* 7/6] 8° Warne 74

" Peasant Life in West of England [descriptive] *o.p.* [*pb.* 10/6] c 8° Low [72] 80

" British Rural Life and Labour 10/6 *n.* 8° P. S. King & Son 11

HEATH, Rich. The English Peasant [Reformer's Bookshelf] 3/6 c 8° Unwin 93
Sketches of peasant-life and homes in a Yorks. dale, fens of Linc., on Surrey commons and Devon gardens, etc.

JACKS, L. P. Mad Shepherds; and other human studies 4/6 *n.* c 8° Williams 10
Admirable studies in the life—and religion—of the rustic poor.

JEFFERIES, Rich. The Toilers of the Field 3/6 ($1·25) c 8° Longman [92]

KEBBEL, T. E. The Agricultural Labourer 2/6 c 8° Sonnenschein [70] 07
$1 Scribner, *N.Y.* [Social Science Series.] A summary of the Engl. agric. labourer's position.

REYNOLDS, Steph. A Poor Man's House 6/ ($1·50) c 8° Lane 08

ROGERS, Prf. J. E. Thorold —*ut* **D** § 117*

SMITH, Edw. The Peasant's Home: 1760–1875 [Howard Prize Essay] *o.p.* [*pb.* 3/6] s 8° Stanford 76

**Allotments and Small Holdings**

GRANT, Corrie The Small Holdings Handbook 1/ c 8° Arrowsmith, *Bristol* 08

GREEN, F. E. The Book of the Small Holding; photos. [practical] 3/ *n.* c 8° Lane 08

GREEN, J. L. Allotments & Small Holdings [Social Science Ser.] 2/6 c 8° Sonnenschein 96
$1 Scribner, *N.Y.* Practical and illustrative, with discussion of the law of the subject.

JEBB, [Miss] L. The Small Holdings of England 10/6 *n.* 8° Murray 07
A survey of various existing systems.

JOHNSON, A. H. Disappearance of the Small Landowner [Ford Lects.] 5/ *n.* ($1·75) c 8° Clar. Press 09
Utilizes the Land-tax assessmts. in the hands of local authorities, dating back in some counties to 1746.

PRATT, E. A. Small Holders: what they must do to succeed 2/ *n.* 8° King 09

Report fr. Departmental Committee on Small Holdings in Great Britain 4/11 f° Wyman 07
Parl. Blue-Book. Minutes of evidence, appendices, and index.

**Banks, Agricultural** —*v.* **D** § 127*

**Commons, Footpaths, Rights of Way** —*for* Law, *v.* **D** § 78

EVERSLEY, L'd Commons, Forests, and Footpaths 2/ *n.* 8° Cassell [ ] 10

HILL, Octavia Our Common Land; and other Essays [plea f. their preservn.] 3/6 c 8° Macmillan 77

HUNTER, Sir Rob. Footpaths & Commons, & Parish & Distr. Councils 7/6 8° Eyre & Spottiswoode 96
Sets forth the law governg. preservn. of footpaths, road-side wastes, commons, and village-greens, and the duties and powers of the Councils.

" The Preservation of Open Spaces, and of Footpaths and other Rights of Way 7/6 8° Eyre & Spottiswoode 96
Treats of the several descrns. of land wh. are subj. to common rts., and of these rts. as means by wh. such lands may be protected fr. enclosure. The law of footpaths is set out, and attention drawn to var. exceptional ways, such as fords and towing-paths, and the use of cliffs and foreshores of the country and of its rivers and lakes. Author writes as both lawyer and member of the various protective Societies.

LEFEVRE, G. Shaw English Commons and Forests 10/6 8° Cassell 94
Account of the battle dur. prev. 30 yrs. for public rts. over commons and forests, by the most active member of the Commons Preservation Soc., who helped the cause more actively in Parl. than any one exc. late Prf. FAWCETT.

SLATER, Dr G. The English Peasantry and the Enclosure of Common Fields 10/6 *n.* 8° Constable 07
Histor. inquiry into causes, circumstances, and conseqs. of the var. Enclosure Acts. Argues th. princ. of collective ownersh. of soil must be estab. (or re-estab.), and agric. co-opern. revived in terms suitable to mod. condns.

**Garden Cities** —*v. also* **D** § 124, *s.v.* City Development

ADAMS, T. The Garden City and Agriculture 1/ *n.* c 8° Simpkin 05

HALL, Bolton A Little Land and a Living [Amer. condns.] $1 c 8° Arcadia Press, *N.Y.* 08

HOWARD, Eben. Garden Cities of To-morrow 1/6 *n.* c 8° Sonnenschein [98] 02
The pioneer book. First edn. (1898) was pubd. *sub tit. To-morrow, a Peaceful Pathway to Real Reform.*

SENNETT, A. R. Garden Cities in Theory and Practice, 2 vols.; ill. 21/ *n.* 8° G. Allen 05

**Land Values, Taxation of** —*v.* **D** § 117

**Nationalization of Land** —*v.* **D** § 142

**Rent** —*for* Interest *v.* **D** § 118

GEORGE, Hy. —*in his* Progress and Poverty, *ut sup.*

JOHNSON, A. S. Rent in Modern Econ. Theory [Am. Ec. Ass.; 2/6 Sonnenschein] 75 c. *n.* 8° Macmillan, *N.Y.* 02

NICHOLSON, Prf. J. S. Tenant's Gain not Landlord's Loss 5/ c 8° Douglas, *Edin.* 83

WALKER, Prf. F. A. Land and its Rent [3/6 Clar. Press] 75 c. 12° Little & Brown, *Boston* 83

**Rural Exodus; Return to the Land** —*for* Growth & Influence of Cities *v.* **D** § 124

CADBURY (G.) + BRYAN (T.)—*in their* The Land and the Landless, *ut sup.*

*Daily News* Special Commissioner [G. F. MILLIN] Life in our Villages 1/ c 8° Cassell [91] 91
A series of letters to the *Daily News*, written in the autumn of 1891. *Vide* MILLIN, *inf.*

FORDHAM, Montague Mother Earth: proposal f. reconstrn. of country life 5/ *n.* c 8° Simpkin [08] 08
Reviews pres. positn. of agric. and organizns. in var. pts. of country affectg. it, urging State interferce. in admin. of markets, wages, etc.

GILMAN, B. Back to the Soil $1·25 c 8° Page, *N.Y.*

GRAHAM, P. A. The Rural Exodus [Social Questions of To-day] 2/6 c 8° Methuen 92
Interesting chaps. on the causes at work in the migration of villagers to the great cities.

GREEN, J. L. Rural Industries of England; Introd. by Jesse Collings *o.p.* c 8° Marlborough 95
A carefully wr. acc., treatg. subj. historically and practically. Main object is to revive industries wh. have ceased to exist, and thus to revivify Engl. village-life. Other chaps. are histor. fr. times of Romans onwards.

HAGGARD, H. Rider The Poor and the Land; ill. 2/ (75 c.) c 8° Longman 05
The author's report on Salv. Army Land Colonies in Amer., w. addn. of Introd. and illns. Incls. descrn. of two interestg. attempts (so far unsuccessful) to settle the town-dweller as an indep. freeholder on the land—Fort Romie (S. Calif.) and Fort Amity (Colorado).

HUBERT, P. G., jun. Liberty and a Living $1 (1/6) 16° Putnam 89
Record of a successful attempt 'to secure bread and butter, sunshine and content, by gardeng., fishg. and huntg.', by an Am. journalist, disciple of THOREAU. Not a serious contribn. to the question.

MASTERMAN, C. F. G. [ed.] To Colonize England 2/6 *n.* c 8° Unwin 07
A colln. of papers, by var. wrs., on recent rural investigns., on rural depopn., and on a policy of land-reform.

MÉLINE, Senator Jules The Return to the Land [tr.] 5/*n.* c 8° Chapman 06
By leader of Moderate Repubns. in France, Min. of Agric. 1883-5, etc. Fch. condns. mostly regarded. Urges return to the land.

MILLIN, G. F. The Village Problem [Social Science Series] 2/6 c 8° Sonnenschein 02
$1 Scribner, *N.Y.* A study of depopulation of the villages. *Vide* also *Daily News, sup.*

MOORE, Harold E. Back to the Land [Social Questions] 2/6 c 8° Methuen 93
On rural depopulation, allotments, labour colonies, co-oper. agric., Salvation Army estate, *etc.*

PEDDER, Lt.-Col. D. C. Where Men Decay: present rural conditions 1/ c 8° Fifield [07] 09
Nine repr. mag. arts. The labourer 'wants Home and Hope. And Land monopoly denies them both'.

*United States*

PLUNKETT, Sir Hor. The Rural Problem of the United States 5/*n.* c 8° Macmillan 10
An excellent statement of the gist of the case for the reconstruction of country-life.

**Taxation of Land Values; Single Tax**—*v.* **D** § 117

**Unearned Increment**

DAWSON, W. H. The Unearned Increment [Social Science Series] 2/6 c 8° Sonnenschein [90]
$1 Scribner, *N.Y.* A moderate and judicious little treatise, dealg. w. concrete phenomena (mainly Engl.), and urging diversn. of Unearned Incr. into publ. channels.

FERRIS, A. J. Pauperising the Rich 7/6 8° Headley 99
On the significance of unearned wealth to owners and to Society.

MALLET, Sir Louis —*in his* Free Exchange, *ut* **D** § 114

PHIPSON, C. B. —*in his* Redemption of Labour *ut sup.*
Contains some original and forcible remarks about Unearned Increment.

**Wages, Agricultural** —*v.* **D** § 118

## 120: CO-OPERATION; TRADES-UNIONS; BLDG. & FRIENDLY SOCIETIES, ETC.

*Bibliography.* Internatl. Co-operative Alliance: Internatl. Co-operative Bibliography 7/6 *n.* r 8° P. S. King & Son 06
A classified bibliography of 5,761 entries on Co-operation and Profit-sharing.

ACLAND (A. H. D.) + JONES (B.) Working Men Co-operators [acc. of Artiz. Co-op. Movem. in Gt. Brit.] 1/ 12° Cassell [84] 92

AVES, Ern. Co-operative Industry 5/*n.* c 8° Methuen 07
Regards Co-opern. as a form of productive and distributive industry, and deals w. its limitns. Spec. sectns. on Agric. Co-opern.

BAERNREITHER, Dr J. M. Engl. Associatns. of Workg. Men, tr. Alice Taylor 10/6 8° Sonnenschein [89] 91

BELL, R. Trade Unionism [Social Problems Series] 1/*n.* c 8° Jack 07

BOLEN, Geo. Getting a Living $2 *n.* (8/6 *n.*) 8° Macmillan 03
A valuable compiln. on subj. of Trades-unionism, generally sympathetic; deals also w. probs. of wealth and poverty, profits and wages. Conts. a mass of informn. on Amer. and Brit. condns., and some of other Europ. countries.

BRABROOK, E. W. Provident Societies and Industrial Welfare 2/6 c 8° Blackie 98
A good little bk., dealg. fully w. subj., inclg. Trades-unions, Savings-Banks, Old-age Pensions, etc.

BURKE, W. M. History and Functions of Central Labor Unions $1 *n.* 8° Macmillan *N.Y.* 99
[Columbia Univ. Studies.] An accurate history of the Trades-Union Congress, and Amer. Labor Federation.

COMMONS, J. R. [ed.] Trade Unionism and Labor Problems $2·50 (8/6) 8° Ginn 05

Co-operative Congress: Annual Report [1910 is 47th Ann. Rept.] 1/ 8° Co-op. Prg. Soc., *Mancs.* [69] *ann.*

„ Wholesale Society: Annual 4/ 8° Co-op. Wholes. Soc., *Mancs.* [80] *ann.*

DRAGE, Geoff. Trade Unions [Bks. on Business] 2/6 *n.* c 8° Methuen 05

ELIOT, Prf. C. W. Future of Trades-Unionism and Capitalism [Larwill Lects.] (4/) c 8° Putnam 10

ELY, Prf. R. T. Studs. in Evoln. of Industr. Society [Citizen's Lib.] $1·25 *n.* (5/*n.*) c 8° Macmillan 03

FAWCETT, Prf. Hy. —*his* Pauperism [*ut* **D** § 127] conts. gd. ch. on Co-operative and Industrial Partnership

FAY, Dr C. R. Co-operation at Home and Abroad 10/6 *n.* 8° P. S. King & Son 09
A careful descrn. and anal. of co-oper. systs. in Engl. and princ. Continental States, under 4 heads (1) Banks, (2) Agric. Socs., (3) Workers' Socs., (4) Stores. Concludes that co-opern. is not the negatn. of competitn., or the herald of Socialism, nor yet a means to combat it, but is centred round an orig. and common impulse.

HARRISON, Fredc. —*in his* National and Social Problems, *ut* **D** § 114

HOBHOUSE, L. T. The Labour Movement [Reformer's Book-Shelf] 3/6 c 8° Unwin [93] 05
On *Aims of Labr., Trade-Unionism, Co-opern.* (both of wh. it favours), *Distribn. of Wealth, Control of Industry.* By a disciple of T. H. GREEN, belonging to Schl. whose leadg. tenet is that the problem of to-day is Distribn. not Productn., and that better distributn. requires active interventn. of State at every turn. Full of moral earnestness.

HOLYOAKE, G. J. The History of Co-operation in England, 2 vols. 21/ 8° Unwin [75-9] 06
i: *The Pioneer Period* [1812-44]; ii: *The Constructive Period* [1845-78].

„ Hist. of the Rochdale Pioneers: 1844-1892 [Social Science Ser.] 2/6 c 8° Sonnenschein [72]
$1 Scribner, *N.Y.* A new edn. of *Thirty-one Years of Co-operation*, brought down to the year 1892.

„ Self-Help One Hundred Years ago [Social Science Ser.] 2/6 c 8° Sonnenschein [88]
$1 Scribner, *N.Y.* An acc. of early devices for self-help: Bp. S. BARRINGTON [1734-1826], Ct. RUMFORD [1752-1814]; Sir T. BERNARD [1729-79]. Author was a worker on behalf of co-operation all his long life, and writes as a zealous advocate, supplying much val. material.

HOLYOAKE, G. H. Co-operative Movement To-day [Social Questions of To-day] 2/6 c 8° Methuen 91
A sensible and intelligent acc. of nature, growth, and extent of co-opern. fr. pt.-of-view of both distribn. and industry.

" Sixty Yrs. of an Agitator's Life—*ut* **D** § 125

" —*in his* Bygones Worth Remembering—*ut* **D** § 125

HOWELL, Geo. Hist. of Conflict between Capital and Labour—*ut* **D** § 118
A hist. and review of the Trades-Unions of Gt. Brit. fr. the Trades-Unionist pt.-of-view.

" Trade Unionism, New and Old [Social Questions of To-day] 2/6 c 8° Methuen 91
A sort of outline of former bk., tho' more directly concerned w. later developmts. of Trades-Unionism, esp. the new Unions, tow. wh. he is very hostile, on acc. of the general favour w. wh. they regard strikes. Shows that 14 of the chief Unions have expended £7,000,000 in provident benefits, while on strikes they have spent only £500,000. Clings to BRENTANO's theory of a long and bitter conflict bet. merchant and craft-gilds, though GROSS [*ut inf.*] finds no evidence for it.

" Labour Legisln., Labour Movemts., and Labour Leaders—*ut* **D** § 118

HUGHES (T.) + NEALE (E. V.) [eds.] Manual for Co-operators 2/6 8° Co-oper. Union, *Mancs.* [81]
The standard English authority, by two leaders in co-operation. Latter died 1892.

JONES, Benj. Co-operative Prodn.; w. Pref. by A. H. Dyke Acland, 2 v. 15/ ($3·75) c 8° Clar. Press 94
A detailed hist. of the experimts. in Co-operative *Production* in every branch of industry wh. have been made dur. 19th cent., and of the success or failure (mostly the latter) by wh. they have been attended—the first adequate book on the subj., the previous good literature of the kind bg. limited to Co-oper. *Distribution*. The last 4 ch. contain author's main conclusns., resultg. in favr. of State and Municipal Socialism, inclg. nationalizn. of Rys., Ports, and Docks.

KROPOTKIN, Pr'ce Mutual Aid—*ut* **D** § 126

Labour Assoc. for Promoting Co-oper. Production: Reports —93 *in prg.*
The Assoc.—to which are affiliated 25 manufg. or 'productive' socs.—seeks to estab. workshops in wh. workers share in profits and participate in managemt.; being thus sharply distinguished fr. the 'Co-oper. Workshops', wh. are merely organizns. of stores employing wage-labr., and also fr. the 'Co-oper. Mills', wh. are nothing but organizns. of small capitalists hiring labr. on ordinary compet. terms.

LLOYD, H. D. Labour Co-partnership $1 12° Harper, *N.Y.* 98
Notes of a visit to co-operative workshops in Great Britain and in Ireland.

MACGREGOR, D. H. Industrial Combination 7/6 *n.* 8° Bell 06
$2·50 *n.* Macmillan, *N.Y.* Deals w. factors of competing strength in order to study effect of combinatn. on ea. of them; considers pres.-day condns. wh. have fostered industr. combins., and gives brief disquisitn. on some questns. of publ. expediency.

MOFFAT, R. S. Economy of Consumption [commerc. crises & trades-unions] 18/ 8° Paul 78

de PARIS, Comte Trades Unions of Engl. [tr.], ed. T. Hughes *o.p.* [*pb.* 7/6] c 8° Smith & Elder 90

PIZZAMIGLIO, Dr L. Distribg. Co-oper. Socs.: essay on soc. econ. [tr.] [Soc. Sci. Ser.] 2/6 c 8° Sonnenschein 91
$1 Scribner, *N.Y.* Brings together and groups a wide array of facts and statistics, Engl., Contin., and Amer., fr. trustworthy sources.

POTTER, Beatrice [Mrs Sid. WEBB] Co-operative Movemt. in Gt. Brit. [Soc. Sci. Ser.] 2/6 c 8° Sonnenschein [91] 10
$1 Scribner, *N.Y.* Deals w. relns. wh., in opinion of author, ought to exist betw. Trades-Unions and Co-oper. Socs. and the State. The ablest and most philosophic analysis of the whole movement.

PRATT, E. A. Trade Unionism and British Industry 5/ *n.* c 8° Murray 04
Reprint of *Times* articles, w. Introd., on the crisis in Brit. industry. A weighty and valuable criticism of trades-unions.

RANSOME, J. S. Modern Labour: a review of the Labour Question 2/ 8° Eyre & Spottiswoode 95
A temperate and fairly-written statement of the case against Trades-Unionism.

RUEGG (A. H.) + COHEN (H.) Present and Future of Trade Unions 1/6 *n.* 8° Butterworth 06

SADLER, M. E., *etc.* Lectures on Co-operative Life 1/6 c 8° Co-oper. Prtg. Co. 89

v. SCHULZE-GAEVERNITZ, Prf. G. Social Peace [tr.]; Introd. by Graham Wallas 3/6 c 8° Sonnenschein 93
$1.25 Scribner, *N.Y.* [Soc. Sci. Ser.] An important study of Trades Union movemt. in Engl. Deals w. the many forms—econ., polit. and moral—in wh. the general movemt. tow. social unity in Engl. presents itself to an acute foreign observer. Pt. i is a general view of industr. condns. at beginning of 19 cent.; Pt. ii treats of Evolution of the Great Industry (patriarchal system, factory legisl., freedom of combination, community of interest betw. workman and employer—the textile industries, coal, iron), the Dock Strike of '89, *etc.*

SMITH, E. J. The New Trades Combination Movement 2/ c 8° Rivington 99

SMITH, Dr S. G. The Industrial Conflict $1 *n.* (3/6 *n.*) 12° Revell 07

Statistics of Co-operative Societies in Various Countries 10/ 4° P. S. King & Son 98
Prepared by the Statistical Committee of the International Co-operative Alliance.

THORNTON, W. T. On Labour—*ut* **D** § 118 [informn. ab. trades-unions]

THURLOW, Hon. T. J. Trades Unions Abroad; w. hints *o.p.* [*pb.* 9/] r 8° Harrison 71

WEBB, Catherine [ed.] Industrial Co-operation 2/6 *n.* c 8° Co-oper. Union, *Mancs.* 04
A textbk., by var. wrs., for candidates in the Co-op. Union exams. Hist., theory, and practice of co-opern.

*WEBB, Sid. + Beatr. History of Trade Unionism 7/6 *n.* ($2·60 *n.*) 8° Longman [94] 11
A valuable and compreh. hist. of growth and developmt. of Trades-Union movemt. in United Kingd. fr. 1700 to pres. day, founded largely on hitherto unpubd. material. A good deal of attention is incidentally given to the polit. hist. of the Engl. working-class dur. period. Full bibliogr.

* " Industrial Democracy 12/ *n.* ($4 *n.*) 8° Longman [98] 01
An economic defence of collective bargaining, outlining future industr. developmt. thro' Trade-Unionism.

" Problems of Modern Industry 5/ *n.* ($2·50) 8° Longman [98] 02
A valuable discussion of the latest Trade-Union problems and developments.

**Australia; New Zealand** —*v. also* **D** § 118, *s.v.* Arbitration, etc.

AVES, Ern. Wages Boards & Industr. Conciln. in Aust. & N.Z. 1/10 8° P. S. King & Son 08

LLOYD, H. D. A Country without Strikes $1 *n.* 12° Doubleday, *N.Y.* 00
An account of anti-strike legislation and its results in N.Z.

**Switzerland**

DAWSON, W. H. —*in his* Social Switzerland, *ut* **E** § 28: [chap. on Organization of Labour]

**United States**

ADAMS, Prf. H. B. [ed.] History of Co-operation in U.S. [by several contributors: Johns Hopkins Univ. Stud.] *o.p.* 8° Macmillan 89

AVELING, Dr E. + E. M. Working-class Movem. in Amer. [Soc. Sci. Ser.] 2/6 c 8° Sonnenschein [87] 91
$1 Scribner, *N.Y.* Gives a good idea of the movemt. in U.S. and of the various organizns. wh. have been formed.

BARNARD, C. Co-operation as a Business [results of co-oper. in U.S. & Eur.] $1 16° Putnam, *N.Y.* 81

BEMIS, Dr E. W. Co-operation in New England $1 8° Macmillan, *N.Y.* 86
2/6 Sonnenschein. [Pubns. of Amer. Econ. Assoc.] Historical; from 1842 (Brook Farm) onwards.

GROAT, G. G. Trade Unions & the Law in N.Y. [Col. Univ. Studs.] $1 *n.* 8° Macmillan, *N.Y.* 04

HOLLANDER (Dr J. H.) + BARNETT (Dr G. E.) Studies in Amer. Trade Unionism $2·75 *n.* Holt, *N.Y.* 06
12/ *n.* Hodder. The first instalmt. of an elabor. inquiry undertaken by the Econ. Seminary of Johns Hopk. Univ.

KIRK, Wm. National Labour Federatns. in U.S. [J. H. Univ. Studs.] Johns Hopk. Pr., *Baltimore* 06

MCNEILL (G. E.) + GEORGE (Hy.) *etc.* The Labor Movement $3·75 8° Bridgman, *Boston.* 86
Chiefly deals w. hist. of organizns. of labour, wr. by Am. representatives of leadg. trades; w. 3 chs. on hist. of labour.

**Co-operative Banking** —*v.* **D** § 127*

**Co-operative Farming Experiments**

CRAIG, E. T. The Irish Land and Labour Question *o.p.* [*pb.* 2/6] c 8° Trübner 82
Hist., by a disciple of Rob. OWEN, of Ralahine Farm (Co. Clare) owned by Mr J. Scott VANDELEUR, and in 1830 let by him to his tenants as a whole at a rental of £700 p.a. (618 acres, 268 of wh. under tillage), Mr V. finding necessary capital for bldgs., plant, stock, etc. The Soc. was managed by a committee of 9 elected by ballot; and the experimt. proved a success, financially and socially, until 1833, when it came to an end by flight of Mr. V., who had ruined himself by gambling.

PARE, Wm. Co-oper. Agriculture: solutn. of land questn. *o.p.* [*pb.* 3/6] c 8° Longman 79

STUBBS, [Bp] C. W. The Land & the Labours [Social Science Ser.] 2/6 c 8° Sonnenschein [83]
$1 Scribner, *N.Y.* A record of a Broad-Church clergyman's successful experimts. in Cottage Farmg. and Co-op. Agric. on his glebe-land.

**Monopolies** and **Trusts** —*for* Law *v.* **D** § 93*, **D** § 117*, *s.v.* Oil Trade [Standard Oil Co.]

*Bibliography.* Library of Congress: List of Books rel. to Trusts $1 4° Gov. Prg. Off., *Washgtn.* [ ] 07

" List of More Recent Works on Federal Control of Commerce and Corporations 15 c. 4° Gov. Prg. Off., *Washgtn.* 07

Amer. Econ. Ass. 3 Papers on Trusts—*in* Pubns., Ser. iii, vol. i, *ut* **D** § 114

BAKER, C. W. Monopolies and the People [Questns. of Day] $1·25 (6/) 12° Putnam [89] 99
Shows prevalence of monop. in U.S. by extens. surv. of Am. trade and industry; discus. natl. & artific. monops., competn., etc., & suggests remedies.

BERGLUND, A. The U.S. Steel Corporation [Col. Univ. Studs.] $1·50 *n.* 8° Macmillan, *N.Y.* 07

BOLEN, G. L. Plain Facts as to Trusts and the Tariff $1·50 *n.* (6/6 *n.*) c 8° Macmillan 02

BRIDGE, J. H. [ed.] The Trust: its work $1·25 *n.* c 8° Doubleday, *N.Y.* 02
8 essays, by var. wrs., on different aspects of the Trust. Bibliography of 28 pp.

CLARK, Prf. J. B. The Control of Trusts 60 c. *n.* (2/6 *n.*) c 8° Macmillan 01

" The Problem of Monopoly $1·25 *n.* (5/ *n.*) c 8° Macmillan 04
A study of a grave danger and of the national mode of averting it.

COLLIER, W. M. The Trusts: what can we do w. them? $1·25 c 8° Twent. Cent. Pb. Co., *Chicago* 00

COOK, W. W. Trusts 50 c. 12° Strouse, *N.Y.* 88

*Daily News* Special Commissioner [G. F. MILLIN] The Social Horizon [Social Science Ser.] 2/6 c 8° Sonnenschein [92]
$1 Scribner, *N.Y.* Graphically paints the almost irresistible tendency of all mod. undertakings tow. monopoly, showg. how small men are being squeezed out and great bodies of capitalists drawing every undertaking more and more within a circumscribed area.

DAVIS, J. P. Corporations, 2 vols.—*ut* **D** § 31

DAY, Dr J. R. The Raid on Prosperity $1·50 (6/ *n.*) 8° Appleton 07
A bold and trenchant attack on 'anti-capitalism' in Amer. and ROOSEFELT's campaign agst. Trusts, defendg. the latter, espec. the Standard Oil Co., the most denounced of them all. By the Chancellor of Syracuse University.

DOS PASSOS, J. R. Commercial Trusts: rights of aggregated capital $1 (5/) c 8° Putnam 01
[Questions of the Day.] An argument objecting to special legislation agst. trusts.

ELY, Prf. R. T. Monopolies and Trusts $1·25 *n.* (5/ *n.*) c 8° Macmillan 00
Includes a study of the question of public control of monopolies.

" —*in his* Problems of To-day, *ut* **D** § 114

GUNTON, G. Trusts and the Public $1 12° Appleton, *N.Y.* [00] 01

v. HALLÉ, E. Trusts or Industrial Combinations and Coalitions in U.S. $1·25 (5/ *n.*) c 8° Macmillan 95
A valuable, and on the whole impartial, acc., no extreme partizan position bg. taken up. Appendices [=over half vol.] cont. copies of Trust agreements, legisl. Acts, contracts, and other valuable documents.

HERRICK, Clay Trust Companies: organizn., growth & managemt. $4 *n.* 8° Bankers' Pb. Co., *N.Y.* 09

HIRST, F. W. Monopolies, Trusts, and Kartells [Bks. on Business] 2/6 *n.* c 8° Methuen 05

JEANS, J. S. Trusts, Pools, and Corners [Soc. Questns. of To-day] 2/6 c 8° Methuen 94

JENKS, Prf. J. W. The Trust Problem $1 *n.* 12° McClure, *N.Y.* [00] 03
5/ *n.* Putnam, *Lond.* Clear and readable: gives arguments for and agst. Trusts, deciding on the whole agst. them.

JOHNSON, Dr E. R. The Relation of Taxation to Monopolies 8° Amer. Acad. of Pol. Sci., *Phila.* 95

KIRKBRIDE (J. B.) + STERRET (J. E.) The Modern Trust Company $2·50 *n.* (10/6 *n.*) c 8° Macmillan 05

LE ROSSIGNOL, Prf. J. E. Monopolies Past and Present [Lib. of Economics] $1·25 12° Crowell, *N.Y.* 01

LEVY, Prf. Hermann Monopoly and Competition: study in Engl. indust. organizn. 10/ *n.* 8° Macmillan 11

LLOYD, H. D. Wealth against Commonwealth $1 12° Harper, *N.Y.* 94
A racy attack upon unscrupulous Trusts and other trade-combinations. Deals spec. w. Standard Oil Co.

MACROSTY, H. W. Trusts and the State [$1·50 *n.* Dutton] 5/ c 8° Richards 01
Deals w. trusts fr. Fabian standpt. Half the bk. is occupied w. Engl. econ. hist., co-operatn., etc.

" The Trust Movement in British Industry 9/ *n.* ($2·50 *n.*) 8° Longman 07
A detailed surv. of industrs. of U.K., w. spec. refer. to amalgamns. and assocns. in them: and considern. of nature and signific. of these combinatns.

MEADE, E. S. Financial Aspects of the Trust Problem 50 c. 8° Am. Acad. of Pol. Sci., *Phila.* 00

" Trust Finance $1·25 *n.* (5/ *n.*) 12° Appleton, 03

MUSSEY, H. R. Combination in the Mining Industry $1 *n.* 8° Macmillan, *N.Y.* 05
4/ P. S. King. [Columbia Univ. Studies.] A study of concentration in Lake Superior Iron Ore production.

NELSON, J. H. [ed.] The Inter-State Commerce Commission, 1908—*ut* **D** § 63
Incls. the Sherman Anti-Trust Act.

PRICE, Dr W. H. Engl. Patents of Monopoly, vol. i
[Harv. Ec. Studs.; 6/ *n.* Constable] $1·50 *n.* 8° Houghton, *Boston* 06

RIPLEY, Prf. W. Z. [ed.] Trusts, Pools, and Corporations $1·80 8° Ginn, *Boston* 05
Colln. of papers by var. wrs. intended for econ. students and to influence publ. opin. in favr. of publ. control.

[ROOSEVELT, Theod.] The Roosevelt Policy; w. Introd. A. Carnegie, 2 vols.
*n.p.* 12° Current Lit. Pb. Co., *N.Y.* 08
Speeches, letters, and State-papers, rel. to corporate wealth and closely-allied topics.

SPELLING, T. C. Treatise on Trusts and Monopolies—*ut* **D** § 93*

" Bossism and Monopoly [$1·50 *n.* Appleton, *N.Y.*] 7/6 c 8° Unwin 06

STICKNEY, Alb. State Control of Trade and Commerce $2·25 8° Baker, *N.Y.* 97
Contends th. the view th. combinatns. by indivs. to raise prices is either injurious to trade or an act in restraint of trade is incorrect fr. a purely legal pt.-of-view.

TARBELL, Ida M. —*in her* History of the Standard Oil Company, *ut* **D** § 117* [also other bks. there].

WALKER, F. Monopolistic Combinations in German Coal Industry
[Am. Ec. Ass.; 5/ Sonnenschein] $1·25 *n.* 8° Macmillan, *N.Y.* 04

*Municipal Monopolies* —*v.* **D** § 124

**Profit-Sharing**

BUSHILL, T. W. Profit-sharing & the Labour Question [Social Questns. of To-day] 2/6 c 8° Methuen 93
By a profit-sharg. employer, contg. acc. of syst. practised by him at Coventry, his cross-exam. bef. Lab. Comm., etc.

GILMAN, N. P. Profit Sharing between Employer and Employé $1·75 c 8° Houghton, *Boston* 89

" A Dividend to Labour 7/6 Macmillan] $1·75 c 8° Houghton, *Boston* 99
An account of profit-sharing methods now in use betw. many employers and their workmen.

" Methods of Industrial Peace —*ut* **D** § 118, *s. v.* Arbitration.

GODIN, J. B. A. The Association of Capital with Labor [tr.] 50 c. 8° Soc. Science Assoc., *N.Y.* 81
The laws and regulatns. of mutual assurance, regulatg. the Social Palace of GODIN ET CIE (iron foundry) at Guise.

" Social Solutions, tr. Marie Howland $1·50 12° Lovell, *N.Y.* 86
These essays were written in 1870—ten years before the legal association of GODIN ET CIE was incorporated.

Twenty-eight Years of Co-partnership at Guise [tr.] 6*d.* *n.* c 8° Lab. Co-p. Assoc. 09

RAWSON, H. G. [ed.] Profit-sharing Precedents; w. notes [legal cases] 6/ c 8° Stevens 91

Report on Profit-sharing [Blue-Bk., by J. Lowrey Whittle] 4½*d.* 8° Eyre & Spottiswoode 91
With list of firms in England, France and U.S. wh. had at that date adopted the system.

Report on Profit-Sharing [Blue-Bk., by D. F. Schloss] 10*d.* 8° Eyre & Spottiswoode 94

TAYLOR, Sedley Profit Sharing betw. Capital and Labour 2/6 c 8° Paul 84
Contains an appendix on the Whitewood Collieries (conducted on co-operative principles).

WRIGHT, Carroll D. Profit-Sharing [repr. fr. 7th Annual Rept.] 8° Bureau of Statcs. of Labor, *Boston* 86

**Relation of Labour Combinations to Law**

BRENTANO, Prf. L. Relation of Labour to Law of To-day [tr.]; w. Introd. $1·50 (6/) f 8° Putnam 91
A bad tr. of a compact little treatise, wh. conts. all main positions of the author of the famous *Die Arbeitergilden der Gegenwart*, 2 vols. (12*m.* 8° Duncker-*Leipz.* '71–2). Regards Tr. Unions as an inevit. outcome of mod. industr. condns., furnishg. a hope that positn. of masses may be improved without a violent reconstrn. of society. The spec. originality of the *Arbeitergilden*, wr. when author was 25 yrs. old, consisted in its applicn. to Tr. Unions of the historic method, wh. has yielded such valuable results on var. econ. questns. and its conseq. tracing of their pedigree in Teutonic world far back into Mid. Ages, showg. analogy of social movemts of to-day w. those of former days.

**Strikes** —*v. also sup.*, *s.v.* New Zealand (LLOYD)

CLAY, Sir Arth. Syndicalism and Labour 6/ *n.* c 8° Murray 11

CROSBY, O. T. Strikes [Questions of Day] $1·25 (5/ *n.*) c 8° Putnam 10

GUYOT, Yves Labour, Socialism, and Strikes [tr.]—*ut* **D** § 126

HALL, Dr F. S. Sympathetic Strikes & Lockouts [4/ P. S. King] $1 *n.* 8° Macmillan, *N.Y.* 98
[Columb. Univ. Studs.] Facts and theories of London Dock Strike 1891, Chicago Strike 1894, etc. Bibliogr.

NICHOLSON, Prf. J. S. Strikes and Social Problems [$1·25 Macmillan, *N.Y.*] 3/6 c 8° Black 96
First essay is on *Strikes and a Living Wage*; wholly polemical, fr. pt.-of-view of advocates of free competitn. and industr. liberty.

*Great Britain*

Board of Trade: Report on Strikes and Lock-outs of the Year 8° Eyre & Spottiswoode *ann.*

MAVOR, Prf. Jas. The Scotch Railway Strike [1891] [acc. & 'lessons'] 1/ c 8° Brown, *Edin.* 91
NASH (V.) + SMITH (H. Ll.) The Story of the Dockers' Strike [1889] 1/ c 8° Unwin 90

*United States*

ASHLEY, Prf. W. J. The Railroad Strike of 1894 10 c. 8° Church Soc. Union, *Cambr.*, *Mass* 95
DACUS, J. A. Annals of the Great Strikes in U.S. $1 12° Goodman, *Chicago* 77
WRIGHT, Carroll D. Strikes and Lock-outs [3rd Rept. of Commr. of Labor; pp. 1172] *gratis* 8° Govt. Prtg. Wks., *Washington* 88
" The Chicago Strike [Am. Econ. Ass.] $1 *n.* 8° Macmillan

**Building, Provident, and Loan Societies**—*for* Law *v.* **D** § 21

BRAYBROOK, Sir Edw. Building Societies 1/ *n.* c 8° P. S. King & Son 06
A popular treatise, advocatg. their developmt. and extension, by late Chief Registrar of Friendly Socs.
" Provident Societies and Industrial Welfare [Victor. Era Ser.] 2/6 c 8° Blackie 98
Building Societies Directory 5/ c 8° *Office* [84] *ann.*
DAVIS, H. F. A. Building Societies: theory, pract. and management 3/6 8° Sweet 87
DEXTER, S. Treat. on Co-oper. Savings & Loan Assocns. $1·50 12° Appleton, *N.Y.* [89] 91
LOWE, C. J. Building Soc. Movemt. [Bristol and W. of Engl.] 3/6 8° Simpkin 01
MILLAR, T. J. Building Society Finance and Statistics 3/6 *n.* 8° Clark, *Edin.* 05
ROSENTHAL, H. S. Manl. f. Bldg. & Loan Assoc. [hist., meths., etc.] $1·50 12° Rosenthal, *Cincinnati* 88
SCRATCHLEY, A. Pract. Treat. on Bldg. Socs., Investmt. & Trust Socs. 25/ 8° Layton [49] 87
" Further Treatise on Building Societies 10/6 8° Layton [ ]
WRIGHT, Carroll D. Buildg. and Loan Assocns. [9th Ann. Rept. of Com'r of Labor] 8° Govt. Prtg. Off., *Washgtn.* 93

**Friendly Societies (Oddfellows,** *etc.*)—*for* Law, *v.* **D** § 21

ANSELL, Chas. Treatise on Friendly Societies; w. numerous tables 5/ 8° Layton 35
SCRATCHLEY, A. Pract. Treat. on Life Assur. and Friendly Societies 27/6 8° Layton [ ] 87
WILKINSON, Rev. J. F. The Friendly Society Movement *o.p.* [*pb.* 2/6] c 8° Longman 85
" The Blackley National Insurance Scheme—*ut* **D** § 127*
" Mutual Thrift [Social Questions of To-day] 2/6 c 8° Methuen 92
A handbk. to the hist. of Friendly Socs.: Mancs. Unity, Foresters, Hearts of Oak, etc., etc.

*Girls' Friendly Society*

MONEY, Agnes L. History of the Girls' Friendly Society; ill. 2/6 c 8° Wells Gardner 97

*Oddfellows*

Complete Manual of Odd-Fellowship 7/6 c 8° Hogg,
DONALDSON, P. Odd Fellows' Text Bk. & Manual, ed. G. Bertram; ill. $2 12° Moss, *Phila.* [6–] 76
" Odd Fellows' Pocket Compan., ed. I. D. Williamson $1·50 18° Carroll, *Cincinnati* [62] 76
SPRY, Jas. The Oddfellows' Text Book 76

**Working-People's and Boy's Clubs**

BUCK, Winifred Boys' Self-governing Club $1 *n.* (4/6 *n.*); 50 c. *n.* c 8° Macmillan 03
CALKINS, Raymond [ed.] Substitutes for the Saloon $1·30 *n.* c 8° Houghton, *Boston* 01
An investign. by a Committee of fifty. Bibliography (2 pp.).
COIT, Dr Stanton Neighbourhood Guilds [Soc. Sci. Ser.; $1 Scribner, *N.Y.*] 2/6 c 8° Sonnenschein [91]
NEUMAN, B. P. The Boy's Club in Theory and Practice 2/6 c 8° Nutt 00
RUSSELL (C. E. B.) + RIGBY (L. M.) Working Lads' Clubs [practical wkg., etc.] 5/ *n.* ($1·50 *n.*) c 8° Macmillan 08
SOLLY, Rev. Hy. Working Men's Social Clubs and Educ. Institns. 3/6 c 8° Simpkin [67] 05
STANLEY, Maude Clubs for Working Girls 6/ ($1·50) c 8° Macmillan [89] 92
Based upon Miss STANLEY's own experience in managemt. of Wrkg. Girls' clubs; w. numerous remarks on wrkg. girls in other relatns.
WHITEHOUSE, J. H. The Boys' Club [posn. in social progress] 6*d.* *n.* c 8° Nutt 06

**Biography of Co-operators** —*v.* **D** § 125

**Gilds; Livery Companies**

*Bibliography:* GROSS, Dr Chas.—*his* Bibliogr. of Brit. Municipal Hist., *ut* **D** § 124: incls. Gilds

BRENTANO, Prf Lujo On Hist. & Devel. of Guilds and Origin of Trades Unions [tr.] *o.p.* [*pb.* 3/6] c 8° Trübner 70
Repr. of *Introd.* to TOULMIN SMITH [*ut inf.*]. Origin of Guilds, Religions, and Social Glds., Town Glds., Craft Glds., Trades Unions.
GROSS, Dr Chas. The Gild Merchant: contribn. to Brit. municipal hist., 2 v. 24/ 8° Clar. Press 90
A thoroughly sound piece of work, the first formal attempt w. any systematic method since BRENTANO [*ut sup.*] to deal w. place in mediaeval civil life of almost all Engl. towns occup. by trade gilds. Eccles. and social gilds (w. wh. Engl. had little to do) are not treated, but craft-gilds are

incid. discussed. To the acc. of Gild Mercht. several essays are added by way of Appendix (*Affiliation of Mediaeval Boroughs* and others almost equally valuable); and vol. ii is filled w. 'proofs and illns.', *i.e.* a ser. of documts. extr. fr. pub. records, notices in county hists., charters, compotus accts., etc. The two most import. chs. (*Distinction betw. Gild and Borough* and *Influence of Gild upon Munic. Constitn.*) clearly prove that the Gild fr. very beginning was a separate entity, not to be confounded w. the Borough. Good Index and glossary.

HIBBERT, F. A. Influence and Development of English Gilds *o.p.* [*pb.* 3/] c 8° Camb. Press 91
[Cambr. Histor. Essays.] Illustrated by the hist. of the craft-gilds of Shrewsbury.

KRAMER, Stella English Craft Gilds & the Govt. [Columb. Univ. Studies] $1 *n.* 8° Macmillan, *N.Y.* 05
By an indep. young scholar: contentious, its chief pt. bg. that craft-gilds continued to flourish throughout Tudor period, and that Tudor legisln. was directed not to their injury but to removal of abuses.

PENTY, A. J. The Restoration of the Guild System—*ut* **D** § 126

SELIGMAN, Prf. E. R. A. Two Chaps. in Mediæval Guilds of England [Am. Ec. Ass.: 2/6 Sonnenschein] 75 c. *n.* 8° Macmillan, *N.Y.* 87

SMITH, [Joshua] Toulmin English Guilds: their ordinances [w. Introd. by Brentano, *ut sup.*] 21/ 8° E. Eng. Tex. Soc. (Paul) 70
Conts. the orig. ordinances of more than 100 early English guilds, fr. MSS. of 14 and 15 cents.; w. notes, introd., and glossary.

SMITH, Lucy Toulmin —*article* Guild, *in* Encyclo. Brit., vol. xi [*ut* **K** § 1]

WALFORD, Cornelius Guilds: origin, constitution, objects, later history *o.p.* [*pb.* 7/6] 8° Redway [88] 89

WAY, T. R. [artist] Ancient Halls of City Guilds; w. l'r pr. P. Norman 31/6 *n.* 4° Bell 03

*London: Collectively*

ARUNDELL, Thos. Histor. Reminisc. of City of Lond. & its Livery Cos. *o.p.* [*pb.* 15/] 8° Bentley 69

DITCHFIELD, P. H. The City Companies of London and their Good Works 21/ *n.* 4° Dent 04
A record of their hist., charity and treasure. Ill. A. R. Quinton.

FIRTH, J. F. B. —*ut* **D** § 124

" Reform of Lond. Govt. & City Guilds [Imper. Parl. Ser.] 1/ c 8° Sonnenschein 87

HAZLITT, W. C. The Livery Companies of the City of London; ill. 25/ *n.* r 8° Sonnenschein 92
$10·50 Macmillan, *N.Y.* Only 750 printed and 100 on *L.P.* at 63/ *n.* A compreh. hist. of their origin, character, developmt., and social and polit. importance; w. acc. of all those Gilds wh. have not survived or have been merged into other Cos.

HERBERT, Wm. Hist. of the Livery Companies of Lond, 2 v. *o.p.* [*pb.* 16/] r 8° Bohn [36–7] 46

Reports of City of London Livery Cos. Commission; w. Appendix, 5 vols. f° *o.p.* Eyre & Spottiswoode 84
A Blue-Book, contg. much informn. ab. Lond. Cos., and also facts rel. to gilds of foreign countries.

UNWIN, Geo. The Gilds and Companies of London [Antiquary's Bks.] 7/6 *n.* 8° Methuen 08
$2 *n.* Scribner, *N.Y.* Deals exhaustively w. institn. of trade or occupation gild in general, its orig. and developmt.—not spec. hist. of the Companies.

Vindication of the Lond. Livery Companies [evid. bef. Roy. Comm.] *o.p.* r 8° Gilbert & Rivington 85

WELCH, Chas. —*in his* Modern History of the City of London, *ut* **E** § 17

*Individually*

*Armourers' and Brasiers' Co.:* Account of. By T. Morley 4° *priv. prin.* 78

*Barber-Surgeons' Co.:* Annals of. By Sidney Young; ill. 42/ 4° Blades 90
One of the best histories of a City Company yet published.

*Blacksmiths' Co.:* Blacksmiths' Co. By T. C. Noble—*appended to his* Ironmongers' Co., *ut inf.*

*Carpenters' Co.:* Hist. Acc. of. By E. B. Jupp, ed. W. W. Pocock; ill. 10/6 8° Pickering & Chatto [48] 87

*Clockmakers' Co.:* Some Account of. By S. E. Atkins + W. H. Overall; pl. r 8° *priv. prin.* 81

*Clothworkers' Co.:* Charters & Letters Patent, granted by the Kings & Queens of England 4° *priv. prin.* 81

" Ordinances; w. those of the Fullers and Shearmen 4° *priv. prin.* 81
Privately re-issued *sub tit.* '*The Government of the Fullers, Shearmen, and Cloth Workers of London*'. Sq. cr. 8° '81.

*Coopers' Co.:* Histor. Memoranda, Charters, etc. [1396–1848]. By J. F. Firth; pl. *o.p.* 8° *London* 48

*Founders' Co.:* Annals of; w. notes & ill. By W. M. Williams; pl. (some col.) 8° *priv. prin.* 67

*Girdlers' Co.:* Historical Account of. By W. Dumville Smyth [popular] 7/6 *n.* 8° Chiswick Press 05

*Goldsmiths' Co.:* CHAFFERS, Wm.—*his* Gilda Aurifabrorum [*ut* **I** § 114] *conts. histor. acc. of the Co.*

" History of the Worshipful Company of Goldsmiths *o.p.* 8° Adlard 37

*Grocers' Co.:* Some Account of. By B. J. B. Heath; ill. *o.p.* 4° *priv. prin.* [29] 69

" Facs. of 1st Vol. of MS. Archives, ed. J. A. Kingdon, 2 vols. [1345–1463; w. photos.] r 8° *priv. prin.* 88

*Hon. Artillery Co.:* Hist. of. By Cpt. G. A. Raikes, 2 v.; col. pl. & maps *o.p.* [*pb.* 63/] 8° Bentley 78–9

*Ironmongers' Co.:* Some Account of. By J. Nicholl; ill. 4° *priv. prin.* [51] 66

" History of A.D. 1351–1889. By T. C. Noble; ill. G. Cruikshank r 8° *priv. prin.* 89

*Leathersellers' Co.:* History and Antiquities of. By W. H. Black; pl. r 4° *priv. prin.* 70–1

*Marblers' Co.:* The Company of Marblers. By E. Conder—*appended to his* Records of Hole Crafte of Masons, *ut* **A** § 94

*Masons' Co.:* Hole Crafte of Masons. By E. Conder—*ut* **A** § 94

*Mercers' Co.:* Charters, Ordinances and Bye-laws [tr. of Latin charters added] f° *priv. prin.* 81

*Merchant Taylors' Co.:* Memorials of Guild of. By C. M. Clode; pl. r 8° *priv. prin.* 75

" Early History of the. By C. M. Clode, 2 vols. r 8° *priv. prin.* 88

*Needlemakers' Co.:* The Company of Needlemakers. By Coles s 4° *priv. prin.* 74

*Parish Clerks' Co.:* Some Account of Parish Clerks. By Rev. J. Christie 4° *priv. prin.* 93
*Paviors' Co.:* History of. By Chas. Welch 4° *priv. prin.* 10
*Pewterers' Co.:* History of. By Chas. Welch, 2 vols. [1348–1760] 42/*n.* r 8° Blades 03
*Saddlers' Co.:* Descr. and Histor. Acc. of. By J. W. Sherwell; pl. *priv. prin.* 89
*Skinners' Co.:* Hist. and Antiq. of. By J. F. Wadmore; ill. 8° Blades [76] 03
Enlarged and revised edn. of paper wh. app. in *Trsns. Lond. and Middlesex Arch. Soc.*, 1876, suppl. by extrs. fr. Ct. Bks. and Wardens' Accounts.
*Stationers' Co.:* Records of. Ed. C. R. Rivington 2/6 8° Nichols 83
*Vintners' Co.:* The Vintners' Co. By T. Milbourn; pl. and ill. 4° *priv. prin.* 88
*Waterman's Co.:* History and Origin of Co. of Watermen and Lightermen. By Hy. Humpherus, 3 vols.; pl. 8° *priv. prin. n.d.* [87 *sqq.*]
*Wheelwrights' Co.:* Account of. By J. B. Scott; ill. 4° *priv. prin.* 84
*Wyre-Drawers', Gold and Silver, Co.:* Gold and Silver Wyre-Drawers' Co. By Hor. Stewart; ill. 4° *priv. prin.* 91

*Aberdeen*
BAIN, Eben. Merchant and Craft Guilds: hist. of Aberd. Incorp. Trades; ill. 7/6 8° 87
BULLOCH, J. The Pynours: hist. notes on anc. Aberd. craft [Shore Porters] 2/6 c 8° *priv. prin.*

*Bristol*
FOX Account of the Merchant Taylors of Bristol; pl. s 4° *priv. prin.* 80
LATIMER, Jno. Hist. of Society of Merchant Venturers of Bristol *subscr.* 21/r 8° Arrowsmith, *Bristol* 03
Of value for hist. of sea-traffic of Engl. Gives also acc. of Bristol gilds from earliest times.

*Dundee*
WARDEN, A. J. Burgh Laws of Dundee 6/6 8° Kidd, *Dundee* 72
Conts. the hist., statutes and proceedings of the gilds, merchants, and fraternities of craftsmen.

*Dunfermline*
THOMSON, Dan. The Weaver's Craft: hist. of Weaver's Incorpn. of Dunf. 8° Gardner, *Paisley* 03
A good, tho' somewhat discursive acc., based on orig. documts. Throws light on soc. and industr. condn. of Scotl. of the period.

*Edinburgh*
COLSTON, Jas. The Guildry of Edinburgh: is it an incorporation? 12/6 4° Colston, *Edin.* 87.
Discusses orig. and hist. of several Scottish gilds; but main object is to prove that Edinb. is a corporate body—a moot point for a long period.
,, The Incorporated Trades of Edinburgh s 4° *priv. prin.* Colston, *Edin.* 91
Acc. of incorpn. of Chirurgeons (and Barbouris), Hammermen, Goldsmythis, Baxters, Fleschouris, Mary's Chapel, Skinners and Furriers, Cordwainers, Talzouris, Wobstaris, Waekaris, Bonnet-Makers. With introd. ch. on rise and progr. of munic. govt. in Edin., and App. on other crafts.
JOHNSTON, A. Keith Histor. Notes rel. to Merchant Co. of Edinb. 4° *priv. press of* P. Lawson, *Edin.* 62
SMITH, Jno. The Hammermen of Edin. & their Altar in St Giles [1494–1558] 10/6 *n.* 8° Hay, *Edin.* 07

*Glasgow*
Merchants' House at Glasgow (The): origin, constitn. and property, etc.; ill. 4° *priv. prin.* 66

*Kingston-upon-Hull*
LAMBERT, Dr J. M. Two Thousand Years of Gild Life; ill. 18/8° Brown, *Hull* 91
Gives the 'compositns.' and ordinances *in extenso* of the 15 craft gilds and tradg. cos. of Kingston fr. 14 [but mostly 17] to 18 cents.; w. 10 chs. discussg. sociolog. theories as to orig. of gilds (favourg. Roman theory of gild-origin), influ. of Fch. commune on Engl. towns, gild mercht., etc. The colln. of ordinances is of gt. value, but orig. pt. has little scientific importance.

*Norwich*
HUDSON, Rev. J. The Wards of City of Norwich: origin & history 5/4° Jarrold, *Norwich* 92

*Preston*
ABRAM, W. A. Memorials of the Preston Guilds [to 1862] 4° *Preston* 82

*Sheffield*
LEADER, R. E. History of the Sheffield Cutlers' Co., vol. i *priv. prin.* 05

*Shrewsbury* —*v.* HIBBERT, *sup.*

*Warwickshire*
SMITH, Miss Lucy Toulmin —*in* Andrews' [ed.] Bygone Warwickshire, *ut* **E** § 17
An interestg. art. on Holy Cross, Birm., one of most distinguished of 14-cent. gilds. Also art. by W. G. FRETTON on *Trading Gilds. of Coventry.*

*Italy: Florence*
STALEY, Edgcumbe The Guilds of Florence; ill. 16/*n.* r 8° Methuen 06
$5 *n.* McClurg, *Chicago.* A full and attractive acc., histor., industr., and polit., of the innumerable gilds, wh. were at once cause of much of Florentine greatness and the flower of Florentine traditns., spreadg. their network over the busy township, ea. a self-contained republic w. its own officers, judges, institns., and charities.

*China*
MORSE, H. B. The Gilds of China; 2 ill. $1·20 *n.* (3/6 *n.*) 8° Longman 09
With an acc. of the gild-mercht. or Co-Hong of Canton. Important, because the gild-syst. is now in full wrkg. order in China, and as efficient as it was in Engl. at height of its power.

## 121 : POPULATION ; EMIGRATION ; IMMIGRATION (ALIENS)

**Population**

ALISON, Sir Archib. Principles of Population & their Connection with Human Happiness, 2 vols. [a reply to Malthus] *o.p.* [*pb.* 30/] 8° Blackwood 40

BAILEY, W. B. Modern Social Conditions ; ill. $3 *n.* 8° Century Co., *N.Y.* 07
A statistical study of births, marriages, and deaths, w. spec. ref. to U.S.

BOURNE, Steph. Trade, Population, and Food [ser. of statist. papers] *o.p.* [*pb.* 12/] 8° Bell 81

BROWNELL, Miss Significance of a Decreasing Birth Rate 35 c. 8° Am. Acad. Pol. Sci., *Phila.* 94

CRACKANTHORPE, Montague Population and Progress 2/6 *n.* 8° Chapman 07
Expounds the view on questn. of birth-rate w. wh. author is identified—of 'purposive selection' operatg. by what he calls 'the voluntary principle', in rel. to (1) Individual Liberty, (2) Morality, (3) National Welfare, (4) Woman Suffrage, (5) War.

CUNNINGHAM, Dr W. The Malthusian Principle—*in his* The Path towards Knowledge, *ut* **D** § 114

DE QUINCEY, Thos. Malthus on Population, etc.—*in his* Writings, vol. ix [*ut* **K** § 83]

GODWIN, Wm. On Population : power of increase in numbers of mankind *o.p.* 8° *London* 20
An early reply to MALTHUS.

HADLEY, Dr A. T. Population and Capital [Am. Econ. Assoc.] $1 *n.* 8° Macmillan, *N.Y.*

MALTHUS, T. R. [1776–1834] Essay on Princ. of Populn., ed. G. T. Bettany 5/ ($2) 8° Ward & Lock [03] 90
On evils and means of checkg. over-populn., w. a view of its past and pres. effects on human happiness. His conclusns. have not by any means been generally accepted, but some of his investigns. have been of the greatest value, and no student of the subj. can afford to neglect his bk. The first edn. (a mere sketch) appeared anon. in 1798. Above is repr. of 6th (1816), the last author himself revised.

,, Parallel Chapters fr. 1st and 2nd Eds. of above [Econ. Classics] 3/ *n.* (75 c.) 12° Macmillan 95
Gives a fair idea of the main points of MALTHUS' theories. After the 2nd edn. the text remained substantially unaltered.

Bonar, Dr J. Malthus and his Work 12/6 ($4) 8° Macmillan 85

Kirkup, T. —*article* Malthus, *in* Encyclo. Brit., 9th edn., vol. xv [*ut* **K** § 1]

Ricardo, Dav. Letters to Malthus, ed. Dr J. Bonar—*ut* **D** § 114

NITTI, Prf. F. S. Population & the Social System [tr.] [Social Science Series] 2/6 c 8° Sonnenschein 94
$1 Scribner, *N.Y.* An accurate and minute study.

PAULIN, G. —*in his* No Struggle for Existence, *ut* **H** § 43
Incl. a criticism of Malthusianism and a statemt. of law and populn., wh. he finds in the reguln. of marriages acc. to ability of indivs. to find means to support a family, this ability dependg. on state of labr. market.

ROSCHER, Wm. —*in his* Principles of Political Economy [tr.], *ut* **D** § 114

SMITH, W. Rose The Growth of Nations 3/6 c 8° Sonnenschein 10
A histor. investign. of growth of populn., with the chief causes, and the factors wh. effect populn.

SPENCER, Herb. —*in his* Principles of Biology, vol. ii, pp. 289 *sqq.* [*ut* **H** § 43]

STANGELAND, C. E. Pre-Malthusian Doctrines of Population [Columbia Univ. Studs. ; 10/ *n.* P. S. King] $2·50 *n.* 8° Macmillan, *N.Y.* 04

TENNEY, A. A. Social Democracy and Population [Col. Univ. Studs. ; P. S. King & Son] 75 c. *n.* 8° Macmillan, *N.Y.* 07

THORNTON, W. T. Over-Population and its Remedy *o.p.* [*pb.* 10/6] 8° Longman 45

USSHER, R. Neo-Malthusianism : its economy and morality 6/ c 8° Gibbings 98

WHETHAM, W. C. D. + Cath. D. [Mrs] The Family and the Nation—*ut* **H** § 42
Incl. treatmt. of the subj. of the diminished birth-rate in the upper and the middle classes.

*Statistics* —*v. also* **D** § 148, *s.v.* Statistics

LONGSTAFFE, Dr G. B. Studies in Statistics ; w. 30 maps and diagrams 21/ *n.* r 8° Stanford 91
Central portion of bk. is occup. w. growth of populn. in differ. pts. of world (omittg. Asia and others), dealg. w. growth of ea. total populn., and w. the proportns. and changes in proportns. of its constit. elements. [Finds that in U.S. *c.* 62 % of inhabs. are of Ang.-Am. origin, the colonies contrastg. less favourably w. U.S. in respect of homogeneity]. Rest of wk., wh. is throughout scientific in spirit, is on miscell. social, polit., and medical statistics.

MAYO-SMITH, Prf. Richm. Statistics and Sociology [=Population Statistics]—*ut* **D** § 148

**Great Britain :** *Census* —*for* Illegitimacy *v.* **D** § 133

Census of England and Wales, 1891 : 11 vols. [Blue Books] 25/9½ f° 91 *sqq.*

Booth, Chas. [ed.] —*in his* Life and Labour, vols. v–viii, *ut* **D** § 118 [1895–6 edn.]

Sanders, W. Digest of Results of Census of 1901 [in tabular form] 3/6 *n.* 8° Layton 03

SPENCER (M. G.) + FALK (H. J.) Employment Pictures fr. the Census ; 60 diagrs. [occupatns.] 2/6 *n.* 8° P. S. King & Son 07

**United States :** *Census* —*for* Negro Question *v.* **D** § 130

Abstract of 12th Census [1900]. Ed. S. N. D. North + W. F. Willcox, etc. 30 c. 8° Govt. Prtg. Off., *Washington* 02

Amer. Econ. Assoc. : Critical Essays on Federal Census, by Members $2 *n.* 8° Macmillan, *N.Y.* 99

Committee on Scope of 12th U.S. Census : Report [Amer. Econ. Assoc.] 25 c. 8° Macmillan, *N.Y.* 98

Scope and Method of the Twelfth Census [Am. Econ. Ass.] $2 *n.* 8° Macmillan, *N.Y.* 99
7/ Sonnenschein. A critical discussion by some 20 statistical experts.

MERRIAM, W. R. Amer. Census-taking fr. First Census of U.S. *gratis* 8° Govt. Prg. Off., *Washgtn.* 05

WILLCOX, Dr W. F. Density of Population of U.S.
[Am. Ec. Ass.; 2/6 Sonnenschein] 50 c. *n.* 8° Macmillan, *N.Y.* 97
„ Area & Populn. at 11th Census [Amer. Econ. Assoc.] 50 c. *n.* 8° Macmillan, *N.Y.* 97

**Eugenics** — *v.* **H** § 43 **Vital Statistics** — *v.* **D** § 151

**Emigration, British:** *General Works*

BADEN-POWELL, [Sir] G. State-Aid and State-Interference *o.p.* [*pb.* 9/] c 8° Chapman 82
„ New Homes for the Old Country [Australia & N.Z.] *o.p.* [*pb.* 21/] 8° Bentley 72
„ Protection and Bad Times [w. spec. ref. to Engl. colonizatn.] *o.p.* [*pb.* 6/] 8° Trübner 79
GWYNN, H. A. Proper Distribn. of Populn. of Empire—*in* Compatriots' Club Lects., *ut* **D** § 122

*Emigration to America and Canada*

HUGHES, Thos. Rugby, Tennessee [acc. of Engl. settlemt. there] *o.p.* [*pb.* 4/6] c 8° Macmillan 81
RITCHIE, J. E. To Canada w. Emigrants: record of experience; ill. *o.p.* [*pb.* 7/6] 8° Unwin 85

*Irish Emigration* —*for* Irish in America, Australia, etc., *v.* **E** § 20

DUFFERIN, L'd [*now* Marq.] Irish Emigration and Tenure of Land *o.p.* [*pb.* 10/6] 8° Willis 67

**United States**

*MAYO-SMITH, Prf. R. Emigration & Immigration: study in soc. sci. $1·50 c 8° Scribner, *N.Y.* [90] 92
7/6 Unwin. Histor. and statist., w. discussn. of polit., soc., and econ. effects. A suggestive bk. (best on subject), full of statistics, w. bibliogr.

**Immigration**

*Bibliography:* Library of Congress: List of Bks. on Immigrn. 15 c. 4° Govt. Prg. Off., *Washington* 07

WHELPLEY, J. D. The Problem of the Immigrant 10/6 *n.* 8° Chapman 05
$3 *n.* Dutton, *N.Y.* Collects and compares the laws rel. to immigrn. of aliens and emigrn. (where extant) of natives of 13 Europ. countries, as well as Gt. Brit., her Colonies, and U.S. Opposed to unrestricted immigrn.

*Great Britain*

BOOTH, Chas. —*in his* Life and Labour of People of London, vols. i and iii [*ut* **D** § 118]
BRADSHAW (F.) + EMANUEL (C.) Alien Immigration 2/6 *n.* c 8° Pitman 04
Deals, pro and con., w. the question of imposing restrictions on immigration.
CUNNINGHAM, Dr W. Alien Immigrants to England
[Soc. Engl. Ser.; $1·25 Macmillan, *N.Y.*] 4/6 c 8° Sonnenschein 98
EVANS-GORDON, W. The Alien Immigrant; map and ill. 6/ *n.* c 8° Heinemann 03
Deals w. immigration into Engl., by a member of Royal Commission on subj. Somewhat anti-Semitic.
HOBSON, J. A. —*in his* Problems of Poverty, *ut* **D** § 127
KIRK, R. E. G. + E. F. [eds.] Returns of Aliens in Lond., Hy. viii to Jas. i, 3 v.
ea. 21/; Index 4° Huguenot Soc. 00–7; 08
LANDA, M. J. The Alien Problem and its Remedy 5/ *n.* c 8° P. S. King & Son 11
PAGE, Wm. [ed.] Letters of Denization and Acts of Naturalization for Aliens in England, 1509–1603 21/ 4° Huguenot Soc. 93
WHITE, Arnold [ed.] The Modern Jew—*ut* **D** § 12 [anti-immigration; anti-Semitic]
„ The Destitute Alien in Gt. Britain [Social Science Ser.] 2/6 c 8° Sonnenschein 92
$1 Scribner, *N.Y.* A symposium by var. wrs., incl. a paper on the Huguenots (by C. B. SHAW).
WILKINS, W. H. The Alien Invasion [Social Questions of To-day] 2/6 c 8° Methuen 92

*Immigration into London* —*for* Australians *v.* **E** § 65; *for* Jews *v.* **A** § 12, **D** § 127

*Immigration into America*

BALCH, Emily G. Our Slavic Fellow Citizens $2·50 8° Charity Pbs. Com., *N.Y.* 10
A valuable wk., based on first-hd. inquiry in Eur. and Amer., its ultimate object bg. to examine the condns. in wh. the Slavic immigrant lives when he has reached U.S., and how far he remains the same man that he was when at home.
BROMWELL, W. J. Immigration into the United States: 1819–55 $1·50 8° *New York* 56
CHETWOOD, Jno. Immigration Fallacies [urges restrictive legisln.] 60 c. 16° Arena Pb. Co., *N.Y.* 96
COMMONS, Prf. J. R. Races and Immigrants in America $1·25 *n.* (6/6 *n.*) 8° Macmillan 07
Deals w. the diff. races of wh. Amer. people is made up and their relns. in industry, civic life, crime, poverty, etc.
FAIRCHILD, H. P. Greek Immigration to the United States [8/6 *n.* Clar. Pr.] $2 8° Univ. of Yale 11
FLOM, G. T. Chapters on Scandinavian Immigration to Iowa; maps $1 4° State Hist. Soc., *Iowa* 07
GIBSON, Otis The Chinese in America $1·50 16° Hitchcock, *Cincinnati* 77
HALL, Prescott F. Immigration & its Effects upon U.S. [6/ *n.* Bell] $1·50 *n.* c 8° Holt, *N.Y.* 06
[Amer. Public Problems.] Of considerable value for its discussn. of the racial effects of immigration.
LORD, E., *& others* The Italian in America; ill. $1·50 8° Buck, *N.Y.* 05
*MAYO-SMITH, Prf. R. Emigration and Immigration—*ut sup.*
PROPER, E. E. Colonial Immigration Laws [Col. Univ. Studs.] 75 c. *n.* 8° Macmillan, *N.Y.*
SANDERSON, J. P. Republican Landmarks
[views of Am. statesmen on for. immigr.] $1·50 8° Lippincott, *Phila.* 56
SENNER, J. H. The Immigration Question 25 c. 12° Am. Acad. of Pol. Sci., *Phila.* 9

SEWARD, G. F. Chinese Immigrn. in its Social and Economical Aspects $2·50 12° Scribner, *N.Y.* 81

SHERARD, R. H. The Closed Door *o.p.* [*pb.* 3/6 *n.*] c 8° Digby & Long 02
A descrip. of the treatment of pauper immigrants at N.Y.

U.S. Industrial Commission: Reports on Immigration $1 8° Govt. Prtg. Off., *Washington* 01

**Infant Mortality** —*v. also* **D** § 151

BLAGG, Helen M. Statistical Analysis of Infant Mortality [w. causes] 1/ *n.* 8° P. S. King & Son 10

NEWMAN, Dr G. Infant Mortality: a social problem 7/6 *n.* c 8° Methuen 06

**Colonization** —*v.* **D** § 136

## 122: INTERNATIONAL TRADE; TARIFF (FREE TRADE AND PROTECTION).

AGACY, H. A. Free Trade, Protection, Dumping, Preferential Tariffs 2/6 *n.* ($1 *n.*) r 8° Longman 03

BOLEN, G. L. Plain Facts as to the Trusts and the Tariff—*ut* **D** § 118

BOWLEY, A. L. Statistical Studies rel. to National Progress since 1882—*ut* **D** § 148

BOYD, R. R. The World's Tariffs & Brit. System of State Aid 2/6 c 8° *Pall Mall* Press 08

FISK, Prf. G. M. International Commercial Policies $1·25 *n.* (5/ *n.*) c 8° Macmillan 08
With special reference to the United States. A text-book.

FURBER, H. W. [ed.] Which? Protection, Free Trade, or Revenue Reform $2 Park Pb. Co., *Hartford* 84
Forty chs. contg. speeches, articles, extrs. fr. bks., etc., of as many leading authorities on all sides, Amer., Engl., French.

GASTRELL, W. S. H. Our Trade in the World in rel. to Foreign Competition, 1885–95 6/ r 8° Chapman 97
Facts gathered without bias fr. offic. sources showg. that commerc. supremacy of Gt. Brit. is less assured than formerly.

HILLIER, Dr A. P. The Commonweal: study of feder. syst. of pol. econ. $1·50 *n.* (4/6 *n.*) c 8° Longman 09
Deals w. the premises on wh. the argumts. for and agst. the policy of Tariff Reform are based, exhibg. the manner in wh. certain great federatns. have secured many of the advantages of Free Trade over large areas, more or less conserved by an outer wall of tariffs.

NORTH, Sir Dudley Discourses upon Trade
[Reprs. of Econ. Tracts] 50 c. 8° Johns Hopk. Univ., *Baltim.* [1691] 07

PIERCE, Franklin The Tariff and the Trusts $1·50 *n.* (6/6 *n.*) 12° Macmillan 07

Tariffs, Reciprocity, and Foreign Trade $1 4° Am. Acad. of Pol. Sci. 07

*British Colonies*

FUCHS, C. J. Trade Policy of Gt. Brit. and her Colonies since 1860 [tr.] 7/6 *n.* ($2·50 *n.*) c 8° Macmillan 05

ROOT, J. W. Colonial Tariffs 7/6 *n.* 8° J. W. Root, *Liverpool* 06

*Canada*

CHOMLEY, C. H. Protection in Canada and Australasia 3/6 *n.* c 8° P. S. King & Son 04

McLEAN, S. J. Tariff History of Canada [Toronto Univ. Studs.] 8° Warwick, *Toronto* 95
A clear and succinct acc. of developmt. of Canad. tariff syst. fr. period immed. bef. formatn. of Dominion to 1895, showing change fr. 'Revenue Duties' to 'Protective Duties' wh. accomp. growth of a natl. spirit of consolidatn.

MONTAGUE (Hon. E. S.) + HERBERT (B., L'd LUCAS) Canada and the Empire: exam. of trade-prefs.
3/6 *n.* c 8° P. S King & Son 04

PORRITT, Edw. Sixty Years of Protection in Canada 5/ *n.* ($1·50 *n.*) c 8° Macmillan 08
Hist. of tariffs and bounties, and of federal provinc., and munic. largesse to industry, fr. 1846 to 1907, w. some acc., of trade relns. betw. Canada and the U.S. fr. 1806.

**India**

LETHBRIDGE, Sir Roper India and Imperial Preference 2/6 *n.* (90 c. *n.*) c 8° Longman 07
A concise and lucid wk. by a scholar and man of affairs, supportg. Imperial preference. With statistical tables.

SMITH, Prf. H. B. Lees India and the Tariff Problem [lectures] 3/6 *n.* c 8° Constable 09
Exams. industrs. of Ind. and finds th. Ind. has little to gain or lose by pref. tariffs, while Brit. trade will suffer severely.

WEBB, M. de P. India and the Empire 3/6 *n.* ($1·20 *n.*) c 8° Longman 08
A consideration of the tariff problem. Introd. by Sir E. F. LAW.

**History** —*v. also* **D** §§ 117, 117*

ASHLEY, Percy Modern Tariff History [$3 *n.* Dutton] 10/6 *n.* 8° Murray [04] 10
Shewing the origin and growth of tariffs in Germany, France, and the U.S. Introd. by R. B. HALDANE.

*Shipping Subsidies*

MECKER, R. History and Theory of Shipping Subsidies
[Am. Ec. Ass.; 3/6 Sonnenschein] $1 *n.* 8° Macmillan, *N.Y.* 05

*Great Britain*

ATTON (H.) + HOLLAND (H. H.) The King's Customs; ill.—*ut* **D** § 117
$3·50 *n.* Dutton, *N.Y.* An acc. of maritime revenue and contraband traffic in Engl., Scotl., and Irel., fr. earliest times to 1800.

BISSETT, A. Notes on the Anti-Corn-Law Struggle [Free Trade] 9/ 8° Williams 84

BRASSEY, T. A., L'd Sixty Yrs. of Progr. & the New Fiscal Policy 2/6 *n.* ($1·25 *n.*) c 8° Longman [04] 06

CUNNINGHAM, Dr Wm. Rise and Decline of Free Trade Movement 2/6 *n.* c 8° Camb. Press 04
60 c. *n.* Putnam, *N.Y.* An adverse criticism of Free Trade, the advocacy of Protection being involved implicitly.

MILLS, J. S. Landmarks of British Fiscal History [40 c. *n.* Macmillan] 1/ *n.* c 8° Black 07

MONGREDIEN, A. History of Free Trade Movemt. in Engld. [Free Trade] 1/ c 8° Cassell [81] 97

NICHOLSON, Prf. J. S. —*in his* History of the English Corn Laws, *ut* **D** § 117*

NOBLE, Jno. Fiscal Legislation [Free Trade] 7/6 8° Longman 67
Acc. of period 1842–65, dur. wh. Gt. Brit. gave up a Protective and adopted a Fr. Tr. policy, repealg. Navigatn. Laws, etc.

TRUMBULL, M. M. Free Trade Struggle in England [296 pp.] 25 c. c 8° Open Ct. Pb. Co., *Chic.* [84] 95
1/6. Paul [Relig. of Science Lib.] See note on him in D § 118. A good summary, by an uncompromising Free-trader, of econ. hist. of struggle in Engl. fr. 1838 to 1846 (*i.e.* fr. formation of Anti-Corn-Law League to final overthrow of Protective syst.) applied to Amer., on theory that history repeats itself and that the condns. are the same.

*United States*

ELLIOTT, Dr O. L. Tariff Controversy in the U.S., 1789–1833 $1 8° Leland Stanford Univ., *Paolo Alto* 92
A hist. of the rise of Amer. protect. beginning w. the colonial period and continuing w. greater detail after 1789.

GOSS, J. D. Hist. of Tariff Administr. in U.S. $1 *n.* 8° Macmillan, *N.Y.* 91
[Columbia Univ. Studies.] From Colonial times to the McKinley Administration Bill.

HILL, W. First Stages of Tariff Policy of U.S.
[Am. Ec. Ass.; 3/6 Sonnenschein] $1 *n.* 8° Macmillan, *N.Y.* 93

LOW, A. Maurice Protection in the United States [3/6 *n.* P. S. King & Son] c 8° *N.Y.* 04
A study of orig. and growth of Amer. tariff syst., and its social and econ. influences.

McKINLEY, W. Tariff: review of legisl. of U.S. fr. 1812 to 1896 $1·50 (7/6) r 8° Putnam [96] 04

RABBENO, Prf. Ugo Am. Commer. Policy: 3 hist. ess. [tr. (fr. Ital.)] 12/*n.* ($3·25) 8° Macmillan [95] 95
Hist. of orig. and growth of mod. Am. commerc. policy fr. estab. by England of Navigation Acts in N.-Am. Cols. to 1895. Sums up to effect that whilst in Engl. advantages of Fr. Tr. are most obvious and harm that wd. be done by Prot. the greatest, in U.S. reverse is the case, tho' even to U.S. Prot. is injurious.

STANWOOD, Edw. Am. Tariff Controvs. in 19 Cent., 2 v. [18/*n.* Constable] $5 *n.* 8° Houghton, *Boston* 03

SUMNER, Prf. W. G. Lectures on History of Protection in U.S. [Free Trade] 75 c. 8° Putnam, *N.Y.* 77
An outline of the history of the tariff, w. discussions of the chief Protective arguments.

TAUSSIG, Prf. F. W. Tariff History of the United States $1·25 (5/*n.*) c 8° Putnam [88] 10
[Questions of the Day.] A series of essays (Free Trade), dealing with the period 1789–1909.

THOMPSON, R. W. History of Protective Tariff Laws [Protectionist] $2 8° Peale, *Chicago* 88

*France*

MEREDITH, H. O. Protection in France 3/6 *n.* c 8° P. S. King & Son 04

*Germany*

DAWSON, W. H. Protection in Germany 3/6 *n.* c 8° P. S. King & Son 04
A history of German fiscal policy during the nineteenth century.

**Free Trade** The Free Trade System is advocated by CAIRNES, FAWCETT, McCULLOCH, MILL, PERRY, PRICE, RICARDO, ROGERS, SAY, SMITH, WALKER, *in* D § 114; and in the Works of CALHOUN, WOODBURY, *etc.*, *in* F §§ 73–4.

ALLEN, J. H. Tariff & its Evils: protection wh. does not protect [Q. of Day] $1 c 8° Putnam, *N.Y.* 88

ARMITAGE-SMITH, G. The Free-Trade Movement and its Results 2/6 c 8° Blackie [98] 03
$1·25 Stone, *Chicago.* [Victorian Era Series.] A good popular account.

ATKINSON, Dr Edw. The Distribution of Products $1·25 8° Putnam, *N.Y.* [86] 87

" Taxation and Work—*ut* **D** § 117: on the tariff and currency

AVEBURY, L'd Free Trade 2/6 ($1·60 *n.*) 8° Macmillan [04] 05

" Our Fiscal Policy—*in his* Essays and Addresses: 1900–3 7/6 *n.* ($3) 8° Macmillan 03

BADEN-POWELL, Sir G. Protection and Bad Times, *and* State Aid—*ut* **D** § 121

BASTABLE, Prf. C. F. Theory of Internat. Trade; w. applicns. to econ. policy
3/6 *n.* ($1·25 *n.*) c 8° Macmillan [87] 03

" The Commerce of Nations [Social Questions of To-day] 2/6 c 8° Methuen [92] 99
In 17 chs.: i–iii introd., iv–x histor., xi–xvii dealg. w. Protectn., Reciprocity and Commerc. Federatn. Object of bk. is to refute Prot. doctrs.

BASTIAT, F. Fallacies of Protection, tr. Dr P. J. Stirling 1/*n.* 8° Cassell 09
Another edn. 3/6 c 8° Unwin '09. ($1 *n.* Putnam, *N.Y.*) A brilliant, incisive and vigorous essay; tr of his *Sophismes Économiques.*

BRIDGMAN, R. L. Passing of the Tariff $1·20 *n.* c 8° Sherman, *Boston* 09
3/6 *n.* Unwin. By an Amer. journalist, attacking Protectionist system of U.S., wh. it explains.

BRIGHT, Jno. —*in his* Speeches, *and* Public Addresses, *ut* **F** § 26

BUTT, Is. [1813–79; Ir.] Protection and Free Trade
[brief & cogent statemt. of main facts] $1·25 12° Putnam, *N.Y.* 75

BUXTON, Syd. Arguments on either side of the Fiscal Question 1/*n.* c 8° Murray 04

CHAPMAN, Prf. S. J. Hist. of Trade betw. U.K. and U.S.
[Soc. Sci. Ser.; $1 Scrib., *N.Y.*] 2/6 c 8° Sonnenschein 99
With special reference to the effect of tariffs.

" Free Trade League [reply to *Rept.* of Tariff Commn.] 1/*n.* 8° Sherratt, *Mancs.* 05

COBDEN, Rich. [1804–65] —*in his* Political Writings, *and* Speeches, ed. J. Bright, *ut* **F** § 27

" Speeches on Free Trade 6*d.* (25 c. *n.*) 12° Macmillan 03

Ashworth, H. Recollections of Cobden and Anti-Corn Law League 5/ c 8° Cassell [77] 79

Axon, Dr W. E. A. Cobden as a Citizen: chap. in Manchester history; ill. 21/*n.* 8° Unwin 07
Contns. a facs. of Cobden's pamphlet *Incorporate your Borough!*, and a full bibliography.

Cunningham, Dr W. Richard Cobden and Adam Smith [2 lectures] 1/ 8° Tariff Reform League 04
Leroy-Beaulieu, P., *etc.* Richard Cobden and the Jubilee of Free Trade 3/6 c 8° Unwin 96
*Morley, Jno. [L'd] Life of Richard Cobden—*ut* **F** § 27
One of the best biographies in the English language.
Rogers, Prf. J. E. T. Richard Cobden & Modern Political Opinion *o.p.* [*pb.* 10/6] 8° Macmillan 73
Schwabe, Mrs Salis Reminiscences of Rich. Cobden. Ed. L'd Farrer 16/ 8° Unwin 95
Passages fr. COBDEN's letters and speeches, and his friends' letters. Interesting.

Cobden Club Fact *v.* Fiction, 1/ *n.*; Tariff Makers [sequel] 1/ *n.* 8° Cassell 04; 09
Also a number of Free Trade pamphlets and tracts.

Cox, Har. The United Kingdom and its Trade—*ut* **D** § 148
,, [ed.] British Industries under Free Trade: essays by experts 3/6 c 8° Unwin [03]
[Reformer's Bkshelf.] Discusses effect of our fiscal system upon several important industries separately.

Cox, S. S. Free Land and Free Trade—*ut* **D** § 119
ELY, Prf. R. T. —*in his* Problems of To-day, *ut* **D** § 114
FARQUHAR, A. B. + H. Economic and Industrial Delusions $1·50 c 8° Putnam, *N.Y.* 91
FARRER, Sir T. H. Free Trade *versus* Fair Trade, ed. C. H. Chomley 5/ c 8° Free Trade Union [82] 04
,, The State in its relation to Trade [Engl. Citizen Ser.] 3/6 ($1) c 8° Macmillan [83] 02
FAWCETT, Prf. Hy. Free Trade and Protection 3/6 c 8° Macmillan [78] 85
An inquiry into the causes wh. have retarded general adoptn. of Free Trade in Engl.: discusses also fully the Amer. argumts. for Protection.

Financial Reform Almanac [*ut* **D** § 119]—conts. information on English Tariff
Free Trade Congress, 1908: Report of the Proceedings 5/ *n.* 8° Cobden Club 08
GEORGE, Hy. Protection or Free Trade? [labour interest; 1/6 c 8° Paul] $1 12° Doubleday, *N.Y.* [86]
GRAHAM, Wm. Tree Trade and the Empire 1/6 *n.* c 8° Paul 04
GROSVENOR, W. M. Does Protection Protect? [thoro' statist. exam.] *o.p.* [*pb.* $2·50] 8° Appleton, *N.Y.* 70
GUYOT, Yves —*in his* Principles of Social Economy, *ut* **D** § 125
,, The Comedy of Protection, tr. M. A. Hamilton 6/ c 8° Hodder 06
HALL, Bolton [ed.] —*in his* Who pays your Taxes?, *ut* **D** § 117
HERVEY, M. M. —*in his* Trade Policy of Imperial Federation, *ut* **D** § 136
HIRST, F. W. [ed.] Free Trade & other fundam. Doctrs. of Manchester School 5/ *n.* c 8° Harper 03
Selns. fr. speeches of COBDEN, BRIGHT, L'd FARRER, and others.

HOBSON, J. A. International Trade: study of econ. principles 2/6 *n.* c 8° Methuen 04
Shows clearly the applicn. of econ. principles to questns. of Free Trade and Preferential and Protective Tariffs.

Internat. Free-Trade Congress: Report of Proceedings [652 pp.] 5/ *n.* 8° Cobden Club 08
MACNAMARA, T. J. Tariff Reform and the Working Man 2/6 c 8° Hodder 10
MALLET, Sir Edw. —*in his* Free Exchange, *ut* **D** § 114
MASSINGHAM, H. W. [ed.] Labour and Protection [Reformer's Bookshelf] 3/6 c 8° Unwin [03]
8 essays: by Jno. BURNS, J. A. HOBSON, G. J. HOLYOAKE, B. S. ROWNTREE, and 4 other writers, presentg. Fr. Tr. case fr. wkg.-man's pt.-of-view.

MEDLEY, G. W. Pamphlets and Addresses [pubd. f. Cobden Club] 3/6 c 8° Cassel 99
MONEY, L. G. Chiozza Elements of the Fiscal Problem 3/6 *n.* 8° P. S. King & Son 03
,, Fiscal Dictionary 5/ *n.* 8° Methuen 09
Alphab. arrgd. headgs. of almost every industry and trade, etc., w. Free Trade Moral to each.

NEALE, J. H. Inquiry into Principles of Free Trade 1/ 8° P. S. King & Son [ ] 03
PERRIS, G. H. The Protectionist Peril [admirable Fr. Tr. statemt.] 1/ 8° Methuen 03
PERRY, A. L. —*in his* Elements of Pol. Econ. [*ut* **D** § 114] [by a disciple of Bastiat]
REA, Russell Free Trade in Being 2/6 *n.* c 8° Macmillan 08
Colln. of lects., arts., and letters, by a shipowner dur. 1903–8, formg. record of his fight w. Tariff-Reformers. Also *Insular Free Trade.* 6d. Cassell '08

ROBERTSON, J. M. Trade & Tariffs [$1·50 *n.* Macmillan, *N.Y. v. also* Amery, *inf.*] 3/6 *n.* c 8° Black 08
ROGERS, Prf. J. E. Thorold —*article* Free Trade, *in* Encyclo. Brit., vol. ix [*ut* **K** § 1]
SCHOENHOF, J. Destruct. Influ. of Tariff on Manuf. & Commerce [Quest. of Day] 75 c. (3/) 12° Putnam 84
SHAW, G. B., *etc.* Fabianism & the Fiscal Question: an alternative policy 1/ 8° Fabian Soc. 04
SMART, Prf. Wm. Return to Protection: re-statemt. of case for free-trade 3/6 *n.* 8° Macmillan [04] 06
SMITH, Adam [1723–90] Free Trade and Protection = Wealth of Nations, Bks. iv and v., chs. 2–3, ed. T. A. Ingram 1/ c 8° Routledge [1776] 03
STRANGE, D. The Farmer's Tariff Manual [Questions of the Day] $1·25 (5/) Putnam 92
A popular presentation of the usual arguments against Protection; by a farmer.

SUMNER, W. G. Protectionism: the 'ism' wh. teaches that waste makes wealth $1 16° Holt, *N.Y.* 85
TAUSSIG, Prf. F. W. Protection of Young Industries in U.S. [Questns. of Day] 75 c. 8° Putnam, *N.Y.* 84
,, [ed.] State Papers and Speeches on Tariff; w. Introd. $1 *n.* 8° Harvard Univ., *Cambr.*, *Mass.* 92

TROUP, C. E. Future Work of Free Trade in Engl. Legisln. [f. Cobden Club] 3/6 8° Unwin 84
VILLIERS, C. P. Free Trade Speeches, ed. by Membrs. of Cobd. Club 2/6 c 8° Paul [83] 84
WELLS, Dav. A. —*in his* Practical Economics, *ut* **D** § 117
WEST, Sir Edw. The Price of Corn and Wages of Labour 8° Johns Hopk. Un. Pr., *Baltim.* [181–]
The tract wh. suggested the precise plan upon which CANNING's Corn Bill was framed.
WISE, B. R. Facts & Fallacies of Mod. Protectn. [Cobd. Cl. Prize Ess.] 2/6 c 8° Trübner 79
,, Industrial Freedom: a study in politics 5/ ($2·50) c 8° Cassell 92
Author, a friend of TOYNBEE, was Att.-Gen. of N.S.W., where he fought battle for Fr. Tr.: his argumts., tho' interestg., are not applic. to Engl. sitn. Useful statistics in Appendix.

**Protectionist** The Protective System is advocated in the works of ADAMS, CLAY, HAMILTON, JACKSON, JEFFERSON, MADISON, MONROE, WASHINGTON, WEBSTER, etc.—v. F §§ 73–4.

AMERY, L. S. Fundamental Fallacies of Free Trade [4 addresses] 1/c 8° Tariff Ref. League [06] 10
,, + ROBERTSON (J. M.) The Gt. Questn.: Tariff Reform or Fr. Tr. [pro & con.] 1/*n.* c 8° Pitman 09
ASHLEY, Prf. W. J. The Tariff Problem 3/6 *n.* c 8° P. S. King & Son [03] 04
,, —*in his* Surveys, Historic and Economic, *ut* **D** § 118
,, [ed.] British Industries: a series of general reviews —*ut* **D** § 117*
A useful volume, w. articles on iron, steel, cotton, woollen, etc., of spec. value. Many of them lean tow. Protectionist side.
BALFOUR, A. J. Fiscal Reform 3/6 *n.* ($1·25 *n.*) 8° Longman 06
Speeches del. June 1880 to Dec. 1905; w. repr. of *Economic Notes on Insular Fr. Tr.* [1903] and corresp. w. CHAMBERLAIN, Sept. '03.
BOWEN, Fcs. —*in his* American Political Economy, *ut* **D** § 114
BYLES, Sir J. B. Sophisms of Free Trade and Popular Polit. Econ. Examined 3/6 *n.* c 8° Lane [49] 03
Powerful, but out of date. Introd. and notes by W. S. LILLY and C. S. DEVAS.
BYNG, G. Protection [a manufacturer's crit. of Fr. Tr.] 3/6 8° Eyre & Spottiswoode 06
CAILLARD, Sir Vincent H. P. Imperial Fiscal Reform 3/6 *n.* c 8° Arnold 03
An able wk., by one of inventors of the Chamberlain policy of protection. Puts the views of older economists clearly into contrast w. pres. condns.
CAREY, H. C. Harmony of Interests: agric., manufg., and commerc. $1·50 8° Baird, *Phila.* [51] 83
,, —*in his* Principles of Social Science, *ut* **D** § 125
,, Unity of Law as exhibited in relations of Physical, Social, Mental, and Moral Science $3·50 8° Baird, *Phila.* 73
In the two latter works he takes the broader ground of all the relations of man to man and his surroundings.
CASTBERG, P. H. Production: a study in economics [tr. fr. Norwegian] 10/6 8° Sonnenschein 08
By a Norweg. bank-manager, who has studied economics of industry in direct contact w. its actualities. Moderate Protectionist stdpt., Norway bg. a Fr.-Tr. country w. tendency tow. Prot. Covers whole field of Distribn. and Exch. Its method is to follow hist. of products in hands of successive holders, pointg. out commercially the princs. of processes involved.
CHAMBERLAIN, Jos. Imperial Union and Tariff Reform [speeches of 1903] 1/*n.* 8° De La More Pr. [03] 11
Compatriots' Club: Lectures, Ser. i 8/6 *n.* ($2·75 *n.*) 8° Macmillan 05
A kind of offcl. manifesto of the group who form the intellectual centre of the Tariff Reform movemt., Prf. ASHLEY, Dr CUNNINGHAM, H. W. WILSON, Sir Vincent CAILLARD, Sir Jno. COCKBURN, J. W. HILLS, H. A. GWYNNE, GARVIN (*Princs. of Constructive Econcs. as appl. to Maintenance of Empire*). Presentatn. of the case by its ablest adherents.
COOPER, Sir Wm. E. Britain for the Briton 10/6 *n.* 8° Smith & Elder 10
CUNNINGHAM, Dr W. Wisdom of the Wise: 3 lects. on Fr. Tr. Imperialism [60 c. *n.* Putnam, *N.Y.*] 2/*n.* c 8° Camb. Press 06
,, The Case against Free Trade 2/6 *n.* c 8° Murray 11
CURTISS, Geo. B. Protection and Prosperity: acc. of Tariff legisln. and its effect in Eur. and America $3·75 r 8° Pan-Amer. Pb. Co., *N.Y.* 96
A very compreh. statemt. of case for Prot. Full of facts, industriously compiled, and obviously honest, but of small philosophic merit. Introdn. in 3 Pts. by Wm. MCKINLEY, Levi P. MORTON, and T. B. REED.
DENSLOW, Van Buren —*in his* Principles of Economic Philosophy, *ut* **D** § 114
DIETZEL, H. Retaliatory Duties, tr. D. W. Simon + W. O. Brigstocke 2/6 *n.* c 8° Unwin 04
GASKELL, T. P. Free Trade a Failure from the First 2/*n.* (70 c. *n.*) 8° Macmillan 03
GILL, Rich. Free Trade; inquiry into nature of its operations 7/6 c 8° Blackwood 87
GREELEY, Hor. Essays designed to Elucidate Sci. of Polit. Econ. $1 16° Porter, *Phila.* [69] 77
HOYT, H. M. Protection *v.* Free Trade [validity & opern. of U.S. duties] 50 c. 12° Appleton [86] 88
KELLEY, W. D. Speeches, Addresses, & Letters on Industr. & Financ. Questns. $2·50 8° Baird, *Phila.* 72
KIRKUP, Thos. Progress & the Fiscal Problem [$1·40 Macmillan, *N.Y.*] 3/6 *n.* c 8° Black 04
LIST, F. —*in his* National System of Political Economy [tr.], *ut* **D** § 114
Regarded as the basis of the Zollverein; of great influence in Germany. Am. tr. was pub. $2 r 8° *Phila.* '56, w. essay and notes S. COLWELL.
Hirst, M. E. Life of Friedrich List [$2 *n.* Scribner, *N.Y.*] 7/6 *n.* 8° Smith & Elder 09
A scholarly presentmt. of the career and wks. of 'the Father of Protectionism'. An excellent summary of his econ. doctrs. is followed by selns. fr. his wrgs. illustrg. his 2 main theses, that of the 3 stages in evoln. of natl. industry, and the distinctn. betw. indiv., polit., and cosmopol. economy.
MCKINLEY, Wm. —*in his* Speeches & Addresses, compiled by J. P. Smith $2 12° Appleton, *N.Y.* 93
MOLESWORTH, Sir G. L. Our Empire under Protection and Free Trade 1/c 8° Ward & Lock 02
,, —*in his* Economic and Fiscal Facts and Falacies, *ut* **D** § 118
PATTEN, Prf. S. N. The Economic Basis of Protection $1 (5/) 12° Lippincott, *Phila.* 90
'Whether we shall have a static or dynamic society is really the centre of the discussion about the Tariff'.
,, —*in his* Theory of Prosperity $1·25 *n.* c 8° Macmillan, *N.Y.* 02

PIGOU, Dn A. C. Protective and Preferential Import Duties 2/6 *n.* ($1 *n.*) c 8° Macmillan 06

RICE, D. Hall Protective Philosophy $1·50 16° Reed, *Boston* 91
A discussion of the principles of Amer. Protectionist system as embodied in the McKinley Bill.

ROSCHER, W. —*in his* Principles of Political Economy, *ut* **D** § 114

SMITH, E. Peshine —*in his* Manual of Political Economy $1·25 12° Baird, *Phila.* [53] 73

SYME, Dav. —*in his* Outlines of Industrial Science 6/ c 8° Paul [76] 77

Tariff Commission: Report and Summary of Evidence, etc. 4° P. S. King & Son 04 *sqq.*, *in prg.*

Chapman, Prf. S. J. Free Trade League [reply to above Rept. on Cotton industry] 1/ *n.* 8° Sherratt, *Mancs.* 05

Tariff Reform League: Speaker's Handbook 1/ c 8° T. R. League, 7, *Victoria St., Lond., S.W. ann.*

THOMPSON, R. E. —*in his* Polit. Economy [w. spec. ref. to industr. hist.] $1·50 12° Porter, *Phila.* [75] 82
Forms a third and revised edn. of his *Social Science and National Economy.*

„ Protection to Home Industry [4 lects. at Harvard] $1 8° Am. Prot. Tariff League, *N.Y.* [86] 08

„ —*in his* Social Science and National Economy $1·50 12° Porter, *Phila.* 75

TRYON, Capt. G. C. Tariff Reform [brief statemt. of case for] 2/6 *n.* 8° *Natl. Rev.* Off. 09

WATSON, J. R. Case for Tariff Reform [colln. of addresses] 2/6 *n.* c 8° Smith, *Glasgow* 09

WELSFORD, J. W. The Strength of Nations 5/ *n.* ($1·75 *n.*) 8° Longman 07
An argument in the light of history, being a review of the fiscal question by a Protectionist.

WILLIAMS, E. E. The Foreigner in the Farmyard [plea f. Protection] 2/6 c 8° Heinemann 97

„ The Case for Protection 5/ c 8° Richards 99

**Reciprocity:** LAUGHLIN (J. L.) + WILLIS (H. P.) Reciprocity $2 *n.* c 8° Baker & Taylor, *N.Y.* 03

## 123: CRIMINOLOGY; PENOLOGY; POLICE; PRISONS

**Bibliography:** HENDERSON (Prf. C. R.) —*in his* Introduction, *ut inf.*

MACDONALD, A. —*in his* Abnormal Man, and Plan for Study of Man, *ut inf.*
Former conts. an elaborate biography (227 pp.) of crime (English and foreign bks. and mag.-arts.); latter a bibl. of child-study.

WIGMORE, J. H. Prelim. Bibliogr. of Mod. Crim. Law and Criminology 65 c. 8° Northw. Univ., *Chic.* 09

**Criminology; Penology** —*v. also* **D** § 32: Criminal Law

ANDERSON, Sir Rob. Criminals and Crime: some facts and suggestions 5/ *n.* 8° Nisbet 07
Utilizes his wide experience in crim. investign. to advocate reforms and to establish doctr. that all princ. offences agst. property are wk. of small bands of profess. criminals, and that the profess. criminal is the creature of our punishmt.-of-crime syst.

ARNOLD, G. F. Psychology applied to Legal Evidence, etc. 12/ *n.* 8° Thacker 07
A criticism, in a scientific spirit (but somewhat doctrinaire), of certain fundam. legal notions, and applicn. to them of the teachgs. of descript. psychol. as a test of the justice and consistency of legal maxims and decisns.

ASCHAFFENBURG, G. Crime and its Repression [tr.] [Mod. Crim. Sci. Ser.] 14/ *n.* 8° Heinemann 11

BAKER, T. B. War with Crime [crime, reformatories, prisons, etc.] 12/6 8° Longman 89

BECCARIA, C. B. [1738–94] Essay on Crimes and Punishments [tr.] [*v.* Farrar *inf.*] $3 12° Little, *Albany, N.Y.* [01] 72
VOLTAIRE, who wr. a comm. on this bk. (1st Engl. tr., w. this comm. 1767), said that by it BECCARIA had made himself a benefactor of all mankind. It has been tr. into 22 languages.

BENTHAM, Jer. [1748–1832] The Rationale of Punishment *o.p.* [*w.* 7/6] 8° *London* 30

BOIES, H. M. Prisoners and Paupers; ill. $1·50 (7/6) 8° Putnam 93
A careful study of abnormal increase of criminals and burden of pauperism in U.S.; w. considern. of causes and remedies. Author, a member of Bd. of Pub. Charities, wd. impose stern restrictns. on foreign immigrn. and on marriage—or destruction of means of reprodn. in both sexes: 'this is simplest, easiest, and most effectual solutn. of whole difficulty (p. 270)'; 'fr. criminals and paupers can only come criminal and paupers (p. 268)'.

„ Science of Penology: defence of society against crime $3·50 *n.* (15/ *n.*) 8° Putnam 02

BONGER, Dr W. A. Criminality and Economic Conditions [tr.] [Mod. Crim. Sci. Ser.] 20/ *n.* 8° Heinemann 11

CARPENTER, Edw. Prisons, Police, and Punishment 2/ *n.* c 8° Fifield [05] 07
An inquiry into the causes and treatment of crime and criminals. Humanitarian; suggestive.

CARPENTER, Mary Our Convicts, 2 vols. [of historical value] *o.p.* [*pb.* 7/ ea.] 8° Longman 64

CHRISTISON, Dr J. S. Crime and Criminals $1·25 12° Keener Co., *Chicago* [97] 99
A study of the criminal mind. Follows LOMBROSO, but a series of articles—not a systematic treatise.

COX, E. W. Princs. of Punishmt. as appl. in admin. of Crim. Law—*ut* **D** § 32

DE QUINCEY, T. [1785–1859] Murder consid. as one of the Fine Arts [1827]—*in his* Wks., v. xiii, *ut* **K** § 89

DE QUIROS, C. Bernaldo Mod. Theories of Criminality [tr.] [Mod. Crim. Sci. Ser.] 14/ *n.* 8° Heinemann 11

DRÄHMS, Rev. Aug. The Criminal; w. Intro. by Lombroso $2 (8/6) c 8° Macmillan 00
A study on LOMBROSO's lines by the Resident Chaplain of San Quentin prison, California.

DU CANE, Col. Sir E. F. Punishmt. and Prev. of Crime [Engl. Cit.] *o.p.* [*pb.* 3/6] c 8° Macm. [85] 93

DUGDALE, R. L. The Jukes: study in crime, pauperism, disease, & heredity $1 (4/) 12° Putnam [77] 86

ELLIS, Havelock The Criminal; 40 ill. [Contemp. Sci. Ser.] 6/ c 8° Walter Scott [90] 03
$1·50 Scribner, *N.Y.* Account of results attained by crim. anthropol. in Italy, Germy., France, Engl., and U.S.; w. criticism.

FARRER, J. A. Crimes and Punishments [incl. a tr. of Beccaria, *ut sup.*] *o.p.* [*pb.* 6/] p 8° Chatto 80

FERRI, Prf. E. Criminal Sociology [tr.], ed. W. D. Morrison 6/ c 8° Unwin 95
$1·50 Appleton, *N.Y.* Deals w. the condns. wh. produce the crim. populn., and meths. whereby it may be diminished. Causes of crime divided into 2 main classes, (1) Indiv., (2) Social.
,, Criminal Sociology, tr. J. I. Kelly [Mod. Crim. Sci. Ser.] 20/ *n.* 8° Heinemann 11
,, Positive School of Criminology [tr.] [3 lects.] 50 c. 8° Kerr, *Chicago* 06
de FLEURI, Maur. The Criminal Mind [tr.] *o.p.* [*pb.* 3/6 *n.*] c 8° Downey 01
A sensible account of the subject, w. forecast as to legislation, etc., in the future.
GAROFALO, R. Criminology [tr.] [Mod. Crim. Science Ser.] 16/ 8° Heinemann 11
GOLL, Aug. Criminal Types in Shakespeare 5/ *n.* c 8° Methuen 09
Analyses types fr. SHAKESPEARE, showg. step by step the minds at work, and givg. a new insight into criminal methods.
GREEN, S. M. Crime: nature, causes, treatment, and prevention $2 (10/6) 8° Lippincott, *Phila.* 89
GROSS, Hans Criminal Psychology [tr.] [Mod. Crim. Sci. Ser.] 17/ *n.* 8° Heinemann 11
HALL, A. C. Crime in rel. to Soc. Progr. [Col. Univ. Studs.; 14/ P. S. King] $3 *n.* 8° Macmillan, *N.Y.* 02
HAMON, A. Universal Illusion of Free Will and Criminal Responsibility *o.p.* [*pb.* 3/6 *n.*] r 8° Univ. Pr. 99
HENDERSON, Prf. C. R. Introd. to Study of Depend., Defect. & Delinq. Classes $1·50 c 8° Heath, *Boston* [93] 02
Largely American. With good bibliographical references to the various sections (English and foreign bks.).
HOOK, Alf. —*in his* Humanity and its Problems, *ut* **F** § 4
KELLOR, F. A. Experimental Sociology $2 *n.* (8/6 *n.*) 8° Macmillan 02
A study by 'laboratory methods' of crime and criminals, w. pract. suggestions.
LOMBROSO, Prf. C. The Female Offender [tr.], ed. W. D. Morrison, w. Introd.; ill. 6/ c 8° Unwin 95
$1·50 Appleton, *N.Y.* Applicn. of the anthropolog. method, examg. whether, and to what extent, the female criminal differs fr. average woman in bodily and mental characteristics, arrivg. at many interesting conclusns. There is no Engl. tr. of his *L'Uomo Delinquente* [3 v. & Atlas, 5th edn. 8° Turin ('89) '96–97]; Fch. tr. by REGNIER+BOURNET, w. Atlas, 8° *Paris* '87.
,, Criminal Anthropology—in vol. xii of Stedman's 'Twentieth Century Practice', *ut* **H*** § 16
,, Crime: causes and remedy [tr.] [Mod. Crim. Sci. Ser.] 16/ *n.* 8° Heinemann 11
Ferrero, Gina L. [dau.] Criminal Man [summary of Lombroso] 6/ *n.* c 8° Putnam 11
LYDSTON, Prf. G. F. The Diseases of Society; ill. (15/ *n.*) 8° Lippincott 10
'The Vice and Crime Problem', by the Prf. of Criminal Anthropology., Chicago Kent College of Law.
MACDONALD, Arth. Abnormal Man $2 8° Lowdermilk, *Washgtn.* 93
Essays on education and crime and related subjects, w. digests of literature and bibliography.
,, Criminology; w. Introd. Prf. C. Lombroso $2 8° Funk, *N.Y.* 93
Valu. psychol. & scient. study in criminol., general & special. First Pt. conts. summary of opins. of LOMBROSO & followers on phys. side of crime.
,, Abnormal Woman $1·25 8° Author 95
,, Plan for the Study of Man *n.p.* 8° Govt. Press, *Washington* 02
W. refer. to Bills to establ. a laboratory for study of criminal, pauper, and defective classes.
,, Hearing on the Bill *n.p.* 8° Govt. Press, *Washington* 03
,, Statistics of Crime, Suicide, etc.; w. bibliography *n.p.* 8° Govt. Press, *Washington* 03
,, Man & Abnormal Man, incl. Study of Children; ill. 40 c. 8° Govt. Press, *Washington* 05
,, Juvenile Crime & Reformation, incl. Stigmata of Degeneration 50 c. 8° Govt. Press, *Washington* 08
,, Study of the Criminal, Pauper, & Defective Classes 25 c. 8° Govt. Press, *Washington* 08
McKIM, W. D. Heredity and Human Progress $1·50 *n.* c 8° Putnam, *N.Y.* 00
Refers social evils to heredity, and would cure them by wholesale destruction of the defective.
MERCIER, Dr Chas. Criminal Responsibility 7/6 *n.* ($2·50) 8° Clar. Press 05
,, Crime and Insanity [Home Univ. Lib.] 1/ *n.* s 8° Williams 11
MORRISON, Rev. W. Douglas Crime and its Causes [Soc. Sci. Ser.] 2/6 c 8° Sonnenschein [91] 09
$1 Scribner *N.Y.* Based on exam. of recent ideas of Engl. and Contin. wrs. (esp. Italns.), and exper. of 14 yrs.' prison-wk. as Chaplain.
MÜNSTERBERG, Prf. Hugo Psychology and Crime [5/ *n.* Unwin] c 8° $2·50 *n.* 12° McClure, *N.Y.* 08
Amer. edn. *sub tit. On the Witness Stand.* A highly suggestive vol. showing, in a ser. of pop.-wr. chs. w. descrns. of experimts., (1) untrustworthiness of human perceptn. and memory, and hence of legal evidence; (2) how psychol. methods may be utilized for detectn. of guilt or innocence.
PARMELEE, Maur. Principles of Anthropology and Sociology in their relation to Criminal Procedure [Citizens' Lib.] $1·25 *n.* (5/ *n.*) c 8° Macmillan 08
PARSONS, P. A. Responsibility for Crime [Columb. Univ. Studs.] $1·50 *n.* 8° Macmillan, *N.Y.* 09
RYLANDS, L. G. Crime: its causes and remedy 6/ 8° Unwin 88
SALEILLES, Prf. R. Individualisation of Punishment [tr.] [Mod. Crim. Sci. Ser.] 16/ *n.* 8° Heinemann 11
SMITH, Adam [1723–90] Lectures on Justice, Police, Revenue, and Arms—*ut* **D** § 114
SUTHERLAND, Dr J. F. Recidivism: habitual criminality and petty delinquency 3/ *n.* 8° Green, *Edin.* 08
TARDE, Gabriel Penal Philosophy [tr.] [Mod. Crim. Sci. Ser.] 20/ *n.* 8° Heinemann 11
WHITEWAY, A. R. Recent Object Lessons in Penal Science [w. bibl.] 3/6 *n.* c 8° Sonnenschein 02
WILSON, Dr A. Education, Personality, and Crime; ill. 7/6 *n.* 8° Greening 08
Conts. a mass of informn. on biolog., physiolog., and sociolog. aspects of the subj.—heredity, fertilizn., environmt., the brain, responsibility, personality, degenerates, criminal characteristics; w. App. of statist. tables of measuremts. of criminals and others.
WILSON, Dr G. R. Clinical Studies in Vice and Insanity 7/6 *n.* 8° Clay, *Edin.* 99

**Juvenile Crime:** BEGGS (Thos.) Extent and Causes of Juv. Depravity *o.p.* [*pb.* 5/] 8° Gilpin 49
CARPENTER, Mary Juvenile Delinquents: their condition and treatment *o.p.* [*pb.* 6/] f 8° Bennet 53
DAY, S. P. Juvenile Crime: its causes, character, and cure *o.p.* [*pb.* 10/6] 8° Hope 58
FOLKS, H. Care of Destitute, Neglected, and Delinquent Children—*ut* **D** § 127, *s.v.* Children

HILL (M. D.) + CORNWALLIS Prize Essays on Juvenile Delinquency *o.p.* [*pb.* 6/] p 8° Smith & Elder 53

MACDONALD, Arth. —*ut supra*

MOLL, Dr. The Sexual Life of the Child [tr.] [on crim. psychol.] 15/ *n.* 8° G. Allen 11

MORRISON, Rev. W. Douglas Juvenile Offenders [Reformer's Bookshelf] 3/6 c 8° Unwin [96]
$1·50 Appleton, *N.Y.* Extent and char. of juv. crime, shewg. effects of heredity, sex, and age on crim. tendencies, phys. and mental characteristics of juvenile offender, his parental, social, and econ. condns., and the institns. in existence and methods f. reclaiming him.

RUSSELL (C. E. B.) + RIGBY (L. M.) The Making of the Criminal 3/6 *n.* ($1·25 *n.*) c 8° Macmillan 06
Based on experience gained among juvenile delinquents in Mancs. Has suggestive chs. on compar. methods of dealing w. youthful criminals.

" Young Gaol Birds [tales fr. Mancs life] 3/6 *n.* c 8° Macmillan 10

TRAVIS, T. The Young Malefactor: study in juv. delinquency, its causes and treatmt.; ill. $1·50 *n.* 8° Crowell, *N.Y.* 08
Introd. by Judge B. B. LINDSEY. An astounding array of facts on the child-criminal based on 6 yrs. investign. in Amer. and Eur. Author does not accept LOMBROSO's theories, does not believe in the congenital criminal, tho' he does believe in heredity, and quotes the remarkable case of the JUKE family, wh. cost N.Y. State £250,000 (*v. sup., s.n.* DUGDALE).

WAUGH, Rev. B. The Gaol Cradle and who Rocks it. *o.p.* [*pb.* 2] c 8° Isbister [73] 80
An eloquent plea for the abolition of juvenile imprisonment.

*Reformatory Schools* —*v.* **D** § 169

**Detection of Crime; Forgery**

AMES, D. T. On Forgery, its Detection and Illustration $3 8° Bancroft, *San Francisco* 00
Illustrated, with particulars of numerous *causes célèbres.*

BAILEY, W. H. The Detective Faculty [fr. judicial records] $1·50 12° Clarke, *Cincinnati* 96

BERTILLON, A. Identifn. of Crim. Classes by Anthropometr. Meth. [tr.] [12 pp.] 8° *London* 89

BLACKBURN (D.) + CADDELL (Capt. W.) The Detection of Forgery 6/ *n.* 8° Layton 09
A practical manual for the use of bankers, solicitors, etc.

ELLIS, Miriam A. The Human Ear: its identification, etc. 3/6 *n.* 8° Black 00
A proposal to identify criminals by the ear; scheme of classification of ears, etc.

FAULDS, Hy. Guide to Finger-print Identification 5/ c 8° Wood, *Henley* 05

GALTON, Fcs. Finger Prints, *o.p.* [*pb.* 6/ *n.*]; Deciphermt. of Blurred Finger Prints [suppl.] 2/6 *n.* 8° Macmillan 92; 93

" Finger-print Directories 5/ *n.* 8° Macmillan 95

" —*in his* Memories of my Life; ill. 10/6 *n.* 8° Methuen 08

GROSS, Dr Hans Criminal Investigation: pract. hdbk. for magistrates, etc. [tr.] ill. 30/*n.* 8° Specialist Pr. 07
An exhaustive manl. f. crim. investigators. Pt. i sets forth general princs., etc.; ii–iii deal w. topics and handicrafts the investigator shd. know; iv treats of methods of criminals. Appendix (36 pp.) conts. Authorities.

*HENRY, Sir E. R. Classification and Uses of Finger-prints; ill. 2/ 8° Wyman [00] 06
The best exposition of the system (first brot. to attention by Fcs. GALTON) wh. has replaced the BERTILLON syst. of anthropometry, now thoroughly discredited by experts.

**Capital Punishment**

COPINGER, W. A. Essay on the Abolition of Capital Punishment *o.p.* [*pb.* 2/] 8° Stevens & Haynes 76

HOBART, L'd On Capital Punishment for Murder [1861]—*in his* Essays, vol. ii 2 vols. *o.p.* [*pb.* 25/] 8° Macmillan 85

MACMASTER, Rev. J. The Divine Purpose of Capital Punishment 6/ c 8° Paul 92
A defence of hanging on authority of *Genesis.* A medley of Bible texts, types, allegories, etc.

MOIR, J. M. On Capl. Punishmt. [based on Mittermaier's *Todesstrafe*] *o.p.* [*pb.* 6/] c 8° Smith & Elder 65

OLDFIELD, J. The Penalty of Death: problem of capital punishment 3/6 *n.* c 8° Bell 01

PALM, A. J. The Death Penalty [Questions of the Day] $1·25 (5/) c 8° Putnam 91

ROMILLY, H. The Punishment of Death [the best treatise] 9/ c 8° Murray 86

SMITH, Rev. Syd. Punishment of Death and Moral Responsibility [1849]—*in his* Works, *ut* **K** § 89
Not contained in Ward & Lock's 3/6 edition of his works.

STEPHEN, Sir J. F. —*in his* Criminal Law, *ut* **D** § 32

TALLACK, W. T. Penological & Preventive Princs. [w. spec. ref. to Eur. & Amer.] 8/ 8° Wertheimer [89] 96
A good argumt. in favour of Capital Punishmt. on grounds that Imprisonmt. for Life is too severe a penalty.

*Corporal Punishment in Schools*—*v.* **D** § 170

**Flagellation** (religious, erotic, etc.)

COOPER, W. M. Flagellation & Flagellants: hist. of the rod; ill. 7/6 c 8° W. Reeves [69] 98

Flagellation in France: fr. a medical and histor. standpt. Carrington, *Brussels* 98

'RÉAL, Ant.' [=F. F. F. MICHEL] Story of the Stick [tr.]; ill. $1·50 s 8° Bouton, *N.Y.* 92

**History of Crime and of Treatment of Criminals**—*for* Trials *v.* **D** § 6

ADAM, H. L. The Story of Crime; 54 ill. 12/6 *n.* 8° Laurie 08
Consists mainly of police-ct. gossip on prisons and prison-life, w. letters of criminals, curiosities of evid., scenes in ct., etc.

DUMAS, Alex. Celebrated Crimes [tr.], 4 vols. ea. 6/ c 8° Methuen [96] 07–8
Ea. $1·75 Macmillan, *N.Y.* i: *Crimes of the Borgias, and others*; ii: *Crimes of Urbain Grandier, and others*; iii: *Crimes of Marquise de Brinvilliers and others*; iv: *Crimes of Ali Pacha, and others.*

ELDRIDGE (B. P.) + WATTS (W. B.) Our Rival, the Rascal: conflict between criminals of this age and the police $3 8° Pemberton, *Boston* 97

FORSTER, Jos. Studies in Black and Red [30 tales of notable crimes] 3/6 c 8° Ward & Downey 96

GRIFFITHS, Maj. A. Mysteries of Police and Crime, 2 vols. 21/8° Cassell 98

HOYLE, Wm. Crime in England & Wales in 19 Cent. [histor. and crit.] 2/6 8° E. Wilson 76

PELHAM, Camden Chronicles of Crime, 2 vols.; ill. 15/8° Miles [41] 86
A kind of supplemt. to *The Newgate Calendar*, fr. 'earliest times' to 1841. 52 steel pl. by 'PHIZ' (H. K. BROWNE). The last edn. of the *Newgate Calendar* itself, ed. A. KNAPP + W. BALDWIN, was pubd. in 4 vols., 8°, 1824–8.

PIKE, L. O. History of Crime in England, 2 vols. *o.p.* [*pb.* 18/ea.] 8° Smith & Elder 73–6
In rel. to civil life and civilizn.: fr. pub. recs. and contemp. documts. Vol. i: *Roman Invasn. to Hy. vii*; ii: *Hy vii to Pres. Time.*

QUINTON, Dr R. F. Crime and Criminals: 1876–1910 4/6 *n.* c 8° Longman 10
An outl. of princ. changes wh. have taken place since Prison Act 1877 (when all the local prisons of Engl. and Wales became vested in Sec. of State f. Home Dept.) in our meths. of repressg. crime and dealg. w. criminals. By late Govr. of Holloway Prison.

*India*

ADAM, H. L. Oriental Crime; ill. 7/6 *n.* 8° Laurie 08
A study of crime, police, and prison-life in India. Fairly well compiled: w. 'true stories'.

" The Indian Criminal 10/6 *n.* 8° Milne 09
A pop. bk. on the Ind. penal syst., the Eastern prisoner, ry.-thieves, dacoity, Khaikarees, etc.

COX, Sir Edm. Police and Crime in India; ill. 12/6 *n.* 8° Stanley Paul 11

CRAWFORD, A. T. Reminiscences of an Indian Police Official *o.p.* [*pb.* 16/] 8° Low 94
Conts. many interestg. stories of crime and its punishmt., concludg. w. an urgent plea f. police reform in India.

HERVEY, Gen. C. Some Records of Crime: diary of a year [1867], 2 vols. 30/8° Low 92
By Gen. Superint. of operatns. f. suppressn. of Thuggee and Dacoity. 1,000 pp. full of grim records of usual and unusual crimes, composed of extrs. fr. confessns. of criminals spared on condn. of treachery to associates, of comments thereon, and of quotns. fr. offic. repts.

*France*

FUNCK-BRENTANO, F. Princes & Poisoners: studs. of Ct. of Louis xiv [tr.]; ports. 6/c 8° Duckworth 01
Conts. an acc. of the 'epidemic' wh. overtook Paris in the seventeenth century.

GORON, M. F. The World of Crime [tr.], ed. A. Keysey 3/6 c 8° Hurst & Blackett 07
Thirteen true detective-stories, by a former chief of the Paris detective police.

IRVING, H. B. Studies of French Criminals of the 19th Century 10/*n.* r 8° Heinemann 01
$2·50 Brentano, *N.Y.* Budget of horrors (murders by TROPPMANN, PRANZINI, PRADO, RAVACHOL, HENRY, etc.): more sensational than instructive.

PROAL, Judge Louis [Puy de Dôme] Passion and Criminality in France [tr.]
[study of jealousy and crimes of love] 21/*n.* 8° Brit. Bibliophiles' Soc., *Brussels* 10

SPICER, Hy. Judicial Dramas: romance of Fch. criminal law *o.p.* [*pb.* 15/] 8° Tinsley 72

*America*

BOIES, H. M. Prisoners and Paupers—*ut sup.*

BRACE, C. L. The Dangerous Classes of New York $1·25 12° Wynkoop, *N.Y.* [ ] 88

BYRNES, Thos. The Professional Criminals of Amer. [202 photos. of crimins.] $5 4° Dillingham, *N.Y.* 86

PINKERTON, Allan Professional Thieves and the Detectives $1·50 8° Dillingham, *N.Y.* 90

TRAIN, Arth. True Stories of Crime fr. the District-Attorney's Office $1·50 12° Scribner, *N.Y.* 08
6/*n.* Laurie. 13 narratives of crime, by an Amer. lawyer, who conducted most of the prosecutns. himself.

**History of Punishment**

ANDREWS, Wm. Bygone Punishments [antiquarian pt.-of-view] 7/6 8° Andrews, *Hull* [90] 98

EARLE, Alice M. Curious Punishments of Bygone Days; ill. $1·50 12° Stone, *Chicago* 96

EVANS, E. P. The Criminal Prosecution & Capital Punishment of Animals—*ut* **C** § 70
$2·50 *n.* Dutton, *N.Y.* Account of a curious phase of criminal and ecclesiastical law in the Middle Ages.

WHITEWAY, A. R. Recent Object Lessons in Penal Science; w. bibliogr.
[$1·25 *n.* Dutton, *N.Y.*] 3/6 c 8° Sonnenschein 02

WINES, Dr F. H. Punishment and Reformation [Lib. of Economics] $1·75 12° Crowell, *N.Y.* 95
6/ Sonnenschein. A historical sketch of the rise of the penitentiary system.

*Hanging in Chains*

HARTSHORNE, A. Hanging in Chains; ill. 4/6 c 8° Unwin 91
A ghastly but interestg. vol., w. reprodns. of rude cuts wh. have perpetuated the gibbet and gibbet-irons. Gibbeting alive in chains was first recogn. by Act of Parl. in 1752, tho' the practice had been common for ages before. Last case was that of COOK (Leics. 1834), when custom was abol. by statute.

*Lynching; Lynch-law*

BANCROFT, H. H. Popular Tribunals = History of the Pacific States, vols. xxxi-ii [*ut* **E** § 56]

CUTLER, Dr J. E. Investig. into History of Lynching in U.S. $1·50 (6/*n.*) c 8° Longman 05

*Tyburn*

MARKS, Alf. Tyburn Tree: its history and annals; ill. 15/*n.* 8° Brown & Langham 08
The result of exhaustive research on the hist. of the Tyburn Gibbet, its origin, victims, the hangman, etc., w. 'annals' in chronol. order fr. 1177 to 1783, date of last execution. Valuable series of reprodns. fr. old prints.

**Biography**: *Criminals; Malefactors; Scoundrels—v. also* **D** § 6: Trials

BERREY, R. J. P. The Bye-Ways of Crime; ill. 2/6 c 8° Greening
Curious information on the ways of thieves, etc.

BLEACKLEY, H. Some Distinguished Victims of the Scaffold; ill. 10/6 *n.* Paul 05
Covers 1751 to 1824, and deals graphically and somewhat flippantly w. Mary BLANDY, the PERREAUS, w. W. RYLAND, Governor WALL, Jno. HADFIELD and Hy. FAUNTLEROY. Gives documentary matter and careful bibliogrs. of contemp. literature.

GRIFFITHS, Maj. A. Criminals I have Known; ill. 6/c 8° Chapman 95
Entertaining stories of crime and criminals, based on the author's experience.

GRIFFITHS, Maj. A. Mysteries of Police and Crime, 2 vols. 21/ 8° Cassell 98
$5 Putnam, N.Y. Engl. and Amer. narratives mainly; includes anecdotes of author's own experience of criminals.

SECCOMBE, T. [ed.] Lives of Twelve Bad Men 6/ c 8° Unwin [94] 95
$3·50 Putnam, N.Y. Bothwell, Hopkins, Judge Jeffreys, Tit. Oates, L'd Lovat, Jon. Wild, 'Fighting Fitzgerald', Wainewright, etc.

SMITH, Lt.-Col. Sir Hy. From Constable to Commissioner 7/6 n. c 8° Chatto 10
Reminiscs. of wk. of City of Lond. Police, incl. author's share in futile attempt to find 'JACK THE RIPPER'; w. remarks on golf (wh. author enjoys distinctn. of hg. given up), racing, deer-stalkg., huntg., dogs, R. L. STEVENSON (his cousin), etc.

VINCENT, Arth. [ed.] Lives of Twelve Bad Women; ill. 6/ 8° Unwin [97] 98
$4 Page, *Boston*. Alice Perrers, Alice Arden (Shakesp.'s type of bad woman), My. Frith ('Moll Cutpurse'), C'ess of Somerset, D'ess of Cleveland, Mary Young, Teresia Constantia Phillips, Miss Chudleigh, Mrs Brownrigg, Eliz. Canning, My. Bateman, Mary A. Clarke. Unwholesome reading, its contents being connected in nothing but unity in sex and worthlessness. A variation of *The Newgate Calendar* style of literature.

WHIBLEY, Chas. A Book of Scoundrels 7/6 c 8° Heinemann 97
$2·50 Macmillan, N.Y. A fantastic eulogy of highwayman, burglar, and pickpocket, in form of a ser. of biogrs. of the leading professors of those arts. DE QUINCEY'S *Murder Considered as one of the Fine Arts* set the fashion in this class of literature, but this book lacks his attractive irony.

*Bushrangers* —*v. also* **E** § 65, *s.v.* Bush Life

BOXALL, G. E. Story of the Australian Bushrangers 3/6 c 8° Sonnenschein 99

HARE, F. A. Last of the Bushrangers; ill. 3/6 c 8° Hurst [92] 94
An account of the capture of the Kelly gang.

WHITE, H. A. [Austral.] Tales of Crime & Criminals in Australia *o.p.* [*pb.* 6/] c 8° Ward & Downey 94
A colln. of exciting narrs. of crime, incl. full acc. of KELLY and his gang, by a late Gov. of Ballarat Gaol.

*Highwaymen*

HARPER, C. G. Half-Hours with the Highwaymen, 2 vols.; ill. 42/ *n.* 8° Chapman 08
$16·80 *n.* Scribner, N.Y. The author's numerous other bks. on coaching [in I § 148] cont. frequent refs. to these fly-by-nights.

*Monetary Crimes*

DELMAR, Alex. History of Monetary Crimes; ill. $1 8° Hackensack, *New Jersey* 01

*Pirates* —*for Buccaneers v.* **E** § 54

BIDDULPH, Col. J. The Pirates of Malabar, etc.—*ut* **E** § 35

POOLE, S. Lane The Barbary Corsairs [Story of Natns.; $1·50 Putnam, *N.Y.*] 5/ c 8° Unwin [90]

*Poisoners* —*v. also* FUNCK-BRENTANO, *sup.*

THOMPSON, C. J. S. Poison Romance and Poison Mysteries 2/6 c 8° Scientific Press [ ] 02

*Privateering*

LAUGHTON, Prf. J. K. —*in his* Studies in Naval History [14–18 cents.], *ut* **F** § 30

NORMAN, C. B. —*in his* The Corsairs of France [17–19 cents.], *ut* **F** § 48

*Smugglers* —*v.* **D** § 117

*Criminals, Individually*

Autobiography of a Thief, ed. H. Hapgood $1·50 (6/) c 8° Putnam 04
A human documt.: an almost unrelievedly sordid, dismal narrative, largely in his own words.

BURKE (W.) [1792–1829] & HARE (W.) History of, and of the Resurrectionist Times. By G. Macgregor; ill. 7/6 8° Morison, *Glasgow* 84

CAMERON, Jane Memoirs of. By a Prison Matron, 2 vols. *o.p.* [*pb.* 21/] c 8° Hurst 64

LESURQUES. Exoffon (A.) The Lyons Mail, tr. R. H. Sherard 6/ c 8° Greening 03
A full acc. of the circumstances of the case, and a convincing proof of the guilt of LESURQUES.

**Police Courts:** *London:* Central Criminal Court (The); ill 168/ Eyre & Spottiswoode 10

'DOGBERRY' [ed. & ill.] Humours and Oddities of the London Police Courts; ill. [1800–1894] 2/6 c 8° Leadenhall Press 94

GAMON, H. R. P. The London Police Court, To-day and To-morrow 3/6 *n.* c 8° Dent 07
A valuable wk.—an investigation of police courts for the authorities of Toynbee Hall. Introd. by Canon BARNETT.

GREENWOOD, Jas. The Prisoner in the Dock 3/6 c 8° Chatto 02
Chatty articles, giving results of the author's observations in London police courts.

HOLMES, Thos. Pictures and Problems from London Police Courts 3/6 c 8° Arnold [00] 02

,, Known to the Police 10/6 *n.* 8° Arnold 08
Former $1·25, latter $3 *n.* Longman, N.Y. By a late Police Ct. missionary, now Sec. to Howard Assoc. Results of long experience of criminals.

TRAIN, A. The Prisoner at the Bar [8/6 Laurie] $1·50 12° Scribner, *N.Y.* [06] 08

*Bow Street Police Office*

**Police Dogs:** RICHARDSON, Maj. E. H. War, Police, and Watch Dogs—*ut* **I** § 15

FITZGERALD, Percy Chronicles of Bow Street Police Office, 2 vols.; ill. 21/ 8° Chapman 88

**Police Magistrates:** Biography of—*v.* **D** § 7

**Prisons**

GRIFFITHS, Maj. A. Secrets of the Prison House, 2 vols.; ill. 30/ 8° Chapman 94
Interestg. gaol-studies and sketches, by ex-Gov. of Wormwood Scrubbs and one of H.M.I.'s of Prisons, contg. a tolerably full acc. of foreign penal systs., incl. Amer., Russ., Moorish, Chinese, New Caledonian, etc., w. mass of observns. on crim. psychol. Opposed to LOMBROSO's theories of penology, and, though humane, by no means 'humanitarian'.

WINES, E. C. State of Prisons & Child-saving Institutions of World $5 8° Wilson, *Cambridge, Mass.* 80

*London* —*v. also* Police Cts., *sup.*, *s.n.* Central Crim. Ct. [Newg., Fleet, etc.]

MAYHEW (H.) + BINNY (J.) Criminal Prisons of London & Scenes of Prison Life ; ill. 10/6 i 8° Griffin 62

*Fleet (The)*

ASHTON, Jno. The Fleet, its River, Prison, and Marriages ; ill. 7/6 c 8° Unwin [88] 89

JESSOPP, Dr A. The Oeconomy of the Fleet [acc. of prison, *temp.* Jas. i] 7/6 s 4° Camden Soc. 80

*Millbank*

GRIFFITHS, Maj. A. Memorials of Millbank ; ill. 6/ 8° Chapman [75] 84

*Newgate ; Old Bailey*

GORDON, Chas. The Old Bailey and Newgate [$5 *n.* Pott, *N.Y.*] 21/ 8° Unwin 02

GRIFFITHS, Maj. A. Chronicles of Newgate ; ill. 6/ 8° Chapman [84] 95

*Dartmoor*

THOMSON, B. The Story of Dartmoor Prison 3/6 c 8° Heinemann 07

*Austria*

PELLICO, Silvio [1788–1854] Memoirs, tr. F. J. Crowest ; w. text [Le Mie Prigioni] 3/6 c 8° Walter Scott

*France*

BINGHAM, Cpt. D. A. The Bastile, its History and Chronicles, 2 vols., ill. 32/ 8° Chapman 88

DAVENPORT, R. A. Hist. of the Bastile and its Principal Captives 3/6 8° Routledge [4–]
$1·50 Dutton, *N.Y.* Appended is a *History of the Man in the Iron Mask.*

FUNCK-BRENTANO, F. Legends of the Bastille [tr.] ; ill. *o.p.* [*pb.* 6/] c 8° Ward & Downey 99
$1·75 Scribner, *N.Y.* Introd. by Victorien SARDOU. An attempt to 'whitewash' the Bastille.

HOPKINS, T. Dungeons of Old Paris : romance of celebr. prisons ; ill. $1·75 (7/6) 12° Putnam, *N.Y.* 97

*Malay : Singapore ; etc.*

MCNAIR (J. F. A.) + BAYLISS (W. D.) Prisoners their own Warders ; ill. & maps 10/6 8° Constable 99
An account of Singapore convict-prison, 1825–73 ; w. hist. of convict establmt. at Bencoolen, Penang, Malacca, fr. 1797.

*Russia*, and *Siberia* —*v. also* **E** §§ 25 and 39

DEUTSCH, L. Sixteen Years in Siberia [tr.], 2 vols ; ill.—*ut* **E** § 39

DE WINDT, Harry —*in his* Siberia as it is, *ut* **E** § 39
A futile attempt to counteract effects of KENNAN's bk. : wr. in good faith, though commonly charged w. bg. inspired by Russ. govt.

DOSTOIEFFSKY, FÉDOR Prison Life in Siberia, tr. H. S. Edwards *o.p.* [*pb.* 6/] c 8° Maxwell 87
Another tr. of the orig. [*House of the Dead*], by Marie v. THILO, was pubd. *s. tit. Buried Alive*, 10/6 c 8° Longman '81.

HOWARD, B. Prisoners of Russia [conv. life in Sakhalien & Sib.] $1·40 *n.* 12° Appleton, *N.Y.* 02

KENNAN, Geo. Siberia and the Exile System, 2 vols. ; ill. $6 8° Century Co., *N.Y.* 91
Author went out to Russia in 1885, an avowed defender of the Govt., and he was not quick to change his views ; his pictures here of the treatmt. of prisoners (not only political) are horrible to the last degree, and evidently truthful. Profusely and well ill.

KROPOTKIN, Pr'ce In Russian and French Prisons *o.p.* [*pb.* 7/6] c 8° Ward & Downey 87

SIMPSON, J. Y. Side-Lights on Siberia ; ill. [railrd., prisons, exile-syst.]—*ut* **E** § 39

YOUVATSHEV, J. P. The Russian Bastille ; or, the Schlusselburg Fortress [tr.] ; ill. 7/6 *n.* 8° Chatto 08

*United States*

FALKNER, Prf. R. P. [ed.] Statistics of Prisoners 50 c. 12° Amer. Acad. of Pol. & Soc. Sci., *Phila.* 93
Data (coll. by Wardens' Asso. of U.S. and Canada) rel. to *c.* 10,000 prisoners, w. analysis of the main results.

POWELL, Cpt. J. C. The American Siberia 50 c. 12° H. J. Smith, *Chicago* 91
Descr. of 14 yrs. in convict-camps of Florida, by the Cpt. of the Camp. A dreadful picture of the miseries and tortures of the convicts, worthy of Mid. Ages. Chiefly occup., however, w. escapes of prisoners and chasing of runaways by hounds.

*Elmira State Reformatory, New York*

New York State Reformatory at Elmira, Year-Bk. i *sqq.* 8° State Reformatory Pr., *N.Y.* 77 *sqq.*

WINTER, Alex. The N.Y. State Reformatory at Elmira [Social Science Ser.] 2/6 c 8° Sonnenschein 91
$1 Scribner, *N.Y.* An interesting account of the prison-reformatory experim., wh. aims at curing rather than punishing first offenders betw. 16 and 30 yrs. of age, by a syst. of educ. and discipline carried on by means of marks for labour, good conduct, and proficiency in study. Preface by Havelock ELLIS.

**Prison Labour :** Commissr. of Labor [Carroll D. WRIGHT] Second Rept. : Convict Labor in U.S. *gratis* 8° Govt. Prtg. Off., *Washgtn.* 87

MERIWETHER, L. —*in his* Afloat and Ashore on the Mediterranean, *ut* **E** § 11
Conts. suggestive facts and comments on convict labr. in Eur. and Am. Author has held post of Commissr. of Labr. Statistics for State of Missouri.

**Prison and Convict Life**

HORSLEY, Rev. J. W. Jottings from Jail : notes and papers on prison life 3/6 c 8° Unwin 87

„ Prisons and Prisoners 3/6 c 8° Pearson 98
On prison-life, reform, etc., by a Prison Chaplain : partly descriptive, partly controversial.

'No. 7' Twenty-Five Years in Seventeen Prisons ; ill. 3/6 c 8° Robinson 02
Apparently a genuine record ; w. much criticism of prison-methods.

ROBINSON, F. W. Female Life in Prison 2/6 c 8° Griffith & Farran [62] 92

„ Prison Characters drawn from Life 2/6 c 8° Griffith & Farran [ ] 92

SCOUGAL, Fces. Prisons and their Inmates : scenes fr. a silent world 2/ c 8° Blackwood 91

WILDE, Oscar —*v.* **K** § 89

*Australia*

BECKE, Louis — Old Convict Days — 6/ c 8° Unwin 99
Description of convict-life in Van Diemen's Land (Tasmania) 60 years ago.

„ +JEFFERY (Walt.) — A First Fleet Family — 6/ c 8° Unwin 96
Story of colonizn. of N.S.W., w. sketches of felon colonists and their governors. Thin thread of fictn. runs thro' it.

*New Caledonia*

GRIFFITH, Geo. — In an Unknown Prison Land ; ill. — 12 / *n.* 8° Hutchinson 01
Account of convicts and colonists in New Caledonia, w. jottings on the journey there and back.

„ — Sidelights on Convict Life ; ill. — 6/ c 8° Long 03
Author has had spec. facilities granted to him for writing of our convict estabmnts., and has also examd. the Fch. penal settlemt. of New Caledonia.

**Insurance and Crime**

CAMPBELL, A. C. — Insurance and Crime — $2·50 *n.* (10/6) 8° Putnam 02

**Political Crime and Political Prisoners**

PROAL, Judge L. — Political Crime [tr.] — [$1·50 Appleton, *N.Y.*] 6/ c 8° Unwin 98
A not very successful attempt to investigate crimes [war, corruption, etc.] committed in name of govt.

**Prisoners after Release from Gaol**

BOOTH, Maud B. C. — After Prison—What ? — 3/6 *n.* ($1·25 *n.*) c 8° Revell [03] 08

**Reformatories** — *v.* **D** § 169

**Prison Reformers**

BUXTON, Sir T. Fowell [1786–1845] Memoirs & Correspce. By C. Buxton *o.p.* [*pb.* 5/] p 8° Murray [48] 72

FRY, Elizab. [1780–1845]

- Ashby, J. M. — Elizabeth Fry — [Friends' Biog. Ser.] 1 / *n.* c 8° Headley 92
- Corder, S. — Life of Elizabeth Fry — [compiled fr. her jls.] 5 / *n.* c 8° Headley
- Cresswell, Fcs. — Memr. of E. Fry, *o.p.* [*pb.* 8/6] ; Abgd. [by her dau.] *o.p.* [*pb.* 3/6] c 8° Nisbet 56 ; 68
- Pitman, Mrs E. R. — Elizabeth Fry — [Eminent Women Series] 1 / p 8° W. H. Allen [84] 95

HILL, Fredc. [b. 1803 ; Inspector of Scottish Prisons]—*v.* **F** § 27

HOWARD, Jno. [1726–90]

- Dixon, W. Hepworth — John Howard and the Prison World of Europe *o.p.* [*pb.* 6/] 12° Jackson [49] 50
- Gibson, E. C. S. — Life of John Howard ; ill. — [Oxford Biogs.] 2/6 *n.* f 8° Methuen 01
- Stoughton, Dr J. — John Howard and his Friends — 7/6 c 8° Hodder 84

PELLICO, Silvio [1788–1854]

- Falletti, Marchesa Giulia — Silvio Pellico [tr.] — *o.p.* c 8° Bentley 66
A useful account of PELLICO, author of *Le Mie Prègioni*, and reformer of Turin prisons.

SKENE, Felicia M. F. [1821–99] Felicia Skene, of Oxford. By E. C. Rickards ; ill. 10/6 *n.* c 8° Murray 02
Known for her work in county gaols, etc.

**Police** — *for* Police Law *v.* **D** § 67

ADAM, H. L. — The Police Encyclopædia, 8 vols. ; ill. — ea. 5/ *n.* 8° Routledge 11

FREUND, Ernst. — The Police Power — $6 *n.* r 8° Univ. Press, *Chicago*

FULD, L. F. — Police Administration — $3 *n.* (12/6 *n.*) 8° Putnam 10
A valuable critical study of police organizations in U.S. and in Europe.

HALE, G. W. *etc.* — Police and Prison Cyclopædia — $4 r 8° Richardson, *Boston* 94
21/ Eyre & Spottiswoode. Details of police and prison syst. in U.S., prison-discipline, managemt., punishmts., food, statistics, Cts., etc.

MAITLAND, F. W. — Justice and Police — [English Citizen Series] *o.p.* [*pb.* 3/6] c 8° Macmillan 85

Metropolitan Police (The) — [ser. of arts. repr. fr. *Times*] 6*d.* 8° *Times* Book Club 09

TIEDEMAN, C. O. — Treatise on the Limitation of Police Power in U.S. — $6 8° Thomas, *St Louis* 86
From both the civil and the criminal aspects.

*History*

LEE, Capt. W. L. M. — History of Police in England — 7/6 c 8° Methuen 02
The only wk. giving an acc. of institns. for the maintenance of order fr. earliest times to the present.

*Australia :* HAYDON (A. L.) The Trooper Police of Australia ; ill. — 10/6 *n.* m 8° Melrose 11

KENNEDY, E. — Black Police of Queensland ; ill. — 10/6 *n.* 8° Murray 02
Reminiscences of official work and personal adventures in the early days of the Colony.

*Canada : Royal North-West Mounted Police*

DONKIN, J. G. — Trooper and Redskin — [life in N.-W. Police, 1884–8] 8/6 r 8° Low 89

HAYDON, A. L. — The Riders of the Plains ; ill. — 10/6 *n.* m 8° Melrose 10
An authoritative record of this fine force, based on official documts., by one who has been in close touch w. the corps.

**Detectives**

MURRAY, J. W. Incidents in the Life of : memoirs of a great detective ; ed. V. Speer ; ill. — [10/ *n.* Heinemann] $2 *n.* 8° Baker, *N.Y.* 05

PINKERTON, Allan — Professional Thieves and the Detectives — $1·50 12° Dillingham, *N.Y.* 90

**Executioners**

SANSON FAMILY Memrs. of: fr. priv. documts. [1688–1847]. By H. Sanson [tr.] 3/6 c 8° Chatto [76] 82
Memrs. of the Fch. family of executioners. Conts. lucid acc. of most notable *causes célèbres* fr. time of Louis XIV to a recent period.

## 124 : LOCAL AND MUNICIPAL GOVERNMENT AND TAXATION

*Vide also* **D** §§ 67, 91, 135 : Law of Taxation, **D** § 117 : Imperial Finance and Taxation

**Bibliography**

BROOKS, R. C. Municipal Affairs : bibliography [a subject-index ; 6/ *n.* King] $1·50 8° Reform Club, *N.Y.* 02

GOMME, G. Laur. Literature of Local Institns. [annot. bibliogr. ; Bk.-Lover's Lib.] 4/6 f 8° Stock [86] 91

GROSS, Dr Chas. Bibliography of British Municipal History $2·50 *n.* (12/) 8° Longman 98
[Harvard Historical Studies.] Classif., annot. and freely indexed. Includes also Gilds and Parliamentary Representation.

Lib. of Congress : Select hist. of Books on Municipal Affairs, ed. A. P. C. Griffin
10 c. 4° Govt. Printing Off., *Washington* 06

WELCH, Chas. Notes on London Municipal Literature—*ut* **E** § 17

**Generally ; Europe**

ASHLEY, Percy Local and Central Government 10/6 *n.* 8° Murray 06
A valuable study of England in comparison w. France, Prussia, and U.S. by a lecturer at Lond. Schl. of Economics, contg. *inter alia* acc. of reforms of BISMARCK and von MIQUEL and hist. of Fch. centralization. *Vide* also in his *Surveys* —*ut* **D** § 114.

CLEVELAND, Dr F. A. Chapters on Municipal Administrn. & Accounting $2 *n.* (7/6 *n.*) c 8° Longman 09
By Director of Bureau of Munic. Research, *N.Y.* Wr. mainly for Amer. readers.

Corporations and Public Welfare. By many authorities $1·50 8° Acad. of Pol. Sci., *Phila.* 00
Deals with all aspects of municipal activity.

ELY, Prf. R. T. The Coming City [reforms, etc.] 60 c. *n.* c 8° Crowell, *N.Y.* 02

FAIRLIE, Prf. J. A. Essays in Municipal Administration $2·50 *n.* (10/6 *n.*) 8° Macmillan [01] 08
A moderate study of munic. tradg. and other munic. activities, dealg. largely w. Amer., but 4 chs. devoted to Gt. Brit. and other Eur. cities.

GOMME, G. Laur. Lectures on the Principles of Local Government 12/ 8° Constable 97

GOODNOW, Prf. F. J. Municipal Problems $1·50 (6/6 *n.*) 12° Macmillan 97
[Columbia Univ. Studs.] Exams. probl. of effective and pure munic. govt. Much informatn. ab. Engl. towns.

,, Politics and Administration $1·50 *n.* 8° Macmillan, *N.Y.* 00

,, Municipal Government $3 *n.* 8° Century Co., *N.Y.* 09

GRICE, J. W. Review of the Relations betw. Central and Local Authorities in Engl., Frce., Belg., and Prussia dur. 19 Cent. 10/6 *n.* 8° P. S. King & Son 10

HAW, Geo. To-day's Work : munic. govt. the hope of democracy 2/6 *n.* c 8° *Clarion* Co. 01

JOWETT, F. W. The Socialist and the City [Labr. Ideal Ser.] 1/ *n.* c 8° G. Allen 07

Municipal Program (A) : Propositions for Municipal Reform, by the National League
$1·00 *n.* 12mo Macmillan, *N.Y.* 00

MUNRO, Prf. W. B. The Government of European Cities $2·50 *n.* (10/6 *n.*) 8° Macmillan 09
An excellent guide to civic affairs, comparing municipal administration of America w. those of France, of Prussia (incidentally of Germy.) and of Engl. (incid. of Scotld.). Does not deal w. munic. taxation.

NEWMAN, Dr Geo. Service of the State [Social Service Hdbks.] 1/6 *n.* c 8° Headley 07

ROWE, Prf. L. S. Problems of City Government $1·50 *n.* c 8° Appleton, *N.Y.* 09
[Pubns. of Univ. of Pennsylvania.] An anal. of the general princs. involved in growth of a city, tracg. hist. of munic. govt. fr. earliest to mod. times. Latter (larger) pt. of bk. devoted to munic. ownership.

SHAW, Dr A. Municipal Govt. in Continental Europe $2 *n.* 8° Macmillan *N.Y.* [96] 01
7/6 *n.* Unwin. An able wk. The ch. entitled *The British System in Operation* is one of the best accs. of our syst. of munic. electns.

WHINERY, S. Municipal Public Works : inceptn., constrn., managmt. $1·50 *n.* (6/ *n.*) c 8° Macmillan 03

WILCOX, D. F. Municipal Franchises, vols. i–ii [ea. 21/ *n.* Constable] ea. $5 8° Gervaise Pr., *N.Y.* 10

WILLARD, C. D. City Government for Young People 50 c. *n.* (2/6 *n.*) c 8° Macmillan 06

**Municipal Law, Parish Councils**—*v.* **D** § 67

**City Development, and Planning**—*v. also* **D** § 119, *s.v.* Garden Cities

BENTLEY (E. G.) + TAYLOR (S. P.) Town Planning Schemes : pract. guide 5/ *n* 8° Philip 11

GEDDES, Prf. Patr. City Development : study of parks, gardens, and culture instits.
21/ *n.* 8° Geddes & Colleagues, *Edin.* 04
A valuable report on the possibilities of Pittencrieff Park, wr. at request of Carnegie Dunfermline Trust. Well ill.

HORSFALL, T. C. The Example of Germany [Mancs. Univ. Pbs.] 1/ *n.* c 8° Sherratt, *Mancs.* 04
Sets forth Germ. munic. methods of controlling developmt. of city-suburbs—bdg.-sites and houses.

MEAKIN, Budgett Model Factories and Villages—*ut* **D** § 127, *s.v.* Housing of Poor

ROBINSON, C. M. Improvements in Towns and Cities $1·25 *n.* (5/ *n.*) c 8° Putnam 01

TRIGGS, H. Inigo Town Planning, Past, Present, and Possible ; ill. 15/ *n.* r 8° Methuen 09

UNWIN, Raymond Town Planning in Practice 21/ *n.* r 8° Unwin 09

WHITEHOUSE, J. H. Problems of a Scottish Provincial Town 3/6 *n.* c 8° G. Allen 05
Study of an average-sized town, w. detailed suggestions for a reconstructive policy. Bibliogr.

**Finance :** GRICE (J. W.) National and Local Finance—*ut* **D** § 117

WEBB, Sid. Grants in Aid : a criticism and a proposal 5/ *n.* 8° Longman 11

**Growth and Influence of Cities**

JAMES, Prf. Edm. The Growth of Great Cities 25 c. 8° Acad. of Pol. Sci., *Phila.* 99
Not concerned with causes, but with general statistics.

STRONG, Rev. Josiah The Twentieth Century City 25 c. 12° Baker & Taylor, *N.Y.* 98

,, Challenge of the City [Story of the Churches] $1 *n.* 12° Baker & Taylor, *N.Y.* 08
Argues that, since conserv. influences grow weaker as the city grows larger and since the town populn. under existg. condns. is degenerating, the city will eventually control the nation greatly to its disadvantage and peril. Proposes a compreh. plan for religious work jointly betw. the Xtn. denominatns.

WEBER, A. F. The Growth of Cities in Nineteenth Century $3·50 *n.* 8° Macmillan, *N.Y.* 99
16/ P. S. King & Co. [Columbia University Studies.] A statistical study.

**Municipal Engineering and Sanitation**—*v. also* **I** § 8

BAKER, M. N. Municipal Engineering and Sanitation $1·25 *n.* (5/ *n.*) c 8° Macmillan 02

CHAPIN, C. V. Municipal Sanitatn. in U.S. ; ill. [25/ P. S. King & Son] $5 r 8° Snow, *Providence, R.I.* 01

GOODHUE, W. F. Municipal Improvements : manl. of methods $1·75 c 8° Wiley, *N.Y.* [ ] 03

**England**

ASHLEY, Percy Local Government [Shilling Scientific Series] 1/ *n.* c 8° Jack 05

CHALMERS, M. D. Local Government [English Citizen Series] *o.p.* [*pb.* 3/6] c 8° Macmillan [83] 93

,, The same, Series ii *o.p.* [*pb.* 15/] 8° Macmillan [71–2] 75
The second Ser. presents the best view of systems of Scotl., Irel., Austral., Holland, Belg., France, Russia, Spain.

CHAPMAN, Prf. S. J. Local Government & State Aid [Social Science Ser.] 2/6 c 8° Sonnenschein 99
$1 Scribner, *N.Y.* Essay on effect of loc. admin. and fin. on paymt. to loc. authorits. of cert. impl. taxes.

County Councils, Municipal Corporations, and Local Authorities Companion 10/6 8° Kelly 89 *sqq., ann.*
Statistical information, with historical notes : complete lists of officials, etc.

DOLMAN, F. Municipalities at Work [Social Questions] 2/6 c 8° Methuen 95
Account of municipal policies of B'ham, Mancs., L'pool, Glasgow, Bradfd., and Leeds. Introd. Sir J. HUTTON.

DYKES, D. C. Scottish Local Government [expository lects.] 1/ *n.* c. 8° Oliphant, *Edin.* 07

GOMME, G. Laur. Index of Municipal Offices ; w. histor. introd. [Index Soc.] 10/6 s 4° Longman 79

GOSCHEN, G. J. Reports and Speeches on Local Taxation *o.p.* [*pb.* 5/] r 8° Macmillan 72

HOWE, F. C. The British City : beginnings of democracy 7/6 *n.* c 8° Unwin 07

JENKS, Prf. Edw. An Outline of Engl. Local Govt. 2/6 *n.* c 8° Methuen [94] 07
An excellent little treatise—lucid, orderly and intelligent ; based on a course of 'lay lects.' at Univ. Coll., L'pool.

LAUDER, A. E. The Municipal Manual 3/6 *n.* c 8° P. S. King & Son 07
A useful attempt to provide a popular introdn. to the scheme of Engl. local govt. and descrn. of constitn. and functns. of urban authorities.

LOWELL, Prf. A. L. The Government of England, 2 vols.—*ut* **D** § 140

MALTBIE, M. R. English Local Govt. of To-day [Col. Univ. Contribs.] $2 *n.* 8° Macmillan, *N.Y.* 97

,, British Cities & their Problems [Citizens' Library] $1·25 *n.* (5/ *n.*) 12° Macmillan

MAXWELL, R. C. English Local Government [Temple Primers ; 40 c. *n.* Macm., *N.Y.*] 1/ *n.* 12° Dent 05

MEREWETHER (H. A.) + STEPHENS (A. J.) Hist. of the Boroughs & Municipal Corporations in U.K., 3 v. *o.p.* r 8° *London* 35
From the earliest to the present time. The standard authority.

Municipal Year-Book of the United Kingdom : ed. R. Donald 7/6 *n.* 8° E. Lloyd *ann.*

ODGERS (Dr W. B.) + NALDRETT (E. J.) Local Govt. [Engl. Citizen Ser.] 3/6 ($1) c 8° Macmillan [99] 07
Replaces CHALMERS' book [*ut sup.*] in the same series.

PROBYN, J. W. [ed.] Local Government and Taxation [Cobden Club Essays] 15/ 8° Cassell 75

,, Local Govern. and Taxatn. in U.K. [Cobden Club Essays] 5/ c 8° Cassell 82

RATHBONE (W.) + PELL (A.) + MONTAGUE (F. C.) Local Govern. and Taxation [Imp. Parl. Ser.] 1/ c 8° Sonnenschein 85

REDLICH, Prf. J. Local Govt. in England [tr.], 2 vols. 21/ *n.* ($6·50 *n.*) 8° Macmillan 03
An able, critical, and exhaustive work, though with political bias. Additions by F. W. HIRST.

SHAW, Dr A. Municipal Government in Great Britain [7/6 *n.* Unwin] $2 *n.* 8° Macmillan, *N.Y.* [95] 01
A readable and stimulatg. bk. After a general acc. of rise of Brit. towns and of the Brit. syst. in operatn., separate studies of Glasgow, Mancs., and B'ham follow, succeeded by ch. on social activities of Brit. towns and 2 chs. on govt. of London.

SKEEL, C. A. J. Council in the Marches : study in local government 7/6 8° Rees 04

SUTHERS, R. B. Mind your own Business 2/6 *n.* c 8° *Clarion* Press 05
Full of facts and statistics popularly and, despite its title, well stated.

*London* —*v. also* **D** § 67

FIRTH, J. F. B. Municipal London *o.p.* [*pb.* 25/] *r.* 8° Longman 76

HOPKINS, A. B. The Boroughs of the Metropolis [hdbk. to Act of 1899] 7/6 *n.* 8° Bemrose 00

LLOYD, Jno. London Municipal Govt.: hist. of a gt. reform 21/ *n.* r 4° P. S. King & Son 10
Hist. of the movemt. (1880–8) wh. resulted in passing the Lond. Govt. Act 1888 and consequent establishmt. of L.C.C., by Hon. Sec. of Munic. Reform League. 21 illns.

London County Council: London Statistics, vols. i–xix; maps, etc. ea. 5/ P. S. King & Son 95–09 *in prg.*

London Reform Union: London To-day and To-morrow [proposals f. reform of govt.] 1/ 8° P. S. King & Son 08

SCHOOLING, J. H. London County Council Finance 2/6 *n.* 8° Murray 07
From the beginning to March 1907; 57 tables and 21 diagrams.

SEAGER, J. R. Government of London under Act of 1899 2/6 c 8° P. S. King & Son 99

WEBB, Sid. The London Programme [Social Science Series] 2/6 c 8° Sonnenschein [91]
$1 Scribner, *N.Y.* Also cheap edn. 1/ (no Amer. ch. edn.). Practically a compl. text-bk. of Lond. Liberal Programme; w. concl. ch. *London as it might be.*

WHELEN, F. London Government [impartial] 3/6 c 8° Richards 98

WRIGHT (R. S.) + HOBHOUSE (H.) Outline of Local Government and Local Taxation in England and Wales 7/6 8° P. S. King & Son [ ] 06

*Traffic*

Royal Commission on London Traffic: Report, Evidence, etc., 8 vols.; maps £8 4*s.* 8*d.* f° Wyman 05–6

*Water-supply*

RICHARDS (H. C.) + PAYNE (W. H. C.) London Water Supply, ed. J. P. H. Soper 6/ *n.* 8° P. S. King & Son [ ] 99
A compendium of hist., law, and transactns. rel. to Metrop. Water Cos. fr. earliest times.

SHADWELL, Arth. The London Water Supply 5/ ($1·75) c. 8° Longman 99

SISLEY, Dr Rich. The London Water Supply; maps and plans 21/ 4° Scientific Press 99

*Norwich*

HAWKINS, C. B. Norwich: a social study 5/ *n.* c 8° Warner 10
Industries, condns. of labour, unemploymt., pauperism, finance, charities, relig. life, etc.

**Scotland**

ATKINSON, Mabel Local Government in Scotland 5/ *n.* c 8° Blackwood 04

WHITEHOUSE, J. H. Problems of a Scottish Provincial Town 3/6 *n.* c 8° G. Allen 05

*Glasgow*

BELL (J.) + PATON (J.) Glasgow, its Munic. Organizn. & Administrn. 21/ *n.* 8° MacLehose, *Glasgow* 96

*Ireland:* CLANCY (J. J.) Handbk. of Local Govt. in Ireland 7/6 r 8° Sealy, *Dublin* 01

**Germany**

JAMES, E. J. Municipal Administration in Germany [Halle] 50 c. 8° Univ. Press, *Chicago* 01

LUNN, Dr H. S. Municipal Lessons from Southern Germany; ill. 2/ 8° Unwin 08
Observns. of a visit in 1907 to Frankft., Nurembg., Munich, Heidelbg., Mannheim, Königswinter, Cologne.

POLLARD, Jas. A Study in Municipal Government: Corporation of Berlin 3/6 c 8° Blackwood 94

**United States**

CLEVELAND, Dr F. A. Chapters on Munic. Administrn. and Accounting $2 *n.* (7/6 *n.*) c 8° Longman 09

CLOW, F. R. Compar. Study of City Finances [Am. Econ. Ass.; 3/6 Sonnenschein] $1 *n.* 8° Macmillan, *N.Y.* 01

EATON, Hon. D. B. The Government of Municipalities $4 *n.* (17/) 8° Macmillan 99
A thorough and constr. crit. of Amer. municipalities; deals especially with 'Tammany'.

GOODNOW, Prf. F. J. Municipal Home Rule: study in administration—*ut* **D** § 67
[Columbia Univ. Studs.] A somewhat abstruse expositn. of the technicalities of Amer. munic. law, w. Introd. and final ch. on the broad characteristics of local govt. in general, comparing Amer. w. Brit. and contin. methods.

" City Govt. in the United States $1·25 *n.* c 8° Century Co., *N.Y.* 05

Johns Hopkins University Studies—*ut* **D** § 114

ROSEWATER, Dr V. Special Assessments: study in munic. finance [Col. Univ. Studs.] $1 *n.* 8° Macmillan, *N.Y.* [93] 98

STEFFENS, L. The Shame of the Cities 5/ *n.* c 8° Heinemann 04
A systematic enquiry into the state of municipal politics in the large Amer. cities, showing an almost incredible picture of corruption.

TOLMAN, Dr W. H. Municipal Reform Movement $1 12° Revell, *N.Y.* 95
A system. hdbk. sketchg. city-functns., describg. 58 city reform-clubs, 13 general organizns. for civic improvemt., 8 women's reform-clubs and methods and organizn. of City Vigilance League.

WILCOX, D. F. The Amer. City: study in democracy [Citizens' Lib.] $1·25 *n.* (5/ *n.*) c 8° Macmillan 04

" A Study of City Government $1·50 *n.* c 8° Macmillan 97

ZUEBLIN, Prf. C. Amer. Municip. Progress: chaps. in munic. sociology $1·25 *n.* (5/ *n.*) c 8° Macmillan 02
[Citizens' Lib.] A good and comprehensive account of municipal activities.

" A Decade of Civic Development $1·25 *n.* c 8° Univ. Press, *Chicago* 05

*Massachussetts*

ALLINSON (E. P.) + PENROSE (B.) Philadelphia : 1681–1887 $3 8° Johns Hopk. Univ. Pr., *Baltim.* 87

WHITTEN, R. H. Public Admin. in Massachussetts [Col. Univ. Studs.] $1 *n.* 8° Macmillan, *N.Y.* 97
On the relation of Central to Local activity.

*Michigan and Ohio*

WILCOX, Dr D. F. Municipal Govt. in Michigan & Ohio [Col. Univ. Studs.] $1 *n.* 8° Macmillan, *N.Y.* 96

*New York*

COLER, B. S. Municipal Government . . . of New York $1 12° Appleton, *N.Y.* 00
Chiefly valuable for its crit. of the Greater N.Y. Charter ; by a former Comptroller of N.Y.

DURAND, Prf. E. D. The Finances of New York City $2 (7/6) 8° Macmillan, *N.Y.* 98
A good account of the Tammany mismanagement and its consequences.

FAIRLIE, Prf. J. A. Centralisn. of Administratn. in N.Y. State [Col. Univ. Studs.] $1 *n.* 8° Macm., *N.Y.* 98

HODDER, A. A Fight for the City $1·50 *n.* (6/ *n.*) c 8° Macmillan, *N.Y.* 03
A brightly written acc. of a campaign against Tammany in N.Y.

*Providence, Rhode Island*

KIRK, Prf. Wm. [ed.] A Modern City : Providence, Rhode Isl. & its activities ; ill.
[by var. wrs.] $2·50 *n.* 8° Univ. Press, *Chicago* 09

**History** —*v. also* **F** § 17

FORDHAM, E. Mary Evolution of Local and Imperial Govt. fr. Teutonic Conquest 6/ *n.* c 8° Knight 03
Mainly historical, followed by a good short acc. of positn. of women in local govt. in pres. day.

SMITH, J. Toulmin The Parish *pub.* 18/ ; *red.* to 9/ 8° Sweet 57

THOMPSON, J. Essay on English Municipal History *o.p.* [*pb.* 5/] p 8° Longman 67

VINE, J. R. S. Engl. Munic. Institns. : growth & developmt. [statist. : 1835–79] 10/6 r 8° Waterlow 79

*WEBB, Sid. + Beatr. English Local Government from the Revolution to Municipal Corporations
Act : The Manor and the Borough, Pts. i–ii 8° Longman 06–8

i : *The Parish and the Council*, 16/ *n.* ($4 *n.*) ; ii : *The Manor and the Borough*, 2 vols. 25/ *n.* ($7 *n.*). A minute and luminous investign. crowded w. detail—conducted not in spirit of the antiquary but w. eye to realities of interest to the politician, the historian, and the economist—of a vast mass of prtd. and MS. matl., exhibitg. the local institns. at work (fr. 1689 to 1834–5) : casts a flood of light on a buried Engld. Pt. i describes those pts. of the organizn. of local admin. wh., by reason of their comprehensiveness and uniformity, may be regarded as 'national' ; ii–iii deal w. the exceptns. to this natl. system, e.g. those exemptns., immunities, and franchises wh. enabled the inhabitants of partic. localities to exclude the authority of the county at large, and to thus enjoy self-govt. ; iv will be devoted to specialized authorities, e.g. Turnpike Trustees, and Street Commissioners.

*Beverley :* LEACH (A. E.) [ed.] Beverley Town Documents—*ut* **D** § 5 [14–15 cents.]

*Cambridge*

*MAITLAND, Prf. F. W. Township & Borough [$2·50 *n.* Putn., *N.Y.* ; Ford Lects.] 10/ r 8° Camb. Pr. 98

*Glasgow*

BELL (Sir J.) + PATON (J.) Glasgow : its munic. organisatn. & admin. ; ill. 21/ *n.* 4° MacLehose, *Glasg.* 96

Corporn. of Glasgow Municipal Enterprise : Glasgow 2/ *n.* c 8° Anderson, *Glasgow* 04
A souvenir of 22nd Congress of Sanit. Institute, 1894. Acc. of the most advanced municipality in Gt. Brit.

*Leicester :* BATESON (Mary) Records of Borough of Leicester, 3 vols.—*ut* **E** § 17, *s.v.* Leicester

*Liverpool*

MUIR (Prf. R.) + PLATT (Edith M.) Hist. of Municipal Govt. in Liverpool [to 1835] 21/ *n.* 4° Williams 06
In 2 Pts., the latter (and longer) bg. a colln. of charters, leases, etc., in Lat., Norm.-Fch., and Engl., w. transcriptns., trs., and notes (by PLATT), the former (by MUIR) consistg. of a long narrative Introd. on hist. of developmt. of munic. govt. in L'pool.

*London* —*v. also* **E** § 17

BEAVEN, Rev. A. B. The Aldermen of the City of London, 2 vols. [1278 *sqq.*] 21/ *n.* 8° Eden Fisher 08

BIRCH, W. de G. [ed.] Histor. Charters & Constit. Documents of City of London 5/ r 8° Whiting [84] 87

GOMME, G. Laur. The Governance of London 15/ *n.* 8° Unwin 07
Roman London, in wh. he finds the key to hist. of the City, and that of Norman and Plantagenet London.

NORTON, Geo. Comm. on Hist., Constitn. & Chart. Franch. of C. of Lond. *o.p.* [*pb.* 14/] 8° Longm. [28] 69

ROUND, J. Hor. The Commune of London, and other Studies 12/6 *n.* 8° Constable 99

WEBB, Sid. + Beatr. —hist. of Corporn. of City of Lond., *in their* Engl. Local Govt., *sup.*

*Southampton*

HEARNSHAW, Dr F. J. C. Leet Jurisdiction in England, espec. as ill. by the Records of the Court
Leet of Southampton 21/ r 8° Cox & Sharland, *S'hptn.* 08
A careful study, prefaced by a valuable histor. acc. of the Court Leet generally, bringing out the striking differences betw. the legal theories of these Cts. and their actual workg.

*Wirral* (Cheshire)

STEWART-BROWN (R.) The Wapentake of Wirral ; ill. 10/6 *n.* 4° Young, *L'pool* 07
Conts. aln ost unbroken informn. as to the Hundred Ct. of Wirral fr. 1352 to its abolitn. in 1856.

*United States*

HOWARD, Prf. G. E. Introd. to Local Constit. Hist of U.S., v. i $3 8° Johns Hopk. Univ. Pr., *Baltim.*, 89
This vol. deals w. the Development of the Township, Hundred, and Shire.

**Police**—*v.* **D** § 123 **Public Health**—*v.* **H*** § 55 **Rating and Taxation**—*for* Law *v.* **D** § 67

*England*

BAKER, C. Ashmore — Rates — 2/6 *n.* 4° P. S. King & Son 10
Outl. and comparison of revenue and expenditure of Boroughs and Urban Distr. C'cils of 10,000 or more inhabs. (Engl. and Wales).

BLUNDEN, G. H. — Local Taxation and Finance [$1 Scribner, *N.Y.*] 2/6 c 8° Sonnenschein 95

BOYLE (E.) + DAVIES (G. H.) Principles of Rating—*ut* **D** § 67, *s.v.* Rating

GRAHAM, J. C. — Taxation, Local & Imperial, & Local Govt., ed. M. D. Warmington 2/ c 8° P. S. King & Son [95] 99

HALL, Bolton [ed.] — Who Pays your Taxes? [Questions of the Day] $1·25 (4/) 12° Putnam 92
Colln. of essays by var. wrs. (incl. one by Dr. WELLS, the well-known free-trader) attackg. pres. syst. of U.S. local taxatn.

NICHOLSON, Prf. J. S. — Rates and Taxes as affecting Agriculture—*ut* **D** § 117

O'MEARA, J. J. — Municipal Taxation at Home and Abroad, Local Govt. Indebtedness and Valuation 7/6 c 8° Cassell 94
Colln. of a gt. number of facts and figs. rel. to Gt. Brit., the Colonies, the Continent, and America: w. discussn. of princs. and statistics.

ROW-FOGO, J. — Reform of Local Taxation in England 6/ *n.* c 8° Macmillan 02
A thorough examination based on the Report of the Royal Commission.

SARGANT, C. H. — Urban Rating *o.p.* [*pb.* 6/] 8° Longman 90

*London*

LANGE, M. E. — Local Taxation in London; pref. by L'd Welby 1/ *n.* 8° P. S. King & Son 06

*History*

CANNAN, Edwin — The History of Local Rates in England 2/6 *n.* c 8° P. S. King & Son 96
A very good little bk., giving hist. of cases by wh. rating has been brgt. to its pres. certain form and all traces of rating of personality got rid of.

*History: Scotland*

TURNER, S. H. — History of Local Taxation in Scotland 5/ *n.* 8° Blackwood 08

**Municipal Ownership, Monopolies, Trading**

AVEBURY, L'd — On Municipal and National Trading [adverse] 2/6 ($1) 8° Macmillan [06] 07

BEMIS, E. W. — Municipal Monopolies [Lib. of Economics; copious statistics] $2 12° Crowell, *N.Y.* 99

CARR, C. T. — Collective Ownership otherwise than by Corporations or Trusts [Yorke Prize Essay; $1·50 *n.* Putnam, *N.Y.*] 5/ *n.* 8° Camb. Press 07

DARWIN, Maj. Leon. — Municipal Trade: advantages and disadvs. [$3·50 *n.* Dutton, *N.Y.*] 12/ *n.* 8° Murray [03] 07

,, — Municipal Ownership 2/6 *n.* c 8° Murray 07
4 lectures at Harvard on the dangers of direct employmt. of labour and municipal ownership.

DAVIES, D. H. — The Cost of Municipal Trading [an address] 2/ i 8° P. S. King & Son 99

HAW, G. — To-day's Work—*ut sup.* [strongly Progressive]

MEYER, Prf. H. R. — Government Regulation of Railway Rates $1·50 *n.* (6/6 *n.*) c 8° Macmillan 05

,, — Municipal Ownership in Great Britain $1·50 *n.* (6/6 *n.*) c 8° Macmillan 06

,, — The British State Telegraphs $1·50 *n.* (6/6 *n.*) c 8° Macmillan 07

,, — Public Ownership & the Telephone in Great Britain $1·50 *n.* (6/6 *n.*) c 8° Macmillan 07
By a critic adverse to public ownership, sometime assist. Prf. of Pol. Econ. in Univ. of Chicago.

National Civic Federn. Commissn.: Report on Publ. Ownership and Operatn., vols. i–iii 39/6 r 8° P. S King & Son 08
Data gathered in U.K. and Amer. by 25 expert accountants, engineers, economists, etc., on Gas, Water, Electric Lighting and Power, and Tramways.

POND, O. L. — Municipal Control of Public Utilities [Columb. Univ. Studs.] $1 *n.* 8° Macmillan 07

PORTER, Hon. Rob. P. — The Dangers of Municipal Trading [2/6 *n.* Routledge] $1·80 *n.* c 8° Century Co., *N.Y.* 07
Pays spec. attention to Gt. Brit., tho' touchg. on other countries, w. spec. chs. on Austral. and Russia. Gives brief hist. of munic. ownership here and sets out certain serious aspects of munic. positn. w. view of indicatg. prob. effects of extensn. of syst. in U.S.

Relation of Mod. Municipalities to Quasi-Public Wks. [Am. Ec. Ass.; 2/6 Sonnenschein] 75 c. *n.* 8° Macm., *N.Y.* 88

ROWE, Prf. L. S. — —*in his* Problems of City Government, *ut sup.*

SHAW, G. Bern. — Commonsense of Munic. Tradg. [Fabian Socialist Ser.] 1/ *n.* c 8° Fifield [04] 08

TOWLER, W. G. — Socialism in Local Government [$1·50 *n.* Macmillan, *N.Y.*] 2/6 *n.* c 8° G. Allen [08] 09
By the Sec. to London Munic. Soc., organized in 1894 to oppose 'Progressive Socialist' politics of L.C.C.

*Gas*

BEMIS, Dr Edw. W. — Munic. Ownership of Gas in U.S. [Am. Ec. Ass.; 2/6 Sonnenschein] $1 *n.* 8° Macmillan, *N.Y.* 90

JAMES, Dr E. J. — Reln. of Mod. Municipality to Gas Supply [Am. Ec. Ass.; 2/6 Sonnenschein] 75 c. *n.* 8° Macmillan, *N.Y.* 86

**Fires and Fire-Brigades** —*for* Fire-Engine Construction *v.* **I** § 12

BRAIDWOOD, J. S. — Fire, its Prevention and Extinguishing 2/6 *n.* 8° Bell (C. & E. Layton) 66

British Fire Prevention Committee: Publications, vols. i–*sqq.* 1, *Waterloo Pl., Lond.* 98 *sqq.*

MUNDELL — Stories of the Fire Brigade [popular] 1/6 c 8° Partridge 99
ORTON-SMITH, H. — Fire Brigades : constitn., rts., respons. [U.K.] 5/ 8° C. & E. Layton [ ]
ROCKWELL, Gen. — *—article* Fire Extinction, *in* Encyclo. Brit., ed. 9, vol. ix, *ut* **K** § 1
SACHS, E. O. — Fires and Public Entertainments 12/6 *n.* 8° Layton 98
Statistics of all known fires in public buildings wh. were attended by serious loss of life. Some 1100 dur. past 100 yrs.
,, — Facts on Fire Prevention, 2 vols. ; fully ill. 25/ *n.* l 8° Batsford 02
A valuable contribution to the art of fire-proof construction.
,, — Urban Fire Protection 1/ 8° Batsford 95
,, — What is Fire Protection ? 1/ *n.* 8° Fire Prot. Prev. Com. [97] 99
SHAW, Cpt. E. M. — Fire Protection : organizn., wkg., etc., of Lond. Fire Brigade 5/ *n.* 8° Layton [77]
,, — Fire Surveys and Risks : summary of principles 5/ 8° Wilson [72] 82
,, — Fires in Theatres 3/ p 8° Spon [76] 89
YOUNG, C. F. T. — Fires, Fire Engines, and Fire Brigades ; ill. *o.p.* [*pb.* 24/] 8° Lockwood 66

*United States*

COSTELLO, A. E. — Our Firemen : hist. of N.Y. Fire Departmts., Volunteer and Paid ; ill. $6 8° Costello, *N.Y.* 87
DOWNES, A. M. — Fire Fighters and their Pets ; ill. $1·50 8° Harper 07
FORD, J. L. — The Third Alarm ; ill. [story of N.Y. fire dept.] $1 12° Brentano, *N.Y.* [93] 07
GERHARD, W. P. — Theatre Fires and Panics $1·50 c 8° Wiley, *N.Y.* 96
HILL, C. T. — Fighting a Fire $1·50 c 8° Century Co., *N.Y.* 97
ROPER, S. — Instructions for Engineers and Firemen $2 c 8° McKay, *Phila.*
WAKEMAN, W. H. — Practical Guide for Firemen 75 c. 12° Am. Indust. Pb. Co., *Bridgept.* 96

**Smoke Problem**

GRAHAM, J. W. — Destruction of Daylight : study in smoke probl. 2/6 *n.* f 8° G. Allen 07

# XI : Social Economy

## 125 : GENERAL AND COLLECTIVE TREATISES, ETC.

**Bibliography and Study** —*v.* **D** § 114 ; *also* Fairbanks, *and* Giddings, *Principles, inf.*

**Encyclopaedia**

BLISS (W. D. P.) + BINDER (Dr R. M.) New Encyclopaedia of Social Reform—*ut* **D** § 114

**Series** —*v.* **D** § 114

**Systematic, Critical, and Historical Treatises**

ADDAMS, Jane — Democracy and Social Ethics—*ut* **D** § 139, *s.v.* Democracy
,, — Newer Ideals of Peace [Citizens' Lib.] $1·25 *n.* (5/ *n.*) c 8° Macmillan 07
Traces the displacemt. of milit. ideals of patriotism by 'a new humanitarianism' an enlightened industrialism, dealg. mainly w. probls. of Amer. city-govt., immigrn., labour, child-protectn., women. By one of the founders of the Hull Ho. Social Settlement.
ARNOLD, Arth. — Social Politics *o.p.* [*pb.* 14/] 8° Paul 78
ARNOLD, Mat. — Culture & Anarchy : polit. & social criticism 2/6 c 8° Smith & Elder [69] 89
BASCOM, Dr Jno. — Sociology : a treatise [popular] $1·50 (6/) 12° Putnam, *N.Y.* 87
,, — Social Theory : grouping of social facts & principles $1·75 12° Crowell, *N.Y.* 95
[Lib. of Economics.] A compact bk., econ. theory bg. incl. within its scope. Mainly designed as a text book.
BLACKMAN, F. W. — Elements of Sociology [Citizen's Library] $1·25 *n.* (7/6) 12° Macmillan 05
CAREY, H. C. — Past, Present and Future $2·50 8° Baird, *Phila.* 48
,, — Principles of Soc. Sci., 3 v., 8° $10 ; Abridgmt., 1 v. $2 12° Baird, *Phila.* [59] 73 ; [74] 79
,, — Miscellaneous Works ; w. Memoir by W. Elder, 2 vols. $6 8° Baird, *Phila.* 83
,, — Unity of Law, *and* Harmony of Interests—*ut* **D** § 122
CARVER, (T. N.) + WELLS (D.A.) Sociol. and Social Progress [selns. in Econcs.] $2·75 (12/6) 8° Ginn 06
COLEMAN, Jas. M. — Social Ethics : nature & ethics of the State $1·25 *n.* c 8° Baker & Taylor, *N.Y.* 03
COMTE, Aug. [1793–1857] — Positive Philosophy—*ut* **C** § 23
COOLEY, C. H. — Social Organization : study of the larger mind $1·50 *n.* 8° Scribner, *N.Y.* 09
CROWELL, Dr J. F. — Logical Process of Social Development $1·75 c 8° Holt, *N.Y.* 98
A hypothesis that social progress is the result of the selective survival of sociological types.
DARDANO, Lorenzo — Elements of Social Science and Political Economy [tr.] 3/6 8° Gill, *Dublin* 09
Tr. of an Italian Roman-Catholic text-book for colleges and schools.
DEALEY, J. Q. — Sociology : simple teachings and applications $1·50 8° Silver, *N.Y.* 09
,, + WARD (L. F.) Text Book of Sociology $1·30 *n.* (6/ *n.*) c 8° Macmillan 05
A clear and concise statemt. of field of sociol., its scient. basis, its princs. as far as these at present known, and its purposes.

DICKINSON, G. Lowes — Justice and Liberty [$1·20 McClure, *N.Y.*] 4/6 *n.* c 8° Dent 08
A discussn., in dialogue-form (by a professor, a banker, and a gentleman of leisure), of first princs. underlying current polit. and social controversy. May be advantageously read w. WALLIS, *inf.*

FAIRBANKS, Arth. — Introduction to Sociology [E. & F. Philos. Lib.] 7/6 p 8° Paul [96] 01
$1·50 *n.* Scribner, *N.Y.* A student's manual, with a good bibliography. [Philos. Lib.]

FOURIER, Chas. — Selections from [tr.] [Soc. Sci. Ser.; $1 Scribner, *N.Y.*] 2/6 c 8° Sonnenschein 01
" — Theory of Social Organization [tr.] $1·50 12° Truth Seeker Co., *N.Y.* 86

GEORGE, Hy. — —*v.* **D** § 119

GEORGE, W. L. — Engines of Social Progress 5/*n.* c 8° Black 07
$2 *n.* Macmillan, *N.Y.* Account of social betterment-schemes in Great Britain.

GIDDINGS, Prf. F. H. — The Theory of Sociology $1 16° Amer. Acad. of Pol. Sci., *Phila.* 94
" — Principles of Sociology [Columbia Univ. Studs.] $3 *n.* (12/6 *n.*) 8° Macmillan 96
Compreh. and instructive, formg. a useful introd. to the new science. The most interesting lines of sociolog. inquiry are indicated, the best results collected, crit. exam., and scientif. arrngd. Bk. i discusses province of sociolog. and its logical meths. of research, is descriptive and classificatory, iii investigates hist. of society, iv formulates ultimate causes and laws of social evol. (objectively a conflict of phys. forces tendg. to equilibrium, subjectively the productn. of personality and of forms of assocn. that partly result fr. and partly determine characters of human beings).
" — Theory of Socialization: syllabus of princs. of sociology 60 c. *n.* (2/6 *n.*) 8° Macmillan 96
" — Elements of Sociology $1·25 (6/*n.*) c 8° Macmillan [98] 08
A clear outline, mainly intended for college-use; somewhat dogmatic. Gives bks. for parallel reading at ends of chs.
" — Inductive Sociology $2 *n.* (8/6 *n.*) 8° Macmillan 01
Presents a scheme for the study of social facts by the inductive method.
" [ed.] — Readings in Descriptive & Historical Sociology $1·60 *n.* (7/*n.*) 8° Macmillan 07

GRINNELL, W. M. — Social Theories and Social Facts [Questns. of Day] $1 (4/) c 8° Putnam 05

GRAHAM, Prf. W. — The Social Problem 14/ 8° Paul 86
Distribution of wealth and work, capital and labour, etc.

GUMPLOWICZ, Prf. L. — Outlines of Sociology, tr. Dr F. W. Moore $1 8° Amer. Acad. of Pol. Sci., *Phila.* 98

GUNTON, Geo. — Principles of Social Economics $1·75 (7/6) c 8° Putnam 91
Inductively consid. and pract. applied, w. crits. of current theories. Defines soc. progress as lying in an ever-increasg. consumptn. of wealth by the masses, no gt. industr. enterprises bg. likely to be very successful unless catering for the multitude. Progr. in politics and society is marked by the tendency to increase the sovereignty of the indiv. and diminish the arbitrary authority of the State by establishg. greater democracy of administration'. In economics it is the 'tendency to centralize industr. admin. and responsibility, de-individualize the labourer as a producer, and socialize the results in better and cheaper products'.

GUYOT, Yves — Principles of Social Economy [tr.] 3/6 c 8° Sonnenschein [84]
$1·25 Scribner, *N.Y.* [Social Science Series, Double Vol.].

HAMERTON, P. G. — Human Intercourse 8/6 c 8° Macmillan 84

HENDERSON, Prf. C. R. — The Social Spirit in America $1·50 12° Scott, *Chicago* [97] 01
[Chautauqua Rg. Circle Liter.] An excellent popular survey of American social needs.
" — Social Elements: institutions, character, progress $1·50 *n.* c 8° Scribner, *N.Y.* 98
A popular study of Amer. condns., w. an explanation of methods of sociological study.
" — Practical Sociology in the Service of Social Ethics 25 c. *n.* 4° Univ. Press, *Chicago* 03

HOBSON, J. A. — The Social Problem [$2 *n.* Pott, *N.Y.*] 2/6 *n.* c 8° Nisbet [01] 04
Largely an argument for Socialistic modifications in the state of society.
" — A Modern Outlook: study of Engl. & Am. tendencies 5/*n.* c 8° Herbert & Daniel 10
Reprs. of the 'middle' arts. of *The Nation*; a series of fresh pprs. by a Radical intellectual, who, at times forgetting his *rôle*, displays a robust sanity and candour. Spec. good arts. on Abraham LINCOLN and Saml. BUTLER.

HYSLOP, J. H. — The Science of Sociology 50 c. *n.* r 8° Univ. Press, *Chicago* 01

INGRAM, Dr J. K. — The Final Transition 2/6 *n.* c 8° Black [05]

JEVONS, Prf. W. Stanley — Methods of Social Reform 10/*n.* 8° Macmillan [83]

JONES, Prf. H. — The Social Organism—*in* Seth + Haldane [eds.] Essays in Philos. Criticism, *ut* **C** § 1

KELLEY, Flor. — Some Ethical Gains through Legislation [Citizens' Lib.] $1·25 *n.* (5/*n.*) 12° Macmillan 05

KELLY, E. — Government; or Human Evolution, 2 vols. $4 (10/6) c 8° Longman 00–1
Deals w. evoln. of human govt. and meaning of justice, w. individualism and collectivism, arguing that the latter is best means of securing justice

KIDD, Benj. — Social Evolution; *and* Principles of Western Civilization—*ut* **F** § 2

LANE, Mich. A. — The Level of Social Motion—*ut* **D** § 134

LLURIA, Dr Enrique — Superorganic Evolution, tr. Rachel Challice + D. H. Lambert 7/6 *n.* Williams 10
By a Monist, offerg. a specific for the miseries of the world in the abolitn. of private property, the forsakg. of worship of money for worsh. of Nature, etc., when, as 'LEWIS CARROLL' puts it, 'brain, and brain alone, shall rule the world'.

LORIA, A. — The Economic Foundations of Society [tr.] 3/6 c 8° Sonnenschein 99
$1·25 Scribner, *N.Y.* [Social Sci. Ser., Double Vol.] Accounts for orig. of all social institns. on economic grounds.

MACKENZIE, Prf. J. S. — Introduction to Social Philosophy 7/6 c 8° MacLehose, *Glasgow* [90] 95
$1·75 *n.* Macmillan, *N.Y.* [Shaw Fellowship Lects.] Compreh. and philosophic (neo-Kantian), seekg. to develop and apply a metaphysic of social life, as disting. fr. an empirical social science. Interestingly wr. and aboundg. in felicities of expressn. and epigram.

MOFFAT, R. S. — Economy of Consumption—*v.* **D** § 120

de MOLINARI, G. — Religion, tr. Walt. K. Firminger 2/6 c 8° Sonnenschein 94
$1 Macmillan, *N.Y.* Traces progressive developmt. of relig. feeling in strict conn. w. econ. evoln. of society. Strongly anti-socialistic.

MOORE, J. — The New Ethics 3/6 *n.* 8° Bell 07

PATTEN, Prf. S. N. Theory of Soc. Forces [study of soc. evoln.] $1 8° Amer. Acad. of Pol. Sci., *Phila.* 96
,, Heredity and Social Progress $1·25 *n.* (5 / *n.*) c 8° Macmillan 03
,, New Basis of Civilization [Am. Soc. Progr. Ser.] $1 *n.* (4/6 *n.*) c 8° Macmillan 07
PEABODY, Dr F. G. The Approach to the Social Question $1·25 *n.* (5 / *n.*) c 8° Macmillan 09
PHIPSON, C. B. The Science of Civilisation 10/6 *n.* 8° Sonnenschein 00
The principles of agricultural, industrial, and commercial prosperity.
PULSKY, Prf. A. Theory of Law and Civil Society [tr.]—*ut* **D** § 1
ROGERS, Prf. J. E. Thorold Social Economy [elementary] 1/; Amer. ed. 75 c. 12° Cassell 72; *N.Y.* 76
ROSS, E. A. Social Control $1·25 *n.* (5 / *n.*) 12° Macmillan [01] 04
A survey of the foundation of order.
,, The Foundations of Sociology [Citizens' Lib.] $1·25 *n.* (5 / *n.*) c 8° Macmillan 05
RUSKIN, Jno. —*v.* **D** § 114
SALEEBY, Dr C. W. Sociology [Scientific Series] 1 / *n.* c 8° Jack 05
SANTAYANA, Prf. Geo. Life of Reason, vol. ii: Reason in Society—*ut* **C** § 69
SMALL, Dr A. W. General Sociology [18 / *n.* Unwin] $4 *n.* 8° Univ. Press, *Chicago* 05
Account of the main development in sociological theory fr. Herb. SPENCER to RATZENHOFER.
,, + VINCENT (G. E.) Introduction to the Study of Society $1·80 c 8° Amer. Bk. Co., *N.Y.* 94
SPENCER, Herb. The Study of Sociology [Internat. Scient. Series] 5 / c 8° Paul [73]
$1·50 Appleton, *N.Y.* Lays down scope, utility, and method of the science. 8° edn., to range w. other works [*ut* **C** § 62] 10/6, 8° Williams [80].
,, The Principles of Sociology, 3 vols., *and* Descriptive Sociology, vols. i–viii—*ut* **C** § 62
,, Social Statics—*ut* **D** § 134
STUCKENBERG, Dr J. H. W. Introduction to the Study of Sociology $1·50 c 8° Armstrong, *N.Y.* 98
9/ Hodder. Intended for the beginner, but somewhat advanced. Contains much bibliographical matter.
,, Sociology, the Science of Human Society, 2 vols. $4·50 *n.* (21 / *n.*) 8° Putnam 03
TARDE, G. Social Laws, tr. H. C. Warren $1·25 (5 /) gl 8° Macmillan 99
,, Laws of Imitation, tr. E. C. Parsons $3 *n.* 8° Holt, *N.Y.* 03
A study of social structure based on fundam. thesis th. 'society is imitn.', and 'began on day when one man first copied another'.
TENNEY, E. P. Contrasts in Social Progress $2·50 *n.* (10 /6 *n.*) 8° Longman 07
THOMPSON, D. G. Social Progress [conditions and promotion of] $2 (7 /6) 8° Longman 88
TOPINARD, Paul Science and Faith [tr.] $1·50 8° *Open Ct.* Pb. Co., *Chicago* 99
6/6 *n.* Paul. A study of social evolution. Man as an animal and man as a member of society.
WARD, Lester F. Dynamic Sociology, or Applied Social Science; 2 vols. $4 s 8° Appleton, *N.Y.* [83] 97
In favour of a great extension of coercive agency and governmt. control in the work of social progress.
,, The Psychic Factors of Civilization $2·50 (8 /6 *n.*) 8° Ginn [93] 06
As agst. the treatmt. of Society as a living organism and the laws of Productn., Distributn., and Consumptn. as analog. to processes of nutritn., circulatn., and assimilatn., author sets forth a *psychological* economy, a philosophy of mind, as the primary motive power of world in all things above level of purely anim. life. In 3 Pts. (1) *Subjective Factors* [true forces of Society are psychic = subjective side of mind, viz. Feeling]; (2) *Objective Factors* [directive agent wh. controls social forces is psychic = objective side of mind, viz. Thought]; (3) *Social Synthesis of the Factors* [showg. how social forces und. control of the directive agent have establ. Society, raised it up to its pres. state, and are carrying it forward to its ultimate destiny.
,, Outlines of Sociology $2 (7 /6 *n.*) c 8° Macmillan 98
12 papers, valuable for discussn. of place of sociology am. the sciences, and of the reln. of sociol. and evol.
,, Pure Sociology: orig. & spontan. developmt. of society $4 *n.* (17 /) 8° Macmillan 03
A striking work, maintaining the superiority of the female sex.
,, Applied Sociology $2·50 8° Ginn, *Boston* 06
WATT, W. A. The Theory of Contract in its Social Light 3 / 8° Clark, *Edin.* 97
,, A Study of Social Morality 6 / 8° Clark, *Edin.* 01
Does not expound any definite philosophy, but states various points wh. cannot be ignored in conn. w. social organization.
WILLOUGHBY, Dr W. W. Social Justice: a critical essay $3 *n.* (12 /6 *n.*) 8° Macmillan 00
WRIGHT, Dr C. D. Outline of Practical Sociology [Amer. Citizen Ser.] $2 7/6 *n.* c 8° Longman [99] 09
A popular treatment of social questions from a practical American point-of-view.
ZIEGLER, Prf. Theod. Social Ethics: outlines of a doctrine of morals [tr.] 3 / c 8° Williams 92

**Collective Essays, etc.**

American Sociological Soc.: Publications, vols. i–iii ea. $1·50 *n.* 8° Univ. Press, *Chicago*
Vol. i: *Papers and Procgs. 1st Ann. Mtg.*; ii: *Social Conflicts* [papers]; iii: *The Family.*
BAKER, J. H. American Problems: essays and addresses $1·20 *n.* (4 / *n.*) c 8° Longman 07
By Pres. of Univ. of Colorado. Grouped under hgs. *Ideals, Sociological Problems, Education.*
BARNETT, Can. + Mrs S. A. Towards Social Reform [$1·50 *n.* Macmillan, *N.Y.*] 5 / *n.* c 8° Unwin 08
Repr. papers showg. growth of soc. activity as reg. Unemploymt., Charit. Relief, Poor Law Meths., and Recreatn. Optimistic.
BOSANQUET, Dr Bern. Essays and Addresses, *and* The Civilization of Christendom—*ut* **A** § 8
,, [ed.] Aspects of the Social Problem 2 /6 *n.* c 8° Macmillan 95
A colln. of valuable facts and opinions by trained observers in the social field. Some arts. are reprs.
,, Helen [=Mrs Bern.] The Standard of Life; & other Reprinted Essays 8 /6 *n.* 8° Macmillan [98] 06
A useful contribn. to discussn., in pop. form and lang., of several soc. probls., e.g. burden of small debts, educn. of women, lines of industr. conflicts, industr. traing. of women, psych. of soc. progress.

Brooklyn Ethical Assoc.: Sociology [17 popular papers] $2 c 8° Kerr, *Chicago* 91
,, Factors in American Civilization $2 c 8° Kerr, *Chicago* 93
14 popular lectures and discussions in applied sociology.

BROOKS, J. G. The Social Unrest $1·50 *n.* (6/ *n.*) c 8° Macmillan 03
Describes the pres. condn. of social instability in Amer., and gives much useful inform . as to Socialism on Continent.

BROWNE, J. H. Balfour Essays, Critical and Political, 2 vols. 15/ *n.* ($5 *n.*) 8° Longman 07
Reprints of essays, by a leading K.C., mostly contributed to *Westminster Review* between 1876 and 1886.

CARNEGIE, Andr. Problems of To-day: wealth, labour, socialism
[$1·40 Doubleday, *N.Y.*] 2/6 *n.* c 8° Geo. Allen 08

CARPENTER, Edw. —*ut* **D** § 126

CUNNINGHAM, Dr W. The Path towards Knowledge 4/6 c 8° Methuen 91
Essays on *Marriage and Population, Socialism, Positivism. Education, Civil Obedience*, etc.

DOLE, C. F. The Ethics of Progress [6/ *n.* Williams] $1·50 8° Crowell, *N.Y.* 09
*Ethics and Evolution, Conscience and the Right, Moral Evil, Probls. of Human Nature, Realm of Casuistry*, etc.

ELY, Prf. R. T. Studies in Evolution of Industr. Soc. [Citizens' Lib.] $1·25 *n.* (5/ *n.*) c 8° Macmillan 03

FAWCETT, Prf. + [Mrs] M. G. Essays and Lectures on Political and Social Subjects—*ut* **D** § 114

GLADDEN, Dr Washington Social Facts and Forces $1·25 (3/6) c 8° Putnam 98
Discusses the ethical bearing of many modern American institutions.

GODKIN, E. L. Reflections and Comments: 1865–95 $2 c 8° Scribner, *N.Y.* 96
7/6 Constable. Deals w. the principal non-political topics wh. have attracted attention of Amer. public.

GRAHAM, R. B. Cunningham Progress; and other Sketches 6/ c 8° Duckworth 05

GRAY, B. Kirkman
Binns, H. B. [ed.] A Modern Humanist: miscell. papers of B. K. Gray c 8° Fifield 10
Papers dealg. chfly. w. Lond. social probls., by an active, independent, social worker.

GREGG, W. R. Literary and Social Judgments, 2 vols.—*ut* **K** § 17

HADLEY, Prf. A. T. Standards of Public Morality [Am. Soc. Progr. Ser.] $1 *n.* (4/6 *n.*) 8° Macmillan 07
Kennedy lects., arranged by the Charity Organization Society of New York.

HARPER, J. W. The Foundations of Society 6/ c 8° Ward & Lock 99

HARRIS, Dr Geo. Inequality and Progress $1·25 16° Houghton, *Boston* 97

HARRISON, Fredc. National and Social Problems—*ut* **D** § 114
,, Realities & Ideals: social, polit., literary, & artistic 7/6 *n.* ($1·75 *n.*) c 8° Macmillan 08

HUEFFER, Ford Madox The Soul of London 5/ *n.* 16° Rivers 05
,, The Heart of the Country 5/ *n.* 16° Rivers 06
,, The Spirit of the People 5/ *n.* 16° Rivers 07
'Small projections of a view of modern life'.

HUXLEY, Prf. T. H. Social Diseases [1891]—*in his* Essays, vol. ix, *ut* **K** § 83

JONES, Prf. Hy. The Working Faith of the Social Reformer, & other Essays 7/6 *n.* c 8° Macmillan 10
A brilliant attempt to establish a philosophy of social life, by an Idealist, auth. of *Idealism as a Practical Creed* [*ut* **C** § 69].

LAING, Sam. Problems of the Future; and other Essays 3/6 8° Chapman [89] 90

LILLY, W. S. On Shibboleths 12/ 8° Chapman 92
Mr LILLY's 7 'shibboleths' are Progress, Liberty, the People, Publ. Opin., Educn., Women's Rts.. and Supply and Demand. Interestg. essays, forcibly stated; but author, a R.-C. in belief, traing. and culture, is a true Sophist in Platonic sense, hg. appearance of knowl. without reality of it (title itself uses 'shibboleths' in a wrong sense).

LOCH, C. S. [ed.] Methods of Social Advance—*ut* **D** § 128
Short studies in social practice, by various writers.

MCCLELLAND, J. Social Science and Social Schemes 3/6 c 8° Sonnenschein 96
A vigorous protest agst. some princ. assumptns. made by authors of soc. Utopias, wrs. on labr., capital, equality, etc.

MACDONALD, Dr G. Ethics of Revolt 5/ *n.* c 8° Duckworth 08
Lectures, mainly to working men, on *Vivisectn., Destiny of Man, Control of Matter, Control of Environmt.*, etc.

MACKENZIE, Dr J. S. Lectures on Humanism, w. spec. ref. to its beargs. on Sociology—*ut* **C** § 69

MACMILLAN, Prf. M. Promotion of General Happiness
[Utilitarian; Soc. Sci. Ser.; $1 Scribner, *N.Y.*] 2/6 c 8° Sonnenschein 90

MACPHAIL, Andr. Essays in Fallacy 6/ *n.* c 8° Longman 10
*The American Woman* [*ut* **D** § 132], *Psychology of Suffragette* [*ut ib.*], *The Fallacy in Educn., The Fallacy in Theology.*

MALLOCK, W. H. Classes and Masses—*ut* **D** § 118

MEATH, EARL OF Social Arrows, 5/; Popular Edition 1/ c 8° Longman [86] 87; 87
Open spaces; assocns. for yg. men, women, and children; over-populn.; shop assists., etc. Pub. when auth. was L'd BRABAZON.
,, + C'ess of Social Aims 6/ c 8° Wells Gardner 93
A colln. of papers on social reform and social experiments, repr. fr. magazines. No political animus.

MONEY, L. G. Chiozza Social and Industrial Problems 5/ *n.* 8° Methuen 08
Papers in amplificn. of above, on current problems in sociol., politics, industry, and taxatn.

MORISON, J. Cotter The Service of Man—*ut* **A** § 7 [Positivist]

MOZLEY, Anne —*in her* Essays from 'Blackwood,' *ut* **K** § 83

MUIRHEAD, Prf. J. H. Philosophy of Life; and other Essays—*ut* **C** § 70

MÜNSTERBERG, Prf. H. Problems of To-day: fr. pt. of view of a psychologist [7/6 *n.* Unwin] 8° 10
*The Fear of Nerves, Choice of a Vocatn., Temperce. Questn., Spiritualism, The Markt and Psychology, The World Language*, and 3 other essays.

NASH, Prf. H. S. The Genesis of the Social Conscience—*ut* **A** § 113
Seeks to show how the establishmt. of Xtianity in Europe foreordained the Social question.

O., S. G. [=Rev. L'd S. G. OSBORNE] Letters, ed. Arnold White, 2 vols. 42/ 8° Griffith 91
Repr. fr. *Times*, 1846 onw. Deals w. many of social wrongs and topics of the day in a trenchant and fearless nanner.

PEARSON, Prf. Karl Chances of Death & other Studies in Evolution, 2 v.; ill. 25/ 8° Arnold 97
$8 Lane, *N.Y.* i: *Chances of Death* [*ut* **A** § 128], *Scient. Aspect of Monte Carlo Roulette* [*ut* **H** § 7], *Reproductive Selection., Socialism and Natl. Selectn., Politics and Science, Reaction, Woman and Labour* [*ut* **D** § 132], *Variatn. in Man and Woman* [*ut* **H** § 100]; ii: *Woman as Witch, Ashiepattle or Hans seeks his Luck, Kindred Group Marrn.* [*ut* **F** § 5], *Germ. Passion Play* [*ut* **K** § 82]. The fundamental note running thro' all the essays is an endeavour to see all phenomena, physical and social, as a connected growth, and to describe them in the briefest formula possible.

PLAYFAIR, Sir Lyon Subjects of Social Welfare [pub. health, natl. wealth, educn.] 7/6 c 8° Cassell 89

RITCHIE, Prf. D. G. Studies in Political and Social Ethics—*ut* **D** § 134

RUNCIMAN, Jas. Joints in our Social Armour 5/ c 8° Hodder 90
*Drink, War, Friendships, Disasters at Sea, Dandies, Ethics of Turf, Bad Company, Good Compauy, 'Sport'*, etc.

" Ethics of Drink; and other Social Questions [bright & sensible] 3/6 c 8° Hodder 92

" Side Lights [posthum.; memoir by Grant Allen] 5/ c 8° Unwin 93

SCUDDER, V. D. Social Ideals in English Letters $1·75 c 8° Houghton, *Boston* 98
A survey of the social ideas of English writers fr. LANGLAND to present day.

SEAGER, Prf. H. R. Social Insurance: program. of social reform $1 *n.* (4/6 *n.*) c 8° Macmillan 10

SIDGWICK, Prf. Hy. —*in his* Miscellaneous Essays and Addresses, *ut* **C** § 1

SMITH, Prf. Goldwin Essays on Questions of the Day—*ut* **D** § 142

Sociological Society: Sociological Papers r 8° Macmillan 04–6 *in prg.*
i: Papers by Fcs. GALTON, E. WESTERMARCK, P. GEDDES, E. DURKHEIM, H. H. MANN, V. V. BRANFORD, Introd. Jas. BRYCE, 10/6 ($3); ii: by GALTON (*Eugenics*—*ut* **H** § 43), GEDDES, M. E. SADLER, WESTERMARCK, HÖFFDING, BRIDGES, STUART-GLENNIE, 10/6 ($3); iii: by G. A. REID, J. A. THOMSON, A. E. CRAWFORD, W. H. BEVERIDGE, J. A. HOBSON, H. Rider HAGGARD, etc., 10/6 *n.* ($3·25 *n.*).

STEPHEN, Sir Leslie Social Rights and Duties, 2 vols.—*ut* **C** § 70 [9/; misprinted there]

WALLACE, A. Russel Studies Scientific and Social, 2 vols.—*ut* **H** § 43

WHITE, Arn. Problems of a Great City [emigr., drink, socialism, etc.] *o.p.* [*pb.* 2/6] c 8° Remington [86] 87

" Tries at Truth: essays on social subjects 2/6 c 8° Isbister (Pitman) [91] 95
*Pauper Immigration, Thrift, Strikes, Sweating, Colonization, Amusemts., Overcrowding, Booth's Scheme*, etc.

" The Views of 'Vanoc' 5/ *n.* f 8° Paul 10
Seln. of essays contrib. over the pseudon. 'VANOC' to front page of *The Referee.*

WOODS, Rob. A. English Social Movements $1·50 c 8° Scribner, *N.Y.* [91] 95
2/6 Sonnenschein. A sketch of several of the chief social movemts. in Engl. at the present time. Now somewhat out of date.

**History of Civilization**—*v.* **F** § 4 **Political Philosophy**—*v.* **D** § 134 **Primitive and Early Society**—*v.* **F** § 5
**Social Results of Early Christianity**—*v.* **A** § 51 (esp. SCHMIDT) **Utopias, Social**—*v.* **D** § 134

### Biography, etc., of Social and Political Reformers

*Collectively:* CLAYTON (Jos.) Leaders of the People [17 biographies] 12/6 *n.* 8° Secker 10

GIBBINS, H. de B. English Social Reformers 2/6 c 8° Methuen [92] 02
John BALL, WESLEY, Sir Thos. MORE, WILBERFORCE, the Factory Reformers, CARLYLE, KINGSLEY, RUSKIN, etc.

LINTON, W. J. European Republicans: recollns. of Mazzini & his friends *o.p.* [*pb.* 10/6] 8° Lawrence 92
MAZZINI, RUFFINI and the BANDIERAS, LAMENNAIS, PESTEL and RYLÉIEFF, HERZEN, KONARSKI, DARASZ, STOLZMAN, WORCELL.

" Memories *o.p.* [*pb.* 10/6] 8° Lawrence 95
Of chief interest for its remins. of older Radicals, Chartists, and Contin. Repubns. (incl. MAZZINI).

ROBERTSON, J. M. Modern Humanists [Social Science Series] 2/6 c 8° Sonnenschein [91] 95
$1 Scribner, *N.Y.* Sociolog. studies of CARLYLE, MILL, EMERSON, ARNOLD, RUSKIN, and SPENCER; w. epilogue on Social Reconstrn.

" Pioneer Humanists—*ut* **C** § 4

*Individually* —*v. also* **D** § 139, *s.v.* Biography of Chartists

BAMFORD, Sam. [Chartist; 1788–1872] Passages in Life of a Radical, ed. H. Dunckley, 2 v.
[Reformer's Bkshelf] ea. 3/6 c 8° Unwin [41] 94

Espinasse, F. Life of S. Bamford—*in his* Lancashire Worthies, Ser. ii, *ut* **E** § 17

BRADLAUGH, Chas. [1833–91]—*v.* **F** § 27

BUCKLEY, Jno. —*v.* **D** § 122

BURT, Thos. [M. P.]

Watson, A. A Great Labour Leader: life of T. Burt 15/ *n.* 8° Brown & Langham 08

COBBETT, Wm. [1762–1835] —*v.* **F** § 27

COBDEN, Rich. [1804–65] —*v.* **F** § 27

DENISON, Edw. [1840–70] Letters. Ed. Sir B. Leighton 1/ f 8° Isbister [75] 84

FOX, W. J. [1786–1864]

Garnet, Rich. + Edw. Life of W. J. Fox, Public Teacher & Social Reformer; ill. 16/ *n.* 8° Lane 10
Based on material coll. by late Mrs Bridell Fox [dau.]. A satisfactory life of the ex-Unit.-minister, lecturer, journalist, and M.P. for Oldham, founder of South Place Chapel (1824) [for hist. of S. Place Ethical Soc., its successor, *v.* **A** § 8].

HOGG, Quintin [1845–1903; fdr. of Polytechnic] Life of. By Ethel M. Hogg; ill. 3/6 *n.* 8° Constable [04] 06

HOLYOAKE, G. J. [1817–1906] Sixty Years of an Agitator's Life, 2 vols.
[Reformer's Bkshlf.] ea. 3/6 c 8° Unwin [92] 93
Autobi. acc. of his experis. as Co-operator, Freethinker, Radical politician. He was concerned in repeal of Corn Laws, was energetic Chartist and strenuous oppon. of newsp. tax; and the bk. conts. notices rel. to Ern. JONES, the Chartist; Thos. SCOTT, friend of COLENSO; Jno. BRIGHT; GARIBALDI; W. E. FORSTER; Leigh HUNT; Fcs. PLACE; OWEN family; w. new letters of LANDOR.

,, Bygones Worth Remembering, 2 vols. [Reformer's Bksh.] 3/6 c 8° Unwin [05]

Goss, C. W. F. Descriptive Bibliography of Writings of Holyoake [w. sk. of life] 5/ n. c 8° Crowther 08

McCabe, Jos. Life and Letters of G. J. Holyoake, 2 vols. 16/ n. 8° Watts 08
Repeats much th. is cont. in *Sixty Yrs.* and *Bygones*, and adds a good deal that is new, welding the whole into a complete history of the 'unswerving champion for nearly 70 yrs. of the people's rights'. Bibliogr. by Goss.

LOVETT, Wm. [Chartist; 1800–87] Life and Struggles *o.p.* [*pb.* 5/] c 8° Paul 76

MAZZINI, Jos. [1805–72] —*v. also* **D** § 139

King, Bolton Mazzini 4/6 *n.* c 8° Dent 03

Linton, W. J. —*in his* European Republicans, *and* Memories, *ut sup.*

V[enturi], E. A. Mazzini: a memoir [*repr. fr.* Thoughts on Democr., *ut* **D** § 139] 6*d.* 8° Alexander [74] 84

OWEN, Rob. [1771–1858] —*v.* **D** § 126

PAINE, Thos. [1737–1807] —*for his* Writings *v.* **D** § 139

Conway, Moncure D. Life of Thomas Paine, 2 vols.; ill. $5 (25/) 8° Putnam 92
Ch. Edn. [unabgd.] 2/6 *n.* Watts '09. Hist. of his career—liter., polit., and relig.—in Engl., Frce., and Amer. Incl. sketch of PAINE by Wm. COBBETT (hitherto unpub.). Overzealous to present its subj. as a hero, tho' clearly shows that he was not the vulgar, dissolute, blasphemous, and unscrupulous 'TOM PAINE' of popular traditn.

PLACE, Fcs. [1771–1854] —*v.* **F** § 27 [pioneer of Mod. Trade-Unionism]

RUSKIN, Jno. [1819–1900] —*v.* **K** § 24 (HOBSON)

SMITH, Geo., of Coalville [1831–95]

Hodder, Edwin George Smith of Coalville: story of an enthusiast 5/ c 8° Nisbet 96
Life of the man whose labrs. on beh. of children employed in brick-yds., canal-boats, and gypsy-vans led to important legisln.

TOYNBEE, Arnold [1852–83] —*v.* **D** § 128

TWINING, Louisa [1820– ] Recollections of Life and Work 15/ 8° Arnold 93
Life of one who took an active pt. in many of the gt. soc. movemts. of 50 yrs. over wh. her Recollns. extend. Early chs. give quaint informatn. ab. her city-life and its surroundgs. dur. her girlhd., and the old-fashioned traing. she received. For her *Workhouse Visiting*, *v.* **D** § 128.

WATSON, Jas. [Chartist and Free-Press Agitator; 1799–1874]

Linton, W. J. James Watson: a memoir *o.p.* [*pb.* 3/] c 8° A. Heywood, *Mancs.* 80

WILSON, Jno. [M. P.] Memoirs of a Labour Leader 5/ *n.* c 8° Unwin 10
Autobiogr. of one who fr. an untutored pit-boy worked his way up to positn. of a Labour Leader.

*Economists*—*v.* **D** § 114 *Slave Emancipators*—*v.* **D** § 130 *Temperance Reformers*—*v.* **D** § 131

*Philanthropists*—*v.* **D** § 128 *Socialists*—*v.* **D** § 126 *Workers among the Poor*—*v.* **D** § 127

*Prison Reformers*—*v.* **D** § 123

**Cities, Growth and Influence of**—*v.* **D** § 124

**Degeneration** —*v.* **C** § 71

**Evolution and Sociology; Biology and Sociology**

BOUGLÉ, Prf. Darwinism and Sociology—*in* Seward [ed.], Darwin and Mod. Science, *ut* **H** § 43

CHATTERTON-HILL, G. Heredity and Selection in Sociology 12/6 *n.* 8° Black 08
An elabor. wk., applying Darwinism and the New Darwinism to social problems. In 3 Pts., (1) *The Theory of Descent* [doctr. of species], (2) *Social Pathology* [effect of certain phenomena, e.g. suicide, insanity, altruism, on soc. life], (3) *Actual Condns. of Social Selection.*

HAYCRAFT, Prf. J. B. Darwinism & Race Progress [Social Science Ser.] 2/6 c 8° Sonnenschein 95
$1 Scribner, *N.Y.* Considers the problem of the 'survival of the unfit', etc.

MASSART (J.) + VANDERVELDE (E.) Parasitism, Organic and Social [tr.]
[Soc. Science Ser.] 2/6 c 8° Sonnenschein 96
$1 Scribner, *N.Y.* A comparison of parasitism in animal world w. parasitism in world of man.

*Eugenics* —*v.* **H** § 43

**Family (The)** —*for* histor. and ethnograph. wks. *v.* **F** § 5

American Sociological Soc.: Publications, vol. iii: The Family—*ut sup.*, *s.v.* Collective Essays

BOSANQUET, Helen [=Mrs Bern.] The Family 8/6 *n.* ($2·75 *n.*) 8° Macmillan 06
A sketch of this wide subj., in two Pts. (1) historical, tracg. family in itself and in its relns. to society and State, fr. patriarchal times, (2) modern, discussg. functn. and constitn. of family in mod. condns. Full of suggestive reflectns. and delicate observns.

,, —*in her* The Strength of the People, *ut* **D** § 127, *s.v.* Poor-Law

HAGAR, F. N. The American Family: a sociological problem $1·50 8° University Pb. Soc., *N.Y.* 05

LAUNSBACH, C. W. L. State and Family in Early Rome $2·50 *n.* 8° Macmillan 08

PARSONS, Mrs E. C. The Family: ethnograph. and histor. outline $3 *n.* (12/6 *n.*) 8° Putnam 06

RIIS, Jac. A. Peril and Preservation of the Home; ill. $1 *n.* c 8° Jacobs, *Phila.* 03

,, The Making of an American; ill. $2 *n.* (8/6 *n.*) 8° Macmillan 01

WELLS, H. G. Socialism and the Family [50 c. *n.* Ball Pb. Co., *Boston*] 1/ *n.* c 8° Fifield 06
Advocates State-subsidization of motherhood.

**Social Psychology ; Psychology of Peoples**—*v. also* **D** § 114, *s.v.* Formatn. of Publ. Opin., **F** § 2, **F** § 5

BALDWIN, Prf. J. M. Social and Ethical Interpretations—*ut* **C** § 71
,, The Individual and Society : psychol. and sociology [6/6 *n.* Rebman] c 8° 11

BOSANQUET, Dr Bern. Psychology of the Moral Self—*ut* **C** § 71

BOUTMY, Emile The English People, tr. E. English 16/ 8° Unwin 04
A good study of Engl. political psychology. Introd by J. E. C. BODLEY.

BRINTON, Prf. D. G. Basis of Social Relations : study in ethnic psychology $1·50 *n.* 8° Putnam, *N.Y.* 02
8/ *n.* Murray. Deals with the mental traits of different human groups—' ethnic psychology '.

BRYCE, Jas. Relatns. of Advanced and Backward Races of Mankind [Romanes Lect.] 2/ *n.* (70 c.) 8° Clar. Press 02

DAVIS, Dr M. M. Psychol. Interpretns. of Society [Columb. Univ. Studs.] $2·50 8° Longman, *N.Y.* 09

DEWE, Prf. J. A. Psychology of Politics and History—*ut* **F** § 2

DUPRAT, G. L. Morals : treat. on psycho-sociolog. bases of ethics [tr.]—*ut* **C** § 70

HAYDEN, E. A. The Social Will [Psychological Monographs] $1 8° Johns Hopk. Univ., *Baltimore* 09

LEBON, Gust. The Crowd : study of the popular mind 6/ c 8° Unwin [96] 03
$1·50 *n.* Macmillan, *N.Y.* A psychol. study of th. train of emotn. wh. makes vast nos. of people act simultaneously, and which is expressed sometimes by phys. panic, sometimes by polit. revolutn. 'In the crowds it is stupidity and not mother-wit that is accumulated'. Laments th. the world is not govd. by reason.

,, The Psychology of Peoples [tr.] 6/ c 8° Unwin 98
$1·50 *n.* Macmillan, *N.Y.* On the influence of the psychology of peoples on their evoln.

,, The Psychology of Socialism [$3 *n.* Macmillan, *N.Y.*] 16/ c 8° Unwin 99
Shows how Socialism is not an economic system based on reasoning, but a new religion, adopted by an act of faith, and as such altogether impervious to the attacks of logic.

McDOUGALL, W. Introduction to Social Psychology [$1·50 *n.* Luce, *Boston*] 5/ *n.* c 8° Methuen 08
Defines the motive forces that underlie all activities of indivs. and of societies, and way in wh. they become organized in indiv. mind and in society.

PATTEN, Prf. S. N. Relation of Sociology to Psychology 25 c. 8° Am. Acad. of Pol. Sci., *Phila.* 96

ROSS, Prf. E. A. Social Psychology : an outline & source-bk. $1·50 *n.* (6/6 *n.*) c 8° Macmillan 08
An attempt to deal systematically w. soc. psychol., whose functn. is to study 'the psychic planes and currents that come into existence among men in conseq. of their association'. Chs. on *Suggestibility, Mob Mind, Fashion, Conventionality* (5 chs.), *Custom, Disequilibration,* etc.

WALLAS, Graham Human Nature in Politics [$1·50 *n.* Houghton, Boston] 6/ 8° Constable 08
A stimulating bk., by an Oxford man, now Lecturer at Lond. Schl. of Economics ; full of apt instances and comparisons. Should be read at same time as *Justice and Liberty* [*ut supra*] by G. L. DICKINSON, a Cambr. man, by way of contrast, the two supplementg. ea. other, catchg. ea. other out, and settg. ea. other off.

WARD, Lester F. The Psychic Factors of Civilization—*ut sup.*

*Social Psychology of Sex* —*v.* **D** § 132

**Statistics, Social and Economic** —v. **D** § 148

## 126 : SOCIALISM ; COMMUNISM ; COLLECTIVISM ; ANARCHISM ; NIHILISM

**Bibliography**

AMES, H. The Red God [a literary survey of Socialism] 2/ *n.* 8° Ouseley 07

BARKER, J. Ellis —*in his* British Socialism, *ut inf.* [over 1,000 bks. and pamphlets]

STAMMHAMMER, Jos. Bibliographie des Social-Politik 18*m.* r 8° Fischer, *Jena* 97

**Historical ; Descriptive**

BLISS, W. P. Handbook of Socialism [Soc. Sci. Ser. ; Double Vol.] 3/6 c 8° Sonnenschein [95] 07
$1·25 Scribner, *N.Y.* A manl. of Socialism as it is, not as it might be—its nature, hist. (over world), w. biogrs. and bibliogr.

BROOKS, J. G. The Socialist Unrest—*ut* **D** § 125
Valuable studies in the Labour and Socialistic movements.

ENSOR, R. C. K. Modern Socialism $1·50 *n.* (5/ *n.*) Ch. Edn. 25 c. (1/) c 8° Harper [07] 10
Aims and recommendns. of Socialist bodies of world as set forth in their speeches, wrgs., and programmes.

GONNER, Prf. E. C. K. The Socialist State 2/6 c 8° Walter Scott 95
Aim is 'to facilitate serious and fruitful study [of Socialism] by a delimitn. of ground it shd. cover and by implied suggestn. th. a final judgmt. must be arrived at, not on one aspect or on one presentmt. of case, but after even-minded review of whole complex medley of interests, difficulties, dangers, and advantages'. Object well achieved, judicial fairness bg. key-note of bk.

GRAHAM, Prf. W. Socialism, New and Old [Internat. Scientific Series] 5/ c 8° Paul [91]
$1·75. Appleton, *N.Y.* Histor. and critical, 'fr. Moses to Marx'. Histor. pt. is inferior to RAE's, and even to de LAVELEYE's, but criticism is good, and attempt to conceive how things wd. constit. themselves under a collectivist *régime* is valuable. A candid study of 'the truth in Socialism'.

HILLQUIT, Morris Socialism in Theory and Practice $1·50 *n.* (6/6 *n.*) c 8° Macmillan 09

HUNTER, Rob. Socialists at Work ; ill. $1·50 *n.* (6/6) ; paper 25 c. *n.* c 8° Macmillan 08
A close and sympathetic study of the facts of the Socialist movemt., w. spec. ref. to Germy., Italy, Frce., Engl., and Belg., w. Suppl. Chap. (by Chas. LAPWORTH) on other countries.

KAUTSKY, Karl Communism in Centr. Europe in time of Reformation [tr.] 16/ 8° Unwin 97

KIRKUP, Thos. An Inquiry into Socialism 4/6 *n.* ($1·40 *n.*) c 8° Longman [87] 07
An attempt to discover wh. is endurg. and beneficent in Socialist movemt. by study of forces, princs., and tendencies at wk. in pres. stage of historic evoln. Orig. contrib. to 9th edn. of *Encycl. Brit.* [*ut* **K** § 1]. Cf. also his arts. *Rob. Owen* and *St Simon* there.

,, A History of Socialism 7/6 *n.* c 8° Black [92] 06
$2·25 *n.* Macmillan, *N.Y.* A temperate, sympathetic, and well-balanced est. of histor. developmt. of Socialism, and an est. and crit. of movemt. as whole. Author gives in his adherence to wh. he terms a 'rational Socialism', thinkg. th. 'society shd. control industry in its own interests'.

,, A Primer of Socialism [40 c. *n.* Macmillan, *N.Y.*] 1/ *n.* c 8° Black 08

LEBON, Gust. The Psychology of Socialism [tr.]—*v.* **D** § 125, *s.v.* Social Psychology

LONDON, Jack War of the Classes [3/6 *n.* Heinemann] $1·50 *n.*; Ch. Edn. 25 c. c 8° Macmillan [05] 05

MENGER, Prf. A. The Right to the Whole Produce of Labour [tr.] 6/ *n.* ($2 *n.*) c 8° Macmillan 99
Introd. and bibliogr. by Prf. H. S. FOXWELL. Gives a hist. of early Engl. Socialists, w. acc. of their wks. Analyses Socialistic theories of natural rts., and gives orig. and developmt. of theory of labour's claim to whole product of industry.

MORRIS (Wm.) + BAX (E. B.) Socialism, its Growth and Outcome [Soc. Sci. Ser.; Doub. Vol.] 3/6 c 8° Sonnenschein [93]
$1·25. Scribner, *N.Y.* Having built up a 'practical' Utopia, MORRIS here—in collab. w. BAX—deals w. his subj. fr. a histor. pt.-of-view, providg. a continuous sketch of developmt. of hist. in rel. to Socialism. A moderate and temperate bk., fr. Socialist side.

*RAE, Jno. Contemporary Socialism [$2·50 *n.* Scribner, *N.Y.*] 10/6 8° Sonnenschein [84] 08
By far the best, most compreh. and philos. bk. on its subj., statg. and criticizg. in a masterly fashion doctrs. of LASSALLE, MARX, Carl. MARLO, *The Socialists of the Chair, The Christian Socialists, Anarchism, Russ. Nihilism. Socialism, State Socialism, Agrarian Socialism of Hy. George*; w. *Introd. Chap.* and ch. on *Progress and Present Position of Socialism.*

SOMBART, Prf. Werner Socialism & Social Movement in 19 Cent., tr. Dr M. Epstein 3/6 *n.* c 8° Dent 09
$1·50 *n.* Dutton, *N.Y.* Tr. fr. 6th Germ. edn., four times as large as the first [pb. 1896, Engl. tr. $1·25 (5/) Putnam '98]. A clear, impartial exam. of growth and aims of Socialism, by an Individualist w. Socialist inclinations.

STODDART, Jane T. The New Socialism: an impartial inquiry 5/ *n.* 8° Hodder 09
Conts. much informn. and many citations, arrgd. acc. to no clear order, but formg. a useful index to a mass of little-known literature.

TUGAN-BARANOWSKY, Dr M. Modern Socialism in its Historic Development [tr.] 3/6 c 8° Sonnenschein 10

WOOLSEY, Theod. D. Communism and Socialism [in hist. and theory, esp. German; 7/6 Low] $1·50 *n.* c 8° Scribner, *N.Y.* 79

WRIXON, Sir Hy. Socialism: notes on a political tour 10/6 ($3) 8° Macmillan 96
A full and fair survey of Socialism and movemts. tow. Socialism in Engld., Canada, and U.S. Auth. was commissioned by Govt. of Victoria to make observns. on 'some publ. questns. th. interested and concerned us colonists in common w. all more progressive communities of the world'.

*England*

ARNOLD-FORSTER, H. O. English Socialism of To-day [$1·25 *n.* Dutton, *N.Y.*] 2/6 *n.* c 8° Smith & Elder [08] 08
An exam. of its teachings and aims, repr. fr. arts. to *The Standard.* Popular; useful.

BARKER, J. Ellis British Socialism: doctrs., policy, aim, etc. 10/6 *n.* 8° Smith & Elder 08
$3 *n.* Scribner, *N.Y.* A vigorous attack on the tchg. of mod. Socialism in rel. to a gt. variety of subjs. based on a very wide exam. of the liter. of the subj. An admirable compendium of Brit. Socialism. Appendices giving offic. progrs. of Socialist organizms.; and a bibliogr.

DICEY, Prf. A. V. Law & Public Opinion in Engld. in XIX Cent. 10/6 *n.* ($3 *n.*) 8° Macmillan 05
A survey of the socialistic tendency of 19-cent. legisln. in response to demands of publ. opinion.

VILLIERS, Brougham The Socialist Movement in England 2/6 *n.* c 8° Unwin [08] 10
An attempt, by one who defends central aim of Socialism, to make clear what Labr.-Socialist party is, and to suggest its prob. influence on near, and more distant, future. More political than *doctrinaire.* Bibliogr.

WEBB, Sid. Socialism in England [Social Science Series] 2/6 c 8° Sonnenschein [90]
$1 Scribner, *N.Y.* A brief account of contemp. Engl. socialism, fr. the Fabian standpt. Now somewhat out-of-date.

*New Lanark Establishment; Orbiston Community*

CULLEN, Alex. Adventures in Socialism 7/6 *n.* c 8° Black 10
The first authentic acc. of Orbiston Community (founded by A. J. HAMILTON and Abram COMBE), based on priv. jls. and other orig. documts. rel. to these two communities in possessn. of L'd HAMILTON of Dalzell, gr'son of HAMILTON. New Lan. Estab. is dealt w. in Rob. OWEN's autobiogr. [*ut inf.*].

*Australia and New Zealand*

BATES, Helen P. Australian Experiments in Industry [by a moder. supporter] 25 c. 8° Acad. of Pol. Sci., *Phila.* 98

REEVES, W. P. State Experiments in Australia and New Zealand, 2 vols. 24/ *n.* 8° Richards 02
A good account, by Agent-Gen. f. N. Zeal., a supporter of State-interference. Period 1881–1902. Maps.

ST LEDGER, A. Australian Socialism 4/6 *n.* ($1·50 *n.*) c 8° Macmillan 09
Histor. sketch of its orig. and developmts., by Senator for State of Queensl. in Commonwealth Parlt., showg. issues of Socialism th. have been disguised fr. Austral. public and servg. as warning to Brit. workers.

*France*

BALSILLIE, Dav. The Lesson of the Revolution 2/6 c 8° Black 90
A criticism of past and present tendencies in the state of society in England.

BAX, E. Belfort Story of the French Revolution [Social Science Series] 2/6 c 8° Sonnenschein [91]
$1 Scribner, *N.Y.* From a strongly Socialist point-of-view.

BOOTH, A. J. St Simon [1760–1825] & St Simonians [Socialism in Frce.] *o.p.* [*pb.* 7/6] 8° Longman 71

ELY, Prf. R. T. French and German Socialism in Modern Times [6/ Paul] 75 c., Ch. Edn. 25 c. 8° Harper, *N.Y.* [83] 86

GAULLIER, Hy. The Paternal State in France and Germany $1·25 c 8° Harper 98
A bitter attack on modern State activities in France and Germany.

GRONLUND, Laur. Ça Ira: Danton in Fch. Revoln. [study of Fch. Socialism] $1·50 12° Lee & Shepard, *Bost.* 88

GUTHRIE, Dr W. B. Socialism before the French Revolution $1·50 *n.* (6/6 *n.*) c 8° Macmillan 07
Incl. an able Introd., w. a bibliogr. and a general apprecn. of early Socialistic theories, fr. Plato downwards.

KROPOTKIN, Pr'ce P. A. The Great French Revolution: 1789–93 6/ *n.* c 8° Heinemann 09

LISSAGARAY, P. O. Hist. of the Commune of Paris [tr.] [Socialist standpt.] 10/6 8° Reeves & Turner 86

PAINE, Thos. [1737–1809] The Rights of Man—*ut* **D** § 139
An answer to BURKE's *Reflections on the French Revolution* [*ut* **F** § 48].

PEIXOTTO, Jessica B. French Revoln. & Modern French Socialism [Lib. of Economics] $1·50 12° Crowell, *N.Y.* 01

ROCQUAIN, F. The Revolutionary Spirit preceding the Fch. Revoln. [tr.]—*ut* **F** § 49

SANBORN, A. F. Paris and the Social Revolution ; ill. V. Trowbridge 16/ *n.* 8° Hutchinson 05
$3·50 *n.* Small, *Boston.* A study of the revol. elements in the various classes of Parisian society.

*Germany* —*v. also sup.* WOOLSEY, and *s.v.* France (GAULLIER)

*Reformation*

BAX, E. Belfort Social Side of the Reformation, 3 vols. [Macmillan, *N.Y.*] s 8° Sonnenschein 94–03
i: *Germ. Society at Close of Mid. Ages*, 5/ ($1·75) ; ii : *Peasants' War*, 5/ ($2) ; iii : *Rise and Fall of Anabaptists*, 6/ ($2). Socialist stdpt.

*Modern and Contemporary :* DAHLINGER (C. W.) The German Revolution of 1849 $1 35 *n.* (7/6) c 8° Putnam 03

DAWSON, W. H. Bismarck & State Socialism [Social Science Series] 2/6 c 8° Sonnenschein [90]
$1 Scribner, *N.Y.* A succinct and well-digested acc. of Germ. social and econ. legisln. fr. 1870 to 1890.

„ German Socialism & Ferdinand Lassalle [Social Sci. Ser.] 2/6 c 8° Sonnenschein [88] 91
$1 Scribner, *N.Y.* A good biograph. hist. of the Germ. Socialist movemts. of 19th cent.

MARX, Karl Revolution and Counter-Revolution : Germany in 1848, tr. Elean. Marx Aveling [$1 Scribner, *N.Y.* ; Soc. Sci. Ser.] 2/6 c 8° Sonnenschein [94]

RUSSELL, Bertrand German Social Democracy 3/6 ($1 *n.*) c 8° Longman 97
A fair sketch of hist. of movemt. c. 1865–95, w. good accs. of MARX and LASSALLE. Ch. on *Woman Questn. in Germy.* by Mrs B. RUSSELL.

*Greece*

SHEBBEARE, C. J. Greek Theory of State and Nonconformist Conscience 2/6 c 8° Methuen 95
'A Socialistic Defence of some Ancient Institns.'—notably the Ho. of Lds. and the Establ. Church. Whimsical (perhaps ironical).

*United States*

ELY, Prf. R. T. Recent American Socialism 75 c. 8° Johns Hopk. Univ. Press, *Baltimore* 85

HILLQUIT, Morris History of Socialism in United States $1·50 *n.* (6/) 8° Funk & Wagnalls [03] 09

HINDS, W. A. American Communities & Co-operative Colonies ; ill. $1·50 12° Kerr, *Chicago* [78] 08
Early cols. at Jamestown and Plymouth, and Moravian Settlements ; Ephrata Community, Snow Hill, Jemima Wilkinson, Shakers, Harmonists' Zoarists, Owenites, Perfectionists, Hopedales, Fourieristics, Brook Farm, N. Am. Phalanx, Fruitlands, Skaneateles, Amana Community, Bethel-Aurora, Icarians, Second Adventists, Nazians, Bruederhofists, Brotherhd. of New Life, Woman's Commonwealth, Shalam, Topobolampo, Kore. shans, Altruists, Ruskinites, Fairhope Assoc., Roycrofters, Straightedgers, House of David, Temple home, Helicon home, fellowsh. farm assocns., etc.

JAMES, H. A. Communism in America $1 s 4° Holt, *N.Y.* 79

LOCKWOOD, G. B. New Harmony Communities ; 22 pl. & ports. $2·50 8° *Chronicle* Co., *Marion, Ind.* 02

KAUFFMANN, Rev. M. Utopias : schemes for soc. improv. fr. More to Marx—*ut* **D** § 134, *s.v.* Ideal C'wealths

NORDHOFF, Chas. The Communistic Societies of the United States ; ill $4 8° Harper, *N.Y.* 75
*O.p.* [*pb.* 15/] Murray. Acc. of author's visits to chief communistic socs. of U.S., describg. their soc. and relig. creeds and practices, and industr. and financ. arrgmts. Economists, Zoarites, Shakers, the Amana, Oneida, Bethel, Aurora, Icarian and other socs.

NOYES, J. H. History of American Socialisms $3·50 8° Lippincott, *Phila.* 70
5/ Reeves. A collection of facts, with interpretation and generalization by the inductive method.

SHAW, Alb. Icaria : a chapter in history of communism $1 12° Putnam, *N.Y.* 84
An impartial hist. of communes wh. have attempted to realize the rational democratic communism of the Utopian philosophers.

*Brook Farm* —*v. also* **D** § 120 (BEMIS)

CODMAN, J. T. History of the Brook Farm $2 c 8° Arena Pb. Co., *Boston* 94

CURTIS, G. W. [1824–92] Early Letters to J. S. Dwight [Brk. Farm & Concord] $1·50 c 8° Harper, *N.Y.* 98

Cary, E. G. W. Curtis [Amer. Men of Letters ; 4/6 *n.* Constable] $1·25 Houghton, *Boston* 94

DWIGHT, J. S. [1813–93] J. S. Dwight : a biography. By G. W. Cooke $2 c 8° Small, *Boston* 99
Acc. of the Saturday Club, of life at Brook Farm ; w. letters of interest fr. contemporaries.

HAWTHORNE, Nat. [1804–64]—*for his* Life *v.* **K** § 29

RIPLEY, Geo. [1802–80] : Frothingham (O. B.) George Ripley [Amer. Men of Letters ; 4/6 *n.* Constable] $1·25 c 8° Houghton, *Boston* 83

SWIFT, Lindsay Brook Farm : its members, scholars, visitors $1·25 Macmillan, *N.Y.* 00

*Oneida :* EASTLAKE (Alan) The Oneida Community 2/6 *n.* c 8° Redway (Paul) 00

SMITH, Prf. Goldwin Oneida—*in his* Essays on Questions of the Day, *ut* **D** § 142

*Africa :* KIDD (Dudley) Kafir Socialism—*ut* **E** § 41

**Biography :** *Collectively*

TAYLOR, G. R. S. Leaders of Socialism 1/ *n.* c 8° *New Age* Press 08
Accounts of 13 leaders, from Rob. OWEN to R. BLATCHFORD, by a Revolutionist, who is very scornful of the 'creeping' methods of the Fabians.

TAYLOR, Ida A. Revolutionary Types ; Introd. by R. B. Cunningham-Graham 7/6 *n.* 8° Duckworth 04
Nine biograph. sketches of typical revolutionaries ; w. conclusn. surveyg. positn. of the revolutionary.

*Individually :* HYNDMAN (H. M.) Record of an Adventurous Life 15/ *n.* 8° Macmillan 11

KINGSLEY, Can. Chas. [Christian Socialist]—*v.* **K** § 24 (KAUFMANN ; STUBBS)

LASSALLE, Ferd. [1825–64]

Bernstein, Edw. Ferdinand Lassalle as a Social Reformer [fr.] [Soc. Sci. Ser.] 2/6 c 8° Sonnenschein 93
$1 Scribner, *N.Y.* Serves as a useful complemt. to DAWSON's book. Author, a thorough-going Social Democrat and a 'philosophic Socialist' seeks to shew th. LASSALLE did not differ fundamentally fr. MARX and his followers. To non-socialists chief pt. in bk. is author's practical abandonmt. of MARX's theory of value.

Brandes, Dr Geo. Ferdinand Lassalle [tr.] 6/ *n.* c 8° Heinemann 11

Dawson, W. H. — German Socialism and Ferdinand Lassalle—*ut sup.*

Evans, Mrs — Eliz. Ferd. Lassalle and Helene von Dönniges — 1 / c 8° Sonnenschein 97

Meredith, Geo. — —*in his* The Tragic Comedians [fiction], *ut* **K** § 50

Edn. w. Introd. by Clement SHORTER conts. a bibliography of LASSALLE literature.

v. RACOWITZA, Pr'ess Helene

Mar, Cecil [tr.] — Princess Helene von Racowitza: an autobiography: tr. 12/6 *n.* 8° Constable 10

*My Connection with Lassalle* (pb. ab. 30 yrs. ago) recounts leadg. episode in this autobiogr., wh. closed w. d. of LASSALLE (1864) in a duel w. Yanko von RACOWITZA, formg. the theme of MEREDITH'S *Tragic Comedians*. The pres. bk. incl. this, and tells the story of her whole career. She is now wife of Bar. SERGE VON SCHEWITZ.

MORRIS, Wm. [1834–96] — —*v.* **K** § 24

OWEN, Rob. [1771–1858] — Life of. Written by himself [w. selns. fr. wrgs.] *o.p.* [*pb.* 10/] c 8° Wilson 57

Booth, A. J. — Robert Owen, the Founder of Socialism in England *o.p.* [*pb.* 5/] p 8° Trübner 69

Cullen, Alex — Adventures in Socialism — 7/6 *n.* 8° Black 10

Narr. of the organizn. on philanthropic and educ. princs. by OWEN of the Lanark Mills on the falls of the Clyde and of the attempt wh. sprang fr. it to form a model community at Orbiston, nr. Motherwell, made by Archib. HAMILTON and Abram COMBE.

Davies, R. E. — Life of Robert Owen, Philanthropist and Social Reformer 1/6 *n.* 16° Sutton 07

Jones, Lloyd — Life, Times, and Labours. of Robert Owen [Soc. Sci. Ser.; $1·25 Scribner, *N.Y.*] 3/6 c 8° Sonnenschein [90] 00

Podmore, Fk. — Robert Owen, a Biography, 2 vols.; ill. — 24/ *n.* 8° Hutchinson 06

Sargant, W. L. — Robert Owen and his Philosophy — *o.p.* [*pb.* 10/6] c 8° Smith & Elder 60

Seligman, Prf. E. R. A. — Owen and the Christian Socialists — 8° Ginn, *Boston* 86

45 pp., reprinted from *Political Science Quarterly*. Contains a bibliography of OWEN and the Christian Socialists.

RODBERTUS J. Carl [1805–75]

Gonner, Prf. E. C. K. — The Social Philosophy of Rodbertus — 7/6 *n.* ($2·50 *n.*) c 8° Macmillan 99

Good expositn.—the first in English—of social and econ. tchg. of a thoroughgoing Socialist with a high reputn. in Germy, tho' little heard of here

ST SIMON [1760–1825] — —*v. sup.*, *s.v.* France (BOOTH)

SHAW, Bernard

Chesterton, G. K. — G. Bernard Shaw — 5/ *n.* ($1·50 *n.*) c 8° Lane 09

Deacon, [Miss] R. M. — Bernard Shaw as Artist-Philosopher — [expository] 1/ *n.* f 8° Fifield 10

Jackson, Holbrook — Bernard Shaw: a monograph — 1/ *n.* c 8° Richards 09

VINCENT, Monsieur [17-cent. Christian Social Reformer]

Adderley, Rev. J. — Monsieur Vincent — [$1·25 Longman, *N.Y.*] 3/6 c 8° Arnold 01

WINSTANLEY, Gerrard — —*ut* **A** § 89

W., Digger and mystic, was also a Communist and Social Reformer; his *Laws for a Free Commonwealth* are given here in Appendix 3.]

## Constructive and Systematic

BAX, E. Belfort — The Religion of Socialism [Soc. Science Series] 2/6 c 8° Sonnenschein [87] 08

$1 Scribner, *N.Y.* 11 well-wr. essays on *Universal Hist.*, *Socialism and Relign.*, *Mod. Revoln.*, *Conscience and Commerce*, *Unscientific Socialism*, *Bourgeois Ideals*, etc. Also 1/.

„ — The Ethics of Socialism [Social Science Series] 2/6 c 8° Sonnenschein [89] 08

$1 Scribner, *N.Y.* 14 essays on *The New Ethic*, *Revoln. of 19 Cent.*, *Crim. Law under Socialism*, '*Justice*', *Mod. Cant*, *Men* v. *Classes*, etc. Also 1/.

„ — Outlooks from the New Standpoint [Soc. Sci. Ser.] 2/6 c 8° Sonnenschein [91]

$1 Scribner, *N.Y.* 11 essays on '*The Orator of the Human Race*' [J. B. CLOOTS (1755–94)], *Decay of Pagan Thought*, *Curse of Law*, *Pract. Ethics*, *Marriage*, etc.

„ — Essays in Socialism, New and Old — [also 6*d.*] 5/ *n.* c 8° Richards 07

About a third are reprinted from his *Outspoken Essays* [12 papers], 2/6 c 8° W. Reeves '97.

BELLAMY, Edw. — Looking Backward—*ut* **D** § 134

„ — Equality — [2/ Heinemann] 50 c. 12° Appleton, *N.Y.* [97] 02

Sanders, G. A. — Reality; or Law & Order *v.* Anarchy & Socialism $2 8° Burrows, *Cleveland* 98

A reply to the above two books.

BERNARD, H. M. — The Scientific Basis of Socialism — 1/ *n.* c 8° *New Age* Press 09

BERNSTEIN, Edw. — Evolutionary Socialism: a criticism and affirmation [tr.] 1/6 *n.* c 8° Natl. Labr. Pr., *Salford, Mancs.* 10

$1 *n.* Huebsch, *N.Y.* [Socialist Lib.] Of some histor. importce.: expangn. of letter by author pointg. out th. the Marxian forecast of collapse of the *bourgeois* econ. is not bg. fulfilled, and th. the no. of members of the possessing classes is to-day not smaller but larger than in MARX'S time—thus discreditg. the so-called scientific basis of Socialism, and earng. for author the enmity of the thoroughgoing Marxians.

BLATCHFORD, Rob. ['NUNQUAM'] Merrie England [10 c. Kerr, Chicago] 1/; 3*d.* c 8° *Clarion* Off. [94]

Replied to by 'NEMO', Labour and Luxury, 1/ c 8° Walter Scott '95.

„ — Britain for the British — 2/6 *n.*; 3*d.* c 8° *Clarion* Off. 02

„ — Not Guilty: defence of the bottom dog — 2/6 *n.*; 6*d.* c 8° *Clarion* Off. 06

Wilson, H. A. — Failure of Modern Socialism — [reply to above] 3/6 c 8° Drane 07

CARPENTER, Edw. — Civilisation, its Cause and Cure; and other Essays [Social Science Ser.] 2/6 c 8° Sonnenschein [89] 08

$1 Scribner, *N.Y.* Well-wr., interesting essays on *Civilizn.*, *etc.*, *Mod. Science*, *Science of Future* [a forecast], *Defence of Criminals*, *Exfoliatn.*: *Lamarck* v. *Darwin*, *Custom*. Also 1/.

„ — England's Ideal; and other Essays [Social Science Series] 2/6 c 8° Sonnenschein [87]

$1 Scribner, *N.Y.* *England's Ideal*, *Money-Lending*, *Social Progress and Indiv. Effort*, *Desirable Mansions*, *Simplification of Life*, *Does it pay?* *Trade*, *Private Property*, *The Enchanted Thicket*. Also 1/.

CLAPPERTON, Jane H. Scientific Meliorism and the Evolution of Happiness 8/6 c 8° Paul 85
One of the more influential books of the earlier epoch in the literature.

,, A Vision of the Future 3/6 c 8° Sonnenschein 05
Restates author's belief in the future, when Society shall have been reorganized for the provision of individual happiness of an ethical character.

ENGELS, Fredk. Socialism, Utopian & Scientific [tr.] [Soc. Sci. Ser.] 2/6 c 8° Sonnenschein [92] 08
$1 Scribner, *N.Y.* A strikg. defence of 'historical materialism', *i.e.* th. view of course of hist. wh. seeks ultim. cause and gt. movg. power of all import. histor. events in econ. developmt. of soc., in modes of productn. and exch., in conseq. divisn. of soc. into classes, and in struggle of these classes agst. ea. other. Appendix on *The Mark*.

Fabian Socialist Series ea. 6*d. n.*, 1/*n.* c 8° Fifield 08–9 *in prg.*
i: *Socialism and Religion.* Rev. S. H. HEADLAM + P. DEARMER + J. CLIFFORD
ii: *Socialism and Agriculture.* E. CARPENTER + T. S. DYMOND + Col. PEDDER
iii: *Socialism and Individualism.* S. WEBB + S. BALL + Bern. SHAW + Sir O. LODGE
iv: *Basis and Policy of Socialism.* S. WEBB + Fabian Soc.
v: *Commonsense of Munic. Trading* [*ut* D § 124]. B. SHAW
vi: *Socialism and National Minimum.* Mrs S. WEBB + Miss B. L. HUTCHINS + Fabian Soc.
vii: *Wastage of Child Life.* [*ut* D § 118] Dr J. JOHNSTON

Fabian Society: Fabian Essays, ed. G. Bernard Shaw 6*d. n.* 8° Walter Scott [90] 09
50 *c. n.* Ball Pb. Co., *Boston.* Seven essays by EDR., Sid. WEBB, Wm. CLARK, Syd. OLIVIER, Annie BESANT, Graham WALLAS, Hubert BLAND, comprising an account of the basis of the Socialism of the Fabian Soc. Wr. w. conspicuous ability, it has been equally attacked and eulogized.

,, Tracts: a series of 1*d.* tracts, in 1 vol. 4/6 *n.* c 8° Fabian Soc.

FERRI, E. Socialism and Positive Science, tr. Edith C. Harvey [Socialist Lib.] 1/6 *n.* c 8° Natl. Labr. Pr., *Salford, Mancs.* 06
Darwin, Spencer, Marx. Another tr. (by R. Rives La Monte) *s.t. Socialism and Modern Science,* $1 Kerr, *Chicago* [00] 09 [4/6 *n.* Paul].

GEORGE, Hy. —*for his expositions of his Agrarian Socialism, v.* **D** § 119

GRONLUND, Laur. The Co-operative Commonwealth—[Social Sci. Ser.] 2/6 c 8° Sonnenschein [84] 91
$1 Lee & Shepard, *Boston.* From the standpoint of MARX. Moderate. Cheap edn., 1/ (50 c.).

,, Our Destiny 50 c. c 8° Lee & Shep., *Boston* [91]
2/6 Sonnenschein. [Soc. Sci. Ser.] On influence of 'Nationalism' [= Amer. Socialism] on morals and religions. A vigorous little book.

,, The New Economy: a peaceable solution $1·25 c 8° Stone, *Chicago* 98
Proposes a vast number of Socialistic changes in American institutions.

HERVÉ, Gust. My Country Right or Wrong, tr. G. Bowman 3/6 *n.* c 8° Fifield 10
With Pref. by E. B. BAX. A noble protest against that fraudulent counterfeit of a moral principle called patriotism'. Author's object—in spite of title—is to show that a country is never right, and to overthrow the 'Patriot Socialists', who maintain that they will defend their country if attacked.

HOBSON, J. A. The Social Problem—*ut* **D** § 125; for his other wks. *v.* General Index

HYNDMAN, H. M. The Historical Basis of Socialism in England *o.p.* [*pb.* 8/6] 8° Paul 83
One of the earlier treatises wh. had most success in bringing in converts to Socialism.

,, The Economics of Socialism 3/ c 8° *Twentieth Cent.* Press 96
7 lects. (6 del. for Soc. Democr. Fedn.) seekg. to rehabilitate Marxian theory of value.

,, The Time of Transition; or, Hope for Humanity 6/ c 8° *New Cent.* Press 00

JAURÈS, Jean L. Studies in Socialism [tr.] [$1 *n.* Putnam, *N.Y.*] 1/6 *n.* c 8° Natl. Labr. Pr., *Salford, Mancs.* [06] 09

KAUTSKY, Karl The Social Revolution [tr.] [Standard Socialist Ser.] 50 c. c 8° Kerr, *Chicago* 03

KELLY, Edm. Government or Human Evolution [*ut* **D** § 134, vol. ii: *Individualism and Collectivism*

,, Twentieth Century Socialism $1·75 *n.* (7/6 *n.*) c 8° Longman 10
By late Lecturer on Munic. Govt. in Columbia Univ., a convert to Collectivism a few yrs. before his death.

KEMPNER, N. Common Sense Socialism [a popular exposn. of princs.] 7/6 8° Sonnenschein 87

Labour Ideal (The): ser. of bks. on social questions ea. 1/*n.* f 8° G. Allen 07 *sqq.*, *in prg.*
i: *Fr. Serfdom to Socialism* J. Keir HARDIE
ii: *The Socialist's Budget* [*ut inf.*] Pp. SNOWDEN
iii: *Labour and the Empire* J. R. MACDONALD
iv: *The Socialist's Church* [*ut inf.*] Rev. Stewart D. HEADLAM
v: *The Woman Socialist* Ethel SNOWDEN
vi: *The Socialist and the City* [*ut* **D** § 124] F. W. JOWETT

MACDONALD, J. Ramsay [M.P.] Socialism [Social Problems Series] 1/*n.* c 8° Jack 07

,, —*v.* Socialist Library, *inf.*
Socialism is, for the author, a programme of gradual reform effected by recognized political machinery, springing partly fr. necessities of econ. change, partly fr. revolt agst. chaos and injustice of pres. condns., and based fundam. on conceptn. of society as an organism w. individuals as cells in that organism.

MARX, Karl [1818–83] Capital [tr.], ed. F. Engels, 2 vols. ea. 10/6 8° Sonnenschein [86] 07; 07
Ea. $2 Kerr, *Chicago.* The most influential systematic wk. in economics yet wr. by any Socialist—the chief foundatn.-stone on wh. Socialist propaganda was based: its Theory of Value, however, has been long since abandoned by more intelligent Socialists, and is indeed as good as dropped in the 2nd (posth.) vol., which was left by author in chaotic state and has been put (more or less) into shape by ENGELS.

,, The same; vol. iii [tr.] 10/6 8° Indep. Lab. Pty. 09

,, Manifesto of the Cummunist Party [tr.], ed. F. Engels 50 c. c 8° Kerr, *Chicago* 08

Aveling, Dr Edw. Student's Marx [epitome; Soc. Sci. Ser.; Scrib., *N.Y.*] [also 1/] 2/6 c 8° Sonnenschein [91]

v. Böhm-Bawerk, Prf. E. Karl Marx and the Close of his System [tr.] 6/ c 8° Unwin 98
$1·60 *n.* Macmillan, *N.Y.* A powerful crit. of inherent contradictn. involved in MARX's analytic economics. Author thinks that, while the syst. of MARX is at an end, Socialism does not, as a general doctr., depend on Marxian anal. of Value.

Boudin, L. B. Theoretical System of Marx in Light of Recent Criticism $1 12° Kerr, *Chic.* 07

Deville, G. The People's Marx [an epitome; Internat. Lib.] 6/*n.* c 8° Paul 05

Spargo, J. Karl Marx: his life and work $2·50 *n.* 8° Huebsch, *N.Y.* 10

Untermann, E. Marxian Economics: pop. introduction to Marx's 'Capital' $1 c 8° Kerr, *Chicago* 07

MASTERMAN, C. F. G. In Peril of Change: essays wr. in time of tranquillity [$1·50 Huebsch, *N.Y.*] 6/ c 8° Unwin 05

" The Condition of England—*ut* **D** § 117*

MATHEWS, Dr B. C. Our Irrational Distribution of Wealth $1·25 *n.* (5/ *n.*) c 8° Putnam 08

MONEY, L. G. Chiozza Riches and Poverty 5/ *n.* 8° Methuen [05] 11
Thesis: nearly one half entire income of U.K. is enjoyed by one-ninth of populn., and more than one-third by less than one-thirtieth; that this 'error of distribn.' shd. be corrected by a graduated Income-Tax and more severely graduated Death-Duties. Many social evils discussed, and the remedy of publ. control, publ. expendre., publ. enterprise applied to each.

MORRIS, Wm. Signs of Change [seven lectures] 4/6 ($1·50) p 8° Longman [88]

" Letters on Socialism [only 34 copies prtd.] [*w.* 21 /] c 8° *priv. prin.* 94
[Ashley Lib. of Priv. Prtd. Bks.] Letters addressed to Rev. Geo. BAINTON, of Coventry.

PEARSON, Prf. Karl —*in his* The Ethic of Freethought, *ut* **A** § 8

PRUDHON, P. J. [1809–65] —*v. inf.*, *s.v.* Anarchism

ROUSSEAU, J.-J. [1712–78] The Social Contract [tr.]—*ut* **F** § 49

SHAW, G. Bernard —*in his* Quintessence of Ibsenism, *ut* **K** § 41

" Fabianism and the Empire 1/ c 8° Richards 00
An electn.-manifesto, givg. Fabian views on chief questns. of day. *V.* also *Fabian Socialist Essays* and Fabian Soc., *sup.*

SINCLAIR, Upton The Industrial Republic [$1·25 *n.* Doubleday, *N. Y.*] 6/ c 8° Heinemann 07
A study of America 10 yrs. hence—a mixture of facts, dreams, and prophecy.

SNOWDEN, P. [M.P.] The Socialist's Budget [Labour Ideal Series] 1/ *n.* 12° G. Allen 07

Socialist Library: ed. J. Ramsay Macdonald [M.P.] ea. 1/6 *n.* c 8° Natl. Labr. Pr., *Salford, Mancs.* 06–10 *in prg.*

i: *Socialism and Positive Science* [tr.] [*ut sup.*] E. FERRI
ii: *Socialism and Society* MACDONALD
iii: *Studies in Socialism* [*ut sup.*] Jean JAURÈS
iv: *White Capital and Coloured Labour* [*ut* **D** § 130] S. OLIVIER
v: *Collectivism and Industr. Evolution* E. VANDERVELDE [tr.]
vi *Socialism and the Drink Questn.* [*ut* **D** § 131] Pp. SNOWDEN [M.P.]
vii: *Evolutionary Socialism* [tr.] [*ut sup.*] E. BERNSTEIN
viii: *Socialism and Government*, 2 Pts. MACDONALD
ix: *The Coming Force* [the Labr. Movemt.] F. H. ROSE
Extra vol. i: *The Revoln. in the Baltic Provinces of Russia* E. O. F. AMES
*Socialism and Foreign Affairs* H. N. BRAILSFORD, *in prep.*
*India* J. Keir HARDIE, *in prep.*

SPARGO, Jno. Socialism: summary and interpretn. of soct. princs. $1·25 *n.* (5/ *n.*) c 8° Macmillan [06] 09
A good exposition of the question of economic reform fr. the Socialist standpoint.

" The Socialists: who they are and what they stand for 50 c. 16° Kerr, *Chicago* 06

" The Common Sense of Socialism $1; 25 c. c 8° Kerr, *Chicago* 08

" The Substance of Socialism $1 *n.* c 8° Huebsch, *N.Y.* 09

SUTHERS, R. B. Common Objections to Socialism Answered 1/ *n.* c 8° *Clarion* Press 08

TOWLER, W. G. Socialism in Local Government—*ut* **D** § 124

Towards a Social Policy: suggestions for constructive reform 1/ *n.* c 8° Rivers 05
Reprs. fr. *The Speaker* of anon. articles [by L. T. HOBHOUSE, C. F. G. MASTERMAN, J. A. HOBSON, J. L. HAMMOND, and others].

WEBB, Sid. Difficulties of Individualism, *and* Socialism, True and False—*in his* Problems of Mod. Industry, *ut* **D** § 118

" *etc.* Socialism and Individualism 1/ *n.* 12° Fifield 08

WELLS, H. G. Anticipations of Reaction of Mechanical and Scientific Progress upon Human Life and Thought 2/ c 8° Chapman [02]
$1·80 Harper, *N.Y.* (1) *Locomotion in 20th Cent.*, (2) *Probable Diffusion of Great Cities*, (3) *Developing Social Elements*, (4) *Certain Social Reactions* [home-life, marrge., etc.], (5) *Life-history of Democracy*, (6) *War in 20th Cent.*, (7) *Conflict of Languages*, (8) *The Larger Synthesis* [rise of world-republic], (9) *Faith, Morals, and Publ. Policy in 20th Cent.* Also 6d.

" Discovery of Future [disc. del. to Roy. Institn.] 2/ c 8° Unwin 02

" Mankind in the Making; *and* A Modern Utopia—*ut* **D** § 134

" The Future of America [$2 *n.* Harper, *N.Y.*] 10/6 *n.* 8° Chapman 06
Impressions and reflections of an American tour. Social, economic, and material condns.

" New Worlds for Old [$1·50 *n.* Macmillan, *N.Y.*] 6/ c 8° Constable 08
Discusses case for and agst. Socialism, and indicates lines of advance tow. author's ideal. Full of clever, diffuse wrg., and too much occupied w. 'his own personal dream' to admit the bk. to much scientific value. Also 1/ *n.*

" First and Last Things: confessn. of faith and rule of life 4/6 *n.* c 8° Constable 08
$1·50 *n.* Putnam, *N.Y.* An exposn. of author's personal views on place and purpose of a human being in the world.

" Socialism and the Family—*ut* **D** § 125

*Nationalization of Health* —*v.* **D** § 142

*Christian Socialism; Christianity and Sociology—v. also* **A** §§ 45, 113

ABRAHAM, Rev. W. H. Studies of a Socialist Parson 3/6 c 8° Simpkin 92

ADDERLEY, Rev. J. Looking Upward: introd. to study of soc. questns. 3/6 c 8° Wells Gardner 96

" The Parson in Politics 1/ c 8° Jackson, *Leeds* 10

BARNETT, Can. + Mrs S. A. Practicable Socialism [ess. on soc. reform] 6/ ($1·50) c 8° Longman [88] 94

BARRY, Bp A. Lectures on Christianity and Socialism 3/6 c 8° Cassell 90

CHRISTIAN SOCIAL UNION: Pubns. 102, *Adelaide Rd., London*

CONE, Dr Orello Rich and Poor in the New Testament—*ut* **A** § 45
A study in prim. Xtn. doctr. of earthly possessns. Higher-critical in method; individualistic in spirit.

CRAFTS, Rev. W. F. Pract. Christian Sociology; ill. [lects.] $1·50 *n.* (6/) c 8° Funk & Wagnalls [95] 07
Tempce., Sabbath-reform. gamblg., purity, civ. serv., munic. ref., educn., immigrn., divorce, woman suffr., etc.

CUNNINGHAM, Dr W. Modern Civilization in some of its Economic Aspects—*ut* **F** § 4

„ Christianity and Social Questions [Studies in Theology] 2/6 *n.* c 8° Duckworth 10

ELY, Prf. R. T. Socialism: nature, strength, and weakness 6/ c 8° Sonnenschein 94

„ Socialism & Social Reform [Lib. of Economics] $1·50 12° Crowell, *N.Y.* [94] 95

GLADDEN, Rev. Washington Christianity & Socialism [*v. also* **A** § 113] $1 *n.* 12° Eaton & Mains, *N.Y.* 05

GUILD OF ST MATTHEW: Pubns. 376, *Strand, London, W.C.*

HAND, Rev. J. E. [ed.] Good Citizenship; pref. by Bp C. Gore 6/ *n.* c 8° G. Allen 99
$1·50 F. P. Harper, *N.Y.* Twenty-three Chr.-Socialist essays on social, personal, and econ. probls. and obligations.

HAW, Geo. [ed.] Christianity & the Working Classes [by var. wrs.] 3/6 *n.* ($1·50 *n.*) c 8° Macmillan 06

HEADLAM, Rev. S. D. The Socialist's Church [Labour Ideal Series] 1/ *n.* 12° G. Allen 07

„ *etc.* Socialism and Religion—*ut sup.*, *s.n.* Fabian Socialist Series

HENDERSON, Prf. C. R. Social Duties from the Christian Point of View $1·25 8° Univ. Press, *Chicago* 09

KAUFMANN, Rev. M. Christian Socialism 4/6 c 8° Paul 88

„ Social Development under Christian Influence [Donnellan Lects.] 5/ 8° Hodges, *Dublin* 00

KENWORTHY, J. C. From Bondage to Brotherhood: a message to the workers 1/ c 8° Walter Scott 94

KINGSLEY, Can. Chas. —*in his novels* Alton Locke *and* Yeast, *ut* **K** § 50

LIBERAL CHRISTIAN LEAGUE: Pubns. *King's Weight Co., Duke St., Lond., W.*

MAURICE, Rev. F. D. Social Morality—*ut* **A** § 3

[MILLIN, G. F.] Commerce & Christianity [agst. competitive syst.] 3/6 c 8° Sonnenschein 00

MUIR, W. Christianity and Labour 6/ c 8° Hodder 10

NEWTON, Rev. R. Heber Social Studies $1·60 (3/6) 16° Putnam, *N.Y.* 87
By Pastor of Prot. Ep. Ch. of All Souls, N.Y. Reviews labr.-questn., co-oper., intempce., moral educn., socialism, communism.

NOEL, Rev. Conrad Socialism in Church History 5/ *n.* c 8° Palmer 10

RAE, Jno. The Christian Socialists = ch. ix *of his* Contemporary Socialism, *ut sup.*

STUBBS, Bp C. W. A Creed for Christian Socialists [*v.* also **A** § 109] 1/ c 8° W. Reeves 97

„ Kingsley and the Christian Social Movement—*ut* **K** § 24

Student Christian Movement: Pubns. [pamphlets] 93, *Chancery Lane, London*

WESTCOTT, Bp B. F. Social Aspects of Christianity—*ut* **A** § 113

WOODWORTH, A. V. Christn. Socialism in Engl. [Soc. Sci. Ser.; $1 Scrib., *N.Y.*] 2/6 c 8° Sonnenschein 03

*Roman Catholic*

NITTI, Prf. F. S. Catholic Socialism [tr. fr. Ital.]; Introd. D. G. Ritchie 10/6 8° Sonnenschein [95] 08
$2·75 *n.* Macmillan, *N.Y.* A v. compreh. study of Cath. Socialism and of relns. of Papacy to the social questn., contg. mass of informn. & materl. (esp. as regs. Continent) not otherwise accessible in Engl. Xtn. Socialism receives share of treatmt.

SODERINI, Ct. Ed. Socialism and Catholicism [tr.]; Introd. Card. Vaughan 6/ ($2) c 8° Longman 96
A full commentary on Papal Encyclical *Rerum Novarum*: amg. documts. in Appendix are Ital. verns. of Encyclicals on *Socialism, Polit. Power, Constitn. of Xtn. States, Chief Duties of Xtn. Citizens, Labour.* On the whole, moderate and sensible.

**Anti-Socialist [wholly or partly]; Individualist**—*v. also* **D** § 135, *s.v.* Liberty

BAIN, F. W. Occam's Razor 4/6 c 8° Parker 90
The razor of a new OCCAM appl. to pol. econ., condns. of progress, Socialism, politics. The refutn. of Socialism, attackg. central posns. of MARX and LASSALLE, particularly logical and methodical.

BASTIAT, Fred. Economic Harmonies, tr. P. J. Stirling *o.p.* [*pb.* 7/6] c 8° Murray 60
The second pt. of the wk. was never wr. owing to author's d. in 1850. The bk. forms the last incarnatn. of thorough-going economic optimistic *laissez-faire*, singularly out of harmony w. all mod. polit. thought. Lucid, but not profound.

BOSANQUET, Dr Bern. —*in his* Civilization of Christendom, and other Studies, *ut* **A** § 8
Conts. two excellent papers on the *Antithesis betw. Individualism and Socialism Philosophically Considered; Liberty and Legislation.*

„ —*in his* Essays and Addresses, *ut* **A** § 8

BUCHANAN, Rob. The Coming Terror; and other Essays and Letters 12/6 8° Heinemann [91] 91
$2·50 U.S. Book Co., *N.Y.* Repr. of newsp. letters, exhibitg. and denouncg. var. phases of the 'coming terror', i.e. 'submergence of indiv. freed. and activity beneath the waves of polit. and soc. anarchy'. While rejecting the New Socialism, the author claims to be a true Socialist, 'a man eager for the common good', wh. 'can only be attained by complete freedom'.

BURKE, Edm. [1729–97] Vindication of the Claims of Natural Society 1/ *n.* f 8° Fifield [1756]
Also in his *Works*, vol. i [*ut* **K** § 89]. Shows the evils inherent in all State governments.

CATHREIN, Rev. Victor Socialism Exposed & Refuted [tr. fr. Germ.] $1·25 *n.* 12° Benziger, *N.Y.* [92] 02
A Jesuit's criticism. Tr. of pt. of his *Der Socialismus*, extr. fr. vol. i of his *Moral-Philosophie.*

COOPER, Sir Wm. E. Socialism and its Perils 2/6 *n.* c 8° Nash 08
A trenchant exposure of the 'fallacies and perils' of the various Socialistic doctrines.

DAWBARN, C. Y. C. Liberty and Progress 9/ *n.* ($3 *n.*) 8° Longman 09
By a disciple of BENTHAM, whose saying 'Poverty is not the work of the laws: it is the primitive condition of the human race' represents his standpt. Shows how improvemt. of positn. of poorer classes can be secured only by increasg. efficiency of lab., to wh. 3 factors contrib. (1) increase of capital, (2) improvemt. of organizn., (3) improvemt. of labourer himself. *Vide* also **D** § 118.

„ The Social Contract 3/6 *n.* 8° Longman 10
More particularly in relation to taxation: practically a complement to above.

DICKINSON, G. Lowes Modern Symposium—*ut* **D** § 134; Justice and Liberty—*ut* **D** § 125

DONISTHORPE, Wordsworth Principles of Plutology, the Science of Wealth 7/6 8° Williams 76

,, Individualism, a System of Politics *o.p.* [*pb.* 14/] 8° Macmillan 89

Polemic rather than apologetic, tho' his main object is to present a system—a kind of philosophical peaceable anarchism dispensing w. the State—wh. he does w. indifferent success.

,, Law in a Free State 5/*n.* ($2) c 8° Macmillan 95

The Empire of the Individual consists of all those moral or "natural" rights wh. have not been taken away for the general good, and all those civil rights wh. have been conferred upon him (the indiv.) by the State in exch. for the rts. of wh. he has been deprived'. Incisive, thoroughgoing, original in outlook, and caustic in expressn., tho' essentially wayward and paradoxical: author has been called 'the Bernard Shaw of Individualism'.

DRESSER, H. W. Voices of Freedom $1·25 (5/) c 8° Putnam 00

FAWCETT, Prf. Hy. + [Mrs] M. G.—*in their* Essays & Lectures on Political & Social Subjects, *ut* **D** § 114

FELL, E. F. B. The Foundations of Liberty—*ut* **D** § 135

Points out th. essence of Socialism consists in compl. mergence of indiv. in the whole, and in denial of the *a priori* or natural rts. of the Person.

FITE, Warner Individualism [four lectures] 6/6 *n.* 8° Longman 11

FLINT, Prf. R. Socialism [$3·25 Lippincott, *Phila.*] 7/6 8° Pitman [95] 08

A large bk. of somewhat small value, findg. th. 'the true doctr. of society' lies somewhere betw. 'Socialism and Individualism, yet is larger than either', and must incl. the truth, while excluding the error, of both.

GILMAN, N. P. Socialism & the American Spirit [6/6 Macmillan] $1·50 c 8° Houghton, *Boston* [93] 00

A discriminatn. betw. var. forms of Individualism and Socialism, w. obj. of showg. th. Amer. spirit [characteristics of wh. he regards as (1) love of pers. liberty, (2) pract. conservatism, (3) enterprise, (4) love of competitn., (5) pub. spirit] is unlikely to carry into pract. any extreme form of either.

GREG, W. R. Mistaken Aims & Unattainable Ideas of the Artisan Classes *o.p.* [*pb.* 10/8] 8° Trübner 76

GUYOT, Yves The Tyranny of Socialism [tr.], ed. J. M. Levy [Soc. Sci. Ser.] 2/6 c 8° Sonnenschein 94

$1 Scribner, *N.Y.* A strong attack on Socialism (chfly. Fch. and Germ.), takg. for its motto LEDRU-ROLLIN's saying th. Socialism may be defined as the State substitutg. itself for individual liberty, and developg. thereby into the most terrible of tyrants.

,, Labour, Socialism, and Strikes [tr.]—*ut* **D** § 118

,, Socialistic Fallacies [tr.] 6/*n.* c 8° Cope & Fenwick 10

A careful investigation of the history and facts of the subject.

HAKE (A. Egmont) + WESSLAU (O. E.) The Coming Individualism 14/ 8° Constable 96

$4 Macmillan, *N.Y.* A mere restatemt. of the familiar argumts. in favr. of Individualism as agst. State Control—too general to be of much value.

HEADLAM, F. W. Darwinism and Modern Socialism 5/*n.* c 8° Methuen 09

A convinced follower of DARWIN and WEISMANN, he regards mod. civilizn. as based on struggle f. existce.—if this, 'exc. so far as it depends on disease' were abol., the life of the nation wd. be sapped. Socialism, in so far as it abolishes competn., is therefore no remedy f. our evils. Pt. ii deals w. Socialism of early communities, iii is a histor. review of its growth, iv is devoted to mod. probs. Practical and tolerant.

HILL, Wm. Socialism and Sense: a Radical review 1/c 8° Walter Scott 95

An incisive crit. of some extravagances of mod. Socialism, followed by exposn. of altern. 'Radical' princs.

HEADLEY, F. W. Darwinism and Modern Socialism 5/*n.* c 8° Methuen 09

HIRSCH, M. Democracy *versus* Socialism—*ut* **D** § 139

IRESON, Fk. The People's Progress: study of facts of natl. wealth 2/6 8° Murray 10

By a pronounced Individualist, discussg. extent to wh. artisan-class has benefited by progr. of last 60 yrs., [and possibility of gain to that class by Socialistic redistribn. of our natl. income.

JEVONS, Prf. W. S. The State in rel. to Labour [Engl. Citizen Ser.] 2/6 ($1) c 8° Macmillan [82] 10

'To explain why, in general, we uphold the rule of *laisser faire*, and yet in many cases invoke the interference of central authorities'.

JUDGE, Mark H. [ed.] Political Socialism [chiefly political] 1/*n.* c 8° P. S. King & Son 08

A colln. of papers by L'd BALFOUR OF BURLEIGH, L'd Hugh CECIL, Percy WYNDHAM, and others.

KAUFFMANN, Rev. M. Socialism Considered: its nat., dangers and remedies *o.p.* [*pb.* 7/6] c 8° H. S. King 74

,, Socialism and Communism 2/c 8° S.P.C.K. 83

,, Socialism & Modern Thought [Soc. Questns. of To-day] 2/6 c 8° Methuen 95

$1 Scribner, *N.Y.* Not very definite or instructive, and somewhat dully wr. Quotes freely fr. wks. of Socialists and appends own comments.

KNOTT, Y. Conservative Socialism [exposes dangers, & suggests remedy] 1/*n.* c 8° Sonnenschein [09] 10

de LAVELEYE, E. The Socialism of To-day, tr. G. H. Orpen *o.p.* [*pb.* 6/] c 8° Field & Tuer 84

LAYCOCK, F. U. Economics and Socialism—*ut* **D** § 119

An attempt to establish the fallacy of Socialism and the beneficence of the Single Tax.

LECKY, W. E. H. —*in his* Democracy and Liberty, *ut* **D** § 139

The 2 chs. *Socialism* and *Labour-Problems* afford an admir. concise and consec. review of course of thought and legisln. in these spheres.

LE ROSSIGNOL, J. E. Orthodox Socialism [Library of Economics] $1 *n.* 12° Crowell, *N.Y.* 07

LEROY-BEAULIEU, Paul Collectivism, tr. & abgd. Sir Arth. Clay 10/6 *n.* 8° Murray 08

$3 *n.* Dutton, *N.Y.* An excell. wr., painstakg., and compreh. wk., showg. how entirely strength of Socialism lies in sentimt., how impract. are its ultim. ideals, and how little support it receives fr. solid argumt. and reason.

,, —*in his* Papacy, Socialism, and Democracy, *ut* **D** § 119

LEVY, J. H. Short Studies in Economic Subjects 1/6 *n.* c 8° Personal Rts. Assoc. 03

[Personal Rights Ser., vol. i.] Introdn. to study of economics fr. pt.-of-view of those who wd. minimize State interference.

,, + Miss A. GOFF Politics and Disease [Pers. Rts. Ser., vol. iii] 3/6 *n.* c 8° P. S. King & Son 06

Pt. i (by LEVY): *Vivisectn. and Vaccin., C.D.A., Lunacy Laws*, etc., conclg. th. the State has gone wrong thro' disregard of pers. rts. Pt. ii (GOFF). shows how same disregard has oper. to detrimt. of hospital-managmt.

Liberty and Proeprty Defence League: *Pamphlets* 25, Victoria St., *Lond.*, *S.W.*

MACKAIL, J. W. Parting of the Ways: an address 2/6 *n.* 8° Hammersmith Pb. Soc. 03

,, Socialism and Politics 2/6 *n.* 8° Hammersmith Pb. Soc. 03

MACKAY, Thos. [ed.] A Plea for Liberty; w. Introd. by Herb. Spencer 2/8° Murray [91] 92
$2·25 Appleton, *N.Y.* *From Freedom to Bondage* (Herb. SPENCER); *Impract. of Socialism* (E. S. ROBERTSON); *Limits of Liberty* (W. DONISTHORPE); *True Line of Deliverance* (Aub. HERBERT); *Liberty for Labr.* (G. HOWELL); *State Socialism in Antipodes* (C. FAIRFIELD); *Post Office* (F. MILLAR); *State Pensns.* (C. J. RADLEY); and 5 other papers—all directed agst. Socialism and Socialistic legisln., fr. the *laissez faire* and Individualist. standpt.

,, Methods of Social Reform; essays crit. and constr.—*ut* **D** § 127, *s.v.* Poor Law
Opens and concludes with anti-Socialistic polemics.

,, [ed.] A Policy of Free Exchange 12/8° Murray 96
$4 Appleton, *N.Y.* *State in rel. to Rys.* (W. M. ACKWORTH); *State Socialism in Austral.* (J. W. FORTESCUE); *Infl. of State Borrowg. in Commerc. Crises* (W. HOOPER); *Law of Trade Combinatns.* (A. LYTTELTON); *Interest of Wkg.-Class in Free Exch.* (EDR.); *Science of Economics* (H. D. MACLEOD); *Coming Industr. Strife* (W. MAITLAND); *Progression and Taxatn.* (B. MALLET); *Natl. Workshops* (St Loe STRACHEY).

MCKECHNIE, W. S. The State and the Individual 10/6 *n.* 8° MacLehose, *Glasgow* 96
$3 *n.* Macmillan, *N.Y.* Introd. to polit. science, w. useful summaries of argumts. *pro* and *con* in main pts. at issue betw. socialism and individualism.

MALLOCK, W. H. Social Equality: a study in a missing science *o.p.* [*pb.* 6/] c 8° Bentley [82] 85
$1 Fenno, *N.Y.* The argumt. is to show that the one great incentive to wealth-producing labour is the desire for social inequality.

,, Property and Progress: inq. into present soc. agitn. [$1 Fenno, *N.Y.*] 6/c 8° Murray 84

,, Labour and the Popular Welfare 1/c 8° Black [93] 95
·90 c. Macmillan, *N.Y.* Combats militant Collectivism, analyzg. relns. betw. Capital and Labr., his main argumt. bg. th. chief productive agent in mod. world is not labr. but ability, wh. is the vital element of capital and therefore inseparable fr. it. Wr. mainly for the 'classes'.

,, Classes and Masses—*ut* **D** § 118 *and* Aristocracy and Evolution, *ut* **D** § 129

,, A Critical Examination of Socialism 6/; Ch. Edn. 1/*n.* c 8° Murray 08; 08
$2 *n.* Harper, *N.Y.* A brilliant and trenchant 'exam. of the false princs. and deficient conceptns. of fact wh. lie at the root, and form the sole distinguishing feature, of all forms of Socialism', i.e. the importce. of ability and the need of a directg. mind to render manual labour successful.

Smith, C. D. National Monopolies in rel. to Soc. Democr. [reply to above] 2/6 *n.* c 8° Fifield 09

MAYNE, Jno. Dawson Triumph of Socialism and How it Succeeded 1/c 8° Sonnenschein 08
A racy descrn. of the Socialist triumph at electns. of 1912, and its disastrous results at home and abroad.

MILL, Jno. Stuart On Liberty—*ut* **D** § 135

DE MOLINARI, G. —*in his* Religion [tr.], *ut* **D** § 125

MORLEY, Jno. [L'd] —*in his* Compromise, *ut* **K** § 89

,, Society of To-morrow: a forecast [tr.] 6/c 8° Unwin 04

NAQUET, A. Collectivism and Socialism, tr. Wm. Heaford [Soc. Sci. Ser.] 2/6 c 8° Sonnenschein 91
$1 Scribner, *N.Y.* An admir. criticism of the Socialism of MARX and LASSALLE; very lucid and acute—one of most effective refutns.

NICHOLSON, Prf. J. S. Historical Progress and Ideal Socialism 1/6 c 8° Black [94] 95

,, Strikes and Social Problems—*ut* **D** § 120

PEARSON, Dr C. H. —*in his* National Life and Character, *ut* **D** § 125

PENTY, Arth. J. The Restoration of the Gild System 3/6 *n.* i 16° Sonnenschein 06
In place of Socialism of orthodox type, suggests restoratn. of Gild syst. as a solutn. of industr. probls.

RAINE, G. E Present-day Socialism, & Problem of the Unemployed 2/6 *n.* c 8° Nash [08] 09

,, + ELGEE (P. C.) Case against Socialism; pref. by A. J. Balfour [$1·50 *n.* Macmillan, *N.Y.*] 5/*n.* c 8° G. Allen 08
A compilation of arguments, facts, and figures intended for political speakers.

RICHTER, Eug. Pictures of the Socialistic Future [tr.]—*ut* **D** § 134

SALEEBY, C. W. Individualism and Collectivism [4 pop. lects.; Spencerian] 2/c 8° Williams 06

SCHÄFFLE, Dr A. Quintessence of Socialism [tr.], w. Introd. B. Bosanquet [Social Science Ser.] 2/6 c 8° Sonnenschein [89]
$1 Scribner, *N.Y.* A very good little bk., explaing. and scientifi. treatg. scheme of Collectivism: lucid, fair, and brief—but adverse. Also 1/.

,, Impossibility of Social Democracy [tr.]; w. Introd. Bosanquet [Soc. Sci. Ser.] 3/6 c 8° Sonnenschein [91]
$1·25 Scribner, *N.Y.* Contin. of above, showg. that Soc. Democ. is 'once for all impossible' as positive pract. programme of new order of society

,, Theory and Policy of Labour Protection [Soc. Sci. Ser.] 2/6 c 8° Sonnenschein 93
$1 Scribner, *N.Y.* A developmt. of ideas in above, contg. an attempt to systematize a conservative programme of reform, and inclg. a discussn. of Maximum Wkg. Day.

SIMONSON, Prf. G. Plain Exam. of Socialism [Soc. Sci. Ser.; $1 Scrib., *N.Y.*] 2/6 c 8° Sonnenschein [01]

SMITH, Bruce Liberty and Liberalism 6/c 8° Longman 87
A protest agst. the 'growing tendency towards undue state interference'. 700 pp.

SMITH, H. Llew. Economic Aspects of State Socialism [Cobden Prize Essay] 3/6 c 8° Simpkin 87

SPENCER, Herb. Social Statics; *and* Man *versus* the State—*ut* **D** § 134; Justice—*ut* **C** § 62

STRACHEY, J. St Loe The Problems and Perils of Socialism 6*d.* (25 c. *n.*) 8° Macmillan 08
'Letters to a Working Man' on the evils of Socialism: repr. fr. *The Spectator*.

Smith, C. D. Socialism: a Solution & Safeguard [reply to above, letter by letter] 6*d.* *n.* c 8° Fifield 08

SUMNER, W. G. What Social Classes Owe to Each Other 60 c. 16° Harper, *N.Y.* 84
3/6 Paul. Maintains that they owe to each other not interference but simply justice. Strongly individualistic.

DE TUNZELMANN, G. W. The Superstition called Socialism 5/*n.* c 8° G. Allen 11

WILSON, W. Lawler The Menace of Socialism 6/*n.* c 8° Richards 09
Destructive criticism of Socialism. Author's remedy for evils of the time is not State Socialism, but 'State Actionism'.

WRIXON, Sir Hy. The Pattern Nation: Socialism, source, drift, outcome 3/*n.* ($1 *n.*) c 8° Macm. [06] 07
A discussn. of the problem as to what the poor will do with the rich, when govt. by majority has become a fact. Forms on the whole a careful and well-considered indictmt. of Socialism.

**Anarchism :** *Historical ; Descriptive ; Critical*

BREWSTER, H. B. Thieves of Anarchy and of Law : a midnight debate 5 / c 8° Williams 87

DUBOIS, Félix The Anarchist Peril, tr. Ralph Derechef ; ill. 5 / c 8° Unwin 94
A compreh. and fair sketch of hist. of Anarchism dur. 20 yrs. endg. 1894 ; i.e. since it took pract. shape out of rivalry betw. BAKUNIN and MARX ; w. statemts., deriv. fr. wrgs. of literary Anarchists, of its theoret. foundatn. and intentn. The Anarch. doctr. is (*A*) *Negative* : all things are at an end (1) There is an end to Property, (2) There is an end to all distinctions of Country, (3) There is an end to the State ; (*B*) *Affirmative* : (1) Do what you choose ; (2) Everything is everybody's. The facs. ill. fr. Anarch. propaganda are interestg. Tr. adds a ch. on *Anarchism in Engl.*

HART, W. C. Confessions of an Anarchist 2/6 *n.* c 8° Richards 06

LATOUCHE, Pet. Anarchy ; ports. and ill. 6/ c 8° Everett 08
A fair exposn. of methods and aims of Anarchism, wh. author neither defends nor denounces.

MEREDITH, Isabel A Girl among the Anarchists 6/ c 8° Duckworth 03
Provides an interesting view of Anarchists and their aims from the inside.

RAE, Jno. Anarchism, *and* Russian Nihilism = chs. viii & ix *of his* Contemporary Socialism, *ut sup.*

SALTER, W. M. Anarchy or Government [Lib. of Economics] $1·75 12° Crowell, *N.Y.* 95
Arrives at concln. th. govt. is necess. now, but th., as soc. consciousness is perfected, it will tend to disappear and Anarchy reign in its stead.

SCHAACK, M. J. M. Anarchy and Anarchists ; ports. & ill. [16/ Low] $3·50 r 8° Schulte, *Chicago* 89
A hist. of the Red Terror and Social Revoln. in Amer. and Eur. : Communism, Socialism, and Nihilism in doctrine and in deed.

SHAW, G. Bernard The Impossibilities of Anarchism 3*d.* c 8° Fabian Soc.

ZENKER, E. V. Anarchism : crit. and hist. of anarchist theory [tr.] 7/6 8° Methuen 98
$1·50 Putnam, *N.Y.* Excellent as a history ; sometimes unfair in criticism.

*Constructive and Systematic*

BAKUNIN, M. God and the State, tr. B. R. Tucker 12° Tucker, *Boston* 83

ELTZBACHER, Dr Paul Anarchism, tr. S. T. Byington ; 7 pots. [6/6 *n.* Fifield] $1·50 s 8° Tucker, *N.Y.* 08
7 chs., compiled fr. wrgs. of GODWIN, PROUDHON, STIRNER, BAKUNIN, KROPOTKIN, TUCKER, TOLSTOI, forms most valuable pt. of the bk. 2 others at beg. and 2 at end are orig. contribns. by author.

GOLDMAN, Emma Anarchism ; and other essays
[4/6 *n.* Fifield] $1 *n.* c 8° Mother Earth Pb. Co., *N.Y.* [10] 11

KROPOTKIN, Pr'ce P. A. Memoirs of a Revolutionist [$2 Houghton, *Bost.*] 3/6 c 8° Sonnenschein [99] 08
Ostensibly autobiographical, it really gives a vivid picture of modern Russian social conditions.

„ Mutual Aid : a factor in evolution 3/6 8° Heinemann [02] 04
$2·50 *n.* McClure, *N.Y.* Expls. by many examples the lge. extent to wh. mutual aid replaces competitn. amg. animals and differ. scales of human race. *Pace* HUXLEY and SPENCER, who thot. that considern. of nat. world leads to sternest individualism, K. tries to show th. there is an equally good argumt. in opposite directn.

„ The Conquest of Bread 10/6 *n.* 8° Chapman 07
$1 *n.* Putnam, *N.Y.* A v. interestg. exposn. of gospel of Anarchy, by a theoret. Anarchist w. an infinite trust in human nature, who believes th. ' the social revoln.' will soon be upon us. Draws a charming pict. of social life when every one acts as he shd. and govt. is therefore abolished, free agreemt takg. its place. Throughout emphasizg. the princ. of freedom, the syst. comes into irreconcilable conflict w. Socialism, wh. is the negatn. of freedom, relying upon absol. control by ' the State '.

„ —*in his* In Russian and French Prisons, *ut* **D** § 123

MACKAY, J. H. [tr.] Anarchists' Picture of Civilisn. at End 19 Cent. [tr.]
50 c. 12° Humboldt Pb. Co., *N.Y.* 93

PRUDHON, P. J. [1809–65] Complete Works, tr. B. R. Tucker Tucker, *Boston* 76–88
Vol. i: *What is Property?* $4; iv: *System of Economic Contradictions*, vol. i, $3·50. Greater pt. of vol. devoted to questns. of labour, machinery, competitn., and monopoly. Based on denial of God.

„ What is Property [tr.] [Humboldt Lib. of Science] $2 8° Humboldt Pb. Co., *N.Y.*, *n.d.*

' STIRNER, Max ' [= J. K. SCHMIDT] Ego & his Own [tr.] ; Introd. J. L. Walker $1·50 c 8° Tucker, *N.Y.* 07
6/6 *n.* Fifield. The first Engl. tr. of this work of the German anarchist [b. 1806, d. 1856].

THOREAU, H. D. [1817–62] Civil Disobedience—*in his* Anti-Slavery and Reform Papers, *ut* **D** § 130

**Nihilism, & Russian Revolutionary Movement**—*v. also* **E** § 25

DEUTSCH, Leo Sixteen Years in Siberia [tr.]—*ut* **D** § 123

FRASER, J. F. —*in his* Red Russia, *ut* **E** § 25

GANZ, H. Downfall of Russia : behind the scenes 6/ c 8° Hodder 04

JOUBERT, Carl Fall of Tsardom [$2 *n.* Lippincott, *Phila.*] 7/6 8° Nash 05

„ Truth ab. Tsar and Present State of Russia 7/6 8° Nash 05

„ Russia as it really is [$2 *n.* Lippinc., *Phila.*] 7/6 8° ; Ch. Ed. 1/ c 8° Nash [04] 05 ; 05

NEVINSON, H. W. Dawn in Russia : scenes in Russian revoln. ; ill. 7/6 *n.* ($2·25 *n.*) 8° Harper 06

NOBLE, E. Russian Revolt : causes, conditions, prospects *o.p.* [*pb.* 5/] c 8° Longman 85

PARES, B. Russia and Reform—*ut* **E** § 25

PERRIS, G. H. Russia in Revolution [$3 *n.* Brentano, *N.Y.*] 10/6 *n.* 8° Chapman [05] 05

' STEPNIAK, Sergius ' Underground Russia [tr.] [sketches of Nihilists] 3/6 c 8° Smith & Elder [83] 96

„ —*in his* Russia under the Tsars, *ut* **E** § 25

„ Russian Storm Cloud—*ut* **E** § 25
Russia in her relations to neighbouring States.

„ Nihilism as it is : pamphlets, tr. E. L. Voynich *o.p.* [*pb.* 3/6] c 8° Unwin 94
Reformer's Lib.] Besides SLEPNIAK's pamphs., are incl. F. VOLKHOVSKY's *Claims of Russn. Liberals*, tr. of letter sent by Russ. Revol. Exec. Comm. to ALEX. III on his accessn. (10 Mch. 1881) and of memorandum pres. to L. MELIKOFF by 25 leadg. Liberals of Moscow in Mch. '80, and Introd. by Dr G. Spence WATSON. Whole forms a clear statemt. of demands of Russn. Nihilists—wh. to Western ears seem unexpectedly moderate.

THOMPSON, Herb. Russian Politics; 5 maps [$2 Holt, *N.Y.*] 16/ 8° Unwin 96
By a member of Soc. of Friends of Russian Freedom, whose object is 'to further the cause of polit. and relig. liberty in Russia by legal and legitimate means'. This bk. is propagandist, and, tho' honest and well-meaning, merely a one-sided view of Russian politics.

TOLSTOY, C't L. N. End of the Age [tr.]; *and* Crisis in Russia [tr.] 2/ 8° Heinemann 06
" The Kingdom of God is Within us [tr.] 2/6 c 8° W. Scott 94
An eloq. denuncn. of tyranny of strong over weak, and defence of his relig. and social creed. For his *Life v.* **K** § 40.
" What Shall we Do? 6*d. n.* c 8° Free Age Press *n.d.*

TRUBETZKOI, Pr'ce Mich. Out of Chaos: a personal story of the revoln. in Russia [$2 Longman, *N.Y.*] 6/ c 8° Arnold 07

TURQUÉNIEFF, Ivan Fathers and Sons—*ut* **K** § 56
A striking Russian novel, which first introduced the word 'Nihilist'.

ULAR, A. Russia from Within [$1·75 *n.* Holt, *N.Y.*] 8/6 *n.* 8° Heinemann 05

WALLING, W. E. Russia's Message: true world-impost of the Revoln.; ill. $3 *n.* 8° Doubleday, *N.Y.* 09
12/6 *n.* Fifield. By a wr. on labr.-questns., who has been 'in touch w. the most conspirative of revol. organizns.' in Russia.

ZILLIACUS, C't Russian Revolutionary Movement [$2·50 *n.* Dutton, *N.Y.*] 7/6 *n.* 8° Rivers 05

## 127: PAUPERISM; POOR LAW; LIFE AND CONDITION OF THE POOR

### Pauperism: Causes and Remedies

BLACKLEY, Rev. W. S. Essays on Pauperism *o.p.* [*pb.* 1/] 16° Paul 80

BOOTH, 'Gen.' Wm. In Darkest England and the Way Out—*ut* **A** § 91

BOSANQUET, Dr B. [ed.] Aspects of the Social Problem—*ut* **D** § 125
The 18 papers deal largely w. pauperism—as a whole emphasize importce. of character in the problem.

CHALMERS, Thos. —*in his* Collected Works, *ut* **A** § 3
Abound in comprehensive suggestions on the causes and cure of pauperism and vice—*v.* espec. vols. xiv, xv, xix–xxi.
" Dr. Chalmers and Poor Laws 2/ c 8° Douglas, *Edin.* 11

DEVINE, E. T. Principles of Relief $2 *n.* (8/6 *n.*) c 8° Macmillan 05
" Efficiency & Relief: programme of soc. wk. [Col. Univ. Pr.] 75 c. *n.* (3/ *n.*) c 8° Macmillan 06
" Misery and its Causes [Amer. Social Progr. Ser.] $1·25 *n.* (5/ *n.*) c 8° Macmillan 09

FAWCETT, Prf. Hy. Pauperism, its Causes and Remedies *o.p.* [*pb.* 5/6] c 8° Macmillan 71

GODARD, J. G. Poverty, its Genesis and Exodus [Soc. Sci. Series] 2/6 c 8° Sonnenschein [92]
$1 Scribner, *N.Y.* Inquiry into causes of poverty and method of their removal. Socialist standpoint.

HENDERSON, Prf. C. R. Introd. to Study of Dependent, Defective and Delinquent Classes—*ut* **D** § 123

HOBSON, J. A. Problems of Poverty [Social Questions of To-day] 2/6 c 8° Methuen [91] 06
$1 *n.* Scribner, *N.Y.* A suggestive inquiry into measure of poverty, effects of machinery on condn. of wkg.-classes, influx of populn. into towns, sweatg. system, over-supply of low-skilled labr., industr. condn. of women wkrs., moral effects of poverty, socialistic legisln., etc.

MCCARTHY, C. The Causes of Poverty [of small value] 2/ *n.* c 8° P. S. King & Son 08

Manufacture of Paupers: a protest and a policy; Introd. J. St Loe Strachey 2/6 *n.* c 8° Murray 06
13 papers by 9 wrs., repr. fr. *Spectator*, dealg. w. differ. forms of that tendency to discourage self-reliant effort and teach dependce. on others wh. has been steadily gatherg. way under Socialistic influence.

WALKER, Thos. [1784–1836] The Original [Morley's Univ. Lib.; 35 c. *n.* Dutton, *N.Y.*] 1/ c 8° Routledge [36] 87
" The same, arranged on a new plan *o.p.* [*pb.* 3/6] c 8° Ward & Downey [36] 87
Contains essays on beggars, paupers, poor-laws, etc. Author was a police-magistrate.

WEBB, Sid. + Beatr. The Prevention of Destitution 6/ *n.* c 8° Longman 11
Incls. good ch. on Natl. Insurce., opposg. new Ins. Bill as it stands.

### Life and State of Poor Generally; United Kingdom —*v. also* **D** § 118; *for* Missions to Poor *v.* **A** § 106

CORNFORD, L. C. Canker at the Heart [studs. in life of poor] 3/6 *n.* c 8° Richards 05

COTTERILL, C. C. Human Justice for those at the Bottom [fragmt.] 2/6 *n.* c 8° Smith & Elder 07

CUNNINGHAM, Dav. Conditions of Social Well-being 10/6 8° Longman 78
Inquiries into material and social positn. of populns. of Europe and America (esp. Gt. Brit. and Irel.).

EDEN, Sir Fredk. M. The State of the Poor, 3 vols. *scarce* [*w.* £9] 4° *London* 1797
A hist. of labrg. classes of Engl. fr. Conq. to 1797, givg. details of diet, dress, fuel, habit., etc.; w. bibliogr. of early bks. on subj.

'German Coal-Miner, A' [Ern. DÜCKERSHOFF] How Engl. Workman Lives [tr.] 1/ c 8° P. S. King & Son 99

GHENT, W. J. Mass and Class: survey of social divisions $1·25 *n.* (5/ *n.*) c 8° Macmillan 04

Heart of the Empire (The): problems of modern City life in England 2/6 *n.* c 8° Unwin [01] 02
Essays by Cambridge men, attemptg. to define a new progressive positn. in view of changed conditions.

HIGGS, Mary Glimpses into the Abyss 3/6 *n.* c 8° P. S. King & Son 06
Acc. of the author's exploratns., disguised as a tramp, amg. the destitute in lodging-houses, tramp-wards, and shelters of Hadleigh, West Ham, Yorks, Lancs, Lond., etc. Pp. 1–86 are an essay on *Vagrancy*.

KAY, Jos. Social Condn. of People of Engl. and Europe, 2 vols.—*ut* **D** § 118

LOANE, Miss M. The Queen's Poor [$1·25 Longman, *N.Y.*] 3/6 c 8° Arnold [05] 06
*Husb. and Wife am. Poor; Relign. of Respectable Poor; Childr. of Poor; State-spread Tables* [impeachmt. of cry for free-food]; etc.
" The Next Street but One [London; $1·25 Longman, *N.Y.*] 6/ c 8° Arnold 07
" From their Point of View [$2 Longman, *N.Y.*] 6/ c 8° Arnold 08
" An Englishman's Castle [$2 Longman, *N.Y.*] 6/ c 8° Arnold 09
12 papers on *Position of Wife in Wkg.-cl. Home, Pleasures of the Poor, Domestic Legislation, The Fatigued Philanthropist*, etc.

LOANE, Miss M. Neighbours and Friends [$2 Longman, *N.Y.*] 6/ c 8° Arnold 10
A series of excell. bks. (by a District Nurse) made up of papers on aspects of the life, ideals, etc., of poor, based on wide experience in gt. cities, sympath. set forth and disting. by robust commonsense and a lively humour. Full of good stories and racy reflectns.

,, The Common Growth [$2 Longman, *N.Y.*] 6/ c 8° Arnold 11

MACKAY, Thos. The English Poor : sketch of social & economic history 7/6 c 8° Murray 89

MALVERY, Olive C. [Mrs A. MACKIRDY] The Soul Market [$1·50 McClure, *N.Y.*] 6/ c 8° Hutchinson 07
Acc. of experimts. of author [a reciter] as street-singer, factory-girl, jam-maker [the British 'jungle'], coffee-shop waitress, in Engl. and U.S., revealg. many abuses fr. an 'inside' pt.-of-view.

MASTERMAN, C. F. G. From the Abyss 1/ *n.* c 8° Dent 03

NICHOLLS, Sir Geo. —*in his* History of the English Poor Law, *ut inf.*

NORTHROP, W. B. Wealth and Want 5/ *n.* c 8° Griffiths 09
Facts rel. to condn. of poor, contrasted w. those rel. to rich, in parallel photographs. Bibliogrs.

REYNOLDS, Steph. A Poor Man's House 6/ ($1·50) c 8° Lane 08
A jl. and letters, presentg. picture of a typical poor Devon fisherman's house and life.

REASON, Will Poverty ; Pref. L. G. Chiozza Money [Soc. Serv. Hdbks.] 1/ *n.* c 8° Headley 09

,, [ed.] Our Industrial Outcasts [by membrs. of Xtn. Soc. B'hood] 2/ c 8° Melrose 05

SHERARD, R. H. The Cry of the Poor 3/6 c 8° Digby & Long 01
Acc. of a 3 months' tour among outcasts of United Kingdom. For his *White Slaves* v. D § 118.

SPENCER, M. Social Degradation 1/ *n.* c 8° Studt. Xtn. Movemt., 93–4 *Chancery La., Lond.* 08
A study of Engl. poverty fr. pt.-of-view of the Christian ideal.

WOODS, R. A., *etc.* Poor in Gt. Cities : probs. & wh. is doing to solve them $3 8° Scribner, *N.Y.* 95
12/ Paul. With contribn. by J. RIIS, O. CRAIG, W. T. ELSING, W. PARSONS, E. J. WENDELL, Sir W. BESANT, and others. Deals chiefly with American cities ; but has good articles on London.

*Children* —*for* Child Labour *v.* **D** § 118 ; *for* Boarding-out *v. inf.*, *s.v.* Workhouses

DENDY, Hel. [=Mrs B. BOSANQUET] Children of Workg. London—*in* Bosanquet [ed.], Aspects, *ut* **D** § 125

GORST, Sir Jno. E. The Children of the Nation [New Lib. of Medicine] 7/6 *n.* c 8° Methuen 07
Deals w. phys. condn. of childr. of poorer classes—not in scientific spirit, but in that of ardent reformer.

HEATH, H. Llew. The Infant, the Parent, and the State 3/6 *n.* c 8° P. S. King & Son 07
On social & other condns. militatg. agst. healthy infancy & ideal parenthd., & steps required to reduce infant-mortality & ensure vigorous childhd.

SPARGO, Jno. The Bitter Cry of the Children ; ill. [Amer. children] $1·50 *n.* (6/6 *n.*) c 8° Macmillan 06

TUCKWELL, Gertr. The State and its Children [Social Questions of To-day] 2/6 c 8° Methuen 94
$1 *n.* Scribner, *N.Y.* Discusses Reformatories and Industr. Schls., Truant Schls., Workhouse Schls., Workh. Childr., and other schemes of dealg. w. childr., Canal and Van Childr., Circus and Theatre Childr., 'Half-Timers', *etc.*

URWICK, E. J. [ed.] Studies of Boy Life in our Cities 3/6 *n.* c 8° Dent 04
Essays by var. wrs. for Toynbee Trust on life of London working-boy.

*United States* —*v. inf.* (RIIS) and **D** § 128 (FOLKS)

*London*

*BOOTH, Chas. [ed.] Life and Labour of the People in London—*ut* **D** § 118

BOSANQUET, Hel. [Mrs B.] Rich and Poor 3/6 *n.* ($1·50) c 8° Macmillan [96] 98
An excellent introdn. to work amg. poor. Gives a vivid picture of their life, the institns., shops, costers, curates, mothers' mtgs., etc. The East End district dealt w. conts. 122,000 inhabs., w. 13,680 houses [c. 9 per house], and the analysis of social condns. in this closely-packed multitude is minute and profoundly interesting. Pervaded w. a broad spirit of pract. wisdom. Emphasizes importance of self-help.

,, The Standard of Life, and other Studies 8/6 *n.* c 8° Macmillan [98] 06
About one-third of bk. is occup. w. discussn. of stand. of life and explan. of its actual wkg. as a basis of econ. progress. Other papers : *Psychol. of Social Progress, Burden of Small Debts, Educn. of Women, Industr. Training of Women*, etc.

FREE, Rev. Rich. Seven Years Hard 5/ *n.* c 8° Heinemann 04
$1·50 *n.* Dutton, *N.Y.* An unconventional descrn. of life in East End of London by one of the working clergy.

GREENWOOD, J. ['The Amateur Casual'] The Seven Curses of London *o.p.* [*pb.* 7/6] p 8° Rivers 69

,, Low Life Depths ; Wilds of London both *o.p.* [ea. *pb.* 7/6] p 8° Chatto 74 ; 74

HALLIFAX, Sid. Annals of a Doss-House 2/6 c 8° G. Allen 00

HOWARTH (E. G.) + WILSON (Mona) West Ham : study in soc. and industr. probls.—*ut* **D** § 118

KING, H. Savage London [River-side life and London dens] *o.p.* [*pb.* 6/] c 8° Low 88

LAW, John' [=Miss HARKNESS] Toilers in London [female labour] 3/6 c 8° Hodder 89
Flower-girls, matchbox-mkrs., servts., factory-girls, shirt-mkrs., barmds., 'sweaters', laundresses, sempstresses, shoemkrs., etc.

LAWLER, O'Dermid W. East London Visions 6/ *n.* c 8° Longman 10
Author descrs. his early life as East-Ender born and bred, and gradual revelatn. to him of a higher life.

LONDON, Jack The People of the Abyss [East London ; 6/ Pitman] $2 *n.* c 8° Macmillan, *N.Y.* 03

MACKRAY, Rob. Night-side of London ; 65 ill. Tom Browne 1/ *n.* c 8° Laurie

MAYHEW, Hy. History of London Labour and London Poor, 3 vols. ; ill. ea. 4/6 r 8° Griffin [51] 67
Street-sellers, street-buyers, street-performers, etc. Extra vol. : *Non-workers, prostitutes, thieves, beggars*, etc.—v. D § 133.

PATERSON, Alex. Across the Bridges : soc. life in S. London 6/ c 8° Arnold 11

READE, Amos Life in the Cut ; ill. [canal and barge life] 2/ c 8° Sonnenschein [88] 89

SHERWELL, Arth. Life in West London : a study and a contrast 2/6 c 8° Methuen [97]
[Soc. Questns. of To-day. A valuable study of poverty, overcrowdg., rent, casual and season labour, marriage, gambling, intemperance, etc.

SIMS, G. R. How the Poor Live ; *and* Horrible London—in 1 vol. 1/ c 8° Chatto [83–9] 98

STALLARD, J. H. London Pauperism among Jews and Christians *o.p.* [*pb.* 12/] 8° Saunders 67

WILLIAMS, Montagu Round London 3/6 c 8° Macmillan [92] 93
A record of keen observn. of the 'Poor Man's Magistrate', one of the most successful defenders of criminals. In two Pts. : (1) *Down East*, (2) *Up West*. With suggestns. for amelioratn. of condn. of poor.

*Aliens* —*v.* **D** § 121 ; *Jews*—*v.* **A** § 12

*York*

ROWNTREE, B. S. Poverty : a study of town life 1/*n.* c 8° Macmillan [01] 06
A valuable acc. of the poor of York, on the lines of Booth's *Life and Labour of People in London.* 426 pp.

*Scotland : Dundee ; Edinburgh*

PATON (D. N.) + DUNLOP (J. C.) + INGLIS (Maud) Study of Diet of Lab. Classes in Edin. 4/*n.* obl 8° Schulze, *Edin.* 01

Rept. of Investign. into Soc. Condns. in Dundee, ed. Mona Wilson, Pts. i–ii 1/6 8° Leng, *Dundee* 05 *in prg.*

*France : Paris :* D'AUVERGNE (E. B.) Night-side of Paris ; 24 pl. 10/6 *n.* 8° Laurie 11

**United States**

BAKER, Dr J. H. —*in his* American Problems $1·20 *n.* (4/*n.*) c 8° Longman 07
By Presidt. of Univ. of Colorado. Grouped under headings *Ideals, Sociological Problems, Education.*

BOIES, H. M. Prisoners and Paupers—*ut* **D** § 123

CAMPBELL, [Mrs] Hel. Prisoners of Poverty [women-wrkrs. of N.Y. ; trades, wages, etc.] Humboldt Pb. Co., *N.Y.* [87] 93

HAPGOOD, Hutchins The Spirit of the Ghetto ; ill. $1·25 *n.* (6/) c 8° Funk & Wagnalls [02] 09
Well catches the elusive spirit of the N.Y. ghetto, a Jewish quarter subtly and strangely Americanized.

„ Types from City Streets $1·50 (6/) c 8° Funk & Wagnalls 10
A candid, sympath., and joyous picture of East End of N.Y. Despite the absence of charit. organizns. in N.Y.—perhaps because of it—the hopeless and helpless misery of the Old World cities does not exist there, Tammany's influ. alone providg. a meal in exch. for a vote. Incidentally this bk. conts. a valuable explan. of this influ. over the whole life of an Am. citizen.

HUNTER, Rob Poverty $1·50 *n.* (6/6 *n.*) ; paper 25 c. *n.* c 8° Macmillan, *N.Y.* 04
Study in effects of unemploymt., long hours, and underpd. employmt. in towns of U.S.

NEEDHAM, G. C. Street Arabs and Gutter Snipes $2·50 c 8° Guernsey, *Boston* 84
The pathetic and humorous side of young vagabond life in great cities, w. records of wk. f. their reclamation.

WRIGHT, Carroll D. Slums of Baltim., Chic., N.Y., Phila. [7th Rept. of Com'r. of Lab.] *gratis* 8° Govt. Prtg. Off., *Washgtn.* 94

*Boston* : WOODS, R. A. [ed.] The City Wilderness [poor in Boston] $1·50 c 8° Houghton, *Boston* 99

*Chicago :* ADDAMS (Jane) Twenty Years at Hull House ; ill. (10/6 *n.*) 8° Macmillan 11

Chicago's Dark Places : investigns. by a corps of spec.-appointed commissioners $1 f 8° Craig Pr., *Chic.* 91

Hull-House Maps and Papers. By Residents of Hull-House, Chicago ; maps $2·50 12° Crowell, *N.Y.* 95
[Lib. of Economics.] A presentation of nationalities and wages in a congested district of Chicago.

*New York*

BRACE, Rev. C. L. Dangerous Classes of N.Y. [20 yrs. wk. amg. them] $1·25 12° Wynkoop, *N.Y.* [72] 80

HADLEY, Sam. H. Down in Water Street [social work] $1 *n.* 3/6 *n.* c 8° Revell, *Chicago* 02

JONES, T. J. Sociology of a N.Y. City Block [Col. Univ. Studs.] $1 *n.* 8° Macmillan, *N.Y.* 04

RIIS, Jac. A. How the Other Half Lives ; ill. [chfly. on N.Y. housing] $1·25 12° Scribner, *N.Y.* [90] 03

„ The Battle with the Slum : a 10 yrs' war rewritten ; ill. $2 *n.* (8/6 *n.*) 8° Macmillan [00] 02

„ The Children of the Poor $2·50 8° Scribner, *N.Y.* [92] 02

„ Out of Mulberry Street $1·25 c 8° Century Co., *N.Y.* 99

„ A Ten Years' War ; ill. $1·50 c 8° Houghton, *Boston* 00

„ Children of the Tenements ; ill. $1·50 (6/) c 8° Macmillan, *N.Y.* 03
Author, a Dane by birth, has for 30 yrs. been a N.Y. Police Headqrs. reporter for the Associated Press. His bks. cont. useful descrns. of life in lower quarters of N.Y. City, but are somewhat journalistic and the accs. are in some cases (admittedly) 'cooked', though true to life.

*Salvation Army Work* —*v.* **A** § 91, *s.v.* Salvation Army

**Social Settlements :** BARNETT (Can. + Mrs S. A.) —*in their* Practical Socialism, *ut* **D** § 126

BOOTH, Chas. —*in his* Life and Labour of People in London, Ser. iii, *ut* **D** § 118

HENDERSON, Prf. C. R. Social Settlements [Hdbks. for Practical Workers] 50 c. c 8° Lentilhon, *N.Y.* 99
Pt. i: *Historical*, w. chronol. lists of University, etc., Settlements; ii : *Theory and Methods of Settlement Work.*

HODSON, Miss A. L. Letters from a Settlement [$1·50 Longman, *N.Y.*] 4/6 *n.* c 8° Arnold 09

KNAPP, J. M. [ed.] The Universities and the Social Problem 5/ c 8° Rivington 95
Short accs. of the Univ. settlemts. in East End by var. wrs. conn. w. them. Introd. by Sir J. GORST.

REASON, W. [ed.] University and Social Settlements [Soc. Questions of To-day] 2/6 c 8° Methuen 98
Papers by persons with practical experience on aspects and uses of University Settlement work.

TOYNBEE, Arnold —*for his* Life *v.* **D** § 128

WOODS, R. A. [ed.] Americans in Process : a settlement study $1·50 *n.* c 8° Houghton, *Boston* 02

**Worker's Manuals** —*v. also sup., s.nn.* BOSANQUET (H.), LUBBOCK

BELL, Rev. G. M. [ed.] Social Service : hdbk. for workers & visitors 1/6 *n.* (60 c.) c 8° Longman 09
By var. wrs., incl. Can. + Mrs S. A. BARNETT. App. (55 pp.) gives list of charit. agencies available.

CONYNGTON, M. How to Help $1·50 *n.* c 8° Macmillan, *N.Y.* [06] 09

HALDANE, Rev. J. B. Social Worker's Guide [by c. 50 contribrs.] 3/6 *n.* c 8° Pitman 11

RICHMOND, M. E. Friendly Visiting among the Poor—*ut* **A** § 106

TUCKWELL (Gert. M.) + SMITH (Const.) Worker's Hdbk. [Soc. Questns.] 2/6 *n.* c 8° Duckworth [08]
Provides informn. (for wkg.-classes and workers am. them) on laws, regulns., and voluntary agencies f. protectn. and ameliorn. of worker's life fr. childhd. to old age, and on claims wh. he, as a citizen, has to fulfil.

**Poor in New Testament** —*v.* **A** § 45 (CONE)

**Poor Law; Poor Relief** —*for* Poor Law *v.* **D** § 67; *for* Aged Poor *v.* **D** § 127*

*History of English Poor Law*

ASCHROTT, Dr P. F. The English Poor Law System, Past & Present [tr.] 10/6 8° Knight [88] 02
Conts. vast mass of detail since 1535, mostly accurate. Introd. by Prf. Hy. SIDGWICK, and ch. on *Old Age Pensns.* by the tr., H. Preston THOMAS.

LEONARD, E. M. Early History of English Poor Relief 7/6 *n.* 8° Camb. Press 00
$2·25 *n.* Putnam, *N.Y.* A valuable suppl. to EDEN and to NICHOLLS, using much hitherto untouched materl. Appendices cont. illust. documts.

MACKAY, Thos. History of English Poor Law: 1834–98 10/6 *n.* 8° P. S. King & Son 99
$6·50 Putnam, *N.Y.* A continuation of NICHOLLS [*ut inf.*].

MONTAGUE, F. C. The Old Poor Law and the New Socialism *o.p.* c 8° Cobden Club (Cassell) 86

NICHOLLS, Sir Geo. History of the English Poor Law 10/6 *n.* 8° P. S. King & Son [54] 04
$10 Putnam, *N.Y.* The standard wk., givg. a complete acc., within well-defined limits of the hist. of the Poor Law in conn. w. legisln and other circumstances affectg. condn. of people, throwg. much light on abuses of the old syst. Covers period A.D 924–1853 Contin. by Thos. MACKAY, *ut sup.* The 3 vols. together, 15/ *n.*

" History of the Irish Poor Law *o.p.* [*pb.* 7/] 8° Murray 55

" History of the Scotch Poor Laws *o.p.* [*pb.* 6/] 8° Murray 56

*United Kingdom*

BOSANQUET, Hel. [Mrs. B.] The Strength of the People 8/6 *n.* ($2·75 *n.*) 8° Macmillan [02] 02
The strength of the people is character (espec. as created or modif. by tyranny of interest), mainly distinguished by indepndce. The family is the unit tow. preservn. of wh. all efforts shd. be directed and its econ. independence the goal of all social endeavour. Auth. demonstrs. how this can be attained from the Chalmers experimt. in Glasgow, and how it can be frustrated fr. records of Poor Law. To this test all pres. social movemts. are brought—Old-age Pensns., feedg. and clothg. of schl.-childr., out-relief, etc.

CHANCE, Sir Wm. Better Administration of the Poor Law 6/ c 8° Sonnenschein 95
[Charity Org. Ser.] Conts. much informn. on hist. and first princs. of Poor Law, condns. of good admin., indoor and outdoor relief, medical help, relief of able-bodied, etc., carefully classif., and w. pros and cons fairly stated. Statist. Appendices.

" Our Treatment of the Poor 2/6 c 8° P. S. King & Son [99]

FOWLE, Rev. T. W. The Poor Law [English Citizen Series] 2/6 ($1) c 8° Macmillan [81]
A useful little bk., contg. a lucid though rather sketchy statemt. of hist. and principles of the Poor Law.

FULLER, S. D. Charity and Poor Law [handy discussn. of poor-law] 1/ c 8° Sonnenschein 01

LOCH, C. S. Controversial Points in Admin. of Poor Relief—*in* Bosanquet [ed.], Aspects, *ut* **D** § 125

LONSDALE, Sophia The English Poor Laws: hist., princs., admin. 1/ *n.* c 8° P. S. King & Son [97] 02

LUBBOCK, Gertr. Some Poor Relief Questions: manl. f. adminrs. & workers 7/6 c 8° Murray 95
Gives the argumts. for and agst. pres. law and var. proposed changes in it, on plan of Syd. BUXTON's *Hdbk. of Polit. Questns.* [*ut* **D** § 142]; *Out-door and Indoor Relief, Old-age Pensns., Provisn. of Meals, and Charit. Relief.*

MACKAY, Thos. Methods of Social Reform: essays crit. & constructive 7/6 c 8° Murray 96
Makes out a strong case agst. further 'endowmt. of poverty'. Chief interest in the bk. is author's profound belief in man's natural capacity for improvemt. and in the varied and effective meths. by wh. he illustrates it.

" Public Relief of the Poor [hist. and crit. lects.] 2/6 *n.* c 8° Murray 01

MILLS, Rev. H. V. Poverty and the State [w. full statemt. of Home Colon. scheme] 6/ c 8° Paul 86

PASHLEY, Rob. Pauperism and the Poor Laws [still of value] *o.p.* [*pb.* 10/6] 8° Longman 52

PEEK, Fcs. Social Wreckage: review of laws as they affect the poor *o.p.* [*pb.* 3/6] c 8° Isbister [83] 93

Poor Law Commission of 1834: Report [Blue-Book] 1/8 f° Wyman [34] 05
Repr. of the famous Rept. wh. led to new Poor Law syst. The 'most magnificent State Paper in existence'.

Poor Law Conferences: ea. Conference 1/; Annual Vol. 12/ *n.* 8° P. S. King & Son *ann.*

Poor Law Reform Assoc.: Pubns. [pamphlets] *Hyde Vale, Greenwich, Kent*

Royal Commission on Poor Laws and Relief of Distress, 1909: Reports and Appendices [ab. 50 in all] P. S. King & Son 09–10
The *Majority Report*, 2 vols., 2/3; *Minority Report*, 1 vol., 1/9. Pocket Edn., 2 vols., ea. 1/. Nat. Com. f. Prev. of Destitn., 37 Norf. St., Strand, Lond.
A convenient pamphlet, contg. the long summary of the *Rept.* w. that of the voluminous *Minority Rept.* is pubd. 4*d.* *Times* Office.

BARNETT, Can. S. A. New Poor Law or No Poor Law 1/ *n.* c 8° Dent 09

BOOTH, Chas. Poor Law Reform; map 1/ *n.* c 8° Macmillan 10
Memoranda submitted to the Poor Law Commission, w. Appendix by Dr A. DOWNES and Octavia HILL.

BOSANQUET, Hel. [Mrs B.] The Poor Law Report of 1909 3/6 *n.* c 8° Macmillan 09
A summary explaing. defects of pres. syst. and princ. recommendns. of the Comm. as reg. Engl. and Wales.

CHANCE, Sir Wm. Poor Law Reform: Via tertia: case for the guardians 1/ *n.* 8° P. S. King & Son 10

JONES, Thos. Pauperism and Poverty 09
A summary and exposition of the results reached by the Commission.

MUIRHEAD, Prf. J. H. By What Authority? 2/ *n.* 8° P. S. King & Son 09
On the princs. in common, and those at issue, in Repts. of Poor Law Comm. Introd. by Sir Oliver LODGE.

New Poor Law or No Poor Law?; w. Introd. Can. S. A. Barnett 1/ *n.* c 8° Longman 09
An epitome of the Majority and the Minority *Repts.*, with some slight comment.

Salvation Army (The) and Poor Law Reform [evidence of 'Gen.' Booth] 1/ *n.* 8° Salvation Army 09

WEBB, Sid. + Beatr. [eds.] The Minority Report of the Poor Law Commission, 2 Pts. 12/6 *n.* ($4·25 *n.*) 8° Longman 09
Pt. i: *Break-up of the Poor Law*, 7/6 *n.* ($2·50 *n.*); ii: *Public Organization of the Labour Markt*, 5/*n.* ($1·75 *n.*); w. Introd. Pt. i. concls. w. a Scheme of Reform of novel and far-reachg. character, elab. wkd. out, involvg. abolitn. of Workhouse and disappearance of the Poor Law. Pt. ii concls. w. Proposals for Reform, givg. in detail the Minority's plan for solvg. whole problem of Unemploymt. *Vide* also their *Engl. Poor Law Policy* [*inf.*].

WEBB, Sid. Reform of the Poor Law—*in* Problems of Modern Industry, *ut* **D** § 118

" + Beatr. English Poor Law Policy 7/6 *n.* ($2·50 *n.*) 8° Longman 10
Detailed anal. of policy of Parlt. & Loc. Govt. Bd. fr. '34 to pres. time, w. 4 chs. analyzing the *Maj. and Minor Repts.*, and explg. the pts. at issue.

*Children; 'Boarding-out'*

AVELING, H. F. The Boarding-out System and Protection of Children 1/6 8° Sonnenschein 90

CHANCE, Sir Wm. Children under the Poor Law 7/6 c 8° Sonnenschein 97
Introd. ch. on hist. of subj. fr. 1834 to 1897, w. chs. on Workh.-schls., Distr. and Separ. Schls., Cottage Home Schls., Detached Homes, Publ. Elem Schls., Boardg.-out, later employmt., 'after-care', criticism of recent reforms, etc. Appendices.

DARROCH, Prf. Alex. The Children [Social Problems Series] 1/*n.* c 8° Jack 07

FOLKS, H. Care of Destit., Neglected, and Delinquent Childr. $1 *n.* 12° Macmillan 02

HILL, Flor. Davenport Children of the State, ed. Fanny Fowke 6/ c 8° Macmillan [68] 89
On training of juvenile paupers: advocates boardg.-out by depictg. other systs. in blackest colours.

LEACH, R. A. Pauper Children: their education and training—*ut* **D** § 67

SKELTON, J. Boarding out of Pauper Children in Scotland 3/6 p 8° Blackwood 76

SMEDLEY, Menella B. Boarding out in Pauper Schools, esp. for girls *o.p.* [*pb.* 3/6] c 8° H. S. King 75

TREVELYAN, Rev. W. F. Some Results of Boardg.-out Poor-Law Children 2/*n.* c 8° P. S. King & Son 03

TUCKWELL, Gertr. M. The State and its Children [Soc. Questns. of To-day] 2/6 c 8° Methuen 94

*Relieving Officer*

DUMSDAY, W. H. The Relieving Officer's Handbook [practical guide] 6/ c 8° Hadden 02

SYMONDS, J. F. The Relieving Officer: his duties 3/6 *n.* p. 8° Butterworth 04

*United States: Connecticut*

CAPEN, E. W. Hist. Devel. of Poor Law of Conn. [Col. Univ. Studs.] $3 *n.* 8° Macmillan, *N.Y.* 05

*Massachusetts; New York*

CUMMINGS, J. Poor Laws of Mass. & N.Y. [Am. Ec. Ass.; 2/6 Sonnenschein] 75 c *n.* 8° Macm., *N.Y.* 95

*Europe*

CARLILE, Rev. W. + V. W. Continental Outcast; ill. [land colonies, poor-law relief] 2/*n.* c 8° Unwin 06

SELLERS, Edith Foreign Solutions of Poor Law Problems 2/6 *n.* 8° H. Marshall 08
8 essays, on Hungary, Austria, Germany (exclg. Elberfeld), Belgium, Balkans, Denmark, Russia.

*Denmark*

SELLERS, Edith The Danish Poor Relief System 2/*n.* c 8° P. S. King & Son 04
Acc. of the Danish system, held up as a model for England.

*Germany*

DOYLE, A. The Poor Law System of Elberfeld *o.p.* 12° *London* 71
A good account of this famous system, which has set the pattern for so many other places.

SUTTER, Julie A Colony of Mercy: social Xty. at work [tr.] 1/*n.* c 8° Johnson [93] 04
A glowing description of the working of the epileptic colony of Bethel, at Wilhelmsdorf, nr. Bielefeld.

" Britain's Next Campaign [tr.] [Elberfeld syst.] 1/*n.* c 8° Johnson [01] 04

**Workhouses: Inmates, Officers, etc.**—*for* 'Boarding-out' *v. sup.*, *s.v.* Poor Law

DAVEY, Syd. The Law relating to Casual Paupers 2/6 8° Hadden 00
Intended for masters of workhouses, etc.: useful also to magistrates.

GREENWOOD, J. The Amateur Casual [repr. fr. 'Pall Mall Gazette'] *o.p.* [*pb.* 6*d.*] 12° Diprose [66] 77
An account of a visit to a workhouse by a well-known journalist in the disguise of a pauper.

HART, Dr G. The Sick-Poor in Workhouses, 2 vols. *o.p.* 8° Smith & Elder 95
Rept. on nursg. and admin. of provincial workhouses, by spec. commissr. of *Brit. Medical Journal.*

HARTILL, Rev. Is. Work among the Poor of London 1/*n.* c 8° Stock 07
Deals w. relief of poor in West and East London in workhouse infirmaries and by institutions. Spec. ch. on Children.

Indoor Paupers: by One of Them 1/f 8° Chatto 86

*Poor Law Officers' Jl.*, Edrs. of Government of the Workhouse [excellent little manual] 1/8° *Office* 94

ROGERS, Dr Jos. Remins. of a Workhouse Medical Officer, ed. J. E. Thorold Rogers 7/6 c 8° Unwin 89

SHEEN, Alf. The Workhouse and its Medical Officer 2/6 c 8° Wright, *Bristol* [90] 90

TWINING, Louisa W'khouses & Pauperism [Soc. Questns. of To-day; $1 Scrib., *N.Y.*] 2/6 c 8° Methuen 98
Expercs. fr. 1853 to 1897. Incl. also matter on women's wk. in the administration of the Poor Law.

" Recollns. of Workhouse Visiting [also in her *Recollns.*, *ut* **D** § 125] 3/6 Paul 80

**Housing of the Poor**: *United Kingdom*—*for* Law *v.* **D** § 67, *s.v.* Artizan's Dwellgs.; *for* Building *v.* **I** § 122

ALDEN (P.) + HAYWARD (E. E.) Housing [Social Service Handbks.] 1/6 *n.* c 8° Headley 07

ALLAN, F. J. Housing of the Working Classes 7/6 8° Butterworth [98] 01

BOOTH, Chas. —*in his* Life and Labour of People in London, vols. iii and ix, *ut* **D** § 118

BOWMAKER, Dr Edw. The Housing of the Working Classes [Soc. Questns. of To-day] 2/6 c 8° Methuen 96
Regards the subj. largely fr. sanit. and building side, and attaches much importance to Act of 1890. A good book.

Committee (Select) on Artizans' and Labourers' Dwellings: Reports [Blue Bks.] s f° Wyman 81–2

,, on Town Holdings: Reports [Blue Bks.; w. Index] s f° Wyman 90

,, on Housing of Wkg. Cl. Acts Amendmt. Bill [Blue Bk.] s f° Wyman 06–7

Commission (Royal) on Housing of Wkg. Classes [in U.K.]: Reports, 2 vols. [vol. ii. =Evidence] [Blue Bks.] s f° Wyman 85

CROTCH, W. W. Cottage Homes of England [agst. hsg.-syst. in rural distrs.] 1/*n.* c 8° Industrial Pb. Co. [2nd ed. 01] 08

DEWSNUP, Prf. E. R. The Housing Problem in England 5/*n.* 8° Sherratt, *Mancs.* 07
[Mancs. University Pubns.] The statistics, legislation, and policy of the English housing problem.

HAW, Geo. No Room to Live [repr. fr. 'The Daily News'] 2/6 c 8° Wells Gardner [99] 00

,, Britain's Homes 2/6 *n.* c 8° *Clarion* Co. 02

HILL, Octavia The Homes of the London Poor *o.p.* [*pb.* 1/] c 8° Macmillan [75] 83
Acc. of her pioneer wk. of rent-collectg. and slum-improvemt. for RUSKIN; w. geneal chapters.

HORSFALL, T. C. Improvemt. of Dwellings of the People 1/*n.* c 8° Sherratt, *Mancs.* 04

HOWARTH (E. G.) + WILSON (Mona)—*in their* West Ham, *ut* **D** § 118

KAUFMANN, Rev. M. Housing of the Working Classes [Social Problems Ser.] 1/*n.* c 8° Jack 07

MARR, T. C. Housing Condns. of Manchester & Salford; ill. 1/*n.* c 8° Sherratt, *Mancs.* 04

MEAKIN, Budgett Model Factories and Villages 7/6 c 8° Unwin 05
Descrn. of efforts tow. ideal condns. of labr. and housing, sel. fr. Engl., U.S., and a few fr. Continent.

NETTLEFOLD, J. S. Housing by Voluntary Enterprise 2/8° Garden City Press 08

PARSONS, Jas. Housing by Voluntary Enterprise 2/6 *n.* c 8° P. S. King & Son 03
Chfly. an exam. of argumts. concerning provision of dwg.-houses by Municipal authorities.

Report on Housing of Working Classes [Blue-Bk.] 8*d.* f° Wyman 89

SMITH, Alf. The Housing Question: 1855–1900 1/c 8° Sonnenschein 00

SMITH, Edw. The Peasant's Home: 1760–1875 3/6 p 8° Stanford 76

STEWART The Housing Question in London: 1855–1900 9/f 8° P. S. King & Son 00
A full hist. of work done by Metrop. Bd. of Wks. and by L.C.C.; w. summary of Acts of Parliament.

SYKES, J. F. J. [M. D.] Public Health & Housing; diagrs. [Milroy Lects.] 5/*n.* c 8° P. S. King & Son 01

THOMPSON, Alderm. W. The Housing Handbook, Up-to-date 3/6 *n.* 8° P. S. King & Son [03] 07
A cpl. statemt. of the facts, list. of authorits. interested, and tables shewg. what has been done by each.

,, Hdbk. to Housing and Town Planning Act 1/*n.* 8° P. S. King & Son 10

WILLIS, W. A. Housg. and Town Planng. in Gt. Br.; w. Act 1909 7/6 8° Butterworth 10

WORTHINGTON, T. Locke Dwellings of the Poor in Large Towns; ill. 2/6 c 8° Sonnenschein [93] 01
$1 Scribner, *N.Y.* [Social Science Ser.] An excellent practical little bk., comprehensive and eminently rational.

*United States*

BOGART, E. L. Housing of Working People in Yonkers [Am. Econ. Ass.] 50 c. *n.* 8° Macmillan, *N.Y.* 98

DE FOREST (R. W.) + VEILLER (L.) [eds.] The Tenement House Problem, 2 vols.; ill. $6 *n.* (25/*n.*) 8° Macmillan, *N.Y.* 04

REYNOLDS, M. T. Housing of the Poor in American Cities [Am. Econ. Ass.; 2/6 Sonnenschein] $1 *n.* 8° Macmillan, *N.Y.* 93

RIIS, Jac. A. Children of the Tenements—*ut sup.*

*Germany*

HORSFALL, T. C. Improvemts. of Dwellgs. & Surroundgs. of People: Example of Germy. 1/*n.* r 8° Sherratt, *Mancs.* [04] 05

**Pauper Litigation**

SPRIGGE, J. J. Shortcomings of the Machinery for Pauper Litigation 3/8° Williams [93] 93

**Pauper Lunatics**

DAVEY, S. The Law relating to Pauper Lunatics 6/*n.* c 8° Poor Law Pbns. Co. [ ] 10

**Vagrants; Tramps; Beggars; etc.**

CHANDLER, F. W. The Literature of Roguery—*ut* **K** § 19

CRAWFORD, J. H. Autobiography of a Tramp 5/*n.* ($1·50) c 8° Longman 00

DAVIES, W. H. Autobiography of a Super-tramp; Pref. by Bern. Shaw 6/c 8° Fifield 08
By a genuine tramp, who has tramped it up hill and down dale in Amer. and in Engl. slums, who has known the agonies of starvn., acquired art of begging, companionized w. thieves, vagrants, mendicants. Its freshness of outlook and spontaneity of expressn., wholly free fr. cant, render it an interestg. 'human documt.' His first appearance in print was as auth. of *The Soul's Destroyer*, a poem wh. was recd. w. a chorus of discriminatg. praise.

,, Beggars 6/c 8° Duckworth 09
A collection of papers about beggars and their characteristics.

DAWSON, W. H. The Vagrancy Problem 5/ n. c 8° P. S. King & Son 10
Plea for measures of restraint; w. study of Germ., Belg., and Swiss Detention Colonies and Labr. Houses.

EDWARDES, Tickner- Lift Luck on Southern Roads 6/ c 8° Methuen 10

'FLYNT, Josiah' [=J. F. WILLARD] Tramping with Tramps; ill. [6/ Unwin] $1·50 c 8° Century Co., *N.Y.* 00
Valuable studies and sketches of vagabond life, chfly. of Amer. tramps, based on author's experimts. as an amateur.

" Notes of an Itinerant Policeman $1·25 c 8° Page, *Boston* 00

" The Little Brother: story of tramp-life $1·50 c 8° Century Co., *N.Y.* 02

FRANCK, H. A. A Vagabond Journey round the World; 109 ills. 15/ n. 8° Unwin 10

HIGGS, Mary —*in her* Glimpses into the Abyss, *ut sup.* [86 pp. on Vagrancy]

JUSSERAND, J. J. —*in his* English Wayfaring Life in Mid. Ages [14 cent.], *ut* **F** § 21

MEEK, Geo., Bath Chairman. By Himself. Ed. H. G. Wells 6/ c 8° Constable 10
An autobiography of a somewhat dull bath-chairman (who saw the world, incl. U.S.)—the product of free libraries and cheap reprs., as opposed to Mr. SHAW's 'Supertramp' (*sup.*), who had a touch of the BORROW spirit in him.

RIBTON-TURNER, C. J. Hist. of Vagrants and Vagrancy, Beggars, etc.; ill. [European] 21/ 8° Chapman 87

STEVENSON, R. L. Beggars—*in his* Works, vol. xv (1907), *ut* **K** § 89

*Paris:* PAULIAN (Louis) The Beggars of Paris, tr. L'y Herschell 1/ (60 c.) c 8° Arnold 97
Amusing anecdotes; with a scheme for the suppression of begging as a trade.

**Reformatory and Pauper Education**—*v.* **D** § 169

## 127*: THRIFT; INSURANCE; OLD-AGE PENSIONS

BARLOWE, Dr C. A. M. [ed.] The Old-Age Pensions Act, 1908; w. notes—*ut* **D** § 23

BLACKLEY, M. J. J. Thrift and Natl. Insurce. as Security agst. Pauperism 1/ n. 12° Paul 06
With Memr. of Can. W. L. BLACKLEY, and repr. of his essays, incl. *Thrift and Independence* [1884], wh. reviews Friendly and similar Socs., and proposes scheme compellg. young to deposit a sum, say £6 10*s.*, bef. they are 21. *V.* WILKINSON, *inf.*

BOOTH, Chas. Pauperism and Endowment of Old Age 5/ ($1·25) c 8° Macmillan 92
After disposg. of BLACKLEY's and of CHAMBERLAIN's schemes by figs. and reasons, states his own, i.e. th. subseq. adopted for Old Age Pensns. Also 6*d*

" The Aged Poor in England and Wales—Condition 8/6 n. ($3·50) 8° Macmillan 94
Presents bare facts of case, w. view to renderg. more profble. a study of '648 separate lessons in admin.,' suppl. by Poor-law Unions of Engl. & Wales.

" Old Age Pensions and the Aged Poor: a proposal 2/ n. 8° Macmillan [99] 07

BROWN, Mary W. The Development of Thrift $1 (3/6 n.) c 8° Macmillan 99
Describes practically the approved schemes for assisting in the saving of money: savings-banks, clubs, etc.

CHANCE, Sir Wm. Our Treatment of Poor [*ut* **D** § 127]: conts. attack on old-age pensions

Charity Organisn. Soc.: Insurance & Saving, ed. C. S. Loch [Charity Organ. Ser.] 2/6 c 8° Sonnenschein 92
Rept. to the Soc. on existg. opports. f. wkg.-class thrift, w. Introd. (pp. 48) on *Poor Law as Obstacle to Thrift and Vol. Insurance*, by T. MACKAY.

DRAGE, Geoffrey The Problem of the Aged Poor 6/ c 8° Black 95
A readable summary of evid. given bef. Roy. Comm. [*ut* **D** § 118], w. accs. of argumts. of other wrs.

GONNER, Prf. E. C. K. Interest and Saving 3/6 n. ($1·25 n.) c 8° Macmillan 06

LECKY, W. E. H. Old-age Pensions [repr. fr. 'The Forum'] 6*d.* n. (25 c.) c 8° Longman 08
Reprinted in his *Historical and Political Essays*—*ut* **F** § 1.

LEWIS, Fk. W. State Insurance, a Social and Industrial Need 5/ n. c 8° Constable 09
$1·25 n. Houghton, *Boston.* Deals generally, and ably, w. the subj.—esp. w. Germany, America, Great Britain and Colonies.

LOCH, C. S. Old-Age Pensions and Pauperism [anti] 1/ 8° Sonnenschein 93

" Pauperism and Old Age Pensions—*in* Bosanquet [ed.], *Aspects*, *ut* **D** § 125

MACKAY, Thos. Working-Class Insurance [*v. also* Char. Org. Soc., *sup.*] 1/ 8° Stanford 92

MAYET, Prf. P. Agric. Insurance in Organic conn. w. Savings Banks, Land Credit and Commutation of Debts [tr.] [$3·50 Macm., *N.Y.*] 10/6 8° Sonnenschein 93

METCALFE, J. Case f. Universal Old Age Pensns.; Introd. Chas. Booth 2/6 n. c 8° Simpkin 99

Old-Age Pensions: collection of short papers 2/6 n. ($1) 8° Macmillan 03

Old Age Pensions: are they Desirable? [*pro* by F. Rogers, *con.* by Millar] 2/6 n. c 8° Pitman 03

ROBERTSON, J. M. The Fallacy of Saving [Soc. Sci. Ser.; $1 Scribner, *N.Y.*] 2/6 c 8° Sonnenschein 92
Pt. i is an exposn. and crit. of views of economists bef. and after MILL; ii is a *Practical Solution*, summg. up in favr. of (1) reform of taxn. w. primary end of paying off Natl. Debt, (2) public wks., to employ labr. thrown out as result of liquidn. of the Debt, (3) natl. syst. of pensions.

Royal Commission on the Aged Poor: minutes, etc., 3 vols. [Blue-Books] f° Wyman 95

SCHLOSS, D. F. Insurance against Unemployment [w. bibliogr.] 3/6 n. c 8° P. S. King & Son 09
Brings down to date his *Report to the Board of Trade on Agencies and Methods for dealing with Unemployed in certain Foreign Countries* (1904). Deals with State-subsidized insurance schemes only.

SPENDER, J. A. The State and Pensions in Old Age [Soc. Sci. Series] 2/6 c 8° Sonnenschein [92] 00
$1 Scribner, *N.Y.* Incl. a study of wkg.-classes in old age, and attempt to ascertain time of life when wages begin to decline in chief trades and rapidity w. wh. they fall in later life. 2 chs. on Foreign Pensn. Schemes.

STEAD, Fcs. H. How Old Age Pensions Began to Be 2/6 n. c 8° Methuen 09

SUTHERLAND, Wm. Old-Age Pensions in Theory and Practice 3/6 n. 8° Methuen 07
Gives a full view of many leadg. schemes, inclg. foreign, statg. advantages and drawbacks.

Thrift Manual: Pref. by Sir E. Brabrook [for primary-schl. use] 2/ n. 8° P. S. King & Son 08
11 pprs., by var. authorities, repr. fr. *Charity Organisn. Review.*

WILKINSON, Rev. J. Frome The Blackley National Insurance Scheme [a criticism] 1/8° Sonnenschein 87

,, Pensions & Pauperism [cf. also his 'Mutual Thrift', *ut* **D** § 120] 1/c 8° Methuen 92

WILLOUGHBY, W. F. Working Men's Insurance [Lib. of Economics] $1·75 12° Crowell, *N.Y.* 98
A clear, if not always up-to-date, acc. of experience in insurce. meths. and legisln. in civilized countries, w. ch. on Ins. agst. Unemploymt. and Swiss experimts. therein.

*United States*

BETTS, L. W. The Leaven in a Great City $1·50 *n.* c 8° Dodd & Mead, *N.Y.* 02
Shows how stand. of livg. is continually rising in N.Y. thro' efforts of crowded populn. of frugal and industr. poor.

HENDERSON, C. R. Industrial Insurance in United States [9/ *n.* Unwin] $2 *n.* 8° Univ. Press, *Chicago* 09
Substantially an abgmt. for Amer. public of Dr ZACHER'S *Die Arbeiter-Versicherung i. d. Vereinigt. Staaten v. N. A.*, Pt. 17 of his *Die Arbeiter-Versicherung im Auslande.* Incl. a summary of Europ. laws, bibliogr., and Appendices of actual schemes by firms and corporations.

*Germany*

BROOKS, J. G. Compulsory Insurance in Germany Govt. Prg. Off., *Washington* 93
An admirable Report to Commiss'r of Labor, thoughtful and dispassionate, commencg. w. an acc. of the successive laws of insurance agst. sickness, accident, and old age and infirmity.

DAWSON, W. H. —*in his* Bismarck & State Socialism, *ut* **D** § 126 [Germ. old-age insur. laws]

HOOPER, E. G. The German State Insurance System 1/*n.* c 8° E. Wilson 08

**Building, Friendly, and Provident Societies**—*v.* **D** § 120

**Co-operative Banks; Agricultural (or Land) Banks**

DEVINE, H. C. People's Co-operative Banks [popular exposn.] 1/*n.* (35 c. *n.*) 8° Cassell 08

WOLFF, H. W. People's Banks: record of soc. and econ. success 6/*n.* 8° P. S. King & Son [93] 10
Advocatg. estab. of credit institns. for deservg. poor, similar to those successfully carried on in Germy., Italy, Switz., Belg., Japan, on princ. that third-class traffic is in aggregate the safest. Gives full descrns. of the two great Germ. systs., that of SCHULZE-DELITZSCH and that of RAFFEISEN (a sort of co-oper. Loan Bank), wh. latter he favours most. 2nd edn. (1896) is substantially a new wk.; and 3rd (1910) a revision thereof.

,, Co-operative Banking: principles and practice 7/6 *n.* 8° P. S. King & Son 07

,, A Co-operative Credit Bank Handbook 1/*n.* 8° P. S. King 09
A revision of the author's *People's Bank Manual* and *Village Bank*, both *o.p.*

**National (Unemployment) Insurance**—*v.* **D** § 151

**Savings Banks** —*for* Law *v.* **D** § 84

BOWIE, Archibald G. The Romance of the Savings Banks 1/6 c 8° Partridge 98

HAMILTON, Prf. J. H. Savings and Savings Institutions [chfly. American] $2·25 *n.* (10/) c 8° Macmillan 02

KEYES, E. W. History of Savings Banks in the U.S., 2 vols. $10 r 8° Rhodes, *N.Y.* 78

LEWINS, W. History of Banks for Savings in Gt. Britain and Ireland 7/6 r 8° Layton [66] 82

PETERS, E. T. Co-oper. Credit Assocns. in cert. Euro. Ctries. = U.S. Govt. Rept., Dep. of Agric., *Washgtn.* 92
A Report on the Savings-banks, etc., of Germany, Austria-Hungary, Italy, and Russia.

SCRATCHLEY, A. Pract. Treatise on Savings Banks [hist. & condn.[ *o.p.* [*pb.* 14/] 8° Longman [52] 63

*Biography*

DUNCAN, Dr Hy. [1774–1846] Dr. Duncan of Ruthwell. By Sophy Hall [g'dau.] 3/6 *n.* c 8° Oliphant 10
A biography of the founder of the Savings Bank system, pubd. in its centenary year.

## 128: STATE AND PRIVATE PHILANTHROPY; CHARITIES; BIOGRAPHY OF PHILANTHROPISTS

**Bibliography**

ADAMS, H. B. Notes on the Literature of Charities 25 c. 8° Johns Hopkins Univ. Pr., *Baltimore* 87

Charity Organisation Soc.: Catalogue of the Library 8° Char. Organizn. Soc. 93

GRANIER, Camille Bibliographie Charitable 17fr.50 8° Guillaumin, *Paris* 91
Describes and catalogues 2,181 wks., not neglecting fiction or poetry. 450 pp., of which Introd. occupies 160 pp.

HENDERSON, Prf. C. R. [ed.] —*in* Modern Methods of Charity, *ut inf.*

**Series**

American Philanthropy of the Nineteenth Century ea. $1 *n.* c 8° Macmillan 02 *in prg.*
FOLKS (H.) *Care of Destitute and Delinquent Children* [*ut* **D** § 127] | LEE (J.) *Constructive and Preventive Philanthropy* [*ut inf.*]

Charity Organisn. Sers.: ed. C. S. Loch [sec. to Lond. Char. Organ. Soc.] ea. 2/6 c 8° Sonnenschein 93 *sqq.*
*Better Admin. of Poor Law* [*ut* **D** § 127] Sir W. CHANCE 6/ | *Better Way of Assistg. Schl. Childr.* | *Epileptic and Crippled Child and Adult* | *Feeble-minded Child and Adult* | *Insurance and Saving* [*ut* **D** § 127]

**History**

FOLKS, H. Care of Destitute, Neglected, & Delinq. Children [historical] 4/6 *n.* c 8° Macmillan 01

GRAY, B. Kirkman History of English Philanthropy 7/6 *n.* 8° P. S. King & Son 05
Fr. Dissoln. of Monasteries (when Charity passed out of immed. directn. and tutelage of Church) to takg. of first census (end 18th cent.). A sound and judicious piece of work.

,, Philanthropy and the State, or Social Politics 7/6 *n.* 8° P. S. King & Son 08
Posth. ed. Eleanor K. GRAY [widow] + B. L. HUTCHINS. A companion wk. to above, describg. the 'transition fr. philanthropy to social politics' wh. 'rests on the breakg. down of the simple old doctr. of individualism'. Cf. also his Miscell. papers in **D** § 125.

LAWRIE, Sir A. C. [ed.] Early Scottish Charities prior to A.D. 1153 10/*n.* 8° MacLehose, *Glasgow* 05

RANDALL, C. D. [ed.] History of Child Saving in U.S. [pp. 315] *o.p.* c 8° Ellis, *Boston* 93

WARNER, Prf. A. G. Evolution of Charities & Charitable Institutions *o.p.* c 8° Appleton, *N.Y.* 93

**Principles; Economics; etc.**—*for* Law *v.* **D** § 23

ADAMS, Prf. H. C. [ed.] Philanthropy & Social Progress [Lib. of Economics] $1·50 12° Crowell, *N.Y.* 93
7 essays del. bef. School of Applied Ethics at Plymouth, Mass., by Jane ADAMS, F'r J. O. S. HUNTINGDON, R. A. WOODS, Prf. F. A. GIDDINGS, Dr B. BOSANQUET. Introd. by EDR.

ALLEN, W. H. Efficient Democracy—*ut* **D** § 139

BARNETT, Can. + Mrs S. A. Practicable Socialism—*ut* **D** § 126

BESANT, Sir Walt. As We Are and as We May Be 6/ c 8° Chatto 03
Twelve essays, nine of which deal with practical philanthropical subjects.

BRACKETT, J. R. Supervision and Education in Charity $1 *n.* (4/6 *n.*) gl 8° Macmillan 03

CARNEGIE, Andr. The Gospel of Wealth [repr. articles; 8/6 *n.* Warne] $2 8° Century Co., *N.Y.* 01

CHALMERS, Dr Thos. [1780–1847] On Charity, arrgd. and ed. N. Masterman; port. 7/6 *n.* 8° Constable 00
A seln. of passages fr. his wrgs. illustrating his social tchg. and pract. wk. One of best and most philos. bks. on subj.

CRAWFORD, Virginia M. Ideals of Charity [addressed to R.-C's.] 2/6 *n.* c 8° Sands 08

DENDY, Hel. [=Mrs B. BOSANQUET] Meaning & Method of Charity—*in* Bosanquet [ed.], *Aspects, ut* **D** § 125

DEVINE, E. T. The Practice of Charity [Hdbks. f. Pract. Wkrs.] 75 c. c 8° Lentilhon, *N.Y.* 01

ELWOOD, C. A. Public Relief & Private Charity in England 75 c. 8° Univ. of Missouri, *Columbia* 02

GHENT, W. J. Our Benevolent Feudalism—*ut* **D** § 118

GILMAN, D. C. [ed.] Organisation of Charities [a report] $1·50 8° Johns Hopk. Univ. Pr., *Baltimore* 94

HENDERSON, C. R., *etc.* Modern Methods of Charity $3·50 *n.* (15/ *n.*) 8° Macmillan 04
Provides in 700 pp., a conspectus of systs. of relief throughout chief countries of Eur., Brit. Emp., and U.S., concludg. w. acc. of Jewish charities. Temperate and impartial. Bibliography.

LEE, J. Constructive & Preventive Philanthropy; Introd. J. A. Riis $1 *n.* (4/6 *n.*) c 8° Macmillan 03
Libra., Savings and Loan Assocns., Bldg. Laws, Home Industries, Vacation Schls., Playgrds., Baths, Clubs, etc.

LOCH, C. S. Charity Organisation [Social Science Series] 2/6 c 8° Sonnenschein [90] 95
$1 Scribner, *N.Y.* An excellent brief manual, giving a sketch indicating not merely the methods and plan of the London Char. Org. Soc., but also enabling the reader to form a conception of the social and other conditns. under which alone, in the author's opin., an organizn. of charity can take root and develop.

,, How to Help Cases of Distress = Introd. *to* Annual Charities Register & Digest—*ut inf.*

,, Charity and Social Life 6/ *n.* c 8° Macmillan 10
Mainly repr. fr. *Suppl.* to *Encyclo. Brit.*, ed. ix (1902). A compreh. review of the stages of charit. thought—primitive, classical, Jewish, and Christian; w. 5 chs. on pres. social needs, and on right and wrong ways of meetg. them. Individualist.

,, [ed.] Methods of Soc. Advance: short studs. in soc. pract. 3/6 *n.* ($1·25 *n.*) c 8° Macmillan 04
By members of Char. Org. Soc. and others, representg. (tho' unofficially) the views of that Society, and sharg. its profound distrust of all communal and State action or interference.

LOWELL, Josephine S. Public Relief & Private Charity [Questns. of Day] *o.p.* [*pb.* 75 c.] c 8° Putnam, *N.Y.* 84

MACKAY, Thos. The State and Charity [Engl. Citizen Ser.] 2/6 ($1) c 8° Macmillan 98
A historical and critical acc. of charities, espec. in Engl. Conservative and individualist.

PATERSON, Arth. Administrn. of Charity [letters repr. fr. 'Times'] 1/ 8° City Council f. Org. of Charity 08
Describes the chaotic state of charity-giving, and proposes an association of subscribers.

ROGERS, Rev. C. F. Charitable Relief [Handbks. for Clergy] 2/6 *n.* (90 c. *n.*) c 8° Longman 04

SPENCER, Herb. Negative Beneficence; *and* Positive Beneficence—*ut* **C** § 62

STEPHENS, W. Walker Higher Life for Working People 3/6 ($1·25) c 8° Longman 99
Discussn. of var. measures for alleviation of poorer-class life: old-age pensns., 8-hrs. day, unhealthy industries, etc.

*Jewish Board of Guardians*

MAGNUS, Laurie The Jewish Board of Guardians; ill. 2/6 *n.* c 8° Jew. Bd. of Gdns. *n.d.* (09)
Hist. of the institn. (wh. first appl. charit. funds to industr. apprenticesh.) and of its makers: 1859–1909.

*Worker's Manuals* —*v.* **D** § 127, *s.v.* Worker's Manuals

**Charitable Institutions: Locally:** *Europe*

DE LIEFDE, Jno. [ed.] The Charities of Europe *o.p.* [*pb.* 5/] c 8° Strahan [65] 72
An impartial acc. of var. systs. adopted, giving details of upwards of 26 institutions visited.

Vagrancy and Public Charities in Foreign Countries [Consular Reports] Govt. Prntg. Off., *Washgtn.* 92

*United Kingdom*

Charitable Ten Thousand: 1905–6 21/ *n.* c 8° Newnham [96] 05
Names and addresses, in alphab. order, of 10,000 living benefactors of charities, interleaved.

Handbook of Catholic Charities, Associations, etc., in Great Britain 1/ 8° Catholic Truth Soc. 94

*London*

FRY, Herb. [ed.] Royal Guide to the London Charities 1/6 c 8° Chatto *ann.*

HOWE, W. F. [ed.] Classified Directory to the Metropolitan Charities 1/ 12° Longman [75] *ann.*

LOCH, C. S. [ed.] Annual Charities Register and Digest [w. good index] 5/ *n.* 8° Longman [85] *ann.*
A classif. register of the London charities, w. digest of information on legal, voluntary, and other means for prevention or relief of distress, and improvemt. of condn. of the poor, and a valuable Introd. [*v. sup.*].

Low & Co., S. [pubs.] Handbook to the Charities of London 1/ c 8° Boothroyd [85] *ann.*

MACDONALD, J. J. The Passmore Edward's Institutions; ill. [nature & aims] 2/6 Strand News Co. 00

*United States*

WARNER, Prf. A. G. American Charities [Lib. of Economics] $2 *n.* 12° Crowell, *N.Y.* [94] 08

*New York*

New York [City] Charities Directory
[classif. and descript. directory; pp. 400] $1 s 8° Charities Org. Soc., *N.Y.* [ ] *ann.*

*Philadelphia*

Civic Club Digest of Educational & Charitable Institns. & Socs. in Philadelphia $1 8° Civic Club, *Phila.* 95

*France*

BALCH, Emily G. Public Assistance of Poor in France
[Am. Ec. Ass.; 2/6 Sonnenschein] $1 *n.* 8° Macmillan, *N.Y.* 93

**Blind; Deaf and Dumb** —*v.* **D** § 169

**Crèches**

Crèches, or Day Nurseries [Offic. Rept. of L.C.C.] 9*d.* c 8° P. S. King & Son 06

HILTON, Mrs Marie [1821–96]

Hilton, W. Deane [son] Marie Hilton: her life and work; port. *o.p.* [*pb.* 7/6] 8° Isbister 97

SUTTER —*in her* Britain's Next Campaign [Elberfeld system], *ut* **D** § 127

**Hospitals and Medical Charities**

BURDETT, Sir Hy. [ed.] Hospital & Charities Annual [$2 *n.* Scrib., *N.Y.*] 10/6 *n.* 8° Scientific Pr. [90] *ann.*
Contg. partics. of over 4,000 institns. of world. Greater pt. of bk. devoted to Hospitals, but much space given to brief dcscrns. of missionary and relig. Socs., institns. for Blind, Deaf and Dumb, Orphanages, Homes, etc. Hospital policy is discussed at length.

RENTOUL, R. R. Reform of our Voluntary Medical Charities 5/ 8° Baillière 91

**Life-Boats**

DIBDIN (J. C.) + AYLING (J.) The Book of the Lifeboat; ill. 4/6 *n.* s 4° Oliphant, *Edin.* 94
A hist. of Lifeboat Saturday Movemt., its first purpose bg. to call public attentn. to financial needs of Lifeboat Institn. Incidentally many deeds of gallantry, described by eye-witnesses, are given.

HAYDON, A. L. The Book of the Lifeboat 3/6 c 8° Pilgrim Press 09
Acc. of Lifeboat Institn. (founded 1824, since wh. date 47,983 lives saved, incl. those by 'shore-boats', fr. the 270 stations), w. many stories of heroic effort and self-sacrifice.

LEWIS, R. History of the Life-boat and its Work *o.p.* [*pb.* 5/] c 8° Macmillan [74] 74

O'CONNOR, W. D. Heroes of the Storm [U.S. life-savg. service] $1·50 c 8° *Boston* 04

RAND, E. A. Fighting the Sea: winter at a life-saving station *o.p.* [*pb.* 3/6] c 8° Burnet 88

*Goodwin Sands*

GATTIE, G. Byng Memorials of Goodwin Sands; ill. [a good little bk.] 6/ c 8° W. H. Allen 90

GILMORE, J. Storm Warriors [life-boat wk. on Goodwin Sands] 3/6 p 8° Macmillan [74]

TREANOR, Rev. T. S. Heroes of the Goodwin Sands; ill. 3/6 c 8° R.T.S. [92] 92

**Clubs for Working Girls and Boys**—*v.* **D** § 120 **Parish Work**—*v.* **A** §§ 107, 113

**Reformatory and Pauper Schools**—*v.* **D** § 169

**Biography of Philanthropists:** *Collectively*

BOLTON, Mrs S. K. Famous Givers and their Gifts $1·50 c 8° Crowell, *N.Y.* 96

BOSANQUET, Dr Bernard Geo. Moore, *and* Jean Leclaire—*in his* Essays and Addresses, *ut* **A** § 8

COCHRANE, Rob. Beneficent and Useful Lives [popular] 2/6 c 8° Chambers 90

DE LIEFDE, Jac. The Romance of Charity *o.p.* [*pb.* 5/] c 8° Strahan 67

JAPP, Dr A. H. Good Men and True; ports. [popular] 6/ c 8° Unwin 90

*Individually*

ASPINALL, Clarke [L'pool philanthropist] Life of. By Walter Lewin; port. 8° *priv. prin.* 92

BARNARDO, Dr Memoir of. By Mrs S. L. Barnardo + J. Marchant 12/ *n.* 8° Hodder 08

BRACE, Rev. C. Loring Life and Letters. By his Daughter [8/6 Low] $2·50 8° Scribner, *N.Y.* 95
BRACE did good service in caring for the waifs and strays of New York.

BURNS, Sir Geo. [Glasg. philanthropist: 1795–1890]

Hodder, Edwin Sir George Burns: his times and friends; port. 14/ 8° Hodder 90

COBBE, Fces. Power [1822–1904] Life of. By Herself 7/6 c 8° Sonnenschein [94] 04
As dau. of squire of Newbridge, nr. Dublin, first 35 yrs. of her life were spent in Irel., of social condn. of wh., in the Forties a good acc. is given, fr. stdpt. of an amiable Tory. This is followed by descrn. of a 'Wanderjahr' in Italy, Egypt, Palestine, and Greece, her wk. w. Miss CARPENTER in the reformatories and ragged schools of Bristol, her wk. w. Miss ELLIOT as workhouse visitor, etc. Two chs., *The Claims of Women* and *The Claims of Brutes*, set forth in detail the pt. she took in Woman's Suffr. and Anti-Vivisectn. movemts.

DIX, Dorothea L. [1802–87] Life of. By Fcs. Tiffany; port. $1·50 12° Houghton, *Boston* 90
Miss DIX revolutionized meths. of caring for insane in U.S.; and succeeded in estabg. State Asylums in nearly every State of Union.

FRY, Lady, of Darlington Life of. By Eliza L. L. B. Orme 3/6 c 8° Hodder 98
A sketch of the public, philanthropic and political side of Lady Fry's Life.

GRANT, Dan. *and* Wm.
Elliot, Rev. W. H. Story of the 'Cheeryble' Grants 5/ *n.* c 8° Sherratt, *Mancs.* 07
Biogrs. of the Lancs. calico prtrs., the originals of DICKENS' Cheeryble Brothers—philanthropists and large employers.

HOWE, Dr S. G. [1801–76] Letters and Journals, ed. L. E. Richards [dau.], 2 vols. ea. $3 *n.* 8° Estes, *Boston* 06–9
Sanborn, F. A. S. G. Howe, the Philanthropist. [Amer. Reformers] $1·50 8° Funk, *N.Y.* 91
HOWE was conn. w. BYRON in liberatg. Greeks, w. emancipn. of negroes in Amer., and organized socs. for blind—his greatest achievemt. bg. his successful treatmt. of Laura BRIDGMAN.

MACGREGOR, Jno. [1825–92]
Hodder, Edwin John MacGregor ('Rob Roy'); ill. 3/6 c 8° Hodder [94] 96
An interesting biography of the well-known canoe-hero, a 'muscular Christian' after the Kingsley model, who devoted entire profits arising fr. his bks. and lectures (latter alone c. £10,000) to charities of best sort.

MONTEFIORE, Sir Moses [1784–1885] Diaries, ed. Dr L. Loewe, 2 vols.; ill. 42/ 8° Griffith 90
Wolf, Lucien Sir Moses Montefiore: a centennial biography 10/6 c 8° Murray 84

MOORE, Geo. [1806–76] Life of. By Dr Sam. Smiles *o.p.* [*pb.* 6/] c 8° Routledge [78] 79

MORLEY, Sam. [1809–86] Life of. By Edwin Hodder; port. 5/ c 8° Hodder [87] 89

MÜLLER, Geo. [*of Bristol*; 1805–98] George Müller. By A. T. Pierson 2/6 *n.* c 8° Nisbet [01] 02

SHAFTESBURY, 7th Earl of [1801–85] Life and Work of. By Edwin Hodder; 8 pl. 3/6 c 8° Cassell [86] 92

TOYNBEE, Arnold [1852–83]
Milner, Alf., L'd Arnold Toynbee 2/6 c 8° Arnold [00] 01
Montague, F. C. Arnold Toynbee: his life & work 50 c. 8° Johns Hopk. Un. Pr., *Baltimore* 89
2/6 Frowde. [Johns Hopk. Univ. Studs.] Conts. also acc. of Toynbee Hall by P. L. GELL, and of Neighbourhd. Guild, *N.Y.*, by C. B. STORER.
Toynbee, Gertr. Joseph & Arnold Toynbee [remins. & letters] 2/6 *n.* c 8° H. J. Glaisher 11

## 129: THE MIDDLE AND UPPER CLASSES; CLUBS AND CLUB-LIFE

GHENT, W. J. Mass and Class—*ut* **D** § 127

PONSONBY, Arth. The Camel and the Needle's Eye 3/6 *n.* c 8° Fifield [ ] 10
An inquiry into the expenditure of the rich and its relation to social disorganization.

MALLOCK, W. H. Aristocracy and Evolution 12/6 8° Black 98
$3 Macmillan, *N.Y.* A study of the rts., origin., and social functns. of the wealthier classes. Much crit. of Socialistic theories.

MARTIN, E. T. The Passing of the Idle Rich [6/ *n.* Hodder] c 8° 11

SEAL, H. The Science of Status: study in sociology 2/ c 8° Williams 96

VEBLEN, Thorstein Theory of the Leisure Class $2 (7/ *n.*) c 8° Macmillan 99
An examination into the position of the leisured class; summing up against its existence. An emminently original wk.

WENDELL, B. The Privileged Classes $1·25 *n.* c 8° Scribner, *N.Y.* 08

**Directory:** *United Kingdom*
Green Book (The): ed. Douglas Sladen + W. Wigmore [the 'Upper Ten'] 5/ *n.* c 8° Whitaker 10

**Clubs and Club Life**

AUSTEN-LEIGH, E. C. [ed.] List of Clubs in all Parts of the World 3/6 obl 16° Spottiswoode [93] *ann.*

IVEY, Lt.-Col. G. J. The Clubs of the World: a general guide *o.p.* [*pb.* 6/] p 8° Harrison [79] 80

*United Kingdom; London*: GRIFFITHS (A.) Clubs and Clubmen 10/6 *n.* 8° Hutchinson 07
Deals chiefly w. pres.-day condns. of London clubs; the histor. sectns. are scrappy.

HATTON, Jos. Club-land; 16 pl. and 33 ill. [Lond. & U.K.] 10/6 4° Virtue

NEVILL (Ralph) London Clubs: history and treasures; 5 col. pl. 7/6 *n.* 8° Chatto 11
" + JERNINGHAM (C. E.) Piccadilly to Pall Mall: manners, morals, man 12/6 *n.* 8° Duckworth 08
Chs. on life, clubs, characters, and social changes in pres. and past, w. many anecdotes and personalia.

ROBINSON, E. F. Early History of Coffee-houses in England; ill. [w. bibl.] 6/ c 8° Paul 93
An interestg. sketch of pt. played by coffee house syst. in life of 17 cent. 1st Lond. one establ. 1652.

TIMBS, Jno. Clubs and Club Life in London; ill. 3/6 c 8° Chatto [66] 98
$1·25 Scribner, *N.Y.* With anecdotes of coffee-houses, hostelries, and taverns, fr. 17th cent. to 1873. Popular; of no great value.

WARD, Sir Spencer Dining Societies of London—*in his* Essays, *ut* **D** § 142

*Athenaeum Club*: WAUGH (F. G.) Athenaeum Club and its Assocns. [a brief sketch] *priv. prin.* 94
WAUGH (F. G.) [ed.] Members of Athenaeum Club fr. its Foundation *priv. prin.* [94] 00

*Beef Steak Club*
ARNOLD, Walt. Life & Death of Sublime Society of Beef Steaks; pl. *o.p.* [*pb.* 10/6] 16° Bradbury 71

*Cogers, Society of*
RAYLEIGH, P. History of Ye Antient Society of Cogers; ill. [1775–1903] 6/ *n.* c 8° Simpkin 03

*Garrick Club*: BARHAM (R. H.) The Garrick Club: notices of former members [by auth. of *Ingoldsby Legds.*] 10/6 *n.* 8° *priv. prin.* 96
FITZGERALD, Percy The Garrick Club; ports. 21/ *n.* 4° Stock 04
An interesting and amusing book; but 'airily and debonnairly' inaccurate in details.

*Kit-Cat* [now *Ranelagh*] *Club*

BARRETT, C. J. History of Bain Elms and the Kit-Cat Club, now the Ranelagh Club; front. [prtd. on one side only] *w.* 21/ 4° *priv. prin.* 89

*Oriental Club*

BAILLIE, Alex. F. The Oriental Club and Hanover Square; ill. 25/ *n.* ($9) 4° Longman 01
Contains much topographical information, in addition to the history of the Club.

*Reform Club*

FAGAN, Louis The Reform Club: its founders and architect; ill. 30/ r 4° Quaritch 87

Hist. of the Reform Club & its Lib.—*incl. in* Catal. of Ref. Club Lib. 10/6 r 8° Smith & Elder [83] 94

*Savage Club*: WATSON (Aaron) The Savage Club; front., 4 col. pl., & c. 64 ill. 21/ *n.* 8° Unwin 07
A medley of history, anecdote, and reminiscence. Conts. a chap. by 'Mark TWAIN'.

*White's*: BURKE (Alg.) The History of White's, 2 v.; 200 pl. (chfly. ports.) 105/ *n.* 4° *priv. prin.* 92
With betting-bk. fr. 1743 to 1878, and list of members fr. 1736 to 1892 (incl. every Prime Min. fr. WALPOLE to PEEL). Only 500 prin.

*Edinburgh*: Book of the Old Edinburgh Club, vols. i–iii 4° T. & A. Constable, *Edin.* 08–11 *ann.*

*Glasgow*: STRANG (Dr J.) Glasgow and its Clubs *o.p.* f 4° Tweed, *Glasgow* [55] 64

**United States**

CROLY, Mrs J. C. History of the Woman's Club Movemt. in America $5 8° H. G. Allen, *N.Y.* 98

*New York*

FAIRFIELD, F. G. The Clubs of New York $2·25 8° Hinton, *N.Y.* 73

**The 'Gentleman'**

BROOKE, Hy. [1708–83] —*in his* The Fool of Quality, *ut* **K** § 50 [educn. of an ideal nobleman]

DEFOE, Dan. [1663–1731] Compleat English Gentleman [*ut* **D** § 161]: *v. note there*

EGAN, Prf. Maur. A Gentleman 4/ *n.* c 8° Burns & Oates 93
A bk. on social ethics and practice, by a Roman-Catholic; w. a ch. on *What to Read.*

FRISWELL, J. Hain The Gentle Life, 2 Ser. ea. 2/6 c 8° Low [64–6] 79
Series i also 1/ *n.* [New Univ. Lib.] Pott 8° Routledge. (50 c. Dutton, *N.Y.*) Essays on formation of character.

HOLE, Dn S. R. The Gentleman—*in his* Addresses to Working Men, *ut* **D** § 118

PALMER, Dr A. Smyth [ed.] What is a Gentleman? 6/ c 8° Routledge 09
$1·50 *n.* Dutton, *N.Y.* A very copious and interestg. colln. of extrs. fr. wrs. of all ages defining or illustratg. the conceptn. of 'gentleman'. A similar, but smaller, colln. by same Edr. was pubd. *sub tit. The Perfect Gentleman o.p.* [*pb.* 2/] f 8° Cassell [92] 95.

PEACHAM, H. The Compleat Gentleman; w. Introd. by G. S. Gordon [Oxford Tudor & Stuart Lib.] 5/ *n.* ($1·75) 12° Clar. Press [1634] 07
Mostly deals in counsels of perfectn., fortified by examples good or bad drawn fr. history (and largely fr. the old moralists, SUETONIUS, PLUTARCH and other Roman biographers. Makes culture (based on leisure) his groundwk.: how diff. fr. mod. 'Popular Educators'.

**The 'Lady'**: PUTNAM (Emily J.) The Lady: signif. phases of her hist.; ill. (10/6 *n.*) 8° Putnam 11
An admirable ser. of studies fr. days of the cave-woman to 'the lady of the Slave-States.' Learned and full of suggestion.

**Luxury** —*v.* **D** § 114

**Simple Life (The)** —*for* Rural Exodus *v.* **D** § 119

BENSON, A. C. The Silent Isle 7/6 *n.* 8° Smith & Elder 10
Sketches some of the details of a simple life—'an experiment in happiness'.

CARPENTER, Edw. Simplification of Life—*in his* England's Ideal, etc., *ut* **D** § 126

" —*in his* Civilization: its cause and cure, *ut* **D** § 126

DAWSON, Dr W. J. The Quest of the Simple Life 6/ c 8° Hodder 03
Reflective and descript. chaps. on life in London, quest f. happiness in country, 'City of the Future', etc.

KEITH, G. S. [M.D.] Plea for a Simpler Life—*ut* **H*** § 55

THOREAU, H. D. Walden, or Life in the Woods—*ut* **K** § 90
A charming acc. of 2 yrs.' sojourn on shore of Walden Pond, where author built himself a shanty, and lived in solitary commun. w. Nature: 'a nullifier of civilizn., who insisted on nibbling his asparagus at the wrong end', said O. W. HOLMES.

" —*in his* Anti-Slavery and Reform Papers, *ut* **D** § 130

WAGNER, C. The Simple Life [tr. fr. Fch.] [$1·25 McClure, *N.Y.*] 3/6 · also 1/, 6*d.* c 8° Pitman [01] 05

WOOLMAN, Jno. [1720–72] Journal—*ut* **A** § 89 [a Quaker classic]

**'Manners'**: *English*

ARMSTRONG, Lucie H. Etiquette Up-to-date 2/6 *n.* c 8° Laurie 08

BELL, Mrs Hugh [L'y] The Minor Moralist [$1·60 *n.* Longman, *N.Y.*] 4/6 *n.* c 8° Arnold 03

BENNETT, E. Amenities of Social Life 3/6 c 8° Stock 87

CAMPBELL, L'y Colin [ed.] Etiquette of Good Society 1/6 *n.* (50 c.) c 8° Cassell [72] 06

GREVILLE, L'y The Gentlewoman in Society [Victoria Library] *o.p.* [*pb.* 6/] c 8° Henry 92

GROVE, L'y The Social Fetich 5/ *n.* 8° Smith & Elder [07] 08
Short papers on social solecisms, the matinée hat, art of hospitality, etc. Some anecdotes.

HARDY, Rev. E. J. Manners Makyth Man [$1·25 Scribner, *N.Y.*] 3/6 16° Unwin [87]
" How to be Happy tho' Civil [$1 *n.* Scribner, *N.Y.*] 5/ *n.* c 8° Unwin 09
HUMPHRY, Mrs [' MADGE,' of *Truth*] Manners for Men ; Manners for Women ea. 1 / c 8° Bowden 97 ; 97
" A Word to Women [50 c. Mansfield, *N.Y.*] 1 / c 8° Bowden 98
Papers on children, home life, chaperons, manners, etc.
JEUNE, L'y [L'y ST HELIER] Lesser Questions *o.p.* [*pb.* 3/6] c 8° Remington [94] 95
*Dinners and Diners, Conversn., Revolt of Daughters* [*ut* D § 132], *Woman of To-day* [*ut ib.*], *Extravagance in Dress, Helping the Fallen, Saving the Innocent, Homes of Poor, Salvatn. Army, The Domestic Servant, Creed of the Poor*, etc.
LANE, Mrs Jno. The Champagne Standard 6/ c 8° Lane [06] 06
Papers on our social manners and foibles : entertaining, racy, pungent yet kindly.
' MEMBER OF THE ARISTOCRACY ' Manners & Rules of Good Society [$1 Scrib., *N.Y.*] 2/6 c 8° Warne [79]
NORTON, H. E. A Book of Courtesy 2/6 c 8° Macmillan 00
A compiln. of anecdotes, for yg. people, illg. good manners and bad manners.
' ONE OF THE ARISTOCRACY ' Etiquette for Women 1 / c 8° Pearson 02

*America*

BUGG, Lelia H. A Lady : manners and social usages $1 16° Benziger, *N.Y.* 93
GREGORY, Eliot Worldly Ways and By-Ways $1·50 c 8° Scribner, *N.Y.* 98
Papers giving a philosophy of fashion, etc., as seen in American society at home and abroad.
HALL, Flor. M. H. Social Customs : a manual of American etiquette $1·75 s 8° Estes, *Boston* [87] 93
" The Correct Thing in Good Society 75 c. *n.* 18° Estes, *Boston* [88] 02
" Social Usages at Washington $1 *n.* 12° Harper 06
HARRISON, Mrs C. C. The Well-bred Girl in Society 50 c. 12° Doubleday, *N.Y.* 98
HOLT, Emily Encyclopaedia of Etiquette ; ill. $2 8° McClure, *N.Y.* 01
KINGSLAND, Mrs Flor. Etiquette for All Occasions $1·50 *n.* 12° Doubleday, *N.Y.* 01
LEARNED, Ellin C. Etiquette of New York To-day $1·25 *n.* 12° Stokes, *N.Y.* 06
SHERWOOD, Mrs M. E. W. Manners and Social Usages $1·25 12° Harper, *N.Y.* [8–] 07
' WOMAN OF FASHION, A ' Etiquette for Americans $1·25 12° Stone, *Chicago* 98

*Conversation*

BELL, Mrs Hugh [L'y] Conversational Openings and Endings 2/6 c 8° Arnold 99
" Wordless Conversation 1 / *n.* c 8° Arnold 04
On the advantages of a syst. of signs, by finger and fan wagging, for the commonplace of conversn.
MAHAFFY, Prf. J. P. Principles of the Art of Conversation 4/6 c 8° Macmillan 87
' MEMBER OF THE ARISTOCRACY, A ' Society Small Talk 2/6 c 8° Warne 97
MORTON, Agnes H. Our Conversational Circle $1·25 16° Century Co., *N.Y.* 98

## 130 : SLAVERY ; THE NEGRO QUESTION ; COLOURED LABOUR

**Bibliography of Slavery**

NIEBOER, Dr H. J. —*his* Slavery [*ut inf.*] conts. bibliogr. list of 700 authorities

**History of Slavery :** *Generally* —*for* Greece *and* Rome *v.* **F** §§ 11 & 12 *resp.*

BROWNLOW, Can. W. R. Lectures on Slavery and Serfdom in Europe 3/6 c 8° Burns & Oates 93
90 c. *n.* Benziger, *N.Y.* Interestg. bk., full of facts on slavery and cognate condns. fr. Xtn. era downwards. Rom. Catholic (unfair to WICLIF)
BUCKLAND, W. W. The Roman Law of Slavery—*ut* **D** § 110
INGRAM, Dr J. K. A History of Slavery and Serfdom 6/ p 8° Black 95
$1·60 *n.* Macmillan, *N.Y.* A concise and useful epitome. After general introdn., traces hist. of institn. thro' medieval serfdom and slavery of more recent times down to 1895, endg. w. ch. on *Slavery and Moham. East.* Enlarged fr. his art. in *Encyclo. Brit.*, 9th edn. [*ut* **K** § 1].
NIEBOER, Dr H. J. Slavery as an Industrial System : ethnological researches 8° Nijhoff, *The Hague* 00
An able study, in English, on prevalence of slavery in all pts. of world, and condns. under wh. it arises.
PATERSON, W. Romaine —*in his* Nemesis of Nations, *ut* **F** § 4
Presents a vivid picture of the effects of slavery on ancient civilization.
VINOGRADOFF, Prf. P. Villainage in England—*ut* **F** § 5

**Race-prejudice** —*v. also* ALSTON, *inf.*

FINOT, Jean Race Prejudice, tr. Flor. Wade-Evans 10/6 *n.* 8° Constable 06
$3 *n.* Dutton, *N.Y.* Attempts, despite the conclusns. of anthropologists, to belittle the distinctns. of origin, colour, and blood, of racial superiority and inferiority. *Vide* note in **E** § 14.
KIDD, Dudley —*in his* Kafir Socialism, *ut* **E** § 41
ROYCE, Prf. Josiah Race Questions, Provincialism, and other Amer. Problems—*ut* **D** § 147
SCHOLES, Dr T. E. S. Glimpses of the Ages, vols. i–ii ea. 12 / *n.* 8° Long 05–8 *in prg.*
Denies the superiority of white races over coloured. Vol. i deals w. mental and physical aspects ; ii w. treatmt. of coloured subjects by Engld. ; iii–iv will complete the moral aspect.
WEALE, B. L. Putnam ' [L. Lenox SIMPSON] The Conflict of Colour $2 *n.* (10 / *n.*) 8° Macmillan 10
With special reference to English-speaking peoples.

**United States** —*v. also* **D** § 147 *and* **F** § 71

ARCHER, Wm. Thro' Afro-America: an Engl. rg. of race-probl. 10/6 *n.* 8° Chapman 10
Acc. of tour in U.S., Cuba, Jamaica, and Panama, mostly repr. fr. Engl. nwspprs. Comes to no conclusns., but inclined to favour formatn. of new State for negroes (declared impossible by many Amer. critics).

BLAIR, L. H. Prosperity of South Dependent on Elevatn. of Negro $1 12° Randolph, *Richmond, Va.* 90

BROUGHAM, Hy., L'd Speeches on Negro Slavery—*in* vol. x *of his* Works, 11 vols., *ut* **K** § 89

BRUCE, P. A. Plantation Negro as a Free Man [Questions of Day] $1·25 8° Putnam 89

BUXTON, T. F. African Slave Trade and its Remedy *o.p.* [*pb.* 5/] 8° Murray 40

CABLE, G. W. The Negro Question 75 c. 12° Scribner, *N.Y.* 90

,, The Silent South [pleads for civil justice for negro] $1 12° Scribner, *N.Y.* [85] 89

CAIRNES, Prf. J. E. Slave Power: character, career, & probable designs *o.p.* [*pb.* 10/6] 8° Macm. [62] 63
An attempt to explain the real issues involved in the Amer. contest of 1861 *sqq.* A singularly lucid book.

CAREY, H. C. The Slave Trade, Domestic and Foreign *o.p.* [*pb.* $2] 8° Baird, *Phila.* 53
Develops the principles under which man advances from slavery to freedom. By a Protectionist writer.

CARLYLE, Thos. Occasional Discourse—*in his* Latter-day Pamphlets, *ut* **K** § 89

CHANNING, W. E. [1780–1842] Slavery; Annexation of Texas; & Emancipation—*in his* Works, *ut* **A** § 95

CLOWES, W. Laird Black America 6/ c 8° Cassell 91
'A study of the ex-slave and his late master', in a series of ten letters to *The Times* (1890–1) by its Special Commissioner.

CONWAY, Moncure D. [1832–1907] Testimonies concerning Slavery *o.p.* [*pb.* 4/] p 8° Chapman [65] 65

DENNETT, R. E. At the Back of the Black Man's Mind—*ut* **E** § 46

DENTON, Dr L. W. Under the Magnolias [probls. of Old Slave States] $1·50 (6/) 8° Funk & Wagnalls 88

DU BOIS, Prf. W. E. B. A Study of the Negro Problem 25 c. 8° Am. Acad. of Pol. Sci., *Phila.* 98

,, Relation of Negroes to Whites in the South 25 c. 8° Am. Acad. of Pol. Sci., *Phila.* 01

,, The Negro Artisan: report of a social study 50 c. 8° Atlanta Univ. Pr., *Atlanta* [02] 03

,, The Souls of Black Folk: essays and sketches $1·20 *n.* 12° McClurg, *Chicago* [03] 05
6/ *n.* Constable. Eloquent and impassioned advocacy of the spiritual rights of his people. Ably describg. the wrongs, ambitions, longings, and despair of negroes of Southern States.

,, [ed.] Health and Physique of the Negro American [report; w. bibliogr.] 75 c. 8° Atlanta Univ. Pr., *Atlanta* 07

,, [ed.] Economic Co-operation among Negro Americans [report] $1 8° Atlanta Univ. Pr., *Atlanta* 08

EASTMAN, H. P. The Negro: origin, history, destiny [pro-Negro] $2 c 8° Eastern Pb. Co., *Boston* 06

FLEMING, W. H. Slavery and Race Problem in the South $1 12° Estes, *Boston* 06

FORTUNE, T. T. Black and White: land, labor, and politics in South $1 16° Fords, *N.Y.* 84
Claims that the Southern problem is not racial or political so much as economic, bg. a protest agst. land-monopoly.

From Servitude to Service [hist. & wk. of S. instns. f. educ. of negro] $1·10 *n.* 12° Am. Unit. Ass., *Boston* 05

HOFFMAN, F. L. Race Traits & Tendencies of Amer. Negro [Am. Ec. Ass.] $1·25 *n.* 8° Macmillan, *N.Y.* 96
5/ Sonnenschein. A compreh. monograph: vital statistics, race-amalgamatn., social and economic conditions and tendencies of Amer. negro. Pessimistic, regarding the race as doomed to extinction.

INGLE, Edw. Southern Side Lights [Lib. of Economics] $1·75 12° Crowell, *N.Y.* 96
A picture of social and economic life in the South a generation before the Civil War.

JOHNSTON, Sir H. H. The Negro in the New World; 4 maps and 391 ill. 21/ *n.* 4° Methuen 10
Embodies results of his study of the colour problem in U.S., West Indies, and Tropical America. Cf. also his *History of a Slave*, ill. 6/ c 8° Paul '89

LINCOLN, Abr. Emancipation Proclamation $4 *n.* Houghton, *Boston* [62] 09

LOWELL, J. R. Anti-slavery Papers, 2 vols. $7·50 *n.* 8° Houghton, *Boston* [*v.y.*] 02

MERRIAM, G. S. The Negro and the Nation [8/ *n.* Bell] $1·75 *n.* p 8° Holt, *N.Y.* 06
A good hist. of Amer. slavery and enfranchisemt., w. spec. chs. to var. statesmen and reformers.

MURPHY, E. G. Problems of the Present South $1·50 *n.*, 25 c. *n.* 12° Macmillan, *N.Y.* 05

,, The Basis of Ascendancy $1·50 *n.* (6/ *n.*) c 8° Longman 09
Treats of the Southern States w. special reference to relns. of negroes w. the whites.

Negro Problem (The): a ser. of arts. by represent. Amer. negroes $1·25 *n.* 12° Pott, *N.Y.* 03

NEWMAN, Prf. F. W. Anglo-Saxon Abolition of Negro Slavery [a lecture] 5/ 8° Paul 89

ODUM, H. W. Social & Mental Traits of the Negro [Col. Un. Studs.] 8° Macmillan, *N.Y.* 10

PARKER, Theod. [1810–60] Discourses on Slavery [1843–58]—*in* vols. v, vi and viii *of his* Works, *ut* **A** § 95

PICKETT, W. P. The Negro Problem: Abraham Lincoln's solution $2·50 *n.* (10/6 *n.*) 8° Putnam 09
Proposes to remove the race gradually fr. country, segregatg. those willing to remain as a subj. populn.

PLATT, O. H., etc. America's Race Problems $1 8° Am. Acad. of Pol. Sci., *Phila.* 01

SHUFELDT, Dr R. W. The Negro, a Menace to Amer. Civilization $1·50 c 8° Badger, *Boston* 07

SIEBERT, W. H. Underground Railroad fr. Slavery to Freedom $4 (17/ *n.*) 8° Macmillan 99

SINCLAIR, Dr W. A. The Aftermath of Slavery $1·50 *n.* 12° Small & Maynard, *Boston* 05
A study of the condn. and environmt. of the Amer. negro. Introd. by Col. T. W. HIGGINSON.

STONE, A. H. Studies in the American Race Problem $2 *n.* c 8° Doubleday, *N.Y.* 08

SUMNER, Chas. —*his* Works [*ut* **F** § 74]: contain important anti-slavery contributions

THOMAS, W. Hannibal The American Negro $2 (7/6 *n.*) c 8° Macmillan 01
A true (and therefore not always pleasant) account of the negro as a free American citizen.

THOREAU, H. D. [1817–62] Anti-Slavery and Reform Papers [Soc. Sci. Ser.] 2/6 c 8° Sonnenschein 90
$1 Scribner, *N.Y.* Sel. and ed. H. S. SALT, w. Introd. on THOREAU.

WASHINGTON, Prc. Booker T. The Future of the American Negro $1·50 c 8° Small & Maynard, *Boston* 99
6/ Putnam, *London*. On the need of education for the negro of the States.

" Up from Slavery [6/ *n.* Unwin] $1·50 c 8° Doubleday, *N.Y.* [01] 02
Autobiogr. of an ex-slave, educ. at Hampton Institute, a schl. for negroes, to wh. he was some yrs. later called upon to return as teacher. In 1881 he began at Tuskegee, in Alabama, under greatest diffics., the wk. for industr. traing. of negroes wh. has made his name famous throughout Amer.

" Working with the Hands; ill. [6/ Richards] $1·50 *n.* c 8° Doubleday 04
Sequel to *Up from Slavery*, treatg. of author's experiences at Tuskegee.

" The Negro in Business; ports. $1·50 8° Hertel, *Chicago* 07

" The Story of the Negro, 2 vols. [10/ *n.* Unwin] $3 *n.* 8° Doubleday, *N.Y.* 09
Narr. of the race fr. early period in Afr., thro' slave-time and emancipn., to pres. day in Amer. Main purpose of bk. is to show how closely negro has intertwined himself w. structure of Amer. life.

" [ed.] Tuskegee and its People; ports. $2 *n.* 8° Appleton, *N.Y.* 05

THRASHER, Max B. Tuskegee: its story and its work $1 12° Small & Maynard, *Boston* 00

" + DU BOIS (Prf. W. E. B.) The Negro in the South $1 *n.* 12° Jacobs, *Phila.* 07
[Wm. Levi Bull Lects.] His economic progress in rel. to his moral and religious development.

WEBSTER, Dan. [1782–1852] Speeches on Slavery—*ut* **F** § 74

WILBERFORCE, Bp. Sam. —*in his* Essays Contrib. to 'Quarterly' (2 vols.), vol. ii, *ut* **K** § 83

*History* —*v. also* **F** § 71

ADAMS, Alice D. Neglected Period of Anti-Slavery in Amer. [1808–31] $1·50 *n.* c 8° Ginn, *Boston* 09

BOTUME, Elijah Hyde First Days among the Contrabands $1·25 12° Lee & Shepard, *Boston* 93
Histor. record of last yr. of Civil War and of effects of dawn of freed. on life of slave, w. sketches of negro-character.

BROWN, W. W. Negro in Amer. Rebellion: heroism & fidelity [1861–5] $2 12° Lee & Shepard, *Boston* 67

BURGESS, Prf. J. W. The Middle Period [*ut* **F** § 70] = chron. of and comm. on the Slavery controversy

CLARKE, Dr J. Freeman Anti-Slavery Days: a sketch of the struggle $1·25 12° Worthington, *N.Y.* 83

CLARKSON, Thos. History of the Slave Trade *o.p.* [*pb.* 15/] 8° Parker 49

DU BOIS, Prf. W. E. Burghardt Suppression of the African Slave Trade to U.S.: 1638–70
[Harvard Historical Studies] $1·50 *n.* (7/6 *n.*) 8° Longman 96
By an ex-slave, b. 1868 in Mass., educ. at Fisk Univ. and Harvard, studied 1892–4 in Berlin, and elected 1894 to Latin professorsh. in Wilberforce Univ., Ohio, a Wesleyan institn., the oldest of schls. for negro youth.

EATON (Gen. J.) + MASON (Ethel O.) Grant, Lincoln, and the Freedmen; ill. $2 *n.* 8° Longman 07
Remins. of the Civil War, w. spec. ref. to wk. for contrabands and freedmen ofIssiss. valley.

FLACK, H. E. Adoption of the Fourteenth Amendment $2 8° Johns Hopkins Pr., *Baltimore* 08

HART, Prf. A. B. Slavery and Abolition [1831–41] = vol. xvi *of his* The Amer. Nation—*ut* **F** § 66

HELPS, Sir Arth. Conquerors of the New World—*ut* **E** § 54 [events wh. led up to slavery]

" Spanish Conquest in Amer., 4 v.—*ut* **E** § 54: in rel. to slavery; *also in* Friends in Council, vol. ii [*ut* **K** § 83]

v. HOLST, Prf. H. —*in his* Constit. and Polit. History, *v.* **D** § 145

KEIFER, Gen. J. W. Slavery and Four Years of War, 2 vols.; ill. $6 (25/) 8° Putnam 00
A political hist. of slavery in U.S., and narrative of author's experiences in Civil War.

McDOUGALL, Marion S. Fugitive Slaves: 1619–1865 [Fay House Monographs] $1 *n.* 8° Ginn, *Boston* 91
A compact acc. of the whole subj. of escapes of slaves, and of legislation to prevent escapes. Full bibliography.

PILLSBURY, P. Acts of Anti-Slavery Apostles $1·50 12° Cupples, *Boston* 84

SMITH, T. C. Liberty and Free Soil Parties in Northwest [1830–61]
[Toppan Prize Essay; Harvard Hist. Studs.] $1·75 *n.* (7/6) 8° Longman 97

" Parties & Slavery [1850–9] = vol. xviii of A.B. Hart's The American Nation, *ut* **F** § 66

SMITH, Wm. Hy. Political History of Slavery, 2 vols. $4·50 *n.* (25/) 8° Putnam 03
Acc. of slavery controversy fr. earliest agitns. in 18 cent. to end of War. Auth. was Priv. Sec. to Pres. HAYES, whose papers he inherited for preparatn. of his Life, but has here used for another purpose. Sets forth attit. and feelgs. of the Middle West. Good Introd. by Whitelaw REID, and final ch. by Prf. HALSEY—the most valuable pts. of the bk.

SPEARS, J. R. History of American Slave Trade; ill. [7/6 Bickers] $2·50 c 8° Scribner, *N.Y.* 01

STEVENS, Wm. The Slave in History: his sorrows and emancipation; ill. 2/ c 8° R.T.S. [04] 07
A popular acc. of slavery, picturesquely and temperately written.

WEEKS, Dr S. B. The Southern Quakers and Slavery—*ut* **A** § 89

WILLEY, Rev. Austin History of Anti-Slavery Cause in State & Nation $2 12° Hoytes, *Portland, Me.* 86

WILLIAMS, G. Hist. of L'pool Privateers and Letters of Marque 12/ *n.* 8° Heinemann 00
Includes an account of the Liverpool slave-trade. Illustrated.

WILLIAMS, G. W. History of Negro Race in America, 2 vols. [1619–1880] $4 8° Putnam, *N.Y.* [83] 85
By the first coloured Member of the Ohio legislature.

History of Negro Troops in War of Rebellion [1861–5] $1·75 8° Harper, *N.Y.* 88

WILSON, Hy. History of Anti-slavery Measures, 2 v. [1861–4] *o.p.* 8° Houghton, *Boston* 64

,, Hist. of Rise & Fall of Slave Power in Amer., 3 v. $9 8° Houghton, *Boston* 72–7

WILSON, J. T. The Black Phalanx; ill. $3 8° Amer. Pb. Co., *Hartford* 88
A history of the negro soldiers of U.S. in wars of 1775–1812 and 1861–5.

*Missouri Compromise* [1820], and its *Repeal* [1854]

DIXON, Mrs S. B. True Hist. of Miss. Compromise and its Repeal $4 8° Clarke, *Cincinnati* 99

RAY, P. O. Repeal of the Missouri Compromise $3·50 *n.* 8° A. H. Clarke, *Cleveland* 09

*Columbia*

TREMAIN, Mary Slavery in District of Columbia $1 c 8° Putnam 92

*Connecticut*

STEINER, B. C. History of Slavery in Connecticut 75 c. 8° Johns Hopk. Univ. Pr., *Baltim.* 93

*Maryland*

BRACKETT, J. R. The Negro in Maryland: study of institution of slavery $2 8° Johns Hopk. Univ. Pr., *Baltimore* 89
[Johns Hopkins University Studies: Extra Vol. (vii)]. A useful bk. for the political student rather than general reader.

,, Notes on Progress of Cold. People of Maryld. since the War $1 Johns Hopk. Univ. Pr., *Baltim.* 90
[J. H. Un. Studs. Supplem. to above], giving statistics on almost every feature of negro's daily life.

*Massachusetts*

DU BOIS, Prf. W. E. B. Philadelphia Negro: a soc. study [Univ. of Penn. Pubs.] $2 8° Appleton, *N.Y.* 00
Social life of negro in Phila., w. report on the negro as domestic servant, by Miss Isab. EATON.

EMILIO, L. F. Hist. of 54th Regt. of Mass. Volunteer Infantry [1863–5] $3 *n.* 8° Boston Bk. Co., *Boston* [91] 94

MOORE, Dr History of Slavery in Massachusetts 8° *Boston* 7–

*Mexico:* TURNER (J. K.) Barbarous Mexico; 48 pl. [indictmt. of slavery] 7/6 *n.* 8° Cassell 11

*New Jersey:* COOLEY (H. S.) Study of Slavery in New Jersey [Johns Hopk. Univ. Studs.] 50 c. 8° Johns Hopk. Univ. Pr., *Baltimore* 96

*North Carolina*

BASSETT, J. S. Slavery and Servitude in North Carolina [J.H.U.S.] 50 c. 8° Johns Hopk. Univ. Pr., *Baltimore* 96

,, Anti-Slavery Leaders of N. Car. [J.H.U.S.] 50 c. 8° Johns Hopk. Univ. Pr., *Baltimore* 98

,, Slavery in North Carolina [J.H.U.S.] 75 c. 8° Johns Hopk. Univ. Pr., *Baltimore* 99

*Virginia*

BALLAGH, J. C. History of Slavery in Virginia $1·50 8° Johns Hopk. Univ. Pr., *Baltimore* 00

DABNEY, R. L. Defence of Virginia *o.p.* [*pb.* $1·50] 12° Hale, *N.Y.* 67

MUNFORD, B. B. Virginia's Attitude toward Slavery & Secession $2 *n.* (9/ *n.*) 8° Longman 09
Presents the Anti-slavery and Union-loving sentimts. wh. pervaded the State, and its effect in mitigatg. the hardships of slavery and in promptg. the emancipn. of thousands of slaves.

**West Indies**

AIMES, H. H. S. History of Slavery in Cuba: 1511–1868 $1·50 *n.* (9/ *n.*) 8° Putnam 07

BUXTON, Chas. Slavery and Freedom in British West Indies *o.p.* [*pb.* 2/6] 12° Longman 60

LIVINGSTONE, W. P. Black Jamaica 6/ c 8° Low 99
A study of evolution of Jamaica negro fr. his first landing: a plea for the black race.

OLIVIER, Sir Syd. White Capital and Coloured Labour [Socialist Lib.] 1/6 *n.* c 8° Natl. Labr. Pr., *Salford, Mancs.* 06
Discusses aspects of probls. wh. arise fr. intercourse betw. Europ. employers and cold., esp. Afric., employees.

PULLEN-BURY, B. Ethiopia in Exile: Jamaica revisited—*ut* **E** § 59

**Africa** —*v. also* **E** §§ 41–50

ALSTON, Leon. The White Man's Work in Asia and Africa 3/ *n.* ($1 *n.*) c 8° Longman 07
[Maitland Prize Essay.] An able and scholarly discussn. of princs. underlying practical relns. of white and coloured races.

BAKER, Sir Sam. W. —*in his* Ismailïa, 2 vols., *ut* **E** § 43

BLYDEN, E. W. Christianity, Islam, and the Negro Race 7/6 8° Whittingham 87
An interesting work by a negro, late Minister Plenipot. of Liberia at Ct. of St James. Introd. by Sam. LEWIS.

CLARKE, R. F. [ed.] Cardinal Lavigerie and the African Slave Trade 14/ ($4·50) 8° Longman 89

COOPER, Jos. The Lost Continent: African slavery and slave trade *o.p.* [*pb.* 6/] c 8° Longman 75

KINLOCH-COOKE, Sir C. Chinese Labour in the Transvaal 1/ 8° Macmillan [ ] 06

MARKHAM, Violet R. A New Era in South Africa 3/6 *n.* 8° Smith & Elder 04
An examination of the Chinese labour-question.

MUNRO, Æ. The Transvaal (Chinese) Labour Problem 1/ c 8° Drane 06

NEAME, L. E. The Asiatic Danger in the Colonies 3/6 c 8° Routledge 07
A plea for the exclusion of masses of Asiatics fr. white colonies at all costs.

DAVIS, A. The Native Problem in South Africa 6/ c 8° Chapman 03

DURHAM, F. A. The Lone Star of Liberia 6/ c 8° Stock 92
Reflections on his own people by a negro (or 'African', as he prefers to be called), w. an account of the experiment to repatriate them.

GESSI, R. Seven Years in the Soudan—*ut* **E** § 43

HUTCHINSON, E. The Slave Trade of East Africa *o.p.* [*pb.* 3/6] 12° Low 74

KIDD, Dudley Kafir Socialism—*v.* **E** § 41

MCPHERSON, Dr J. H. T. African Colonisation [history of Liberia]—*ut* **E** § 46

MAXWELL, J. R. The Negro Question: hints for physical improvement of the race 6/ c 8° Unwin 91
Auth., native of W. Afr. educ. in Engl., pleads for advcemt. of his people, whose 'hideousness' is 'the princ. curse of the race'.

Question of Colour (A): a study of South Africa 6/ *n.* c 8° Blackwood 06
By a negro, wr. fr. pt.-of-view of an educated Christian native belonging to Church of S. Africa.

TILLINGHAST, J. A. Negro in Afr. & Amer. [Am. Ec. Ass.; 5/ Sonnenschein] $1·25 *n.* 8° Macm., *N.Y.* 02

*Portuguese West Africa: Angola; Islds. of San Thome and Principe*

BOURNE, H. R. Fox Slave Traffic in Portuguese Africa 1/ 8° P. S. King & Son 08

CADBURY, W. A. Labour in Portuguese West Africa 2/6 c 8° Routledge 10
Acc. of a visit on beh. of Cadbury Bros., Ltd., the cocoa-manufrs., w. obj. of inquirg. how far promises of reform made by Colonial Minister in Lisbon had been carried out.

MOREL, E. D. Red Rubber; Introd. by Sir H. H. Johnston; 2 maps 3/6 *n.*; *ppr.* 2/6 *n.* c 8° Unwin 06
Story of the 'rubber slave-trade' flourishing on the Congo.

NEVINSON, H. W. A Modern Slavery 6/ ($2 *n.*) 8° Harper 06

**Slave Trading**

CHURCHWARD, W. B. 'Blackbirding' in the South Pacific; ill. 2/ 8° Sonnenschein [88]
Account, in narrative form, of horrors of slave trade in Polynesia, by British ex-Consul at Samoa.

COLOMB, Cpt. P. H. [R.N.] Slave-catching in Indian Ocean; ill. [naval experces.] *o.p.* [*pb.* 21/] 8° Longman 73

MARKHAM, A. H. —*in his* Cruise of the *Rosario*, *ut* **E** § 64

PALMER, G. Kidnapping in the South Seas; ill. *o.p.* [*pb.* 10/6] 8° *Edinburgh* 71

SULIVAN, G. L. Dhow Chasing in Zanzibar Waters, and on Afric. coast [5 yrs.] *o.p.* [*pb.* 16/] 8° Low 73

SWANN, A. J. Fighting the Slave-Hunters in Central Africa; 45 ill. 16/ *n.* 8° Seeley 10
Narrative of advent., travel, and sport, 1882–1909, w. the Lond. Missy. Soc.'s expedn. to Lake Tanganyika, to help undermine the slave-trade round the great lakes. Supplies a good picture of the Arab slave-trade. Introd. by Sir H. H. JOHNSTON. Map.

WAWN, Cpt. W. T. —*in his* South Sea Islanders and Queensld. Labour, *ut* **E** § 63

**Law relating to Slavery** —*v.* **D** § 55

**Biography:** *Negroes*

DOUGLASS, Fred. [1817–95]

Holland, F. M. Frederick Douglass, the Coloured Orator [Amer. Reformers] $1·50 (6/) c 8° Funk, *N.Y.* [91] 07
DOUGLASS wrote accounts of his own life: *Narr. of my Exper. in Slavery, Bost.* '44; and *My Bondage and my Freedom, Rochester* '55.

Washington, Booker T. Frederick Douglass [Amer. Crisis Biographies] $1·25 *n.* c 8° Jacobs, *Phila.* 07

HUTCHINSON FAMILY

Hutchinson, J. W. The Story of the Hutchinsons, 2 vols.; ill. $5 8° Lee & Shepard, *Boston* 96
By the last survivor of the 13 brothers and sisters, giving their story of their lives.

*Slave Emancipators*

HOWE, Dr S. G. [1801–76] —*v.* **D** § 139, *s.v.* Blind

HUME, J. F. The Abolitionists [w. personal memories, 1830–64] $1·25 *n.* (5/) c 8° Putnam 05

MICHAEL, C. D. The Slave and his Champions; ill. 1/6 c 8° Partridge 91
Moderately good short biogrs. of Granville Sharp, Thos. Clarkson, Wm. Wilberforce, Sir T. Fowell Buxton. Quite popular.

*Individually* —*v. also* **F** § 73: Amer. Presidents; **F** § 74: Amer. Statesmen

BROWN, Cpt. Jno. [1800; *exec.* 1859]

Du Bois, Prf. W. E. B. John Brown [Amer. Crisis Biographies] $1·25 *n.* c 8° Jacobs, *Phila.* 09

Sanborn, F. B. Life and Letters of John Brown [elaborate biogr.; 12/6 Low] $2 8° Little & Brown, *Boston* 85

Thoreau, H. D. Plea for John Brown, *and* Last Days of John Brown—*in his* Anti-Slav. Papers, *ut sup.*

BUXTON, Sir T. Fowell [1786–1845] Memoirs and Correspondence of. By Chas. Buxton *o.p.* [*pb.* 5/] p 8° Murray [49] 72

CLARKSON, Thos. [1760–1846] Biography of. By T. Taylor *o.p.* [*pb.* 3/] 12° Hall [47] 47

GARRISON, W. Lloyd [1805–79] Story of Life, told by his Children, 4 vols. [60/ Unwin] $16 8° Century Co., *N.Y.* [85–9] 94

Grimke, A. H. Wm. Lloyd Garrison, the Abolitionist [Amer. Reformers] $1·50 (6/) gl 8° Funk & Wagnalls 91

Johnson, Oliver — William Lloyd Garrison and his Times — $2 12° Houghton, *Boston* [80] 81
Smith, Prf. Goldwin — Wm. Lloyd Garrison: a biographical essay — $1 12° Williamson, *Toronto* 92

GRIMKÉ, Sarah M. [1792–1873] *and* Angelina E. [1805–79]
Birney, Cath. H. — The Grimké Sisters — $1·25 c 8° Lee & Shepard, *Boston* 85

HOWE, Dr S. G. [1801–76] —*v.* **D** § 128

JAY, Wm. [1789–1858] William Jay. By B. Tuckerman [12/6 Osgood] $3·50 8° Dodd & Mead, *N.Y.* 93

PHILLIPS, Wendell [1811–84] Wendell Phillips, the Agitator. By C. Martyn [Amer. Reformers] $1·50 (6/) 12° Funk & Wagnalls 90

STOWE, Mrs Harriet Beecher [auth. of *Uncle Tom's Cabin*, *ut* **K** § 51; 1812–96]—*ut* **K** § 29

SUMNER, Chas. [1811–74] —*v.* **F** § 74

WHITTIER, J. G. [1808–92] —*v.* **K** § 29

WILBERFORCE, Wm. [1759–1833] Private Papers of. Ed. Mrs A. M. Wilberforce; ill. 12/ 8° Unwin 07
Colquhoun, J. C. — William Wilberforce, his Friends and Times — *o.p.* [*pb.* 9/] c 8° Murray [66] 67
Stephen, Sir Jas. — Wilberforce—*in his* Essays, vol. ii, *ut* **A** § 49
Stoughton, Dr J. — Wilberforce — [Men Worth Remembering] 2/6 c 8° Hodder 80
Wilberforce Bp Sam. [son] Life of William Wilberforce — *o.p.* [*pb.* 6/] p 8° Murray [68] 71

## 131: TEMPERANCE AND INTEMPERANCE

**Cyclopædia** —*for* Law *v.* **D** § 67, *s.v.* Licensing

Cyclopædia of Temperance and Prohibition — $3·50 r 8° Funk & Wagnalls, *N.Y.* 91
WAKELEY, J. B. Amer. Temperance Cyclo. of History, Anec. & Illns. $3 12° Funk & Wagnalls, *N.Y.* 75

**Generally**

Amer. Acad. of Polit. Science: Regulation of the Liquor Traffic $1 8° Am. Acad. of Pol. Sci., *Phila.* 08
BARNETT, H. N. — Legal Responsibilities of the Drunkard—*ut* **D** § 39
BARRETT, E. R. — Truth about Intoxicating Drinks — 2/6 c 8° Ideal Pb. Co. [89] 99
The scientific, social, and religious aspects of Total Abstinence. A prize-essay.
BILLINGS, J. S., *etc.* — The Liquor Problem — $1 *n.* 12° Houghton, *Boston* 05
Summary of investigations conducted by a Committee of Fifty from 1893 to 1903.
BURNS, Dr Dawson — Local Option — [Imperial Parliament Series] 1/ c 8° Sonnenschein [85] 09
A concise statemt. of hist. of movemt. and its princs.: an excellent vade-mecum f. tempce. advocate.
CHESHIRE, F. R. — The Scientific Temperance Handbook; ill. — 3/ c 8° Nat. Temper. League 91
A sensible bk., cont. a body of useful information, and not harping too much on the principles themselves.
CLUM, F. D. — Inebriety: its causes, its results, its remedies — $1·25 12° Lippincott, *Phila.* 88
CORNARO, Luigi — Treatise of Temperance and Sobrietie, tr. Herbert, ed. Dr G. S. Saunders c 8° *Eastbourne* [17-] 00
CROSLAND, T. W. H. — The Beautiful Teetotaller — 5/ c 8° Century Press 07
A slashing attack on the teetotal party, by auth. of *The Unspeakable Scot*, *Lovely Woman*, etc.
CUMMING, A. N. Public House Reform [Social Science Ser.; $1 Scribner, *N.Y.*] 2/6 c 8° Sonnenschein 01
ELLIOT (C. W.) + LOW (S.) + CARTER (J. C.) Liquor Problem in Legisl. Aspects $1·50 (6/) c 8° Putnam 97
FANSHAWE, E. L. — Liquor Legislation in the U.S. and Canada — 2/6 ($1) c 8° Cassell 93
An impartial report made on the spot by an Engl. barrister upon the laws and their operation.
FERNALD, J. C. The Economics of Prohibition [statistics of cost] $1·50 8° Funk & Wagnalls, *N.Y.* 90
GARVIE, Rev. A. E. — Ethics of Temperance as Applied to Drink Question — Sunday Sch. Union 96
GOUGH, J. B. [1817–86] 12 Lectures on Temperance [1/ Morgan] 25 c. c 8° Am. Temp. Pb. Ho., *N.Y.* 79
" — Platform Echoes; w. life by L. Abbott; ill. $3·50 8° Worthington, *N.Y.* 85
GRINDROD, R. B. — The Nation's Vice: the claims of temperance — 5/ c 8° Hodder 84
GUSTAFSON, A. — The Foundation of Death: study of the drink question 5/ c 8° Hodder [84] 88
HOYLE, W. — Our National Drink Bill as it affects England 2/6 p 8° Nat. Temp. League 84
INGLE, J. — A Moral Indictment of Teetotalism — 1/ *n.* c 8° Allenson 08
KOREN, Jno. — Economic Aspects of the Liquor Problem — $1·50 c 8° Houghton, *Boston* 99
An able wk., investigatg. reln. of liq. probl. to poverty, negro questn., etc. Bibliogr. *V.* also WINES + KOREN in **D** § 67.
LACEY, W. J. — The Case for Total Abstinence [Prize Essay] 3/6 c 8° Nat. Temp. League 89
LEES, F. R. Text-Book of Temperance [teetotal standpoint] $1·25; 50 c. 12° Nat. Temp. Soc., *N.Y.* 86
LEES (Dr F. R.) + BURNS (Dr D.) The Temperance Bible Commentary *o.p.* c 8° Nat. Temper. Depôt 94
Crit. and exposn. of all passages occurrg. in Bible bearg. on 'Wine' and 'Strong Drink', to ill. princs. of Temp.
LEWIS, Dav. — The Drink Problem and its Solution — 4/6 c 8° Nat. Temp. Depôt 81
MCKENZIE, F. A. — Sober by Act of Parliament [Social Sci. Ser.] 2/6 c 8° Sonnenschein [94]
$1 Scribner, *N.Y.* An unbiassed, concise acc. of results obtd. fr. var. systs. of drink-legisln. at home and abroad.

MAGEE, Bp W. C. —*speeches on* Temp. Questn., *in his* Speeches & Addresses *o.p.* [*pb.* 7/6] 8° Isbister 92
Incl. the famous speech in wh. he made the oft-quoted declarn. : '*If I must take my choice* . . . whether Engl. shd. be free or sober, I declare . . . th. I shd. say it wd. be better th. Engl. shd. be free than th. Engl. should be compulsorily sober. . . . I wld. distinctly prefer freedom to sobriety, bec. w. freedom we mt. in the end obtain sobriety ; but in the other alternative, we shd. inevitably lose both freedom and sobriety'.

MITCHELL, Dr Kate — Drink Question : social and med. aspects [Soc. Sci. Ser. ; $1 Scribner, *N.Y.*] 2/6 c 8° Sonnenschein 89

NEWTON, J. — Our National Drink Bill 1/*n.* c 8° Nisbet 09
Effects on natl. health. Wr. for Natl. Commercial Temperance League.

PATTEN, Prf. S. N. — The Economic Basis of Prohibition 15 c. 8° Am. Acad. of Pol. & Soc. Sci., *Phila.* 93

PEASE, Edw. R. — The Case for Municipal Drink Trade [Socialist] 1/*n.* c 8° P. S. King & Son 04

PEEL, Sid. — Practical Licensing Reform [sensible little bk] 1/6 c 8° Methuen 01

PEREIRA, Bp H. H. — Intemperance [Hdbks. for Clergy] 2/6 *n.* (90 c. *n.*) c 8° Longman 05

PRATT, E. A. — The Licensed Trade : an independent survey 1/*n.* c 8° Murray [07] 07

ROBERTS, Chas. — Time Limit and Local Option : restatemt. of licensg. controv. 1/*n.* 8° P. S. King & Son [08] 10

*ROWNTREE (J.) + SHERWELL (A.) The Temperance Problem and Social Reform 6/ c 8° Hodder [99] 01
$2 Whittaker, *N.Y.* By far the most complete, best-informed, and sanest bk. on the subj. Startg. w. admirable anal. of statistics of the traffic and its effects on community, discussg. the trade as a 'social and polit. menace', proceeds to consider proposed remedies—Prohibn., State monopoly, high licence, the Scand. experimts., etc. Valuable Appendices. Abgd. 6*d. n.*

,, ,, Public Interests or Trade Aggrandisement ? 1/*n.* c 8° P. S. King & Son 04

,, ,, Taxation of the Liquor Trade, vol. i 10/6 *n.* ($3·25 *n.*) 8° Macmillan [06] 08
Vol. i deals w. Publichouses, hotels, restaurants, theatres, railwy.-bars, and clubs.

RUNCIMAN, Jas. —*in his* Joints in Social Armour ; *and* Ethics of Drink, *ut* **D** § 125

SAMSON, G. W. — Divine Law as to Wines [testims. of 'sages, physicns., legislrs.'] $1 12° Lippincott, *Phila.* [80] 86

SANGER, C. P. Place of Compensn. in Temp. Reform [in fav. of Compensn.] 2/6 c 8° P. S. King & Son 01

SHADWELL, Arth. — Drink, Temperance, and Legislation 5/*n.* ($1·75) c 8° Longman 02
Adequate acc. of liquor-probl., advisg. educn. of feelg. of responsibility and moderate legisln. as remedy.

SHERWELL, Arth. — The Drink Peril in Scotland 1/*n.* c 8° Oliphant 03

SITES, C. N. L. — Centralized Admin. of Liq. Laws in Amer. C'wealth [Col. Un. Studs.] $1 *n.* 8° Macmillan, *N.Y.* 99

SMITH, Prf. Goldwin — Prohibition in Canada and United States—*in his* Essays, *ut* **D** § 142

SNOWDEN, P. Socialism & Drink Questn. [Socialist Lib.] 1/6 *n.* c 8° Natl. Labr. Pr., *Salford, Mancs.* 08

SOUTTAR, R. — Alcohol : its place and power in legislation 3/6 c 8° Hodder 04

STARKE, J. — Alcohol : sanctn. f. its use scientifically estabd. $1·50 *n.* (6/) c 8° Putnam 07

THORNE, E. — Heresy of Teetotalism in light of Script., Science, Legisln. 5/ c 8° Simpkin [03] 04

TOMPSON, F. W. — High Licence 1/*n.* 8° Macmillan 09
Facts and figs. rel. to U.K. and U.S. duties compared w. figs. and argumts. in ROWNTREE + SHERWELL'S *Taxn. of Liquor Trade, ut sup.*

United Kingdom Alliance : Pubns. present the side agst. Compensation 20 *Tothill St., Westminster, Lond.*

WARD, Rob. — The Fallacies of Teetotalism : duty of the legislature 7/6 c 8° Simpkin 72

WEEDON, W. B. — The Morality of Prohibitory Liquor Laws $1·25 16° Houghton, *Boston* 86

WHEELER, E. J. — Prohibition : principle, policy, and party 75 c. 8° Funk & Wagnalls, *N.Y.* 89
A good American summary of the case for Prohibition. With Appendix of legal decisions, statistics, etc.

WINES (F. H.) + KOREN (J.) Liquor Problem in Legislative Aspects $1·25 c 8° Houghton, *Boston* 97
5/*n.* Gay & Hancock. Detailed repts. on Maine, Iowa, S. Carol., Mass., Penn., Ohio, Ind., Missouri.

## History

—*for* History of Wines and Wine-trade, *v.* **I** § 37

BRIDGETT, Rev. T. E. — Discipline of Drink [$1·50 Kelly, *Baltimore*] 3/6 c 8° Burns & Oates 76
A histor. inquiry into princ. and practice of Rom.-Cath. Church reg. alcoholic drinks. Introd. by Card. MANNING.

BURNS, Dr Dawson — Temperance History : rise, devel. and exten. 2 v. 10/ 8° Nat. Temp. League 89

,, Temperance in the Victorian Age [1837–97] 1/ c 8° Ideal Pb. Co. 98

ELLISON, Can. H. J. — Sermons and Addresses on Temperance Subjects 5/ c 8° Wells Gardner 95
Contains a full history of the Church Temperance Movement.

FRENCH, R. V. Nineteen Centuries of Drink in Engl. : a history 3/6 c 8° Nat. Temp. League [84] 90

LEWIS, Dav. Drink Traffic in 19th Century : growth & influence 2/6 c 8° Nat. Temp. Depôt 85

National Temperance League
Gourlay, W. National Temperance ; Introd. J. T. Rae [hist. of the N.T.L.] 2/6 c 8° R. J. James 07

SAMUELSON, Jas. — The History of Drink *o.p.* [*pb.* 6/] 8° Trübner [78] 80

STEARNS, J. N. — Temperance in all Nations, 2 vols. $5 8° Nat. Temp. Soc., *N.Y.* 93

WEBB, Sid. + Beatr. Hist. of Liquor Licensing in Engl. [chfly. 1700–1830] 2/6 *n.* ($1) c 8° Longman 03

WINSHILL, P. T. Temperance Movement and its Workers, 4 v. ; *c.* 200 ports. 38/ r 8° Blackie 91
A comprehensive, popular and fairly good hist. of the movemt. in all its aspects fr. the earliest times.

WOOLLEY (J. R.) + JOHNSON (W. E.) Temperance Progress of the Century—*ut inf.*

*United States*

CLARK, G. F. Hist. of Temp. Ref. in Massachusetts : 1813–83 $1·50 12° W. B. Clarke & Co., *Boston* 88

One Hundred Yrs. of Temperance [1785–1885 ; Philadelphia Centennial $3 8° Natl. Temp. Soc., *N.Y.* 86

WOOLLEY (J. R.) + JOHNSON (W. E.) Temperance Progress of the Century 5/ *n.* c 8° Chambers 05

[Nineteenth Cent. Ser.] Mainly hist. of tempce. agitatn. and legisln. in Amer., fr. foundn. of first total-abstin. soc. in 1818 to pres. variegated laws and systs. wh. make liquor legisln. of Am. States such a fruitful field for tempce. experimt.

**Australia**

BOYCE, Fcs. B. The Drink Problem in Australia 3/6 c 8° Nat. Temper. League 93

**Canada**

SMITH, Prf. Goldwin Prohibition in Canada and United States—*in his* Essays, *ut* **D** § 142

**Norway ; Sweden : Gothenberg System**

GOULD, Dr E. R. L. Popular Control of the Liquor Traffic 1/ (50 c.) c 8° Cassell 95

A discussn. of legal basis and practical results of the Gothenburg System, by an advocate of it.

JOHNSON, Jas. The Gothenburg System : what it is & how it works 1/ c 8° C. of E. Temp. Soc. [93] 93

PRATT, E. A. Licensg. & Temperce. in Sw., Norw., Denm. [$1 *n.* Dutton, *N.Y.*] 2/6 *n.* c 8° Murray 07

ROWNTREE (J.) + SHERWELL (Arth.) British ‘Gothenburg’ Experiments and Public House Trusts 2/6 c 8° Hodder [01] 03

,, ,, Public Control of the Liquor Traffic 2/6 *n.* 8° Richards 03

A review of Scandinavian experiments in the light of recent experience.

WALKER, Jno. The Commonwealth as Publican ; diagrs. 2/6 *n.* c 8° Constable 02

An examination and adverse criticism of the Gothenberg System.

WILSON, T. M. Local Option in Norway 1/ c 8° Cassell 91

With an account of the establishment and working of the Soc. for Retailing Ardent Spirits in Bergen.

WRIGHT, Carroll D. Gothenburg System [=5th Spec. Rept. of Com'r of Labor] *gratis* 8° Govt. Prg. Off., *Washgtn.* 93

**Antiquarian books** —*v. also sup., s.v.* History (FRENCH)

‘BICKERDYKE, Jno.’ [=F. C. COOK] Curiosities of Ale and Beer [w. 50 early cuts] *o.p.* [*pb.* 21/] r 8° Sonnenschein [86] 89

DEATH, Jas. Beer of the Bible—*ut* **A** § 47, *s.v.* Beer

Cups and their Customs ; front. *o.p.* [*pb.* 2/6] c 8° Van Voorst [63] 69

Vade Mecum for Malt-Worms : facs. reprint *o.p.* s 4° *London* [1690(?)] *n.d.*

A descrn. of Publ. Houses of Lond., w. quaint cuts of signs, and verses to ea. Date usually assigned to it (there is none on title-p.) is 1690 ; but it must be later than 1702, since one of the signs is th. of ‘The Three Protestant Queens’ = Eliz., Mary, Anne.

**Blue Ribbon Movement**

BLACKWELL, Ern. Booth of Blue Ribbon Movemt. [life of Booth by his secretary] 3/6 c 8° Passmore 83

**Medical and Hereditary Aspect**

BUCKNILL, Dr J. C. Habitual Drunkards and Insane Drunkards *o.p.* [*pb.* 2/6] c 8° Macmillan 78

CUTTEN, Rev. G. B. The Psychology of Alcoholism [$1·50 Scribner, *N.Y.*] 5/ c 8° Walter Scott 07

ELDERTON (Ethel M.) + PEARSON (Prf. K.) Influence of Parental Alcoholism on Offspring 4/ 8° Dulau 10

Concls. th. alcoholism has next to no sensible influ. on health or intelligence of offspring. *Supplt.* [Questns. of Day & Fray] 1/ *n.* '10.

HORSLEY (Sir Vict.) + STURGE (Mary D.) Alcohol and the Human Body [anti-alcohol] 5/ *n.* ($1·50 *n.*) c 8° Macmillan 07

KEELEY, L. E. Non-heredity of Inebriety $1·50 12° Griggs, *Chicago* 96

KELYNACK, T. N. [M.D.] The Alcohol Problem in its Biological Aspect 2/ c 8° R. J. James 05

,, [ed.] The Drink Problem in its Medico-Sociological Aspects 7/6 *n.* 8° Methuen 07

$2·50 Dutton, *N.Y.* [New Lib. of Medicine.] By 14 medical authorities, in 15 chs., on every phase of the subject.

KERR, Dr Norman Inebriety, or Narcomania : etiol., pathol., treatmt., jurisprud. 7/6 *n.* c 8° H. K. Lewis [88] 01

Defines inebriety as a nervous disease allied to insanity. Gives results of legisln. in America and in our Colonies at great length.

MAGNAN, Dr V. On Alcoholism : its various forms and treatment [tr.] 7/6 8° H. K. Lewis 76

PAGET, Sir Jas., T. L. BRUNTON, etc. The Alcohol Question *o.p.* [*pb.* 3/6] c 8° Strahan 79

PALMER, C. F. Inebriety : its source, prevention, cure 2/6 c 8° Oliphant 96

REID, Dr G. Archdall Alcoholism : a study in heredity 6/ *n.* 8° Unwin 01

An original book, holding throughout to the evolutionary and selective point-of-view.

RICHARDSON, Dr B. W. Alcohol, 1/ ; Diseases of Mod. Life, 6/ ; Total Abstin. 3/6 c 8° Macmillan 75–8

RIDGE, Dr J. J. Alcohol and Public Health [physiol. effects] 2/ c 8° H. K. Lewis 94

SULLIVAN, W. C. Alcoholism : chapter in social pathology 3/6 *n.* c 8° Nisbet 06

WILSON, Dr G. R. Drunkenness [Social Sci. Ser. ; $1 Scribner, *N.Y.*] 2/6 c 8° Sonnenschein [93]

Disregarding teetotal questn. altogether, deals purely w. medical and social aspects of questn. Scientific and temperate.

**Biography of Temperance Reformers**

SHERLOCK, F. Illustrious Abstainers 2/6 c 8° Nat. Temp. League 79

*Individually*

CAINE, W. S. [1842–1903] W. S. Caine, M.P. By Jno. Newton; ill. 3/6 8° Nisbet [07] 08

FINCH, J. B. John B. Finch. By F. E. Finch + F. J. Sibley $1·50 12° Funk & Wagnalls, *N.Y.* 88

GOUGH, Jno. B. [1817–86] Autobiogr. and Pers. Recollns.
[1/ Morgan] $3·25 c 8° Nichols, *Springfd., Mass.* [70] 78

,, Sunlight and Shadow: gleanings from my life-wk.
[3/6 Hodder] $3·25 8° Washington, *N.Y.* [80] 88

Martyn, Dr C. Life of J. B. Gough, the Apostle of Cold Water $1·50 (6/) gl 8° Funk & Wagnalls 93

HADDOCK, Rev. Geo. Life of. By F. C. Haddock; ill. $2 (8/) sq 8° Funk & Wagnalls 87

HAYES, Jas. [1820–97] Brief Memoir of. By J. D. Hilton 1/ c 8° Ideal Pb. Co. 98

KIRTON, Dr J. W. John William Kirton, LL.D. By J. J. Ellis 2/6 c 8° Nat. Temp. League 93

LAWSON, Sir Wilf. Sir W. Lawson, a Memoir. By G. W. E. Russell; 3 ports. 7/6 *n.* 8° Smith & Elder 09

LINCOLN, Abraham [1809–65]—*v. also* **F** § 73

The Lincoln Legion [story of Lincoln as total-abst. advocate] $1 (4/) 8° Funk & Wagnalls [86] 87

LIVESEY, Jos. [1794–1884] Life & Teachings of [autob.]. Ed. J. Pearse 3/6 c 8° Nat. Temp. Depôt [85] 87

RIPLEY, Jno. [1822–92] Life & Journeyings of. Ed. M. A. P. Ripley [wife] 2/ c 8° Nat. Temp. League 93

WIGHTMAN, Mrs [1816–98]

Fletcher, Rev. J. M. J. Mrs Wightman, of Shrewsbury; 14 ill. 3/6 *n.* ($1·50 *n.*) c 8° Longman 06
A careful life of a pioneer in temperance wk., author of *Haste to the Rescue*, etc.

WILLARD, Fces. E. [1839–98] Glimpses of 50 Years; ill.
[3/6 Ward & Lock] $2·75 c 8° Women's Temp. Pb. Assoc., *Chicago* 89
Reminiscences of early days of Temperance, Women's Rights, and Social Purity movements.

## 132: WOMAN: HISTORY; POSITION, RIGHTS; EMPLOYMENT; CHARACTERISTICS; DUTIES, ETC.; BIOGRAPHY

**Cyclopaedia:** Every Woman's Cyclopaedia, 48 Pts. ea. 7*d.* r 8° Amalg. Press 10 *in prg.*

JACK, Flor. B. [ed.] The Woman's Book [arrgd. acc. to subjs.] 3/6 *n.* l 8° Jack 11

**History of Woman**

FULLON, Steph. W. History of Woman *o.p.* [*pb.* 5/] c 8° Routledge [55] 60
History of her connexion with religion, civilization, and domestic manners.

GAGE, Matilda J. Woman, Church, and State $2 8° Kerr, *Chicago* 93
'A Historical Account of Women through the Christian Ages'.

JOYCE (T. A.) + THOMAS (N. W.) [eds.] Women of all Nations—*ut* **E** § 3

PUTNAM, Emily J. The Lady—*ut* **D** § 129

REICH, Dr Emil Woman through the Ages, 2 vols.; 36 ill. 21/ *n.* 8° Methuen 08
$7 *n.* Dutton, *N.Y.* Chs. on characteristics, condn., and influ. of Egyptn., Gk., Rom., Byzant., Medieval, and Renaissance women (incl. Joan of Arc and St Teresa) in vol. i; on Engl. and Fch. women of differ. periods, literary women, feminism in 19 cent., and women in Amer. in vol. ii.

SCHUSTER, E. J. The Wife in Ancient and Modern Times 4/6 *n.* c 8° Williams 11

v. SCHWEIGER-LERCHENFELD, A. Woman in all Lands [tr.]; ill. [popular] $6·25 4° Roper, *N.Y.* 80–2

Woman in All Ages and in All Countries, 10 vols.; ill. $125 16° Barrie, *Phila.* 07–8
i: *Greek Women* (M. CARROLL); ii: *Roman Women* (A. BRITTAIN); iii: *Wom. of Early Xty.* (BRITTAIN + CARROLL); iv: *Oriental Wom.* (E. P. POLLARD); v: *Wom. of Mediaeval Frce.* (Pierce BUTLER); vi.: *Wom. of the Romance Countries* (J. R. EFFINGER); vii: *Wom. of Mod. Frce.* (H. P. THIEME); viii: *Wom. of the Teutonic Natns.* (H. SCHOENFELD); ix: *Wom. of Engld.* (B. B. JAMES); x: *Wom. of Amer.* (J. R. LARUS).

WRIGHT, Thos. Womankind in Western Europe; ill.
[earliest times to 17 cent.] *o.p.* [*pb.* 25/] s 4° Groombridge 69

,, —*in his* Domestic Manners & Sentiments in England *o.p.* [*pb.* 21/] s 4° Chapman 61

*England*

HILL, Georgiana Women in Engl. Life fr. Mediaev. to Mod. Times, 2 v. *o.p.* [*pb.* 28/] 8° Bentley 96
An industrious and conscientious compiln., w. much biograph. matter. Best for movemts. of Victorian era.

*France*

KAVANAGH, Julia Woman in France during Eighteenth Cent., 2 vols. *o.p.* [*pb.* 24/] 8° Smith & Elder 50

*Germany:* ECKENSTEIN (Lina) Woman under Monasticism—*ut* **A** § 57, *s.v.* General Works

*Greece; Rome; Early Christian*

BENECKE, E. F. M. —*in his* Antimachus of Colophon and Posn. of Wom. in Gk. Poetry, *ut* **K** § 190

DONALDSON, Prc. Jas. Woman, her Position and Influence in Ancient Greece and Rome,
and among the Early Christians 5/ *n.* ($1·60 *n.*) c 8° Longman 07
A lucid and well-wr. summary of salient facts to be gathered fr. the scattered, and often conflictg., testimonies available—very concise, but w. suggestns. at every step of best material for study, incl. Germ. wrs. Bibliogr. (14 pp.).

PERRY, W. C. Women of Homer; ill. [$2·50 Dodd, *N.Y.*] 6/ c 8° Heinemann 98

*Italy* —*v. also* **F** § 53

BOULTING, W. Woman in Italy; 16 ill. 10/6 *n.* 8° Methuen 10
Fr. 'introdn. of the chivalrous service of love to the appearance of the professional actress', i.e. to end of 16th cent. A detailed picture of female life in medieval Italy.

de MAULDE LA CLAVIÈRE, R. Women of the Renaissance: a study of feminism—*ut* **F** § 14: a v. good bk.

**Women's Place in Primitive Society**—*v.* **F** § 5; **in History of Civilizn.**—*v.* **F** § 4; **Folklore of Women**—*v.* **B** § 3

**Political and Legal Position, etc.**—*for* Laws affecting Married Women *v.* **D** §§ 59–60

ANTHONY, C. The Social and Political Dependence of Woman *o.p.* [*pb.* 3/6] c 8° Longman [67] 80

BAYLES, G. J. Woman and the Law $1·40 *n.* c 8° Century Co., *N.Y.* 01

BEBEL, A. Woman in the Past, Present, and Future [tr.] [Bellamy Lib.] 1/ c 8° W. Reeves [85] 07
30 c. Lovell, *N.Y.* By a representative Germ. Communist, emphasizing the Socialistic objectn. to 'property' in woman as much as to property in anything else. The later Germ. edns. have been considerably expanded.

DAVIES, Dr Emily Thoughts on Some Questions rel. to Women 3/6 *n.* c 8° Bowes, *Camb.* 10
13 repr. papers (1860–1908) by a pioneer and leader in movemt. for advancemt. in posn. of women and their higher educn.

HOUSMAN, Laur. Articles of Faith in the Freedom of Women Fifield *in prep.*

International Congress of Women: 1899, 7 vols. ea. 3/6 *n.* Unwin 00
A storehouse of information on all subjects concerning women.

KEY, Ellen K. S. The Woman Movement [tr. fr. Swedish] 09

LENNARD, T. B. The Position of Women in Law 6/ c 8° Waterlow 83

MILL, J. Stuart The Subjection of Women, ed. Dr Stanton Coit; w. introd. anal. [Also 6*d. n.*] 3/ *n.* (40 c. *n.*) c 8° Longman [69] 06
The bk. that has played the leadg. pt. in recent advancemt. in status of women. Its object was to show th. the then positn. of women was wrong, not merely in details, but in its fundam. princ., viz. the legal subordinatn. of one sex to the other.

Position of Woman, Actual and Ideal [8 pprs. by var. wrs.] 3/6 *n.* c 8° Nisbet 11

WHADCOAT, Gordon C. Every Woman's Own Lawyer [comprehensive] 3/4 *n.* c 8° Unwin 07

WOLLSTONECRAFT (GODWIN), Mary [1759–97] Vindication of Rights of Woman 7/6 c 8° Unwin [1791] 91
Authoress afterw. became wife of Wm. GODWIN and mother of SHELLEY'S 2nd wife. This edn. conts. a crit. Introd. by **Mrs** Hy. FAWCETT, discussg. soc. condn. of women then and now. For her Life *v.* **K** § 24.

„ The same; w. Introd. Eliz. R. Pennell [Scott Lib.] 1/ *n.* c 8° Walter Scott [1791] *n.d.* (92)

*Historical:* CLEVELAND (Arth. R.) Women under English Law 7/6 c 8° Hurst 96
Shows progress of laws in favr. of women fr. landg. of Saxons to pres. time. Readable; but desultory.

LAWRENCE, B. E. History of Laws of Prop. of Married Women in Engld. 5/ 8° Reeves & Turner 84

LECKY, W. E. H. —*in his* History of European Morals, *ut* **F** § 4
Ends w. an essay on influence of Christianity on the positn. of woman in Europe.

MEAKIN, Annette M. B. Woman in Transition 6/ c 8° Methuen 08
A rept. on stage wh. woman-movemt. has reached in its progr. tow. 'full equality of the sexes'.

MORTEN, Honnor Questions for Women (and Men) 2/ c 8° Black 99
A discussion of the changes in position of women during 19th cent. Pref. by Mrs Hy. FAWCETT.

PRATT, Edwin A. Pioneer Women in Victoria's Reign 5/ c 8° Newnes 97
Biogr. sketches of women under heads Emigrn., Higher Educn. of Women, Women Doctors, Nursing, Philanthropy, etc.

STOPES, Charl. C. Brit. Freewomen: their histor. privileges [Soc. Sci. Ser.] 2/6 c 8° Sonnenschein [94] 07
$1 Scribner, *N.Y.* A storehouse of histor. and legal informn. on the feminist movemt. Covers a wide period.

WALLIS-CHAPMAN, Dr A. B. + M. Status of Woman under the English Law 2/6 *n.* 12° Routledge 09
75 c. *n.* Dutton, *N.Y.* Gives a concise and compreh. view of positn. of women, polit., industr., and legal, und. Engl. law since Norm Conq.

*France:* THICKNESSE (Ralph) The Rights and Wrongs of Women, Pt. i Woman Citizen Pb. Co., 10 *in prg.*
Provisns. and wkg. of law of France in different spheres of life as it affects women.

*Germany*

RUSSELL, A. Wom. Questn. in Germy.—*in* B. A. W. Russell's Germ. Social Democracy, *ut* **D** § 126

*India, etc.* —*for* Child Marriage *v.* **D** § 133

ARMSTRONG-HOPKINS, Mrs S. Within the Purdah $1·25 12° Eaton, *N.Y.* 99
By a lady doctor: a good account of the condition of Indian women.

BARNES, Irene H. Behind the Purdah [missionary] $1·50 Crowell, *N.Y.* 98

BILLINGTON, Mary F. Woman in India; ill. *o.p.* [*pb.* 14/] 8° Chapman 95
Reprts. of a ser. of letters contrib. to *Daily Graphic*, contg. much sound, unprejudiced observn. of native Ind. society.

FULLER, Mrs Marcus B. The Wrongs of Indian Womanhood 5/ c 8° Oliphant, *Edin.* 00

MONTGOMERY, Helen B. Western Women in Eastern Lands 2/ c 8° Macmillan 10
A graphic acc. of what is bg. and has to be done f. women in India, China, Japan, and the East generally.

POOL, J. J. Woman's Influence in the East; Introd. by Sir L. Griffin 6/ c 8° Stock 92
Stories of lives of past Queens and Princesses of India (22 in all), wr. to show that woman, even in Eastern lands, amidst seclusion of the zenana, exerts a powerful influence not only on her friends, but on society at large.

RAMABAI SARASVATI The High-caste Hindu Woman 75 c. *n.* 12° Revell 87

SORABJI, Camelia Love & Life behind the Purdah [wrongs of Ind. women] 6/ c 8° Freemantle 02

*United States* —*v. inf.*, *s.v.* Characteristics

**'Rights'; Suffrage**

BLACKBURN, Hel. Women's Suffrage 6/ c 8° Williams 02
Has much to tell of Miss Lydia BECKER: not a complete general account.

MATHEW, A. H. Woman Suffrage [Social Problems Series] 1 / *n.* c 8° Jack 07

OSTROGORSKI, M. Rights of Women [tr.] [Soc. Sci. Ser.; $1 Scribner, *N.Y.*] c 8° 2/6 Sonnenschein 93
Compar. study in hist. and legisln.: unique attempt to collect and reduce to a syst. all available informn. on subj.

*History and Statistics:* COBBE (Fces. Power) —*in her* Life, by Herself, *ut* **D** § 128

ETHELMER, Ellis Woman Free 5 / c 8° Woman's Emancip. Union 93
Hist. of subjectn. and emancipn. of women; w. notes and argumts. in favr. of her general capabilities and equality w. man.

HECKER, Eugene A. Short Hist. of Progress of Women's Rights Putnam *in prep.*

SMITH, W. Sid. Outlines of Woman's Franchise Movemt. in N. Zeald. 2/6 *n.* c 8° Whitcombe; *Christchurch, N.Z.* 05

STANTON (E. C.) + ANTHONY (S. B.) + GAGE (M. J.) History of Woman Suffrage, 4 vols. [to 1885] ea. $5 8° Mann, *Rochester, N.Y.* 81–7

,, [1815–97] Eighty Years & More; 11 ports. [7/6 Unwin] $2 8° Europ. Pb. Co., *N.Y.* 98
Remins., coverg. her life-long wk. for Women's Rights and her connexions and sympathy w. advanced movemts.

STANTON, Th. [ed.] Woman Questn. in Europe [by 24 contributors] $3·50 8° Bardeen, *Syracuse, N.Y.* 84
12/6 Low. Suffr., educn., medicine, industr. movemt. in countries of Europe. A valu. compendium of facts, statistics, meths., and pictures of life.

SUMNER, Dr Helen L. Equal Suffrage in Colorado $2 *n.* (7/6 *n.*) c 8° Harper 09
Gives an answer to every questn. regarding actual workg. of Woman Suffrage in Colorado.

ZIMMERN, Alice Woman's Suffrage in Many Lands 1 / *n.* c 8° 13, *Bream's Bldgs., Lond., E.C.* 09

*Pro:* BLEASE (W. L.) The Emancipation of English Women 6 / *n.* 8° Constable 10

COBBE, Fces. Power The Claims of Women—*in her* Life, by Herself, *ut* **D** § 128

DILKE, Mrs Ashton Woman's Suffrage [Imper. Parliamt. Ser.] 1 / c 8° Sonnenschein 85

FARR, Flor. [Mrs EMERY] Modern Woman: her intentions 2/6 c 8° Palmer 10
'When the vote was refused, the first artillery for the woman's army [of revolt] was forged'.

FAWCETT, Prf. H. + M. G. —*in their* Essays and Lects. on Polit. and Social Subjs., *ut* **D** § 114

GROVE, L'y The Human Woman 5 / *n.* c 8° Smith & Elder 08
Essays in defence of woman suffrage. Show a candid apprecn. of chief argumts. *con.*

JACOBI, Dr Mary Putnam Common Sense' applied to Woman Suffrage [Questions of the Day] $1 (4/) 16° Putnam 94

LAWRENCE, F. W. Pethick Women's Fight for the Vote 1 / *n.* c 8° Woman's Press 10
Acc. of suffragist demand, its justice and necessity, objectns. raised, and history to Conciln. Bill.

MILL, J. Stuart Enfranchisement of Women—*in his* Dissertations, vol. ii, *ut* **C** § 49

PEARSON, Prf. Karl —*in his* Ethic of Freethought, *ut* **A** § 8; *and* Women and Labour, *in his* Chances of Death, etc., vol. i, *ut* **D** § 125

REED, Myrtle The Spinster Book $1·50 *n.* (6/) 12° Putnam 01

SHARP, Evelyn Rebel Women 1 / c 8° Fifield 10
Scenes of a suffragette's experiences—the 'raid', prison, street-speakg., street-sellg., conversion of the 'Anti', etc.

SMEDLEY, Const. Woman, her Position To-day 6*d.* *n.* c 8° *New Age* Press 08

STETSON, Charl. P. Women and Economics—*ut inf.*

SUMNER, Hel. L. Equal Suffrage $2 *n.* 8° Harper, *N.Y.* 09
Results of an investign. in Colorado made for the Collegiate Equal Suffrage League of N.Y. State.

VILLIERS, Brougham [ed.] The Case for Woman's Suffrage 2/6 *n.* c 8° Unwin 07
Essays by 16 wrs. (12 women, 4 men): Flor. BALGARNIE, Eva GORE-BOOTH, J. Keir HARDY, Emmeline and Christabel PANKHURST, Const. SMEDLEY, Edith PALLISER, Mrs FAWCETT, Mrs C. DESPARD, Isr. ZANGWILL, etc.

WOOLSEY, Mrs K. T. Republics *versus* Woman [3/6 Gay & Hancock] $1·25 *n.* c 8° Grafton Pr., *N.Y.* 03
Proclaims that women are less well off in the United States than under the monarchies of Europe.

*Con:* BILLINGTON-GREIG (Teresa) The Militant Suffrage Movement 2/6 *n.* c 8° Palmer 11

BUCKLEY, J. M. Wrong and Peril of Woman Suffrage 75 c. *n.* 12° Revell 09

CREPAZ, Adèle Emancipn. of Women & Prob. Conseqs. [tr.] [Soc. Sci. Ser.] 2/6 c 8° Sonnenschein [93]
$1 Scribner, *N.Y.* [Soc. Sci. Ser.] Pref. Letter W. E. GLADSTONE, who in 1892 pub. *Female Suffrage* [letter to S. Smith, M.P.] 3*d.* 8° Murray '92.

DICEY, Prf. A. V. Letters to a Friend on Votes for Women 1 / *n.* c 8° Murray 09
By a former advocate, now an opponent, of Woman Suffrage. Explains why he changed his mind.

JOHNSON, Mrs Helen Woman and the Republic $1·50 c 8° Appleton, *N.Y.* 97

Man's Case against Giving a Million Votes to Women 1 / 8° Hodder 10

S., M. E. Mixed Herbs: wkg. woman's remonstr. agst. Suffr. Agitn. 2 / *n.* c 8° Low 08

**Employment** —*for* Labouring Classes *v.* **D** § 118

ABBOTT, Edith Women in Industry $2 *n.* (8 / *n.*) 8° Appleton 09
Acc. of growth and developmt. of employmt. of women, discussg. probl. of women's wages and status of wkg.-women to-day. Bibliogr.

BARNETT, Edith A. The Training of Girls for Work 2/6 gl 8° Macmillan 94
Sensible remarks on girls' health, schls., character, househd. wk., professl. wk. and wages, marriage, etc.

BERRY, T. W. Professions for Girls; Pref. by L'y Grove 2/6 *n.* c 8° Unwin 09

CANDEE, Helen C. How Women may Earn a Living $1 (4/6) f 8° Macmillan 00

COLLET, Clara E. Educated Working Women 2 / *n.* c 8° P. S. King & Son 02
Six papers on the economic position of women workers in the middle-classes.

DAVIDSON, Mrs H. C. What our Daughters can do for Themselves 3/6 c 8° Smith & Elder 93

DILKE (L'y) + ABRAHAM (May) + BULLEY (Amy) Women's Work [Social Questions of To-day] 2/6 c 8° Methuen 94
A practical survey of the professional and industrial situation of women.

Education and Professions for Women [by 8 contributors] 5/ *n.* c 8° Chapman 03
*Higher Education; Stage; Art; Teaching; Journalism; Medicine; Public Work; Sanitary Inspecting.*

Englishman's Year-Book and Directory: ed. G. E. Mitton 2/6 *n.* c 8° Black *ann.*

Fingerpost (The): guide to professns. & occupns. of educ. women 1/ 8° Centr. Bureau f. Empl. of Wom. [ ] 08

HIGGS (Mary) + HAYWARD (E. E.) Where shall she Live? 1/6 *n.* c 8° P. S. King & Son 10
By Hon. Secs. of Southern and of Northern Committee of Natl. Assoc. for Working-Women's Lodging Homes.

HODGSON, W. B. Education of Girls, and Employment of Women *o.p.* [*pb.* 3/6] c 8° Trübner [69] 69

KILBOURN, Kath. R. Money-making Occupations for Women $1·50 12° Neale, *Washington* 01

Manuals of Employment for Educ. Women: ed. Christabel Osborn ea. 1/ f 8° Walter Scott 00–01 *in prg.*
i: *Secondary Teaching* (EDR. + Flor. B. LOW); ii: *Elem. Tchg.* (EDR.); iii: *Sick Nursg.* (EDR.); iv: *Medicine* (EDR.).

PFEIFFER, Emily Women and Work [reln. of higher educ. to health] *o.p.* [*pb.* 6/] c 8° Trübner 87

Woman's Library: ed. Ethel M. M. McKenna, 6 vols. ea. 5/ *n.* c 8° Chapman 03
i: *Educn. & Profesns.*; ii: *Needlewk.*; iii: *Nursery & Sick-room*; iv: *Arts & Crafts*; v: *Cookery & Housekpg.*; vi: *Lighter Branches of Agriculture.*

*South Africa*

SMITH, Alys Women Workers and South Africa [employmt.] 1/ *n.* c 8° Paul 03

*Poland:* ZAMOYSKA (C'ess) Ideals in Practice, tr. L'y M. Domvile 2/ *n.* c 8° Art & Book Co. 03
Acc. of women's schl. of domestic economy establd. by her over 20 yrs. ago at Zakopane.

*Agriculture; Gardening* —*v.* **I** § 47

*Journalism*

BENNETT, E. A. Journalism for Women [practical guide] 2/6 *n.* (75 c.) r 16° Lane 98

LOW, Fces, H. Press Work for Women 1/ *n.* c 8° Upcott Gill 04

*Medicine*

BLACKWELL, Dr Eliz. Pioneer Work in Openg. Med. Profn. to Women 6/ ($1·50) c 8° Longman 95

CHADWICK, J. R. Study and Practice of Medicine by Women *o.p.* c 8° Barnes, *N.Y. n.d.* (79)

JEX-BLAKE, Dr Sophia Medical Women: a thesis and a history 5/ c 8° Oliphant, *Edin.* 86

*Teaching* —*v.* **D** § 168

**Woman Compared w. Man; Equality of the Sexes; Psychol. of Woman**—*v.* also **C** § 71, **D** § 133, **H** § 100

DENSMORE, Dr E. [M.D.] Sex Equality $1·50 *n.* c 8° Funk & Wagnalls, *N.Y.* 07
6/ Sonnenschein. The thesis is that of sex-identity, woman and man bg. naturally one and the same in all psychical characters and functions.

ELLIS, Dr Havelock Man and Woman—*ut* **C** § 71
A sane consideration of the subj. fr. a psycholog. and anthropolog. point-of-view.

" Analysis of the Sexual Impulse in Women 21/ *n.* s 8° Soc. of Psychol. Research 04

FERRI, E. —*in his* Socialism and Positive Science [tr.], *ut* **D** § 126

FOUILLÉE, Alf. Woman: a scientific study and defence [tr.] 2/6 c 8° Greening 00

GAMBLE, Eliza B. The Evolution of Woman $1·75 (7/6) c 8° Putnam 94
'An inquiry into the Dogma of her Inferiority to Man'. Anthropological.

GARDENER, Hel. H. Facts and Fictions of Life 50 c. c 8° Fenno, *N.Y.* [93] 95
Discusses woman's character, brain-capacity, moral relns., etc. Claims complete equality w. man.

HANSSON, [Mme] Laura M. The Psychology of Woman [tr. fr. Germ.] s 8° *Paris* 99

'LEE, Vernon' [=Viol. PAGET] Rosny on Econ. Parasitism of Woman—*in her* Gospels of Anarchy, *ut* **D** § 134

MARHOLM, Laura Studies in Psychol. of Woman [tr.] [6/ De La More Pr.] $1·50 c 8° Stone, *Chicago* 99
Sociological. Mainly an attack on the Emancipn. Movemt. and a plea for simple womanliness.

SCHOPENHAUER, Arth. On Women—*in his* Studies in Pessimism [tr.], *ut* **C** § 59
A tremendous and characteristic attack on woman in general, and the Europ. [better to have limited it to Germ.] 'lady' in particular.

STAARS, Dav. The English Woman: studs. in her psychic evoln. [tr.] 9/ *n.* s 8° Smith & Elder 09

STETSON, C. P. [Mrs GILMAN] Woman and Economics; [6*d.* Putn.] $1·50 c 8° Small, *Camb., Mass.* [98] 09
Argumt.: Woman is the only female in anim. world dependent on male f. food (house-service not makg. her econ. indept., as her return in money, luxuries, etc., bears no ratio to her wk. but to her husb.'s power and will). Her econ. dependce., however, is balanced by sexual selectn., wh. provides her not only w. mate but w. livelihood in ratio of her power of attraction, as is case w. no other creature; and hence she has developed along lines of sex rather than of race.

THOMAS, Prf. W. I. Sex and Society [6/6 *n.* Unwin] $1·50 *n.* 12° Univ. Press, *Chicago* 07
Studies in the social psychology of sex.

WEININGER, Otto Sex and Character [tr.]—*ut* **C** § 71
After a parade of learng., shewg. some familiarity w. KANT, SCHOPENHAUER, NIETZSCHE, HUME, LOCKE, etc., concludes th. woman is merely an unintellectual and non-moral organism for perpetn. of the race; supported by discussn. of matters commonly excl. fr. conversation.

*Religion of Woman*

GARDENER, Hel. —*in her* Men, Women, and Gods 50 c. c 8° Truthseeker Co., *N.Y.* [85] 86

McCABE, Jos. The Religion of Woman [Rationalist Press pubn.] 2/6, 6*d.* 8° Watts [05] 05
On the effect of the Christian religion on the life of woman. Introd. by L'y Florence DIXIE.

**Characteristics**

COOK, Mrs E. T. From a Woman's Note-Book 5/ c 8° G. Allen 03
Studies of modern girlhood, and other sketches.

HANSSON, [Mme] Laura M. We Women and our Authors [tr. fr. Germ.] 3/6 *n.* ($1·50) c 8° Lane 98
A study of the conception of woman in wks. of KELLER, IBSEN, TOLSTOY, and other 19th-cent. writers.

JAMESON, Mrs Characteristics of Women: moral, poetical, and historical 3/6 c 8° Routledge [36] 90

LINTON, Mrs E. Lynn Ourselves: essays on women 2/6 f 8° Chatto [69] 84

MICHELET, J. Woman [tr.] 50 c. 12° Dillingham, *N.Y.* [60] 97

SALAMAN, Malcolm C. Woman through a Man's Eye-glass; ill. 3/6 c 8° Heinemann 92
Bright sketches of *Lady Novelist, Domestic Woman, Skittish Old Maid, Awfully Jolly Girl, Little Widow, 'Fin de Siècle' Woman,* etc.

*United States*

BLANC, Mme [Th. BENTZON] Condition of Woman in U.S. [tr.] $1·25 16° Roberts, *Boston* 95
Bright and sympathetic sketches of Amer. women, by a broad-minded Frenchwoman, visiting the States.

FAITHFULL, Emily —*in her* Three Visits to America, *ut* **E** § 56

MACCRACKEN, E. Women of America $1·50 *n.* (6/6 *n.*) c 8° Macmillan 04

MACPHAIL, Andr. The American Woman—*in his* Essays in Fallacy, *ut* **D** § 125

STOCKHAM (Dr Alice B.) + TALBOT (L. H.) Koradine Letters: a girl's own book; ill.
$2·25 12° Alice B. Stockham & Co., *Chicago* 94
Reveals progressively the development of a young girl in body, mind, and spirit.

de VARIGNY, C. The Women of the United States [tr.] $1·25 12° Dodd & Mead, *N.Y.* 95
A sensible, gd.-humoured bk. on mod. Amer. woman, by an enthus. yet not blindly apprec. Frenchman.

'*Modern* (*New*) *Woman*', *The*—*v. also* HANSSON, *sup.*

BURRILL, Katharine Corner Stones 3/6 *n.* c 8° Dent [04]
Advice for girls ('that our daus. may be as corner stones'); w. a racy defence of the modern girl.

COLERIDGE, Christabel R. The Daughters who have not Revolted 1/ f 8° Wells Gardner 94
6 sympath. essays, 'addressed to middle-aged maids', in reply to article *The Revolt of our Daughters*, by Mrs CRACKANTHORPE, in *Nineteenth Century.*

HANSSON, [Mme] Laura M. Modern Women: six psychological studies [tr. fr. Germ.] 3/6 *n.* c 8° Lane 95
$1·25 Roberts, *Boston.* Clever studies of 'George EGERTON,' Sonya KOVALEVSKY, Eleonora DUSE (whom author regards as type of mod. women on the stage), Amalie SKRAM, Marie BASHKIRTSEFF, A. EDGREN LEFFLER.

JEUNE, L'y Revolt of the Daughters, *and* Woman of To-day—*in her* Lesser Questions, *ut* **D** § 129

LINTON, Mrs E. Lynn The Girl of the Period; & other Social Essays, 2 vols. *o.p.* [*pb.* 24/] 8° Bentley 83

**Duties, Influence, etc.**

ADAMS, W. H. Davenport Woman's Work and Worth [popular] 6/6 c 8° Hogg 80

ASHMORE, Ruth Side-Talks with Girls $1 c 8° Scribner, *N.Y.* 95
A bk. of chatty 'gd. advices' to Am. girls; on whole sensible: conts. a gd. deal of wisdom sincerely expressed.

BAKER, L'y Letters to my Girl Friends 2/6 f 8° Wells Gardner 90

BELLAIRS, L'y Gossips with Girls and Maidens, Betrothed & Free 5/ c 8° Blackwood [87] 89

BLAND, Hubert N. Letters to a Daughter [$1·25 Kennerley, *N.Y.*] 3/6 *n.* c 8° Lawrie 06

BUCKLE, H. T. Influ. of Wom. on Progr. of Knowl. [also in *Misc. Bks.*, *ut* **K** § 89] 1/ *n.* 16° Fifield [72]

BUTLER, Josephine [ed.] Woman's Work & Culture [a colln. of essays] *o.p.* [*pb.* 10/6] 8° Macmillan 69

COBBE, Fces. Power The Duties of Women [a course of lectures] 2/6 c 8° Sonnenschein [81] 05

COUTTS, Bar'ss Burdett [ed.] Woman's Mission *o.p.* [*pb.* 10/6] r 8° Low 93
33 Congress Papers on philanthropic wk. of women by var. wrs. Pub. for Brit. Commissn., Chicago exhibition.

[CRAIK, Mrs] A Woman's Thoughts about Women 5/ p 8° Hurst [58] 87

CUNNINGHAM, Dr W. True Womanhood [6 papers; 35 c. Crowell, *N.Y.*] 1/ 8° Sonnenschein 96

ELLIS, Mrs [*née* STRICKLAND] Women of England, 2/; Daughters of England 2/ 12° Biggs [38; 42] 89

„ Wives of England, 2/; Mothers of England 2/ 12° Biggs [43; 43] 89

„ Chapters on Wives *o.p.* [*pb.* 5/] c 8° Bentley 60

GREY, Mrs Wm. Last Words to Girls on Life in School and after School *o.p.* [*pb.* 3/6] c 8° Rivington 89

HARDY, Rev. E. J. The Five Talents of Woman 3/6 c 8° Unwin [88] 94
Sensible and frank advice for girls and young women on the home and social life of women, their work and leisure.

HARRISON, Fredc. —*in his* Realities and Ideals, *ut* **D** § 125

HARVEY, Geo. Women, etc. [by Edr. 'N. Amer. Review'] $1 *n.* (5/ *n.*) c 8° Harper 08

HAWEIS, Rev. H. R. Ideals for Girls 2/6 c 8° Bowden 97
*Talks w. Untidy Girls, Musical Girls, Parochial Girls, Learned Girls, Mannish Girls, Engaged Girls, Brides.*

HAWEIS, Mrs H. R. Words to Women: addresses and essays *o.p.* [*pb.* 5/] c 8° Burnet 00

HIGGINSON, T. W. Commonsense ab. Women [2/6 Sonnenschein] $1·50 12° Lee & Shepard, *Boston* [82] 90

„ Women and Men [new essays] $1 16° Harper, *N.Y.* 88

HOPKINS, Ellice The Power of Womanhood; or Mothers and Sons 3/6 c 8° Wells Gardner [99] 04
Urges mothers to realize that on them is laid the burden of raisg. the moral standard of the world.

MEYER, Annie M. [ed.] Woman's Work in America [7 chs. by var. wrs.] $1·50 c 8° Holt, *N.Y.* 91

NEWTON, Rev. R. Heber Womanhood: lects. on woman's wk. in the world $1·25 12° Putnam, *N.Y.* 79

'O'RELL, Max' [Paul BLOUËT] Her Royal Highness Woman and his Majesty Cupid [$1·50 Abbey Pr., *N.Y.*] 3/6 c 8° Chatto [91] 01

" Rambles in Womanland 3/6 c 8° Chatto & Windus 03
Mainly on love and marriage; by a convinced feminist.

RUSKIN, Jno. Sesame and Lilies: lectures on books, women, etc.—*ut* **K** § 89

" A Letter to Young Girls 1*d.* 12° G. Allen [77]

SANGSTER, Marg. E. Winsome Womanhood: familiar talks; ill. 3/6 *n.* c 8° Oliphant 01

SHEARER, W. J. Talks to Young Women $1 *n.* c 8° Macmillan

WALSH, N. Woman 2/ *n.* c 8° Gill, *Dublin* [04] 04
A Roman-Catholic treatise on the duties of women in the various relations of life.

WHITNEY, Mrs A. D. T. Friendly Letters to Girl Friends [sensible and in tonic spirit] $1·25 16° Houghton, *Boston* 96

WILDE, L'y Social Study *o.p.* [*pb.* 6/] c 8° Ward & Downey 93
On *The Bondage of Women, Genius and Marriage, Social Graces*, amongst other papers.

YONGE, Charlotte M. Womanhood *o.p.* [*pb.* 3/6] c 8° Smith & Innes [77] 89

**Biography**: *for Bibliography*—*v.* **F** § 1, *s.t.* Manuel; *Series*—*v.* **F** § 1

ADAMS, W. H. Davenport Girlhood of Remarkable Women 5/ 8° Sonnenschein [83]

" Englishwomen of the Victorian Era, 2 vols. *o.p.* [*pb.* 12/] c 8° White 84

BEACH, Seth C. Daughters of the Puritans $1·10 *n.* c 8° Am. Unit. Assoc., *Boston* 05

BOLTON, Sar. K. Famous Types of Womanhood; ports. $1·50 12° Crowell, *N.Y.* 92
Popular biogr. sketches of Qu. LOUISE, Mme RECAMIER, Miss DIX, J. LIND, S. WESLEY, H. MARTINEAU, A. B. EDWARDS, Mrs JUDSON.

BROOKS, E. S. Historic Girls: stories of girls who have influenced hist. $1·25 (6/) 8° Putnam [87] 91
ELIZABETH of Tudor, ZENOBIA of Palmyra, CLOTILDA of Burgundy, PULCHERIA of Constantinople, Woo of Hwang-Ho, EDITH of Scotland, JACQUELINE of Holland, CATARINA of Venice, MATAOKA of Powhatan, THERESA of Avila, HELENA of Britain, CHRISTINA of Sweden.

BROWNE, W. H. Famous Women of History $2 12° Arnold, *Phila.* 95
About 3,000 brief biographies and over 1,000 female pseudonyms, w. list of proper names for women and their meanings.

CAREY, Rosa N. Twelve Notable Good Women of Nineteenth Century 6/ c 8° Hutchinson 99
$2 Dutton, *N.Y.* Qu. VICTORIA, F. NIGHTINGALE, E. FRY, Bar'ess BURDETT-COUTTS, PR'ESS OF WALES (now QU. ALEXANDRA), D'ess of TECK, 'Sister DORA', A. WESTON, Grace DARLING, P'ess ALICE, L'y Hy. SOMERSET, F. R. HAVERGAL.

'COOLIDGE, Sus.' [Sar. C. WOOLSEY] An Old Convent School in Paris, and other Papers $1·50 c ° Little & Brown, Boston 95
CATHERINE the Autocrat (CATHER. II of Russ.), Hélène MASSALSKI (afterw. P'ess de SIGNE, finally C'ess POTACKI, of Pold.), Miss EDEN (sister of Ld. AUCKLAND), Duc de ST SIMON.

CORKRAN, Alice Romance of Woman's Influence; ill. 6/ c 8° Blackie 05
Lives of St MONICA, Vittoria COLONNA, Mme GUYON, and others.

DA LIBRA Women Types of To-day: Venus, Juna, Minerva 10/6 *n.* 8° Stock 07
Sketches of characteristics of women of classical times as comp. w. those of present day.

EDWARDS, M. Betham- Six Life Studies; 6 ports. 7/6 c 8° Griffith 80
Fernan CABALLERO (Span. novelist), Alexandrine TINNE (Afric. explorer), Carol. HERSCHEL (astronomer), Marie PAPE-CARPENTIER (educl. reformer) Eliz. CARTER (Gk. scholar), Matilda BETHAM (littérateur and artist).

ELLET, Mrs E. F. Women of the American Revolution, 2 vols. $4 12° Jacobs, *Phila.* [ ] 00

" Queens of American Society 75 c. c 8° Porter & Coates, *Phila.* [67] 86

FAWCETT, Mrs Hy. Some Eminent Women of Our Time 2/6 (75 c.) c 8° Macmillan 89

GREEN-ARMYTAGE, A. J. Maids of Honour: 12 sketches; ports. 10/6 *n.* 8° Blackwood 06
Single women who have disting. themselves in philanth., nursg., poetry, travel, science, prose—H. MORE, M. CARPENTER, C. HERSCHEL, 'SISTER DORA', M. KINGSLEY, A. A. PROCTER, M. NORTH, J. INGELOW, L. ALCOTT, C. ROSSETTI, A. STRICKLAND, M. LAMB.

HANSSON, [Mme] Laura M. Modern Women—*ut sup.*

HAYS, Fces. Women of the Day [a biographical dictionary] 5/ c 8° Chatto 85

HIGGINS, Mrs N. Women of Europe in 15th and 16th Centuries, 2 v. *o.p.* [*pb.* 30/] 8° Hurst 85

HONE, [Mrs] Annie M. Woman's Enterprise and Genius; ports. 3/6 c 8° Hutchinson 93
Deals with ladies who, by their efforts and achievemts., have opened avenues to success for all who desire to employ their time in philanthropic, literary, artistic, musical, exploring, professional, or commercial enterprise.

MENZIES, Sutherland Memoirs of Distinguished Political Women, 2 v. *o.p.* [*pb.* 24/] p 8° H. S. King 73
ANNE DE BOURBON, D'ess of LONGUEVILLE; D'ESS DE CHEVREUSE; PR'ESS PALATINE; Mlle de MONTPENSIER; Mme de MONTBAZON; D'ess of PORTSMOUTH; D'ess of MARLBOROUGH; Sarah JENNINGS.

MILLER, Mrs Fenwick In Ladies' Company *o.p.* [*pb.* 5/] f 8° Ward & Downey 92
Mary SEATON (friend of MARY, Qu. of Scots), D'ess of BERRI, Mrs COCKBURN, Fanny MENDELSSOHN, Carol. HERSCHEL, Ida PFEIFFER.

PRATT, E. A. Pioneer Women in Victoria's Reign—*ut sup.*

SMITH, G. Barnett Women of Renown [19th-century] 7/6 c 8° W. H. Allen 93
F. BREMER, L'y BLESSINGTON, Geo. ELIOT', J. LIND, M. SOMERVILLE, 'G. SAND', M. CARPENTER, L'y MORGAN, RACHEL, L'y H. STANHOPE.

" Noble Womanhood: a series of biographical sketches 5/ c 8° S.P.C.K. 94
P'ESS ALICE, GRAND D'ESS OF HESSE, F. NIGHTINGALE, F. R. HAVERGAL, H. B. STOWE, 'SISTER DORA', L. M. ALCOTT, E. FRY, F. D. HEMANS.

YONGE, Charl. M. Biographies of Good Women [16th–19th cents.] *o.p.* [*pb.* 3/6] c 8° Innes [62] 93

YONGE, Prf. C. D. Seven Heroines of Christendom ; ports. 3/6 c 8° Sonnenschein [79] 

*American Women*

BOLTON, Sarah K. [Am.] Successful Women $1 12° Lothrop, *Boston* 88
M. HARLAND (Mrs TERHUNE), Mrs G. R. ALDEN (' Pansy '), C. BARTON, A. FREEMAN (pres. of Wellesley Coll.), R. BODLEY (dean of Women's Med. Coll., Phila.), etc.

HOLLOWAY, Laura Ladies of the White House [Presidents' wives, 1789–1880] $3·50 12° Bradley, *Phila.* 81

WILLARD (Fces. E.) + LIVERMORE (Mrs M. A.) [eds.] Woman of the Century [biogr. sketches] $10 8° Moulton, *Buffalo, N.Y.* 93

*Artists* —*v. also* **I** §§ 90–98

CLAYTON, [Miss] E. C. English Female Artists, 2 vols. *o.p.* [*pb.* 30/] 8° Tinsley 76

*Authors* —*v.* **K** § 23

*French Women*

FAWCETT, Mrs Hy. Five Famous French Women ; ill. 6/ ($2) c 8° Cassell 05

GEAREY, Carol. French Heroines 5/ c 8° Blackwood 85

*Irish Women*

' BLACKBURNE, E. O. ' [=Mrs E. O. B. CASEY] Illustrious Irishwomen, 2 vols. *o.p.* [*pb.* 28/] 8° Tinsley 77

GERARD, Fces. A. Celebrated Irish Beauties ; ill. [18 cent.] *o.p.* [*pb.* 21/] 8° Ward & Downey 95

,, Some Fair Hibernians [suppl. to above ; 18–19 cents.] *o.p.* [*pb.* 21/] 8° Ward & Downey 97

*Italian Women* —*v.* **F** § 53

*Mothers ; Wives*

ELLIS, Mrs [*née* STRICKLAND] Mothers of Great Men 6/ c 8° Chatto [59] 74

HERBERT, L'y Wives and Mothers in the Olden Times *o.p.* [*pb.* 6/] c 8° Bentley 85

HOLLOWAY, Laura Mothers of Great Men and Women $3 12° Funk & Wagnalls, *N.Y.* 83

*Queens ; Princesses* —*v. also* **F** *passim*

FINCH, Barbara C. Lives of the Princesses of Wales, 3 vols. *o.p.* [*pb.* 31/6] c 8° Remington 83

GREEN, Mrs M. A. E. Lives of Princesses of England, 6 vols.—*ut* **F** § 16

JAMESON, Mrs Memoirs of Celebrated Female Sovereigns 3/6 c 8° Routledge [31] 90

STRICKLAND, Agnes Lives of the Queens of England, 6 vols.—*ut* **F** § 16

,, Lives of Tudor Princesses—*ut* **F** § 32

,, Lives of the Last Four Princesses of the House of Stuart—*ut* **F** § 23

*India* —*v.* POOL, *sup.*

*Saintly Women*

DUNBAR, Agnes B. C. Dictionry. of Saintly Women, 2 v. [ea. $4 *n.* Macmn., *N.Y.*] ea. 10/6 *n.* 8° Bell 04–5

*Scottish Women*

FITTIS, Rob. Scott Heroines of Scotland 6/ c 8° Gardner, *Paisley* 89

GRAHAM, H. J. C. Group of Scottish Women [13–19 cents.] $3·50 *n.* 8° Duffield, *N.Y.* 08

*Soldiers ; Sailors*

CLAYTON, [Miss] E. C. Female Warriors, 2 vols. *o.p.* [*pb.* 18/] 8° Tinsley 79

DOWIE, [Miss] M. M. [ed.] Woman Adventurers ; w. Introd. [Adventure Series] 7/6 c 8° Unwin 93
$1·50 Macmillan, *N.Y.* Mme VELAZQUEZ [' Lieut. Harry T. Bulford, C.S.A.'], Hannah SNELL, Mary Anne TALBOT, and Mrs Christian DAVIES, all of whom disting. themselves by fightg. in men's clothes, takg. pt. in masc. orgies, even prosecutg. amours w. their own sex. [SNELL's autobiogr. is cont. in Adventure Ser., *sub tit. The Female Soldier, ut* **E** § 5].

VIZETELLY, Edw. The Warrior Woman 2/6 c 8° Treherne 02
Studies of women-warriors, sailors, etc., from Middle Ages to present time : good biographical matter.

*Individually* [lives not otherwise classed in this bk.]

ALICE, Princess Biographical Sketch and Letters of 12/ c 8° Murray 84

BOWNE, Eliza Southgate A Girl's Life 80 Yrs. Ago ; ports. & ill. [selns. fr. her letters] 12/ f 4° Chapman 89

BUNSEN, Baroness Life and Letters of, ed. A. J. C. Hare, 2 vols. *o.p.* [*pb.* 21/ ; *w.* 7/6] c 8° Daldy 78

BUTLER, Josephine [1828–1907]—*v.* **D** § 133

CARPENTER, Mary [1807–77] Life and Work of. By Rev. J. E. Carpenter ; port. 6/ 8° Macmillan [79] 82

CHARLOTTE of WALES, Princess. Brief Memoir of. By Lady Weigall ; portrait 8/6 c 8° Murray [74] 74

' DORA, Sister ' [=Dor. PATTISON ; 1832–78] : a biogr. By Marg. Lonsdale ; port. 2/6 c 8° Paul [80] 81

FOX, Carol. [1819–71] Memories of Old Friends 7/6 c 8° Smith & Elder [81] 83
Extrs. fr. her *Journals* 1835–71 : she was a friend of J. S. MILL, Jno. STERLING, and CARLYLE.

FRY, L'y Lady Fry of Darlington. By E. Orme 3/6 c 8° Hodder 98
A sketch of the life of a late vice-pres. of Women's Nat. Lib. Assoc., and well-known philanthropist.

JONES, Agnes Eliz. Memorials of. By her Sister ; portrait 3/6 s 8° Nisbet [72] 81

KOVALEVSKY, Sonya [1850–91]

Leffler [Edgren], Anna C. Sonia Kovalevsky: biography and autobiography, tr. Louise v. Cossel; 4 ports. [$1·25 Macmillan, *N.Y.*] 3/6 c 8° W. Scott 95

„ Sonya Kovalevsky: her recollns. of childhood; w. a biography; former tr. Isab. F. Hapgood, latter tr. A. M. Clive Bayley; ill. c 8° 6/ Unwin 95

$1·75 Century Co., *N.Y.* An extraordinary life of a passionate, impulsive, changeable, jealous, introspective woman, a Slav of the Slavs, gifted w. great mathematical powers, a favourite pupil of WEIERSTRASS, a deputy Professor at Stockholm and gainer of the Prix Bordin (Paris Acad. of Sciences).

ST HELIER, L'y Memories of Fifty Years [$4·20 *n.* Longman, *N.Y.*] 15/ *n.* 8° Arnold 09

SHORE, Emily Journal of 6/ c 8° Paul 91

The *Journal*, begun when the writer was under 12 and ending when she was 20, is a good record of what a talented girl with a passion for observation, information and literary labour was capable of before the days of High Schools. It is a sel. only, the MS. occupying 12 8vo vols.

TAIT, Cath. and Craufurd [wife and son of late Abp. of Canterbury]. Ed. [Can.] W. Benham 2/6 c 8° Macmillan [79] 82

WILLARD, Mary

Willard, Fces. E. Nineteen Beautiful Years: sketches of a girl's life 75 c. 12° Revell, *N.Y.* [77] 92

## 133: RELATION OF THE SEXES: LOVE; MARRIAGE; DIVORCE, ETC.

**Love; Courtship** —*for* Psychol. of Sex and Hist. of Love *v.* **C** § 71, **D** § 132, *s.v.* Woman cpd. w. Man

CORBIN, Carol. F. A Woman's Philosophy of Love $1·50 c 8° Lee & Shepard, *Boston* 93

DEVEREUX, G. R. N. Lover's Guide to Courtship and Marriage 1/ c 8° Pearson 02

DURING, Julia Amor in Society [a clever and vigorous bk.] $1·50 12° *Phila.* 93

GORST, H. E. The Philosophy of Making Love 5/ c 8° Cassell 08

Reflectns. on need of truer sympathy and freer expressn. of sentimts. betw. the sexes, etc. 'The whole argumt. has been designed as a protest agst. the pernicious custom of readg. immorality into everything that does not spell marriage'.

GREENWOOD, Fredk. The Lover's Lexicon 6/ ($1·50) c 8° Macmillan 93

'A Handbk. for Novelists, Playwrights, Philosophers, and Minor Poets; but especially for the Enamoured'. Genially sentimental imitatns. of 18-cent. models: subtle in humour, occas. ironical; but always serious, the exact opposite of BOURGET'S *Physiologie de l'Amour*.

HARDY, Rev. E. J. The Love Affairs of Some Famous Men [6/ Unwin] $1·50 c 8° Stokes, *N.Y.* 97

„ Love, Courtship, and Marriage 3/6 c 8° Chatto 01

HAULTAIN, Arnold Hints for Lovers 4/6 *n.* c 8° Constable 10

KEY, Ellen Love and Marriage [tr. fr. Swedish] 6/ *n.* c 8° Putnam 11

PICO DELLA MIRANDOLA, G. F. [1463–94] Platonick Discourse upon Love, tr. T. Stanley $6 *n.* r 8° Merrymount Press, *Boston* [1651] 10

[Humanists' Library—*v.* **K** § 1.] Edited by E. J. GARDNER.

RAND, Kath. E. Childhd. of an Affinity—*ut* **D** § 162 [early sex-attraction]

SPINGARN, J. E. Chivalric Ideals & Renaissance Books of Love $6 *n.* r 8° Merrymount Pr., *Bost.*, *in prep.*

[Humanists' Lib.] Announcement appeared too late for inclusion in **C** § 71.

STEVENS, A. How Men Propose: the fatal question and answer. 6/ c 8° Unwin 89

WORLAND, F. E. Love, Sacred and Profane 3/6 *n.* f 8° Daniel 07

*Kiss, The:* NYROP (Prf. Chris.) The Kiss and its History [tr. fr. Danish] 7/6 *n.* c 8° Sands 01

A scholarly treatise, replete w. apt illustration and quotn. in verse and in prose.

*Pedagogic Aspect* —*v.* **D** § 167, *s.v.* Moral Education

*Platonic Love:* FLETCHER (J. B.) Religion of Beauty in Woman; & other essays on Platonic Love in poetry and society 5/6 *n.* gl 8° Macmillan 11

**Marriage; Divorce**

BINGHAM, J. F. Christian Marriage $2 c 8° Dutton, *N.Y.* [ ] 01

BRABY, Maud C. Modern Marriage and How to Bear it 3/6 *n.* c 8° Laurie 08

Good advice, brightly conveyed, but rather too much of the 'mutual dissatisfactn. of the sexes' in it.

BROOKS, E. C. H. Marriage and Marriages 4/ *n.* c 8° Longman 03

CAIRD, Mona Morality of Marriage; and other Essays [on woman] *o.p.* [*pb.* 6/] c 8° Redway 97

CHAPMAN, Elizabeth R. Marriage Questions in Mod. Fiction; & other Essays 3/6 *n.* ($1·50) c 8° Lane 97

A series of essays of a conservative character on marriage, divorce, and kindred questions.

COOK, Mrs E. T. The Bride's Book [$1·50 *n.* Dutton, *N.Y.*] 6/ c 8° Hodder 01

CORIN, Jas. Mating, Marriage, and Status of Woman 2/6 *n.* c 8° W. Scott 10

On the relns. of human male and female fr. a zoolog. pt.-of-view, workg. in the idea th. the positn. now occup. by man is due to his managemt. of his affairs on differ. lines fr. those taken by the anthropoid apes—his nearest competitors.

GRAY, Dr G. Z. Husband and Wife: the theory of marriage and its consequences $1 16° Houghton, *Boston* [85] 86

HAMILTON, Cicely Marriage as a Trade 6/ c 8° Chapman 09

Analysis of mod. conventns.; w. suggestns. th. woman has other activities open to her besides marriage.

HARDY, Rev. E. J. How to be Happy though Married 1/ 16° Unwin [85] 94

HENSON, Can. Hensley Christian Marriage 1/6 *n.* c 8° Cassell 07

LICHTENBERGER, Dr J. P. Divorce: study in social causation [Col. Un. Sts.] $1·50 8° Macm., *N.Y.* 09

LUCKOCK, Dn H. M. History of Marriage, Jewish and Christian 6/ ($1·75) c 8° Longman 94
In rel. to Divorce and certain forbidden degrees, takg. strictest view on both points. An elab. theolog. and eccles. argumt., dogmatic in tone and in some cases founded on rather dubious premisses.

MANTEGAZZA, Prf. P. Art of Taking a Wife [tr. fr. Ital.] 3/6 f 8° Gay & Hancock [94] 96

" Art of Choosing a Husband [tr. fr. Ital.] 3/6 f 8° Gay & Hancock 04

Modern Marriage Market: a discussion; ports. 2/ c 8° Hutchinson 98
By Marie CORELLI, L'y JEUNE (ST HELIER), Flora A. STEEL, and C'ess of MALMESBURY.

'PHILANTHROPUS' The Institution of Marriage in the United Kingdom 10/6 c 8° E. Wilson 79

POMEROY, Dr H. S. The Ethics of Marriage $1 (4/) 8° Funk & Wagnalls 88

POST, L. F. Ethical Principles of Marriage & Divorce [5/ Paul] $1 *n.* c 8° Public Pb. Co., *Chicago* 06

Question of Divorce (The): an essay [argues for reform] 2/ *n.* s 8° Richards 03

QUILTER, Harry [ed.] Is Marriage a Failure? [repr. fr. 'Dy. Telegraph'] 1/ c 8° Sonnenschein 88
Correspce. aroused by art. in *Westmr. Rev.* by Mrs Mona CAIRD. Interesting as key to Engl. middle-class mind and experience.

SWAN, Annie S. Courtship and Marriage, and the Gentle Art of Home-making 1/6 c 8° Hutchinson 93

WATKINS, Rev. O. D. Holy Matrimony: treat. on divine laws of marriage 10/6 *n.* 8° Rivington [95] 07

WILKINS, Dr H. J. History of Divorce and Remarriage 3/6 *n.* ($1·25 *n.*) c 8° Longman 10

*Roman Catholic; Mixed Marriages*

FEIJE, H. J. De Impedimentis et Dispensationibus Matrimonialibus $3·75 *n.* 8° Benziger, *N.Y.*

HUMPHREY, Rev. Wm. Christian Marriage [by a Jesuit] 1/6 f 8° Paul 86

KANE, F'r Rob. [S.-J.] The Plain Gold Ring: lectures 2/6 *n.* (90 c. *n.*) c 8° Longman 10

LAMBING, Dr A. A. Plain Sermons on Mixed Marriages [1/6 Washbourne] 25 c. c 8° Pustet, *N.Y.* 88

MONTSABRÉ, Père Marriage, tr. M. Hopper [Am.] [4/6 *n.* Washbourne] $1 *n.* 12° Benziger, *N.Y.* 90
Conferences on marriage and divorce deliv. in Cathedral of Notre Dame, Paris; author has preached the Lenten conferences there since 1872.

SMITH, Dr S. B. Marriage Process in U.S. [12/ *n.* Burns & Oates] 8° *priv. prin.* 93

ULLATHORNE, Bp W. B. Instruction on Mixed Marriages [25 c. Benziger, *N.Y.*] 16° Art & Bk. Co.

YOST, Casper S. The Making of a Successful Husband [2/6 *n.* Collier] $1 c 8° Dillingham, *N.Y.* 07

" The Making of a Successful Wife [2/6 *n.* Collier] $1 c 8° Dillingham, *N.Y.* 07
Sub titles are resp. *Letters of a Happily Married Man to his Son*, and of *Letters of a Father to his Daughter*: racy, and shrewd.

*Socialist Theory* —*v. also* **D** § 126, *passim*

SHAW, G. Bernard Preface (on Marrge. and Divorce) *to* Getting Married—*ut* **K** § 80

*United States*

Comm'r. of Labor [C. D. WRIGHT] Rept. on Marriage & Divorce in U.S.: 1867-86
*gratis* 8° Govt. Prtg. Off., *Washgtn.* 89
An important statist. wk., commenced in 1879 by U.S. Commissioner of Labor, and since continued under provisn. of statute.

CONVERS, D. Marr. & Div. in U.S. as they are & as they ought to be $1·25 16° Lippincott, *Phila.* [89] 94

ROGERS, Anna A. Why Amer. Marriages Fail; & other Papers $1·25 c 8° Houghton, *Boston* 10
4/6 *n.* Constable. Six papers contg. some shrewd criticisms of Amer. social, domestic, and educational life.

SNYDER, W. L. The Geography of Marriage $1·50 12° Putnam, *N.Y.* 89
On the legal perplexities of marriage in the United States.

de VARIGNY, C. —*in his* The Women of the United States, *ut* **D** § 132

*Jewish* —*v.* **A** § 12, *s.v.* Law

*Law of Marriage and Divorce* —*v.* **D** § 59 *Marriage and Heredity*—*v.* **H** § 43, *s.v.* Eugenics

**Near-of-Kin**

ARNER, Dr G. B. L. Consang. Marrges. in Am. Populn. [Col. Univ. Studs.] 75 c. 8° Macm., *N.Y.* 08

DARAB DASTUR PESHOTAN SUNJANA Next-of-Kin Marriages in Old Iran *o.p.* [*pb.* 3/] c 8° Trübner 88

HUTH, A. H. The Marriage of Near Kin 7/6 r 8° Longman [75] 87
Gives a comprehensive view of the *pros* and *cons* of marriage between blood relations, consid. w. respect to the law of nations, result of experience and doctrines of biologists.

" Index to Bks. and Papers on Marriage betw. Near Kin [1879] *appended to above bk.*

MORGAN, L. H. Systems of Consanguinity and Affinity—*ut* **F** § 5

**Antiquarian Books** —*for* History *v.* **F** § 5; *for* Customs *v.* **B** § 3

ASHTON, J. The Fleet, its River, Prison, and Marriages—*ut* **D** § 123

JEAFFRESON, J. Cordy Brides and Bridals, 2 vols. *o.p.* [*pb.* 30/] 8° Hurst 72

JONES, W. —*in his* Finger-Ring Lore, *ut* **I** § 115 7/6 c 8° Chatto [76] 90

SOUTHGATE, Hy. [ed.] The Bridal Bouquet 12/6 s 4° Lockwood [82]
Selections fr. Homer to Swinburne, in prose and verse.

*Scottish*

WALTON, F. P. Scotch Marriages, Regular and Irregular 2/6 c 8° Green, *Edin.* 93
Conts. full particulars of Scottish irregular marriages, of which 3 kinds are recognized by the law of Scotl., (1) by declarn. of consent, (2) by promise *subsequente copula* (at one time the law of nearly all Europe), (3) by habit and repute.

**Child-Marriage**

BEHRAMJI M. MALABARI [ed.] Infant Marriage and Enforced Widowhood in India 3/6 s f° *Bombay* 87
A colln. of opins. *pro* and *con.* recd. by EDR. fr. representative Hindus and official and other authorities. For Life of B. *v.* F § 62.

FURNIVALL, F. J. [ed.] Child Marrgs., Divorces, etc., in Dio. of Chester [1561–6] 8° E. E. Text Soc. (Paul) 97

PETROCOKINO, J. T. Enforced Widowhood 6*d.* 8° Unwin 92
A strong appeal to Engl. readers in favour of aboln. of Child Marr. and Enforced Widowhood in India.

**Prostitution, Social Purity, etc.** —*for* Law *v.* **D** § 67, *s.v.* Public Health

ACTON, W. Prostitution Considered: moral, social, sanitary aspects *o.p.* [*pb.* 12/] 8° Churchill [57] 70

AMOS, Prf. Sheldon [ed.] Laws for Prohibition, Regulation, and Licensg. of Vice—*ut* **D** § 67

BEALE, Prf. Lionel Our Morality & the Moral Question [chfly. fr. medical side] 3/6 c 8° Churchill [89] 93

BLACKWELL, Dr Eliz. Moral Education of the Young 2/ 12° Hatchard [78] 82

" The Human Element in Sex 2/6 c 8° Churchill [82] 94

" Essays in Medical Sociology, 2 vols. 7/ c 8° Bell 02
Incls. above two, and others on *Rescue Work, C.D.A., Purchase of Women,* etc.

BLOCH, I. —*in his* Sexual Life in rel. to Modern Civilizn. [tr.] 21/ *n.* 8° Rebman 08

BUTLER, Josephine E. [1828–1907] Personal Reminiscences of a Great Crusade 7/6 8° H. Marshall 96

" Autobiograph. Memoir. Ed. G. W. + Lucy A. Johnson; ports. 6/ *n.* 8° Arrowsmith, *Bristol* 09
Acc. of her life-long wk. on beh. of social purity and fallen women, made up fr. her life of her husband [*ut* A § 62], her *Personal Remins.*, and other wrgs. Bibliogr. (5 pp.) of her pubns. (in Engl., Fch., Germ.).

GIBSON, J. W. Social Purity $1·75 8° Nichols Press, *Lynn, Mass.* 03

GOODNOW, Eliz. The Market for Souls [3/6 *n.* Palmer] $1·25 *n.* c 8° Kennerley, *N.Y.* 10

LOMBROSO, Prf. C. —*in his* The Female Offender [tr.], *ut* **D** § 123

LYDSTON, Prf. G. F. —*in his* The Diseases of Society, *ut* **D** § 123

MARCHANT, Jas. Social Hygienics: a new crusade 1/ c 8° Sonnenschein 09
Pubd. fr. Natl. Social Purity Crusade, wr. by its Director. Pref. by H. J. GLADSTONE, M.P.

" [ed.] Public Morals [20 arts. by var. wrs.] 1/ *n.* c 8° Morgan & Scott 02

MAYHEW, Hy. London Labour and London Poor: Extra Vol. 10/6 8° Griffin 62
This (the 4th) vol. deals with Prostitutes, Thieves, Beggars, etc. For vols. i–iii *v.* D § 127.

MERRICK, Rev. G. P. Work among the Fallen; intro. Archd. F. W. Farrar 1/ c 8° Ward & Lock 91
By the chaplain of Newgate—late chap. of H.M. Prison, Millbank [abolished,(1893)]—describing his work at Millbank among female prisoners.

MORROW, P. A. Social Diseases and Marriage: social prophylaxis $3·50 *n.* (14/ *n.*) 8° Appleton 04

Nation's Morals (The) [procgs. of Publ. Morals Confer., Lond. 1910] 6/ *n.* 8° Cassell 09

New Godiva (The); and other Studies 3/6 c 8° Unwin [85] 86

POWELL, A. M. State Regulation of Vice $1 12° Wood & Holbrook, *N.Y.* 78

SANGER, W. W. History of Prostitution: extent, causes, effects $2 8° Med. Pb. Co. *N.Y.* [58] 98

SCOTT, Benj. A State Iniquity: its rise, extension, and overthrow 3/6 c 8° Paul 90
A history of the system of State-regulated vice; strongly antagonistic to the Engl. C.D.A., whose doom it foresees.

SIMS, G. R. London by Night 6*d.* c 8° Greening 06

*Chicago*

STEAD, W. T. If Christ came to Chicago [im-morals of Chicago] 1/ c 8° *Review of Reviews* Off. [94] 94

*New York*

Social Evil (The): w. spec. ref. to condns. in N.Y. [Questns. of Day] $1·25 *n.* (5/ *n.*) c 8° Putnam [02] 03
Result of an investigatn. undertaken by a committee of 15; much informn. also ab. condns. in Europe.

WARDLAW, Dr Ralph Lectures on Female Prostitution *o.p.* [*pb.* 2/6] c 8° Jackson [42] 43

*China; Japan*

COLTMAN, R. —*in his* The Chinese [*ut* **C** § 34]: treats Chinese prostitn. at length

De BECKER, J. E. The Nightless City: hist. of Yoshi-wara Yukwaku 8° Maruya, *Tokio* [99] 06
A study of the social evil in Japan. 1st edn. pubd. anonymously.

HUMBERT, Aimé —*in his* Japan and the Japanese [tr.], *ut* **E** § 37

MITFORD, A. B. The Yoshiwara of Yedo—*in his* Tales of Old Japan, *ut* **B** § 37

NORMAN, Sir Hy. —*in his* Real Japan, *ut* **E** § 37

# XII: Science of Politics

## 134: POLITICAL PHILOSOPHY

**Bibliography** —*v. also* **D** § 114 and *inf.*, *s.nn.* DUNNING, WOOLSEY

BLAKEY, Rob. History of Political Literature from the Earliest Times, 2 v. *o.p.* [*pb.* 24/] 8° Bentley 55
1400–1700. Greece, Rome, Xtn. F'rs, Schoolmen, Mid. Ages; Gt. Brit., France, Italy, Germy., etc., Spain, Port. Of no great value now.

BLUNTSCHLI, J. K. —*in the notes to his* Theory of the State, *ut inf.*

**Dictionaries** —*v. also* **D** § 114

FOSTER, E. Cyclopædia of Civil Government $2·50 8° College Pb. Co., *Chicago* 08

Political Cyclopædia, 4 vols. [Bohn's Lib.; ea. $1 *n.* Macmillan] ea. 3/6 c 8° Bell [48]

**History of Political Theory, and of Politics**—*v.* also **D** § 114, *s.v.* History of Economic Theory

CARLYLE, R. W. + A. J. Mediæval Political Theory in the West, v. i–ii ea. 15 / *n.* 8° Blackwood 03–9

DUNNING, Prf. W. A. A History of Political Theories, v. i–ii $5 *n.* (20/6 *n.*) 8° Macmillan 02–5
i: *Ancient and Mediaeval* [fr. Gk. idea of the State to MACHIAVELLI], $2·50 *n.* (10/ *n.*); ii: *From Luther to Montesquieu*, $2·50 *n.* (10/6 *n.*). A sound and conscientious wk. Good index and bibliogr.

FIGGIS, Rev. J. N. Studies of Polit. Thought fr. Gerson to Grotius; 1414–1625 3/6 *n.* c 8° Camb. Press 07
$1·10 *n.* Putnam, *N.Y.* 7 excellent lects., discussg. C'cil of Constance (represg. a movemt. supported by GERSON and others to raise mediaev. theory of a lim. monarchy to its highest power); its failure, and Papalist reaction; LUTHER and MACHIAVELLI; wrgs. of *Politiques* at close of 16 cent., and relig. toleratn.; Huguenots, Presbytns. and others who, to protect themselves, formulated theories of natl. right and derived fr. feudalism idea of the orig. compact; syst. of Jesuits, and its sequel in resistce. of Pr. of SPAIN and estab. in Netherlds. of 'a centre of light whence polit. educn. of 17 cent. largely proceeded'.

GIERKE, Prf. Otto Political Theories of Middle Age, tr. Prf. F. W. Maitland 10 / r 8° Camb. Press 00
$2·50 *n.* Putnam, *N.Y.* With an Introd. by MAITLAND. Probably the most complete study of the subj. in existence.

GOOCH, G. P. Annals of Politics and Culture; Introd. by L'd Acton [$2·25 *n.* Putnam, *N.Y.*] 7/6 *n.* 8° Camb. Press 01

JENKS, Prf. Edw. History of Politics [Temple Primers; 40 c. *n.* Macmillan, *N.Y.*] 1 / *n.* pott 8° Dent 00
An excellent little summary of polit. action: *Savage Society, Patriarchal Society, Modern (Political) Society.*

,, Law and Politics in the Middle Ages 12 / 8° Murray 98
$2·75 *n.* Holt, *N.Y.* With a useful Synoptic Table of Sources.

MACPHERSON, Hector A Century of Political Development 3/6 *n.* c 8° Blackwood 08
A brief *résumé* of hist. of polit. science and theory in Engld., fr. days of BURKE to pres. time. Valuable as a judicious and dispassionate criticism of modern political ideals.

MAITLAND, Prf. F. W. —*in his* Collected Papers, 3 vols., *ut* **F** § 1

MERRIAM, C. E. History of American Political Theories $1·50 *n.* (6/ *n.*) c 8° Macmillan 03

POLLOCK, Sir Fredk. Introduction to Hist. of Science of Politics 2/6 (75 c.) c 8° Macmillan [90] 11
A brief histor. sketch of devel. of certain polit. ideas (e.g. theories of sovereignty, of orig. of civil soc.) fr. PLATO to Justice STEPHEN. Agreeably wr

SIDGWICK, Prf. Hy. Development of European Polity—*ut* **F** § 15

TREMENHEERE, H. S. Manual of the Principles of Government 5/ c 8° Paul [52] 82
1st edn. (1852) pb. *s.t. Polit. Experience of Ancients in its Bearg. upon Mod. Times.* Scrappy; but useful on account of its extracts and analyses.

WILLOUGHBY, Dr W. W. Political Theories of the Ancient World $2 *n.* (6/ *n.*) c 8° Longman 03
Brings together in handy form the conclusns. of many mod. philosrs. and historns. on developmt. of polit. theory in Greece and Rome. Chiefly occupied w. acc. of theories of PLATO and ARISTOTLE and of early Roman law.

*Greek and Roman* —*v. also* **C** §§ 2 *sqq.*

*Selections:* GRAHAM (Prf. W.) [ed.] English Political Philosophy fr. Hobbes to Maine 10/6 *n.* 8° Arnold 99
$3 *n.* Holt, *N.Y.* Abstracts of polit. wrgs. of HOBBES, LOCKE, BURKE, BENTHAM, MILL, MAINE; w. instructive criticisms.

**Systematic Works:** AMOS (Prf. Sheldon) The Science of Politics [Internat. Scientific Ser.] 5/ c 8° Paul [83]
$1·75 Appleton, *N.Y.* Of no very great value; suggestive, but scrappy, unsystematic, and ill expressed.

ARISTOTLE [B.C. 385–322] Politics [tr.]—*ut* **C** § 9
The foundation of all later discussion on the constitution of the State. Ethical.

BAGEHOT, Walt. Physics and Politics [Internat. Scientific Ser.] 5/ c 8° Paul [73]
$1·50 Appleton, *N.Y.* An extremely interestg. pop. bk., applying meths. of DARWIN ('Natural Selection' and 'Inheritance') to some elem. probls. of polit. science. Ch. edn. 3/6 [Paternoster Lib.].

BENTHAM, Jer. [1747–1832] Fragment on Government [1776]; ed. F. C. Montague; w. Introd. 7/6 ($2) 8° Clar. Press 91
Introd. is an admirable crit. of BENTHAM and statemt. of his place in hist. of thought, and of signific. of this treat. as a contribn. to polit. philos. The *Fragm.* was pub. anon. in 1776 (when BENTHAM was in his 29th yr.), and was a polemic agst. the views of BLACKSTONE, whose polit. opins. he abhorred, whilst admirg. his jurisprudence.

BENTLEY, A. F. The Process of Government $3 *n.* 8° Univ. Press, *Chicago* 08

BLUNTSCHLI, Prf. J. K. Theory of the State [tr.] 8/6 ($3) c 8° Clar. Press [85] 92

BOSANQUET, Dr Bernard The Philosophical Theory of the State 10/ *n.* ($3·25 *n.*) 8° Macmillan 99
An important wk., somewhat on HEGEL's lines, already a classic in philos. literature; constr. on large and simple lines yet by no means easy rdg.

BROUGHAM, Hy., L'd Political Philosophy, 3 vols. *o.p.* [*pb.* 31/6] 8° Bell [40]
*Monarchical Government; Democratic and Mixed Government; Aristocratic Government.*

BURGESS, Prf. J. W. Political Science & Comparative Constit. Law, 2 v. $5 8° Ginn, *Boston* [90] 02
25/ Arnold. In 2 Pts. (not coinciding w. the vols.): first dealg. w. nature of the Nation, regardg. it is a purely ethnolog. concept, idea of State, its orig. and var. forms, and forms of govt.; second (and more valuable) consistg. of a compar. of the 4 leadg. constits. of world (U.K., U.S., Frce., Germy.) in their organizn., in the amt. of civil lib. they allow to citizens, and in their legisln. A really valuable contribn. to an independent and inductive science of politics.

CICERO [B.C. 106–43] Republic—*ut* **K** § 218

COKER, Dr F. W. Organismic Theories of the State [Col. Univ. Studs.] $1·50 *n.* 8° Macmillan, *N.Y.* 10

COMTE, Aug. [1793–1857] Positive Philosophy, tr. Harriet Martineau—*ut* **C** § 23

CROZIER, Dr J. B. Sociology applied to Practical Politics 9/ *n.* 8° Longman 11
Cf. also his *Hist. of Intell. Developmt.*, vol. iii., *ut* **F** § 4.

DICKINSON, G. Lowes A Modern Symposium [$1 *n.* McClure, *N.Y.*] 2/6 *n.* c 8° Johnson 05

ELIOT, Sir Jno. [1590–1632] De Jure Majestatis; pol. treatises on govt., 2 v. 4° *priv. prin.* [1628–30] 82
With *Letter-Book* [1625–32]. Ed. for Earl of ST GERMANS, w. introds., notes, and ill., by Dr A. B. GROSART, who has also ed. for the same nobleman ELIOT's *The Monarchie of Man*, 2 vols., '79, and *The Apologie of Socrates* and *Negotium*, 2 vols. '81. Only 100 of ea. printed.

ELYOT, Sir Thos. [1499–1546] The Boke named the Governour—*ut* **D** § 161.

FICHTE, J. G. [1762–1814] The Science of Rights [tr.]—*ut* **D** § 1

FISKE, Prf. Jno. American Political Ideas $1 c 8° Harper, *N.Y.* 85
Viewed fr. the standpoint of Universal History. General in character: an admirable little book.

FORMAN, S. E. Essentials in Civil Government 60 c. 12° Am. Bk. Co., *N.Y.* [02] 09

FREDERICK THE GREAT [1712–86] On Kingcraft, ed. fr. orig. MS. by Sir J. W. Whittall 7/6 *n.* 8° Longman 01

FREEMAN, Prf. E. A. —*in his* Comparative Politics, *ut* **F** § 5

„ Introd. *to his* History of Federal Government, vol. i, *ut* **D** § 139

„ —*some of his* Historical Essays, *ut* **F** § 1

GETTELL, Prf. R. G. Introduction to Political Science ($2) 8° Ginn 11

GODWIN, Wm. [1756–1836] Political Justice: On Property, ed. H. S. Salt [Soc. Sci. Ser.] 2/6 c 8° Sonnenschein [1793] 90

$1 Scribner, *N.Y.* Repr. of conclg. portn. of *Enquiry concg. Pol. Justice: On Prop.*, wh. GODWIN regards as 'the key-stone th. completes the fabric of polit. justice'. On its appearce. the bk. exercised a gt. influ. on philos. mind of the country. It is essentially a moral treatise, conc. 'the adoptn. of any princ. of morality and truth into the practice of a community'.

GREEN, Prf. T. H. [1836–82] Lects. on Principles of Political Obligation 5/ ($1·75) 8° Longman 95

Ed. Dr Bern. BOSANQUET. Repr. fr. his *Coll. Wks.* [*ut* **C** § 29], w. his *Lect. on Freedom* prefixed. The 2 form a excell. mod. specimen of combined crit. and constructive wk. in polit. philos. Author's theory is in main ARISTOTLE'S, w. a fuller meang.: that a man who is not a member of an organized State is not a man at all; that all rts. of man are social rts. and attach to him as a member of a definite soc.; that the State is thus more than an arrangemt. for restriction or coercion, or an agency for doing things collectively wh. can be conveniently done individually; that it has positive as well as negative functns., and aims at nothing less than the formatn. of perfect indivs. The theory is applied to War, Punishment, Property, the Promotion of Morality, the Family; and detailed criticisms of SPINOZA, HOBBES, LOCKE, and ROUSSEAU are incl. *Introd.* (25 pp.) presents author's discussion of *The Dift. Senses of 'Freedom' as Appl. to Will and to the Moral Progress of Man.*

Muirhead, Prf. J. H. The Service of the State, *ut* **D** § 135 [4 lects. on T. H. Green]

GROTIUS, Hugo [1583–1645] De Jure Belli et Pacis—*ut* **D** § 113

HAMMOND, B. E. Outlines of Comparative Politics 7/6 c 8° Rivington 03

Seeks to prove historically (HOMER to pres. times) that polit. communities alike in non-governmental qualities (e.g. habitat, environmt., pursuits, econ. condn., concentrn. in city or dispersion over wide area and in homogen. or heterogen. char. of inhabts.) are also alike in forms of their govt.

HARRISON, Fredc. Order and Progress [*Govt.; Studs. of Polit. Crises*] *o.p.* [*pb.* 14/] 8° Longman 75

HELPS, [Sir] Arth. Thoughts upon Government *o.p.* [*pb.* 9/6] 8° Bell 72

HILDRETH, R. Theory of Politics; inq. into foundatn. of govts., etc. *o.p.* [*pb.* $1·50] 12° Harper, *N.Y.* 54

HILLIER, Dr A. P. The Commonweal—*ut* **D** § 122

HOBBES, Thos. [1588–1679] Leviathan: matter, form, and power of a commonwealth, ecclesiastic and civil, ed. A. R. Waller 4/6 c 8° Camb. Press [1651] 04

$1·50 Putnam, *N.Y.* [Camb. Engl. Classics.]

„ The same, ed. W. G. Pogson Smith; w. Essay 2/6 *n.* (85 c.) c 8° Clar. Press [1651] 09

„ The same [50 c. Dutton, *N.Y.*] [New Universal Lib.] 1/*n.* pott 8° Routledge [1651] 07

Campion, W. J. H. Outlines of Lects. on Pol. Sci. [review of Hobbes] 1/6 8° Simpkin [9–] 05

HOFFMAN, Prf. F. S. Sphere of the State; people as body politic $1·50 (6/) c 8° Putnam 94

KANT, Imman. [1724–1804] Principles of Politics, tr. Prf. W. Hastie; w. Introd. 2/6 c 8° Clark, *Edin.* [89] 91

$1 *n.* Scribner, *N.Y.* Includes the celebrated essay on *Perpetual Peace* [*ut* **D** § 138] and *Principle of Federation.*

KELLY, Edm. Government, or Human Evolution, 2 vols. $4 (18/ *n.*) c 8° Longman 00–1

i: *Justice*, $1·50 (7/6 *n.*); ii: *Individualism and Collectivism* [*ut* **D** § 126], $2·50 (10/6 *n.*).

KINNEAR, J. Boyd Principles of Civil Government *o.p.* [*pb.* 7/6] c 8° Smith & Elder 87

*Representative System, Nationality, Federation, Local and Party Government*, etc. Clear, untechnical, philosophic, and unbiassed.

LEACOCK, Dr S. B. Elements of Political Science $1·75 *n.* 12° Houghton, *Boston* 06

7/6 *n.* Constable. Accurate and well-informed, though somewhat conventional.

LEROY-BEAULIEU, P. Modern State in rel. to Soc. [tr.] [Soc. Sci. Ser.] 2/6 c 8° Sonnenschein [91]

$1 Scribner, *N.Y.* An acute and suggestive analysis of the relns. of mod. State to Society and to the Individual. Individualistic standpt.

LEWIS, Sir G. Cornewall Remarks on Use and Abuse of Polit. Terms, ed. Thos. Raleigh 3/6 (90 c.) c 8° Clar. Press [32] 98

„ Methods of Observn. and Reasong. in Politics, 2 v. *o.p.* [*pb.* 28/] 8° Parker 52

LILLY, W. S. First Principles in Politics 5/*n.* 8° Murray [99] 07

An attempt, of questionable success, to investigate the principles wh. underlie all political action.

LOCKE, Jno. [1632–1704] On Civil Government 1/c 8° Routledge [1690]

35 c. *n.* Dutton, *N.Y.* [Morley's Universal Lib.] Includes also *On Toleration* [*ut* **A** § 113].

MACHIAVELLI, Niccolò [1469–1527] Il Principe, ed. L. A. Burd—*ut* **C** § 46

„ The Prince, tr. N. H. Thomson [Oxf. Lib. of Trs.] 3/6 *n.* ($1) f 8° Clar. Press [82] 97

„ „ tr. Luigi Ricci [World's Classics] 1/*n.* (40 c.) pott 8° Frowde 03

„ „ tr. W. K. Marriott [Everyman's Lib.; 35 c. *n.* Dutton, *N.Y.*] 1/*n.* f 8° Dent 08

„ „ and other Pieces: tr. [1674] [Morley's Univ. Lib.; 35 c. *n.* Dutton, *N.Y.*] 1/c 8° Routledge [83]

The 'other pieces' are *Life of Castruccio Castracani, Murder of Vitelli, Marriage of Belphegor, State of France, State of Germany.* For Life and Criticism, etc., of MACHIAVELLI *v.* **C** § 46.

MCKECHNIE, W. S. The State and the Individual—*ut* **D** § 126

MACKENZIE, Prf. J. S. Introduction to Social Philosophy—*ut* **D** § 125

MILL, Jno. Stuart —*v.* **C** § 49

MONTESQUIEU, C. de S., Bar. [1689–1755] Spirit of the Laws [1751] [tr.] 2 vols.—*ut* **F** § 2

MORLEY, L'd Miscellanies, ser. iv.—*ut* **K** § 89

MULFORD, Elisha — The Nation; foundns. of civil order and polit. life $2·50 8° Houghton, *Boston* [72] 98
Relates to the United States. Influenced by Hegel and Christianity. Learned, and still of value.

PLATO [B.C. 427–348] — Epinomis, Leges, Politicus, Republic—*v.* **K** § 194 and **C** § 8

PLUTARCH [c. 46–c. 120] — Moralia—*v.* **K** § 192

RALEIGH, T. — Elementary Politics [gd. introd. to pol. philos.] 1/ 12° Frowde 86

ROBERTSON, J. M. — Introduction to English Politics *o.p.* [*pb.* 10/6 *n.*] r 8° Richards 00

ROSS, Dr E. A. Social Control; survey of foundns. of order [Citiz.Lib.] $1·25 *n.* (5/*n.*) c 8° Macmillan Co. 02

ROUSSEAU, J. J. [1712–78] The Social Contract [tr.]—*ut* **F** § 49
Of considerable interest to the student of the principles of political obligation. *Vide* **F** § 49.

SEELEY, Sir J. R. — Introduction to Political Science [Eversley Ser.] 5/ ($1·50) gl 8° Macmillan [96] 02
Lects., repreeg. more fully and systemat. than any of his wrgs. his general view of true aims and meths. of histor. study, viz. (1) that rt. meth. of studying polit. sci. is an essentially histor. meth., (2) that rt. meth. of studying polit. hist. is to study it as materl. for polit. science, i.e., 'polit. science without hist. has no root'.

SERA, Dr. G. [M.D.] — On the Track of Life [tr. (fr. Ital.)] 7/6 *n.* 8° Lane 10
'The Immorality of Morality': an attempt to 'estab. our conceptn. of social life on its orig. basis'. Holds th. diffusn. of democratic princs. is vulgarizg. science and art, and th. pres. soc. condns., esp. work and Xtn. tchg., are leadg. to intell. and moral degeneratn.

SIDGWICK, Prf. Hy. — The Elements of Politics 14/ *n.* ($4 *n.*) 8° Macmillan [91] 97
Avowedly constructed on lines of BENTHAM and MILL, it expounds, in as syst. a form as subj. matter (at present) admits of the chief gen. considns. that enter into rational discussn. of polit. questns. in mod. States (jurisprud., art of legisln., internat. morality, and constit. law or politics in its restricted sense). An important wk., at once luminous, profound, and stimulating. SIDGWICK, before all things a moralist, treats politics as a theory not of what is but of what should be.

SPELMAN, Wm. — Dialoge or Confabulation between Two Travellers 4° Roxburghe Club 96
'Treateth of Civile and Pollitike Gouvernement in Dyvers Kingdomes and Countries'. By uncle of the antiquary; ed. Sutton PICKERING.

SPENCER, Herb. — Social Statics 10/ 8° Williams [51] 92
An elementary analysis and discussion of 'rights'. In *Justice* [*ut* **C** § 62] author withdrew his views on priv. property in land as stated in 1st edn. of this bk. The above edn. incls. a repr. of *The Man versus the State* [anti-Socialistic].

" — *—some of his* Essays, 3 vols., *ut* **C** § 62

de SPINOZA, Bened. [1632–77] Tractatus Politicus, *and* Tract. Theologico-politicus—*ut* **C** § 63

WALTHEW, G. W. — The Philosophy of Government $1·25 (5/) c 8° Putnam 98
Sets up a combination of American and English systems as the ideal: of small philosophical value.

WILLOUGHBY, Dr W. W. — Examination of the Nature of the State $3 *n.* 8° Macmillan [96] 03
A philosophico-speculative treat. on rational orig. of the State, its essential attribs., powers, and aims, nature of sovereignty and its locatn. in body politic, nature of positive law, and other such theoret. questns. The 'Federal', or 'Composite', State is spec. analysed.

" — Social Justice; a critical essay $3 *n.* (12/6 *n.*) 8° Macmillan 00

WILSON, Sir Roland K. — The Province of the State [anti-Socialistic] 7/6 *n.* 8° P. S. King & Son 11

WILSON, Dr Woodrow — The State; elements of histor. & practical politics $2 8° Heath, *Boston* [89] 99
Exhibits the actual organization and admin. practice of the chief modern govts. in proper relns. w. the practice of govts. of the past, and w. general principles of jurisprudence and politics as developed by historical criticism. An excellent book.

WOOD, Fredk. — Government and the State $2 8° Putnam 03
A volume of abstract political philosophy, on unorthodox lines.

WOOLSEY, Dr T. D. — Political Science; State theoret. and pract. consid., 2 v. $5 8° Scribner, *N.Y.* [77] 93
A good systematic treatise; its historical part especially instructive. Standard.

## Collected Essays on Political Philosophy

BRADLEY, F. H. — *—in his* Ethical Studies, *ut* **C** § 70

Brooklyn Ethical Soc.: Man and the State [17 lectures] $2 12° Kerr, *Chicago* 92
All popular, and some of consid. value, *e.g.* Dr E. B. ANDREWS, *Duty of Public Spirit*, Dr L. G. JANES, *Probl. of City Govt.*

BURKE, Edm. [1729–97] — *—in his* Works, *ut* **K** § 89
'On the whole, for those who can make the needful corrections, what distinguishes these writings is their profoundly permanent, fruitful, philosophical truth'—Mat. ARNOLD.

CAIRNES, Prf. J. E. — Political Essays 10/6 8° Macmillan 73
*Colonization and Colonial Govt., The Revolution in America, International Law, Protection, Free Trade*, etc.

CHAPMAN, J. Jay — Causes and Consequences; *and* Practical Agitation—*ut* **D** § 139

HUXLEY, Prf. T. H. — Administrative Nihilism [on theory of govt.]; *and* Government—*in his* Coll. Essays, vol. i, *ut* **K** § 83

KENT, C. B. R. — Essays in Politics 5/ c 8° Paul 91
*Sovereignty, Fed. Govt., Polit. Institns. of Switz., Progr. of Masses, Science and Politics*, etc. Sober, if not very orig. essays fr. constit. and histor. stdpt.

LAUGHLIN, J. L. — Latter-day Problems $1·50 *n.* 12° Scribner, *N.Y.* 09

LECKY, W. E. H. — Historical and Political Essays—*ut* **F** § 1

'LEE, Vernon' [= Violet PAGET] Gospels of Anarchy, and Other Contemp. Studies 10/6 *n.* 8° Unwin 08
*Deterioratn. of Soul; Tolstoy as Prophet; Nietzsche and 'Will to Power'* [*ut* **C** § 51*]; *Prf. James and 'Will to Believe'; Rosny on the Economic Parasitism of Woman; Ruskin as Reformer; On Modern Utopias* [*ut* **D** § 134]. WHITMAN, EMERSON, RUSKIN, IBSEN, etc. Together form a critical survey of some 'prophets' of 19th cent., by an acute antipathetic Darwinian.

LESLIE, Prf. T. E. Cliffe- — Essays in Political and Moral Philosophy—*ut* **D** § 114

LIEBER, Prf. Fr. — Manual of Political Ethics, ed. T. D. Woolsey, 2 v. $5·50 8° Lippincott, *Phila.* [38–9] 75

" — Miscellaneous Writings, 2 v. [collected articles, etc.] $6 8° Lippincott, *Phila.* 81

" — Legal and Political Hermeneutics—*ut* **D** § 1 [prolix but valuable]

LOWELL, Prf. A. L. — Essays on Government $1·25 12° Houghton, *Boston* 89

MACPHAIL, Andr. — Essays in Politics 6/ *n.* ($1·80 *n.*) c 8° Longman 09
*Patience of Engld.; Loyalty—to What?; The Dominion and the Spirit; What Can Canada Do?; New Lamps for Old; A Patent Anomaly; Protectn. and Politics; Why the Conservatives Failed; Psychol. of Canada; Brit. Diplomacy and Canada.*

RITCHIE, Prf. D. G. Principles of State Interference [Soc. Sci. Series] 2/6 c 8° Sonnenschein [91]
$1 Scribner, *N.Y.* 4 valuable essays tow. a constructive philosophy of the State. First two devoted to criticism of SPENCER, revealg. his weak points, 3rd takes up MILL's *Liberty* [exceedingly suggestive]; 4th is on polit. philos. of T. H. GREEN.

,, Darwinism and Politics [Social Science Series] 2/6 c 8° Sonnenschein [89]
$1 Scribner, *N.Y.* A very interestg. applicn. of evoln. to sociology, in form of essays on *The 'Struggle for Existence' in Malthus and Darwin, Evol. Theory as appl. to Society by Darwin, Strauss, Spencer, Maine, and Clodd, 'Survival of the Fittest', Does Heredity support Aristocracy?, Why fix Ideas in Institns.?, Nat. Seln. and Hist. of Institns.*, etc.
Argues th. 'survival of the fittest' does not necessarily mean 'survival of the best', and th. the doctr. cannot therefore be appl. as a sanctn. for competition.

,, —*in his* Darwin and Hegel, w. other Studies, *ut* **C** § 4 (where contents given)

,, Studies in Political & Social Ethics [Ethical Lib.; $1·50 Macm., *N.Y.*] 4/6 c 8° Sonnenschein 02

SETH [PRINGLE-PATTISON] (Prf. A.) + HALDANE (R. B.) [eds.] Essays in Philosophical Criticism—*ut* **C** § 1

SIDGWICK, Prf. Hy. Miscellaneous Essays and Addresses—*ut* **D** § 114

WILSON, Dr Woodrow An Old Master, and other Political Essays $1 12° Scribner, *N.Y.* 93
5 essays: *An Old Master* [Adam SMITH], *Study of Politics, Political Sovereignty, Character of Democracy in U.S., Govt. under the Constitn.*

**Biography and Criticism:** *Collectively*

MACCUNN, Prf. J. Six Radical Thinkers 6/*n.* c 8° Arnold 07
$1·70 *n.* Longman, *N.Y.* BENTHAM, J. S. MILL, COBDEN, CARLYLE, MAZZINI, T. H. GREEN. Lives interestg., but treatmt. of polit. philos. not v. satisfactory.

PRINGLE-PATTISON, Prf. A. Seth The Philosophical Radicals; and other Essays—*ut* **C** § 4

WADIA, Prf. P. A. The Philosophers and the French Revolution 2/6 c 8° Sonnenschein 05
$1 Scribner, *N.Y.* [Social Science Series.]

*Individually* —*v.* **D** §§ 114, 125

**Formation of Political Opinion**

CRUMP, A. Short Inquiry into Formatn. of Political Opinion *o.p.* [*pb.* 7/6] 8° Longman [85] 88
From the reign of the great families to the advent of democracy.

KYDD, S. Sketch of the Growth of Public Opinion $1 8° Armstrong, *N.Y.* 88

**Constitutions: Collectively** —*v.* **D** § 144

**Natural Rights** —*v.* **D** § 1

**Political and Social Psychology**—*v.* **D** § 125

**Series** —*v.* **D** § 114

**Ideal Commonwealths (Utopias) and Social Forecasts**—*for* schemes put into practice *v.* **D** § 126

*Collectively*

KAUFMANN, Rev. M. Utopias, from More to Marx *o.p.* [*pb.* 5/] c 8° Paul 79

MORLEY, Prf. Hy. [ed.] Ideal Commonwlths.; w. Introd. [Morley's Univ. Lib.] 1/c 8° Routledge [85]
35 c. *n.* Dutton, *N.Y.* PLUTARCH'S *Lycurgus*, MORE'S *Utopia*, BACON'S *New Atlantis*, CAMPANELLA'S *City of the Sun*, and a fragmt. of HALL'S *Mundus Alter et Idem.*

*Individually*

ASHBEE, C. R. The Building of Thelema 4/6 *n.* c 8° Dent
A novel, preachg. MORRIS' gospel, tho' PLATO'S *Repub.* and other more mod. Utopias are laid und. contribn. Thelema is not something wh. is, but wh. is always coming, not a place where happiness has been achieved, but a place in the age-long bldg. of wh. happiness is to be found.

AUGUSTINE, St [354–430] De Civitate Dei [and trs.]—*ut* **A** § 55

BACON, Fcs., L'd [1561–1626] The New Atlantis, ed. G. C. Moore-Smith 1/6 f 8° Camb. Press [1627] 01
40 c. *n.* Putnam, *N.Y.* [Pitt Press Series.] With Introd. and notes. Also in World's Classics, 1/*n.* (35 c.) pott 8° Clar. Press '06; in Morley's *Ideal C'wealths* [*sup.*], and in Bacon's *Works* [*ut* **C** § 16].
An (unfinished) acc. of a land discovered in the Pacific, inhab. by a people of higher civilizn. than that of Europe. Embodies a good deal of BACON'S philos. and some suggestns. wh. have since borne fruit (e.g. the utility of scientific academies).

BALMFORTH, R. The New Reformation & its rel. to Moral & Soc. Probls. 2/6 c 8° Sonnenschein [93]
$1 Scribner, *N.Y.* [Soc. Sci. Ser.] Deals w. what will, in author's view, be the prob. future developmt. of relig. thought and life: largely sociological.

BELLAMY, Edw. Looking Backward, 2000–1887; a romance 50 c. c 8° Houghton, *Boston* [88]
1/ Routledge. A socialistic prophetic sketch, picturing an ideal commonwealth in yr. 2000. Excited a great deal of popular interest on its appearance, a Bellamy club having been formed at Boston to propagate its 'principles'.

BLATCHFORD, R. The Sorcery Shop 1/6 c 8° *Clarion* Office 09

CLAPPERTON, Jane H. Vision of Future, based on Ethical Princs. 3/6 c 8° Sonnenschein 04

DANTE, Aligheri [1265–1321] De Monarchia, tr.—*in* Church's 'Dante', *ut* **K** § 39

HALL, Bp Jos. [1574–1656] Mundus Alter et Idem, ed. H. J. Anderson 2/ c 8° Bell [1607] 08
A sportive invention of a Royalist, who in 1641 was made Bp of Norwich, satirizing the vices of various nations, esp. Engl. and Germy. Crapulia is an ideal world, divided into regions answerg. to man's chief weaknesses or vices. This edn. is prep. for school-use, w. Vocab. (65 pp.) and notes.

,, tr. Dr Wm. King—*in* Morley, Prf. H. [ed.] Ideal Commonwealths, *ut sup.*

'HARDING, Ellison' [=Edm. KELLY] The Woman who Vowed 6/ c 8° Unwin 08

HARRINGTON, Jas. [1664–93] Oceana; w. Pref. by Prf. H. Morley 1/ c 8° Routledge [1656] 87
35 c. *n.* Dutton, *N.Y.* [Morley's Universal Lib.] An ideal republic. Influenced by PLATO.

HAYES, F. W. Great Revolution of 1905: story of the phalanx 1/ c 8° W. Reeves 93

HERBERT, E. G. Newaera: a socialist romance 6/*n.* c 8° P. S. King & Son 10
Pt. i: *The Discussion*; ii: *The Preparation*; iii: *The Realization*—a reductio ad absurdum.

HERTZKA, Dr Th. Freeland; a social anticipation [tr.] 6/ c 8° Chatto 91
$1 Appleton, *N.Y.* By a well-known Viennese polit. economist, 'a high priest of the Mancs. School'. The bk. at once resulted in several socs. bg. formed in differ. pts. of Germ. and Austria for formatn. of a colony, in wh. author's views may be practically tested.

HUME, Dav. [1711–76] Perfect Commonwealth—*in his* Essays, vol. i, *ut* **C** § 38

KROPOTKIN, Pr'ce —*in his* Conquest of Bread—*ut* **D** § 126, *s.v.* Anarchism [v. note there]

LANE, M. A. The Level of Social Motion $2 *n.* (8/6 *n.*) c 8° Macmillan 02
A prophecy of the future condition of society—Equality.

L'ESTRANGE, Miles What we are Coming to 2/6 c 8° Douglas, *Edin.* 92
A forecast of Engl. *tempora* and *mores* a generation hence. Of the *Looking Backward* type, but of opposite intention.

'MILLER, Joaquin' [C. H. MILLER] The Building of the City Beautiful $1·50 12° Stone, *Chicago* 93

MORE, Sir Thos. [1480–1535] Utopia, Lat. original [1516]; tr. Ralph Robinson [1551]
A sketch of a State based on the principles of community of property and consequent uselessness of money. Introduced the word 'Utopia.'

*Text and Tr.:* *ed. Rev. J. N. Lupton; 3 facss. 10/6 *n.* ($3·50) 8° Clar. Press 95
A scholarly edition, of both the Latin text (fr. edn. revised by author and pubd. by FROBEN at Basle in 1518) and the first Engl. tr., by Ralph ROBYNSON in 1551, w. var. rgs., additional trs., an Introd. (biographical and comparing the *Utopia* w. other ideal commonwealths), admirable and copious notes, a glossary to ROBYNSON'S quaint English, and Index.

,, hrsg. Prfs. V. Michels + Th. Ziegler; 2 pl. 3*m*.60 s 8° Weidmann, *Berlin* 95
[Latein. Litteratur-Denkmäler d. 15–16 Jahrh.] Based on the *ed. princeps* (Th. Martin, *Louvain* 1516)—an erroneous text, w. a very suggestive *Einleitung* (by ZIEGLER), contg. a mass of detailed informatn. on the subject-matter of the *Utopia*, and (by MICHELS) a short life of MORE, an acc. of early edns., a few notes and crit. apparatus.

Sampson, Geo. [ed.] More's Utopia; w. Introd. and Notes [Bohn's Lib.] 5/ c 8° Bell 10
$1·25 *n.* Macmillan, *N.Y.* Text of 1st edn., w. ROBINSON'S tr. Conts. also ROPER'S *Life of More* and *More's Letters to Margaret Roper.* Bibliogr.

*Tr. Robinson:* Reprint of 1st edn. [1551] *o.p.* s 4° Kelmscott Press 93
A very handsome edn., in antique type designed by Wm. MORRIS. Only 300 copies printed.

Reprint of 2nd edn. [1556]; 3 pl. [Chiswick Library of Noble Wrs.] 42/ *n.* s f° Bell 03
Finely printed. With the *Life of More*, by Wm. ROPER [his son-in-law], freshly ed. fr. the 4 Harl. MSS. in Brit. Mus. by Geo. SAMPSON, and MORE'S *Letters to Margaret Roper and others*, repr. fr. RASTELL'S edn. of More's *English Works.*

Adams, Maur. [ed.] More's Utopia; w. Introd. [Scott Lib.] 1/ *n.* c 8° Walter Scott [90]
Contains also *Edward V* and ROPER'S *Life of More.*

Arber, Edw. [ed.] More's Utopia; repr. of 2nd edn.
[Arber's Reprints; 35 c. *n.* Macm., *N.Y.*] 1/ *n.* f 8° Constable [69]

Collins, Prf. J. Churton [ed.] More's Utopia; repr. of 1st edn.; w. Introd. and Notes
3/6 *n.* (90 c.) c 8° Clar. Press 04

Cotterill, H. B. [ed.] More's Utopia; w. Introd. and Notes 2/6 gl 8° Macmillan 08

Dibdin, Rev. T. F. [ed.] More's Utopia, 2 v.; w. Introd. & Notes *o.p.* 8° Roberts, *Boston, Eng.* [08] 78

Latimer, T. [ed.] More's Utopia; w. Introd. and Notes 1/4 c 8° Rivington 00

Lumby, Dr J. R. [ed.] More's Utopia; w. Introd. and Notes
[50 c. *n.* Putnam, *N.Y.*] 3/6 c 8° Camb. Press [79] 97

Salmon, Dav. [ed.] More's Utopia; w. Introd. and Notes 2/6 *n.* c 8° Ralph & Holland 08

Cheap edns. of text of the tr. are also pubd. in Temple Classics 1/6 *n.* 18° Dent (50 c. Macmillan, *N.Y.*); King's Classics 1/6 *n.* Chatto; Natl. Lib. 6*d. n.* (40 c.) 18° Cassell.

MORRIS, Wm. News from Nowhere; an epoch of rest 1/6 (60 c.) 16° Longman [91]

,, The same; Kelmscott Press edn. [300 printed] *o.p.* s 4° Kelmscott Press 92
The poet and socialist here shows us how he wld. have us live, and what is his conceptn. of the *mens sana in corpore sano.* Excellently wr. and highly poetical.

,, A Dream of John Ball; *and* A King's Lesson 2/ *n.* ($1) 16° Longman [88] 03

NEWTE, H. W. C. The Master Beast'; A.D. 1888–2020 3/6 *n.* c 8° Rebman 08
A novel, picturg. the ruthless tyranny inflicted on Brit. people by Socialism in 2020.

PEARSON, Dr C. H. National Life and Character; a forecast 5/ *n.* ($2 *n.*) c 8° Macmillan [93] 94
A very striking forecast made in 1893. Pointed out th. the social and intell. forces at wk. amg. higher races of mankind were tendg. and wld. increasingly tend tow. a state of equilibrium (rather than an ever-expandg. ideal), owg. to adoptn. of State Socialism, wh. ultimately wld. prevail everywhere, favoured by the gen. extensn. of milit. service and growth of large towns; and that, tho' the new society wld. gain by an increased patriotism, family-life wld. be to a large extent broken up and indiv. character lose in self-reliance more than it wld. gain in sobriety.

PLATO [B.C. 427–348] Republic—*ut* **C** § 8

Stewart, Prf. J. A. The Atlantis Myth—*in his* Myths of Plato, *ut* **C** § 8
Account (13 pp.) of the contents of the myth as sketched by Critias in the *Timæus.*

Reign of George vi, 1900–1925: a forecast, ed. Prf. C. W. C. Oman 2/6 c 8° Rivington [1763] 99
An interesting example of a historical forecast, orig. wr. in 1763. Preface by OMAN.

RENOUVIER, Chas. Uchronie

Whittaker, Thos. —acc. of above in his Essays and Notices, *ut* **C** § 1
An attempt to rewrite past hist. as it might have been on certain hypotheses.

RICHTER, Eug. Pictures of the Socialistic Future [tr.] 1/ *n.* c 8° Sonnenschein [93] 07
A striking picture of 'the coming Socialistic revolution' and its results, in form of Diary of an ardent Socialist who gradually becomes disillusionized.

RUSSELL, T. Baron A Hundred Years Hence $1·50 *n.* c 8° McClurg, *Chicago* 05
7/6 Unwin. A serious forecast, based on acute observn. and untrammelled by prejudice, by a very sanguine optimist. War will be abolished, intelligence will rule, wealth will be organized not by Socialism but by Co-opern., advts. will be more extensive but wr. by trained wrs. using argumt. not puff, leisure and intell. enjoymt. will have replaced pressure, wine and flesh will have been abjured; educn. will be 'mixed', and so on.

SEDGWICK, W. Man and his Future; glimpse fr. fields of science 8/6 *n.* 8° Laurie 08

SINCLAIR, Upton The Industrial Republic—*ut* **D** § 126

STANLEY, Wm. The Case of Theodore Fox: his prophecies of period 1900–1950:
a political Utopia 2/6 sq 12° Truslove 03

TARDE, Gabriel — Underground Man — 3/6 *n.* c 8° Duckworth 05

WELLS, H. G. — Anticipations—*ut* **D** § 126
Maps out the developmt. of the human world as conceived by the vivid imagination of a man with a scientific mind. Also 6*d*., '04.

,, — Mankind in the Making [$1·50 *n.* Scribner, *N.Y.*] 3/6 c 8° Chapman [03]
A complement to above, applying the same princs. to the traing. and developmt. of the pres. generation: sociological, economic, and political. Its design is to formulate the princs. wh. shall guide a new republic—an ideal State. Also 6*d*.

,, — A Modern Utopia; ill. [$1·50 *n.* Scribner, *N.Y.*] 7/6 c 8° Chapman [05]
Under a thin veil of fictn., compls. the trilogy of WELLS' bks. contg. his views on society of future. His Utopia is a World-State (not a mere city like PLATO's) w. a world-lang. State is govd. by 'voluntary nobility', w. 4 classes in it, the Poietic, the Kinetic, the Dull, the Base: former two 'constitute the living tissue of the State; latter are the fulcra and resistances—the bone and cover of its body'. Caste has no place—it is evoln. of fittest th. counts. Govt. is in hands of 'Samurai'—volunteers, leadg. a life fixed for them by system wh. interdicts tobacco, wine, meat, usury, acting, singing, etc., and enforces chastity, but not necess. celibacy. Motherhd. subsidized; no 'human stud-farms', but marrges. licensed only after due inquiry; and so on. An interestg. and suggestive wk. *Cf.* also his *Discovery of the Future* and *New Worlds for Old*, *ut* **D** § 126.

'LEE, Vernon' [=Violet PAGET] On Modern Utopias; an open letter to Mr H. G. Wells—*in her* Gospels of Anarchy, *ut sup.*

## 135 : CIVICS ; CITIZENSHIP ; CIVIL LIBERTY ; ELECTORAL SYSTEM ; REPRESENTATION ; FREEDOM OF PRESS

### Generally ; United Kingdom

ARNOLD-FORSTER, H. O. — The Citizen Reader — 1/6 c 8° Cassell [ ]
A good little school-bk., describg. in simple language how the internal affairs of the country are managed.

,, — Laws of Every-day Life [summary of econ. & pol. laws] 1/6 c 8° Cassell [85]

ASTON, W. D. — Elements of Duties and Rights of Citizenship — 1/6 c 8° Clive [06] 07

BRYCE, Jas. — The Hindrances of Good Citizenship — 6/ *n.* c 8° Frowde 09
$1·15 *n.* Yale Univ. Pr., *New Haven.* Dodge Lects.: on *Indolence, Priv. Self-interest, Party Spirit, How to Overcome the Obstacles.*

Citizen and the State (The); 2 Pts. — ea. 1/6 gl 8° Macmillan 95
Pt. I: E. J. MATHEW, *Representative Government*; II: S. St Loe STRACHEY, *The Empire; industrial and social life.*

HAND, J. E. [ed.] — Good Citizenship — 6/ *n.* c 8° G. Allen 99
$1·50 F. P. Harper, *N.Y.* 23 essays on social, personal, and econ. problems and obligns., by var. wrs. Xtn. Soc. Union pt.-of-view.

,, [ed.] — Science in Public Affairs; pref. by R. B. Haldane — 5/ *n.* c 8° G. Allen 06

HODGSON, Geraldine — Life of the State [lects. on civics to all girls] 2/6 c 8° H. Marshall 03

HORNE, C. S. — The Model Citizen — 2/ *n.* c 8° Law 05

HUGHES, C. E. — Conditions of Progress in Democratic Govt. — 6/ *n.* c 8° Frowde 10
$1·15 *n.* Yale Univ. Press, *New Haven.* Lects., by a N.Y. lawyer, on the responsibility of citizenship. Uniform w. BRYCE, *sup.*

HUGHES, R. E. — Making of Citizens; study in compar. educn.—*ut* **D** § 156

KEEBLE, S. E. [ed.] — The Citizen of To-morrow [15 essays by var. wrs.] 2/ *n.* c 8° Kelly [ ] 06

MACCUNN, Prf. J. — Ethics of Citizenship [$1 *n.* Macmillan, *N.Y.*] 2/6 *n.* c 8° MacLehose, *Glasgow* [94] 07
An excellent popular manual, connecting some leading aspects of democratic citizenship w. ethical facts and beliefs.

MALDEN, H. E. — The Life and Duties of a Citizen — 1/6 c 8° Methuen 94

MILLS, W. T. — The Science of Politics — $1; 50 c. (4/) 8° Funk & Wagnalls 87
On the citizen as an active and effective part of Government.

MUIRHEAD, Prf. J. H. — The Service of the State — 3/6 *n.* c 8° Murray 08
Four stimulating lectures on the political teaching of T. H. GREEN [*v.* **D** § 134].

NEWLAND, H. O. — Short History of Citizenship; introd. to sociology — 2/6 *n.* c 8° Stock 04

,, — The Model Citizen; rights and duties; ill. — 1/6 c 8° Pitman 07

PEAKER, F. — British Citizenship; its rights and duties — 2/ c 8° Ralph & Holland 06

PORRITT, Edw. — The Englishman at Home [Lib. of Economics] $1·75 12° Crowell, *N.Y.* 94
Rights and duties. Primarily written for Amer. readers, yet of value to Englishmen also.

RITCHIE, Prf. D. G. — —*in his* Studies in Political and Social Ethics, *ut* **D** § 134

ROGERS, Prf. J. E. Thorold — The Engl. Citizen [rts. & duties of the citizen; popular] 1/ c 8° S.P.C.K. 85

ROOT, Elihu — Citizen's Part in Government — $1 *n.* 12° Scribner, *N.Y.* 07
[Yale Lects. on Responsibilities of Citizenship.]

TAFT, W. H. — Four Aspects of Civic Duty — $1 *n.* 12° Scribner, *N.Y.* 06

TAYLER, Jas. — The Public Man; his duties, powers, and privileges 3/6 *n.* c 8° E. Wilson 97
Acc. of the var. publ. positns. open to citizens of Britain and informn. as to transactn. of publ. business. Not much detail.

THOMAS, W. Beach [ed.] — Our Civic Life — [Citizen Books] 1/ *n.* c 8° Rivers 09

TROTTER, W. F. — The Citizen and his Duties — [Social Problems Ser.] 1/ *n.* c 8° Jack 07

*United States* — —*v. also* **D** § 145

ABBOTT, Dr Lyman — America in the Making — [Yale Lects.] $1·15 (6/ *n.*) 8° Clar. Press 11

ASHLEY, R. L. — Government and the Citizen — 70 c. *n.* c 8° Macmillan, *N.Y.*

,, — American Federal State—*ut* **D** § 145

BOYNTON, F. D. — School Civics: orig. sc. of U.S. govt. — $1 (4/6) c 8° Ginn 04

BROOKS, E. S. — Century Book for Young Americans; ill. [elementary] $1·50 c 8° Scribner, *N.Y.* 94

BREWER, D. J. — American Citizenship — [Yale lectures] 75 c. *n.* 12° Scribner, *N.Y.* 02

CLARK, F. H. Outlines of Civics
[suppl. to Bryce's 'Amer. C'wealth'] 75 c. *n.* (3/6 *n.*) c 8° Macmillan [ ] 99

CURTIS, G. W. Works, ed. Chas. Eliot Norton, vol. i $3 8° Harper, *N.Y.* [*v.y.*] 93
This vol. conts. his Orations and Addresses on principles and character of Am. institns. and Duties of Amer. citizens.

DOLE, C. F. The American Citizen $1 12° Heath, *Boston* 91

FORD, W. C. American Citizen's Manual, 2 Pts. ea. 75 c.; in 1 vol. $1·25
[Questns. of Day] c 8° Putnam, *N.Y.* [82–3] 86

FORMAN, S. E. Advanced Civics; spirit, form, & functns. of Am. govt. $1·25 *n.* 12° Century Co., *N.Y.* 05

" First Lessons in Civics 60 c. *n.* 12° Am. Bk. Co., *N.Y.* [98] 07

HADLEY, Dr A. T. The Education of an American Citizen $1·50 *n.* c 8° Scribner, *N.Y.* 01

HOLT, H. Talks on Civics $1·25 *n.* c 8° Macmillan 01

" On the Civic Relations $1·75 *n.* c 8° Houghton, *Boston* 07

JENKS, Prf. J. W. Citizenship and the Schools [6/ *n.* Bell] $1·25 *n.* c 8° Holt, *N.Y.* 06
Addresses and essays on nature of public life and public duty, and best ways of traing. childr. for useful citizens.

MCCLEARY, J. T. Studies in Civics $1 12° Amer. Book Co., *N.Y.* 95

MORSE, A. P. A Treatise on Citizenship $4 8° Little & Brown, *Boston* 81

POTTER, Bp H.C. The Citizen in rel. to Industr. Situation [Yale lects.] $1 *n.* c 8° Scribner, *N.Y.* 02

SHALER, Prf. N. S. The Citizen; study of indiv. and govt. [6/ *n.* Constable] c 8° Houghton, *Boston* 04

SHERMAN, W. H. Civics; studies in American citizenship, 2 Pts. 90 c. *n.* (4/ *n.*) Macmillan 05

WILLOUGHBY, Dr W. W. Rights and Duties of American Citizenship $1 12° Am. Book Co., *N.Y.* 99
A book for higher schools. Pt. i: *Political Science Generally*; ii: *Description of U.S. Government.*

WISE, J. S. Treat. on Amer. Citizenship; studs. in constit. law $3 8° Thompson, *Northport* 06

*Teaching of Civics* —*v.* **D** § 167

**Civil Liberty**

BOSANQUET, Dr Bernard Liberty and Legislation—*in his* Civilizn. of Christianity, *ut* **A** § 8

CECIL, L'd Hugh Liberty and Authority 2/6 *n.* c 8° Arnold 10
An Address to Assoc. Students of Edinb. Univ. mainly on MILL and Mat. ARNOLD.

DAWBARN, C. Y. C. Liberty and Progress—*ut* **D** § 118

DICKINSON, G. Lowes Justice and Liberty—*v.* **D** § 125

DYMOND, Jon. H. [1796–1828; Quaker] Essays on Princs. of Morality, & on Priv. & Polit.
Rts. & Obligations of Mankind *o.p* [*pb.* 5/] c 8° Routledge [29] 85

" Essays on the Principles of Morality 1/ *n.* 8° Headley [29] 94
John BRIGHT said 'I know of no better bk. in our language dealing w. morals as appl. to nations than DYMOND's *Essays*'.

FELL, E. F. B. The Foundations of Liberty 6/ c 8° Methuen 08
Thesis: Liberty is based not on utilitn. induction but an *a priori* moral claim arisg. fr. Personality, wh. involves moral responsibility and wh. is realized and developed by Family on one hd. and Polit. Nation on other. Distings. this doctr. ('Personalism') fr. Indiv'm and Socialism, to wh. much crit. is devoted.

v. HUMBOLDT, Bar. W. The Sphere and Duties of Government [tr.] *o.p.* [*pb.* 5/] c 8° Chapman 54
An excellent essay on the limits of the activity of the State.

JELLINEK, G. Declarn. of Rts. of Man and of Citizens [tr.] 75 c. *n.* 12° Holt, *N.Y.* 01

JEPHSON, H. The Platform, 2 vols.—*ut* **D** § 139

LACEY, G. Liberty and Law 12/ 8° Sonnenschein 88

LIEBER, Fcs. On Civil Liberty & Self-Govt., ed. T. D. Woolsey $3·15 *n.* r 8° Lippincott, *Phila.* [53] 83
A valuable book, of a standard character; comprehensive and trustworthy.

MEDLEY, D. J. Liberty of Subject = a sectn. of his 'Manl. of Engl. Constit. History'—*ut* **F** § 17
Treats the history of the subject concisely and well.

MILL, J. Stuart On Liberty 1/4 (50 c.) c 8° Longman [59]

" On Liberty; w. Introd. Prf. A. Seth Pringle-Pattison
[Bks. th Marked Epochs] 2/6 *n.* c 8° Routledge [59] 10
Also in New Univ. Lib. 1/ *n.* pott 8° Routledge (50 c. Dutton, *N.Y.*); Scott Lib. 1/6. *Vide* STEPHEN, *inf.* *Cf. also* his '*Utilitarianism*' [*ut* **C** § 49].

Buckle, H. T. Mill on Liberty—*in his* Miscellaneous Works, vol. i, *ut* **K** § 89

MONTAGUE, F. C. Limits of Individual Liberty *o.p.* [*pb.* 10/6] 8° Rivington 85

MORISON, Dr Milton and Liberty—*ut* **K** § 24

MORLEY, Jno. [L'd] On Compromise = Collected Wks., vol. iii—*ut* **K** § 89
On the lines of MILL's *On Liberty*, treating the question of compromise between principle and expediency.

NEVINSON, H. W. Essays in Freedom 6/ *n.* c 8° Duckworth 09

PAINE, Thos. The Rights of Man—*ut* **D** § 139

PATERSON, J. Comm. on Lib. of Subject & Laws of Engl., 2 vols. *o.p.* [*pb.* 21/] c 8° Macmillan [77] 80

" Liberty of Press, Speech, & Public Worship *o.p.* [*pb.* 12/] c 8° Macmillan 80

SPENCER, Herb. —*v.* **D** § 134 [cf. Maitland (F. W.) *in his* Coll. Papers, 3 v., *ut* **F** § 1]

STEPHEN, Sir J. F. Liberty, Fraternity, Equality 14 / 8° Smith & Elder [73] 74
A criticism of MILL's theories, and an attempt to re-analyse and re-state them.

*Anti-State-interference* —*v.* **D** § 126, *s.v.* Anti-Socialist

**History of Liberty**

ACTON, L'd The History of Freedom ; and other Essays—*ut* **F** § 1

FISKE, Prf. Jno. Beginnings of New England [7/6 Macmillan] $2 c 8° Houghton, *Boston* 89
On the Puritan theocracy in its relations to Civil and Religious Liberty.

HILL, Mabel [ed.] Liberty Documents, ed. A. B. Hart $2 (7/6 *n.*) 8° Longman 01
Contemporary exposition and critical comments, drawn fr. various writers, fr. HENRY I. onwards (tr., where non-English), w. full hist. crit. notes, etc.

HOLLAND, F. M. Liberty in the Nineteenth Century $1·25 (7/6) c 8° Putnam 99

HOSMER, Prf. J. K. —*in his* Short History of Anglo-Saxon Freedom, *ut* **F** § 18

MACKINNON, Dr Jas. A History of Modern Liberty, vols. i–iii 45/ *n.* ($15 *n.*) 8° Longman 06–8 *in prg.*
A useful compiln. fr. good sources, vigorously wr. i: *Introd.* (Origins, Mid. Ages); ii: *Age of Reformation* : iii: *Struggle w. the Stuarts* (1603–47) [i–ii, 30/ *n.* ($10 *n.*); iii, 15/ *n.* ($5) *n.*). Vol. i treats the movemts. tow. polit., munic., and social emancipn. in Mid Ages; ii deals w. movemts. in favr. of intellect. and relig. emancipn. (Renaissance and Reformn.); iii is a satisfactory and fair histor. narr. of the 17 cent. constit. struggle [for other bks. on wh. *v.* **F** § 23]. Ea. vol. separately indexed.

MORRIS, M. F. Hist. of Developmt. of Constit. & Civil Liberty $2 8° Morrison, *Washington* 98

SCHERGER, G. L. The Evolution of Modern Liberty 5/ *n.* ($1·10 *n.*) c 8° Longman 04

**Representation ; Repres. Govt. ; Electoral System :** *Europe—for* Law *v.* **D** § 40

GUIZOT, F. P. G. History and Origin of Representative Govt. in Europe [tr.] 3/6 c 8° Bell [52] 61
[Bohn's Lib.] 50 lects. del. in 1820, but not pub. till after 1848 Revoln. Pt. ii devoted to England exclusively, fr. Norman Conquest to Tudors. Lects. 6–26 examine the early legislative assemblies of the Continent.

*United Kingdom*

*Bibliography :* GROSS, Dr Chas.—*in his* Bibliogr. of Brit. Municipal Hist., *ut* **D** § 124

AVEBURY, L'd Representation [theoretical ; Imper. Parlmt. Ser.] 1/ c 8° Sonnenschein [85] 06

HARE, Thos. Electn. of Representatives ; Parliamentary & Municipal *o.p.* [*pb.* 10/] 8° Longman [59] 73

ILBERT, Sir C. P. Legislative Methods and Forms 16/ ($4) 8° Clar. Press 01

KING, Jos. Electoral Reform [pros and cons of reform] 2/6 *n.* c 8° Unwin 08

LIEBER, Fcs. On Civil Liberty and Self-Government—*ut sup.*

MILL, J. Stuart Considerations on Representative Government 2/ (75 c.) c 8° Longman [61]
Also 1/ *n.* [New Univ. Lib.] pott 8° Routledge 05 (50 c. Dutton, *N.Y.*). Conts. Index (here first added).

POWELL, Ellis T. Essentials of Self-Government (Engl. & Wales) 4/6 *n.* ($1·50 *n.*) 8° Longman 09
A compreh. survey of the electoral mechanism as the foundn. of polit. power and a potent instrumt. of social and intell. evoln., elaborg. in gt. detail a syst. of wh. main features are insep. assocn. of obligns. w. electoral rts., without distinctn. of sex. Introd. (29 pp.) criticizes pres. syst. of 'electoral impotence'.

SPENCER, Herb. Representative Government—*in his* Essays, vol. ii, *ut* **C** § 62

SYME, Dav. Representative Govt. in England ; its faults & failures 6/ c 8° Paul [82] 82

WALPOLE, Spencer The Electorate and the Legislature [Engl. Citizen Ser.] 2/6 ($1) c 8° Macmillan [81]

*History of Elections* —*for* Reform Bills *v.* **D** § 140, **F** § 17

COX, Homersham Antient Parliamentary Elections *o.p.* [*pb.* 8/6] 8° Longman 68
A history, showing how parliaments were constituted and representatives elected.

GREGO, Jos. History of Parliamentary Elections & Electioneering in Old Days 7/6 8° Chatto [86] 92
With 92 cuts der. fr. contemp. prints, squibs, lampoons, etc. An interesting account of what the masses believed or their leaders wished them to believe, full of local colour and detail : 1660–1857.

*United States*

BISHOP, C. F. History of Elections in the American Colonies $2 *n.* 8° Macmillan, *N.Y.* 93

DALLINGER, F. W. Nominatns. f. Elective Office in U.S. $1·50 *n.* (7/6) 8° Longman 97
[Harvard Hist. Studies.] A brief hist. and descrn. of caucus and nominatg. conventn. in U.S.; w. suggested remedies.

DOUGHERTY, J. H. Electoral System of the United States $2 *n.* (9/ *n.*) 8° Putnam 06

FULLER, R. H. Government of the People $1 *n.* (4/6 *n.*) c 8° Macmillan 08
Descrn. of laws and customs regulatg. election-syst. and formatn. and control of polit. parties in U.S.

HAYNES, Prf. G. H. Representation in State Legislatures 75 c. 8° Acad. of Pol. Sci., *Phila.* 00

" Representation in New England Legislatures 15 c. 8° Acad. of Pol. Sci., *Phila.* 00

" The Election of Senators [6/ *n.* Bell] $1·50 *n.* c 8° Holt, *N.Y.* 06

GRIFFITH, E. C. Rise & Development of the Gerrymander ; maps $1·25 8° Scott, *Chicago* 07

MCKNIGHT, D. A. The Electoral System of the United States $3 8° Lippincott, *Phila.* 78
A critical and historical exposition of the principles.

MCMILLAN, D. C. Elective Franchise in U.S. [clear and logical] $1 12° Putnam, *N.Y.* 80

MERRIAM, Prf. C. E. Primary Elections $1·25 *n.* 12° Univ. Press, *Chicago* 08
Traces developmt. of legal reguln. of party primaries fr. 1866 to 1908, and sums up pres. tendencies.

O'NEIL, C. A. American Electoral System [character and history] $1·50 12° Putnam, *N.Y.* 87

STANWOOD, E. History of the Presidency $2·50 12° Houghton, *Boston* [84] 98
A rewr. edn. of his *Hist. of Presidential Elections.* An impartial and accurate account.

STERN, E. S. Repres. Govt. & Personal Represn. [based on Hare] *o.p.* [*pb.* $1·75] 8° *Philadelphia* 71

*Caucus System*

BRANSON, Dr W. J. The Philadelphia Nominating System 25 c. 8° Acad. of Pol. Sci., *Phila.* 99
A careful account of Amer. Caucus System at its most important point.

LAWTON, G. W. Amer. Caucus Syst.; orig., purpose, utility [Questns. of Day] $1 12° Putnam, *N.Y.* 85

WHITRIDGE, F. W. The Caucus System; an essay [Economic Tracts] 25 c. 12° Putnam, *N.Y.* 82

**Proportional Representation**

ASHWORTH, T. R. + H. P. C. Proportional Representn. applied to Party Govt. 5/ *n.* c 8° Sonnenschein 11

BUCKALEW, C. R. Proportional Representation, ed. J. G. Feese $3 8° Campbell, *Phila.* 72

COMMONS, Prf. J. R. Proportional Representation [Lib. of Economics] $1·25 (5/ *n.*) c 8° Macmillan [96] 07
By an ardent member of the Prop. Repres. League. The fullest and fairest explan. of the diff. systs. in English. *La Representation Proportionelle* [1888] by Soc. for Study of Prop. Repres. in Paris is also a very good bk., and conts. more histor. matter, but is not so practical or so up-to-date.

HUMPHREYS, J. H. Proportional Representation 5/ *n.* c 8° Methuen 11
Descrs. syst. of legisn. wh. obtains in several Continental countries and in some of our Colonies.

**Referendum**

DEPLOIGE, S. Referendum in Switzerland [tr.] [Studs. in Econcs.] $2·25 *n.* (7/6 *n.*) c 8° Longman 98
Contains also a tr. of J. van den HEUVEL'S *Referendum in Belgium.*

OBERHOLTZER, E. P. The Referendum in America $2 c 8° Scribner, *N.Y.* [93] 00

SULLIVAN, J. W. Direct Legisln. of Citizenship through Initiative and Referendum 75 c. 8° Humboldt Pb. Co., *N.Y.* [92] 93

**Woman Suffrage** —*v.* **D** § 132

**Freedom of the Press** —*v. also sup., s.n.* PATERSON

BENTHAM, Jer. [1748–1832] Liberty of the Press—*in his* Works, vol. ii, *ut* **C** § 18 [Spain]

CARLILE, Rich. [1790–1843]

Campbell, Theophila Carlile [dau.] Life of Richard Carlile; 2 ports. 6/ *n.* c 8° Bonner 99

COLLET, C. D. Hist. of Taxes on Knowledge; origin and repeal, 2 vols. 16/ c 8° Unwin 00
History of the Stamp and other Acts wh. hindered circuln. of newspapers fr. Qu. ANNE'S rn. to 1869.

DUNIWAY, C. A. Developmt. of Fr. of Pr. in Mass. [Harv. Hist. Studs.] $1·50 *n.* (7/6) 8° Longman 06

HUNT, F. K. —*in his* The Fourth Estate, 2 vols., *ut* **K** § 26 [hist. of newspapers, and freed. of press]

LINTON, W. J. James Watson [memoir of a free-press agitator] 2/ c 8° Truelove 79

MILTON, Jno. [1608–74] Areopagitica, ed. H. B. Cotterill [Engl. Classics] 2/ (50 c. *n.*) c 8° Macmillan [1664] 04
MILTON'S best prose wk.—a close and conclusive vindicn. of liberty of the press. Also in Temple Classics 1/6 *n.* f 8° Dent (50 c. Macm., *N.Y.*) '00; Natl. Lib. 6*d.*, 18° Cassell; ed. W. H. D. Rouse 6*d.* Blackie '10; Arber's Reprts. 1/ *n.* f 8° Constable (35 c. *n.* Macm., *N.Y.*).

ROUTLEDGE, Jas. Chapters on the History of Popular Progress *o.p.* [*pb.* 16/] 8° Macmillan 76
Chiefly in relation to Freedom of the Press and Trial by Jury in England, 1660–1820; w. applicn. to later years.

SCHROEDER, T. [ed.] Free Press Anthology $2 8° Free Speech League, *N.Y.* 09

*Index Expurgatorius* —*v.* **K** § 5*

**Freedom of Religious Opinion**—*v.* **A** § 113, *s.v.* Toleration

**Trial by Jury** —*v. also sup., s.n.* ROUTLEDGE; *for* History *v.* **D** § 5; *for* Law *v.* **D** § 109

ROLLINS, D. [ed.] The Englishman's Right [dialogue in rel. to trial by jury] $1 12° *Boston* [1772] 83

## 136: COLONIZATION; COLONIAL POLICY

BIGELOW, Poulteney The Children of the Nations $2 *n.* 8° McClure, *N.Y.* 91
10/ Heinemann. Colonizn. and its probls.; with more reference to Spanish colonizn. of Amer. than to British colonies.

BROUGHAM, Hy., L'd Colonial Policy of European Powers—*in his* Works, *ut* **K** § 89 [chiefly American]

CAIRNES, Prf. J. E. Colonizn. and Colonial Govt.—*in his* Essays in Polit. Econ., *ut* **D** § 114

IRELAND, Alleyne Tropical Colonization [excell. tables of statistics] $2 (7/6 *n.*) 8° Macmillan 98
A study of probls. of Tropical Colonizn., w. spec. ref. to those facing United States in her new possessions.

" Far Eastern Tropics; studies in administration of tropical dependencies [$2 *n.* Houghton, *Boston*] 7/6 *n.* c 8° Constable 05

" Report on Colon. Admin. in Far East, vols. i–ii 8° Constable 07
Ea. $12·50 *n.* Houghton, *Bost.* Vols. i–ii: *Province of Burma*; w. maps, tables, etc. To occupy 12 vols., incl. Brit., Fch., Dutch, and Amer. colonial meths.—Burma, Brit. N. Borneo, Sarawak, Hongkong, Str. Settlemts., Fed. Malay States, Tonkin, Annam, Cochin China, Cambodia, Laos, Java, and Philippines.

KELLER, A. J. Colonization; study of fdg. of new societies $3 8° Ginn, *Boston* 08

KIDD, Benj. The Control of the Tropics 3/ *n.* (75 c.) c 8° Macmillan 98
A study of economic condns. likely to govern the administration of tropical regions in the future.

LEWIS, Sir G. Cornewall Essay on Government of Dependencies, ed. C. P. Lucas 14/ ($3·50) 8° Clar. Press [41–2] 91
Embodies a mass of histor. and polit. informn., clearly and impartially put together by a pract. statesman and polit. philosopher.

MERIVALE, Herman — Lectures on Colonization and Colonies [del. at Oxon. '39–'41] *o.p.* [*pb.* 18/] 8° Longman [41] 61

PAYNE, E. J. — Colonies and Colonial Federations [Engl. Citizen Ser.] 3/6 c 8° Macmillan [05]

PEARSON, C. H. — *in his* National Life and Character, *ut* **D** § 134

REINSCH, Prf. P. S. — Colonial Government [Citizen's Lib.] $1·25 *n.* (5/*n.*) c 8° Macmillan 02
A sketch of colonial policy of the various powers. Probls. examined largely fr. Brit. pt.-of-view.

,, — Colonial Administration [Citizen's Lib.] $1·25 *n.* (5/*n.*) c 8° Macmillan 05
Introd., educn. and gen. improvemt., finance, currency and bkg., commerce, means of transport, land-policy, labour, defence, police, etc.

SNOW, A. H. — The Administration of Dependencies $3·50 *n.* (15/*n.*) 8° Putnam 02
Deals chiefly w. Amer. condns., historically and crit.; but also has much of value on Brit. col. policy and impl. federatn.

**British Empire** —*v. also* **D** § 143, **E** § 21, **F** § 33

ADDERLEY, Sir C. B. [=L'd NORTON] Colonial Policy and History *o.p.* [*pb.* 9/] 8° Stanford 69

BARKER, J. Ellis — Great and Greater Britain 10/6 *n.* 8° Smith & Elder [09] 10

BEDWELL, C. E. A. [ed.] — The Legislation of the Empire, 4 vols.—*ut* **D** § 107

BOWEN, Sir Geo. F. — *in his* Thirty Years of Colonial Govt., *ut* **E** § 65 [chiefly Australia]

BRUCE, Sir Chas. — The Broad Stone of Empire, 2 vols.; maps 30/*n.* 8° Macmillan 10
A substantial wk. on admin. of Crown Colonies, w. summary of their hist., organizn., resources, etc.

CALDECOTT, Alf. — English Colonisation and Empire [Univ. Extens. Manls.] 3/6 c 8° Murray 91
$1 *n.* Scribner, *N.Y.* Calls attention to crisis wh. he thinks has been reached in hist. of the Empire; incl. India and U.S.

COTTON (J. S.) + PAYNE (E. J.) Colonies [English Citizen Series] *o.p.* [*pb.* 3/6] c 8° Macmillan 83

DILKE, Sir Chas. W. — Problems of Greater Britain; maps 12/6 ($4 *n.*) c 8° Macmillan [90] 90
An important study of compar. politics, and survey of polit. and social questns. of entire Empire. Not to be confused w. his *Greater Britain* [*ut* **E** § 21], wh. is a record of travel fr. sight-seeing pt.-of-view rather than that of polit. and social observn. and comparison.

,, — The British Empire—*ut* **E** § 21

DUFFERIN, Earl — Speeches during Last 30 Years [incl. the Canadian] *o.p.* [*pb.* 12/] 8° Murray 82

Essays in Colonial Finance. By Var. Wrs. [Am. Ec. Ass.; 6/ Sonnenschein] $1·50 *n.* 8° Macm., *N.Y.* 00

GRESWELL, Rev. W. P. — Outlines of British Colonization 6/ c 8° Rivington 93
Full of historical and other information concerning our colonial Empire. Introd. by Lord BRASSEY.

HEARN, Hon. W. E. — *his* Govt. of England [*ut* **D** § 140] conts. lect. *Colonies and Mother Country*

JEBB, Rich. — The Imperial Conference: a history & study, 2 vols. 25/*n.* 8° Longman 11

KEITH, Arth. B. — Responsible Government in the Dominions 10/ 8° Stevens 09
An important wk., discussg. wisely and w. full knowl. main constitl. points. Concls. that in long run fabric of the Empire will have to be altered, and certain privileges of Dominions (e.g. treat-mkg. power) conceded.

MEAKIN, W. — Life of an Empire 6/*n.* 8° Unwin 07

MOLESWORTH, Sir Wm. — Selected Speeches on Questions rel. to Colonial Policy 15/*n.* 8° Murray 03
Ed. by Hugh EGERTON. Speeches 1836–1853: of no special present-day value.

PARKES, Sir Hy. — Speeches on Various Occasions [1848–74; conn. w. N.S.W.] 14/ 8° *Melbourne* 76

ROSEBERY, Earl of — Questions of Empire [a Rectorial Address] 1/ 8° Humphreys 00

SEELEY, Sir J. R. — The Expansion of England—*ut* **F** § 33
2 courses of lects. Holds that expansion of Engl. in Amer. and India is the dominant historical fact of last 3 cents.

TEMPLE, Sir Rich. — Cosmopolitan Essays; maps *o.p.* [*pb.* 16/] 8° Chapman 86
*Position of British Empire; Imperial Federation; Prospects of Canada; Burmah; India; Congo; America, etc.*

WHITE, Arnold — Efficiency and Empire 6/ c 8° Methuen 01
A general indictment of our political system and government offices and officials. Powerful but unreasonable.

WILSON, A. J. — An Empire in Pawn—*ut* **D** § 117

*History*—*v.* **F** § 33 *Commercial Policy*—*v.* **D** § 122 *Imperial Defence*—*v.* **D** § 138

**Imperial Federation**

BÉRARD, Vict. — British Imperialism & Commercial Supremacy [tr.] 7/6 *n.* ($2·60 *n.*) 8° Longman 06
By a brilliant Fch. journalist, wr. in 1900. Based largely on figures now hopelessly out of date.

BRASSEY, L'd — Papers & Addresses on Impl. Federn. and Colonisation 5/ c 8° Longman 94
Reprints of addresses and magazine articles from 1880 to 1894. Ed. A. H. LORING + R. J. BEADON.

BRASSEY, T. A. — Problems of Empire; Pref. by Dr G. R. Parkin 6/*n.* r 8° Humphreys 04

BUTLER-JOHNSTONE, H. M. Imperial Federation and Policy 2/6 c 8° G. Allen 02
Leading articles, written in 1896 and now mostly out of date. Favourable to Imperial Federation.

CUNINGHAM, G. C. [Canad.] A Scheme for Imperial Federation 3/6 ($1·25) c 8° Longman 95
The 'scheme' is the creation of a Senate for the Empire. 3 arts. repr. fr. *Westminster Review*, 1879.

DAVIDSON, J. — Commercial Federation and Colonial Trade Policy [Social Science Series; $1 Scribner, *N.Y.*] 2/6 c 8° Sonnenschein 00

DENISON, Col. G. T. — The Struggle for Imperial Unity 8/6 *n.* ($2·25 *n.*) c 8° Macmillan 09
Recollns. of the author's career of 40 yrs. in Canada as keen supporter of Imp. unity and pref. tariffs.

FABIAN SOCIETY: Fabianism and the Empire: a manifesto; ed. G. B. Shaw 1/*n.* c 8° Fabian Soc. 00

Frame-work of Union (The) 6/ 8° *Cape Times* Off., *Cape Town* 08
Comparison of some Union Constitns.—Canada, Austral., Germy., U.S.; w. Provisions. Iss. for Closer Union Soc.

FRANKLYN, H. Mortimer — The Unit of Imperial Federation *o.p.* [*pb.* 10/6] 8° Sonnenschein 87

GIDDINGS, Prf. F. H. — Democracy and Empire—*ut* **D** § 139

GOLDMAN, C. S. [ed.] The Empire and the Century; essays on imper. probls. 21/n. 8° Murray 05
Essays by var. wrs. of all opinions—GARVIN, St Loe STRACHEY, MONYPENNY, AMERY, WISE, Sir J. COCKBURN, PARKIN, Bern. HOLLAND, Rich. JEBB, etc. The dominant strain is preferential. 7 maps.

HALDANE, R. B. Imperial Federation—*in his* Education and Empire—*ut* **D** § 155

HERTZ, G. B. The Old Colonial System 7/6 n. 8° Sherratt, *Mancs.* 05

,, British Imperialism in the Eighteenth Century 6/n. Constable 08

HERVEY, M. M. Trade Policy of Impl. Feder. [Social Science Ser.] 2/6 c 8° Sonnenschein 92
$1 Scribner, *N.Y.* Favours a 'Commercial Union' betw. Engl. and her Colonies, in advance of a polit. union. From an Austral. standpt.

HIRST, F. W., etc. Liberalism and the Empire 3/6 n. c 8° Brinsley Johnson 00
*Imperialism and Finance* (HIRST); *Exploitn. of Inferior Races* (Gilb. MURRAY); *Colon. and Foreign Policy* (J. L. HAMMOND).

HOBSON, J. A. Imperialism; a study; maps and diagrs. 2/6 n. c 8° Constable [02] 05
An armoury of arguments for anti-jingoites, very capably brought together.

HOLLAND, Bernard Imperium et Libertas 12/6 n. 8° Arnold 01
$4 Longman, *N.Y.* An able study of Imperial Federation, Home Rule, and allied questions.

JEBB, Rich. Studies in Colonial Nationalism 12/6 n. 8° Arnold 05
$3·50 n. Longman, *N.Y.* A good book.

JESSETT, Montague G. The Bond of Empire [imp. fedn., trade, defence] 6/ c 8° Low 02

KINNEAR, J. Boyd —*in his* Princ. of Civil Govt. [*ut* **D** § 134]: good chaps. on Federation

LORNE, Marq. of [*now* Dke. of ARGYLL] Imperial Federation [Impl. Parl. Ser.] 1/ c 8° Sonnenschein [85] 91

MARTIN, A. P. Australia & the Empire [by late edr. *Melb. Rev.*] 7/6 c 8° Douglas, *Edin.* 89

MILNER, Visc. Constructive Imperialism [5 speeches] 1/n. 8° *Natl. Review* Off. 08

,, Imperial Unity [speeches in Canada, 1908] 2/6 c 8° Hodder 07

NICHOLSON, Prf. J. S. A Project of Empire 7/6 n. 8° Macmillan 09
A crit. study of economics of Imperialism, w. spec. ref. to ideas of Adam SMITH, who said 'This Empire has hitherto existed in imagination only. It has hitherto been not an empire, but a project of empire.' N. shows that, if we accept SMITH's tests, the Empire is still 'a golden dream'.

NORTON, L'd Imper. Fellowship of Self-governed Brit. Colonies 2/6 c 8° Rivington 03

PARKIN, Dr G. R. Imperial Federation; the problem of national unity 4/6 ($1·25) c 8° Macmillan 92
A thoughtful and able statemt. of case for Imp. Fed., by an enthusiastic believer in ideal of natl. organic unity.

PULSFORD, E. Commerce and the Empire 3/6 c 8° Cassell 03

ROBERTSON, J. M. Patriotism and Empire 3/6 c 8° Richards [99] 00
On the topics of ***Patriotism, Militarism,*** and ***Imperialism***; w. much unfavourable criticism of two last.

SILBURN, P. A. B. The Governance of Empire 9/n. 8° Longman 10
A Colonial view of the Imperial idea, by a member of Legisl. Assembly of Natal. Favourable to Imp. Fedn.

de THIERRY, C. Imperialism 2/ c 8° Duckworth 98
An analysis of the idea of imperialism in England. Introd. by W. E. HENLEY.

WHITE, A. Silva [ed.] Britannic Confederation [6 arts. by var. wrs.] 1/ c 8° Philip [92] 93

YOUNG, F. [ed.] Federation of Great Britain and her Colonies 12/ 8° Silver 76

**Africa**

SCHREINER, Olive Closer Union 1/n. s 8° Fifield 09

**Australia** —*v. also* **E** § 65

COCKBURN, Sir Jno. Australian Federation; Pref. by C. W. Dilke 2/6 n. c 8° Marshall 01

MOORE, Prf. W. H. —*in his* Commonwealth of Australia, *ut* **D** § 143

REEVES, W. Pember —*in his* State Experiments in Australia and New Zealand, 2 vols., *ut* **D** § 126

*Grey, Sir Geo.* —*in* Henderson's Sir George Grey, *ut* **E** § 65
A valuable contribn. to imperial history and to the philosophy of imperialism.

**Canada**

DOUGLAS, Jas. Canad. Indep., Annexn. [by U. S.], and Brit. Impl. Federn.—*ut* **D** § 143

EWART, J. S. Kingd. of Canada, Imperial Federation, & other Essays Morang, *Toronto* 08
Essays by a Canadian lawyer, advocate for Canada's future: 'nationhood; self-control; polit. equal. w. U.K., instd. of subordin. and subserviency to Colon. Off.; Kingd. of Canada, inst. of one of many "Dominions beyond the Seas" . . . increase by these means of Imper. sympathy and friendship and brotherhood'

LAWSON, W. R. Canada and the Empire 6/n. c 8° Blackwood 11

*MACPHAIL, Andr. Essays in Politics 6/n. ($1·80 n.) c 8° Longman 09
Excellent essays on Canada's place in the Empire, English relns. w. her, her Patent-law, etc.

MONTAGUE (E. S.) + HERBERT (B.) Canada and the Empire—*ut* **D** § 122: exam. of trade-preferences

MUNRO, Prf. W. B. The Seignorial System in Canada [Harv. Hist. Studs.] $2 n. (10/6) 8° Longman 07
A study of French colonial policy, based on contemporary documents.

SMITH, Prf. Goldwin —*in his* Canada and the Canadian Question, *ut* **D** § 143

YOUNG, Sir F. A Pioneer of Imper. Federn. in Canada—*ut* **E** § 55

**China, etc.**

des VŒUX, Sir J. W. —*in his* My Colonial Service, 2 vols., *ut* **E** § 61

**India** —*v. also* **E** § 33; **E** § 35, *s.v.* Administration

ADYE, Sir Jno. Indian Frontier Policy; an historical sketch 3/6 8° Smith & Elder 97
Not a full or complete sketch: adverse criticism of recent policy. Map.

BRUCE, Rich. The Forward Policy and its Results 15/ *n.* ($5) 8° Longman 00
An account, by an experienced official, of British difficulties on the Afghan border, w. their causes.

*CHAILLEY, Jos. Administrative Problems of British India, tr. Sir W. Meyer 10/ *n.* 8° Macmillan 10
A scholarly, dispassionate, and compreh. pronouncemt. on Brit. rule in India by a Fch. critic. Condemns the idea of abandong. the old policy of reliance on nobles and gentry and granting higher powers to native 'competition wallahs' blessed only w. theoret. knowl.

*CHESNEY, Gen. Sir Geo. Indian Polity; map 21/ ($6) 8° Longman [68] 94
A view of the system of administration in India. Has had great influence. Now somewhat out of date.

CHIROL, Valentine Indian Unrest [repr. fr. 'Times'] 5/ *n.* 8° Macmillan 10

ILBERT, Sir C. P. The Government of India 10/6 *n.* ($3·4c) 8° Clar. Press [98] 07
A clear, concise statemt. of legal positn. and powers of the Brit. Govt. in India.

LETHBRIDGE, Sir Roper India & Imperial Preference [w. statist· tables] 2/6 *n.* (90 c. *n.*) c 8° Longman 07

LILLY, W. S. India and its Problems 7/6 *n.* 8° Sands 02

LOW, Sid. Vision of India; dur. tour of Prince of Wales 10/6 *n.* 8° Smith & Elder 06
A notable and accurate record of the impressions of a casual visitor. Ill.

MACDONALD, J. Ramsay The Awakening of India [repr. fr.' Dy. Chron.'] 6/ c 8° Hodder 10

MITRA, S. M. Indian Problems 7/6 *n.* 8° Murray 08
By a native practisg. advocate, wrg. as a loyal Indian opposed to aspiratns. of Ind. Nat. Congress, appreciatg. benefits of Brit. rule, but urging more regard for Ind. ideals.

MORISON, Theod. Imper. Rule in India; princs. proper to Govt. of dependencies 3/6 c 8° Constable 99

MORLEY, Visc. Indian Speeches; 1907–1909 2/6 *n.* 8° Macmillan 09

NAOROJI, Dadhabai Poverty and Un-British Rule in India 10/6 8° Sonnenschein 01

O'DONNELL, J. C. The Causes of Present Discontent in India 2/6 *n.* c 8° Unwin 08

*STRACHEY, Sir Jno. India, its Administration and Progress 10/ *n.* r 8° Macmillan [88] 11
Ed. Sir T. W. HOLDERNESS. By far the best conspectus of the Indian Empire and its problems.

TUPPER, C. L. Our Indian Protectorate *o.p.* [*pb.* 16/] 8° Longman 93
On relns. betw. our govt. and so-called feudatory States, fr. pt.-of-view of internat. law; wr. w. skill and a large knowl. of Anglo-Ind. customs and laws. Emphasizes advants. of native rule, when fairly well conducted, and its likelihood of its greater popularity than Brit. admin. Concl. w. essay on *India and Imper. Federn.*

**New Zealand** —*v. also* **E** § 66

DOUGLAS, Sir A. P. The Dominion of New Zealand [All Red Series] 7/6 *n.* 8° Pitman 09
Not a guide-bk. or a statistical record so much as an introd. to study of Imperial questions.

IRVINE, R. F. + ALPERS (O. T. J.)—*in their* Progress of New Zealand, *ut* **E** § 66

LLOYD, H. D. —*in his* Newest England: notes of a democratic traveller, *ut* **E** § 66

REEVES, W. Pember —*in his* The Long White Cloud, *ut* **E** § 66

SCHOLEFIELD, Guy H. New Zealand in Evolution; industr., econ., political 10/6 *n.* 8° Unwin 09
Survey of condn. of the Colony wh. has been called 'the economic laboratory of the world' Ill.

**United States** —*v. also* **D** § 146

ADAMS, Brooks The New Empire; maps $1·50 *n.* (6/ *n.*) c 8° Macmillan 02
A prophecy of the future greatness of the United States, with comparisons w. Great Britain, etc.

Am. Acad. of Polit. & Soc. Sci.: Amer. Col. Policy & Administration $1 8° Am. Ac. Pol. Sci., *Phila.* 07

COLQUHOUN, A. R. —*in his* Greater America, *ut* **E** § 52

JORDAN, Dr D. S. Imperial Democracy—*ut* **D** § 139
Written at the time of the struggle with the Philippines; unfavourable to U.S. policy in the Philippines.

RABBENO, Prf. Ugo The American Commercial Policy—*ut* **D** § 122

SMITH, Goldwin Commonwealth or Empire 2/6 *n.* (60 c. *n.*) c 8° Macmillan 02
A pessimistic view of recent tendencies of plutocracy, militarism, and imperialism in the United States.

SNOW, A. H. The Administration of Dependencies—*ut sup.*

WILLOUGHBY, W. Franklin Territories and Dependencies of U.S. $1·25 *n.* 12° Century Co., *N.Y.* 05

**France** —*v.* **E** §§ 34, 36; **F** § 50

## 137: CIVIL SERVICE

**British** —*for* C. S. Examinations *v.* **D** § 168

BRYANT, W. C. Rise and Constitution of the Civil Service *o.p.* [*pb.* 4/] c 8° Chapman 76

MARVIN, Chas. Our Public Offices; how we are governed; ill. [satirical] 2/6 c 8° Sonnenschein [79] 84

*Guides to Employment*

CARR, E. A. How to Enter the Civil Service [w. exam. pprs.] 2/6 c 8° Richards 02

GIBSON, J. Guide to the Civil Service [Start in Life Ser.] 3/6 c 8° Hodder 03

Guide to Employment in the Civil Service 3/6 c 8° Cassell 83

JOHNSTON, R. Civil Service Guide; particulars of every office 3/6 12° Longman [ ]

*Foreign Office*

HERTSLET, Sir Edw. Recollections of the Old Foreign Office 12/ *n.* 8° Murray 01
Record of matters pertaining to the Office in the 19th century by the Librarian [1857-96].

*Post Office*

BAINES, F. E. Forty Years at the Post Office, 1850–1890, 2 vols.; ill. *o.p.* [*pb.* 21/] c 8° Bentley 95
Historical, descriptive, and anecdotal, drawing a faithful picture of the inner life of the P.O., its posts and its telegraphs.

„ On the Track of the Mail Coach *o.p.* [*pb.* 7/6] c 8° Bentley 95
Sequel to above. Full of anecdotes of the Mail Coach era.

BLACKWOOD, Sir S. A. [Finan. Sec. to P.O.] Life—*ut* **F** § 27

HILL, Sir Rowland [1795–1879] Life of. By Dr G. Birkbeck Hill *o.p.* [*pb.* 16/] 8° De La Rue [80] 81

Smyth, Mrs E. C. [dau.] Sir Rowland Hill: story of a great reform [$1·65 Wessels, *Brooklyn*] 3/6 c 8° Unwin [07] 09

HYAMSON, A. M. The Humour of the Post Office; facss. 1/*n.* c 8° Routledge 09

HYDE, J. Wilson The Royal Mail: curiosities & romance; ill. *o.p.* [*pb.* 6/] c 8° Blackwood [85] 89

„ The Post Office in Grant and Farm 5/ c 8° Black 94
$1·75 Macmillan, *N.Y.* Accurate, based largely on State Pprs. and offic. records rel. to working of the P.O. fr. its beginnings in the patent granted by Qu. ELIZABETH (1590) to close of 17th century.

JOYCE, Herb. History of the Post Office *o.p.* [*pb.* 16/] 8° Bentley 93
An unpretentious acc. of rise and progress of P.O. fr. its estabmt. down to 1836. By one of Secretaries.

LEWINS, W. Her Majesty's Mails [histor. and descr. acc. of P.O.] *o.p.* [*pb.* 6/] c 8° Low [64] 65

NORWAY, A. H. Hist. of Post Office Packet Service: 1793–1815; ill. 8/6 *n.* ($3·50) c 8° Macmillan 95
Hist. of postal packet system (fr. records chiefly official) in time of our last great wars w. Continent and U.S. By far greater pt. of the service centred in port of Falmouth. A very interesting bk., w. many accs. of sea fights, escapes and victories.

Post Office (The): an historical summary 8° H. M. Stationery Office 11

RAIKES, H. C. [1838–91; Post-Master Gen.] Life & Letters. By H. St J. Raikes 10/*n.* ($4) 8° Macmillan 98

SWIFT, H. G. History of Postal Agitation [1850–1900] 3/6 c 8° Pearson 00

TOMBS, R. C. The King's Post: historical facts 3/6 c 8° Simpkin 07

*Colonial:* LOWELL (A. L.) Colonial Civil Service $1·50 c 8° Macmillan 00
Incl. an account of the East India College at Haileybury.

**United States** —*fr.* C. S. Examinations, *v.* **D** § 168

CURTIS, G. W. Orations and Addresses, vol. ii: Addresses and Reports on Reform of the Civil Service of U.S.—*ut* **K** § 90

EATON, D. B. Literature of Civil Service Reform in United States 20 c. 12° *New York* 81

„ Civil Service in Great Britain 25 c. 4° Harper, *N.Y.* [79] 81
A history of abuses and reforms, and their bearings on American politics.

EWART (J. A.) + FILED (W. S.) + MORRISON (A. H.) Civil Service Manual, 3 vols. $2·50 c 8° Home Corr. Sch., *Springfd.* 08

FISH, Dr C. R. Civil Service & the Patronage [Harv. Hist. Studs.] $2 *n.* (10/6 *n.*) 8° Longman 05

FOLTZ, E. B. K. The Federal Civil Service as a Career $1·50 *n.* (6/) c 8° Putnam 09
By an Amer. Civil Servt. Covers a wide field, and shows fully the business meths. of the natl. govt.

FOULKES, W. D. Civil Serv. Reform: its later aspects [Econ. Tracts] 10 c. 12° Soc. f. Polit. Ed., *N.Y.* 90

JAMESON, T. A. [ed.] The Civil Service [rept. of Sel. Comm. on Retrenchmt.] 75 c. 8° Govt. Prg. Off., *Washgtn.* 86

*Post Office*

COWLES, J. L. A Gen. Freight & Passgr. Post [Questns. of Day] $1·25 (5/) c 8° Putnam 96

CUSHING, M. Story of our Post Office *subscr.* $3·75 8° Thayer, *Boston* 93

HUEBNER, F. C. Our Postal System $3·50 8° Beall, *Washington* 06

**Rome (Ancient)** —*v.* **F** § 12

## 138: INTERNATIONAL RELATIONS; PEACE AND WAR

### International Relations

International Policy: essays on the foreign relations of England 2/6 c 8° Reeves & Turner [ ] 84
By Six Positivists. *The West* (Dr R. CONGREVE), *England and France* (F. HARRISON), *England and the Sea* (Prf. E. S. BEESLY), *England and India* (E. H. PEMBER), *England and China* (Dr J. H. BRIDGES), *England and Uncivilized Communities* (H. D. HUTTON).

LUND, J. K. England and Continental Powers: questns. of for. policy 2/6 c 8° Sonnenschein 94

MAHAN, Adm. A. T. Retrospect & Prospect [8/6 *n.* Low] $1·60 *n.* c 8° Little & Brown, *Boston* 02
Studies in international relations, naval and political.

WALPOLE, Spencer Foreign Relations [English Citizen Ser.] *o.p.* [*pb.* 3/6] c 8° Macmillan [82] 93
A hist. of for. relns. bef. and after 1815, w. chs. on Ambassrs. and Consuls. Clear, and rigidly impartial.

WILKINSON, Prf. H. Spenser The Great Alternative; plea for a national policy 6/ 8° Constable [94] 02
The Alternative is betw. first place am. nations of world—and last betw. leadership of human race and loss of the Empire and of all but the shadow of independence.

„ The Nation's Awakening; essays tow. a natl. policy 5/ 8° Constable 96
A further colln. of repr. newsppr. arts., etc.—both serious attempts tow. a solutn. of the probl. of our Natl. developmt. and destiny.

*Frontiers*

ADYE, Sir Jno. —*in his* Indian Frontier Policy and its Results, *ut* **D** § 136 [Afghan border]

CURZON of Kedleston, L'd Frontiers [Romanes Lect.; historico-critical] 2/*n.* 8° Clar. Press 07

HOLDITCH, Col. Sir Thos. —*in his* Gates of India, *ut* **E** § 35

*England and America* —*v. also* **D** § 146

ADAMS, Prf. G. B. Why Americans Dislike Engld. [Belles-Lettres Ser.] 30 c. 16° Altemus, *Phila. n.d.* (96)
Whilst acknowledging existence of wide-spread dislike, regards it as 'in the main a really mistaken feeling . . . in every regard to be deplored'.

America and Europe: a study of international relations [Questions of Day] $1 12° Putnam 96
(1) *Relns. betw. U.S. and Gt. Brit.* (D. A. WELLS), (2) *True Monroe Doctr.* (E. J. PHELPS) [*ut* **D** § 147], (3) *Arbitrn. in Internat. Disputes* (C. SCHURZ).

*England and Germany*

'French Staff Officer (A)' The German Invasion of England 1/*n.* 8° Nutt 10
An anal. of its possibilities. Impartial and non-sensational. Pref. deals w. the converse problem.

THIRLMERE, Rowl. The Clash of Empires 2/6 *n.* c 8° Heinemann 07
Inspired by a belief in the danger fr. Germy. and her growing strength. Discusses naval and fiscal policy (Protectionist).

'VIGILANS SED ÆQUUS' German Ambitions as they Affect Britain & U.S. 2/6 *n.* c 8° Smith & Elder 03
A series of striking papers, orig. contrib. to *The Spectator.* The *nom de plume* gives keynote to pt.-of-view.

*England and Portugal*

SARMENTO, Gen. J. E. De Moraes Anglo-Portug. Alliance and Coast Defence [tr.] 5/*n.* 8° Rees 08
A valuable discussn. of alliances, condns. of naval warfare and coast-defence. Considers th., in case of Europ. War, the A.-P. alliance wld. exercise a real influ. on naval strategy.

## War and Peace

*Bibliography:* HIRST, F. W. A Library of Peace and War [best 100 bks.] 1/*n.* 8° *Speaker* Pb. Co. 07

Arbiter in Council (The) 10/*n.* ($2·50 *n.*) 8° Macmillan 06
Discussns. at a conference, reported and pubd. in bk.-form, on *Causes and Conseqs. of War; Mod. Warfare; Private War and the Duel; Cruelty; Perpetual Peace,* or *Federn. of World; Plea for Arbitrn.; Polit. Econ. of War; Christianity and War.*

## Peace Arguments, etc.

ANGELL, Norman Europe's Optical Illusion 2/6 c 8° Simpkin 09
Advocates an anti-armament league. 'It has become a physical impossibility for any nation to benefit by military conquest'.

" The Great Illusion [enlargemt. of above] 2/6 *n.* c 8° Heinemann 10

ARNOLDSON, K. P. Pax Mundi [tr.]; w. Introd. by Bp of Durham 2/6 c 8° Sonnenschein 92
Acc. of progress of movemt. for Peace by means of Arbitration, Neutralizn., Intern. Law and Disarmamt. By a Swedish M.P.

CARLSEN, Wilh. War as it is, tr. (fr. Danish) P. H. Peckover; 46 ill. 1/, *cl.* 2/ c 8° Sonnenschein 92
Descrns., by pen and pencil, of the horrors of war.

CHANNING, W. E. [1780–1842] Discourses on War; w. Introd. E. D. Mead 50 c. 12° Ginn, *Boston* [*v.y.*] 03

'COBDEN CLUB': Burden of Armaments [plea for retrenchmt.] 3/6 c 8° Unwin 05

DYMOND, Jon. H. [1796–1828] War; an essay; w. Introd. by Jno. Bright [thoughtful; by a Quaker] 1/c 8° Heywood, *Mancs.* [23] 89

" —*in his* Essays on the Princs. of Morality, etc., *ut* **D** § 135

JONES, Russell Lowell Internat. Arbitrn. as Substitute for War [prize-ess.] 5/*n.* 8° Univ. Press, *St Andrews* 08

HOLLAND, Can. H. Scott War—*in his* Pleas and Claims for Christ, *ut* **A** § 109

KANT, Imman. [1724–1804] Perpetual Peace [1795], tr. M. C. Smith; w. notes 2/6 c 8° Sonnenschein 03
Extracted fr. his *Principles of Politics* [*ut* **D** § 134]. Introd. by Prf. R. LATTA.

KRAUSE, K. C. F. The Ideal of Humanity and Universal Federation [tr.] 3/c 8° Clark, *Edin.* 01

PEACE SOCIETY: Pubns. [pamphlets] 47 *New Broad St., London*

RICHET, C. Peace and War, tr. Marian Edwardes 1/*n.* f 8° Dent 06

RITCHIE, Prf. D. G. —*in his* Studies in Political and Social Ethics, *ut* **D** § 134

TAYLOR, Hugh Morality of Nations: study in evoln. of ethics 6/c 8° Paul 88

TOLSTOY, C't The Kingdom of God is Within you, tr. L. Wiener 3/6 *n.* c 8° Dent 05
$1·50 Estes, *Boston.* A forcible bklet. on folly and wickedness of war. Tr. Miss DELANO, 2/6 c 8° W. Scott.

UNIVERSAL CONGRESS OF PEACE: Official Rept. of the 17th Congr. 5/*n.* 8° Nat. Council of Peace Socs. 08

WALSH, Rev. Walt. Moral Damage of War [90 c. *n.* Ginn, *Bost.*] 3/6 *n.* c 8° Brimley Johnson 02

*Biography*

CREMER, Sir Randal [1828–1908] Sir A. Cremer: life and works. By Howard Evans 5/*n.* 8° Unwin 09
A life of one of the pioneers of the Peace movement.

RICHARD, Hy. [1812–88; the 'Apostle of Peace'; prominent member of Peace Soc.]

Appleton, Lewis Memoirs of Henry Richard *o.p.* [*pb.* 7/6] c 8° Trübner 89

Miall, C. S. Henry Richard, M.P.: a biography; port. 7/6 s 8° Cassell 89

*Fiction*

v. SUTTNER, B'ess Bertha Lay Down Your Arms; an autobiogr. [tr.] 2/6 (75 c.) c 8° Longman [93] 94
A tr. (by T. HOLMES) of *Die Waffen Nieder!*—a romance wh. attained some success in Germy. As fiction weak, but as an attempt to rouse attention to the evils of war and possibility of findg. remedy in arbitrn. tribunals and mutual disarmamt. it has some value. Am. tr. by Alice A. ABBOTT. $1·50 12° McClurg, *Chicago* [92] 07.

*International Arbitration*

*Bibliography:* TRUEBLOOD, B. F. Federation of the World $1 c 8° Houghton, *Boston* 99

ALDERSON, A. W. Extinction in Perpetuity of Armamts. & War 7/6 *n.* 8° P. S. King & Son 08

American Conference on International Arbitration [procdgs. and addresses] $1·50 8° Baker, *N.Y.* 96

BALCH, T. International Courts of Arbitration 75 c. 8° Coates, *Phila.* 99

DARBY, Dr W. E. [ed.] International Tribunals 15/ *n.* 8° Dent [97] 04
A colln. of var. schemes propounded, and of instances since 1815.

JONES, Russell Lowell International Arbitration as Substitute for War 5/ *n.* c 8° Simpkin 08
Univ. of St Andrews Rector's Prize Essay. Pref. by Dr B. BOSANQUET.

SCHURZ, Carl Arbitrn. in Internatl. Disputes—*in* Amer. and Europe, *ut sup.* [a plea for it]

*Hague Conferences* —*v.* **D** § 113

**War** —*v. also* **D** § 113, *s.v.* War

AMOS, Prf. Sheldon Political and Legal Remedies for War—*ut* **D** § 113

BETHUNE-BAKER, J. F. Influence of Christianity on War 5/ 8° Macmillan 89
[Burney Prize Essay]. Historical; from beginning of the Christian era onwards.

BLOCH, I. S. Is War now Impossible? [tr.]; ill. and maps 6/ c 8° Richards 00
Issued in 1899 *s.t. Mod. Weapons and Mod. War* (dated 1900). Auth. is a Russ. banker, and prepared his monumental wk. on mod. war in all aspects and details (6 vols. 4to, ea. of c. 1,000 pp.) in a cool scient. spirit of inquiry, logically marshallg. his facts and figs., and provg. beyond dispute th. a gt. Europ. war wd. mean natl. suicide for all Europ. peoples. This vol. = tr. of 6th (last) of orig. sums up conclusns. of prev. five vols. Pref. by W. T. STEAD.

,, Future of War: in its techn., econ., and polit. relns. [tr.] 60 c. 12° Ginn, *Boston* [99] 02

v. CLAUSEWITZ, Carl On War [tr.], 3 vols.—*ut* **I** § 15 [a philosophical analysis of war]

ERASMUS, Desiderius [1466–1536] Against War [tr.], ed. J. W. Mackail [Humanist's Lib.] $6 *n.* 8° Merrymount Pr., *Boston* 07

,, Treatise on War [tr.] [Humanist's Lib.] $6 *n.* 8° Merrymount Pr., *Boston* 08

FERRERO, Guglielmo Militarism [tr. (fr. Ital.)] [$3·50 Page, *Boston*] 12/ 8° Ward & Lock 02
A remarkable essay—a hist. study of militarism tendg. now tow. recognitn. of peace as a necessary condn. of progress. Prev. tr. by Helen ZIMMERN [*o.p.* (*pb.* 15/ *n.*) 8° Innes '99].

v. der GOLTZ, Bar. The Nation in Arms, tr. P. A. Ashworth 7/6 *n.* 8° Rees 03

GROTIUS, Hugo —*v.* **D** § 113

MAHAN, Cpt. A. T. Some Neglected Aspects of War; etc. [6/ *n.* Low] $1·50 *n.* c 8° Little & Brown, *Boston* 07
Repr. arts. fr. reviews. Incl. also *The Power that Makes for Peace* by H. S. PRITCHETT, and *The Capture of Private Property at Sea* by Julian S. CORBETT. *V.* also his *Retrospect and Prospect* [*sup.*] and General Index.

MAUDE, Col. F. N. War and the World's Life; map and diagrs. 12/6 *n.* 8° Smith & Elder 07
Marked by ardent militarism, exhibtg. the necessity, even desirability fr. certain aspects, of war for the well-being of a Nation, and for England the unique advantage of the Volunteer system as at present constituted. By a Volunteer officer.

PEARSON, Prf. Karl National Life from the Standpoint of Science 1/6 *n.* c 8° Black 01
A reprinted lecture, arguing from an evolutionary point-of-view in favour of war, etc.

RUSKIN, Jno. —*in his* Crown of Wild Olive, *ut* **K** § 89

WARAKER, Prf. T. Naval Warfare of the Future 5/ c 8° Sonnenschein 92
A consideration of the Declarn. of Paris, 1856; its obligation and its operation upon maritime belligerents.

WILKINSON, Prf. H. Spenser War and Policy [$3·50 Dodd & Mead, *N.Y.*] 15/ 8° Constable 00
A colln. of erudite and sound newsppr. arts., etc. (1885 to 1900) on milit. hist., biogr., strategy, defence of London, Boer War, *Trifig. w. Natl. Defence, Art of Going to War, Character of Mod. War, Evoln. not Revoln. in Mod. Warfare*, etc., w. unity of purpose running thro' whole, but much repetitn.

*Neutrality* —*v.* **D** § 113, *s.v.* Neutrality

*War and Commerce* —*v. also* **D** § 113

DANSON, J. T. Our Next War in its Commercial Aspects 7/6 c 8° E. Wilson 94
Its chief value consists in the account of war premiums paid at Lloyd's from 1805 to 1816.

,, Our Commerce in War, and How to Protect it 3/6 *n.* c 8° Blades 97
A proposal th. we should give notice that in future we will not in time of war seize private property at sea, nor allow it to be seized, relying on the generosity of other Powers to impose upon themselves a similar self-denying ordinance!

PHILLIPSON, Dr C. Effect of War on Contracts and Trading Assocns.—*ut* **D** § 113

*War and Finance*

HAMILTON-GRACE, Cpt R. S. Finance and War [historical and financial] 2/6 *n.* 8° Rees 10

*War and Food-Supply*

MARSTON, R. B. War, Famine, and our Food-Supply [urges storage of wheat] 2/6 c 8° Low 97

*War and Labour*

ANITCHKOW, M. War and Labour [$5 Longman, *N.Y.*] 18/ 8° Constable 00
$5 Longman, *N.Y.* An able plea for cessation of war and explanation of means to that end.

*War: its Effect on Property* —*v.* **D** § 113, *s.v.* War

*War and Representative Government*

ROSS, Maj. Chas. Representative Government and War 10/6 *n.* 8° Hutchinson 03

**Army Reform** —*for* Statistics, etc., **I** § 14

AMERY, L. S. Problem of British Army [repr. of l'rs. to 'Times'] 6/ *n.* c 8° Arnold 03
ARNOLD-FORSTER, H. O. War Office, Army, and Empire [reprs. fr. newspprs.] 1/6 c 8° Cassell 00
„ Army Letters [repr. of letters to 'Times'] 3/6 c 8° Arnold 98
DILKE, Sir Chas. W. Army Reform *o.p.* [*pb.* 2/6] c 8° Service 98
HALDANE, R. B. Army Reform and other Addresses 7/6 *n.* c 8° Unwin 07
MAXSE, Cpt Our Military Problem: for Civilian readers [repr. fr. 'Nat. Rev.'] 1/ *n.* c 8° Dent 96
ROBERTS, Earl A Nation in Arms [speeches on army-reform] 1/ *n.* c 8° Murray 07
ROPER-CALDBECK, Maj. W. The Nation and the Army 2/6 *n.* c 8° Richards 10
v. SOSNOSKY, Th. England's Danger: future of Brit. Army reform [tr.] 7/6 c 8° Chapman 01
With 12 statist. tables showg. strength and distribn. of army at home and abroad, and 4 maps. From pt.-of-view of a foreigner well conversant w. workgs. and strength of all Europ. armies.

*Conscription*

HAMILTON, Gen. Sir Ian Compulsory Service 2/6 *n.* c 8° Murray [10] 11
MAUDE, F. N. Voluntary versus Compulsory Service 5/ 8° Stanford 97
SHEE, G. F. The Briton's First Duty [case for conscription] 6/ c 8° Richards 01

**Navy** —*for* Influence of Sea Power *v.* **F** § 2; *for* Statistics *v.* **I** § 20

'BARFLEUR' [Vice-Adm. Sir Reg. CUSTANCE] Naval Policy: plea for the study of war 7/6 *n.* c 8° Blackwood 07
A sustained indictmt. of the policy of the Admiralty and its immed. predecessor. In spite of its frequent carping and crit. of comparatively trivial points, full of valuable comment and suggestion.
HURD, A. S. The British Fleet: is it sufficient and efficient 1/ c 8° Blackwood 01
„ Naval Efficiency: war-readiness of the fleet 7/6 c 8° Blackwood 02
STEEVENS, G. W. Naval Policy: w. acc. of Engl. and foreign war-ships 6/ 8° Methuen 96
WILKINSON, Prf. H. Spenser Command of the Sea; *and* Brain of the Navy 2/6 c 8° Constable [94; 95] 00
$1·25 Dodd & Mead, *N.Y.* Former expounds meang. of strateg. expressn. 'Command of the Sea.' and its bearg. on naval policy of Engl.; latter is an appeal for reform of Admiralty, w. suggestns. for a 'Forethought Dept.' and plan for its admin.

**Imperial Defence**

ARNOLD-FORSTER, H. O. Military Needs and Military Policy 3/6 *n.* c 8° Smith & Elder 09
CARNARVON, 4th Earl of The Defence of the Empire; map 5/ c 8° Murray 97
A seln. fr. his letters and speeches, ed. Lt.-Col. Sir G. S. CLARKE.
CLARKE, Sir Geo. S. Imperial Defence [Imperial Lib.] *o.p.* [*pb.* 7/6] 8° Imperial Press 97
COLOMB, Adm. P. H. Essays on Naval Defence; plans 6/ c 8° W. H. Allen [ ] 96
CORNFORD, L. C. The Defenceless Islands 2/6 *n.* c 8° Richards 06
Study of soc. and industr. condn. of G.B. and I., and of effect on them of outbreak of a maritime war.
DILKE, Sir Chas. W. Present Positn. of Europ. Politics: Europe in 1887 12/ 8° Chapman 87
„ The British Army [repr. fr. Fortn. Rev.] 12/ 8° Chapman 88
Its present state, compared w. other armies of the Continent; National Defence, etc.
„ + WILKINSON (Spenser) Imperial Defence 2/6 c 8° Constable [92] 97
$1·25 New Amsterd. Bk. Co., *N.Y.* A clear treatise on higher policy of defence, refuting views of the 'peace at any price.'
FOX, Fk. Ramparts of Empire 5/ *n.* c 8° Black 10
An excellent popular bk. on navy of to-day, and eloquent argumt. for syst. of naval defence.
HAMLEY, Sir E. H. National Defence [articles and speeches] 6/ 8° Blackwood 89
KNYVETT, Sir H. Defence of the Realme [Tudor & Stuart Lib.] 5/ *n.* ($1·75) c 8° Clar. Press [1596] 06
Here first printed fr. MS. in the Chetham Lib., Mancs.; w. Introd. by Chas. HUGHES.
MAURICE, Maj.-Gen. Sir J. F. National Defences [Engl. Citizen Ser.] 2/6 ($1) c 8° Macmillan 97
MAURICE, [Sir] Fred. The Balance of Military Power in Europe [repr. fr. *Blackwood's Mag.*] 6/ c 8° Blackwood 88
An exam. of war-resources of Gt. Brit. and Continental States: in part reply to DILKE, *sup.*
MAY, Lt.-Col. E. S. Principles and Problems of Imperial Defence 7/6 *n.* 8° Sonnenschein 03
MURRAY, Col. A. M. Imperial Outposts fr. Strateg. and Commerc. Aspect; ill. 12/ 8° Murray 07
Acc. of jy. to Japan *via* Gib., Suez, Colombo, Singap., Hong-Kong, Shang.; w. spec. ref. to the Jap. Alliance.
ROBERTS, Earl Speeches and Letters on Imperial Defence 1/ *n.* f 8° Simpkin 09
ROSS, Maj. Chas. The Problem of National Defence 12/ *n.* 8° Hutchinson 07
SILBURN, P. A. B. The Colonies and Imperial Defence 6/ ($2) c 8° Longman 09
Wr. to teach Impl. responsibilty, and to arouse Home and Colonial publics to more complete defence.
'Times,' Milit. Correspt. to [Col. REPINGTON] Imperial Strategy; maps 21/ *n.* 8° Murray 06
An important wk., partly repr. fr. *Times, Blackwood's Mag.*, etc. The subjs. most prominent are the Defence of India, and warlike action on pt. of Engld. to prevent mouths of Rhine, etc., in Low Countries fallg. into hands of Germy.
WILKINSON, Prf. H. Spenser Britain at Bay 6/ *n.* 8° Constable 09
A powerful presentmt. of dangers wh. beset Engl., and of insufficiency of her preparns. to meet them.
*Australia:* CRAIG (G. C.) The Federal Defence of Australia 5/ 8° Clowes 97

SCRATCHLEY (Sir P.) + KINLOCH-COOKE (C.) Australian Defences and New Guinea—*ut* **E** § 64

**War Forecasts**

COLOMB, Adm. P. H., etc. The Great War of 189–: a forecast; ill. 12/6 8° Heinemann 92
Papers by Adm. COLOMB, Gen. J. F. MAURICE, Col. F. N. MAUDE, Archib. FORBES, Chas. LOWE, D. Christie MURRAY and F. SCUDAMORE, repr. fr. *Black and White*, forecastg. course and issues of the gt. struggles wh. many believe will convulse the world in a not distant future. Milit. and naval operns.: Engld. almost always victorious. Of th. class of *The Battle of Dorking* and other Chauvinist publications, wh., by causing bad blood, do more harm than good.

EARDLEY-WILMOT, Cpt [R.N.] The Next Naval War 1/8° Stanford [94] 94
Acc. of imag. war betw. Engl. and Frce.: former (owing to unpreparedness) has to call in Triple Allce. to avoid cpl. disaster.

GRIFFITH, Geo. The World Peril of 1910 [introduces livg. people] 6/ c 8° White 10

LE QUEUX, Wm. The Great War in England in 1897; ill. 3/6 c 8° White [94] 97
A highly sensational descrn. of a war betw. Frce. and Russia agst. Engl. aided by Indian and Colon. troops and Frce. by Germy., in which England after getting terribly mauled, scores a tremendous and final victory off Dungeness.

'SEESTERN' Armageddon: 1907, tr. [fr. Germ.] G. M. Fox-Davies 6/ c 8° Paul 06

**Eastern Question (Far East, *and* Near East)**—*v. also* **E** §§ 29, 31, 33, 34, 37, 38; **F** § 60

*Bibliography*: BENGESCO, G. La Question d'Orient Lacomblez, *Brussels* 01

ARGYLL, Duke of Our Responsibilities for Turkey 3/6 c 8° Murray 96

BONSAL, Steph. [ed.] The Golden Horseshoe [the Pacific and China] ($1·50) c 8° Macmillan, *N.Y.* 00

BOULGER, D. C. Central Asian Questions—*ut* **E** § 33

BUXTON, C. Roden Turkey in Revolution 7/6 *n.* 8° Unwin 09

BUXTON, Noel Europe and the Turks 2/6 *n.* c 8° Murray 07

CHIROL, Valentine The Far Eastern Question [bas. on l'rs to 'Times'] 8/6 *n.* 8° Macmillan 96
Shows how war has laid bare the rottenness of China under a venerable cloak of an anc. civilizn., and disposes of her (theoret.) vast latent power.

,, The Middle Eastern Question [l'rs to 'Times'] 18/ *n.* r 8° Murray 03
Shows how Engl. policy has been to maintain a fictitious integrity and independence of Turkey, China, and Persia, under cover of wh. Russia has now substituted herself for these powers who have become her 'paid hall-porters'.

COATES, Lt.-Col. C. China and the Open Door 2/6 c 8° Taylor, *Bristol* 99

COLQUHOUN, A. R. Russia against India: the struggle for Asia 5/ ($1·50) c 8° Harper 00
On relative positns. of Russia and Engl. tow. India, China, and the East generally.

,, The Mastery of the Pacific; maps and ill. 18/ *n.* 8° Heinemann 02
Incl. some amt. of descrn. and hist., but chiefly valuable as a study of the polit. situation in 1902.

COTES, Everard Signs and Portraits in the Far East 7/6 *n.* 8° Methuen 07

COWEN, Jos. Speeches on Near Eastern Questn., etc. 2/6 *n.* 8° Reid, *Newcastle* 09

CURZON OF KEDLESTON, L'd Problems of Far East—*ut* **E** § 37

DOUGLAS, Sir R. K. Europe and the Far East 7/6 8° Camb. Press 05
$2 *n.* Putnam, *N.Y.* [Cambridge Historical Series.]

HAMILTON, Angus Problems of the Middle East 12/6 *n.* 8° Nash 09
'Young Turks', Persia, Bagdad Railway, Anglo-Russn. Conventn., Afghanistan, Hedjaz Ry., Korea.

HART, Sir Rob. 'These from the Land of Sinim' [Chinese questn.] 6/ 8° Chapman [02] 03

HOLCOMBE, Rev. Chester The Real Chinese Question $1·50 c 8° Dodd & Mead *N.Y.* 01
6/ Methuen. A distorted pro-Chinese statemt.: everything Chinese right, everything British wrong. Rabid on opium-question.

HOLLAND, Prf. T. E. The European Concert in Eastern Question—*ut* **D** § 113 [colln. of treaties, etc.]

KRAUSSE, Alexis The Far East: its history and its question 18/ 8° Richards 03
Hist. of opening of the Far East, w. study of its situation in 1900. Bibliography.

LEROY-BEAULIEU, Pierre The Awakening of the East [tr.] 6/ c 8° Heinemann 00
Siberia, Japan, China. An impartial, but not very profound, study of conditns., w. remarks on policy.

MAHAN, Cpt A. T. Problem of Asia & its Effect on Intern. Policies $2 8° Little & Brown, *Boston* 00
10/6 *n.* Low. Repr. arts. fr. *Harper's Mag.* and *N. Amer. Rev.* on the politics of Asia. Of no great value.

MARX, Karl The Eastern Question—*ut* **F** § 31

PALGRAVE, W. G. Essays on Eastern Questions *o.p.* [*pb.* 10/6] 8° Macmillan 72

POPOWSKI, Josef The Rival Powers in Central Asia *o.p.* [*pb.* 12/6] 8° Low 93

RAWLINSON, Maj.-Gen. Sir H. C. England and Russia in the East *o.p.* [*pb.* 12/] 8° Murray [75] 75

REINSCH, Prf. P. S. World Politics at End of Nineteenth Cent. $1·25 *n.* (5/ *n.*) c 8° Macmillan 00
[Citizen's Lib.] A study of the Chinese question in its international relations.

SOREL, Alb. The Eastern Question in the Eighteenth Century [tr.]—*ut* **F** § 55

STRATHEDEN AND CAMPBELL, L'd Speeches on the Eastern Question 12/ 8° Murray 94

TOWNSHEND, Meredith Asia and Europe 5/ *n.* c 8° Constable [01] 05

UPWARD, Allen The East End of Europe; ill. 12/ *n.* 8° Murray 08
Rept. of an unofficial mission to the European provinces of Turkey on eve of the revolution.

VAMBERY, A. Western Culture in Eastern Lands 12/ *n.* 8° Murray 06
A comparison of the methods adopted by England and Russia in the Middle East.

VILLARI, Luigi [ed.] The Balkan Question [by var. wrs.] 10/6 *n.* 8° Unwin 05

'WEALE, B. L. Putnam' [=B. L. SIMPSON] The Coming Struggle in Eastern Asia
12/6 ($3·50 *n.*) 8° Macmillan [08] 09

**International Law ; Treatises**—*v.* **D** § 113
**International Trade** —*v.* **D** § 149, **D** § 122

## 139 : POLITICAL INSTITUTIONS : DEMOCRACY ; FEDERAL GOVERNMENT

**Collectively :** *Administrative Government*

GOODNOW, Prf. F. J. Comparative Administrative Law, 2 vols. ea. $2·50 (12/6 *n.*) Studt's. Edn. $3 *n.* 8° Putnam 93
Pt. I: *Organization*; II: *Legal Relations*. The most important serious attempt to systematize the study of the subject wh. has yet appeared, analysing the admin. systems—national and local—of U.S., Engl., France, and Germany.

„ Politics and Administration—*ut* **D** § 146

SPENCER, Herb. Political Institutions [=Principles of Sociology, v. ii, Pt. 2]—*ut* **C** § 62

**Primitive** —*v.* **F** § 5 ; **Greece and Rome** *v.* **F** §§ 10, 12

**Monarchy ; Sovereignty ; Divine Right of Kings**

FIGGIS, J. N. Theory of Divine Rt. of Kgs. [Camb. Hist. Ess. ; $1·25 Putn., *N.Y.*] 4/6 c 8° Camb. Press 96

MERRIAM, C. E. *jun.* History of the Theory of Sovereignty since Rousseau [Columbia Univ. Studies] $1·50 *n.* 8° Macmillan, *N.Y.* 00

POLLOCK, Sir Fredk. —*in his* Introduction to the History of Politics, *ut* **D** § 134

**Federal Government** —*v. also* **D** § 145

AMES, H. V. [ed.] State Documts. on Federal Relations : the States and U.S. [Univ. of Penn. pubns.] $1·75 12° Longman 07

BASSETT, J. S. The Federalist System : 1789–1801 = Hart, A. B. [ed.] American Nation, vol. xi [*ut* **F** § 66]

FREEMAN, Prf. E. A. —*in his* Federal Govt. in Greece and Italy, ed. J. B. Bury 12/6 8° Macmillan [63] 93
A scholarly acc. of the efforts made to 'nationalize' the several States, and of the difficulties met with in the attempts.

HAMILTON, Alex. The Federalist—*ut* **D** § 145

HART, Prf. A. B. Introd. to Study of Federal Govt. [Harvard Hist. Monogrs.] $1 8° Ginn, *Boston* 91
Partly histor. acc., partly analysis of constits. of U.S., Switzerl., Germy., Canada (w. few wds. on S. and Cent. Amer.). Bibliogr.

**Democracy** —*v. also* **D** §§ 126, 134, 135

ADDAMS, Jane Democracy and Social Ethics [Citizen's Lib.] $1.25 *n.* (5/ *n.*) c 8° Macmillan 02
A study of the increasing social responsibilities of certain classes or groups of people under democratic government.

„ Newer Ideals of Peace $1·25 n. (5/ *n.*) c 8° Macmillan 07

ALLEN, W. H. Efficient Democracy ; ill. $2 *n.* c 8° Dodd & Mead, *N.Y.* 07

ARNOLD, Matt. —*article* Democracy, *in his* Mixed Essays, *ut* **K** § 83

BUTLER, N. M. True and False Democracy $1 *n.* (4/6 *n.*) c 8° Macmillan 07

CARPENTER, Edw. England's Ideal ; and other Papers—*ut* **D** § 126

„ Towards Democracy [$1 *n.* Small, *Boston*] 3/6 *n.* c 8° Sonnenschein [81] 05

CARNEGIE, Andr. Triumphant Democracy 1/6 c 8° Low [86]

COIT, Dr Stanton [ed.] Ethical Democracy ; essays in social dynamics 6/ c 8° Richards 00
Issued for Soc. of Ethical Propagandists. Essays on importance of ethical standards in commerce, educn., family-life, liter., etc.

DOLE, C. F. The Spirit of Democracy $2 *n.* c 8° Crowell, *N.Y.* 06

DYE, J. T. Ideals of Democracy 90 c. *n.* 12° Bobbs-Merrill, *Indianapolis* 09

FERGUSON, C. The Religion of Democracy $1 12° Funk & Wagnalls, *N.Y.* 00

GODKIN, E. L. Problems of Modern Democracy $2 c 8° Scribner, *N.Y.* 96
7/6 Constable. An admirable coll. of essays, repr. fr. *N. Amer. Rev.*, and other periodicals. Author has faith in princs. of democr., but is not blind to the faults wh. it develops. The 3 most suggestive papers are on cost of Socialism, Currency questn., and sorrows of Amer. millionaire.

„ Unforeseen Tendencies of Democracy [6/ *n.* Constable] $2 c 8° Houghton, *Boston* 98
A calm view of democracy, surveying evoln. of the boss, decline of legislature, increasg. diffics. of munic. govt., and describg. some of departures democr. has made fr. ways earlier promoters expected it to follow.

„ Reflections & Comments : 1865–95 [7/6 Constable] $2 c 8° Scribner, *N.Y.* 95

HADLEY, Prf. A. T. Relations between Freedom and Responsibility in the Evolution of Democratic Government [Yale Lectures] $1 *n.* c 8° Scribner, *N.Y.* 03

HARRISON, Fredc. —*in his* Order and Progress, *ut* **D** § 134

HARWOOD, G. The Coming Democracy 6/ c 8° Macmillan 82

HILL, Dr R. T. The Public Domain & Democracy [Col. Univ. Studs.] $2 *n.* 8° Macmillan, *N.Y.* 10

HIRSCH, M. Democracy versus Socialism $3·25 *n.* (10/ *n.*) r 8° Macmillan 01
Critical exam. of Socialism as remedy for social injustice—an exposn. of Single Tax doctr.

HOBHOUSE, L. T. Democracy and Reaction [$1·50 Putnam, *N.Y.*] 5/ c 8° Unwin 04
Arts. repr. mostly fr. *The Speaker*. Attaches much importce. to a supposed sudden and compl. change of polit. thought in 1903.

„ Liberalism [Home Univ. Lib.] 1/ *n.* s 8° Williams 11

HOBSON, J. A. The Crisis of Liberalism : new issue of democracy 6/ *n.* 8° P. S. King & Son 09

„ New Issues of Democracy 6/ *n.* 8° P. S. King & Son 11

HOSMER, G. W. The People and Politics $3 8° Houghton, *Boston* 83
On the structure of States and the significance and relation of political forms.

HOWE, F. C. Privilege and Democracy [7/6 *n.* Unwin] 10
Presents certain vital problems wh. the democracy of future will, in author's opinion, have to solve. By a follower of Hy. GEORGE.

HUGHES, C. E. Conditions of Progress in Democratic Government—*ut* **D** § 135

HYSLOP, Prf. J. H. Democracy: a study of government [an indictmt.] $1·50 c 8° Scribner, *N.Y.* 99

INGERSOLL, Chas. J. Fears for Democracy [fr. Amer. pt.-of-view] $1·25 8° *Philadelphia* [75] 86

JORDAN, D. S. Imperial Democracy $1·50 c 8° Appleton, *N.Y.* 99
On the rel. of govt. by the people to the demands of a vigorous foreign policy.

LEBON, Gust. The Crowd [tr.]—*ut* **D** § 125

LECKY, W. E. H. Democracy and Liberty, 2 vols. 36/ ($5) 8°; 1 v. 10/ *n.* c 8° Longman [96] 99
Not an indictmt. of democr., but unsparing crit. of its shortcomgs. and frank proclamatn. of disillusns. of its apostles. Conts. a mass of informn. formg. a veritable encyclopaedia, on the polit. probls. of recent times: *Nationalities, Socialism, Trades Unions and other Labour Questions Relig. Liberty, Irish Land, Women Suffrage, Sunday-keeping, Gambling, Drink, Marriage and Divorce*, etc. In 1899 edn. large pt. of *Introd.* is occup. by brilliant sketch of W. E. GLADSTONE (sep. pubd. 2/).

LEROY-BEAULIEU, Paul Papacy, Socialism, and Democracy [tr.]—*ut* **D** § 119

LINTON, W. J. The English Repub., ed. K. Parkes; w. Introd. and notes 2/6 c 8° Sonnenschein [51]
$1 Scribner, *N.Y.* [Soc. Science Ser.] Selns. fr. the 4 pubd. vols. of *Engl. Repub.*, a periodical ed.—and mostly wr.—by LINTON [vol. i, Watson, *Lond.* 51; ii, *Leeds* '52–3; iii, Linton's priv. press, *Coniston* '54; iv (only Jan.-Apl. 15] *ib.* '55]. Comprises a fairly compl. exposn. of Republicanism.

LOWELL, A. L. Public Opinion and Popular Government [Am. Citizen Ser.] Longman, *N.Y. in prep.*

LOWELL, J. Russell Democracy 15 c. *n.* 12° Houghton, *Boston* [87] 98

„ Democracy; and other Essays 6/ c 8° Macmillan 87

McVEY, F. L. The Populist Movement 50 c. *n.* c 8° Macmillan 96

MAINE, Sir H. S. Popular Government [4 essays; repr. fr. 'Quart. Rev.'] 2/6 *n.* c 8° Murray [85] 09
*Prospects of Popular Government; Nature of Democracy; Age of Progress; Constitution of United States.*

MAZZINI, G. Life and Writings, 6 vols. ea. 4/6 c 8° Smith & Elder [69] 90–1
Vols. i, iii, and v, *Autobiographical and Political*; ii, iv, and vi, *Critical and Literary.*

„ Thoughts on Democracy; Duties of Man—*cont. in* Mazzini; a memoir, by E. A. V[enturi] 6*d.* 8° Alexander [75] 84

„ Essays [Camelot Series] 1/ 16° Walter Scott [87]
*Faith & Future; Lamennais; Byron & Goethe; On Carlyle's 'Fch. Revol.'; Europe: Cond. & Prospects; Renan; Minor Wks. of Dante*; etc.

„ Duties of Man; & other Essays [35 c. *n.* Dutton, *N.Y.*; Everym. Lib.] 1/ *n.* 12° Dent [62] 07

„ God and the People!, ed. [Bp.] W. Stubbs 3/6 c 8° [91] 96
Selns. fr. the writings of MAZZINI illustrating the religious creed of a democrat, arranged in 'creed form'. With bibliography.

MORLEY, Jno. Visc. —*in his* Miscellanies, ser. iv, *ut* **K** § 89

OSTROGORSKI, M. Democracy & Organization of Political Parties [tr.], 2 v. 25/ *n.* ($6 *n.*) 8° Macmillan 02
A full study of the party-system and its workings in Great Britain and U.S. With Introd. by Jas. BRYCE.

PAINE, Thos. [1737–1809] Writings, ed. Moncure D. Conway, 4 v. ea. $2·50 (12/6) 8° Putnam [*v.y.*] 93–6
Vol. i covers period of Amer. Revoln. [1763–89], ii consists mainly of *Rts. of Man* [1791–2], iii–iv of his relig. wrgs., some essays on Am. affairs, and his poems. For CONWAY'S *Life of Paine v.* **D** § 125.
The best previous edn. of the *Works* is WATSON'S, in 2 vols. f 8° 1881, wh. lacks at least 20 good essays.

„ Age of Reason, ed. M. D. Conway; w. Introd. & notes $1·25 (3/6) 8° Putnam [1793]
Repr. fr. vol. i of *Writings, sup.* Also w. biogr. Introd. by J. M. ROBERTSON, 6*d.*, Watts.

„ Rights of Man, ed. M. D. Conway; w. Introd. and notes $1 8°. Putnam [1790] 95
A reply to BURKE'S attack on the French Revolution. Repr. fr. vol. i of *Writings, sup.* Also ed. Hypatia B. BONNER, 6*d.*, Watts.

POST, Louis F. The Ethics of Democracy $2 *n.* 12° Moody Pb. Co., *N.Y.* 03

REED, Milton The Democratic Ideal 75 c. *n.* 12° Am. Unit. Ass., *Boston* 07

SANDERS, W. Political Reorganization of the People [Ethical Ser.] 1/6 *n.* c 8° Sonnenschein 02

SMYTHE, W. E. Constructive Democracy $1.50 *n.* (6/6 *n.*) c 8° Macmillan 05

STEPHEN, Can. Reg. Democracy and Character [Moorhouse Lects. (seven)] 5/ c 8° Williams 08

STICKNEY, A. Democratic Government; A True Republic ea. $1 12° Harper, *N.Y.* 79; 79

„ Organized Democracy $1 12° Houghton, *Boston* 06

STUBBS, [Bp] C. W. Christ and Democracy—*ut* **A** § 109

TENNEY, A. A. Social Democracy and Population—*ut* **D** § 121

TRIGGS, Oscar L. The Changing Order: study of democracy $1 12° Kerr, *Chicago* [05] 06

WALLAS, Graham Human Nature in Politics—*ut* **D** § 125

WEBB, Sid. & Beatr. Industrial Democracy—*ut* **D** § 120

WHITE, Arnold English Democracy: its promises and perils 3/6 c 8° Sonnenschein [94] 95
Suggestive, but rather discursive essays: regards the 'perils' as more obvious than the 'promises'.

WHITE, Wm. Allen The Old Order Changeth: view of Am. democr. $1·25 *n.* (5/ *n.*) c 8° Macmillan 10

WHITTAKER, Thos. The Liberal State: a speculation [philosophical] 2/6 *n.* c 8° Watts

WRIXON, Sir Hy. Jacob Shumate: or the People's March, 2 vols. 21/ *n.* 8° Macmillan 03

**History**: *Generally; Europe*

CAPEN, Nahum History of Democracy; or Political Progress $5 r 8° Am. Pb. Co., *Hartford* 75

FREEMAN, Prf. E. A. —*in his* Comparative Politics, *ut* **F** § 5

MANN, Hy. Ancient and Mediæval Republics $3 8° Barnes, *N.Y.* 79
A review of their institutions, and the causes of their decline and fall.

MAY, Sir T. Erskine Democracy in Europe : a history, 2 vols. *o.p.* [*pb.* 32/] 8° Longman 77

PRINGLE-PATTISON, Prf. A. Seth The Philosophical Radicals, and other Essays—*ut* **C** § 4

SEARS, Prc. E. H. Outline of Political Growth in Nineteenth Century $3 *n.* 8° Macmillan 00
An outline of the growth of democracy rather than of political growth : not an original work.

*England*

BORGEAUD, Dr C. Rise of Mod. Democr. in Old & New Engl. [tr.] 2/6 c 8° Sonnenschein [94]
$1 Scribner, *N.Y.* [Soc. Sci. Ser.] Excellent constit. studies on Puritan and Commonwealth period, and Connecticut, Mass. and Rhode Island. Introd. by C. H. FIRTH.

BRIGHT, Can. J. F. The Growth of Democracy [in England ; 1837–80] *o.p.* [*pb.* 6/] c 8° Rivington 82

CLAYTON, Jos. Leaders of the People ; ill. 12/6 *n.* 8° Secker 10
Studies in democratic history from the 12th century to the Chartist Movement.

GOOCH, G. P. Hist. of Engl. Democratic Ideas in 17th Cent. 5/ c 8° Camb. Press 98
$1·50 *n.* Putnam, *N.Y.* [Thirlwall Dissertn. ; Camb. Histor. Essays]. Study of democr. movemt. bound up w. the Puritan revoln.

ROSE, Dr J. Holland The Rise of Democracy [$1·25 Stone, *Chicago*] 2/6 c 8° Blackie 97
[Victorian Era. Series.] A moderate and accurate account of the rise of democratic power in England.

*Chartist Movement :* 1838–48 : CARLYLE (Thos.) Chartism [1839]—*in his* Essays, vol. v, *ut* **K** § 89

CHADWICK, W. H. [1829–1908] NEWBOULD (T. P.) Pages fr. a Life of Strife [recollns of Chadwick] 1/ *n.* c 8° Palmer 11

GAMMAGE, Dr R. G. History of the Chartist Movement ; ill. 15/ *n.* 8° Browne, *Newc.* 94
The fullest and most authentic acc. of the movemt., wr. fr. intimate knowl., tho' by no means a model histor. wk. The 'People's Charter' consisted of 6 points : (1) Manhood Suffrage, (2) Equal Electoral Districts, (3) Vote by Ballot, (4) Annual Parlts., (5) Abolitn. of Property-qualification for M.P.'s, (6) Payment of Members.

JEPHSON, Hy. —*in his* The Platform, vol. ii, *ut inf.*

Trials (State), Reports of, ed. Macdonnel + Wallis, vol. vi—*ut* **D** § 6 [FUSSELL, WILLIAMS, VERNON & E. JONES]

*Biography of Chartists* —*v. also* **D** § 125 (LOVETT, WATSON)

COOPER, Thos. [1805–92] Life of. By Himself *o.p.* [*pb.* 3/6] c 8° Hodder [72] 80

LINTON, W. J. [1812–98] Memories *o.p.* [*pb.* 10/6] 8° Laurence & Bullen 95

STEPHENS, J. R. [1805–79] Life of. By G. J. Holyoake *o.p.* [*pb.* 3/] c 8° Williams 81

VINCENT, H. [1813–78] H. Vincent : a biogr. sketch. By W. Dorling 2/ c 8° J. Clarke 79

*France*

ADAMS, Prf. C. K. Democracy and Monarchy in France $2·50 12° Holt, *N.Y.* 74
From the Revolution to the end of the Second Empire.

GUIZOT, F. P. G. Democracy in France [tr.] *o.p.* [*pb.* 3/6] c 8° Murray 49

*Switzerland* —*v.* **D** § 144, **F** § 59

*United States* —*v.* **D** § 145

BANCROFT, H. H. Popular Tribunals, 2 vols. = Hist. of Pacific States of N. Am., vols. 31–32—*ut* **E** § 56
On Vigilance Committees, and right of a community to take administration of justice into its own hands.

BRADFORD, Gamaliel The Lesson of Popular Government, 2 vols. $4 (15/ *n.*) c 8° Macmillan 99
Some acc. of the govt. of U.S., from wh. conclusions favourable, on the whole, to democracy, are drawn.

*BRYCE, J. The American Commonwealth, 3 vols.—*ut* **F** § 66

CHAPMAN, Jno. Jay Causes and Consequences $1·25 12° Moffat, *N.Y.* [98] 09
Engl. edn. *sub tit.* '*Government and Democracy, and Other Essays*', 3/6 Nutt. Essay on *Politics* conts. perhaps clearest and most convincing study of Amer. munic. corruption in existence. The other essays are occup. w. sketching a syst. of polit. and social philosophy.

" Practical Agitation—*ut* **D** § 147

CLEVELAND, F. A. Growth of Democracy in the United States $1·50 c 8° Quadrangle Press, *Chicago* 99

GIDDINGS, Prf. F. H. Democracy and Empire $2·50 (8/6 *n.*) 12° Macmillan, *N.Y.* 00
Occupied with the ethical foundations of democracy, and the development of the United States towards Imperialism.

GODKIN, E. L. Unforeseen Tendencies of Democracy—*ut sup.*

MOSES, Prf. Bernard Democracy and Social Growth in America $1 (4/) c 8° Putnam 99
Prophesies the development of democracy towards a highly centralized form of government.

de TOCQUEVILLE, Alexis Democracy in America, tr. Hy. Reeve, 2 v. $5 8° Century Co., *N.Y.* [35–40] 98
Revised by F. BOWEN, w. Introd. by Prf. D. C. GILMAN. Includes a bibliographical note. One of the few treatises on the philosophy of politics wh. have achieved the rank of a classic.

The same ; w. Introd. J. T. Morgan + J. J. Ingalls, 2 vols. ; ill. $3·50 8° Lamb Pb. Co., *N.Y.* [35–40] 08

*Australia*

BROWN, Prf. W. Jethro The New Democracy : a political study $2 (7/6) 8° Macmillan 99
Treats of the 'Hore' scheme in Tasmania, the Referendum, the Australian Commonwealth, and Democracy generally.

*Canada*

BOURINOT, J. G. Federal Government in Canada $1 8° Johns Hopk. Un. Pr., *Baltimore* 89

**The Platform :** *its history, position, and power*

JEPHSON, Hy. The Platform : its rise and progress, 2 vols. 21/ *n.* ($4) 8° Macmillan [92] 92
Vol. i. descs. the long struggle dur. rns. of GEO. iii and iv for rts. of publ. mtg. and free speech ; vol. ii traces progress of platform fr. 1st Reform Act down to Reform agitn. of 1884, conclg. w. exam. of positn. and power of platform as one of the gt. polit. institns. of the country in pres. day. It is amply ill. (perhaps over-fully) fr. contemp. speeches. Chartist movt. fully treated in vol. ii.

## 140 : CONSTITUTION OF GREAT BRITAIN AND IRELAND

**Constitution and Administration**—*for* elem. treatises *v. also* **D** § 135

AMOS, Prf. Sheldon — Primer of the English Constitution and Government 6/ c 8° Longman [73] 77

ANSON, Sir W. R. — —*his* Law and Custom of the Constitution [*ut* **D** § 27] : of special value here

BAGEHOT, Walt. — The English Constitution and other Essays 7/6 c 8° Paul [67] 03
$2 Appleton, *N.Y.* Also [Paternoster Lib.] 3/6 Paul. A keen, philos. expositn. of principles. The other Essays are : *Character of L'd Brougham, Character of Sir R. Peel.*

BOUTMY, Prof. Emile — The English Constitn. [tr.] ; w. Introd. Sir F. Pollock 6/ ($1·75) c 8° Macmillan 91
A good concise view of developmt. of our Constitn. on the social and econom. sides, fr. a Fch. pt.-of-view ; not a system. treatise, but rather a brilliant essay. Almost ignores Ang.-Sax. period, but lays great emphasis on social changes of 18th cent.

COURTNEY, Leon. H. — The Working Constitution of U.K. and its Outgrowths 7/6 *n.* 8° Dent 01
$2 *n.* Macmillan, *N.Y.* An excellent work, suitable as a textbook for the beginner, or as a book of reference.

„ — Working Constitn. of U.K. and its Outgrowths [Temple Primers] 1/ *n.* 12° Dent 05
40 c. *n.* Macmillan, *N.Y.* Abridgmt. of above by Geo. UNWIN. Pt. iii deals w. the Empire outside the U.K.

COX, Homersham — Institutions of the English Government *o.p.* [*pb.* 24/] 8° Sweet 63

DICEY, Prf. A. V. — Introduction to Study of Law of the Constitution—*ut* **D** § 27
An excellent introductory bk. on the Constitution ; w. analysis of the U.S. constitution.

DORMAN, Marcus — The Mind of the Nation 12/ *n.* 8° Paul 00
Mainly a description of the British constitution and a history of British politics.

FISCHEL, E. — The English Constitution [tr. fr. German] *o.p.* [*pb.* 14/] 8° Bosworth 63
Much less interesting than BAGEHOT's book, but a good companion to it. While B. discusses principles, F. describes forms.

de FONBLANQUE, A. — How we are Governed : crown, senate, bench [popular] 1/6 c 8° Warne [58] 89

FORTESQUE, Sir J. [d. *c.* 1480] Governance of England : difference between absolute and limited monarchy, ed. C. Plummer 12/6 ($3·25) 8° Clar. Press 85
A reprint of the earliest English Constitutional treatise, w. valuable Introd. (105 pp.) and notes (188 pp.). First pub. fr. the MS. in 1714. A thoroughly practical treatise, wh. greatly increases its present value.

FRAILL, H. D. — Central Government, ed. Sir H. Craik [Engl. Citizen] 3/6 c 8° Macmillan [81] 92

GOODNOW, Prf. F. J. — —*v.* **D** § 139

HEARN, Prf. W. E. [Austral.] Govmt. of Engl. : its struct. & developmt. *o.p.* [*pb.* 16/] 8° Longman [67] 87

HOGAN, Dr A. E. — Governmt. of U.K., its Colonies, and Dependencies 2/6 c 8° Clive 08

LOW, Sid. — The Governance of England 3/6 *n.* 8° Unwin [04] 06
Study of realities of Engl. govt., examg. how system works and comparg. facts w. conventional theories and legal fictions.

LOWELL, Prf. A. L. — The Government of England, 2 vols. $4 *n.* (17/ *n.*) 8° Macmillan 08
An impartial, detached, and very comprehensive acc. of how Engld. is ruled and rules herself—already a standard wk. Noteworthy for the author's mastery of its subj. and his capacity for polit. speculation. A sort of counterpt. to BRYCE's *American Commonwealth* [*ut* **D** § 145].

MACY, Prf. Jesse — The English Constitution $2 *n.* (8/6 *n.*) c 8° Macmillan [97] 03
A commentary on the nature and growth of the English constitn., intended primarily for Amer. readers.

MARRIOTT, J. A. R. — English Political Institutions 4/6 ($1·10) c 8° Clar. Press 10

MORAN, Prf. T. F. — Theory and Practice of the English Government $1·20 *n.* (5/ *n.*) c 8° Longman 03

SERGEANT, Lewis [ed.] — —*in his* Government Handbook 10/6 p 8° Unwin [88–] 91 *not cont.*
The forms and methods of Govt. in Gt. Brit., Colonies, and Foreign Countries. Pub. for 1888 and '89 at 6/, 1890 at 10/6.

SMITH, Sir T. [1513–77] — De Republica Anglorum [1583], ed. L. Alston 4/ *n.* c 8° Camb. Press 06
$1·25 *n.* Putnam, *N.Y.* 'A Discourse on the Commonwealth of England' [in English]. Pref. by Prf. F. W. MAITLAND.

TODD, Dr Alphæus — Parliamentary Govt. in England, ed. Spencer Walpole, 2 v. 15/ c 8° Low [67–9] 92
Provides a good insight into machinery of Engl. govt. in all its parts. By ex-Librn. of Canadian Parlt.

TRAIL, H. D. — Central Government [Engl. Citizen Ser.] 3/6 c 8° Macmillan 92

*Statistics :* Statesman's Year Book —*ut* **D** § 148

**Parliamentary Reform ; Reform Bills and Acts**

BAGEHOT, Walt. — Essays on Parliamentary Reform [Paternoster Lib.] 3/6 c 8° Paul [83] 91

BEACONSFIELD, Earl of — Speeches on Parliamentary Reform [1848–66] *o.p.* [*pb.* 12/] 8° Longman [67] 67

GREY, Earl — Parliamy. Govmt. w. reg. to Parly. Ref. [Ref. Bills '59 & '61] *o.p.* [*pb.* 9/] 8° Murray [62] 67

GROTE, Geo. — Essentials of Parliamy. Reform [1831]—*repr. in his* Minor Works [posth.], *ut* **K** § 89
A vigorous assertion of the broadest principles of popular representation.

HARRISON, Fredc. — —*in his* Order and Progress, 2 vols., *ut* **D** § 134

HEATON, W. — The Three Reforms of Parliament [1830–85] 5/ c 8° Unwin 85

MILL, Jno. Stuart — Thoughts on Parliamentary Reform—*in his* Dissertations, vol. iii, *ut* **C** § 49

MURDOCH, Jas. — Constitutional Reform in Great Britain and Ireland 7/6 c 8° Blackie 85
With an account of the three great measures of 1832, 1867, and 1884.

SPENCER, Herb. — Parliamentary Reform—*in his* Essays, vol. iii, *ut* **C** § 62

TORRENS, W. T. M. — Reform of Procedure in Parliament *o.p.* [*pb.* 5/] c 8° W. H. Allen [81] 81

*History of Reform Bills*

COX, Homersham — History of the Reform Bills of 1866–7 *o.p.* [*pb.* 7/6] 8° Longman 68
The best account, fr. the Liberal side, of the Reform under the Derby-Disraeli government, but strongly partisan.

JEPHSON, Hy. —*in his* The Platform, *ut* **D** § 139
MOLESWORTH, Rev. W. N. History of the Reform Bill [1832] *o.p.* [*pb.* 10/6] 8° Chapman [65] 66
**Constitutional Law**—*v.* **D** § 27 **Constitl. Hist., and Hist. of Parlt.**—*v.* **F** § 17

## 141 : POLITICAL HIST. OF GT. BRIT. ; HIST. OF PARLIAMENT—*v.* F § 17

## 142 : BRITISH POLITICS : RECENT AND CONTEMPORARY

*Vide also* **D** §§ 125–133 *passim, and* **F** § 27. *For* Political History *v.* **F** § 17*

ARNOLD, Mat. Culture and Anarchy 2/6 c 8° Smith & Elder [69]
$1·50 Macmillan, *N.Y.* An 'essay in political and social criticism'.
BOUTMY, Emile The English People [tr.]—*ut* **D** § 125
BRASSEY, L'd Papers & Addresses, vol. iv: Polit. & Miscell., 1861–94 5/ ($1·75) c 8° Longman 95
BRODRICK, Hon. G. C. Political Studies 14/ 8° Paul 79
BUXTON, Syd. Handbook to Political Questions of the Day 12/ *n.* 8° Murray [81] 03
An excellent presentation, in tabulated form, of the *pros* and *cons.* of many of the chief current political problems.
DUFF, [Sir] M. E. Grant Miscellanies, Political and Literary *o.p.* [*pb.* 10/6] 8° Macmillan 79
ESHER, Visc. To-day and To-morrow; and other Essays 7/6 *n.* 8° Murray 10
A seln. of essays and lects. wr. or deliv. dur. past 20 yrs., chfly. of Imperl. and national concern.
FAWCETT, Prf. Hy. Speeches on Some Current Political Questions *o.p.* [*pb.* 10/6] 8° Macmillan 73
*Indian Finance, Birmingham League, Nine Hrs.' Bill, Electn. Expenses, Women's Suffr., Household Suffr., Irish Univ. Educn.*, etc.
,, +[Mrs] M. G. Essays and Lectures on Political and Social Subjects—*ut* **D** § 114
GLADSTONE, W. E. Speeches and Public Addresses—*ut* **F** § 27
GREG, W. R. Political Problems of our Age and Country *o.p.* [*pb.* 10/6] 8° Trübner 70
,, Rocks Ahead; or, the Warnings of Cassandra *o.p.* [*pb.* 9/] 8° Trübner [74] 74
,, Miscellaneous Essays: 2 Series *o.p.* [*pb.* 7/6 ea.] 8° Trübner 81–4
Imperial Parliament Series: series of short books, ed. Syd. C. Buxton ea. 1/ c 8° Sonnenschein [85–8]
Deals with the rights and responsibilities of citizens as Reformers think they should be; contrib. to exclusively by Members of Parliament.
*Church Reform* GREY + FREMANTLE | *Leaseh. Enfranchisemt.* BROADHURST + REID | *London Govt.* [*ut* **D** § 120] J. F. B. FIRTH
*Disestablishmt.* [*ut* **A** § 112] Richard + C. WILLIAMS | *Local Govt.* [*ut* **D** § 124] W. RATHBONE + A. PELL + F. C. MONTAGUE | *Representation* [*ut* **D** § 135] L'd AVEBURY
*England and Russia* W. E. BAXTER | *Local Option* [*ut* **D** § 131] Dr DAWSON BURNS | *Woman Suffrage* [*ut* **D** § 132] Mrs A. DILKE + W. WOODALL
*Imper. Federatn.* [*ut* **D** § 136] MARQ. OF LORNE
KENT, C. B. Roylance Essays in Politics—*ut* **D** § 134
LOWELL, J. R. Political Essays [7/6 Macmillan] $1·50 12° Houghton, *Boston* 88
LUBBOCK, Sir Jno. [L'd AVEBURY] Addresses, Political and Educational 8/6 8° Macmillan 79
MACPHAIL, Andr. Essays in Politics—*ut* **D** § 136
MORLEY, Jno. [L'd] Miscellanies, etc.—*ut* **K** § 89
Pros and Cons: digest of ab. 300 questns., soc., polit., and relig. 1/ *n.*; cl. 1/6 *n.* c 8° Routledge [99] 10
A v. useful bk. for debaters. For Amer. counterpt. *v.* **D** § 147, *s.nn.* BROOKINGS + RINGWALT.
ROBERTSON, J. M. Introduction to English Politics 10/6 *n.* 8° Richards 00
A survey of polit. growth in anc. and mod. times, intended as an introd. to a projected ser. of studies of Engl. statesmen.
SALISBURY, [3rd] Marq. of Essays: Foreign Politics [$2 *n.* Dutton, *N.Y.*] 6/ *n.* c 8° Murray 05
SMITH, Prf. Goldwin Essays on Questions of Day, Polit. & Social 9/ ($2·25) c 8° Macmillan [94] 94
Magazine arts. by an 'Old Liberal': *Social and Industr. Revoln.; Utopian Visions; Disestablishment; Polit. Crisis in Engl.; The Empire; Woman Suffr.; Jewish Questn.; Irish Questn.; Prohibn. in Canada and U.S. Appendix on Oneida Co. and Amer. Socialism.*
WALPOLE, Sir Spencer Essays, Political and Biographical, ed. Fcs. Holland 10/6 *n.* 8° Unwin 08
WHATES, H. [ed.] The Politician's Handbook, vols. i–iv ea. 6/ r 8° Vacher 99–02 *not cont.*
A useful, well-ed., digest of the Blue-Bks. and other parly. papers and govt. documts. of the previous yr.

**Political Parties** —*for* History of Political Parties *v.* **F** § 17*
BELLOC (Hilaire) + CHISTERTON (Cecil) The Party System 3/6 *n.* c 8° Swift 11
A protest agst. the unreality of Party Politics, 'exposing' the sham fight kept up betw. the two Front Benches, and the ways in wh. they have captured the control of Parlt., and eliminated the Private Member.

*Liberal; Radical* —*v. also* **D** § 139, *s.v.* Democracy
SAMUEL, Herb. Liberalism: its principles and proposals 5/ c 8° Richards 02
SIX OXFORD MEN Essays in Liberalism 3/6 c 8° Cassell 97
A defence of Liberalism, pleadg. for the deductive meth. in politics as agst. hand-to-mouth opportunism. By H. BELLOC, F. W. HIRST, J. J. A. SIMON, J. S. PHILLIMORE, J. L. HAMMOND, J. P. MACDONELL. Home Rule and Natl. Defence probls. not treated!
WATSON, R. Spence National Liberal Federation [fr. commencemt. to 1906] 5/ c 8° Unwin 07
WHITTAKER, Thos. The Liberal State: a speculation 2/6 *n.* c 8° Watts 07

*Annuals*

Financial Reform Almanack and Year Book 1/ *n.* c 8° *Morning Leader* Off. *ann.*
Liberal Year-Book 1/ *n.* c 8° Lib. Pubn. Dept. 05 *sqq.*, *ann.*

Reformer's Year-Book: ed. C. D. Sharp 1/ n. c 8° *New Age* Press 06 *sqq., ann.*

*Unionist ; Conservative*

MALMESBURY, L'd [ed.] The New Order: studies in Unionist policy 12/6 n. 8° Griffiths 08

Colln. of 15 papers by var. wrs., of v. varying quality and no uniform standpt., yet in spirit consistent w. Unionist tradns.

**Education Question** —*v.* D § 157

**Fisheries Question**

DORAN, J. I. Our Fishery Rights in N. Atlantic [claims jt. ownersh. w. Eng.] $1 8° Allen, *Phila.* 88

HARVEY, Dr. M. —*his* Newfoundland as it is [*ut* E § 55] gives full informn. on Newfdld. fishery in 1894

HAYNES, T. H. International Fisheries Disputes; 4 maps 1/ 8° Cassell 91

ISHAM, Chas. The Fishery Question [hist. and anal. of issues; Questns. of Day] 75 c. 12° Putnam, *N.Y.* 87

de RICCI, J. H. The Fisheries Dispute and Annexation of Canada 6/ c 8° Low 88

SNOW, Freeman —*his* Cases on Internatl. Law [*ut* D § 113] gives acc. of Behr. Sea Arbitrn. 1893

*Times* Correspondent Behring Sea Arbitration: letters to the 'Times' [with the award] 2/6 c 8° Clowes 93

An authentic record of the Arbitration (Paris) proceedings, w. caustic comment on their leading incidents.

For the earlier writings, *v.* wks. of ADAMS (J., J. Q., and S.), FRANKLIN, GALLATIN, HAMILTON, JEFFERSON, MADISON, SEAWARD, WEBSTER, *ut* F §§ 73–4; and life of L'd SHELBURNE *ut* F § 25.

**House of Lords; Second Chambers** —*for* History of the House of Lords *v.* F § 17

CHARLEY, Sir Wm. Crusade agst. the House of Lords [vindicn.; C. of E. stdpt.] 7/6 c 8° Low 95

HOUFE, C. A. Question of the Houses [a vindicn., w. sugg. reform] 2/6 12° Constable 95

MCKECHNIE, Dr W. S. The Reform of the House of Lords 2/6 n. c 8° MacLehose, *Glasgow* 08

MACPHERSON, W. C. [Austral.] The Baronage and the Senate 16/ 8° Murray 93

Defence of Ho. of L'ds, in form of a prolonged polit. pamphlet, tracg. orig. and constitn. of existg. peerage, explg. true positn. and *raison d'être* of a Second Chamber, and contraveng. radical case agst. it; offering suggestns. for reform and expansion, chfly. fr. Colon. pt.-of-view.

MARRIOTT, J. A. R. Second Chambers: an inductive study 5/ n. ($1·75) 8° Clar. Press 10

A calm and judicious comparative study of whole questn. of a Second Chamber, makg. its appeal to history. Advocates correction, not destruction.

MORGAN, Prf. J. H. The House of Lords and the Constitution 1/ n. c 8° Methuen 10

MUIR, Ramsey Peers and Bureaucrats: two problems of English government 4/6 n. c 8° Constable 10

SHEBBEARE, Chas. J. —*in his* Greek Theory of State and the Nonconformist Conscience, *ut* D § 126

SPALDING, T. A. House of Lords: retrospect and forecast [controversial; Radical] *o.p.* [*pb.* 3/6] 8° Unwin [93] 94

STEAD, W. T. Peers or People? [anti-Ho. of L'ds] 2/6 n. c 8° Unwin 07

TEMPERLEY, H. W. V. Senates and Upper Chambers 4/6 n. c 8° Constable 10

A survey of Upper Chbrs. of Engl.-spkg. world and Continent; w. useful Appendices and notes. Bibliography.

WONTNER, Adrian The Lords: their history and powers 1/ n. 8° P. S. King & Son 10

Emphasizes difference. betw. legal rts. and constit. practice, showg. how this difference. bears on relns. of the Houses.

**Irish (Home-Rule) Question** —*for* Hist., etc., of Irel. since the Union, *v.* F § 45

*Home-Rule side*

BRYCE, Jas. Handbook of Home Rule [repr. articles] 1/ c 8° Paul

GLADSTONE, W. E. —*in his* Speeches and Public Addresses, *ut* F § 27

" Special Aspects of Ir. Questn.: reflectns. in and since 1886 [reprs.] 3/6 c 8° Murray 92

GWYNN, Steph. To-day and To-morrow in Ireland [repr. essays] 5/ n. c 8° Hodges, *Dublin* 03

MCCARTHY, J. H. The Case for Home Rule 5/ c 8° Chatto 87

MCCARTHY, M. F. J. Irish Land and Irish Liberty: a study of the new lords of the soil 7/6 n. 8° Robt. Scott 11

MACKNIGHT, Thos. —*in his* Ulster as it is, *ut* E § 20 [authr. adopted H. Rule w. Gladstone]

MACNEILL, J. G. Swift Titled Corruption: sordid orig. of some Irish peerages 3/6 c 8° Unwin 94

[Reformers' Bookshelf.] An 'argument' for the Repeal of the Union.

MULHOLLAND, J. S. The Predominant Partner: his rts. and duties 2/6 n. 8° Sealy, *Dublin* 09

A review of the past and present relations of England to Ireland.

O'BRIEN, R. B. Irish Wrongs and English Remedies 5/ c 8° Paul 87

" Irish Ideas [papers read before young Irishmen] 2/6 c 8° Longman 93

" Wm. An Olive Branch in Ireland and its History 10/ n. c 8° Macmillan 10

Tells the story of the author's latest attempt to settle the Irish question.

'PAT' Economics for Irishmen 1/ n. 8° Maunsel, *Dublin* 06

" The Sorrows of Ireland [repr. fr. 'Sat. Rev.'] 1/ n. 8° West Strand Pb. Co. 07

REDMOND, Jno. Home Rule Speeches: 1886–1910, ed. R. B. O'Brien 7/6 n. 8° Unwin 10

All the speeches bear on Home Rule, treating the subj. fr. every point-of-view.

ROBERTSON, J. M. The Saxon and the Celt *o.p.* [*pb.* 1/ n.] 8° University Press 97

RUSSELL, Sir Chas. [L'd RUSSELL OF KILLOWEN] New Views on Ireland: Irish land grievances and remedies 2/6 ($1) c 8° Macmillan 81

*Dublin Castle:* O'BRIEN (R. Barry) Dublin Castle and the Irish People 7/6 n. 8° Paul 09

Hist., admin., and character of Dublin Castle and the var. boards and depts. in connex. w. it. By a Home-Ruler.

*Unionist side*

ARGYLL, D'ke of Irish Nationalism: an appeal to history 3/6 c 8° Murray 93

Reply to the 'inflated fable', that Irel. was a happy and prosperous country until the brutal Engl. conq. her 7 cents. ago.

ARNOLD, Mat. Irish Essays; and Others 2/6 c 8° Smith & Elder [82] 91

*Incompatibles, An Unregarded Irish Grievance, Future of Liberalism, Ecce! convertimur ad gentes,* etc.

BADEN POWELL, Sir Geo. Saving of Ireland [industr., financ., polit.] 7/6 8° Blackwood 98

CHAMBERLAIN, Jos. Home Rule and the Irish Question [speeches 1881–5] 1/ c 8° Sonnenschein 87

" A New Unionist Policy 1/ c 8° Sonnenschein 88

" Speeches on Irish Question betw. 1887 and 1890 1/ c 8° Sonnenschein 91

DARYL, Philippe Ireland's Disease: notes and impressions [tr.] *o.p.* [*pb.* 3/6] c 8° Routledge 87

DICEY, Prf. A. V. England's Case against Home Rule 7/6 p 8° Murray [86] 87

" Letters on Unionist Delusions [repr. fr. 'The Spectator] 2/6 c 8° Macmillan 87

" A Leap in the Dark; or, Our New Constitution 3/6 c 8° Murray 93

Exam. and crit. of Home-Rule Bill, seekg. to show th. it 'conts. in reality a new constitn. for whole U.K.', and that this constitn. must injure both Engl. and Irel.

GRAVES, Chas. L. The Blarney Ballads; ill. G. R. Halkett 5/ f 4° Sonnenschein [88] 89

" The Red above the Green; ill. Linley Sambourne 5/ f 4° Sonnenschein 89

Two very clever collections of original political squibs in verse; from the Unionist side.

HURLBURT, H. W. Ireland under Coercion $1·75 c 8° Houghton, *Boston* 88

2/ Douglas, *Edin.* The diary of an American on an inspection-visit to Ireland.

INGRAM, Dr T. D. Hist. of Legislative Union betw. G. B. and Irel. [defence of Union] 10/6 8° Macmillan 87

" Two Chapters of Irish History 6/ c 8° Macmillan 89

Attack on Irish Parlt. of JAMES ii, and apology for violatn. of Treaty of Limerick [1691]. Both strongly Unionist.

IWAN-MÜLLER, E. B. Ireland To-day and To-morrow [repr. fr. 'Dy. Telegr.'] 3/6 n. c 8° Chapman 07

LLOYD, Clifford Ireland under the Land League: narrat. of person. exper.—*ut* F § 45

MORRIS, W. O'Connor Present Irish Questions 6/ c 8° Richards 01

From a Unionist (but anti-Dublin-Castle) point-of-view.

'PACIFICUS' Federalism and Home Rule [repr. letters to *The Times*] 2/6 n. c 8° Murray 10

POLLOCK, Sir Fredk. Home Rule and Imperial Sovereignty—*in his* Oxford Lectures and other Discourses, *ut* D § 1

Orig. pub. in a volume, entitled, *The Truth about Home Rule,* 1/ c 8° Blackwood '88.

SPALDING, T. A. Federation and Empire *o.p.* [*pb.* 10/6 n.] 8° Henry 96

An argument and scheme for the transformation of the government of Great Britain and Ireland into Federal form.

*Times (The)* The Parnellite Split [repr. fr. 'The Times'; w. Introd.] 3/6 8° Wright 91

Unknown Power behind the Nationalist Party 5/ n. c 8° Sonnenschein 07

*'Times' Parnell Commission* [1888–9]

DAVITT, Mich. Speech in Defence of the Land League [Home-Rule] 5/ c 8° Paul 89

DICEY, Prf. A. V. The Verdict; tract on its political significance [anti-Home-Rule] 2/6 8° Cassell 90

JAMES, Sir Hy. Work of the Irish Leagues [repr. fr. 'Times', replying on Parnell Comm. Inquiry] 6/ c 8° Cassell 90

LE CARON, Maj. Twenty-five Years in the Secret Service 2/6 8° Heinemann [92] 93

The recollns. of a spy, drawing v. unfavourable pictures of the Irish-Amer. leaders. Not an edifying bk. fr. any pt.-of-view.

RUSSELL, Sir Chas. [L'd RUSSELL OF KILLOWEN] Opening Speech delivered in Parnell Commission Inquiry 2/ (75 c.) 8° Macmillan [89] 89

The opening speech for the defence: one of the most elaborate forensic efforts of the 19th century.

*Times* Report of the Proceedings before the Special Commission, 4 vols. [incl. James, *sup.*] 50/ 4° *Times* Office 90

**Health Nationalization (Municipalization)**
ELLIS, Havelock — The Nationalization of Health — 3/6 c 8° Unwin 92
$1·25 Putnam, *N.Y.* A crit. of pres. condn. of hospitals, and plea for municipalizn. or nationalizn. of almost whole of care of health and sickness
WEBB, Sid. + Beatr. — The State and the Doctor — 6/ *n.* 8° Longman 10
A plea for the socialization of medical treatment by means of a vast gratuitous State service.

**Land Nationalization**
ARNOLD, Arth. — —*in his* Social Politics, *ut* **D** § 125
COX, Har. — Land Nationalization — [Social Questns. of To-day ; critical] 2/6 c 8° Methuen 92
GEORGE, Hy. — Progress and Poverty, etc.—*ut* **D** § 119
WALLACE, Dr A. R. — Land Nationalisation : its necessity and aims — [Soc. Sci. Ser.] 2/6 c 8° Sonnenschein [82]
$1. Scribner, *N.Y.* Compar. of syst. of landld. and tenant w. that of occupying ownership in their influence on well-being of people. Bibliogr. Cf. also his *Studies*, vol. ii, *ut* **H** § 43.

**Municipal Ownership and Trading** —*v.* **D** § 124

**National Insurance** —*v.* **D** § 151

**Railway Nationalization** —*for* U.S.A. *v.* **D** § 145 ; *for* Switzerl. *v.* **D** § 144 : *v. also* **D** § 152
ACKWORTH, W. M. — —*in his* Elements of Railway Economics—*ut* **D** § 152
„ — The State in rel. to Rys.—*in* Mackay [ed.] Policy of Free Exchange, *ut* **D** § 126
CUNNINGHAM, W. — Railway Nationalization — 2/6 *n.* 8° Author, *Dunfermline* [ ] 06
DAVIES, A. E. — The Nationalization of Railways — [pros and cons] 1/ *n.* c 8° Black 08
EDWARDS, Clement — Railway Nationalization — [Soc. Questns. of To-day] 2/6 *n.* c 8° Methuen [98] 07
Acc. of foreign and colonial experimts. in ry. nationalizn., w. discussn. of probls. involved in Britain.
HOLE, Jas. — National Railways — [argumt. for State purchase] 4/ *n.* c 8° Cassell 95
JEVONS, Prf. W. Stanley — Railways and State—*in his* Methods of Social Reform, *ut* **D** § 125
MEYER, Prf. H. R. — —*ut* **D** § 124 [adverse to public ownership]
PRATT, A. E. — Railways and Nationalisation — 2/6 *n.* c 8° P. S. King & Son 08
„ — State Railways : object lessns. fr. other lands — 1/ *n.* 8° P. S. King & Son 07
Tr. of 2 arts. by M. PESCHAUD ptg. out evils of Belg. State managemt. ; w. essay in support (Denm., It., Australasia).
WARING, Chas. — State Purchase of Railways — 5/ 8° Chapman 87

**Telegraph and Telephone Nationalization**—*v.* **D** § 124 (MEYER)

**Woman Suffrage**—*v.* **D** § 132

## 143 : CONSTITUTION AND POLITICS OF BRITISH COLONIES

For Constitutional History and Political History of British Colonies Collectively, *v.* **F** § 33

**Collectively** —*v. also* **D** § 136
BRYCE, Jas. — —*in his* Studies in History and Jurisprudence, *ut* **F** § 1
COURTNEY, L. H. — —*in his* Working Constitution of U.K. (both bks.), *ut* **D** § 140
CREASY, Sir Edw. — Imperial and Colonial Constitns. of English Empire *o.p.* [*pb.* 15/] 8° Longman 72
EGERTON, H. E. — Federations and Unions within the British Empire 8/6 *n.* ($2·90) 8° Clar. Press 11
GRESWELL, Rev. W. P. — Growth and Administration of the British Colonies : 1837–97—*ut* **F** § 33
JENKYNS, Sir H. — British Rule and Jurisdiction beyond the Seas—*ut* **D** § 113
KEITH, A. B. — Responsible Government in the Dominions—*ut* **D** § 136
MILLS, A. — Colonial Constitutions — *o.p.* [*pb.* 14/] 8° Murray [56] 91
TODD, Dr Alphæus — Parliamentary Government in British Colonies *o.p.* [*pb.* 21/] 8° Longman 80
TROTTER, W. F. — The Government of Greater Britain — 1/ *n.* 12° Dent 05
40 c. *n.* Macmillan, *N.Y.* The 3rd pt. COURTNEY's bk. in same series [*ut* **D** § 140] deals w. the subj. much better.

*Colonial Law*—*v.* **D** § 107 *Relation of Colonies to Gt. Britain*—*v.* **D** § 136

**America, North** —*for* Hist. of Brit. Colonies in America *v.* **F** § 67

**Australia ; New Zealand** —*v. also* **E** §§ 65–67
ALLIN, C. D. — The Early Federation Movement in Australia 8° Br. Whig Pb. Co., *Kingston, Canada* 07
BOWEN, Sir G. F. — —*in his* Thirty Years of Colonial Government, *ut* **E** § 65
BRYCE, Jas. — Constitn. of C'wealth of Australia—*in his* Studies in Hist. & Jurisprud., *ut* **F** § 1
GARRAN, R. R. — The Coming Commonwealth : hdbk. of federal govt. 7/6 8° Angus & Robertson, *Melb.* 97
An introd. to study of systs. of Fed. Govt. in all countries. Regards Federated Australia as ' a foregone conclusion '.
MOORE, Prf. W. H. — Constitution of Commonwealth of Australia — 30/ *n.* 8° Murray [02] 10
Gives documents in full, with tables of cases and statutes.
„ — The Commonwealth of Australia — 8° Robertson, *Melbourne* 97
Four lectures on the Australian Constitution Bill of 1897.
QUICK (Dr J.) + GARRAN (R. R.) Annotated Constitution of Austral. Commonwealth — 36/ *n.* r 8° Angus & Robertson, *Melb.* 01
A valuable analyt., histor., legal, and polit. commentary of the Constitution. 1,000 pp., first 250 an histor. Introdn. in 4 Pts. (1) *Anc. Colonies*, (2) *Mod. Cols.*, (3) *Col. Govt. in Austral.*, (4) *The Federal Movemt. in Austral.*
REEVES, W. P. — State Experiments in Australia and New Zealand, 2 vols.—*ut* **D** § 126
TEECE, R. C. — Comparison of Federal Constitns. of Canada and Australia—*ut inf.*

*New South Wales*
BUCHANAN, D. — Speeches deliv. in Parliament of N.S.W. and Elsewhere 7/6 s 8° 86
PARKES, Sir Hy. — Fifty Years in the Making of Australian History—*ut* **E** § 66

*South Australia* —*for* Constitutional History, *v.* **E** § 66
BLACKMORE [ed.] — Law of the Constitution of South Australia — 8° Govt. Press, *Adelaide* 94
A collection of Imperial statutes and local Acts relating to government of the colony.

*Victoria*
JENKS, Prf. Edw. — The Government of Victoria — 14/ ($4) 8° Macmillan 91
A lucid and exhaustive acc., followg. the gradation of authority fr. Govt. down to petty constable. Enlarged fr. Melb. Univ. lects.

**Canada :** *Constitution* —*v. also* **D** § 27 ; *for* Constitutional History *v.* **F** § 67

BOURINOT, Sir J. G. [Canad.] Federal Govt. in Canada [J. H. Univ. Studs.] $1 8° Johns Hopk. Pr., *Baltim.* 89

,, How Canada is Governed $1 c 8° Copp Clark, *Toronto* [95] 02
A lucid review of public institns. of Canada, executive, legisl., judicial, and munic., w. histor. outline of origin and developmt.

CARNARVON, Earl of Speeches on Canadian Affairs, ed, Sir R. Herbert 7/6 *n.* c 8° Murray 02

DOUGLAS, Jas. [Canad.] Canadian Independence, Annexation and Brit. Imperial Federn. 75 c. (3/6) c 8° Putnam 94
[Questions of the Day.] Opposed to the annexation of Canada by the United States.

DOUTRE, J. [Canad. ; ed.] Constitn. of Canada : Brit. N.-Am. Act. 1867 interpreted 30/ r 8° *Montreal* 87

HOLLAND, B. —*in his* Imperium et Libertas, *ut* **D** § 136

HOUSTON, Wm. [Canad. ; ed.] Documents illustrative of Canadian Constitution 8° Carswell, *Toronto* 91
By Librn. of Ontario Provincial Legislature. From the establishmt. of English rule (1713) to 1878. Notes and Appendix. Useful.

MUNRO, Prf. J. E. C. Constitn. of Canada [comprehensive ; $2·60 *n.* Putnam, *N.Y.*] 10/ 8° Camb. Pr. 89

TEECE, R. C. Comparison of Federal Constitns. of Canada and Australia 5/ r 8° W. E. Smith, *Sydney* 02

*Politics* —*for* Political History *v.* **F** § 67

BOURINOT, Sir J. G. [Canad.] Canadian Studies in Comparative Politics 8° Dawson, *Montreal* 91
An important bk. for the Imperial politician. *English Character of Canad. Institns.* ; *Comparison betw. Polit. Systs. of Canada and U.S.* ; *Federal Govt. in Switzerld. comp. w. that of Canada.* By Clerk to Canadian House of Commons.

MACPHAIL, Andr. Essays in Politics—*ut* **D** § 136

PARKIN, Dr G. R. The Great Dominion : studies of Canada 6/ ($1·75) c 8° Macmillan 95
An enlargemt. of a series of letters to *The Times*, the outcome of 2 visits (1892–3, 1894) : useful studies of the most significant condns. of Canad. life, of Canad. ' problems ', and the external relns. of the Colony.

SMITH, Prf. Goldwin Canada and the Canadian Question ; map 8/ *n.* ($2) 8° Macmillan 91
Author opines that, by opern. of polit. gravity (geogr., commerce, race, lang., instits., *etc.*), Canada must event. fall into U.S.

*Fisheries* —*v.* **D** § 142

**India** —*v.* **D** § 136 ; **E** § 35, *s.v.* Administration

**Nova Scotia**

HOWE, Jos. Speeches and Letters, ed. J. A. Chisholm 8° *Morning Chron.* Off., Halifax, *N.S. in prep.*
To incl. all the materl. of the 1858 edn., w. speeches and letters 1858–1873, the yr. of his death.

**South Africa :** *Constitution ; Politics*—*v. also* **E** §§ 49–50

BRAND, R. H. The Union of South Africa 6/ *n.* ($2) 8° Clar. Press 09
Gives a short sketch of the leading features of the S. African Constitution, w. hist. of the movemt. tow. union.

BROWNE, J. H. B. South Africa : glance at curr. condns. & politics 7/6 *n.* ($2·50) 8° Longman 05

BRYCE, Jas. Two S. Afr. Constitns. [Transv., Or. Fr. St.]—*in his* Studies in Hist. & Jurispr., *ut* **F** § 1

,, —*in his* Impressions of South Africa, *ut* **E** §§ 49–50

BUCHAN, J. African Colony : studies in the reconstruction 15/ *n.* r 8° Blackwood 03

BUTLER, Sir W. F. From Naboth's Vineyard 5/ *n.* c 8° Chapman 07
Impressions during a fourth visit undertaken for *The Tribune* (newspaper).

COLQUHOUN, A. R. Africander Land 16/ *n.* 8° Murray 06

FLETCHER-VANE, P. Pax Britannica in S. Africa ; ill. and plans 10/6 *n.* 8° Constable 05

FREEMANTLE, H. E. S. The New Nation 5/ *n.* c 8° Ouseley 09
An excellent bk. on the framing and the effect of the S. African Constitution.

Government of South Africa, 5 Pts. ea. 1/ 8° Central News Agency 08

HOBSON, J. A. The War in South Africa—*ut* **F** § 31

MACKENZIE, J. Austral Africa, 2 vols.—*ut* **E** § 50

METHUEN, A. M. S. Peace or War in South Africa 1/ c 8° Methuen 01

ROBERTSON, J. M. Wrecking the Empire 5/ 8° Richards 01

SCHREINER, Olive An English S. African's View of the Situation 1/ c 8° Hodder 99

*Coloured Labour* —*v.* **D** § 130

## 144 : CONSTITUTIONS AND POLITICS OF MODERN CONTINENTAL EUROPE

**Collectively**

ALSTON, Leon. Modern Constitutions in Outline 2/6 *n.* (90 c.) c 8° Longman 05

BORGEAUD, Dr C. Adoptn. & Amendmt. of Constitns. of Eur. & Amer. [tr.] $2 *n.* (8/6 *n.*) Macmillan 95
A useful bk., inclg. a pract. discussn. on Revisn. of Written Constitns. Obtd. *prix Rossi* of Paris Univ. '92.

DILKE, Sir Chas. W. Present Position of Eur. Politics [repr. fr. ' Fortn. Rev. '] 12/ 8° Chapman 87

DODD, W. F. [ed.] Modern Constitutions, 2 v. [20/ *n.* Camb. Pr.] $5 *n.* 8° Univ. Press, *Chicago* 09
Colln. of constitns. or fundamental laws of Argentina, Austral., Austria-Hung., Belg., Brazil, Canada, Chile, Denm., Frce., Germy., Italy, Jap., Mexico, N'lands, Norw., Portug., Russia, Spain, Swed., Switzerl., and U.S.—foreign texts in English. Introd., notes, bibliographies.

DUFF, [Sir] M. E. Grant Studies on European Politics *o.p.* [*pb.* 10/6] 8° *Edinburgh* 66
LOWELL, A. L. Governments and Parties in Continental Europe, 2 vols. $5 8° Houghton, *Boston* [96] 00
21/ Longman. First-hand descrns. of the governmental machinery (espec. admin. and legislative) of France, Germany, Switzerl., Austria-Hungary, Italy, showg. wherein these govts. differ fr. ea. other and fr. that of U.S. Appendix conts. Constitns. in orig. langs.
MAY, T. E. Democracy in Europe—*ut* **D** § 139
SIDGWICK, Prf. Hy. Development of European Polity—*ut* **F** § 15
WILSON, Dr Woodrow The State—*ut* **D** § 134

**Austria-Hungary**
COLDSTREAM, J. P. The Institutions of Austria 2/ f 8° Constable 95

**Belgium** —*for* Referendum *v.* **D** § 135
VINCENT, Dr J. M. [tr.] Constitn. of Belgium: tr. [Ser. of Constitns.] 50 c. 8° Am. Ac. of Pol. Sci., *Phila.*
,, Government in Belgium [Citizen's Lib.] $1·25 *n.* (5/ *n.*) c 8° Macmillan 00

**Finland**
MECHELIN, L. Finland and the Public Law [tr.] [conts. gd. view of constitn.] 2/6 c 8° Chapman 89

**France**
*BODLEY, J. E. C. —*in his* France, *ut* **F** § 50
Bk. ii: *The Constitn. and Chief Aim of the State*, bk. iv: *Political Parties*. See note in **F** § 50.
CURRIER, Prf. C. F. A. [tr.] Constit. and Organic Laws of France: 1875–89: tr. [Ser. of Constitns.] 50 c. 8° Am. Ac. of Pol. Sci., *Phila.* 93
GAULLIER, H. The Paternal State in France and Germany $1·25 (5/) c 8° Harper 98
LOCKWOOD, H. C. —*in his* Constitutional History of France, *ut* **F** § 47

**Germany** (incl. **Prussia**): *Constitution—v. also* **E** § 15
BERRY, R. M. Germany of the Germans; ill. 6/ c 8° P. S. King & Son
*Constitn., Prussia's Preponderance, Impl. Parlt., Army, Navy, Insurance, Unemployed, Women's Positn., The Press, etc.*
HOWARD, Dr B. E. The German Empire $2 *n.* (8/6 *n.*) c 8° Macmillan 06
Deals w. foundn. of the mod. Emp., and powers and functns. of the differ. elements wh. compose it (the Constitn.).
JAMES, E. J. [tr.] Federal Constitution of Germany: tr. 50 c. 12° Univ. of Penn., *Phila.* 90
NICOLSON, A. Sketch of Germ. Constitn. [& events in Germy. 1815–71] *o.p.* [*pb.* 5/] 8° Longman 75
ROBINSON, Dr J. Harvey The German Bundesrath [Univ. of Pa. Pbs.] 75 c. 8° Ginn, *Boston* 91
Study in compar. constit. law, based on the *Bundesrath*, the centre and core of existg. form of govt. in Germy. and an instructive example of institutional evoln.
,, tr.] Constitn. of Prussia: tr. [Ser. of Constitns.] 50 c. 8° Am. Ac. of Pol. Sci., *Phila.*
TURNER, S. E. Sketch of the Germanic Constitution $1·25 (5/) c 8° Putnam 88
From the Cimbri and Teutones (about 113 B.C.) to the abdication of FRANCIS II in A.D. 1806.
'VERITAS' The German Empire of To-day 6/ *n.* ($2·25) c 8° Longman 02
An admirable elementary bk. on the formation and development of modern Germany.

*Politics, etc.*
BARKER, J. Ellis Modern Germany 10/6 *n.* 8° Smith & Elder [07] 09
$3 *n.* Dutton, *N.Y.* Her polit. and econ. problems, foreign and domestic policy, ambitions, and causes of success. 583 pp.
DAWSON, W. H. Germany—*ut* **E** § 15
GAULLIEUR, H. The Paternal State in France and Germany—*ut sup.*
Pan-Germanic Doctrine: study of Germ. polit. aims and aspiratns. 10/6 8° Harper 04

**Italy**
LINDSAY (Prf. S. M.) + ROE (Prf. L. S.) [trs.] Constitn. of Italy: tr. [Ser. of Consns.] 50 c. 8° Am. Ac. of Pol. Sci., *Phila.* 94

**Russia** —*for* Nihilism *v.* **D** § 126
KOVALEVSKY, Maxime Russian Political Institutions; maps $1·50 *n.* c 8° Univ. Press, *Chicago* 02
THOMPSON, Herb. M. Russian Politics; 5 maps [mainly a compiln.] 16/ 8° Unwin 95

**Spain**
CURRY, J. L. M. Constitutional Government in Spain [a sketch only] $1 16° Harper, *N.Y.* 89

**Switzerland** —*for* Constitutional and Polit. Hist. *v.* **F** § 59
ADAMS (Sir F. O.) + CUNNINGHAM (C. D.) The Swiss Confederation—*ut* **F** § 59
JAMES, E. J. [tr.] Federal Constitution of Switzerland: tr. 50 c. 12° Univ. of Penn., *Phila.* 91
LLOYD, H. D. The Swiss Democracy: study of a sovereign people 6/ *n.* c 8° Unwin 07
$1·50 *n.* Doubleday, *N.Y.* Rough notes on Switzerld., by an Amer., posthum. expanded into a bk. by J. A. HOBSON, who writes: 'Happy Switzerland! It has no coast, no navy, no colonies, no empire, no masses, no new wealth and very little old wealth, no trusts, and no departmental stores, no policy of territorial expansion'—wh. gives the pt.-of-view of the bk.
MOSES, Prf. B. Federal Govt. of Switzerl.: ess. on the constitn. $1·50 12° Pacific Press, *Oakland, Cal.* 89

RICHMAN, Irvin, B. Appenzell: pure democracy and pastoral life 5/ c 8° Longman 95
An excellent historical and descriptive account of institutions, history, social life, etc.

VINCENT, Dr J. M. State & Federal Govt. in Switz. [J. H. Univ. Sts.] $1·50 8° Johns Hopk. Pr., *Baltim.* 90
A clear and exhaustive statemt. of the facts, spec. interestg. on reln. of exec. to legislative, and on Referendum.

,, Government in Switzerland [Citizens' Lib.] $1·75 *n.* (5/ *n.*) c 8° Macmillan 00
An exhaustive expositn. of whole framewk. and admin. of the Swiss government.

WINCHESTER, Boyd The Swiss Republic $2 (10/6) 8° Lippincott, *Phila.* 91

*Railway Nationalization* —*for* Gt. Brit. *v.* **D** § 142; *for* U.S.A. *v.* **D** § 147

MICHELI, H. State Purch. of Rys. in Switzerl. [tr.] [Am. Ec. Ass.] 50 c. *n.* 8° Macmillan 98

VIETLER, Dr Hans Reguln. and Nationalizn. of the Swiss Railway 99
A historical acc. of the important political movemt. wh. nationalized the Swiss railways.

*Referendum* —*v.* **D** § 135

## 145: CONSTITUTION OF THE UNITED STATES

For Elementary treatises *v.* **D** § 135; *for* Constitutional History and Political History *v.* **F** § 69; *for* Constitutional Law *v.* **D** § 27

### Constitution and Administration

ALDEN, J. Science of Government [in conn. w. Am. institns.] $1·50 12° Sheldon, *N.Y.* 74

AMES, Dr H. V. [ed.] State Documents on Federal Relations $1·50 8° Univ. of Penn., *Phila.* 00

ANDREWS, Dr I. W. Manual of Constitution of U.S. [schl.-bk.] $1 12° Amer. Bk. Co. *N.Y.* [74] 00

ASHLEY, Roscoe L. The American Federal State $2 *n.* (8/6 *n.*) 8° Macmillan 02
An exhaustive handbook on American politics, intended for school and college use. Bibliographies.

,, American Government $1 *n.* (4/6 *n.*) c 8° Macmillan [03] 08

BANNATYNE, D. J. Hdbk. of Republican Institutions of U.S. [7/6 Blackwood] $3 8° Scribner, *N.Y.* 87

BEARD, Prf. C. A. [ed.] Readings in Amer. Government and Politics $1·90 *n.* (9/ *n.*) c 8° Macmillan 09
Pt. i deals w. Histor. Foundns.; ii w. Feder. Govt. in its var. aspects; iii w. State Govt.

BONDY, Wm. Separation of Governmental Powers in History, Theory, and in the Constitution [Columbia Coll. Studs.] $1 8° Columbia Coll., *N.Y.* 96
An exhaustive discussn. of the rel. existing betw. exec., legisl., and judicial powers in Am. constitn. The questn. of checks and balances is exam. both as an abstract questn. of polit. science and in its actual opern.

BROOKS, Noah How the Republic is Governed 75 c. *n.* 16° Scribner, *N.Y.* 95
A simple, compact, and brief descrn. of U.S. govt., w. appendix of Declaration of Independence and Constitution.

*BRYCE, Prf. Jas. The American Commonwealth, 2 vols. 21/ *n.* ($4 *n.*) c 8° Macmillan [88] 11
By far the best general descrn. (and criticism) of the several Federal authorities, the President, Congress and Cts.-of-law, and the constitn. and wkg. of the State govts., paying much attention to munic., industr., and social probls. Abgd. edn. [for Amer. schls.] $1·75 *n.* Macm., *N.Y.* [96] 06. The 1911 edn. is completely revised and 4 new chapters are added.

,, Constitn. of U.S. as seen in the Past—*in his* Studies, *ut* **F** § 1
Has special reference to the forecasts of HAMILTON and DE TOCQUEVILLE.

BULLITT, W. G. Review of Constitution of United States $2 8° Clarke, *Cincinnati* 99

BURGESS, Prf. J. W. Political Science and Comparative Constitutional Law—*ut* **D** § 134

CLARK, F. H. Outlines of Civics 75 c. *n.* 8° Macmillan, *N.Y.* 99
A Supplement to the abridged edition of Bryce's *American Commonwealth* [*sup.*].

COCKER, W. J. The Govt. of U.S. [elem., clear, concise] 75 c. 16° Harper, *N.Y.* 89

COHN, M. M. Introduction to the Study of the Constitution $1·50 8° Johns Hopk. Univ. Pr., *Baltimore* 92

COXE, Brinton Essay on Judicial Power and Unconstitutional Legislation $3 8° Kay, *Phila.* 94
An elabor. exam., histor., and juridical, of an important and characteristic provision of Amer. constitn. A valuable treatise.

FAIRLIE, J. A. National Administration of the U.S. $2 *n.* (10/6 *n.*) 8° Macmillan 05

FISKE, Prf. Jno. Civil Government in U.S. w. ref. to its Origins $1 *n.* 12° Houghton, *Boston* [90] 04
6/6 Macmillan. A concise manl., historical in method; for school-use. *Articles of Federn.*, *Constitn. of U.S.*, and *Magna Carta*, in App.

FLANDERS, Hy. Exposition of the Constitution of United States $1·75 12° Johnson, *Phila.* [73] 86

FORD, P. L. ed.] Essays on Constitution of United States $5 8° Histor. Prtg. Club, *Brooklyn, N.Y.* 92
Reprints of a colln. of essays orig. published betw. 1787 and 1788 dur. discussion of the Constitn. by the people.

FOSTER, Roger Commentaries, Historical and Juridical, on U.S. Constitn., vol. i $4·50 8° Boston Bk. Co., *Boston* 96

GAUSS, H. C. American Govt.: organizn. and officials $5 8° Hamersly, *N.Y.* 08

HAMILTON (J.) + HAY (J.) + MADISON (J.) The Federalist [1787], ed. H. Cabot Lodge [10/6 Unwin] $1·50 8° Putnam, *N.Y.* [88] 02

,, The same, ed. P. L. Ford; w. notes and App. $2·50 c 8° Holt, *N.Y.* 98

,, The same, ed. Prf. Goldwin Smith; w. Introd. $1·75 8° Lamb Pb. Co., *N.Y.* [ ] 08
A commentary on 1787 constitn. of U.S. in form of series of essays, 'written at the very birth of the Union by those who watched its cradle'. Vide Sir J. F. STEPHEN'S *The Federalist*, in *Horae Sabb.*, vol. ii [*ut* **K** § 83]

HARRISON, B. J. This Country of Ours [3/6 Nutt] $1·50 *n.* c 8° Scribner, *N.Y.* 97
An excellent account in small compass. Constitution printed in Appendix.

HART, Dr A. B. Practical Essays on American Government $1·50 (6/) c 8° Longman 93

,, Actual Govt. as appl. und. Amer. Condns.; maps [Am. Citizen Ser.] $2·25 c 8° Longman, *N.Y.* 03

HICKEY, W. [ed.] Constitution of United States, ed. A. Cumings $2·50 12° Murphy, *Baltimore* [7th ed. 54] 78

*Proceedings of the Continental Congress; Declaration of Independency*, etc., with alphab. analysis.

HOUGH, F. B. American Constitutions, 2 vols. ea. $7·50 8° Weed, *Albany, N.Y.* 72

The Constitution of each State, with articles of confederation.

HOXIE, C. De F. How the People Rule: civics f. boys and girls 40 c. *n.* c 8° Silver, *N.Y.* 03

JOHNSTON, Prf. Alex. History and Constitution of the United States—*ut* **F** § 69

LAMPHERE, G. N. The United States Governmt. [organization & working] $2·50 8° Lippincott, *Phila.* 80

LANDON, J. S. Constitutional History & Government in the U.S. $3 8° Houghton, *Boston* [89] 00

LINCOLN, C. Z. The Fundamentals of Amer. Govt. $3 8° Lawyers' Co-op. Pb. Co., *Rochester, N.Y.* 07

Incl. the gt. documts. on wh. institns. of Amer. are founded, and Statutes rel. to naturalizn. and expatriatn.

LOBINGER, Dr C. S. The People's Law: pop. participn. in law-mkg. $4 *n.* (17/ *n.*) 8° Macmillan 10

An investign. of hist. of the var. States of the Union, the developmt. of constitns. and of law-mkg. in light of pop. ratificatn. thereof, w. histor. chs. on same topic in other countries.

McKEE, T. H. [ed.] The Constitution of the United States Govt. Press, *Washington* 99

Includes text of Constitution, Jefferson's *Manual*, rules of the House of Representatives, etc.

MACY, Prf. Jesse Our Govt.: how it grew, what it does, how it does it 75 c. 12° Ginn, *Boston* [86]

A concise account, in form of a school-bk. Appendix of *Articles of Confedern.* and the Constitn. of U.S.

MAINE, Sir Hy. —*in his* Popular Government [*ut* **D** § 139]: *article* 4: Constitn. of U.S.

MOSES, Bern. Government of United States [20th-Cent. Textbks.] $1·05 *n.* Appleton 06

MULFORD, E. The Nation—*v.* **D** § 134

PASCHAL, G. W. Constitn. of U.S. Defined and Annotated $3 8° Morrison, *Washington* [2nd ed. 68] 76

POORE, B. P. [ed.] Fed. and State Constns., Colon. Charters, and Organic Laws, 2 v. $7 r 8° *Washington* [77] 78

SANFORD, A. H. Government in State and Nation $1 *n.* 12° Scribner, *N.Y.* 01

,, + JAMES (J. A.) Our Government 75 c. *n.* 12° Scribner, *N.Y.* 03

SCHOULER, Dr Jas. Constitutional Studies $1·50 8° Dodd & Mead, *N.Y.* 97

Ship of State (The) By Those at the Helm 75 c. c 8° Ginn, *Boston* 03

12 papers by T. ROOSEVELT, H. C. LODGE, T. B. REED, D. J. BREWER, J. D. LONG, and others. For older boys and girls.

SMITH, J. A. Spirit of Amer. Government [Citizens' Lib.] $1·25 (5/ *n.*) c 8° Macmillan 07

SPEER, Judge Emery Lectures on Constitution of United States 8° Burke Co., *Macon, Georgia* 98

By a Southern who is at the same time a strong supporter of Federal ideas.

STIMSON, Prf. F. J. American Constitution: the national powers, rts. of the States, liberties of the people [Lowell Lects. '07] $1·25 *n.* 12° Scribner, *N.Y.* 08

STORY, Jos. Commentaries on Constitn. of U.S., ed. M. M. Bigelow, 2 v. $12 8° Little & Brown, *Boston* [33] 91

With a prelim. review of the constitutional history of the Colonies and States before adoption of the constitution.

,, Familiar Exposition of Constitution of the United States 90 c. 12° Harper, *N.Y.* [74] 90

THOMPSON, D. G. Politics in a Democracy: an essay $1·25 (5/) c 8° Longman 93

Gives some account of methods of government in a democracy as exemplified by that of U.S. Optimistic.

TIEDEMAN, C. G. The Unwritten Constitution of the United States $1 (4/) 12° Putnam 90

Shows how Public Opinion has given all the importance of written law to certain rulings in U.S. govt., and these are presented and discussed.

de TOCQUEVILLE, Alexis Democracy in America [tr.]—*ut* **D** § 139

WILLOUGHBY, W. W. + W. F. Government and Administration of the U.S. 75 c. 8° Johns Hopkins Univ. Pr., *Baltimore* 91

WILSON, Dr Woodrow State and Federal Governments of U.S. 50 c. 12° Heath, *Boston* 90

,, Congressional Government $1·25 c 8° Houghton, *Boston* 96

WOODBURN, J. A. The American Republic and its Government $2 *n.* (9/ *n.*) 8° Putnam 03

An analysis, with an account of principles.

**Congress**

BAILEY, E. A. Among the Law Makers, ed. Edm. Alton $1·50 c 8° Scribner, *N.Y.* 86

Gives a good popular inside view of the workings of Congress; w. personal sketches.

MACCONACHIE, Dr L. G. Congressional Committees [Lib. of Economics] $1·75 12° Crowell, *N.Y.* 98

A study of one of the newer features of American constitutional development.

WILSON, Dr Woodrow Congressional Government $1·25 12° Houghton, *Boston* [92] 96

**Executive Departments**

ELMES, Webster The Executive Departments of U.S. at Washington $2 12° Morrison, *Washington* 79

The powers, functions, and duties of the Heads of Departments, Bureaus, and Divisions.

**Referendum** —*v.* **D** § 135

**Speaker of the House of Representatives**

FOLLETT, M. P. The Speaker of the House of Representatives $1·75 c 8° Longman 02

**Illinois**

GREENE, E. B. Government of Illinois [Hdbks. of Am. Govt.] 75 c. *n.* c 8° Macmillan, *N.Y.*

**Indiana**

RAWLES, W. A. Centralizg. Tendencies in Admin. of Indiana [Col. Un. St.] $2·50 *n.* 8° Macmillan, *N.Y.* 03

**Iowa**

BOWMAN, H. M. The Administration of Iowa [Col. Univ. Studs.] $1·50 *n.* 8° Macmillan, *N.Y.* 03

**Maine**

MACDONALD, W. Government of Maine [Hdbks. of Am. Govt.] 75 c. *n.* c 8° Macmillan, *N.Y.* 02

**Massachusetts**

CUSHING, H. A. Hist. of Transition fr. Provinc. to C'w. Govt. in Mass. [Col. Univ. Studies] $2 *n.* 8° Macmillan, *N.Y.* 96
WHITTEN, R. H. Public Administration in Massachusetts [Col. Univ. Studs.] $1 *n.* 8° Macmillan, *N.Y.* 98

**Minnesota**

MCVEY, F. L. Government of Minnesota [Hdbks. of Am. Govt.] 75 c. *n.* c 8° Macmillan, *N.Y.* 01

**New York State**

FAIRLIE, J. A. Centralizn. in Admin. in N.Y. State [Col. Un. Studs.] $1 *n.* 8° Macmillan, *N.Y.* 98
MOREY, W. C. Government of New York [Hdbks. of Am. Govt.] 75 c. *n.* c 8° Macmillan, *N.Y.* 02
SCISCO, L. D. Political Nativism in N.Y. State [Col. Un. Studs.] $2 *n.* 8° Macmillan, *N.Y.* 01

**Ohio**

ORTH, S. P. Centralizn. of Admin. in Ohio [Col. Un. Studs.] $1·50 *n.* 8° Macmillan, *N.Y.* 03
SIEBERT, W. H. Government of Ohio [Hdbks. of Am. Govt.] 75 c. *n.* c 8° Macmillan, *N.Y.*

**Pennsylvania**

SHEPARD, W. R. Hist. of Proprietary Govt. in Pennsylvania $4 *n.* 8° Macmillan, *N.Y.*

## 146 : POLITICS OF THE UNITED STATES : RECENT AND CONTEMPORARY

BAKER, Dr J. H. American Problems—*v.* **D** § 127

BROOKINGS (W. Du B.) + RINGWALT (R. C.) Briefs for Debate on Current Topics 6/ ($1·25) c 8° Longman 96
75 topics, polit., econ., and social, ea. w. suggestns. and bibliogr. refs. For Engl. counterpt. *v.* **D** § 142, *s. tit. Pros and Cons.*

BROWN (E.) + STRAUSS (A.) Dictionary of American Politics $1·25 8° Burt, *N.Y.* [88] 07

CHAPMAN, J. Jay Practical Agitation $1·25 12° Moffat, *N.Y.* [00] 09
3/6 Nutt. An attack on dishonesty of Amer. public life, w. suggestions towards a remedy.

CLEVELAND, Grover [ex-Pres.] Presidential Problems $1·50 (7/6 *n.*) 8° Putnam 04
*Indepce. of the Executive; Action of Govt. in Chicago Strike of* 1894 ; *The Bond Issues; Venezuela Boundary Controversy.*

COOLIDGE, A. C. The United States as a World Power $2 *n.* (8/6 *n.*) 8° Macmillan 08

DRAPER, Dr J. W. Thoughts on Future Civil Policy of America $2 12° Harper, *N.Y.* [65] 75

FISKE, Prf. Jno. American Political Ideas—*ut* **D** § 134

'FLYNT, Josiah' [J. F. WILLARD] The World of Graft $1·25 c 8° McClure, *N.Y.* 01

FORD, H. J. The Rise and Growth of American Politics $1·50 c 8° Macmillan 99
Less of a narrative than a careful examination and criticism.

FRANKLIN, F. People & Problems: addresses & editorials [6/ *n.* Bell] $1·50 *n.* c 8° Holt, *N.Y.* 08

GOODNOW, F. J. Politics and Administration: a study of govt. $1·50 *n.* (6/6 *n.*) c 8° Macmillan 00
An optimistic view of political corruption in the United States.

HOPKINS, C. T. Manual of American Ideals [good elem. bk.] $2·25 8° Bancroft, *San Francisco* 73

MONTGOMERY, H. E. Vital American Problems [Questions of Day] $1·50 *n.* (6/ *n.*) c 8° Putnam 08
Suggested solutions of the Trust, the Labour, and the Negro problems.

NORDHOFF, Chas. Politics for Young Americans [good elem. bk.] 75 c. 12° Harper, *N.Y.* [77] 99

ROOSEVELT, Theod. [ex-Pres.] Amer. Ideals; & other Essays, Social & Polit., 2 v. ea. $6 c 8° Putnam [98] 07
Chiefly occupied with American political life, but not with practical politics.

„ Addresses and Presidential Messages, 2 vols. (ea. 6/) c 8° Putnam [*v.y.*]

„ The Roosevelt Policy—*ut* **D** § 118

ROYCE, Prf. Josiah Race Questions, Provincialism, and other Amer. Problems $1·25 *n.* (5/ *n.*) c 8° Macmillan 08

SHAW, Alb. Polit. Problems of Amer. Developmt. [Col. Un. Lects.] $1·50 *n.* (7/6 *n.*) 8° Macmillan 07

SMITH, Prf. Goldwin —*in his* Essays on Questions of the Day, *ut* **D** § 142

TAFT, W. H. [Pres.] Political Issues and Outlooks [5/ Heinemann] c 8° 10

WOODBURN, J. A. Polit. Parties and Party Probls. in U.S. $2 *n.* (9/ *n.*) 8° Putnam 03

**Annexation**

RANDOLPH, C. F. The Law and Policy of Annexation $3 (9/ *n.*) 8° Longman 01
With spec. ref. to the Philippines and the status of Cuba. Opposed to principle of annexation.

**Atlas:** HEWES, (F. W.) Citizen's Atlas of American Politics [1789–1888] $2 f° Scribner, *N.Y.* 88
With col. maps, illustrating Presid. Elections, Foreign populn., Distribu. of manufactures, Distribn. of wool-produce.

**Foreign Policy & Relations; Monroe Doctrine**—*v. also* **D** § 136, **D** § 113, *s.v.* Monroe Doctrine

AMER. ACAD. OF POL. & SOC. SCIENCE: The Foreign Policy of U.S. $1 8° Am. Acad. of Pol. Sci., Phila. 99

'DIPLOMATIST, A' American Policy Foreign [5/ *n.* Constable] $1·25 *n.* c 8° Houghton, *Boston* 00

**Foster**, J. W. — A Century of American Diplomacy $3·50 8° Houghton, *Boston* 01
A review of the foreign relations of U S. 1777–1876. Ch. on Monroe Doctr. incls. the Venezuela dispute.

" — American Diplomacy in the Orient [suppl. to above] $3 *n.* 8° Houghton, *Boston* 03

" — Practice of Diplomacy as illustrated by Foreign Relns. of U.S. [12/6 *n.* Constable] $3 *n.* 8° Houghton *Boston* 07

**Griffis**, W. E. — America in the East: probls. of The Pacific $1·50 12° Barnes, *N.Y.* 99

**Hart**, Prf. A. B. — The Foundations of American Foreign Policy $1·50 *n.* (6/) c 8° Macmillan 01

**Henderson**, J. B., jun. — American Diplomatic Questions $3·50 *n.* (14/ *n.*) 8° Macmillan 01
*Fur Seals and Behr. Sea Award, Interoceanic Canal Problem, U.S. and Samoa, Monroe Doctr., N. Coast Fisheries.*

**Latanè**, Prf. J. H. — Diplom. Relations of U.S. & Spanish America $1·50 8° John Hopk. Univ., *Baltim.* 00
Deals with the Monroe Doctrine, the Panama question, etc.

**Mahan**, Adm. A. T. — The Interest of America in Internatl. Conditions $1·50 *n.* c 8° Little & Brown, *Bost.* 10
7/6 *n.* Low. *Orig. and Char. of Pres. Internat. Groupgs. in Eur.; Predomce. of Germy. in Eur., Relns. betw. East and West, The Open Door.*

**Woolsey**, Prf. T. S. — America's Forn. Policy [internat. law pt.-of-view] $1·25 c 8° Century Co., *N.Y.* 98

**Party Organization and Machinery**

**Macy**, Prf. Jesse — Party Organizn. and Machinery [Am. State Ser.; 6/ *n.* Unwin] c 8° 04

**Political Terms**

**Norton**, C. L. — Political Americanisms $1 (2/6) f 8° Longman 91
A glossary of terms current at different periods in American politics.

**Railway Nationalization** —*for* Gt. Britain *v.* **D** § 142; *for* Switzerl. *v.* **D** § 144

**Cowles**, J. L. — A General Freight and Passenger Post—*ut* **D** § 137 [scheme for Nationalizn.]

**Dixon**, F. H. — State Railway Control [w. hist. of devel. in Iowa] $1·75 c 8° Crowell, *N.Y.* 96

**Lewis**, G. H. — National Consolidation of the Railways of U.S. $1·50 12° Dodd & Mead, *N.Y.* 93

**Million**, J. W. — State Aid to Railways in Missouri [Econ. Studies] $1·75 *n.* 8° Univ. Press, *Chicago* 01

**v. Wagenen**, Judge A. — Government Ownership of Railways [pro] $1·50 (6/) c 8° Putnam 10

**Shipping Question**

**Bates**, W. W. — The Amer. Marine: shpg. questn. in hist. and politics $4 8° Houghton, *Boston* 93

## 147: CONSTITUTIONS OF MEXICO, AND OF SOUTH AMERICA

**Mexico**

**Moses**, Prf. Bern. [tr.] — Constitn. of U.S. of Mexico: tr. [Ser. of Constitns.] 35 c. 8° Am. Ac. of Pol. Sci., *Phila.* 93

**South America**

**Wallace**, Eliz. — Constitn. of Argentine Repub. and U.S. of Brazil 50 c. 8° Univ. Press, *Chicago* 9–

*Columbia*

**Moses**, Prf. Bern. [tr.] — Constitn. of Repub. of Columbia: tr. [Ser. of Constitns.] 50 c. 8° Am. Ac. of Pol. Sci., *Phila.* 93

# XIII: Commerce and Trade

## 148: DICTIONARIES; SERIES; STATISTICS; COMMERCIAL GEOGRAPHY

**Dictionaries**

**Beeton**, S. O. — Dictionary of Industries and Commerce; ill. [popular] 7/6 r 8° Ward & Lock 88

**de Colange**, L. — Dictionary of Commerce [tr.], 2 vols. ea. $6·75 r 8° Estes, *Boston* 80

**Homans**, I. S. + I. S., jun. — Cyclopædia of Commerce & Commercial Navigtn. $7·50 r 8° Harper, *N.Y.* 7–

**McCulloch**, J. R. — Dictionary of Commerce and Commercial Navigation, ed. H. G. Reid [pract., theoret., historical] *o.p.* [*pb.* 63/] m 8° Longman [32] 82

*Dictionaries, etc., of Commercial Terms*—*v.* **D** § 150

**Commercial Treaties**—*v.* **D** § 113. **History of Commerce**—*v.* **D** § 117*

**Series**

Books on Business ea. 2/6 *n.* c 8° Methuen *in prg.*

*Advertising* [*ut* **D** § 150] C. G. Moran
*Agriculture* [*ut* **I** § 25] A. G. L. Rogers
*Automobile Industry* [*ut* **I** § 12*] G. de Holden-Stone
*Brewing Industry* [*ut* **I** § 60] J. L. Baker
*Civil Engineering* [*ut* **I** § 3] T. C. Fidler
*Cotton Industry* [*ut* **D** § 117*] S. J. Chapman
*Electrical Industry* [*ut* **I** § 11] A. G. White
*Insurance* [*ut* **D** § 151] A. J. Wilson
*Iron Trade* [*ut* **I** § 81] J. S. Jeans
*Law in Business* [*ut* **D** § 63] H. A. Wilson
*Mining and Mining Investmts.* [*ut* **I** § 79] 'A. Moil'
*Money Market* [*ut* **D** § 115] F. Straker
*Monopolies, Trusts, etc.* [*ut* **D** § 120] F. W. Hirst
*Ports and Docks* [*ut* **D** § 149] D. Owen
*Railways* [*ut* **D** § 152] E. R. McDermott
*Shipbuilding* [*ut* **I** § 23] D. Pollock
*Stock Exchange* [*ut* **D** § 153] C. Duguid
*Trade Unions* [*ut* **D** § 120] G. Drage

Harper's [pubs.] International Commercial Series ea. 3/6 c 8° Harper 02

Cox (Har.), *United Kingdom and its Trade* [*ut inf.*] | Morris (J.), *Japan and its Trade* [*ut inf.*] | Pogson (G. A.), *Germany and her Trade* [*ut inf.*]

METHUEN'S [pub.] Commercial Series: ed. Dr H. De B. Gibbins c 8° Methuen *v.y.*

*Arithmetic: Short Commerc.* F. G. TAYLOR 1/6 | *Book-keeping, Princs. of* [*ut* D § 150] J. E. B. MCALLEN 2/ | *Brit. Commerce and Colonizn.* [*ut* D § 117*] GIBBINS 2/ | *Commercial Education* [*ut* D § 168] E. E. WHITFIELD 5/ | *Commerc. Geogr. of Br. Empire* [*ut inf.*] L. W. LYDE 2/ | *Comm. Geogr. of Foreign Nations* [*ut inf.*] F. C. BOON 2/ | *Economics of Commerce* [*ut* D § 149] GIBBINS 1/6 | *Entr. Guide to Profns. and Bus.* [*ut* D § 150] H. JONES 1/6 | *Examination Papers: Commercial* GIBBINS 1/6 | *French Commerc. Corresp.* [*ut* D § 150] S. E. BALLY 2/ | *French Commerc. Reader* [*ut* D § 150] BALLY 2/ | *German Commerc. Correspondence* BALLY 2/6 | *German Commerc. Reader* BALLY 2/ | *Law: Commercial* [*ut* D § 63] W. D. EDWARDS 2/ | *Precis Wrig. and-Off. Corresp.* [*ut* D § 150] WHITFIELD 2/ | *Primer of Business* [*ut* D § 150] S. JACKSON 1/6

**Statistics of Trade, etc.** —*for* General Statistics *v.* **K** § 2, **E** *passim*

*Bibliography* Royal Statistical Society's Library Catalogue, 2 vols. r 8° Statistical Soc. [59] 08

Bd. of Trade: Statist. Abstract for Foreign Countries, nos. 1–27 [Blue-Bks.] ea. *c.* 1/6 8° Wyman *in prg.*

BOURNE, Steph. Trade, Population, and Food [ser. of statist. papers] *o.p.* [*pb.* 12/] 8° Bell 81

BOWLEY, A. L. Elements of Statistics; diagrs. 10/6 *n.* 8° P. S. King & Son [01] 08
A good textbook, for the use of students, actuaries, bankers, etc.

,, Elementary Manual of Statistics 5/ *n.* c 8° P. S. King & Son 10

DANSON, J. T. Economic and Statistical Studies: 1840–90 2/ *n.* 4° Unwin 06
Ser. of statist. diagrs. and 2 pprs., (1) changes in condn. of people 1839 and 1847, (2) commerc. progr. of Colonies 1827–46.

ELDERTON, W. P. + Ethel M. Primer of Statistics [general statistics] 1/6 *n.* c 8° Black 09

FENN, Chas. On the Funds—*ut* **D** § 153

GIFFEN, Rob. —*in his* Essays; *and* Economic Enquiries, *ut* **D** § 117

JEVONS, H. Stanley The Sun's Heat and Trade Activity 2/ r 8° P. S. King & Son
A tentative attempt to show that periodic variatn. of sun's condn. really has some effect on activity of world's industry and commerce.

KOLB, G. T. The Condition of Nations [tr.] [social and polit. statistics] *o.p.* [*pb.* 42/] r 8° Bell 80

MACGREGOR, J. Commercial Statistics, including Treaties, 5 vols. *o.p.* [*pb.* 150/] r 8° Whittaker 44–50

*MAYO-SMITH, Prf. R. The Science of Statistics, 2 vols. *o.p.* [*pb.* 12/6 *n.* ea.] 8° Macmillan 95–9
i: *Statistics and Sociology* [population statcs.]; ii: *Statistics and Economics* [commerce, trade, finance, econ. social life generally]. An elab. wk.

MULHALL, M. G. Progress of World since beg. of 19th Century *o.p.* [*pb.* 12/6] 8° Stanford 80

,, Balance Sheet of the World: 1870–80 *o.p.* [*pb.* 6/] c 8° Stanford 81

* ,, Dictionary of Statistics 21/ *n.* r 8° Routledge [83]
$7 *n.* Dutton, *N.Y.* The standard dictionary; very comprehensive. Fourth edn. For Supplement [to 1910] *v.* WEBB, *inf.*

,, Industries and Wealth of Nations; 32 diagrs. 8/6 ($3) c 8° Longman 96
An excellent collection of facts and statistics relating to all the chief nations of the world.

Statesman's Year-Book: ed. J. Scott Keltie + I. P. A. Renwick 10/6 *n.* ($3) c 8° Macmillan 63 *sqq., ann.*
An invaluable 'Statistical and Historical Annual of the States of the World', indispensable to statesman, politician, publicist, and statistician.

WAKEFIELD, C. G. Future Trade in the Far East; maps, etc. 7/6 c 8° Whittaker 96
Chiefly statist. informn. conc. pres. trade of principal ports of Far East, incl. India. Introd. ch. on Trans-Siberian Ry.

WALKER, Prf. F. A. Discussions in Economics and Statistics, 2 vols.—*ut* **D** § 114

*WEBB, A. D. The New Dictionary of Statistics 21/ *n.* r 8° Routledge 11
Dutton, *N.Y.* A complement to MULHALL: Fourth Edn [*ut sup.*], bringing all the statistics down to date.

WEBSTER, R. G. Trade of the World [pres. systs. examined] *o.p.* [*pb.* 10/6] 8° W. H. Allen 80

WELTON, T. A. England's Recent Progress: investign. of statistics 10/6 *n.* 8° Chapman 11

WILSON, A. J. Resources of Mod. Countries, 2 v. [wealth, debts, resources] *o.p.* [*pb.* 24/] 8° Longman 78

*Principles and Method of Statistics*—*v.* **K** § 2

*Statistics of Insurance v.* **D** § 151, *of Land Distribn. v.* **D** § 119, *of Populn. v.* **D** § 121, *Vital Statcs. v.* **D** § 151
*For Statcs. of other special subjs. v.* General Index

**United Kingdom** —*v. also* **D** § 117*

Bd. of Trade: Statist. Abstract f. U.K. for last 15 Yrs., nos. 1–53 [Blue-Bk.] ea. *c.* 1/3 8° Wyman *in prg.*

BOWLEY, A. L. Statist. Studies rel. to Natl. Progress since 1882 2/ *n.* c 8° P. S. King & Son 04

British Trade Bk.: ed. J. H. Schooling, vol. iii [yrs. 1880–1905]; 221 tables 10/6 *n.* m 8° Murray 08 *bienn.*
Shows clearly and compendiously course of Brit. and internatl. commerce, w. bearg. on our internal trade and industries.

Business Prospects Year Book: vol. iv [forecasts of tr.-movemts.] 5/ 8° Bus. Statistics Pb. Co., 10 *ann.*

COX, Har. United Kingdom and its Trade [Intern. Comm. Ser.] 3/6 c 8° Harper 02
A good compiln. fr. statistics of trade and matters bearg. on trade, e.g. publ. income, expendre., debt.

DRAGE, Geoff. The Imperial Organization of Trade 10/6 *n.* 8° Smith & Elder 11

DYMES, T. J. Handbook of the Trade of United Kingdom 3/6 c 8° Stock 89

GASTRELL, W. S. H. Our Trade in World in rel. to Foreign Competitn.—*ut* **D** § 122

ROOT, J. W. Trade Relations of the British Empire 10/6 *n.* 8° J. W. Root, *L'pool* [03] 04

**British Colonies** —*v. also* **D** § 117*, *s.v.* 18th Cent. to Present Day, *and* **D** § 136

Bd. of Trade: Statist. Abstract for Colonial and other Possessns. of U.K., nos. 1–30 [Blue-Bk.] ea. *c.* 1/9 8° Wyman *in prg.*

Statist. Tables rel. to Colon. and other Possessns. of U.K., Pts. 1–26 [Blue-Bk.] *v. pp.* 8° Wyman *in prg.*

*Australasia*
MORGAN, B. H. Trade and Industry of Australasia; ill. 6/ *n.* 8° Eyre & Spottiswoode 09
A Report, by the spec. commissioner sent by the Manufacturers' Assocn. for Gt. Britain.
*Australia* —*v.* **E** § 65
*Canada* —*v. also* **E** § 55; *for* Fiscal Policy *v.* **D** § 122
BARRETT, R. J. Canada's Century: progress and resources; ill. 6/ *n.* 8° *Financier* Off. 07
BIGGAR, H. P. Early Trading Companies of New France—*ut* **D** § 117*
Canada Year Book 8° Parmelee, *Ottawa ann.*
FRASER, J. F. —*in his* Canada as it is, *ut* **E** § 55
GRANGE, H. The English Farmer in Canada 3/6 *n.* c 8° Blackie 04
Notes and observns. on Canada as a field f. Brit. capital and labour, by a pract. farmer.
HOBSON, J. A. —*in his* Canada To-day, **E** § 55
JEANS, J. S. Canada's Resources and Possibilities; ill. 15/ *n.* r 8° Brit. Iron Tr. Assoc. 05
With special reference to the iron and allied industries, and increase of trade with Mother-country.
PARKIN, G. R. —*in his* The Great Dominion: studies of Canada, *ut* **D** § 143
*South Africa*: JENKIN (T. N.) The General Trades of South Africa; ill. 10/ *n.* 8° P. S. King & Son 01
**United States** —*v. also* **D** § 117*
HATFIELD, H. R. [ed.] American Commerce and Finance—*ut* **D** § 117
NELSON, H. L. The United States and its Trade 50 c. (3/6) c 8° Harper 02
PATTON, J. H. National Resources of the United States $3 (15/) 8° Appleton [88] 94
World Almanac and Encyclopædia 25 c. c 8° Press Pub. Co. *ann.*
Very useful for recent statistics, election returns, etc., of U.S. Incl. other countries.
**Germany**: HOWARD (E. D.) Cause and Extent of the Recent Industrial Progress of Germany [4/6 *n.* Constable] $1 *n.* 8° Houghton, *Boston* 07
POGSON, G. A. Germany and its Trade [Intern. Comm. Ser.] 3/6 c 8° Harper [02] 03
**China** —*v. also* **D** § 117*, **E** § 34
JERNIGAN, T. R. China's Business Methods and Policy [12/ *n.* Unwin] 8° 04
,, China in Law and Commerce $2 *n.* (10/6 *n.*) 8° Macmillan 05
MORSE, Hosea B. Trade & Administration of Chinese Emp.; maps & ill. 7/6 *n.* ($2·50 *n.*) 8° Longman 08
,, The Gilds of China—*ut* **D** § 120
SARGENT, A. J. Anglo-Chin. Commerce & Diplomacy [chfly. 19 cent.] 12/6 *n.* ($4·15) 8° Clar. Press 07
**Japan** —*v. also* **D** § 117*, **E** § 37
BRINKLEY, F. —*in his* Japan and China, vol. vi, *ut* **E** § 37
COCKS, Rich. [17 cent.] Diary, ed. Maunde Thompson, 2 vols.—*ut* **E** § 37
MASUDA, Takashi Japan; its Commercial Development 2/6 *n.* c 8° Sisley 08
MORRIS, J. Japan and its Trade [Intern. Commerc. Ser.] 3/6 c 8° Harper 02
**Commercial Education** —*v.* **D** § 168
**Commercial Geography**
BOON, F. C. Commerc. Geogr. of Foreign Nations [Commerc. Ser.] 2/ c 8° Methuen 01
CHANTILLON Essai sur le Commerce $1·50 8° Ellis, *Boston* [1755] 93
An important wk., hitherto practically inaccessible. Repr. page for page fr. 1755 edn., for Harvard University.
*CHISHOLM, G. G. Handbook of Commercial Geography; 38 maps 15/ *n.* ($4·80) 8° Longman [89] 10
,, Smaller Commercial Geography 3/6 (90 c.) c 8° Longman [90] 05
GANNETT (H.) + GARRISON (C. L.) + HOUSTON (Dr E. J.) Commercial Geography; maps and ill. [6/ *n.* Philip; for commerc. schls.] $1·25 c 8° Am. Bk. Co., *N.Y.* 05
GONNER, Prf. E. C. K. Commerc. Geography [Elem. Commerc. Class-Bks.] 3/ (75 c. *n.*) gl 8° Macmillan 94
In 3 Pts. (1) *Commerc. Geogr. and its Princs.*, (2) *Geogr. of Chief Products and Others*, (3) *Agric., Industries, and Commerce of var. Countries.*
KELTIE, J. Scott Applied Geography: 11 col. maps and diags. 3/6 c 8° Philip 90
LYDE, Prf. L. W. Commercial Geography of Brit. Empire [Commerc. Ser.] 2/ c 8° Methuen [93]
,, Man and his Markets; ill. 2/ (50 c. *n.*) gl 8° Macmillan 96
,, Short Commercial Geography 3/ c 8° Black [03] 06
MILL, Dr H. R. Elementary Commerc. Geography [40 c. *n.* Putnam, *N.Y.*] 1/6 12° Camb. Press [88] 06
,, New Lands: resources & prospective advantages; 10 maps 5/ c 8° Griffin 00
REDWAY, J. W. Commercial Geography; ill. & maps (15 col.) $1·25 *n.* c 8° Scribner, *N.Y.* 03
SMITH, Rev. F. Brief Introduction to Commercial Geography 1/9 c 8° Blackie 03
TROTTER, S. Geography of Commerce; 85 maps & 16 pl. $1·10 *n.* (5/ *n.*) c 8° Macmillan 03
YEATS, Dr J. The Golden Gates of Trade; col. map 4/6 c 8° Philip 90
An introduction to the study of mercantile economy and the science of commerce.

ZEHDEN, C. Commercial Geography, tr. Findlay Muirhead [comprehensive] 5/ c 8° Blackie [89] 93

*Atlases; Maps*

BARTHOLOMEW, J. G. Atlas of Commercial Geography [to accomp. Mill, *supra*] Camb. Press 89
,, Atlas of the World's Commerce [176 maps and descr. text] 21/ *n.* f° Newnes 07
GIBBINS, H. de B. Atlas of Commercial Geography [48 maps, w. l'rpr.] 5/ 4° Johnston
JOHNSTON, W. & A. K. [pubs.] Commercial and Library Chart of World 63/ 6 by 4 ft. 8° Johnston
HASTINGS, E. J. Statist. Atlas of Commercial Geogr. [impts., expts., produce] 2/6 s 4° Johnston 87
L'ESTRANGE, P. H. Philip's Progressive Atlas of Commerc. Geogr. 3/6 *n.* 8° Philip
M. P. Atlas: maps showg. commerc. and polit. interests of Brit. Emp. over world 25/ *n.* f° Johnston 06
PHILIP & SON [pubs.] Commercial Atlas of the World 126/ f° Philip 10
SAVAGE, R. F. Atlas of Commercial Geography 5/ *n.* 4° Johnston 05
YEATS, Dr J. Map Studies of the Mercantile World 4/6 c 8° Philip 90
Six charts exhibiting the natural and manufactured products of Europe, Asia, Africa, Amer., Oceania, and Brit. Colonies.

*British Industrial Rivers*

Industrial Rivers of the United Kingdom. By various experts; ill. 7/6 8° Unwin 88

**Biography: Collectively** —*v. also* **I** § 2

ALLEN, Grant Biographies of Working Men [People's Library] 1/ c 8° S.P.C.K. 84
BOURNE, H. R. Fox Engl. Merchants: memrs. in ill. of progr. of Br. commerce 3/6 c 8° Chatto [66] 98
,, Famous London Merchants, 2/6; Romance of Trade 3/6 c 8° Cassell [61] 76; [71] 71
BRIDGE, J. H. Carnegie Millions and the Men who made them: inside hist. of Carnegie Steel Co. [21/ Limpus] $2 *n.* 8° Aldine Bk. Co., *N.Y.* 03
BRYANT, E. A. A New Self Help; ill. [successful men and women] 5/ *n.* 8° Cassell 08
BURNLEY, Jas. Fortunes made in Business, 3 v. [biogr. sketches] *o.p.* [*pb.* 48/] 8° Low 84–7
,, Summits of Success [business-men] 6/ 1 8° Richards 01
,, Millionaires and Kings of Enterprise; ill. 21/ *n.* 8° Roy. 03
Lives of American millionaires. Former $1·50 *n.*, latter $6 *n.* Lippincott, *Phila.*
CASSON, N. H. Romance of Steel: story of 1,000 millionaires—*ut* **D** § 117*
HALL, Thornton Roads to Riches: romance of money-making 3/6 *n.* c 8° Laurie 09
JEANS, W. S. Creators of the Age of Steel 7/6 8° Chapman 84
SIEMENS, BESSEMER, WHITWORTH, BROWN, etc.
JONES, Maj. Heroes of Industry: original biographies; 16 ports. 7/6 8° Low 89
MARDEN, Orison S. Pushing to the Front: success under difficulties $1·50 c 8° Crowell, *N.Y.* 99
5/ Gay & Hancock. Anecdotes and sayings of eminent and successful men and women. 24 ports.
PRATT, Edwin A. Notable Masters of Men; ports. 3/6 c 8° Melrose 01
Lives of BIRKBECK, Sir G. WILLIAMS, CARNEGIE, Jas. TYSEN, somewhat on the lines of SMILES' bks.
,, Successful Lives of Modern Times; ports. 3/6 c 8° Melrose 06
RITCHIE, J. E. Famous City Men [19th century] *o.p.* [*pb.* 10/6] 8° Tinsley 84
SCOVILLE Old Merchants of New York, 4 vols. $7 12° Miller, *N.Y.* [ ] 76
SMILES, Dr Sam. Industrial Biography [iron-workers & tool-makers] 3/6 c 8° Murray [63]
,, Life and Labour: characteristics of indust., culture, genius 3/6 c 8° Murray 87
,, Lives of the Engineers—*v.* **I** § 2
,, Men of Invention and Industry; ill. 3/6 c 8° Murray [84]
,, Character: a bk. of noble characteristics; ill. 3/6; 2/ *n.* c 8° Murray [71] 08
,, Duty; w. ill. of courage, patience, endurance; ill. 3/6; 2/ *n.* c 8° Murray [80] 08
,, Self-Help: illns. of conduct and perseverance; ill. 3/6; 2/ *n.* c 8° Murray [59] 08
,, Thrift: a bk. of domestic counsel; ill. 3/6; 2/ *n.* c 8° Murray [75] 08

*Shoemakers*

WINKS, W. E. Lives of Illustrious Shoemakers; 9 ports. 25 c. c 8° Funk & Wagnalls, *N.Y.* 83
7/6 Low. Includes Noah WORCESTER, J. G. WHITTIER, Rob. BLOOMFIELD, Jas. LACKINGTON, etc.

**Individually** —*v. also* **I** § 2

ALLEN, Wm. The Spitalfields Weaver. By J. Fayle; ill. 4/6 8° Hodder 85
BURN, Jas. [1802–82] The Beggar Boy: autobiogr. of Jas. Burn 7/6 c 8° Hodder 82
CARNEGIE, Andr. From Telegraph Boy to Millionaire. By B. Alderson; ill. 2/6 c 8° Pearson 02
DAVIES, W. H. Autobiography of a Super-Tramp—*ut* **D** § 127
DICK, Rob. [1811–66; baker & naturalist of Thurso] Life of. By S. Smiles; ill. 3/6 c 8° Murray [78] 97

DUNCAN, Jno. [1794–1881; Scotch weaver & botanist] Life of. By W. Jolly 9/ c 8° Paul [83] 83
EDWARD, Thos. [1814–86; shoemaker & naturalist of Banff] Life of. By S. Smiles; ill. 3/6 c 8° Murray [79] 97
GRESHAM, Sir Thos. [1519(?)–79]
Burgon, Dn. J. W. Life and Times of Sir T. Gresham, 2 vols.; ill. *o.p.* [*pb.* 30/] 8° Jennings 39
HARVEY, Jas. From Suffolk Lad to London Merchant. By Rev. A. J. Harvey 2/ c 8° Arrowsmith, *Bristol* 01
HILLOCKS, Rev. J. I. Hard Battles for Life and Usefulness; ill. 3/6 c 8° Houlston [84] 88
IRVINE, Alex. From the Bottom up 6/ *n.* c 8° Heinemann 10
MEEK, Geo. [Bath-Chairman]—*ut* **D** § 127
MERCER, Jno. [1791–1866; self-taught chemical philosr.] Life of. By E. A. Parnell 7/6 c 8° Longman 86
MILLS, Jno. Threads fr. the Life of; ed. Mrs Mills [wife] 6/ *n.* c 8° Sherratt, *Mancs.* 99
Life of a banker, author of *Vox Humana* [2/ *n.* Sherratt, *Mancs.*]; with his wife's early recollections.
MOORE, Geo. [1806–76; merchant and philanthropist] Life of. By Dr Samuel Smiles *o.p.* [*pb.* 6/] c 8° Routledge [78] 79
ROTHSCHILDS, The By Jno. Reeves; ports. 7/6 c 8° Low 87
The London, Paris, and Vienna branches of the family.
SKIPSEY, Jos. Joseph Skipsey. By R. Spence Watson 2/6 *n.* c 8° Unwin 09
STRATHCONA, L'd Story of his Life. By Beckles Willson [public life] 7/6 c 8° Methuen 02
TAYLOR, Peter Autobiography 3/6 c 8° Gardner, *Paisley* 03
Autobiography of a Scottish workman who rose to be a manufacturer.
'WORKING MAN (A)' Reminiscences of a Stonemason 6/ *n.* c 8° Murray 08
Recollns. of a factory-boy who emigr. to Amer., settg. forth past and pres. industr. probls.
YOUNGER, Jno. [1785–1860; shoemaker of St Boswell's] Autobiography *o.p.* [*pb.* 7/6] c 8° *Edinburgh* 81

## 149: ECONOMY OF TRADE; SHIPPING

**British** —*for* Depression in Trade *v.* **D** § 118
FARRER, Sir T. H. The State in its Relation to Trade—*ut* **D** § 122
GIBBINS, H. de B. Economics of Commerce [Commerc. Series; simple] 1/6 c 8° Methuen 94
LORIMER, G. H. Letters from a Self-made Mercht. to his son; ill. $1·50 c 8° Small, *Camb., Mass.* [03] 06
" Old Gorgon Graham: more letters; ill. $1·50 c 8° Small, *Camb., Mass.* 05
Former 3/6, latter 6/ Methuen. Exceedingly shrewd and facetious advice; typically American.
VEBLEN, Thornstein The Theory of Business Enterprise $1·50 *n.* c 8° Scribner, *N.Y.* 04
*Foreign Competition* —*v. also* **D** §§ 118, 122
FURNESS, Sir Christopher The American Invasion; ill. [anti-Protectionist] 1/ *n.* c 8° Simpkin 02
GASTRELL, W. S. H. Our Trade in World in rel. to For. Competn. 6/ 8° Chapman 97
McKENZIE, F. A. The American Invaders 2/6 *n.* c 8° Richards 02
Carefully compiled acc. of Amer. enterprise in mechanics, engineering, literature, etc., in England.
WILLIAMS, E. E. Made in Germany [alarmist] 1/ c 8° Heinemann [96] 97
Medley, G. W. The German Bogey [Cobden Club reply to above] 6*d.* c 8° Cassell 96
**Trade: International** —*for* Free Trade and Protection *v.* **D** § 122
BASTABLE, Prf. C. F. Theory of Internatl. Trade, *and* Commerce of Natns.—*ut* **D** § 122
CAIRNES, Prf. J. E. —*in his* Some Leading Principles of Political Economy, *ut* **D** § 114
FISK, G. M. Internatl. Commerc. Policies w. spec. ref. to U.S. [Citiz. Lib.]—*ut* **D** § 122
HOBSON, J. A. International Trade—*ut* **I** § 122 [applicn. of econ. principles]
PHEAR, Sir J. B. Internatl. Trade, and Reln. betw. Exports and Imports *o.p.* [*pb.* 2/6] c 8° Macmillan 81
**Commercial Policy**—*v.* **D** §§ 136, 122 **Mercantile Law**—*v.* **D** § 63 **Treaties and Tariffs**—*v.* **D** § 113
**Shipping** —*v. also* **I** § 23*
CALVERT, Alf. Shipping Office Organizn., Managemt., and Accounts 5/ *n.* 8° Pitman
COOLEY, C. H. Theory of Transportation [Am. Econ. Ass.; 2/6 Sonnenschein] 75 c. *n.* 8° Macmillan, *N.Y.* 94
HALL (Arnold) + HEYWOOD (F.) Shipping [guide to routine] 1/ *n.* 8° Pitman 09
JOHNSON, E. R. Ocean and Inland Water Transportation $1·50 *n.* (6/ *n.*) c 8° Appleton 06
SMITH, J. Russell Organization of Ocean Commerce [Univ. of Penn. Studs.] $1·50 4° Appleton, *N.Y.* 05
URQUHART, G. D. Dues & Charges on Shpg. in Foreign & Col. Ports 40/ *n.* r 8° Philip [92] 10
Incls. ab. 3,000 ports. In this edn. a short article on commerce, currency, etc., is added to ea. country.

*Ports, Docks, etc.*
OWEN, Douglas — Ports and Docks [Books on Business] 2/6 *n.* c 8° Methuen 04
TURNBULL — Dock and Port Charges of the U.K. 21/ *n.* 8° Potts, *N. Shields* (Philip) [85] 10
*Lloyd's* —*v.* **D** § 151
*Port of London*
BARLOW (C. A. M.) + LEESE (W. H.) [eds.] Port of London Act, 1908 20/ *n.* r 8° E. Wilson 09
Port of London (The) and the Thames Barrage; maps and pl. [by 5 wrs.] 12/6 *n.* 4° Sonnenschein 07
*Trinity House*
BARRETT, C. R. B. — The Trinity House of Deptford Strond; ill. by author 12/6 *n.* 4° Sidgwick 93
An excellent hist. of the corporatn., skilfully compiled fr. the records. Does not deal w. constit. and econ. aspects.
MAYO, W. H. — Trinity House, London, Past and Present; ill. 5/ *n.* c 8° Smith & Elder 05
*Shipping Subsidies*
MEEKER, R. History of Shipping Subsidies [Am. Ec. Ass.; 3/6 Sonnenschein] $1 *n.* 8° Macmillan, *N.Y.* 05

## 150: PRINCIPLES AND PRACTICE OF BUSINESS

*Vide also* **D** § 168, *s.v.* Commercial Education

AVEBURY, L'd, etc. — King's Weigh House Lectures to Business Men 2/6 c 8° Macmillan 01
Lects. on practical commercial subjs. deliv. at the King's Weigh House, Grosvenor Square, London, 1900–1.
BOYLE, Sir Courtenay — Hints on Conduct of Business, Public and Private 3/6 c 8° Macmillan 00
An admirable guide to the duties of a secretary or higher official.
CARNEGIE, Andr. — The Empire of Business 2/6 *n.* r 8° Harper [01]
$3 Doubleday, *N.Y.* Seventeen reprinted papers.
CLEMSON, H. — Methods and Machinery of Business [exchgs. and insur.] 5/ *n.* c 8° Butterworth 07
CLOW, F. R. — Introduction to the Study of Commerce $1·25 *n.* c 8° Silver, *N.Y.* 01
Treats economic principles as illustrated in commercial life.
COOKE, H. O. S. — Success in the Office: clerkship made easy 2/ *n.* 12° Simpkin 07
CORDINGLEY, W. G. — The Counting House Guide 7/6 c 8° E. Wilson 01
Intended to replace TATE'S *Guide* [*ut inf.*], now out of date: gives copies of all chief documents used in commerce.
" — First Year of Office Work 2/ *n.* 12° E. Wilson 03
Counting House Routine: 1st Yr's Course, 1/; Second Yr's Course 1/6 c 8° Pitman
DAVIES, A. E. — Business Customs and Practice on the Continent 2/6 *n.* c 8° Pitman 08
DICKSEE (Prf. L. R.) + BLAIR (H. E.) Office Organization and Management; ill. 5/ *n.* 8° Pitman 06
" — Business Organization 5/ c 8° Longman 10
DOUGLAS, Gavin — How to Make Money [Dutton, *N.Y.*] 1/ c 8° Routledge 10
DUNCAN, J. C. — The Principles of Industrial Management $2 *n.* (7/6 *n.*) c 8° Appleton 10
ELGIE, T. H. — Commercial Efficiency: manl. of modern methods 1/ *n.* c 8° E. Wilson [04] 05
FIELDHOUSE, A. — Student's Business Methods, or Commercial Practice 2/6 c 8° Simpkin [06] 09
GAMBARO, Prf. R. — Lessons in Commerce, ed. Prf. J. Gault 3/6 c 8° Lockwood [92] 02
A text-bk., wr. in English by the author (of Genoa), and first issued in Italy, for use of Engl. studts. there. Comprehensive.
GAMBLE, W. — Business of Life: straight talks on business 1/ *n.* 12° Pitman 07
GRAHAM (J.) + OLIVER (G. A. S.) French Commercial Practice; German Commercial Practice; Spanish Commercial Practice c 8° Macmillan 04–7
Each in 2 Pts. (i) *Home Trade*, 2/6 (60 c. *n.*); (ii) *Export and Import*, 4/6 ($1·25 *n.*).
HATFIELD, H. R. — Lectures on Commerce $1·50 *n.* s 8° Univ. Press, *Chicago* 04
HEELIS, F. — Mod. Commercial Practice: Home Trade 2/ (50 c. *n.*) c 8° Macmillan 04
HELPS, Sir Arth. — Essays written in Intervals of Business gl 8° Macmillan [41] 89
*On the Transaction of Business, Choice and Managemt. of Agents, Treatment of Suitors*, and other practical essays.
HOOPER (F.) + GRAHAM (J.) Modern Business Methods: Home Trade, 2/6 ($1); Impt. and Expt. Trade 3/6 ($1) 8° Macmillan 98–9
JACKSON, S. — A Primer of Business [Commerc. Ser.] 1/6 c 8° Methuen 94
JOHNSON, Geo. — Mercantile Practice 2/6 *n.* c 8° E. Wilson 97
JONES, H. — Entrance Guide to Professions and Business [Commerc. Ser.] 1/6 c 8° Methuen 98
KNOOP, Douglas — American Business Enterprise [Mancs. Univ.] 1/6 *n.* 8° Sherratt, *Mancs.* 07
A *Report*, by a Gartside Scholar, of a nine-months tour in U.S. (and Canada).
MALET, Sir E., *etc.* — Unwritten Laws and Ideals of Active Careers 7/6 c 8° Smith & Elder 00
Acc. of the 'customary' rules wh. obtain and are binding in certain professions.
PITMAN'S [pubs.] — Manual of Business Training; 57 maps and facss. 2/6 c 8° Pitman
" — Office Desk Book; w. tables and ready reckoner 1/ *n.* c 8° Pitman *n.d.*
PLATT, Jas. — Business [quite popular] 1/ c 8° Simpkin [75]
SLATER, J. A. [ed.] — Pitman's Business Man's Guide 3/6 *n.* c 8° Pitman [03] 06
SPARLING, S. E. Introduction to Business Organization [Citizen's Lib.] $1·25 *n.* (5/ *n.*) c 8° Macmillan 07

SUTHERLAND, Alex. Manual of Commercial Instruction 2/6 (90 c.) c 8° Longman 92
An attempt to teach 'just so much of commercial knowledge as ought to be current in all classes of society'.

TATE, W. Countinghouse Guide—*v.* Cordingley, *sup.*

TURNER, B. B. Handbook of Commerce and Banking [elementary] 1/ c 8° Sonnenschein [89] 07

WARREN, Algernon Commercial Knowledge: methods and transactions 2/6 c 8° Murray 01

WARREN, W. P. Thoughts on Business [shrewd advice; classified; 1/ *n.* Nash] $1·25 c 8° Forbes, *Chicago* 07

*Encyclopaedia:* Business Encyclopaedia and Legal Adviser, ed. W. S. M. Knight, 6 vols.; ill. ea. 7/6 *n.* 8° Caxton Pb. Co., 02–3

**Advertizing:** BRIDGEWATER (H.) Advertising 1/ *n.* c 8° Pitman

CALKINS (E. E.) + HOLDEN (R.) Modern Advertizing $1·50 *n.* (6/ *n.*) c 8° Appleton 05

de CASTAREDE, L. Money-Making by Ad-Writing 10/6 *n.* c 8° Neuman 05

MARES, G. C. Advertising that Tells [advg. in small way] 1/ *n.* c 8° Pitman 07

MORAM, C. G. The Business of Advertizing [Bks. on Business] 2/6 *n.* c 8° Methuen 05

SCOTT, Prf. W. Dill Theory & Practice of Advertising; 61 ill. [6/ *n.* Pitman] $2 *n.* 8° Small, *Boston* 08

,, Psychology of Advertising; 67 ill. [6/ *n.* Pitman] $2 *n.* 8° Small, *Boston* 08
Two valuable treatises, by the Director of the Psychological Laboratory of North-Western Univ., U.S.A.

SPIERS, E. A. Art of Publicity and its Applicn. to Business 5/ *n.* c 8° Unwin 10

de WEESE, Truman A. Principles of Practical Publicity; 43 pl. $2 c 8° Matthews, *N.Y.* 06
7/6 *n.* Pitman. Author was in charge of Publicity Dept. of the Louisiana Purchase Exposition (1904).

*History*

LEWIS, Lawrence [ed.] Advertisements in 'The Spectator' [6/ *n.* Constable] $2 8° Houghton, *Boston* 09
A study of the social life of Engl. in Qu. Anne's days, and an illn. of the origins of the art of advertizing.

SAMPSON, H. Hist. of Advertising fr. Earliest Times; ill. [$2·75 Scrib., *N.Y.*] 7/6 c 8° Chatto 74

*Decorative Posters* —*v.* I § 111

*Press Directories:* American Newspaper Annual $5 *n.* 8° Ayer, *Phila.* [80] *ann.*

MITCHELL [pub.] Newspaper Press Directory and Advertisers' Guide 2/ 4° Mitchell [45] *ann.*

SELL [pub.] Dictionary of the World's Progress [directory of world's press] 2/6 i 8° Sell *ann.*

WILLING'S [pubs.] Press Guide 1/ f 8° Willing *ann.*

**Banking** — *v.* **D** § 116

**Book-keeping; Accountancy; Auditing**—*for* teaching of book-kpg. *v.* **D** § 167

*Bibliography:* BECKETT, Thos. The Accountant's Assistant 6/ *n.* c 8° Gee 01
An index to accountancy lects. and articles in *The Accountant* and *The Accountant's Journal.*

Accountants' Library: vols. i–li *v.pp.* 8° Gee *v.y.*, *in prg.*

*Agric. Accs. and Income Tax* T. W. MEATS 5/ *n.*
*Auctioneers' Accounts* L. R. DICKSEE 3/6 *n.*
*Bakers' Accounts* F. MEGGISON 5/ *n.*
*Bank Bkkpg. and Accs.* J. A. MEELBOOM + C. F. HANNAFORD 5/ *n.*
*Brewers' and Bottlers' Accs.* H. LANHAM 10/6 *n.*
*Brickmakers' Accounts* W. H. FOX 3/6 *n.*
*Builders' Accounts* J. A. WALBANK 3/6 *n.*
*Building Societies' Accs.* W. C. GRANT-SMITH 3/6 *n.*
*Colliery Accounts* Jno. MANN 5/ *n.*
*Co-operative Societies' Accs.* F. H. SUGDEN 5/ *n.*
*Cotton Spinners' Accounts* W. MOSS 5/ *n.*
*Dairy Accounts* F. ROWLAND 3/6 *n.*
*Depreciation, Reserves, etc.* L. R. DICKSEE 3/6 *n.*
*Drapers', etc., Accounts* G. H. RICHARDSON 5/ *n.*
*Electric Lighting Accs.* G. JOHNSON 5/ *n.*
*Engineers' and Shipbuilders' Accs.* F. G. BURTON 3/6 *n.*
*Fishing Industry Accounts* Chas. WILLIAMSON 3/6 *n.*
*Fraud in Accounts* EDITOR 3/6 *n.*
*Friendly Societies' Accs.* E. Furnival JONES 5/ *n.*
*Gas Accounts* EDITOR 5/ *n.*
*Grain, Flour, etc., Merchts.' Accs.* G. JOHNSON 3/6 *n.*
*Hôtel Accounts* L. R. DICKSEE 3/6 *n.*
*Insurance Cos.' Accounts* E. A. TYLER 10/6 *n.*
*Jewellers' Accounts* Allen EDWARDS 5/ *n.*
*Laundry Accounts* F. J. LIVESEY 3/6 *n.*
*Medical Practitioners' Accs.* J. H. MAY 3/6 *n.*
*Miner. Water Manufrs.' Accs.* J. LUND + G. H. RICHARDSON 3/6 *n.*
*Mining (Austral.) Cos.' Accs.* D. GODDEN + W. N. ROBERTSON 3/6 *n.*
*Multiple Cost Accounts* H. S. GARRY 3/6 *n.*
*Multiple Shop Accounts* J. HAZELIP 3/6 *n.*
*Municipal Accounts* J. ALCOCK 10/6 *n.*
*Pawnbrokers' Accounts* F. THORNTON + J. H. MAY 3/6 *n.*
*Polytechnic Accounts* H. C. MARSHALL 3/6 *n.*
*Printers' Accounts* H. LAKIN-SMITH 3/6 *n.*
*Process Cost Accounts* H. S. GARRY 5/ *n.*
*Quarry Accounts* J. G. P. IBOTSON 3/6 *n.*
*Shipping Accounts* R. R. DALY 3/6 *n.*
*Single Cost Accounts* G. A. MITCHELL 5/ *n.*
*Solicitors' Accounts* L. R. DICKSEE 3/6 *n.*
*Stockbrokers' Accounts* W. D. CALLAWAY 3/6 *n.*
*Terminal Cost Accounts* A. G. NISBET 3/6 *n.*
*Theatre Accounts* W. H. CHANTREY 3/6 *n.*
*Timber Merchants' Acc.* E. E. SMITH 3/6 *n.*
*Tramway Accounts* McCOLL 10/6 *n.*
*Tramway Bkkpg. and Accs.* Donald McCOLL 2/6 *n.*
*Trustees', Liquidators', and Receivers' Accounts.* S. S. DAWSON + H. R. GRAVES 3/6 *n.*
*Underwriters' Accounts* E. E. SPICER + E. C. PEGLER 5/ *n.*
*Urban Distr. Council's Accs.* F. S. ECKERSLEY 5/ *n.*
*Water Companies' Accs.* F. KEY 3/6 *n.*
*Wine Merchants' Accs.* A. SABIN 5/ *n.*
*Woollen, etc., Accounts* J. MACKIE 3/6 *n.*

To subscribers for 20 or more vols. 3/6 vols. charged 2/6, 5/ charged 3/9, 10/6 charged 5/.

Accountants' Manual: vols. i–xi ea. 12/6 *n.* 8° Gee 84–08 *bienn*
A fund of informn. on var. points of practice and law rel. to accountancy, cont. in questns. and ansrs. of the Institute exams.

ADGIE, W. Modern Book-keeping and Accounts 5/ c 8° Macmillan 01–4
Also in 3 Pts., i: *Elementary*, 1/6; ii: *Intermediate*, 2/6; iii: *Advanced*, 2/6. *Key* to each, 2/6 *n.* ea.

CARLILL, J. A. Principles of Parnassus 3/6 *n.* 8° Gee

CARTER, F. H. Practical Book-keeping, ed. F. W. Carter 8/6 8° Bell & Bradfute, *Edin.* [73] 90

CROPPER, L. C. Bookkeeping and Accounts 3/6 *n.* 8° Gee

DAWSON, S. S. The Accountant's Compendium 25/ *n.* 4° Gee [98] 08
A lexicon, contg. c. 1,500 articles of interest to accountants, secretaries, head-clerks, etc.

DAY, Clarence M. Accounting Practice $6 *n.* (25/ *n.*) m 8° Appleton 08

*DICKSEE, Prf. L. R. A B C of Bookkeeping 2/ (80 c.) f 8° Longman 08
" Advanced Accounting [App. on Law by J. E. G. de Montmorency] 21/ *n.* 4° Gee 03
* " Bookkeeping for Accountant Students 10/6 *n.* 8° Gee [ ] 06
" Student's Guide to Accountancy 2/6 *n.* 8° Gee [ ]
ELWORTHY (W. R.) + CAMPLING (C. C.) Book-keeping for Traders, Manufrs., etc. 4/6 *n.* 8° Jordan [00] 04
Encyclopaedia of Accounting, 8 vols. ea. 20/ *n.* 8° Green, *Edin.* 03–4
FIELDHOUSE, A. Student's Complete Commercial Book-kpg., 4/; Key, 16/ *n.* c 8° Simpkin [98] 08 ; 09
" Student's Advanced Book-keeping 3/ 8° Simpkin [9–] 07
Forms and Precedents for Accountants, 2 vols. ea. 20/ r 8° Green, *Edin.* 07
GREENDLINGER, L. Accountancy Problems 21/6 *n.* 8° Gee
Partnership accs., theory of accs., auditing, commercial law, etc.
HAMILTON (Sir R. G.) + BALL (J.) Book-keeping 2/ (50 c.) 12° Clar. Press [69] 85
HATFIELD, H. R. Modern Accounting $1 75 *n.* (7/6 *n.*) t 8° Appleton 09
HAWKINS, L. W. Book-keeping: princs. and pract. of double-entry 5/ *n.* 8° Good 05
" Cost Accounts 5/ *n.* 8° Gee 05
HAY, G. H. Princs. of Check Figure Systems for Accountants 7/6 *n.* c 8° Gee 08
HOLAH, E. Double Entry: principle of perfect book-kpg. 2/ *n.* c 8° E. Wilson [82] 03
HUNTER, Rev. Jno. Self-Instruction in Book-keeping, 2/; Key, 2/6 12° Longman [71] 78
" Progressive Exercises in Bookkpg. by Doub. Entry, 1/6; Key, 2/6 12° Longman [ ]
IRESON, F. Text-Book of Book-Keeping 3/6 8° Macmillan 00
JACKSON, Geo. Practical System of Book-keeping, ed. H. T. Easton 5/ *n.* 8° E. Wilson [ ] 01
" Check Journal upon Principle of Double Entry 5/ 8° Wilson [ ] 87
JENKINSON, M. W. Cost Accounts for Small Manufacturers 2/6 8° Gee 07
" Book-Kpg. & Accounting 16/ *n.* 8°; Elements of Bkkpg. 1/6 c 8° l 8° Arnold 10 ; 07
JOHNSON, Geo. Book-keeping and Accounts; w. notes on auditing 7/6 *n.* 8° E. Wilson 05
LISLE, Geo. Accounting in Theory and Practice 15/ *n.* 8° Green, *Edin.* [06] 09
MCALLEN, J. E. B. Princs. of Bk-kpg. by Doub. Entry [Comm. Ser.] 2/ c 8° Methuen 99
MILLAR, T. J. Managemt. Book-kpg. f. manuf., wholesaler, and retailer 5/ *n.* c 8° C. & E. Layton
MINCK, O. R. F. Text-book of Book-keeping, ed. Jos. Stiles 2/6 c 8° Philip [93] 02
MOLE, A. C. Student's Epitome of Accountancy and Bk.-kpg. 3/6 *n.* 8° W. Mole, *Meml. Hall, Lond.* 08
NIXON, Alf. Advanced Bookkeeping [w. questns. & exx.] 3/6 c 8° Longman 94
" + STAGG (J. H.) Accounting and Banking [Commercial Series] 10/6 ($3) r 8° Longman 07
PITMAN'S [pub.] Primer of Book-keeping, 1/; Exercs., 6*d.*; Key, 1/ c 8° Pitman 99–00
" Book-keeping Simplified, 2/6; Answers, 1/ c 8° Pitman [ ] 08–8
" Advanced Bookkeeping, 2/6; Answers, 1/ c 8° Pitman 00
" Complete Book-keeping, 3/6; Answers, 2/6 c 8° Pitman [04] 08
PIXLEY, F. W. Accountancy [a careful pract. treatise] 5/ *n.* 8° Pitman 08
" + WILSON (J.) Book-keeping 2/6 c 8° Sonnenschein 92
PORRITT (H. W.) + NICKLIN (W.) Book-keeping for Retailers 1/ *n.* c 8° Pitman
ROBERTSON (W. A.) + ROSS (F. A.) Actuarial Theory 21/ *n.* 8° Oliver & Boyd, *Edin.* 07
SNAILUM, W. W. Fifteen Studies in Book-keeping [$1 *n.* Putnam, *N.Y.*] 3/6 *n.* c 8° Camb. Press 00
SPICER (E. E.) + PEGLER (E. C.) Book-Keeping and Accounts 15/6 *n.* 4° Lynch 08
STRACHAN, W. Cost Accounts: key to economy in manuf. 3/6 *n.* 8° Stevens & Haynes [ ] 04
THOMSON, Prf. A. W. Textbk. of Princs. and Practice of Book-keeping 5/ c 8° Bell 87
THORNTON, Jas. First Lessons in Book-keeping, 2/6 c 8°; Key, 10/6 4° Macmillan [79]
" Manual of Book-Keeping [Commercial Class-Books] 7/6 ($1·75 *n.*) c 8° Macmillan 95
The best book on the subject—the theory intelligently explained and the practice clearly illustrated.
" Primer of Book-keeping, 1/; Key, 2/6 pott 8° Macmillan 90
" + S. W. Book-keeping for Business Men 3/6 c 8° Macmillan 01
VAN DE LINDE, Gérard Book-keeping and other Papers 7/6 *n.* 8° Gee [91] 04
WARDHAUGH, J. B. The Accountant's Digest 10/ *n.* 8° Green, *Edin.* [ ] 10
WHATLEY, G. E. Stuart Accountant's and Bookkeeper's Vade Mecum 7/6 8° Gee
*History:* BROWN (Rich.) History of Accounting and Accountants 10/6 *n.* r 8° Jack, *Edin.* 05
HEAPS, J. W. The Antiquity of Bookkeeping 1/ *n.* 8° Gee

WORTHINGTON, B. — Professional Accountants — 2/6 *n.* 8° Gee
A histor. survey of the professn. in Engld. fr. its beginning to present time.

*Auditing*

CUTFORTH, A. E. — Audits — 6/6 *n.* 8° Gee [08] 10
*DICKSEE, Prf. L. R. — Auditing: practical manual for auditors — 21/ *n.* 8° Gee [3rd ed. 98] 09
*PIXLEY, F. W. — Auditors: duties and responsibilities, 2 vols.—*ut* **D** § 14

*Balance Sheet*

'Chartered Accountant (A)' — How to Understand the Balance Sheet, etc. — 2/6 *n.* 8° Jordan 03
GOUGH, T. H. — Balance Sheets and How to Read Them — 1/ *n.* c 8° Simpkin 06
MACKENZIE, V. St Clair — The Modern Balance Sheet — 2/6 *n.* c 8° E. Wilson 08
PIXLEY, F. W. — How to Read a Balance Sheet — 6*d.* *n.* 8° Gee [ ]

*Boot and Shoe Trade Accountancy*

HEADLY, L. C. — Boot and Shoe Costings — 2/6 *n.* 8° Gee

*Chartered Accountant's Charges*

PIXLEY, F. W. — Chart. Accountants' Charges and Law rel. thereto — 10/6 *n.* 8° Gee

*Colliery Accountancy* —*v. also* Accountants' Lib., *sup.*

MONKHOUSE, GODDARD & Co. — Colliery Book-keeping — 5/ *n.* 4° Simpkin 05

*Company Secretaries' Accountancy—v. also* **D** § 26

DICKSEE, Prf. L. R. — Book-keeping for Company Secretaries — 5/ *n.* 8° Gee [ ]

*Executors, Administrators, Trustees Accountancy—v. also* Accountants' Lib., *sup.* and **D** § 100

CALDICOTT, O. H. — Executorship Accounts — 3/6 *n.* 8° Gee [ ]
CARTER, R. N. — Students' Guide to Executorship Accounts — 5/ *n.* 8° Gee
GOTTSBERGER, F. — Accountant's Guide for Exors., Admins., etc. — $5 4° Peck, *N.Y.* 02
HAWKINS, T. W. — Bookkeeping for Executors and Trustees — 3/6 *n.* 8° Gee
WHINNEY (F., jun.) + van NECK (A. P.) — Executorship Law and Accounts — 7/6 *n.* 8° Gee [ ]

*Factory Accountancy*

GARCKE (E.) + FELLS (J. M.) — Factory Accounts: principles and practice — 7/6 *n.* c 8° Gee [ ]

*Farmers', etc., Accountancy*

KERSEY, H. W. — Bkkpg. f. Farmers, Mkt.-gdnrs., and Dairymen — 1/6 *n.* 4° Headley 07

*Gas Company Accountancy* —*v. also* Accountants' Lib., *sup.*

BREARLEY (J. H.) + TAYLOR (B.) — Gas Companies' Bookkeeping — 12/6 *n.* 4° Gee

*Hôtel Accountancy* —*v. also* Accountants' Lib., *sup.*

PITMAN'S [pub.] — Hôtel Book-keeping — 2/6 c 8° Pitman 07

*Income Tax Accountancy*

Income Tax Accounts and How to Prepare Them — 2/ c 8° Pitman

*Investment and Loan Societies' Accountancy*

BROWN (D. J. A.) + THOMAS (E.) — Investment and Loan Societies' Accounts — 5/ *n.* 8° Gee

*Mining Accountancy* —*v. also* Accountants' Lib., *sup.*

LAWN, J. G. — Mine Accounts and Mining Book-keeping — 10/6 8° Griffin [97] 09
WALLACE, D. — Simple Mine Accounting — 4/6 *n.* 8° Hill Pub. Co. 08

*Municipal Accountancy*

CLEVELAND, Dr F. A. — Chapters on Municipal Administrn. and Accounting—*ut* **D** § 124
COLLINS, A. — Municipal Internal Audit — 3/6 *n.* 8° Gee 04
,, — Local Authorities' Accounts [organizn. and audit] — 12/6 *n.* 8° Gee
EVANS, J. M. — Exemplifcn. of Syst. of Accs. f. Urb. and Rural Dist. Councils — 21/ *n.* 8° Butterworth 97

*Newspaper Accountancy*

COMINS, Chas. — Newspaper Book-Keeping and Accounts — 12/6 *n.* 8° Hadden 95
NORTON (B. J.) + FEASEY (G. T.) — Newspaper Accounts — 10/ *n.* 8° Gee

*Personal and Domestic Accountancy*

IBOTSON, J. G. P. — Personal and Domestic Accounts — 1/ *n.* 8° Gee

*Printers' Accountancy* —*v. also* Accountants' Lib., *sup.*

WILD, J. A. — Cost of Production [printg. and allied trades] — 10/6 *n.* 8° Gee

*Publishers' Accountancy*

ALLEN, C. E. — Publishers' Accounts — 2/6 *n.* 8° Gee 97

*Railway Accountancy*

ANDERSON, A. C. A Digest of Railway Accounts 3/6 *n.* 8° Gee

FISHER, J. A. Railway Accounts and Finance 10/6 *n.* 8° G. Allen [91] 11

*Retail Traders' and Shopkeepers' Accountancy*

FINDLAY, Jas. Bookkeeping for Retail Traders 3/ *n.* 8° Gee

PORRITT (H. W.) + NICKLIN (W.) Book-keeping for Retailers 1/ *n.* c 8° Pitman 09

QUIN, S. B. Shopkeepers' Accounts 2/6 *n.* 8° Gee [ ]

*Solicitors' Book-keeping* —*v.* **D** § 53

*Stock Exchange* —*v. also* Accountants' Lib., *sup.*

WARNER, Rob. Stock Exchange Book-keeping 2/6 *n.* c 8° E. Wilson

*Theatrical Accountancy* —*v. also* Accountants' Lib., *sup.*

SMEDLEY, C. E. Theatrical Accounts [w. model forms] 3/6 8° *Era* Office 09

**Card Indexing**

KAISER, J. The Card System at the Office [v. comprehensive] 5/ *n.* 8° McCorquodale 10

**Commercial Codes**

A B C Universal Commercial Code. By W. Clauson-Thue 20/ r 8° E. Wilson
AGER, G. Simplex Standard Telegram Code [205,500 wds.] 105/ 4° E. Wilson
" Duplex Combination Standard Code [150,000 wds.] 84/ 4° E. Wilson
" Extension Duplex Code [45,000 addtl. wds.] 21/ 4° E. Wilson
" Standard Telegram Code [100,000 wds.] 63/ 4° E. Wilson 81
" Telegram Code [56,000 words] 42/ 4° E. Wilson [ ]
" Alphabetical Telegram Code 25/ 4° E. Wilson
The code-words in sequence to the 150,000 words in *Duplex Standard Code.*
" Telegraphic Primer [19,000 Engl. and 12,000 Dutch wds.] 12/6 4° E. Wilson 80
" General and Social Code [for travellers, bankers, etc.] 10/6 8° E. Wilson
BENTLEY Complete Phrase Code 84 /*n.* E. Wilson
BERNE Official Vocubulary, 1894 E. Wilson 95
BISHOP Travellers' Telegraph Code [for tourists] 1/ *n.* E. Wilson
BROOMHALL Comprehensive Cipher Code [170,000 phrases] 73/6 4° E. Wilson
" Standard Shipping Code 60/ *n.* 4° E. Wilson
Figure Code for Stocks and Shares [f. use w. Berne 'Offic. Vocab.'] 42/ 4° E. Wilson
HARTFIELD Wall Street Code [467,000 wds.] 42/ *n.* 4° E. Wilson
HAWKE, W. H. Premier Cypher Telegr. Code [120,000 wds. and phr.] 10/6 *n.* 4° E. Wilson 07
" 100,000 Word Supplement to above 10/6 *n.* 4° E. Wilson
" Premier Code Condenser [figure-key to above] 10/6 *n.* 4° E. Wilson
KOLKENBECK Ideal Code Condenser [a 13-fig. code] 21/ *n.* 4° E. Wilson
McNICOL Nine-Figure Code [1,000,000,000 pronounceable wds.] 2 copies £20 *n.* 4° E. Wilson
Official Vocabulary in Terminational Order 40/ *n.* 4° E. Wilson
PIERON Code Condenser, 4 Pts. ea. 30/ *n.* 4° E. Wilson
*English, French, Spanish, German.*
SCOTT Shipowners' Telegraphic Code 52/6 4° E. Wilson [ ] 06
VOLLERS Nine-Figure System 40/ *n.* 4° E. Wilson
1,000,000,000 pronounceable wds., ea. in 10 letters, in accord. w. Lond. Telegr. Conference, 1903.
WATKINS Ship-broker's Telegraphic Code 147/ *n.* 4° E. Wilson
Western Union Telegraphic Code: Universal Edn. 60/ *n.* 4° E. Wilson
WHITELAW Telegraph Cyphers 4° E. Wilson
*Fch., Span., Port., Ital., Latin* (200,000 wds.), ea. 150/ *n.*; *English* (53,000), 50/ *n.*; *Germ.* (42,600), 50/ *n.*; *Dutch* (40,000), 50/ *n.*
" 400,000 Cyphers in one Alphabetical Order £12 10/ 4° E. Wilson
" 401,000,000 Pronounceable Words, all of 10 Letters 150/ 4° E. Wilson

**Commercial Education** —*v.* **D** § 169

**Commercial Forms**

CORDINGLEY, W. G. Counting-House Guide: commercial documents 7/6 *n.* 8° E. Wilson 01

WATERSTON, W. Manual of Commerce: commercial forms 3/6 12° *Edinburgh* [ ] 84

**Commercial Language** —*for* Dictionaries *v.* **K** §§ 230–270, *passim*

*Abbreviations* (*Commercial*) —*for* Abbreviations Generally *v.* **K** § 2

CORDINGLEY, W. G. Dict. of Abbrevns. used in Mercant. Transns. 1/ *n.* f 8° E. Wilson 02

*Correspondence* (*Commercial*)—*for* Volapük, Esperanto, etc., *v.* **K** § 286

ADAM, Prc. Jno. Commercial Correspondence [elementary; 92 pp.] 3/ r 8° Longman [86] 98

ALTMAIER, C. L. Commercial Correspondence and Postal Information 3/6 *n.* (60 c. *n.*) c 8° Macmillan 04

ANDERSON, W. Practical Mercantile Correspondence 3/6 c 8° Paul [69] 89

BAKER, C. E. Foreign Commerc. Correspondent [Engl., Fch., Germ., Ital., Span.] 5/ c 8° Lockwood 88

BALLY, S. E. French Comm. Corresp., 2/; Fch. Com. Reader, 2/ [Comm. Ser.] c 8° Methuen 93–5

" German Comm. corresp., 2/6; Germ. Com. Reader, 2/ [Comm. Ser.] c 8° Methuen 96–00

Commercial Correspondence in 9 Languages ea. 2/6 12° Nutt *v.y.*
Dutch, Engl., Fch., Germ., It., Port., Russn., Span., Swed. The letters bg. the same, page for page, ea. serves as Key to the others.

CORNETT, W. N. Portuguese Comm. Corr.; Spanish Comm. Corr. ea. 2/ *n.* c 8° Hirschfeld 05; 05

COUMBE, E. H. Manual of Commercial Correspondence 2/6 *n.* c 8° E. Wilson [99] 01

DAVIES, A. E. Foreign Correspondent for Business Purposes 1/6 *n.* c 8° Pitman [04] 05

GLAUSER, C. French Commercial Correspondence 4/6 c 8° Murray 02

GRAHAM (J.) + OLIVER (G. A. S.) Foreign Trader's Correspondence Hdbk. 3/6 (75 c. *n.*) c 8° Macmillan 05

HOSSFELD Engl.-Fch. Correspondent; Eng.-Germ. Corr.; Eng.-Span. Corr. ea. 2/ n. c 8° Hirschfeld
PARKYN, W. A. The Language of Commerce, 2 vols. [w. test-pprs.] ea. 1/6 c 8° Simpkin 06
PITMAN'S [pub.] International Mercantile Letters ea. 2/6 c 8° Pitman 08
*English; English-French; English-German; English-Italian; English-Portuguese.*
,, [pub.] Dictionary of Commerc. Corresp. [Engl., Fch., Germ., Sp., Ital.] 5/6 n. 8° Pitman 11
,, [pub.] Comm. Corr., in Fch., 2/6; in Germ., 2/6; in Span., 3/6 c 8° Pitman
SCHOLL Dictionary of Commercial Correspondence, 3 vols. ea. 12/ 8° Hachette 86
SIMON (L.) + VOGEL (C.), etc. Practical Mercantile Correspondence ea. 3/ *or* 4/6 c 8° Whittaker 87
*Engl., w. Germ. notes, 3/; Engl., w. Fch. notes, 4/6; Germ., w. Engl. notes, 3/; French, w. Engl. notes, 4/6.*
WHITFIELD, E. E. Précis Writing and Office Corresp. [Commerc. Ser.] 2/ c 8° Methuen 97

*Terms and Phrases* (*Commercial*)

BITHELL, R. Counting-house Dictionary [technical terms] 2/6 c 8° Routledge [82] 03
CORDINGLEY, W. G. London Commercial Dictionary [trade-terms] 2/6 n. c 8° E. Wilson 07
GRAHAM (J.) + OLIVER (G. A. S.) Foreign Trader's Dict. [Eng., Germ., Fch., Span.] 3/6 ($1) c 8° Macm. 06
PITMAN'S [pub.] Business Terms and Phrases [Engl., Fch., Germ., Span.] 2/6 c 8° Pitman

**Salesmanship**

CORBION (W. H.) + GRIMSDALE (G. E.) Salesmanship 2/6 n. c 8° Pitman 08
Intended for the shop-assistant, commercial traveller, and agent.
RITTENBERG, Max Selling Schemes for Retailers 1/ c 8° Routledge 10

**Commercial Travellers**

ALLEN, A. P. Ambassadors of Commerce [their duties, etc.] 3/6 c 8° Unwin 85
GRIEVE, E. B. How to Become a Commercial Traveller 1/ f 8° Unwin 03
WARREN, Algernon Commercial Travelling: its features, past and present 6/ c 8° Unwin 04

**Shorthand** —*v.* **K** § 100

**Telegraphic Addresses**

SELL [pub.] Directory of Registered Telegraphic Addresses 21/ r 8° Sell [94] *ann.*

**Type-writing**

MARES, G. C. History of the Typewriter 6/ n. 8° Pitman 09
MORTON, A. E. Modern Typewrg. & Manl. of Office Procedure; ill. 2/6 r 8° Pitman [03] 03
,, Teacher's Handbook and Key to above 2/6 r 8° Pitman 03
,, Practical Typewriting and Examination Guide 2/6 r 8° Pitman 07
SMITH, C. E. Practical Course in Touch Typewriting 1/6 (50 c.) 4° Pitman [93] 09

**Valuations** —*v. also* **D** § 78; *for* Valuation Tables *v.* **D** § 154

ESDALE, Marcus How Property is Valued [popular] 6/ n. 8° Cable Prg. & Pb. Co. 09

## 151 : INSURANCE

**Encyclopaedias; Directories**

Amer. Encyclopaedic Lib. Assoc.: Internatl. Insurce. Encyclo., 7 v. [147/ Layton] Am. Encyc. Lib. Ass.
BOURNE'S Insurance Directory [prev. to '09 5/ n. E. Wilson] 7/6 n. 8° Insur. Pb. Co. *ann.*
Insurance Blue-book and Guide 2/ n. 8° Dawbarn & Ward (Routledge) *ann.*
WALFORD, Cornelius The Insurce. Cyclop., v. i–v & Pt. 1 of vi red. to 42/ n. r 8° C. & E. Layton 72–80
Terms, biography, bibliogr., hist. of offices. Comprises A–Ha; will not be continued.
Who's Who in Insurance: an international year-bk. [25/ C. & E. Layton] 8° Singer, *N.Y.* *ann.*
Full for United States; Gt. Britain, where insurance is more developed and more successfully carried out, less well represented.

**Actuarial Theory**

DAWSON, M. M. Practical Lessons in Actuarial Science, 2 vols. $7 8° Spectator Co., *N.Y.* [ ] 05
*KING, Geo. Theory of Finance: treatise on doctrine of interest and annuities-certain 4/ 8° C. & E. Layton [ ]
*ROBERTSON (W. A.) + ROSS (F. A.) Actuarial Theory 21/ n. 8° Oliver & Boyd, *Edin.* 07
Intended for studts. preparg. for the Second Exams. of Inst. of Actuaries and Faculty of Actuaries in Scotland.
WHITTALL, W. J. H. Elementary Lecture on Theory of Life Assurance 2/ n. 8° C. & E. Layton
WILLETT, A. H. Econ. Theory of Risk & Insurce. [Col. Univ. Studs.] $1·50 n. 8° Macmillan, *N.Y.* 02

*History*

DEUCHAR, J. J. W. Sketch of Hist. of Science of Life Contingencies 2/ 8° C. & E. Layton

**Insurance Generally**

ACTUARIAL Soc. of Glasgow: Transactions, vol. i, *o.p.*; ii–iv, ea. 15/; v, 20/ m 8° C. & E. Layton *in prg.*

COX, Chas. How to Choose your Insurance Company 2/6 c 8° Argus Prg. Co. 01
EKE, J. A. Elements of Insurance [all kinds of insurance] 1/ *n.* (50 c.) c 8° Pitman 09
FACULTY OF ACTUARIES IN SCOTLAND : Transactions, v. i–ii, ea. 21/; iii–iv, 15/ m 8° C. & E. Layton *in prg.*
HENDERSON, E. P. Insurance Question Plainly Treated 1/ *n.* 8° E. Wilson 00
HUEBNER, Solomon Property Insurance $2 *n.* (7/6 *n.*) c 8° Appleton
INSTITUTE OF ACTUARIES : Journal, v. i–xlii, ea. 12/; xliii, 14/; Index i–xl, 5/ m 8° C. & E. Layton *in prg.*
Insurance : a series of papers $1·25 8° Am. Acad. of Pol. Sci., *Phila.* 06
INSURANCE INSTITUTE OF G.B. AND I. : Journal, vols. i–ii, *o.p.*; iii–iv, ea. 5/ *n.*; v–xii, ea. 6/ *n.* C. & E. Layton *in prg.*
INSURANCE SOC. OF EDINB. : Transactions, vol. i, 5/; ii–v, ea. 3/ 8° C. & E. Layton *ann.*
Internatl. Actuarial Congress, Second [1898] : Transactions 30/ *n.* r 8° C. & E. Layton 98
WILSON, A. J. The Business of Insurance [Books on Business] 2/6 *n.* c 8° Methuen 04
YOUNG, T. E. Insurance : pract. expositn. f. studt. and business-man 5/ *n.* 8° Pitman [03] 06
,, + MASTERS (R.) Insur. Office Organizn., Managemt., and Accounts 3/6 *n.* 8° Pitman [04]
ZARTMAN, L. W. [ed.] Yale Readings in Insurance, 2 vols. ea. $2·25 *n.* 8° Yale Univ. Press 09

*History: United States: Philadelphia*

FOWLER, J. A. Hist. of Insur. in Philadelphia for 2 Cents. [1683–1882] $10 8° Review Pb. Co., *Phila.* 83

**Life and Annuity Insurance** —*for* Annuity Tables *v.* **D** § 154

ACKLAND (T. G.) + HARDY (G. F.) Graduated Exercises and Examples 10/6 *n.* 8° C. & E. Layton 89
For the use of students of the Institute of Actuaries *Text-Book*, *ut inf.*
BROCKBANK, E. M. Life Insurance and Gen. Practice [Oxfd. Med. Pbs.] 7/6 *n.* c 8° Frowde 08
DAWSON, M. M. Elements of Life Insurance $2 8° Spectator Co., *N.Y.* 94
,, The Business of Life Insurance $1·50 *n.* c 8° Barnes, *N.Y.* 05
EAGLE, P. A. Life Assurance Manual 5/6 8° Layton
FACKLER, E. B. Notes on Life Insurance $3 8° Spectator Co., *N.Y.* 07
GREENE, C. L. Medical Examination for Life Insurance $4 *n.* 8° Blakiston, *Phila.* [00] 05
*Institute of Actuaries Text-Book of Princs. of Interest, Life Annuities, and Assurances, and their Pract. Applicn. C. & E. Layton
Pt. i : *Interest (incl. Annuities—Certain)*, by Ralph TODHUNTER, 10/6 [82]; *Life Contingencies (incl. Life Annuities and Assurances)*, by Geo. KING, 31/6 [87].
POLLOCK (J. E.) + CHISHOLM (J.) Medical Hdbk. of Life Ass. [for med. officers] 7/6 c 8° Cassell 89
SMITH, G. W. Notes on Life Insurance $2 8° Spectator Co., *N.Y.*
WALFORD, Cornelius Insurance Guide and Hand-Book [Life] 7/6 8° C. & E. Layton [ ] 67
WILLARD, C. E. A B C of Life Insurance $1 8° Spectator Co., *N.Y.* [ ]
WILLEY, Nathan Princs. & Pract. of Life Assurance [$5 Spectator Co., *N.Y.*] 5/ r 8° C. & E. Layton 85
WILSON, A. J. Plain Advice about Life Insurance 1/ f 8° E. Wilson [93] 97
Attacks Life Insur. *as investmt.*, showing clearly that investor had better make his own investmts. than entrust them to any corpn. wh. professes to do more for him than he can do for himself. Pt. ii devoted to attack on Amer. life-offices.

*Life Insurance Companies*

ALEXANDER, W. The Life Insurance Company $1·50 *n.* (6/ *n.*) c 8° Appleton, 05
American Life Insurance Cos. : charters of 46 companies $5 8° Spectator Co., *N.Y.* 06
HARDING, H. R. Life Assurance Offices and their Investments 10/ *n.* 4° C. & E. Layton
ZARTMAN, Dr L. W. Investments of Life Insurance Cos. [5/ *n.* Bell] $1·25 *n.* c 8° Holt, *N.Y.* 06

*Medical Examination for Life Assurance*

ALLEN, Dr J. A. Medical Examinations for Life Insurance $2 8° Spectator Co., *N.Y.*
HALL, F. de H. Medical Exam. for Life Assurce.; seln. of an office 4/ *n.* c 8° Wright, Bristol [ ] 03
KEATING, Dr J. M. How to Examine for Life Insurance [8/ Saunders] r 8° [ ]
STILLMAN, Dr C. F. Life Insurance Examiner $3 8° Spectator Co., *N.Y.*

**Vital Statistics** —*v. also* **D** § 148

ANSELL, C., jun. Rate of Mortality at Early Periods of Life 10/6 r 8° C. & E. Layton
,, Rate of Mortality in Upper and Profess. Classes *o.p.* 8° C. & E. Layton 74
BRINTON, Dr W. On Medical Selection of Lives for Assurance 2/ 12° C. & E. Layton [ ]
British Officers' Life Tables (1893) : Aggregate Tables, Whole-life participg. assces., male 42/ *n.* 4° C. & E. Layton
,, Annuity Tables (1893) : Life Annuitants, male and female 31/6 *n.* 4° C. & E. Layton
,, Life Tables (1893) : Whole-life particg. and non-part. assces., male 42/ *n.* 4° C. & E. Layton
,, Life Tables (1893) : Princs. and Meths. in Compiln. of Date 15/ *n.* 4° C. & E. Layton

FARR, Wm. Vital Statistics, ed. Noel A. Humphreys 30/1 8° Sanitary Inst. 85
Selections from his historical reports and writings: a memorial volume.

HARDY, G. F. Theory of Construction of Tables of Mortality, etc. [lects.] 7/6 8° C. & E. Layton 05

HEWAT, Archib. Investign. of Marrge. & Mortal. of Scottish Ministers 5/ 8° C. & E. Layton

,, Marrge. & Mortal. of Widows' Fund of Scottish Banks 2/6 8° C. & E. Layton 96

Institute of Actuaries: Combined Experience of Life Annuitants: 1863–93 21/ *n.* 4° C. & E. Layton

,, Combined Experience of Assured Lives: 1863–93, 3 Pts. ea. 21/ *n.* 4° C. & E. Layton
*Endowmt. Assces. and Minor Classes* (males and fem.); *Whole-life Assces.; Males; Ditto: Females.*

MEIKLE, Jas. Observns. on Rate of Mortality of Assured Lives as exper'ced. by 10 Cos. in Scotl. 1815–63 42/ *n.* r 8° C. & E. Layton

NEISON, F. G. P. Vital Statistics 21/ *n.* 4° C. & E. Layton [46]
A developmt. of rates of mortality and laws of sickness, w. study of influences of locality, occupn., habits, etc.

*NEWSHOLME, Dr A. Vital Statistics: handbk. for students; w. diagrs., bibl., etc. 7/6 *n.* c 8° Sonnenschein [89] 99

NICOL, Jas. Vital, Social, and Econ. Statistics of Glasgow: 1885–91 3/6 *n.* 8° MacLehose, *Glasgow* 91

PEARSON, Prf. Karl —*in his* Chances of Death and other Studies, *ut* **D** § 125

WATSON, A. W. Sickness & Mort. Experce. of Order of Oddfellows: 1893–7 21/ *n.* 8° C. & E. Layton

*Infant Mortality* (social aspect)—*v.* **D** § 121 *Longevity, Centenarians*—*v.* **H** § 100

*History of Life Insurance*

HENDRICK, B. J. Story of Life Insurance [American; 3/6 *n.* Heinemann] $1·20 *n.* McClure, *N.Y.* 07

**Tables** —*v. also* **D** § 154

BOWSER, W. A. Valuation and other Tables [Inst. of Actuaries] 10/6 r 8° C. & E. Layton

,, Friendly Societies' Valuation and other Tables 21/ 4° C. & E. Layton

CARMENT, D. Table showg. Value at end of any No. of Yrs. of Policy of £100 at Death, etc. 10/6 8° C. & E. Layton [ ]

CHISHOLM, D. Commutation Tables for Jt. Annuity and Surviv. Assurce., 2 vols. *o.p.* [*pb.* 105/] r 8° C. & E. Layton

CHISHOLM, J. Tables f. Findg. Values of Policies of all Durations 31/6 r 8° C. & E. Layton

COLQUHOUN, E. Valuation and other Tables 21/ *n.* C. & E. Layton
Based on the Inst. of Actuaries' Mortality Experience.

DAVIES, G. Treatise on Annuities [with numerous tables] 10/6 8° C. & E. Layton

DOUGHARTY, H. Annuities and Sinking Funds [tables & notes] 2/6 *n.* 8° E. Wilson 05

FARR, Wm. English Life Tables; w. Introd. *o.p.* [*pb.* 42/] i 8° Harrison 64

FINLAISON, A. J. Joint-Life Annuity Tables for Both Sexes 10/6 m 8° Inst. of Acts (Layton)

GRAY, P. Tables and Formulæ for Computation of Life Contingencies 15/ 8° C. & E. Layton

,, + SMITH + ORCHARD Ass. & Ann. Tables acc. to Carlisle Rate @ 3% 10/6 8° C. & E. Layton

HENRY, J. The Government Annuity Tables, 6 vols. 336/ C. & E. Layton

KING (Geo.) + WHITTALL (W. J. H.) Valuation and other Tables 21/ *n.* C. & E. Layton
Deduced fr. the Institute of Actuaries' Mortality Experience, *ut supra.*

MANLY, H. W. Tables on Basis of $H^m$ 3, 3½, and 4% for Convertg. Whole-life Policies into Endowmt. Assurances, 3 cards 42/ 2 ft. 1 × 1 ft. 8 C. & E. Layton

MARR, T. Terminable Annuity Tables 10/6 8° C. & E. Layton

OAKES, Lt.-Col. W. H. Tables for Findg. Intermed. Rates of Int. in Annuity-certain 10/6 *n.* 8° C. & E. Layton
W. an extra col. of multipliers, by aid of wh. the rate of int. in an annuity can be found fr. pres. value of an annuity of £1 for any number of yrs. or periods up to 100.

ROTHERY (H. J.) + RYAN (G. H.) Premium Conversion Tables 21/ *n.* 8° C. & E. Layton
For findg. single and ann. prems. correspg. to given annuity-values at certain rates of interest.

Short Collection of Actuarial Tables [Instit. of Actuaries] 3/6 8° C. & E. Layton

SPRAGUE, T. B. Select Life Tables deduced fr. I. of A.'s Experce. [I. of Acts.] 21/ m 8° C. & E. Layton

TAYLOR, F. J. C. Tables of Annuities & Premiums at 3½% Interest 21/ *n.* 8° C. & E. Layton

TYLER, F. W. Prem. & Int. Calculator for Fractl. Pts. of 1 Yr. 63/ r 8° C. & E. Layton

WRIGHT, Hon. E. Life Valuation Tables 210/ 4° C. & E. Layton

**Fire Insurance; Average**

ATKINS, R. The Average Clause: hints on settlement of claims 5/ c 8° C. & E. Layton

COLES (W. S.) + BELL (H. S.) Fire Insurance Handbk. [risks alphab. arrgd.] 15/ *n.* 8° C. & E. Layton

HARE, F. A. C. Fire Risks: the various kinds [alphab. arranged] 15/ 8° C. & E. Layton 86

HORE, W. H. Remarks on the Apportionment of Fire Losses 7/6 *n.* 8° C. & E. Layton

KITCHIN, F. H. Principles and Finance of Fire Insurance 6/ *n.* c 8° E. Wilson 04
LAIRD, Jno. + Jas. Theory & Practice of Fire Loss Apportionments 7/6 *n.* l 8° Green, *Edin.* 09
MILNES, T. J. Fire Loss Settlements and Condns. of Fire Ins. Policies 3/6 *n.* c 8° C. & E. Layton
v. SCHWARZ, Dr Fire and Explosion Risks [tr.] 16/ 8° Griffin 04
WEED, S. R. Handbook of Fire Insurance $1·50 8° Spectator Co., *N.Y.*

*History*

RELTON, F. B. Account of Fire Insurance Companies and Schemes, etc. 25/ *n.* r 8° Sonnenschein 93
Acc. of Cos. and schemes estab. or projected in G.B. and I. dur. 17–18 cents., w. life of Chas. POVEY, projector of Sun Fire Office, and hist. of that Co. Conts. many particulars of various schemes not noticed in WALFORD's *Insur. Cyclo.* [*ut sup.*].

*Underwriting*

CAMPBELL, D. A. Fire Underwriter's Companion 10/6 8° Layton
GRISWOLD, J. Fire Underwriter's Text-Book $10 8° Wilson-Smith, *Montreal* 89

**Marine Insurance**

GOW, Dr Wm. Marine Insurance: a handbk. [Commerc. Class-Bks.] 5/ ($1·50) gl 8° Macmillan [95] 09
MCARTHUR, C. Policy of Marine Insurance [popular] 3/6 8° Layton
TEMPLEMAN, F. Marine Insurance: its principles and practice 3/6 c 8° Macdonald [ ] 09
*Lloyd's:* GREY (H. M.) Lloyd's Yesterday and To-day; ill. [popular descrn.] 5/ 8° Hadden 93
MARTIN, Fred. History of Lloyd's and of Marine Insurance in Gt. Brit. *o.p.* [*pb.* 14/] 8° Macmillan 76
Contains an Appendix relating to the statistics of marine insurance.

**Accidents, Insurance against**

FOOT, Alf. Pract. of Insur. agst. Accidts. and Employers' Liability 5/ c 8° Smith & Ebbs [ ] 09

**Burglary Insurance:** MCMILLAN (F. D.) Outlines of Burglary Insurance 5/ *n.* 8° C. & E. Layton

**National (Unemployment) Insurance** —*v. also* **D** § 127 (WEBB, Prevention of Destitution)

GIBBON, I. G. Unemployment Insurance: a study of schemes 6/ *n.* c 8° P. S. King & Son 11
HENDERSON, C. R. Industr. Insurce. in U.S. [8/ *n.* Camb. Press] 8° Univ. Press, *Chicago* [09] 11
SCHLOSS, D. F. Insurance against Unemployment 3/6 *n.* c 8° P. S. King & Son 09

**Law of Insurance** —*v.* **D** § 50

## 152: RAILWAYS

**Bibliography**

COTTEREL, S. Hdbk. to Pubns. on Rise and Developmt. of Ry. System 1/ 8° Baker, *Birm.* 93
Hopkins Railway Library: Catalogue. By F. J. Teggart $1·25 Leland Stanfd. Jun. Univ., *Paolo Alto* 95
Lib. of Congress, Washington: List of Bks. rel. to Railways [131 pp.] 15 c. 4° Govt. Press, *Washington* 04

**Terms:** SERRAILLIER L. Railway Technical Vocabulary 7/6 *n.* 8° Whittaker
5,000 French, English, and American technical expressns. rel. to managemt., constrn., and working of rys.

**History; Description**

**England**

ACWORTH, W. M. The Railways of England; 67 ill. 10/6 8° Murray [89] 00
$6 Scribner, *N.Y.* A good popular account of the chief English railways.

GORDON, W. J. The Story of Our Railways; ill. [juvenile] 1/6 c 8° R.T.S. 96
" Our Home Railways, in 12 Pts. [popular] ea. 9*d.* 8° Warne 10 *in prg.*
" Everyday Life on the Railroad; ill. [popular; 75 c. Revell, *N.Y.*] 2/ c 8° R.T.S. 92
GRINLING, C. H. Ways of Our Railways; 200 ill. 5/ *n.* 8° Ward & Lock [05] 10
PARSLOE, J. Our Railways: sketches, historical and descriptive 6/ c 8° Paul 78
PEASE, Edw. [1767–1858] Diaries, ed. Sir A. E. Pease [gt. gr'son] 7/6 *n.* 8° Headley 07
PEASE, Hy. [1807–81] Short Hist. of Hy. Pease. By M. H. Pease; ill. 2/6 c 8° Headley [97] 98
PENDLETON, Jno. Our Railways, 2 vols.; ill. 12/ c 8° Cassell [94] 96
A readable and pleasant, though rather discursive, popular hist. of the chief British lines and of the progress of railway enterprise.

PRATT, E. A. Hist. of Inld. Transport and Commicn. in Engld. 6/ *n.* c 8° Paul 11
Round the Works of our Great Railways. By Various Writers; ill. [popular] 3/6 8° Arnold 93
WILLIAMS, F. S. Our Iron Roads: history, construction, and admin. *o.p.* [*pb.* 8/6] 8° Bentley [52] 88

*Great Northern Railway*

GRINLING, C. H. History of Great Northern Railway; maps & ill. [1845–95] 10/6 8° Methuen [98] 03

*Great Western Railway*

SEKON, G. A. Hist. of the G.W.R., revised F. G. Saunders; ill. 7/6 8° Digby [95] 95
A chronicle of the 'Broad Gauge' or that part of the G.W.R. which was formerly 'Broad Guage', laboriously compiled.

*Midland Railway*

STRETTON, C. E. History of the Midland Railway; ill. 12/6 8° Methuen 01

WILLIAMS, F. S. History of the Midland Railway: rise and progress *o.p.* [*pb.* 6/] p 8° Bentley [76] 88

**Scotland**

ACWORTH, W. M. The Railways of Scotland 5/ c 8° Murray 90

**France**

MONKSWELL, L'd French Railways; ill. [descriptive] 3/6 *n.* c 8° Smith & Elder 11

**United States** —*v. also* **I** § 4

CARTER, C. F. When Railroads were New; ill. [8/ *n.* Bell] $2 *n.* 8° Holt, *N.Y.* 09
A popular account of early railway enterprise in the United States.

COOLEY, T. M. [ed.] The Railways of America; 200 ill. $6 l 8° Scribner, *N.Y.* 89
31/6 Murray. Constrn., developmt., managemt., and appliances. Popular. Each chap. by an American specialist.

CRAM, G. F. Standard Amer. Railway System and Atlas $12·50 f° Cram, *Chicago* [04] 08

DIXON, F. H. State Railroad Control [w. hist. in Iowa] $1·75 c 8° Crowell, *N.Y.* 96

DORSEY, E. B. English and American Railroads Compared; pl. $1·50 8° Wiley, *N.Y.* 87

HINE, C. De Lano Letters fr. an Old R'y Official to his Son 8° *Railway Age, Chicago* 05
Conts. many interesting, shrewd, and valuable points and suggestions for railway-men and managers.

POOR, H. V. Manual of the Railroads of the United States—*ut* **D** § 153

POOR, J. A. First Internat. Ry. and Colonizn. of New Engl. $3 8° Putnam, *N.Y.* 92

PRATT, A. E. American Railways [partly repr. fr. 'Times'] 3/6 *n.* ($1·25 *n.*) c 8° Macmillan 03

Railways of America. By var. wrs. Introd. Cooley; ill. 31/6 r 8° Murray 90

VROOMAN, C. S. Amer. Ry. Probls. in light of Eur. Experience (6/ *n.*) c 8° Clar. Press 10

WARMAN, C. Story of the Railroad; ill. [Story of West Ser.] $1·50 c 8° Appleton, *N.Y.* 98

*Cincinnati Southern Railway*

BOYDEN, H. P. Beginnings of Cincinnati Southern Ry. [1869–78] 50 c. c 8° Clarke, *Cincinnati* [01] 02

HOLLANDER, J. H. Cincinnati Southern Ry.: study in munic. activity $1 8° Johns Hopk. Pr., *Baltim.* 94

*Northern Pacific Railroad*

SMALLEY, E. V. History of Northern Pacific Railroad; ill. [1834–83] $3 8° Putnam, *N.Y.* 83

*Pennsylvania Railroad*

DREDGE, Jas. The Pennsylvania Railroad i 4° Wiley, *N.Y.* 79
52/6 l 4° *Engineering* Office. Organization, construction, and management. Fully illustrated.

*Union Pacific Railway*

DAVIS, Dr J. P. Union Pacific Ry. [politics, hist., economics] $2 8° Griggs, *Chicago* 94

" Union Pac. Ry. [paymt. of ry.-loan; Am. Ac. Pol. Sci.] 8° Macmillan, *N.Y.* 96

WHITE, Hy. Kirke History of the Union Pacific Railway $1·50 *n.* 8° Univ. Press, *Chicago* 95
[Chicago Univ. Econ. Studies.] A history of the ry. and of its peculiar relns. w. the U.S. govt.

**China**

KENT, P. H. Railway Enterprise in China; maps [orig. and devel.] 12/6 *n.* 8° Arnold 07

**Siberia**

RUSSIAN MINISTRY OF WAYS: Guide to Great Siberian Ry.; 7 maps and 362 ill. 18/ *n.* r 8° Stanford

**Statistics; 'Records'**

ALEXANDER, J. F. B. Runs in Three Continents 7/6 *n.* 8° Stock 00
Records of actual performances on European, Canadian, and other railways.

FOXWELL (T. C.) + FARRER (E.) Express Trains: English and Foreign; maps [statist. acc.] 6/ 8° Smith & Elder 89

MINOT, R. S. Railway Travel. in Europe & Amer. [25 statist. tables] 50 c. 8° Williams, *Boston* 82

**Economics; Administration**—*v. also* **I** § 4; *for* Finance, etc., *v.* **D** § 153

ACWORTH, W. M. Elements of Railway Economics 2/ *n.* (70 c.) c 8° Clar. Press 05

ADAMS, C. F., jun. Railroads & Railroad Quests. [ownership, use, admin.] $2·25 12° Putnam, *N.Y.* [75] 78

ALEXANDER, E. P. Ry. Practice: princs. & sugg. reforms [Questns. of Day] 75 c. 8° Putnam, *N.Y.* 87

ASHLEY, Ossian D. Railways and their Employés 8° *Railway Age* Off., *Chicago* 95
14 papers on the real and ideal relns. of railways to their employés, w. stray critical chaps. on Socialism thrown in.

BOLLAND, W. Railways and the Nation: probls. and possibilities [Sociolog. Ser.] 1/ *n.* c 8° Unwin 09

BONHAM, J. M. Railway Secrecy & Trusts [Questions of the Day] $1·25 (4/) c 8° Putnam 90
Analysis of chief evils of railway management in U.S. in rel. to interstate legislation.

JAMES, Dr E. J. The Railway Question [Johns Hopk. Univ. Studs.; 2/6 Sonnenschein] 75 c. *n.* 8° Macmillan, *N.Y.* 87

JEANS, J. S. Railway Problems: econ. condns. of ry. wkg. in diff. countries 12/6 ($4·25) 8° Longman 87
State control; cost of transport comp. w. rates; inland navign.; effect of cheap transport; ry. finance; rys. as investmts., etc., w. 220 statist. tables
LANGSTROTH, C. S. Railway Co-operation [Univ. of Penn. Studies] $1 8° Appleton, *N.Y.* 99
LARRABEE, W. Railroad Question: historical and practical treatise $1·50 12° Schulte, *Chicago* 93
MCDERMOTT, E. R. Railways [Books on Business] 2/6 *n.* c 8° Methuen 04
MORRIS, Roy Railroad Administration; 24 charts $2 *n.* (7/6 *n.*) 8° Appleton 11
RIPLEY, W. Z. [ed.] Railway Problems [Selns. and Docums. in Econcs.] $2·25 8° Ginn, *Boston* 07
STICKNEY, A. B. The Railway Problem; diagrs. (some col.) $2 12° Merrill, St Paul, *Minn.* 91
*India:* BELL (Hor.) Railway Policy in India; map [historical] 16/ 8° Rivington 94
GEORGE, E. Monson Railways in India: economic construction and management 2/6 c 8° E. Wilson 95
MACGEORGE, G. M. —*in his* Ways and Works in India, *ut* I § 3
*Continent of Europe*
Continental Railway Investigations [Belg., France, Italy] 2/4 8° P. S. King & Son
PRATT, E. A. German *v.* British Railways 1/ *n.* 8° P. S. King & Son 07

**Finance** —*v.* **D** § 153, *s.v.* Railways

**Organization; Management; Working** *v. also* **I** § 4
DEWSNUP, E. R. [ed.] Ry. Organizn. & Working [lects.; 9/ *n.* Unwin] $2 *n.* s 8° Univ. Press, *Chicago* 07
DIACOMIDIS, J. D. Statist. Tables of Wkg. of Rys. in Var. Countries 16/ *n.* 4° Spon [ ] 06
FINDLAY, Sir Geo. Working and Management of an English Railway; ill. 7/6 c 8° Whittaker [89]
$1 Macmillan, *N.Y.* By the General Manager of the London and North-Western Railway. A very good book.
HAINES, H. S. American Railway Management 10/6 c 8° Chapman 98
HAMBLEN, H. E. The General Manager's Story $1·50 c 8° Macmillan 98
In the form of fiction; but records many real experiences.
KEMPTHORNE, W. O. Principles of Railway Stores Management 10/6 *n.* 8° Spon 07
MITTON, Geo. The Book of the Railway; ill. [descriptive] 6/ c 8° Black 10
ROSS, H. M. British Railways: their organisation and management 5/ *n.* c 8° Arnold 04
*Accidents* —*v.* **I** § 4

**Rates** —*for* Law of Rating *v.* **D** § 67, *s.v.* Rating
ACWORTH, W. M. Railways and Traders [rates in theory and practice] 1/ c 8° Murray [91] 91
COTSWORTH, M. B. Railway Maximum Rates and Charges 6/6 18° Bemrose 92
DARLINGTON, H. R. Railway Rates and Carriage of Merchandize by Railway 25/ 8° Stevens 93
Incl. Provis. Orders of Bd. of Trade as sanct. by Parlt.. classifcn. of traffic and schedule of maximum rates and charges applic. to rys. of Gt. Brit.
GRAY, J. W. Railway Rate Handbooks 25/ *n.* l 8° Tapp & Toothill, *Leeds v.y.*
20 edns., ea. for a leadg. town in Gt. Brit., are pubd., shewg. rates betw. diff. centres, etc.
GRIERSON, J. Railway Rates: English and foreign 5/ 8° Stanford 86
HORROCKS, Jos. Railway Rates 21/ 8° Sonnenschein 09
An elaborate method of calculating equitable rates and charges for merchandise carried on railways.
JOHNSON (Dr E. R.) + HUEBNER (Dr G. G.) Railroad Traffic and Rates $5 *n.* (21/ *n.*) 8° Appleton 11
KIRKMAN, M. M. Railway Rates and Government Control $2·50 12° Rand & McNally, *Chicago* 92
MEYER, Prf. H. R. Government Regulation of Railway Rates—*ut* **D** § 124
PRATT, E. A. Railways and their Rates [$1·50 *n.* Dutton, *N.Y.*] 5/ *n.* c 8° Murray 05
Presents the case for the Railways. With Appendix on the British Canal problem.
PLEIGMAN, Prf. E. R. A. Railway Tariffs and the Inter-state Commerce Law 50 c. 8° Ginn, *Boston* 87
Explains the theory of rates. Defends 'pools'. Refers to all the principal foreign literature on the subject.
SMALLEY, H. S. Railrd. Rate Control [Am. Econ. Ass.; 3/6 Sonnenschein] $1 *n.* c 8° Macmillan, *N.Y.* 06
WAGHORN, T. Railways and Traders: the Traders' Case 4/ *n.* c 8° E. Wilson 07

**State and the Railways; Legislation**—*for* Law *v.* **D** § 81
CLARK, Dr F. C. State Railroad Commissions [Am. Ec. Ass.; 2/6 Sonnenschein] 75 c *n.* 8° Macm. *N.Y.* 90
DABNEY, W. D. Public Regulation of Railways [Questions of Day] $1·25 (5/) 12° Putnam 89
DIXON, Dr Fk. H. State Railroad Control [Libr. of Economics] $1·75 c 8° Crowell, *N.Y.* 96
Introdn. by Prf. H. C. ADAMS, who believes th. the solution of the Ry. Questn. must come about thro' ry. reguln. by Commissions, or Govt. ownership, latter meth. bg. rejected as undesirable.
HAINES, H. S. Restrictive Railway Legislation $1 *n.* (5/) c 8° Macmillan 05
HENDRICK Railway Control by Commissions [Questions of Day] $1 (4/) c 8° Putnam
HUDSON, J. F. The Railways and the Republic $2 8° Harper, *N.Y.* 86
MEYER, B. H. Railway Legislation in U.S. [Citizens' Lib.] $1·25 *n.* (5/ *n.*) c 8° Macmillan 03
*Progress of Railway Legislation; Past and Future of Inter-State Commission.*
MILLION, J. W. State Aid to Rys. in Mo. [Chic. Un. Econ. Studs.] $1·75 *n.* 8° Univ. Pr., *Chicago* 96

*State Purchase ; Nationalization*—*v.* **D** §§ 142, 146

**Transportation ; Traffic** —*v. also sup., s.v.* Rates (JOHNSON)

COOLEY, Dr C. H. Theory of Transportn. [Am. Ec. Ass. ; 2/6 Sonnenschein] 75 c. *n.* 8° Macm., *N.Y.* 95

HADLEY, Dr A. T. Railroad Transportation : hist. and laws [a v. good bk.] $1·50 12° Putnam, *N.Y* [85] 03

JOHNSON, Dr E. R. American Railway Transportation $1·50 *n.* (6/ *n.*) c 8° Appleton [03] 08
The best Am. bk. : ownersh., managemt., monopoly and competn., rates, fares, etc. Bibliogr.

" Elements of Transportation $1·50 *n.* (6/ *n.*) c 8° Appleton 11

McCAIN, C. C. Compendium of Transportation Theories $2 8° Kensington Pb. Co., *Washington* 93

McPHERSON, Logan The Working of the Railroads [6/ *n.* Bell] $1·50 *n.* p 8° Holt, *N.Y.* 07
A course of lects. on transportation del. at Johns Hopkins Univ. Amer. condns. kept in view.

" Transportation in Europe [5/ *n.* Constable] p 8° 11

NEWCOMB, H. T. Railway Economics [transportation questns.] $1 8° *Railway World* Pb. Co., *N.Y.* 98

RINGWALT (J. L.) Developmt. of Transn. Syst. in U.S.; 50 pl. [fr. earliest times] $7·50 f° Ringwalt, *N.Y.* 88

WEYL, W. E. Passenger Traffic in Rys. [Univ. of Penn. Studies] $1·50 8° Appleton, *N.Y.* [01] 02

WILLIAMS, S. C. The Economics of Railway Transport 3/6 *n.* c 8° Macmillan 09

**Accounts**—*v.* **D** § 150 **Engineering**—*v.* **I** § 4 **Law**—*v.* **D** §§ 81, 63

**Prospecting :** RAPIER (R. C.) Remunerative Railways in New Countries 15/ 8° Spon 78

**Railway Shares, etc., as Investments**—*v.* **D** § 153

## 153 : STOCKS AND SHARES

**Theory of Speculation and Fluctuations**—*v. also* **D** §§ 115, 116

BABSON, R. W. Business Barometers used in Forecasting Trade and Security Prices : textbk. of appl. economics [E. Wilson] $2 16° Auth., *Wellesley Hills, Mass.* [09] 10

BURN, Jos. Stock Exch. Investmts. in Theory and Practice 10/6 *n.* 8° C. & E. Layton

CRUMP, Arth. Theory of Stock Exchange Speculation *o.p.* [*pb.* 10/6] 8° Longman 75

ELLIS, A. Rationale of Market Fluctuations 7/6 8° E. Wilson [ ] 79

EMERY, Dr H. C. Speculn. on Stk. and Produce Exchs. of U.S. $1·50 *n.* 8° Macmillan, *N.Y.* 96
[Columbia Univ. Studies.] Occupied with the economic function of the exchange.

GIFFEN [Sir] Rob. Stock Exchange Securities : causes of their fluctuation 8/6 8° Bell [77] 79

**London Stock Exchange** —*for* Rules and Law *v.* **D** § 88

AUBREY, Dr W. H. S. St. Exch. Investmts. : theory, meths., pract., results 5/ Simpkin [96] 96
A popular, practical treatise on usages of Brokers and Jobber, Cover System, Settlemts., Transfers, Fluctuatns., *etc.*

CLARE, Geo. Money-Market Primer and Key to the Exchanges—*ut* **D** § 116

" The London Daily Stock & Share List [lectures] 1/6 c 8° C. & E. Layton

CORDINGLEY, W. G. Guide to the Stock Exchange 2/ *n.* c 8° E. Wilson 01

DUGUID, Chas. How to Read the Money Article 2/6 *n.* c 8° E. Wilson [01] 05

" The Stock Exchange [Books on Business] 2/6 *n.* c 8° Methuen 04

HIRST, Fcs. The London Stock Exchange [Home Univ. Lib.] 1/ *n.* c 8° Williams 11

INGALL (G. D.) + WITHERS (G.) The Stock Exchange 5/ *n.* c 8° Arnold 04

POLEY (A. P.) + GOULD (F. C.) Hist., Law, and Pract. of Stock Exchange 5/ *n.* 8° Pitman 07

WARREN, H. How to Deal with your Broker 3/6 c 8° Sonnenschein 05

*History of the London Stock Exchange*—*v. also* POLEY + GOULD, *sup.*

DUGUID, Chas. Story of the Stock Exchange : history and position ; ill. 6/ c 8° Richards 01
The best account. Enlarged from essay in *The Stock Exchange* in 1900, £15 (Spottiswoode), a copiously ill. work.

FRANCIS, J. Chronicles of the Stock Exchange [standard] *o.p.* [*pb.* 21/] 8° Willoughby 49

GIBSON, G. R. Stock Exchs. of Lond., Paris & N.Y. ; ill. [compar. & hist.] $1 12° Putnam, *N.Y.* 89

*'Options'*

HIGGINS, L. R. The Put-and-Call 3/6 *n.* 8° E. Wilson 96

*Terms* —*v. also* THORPE, *inf.*

CORDINGLEY, W. G. Dictionary of Stock Exchange Terms 2/6 *n.* c 8° E. Wilson 01

WILSON, A. J. Glossary of Slang, etc., in use in St. Exch. and Money Market—*ut* **K** § 241

*Values ; Prices*

CRUMP, Arth. Key to Lond. Money Market [Bk. of Engl. wkly. retns., *etc.*] 21/ 8° Longman [72] 77

" Key to Positn. and Progress of Lond. Jt.-Stk. Banks dur. 21 Years—*ut* **D** § 115

*FENN, Chas. On the Funds, ed. S. F. Van Oss + H. H. Bassett 15/ 8° E. Wilson [ ] 98
Details and histories of the Debts, Budgets, and Foreign Trade of all Nations ; with statistics elucidatg. financ. and econ. progress and positn. of the various countries.

GIBSON, A. H. The Fall in Consols and other Investmts. since 1897 5/ *n.* 8° Jackson, *Halifax* 07
Investign. into causes of rise fr. 1875 to 1897, and the fall since: former attrib. to increasg. excess of impts. over expts. per head of populn. and extensive purchasg. of consols on Savgs. Bk. acc.; latter to absence or reversal of these factors.

MATHIESON (F. C.) & SONS Handbook for Investors 2/6 *n.* 8° E. Wilson *ann.*
A pocket record of Stock Exch. prices and of divs. for previous 10 yrs. of 2,000 securities.

" Stock Exch. Ten-Yr. Record of Prices and Dividends 10/ *n.* i 8° E. Wilson 10

" Highest and Lowest Prices and Divs. of past 6 Yrs. 2/6 *n.* 8° E. Wilson 86 *sqq., ann.*

*SKINNER, T. [ed.] Stock Exchange Year Book [hist. and positn. of securities] 31/6 r 8° Office *ann.*

*Stock Exchange Official Intelligencer 50/ 4° Spottiswoode *ann.*

**New York Stock Exchange (Wall Street)**

CLEWS, Dr H. Fifty Years in Wall Street—*ut* **D** § 115

" The Wall Street Point of View $1·50 12° Silver, *N.Y.* 01

CONANT, C. A. Wall Street and the Country $1·25 (5/ *n.*) c 8° Putnam 04

NORTON, J. P. Statist. Studies in N.Y. Money Market [Yale Univ. Pbs.] $1 *n.* (6/ *n.*) 8° Macmillan 02

PRATT, S. S. The Work of Wall Street $1·25 *n.* (6/ *n.*) c 8° Appleton 03

**Investments**

'Banker's Daughter (A)' First Lessons in Business Matters 1/ c 8° Macmillan 93

GABBOTT, E. R. How to Invest Money 1/ *n.* 12° E. Wilson [92] 05

HADDEN, R. Investor's Adviser 5/ c 8° Harrison [94] 05

LOWENFELD, H. All about Investment 5/ *n.* 8° *Financ. Rev. of Reviews* 09

" Investment Practically Considered [repr. arts.] 5/ *n.* 8° *Financ. Rev. of Reviews* 09

" The Investment of Trust Funds 2/6 *n.* 8° Investmt. Registry 07

LOWNHAUPT, F. Investment Bonds: issue and relationships $1·75 *n.* (7/6) 8° Putnam 08

THORPE, C. H. How to Invest and How to Speculate 5/ c 8° Richards 01
Details of Stock Exch. business, and main classes of securities; w. Glossary of Terms.

*WITHERS, Hartley Stocks and Shares Smith & Elder *in prep.*
On various aspects of the securities in wh. people invest and speculate, and the cos. that produce them.

*Banks* —*v.* **D** § 116

*Industrials:* POOR (H. V.) Manual of Industrials [31/6 E. Wilson] 1 8° Poor, *N.Y.*

*Mines* —*v. also* **I** § 79

GABBOTT, E. R. How to Invest in Mines: mine, company and market 2/6 c 8° E. Wilson [93] 96
*Punch's* advice to those about to marry, *Don't!* may be safely applied here.

'MOIL, A' Mining and Mining Investments—*ut* **I** § 79

SKINNER, W. R. The Mining Manual 21/ 8° Simpkin [93] *ann.*

*Railways* —*for* Law of Ry. Securities *v.* **D** § 85

BRADSHAW'S Railway Manual and Shareholder's Guide 12/ 8° *Bradshaw Ho., Surrey St., Strand* [47] *ann.*
Past hist. and pres. financial positn. of every ry. in wh. Brit. capital is interested both at home and abroad.

CLEVELAND (Dr F. A.) + POWELL (F. W.) Railrd. Promotion and Capilizn. in U.S. $2 *n.* (7/6 *n.*) c 8° Longman 09
Both a history and a description of railway financial methods in U.S. Good bibliography on hist. and finance.

POOR, H. V. [ed.] Manual of Railroads of U.S., Can., & Mexico $7·50 l 8° Poor, *N.Y.* [67 *sqq.*] *ann.*
45/ *n.* E. Wilson. Route, mileage, stocks, bonds, debt, costs, traffic, earnings, divs., directors, etc.

SNYDER, Carl American Railways as Investments $3·20 *n.* 8° Moody Corpn., *N.Y.* 07

STEVENS, W. J. Home Railways as Investments; w. tables 2/6 *n.* c 8° E. Wilson 96

" Investment and Speculation in British Railways 4/ *n.* c 8° E. Wilson 02

VAN OSS, S. F. American Railroads as Investments; maps $4 8° Putnam, *N.Y.* 93
16/ E. Wilson. Sketches of leading American lines and railroad policy and prospects: a valuable book for investors.

WALL, W. W. British Railway Finance: guide to investors 6/ *n.* c 8° Richards 02
A full account, generally and individually, of the financial position of British Railways.

" How to Invest in Railways 6/ *n.* c 8° Richards 03

**Gambling; 'Futures'; Options**—*for* Ethical Aspect *v.* **A** § 113; Mathematical **H** § 7

RÜHLAND, Dr G. Ruin of World's Agriculture and Trade [tr.] 2/ r 8° Low 96
On international fictitious dealings in 'futures' of agricultural produce and silver.

SMITH, C. W. The S. African War and the 'Bear' Operation 2/ *n.* c 8° P. S. King & Son 02

" International Commercial and Financial Gambling 6*d.* *n.* 4° P. S. King & Son [06] 10
A manifesto against 'options' and 'futures', pleading for international legislation.

## 154: TABLES (MATHEMATICAL AND MONEY); WEIGHTS AND MEASURES

**Exchange Tables**

BARTLETT-AMATI, L. Banking and Commercial Tables between Gt. Britain and all other Pts. of the World 10/ *n.* r 8° Simpkin 04

COHN, M. Tables of Exchange [Engl., Frce., Belg., Switz., It.] 10/6 8° E. Wilson 72
DEUTSCH, Hy. Arbitrage in Bullion, Coins, Bills, Stocks, Shares, and Options 10/6 *n.* 8° E. Wilson
LECOFFRE, A. General Tables of Exchange 15/ *n.* r 8° McCorquodale
Francs, lire, Marks, $, Kronen, florins, kronos, pesetas, rupees, milreis—all into £.
REUTZSCH, B. J. Enlarged Exchange Tables 15/ 8° Roberts 84
,, Exchange and Bullion Tables 21/ 8° Roberts 84
TATE Modern Cambist, ed. H. T. Easton 12/ *n.* 8° E. Wilson [ ]
A manual of foreign exchanges and bullion, w. monetary systems of the world.

*American Currency*
American Exchange Rates [fr. $4·75 to $4·95] 40/ *n.* r 8° E. Wilson
HEAVINGHAM, E. L. Dollar Exchange Tables [$2 *n.* Dutton, *N.Y.*] 7/6 *n.* 8° Routledge 04
Dollars fr. 4/ to 4/2 pr. $ by 1-32*d.* per $; and fr. $4·80 to $4·90 pr. £ by ½ cent per £.
LECOFFRE, A. Tables of Exch. betw. U.S.A. and Gt. Britain 25/ *n.* r 8° McCorquodale [ ] 09
Dollars (in cents) to Engl. money at rates fr. $4·75 to $4·95 per £, advancg. by 1-16 cent; Engl. money to dollars (in cents) as above; dollars to Engl. money (in pence) at fr. 48 to 50 pence per $, by 1-32*d.*; Engl. money to dollars (in pence) as above, by 1-32*d.* 1 c. to $300,000, 1*d.* to £40,000 resp.
NORMAN, J. H. Universal Cambist 12/6 *n.* 8° E. Wilson
For. and Col. exchgs. of 7 monetary and currency intermediaries, etc.
SCHULTZ, C. W. H. Universal American Dollar Exch. Tables 10/6 *n.* 8° E. Wilson 74
From $4·80 to $4·90 per £, and fr. 3/10 to 4/6 per $; w. introd. ch. on coinages and exchanges of world.
,, Universal Dollar Tables: U.S. Edition 21/ *n.* 8° E. Wilson
Covers all exchanges betw. U.S. and Gt. Brit., Frce., Belg., Switzerl., Italy, Spain, Germany.

*South-American Currency*
GARRATT, Jno. Exchange Tables [S. Amer. and Brit. currency] 10/6 *n.* 8° E. Wilson

*Eastern Currencies: India, China, etc.*
LECOFFRE, A. Tables of Exch. for Eng. Money w. Eastern Currencies 21/ *n.* r 8° McCorquodale
Sterling into rupees at rates fr. 1/3½ to 1/4 23-32, advancg. by 1-32*d.*; rupees into sterlg. at above rates by 1-32*d.*; Engl. into yens, piastres and taels, at fr. 1/9 to 3/3 15-16, advcg. by 1-16*d.*; yens, etc., into Engl. at above rates, advcg. by 1-16*d.*
MERCES, F. A. D. Indian Exchange Tables 15/ *n.* 8° Thacker, *Calcutta* (E. Wilson) [80]
Engl. money into Ind. currency (and *vice versa*), calc. f. every 32nd of 1*d.*; 1/ to 1/6.
REUTZSCH, B. J. Indian Exchange Tables 15/ 8° Roberts [ ] 83
RUTTER, H. Exchange Tables betw. England, India, and China 30/ r 8° E. Wilson [ ] 76

*French, Belgian, and Swiss Currencies*
LECOFFRE, A. Tables of Exch. betw. Fce., Belg., Sw. & G.B. 21/ *n.* r 8° McCorquodale

*German, Austrian, and Dutch Currencies*
LECOFFRE, A. Tables of Exch. betw. Germany & Gt. Brit. 15/ *n.* 8° McCorquodale [ ] 09
Germ. to Engl. money at fr. 20·30 to 20·70 mks. per £, showg. value fr. 1 pfg. to 300,000 mks., advcg. by ¼ pfg.
,, Tables of Exch. betw. Austria, Holland, and Gt. Brit. 15/ *n.* 8° McCorquodale ] 09
Austrian and Dutch florins (in krs. or cents) to Engl. money at rates fr. 11·90 to 12·40 fl. per £, advcg. by ¼ kr. (or cent); Dutch florins (in stivers to Engl. at rates fr. 12 to 12·8 stivers, advcg. by ⅛ st.; Engl. money to Dutch fls. (in sts.) at above rates, advcg. by ⅛ st. 1 fl. to 100,000, 1*d.* to £5,000 resp.
SCHULTZ, C. W. H. English-German Exchange Tables 5/ *n.* 8° E. Wilson
20 to 21 Marks per £, by ·025 Mark per £ progressively.

*Russian Currency*
KOSCKY, G. Tables of Exch. betw. Russia and Gt. Brit. 6/6 *n.* 8° E. Wilson
Engl. money into roubles and kopecks and Russ. into £; 90–100 roubles, by 5 kopecks.

**Insurance Tables** —*v.* **D** § 151

**Interest; Annuities**
ARCHER, J. A. Tables for Repayment of Loans, etc. 17/6 *n.* r 8° Shaw [ ] 06
,, Compd. Interest Annuity and Sinkg. Fd. Tables 8/6 *n.* r 8° Shaw 07
BLAKE, J. Tables for Conversion of 5% Int. fr. $\frac{1}{16}$*d.* to 7% 12/6 8° Longman 90
BOOTH (A. A.) + GRAINGER (M. A.) Diagr. f. Calculg. Yield on Redeemable Stocks 10/6 *n.* E. Wilson 96
A useful diagram, by means of which, and a ruler, value of stock can be at once reduced to par.
BOSANQUET, Bern. T. Universal Simple Interest Tables 21/ 8° E. Wilson
Any sum at 100 rates fr. ¼ to 12¼%; also any sum for one day at above rates: to £50,000,000.
CROSBIE (A.) + LAW (W. C.) Tables for Conversn. of Products into Interest [29 rates] 12/6 *n.* r 8° E. Wilson [ ]
From 1 to 8 per cent. incl., proceedg. by quarter rates.
DOUGHARTY, H. Annuities & Sinkg. Fds. Simp. & Comp. Int. Tables 2/6 *n.* 8° E. Wilson
GILBERT, E. W. Tables of Interest [by ⅛ fr. ⅛% to 4%, 1 to 60 days, £1–100,000] 30/ 8° Hodder 81
,, Tables of Interest from 4⅛ to 5% 6/6 8° Hodder
,, Tables of Interest at 5% [£1–100,000, 1–125 days] 36/ 8° Hodder 83
GUMERSALL, T. B. Interest and Disc. Tables [2½–5%, 1–365 days, £1–20,000] 10/6 *n.* 8° E. Wilson [ ]
HANNYNGTON, Maj.-Gen. Interest Tables for all Rates 10/6 r 8° C. & E. Layton
Especially applicable to mutations of interest and varying balances.

HEATON, Jno. Interest Tables [1 to 5%, £1–100, 1–100 dys.] 3/6 c 8° Routledge *n.d.*
KING, Jos. Interest Tables at 5% [£1–10,000, 1–365 days] 7/6 m 8° Bell [ ] 90
*LAURIE, Jas. Tables of Simple Interest 21/ m 8° Routledge [ ] 08
At 5, 4½, 4, 3½, 3, 2½, and ½% per ann., 1 to 365 days; also Tables of Comp. Int., and of Brokerage, ⅛ to 10%.
" High Rate Tables of Interest [5–9½%] 7/6 8° Routledge [87]
" Compound Interest Tables 21/ 8° Bell [ ] 73
LECOFFRE, A. Universal Interest Tables at 5% [£1 to £100,000] 21/ *n.* r 8° McCorquodale
Also at 5% the interest fr. 1 to 100 and their multiples by 10, 100, 1,000, and 10,000 on any foreign money.
LEWIS, W. Tables for Finding the Number of Days 12/6 8° E. Wilson 74
OAKES, Lt.-Col. W. H. Tables of Comp. Int. [by ⅛ fr. ¾% to 10%, 1–100 yrs.] 42/ 8° C. & E. Layton 76
" Loans Payable by Drawings and Debent. Int. Tables 10/6 *n.* 8° C. & E. Layton
" Tables for Finding Half-yrly. Rate of Interest. fr. 1¼% upw. realized on Stock or Bonds bearg. 1½ to 3% hf.-yrly. int. 10/6 *n.* i 8° C. & E. Layton
OPPENHEIM, F. Universal Interest Tables [1/16 to 6%, by 1/16, 1 yr.] 4/ *n.* 8° E. Wilson
RANCE, T. G. Tables of Compound Interest [by ¼ fr. ¼% to 10%, 1–100 yrs.] 21/ r 8° C. & E. Layton
READER, Thos. Time Tables on New and Simplified Plan 2/6 *n.* ($1) c 8° Longman
Show no. of days fr. every day in yr. to any other day, for any period up to 365 days.
RUTTER, H. General Interest Tables [1–12%] 10/6 *n.* 8° E. Wilson
Dollars, frcs., milreis, etc., adapted to Engl. and Indian currency; 1 to 12% on decimal system.
STUBBINS, T. K. Tables of Present Value of Annuities payable by Monthly, Quarterly, and ½-yrly. Instalmts. at fr. 3 to 8% 6/ 8° C. & E. Layton [ ]
WILHELM, J. Comprehensive Tables of Compound Interest 2/6 obl. 8° E. Wilson 93
On £1, £5, £25, £50, £75 and £100, shewg. accumulns. yr. by yr. for 50 yrs. at rates of int. fr. 1 (progressg. ½) to 5%.

**Measures and Weights** —*v. also* **H** § 10; *for* Law *v.* **D** § 99
BROWNE, Dr W. A. Merchant's Book of Money, Weights, and Measures [w. Engl. equivalents] 5/ f 8° Stanford [6–] 92
CHADWICK, Wm. The Number, Weight, and Fractional Calculator 18/ 8° Lockwood [86] 90
CHANEY, H. J. Our Weights and Measures; 11 pl., and several ill. 7/6 8° Eyre & Spottiswoode 97
A practical treatise on the standard wts. and measures in use in Brit. Empire; contg. also acc. of Metric System.
CHISHOLM, H. W. On the Science of Weighing and Measuring *o.p.* [*pb.* 4/6] 12° Macmillan 77
CLARKE, F. W. Weights, Measures, & Money of all Nations $1·50 8° Appleton, *N.Y.* [75] 91
CLARKE, Latimer Dictionary of Metric Measures 6/ c 8° Spon 91
A very full colln. of tables, alphab. arrgd., for conversion of wts., meas., moneys, and various physical magnitudes. In each case not only the coverting factor is given, but also its reciprocal and its logarithm.
DONISTHORPE, Wordsworth System of Measures of Length, Area, Bulk, Weight, Value, Force, etc. 4° *priv. prin.* 95
*Method of Metrology, Modern English Standards, French System, Old Pipe Scale, Greek and Roman Measures, Metric System, Basic System, etc.*, with their various histories.
HATCH (Dr F. H.) + VALLENTINE (E. J.) Weights and Measures of International Commerce: tables and equivalents 2/6 *n.* 8° Macmillan 07
NEWDEGATE, A. L. British and Metric Weights and Measures 5/ c 8° Spon 71
NOEL, E. Science of Metrology: natural weights and measures 2/6 8° Stanford 90
RUTTER, H. Metrical System and Weights and Measures Tables 4/ 8° E. Wilson
SIDDONS (A. W.) + VASSALL (A.) Practical Measurements [Putnam, *N.Y.*] 1/6 8° Camb. Press 10
SMITH, Prf. R. H. Measurement Conversions, English and French 7/6 4° 98
28 tables shewg. conversions for different units of lengths, areas, volumes, weights, horse-power, etc.
WATSON, Col. Sir C. M. Brit. Wts. & Meas. as Descr. in Laws fr. Ang. Sax. Times 2/6 *n.* c 8° Murray 10
WOOLHOUSE, W. S. B. Measures, Wts., and Moneys of all Nations 2/6 f 8° Lockwood [ ] 91
[Weale's Series.] 80 c. Van Nostrand, *N.Y.*

**Metric System**—*v. also* **H** § 10: ANTHONY (E.) Enquiry into & Explan. of Decimal Coinage & Metric System of Weights and Measures 2/6 *n.* 4° Routledge [05] 05
ARNOLD-FORSTER, H. O. Coming of the Kilogram [Cheap Edn. 6*d.*] 2/6 ($1) c 8° Cassell 00
DELBOS, Leon The Metric System 2/ c 8° Methuen 00
JACKSON, S. The Metric System in Theory and Practice 1/ c 8° Allman 00
PERKIN, F. M. Metric and Brit. Systs. of Wts., Meas., and Coinage 1/6 *n.* 8° Whittaker 07
SMITH, J. Hamblin Elementary Treatise on the Metric System 2/ (75 c.) c 8° Longman 97
SPENCER, Herb. The Metric System 6*d.* 8° Williams 96
Repr. of 3 letters to *The Times*, advocating the reorganization of our system of numeration on the duodecimal system.
WAGSTAFF, Prf. W. H. Metric Wts. and Meas. compared with Imperial 1/6 c 8° Whittaker 96
4 lectures delivered at Gresham College; a good popular account.

*History of Weights and Measures and of Metric System*—*v. also* DONISTHORPE, *sup.*

HALLOCK (W.) + WADE (H. T.) Outlines of the Evolution of Weights and Measures and the Metric System 10/*n.* ($2·25 *n.*) 8° Macmillan 06

RIDGEWAY, Prof. Wm. Origin of Metallic Currency and Weight Standards—*ut* **G** § 20

WARREN, Lt.-Gen. Sir Chas. The Ancient Cubit & Our Weights & Measures 5/9 8° Palestine Exp. Fund 03
Attempts to show that al. wts. and meas. now in use (exc. the metric) are derived fr. the orig. double cubit cubed of Babylonia.

**Mathematical Tables**

CUNNINGHAM, Lt.-Col. A Binary Canon 15/ 4° Taylor & Francis 01
Gives residues of powers of 2 for divisors under 1,000, and indices to residues. Prepared under ausp. of Brit. Assoc.

GALBRAITH (A.) + HAUGHTON (S.) Manual of Mathematical Tables 3/6 12° Cassell

LAW (H.) + YOUNG (J. R.) Mathematical Tables 4/ c 8° Lockwood [ ] 79

PRYDE, J. Mathematical Tables 4/6 c 8° Chambers [ ] 78

*Logarithms*

HANNYNGTON, Maj.-Gen. Table of Logs. & Anti-Logs. [4 figs.; 1–10,000] 5/*n.* m 8° C. & E. Layton

SANG, E. New Table of Seven-place Logarithms [20·000–200·000] 21/i 8° Layton

SCOTT, E. Erskine 2 Tables of Logarithms to Natural Nos. [1–99,999] 42/*n.* r 8° C. & E. Layton [ ]

" Short Table of Logs. and Anti-Logs. [to 10 places] 10/*n.* r 8° C. & E. Layton

" Improved Table of Five-figure Logarithms 7/6 *n.* 8° C. & E. Layton

SHORTREDE, R. Logarithms of Sines and Tangents [for every second] 30/ r 8° C. & E. Layton [ ]

*Products and Quotients*

CRELLE, A. L. Tables for givg. Prods. and Quots. [18/ Layton; 2 nos. up to 1,000] 15 *m.* 4° G. Reimer, *Berlin* [ ] 95

LAUNDY, S. L. Table of Products by Factors [1–9, up to 100,000] 5/ r 4° C. & E. Layton

*Quarter-Squares*

BLATER, Jos. Table of Quarter-Squares [1–200,000: for sq. roots] 21/ r 4° Trübner (Paul) 88

LAUNDY, S. L. Table of Quarter-Squares of Integer Nos. [up to 100,000] 21/*n.* r 8° C. & E. Layton

*Reciprocals of Numbers*

OAKES, Lt.-Col. W. H. Table of Reciprocs. of Nos. [1–100,000; w. diffces.] 21/*n.* r 8° C. & E. Layton 65

*Traverse Tables* —*v.* **I** § 7

**Ready Reckoners**

COTSWORTH, M. B. The Railway and Traders' Calculator 10/6 4° McCorquodale [ ] 02

*HEATON, Jno. Enlarged Ready Reckoner [135,000 calculns.] 2/6 c 8° Routledge [ ] *n.d.*

HOTSON, W. C. General Ready Reckoner, 2 vols., ea. 8/6; Suppl. 2/6 8° Butterworth [ ]

KLEIN, R. The Quick Calculator: in 4 languages 2/6 *n.* obl. 64° Routledge [05] 09

MASTERS Ready Reckoner [63,000 calculns.] 1/; 2/6 12° Routledge [ ] *n.dd.*

MERCES, F. A. D. Indian Ready Reckoner 25/*n.* 8° E. Wilson [ ]
Tables of rates by no., quantity, wt., etc., at rates fr. ½ pie to 250 rs., etc.

National Ready Reckoner 5/ f 8° Collins [ ] 01

**Valuation Tables; Tables for Purchase of Estates**—*for* Principles of Valuation *v.* **D** § 150

BIDEN, W. D. Rules, Formulæ, and Tables f. Valn. of Estates 12/ 8° C. & E. Layton

" Practical Rules for Valuers [chiefly of estates] 1/6 12° C. & E. Layton

INWOOD, W. Tables for Purchasing of Estates, ed. Thoman 8/ 12° C. & E. Layton [ ] 04

WILLICH, C. M. Popular Tables, ed. H. Bence Jones 10/6 c 8° Longman [ ]
Tables for ascertaing. value of lifehold, leasehold, and Church property, the public funds, etc.

*Bonds*

CROAD, H. J. How to Value Bonds, by Meth. of U.S. Treasy. Dept. [42/*n.* Layton]
Any bond runng. fr. ½ yr. to 50 yrs. (int. payable ½-yrly.) can be valued to realize 1 to 10% rising by ⅛% fr. 1 to 7% by ¼% fr. 7½ to 10%.

# XIV: Education

## I: Comprehensive Works on Pedagogy

### 155: BIBLIOGRAPHY; CYCLOPÆDIAS; ENCYCLOPÆDIAS

**Bibliography** —*v. also* **D** § 156 (CUBBERLEY)

HALL (Prf. G. S.) + MANSFIELD (J. M.) Hints tow. a Bibliogr. of Educn. [Pedagog. Lib.] $1·50 c 8° Heath, *Boston* [87] 93

KLINKHARDT, Jul. Bibliotheca Pedagogica [German bks.] 8° Klinkhardt, *Lpz.* 9–
LOCKE, Geo. H. Bibliography of Secondary Education 25 c. *n.* r 8° Univ. Press, *Chicago*
*MONROE, Prf. W. S. Bibliography of Education (8/6) c 8° Appleton [97] 07
[Internat. Educ. Series.] Classified; with occasional notes. About 3,200 books and pamphlets; no prices. Ends w. 1897.
*Musée Pédagogique, Paris: Catal. By Bonet-Maury; 2 v. & Suppl. Impr. Nat. (Hachette), *Paris* 86–9
The fullest bibliogr. of educl. bks. hitherto pubd. in any country—some 50,000 wks., largely French.
NATL. EDUC. ASSOC.: Index to Pubns. of First Fifty Yrs [1857–1906] 8° Nat. Ed. Ass., *Winona, Minn.* 07
SONNENSCHEIN, Wm. Swan Bibliogr. of Pedagogy—*appended* to Sonnenschein's Cyclo. of Educ., *ut inf.*
WYER (J. I.) + BROWN (Mary G.) Bibliography of Education
[repr. fr. 'Educ. Rev.'] 8° Columb. Univ., *N.Y.* 00 *sqq., ann.*

*Sixteenth Century*

BUISSON, Ferd. [ed.] Repertoire d. Ouvrages Pédag. d. 16e Siède [p. 733] 8° Hachette, *Paris*

*Periodical and School-Programme Literature*

SCHULZE, C. Syst. Uebers. d. in Zschr., Program. [*etc.*] Aufsätze üb. Päd. 3*m*·60 8° Meyer, *Hanover* 87
[Pädag. Bibl.] A useful list of the more valuable essays on pedagogy wh. appeared in journals, *etc.*, fr. 1880 to 1886.
VARNHAGEN, Herm. —*in his* Systematisches Verzeichniss d. Programmabhandlungen, *etc.*, *ut* **K** § 92
Pp. 227–229 are devoted to *Pädagogik u. Methodik*: general treatment, and English and Romance philology.
U. S. Bureau of Educ. Catal. of Educational Literature *n.p.* 8° Bur. of Educ., *Washington* 92 *sqq.*
An analytical index to BARNARD's Amer. Journal of Educn., 31 vols. [1855–81, when it was discont.].

*Books for School Libraries* —*v.* **K** § 10

## Cyclopædias

KIDDLE (H.) + SCHEM (A. J.) Cyclopædia of Education $4 m 8° Steiger, *N.Y.* [77] 83
Deals almost exclusively w. Amer. and Brit. subjs.; somewhat restricted in scope. Statistical pt. [by SCHEM] of chief value.
" + " Dictionary of Education [abdgmt. of above] $1·50 8° Steiger, *N.Y.* 81
The *Yearbook of Education*, ed. by same, for 1878 and 1879 [ea. $1·25, Steiger, *N.Y.* '78–9] supplement above.
LAURIE, A. P. [ed.] The Teacher's Encyclopædia, vol. i; ill. (some col.) 8° Caxton Pb. Co. 11 *in prg.*
MONROE, Dr Paul [ed.] Cyclopædia of Education, v. i [A-Chu]; ill. (21/ *n.*) i 8° Macmillan 11 *in prg.*
An important and comprehensive wk., ed. by departmental edrs. and contrib. to by over 1,000 contribrs.
SONNENSCHEIN & Co. [pubs.] Cyclopædia of Education, ed. A. E. Fletcher, rev. M. E. John
2/6 *n.* m 8° Sonnenschein [88] 06
$1 *n.* Macmillan, *N.Y.* 530 double-col. pp. The best small general cyclo. Appendix conts. *Bibliography of Education* (31 pp.).

*Directory of Universities*

Minerva: Jahrbuch d. Universitäten d. Welt, hrsg. Dr R. Kukula + K. Trübner
12° Trübner, *Strassb.* 92 *sqq., ann.*
An academic directory of all Univs. of world, in alphab. order, w. statistics, teaching staff and general nominal index at end.

## Collected Essays —*v. also* **D** § 161, *passim*

ANDERSON, Martin B. Papers and Addresses, ed. Dr W. C. Morey, 2 v.
$2·50 c 8° Am. Bapt. Pb. Soc., *Phila.* 95
By the late President of the Univ. of Rochester. The 1st group (of 5) consists of educ. papers and addresses.
ARMSTRONG, Prf. H. E. Teachg. of Scient. Method and other Papers on Educ. 6/ ($1·50 *n.*) c 8° Macm. 03
AVEBURY, L'd Addresses, Political and Educational—*ut* **D** § 142
'AZARIAS, B'r' [P. F. MULLANY; R.-C.] Essays, vol. i: Educational—*ut* **A** § 97
*Cloistral Schls.*; *The Palatine Schl.*; *Mediaev. Univ. Life*; *Univ. colleges, orig. and meths.*; *Primary Schl. in Mid. Ages*; etc.
BAKER, J. H. Education and Life: papers and addresses 4/6 ($1·25) c 8° Longman 01
BROWN, Elmer E. Governmt. by Influence and other Addresses $1·35 *n.* (5/ *n.*) 8° Longman 10
14 addresses on Amer. educ. questns or deliv. at Amer. univs., by Comm'r of Educ. of U.S.A.
BUTLER, Prf. N. M. Meaning of Education & other Essays & Addr. $1 (4/6) c 8° Macmillan [98] 05
The other ess. are:—*What Knowl. is of most Worth?*; *Is there a New Educ.?*; *Democracy and Educ.*; *The Amer. College and Amer. Univ*; *Functn. of Second. Schl.*; *Reform of Second. Educ. in U.S.*
CREIGHTON, Bp M. Thoughts on Education [speeches & serms.] 5/ *n.* ($1·60 *n.*) c 8° Longman 02
DEWEY, Jno. School & Child: seln. fr. educ. essays, ed. J. J. Findlay 1/ *n.* 12° Blackie 07
ELIOT, C. W. Educational Reform [addresses 1869–97] $2 c 8° Century Co., *N.Y.* 98
Essays, Mock Essays, and Character Sketches 6/ c 8° *Jl. of Educ.* Off. 98
24 essays by var. wrs., repr. f. *Jl. of Educ.*; w. contribns. by Hon. L. A. TOLLEMACHE. 'Esoteric pedagogics have been eschewed'.
GILDERSLEEVE, B. L. Essays and Studies $3·50 (14/) sq 8° Putnam 90
The educ. essays are on *Limits of Culture*, *Classics and Colleges*, *Univ. Work in America*, *Grammar and Æsthetics*.
HALDANE, R. B. Education and Empire 5/ *n.* c 8° Murray 02
Thoughtful addresses on *German and British Educn.*, *Schools and Universities in Scotld.*, *Imperial Federn.*, etc.
HALE, E. E. Addresses and Essays on Hist., Educ., Govt. [=Wks., vol. viii]
$1·50 c 8° Little & Brown, *Boston* [v.y.] 00
HENDERSON, C. H. Education and the Larger Life $1·30 *n.* c 8° Houghton, *Boston* 02
*Point of View*; *The Social Purpose*; *Source of Power*; *Organic Educ.*; *Cause and Effect*; *Childhd.*; *Youth*; *Holidays*; *At the Univ.*; *The Experimental Life*; *The Agents of the Social Purpose*. Main value lies in its sincere and inspiring idealism.

**Huxley**, Prf. T. H. Science and Education = Collected Essays, vol. iii, *ut* **K** § 83
*Jos. Priestley* [1874]; *Educ. Value of Nat. Hist. Sciences* ['54]; *Emancipn.*; *Black and White* [higher educ. of girls; '65]; *A Liberal Educ.* ['68]; *Scient. Educ.* ['69]; *Science and Culture* ['80]; *Sci. and Art in rel. to Educ.* ['82]; *Universities: Actual and Ideal* ['74]; *On Univ. Educ.* ['76]; *Study of Biology* ['76]; *Elem. Instrn. in Physiol.* ['77]; *On Medical Educ.* ['70]; *State and Med. Professns.* ['84]; *Conn. of Biol. and Med.* ['81]; *Schl. Boards* ['70]; *Techn. Educ.* ['77]; *Addr. on Techn. Educ.* ['87].

**Ladd**, Prf. G. T. Essays on the Higher Education $1 *n.* c 8° Scribner, *N.Y.* 99
*Amer. Educn.*; *Developmt. of Am. University*; *The Fitting School in Education, Old and New*; *A Modern Liberal Educn.*

**Laurie**, Prf. S. S. Occasional Addresses on Educ. Subjs. [theory & biogr.] *o.p.* [*pb.* 5/] c 8° Camb. Press 88

**Lockyer**, Sir N. Education and National Progress 5/ *n.* 8° Macmillan 06
Essays and addresses, from 1870 to 1905; w. Introd. by R. B. Haldane.

**Muir**, R. J. Ruskin Revised, and other Papers on Educn. 2/ 8° Oliver & Boyd, *Edin.* 97

**Rooper**, T. G. [H.M.I.] Essays and Lects. on Current Educl. Topics 6/ c 8° Brown, *Hull* 96
,, School and Home Life: essays on curr. educ. topics 3/6 *n.* c 8° Brown, *Hull* 99
,, Educational Studies and Addresses 2/6 *n.* c 8° Blackie 02
,, Selected Writings, ed. R. G. Tatton 7/6 *n.* 8° Blackie 07

**Seehan**, Can. P. A. [R.-C.] Early Essays and Lectures 6/ *n.* ($1·60 *n.*) c 8° Longman 06
Mag. arts. on a variety of topics: *Relig. Instrn.*, *Germ. Univs.* (3 essays), *Character*, etc.

**Smith**, Arnold W. Educn. & Ethics, & other Essays on Educ. Subjs. 2/ *n.* c 8° St George Pr., *Birm.* 06
*The Human Boy, Discipline, Pedagogue in Fact and Fictn., Conflict of Studies, Modern University.*

**Tarver**, J. C. Debateable Claims: essays on secondary educn. 6/ c 8° Constable 98
,, Some Observations of a Foster Parent 6/ c 8° Constable 97
Readable and clever discursive essays on schls., masters, boys, and much th. concerns each of them.

**Walker**, F. A. Discussions in Education, ed. J. P. Munroe $3 8° Holt, *N.Y.* 99

**Wilkinson**, Prf. Spencer [ed.] The Nation's Need: chapters on educn. 6/ c 8° Constable 03
By var. wrs. *Elem. Educn.* (Marvin + Graham Wallas); *Girls' Primary Educn.* (Cath. I. Dodd); *Higher Educn. in Frce.* (Hartog); *Do. in Germy.* (Findlater); *Engl. Secondary Schls.* (Findlater); *Public Schls.* (J. C. Tarver); *Univs.* (H. C. Mackinder); *Tchg. of Mod. Langs.* (Breul).

## Series

**American Teachers Series: ed. Dr Jas. E. Russell** ea. $1·50 (6/ *n.*) c 8° Longman *v.y.*

Bourne (H. E.), *Tchg. of Hist. and Civics* [*ut* **D** § 167]
Carpenter (G R.) + Baker (F. T.), *Tchg. of Engl.* [*ut* **D** § 167].
Lloyd (F. E.) + Bigelow (M. A.), *Tchg. of Biology* [*ut* **D** § 167]
Richards (C. R.), *Manual Training* [*ut* **I** § 167]
Smith (Alex.), *Tchg. of Chem. and Phys.* [*ut* **D** § 167]
Young (J. W. A.), *Tchg. of Mathemas.*, 2 Pts. [*ut* **D** § 167]

**Columbia Univ.: Contribns. to Philos., Psychol., and Education** *v.p.* 8° Macmillan, *N.Y.* 94 *sqq., in prg.*

i–v (philosophical)—*v.* **C** § 1
vi (1–4) *Educat. Legisln. and Administns. in Colonies* E. W. Clews $2 *n.*
vii (1) *Educn. of the Pueblo Child* F. C. Spencer 75 c. *n.*
(2) *Econ. Aspect of Teachers' Salaries* C. B. Dyke $1 *n.*
(3) *Education in India* W. L. Chamberlain 75 c. *n.*
(4) *Horace Mann in Ohio* G. A. Hubbell 50 c. *n.*
viii (1) *Imitation in Educ.* J. N. Deahl *o.p.* [*pb.* 60 c. *n.*]
(2) *Histor. Developmt. of School Reading Books* *o.p.*
(3–4) *Notes on Child Study* E. L. Thorndike $1 *n.*
ix–x (philosophical)—*v.* **C** § 1
xi (1) *School Administrn. and Munic. Govt.* F. Rollins 75 c. *n.*
(2) *Heredity, Correlation and Sex Differences in School Abilities* E. L. Thorndike 50 c. *n.*
(3–4) *College Admission Requirements* E. C. Broome $1 *n.*
xii (1–4) *Professl. Training of Secondary Teachers in U.S.* G. W. A. Lucky $2·50 *n.*

**Education Library** *v.p.* c 8° Paul [81–8] *v.y.*

Browning (O.), *Hist. of Educ. Theories* [*ut* **D** § 156] 3/6
Landon (J.), *School Management* [*ut* **D** § 170] 6/
Laurie (S. S.), *J. A. Comenius* *o.p.*
Not repr. in the ser., but by Camb. Press [*ut* **D** § 161].
Magnus (Sir Pp.), *Industrial Education* [*ut* **D** § 167] 6/
Mahaffy (Prf. J. P.), *Old Greek Education* [*ut* **D** § 157] 3/6

**Great Educators, The** [ea. $1 *n.* Scribner, *N.Y.*] ea. 5/ c 8° Heinemann 92 *sqq., in prg.*

*Abelard* [*ut* **D** § 161] J. G. Compayré
*Alcuin* [*ut* **D** § 161] A. F. West
*Aristotle* [*ut* **D** § 157] Dr T. Davidson
*Arnold* (*T. and M.*) [*ut* **D** § 161] Sir J. Fitch
*Froebel, Friedrich* [*ut* **D** § 165] H. C. Bowen
*Herbart* [*ut* **C** § 161] Dr C. De Garmo
*Loyola, Ignatius* [*ut* **D** § 161] Rev. T. Hughes
*Mann, Horace* [*ut* **D** § 161] B. A. Hinsdale
*Pestalozzi* [*ut* **D** § 161] A. Pinloche
*Rousseau* [*ut* **D** § 161] T. Davidson
A series of biographies, with concise accounts of the associated movements.

**International Education Series: ed. Dr W. T. Harris** ea. $1·50 (6/) c 8° Appleton 87 *sqq., in prg.*

Adler (F.), *Moral Instrn. of Childr.* [*ut* **D** § 167]
Baldwin (J.), *Psychol. and Educ.* [*ut* **D** § 162]
,, *Psych. appl. to Art of Tchg.* [*ut* **D** § 162]
,, *School Managemt.* [*ut* **D** § 170]
Blow (Sus. E.), *Letters to a Mother* [*ut* **D** § 164]
,, *Symbolic Education* [*ut* **D** § 165]
,, *Educ. Issues in Kg.* [*ut* **D** § 165]
,, + Eliot (H. R.), *Mottoes and Comms. of Froebel's Mother-Play* [*ut* **D** § 165]
Bolton (Dr F. E.), *Second. Schl. Syst.* [*ut* **D** § 157]
Boone (Prf. R. G.), *Hist. of Educ. in U.S.* [*ut* **D** § 157]
Compayré (G.), *Developmt. of Child* [tr.] [*ut* **C** § 71]
,, *Later Infancy of Child* [*ut* **D** § 162] $1·20 *n.* (5/ *n.*)
Davidson (T.), *Educn. of Gk. People* [*ut* **D** § 157]
Fouillée (A.), *Educ. fr. Natl. Stdpt.* [tr.] [*ut* **D** § 163]
Froebel (F.), *Educ. of Man* [tr.] [*ut* **D** § 165]
,, *Educ. by Developmt.* [tr.] [*ut* **D** § 165]
,, *Laws for All Teachers* [tr.] [*ut* **D** § 165]
,, *Mother-Play* [tr.] [*ut* **D** § 165]
,, *Pedagogics of Kindergarten* [tr.] [*ut* **D** § 165]
Greenough (J. C.), *Evoln. of Elem. Schls.* [*ut* **D** § 157] $1·20 *n.* (5/ *n.*)
Greenwood (J. M.), *Princs. of Education* [*ut* **D** § 170] $1 (4/6)
,, + de Guimps (R.), *Pestalozzi* [tr.] [*ut* **D** § 161]
Harris (W. T.), *Psychologic Foundng. of Educ.* [*ut* **D** § 162]
Herbart (J. F.), *ABC of Sense-Perceptn.* [tr.] [*ut* **D** § 161]
,, *Textbk. in Psychology* [tr.] [*ut* **D** § 162]
Hinsdale (B. A.), *How to Study History* [*ut* **D** § 167]
,, *Teaching the Language-Arts* [*ut* **D** § 167]
Howe (E. G.), *Advanced Elementary Science* [*ut* **D** § 167]
,, *Systematic Science Tchg.* [*ut* **D** § 167]
Howland (G.), *Prac. Hints to Tchrs.* [*ut* **D** § 170] $1 (4/6)
Hughes (J. L.), *Dickens as an Educator* [*ut* **K** § 24]
Johonnot (J.), *Princs. and Pract. of Tchg.* [*ut* **D** § 170]
Judd (C. F.), *Genetic Psychol. f. Tchrs.* [*ut* **D** § 162]
†Kay (D.), *Memory* [*ut* **D** § 163]
Klemm (L. R.), *European Schools* [*ut* **D** § 156] $2 (8/6)
Lange (Hel.), *Higher Educ of Women* [tr.] [*ut* **D** § 168] $1 (4/6)
†Laurie (S. S.), *Rise of Universities* [*ut* **D** § 157]
McLellan (J. A.) + Dewey (J.), *Psychol. of Number* [*ut* **D** § 167]
Martin (G. H.), *Massach. Pub.-Sch. Syst.* [*ut* **D** § 157]
Monroe (W. H.), *Bibliogr. of Educn.* [*ut* **D** § 155]
,, (P.), *Thomas Plättner* [*ut* **D** § 161] $1·20 (5/ *n.*)
de Montaigne (M. E.), *Educ. of Children* [tr.] [*ut* **D** § 161]
Morrison (G. B.), *Ventiln. of Schl. Bldgs.* [*ut* **D** § 171] 75 c. (3/6)
Painter (F. V. N.), *Hist. of Educn.* [*ut* **D** § 156]
Parker (F. W.), *How to Study Geography* [*ut* **D** § 167]
Pickard (J. L.), *School Supervision* [*ut* **D** § 170] $1 (4/6)
Preyer (W.), *Mind of Child* [tr.] i.: *Senses and Will*, ii.: *Devel. of Intellect* [*ut* **C** § 71]
†Quick (R. H.), *Educational Reformers* [*ut* **D** § 156]
Rosenkranz (J. K.), *Philos. of Educ.* [tr.] [*ut* **D** § 161]
Ross (G. W.), *Schl. Syst. of Ontario* [*ut* **D** § 157] $1 (4/6)
Rousseau (J. J.), *Emile* [tr.] [*ut* **D** § 161]
Search (P. W.), *An Ideal School* $1·20 *n.* (5/ *n.*)
Sheldon (H. D.), *Student Life* [*ut* **D** § 158] $1·20 *n.* (5/ *n.*)
Sharpless (Is.), *English Education* [*ut* **D** § 157] $1 (4/6)
Taylor (A. R.), *Study of the Child* [*ut* **C** § 71]
Ware (Fabian), *Educ. Foundns. of Trade* [*ut* **D** § 167] (5/ *n.*)

† Not saleable in Engld., bg. Eng. copyrt. bks.

LIPPINCOTT'S [pubs.] Educational Series: ed. Dr M. G. Brumbaugh, vols. i–vii
ea. $1·25 12° Lippincott, *Phila.* 02 *sqq., in prg.*

i: *Thinking and Learning to Think* Dr N. C. SCHAEFFER
ii: *Two Cents. of Penns. Hist.* [*ut* **D** § 157] Dr I. SHARPLESS
iii: *History of Education* [*ut* **D** § 156] E. L. KEMP
iv: *Educ. Theory of Kant* [*ut* **D** § 161] E. F. BUCKNER
v: *The Recitation* [*ut* **D** § 167] S. HAMILTON
vi: *The Educatl. Process* A. C. FLESHMAN
vii: *Study of Nature* [*ut* **D** § 167] S. C. SCHMUCKER

MACMILLAN [pubs.] Pedagogical Lib. (The): 16 vols. [sold in sets only] $12 *n.* c 8° Macmillan, *N.Y.*

BUTLER (N. M.), *Meaning of Educn.*
CHUBB (P.), *Teaching of English* [*ut* **D** § 167]
DE GARMO (C.), *Interest and Educn.* [*ut* **D** § 163]
HORNE (H. H.), *Philosophy of Educn.* [*ut* **D** § 161]
KIRKPATRICK (E. A.), *Fundams. of Child Study* [*ut* **C** § 71]
MCMURRY (C. A.), *Elems. of Gen. Method* [*ut* **D** § 163*]
„ + F. M., *Method of the Recitn.* [*ut* **D** § 167]
MCMURRAY (C. A.), *Spec. Meth. in Geogr.* [*ut* **D** § 167]
„ *Special Meth. in History* [*ut* **D** § 167]
„ *Special Meth. in Science* [*ut* **D** § 167]
ROWE (S. H.), *Phys. Nature of Child*
ROYCE (J.), *Outlines of Psychol.* [*ut* **D** § 162]
SHAW (E. R.), *School Hygiene* [*ut* **D** § 171]
SMITH (D. E.), *Tchg. of Elem. Mathcs.* [*ut* **D** § 167]

Monographs on Education ea. 25 c. 12° Heath, *Boston* 86 *sqq., in prg.*

GENUNG (J. F.), *Rhetoric* [*ut* **D** § 167]
HALL (G. S.), *Schl. Readg.* [*ut* **D** § 167]
HUFFCUT (E. W.), *English in Prep. Schls.* [*ut* **D** § 167]
MORRIS (E. P.), *Study of Latin* [*ut* **D** § 167]
PHILLIPS ( ), *History and Literature* 15 c.
RICE (W. N.), *Science Teaching* [*ut* **D** § 167]
SAFFORD (T. E.), *Mathem. Teachg.* [*ut* **D** § 167]
WILLIAMS (G. H.), *Petrography* [*ut* **D** § 167]
WOODWARD (F. C.), *Engl. in Schls.* [*ut* **D** § 167]
WOODWARD (C. M.), *Manual Training* [*ut* **D** § 167]

National Soc. for Scientific Study of Educn. (*form.* Natl. Herbart Soc.) Pubns. 8° Univ. Press, *Chicago*
Natl. Herb. Soc., *Yearbooks* i–v, ea. 75 c. *n.*, *Suppls.*, ea. 25 c. *n.*: the 5 *Yrbks.* and 6 *Suppls.* $5 *n.* '95–9; Nat. Soc., *Yrbks.* i–viii, ea. in 2 Pts., ea. Pt. 50 c. *n.* to 75 c. *n.* '02–9 *in prg.*

Pedagogical Library c 8° Heath, *Boston* 83 *sqq., in prg.*

ADAM (J.), *Herbartian Psych. Applied* [*ut* **D** § 161] $1
ASCHAM (R.), *The Scholemaster* [*ut* **D** § 161] $1·25
BARNES (Mary S.), *Historical Method* [*ut* **D** § 167] 60 c.
BARRETT, *Pract. Pedagogy* $1
BURRAGE + BAILEY, *Schl. Sanitn.* [*ut* **D** § 171] $1·50
CHANCELLOR (W. E.), *Our Schools* [*ut* **D** § 157] $1·50
„ *Our City Schools* [*ut* **D** § 157] $1·25
CLOYD, *Benj. Franklin and Educ.* $1
COMENIUS (J. A.), *Schl. of Infancy* [tr.] [*ut* **D** § 161] $1
COMPAYRÉ (G.), *Hist. of Pedagogy* [tr.] [*ut* **D** § 156] $1·75
„ *Lects. on Pedagogy* [tr.] [*ut* **D** § 161] $1·75
„ *Psychol. appl. to Educ.* [*ut* **D** § 162] 90 c.
DAVENPORT, *Educ. for Efficiency* $1
DE GARMO (C.), *Essentials of Method* [*ut* **D** § 163*] 65 c.
†GILL (J.), *Systems of Educ.* [*ut* **D** § 157] $3·25
HALL (G. S.) [ed.], *Tchg. Hist.* [*ut* **D** § 167] $1·50
„ + MANSFIELD (J. M.), *Bibliogr. of Educ.* [*ut* **D** § 155] $1
†HERBART (J.), *Introd. to Educ.* [tr.] [*ut* **D** § 161] $1
† „ *Science of Educ.* [tr.] [*ut* **D** § 161] $1
HERTFORD (W. H.), *Student's Froebel* [*ut* **D** § 165] 75 c.
HOLLIS, *Oswego Movemt.* $1
HOLLISTER, *High Schl. Admin.* [*ut* **D** § 157] $1·50
KANT (I.), *On Education* [tr.] [*ut* **D** § 161] 75 c.
LAING, *Manl. of Readg.* $1
LANGE (K.), *Apperception* [tr.] [*ut* **D** § 162] $1
LEFEVRE (A.), *Number and its Algebra* [*ut* **D** § 167] $1·25
LINDNER (G. A.), *Psychology* [tr.] [*ut* **D** § 162] $1
LUKEN, *Thought and Memory* [*ut* **D** § 163] $1
*MALLESON (Mrs F.), *Early Trg. of Childr.* [*ut* **D** § 166] 75 c.
MARWEDEL, *Conscious Motherhood* $2
*Meths. of Tchg. Mod. Langs.* [*ut* **D** § 167] 90 c.
MUNROE (J. P.), *Educl. Ideal* [*ut* **D** § 156] $1
*NEWSHOLME (A.), *School Hygiene* [*ut* **D** § 171] 75 c.
PAYNE (W. M.), *Engl. in Am. Univs.* [*ut* **D** § 167] $1
PEABODY (E. P.), *Lects. to Kindergartners* [*ut* **D** § 165] $1
PESTALOZZI (J. H.), *Leonard and Gert.* [tr.] [*ut* **D** § 161] 90 c.
RADESTOCK (P.), *Habit* [tr.] [*ut* **D** § 163] 75 c.
ROSMINI (A. S.), *Meth. appl. to Educ.* [tr.] [*ut* **D** § 161] $1·50
ROUSSEAU (J. J.), *Emile* [tr.] [*ut* **D** § 161] 90 c.
RUSSELL (E. H.), *Child Observations* [*ut* **D** § 162] $1·50
SCOTT, *Nature Study and the Child* [*ut* **D** § 167] $1·50
„ *Organic Education* $1·25
SEIDEL (R.), *Industr. Instruction* [tr.] [*ut* **D** § 167] $1
SHELDON-BARNES, *Historic Method* [*ut* **D** § 157] 90 c.
TAYLOR, *Syllabus of Hist. of Educ.* [*ut* **D** § 156] $1
THOMPSON (D. W.), *Day-Dreams of a Schlmaster.* [*ut* **D** § 167] $1·25
TRACY, *Psychol. of Childhd.* [*ut* **D** § 162] 90 c.
UFER (C.), *Introd. to Ped. of Herbart* [*ut* **D** § 161] 90 c.

† = Not available in Engld. in this edn., bg. an Engl. copyrt. bk.

Pioneers in Education [ea. 2/6 *n.* Harrap] ea. 90 c. *n.* c 8° Crowell, *N.Y.*

*Herbart and Education* J. G. COMPAYRÉ
*Montaigne and Education* COMPAYRÉ
*Pestalozzi and Elem. Educn.* COMPAYRÉ
*Rousseau and Education* COMPAYRÉ
*Spencer (Herb.) and Scient. Educn.* COMPAYRÉ

University of Chicago Contributions to Education, 6 Pts. in 1 vol. $1·50 *n.* 12° Univ. Press, *Chicago, v.y.*

DEWEY (Jno.), *Child and Curriculum* 25 c. *n.*
„ *Education Situation* 50 c. *n.*
DEWEY (Jno.), *Psychology and Social Practice* 25 c. *n.*
YOUNG (Ella F.), *Ethics in the School* 25 c. *n.*
„ *Isolation in the School* 50 c. *n.*
„ *Some Types of Educ. Theory* 25 c. *n.*

# II: History and Biography of Pedagogy

## 156: HISTORY AND METHODS OF PEDAGOGY (*a*): GENERALLY

### General History of Education

BARNARD, Dr Hy. [ed.] National Education in Europe *o.p.* 8° *Hartford* [54] 70

BROWNING, Oscar Introduction to History of Educational Theories 3/6 c 8° Paul [81]
From the Greeks to KANT, FICHTE, HERBART, and the English Public School.

CLOUGH, G. Benson Short History of Education 1/6 c 8° Ralph & Holland [04] 05

COMPAYRÉ, Prf. Gabriel History of Pedagogy, tr. Prf. W. H. Payne $1·75 c 8° Heath, *Boston* [86]
6/ Sonnenschein. The best universal history in English; concise and comprehensive. Introd., notes, and index by the translator.

CUBBERLEY, E. P. Syllabus of Lects. on Hist. of Educn., 2 v. [w. bibliogrs.] $2·50 *n.* c 8° Macmillan, *N.Y.* 02

DAVIDSON, Thos. A History of Education $1 *n.* c 8° Scribner, *N.Y.* 00
5/ *n.* Constable. A wk. of great scope, tracing the progress of educn.—'conscious evolut'cn'—fr. savage times to present day.

DONALDSON, Jas. History of Education *o.p.* 8° Murray 95

DRAPER, J. W. —*in his* Hist. of Intellectual Developmt. in Europe, *ut* **F** § 2

HAILMAN, W. N. History of Pedagogy 60 c. c 8° Amer. Bk. Co., *N.Y.* 94

KEMP, E. L. History of Education [Lippincott's Educ. Ser.] $1·25 12° Lippincott, *Phila.* 02
Singles out events wh. ill. most clearly the genesis and evoln. of existing systs. and method.

MONROE, Paul Text-Book of History of Education $1·90 *n.* (8/*n.*) 8° Macmillan 05

„ Brief Course in History of Education; ill. $1·25 *n.* (5/*n.*) c 8° Macmillan 07
Condensn. of above. Both treat, in chronol. order, the princs. underlying educ. systs. and meths. of instrn. of chief nations fr. primitive to pres. times. Useful, but dry, in spite of biograph. sketches.

PAINTER, Prf. F. V. N. History of Education [Internat. Educ. Series] $1·50 (6/) c 8° Appleton 87

PAYNE, Jos. Lects. on Hist. of Educn., ed. Dr J. F. Payne; ill. [=Wks., vol. ii] 10/6 c 8° Longman 92
Del. at Coll. of Preceptors c. 1870; posth. pubd. Of considerable value. Repr. of *A Visit to German Schools* [*ut* **D** § 15 7] is added.

SEELEY, Levi History of Education $1·25 12° Amer. Bk. Co., *N.Y.* 99

SHOUP, W. J. The History and Science of Education $1 c 8° Amer. Bk. Co., *N.Y.* 91

TAYLOR Syllabus of History of Education [Pedag. Lib.] $1 c 8° Heath, *Boston*

**Ancient; Early Oriental Nations**

GRAVES, Prf. F. P. History of Education before the Middle Ages $1·10 *n.* (5/*n.*) 8° Macmillan 09
A text-bk. presentg. the subj. as worked out in the class-room, w. lists of bks. for supplem. reading.

HOBHOUSE, W. Theory and Practice of Ancient Education 2/ 8° *Oxford* 85

LAURIE, Prf. S. S. Histor. Survey of Pre-Christian Education 7/6 ($2) 8° Longman [95] 00
A valuable attempt to supply a philosophy of educ. hist. of pre-Xtn. times: Egyptn., Arab., Babyl., Assyr., Phoenic., Hebr., Chin., Hindu, Medo-Pers., Gk., and Roman. Facts derived fr. best authorities (duly acknowledged).

**China**

de GROOT, J. J. M. —*in his* The Religious System of China, *ut* **A** § 10

DOOLITTLE, J. —*in his* Social Life of the Chinese; chs. xv., xvi, xvii, *ut* **E** § 34

FIELDE, Adèle M. —*in her* A Corner of Cathay, *ut* **E** § 34

MARTIN, W. A. P. The Chinese: their educn., philosophy, & letters $1·75 12° Harper, *N.Y.* 81

WILLIAMS, S. Wells —*in his* The Middle Kingdom, *ut* **E** § 34
Chapters ix–xii of vol. i (pp. 519–723) deal with the education and literature of the Chinese.

YAN PHON LEE When I was a Boy in China 60 c. c 8° Lothrop, *Boston* 87
A very readable bk., with a chapter on schools and school-life.

**Egypt (Ancient)** —*v. also* **F** § 8

KINGSLEY, Can. C. Alexandria and her Schools—*ut* **C** § 15

MASPERO, G. —*in his* The Dawn of Civilization [tr.], *ut* **F** § 5
Conts. a good deal of matter bearing on educn. among the anc. Egyptians and Chaldeans.

" —*in his* Life in Ancient Egypt and Assyria, *ut* **F** § 8
Includes, among other matter of interest here, a ch. on ASSURBANIPAL's library.

RAWLINSON, Can. G. —*in his* Moses, *ut* **A** § 25 [ch. iv on Egyptn. educn.]

**Greece and Rome** —*v. also* **D** § 160

BECKER, W. A. —*in his* Charicles [tr.] *and* Gallus [tr.], *ut* **F** §§ 11–12 [antiquated; but helpful]

BUTCHER, Prf. S. H. —*in his* Aspects of Greek Genius, *ut* **K** § 187

CAPES, W. W. University Life in Ancient Athens [Oxford lects.] *o.p.* [*pb.* 5/] c 8° Longman 77

CLARKE, Dr Geo. Education of Children at Rome [interesting] *o.p.* [*pb.* 3/] 32° Macmillan 96

DAVIDSON, Dr Thos. Aristotle and Ancient Educatl. Ideals [Gt. Educators] $1 *n.* c 8° Scribner, *N.Y.* 92
5/ Heinemann. ARISTOTLE occupies ab. one-fifth of bk.; rest devoted to Gk. educ. bef. him, and to some earlier and later theories. Fairly good but discursive.

" Educn. of Gk. People, and its Influ. on Civilizn. $1·50 (6/) c 8° Appleton 94
[Internat. Educ. Ser.] Gives prominence to differ. stages in growth of Gk. polit., ethical, and relig. consciousness.

FREEMAN, Kenneth J. Schools of Hellas, ed. M. J. Rendall; ill. 4/*n.* ($1·90 *n.*) 8° Macmillan [07] 07
An essay on pract. and theory of Gk. educn. fr. B.C. 600–300, presentg. a fairly complete acc. of the educl. systs. Ill. fr. Gk. vases.

GREGORY OF NAZIANZUM [329(?)–391] Panegyric on S. Basil—*in his* Select Orations & Letters [tr.], *ut* **A** § 55
With his highly interesting description of the friends' student-life at Athens.

HATCH, Dr Edwin —*in his* Influence of Gk. Ideas upon the Christian Church, *ut* **A** § 119
Lect. ii gives an interesting acc. of Greek education, its methods, subjects, and teachers.

LANE, Prf. F. H. Elementary Greek Education 50 c. 12° Bardeen, *Syracuse, N.Y.* 95

LAURIE, Prf. S. S. —*in his* Historical Survey of Pre-Christian Education, *ut sup.*

LUCIAN [*c.* 120–*c.* 200] Anacharsis [tr.]—*ut* **D** § 160

MAHAFFY, Prf. J. P. Old Greek Education 3/6 c 8° Paul [81] 83
Follows the order of the pupil's age; based on GRASBERGER, *supra.*

MONROE, Paul [ed.] Source-Book of Hist. of Educn.: Gk. and Rom. Period $2·25 *n.* (10/*n.*) c 8° Macmillan 01
Tr. selns. (often fr. very inferior sources) fr. Gk. and Rom. wrs. on educn.; w. brief Introdns.

NETTLESHIP, Prf. Hy. —*in his* Lectures on Lat. Literature and Scholarship, *ut* **K** § 211

WILKINS, Prf. A. S. National Education in Greece in Fourth Cent. B.C. *o.p.* [*pb.* 5/] c 8° Isbister 73
A succinct view of the educational theories of PLATO and ARISTOTLE.

" Roman Education 2/*m.* c 8° Camb. Press 05
60 c. *n.* Putnam, *N.Y.* Brings tog. much varied informn. fr. bks. of BERNHARDY, HULSEBOS, GRASBERGER, MARQUHARDT, JULLIEN.

XENOPHON [B.C. *c.* 431–*c.* 355] Cyropaedia—*ut* **D** § 160
A good authority on education among the Persians and Spartans.

*Games; Gymnastics* —*v. also* **F** § 11

SONNENSCHEIN, Prf. E. A. The Greek Games—*in his* Ideals of Culture 2/6 c 8° Sonnenschein 91
*Games of the Nursery; Gymnastic Exercises of the School; Agonistic Exercises and Social Games of Mature Life.*

**India** —*v.* **D** § 157, *s.v.* India

**Jews (Ancient)** —*v. also* **A** § 12, **F** § 7

EDERSHEIM, Dr A. —*in his* Sketches of Jewish Social Life in the Days of Christ, *ut* **A** § 46
Touches on education. By a learned converted Jew.

FENTON, Jno. —*in his* Early Hebrew Life, *ut* **F** § 7 [incls. acc. of education]

LEIPZIGER, H. M. Education of the Jews [Educl. Monogrs.] 20 c. 8° College f. Tchrs., *N.Y.* 90

SPIERS, B. The School System of the Talmud—*ut* **A** § 12

**Persia**

ARBUTHNOT, F. F. —*in his* Persian Portraits, *ut* **F** § 64

Dabistan, or School of Manners [tr.]—*ut* **K** § 134

RAGOZIN, Z. A. —*in his* Story of Media, Babylonia, and Persia, *ut* **F** § 9

XENOPHON [B.C. *c.* 431–*c.* 355] Cyropaedia—*ut sup.*, *s.v.* Greece and Rome

**Primitive Christian** —*v. also* **A** § 51

HODGSON, Geraldine Primitive Christian Education 4/6 *n.* 8° Clark, *Edin.* 06
Indicates the *rôle* played by the prim. Xtns. in educn.: traverses view that early Xty. was its deadly foe.

TACITUS [A.D. 54–*post* 117] Works—*ut* **K** § 215
Conts. valuable material on intellectual condn. of the people at beginning of Xtn. era.

**Medieval; Renaissance** —*v. also* **F** §§ 13–14

ASSER —*in his* Life of Alfred the Great [tr.], *ut* **F** § 18

BRYCE, Jas. —*in his* The Holy Roman Empire, *ut* **A** § 56

BURCKHARDT, J. G. —*in his* Civilization of Period of Renaissance in Italy [tr.], *ut* **F** § 53

COMPAYRÉ, Prf. J. G. Abelard and Orig. and Early Hist. of Universities [tr.]—*ut* **D** § 161

DRANE, Augusta T. Christian Schools and Scholars 12/6 8° Burns & Oates [67] 81
By a Roman-Catholic; educational sketches, fr. orig. Latin sources, extendg. fr. Christian era to Council of Trent.

EGINHARD [9 cent.] Life of Karl the Great (Charlemagne) [tr.] *ut* **F** § 51
Conts. one of the best accounts of the educational condns. of the period.

HEALY, Dr Jno. Insula Sanctorum et Doctorum—*ut inf.*, *s.v.* Ireland

KIRKPATRICK, Prf. Jno. The University of Bologna—*ut inf.*, *s.v.* Italy

LACROIX, Paul —*in his* Science and Literature in Middle Ages [tr.], *ut* **F** § 14
Contains much valuable material bearg. on intellectual activities of Mid. Ages.

LAURIE, Prf. S. S. Lects. on Rise and Early Constitn. of Universities 6/ c 8° Paul 86
$1·50 Appleton, *N.Y.* Contains an excellent survey of medieval education.

MULLINGER, J. Bass The Schools of Charles the Great *o.p.* [*pb.* 7/6] 8° Longman 77
Account of the restoration of education in the ninth century.

NEWMAN, Card. J. H. Rise and Progress of Universities *o.p.* [*pb.* 6/] c 8° Pickering 72

OZANAM, A. F. —*in his* History of Civilization in Fifth Century [tr.], 2 vols., *ut* **F** § 4

*RASHDALL, Dr Hastings Universities of Europe in Middle Ages, 2 vols. *o.p.* [*pb.* 45/] m 8° Clar. Press 95
Vol. i: *Salerno, Bologna, Paris*; ii, Pt. 1: *Italy, Spain, France, Germany, Scotland*, etc.; 2: *English Universities; Student Life.* By far most import. and weighty contribn. to gen. hist. of Europ. learng. dur. Mid. Ages th. has yet appeared in English. Sources indicated in footnotes. Maps & ill.

SYMONDS, J. A. —*in his* History of the Renaissance in Italy, *ut* **F** § 53

WATSON, F. Curriculum in Engl. Schls. in 17th Cent.—*in* Trns. of Bibliogr. Soc., vol. vi, *ut* **K** § 3

WEST, A. F. Alcuin and the Rise of the Christian Schools—*ut* **D** § 161

WOODWARD, Prf. W. H. Vittorino da Feltre, and other Humanist Educators 6/ c 8° Camb. Press 97
$1·60 *n.* Putnam, *N.Y.* An interestg. and scholarly acc. of DA FELTRE, who, hg. been Prf. at Padua and a schoolmr. at Venice, fr. 1423–46 (his death), estab. at Mantua the first great School of Renaiss., the typical schl. of the Humanities, the spirit, curriculum, and meth. of wh. formed a landmk. in hist. of class. tchg. Trs. of 4 noteworthy treatises of period are added, tog. w. a valuable General View of educn. as conceived by the early Humanist scholars.

,, Studies in Education during Age of Renaissance 4/6 *n.* c 8° Camb. Press 07
50 c. *n.* Putnam, *N.Y.* Cover the period 1400–1600.

,, [ed.] Contribns. to Hist. of Educ. in Mediaev. & Mod, Europe, 5 v. c 8° Camb. Press 07 *in prg.*
i: *Mediaeval Schls. and Univs.* *in prep.* | iii: *Pioneers of Mod. Educ.* [*ut inf.*] J. W. ADAMSON | iv: *Theory and Pract. of Educ. in 18 Cent.* Foster WATSON, *in prep.*
ii: *Studies in Educ. dur. Renaiss.* [*ut sup.*] EDR. | v: *Educn. in 19 cent.* *in prep.*

*Scholastic Age* —*v. also* **A** § 119

**Modern; Contemporary**

BARNARD, H. [ed.] National Education, 3 vols. ea. $3·50 m 8° Steiger, *N.Y.* 72
i: Germ.; ii: Switz., Frce., Belg., Holl., Denm., Norw., Swed., Russ., Grce., Turk., It., Port., Sp.; iii: Gt. Brit., Amer.

GRASBY, W. C. [Austral.] Teaching in Three Continents [Am., Eur., Austr.] 6/ ($1·50) c 8° Cassell 91

HOYT, C. O. Studies in the History of Modern Education $1·50 c 8° Silver, *N.Y.* 08

HUGHES, R. E. Schools at Home and Abroad 4/6 c 8° Sonnenschein 01

KLEMM, Dr L. R. European Schools; ill. [Internatl. Educ. Series] c 8° $2 (8/6) Appleton [89] 97
Account of the author's visit to schools of Germany (espec. good), France, Austria, and Switzerland.

LAISHLEY, R. Rept. on State Educn. in Gt. Brit., Frce., Switz., U.S., etc. 8° *Wellington, N.Z.* 86

LAURIE, Prf. S. S. Studies in Hist. of Educ. Opinion fr. Renaissance 6/ c 8° Camb. Press 03
$1·50 *n.* Putnam, *N.Y.* Repr. lects., giving accs. and criticisms of COMENIUS, PESTALOZZI, SPENCER, etc.

MUNROE, J. P. The Educational Ideal [Pedag. Lib.] $1 c 8° Heath, *Boston* 95
Outl. of growth in mod. times of the educ. ideal, in a successn. of sketches of educationists: RABELAIS, BACON, COMENIUS, MONTAIGNE and LOCKE, Jansenists and FÉNELON, ROUSSEAU, PESTALOZZI, FROEBEL; *Women in Educn.*

WILLIAMS, S. G. Hist. of Mod. Educn. [Renaiss. to pres. day] $1·50 8° Bardeen, *Syracuse, N.Y.* [92] 96
Lects. deliv. in class-room. Employs comparative method; internat. in scope. Of no great value, but fair in statemt. of principles.

*Nineteenth and Twentieth Centuries*

HUGHES (J. L.) + KLEMM (L. R.) Progr. of Educn. in the Cent. [XIX Cent. Ser.] 5/ *n.* c 8° Chambers 07

HUGHES, R. E. The Making of Citizens [Cont. Science Ser.] 6/ c 8° Walter Scott 02
$1·50 Scribner, *N.Y.* Clear acc. of exact positn. of educn. in Eng., Germy., Frce, & U.S.; contrastg. points of diff. in their systs; w. statistics.

ROBERTS, Dr R. D. [ed.] Education in the Nineteenth Century 4/ c 8° Camb. Press 01
$1 *n.* Putnam, *N.Y.* 13 papers (mostly Univ. Extensn. lects.) by experts, on var. phases of educ. hist. 1801–1900.

**Biography and Criticism:** *Collectively—for* Individuals, *v.* **D** § 161, *passim*

ADAMS, W. H. D. A Book of Earnest Lives 3/6 8° Sonnenschein [83]
Popular lives of COLET, ASCHAM, Mary MONTAGU, SWIFT, LANCASTER, BELL, OBERLIN, ARNOLD.

ADAMSON, Prf. J. W. Pioneers of Modern Education: 1600–1700
[$1·50 *n.* Putn., *N.Y.*] 4/6 *n.* c 8° Camb. Press 05

COLVILLE, Dr Jas. Some Old-fashioned Educationists 2/ *n.* c 8° Green, *Edin.* 07

HODGSON, Geraldine Studies in French Educ. fr. Rabelais to Rousseau 3/6 *n.* c 8° Camb. Press 08
$1·10 *n.* Putnam, *N.Y.* A sensible and careful acc., endg. w. notice of Mme. d'EPINAY's ideal of female educ.

HOW, F. D. Six Great Schoolmasters; ports. and ill. 7/6 8° Methuen 04
HAWTREY (Eton), KENNEDY (Shrewsbury), MOBERLY (Winchester), VAUGHAN (Harrow), TEMPLE (Rugby), BRADLEY (Marlborough), all of whom worked betw. 1835 and 1865. Shows how the 2 gt. influences of those times—life of ARNOLD and public opinion—gradually brot. ab. an extraord. improvemt. in publ. schl. life.

KAY, Dav. Education and Educators—*ut* **D** § 159*

LANG, Ossian H. Great Teachers of Four Centuries [cram-bk.] 25 c. 12° Kellogg 95

LEITCH, J. Muir Practical Educationists and their Systems of Teaching 6/ c 8° MacLehose, *Glasgow* 75
Excellent lects. on LOCKE, PESTALOZZI, BELL, LANCASTER, WILDERSPIN, STOW, Herb. SPENCER.

PATTISON, Rev. Mark J. J. Scaliger [1540–1609], *and* Isaac Casaubon [1559–1609]—*in his* Essays, 2 vols., *ut* **K** § 83. For his *Life of Casaubon—v.* **K** § 174

*QUICK, Rev. R. H. Essays on Educational Reformers 3/6 c 8° Longman [68] 93
$1·50 [Intern. Educ. Ser.] Appleton, *N.Y.* *Jesuits; Ascham, Montaigne, Ratich, Milton; Comenius; Locke; Rousseau's 'Emile'; Basedow; Pestalozzi; Jacotot; Herb. Spencer; About Teaching Children; Moral and Religious Education; Renaissance, Sturm, Rabelais, Montaigne, Mulcaster, Port Royalists, Froebel.* There are 3 other Amer. edns. on the Amer. market—all incomplete and unauthorized.

**History of the Philosophy of Pedagogics**—*v. also sup.* (LAURIE's Pre-Christian Educn.)

BENNETT, Dr C. W. History of the Philosophy of Pedagogics 50 c. 12° Bardeen, *Syracuse, N.Y.* [77] 93

## 157: HISTORY AND BIOGRAPHY OF PEDAGOGY (*b*): ACCORDING TO COUNTRIES

**Australia**

BARFF, H. E. Short Histor. Account of University of Sydney; ill. 8° Angus & Robertson, *Sydney* 03

PEARSON, C. H. [Fellow of Oriel; Educ. Minister in Vict.] Rept. on Educ. in Victoria. 8° *Melbourne* 78

Stebbing, W. C. H. Pearson: memls. by himself, wife, and friends 14/ ($4 *n.*) r 8° Longman 00

Special Reports on Educational Subjects, vol. v—*ut* **D** § 163*

RUSSELL, Jno. —*in his* The Schools of Greater Brit. [fr. official sources] 3/6 c 8° Collins 88

**Austria** —*v.* Germany, *inf.*

**Bulgaria**

DICEY, Prf. Edw. —*chapter on* Public Education, *in his* The Peasant State, *ut* **E** § 29

**Canada**

BIGGAR, E. B. Educational System of the Province of Ontario [Govt. pub.] 8° *Toronto* 86

DAWSON, Sir J. Wm. Fifty Years of Work in Canada c 8° Ballantyne 01
An autobiographical account of the life of the Principal of McGill University, Montreal, 1855–93.

Education in Canada —*in* Special Reports on Educational Subjects, vol. iv, *ut* **D** § 164

FRASER, Rev. Jas. Report to the Schools Inquiry Commission [Blue-Book] 8° Eyre & Spottiswoode 67

HODGINS, Dr J. G. Documentary Hist. of Educn. in Upper Canada, vols. i–ii
ea. $1 r 8° Briggs, *Toronto* 94 *in prg.*

MILLAR, Jno. Educational System of the Province of Ontario [pp. 114] 8° Warwick, *Toronto* 93

ROSS, Dr G. W. [Minister of Educ., Ont.] History of School System of Ontario
[Int. Educ. Ser.] $1 (4/6) 12° Appleton 96
History, organizn., and managemt., uniform exams., training of teachers (in public and high schools), supervision by Educ. Dept.

RUSSELL, Jno. —*in his* The Schools of Greater Britain, *ut sup.* [fr. official sources]

*Queen's College, Kingston, Ontario*

GRANT, Geo. M. Life of. By W. L. Grant + F. Hamilton 12/6 *n.* 8° Jack 05

*Toronto Univ.:* Univ. of Toronto and its Colleges: 1827–1906; ill. [by var. wrs.] Univ. Library, *Toronto* 07

**France:** *Description, Criticism*

PARSONS, J. R. *jun.* French Schools through American Eyes $1 8° Bardeen, *Syracuse, N.Y.* 92

Special Reports on Educational Subjects, vol. i, ii, iii, vii—*ut* **D** § 163*

TEEGAN, Prf. T. H. Elementary Education in France 5/ c 8° Simpkin 92

A clear and compreh. acc. of Fch. pop. educ. and of changes wh. have led up to it fr. the first attempts at founding it 'in the stormy days of the Revoln.'; w. details as to traing., appoinmt., and salaries of teachers, inspectors, profs., *etc.*, and interestg. acc. of life in Superior Normal Coll. of St Cloud.

*History*

BARNARD, H. [ed.] French Pedagogy [coll. arts. by var. wrs.] $3·50 m 8° *Hartford n.d.*

,, English, French, and other Teachers $3·50 m 8° *Hartford n.d.*

HODGSON, Geraldine Studies in French Education fr. Rabelais to Rousseau—*ut* **D** § 156

DE LIGNE, P'ess —*in the* Memoirs of [tr.], *ut* **F** § 48

Contains a good picture of 18-century Convent education, w. account of the studies, punishmts., rewards, and games.

*University of Paris; Colleges*

BOYLE, Rev. Patr. The Irish College in Paris (1578–1901) 4/ c 8° Art & Bk. Co. 01

Several interesting orig. documts. are printed, and particulars of other Irish colleges in France given.

Record of Visit of University of Paris to University of London, 1906 5/ *n.* 8° Murray 07

*Popular Education*

ARNOLD, Mat. Popular Educn. of France, Holland, and Switzerld. *o.p.* [*pb.* 10/] 8° Longman 61

*Secondary Education*

ARNOLD, Mat. A French Eton: middle-class education and the State 6/ c 8° Macmillan [64] 92

To this edn. is added that pt. of the author's *Schools and Universities on the Continent* which relate to France (1st pub. 1868).

FARINGDON, Dr F. E. French Secondary Schools (7/6 *n.*) 8° Longman 10

Conts. much informn. on origin, developmt., and pres. organizn. Bibliography (20 pp.).

*Port Royalists* [16th cent.] —*v. also* **A** § 101, *s.v.* Jansenists

CADET, Félix [ed.] Port-Royal Education, tr. A. D. Jones 4/6 c 8° Sonnenschein 98

$1·50 Bardeen, *Syracuse, N.Y.* Extracts from the Port Royal writers, translated; with Introduction (67 pp.).

**Germany; Austria:** *Generally; Miscellaneous Works*

BARNARD, Dr Hy. [ed.] German Pedagogy [coll. arts. by var. wrs.] $3·50 m 8° *Hartford n.d.* (76)

,, Memrs. of Eminent Teachers and Educators of Germy. $3·50 m 8° Brownell, *N.Y. n.d.* (63)

BEATTY, Dr H. M. Education in a Prussian Town [Wiesbaden] 1/ 8° Blackie 07

DAVIS, G. B. Report on Schools in Germany and Switzerland 8° Houghton, *Birmingham* 79

DONALDSON, Jas. Lects. on Hist. of Educn. in Prussia & England *o.p.* [*pb.* 3/6] c 8° Black 74

Education in Germany, *&* in Baden—*in* Special Reports on Educ. Subjs., vols. i, ix *&* iii, *ut* **D** § 163*

HAUFE, Dr Ewald Passages from Life of an Educational Free-lance [tr.] 3/ *n.* c 8° Pitman 02

HUGHES, R. E. —*in his* The Making of Citizens, *ut* **D** § 156

HURST, Rev. J. F. Life and Liter. in Fatherld. [schls., educn., etc.] $2·25 8° Scribner, *N.Y.* [74] 76

KLEMM, Dr L. R. —*in his* European Schools, *ut sup.*

LEXIS, Dr W. Hist. and Organizn. of Publ. Educ. in Germ. Emp. [tr.] 3/6 *n.* 8° Asher 04

*PAULSEN, Prf. Friedr. German Education, Past and Present [tr.] 5/ 8° Unwin 08

Deals more fully w. 'past' than 'present'. First 10 pp., *Terminological Notes*, tr. and explain Germ. educ. terms.

MANN, T. My German Schools and Schoolmasters *o.p.* [*pb.* 1/6] f 8° Ward 59

PAYNE, Prf. Jos. A Visit to German Schools *o.p.* [*pb.* 4/6] c 8° Paul 76

Reprinted in his *Lectures on the History of Education*, *ut* **D** § 156.

PRINCE, Dr J. T. Methods of Instrn. and Organisn. in Schls. of Germy. $1 12° Lee & Shepard, *Boston* 92

An epitome of all grades of schls. in Germy.—*Gymnasium, Realschule, Realgymnasium, Progymnasium, Realprogymnasium, Oberrealschule, Höhere Burgerschule.*

SIDGWICK, Mrs Alf. —*in her* Home Life in Germany, *ut* **E** § 15

WINCH, W. H. Notes on German Schools 6/ ($1·50 *n.*) c 8° Longman 04

With special reference to curriculum and methods of instruction.

*History and Biography: Collectively—for* Individuals *v.* **D** § 161, *passim*

BARNARD, H. [ed.] German Educational Reformers and Teachers [tr.] $3·50 m 8° *Hartford n.d.*

,, National Education in German States [tr.] $3·50 m 8° *Hartford n.d.*

Trs. of vols. i–ii of Prf. K. v. RAUMER'S *Gesch. d. Pädagogik*, hrsg. G. LUTHHOLZ (fr. Dante; 5 Pts. 34 *m.* 8° Bertelsmann, *Gütersloh* [42]).

PAWLE, C. D. Sketch of History of Education in Germany 8° Allingham, *Reigate* 02

SEELEY, [Sir] J. R. —*his* Life of Stein, 3 vols. [*ut* **F** § 51]: conts. admir. acc. of Stein's educ. reforms

*Elementary Schools: Volksschule, etc.; History and Methods—v. also* **D** § 166

ANDREW, Geo. [H.M.I.] Rept. on Gemeinde-Schulen of Berl. & Charlottenb. [Blue-Bk.] Wyman 04
ARNOLD, Mat. [H.M.I.] Special Report on Certain Points conn. w. Elem. Educn. in Germy., Switzerl., and France [Blue-Bk.] Wyman 86
BARNARD, H. [ed.] National Education in German States [tr.]—*ut sup.*
BASHFORD, J. L. Elementary Education in Saxony *o.p.* [*pb.* 1/] 8° Low 81
ENDEAN, J. Russell The Public Education of Austria 6*d.* 8° Simpkin 88
PERRY, C. C. Reports on German Elem. Schools & Training Colleges 5/ c 8° Rivington 87
SEELEY, Levi Common School Syst. of Germany & its Lessons $1·50 12° Kellogg, *N.Y.* 96
A full description of the elementary-school system of Prussia (only). Statistics out of date.

*Secondary Schools; Gymnasia*

ARNOLD, Mat. [H.M.I.] Higher Schools & Universities in Germany *o.p.* [*pb.* 6/] c 8° Macmillan [68] 92
Repubn. of that portion of his *Schools and Universities on the Continent* [10/6 *id.* '68] wh. relates to Germany.
BARNARD, Dr Hy. [ed.] Classical Gymnasia—*in his* National Education in Europe, *ut* **D** § 156
BIRD, Chas. Higher Education in Germany and England 2/6 c 8° Paul 84
BOLTON, Dr F. E. The Secondary School System of Germany $1·50 (6/) 12° Appleton 00
RUSSELL, Dr J. E. German Higher Schools $2·50 (7/6 *n.*) c 8° Longman [99] 05
A mass of facts, historical and descriptive, rel. to history and organizn. of Germ. secondary educn.

*Universities and Colleges; Collectively*

ARNOLD, Mat. —*in his* Higher Schools and Universities in Germany, *ut sup.*
CONRAD, J. German Universities for Last Fifty Years [tr.] [statistical] 10/6 c 8° *Glasgow* 85
DIDON, F'r —*in his* The Germans [tr.; *ut* **E** § 15] conts. chs. on the Universities
ERMAN (W.) + HORN (E.) Bibliogr. d. Deut. Universitäten, Pt. i. ; ii, 40 *m.*; iii, 8° Teubner, *Lpz.* -05
HART, Prf. J. M. German Universities *o.p.* [*pb.* $1·75] 12° Putnam, *N.Y.* 74
A comparison with English and American universities; from personal observation.
*PAULSEN, Prf. Friedr. German Universities: character and histor. developmt. [tr.] $1·50 (7/ *n.*) c 8° Macmillan 95
An admirable outl. of hist. and character of Germ. Univ., tr. fr. Introd. part of *Die Deutschen Universitäten*, pubd. under direcn. of Germ. Govt. in conn. w. her educat. exhibit at Columbian Exhibn., Chicago, 1893. Statistics and bibliogr.
* ,, The German Universities and University Study $3 *n.* 8° Scribner, *N.Y.* 06
15/ *n.* Longman. The standard authority; in 5 sectns. (1) Historical; (2) Place of univ. in publ. life—their relns. to State, society, Church; (3) univ. teachers; (4) students; (5) the 4 teaching faculties—theol., law, medicine, philos. (last incl. liter., hist., science, math.). Describes their character, and criticizes certain features of recent developmts. A monumental wk., full of suggestion.
Bode, Dr Mabel German Universities [review of above bk.] 1/ *n.* 8° P. S. King & Son
SCHAFF, Dr Pp. Germany: its universities, theology, and religion—*ut* **A** § 64
SHEEHAN, Can. P. A. [R.-C.] 3 *essays on* Germ. Univs., *in his* Early Essays and Lectures, *ut* **D** § 155

*Student Life*

CORNELIUS, Dr Student Life of Germany, tr. [fr. unpb. MS.] Wm. Howitt *o.p.* [*pb.* 10/6] 8° Routledge 41
MAYHEW, Hy. —*in his* Life and Manners as seen in Saxony, *ut* **E** § 15
Contains an account of student life and customs at the University of Jena.
ROBERTSON, Dr W. B. German Student Life—*in his* Martin Luther and Two Other Lects., *ut* **A** § 64
STEFFENS, H. German University Life [tr.] *o.p.* [*pb.* $1·25] 12° Lippincott, *Phila.* 74
The story of his career as a student and as a professor.

## Great Britain

*History: Generally*

BARNARD, Hy. [ed.] English Pedagogy, 2 Ser. [coll. arts. by var. wrs.] ea. $3·50 m 8° *Hartford* [66] 76
,, English, French, and other Teachers $3·50 m 8° *Hartford n.d.*
GILL, Jno. Systems of Education [English; Ascham to Hor. Grant] *o.p.* [*pb.* 2/6] 12° Longman 76
$3·25 [Pedag. Lib.] Heath, *Boston.* Incl. a good brief account of the BELL-LANCASTER monitorial system. A. BELL'S *Mutual Tuition and Moral Discipline* was pub. by Roake, *Lond.* 1823; J. LANCASTER'S *Improvements in Educn.* by Darton, *Lond.* 1803.
GREEN, Mrs J. R. —*in her* Town Life in the Fifteenth Century, *ut* **F** § 21
*LEACH, A. F. English Schools at the Reformation, 1546–8 12/ *n.* 8° Constable 96
A most valuable wk., breakg. new ground, and showg. beyond discussn. th. before the Reformn. there was a widespread and effective provisn. in Engld. f. secondary educn., and t. this syst. was greatly damaged by Edw. vi (hitherto regarded as one of the gt. fdrs. of Gram. Schls.), who, by his Ministers, destroyed or despoiled 259 schls. (of wh. 193 Gram. Schls.). Incl. histor. acc. of differ. kinds of schls. at time of Edw. vi, w. typical illns. of 7 kinds. Pt. ii (300 pp.) consists of extrs. fr. Commissrs.' Returns und. Chantries Acts of 37 Hy. viii and 1 Edw. vi. Index.
,, [ed.] Early Yorkshire Schools, vols. i–ii. Yorks Archaeol. Soc. 00–3
Vol. i. deals with schools at York, Ripon, and Beverley. Based on all available documts.
,, [ed.] Educational Charters and Documents: 598–1909 10/ *n.* c 8° Camb. Press 11
Putnam, *N.Y.* Does for educl. hist. what STUBBS' *Select Charters* did for constitl. history.
MAGNUS, Sir Pp. Educational Aims and Efforts: 1880–1910 7/6 *n.* 8° Longman 10
Pt. i: *Introductory; Progress in Elem. Educ.; Probls. of Secondary Educ.; Schemes f. Reorganizg. Lond. Univ.; Techn. Instrn. Movemt.; Soc. Changes and Schl. Wk.;* ii: Repr. arts. and addresses on Manl. and Industr. Traing., Handwk., etc.
MARK, H. T. Outl. of Hist. of Educ. Theories in Engld. 1/6 *n.* c 8° Sonnenschein [99] 03

de MONTMORENCY, J. E. G. State Intervention in English Education 5 / n. c 8° Camb. Press 02
$1·50 n. Putnam, N.Y. From Saxon times to 1833, when Parliamy. moneys were first voted f. educ. purposes. An exam. of orig. documts.

WATSON, Prf. Foster The English Grammar Schools to 1660 6 / n. c 8° Camb. Press 08
$2 n. Putnam, N.Y. An interestg. bk., presentg. an acc. of workg. of schls. in Eng. dur. Reformn., Renaissce., and Puritan period (as well as of courses of University educn.), incl. curricula, daily life of childr., youths, and yg. men at home and at schl. or college.

,, Beginnings of Teachg. of Modern Subjs. in Engld. 7 /6 n. 8° Pitman 09
A useful, tho' not very interestg., bk., consistg. of a mass of quotns. rather th. a continuous narrative. The 'beginnings' were mostly laid in 16–17 cents. Much bibliogr. matter.

*Methods; Systems; Description; Criticism*

BALFOUR, Graham Educational Systems of Great Britain and Ireland 7 /6 n. ($2·50) c. 8° Clar. Press [98] 06
An accurate, comprehensive book on elem., secondary, and higher educn., based on docum. authority. Quite impartial.

LAWSON, W. R. John Bull and his Schools 5 / n. c 8° Blackwood 08
'A book for parents, ratepayers, and men of business'. Impressed by the inadequacy of results of Brit. educl. institns.

MAGNUS, Laurie [ed.] National Education: ess. tow. constructive policy 7 /6 n. 8° Murray 01
A symposium dealing with various educational subjects; w. a bibliographical note.

SHARPLESS, Dr I. Engl. Educn. in Elem. and Second. Schls. [Int. Ed. Ser.] $1 (4 /6) c 8° Appleton 92
Descrn. of Engl. elem., second., and publ. schls., by Pres. of Haverford Coll., Penn. On the whole highly laudatory.

WIESE, Dr L. German Letters on English Education [tr.] o.p. [pb. 5 /] c 8° Collins 77

*Elementary* —*v. also* **D** §§ 165–166

ADAMS, F. History of Elementary School Contest in England 6 / c 8° Chapman 82

*ARNOLD, Mat. Reports on Elem. Schools, ed. Sir F. R. Sandford 1 / c 8° Wyman [89] 08
Reports of 1852–82. Issued by Bd. of Educn. for offic. use. Conts. some new matter, e.g. ARNOLD'S impressns. of FITCH.

GREEN, T. H. Elementary School System—*in his* Works, vol. iii, *ut* **C** § 29

GREENHOUGH, J. C. Evoln. of Elem. Schls. of Gt. Brit. [Int. Educ. Ser.] $1·20 n. (5 / n.) c 8° Appleton

HOLMAN, H. English National Education [Victorian Era Ser.] 2 /6 c 8° Blackie 98
$1·25 Stone, *Chicago*. A sketch of rise in and progress dur. 19th cent. of Public Elem. Schools in Engld.

Report of the Education Department [Blue-Books] f° Eyre & Spottiswoode 39 *sqq., in prg.*

,, General Digest of Endowed Charities [Blue-Books] f° Eyre & Spottiswoode 67–76
Constitutes a sort of Domesday-Bk. of foundns., showg. a total income of £2,200,000 (not incl. newer charities) fr. Primary Schls. to Univs. *Vide* also the Reports of L'd BROUGHAM'S Commissrs. at work fr. 1818 to 1837, 38 vols. f°.

,, of Special Committee on Subj. & Modes of Instr. in Bd. Schls. [Blue-Bks.] f° Eyre & Spottiswoode 88

,, Royal Commission on Wrkg. of Educ. Acts, Rept. 5 /6; Evid. 10 v. 48 /1 [Blue-Bks.] f° Eyre & Spottiswoode 88

,, Commissioners on Popular Education, 6 vols. [Blue-Books] 18 /3 f° Eyre & Spottiswoode 61

,, the School Inquiry Commission, 21 vols. [Blue-Books] 69 /3 f° Eyre & Spottiswoode 68–9

,, Commission on Technical Education—*v.* **D** § 167, *s.v.* Technical Education

STANLEY, Hon. E. L. Our National Education [hopeful, but incomplete] 2 /6 c 8° Nisbet 99

WINCH, W. H. Problems in Education 4 /6 c 8° Sonnenschein 00

*British and Foreign School Society*

BINNS, H. B. A Century of Educn. [centenn. hist. of B. & F. S. S.] 5 / n. c 8° Dent 08

*London School Board; London County Council*

JEPHSON, A. W. My Work in London 3 /6 n. c 8° Pitman 10

MORLEY, Chas. Studies in Board Schools 6 / c 8° Smith & Elder 97
A ser. of sketches, repr. fr. *Daily News*, of London schools and scholars as they actually are.

PHILPOTT, H. B. London at School 6 / c 8° Unwin 04
An interestg. acc. of Lond. Schl. Bd. fr. its establmt. in 1870 to 1904, by an ex-scholar in one of its schls.

SPALDING (T. A.) + CANNEY (T. S. A.) The Work of the London School Board 5 / 4° P. S. King & Son 00
A descriptive work, prepared for the Paris Exhibition.

WEBB, Sid. London Education 2 /6 n. c 8° Longman 04
A clear acc. of the existg. educatl. needs of the metropolis, and of contemp. schemes of reform.

*School Inspection* —*v. also inf., s.v.* Scotland (KERR)

SNEYD-KYNNERSLEY, E. M. H.M.I.: passages in life of an Insp. of Schls. 8 /6 n. 8° Macmillan 08
A valuable acc. of schl.-inspectn., by one who began in 1871 and 'watched the cradle and followed the hearse' of the Schl. Bds.

*Education Question*

CARNEGIE, W. H. The Church and the Schools 2 / f 8° Wells Gardner 05

EGERTON, H. Maintenance of Denominational Teaching 1 /6 n. c 8° G. Allen 05

GLANCEY, Rev. M. F. Catholics and the Education Question 8° Cath. Truth Soc. 02

GREGORY, Dn Rob. Elementary Education [histor. and controversial] 3 /6 c 8° National Soc. 95

HENSON, Can. Hensley H. Education Act and After [appeal to nonconformists] 1 / c 8° Methuen 03

McCOLL, Can. M. Educ. Quest. and Liberal Party [advocs. denom. tchg.] 2 /6 ($1) 8° Longman 02

MOBERLY, Prf. R. C. Undenominationalism as Princ. of Prim. Educ. 1 / n. 8° Murray 02

National Education Assoc.: Pamphlets *Caxton Ho., Westminster*

PICTON, J. Allanson — The Bible in School: a questn. of ethics — 1/ c 8° Watts 01

Towards Educational Peace — 1/ n. (36 c. n.) r 8° Longman 10
A plan of re-settlemt. issued by the Executive Committee of the Educational Settlement Committee.

*Continuation Schools, etc.*

ROWNTREE (J. W.) + BINNS (H. B.) Adult School Movement in History — 2/ s 4° Headley 03

SADLER, Prf. M. E. [ed.] — Continuation Schools in England & Elsewhere — 8/6 n. 8° Sherratt, *Mancs.* 07
[Mancs. Univ. Pbs.] *Histor. Review* (104 pp.) by SADLER, w. 24 chs. dealg. w. subj. fr. var. aspects, Engl., Scottish, Dan., Germ., Swiss, Fch., U.S.

*Working Men's College, London*

DAVIES, Rev. J. Llew. [ed.] The Working Men's College: 1854–1904 — 4/ n. c 8° Macmillan 04
Interestg. chs. by var. wrs. on the progr., influ., early troubles, etc., of this institn., wh. has played an important part in the sociolog. evolution of the past half-century.

*Preparatory Schools*

Preparatory Schools for Boys—*in* Special Reports on Educatl. Subjects, vol. vi, *ut* **D** § 163*

*Secondary Education; Public Schools; Private Colleges, etc.*

COOKSON, Chr. [ed.] Essays on Secondary Educn. [by var. wrs.; practical] 4/6 ($1·10) c 8° Clar. Press 98

COULTON, G. G. — Public Schools and Public Needs — 5/ n. c 8° Simpkin 01
Suggestns. for reform. Deals chiefly w. teaching of English and other modern languages.

JACOB, H. P. — Public School Life in England — 8° Mercantile Press, *Karachi* 93
An enthusiastic descr. of methods, achievemts., and merits of Engl. pub. schls. [thirty], by an Educ. Inspector in Sind. Conts. a repr. of Sir Hy. SIDNEY's letter to his son [afterw. Sir P. SIDNEY]—*ut inf., s.v.* Shrewsbury School.

'KAPPA' — Let Youth but Know — 3/6 n. c 8° Methuen 05
A criticism of publ.-schl. and univ. educn.: 'a plea for reason'. Repr. fr. *Westmr. Gazette.*

LEIGHTON, R. L. — The Boy and his School — 2/6 n. c 8° Murray 05
A suggestive essay on condns. and mistakes of our syst. of second. educn., by H.M. of Bristol Gram. Schl.

NORWOOD (C.) + HOPE (A. H.) The Higher Education of Boys in England — 12/ n. 8° Murray 09
Sets forth a majestic scheme of reform, based on a wide investign. incl. State responsibility in the conduct of every public school; with a number of essays by var. hands, wh.—apart fr. the main thesis of the authors—are of considerable value.

PELLATT, T. — Public Schools and Public Opinion — 2/6 n. ($1) c 8° Longman 04
An *apologia* for certain methods in English Higher Education.

SCOTT, R. P. [ed.] — What is Secondary Education? — [by var. wrs.] 2/6 c 8° Rivington 99

TURNER, J. C. — Debateable Claims: essays on secondary educn. — 6/ c 8° Constable 98
Deals almost wholly with English secondary education and its possibilities.

WARE, Fabian — Educational Reform — 2/6 Methuen 00
Chiefly concerned w. possibilities of reform in secondary educn. opened up by 1899 Act.

*Scholarship System*

SADLER (Prf. M. E.) + SMITH (H. Bompas) The English Scholarship System, in rel. w. Secondary Schools for Boys and Girls — Longman *in prep.*

**Schools:** *History; Description; Statistics*

BISSON, F. S. de C. [ed.] — Our Schools & Colleges: vol. i [Boys] 21/6; vol. ii [Girls] *o.p.* [*pb.* 7/6] c 8° Simpkin [72] 84

CARTER, Vivian — Our Great Public Schools; ill. — 10/6 n. 8° Treherne 11

CORBIN, Jno. — Schoolboy Life in England; ill. — $1·25 c 8° Harper, *N.Y.* 97
A friendly criticism of life at Eton, Harrow, Rugby, and Winchester.

Great Public Schools; *c.* 100 ill. — [by various writers] 6/ i 16° Arnold 93
Descrns., w. good illns., of Eton, Harrow, Wincs., Rugby, Westmr., Marlbro', Cheltenham, Haileyby., Clifton, Charterhouse.

MINCHIN, J. G. C. — Our Public Schools — 6/ c 8° Sonnenschein 01
Eton, Harrow, Rugby, Charterhouse, Winchester, Westminster, Merchant Taylors', St Paul's. An interestg. compiln.

Our Public Schools — [Eton, Harrow, Wincs., Rugby, Westmr., Marlboro', Charterh.] 6/ c 8° Paul 81

PASCOE, C. E. [ed.] — Everyday Life in our Public Schools — 3/6 c 8° Griffith [81] 83
A series of sketches by head scholars of 7 chief publ. schls., w. Merch. Taylors' and Christ's Hosp. added; also glossary of schl.-terms.

„ — Practical Handbk. to Principal Schools of Engld. *o.p.* [*pb.* 3/6] f 8° Low [77] 78

Preparatory Schools for Boys—*in* Special Reports on Educational Subjects, vol. vi, *ut* **D** § 163*
A most valuable account of a hitherto undescribed class of schools.

Public Schools from Within (The) — 3/6 c 8° Low 07
32 essays by 22 contribrs. (mostly schlmasters.) on *Class Room and Auxil. Studies; Moral and Social Influs.; Phys. Culture; Hist. and Descriptive; Miscellaneous.*

Public Schools (The): with notes on their history and traditions — 8/6 f 8° Blackwood 67
Winchester, Westminster, Shrewsbury, Harrow, Rugby. By the author of *Etoniana* [*inf.*].

Royal Commission on Revenues, Managemt. of Certain Colleges and Schls. and Studies pursued: Report, 4 Pts. — [Blue-Bks.] 20/ f° Wyman 64
Eton, Wincs., Westmr., Charterh., St Paul's, Merch. Taylors', Harrow, Rugby, Shrewsby. Appendices consist of valuable pprs. on Higher Educn. by W. E. GLADSTONE, Dr W. WHEWELL, Sir J. HERSCHELL, Sir J. G. Shaw LEFEVRE, Archd. G. A. DENISON, etc.

STAUNTON, Howard — The Great Schools of England; ill. — *o.p.* [*pb.* 7/6] c 8° Strahan [65] 69

*Directory:* Public Schls. Yr.-Bk. & Preparatory Schls. Yr.-Bk. — 3/6 n. c 8° Sonnenschein 89 *sqq., ann.*

Schoolmasters' Year-Book and Directory — 7/6 n. c 8° Sonnenschein 02 *sqq., ann*

*Abbotsholme*

REDDIE, Dr Cecil — Abbotsholme; 2 ports. and 32 ill. [640 pp.] 10/6 *n.* c 8° G. Allen 00
Ill-arrgd., but conts. a good deal of informn. on organizn. of 'a normal tertiary schl. for boys of 11 to 18, bel. to the Directing Classes'.

*Ackworth School* [Quaker]

NODAL, J. H. — Bibliography, Biogr. and Topogr., of Ackworth School 2/6 *n.* 8° Nodal, *Mancs.* 90

'W.' — Between the Cupolas [recollns. of Ackworth Schl.] 2/6 *n.* c 8° Headley 05

*Addiscombe College*

VIBART, Col. H. M. — Addiscombe: its heroes and men of note; ill. [to its close in 1861] 21/ *n.* 4° Constable 94

*Blackburn Grammar School*

GARSTANG, J. — History of Blackburn Grammar School 8° N.E. Lancs Press Co., *Blackburn* 98

STOCKS, G. A. [ed.] — The Records of Blackburn Grammar School, 3 vols. s 4° Chetham Soc. 09

*Blundell's School*

BANKS, M. L. — Blundell's Worthies 7/6 *n.* 4° Chatto 04

SNELL, F. J. — —*his* Chronicles of Twyford [*ut* **E** § 17, *s.v.* Devon]: *conts. a hist. of Blundell's*

" — Early Associations of Abp. Temple; 17 ill. 6/ *n.* c 8° Hutchinson 04
A record of Blundell's and its neighbourhood.

*Bradfield College*

Bradfield College Register: 1871–8, ea. 1/ c 8°; 1879–1888, in 1 vol. 2/6 s 4° Rivgtn. 72–9; Blackwell, *Readg.* 84–8

LEACH, A. F. [ed.] — History of Bradfield College [by old Bradf. boys] 10/6 *n.* ($4·20) 8° Clar. Press 00

*Canterbury School* (*'King's School, Canterbury'*)

WOODRUFF (H. E.) + CAPE (H. J.) Schola Regia Cantuarensis Mitchell & Hughes 09
Claims (with St Peter's School, York) to be the oldest school in England.

*Charterhouse School* — —*for* the Charterhouse, London, *v.* **E** § 17

BARRETT, C. R. B. — Charterhouse: 1611–1895; etchg. and *c.* 40 ill. [text of no value] *o.p.* [*pb.* 6/ *n.*] s 4° Bliss 95

BROWN, Dr W. Haig — Charterhouse, Past and Present [a short history] 7/ c 8° Simpkin 79

" — Carthusian Memories and other Verses 5/ *n.* ($1·60 *n.*) 12° Longman 05
Schl. songs, prologues, hymns, trs. (Lat., Gk., Fch., Germ.), miscell. poems, etc.

EARDLEY-WILMOT (E. P.) + STREATFEILD (E. C.) Charterhouse, Old and New; ill. *o.p.* [*pb.* 12/6 *n.*] 8° Nimmo 95
Acc. of School fr. its foundn. to date of removal to Godalming, w. curious descrn. of life and games of the scholars, notices of Old Carthusians, *etc.*, by EARDLEY-WILMOT; and a second pt., by STREATFEILD (of much inferior value) on the School at Godalming.

MOZLEY, Rev. Thos. — —*in* vol. i [pp. 373–436] *of his* Remin. of Towns, Villages, and Schools, *ut* **E** § 16

PARISH, Rev. W. D. [ed.] — List of Carthusians: 1800–79 8° *Lewes* 79

TOD, A. H. — Charterhouse; 57 ill. [Hdbks. to Gt. Pub. Schls.] 3/6 *n.* c 8° Bell 00
One chapter is historical: the rest is devoted to school-life in the present, school-expenses, etc.

*Biography*

BROWN, Dr Wm. Haig [HM. 1863–97; d. 1906]

Brown, Har. E. Haig [ed.] Wm. Haig Brown of Charterhouse 7/6 *n.* 8° Macmillan 08
A short biographical memoir, wr. by some of his pupils, and ed. by his son.

*Cheltenham College*

HUNTER, A. A. [ed.] — Cheltenham College Register 1841–89; 16 photos 21/ i 8° Bell 90
Conts. a history of the College, and an architectural description of the buildings.

PRUEN (G. G.) + CADE (F. J.) + HUNTER (A. A.) [eds.] Cheltenham College Jubilee: 1891 10/6 i 8° Darter, *Cheltenham* 91

*Biography*

BUTLER, Can. Geo. [1820–90] Recollections of. By Josephine E. Butler [wife]—*ut* **A** § 62

*Chigwell School*

SWALLOW, Can. [ed.] — Chigwell Register; w. hist. acc. of school 8° Phelp 07

*Christ's Hospital*

BLANCH, W. H. — Blue-coat Boys: schl. life in Christ's Hosp. *o.p.* [*pb.* 1/] c 8° E. W. Allen 77

Eight Years a Blue-coat Boy: Dundalker's narrative of fact 1/ f 8° Dean 77

JOHNSON, R. Brimley [ed.] Christ's Hospital: recollns. of Lamb, Coleridge, and Leigh Hunt; ill. 2/ c 8° G. Allen [96] 02
Passages ab. their old school extr. fr. LAMB'S *Essays of Elia*, COLERIDGE'S *Biographia Liter.*, *Table Talk*, etc., and HUNT'S *Autobiogr.*

PEARCE, Rev. E. H. — Annals of Christ's Hospital; ill. 7/6 8° Methuen 01
An excellent account based on original documents; well illustrated.

S., A. O. — Ups and Downs of a Blue-coat Boy *o.p.* [*pb.* 3/6] c 8° Houlston 76

WICKHAM, Geo. — Blue-coat Boy's Recollns. of Hertford School *o.p.* [*pb.* 2/6] c 8° Harvey 41

*Clifton College*

Clifton College: Brown's House: 1864–95, 5 Pts. 8° *priv. prin.* 77–95

Clifton College Twenty-five Years Ago [diary of a fag] 7/6 *n.* c 8° Robinson 04

OAKELEY, E. M. Clifton College: 1860–1897 8° *priv. prin.* 97

*Derby School*

TACCHELLA, B. [ed.] Derby School Register: 1570–1901 8° Bemrose 02
A register of the *alumni* of the foundation, tabulated under the names of headmasters.

*Dulwich College*

BLANCH, W. H. Dulwich College & Edw. Alleyn: short hist.: ill. *o.p.* [*pb.* 3/6] 8° E. W. Allen 77

YOUNG, Wm. History of Dulwich College, 2 vols.; fully ill. 63/r 4° T. B. Bumpus 89
By one of the Govs. of the Coll. A full and excellent hist. of the school; contg. also a hist. of the Picture Gallery, a descr. of the neighbourhd. and a life of Edw. ALLEYN [1566–1626], w. transcript fr. his *Diary* [1617–22] and hist. of the Fortune Theatre. Portraits, illns. and facs. of MSS.

*Durham School*

LEACH, A. F. [ed] Register of Durham School 8° Surtees Soc. *in prep.*

*Elizabeth College, Guernsey*

DURAND, Col. C. J., etc. Elizabeth Coll. Register: 1824–73 [another vol. in prep.] 8° Clarke, *Guernsey* 98

*Eton College*

*Bibliography:* HARCOURT, L. Vernon An Eton Bibliography 8/6 *n.* 4° Humphreys [98] 02

*History; Register; Description*

CLUTTON-BROCK, A. Eton; 46 ill. [Hdbks. to Gt. Pub. Schls.] 3/6 *n.* c 8° Bell 00
Partly historical; partly descriptive of the school at the present day.

CUST, Lion. History of Eton College; ill. 2/6 4° Duckworth [99] 09
A fresh treatment on the lines of LYTE's book, *inf.* Many biographical particulars.

Eton Register: Pts. i–v [1841–89] 8° Spottiswoode, *Eton* 03–8 *in prg.*

GAMBIER-PARRY, Maj. Annals of an Eton House; ill. 15/*n.* 8° Murray 07
Hist. of 'Evans's', the last of the Dame's houses at Eton. All the boardg.-houses at Eton were orig. kept by ladies for their own profit. Wm. EVANS (joined 1818) made new departure in startg. a Dame's [= non-tutorial] house to be run for good of its inmates, and, tho' it nearly ruined him financially, it was a gt. success fr. the first. EVANS d. 1855, and was succeeded by his daus. Anne (d. 1871) and Jane (d. 1906), latter of whom exercised gt. influence. Evans's is now no more.

HORNBY, J. J. Walks round about Eton and Eton Buildings; ill. 7/6 c 8° Drake, *Eton* 95

LEIGH, R. A. Austen [ed.] Eton College Lists: 1678–1790 15/1 8° Spottiswoode, *Eton* 07

*LYTE, Sir H. C. Maxwell History of Eton College; ill. [1440–1910] 21/*n.* r 8° Macmillan [75] 11
Fourth edn. of the standard hist. of Eton, ea. successive edn. addg. whatever Eton lore may have been brot. to light, and continuing hist. to date.

RIMMER, Alf. —*in his* Rambles round Eton and Harrow, *ut* **E** § 17, *s.v.* Bucks

STAPYLTON, H. E. Chetwynd [ed.] Eton School Lists: 1791 to 1877; w. notes and index 30/s 4° Drake, *Eton* [64] 90

" [ed.] Eton School Lists from 1853 to 1892; w. notes & index 21/*n.* s 4° Simpkin 00

STERRY, Wasey Annals of King's Coll. of Lady of Eton beside Windsor 7/6 8° Methuen 98
Readable, w. good stories of masters and boys, incl. the best in print of early days of the Eton Society or 'Pop'. Ill.

WILLIS (R.) + CLARK (J. W.) Architect. Hist. of Cambr. and Eton—*ut inf.*, *s.v.* Cambridge

*Biography: Collectively*

BENSON, A. C. Fasti Etonenses 15/*n.* 8° Drake, *Eton* 00
A valuable series of biographies of celebrated Etonians, in chronological order, formg. a hist. of the College.

CREASY, Sir E. S. Memoirs of Celebrated Etonians; 12 ports. and 1 pl. 7/6 c 8° Chatto [50] 76
WELLINGTON, LYTTLETON, BOLINGBROKE, Hor. WALPOLE, NORTH, WELLESLEY, PORSON, Sir Rob. WALPOLE, GRAY, PITT, *etc.*

JESSE, J. H. Memoirs of Celebrated Etonians, 2 vols. *o.p.* [*pb.* 28/] 8° Bentley 75

*Individually*

HAWTREY, Dr E. C. [1789–1862] Memoir of. By Rev. F. St John Thackeray; ill. 7/6 s 8° Bell 96
A good sketch of the HM. (later Provost) of Eton and his reform-wk. in the schl., in successn. to KEATE.

*Portraits; Frescoes*

CUST, Lionel Eton College Portraits; w. 100 reprodns. £5 5/ 4° Spottiswoode, *Eton* 10
Catal. of the colln. of ports. of distinguished boys wh. hang in the Provost's lodge—presented over 100 yrs. in place of the usual leaving-fee. Incl. examples of ROMNEY, GAINSBOROUGH, and REYNOLDS.

JAMES, Dr M. R. The Frescoes in Chapel at Eton College; ill. 7/6 *n.* 4° Spottiswoode, *Eton* 07

*Reminiscences*

BANKES, G. Nugent A Day of my Life at Eton 1/c 8° Low [77] 89

" About Some Fellows 1/c 8° Low [78]

" An Eton Boy's Letters 5/c 8° Cassell 01
A series of letters to his relations and friends, giving an accurate delineation of Eton life, its manners and customs.

BROWNING, Oscar Memories of 60 Yrs. at Eton, Cambr., etc.; ill. 14/*n.* 8° Lane [10] 10

COLERIDGE, A. Duke Eton in the Forties; ill. 6/c 8° Bentley [96] 98
Eton under HAWTREY, fr. the 'College' pt.-of-view. Author was one of last tenants of 'Long Chamber', the famous dormitory—at its best 'a rough barrack', at its worst 'a chamber of horrors'. In 1898 edn. new illus. replace the poor ones of 1st (1896) edn.

E., O. Eton under Hornby [many good stories] 3/6 *n.* c 8° Fifield 10
Etoniana, Ancient and Modern: notes on hist. and tradns. of the college *o.p.* [*pb.* 5/] c 8° Blackwood 65
By W. L. COLLINS.
GREEN, W. C. Memories of Eton and King's 2/6 *n.* c 8° Spottiswoode, *Eton* 05
LUBBOCK, Alf. Memories of Eton and Etonians; ill. 9/8° Murray 99
A series of rather confused reminiscs. of the yrs. 1854–63, and of subseq. cricket to 1874.
M., C. H. Recollections of an Eton Colleger: 1898–1902 5/*n.* c 8° Spottiswoode, *Eton* 05
'OLD COLLEGER (An)' Eton of Old, or Eighty Years since; ill. *o.p.* [*pb.* 15/] 4° Griffith & Farran 92
Presents a capital picture of the College in the yrs. 1820–30; w. acc. of the famous KEATE.
'OLD ETONIAN (An)' Eton Memories; 13 ill. by author 10/6 *n.* 8° Lane 09
By Rev. W. H. TUCKER. Eton in the 'twenties, under KEATE, fr. pt.-of-view of oppidans fr. wealthy homes.
RICHARDS, J. Brinsley Seven Years of my Life at Eton [1857–64] *o.p.* [*pb.* 6/] c 8° Bentley [83] 85
WILKINSON, Rev. C. A. Reminiscences of Eton [in Keate's time] 6/c 8° Hurst 87
*Glossary:* STONE (C. R.) Eton Glossary 1/*n.* c 8° Spottiswoode, *Eton* 02
*Anthologies:* AINGER, A. C. Eton Songs set to Mus. by [Sir] Jos. Barnby; ill. 30/4° Leadenhall Press 91
,, [ed.] Eton in Prose and Verse 63/*n.* 34° Hodder 10

*Felstead School*

SARGEAUNT, Jno. History of Felstead School [fr. its foundn. in 1564] 4/*n.* 8° Durrant, *Chelmsford* 90

*Haileybury College*

MILFORD, Rev. L. S. Haileybury College, Past and Present; ill. 10/6 *n.* 8° Unwin 09
,, [ed.] Haileybury Register [1862–87] 7/6 4° Austin, *Hertford* [87] 91
MONIER-WILLIAMS (Sir M.) + WIGRAM (P.) [eds.] Memorls. of Old Haileybury; ill. 21/*n.* 4° Constable 93

*Harrow School*

HOWSON (E. W.) + WARNER (G. T.) [ed.] Harrow School; ill. Herb. Marshall 21/*n.* 4° Arnold 98
A series of separate papers, by various writers, on various aspects of Harrow life. *L. P.* (150 copies) 63/*n.*
MINCHIN, J. G. C. Old Harrow Days; ill. [reminisc. 1864 onwards] 5/c 8° Methuen [97] 98
RIMMER, Alf. —*in his* Rambles round Eton and Harrow, *ut* **E** § 16, *s.v.* Bucks
THORNTON, P. M. Harrow School and its Surroundings; ill. *o.p.* [*pb.* 15/] 8° W. H. Allen 85
WELCH, R. Courtenay [ed.] Harrow School Register, ed. M. G. Dauglish: 1801–1900 15/*n.* 8° Longman [81] 01
WILLIAMS, J. Fischer Harrow; 48 ill. [Hdbks. to Gt. Pub. Schls.] 3/6 *n.* c 8° Bell 01
A valuable account, historical and contemporary: mostly compiled.
*Biography:* BOWEN (Edw.) Edw. Bowen, a Memoir. By Rev. W. E. Bowen 12/6 *n.* ($5) 8° Longman 02
Appendices cont. several of his essays, songs, verses, etc.
SMITH, Reg. Bosworth [1839–1908]
Grogan, L'y Reginald Bosworth Smith 10/6 *n.* 8° Nisbet 09

*Louth: Free School of King Edward VI*—*v.* **E** § 17, *s.v.* Lincs (GOULDING)

*Marlborough College*

BRADLEY (A. G.) + CHAMPNEYS (A. C.) + BAINES (J. W.) Hist. of Marlborough College; ill. 7/6 *n.* c 8° Murray 93
Gives an interesting acc. of the early hist. of the town, of the Marq. of HERTFORD's house (wh. still forms pt. of the schl. buildings), of the early struggles of the College, chaps. on games, rifle corps, and nat. hist. society.
HULME, F. E. Town, College, & Neighbourhood of Marlborough; ill. *o.p.* [*pb.* 6/] c 8° Stanford 81
LOCKWOOD, E. Early Days of Marlborough College; ill. 10/6 *n.* 4° Simpkin 93
Author entered Marlb. at its foundn. (1843), and his recollns. of its earliest days under Dr WILKINSON are very gloomy. Poorly written.
MANT, Rev. Newton Account of New Chapel at Marlborough School; ill. *o.p.* [*pb.* 6/] c 8° W. H. Allen 91
SIMPKINSON, H. W. [ed.] Register of Marlborough College 10/6 8° Leader, *College, Marlbro'* 90

*Merchant Taylors' School*

BAKER, Dr Wm. [ed.] Merchant Taylors' School Register: 1871–1900 8° R. Clay & Sons 08
Chronol. list, w. biogr. notices, of all who entered the schl. under BAKER's headmastersh., w. notices of earlier boys brot. down to date.
ROBINSON, C. J. [ed.] Register of Schlrs. adm. to M. T. Sch., 1562–1874 2 v. 42/– r 8° Farncombe 82–3

*Mill Hill School*

JAMES, N. G. B. History of Mill Hill School: 1807–1907 7/6 *n.* 8° Melrose 09

*Penketh School* [Quaker]

HODGSON, Jos. S. History of Penketh School; ports. and ill. 5/*n.* 8° Headley 07

*Radley, St. Peter's College*

RAIKES, Rev. T. D., *etc.* Sicut Columbae: 50 yrs. of St Peter's Coll., Radley 10/*n.* 8° Parker, *Oxford* 97
By Old Radleians. Of considerable interest in connexion with the Oxford Movement.

*Repton School*

HIPKINS, Rev. F. C. Hist. of Repton & Neighbhb.; ill. [incl. Schl.] 4/6 *n.* c 8° Lawrence, *Repton* [ ] 99

*Rossall School*

BEECHEY, Can. St Vinc. Rise & Progr. of Rossall Schl. [by fdr. of the schl. (1844)] 2/6 c 8° Skeffington 94

Rossall Register: 1884–89 89

ROWBOTHAM, J. F. History of Rossall School; ill. 10/ 8° J. Heywood, *Mancs.* 95

*Rugby School*

ARBUTHNOT, Sir A. J. [1822–1907] Memories of Rugby and India; ports. 15/ *n.* 8° Unwin 10
Rugby under ARNOLD; also Haileybury 1840–1; w. Ind. career to retiremt. fr. Vice-Regal Council in 1880.

BLOXAM, M. H. Rugby, the Schl. and Neighbhd., ed. Rev. W. H. Payne-Smith 7/6 *n.* 8° Whittaker 90
Throws a good deal of light on state of educ. in Engl. in first quarter of 19 cent.; and his letters to Dr JAMES (here reprod.) furnish lively pict. of Rugby 100 yrs. ago, no. of classes, authors read, etc. A colln. of matls. rather th. a history.

BRADBY, H. C. Rugby; 44 ill. [Hdbks. to Gt. Pub. Schls.] 3/6 *n.* c 8° Bell 00

BRADLEY, A. G. —*his* Avon and Shakesp. Country [*ut* **E** § 17]: conts. good acc. of Rugby

GOULBURN, Dn E. M. Book of Rugby School [history and life] *o.p.* c 8° 56

RIMMER, Alf. —*in his* Rambles round Rugby, *ut* **E** § 17, *s.v.* Warwickshire

ROUSE, Rev. W. H. D. History of Rugby School; ill. [Engl. Pub. Schls.] 2/6 *n.* s 4° Duckworth [98] 09
The best history of the school, dealg. much more soundly w. the early hist. than any other bk.

Rugby School Register: 1675–1874, vol. i, 8/6; ii, 6/ in 1 vol. 10/ 8° Rivington 81–96
With annotations and index. A previous *Register* [1675–1867] was pub., 7/6 8° Whittaker, '67.

SELFE, Col. Syd. Chapters fr. History of Rugby School c 8° Lawrence, *Rugby* 10
Rugby under JAMES (1778–94), WOOLL (1807–28), TAIT (1842–50), ARNOLD. Incls. an enlarged repr. of his *Notes on Characters and Incidents in 'Tom Brown's Schooldays'* (1909).

*Biography*

ARNOLD, Dr Thos. [1795–1842]

Findlay, J. J. [ed.] Arnold of Rugby: his school-life & contribns. to educn. 5/ c 8° Camb. Pr. 97
$1·25 *n.* Putnam, *N.Y.* A seln. of passages fr. STANLEY'S *Life* and fr. ARNOLD'S own Serms. and Essays, w. connectg. passages by Edr.

Fitch, Sir Josh. T. & M. Arnold, & their Influ. on Engl. Educn. 5/ c 8° Heinemann 97
$1 *n.* Scribner, *N.Y.* [Gt. Educators.]. An excellent summary of what has been said before about Thos. ARNOLD, but conts. little that is new.

Selfe, Rose E. Dr Arnold of Rugby [World Workers; quite popular] 1/ c 8° Cassell 89

*Stanley, Dn A. P. Life & Corresp. of T. Arnold; Pref. Sir J. Fitch; ill. 2/6 c 8° Murray [47] 04
One of the best biogrs. in the language. Ch. edns.: 2/ [Minerva Lib.] Ward & Lock; Abgd. 1/ *n.* [Lib. of Stand. Biogrs.] Hutchinson '03.

Worboise, Emma J. Life of Dr Arnold [quite popular] *o.p.* [*pb.* 3/6] c 8° Isbister [6–] 85

*St Edmund's College, Ware, Herts* [Roman-Catholic School: founded 1795]

WARD, Rev. Bern. Hist. of St Edmund's Coll., Old Hall; ill. [by its president] 10/6 8° Paul 93

*St Paul's School*

GARDINER, Rev. R. B. [ed.] Admissn. Regrs. of St. Paul's Schl.: 1748–1876, 31/6; 1876–1905, 21/ *n.* r 8° Bell 84; 06

McDONNELL, M. F. J. History of St Paul's School; 48 ports. and ill. 12/6 *n.* 8° Chapman 09
An adequate piece of wk.—the first history pubd. of the school. Well ill.

*Biography*

COLET, Dn Jno. [1466–1519; founder of St Paul's School]—*v.* **A** § 62

*Sandhurst*

MOCKLER-FERRYMAN, Maj. A. F. Annals of Sandhurst; 12 ill. 10/ *n.* r 8° Heinemann 00
Largely records of Sandhurst athletics; with offical regulations, etc.

*Sedbergh School*

AINSLIE, R. St John Sedbergh School Songs 8° Jackson, *Leeds* 97

Sedbergh School Register: 1546–1895

*Sherborne*

HARPER, Dr H. D. Memoir of. By L. V. Lester 5/ c 8° Longman 96

*Shrewsbury School*

AUDEN, J. E. Shrewsbury School Register: 1798–1898 8° Woodall, *Oswestry* 98

CALVERT, Dr [ed.] Register of Shrewsbury School: 1562–1635 8° *priv. prin.*

FISHER, G. W. Annals of Shrewsbury School, ed. J. S. Hill; 34 pl. 10/6 8° Methuen 99

GRETTON, Dr F. E.—*in his* Memory's Hark-back thro' Half a Cent. [1808–59] *o.p.* [*pb.* 12/] 8° Bentley 89

Shrewsbury School: a history; 26 ill. [fr. Blakeway MSS., etc.] *o.p.* 4° 89

SIDNEY, Sir Hy. [16 cent.] Very Godly Letter unto Phillip Sidney, his Sonne—*in* Jacob's Public School Life, *ut sup.*
Written to young SIDNEY [afterw. Sir Pp. SIDNEY] while 'at schoole in the towne of Shrewsbury'. Orig. pub. in 1591, 18 pp. s 8°, prtd. by T. Dawson; later repr. (fr. orig. MS.) in vol. ix of *Harleian Miscellany*, and in *Sidney State Papers*, ed. A. COLLINS (fr. origs. at Penshurst), 2 vols. f° *Lond.* 1746.

*Biography*

BUTLER, Dr Sam. [1774–1840; HM. 1798–1836, *afterw.* Bp of Lichfield]

Butler, Sam. [gr'son] Life and Letters of Samuel Butler, D.D., 2 vols. 24/ 8° Murray 96
A vivid portrait of the man as a schoolmaster and a divine; much valueless correspce. included.

*Sidcot School* [Quaker]

KNIGHT, Fcs. A. History of Sidcot School [1808–1908] 6/*n.* i 16° Dent 08

*Stonyhurst* [' the Catholic Eton '; founded 1794 by Jesuit fathers fr. Liége]

FITZGERALD, Percy Stonyhurst Memories [rather trivial and egotistical] *o.p.* [*pb.* 6/] c 8° Bentley 95

GERARD, Rev. Jno. Stonyhurst College, its Life beyond the Seas 1592–1794, and on English Soil 1794–1894 12/6 4° Burns & Oates 94

GRUGGEN (Rev. G.) + KEATING (Rev. J.) Stonyhurst, its History and Life; ill. 7/6 8° Paul 01

HEWITSON, Anth. [' ATTICUS '] Stonyhurst College: its past and present 10/6 *n.* 8° *Preston* (Burns & Oates) [70]

RIMMER, Alf. Stonyhurst Illustrated; 32 pl. 31/6 i 4° Burns & Oates 84

*Tonbridge School*

HUGHES-HUGHES, W. O. [ed.] Register of Tonbridge School: 1820–93 *o.p.* [*pb.* 6/] 8° Bentley 93

The School, tho' founded (by Andr. JUDDE) ab. reign of Edward vi, has no earlier register.

RIVINGTON, S. History of Tonbridge School [from 1553] 12/6 *n.* 8° Rivington [69] 98

*University College School, London*

FELKIN, F. W. From Gower Street to Frognal [short hist.: 1830–1907] 1/*n.* 8° Fairbairns 09

ORME, Temple [ed.] Register of Univ. Coll. Schl., Lond.: 1831–91 10/6 *n.* 8° Lawrence & Bullen *n.d.* (91)

*Uppingham School*

OLD BOY (An) ' Early Days at Uppingham under Thring 3/6 *n.* ($1·50) c 8° Macmillan 04

Uppingham School Roll: 1824–1905 8/6 *n.* 8° Stanford [94] 06

*Biography*

THRING, Rev. Edw. [1821–87; HM.]

Parkin, Geo. R. Edward Thring, Headmaster of Uppingham; ill. 6/ c 8° Macmillan [98] 00

Rawnsley, Rev. H. D. Edward Thring, Teacher and Poet 3/6 c 8° Unwin 89

Skrine, Rev. J. H. Memoir of Edward Thring *o.p.* [*pb.* 6/] c 8° Macmillan 90

Mr SKRINE was first a boy, and later an assistant master, at Uppingham, under THRING.

*Wakefield Grammar School*

PEACOCK History of Wakefield Grammar School; pl. 92

*Warwick School*

LEACH, A. F. History of Warwick School; ports. and ill. 10/6 *n.* 8° Constable 06

A scholarly wk., incl. much informn., based on docum. sources, in the Colleg. Church, gilds, and borough.

*Westminster School* [*St Peter's College*]

AIRY, Reg. Westminster; 51 ill. [Hdbks. to Gt. Pub. Schls.] 3/6 *n.* c 8° Bell 02

BARKER (G. F. R.) + STENNING (A. H.) [eds.] Westminster School Register: 1764–1883 10/6 *n.*; Suppl. 1/*n.* r 8° Macmillan 92–4

FORSHALL, F. H. Westminster School, Past and Present; pl. *o.p.* [*pb.* 21/] 8° Wyman 84

MARKHAM, Cpt. F. Recollns. of a Town Boy at Westmr. 10/6 8° Arnold 03

Westminster under LIDDELL. Deals chiefly w. the lighter side of schl.-life. Illustrations by the author.

SARGEAUNT, Jno. Annals of Westminster School; 31 pl. 7/6 8° Methuen 98

A good account, from Elizabethan to present times; w. Appendices.

*Biography*

BUSBY, Dr Rich. [1606–95; Headmaster]

Barker, G. F. R. Memoir of Rich. Busby, D.D.; 7 ports., views, etc. 21/*n.* 4° Lawrence & Bullen 95

An account of BUSBY's life (of wh. very little is known), BAGSHAWE's quarrel with him, his Account-book (w. a facs. page), his will, etc., and a short but interestg. descrn. of school-life at Westmr. in 17 cent. 320 printed.

*Westminster Grey Coat Hospital* [now a Girls' School]

DAY, [Miss] E. S. An Old Westminster Endowment 3/*n.* c 8° Rees 02

*Winchester College* —*v. also* **E** § 17, *s.v.* Hampshire

ADAMS, Rev. H. C. Wykehamica: history of Winchester College, etc. 10/6 c 8° Parker 78

LEACH, Arth. F. History of Winchester College [Engl. Publ. Schls.] 6/*n.* c 8° Duckworth 99

500 pp. Illustrated. An excellent account.

WARNER, R. T. Winchester; 46 ill. [Hdbks. to Gt. Pub. Schls.] 3/6 *n.* c 8° Bell 01

Mainly descriptive, but includes a historical account; much from original documents.

*Biography*

DEANE, Christopher: WATSON (E. H. L.) Christ. Deane: a character study 6/ c 8° E. Matthews 01

Life at Winchester and at Cambridge.

RIDDING, Bp Geo. [d. 1904]

Ridding, L'y Laura [wife] George Ridding, Schoolmaster and Bishop; ill. 15/*n.* 8° Arnold 08

An interestg. life of the HM. [1866–84], to whom was accorded the title of ' second founder '; later Bp of Southwell [1884–1904].

WYKEHAM, WILLIAM OF [1324–1404]—*v. also* **A** § 62 (LOWTH, MOBERLY)

Walcott, M. E. C. William of Wykeham and his Colleges *o.p.* [*pb.* 14/] 8° Whittaker 52

*Registers*

HOLGATE, C. W. [ed.] Wincs. Coll., 1836–1906: a register, ed. J. B. Wainewright 8° Wells, *Wincs.* [91] 07

,, [ed.] Winchester Long Rolls: 1653–1812, 2 vols. ea. 10/*n.* 8° Wells, *Wincs.* 99–04
With Introd. and notes. Vol. ii conts. brief memr. of Edr., a thoro' student and devoted Wykehamist (d. 1903, aged 45).

,, [ed.] Winchester Commoners: 1800–35; w. Introd. & notes 1/c 8° Brown, *Salisbury* 93

,, [ed.] Roll of Names & Addresses of Old Wykehamists [pp. 380] 8° *priv. prin.* 00

KIRBY, T. F. [ed.] Winchester Scholars: wardens, fellows, scholars; w. notes 10/6 8° Frowde 88

,, Annals of Wincs. College fr. Foundn. [1382] to 1887 15/ 8° Frowde 92

*Reminiscences*

MANSFIELD, R. Blachford School Life at Wincs. Coll., 1835–40; cuts and 12 col. pl. 6/c 8° Nutt [66] 93
Gives on the whole a pleasanter picture than TUCKWELL [both were in College]. Conts. a *Glossary of School Terms* (not so good as WRENCH, *inf.*).

TUCKWELL, Rev. W. The Ancient Ways: Wincs. 50 years ago; ill. 4/6 ($1·50) c 8° Macmillan 93
Interestg. papers on *The Candlestick, The Junior, Manners and Customs, Men.* An honest bk., clearly showg. th. in the forties the schl. had a tradn. of slavery and did not fail to enforce it. L'd SELBORNE [in his paper in *Wincs. College, inf.*] is almost the only other Old Wykehamist who has wr. candidly ab. the schl. as it was.

Winchester College: 1393–1893. By Old Wykehamists; ill. Herb. Marshall 25/*n.* 4° Arnold 93
Quincent. Memorial Vol. Among contribrs. are L'd SELBORNE, Bp of SOUTHWELL, Dn KITCHIN, Dr FEARON [late HM.].

*Slang; Place-names* —*v. also sup. s.n.* MANSFIELD

'THREE BEETLEITES' Winchester College Notions, 2 vols. ea. 4/6*n.* 8° Wells, *Winchester* [01] 11; 11
A dict. of words and place-names in use at Wincs. Coll. Vol. ii gives examples and derivations.

WRENCH, R. G. K. [ed.] Winchester Word-Book: a collection of past & present notions 2/6 s 4° Nutt 91
Traces the etymology and dialectical usage of the slang words. Very well compiled and edited.

*Mission* —*v.* **A** § 106 (DOLLING)

**British Colonies: Generally**

RUSSELL, Jno. Schools of Greater Brit.: educ. syst. of Colonies & India—*ut sup., s.v.* Australia

**Universities:** *Collectively*

CAMPBELL, Prf. Lewis Nationalization of the Old English Universities 7/6 c 8° Chapman 01
Traces the growth of Oxford and Cambridge from exclusiveness to a national position.

HUBER, Prf. V. A. The English Universities [tr.], 2 vols. in 3; ill. *o.p.* [*pb.* 50/] 8° Pickering 43
i: 12th Cent. to d. of Eliz.; ii: to 1843; iii: Constitn. of Univs., Student Life. A compiln. of considerable research, but much irrelevancy, no histor. order, and prejudiced. Tr. Prf. F. W. NEWMAN; 52 ports. and pl. of founders, celebr. scholars, scenes of Univ. life, etc.

Oxford and Cambridge Year Book: ed. A. W. Holland ea. 5/*n.* c 8° Sonnenschein [04] 05 *not cont.*
i: *Oxford*; ii: *Cambridge*. Gives degrees and other distinctns., w. pres. occupns. and addresses of all then (1905) living who have graduated or wh. were then entitled to graduate.

Report of H.M. Commissioners on Property and Incomes of Oxfd. and Camb., 2 v. [Blue-Bks.] f° Eyre & Spottiswoode 74

WORDSWORTH, Bp C. Social Life at Engl. Universities in 18th Cent. *o.p.* [*pb.* 15/] 8° Bell 74

,, Scholæ Academicæ 15/ 8° Camb. Press 77
$2·75 *n.* Putnam, *N.Y.* An account of studies at English Universities in the 18th century.

*University and College Verse* —*v.* **K** § 66 *University Education*—*v.* **D** § 168

**Cambridge University:** *Collectively* —*v. also* **D** § 168, *and* **E** § 17, *s.v.* Cambridgeshire

ATKINSON, T. D. Cambridge Illustrated & Described; 30 pl., maps & ill. 12/6*n.* 8° Macmillan 98
Acc. of the Univ. and ea. of its Colleges, as well as of the Town, incl. its early hist.

Book of Matriculations and Degrees, 1851–1900 15/ 8° Camb. Press 02
$4 *n.* Putnam, *N.Y.* The first book of the kind issued in English, in place of Latin.

BREUL, Dr Karl Students' Life and Work in Cambridge [2 lectures] 1/*n.* gl 8° Bowes, *Camb.* [08] 10

BRISTED, C. A. Five Years in an Engl. University *o.p.* [*pb.* $2·25] 12° Putnam, *N.Y.* [ ] 74
Account of the social life of Cambridge in 1842–7, by an American student.

CLARK, J. W. Cambridge—*ut* **E** § 17, *s.v.* Cambridgeshire

,, Concise Guide to Cambridge 1/9 f 8° Bowes, *Camb.* [98] 02
Under the guise of four walks about the town.

,, Old Friends at Cambridge and Elsewhere 6/c 8° Macmillan 00
Biographical sketches of Dr WHEWELL, Bp THIRLWALL, L'd HOUGHTON, E. H. PALMER, F. M. BALFOUR, Hy. BRADSHAW, W. H. THOMPSON, C. TROTTER, Richard OKES, H. R. LUARD, and Prf. OWEN.

,, [ed.] Letters Patent of Eliz. and Jas i addressed to Univ. Camb. 2/6 8° Camb. Pr. 92
75 c. *n.* Putnam, *N.Y.* With other documents, and trs. of ELIZABETH's letters.

,, [ed.] Endowmts. of Univ. of Camb. [$3·50 *n.* Putn., *N.Y.*] 10/6*n.* 8° Camb. Press 04

,, [ed.] Ordinances of Univ. of Camb. [$2 *n.* Putnam., *N.Y.*] 7/6 8° Camb. Pr. [85] 04

COOPER, C. H. Annals of Cambridge, vols. i–iv *o.p.* 8° *priv. prin.* 42–52

,, The same, vol. v, ed. Dr J. W. Cooper 18/*n.* 8° Camb. Press 08
Putnam, *N.Y.* Covers the period 1850–6, w. addns. and corrns. to vols. i–iv, and Index to the 5 vols. A Suppl. Vol. is in prep.

,, Memorials of Cambridge, 3 vols.; pl. *o.p.* [*pb.* 25/ ea.] 8° Macmillan 80

COOPER, C. H. + T. Athenæ Cantabrigienses, vols. i–ii [1500–1609] *o.p.* [*pb.* 36/] 8° Macmillan 58–61
Authors' intention was to have compiled a wk. of similar scope to Ant. à WOOD'S *Athenæ*, but death prevented its fulfilmt. As the pt. wr., however, incl. whole of Tudor period and so much of Stuart as covers the preparatn. of the *Authorized Version* it conts. many biogrs. and biogr. notices (some 1,400 in all) of importance and interest.

Grace Books: Bk. A: 1454–88, ed. S. M. Leathes [Luard Memorial Ser.] 21/*n.* 8° Deighton, *Camb.* 98
,, Bk. B, Pt. i: 1488–1511; Pt. ii: 1511–44; Introds. Mary Bateson ea. 21/*n.* 8° Camb. Press 03–5
,, Bk. Γ: 1501–42, ed. W. G. Searle 21/*n.* 8° Camb. Press 08
$6 *n.* Putnam, *N.Y.* Proctors' accounts and other records of the University.

HARVEY, Gabr. [1545–1630] Diary and Letter-Bk., ed. E. J. L. Scott [1573–80] 5/s 4° Camden Soc. 84
Throws some light on University life at Cambridge in the days of ELIZABETH.

HARVEY, W. J. [ed.] Alumni Cantabrigienses *priv. prin., in prg.*
Transcript of Cambr. matrics. & admissns. to colls., on plan of FOSTER'S *Oxford Matrics. ut inf.* To occupy some 21 v. In ea. case brot. down to 1800.

HOPE, W. H. St John Seals and Armorial Insignia of Univ. and Colls. of Camb.—*ut* **G** § 21

LOGGAN, Dav. Cantabrigia Illustrata, ed. J. W. Clark; w. notes 42/*n.* f° Bowes, *Camb.* [1690] 05
Minutely accur. views of Camb. Univ. and Town at close of 17 cent., after the extensive bldg. operns. carried out in rns. of the Tudors and Stuarts, and when BENTLEY was fightg. his enemies and crushg. the wits of Oxfd. and Hy. ESMOND learng. the *botte de Jésuite* fr. his old fencg.-master. Introd. and notes by CLARK.

LUARD, H. R. [ed.] Graduati Cantabrigienses 1800–84 [$3 *n.* Putnam, *N.Y.*] 12/6 8° Camb. Press [73] 85

MULLINGER, J. Bass Univ. of Camb. fr. Earliest Times to 1535 [$3 *n.* Putn., *N.Y.*] 12/8° Camb. Press 73
,, Univ. of Camb. fr. 1535 to Accn. of Chas. i [$4·50 *n.* Putn., *N.Y.* 18/8° Camb. Press 84
,, Hist. of Univ. of Cambridge [Epochs of Church Hist.] 2/6 (80 c.) f 8° Longman 88

NEALE, C. M. [ed.] Honours Register of Univ. of Cambr., 2 Pts. ea. 10/*n.* s 4° Hitchcock, *Streatham* 00–2
From 1246 to date; alphab. arranged. Pts. i–ii A–KINGSLEY. Women students included. Notes.
,, Senior Wranglers: 1748–1907; w. biogr. notes 2/6 *n.* 8° Groom, *Bury St Edmunds* 07
,, [ed.] Early Honour Lists of Univ. Camb.: 1498–1747; w. notes 6/*n.* Groom, *Bury St Edmunds* 09

SANDYS, Dr J. E. Orationes et Epistolae Cantabrigienses: 1876–1909 10/*n.* ($3 *n.*) 4° Macmillan 01

Statutes for the Univ. of Camb. and Colleges: 1878–82 [$4 *n.* Putnam, *N.Y.*] 16/8° Camb. Press 83
,, of the University of Cambridge [$1 *n.* Putnam, *N.Y.*] 3/6 8° Camb. Press [ ]

Students' Handbook to University and Colleges of Cambridge 3/*n.* c 8° Camb. Press [02] 07
$1 *n.* Putnam, *N.Y.* A full acc. of teaching staff, admission, expenses, scholarships, prizes, exams., etc.

THOMPSON, A. H. Cambridge and its Colleges; ill. 3/18° Methuen 98

TUKER, M. A. R. Cambridge; col. pl. W. Matthison [$6 *n.* Macmillan, *N.Y.*] 20/*n.* sq 8° Black 07

*WILLIS (R.) + CLARK (J. W.) Architectural Hist. of Univ. of Camb. and Colleges of Cambridge and Eton, 4 vols. 84/*n.* r 8° Camb. Press 86
$25 *n.* Putnam, *N.Y.* By no means so restricted in its scope as its title indicates. Vol. iv contains maps, plans, and plates.

*Amateur Drama*

BURNAND, [Sir] F. C. The A. D. C. [reminiscences] *o.p.* [*pb.* 10/6] 8° Chapman [79] 80

Club Law: ed. Prf. G. C. Moore Smith; w. Introd. and notes 6/*n.* s 4° Camb. Press 07
$2 *n.* Putnam, *N.Y.* A comedy acted in Clare Hall c. 1599–1600. Here first prtd. fr. the MS. in St John's Coll.

Hymenæus: ed. Prf. G. C. Moore Smith; w. Introd. and Notes 2/6 *n.* s 4° Camb. Press 09
$1·10 *n.* Putnam, *N.Y.* A comedy acted at St John's 1578–9; based on 10th story of Fourth Day of BOCCACCIO'S *Decameron*.

Worke for Cvtlers: ed. A. Forbes Sieveking; Introd. A. W. Ward 5/*n.* s 4° Camb. Press 04
$1·50 *n.* Putnam, *N.Y.* A 'merry dialogue betw. Sword, Rapier, and Dagger'; acted 1615.

*Anthology*

KELLETT, E. E. [ed.] A Book of Cambridge Verse [Chaucer to 20 cent.] 6/*n.* c 8° Camb. Press 11

WHIBLEY, C. [ed.] In Cap and Gown—*ut* **K** § 66

*Magazines—v.* **K** § 26 *Oxford and Cambridge Boat-Race—v.* **I** § 153

*Christ's College*

PEILE, Dr Jno. History of Christ's College [College Histories] 5/*n.* c 8° Hutchinson 01
,, [ed.] Biographical Register of Christ's College: 1505–1905, vol. i 8° *priv. prin.* 10

*Clare College*

WARDALE, J. R. History of Clare College [College Histories] 5/*n.* c 8° Hutchinson 00

*Corpus Christi College*

MASTERS, Rob. Hist. of Corp. Chr. Coll., ed. J. Lamb; 6 pl. *o.p.* [*pb.* 31/6] 4° Murray [1753] 31

STOKES, Rev. H. P. Corpus Christi College [College Histories] 5/*n.* c 8° Hutchinson 98
Well indexed.

*Downing College*

STEVENS, Rev. H. W. P. Downing College [College Histories] 5/*n.* c 8° Hutchinson 99

*Emmanuel College*

SHUCKBURGH, E. S. Emmanuel College [College Histories] 5/*n.* c 8° Hutchinson 04

*Gonville and Caius Colleges*

VENN, Dr Jno. Biograph. Hist. of Gonville & Caius Coll.; ill., 3 vols. 52/6 *n.* 8° Camb. Press 98–02
Ea. 20/ *n.* (ea. $8 *n.* Putnam, *N.Y.*). i: List of Membrs., w. notes, 1349–1713; ii: 1713–1897; iii: Biogrs., bldgs., deeds, etc.

,, Caius College [College Histories] 5/ *n.* c 8° Hutchinson 01

,, + S. C. [eds.] Admissions to Gonville and Caius Colls. [1558–1678–9; $4 *n.* Putn., *N.Y.*] 10/ 8° Camb. Press 87

*King's College*

FAY, C. R. King's College, Cambridge; ill. [College Monographs] 2/ *n.* 12° Dent 06

LEIGH, A. Austen King's College, Cambridge [College Histories] 5/ *n.* c 8° Hutchinson 99

Leigh, W. Austen [bro'] Augustus Austen Leigh: record of coll. reform 8/6 *n.* c 8° Smith & Elder 06
Life of the late Provost (d. 1905), a gr'd-neph. of Jane AUSTEN; entd. Eton 1852 and passed on to King's.

*Peterhouse*

WALKER, T. A. Peterhouse, Univ. of Cambridge [College Histories] 5/ *n.* c 8° Hutchinson 06

*Queen's College*

GRAY, J. H. History of Queen's College 5/ *n.* c 8° Hutchinson 00

*St Catherine's College*

BROWNE, Bp G. F. St Catherine's College, Cambridge [Coll. Histories] 5/ *n.* c 8° Hutchinson 03

*St John's College*

BAKER, Thos. History of College of St John, 2 vols. 24/ 8° Camb. Press 69
$6 *n.* Putnam, *N.Y.* Edited, w. elaborate notes, by Prf. J. E. B. MAYOR. Author was an 'Ejected Fellow'.

MAYOR, Prf. Jno. E. B. [ed.] Admissns. to Coll. of St. John, Camb., pts. i–ii [Jan. 1629–30–Jy. 1715] 10/6 *n.* 8° Deighton, *Camb.* 82; 93

MULLINGER, J. Bass St John's College, Cambridge [College Histories] 5/ *n.* c 8° Hutchinson 01

SCOTT, R. F. Notes fr. Records of St John's Coll., Cambridge 8° *priv. prin.*, *Camb.* 89–99

,, St John's College, Cambridge; ill. [College Monographs] 2/ *n.* 12° Dent 06

*Selwyn College*

BROWN, A. L. Selwyn College, Cambridge [College Histories] 5/ *n.* c 8° Hutchinson 06

*Sidney Sussex College*

EDWARDS, G. M. Sidney Sussex College [College Histories] 5/ *n.* c 8° Hutchinson 99

*Trinity College*

BALL, W. W. Rouse Notes on History Trinity College, Cambridge 2/6 *n.* c 8° Macmillan 99

,, Trinity College, Cambridge; ill. [College Monographs] 2/ *n.* 12° Dent 06

,, + VENN (T. A.) [eds.] Admissions to Trinity College, Camb.: 1801–50 21/ *n.* 8° Macmillan 11

BLAKISTON, H. E. D. Trinity College, Cambridge [College Histories] 5/ *n.* c 8° Hutchinson 98

CAROË, W. D. King's Hostel, Trinity College, Cambridge 10/6 *n.* 8° Deighton, *Camb.* 09
History of King's Hostel, the nucleus of Trinity College; dates back to 1334.

*Trinity Hall*

MALDEN, H. E. Trinity Hall [College Histories] 5/ *n.* c 8° Hutchinson 02

**Durham University**

FOWLER, Can. J. T. Durham Univ.: earlier foundns. & pres. colls. [Coll. Hists.] 5/ *n.* c 8° Hutchinson 04

**London University**

ALLCHIN, Dr W. H. Reconstruction of London University, Pts. i–ii 7/6 *n.* i 8° Wyman 05–11

**Oxford University** —*v. also* **D** § 168, *and* **E** § 17, *s.v.* Oxfordshire

ANSTEY, Rev. Hy. [ed.] Munimenta Academica, 2 Pts. ea. 10/ r 8° Rolls Series 68
Documents illustrating academic life and studies at Oxford.

,, [ed.] Epistolae Academicae Oxon., 2 Pts. 21/ *n.* r° Oxford Hist. Soc. 98–00
Documents, Latin and English, of the 15th cent., mostly referring to business matters, with abstracts and introduction.

BEDFORD, Rev. W. K. R. Outcomes of Old Oxford; ill. [life 50 yrs. previous] *o.p.* [*pb.* 3/6 *n.*] c 8° Robinson 99

BOASE (Rev. C. W.) + CLARK (Rev. A.) [eds.] Register of University of Oxford, 2 vols. in 5 Pts. [1449–1622] 86/ *n.* 8° Oxford Histor. Soc. 85–9

BOURGET, Paul Some Impressions of Oxford [tr.]; ill. 3/ *n.* 12° H. W. Bell 02

BRODRICK, Hon. G. C. Hist. of Univ. of Oxford [Epochs of Church Hist.] 2/6 (80 c.) f 8° Longman 86

BURROWS, Prf. Montagu [ed.] Puritan Visitation of the University of Oxford 10/ s 4° Camden Soc. 8–

Catalogue of Oxford Graduates: 1659–1850 7/6 ($1·90) 8° Clar. Press 51

CLARK, Rev. Andr. [ed.] Colleges of Oxford: history & tradns. [by var. wrs.] 18/ 8° Methuen [91] 93

Compotus Manualis ad Usum Oxoniensium—*v.* Wordsworth, *inf.*

COUCH, Lilian M. Quiller [ed.] Reminiscences of Oxford by Oxford Men 17/ *n.* 8° Oxford Hist. Soc. 92
An interesting colln. of papers by a variety of writers from 1559–1850, giving various impressns. wh. college-life made on them.

DURAND, R. A. Oxford, its Buildings and Gardens; 32 col. pl. 21/ *n.* 4° Richards 10

FOSTER, Jos. [ed.] Oxford Men and their Colleges; w notes; ports. 63/ *n.* 4° Parker 93
Directory of Oxf. men of the period, w. their biogs., record of schls., honours, and degrees, and ser. of views of Oxf. bldgs., new and old, incl. fairly good (reduced) reprodns. fr. LOGGAN's *Oxonia Illustrata* [f° Oxon. 1675], BEREBLOCK [1566], (curious), ACKERMAN's *Hist. of Univ. of Oxford* (2 v., 4° Lond. 1815], J. INGRAM's *Memls. of Oxford* [*ut inf.*], etc. First pt. conts. histor. acc. of ea. college by var. wrs. The *Record of Honours* is issued separ. *sub tit. Oxford Men* 1880–92, 31/6 *n.*

,, [ed.] Alumni Oxonienses, 8 vols. [1500–1886] 16 gs. r 8° Parker 87–91
Contin. of Ant. à WOOD's *Athenæ*, *ut inf.*, and *Fasti*, giving parentage, birthplace, and yr., and record of degrees of all members fr. 1715 to 1886.

GLADSTONE, W. E. The Romanes Lecture, 1892: an academic sketch 2/ 8° Clar. Press 92
Gives a historical sketch of the University of Oxford.

GODLEY, A. D. Aspects of Modern Oxford 2/ *n.* s 8° Seeley [94] 09

,, Oxford in the Eighteenth Century 7/6 *n.* c 8° Methuen 08
An *apologia* for 18th-cent. Oxford, providg. an entertaining view of the Univ., its colls., tchg., fellowshs., coll.-life and discipl., exercises, exams., reforms and reformers, politics and persecutions, the streets—deriv. mainly fr. contemp. literature. Full of informn. App. gives a sort of *Who's Who* of Heads of Colleges.

GREEN, J. R. Oxford Studies, ed. Mrs J. R. Green + Kate Norgate; w. notes 4/ *n.* gl 8° Macmillan 01
[Eversley Ser.] *Early Hist. of Oxfd.*; 22 pprs. on *Oxfd. dur. 18 Cent.*; and 2 on *Young Oxfd.* and *Oxfd. as it is.*

,, + ROBERSON (Rev. Geo.) Studies in Oxford Hist., ed. C. L. Stainer 21/ *n.* 8° Oxfd. Histor. Soc. 01
Conts. same as above, without the notes, but, in addn., 12 papers by ROBERSON.

,, Mrs J. R. —*in her* Town Life in the Fifteenth Century, 2 vols., *ut* **F** § 21

GRIBBLE, Fcs. The Romance of the Oxford Colleges; 17 pl. 6/ c 8° Mills & Boon 10
Commemorates the worthies of ea. College in successn., fr. Elizabethan SAVILE, of Merton, down to GOLDBERG, of Linc., a sporting journalist.

HEARNE, Thos. [1678–1735] Remarks and Collections, ed. C. E. Doble—*ut* **G** § 30

Historical Register of the University of Oxford [suppl. to the *Calendar*] 7/6 ($1·90) c 8° Clar. Press [88] 00
Alph. index to Univ. Hons., w. name of every grad. who recd. Univ. distinctn. fr. foundn. to 1900, w. a record of career.

HULTON, S. F. Rixæ Oxonienses; 6 ill. fr. Skelton 5/ c 8° Blackwell, *Oxon.* 92
The 'Battles of the Nations', Town and Gown rows and polit. riots of older Oxford, pract. all extr. fr. Ant. à WOOD, HEARNE, and PRIDEAUX.

,, [ed.] The Clerk of Oxford in Fiction 10/6 *n.* 8° Methuen 09
Ser. of extrs. fr. CHAUCER, medieval manls. of wit, Overbury's *Characters*, Earle's *Microcosmogr.*, essays of STEELE, AMHERST, JOHNSON, etc., w. running commentary—illg. Oxfd.'s view of the world and the world's view of Oxfd.

HUTTON, Laur. Literary Landmarks of Oxford; ill. 5/ *n.* c 8° Richards 03

INGRAM, J. Memorials of Oxford, 2 vols.; ill. *o.p.* [*pb.* 30/] 8° Parker [33–7] 47
An historical sketch of each College, w. numerous illns. by LE KEUX.

LANG, Andr. Oxford: historical and descriptive notes; ill. 6/ c 8° Seeley [80] 05

LITTLE, A. G. The Grey Friars in Oxford—*ut* **A** § 57

LYTE, H. C. Maxwell History of the University of Oxford [to 1530 only] 16/ 8° Macmillan 86

MARRIOTT, J. A. R. Oxford and its Place in National History [lecture] 1/ *n.* 8° Simpkin 07

NEWMAN, Card. J. Hy. —*in his* Letters and Correspondence, *ut* **A** § 98
Gives a charming picture of Oxford eighty yrs. ago.

OGLE, Oct. [ed.] Royal Letters to Oxford 15/ *n.* r 8° Parker 92
Charters, inquisitions, warrants, orders in council, etc., dating fr. a charter of Kg. STEPHEN (*c.* 1136) and ending w. 1700.

Oxford Historical Soc.: Publications *v.pp.* 8° Frowde 84 *sqq.*, *in prg.*

ANSTEY (Rev. H.) [ed.], *Epistt. Acad. Oxon.*, Pt. i [*ut sup.*] 21/ *n.*
*Brasenose Coll. Monogrs.*, 2 v. in 3 Pts. [*ut inf.*] 21/ *n.*
*Brasenose Coll. Register* [*ut inf.*] 15/ *n.*
BLOXAM (Dr J. R.), *Magdalen Coll. and Jas. ii* [*ut inf.*] 16/ *n.*
BOASE (Rev. C. W.) [ed.], *Regr. of Exet. Coll.* [*ut inf.*] 15/*n.*
,, + CLARK (Rev. A.) [eds.], *Regr. of Univ. of Oxf.*, 2 v. in 5 Pts. [*ut sup.*] 86/ *n.*
BRODRICK (G. C.), *Memls. of Merton Coll.* [*ut inf.*] 16/*n.*
*Collectanea*, Ser. i–iv [*ut inf.*] ea. 16/ *n.*
COUCH (Lilian M. Q.) [ed.], *Remin. of Oxf.* [*ut sup.*] 17/ *n.*
DOBLE (C. E.) [ed.], *Place Names in Oxford* [*ut* **E** § 17] *in prep.*
FOWLER (Dr T.), *Hist. of Corpus* [*ut inf.*]
GREEN (J. R.), *Studies in Oxfd. Hist.* [*ut sup.*] 21/ *n.*
HEARNE (T.), *Remarks and Collns.*, Ser. i–viii [*ut* **G** § 30]
HURST (H.), *Oxford Topography* [*ut* **E** § 17] 21/ *n.*
LITTLE (A. G.), *Grey Friars in Oxford* [*ut* **A** § 57] 16/ *n.*
MACLEANE (Rev. D.), *Hist. of Pembr. Coll.* [*ut inf.*] 21/ *n.*
MADAN (F.), *Early Oxfd. Press* [*ut* **K** § 12] 18/ *n.*
PARKER (J.), *Early Hist. of Oxf.* [*ut inf.*] 20/ *n.*
PHILLIMORE (W. P. W.) [ed.], *Wills of Berks* [*ut* **G** § 22] 10/ *n.*
PLUMMER (Rev. C.) [ed.], *Elizab. Oxford* [*ut inf.*] 10/ *n.*
RADCLIFFE (R.) and JAMES (J.), *Letters* [*ut inf.*] 15/ *n.*
ROGERS (J. E. T.) [ed.], *Oxford City Documts.* [*ut* **E** § 17] 12/ *n.*
SALTER (Rev. H. E.) [ed.], *Abbey of Eynsham*, 2 v. [*ut* **E** § 17] ea. 31/6 *n.*
STAINER (C. L.), *Oxfd. Silver Pennies* [*ut* **G** § 20] 21/ *n.*
STAPLETON (Mrs B.), *Three Oxfordsh. Parishes* [*ut* **E** § 17] 17/ *n.*
WIGRAM (Rev. S. R.) [ed.], *Chartulary of St Frideswides*, 2 v. [*ut* **E** § 17] 42/ *n.*
WOOD (Ant. à), *City of Oxford* 3 v. [*ut* **E** § 17] 66/ *n.*
,, *Life and Times*, 5 vols. [*ut* **G** § 30] 106/ *n.*
WORDSWORTH (Rev. C.), *Ancient Kalendar* [*ut inf.*] 31/6 *n.*

Oxford Historical Soc.: Collectanea, Series i, ed. C. R L. Fletcher; 2 ill. 16/ *n.* 8° Oxford Histor. Soc. 85
Letters of 14 cent. rel. to Oxfd.; Catal. of Oriel Coll. Lib. in 14 cent.; acc.-bk. of Jno. DORNE, bkslr. in Oxon., 1520; etc., ed. by var. scholars.

,, Collectanea, Series ii, ed. Prf. Montagu Burrows 16/ *n.* 8° Oxford Histor. Soc. 90
*Oxford Market*; *Univ. in 12 Cent.*; *Friars Preachers in Univ.*; *Jews in Oxford*; LINACRE's *Catal. of Grocyn's Bks.* (w. memr. of GROCYN); *notes*, etc., on Jno. DORNE, etc.

,, Collectanea, Series iii, ed. Prf. Montagu Burrows 21/ *n.* 8° Oxford Histor. Soc. 96
Papers on academic, collegiate, and liter. hist. of Oxfd.: Rev. H. BLAKISTON in *The Coll. of Monks of Durham studying at Oxfd.* (Durh. Coll. preceded Trin. on same site); *Wykeham's Bks. at New Coll.*; *Dr Newton and Hertf. Coll.* [18 cent.]; *Parly. Petitns. rel. to Oxfd.* [13–15 cents.]; *Poems rel. to Town and Gown*, 10 *Feb.* 1354–5 [most terrible of Town and Gown rows], and contemp. poem by TRYUYTLAM, *De Laude Univ. Oxon.*; *Corresp. betw. 2nd Earl of Clarendon and 1st Earl of Abingdon*; *Charles, Earl of Stanhope, and Oxford Univ. Press.*

,, Collectanea, Series iv, ed. by Committee of O.H.S. 31/6 *n.* 8° Oxf. Histor. Soc. 05
*Descrn. of Oxfd. fr. Hundred Rolls*; *Oxfd. Church Notes* (Rich. SYMONDS, 1643–4); *Consecrns. of 3 Coll. Chapels*; THOS. BASKERVILLE's *Acc. of Oxfd. c.* 1670–1700, ed. H. BASKERVILLE; *Coachg. in and out of Oxfd.* 1820–40; etc.

PARKER, Jas. The Early History of Oxford; 3 ill. [727–1100] 20/ *n.* 8° Oxford Histor. Soc. 85
A full acc. of all existing records, espec. Domesday survey, w. appendix of orig. Latin and A.-S. passages.

PATTISON, Rev. Mark Oxford Studies; *and* Chapter of Univ. Hist., etc.—*in his* Essays, 2 vols., *ut* **K** § 83

PLUMMER, Rev. C. [ed.] Elizabethan Oxford 10/ *n.* 8° Oxford Histor. Soc. 86
Reprints of rare tracts: Nic. FIERBERTI, *Oxon. Acad. Descriptio* [1602]; Leon. HUTTON, *Antiq. of Oxf.*; *Qu. Eliz. at Oxf.* [1566]; Pp. STRINGER's *Qu. Eliz. at Oxf.* [1592], *etc.*

PRIDEAUX, Dr H. [1648–1724] Letters, ed. E. Maunde Thompson 5/ s 4° Camden Soc. 75
Conts. amusing descrns. of Oxf. life at close of 17th and beginning of 18th century.

PYCROFT, Jas. Oxford Memories: retrospect after fifty years; 2 vols. *o.p.* [*pb.* 24/] 8° Bentley 86
An interesting record of how Oxford looked to an observant undergraduate in the thirties.

ROGERS, Prf. J. E. Thorold [ed.]—*in his* Oxford City Documents, *ut* **E** § 17 [*v.* note thereto]

de SÉLINCOURT, Hugh Oxford fr. Within; 12 col. & 8 sepia ill. by Yoshio Markino 7/6 *n.* 8° Chatto 10
Readable gossip ab. educ., sports, drama, etc.; w. impressionist pictures.

SMITH, Prf. Goldwin Oxford and her Colleges: a view from the Radcliffe Library; 16 ill. fr. photos. 6/ ($1) 16° Macmillan 94
An outline, chatty description for the use of American tourist-visitors.

'SOME OXFORD TUTORS' Oxford and the Nation [repr. fr. 'The Times'] 1/ c 8° *Times* Off. 07

Statuta Universitatis Oxoniensis, 1907 5/ ($1·25) 8° Clar. Press 07

Statutes made by Commrs. for Univ. of Oxfd. and Colleges, 1877, 12/6 ($3·25); Suppl. 2/6 (60 c.) 8° Clar. Press 78; 88

STEDMAN, A. M. M. Oxford: its social and intellectual life 7/6 c 8° Trübner 78

,, [ed.] Oxford: its life and schools 7/6 c 8° Bell 87
A kind of guide-book, comp. by college and private tutors, to hist. of the Univ., expenses, rewards, etc.

Student's Handbook to the Univ. of Oxford [by Dr Edwin Hatch] 2/6 *n.* (75 c.) c 8° Clar. Press [73] 06

TUCKWELL, Rev. W. Reminiscences of Oxford; 16 ill. 6/ *n.* c 8° Smith & Elder [00] 07
An entertaining book of reminiscences from 1830 onwards; full of good stories.

WELLS, J. [ed.] Oxford and Oxford Life [by var. wrs.] 3/6 c 8° Methuen 92
Life at Oxford, estimate of expenses, review of recent changes, chaps. on Women's Educn., Univ. Extension.

,, Oxford and its Colleges; ill. [excellent guide-bk.] 3/ f 8° Methuen 97

A WOOD, Anth. [1632–95] Athenæ Oxonienses: hist. of writers and bps. educ. at Oxfd. fr. 1500 to 1695 [1721], ed. Dr P. Bliss, 4 vols. *o.p.* [*w.* £15] 4° *London* [1691–2] 13–20
A valuable body of English biography, containing upwards of 2,200 lives.

WORDSWORTH, Can. Christ. [ed.] The Ancient Kalendar of Univ. of Oxfd. 31/6 *n.* 8° Oxford Histor. Soc. 04
Text of the *Compotus Manualis* (edn. 1520), the textbk. for Arts studts., of wh. only one copy is known to exist, w. annot. text of princ. MSS. of the *Anc. Kalendar* as found in the old proctorial bks., etc., wr. c. 1400. Bibliogr. of the *Compotus* (prtd. at least 30 times betw. 1486 and 1529) and of bks., etc., treatg. of it.

*Anthologies (Verse and Prose)*

BALL, Oona H. [ed.] The Oxford Garland [prose and verse] 2/6 *n.* 16° Sidgwick 09

FIRTH, J. B. [ed.] Minstrelsy of Isis; ill. (old views) 6 *n.* c 8° Chapman 08
A good colln. of poems, old and new, rel. to Oxford and various phases of Oxford life.

HULTON, S. F. [ed.] The Clerk of Oxford in Fiction—*ut sup.*

SECCOMBE (T.) + SCOTT (H. S.) [eds.] In Praise of Oxford, vol. i 6/ *n.* m. 8° Constable 10

KNIGHT, Prf. Wm. [ed.] The Glamour of Oxford [verse and prose] 6/ *n.* c 8° Blackwell, *Oxon.*, 11

*Magazines* —*v.* **K** § 26

*Oxford University Dramatic Society*

MACKINNON, Alan The Oxford Amateurs; many ports. 16/ *n.* 8° Chapman 10
Sketch of Middle Ages; then fully fr. middle 19th cent. onwards, incl. the Philothespians, the O.U.D.S., and mod. revival.

*Portraits*

ROTHENSTEIN, Will [artist] Oxf. Characters: 24 lithogr. ports.; w. text F. York Powell 126/ *n.* f° Lane 93–6

*Coins*—*v.* **G** § 20 *Postage Stamps*—*v.* **G** § 27 *Sports*—*v.* **I** *passim*

*All Souls' College*

BURROWS, Prf. Montagu Worthies of All Souls' [1362–1874] *o.p.* [*pb.* 14/] 8° Macmillan 74

ROBERTSON, C. Grant All Souls' College; 9 pl. [College Histories] 5/ *n.* c 8° Hutchinson 99

*Balliol College*

DAVIS, H. W. Carless Balliol College; ill. [College Histories] 5/ *n.* c 8° Hutchinson 99

DE PARAVICINI, Fces. Early History of Balliol College, Oxford 12/ 8° Paul 91
Pleasant gossip ab. John de BALLIOL & Devorguilla, his wife, & other early benefactors. Ends ab. time of Reformation. By wife of a Coll. Tutor.

*Biography*

JOWETT, Dr Benj. [1817–93] Letters, ed. Ev. Abbott + Lew. Campbell, 3 v. 48/ 8° Murray 97–9

Tollemache, Lion. Benj. Jowett, Master of Balliol: a personal memoir 3/6 c 8° Arnold [95] 95

*Brasenose College*

Brasenose Coll. Quartercentenary Monogrs., v. i–ii (2 Pts.) [Oxf. Hist. Soc.] 21/ *n.* 8° Blackwell, *Oxon.* 09
Vol. i: *General*, edd. F. MADAN + A. J. BUTLER + E. W. ALLFREY; ii: *Special Periods*, edd. I. S. LEADAM + R. W. JEFFERY + G. H. WAKELING + R. LODGE + H. C. WACE, etc. Well ill. and copiously indexed.

Brasenose College Register: 1509–1909, ed. Dr Heberden, 2 vols. 15/ 8° Blackwell, *Oxon.* 09
Supplements BUCKLEY + MADAN by annotations fr. the Registers and fr. various fresh sources.

BUCKLEY (Rev. W. E.) + MADAN (F.) [eds.] Calendar of Brasenose College 88
BUCHAN, J. Brasenose College [College Histories] 5 / *n.* c 8° Hutchinson 98

*Christ Church*

ASTON, J. (artist) Sketches of Christ Church, Oxford [drawings] 3 /6 4° Methuen 01
CHANCELLOR, E. B. Christ Church, Oxford ; ill. V. R. Prince 10 /6 4° Bemrose 91
THOMPSON, Rev. H. L. Christ Church, Oxford [College Histories] 5 / *n.* c 8° Hutchinson 00

*Biography*

LIDDELL, Dn H. G. [1811–98] —*v.* **A** § 62

*Corpus Christi College*

FOWLER, Dr Thos. History of Corpus Christi College [by the President] 20 / *n.* 8° Oxford Histor. Soc. 93
An excellent bk., incl. careful life of founder of the Coll., Bp FOXE, notices of princ. benefrs., tog. w. Apps. consistg. of elabr. register (chron. arrgd.) of every Scholar fr. foundn., list of Readers, Prfs., Chaplains, Clerks, Choristers, Exhibtrs., Commrs, even Coll. servants.
„ Corpus Christi [Coll. Hists. ; abdgmt. of above] 5 / *n.* c 8° Hutchinson 98

*Exeter College*

BOASE, Rev. C. W. [ed.] Regr. of Rectors, Fellows, etc., of Ex. Coll., Oxon. 15 / *n.* 8° Oxf. Hist. Soc. [79] 94
The 1894 edn. incl. a lengthy hist. of the Coll., tho' omits some partlrs. wh. 1879 edn. gave of the founder, Bp STAPELDON.
„ [ed.] Registrum Collegii Exoniensis, Pt. ii : Commoners [chron. arrgd.] 8° *priv. prin.* 94
STRIDE, W. K. Exeter College, Oxford [College Histories] 5 / *n.* c 8° Hutchinson 00

*Hertford College*

HAMILTON, S. G. Hertford College, Oxford [College Histories] 5 / *n.* c 8° Hutchinson 03

*Jesus College*

HARDY, E. G. Jesus College, Oxford ; ill. [College Histories] 5 / *n.* c 8° Hutchinson 99
Includes a hist of Fellows from the beginning, with much biographical matter.
HARPER, Dr Hugo D. [b. 1821] Memoir of. By L. V. Lester 5 / c 8° Longman 97

*Lincoln College*

CLARK, Rev. Andr. Lincoln College, Oxford [College Histories] 5 / *n.* c 8° Hutchinson 98

*Magdalen College*

BLOXAM, Dr J. R. [ed.] Magdalen Coll. & King James II [documts. 1686–88] 16 / *n.* 8° Ox. Histor. Soc. 86
BLOXAM, Dr M. H. [ed.] Register of Magdalen College, Oxford, 7 vols. 5–
Arranged under a minute classification of ranks, commencing from the bottom, the choristers, and not reaching to the Fellows.
GLASGOW, E. (artist) Sketches of Magdalen College, Oxford [drawings] 5 / *n.* i 8° Dent 01
MACRAY, Dr W. D. [ed.] Register of St Mary Magdalen, New Ser., vols. i–vi ea. 7 /6 *n.* ($2·50) 8° Clar. Press 94–09
A continuation of BLOXAM, *sup.*, to 1880. Edited w. scholarly exactness and amplitude.
WARREN, Dr T. H. Magdalen College, Oxford ; ill. [College Monographs] 21 / *n.* 12° Dent 07
WILSON, Rev. H. A. Magdalen College, Oxford [College Histories] 5 / *n.* c 8° Hutchinson 99

*Manchester College*

Manchester College, Oxford : proceedings and addresses at opening [1893] ; 6 ill. 5 / *n.* r 8° Longman 94

*Mansfield College*

Mansfield College, Oxford : its origin and opening [1889] 10 /6 8° J. Clarke 90

*Merton College*

BRODRICK, Dr G. C. [ed.] Memorials of Merton College 16 / *n.* 8° Oxford Histor. Soc. 85
A history of the College and list of Fellows ; w. biographical notices of Wardens and Fellows.
HENDERSON, B. W. History of Merton College [College Histories] 5 / *n.* c 8° Hutchinson 99
WHITE, H. T. Merton College, Oxford ; ill. [College Monographs] 2 / *n.* 12° Dent 06
*Biography :* NARES, Dr Edw. [1762–1841] A Versatile Professor. By Rev. G. C. White 5 / *n.* c 8° Brimley Johnson 03
À WOOD, Anth. [1632–95] Life and Times of—*v.* **G** § 30

*New College*

GEORGE, Hereford B. New College : 1856–1906 2 /6 *n.* ($1) c 8° Clar. Press 06
By the Senior Fellow, who has been in almost continuous residence for 50 years.
PRICKARD, A. O. New College, Oxford ; ill. [College Monographs] 2 / *n.* 12° Dent 06
RASHDALL (Rev. H.) + RAIT (R. S.) New College, Oxford [College Histories] 5 / *n.* c 8° Hutchinson 01
RONALDSON, T. M. [artist] Drawings of New Coll. Oxf. ; Introd. C. L. Woolley 6 / *n.* 4° Blackwell, *Oxford* 06

*Oriel College*

MOZLEY, Rev. T. Reminiscences of Oriel and Oxford Movemt., 2 vols. *o.p.* [*pb.* 18 /] c 8° Longman 82
RANNIE, D. W. Oriel College, Oxford [College Histories] 5 / *n.* c 8° Hutchinson 00

SHADWELL, C. L. [ed.] Registrum Orielense, 2 vols. [1500–1900] 25/ *n*. ($8·30) 8° Clar. Press 93–03

*Pembroke College*

MACLEANE, Rev. Dougl. History of Pembroke College, Oxford 21/ *n*. 8° Oxford Histor. Soc. 97
A very full account of the College, w. much biographical matter.

„ Pembroke College, Oxford [College Histories] 5/ *n*. c 8° Hutchinson 00

*Biography:* HILL, Dr G. Birkbeck Letters, ed. Lucy Crump [dau.] 12/6 *n*. 8° Arnold 06

*Queen's College:* MAGRATH (J. R.) [ed.] Obituary Bk. of Qu. Coll., Oxford 8° Oxf. Hist. Soc. 11

RADCLIFFE (Rich.) + JAMES (Jno.) Letters, ed. Marg. Evans [1749–83] 15/ *n*. 8° Oxford Histor. Soc. 88

*St John's College*

HUTTON, Rev. W. H. St John Baptist College, Oxford [College Hists.] 5/ *n*. c 8° Hutchinson 98

*Trinity College*

BLAKISTON, Rev. H. E. P. Trinity College [College Histories] 5/ *n*. c 8° Hutchinson 00

*University College*

CARR, W. University College, Oxford [College Histories] 5/ *n*. c 8° Hutchinson 02

MACAN, Dr R. W. History of University College Oxford Oxford Histor. Soc. *in prep.*

*Wadham College*

GARDINER, Rev. R. B. [ed.] Registers of Wadham College, 2 Pts. [1613–1871; w. notes] ea. 21/ 8° Bell 89–95

GLASGOW, E. [artist] Sketches of Wadham College, Oxford [drawings] 2/6 *n*. 4° Methuen 00

JACKSON, T. G. Wadham Coll., Oxford: its foundn., archit. & hist.; ill. 42/ *n*. ($12·75) 4° Clar. Press 93
A beautiful volume; spec. attentn. paid to the college bldgs. Conts. also acc. of family of WADHAM, and their seats in Somerset and Devon.

*Worcester College*

DANIEL (Rev. C. H.) + BARKER (W. R.) Worcester College, Oxford [Coll. Hists.] 5/ *n*. c 8° Hutchinson 00

*Victoria University, Manchester; Owens College, Manchester*

HARTOG, F. J. [ed.] The Owens College, Manchester; profusely ill. 8° Cornish, *Mancs.* 01
A full descrn. of the various departmts., and record of benefactions, donations, etc.

SMITH, J. F. [ed.] Admission Register of Mancs. School, 3 vols. in 4 Pts. s 4° Chetham Soc. 66–74

THOMPSON, Jos. Owens College, its Foundation and Growth 18/ 8° Cornish, *Mancs.* [86] 86

**University Extension** —*v.* **D** § 168

## Scotland

BALFOUR, Graham —*in his* Educational Systems of Gt. Britain and Ireland, *ut sup.*

CLARKE, J. Short Studies in Education in Scotland 3/6 *n*. ($1·20 *n*.) c 8° Longman 04

CRAIG, G. A. From Parish School to University; and other papers 3/6 *n*. c 8° Simpkins 99
'Memories and Scottish characteristics of forty years since'.

EDGAR, Jno. History of Early Scottish Education 10/6 8° Thin, *Edin.* 93
Interestg. acc. of Scott. educn. up to Reformn., fr. a national pt.-of-view, and in conn. w. other intellectual forces at wk. within the nation.

GRANT, Jas. Hist. of Burgh & Parish Schls. of Scotl. [a gd. bk.] *o.p.* [*pb.* 10/6] r 8° Collins 76

KERR, Dr Jno. Scottish Education, School and University 6/ *n*. 8° Camb. Press 10
$2 *n*. Putnam, *N.Y.* From early times to 1908. Skilfully arrgd. facts, formg. a readable narrative.

STRONG, J. Hist. of Secondary Educn. in Scotld. [early times to 1908] 7/6 *n*. ($2·50) 8° Clar. Press 09

WRIGHT, A. Hist. of Educn. of Old Parish Schls. of Scotld. 4/ c 8° Menzies, *Edin.* 98

*Reports*

Report of the Commission on Endowed Schools and Hospitals in Scotland Eyre & Spottiswoode 73

Reports of the Scotch Education Department Eyre & Spottiswoode 72 *sqq.*

Reports of the Commission of Inquiry on Schools in Scotland Eyre & Spottiswoode 65 *sqq.*

Report of the Committee of Council on Education in Scotland 2/8 Eyre & Spottiswoode 97

Report of the Royal Commission on Science and Art Eyre & Spottiswoode 66

Report of the Select Committee on Education, Science and Art Eyre & Spottiswoode 84

Reports of the Commission on Endowed Institutions in Scotland Eyre & Spottiswoode 80–1

Reports of the Scottish Educational Endowment Commissioners Eyre & Spottiswoode 82 *sqq.*

Reports of the Board of Education in Scotland Eyre & Spottiswoode 73 *sqq.*

*Biography and Reminiscences*

KERR, Dr Jno. Memories, Grave and Gay; ill. 2/6 *n*. c 8° Blackwood [02] 03
Forty years' experience as a school inspector.

„ Other Memories, Old and New 3/6 *n*. c 8° Blackwood 04

MILLER, Hugh [1802–56] My Schools & Schoolmasters; ill. [cheap edn., 1/] 3/6 c 8° Nimmo, *Edin.* [54] 07

SHAW, Jas., of Tynoon, Dumfriesshire

Wallace, R. A Country Schoolmaster 6/ c 8° Oliver & Boyd 99

STEWART, Agnes G. The Academic Gregories [Famous Scots] 1/6 c 8° Oliphant, *Edin.* 01

An account of the wonderful GREGORY family and the Scottish Professors who are members of it.

*Edinburgh: High School*

STEVEN, Dr Wm. History of High School of Edin. fr. 16th Cent. *o.p.* [*pb.* 7/6] 8° McLachlan, *Edin.* 49

*Loretto School:* TRISTRAM (H. B.) Loretto School; ill. 7/6 *n.* 8° Unwin 11

Fettes College Register *Edin.* 90

*George Heriot's Hospital* [now a secondary day-schl. for boys]

GUNN, C. B. George Heriot's Hospital 7/6 *n.* 8° Livingstone, *Edin.* 02

*Loretto School:* TRISTRAM (H. B.) Loretto School; ill. 7/6 *n.* 8° Unwin 11

ALMOND, Hely Hutchinson

Mackenzie, Rev. R. J. Almond of Loretto: life and sel. of letters 12/6 *n.* 8° Constable 05

The story of ALMOND's struggle f. freedom in dress, and rationality in reg. to food, sleep, exercise—and punishment.

*Paisley Grammar School*

BROWN, Rob. Hist. of Paisley Gram. Schl.; 48 ports., etc. [fr. foundn. in 1576] 8° Gardner, *Paisley* 75

*Stirling High School*

HUTCHINSON, A. F. History of the High School of Stirling 21/ 4° Mackay, *Stirling* 04

**Universities: Collectively**

HUTTON, Laur. Literary Landmarks of Scottish Universities; ill. 5/ *n.* c 8° Putnam 04

Only a moderately good compiln., with notable omissns. Much space on Univ. constitns. and transatlantic comparisons.

*Aberdeen: Marischal College and University*

ANDERSON, P. J. Collns. tow. Bibliogr. of Univ. of Aberdeen; 12 facss. 10/6 4° Bibliogr. Soc., *Edin.* 08

„ [ed.] Fasti Acad. Mariscallanae. 3 vols.; pl. 52/6 4° New Spalding Club 89–98

Selns. fr. Records of Marischal Coll. and Univ., 1593–1860. Vol. i: *Endowmts.*; ii: *Officers, Graduates, Alumni*; iii; *Index to vol. ii.*

„ [ed.] Officers & Graduates of King's Coll., Aberd.: 1495–1860 4° New Spalding Club 93

„ [ed.] Rectorial Addresses del. in Univs. of Aberd.: 1835–1900 [Ab. Univ. Studs.] 10/6 8 Univ. Pr., *Aberd.* 02

„ [ed.] Roll of Alumni of King's Coll., Aberd.: 1596–1860 [Aberd. Univ. Studs.] 7/6 r 8° Univ. Press, *Aberd.* 00

„ [ed.] Record of Celebrn. of Quatercent. of Univ. Aberd.; ill. Univ. Press, *Aberdeen* 07

„ [ed.] Records of the Aberdeen Univ. Commission: 1716–7 2/ 8° Milne, *Aberd.* 00

„ [ed.] Studies in Hist. & Devel. of Univ. Aberd. [Ab. Un. Studs.] 10/6 8° Univ. Press, *Aberd.* 06

Aurora Borealis Academica 12/6 8° Univ. Press, *Aberdeen* 99

30 papers on Professors and others connected with Aberdeen University since 1860.

BULLOCH, J. M. History of the University of Aberdeen: 1495–1895 4/6 c 8° Hodder & Stoughton 95

ELPHINSTONE, Wm. [1431–1514] Life. By Hector Boece [1465–1536; first Rector]—*v.* **A** § 71

INNES, Cosmo [ed.] Fasti Aberdonenses [sel. fr. records of Univ. & King's Coll.; 1494–1854] 4° Spalding Club 54

JOHNSTON, Col. W. Calendar of Univ. of Aberd. 1860–1 & 1863–4 3/6 c 8° Univ. Press, *Aberdeen* 90

„ [ed.] Acc. of Last Bajans of King's & Marischal Coll. of Aberd. 21/ 4° Adelphi Press, *Aberd.* 99

„ [ed.] Roll of Graduates of Univ. Aberd.: 1860–1900 [Ab. Univ. Studs.] 10/6 8° Univ. Pr., *Aberd.* 06

RAIT, R. S. History of Universities of Aberdeen [Marischal & King's] 4/ *n.* 8° Bisset, *Aberdeen* 95

A lucid and solid piece of work, but too long.

SHEWAN, Alex. Meminisse Juvat; 18 pl. 21/ 8° Univ. Press, *Aberdeen* 05

A 'class-record' of King's Coll., 1866–70, w. other recollns. of the coll., its staff, studts., etc., of that period.

*Edinburgh University*

ANDERSON, P. J. [ed.] Laing Charters belonging to Univ. Edinb. Calendar: A.D. 854–1837 32/ *n.* i 8° Thin, *Edin.* 99

DALZEL, A. History of University of Edinburgh, 2 vols. *o.p.* [*pb.* 21/] 8° *Edinburgh* 62

GRANT, Sir Alex. Story of Univ. of Edinb. dur. first 300 Yrs., 2 v.; ill. *o.p.* [*pb.* 36/] 8° Longman 84

HOLE, Wm. [artist] Quasi Cursores *o.p.* i 4° Douglas, *Edin.* 84

64 portraits (on 49 etched plates) of High Officers and Professors of Univ. of Edinburgh.

WALKER, A. Stodart [ed.] Rectorial Addresses [1858–1900] 7/6 *n.* 8° Richards 00

*Biography*

FORBES, Prf. E. Life of. By Dr G. Wilson + J. Geikie [*conts. gd. pict. of life at Ed. Un.*] *o.p.* [*pb.* 14/] 8° Macmillan 61

*Glasgow University.*

ADDISON, W. I. [ed.] Roll of Graduates of Univ. Glasg. 1727–1897 ; w. notes 21 / *n.* 4° MacLehose, *Glasg.* 98

„ Snell Exhibitions fr. Univ. Glasg. to Balliol Coll., Oxfd. : 1697–1900 7/6 *n.* i 8° MacLehose, *Glasgow* 01

A learned investigation of particulars regarding the founder and holders of these scholarships.

COUTTS, Jas. History of the University of Glasgow ; ill. 21 / *n.* 4° MacLehose, *Glasgow* 09

INNES (C.) + ROBERTSON (J.) [eds.] Monumenta Almae Univ. Glasg., 4 vols. 4° Maitland Club 54

Chronolog. list of graduates. Fr. the foundation, A.D. 1450 to 1727. Continued by ADDISON, *sup.*

MACLEAN, Neal N. Life at a Northern University [Glasgow Univ.] *o.p.* [*pb.* 5 /] c 8° Marr, *Glasgow* 74

Record of the Ninth Jubilee of the University of Glasgow 5 / *n.* 8° MacLehose, *Glasgow* 02

STEWART, Prf. Wm. [ed.] University of Glasgow, Old & New ; ill. 105 / *n.* i 4° MacLehose, *Glasgow* 91

Excellently got up, w. 39 pl. (72 ports. of members of Senate 1869–90 and of Univ. officers) and 35 views of Old Coll. and New Coll.

*Biography*

STORY, Prc. Rob. Herb. [d. 1907] Life of. By his Daughters ; ports. 10 /6 *n.* 8° MacLehose, *Glasgow* 09

VEITCH, Prf. Jno. [1829–94] Memoir of. By Mary R. L. Bryce—*ut* **C** § 4

*St Andrew's University*

ANDERSON, J. Maitland Heraldry of St Andrew's University—*ut* **G** § 23

„ [ed.] Matriculation Roll of Univ. of St Andrew's : 1747–1897 18 / *n.* 8° Blackwood 05

BOYD, Rev. A. K. H. Twenty-five Years at St Andrew's, 2 vols. [1865–90] 27 / 8° Longman 92–3

KERR, D. R. —*his* St Andrew's in 1645–46 [*ut* **E** § 19] throws light on hist. of University

KNIGHT, Prf. Wm. [ed.] Rectorial Addresses of University of St Andrew's, 1863–93 ; with Introduction 10 /6 8° Black 94

**Ireland**

BALFOUR, Graham —*in his* Educational Systems of Gt. Britain and Ireland, *ut sup.*

DOYLE, Dr Thos. Essay on Educn. and State of Irel., ed. W. F. Fitzpatrick 2/6 c 8° Gill, *Dublin* 80

HEALY, Dr Jno. Insula Sanctorum et Doctorum ; map and index 7 /6 r 8° Sealy, *Dublin* [90] 01

An exhaustive acc. (in English) of anc. schls. and scholars of Irel., fr. time of St PATRICK to Anglo-Norm. invasn. of Ireld.

Hesperica Famina (The) : ed. F. J. H. Jenkinson ; w. Introd. 6 / *n.* 8° Camb. Press 09

Putnam, *N.Y.* A cryptic composn. in medieval Latin by Irish monk of 7th cent. Affords a pict. of daily life in Irish school ab. 6th or 7th cent.

MADDEN, Justice D. H. Passages in Early Hist. of Classical Learng. in Irel. 2/6 *n.* c 8° Longman 08

O'DONNELL, Fk. H. The Ruin of Education in Ireland 5 / *n.* 8° Nutt [02] 03

A spirited protest agst. the scheme for a Catholic University in Ireld., by a staunch Roman-Catholic.

Report of the Commissioners of National Education Eyre & Spottiswoode 34 *sqq., in prg.*

Evidence taken before the Committee of House of Lords on Educ. in Ireland Eyre & Spottiswoode 37

„ taken by the Committee of the House of Commons Eyre & Spottiswoode 37

„ taken by the Committee of the House of Lords Eyre & Spottiswoode 37

Report of the Royal Commission on Science and Art Eyre & Spottiswoode 66

„ of the Royal Commission on Primary Educ. in Ireland [Powis] Eyre & Spottiswoode 68–70

„ of the Select Committee on Education, Science, and Art Eyre & Spottiswoode 84

„ of the Royal Commission on Industrial and Reformatory Schools Eyre & Spottiswoode 84

„ of the Royal Commission on Education Erye & Spottiswoode 87

„ of the Royal Commission on the Deaf, Dumb, and Blind—*ut* **D** § 169

Special Reports on Educational Subjects, vol. i—*ut* **D** § 163*

*Downside*

BIRT, Dom H. N. Downside : hist. of St Gregory's School ; 25 ill. 6 / *n.* 8° Paul 02

An account of the school from its commencement at Douay to the present time.

SNOW, Abbot Sketches of Old Downside 5 / *n.* 8° Sands 03

*Dublin University (Trinity College)*

Book of Trinity College, Dublin ; 70 ill. [1591–1891] *o.p.* [*pb.* 21 /] 4° Marcus Ward 92

By several well-known contribrs., incl. Prf. J. P. MAHAFFY, Dr J. W. STUBBS, Dr ABBOTT, Sir R. BALL, Prf. WRIGHT, etc. Rather an ill. gift bk. than a very serious work.

Catalogue of Graduates who have Passed to Degrees, 3 v. [1595–1905] 8° *Dublin* 69–06

DIXON, Prf. W. McNeile Trinity College, Dublin [College Histories] 5 / *n.* c 8° Hutchinson 02

A very readable account, not in any way controversial.

MAHAFFY, Prf. J. P. An Epoch in Irish History [1591–1660] 16/ 8° Unwin [03] 06

An account of Trinity College, Dublin, its foundations and early fortunes. Introd. deals w. sources.

OLDHAM, C. H. Trinity College Pictorial ; profusely ill. [tercenten. vol.] 2/6 c 8° Thom, *Dublin* 92

Records of Tercentenary Festival of Univ. of Dublin held 5 to 8 July, 1892 10 /6 4° Hodges, *Dublin* 94

STUBBS, Dr J. W. History of the University of Dublin 12 /6 8° Hodges, *Dublin* 89

The standard history. From the foundation to end of 18th century ; w. orig. (hitherto unpubd.) documts.

STUBBS, Dr. J. W. [ed.] Abp Adam Loftus & the Foundation of Trin. Coll., Dubl. 1/ 8° Hodges, *Dublin* 92
Abp LOFTUS' speeches on var. occasions as preserved in a MS. in the Library of Armagh, now first printed: w. Introduction by STUBBS.

TAYLOR, W. B. S. History of the University of Dublin; p.. (some col.) *o.p.* [*pb.* 21/] 8° Bohn 45
Chiefly valuable as giving the Parliamentary history of the College, and for its biogr. notices.

Trinity College, Dublin: Speeches of Public Orators 5/1 8° Hodges, *Dublin* 09

URWICK, Wm. Early History of Trin. Coll., Dublin: 1591–1660 [tercent. vol.] 1/ 8° Unwin 92

*Blue Coat School, Dublin*

FALKINER, Sir R. Foundn. of Hosp. & Free Schl. of Chas. ii, Oxmantown 7/6 8° Sealey, *Dublin* 06
From its foundn. in 1668 to 1840, when its govt. by the City of Dublin ceased.

*Kildare Place Society*

MOORE, Dr H. Kingsmill An Unwritten Chapter in Hist. of Educn. 7/6 *n.* 8° Macmillan 04
History of the Kild. Pl. Soc. for educn. of the poor, fr. 1811 to 1831, by its Principal.

*Maynooth College* [Roman-Catholic]

HEALY, Bp J. Maynooth Coll.: centen. hist.; 200 ill. [1795–1895] 21/ *n.* 4° Browne & Nolan, *Dublin* 95
An enormous wk. in size, tho' little more than a huge party-pamphlet, rehearsg. all injustices, imag. and real, laid to charge of Protest. Engld. by R.-C. Ireld., rather than vindicatg. Maynooth College—as a result, fortifyg. the prejudiced instead of convincg. the unprejudiced.

*Paris, Irish College in* —*v.* France, *sup.*

**Wales**

MORGAN, Rev. J. V. Welsh Political and Educatl. Leaders in Victorian Era 16/ 8° Nisbet 08

*Universities; Llantwit Major*

DAVIES (W. C.) + JONES (W. L.) Univ. of Wales & Constituent Colls. [Coll. Hists.] 5/ *n.* c 8° Hutchinson 05

FRYER, Dr A. C. Llantwit Major; views 4/6 c 8° Stock 93
Acc. of a 5th cent. Welsh Univ., w. sketch of line of study that may have been carried on there, and lives of men educ. there.

**Holland; Belgium** —*v. also* **D** § 156, *and* France, *sup.* (ARNOLD)

Elementary and Middle Class Instruction in the Netherlands [pp. 173] 8° Sijthoff, *Leyden* 76

*Leyden University*

PEACOCK, Edw. [*ed.*] English-speaking Students of Leyden University 10/6 8° Index Soc. (Longman) 83

**India**

ALI, Syed Amir English Education in India c 8° *Madras* 02
An inquiry into the 'failure of University education' in India. 66 pp.

ALSTON, Prf. Leon. Education and Citizenship in India 4/6 *n.* ($1·25 *n.*) c 8° Longman 10

CARPENTER, Mary Education in India, 2 vols. *o.p.* [*pb.* 18/] 8° Longman 68

COTTON, J. S. [ed.] Moral and Material Progress and Condn. of India Eyre & Spottiswoode 85–9
[Blue Bks.] With special reference to the *Report* of the Education Commission.

CROFT, Sir Alf. Review of Education in India in 1886 8° Govt. Press, *Bengal* 88

KERR, J. Review of Publ. Instrn. in Bengal Presid., 2 vols. [1835–51] *o.p.* [*pb.* 8/6] 8° W. H. Allen 53

LEITNER, Dr G. W. History of Indigenous Oriental Education £5 f° Govt. Prg. Off., *Calc.* 82
More particularly in the Punjaub, since the annexation.

LETHBRIDGE, Sir Roper Higher Education in India [English schools] *o.p.* [*pb.* 7/6] c 8° W. H. Allen 82

MAHMOOD, Syed Hist. of Engl. Educn. in India [1781–1893] s 4° *Aligarh* 95

ORANGE, H. W. Progress of Educn. in India: 1902–7, 2 vols. [Blue-Bks.] 3/9 Wyman 09

RUSSELL, J. —*in his* Schools of Greater Britain, *ut sup.*, *s.v.* Australia

SATTHIANADHA, Prf. S. History of Education in the Madras Presidency 8° Srinivasa, *Madras* 94
The first attempt at a continuous hist. of educ. operns. in Madras Pres., by one who was First Assistant to Director of Pub. Instn. in Madras.

STRATTON, A. W. —*in his* Letters from India, *ut* **E** § 35
Some of the letters deal in interestg. way w. Univ. life in N. India, class of native scholars, etc.

THOMAS, F. W. Hist. and Prospects of Brit. Educn. in India 4/6 8° Brighton, *Camb.* 91
[Lebas Prize Essay. Conts. a good deal of compressed information, fr. a variety of sources, in readable form.

*Mayo College*

SHERRING, Herb. The Mayo College, 2 vols. 15/ 8° Thacker, *Calcutta* 97
Descriptive, historical, and statistical account of the 'Indian Eton' fr. 1875 to 1895.

**Italy** —*v. also* **D** § 156, *s.v.* Renaissance (WOODWARD)

*Bologna University*

KIRKPATRICK, Prf. Jno. University of Bologna [acc. of Octocent. Festival, 1888] 3/6 c 8° Thin, *Edin.* 88

**Japan**

Education in Japan [Bureau of Educn.] *n.p.* 8° Govt. Prtg. Off., *Washington* 85

Education in Japan: letters addr. by Americans to Arinori Mori [Jap. Ambass. to U.S.]
$1·50 12° Appleton, *N.Y.* 76

ENOMATO, Takeali Outlines of Modern Educn. in Japan 8° Dept. of Educn., *Tokyo* 88

GRIFFIS W. E. Education in Japan [Bureau of Educn.] *n.p.* 8° Govt. Prtg. Off., *Washington* 75

KIKUCHI, Bar. Dairoku — Japanese Education — 5/*n.* 8° Murray 09
Gives a clear insight into wkg. of Jap. Educn. Dept., and definitn. of different grades of schools, etc.

'LAURIE, André' [=Pascal GROUSSET] Schoolboy Days in Japan [tr.] $1 12° Estes & Lauriat, *Boston* 95

Outline History of Japanese Education — [prepared for Phila. Exhibn.] 12° *New York* 76

Outlines of Modern Education in Japan: translated — 8° Dept. of Educn., *Tokyo* 93

SHARP, W. H. — Educational System of Japan — [Occasional Repts., No. 3] 5/ 8° Unwin 07

**Jews (Ancient)** —*v.* **D** § 156

**Russia**

Education in Russia = Special Reports on Educl. Subjs., vol. xxiii—*ut* **D** § 163*

LAURIE, André — Schoolboy Days in Russia, tr. Laura E. Kendall $1 c 8° Estes & Lauriat, *Boston* 92

Russian Ministry of Education (The) — [best acc. in English; pp. 64] 8° *St Petersburg* 93

STEPNIAK, S. —*in his* The Russian Peasantry, *ut* **E** § 25

TIKHOMIROV, L. —*in his* Russia, Political and Social, 2 vols., *ut* **K** § 40

**Scandinavia**

ANDREWS (C. G.) + GADE (G.) Publ. Instrn. in Swed. & Norway [Bur. of Educ.; pp. 48] *Washington* 71

FRIES, Ellen [ed.] — Repts. fr. Swed. Ladies' Comm. to Worlds Exposn. — 8° *Stockholm* 93

HEALEY, Eliz. — Educ. Systs. of Swed., Norw. and Denm. [chfly. girls] 6*d.* 8° Taylor & Francis 93

**Switzerland** —*v. also* France, *sup.* (ARNOLD), *and* Germany, *sup.*

BARNARD, H. [ed.] — Swiss Teachers and Educators — [by var. wrs.] $3·50 m 8° *Hartford n.d.*

,, [ed.] — Swiss Pedagogy — [by var. wrs.] $3·50 m 8° *Hartford n.d.*

DAVIS, G. B. — Report on Schools in Germany and Switzerland—*ut sup.*, *s.v.* Germany

Special Reports on Educational Subjects, vols. iii, viii—*ut* **D** § 163*

**United States:** *Description; Criticism*

BARNARD, H. [ed.] — American Pedagogy [collected arts. by var. writers] $3·50 8° *Hartford n.d.*

,, — Memoirs of American Teachers & Educators, 2 Ser. ea. $3·50 8° *Hartford n.d.*

,, — Benefactors of American Education — $3·50 8° *Hartford n.d.*

BURSTALL, Sara A. — Impressions of American Education in 1908 4/6 ($1·25 *n.*) c 8° Longman 09
A very interestg. investign., full of shrewd observns., by a competent critic. Much attentn. to girls' educn.

Carnegie Foundation for Advancement of Teaching: Bulletins
Carnegie Foundn., 576 *5th Ave., N.Y.* 08 *sqq., in prg.*

CHANCELLOR, W. E. — American Schools: admin. & supervisn. [Ped. Lib.] $1·50 c 8° Heath, *Boston* 05
A pract. treat. on mod. Am. educ. polity, fr. pt.-of-view of the manager; chfly. smaller schls. and schl.-systems.

,, — Our City Schools — [Pedag. Lib.] $1·25 c 8° Heath, *Boston*

Education in United States 2 Pts. — Pt. i, 2/3; ii, 2/6 8° Eyre & Spottiswoode
[Blue Books.] i: *Public Schools and Training of Teachers*; ii: *Secondary Schools, Universities, etc.*

FITCH, Dr [Sir] J. G. — Notes on American Schools and Training Colleges 2/6 (60 c. *n.*) gl 8° Macmillan 90
Repr. fr. *Report of English Education Dept. fr.* 1888–9 [Blue-Bk.]. A valuable little book.

Gilchrist Trust: Reports to the Trustees — *v.pp.* c 8° Sonnenschein *v.y.*

BRAMWELL (Amy B.) + HUGHES (H. M.) *Training of Teachers in U.S.* [*ut* D § 170]. 3/6
BURSTALL (Sar. A.), *Educ. of Girls in U.S.* [*ut* D § 168] 3/6
PAGE (Mary H.), *Graded Schools of U.S.* 2/
ZIMMERN (Alice), *Methods of Educ. in U.S.* [*ut* D § 164] 3/6

FRASER, Rev. Jas. — Report to Schools Inquiry Commissioners [Blue Book] Eyre & Spottisw. 67

MARK, H. T. — Individuality & Moral Aim in Amer. Educn. 6/ ($1·50 *n.*) c 8° Longman 01

Report of the Commissioner of Education, U.S.A., vols. i–xxxiii — Govt. Prtg. Off., *Washington* 68 *sqq.*

,, of the Massachusetts Board of Education. By Hor. Mann, 12 vols. — *Boston* 38–49

,, The same, abgd. & ed. G. C. Mann, 4 v.; w. Life, 5 v.—*ut* **D** § 161

ROBSON, E. S. A. — Report of a Visit to Am. Educl. Institns. — 1/*n.* r 8° Sherratt, *Mancs.* 05

Special Reports on Educational Subjects, vols. x, xi—*ut* **D** § 163*

*History*

BOONE, Prf. R. G. — Hist. of Educn. in U.S. [Intern. Educ. Ser.] $1·50 (6/) c 8° Appleton 89

CAMPBELL, Douglas —*in his* The Puritan in Holland, Engld., and America, *ut* **A** § 88
Traces growth of Engl., Dutch, and French ideals in America: of considerable importance here.

DEXTER, E. G. — History of Education in United States — $2 *n.* (8/6 *n.*) c 8° Macmillan 04

HARRIS, Dr W. T. — ch. on Education—*in* Shaler [ed.] The United States of America, *ut* **E** § 52

*Elementary Education; Common Schools; Free Schools*

ADAMS, Fcs. — Free School System of United States — *o.p.* [*pb.* 9/] 8° Chapman 75

ANDERSON, Dr L. F. — History of Common School Education [6/ Bell] $1·25 c 8° Holt, *N.Y.* 09
Deals also largely with English and European educational history.

BOESE, T. Public Educn. in City of N.Y. [hist., condn., statistics] *o.p.* c 8° *New York* 69
BURTON, W. E. The District School as it was $1·25 12° Lee & Shepard, *Boston* [50] 99
CLEWS, E. W. Educ. Legisln. & Admin. of Colonial Govts. [Col. Univ. Pbs.] $2 *n.* 8° Macmillan, *N.Y.* 99
CUSTIS, J. T. Public Schools of Philadelphia ; ill. [hist., biogr., statist.] $5 f° *Philadelphia* 97
DUTTON (Prf. S. T.) + SNEDDEN (Prf. D.) Admin. of Publ. Educn. in U.S. $1·75 *n.* (7/6 *n.*) c 8° Macm. 08
MARTIN, G. H. Evoln. of Massach. Pub.-Schl. Syst. [Int. Ed. Ser.] $1·50 (6/) c 8° Appleton 94
PALMER, A. E. New York Public Schl. [hist. of free educ. in N.Y. City] $1 *n.* (4/6 *n.*) c 8° Macmillan 05
PHILBRICK, J. D. City School Systems in U.S. [Bureau of Educ.] *n.p.* 8° Govt. Prtg. Off., *Washington* 85
RANDALL, S. S. Hist. of Common Schl. Syst. of State of N.Y. [1795–1870] *o.p.* [*pb.* $3] 8° Ivison, *N.Y.* 71
RUSSELL, A. T. History of the Common Schools of Florida, etc. *o.p.* 8° *Tallahassee* 84
STOCKWELL, T. B. History of Public Education in Rhode Island *o.p.* 8° *Providence* 76
SWETT, J. Centennial Hist. of Publ. Schl. Syst. of California $2 8° Bancroft, *San Francisco* 76
WHITFORD, W. C. Historical Sketch of Education in Wisconsin *o.p.* 12° *Madison* 76
*Negro Schools* —*v.* **D** § 130

*Higher Education ; Colleges ; Universities*

BIRDSEYE, C. F. Reorganization of our Colleges [7/6 *n.* Simpkin] 8° Baker & Taylor, *N.Y.* 10
" Individual Training in our Colleges $1·75 *n.* (7/6 *n.*) c 8° Macmillan 07
BLAKE, Sophia Jex A Visit to American Schools and Colleges *o.p.* [*pb.* 6/] c 8° Macmillan 67
BOWDEN-SMITH, [Miss] A. G. An Engl. Student's Wander-Year in America 5/ *n.* c 8° Arnold 10
BROOK, A. T. American State Universities [origin, progress, etc.] r 8° *Cincinnati* 75
BROWN, E. E. Making of our Middle Schools [w. bibliogr.] $3 (10/6 *n.*) c 8° Longman 03
BROWN, Dr J. F. The American High School $1·40 *n.* (6/ *n.*) c 8° Macmillan 09
CANFIELD, J. H. The College Student and his Problems $1 *n.* (4/6 *n.*) c 8° Macmillan 02
[Personal Problem Series.] Selection of College, expenses, *curricula*, subjects, etc. Full of excellent advice.
DE GARMO, Dr C. Principles of Secondary Education, 3 vols. c 8° Macmillan 07 *in prg.*
i: *Studies* $1·25 *n.* (5/ *n.*) ; ii: *Processes of Instruction* $1 *n.* (4/6 *n.*) ; iii: *Processes of Training, in prep.*
Four American Universities ; ill. [Harvard ; Yale ; Princeton ; Columbia] $3·50 s 4° Harper, *N.Y.* 95
GILMAN, D. C. University Problems in the United States $2 8° Century Co., *N.Y.* 98
Addresses, settg. forth ideal of a University and its rel. to modern life.
HAMMOND, C. W. New England Academies and Classical Schools *Washington* 68
HARPER, Pres. W. R. Trend of Higher Educ. in Amer. [7/6 *n.* Unwin] $1·50 *n.* 12° Univ. Pr., *Chicago* 05
Collected essays and addresses, by the President of the University of Chicago.
HART, Prf. A. B. Studies in American Education $1·25 (5/) 12° Longman 95
HOLLISTER High School Administration [Pedag. Lib.] $1·50 c 8° Heath, *Boston*
LADD, Prf. G. T. Essays on the Higher Education $1 *n.* 12° Scribner, *N.Y.* 99
PORTER, Prf. Noah American Colleges and the American Public $1·50 12° Scribner, *N.Y.* [70] 83
RICHARDSON (C. F.) + CLARK (H. A.) The College Bk. [24 of older Colleges] $15 4° Houghton, *Boston* 78
RISK, R. K. America at College, as seen by Scots Graduate 3/6 *n.* c 8° Smith, *Glasgow* 08
A bright journalistic acc. of a visit to some dozen representative Universities and Colleges of U.S.
SLOSSON, Dr E. E. Great American Universities ; ill. $2·50 *n.* (10/6 *n.*) 8° Macmillan 10
Descrs., compares, and criticizes constitns. of 14 American Universities.
TENBROOK, Andr. American State Univs. : origin and progress $3·50 8° Clarke, *Cincinnati* 75
THWING, C. F. American Colleges : students & work [popular essays] $1·25 16° Putnam, *N.Y.* 78
" The American College in American Life $1·50 (6/) c 8° Putnam 97
" History of Higher Education in America $3 *n.* (12/6 *n.*) 8° Appleton 06
WAYLAND, Fcs. Thoughts on Present Collegiate Syst. in U.S. *o.p.* 16° Gould, *Boston* 42

*Student Life*

BAIRD, W. R. American College Fraternities $2 12° Downs, *N.Y.* [79] 90
A descriptive analysis of the Society System in United States Colleges.
BARNARD, Dr H. [ed.] True Student Life [selns. fr. eminent wrs.] $3·50 8° *Hartford* 72
OSGOOD, Sam. Student Life : letters and recollections $1 12° Miller, *N.Y.* 61
SHELDON, Dr H. D. Student Life & Customs [Intern. Educ. Ser.] $1·20 *n.* (5/ *n.*) c 8° Appleton 02

**According to Colleges and Universities**

*Amherst College*

CUTTING, G. R. Student Life at Amherst College *o.p.* 12° *Amherst* 71
HITCHCOCK, E. Autobiography : remins. of Amherst Coll. ; ill. *o.p.* [*pb.* $1·75] 12° *Northampton, Mass.* 63
TYLER, W. S. Hist. of Amherst Coll. from 1821 to 1891 $1·50 c 8° Hitchcock, *N.Y.* [73] 95

*Bowdoin College*

CLEVELAND (N.) + PACKARD (A. S.) Hist. of Bowdoin Coll.; w. biogr. sketches [1806–79] $5 8° Houghton, *Boston* 82

*Brown University*

BURSAGE, H. S. Brown University in the Civil War o.p. 8° *Providence* 68

Sketch of the History and Present Organisation of Brown University o.p. 8° *Providence* 61

WAYLAND, Fcs. [1796–1865] Life—*v.* **A** § 79

*California University*

JONES, W. C. Hist. of Univ. of California: 1868–1901 $5 f° Berkeley Bk. Store, *Berkeley, Cal.* [95] 02

WILLEY, S. H. History of the College of California 8° Carson, *San Francisco* 87

*Columbia University* (*College*)

History of Columbia University; ill. [1754–1904] $2·50 *n.* 8° Macmillan, *N.Y.* 05

MOORE, Dr N. F. Historical Sketch of Columbia College o.p. 12° *New York* 46

*Biography*: BARNARD, Pres. F. A. P. [10th Pres.; 1809–89] Life of. By Jno. Fulton $4 (14/) 8° Macm. 96

Van AMRINGEL, J. H. Historical Sketch of Columbia College [1754–1876] *pr. pr.* (*Columbia Coll.*) 76

*Cornell University*

PERKINS, F. C. Cornell Univ.: general and technical courses; ill. $1·50 obl 16° Wiley, *N.Y.* 91

SCHURMAN, J. G. A Generation of Cornell: 1868–98 75 c. 12° Putnam, *N.Y.* 98

*Dartmouth College*

CHASE, Fred. Hist. of Dartmouth Coll. & Town of Hanover, [posth.] ed. J. K. Lord vol. i [to 1815] [in 2 vols.] $3·50 8° Wilson, *Cambr., Mass.* 91

CROSBY, N. First Half-Century at Dartmouth College 25 c. 12° *Hanover, U.S.* 76

SMITH, B. P. History of Dartmouth College $5 8° Houghton, *Boston* 78

*Harvard University*

ATTWOOD, F. G. [art.] Manners & Customs of ye Harv. Students [26 cartoons] $1·50 4° Houghton, *Bost.* 78

BUSH, Geo. G. Harvard, the First American University; ill. $1·25 16° Cupples, *Boston* 86

ELIOT, Chas. W. [President 1869–1909]

Kühnemann, Prf. E. Charles W. Eliot; port. [4/6 *n.* Constable] $1 *n.* c 8° Houghton, *Boston* 09

HARVARD, Jno. [1607–38; founder]

Shelley, H. C. John Harvard and his Times; 24 pl. $2 *n.* p 8° Little & Brown, *Boston* 07

7/6 *n.* Smith & Elder. A pleasant narrative of the life of the founder of the oldest of the Amer. Univs., wh. he orig. endowed w. £400 (half his property) and his library: it is now in rect. of an average of £100,000 a year.

HIGGINSON, T. W. [ed.] Harvard Memorial Biographies, 2 vols. o.p. 8° *Cambridge, U.S.* 67

HILL, Dr G. Birkbeck Harvard College, by an Oxonian [sympathetic] 9/ c 8° Macmillan 95

PEABODY, Dr A. P. Harvard Reminiscences [biogr. sketches, 1776–1831] $1·25 12° Ticknor, *Bost.* 88

" Harvard Graduates whom I have Known $1·25 12° Houghton, *Boston* 90

POST, W. K. Harvard Stories: sketches of the Undergraduate $1·50 (6/) 12° Putnam [94] 97

Incl. a very good account of the boat race betw. Harvard and Yale.

QUINCY, Josiah Hist. of Harvard University, 2 vols. [standard] o.p. 8° *Cambridge, Mass.* 40

SIBLEY, J. L. Biogr. Sketches of Graduates of Harvard [1647–1858] $5 8° Sever, *Cambridge, Mass.* 74

TRIPP, G. H. Student Life at Harvard $1·75 c 8° Lockwood, *Boston* [76] 77

VAILLE (F. O.) + CLARK (H. A.) [eds.] Harvard Book, 2 vols. [history, etc., by var. wrs.] $30 4° Houghton, *Boston* [75] 79

WINSOR, Justin [ed.] Record of 250th Anniv. of Harv. Coll., 2 vols. Wilson, *Cambridge, Mass.* 87

*Haverford College*

GARRETT, P. C. [ed.] History of Haverford College [1830–90] 8° Porter, *Phila.* 92

*Johns Hopkins University*

ADAMS, H. B. —*in* Johns Hopkins University Studies 8° Johns Hopk. Press, *Baltimore*

GILMAN, D. C. Launchg. of a Univ. [=J. H. Univ.]; & other Papers $2·50 *n.* 8° Dodd & Mead, *N.Y.* 06

STEINER (B. C.) + GILMAN (D. C.) Hist. of Higher Ed. in Maryl. and J. H. U. [J. H. U. Studs.] 50 c. J. H. Un. Press, *Baltim.* 91

*Kenyon College*

BODINE, W. B. Kenyon College [a history of the College] 8° *Columbus, Ohio* 91

*Lowell Institute, Boston*

SMITH, Harriette K. History of the Lowell Institute [biographical] $1 12° Lawson, *Boston* 98

*Madison University*

First Half-Century of Madison University [1819–69] 8° *New York* 72

*Marietta College*

ANDREWS, J. W. Historical Sketch of Marietta College [by its President] 8° *Cincinnati* 76

*Michigan University*

ANDERSON, Olive S. L. ['Iola'] An American Girl in a Boy's College $1·25 12° Appleton, *N.Y.* 78
Author was one of first of her sex to enter Univ. of Mich. (1875), and gives an acc. of the beginnings of co-educn. there. Her novel is virtually an autobiogr. and her characters real persons.

DEMMON, I. N., etc. Semicenten. Celebrn. of Univ. of Mich. 8° *Ann Arbor* 88

FARRAND, E. M. History of the University of Michigan $1·60 12° Register Pb. Ho., *Ann Arbor* 85

TENBROOK, Andr. Amer. State Univs. [*ut sup.*] conts. partic. acc. of hist. of Mich. Univ.

*Muhlenberg College*

OCHSENFORD, S. E. Muhlenberg College [w. record of its men] $3 8° *Muhlenberg* 92

*New York City College ; and University*

HOUGH, F. B. Historical and Statistical Record of Univ. of State of New York during 1784 to 1884 Weed, *Albany, N.Y.* 85

ROSENTHAL (P. J.) + HORNE (C. F.) [eds.] City College : memories of 60 yrs. $5 *n.* (21 / *n.*) r 8° Putnam 07

*North Carolina*

BATTLE, K. P. Sketches of Hist. of Univ. of N. Carolina 8° *Chapel Hill, N.C.* 89

*Pennsylvania University*

MCMASTER, J. B. The University of Pennsylvania Illustrated obl 8° 97

MONTGOMERY, T. H. History of Univ. of Pennsylvania [foundn. to 1770] $5 8° *Philadelphia* 87

SHARPLESS, Dr Is. Two Cents. of Pennsylv. Hist. [Lippincott's Educ. Ser.] $1·25 12° Lippincott, *Phila.* 00

SMITH, Dr W. Life & Correspondence, ed. H. W. Smith [gr.-g'son], 2 vols. $10 8° Hammond, *Phila.* 77–9

THORPE, F. N. Benj. Franklin & Univ. of Penn. [Bureau of Educ.] *n.p.* Govt. Prtg. Off., *Washgtn.* 93

WOOD, Dr Geo. B. Early Hist. of the Univ. of Penn. ; ill. [1749–1827] 8° [83] 96

*Princeton Col.:* ALEXANDER (J. W.) Princeton, Old & New [recollns.of undergr.life] $1·25 12° Putnam, *N.Y.* 98

ALEXANDER, S. D. Biogr. Sketches of Founder & Princ. Alumni of the Log College *o.p.* 8° *Phila.* 51
The Log College, founded by Wm. TENNENT in 1739, was the beginning of Princeton University.

„ Princeton College dur. 18th Cent. [sketches of individuals] *o.p.* c 8° Randolph, *N.Y. n.d.* (72)

FITHIAN, P. V. Journal and Letters, ed. J. R. Williams ; ill. $3 *n.* 8° Univ. of Princeton 01
FITHIAN was a student at Princeton 1770–2, tutor at Nomini Hall, Virginia, 1773–4.

HAGEMAN, J. F. History of Princeton and its Institutions, 2 vols. $8 8° Lippincott, *Phila.* 79

MACLEAN, J. History of College of New Jersey, 2 vols. [1746–1854] $7 8° Lippincott, *Phila.* 77

Princeton Book (The) : history, organizn., and pres. condn. of the college $18 4° Houghton, *Boston* 80

WALLACE, G. R. Princeton Sketches : story of Nassau Hall $2 8° Putnam, *N.Y.* 93

*St John's College, Fordham, N.Y.* [Roman-Catholic]

TAAFFE, T. G. History of St John's Coll., Fordham, N.Y. ; ill. $2 *n.* 8° Cath. Pb. Soc., *N.Y.* 91

*St Louis University*

HILL, Walt. H. Historical Sketch of St Louis University Fox, *St Louis* 79
Incl. an account of the origin of the Jesuit society in Missouri.

*South Carolina College*

LABORDE, M. History of the South Carolina College *o.p.* 8° *Charleston* 74

*Tennessee University*

SANFORD, E. T. Blount College and Univ. of Tennessee [historical] *Knoxville, Tenn.* 94

WHITE, Moses Early Hist. of Univ. of Tennessee [80 pp.] *Knoxville, Tenn.* 79

*Vermont University*

HUNTINGDON, C. A. University of Vermont Fifty Years Ago Whitney, *Burlington* 92

*Virginia University, etc.*

ADAMS, Prf. H. B. College of William and Mary [founded 1693] [Bureau of Educ.] *n.p.* Govt. Prtg. Off., *Washington* 87

„ Thomas Jefferson & Univ. of Virginia [Bureau of Educ.] *n.p.* Govt. Prtg. Off., *Washington* 88

JEFFERSON (T.) + CUBELL (J. C.) Early History of the University of Virginia *o.p.* 8° *Richmond* 56
Of considerable historical value.

Sketch of the History of the University of Virginia 8° *Richmond* 85

*Williams College*

DURFEE, Calvin A History of Williams College *o.p.* 8° Williams, *Boston* 60

**Williams College : 1793–1893** 8° Wilson, *Cambridge, Mass.* 94

***Wisconsin University, etc.***

CARPENTER, S. H. Histor. Sketch of the Univ. of Wisconsin [1849–76] 8° *Madison* 76

CHAPIN, A. L. Historical Sketches of the Colleges of Wisconsin 8° *Madison* 76

Historical Sketch of the University of Wisconsin [1849–76] 8° *Madison* 76

***Yale University (College)***

BAGG, L. H. Four Years at Yale [by a graduate of Yale] 8° *New Haven* 71

BALDWIN, Eben. History of Yale College [to 1838] *o.p.* 8° Noyes, *New Haven* 41

BEERS, Prf. H. A. Ways of Yale in Consulship of Plaucus 50 c. 16° *New York* 95
Personal reminiscences of Yale thirty to forty years ago, with stories of student-life and fun.

CAMP (W.) + WELCH (L. S.) [eds.] Yale, his Campus, Class-rooms, & Athletics $2·50 c 8° Page, *N.Y.* 99
A very full account by various hands; especially strong on the athletic side. 100 illns.

DEXTER, E. B. Biogr. Sketches of Graduates of Yale, w. Annals of Coll. Hist. [1701–45] $5 *n.* 8° Holt, *N.Y.* 85

,, Sketch of the History of Yale University $1·25 12° Holt, *N.Y.* 87

KINGSLEY, W. L. [ed.] Yale College : sketch of its history, 2 vols. ; ill. $37 4° Holt, *N.Y.* 79

PORTER, Jno. A. [ed.] Sketches of Yale Life [fr. college mags., etc.] Arlington Pb. Co., *Washgtn.* 86

PORTER, Dr Noah [1811–92 ; President]
Merriman, F. S. [ed.] Dr Noah Porter : meml. by his friends c 8° 93

REYNOLDS, J. B. Two Centuries of Christian Activity at Yale $1·50 (7/6) c 8° Putnam 01

WOOD, Jno. Seym. Yale Yarns : sketches of life at Yale [15 short stories] $1 12° Putnam, *N.Y.* 95

Yale College : record of bicenten. celebrn. [Oct. 20–3, 1901] $5 *n.* 4° Yale Univ. 02

**According to States**

*Alabama* : CLARK (Willis G.) History of Education in Alabama [Bureau of Educ.] *n.p.* Govt. Prtg. Off., *Washgtn.* 89
*Connecticut* : STEINER (B. C.) History of Education in Connecticut [Bureau of Educ.] *n.p.* Govt. Prtg. Off., *Washgtn.* 93
*Delaware* : POWELL (L. P.) History of Education in Delaware [Bureau of Educ.] *n.p.* Govt. Prtg. Off., *Washgtn.* 93
*Florida* : BUSH (R. G.) History of Education in Florida [Bureau of Educ.] *n.p.* Govt. Prtg. Off., *Washgtn.* 88
*Georgia* : JONES (C. E.) Education in Georgia [Bureau of Educ.] *n.p.* Govt. Prtg. Off., *Washgtn.*
*Indiana* : BOONE (Prf. R. G.) History of Education in Indiana c 8° Appleton, *N.Y.*
SMART, Jas. H. Indiana Schools and the Men who have Worked them Wilson, *Cincinnati* 76
WOODBURN, J. A. Higher Education in Indiana [Bureau of Educ.] *n.p.* Govt. Prtg. Off., *Washgtn.* 91
*Iowa* : PARKER (L. F.) Higher Education in Iowa [Bureau of Educ.] *n.p.* Govt. Prtg. Off., *Washgtn.* 93
*Kansas* : MACDONALD (Jno.) [ed.] Columbian History of Education in Kansas *Topeka* 93
*Maryland* : STEINER (B. C.) Hist. of Educ. in Maryland [Bureau of Educ.] *n.p.* Govt. Prtg. Off., *Washgtn.* 94
*Massachusetts* : BUSH (G. G.) Hist. of Higher Educ. in Massa. [Bureau of Educ.] *n.p.* 8° Govt. Prtg. Off., *Washgtn.* 91
EMERSON (J. B.) Education in Massachusetts [early legisln. and hist.] *Boston* 69
*Michigan* : MCLAUGHLIN (Prf. A. C.) Hist. of Higher Educ. in Mich. [Bur. of Ed.] *n.p.* 8° Govt. Prtg. Off., *Washgtn.* 91
SMITH, Wm. L. Historical Sketches of Education in Michigan *Lansing* 81
*North Carolina* : SMITH (C. Lee) History of Education in N. Carolina [Bureau of Educ.] *n.p.* Govt. Prtg. Off., *Washgtn.* 88
*Ohio* : KNIGHT (G. W.) + COMMONS (J. R.) Hist. of Higher Educ. in Ohio [Bur. of Educ.] *n.p.* 8° Govt. Prtg. Off., *Washgtn.* 91
*Pennsylvania* : WICKERSHAM (J. P.) History of Education in Pennsylvania $3 8° Inquirer Pb. Co., *Lancaster, Pa.* 86
From time of settlement of Swedes on the Delaware to 1886. Best State hist. of educn. yet wr.
*Rhode Island* : TOLMAN (W. H.) Hist. of Higher Educn. in Rhode Isl. [Bur. of Educ.] Govt. Prtg. Off., *Washgtn.* 94
*South Carolina* : MERRIWETHER (C.) Hist. of Higher Educn. in S. Carol. [Bur. of Ed.] *n.p.* Govt. Prtg. Off., *Washgtn.* 88
*Tennessee* : MERRIAM (L. S.) Higher Education in Tennessee [Bureau of Educ.] *n.p.* Govt. Prtg. Off., *Washgtn.* 93
*Virginia* : MAYO (A. D.) Education in South-western Virginia [Bureau of Educ.] *n.p.* Govt. Prtg. Off., *Washgtn.* 94
*Wisconsin* : ALLEN (W. F.) + SPENCER (D. E.) Higher Educn. in Wisconsin [Bureau of Educ.] *n.p.* Govt. Prtg. Off., *Washgtn.* 89
STERNS, J. W. [ed.] Columbian History of Education in Wisconsin $8 8° Caspar, *Milwaukee* 93

### 158 : STUDENT LIFE : SCHOOL AND UNIVERSITY—classed with D § 157 *passim*.

---

## III : The State in Relation to Education

### 159 : EDUCATIONAL LAW ; EDUCATIONAL CODES

BARNARD, H. [ed.] School Codes, State, Municipal, Institutional $3·50 m 8° *Hartford n.d.*

SONNENSCHEIN, A. [tr.] Educational Codes of For. Countries : translated 3/6 c 8° Sonnenschein [82] 89
Codes of Austria, Belg., Germy., Italy, Switz., S. Australia, etc., w. geogr. directns. of Pruss. R. Cadet Corps. Introd. and notes.

**Great Britain**

BAKER, C. E. Local Education : manl. f. boro' and urban councils 5/ *n.* 8° Black 03

BARLOW (M.) + MACAN (H.) [eds.] Education Act, 1902 ; w. notes 3/6 *n.* c 8° Butterworth [02] 03

CASSON (W. A.) + WHITELEY (E. C.) [eds.] Education Act, 1902 ; w. notes 7/6 *n.* 8° Knight [02] 03

CUTLER (E.) + LYNN (H.) The Teacher's Legal Guide 3/6 c 8° Gill 93

DISNEY, H. W. The Law relating to Schoolmasters 2/6 c 8° Arnold 93

DUMSDALE (W. H.) + MOTHERSOLE (H.) The Law of Education [v. comprehensive] 42/ r 8° Hadden 04

Elementary Educn. Acts : Reports of Royal Commission ; vols. i–iv, and Supplement f° Eyre & Spottiswoode 87–8

GLEN, W. C. [ed.] Elementary Educn. Acts: w. notes [1870, 73, 74, 75, 80] 10/6 12° Shaw [71] 81
JONES (G. E.) + SYKES (J. C. G.) Law of Public Educn. in Engld. and Wales 21/ n. 8° Rivington [03] 04
KNIGHT & Co. [pubs.] Elementary School Manager's Handbook 2/6 n. c 8° Knight 03
„ Handbk. for Members of Education Committees 3/6 n. c 8° Knight 03
MACLEAN, A. H. H. Law conc. Secondary and Preparatory Schools 15/ n. 8° Jordan 09
ORGAN, T. A. Law rel. to Schools and Teachers 8/6 n. 8°; 2/6 n. c 8° Arnold, *Leeds* 00
A valuable and comprehensive account of law, espec. as affecting Public Elementary Schools.
„ + THOMAS (A. A.) [eds.] Education Law: Acts 1870–1902, etc. 12/6 n. c 8° Butterworth 03
OWEN, Sir Hugh [ed.] Elem. Educn. Acts: 1870–1902; w. Introd. & notes 21/ n. 8° Knight [71] 03
STEINTHAL, A. E. [ed.] Elementary Educn. Act 1891; w. Introd. and notes 2/6 n. c 8° Sweet 91
TAYLOR, G. R. S. [ed.] Educn. Acts, 1902 (Engl. and Wales) and 1903 (Lond.); w. notes 1/ 8° Routledge [03] 04
TROWER, C. F. [ed.] Law of Building Churches, Parsonages, and Schools 9/ 8° Butterworth 74
WILLIAMS, Jas. Education [Manuals of Practical Law] 5/ c 8° Black 92
$1·50 Macmillan, *N.Y.* Very comprehensive, incl. pub. and priv. schls., techn. and profess. educ., reformatories, etc.; w. cases and authorities.
WILLSON, W. R. The Law of Education 21/ 8° Gee 03
WYATT, C. H. Companion to the Education Acts 1870–1902 7/6 n. 8° Wyatt, *Mancs.* 03
Summary of 1902 Act. Articles on work of new authorities, forms, regulations, etc.

*Reformatory and Industrial Schools*

HORNBY, F. P. [ed.] The Reformatory and Industrial Schools Acts 5/ 8° Eyre & Spottiswoode 97

*Secondary Education*

Secondary Education: handbk. to Bd. of Educn. Act, 1899 4/6 c 8° Knight 00

*Universities*

GAMLEN, W. B. [ed.] Universities & College Estates Acts, 1858–80, 1898 2/6 (60 c.) 8° Clar. Press 98
GRIFFITHS, Jno. [ed.] Enactmts. in Parlt. conc. Univs. of Oxfd. & Camb. 12/ ($3) 8° Clar. Press 69
MORTON, J. N. Analysis of Universities (Scotl.) Act 1889 [w. the Act itself] 3/ 8° Blackwood 90
SKENE, W. B. [ed.] Acts rel. to Oxford and Cambridge and Colleges in Sale, Acquisition, and Administration of Property 7/6 8° Sweet 94
WILLIAMS, Dr J. The Law of the Universities 10/6 8° Butterworth 09

**Scotland**

GRAHAM, J. E. [ed.] Manual of Acts rel. to Educn. in Scotland 18/ c 8° Blackwood 02
KERR, J. [ed.] Vade Mecum of Scottish Educn. [annotated Code] 1/ n. 8° Nelson 99
MURRAY, S. M. [ed.] Short Manual of Educn. (Scotld.) Act, 1908 1/ n. 8° Blackie 09
SELLAR, A. C. [ed.] Law rel. to Educn. Acts in Scotl., ed. J. E. Graham 12/6 8° Blackwood [72] 94

**Wales**

HUGHES Welsh Intermediate Schools 7/6 8° Butterworth 98

**Germany and Austria**

Prussian Code (The) in its Present Form: translated 2/6 c 8° Paul 79

**United States**

BARDEEN, C. W. [ed.] Common Schl. Law for Common Schl. Teachers 75 c. 16° Bardeen, *Syracuse, N.Y.* [75] 88
BARNARD, H. [ed.] School Codes: State, municipal, institutional $3·50 m 8° *Hartford* 73
BURKE, F. Treatise on the Law of Public Schools $1 12° *New York* 80
KEYES, E. W. [ed.] Laws of N. York rel. to Common Schls.; w. notes $4 Bardeen, *Syracuse, N.Y.* [79] 88
KIRK, J. E. [ed.] Code of Public Instruction of State of New York $4 8° *New York* 88
TAYLOR, I. Public-School Law of the United States $5 8° Crane, *Topeka, Kan.* 92

*Colonies*

CLEWS, E. W. Educatl. Legisln. and Admin. in the Colonies [Columbia Univ. Contribs.] $2 n. 8° Macmillan, *N.Y.* 99

## 159*: SOCIOLOGICAL ASPECTS OF EDUCATION

BAKER, Pres. J. H. Education and Life $1·25 c 8° Longman, *N.Y.* 00
Papers and addresses by the President of Colorado Univ.; some dealing with aspects of education; others with the ideal life.
BRYANT, Dr Sophie Educational Ends: the ideal of personal development *o.p.* [*pb.* 6/] c 8° Longman 87
CHANCELLOR, W. E. Theory of Motives, Ideals, & Values in Educn. $1·75 n. 8° Houghton, *Boston* 07

CONWAY, F'r J. [S.-J.] The State Last 25 c *n.* 16° Pustet, *N.Y.* 92
Reply to Dr BOUQUILLON's pamph. *Education : to whom does it belong?* Denies to State a monop. in educn., and even the rt. to estab. a standard of educn. The argumts. manifest the scholarsh. wh. has always characterized the Society of Jesus.

CRAIK, Sir Hy. The State in rel. to Education [Engl. Citizen Ser.] 2/6 ($1) c 8° Macmillan [84]
An admirable sketch of historical development of Governmental policy with regard to Education.

DEWEY, Prf. J. School and Society [3/ *n.* P. S. King ; 3 lects.] $1 12° Univ. Press, *Chicago* [oo] 01

DUTTON, S. T. Social Phases of Educn. in Schl. and Home $1·25 *n.* (5/) c 8° Macmillan 99

FOUILLÉE, Alf. Education fr. a National Standpt. [tr.] [Int. Ed. Ser.] $1·50 (6/) c 8° Appleton 92
Maints. th. chief matl. of educn. must be human, its form and subst. the Humanities (wh. thus take w. him place assigned by SPENCER to science), not bec. they are of most pract. worth but bec. a knowl. of them is the essential requisite to living well as indivs. and as nations. Wr. w. enthusiasm and eloquence. Well tr. by W. J. GREENSTREET.

HANUS, Prf. P. H. Educational Aims & Educl. Values [repr. pprs.] $1 (4/6) c 8° Macmillan, *N.Y.* 99

HARPER, J. Wilson Education and Social Life 4/6 *n.* c 8° Pitman 07

HENDERSON, C. H. Education and the Larger Life $1·30 *n.* 8° Houghton, *Boston* 02
Education as furthering the progress of civilization : and an advocacy of practical methods.

KAY, DAV. Education and Educators 7/6 c 8° Paul 83
*Meangs., Nature and Importce., and Hered. Effects of Educn. ; Educn. and the State ; Educn. and Religion ; Diff. Kinds of Educators.*

de MONTMORENCY, J. E. G. National Education and National Life 3/ c 8° Sonnenschein 06

MÜLLER, Mich. [R.-C.] Public School Education $1·50 c 8° Sadlier, *N.Y.* 75
Exposn. of evil conseqs. of publ.-schl. educn., and denial of rt. of State to educate.

O'SHEA, M. V. Education as Adjustment $1·50 (6/) c 8° Longman 04
Educational theory viewed in the light of contemporary thought.

" Dynamic Factors in Education $1·25 *n.* (5/ *n.*) c 8° Macmillan 06

PLAYFAIR, Sir Lyon —*in his* Subjects of Social Welfare, *ut* **D** § 125

SADLER, Mrs S. H. [R.-C.] Higher Educn. of Young [soc., domest., relig.] 3/6 c 8° Routledge [ ] 07

SHARPLESS, Is. Reln. of State to Educ. in Eng. & Am. 25 c. 8° Am. Acad. of Pol. Sci., *Phila.* 93

TAYLOR, C. E. How Far shd. State Undertake to Educate [pp. 48] c 8° Edwards, *Raleigh* 94

VINCENT, Prf. G. E. The Social Mind and Education $1·25 c 8° Macmillan, *N.Y.* 97
A valuable exposition of the relation of sociology to pedagogy.

*Education in rel. to Crime*—*v.* **D** § 123 *Educn. in rel. to Heredy*—*v.* **D** § 159*
*Philanthropy*—*v.* **D** § 128 ; *Home-Missions*—*v.* **A** § 106 ; *Settlements*—*v.* **D** § 127

---

# IV : Systematic Pedagogy : Generally

## 160 : SYSTEMATIC PEDAGOGY (*a*) : ANCIENT

Including BIOGRAPHY & CRITICISM OF WRITERS (*v. also* **C** §§ 2–15). For History of Gk. & Rom. Educn. *v.* **D** § 156

ARISTOTLE [B.C. 385–322] Nicomachæan Ethics ; Politics ; Rhetoric ; Economics—*passim, ut* **C** § 9, **K** § 194

" On Education, ed. and tr. Prf. Jno. Burnet—*ut* **C** § 9
Translated extracts fr. the *Ethics* and *Politics*, giving ARISTOTLE's ideas on education ; w. notes.

Davidson, Dr Thos. Aristotle and the Educational Ideals—*ut* **D** § 156, *s.v.* Greek and Roman

CICERO [B.C. 106–43] De Oratore—*ut* **K** § 220

CORNIFICIUS [B.C. 1 cent.] Rhetorica [ad Herennium]—*ut* **K** § 220

ISOCRATES [B.C. 436–338] Orationes—*ut* **K** § 193
Oratio xiii : against the Sophists and their methods ; Oratio xv : on the antidosis, or theory of practical culture.

LUCIAN [A.D. *c.* 120–*c.* 200] Anacharsis vel de Gymnasiis, tr. Dr C. E. Lowrey *sub tit.* Physical Educ. among the Greeks ; w. comments [Bur. of Educn.] *n.p.* 8° Govt. Prtg. Off., *Washgtn.* 92

PHILOSTRATUS THE ELDER [2–3 cent.] Libellus de Arte Gymnastica

PLATO [B.C. 427–348] Dialogues : The Republic ; The Laws—*passim, ut* **C** § 8

Adamson, J. E. Theory of Educn. in Plato's 'Republic' [$1·10 *n.* Macm., *N.Y.*] 4/6 c 8° Sonnenschein 03

Bosanquet, Prf. Bern. [tr.] Education of the Young in 'Republic' of Plato 2/6 c 8° Camb. Press 00
70 c. *n.* Putnam, *N.Y.* Tr. of *Repub.*, Bk. ii, 9 to Bk. iv ; w. scholarly Introd. and valuable notes. Intended for use of those who have no Greek.

Grote, Geo. Plato and other Companions of Socrates, 4 vols.—*ut* **C** § 8

Nettleship, R. L. Theory of Educn. in 'Repub.' of Plato—*in* Hellenica, *ut* **C** § 3 [repr. 50 c. *n.* Univ. of Chic. '07]

Packard, L. F. Studies in Greek Thought : essays [Plato's system of educn.] $1 12° Ginn, *Boston* 86

Wilkins, Prf. A. S. Natl. Educn. in Greece in 4th Cent. [Plato & Aristotle] *o.p.* [*pb.* 5/] c 8° Isbister 73

v. Zeller, Ed. Socrates and the Socratic School [tr.]—*ut* **C** § 7

PLUTARCH [A.D. 46–120] Morals, *passim*—*ut* **C** § 15

QUINTILIAN [*c.* 35–97] Institutes of Oratory—*ut* **K** § 220

TACITUS [*c.* 54–*c.* 117] Dialogus de Oratoribus—*ut* **K** § 220

XENOPHON [B.C. *c.* 431–*c.* 355] Cyropædia—*ut* **K** § 192 : education and life of Cyrus
A good authority on education among the Persians and Spartans.

" Œconomicus—*ut* **K** § 192 : education of a wife for the household

## 161: SYSTEMATIC PEDAGOGY (*b*): MEDIEVAL AND MODERN

Including BIOGRAPHY AND CRITICISM OF WRITERS, and Miscellaneous Works by them

ABELARD [Pierre ABAILARD ; 1079–1142] [$1 *n.* Scribner, *N.Y.* ; Gt. Educators] 5 / c 8° Heinemann 93
Orig., organizn., course of study and meths. of tchg., general spirit, and influ. ABELARD occupies but little space. Bibliogr.

ALCUIN [735–804]

Gaskoin, C. J. B. Alcuin, Life and Work—*ut* **A** § 62
Accurate and scholarly. Give a good idea of the theol. controversies of time, and of ALCUIN's influ. and amazg. versatility.

West, Prf. A. F. Alcuin and Rise of Christian Schools [Gt. Educators] 5 / c 8° Heinemann 92
$1 *n.* Scribner, *N.Y.* Gives a gd. pop. acc. of rise of free schls. founded by CHARLEMAGNE, told chfly. in words of ALCUIN, the Engl. prelate (who is by some thought to have induced the great king to undertake them). Conts. a useful sketch of ALCUIN's forerunners.

ARNOLD Dr Thos. [1795–1842]—*v.* **D** § 157, *s.v.* Rugby School

ASCHAM, Rog. [1515–68] The Scholemaster, ed. Prf. J. E. B. Mayor [Bohn's Cheap Ser.] 1 / f 8° Bell [1570] 84

„ The same : text only [35 c. *n.* Macmillan, *N.Y.* ; Arber's Reprts.] 1 / *n.* f 8° Constable [1570]
Also in Cassell's Little Classics, *7d. n.*, and in his *Works*, ed. GILES, 4 v., *ut* **K** § 89, wh. conts. a satisf. Life of ASCHAM. 'It contains, perhaps, the best advice that was ever given for the study of languages'.—Saml. JOHNSON.

Quick, Rev. R. H. —*in his* Essays on Educational Reformers, *ut* **D** § 155

BACON, Frcs., L'd [1561–1626] Advancement of Learning *and* Life [and Criticism]—*v.* **C** § 16

BAIN, Prf. Alex. [1810–77] Education as a Science [Internat. Scient. Ser.] 5 / c 8° Kegan Paul [79] 92
$1·75 Appleton, *N.Y.* Notable for its studied analysis and minute scholarship.

„ Practical Essays 2/ c 8° Longman 84
$1·50 Appleton, *N.Y.* *Civil Service Exams.* ; *Classical Controv.* ; *Metaphysics and Debatg. Socs.* ; *University Ideal Past and Pres.* ; *Art of Study, etc.*

BASEDOW, J. [1723–90] QUICK (Rev. R. H.)—*in his* Essays on Educational Reformers, *ut* **D** § 155

BELL, Dr Andr. [1753–1832]

Meiklejohn, Prf. J. M. D. An Old Educational Reformer [Bell] *o.p.* [*pb.* 3 /6] c 8° Blackwood 81

BENEKE, F. E. [1798–1854] —*v.* **C** § 71

COMBE, Geo. [1788–1858] Discussions on Education [pp. 232] 1 / f 8° Cassell [3rd edn. 48] 94

„ Education, its Principles and Practice, ed. W. Jolly *o.p.* [*pb.* 15 /] 8° Macmillan 79

COMENIUS, Bp J. A. [1592–1671] Magna Didactica : ex ed. Amstelod. 1657 ed. F. C. Hultgren, 2 Pts. 5 m. 8° Siegismund, *Lpz.* 94

„ The same, ed. and tr. M. W. Keatinge, *s.t.* The Great Didactic, vol. i : Tr., 7 /6 *n.* ; ii : Text 4 /6 *n.* c 8° Black [96] 11
Ea. $1·75 *n.* Macmillan, *N.Y.* The text is ed. fr. the Lat. orig. in Advoc. Lib., Edin., the tr. is the first complete Engl. versn. of the book, wh. embodies its author's most mature opinions. Biogr., histor., and crit. Introds. ; well tr.

„ Orbis Pictus [w. facs. reprod. of orig. pict.] $3 8° Bardeen, *Syracuse, N.Y.* [1658] 87
The first picture-book for children ever pubd. The Latin text is from the edn. of 1658, the Engl. tr. from that of 1727.

„ School of Infancy, tr. W. S. Monroe ; w. Introd. and notes $1 c 8° Heath, *Boston* 96
[Pedag. Lib.] An essay on educn. of children dur. first 6 yrs. Prev. tr. D. BENHAM in 1858, w. a *Life* of COMENIUS (perhaps the best).

Butler, N. M. Place of Comenius in Hist. of Educn. [pp. 20] 20 c. 16° Bardeen, *Syracuse, N.Y.* 92

Lang, O. H. Comenius : life and princs. of educn. [pp. 26] 25 c. 12° Kellogg, *N.Y.*

Laurie, Prf. S. S. J. A. Comenius, his Life and Educ. Works 3 /6 c 8° Camb. Press [81] 99
$1 *n.* Putnam, *N.Y.* Includes a very full critical analysis of *The Great Didactic.*

Monroe, Prf. W. S. Comenius and the Beginnings of Educational Reform [Great Educators ; 5 / Heinemann] $1 *n.* c 8° Scribner, *N.Y.* 00

Quick, Rev. R. H. —*in his* Essays on Educational Reformers, *ut* **D** § 155

COMPAYRÉ, Prf. G. Lectures on Pedagogy, Theoretical & Practical [tr.] $1·60 c 8° Heath, *Boston* 87
[Pedag. Lib.] One of the best bks. on the theory and practice of teaching.

DE BRATH, Stanley The Foundations of Success 2 /6 c 8° Philip 96
A stimulating little bk., givg. a summary of princs. of a 'rational' educn., and proposg. to estab. an assoc. of 60 members at £200 ea. for foundg. a new schl. for 250 boys (capital to be repd. fr. sinking fund).

DEFOE, Dan. [1663–1731 Compleat English Gentleman, ed. Dr Karl D. Bülbring 12 / m 8° Nutt 90
Now ed. for first time fr. author's MS. in Brit. Mus. [Add. MSS., 32,555], w. elab. Introd. (76 pp.) on hist. of word 'Gentleman' and on educn. of Gentry in former times, notes [9 pp.] and Index [7 pp.], wr. to show necessity of educg. not only younger sons of gentry (as was the custom) but also heirs to the estates, where culture was in Defoe's time entirely neglected in favr. of sports. Of gt. interest, but of course of no pres. pract. value.

„ Of Royall Educacion : a fragmentary treatise, ed. Bülbring 1 / *n.* 8° Nutt 95
Forms a Supplement to above. Of small pedagogic interest, consistg. mainly of examples of want of care in educn. of princes and nobles. Introd. and notes.

DRESSER, H. W. Education and the Philosophical Ideal $1·25 (5 /) c 8° Putnam 00

ELYOT, Sir Thos. [1499–1546] The Boke named the Governour, ed. H. H. S. Croft, 2 vols. [w. Life of Elyot] *o.p.* [*pb.* 50 /] s 4° Paul [1531] 83

„ The same, ed. Prf. E. Arber *o.p.* [*pb.* 5 /] f 8° Arber, *Birm. n.d.*

„ The same, *s.t.* The Gouernour, ed. Prf. Foster Watson 1 / *n.* s 8° Dent 07
35 c. *n.* Dutton, *N.Y.* [Everyman's Lib.] With Introduction and notes. ELYOT's chief wk., bg. a prose treatise on educn., generous and wise in tone, opposing, amongst other things, the custom of ill-treatg. schoolboys. He also tr. PLUTARCH's treatise on educn.

EMERSON, R. W. [1803–82] Education : an essay [also in his *Wks.*, *ut* **K** § 90] 15 c. *n.* 12° Houghton, *Boston* [ ] 09

ERASMUS, Desiderius [1466–1536]
Woodward, Prf. W. H. Erasmus Concerning Aim & Method of Education 4/ *n.* c 8° Camb. Press 04
$1·30 *n.* Putnam, *N.Y.* An excellent statemt. and criticism of Erasmus' views on educn.
EVE (H. W.) + SIDGWICK (A.) + ABBOTT (E. A.) Three Lectures on Practice of Educn.
*o.p.* [*pb.* 2/] p 8° Camb. Press 83
*On Marking; Stimulus; The Teaching of Latin Verse Composition.*
FICHTE, J. G. [1762–1814] On Nature of Scholar [tr.]—*in his* Popular Writings, 2 vols., *ut* **C** § 28
FITCH, Sir Joshua Art of Teaching, ed. Rev. F. Johnson [a lecture] 1/ *n.* S.S.U. [*c.* 60] 08
" Educational Aims and Methods 5/ c 8° Camb. Press 00
Misc. pprs., of varying values, inclg. studies of SOCRATES, ASCHAM, THRING, LANCASTER, PESTALOZZI.
" Lectures on Teaching [15 lects. at Cambridge] 5/ c 8° Camb. Press [80] 01
$1·25 Kellogg, *N.Y.* Practical. Sums up the best current thought on teaching. Topical treatment.
Arnold, Matt. —impressions of Fitch, *in his* Reports on Elementary Schools, *ut* **D** § 157
Lilley, Rev. A. L. Sir Joshua Fitch: acc. of his life and work 7/6 *n.* 8° Arnold 06
FRANCKE, A. H. [1663–1727] Life of. Tr. S. Jackson, fr. German *o.p.* c 8° Seeley 87
FROEBEL, Friedr. [1782–1852]—*v.* **D** § 164
GANE, Douglas M. Building of the Intellect 5/ c 8° Stock 97
HARRIS, Dr W. T., etc. Report of the Committee of Fifteen *o.p.* 8° New Eng. Pb. Co., *Boston* 95
A valuable Report on the principles of educn. as embodied in the course of study.
HEGEL, G. W. F. [1770–1831]
Luqueer, F. L. Hegel as Educator [Columb. Univ. Contribs.] $1 *n.* 8° Macmillan, *N.Y.* 95
Mackenzie, Prf. Millicent Hegel's Educational Theory and Practice 3/ *n.* c 8° Sonnenschein 09
A good intelligible acc. of H.'s contribn. to educn.; Introd. by Prf. J. S. MACKENZIE, and a short Life.
HERBART, J. F. [1776–1841] The Science of Education *and* The Æsthetic Revelation of the World,
tr. H. M. + E. Felkin 4/6 c 8° Sonnenschein [92] 10
$1 [Pedag. Lib.] Heath, *Boston.* Tr. of *Allgemeine Pädagogik*, w. Introd. (56 pp.) formg. a sort of biograph. commentary. Orig. pub. in 1806, the wk. is the foundation-stone of Germ. scientific pedagogics, and has had a vast influence, evinced by the compreh. bibliogr. of Herbartian liter. appended to VAN LIEW's tr. of REIN's *Pädagogik* [*ut inf.*]. Acc. to H. the main obj. of educn. is formatn. of Character. His test of quality of knowl. is Interest, wh. he analyses as bg. of 2 kinds: I, the interests conn. w. knowl. (*a*, the Empirical, e.g. kindergarten, *b*, the Speculative, *c*, the Æsthetic); II, those conn. w. Intercourse or Sympathy (*a*, Personal Sympathy w. Individuals, *b*, the Social Interest, *c*, the Religious Interest).
" A B C of Sense Perception, *&* Minor Pedag. Wks., tr. W. J. Eckoff,
w. notes & comm. [Int. Ed. Ser.] $1·50 (6/) c 8° Appleton 96
" Application of Psychology to Education [tr.] 4/6 c 8° Sonnenschein 98
$1·50 *n.* Scribner, *N.Y.* Tr. Beatrice C. MULLINER; w. Introd. and 5 plates.
" Letters and Lectures on Pedagogy, tr. H. M. + E. Felkin
[$1·75 Bardeen, *Syracuse, N.Y.*] 4/6 c 8° Sonnenschein [99] 07
" Same, tr. Dr A. F. Lange, *s.t.* Outlines of Educl. Doctrine $1·25 *n.* (5/ *n.*) c 8° Macmillan 01
" Textbook in Psychology, tr. M. K. Smith [Int. Ed. Ser.] $1 (4/6) c 8° Appleton 91
Adams, Rev. Jno. Herbartian Psychology appl. to Education $1 c 8° Heath, *Boston* [97] 00
[Pedag. Lib.] A bright little book, intelligently and racily expounding HERBART's psychology.
Cole, P. R. Herbart & Froebel: attempt at synthesis [Col. Univ. Studs.] $1 *n.* 8° Macmillan, *N.Y.* 07
Compayré, Prf. G. Herbart and Educn. by Instruction [tr.] 90 c. *n.* c 8° Crowell, *N.Y.* 07
2/6 *n.* Harrap. [Pioneers in Education.]
Darroch, Alex. Herbart & the Herbartian Theory of Educ. [critical] 3/6 *n.* ($1·20 *n.*) c 8° Longman 03
Davidson, Jno. New Interpretn. of Herbart's Psychol. & Educ. Theory 5/ *n.* 8° Blackwood 06
Interpreted thro' the philosophy of LEIBNIZ.
De Garmo, Dr C. Herbart and the Herbartians [Gt. Educators] $1 *n.* c 8° Scribner, *N.Y.* 95
5/ Heinemann. Lucid and suggestive, contg. acc. of HERBART's life and wk., psychol. and ethics, w. chap. on what PESTALOZZI left HERBART to do, and the best acc. we have of the developmts. of his wk. in hands of his successors (ZILLER, STOY, REIN, LANGE). Bibliography.
Dodd, Cath. I. Introduction to Herbartian Princs. of Teachg. 4/6 c 8° Sonnenschein [01] 05
With an Introd. by Prf. W. REIN [tr.].
*Felkin, H. M. + Emmie Introduction to Herbart's 'Sci. of Educn.' 4/6 c 8° Sonnenschein [95]
$1 [Pedag. Lib.] Heath, *Boston.* An admirable Introd. to a very difficult bk., the examples illustrg. H.'s positns. bg. largely supplied fr. Engl. sources. The most comprehensive exposition in English.
Fennell, M., *etc.* Notes of Lessons on Herbartian Method 3/6 ($1·10) c 8° Longman 02
Hayward, Dr F. H. Meang. of Educn. as interpr. by Herbart 2/ *n.* c 8° Ralph & Holland 07
" Science of Educn. (the Secret of Herbart) 6*d.* 8° Watts 07
" The Student's Herbart: an educl. monograph 1/6 *n.* c 8° Sonnenschein [02] 08
A brief explanation of the Herbartian principles.
" + THOMAS (M. E.) Critics of Herbartianism 4/6 c 8° Sonnenschein 03
Ufer, Chr. Introduction to the Pedagogy of Herbart [tr.] 90 c. c 8° Heath, *Boston* 94
[Pedag. Lib.] Ed. by Dr C. DE GARMO, pub. und. ausp. of Am. Herbart Club. Concise and useful; its illustrations are, however, all German.
HEWETT, Edwin C. Treatise on Pedagogy f. Yg. Teachers 85 c. c 8° Am. Bk. Co., *N.Y.* 94
HORNE, Prf. H. H. The Philosophy of Education $1·75 *n.* (7/6 *n.*) c 8° Macmillan 04
HUNTINGTON, F. D. Unconscious Tuition [pp. 41] 15 c. c 8° Kellogg, *N.Y.* 88
'A modern educational classic'.—W. S. MONROE.

HUXLEY, Prf. T. H. —*in his* Lay Sermons, Addresses and Reviews, *ut* **H** § 42
*A Liberal Education; A Scientific Educn.; Educl. Value of Natural Hist.; Study of Zoology*, etc.

,, —*in his* Science and Culture, and other Essays, *ut* **H** § 42
*Universities, Actual and Ideal; Technical Education: Elementary Instruction in Physiology.*

INGRAM, Prf. J. K. Practical Morals: treatise on universal educn.—*ut* **C** § 23
An application of the Positivist doctrine to the problem of educn.

JACOTOT, J. J. [1770–1840] —*cf.* Payne, *in his* Lects. [*inf.*], Quick, *in his* Essays [*ut* **D** § 155]

JEFFERSON, Thos. [1743–1826; President U.S. 1801, 1805]

Henderson, J. C. Thomas Jefferson's Views on Public Education $1·75 (7/6) 8° Putnam 90

JOHONNOT, J. [1823–88] Principles and Practice of Teaching [tr.] $1·50 8° Appleton, *N.Y.* [78] 91

KANT, Immanuel [1724–1804] On Education, tr. Annette Churton 2/6 *n.* c 8° Paul 00
75 c. [Pedag. Lib.] Heath, *Boston.* With Introd. by Mrs Rhys DAVIDS. Tr. of KANT's notes for lects. [*Ueber Pädagogik.*]

,, Educational Theory [tr.]; w. Introd. [L'cotts Ed. Ser.] $1·25 12° Lippincott, *Phila.* 08

KING, H. C. Personal and Ideal Elements in Educn. $1·50 *n.* (6/6 *n.*) c 8° Macmillan 05

LAURIE, Prf. S. S. Handbk. to Lectures on Theory & Art of Educn. 2/ f 8° Thin, *Edin.* [78] 79

,, Training of Teachers, and Methods of Instruction 6/ 8° Camb. Press [82] 01
$1·50 *n.* Putnam, *N.Y.* *Primary Instruction; Montaigne; Educatl. Wants of Scotland; Secondary and High Schools.*

,, Occasional Addresses on Educational Subjects—*ut* **D** § 155

LESSING, G. E. [1729–81] Education of the Human Race, tr. Rev. F. W. Robertson—*ut* **C** § 42

LOCKE, Jno. [1632–1704] Some Thoughts concerning Educn. [1693], ed. Rev. R. H. Quick 3/6 c 8° Camb. Press [80]
$1 *n.* Putnam, *N.Y.* With Introduction and notes. The best edition.

,, The same, ed. Can. Evan Daniel 4/ c 8° National Soc. [80] 89

,, The same, *s.t.* How to Bring up your Children 1/ *n.* f 8° Low 02
Of all LOCKE's works the most universally approved. Familiar in style, aboundg. in repetitns., and a little disconnected, yet a golden treatise, the very incarnatn. of good sense and right feeling.

,, Conduct of the Understanding [1690], ed. Dr Thos. Fowler; w. Introd. and notes 2/6 (60 c.) f 8° Clar. Press [82] 91
'I cannot think any parent or instructor justified in neglecting to put this little treatise in the hands of a boy about the time when the reasoning faculties become developed'.—Hallam, *Liter. of Eur.* For Life, etc., *v.* LEITCH & QUICK in **D** § 156; also **C** § 44.

LOYOLA, Ignatius [1491–1556]

Hughes, F'r T. [S.-J.] Loyola & the Educl. Syst. of Jesuits [Gt. Educators] $1 *n.* c 8° Scribner, *N.Y.* 92
5/ Heinemann. An interestg. and fair bk. on LOYOLA, one of outstanding figures in hist. biogr. and the educl. syst. of Jesuits, the most remarkable of all studies in pedagogic organizm., wh. has fr. first paid greatest attentn. to traing. of teachers.

LUBBOCK, Sir Jno. [L'd AVEBURY] Addresses, Political and Educational—*ut* **D** § 142

LYTTELTON, Rev. E. [ed.] Thirteen Essays on Education 7/6 c 8° Rivington 91
13 papers by a small body of professl. tchrs. who call themselves 'The Thirteen', and who met for discussn. of educl. subjs.

MACVICAR, Dr Malcolm [Canad.] Principles of Education 70 c. c 8° Ginn, *Boston* 93
2/6 Arnold. Brief statemt. of leadg. proposns. conc. nature and processes of educn. leading up, finally, to traing. necessary for a teacher.

MANN, Hor. [1796–1859] Life & Works, ed. G. C. Mann [son], 5 v. $12·50 *n.* c 8° Lee & Shepard, *Boston* 91
Vol. i: *Life*, by Mary MANN [wife] [(1881) 88]; ii–iv: *Lects. and Ten Reports* [1837–52] *on Educn.* [1872]; *Essays and Miscell. Papers.*

Hinsdale, Prf. B. A. Horace Mann and the Common School Revival $1 *n.* c 8° Scribner 98
5/ Heinemann. [Gt. Educators.] An admirable acc.: valuable for history of elem. educn. in America.

Winship, A. E. Horace Mann, Educator *o.p.* c 8° New Eng. Pb. Co., *Boston* 96

MATTHEWS, F. H. Princs. of Intellectual Education [75 c. *n.* Putnam, *N.Y.*] 2/6 *n.* c 8° Camb. Press 07

MILTON, Jno. [1608–74] Treatise on Education [1673], ed. O. Browning 2/ f 8° Camb. Press [83] 90
50 c. *n.* Putnam, *N.Y.* [Pitt Press Series.] With Introd. and notes. 'The noble moral glow th. pervades it, the mood of magnanimity in wh. it is conceived and wr., and the faith it inculcates in the powers of the yg. human spirit, if rightly nurtured and directed, are merits everlasting'.—MASSON.

,, Tractate on Educn., ed. Prf. E. E. Morris [Austral.] [Engl. Classics] 1/9 (40 c. *n.*) gl 8° Macmillan 95
With Introd. (35 pp.) and notes (22 pp.). MORRIS' treatmt. is literary, BROWNING's pedagogic. The *Tractate* itself is well worth reading in these days of *multa non multum.*

,, Tractate to Hartlib *o.p.* [*pb.* 2/] c 8° Camb. Press 83

,, Letter on Education [w. Areopagitica, etc.; Natl. Lib.] 6*d.* 18° Cassell 88

Dircks, H. Samuel Hartlib: a biographical memoir [pp. 124] *o.p.* c 8° Bardeen, *Syracuse, N.Y.* 60

Quick, Rev. R. H. —*in his* Essays on Educational Reformers, *ut* **D** § 156

de MONTAIGNE, Michel [1533–92] Essays [1580]—*ut* **C** § 50 (where also are Life and Criticism)

,, The Education of Children [tr.] [Ariel Booklets] 50 c. (1/6 *n.*) 18° Putnam [91] 07

Compayré, J. G. Montaigne and Educ. of Judgmt. [Pioneers in Ed.; 2/6 *n.* Harrap] 90 c. *n.* 12° Crowell, *N.Y.* 07

Rector, L. E. [tr.] Montaigne's Educ. of Child [tr. selns.; Int. Ed. Ser.] $1 (4/6) c 8° Appleton 99

MULCASTER, Rich. [1532–1611] Educl. Writings, abgd. J. Oliphant 3/6 *n.* c 8° MacLehose, *Glasgow* 03
Conts. the principal parts of the *Positions* and the *Elementarie* (slightly modernized), w. a critical estimate.

MULCASTER, Rich. Positions [1581] *o.p.* [*pb.* 10/6] 8° *priv. prin.* (R. H. Quick, *Redhill*) 88
Treats of the 3 parts of educn. given resp. in the elem. and grammar schl. and the universities, espec. the 2 former; best on the first; in wh. he advocates tchg. of rg., wrg., drawg., and music. One of the earliest Engl. treatises on educn.

Watson, Prf. Foster Mulcaster and his 'Elementarie' pp. 20 [*o.p.*] 8° Hodgson 93

PAYNE, Prf. Jos. [1808–76] Lects. on Sci. & Art of Educ., ed. R. H. Quick 14/ ($3·50) 8° Longman [80] 83
PAYNE was the first prof. of science and art of educn. at Coll. of Preceptors. Chief contents of this volume are: *Curriculum of Modn. Educ.* [1st pub. 1866]; *Training of Teacher* ['73]; *Theories of Teaching* ['68]; *Coll. of Preceptors* ['68]; *True Foundn. of Science Tchg.* ['73]; *Jacotot: life and system* ['67]; *Visit to Germ. Schls.* ['76]. Am. edns. (1) Small, *Boston*; (2) 50 c. Bardeen, *Syr., N.Y.* '85; (3) $1 Kellogg, *N.Y.* [84] 87.

PAYNE, Prf. W. H. Contribns. to Science of Educn. [6/ Blackie] $1·25 c 8° Amer. Bk. Co., *N.Y.* 86

PESTALOZZI, J. H. [1746–1827] How Gertrude Teaches her Children [tr.] 3/ c 8° Sonnenschein [94] 07
An attempt to help mothers to teach their own children, and an account of the method. Ed. E. COOKE.

" Leonard and Gertrude [tr. and abgd.] [Pedag. Lib.] 85 c. c 8° Heath, *Boston* [85] 92

" Letters on Early Educn. addr. to J. P. Greaves [tr.] $1 12° Bardeen, *Syracuse, N.Y.* [27]
Repr. of the Engl. edn. (1827) of the famous letters wr. for GREAVES in 1818 and tr. by his friend Dr WORMS.

*Bibliography:* Katal. d. Bibl. d. Pestalozzianums zu Zürich 8° Ruegg, *Zürich* 94

Barnard, Dr Hy. [ed.] Pestalozzi and Pestalozzianism $3·50 m 8° Brownell, *Hartford* [59] 62
A miscellaneous colln. of repr. papers on his life, principles and methods, w. some trss. from his wks., pts. of *Leon. and Gert.*, *Evening Hour of a Hermit*, the *Swan Song*, selns. fr. *Christopher and Elsie*.

Compayré, Prf. G. Pestalozzi and Elem. Educ. [tr.]
[2/6 *n.* Harrap; Pioneers in Educ.] 90 c. *n.* 12° Crowell, *N.Y.* 07

*de Guimps, R. Pestalozzi, his Life and Works, tr. J. Russell 6/ c 8° Sonnenschein [89] 08
$1·50 Appleton, *N.Y.* Tr. fr. the 2nd edn. The tr. in the Internat. Educn. Ser. [*ut* D § 155] is fr. the 1st edn., and of much less value.

Hayward, Dr F. H. Educatl. Ideas of Pestalozzi & Froebel [Norm. Tut. Ser.] 2/ c 8° Simpkin 04

Holman, Prf. H. Pestalozzi: acc. of his life and work 3/ *n.* (75 c.) c 8° Longman 08

Krüsi, Hermann Pestalozzi, his Life, Work, and Influence $1·20 12° Amer. Bk. Co., *N.Y.* [75] 03

Leitch, J. Muir —*in his* Practical Educationists, *ut* **D** § 156

Pinloche, A. Pestalozzi and the Foundation of the Modern Elementary School
[Great Educators; 5/ Heinemann] $1 *n.* c 8° Scribner, *N.Y.* 01

Quick, Rev. R. H. —*in his* Essays on Educational Reformers, *ut* **D** § 156

v. Raumer, K. Life and System of Pestalozzi, tr. J. Tilleard *o.p.* 8° Longman 55

Russell, J. Student's Pestalozzi [brief acc. of life and wk.] 1/6 c 8° Sonnenschein [88]

PLÄTTER, Thos.

Monroe, Paul T. Plätter & Educ. Renaissce. of 16 Cent. [Int. Ed. Ser.] $1·50 *n.* (5/ *n.*) c 8° Appleton 04

PUTNAM, Prf. Dan. Manual of Pedagogics $1·50 12° Silver, *Boston* 95
Semi-popular and elementary in character: intended for young teachers.

QUICK, Rev. R. H. [1831–91]

Storr, Fcs. Life and Remains of Rev. R. H. Quick; port. 7/6 c 8° Camb. Press 99
Incl. many extrs. fr. the 'forty notebooks' wh. QUICK is said to have left.

RABELAIS, Fr. [1495–1553] Readings in Rabelais, tr. [Sir] Walter Besant—*ut* **K** § 53
'Lessons to teach wh. concern humanity in all ages, and shall be read w. profit until the Golden Age comes back again, and then we shall all be educd. like Gargantua'.—BESANT.

RATICH, W. [1571–1635] —*v.* Quick, *in his* Essays on Educatl. Reformers, *ut* **D** § 156

RAYMONT, T. Principles of Education 4/6 ($1·40) c 8° Longman 04

REIN, Prf. W. Outlines of Pedagogics, tr. C. C. + Ida Van Liew $1 c 8° Bardeen, *Syracuse, N.Y.* [93] 95
3/ Sonnenschein. A compreh. and succinct acc. of entire Herb. syst. of pedagogics; w. elab. bibliogr. of Herb. liter. [15 pp.].

RICHTER, Jean [Paul [1763–1825] Levana; or, Doctrine of Educn. [tr.]
[Bohn's Lib.; $1 *n.* Macmillan, *N.Y.*] 3/6 c 8° Bell [76] 86

" Levana for English readers, tr. and ed. Susan Wood 3/ c 8° Sonnenschein 87
Extrs. w. running comm. and eluc. links. The wk. claims to be only a fragmt., but its spirit is broad and generous.

ROSENKRANZ, Prf. K. Philosophy of Educn., tr. Anna C. Brackett $1·50 (6/) c 8° Appleton [72] 87
[Intern. Educ. Ser.] A profound and thoughtful bk. on the philos. of educn. Hegelian. Comm. and anal. by Dr W. T. HARRIS.

ROSMINI, Ant. Serbati [1797–1855] Ruling Princ. of Method applied to Educ. [tr.]
[Ped. Lib.] $1·50 c 8° Heath, *Boston* 87
Tr. from Italian by Mrs WM. GREY. For ROSMINI-SERBATI's philosophical wks. *v.* **C** § 55.

ROUSSEAU, J. J. [1712–78] Emile, tr. W. H. Payne [Intern. Educ. Ser.] $1·50 (6/) c 8° Appleton 93

" The same, tr. E. Worthington [extrs.; w. notes; Ped. Lib.] 25 c. c 8° Heath, *Boston* [85] 88
'There are fifty pages of the Emile that should be bound in velvet and gold'.—VOLTAIRE.

Compayré, Prf. G. Rousseau and Educ. fr. Nature
[2/6 *n.* Harrap; Pion. in Educ.] 90 c. *n.* 12° Crowell, *N.Y.* 07

Davidson, Thos. Rousseau and Education according to Nature $1 *n.* c 8° Scribner, *N.Y.* 98
5/ Heinemann. [Great Educators.] A full study of ROUSSEAU's educational ideas and influence.

Morley, Jno. [L'd] Life of Rousseau—*ut* **C** § 56
Ch. xiii conts. an excellent account of ROUSSEAU's educational theories.

Quick, Rev. R. H. —*in his* Essays on Educational Reformers, *ut* **D** § 156

RUSKIN, Jno. [1819–1900]

Jolly, Wm. Ruskin on Education 1/ c 8° G. Allen [94] 07

A series of articles on RUSKIN's opinions on education, by a strong Ruskinian; w. extrs. fr. RUSKIN's writings.

SKRINE, J. Huntley Pastor Agnorum: a schoolmaster's afterthoughts 5/ ($1·60 *n.*) c 8° Longman 02

Contains much of value to educationists, though not in form a book on educational theory.

*SPENCER, Herb. [1820–1903] Education: Intellectual, Moral, and Physical 1/ *n.* c 8° Williams [61] 11

This edn. was reset and improved in typography. This bk. has come to be regarded as *the* 'English' utterance on educn., coming not fr. academical groves, and appealg. to the democracy—commonsense to the core. 'If it does not yet cont. a perfect and fully worked out theory of educ. it is at least a vigorous effort and a notable step tow. a rational pedagogy'.—COMPAYRÉ. Ch. Edn. 6*d.* Watts '03.

" —*in his* Essays, Scientific, Political, and Speculative, 3 vols., *ut* **C** § 62

Compayré, Prf. G. Spencer & Scient. Ed. [2/6 *n.* Harrap; Pioneers of Ed.] 90 c. *n.* c 8° Crowell, *N.Y.* 07

*Vide* also LEITCH's *Pract. Educationists* [*ut* **D** § 156], and QUICK, *Essays* [*ut* **D** § 156]. For other bks. on SPENCER *v.* **C** § 62.

SPURZHEIM, J. G. [1776–1832] Education: elems., princ. found. on nature of man [tr.] *o.p.* [*pb.* $1·25] 12° Wells, *N.Y.* [36] 47

STOW, Dav. [1793–1864] The Training System in Glasgow Model Schls. *o.p.* [*pb.* 6/6] 8° Longman [36] 59

Fraser, Wm. Memoir of the Life of David Stow *o.p.* [*pb.* 5/] c 8° Nisbet 68

Leitch, J. Muir —*in his* Practical Educationists, *ut* **D** § 156

THRING, Rev. Edw. [1821–87] Addresses [*for* Life *v.* **D** § 157, *s.v.* Uppingham] 5/ c 8° Unwin 89

" Theory and Practice of Teaching [$1 *n.* Putnam, *N.Y.*] 4/6 c 8° Camb. Press [83] 85

" Education and School *o.p.* [*pb.* 6/] c 8° Macmillan [67] 67

VICO, G. B. [1668–1744] —*v.* **C** § 65

WIDGERY, Wm. Hy. William Henry Widgery. Ed. W. K. Hill 3/ *n.* c 8° Nutt 94

Selns. fr. his wrgs., contg. a good deal of suggestive matter, often original; w. full Memoir.

WILDERSPIN, S. [1792–1866] System of Education [tr.] *o.p.* 8° *London* 70

" Infant Education [tr.] [poor children; to 7 years old] *o.p.* c 8° *London* [34] 75

Leitch, J. Muir —*in his* Practical Educationists, *ut* **D** § 156

---

# V: Pedagogical Psychology and Ethics

## 162: PEDAGOGICAL PSYCHOLOGY AND ETHICS (*a*): GENERALLY; CHILD-STUDY

*For* Treatises on Pure Psychology *v.* **C** § 71

*Bibliography* —*v.* **C** § 71

BAKER, J. H. Elem. Psychology, w. pract. applicns. to educ. & conduct $1 c 8° Maynard, *N.Y.* 90

BALDWIN, Dr Jos. Elementary Psychology & Education [Int. Ed. Ser.] $1 (4/6) c 8° Appleton [87] 91

" Psychology appl. to Art of Tchg. [Int. Ed. Ser.] $1·50 (6/) c 8° Appleton 92

BAYLEY, Dr W. C. The Educative Process $1·25 *n.* (5/ *n.*) c 8° Macmillan 05

A valuable presentn. of 'the basal principles of the educative process'.

BOOLE, Mary E. Preparation of the Child for Science—*ut* **D** § 167, *s.v.* Sciences

COMPAYRÉ, Prf. G. Elements of Psychology, tr. W. H. Payne $1 12° Lee & Shepard, *Boston* [90] 95

Especially adapted to the needs of young teachers.

" Psychology appl. to Education, tr. Payne [Pedag. Lib.] 90 c. c 8° Heath, *Boston* 94

Summary of educ. princs. deduced fr. psychol., admirably arrgd. and proportioned, but highly condensed and therefore stiff readg.

" Intellectual and Moral Developmt. of Child [tr.]—*ut* **C** § 71

DEXTER (T. F. G.) + GARLICK (A. H.) Psychology in the Schoolroom $1·50 (4/6) c 8° Longman 98

Comprehensive, but not always accurate on the psychological side.

DONALDSON, Prf. H. H. The Growth of the Brain—*ut* **C** § 71

HALL, Prf. G. Stanley Adolescence, 2 vols.—*ut* **C** § 71

The standard bk. on psychol. of youth and its relns. to physiol., anthropol., sociol., sex, religion, crime, educn. Constructive, abounding in facts and suggestions.

" Youth: its educn., regimen, hygiene [abgmt. of above] $1·50 *n.* (6/ *n.*) c 8° Appleton 07

HARRIS, Dr W. T. Psychologic Foundations of Education $1·50 (6/) c 8° Appleton 97

[Internat. Education Series.] A striking and comprehensive treatment.

*HERBART, J. F. Textbook in Psychology [tr.] and other works, *v.* **D** § 161

HOFFMANN, U. J. Science of Mind applied to Teaching; ill. $1·50 c 8° Fowler, *N.Y.* 85

HOPKINS, Louisa P. Educational Psychology: for parents and teachers 50 c. 12° Lee & Shepard, *Bost.* 87

HORNE, Prf. H. H. Psychological Principles of Education $1·75 *n.* (7/6 *n.*) c 8° Macmillan 06

JAMES, Prf. Wm. Talks to Teachers on Psychology $1·50 *n.* 8° Holt, *N.Y.* [99] 07

4/6 Longman. Couched in clearest and simplest English and well ill. by exx. drawn fr. common observn.

JUDD, C. F. Genetic Psychology for Teachers [Intern. Educ. Ser.] $1·20 *n.* (5/ *n.*) c 8° Appleton 03

**Laurie**, Prf. S. S. The Institutes of Education 6/6 8° Oliver & Boyd, *Edin.* [92] 09
$1·90 *n.* Macmillan, *N.Y.* 'An introduction to rational psychology', mainly of the text-bk. order, in pts. merely in outline, but the philosoph. groundwk. treated in full. Regards Will as the essential subject of educ., whose end is morality—morality being a state of will.

**Lindner**, Dr G. A. Manual of Empirical Psychology, tr. C. De Garmo $1 12° Heath, *Boston* 89
[Pedagogic Lib.] A good compact manual of psychology fr. the Herbartian standpoint.

**McLellan**, J. A. Applied Psychology $1·25 12° Educ. Pb. Co., *Boston* 89
Based on the *Psychology* of Prf. J. Dewey [*ut* **C** § 71]. A good and suggestive bk. for teachers.

**Maher**, Mich. [R.-C.] Psychology [Stonyhurst Philos. Ser.] 6/6 ($1·75 *n.*) c 8° Longman 90
The best Roman-Cath. bk. on the subject: sober, and scholarly.

Mancs. Univ.: Demonstrn. Schls. Record, No. 1. By J. J. Findlay 1/6 *n.* 8° Sherratt, *Mancs.* 08 *in prg.*

**Morgan**, Prf. C. Lloyd Psychology for Teachers; pref. by [Sir] J. G. Fitch 4/6 c 8° Arnold [94] 06
$1 Scribner, *N.Y.* A series of lects., epitomizing author's *Introd. to Comparative Psychology* [*ut* **C** § 71]. With additional studies.

**Münsterberg**, Prf. Hugo Psychology and the Teacher $1·50 (6/ *n.*) c 8° Appleton 09
[Pubns. of Univ. of Pennsylv.] Renders serviceable f. educ. purposes latest developmts. of psychol. laboratory.

**Oppenheim**, Dr N. Mental Growth & Control [Pers. Probl. Ser.] $1 *n.* (4/6 *n.*) c 8° Macmillan 02
Relates both physiol. and psychol. to growth of character, developmt. of mental power, educ. of imagin., control of emotns., traing. of reason, and guidance of will.

**Roark**, Prf. R. N. Psychology in Education $1 12° Amer. Book Co., *N.Y.* 95
An orderly and clear outline, suitable for the use of young teachers and Training Colleges.

**Royce**, J. Outlines of Psychology [Macm.'s Pedag. Lib.]—*ut* **C** § 71

**Schulte**, Dr R. Experimental Pyschology and Pedagogy [tr.]; ill. 15/ *n.* 8° G. Allen 11

***Sully**, Prf. Jas. Outlines of Psychology; *and* Teacher's Handbk. of Psychology—*ut* **C** § 71

**Thorndike**, E. Lee Principles of Teaching based on Psychology [6/6 *n.* Paul] $1·25 12° Seiler, *N.Y.* 06

**Wall**, Geo. Natural History of Thought [mainly educational] *o.p.* [*pb.* 12/6] 8° Trübner 89

**Warner**, Fcs. [*M.D.*] Lects. on Growth and Trg. of Mental Faculty [90 c. *n.* Putn., *N.Y.*] 4/6 c 8° Camb. Pr. 90

**Welton**, Prf. J. The Psychology of Education [v. readable] 7/6 *n.* 8° Macmillan 11

**Child-study** —*v. also* **C** § 71, *s.v.* Infant Psychol.; *and* **D** § 164

**Alcott** (Louisa M.) + **Pratt** (Anna B. A.) Comic Tragedies $1·50 c 8° Roberts, *Boston* 93
A colln. of dramas wr. by girls: interestg. for a study of dramatic activity in yg. people.

**Allen**, Mrs A. W. Home, School, and Vacation $1·25 *n.* c 8° Houghton, *Boston* 07

**Baldwin**, Prf. J. M. Mental Development in the Child and the Race—*ut* **C** § 71

**Barnes**, Prf. Earl Child Study, no. i–vii 8° Stanford Univ., *California* 93–5
A series of suggestive papers on child-study, of from 4 to 22 pp. each.

,, [ed.] Studies in Education $1·50 8° Stanford Univ., *California* 96–7
A series of 10 numbers, consisting of articles on Child-study and the History of Education.

**Bashkirtseff**, Marie Journal [tr.], *and* Letters—*ut* **K** § 35
Of some value as an introspective study of early girlhood. Vide note in **K** § 35.

**Birney**, Alice McL. Childhood; Introd. by Prf. G. S. Hall $1 *n.* 12° Stokes, *N.Y.* 05

**Brown**, Elmer E. [ed.] Notes on Children's Drawings 50 c. c 8° Univ. of Calif., *Berkeley* 97

**Bulow**, B'ess v. Marenholtz The Child and the Child Nature [tr.]—*ut* **D** § 165

**Burke**, C. E. Child Study & Education [75 c. Benziger, *N.Y.*] 2/ *n.* f 8° Browne & Nolan, *Dublin* 08
Forcible practical papers on guidg. princs. of moral and intell. traing. of children at home and at school. Emphasizes importance of child-study by parents.

**Carus**, Dr Paul Our Children $1 *n.* 8° *Open Ct.* Pb. Co., *Chicago* 07
4/6 *n.* Paul. Hints for parents and teachers.

**Chamberlain**, Dr A. F. The Child: study in evoln. of man—*ut* **C** § 71

,, The Child and Childhood in Folk-thought—*ut* **B** § 3

Child-Study Society: The Paidologist *Parkes Museum, Margaret St., Lond. qrtly.*

**Compayré**, Prf. G. Developmt. of Child in Later Infancy [tr.] [Int. Ed. Ser.] $1·20 *n.* (5/ *n.*) c 8° Appleton 02
Shd. have been classed in **C** § 71, w. author's *Intellectual and Moral Developmt. of Child*, of wh. it is the Second Pt.

**Crafts**, W. F. Childhood: the text-book of the age $1·50 c 8° Lee & Shepard, *Boston* 95
Fragmentary observations, based largely on Sunday-school experiences.

**Drummond**, W. B. Introduction to Child Study [$1·70 *n.* Longman, *N.Y.*] 6/ *n.* c 8° Arnold 07

**Dupanloup**, F'r F. A. P. The Child, tr. Kate Anderson—*ut* **C** § 71
A Rom.-Cath. treatmt. of the subj., wr. in early 19th cent., expoundg. a pt.-of-view different fr. that taken to-day.

**Gordy** (J. P.) + **Burnham** (W. H.) Apprenticeship and Study of Children *o.p.* c 8° *Boston* 93

**Grinnell**, Eliz. How John and I Brought up the Child 80 c. c 8° Am. S.S. Union, *Phila.* 91

**Hall**, Prf. G. Stanley Contents of Children's Minds [pp. 56] 25 c. 12° Kellogg, *N.Y.* 93

**Home**, H. The Child Mind: study in elem. ethology 1/6 *n.* 12° E. Mathews 06

Illinois Society for Child Study: Transactions, ed. C. C. Van Liew *Illinois in prg.*

Internatl. Congr. of Hygiene & Demography: Infancy, Childhd., & Schl.-life 8° Eyre & Spottiswoode 92
Conts. several papers bearing on the experimental study of children.

**Key**, Ellen Education of the Child, tr. [fr. Swedish] 50 c. (2/6 *n.*) c 8° Putnam 10

**King**, Irving The Psychology of Child Development $1 *n.* 12° Univ. Press, *Chicago* 03

KIRKPATRICK, E. A. Fundamentals of Child Study—*ut* **C** § 71
A discussn. of instincts and other factors in human developmt., w. practical applicns.

MACDONALD, Arth. The Experimental Study of Children *n.p.* Govt. Prg. Office, *Washington* 99

MANGOLD, Dr G. B. Child Problems [Citizen's Lib.] $1 *n.* (5/ *n.*) c 8° Macmillan 10

MEYER, Bertha The Child, Physically and Mentally [tr.] 50 c. Holbrook, *N.Y. n.d.* (93)

MOORE, Kathl. C. The Development of a Child *o p.* c 8° Macmillan, *N.Y.* 96
A painstaking study of a child, by its mother.

OPPENHEIM, Dr N. The Development of the Child—*ut* **C** § 71
By a hospital-physician. Much physiolog. matter; but many good educatl. hints as well.

OUROUSSOV, Mary Education from the Cradle [tr.] [for yg. mothers] 2/6 f 8° Bell 90

PREYER, Prf. W. Mind of the Child [tr.], *and* Mental Developmt. of the Child [tr.]—*ut* **C** § 71

RAND, Kath. E. The Childhood of an Affinity 50 c. 12° Arena Pb. Co., *Boston* 93
A retrospective study on early sex-attraction.

RUSSELL, E. H. Child Observations—*ut* **D** § 163, *s.v.* Imitation

SCUDDER, Hor. E. Childhood in Literature and Art: a study $1·25 c 8° Houghton, *Boston* 94
A literary treatmt. of child-nature. Incl. observns. on literature for children.

SHINN, Millicent W. Notes on Developmt. of a Child, Pts. i–ii, ea. 25 c.; iii–iv, 70 c. 8° Univ. of Calif., *Berkeley* 93–9
[Univ. of Calif. Studies.] Valuable classif. notes on a single child dur. her first 3 yrs. of life.

" Biography of a Baby $1·50 c 8° Houghton, *Boston* 00

SOWERBY, Millic. + Githa Childhood; ill. $1·50 8° Duffield, *N.Y.* 07

*SULLY, Prf. Jas. Studies of Childhood; *and* Children's Ways—*ut* **C** § 71

TAYLOR, Dr Alb. R. The Study of the Child—*ut* **C** § 71

THORNDIKE, E. Lee Notes on Child Study [Col. Univ. Contribs.] $1 *n.* 8° Macmillan [01] 03

TRACY, Fredk. Psychology of Childhood [Pedag. Lib.] 90 c. c 8° Heath, *Boston* 95

TYLER, J. M. Growth and Education $1·50 *n.* 12° Houghton, *Boston* 07

URWICK, W. E. The Child's Mind, its Growth and Training 4/6 *n.* c 8° Arnold 07
$1·50 Longman, *N.Y.* Process of mind-growth in conn. w. mechanism and processes of learng., reasong., etc. Genetic method.

WARNER, Fcs. [*M.D.*] The Children: how to study them [mainly phys. condns.] 1/6 f 8° Hodgson [87] 96

" Growth and Means of Traing. Mental Faculties *o.p.* c 8° Macmillan 90

" Study of Children and their School Training 4/6 *n.* ($1 *n.*) c 8° Macmillan 97
Emphasizes importance of physical nature of child as factor in traing. *V.* also **D** § 163, *s.v.* Brain, etc.

WASHBURNE, Mrs M. F. The Study of Child Life $1·50 *n.* 12° Am. Sch. of Home Econcs., *Chicago* 07

" The Mother's Year-Book; ill. $1·25 *n.* (5/ *n.*) 12° Macmillan 08
Applicns. of results of scientific child-study to probls. of 1st yr. of childhood.

WIGGIN, [Mrs] Kate D. Children's Rights—*ut* **D** § 165

WINSHIP (A. E.) + MONROE (W. S.) + STOWELL (Agn.) Child Study [31 pp.] *o.p.* New Engl. Pb. Co., *Bost.* 97

Yale Psychol. Laboratory: Studies, ed. Prf. E. W. Scripture, 6 vols.—*ut* **C** § 71
Incl. several papers of considerable value on child-research, mental and physical.

**Children: *Generally*** —*for* The Child in Ethnology *v.* **E** § 3

COOPER, Edw. H. The Twentieth-Century Child 6/ ($1·50) c 8° Lane [05] 05
A fresh, unconventional bk.; excellent reading, interspersed with humour.

DU BOIS, Patterson Beckonings of Little Hands [8 studs. of child-life] $1·25 c 8° Wattles, *Phila.* 95

GODFREY, Elizab. English Children in the Olden Time; 32 ill. 7/6 *n.* 8° Methuen [07]
A study of childhd. in Engld. fr. earliest times of wh. record remains to Victorian era. Characteristics, games, toys, dress, schooling, breeding. Several quaint tales and notes.

*GRAHAME, Kenneth The Golden Age; *and* Dream Days [ea. 1/ *n.* Nelson] ea. 3/6 *n.* c 8° Lane [04]

" The same bks.: ill. Maxfield Parrish ea. 7/6 *n.* (2 v. $5 *n.*) 8° Lane 06
The former espec. is a fascinatg. bk.: sketches of child-life w. all its fancies and illusions, brimming over w. humour.

HARKER, L. A. Romance of the Nursery 5/ *n.* ($1·25 *n.*) c 8° Lane 02

" The Little People 5/ ($1·25 *n.*) c 8° Lane 03
17 stories about children, full of the subtler side of child-character.

KELLY, Myra Little Aliens; 8 ill. $ 1·50 (6/) c 8° Longman 10
A ser. of stories based on experiences of a N.Y. teacher amg. poor Jewish and other school-children.

'LOTI, Pierre' [= L. M. J. VIAUD] The Romance of a Child [tr.] 25 c. c 8° Rand, *Chicago* 91
A suggestive reminiscent study of childhood.

MEYNELL, Alice The Children 3/6 *n.* ($1·25) c 8° Lane 96
Graceful essays on aspects of child-life, by one who knows the child 'through and through'.

PAGET, Steph. The Young People [charming essays] 3/6 *n.* c 8° Macmillan [ ] 11

SKRINE, Mary J. H. The World's Delight 6/ ($1·50) c 8° Lane 01
Studies of children of all classes and temperaments.

SMITH, Theodate L. [ed.] Aspects of Child Life and Education $1·50 *n.* c 8° Ginn, *Boston* 07
A colln. of papers, by Prf. G. Stanley HALL and his pupils, on childhd., its doings, sayings, thinkings, inclg. *On the Contents of Children's Minds on Entering Schl.* (by HALL).

SOWERBY, Githa Childhood; ill. by Millicent Sowerby 3/6 *n.* r 8° Chatto 07

TOLSTOY, C't L. N. Childhood, Boyhood, Youth [tr. fr. Russn.]—*ut* **K** § 56

WHITTIER, J. Greenleaf Child Life in Prose; ill. $1·50 c 8° Houghton, *Boston* 89

*America*

EARLE, Alice M. Child-life in Colonial Days—*ut* **F** § 67

*Japan* —*v. also* **E** § 37

BRAMHALL, M. St John The Wee Ones of Japan; ill. $1 16° Harper, *N.Y.* 94
A readable acc. of Japanese children. Useful for comparison.

**Child in Art** —*v.* **I** § 82

**Children's Sayings, etc.**

BARKER, H. J. Original English as wr. by Little Ones at Schl. 1/ f 8° Jarrold, *Norwich* 89

" Our Boys & Girls at Schl. 1/; Comic Schl. Tales 6*d.* f 8° Jarrold, *Norwich* 91; 06

" Merry Moments with Scholars 1/ *n.* c 8° Harper 09

HARRISON, W. Children, their Thoughts, Words, and Ways 2/6 c 8° J. Heywood, *Mancs.* [00] 04
A good collection of stories, anecdotes, and other matters relating to child-life.

PAUL, H. Clever Things said by Children *o.p.* c 8° *London* 82

SHEARER, D. Juvenile Wit and Humour 1/ c 8° *Edinburgh* [81] 81

SHEELY, Aaron Anecdotes and Humors of School Life $1·50 c 8° Bardeen, *Syracuse, N.Y.* 89

**Early School-Books**

A B C both in Engl. and Latin: ed. E. W. Shuckburgh 4/6 12° Stock [1538] 89
A facs. reprodn. of the earliest English reading-book.

Babees Book: early Engl. meals and manners 12/ 8° E. Engl. Text Soc. 67
With a Preface (*Education in Early England*) by Dr F. J. FURNIVALL. Modernized edn., ed. Edith RICKERT, 5/ *n.* 16° Chatto '08

BRADSHAW, Hy. On the A B C as Authorized Sch.-bk. in 16 Cent.—*in his* Coll. Papers, *ut* **K** § 3
This was a first bk. for childr., contg. not only alphabet but also elemts. of relig. instrn. BRADSHAW draws attentn. to edns. fr. 1538–88, and shows that something v. like it existed down to 1852 in Estab. Ch. of Scotl. An interesting contribn. to hist. of mediev. schl.-bks.

COMENIUS, Bp J. A. [1592–1671] Orbis Pictus—*ut* **D** § 161

FIELD, Mrs E. M. —*in her* The Child and his Book 6/ c 8° Wells Gardner [91] 92
Tho' this study is purely literary and fr. the outside, it is full of interest to studt. of hist. of Engl. educn. Commencg. w. earliest times (Druids !) and passg. thro' Mid. Ages to Puritan times, when children all became 'miserable little sinners', it ends at 1826; since wh. time author wisely refrains fr. mentiong. more than a few names. Her bk. forms excellent *mémoires pour servir*, and is v. interesting.

HAZLITT, W. Carew Schools, School Books, and Schoolmasters 7/6 c 8° Jarvis 87

JOHNSON, Clifton Old-Time Schools and School Books; facss. $2 *n.* (8/6 *n.*) c 8° Macmillan 04
Mainly on the old schls. and schoolbks. of Massachusetts, w. notes on those of other States.

New England Primer: ed. P. L. Ford $1·50 8° Dodd & Mead, *N.Y.* [97] 99
Reprint of the earliest edn., with illns. in facs., etc., and a history of its development.

TRUMBULL, J. H. The New England Primer and its Predecessors *Phila.* 82

TUER, And. W. History of the Horn Book; facs. ill. 6/ *n.* 4° Leadenhall Press [96] 97
The first edn., in 2 vols., 4° (42/ *n.*), is far the better. Incls. accs. of the A B C, the *Primer*, wooden and cardbd. battledores, samplers, gingerbread horn-bks., and tin alphabet book-rims.

Zodiacus Vitae: or Marcellus Palingenius Stellatus 2/ *n.* c 8° Wellby 08
Ed. Prf. Foster WATSON. Acc. (without a repr., but w. quotns. fr. GOOGE's tr.) of an old schoolbk. used in Engl. and foreign schls. in time of ELIZABETH—a satire on life, on Lat. hexameters, contg. a mass of classical learning: ea. of the 12 Bks. called after a sign of the zodiac.

## 163: PEDAGOGICAL PSYCHOLOGY AND ETHICS (*b*): SPECIAL DEPARTMENTS

**Apperception**

*LANGE, Dr Karl On Apperception [tr.], ed. C. De Garmo [Pedag. Lib.] $1 c 8° Heath, *Boston* 94
A very able bk. To Author belongs credit of elucidg. a psychol. method by wh. every probl. of the schoolroom can be directly examined. Strongly Herbartian. Apperception is Perception *plus* the connotations wh. become added to Perception, and this bk. is an applicn. of theory of Apperception to educn., as valuable to parent as to teacher who is responsible for children w. only 6 hours a day agst. former's 18—and the holidays.

ROOPER, T. G. Apperception; or Pot of Green Feathers [pp. 52; 50 c. Bardeen, *Syracuse*] 91

**Attention** —*v. also* **C** § 71, *s.v.* Attention (PILLSBURY, RIBOT, TITCHENER)

AIKEN, Cath. Methods of Mind Traing.: attentn. & memory $1 12° Am. Bk. Co., *N.Y.* 95

ARNOLD, Dr Felix Attention and Interest $1 *n.* (4/6 *n.*) c 8° Macmillan 10

HUGHES, J. L. [Canad.] Securing and Retaining Attention 50 c. 16° Kellogg, *N.Y.* [ ] 93

**Brain; Nervous System** —*v. also* **C** § 71

BROWNE, Sir J. Crichton Education and the Nervous System *o.p.* c 8° Cassell 84

HALLECK, R. Post The Education of the Central Nervous System $1 *n.* (5/ *n.*) c 8° Macmillan 96
'A study of Foundations, espec. of Sensory and Motor Training', an applicn. to pract. wk. of educn. of principle that nerve-cells are plastic only at a cert. period and must be trained then or not at all.

" Psychology and Psychic Culture—*ut* **C** § 71

WARNER, Dr Fcs. Nervous Syst. of Child: growth & health in educn. 4/6 *n.* ($1 *n.*) c 8° Macmillan 00

**Character** —*v. also* **A** § 113, *s.v.* Character

BAIN, Prf. Alex. Study of Character—*ut* **C** § 17

CLARK, H. W. Studies in the Making of Character 2 / *n.* c 8° R. Scott 10
ELLIS, F. H. Character Forming in School 3 / (90 c.) c 8° Longman 07
LEIGHTON, Prf. Gerald The Greatest Life 5 / *n.* c 8° Duckworth 08
Orig. and devel. of character. Advances theory th. all developmt., phys., ment., mor., and spiritual, is govd. by one law.
MACCUNN, Prf. Jno. Making of Character [educ. aspects of ethics] 2 /6 c 8° Camb. Press 00
MASON, Charl. M. Some Studies in Formn. of Character [Home Educ. Ser.] 3 /6 *n.* c 8° Paul 06
SCHOFIELD, Dr A. T. The Springs of Character [popular] 3 /6 8° Hodder 01
SOULSBY, Lucy H. M. Stray Thoughts on Character—*ut* **A** § 113, *s.v.* Character

**Concentration**

MILES, Eust. H. Power of Concentration: how to acquire it 3 /6 *n.* f 8° Methuen 07
PARKER, Col. F. W. Talks in Pedagogics: outline of theory of concentration [suggestive] $1·50 12° Kellogg, *N.Y. n.d.* (94)

**Emotions; Passion**

ABERCROMBIE, J. Philos. of the Moral Feelings, ed. Jac. Abbott [Engl. edn. *o.p.*] $1·05 12° Collins, *N.Y.* [ ] 74
BOOLE, Mary E. The Forging of Passion into Power 5 / *n.* 8° Daniel 10
Attempts to show how the normal and abnormal passions may be turned to good use. Vague, but often suggestive.
BRAY, Chas. Education of the Feelings
COBBE, Fces. P. Educn. of the Emotions—*in her* Scient. Spirit of the Age [essays] *o.p.* [*pb.* 6 /] c 8° Smith & Elder 88

**Eugenics** *v.* **H** § 43

**Habit**

RADESTOCK, Dr P. Habit and its Importce. in Educ. [tr.] [empirical; Ped. Lib.] 65 c. 12° Heath, *Boston* [82] 87
ROWE, Dr Stuart H. Habit-Formation & the Science of Teaching $1·50 *n.* (6 / *n.*) c 8° Longman 09
Based on an investign. of the formative value of Latin and Greek.

**Heredity** —*v. also* **C** § 71, **H** § 42

FOUILLÉE, Alf. Education fr. a National Standpoint [tr.]—*ut* **D** § 159*
Whil following the lines of GUYAU, it is more restricted to the practical problems.
GUYAU, J. M. Educ. and Heredity: a study in sociology [tr.] 3 /6 c 8° Walter Scott 91
$1·25 Scribner, *N.Y.* [Cont. Sci. Ser.] A useful contrib. to pract. pedagogics, w. excellent Introd. by Prf. G. F. STOUT.
HAYWARD, Dr F. H. Education and the Heredity Spectre 1 / *n.* c 8° Watts 08
An able vindicn. of Herbartian doctr., urging importce. of ideas as true startg.-pt. for educ. practice.
ROYCE, Sam. Deterioration and Race Education $2·50 c 8° Lee & Shepard, *Boston* 78

**Imagination**

GOSCHEN, J. G. Cultivation and Use of the Imagination [an address] 2 /6 c 8° Arnold 93
HINTON, C. Howard The Education of the Imagination 1 / c 8° Sonnenschein 88
MACMILLAN, Marg. Education through the Imagination 3 /6 c 8° Sonnenschein 04
RHOADES, J. The Training of the Imagination 1 / *n.* 16° Lane 08

**Imitation**

DEAHL, J. N. Imitation in Education [Columb. Univ. Contribs.] *o.p.* [*pb.* 60 c. *n.*] 8° Macmillan, *N.Y.* 00
HASKELL, Ellen M. Imitation in Children [pp. 18] *o.p. Worcester, Mass.* 95
RUSSELL, Prc. E. H. [ed.] Child Observations $1·50 c 8° Heath, *Boston* 96
[Pedagogical Lib.] Ser. 1: *Imitation and Allied Activities.* By Students of the State Normal School, Worcester, Mass.

**Intellectual Powers**

ABERCROMBIE, J. Intellectual Powers, ed. Jacob Abbott [Engl. edn. *o.p.*] $1·05 12° Collins, *N.Y.* [ ] 74

**Interest**

DE GARMO, Dr C. Interest and Education: doctr. of int. and its concrete applicn. $1 *n.* (4 /6 *n.*) c 8° Macmillan 02
OSTERMANN, W. Interest in its rel. to Pedagogy, ed. E. R. Shaw $1 c 8° Kellogg, *N.Y.* 03

**Language**

DEWEY, J. [Am.] The Psychology of Infant Language—*in* The Psychological Review, 1894
POLLOCK, Sir Fredk. An Infant's Progress in Language—*in* Mind, vol. iii [1878], pp. 392–401
TAINE, H. On Acquisition of Language by Children [tr.]—*in* Mind, v. ii [1877], pp. 252–9

**Memory**

COLERIDGE, S. T. Method of Mnemonics 2 / c 8° Griffin [49] *n.d.*

COPNER, Jas. Memoranda Mnemonica 3/6 c 8° Williams 93
A popular psychology of memory, with mnemonic devices.

FULLER, H. H. Art of Memory: pract. syst. of memory culture $3 8° Nat. Pb. Co., *St Paul, Minn.* 98

GREEN, Dr F. W. Edridge Memory and its Cultivation; ill. [Internat. Scient. Ser.] 5/ c 8° Paul 97
$1·50 Appleton, *N.Y.* Not quite up-to-date on the psychological side. The practical rules are good.

,, Memory: its local relations and cultivation 6/ c 8° Baillière [88] 91

KAY, Dav. Memory: what it is, and how to improve it [Int. Sci. Ser.] 6/ c 8° Paul 88
$1·50 Appleton, *N.Y.* W. numerous quotns. fr. sundry metaphys. and psycholog. authorities, who also figure largely in footnotes.

,, The Science of Memory 3/6 c 8° Paul 02

LOISETTE, Prf. A. A. Assimilative Memory: how to attend and never forget $2·50 *n.* (10/6) 8° Funk & Wagnalls 98
The only published account of LOISETTE's system.

LUKENS, H. T. Connection between Thought & Memory [Pedag. Lib.] $1 c 8° Heath, *Boston* 95

MILES, Eust. H. How to Remember: with or without memory systs. 2/6 c 8° Warne 01

PICK, E. Lectures on Memory Culture $1 *n.* 16° Kellogg, *N.Y.* 99

**Observation** —*v. also* **D** § 167, *s.v.* Nature Study

GILL, Jno. Art of Teaching Young Minds to Observe and Think *o.p.* [*pb.* 2/] 12° Longman 72

**Order and Correlation of Studies**

HARRIS, Dr W. T., etc. Rept. on Correln. of Studs. by Committee of 15 *o.p.* Pb. Sch. Pb. Co., *Bloomington* 95

HILL, Dr T. The True Order of Studies $1 12° Putnam, *N.Y.* 76

**Scholar (The)**

FICHTE, J. G. Nature of the Scholar, & its Manifestation—*in his* Popular Writings [tr.], 2 vols., *ut* **C** § 28

**Sex**

CLARKE, Dr E. H. Sex in Education $1·25 12° Houghton, *Boston* 73

**Stimulus**

SIDGWICK, A. On Stimulus [30 c. *n.* Putn., *N.Y.*; repr. fr. Three Lects. on Educn. *ut* **D** § 161] 1/ 12° Camb. Press 89

**Suggestion; Hypnotism**

KEATINGE, M. W. Suggestion in Education [$1·75 *n.* Macmillan, *N.Y.*] 4/6 *n.* 8° Black 07
A sound contribn. to pedag. liter., by a follower of PAULHAN and RIBOT, makg. good use of their (and other) material.

**Thinking; Reasoning** —*v. also* **C** § 71

SCHAEFFER, N. C. Thinking and Learning to Think $1·25 *n.* c 8° Lippincott, *Phila.* 00
[Lippincott's Educ. Ser.] A careful anal. of psychol. bases of good thinking. Clear, and pointedly ill.

---

# VI: Methods of Instruction

## 163*: METHODS: GENERALLY

*Vide also* **D** §§ 156–161

BARNETT, P. A. [ed.] Teaching & Organization: w. spec. ref. to second. schls. 6/6 ($2) c 8° Longman 97
24 papers, by var. wrs., on tchg. of *Classics, Engl. Gram., Mod. Langs., Geogr., Sci., Wrg. and Drawg., Math., Readg. and Spkg.*, w. introd. ch., by EDR., on *Criteria in Educn.* [defence of empiricism].

BOYER, C. C. Modern Methods for Teachers $1·50 8° Lippincott, *Phila.* 09

CRONSON, Bern. Methods in Elem. School Studies $1·25 *n.* 12° Macmillan, *N.Y.* 06

DE GARMO, Dr C. The Essentials of Method [Pedag. Lib.] 65 c. 12° Heath, *Boston* 89
An able little bk. discussg. the essential forms of right meths. in tchg.: mainly psychological (Herbartian).

HOOSE, J. H. Methods of Teaching $1 12° Bardeen, *Syracuse, N.Y.* 79

KIDDLE (Hy.) + HARRISON (F.) + CALKINS (N. A.) How to Teach $1 12° Van Antwerp, *Cincinnati* [77] 94
A graded course of instruction and manual of methods.

MACALISTER, Jas. Manuals of Graded Course of Instruction in the Philadelphia Public Schools, 3 vols. 8° *Philadelphia* 87

MCMURRY, Dr C. A. Elements of General Method [Herbartian] 90 c. *n.* (4/ *n.*) c 8° Macmillan [92] 03

,, Course of Study in Eight Grades, 2 vols. ea. 75 c. (2 v., 6/6 *n.*) c 8° Macmillan 06
The 8 grades of the Amer. Common School, correspg. to the wk. done in Engl. publ. elementary schools.

PARKER, F. W. Notes of Talks on Teaching $1 c 8° Kellogg, *N.Y.* [83] 85
Reported by Leila E. PATRIDGE. On methods of teaching the elementary subjects.

PRINCE, J. T. Courses of Study and Methods of Teaching 85 c. 12° Ginn, *Boston* 88

RAUB, Alb. N. Methods of Teaching [pp. 415] *o.p.* c 8° *Lock Haven* 84

Special Reports on Educational Subjects [Blue-books] *v.pp.* r 8° Wyman 96 *sqq.*, *in prg.*
i: *Educ. in Gt. Brit. and Irel.; Frce.; Germy.; Denmk.; Belg.;* etc., 3/4, '96–7
ii.: *Educ. in Engld. and Wales; Phys. Educ.; Heuristic Meth. of Tchg.; University Educ. in Frce.*, 6/2, '98
iii: *National Organizn. of Educ. in Switz.; Secondary Educ. in Prussia, Baden, and Sweden; Tchg. of Mod. Langs.; Higher Commerc. Educ. in Frce., Germy., and Belg.*, 6d., '98
iv: *Educ. Systs. of Canada, Newfdld., W. Indies*, 4/8, '01
v: *Educ. Systs. of Cape Col., Natal, Australia, N. Zeal., Ceylon, Malta*, 4/, '01
vi: *Prepar. Schls. f. Boys: place in Engl. Second. Educ.*, 2/3½, '00
vii: *Rural Educ. in Frce.*, 1/4, '02
viii: *Educ. in Scandin., Switz., Holland, Hung., etc.*, 3/2, '02
viii (suppl.): *Educ. in Netherl.; Schl. Traing. and Early Employmt. of Lancs. Children*, 5/, '02–3
ix: *Educ. in Germy.*, 2/7, '02
x–xi: *Educ. in U.S.A.*, 2 Pts., 2/3, 2/6, '02
xii: *Educ. Systs. of W. Indies, Centr. Amer., St Helena, Cyprus, Gibr.* 2/, '05.
xiii: *Educ. Systs. of W. Africa, Basutold., S. Rhodesia, E. Afric. Protectorate, Uganda, Mauritius, Seychelles*, 1/8, '05
xiv: *Educ. Systs. of Malay States, Hong Kong, Straits Settlemts., Fiji, Falkld. Isl.*, 1/8, '05
xv–xvi: *Schl. Traing. f. Home Duties of Women*, Pt. i [*U.S.*], 1/9, ii [*Belg., Swed., Norw., Denm., Switz., Fce.*], 1/6, '05–6
xvii: *Schls. Publ. and Priv. in N. of Eur.*, 8d., '07
xviii: *Educ. and Trg. of Fch. Primary Tchr.*, 1/, '07
xix: *Schl. Traing. for Home Duties of Women*, Pt. iii [*Germ., Austr.*], 7½d., '07
xx: *Tchg. of Classics in Sec. Schls. in Germy.*, 9½d., '09
xxi: *Schl. Excursions and Vacation Schls.*, 5½d., '07
xxii: *Provisn. f. Childr. und. Compuls. Schl. Age in Belg., Frce., Germy., Switz.*, 1/3, '09
xxiii: *Educn. in Russia*, 2/5, '09
xxiv: *Secondary Educn. in Frce. in prep.*

SPENCER, Dr Fredc. [ed.] Chapters on the Aims and Practice of Teaching 6/ c 8° Camb. Press 97
*Gk.* (Prf. W. Rhys ROBERTS); *Lat.* (J. L. PATON); *Fch., Germ.* (Edr.); *Engl.* (A. S. WAY); *Hist.* (Prf. J. E. LLOYD); *Geogr.* (H. Y. OLDHAM); *Alg.* (Prf. G. B. MATHEWS); *Geom.* (W. P. WORKMAN); *Phys. Sci.* (Prf. R.W. STEWART); *Chem.* (Prf. H. E. ARMSTRONG); *Botany* (Prf. R. W. PHILIPPS); *Physiol.* (Dr Alex HILL).

SWETT, Jno. Methods of Teaching $1·25 c 8° Harper, *N.Y.* 81
TAYLOR, Jno. Notes of Lessons f. Young Teachers 50 c. *n.* c 8° Schl. Supply Co., *Boston* 89
VAN WIE, C. B. Methods in Common Branches 75 c. c 8° Bardeen, *Syracuse, N.Y.* 86
WELTON (Prf. Jas.) + BLANDFORD (F. G.) Principles and Methods of Teaching 5/6 c 8° Clive [04] 09
WICKERSHAM, J. P. Methods of Instruction $1·25 c 8° Lippincott, *Phila. n.d.*
WINTERBURN, Rosa V. Methods in Teaching [the Stockton meths.] $1·25 *n.* (5/ *n.*) c 8° Macmillan 07
ZIMMERN, Alice Meths. of Educn. in U.S. [Rept. to Gilchr. Trustees] 3/6 c 8° Sonnenschein 94

## 164: METHODS OF INSTRUCTION (*a*): HOME EDUCATION (GENERALLY)

ABBOTT, Dr E. A. Hints on Home Teaching 3/ c 8° Seeley [83] 83
AREY, Mrs H. E. G. Home and School Training 75 c. c 8° Lippincott, *Phila.* 84
BALLIN, Ada S. From Cradle to School [a practical bk.] 3/6 c 8° Constable 02
BARNARD, Amy B. Home Training of Children [practical] 3/6 *n.* Pilgrim Press 10
FITZ, Rachel K. + Dr G. W. Problems of Babyhood $1·25 *n.* f 8° Holt, *N.Y.* 06
3/6 *n.* Bell. On *Building a Constitution*, and *Forming a Character*. Constructive.
GILMAN, Charlotte P. [Mrs STETSON] Concerning Children $1·25 (6/) c 8° Putnam [00]
Advocates new methods of training children, which would almost supersede ordinary home influence.
GORDON, Dr H. Laing The Modern Mother; ill. 6/ *n.* 8° Laurie 09
Grlhd, motherhd., infancy. Heredity, environment, educn., schls, home-trg., etc.
HITCHING, Wilena Home Management: a 3-yrs' course f. schls. 2/6 c 8° Chambers 10
KENNEDY, Jno. The School and the Family: ethics of schl. relns. $1 16° Harper, *N.Y.* 78
LYTTELTON, Rev. E. Mothers and Sons: probls. on home training of boys 3/6 c 8° Macmillan [93] 93
A sensible little bk. dealing in a pract. way w. important quests. in public-schl. boy's educ.
MANN (Mary) + PEABODY (Eliz. P.) The Moral Culture of Infancy $1·25 12° Steiger, *N.Y.* [69] 74
MARTINEAU, Harriet Household Education [$1·25 Houghton, *Boston*] 2/6 12° Smith & Elder [49] 76
MASON, Charl. M. Home Education Series, vols. i–iv ea. 3/6 *n.* c 8° Paul [86–06] *v.y.*
*Home Education* [lectures]; *Parents and Children*; *Ourselves*; *School Education*.
MOSHER, Martha B. Child Culture in the Home $1 12° Revell, *N.Y.* 98
3/6 Low. 16 practical chapters; not original, but well expressed.
PEABODY, Eliz. P. The Home, Kindergarten and Primary School $1 *n.* 12° Heath, *Boston* 86
3/ Sonnenschein. Introd. by Eliz. A. MANNING.
PESTALOZZI, J. H. [1746–1827] How Gertrude Teachers her Children [tr.]—*ut* **D** § 161
SHIRREFF, Emily A. Home Educn.; *and* Kindergarten at Home—*ut* **D** § 165
TAYLOR, Isaac Home Education *o.p.* [*pb.* 5/] c 8° Bell [38] 67

## 165: METHODS OF INSTRUCTION (*b*): KINDERGARTEN

**Bibliography:** WALTER (L.) Die Fröbel-Literatur 2m.40 8° Huhle, *Dresden* 81
A list of KG. books since 1838, classified both chronologically and by standpoint of writers.

### Theoretical, Expository, Historical

BALLIN (Ada S.) + WELLDON (E. A.) Kindergarten System Explained 3/6 4° F. L. Ballin [ ] 03
BARNARD, Dr Hy. [ed.] Kindergarten and Child Culture Papers [by var. wrs.] $3·50 m 8° *Hartford* 84
BLOW, Susan E. Letters to a Mother on Philos. of Froebel [Int. Ed. Ser.] $1·50 (6/) c 8° Appleton 99
" Educational Issues in Kindergarten [Int. Educ. Ser.] $1·50 *n.* (6/) c 8° Appleton 08

**BÜLOW**, B'ess v. Marenholtz The Child and Child Nature, tr. Alice M. Christie 3/ c 8° Sonnenschein [79]
,, Hand-work & Head-work: reln. to one another [tr.] 3/ c 8° Sonnenschein 83
,, The New Educn. by Work, acc. to Froebel's Meth. [tr.] *o.p.* c 8° *Camden* 76
Bülow-Wendhausen, B'ess v. [niece] Life of B'ess v. Marenholtz Bülow [tr.], 2 v. $3·50 *n.* 8° Harison, *N.Y.* 02
FERRIS, Carrie S. Sunday Kindergarten: Game, Gift, Story $10·25 *n.* 8° Univ. Press, *Chicago*
FROEBEL, Friedr. [1782–1852] Autobiography, tr. H. K. Moore + Em. Michaëlis [$1 Bardeen, *Syr.*] 3/ c 8° Sonnenschein [86] 09
,, Educn. of Man, tr. W. N. Hailman; w. notes $1·50 (6/) c 8° Appleton [87] 06
[Internat. Educ. Ser.] Measures every educational activity by its influence on character.
,, ,, tr. W. H. Herford, *s.t.* The Student's Froebel, 2 Pts. ea. 2/6 c 8° Pitman 93–4
75 c. [Pedag. Lib.] Heath, *Boston*. Passages adapted fr. *Die Erziehung der Menschheit.* Pt. i: *Theory of Educ.*: ii: *Pract. of Educ.*
,, Letters on the Kindergarten, tr. E. Michaëlis + H. K. Moore 3/ c 8° Sonnenschein [89]
$1·50. Bardeen, *Syracuse, N.Y.* An interesting and compreh. colln. of his letters, dating fr. 1838 to 1852, and all rel. to the KG. and its principles.
,, Letters, ed. A. H. Heinemann; w. notes $1·25 12° Lee & Shepard, *Boston* 93
,, Pedagogics of the Kindergarten, tr. Josephine Jarvis, 2 Pts. ea. $1·50 c 8° Appleton 95–9
[Intern. Educ. Ser.] Tr. of the essays of FROEBEL coll. by Wichard LANGE, *s.t. Die Pädagogik des Kindergartens* (Berlin '61). Its chief value is its thoroughgoing discussn. of the first five 'Gifts'.
Bowen, H. C. Froebel and Educn. by Self-Activity [Gt. Educrs.; $1 *n.* Scrib., *N.Y.*] 5/ c 8° Heinemann [92] 03
Bülow, Bar'ess v. Marenholtz Reminiscences of Froebel, tr. Mrs Horace Mann $1·20 c 8° Lee & Shepard, *Boston* [77] 82
Cole, P. R. Herbart and Froebel: an attempt at sythesis—*ut* **D** § 161, *s.v.* Herbart
Ebers, Geo. Story of my Life fr. Childhood to Manhood [tr.] $1·25 c 8° Appleton, *N.Y.* 93
Incl. a full acc. of FROEBEL and his institution at Keilhau.
Hanschmann, A. B. Froebel: developmt. of his ideas in his life [tr.] 5/ c 8° Sonnenschein [97] 05
Hayward, Dr F. H. Educational Ideas of Pestalozzi and Froebel—*ut* **D** § 161, *s.v.* Pestalozzi
Shirreff, Emily A. Froebel: sketch of life, w. his letters [tr.] to his wife 2/ c 8° Chapman [77] 87
Snider, D. J. Life of Froebel, Founder of the Kindergarten $1·25 8° Sigma Pb. Co., *St Louis* 00
White, Jessie The Educational Ideas of Froebel 1/ f 8° Clive 05
Froebel Society: Essays on Kindergarten deliv. bef. Froebel Society 3/ c 8° Sonnenschein [80] 92
By Emily SHIRREFF, Anna BUCKLAND, Mrs. HOGGAN, H. Keatley MOORE, Eleanor HEERWART, etc.
HAILMAN, W. N. KG. Culture in Family & KG. [chfly. f. mothers] 75 c. 12° Am. Bk. Co., *N.Y.* [73]
HUGHES, J. L. [Canad.] Froebel's Educatl. Laws f. all Tchrs. [Int. Ed. Ser.] $1·50 (6/) c 8° Appleton 97
LEWIS, Ellen 'A.L.' Scheme of Advanced Kindergarten, Pts. i–iii 2/, 2/, 2/6 *n.* 4° Arnold, *Leeds* 94, 95, 01
LYSCHINSKA (Mary J.) + MONTEFIORE (Theresa G.) Ethical Teachgs. of Froebel [2 essays] 2/6 c 8° Paul 89
PEABODY, Eliz. P. Lectures in Traing. Schls. for Kindergartners [Pedag. Lib.] $1 c 8° Heath, *Boston* 93
,, The Home, the Kindergarten, and the School—*ut* **D** § 164
PESTALOZZI, J. H. —*v.* **D** § 161
POULSSON, Emilie Love and Law in Child Training Milton Bradley, *Springfd.* 00
SHIRREFF, Emily A. The Kindergarten: principles of Froebel's system 1/4 c 8° Sonnenschein [76] 87
,, Home Education in rel. to the Kindergarten 1/6 12° Chapman 84
,, Kindergarten at Home: pract. hdbk. f. mothers 3/6 c 8° Clive [84] 03
SMITH, Nora A. The Children of the Future [$1 Hougton, *Boston*] 3/6 *n.* c 8° Constable
VANDERWALKER, Nina C. The Kindergarten in American Education $1·25 *n.* (5/ *n.*) c 8° Macmillan 08
WIGGIN, [Mrs] Kate D. Children's Rights: a bk. of nursery logic $1 16° Houghton, *Boston* [92]
Readable essays on *Children's Playthings, What shall Children read?, Other People's Children, Rel. of K.-G. to School,* arguing strongly in favour of KG.
,, The Kindergarten $1 16° Harper, *N.Y.* 93
,, + SMITH (Nora A.; sister) The Republic of Childhood, 3 vols. ea. $1 c 8° Houghton, *Bost.* 95–6
Each 5/ Gay. i: *Froebel's Gifts*; ii: *Froebel's Occupns.*; iii: *KG. Princs. and Practice.* Full of valuable hints.

**Practical**

BATES, Loïs Kindergarten Guide; 16 col. pl. & 200 ill. [purely practical] 6/ ($1·50) c 8° Longman 97
FERRIS, Carrie S. Sunday Kindergarten: game, gift, story; ill. $1·25 *n.* 8° Univ. Pr., *Chicago* 09
GOLDAMMER, H. The Kindergarten: guide to Froebel's syst. [tr.]; ill. [10/6 Williams] 10m. 8° Habel, *Berlin* 85
KÖHLER, Aug. Die Praxis des Kindergartens, 3 vols.; 361 pl. ea. 4m.60 8° *Weimar* [70–76] 76–82
The same, tr. Mary Gurney, pt. i [First Gifts]; ill. 2/6 4° Myers [77] 90

KRAUS-BOELTE (Maria) + KRAUS (Jno.) Kindergarten Guide, 10 Pts.; ill. ea. 35 c. to $1 8° Steiger, *N.Y.* 77–92

LYSCHINSKA, Mary — Principles of the Kindergarten, ill. — 4/6 s 8° Pitman [80] 86

NEWMAN, Carrie S. — The Kindergarten in the Home; ill. — $1·50 c 8° Page, *Boston* 09

WIEBE, Prf. E. — The Paradise of Childhood — $2 4° Milton Bradley, *Springfd.* [7–] 96
A manual of instruction and practical guide to the KG.; 74 good plates.

**Music; Songs; Games**

BATES, Lois — Games w. Music, Actn. Songs, and Guessg. Rhymes — 2/6 (80 c.) c 8° Longman 01

BERRY (Ada) + MICHAËLIS (Em.) — Kindergarten Songs and Games — 1/6 c 8° Myers [ ]

CAMERON, Marg. — Games, Songs, and Recitations for the Kindergarten — 2/ 4° Simpkin 99

CURWEN, J. — Songs and Tunes for Education — [tonic-solfa] 3/ r 8° Curwen [ ] 00

FROEBEL, Friedr. — Mothers' Songs and Games, tr. Fces. + Emily Lord; ill. — 7/6 8° Rice [85] 95
Tr. of *Mutter-u. Kose-Lieder.* Conts. all orig. ill. (of wh. 46 full-page), and orig. music (80 pp.), rearrgd. f. children's voices, w. pianof. accomp.

" — The same, *s.t.* Mother-Play, tr. and ed. Henrietta R. Eliot + Sus. E. Blow, 2 v. ea. $1·50 (6/) c 8° Appleton 95; 95
[Intern. Educ. Ser.] i: *The Mottoes and Commentaries* [verse tr., by ELIOT; chfly. for mothers and tchrs.]; ii: *The Songs and Music* [by BLOW] is the children's bk.

" — The same, tr. Fannie E. Dwight + J. Jarvis — $2 f° Lee & Shepard, *Boston* 78

Blow, Susan E. — Symbolic Education — [Intern. Educ. Ser.] $1·50 (6/) c 8° Appleton 94
A discussn. of foundns. of philos. of FROEBEL as found in *Mothers' Songs and Games*, w. view to shew. claims of KG. as a corner-stone of educn.

GARDINER, Alfonzo [ed.] — Songs, Recitations for Kindergarten, etc. — 2/6 *n.* 4° Simpkin 04

HAILMAN, E. L. — Songs, Games, and Rhymes for Kindergarten — $1·75 12° Milton Bradley, *Springfd.* 87

HEERWART, Eleonore — Music for the Kindergarten — 2/6 8° Boosey 77

HIDDEN, J. A. — Garden Game and other Songs — 75 c. 8° Milton Bradley, *Springfd.* 09

HUBBARD, Clara B. — Merry Songs and Games — [for Kindergartens] $3 8° Balmer, *St Louis* 81

HUMPHREYS, Jennett — Laugh and Learn — [nursery lessons and games] 2/6 r 16° Blackie [ ] 01

JAMES, F. — Infant School Songs, 5/; Imperial Action Songs, 3/6 — 8° Curwen 85; 89

KRIEGE, Alma L. — Rhymes and Tales for KG. and Nursery — 50 c. c 8° Steiger, *N.Y.* 76

MULLEY (Jane) + TABRAM (M. E.) — Songs and Games for our Little Ones — 1/ c 8° Sonnenschein [81]

PEARSON (W. W.) — Action Songs f. Schl. and Concert — [wds. by E. Oxenford] 2/6 8° Simpkin 03

**Sloyd** — *v. inf., s.v.* Technical Education, etc.

## 166: METHODS OF INSTRUCTION (*c*): PRIMARY EDUCATION; INFANT SCHOOL

BEEBE, Kath. — The First School Year — [pp. 147] *o.p.* c 8° Werner, *Chicago* 95

BÉESAU, Amable — The Spirit of Education [tr.] — $1·25 c 8° Bardeen, *Syracuse, N.Y.* 81

BROWN, Mabel A. — Child Life in our Schools; ill. — 3/6 *n.* 4° Philip [06] 07
A manual of method for teachers in infant-schools.

CURRIE, Jas. — Princs. and Pract. of Early and Infant School Educn. $1·25 16° Kellogg, *N.Y.* 87

GUNN, J. — The Infant School: principles and methods — 3/6 c 8° Nelson 04

HAGMANN, J. G. — Reforms in Primary Education [tr.] — 2/6 *n.* c 8° Williams 06

HAILMAN, W. N. — Primary Methods — 75 c. c 8° Barnes, *N.Y.* 87

HOARE, Mrs — Hints on Early Education — 1/6 12° S.P.C.K. [20] 05

JACOBI, Mary Putnam — Physiolog. Notes on Primary Educ., and Study of Lang. — $1 (4/) c 8° Putnam, *N.Y.* 89

LAURIE, Prf. S. S. — Primary Instruction in relation to Education — 4/ c 8° Simpkin [67] 99

" — Education and Primary Instruction — 3/6 c 8° Thin, *Edin.* [84]

MCMILLAN, Marg. — Early Childhood; 5 ill. — 3/6 c 8° Sonnenschein 00
A sensible book: includes remarks on Oral Training, Arm and Manual Training, Literature and Children, etc.

MALLESON, Mrs Fk. — Notes on the Early Training of Children — 1/ c 8° Sonnenschein [84] 86
Amer. edn. in Pedag. Lib. 75 c. Heath, *Boston.* Sound and practical advice.

NORRIS, Rev. W. F. — Elementary Schools [Handbks. f. the Clergy] 2/6 *n.* (90 c. *n.*) c 8° Longman 04

PERRY, Arth. C. — Problems of the Elementary School — (5/ *n.*) 8° Appleton 10
Organization of the elementary school and relation thereto of the curriculum and moral training.

PLAISTED, Laura L. — The Early Education of Children; ill. — 4/6 *n.* ($1·50) c 8° Clar. Press 09
A bk. for the teacher, showg. in detail the applicn. of princs., examples of wk., methods, and curricula. A good bk.

QUICK, Rev. R. H. — Thoughts and Suggestions about Teaching Children—*in his* Essays, *ut* **D** § 156

SALMON (D.) + HINDSHAW (Winif.) Infant Schools: history and theory — 4/6 ($1·50 *n.*) c 8° Longman 04

SINCLAIR, S. B. — The First Year at School — 70 c. c 8° Kellogg, *N.Y.* 94

## 167: METHODS OF INSTRUCTION (*d*): SPECIAL SUBJECTS

**Agriculture** — *v. also* **I** § 24

AIKMAN, C. M. — Agric. Educn. in this Country and Abroad — [pp. 22] *o.p.* 8° *Glasgow* 89

BRICKER, G. A. — Teaching of Agriculture in the High School — (4/6 *n.*) c 8° Macmillan 11

DAVIS, Benj. M. — Recent Development of Agricultural Education 8° Univ. Press, *Chicago in prep.*

JEWELL, J. R. Agric. Educatn., incl. Nature Study [doctor's thesis] *n.p.* 8° Govt. Prg. Off., *Washington* 07

SOMERVILLE, Prf. W. Beargs. of Educ. & Sci. in Pract. Agric. [30 c. *n.* Putn., *N.Y.*] 1/ 8° Camb. Press 00

" — Place of Rural Econy. in a Univ. Curriculum — 1/ *n.* (35 c.) 8° Clar. Press 07

WALLACE, R. Agricultural Education [pp. 23] *o.p.* 8° *Edinburgh* 85
WRIGHTSON, Prf. J. Princs. of Agric. Practice as an Instructional Subj. 5/ c 8° Chapman [88] 90
**Architecture:** Institute of British Architecture Papers on Education [pp. 84] 8° Inst. of Brit. Architecture 87
SHAW (R. Norman) + JACKSON (T. G.) [eds.] Architecture a Profession or an Art 9/ 8° Murray 92
Thirteen short essays, by various writers, on the qualifications and training of architects. A useful book.
TRAVERS, W. J. Architectural Education [history; & reforms] 4/ *n.* 8° Harrison & Jehring 08
**Arithmetic; Algebra; Number**—*v. also* Mathematics, *inf.*
CROOK, C. W. Notes of Lessons on Arithc., Mensurn., Pract. Geom., 2 v. ea. 3/ c 8° Pitman 08
FITCH, [Sir] J. G. Methods of Teaching Arithmetic [pp. 36] *o.p.* c 8° *London* 72
GRUBE, A. W. Method of Teaching Arithmetic [tr.] [heuristic meth.] c 8° Kellogg, *N.Y.* 89
Badanes, S. Falsity of Grube Meth. of Tchg. Arithc. [pp. 47] *o.p.* c 8° *New York* 95
Seeley, Levi Grube's Method Explained and Illustrated $1 12° Kellogg, *N.Y.* 88
Soldan, Louis Grube's Method: two essays 30 c. c 8° Winchell, *Chicago* 78
HARTLEY, J. A. [Austral.] Teacher's Manual of Elementary Arithmetic c 8° *Adelaide* 87
HOOSE, J. H. Pestalozzian First-Year Arithmetic 50 c. c 8° Bardeen, *Syracuse, N.Y.* 82
HUNTER, J. H. Short Methods in Arithmetic *o.p.* c 8° Longman 84
JACKMAN, W. S. Number Work in Nature Study *o.p.* c 8° *Chicago* 93
LANGLEY, E. M. A Treatise on Computation 3/6 ($1) c 8° Longman 95
A useful bk., givg. acc. of chief general meths. for arriving at rapidity of numerical calculations.
LEFEVRE, Arth. Number and its Algebra [Pedagogical Lib.] $1·25 c 8° Heath, *Boston* 96
LIVERSEY, T. J. How to Teach Arithmetic [pp. 95] *o.p.* c 8° *London* 80
McLELLAN (J. A.) + DEWEY (J.) The Psychology of Number [Intern. Ed. Ser.] $1·50 (6/) c 8° Appleton 95
With its applications to methods of teaching arithmetic.
McMURRY, C. A. Special Method in Arithmetic 70 c. *n.* (3/ *n.*) c 8° Macmillan 05
MARTIN, J. L. Teaching of Pract. Arithmetic to Junior Classes 2/6 c 8° Harrap 08
NORMAN, J. S. The Teaching of Arithc. to Simple Proportion 1/ *n.* c 8° Sonnenschein 08
PALIN, E. F. The Best Methods of Teaching Arithmetic 1/ c 8° Harrison, *Ripon* 90
REED (E. M.) + WENTWORTH (G. A.) First Steps in Number 90 c. c 8° Ginn, *Boston* 87
REINER, C. Lessns. in Number as given in a Pestalozzian Schl. *o.p.* c 8° Bardeen, *Syracuse, N.Y.* 93
SONNENSCHEIN, Edith A. The Elements of Number, Pts. i, ii, v 2*d.*, 2*d.*, 1/ c 8° Sonnenschein 97
SPEER, W. W. Primary Arithmetic: for use of teachers 40 c. c 8° Ginn, *Boston* 96
**Army, Education for the** —*v.* Military, *inf.*
**Art: Generally** —*v. also sup., s.v.* Architecture; *inf., s.v.* Drawing
BROWN, Prf. G. Baldwin Fine Art as Branch of University Study c 8° *Edinburgh* 81
CHESNAU, E. Education of an Artist [tr.]; ill. [Fine Art Lib.] 5/ c 8° Cassell 86
COUTURE, Thos. Conversations on Art Methods $1·25 c 8° Putnam, *N.Y.* 79
CRANE, Walt. Relation of Art to Education and Life *o.p.* c 8° Leek Press 93
DAVIDSON, Thos. The Place of Art in Education [a lecture] 24 c. 16° Ginn, *Boston* 85
HIND, C. L. Education of an Artist; ill. [$2·50 Macmillan, *N.Y.*] 7/6 *n.* 8° Black 06
HOLLAND, Chas. Design for Schools: hdbk. for teachers; ill. 6/ *n.* ($1·90 *n.*) r 8° Macmillan 02
HULME, Prf. F. E. Art Instruction in England *o.p.* [*pb.* 3/6] f 8° Longman 87
LANGL, Jos. Modern Art Education, tr. S. R. Köhler 75 c. c 8° Prang, *Boston* 75
Austrian Offic. Rept. at Vienna Exhib. 1873. On the pract. and æsthet. culture of mod. art-educ.
PAPWORTH, W. A. Art Education [pp. 76] *o.p.* c 8° *London* 89
PARTRIDGE, W. O. Art for America $1 c 8° Roberts, *Boston* 94
SMITH, Walt. Art Education: scholastic & industrial; ill. *o.p.* [*pb.* $5] 8° Houghton, *Boston* 72
TADD, J. L. New Methods in Education—*ut* **D** § 167, *s.v.* Manual Training
TAYLOR, Edw. R. Elementary Art Teaching; w. 600 diagrs. & ill. (good) 10/6 i 8° Chapman [91] 94
**Biology** —*v.* Sciences, Natural, *inf.*
**Book-keeping** —*v. also* **D** § 150, *s.v.* Book-keeping
PORRITT (H. W.) + NICKLIN (W.) How to Teach Book-keeping 2/6 *n.* c 8° Pitman 05
**Botany**—*v.* Sciences, Natural, *inf.* **Chemistry**—*v.* Sciences, Natural, *inf.*
**Civics** —*v. also* **D** § 135
BOURNE, H. E. The Teaching of History and Civics—*ut inf., s.v.* History 05

DARROCH, A. The Children: some educ. probls. [Soc. Probls. Ser.] 1/*n*. c 8° Jack 07
An introd. to the latest educational methods for fitting children for citizenship.

HUGHES, E. H. The Teaching of Citizenship $1·25 12° Wilde, *Boston* 09

JENKS, J. W. Citizenship and the Schools $1·25 *n*. c 8° Holt, *N.Y.* 06

SEELEY, Sir J. R. The Teaching of Politics—*in his* Lectures [1870], *ut* **F** § 1

WATERMAN, S. D. Practical Aids to Teaching of Civics 60 c. 12° Whitaker, *San Francisco* 09

**Classics** —*v*. Languages, Ancient, *inf*.

**Co-education** —*v*. **D** § 168, *s.v.* Women and Girls **Commercial** —*v*. **D** § 168

**Domestic Economy**

BIDDER (Marion G.) + BADDELY (Flor.) Domestic Economy in Theory and Practice [$1·10 *n*. Putn., *N.Y.*] 4/6 *n*. c 8° Camb. Press 01

MAJOR, H. Teacher's Manual of Lessons on Dom. Econ. 4/6 c 8° Blackie 93

" Domestic Economy for Teachers 3/*n*. c 8° Newmann 99

MURCHÉ, V. T. Tchr's. Manl. of Obj. Lessns. in Dom. Econ. i, 2/6; ii, 3/ gl 8° Macmillan 98

NEWSHOLME (Dr A.) + SCOTT (Marg. E.) Domestic Economy: laws of health in appl. to home life and wk.; ill. 3/6 c 8° Sonnenschein [92]

PAUL, F. T. Text-Book of Domestic Economy, 2 Pts.; ill. ea. 2/; in 1 vol. 4/ c 8° Longman 93

**Drawing; Colour** —*v. also sup., s.v.* Art: Generally

ABLETT, T. R. How to Teach Drawing in Elementary Schools 1/6 c 8° Blackie 89

BAILEY, H. T. A First Year of Drawing; ill. 75 c. 8° Educ. Pb. Co., *Boston* 94

BRADLEY, Milton Elementary Color; Introd. Hy. Lefavour; ill. 25 c. 12° Milton Bradley, *Springfd.* 95

" [ed.] Color in the Schoolroom [colr. as a schl. study] $1 c 8° Milton Bradley, *Springfd.* 91

BRANCH, E. A. Freehand Drawg. for Teachers & Art Studts.; 28 ill. 2/6 *n*. 4° Ralph & Holland 05

CAVÉ, Marie E. Cavé Meth. of Learng. to Draw fr. Memory *o.p.* [*pb.* $1] 12° Putnam, *N.Y.* 71

CLARKE, I. Edwards Drawing in the Public Schools [Bur. of Educ.] *n.p.* Govt. Prtg. Off., *Washgtn.* 85

GARDINER, A. Elementary Drawing under Bd. of Education 5/ c 8° J. Heywood, *Mancs.* [ ] 01

HOWIE, R. Y. Self-Educator in Drawing 2/6 c 8° Hodder 03

MOODY, F. W. Lectures and Lessons on Art; diagrs. 3/6 c 8° Bell [73] 80
Of spec. value for beginners in decorative composn. design, draperies, and posing of figures.

MORRIS, J. H. The Teaching of Drawing 4/6 ($1·50) c 8° Longman 93

PRANG (L.) + HICKS (Mary W.) + CLARK (J. S.) Suggns. f. Instrn. in Color; ill. $1 12° Prang, *Boston* 95
Suggestive as correlating colour-study and literature.

*Blackboard Drawing; Free-arm Drawing*—*v. also* **I** § 104

LYDON, F. F. Ambidextrous & Free-Arm Blackboard Drawing & Design 3/4 4° Philip 07

PIERCE, R. F. Y. Pictured Truth: hdbk. of b'b. drwg. & obj.-lessns. 75 c. (3/6 *n*.) c 8° Revell 03

SEABY, A. W. Blackboard Drawing 3/6 *n*. 4° Nelson 02

SPARKES, W. E. Blackboard Drawing; 52 pl. [hints on sktchg. natl. forms] 5/ 4° Cassell 98

STEPHENS, H. H. Blackboard and Free-arm Drawing; ill. 4/6 *n*. 4° Blackie 06

STEVENS, J. H. Free-arm Drawing for Infants: 40 col. pl., w. instrns. 3/6 *n*. i 8° Philip 00

SWANNELL, M. Blackboard Drawing; ill. 4/6 r 4° Macmillan 98

*Brush Drawing*

NICOL, J. W. Brush Drawing: hdbk. f. teachers and studts. 7/6 *n*. 4° Blackie 02

YEATS, Eliz. C. Brushwork Studies of Flowrs., Fruit, Animals; 27 ill. 6/*n*. obl 4° Philip 98

" Elementary Brushwork Studies; 24 ill. 5/*n*. obl 4° Philip 99

*Geometrical Drawing* —*v*. **I** § 7

**Elocution; Rhetoric** —*v. also* **K** § 86

GENUNG, Prf. J. F. Study of Rhetoric in College & Course [Monogrs. on Educ.] 25 c. 12° Heath, *Boston* 87

**English Language and Literature**—*v. also inf., s.v.* Languages and Literature, Modern

ABBOTT, Dr E. A. Teaching of Eng. Lit.—*in* Lects. on Educ. bef. Coll. of Preceptors *o.p.* 8° Longman 71

AMES, P. W. Address on Study of English Literature 1/6 8° Asher 98

BADLAM, Anna B. Suggestive Lessns. in Lang. and Readg. $1·50 c 8° Heath, *Boston* 87

BAIN, Prf. Alex. On Teaching English [w. detailed examples] 2/6 c 8° Longman 87

BATES, Arlo Talks on Teaching Literature $1·30 *n*. c 8° Houghton, *Boston* 06

BOWEN, H. Courthope English Literature Teaching in Schools [2 lects.] 1/6 c 8° Rivington 91

BRACKENBURY, Laura The Teaching of Grammar 2/ c 8° Murray 09

CARPENTER (G. R.) + BAKER (F. T.) + SCOTT (F. W.) Teaching of English in Elementary and Secondary Schools $1·50 (6/ *n.*) c 8° Longman 03
[Amer. Teachers Ser.] Full treatmt. of the subj., fr. Amer. pt.-of-view. Bibliogr. index at end.

CHUBB, P. Teachg. of English [Macmillan's Pedag. Lib.] $1 *n.* (4/6 *n.*) c 8° Macmillan, *N.Y.* 02

COLLINS, Prf. J. Churton The Study of English Literature 4/6 ($1) c 8° Macmillan 91
A plea for its recognitn. and organizn. at the Univs., attackg. them for their policy tow. its study.

COMENIUS, Bp J. A. [1592–1671] Orbis Pictus [tr.]—*ut* **D** § 161

CORNFORD, L. Cope English Composition: manl. of theory and practice 3/6 c 8° Nutt 00

GAYLEY (C. M.)+BRADLEY (C. B.) English in Secondary Schls. [pp. 68] *o.p.* c 8° Univ. of Calif., *Berkeley* 94

GOW, Dr Jas. Method of English chiefly for Secondary Schools 2/ (60 c.) c 8° Macmillan 92

HINSDALE, Dr B. A. Teaching the Language-Arts [Internat. Educ. Ser.] $1 (4/6) c 8° Appleton 96

HOOKER, E. R. Study Book in English Literature 75 c. c 8° Heath, *Boston* 10
Very useful; chronol. arrgd. and tabuld. (1) Bibliogr., (2) List of readg., (3) Notes to tchr., (4) Topics f. study, (5) Essay-subjs.

HUFFCUT, E. W. English in Preparatory Schools [Monogrs. on Educn.] 25 c. 12° Heath, *Boston* 88

HUDSON, Prf. H. N. Essays on the Study of Shakespeare 25 c. sq 16° Ginn, *Boston* 83
*English in Schools; Shakespeare as a Text-Book; How to Use Shakespeare in Schools. Preface* to his new edn. of *Hamlet.*

MCMURRY, C. A. Special Method in Readg. of Compl. Engl. Classics 75 c. *n.* (3/6 *n.*) c 8° Macm. [94] 03

" Spec. Meth. in Rg. in the Grades $1·25 *n.* (5/ *n.*) c 8° Macmillan 08

MARCH, F. A. Method of Philological Study of English Language 75 c. 12° Harper, *N.Y.* 7–

PATTEE, F. L. Literature in the Public Schools 20 c. c 8° Bardeen, *Syracuse, N.Y.* 91

PAYNE, Prf. W. M. [ed.] English in American Universities [Pedagogical Lib.] $1 12° Heath, *Boston* 96
A series of papers, by Professors of English in 18 Amer. Universities.

ROBERTS (A. E.) + BARTER (A.) The Teaching of English [practical] 2/6 *n.* c 8° Blackie 08

ROLFE, Dr W. J. Elementary Study of English: hints to teachers 36 c. 12° Harper, *N.Y.* 96

SCUDDER, Hor. E. Literature in School 15 c. c 8° Houghton, *Boston* 88

SIDGWICK, Prf. A. On the Teaching of Composition [a lecture] 1/6 12° Rivington 89

THOMPSON, Maur. How to Study Literature—*in* Hart's How to Study, etc., *ut inf., s.v.* History

WILLIAMS, M. Atkinson Rept. on Tchg. of Engl. in U.S. [Gilchrist Rept.] 2/ *n.* c 8° Sonnenschein 08

WILLIAMS, R. Lingua Materna: chs. on schl. tchg. of English 3/6 c 8° Arnold 05

WOODWARD, F. C. English in the Schools [Monogrs. on Educ.] 25 c. c 8° Heath, *Boston* 87

*Composition; Essay-Writing; Précis-Writing*

CORNFORD, L. Cope Essay Writing for Schools [w. examples] 4/6 c 8° Murray 03

FORBES, A. W. Holmes Practical Essay-Writing 1/6 c 8° Sonnenschein [88]

HARTOG (J. P.) + LANGDON (Amy H.) The Writing of English [practical] 2/6 (60 c.) c 8° Clar. Press 07

JACKSON (T. C.) + BRIGGS (J.) Text-Book of Précis-Writing [Univ. Tutorial Ser.] 2/6 c 8° Clive 05

MILES, Eust. H. How to Prepare Essays, Lects., Bks., Speeches, etc. 6/ *n.* c 8° Rivington 00

MILLER, Jas. W. English Composition and Essay-Writing 2/ c 8° Longman 10

SKIPTON, H. S. The Essay Writer: on essays & how to write them [cram-bk.] 2/6 f 8° Lockwood [89] 90

*Reading: Primary*

DALE, Nellie On the Teaching of English Reading 2/6 c 8° Dent 99
For use with the author's series of *Readers. Further Notes on Tchg. of Engl. Reading*, 3/ *n.* c 8° Philip 02.

FARNUM, G. L. Sentence Meth. of Tchg. Rg., Wrg., & Spg. *o.p.* c 8° Bardeen, *Syracuse, N.Y.* 87

HALL, Prf. G. S. How to Teach Readg. & What to Rd. in Schls. [Monogrs. on Ed.] 25 c. c 8° Heath, *Boston* 87

HUEY, E. B. Psychology and Pedagogy of Reading $1·40 *n.* (6/ *n.*) c 8° Macmillan 08
Expansn. of a thesis for Dr's degree. Incls. review of hist. of rg., and wrg., and of methods of tchg.

MCMURRY, C. A. Special Meth. in Primary Rg. & Oral Wk. 60 c. *n.* (2/6 *n.*) c 8° Macmillan 03

SONNENSCHEIN, A. Teacher's Companion to Reading in a Twelvemonth 1/ c 8° Routledge [01] 10
For use with author's series of readers entitled *Reading in a Twelvemonth*, 4 Pts. in 3 vols. (10d., 10d., 1/), broken up into Primers i–viii (ea. 3d.), ix (6d.).

SPAULDING (Dr F. E.) + BRYCE (Cath. T.) Learng. to Read: manl. f. tchrs. 60 c. 12° Newson, *N.Y.* 07

SPEAR, Mary A. Preparing to Read; ill. [a good bk.] 50 c. 12° New Eng. Pb. Co., *Boston* 91

*Horn-book—v.* **D** § 162 *Spelling Reform—v. inf.*

*Reading: Higher; Reading as an Art*

HALL, Prf. G. Stanley School Reading: how & what? [Monogrs. on Educn.] 25 c. c 8° Heath, *Boston* 87

LEE, G. S. The Child & the Book [repr. of Lost Art of Rg.] $1·50 *n.* (6/) c 8° Putnam [02] 07

LEGOUVÉ, Ernest The Art of Reading [tr.]; w. notes $1·25 12° Lippincott, *Phila.* [79] 84

" Reading as a Fine Art [tr. A. L. Alger] 50 c. 12° Penn Pb. Co., *Phila.* [79] 86
Two different trs. of his *L'Art de la Lecture*: the former the better.

*Choice of Books—v.* **K** § 10 *Use of School Libraries—v.* **K** § 16*

*Spelling: Spelling Reform —v. also* **K** § 238

ALLEN, F. S. Apropos of Spg. Reform; Princs. of Sp. Ref. ea. 50 c. 8° Bradley & White, *N.Y.* 07; 07

BELL, A. M. Faults of Speech: self-instructor and teacher's manual 2/6 18° Trübner 80

ELLIS, A. J. A Plea for Phonetic Spelling *o.p.* [*pb.* 1/6] 8° Pitman 48

GLADSTONE, Dr J. H. Spelling Reform fr. an Educational Point of View 1/6 c 8° Macmillan 78

GOODARD, F. B. The Art of Spelling c 8° Baker, *N.Y.* 89

LOUNSBURY, Prf. T. R. English Spelling and Spelling Reform [by advocate of reform] $1. 25 *n.* (6/ *n.*) c 8° Harper 09

MARCH, F. A. The Spelling Reform [Bureau of Educn.] *n.p.* Govt. Prtg. Off., *Washington* 93

MÜLLER, Prf. Max On Spelling [reform] [pp. 46] *o.p.* c 8° Pitman, *n.d.* (80)

PITMAN, [Sir] Is. Plea for Spelling Reform [phonographic pt.-of-view] c 8° Pitman

SKEAT, Prf. W. W. The Problem of Spelling Reform 1/ *n.* (25 c.) 8° Clar. Press 06

SWEET, Hy. Handbk. of Phonetics & Princs. of Spellg. Reform *o.p.* [*pb.* 4/6] f 8° Clar. Press 77
Contains a popular exposition of the principles of Spelling Reform.

**French Language** *—v. also inf., s.v.* Languages and Literature, Modern

JEFFREY, P. Shaw The Study of Colloquial and Literary French 5/ c 8° Whittaker 99
Founded on Germ. wk. of KOSCHWITZ. Lists of the authorities in every dept., particulars of exams., methods of study; good bibliography.

RIPPMANN, Prf. W. Hints on Teaching French [Mod. Lang. Ser.] 1/6 12° Dent 98

**Gardening** *—v. also* Nature-Study, *inf.*

ELFORD (P.) + HEATON (S.) Practical School Gardening; ill. [f. teachers] 2/ *n.* (70 c. *n.*) c 8° Clar. Press 09

LATTER, Lucy R. School Gardening for Little Children [hints to tchrs.] 2/6 *n.* c 8° Sonnenschein 06

WATKINS (W. E.) + SOWMAN (A.) School Gardening; 25 ill. 2/6 c 8° Philip 05

**Geography** *—v. also* **E** § 2

*Bibliography:* MILL (Dr H. R.) Guide to Geogr. Bks. and Appliances 4/6 c 8° Philip [08] 10
New edn. of MILL'S *Hints to Tchrs. and Studts. on Choice of Geogr. Bks.*, prep. J. F. UNSTEAD + N. E. MACMUNN, ed. Dr A. J. HERBERTSON.

ARCHER (Prf. R. L.) + LEWIS (W. J.) + CHAPMAN (A. E.) Tchg. of Geogr. in Elem. Schls. 3/6 *n.* c 8° Black 10

BAKER, W. G. Realistic Elem. Geogr. taught by Picture and Plan 1/9 c 8° Blackie 89
On lines of Germ. plan of vivifying study of geogr. by means of classified pictures.

BLAKISTON, J. R. How to Teach Geography *o.p.* c 8° Griffith & Farran 86

CARVER, Elvira How to Teach Geography 50 c. 12° Educ. Pb. Co., *Boston* 95

CROCKER, Lucretia Meths. of Teaching Geography [notes of lessons] 60 c. 12° Schl. Supply. Co., *Boston* 84

DAVIS, Wm. Morris Geographical Illustrations c 8° Camb., *Mass.* 95
Based on phys. features of southern New Engld. Rich in suggestns. f. tchg. relns. of geogr. forms.

„ etc. Report on Govt. Maps for Use of Schls. [v. useful] 30 c. 8° Holt, *N.Y.* 94

FRYE, A. E. The Child and Nature $1·25 12° Ginn, *Boston* 88
Method of teaching geography with sand-modelling.

„ How to Teach Primary Geography 60 c. 12° Ginn, *Boston* 96

„ Teacher's Manual of Methods in Geography 50 c. 12° Ginn, *Boston* 96

GEIKIE, Prf. A. Teaching of Geography: principles & methods 2/ (60 c. *n.*) 12° Macmillan 87
Advocates the claims of geography as an educational discipline of a high order.

„ *—in his* Fragments of Earth-Lore, *ut* **H** § 31
The first paper is a plea for the more intelligent and far-sighted meth. of teaching geography.

GEOGRAPH. ASSOCN., Members of Lectures on Teaching of Geography 1/ *n.* 8° Philip 09

GRIFFIN, Ida L. Topical Geography; w. methods 50 c. c 8° Bardeen, *Syracuse, N.Y.* 91

GUYOT, Arnold Geographical Teaching [tr.] *o.p.* c 8° Scribner, *N.Y.* 66
Full of suggestion. Emphasizes study of nature before symbols, and importance of topical study.

„ The Earth and Man, tr. C. C. Felton; maps $1·75 c 8° Scribner, *N.Y.* [49] 90
Tho' pubd. in 1849, still full of inspirn. for tchr. Strong on rel. of earth's slopes to human developmt.

v. HUMBOLDT, Alex. *—in his* Cosmos [tr.], 5 vols., *ut* **H** § 25

JOLLY, W. Realistic Teaching of Geography [its principles] 1/ 12° Blackie 87

KELLOGG, A. M. Geography by Map Drawing 50 c. 16° Kellogg, *N.Y.* 93

*KELTIE, J. S., etc. Rept. of Progs. of R.G.S. in ref. to Improvemt. of Geog. Edu. [pp. 343] *o.p.* 8° Murray 86
Avaluable Rept. (by KELTIE) on tchg. geogr. on Continent, in U.S., and Canada, a bibliogr. of geogr., and 4 lects. (1) *Aims and Meths. of Geogr. Educn.* (E. G. RAVENSTEIN), (2) *Appliances in Tchg. Geogr.* (EDR.), (3) *Geogr. in rel. to Hist.* (JAS. BRYCE), (4) *Scient. Aspects of Geogr. Educn.* (H. N. MOSELEY).

KING, C. F. Methods and Aids in Geography $1·60 *n.* 12° Lee & Shepard, *Boston* 89

LYDE, L. W. The Teaching of Geography 1/ *n.* c 8° Blackie 09

MCMURRY, C. A. Teacher's Manual of Method in Geography 40 c. *n.* (2/6) 4° Macmillan 02

„ Spec. Method. in Geogr. [Macm.'s Pedag. Lib.] 70 c. *n.* (3/ *n.*) c 8° Macmillan, *N.Y.* [94] 03

„ Excursions and Lessons in Home Geography 50 c. *n.* (2/6) c 8° Macmillan 04

MALTBY, A. E. Map Modelling in Geogr. and History; ill. $1·25 8° Kellogg, *N.Y.* 95
MARSH, Lewis Notes of Lessons on Geography, 2 vols. ea. 3/ c 8° Pitman 08
MORTON, Eliza H., etc. Modern Methods in Geography *o.p.* c 8° Educ. Pb. Co., *Boston* 90
MURCHÉ, V. T. Teacher's Manl. of Object Lessons in Geography 3/6 c 8° Macmillan 02
NICHOLS, W. F. Topics in Geography 65 c. c 8° Heath, *Boston* 90
PARKER, Fcs. W. How to Study Geography [Intern. Educ. Ser.] $1·50 (6/) c 8° Appleton 89
PULLING, F. S. The Teaching of Geography and History *o.p.* c 8° *London* 82
REDWAY, J. W. New Basis f. Geography: manl. f. the teacher $1 *n.* (4/6 *n.*) c 8° Macmillan 01
Seeks to set forth the relns. betw. human activities and geographical environment.
REYNOLDS, Joan B. Teaching of Geogr. in Switzerld. and N. Italy 2/6 c 8° Camb. Press 00
60 c. *n.* Putnam, *N.Y.* A Report to the Gilchrist Trustees, 1898.
ROYAL GEOGRAPH. SOC.: Report of Procgs. in ref. to Improvemt. of Geog. Educn. 3/6 m 8° Murray
" Syllabus of Instruction in Geography [pp. 17] *gratis* R. G. S., 1, *Savile Row, London*
SONNENSCHEIN, A. [ed.] Regulns. f. Tchg. Geogr. in Prussian Cadet Corps—*in his* Foreign Codes, *ut* **D** § 159
SUTHERLAND, W. J. The Teaching of Geography $1·50 *n.* c 8° Scott, *Chicago* 09
TROTTER, Spencer Lessons in the New Geography $1 c 8° Heath, *Boston*
WICKS (J. F.) + BOYER (J. M.) How to Study & Teach Geogr., 2 v. 50 c., 75 c. 12° Flanagan, *Chicago* 95
WILKINS, Eva D. Descr. Geogr. taught by Map Drawing; 9 maps $1·50 Bardeen, *Syracuse, N.Y.* 93
*Map-making* —*v.* **E** § 2

**Geology** —*v.* Sciences, Natural, *inf.*

**Geometry**

HANUS, Paul H. Geometry in the Grammar Schools 25 c. c 8° Heath, *Boston* 93
ILES, Geo. A Class in Geometry: lessns. in obsn. & experimt. 30 c. 16° Kellogg, *N.Y.* 94
MACDONALD, J. W. Study of Geometry in Secondary Schools [pp. 137] c 8° *Boston* 89
PETCH, T. Plane Geometry adapted to Heuristic Meths. of Tchg. 1/6 c 8° Arnold 03

**German Language** —*v. also inf., s.v.* Languages and Literature, Modern

MUSGRAVE, Curt Abel The Caricature of German in English Schools 1/ c 8° Rice 93
An objection to the inaccuracies in certain school text-bks. on German grammar, etc.
RIPPMANN, Prf. W. Hints on Teaching German [the 'new' meth.] 1/6 12° Dent [99] 06

**Girls, Education of** —*v.* **D** § 168, *s.v.* Women **Gymnastics** —*v.* Physical Education, *inf.*

**Handwriting**

*JACKSON, Jno. Theory and Practice of Handwriting; ill. 5/ 8° Simpkin [93] 04
By the originator of the system of Upright Penmanship.
" Ambidexterity: two handedness and two brainedness 6/ *n.* 8° Paul 05
" Left Handwriting: complete practical course 2/6 obl 4° Simpkin 05

**History** —*v. also* **F** § 3

ACTON, L'd Lecture on the Study of History 2/6 (75 c. *n.*) f. 8° Macmillan 95
Advocates the ethical aim. Cf. also his *Germ. Schls. of Hist.*—in his *Historical Essays*, *ut* **F** § 1.
ADAMS, Prf. C. K. —*in his* Manl. of Hist. Liter. [*ut* **F** § 1] are suggestions as to methods & courses
ADAMS, Prf., H. B. Meths. of Histor. Study [Johns Hopk. Univ. Studs.] 50 c. 8° J. H. Univ. Press, *N.Y.* 84
" Study of Hist. in Am. Colls. and Univs. 8° Govt. Prtg. Off., *Washington* 87
[Bureau of Educn.] Describes actual courses given at date of pubn.
ALLEN, Prf. J. W. The Place of History in Education 5/ *n.* c 8° Blackwood 09
A suggestive inquiry into the subj.-matter of hist., mod. meths. of tchg. it, and its educatl. value.
ALLEN, W. F. History Topics [for high-schls. and colleges] 25 c. 12° Heath, *Boston* 86
ARCHBOLD, W. A. J. Essays on Tchg. of History *o.p.* [*pb.* 2/6 *n.*] c 8° Camb. Press 02
ATKINSON, W. P. On History and the Study of History 50 c. 16° Roberts, *Boston* 84
BARNES, Prf. Mary S. Teachers' Manual to General History c 8° Heath, *Boston* 94
" Teachers' Manual to American History 60 c. 12° Heath, *Boston* 93
" Studies in Historical Method [Pedag. Lib.] 90 c. 12° Heath, *Boston* 96
Approaches subj. inductively, by studies in histor. sense in children and savages, and survey of the hist. of history.
BOURNE, H. E. The Teaching of History and Civics $1·50 (6/ *n.*) 8° Longman 02
[Amer. Teacher's Ser.] A complete treatmt. of the subj., in both elem. and secondary schls. Good bibliographies.
BROWNING, Oscar The Teaching of History in Schools [pp. 20] c 8° *London* 87
DIESTERWEG, F. A. W. Instruction in History [tr.] [fr. his *Wegweiser*] 8° *Boston* 85
DODGE, Eva Teachg. of Hist. in Girls' Schls. in N. & Cent. Germy.
[Gilchr. Rept.] 1/6 *n.* 8° Sherratt, *Mancs.* 08

DROYSEN, Prf. J. G. Outlines of the Principles of History [tr.] $1·10 12° Ginn, *Boston* 93
Tr. of his *Grundriss der Historik*, a syllabus of admirable lects. on the encyclopædia and methodology of history.

Essays on the Teaching of History [75 c. *n.* Putnam, *N.Y.*] 2/6 *n.* c 8° Camb. Press 02
By F. W. MAITLAND, H. M. GWATKIN, R. L. POOLE, W. E. HEITLAND, W. CUNNINGHAM, J. R. TANNER, W. H. WOODWARD, C. H. K. MARTEN, W. J. ASHLEY.

FIRTH, Prf. C. H. Plea for Historical Teachg. of History 1/ *n.* (35 c. *n.*) 8° Clar. Press 04

FOSTER, Fk. H. Seminary Meth. of Orig. Study in Historical Sciences $1 12° Scribner, *N.Y.* 88

FREDERICQ, Prf. P. Study of Hist. in Germ. and Frce. [tr.] [J. H. Univ. Studs.] $1 8° Johns Hopk. Univ. Pr., *Baltim.* 90

„ Study of Hist. in Holld. and Belg. [tr.] [J. H. Univ. Sts.] 50 c. 8° Johns Hopk. Univ. Pr., *Baltim.* 90

„ Study of History in Engld. and Scotl. [J. H. [tr.] Un. Sts.] 25 c. 8° Johns Hopk. Univ. Pr., *Baltim.* 87

FREEMAN, Prf. E. A. The Unity of History—*appended to his* Comparative Politics, *ut* **F** § 5

„ How the Study of History is Let and Hindered [pp. 32] *o.p.* 8° Macmillan 76

„ Methods of Historical Study [8 Oxf. lects. '85–6] 10/6 8° Macmillan 86

„ The Office of the Historical Professor [an Oxford lecture] 2/ c 8° Macmillan 84
All above discuss the large principles governing the study of history.

FROUDE, J. A. Sci. of Hist., *and* Scient. Meth. appl. to Hist.—*in his* Short Studies, vols. i–ii, *ut* **F** § 1

HALL, Prf. G. S. [ed.] Meths. of Teaching & Studying Hist. [Pedag. Lib.] $1·30 12° Heath, *Boston* [83]
Gives the opinions and modes of instruction (actual or ideal) of many teachers, Amer. and English.

HINSDALE, Dr B. A. How to Study and Teach History [chfly. Am. hist.] 75 c. 12° Appleton, *N.Y.* 94

JÄGER, Oskar Teaching of History [tr.]; pref. by C. H. Firth 3/6 *n.* c 8° Blackwell, *Oxon.* 08
A descrn. of the method of tchg. history, both classical and modern, in Prussian schools.

KEATINGE, M. W. Studies in the Teaching of History 4/6 *n.* 8° Black 10

MCMURRY, C. A. Special Method in Hist. [Macm.'s Pedag. Lib.] 70 c. *n.* (3/ *n.*) c 8° Macmillan, *N.Y.* 03

MACE, Prf. W. H. Method in History: for teachers and students $1·10 c 8° Ginn, *Boston* 97

MORISON, J. Cotter —*article* History *in* Encyclo. Brit., 9th edn., vol. xii [*ut* **K** § 1]

OMAN, C. W. C. Inaugural Lecture on Study of History 1/ *n.* (35 c.) 8° Clar. Press 06

PEARSON, Dr C. H. Teaching of History in State Schools—*in his* Reviews and Crit. Essays, *ut* **K** § 83
A valuable lecture by the author of *National Life and Character* [*ut* **D** § 134].

SEELEY, Prf. J. R. *article* Teaching of History—*in* Hall [ed.], Meths. of Teaching History, *ut sup.*
Advocates the scientific and sociolog. in lieu of chronolog. and purely liter. method.

SMITH, Prf. Goldwin Lectures on the Study of History *o.p.* [*pb.* 3/6] s 8° Parker [61] 65
Oxford lects. 1859–61. Conts. good, but now somewhat antiquated, refs. to books and parts of books.

SORLEY, Prf. W. R. The Historical Method—*in* Seth [ed.], Essays in Philos. Criticism, *ut* **C** § 1

Study of History in Schools: rept. to Amer. Hist. Assoc. by Com'ee of 7 50 c. *n.* (2/ *n.*) c 8° Macmillan 99

WELLS, J. Teaching of History in Schools [a lecture] 6*d.* 12° Methuen 92

WITHERS, H. L. Teaching of History; and other Papers 4/6 *n.* c 8° Sherratt, *Mancs.* 04

WOODS, M. E. Report on Tchg. of Hist. in Germy. and Belgium 2/ 8° Macmillan 02

**Kindergarten** —*v.* **D** § 164

**Languages (Ancient); Humanities** *v.* **Modern Subjects**—*v. also* **D** § 169, *s.v.* University Educ.

ASCHAM, Rog. [1515–68] —*in his* The Scholemaster, *ut* **D** § 161

ASHMORE, S. G. The Classics and Modern Training $1·25 *n.* (5/ *n.*) c 8° Putnam 05

BABBITT, Irving Literature and the Amer. College $1·25 *n.* c 8° Houghton, *Boston* 08
5/ *n.* Constable. Essays in defence of the humanities; mostly repr. fr. magazines.

BAIN, Prf. Alex. The Classical Controversy—*in his* Practical Essays, *ut* **D** § 161

BENNETT (C. E.) + BRISTOL (G. P.) Teachg. of Lat. & Gk. in Second. Schl. ($1·50) 5/ *n.* c 8° Longman 01

CURZON OF KEDLESTON, L'd Principles and Methods of University Reform 2/6 *n.* (85 c.) 8° Clar. Press 09

FARRAR, F. W. [ed.] Essays on a Liberal Education *o.p.* [*pb.* 10/6] 8° Macmillan [67] 68
Contribns. by C. S. PARKER, H. SIDGWICK, J. R. SEELEY, E. E. BOWEN, F. W. FARRAR, J. M. WILSON, J. W. HALES, W. JOHNSON, L. HOUGHTON.

FOUILLÉE, Alf. —*in his* Education from a National Standpoint [tr.], *ut* **D** § 161
Enthusiastically advocates retention of classics (esp. Latin) in the higher schls. of France.

GARDNER, Prf. Percy Oxford at the Cross Roads 2/6 *n.* c 8° Black 03
A criticism of present course of Litterae Humaniores at Oxford, w. suggestions for amendment.

HALE, Prf. W. G. Aims and Methods in Classical Study [an address] 25 c. 12° Ginn, *Boston* 88

HOFMANN, Prf. A. W. Question of Division of the Philosophical Faculty 25 c. 12° Ginn, *Boston* [83] 83
A Report, incorporating the opinions of many German professors.

IRWIN, Sid. T. Why we Learn Latin and Greek 1/ c 8° Constable 04

JEBB, Prf. R. C. Humanism in Education [1899]—*in his* Essays, *ut* **K** § 168

LEVERSON, Dr M. R. Thoughts on Institns. of Higher Educ. [combats 'classical fetich'] 50 c. 12° Huebsch, *N.Y.* [ ] 93

MACH, Prf. Ernst —*in his* Essays [tr.], *ut* **H** § 10
*On the Relative Educational Value of the Classics and the Mathematico-Physical Sciences.*

MÜLLER, Prf. F. Max Three Lects. on Science of Lang. and its Place in General Educn. [75 c. Open Ct. Pb. Co., *Chic.*] 2/ c 8° Longman [89] 89

NETTLESHIP, Prf. Hy. Moral Influ. of Liter.; & Class. Educ. in Past & Pres. 1/6 c 8° Percival 90
Two pop. addresses, the second of wh. is a powerful apology for the retention of classics.

ROLLESTON, Prf. G. Relative Value of Class. and Scient. Training—*in his* Scient. Papers, vol. ii, pp. 716–722, *ut* **H** § 73

ROWE, Dr Stuart H. Habit-Formation and the Science of Teaching—*ut* **D** § 163

TAYLOR, S. H. The Method of Classical Study $1·25 12° Thompson, *Boston* 61

,, Classical Study $2 12° Draper, *Andover* 70
Value of class-study ill. by selns. fr. wrtgs. of scholars. Reply to YOUMAN, *Culture demanded by Modern Life, ut inf., s.v.* Sciences.

Teaching of Classics in Germany = Special Reports on Educl. Subjs., vol. xx—*ut* **D** § 163*

WOODWARD, W. H. —*in his* Vittorino da Feltre: *ut* **D** § 156
Forms an admirable introduction to the history of classical teaching. Cf. also SANDYS, *Hist. of Classical Scholarship*, 3 vols., *ut* **K** § 167.

## Greek

ADAMS, C. F. A College Fetich [Greek] [an address] 25 c. 8° Lee & Shepard, *Boston* [83] 93

BREUL, Prf. Karl. Greek & its Humanistic Alternatives in 'Little Go' 1/ *n.* 8° Heffer, *Cambridge* 05

CLARK, Prf. E. C. Greek and other Studies at Cambridge 6*d.* c 8° Bowes, *Camb.* 91
Recognizes value of Gk. in a liberal educn., but argues that knowl. of it required at present is only a sham.

CORNFORD, F. M. Cambr. Class. Course: ess. in antic. of further reform 1/ *n.* 8° Heffer, *Cambridge* 03

KENNEDY, Prf. Jno. Must Greek Go? [pp. 66] 50 c. c 8° Bardeen, *Syracuse, N.Y.* 94

LYTTELTON, Rev. E. [ed.] —*in his* Thirteen Essays on Education, *ut* **D** § 161
*In Behalf of Greek* (by FIELD); *Compulsory Greek* (EDITOR); *Teachg. of Greek* (M. J. RENDALL).

MAYOR, Prf. Jno. E. B. Mutato Nomine [protest agst. exclusn. of Gk.] 6*d.* 8° Bowes, *Camb.* 91

MURRAY, Prf. G. G. A. Place of Greek in Education *o.p.* 8° MacLehose, *Glasgow* 89

SNOW, T. C. How to Save Greek 2/ *n.* 8° Blackwell, *Oxon.* 10

STEPHEN, J. K. The Living Languages [defence of compulsory Gk.] 1/ c 8° Bowes, *Camb.* 91

## Latin

ABBOTT, Dr E. A. Latin Verse—*in* Eve + Sidgwick + Abbott, Three Lectures on Teaching, *ut* **D** § 161

HALE, Prf. W. G. Art of Reading Latin: how to teach it 25 c. s 8° Ginn, *Boston* 87

HORWELL, H. W. Right Meth. of Studying Latin Classics 1/ 8° *Oxford* 87

JONES, W. H. S. The Teaching of Latin [Lib. of Pedagogics] 1/ *n.* f 8° Blackie 05

LYTTLETON, Hon. E. Are we to go on with Latin Verse? [defence] 3/6 c 8° Longman 97

MORRIS, Prf. E. P. Study of Latin in Preparatory Course [Monogrs. on Educ.] 25 c. c 8° Heath, *Boston* 87

TARVER, J. C. —*in his* Some Observations of a Foster Parent, *ut* **D** § 155
Contains a sane defence of Latin as a pedagogic instrument.

THOMPSON, Darcy W. Day Dreams of a Schoolmaster 5/ c 8° Isbister [64] 98
Amer edn. in Pedag. Lib. $1·25, Heath, *Boston.* A very suggestive book.

## Languages and Literature (Modern)

BREBNER, Mary Method of Teaching, Modern Languages in Germy. [Gilchr. Rept.; 40 c. Putnam, *N.Y.*] 1/6 c 8° Camb. Press 98

BRERETON, Cloudesley Teaching of Modern Languages [Lib. of Pedagogics] 1/ *n.* f 8° Blackie 05

BREUL, Prf. Karl Teachg. of Mod. Langs. and Traing. of Tchrs. [60 c. *n.* Putn., *N.Y.*] 2/ *n.* c 8° Camb. Press [98] 06

BREYMANN, Prf. H. Bearing of Study of Modern Languages on Education *o.p.* 8° *Manchester* 71

COLBECK, C. On Teaching Modern Languages: theory & practice *o.p.* [*pb.* 2/] 12° Camb. Press 87

COMFORT, G. F. Modern Languages in Education 25 c. 8° Bardeen, *Syracuse, N.Y.* 86

CORSON, Prf. Hiram Aims of Literary Study· [repr. fr. *Poet Lore*] 75 c. *n.* (3/) pott 8° Macmillan 95

DAWES, T. R. Bilingual Teaching in Belgium 2/ c 8° Camb. Press 02
50 c. *n.* Putnam, *N.Y.* A Report to the Gilchrist Trustees.

GIBBON, E. Essays on the Study of Literature—*in his* Miscellaneous Works, *ut* **K** § 89

GIRARD, F'r The Mother Tongue, tr. Vis. Ebrington *o.p.* [*pb.* 5/] f 8° Parker 47
A work of mature thought, summing up a whole life-time of labour.

GOUIN, Prf. Frç. Art of Teaching and Studying Languages [tr.] 7/6 c 8° Philip [92] 92
A 'new method' lighted on by chance, claimg. to have discov. an infallible 'royal road'. It was much puffed in the press and considerably read.

HILL, Dr G. Birkbeck Writers and Readers [$1·75 Putnam, *N.Y.*] 2/6 c 8° Unwin [91] 92
Six lects., 4 dealg. w. Revolns. in Literary Taste, 2 w. study of liter. as pt. of educn. Pleasant and chatty.

HINSDALE, Dr B. A. Teaching the Language Arts $1 12° Appleton, *N.Y.* 96
[Internatl. Educ. Ser.] Speech, reading, composition.

HORNER, Prf. R. Tchg. of Mod. Langs. in Schls., adapted D. T. Holmes 2/ *n.* c 8° Gardner, *Paisley* 03
*JESPERSEN, Prf. Otto How to Teach a Foreign Language [tr.] 3/6 c 8° Sonnenschein 04
90 c. *n.* Macmillan, *N.Y.* Very suggestive.
*LAURIE, Prf. S. S. Language & Linguistic Method in the School 4/ c 8° Oliver & Boyd, *Edin.* [90] 03
LOWELL, J. R. Study of Mod. Langs.—*in his* Latest Literary Essays, *ut* **K** § 18
Methods of Teaching Modern Languages [Pedag. Lib.] 90 c. c 8° Heath, *Boston* 93
13 addresses and arts. by var. Amer. prfs.: those on Fch. and Germ. espec. good.
*Modern Language Assoc.: Transactions 8° *Baltimore* 86 *sqq.*
Full of most valuable papers on the teaching of modern languages.
MORLEY, Jno., L'd The Study of Literature [an address] 1/6 (50 c.) c 8° Macmillan 87
NETTLESHIP, Prf. Hy. Study of Modern Languages at Oxford [pp. 20] *o.p.* 8° *Oxford* 87
O'SHEA, Prf. M. V. Linguistic Development and Education $1·25 *n.* (5/ *n.*) c 8° Macmillan 07
Summary of observns. and experimts. in ling. traing. of children and investign. of methods in Amer. and elsewhere.
QUICK, Rev. R. H. First Steps in Tchg. a Foreign Lang. *o.p.* c 8° Nutt 75
STRONG, Prf. H. A. Methods of Teachg. Mod. Langs. in Belgium [a rept.] 6*d.* 8° Eyre & Spottiswoode 93
SWEET, Prf. H. Practical Study of Languages [tables and ill. quotns.] 6/ *n.* 8° Dent 99
WIDGERY, W. H. Teaching of Languages in Schools [suggestive] 1/ *n.* c 8° Nutt [88] 03

**Law** —*v.* **D** § 168 **Manual Training** —*v. inf., s.v.* Technical Education, etc.

**Mathematics** —*v. also sup., svv.* Arithmetic, Geometry
BALL, W. W. Rouse History of Study of Mathematics at Cambridge—*ut* **H** § 5
BRANFORD, Benchara Study of Mathematical Education 4/6 ($1·10) Clar. Press 08
A valuable bk., based on 20 yrs.' experience, advocatg. (w. reasons given) reform. Incls. Arithc.
CAJORI, Prf. Florian A Hist. of Elem. Math. in U.S.; w. hints on meths. of tchg.—*ut* **H** § 5
De MORGAN, Prf. A. On Study and Difficulties. of Mathematics
[4/6 *n.* Paul] $1·25 *n.* c 8° Open Ct. Pb. Co., *Chicago* [ ] 09
HAMILTON, Sir Wm. Study of Mathem. as an Exerc. of Mind [1836]—*in his* Discussns., *ut* **C** § 30
HORNBROOK, Adelia R. Laboratory Meths. of Tchg. Math. in Sec. Schls.
[16 pp.] *o.p.* c 8° Am. Bk. Co., *N.Y.* 95
LODGE, Sir Oliver Easy Mathematics, chfly. Arithc. [hints to tchrs.] 4/6 ($1·10 *n.*) 8° Macmillan 05
SAFFORD, Dr T. H. Mathem. Teachg. & its Mod. Methods [Monogrs. on Educ.] 25 c. 12° Heath, *Boston* 87
SMITH, D. E. Teachg. of Elem. Mathematics [Macm.'s Pedag. Lib.] $1 *n.* (4/6 *n.*) c 8° Macmillan, *N.Y.* 00
YOUNG, J. W. A. Teachg. of Mathcs. in Elem. and Second. Schl.
[Am. Tchrs' Ser.] $1·50 *n.* (6/ *n.*) c 8° Longman 07
" Teachg. of Mathcs. in Higher Schls. of Prussia [Am. Tchrs' Ser.] 80 c. *n.* (2/6 *n.*) c 8° Longman 00

**Medicine; Surgery** —*v.* **D** § 168 **Mineralogy** —*v.* Sciences, Natural, *inf.*

**Moral Education** —*v. also inf., s.vv.* Relig. Educn.; Serms. to Schoolboys; *and* **A** § 8, *s.v.* Ethical Relig.
ABBOTT, Jac. The Teacher: moral influences employed, etc. $1·75 c 8° Harper, *N.Y.* [ ]
ADLER, Dr Felix The Moral Instruction of Children [Internat. Ed. Ser.] $1·50 (6/) c 8° Appleton [92] 95
By Pres. of N.Y. Ethical Soc. Deals w. whole of schl.-life, fr. 6 to 16 yrs., w. hints for courses of lessns. on laws of conduct.
BRYANT, Dr Sophie Short Studies in Character 4/6 c 8° Sonnenschein 94
" Teachg. of Morality in Family and School 3/ c 8° Sonnenschein 97
Former $1·50, latter $1·25 Macmillan, *N.Y.* Both vols. of Ethical Library.
" —*in her* Educational Ends: ideal of personal development, *ut* **D** § 159*
BUCHANAN, J. R. Moral Education: its laws and methods $1·50 12° Green, *N.Y.* [82] 83
CABOT, Ella Lyman Every-day Ethics [5/ *n.* Bell] $1·25 c 8° Holt, *N.Y.* 06
Intended for schl.-use. Discusses the living issues already present to girls and boys of 13 to 18 yrs. old. Key for tchrs. at end.
DAWSON, G. E. The Child and his Religion [suggestive] 75 c. *n.* 16° Univ. Press, *Chicago* 09
DE GARMO, Dr C. Ethical Training in Public Schools 25 c. 8° Am. Acad. of Pol. Sci., *Phila.*
Sketches of the five fundamental ideas of Herbartian ethics, and adds a sixth: 'the doctrine of service'.
DU BOIS, Patterson Natural Way in Moral Educn.: 4 modes of nurture $1·25 *n.* (5/ *n.*) 12° Revell 03
GALLWEY, F'r Peter [ed.] Pract. Notes on Moral Training [Rom.-Catholic] 2/6 8° Burns & Oates [79] 87
GILMAN (N. P.) + JACKSON (E. P.) Laws of Daily Conduct; *and* Character Building
$1·50 12° Houghton, *Boston* 92
These 2 essays divided the prize offered by the Amer. Secular Union for the 'essay, treatise, or manual adapted to aid and assist teachers in our free public schls.'. GILMAN is less directly stimulating, but more theoretical, than JACKSON.
GOULD, F. J. Conduct Stories: for moral instrn. of Children 2/6 *n.* c 8° Sonnenschein 10
" Life and Manners: stories for moral instruction 2/6 *n.* c 8° Sonnenschein 06
" Stories for Moral Instruction 2/ c 8° Watts 09
GRIGGS, Edw. H. Moral Education [9/ *n.* Gay & Hancock] c 8° Huebsch, *N.Y.* [ ] 05

HART, J. K. Critical Study of Current Theories of Moral Educn. Univ. Press, *Chicago, in prep.*
HAYWARD, Dr F. H. Reform of Moral and Biblical Education 4/6 c 8° Sonnenschein 03
INGRAM, Prf. J. K. Practical Morals: treat. on universal educn.—*ut* **C** § 23 [Positivist]
International Moral Educ. Congress: Papers on Moral Education 5/*n.* 8° Nutt 08
JOCELINE, Eliz. Mother's Legacy to her Unborn Child 4/6 16° Macmillan [1624] 94
A repr. of 6th ed. [1632], w. Intro. Bp. of ROCHESTER. Written in 1622 by a mother for a child whose birth caused her own death, and 1st pub. 1624, last 1853. Full of earnest piety, and quiet womanly counsel and commonsense.
LESSING, G. E. Education of the Human Race, tr. Rev. F. W. Robertson 2/6 f 8° Paul [72] 96
MCCUNN, Prf. Jno. The Making of Character 2/6 c 8° Camb. Press 00
Occup. more w. moral theory th. pract. morals of schl.-life. For other bks. on Character *v.* **A** § 113, *s.v.* character, where this shd. have been incl.
MARK, H. Thistleton The Teacher and the Child: mor. and rel. tchg. 1/6 c 8° Unwin 02
75 c. Revell, *N.Y.* Chiefly for teachers in Sunday and Night Schools.
MATTHEWS, F. H. Dialogue on Moral Education 3/6 c 8° Sonnenschein 98
MAYOR, H. Moral Instruction: in accordce. w. Code requiremts. 1/*n.* c 8° Blackie 07
Moral Training in the Public Schools: California Prize-Essays $1·50 12° Ginn, *Boston* 07
By C. E. RUGH, T. P. STEVENSON, Prf. E. D. STARBUCK, F. CRAMER, and Prc. G. E. MYERS.
PEABODY, Eliz. P. Record of Mr. Alcott's School *o.p.* [*pb.* $1·50] c 8° Roberts, *Boston* [ ] 74
Acc. of the principles and methods of moral culture adopted in his school.
Practical Notes on Moral Training [Roman Catholic] 2/6 c 8° Burns & Oates
QUICK, Rev. R. H. Remarks about Moral and Religious Education—*in his* Essays, *ut* **D** § 155
*SADLER, Prf. M. E. [ed.] Moral Instruction and Training in Schools, 2 vols.
ea. 5/*n.* (ea. $1·50 *n.*) c 8° Longman 08
Report of an internatl. inquiry, coverg. an immense ground, extendg. fr. Japan to N. Zeal., and fr. Eton to Reformatory Schls. By 80 contribrs., of widely differ. pts.-of-view, consistg. of essays on aspects of questn. and informn. on meths. and results. i: *U.K.*; ii: *Foreign and Colonial.*
SHELDON, W. L. An Ethical Sunday School 3/ c 8° Sonnenschein 00
$1·25 Macmillan, *N.Y.* [Ethical Library.] A scheme for moral instruction.
SPILLER, Gust. Rept. on Moral Instrn. and Traing. in Eighteen Countries 3/6 *n.* 8° Watts 09
By the organizer of the Internat. Moral Educn. Committee. Much informn., inclg. survey of the ethical portions of Protestant, Roman-Catholic, and Jewish instruction-manuals.
STOW, Dav. Moral Training and the Training System in Glasgow *o.p.* 8° Longman 41
WELTON (J.) + BLANDFORD (F. G.) Principles and Methods of Moral Training 3/6 c 8° Clive 09

*Elementary Manuals of Ethics* (suitable for General Readers or School use)

ALLEN, Jos. Text-book of Ethics f. Schls. & Bible-classes 60 c. 12° Barnes, *N.Y.* [64] 69
COMEGYS, B. B. A Primer of Ethics 50 c. 12° Ginn, *Boston* 91
Based on Jac. ABBOTT's once-noted *Rollo Code of Morals.*
EVERETT, Prf. C. C. Ethics for Young People 60 c. 12° Ginn, *Boston* 92
SEELYE, Rev. J. H. Duty: a book for Schools 30 c. 12° Ginn, *Boston* 91
Bases ethics on religion. Designed to aid in the formation of character.

*Sex*

HIME, Dr M. C. Schoolboys' Special Immorality [indictmt. of cubicle syst.] 6*d. n.* 8° Churchill 99
LYTTELTON, Rev. Edw. Training of Young in Laws of Sex [frank] 2/6 *n.* ($1) c 8° Longman 00
MILES, Eust. H. A Boy's Control and Self Expression 3/6 *n.* c 8° Celtic Press [ ] 07
*Character, Training of* —*v. also* **A** § 113, *s.v.* Character
*'Gentleman', The* —*v.* **D** § 129

**Music; Singing** —*for* KG. Music *v.* **D** § 165; Voice, *v. inf.*; Tonic Sol-Fa *v.* **I** § 132

BACH, A. B. On Musical Education and Vocal Culture 5/ c 8° Blackwood [81] 83
BROOKS, Edw. Special Report on Teaching Music *o.p.* c 8° *Phila.* 95
CURWEN, Jno. Teacher's Manual of Tonic Sol-fa Method 5/ 4° Curwen [75]
DICKS, E. A. Handbk. of Examinations in Music [questns. and ansrs.] 3/6 8° Novello 98
EASTMAN, Edith V. Musical Education and Musical Art $1·25 16° Damrell, *Boston* 93
ELSON, L. C. Realm of Music [hist. & educatl.] $1·50 12° New Eng. Conserv. of Mus., *Bost.* 92
FAY, Amy Music Study in Germany 4/6 c 8° Macmillan 86
FISHER, Hy. The Musical Profession 6/ c 8° Curwen 88
HOSKINS, A. B. Singing in Schools: compl. course of pract. teaching 2/ 8° Bemrose 85
HULLAH, Jno. Time and Tune in the Elementary School *o.p.* [*pb.* 2/6] 12° Longman 74
" Method of Teaching Singing *o.p.* c 8° Longman 80
MASON (Lowell) + SEWARD (T. F.) The Pestalozzian Music Teacher $2 l 8° Ditson, *Boston* 71
MILLS, E. Study of Music as a Means of Education 1/*n.* f 8° Simpkin 05
PRATT, W. S. Music as a University Study *o.p.* c 8° *Chicago* 94

PRENTICE, Ridley — The Musician: a guide to pianoforte students; 6 grades ea. 2/ 16° Curwen [83–6] 97
Lists of pieces to be studied, arranged in order of difficulty, w. full critical analysis of many and helps to analysis of the rest.

TILDEN, W. S. — Papers on School Music [pp. 38] *o.p.* c 8° New Eng. Pb. Co., *Boston* 89

WARREN, Chas., etc. — Study of Music in Publ. Schls. [Bur. of Educ.] *n.p.* Govt. Prtg. Off., *Washgtn.* 86

WATKINS, A. — Singing in Elementary Schools [lects. to teachers] 1/ 8° Curwen 85

ZUCHTMANN (F.) + KIRTLAND (E. L.) Amer. Music System: tchr's manl. *o.p.* 8° King, *Springfd., Mass.* 93

**Nature-study** — *v. also inf., s.vv.* Object-lessons; Sciences; **H** §§ 45, 51, 76

BAILEY, Prf. L. H. — The Nature-Study Idea; ill. $1·25 *n.* (4/6 *n.*) c 8° Macmillan [03] 09

BUCHANAN, H. B. M. — Country Reader for Schools; ill.: Senior, i–ii, ea. 1/6; iii, 2/; Junr., i, 1/; ii, 1/2; iii, 1/4 gl 8° Macmillan 01–4

„ + GREGORY (R. R. C.) Lessons on County Life; ill. 3/6 c 8° Macmillan 03

BURTON, W. J. P. — Schemes of Nature Study for Schools 1/ *n.* c 8° Simpkin 03

CUMMINGS, H. H. — Nature Study by Grades; ill. $1 12° Amer. Bk. Co., *N.Y.* 09

DODD, Cath. I. — Nature Studies and Fairy Tales 3/6 c 8° Nelson 04

GEE, W. — Short Studies in Nature Knowledge $1·10 *n.* c 8° Macmillan, *N.Y.* 95

HILL (M. D.) + WEBB (W. M.) Eton Nature Study, 2 Pts.; 250 ill. ea. 3/6 *n.* sq 8° Duckworth 03–4

HOARE, T. W. — How to Teach Nature Study: pract. guide to tchrs. 3/6 *n.* 10

HODGE, Prf. C. F. — Nature Study and Life; ill. $1·65 12° Ginn, *Boston* 02

HOLTZ, F. L. — Nature Study; ill. $1·50 *n.* 12° Scribner, *N.Y.* 08

HOPKINS, Louisa P. — Observation Lessons in the Primary Schls. 20 c. 12° Lee & Shepard, *Boston* 90

JACKMAN, W. S. — Nature Study for the Common Schools $1·20 *n.* 12° Holt, *N.Y.* 92

„ — Field Work for Nature Study *o.p.* c 8° Werner, *Chicago* 94

„ — Nature Study and Related Subjects *o.p.* c 8° Werner, *Chicago* 95

LANGE, D. — Hndbk. of Nature Study for Pupils and Teachers $1 *n.* (5/) c 8° Macmillan 03

LONG, C. R. — Aim and Method of Nature Study 1/ c 8° Macmillan 05

MACKIE, A. — Nature Knowledge in Modern Poetry 2/6 *n.* ($1) c 8° Longman 06
Chaps. on TENNYSON, WORDSWORTH, Mat. ARNOLD, LOWELL, as exponents of nature-study.

MCMURRY, Mrs L. B. — Nature Study Lessons for Primary Grades 60 c. *n.* (2/6 *n.*) c 8° Macmillan 05

MEDD, J. C. — The Educational Value of Nature Study 03

MORGAN, Prf. C. Lloyd — The Interpretation of Nature 2/ *n.* 12° Arrowsmith, *Bristol* 05

MUNDY, Randal — Primer of Biology and Nature Study 2/6 *n.* c 8° Ralph & Holland [04] 07

MURCHÉ, V. T. — Tchr's. Manl. of Obj. Lessns. in Nat. Knowl, 3 Pts. 1/6, 2/, 2/6 gl 8° Macmillan *v.y.*

Nature Study Exhibition: Official Report 2/6 *n.* 8° Blackie 03
Report of the judges, report on the exhibition [very valuable], and papers read at conferences.

PAYNE, F. O. — 100 Lessns. in Nat. Stud. around my Schl. $1 12° Kellogg, *N.Y.* *n.d.* (95)

PYCRAFT (W. P.) + KELMAN (Janet H.) Nature Study on the Blackboard, vol. i: Plant Life; well ill. [to occupy 3 vols.] 7/6 *n.* 8° Caxton Pb. Co. 10 *in prg.*

RENNIE, Dr Jno. — The Aims and Methods of Nature Study 3/6 c 8° Clive 10

SCHMUCKER, S. C. — Study of Nature; ill. [Lippincott's Educ. Ser.] $1·25 12° Lippincott, *Phila.* 08

SCOTT, C. B. — Nature Study and the Child [Pedag. Lib.] $1·50 (6/) c 8° Heath, *Boston* 01

TADD, J. L. — New Methods in Education—*ut sup., s.v.* Technical Education

WARD, H. E. — Helpful Notes on Nature-Study 3/6 *n.* c 8° Simpkin 07

WATTS (F.) + FREEMAN (W. G.) Nature Teachg.: bas. on princs. of agric. 3/6 c 8° Murray 04

WILSON, D. C. — Nature Study & the Teacher; 153 blackbd. studies 2/ *n.* c 8° Charles & Dible 03

WILSON, Lucy L. W. — Nature Study in Elem. Schls.: manl. f. tchrs. 90 c. *n.* (3/6) gl 8° Macmillan 98

YOUMANS, Eliza L. — First Book of Botany—*ut inf., s.v.* Sciences: Botany [*v.* note there]

**Needlework; Knitting; Cutting-out**

BRANT, Eliz. M. — System. Cutting-out fr. Units of Measurement 2/ c 8° Sonnenschein 84

BRIETZCKE (Hel. K.) + ROOPER (Emily F.) Manl. of Collective Lessns. in Plain Needlewk. and Knitting; ill. 3/6 c 8° Sonnenschein 85

GLAISTER, Eliz. — Needlework [Art at Home Ser.] 2/6 c 8° Macmillan 80

HAPGOOD, O. C. — School Needlework: Teacher's Edn.; ill. [a good bk.] 85 c. 12° Ginn, *Boston* 93

ROSEVEAR, Eliz. — Textbk. of Needlewk., etc.; ill. [incl. methods] 6/ ($1·75) c 8° Macmillan 93

SMITH, Amy K. — Needlework for Student Teachers; 136 diagrs. 3/6 *n.* 8° City of Lond. Bk. Depôt

**Number** — Arithmetic, *sup.*

**Object Lessons** —*v. also sup., s.v.* Drawing (Blackboard), *inf., s.v.* Sciences

BARNARD, Dr Hy. [ed.] Object Teaching and Oral Lessons $3·50 m 8° *Hartford* 80
CALKINS, N. A. Manual of Object Teaching; with illustr. lessons $1·25 12° Harper, *N.Y.* 82
CANN, A. L. Notes on Object Lesson Teaching [w. 120 model-lessns.] 4/6 c 8° Simpkin 02
DOVE, Mrs E. E. Illustrated Object Lesson Book for Infants 1/6 c 8° Simpkin 00
MAYO, Eliz. Lessons on Objects [Pestalozzian] 3/6 c 8° Seeley [ ] 74
MORRISON, T. Object Lessons and How to Teach them 1/6 12° Collins 87
PARK, A. Teacher's Manual of Object Lessons; ill 5/ c 8° Heywood, *Mancs.* [73]
PERNOT (A.) + AKEHURST (F. E.) Teaching of Picture: Obj. Lessns. and Grammar; ill 3/6 *n.* 8° A. Owen [04] 04
RICKS, G. Object Lessns. & How to Give them, 2 Ser. [ea. 90 c. Heath, *Bost.*] ea. 3/6 p 8° Pitman [85] 87
" Natural History Object Lessons [$1·50 Heath, *Bost.*] 4/6 c 8° Pitman 88
ROOPER, W. + H. Manual of Object Lessons; ill. 3/6 c 8° Sonnenschein [83]

**Physical Education; Gymnastics**—*v. also* **I** § 164

ALEXANDER, A. Healthful Exercises for Girls; *c.* 200 ill. 2/6 c 8° Philip [85] 93
" Modern Gymnastic Exercises; ill. Pt. i [Elem.] 3/6; ii [Advanced] 5/ 8° Philip [87] 01; 90
" Physical Drill of all Nations; illns., music, and exx. 3/6 8° Philip 93
" New Games and Sports for Schls., Clubs, & Gymnasia 3/6 8° Philip 95
ALLEN, Nathan Physical Developmt.: laws govg. human syst. $2·50 12° Lee & Shepard, *Boston* 88
ANGERSTEIN (Dr E.) + ECKER (G.) Home Gymnastics for Well and Sick [tr.]; ill. $1·50 8° Houghton, *Boston* 89
BANCROFT, Jessie H. School Gymnastics with Light Apparatus $1·75 12° Heath, *Boston* 00
BARROWS, Isab. [ed.] Physical Training [by various writers; pp. 135] *o.p.* c 8° Ellis, *Boston* 90
BISHOP, Emily M. Self-expression and Health [Delsarte system] $1 16° *Chautauqua* 93
BISSELL, Dr Mary T. Physical Developmt. and Exercises for Women [Portia Ser.] $1·25 12° Dodd & Mead, *N.Y.* 91
BROMAN, Allan School Gymnastics on the Swedish System *o.p.* c 8° Bale 95
CHESTERTON, Thos. Theory of Phys. Educn. in Elem. Schools [cram-bk.] 3/ *n.* c 8° Gale & Polden [95] 00
CRUDEN, G. Manl. of Physical Culture and Musical Drill 3/6 c 8° Simpkin [89] 01
DUDLEY (Gert.) + KELLOR (Fces. A.) Athletic Games in Educn. of Women [5/ *n.* Bell] $1·25 *n.* c 8° Holt, *N.Y.* 09
GALBRAITH, Dr Anna M. Hygiene and Physical Culture for Women $1·75 12° Dodd & Mead, *N.Y.* 95
HARTELIUS, T. J. Home Gymnastics for Old & Young [tr. fr. Swedish] 1/6 c 8° Pitman [81] 06
HARTWELL, E. M. Phys. Traing. in Amer. Colleges & Universities *n.p.* Govt. Prtg. Off., *Washington* 86
HARVEY, F. J. Teacher's Manual of Physical Exercises *o.p.* [*pb.* 3/6] obl. Longman 94
JAMES, Alice R. Girls' Physical Training; ill. [with music] 7/6 ($1·75 *n.*) 4° Macmillan 98
JOHNSON, Theodora Swedish System of Physical Education; 27 ill. 3/6 *n.* c 8° Wright, *Bristol* [97] 99
JOLLY, Wm. Physical Education for Common Schools *o.p.* c 8° Laurie 81
KOCH, C. F., etc. Essays conc. German Syst. of Gymnastics [tr.] [9 papers] c 8° Freidenker Pb. Co., *Milwaukee n.d.*
LAGRANGE, Dr F. The Physiology of Physical Exercises—*ut* **I** § 167
LENNOX (Dr B.) + STURROCK (A.) Elements of Phys. Educn.; ill. [a tchr's manl.] 4/ c 8° Blackwood 98
LING, Dr Swedish Gymnastics for Schools 1/6 4° Hachette 85
LISHMAN, J. Drill Book for Elementary Schools 7/6 ($2·50) 8° Longman 01
*MACLAREN, Arch. Physical Education: theoret. and pract.; ill. Wallace Maclaren; 400 ill. 8/6 *n.* ($2·60) c 8° Clar. Press [69] 95
" Training in Theory and Practice *o.p.* [*pb.* 6/6] c 8° Clar. Press [66] 74
MÉLIO, G. Manual of Swedish Drill 1/6 c 8° Low 89
MORRIS, Dr R. Anna Physical Education in the Public Schools $1 8° Amer. Bk. Co., *N.Y.* 92
An eclectic syst. of exx., incl. Delsartean princs. of executn. and expressn. establ. by Fcs. DELSARTE [1811–71], a contemp. of LING, his syst. bg. however artistic and emotional whilst LING's claims to be strictly scientific (and conseq. wearisome in the extreme).
NISSEN, Hartvig A B C of Swed. Syst. of Educl. Gymnastics 75 c. *n.* 12° Educ. Pb. Co., *Boston* 92
" Rational Home Gymnastics; ill. $1 16° Badger, *Boston* 98
Largely made up of good illustrations, with sufficient explanatory letterpress.
NOAKES, Sergt.-Maj. System of Free Gymnastics and Dumb Bell Drill 1/6 32° Gale [ ] 94

OXLEY, Chas.  Manual of Drill and Phys. Exercises ; ill.  [w. music] 4/6 8° Blackie 95
POSSE, Bar. Nils  Swedish System of Educatl. Gymnastics [tr.] ; ill. $2 *n.* 8° Lee & Shepard, *Boston* 90
„  Spec. Kinesiology of Educ. Gymnastics ; 267 ill. [12/6 *n.* Bird] $3 8° Lee & Shepard [90] 07
„  Handbook of School Gymnastics  [2/6 *n.* Paul] 50 c. 16° Lee & Shepard 92
ROBERTS, Chas. [ed.]  Papers on Physical Education, Ser. i  [by var. wrs.] 4/ r 8° Bell 91
ROBERTS, E. A.  Handbook of Free-standing Gymnastics  3/6 *n.* r 8° Sherratt, *Mancs.* 05
ROTH, Dr M.  Gymnastic Exercises without Apparatus ; ill. [Ling's syst.] 1/ 8° Myers [64] 93
„  On Neglect of Physical Education and Hygiene  2/ c 8° Baillière 89
SARGENT, D. A.  Physical Education  $1·50 *n.* (6/ *n.*) c 8° Ginn 07
SCHREBER, G. M.  Medical Indoor Gymnastics  3/ *n.* 8° Williams 00
SEYMOUR, H. R.  Physical Training : theory & practice ; ill. 2/6 *n.* c 8° Livingstone, *Edin.* [98] 00
SMILES, Dr Sam.  Physical Educn. of the Young, ed. Sir H. Beevor  2/6 c 8° W. Scott [38] 05
SPALDING (M. H.) + COLLETT (L. L.) The Swedish Drill Teacher  3/6 8° Curwen 10
Special Reports on Educational Subjects, vol. ii : Physical Education—*ut* **D** § 164
STECHER, W. A.  Gymnastics : text-bk. of Germ.-Am. gymn. f. schl.-use ; ill.
$3 4° Lee & Shepard, *Boston* 96
By the Secretary of the Committee on Physical Training of the North American Gymnastic Union.
STREET (Lt. A. G.) + GOODERSON (V. E.) A Handbook of Physical Training  3/6 *n.* 8° Blackie 10
Based on the Swedish drill employed in the Navy.
TREVES, [Sir] Fredk.  Physical Education  2/6 8° Churchill 92
Repr. fr. STEVENSON + MURPHY's [eds.] *Treatise on Hygiene, ut* **H*** § 55.
WALKER, Donald  Manly Exercises ; ill.  [standard ; antiquated] 5/ c 8° Bohn's Lib. [34] 78
WATSON, J. M.  Handbook of Calisthenics and Gymnastics  $2 c 8° Steiger, *N.Y.* [6–] 79
*Greek Gymnastics*—*v.* **D** § 157, *s.v.* Greece and Rome  *Medical Gymnastics*—*v.* **H*** § 56

**Physiology**  —*v.* Sciences, Natural, *inf.*

**Political Economy**  —*v. also* **D** § 114
ASHLEY, Prf. W. J.  The Study of Economic History  8° *priv. prin.* 93
Repr. fr. *Quarterly Journal of Economics*. Holds an even hand betw. the deductive and the histor. schls.
COSSA, Prf. Luigi  Guide to Study of Polit. Econ. [tr.]—*ut* **D** § 114
FALKNER, R. P.  Instruction in Economics in Italy 25 c. 8° Am. Acad. of Pol. Science, *Phila.*
LAUGHLIN, J. L.  Study of Political Economy [hints to studts. and tchrs.] $1 16° Appleton, *N.Y.* 85
PATTEN, Prf. S. N.  Educ. Value of Pol. Econ. [2/6 Sonnenschein] 75 c. 8° Am. Econ. Ass., *Baltimore* 91
RITCHIE, Prf. D. G. [Eng.] Pol. Science at Oxf. [descr. of wk. & courses] 15 c. 8° Am. Ac. of Pol. Sci., *Phila.*
ROWE, Leo S.  Instruction in Public Law & Economics in Germany 35 c 8° Am. Ac. of Pol. Sci., *Phila.*
„  Instruction in French Univs. [espec. pub. law & economics] 25 c 8° Am. Ac. of Pol. Sci., *Phila.*

**Ragged School Education**  —*v.* **D** § 169

**Religious Education**  —*v. also* Moral Education, *sup.*
ABBOTT, E. A.  —*in his* Hints on Home Teaching [*ut* **D** § 164] : conts. an admirable ch. on relig. educn.
ARNOLD, Matt.  Gt. Prophecy of Israel's Restorn. [Isaiah, chs. xl–lxvi]  5/ c 8° Macmillan 75
BELL, Rev. G. C.  Religious Teaching in Secondary Schools  3/6 c 8° Macmillan [97] 98
An attempt to infuse into such teaching more vitality, more intelligence and more appreciation of recent advances in Biblical criticism.
CARNEGIE, Rev. W. H.  Some Principles of Religious Education  2/6 c 8° Murray 96
DRAWBRIDGE, Rev. C. L. Religious Education & How to Improve it 2/ *n.* (50 c. *n.*) c 8° Longman [06] 08
FROTHINGHAM, O. B. [Unit.] Child's Book of Religion  [suggestive] $1 16° Putnam, *N.Y.* [66] 76
GILL, J.  The Art of Religious Instruction  2/6 c 8° Longman [6–] 87
LAYARD, E. B.  Religion in Boyhood : hints in rel. trg. of boys [pp. 79] *o.p.* c 8° Methuen 94
MITCHELL, Rev. A. F.  How to Teach the Bible  [advanced] 2/6 c 8° Williams [06] 06
PALMER, W. Scott  Studies in the Teaching of Religion  1/ *n.* (40 c. *n.*) c 8° Longman 09
SMITH, Martin R.  What I have Taught my Children  3/6 c 8° Williams
SOARES, T. G.  Religious Education  Univ. Press, *Chicago, in prep.*
SPALDING, Bp J. L. [R.-C.] Education and the Higher Life  $1 12° McClurg, *Chicago* 90
„  Means and Ends of Education  75 c. 12° McClurg, *Chicago* 95
A plea for extens. of knowl. and culture along lines of Catholic theol., endg. w. appeal for an Amer. Cath. University.
„  Thoughts and Theories of Life and Education  $1 12° McClurg, *Chicago* 98
STEPHENS, Thos. [ed.]  The Child and Religion  [Crown Theol. Lib.] 6/ c 8° Williams 05
$1·50 *n.* Putnam, *N.Y.* [Crown Theolog. Lib.] Eleven essays by Prf. Hy. JONES, C. F. G. MASTERMAN, Prf. G. T. LADD [Am.], F. R. TENNANT, Dr. J. C. JONES, Can. Hensley HENSON, Rev. R. F. HORTON, Dr G. HILL, Rev. J. J. THORNTON, Rabbi A. A. GREEN, and Dr J. A. BEET—wrs. of various schools of thought.

WARD, Mrs Humphry New Forms of Christian Educn. [no Engl. edn.] 35 c. 12° Crowell, *N.Y.* 98

*Sermons for School-boys—v. inf.* *Sunday School Education—v.* **D** § 168

**Sciences: Natural and Physical:** *Generally*

ARMSTRONG, Prf. H. E. Teachg. of Scient. Method, & other Pprs. on Educ., *ut* **D** § 155

BOOLE, Mary E. Preparation of the Child for Science 2/ (50 c.) c 8° Clar. Press 04

DYER, Dr Hy. Science Teaching in Schls. [an addr. to Glasgow branch of Tchrs' Guild] 2/ c 8° Blackie 93
With insertion of courses at Ecole de Commerce et de Tissage of Lyons and the Public Mercantile Educ. Instit. of Leipzig.

HARRIS, Dr W. T. How to Teach Natural Science in Public Schls. 15 c. 16° Bardeen, *Syracuse, N.Y.*[71]95

HODSON, Dr F. [ed.] Broad Lines in Science Teaching 5/ *n.* 8° Christophers 09
Pprs. by O. LATTER, Prf. SMITHELLS, P. NUNN, Prf. MANN (of Chicago), and EDR. Introd. by Prf. M. E. SADLER.

HOWE, E. G. Advanced Science Tchg.; Systematic Sci. Tchg.
[Int. Ed. Ser.] ea. \$1·50 (6/) c 8° Appleton 94; 95

HUXLEY, Prf. T. H. —*in his* Science and Culture; *and* Lay Sermons, *ut* **H** § 42

" Science and Education—*ut* **D** § 155

LANKESTER, Prf. E. Ray Advancemt. of Science: essays, & addresses *o.p.* [*pb.* 10/6] 8° Macmillan 90

MCMURRY, C. A. Spec. Method in Science [Macm.'s Pedag. Lib.] 75 c. *n.* (3/6 *n.*) Macmillan, *N.Y.* [96] 99

MÜHLBERG, F. Natural Science in Secondary Schools *n.p.* Govt. Prtg. Off., *Washington* 82

MURCHÉ, V. T. Object Lessons in Elementary Science, 7 Stages ea. 2/ gl 8° Macmillan [04–6] *v.y.*

" Tchr's. Manl. of Obj. Lessns. in Elem. Sci. and Geogr.,
i–ii, ea. 1/6 (35 c. *n.*), iii, 1/6 (40 c. *n.*) gl 8° Macmillan 99

Report of the Committee on Science Teaching of America Assoc. f. Advancemt. of Sci. 80

Report of the Royal Commission on Scientific Instruction f° Eyre & Spottiswoode 70 *sqq.*

RICE, Prf. W. N. Science Teaching in the Schools [Monogrs. on Educn.] 25 c. 12° Heath, *Boston* 89
A plea for introduction of elementary science into common schools by an Amer. Prof. of Geology.

ROLLESTON, Prf. G. —*in his* Scientific Papers, vol. ii [1884], *ut* **H** § 73

SONNENSCHEIN, Prf. E. A. —*in his* Ideals of Culture, *ut* **D** § 157, *s.v.* Greece and Rome
The former paper of the two wh. compose the vol. is on *The Relation between Culture and Science.*

SPANTON, J. Preparation for Science Teaching 1/6 12° Griffith & Farran 82

WILSON, Rev. J. M. On Teachg. Nat. Sci. in Schls.—*in* Farrar [ed.], Essays on a Liberal Educn., *ut* **D** § 161

WRIGHT, Prf. Alder The Threshold of Science; ill. 6/ c 8° Griffin [ ] 92

YOUMANS, Eliza L., etc. Culture Demanded by Modern Life \$2 12° Appleton, *N.Y.* [67] 89
A series of addresses and argumts. on the claims of education in science.

*Biology; Zoology*

BURGESS, E. S. Syllabus of Courses in Botany and Zoology *Washington* 84

CAMPBELL, Prf. J. P. Biological Teachg. in Colleges in U.S.
[Bureau of Educ.] *n.p.* 8° Govt. Prtg. Off., *Washgtn.* 91

HAECKEL, Prf. E. Freedom in Science and Teaching [tr.] [reply to Virchow, *inf.*] 5/ 8° Paul 79

LLOYD (F. E.) + BIGELOW (M. A.) Tchg. of Biol. in Second. Schl.
[Am. Tchrs.' Ser.] \$1·50 (6/ *n.*) c 8° Longman

MANTON, Dr W. P. Primary Meths. in Zool. Tchg. f. Tchrs. in Com. Schls.
50 c. 18° Lee & Shepard, *Boston* 88

MIALL, Prf. L. C. —*in his* Thirty Years of Teaching 3/6 (\$1) c 8° Macmillan 97
Incls. papers on miscellaneous educatl. subjects, repr. fr. *The Journal of Education.*

NICHOLSON, H. A. The Study of Biology [pp. 163] *o.p.* c 8° 80

ROLLESTON, Prf. G. Biolog. Training & Studies—*in his* Scientific Papers, v. ii. pp. 846–79, *ut* **H** § 73

VIRCHOW, Prf. R. Freedom of Science in the Modern State [tr.] 2/ f 8° Murray 78
A protest against the teaching of Evolution in lower-grade schools. Replied to by HAECKEL, *ut sup.*

*Botany* —*v. also* Biology, *sup.*

BEAL, W. J. The New Botany: a lecture on teaching *Lansing* 82

HENFREY, Prf. A. The Study of Botany—*in* Youmans' Culture Demanded by Modern Life, *ut sup.*

YOUMANS, Eliza A. First Book of Botany, designed to cultiv. Observing Powers
in Children; ill. 2/6 c 8° Paul [79] 82

*Chemistry*

CLARKE, F. W. Report on Teachg. of Chemistry & Physics in U.S. *n.p.* Govt. Prtg. Off., *Washington* 81

FRANKLAND, Prf. E. How to Teach Chemistry; ill. [6 lectures, 1872] 3/6 c 8° Churchill 75

HUGHES (Miss A. M.) + STERN (Miss R.) Meth. of Tchg. Chemistry in Schls.
[\$1 *n.* Putn., *N.Y.*] 3/ *n.* c 8° Camb. Press 06

REMSEN, Prf. Ira Organic Chemistry—*ut* **H** § 18 [of value f. methods of teaching]

REMSEN, Prf. Ira. Introduction to the Study of Chemistry—*ut* **H** § 18
SMITH (Prf. Alex.) + HALL (Prf. E. H.) Teachg. of Chem. and Physics in Sec. Schls. [Amer. Tchrs.' Ser] $1·50 (6/ *n.*) c 8° Longman 03

*Geology; Mineralogy; Petrology*
EVANS, Ern. How to Study Geology; ill. 3/6 c 8° Sonnenschein 07
SHALER, Prf. N. S. Teachers' Methods in Geology 25 c. 12° Heath, *Boston* 93
WILLIAMS, G. H. Modern Petrography [Monogrs. on Educ.] 25 c. 12° Heath, *Boston* 86
WINCHELL, A. Shall we Teach Geology?: place of geol. in mod. educ. $1 c 8° Griggs, *Chicago* 89
*Mathematical Geography* —*v.* Geography, *sup.*
*Medicine and Surgery* —*v.* **D** § 168
*Nature-study* —*v. sup., s.v.* Nature-study
*Physics* —*v. also* Chemistry, *sup.*
WEAD, C. K. Aims & Meths. of Tchg. Physics [Bur. of Educ.] *n.p.* 8° Govt. Prtg. Off., *Washgtn.* 94

*Physiology; Anatomy*
BOWDITCH, H. P. Hints for Teaching Physiology 20 c. c 8° Heath, *Boston* 91
HUXLEY, Prf. T. H. Elementary Instruction in Physiology—*in his* Science & Culture, *ut* **H** § 42
MACALISTER, Prf. A. History of Study of Anatomy in Cambridge 1/ 8° Camb. Press 91
25 c. *n.* Putnam, *N.Y.* A lecture deliv. at opening of New Anatom. Lecture Room, Camb. (29 Jan. 1891).
MANN, Horace On the Study of Physiology in Schools 25 c. 24° Bardeen, *Syracuse, N.Y.* [69] 72

**Self-culture; Self-education** —*v. also* **A** § 113, *s.v.* Yg. Men (Women), **D** § 129, *s.v.* Gentleman
BEARD, Rev. J. R. Self-Culture: what, how, and when to learn 3/6 c 8° *Manchester* [60] 75
BLACKIE, Prf. J. S. On Self-Culture: intellectual, physical, and moral 2/6 12° Douglas, *Ed.* [74] 86
CHANNINGS, W. E. [1780–1842] Self-Culture 35 c. c 8° Crowell, *N.Y.* [42]
CHESTER, Eliza Chats with Girls on Self-Culture *o.p.* c 8° Dodd & Mead, *N.Y.* 91
CLARKE, Dr J. Freeman Self-Culture: physical, intellectual, & moral $1·50 12° Houghton, *Boston* [81] 92
COBBETT, Wm. Advice to Young Men and incidentally to Young Women [Oxfd. Lib. of Prose and Poetry] 2/6 *n.* (90 c.) c 8° Clar. Press [29] 06
Cheap edn. [Morley's Univ. Lib.]. 1/ c 8° Routledge (35 c. *n.* Dutton, *N.Y.*). Advice to a Youth, to a Yg. Man, to a Lover, to a Husband, to a Father, to a Citizen.
FOSTER, Jno. Essay on the Improvement of Time 3/6 c 8° Bohn's Lib. [ ] 52
HAMERTON, P. G. The Intellectual Life [$1·25 Roberts, *Boston*] 10/6 c 8° Macmillan 73
HOOD, Rev. E. Paxton Self-Formation 2/6 12° Clarke [5–] 83
ROOSEVELT, Theod. [Am.] The Strenuous Life [Readers' Lib.] 3/6 *n.* c 8° Duckworth [02] 11
SAMSON, Dr G. W. A Guide to Self-Education
SIDGWICK, Prf. Hy. Pursuit of Culture—*in his* Practical Essays, *ut* **C** § 70
TODD, Rev. Jno. Student's Manual [35 c. *n.* Dutton, *N.Y.*] 1/ c 8° Routledge [ ]
VENABLE, Prf. W. H. Essays chiefly rel. to Education & Culture $1·50 12° Lee & Shepard, *Boston* 93
,, Let him first be a Man $1·25 12° Lee & Shepard, *Boston* 93
WATERS, Rob. Intellectual Pursuits: culture by self-help $1·25 12° Worthington, *N.Y.* 92
WATTS, Dr Is. [1674–1748] Improvemt. of the Mind [still well worth readg.] 3/6 12° *Edin.* [1741] 68

*Text Books*
CASSELL & Co. [pubs.] New Popular Educator, 8 vols.; ill. ea. 5/ r 8° Cassell 89 *sqq.*
WARD & LOCK [pubs.] Universal Instructor: or self-educn. for all, 3 v.; ill. ea. 7/6 r 8° Ward & Lock 82–4

*Chautauqua Movement* [United States]
RAYMOND, Emily About Chautauqua *o.p.* c 8° *Toledo* 86
VINCENT, J. H. The Chautauqua Movement $1 12° Chautauqua Press, *Chautauqua, N.Y.* 86
*National Home Reading Union* [Gt. Britain] Pamphlets from the Sec., 12, *York Buildings, Adelphi, Lond.*

**Sermons to Schoolboys**
ALMOND, Dr H. H. [*Loretto*] Sermons by a Lay Headmaster 5/ Blackwood; Ser. ii, 3/6 c 8° Sonnenschein 86; 92
ARNOLD, Dr Thos. [*Rugby*] Sermons, 3 Ser. [preached at Rugby] ea. 3/6 c 8° Reeves & Turner [45 *etc.*] 77
,, Sermons on the Christian Life [del. in Rugby Sch.] 5/ c 8° Longman [42] 78
BENSON, [Abp] E. W. [*Wellington*] Sermons Preached in Wellgtn. Coll. Chapel *o.p.* 8° *London* 59
,, Boy Life: its trials, strength, fulness [Wellgtn. serms.] 7/6 c 8° Macmillan [74]
BOUTFLOWER, C. H. [*Aysgarth*] Eight Aysgarth School Sermons 2/6 f 8° Macmillan 00

BRAMSTON, Rev. J. T. [*Wincs.*] Sermons for Boys Pchd. in Wincs. Coll. Chapel 3/6 c 8° Macmillan 90
Twenty-five earnest and scholarly addresses to boys of from 16 to 18: full of 'muscular Christian' teaching.
„ Fratribus: serms. chiefly in Wincs. Coll. Chapel 5/ *n.* c 8° Arnold 03
BUTLER, Dn H. M. [*Harrow*] Sermons Preached at Harrow, 2 Series *o.p.* [*pb.* 7/6 ea.] c 8° Macmillan 61–9
„ Public School Sermons *o.p.* [*pb.* 5/] c 8° Isbister 99
17 serms., all bearg. on life of publ. schls., pchd. at commem. services at Eton, Harr., Marlboro', etc.
BYRDE, Rev. R. A. [*Honiton*] High Aims at School 3/6 c 8° Stock 99
FARRAR, Archd. F. W. [*Marlbro'*] 'In the Days of thy Youth' 9/ c 8° Macmillan [76] 77
FOXELL, Rev. W. J. God's Garden; In a Plain Path ea. 3/6 c 8° Macmillan 96; 97
GLAZEBROOK, Rev. M. G. [*Clifton*] Prospice: serms. in Clift. Coll. Chapel 4/6 *n.* c 8° Rivington 01
HART, Rev. H. G. [*Sedbergh*] Sermons in Sedb. Schl. Chapel: 1883–1900 3/6 f 8° Rivington 02
Harvard Vespers [addresses to studts. by preachers, 1886–8] $1 12° Roberts, *Boston* 88
HUGHES, Thos. Manliness of Christ—*ut* **A** § 123 [serms. to Rugby & Clifton boys, by auth. of *Tom Brown's Schooldays*
JAMES, Dn H. A. [*Rossall*] School Ideals 6/ c 8° Macmillan 87
King's School, Canterb.: Sermons pchd. in Commem. of Founders [1887–96] 3/6 c 8° Longman 97
LUSHINGTON, Rev. F. de W. [*Elstree*] Sermons to Young Boys 3/6 c 8° Murray 01
PERCIVAL, [Bp] J. Some Helps from School Life [Clifton, 1862–79] 3/6 c 8° Longman 97
„ Sermons at Rugby 3/6 *n.* c 8° Nisbet 05
POTTS, Dr A. W. [*Fettes*] School Sermons; w. memoir of author 7/6 c 8° Blackwood 91
RUTHERFORD, Dr W. G. [*Westmr.*] Key to Knowledge [serms. to Westm. boys] 6/ c 8° Macmillan 01
SKRINE, Rev. J. H. [*Glenalmond*] The Heart's Counsel; and other Sermons 3/6 c 8° Skeffington 99
„ The Mountain Mother; and other Sermons 3/6 c 8° Skeffington 02
TEMPLE, [Abp] F. [*Rugby*] Serms. prchd. at Rugby, Ser. i, 4/6; ii–iii, ea. 6/ c 8° Macmillan [67–71] 70–1
THACKERAY, Rev. F. St J. [*Eton*] Sermons prchd. in Eton Coll. Chapel: 1870–97 3/6 c 8° Bell 97
THRING, Rev. Edw. [*Uppingham*] Sermons at Uppingham School, 2 vols. 12/ c 8° Bell 86
VAUGHAN, Dn C. J. [*Harrow*] Memorials of Harrow Sundays 10/6 c 8° Macmillan [59] 85
WELLDON, Rev. J. E. C. [*Harrow*] The Future & Past [Harrow serms. 1885–86] 7/6 c 8° Rivington [87] 88
„ Sermons Preached to Harrow Boys 7/6 c 8° Rivington 87
„ Fire upon the Altar [Harrow serms. '87–90] 7/6 c 8° Rivington 91
„ Youth and Duty [Harrow sermons] 3/6 c 8° R.T.S. 03
WICKHAM, Rev. E. C. [*Wellington*] Wellington College Sermons 6/ c 8° Macmillan 87
WILSON, [Archd.] J. M. [*Clifton*] Sermons in Clifton Coll. Chapel, 2 Ser. ea. 6/ ($1·75) c 8° Macmillan 83

*Roman-Catholic*

BURTON, E. H. [*St Edmund's*; R.-C.] Sermons in St Edmund's Coll. Chapel 5/ c 8° Burns & Oates 04
DOYLE, F. C. [O.S.B.] Lectures to Boys, 3 vols. ea. 7/6 c 8° Washbourne [ ] 00
LUCAS, Herb. [S.-J.] At the Parting of the Ways 3/6 *n.* c 8° Sands 06
„ In the Morning of Life 3/6 *n.* c 8° Sands 04
„ We Preach Christ Crucified 3/6 *n.* c 8° Sands 08

**Shorthand** —*v.* **K** § 100

**Singing**—*v.* Music, *sup.* **Slojd**—*v. inf.*, *s.v.* Technical Education

**Story-telling; Educational Value of the Story**

BRYANT, Sara C. How to Tell Stories to Children [w. stories] 2/6 *n.* c 8° Harrap 10
SHEDLOCK, Marie L. Eastern Stories & Legends [for narratn.; Dutton, *N.Y.*] 1/6 *n.* c 8° Routledge 10
WILTSE, Sara E. Place of the Story in Early Educn.; & other Essays 60 c. 12° Ginn, *Boston* 92

**Technical Educn.; Manual Traing.; Handwork; Wood-work**—*v. also* **D** § 157, *s.v.* Germany (Gymnasia)

ACLAND (A. H. D.) + SMITH (H. Ll.) [eds.] Studies in Second. Educn. [by var. wrs.] 7/6 c 8° Rivington 91
ASHBEE, C. R. Chapters in Workshop Construction and Citizenship; ill. 5/ 8° Guild & Schl. of Handicraft, *Lond.* 95
„ Craftsmanship in Competitive Industry 5/ *n.* 8° Essex Ho. Press 08
A record of the workshops of the Guild of Handicraft, and deductns. fr. their 21 years' experience.
„ [ed.] Manual of the Guild and School of Handicraft 2/6 c 8° Cassell 92
BALLARD, P. B. Handwk. as an Educl. Medium; & other Essays 2/6 *n.* c 8° Sonnenschein 10

BARNARD, Dr Hy. [ed.] Scientific and Industrial Educn. in Europe [Gov. Rept.] $3·50 m 8° Govt. Prtg. Off., *Washington* 70

„ Science and Art: systs., institns., statistics 8° Steiger, *N.Y.* 72

BARROWS, Isab. C. [ed.] A Conference on Manual Training *o.p.* c 8° Ellis, *Boston* 91

BÜLOW, Bar'ess Marenholtz Hand-work & Head-work [tr.] [chfly. in Kin'garten] 3/ c 8° Sonnenschein 83

CLARKE, J. E. Industrial & Art Education in the United States Govt. Prtg. Off., *Washington* 85

Commission on Industr. Educn.: Report to Legisl. of Penn. [pp. 592] *o.p.* 8° Myers, *Harrisburg* 89

„ on Manl. Traing. & Industr. Educn.: Report to Legisl. of Mass. [pp. 320] *o.p.* 8° *Boston* 93

CREASEY, C. R. Technical Education in Evening Schools 3/6 *n.* c 8° Sonnenschein 05

DOPP, Kath. E. Place of Industries in Elem. Educn. [5/ *n.* P. S. King & Son] $1 *n.* 12° Univ. Press, *Chicago* [03] 05

EDGEWORTH, Maria [1767–1849] Treatise on Practical Education *o.p.* 12° *London* [1798]
An Amer. edn. was pubd. by Harper, *N.Y.* in 1849. Written with her father: standard.

GALLOWAY, R. Education, Scientific and Technical *o.p.* [*pb.* 10/6] 8° Trübner 81

GÖTZE, W. Ill. Manl. of Hand and Eye Training; 69 ill. 4/ c 8° Newmann 94
The best exposition of the German system of manual training.

HAM, C. H. Mind & Hand: Manl. Traing. chief factor in educn.; ill. $1·25 12° Am. Bk. Co., *N.Y.* [86] 00
Incls. detailed acc. of Chicago manual-training school. Argues f. man. trg. as pt. of general educn.

HENDERSON (A. W.) + PALEN (H. O.) What and How: handwork. for primary grades $2 8° Milton Bradley, *Springfd.* 09

HUXLEY, Prf. T. H. Technical Education—*in his* Science and Culture, *ut* **H** § 42

LELAND, C. G. Practical Education $2·25 c 8° Van Nostrand, *N.Y.* [88] 89
6/ Whittaker. Treatg. of developmt. of memory, increasg. quickness of perceptn., and traing. construct. faculty. Bibliogr.

LYDON, F. F. Woodwork for Schools: 45 pl. and 55 diagrs. of tools 3/6 *n.* 4° Low 02

MCARTHUR, Arth. Education in relation to Manual Industry $1·50 c 8° Appleton, *N.Y.* 84

MAGNUS, Sir Pp. Industrial Education [Education Lib.] 6/ 8° Paul 88

„ —*in his* Educational Aims and Efforts, *ut* **D** § 157
*Manl. Trg. in Schls.: orig. and purp.* [1894]; *Handwk. and Headwk. in Elem. Schls.* [1903]; *Handwk. in Schl. Life: Domestic Subjs.* [1903]; *Manl. Trg. in rel. to Health* [1891].

NICHOLS, G. W. Art Education as applied to Industry; ill. $4 8° Harper, *N.Y.* 77

MONTAGUE, F. C. Technical Education [pp. 68] *o.p.* 8° 87

PARKS, J. C. Educatl. Woodworking for Home and School; ill. $1 *n.* (4/6 *n.*) Macmillan 10

PERSON, H. S. Industrial Education; diagrs. [3 prize-essays] $1 *n.* 8° Houghton, *Boston* 07

RICHARDS, C. R. Manual Training [Amer. Tchrs.' Ser.] $1·50 (6/ *n.*) c 8° Longman *in prep.*

RICKS, Geo. Manual Training: Woodwork; 275 ill. 7/6 ($1·60 *n.*) 4° Macmillan 98

Royal Commissioners on Technical Instruction: Report [Commission 1881] f° Eyre & Spottiswoode 84
Five Blue-books, of great value. The Report covers the whole of Europe.

SEIDEL, Rob. Industrial Instruction, a necessity [tr.] [Pedag. Lib.] $1 12° Heath, *Boston* 87

SMITH, H. Llew. Report to London County Council on Technical Educn. 5/ c 8° Steel 93

STETSON, C. B. Techn. Educn.: what it is and what Am. Pub. Schls. shd. teach $1·25 12° Houghton, *Boston* [73] 76

STURCH, F. Manual Training (Woodwork): princs. & applicn.; ill. 5/ *n.* s 4° Methuen

TADD, J. Liberty New Methods in Education; 500 ill. $3 *n.* r 8° Orange Judd Co., *Springfd.* [99] 04
8/6 *n.* Paul. Deals comprehensively with manual training and also with Nature-study.

TWINING, T. Technical Training: system of industrial instruction *o.p.* [*pb.* 12/] 8° Macmillan 74

WAKE, Rich. Manual Training: Woodwork; 287 ill. 10/ *n.* 8° Chapman 99

WOODWARD, Dr C. M. Manual Training in Education; ill. [Contemp. Science Series; 3/6 Scott] $1·25 c 8° Scribner, *N.Y.* 90

„ The Manual Training School; ill. [aims, meths., etc.] $2 m 8° Heath, *Boston* 87

WRIGHT, Carroll D. Industrial Education [8th Rept. of Commissioner of Labor] *gratis* 8° Govt. Prtg. Off., *Washgtn.* 92

WYATT, C. J. Manl. of Continuation Schools & Technical Instruction 6/ *n.* c 8° J. Heywood, *Mancs.* 93
A compreh. and trustworthy guide to establmt. and maintenance of day and evg. schls. of techn. instrn., by Clerk to Mancs. Sch.-Bd.

*Textbook*

CASSELL & Co. [pubs.] New Technical Educator, 6 vols.; ill. ea. 3/6 r 8° Cassell 93 *sqq.*
A comprehensive and on the whole excellent work: copiously ill.

*Sloyd* (common incised carving and small carpenter's-wk. for schl. use—*for* Wood-Carving proper *v.* I § 144

BARTER, S. Manual Instruction: Woodwork; 302 ill. 7/6 f 4° Whittaker 92
$2 Macmillan, *N.Y.* The best pt. of the bk., itself good thro'-out, is that on bench-wk., wh. is very thoro' and comprehensive.

CHAPMAN, [Miss] C. Sloyd: handwork as a factor of education Rice 88

FRANZEN, J. A Plea for Slöjd, tr. Anna Strömsten [tr. fr. Swed.] *o.p.* c 8° Philip 91

HOFFMAN, B. B. Sloyd System of Wood Carving $1 c 8° Am. Bk. Co., *N.Y.* 92
**With descrn. of the Eva Rohde models, and sketch of hist. of man.-trg. idea.**

KILBON, G. B. Elementary Woodwork: sixteen lessons; ill. 75 c. 8° Lee & Shepard, *Bost.* 93

MARTINEAU, Gertr. Village Class for Drawg. & Wood Carvg.: hints to tchrs. 2/6 c 8° Longman 91

NELSON, W. Woodwork Course for Boys [good pract. bk.; w. plain diagrs.] 3/6 r 8° Philip 93

PEARSON, J. C. Manual Instruction: woodwork for standards 5, 6 & 7; ill. 10/6 s 4° Philip 93

SALOMON, Otto Theory of Educational Slöjd [tr. (fr. Swedish)] 3/6 c 8° Philip 92

" Teacher's Handbook of Slöjd [tr.]; *c.* 130 ill. & pl. 6/ 8° Philip [92] 94
**Tr. of a stand. Swed. wk. by Director of Nääs Traing. Schl., and pub. und. ausp. of Slöjd Assoc. Intended primarily for tchrs. Regards Sloyd 'as a means of formative educ.', belonging 'purely to *general* educ.'—not as a branch of techn. educ.: 'the objs. wh. the child makes [in the Sloyd class] are equally useful w. those of the carpenter; but, unlike the wk. of the carpenter, the value of the child's wk. does not exist in *them*, but in the *child* that made them'.**

*Birkbeck Schools:* ELLIS, Wm. [1800–81; founder]

Blyth, E. Kell Life of Wm. Ellis, Educl. Reformer and Economist 10/6 8° Paul [89] 92

Godard, J. G. George Birkbeck, Pioneer of Popular Educn. 2/6 c 8° Bemrose [84] 88

*Polytechnic Institutions*

Bayley, Edric The Borough Polytechnic Institute 6/ *n.* l 8° Stock 10

Webb, Syd. Hist. of the London Polytechn. Institns.—*in* Special Reports, vol. ii, *ut* **D** § 163*

*France*

BARNARD, Dr Hy. [ed.] Scientific Schools in France $3·50 m 8° *Hartford n.d.*

SCHOENHOF, J. Techn. Educ. in Europe: France *n.p.* Govt. Prtg. Off., *Washington* 88

TEEGAN, Prf. T. H. Technical Industr., and Commerc. Education in France 5/ c 8° Simpkin 92
**A compreh. hist. of the wonderfully cpl. network of Fch. techn. schls.—describg. training tchrs., w. accs. of industr., comm. and agric. educn.**

THOMPSON, Prf. S. P. Technical Education: apprenticeship schools in France *o.p.* 8° Macmillan 81

*Germany*

FELKIN, H. M. Technical Education in a Saxon town *o.p.* [*pb.* 2/] 8° Paul 81

*Holland*

COUSIN, Victor Education in Holland [tr.] [wkg.-classes and the poor] 8° *London* 78

*India*

SPRING, F. J. E. Technical Education in India [pp. 77] *o.p.* 8° *Calcutta* 87

**Voice Training** —*v. also sup., s.v.* Music

BEHNKE (Emil) + BROWN (Lenox) The Child's Voice [60 pp.] *o.p.* c 8° Marquis, *Chicago* 85
**On its treatment with regard to after-development.**

BROWN (Lenox) + BEHNKE (Emil) Voice, Song, and Speech; ill. $2 c 8° Putnam, *N.Y.* 86

CHATER, Thos. The Scientific Voice, Artistic Singing, Effect. Spkg. 2/6 f 8° Bell 90

DURANT, Geo. Hygiene of the Voice: physiol. and anatomy 6/ 8° Cassell [79] 80

GRIFFITHS, W. H. The Human Voice: its cultivn. and preservn. 2/6 c 8° Philip 92

HOLMES, Gordon Treatise on Vocal Physiol. and Hygiene 6/6 c 8° Churchill [79] 81

HOWARD, F. E. The Child's Voice in Singing $1 12° Werner, *N.Y.* 96

LEIB, W. H. Voices of Children: how made efficient 45 c. 12° Ginn, *Boston* 89

LUNN, Chas. The Philosophy of Voice 2/6 c 8° Baillière [86] 88

MACKENZIE, Sir Morell Hygiene of the Vocal Organs 6/ c 8° Macmillan [86] 88

MACKINLAY, M. Sterling Singing Voice and its Training [Dutton, *N.Y.*] 3/6 *n.* c 8° Routledge 10

SEILER, Emma Voice in Speakg. [tr.]; in Singing [tr.] ea. $1·50 c 8° Lippincott, *Phila.* 75

**Wood-work** —*v. sup., s.v.* Technical Education, etc.

**Writing** —*v. sup., s.v.* Handwriting

## 168: METHODS OF INSTRUCTION (*e*): COURSES AND SYSTEMS OF EDUCATION

**Blind (The)** —*v.* **D** § 169

**Civil Service Examinations:** *United Kingdom*—*v. also* **D** § 137

CATTON, J. Morris A B C of English Civil Service at Home and Abroad 2/ c 8° Sonnenschein 87

CRAWLEY, W. J. C. Handbook of Competitive Examinations 2/6 c 8° Longman [80] 85

EWALD, A. C. Guide to the Civil Service 3/6 c 8° Warne [6–] 69

JOHNSON, R. Guide to the Civil Service 3/6 c 8° Longman [71] 78

*United States*

BOWKER, R. R. Civil Serv. Examinatns. [illns. of purpose & character] 15 c. 12° Soc. f. Pol. Educ., *N.Y.* 87
COMSTOCK, J. M. The Civil Service in U.S. [w. exam. papers] $2 12° Holt, *N.Y.* 85
LEUPP, F. E. How to Prepare for a Civil Serv. Examn. $2 c 8° Hinds, *N.Y.* 99

**Commercial** —*v. also* **D** § 150

HEELIS, F. How to Teach Business Training 2/6 *n.* c 8° Pitman 07
HERRICK, C. A. Meaning and Practice of Commercial Education 5/ *n.* c 8° Macmillan 04
HOOPER (F.) + GRAHAM (J.) Commercial Education at Home & Abroad 6/ ($1·50 *n.*) c 8° Macmillan 01
A complete guide to what has been done: descriptive rather than practical.
JAMES, Edm. J. The Education of Business-Men 50 c. *n.* 8° Univ. Press, *Chicago*
A view of the organizn. and causes of study in commercial High Schools of Europe.
WARE, Fabian Educatl. Foundns. of Trade & Industry [Int. Educ. Ser.] $1·20 *n.* (5/ *n.*) c 8° Appleton 02
A study of the educational methods of our commercial rivals and their results on trade.
WHITFIELD, E. E. School Introduction to the Commercial Sciences 3/6 c 8° Rivington 92
,, Commercial Education in Theory and Practice 5/ c 8° Methuen 01
[Commerc. Ser.] Gives practical proposals tow. the organizn. of commerc. teaching.

**Common School System**: *American*—*v.* **D** § 157, *s.v.* United States **Gymnasia**—*v.* **D** § 157, *s.v.* Germany

**Legal** —*v. also* **D** § 53

BALL, W. W. Rouse Student's Guide to the Bar 2/6 c 8° Macmillan [78] 88
BILLINGS, J. S. Medical Education [pp. 42] *o.p.* 8° Boyle, *Baltimore* 78
BRYCE, Dr Jas. Legal Studies in Univ. of Oxford [valedict. lect.] 1/ *n.* 8° Macmillan 93
FINCH, G. B. Legal Education Aim & Method [40 c. *n.* Putnam, *N.Y.*] 1/ 8° Camb. Press 85
MUNRO, J. E. C. Study of Law in Greece, Rome, and England *o.p.* 8° *Manchester* 82
NAPIER (T. B.) + STEVENSON (R. N.) Practical Guide to the Bar 2/6 c 8° Cox 88
POLLOCK, Sir Fredk. —*in his* Oxford Lectures, and other Discourses, *ut* **D** § 1
Chs. on meths. of jurispr., Engl. opports. in hist. and compar. jurispr., Oxf. law studies, and law libraries.
SMITH, P. A. History of Education for the English Bar *o.p.* [*pb.* 9/] 8° Butterworth 60
THAYER, J. B. Teachg. of Engl. Law at Universities [pp. 18] *o.p.* 8° Little & Brown, *Boston* 95

**Medical and Surgical**: ALLBUTT (Dr T. Clifford) On Professional Education
[chfly. medicine; address] 2/ *n.* (75 c. *n.*) c 8° Macmillan 06
BLENKINSOP, W. H. Student's Handbook of Medical Education *o.p.* [*pb.* 5/] 8° *Cambridge* 81
CARTER, Dr R. B. Traing. of Mind for Study of Medicine *o.p.* 8° *London* 73
CHESTERFIELD, Dr Letters to his Son on Med. as Career, ed. Sir W. B. Dalby 1/ c 8° Longman 94
CLARK, E. C. Cambridge Legal Studies 2/6 f 8° Bell 88
DAVIS, N. S. Contribs. to Hist. of Med. Educn. in U.S. [Bur. of Ed.] *n.p.* Govt. Prtg. Off., *Washgtn.* 77
FLEXNER, A. Medical Education in United States & Canada 1 8° Carnegie Foundn., *N.Y.* 10
First of a ser. of papers on professl. schls. to be issued by Carnegie Foundn., 576 Fifth Ave., N.Y. City. 346 pp.
GARDINER, W. T. Medical Education [pp. 80] *o.p.* 8° *Glasgow* 83
HARDWICKE, H. J. Medical Educn. and Practice in all Pts. of World 10/ 8° Churchill 80
HELMHOLTZ, Prf. H. On Thoughts in Medicine—*in his* Popular Scientific Lectures [tr.], *ut* **H** § 10
HOLMES, Oliver Wendell —*in his* Medical Essays $2 c 8° Houghton, *Boston* 83
Chs. on scholastic and bedside tchg., med. professn. in Mass., med. libraries, etc.
HUN, H. Guide to Amer. Medical Students in Europe [pp. 151] *o.p.* c 8° *New York* 83
HUXLEY, Prf. T. H. Connection of Biolog. Sciences w. Medicine—*in his* Science & Culture, *ut* **H** § 42
,, On Medical Education—*in his* Critiques and Addresses, *ut* **H** § 42
,, —*in his* Science and Education = Collected Essays, vol. iii, *ut* **H** § 83
JORDAN, D. S. The General Education of the Physician *o.p.* c 8° *San Francisco* 91
KEETLEY, C. B. Student's Guide to the Medical Profession *o.p.* [*pb.* 2/6] c 8° Macmillan 78
PEPPER, Wm. Higher Medical Education [pp. 46] *o.p.* c 8° Collins, *Phila.* 77
PUSCHMANN, Dr Th. History of Medical Educn. [tr.]—*ut* **H*** § 1
RAUCH, J. H. Medl. Educn., Med. Colls. etc., in U.S. & Canada [pp. 258] *o.p.* c 8° *Springfield, Ill.* 91
SAWYER, Sir J. Notes on Medical Education 3/ c 8° *Birmingham* 89
WEST, C. Profession of Medicine: Study, Practice, Duties, Rewards 2/6 12° Paul 96
WOOTON, E. Guide to the Medical Profession 2/6 c 8° Upcott Gill 83

*Medical Education for Women*—*v.* **D** § 132

*Dental*: HILL (A.) History of the Reform Movement in Dental Profession in Gt. Brit.
dur. last 20 Yrs. *o.p.* [*pb.* 10/6] c 8° Trübner 77

TURNER, A. Manual of Dental Education *o.p.* [*pb.* 1/] f 8° Livingstone, *Edin.* 61
WETHERBY, I. J. The Past and Future of the Dental Profession *o.p.* c 8° *Boston* 66

*Indian Medical Service*

WEBB, W. W. The Indian Medical Service 5/6 c 8° Thacker 90

**Military Education**

BANNATYNE, Col. J. M. Guide to Promotn. in Infantry, 2 Pts. ea. 7/ c 8° MacLehose, *Glasgow* [62–38] 84–6
BARNARD, Dr Hy. [ed.] Military Schls. & Courses of Instruction in France $3·75 m 8° Steiger, *N.Y.* [62] 72
In France, Germany, Russia, Sweden, Switzerland, etc.
BELLAIRS, Lt.-Gen. Sir Wm. The Military Career; ill. *o.p.b.* [*pb.* 2/6] c 8° W. H. Allen [89] 90
How we Educate our Officers *o.p.* [*pb.* 2/6] c 8° W. H. Allen 84
PRATT, Lt.-Col. Sisson C. Guide to Promotion, 2 Pts. 7/; 6/ c 8° Stanford 92–3
Pt. i: *Ranks of Lieut., Capt. and Maj.*; ii: *Rank of Major* [completed]. On lines of BANNATYNE's bk., *ut sup.*
Report of Director-General of Milit. Educn. on Army Schls. & Libraries [Blue-Bk.] f° Eyre & Spottisw. 77
Royal Commission on Military Education, 1870: Reports [Blue Books] f° Eyre & Spottiswoode
Appended are accounts of foreign systems.
YOUNGHUSBAND, Cpt. G. J. The Queen's Commission 6/ c 8° Murray [91] 92
How to prepare for, obtain, and use the Commission, w. information as to costs, and prospects.

*History: United States*

HANCOCK, H. I. Life at West Point: makg. of an Am. officer; ill. $1·40 12° Putnam 03
An ill. acc. of the famous American military academy of U.S. Very interesting.

**Realschule** —*v.* **D** § 157, *s.v.* Germany

**Roman-Catholic Education** —*v. also* **A** § 99; *for* Ignatius Loyola *v.* **D** § 161

BURNS, J. A. Catholic School System in the United States $1·25 12° Benziger, *N.Y.* 08
PACHTLER, G. M. [ed.] Ratio Studiorum et Institt. Scholast. Soc. Jesu, 4 vols.
ea. 15 m. r 8° Hofmann, *Berlin* 87–94
[Monumenta Germ. Paedag.] The celebr. educl. syst. of Jesuits, drawn up under directn. of ACQUAVIVA, 5th Genl. of the Order. It recd. its final form in 1599. It is fully analysed in Hughes' *Loyola* 1892, *ut* D § 161.
SCHOUPPE, F. X. [R.-C.] Abgd. Course of Religious Instruction [tr.] 3/ c 8° Burns & Oates 89
SCHWICKERATH, F'r R. [S.-J.] Jesuit Education: hist. and principles
[7/6 *n.* Burns] $1·75 *n.* 8° Herder, *St Louis* [03] 05
SHEEHAN, Can. P. A. [R.-C.] Early Essays and Lectures—*ut* **D** § 155

*Port-Royal*—*v.* **A** § 101 *Roman-Catholic Schools and Colleges*—*v.* **D** § 157, *passim*

**Sunday School:** *History; Bibliography*

BROWN, Mariana C. Sunday-School Movements in America $1·25 c 8° Revell, *N.Y.* 01
BULLARD, Rev. Asa Fifty Years with the Sabbath Schools [Amer. schls.] $1·75 12° Lockwood, *Boston* 76
CANDLER, Rev. W. A. History of Sunday Schools [American schls.] 12° Phillips, *N.Y.* 80
DUNCAN, Rev. R. S. History of Sunday Schools
[American Schls.] $1 12° Southern Bapt. Pb. Soc., *Memphis, Tenn.* 7
DUNNING, A. E. The Sunday School Library 60 c. 16° *Publ. Wkly.* Off., *N.Y.* 84
Treats of hist., object, etc., of Sunday Schl., w. appendix contg. a bibliography; 105 pp. in all.
FOOTE, Eliz. L. Librarian of the Sunday School [a good bk.] 35 c. 16° Eaton, *N.Y.* 97
GRAY, Rev. Jas. C. Sunday Schl. World: encyclo. of facts and principles 4/6 c 8° Stock 71
GREENWOOD, Thos. Sunday School and Village Libraries [English only] 1/6 c 8° J. Clarke 92
GROSER, Wm. H. A Hundred Years' Work for Children 2/6 c 8° S.S.U. 03
A good and complete hist. of the wk. of the Sunday School Union, fr. formatn. (1803) to 1903.
HARRIS, J. H. Story of the Sunday School 1/6 c 8° Culley 01
HOWARD, P. E. [ed.] Sunday Schools of the World Around [a Report] 2/6 *n.* c 8° S.S.U. 08
PRAY, L. H. Hist. of Sund. Schls. & of Relig. Educn. [full of facts] *o.p.* Crosby, *Boston* 47

*Biography*

RAIKES, Rob. [1735–1811]
Belcher, Jos. R. Raikes: his Sund.-schls. & his friends [pp. 311] *o.p.* 8° Am. Bapt. Pb. Soc., *Phila.* 59
Gregory, Alf. Robert Raikes, Journalist and Philanthropist *o.p.* c 8° Hodder 77
Harris, J. H. [ed.] Robert Raikes, the Man and his Work; ill. 7/6 8° Arrowsmith 99
Biograph. notes and letters, rather ill-digested; w. results of much investigation on the spot.
" Robert Raikes [Splendid Lives Series] 1/ c 8° S.S.U. 00

*Principles; Methods*

BEARD, Rev. F. The Blackboard in the Sunday School $1·50 12° Haney, *N.Y.* 77
CAPE H. F Modern Sunday School: princ. and practice $1 *n.* (3/ *n.*) c 8° Revell 07

CRAFTS, Rev. W. F. Plain Uses of Blackboard & Slate in S.S. $1 12° Jennings, *Cincinnati* [81] 01

GROTON, W. M., *etc.* Sunday School Teacher's Manual $1 *n.* c 8° Jacobs, *Phila.* 09

HASLETT, S. B. Pedagogical Bible School $1 (5/ *n.*) 8° Revell 04

LAWRANCE, Marion How to Conduct a Sunday School $1·25 *n.* (4/6 *n.*) c 8° Revell [05] 01

MEAD, G. W. Modern Methods in Sunday School Work $1·50 *n.* c 8° Dodd & Mead, *N.Y.* 03

PALMER [KING], Flor. U. One Year of S.S. Lessns.; Secd. Yr.; ill. ea. $1·25 *n.* c 8° Macmillan, *N.Y.* 09

POTTER, Bp. H. C. Principles of Religious [=Sund. Sch.] Education $1·25 c 8° Longman, *N.Y.* 01

SHELDON, W. L. An Ethical Sunday School [Ethical Lib.] $1·25 c 8° Macmillan, *N.Y.* 00
**3/ Sonnenschein. From the 'Ethical Society's' point of view. Incls. some specimen lessons.**

TARBELL, Dr Martha Teacher's Guide to Intern. S.S. Lessons; ill. [5/ Downie] 8° $1·25 Bobbs-Merrill, *Indianapolis* 05

TRUMBULL, Rev. H. C. Teaching & Tchrs. [S.-S.; systematic; 5/ Hodder] $1·50 c 8° Wattles, *Phila.* 84

,, The Sunday School [orig., mission, meths., etc.] $1·50 c 8° Wattles, *Phila.* 88

,, Yale Lectures on the Sunday School *Sund. Schl. Times* Off., *Phila.*

VINCENT, J. H. The Modern Sunday School $1 c 8° Phillips & Hunt, *N.Y.* 87

WELLS, A. R. Sunday School Success: pract. methods $1·25 c 8° Revell, *N.Y.* 98

,, Sunday School Problems $1 12° Wilde, *Boston* 05

**University Education:** *Generally—v. also* **D** § 157, *and* **D** § 167, *s.v.* Languages (Ancient)

ASQUITH, H. H. Ancient Universities & the Modern World [address] 1/ *n.* 8° MacLehose, *Glasgow* 07

BAIN, Prf. Alex. University Ideal—*in his* Practical Essays, *ut* **D** § 161

BARNARD, Dr Hy. [ed.] Universities & Institns. of Super. Instrn. in Differ. Countries $3·50 8° *Hartford* 73

BRODBECK, Dr A. The Ideal of Universities [tr. by author] *o.p.* c 8° Metaphys. Pb. Co., *N.Y.* 96

CAIRD, Prc. Jno. University Addresses [on subjs. of acad. study] 6/ *n.* 8° MacLehose, *Glasgow* 98

CAMPBELL, Prf. Lewis Nationalization of Old English Universities 7/6 c 8° Chapman 01

v. DÖLLINGER, Dr J. J. I. Universities, Past and Present—*in his* Addresses [tr.], *ut* **F** § 1

ELIOT, C. W. [Pres. of Harvard] University Administration $1.50 *n.* 8° Houghton, *Boston* 08
**6/ *n.* Macmillan. Limited to Amer. univs., the majority of wh. are not properly univs. at all, consistg. as they do of single colleges rd. wh. have grown up an under-grad. dept. of appl. science, inclg. agric., engineerg., commerce, and sometimes divinity.**

EMERSON, R. W. Universities—*in his* English Traits, *ut* **E** § 16

GILMAN, Prí D. C. University Problems in the United States [10/6 Unwin] $2 8° Century Co., *N.Y.* 98

HALDANE, R. B. Universities and National Life [3 addresses] 2/6 *n.* c 8° Murray 10

HAMILTON, Sir Wm. University Reform—*in his* Discussions on Philosophy, *ut* **C** § 30
**Incls. also papers: *On Patronage, etc., of Universities; On Reform of Engl. Universities; On State of Engl. Universities.***

HUXLEY, Prf. T. H. Universities, Actual and Ideal—*in his* Science and Culture, *ut* **H** § 42

,, Univ. Educn.—*in his* Amer. Addresses, *ut* **H** § 42 (*also in* Coll. Essays, vol. iii, *ut* **K** § 83)

JEBB, Prf. R. C. Work of Univs. for the Nation, Past & Present 1/ c 8° Camb. Press 93
**50 c. *n.* Putnam, *N.Y.* An inaugural lecture. Repr. in his *Essays* [*ut* K § 168], where also is his *University Educn. and Natl. Life.***

KNAPP, J. M. The Universities and the Social Problem 5/ c 8° Rivington 97

MAGNUS, Sir Pp. —*in his* Educational Aims and Efforts, *ut* **D** § 157
***Schemes for Reorganizing London University; London University in Relation to the Empire.***

MORRIS, Prf. G. S. Univ. Education—*in his* Philosophical Papers, Ser. i, pp. 1–40 *o.p.* 8° *Ann Arbor* 81

MULLINGER, J. Bass *article* Universities—*in the* Encyclo. Brit. xxiii, 9th edn., *ut* **K** § 1

NEWMAN, Card. J. H. The Idea of a University Defined & Illustrated 3/6 ($1·25) 8° Longman [73] 91
**[Silver Lib.] Discourses powerfully enforcg. the true purpose of liberal educn., that it is a pursuit of knowl. for sake of knowl. and not for the value of any of its fruits or applicns., however important. *Univ. Tchg. consid. in Nine Discourses,* bg. Pt. i of above. [Pocket Lib.] 2/ *n.* (75 c *n.*) f 8° Longman 08.**

,, Lectures and Essays on University Subjects 6/ c 8° Burns & Oates 59

,, Office and Work of Universities 6/ c 8° Burns & Oates 56

,, Rise and Progress of Universities—*ut* **D** § 157, *s.v.* Medieval [historical]

,, Scope and Nature of University Education 6/ c 8° Burns & Oates [58] 59

,, The same, ed. A. R. Waller [Cloister Lib.] 2/6 *n.* f 8° Dent [58] 03

,, University Sketches; Introd. G. Sampson [Scott Lib.] 1/6 c 8° W. Scott [56] 02

RAMSAY, Sir Wm. Functions of a University—*in his* Essays, *ut* **H** § 17

SCHAFF, Dr Pp. The University, Past, Present and Future—*in his* Literature and Poetry, *ut* **K** § 17

SEELEY, Sir J. R. A Liberal Education—*in his* Lectures and Essays, *ut* **F** § 1

*Cambridge* —*v. also* **D** § 157, *s.v.* Cambridge

SEDGWICK, Rev. A. A Discourse on the Studies of Cambridge *o.p.* [*pb.* 12/] p 8° *London* [34] 50

WHEWELL, Dr W. Of a Liberal Educn., 3 Pts. *o.p.* [*pb.* 10/] 8° Parker [40–52] 50–2
**W. partic. ref. to studies at Camb. i: *Principles and Recent History*; ii: *Dissensions and Changes*; iii: *Revised Statutes.***

*Oxford* —*v. also* **D** § 157, *s.v.* Oxford
ROGERS, Prf. J. E. Thorold Education in Oxford: methods, aids, rewards *o.p.* [*pb.* 6/] c 8° Clar. Press 61
SMITH, Prf. Goldwin Reorganisation of the University of Oxford *o.p.* [*pb.* 2/] c 8° Parker 68

**University Extension**

ADAMS, Prf. H. B. Seminary Libraries & Univ. Extension 25 c. 8° Johns Hopkins Univ. Pr., *Baltimore* 87
Aspects of Modern Study: University Extension addresses [from 1884 to 1894] 2/6 *n.* c 8° Macmillan 94
By Ld. PLAYFAIR, Can. BROWNE, G. J. GOSCHEN, Jno. MORLEY, Sir Jas. PAGET, Prf. Max MÜLLER, Duke of ARGYLL, Bp. of DURHAM, Prf. R. C. JEBB.
HART, Prf. A. B. Univ. Participation [as substit. f. Univ. Ext.]—*in his* Studs. in Am. Educn., *ut* **D** § 157
JAMES, G. F. Handbook of University Extension $1 8° Am. Soc. of Univ. Tchg., *Boston* 93
MACKINDER (H. J.) + SADLER (M. E.) Univ. Extension, Past, Present, & Future 1/6 c 8° Cassell [90] 92
MOULTON (R. G.) + STUART (J.) The Univ. Extension Movemt. [account of] *o.p.* c 8° Bemrose, *Derby* 85
ROBERTS, Dr R. D. Eighteen Years of University Extension *o.p.* [*pb.* 1/] c 8° Camb. Press 91
STEDMAN, A. M. M. [ed.] —*article in his* Oxford, its Life and Schools, *ut* **D** § 157, *s.v.* Oxford
*University Settlements in East London*—*v.* **D** § 127

**Volksschule** —*v.* **D** § 157, *s.v.* Germany

**Women and Girls** —*v. also* **D** § 132

*Bibliography:* ROLLINS (Mary H.) Contribs. to Bibl. of Higher Educ. of Women Publ. Lib., *Boston* 98
BARNETT, Edith A. The Training of Girls for Work 2/6 f 8° Macmillan 95
A good survey of the subject, with many practical recommendations.
BATESON, Marg. [ed.] Professional Women upon their Professions [interviews] 5/ 8° H. Cox 95
BEALE, Dorothea Addresses to Teachers 1/6 *n.* (50 c.) c 8° Longman 10
12 addresses touchg. many subjs., but dealg. rather w. spiritual outlook, mental traing. and diffics. of tchrs. than giving guidance in method.
,, and others Work and Play in Girls' Schools 7/6 ($2·25) c 8° Longman 98
A full account and explanation of a course of secondary teaching suited for girls.
BOLTON, Sar. K. Social Studies in England [educational] $1 c 8° Lothrop, *Boston n.d.* (85)
BRACKETT, Anna [ed.] The Education of American Girls $1·50 12° Putnam, *N.Y.* 75
A symposium of twelve ladies; evoked by Dr CLARKE's *Sex in Education, ut inf., s.v.* Co-education.
,, [ed.] Women and the Higher Education [by var. wrs.] $1 16° Harper, *N.Y.* 93
BREMNER, [Miss] C. S. Education of Girls and Women in Great Britain 4/6 c 8° Sonnenschein 97
A thorough and moderate work—a repository of information.
BURSTALL, Sar. A. Education of Girls in U.S. [Gilchrist Report] 3/6 c 8° Sonnenschein 94
,, —*in her* Impressions of American Education, *ut* **D** § 157, *s.v.* United States
,, English High Schools for Girls 4/6 ($1·25 *n.*) c 8° Longman 07
,, + DOUGLAS (M. A.) [eds.] Public Schools for Girls [by var. wrs.] 4/6 ($1·25 *n.*) c 8° Longman 10
BUSS, Fces. Mary Leaves from the Note-Books of, ed. Grace Toplis 3/6 gl 8° Macmillan 97
Addresses to girls on Candour, Cheerfulness, Courtesy, Family Love, Honesty, Idleness and Weariness, Self-Control, Youth and Beauty, etc.
BUTLER, Josephine E. Woman's Work and Woman's Culture [essays] *o.p.* [*pb.* 10/6] 8° Macmillan 69
CHESTER, Eliza Chats with Girls on Self-Culture [Portia Series] $1·25 12° Dodd & Mead, *N.Y.* 92
COBBE, Fces. Power Essays on the Pursuits of Women *o.p.* [*pb.* 2/] c 8° Faithfull [63] 66
DAVIES, Emily The Higher Education of Women *o.p.* [*pb.* 3/6] 12° Strahan 66
,, Women in the Universities of Engl. & Scotl. [pamphlet] *o.p.* c 8° Macmillan 96
DUNLOP, O. J. Leaves from a Cambridge Note-Book 2/6 *n.* c 8° Heffer, *Camb.* 08
Essays on Cambridge life by a late student of Girton College.
Education and Professions for Women [by var. wrs.] 5/ c 8° Chapman 03
Female Schools and Education [repr. fr. *Amer. Jl. of Educ.*] $3·50 m 8° *Hartford* 75
FÉNELON, Frç. [1651–1715] Education of Girls [1687], tr. Kate Lupton 55 c. 12° Ginn, *Boston* 90
'A work of gentleness and goodness, pervaded by a spirit of progress'.—COMPAYRÉ.
Girls School Year Book (Public Schools) 2/6 *n.* c 8° Sonnenschein [06 *sqq.*] *ann.*
Pt. i conts. acc. of ab. 130 leadg. publ. schls. for girls in Gt. Brit. and Ireld.; Pt. ii arts. on careers for women.
Girls' Schools—*in* Special Reports on Educational Subjects, vol. ii, *ut* **D** § 163*
GREY, Maria G. [= Mrs. Wm.] On the Education of Women *o.p.* [*pb.* 1/] 8° Ridgway 71
,, Last Words to Girls on Life in Schl. and after Schl. 3/6 c 8° Rivington 89
,, + SHIRREFF (Emily) Thoughts on Self-Culture, addressed to Women *o.p.* [*pb.* 4/6] c 8° Simpkin [71] 72
HIGGINSON, T. W. —*in his* Common Sense about Women, *ut* **D** § 132
HODGSON, Prf. W. B. Education of Girls & Employment of Women *o.p.* [*pb.* 3/6] c 8° Trübner [69] 69
HOWE, Julia Ward [ed.] Sex in Education [replies to Clarke, *sup.*] *o.p.* [*pb.* $1·25] c 8° Roberts, *Boston* 74
LANGE, Helene The Higher Education of Women in Europe [tr.] $1 (4/6) c 8° Appleton 90
[Int. Educ. Ser.] Treats the subj. in a polemical style. The tr. adds some comparative statistics and charts.

MADDISON, Isabel — Hdbk. of Courses open to Women in British, Continental, and Canadian Universities 75 c. *n.* (3/) ; Suppl. 20 c. *n.* (1/*n.*) c 8° Macmillan [96] 99 ; 97
OLIN, Helen R. — The Women of a State University—*ut* **D** § 168
PFEIFFER, Emily — Women & Work [rel. of higher educn. to health] *o.p.* [*pb.* 6/] c 8° Trübner 88
RHYS, Isabel L. — Education of Girls in Switzerland and Bavaria 1/*n.* f 8° Blackie 05
School Traing. for Home Duties of Women, Pts. i–iii=Spec. Reps. on Ed. Subjs., xv–xvi, xix—*ut* **D** § 163*
SCHWARTZ, Julia A. — Vassar Studies $1·50 (3/6) c 8° Putnam 99
SHIRREFF, Emily — Intellectual Education & its Influence on Women *o.p.* [*pb.* 6/] c 8° Smith & Elder 62
" — Princs. of Kindergarten, & Bearing on Higher Educ. of Women—*ut* **D** § 165
SIDGWICK, Mrs Hy. — University Education of Women 6*d.* *n.* 8° Macmillan 97
STANTON, Th. [ed.] — —*in* The Woman Question in Europe, *ut* **D** § 132
TALBOT, Marion — The Education of Women Univ. Press, *Chicago in prep.*
THWING, C. F. — The College Woman $1 c 8° Barnes, *N.Y.* *n.d.* (94)
WARWICK, C'ess of [ed.] — Progress of Women's Education in British Empire 6/ c 8° Longman 98
Victoria Era Exhib. (1897) papers of misc. characters and varying values ; all conn. w. the subject.
WILSON, Arch. J. M. — Three Addresses to Girls at School 1/6 f 8° Rivington 90
WINSLOW, Anna Green — Diary of Boston Schl.-Girl, 1771, ed. Alice M. Earle $1·25 16° Houghton, *Bost.* 92
ZIMMERN, Alice — The Renaissance of Girls' Education in England *o.p.* [*pb.* 5/] c 8° Innes 98
A good survey of the subj. : full account of the progress of last half of 19th century.
*Medicine as a Profession* — —*v.* **D** § 132, *s.v.* Employment : Medicine
*Physical Education of Girls* — —*v.* **D** § 167, *s.v.* Physical Education

*Biography*

BEALE, Dorothea [*Cheltenham* ; d. 1906] Life of. By Eliz. Raikes ; ill. 10/6 *n.* 8° Constable 08
BUSS, Fces. Mary
Ridley, Annie E. — Frances May Buss and her Work for Education 7/6 c 8° Longman 95
CLOUGH, Anne J. [*Newnham*, Camb. ; 1820–92] Memoir of. By Blanche A. Clough 6/ c 8° Arnold [97] 08
PALMER, Alice F. — Life of. By G. H. Palmer [6/ *n.* Constable] $1·50 *n.* 8° Houghton, *Boston* 08
Life, by her husband, of Pres. of Wellesley Coll. 1881–7, Dean of Women at Chicago Univ., etc.
PIPE, Hannah E. [1831–1906] Life and Letters. By Anna M. Stoddart 15/ *n.* 8° Blackwood 10
An interesting life of one of the greater schoolmistresses of the Victorian period—headmistress and owner of 'Laleham', Clapham Park, London.

*Vassar College* [for women]

LOSSING, B. J. — Vassar College and its Founder $4·75 i 8° Alvord, *N.Y.* 67
RAYMOND, J. H. — Vassar College : sketch of its foundn. and aims *o.p.* 8° Green, *N.Y.* 73

**Co-education**

CAMPBELL, D. — Mixed Educn. of Boys and Girls in Engld. and Amer. *o.p.* c 8° Longman 74
CLARKE, Dr E. H. — Sex in Education, or A Fair Chance for Girls $1·25 12° Houghton, *Boston* 73
Comfort, Geo. F. + Anna M. Woman's Educn. and Woman's Health [crit. of above] $1 12° Bardeen, *Syracuse, N.Y.* 74
Duffey, E. B. — No Sex in Educn. : equal chance f. boys & girls $1 16° Stoddart, *Phila.* 74
Greene, W. B. Crit. Comments on Passges. in 'Sex in Educn.' [pp. 30] *o.p.* c 8° Lee & Shepard, *Bost.* 74
GRANT, C. — American Co-education *n.p.* 8° Govt. Prtg. Off., *Washington* 02
HAWTREY, Mabel — The Co-Education of the Sexes 2/6 *n.* c 8° Paul 96
A sensible book, arguing against co-education.
MILLS (Elliott) + TYLEE E. S. — Boy and Girl : shd. they be educ. together? 1/ c 8° Simpkins 06
OLIN, Helen R. — The Women of a State University $1·50 *n.* (6/*n.*) c 8° Putnam 09
An illustration of the working of co-education in the University of Wisconsin.
WOODS, Alice [ed.] — Co-Education : a series of essays 3/*n.* ($1) c 8° Longman 03
Confined to secondary schools ; essays by various hands. Favourable on the whole. Introd. by Prf. M. E. SADLER.
*Michigan Univ.* : ANDERSON (Olive S. L.) An Amer. Girl in a Boys' College—*ut* **D** § 157
*Oberlin College* [a co-educl. institn. in Ohio, founded 1833]
LEONARD, D. L. — The Story of Oberlin $1·50 c 8° Pilgrim Press, *Boston* 98
An account of the community (some 100 instructors and 1,500 studts.), the idea, and the movement.

## 169 : METHODS OF INSTRUCTION (*f*) : CORRECTIVE AND REMEDIAL EDUCATION

**Blind (The)**

*Bibliography* : Perkins Instit. : Cat. of Bks. for Blind [1800 entries] 8° Perkins Inst., *Boston* 07
CAMPBELL, Sir J. F. — *article* Blind—*in* Encyclo. Brit., 9th edn. vol. iii [*ut* **K** § 1]
LEVY, W. Hanks — Blindness and the Blind *o.p.* [*pb.* 7/6] c 8° Chapman 72

Royal Commission: Report on the Blind, Deaf and Mute, 4 vols. 14/7 f° Eyre & Spottiswoode 89
Vol. i: *Report* 1/1; ii: *Appendix* [= lithos. ill. of systs. of tchg.] 4/6; iii: *Minutes of Evidence*, 7/6; iv: *Alphab. Digest*, 1/6. The most exhaustive examination of the care and training of defective children ever printed.

de la SIZERANNE, Maur. The Blind as seen through Blind Eyes [tr.] *o.p.* c 8° Putnam 93
Account, fr. exper. of Valentine HAUY, the well-known friend of blind in France and Russia at end of 18 and beginning of 19 cent., of everyday life of a blind person, w. informn. on latest improvemts. in tchg.

,, The Blind Sisters of St Paul [tr.] 7/6 8° Paul
[Int. Cath. Lib.] On psychol. of blind women, by one herself blind; w. hist. of the community of Blind Sisters of St Paul.

*Practical Works*

ALSTON, Jno. Educn., Employmts., and Internal Arrangemts. adopted at Asylum for Blind, Glasgow; ill. 2/ 8° Low [42] 95

ARMITAGE, T. R. The Education of the Blind [pp. 216] c 8° *London* 86

GALL, J. Histor. Sketch of Orig. & Progr. of Literature f. Blind [pp. 388] *o.p.* 8° *Edinburgh* 34

,, Education of the Blind [chfly. of histor. interest now] *o.p.* 8° *Edinburgh* 37

GUILLÉ, Dr Sebastian Instruction and Amusements of the Blind [tr.]; 23 ill. 5/ 8° Low [19] 94

JAVAL, Dr Emil On Becoming Blind, tr. C. E. Edson $1·25 *n.* f 8° Macmillan 05
Tr. of *Entre Aveugles*—advice to those who have recently lost their sight. By a Fch. doctor, who became blind at 60.

MOON, W. Sight for the Blind, syst. of reading f. the Blind *o.p.* [*pb.* 5/] c 8° Longman 73

PLUMPTRE, Mrs F. H. The 'Braille' System f. the Blind [arrgd. for 'seeing' wrs.] 3/ 4° *Newton Abbott* 90

VINCE Education and Management of Blind Children *o.p.* [*pb.* 1/6] 12° Simpkin 76

*History and Statistics*

ANAGNOS, M. Education of the Blind [historical sketch] 12° Rand, *Boston* 82

,, Kindergarten and Primary School for the Blind *o.p.* 12° *Boston* 86

ILLINGWORTH, W. H. History of the Education of the Blind 3/6 *n.* c 8° Low 10

*Biography of the Blind and Workers for them*

BRIDGMAN, Laura Dewey [Blind, Deaf, and Dumb; 1829–89]

Donaldson, Dr H. H. The Brain of Laura Bridgman—*in* Amer. Jl. of Psychol., Dec. '90
This historical child, notwithstg. loss or grave impairmt. of all senses exc. Touch, managed by help of carefully planned educn. to growinto an intell. moral being.

Howe, Dr S. G. Education of L. Bridgman [pp. 233] *o.p.* c 8° *Boston* 90

Howe (Maud) + Hall (Flor. Howe) Laura Bridgman [7/6 Hodder] c 8° 04
Acc. of her treatmt. and educn. by Dr HOWE, by his daughters. *V.* also HOWE's *Letters and Jls.*, *inf.*

Lamson, Mary S. Life & Education of Laura D. Bridgman $1·50 12° Houghton, *Boston* [78] 81

GILBERT, Eliz. Marg. Maria [1826–85]

Martin, Fces. Elizabeth Gilbert and her Work for the Blind 6/ c 8° Macmillan 87
Life of fdr. (w. W. H. LEVY) of Assoc. f. Promg. Gen. Welf. of Blind; herself rend. blind as child by scarlet fever.

HOWE, Dr S. G. Letters and Journals, 2 vols.—*ut* **D** § 128
In 1832 HOWE, after visit to Eur., retd. to Am., and set ab. workg. for blind, later throwg. hmself into anti-slav. wk.

KELLER, Helen Adams Story of my Life [7/6 Hodder] $1·50 *n.* c 8° Doubleday, *N.Y.* 03

,, My Key of Life, Optimism: an essay f 8° [04] 08
2/6 Pitman. Former is an interestg. acc. of educn. of a blind, deaf, and dumb Amer. girl.

,, The World I Live in; port. [3/6 *n.* Hodder] $1·20 *n.* 12° Century Co., *N.Y.* 08

**Deaf-mutes**

HATTON, J. Deaf-and-Dumb Land *o.p.* s 8° *London n.d.* (87)

LARGE, A. *article* Deaf and Dumb—*in* Encyclo. Brit., 9th edn., vol. vii [*ut* **K** § 1]

SCOTT, Dr W. R. Deaf & Dumb: their educn. & social positn. *o.p.* [*pb.* 7/6] 8° Bell [ ] 70

SEISS, Dr J. A. Children of Silence [pop. acc.; w. meths. of educ.] $1 12° Porter, *Phila.* 87

*History; Statistics*

BELL, Alex. Graham Memr. upon Formn. of a Deaf Variety of Human Race [pp. 83] 8° *Washington* 83

,, Facts and Opinions rel. to the Deaf [pp. 195] 8° Eyre 88

FAY, E. A. [ed.] Procgs. of World's Congr. of Instrs. of Deaf [Chic. '93] *n.p.* Govt. Prtg. Off., *Washgtn.* 93

,, [ed.] Histories of Amer. Schls. for the Deaf: 1817–93, 3 v. 8° Volta Bureau, *Washgtn.* 93
Vol. i: *Public Schls. estab.* 1817–54; ii: *Public Schls.* 1854–1893; iii: *Denom. and Priv. Schls.; Schls. in Can. and Mex.*

HUBBARD, H. W. Deaf-mutism [historical; all ages, to 1894] c 8° 94

Royal Commission: Report—*ut sup.*, *s.v.* Blind

*Biography*

BRIDGMAN, Laura Dewey [1829–89]—*v. sup.*, *s.v.* Blind

GALLAUDET, Rev. Thos. Hopkins [1787–1851; founder of deaf-mute instrn. in Amer.]

Gallaudet, E. M. Life of T. H. Gallaudet $1·75 12° Holt, *N.Y.* 88

KELLER, Helen —*v. sup.*, *s.v.* Blind

*Practical Works*

ADDISON, W. H. Educn. and Training of Deaf-Mutes—*in* Love's Deaf Mutism, *ut* **H*** § 15
ARNOLD, Thos. On Education of the Deaf, ed. A. Farrar 5/ *n.* c 8° Simpkin [81] 01
BELL, Alex. Graham Methods of Teachg. the Deaf in U.S. Gibson, *Washgtn.* 98
BELL, A. M. Visible Speech: science of universal alphabetics *o.p.* [*pb.* 15/] 4° Simpkin 67
GORDON, J. C. [ed.] Education of Deaf Children Volta Bureau, *Washgtn.* 92
" Notes and Observn. on Educ. of Deaf Children Volta Bureau, *Washgtn.* 92
HARTMANN, A. Deafmutism and Education of Deaf-Mutes [tr.] 7/6 s 8° Baillière 81
KINSEY, A. A. Report on Internatl. Congress on Educn. of Deaf *o.p.* [*pb.* 5/] 8° W. H. Allen 80
Report on the Milan Congress: of great value.
VAN PRAAGH, Wm. Lessns. f. Instrn. of Deaf & Dumb Children, 2 Pts. *o.p.* [*pb.* 4/] 12° Trübner 84

**Idiots; Feeble-minded; Crippled, etc.**

BALFOUR OF BURLEIGH, L'd Education of Neglected Children 6*d.* c 8° Blackwood 99
BEECH, Fletcher Treatmt. and Educn. of Mentally Feeble Children *o.p.* c 8° Churchill 92
BRADY, C. Training of Idiotic and Feeble-minded Children *o.p.* 8° *Dublin* 64
Charity Organisation Soc.: Report on the Epileptic and Crippled—*ut* **D** § 128
DOWN, J. Langdon Educn. and Traing. of Feeble in Mind *o.p.* c 8° *London* 77
" Some Mental Affectns. of Childhd. and Youth [lects.] 6/ c 8° Churchill 86
DUNCAN, E. M. Method of Drill and Gymnastics used for Idiots, etc. *o.p.* 8° *London* 61
DUNCAN (P. M.) + MILLARD (W.) Manl. for Classif., Trg., and Educn. of Feeble-minded, Imbecile, and Idiotic *o.p.* 8° *London* 86
FRY, Sir Edw. [ed.] Problem of the Feeble-minded 1/ *n.* 8° P. S. King & Son 09
Abstr. of Rept. of the Roy. Comm.; w. Introd. by FRY and contribs. by Sir F. GALTON, Rev. W. R. INGE, Prf. A. C. PIGOU, Mary DENDY.
JOHNSON, G. E. Contribns. to Pedag. & Psychol. of Feeble-m. Childr. [pp. 51] 8° *Worcester, Mass.* 95
LEPAGE, Dr C. P. Feeblemindedness in Children of School age 5/ *n.* c 8° Univ. Press, *Mancs.* 11
MAENNAL, G. Auxiliary Schls. of Germany [tr.] [6 lects.] *n.p.* Govt. Prtg. Off., *Washington* 07
SCOTT, Dr W. R. Remarks, Theoret. and Pract., on Educ. of Idiots, etc. *o.p.* c 8° *London* 47
Gives an account of the work of SEGUIN at the Bicetre.
SEGUIN, Edw. Idiocy, & its Treatmt. by Physiolog. Meth. [standard] $5 8° Wood, *N.Y.* 66
" Psycho-physiol. Traing. of an Idiotic Hand 30 c. 8° Putnam, *N.Y.* 79
" Psycho-physiol. Traing. of an Idiotic Eye 30 c. 8° Putnam, *N.Y.* 80
SHUTTLEWORTH, G. E. Mentally Deficient Children: their treatmt. & traing. 4/ c 8° H. K. Lewis 95
The best short treatmt. of subj. fr. an educational standpoint.
" Care of the Mentally Feeble Child *o.p.* H. K. Lewis 92
WYNTER, Andr. The Borderland of Insanity $2 8° Putnam, *N.Y.* 75
Conts. a chapter on the training of imbecile children.

*History; Statistics*

FERNALD, W. E. History of the Treatment of the Feeble-Minded *o.p.* c 8° *Boston* 93
A good acc. of what has been done in the United States and elsewhere.
WARNER, Fcs., etc. Feeble-minded Child and Adult *o.p.* c 8° *London* 93
Bureau of Educ., *Washgtn.* Report of an investign. of 50,000 schl.-childr.; w. suggestions.

**Reformatory and Ragged Schools**

BAKER, T. B. —*in his* War with Crime, *ut* **D** § 123
BARNARD, Dr Hy. [ed.] Reformatory Educn. [Eur. & U.S.: by var. wrs.] $1·50 8° *Hartford* 57
BARTLEY, G. C. T. The Schools for the People; pl. *o.p.* [*pb.* 21/] m 8° Bell 71
Acc. of devel. of schls. for defective, delinquent, and dependent children in England up to 1871.
CARPENTER, Mary Reformat. Schls. f. Childr. of Perishg. & Dangerous Classes *o.p.* [*pb.* 5/] f 8° Bennett 51
" Reformat. Pris. Discipl. as devel. by Sir W. Crofton [Irish prisons] *o.p.* [*pb.* 2/6] 12° Longman 79
HILL, Florence Davenpt. —*in her* Children of the State, *ut* **D** § 127, *s.v.* Children
MONTAGUE, C. J. Sixty Years of Waifdom [Ragg. Schl. movemt.] 2/ c 8° C. Murray 04
PIKE, G. H. Pity the Perishing [Rag. Schl. wk. at var. centres] 3/6 c 8° J. Clarke 83
Reports on Reformatory and Industrial Schools [Blue-Books] f° Eyre & Spottiswoode 78, 83, 85
SPENCER (Anna G.) + BIRTWELL (C. W.) [eds.] The Care of Dependent, Neglected, and Wayward Children [pp. 163] *o.p.* 8° *Baltimore* 94
TUCKWELL, Gertr. —*in her* The State and its Children, *ut* **D** § 127, *s.v.* Children
WINES, Dr F. H. —*in his* Punishment and Reformation [U.S.], *ut* **D** § 123

*Biography* —*v. also* **D** § 132 [CARPENTER (M.), 'DORA (Sister)', JONES (A. E.)]

POUNDS, Jno. [1766–1839] Recollections of. By H. Hawkes 4/6 c 8° Williams 84

**Stammering** —*v.* **H*** § 15

## VII: School Management, Discipline, Hygiene, Architecture

### 170: THE TEACHER—*v. also* D § 161

ADAMSON, J. W. [ed.] The Practice of Instruction 4/6 *n.* c 8° National Soc. 07
A treatise on gen. method and curriculum (EDR.), w. contribs. by var. wrs. on spec. depts.

ARNOLD, Dr Felix Textbook of School & Class Management, 2 v. $2·25 *n.* (9/6 *n.*) c 8° Macmillan 08–10
An Amer. bk., vol. i ($1·25 *n.*, 5/ *n.*) dealg. w. co-opern. betw. principal and tchrs., and class-managemt.—the treatmt. of class-managemt. bg. restricted to 'the problem of conduct'; vol. ii ($1 *n.*, 4/6 *n.*) w. Admin. and Hygiene.

BAGLEY, W. C. Educative Process; Class-Room Management ea. $1·25 *n.* (5/ *n.*) c 8° Macmillan 05; 07

BALDWIN, Prf. J. The Art of School Management $1·50 12° Appleton, *N.Y.* 81

,, School Management & School Methods [Intern. Educ. Ser.] $1·50 (6/) c 8° Appleton 97

BARNETT, Prf. P. A. [ed.] Teaching and Organization [by var. wrs.] 6/6 ($2) c 8° Longman 97
W. spec. ref. to Second. Educn.; incls. much on general school-organizn. as well as on teaching.

,, Common Sense in Education and Teaching 6/ ($1·50) c 8° Longman 99
An introd. survey of the mod. educatl. field, w. many useful criticisms.

BENSON, A. C. The Schoolmaster 2/6 *n.* c 8° Murray [02] 08
$1·25 *n.* Putnam, *N.Y.* On the aims and methods of the public-schoolmaster.

BLAKISTON, J. A. The Teacher: hints on school management 2/6 c 8° Macmillan 79

BOARDMAN, J. H. Practical School Method & Organizn. [Normal Tut. Ser.] 5/ *n.* c 8° Simpkin 03

,, + SLEFRIG (S.) Practical School Work [Normal Tut. Ser.] 7/6 *n.* c 8° Simpkin 03

BOYER, Prf. C. C. Principles and Methods of Teaching $1·50 8° Lippincott, *Phila.* 99
A very full treatment; written as a teacher's manual.

BRAY, S. E. School Organization 2/ c 8° Clive 05

BROOKS, E. Normal Methods of Teaching $2·25 12° Sower, *Phila.* [79] 83

CALDERWOOD, Prf. H. On Teaching, its Ends and Means 2/6 f 8° Macmillan [74] 81

COLLAR (G.) + CROOK (C. W.) Schl. Managemt. & Meths. of Instrn. [elem.] 3/6 ($1 *n.*) c 8° Macmillan 01

COWHAM, J. H. School Organization, Hygiene, Discipline, Ethics 3/6 c 8° Simpkin [91] 01

COX (T. A.) + MACDONALD (R. F.) Suggestive Hdbk. of Pract. Schl. Method 3/6 c 8° Blackie 96
Embraces curric. of Engl. publ. elem. schls.—oblig. subjs., class-subjs., obj.-lessns., music, drill, etc.

CRONSON, Bernard Pupil Self-Government: theory & practice; ill. 90 c. *n.* (4/ *n.*) c 8° Macmillan 07

De GRAFF, E. V. Schoolroom Guide to Meths. of Teachg. and Schl. Mangt. [70th ed., re-wr.] $1·50 12° Bardeen, *Syracuse, N.Y.* [78] 94

DEXTER (T. F. G.) + GARLICK (A. H.) Primer of School Method 2/6 (80 c.) c 8° Longman 05

DUTTON, S. T. School Management [practical suggestions] $1 *n.* c 8° Scribner, *N.Y.* 03

FARRAR (F. W.) + POOLE (R. B.) General Aims of the Tchr.; & Form Managemt. 1/6 12° Camb. Press 83
40 c. *n.* Putnam, *N.Y.* Two lectures.

FINDLAY, Dr J. J. Principles of Class Teaching 5/ ($1·25) c 8° Macmillan 02
A suggestive book which criticizes the whole of modern theory on the subject.

FITCH, [Sir] J. G. —*in his* Lectures on Teaching, *ut* D § 161

GILL, J. School Management, 3/; Introd. Textbk. to Schl. Educn. 12° Longman 81; 82

GLADMAN, F. J. School Work: control and teaching 7/6 c 8° Jarrold 86

,, Organization and Principles, 4/; School Method 2/6 c 8° Jarrold *n.d.*

GREENWOOD, Jas. M. Principles of Educn. Pract. Applied [Int. Educ. Ser.] $1 (4/6) c 8° Appleton 87

Guide to the Teaching Profession, 2 Pts. [Normal Tutorial Ser.] 4/ *n.* c 8° Simpkin 06
Pt. i: *Public Elementary Schools* (A. E. IKIN), 2/6 *n.*; ii: *Secondary Schools* (M. LIGHTFOOT), 1/6 *n.*

HAYWARD, Dr F. H. Day and Evg. Schls.: managemt. and organizn. [Ed. Sci. Ser.] 5/ *n.* c 8° Ralph & Holland 10

HINSDALE, Dr B. A. Art of Study: science and art of teaching $1 12° Am. Bk. Co., *N.Y.* 00

HOLBROOK, Alf. Normal Methods of Teaching $1·50 12° Barnes, *N.Y.* [75] 76

HOWLAND, Geo. Practical Hints to Teachers [Internat. Educ. Ser.] $1 (4/6) c 8° Appleton 90

HUGHES, J. L. [Canad.] Mistakes in Teaching 50 c. 16° Kellogg, *N.Y.* [86] 95

Incorp. Assoc. of Assist. Masters: Report on Conditions of Service of Teachers in Engl. and Foreign Secondary Schools [w. bibliography] 2/ c 8° Bell 10

J., W. [Wm. CORY (*later* JOHNSON); 1823–92] Hints for Eton Masters 1/ *n.* (35 c.) 8° Clar. Press [62] 98
By the author of *Ionica.* On relns. betw. a form-master and the boys who are 'up to him', etc.

JOHONNOT, Jas. Principles & Practice of Teaching [Int. Educ. Ser.] $1·50 (6/) c 8° Appleton 86

JOYCE, P. W. Handbk. of Schl. Managemt. and Meths. of Teachg. 3/6 12° Simpkin [63] 87

KELLOGG, Amos M. School Management: pract. guide to tchr. 75 c. 16° Kellogg, *N.Y.* 84

KENNEDY, Jno. School and Family [ethics of schl. relns.] $1 16° Harper, *N.Y.* 78

KLEMM, Dr L. R. Chips fr. a Teacher's Workshop [repr. articles, etc.] $1·50 c 8° Lee & Shepard, *Boston* 88
LANDON, Jos. School Management [Education Library] 6/ c 8° Paul [83] 88
,, Principles and Practice of Teaching and Class Managemt. 5/ c 8° Holden, *L'pl.* 94
A good pract. bk., dealg. mainly w. oral tchg., discussg. 'teaching devices', and expoundg. princs. of class-management.
LODGE, Sir Oliver School Teaching and School Reform 3/ c 8° Williams 05
A course of 4 lects. on curricula and methods. Iconoclastic; but sensible.
MCMURRY, C. A. Elements of General Method 90 c. *n.* (4/ *n.*) c 8° Macmillan [ ] 03
MCMURRY, F. M. How to Study and Teaching how to Study $1·25 *n.* 12° Houghton, *Boston* 09
OGDEN, Jno. The Art of Teaching $1 12° Am. Bk. Co., *N.Y.*
PAGE, Dav. P. Theory and Practice of Teaching $1·50 s 8° Bardeen, *Syracuse, N.Y.* [47] 93
PALMER, G. H. + Mrs A. E. F. The Teacher $1·50 *n.* 8° Houghton, *Boston* 08
PARKER, F. W. Talks on Teaching $1 c 8° Kellogg, *N.Y.* [83] 03
PRINCE, J. J. School Management & Method in Theory & Practice 3/6 f 8° Heywood, *Mancs.* [79] 89
RAYMOND, Prf. T. The Principles of Education [schl.-managemt.] 4/6 ($1·40) c 8° Longman 04
RICKARD (J.) + TAYLOR (A. H.) Notes of Lessons: their preparation, etc. 2/6 c 8° Bell [8–]
ROBINSON, R. Teacher's Manual of Method and Organization 3/6 c 8° Longman [63] 84
SALMON, Prf. Dav. The Art of Teaching 3/6 ($1·25) c 8° Longman 98
A practical guide to method in the most important subjects; with some historical remarks.
SHAW (E. R.) + DONNELL (W.) School Devices [ways & suggestns. for tchrs.] $1·25 c 8° Kellogg, *N.Y.* 86
SOUTHWICK, A. P. Quiz Bk. of Theory & Pract. of Teaching $1 12° Bardeen, *Syracuse, N.Y.* [84] 87
SMITH, H. Bompas Boys and their Management in School 2/6 *n.* (90 c. *n.*) c 8° Longman 05
TATE, W. The Philosophy of Education, ed. F. W. Parker $1·50 8° Bardeen, *Syracuse, N.Y.* [ ] 84
TOMPKINS, Arnold The Philosophy of School Management 75 c. c 8° Ginn, *Boston* 95
TRUMBULL, H. C. Teaching and Teachers—*v.* **D** § 165, *s.v.* Sunday School
WEDGWOOD, J. The Nineteenth Century Teacher; & other Essays $3 *n.* 8° Doran, *N.Y.* 09
WIGGIN (H. R. R.) + GRAVES (A. P.) Elementary School Manager *o.p.* [*pb.* 5/] c 8° Isbister [79] 83
WELTON, J. Principles and Methods of Teaching 4/6 c 8° Clive 06
WENHAM (J. G.) + RICHARDS (W. J. B.) [eds.] The Schl. Manager [Rom. Cath.] 4/ St Anselm's Soc. [78] 92
WHITE, Emerson E. School Management $1 c 8° Amer. Bk. Co., *N.Y.* 93
,, The Art of Teaching $1 c 8° Amer. Bk. Co., *N.Y.* 01

**Corporal Punishment**

ADDERLY, C. National Education and Punishments *o.p.* c 8° Longman 74
COBB, Lyman The Evil Tendencies of Corporal Punishment *o.p.* c 8° Newman, *N.Y.* 47
In families and in schools. An exhaustive treatmt. of the subject.
HUMPHREYS, R. C. Corporal Punishment [pp. 26] *o.p.* c 8° Ellis, *Boston* 92
JONES, A. The Philosophy of Corporal Punishment *o.p.* c 8° Constable 59
Massachusetts: Rept. on Abolitn. of Corp. Pun. in Publ. Schls. [pp. 48] *o.p.* 8° Wright, *Boston* 68
New York City: Report on Corporal Punishment [pp. 34] 8° Bd. of Educn., *N.Y.* 77

**Curriculum**

BRYANT, Dr Sophie Curriculum of Girls' Schools [Blue-Bk.] Eyre & Spottiswoode 98
DEWEY, Prf. J. The Child and the Curriculum 25 c. *n.* 12° Univ. Press, *Chicago* 02
DODD, Cath. I. The Child and the Curriculum 2/6 c 8° Sonnenschein 06
HAYWARD, Dr F. H. The Primary Curriculum [Herbartian] 4/ *n.* c 8° Ralph & Holland 09
LODGE, Sir Oliver —*in his* School Teaching and School Reform, *ut sup.*
LYTTELTON, Rev. Edw. Schoolboys and Schoolwork 3/6 ($1·25) c 8° Longman 09
On the principles of a rational curriculum for boys in Public Schools.
PAYNE, Jos. Curriculum of Mod. Educ.—*in his* Lects. on Science & Art of Tchg., *ut* **D** § 161
THOMPSON, H. M. Essays in Revolt: what should be taught at school 2/6 *n.* c 8° Dent 05

**Discipline**

HOLBROOK, Alf. School Management [discipline] $1·50 8° Stevens, *N.Y.* 70
HUGHES, J. L. [Canad.] How to Keep Order 50 c. 16° Kellogg, *N.Y.* [88] 95
JEWELL, F. S. School Government: facts, princs., applicn. *o.p.* [*pb.* $1·50] 12° *New York n.d.* (66)
RAUB, Alb. N. School Management [discipline] 50 c. 12° *New Haven* 80
SIDGWICK, Prf. A. Form Discipline [lectures to teachers] 1/6 8° Rivington [86] 87

**Examinations**

FERREE, Barr [ed.] Educn. and Examination [pprs. by Am. wrs.] 25 c. 12° Scott Pb. Co., *N.Y.* 89
HARRISON, Fredc. —*in his* Realities and Ideals, *ut* **D** § 125
HERBERT, Auberon [ed.] Sacrifice of Education to Examination [repr. fr. *XIX Cent.*] 2/ 8° Williams 89
JEVONS, Prf. W. Stanley 'Cram'—*in his* Methods of Social Reform, *ut* **D** § 125
LANKESTER, Prf. E. Ray Examinations [1888]—*in his* Advancement of Science, *ut* **D** § 167, *s.v.* Sciences
LATHAM, Hy. On Action of Examinations as Means of Selection 10/6 c 8° Deighton, *Camb.* 77
$1·20 Lee & Shepard, *Boston*. A standard work.
MURRAY, Dav. The Use and Abuse of Examinations c 8° Bardeen, *Syracuse, N.Y.* 80
POLLOCK, Sir Fredk. Examinations & Education—*in his* Oxford Lects. & other Discourses, *ut* **D** § 1
Repr. of a well-known article, in wh. he denounces greater pt. of existg. compet. syst. as 'Machinery run mad'.
ROLLESTON, Prf. G. The Examination System—*in his* Scient. Papers, vol. ii, pp. 907–915, *ut* **H** § 73
TODHUNTER, Is. The Conflict of Studies and other Essays *o.p.* [*pb.* 10/6] 8° Macmillan 73

**Inspection**

—*for* Medical Inspection *v.* **D** § 171
FEARON, D. R. School Inspection 2/6 12° Macmillan [76] 87

**Marking**

SIDGWICK, A. Marking—*in* Eve + Sidgwick + Abbott, Three Lects. on Teaching, *ut* **D** § 161

**Play; Games**

ARCHIBALD, G. H. The Power of Play in Child Culture 2/6 *n.* c 8° Melrose 05
BARKER, J. S. Games for the Playground; 25 ill. 2/ c 8° Longman 10
JOHNSON, Geo. E. Education by Play and Games [w. bibliogr.] 90 c. c 8° Ginn 07
Theoretical and historical, w. a course of plays and games divided into 5 periods, fr. birth to age of 15.
SMITH, H. M. In Playtime 3/6 *n.* 12° Chapman 07
,, Playmates: studies in child-life 2/6 *n.* c 8° Masters 07
STRACHAN, Jno. What is Play? its bearg. on educ. and traing. *o.p.* [*pb.* 1/] c 8° Douglas, *Edin.* 77

**Supervision**

PAYNE, Prf. W. H. Chapters on School Supervision $1 12° Am. Bk. Co., *N.Y.* [76] 94
Unique as a guide to superintendts. in the distrib. of pupils and of studies in graded City schools.
PICKARD, Dr J. L. School Supervision [Internat. Educ. Ser.] $1 (4/6) c 8° Appleton 90

**Characteristics, etc., of the Teacher**

EGGLETON, Edw. [ed.] The Schoolmaster in Literature $1·40 c 8° Amer. Bk. Co., *N.Y. n.d.* (92)
Selns. fr. ASCHAM; MOLIÈRE, ROUSSEAU, COWPER, GOETHE, PESTALOZZI, PAGE, DICKENS, IRVING, 'Geo. ELIOT', etc.
RHYS, J. The Modern Pedagogue: rustic reminiscences, 2 vols. *op.* [*pb.* 21/] p 8° Saunders 68
Schoolmaster (The) in Comedy and Satire [Rabelais, etc.] $1·40 c 8° Amer. Bk. Co., *N.Y. n.d.* (94)
SKRINE, J. Huntley Pastor Agnorum: a schoolmaster's afterthoughts 5/ *n.* ($1·60 *n.*) c 8° Longman 02
A suggestive picture of the author's ideal of the schoolmaster, by late H.M. of Glenalmond.

**Teaching as a Career**

FINDLAY, Dr J. J. Teaching as a Career for University Men 1/6 c 8° Rivington 89
HART, Prf. A. B. Has the Teacher a Profession?—*in his* Studies in Amer. Educn., *ut* **D** § 157
MULLIGAN, J. Is Teaching a Profession? [pp. 23] *o.p.* 8° *Glasgow* 89

**Training of Teachers; Normal Schools**

ATKINSON, F. W. Professional Prep. of Second. Tchrs. in U.S. [pp. 64] 8° Breitkoff, *Lpz.* 93
BARNARD, Dr Hy. Normal Schls. and other Institns. f. Ed. of Tchrs. *o.p.* m 8° *Hartford* 51
BARNES, H. Training Colleges for Schoolmistresses [English; pp. 282] *o.p.* c 8° Barnes, *N.Y.*
BATES, S. P. Method of Teachers' Institutes and Theory of Educn. *o.p.* [*pb.* 75 c.] 12° Barnes, *N.Y.* 62
BRAMWELL (Amy B.) + HUGHES (H. M.) Training of Teachers in U.S.
[Gilchrist Rept.] 3/6 c 8° Sonnenschein 94
COX (J. W.) + MCHUGH (J. V.) Hist. of Illinois State Normal Univ. [pp. 255] 8° Normal Univ., *Ill.* 82
EATON, Jno. [ed.] Training of Tchrs. in Germany [Bureau of Educn.] *n.p.* 8° Govt. Prtg. Off., *Washgtn.* 78
GORDY, J. P. Rise and Growth of Normal School Idea in U.S.
[Bur. of Ed.] *n.p.* 8° Govt. Prtg. Off., *Washgtn.* 91
GRAY, T. J. Meths. of Instrn. & Courses of Study in Norm. Schls. 15 c. 8° Bardeen, *Syracuse, N.Y.* 89
JOLLY, W. The Professional Training of Teachers *o.p.* 8° *London* 74
LAURIE, Prf. S. S. The Training of Teachers and Methods of Instruction—*ut* **D** § 161
Also *Training of Teachers*. [Inaug. lect.] 1/ 8° Sherratt, *Mancs.* 03.
RIGG, J. H. Public Elementary Education and Training Colleges c 8° *London* 88
ROSS, D. Education as a University Subject *o.p.* c 8° *Glasgow* 83

SEAVER, E. P. The Professional Training of Teachers [pp. 21] *o.p.* c 8° *Concord* 91
SMART, Jas. H. Teachers' Institutes [Bureau of Educn.; pp. 206] *n.p.* 8° Govt. Prtg. Off., *Washgtn.* 85
STOW, Dav. [1793–1864] The Training System of Education *o.p.* [*pb.* 6/6] 8° Longman [36] 59
Incl. *Normal Seminaries for Training Teachers.* Of historical interest.

*Austria; France*
Educn. & Traing. of French Primary Schl. Tchr.=Spec. Repts. on Educ. Subjs., vol. xviii—*ut* **D** § 163*
HANNAK, E. The Training of Teachers in Austria 20 c. 8° Industr. Ed. Assoc., *N.Y.* 89

**Self-Culture** —*v.* **D** § 165

## 171: SCHOOL MANAGEMENT; HYGIENE

*Bibliography:* BAGINSKY (A.) Handbuch der Schulhygiene; 104 ill. 14m. 8° Enke, *Stuttgart* [73] 83
Contains elaborate bibliographies (chiefly of foreign bks.), topically classified.

BURNHAM, W. H. Outlines of School Hygiene [a good bk.] c 8° Worcester, *Mass.* 92
BURRAGE (S.) + BAILEY (H. T.) School Sanitation and Decoration; ill. $1·50 c 8° Heath, *Boston* 00
CARPENTER, Dr A. Principles and Practice of School Hygiene; ill. 4/6 c 8° W. H. Allen [86] 94
COLLINS, H. Beale The Hygiene of Schools and Scholars 2/ c 8° Ralph & Holland 02
CROWLEY, Dr R. H. The Hygiene of School Life 3/6 *n.* c 8° Methuen 09
DUKES, Dr Clement Health at School: mental, moral, and physical aspects 10/6 *n.* c 8° Rivington [88] 05
Edin. Charity Organ. Soc.: Rept. on Phys. Condn. of 1,400 Schl. Childr. in Edin. 5/ *n.* r 4° P. S. King & Son
ELKINGTON, J. S. C. Health in the School: hygiene for teachers 2/ *n.* c 8° Blackie 07
EVANS, E. The Student's Hygiene; ill. 3/6 c 8° Sonnenschein 06
FARQUHARSON, Dr R. School Hygiene and Diseases of School Life 7/6 c 8° Smith & Elder 85
FORSYTH, Dr Dav. —*in his* Children in Health and Disease, *ut* **H*** § 48
HALL, G. S. Truth, its Education, Regimen, and Hygiene—*ut* **D** § 162
HOPE (Prf. E. W.) + BROWNE (E. A.) Manual of School Hygiene; ill. [$1 *n.* Putnam, *N.Y.*] 3/6 c 8° Camb. Press 01
KINGSLEY, Can. Chas. Health and Education [$1·75 Appleton, *N.Y.*] 6/ c 8° Macmillan [74] 79
LYSTER, R. A. School Hygiene [University Tutorial Ser.] 3/6 c 8° Clive 08
MACMILLAN, Marg. Labour and Childhood 3/6 c 8° Sonnenschein 07
On wk. of the schl.-doctor, hyg. of instrn., and connexion betw. wk. of artisan, the doctor, and the physiologist.
" The Child and the State Nat. Labr. Press, *Mancs.* 11
NEWSHOLME (Dr A.) + PAKES (W. C. C.) School Hygiene: laws of health in rel. to schl. life; ill. 3/ c 8° Sonnenschein [87] 04
Amer. edn. in Pedagogical Lib. 75 c. Heath, *Boston.* A good class-book.
PORTER, Dr Chas. School Hygiene and Laws of Health; ill. 3/6 ($1·25) c 8° Longman 06
RAVENHILL, Alice Lessons in Pract. Hygiene: for use in schls. 5/ *n.* c 8° Arnold, *Leeds* 07
SHAW, Prf. E. R. School Hygiene [Macmillan's Pedag. Lib.] $1 *n.* (4/6 *n.*) c 8° Macmillan, *N.Y.* 01
YOUNG, A. G. School Hygiene and Schoolhouses—*ut inf.*, *s.v.* Ventilation, etc.

**Diet**
DUKES, Dr Clement Essentials of School Diet [good, practical manl.] 6/ *n.* c 8° Rivington [91] 99
RICHARDS (Ellen H.) + TALBOT (Marion) Food as a Factor in Student Life 25 c. 8° Univ. Pr., *Chicago* 94

**Eyesight**
CALHOUN, A. W. Effects of Student Life upon the Eyesight *n.p.* Govt. Prtg. Off., *Washington* 81
CARTER, R. Brudenell Eye-sight in Schools [a paper] *o.p.* [*pb.* 1/] c 8° Macmillan 85
CASTLE, Dr F. D. Hygiene of Eye; w. spec. ref. to schools 25 c. 8° Am. Acad. Pol. Sci., *Phila.*
COHN, Herm. Hygiene of the Eye in Schools 10/6 r 8° Simpkin 86
LIEBRICH, Dr R. School Life: its influence on sight and figure 1/ 8° Churchill [77] 78
MAGENNIS, E. Eyesight of School Children 6*d.* c 8° Wright, *Bristol* 02
SNELL, Simeon Eye-sight & School Life; ill. [by an ophthalmologist] 2/6 8° Wright, *Bristol* 95

**Fatigue**
MOSSO, Prf. A. Fatigue, tr. M. + W. B. Drummond; diagrs. 4/6 c 8° Sonnenschein 03

**Medical Inspection**
KELYNACK, Dr T. N. [ed.] Medical Examination of Schls. and Scholars 10/6 *n.* 8° P. S. King & Son 10
32 essays, by var. experts of Brit., Amer., and the more progressive countries of the Continent.
MACKENZIE, Dr W. L. Health of the School Child [med. supervisn.] 2/6 c 8° Methuen 06
" + MATTHEW (Dr E.) Medical Inspection of Schl. Children 10/6 *n.* 8° Hodge, *Glasgow* 04

Medical Inspection and Feeding of Children, 2 vols. 4/3 Wyman 05
The Rept. of the Internat. Departmental Committee on Childr. attendg. Elem. Schls. i: *Report*, 1/3; ii: *Evidence, etc.*, 3/.

ROBERTS, Chas. Med. Inspection of & Phys. Educn. in Schools 2/ *n.* m 8° Bale & Sons 96

STEVEN, E. M. Medical Supervision in Schools 5/ *n.* c 8° Baillière 10

**Open-air Schools**

AYRES, Dr L. P. Open Air Schools 10
By the founder of the first outdoor schl. in Amer.—in Porto Rico, 1904.

**Over-Pressure**

ARMSTRONG, Rev. R. A. The Overstrain in Education [pp. 38] *o.p.* c 8° *London* 83

DE BRATH (S.) + BEATTY (F.) Over-Pressure 3/6 c 8° Philip 99
Critical, and urges remedies for the evil in the shape of a better arranged curriculum, etc.

BROWNE, Dr J. Crichton Rept. on Over-Pressure [*v. also* Hertel, *infra*] [blue-bk.] Eyre & Spottiswoode 85

BUXTON, Syd. Over-Pressure and Elementary Education 1/ c 8° Sonnenschein 85

DONALDSON, Prf. Hy. Herb.—*in his* The Growth of the Brain, *ut* **D** § 162

DUKES, Dr Clement Work and Overwork in rel. to Health and Schools 1/ 8° Rivington 93
An address by one who believes that much harm is being done to health by over-competition in schools and the multiplication of examination subject.

HERTEL, Dr Over-Pressure in the High Schools of Denmark [tr. fr. Danish] 3/6 c 8° Macmillan 85
Based on a study of several hundred Copenhagen children; w. valuable intro. of 40 pp. by Dr Crichton BROWNE.

HOLBROOK, M. L. [ed.] Hygiene of the Brain [letters fr. emin. wrs.] 30 c. 12° Lovell, *N.Y.* [84] 90

SONNENSCHEIN, A. The Truth about Elementary Education *o.p.* [*pb.* 6*d.* 8° Sonnenschein 86

**Ventilation; Warming; Sanitation**

JACOB, E. H. Ventiln. and Warmg. of Houses, Schls., etc.; ill. 30 c. 16° Young, *N.Y.* 94

MORRISON, G. B. Ventilation & Warming of Schl. Bldgs.; ill. [Int. Ed. Ser.] 75 c. (3/6) c 8° Appleton 87

YOUNG, A. G. School Hygiene and Schoolhouses [pp. 399] *o.p.* 8° *Augusta* 92
The 7th Annual Rept. of State Bd. of Health of Maine. Valuable.

## 172: SCHOOL ARCHITECTURE, FURNITURE, APPLIANCES, ETC.

**Architecture**

BARNARD, Dr Hy. [ed.] School Architecture; 300 ill.
[misc. pprs. by var. wrs.] $3·50 m 8° Norton, *N.Y.* [ ] 63

BICKELL, A. J. School-House and Church Architecture; ill. *o.p.* [*pb.* 15/] 4° Trübner 77

BRIGGS, W. R. Modern American School Buildings; 89 ill. $4 8° Wiley, *N.Y.* 99
A practical designer's book.

CLARK, T. M. Rural School Architecture [Bureau of Educn.] *n.p.* Govt. Prtg. Off., *Washgtn.* 80

*CLAY, Felix Modern School Buildings, Elem. & Secondary; 400 ill. 25/ *n.* i 8° Batsford [02] 06

EVELETH, S. F. Schoolhouse Architecture; 67 pl. [text is 14 pp.] $6 4° Woodward, *N.Y.* *n.d.* (70)

GARDNER, E. C. Town & Country Schl. Bldgs. [designs, plans & descrns.] $2·50 8° Kellogg, *N.Y.* 86

HODGINS, J. G. [Canad.] Hints & Suggns. on Schl. Archit. & Hygiene; ill. 8° Educ Dept., *Toronto* 86

,, The Schoolhouse: archit. and arrgmts. *o.p.* 8° Copp, *Toronto* 76

JOHONNOT, J. Schl. Houses, w. archit. designs by S. E. Hewes *o.p.* [*pb.* $3] 8° Schermerhorn, *N.Y.* [71] 72

ROBINS, E. C. Technical School and College Buildings; 99 pl. 18/ *n.* 4° Batsford [77] 87
The 1st edn. [1877], of wh. the three papers in this reprint formed the nucleus, was pub. at 50/, 4° Whittaker, and is now scarce.

ROBSON, E. R. School Architecture: planning, designing, building, etc. 18/ r 8° Murray [74] 77
By the architect to the London School Board.

School Infirmaries: Construction and Maintenance of 1/ 8° Churchill 88

**Furniture and Appliances** —*v. also* **D** § 165, *s.v.* Geography

FITCH, J. G. Schoolroom & its Appliances—*in his* Lects. on Teaching, pp. 64–89, *ut* **D** § 161

HOLBROOK, Josiah Apparatus for Schools, Academies, etc. 8° Butts, *Boston n.d.*

ROBRICK, G. A. School Furniture: treat. on its constrn. [pp. 18] c 8° *Boston* 87

,, Hygienic Requirements of School Furniture c 8° *New York* 92

**Library** —*for* Choice of Books *v.* **K** § 10

BARNARD, Dr Hy. School, District, Town, & Village Libraries [organ. & managemt.] $1·50 8° *Hartford* 54

# CLASS E: GEOGRAPHY

## (ETHNOGRAPHY, TRAVEL, TOPOGRAPHY, LOCAL HISTORY)

## I: Universal and Comprehensive Works

### 1: BIBLIOGRAPHY; DICTIONARIES; GAZETTEERS

**Bibliography**

Bibliographie Géographique Annuelle 5 fr. 8° Colin, *Paris, ann.*
Presented to subscribers to the *Annales de Géographie*. Selected bks., classified.

BRUNET, J. C. Dictionnaire de Géographie [suppl. to his *Manuel du Libraire*] r 8° *Paris* 78

CHEVALIER, C. U. J. Répertoire d. Sources Hist. du Moyen-Age: Topobibliographie, 2 Pts. 8° *Paris* 94–03

ENGELMANN, W. [ed.] Bibliotheca Geographica [Germ. bks. only: 1750 to 1856] 12 m. 8° Engelmann, *Lp.* 58

FROMM, E. Geschichte und Geographie [chfly. foreign bks.; 1820–82] 8 m. 4° Weigel, *Leipzig* 87

GESELLSCH. F. ERDKUNDE, Berlin: Bibliotheca Geographica ea. 8 m. 8° Kühl, *Berlin* 95 *sqq., ann.*
A very comprehensive annual list of all geogr. bks. and contribns. to jls. of world of the yr. Pubd. in contin. of that wh. the late Dr KONER used to contribute to the Society's *Zeitschrift*.

,, Katalog der Bibliothek 8° *Dinse* 03

MARKHAM, [Sir] C. R. Fifty Years' Work of the R. Geogr. Soc. 4/ 8° Murray 81
Conts. a cpl. classif. Index to *Journal* and *Proceedgs.* of the Society. Vols. since 1879 are indexed.

MILL, Dr H. R. Guide to Geogr. Bks. and Appliances, prep. by J. F. Unstead + N. E. MacMunn —*ut* **D** § 167, *s.v.* Geography

PETHERICK, E. A. Index to the Literature of Geography; facss. *o.p.* [*pb.* 42/] r 8° Murray [82] 86
Catal. of York Gate Lib., Regent's Pk., Lond., formed by Mr S. W. SILVER: 5,000 vols. and pamphlets.

ROYAL GEOGRAPH. SOC. Catalogue of Library, ed. Dr H. R. Mill [over 800 pp.] 5/ 8° Murray [52] 95

,, General Index to First 20 vols. of Journal [1893–1902] 10/6 *n.* r 8° Stanford

ROYAL SOCIETY OF LONDON: International Bibliogr.: Geography, vol. i 8° Royal Soc. 03 *in prg.*

VIVIEN DE SAINT MARTIN (P.) + ROUSSELET (L.)—*in their* Nouveau Dictionnaire, *ut inf.*

**Dictionaries; Gazetteers (Universal)**

BARTHOLOMEW, J. Pocket Gazetteer of World [convenient little bk.] 2/6 32° Walker 88

BLAIKIE, Dr W. G. Imperial Gazetteer: general dict. of geogr., 2 vols.; ill. 95/ i 8° Blackie 78

BRYCE (J.) + JOHNSTON (K.) Library Cyclo. of Geogr.: descr., phys., polit., hist.; ill. 15/ r 8° Collins [56] 80

CHAMBERS, W. & R. [pubs.] Concise Gazetteer of World [good pop. bk.] 6/ *n.* c 8° Chambers 94

CHAMPLIN, J. D. jun. Yg. Folks' Cyclo. of Persons and Places; ill. $2·50 8° Holt, *N.Y.* [90] 00

CHISHOLM, G. C. [ed.] Longman's Gazetteer of the World 18/ *n.* ($6·40 *n.*) i 8° Longman [95] 02
A monumt. of accuracy and industry; but now somewhat out-of-date. 1902 edn. is merely a cheaper re-issue of that of 1895. Authoritative on spellg. and pronuncn. 2,000 closely-prtd. dble.-col. pp.

HEILPRIN, A. & L. [eds.] Lippincott's New Gazetteer of World $10 *n.* (42/ *n.*) i 8° Lippincott [55] 06
Formerly ed. J. THOMAS + BALDWIN. 100,000 places; pronouncing; concise and well up-to-date (1906).

McCULLOCH, J. R. Dictionary of Commerce and Commerc. Navign., ed. H. G. Reid—*ut* **D** § 148

MAUNDER, S. Treasury of Geogr.: phys., hist., descr., pol.; ill. ($1·75) 6/ 12° Longman [56]

PATRICK, D. Chambers' Concise Gazetteer of the World 6/ *n.* c 8° Chambers 06

*VIVIEN DE SAINT MARTIN (P.) + ROUSSELET (L.) Nouveau Dict. de Géogr. Univ., 8 vols., 250 fr.; Suppl., 2 v., 44 fr. l 8° Hachette, *Paris* 79–95; 97–00
Notices every town of at least 1,000 inhabs.; deals fully w. phys., polit., and econ. geogr. and ethnol. No maps; full bibliographies under ea. headg.

*Latin Names*

DESCHAMPS, P. Dict. de Géogr. Ancienne et Moderne *o.p.* 8° *Paris* 70

GRÄSSE, J. G. T. Orbis Latinus 5m.50 8° Schönfeld, *Dresden* 61

*Terms (Geographical)*

KNOX, A. Glossary of Geogr. and Topogr. Terms 15/ c 8° Stanford 04
$5·50 *n.* Lippincott, *Phila.* Suppl. vol. to compend. of Geogr. [*ut* **E** § 2]. Incl. also wds. of freq. occurrce. in composn. of geogr. terms and place-names.

**Geographic Orthography**

CHISHOLM, G. C. Pronouncg. Vocab. of Mod. Geograph. Names 1/6 f 8° Blackie 85

MENDENHALL, T. C., etc. 1st *and* 2nd Repts. of U.S. Bd. on Geogr. Names *n.pp.* 8° Govt. Prtg. Off., *Washington* 92–5
The standard authority as to usage and spelling of geogr. names in pubns. of U.S. govt.

## 2: PHYSICAL, DESCRIPTIVE, AND COMPARATIVE GEOGRAPHY; SERIES

**Generally** —*v. also* **H** §§ 25–30: Physiography; **H** §§ 31–41: Geology

ARNOLD-FORSTER, H. O. This World of Ours; maps 2/6 c 8° Cassell [91]
A vivid, clear, and stimulatg. little schl.-bk. on phys. geogr. of the earth.

ARRHENIUS, S. Worlds in the Making [tr.]—*ut* **H** § 21

BIRD, Chas. School Geography [a good schl.-bk.] 2/6 c 8° Whittaker 98

BROWN, Dr Rob. Countries of World, 6 vols.; fully ill. ea. 6/ ($2·25) 4° Cassell [*n.d.*] (77–81) 98–9
A fairly good popular work, more discursive and less systematic than RECLUS [*inf.*].

,, [ed.] Our Earth and its Story, 3 vols.; fully ill. ea. 5/ ($2) r 8° Cassell [88–9] 99

CHISHOLM, G. C. Longman's School Geogr.; 61 maps [best bk. on new lines] 3/6 ($1·50) 8° Longman

CLYDE, J. School Geography; maps [best bk. on old lines] 4/ f 8° Oliver & Boyd, *Edin.* [6–]

CONN, Prf. H. W. The Living World: whence it came, whither drifting $1·25 (5/) c 8° Putnam 91
A useful little bk.—semi-scientific, involvg. some prelim. knowl. of biol. and geology.

DODGE, R. E. Elementary Geogr., 65 c.; Advanced Geogr., $1·20 c 8° Rand, *Chicago* 07; 07

FRYE, A. E. Primary Geogr.; ill. 65 c. (3/); Compl. Geogr.; ill. $1·25 (6/) 4° Ginn, *Boston* 94–5

,, Elems. of Geogr.; ill. 65 c. (3/); Gram. Schl. Geogr.; ill. $1·25 (6/) 4° Ginn, *Boston*

GEIKIE, Prf. Jas. —*in his* Fragments of Earth Lore, *ut* **H** § 31

GEIKIE, Sir Arch. Elem. Lessns. in Phys. Geogr., 4/6; Primer, 1/ Macmillan [80] 00; [80]

GREGORY, Prf. J. W. Geography: structural, physical, comparative 6/ *n.* c 8° Blackie 08
A good textbook for senior students; w. a series of coloured maps and 32 black-and-white sketch-maps. Based on SUESS, *inf.*

HAUGHTON, Prf. S. Six Lectures on Physical Geography [dcl. 1876] 12/6 8° Dubl. Univ. Press 80

HEATON, E. W. A Scientific Geography; sketch-maps 5/ *n.* c 8° Ralph & Holland 08
Geography as viewed by a geologist; w. full treatmt. of geological factors and good sketch-maps.

HERBERTSON, A. J. Illustrated School Geography 5/ 4° Arnold [98] 04
Copiously and well ill.—a textbk., picture-bk., and atlas combined.

,, Oxford Geographies: Prelim. Geogr., 40 c. (1/6); Junr. Geogr., 50 c. (2/); Senr. Geogr., 60 c. (4/) c 8° Clar. Press 06–7
*Prel.* is mainly descriptive; *Junr.* has a more definitely causal treatmt., emphasizg. econ. condns.; *Senr.* emphasizes histor. geogr. Ea. w. ser. of good diagrammatic maps.

HINMAN, Russell Eclectic Physical Geography; maps & ill. $1 *n.* c 8° Amer. Bk. Co., *Cincinnati* 88
5/ Low. A clear, methodical, and intelligible elementary physical geography.

HUGHES (W.)+WILLIAMS (J. F.) Compendium of Mod. Geogr. [phys., polit., commerc.] 10/6 c 8° Philip 94

HULL, Prf. E. Text-Bk. of Phys. Geogr.; maps [strictly geographical] *o.p.* [*pb.* 5/] c 8° Deacon 89

v. HUMBOLDT, Bar. A. [1769–1859] Cosmos: phys. descr. of universe, 5 vols. [tr.] 19/ c 8° Bell [49]
$6 *n.* Macmillan, *N.Y.* [Bohn's Lib.] All anim. life the result of harmonious and correlated forces.

,, Views of Nature [tr.] [$1·50 *n.* Macm., *N.Y.*] [Bohn's Lib.] 5/ c 8° Bell [50]

*HUXLEY, Prf. T. H. Physiography, ed. Prf. R. A. Gregory; ill. 4/6 ($1·10 *n.*) gl 8° Macmillan [80] 04
The earliest wk. of the kind in English: still the most satisfactory, on the whole.

JOHNSTON, K., jun. School Physical and Descriptive Geogr.; maps & ill. 6/ c 8° Stanford [81] 92
Abgd. fr. his *Physical, Historical, Political, and Descriptive Geography*—*ut* **E** § 9. Revised by A. H. KEANE.

KING, C. F. Elem. Geogr., 65 c. *n.*; Advanced Geogr., $1·25 *n.* 12° Scribner, *N.Y.* 03–4

LESTRANGE, P. H. Progressive Course of Comparative Geography on the Concentric System; 172 col. maps and diagrs. and many ill. 6/ *n.* 4° Philip
Separ.: *Atlas*, 3/6 *n.*; *Text*, 3/6 *n.* The maps and ill. are chief features of bk. *Junior Course*, 3/6 *n.* 8° *id.* '07. Tchr's Hdbk., 5/ *n.*, '11.

LYDE, Prf. L. W. School Geogr. of World; ill. [$1 *n.* Macm., *N.Y.*] 3/6 s 8° Black 03

POUCHET, F. A. The Universe: infinitely great & inf. little [tr.]; 270 ill. 7/6 8° Blackie [69] 89

MACKAY, Rev. A. Manual of Modern Geogr.: mathem., phys., polit. 7/6 c 8° Blackwood [70–1] 88

MACKINDER, H. J. Elementary Studies in Geography, 4 vols. ea. 2/ c 8° Philip
i: *Our Own Islands*; ii: *Lands beyond the Channel*; iii: *Distant Lands*; iv: *Lands of Mod. World.*

MALTE-BRUN, C. Universal Geography [tr.], 10 vols. *o.p.* 8° Black 52–5
Of equal histor. importce. w. RITTER [*inf.*], and more intrinsically valuable, as its matter was of later accumuln. and more accurate. It is very readable. An abgmt. by J. LAURIE was pubd. in 8° Black '42, new edn. 15/ Bohn '51.

MILL, Dr H. R. Elem. Class-Bk. of General Geogr.; ill. [Geogr. Ser.] 3/6 (90 c. *n.*) c 8° Macmillan 89

,, [ed.] International Geography; 488 maps & ill. [1118 pp.] 12/ *n.* 8° Macmillan [99] 07
$3·50 Appleton, *N.Y.* By 70 Brit. and for. specialists on a uniform plan. Pt. i consists of essays on princs. of geogr.; ii of detailed survey of earth. The best comprehensive bk. in English—thorough, accurate, concise. Issued also in Sectns.: *Princs. of Geogr.* 1/6; i: *Brit. Isl.*, 1/; ii: *Europe*, 2/6; iii: *Asia*, 2/; iv: *Austral.*, 1/6; v: *N. and Cent. Amer., W. Ind.*, 2/ (90 c. *n.*); vi: *S. Amer.*, 1/6; vii: *Africa*, 2/.

,, Elem. Class-Bk. of Gen. Geogr. [gd. schl.-bk.] 3/6 (90 c. *n.*) c 8° Macmillan 04

MILL, Dr H. R. The Realm of Nature; 19 maps and 68 ill. 5/ c 8° Murray [92]
$1·50 *n.* Scribner, *N.Y.* [Univ. Extensn. Manls.] A v. gd. bk., furnishg. much informn. in v. readable form.

MONCRIEFF, A. R. Hope The World of To-day, 6 v.; maps & ill. *subscr.* 48/ *n.* 4° Gresham Pb. Co. 05–6
A well-wr. popular survey of lands and peoples of globe as seen in travel and commerce. Well ill. fr. photos.

RECLUS, Élisée Universal Geography [tr.], 19 vols.; 110 col. maps and copious ill. ea. 21/ i 8° Virtue [71 *sqq.*] 78–94
Deals w. whole world on a uniform plan. In pts. out of date, but valuable for its vivid descrns. of a living world. The general introd. vol. is entitled *The Earth and its Inhabitants.*

REDWAY (J. W.) + HINMAN (R.) Natural Introductory Geography 60 c. 12° Am. Bk. Co., *N.Y.* 07
,, ,, Natural School Geography $1·25 12° Am. Bk. Co., *N.Y.* 07

REICH, Dr Emil Hdbk. of Geography: descriptive and mathem., 2 vols. 12/6 *n.* 8° Duckworth 08
With 10 maps and some figs. Vol. ii [*Mathem. Geogr.*] of considerable value; i of next to no value.

REYNOLDS, Joan B. Regional Geographies; maps and ill. ea. 2/ c 8° Black 04 *sqq.*
*Brit. Isles; Europe; The Americas; Africa and Australia; Asia.* Ea. 128 pp.; well ill.

RITTER, Carl Comparative Geography, tr. W. L. Gage *o.p.* c 8° Am. Bk. Co., *N.Y.* 95
3/6 Blackwood. A tr. of a few of his essays.

,, Geographical Studies, tr. W. L. Gage *o.p.* c 8° Am. Bk. Co., *N.Y.* 95
Conts. a sketch of life of RITTER, tr. of the *Introd.* to his *Erdkunde* (his masterpiece), and var. essays. His *Erdkunde im Verhältnisse zur Natur u. Gesch. d. Menschen* [18 vols., 8° G. Reimer, *Berlin* 1822–59] made an epoch in study of geogr., first placg. it on a sound scientific basis of ascertained fact, analysis, and classificn., kneadg. the whole into an organic whole, united by the principle of causality; its method, however, bg. pre-Darwinian, is teleological.

SHALER, Prf. N. S. Aspects of the Earth; 100 ill. [16/ Smith & Elder] $2·50 *n.* 8° Scribner, *N.Y.* 89

**SMITH, Bernard** **Physical Geography; 220 ill. and maps** **3/6 c 8° Black 11**

SOMERVILLE, Mary Physical Geography, ed. Rev. J. Richardson 9/ p 8° Murray [48] 77

STEPHENSON, J. H. N. Elems. of Geogr., Pt. i: General Geogr.; 11 maps & 53 ill. 3/6 c 8° Stanford 08

STRACHEY, Gen. R. Lectures on Geography [del. at Camb.] 4/6 c 8° Macmillan 88
A useful summary of what subjects are incl. in geography for the modern student by then Pres. R.G.S.

*SUESS, Prf. E. The Face of the Earth [tr.], vols. i–iv—*ut* **H** § 31

TARR (R. S.) + MCMURRY (F. M.) Geography in Three Books, 3 Pts. $2·10 *n.* (12/6) c 8° Macmillan 00–1
i: *Home Geogr., and Earth as a Whole,* 60 c. *n.* (3/6); ii: *North America,* 75 c. *n.* (4/6); iii: *Europe, and other Continents,* 75 c. *n.* (4/6).

THORNTON, J. Advanced Physiography; maps and ill. 4/6 ($1·40) c 8° Longman 90

**UNSTEAD (J. F.) + TAYLOR (E. G. R.) General & Regional Geogr. for Students; 140 maps 6/ 8° Philip 11**

### Astronomical (Mathematical) Geography; Geodesy—*v. also* H § 21, I § 7

CLARKE, A. R. Geodesy; ill. 12/6 8° Clar. Press 80
A book for the mathematician on meths. of exact surveying, measuremt. of the earth and determination of its figure.

GORE, J. Howard Geodesy; ill. [Scientific Handbks.] 5/ c 8° Heinemann 91
A concise and careful hist. of the measuremts. of terrestr. degrees fr. days of Eratosthenes to pres. time.

HERSCHELL, Sir Jno. —*in his* Outlines of Astronomy [*ut* **H** § 21]: clear instrns.

JOHNSON, Prf. Willis E. Mathem. Geogr.; 127 ill. & gloss. [5/ *n.* Philip] $1 c 8° Am. Bk. Co., *N.Y.* [08]

REICH, Dr Emil —vol. ii of his Handbook of Geography, *ut sup.*
Shows how geomet. sitn. of a town or hill on globe is correctly determined and how located on map.

ROYAL GEOGRAPH. SOC. —*in* Hints to Travellers, 2 vols. [*ut* **E** § 5]: practical instrns.

***Map-making*** *v. also* **D** § 167, *s.v.* Geography (KELLOGG; MALTBY; WILKINS); *for* Maps *v.* **E** § 4

ELDERTON, W. A. Maps and Map Drawing [Macm's. Geogr. Ser.] 1/ (35 c. *n.*) pott 8° Macmillan 90

MORRISON, G. J. Maps, their Uses and Construction; 45 ill. 5/ *n.* 8° Stanford [01] 11
A very clear and simple acc. of 8 common map-projections, their principles and construction.

REEVES, E. A. Maps and Map-Making; ill. [bas. on lects.] 8/ 8° Roy. Geograph. Soc. 10

WHITE, T. Pilkington —*in his* The Ordnance Survey of United Kingdom, *ut* **E** § 16

### Commercial Geography —*v. also* D § 148

### Economic Geography; Relations of History and Geography

FREEMAN, Prf. E. A. Historical Geography of Europe, 2 vols.—*ut* **F** § 15
Treats of geography as influenced by history, and hist. as influenced by geogr. Incl. Greece, Rome, Modern Europe.

GEORGE, Rev. H. B. Relations of Geography and History; 2 maps 4/6 ($1·10) c 8° Clar. Press [01] 07
Best Engl. acc. of influ. of geogr. features on hist. events. Pt. ii deals w. Eur. countries in detail.

GUYOT, Arnold The Earth and Man [tr.]—*ut* **D** § 167, *s.v.* Geography [w. note]

HERBERTSON, R. J. + F. D. Man and his Work; ill. 1/6 c 8° Black [99]
60 c. *n.* Macmillan, *N.Y.* On influ. of geogr. on occupns. of man and influ. of occupns. on his life.

**HILLIARD, G. S. The Connection between Geography & History [pp. 43] *o.p.* c 8° Ticknor, *Boston* 46**

KELTIE, Dr J. Scott Applied Geography 2/6 c 8° Philip [90] 08
Strong in showing the bearings of geogr. knowledge on human interests.

KIRCHHOFF, Prf. A. Man and Earth 1/ *n.* pott 8° Routledge 06
50 c. Dutton, *N.Y.* [New Univ. Lib.] A good popular treatise on the reciprocal relns. and influences of man and his environmt. formg. a suitable introductory bk. on the subject.

MARSH, G. P. The Earth as Modified by Human Action $4·50 8° Scribner, *N.Y.* [64] 74
New edn. of *Man and Nature.* A suggestive bk., but no longer in touch with modern results.

PROTHEROE, Ern. The Dominion of Man; 32 pl. 2/ c 8° Methuen 06
Showg. what man, espec. the Briton, is by his labour doing in his world heritage.

RATZEL, Prf. F. —*in his* Anthropogeographie, *and* Anthropolog. Geographie, *ut* **E** § 3 [note]

*Transportation—v. also* **D** § 152, *s.v.* Transportation

JOHNSON, E. R. Oceanic and Inld. Waterway Transportation $1·50 *n.* c 8° Appleton, *N.Y.*

**Cities; Towns; Capitals; Streets; Buildings**

Capitals of the World: by var. wrs. [tr.], 2 vols.; ill. [of 'gift-bk.' order] $10 r 8° Harper, *N.Y.* 92

Great Streets of the World; c. 100 ill. [by var. contributors] $4 r 8° Scribner, *N.Y.* 92
Picts. of characteristic life of *Broadway, Piccadilly, Unter den Linden, Corso, Grand Canal, Névsky Prospekt.*

Historic Towns: ed. E. A. Freeman + Rev. W. Hunt; maps & plans ea. 3/6 ($1·25) c 8° Longman 87–9
*Boston, U.S.* [*ut* **E** § 57] H. C. LODGE | *Bristol* [*ut* **E** § 17] Rev. W. HUNT | *Carlisle* [*ut* **E** § 17] Bp. M. CREIGHTON | *Cinque Ports* [*ut sup.*] Prf. M. BURROWS | *Colchester* [*ut* **E** § 17] Rev. E. M. CUTTS | *Exeter* [*ut* **E** § 17] E. A. FREEMAN | *London* [*ut* **E** § 17] Rev. W. J. LOFTIE | *New York* [*ut* **E** § 57] TH. ROOSEVELT | *Oxford* [*ut* **E** § 17] Rev. C. W. BOASE | *Winchester* [*ut* **E** § 17] Dn. G. W. KITCHIN | *York* [*ut* **E** § 17] Rev. J. RAINE

HODDER, Edwin [ed.] Cities of World: orig., progr., aspects, 4 vols.; ill. ea. 7/6 4° Cassell 82–9

Mediaeval Towns Series —*v.* **E** § 11

RITCHIE, J. E. The Cities of the Dawn; 31 ill. 5/ c 8° Unwin 97
Naples, Athens, Pompeii, Constantinople, Smyrna, Jaffa, Jerusalem, Alexandria, Cairo, etc.

SINGLETON, Esther [ed.] Turrets, Towers and Temples; 48 ill. $2 8° Dodd & Mead, *N.Y.* 98
Passages selected fr. English and tr. fr. foreign literature describing great buildings.

**Islands**

KELLOG, Mrs E. M. Australia and Islds. of the Sea 68 c. *n.* c 8° Silver, *N.Y.* 97
[World and its People.] Incl. all import. islds. and groups of islds. exc. Brit. Isles and Japan.

**Rivers**

STEAD, R. Adventures on Great Rivers; ill. [travel and sport] 5/ c 8° Seeley 06

**Scenery**

BLACK, A. & C. [pbs.] Beautiful Books—*ut* **E** § 16, *s.v.* Series

MENPES, Mortimer [artist] World Pictures; w. text by Dorothy Menpes 20/ *n.* sq 8° Black 02
A brilliant series of pictures (many col.) of well-known places all over world.

Pen and Pencil Series [ea. $3·20 Revell, *N.Y.*] ea. 8/ i 8° R.T.S. 74–94
*Amer. Pictures* [*ut* **E** § 52] Rev. S. MANNING | *Austral. Pictures* [*ut* **E** § 65] H. WILLOUGHBY | *Bible Lands, Picts. fr.* [*ut* **E** § 30] S. G. GREEN | *Bohemia Pictures* [*ut* **E** § 12] J. BAKER | *Canad. Pictures* [*ut* **E** § 55] Marq. of LORNE | *Engl. Pictures* [*ut* **E** § 16] MANNING + GREEN | *French Pictures* [*ut* **E** § 14] GREEN | *Germ. Fatherld., Picts. fr.* [*ut* **E** § 15] GREEN | *Greek Pictures* [*ut* **E** § 22] Prf. J. P. MAHAFFY | *Holland, Picts. fr.* [*ut* **E** § 13] R. LOVETT | *Indian Pictures* [*ut* **E** § 35] Rev. W. URWICK | *Irish Pictures* [*ut* **E** § 20] Rich. LOVETT | *Italian Pictures* [*ut* **E** § 24] MANNING | *London Pictures* [*ut* **E** § 17] LOVETT | *Norwegian Pictures* [*ut* **E** § 26] LOVETT | [Palestine] *Those Holy Fields* [*ut* **E** § 30] MANNING | *Pharaohs, Land of* [*ut* **E** § 42] MANNING | *Russian Pictures* [*ut* **E** § 25] Thos. MICHELL | *Scottish Pictures* [*ut* **E** § 19] GREEN | *Sea Pictures* [*ut* **H** § 27] Dr J. MACAULAY | *Swiss Pictures* [*ut* **E** § 28] MANNING | *United States Picts.* [*ut* **E** § 56] LOVETT | *Welsh Pictures* [*ut* **E** § 18] LOVETT

REYNOLDS, Joan B. [ed.] World Pictures: an elem. pictorial geogr. 2/ 8° Black [01] 04
A series of picts. of important types of scenery and correspg. condns. of human life; w. text.

Wonders of the World; marvels of nature and of man, 2 v.; 1000 ill. 25/ *n.* 4° Hutchinson 11

*Study of Scenery*: AVEBURY (L'd) The Scenery of England—*ut* **E** § 16

GEIKIE, Sir Arch. The Scenery of Scotland—*ut* **E** § 19

" Landscape in History; and other Essays 8/6 *n.* ($2·75 *n.*) 8° Macmillan 05

MARR, J. E. The Scientific Study of Scenery; 21 ill. 6/ c 8° Methuen [99] 00
$1 New Amst. Bk. Co., *N.Y.* A good elem. treat. on geomorphology for geographers, givg. an excellent notion to the general reader of the laws wh. have controlled the productn. of the earth's principal scenic features.

**Sea; Ocean** —*v. also* **H** § 27, 44

BULLEN, Fk. T. Our Heritage the Sea; front. 6/ c 8° Smith & Elder 06
The sea as 'reservoir of health', source of food supply, univ. highway, battlefd., winds, clouds, tides, etc.

CONRAD, Jos. The Mirror of the Sea 6/ c 8° Methuen 06
An admirable and subtle study of the sea, remarkable for its quality and fine temper, by one who knows it fr. personal contact in all its moods and aspects, and writes w. an unerring eye for the romantic and the beautiful.

HARTWIG, Dr G. The Sea and its Living Wonders—*ut* **H** § 45

HUXLEY, Prf. T. H. Problems of the Deep Sea—*in his* Collected Essays, vol. viii, *ut* **K** § 83

INGERSOLL, Ern. Book of the Ocean; ill. $1·50 c 8° Century Co., *N.Y.* [98] 03
Ocean currents, early voyages, naval battles, ships, rigging, sea-animals, etc.

MAURY, M. F. [1806–73] Physical Geography of the Sea; diagrs. *o.p.* [*pb.* 4/] c 8° Nelson [2nd ed. 55] 83
Antiquated scientifically, but noteworthy historically. Vivid descriptions.

RECLUS, Elisée Ocean, Atmosphere, and Life [tr.], ed. A. H. Keane; ill. 21/ i 8° Virtue 87

SHAW (Cpt. F. H.) + ROBINSON (E. H.) [eds.] The Sea and its Story, 24 Pts.; fully ill. ea. 7*d.* i 8° Cassell 10 *in prg.*

**Series**

Cambridge Geographical Series: ed. Dr F. H. H. Guillemard; ill. [Putnam, *N.Y.*] *v.pp.* c 8° Camb. Press 03 *sqq.*, *in prg.*
CLEMOW (Dr F. G.), *Geogr. of Disease* [*ut* **H** § 14] 15/ ($4 *n.*) | KEANE (A. H.), *Ethnology* [*ut* **E** § 3] 10/6 ($2·60 *n.*) | " *Man, Past and Present* [*ut* **E** § 3] 12/ ($3 *n.*) | LE STRANGE (G.), *Lands of Eastern Caliphate* [*ut* **E** § 30] 15/ ($4 *n.*) | LYDEKKER (R.), *Geogr. Hist. of Mammals* [*ut* **H** § 71] 10/6 ($2·60 *n.*) | MAGUIRE (T. M.), *Outls. of Military Geogr.* [*ut* **E** § 18] 10/6 ($2·50 *n.*) | TOZER (H. F.), *Hist. of Anc. Geogr.* [*ut* **E** § 10] 10/6 ($2·60 *n.*)

Descrip. Geographies fr. Orig. Sources, ed. A. J. + F. D. Herbertson ; ill. ea. 2/6 c 8° Black 03 *sqq., in prg.*
60 c. *n.* to 90 c. *n.* ea. Macmillan, *N.Y.* *Eur.* ; *Asia* ; *Africa* ; *Austr. and Occania* ; *N. Amer.* ; *Cent. and S. Amer.* ; *Brit. Emp.* ; *Brit. Isles* (ed. Lettice JOWETT). Collns. of graphic descrns. of pts. of world fr. wrgs. of explorers and travellers, w. Introds. and notes.

Geographical Congress, Sixth Internatl. : Report ; maps & ill. [Lond. 1895] 21/ m 8° R.G.S. (Murray) 95

Hakluyt Soc. : Publications —*v.* **E** § 5

Our Neighbours —*v.* **E** § 11

Our Neighbours at Home ; ill. ea. 5/ *n.* c 8° Newnes *v.y.*
*America at Home* [*ut* **E** § 56] A. M. LOW | *New Zealand at Home* [*ut* **E** § 67] R. A. LOUGNAN | *Norway at Home* [*ut* **E** § 26] Rev. T. B. WILLSON | *South Africa at Home* [*ut* **E** § 50] R. H. FULLER

Peeps at Many Lands : 35 vols. ; col. ill. ea. 1/6 *n.* c 8° Black 07 *sqq.*
Brightly-written accounts of peoples and of countries. *Belg.* ; *Burma* ; *Canada* ; *China* ; *Corsica* ; *Egypt* ; *Engl.* ; *Finl.* ; *Frce.* ; *Germy.* ; *Greece* ; *Holland* ; *Holy Ld.* ; *Iceld.* ; *India* ; *Ireld.* ; *Italy* ; *Jamaica* ; *Japan* ; *Morocco* ; *N. Zeald.* ; *Norw.* ; *Portug.* ; *Scotl.* ; *Siam* ; *S. Afr.* ; *S. Seas* ; *Switzerl.*

Peeps at the World : col. ill. 3/6 *n.* c 8° Black 08

*Regions of World : geogr. memoirs, ed. H. J. Mackinder, 12 v. ; maps ea. 7/6 *n.* ($2) 8° Clar. Press 02 *sqq.*
*Africa* Dr J. S. KELTIE, *in prep.* | *America, North* [*ut* **E** § 52] J. RUSSELL | *Britain and Brit. Seas* [*ut* **E** § 16] EDR. | *Europe, Central* [*ut* **E** § 11] J. PARTSCH | *Far East* [*ut* **E** § 31] Arch. LITTLE | *India* [*ut* **E** § 35] Sir Thos. HOLDITCH | *Mediterranean and France* E. RÉCLUS, *in prep.* | *Nearer East* [*ut* **E** § 29] D. G. HOGARTH

STANFORD, E. [pub.] Compendium of Geogr. & Travel, 13 v. ; maps & ill. ea. 15/ 8° Stanford [79–85] 95–07
*Africa*, 2 vols. [*ut* **E** § 41] Prf. A. H. KEANE | *America : Central and South*, 2 v. [*ut* **E** §§ 58, 60] KEANE | „ *North*, 2 vols. [*ut* **E** §§ 55, 56] S. E. DAWSON ; H. GANNETT | *Asia*, 2 vols. [*ut* **E** § 31] KEANE | *Australasia*, 2 vols. [*ut* **E** § 62] J. W. GREGORY ; F. H. GUILLEMARD | *Europe*, 2 vols. [*ut* **E** § 11] G. C. CHISHOLM | *Glossary of Geogr. Terms* [*ut* **E** § 1] A. KNOX
Ea. vol. $5·50 *n.* Lippincott, Phila., originally based on HELLWALD'S *Die Erde und ihre Völker.* Fully illustrated and semi-popular.

**Etymological Geogr.** inclg. **Pronunciation**—*v.* **K** § 120 **Methods of Teaching Geogr.**—*v.* **D** § 167, *s.v.* Geogr.

**Physical Geography**—*v.* **H** §§ 25–30 ; Faunas §§ 101–6 ; Floras §§ 62–9 ; Geology §§ 35–41

## 3 : ETHNOLOGY : GENERAL TREATISES

For the Ethnology of Individual Countries *v.* the Countries ; for Physical History of Man *v.* **H** § 100 ; for Primitive Society, *v.* **F** § 5 ; for History of Civilization, *v.* **F** § 4

### Bibliography ; Scope and Content ; History

DIESERUD, J. Scope and Content of Science of Anthropology $2 *n.* c 8° *Open Ct.* Pb. Co., *Chicago* 08
8/6 *n.* Paul. Histor. review, a most elab. classificn., annot. bibliogr. ; pubns. of anthrop. societies.

HADDON, A. C. History of Anthropology 1/ *n.* c 8° Watts 10

RIPLEY, Prf. W. Z. Bibliogr. of Anthrop. and Ethnol. of Europe—*ut inf.*

THOMAS, Prf. W. I. [ed.] Source Book for Social Origins $4·50 *n.* 8° Univ. Press, *Chicago* 09
In 7 Pts. (1) *Anthropogeography, Prim. Economics* ; (2) *Prim. Mind and Educn.* ; (3) *Early Marriage* ; (4) *Invention and Technol.* ; (5) *Art, Ornamt. Decorn.* ; (6) *Magic, Religion, etc.* ; (7) *Soc. Organizn.* By BOAS, TYLER, WESTERMARCK, SPENCER AND GILLEN, HADDON, RIVERS. Valuable bibliogrs. occupy 111 pp., 1 to ea. Pt. and a final one arrgd. by races.

### Generally

BETTANY, G. T. The World's Inhabitants ; ill. 7/6 r 8° Ward & Lock [88] 97
A quite popular account of mankind, animals, and plants of the world.

BRACE, C. L. The Races of the Old World *o.p.* [*pb.* $2·50] c 8° Scribner, *N.Y.* [63] 71

BRINTON, Prf. D. G. Races and Peoples : lects. on science of ethnogr. $1·50 c 8° McKay, *Phila.* [90] 01

BROWN, Dr R. Peoples of World, 6 v. ; ill.
[new ed. of *Races of Mankd.*] ea. 7/6 ($1·50) r 8° Cassell [73–6] 82–6

BRYCE, Jas. Relns. of Advcd. & Backwd. Races of Man [Romanes Lect.] 2/ *n.* (70 c.) 8° Clar. Press 02

DENIKER, Jos. Races of Man : outl. of ethnography ; ill. 6/ c 8° W. Scott 00
$1·50 Scribner, *N.Y.* [Contemp. Science Ser.] First pt. deals w. anthropol., second w. ethnol. : a trustworthy summary of essential facts, drawn fr. 500 authors. 176 ill. and 2 maps.

DUCKWORTH, W. L. N. Morphology and Anthropology—*ut* **H** § 100

ELLIOTT, G. F. Scott The Romance of Savage Life ; ill. 5/ c 8° Seeley 07
A popular acc. of customs, occupns., beliefs, arts, crafts, games, etc., of primitive man.

FIGUIER, Louis The Human Race [tr.] ; ill. [popular ; antiquated] 3/6 c 8° Cassell [72] 82

HABERLANDT, Dr M. Ethnology ; ill. [Temple Primers ; 40 c. Macm., *N.Y.*] 1/ *n.* 12° Dent 00

HASTINGS (Dr J.) + SELBIE (Dr J. A.) [eds.]—*in their* Encyclo. of Religion and Ethics, *ut* **A** § 49
Deals fully with subjects of ethnological and anthropological interest.

HADDON, Prf. A. C. The Study of Man ; 48 ill. and diagrs. 6/ c 8° Murray 98
$2 Putnam, *N.Y.* [Progr. Sci. Ser.] Detached studies on anthropol. byways—the Bertillon syst., hair-colour, eye-colour, craniol. and nasal measuremts., games, toys, etc.

„ The Races of Man [summary of facts] 1/ *n.* c 8 Milner 09

HEWITT, J. F. Ruling Races of Prehistoric Times, 2 vols.—*ut* **E** § 35, *s.v.* Ethnology

HUTCHINSON (H. N.) + GREGORY (J. W.) + LYDEKKER (R.) The Living Races of Mankind
21/ *n.* 4° Hutchinson *n.d.* (01–2)
A copious series of 648 excellent illns. photogr. fr. life, accomp. by readable popular text. Forms vols. iv–v of *People's Nat. Hist.*

HUXLEY, Prf. T. H. Methods and Results of Ethnology—*in his* Coll. Essays, vol. vii, *ut* **K** § 83

KEANE, Dr A. H. Ethnology; ill. [Cambridge Geogr. Ser.] 10/6 c 8° Camb. Press [96] 01
$2·60 *n.* Putnam, *N.Y.* The best systematic treat. Pt. i deals w. fundam. ethnical probls., ii classifies races of men into primary ethnical groups. Useful bibliogr. refs.

" Man, Past and Present; 15 ill. 12/ c 8° Camb. Press 99
$3 *n.* Putnam, *N.Y.* Sequel to above, giving narrative of developmt. of man and races of men.

" The World's Peoples: 270 ill. 6/ *n.* c 8° Hutchinson 08
An admirably succinct, pop., yet very detailed, acc. of bodily and mental characters, beliefs, tradns., institns., etc., of races of world. Ill. of racial types (fr. life) very good. Assigns the common ancestor, *Pithecus erectus* (w. gorilla and chimpanzee as poor relations) to Pliocene period, in Java.

KINGSLEY, Prf. J. S. Standard Natural History, vol. vi—*ut* **H** § 76
This vol., dealg. w. nat. hist. of man, is founded on F. A. H. v. HELLWALD'S *Naturgesch. des Menschen* [2 v.; ill. 27 m. 50 8° Spemann, *Stuttgt.* 82–5].

LEFÈVRE, Prf. A. F. Race and Language 5/ c 8° Paul 94
$1·50 Appleton, *N.Y.* [Internat. Scientific Ser.] No longer up-to-date.

LETOURNEAU, Dr C. Sociology based on Ethnography [tr.] 3/6 8° Chapman 93
An able wk.: carries the study of race-origins to new conclusions.

NOTT (J. C.) + GLIDDON (G. R.) Types of Mankind; col. ill. *o.p.* [*pb.* $5] r 8° Lippincott, *Phila.* [54] 68

" " Indigenous Races of the Earth; col. pl. & ill. *o.p.* [*pb.* $5] r 8° Lippincott, *Phila.* 57

PESCHEL, Dr O. F. Races of Man and their Geogr. Distribn. [tr.] 9/ c 8° Paul [76] 81

PICKERING, Dr C. Races of Man and their Geogr. Distribn.; pl. 5/ c 8° Bell [49] 50
$1·50 *n.* Macmillan, *N.Y.* [Bohn's Lib.] Once very popular; now quite superseded.

PRICHARD, Dr J. C. Researches into Phys. Hist. of Man, 5 v.; col. pl. *o.p.* [*pb.* 82/] 8° Sherwood [13] 36–7

" Illustrations to the same *o.p.* [*pb.* 18/] 8° Baillière 44

" Nat. Hist. of Man, ed. E. Norris, 2 v.; pl. and ill. *o.p.* [*pb.* 38/] r 8° Baillière [43] 55
PRICHARD was first wr. who attempted to estab. ethnol. on a purely inductive basis. In fav. of unity of hum. species.

de QUATREFAGES, J. L. A. The Human Species [tr.] 5/ c 8° Paul [79] 81
$1·50 Appleton, *N.Y.* [Internat. Scientific Ser.] Largely antiquated.

*RATZEL, Prf. F. History of Mankind, tr. A. J. Butler, 3 vols.; ill. ea. 12/ *n.* ($4 *n.*) r 8° Macmillan 96–8
A very full and authoritative popular wk., tr. fr. 2nd edn. (1894) of *Völkerkunde* [1885–8]. Col. pl., maps, and c. 3,000 good ports. of typical members of var. races and specs. of workmanship of primitive peoples. The author's *Anthropogeographie*, 2 vols. [ea. 15 m. 8° Engelhorn, *Stuttgt.* 82–91] has not been tr. It is an import. bk. on the relns. of human race to the earth, on characteristics of peoples, and on dependence of hist. on geography. Cf. also his *Anthropologische Geographie* [10 m. 8° *id.*].

SMITHSONIAN INSTITUTION: Annual Repts., *sqq.*; ill. *n. pp.* 4° Govt. Prtg. Off., *Washgtn.* 78 *sqq.*, *in prg.*

SPENCER, Herb. [ed.] Descriptive Sociology—*ut* **C** § 62
A colln., in tabular form, of a mass of facts and observns. servg. as data for the science.

WESTERMARCK, Dr E. The Origin and Development of Moral Ideas, 2 vols.—*ut* **C** § 70

WILSON, Sir Dan. The Lost Atlantis and other Studies 15/ 8° Douglas, *Edin.* 91
$4 Macmillan, *N.Y.* *Lost Atlantis; The Vinland of Northmen; Trade and Commerce in Stone Age; Pre-Aryan Amer. Man.; Æsthetic Faculty in Aborig. Races; The Huron-Iroquois: a Typical Race; Hybridity and Heredity; Relative Racial Brain-Weight and Size.*

WOOD, Rev. J. G. The Natural History of Man, 2 vols.; copiously ill. 14/ r 8° Routledge 68–70

" Man and his Handiwork; 500 ill. [popular] 10/6 c 8° S.P.C.K. 86
An attempt to trace the history of the human race thro' its weapons and utensils at different periods.

World & its Peoples Photographed & Descr.; 114 Maps & c. 1,000 ill. $10 f° Rand & McNally, *Chicago* 06

**Anthropology and Classics:** MARETT (R. R.) [ed.] Anthropology & the Classics 6/ *n.* ($2) 8° Clar. Press 08
Course of 6 lects. del. at Oxon., aimg. to show that anthropologists and humanists are engaged in concerted operns.—'the proper study of mankind'. A. J. EVANS, *Eur. Diffusn. of Pictography and its Beargs. on Orig. of Script*; Andr. LANG, *Homer and Anthrop.*; Gilb. MURRAY, *Anthrop. in Gk. Epic outside Homer*; F. B. JEVONS, *Græco-Ital. Magic*; J. L. MYRES, *Herodotus and Anthrop.*; W. W. FOWLER, *Roman Festivals* [a good study on *Lustratio*].

**Child in Ethnology (The)** —*v. also* **B** § 3, *s.v.* Customs (Children); **D** § 162

JACKSON, Mrs Nevill Toys of other Days; ill. [*Country Life* Lib.] 21/ *n.* 4° *County Life* Off. 08
A hist. of playthings of children fr. prehistoric times to first half of 19th century.

MILN, Louise J. Little Folk of Many Lands; pl. $2·50 *n.* c 8° Scribner, *N.Y.* [99] 02
An unequal attempt to describe the children of the var. peoples of the world.

TRUMBULL, H. Clay [ed.] Child Life in Many Lands; ill. $1 *n.* (3/6) c 8° Revell 03

Wide World (The) [child-life in Jap., Eg., Eur., S. Am., etc.] 25 c. 12° Ginn, *Boston* 02

**Folklore, etc.** —*v.* **B** §§ 1 *sqq.*

**Number Concept** —*v.* **C** § 71

**Pigmies**—*v. also* **B** § 5*, **E** § 48 (BURROWS, DUCHAILLU, GEIL, LLOYD, OLUFSEN)

HALIBURTON, R. G. 'The Holy Land of Punt': racial dwarfs in the Atlas and Pyrenees, etc. 8° 93

" Survival of Dwarf Races in New World [pamphlet] 8° 94

" How a Race of Pygmies was Found in N. Afr. & Spain; & pprs. on other subjs. 1 8° *Toronto* 97

de QUATREFAGES, Prf. A. The Pigmies, tr. F. Starr; 6 pl. $1·75 c 8° Appleton, *N.Y.* 95
6/ *n.* Macmillan. A treatise, histor. and anthropol., on the pigmy races of Malaysia and Africa, their habits, characteristics, and legends attached to them. Does not incl. the recently discov. neolithic pigmy.

TYSON, Dr Edw. [17 cent.] Philolog. Essay conc. Pygmies of Ancients, ed. B. C. Windle 6/ *n.* c 8° Nutt 95
Bibl. de Carabas.] Almost equally divided betw. Edr's. *Introd.* and repr. of TYSON's tractate, orig. [A.D. 1699] appended to his *Anatomie of a Pygmie*, wh. 'pygmie' was a certain chimpanzee whose skeleton is now in Nat. Hist. Mus., S. Kens. The *Introd.* conts. a survey of the var. dwarfish races known to science, story, and legend.

**Women** —*v. also* **B** § 3, *s.v.* Customs (Women)

JOYCE (T. A.) + THOMAS (N. W.) [eds.] Women of all Nations, 2 vols.; ill. ea. 15/*n.* r 8° Cassell 08–9
A popular record of their characteristics, habits, customs and influence, by a variety of contributors. 25 col. pl. and 625 ill. Ch. Edn. 6/*n.* '10.

**Races of Europe: Generally**—*for* Origin of Aryans, *v.* **F** § 5

LATHAM, Dr R. G. The Nationalities of Europe, 2 vols. [antiquated] *o.p.* [*pb.* 32/] 8° Bentley 63

RIPLEY, Prf. W. Z. The Races of Europe: a sociological study; ill. $6 8° Appleton, *N.Y.* 00
18/*n.* Paul. A very valuable and lucid survey of origins and phys. characteristics of var. Europ. peoples; w. 86 maps and diagrs. and 222 portrait types. The Bibliogr. mentioned above, tho' bnd. separ., is incl. in above price.

**Races of the Old Testament** —*v.* **A** § 47 (SAYCE)

**Mediterranean Race:** SERGI (Prf. G.) The Mediterranean Race; 93 ill. 6/ c 8° W. Scott 01
$1·50 Scribner, *N.Y.* [Contemp. Sci. Ser.] The most complete acc. of author's views on North-Afr. orig. of the European races.

**Anthropol. Research (Guides to)**—*v.* **E** § 8 **Ethnology in Folklore**—*v.* **B** § 1 **Primitive Society**—*v.* **F** § 5

**Relation betw. Race and Nationality**—*v.* **F** § 2 **Tattooing**—*v.* **E** § 67

## 4: GENERAL ATLASES; MAPS

**Bibliography**

British Museum: Catalogue of MS. Maps, Charts, and Plans, 2 vols. 20/ 8° Brit. Museum 44

,, Catalogue of Prtd. Maps, Plans, and Charts, 2 vols. 126/ 4° Brit. Museum 85
Excepts: *World*, 2/6; *England*, 1/6; *London*, 2/.

,, Catal. of Geogr. Colln. in Lib. of Geo. iii, 2 vols. *o.p.* [*pb.* 24/] 8° Brit. Museum 29

RAVENSTEIN, E. G. A Life's Work: cat. of maps, bks., and papers: 1853–1908 *priv. prin.* 08

**Historical:** *General and Ancient*—*v.* **F** § 1; *Europe v.* **F** § 15; *Engl. v.* **F** § 16; *Brit. Cols. v.* **F** § 33

**Modern; General**

v. ANDREE, R. Allgemeiner Handatlas 24*m.* f°
An excellent atlas. For the English version *v.* '*Times*' *Atlas*, *infra.*

BARTHOLOMEW, Jno. [1831–93] Lib. Reference Atlas of World [84 maps] *o.p.* [*pb.* 52/6 *n.*] f° Macmillan 90

,, Pocket Atlas of World; Brit. Colon. Pocket Atlas ea. 2/6 18° Walker [87]
Ea. w. 54 maps. Two very convenient, well printed, little coloured atlases; w. copious and accurate indexes.

BARTHOLOMEW, Jno. G. [son] Internat. Studt.'s Atl. of Mod. Geogr. [105 maps] *o.p.* [*pb.* 6/*n.*] 4° Newnes 02

,, Twentieth Century Citizen's Atlas [156 maps] 21/*n.* f° Hodder 02
The best guinea atlas in the English market. Strong on British Empire.

,, Cassell's Atlas [88 maps] 12/6 *n.* r 8° Cassell 09

,, Handy Reference Atlas [160 maps] 7/6 c 8° Walker [ ] 08
A very convenient and accurate concise atlas on a small scale.

,, Graphic Atlas of the World 5/*n.* i 8° Walker [ ]

,, The Comparative Atlas [64 maps] 2/6 Meiklejohn

,, Survey Atlas of England & Wales [84 maps] 70/*n.* f° Geogr. Inst., *Edin.* 05

CASSELL & Co. [pbs.] Cassell's Atlas [88 maps] 12/6 *n.* 4° Cassell 09

CHISHOLM, G. C. Longman's New School Atlas 12/6 4° Longman

,, Longman's New Five-shilling Atlas [32 maps] 5/ ($1·50) i 8° Longman

DEBES, E. Neuer Handatlas 20 m. Wagner & Debes, *Lpz.* [ ]
61 lge. and 124 inset maps. Clear and accurate. Ea. map may be purchased separately.

,, + KIRCHHOFF (A.) + KROPASCHECK Schulatlas 5 m. 4° Wagner & Debes, *Lpz.*
Other good Germ. schl.-atlases are by DIERCKE + GAEBLER (6 m. Westermann, *Brunsw.*), LEHMANN + SCOBEL (5 m. Velhagen, *Lpz.*) •SYDOW-WAGNER (5 m. J. Perthes, *Gotha*).

ELTON, E. F. The Class-room Atlas [48 maps] 5/*n.* r 4° Johnston [ ] 08
A good schl.-bk.: Physical, Political, Biblical, and Classical.

HABENECHT Taschen-Atlas 4° J. Perthes, *Gotha* [ ] *ann.*

JOHNSTON, Dr A. Keith Royal Atlas of Modern Geography [57 maps] 126/ r f° Johnston [61] 11
At one time the best English atlas; clearly printed, and revised to 1906. Incl. 104 inset maps and plans.

,, Handy Royal Atlas of Mod. Geogr. [52 maps] 25/ i 4° Johnston [67] 10
An excellent and really handy adaptation of the above. Separ. maps, 1/6 ea.

JOHNSTON, W. & A. K. [pubs.] The Victoria Regina Atlas [200 maps] 21/ r 4° Johnston [ ] 01
Conts. many place-names and plans of cities, w. physical and topograph. maps.

,, The Unrivalled Atlas [40 maps] 3/6 r 8° Johnston [ ] 07

,, The Cosmographic Atlas [comprehensive] 21/ f° Johnston

KELTIE (J. S.) + MACKINDER (H. J.) + RAVENSTEIN (E. G.) Philip's Systematic Atlas 15/ r 8° Philip 94
An excellent Atlas for teachers, w. c. 250 maps on 52 pl. School Edn., w. 41 of the pl., 10/6.

,, Johnston's World Wide Atlas [128 col. maps] 7/6 r 4° Johnston [ ] 10

KIEPERT, H. Grosser Hand-Atlas [45 maps] 40 m. f° G. Reimer, *Berlin*
One of the best of the larger German atlases: quite trustworthy.

PHILIP, G., jun. Philip's New Handy General Atlas [160 maps on 70 pl.] 21/ *n.* c f° Philip [97] 05
A very good and well-prtd. general reference-atlas. British Empire in detail.

" The Harmsworth Atlas and Gazetteer [500 maps] 40/ *n.* f° Amalg. Press 07

" Mod. School Atlas of Comparative Geogr. [64 maps] 3/6 4° Philip 09

PHILIP & SON [pubs.] Imperial Atlas of the World [80 maps] £8 i f° Philip [64] 10

" New General Atlas £4 i f° Philip 10

" New General Atlas of World 21/ *n.* c f° Philip [ ] 11

" New Popular Atlas [48 maps] 3/6 4° Philip 10

" New Schl. Atlas of Comparative Geogr. [97 maps] 2/6 8° Philip 09

RAND, MCNALLY & Co. [pubs.] Imperial Atlas of the World $2·50 4° Rand, *Chicago*

RAVENSTEIN, E. G. Philip's Handy Volume Atlas [72 maps] 3/6 s 8° Philip 10
A good pocket-atlas; with valuable and concise text.

SCHRADER (F.) + GALLOUÉDEC (L.) Atlas Classique de Géogr. Anc. et Mod. 7 fr. 50 l 8° Hachette, *Paris* 09

" + PRUDENT (F.) + ANTHOINE (E.) Atlas de Géogr. Mod. 25 fr. f° Hachette, *Paris*
60 coloured maps, w. 600-black-and white charts, etc.

STANFORD, E. [pub.] London Atlas of Universal Geog. [110 maps] £12 i f° Stanford [82] 04

" London Atlas of Universal Geogr.: Quarto Edn. [50 maps] 25/ i 4° Stanford [82]

" Octavo Atlas of Modern Geography [50 maps] 25/ r 8° Stanford [ ] 06
A well and clearly printed atlas for general reference purposes.

" Handy Atlas of Modern Geography [30 maps] 10/6 r 8° Stanford [92] 06
Well printed and convenient: useful for place-names and political divisions.

*STIELER, Ad. [ed.] Atlas of Mod. Geogr.: Engl. Edn. [100 maps] 46 m. f° J. Perthes, *Gotha* (17–22] 09
The atlas wh. most frequently continues to be constructed throughout fr. orig. matls. on scient. princs. Has for long held foremost place amongst *all* atlases. There are edns. also in Germ. (the orig.), Fch., Ital., Span., diffces. bg. only in titles, etc., of maps. The sheets may be purchased separately, and thus the best local maps may be obtained at trifling cost.

*Times* Atlas: 117 maps (on 118 pp.), w. excellent index of 150,000 names 27/6 f° *Times* Office [95] 00
An excellent and exceedingly cheap General Atlas, spec. strong on Brit. Cols. and Possessns. It is based on ANDREE's *Handatlas*, and prtd. fr. plates of Cassell's *Universal Atlas*, many improvemts. hg. been introd. Index is a laborious performce.; and, as uniformity of spellg. has been introd., it is also valuable f. general ref. purposes.

VIDAL DE LA BLACHE, P. Atlas Générale: Historique et Géographique 30 fr. f° Colin, *Paris* [ ] 09
A very good atlas for general use, w. 420 maps and plans. The 2 Pts. may be bot. separately, ea. 15 fr.

VIVIEN DE ST MARTIN + SCHRADER Atlas Universelle de Géographie, Maps i–lxx
ea. 2 fr. f° Hachette, *Paris* 74 *in prg.*
To consist of 90 maps in all. Very detailed and excellently engraved.

*British Empire* —*v.* **E** § 21

**Cartography; Maps** —*for* Map-making *v.* **E** § 2, *s.v.* Mathematical Geogr.

MERCATOR, Gerh. [G. KAUFFMANN, 1512–94] Three Maps 60 m. r f° Kühl, *Berlin* 91
*Eur.* (1554) 15 shs.; *Brit. Isl.* (1564) 8 shs.; *World* [w. Amer.] (1569) 18 shs. Facs. reprs. fr. hitherto unkn. origs. in lib. of Breslau Univ.

NORDENSKIÖLD, Bar. A. E. [ed.] Facsimile Atlas of Oldest History of Cartography 89
Folio reprodns. of 51 maps prtd. before 1600, w. descr. letterpress and other ill.

*For* **Atlases of Commercial Geogr.** *v.* **D** § 148; **Geol.** *v.* **H** § 31; **Meteorol., Oceans** *v.* **H** § 29, § 27; **Physical Geogr.** *v.* **H** § 25

## 5: COLLECTIONS OF VOYAGES, TRAVELS, AND ADVENTURES. SERIES

### Early Collections

DE BRY, J. T. [ed.] Collectiones Peregrin. in Indiam Occident. et Orient., 13 Pts. *Frankfort* 1590–1634

Crawford, Earl of Collns. and Notes, No. 3: Voyages of de Bry; 33 pl. 63/ 4° Quaritch

CHURCHILL, A. + J. [eds.] Colln. of Voys. & Travels, 8 vols.; maps and pl. f° *London* [1707–47] 1752

*HAKLUYT, Rich. [ed.] Principal Navigns., Voyages, Traffiques, and Discovs. of Engl. Nation; w. Essay by Prf. W. Raleigh, 12 vols. *o.p.* [*pb.* 12/6 *n.* ea.] 8° MacLehose, *Glasgow* [1598–1600] 03–5
[Elizab. Travels Ser.] An invaluable colln., commencg. w. Kg. ARTHUR and endg. w. 1590. A very handsome repr. of 1st edn., w. copious Index and Life of HAKLUYT by Prf. W. RALEIGH. Issued also as vols. i–xx of Extra Ser. of Hakluyt Soc. A cheap repr. of same edn. in 8 vols. [Everyman's Lib.] ea. 1/ *n.*, pott 8° Dent 08 (35 c. *n.* Dutton, *N.Y.*).

HAKLUYT SOCIETY: Publications *ann. subscr.* (2 vols.) 21/ 8° Hakluyt Society 47 *sqq. in prg.*

SERIES I (1847–98).

de ACOSTA (J.), *Hist. of Indies* [tr.], 2 v. [*ut* **E** § 59] C. R. MARKHAM 80
AL FASI [= LEO AFRICANUS], *Africa*, 3 v. [tr.] [*ut* **E** § 41] 96
de AZURARA (G. E.), *Guinea* [tr.], 3 v. [*ut* **E** § 46] ed. C. R. BEAZLEY + E. PRESTAGE 96–8
ALVAREZ (F.), *Port. Emb. to Abyss.* [tr.] [*ut* **E** § 44] L'd STANLEY OF ALDERLEY 81
de ANDAGOYA (P.), *Narrative* [*ut* **E** § 61], tr. C. R. MARKHAM 65
ASHER (G. M.) [ed.], *Hy. Hudson* [*ut* **E** § 68] 60
BAFFIN (W.), *Voyages* [*ut* **E** § 68] C. R. MARKHAM 81
BARBARO (J.) *and* CONTARINI (A.), *Tana and Persia* [*ut* **E** § 38] ed. L'd STANLEY OF ALDERLEY 73
BARBOSA (D.), *E. Africa and Malabar* [*ut* **E** § 65] tr. H. STANLEY 66
BENZONI (G.), *Hist. of New World* [*ut* **E** § 54] tr. Adm. W. H. SMYTH 57
BONTIER (P.) + le VERRIER (J.), *Canarians* [*ut* **E** § 46] tr. R. H. MAJOR 72
BUTLER (Cpt. N.), *Hist. of Bermudas* [*ut* **E** § 55] Sir J. H. LEFROY 81
CHAMPLAIN (S.), *Voy. to W. Indies* [*ut* **E** § 59] A. WILMERE 59
de CLAVIGO (R. G.), *Embassy to Timour* [*ut* **E** § 33] C. R. MARKHAM 59
COATS (Cpt. W.), *of Hudson Bay* [*ut* **E** § 68] [Sir] J. BARROW 52
COCKS (R.), *Diary in Japan*, 2 v. [*ut* **E** § 37] E. M. THOMPSON 83
COLUMBUS (Chr.), *Select Letters* [*ut* **E** § 54] tr. R. H. MAJOR [47] 70
" *Jl. dur. First Voy., etc.* [*ut* **E** § 54] tr. C. R. MARKHAM 93
CORREA (C.), *Voys. of Vasco da Gama* [*ut* **E** § 35] tr. L'd STANLEY OF ALDERLEY 69
CORTES (H.), *Fifth Letter* [*ut* **E** § 58] tr. P. de GAYANGOS 68
COSMAS INDICOPLEUSTES, *Topographia Christ.* [*ut* **E** § 30] tr. J. W. MCCRINDLE 97

da GAMA (Vasco), *Jl. of 1st Voyage* [*ut* E § 35] tr. E. G. RAVENSTEIN 98
DALLAM (T.) *and* COVEL (J.), *Voys. in Levant* [*ut* E § 29] J. T. BENT 93
DALBOQUERQUE (A.), *Comms.* [tr.], 4 v. [*ut* E § 35] W. De G. BIRCH 75–84
DAVIS (J.), *Voyages and Works* [*ut* E § 68] Cpt. A. H. MARKHAM 80
DOMINIGUEZ (L. L.) [ed.], *La Plata* [*ut* E § 60] 91
DRAKE (Sir F.), *World Encompassed* [*ut* E § 61] W. S. W. VAUX 55
FLETCHER (G.), *Russia* [*ut* E § 25] E. A. BOND 56
FOXE (Cpt. L.) *and* JAMES (Cpt. T.), *Hudson's Bay* [*ut* E § 55] M. CHRISTY 93
FROBISHER (Sir M.), *Three Voyages* [*ut* E § 68] Adm. COLLINSON 67
GAIRDNER (J.) [ed.], *Sailg. Directns. f. Circumnavign. of Engl'd.* 88
GALVANO (A.), *Discovs. of World* [*ut* E § 7] Adm. BETHUNE 62
de GAMBOA (P. S.), *Voyages* [*ut* E § 61] tr. Sir C. R. MARKHAM 94
GOSCH (C. C. A.) [ed.], *Danish Arctic Expedns.*, 2 v. [*ut* E § 68]
de GUZMAN (A. E.), *Life of* tr. C. R. MARKHAM 62
HAKLUYT (R.) [ed.], *Disc. of Amer.* [*ut* E § 54 J. W. JONES *o.p.* 50
HAWKINS (Sir R.), *South Sea: 1593* [*ut* E § 62] Cpt. C. R. D. BETHUNE *o.p.* 48
„ The same [*ut* E § 62] C. R. MARKHAM 78
HEDGES (W.), *Diary in Bengal, etc.*, 3 v. [*ut* E § 35] Col. H. YULE 87–9
v. HERBERTSTEIN (Bar. S.), *Russia*, 2 v. [*ut* E § 25] tr. R. H. MAJOR *o.p.* 51–2
HUES (R.), *Tractatus de Globis* [*ut* I § 19] ed. C. R. MARKHAM 89
JENKINSON (A.), etc., *Russia and Persia*, 2 v. [*ut* E § 25] E. D. MORGAN + C. H. COOTE 86
JORDANUS, *Mirabilia Descripta* [*ut* E § 31] tr. Col. H. YULE 63
LANCASTER (Sir J.), *Voyages* [*ut* E § 35] C. R. MARKHAM 77
LEGUAT (F.), *Voy. to Rodriguez* [*ut* E § 41] Cpt. S. P. OLIVER 91
de LEON (C.), *Travs. in 1532–50* [*ut* E § 61] tr. C. R. MARKHAM 64
„ *Sec. Pt. of Chron. of Peru* [*ut* E § 61] tr. same 83
van LINSCHOTEN (J. H.), *E. Indies* [tr.] [*ut* E § 35] A. C. BURNELL + P. A. TIELE 85
MAGELLAN (F.), *First Voyage* [*ut* E § 7] ed. L'd STANLEY OF ALDERLEY 74
MAJOR (R. H.) [ed.], *Terra Australis* [*ut* E § 65] 59
„ [ed.], *India in 15 Cent.* [*ut* E § 35] 57
*Map of Peru* 79
„ *of the World: 1600* [ill. Davis' voyages] 78
MARKHAM (C. R.) [tr.], *Repts. on Disc. of Peru* [*ut* E § 61] 72
„ [tr.], *Rites of Incas* [*ut* E § 53] 73
MARTEN (F.), *Spitzbergen and Greenld.* [*ut* E § 69] A. WHITE 55
MAYNARDE (T.), *Sir Fcs. Drake* [*ut* E § 58] W. D. COOLEY 49
de MENDOZA (J. G.), *Hist. of China* [tr. R. PARKE], 2 v. [*ut* E § 34] Sir G. T. STAUNTON 53–4
MIDDLETON (Sir H.), *Bantam and Maluco Isls.* [*ut* E § 36] *o.p.* B. CORNEY 55
de MORGA (A.), *Philippine Islands* [*ut* E § 36] tr. L'd STANLEY OF ALDERLEY 68
d'ORLEANS (J.), *Tartar Conquerors of China* [tr.] [*ut* F § 61] *o.p.* R. H. MAJOR 54
PYRARD (F.), *Voys. to E. Indies*, 2 v. in 3 Pts. [*ut* E § 36] tr. A. GRAY + H. C. P. BELL 87–9
RALEIGH (Sir W.), *Discoverie of Guiana* [*ut* E § 61] Sir R. H. SCHOMBURK *o.p.* 48
RUNDALL (T.) [ed.], *Early Voyages tow. N.-W. Cathay and India* [*ut* E § 68] *o.p.* 49
RUNDELL (T.) [ed.], *Docums. on Japan* [*ut* E § 37] *o.p.* 50
SALIL-IBN-RAZÎK *Imâms of 'Omân* tr. G. P. BADGER 71
SCHILTBERGER (J.), *Bondage and Travels* [*ut* E § 7] tr. J. B. TELFER 79
SIMON (P.), *Exped. of Ursua* [*ut* E § 36] tr. W. BOLLAERT 61
[? SMITH (Cpt. J.)], *Hist. of Bermudas* [*ut* E § 55] Gen. Sir J. H. LEFROY 82
de SOTO (F.), *Discov. Florida* [tr. Hakluyt] [*ut* E § 57] W. B. RYE 51
STADE (H.), *Captivity in 1547–55* [*ut* E § 61] tr. A. TOOTAL 74
STRACHEY (W.) [ed.], *Travaile into Virginia* [*ut* E § 54] *o.p.* 51
de la VALLE (P.), *Travels to India* [tr.] [*ut* E § 35] E. GREY 92
di VARTHEMA (L.), *Travels in 16 Cent.* [*ut* E § 30] tr. J. W. JONES 63
de VEER (Gerrit), *Voys. to Cathay* [*ut* E § 68] ed. Dr C. T. BEKE *o.p.* 53
„ The same [*ut* E § 68] ed. K. BEYNEN 76
de la VEGA (G.), Inca *Valley of Amazons* [*ut* E § 60] tr. C. R. MARKHAM 59
„ *Commentaries of Yncas*, 2 v. [*ut* E § 61] tr. C. R. MARKHAM 69–71
VESPUCCI (A.), *Letters*, tr. Sir C. R. MARKHAM [*ut* E § 54] 94
YULE (Col. H.) [ed.], *Cathay and Way Thither*, 2 v. [*ut* E § 34] *o.p.* 66
ZENO (N. *and* A.), *Voyages* [*ut* E § 68] tr. R. H. MAJOR 73

SERIES II (1899 *sqq.*).

BATTELL (Andr.), *Strange Advents.* [*ut* E § 48] ed. E. R. RAVENSTEIN 00
BOWREY (T.), *Countries rd. Bengal* [*ut* E § 35] ed. Sir R. C. TEMPLE 03
CASTANHOSO + BERMUDEZ, *Exp. to Abyss.* [*ut* E § 44] *o.p.* ed. R. S. WHITEWAY 02
DIAZ DEL CASTILLO (B.), *New Spain*, 3 v. [*ut* E § 57*] ed. G. GARCÍA [tr.] 08–10
CONWAY (Sir M.) [ed.], *Voys. to Spitzbergen* [*ut* E § 68] 02
DUDLEY (Sir R.), *West Indies* [*ut* E § 59] ed. G. F. WARNER 99
de ESPINOSA (A.), *Guanches of Tenerife* [*ut* E § 46] tr. Sir C. R. MARKHAM 07
FRYER (J.), *East Indies and Persia* [*ut* E § 36] ed. W. CROOKE 09
de GAMBOA (P. S.), *Hist. of Incas*, 2 v. [*ut* E § 53] tr. Sir C. R. MARKHAM 07
GONZALEZ (D. F.), *Voyage* [*ut* E § 64] tr. B. G. CORNEY 08
van 's GRAVESANDE (Storm), *Brit. Guiana*, 2 v. [*ut* E § 61] ed. C. A. HARRIS + J. A. J. DE VILLIERS 11
JOURDAIN (J.), *Jl. of Voy. to E. Indies* [*ut* E § 35] ed. W. FOSTER 05
MARKHAM (Sir C. R.) [ed.], *Magellan's Strait* [*ut* E § 61] 11
MENDANA, *Solomon Isld.*, 2 v. [*ut* E § 64] *o.p.* ed. L'd AMHERST + B. THOMSON 01
MUNDY (P.), *Travels in Eur.* [*ut* E § 11] ed. Sir R. C. TEMPLE 05
de QUIROS (P. F.), *Voyages: 1595–1606*, 2 v. [*ut* E § 64] tr. Sir C. R. MARKHAM 04
ROE (Sir T.), *Court of Mogul*, 2 v. [*ut* E § 35] ed. W. FOSTER 99
SARIS (Cpt. J.), *Voy. to Japan* [*ut* E § 37] ed. Sir E. M. SATOW 00
van SPIELBERGEN (J.), *E. and W. Ind. Mirror* [*ut* E § 7] tr. J. A. J. DE VILLIERS 06
TEIXEIRA (P.), *India to Italy* [*ut* E § 7] *o.p.* tr. W. F. SINCLAIR 01
WILLIAM OF RUBRUCK *and* JOHN OF PIAU DE CARPINE, *Tartary* [*ut* E § 39] *o.p.* tr. W. W. ROCKHILL 00

EXTRA SERIES.

i–xii: HAKLUYT (R.), *Voyages*, 12 v.—*ut inf.*
xiii: JOHN DE PIANO CARPINI *and* WILLIAM DE RUBRUQUIS, *Texts and Verns.* [*ut* E § 39] *o.p.* ed. C. R. BEAZLEY
xiv–xxx: PURCHAS (S.), *Hakluytus Posthumus*, 20 v.—*ut inf.*

Harleian Colln. of Voys. and Travels not before coll. in Engl., 2 v.; maps and pl. f° *London* 1745

KERR, Rob. [ed.] Collection of Voyages & Travels, 17 vols. *o.p.* [*pb.* £10 4/] 8° Baldwin 11–25

NAVY RECORDS SOCIETY: Publications—*ut* F § 28

Original Narratives of Early American History [Series]—*ut* E § 54

PINKERTON, Jno. [ed.] Voyages and Travels, 17 vols. *o.p.* [*pb.* £37 16/] 4° Longman 1808–14

*PURCHAS, Sam. [ed.] Hakluytus Posthumus, or Purchas, his Pilgrimes, 20 vols.; facs. maps and ill. ea. 12/6 *n.* 8° MacLehose, *Glasgow* [1625] 05–6
[Elizab. Travels Ser.] A worthy repr. of 1st edn., a most important 'History of the World in Sea Voyages and Lande Travells by Englishmen and others'. Vol. xx is *Index*. Issued also as vols. xiv–xxxiii of Extra Ser. of Hakluyt Soc.

## Modern Collections

BATES, H. W. [ed.] Illustrated Travels: record of discovery, geography, and adventure, 6 vols.; fully ill. [popular] ea. 15/ r 4° Cassell *n.d.* (69–81)

BEAZLEY, C. R. [ed.] Voyages and Travels mainly dur. 16 and 17 Cents., 2 v. [Engl. Garner] ea. 4/ *n.* c 8° Constable 03

CASSELL & Co. [pubs.] The World of Adventure, 3 vols.; ill. ea. 9/ 4° Cassell 89–91
A popular colln. of true tales of adventure by land and sea, every age and country bg. laid under contribn.

CUNDALL, Jos. [ed.] Tales of Advent. and of Travel 50 Yrs. Ago; 20 pl. 12/6 p 8° Low 92
Amongst authors drawn on are COLERIDGE, Sir W. SCOTT, BYRON, HOWITT, THACKERAY, DICKENS, 'Barry CORNWALL', Duke of RUTLAND [then L'd J. MANNERS].

HYAMSON, A. M. [ed.] Elizabethan Adventurers on Spanish Main; 8 pl. [fr. Hakluyt] 3/6 c 8° Routledge 11
HAWKINS, DRAKE, OXENHAM, BARKER, CANDISH, GRENVILLE, RALEIGH; spelling modernized.

JOHNSON, R. Brimley [ed.] Voyages of Famous Brit. Seamen [fr. Hakluyt] 1/ 12° Dent 07

MORRIS, Chas. [ed.] Half-hrs. of Travel at Home & Abroad, 4 v.; ill. $10 c 8° Lippincott, *Phila.* 97

PAYNE, E. J. [ed.] Voys. of Elizab. Seamen to Amer. [fr. Hakluyt] 5/ ($1·10) c 8° Abgd. 4/6 (60 c.) Clar. Press [80–00] 07
Selns. fr. 2 Ser. pb. 1880, '93, '00, HAWKINS, FROBISHER, DRAKE, GILBERT, AMADAS, etc. Ed. C. R. BEAZLEY.

PURVES, D. L. [ed.] English Circumnavigators: most remarkable voys. rd. world 5/ c 8° Nimmo 74
Conts. DRAKE'S *World Encompassed* (1628); DAMPIER'S *New Voyage* (1697); ANSON'S *Voyage* (1741–4); COOK'S *Voyages* (1768–80).

VERNE, Jules — Celebrated Travels [tr.], 3 vols.; ill. — *o.p.* [*pb.* 12/6 ea.] 8° Low 79–81
i: *Exploration of the World*; ii: *Great Navigators of 18th Century*; iii: *Great Explorers of 19th Century.*

**Series**

Adventure Series; ill. — [mostly edited reprs.] 3/6 c 8° Unwin 91 *sqq.*

BECKWOURTH (J. P.), *Life and Advents.* [ut E § 53] — C. G. LELAND
de BENYOWSKY (Ct), *Memrs. and Travels* [tr.] [ut E § 31] — S. P. OLIVER
CABLE (G. W.), *Famous Advents. and Prison Escapes of Civil War* (7/6)
CARLYON-JENKINS (Mrs C.) [ed.], *Hard Life in the Colonies* — *o.p.*
The emigrants who wrote these letters [c. 1870] were A. C. + G. C. Jenkins and H. K. Dunbar. China, Melb., Calc., N. Zeal.
[CHOYCE (J.)], *Log of a Jack Tar* — V. LOVETT CAMERON
Printed fr. orig. MS. With [the Irish Cpt.] *O'Brien's Captivity in Frce.* added.
COMPTON (H.), *Milit. Advents. in Hindustan* [ut E § 35]
DOWIE (M. Muriel) [ed.], *Women Adventurers* [ut D § 132] — *o.p.*
DRURY (R.), *Jl. in Madagascar* [ut E § 51] — S. P. OLIVER
EASTWICK (Cpt. R. W.), *A Master Mariner* [ut E § 35] — H. COMPTON
KOLOKOTRONES, *Klepht and Warrior* [tr. fr. Gk.]
*Missing Friends* [ut E § 66]
PELLOW (T.), *Adventures* [ut E § 45] — R. BROWN
PINTO (F. M.), *Voyages and Advents.* [ut E § 36] — A. VAMBERY
PYLE (H.) [ed.], *Buccaneers of America* [ut E § 54]
ROCHE (J. J.), *Story of Filibusters* [ut F § 70] — (5/)
SHIPP (J.), *Military Career* — Maj. H. M. CHICHESTER
SNELL (Hannah), *The Female Soldier* — *o.p.*
Served [as 'Jas. Gray'] in infantry and marines, and was present at capture of Carlisle in rebelln. of 1745, and afterw. at siege of Pondicherry.
TRELAWNY (E. J.), *Advts. of a Younger Son* — E. GARNETT [ut K § 24]
VILLARS (P.) [ed.], *Escapes of Latude and Casanova fr. Prison* — (5/)
WATSON (W.), *Advents. of Blockade Runner* [ut F § 71]

Elizabethan Travel Series; ill — ea. 12/6 *n.* 8° MacLehose, *Glasgow* [*v.y.*] 03 *sqq., in prg.*

CORYAT (T.), *Crudities*, 2 v. [ut E § 11]
HAKLUYT (R.), *Voyages*, 20 v. [ut sup.]
KAEMPFER (E.), *Hist. of Japan* [tr.], 3 v. [ut E § 37]
LITHGOW (W.), *Travels* [ut E § 6]
MORYSON (F.). *Itinerary*, 4 vols. [ut E § 11]
PURCHAS (S.), *Voyages*, 20 v. [ut sup.]
SMITH (Cpt. J.), *Travels*, 2 v. [ut E § 54]

## 6: BIOGRAPHY OF VOYAGERS AND DISCOVERERS: COLLECTIVELY

**Series**

Story of Exploration: ed. Dr J. Scott Keltie—*v.* **E** § 9

World's Great Explorers and Explorations: ed. J. S. Keltie + H. J. Mackinder + E. G. Ravenstein; maps and ill. — ea. 3/6 c 8° Philip 89 *sqq.*

Ea. $1·25 Dodd & Mead, *N.Y.*
*Columbus* [ut E § 54] — C. R. MARKHAM
*Davis (Jno.)* [ut E § 68] — C. R. MARKHAM
*Franklin (Sir Jno.)* [ut E § 68] — Cpt. A. H. MARKHAM
*Livingstone (Dr)* [ut E § 41] — H. H. JOHNSON
*Magellan (Ferd.)* [ut E § 61] — F. H. H. GUILLEMARD
*Palestine* [ut E § 30] — Maj. C. R. CONDER
*Park (Mungo)* [ut E § 46] — JOS. THOMSON

**Individual Writers** —*v. also* **F** § 30

BOLTON, Sarah K. Famous Voyagers and Explorers [popular; 3/6 Hodder] 75 c. c 8° Crowell, *N.Y.* [93]
COLUMBUS; Marco POLO; MAGELLAN; RALEIGH; FRANKLIN, KANE, C. F. HALL, etc.; LIVINGSTONE; PERRY, GREELY, etc.

Early English Voyagers — [Drake, Cavendish, Dampier] 5/ c 8° Nelson 87
Appears to be a reprint of a book originally published in 1831; but not so stated. Quite popular.

FRITH, Hy. — Romance of Navigation: earliest times to 18 cent.; ill. — 3/6 c 8° Ward & Lock 93

GREELY, Gen. A. W. — Men of Achievement: Explorers and Travellers — $2 *n.* 8° Scribner, *N.Y.* 93
8/6 Low. Limited to American explorers, with DU CHAILLU and STANLEY.

HOWELLS, W. D. [ed.] — Lib. of Universal Advent. by Sea and Land — $5·75 8° Harper, *N.Y.* 88
Orig. narrs. of personal prowess and peril fr. A.D. 79 to 1888.

JOHNSON, W. H. — The World's Discoverers — $1·50 c 8° Little & Brown, *Boston* 00

KINGSLEY, Hy. — Tales of Old Travel Renarrated; ill. [popular] 3/6 ($1·50) c 8° Macmillan [69] 91
Marco POLO, COLUMBUS, Vasco da GAMA, MAGELLAN, VERRAZANO, FROBISHER, DAVIS, DRAKE, HUDSON, and Arctic.

KINGSTON (W. H. G.) + FRITH (Hy.) Notable Voyagers, ed. Edw. Latham; col. pl. and ill. — 5/ c 8° Routledge [79] 04
$2 Dutton, *N.Y.* Interesting sketches; from COLUMBUS to NANSEN.

MARKHAM, C. R. — Famous Sailors of Former Times — [popular] 2/6 c 8° Cassell [85] 86

RALEIGH, Prf. Walt. — The English Voyages of the 16th Century 4/6 *n.* c 8° MacLehose, *Glasgow* 06
$1·25 *n.* Macmillan, *N.Y.* Chs. on *The Voyagers*; *Hakluyt*; *Influ. of the Voys. on Poetry and Imaginatn.* Repr. fr. his edn. of HAKLUYT [ut E § 5]

STATHAM, Com'r E. P. — Privateers and Privateering; 8 pl. — 7/6 *n.* 8° Hutchinson 10
True stories of pluck and daring of Brit., Fch., and Amer. sailors, addicted to patriotism and plunder. Middle 16th to early 19th cent.

STOCKTON, F. R. — Buccaneers and Pirates of our Coasts — $1·50 (6/) c 8° Macmillan 98
[Stories fr. Amer. Hist.] Chiefly West Indies and Spanish Main. Picturesquely written.

TOWLE, G. M. — Yg. Folk's Heroes of History, 6 v.; ill. — ea. $1·25; Schl. Edn., ea. 60 c. 12° Lee & Shepard, *Bost.* 78–83; 88
DRAKE, da GAMA, MAGELLAN, MARCO POLO, RALEIGH.

## 7: VOYAGES ROUND THE WORLD AND TRAVELS OVER LARGE AREAS

*Other voyages are entered under the regions to which they more particularly refer*

**Early Travels**

ANSON, G. A., L'd [1697–1762] Voyage rd. World [1740–4; Everym. Lib.; 35 c. *n.* Dutton, *N.Y.*] — 1/ *n.* s 8° Dent [1748] 11

COOK, Capt. Jas. [1728–79] Three Voyages rd. the World, ed. Lt. C. R. Low — 5/ 8° Routledge [1768–84]
$2 Dutton, *N.Y.* With coloured pl. and ill. Also Cheap Edns. 3/6 ($1·50); 2/.

" — Voyages, ed. Sir J. Barrow; 8 col. pl. [$1·50 *n.* Macm., *N.Y.*] 3/6 c 8° Black 04

" — Voyages, ed. A. Kippis — [thin-paper edn.] 3/ *n.* p 8° Newnes 05

" — Voyages of Discovery [35 c. *n.* Dutton, *N.Y.*; Everyman's Lib.] 1/ *n.* pott 8° Dent 06

COOK, Capt. Jas. Jl. of First Voyage rd. World; maps, charts, & facss. 21/ r 8° Stock 93
A literal transcrn. of orig. MS. by Cpt. W. J. L. WHARTON, w. Introd. and notes. The first time the *Jl.* has been pubd. *in extenso*; but it does not add much to our knowl. It is that of the first voy. made 1768–71 in *Endeavour*, a Whitby collier, in wh. New Zeal. and E. Coast of Australia were first explored.

Banks, Sir Jos. [1743–1820] Journal during Capt. Cook's First Voyage—*ut* **H** § 44

Besant, [Sir] Walt. Captain Cook [Engl. Men of Action] 2/6 (60 c.) c 8° Macmillan 89
An apprecn. of COOK's positn. amongst his contemporaries and estimate of his character and value of his wk.

Jones, M. Story of Capt. Cook's Voyages round World 5/ 12° Cassell [70]

*Kitson, Arth. Capt. James Cook, 'the Circumnavigator'; maps and ill. 15/ *n.* 8° Murray 07
$4·50 *n.* Dutton, *N.Y.* A complete and unvarnished narr. of the 3 voyages, prep. fr. COOK's own jls. and other orig. sources—the first attempt at a crit. memoir on the navigr. and his wk. since that by Dr A. KIPPIS' *Life of Cook* [1788], until now the chief authority. Incl. a val. track-chart.

DAMPIER, Wm. [1652–1715] Voyages, ed. Jno. Masefield, 2 v.; maps & ill. 25/ *n.* 8° Richards 06
An excellent edn., after the early edns.; w. notes and most of orig. maps and ill., and a biograph. and crit. study of DAMPIER's life and wks.

,, Voyage rd. World, w. Introd. Rob. Steele [school-bk.] 10*d. n.* f 8° Rivington 93

Russell, W. Clark Dampier [Engl. Men of Action] 2/6 (60 c.) c 8° Macmillan 89

DRAKE, Sir Fcs. [ ] —*v.* **E** § 61

GALVANO, Ant. Discoveries of the World, unto 1555, ed. Adm. Bethune 8° Hakluyt Soc. 62
First published by HAKLUYT [1601]; contains the original Portuguese text and revised tr.

da GUZMAN, A. E. Life & Acts [1518–43], tr. by [Sir] C. R. Markham, w. Introd. 8° Hakluyt Society 62

LITHGOW, Wm. [1582–1645] Totall Discourse of the Rare Adventures and Painefull Peregrinations of long 19 Yeares Travayles 12/6 *n.* MacLehose, *Glasgow* [1614] 06
$3·25 *n.* Macmillan, *N.Y.* [Elizab. Travels Ser.] 'From Scotland to the most famous kingdomes in Europe, Asia, and Affrica. Perfited by three deare bought Voyages, in Surveighing of forty eight Kingdomes ancient and moderne'. A sumptuous edn.

MAGELLAN, Ferd. [1480–1521] First Voyage round the World [tr.] 8° Hakluyt Society 74
Tr. fr. PIGAFETTA and other contemporary wrs. by L'd STANLEY OF ALDERLEY, w. notes, etc.

Guillemard, Dr F. H. H. Magellan and the First Circumnavign. 3/6 c 8° Philip 90
$1·25 Dodd & Mead, *N.Y.* [World's Gt. Explorers.] A good popular account, w. 4 maps and 21 ill.

Pigafetta, A. Magellan's Voyage around World, ed. J. A. Robertson, w. tr.; 2 vols. $7·50 *n.* 8° A. H. Clark Co., *Cleveland* 06
36/ *n.* Paul. An excellent, well-equipped edn. of cpl. text fr. orig. Ambrosian MS.; w. Engl. tr., notes, bibliogr., and index.

SCHILTBERGER, Joh. [14–15 cent.] Bondage and Travs. of in Eur., As. & Afr. [tr.], ed. K. F. Neumann 8° Hakluyt Soc. 79

van SPEILBERGEN, Joris East & West Indian Mirror [tr.], ed. J. A. J. De Villiers 8° Hakluyt Society 06
Acc. of his voyage rd. world in 1614–7. Incls. Austral. navigns. of Jac. Le Mair [tr.]. Maps, 26 ill., and bibliogr.

TEIXEIRA, Pedro Jy. fr. India to Italy by Land [tr.] [1604–5] *o.p.* 8° Hakluyt Society 01

VESPUCCI, Amerigo [1451–1512]—*v.* **E** § 54

**Modern** —*v. also* **I** § 153: Yachting; **I** § 148*: Motoring; **I** § 149: Cycling; and *for* Scientific Voys. *v.* **H** § 44

AGASSIZ, A. Three Cruises of the *Blake*, 2 vols.; ill. $8 8° Houghton, *Boston* [88] 01
42/ Low. The *Blake*, of U.S. Coast Surv., made 3 cruises (1877–8, '78–9, '80) to Strts. of Florida, Yucatan Bank, Gf. of Mex., Caribb. Sea, and alg. Atl. coast. A valuable account of oceanic research.

de AMICIS, Edm. On Blue Water [tr. (fr. Ital.)] $2·25 c 8° Putnam, *N.Y.* 97
Voyage fr. Genoa to Buenos Ayres. Mainly a study of human nature in cabin and steerage.

'Anglo-Indian Globe-Trotter' Farthest East and South and West; 12 pl. 15/ 8° W. H. Allen 92
Notes of a journey from India to England, thro' Japan, Australasia, and America.

ARNOLD, Sir Edwin Wandering Words; 23 pl. & 22 ill. [Egypt, Asia] *o.p.* [*pb.* 18/] 8° Longman 94

,, East and West; 41 ill. [Egypt, Ind., Japan] *o.p.* [*pb.* 18/] 8° Longman 96

,, Seas and Lands; 42 pl. and 29 ill. [Silver Lib.] 3/6 c 8° Longman [91] 94
$3, 8°. Above three bks. were orig. pub. in *Daily Telegraph*. All are lively and full of information.

AUBERTIN, J. J. Wanderings and Wonderings; map 8/6 c 8° Paul 92
Japan, Corea, Formosa, Manila, Tientsin, Wall of China, Pnom Penh (capital of Cambodia) and R. Mecon (where CAMOENS swam ashore w. his poems in one hand), Kashmir, Darjeeling, Austral., N.Z., U.S.—occupying 3 yrs. Wr. as l'rs to friends.

*Bacchante*, H.M.S. Cruise of H.M.S. *Bacchante*, 2 vols., maps & ill. 52/6 m 8° Macmillan 86
1879–82. From journals, etc., of Prince ALBERT VICTOR and Prince GEORGE OF WALES, w. addns. by Can. J. N. DIXON.

BADEN-POWELL, Lt. B. F. S. In Savage Isles & Settled Lands; maps & ill. *o.p.* [*pb.* 21/] 8° Bentley 92
Egypt, Ceyl., Ind., Austral., N.Z., Java, Sts. Settlemts., N. Guinea, Borneo, Tonga, Samoa, Sandw. Isl., U.S.: 1888–1891.

BARROWS, J. H. A World-Pilgrimage, ed. M. E. Barrows [letters] $1 c 8° McClurg, *Chicago* 97

BELCHER, Adm. Sir E. Voy. rd. World in H.M.S. *Sulphur*, 2 vols. [1836–42] *o.p.* [*pb.* 36/] 8° Colburn 43

,, Voy. of H.M.S. *Samarang*, 2 vols. [E. Archipel.; 1843–6] *o.p.* [*pb.* 36/] 8° Lovell Reeve 48

,, Voy. in H.M.S. *Assistance*, 2 vols. [1852–4] *o.p.* [*pb.* 36/] r 8° Lovell Reeve 55

BRASSEY, Annie, L'y A Voyage in the *Sunbeam*; 66 ill. [Silver Lib.] 3/6 c 8° Longman [78]
$2 Holt, *N.Y.* Fr. Engl., *via* Madeira, C. de Verde, Rio de Janeiro, Sts. of Magellan, Chili, S. Sea, Sandw. Isls., Jap., China, Ceyl., Medit. Schl. Ed. 37 ill. 2/ (75 c. Longm., *N.Y.*) [80].

,, In the Trades, the Tropics, & 'Roaring Forties'; 220 ill. $2·50 Holt, *N.Y.*] 7/6 c 8° Longman [85] 86

,, Last Voyage in *Sunbeam*; ill. [Ind. and Austr.; [1887] *p.* [*pb.* 21/] 8° Longman [ ] 89

BRASSEY, Thos., L'd Voyages & Travels, ed. Cpt. S. Eardley-Wilmot, 2 v. *o.p.* [*pb.* 10/] c 8° Longman 95
Acc. of his impressns. of var. countries on var. jys. [1862–94], many in *Sunbeam*, w. observns. on navign., Imp. Fedn., land-tenures, etc. Maps.

BREHM, A. E. From North Pole to Equator [tr.]; 83 ill. 21/ r 8° Blackie 96
$6 Scribner, *N.Y.* Colln. of sketches of wild life, scenery, and travel in var. pts. of world, esp. Asia and Afr. Ed. J. A. THOMSON.

BRUCE, Maj. C. Dalrymple In the Footsteps of Marco Polo—*ut* **E** § 33

BULLEN, Fk. T. Cruise of the *Cachalot* rd. World; 8 pl. 3/6 c 8° Smith & Elder [98] 05
$1·50 Appleton, *N.Y.* A graphic picture of meths., dangers, and delights of sperm-whale hunting.

" The Log of a Sea-Waif; 8 ill. 3/6 c 8° Smith & Elder [99]
$1·50 Appleton, *N.Y.* Recounts his earliest advents. on the deep, begun when less than 12 yrs. old.

" Back to Sunny Seas; 8 pl. 6/ c 8° Smith & Elder 05

BURTON, Sir R. F. Wanderings on Three Continents; ill. 16/ *n.* 8° Hutchinson 01
Reprinted lectures dealing with BURTON's travels and experiences 1853–70, ed. by W. H. WILKINS, with notes.

CAINE, W. S. A Trip round the World; ill. [1887–8] 3/6 c 8° Routledge [88]

CLEMENS, S. L. [' Mark TWAIN '] Following the Equator $2 c 8° Harper, *N.Y.* 03
An able and picturesque narrative, notable for its good sense and good humour.

COLQUHOUN, Ethel Two on their Travels; ill. (some col.) by author 10/ *n.* 8° Heinemann 02

*DARWIN, Chas. A Naturalist's Voyage round the World—*ut* **H** § 44

DEL MAR, Walt. Around the World through Japan; ill. 12/6 *n.* r 8° Black [03] 04
$3 *n.* Macmillan, *N.Y.* Excellent impressionist record of recent travel thro' Ceyl., Java, China, Japan (last v. fully treated).

DEWAR, Cpt. J. C. Voyage of *Nyanza*, R.N.Y.C.; map and ill. 21/ 8° Blackwood 92
A thoroughly interesting acc. of a 3 years cruise [1887–90] in a schooner yacht in Atlantic and Pacific, wrecked at Ponapi.

DE WINDT, Harry From Paris to New York by Land; maps and ill. 12/6 *n.* 8° Newnes 03
Narr. of overland jy. thro' Russia, Siberia, Alaska, etc.: good acc. of Siberian convict-settlements.

" My Restless Life 7/6 *n.* 8° Richards 09
Sarawak [pres. Rajah is author's bro'-in-law], London, Melb. to China, Siberian prisons, Monte Carlo as it was, etc.

DUFF, Sir M. E. Grant Notes from a Diary, 14 vols.—*ut* **F** § 27
Contains many notes on travel in the East of Europe and in Asia, especially India.

GUILLEMARD, Dr F. H. H. Cruise of the *Marchesa*; ill. *o.p.* [*pb.* 21/] 8° Murray [86] 89
To Kamschatska and New Guinea; w. notices of Formosa, Liu Kiu, islands of Malay Archipelago, etc.

HAWEIS, Rev. H. R. Travel and Talk, 1885–1893–95, 2 vols.; 2 ports. 12/ c 8° Chatto [96] 97
A fluent narrative of 100,000 miles of travel in Amer., Australia, N.Z., the Pacific, etc.

HUGHES, Thos. Vacation Rambles 6/ c 8° Macmillan 95
Good tempered, cheerful holiday pprs., 1862–1895, orig. contrib. *sub nom.* 'Vacuus Viator' to *Spectator*. Turk., Grce., Normy., and other regns. of Frce., Can., U.S.

JAMES, Lion. Side Tracks and Bridle Paths 6/ c 8° Blackwood 09
Persia, India, Russia, South Africa, Germany, Turkey, England.

JEBB, Jno. Gladwyn Life and Advents. of. By Mrs J. G. Jebb [widow] 10/6 s 8° Blackwood 94
An interestg. acc. of a life of varied advent., in Ind., Nicar., U.S., Brazil, Rockies, Mex.: a bk. for explorers and sportsmen.

JERNINGHAM, Sir Hubert From West to East; 2 maps and 24 pl. 15/ *n.* 8° Murray 07
Globe-trottg. Dec., 1905–May 1906; best on Japan, Manchuria, Corea: home *via* Honolulu and U.S.

KIPLING, Rudyard From Sea to Sea: letters of travel, 2 vols. ea. 5/ *n.* f 8° Macmillan [00]
$2 Doubleday, *N.Y.* Brilliant letters of travel wr. for Indian papers, 1887–9, fr. pts. of India, Burmah, Japan, and America.

NORTH, Marianne [*d.* 1890] Recollections of a Happy Life, 2 vols. 17/ *n.* ($7) c 8° Macmillan 92
Charmg. record of a traveller-botanist's experces., ed. Mrs J. A. SYMONDS [her sis.]. Miss NORTH, a lineal desct. of Roger NORTH, visited N. Am., W. Indies, Calif., Japan, Java, Borneo, Ceyl., Ind., Austr., N. Z., Tasm., S. Afr., Seychelles, Chili—paintg. flowerg. plts. of world in actual habitats. She bequeathed her wonderful colln. of ptgs. to the nation, and built a gallery for it at Kew Gdns.

" Some Further Recollections of a Happy Life 8/6 *n.* ($3·50) c 8° Macmillan 93
Earlier recollns. than precedg., sel. fr. her jls. Ed. by same. Pyrenees and Spain, Egypt, Palestine, Mentone, Switz.: 1859–69.

*Novara* [Austrian frigate: 1857–9]

Scherzer, Dr Karl Circumnavign. of Globe by *Novara* [tr.], 3 vols.; maps and ill. *o.p.* [*pb.* £3] r 8° Saunders 61–3

OOKHTOMSKY, Pr'ce E. Travels in East of Nicholas ii, when Cesarewitch [tr.], ed. Sir G. Birdwood, 2 vols.; c. 500 ill. 105/ *n.* 4° Constable 96–00
Wr. by order of NICH. ii, describg. his travs. 1890–1: Egypt und. Brit. rule, Ind., China, Japan, Siberia. Profusely ill. (largely architect.); letterpress partly of gazette kind (accs. of cerems., etc.), partly of better guide-bk. kind. A bk. for the drawg.-room rather than the study.

*Ophir* (The): Voyage 1901

Knight, E. F. With the Royal Tour; map and 16 ill. 5/ *n.* ($2) c 8° Longman 02
Abridgment of letters written to *The Morning Post*: a pleasant, readable account.

Maxwell, Wm. With the *Ophir* round the Empire; 24 ill. 6/ c 8° Cassell 02
Letters, partly re-written, by the special correspondent of *The Standard*.

Wallace, Sir Don. M. The Web of Empire 21/ *n.* ($6·50 *n.*) 8° Macmillan 02
Cheap Edn. 1/6. The 'authorized', and at the same time fullest, account of the tour.

Watson, Jos. The Queen's Wish: with the *Ophir*, etc. 12/6 *n.* 8° Hutchinson 02
By Reuter's correspondent; text perhaps inferior to WALLACE's. Excellent illns.

SLOCUM, Cpt. Josh. Sailing alone around the World; 63 ill. $2 8° Century Co., *N.Y.* 00
Narrative of the author's solitary voyage of 46,000 miles in the sloop *Spray*.

STEVENSON, R. L. The Amateur Emigrant: Clyde to Sandy Hook—*in his* Works, *ut* **K** § 89
$1·25 Scribner, *N.Y.* Jy. acr. Atlantic as 2nd-cabin passgr. Full of sanity and wholesome views of life.

" Essays of Travel 2/ *n.* c 8° Chatto [05] 09

THOMPSON, F. D. In the Track of the Sun; ill. $6 r 8° Appleton, *N.Y.* 94
25/ Heinemann. Acc. of a seven-months' tour fr. N.Y. westwd., *via* Japan, China, Ind., Egypt, Palest., It., Engl., and home. Finely ill.

TREVES, Sir Fredk. The Other Side of the Lantern; 40 pl. 6/ *n.* c 8° Cassell [05] 06
Account of trip rd. world, fresh in outlook, keen in observn., and vigorous in description.

VANDERVELL, Harry A Shuttle of an Empire's Loom 6/ c 8° Blackwood 99
A plain, matter-of-fact acc. of a 5-months' voyage rd. world by a landsman shipped as a fo'c's'le hand.

## 8 : ART OF TRAVEL ; MANUALS FOR TRAVELLERS AND EXPLORERS

ADAMS (A.) + BAIKIE (W.) + BARRON (C.) Manl. of Nat. Hist. for Use of Travellers *o.p.* [*pb.* 21/] p 8° Van Voorst 54

GALTON, Fcs. Art of Travel: hints on shifts in wild countries; ill. 7/6 12° Murray [55] 76

HERSCHEL, Sir J. F. W. Admiralty Manl. of Scient. Inquiry, ed. Sir R. S. Ball; map *o.p.* [*pb.* 3/6] p 8° Murray [49] 86

JONES, Mary C. European Travel for Women [f. Amer. women] $1 *n.* (4/6) gl 8° Macmillan, *N.Y.* 00

KNOX, T. W. How to Travel: hints, advice, suggestions [popular] 75 c. 16° Putnam, *N.Y.* [80] 87

LORD (W. B.) + BAINES (T.) Shifts & Expedts. of Camp Life, Travel, & Explorn. 30/ r 8° Cox [68] 76

*ROY. GEOGRAPH. SOC.: Hints to Travellers, Scientific & General, 2 v. 15/ *n.* c 8° Roy. Geogr. Soc. [54] 06
Ed. E. A. REEVES. The 8th edn. (1901) was ed. by Jno. COLES; the 6th (1889) by D. W. FRESHFIELD + Cpt. W. J. L. WHARTON.

,, Antarctic Manual, ed. Geo. Murray 15/ *n.* r 8° Murray 01
Prepared for the use of the expedition of 1901. Pref. Sir C. R. MARKHAM.

### Anthropological Research

Anthrop. Inst.: Notes & Queries on Anthropology. By Dr J. G. Garson + C. H. Read 5/ c 8° Anthrop. Inst. [75] 92

KELLER, Prf. A. G. Queries in Ethnography 2/ *n.* (50 c.) f 8° Longman 03
70 pp. A useful manual for the collector of ethnographic data.

RIVERS, W. H. R. —*in his* The Todas, *ut* **E** § 35, *s.v.* Ethnology (*v.* note there)

## 9 : HISTORY OF EXPLORATION AND DISCOVERY : GENERALLY

### Generally

*BEAZLEY, C. R. The Dawn of Mod. Geography, 3 v.; maps & ill. 50/ *n.* ($16·50) 8° Clar. Press 97–06
Vol. i. covers hist. of explorn. and geogr. science fr. Fall of Rom. Emp. (where BUNBURY ends) to A.D. 900; ii fr. 900 to 1260; iii ends w. the early 15th cent. A exhaustive and interestg. wk. Vols. i–ii ea. 15/ *n.* ($5), iii 20/ *n.* ($6·50).

JACOBS, Jos. The Story of Geographical Discovery; 24 maps 1/ c 8° Newnes 98
35 c. *n.* Appleton, *N.Y.* [Lib. of Useful Stories.] A good condensed popular account. Earliest times to NANSEN.

*JOHNSTON, Keith, jun. Physical, Historical, Polit., and Descr. Geogr.; maps 12/ 8° Stanford [81] 08
An excellent record of geograph. discovery and settlemt., ill. by a ser. of col. maps, formg. the best hist. of geography for Engl. readers. Germ. readers shd. consult C. RITTER's *Geschichte d. Erdkunde u. d. Entdeckungen*, hrsg. H. A. DANIEL [5 m. 50 8° G. Reimer, *Berl.* 61]. Repr. fr. above: *Sketch of Historical Geogr.*, 3/6 *n. id.* '09, inclg. an apprecn. of the yg. author (d. 1879) by Sir Clement MARKHAM. Abgd. fr. above: *Schl. Phys. and Descr. Geogr.*—*ut* **E** § 2.

KEANE, Jno. The Evolution of Geography; 19 maps and 7 ill. 6/ c 8° Stanford 99
Mainly conc. w. discov. of shape of world and distribn. of land and water, fr. earliest times to first circumnavign. [1522].

LEE, Alb. The World's Exploration Story; ill. [popular] 5/ *n.* c 8° Melrose 06

Story of Exploration (The): ed. Dr J. Scott Keltie; maps & ill. ea. 4/6 *n.* c 8° Rivers 03 *sqq.*, *in prg.*
*Arabia, Penetrn. of* [*ut* **E** § 32] D. G. HOGARTH | *Nile Quest (The)* [*ut* **E** § 43] Sir H. JOHNSTON | *South Pole, Siege of* [*ut* **E** § 69] Dr H. R. MILL
*Further India* [*ut* **E** § 36] Hugh CLIFFORD | *St Lawrence Basin* [*ut* **E** § 54] Dr S. E. DAWSON | *Tibet the Mysterious* [*ut* **E** § 34] Sir T. HOLDICH
A history of discovery fr. earliest records to date, in monographs.

WILLIAMS, Archib. The Romance of Exploration, 2 Series; maps & ill. ea. 5/ c 8° Seeley 04–6
Ser. i: *Romance of Early Exploration*; ii: *Romance of Modern Exploration*.

**Ancient**—*for* Geogr. of Early Nations *v. also* **F** *passim*; *for* Atlases *v.* **E** § 4

BEVAN, [Can.] W. L. Student's Manl. of Anc. Geogr., 7/6; Small Edn. 3/6 p 8° Murray [64] 81; 72

*BUNBURY, Sir E. H. Hist. of Anc. Geogr. am. Gks. and Roms., 2 vols. 21/ 8° Murray [79] 84
A very valuable and compreh. wk., beg. w. Argonauts and Homeric geogr., and endg. w. Fall of Rom. Emp. Maps and ill.

COOLEY, W. D. Hist. of Maritime & Inland Discovery, 3 vols. *o.p.* f 8° *London* 30–1
[Lardner's Cyclo.] i: *Geogr. of Ancts. and of Mid. Ages*; ii: *Mod. Voys.: Columbus to Anson*; iii: *Cook, La Perouse, Parry, Ross, Humboldt*, etc.

HEEREN, Prf. A. H. L. Historical Researches, *and* Manl. of Anc. Hist.—*ut* **F** § 6

KIEPERT, H. Manual of Ancient Geography [tr.] [classical] *o.p.* [*pb.* 5/] c 8° Macmillan 81

TOZER, Rev. H. F. Primer of Classical Geography [Primer Series] 1/ 18° Macmillan 78

,, History of Ancient Geography; 10 maps 10/6 c 8° Camb. Press 97
$2·60 *n.* Putnam, *N.Y.* [Camb. Geogr. Ser.] An excellent summary of classical geography, dealg. largely w. explorn. Covers same period as BUNBURY, on wh. the bk. is largely based.

*Dictionary*: SMITH, Sir W. [ed.] Dict. of Gk. & Rom. Geogr., 2 vols.; 535 ill. 56/ m 8° Murray [54–7] 78

### Medieval

BRETSCHNEIDER, Dr E. [ed. & tr.] Ess. on Intercourse of Chinese w. Western Countries—*ut* **D** § 117*

,, Mediæv. Researches fr. E. Asiatic Sources, 2 vols.—*ut* **E** § 31
Bears clear testimy. to state of geogr. knowl. of Western countries possessed by Chinese scholars fr. 13 to 17 cents.

**Modern**—*for* British Empire *v.* **E** § 21

ROBERTS, C. G. D. Discoveries and Explorations of the Century c 8° 06
5/ *n.* Chambers. [Nineteenth Century Ser.] A good popular account.

## 10: ANCIENT, MEDIEVAL, AND MODERN GEOGRAPHERS

**Ancient:** *Arabian—v.* **K** § 115; *Greek—v.* **K** § 192; *Roman—v.* **K** § 216

**Medieval**

ALFRED THE GREAT [849–901] Descrn. of Europe & Voys. of Ohthere & Wulstan, tr. J. Bosworth *o.p.* [*pb.* 8/] 8° Longman 55

„ Voyages of Ohthere and Wulstan [National Lib.] 6*d.* 18° Cassell 89

BARTHOLOMEW ANGLICUS [Barth. de GLANVILLA; 13 cent.] Mediæval Lore [tr.]—*ut* **B** § 3 (STEEL)

BEHAIM, Martin [15 cent.] Martin Behaim. By E. G. Ravenstein; maps and ill. 63/*n.* 4° Philip 08
A fairly exhaustive memr. on BEHAIM's life and his globe, w. maps, ill., and a facs. of his globe.

Mappa Mundi [Hereford Cathedral; 13 cent.]: facsimile *priv. prin.* 72

Benedict, Dr R. D. The Hereford Map and Legend of St Brendan

Bevan (W. L.) + Phillott (H. W.) Mediaeval Geography: essay in ill. of the Mappa Mundi; 3 photos. *o.p.* [*pb.* 4/] 8° Jakeman, *Herefd.* 73
The Introdn. deals w. general princs. of med. geogr., and val. appliances at hand for its study. The body gives a cpl. transcript of contents of the map, and seeks to identify and explain meang. of names and legends, and to trace sovrces whence the cartographer drew his materials.

**Modern**

RENNELL, Maj. Jas. [1742–1830]

Markham, Sir C. R. Maj. J. Rennell and Rise of Mod. Engl. Geogr. *o.p.* c 8° Cassell 95

RITTER, Carl [1779–1859] Life of. By W. L. Gage *o.p.* [*pb.* $2] c 8° Scribner, *N.Y.* 67

---

# II: Historical Geography

—*v.* **E** § 2; Europe *v.* **E** § 11; for separate countries, etc., *v.* their names

---

# III: Geography, etc., of Europe

## 11: EUROPE: GENERALLY

**Early Travel and Accounts**

BENJAMIN OF TUDELA [12 cent.] Itinerary: text, w. tr. and comm. M. N. Adler 5/*n.* ($2) 8° Frowde 07
Catalonia, S. Frce., Italy, Greece, Levant, Syria, Palest., Bagdad, and back *via* Khuzistan, Ind. Ocean, Yemen, Egypt, Sicily. 1160–73 (? 1165–71). Chief value lies in its full statemts. of nos. and condn. of Jews in pts. visited. Facss.

COCKERELL, C. R. Travels in Southern Europe and Levant—*ut* **E** § 29

CORYAT, Thos. [1577–1617] Coryat's Crudities hastily Gobbled up in Five Months Travells, 2 vols.; facs. ill. 25/*n.* 8° MacLehose, *Glasgow* [1611] 05
[Elizab. Travels Ser.] Travels dur. 1608 in Frce., Savoy, Italy, Rhetia (Grisons), Helvetia, High Germy., and Netherlds. One of the most popular travel-bks. of the 17th century. Quaint, yet full of informn.

FRYE, Maj. W. E. [1784–1853] After Waterloo, ed. Salomon Reinach; w. notes 10/*n.* 8° Heinemann 08
Reminces. of European travel (exceptg. Russia) in 1815–9, in form of letters to an imaginary correspondent.

HOWELL, Jas. [1594–1666] Instructions for Forreine Travel 1/*n.* s 8° Constable [1642] 69
[Arber's Reprs.] Repr. fr. 2nd edn. [1650]. First Engl. hdbk. for 'the Continent'.

MAYNE, Jno. Journal, ed. Jno. Mayne Colles [gr'son]; 16 ill. 12/6 *n.* ($4 *n.*) 8° Lane 09
Journal of a driving-tour to Naples and back, on the reopening of Europe after the fall of NAPOLEON in 1814.

de MONTAIGNE, M. E. [1533–92] Journal of Travels in Italy, etc.—*ut* **E** § 24

MORYSON, Fynes [1566–1629] Itinerary, 4 vols.; maps [Elizab. Travels Ser.] ea. 12/6 *n.* 8° MacLehose, *Glasgow* [1617] 07–8
First repr. since 1st edn. of 1617. 'Ten Yeeres Travel through the Twelve Dominions of Germany, Bohmerland, Sweitzerland, Netherlands, Denmark, Poland, Italy, Turkey, France, England, Scotland, and Ireland'. Pt. i is a jl. of his travels; ii a hist. of TYRONE's rebelln. (incl. valuable State documents and details); iii consists of essays on advants. of travel, Eur. topography, natl. costume, character, etc.

Hughes, Chas. [ed.] Shakespeare's Europe: unpub. chs. of Moryson's 'Itin.' 15/*n.* 8° Sherratt, *Mancs.* 03
Excerpts fr. Pt. iv (hitherto unpb., fr. MS. at Corp. Chr. Coll., Oxon.). Deals w. Germy., Switz., and Netherl.; w. good Life of MORYSON.

MUNDY, Peter [17 cent.] Travels in Eur. and Asia: 1608–67, vol. i: Europe, ed. Sir R. C. Temple; 3 maps, 3 ill., and bibliogr. 8° Hakluyt Soc. 07

RERESBY, Sir Jno. [1634–89] Memrs. and Travels [Dryden Ho. Memrs.] 3/6 *n.* s 8° Paul [1734; 1813] 04

*Modern Writer:* SHAND (A. Innes) Old Time Travel 12/*n.* 8° Murray 03
$3·50 *n.* Dutton, *N.Y.* Pleasant memory-pictures of old times and old ways, mostly in Western Europe, 50 yrs. ago.

**General Geography and Topography; Manuals**—*v. also* **E** § 2

CASSELL & Co. [pubs.] Picturesque Europe, 5 vols.; 13 steel pl. & 200 ill. ea. 18/ 4° Cassell [76–9] 82–6

*CHISHOLM, G. G. Europe, 2 v.; maps & ill. [Compendium of Geogr.] ea. 15/ c 8° Stanford [85] 99–02
Vol. i: *Countries of Mainld. excl. N.-W.*; ii: *British Isles, Scandinavia, Denm., Low Countries.* The best comprehensive geogr. of Europe in English, paying spec. attention to economic historical geogr.

*PARTSCH, Prf. Jos. Central Europe [tr.]; maps & ill. [Regions of World] 7/6 *n.* ($2) 8° Clar. Press 03
The best general bk. in English on Cent. Eur. (incl. Servia, Bulg., Roumania), tho' fr. Germ. pt.-of-view. Very detailed.

RECLUS, Élisée — Universal Geography: Europe [tr.], 5 vols.—*ut* **E** § 2
REYNOLDS, J. B. — Europe — [good school-bk.] 2/ c 8° Black 05
SIME, Jas. — Geography of Europe; ill. — 3/ (80 c. *n.*) f 8° Macmillan 90

**Historical Geography**—*v. also* **F** § 15

*LUCAS, [Sir] C. P. — Mediterr. and Eastern Colonies [= Hist. Geogr., vol. i], ed. R. E. Stubbs; 13 maps — 5/ ($1·25) c 8° Clar. Press [88] 06

**Recent Travel and Description**

ALDRICH, T. B. — From Ponkapog to Pesth — $1·50 c 8° Houghton, *Boston* 83
ALLEN, Grant [Eng.] — The European Tour — $1·25 c 8° Dodd, *N.Y.* 02
BELLOC, Hilaire — Hills and the Sea — [impressionist descrns.] 6/ c 8° Methuen [06] 10
„ — The Path to Rome; 80 ill. — 7/6 *n.* c 8° G. Allen 02
$2 *n.* Longman. High-spirited acc. of walk to Rome fr. Toul (Lorraine), acr. the Jura, Alps, and Apennines. Good descrns. Also 1/ *n.* f 8° Nelson.
HAMILTON, Pet. — Rambles in Historic Lands — $1·75 (7/6) c 8° Putnam 93
Belgium, Germany, Switzerland, Italy, France, England.
JAMES, Hy. — Portraits of Places — $1·50 c 8° Houghton, *Boston* 83
Engl., France, Italy; w. delicate observns. of things th. wld. escape most people.
„ — Transatlantic Sketches — $2 c 8° Houghton, *Boston* 03
Sensitive impressns. of Chester, Lichfd., Warw., N. Devon, Wells, Salisb.; Switz.; Milan, Venice, Rome, Siena, Florence, Tuscan cities, Ravenna; The Splügen, Hombg., Darmstadt; Holl.; Belg.
KNOX, T. W. — Boy Travellers in N. Eur.; . . in S. Eur. — ea. $2 c 8° Harper, *N.Y.* 92–4
(1) Visits to Holl., Pruss., Denm., Norw.; (2) It., S. Frce., Spain, Gibr., Sicily, Malta.
'LEE, Vernon' [= Violet PAGET] — Genius Loci: notes on places — 3/6 *n.* ($1·25 *n.*) c 8° Lane [99] 07
A glorified guide-bk. Augsbg., Tuscany, Touraine, Siena, Fribourg, Venice, Bayeux, etc.
LONGFELLOW, H. W. — Outre-mer: pilgrimage beyond the sea — $1·50 c 8° Houghton, *Boston* [50]
Also [Home Lib.] $1 12° Burt, *N.Y.* '02; 60 c. 12° Hurst, *N.Y.* '03. Travels in France, Spain, Italy.
LOOMIS, L. C. — Index Guide to Travel and Art-Study in Eur. — $3 c 8° Scribner, *N.Y.* 90
STOCKTON, Fk. R. — Personally Conducted; ill. J. Pennell, etc. — $2 c 8° Scribner, *N.Y.* 89
TAYLOR, Bayard — Views a-foot: Eur. seen w. knapsack & staff — $1·50 c 8° Putnam, *N.Y.* [46]
Ill. Edn. $1·75, 8°. Two yrs.' travel on foot thro' Germy., Italy, France, spendg. $500 earned on road.
„ — By-Ways of Europe — $1·50 c 8° Putnam, *N.Y.* [69]
WARNER, C. D. — Saunterings — $1 c 8° Houghton, *Boston* 00
Record of travel in Engld., France, Belg., Holland, Switzerld., Bavaria, Italy.

*Cycling*—*v.* **I** § 149; *Motoring v.* **I** § 148*; *Pedestrianism v.* **I** § 149*

**Series**

Our Neighbours: life in town and country; ill. — ea. 3/6 *n.* c 8° Newnes *v.y.*
Deals w. intell. life, manners and customs, industr., rural, relig. life, amusemts., etc.

*Austrian Life in Town and Country* [*ut* **E** § 12 — F. H. E. PALMER
*Belgian* [*ut* **E** § 13] — D. C. BOULGER
*Danish* [*ut* **E** § 26] — J. BRÖCHNER
*French* [*ut* **E** § 14] — Hannah LYNCH
*Greek* [*ut* **E** § 22] — W. MILLER
*Italian* [*ut* **E** § 24] — Luigi VILLARI
*Russian* [*ut* **E** § 25] — F. H. E. PALMER
*Spanish* [*ut* **E** § 27] — L. HIGGIN
*Swedish* [*ut* **E** § 26] — O. G. v. HEIDENSTAM
*Swiss* [*ut* **E** § 28] — A. T. STORY
*Turkish* [*ut* **E** § 29] — L. M. J. GARNETT

Our Neighbours at Home—*v.* **E** § 2.

Picturesque Places at Home and Abroad; col. and other ill. — ea. 6/ c 8° Methuen *v.y.*

*Cornwall, Days in* [*ut* **E** § 17] — C. Lewis HIND
*East Anglia in Motor Car, Thro'* [*ut* **I** § 148*] — J. E. VINCENT
*Florence and N. Tuscany* [*ut* **E** § 24] — E. HUTTON
*Holland, A Wanderer in* [*ut* **E** § 13] — E. V. LUCAS
*London, A Wanderer in* [*ut* **E** § 17] — E. V. LUCAS
*Naples* [*ut* **E** § 24] — A. H. NORWAY
*Naples Riviera* [*ut* **E** § 24] — H. M. VAUGHAN
*New Forest* [*ut* **E** § 17] — H. G. HUTCHINSON
*Norfolk Broads* [*ut* **E** § 17] — W. H. DULT, etc.
*Norway and its Fjords* [*ut* **E** § 26] — M. A. WYLLIE
*Oxford* [*ut* **E** § 17] — H. C. MINCHIN + Rob. PEEL
*Pyrenees, Bk. of the* [*ut* **E** § 27] — Rev. S. Baring-GOULD
*Rhine, Bk. of the* [*ut* **E** § 15] — Rev. S. Baring-GOULD
*Riviera, Bk. of the* [*ut* **E** § 24] — Rev. S. Baring-GOULD
*Scotland of To day* [*ut* **E** § 19] — HENDERSON + WATT
*Skirts of the Great City* [*ut* **E** § 17] — Mrs A. BELL
*Spain, Cities of* [*ut* **E** § 27] — E. HUTTON
*Umbria, Cities of* [*ut* **E** § 24] — E. HUTTON
*Wiltshire, Round about* [*ut* **E** § 17] — A. G. BRADLEY

**Cities; Towns**

GALLICHAN, W. M. — Old Continental Towns; ill. — [c. 25 towns] 6/ *n.* c 8° Laurie 10

*Mediæval Towns Series — [$1·50 to $2 *n.* Dutton, *N.Y.*] 4/6 *n.* 8° Dent *v.y.*

*Assisi* — Lina Duff GORDON 3/6 *n.* ($1·50)
*Bruges* — E. GILLIATT-SMITH
*Brussels* — E. GILLIATT-SMITH
*Cairo* — S. Lane POOLE
*Cambridge* — Bp C. W. STUBBS
*Chartres.* — Cecil HEADLAM
*Constantinople* — W. H. HUTTON 3/6 *n.* ($1·50)
*Dublin* — D. A. CHART
*Edinburgh* — O. SMEATON
*Ferrara* — Ella NOYES
*Florence* — E. G. GARDNER ($1·75)
*London* — H. B. WHEATLEY ($1·75)
*Milan* — Ella NOYES
*Moscow* — Wirt GERRARE 3/6 *n.* ($1·50)
*Nuremberg* — Cecil HEADLAM 3/6 *n.* ($1·50)
*Oxford* — Cecil HEADLAM
*Padua* — C. FOLIGNO ($2)
*Paris* — Thos. OKEY
*Perugia* — Marg. SYMONDS + L. D. GORDON 3/6 *n.* ($1·50)
*Pisa* — Janet Ross
*Prague* — C't LÜTZOW 3/6 *n.* ($1·50)
*Rome* — Norwood YOUNG ($1·75)
*Rouen* — T. A. COOK ($2)
*Seville* — W. M. GALLICHAN ($1·75)
*Siena* — E. G. GARDNER ($1·75)
*Toledo* — Hannah LYNCH 3/6 *n.* ($1·50)
*Verona* — Alethea WELLS
*Venice* — Thos. OKEY

SYMONS, Arth. — Cities; 8 pl. — 7/6 *n.* 8° Dent 03
'Prose poems' on Rome, Venice, Naples, Seville, Prague, Moscow, Budapest, Belgrade, Sofia, Constantinople.

**Ethnology**—*v.* **E** § 3

**Seas; Rivers; Canals**

MACGREGOR, Jno. 1,000 miles in *Rob Roy* canoe on Rivers and Lakes of Eur.—*ut* **I** § 153

MAXWELL, Don. A Cruise across Europe; 4 maps and 100 ill. 10/6 *n.* ($3 *n.*) 8° Lane 00
Humorous acc. of a freshwater voy. fr. Holl., down Rhine, Ludwigs-Kanal, Danube, to Black Sea.

" Log of the *Griffin*; col. pl. & ill. & 8 maps 10/6 *n.* ($2·50 *n.*) c 8° Lane 05
Acc. of a sailing-trip fr. Switzerland down Limmat and Rhine to the Thames.

*Adriatic Sea* —*for* Austrian side, *v.* **E** § 12; *for* Italian, *v.* **E** § 24

*Baltic Sea*

KNIGHT, F. E. The *Falcon* on the Baltic; ill. [Lond. to Copenh.] 7/6 c 8° W. H. Allen 89

LUCY, H. W. Log of *Tantallon Castle*; ill. [W. E. Gladstone's trip] 6/ c 8° Low 96

MACGREGOR, Jas. The *Rob Roy* on the Baltic—*ut* **I** § 153

*Mediterranean Sea* —*for* Yachting *v.* **I** § 153

BAEDEKER, R. [pb.] The Mediterranean; 87 maps, etc. [Scribner, *N.Y.*] 12/ s 8° Unwin 11

BALL, E. A. Reynolds- Mediterranean Winter Resorts, 2 vols.; maps ea. 3/6 *n.* c 8° Hazell [ ] 08
i: *South Europe*; ii: *North Africa and Mediterr. Islands.* With medical arts. by resident physicians.

BARR, Rob. The Unchanging East [Mediterr.; facetious journalism] 6/ Chatto 00

BLOCK, Wm. Narrative of Cruises in Mediterranean: 1822 6 14/ *n.* 8° Oliver & Boyd, *Edin.* 00
A naval surgeon's notes during the Greek War of Independence. 20 ill.

BROOKS, Noah The Mediterranean Trip; maps and 24 ill. $1·25 *n.* c 8° Scribner, *N.Y.* 95
A guide to the prnc. points on shores of W. Mediterr. and the Levant. Largely historical.

BUTTERWORTH, H. Zig-Zag Journeys on the Mediterranean; ill. $1·50 s 4° Estes & Lauriat, *Boston* 93

CAVAN, Earl of With Yacht and Camera in Eastern Waters; pl. 12/6 8° Low 95
Contains a fine series of photos of harbours and shores of the Mediterranean Sea.

DAVIS, R. H. The Rulers of the Mediterranean; ill. $1·25 c 8° Harper, *N.Y.* 94
An American's holiday trip, describing Gibraltar, Tangier, Cairo, Athens, Constantinople, *etc.*

FLITCH, J. E. C. Mediterranean Moods; maps and 33 ill. $4 *n.* 8° Dutton, *N.Y.* 11

LORENZ, D. E. The Mediterranean Traveller [pract. informn.] $2·50 *n.* 12° Revell, *N.Y.* 05

MACMILLAN & Co. [pubs.] Guide to Eastern; . . to Western Mediterr. ea. 9/ *n.* ($3 *n.*) Macmillan 06; 01

Mediterranean Illustrated. By Authors of 'The Arctic World'; ill. 12/ i 8° Nelson 77

MILLARD, Bruce [ed.] The Mediterranean Cruise [guide-bk.] (9/ *n.*) c 8° Putnam 11

MURRAY, Jno. [pub.] Handbk. to Mediterranean. By R. L. Playfair, 2 Pts. s 8° Stanford [81] 90

Picturesque Mediterranean, 2 vols.; finely ill. 84/ i 4° Cassell 91

WARNER, C. D. A Roundabout Journey $1·50 c 8° Houghton, *Boston* 83
Rd. W. coast of Medit., visitg. Frce., Sic., Malta, Mor., Spain; w. acc. of Bayreuth.

## 12: AUSTRIA-HUNGARY

**Austria-Hungary:** *Generally*

*Atlas:* TRAMPLER Atlas d. Oesterr.-ungar. Monarchie 1 fl. 80 4° *Vienna* 98

BAEDEKER, Karl [pub.] Austria-Hungary; 33 maps and 44 plans 8/ *n.* s 8° Unwin [ ] 05
$2·40 *n.* Scribner, *N.Y.* [Hdbks. f. Travrs.] Incls. Dalmatia, Bosnia, Bucharest, Belgrade, Montenegro.

COLQUHOUN, A. R. + Ethel The Whirlpool of Europe: Austria-Hungary and the Habsburgs; maps and ill. [15/ *n.* Harper, *Lond.*] $3·50 *n.* 8° Dodd & Mead, *N.Y.* 07

DRAGE, Geoffr. Austria-Hungary 21/ 8° Murray 09
The best acc. of modern economic and political condns. of country.

HODGSON, R. L. Wanderings in Unknown Austria; ill. [gossipy] *o.p.* [*pb.* 7/6] s 4° Macmillan 96

KAY, Dav. Austria-Hungary [For. Countries and Brit. Cols.] 3/6 c 8° Low 80

KOHL, J. G. Travels in Austria [tr.] [Foreign Lib.] *o.p.* [*pb.* 11/] 8° Chapman 44
Bohemia, Hungary, Styria, Galicia, Moravia, Bukovina.

MALLESON, Col. G. B. Rivers and Lakes of Austr., Bav., Hung. 3/6 c 8° Chapman 97

PALMER, F. H. E. Austro-Hungarian Life in Town & Country; 26 ill. 3/6 *n.* c 8° Newnes *n.d.* (03)
$1·20 *n.* Putnam, *N.Y.* [Our Europ. Neighbrs.] Best chs. on nationalities and polit. and offic. life.

PATON, A. A. Highlands & Islands of Adriatic, 2 vols.; maps & ill. *o.p.* [*pb.* 32/] 8° Chapman 49

" Histor. Researches on Danube & Adriatic, 2 v. *o.p.* [*pb.* 12/] p 8° Trübner 62
Investigns. into phys. geogr. and ethnogr. of Hung., Transylv., Dalmatia, Croatia, Servia, and Bulgaria.

WHITMAN, Sid. Realms on the Habsburgs 7/6 c 8° Heinemann 93

**Hungary:** *Generally* —*for* Cycling *v.* **I** § 149

ALDEN, Percy [ed.] Hungary of To-day; ill. 7/6 *n.* c 8° Nash 09
Chs. by var. wrs. *Taxation Reform, Laws and Justice, Constitution, Labour Legisln., Agric., Educn.*, etc.

ANSTED, D. T. Hungary & Transylvania [incl. nat. hist. & products] *o.p.* [*pb.* 8/6] 8° W. H. Allen 62

BOVILL, W. B. F. Hungary and the Hungarians; 16 col. pl. & 12 ill. 7/6 *n.* c 8° Methuen 08
Presents 'the Hungarian point of view in a picturesque form'.

BROWNING, H. Ellen A Girl's Wanderings in Hungary; map & 19 ill. 3/6 ($1·25) c 8° Longman [96] 97
A ser. of anecdotes of travel, of small value; but some notes on home-life and folklore worth recording.

EIGHTY CLUB: Hungary, its Peoples, Places, and Politics; 60 ill. 10/6 8° Unwin 07
Account of the journey of the Eighty Club in 1906.

FELBERMANN, Louis Hungary and its People; map [good], & ill. [poor] 7/6 c 8° Griffith 92
A discursive acc. of orig. of people; of 1,000 yrs.' hist. of country, its custs. and tradns.; of Carpathns., Snow Alps; lowlds., etc.

FLETCHER, Marg. Sketches of Life and Character in Hungary; ill. 7/6 c 8° Sonnenschein 92

FORSTER-BOVILL, W. B. Hungary and the Hungarians; 12 col. pl. and 12 ill. 7/6 *n.* 8° Methuen 08
Hungary past and present—her people, her scenery, her customs, her charms.

GINEVER, Flora + C. Arth. [trs.] The Hungarian Question 2/6 *n.* 8° Paul 08
Tr. fr. the wk. of an anon. Hung. publicist, setting forth Hungary's attitude. Histor., econ., ethnograph. pts.-of-view.

PAGET, Jno. Hungary and Transylvania, 2 vols. *o.p.* [*pb.* 18/] 8° Murray [39] 55

PATTERSON, A. J. The Magyars: country & institns., 2 v.; 3 maps *o.p.* [*pb.* 18/] c 8° Smith & Elder 69

*SETON-WATSON, R. W. Racial Problems in Hungary; map & 42 ill. (6 col.) 16/ *n.* 8° Constable 09

STOKES, Adrian + Mrs [artists] Hungary: 75 col. pl.; w. text [$6 *n.* Macm., *N.Y.*] 20/ *n.* sq 8° Black 09

TISSOT, Victor Unknown Hungary [tr. (fr. French)], 2 vols. *o.p.* [*pb.* 21/] c 8° Bentley 81

de VARGHA, J. Hungary: country, people, condns. *free* 8° *Athenæum* Off., *Budapest* 08
Author is Director of Central Statist. Off. of Hung. A useful bk., of 81 pp.

*Adriatic Sea, Shores of the* —*v. also* PATON, *sup.*; *for* Italian side *v.* **E** § 24

BLAKSLEY, Maj.-Gen. J. Footprints of the Lion; & other stories of travel; ill. 6/ 8° W. H. Allen [95] 97
Travels on the shores of the Adriatic where lion of St. Mark once held sway.

*JACKSON, F. H. Shores of Adriatic, Pt. ii: Austrian Side—*ut* **E** § 24 [architect. & archaeol.]

STRANGFORD, Visc't'ss The Eastern Shores of the Adriatic *o.p.* [*pb.* 18/] 8° Bentley 64

*Alps (Austrian)* —*v.* **E** § 128

**Bohemia** —*for* Cycling *v.* **I** § 149; *for* Sport *v.* **I** § 147

BAKER, Jas. Pictures fr. Bohemia: drawn w. pen and pencil; ill. 8/ i 8° R.T.S. 94

LÜTZOW, C't Bohemia: an historical sketch; maps 9/ c 8° Chapman 96

MONROE, W. S. Bohemia & the Cechs; ill. [hist., geog., etc.; 7/6 *n.* Bell] $3 8° Page, *Bost.* 10

**Bosnia-Herzegovina; Dalmatia; Istria**—*v. also* **E** § 29

ASBÓTH, János Official Tour thro' Bosnia & Herzegovina [tr.]; ill. 20/ l 8° Sonnenschein 90
A valuable descr. wk. on antiqs., hist., agrar. condn., relig., folklore, etc. Well ill. w. 33 pl. and 187 cuts.

EVANS, A. J. Thro' Bosnia & Herzegovina on Foot; ill. *o.p.* [*pb.* 18/] 8° Longman [76] 77

" Illyrian Letters *o.p.* [*pb.* 7/6] p 8° Longman 78

HOLBACH, [Mrs] Maude M. Dalmatia: land where east meets west; 50 ill. 5/ *n.* ($1·50 *n.*) 8° Lane 08

" Bosnia & Herzegovina: some wayside wandergs.; 48 ill. 5/ *n.* ($1·50 *n.*) 8° Lane 09

*JACKSON, T. G. Dalmatia: the Quarnero, & Istria, 3 vols.; ill. 42/ ($12·75) 8° Clar. Press 87
Incl. Cettigne and I. of Grado. By far best bk. on districts. Largely archaeol; well ill. w. pl. and text-cuts.

MUNRO, Dr Rob. Rambles & Studies in Bosnia & Dalmatia; ill. 12/6 *n.* 8° Blackwood [95] 00
Interesting travel-sketches, with much archaeological matter. Many illns.

PATON, A. A. —*ut sup.*

ROYLE, Wm. [artist] Dalmatia Illustrata [a bk. of sketches] 12/6 *n.* f° Vinton 00

'SNAFFLE' In the Land of Bora; ill. [1894–6] 15/ 8° Paul 97
Camp-life and sport in Dalmatia and the Herzegovina. The 'Bora' is a wind at times felt fr. extreme N. of Adriatic as far as Albania.

THOMSON, H. C. The Outgoing Turk; 3 maps and 76 ill. 14/ *n.* 8° Heinemann 97
$4 Appleton, *N.Y.* Record of jy. thro' outlying distrs. of Bosn. and Herz., testifyg. to great wk. done in Bosn. by Austrians since occupn. [1878]. The 'outgoing Turk' is the Osmanli official. Descrs. aspirns. of neighbg. peoples—Croats, Serbs, Dalmatns.

WILKINSON, Sir J. G. Dalmatia & Montenegro; w. jy. to Mostar, 2 v. *o.p.* [*pb.* 42/] 8° Murray 48

*Carpathian Mountains*

CROSSE, A. F. Round about the Carpathians; map *o.p.* [*pb.* 12/6] 8° Blackwood 78

Magyar-Land: narr. of travels thro' Carpathns. and Gt. Alfold, 2 v.; ill. *o.p.* [*pb.* 38/] 8° Low 81

MUIR-MACKENZIE (Georgina M.) + IRBY (Miss A. P.) Across the Carpathians *o.p.* 8° Bell 62

NORMAN, Merie Muriel A Girl in the Karpathians 3/6 c 8° Philip [91] 91
$1·50 Cassell, *N.Y.* An interestg. and very readable account of a girl's wanderings in remote districts about the outlying spurs of E. Galicia (Poland), w. useful contribns. on the social life of the people.

**Danube** —*v. also* Paton, *sup.*; *and* **I** § 153

BAKER, Cpt. B. G. The Danube with Pen and Pencil; ill. 15/ *n.* 8° Sonnenschein 11

JERROLD, Walter The Danube; 30 ill. (12 col.) [popular] 10/6 *n.* 8° Methuen 11

MILLET, F. D. The Danube fr. Black Forest to Black Sea; ill. $2·50 8° Harper, *N.Y.* 93
By *D. News* corresp. dur. Russo-Turk. War. Acc. of canoe-trip, full of graphic descrns. of peoples, places, and scenery. Illns. v. good.

**Dolomites** —*for* Climbing *v.* **I** § 165 [where are best bks. on district]

EDWARDS, Amelia B. Untrodden Peaks and Unfrequented Valleys; ill. 7/6 8° Routledge [73] 89
$2·50 Dutton, *N.Y.* The classic book on the Dolomite regions.

HAMER, S. H. The Dolomites; 16 col. pl. H. Rowntree 7/6 *n.* 8° Methuen 10
A pleasant and informing acc. of a walking-tour, w. sectn. on chief summits by W. J. WILLIAMS.

HARE, A. J. C. —*in his* Cities of Northern Italy, *ut* **E** § 24

ROBERTSON, Dr Alex. Through the Dolomites from Venice to Toblach; ill. 7/6 c 8° G. Allen 96
A supplemt. to HARE's bk.—something betw. a guide-book and a book of travel; w. pract. details.

**Transylvania:** BONER (Chas.) Transylvania: products and people *o.p.* [*pb.* 21/] 8° Longman 65

GERARD, Emily The Land beyond the Forest, 2 vols. 25/ 8° Blackwood 88

**Tyrol** —*for* BAEDEKER's Tyrol, *v.* **E** § 28, *s.v.* Eastern Alps

BAILLIE-GROHMANN, W. A. Tyrol and the Tyrolese; ill. *o.p.* [*pb.* 6/] p 8° Longman [76] 77

" Gaddings with a Primitive People [the Tyrolese] *o.p.* [*pb.* 10/6] c 8° Remington [78] 79

* " Tyrol, the Land in the Mountains; maps and ill. 12/6 *n.* 8° Simpkin 07
A scholarly and authoritative acc. of the past and pres. of Tyrol, its peoples and castles. Throws valuable sidelights on econ. condn. of medieval Europe. Illns. fr. old prints and photos.

BUSK, Rachel H. The Valleys of the Tirol—*ut* **B** § 21

COMPTON, E. Harrison [art.] Tyrol; 24 col pl. w. text W. A. Baillie-Grohmann 6/ *n.* c 8° Black 08

HOLLAND, Clive Tyrol and its People; col. ill. and photos. 10/6 *n.* 8° Methuen 09
Pleasant journalistic description of the whole of the Tyrol: hist., assocns., life, character.

MCCRACKAN, W. D. The Fair Land Tyrol; c. 30 ill. [5/ *n.* Duckworth] $1·60 *n.* c 8° Page, *Boston* 05

SCHMIDT (H.) + STIELER (K.) The Bavarian Highlands and Salzkammergut [tr.]—*ut* **E** § 15

WARING, G. E., jun. Tyrol and the Skirt of the Alps; ill. $3 8° Harper, *N.Y.* 79

WHITE, W. Holidays in the Tyrol *o.p.* [*pb.* 14/] c 8° Chapman

*Buda-Pest:* SMITH (F. Berkeley) City of the Magyars; ill. [5/ *n.* Unwin] c 8° 04

*Prague*

LÜTZOW, C't Story of Prague; ill. [Medæv. Towns; $1·50 Dutton, *N.Y.*] 3/6 *n.* f 8° Dent 02

*Vienna*

'ENGLISH OFFICER, AN' Society Recollns. in Paris and Vienna—*ut* **E** § 14, *s.v.* Paris

LANSDALE, Maria H. Vienna and the Viennese; 25 ill. $2·40 *n.* c 8° Coates, *Phila.* 02
Based on V. TISSOT's *Vienne et la Vie Viennoise* [*Paris* '78–88], brot. down to date. People, customs, life, histor. assocns., etc.

LEVETUS, A. S. Imperial Vienna: hist., tradns., art; c. 150 ill. 18/ *n.* ($5 *n.*) 8° Lane 05

REEVE, Dr Hy. Jl. of Residce. in Vienna & Berl., ed. his Son [1805–6] *o.p.* [*pb.* 8/6] p 8° Longman 77

## 13: BELGIUM AND HOLLAND

*Atlas:* BEEKMAN + SCHUILING Schl. Atl. of Netherls. and Possessns. 3 fl. 75 c. 4° Thieme, *Zutphen*
Shows in some detail the peculiar geograph. condns. of the Rhine delta.

*Guide:* BAEDEKER, Karl [pb.] Belg. and Holland; 15 maps and 30 plans 6/ s 8° Unwin [ ] 05
Scribner, *N.Y.* [Handbks. for Travellers.] Includes Luxemburg.

### BELGIUM

**Early Travel**

DÜRER, Alb. [1471–1528] Journeys to Venice and to Low Countries [tr.]—*ut* **E** § 24

SOUTHEY, Rob. [1774–1843] Journal of Tour in Netherlands in 1815 6/ c 8° Heinemann [ ] 03
Diary of journeys thro' Bruges, Ghent, Brussels, Namur, Liége, Aix, Maestricht, Antwerp, etc.

**Modern Description and Travel**

ALLEN, Grant Cities of Belgium [$1·25 *n.* Wessels, *N.Y.*] 3/6 *n.* c 8° Richards 97

BOULGER, D. C. Belgian Life in Town and Country; 24 ill. 3/6 *n.* c 8° Newnes 04

" Belgium and the Belgians [Countries and Peoples] 6/ *n.* c 8° Putnam 11

GEORGE, Ern. [artist] Etchings in Belgium [30 etchings] 21/ i 4° Seeley [77] 86

HOLLAND, Clive The Belgians at Home; ill. and 16 col. pl. 10/6 *n.* 8° Methuen 11

HUET, C. B. Land of Rubens [tr. fr. Dutch] [sort of guide-bk.] 3/6 c 8° Low 88

KING, R. J. Sketches and Studies, Descriptive and Historical *o.p.* [*pb.* 12/] 8° Murray 74

OMOND, G. W. T. Belgium; map and 77 col. pl. 20/ *n.* sq 8° Black 08

" Brabant and East Flanders; 20 col. pl. 7/6 *n.* sq 8° Black 07

" Bruges and West Flanders; 37 col. pl. 7/6 *n.* sq 8° Black 06

" Liége and the Ardennes; 20 col. pl. 7/6 *n.* sq 8° Black 08
(1) $6 *n.*, (2) to (4) ea. $3 *n.* Macmillan, *N.Y.* All the col. pl. by A. FORESTIER. Moderately good texts.

SCUDAMORE, Cyril Belgium and the Belgians 6/ c 8° Blackwood 01
A collection of useful facts and figures relating to Belgian places and institutions.

STEVENSON, R. L. An Inland Voyage; 12 col. pl. and 12 ill. 7/6 *n.* c 8° Chatto [78] 08
$1·25 Scribner, *N.Y.* Ch. Edn. 6/ (50 c.); 2/ *n.* pott 8°. Acc. of a canoe trip fr. Antwerp (Belg.) to Pontoise (Frce.). An *Epilogue* to *An Inland Voyage* is one of the essays in his *Across the Plains, etc.* [*ut* **K** § 89].

STRANG, Wm. [artist] Western Flanders: 10 etchgs., w. text Laur. Binyon 42/ *n.* 4° Unicorn Press 99
TENNENT, Sir J. E. Travels in Belgium, 2 vols. *o.p.* [*pb.* 21/] c 8° Bentley 41
*Ardennes* —*v. also* OMOND, *sup.*
LINDLEY, Percy Walks in the Ardennes; ill. [Luxemb. and Belg.] 1/ obl. Lindley [82]
MACQUOID, [Mrs] Kath. In the Ardennes; ill. 6/ sq 8° Chatto [81] 95
*Bruges:* GILLIAT-SMITH (Em.) Bruges; maps and 50 ill. [Mediaev. Town Ser.] 4/6 *n.* f 8° Dent [01] 05
$1·75 *n.* Dutton, *N.Y.* Not a formal hist., but gives much informn. on developmt. of Bruges and its artistic and architect. hist.
ROBINSON, W. B. Bruges: an historical sketch 4/ 8° Plancke, *Bruges* 00
Compiled from good authorities; notes connecting points with English history, and history of art.
*Cathedrals and Churches* —*v.* **I** § 121
*Rivers* —*v.* **E** § 14 (WARREN + CLEVERLEY)

**HOLLAND**

de AMICIS, Edm. Holland and its People [tr. (fr. Ital.)]; ill. $2 (7/6) 8° Putnam, [80] 93
BIRD, F. S. The Land of Dykes and Windmills *o.p.* [*pb.* 12/6] c 8° Low 82
BOUGHTON (G. H.) + ABBEY (E. A.) Sketching Rambles in Holland; ill. *o.p.* [*pb.* 21/] s 4° Macmillan 84
EDWARDS, G. Wharton Thumb-nail Sketches in Holland $1 f 8° Century Co., *N.Y.* 93
„ Holland of To-day; ill. $6 4° Moffat, *N.Y.* 09
ESQUIROS, Alph. The Dutch at Home [tr.], 2 vols. *o.p.* [*pb.* 18/] c 8° Chapman 61
GRIFFIS, Dr W. E. The American in Holland: sentimental rambles; ill. $1·50 12° Houghton, *Boston* 99
6/ Constable. Tours in the provinces of Holl. in 1869, 91, 92, 95, 98; w. histor. assocns. Map and 16 ill.
HARE, A. J. C. Sketches in Holland & Scandinavia; ill. [$1 Macm., *N.Y.*] 3/ c 8° G. Allen [84] 85
HAVARD, H. Dead Cities of the Zuyder Zee [tr.]; 10 etchgs. *o.p.* [*pb.* 6/] c 8° Bentley [75] 76
„ Picturesque Holland [tr.]; 10 etchgs. and map *o.p.* [*pb.* 16/] 8° Bentley 76
„ In the Heart of Holland [tr.]; 8 etchgs. *o.p.* [*pb.* 15/] 8° Bentley 80
A good acc. of the country as seen dur. a yachting-cruise along its chief waterways.
HOUGH, P. M. Dutch Life in Town and Country; 32 ill. 3/6 *n.* c 8° Newnes 01
$1·20 *n.* Putnam, *N.Y.* [Our Eur. Neighbrs.] A very accurate descrn. of Dutch life in its various phases.
JUNGMAN, Nico + B. Holland: 75 col. pl.; w. l'rpress [$6 *n.* Macm., *N.Y.*] 20/ *n.* sq 8° Black 04
„ The Dutch People; col. pl. [$6 *n.* Macm., *N.Y.*] 20/ *n.* sq 8° Black 11
LOVETT, Rich. Pictures from Holland: drawn w. pen and pencil; 132 ill. 8/ i 8° R.T.S. 87
LUCAS, E. V. A Wanderer in Holland; col. and other ill. 6/ c 8° Methuen [05] 06
$1·75 Macmillan, *N.Y.* A pleasant acc. of a 'pilgrimage', descg. towns, life, galleries, gardns., canals, etc.
MAHAFFY (J. P.) + ROGERS (J. E.) Sketches of Tour thro' Holland and Germany; 85 ill.
*o.p.* [*pb.* 10/6] c 8° Macmillan 89
Deals with parts of the countries not often described.
MELDRUM, D. S. Holland and the Hollanders; map and ill. 6/ 8° Blackwood [99] 99
$2 Dodd, *N.Y.* Ill. after Dutch ptgs. Perhaps the best descrn. of Dutch life and of all pts. of the country.
„ Home Life in Holland; 16 col. pl. 10/6 *n.* 8° Methuen 11
PENFIELD, E. [artist] Holland; col. ill. 10/ *n.* r 8° Hodder 08
POOLE, R. Lane Holland [For. Countries and Brit. Cols.] 3/6 c 8° Low 82
RITCHIE, J. E. On the Track of the Pilgrim Fathers *o.p.* [*pb.* 7/6] c 8° Tinsley 76
ROBINSON, C. E. Cruise of the *Widgeon*; 4 ill. *o.p.* [*pb.* 9/] 8° Chapman 76
700 miles in a 10-ton yacht fr. Swanage to Hambg., thro' Dutch canals, Zuyder Zee, etc.
SALA, G. A. Dutch Pictures, & Pictures done w. a Quill; 8 ill. *o.p.* [*pb.* 2/6] c 8° Vizetelly [82] 87
SOUTHEY, Rob. [1774–1843] Journal of a Tour in Netherlands: 1815—*ut sup.*
TRAHERNE, Mrs A Summer in a Dutch Country House 6/ c 8° Paul 89
TUYN, W. J. [ed.] Old Dutch Towns and Villages of Zuiderzee 21/ 4° Unwin 01
A colln. of line-drwgs. and woodcuts by W. O. J. NIEUWENKAMP and J. G. VELDHEER, w. historical letterpress.
WOOD, Chas. W. Through Holland; ill. *o.p.* [*pb.* 12/] 8° Bentley 77
*Architecture* —*v.* **I** § 121
*Waterways, Friesland Meres, etc.*—*v.* **I** § 153: Boating

## 14: FRANCE; MONACO

**Early Travel**

BROWNE, Mary Diary of a Girl in France in 1821; ill. 9/ *n.* i 16° Murray 05
A quaintly ill. diary of a girl of 14, who travelled w. her parents and 5 bros. and sisters. All seem to have been in agreemt. as to the general inferiority of the foreigner!
FERRIER, Rich. Jl. while Travellg. in Frce. in 1687—*in* Camden Miscellany, vol. ix s 4° Camden Soc. 95
LOCATELLI, S. Voyage [tr.] [1664–5] 8° 05

ROOTS, Wm. Paris in 1814—*ut inf.*, *s.v.* Paris

SMOLLETT, Tobias G. [1721–71] Travels through France & Italy 1/ *n.* (40 c.) pott 8° Clar. Press [1765] 07
[World's Classics.] Introd. Thos. SECCOMBE. L'rs wr. fr. abroad: Boulogne, Paris, Lyons, Nice, Genoa, Rome, etc.

STERNE, Laur. [1713–68] A Sentimental Journey thro' Frce. and Italy—*ut* **K** § 50

YOUNG, Arth. [1741–1820] Travels in France dur. 1787, 1788, 1789, ed. Matilda Betham-Edwards—*ut* **D** § 119

**Recent Travel and Description**—*for* Cycling Tours *v.* **I** § 149; *for* Caravanning *v.* **I** § 148*

ACLAND-TROYTE, Charlotte E. From Pyrenees to Channel in Dog-Cart; pl. 16/ 8° Sonnenschein 87

BARKER, E. Harrison Wayfaring in France; 50 ill. *o.p.* [*pb.* 16/] 8° Bentley 90
Walks thro' the Landes, in Dauphine, in Languedoc, in Brittany, and in Alsace. Specialities field boty. and church archit.

" Wandering by Southern Waters: Eastern Aquitaine; ill. *o.p.* [*pb.* 16/] 8° Bentley 93
Excellent descrn. of a jy. on foot in valleys of Dordogne, Tarn and Lot, w. tribs. and plateaux betw. them.

BELLOC, Hilaire The Path to Rome—*ut* **E** § 11

BETHAM-EDWARDS, Matilda Literary Rambles in France—*ut* **K** § 34

BLACK, C. B. South of France: fr. Loire to Mediterr.; maps 7/6 c 8° Black [88] 89

DARMESTETER, Mme Jas. The Fields of France: essays in sociology c 8° [ ] 04

GRENVILLE-MURRAY, E. C. Round about France *o.p.* [*pb.* 7/6] c 8° Macmillan 78

HAMMERTON, J. A. In the Track of R. L. Stevenson and Elsewhere in Old France; 92 ill. [travel-sketches] 6/ 8° Arrowsmith, *Bristol* 07

HARE, A. J. C. N.-E. Frce.; N.-W. Frce.; S.-E. Frce.; S.-W. Frce. ea. 6/ c 8° G. Allen [90–4] *v.y.*
Ea. $2·50 *n.* Macm., *N.Y.* Admirable guides f. persons of artistic, archit., and eccles. tastes, and for ordin. informn. of travrs. Maps and Ill.

HAWTHORNE, Nat. [1804–64] Passages fr. French and Italian Note-Books [1871]—*ut inf.*

HURLBERT, W. H. France and the Republic; map 18/ ($5) 8° Longman 90
An account of French provinces during the 'centennial year' [1889].

JAMES, Hy. Portraits of Places—*ut* **E** § 11

" A Little Tour in France—*ut inf.*, *s.v.* Touraine

JOHNSON, Clifton Along French Byways; ill. $2 *n.* (8/6 *n.*) Macmillan, *N.Y.* [00] 07
Peasant-life and landscape of rural France; w. good photogr. illns. by the author.

LEBON (Prf. A.) + PELET (Prf. P.) France as it is [tr.]; 3 maps 7/6 c 8° Cassell 88
A valuable little textbk. of Frce., based on its geogr. condns.

'LEE, Vernon' [=Violet PAGET] The Sentimental Traveller: notes on places 3/6 *n.* ($1·50 *n.*) c 8° Lane 08

MUSGRAVE, G. M. Nooks and Corners in Old France, 2 vols. *o.p.* [*pb.* 24/] c 8° Hurst 67

PEIXOTTO, E. C. Through the French Provinces; w. 85 ill. by author 10/6 *n.* 8° Laurie 10

PENNELL, J. + E. R. Our Sentimental Jy. thro' Frce. and Italy 6/ c 8° Longman 88

ROBERTS, [Miss] M. France [For. Countries and Brit. Colonies] 3/6 c 8° Low 81

STOKES, Marg. Three Months in Forests of France; ill. 12/ *n.* 4° Bell 95
A journey in the footsteps of ancient Irish Saints: much information on little-known pts. of Champagne and Picardy, etc.

TAINE, H. A. Journeys thro' France [tr.]; 8 ill. [old-fashioned] 7/6 c 8° Unwin 97
$2·50 Holt, *N.Y.* Notes of travel, descr., polit., and social, in Fch. provinces 1863–6. Unaffected, and graceful.

*Guides:* BAEDEKER, Karl [pb.] France, 2 vols.; 49 maps and 104 plans 16/6 *n.* s 8° Unwin [ ] 09; 07
Scribner, *N.Y.* [Hdbks. f. Travrs.] i: *Northern France* [exclg. Paris], 7/6 *n.* ($2·10 *n.*); ii: *Southern France* [inclg. Corsica], 9/ *n.* ($2·70 *n.*).

MURRAY, Jno. [pub.] Handbook for France, 2 Pts. [pt. i *o.p.*] ea. 7/6 s 8° Stanford [4–] 92

*Motor-Tours* —*v.* **I** § 148*

**Life and People**

BARKER, E. Harrison France of the French; 32 pl. 6/ *n.* c 8° Pitman 08

BETHAM-EDWARDS, Matilda A Year in Western France *o.p.* [*pb.* 10/6] c 8° Longman 77

" Holidays in Eastern France 15/ 8° Hurst 79

" France of To-day: a survey, compar. & retrosp., 2 vols. ea. 7/6 c 8° Rivington 92–4
Ea. $1·25 Lovell, *N.Y.* A survey of agricultural and industrial France, describing what French peasant-life and French farming really are: also life in French country-towns. Unnecessarily controversial (on the Protestant side).

" Anglo-French Reminiscences: 1875–1899 7/6 8° Chapman 00
By a useful, tho' biassed, interpreter of Frce. to Englishmen; w. several good stories. Considers th. whatever is good in Frce. is either Voltairean or Protestant: scathing remarks on convents and confessional.

" Home Life in France; ill. [$2·50 *n.* McClurg, *Chicago*] 6/ c 8° Methuen [05] 07
Households, incomes, childr., recreatns., daily routine, standards and ideals of mid. classes, glaring discrep. betw. Fch. fictn. and family-life, etc. Well ill.

" —*in her* French Men, Women, and Books, *ut* **K** § 33

" Unfrequented France: by river, mead, and-tarn; ill. 10/6 *n.* 8° Chapman 11
Largely made up of extrs. (brot. down to date) fr. *Roof of Frce.* [*inf.*], *Yr. in W. Frce.* [*sup.*], and *Holidays in E. Frce.* [*sup.*].

*BODLEY, J. E. C. —*in his* France, *ut* **F** § 50 [much matter on Fch. social life]

BRACQ, Prf. J. C. France under the Republic 7/6 *n.* 8° Laurie 11

BROWNELL, W. C. French Traits: an essay in comparative criticism $1·50 12° Scribner, *N.Y.* 89
7/ Nutt. A suggestive and penetrating study of the social and moral ideas of French society.

DUCLAUX, Mme. Mary [A. Mary F. ROBINSON] The Fields of France 5/ *n.* c 8° Chapman [03] 04
Charming 'little essays' on the rural economy of France, treated by a learned nature-lover and kindly sociologist. Ill. Edn., w. 20 col. pl. W. B. MACDOUGALL, 21/ *n.* 4° *id.* '05.

FONCIN, Pierre France, ed. and tr. Dr H. H. Kane c 8° Intern. Co., *N.Y.* 02
A short sketch of the history, literature, art, and characteristics of France: written for foreigners.

French Home Life [pprs. repr. fr. *Blackwood's Mag.*] *o.p.* [*pb.* 5/] c 8° Blackwood [73] 74

GEORGE, W. L. France in the Twentieth Century 6/ *n.* c 8° Rivers 08
An unbiassed picture of condns. of soc. life in Frce. to-day, and political basis of its govt.

GRENVILLE-MURRAY, E. C. High Life in France under the Republic *o.p.* [*pb.* 2/6] c 8° Vizetelly [84] 87
Caustic sketches of high-life and society in Paris and the provinces: originally contributed to *The Pall Mall Gazette.*

,, French Pictures in English Chalk, 2 Ser. *o.p.* [*pb.* 7/6 ea.] 8° Smith & Elder 76–8

HAMERTON, P. G. Round My House: rural life in Frce. in Peace & War 3/6 c 8° Seeley [76] 94

,, French and English: a comparison *o.p.* [*pb.* 10/6] c 8° Macmillan 89
$1·50 Little & Brown, *Bost.* Educn., politics, religion, customs, etc. Scarcely does justice to English.

HASSALL, A. The French People [Great Peoples Ser.] 6/ 8° Heinemann 10

HAWTHORNE, Nat. Passages from French and Italian Note Books.
[7/6 Paul; posth.] ea. $2 c 8° Houghton, *Boston* [71] 99

HILLEBRAND, C. France & French in Second Half of 19th Cent. [tr.] 10/6 p 8° Trübner (Paul) 81

JERROLD, Laur. The Real France 5/ *n.* c 8° Lane 10

KLEIN, Abbé Félix An American Student in France [tr.]; 25 ill. $2·50 *n.* c 8° McClurg, *Chicago* 08
By a (late) well-known Fch. Liberal clergyman, nominally by an 'Amer. Student', tho' the disguise is thrown off in the tr. Descrs. picturesque pts. of rural Frce., châteaux, etc.

LYNCH, Hannah French Life in Town and Country; 12 ill. 3/6 *n.* c 8° Newnes 01
$1·20 *n.* Putnam, *N.Y.* [Our Eur. Neighbrs.] An excellent pop. acc. of soc. diversns., educn., army, home-life, etc.

MUSGRAVE, G. M. Ten Days in a French Parsonage, 2 vols. *o.p.* [*pb.* 16/] c 8° Low 64

PROTHERO, Rowl. E. The Pleasant Land of France 10/6 *n.* 8° Murray 08
7 essays (mostly repr. fr. mags., and some out-of-date) on Fch. provincial life, agric., folklore, RABELAIS, Fontainebleau, and mod. poets (w. trs.).

SARTORIS, Adel. [*née* KEMBLE] A Week in a French Country House; ill. 7/6 c 8° Smith & Elder [67] 03

SEGUIN, L. G. [=Mrs STRAHAN] Life in a French Village *o.p.* [*pb.* 2/6] 12° Strahan 79

SMITH, E. Boyd My Village; c. 150 ill. by author $2 12° Scribner, *N.Y.* 96
A lively pict. of life of Fch. peasts. (in a village 30 m. N. of Paris), amg. whom he spent several yrs., livg. their life.

THEURIET, C. A. A. Rustic Life in France [tr.]; ill. $2·50 c 8° Crowell, *N.Y.* 96
At once the descrn. and the threnody of Fch. farm-life, the rustic epic of a passg. race of toilers of field.

UZANNE, Oct. The Frenchwoman of the 19th Cent. [tr.]; col. ill. *o.p.* [*pb.* 42/] r 8° Nimmo (Routledge) 86

VANDAM, A. D. French Men and French Manners; w. Introd. 10/6 c 8° Chapman 95
Stray cuttings fr. old Parisian newspprs. translated into journalistic English.

WENDELL, Prf. Barrett The France of To-day [6/ *n.* Constable] $1·50 *n.* s 8° Scribner, *N.Y.* 07

YVES LE QUERDEC Letters of a Country Vicar [tr.] 5/ c 8° Heinemann 96
Afford an admirable pict. of life in a Fch. village, correspondg. rather to a v. small country-town than to ordin. Engl. village.

### Ethnology

FINOT, Jean —*in his* Race Prejudice [tr.], *ut* **D** § 130
The most interestg. chs. relate to Frce., seekg. to prove, w. a wealth of detail, th. adverse elemts. have gone to make up Fch. people, and in establg. the paradox of D'ARBOIS DE JUBAINVILLE th. there is prob. in Germy. more Gaulish blood than in Frce., and th. the Fch. have become a Germanic people, and the Germanic folk have become Gaulish'.

SPENCER, Herb. Descriptive Sociology: Pt. viii: French Civilization—*ut* **E** § 3

## PROVINCES; DEPARTMENTS; DISTRICTS

**Auvergne:** BARKER (E. Harrison) Through Auvergne 1/6 c 8° Griffith & Farran 84

COSTELLO, Louisa S. A Pilgrimage to Auvergne, 2 vols. *o.p.* [*pb.* 28/] 8° Bentley 42

GOSTLING, Fces. M. Auvergne and its People; ill. and 8 col. pl. 10/6 *n.* 8° Methuen 11

de KANTZOW, Adm. Summer Days in Auvergne; ill. *o.p.* [*pb.* 5/] c 8° Bentley 75

### Aveyron

DAVIES (G. C.) + BROUGHALL (Mrs) Our Home in Aveyron; 12 pl. [peasant life] 15/ 8° Blackwood 89

*Bourbonnais, etc.:* BETHAM-EDWARDS (M.) East of Paris; ill. 7/6 *n.* 8° Hurst 02
$2·50 *n.* Dutton, *N.Y.* Gatinais, Bourbonnais, Champagne.

### Brittany

ATKINSON, Mary J. A Chateau in Brittany; 17 ill. 10/6 *n.* 8° Stanley Paul 11

BELL, Nancy R. E. M. ['N. D'ANVERS'] Picturesque Brittany; col. ill. A. G. Bell 10/6 *n.* 8° Dent 06

BLACKBURN, H. Breton Folk; 170 ill. by R. Caldecott 10/6 sq 8° Low 80

EDWARDS, G. W. Brittany and the Bretons; fully ill. [18/ *n.* Herbert] 8° 11

GOSTLING, Fces. M. The Bretons at Home; 12 col. pl. and 32 ill. 10/6 *n.* 8° Methuen 09
Interesting and sympathetic descrn. of Breton peasant-life, monumts., legends, etc.

GOULD, Rev. S. Baring- A Book of Brittany; 69 ill. 6/ c 8° Methuen 01
Popular chs. on archaeol. and ethnol., w. descrns. and hists. of chief towns and places, and ch. on the Pardons.

HARE, A. J. C. —*in his* Northwestern France, *ut sup.*
HUTCHINSON, T. J. Summer Holidays in Brittany *o.p.* [*pb.* 10/6] c 8° Low 76
LE BRAZ, Anatole The Land of Pardons [tr.]; 50 ill. (10 col.) 6/ *n.* 8° Methuen [06]
Excellent descrns. of the 5 great obligatory festivals of Brittany, w. its real life, customs, legends, etc.
MACQUOID, [Mrs] Kath. S. Through Brittany; ill. 7/6 8° Chatto [77] 81
MACQUOID, T. R. [art.] + K. S. Pictures and Legends fr. Normandy and Brittany—*ut inf., s.v.* Normandy
MENPES, M. [art.] + Dorothy Brittany: 75 col. pl.; w. l'rpr. [$6 *n.* Macm., *N.Y.*] 20/ *n.* sq 8° Black 05
'MILTOUN, Fcs.' [=Milburg F. MANSFIELD] Rambles in Brittany; ill. [scrappy] 6/ *n.* f 8° Duckworth 06
MUSGRAVE, G. M. A Ramble into Brittany, 2 vols. *o.p.* [*pb.* 24/] 8° Hurst 70
PALLISER, Mrs Bury Brittany and its Byeways *o.p.* [*pb.* 12/] c 8° Murray 69
SLADEN, Dougl. B. W. Brittany for Britons; ill. [St. Malo, Dinard, etc.] 2/6 c 8° Black [96] 96
TROLLOPE, T. A. A Summer in Brittany, ed. F. Trollope, 2 vols. *o.p.* [*pb.* 32/] c 8° Colburn 40

**Cevennes Mountains**

BETHAM-EDWARDS, Matilda The Roof of Frce.: or the Causses of the Lozère *o.p.* [*pb.* 12/] 8° Bentley 89
Pleasant descrns. of picturesque districts far from tourist tracks, with observns. on phases of peasant-life.
GOULD, Rev. S. Baring- Book of the Cevennes; map, 8 col. pl., and 40 ill. 6/ c 8° Long 07
*STEVENSON, R. L. Travels with a Donkey in the Cevennes 6/ c 8° Chatto [79] 03
" The same; w. 12 col. pl. and 12 dwgs. Noel Rooke 7/6 *n.* c 8° Chatto 09
Ch. Edn. 2/ *n.* pott 8°. (50 c. *n.* Scribner, *N.Y.*) Acc. of a 12-days trip in the mountains of S. France, startg. fr. Le Monastier (Hte. Loire), crossg. Cevennes, to Alais. Charmingly and observantly wr., but little scenery described.

**Corsica**

BARRY, J. W. Corsican Studies; maps and ill. 6/ *n.* 8° Low [93] 94
Descr. the agriculture of Corsica, social life at Ajaccio, the people, fauna, flora, bandits, etc.
BERGERAT, E. A Wild Sheep Chase [tr.]; 200 ill. 5/ c 8° Seeley 93
$1·75 Macmillan, *N.Y.* An entertaining descrn. of the island and its lawless inhabitants.
CAIRD, L. H. History of Corsica [useful, but dull] 5/ c 8° Unwin 99
CHAPMAN, J. M. Corsica, an Island of Rest; map and 32 ill. 7/6 *n.* 8° Stanford 08
D'ESTE, Marg. Thro' Corsica with a Camera (7/6 *n.*) 8° Putnam
FORDE, Gertr. A Lady's Ride in Corsica, 2 vols.; ill. *o.p.* [*pb.* 21/] c 8° Bentley 80
FORESTER, Thos. Rambles in Corsica and Sardinia; 8 col. pl. *o.p.* [*pb.* 18/] r 8° Bohn [58] 61
A standard wk. on the history, antiquities and then condition of the islands.
GREGOROVIUS, Ferd. Wanderings in Corsica, tr. A. Muir, 2 vols. *o.p.* [*pb.* 7/] c 8° *Edinburgh* 55
" Tour in Corsica, tr. H. Martineau *o.p.* [*pb.* 3/6] 16° Longman 55
RENWICK, G. Romantic Corsica; map and 67 ill. 10/6 *n.* 8° Unwin 09
Topographical and descriptive, w. hist. notes and ch. on Climbing by T. G. OUSTON.
VUILLIER, Gaston The Forgotten Isles [tr.]; 162 ill. by author 16/ 8° Hutchinson 96
$4·50 Appleton, *N.Y.* Travels in Corsica, Sardinia, Majorca, and Minorca.

**Dauphiné:** BONNEY (T. G.) Outl. Sketches in High Alps of Dauphiné *o.p.* [*pb.* 16/] 4° Longman 65
MUSGRAVE, G. M. Pilgrimage into Dauphiné, 2 vols. *o.p.* [*pb.* 21/] c 8° Hurst 57

**Gironde:** SIEVEKING (J. G.) Autumn Impressions of the Gironde; ill. 3/6 *n.* c 8° Digby & Long 10

**Guienne; Aquitaine; Gascony**

BARKER, E. Harrison Two Summers in Guyenne; ill. *o.p.* [*pb.* 16/] 8° Bentley 94
A very good record of travel, in excellent liter. form, thro' a little-kn. region, w. many interestg. histor. excursuses and valuable picts. of rural Fce. 100 yrs. after the Revoln. Picturesque side of subj. also fully developed.
FLOWER, Wickham Aquitaine: Traveller's Tales; ill. J. Pennell 63/ *n.* 4° Chapman 97
GOULD, Rev. S. Baring- The Deserts of Southern France, 2 vols.; ill. 32/ 8° Methuen 94
A mass of ill-arrgd. informn., coverg. much same ground as BARKER'S *Wandgs. by S. Waters* [*ut sup.*] and *Two Summers* [*ut sup.*], where district is much better treated.

**Médoc:** SOMERVILLE (Edith Oe.) + Ross (M.) In the Vine Country; ill. 3/6 c 8° W. H. Allen 93

**Normandy**

BECKE, Louis Sketches from Normandy 6/ c 8° Laurie 06
BLACKBURN, Hy. Picturesque Normandy; ill. *o.p.* [*pb.* 16/] 8° Low 69
" Artistic Travel: 1,000 miles tow. the sun; 130 ill. 7/6 c 8° Low [92] 95
Normandy, Brittany, Pyrenees, Spain, Algeria. Out-of-date repr. magazine articles. Ill. good, but not new.
CAMPBELL, W. F. Life in Normandy, 2 vols. *o.p.* c 8° *Edinburgh* 63
*DEARMER, Percy Highways and Byways in Normandy; map and ill. 6/ ($2) c 8° Macmillan [00] 04
[Highways & Byways Ser.] Espec. valuable for its remarks on architecture: quite comprehensive. Ill. Jos. PENNELL.
FREEMAN, Prf. E. A. Sketches of Travel in Normandy and Maine; 20 ill. *o.p.* [*pb.* 8/6] c 8° Macmillan 97
Holiday arts., orig. contrib. to *Sat. Rev.* or *Guardian.* Historical and archaeol. assocns., and, to less extent, architectural.
HARE, A. J. C. —*in his* Northwestern France, *ut sup.*
HOME, Gordon [artist] Normandy: scenery and romance of anc. towns; ill. 10/6 *n.* 8° Dent 06

JUNGMAN, Nico [art.] Normandy: 40 col. pl., w. l'rpr. G. E. Mitton [$3 *n.* Macm., *N.Y.*] 7/6 *n.* sq 8° Black 05
MACQUOID, [Mrs] Kath. S. Through Normandy; map and 92 ill. 6/ 8° Chatto [74] 95
MACQUOID, T. R. [art.] + K. S. Pictures and Legends fr. Normandy & Brittany; ill. 7/6 8° Chatto 79
'MILTOUN, Fcs.' [=Milburg F. MANSFIELD] Rambles in Normandy; ill. and 9 maps [scrappy] 6/ f 8° Duckworth 05
MUSGRAVE, G. M. A Ramble through Normandy *o.p.* [*pb.* 16/] c 8° Hurst 55
'VADOS' The Belmont Book [life in Norm. and amg. peasts.] 6/ c 8° Smith & Elder 11

**Picardy**

MUSGRAVE, G. M. Bye-Roads and Battle-Fields in Picardy *o.p.* [*pb.* 16/] 8° Bell 61

**Provence** —*v. also* Riviera, *inf.*

ALDEN, Percy Impressions of Provence; ill. L. Lelée + Marj. Nash 12/6 *n.* 8° Nash 10
CAIRD, Mona Romantic Cities of Provence; ill. J. Pennell + E. M. Synge 15/ *n.* 8° Unwin 06
COOK, Theod. A. Old Provence, 2 vols.; ill. $4 *n.* c 8° Scribner, *N.Y.* 05
16/ Rivington. Vol. i devoted to Phœnicns., Gks., and Roms. who have left traces in the district; ii to hist. 1000–1484, when CHARLES OF ANJOU left Provence to Louis XI of France.
DUMAS, Alex. The Speronara [tr.] 3/6 *n.* c 8° Dent 03
Descrn. of a trip to Provence in 1884; the first of series of vols. of the *Impressions de Voyage.*
FORREST, A. S. Tour thro' Old Provence; 108 ill. by author 6/ *n.* c 8° Stanley Paul 11
GOULD, Rev. S. Baring- In Troubadour Land [Provence and Languedoc] 12/6 8° W. H. Allen 91
JANVIER, Thos. An Embassy to Provence—*ut* **K** § 267
" Christmas Kalends of Provence $1·50 *n.* (6/) c 8° Harper 02
Acc. of the country and its customs, manners, and festivals. Wr. w. sympathy and humour.
MACGIBBON, D. Architecture of Provence and the Riviera—*ut* **I** § 121
'MILTOUN, Fcs.' [=M. F. MANSFIELD] Rambles in Provence and on Riviera; ill. [scrappy] 7/6 *n.* c 8° Sisley 07
MISTRAL, Frederi M. —*in his* Memoirs [tr.], *ut* **K** § 267
PENNELL, Jos. + Eliz. R. Play in Provence; c. 100 ill. 6/ c 8° Unwin 92
Descrn. of the life of the people—bull-fights, the ferrade, the water-tournament, etc.

**Pyrenees** —*for* Driving Tours, *v.* **I** § 148

BELLOC, Hilaire The Pyrenees; 12 maps and 46 ill. 7/6 *n.* 8° Methuen 09
Historical, descriptive, reminiscent, anecdotal, practical, geographical, political, and literary.
BILBROUGH, E. J. 'Twixt France and Spain; ill. 7/6 c 8° Low 83
BLACKBURN, Hy. Summer Life at Fch. Watering Places; ill. G. Doré 7/6 c 8° Low [67] 81
HUGO, Victor —*in his* The Alps and Pyrenees [tr.], *ut* **E** § 28
GOULD, Rev. S. Baring- Book of the Pyrenees; 25 ill. 6/ c 8° Methuen 07
RAMOND DE CARBONNIÈRES, Bar. L. F. E. Travels in the Pyrenees [tr.] [standard] *o.p.* 8° *London* 13
RUSSELL, Ct. H. Biarritz and the Basque Countries; map *o.p.* [*pb.* 6/] c 8° Stanford 73
SPENDER (Har.) + SMITH (H. Llew.) Through the High Pyrenees; maps & ill. *o.p.* [*pb.* 16/] 8° Innes 98
Narr. of travel 1896–7 in more remote pts. on both Fch. and Span. sides, incl. visit to Andorra.
TAINE, H. A. Through the Pyrenees [tr.] [descriptive] $2·50 c 8° Houghton, *Boston* 75

**Riviera** (French and Italian); **Alpes Maritimes**—*v. also* Provence, *sup.*

ALFORD, Dn Hy. Riviera: fr. Cannes to Genoa; col. pl. and ill. *o.p.* [*pb.* 42/] r 8° Bell 70
ANSTED, Alex. [artist] Riviera: 20 etchgs. and 40 vigns.; w. notes 25/ *n.* f° Seeley 93
Author of 'Vera' The Maritime Alps and their Seaboard; ill. *o.p.* [*pb.* 21/] 8° Longman 84
BULLOCK-HALL, W. H. The Romans on the Riviera and the Rhone 6/ ($2 *n.*) 8° Macmillan 98
A careful investign. of the whole questn. of Rom. conquest of Liguria and the 'Provincia'.
DEMPSTER, Charlotte L. H. The Maritime Alps, etc. *o.p.* 8° 85
GOULD, Rev. S. Baring- Book of the Riviera; 40 ill. 6/ c 8° Methuen 05
HARE, A. J. C. The Rivieras; 67 ill. by author [guide-bk.] 3/ f 8° G. Allen 97
HOME, Gordon Rivieras of France and Italy [$2·50 Macm., *N.Y.*] 7/6 *n.* 8° Dent 98
LENTHERIC, Chas. Riviera, Ancient and Modern [tr.] [$2 Putnam, *N.Y.*] 7/6 c 8° Unwin 95
A good bk. on archaeology and hist. of the district, wr. professedly for travellers 'with brains'. Good maps and plans.
MACMILLAN, Dr Hugh The Riviera: Eastern and Western; ill. 15/ *n.* s 4° Virtue [85] 02
MILLER, Wm. Wintering in the Riviera; ill. *o.p.* [*pb.* 7/6] p 8° Longman [79] 80
SCOTT, Wm. Rock Villages of the Riviera; 60 ill. 7/6 c 8° Black 98
" The Riviera; 75 col. pl. by author [$6 *n.* Macm., *N.Y.*] 20/ *n.* sq 8° Black 07
STRASBURGER, Prf. E. Rambles on the Riviera [tr.]: 87 col. ill. 21/ *n.* 8° Unwin 06
An important bk. on the flora of the Riviera, by an eminent German professor of botany.

*Bordighera:* HAMILTON (F. F.) Bordighera and W. Riviera [tr.] 7/ c 8° Stanford 83
*Cannes:* BENECKE (Amy M.) [art.] Cannes and its Environs: 40 pl. (16 col.) 10/6 *n.* s 4° G. Allen 08
*Mentone:* WOOLSON (C. F.) Mentone, Cairo, and Corfu $1·75 c 8° Harper, *N.Y.* 96
*Nice:* HOLE (Can. S. R.) Nice and her Neighbours; ill. *o.p.* [*pb.* 16/] sq 8° Low 81

**Monaco** [a principality]
MAYNE, Ethel C. Romance of Monaco & its Rulers; ill. [chfly. historical] 16/ *n.* 8° Hutchinson 10
PEMBERTON, H. History of Monaco, Past and Present *o.p.* [*pb.* 12/] 8° Tinsley 67

**Savoy:** READ (Gen. Meredith) Historic Studies in Vaud, Berne, and Savoy—*ut* **E** § 28
SAINT JOHN, Bayle The Subalpine Kingdom, 2 v. [Savoy, Piedmt., Genoa] *o.p.* [*pb.* 21/] c 8° Chapman 56

**Touraine** —*v. also* Châteaux, *inf.*
JAMES, Hy. A Little Tour in France; 84 ill. Jos. Pennell 6/ c 8° Heinemann [01] 07
$1·50 Houghton, *Boston.* Impressionist descr. of jy. in Touraine and neighbg. districts along beaten tracks. Excellent ill.
LEES, Fredc. A Summer in Touraine; 12 col. pl. and 87 ill. 10/6 *n.* 8° Methuen 09
MACDONELL, Anne Touraine and its Story; ill. and col. pl. 21/ *n.* 8° Dent 06
SUDBURY, Rich. Two Gentlemen in Touraine $3·50 8° Stone, *Chicago* 99

**Vosges Mountains:** LEE (Kath.) Among the Alsatian Mountains—*ut* **E** § 15
BETHAM-EDWARDS, Mat. In the Heart of the Vosges; ill. 10/6 *n.* 8° Chapman 11
WOLFF, H. W. The Country of the Vosges; map *o.p.* [*pb.* 12/] 8° Longman 91
Reminiscs. of a three months jy. on foot, w. curious informn. as to customs, legends, songs, and hist. of people.
" The Watering Places of the Vosges; map *o.p.* [*pb.* 4/6] c 8° Longman 91

**Cathedrals; Churches** —*v.* **I** § 121

**Châteaux; Abbeys**
CHAMPNEY, Eliz. W. Romance of the Renaissance Châteaux; 40 ill. $3 *n.* (15/ *n.*) 8° Putnam 01
" Romance of the Bourbon Châteaux; 47 ill. & col. fr. $3 *n.* (15/ *n.*) 8° Putnam 03
" Romance of the Feudal Châteaux; 40 ill. $3 *n.* (15/ *n.*) 8° Putnam 04
" Romance of the Fch. Abbeys; 61 ill. (2 col.) $3 *n.* (15/ *n.*) 8° Putnam 04
Ea. ill. by photogravures and other illns., w. a medley of legends, assocns., tradns., as text.
COOK, Theod. A. Old Touraine: famous châteaux of France, 2 vols.; ill. $5 c 8° Scribner, *N.Y.* 92
16/ Rivington. Gives an accur. pict. of old life in famous chateaux along valley of Loire; w. itinerary and maps.
GOSTLING, Fces. Rambles among French Châteaux; ill. [Rambles Ser.] 6/ c 8° Mills & Boon 11
LANSDALE, M. H. The Châteaux of Touraine; col. ill. J. Guérin 24/ *n.* 8° Nash 06
LARNED, W. C. Churches and Castles of Mediaeval France—*ut* **I** § 121
'MILTOUN, Fcs.' [=Milburg F. MANSFIELD] Castles and Châteaux of Old Touraine and the Loire Country; ill. 7/6 *n.* c 8° Pitman 07
" Castles & Châteaux of Old Navarre & the Basque Provinces; ill. 7/6 *n.* c 8° Pitman 08
" Castles & Châteaux of Old Burgundy & Border Provs.; ill. 7/6 *n.* c 8° Pitman 10
WADDINGTON, Mary K. Châteaux and Country Life in France; 24 pl. 10/6 *n.* 8° Smith & Elder 08
Chateau-life, country-visits, home of LAFAYETTE, ceremonies, festivals, Xmas in the Valois, etc.
WARD, W. H. [ed.] French Châteaux and Gardens in 16th Cent. 25/ *n.* Batsford 10
A seln. (w. descrns.) of 45 out of 116 drwgs. of plans, elevns., and bird's-eye views, by J. A. du CERCEAU, discov. by Edr. in Brit. Mus. and larger than the engravgs. pb. fr. them in 1576 and 1579.

**Cities; Towns:** COLLINS (W. W.; art.) Cathedr. Cities of Frce.: col. pl., w. l'rpr. 16/ *n.* 8° Heinemann 10
*Autun; Mt. Beauvray:* HAMERTON (P. G.) The Mount; ill. 3/6 c 8° Seeley 97
$2 Roberts, *Boston.* Orig. formed pt. of his *Rd. my House* [*ut sup.*]. The district, sketches of peasantry, etc.
*Avignon:* MARRIAGE (Ellen) Avignon; ill. [Med. Towns; $2 *n.* Dutton, *N.Y.*] 4/6 *n.* f 8° Dent 11
*Falaise:* DODD (Anna B.) Falaise, the Town of the Conqueror; ill. 7/6 c 8° Unwin 01
$2 Little & Brown, *Bost.* Gd. acc. of architect. and hist. of the town, birthpl. of WM. THE CONQ., and of its famous horse-fair.

*Paris* —*for* Paris dur. Fch. Revolution *v.* **F** § 49
*Bibliography:* LACOMBE (P.) Bibl. Parisienne [1600–1880; chron., w. notes] 8° *Paris* 87
ADOLPHUS, F. Some Memories of Paris [pleasant gossip; 1850–87] 6/ c 8° Blackwood 95
ALLEN, Grant Paris [$1·25 *n.* Wessels, *N.Y.*; a guide-book] 3/6 *n.* f 8° Richards [00] 00
de AMICIS, Edm. Studies of Paris [tr. (fr. Italian)] $1·25 c 8° Putnam, *N.Y.* [79] 92
d'AUVERGNE, E. B. The Night Side of Paris; ill. 10/6 *n.* 8° Laurie 09
BAEDEKER, Karl [pub.] Paris & its Environs; maps, etc. [$1·80 *n.* Scrib., *N.Y.*] 6/ *n.* s 8° Unwin [ ] 07
BALL, E. A. Reynolds Paris in its Splendor, 2 vols.; 60 ill. 10/ *n.* 8° Unwin 00
$3 Estes, *Boston.* Impressions of the sights and scenes of Paris and its past and present life.
BELLOC, Hilaire Paris; ill. and 7 maps 6/ c 8° Methuen [02] 07
A detailed sketch of the historical developmt. of Paris.

BINGHAM, Cpt. D. A. Recollections of Paris, 2 vols. *o.p.* [*pb.* 18/] 8° Chapman 96
Person. experces. of a newsppr.-corresp. in Paris, full of anecs. of leadg. men and women of recent times. Incl. long acc. of war of 1870–1, the two sieges, and the Commune, followed by a sectn. 'After the Commune'.

BONDE, B'ess [*née* ROBINSON] Paris in '48, ed. C. E. Warr 8/ *n.* c 8° Murray 03
$2 *n.* Pott, *N.Y.* Letters fr. a resident describing the events of the 1848 Revolution.

CAIN, Georges Nooks and Corners of Old Paris [tr.]; facs. ill. 10/6 *n.* 4° Richards 07
$3·50 *n.* Lippincott, *Phila.* By the Curator of Carnavalet Museum and of the historic collns. of City of Paris. Pref. by V. SARDOU.

„ Walks in Paris [tr.]; 118 ill. 7/6 *n.* 8° Methuen 09
$2 *n.* Macmillan, *N.Y.* An amusing medley of description, gossip, and antiquarian lore.

DAVIS, R. H. About Paris; ill. $1·25 12° Harper, *N.Y.* 95

DESCAVES, L. [ed.] The Color of Paris; ill. $6 *n.* 8° Dodd & Mead, *N.Y.* 09

F., A. M. On the Banks of the Seine 6/ ($2) c 8° Longman 00

DE FOREST, Kath. Paris As It Is; ill. $1·25 *n.* c 8° Doubleday, *N.Y.* 00
3/6 Gay & Hancock. Much interesting matter on life in Paris, disfigured, however, by mistakes and misprints.

EDWARDS, Dr G. F. Old-Time Paris [guide to chief survivals] 2/ *n.* f 8° A. Doubleday 08

EDWARDS, H. Sutherld. Old & New Paris, 2 vols.; ill. [popular descrn.] ea. 9/ r 8° Cassell 93–4

English Girl in Paris (An) 6/ c 8° Lane [02] 04

'ENGLISH OFFICER, AN' Society Recollections in Paris and Vienna; ill. 12/ *n.* 8° Long 07
$3 Appleton, *N.Y.* Cover the period 1879 to 1904.

FOX, Shirley Art-Studt's. Reminiscs. of Paris in '80's; ill. [entertaing.] 10/ 8° Mills & Boon 09

GONCOURT, Les Académiciens The Colour of Paris [tr.]; col. ill. 20/ *n.* 4° Chatto 09
Acc. of insts., hist., women, artists, army, industry., politics, w. col. ill. by a Japanese artist, YOSHIO MARKINO.

HAMERTON, P. G. Paris in Old and Present Times; ill. 2/ c 8° Seeley [85] 06
$3 Little & Brown, *Bost.* A valuable archit. and generally artistic guide to the city: pleasantly written.

HARE, A. J. C. Paris, 2 vols. [$1·75 *n.* Macmillan, *N.Y.*] ea. 3/ s 8° G. Allen [87] 00
Another Amer. edn., *sub tit. Walks in Paris*, $1·25 McKay, *Phila.* '88, w. quotns. fr. Fch. in Engl. tr.

„ Days Near Paris [environs; $2·50 *n.* Macm., *N.Y.*] 6/ c 8° G. Allen [87] *n.d.*

HAYNIE, H. Paris, Past and Present, 2 vols.; ill. $4 *n.* c 8° Stokes, *N.Y.* 02

HEINE, Heinr. [1799–1856] French Affairs: letters fr. Paris [tr.] = Works, vols. vii–viii—*ut* **K** § 91

HESSLING, E. [ed.] Old Paris: histor. bldgs. & their details, 2 vols. ea. $20 4° Hessling, *N.Y.* 05–7
Vol. i: *Romanesque Gothic Period*; ii: *Early Renaissance.* Text in Fch. or German.

HOPKINS, Tighe An Idler in Old France [historical] 7/6 c 8° Hurst 99

HYATT, A. H. [ed.] The Charm of Paris: an anthology 2/ *n.* pott 8° Chatto 09

JACKSON, C. C., L'y Old Paris: its court & literary salons, 2 vols. *o.p.* [*pb.* 24/] p 8° Bentley 78

„ The Old Régime; court, salons, theatres, 2 v. *o.p.* [*pb.* 24/] p 8° Bentley 80

JERROLD, W. Blanchard At Home in Paris, 2 Ser.; 4 vols. *o.p.* [*pb.* 37/] c 8° W. H. Allen 71–84

„ On the Boulevards, 2 vols. *o.p* .[*pb.* 21/] c 8° W. H. Allen 67

LONERGAN, W. F. 40 Years of Paris; 32 ports. [$3·50 *n.* Brentano, *N.Y.*] 10/6 *n.* 8° Unwin 07

LUCAS, E. V. A Wanderer in Paris; 16 col. pl. [$1·75 *n.* Macm., *N.Y.*] 6/ c 8° Methuen 09

MARTIN, B. E. + Charl. M. The Stones of Paris in History & Letters; ill. $2 c 8° Scribner, *N.Y.* [00] 06
7/6 *n.* Smith & Elder. Follows the fragmts. remaing. of walls of Philip Augustus, bringg. to light half-recalled, half-forgotten relics of the past.

MENPES, Mortimer [artist] Paris; w. text Dorothy Menpes; ill. & 24 col. pl. 6/ *n.* sq 8° Black 07
$2 *n.* Macmillan, *N.Y.* Ed. de Luxe, w. 75 col. pl., 42/ *n.* 4° *id.* '09.

'MILTOUN, Fcs.' [=Milburg F. MANSFIELD] Dumas' Paris *o.p.* [*pb.* 7/6 *n.*] c 8° Sisley 07

MURRAY, Jno. [pub.] Handbook for Travrs. in Paris; 15 maps & plans 3/6 c 8° Stanford [ ]

OKEY, T., etc. Paris and its Story; ill. [$6 *n.* Macmillan, *N.Y.*] 21/ *n.* r 8° Dent 04

„ etc. Story of Paris [Mediaev. Towns; $2 *n.* Dutton, *N.Y.*] 4/6 *n.* c 8° Dent 06

PEAT, A. B. N. Gossip from Paris dur. the Second Empire 7/6 *n.* c 8° Paul 03
$2·50 *n.* Appleton, *N.Y.* Correspondence during yrs. 1864–9, selected and ed. A. R. WALLER.

RAPHAEL, J. N. Picts. of Paris & Some Parisns.; ill. [$1·50 *n.* Macm., *N.Y.*] 3/6 *n.* c 8° Black 08

ROBINSON, Wm. The Parks and Gardens of Paris; ill. 18/ 8° Macmillan [69] 78

ROOTS, Wm. Paris in 1814, ed. Sir H. A. Ogle; 30 pl. 7/6 *n.* 4° Reid, *Newcastle* 09

RUTTER, Fk. The Path to Paris—*ut* **I** § 149

SALA, G. A. Paris Herself Again; 350 Fch. ill.
[1878–9; aft. war 1870–1] *o.p.* [*pb.* 2/6] c 8° Vizetelly [79] 87

SHERARD, R. H. Twenty Years in Paris: recollns. of liter. life; 8 ill. 16/ *n.* 8° Hutchinson 05
Personalia ab. LESSEPS, EIFFEL, HAUSSMANN, EDISON, HUGO, DUMAS fils, MAUPASSANT, ZOLA, MALLARMÉ, LOUYS, etc.

„ My Friends the French; w. allusns. to other people; ill. 12/6 *n.* 8° Laurie 09

„ Modern Paris; ill. [reminiscences, etc.] 12/6 *n.* 8° Laurie 11

SMITH, F. Berkeley Parisians Out of Doors $1·50 *n.* (6/) c 8° Funk & Wagnalls 05

STEEVENS, G. W. Glimpses of Three Nations, ed. V. Blackburn 6/ ($1·50) c 8° Dodd & Mead, *N.Y.* 00
6/ Blackwood. A well-known journalist's impressionist sketches of London, Paris, and Berlin.

TAINE, H. A. Notes on Paris, tr. J. A. Stevens; w. notes $2·50 12° Holt, *N.Y.* [68] 88
THACKERAY, W. M. Paris Sketch Book—*ut* **K** § 50
UZANNE, Octave The Modern Parisienne [tr.] 10/ *n.* 8° Heinemann 11
VANDAM, A. D. An Englishman in Paris; *and* My Paris Note-Book—*ut* **F** § 50
" Paris and its Inhabitants—*in his* French Men & French Manners, *ut sup.*
'VASILI, C't Paul' Society in Paris: upper 10,000 [tr.] [ser. of letters] 6/ c 8° Chatto 90
WALTON, W. Paris fr. Earliest Period to Pres. Day, 10 vols.; ill. ea. $3 8° Barrie, *Phila.* 89–03
" Paris Known and Unknown, in Pts. *subscr.* f° Barrie, *Phila.* 98 *sqq.*
WASHBURN (C. C.) + HORNBY (L. G.) Pages fr. Bk. of Paris; 40 ill. [7/6 *n.* Constable] c 8° Houghton, *Bost.* 10
WHITEING, Rich. The Life of Paris [soc., polit., artistic] 6/ c 8° Murray 00
" Paris of To-day; ill. $5 4° Century Co., *N.Y.* 00
WHITING, Lilian Paris the Beautiful; ill. [$2 Little & B., *Bost.*] 10/6 8° Hodder 09
*Art Galleries* —*v.* **I** § 88
*Houses:* HARRISON (W.) Memorable Paris Houses; c. 60 ill. by Fch. artists 6/ c 8° Low 93
*Law Courts*—*v.* **D** § 5 *Prisons*—*v.* **D** § 123
*Quartier Latin*
MACDONALD, J. F. Paris of the Parisians 5/ c 8° Richards 00
$1·50 Lippincott, *Phila.* Paris of the 'Quartiers'.
MORROW, W. C. Bohemian Paris of To-day; 106 ill. 6/ c 8° Chatto 99
$2·50 Lippincott, *Phila.* Pleasant notes of student-life in the Quartier Latin.
MURGET, Henri [1822–61] Bohemians of Latin Quarter [tr.]—*ut* **K** § 53 [a novel]
SMITH, F. Berkeley The Real Latin Quarter; ill. by author $1·20 *n.* (6/) c 8° Funk & Wagnalls 01
" How Paris Amuses Itself; ill. $1·50 *n.* (6/) c 8° Funk & Wagnalls 03
*Rouen* —*for* Cathedrals and Churches *v.* **I** § 121
COOK, Th. A. Story of Rouen; ill. [Mediæv. Towns; $2 *n.* Dutton, *N.Y.*] 4/6 *n.* c 8° Dent 99
*Versailles* —*for the* Gardens *v.* **I** § 46
ARNOTT (J. A.) + WILSON (J.) The Petit Trianon, Versailles, 3 Pts.; pl. ea. 21/ *n.* f° Batsford 07–10
Ea. $9 *n.* Scribner, *N.Y.* A portfo. of fine pl. of measd. dwgs. and photos (w. notes) of whole bldgs., furnit., etc., and acc. of Palace.
BOYD, Mary S. A Versailles Christmas-tide; ill. 6/ c 8° Chatto 01
BRADBY, G. F. The Great Days of Versailles; ports. 10/6 *n.* 8° Smith & Elder 06
$1·75 *n.* Scribner, *N.Y.* Studies fr. Court-life in the later years of LOUIS XIV.
FARMER, J. E. Versailles and the Court of Louis XIV $3·50 *n.* 8° Century Co., *N.Y.* 06
de NOLHAC, Pierre Versailles and the Trianons; col. pl. R. Binet 16/ *n.* r 8° Heinemann 06
$3·50 *n.* Dodd & Mead, *N.Y.* Descrn. of gardens and treasures, signif. in hist. and art, and Ct.-life.

**Inns**

FRAPRIE, F. R. Little Pilgrimages amg. French Inns; map & ill. $2 c 8° Page, *Boston* 04
GIBSON, Chas. Among French Inns [6/ Hodder] $1·60 c 8° Page, *Boston* 06

**Rivers; Valleys**

MOLLOY, J. L. Autumn Holiday on Fch. Rivers; ill. Linley Sambourne 7/6 i 8° Bradbury [74] 79
WARREN (E. P.) + CLEVERLEY (C. F.) Wandergs. of *Beetle* on Rivers of Fce. & Belg.; ill. 7/6 r 8° Griffith 86
*Loire; Seine:* GEORGE (E.) [art.] Etchgs. fr. Loire and S. of Frce.: 20 pl. 42/ f° Murray 74
PEARS, Chas. From the Thames to the Seine—*ut* **I** § 153
RUTTER, Fk. The Path to Paris; 68 ill. 10/6 *n.* ($5 *n.*) 8° Lane 08
Acc. of a cycle-tour along banks of Seine fr. Havre to Paris; w. excursions.
TURNER, J. M. W. [art.] Seine and Loire: 61 steel pl.; w. l'rpress M. B. Huish 42/ 4° Virtue [33–5] 90
*Rhone:* KINGSLEY (Rose) In the Rhone Country; 52 pl. 10/6 *n.* c 8° G. Allen 10
WOOD (C. W.) In Valley of the Rhone; 88 ill. 10/ *n.* ($4) 8° Macmillan [99] 00
Travels in both the French and Swiss (Vaud and Valais) portions of the Rhone valley.
*Saône:* HAMERTON (P. G.) The Saône; 4 maps and 148 ill. J. Pennell 21/ r 8° Seeley 87

**Scenery** —*v. also* GONCOURT, MENPES, and Rivers, *sup.*

GREEN, Rev. S. G. French Pictures: drawn with Pen and Pencil; 150 ill. 8/ i 8° R.T.S. [78] 79
MURRAY, A. H. Hallam [art.] On Road thro' Frce. to Florence; 48 col. pl., w. text H. W. Nevinson + M. Carmichael [$5 *n.* Dutton, *N.Y.*] 21/ *n.* m 8° Murray 04

## 15 : GERMANY

### Early Accounts

v. GOETHE, J. W. [1749–1832] Miscellaneous Travels, L. Dora Schmitz ; tr. ; plan 3/6 c 8° Bell 84
$1 *n.* Macmillan, *N.Y.* [Bohn's Lib.] Letters fr. Switzerl. ; fr. the Fch. campaign of 1792 ; siege of Mainz ; tour on Rhine, Maine, and Neckar 1814–5.

HEINE, Heinr. [1799–1856] Germany, tr. C. G. Leland = Works, vols. v–vi—*ut* **K** § 91
Intended to supplemt. Mme DE STAEL'S *Germany*, dealg. w. relig., philos., and *belles lettres*. Of small value now (or at any time) for its facts, tho' an excellent piece of literary wk., full of wit and humour. Its pt.-of-view is political (anti-Catholic). Poorly tr.

de MONTAIGNE, M. [1533–92] Jl. of Travs. in Italy by way of Switz. and Germy. [tr.], 3 v. 15/ *n.* c 8° Murray 03
Accounts of institutions, rather than pictorial impressions. The only English tr. since 1842.

de STAEL, Mme [1766–1817] Germany, tr. O. W. Wright ; w. notes $2·50 c 8° Houghton, *Boston* [71]

### Guides

BAEDEKER, Karl [pub.] Germany, 2 Pts. ; 79 maps & 98 plans 14/ *n.* ($4·20 *n.*) s 8° Unwin [ ] 09 ; 07
Scribner, *N.Y.* i : *Northern Germany*, 8/ *n.* ($2·40 *n.*) ; ii : *Southern Germy.*, 6/ *n.* ($1·80 *n.*). *Vide* also *Berlin* and *Rhine, inf.*

MURRAY, Jno. [pub.] Germany, 2 Pts. (3 vols.) ; maps and plans p 8° Stanford [3–] 86–10
Pt. i : *Northern Germany and the Rhine*, 8/ ; ii : *Southern Germany and Austria*, 43 maps and plans, 6/.

### Life ; People ; Economic Condition, etc.—*v. also* D § 144, *s.v.* Germany

BAKER, R. S. Seen in Germany ; ill. $2 8° McClure & Phillips, *N.Y.* 02
5/ Harper, *Lond.* A fresh study of Kaiser, soldier, workman, industries, student-life, etc.

BARKER, J. Ellis Modern Germany—*ut* **D** § 144

BERRY, Rob. M. Germany of the Germans—*ut* **D** § 144

BIGELOW, Poultney The Borderland of Czar and Kaiser ; ill. $2 8° Harper, *N.Y.* 95
7/6 *n.* Gay & Hancock. Much trustworthy information on the German and Russian military systems.

" The German Emperor & his Eastern Neighbrs. [3/ Cassell] 75 c. c 8° Webster, *N.Y.* 92

DAWSON, W. H. Germany and the Germans, 2 vols. 26/ 8° Chapman 94
A ser. of lively chs. on Germ. life, instits., culture, relig., politics and parties—journalistic rather than literary.

" Germany at Home 5/ c 8° Hodder [01] 08
Much exact informn. on Germ. life. 1st edn. (1901) pub. *sub tit.* '*German Life in Town and Country*' [Our Eur. Neighbrs.].

DIDON, Abbé H. N. The Germans, tr. R. L. de Beaufort 7/6 p 8° Blackwood 84

ELZBACHER, O. Mod. Germany [mainly political ; $2·50 *n.* Dutton, *N.Y.*] 7/6 *n.* c 8° Smith & Elder 05

FRANCKE, Prf. Kuno Glimpses of Modern German Culture $1·25 c 8° Dodd & Mead, *N.Y.* 98
Takes on the whole an optimistic view of Germany's position and future.

" Germ. Ideals of To-day & other Ess. on Germ. Culture $1·50 *n.* c 8° Houghton, *Boston* 07

FREYTAG, Gust. Pictures of Germ. Life in 15–17 Cent. [tr.], 2 vols. *o.p.* [*pb.* 21/] c 8° Chapman 62

" Pictures of Germ. Life in 18–19 Cent. [tr.], 2 vols. *o.p.* [*pb.* 21/] c 8° Chapman 63

German Home Life [repr. arts. fr. 'Fraser's Mag.'] *o.p.* [*pb.* 6/] c 8° Longman [76] 76

GOSTWICK, J. German Culture & Christianity : 1770–1880 *o.p.* [*pb.* 10/6] 8° Norgate [82] 89

GOULD, Rev. S. Baring- Germany, Past and Present 7/6 p 8° Paul [79] 81
Contains a good view of the social institutions and customs of Germany.

" Germany [Foreign Countries and Brit. Cols.] 3/6 c 8° Low 83

MAYHEW, Hy. German Life and Manners in Saxony *o.p.* [*pb.* 7/] c 8° W. H. Allen [69] 65

Pan-Germanic Doctrine (The) : study of Germ. polit. aims and aspirns. ; maps 10/6 8° Harper 04

v. SCHIERBRAND, W. Germany, the Weldg. of a World-Power $1 *n.* 8° Doubleday, *N.Y.* [02] 10
Chs. on social, poltical and commercial affairs, German colonies, the Kaiser'personality, etc.

SIDGWICK, Mrs Alf. Home Life in Germany ; 16 pl. 10/6 *n.* 8° Methuen 08
$1·75 *n.* Macmillan, *N.Y.* An interestg. picture of the more intimate and small details of soc. and domestic life : the nursery, schoolroom, youth at Univ., peasant, town-poor, Sunday amusemts., shops, inns, food, expenses, courtship, marrge., etc.

SINGLETON, Esther [ed.] Germany as Described by Great Writers $1·60 *n.* c 8° Dodd & Mead, *N.Y.* 07

STEEVENS, G. W. Glimpses of Three Nations, ed. V. Blackburn—*ut* **E** § 14, *s.v.* Paris

VARNHAGEN v. ENSE, C. A. L. P. Sketches of German Life & Scenes [tr.] *o.p.* [*pb.* 3/6] c 8° Murray [47] 61

VIZETELLY, H. Berlin und. the New Empire ; ill. [institns., soc. life, etc.], 2 v. *o.p.* [*pb.* 30/] 8° Tinsley 79

WHITMAN, Sid. Imperial Germany : crit. study of fact & character 3/6 c 8° Heinemann [89] 91
75 c. Chautauqua Press, '01. Politics, life, educn., aristocr., women, etc.

WYLIE, I. A. R. My German Year [friendly acc. of home-life] 10/6 *n.* 8° Mills & Boon 10

**Art Galleries**—*v.* **I** § 88 **Cathedrals ; Churches**—*v.* **I** § 121

### Rivers and Canals —*for* Boating *v.* I § 153

*Danube* —*v.* **E** § 12

*Moselle :* AUSONIUS, D. M. [4 cent.] Mosella—*ut* **K** § 214 [a 4th-cent. Lat. poem on the river]

GEORGE, Ern. [artist] Etchings of Mosel : 20 etchgs., w. l'rpress *o.p.* [*pb.* 42/] f° Murray 73

*Rhine (The)*

BAEDEKER, Karl [pub.] The Rhine; 52 maps & 29 plans [$2·10 *n.* Scrib., *N.Y.*] 7/ *n.* s 8° Unwin [ ] 06

GOULD, Rev. S. Baring- A Book of the Rhine; ill. 6/ c 8° Methuen [06]

From Cleve to Mainz. Severely historical; w. 8 good col. pl. by Trevor HADDEN, and 48 ill. fr. photos.

LONGFELLOW, H. W. Hyperion [1/ Routledge] 50 c. 16° Houghton, *Boston* [48]

LYTTON, 1st L'd Pilgrims of the Rhine—*ut* **K** § 50

*MACKINDER, H. J. The Rhine; 2 col. maps & c. 50 col. ill. Mrs J. Jardine 20/ *n.* 4° Chatto 08

An excellent descrn. of the country and its past, of the river and its tribs. (Moselle, Meuse, Scheldt) and the pt. they have played in history.

MARRIOTT, C. The Romance of the Rhine; 16 col. pl. 10/6 *n.* 8° Methuen 11

STIELER, K. The Rhine, fr. its Source to the Sea [tr.]; 170 ill. 15/ s 4° Virtue [78] 88

**Scenery:** GREEN (Rev. S. G.) Pictures from the German Fatherland; ill. 8/ i 8° R.T.S. [80] 93

SCHAUFFLER, R. H. [artist] Romantic Germany: 73 col. and plain ill. 12/6 *n.* 8° Hutchinson 10

$3·50 *n.* Century Co., *N.Y.*

**Alsace:** LEE (Kath.) Among the Alsatian Mountains; ill. *o.p.* [*pb.* 9/] c 8° Bentley 83

WOLFF, H. W. —*in his* The Country of the Vosges, *ut* **E** § 14

**Bavaria**

FRAPRIE, F. R. Little Pilgrimages am. Bavarian Inns; ill. $2 c 8° Page, *Boston* 06

With reminiscences of student-life and artist-life in Munich.

SCHMID (H.) + STIELER (K.) Bavarian Highlds. & Salzkammergut [tr.]; ill. *o.p.* [*pb.* 25/] f° Chapman 74

SÉGUIN, L. G. [+Mrs A. STRAHAN] The Country of the Passion Play; ill. 6/ c 8° Chatto [80] 88

*Bayreuth* —*v. also* **I** § 124, *s.v.* Wagner

BARRY, Mrs Milner Bayreuth and Franconian Switzerland; pl. 2/6 c 8° Sonnenschein [87] 88

*Ober-Ammergau* —*v. also* **K** § 82, *s.v.* Passion Play

MILNER, Edith Life in Ober Ammergau: its flowers & legends; ill. 25/ *n.* 8° Ben Johnson, *York* 09

**Black Forest**

HUGHES, C. E. Book of the Black Forest; 2 maps and 21 ill. 7/6 *n.* Methuen 10

Acc. of ramble rd. Baden-Baden, Pforzheim, Wildbad, Freiburg, Donaueschingen, and their hills and valleys.

Moravian Life in the Black Forest; ill. 6/ c 8° Sonnenschein 89

RIDDELL, Mrs J. H. A Mad Tour: rambles on ft. thro' Black Forest *o.p.* [*pb.* 10/6] c 8° Bentley 91

SÉGUIN, L. G. [=Mrs Alex. STRAHAN] The Black Forest; its people and legends 6/ p 8° Hodder [79] 86

WOLFF, H. W. Rambles in the Black Forest *o.p.* [*pb.* 7/6] c 8° Longman 90

A sympathetic descrn. of the men and manners, their houses and condn., legends and romantic lore, of Schwarzwald.

WOOD, Chas. W. In the Black Forest *o.p.* [*pb.* 6/] c 8° Bentley 82

WYLIE, I. A. R. Rambles in Black Forest; ill. [Rambles Ser.] 6/ c 8° Mills & Boon 11

**Eifel Mountains:** MACQUOID (Kath. S. + G. S.) In the Volcanic Eifel; 55 ill. 7/6 8° Hutchinson 96

Travel-gossip, w. many legends conn. w. the old caskes of the district. 3 maps and 55 ill. by T. R. MACQUOID.

**Harz Mountains**

ANDERSEN, Hans Chr. Rambles in Harz, Saxon-Switz., etc. [tr.] *o.p.* [*pb.* 10/6] c 8° Bentley 48

BLACKBURN, Hy. The Harz Mountains: tour in toy country; 40 ill. *o.p.* [*pb.* 12/] 8° Low 73

FORMAN, H. J. In Footprints of Heine; ill. [6/ *n.* Constable] c 8° Houghton, *Boston* 10

HEINE, Heinr. [1799–1856] A Trip to the Brocken, tr. McLintock *o.p.* [*pb.* 3/6] c 8° Macmillan 81

,, Pictures of Travel [tr.], 2 vols. =Works, vols. ii–iii—*ut* **K** § 91 [incl. 'Tour in Harz']

**Heligoland:** BLACK (W. G.) Heligoland and Islands of North Sea *o.p.* [*pb.* 4/] 8° Blackwood 88

Customs, legends, festivals, and folklore of the people; w. sketch of hist., lang., and laws.

**Rügen:** v. ARNIM (C'ess) Adventures of Elizabeth in Rügen; map 6/ ($1·50) c 8° Macmillan 04

A graceful and humorous acc. of a driving-tour through the island.

**Towns**

*Berlin*

BAEDEKER, K. [pub.] Berlin & Environs; 5 maps and 20 plans [90 c. *n.* Scrib., *N.Y.*] 3/ *n.* s 8° Unwin [ ] 08

REEVE, Dr H. Journal of Residence in Vienna and Berlin—*ut* **E** § 12, *s.v.* Vienna

STEEVENS, G. W. —*in his* Glimpses of Three Nations, *ut* **E** § 14, *s.v.* Paris

*Heidelberg:* GODFREY (Eliz.) Heidelberg: its princes and palaces; ill. 12/6 *n.* 8° Richards 06

A good acc. of 'The Hill of the Bilberries' and a story of the Palatinate. The best, however, is Dr Karl PFAFF's *Heidelberg und Umgebung*, 8° Hörning, *Hdlbg.* [97] 02.

*Munich:* WADLEIGH (H. R.) Munich: hist., monumts., art 6/ *n.* c 8° Unwin 10

First hf. on hist. of Bavaria, second on Munich; appendix on Passion Play at Oberammergau. Map and ill.

WILBERFORCE, Edw. Social Life in Munich *o.p.* [*pb.* 10/6] c 8° W. H. Allen [63] 64

*Nuremberg*

BELL, A. G. [art.] + Mrs A. G. Nuremberg: 20 col. pl.; w. l'rpr.
[$2·50 *n.* Macm., *N.Y.*] 7/6 *n.* sq 8° Black 05

HEADLAM, Cecil Story of Nuremberg; 31 ill. [Mediaev. Towns; $1 Dutt., *N.Y.*] 3/6 *n.* c 8° Dent [99]

REE, P. J. Nuremberg and its Art to End of 18th Cent. [tr.]; 123 ill. 4/ *n.* 4° Grevel 05

*Rothenburg:* UHDE-BERNAYS (H.) Rothenburg on the Tauber; ill. 4/ *n.* 8° Grevel 08
Histor. and topogr. acc. of one of the most perfect medieval towns in Europe. It is in Bavaria.

## 16: GREAT BRITAIN AND IRELAND (*a*): GENERALLY

### Bibliography

ANDERSON, J. P. Book of British Topography *o.p.* [*pb.* 25/] i 8° Satchell 81
A catalogue of the topographical books in the British Museum; w. a few short notes.

CALYZER, T. S. [ed.] Britannia: colln. of princ. Latin Authors ref. to Brit. 8° 78

NICHOLS, J. G. The Topographer and Genealogist, 3 vols. *o.p.* [*pb.* 25/] 8° J. R. Smith 46–58
Forms a bibliogr. contin. of his *Collectanea Topogr.* [*ut* G § 22], and conts. a val. colln. of orig. pprs. on Engl. hist., heraldry, customs, etc.

SMITH, A. R. Catalogue of Tracts, Prints, etc., illustrating Top. of England, Wales, Scotland, and Ireland *o.p.* 8° A. R. Smith 78

UPCOTT, W. Bibliogr. Acc. of Princ. Wks. on Eng. Topogr., 3 v.; ill. [*w.* 80/] 8° *London* 18

*Maps* —*v. inf., s.v.* Atlases (Maps)

*Records* (*Local*): CHARITY COMMISSIONERS: Reports, i–lvii [1910] ea. 2½*d.*–4*d.* 8° Wyman 18 *sqq., ann.*
Contain accounts of many documts., such as conveyces. of land and wills, benefitting churches.

COMMITTEE ON LOCAL RECORDS: Report, 6*d.*; Evidence, 2/4 Wyman 00
App. viii to *Rept.* conts. list of publ. and semi-publ. collns. of local recds. rep. on by Hist. MSS. Comm.

GROSS, Dr Chas. —*in his* Sources and Literature of English History, *ut* **F** § 16
For list of local Societies for pubn. of records, w. their pubns., *v.* pp. 15–22; for full bibliogr. of local records *v.* pp. 400–467.

*HISTORICAL MSS. COMMISSION: Reports—*ut* **F** § 16 [*v.* Comm. on Local Records, *sup.*]

### Series

Cambr. County Geogrs.: ed. Dr F. H. H. Guillemard; ea. 2 col. maps ea. 1/6 c 8° Camb. Pr. *v.y., in prg.*
Ea. vol. gives acc. of hist., antiqs., archit., nat. hist., industries, and phys. geogr. For schl. use.

*Gentleman's Magazine* Lib., ed. G. L. Gomme: English Topography, 17 vols. ea. 7/6 8° Stock 91–05
Contains much interesting matter gleaned fr. the old *Gentleman's Mag.* [1731–1868]. Deals w. the counties in alphab. order (2 to 3 in ea. vol.), and w. the localities in ea. county alphab. under county-name. Full indexes of names and subjs. to ea. For other vols. of series *v.* Gen. Index. i: *Beds, Berks, Bucks*; ii: *Cambs, Cumb.*; iii: *Derbysh., Dors.*; iv: *Durh., Gloucs.*; v: *Hants, Hunts*; vi: *Kent, Lancs*; vii: *Leics, Monm.*; viii: *Norf., Northants, Northumb.*; ix: *Notts, Oxf., Rutl.*; x: *Salop, Somers.*; xi: *Staffs, Suff.*; xii: *Surr., Suss.*; xiii: *Warw., Westm., Wilts*; xiv: *Worcs, Yorks*; xv–xvii: *London*, 3 *Pts.*

Heart of England Series: col. pl. ea. 3/6 *n.* s 8° Dent 09–10 *in prg.*
*Heart of England* Edw. THOMAS | *Historic Thames* [*ut. inf.*] Hilaire BELLOC | *South Country* Edw. THOMAS

Highways and Byways Series: ea. fully and well. ill. ea. 6/ ($2 *n.*) c 8° Macmillan *in prg.*
*Berkshire* [*ut* **E** § 17] J. E. VINCENT
*Derbyshire* [*ut* **E** § 17] J. B. FIRTH
*Devon and Cornwall* [*ut* **E** § 17] A. H. NORWAY
*Donegal and Antrim* [*ut* **E** § 20] S. GWYNN
*Dorset* [*ut* **E** § 17] Sir Fredk. TREVES
*East Anglia* [*ut* **E** § 17] W. A. DUTT
*Hampshire* [*ut* **E** § 17] D. H. M. READ
*Hertfordshire* [*ut* **E** § 17] H. W. TOMPKINS
*Kent* [*ut* **E** § 17] W. JERROLD
*Lake District* [*ut* **E** § 17] A. G. BRADLE
*London* [*ut* **E** § 17] Mrs E. T. COOK
*Oxford and Cotswolds* [*ut* **E** § 17] H. A. EVANS
*Surrey* [*ut* **E** § 17] Eric PARKER
*Sussex* [*ut* **E** § 17] E. V. LUCAS
*Wales, North* [*ut* **E** § 17] A. G. BRADLEY
„ *South* [*ut* **E** § 17] A. G. BRADLEY
*Yorkshire* [*ut* **E** § 17] A. H. NORWAY
[*Normandy* [*ut* **E** § 14] P. DEARMER]
A good ser. of topogr. accs. of the counties, w. chief histor., antiq. and associational interests. Well ill. by leadg. artists of the day.

Memorials of the Counties of England: ed. Rev. P. H. Ditchfield; ill. ea. 15/ *n.* 8° G. Allen *in prg.*
A useful ser. of collns. of miscell. topogr. and antiqu. papers by var. wrs., of varying style and merit.
*Old Bucks* [*u* **E** § 17] ed. EDR.
*Old Cheshire* [*ut* **E** § 17] ed. Rev. E. BARBER + EDR.
*Old Derbyshire* [*ut* **E** § 17] ed. Rev J. C. COX
*Old Devonshire* [*ut* **E** § 17] ed. F. J. SNELL
*Old Dorset* [*ut* **E** § 17] ed. T. PERKINS + H. PENTIN
*Old Durham* [*ut* **E** § 17] ed. H. R. LEIGHTON *in prep.*
*Old Essex* [*ut* % § 17] ed. A. C. KELWAY
*Old Hampshire* [*ut* **E** § 17] ed. Rev. G. E. JEAN.
*Old Herefordshire* [*ut* **E** § 17] ed. Rev. Compton READE
*Old Hertfordshire* [*ut* **E** § 17] ed. P. C. STANDING
*Old Kent* [*ut* **E** § 17] ed. EDR. + G. CLINCH
*Old Lancashire*, 2 v. [*ut* **E** § 17] ed. Lt.-Col. H. FISHWICK + EDR.
*Old Leicestershire* [*ut* **E** § 17] ed. Alice DRYDEN *in prep.*
*Old Lincolnshire* [*ut* **E** § 17] ed. Dr E. M. SYMPSON *in prep.*
*Old London*, 2 vols. [*ut* **E** § 17] ed. EDR.
*Old Norfolk* [*ut* **E** § 17] H. J. D. ASTLEY
*Old North Wales* [*ut* **E** § 18] ed. E. A. JONES *in prep.*
*Old Northants* [*ut* **E** § 17] Alice DRYDEN
*Old Oxfordshire* [*ut* **E** § 17] ed. EDR.
*Old Shropshire* [*ut* **E** § 17] ed. T. ANDEN
*Old Somersetshire* [*ut* **E** § 17] ed. F. J. SNELL
*Old Staffordshire* [*ut* **E** § 17] ed. Rev. W. BERESFORD
*Old Surrey* [*ut* **E** § 17] ed. Dr J. C. COX *in prep.*
*Old Sussex* [*ut* **E** § 17] ed. P. D. MUNDY
*Old Warwickshire* [*ut* **E** § 17] ed. Alice DRYDEN
*Old Wiltshire* [*ut* **E** § 17] ed. Alice DRYDEN
*Old Yorkshire* [*ut* **E** § 17] ed. T. M. FALLOW

Popular County Histories ea. 7/6 8° Stock 85 *sqq.*
*Berkshire* [*ut* **E** § 17] Lt.-Col. C. C. COOPER-KING
*Cambridgeshire* [*ut* **E** § 17] [also 3/6 *n.*] Rev. E. CONYBEARE
*Cumberland* [*ut* **E** § 17] R. S. FERGUSON
*Derbyshire* [*ut* **E** § 17] J. PENDLETON
*Devonshire* [*ut* **E** § 17] [also 3/6 *n.*] R. N. WORTH
*Hampshire* [*ut* **E** § 17] T. W. SHORE
*Lancashire* [*ut* **E** § 17] [also 3/6 *n.*] Lt.-Col. H. FISHWICK
*Norfolk* [*ut* **F** § 17] Walt. RYE
*Northumberland* [*ut* **E** § 17] C. J. BATES
*Nottinghamshire* [*ut* **E** § 17] [also 3/6 *n.*] C. BROWN
*Oxfordshire* [*ut* **E** § 17] [also 3/6 *n.*] J. M. FALKNER
*Suffolk* [*ut* **E** § 17] [also 3/6 *n.*] J. J. RAVEN
*Surrey* [*ut* **E** § 17] H. E. MALDEN
*Warwickshire* [*ut* **E** § 17] S. TIMMINS
*Westmoreland* [*ut* **E** § 17] [also 3/6 *n.*] R. S. FERGUSON
Supplies in moderate compass, chief facts and characteristics of the several counties. A useful, popular series.

*Victoria Hist. of the Counties of Engld., vols. i– ; maps & ill. ea. 31/6 *n.* r 8° Constable 06 *sqq., in prg.*
To occupy 184 vols. (incl. *London*, 3 vols.), price per set £291 1/6 *n.* An 'Empire Edn.' is issued on the instalmt. syst. at 42/ *n.* per vol. Of ea. county are given accs. by specialists of its Geol. and palaeontol.; Flora and fauna; Prehist., Roman and Ang.-Sax. remains; Domesd. Bk. and other records; Archit.; Eccles. hist.; Polit. hist.; Hist. of schools; Topogr. accs. of parishes and manors; Agric.; Forestry; Industries, arts., and manufs. Social and econ. hist.; Sport, anc. and mod. Finely and profusely ill. (sometimes in colour) w. maps, views, bldgs., coats-of-arms, brasses, col. glass, etc. The first serious attempt to utilize to the full and on a comprehensive scale our magnificent ser. of natl. and local munimts. by an organized body of experts. Ea. wk. ent. separ. in **E** § 17.

*Beds.* (3 vols.), vols. i–ii
*Berks* (4), vols. i–ii
*Bucks* (4), vols. i–ii
*Cornwall* (4), vol. i
*Cumberl.* (4), vols. i–ii
*Derby* (4), vols. i–ii
*Devon* (4), vol. i
*Dorset* (4), vol. ii
*Durham* (4), vols. i–ii
*Essex* (4), vols. i–ii
*Gloucs.* (4), vol. ii
*Hants* (4), vols. i–iii
*Hereford* (4), vol. i
*Herts* (4), vols. i–ii
*Kent* (5), vol. i
*Lancs* (5), vols. i–iii
*Leics.* (4), vol. i
*Lincs* (4), vol. ii
*London* (3), vol. i
*Norfolk* (6), vols. i–ii
*Northants* (4), vols. i–ii
*Notts* (4), vols. i–ii
*Oxford* (4), vol. ii
*Ruland* (2), vol. i
*Salop* (4), vol. i
*Somerset* (4), vol. i
*Staffs* (4), vol. i
*Suffolk* (4), vol. ii
*Surrey* (4), vols. i–ii
*Sussex* (4), vols. i–ii
*Warwick* (4), vols. i–ii
*Worcs.* (4), vols. i–ii
*Yorks* (8), vol. i

*Supplem. Vols.* (to ea. county : genealog ; ea. 105/ *n.*—*ut* **G** § 22) : *Northamptonshire Families*, ed. O. BARRON, '06 ; *Hertfordshire Families*, ed. D. WARRAND, '07.

**Early Topography** (to 18th Cent.)—*v. also inf.* Engl. as seen by Foreigners, *passim*

CAMDEN, Wm. [1551–1623] Britannia, tr. and enlarged R. Gough, 4 vols. [*w.* £3] f° *London* [1606–7] 1806
Orig. wr. in Lat. and pubd. 1586. Also tr. by Dr Philemon HOLLAND [1610] 1637. The classic wk.

,, Britannia : Surrey & Sussex [repr. fr. Holland's tr., 1610] 7/6 *n.* 4° Fifield 06

Gosse, Edm. Camden's Britannia [1610]—*in his* Gossip in a Library, *ut* **K** § 18

,, Remains concerning Britain [Lib. of Old Authors] *o.p.* [*pb.* 7/6] c 8° J. R. Smith [1605] 70
Repr. of 1674 edn., the best. Langs., names, anograms, armories, apparel, wise speeches, provbs., epitaphs, etc.

FIENNES, Celia Thro' England on a Side-Saddle 12/6 8° Leadenhall Press 88
*Temp.* WILLIAM AND MARY. The Diary of Celia FIENNES, ed. w. an explan. Introd., by Hon. Mrs GRIFFITHS.

HARRISON, Wm. [1536–93] Description of England—*ut* **F** § 22

*LELAND, Jno. [1506–62] Itinerary, ed. Lucy Toulmin-Smith, 5 vols. ; maps s 4° Bell [1617] 07–10
Macmillan, *N.Y.* Vol. i, 18/ *n.* ($6 *n.*) ; ii, 12/ *n.* ($4 *n.*) ; iii, 10/6 *n.* ($3·50 *n.*) ; iv, 12/ *n.* ($4 *n.*) ; v, 18/ *n.* ($6 *n.*). An excellent and scholarly edn., fr. the MSS., of the itinerary thro' Engl. and Wales 'in or about the yrs. 1535–43', by 'the Father of English Topography' ; w. Appendices inclg. extrs. fr. LELAND's *Collectanea*, Indexes, and Glossary. Throws much light on the then vanishg. feudal period. Not prev. ed. since HEARNE's 2nd edn. of 1744 (9 vols., 8°). For Welsh portns. separ. *v.* **E** § 18.

LYSONS, Rev. D. + S. Magna Britannia : concise topogr. acc. of several counties of Gt. Brit., 6 vols. *o.p.* [*pb.* £27 4*s.* ; *w.* £5] 4° *London* 06–22
Usually bnd. into 7 or 8 vols. Vol. i. Beds., Berks, Bucks ; ii. Cambs., Chesh. ; iii. Cornw. ; iv. Cumberl. ; v. Derbysh. ; vi. Devonsh. [All pubd.]

MORYSON, Fynes [1566–1629] Itinerary, 4 vols.—*ut* **E** § 11

NICHOLS, J. Gough [ed.] Collectanea Topographica et Genealogica, 8 vols.—*ut* **G** § 22

POCOCKE, Bp R. [1704–65] Travels thro' Engld., ed. J. J. Cartwright, 2 v. [1750–1760] s 4° Camd. Soc. 88–9

TAYLOR, Jos. Journey to Edenborough [1705], ed. Wm. Cowan 6/ *n.* 8° Brown *Edin.* 04
Here first printed from the original MS. ; w. notes.

*Domesday Book* [survey of WILLIAM I, A.D. 1086]—*ut* **F** § 19

**Modern Topography and Description**—*v. also* **H** §§ 51, 76, *and inf.*, *passim*

ALLEN, Grant Science in Arcady 3/6 c 8° Routledge [92] 04

[BEECHING, Rev. H. C.] Provincial Letters, and other Papers 5/ *n.* c 8° Smith & Elder 06

BELLOC, Hilaire Hills and the Sea 6/ c 8° Methuen 06
Essays on Ely, Lynn, The Fen Country, Sussex, Engl. Channel, North Sea, etc.

COBBETT, Wm. [1762–1835] Rural Rides, ed. Pitt Cobbett, 2 vols. 12/6 c 8° Reeves & Turner [30] 94

,, Rural Rides, sel. & ed. J. H. Lobban [40 c. *n.* Putnam, *N.Y.*] 1/4 c 8° Camb. Press 08
Acc. of jys. on horseback in Surrey, Kent, Sussex, Hants, Berks, Oxfd., Bucks, Wilts, Somerset, Gloucs, Herefd., Salop, Worcs, Staffs, Leics, Hertfd., Essex, Suff., Norf., Cambs, Htgdn., Notts, Lincs, Yorks, Lancs, Durh., Northumb., recordg. acute observns. on economic and rural matters, soil, climate, produce, etc., w. reflectns. on politics : an excellent pict. of contemp. domestic affairs.

CREIGHTON, Bp M. Story of Some [=19] English Shires [accur. ; picturesque] 6/ *n.* r 8° R.T.S. [97] 03

DITCHFIELD, Rev. P. H., etc. The Counties of England, 2 v. ; 150 pl. [hist., antiqs.] 21/ *n.* 8° G. Allen 11

FLETCHER, J. S. The Enchanting North ; ill. (some col.) 2/6 *n.* c 8° Nash 08
Desultory notes on Northumb., Cumberl., Westmorel., Durham, Yorks.

HISSEY, J. J. —*ut inf.*, *s.v.* Roads

JAMES, Hy. Portraits of Places—*ut* **E** § 2

JESSOPP, Dr Aug. Studies by a Recluse : in cloister, town and country—*ut* **F** § 16

JOHNSON, Clifton Among English Hedgerows ; ill. $2 *n.* (8/6 *n.*) c 8° Macmillan [99] 07

LANE-POOLE, Stanley North-West and by North : Irish hills and Engl. dales 3/6 c 8° Simpkin 03

Le GALLIENNE, Rich. Travels in England ; ill. Herb. Railton 6/ ($1·50) c 8° Lane [00] 07
17 travel papers : Selborne, Winchester, Stonehenge, Stratford-on-Avon, Lechlade, etc.

**Geographical Manuals and Textbooks**—*v. also* **H** § 35

Cambridge County Geographies—*ut sup.*, *s.v.* Series

COLLETT, A. K. The Face of England [Citizen Bks. ; popular] 1/ c 8° Rivers

DAVIES, A. Morley The British Isles, 2 vols. 3/6 c 8° Macmillan 09
i : *England and Wales*, 2/6 ; ii : *Scotld. and Irtld.*, 1/. A good schl. bk., on heuristic lines ; w. exercises.

GEIKIE, Prf. Arch. Geography of British Isles [Macmillan's Geogr. Ser.] 1/ 18° Macmillan 89

GREEN, J. R. + Alice S. Short Geogr. of British Islands ; maps 3/6 c 8° Macmillan 89
An 'earth-picture' of surface of country, and acc. of its influ. on history and society life.

HAUGHTON, T. Descriptive, Physical, Industr. & Histor. Geogr. of Engl. & Wales 6/ c 8° Philip 93

HULL, Dr Edw. Contrib. to Physical Hist. of Br. Isles ; 27 maps 12/6 8° Stanford 82

JOWITT, L. Descriptive Geography of the British Isles 2/6 c 8° Black 09

JUKES-BROWN, A. J. The Building of the Brit. Islands ; ill. and 16 col. maps 12 / *n.* c 8° Stanfd. [88] 11
Shows order in wh. diff. pts. of Brit. Isls. emerged, and land-changes th. occurred at diff. periods.

*MACKINDER, H. J. Britain & the British Seas ; 6 maps & 132 ill. 7/6 *n.* ($2) 8° Clar. Press [02] 07
[Regions of the World.] Quite the best bk. fr. the mod. viewpt., presentg. in a most lucid manner a synthetic pict. of Britain's phys. hist., climatol, regional topogr., and histor. and econ. geogr. Strong on influ. of geogr. environmt. on history. A model of the regional treatmt. of a country.

„ Elem. Studies in Geogr., Bk. i : Our Own Islands ; maps & ill. 2 / c 8° Philip [07] 10
An admirable elem. schl.-bk. presentg. many ideas of above wk. adapted for children.

MILL, Dr H. R. [ed.] International Geography, Pt. i : Brit. Isles—*ut* **E** § 2

RAMSAY, Sir A. C. Physical Geology and Geography of Great Britain 10/6 p 8° Stanford [63] 94

RECLUS, Elisée Universal Geography : British Isles [tr.], well ill. 21 / r 8° Virtue 88

REYNOLDS, Joan B. Regional Geography : British Isles ; 85 ill. and diagrs. 2 / 8° Black
A good bk., doing for middle and upper classes what MACKINDER [*ut sup.*] does for advanced students.

RUDLER (F. W.) + CHISHOLM (G. G.) The British Isles—*in their* Europe, *ut* **E** § 11
Physical Features, rivers, geology, soil, climate, flora, fauna, ethnogr., religion, educ., traits, etc., etc.

*Historical Geography* —*v.* **F** § 16

## Guides

BADDELEY (M. J. B.) + WARD (C. S.) Thorough Guide Series ; maps [prices net] s 8° Nelson [*v.y.*] 02–10
*Bath and Bristol* 5/ | *Lake District* 5/ | *Orkney and Shetld.* 1/6 | *Scotland*, 3 vols. 14/ | *Wales*, 3 vols. 9/
*Eastern Counties* 3/6 | *Ireland*, 2 vols. 9/ | *Peak District* 3/ | *Surrey and Sussex* 3/6 | *Yorkshire*, 2 vols. 5/6
*Isle of Wight* 2/6 | *N. Devon and N. Corw.* 3/6 | *S. Devon and S. Cornw.* 4/
Very good for their detailed topography, routes for pedestrians, and coloured contour-maps.

BAEDEKER, Karl Great Britain ; 22 maps and 58 plans 10/6 *n.* s 8° Unwin [87] 10
$3 *n.* Scribner, *N.Y.* Ed. J. Findlay MUIRHEAD. Not very full on Scotland.

BLACK, A. and C. [pubs.] Beautiful Books ; ea. w. col. pl. and maps *v.pp.* sq 8° Black *v.y.*
*V.pp.* Macmillan, *N.Y.* Classified *inf.* and in **E** § 17 accg. to their localities. Chiefly British.

„ [pubs.] Guides ; maps and plans [prices net] *v.pp.* s 8° Black [*v.y.*] 00–10
*Bucks* 1/ | *Devonsh.* 2/6 | *Kent* 2/6 | *Scotld.* 7/6 [ch. ed. 1/] | *Sussex* 2/6
*Channel Islds.* 2/6 | *Dorsetsh.* 2/6 | *Lakes, English* 3/6 [ch. ed. 1/] | *Somerset* 2/6 | *Wales, N. and S.* ea. 3/6
*Cornwall* 2/6 | *Hants* 2/6 | *Surrey* 2/6 | *Also many* Towns.
*Derbysh.* 2/6 | *Ireld.* 5/ [ch. ed. 1/]

DENT & Co., J. M. [pubs.] County Guides, ed. G. A. B. Dewar ea. 4/6 *n.* f 8° Dent *v.y.*
*Hants and I. o. W.* ed. EDR. | *Norfolk* ed. W. A. DUTT | *Surrey* ed. Walt. JERROLD
*Lake Counties* ed. W. G. COLLINGWOOD
Ea. vol. has map, many ill. and plans. Pt. i of ea. deals w. hist. and scenery of the county, ii conts. arts. on nat. hist. and sport, in form of a gazetteer and guide-bk.

Highways and Byways Series—*ut sup.*

Little Guides : maps and ill. ea. 2/6 *n.* s 8° Methuen [*v.y.*] *v.y.*, *in. prg.*
A series of handy manuals on Counties or Districts, ea. contg. Gen. Introd. foll. by antiq. and histor. details of places. Arrgd. alphab. Incl. a few foreign.

MURRAY, Jno. [pub.] English Handbooks for Travellers ; maps and plans *v.pp.* s 8° Stanford [*v.y.*]
*Engl. and Wales*, 12/ ; *Berks*, 6/ ; *Bucks*, 6/ ; *Derby, Notts, Leics, Staff.*, 9/ ; *Hants*, 6/ ; *Herts, Hunts, Beds*, 7/6 ; *Ireld.*, 9/ ; *I. o. W.*, 2/6 ; *Lakes*, 6/ ; *Lancs*, 6/ ; *Lincs*, 7/6 ; *London : Environs*, 2 Pts., 21/ ; *Northants and Rutl.*, 7/6 ; *Oxf.*, 6/ ; *Scotld.*, 10/6 ; *Salop and Chesh.*, 6/ ; *Somerset*, 6/ ; *Surr.*, 6/ ; *Suss.*, 6/ ; *Wales, N. and S.*, ea. 6/ ; *Warw.*, 6/ ; *Wilts and Dors.*, 6/ ; *Yorks*, 14/. [Other vols. at present *o.p.*] A valuable and famous ser. of manls., takg. the districts by railway routes, and dealg. w. their antiquarian, architectural, and historical aspects w. accuracy and learning.

## Antiquities —*v.* G §§ 1*–4

## Atlases ; Maps

BACON, G. W. [ed.] Library Atlas of British Isles [124 maps] 42 / *n.* f° Bacon 09
Based on Ordn. Surv. ; incl. Colon. Supplt., Index-Gazetteer (50,000 names), descrns., etc.

BARTHOLOMEW, J. G. Royal Atlas of England & Wales : 70 col. maps & plans 16 / *n.* f° Newnes 00
A handsome atlas—political, eccles., populn., ry., geol., orograph.

* „ Survey Atlas of England and Wales ; 78 maps & 15 plans 70 / *n.* f° Geogr. Instit., *Edin.* 05
Ordn. Surv. red. to unif. scale of ½ in. to m. ; w. ry., commerc., hist., rainfall, etc., maps, and gloss. of components of place-names.

JOHNSTON, W. & A. K. [pubs.] Modern Atlas of Counties of Engl. and Wales 12/6 i 8° Johnston
58 col. maps, scale 7 miles to the inch. All maps drawn on *same scale.* Ea. map separ., 1*d.*

PHILIP, G. [ed.] Philip's Handy Atlas and Gazetteer of Brit. Isles 7/6 *n.* 4° Philip 09

*Maps :* Ordnance Survey of United Kingdom : maps Stanford [etc.] *v.y.*
(*a*) 1 *in. to m.*, 360 shts., 20 × 15 in., ea. 1/, col. 1/6 ; New Large Sheet Edn., 30 × 22 (shts. 1–97 ready), *in prg.* For Geolog. Edn. *v.* **H** § 35. (*b*) 2 *in. to m.*, 18 × 12, ea. 1/ to 1/6. (*c*) 4 *in. to m.*, 18 shts., 22½ × 16, ea. in outline 1/6 (col. same price) ; the set, folded in case, 60/. (*d*) 6 *in. to m.* (*County Maps*), ea. coverg. c. 6 sq. miles, ea. 1/. (*e*) 25 *in. to m.* (*Parish Maps*), ea. 3/. (*f*) 10½ *ft. to m.* (*Town Plans*), *v.pp.* (2/6 to 6/), Indexes, 3d. to 5d. (*d*) and (*e*) incl. every house and field, palings, footpaths, etc., (*e*) givg. area of ea. enclosure.

Catalogue of Ordn. Surv. Maps, Sectns., and Memrs. 6*d.* 8° Stanford [91]

„ of 6-in. and 25-in. Co. and Town Plans E. & W., 1/6 ; Indexes 1 / 8° Stanford 09

„ of 6-in. and 25-in. Co. Maps and Town Plans Scotl., 1 / ; Indexes 1 / 8° Stanford 09

„ of 6-in. and 25-in. Co. Maps and Town Plans Irel., 1 / ; Indexes 1 / 8° Stanford 09

WHITE, T. P. The Ordnance Survey of the U.K. [hist. and descr.] 5 / c 8° Blackwood 86

## Ethnology ; People —*v. also* **D** § 125, *s.v.* Social Psychology

BEDDOE, Dr J. The Races of Britain 21 / r 8° Trübner (Paul) 86

BOXALL, G. E. The Anglo-Saxon : a study in evolution 6 / c 8° Richards 02
Discusses the development of the Anglo-Saxon spirit in politics, and prophesizes its future progress.

CHADWICK, H. M. The Origin of English Nation ; 4 maps 7/6 *n.* 8° Camb. Press 07
$2·25 *n.* Putnam, *N.Y.* [Camb. Archæol. and Ethnolog. Ser.]

CREIGHTON, Bp Mandell — The English National Character [Romanes Lecture 1896] 2/ 8° Clar. Press 96

DEMOLINS, Edm. — Anglo-Saxon Superiority: to what it is due [tr.] 3/6 8° Leadenhall Press 98
$1·25 c 8° Scribner, *N.Y.* Attributes A.S. superiority to individualism as opposed to the collectivism of French race. A social study.

GOWEN, Aline — Anglo-Saxons and Others $1·50 12° Scribner, *N.Y.* 00
An attempt to point out the weaknesses of the race.

GUMMERE, Prf. Fcs. — Germanic Origins—*ut* **F** § 5

LUBBOCK, Sir [L'd AVEBURY] — The Races of the British Isles 2/6 s 4° Quaritch 87
Repr. of l'rs to *The Times*, w. rejoinders by J. BRYCE, and l'rs in suppt. by D'ke of ARGYLL, J. BEDDOE, HUXLEY, etc.

MACNAMARA, N. C. — Origin and Character of British People; 33 ill. 6/ c 8° Smith & Elder 00
A somewhat rambling work, opposing most previous theories on the subject.

MUNRO, J. — Story of British Race; ill. [Lib. of Usef. Stories] 1/ *n.* 12° Hodder [99] 09

ROBERTSON, C. G. — The Making of the English Nation [Oxford Manuals of English History] Blackie 95
Traces the workings of the various elements which have been combined to make the composite English nation—Iberians, Celts, Romans, Anglo-Saxons, Danes and Normans.

ROBERTSON, J. M. — The Saxon and the Celt—*v.* **D** § 142, *s.v.* Irish (Home-Rule) Question

ROEMER, J. — Origins of the English People, and English Language [compilation] 18/ 8° Bell 88

TILBY, A. Wyatt — The English People Overseas, 6 vols. *v.pp.* c 8° Constable 11 *in prg.*
i: *Amer.-Colonies*: 1584–1763 4/6 *n.* | iii: *Canada*: 1763–1867 6/ *n.* | v: *Australasia* *in prep.*
ii: *India*: 1600–1826 4/6 *n.* | iv: *Amer.-Tropics* *in prep.* | vi: *South-Africa* *in prep.*

*Celtic Ethnology* —*v.* **K** § 279, *s.v.* Linguistic Ethnology

**Gazetteer** —*v. also sup., s.v.* Atlases (BACON)

BARTHOLOMEW, J. G. — Survey Gazetteer of Brit. Isles; 48 maps 17/6 *n.* r 8° Newnes [87] 04
60,000 cities, towns, vills. parishes, etc., w. all Ry. Statns., P. O.'s, Co. Seats, Mills, Mines, Rivers, Lakes, Bays, Islds., Mtns., Ruins, etc.

CASSELL & Co. [pubs.] — Gazetteer of Gt. Brit. & Irel., 6 vols.; ill. & 60 maps ea. 5/ r 8° Cassell [94–8] 00
A useful bk., incl. all parishes and most places needed for ord. ref., much space given to antiqs. Fuller than BARTHOLOMEW.

**Abbeys** —*v. also* **I** §§ 119–20, *and inf., s.v.* Scenery (TURNER)

BONNEY, Rev. T. G. — Abbeys and Churches of Engl. and Wales; ill. *o.p.* [*pb.* 21/] 4° Cassell 87

BEATTIE, Dr W. — Castles and Abbeys of Engl., 2 vols.; 200 ill. 25/ i 8° Virtue [42–51]

CRAM, R. A. — The Ruined Abbeys of Gt. Britain; 67 pl. $2·50 *n.* r 8° Pott, *N.Y.* [06] 10
10/6 *n.* Gay & Hancock. A very well-wr. and well-ill. popular acc. of Beaulieu, Bolton, Byland, Dryburgh, Fountains, Gisburgh, Glastonbury, Jedburgh, Kelso, Kirkstall, Lindisfarne, Malmesbury, Melrose, Rievaulx, Whitby, St Mary's, York, by a prominent Amer. church-architect.

DIXON, H. C. — The Abbeys of Great Britain; 16 pl. 6/ *n.* c 8° Laurie 08
Concise and workmanlike accs. of over 60 abbeys.

DUGDALE, Sir Wm. [1605–86] — Monasticon, 8 vols.; 250 pl. [*pb.* & *w.* £25] f° March [1655–73] 49
The standard history of abbeys, monasteries, hospitals, etc., of England and Wales.

GASQUET, Dom F. A. — The Great Abbeys of England; 60 col. pl. 20/ *n.* s 4° Chatto 08
Col. pl. by Warwick GOBLE of the greater monastic houses of Engl., w. hist. and topogr. accounts by GASQUET.

HOWITT, Wm. + Mary — Ruined Abbeys and Castles of Gt. Brit.; 2 Ser.; photos. *o.p.* [*pb.* 42/] 4° Bennett 61–4

LANG, Elsie M. — Some Old English Abbeys; ill. 2/6 *n.* f 8° Laurie 08
A handy little bk. on Glastonbury, St Albans, Fountains, Tintern, Selby, Furness, Evesham.

TIMBS (J.) + GUNN (A.) — Abbeys, Castles, Anc. Halls of E. & W., 3 v. 10/6 *n.* m 8° Warne [70] 02
Their legendary lore and popular history. With 12 photogravures.

**Battle-Fields: Collectively** —*for* Individual Battles, *v.* **E** § 17, *passim*

BROOKE, R. — Visits to Fields of Battle in Engl. of 15th Cent. *o.p.* [*pb.* 15/] r 8° J. R. Smith 57

**Castles** —*v.* Houses, etc., *inf.*

**Cathedrals; Churches** —*v.* **I** §§ 119–120

**Cinque Ports:** *Collectively*

BURROWS, Prf. Montagu — The Cinque Ports; ill. [Historic Towns Ser.] 3/6 ($1·25) c 8° Longman [88] 95

Historical MSS. Commission: Report IV—*ut* **F** § 16

HUEFFER, Ford Madox — The Cinque Ports: historical and descriptive 63/ *n.* r 4° Blackwood 00
Excellent ill. by Wm. HYDE. History and topography, from a literary point of view.

Table Book of the Cinque Ports 10/6 4° Stock 05
Index to the decrees of the Courts of Brotherhood and Guestling, from 1433 to present time.

*Individually* —*v.* **E** § 17, *s.vv.* Dover, Hastings, Hythe, Romney, Rye, Sandwich, Winchelsea

**Coasts** —*v. also* **E** § 17 *passim*

County Coast Series: maps and ill. ea. 6/ *n.* c 8° Unwin 09 *sqq., in prg.*
*Cornwall Coast* [*ut* E § 17] A. L. SALMON | *Norfolk and Suffolk Coast* [*ut* E § 17] W. A. DUTT | *South Devon and Dorset Coast* [*ut* E § 17] S. HEATH

HARPER, C. G. [Am.] — The Cornish Coast; map and ill. 15/ *n.* 8° Chapman 10

" — The Dorset Coast; map and ill. 15/ *n.* 8° Chapman 05

" — The North Devon Coast; map and ill. 15/ *n.* 8° Chapman 08

" — The South Devon Coast; map and ill. 15/ *n.* 8° Chapman 07

HARPER, C. G. [Am.] The Somerset Coast ; map and ill. 15 / *n.* 8° Chapman 09
Ea. $6 *n.* Scribner, *N.Y.* Descrns. of scenery, bldgs., topogr., histor. assocns., etc., made dur. visits on bicycle and in boat. Ea. ill. by author and fr. old prints.

L'ESTRANGE, A. G. K. From Thames to Tamar : summer on S. coast *o.p.* [*pb.* 15 /] 8° Hurst 73

Round the Coast 10 /6 obl 4° Newnes 96
Large illns. of coast scenery, many of geographical value.

STANFIELD, C. [artist] Coast Scenery of England *o.p.* [*pb.* 21 /] 4° Virtue 73

TURNER, J. M. W. [artist] Coast Scenery—*ut inf.*, *s.v.* Scenery

WILLSON, Beckles Story of Lost England ; ill. 1 / 12° Newnes 02
[Lib. of Useful Stories.] Acc. of losses of English coast-line by erosion ; w. hist. of submerged portions.

*Coast-erosion* —*v.* **I** § 5

**Forests :** *Collectively*

COX, Dr J. C. The Royal Forests of England ; ill. [Antiquary's Bks.] 7/6 *n.* c 8° Methuen 05

GILPIN, Rev. W. [1724–1804] Forest Scenery, ed. F. G. Heath ; ill. [chfly. New Forest] 7/6 c 8° Low [1791] 82

**Harbours ; Sea-ports**

FINDEN, W. + E. Ports, Harbours & Watering Places of Great Britain, 2 vols. ; w. 120 steel pl. 42 / 4° Virtue [38] 42

HOLLAND, Clive From North Foreland to Penzance ; col. pl. M. Randall 12 /6 *n.* 4° Chatto 08
A moderately good, but discursive, acc. of the ports and harbours of the South Coast of England.

RUSKIN, Jno. Harbours of England ; 12 ill. J. M. W. Turner 6 / *n.* c 8° G. Allen [77]
Introd. T. J. WISE. Pocket Ed. 2/6 *n.*, 1/ *n.* Ch. Ed. (w. the ill. red.) 1/ *n.* [New Univ. Lib.] Routledge '07 (50 c. Dutton, *N.Y.*)

**Health and Holiday Resorts** —*v.* **H** * § 57

**Houses, Halls, Mansions, Castles :** *Collectively*—*v. also* Abbeys, *sup.* & **I** §§ 119–20

ALLINGHAM, [Mrs] Helen [art.] Happy England : 80 col. pl., w. l'rpr. by M. B. Huish 20 / *n.* sq 8° Black 03

„ [artist] The Cottage Homes of England : 64 col. pl. 21 / *n.* 4° Arnold 09
Former $6 *n.* Macmillan, *N.Y.* ; latter $7 *n.* Longman, *N.Y.* Excellent 'colour-books'.

BALCH, Eliz. Glimpses of Old English Homes ; 51 ill. 14 / ($3·50) 4° Macmillan 90
Penhurst, Arundel Castle, Hinchinbrooke, Eridge Castle, Chiswick House, Berkeley Castle, Highclere Castle, Osterley Pk.

*CLARK, G. T. Mediaeval Military Archit. in Engl., 2 v. ; 140 ill. 31 /6 8° Wyman 84
This, with MACKENZIE [*ut inf.*] as a supplement, form the best work on the subject in English.

D'AUVERGNE, E. B. The English Castles ; ill. 6/ *n.* c 8° ; Cheap Edn. 1/ *n.* 32° Laurie 08 ; 10

DITCHFIELD, Rev. P. H. The Manor Houses of England ; 150 ill. S. R. Jones 7 /6 r 8° Batsford 10
Deals w. typical examples of different kinds and in different counties ; many little known.

„ Vanishing England ; ill. F. Roe 15/ *n.* sq 8° Methuen 10
A record of all kinds of bldgs. (and social customs) wh. are gradually disappearing.

FEA, Allan Picturesque Old Houses 10 /6 *n.* 8° Bousfield 02
Numerous full-page photo-engravings of old castles, farm-houses, cottages, inns, etc. : letterpress of small value.

„ Secret Chambers and Hiding-Places ; ill. 5 / *n.* 8° Bousfield [01] 04
Historic, romantic, and legendary stories and tradns. about hiding-holes, secret chambers, etc.

„ Nooks and Corners of Old England ; ill. 10 /6 *n.* 8° Nash [07] 08
Old houses in Suffolk, Norfolk, the Midlands, the South-West, Derbysh., Yorks, Salop, Staffs.

„ Old English Houses : record of a random itinerary ; ill. 10 /6 *n.* 8° Secker 10

HALL, S. C. Baronial Halls & Picturesque Edifices of Engl., 2 v. ; pl. *o.p.* [*pb.* 147 /] f° Chapman [48] 58

HARVEY, A. English Castles & Walled Towns ; ill. [Antiquary's Bks.] 7/6 *n.* 8° Methuen 11

Historic Houses of the United Kingdom ; pl. and ill. [24 famous houses] 10 /6 4° Cassell 92

HODGES, Eliz. T. Some Ancient Engl. Homes & their Assocns. ; ill. 10 /6 *n.* s 4° Unwin 95
Largely based on MS. hist. of Berkeley Family wr. early in 17 cent. by Jno. SMYTH, of Nibley, and ed. Sir J. MACLEAN in 1883. An account of 10 old houses, 6 in Gloucs. and 4 Warwickshire—5 of wh. have belonged at one time or another to the great families of BERKELEY and FITZHARDINGE.

HOWITT, Wm. Visits to Remarkable & Notable Places ; ill. 3/6 ($1·25) c 8° Longman [39–41]
Includes visits to old halls, battle-fields, historic fields, places assoc. w. famous poetry, etc.

JEWITT (S. C.) + HALL (Ll.) Stately Homes of England, 2 Ser. ; 380 ill. ea. 21/ r 8° Virtue [74–7] 81

KING, Edw. Munimenta Antiqua : observns. on anc. castles, etc., 4 v. *o.p.* f° *London* 1799–1805

LATHAM, C. [art.] In English Homes ; ill; w. l'rpr. H. A. Tipping, 2 v. ea. 42 / *n.* f° Newnes 07

*MACKENZIE, Sir J. D. Castles of England : their story and structure, 2 vols. ; ill. *subscr.* 63 / *n.* i 8° Heinemann 97
Deals w. 660 castles, many still habitable, many in ruins, others of wh. only their history or site remains. 40 pl., 160 text-ill. and several plans. A valuable suppl. to CLARK'S *Military Architecture* [*ut sup.*].

MALAN, A. H. [ed.] Famous Homes of Great Britain & their Stories ; ill. 21 / *n.* ($7·50) r 8° Putnam 99

„ [ed.] More Famous Homes of Great Britain ; ill. 21 / *n.* ($7·50) r 8° Putnam 02

„ [ed.] Other Famous Homes of Great Britain ; ill. 21 / *n.* ($7·50) r 8° Putnam 02
Many excellent ill. These vols. cont. accs. of all the more important Brit. castles, etc., by the owners themselves in most cases. Repr. fr. *Pall Mall Mag.*

MORRIS, Rev. F. O. The Ancestral Homes of Britain; 40 col. pl. *o.p.* [*pb.* 31/6] 4° Bell 68

" Castles & Halls of England; col. pl. [Ser. ii of above] *o.p.* [*pb.* 31/6] 4° Bell 70

Moss, Fletcher The First [Second, Third, Fourth, and Fifth] Book of Pilgrimage to Old Homes, 5 Ser.; ea. w. c. 200 excellent ill. ea. 21/ *n.* r 8° Authur, *Didsbury* 01–10

NASH, Jos. Mansions of England in Olden Time, ed. C. Holme; 104 ill. 5/ *n.* f° *Studio* Off. [39–49] 06

TRISTRAM, A. Outram Moated Houses; 76 ill. Herb. Railton [25 houses] 12/6 *n.* 8° Methuen 10

TWYCROSS, E. Mansions of Engl. and Wales, 4 vols.; pl. *o.p.* 4° Ackermann 47–50

**Inns**

FRAPRIE, F. R. Little Pilgrimages among English Inns; ill. $2 c 8° Page, *Boston* 04

HACKWOOD, F. W. Inns, Ales, and Drinkg. Custs. of Old Engld.; ill. 10/6 *n.* 8° Unwin 09

HARPER, C. G. [Am.] The Old Inns of Old England, 2 vols.; ill. 42/ *n.* 8° Chapman 06

MASKELL (H. P.) + GREGORY (E. W.) Old Country Inns; ill. 7/6 *n.* 8° Pitman 10
Curious and miscell. informn. conc. inns in var. pts. of the country, espec. in the South.

*London Inns* —*v.* **E** § 17, *s.v.* Middlesex (London)

**Literary and Historical Landmarks**

BATES, Prf. Kath. L. Gretna Green to Land's End $2 *n.* c 8° Crowell, *N.Y.* 08
7/6 *n.* Richards. A literary journey, by an American lady, Prf. of English at Wellesley College.

BOCKETT, F. W. Some Literary Landmarks for Pilgrims on Wheels; ill. 3/6 *n.* f 8° Dent 01
$1·25 Lippincott, *Phila.* Notes of a cyclist's visits to Eversley, Selborne, the homes of SHELLEY, MILTON, Jane AUSTEN, etc.

HUISH, Marcus B. The American's Pilgrim's Way in England; ill. 20/ *n.* s 4° Fine Art Soc. 07
A very handsome vol., wr. round a ser. of 43 col. pl. by Eliz. M. CHETTLE (100 ill., ports., photos., and facss. bg. added), formg. a sort of guide to homes and memorials of founders of Virginia, New Engld., and Pennsylvania.

SALMON, Arth. L. Literary Rambles in the West of England 6/ *n.* c 8° Chatto 06
Cornwall (BORROW), Teignmouth (KEATS), Quantocks (WORDSWORTH), Clevedon (COLERIDGE, TENNYSON), Wilts (JEFFERIES), etc.

SHARP, W. Literary Geography 5/ *n.* 8° *Pall Mall Gaz.* Off. 06

STORY, A. T. American Shrines in England; ill. and 4 col. pl. 6/ c 8° Methuen 08
$2 *n.* Macmillan *N.Y.* 14 chs. on places in Engld. conn. w. WASHINGTONS, FRANKLIN, PENN, Pilgrim F'rs, HARVARDS, etc.

WOLFE, Dr T. F. A Literary Pilgrimage am. Haunts of Brit. Authors $1·25 12° Lippincott, *Phila.* 95

*London*—*v.* **E** § 17 *Oxford*—*v.* **E** § 17 *Edinburgh*—*v.* **E** § 19

**Palaces (Episcopal; Royal)**

English Episcopal Palaces; ill. 8° Constable 10 *in prg.*
Vol. i: *Province of Canterb.*, ed. R. S. RAIT [*ut* E § 17]. To be foll. by *Prov. of York, Roy. Palaces of Engld., of Scotl.* Overflow matter fr. the eccles. portions of *The Victoria County History.*

TOOLEY, Sar. A. Royal Palaces and their Memories; 49 pl. [$4·50 *n.* Wessels, *N.Y.*] 16/ *n.* i 8° Hutchinson 02

VENABLES, Can. E. Episcopal Palaces of England; 120 ill. A. Ansted 21/ *n.* r 8° Isbister 95

**Place-Names**—*v.* **K** § 120 **Parish Registers, Local Genealogy, etc.**—*v.* **G** § 22

**Rivers** —*v. also* **I** § 160: Angling

DEWAR, G. A. B. South Country Trout Streams—*ut* **I** § 160

EDWARDS, E. M. Severn to Tyne: story of six English rivers 2/6 c 8° Wesl. Conf. Off. 90

Industrial Rivers of the United Kingdom. By various experts; ill. 7/6 c 8° Unwin 88
Thames, Mersey, Tyne, Clyde, Wear, Avon, Southampton Water, Humber, Liffey, Usk, Tees, Severn, etc.

LEWIS, Saml., jun. Acc. of Rivers of Engl. and Wales [alphab. arrgd.] *o.p.* [*pb.* 8/6] s 8° Longman 55

PALMER, Sutton [artist] Rivers and Streams of England: 75 col. pl., w. l'rpr. A. G. Bradley [$6 *n.* Macmillan, *N.Y.*] 20/ *n.* 4° Black 09

Rivers of Great Britain: descriptive, historical, pictorial, 3 vols. By var. wrs.; profusely ill ea. 16/ 4° Cassell [89–90] 91–7
i: *The Royal River* [Thames]; ii: *East Coast*; iii: *South and West Coasts.* Pop. descrns. of the rivers and their tributaries.

*Avon* [Warw.]: QUILLER-COUCH (Sir A. T.) Warwickshire Avon; ill. 12/6 c 8° Osgood 92

*Axe* [Devon]: PULMAN (G. P. R.) Book of the Axe—*ut* **I** § 160

*Dart*: BROWN (W.) + CHARLTON (E. W.) River Dart [ser. of etchgs.] 15/ f° Virtue 90

*Dee*: HOWSON (Dn J. S.) + RIMMER (A.) River Dee: aspect & hist.; 93 ill. 7/6 8° Virtue [75] 81

*Granta; Cam*: FARREN (R.) [art.] Granta and Cam [etchgs.; *v.* Thames, *inf.*] 38/ f° Deighton, *Camb.* 80

*Ouse* [Beds]: FOSTER (A. J.) The Ouse 3/6 c 8° S.P.C.K. 92

*Ribble*: DOBSON (W.) Rambles by the Ribble, 3 Ser. ea. 1/ c 8° *Preston* [64] 77–83

*Tamar; Tavy*: BRAY (Mrs) Borders of Tamar and Tavy, 2 vols.—*ut* **B** § 23

*Thames*

BALL, J. Ivo Down the Silver Stream of Thames; col. pl. 1/ s 8° Photochrome Co. 02

BELLOC, Hilaire The Historic Thames; col. pl. A. R. Quinton 3/6 *n.* s 8° Dent [07] 09

BESANT, Sir Walt. Thames ; ill. [Fascin. of Lond. ; 90 c. Macm., *N.Y.*] 1/6 *n.* 12° Black 03
CHURCH, A. J. Isis and Thamesis ; ill. [Oxford to Henley] 16/ r 8° Seeley 85
CORNISH, C. J. The Naturalist on the Thames 7/6 r 8° Seeley 02
DICKENS, Chas., jun. Dictionary of the Thames 1/ 16° Macmillan [79]
FARREN, Rob. [artist] Thames, Isis, and Cam [etchings] *o.p.* [*pb.* 36/] 4° Macmillan 81
HALL, S. C. + Mrs S. C. The Book of the Thames ; ill. *o.p.* [*pb.* 21/] 4° Virtue [59] 78
HASLEHURST, E. W. [artist] The Silvery Thames : 60 col. pl., w. text W. Jerrold 15/6 4° Cooke, *Leeds* 06
HERRING, J. H. [artist] Thames Bridges fr. London to Hampton Court [etchings] 10/6 f° Pinder 85
HUTTON, Rev. W. H. By Thames and Cotswold ; map and c. 100 ill. 10/6 *n.* 8° Constable 03
The recreatns. of an Oxford don : antiquarian, descriptive, w. literary assocns. and allusns.
LAW, D. [artist] The Thames : Oxford to London [20 etchgs.] 31/6 4° Bell 81
LESLIE, G. D. [artist] Our River : artist's life on Thames ; w. 50 ill. 12/6 4° Bradbury [81] 88
LEYLAND, J. Thames Illustrated ; ill. [Richmond to Oxfd.] 10/6 *n.* 4° Newnes [97] 01
MENPES, M. [artist] Historic Thames ; w. l'rpr. G. E. Mitton [$6 *n.* Macm., *N.Y.*] 20/ *n.* sq 8° Black 06
PENNELL, Jos. + Eliz. The Stream of Pleasure ; c. 90 ill. [Oxon. to Lond.] 6/ 4° Unwin 91
ROBERTSON, H. R. [artist] The Upper Thames ; ill. *o.p.* [*pb* 21/] 4° Virtue 74
SENIOR, Wm. Thames fr. Oxfd. to the Tower ; 30 etchgs. F. S. Walker *o.p.* [*pb.* 63/ *n.*] 4° Nimmo (Routledge) 91
Thames (The) and its Story : fr. Cotswold to Nore ; ill. and maps 6/ ($2) c 8° Cassell 06
VINCENT, J. E. The Story of the Thames ; map and 16 pl. 7/6 *n.* s 8° Smith & Elder 09
Historical, literary, and personal assocns. of the river ; w. illns. fr. old pictures.
WACK, H. W. In Thamesland : rambles fr. source to sea ; ill. $3 *n.* (12/6 *n.*) 8° Putnam 06
WAY, T. R. [artist] The Thames fr. Chelsea to the Nore ; text by W. J. Bell 42/ *n.* 4° Lane 06
WYLLIE, W. L. [artist] Tidal Thames : 20 photogrs., w. l'rpr. Grant Allen 42/ *n.* f° Cassell [94] 96
„ [artist] London to the Nore Painted and Descr. [$6 *n.* Macm., *N.Y.*] 20/ sq 8° Black 05
*Tyne :* GUTHRIE (J.) River Tyne : hist. and resources ; ill. 10/6 8° *Newcastle* 80
PALMER, W. J. [artist] The Tyne and Tributaries ; 150 ill. *o.p.* [*pb.* 25/] i 8° Bell 82
*Wye :* HUTTON, Edw. Book of the Wye ; 20 col. pl. A. R. Quinton 7/6 *n.* 8° Methuen 11
PALMER, Sulton [art.] The Wye : 24 col. pl., w. l'rpr. A. G. Bradley 7/6 *n.* sq 8° Black

**Roads** —*v. also* **I** § 148 : Coaching ; **I** § 149 : Cycling ; **I** § 165 : Motoring.

BAINES, F. E. On Track of the Mail : reminiscences *o.p.* [*pb.* 7/6] c 8° Bentley 95
BURNABY, Evelyn A Ride from Land's End to John O'Groats *o.p.* [*pb.* 3/6] c 8° Low 93
COBBTET, Wm. Rural Rides—*ut sup.*, *s.v.* Modern Topography
HARPER, C. G. [Am.] Bath Road : hist., fashion, etc., on old highway 16/ 8° Chapman 99
„ Brighton Road : speed, sport, and hist. 18/ ($6·40 *n.*) 8° Chapman [92] 06
„ Cambridge, Ely, and King's Lynn Road 16/ 8° Chapman 02
„ Cycle Rides round London—*ut* **I** § 149
„ Dover Road : annals of an anc. turnpike 16/ 8° Chapman 95
„ Exeter Road : the West of Engl. highway 16/ ($6·40 *n.*) 8° Chapman 99
„ From Paddington to Penzance 16/ 8° Chatto 93
„ Great North Road : old mail-rd. to Scotl., 2 vols. 32/ 8° Chapman 01
„ Hastings Road & Happy Springs of Tonbridge 16/ ($6·40 *n.*) 8° Chapman 06
„ Holyhead Road : the mail-route to Dublin, 2 v. 32/ ($12·80 *n.*) 8° Chapman 02
„ Manchester and Glasgow Road, 2 vols. 32/ 8° Chapman 07
„ Newmarket, Bury, Thetford, and Cromer Rd. 16/ ($6·40 *n.*) 8° Chapman 04
„ Norwich Road : an E. Anglican highway 16/ 8° Chapman 01
„ Oxford, Gloucs, and Milfd. Haven Road, 2 vols. 32/ ($12) 8° Chapman 05
„ Portsmouth Road and its Tributaries 16/ ($6 *n.*) 8° Chapman 95
Scribner, *N.Y.* (where priced in Amer. money). All deal w. old coach-roads, and throw light on hist. of coachg., old inns, and topogr. of districts traversed. Ea. ill. by author and fr. old prints, etc. Ch. Edns. of *Bath, Brighton, Dover, Exeter, Norwich* and *Portsmouth* Roads, ea. 1/6 *n.* 32° Treherne '06–11.

HISSEY, Jas. Jno. [Am.] Across England in a Dog-Cart ; 20 ill. *o.p.* [*pb.* 16/] 8° Bentley [91] 91
From London to St David's and back.
„ Drive thro' England : 1,000 miles of rd.-travel *o.p.* [*pb.* 16/] 8° Bentley 85
„ An English Holiday with Car and Camera ; ill. 10/ *n.* ($3 *n.*) 8° Macmillan 08
„ On the Box Seat : London to Land's End *o.p.* [*pb.* 16/] 8° Bentley 86

HISSEY, Jas. Jno. [Am.] Over Fen & Wold : thro' fen-country ; 14 pl. & plan 10/ *n.* 8° Macmillan 98
,, A Holiday on the Road : Kent, Sussex, Surrey *o.p.* [*pb.* 16/] 8° Bentley 87
,, An Old-Fashioned Journey in England & Wales ; front. 10/ *n.* 8° Macmillan 84
,, On Southern English Roads ; 16 ill. and plan 10/ *n.* 8° Macmillan 96
,, Through Ten English Counties ; 16 ill. and plan 16/ 8° Bentley 94
Record of a driving tour thro' Surrey, Hants, Wilts, Gloucs, Worcs, Herefordsh., Salop, Warwicksh., Oxfordsh., Bucks.
,, Tour in Phaeton thro' Eastern Counties *o.p.* [*pb.* 16/] 8° Bentley 89
,, Untravelled England ; 24 pl. 10/ *n.* ($4·50 *n.*) 8° Macmillan 06
,, The Charm of the Road : Engl. & Wales ; 28 pl. & map 10/ *n.* 8° Macmillan 10
Accs. of a ser. of driving-tours by an Amer. thro' Engl. counties, w. descrns. of scenery and places traversed. 1906 and 1908 vols. in motor-car.
HUDSON, W. H. Afoot in England 6/ *n.* 8° Hutchinson [09] 11
*Wayfaring* —*v. also* **D** § 127, *s.v.* Vagrancy
DAVIES, R. [ed.] Life of Marmaduke Rawdon, of York, w. notes s 4° Camden Soc. 63
Conts. curious details of travelling in 17th cent. in England as well as in Europe and America.
*JUSSERAND, J. J. English Wayfaring Life in Middle Ages [tr.]—*ut* **F** § 21
*Pilgrims' Way*—*v.* **E** § 17, *s.v.* Kent *Roman Roads* and *Roman Wall*—*v.* **G** § 2

**Sanctuaries**

COX, Dr J. C. Sanctuaries and Sanctuary Seekers of Mediaev. Engld. 15/ *n.* 8° G. Allen 11
DE' MAZZINI, Thos. Jno. Sanctuaries [by Libn., Wm. Salt Lib., Stafford] *o.p.* 1 8° *Stafford* 87

**Scenery** —*v. also sup.*, *s.v.* Coasts

ALLINGHAM, Mrs H. [art.] Happy Engl. : w. l'rpr. M. B. Huish [$6 *n.* Macm., *N.Y.*] 20/ *n.* sq 8° Black 03
Beautiful Britain : scenery and splendours of United Kingdom 21/ l 4° S.P.C.K. 96
196 photographic plates of fine scenes in Gt. Britain ; with explanatory letterpress.
CASSELL & Co. [pubs.] Our Own Country, 6 vols. ; ill. *o.p.* [*pb.* 7/6 ea.] 4° Cassell 79–83
,, [pubs.] Picturesque Europe, vols. i–ii : Gt. Brit. and Irel.—*ut* **E** § 11
,, [pubs.] Brit. Isles, depicted by Pen & Camera, 3 vols. ; ill. (same col.) ea. 21/ *n.* f° Cassell 04–5
EMERSON, P. H. Pictures fr. Life in Field and Fen [20 photogravs.] 63/ f° Bell 87
FOSTER, Birket [art.] Picts. of Engl. Landscape : 30 pl., w. l'rpr. Tom Taylor *o.p.* [*pb.* 21/] r 4° Routledge 63
,, Pictures of Rustic Landscape ; w. selns. ed. Davidson ; 30 ill. *o.p.* [*pb.* 10/6] r 8° Nimmo 95
Great Britain and Ireland : illustrated by pen and pencil [a ' table-bk. '] 28/ r 8° R.T.S. 94
HOWITT, Wm. Rural Life in England ; ill. Bewick + S. Williams *o.p.* [*pb.* 12/6] m 8° Longman [37] 62
Sports, gardens, old houses, farmers, farm servts., habits and amusemts. of the people, inns, etc.
MANNING (S.) + GREEN (Rev. S. G.) Engl. Pictures, drawn w. Pen & Pencil ; ill. 8/ i 8° R.T.S. [77] 89
ORROCK, Jas. [artist] Old England : 80 col. pl., w. text by W. Shaw Sparrow 24/ *n.* 4° Nash 08
Attempt to present Art and Landscape as Social History—influ. of roads and bridges, how they built in old Engl., etc.
TURNER, J. M. W. [art.] Picturesque Views in Engl. and Wales : 96 autotypes, 3 v. *o.p.* [*pb.* 126/] f° Bell [27–35] 72
Also separately : *Landscapes* [40 pl.] 52/6 ; *Castles and Abbeys* [32 pl.] 42/ ; *Coast Scenery* [24 pl.] 31/6.
,, Southern Coast of Engl. : 40 line-engrs., w. Introd. M. B. Huish 73/6 f° Virtue [14–27] 92
Omits dwgs. by other artists than TURNER wh. appd. in orig. wk. ; and orig. l'rpr. by W. COMBE (authr. of *Dr Syntax*) is replaced by descr. notes.
VALENTINE, L. [ed.] Picturesque England : landmks. & hist. haunts ; ill. 10/6 s 4° Warne [90] 93
Selections of descriptions ' in lay and legend, song and story '. Popular and moderately good. 10 photogravs. and 140 ill.

*Preservation of ' Natural ' Monuments*

CONWENTZ, H. Care of Natural Monuments ; 10 ill. 2/6 *n.* c 8° Camb. Press 09
$1 *n.* Putnam, *N.Y.* Classes amg. monumts. exx. of beautiful scenery, characteristic soil formns., rare species of flora and fauna, etc.
*Study of Scenery* —*v. also* **E** § 2, *s.v.* Study of Scenery (MARR)
AVEBURY, L'd The Scenery of England and its Causes ; ill. 6/ ($2·50 *n.*) c 8° Macmillan [02] 04
On relationship betw. form of land and its structure : largely geological. Pleasantly wr. and well ill. Cf. also his *Scenery of Switzerl.* [*ut* **E** § 28].
MACKINTOSH The Scenery of England and Wales
Refers the configuration of England mainly to marine action.

**Seas**

BELLOC, Hilaire Hills and the Sea—*ut sup.*, *s.v.* Modern Topography
RUSSELL, W. Clark [ed.] The British Seas : picturesque notes ; ill. 6/ c 8° Seeley [92] 93
Articles by var. wrs., repr. fr. *The Portfolio*, w. ill. after J. C. HOOK, Hy. MOORE, Colin HUNTER, and others : some very fine.
*North Sea :* WOOD (Walt.) North Sea Fishers & Fighters ; ill. & col. pl. F. H. Mason 10/6 *n.* 8° Paul 11

**Towns ; Streets ; Villages**

ALLEN, Grant County and Town in England ; map 6/ c 8° Richards 01
Deals w. origin of 30 counties and 18 towns, and traces hist. of an imag. town fr. earliest times. Introd. F. York POWELL.
Ancient Cities : ed. B. C. A. Windle ; ill. ea. 4/6 *n.* c 8° Methuen *v.y.*
Ea. vol. a hist. and a guide combined, with an Itinerary appended.

| | | | | | |
|---|---|---|---|---|---|
| *Bristol* [*ut* **E** § 17] | A. HARVEY | *Dublin* [*ut* **E** § 17] | S. A. O. FITZPATRICK | *Shrewsbury* [*ut* **E** § 17] | T. AUDEN |
| *Canterbury* [*ut* **E** § 17] | Dr J. C. COX | *Edinburgh* [*ut* **E** § 17] | M. G. WILLIAMSON | *Wells and Glastonbury* [*ut* **E** § 17] | T. S. HOLMES |
| *Chester* [*ut* **E** § 17] | B. C. A. WINDLE | *Lincoln* [*ut* **E** § 17] | E. M. SYMPSON | | |

ANDREWS, Wm. Old English Towns; ill. [28 towns; Cathedr. Ser.; *v.* Lang, *inf.*] 6/ *n.* c 8° Laurie 09
COLLINS, W. W. [art.] Cathed. Cities of Engl.: 60 col. pl., w. l'rpr. G. Gilbert 16/ *n.* 8° Heinemann 05
DITCHFIELD, Rev. P. H. Story of our English Towns [scrappy] *o.p.* [*pb.* 6/] c 8° Redway 97
DORAN, Dr J. Memories of our Great Towns; 38 ill. [1860–77] 7/6 c 8° Chatto 78
FLENLEY, R. [ed.] Six Town Chronicles of England, ed. fr. MSS. 7/6 *n.* ($2·50) 8° Clar. Press 11
FREEMAN, Prf. E. A. English Towns & Districts; ill. [addresses & essays] *o.p.* [*pb.* 14/] 8° Macmillan 83
Historic Towns Series —*ut* **E** § 2
HOWELLS, W. D. —*ut inf.*, *s.v.* England as Seen by Foreigners
LANG, Elsie M. Old English Towns; ill. [Cathedral Ser.] 6/ *n.* c 8° Laurie 11
Chichester, Ely, Ripon, Exeter, Bristol, L'pl., Dover, etc. Companion to ANDREWS, *sup.*
MOZLEY, Rev. T. Reminiscences of Towns, Villages, & Schools, 2 v. *o.p.* [*pb.* 18/] c 8° Longman 85
RIMMER, A. Ancient Streets and Homesteads; ill. *o.p.* [*pb.* 10/6] 8° Macmillan [77] 79
„ Our Old Country Towns; 54 ill. 3/6 16° Chatto [81] 98

*Villages:* ALLINGHAM (Mrs H.)—*in her* Happy England, *ut sup.*, *s.v.* Scenery
DITCHFIELD, Rev. P. H. English Villages; 100 ill. [antiquarian] 2/6 *n.* c 8° Methuen [02]
„ The Charm of the English Village; 150 ill. S. R. Jones 7/6 *n.* 8° Batsford 08
*Walled Towns* —*v. sup.* Castles

**Social and Rural Life** —*v. also sup.*, *s.v.* Early Topogr., **D** § 117*, **F** §§ 19–27, *passim*
ANDREWS, Wm. [ed.] Bygone England: social studies; ill. 6/ 8° Andrews, *Hull* 92
BESANT, [Sir] Walt. Fifty Years Ago; 144 ill. 5/ c 8° Chatto [88] 92
$2·50 Harper, *N.Y.* Pictures of the year 1837, the people, society, school, tavern, club, etc.
CAPES, W. W. Scenes of Rural Life in Hampshire—*ut* **E** § 17, *s.v.* Hampshire (Bramshott)
COBBETT, Wm. [1762–1835] —*in his* Rural Rides, *ut sup.*, *s.v.* Modern Topography
ELLIS, Annie R. Sylvestra: studies of manners in Engl., 2 v. [1770–1800] 21/ c 8° Bell 82
A quaint and interesting acc. of Engl. university, cathedral, provincial and metrop. life in 18th cent.
ESCOTT, T. H. S. Social Transformations of the Victorian Age 6/ 8° Seeley 97
A rewr. versn. of his *England: its people, polity, and pursuits* [1879], essentially a new wk.: chatty, informg., and marked by genial optimism.
FIENNES, Celia Thro' England in a Side-Saddle [*temp.* Wm. + Mary]—*ut sup.*, *s.v.* Early Topography
FOWLER, J. K. [' Rusticus '] Echoes of Old Country Life; port. and ill. 10/6 i 8° Arnold 92
$2·50. Macmillan, *N.Y.* Recollns. of sports, coaching, posting, early railways, society, politics, farming and country life and manners in middle 19 cent. by the former proprietor of White Hart Hotel and Prebendal Farms, Aylesbury, a prominent shorthorn breeder and poultry breeder.
„ Recollections of Old Country Life 10/6 ($3) 8° Longman 94
„ Records of Old Times; 9 ill. 10/6 8° Chatto 98
Historical, social, political, sporting, and agricultural.
GOLDSMITH, Oliver [1728–74] Citizen of the World, ed. Austin Dobson, 2 v. 10/6 *n.* pott 8° Dent [1762] 91
[Temple Lib.] A scholarly, accur., and pretty little edn., full of illustrative learng. and happy research. Imaginary letters fr. a 'Chinese Philosopher' resident in Lond. to his friends in the East. Contemp. criticism and satire on Engl. life and manners in middle 18th cent.
GOULD, Rev. S. Baring- Old Country Life; 67 ill. 6/ c 8° Methuen [90] 92
$3 Lippincott, *Phila.* Old country-families, co.-houses, co.-dances, co.-parsons, etc. Healthy readg., full of quaint stories.
„ An Old English Home and its Dependencies; ill. 6/ c 8° Methuen 98
A gossipy acc. of old-fashioned rural life, w. pretty sketches by F. B. BOND.
HUTTON, Cath. Reminiscences of a Gentlewoman of the Last Century—*ut* **F** § 26
Contains a lively picture of provincial life in the 18th century.
Inedited Tracts ill. Manners, Opins. and Occupns. of Englishmen in 16–17 Cent.; ill.
[1579–1618] s 4° Roxburghe Lib. 68
KEBBEL, T. E. The Old and the New: English country life 5/ c 8° Blackwood 91
Descrs. the changes of previous generatn. in spirit of *laudator temporis acti:* a sort of 19 cent. reprodn. of BURKE's lament over the Age of Chivalry, dealg. w. country clergy, gentlemen, farmers, peasantry, and concl. w. ch. on 18th cent. as age of repose and tranquillity.
PAULI, Dr Reinhold Pictures of Old England [tr.]—*ut* **F** § 19
RAYMOND, Walt. English Country Life; 16 col. pl. Wilf. Ball 5/ *n.* c 8° Foulis, *Edin.* 10
Intimate sketches of village life (probably in Somerset), sympathetically and lovingly set down.
*Peasant-Life*—*v.* **D** § 119, *s.v.* Agric. Labourer *Shakespeare's Engld.*—*v.* **K** § 24 *Wayfaring*—*v. sup.*, *s.v.* Roads

**England as seen by Foreigners, Scotsmen, Colonials, and Americans**
SMITH, Edw. [ed.] Foreign Visitors to England, & What they have Thought of us
[Bk. Lover's Lib.; 17–18 Cent.] 4/6 f 8° Stock 89

**Scotsmen**
MACRITCHIE, Rev. Wm. Diary of Tour thro' Gt. Britain: 1795 6/ c 8° Stock 97
Plain diary of the jy. of a yg. Scot. fr. Clunie to Lond. and back, by coach and on ft. Ed. w. Introd. and notes Dav. MACRITCHIE [gt. neph.].
MILLER, Hugh [1802–56] First Impressions of England and its People 3/6 c 8° Nimmo, *Edin.* [47] 89
Acc. (w. shrewd observns. on social condns.) of jy. thro' Newc. Doncaster, York, to Midlds. and thro' N.-W.

**Colonials:** *Australians*
ABBOTT, J. H. M. An Outlander in England 6/ c 8° Methuen 05

HOGAN, J. F. The Australian in London and America *o.p.* [*pb.* 6/] c 8° Ward & Downey 89
MACK, Louise An Australian Girl in London [superficial] 6/ c 8° Unwin 02
Old Roof-Tree (The): letters of Ishbel to her Half-bro' Mark Latimer 5/ *n.* ($1·50 *n.*) 8° Longman 06
L'rs. of an Austral. lady, dealg. chfly. w. the 'chaos of misery th. underlies Britain's social syst.'.
PARKES, [Sir] H. Australian Views of England during 1861–2 *o.p.* [*pb.* 3/6] 12° Macmillan 69
*Canadians:* SMITH (Prf. Goldwin) A Trip to England 3/6 (75 c.) 32° Macmillan 92
An admirable summary, for intelligent inquirer, of characteristics of Engl. landscape and history.
Ten Years in Upper Canada in Peace and War [1805–15] 10/6 8° Unwin 91
Letters of Thos. RIDOUT, ed. by Mrs M. EDGAR [dau.]. Give acc. of struggle in Canada dur. war w. U.S., and contain RIDOUT'S descrn. of his stay in Engl. 1811-12, giving a good view of what life in both Lond. and Oxfd. was in those days.

**Americans**

Americans in Europe By One of Them $1 12° Tait, *N.Y.* 93
BROWN, Alice By Oak and Thorn: recd. of Engl. days $1·25 16° Houghton, *Boston* 96
*COLLIER, Price England and the English 7/6 *n.* 8° Duckworth [09] 10
$1·50 *n.* Scribner, *N.Y.* One of best and fairest Amer. estimates of English. By Amer. resident in Engld. Deals mainly w. minor affairs of life.
COOK, Joel England, Picturesque and Descriptive; ill. $5 *n.* 8° Coates, *Phila.* 99
An itinerary (in 10 tours) to most approved localities in Engl. and Wales. Map and 50 excellent photo. pl.
DAVIS, R. H. Our English Cousins; ill. $1·25 c 8° Harper, *N.Y.* 94
The Derby, Ascot, Henley, a general election, undergrad.-life at Oxon., London aspects, etc.
DORR, Julia C. R. The Flower of England's Face [sympathetic sketches] 75 c. (3/) 32° Macmillan 95
,, A Cathedral Pilgrimage—*ut* **I** § 119
DUNCAN, Sara J. An American Girl in London; ill. $1·50 c 8° Appleton, *N.Y.* 91
7/6 Chatto. Satirizes Londoners and London w. much liveliness and some truth. Ch. Edn. 25 c. Rand & McNally, *Chicago* '91.
EMERSON, R. W. English Traits—*ut* **K** § 90
Lectures on the race, ability, manners, truth, character, wealth, religion, etc., of England.
HAWTHORNE, Nat. Our Old Home; *and* Engl. Note Bks. [posth.] [= vols. vii–viii of 'Wks.'] ea. $2 12° Houghton, *Boston* [63–70] 83
,, Our Old Home: Ill. Edn., 2 v.; w. photogravs. $4 8° Houghton, *Bost.* [63] 91
English travel-sketches, wr. dur. his resid. as Am. Consul at Lpl., 1853–7. Ch. Edn., ill. T. E. MACKLIN, 2/6 c 8° W. Scott '94.
HOLMES, Oliver W. Our 100 Days in Europe [repr. fr. 'Harper's Mag.'] $1·50 c 8° Houghton, *Bost.* [87] 93
HOPPIN, Dr J. M. Old England: scenery, art, people $1·75 16° Houghton, *Boston* [67] 90
HOWELLS, W. D. Certain Delightful English Towns; ill. $3 *n.* (10/6) 8° Harper 06
Plymouth, Exeter, Bath, Wells, Bristol, Folkestone, Kent, Oxfd., Chester, Malvern, Worcs, Herefd., etc., w. 'country between'.
,, Seven English Cities $2 *n.* (10/6) 8° Harper 09
Liverpool, Manchester, Sheffield, York, Doncaster, Durham, and Boston.
,, London Films—*ut* **E** § 17, *s.v.* Middlesex (London)
JAMES, Hy. English Hours; 92 ill. Jos. Pennell 10/ *n.* 8° Heinemann 05
$3 Houghton, *Boston.* Apprec. and sympath. crit. [reprs., mostly wr. bef. 1880] by a liter. man resid. in Rye—not a typical Amer.-in-Eur.
JOHNSON, C. Among English Hedgerows; ill. $2 *n.* (8/6 *n.*) c 8° Macmillan 00
Interestg. observns. by an Amer. pedestrian on Engl. rural life and manners, scenery, bldgs., etc.
STILLMAN, W. J. An American's Reverie over London—*in his* Old Rome and the New, *ut* **K** § 84
The impressns. of a cultivated and sympathetic Amer. on enterg. London for first time and on its after-acquaintance.
TYLER, Moses Coit Glimpses of England: social, polit., literary $1·25 (5/) c 8° Putnam 98
WHITE, R. Grant England Without and Within $2 c 8° Houghton, *Boston* [81] 82
Informal, matter-of-course, untouristlike chronicles.
WINTER, Wm. Gray Days and Gold; 12 pl. and 100 ill. $2·50 16° Macmillan [94] 96
A pleasant narrative of a journey to England and Scotland by an American who is almost an Anglomaniac.

**Frenchmen:** 'DARYL (Philippe)' [= P. GROUSSET] Public Life in Engld. [tr.] *o.p.* [*pb.* 2/6] c 8° Routl. 84
ESQUIROS, Alph. English at Home [tr.], Ser. i, 2 v.; Ser. ii–iii, ea. v. *o.p.* [*pb.* 39/] c 8° Chapman 61–3
FAUJAS DE ST FOND, B. Journey thro' Engl. & Scotl. to Hebrides in 1784, tr. [1799], ed. Sir Arch. Geikie; w. memr. of author, 2 vols. 21/ *n.* 8° Hopkins, *Glasgow* 07
d'HUMIÈRES, Vicomte Rob. Through Isle and Empire, tr. A. T. de Mattos 6/ c 8° Heinemann 05
$1·40 *n.* Doubleday, *N.Y.* Acc. of visits to Engld., India and other pts. of the Empire; by a friend to England and the English.
JUSSERAND, J. J. —*in his* English Essays from a French Pen [tr.], *ut* **F** § 16
*A Jy. to Scotld. in* 1435 [based on Rept. of Maître Regnault GIRARD, Kt.]; and tr. of *A Jy. to Engld. in* 1663 [by Saml. SORBIÈRES, friend and admirer of HOBBES]—a bk. much discussed on its first appearance], etc.
LAUGEL, Auguste England, Political and Social, tr. J. M. Hart $1·50 12° Putnam, *N.Y.* 74
MAUREY, Gabr. Across the Channel: life and art in London [tr.] 5/ c 8° G. Allen 96
'O'RELL, Max' [= Paul BLOUET] John Bull and his Island 2/6 c 8° Field & Tuer [83] 85
,, John Bull's Womankind 2/6 c 8° Field & Tuer 84
By a French teacher in London, 'taking off' the English in a good-natured, semi-humorous way.
SAUSAURE, César de A Foreign View of England in the Reigns of Georges I & II 10/6 *n.* c 8° Murray 02
384 pp. Many ill. 16 letters giving an account of London and England in 1725–1729; tr. by Mme. van Muyden.

TAINE, H. A. Notes on England, tr. W. F. Rae [$2·50 Holt, *N.Y.*] 5/ c 8° Chapman [72] 85
A very interestg. record of his visit of 1862, treatg. of home-life, social life, character, amusemts., educn., etc.

VILLARS, P. English Provinces: a picturesque survey [tr.]; 200 ill. *o.p.* [*pb.* 7/6] r 8° Routledge 87

" Scotland & Ireland: a picturesque survey [tr.]; 200 ill. *o.p.* [*pb.* 7/6] r 8° Routledge 87

" Sketches of England [tr.]; ill. Myrbach 21/ 4° Virtue 91
By the then London Correspondent of *Le Journal des Débats.*

VOLTAIRE, F. M. A. Letters on England [tr.] [Cassell's National Lib.] 6*d. n.* (25 c. *n.*) 18° Cassell. [89] 01

Jusserand, J. J. One More Documt. conc. V's Visit to Engl.—*in his* Engl. Essays [tr.], *ut sup.*

**Germans:** BRAND (W. F.) London Life Seen w. Germ. Eyes 2/ *n.* p 8° Siegle [87] 02

HENTZNER, Paul Travels in Engld. dur. rn. of Q. Eliz. [in 1598] 6*d. n.* (25 c. *n.*) 18° Cassell [1629] 89
[Cassell's Natl. Lib.] Orig. wr. in Latin: first tr. for Hor. WALPOLE by Rich. BENTLEY (son of Dr BENTLEY) *Strawb. Hill*, 1757.

KIELMANSEGG, C't F. Diary of a Journey to England: 1761–62; ill. 5/ *n.* ($2) c 8° Longman 02
Account of the experiences of a Hanoverian and his brother, who attended the Coronation of GEORGE iii.

POMERANIA, Pp. Jul., D'ke of [16–17 cent.] Diary of Travels: Engl. portion, ed. Dr v. Bülow + Wilf. Powell 8° Roy. Histor. Soc.
The *Diary*, after having been lost since the times of the Napoleonic wars, was in 1894 discovered in Berlin.

RODENBERG, Julius England: literary & social, fr. Germ. pt.-of-view [tr.] *o.p.* [*pb.* 14/] 8° Bentley 75

RYE, W. B. [ed. & tr.] Engld. as seen by Foreigners in days of Eliz. & Jas. I. *o.p.* [*pb.* 15/] 8° J. R. Smith 65
Trs. of *Journals* of two Dukes of Wirtemberg [1592 and 1610], ill. of Shakespeare, w. tr. extrs. fr. other accs. 1558–1617.

**Russians:** 'Vasili (C't P.)' The World of London [tr.] 6/ c 8° Low 85

**Spaniards; Portuguese**

GONZALES, Man. London in 1731 [Cassell's Nat. Lib.] 6*d. n.* (25 c. *n.*) 18° Cassell 88

MARTINS, Oliveira England of To-day: letters of a traveller [tr.] 5/ c 8° G. Allen 96
Tr. of *A Ingilterra de Hoje* (*Lisbon* 93): a caricature, tho' intended as serious criticism, based on superficial observn. of a poorly equipped critic.

**Swedes**

*KALM, Pehr. Acc. of Visit to Engld. on way to America [tr.] 12/ *n.* ($5) 8° Macmillan 92
KALM, son of a Swedish minister, travd. in Norw., Engl., and Amer. in interests of Roy. Swed. Ac. of Sci. 1747–51. Am. portn. of wk. was tr. into Engl. by Rev. Reinh. FORSTER in 18 cent.; but Engl. portn. is here first tr. It is even of greater interest, prob. transcendg. in completeness and accuracy any similar productn. of its age. His wk. in Engl. was carried on fr. 4 centres: Gravesend, Lond., Woodfd., and Little Gaddesden (Herts.). It is of great value for rural econ. of the country. Ill. and 2 maps.

**Orientals:** *Chinese*

WO CHANG England thro' Chinese Spectacles: extrs. fr. Journal [tr.] 6/ c 8° Cotton Press *n.d.* 97
A Chinaman's criticism of Engl. condns., social, econ., legal, educ., financial, criminal, etc.

YUAN HSIANG-FU Those Foreign Devils, tr. and ed. W. H. Wilkinson 2/6 c 8° Leadenhall Press 91
Views of a Celestial on England and Englishmen; rather prosaic. The edr's notes are the best thing in the bk.

*Indians:* ABDUR RAZZAK Native Officer's Diary [tr.] 8° Higginbotham, *Madras* 95
Tr. of Diary (in Hindustani) of one of 8 non-com. offrs. sel. fr. Ind. cavalry to supply gd.-of-honr. to Qu.-Empress at openg. Imper. Inst. (May '93) and marr. of DUKE OF YORK (July '93). Crude in comp., confused in ideas, but not uninstructive.

BEG, Subadar Mohammad My Jubilee Visit to London [tr.] 3/ 8° Thacker, *Bombay* 99

BHAGVAT SINH JEE, Sir Journal of a Visit to England [1883] s 8° *Bombay* 86

JAGATJIC SINGH, Raja of Kalpurthala My Travels in Europe and Amer.; ports. *o.p.* [*pb.* 21/] 4° Rout. 96
Diary of a yg. Sikh Prince, one of most honoured represves. of gt. feudatories of Brit. Ind. Emp. at openg. of Imper. Inst. and the marr. of D'ke of York. Wr. in excell. Engl,'givg. evidce. of really liberally educ. mind and habits of shrewd observn.

LALA BAIJNATH England and India: impressions of persons and things, Engl. and Indian 8° Jehangir Karani, *Bombay* 94
Conts. a frank but not unfriendly criticism of things English; w. notes on France, Switz., Italy and Ceylon.

MAHTAB, B. C. Impressions: diary of Eur. tour [pp. 102–220 Engl.] 6/ *n.* 8°

MALABARI, Behramji M. The Indian Eye on English Life 3/6 c 8° Constable [93] 94
A v. interestg. acc. of Engl. life and manners as seen by a cultured and observt. Parsee and his servt. 'Crocodile'—friendly but by no means uncrit.: it is in reality what MONTESQUIEU's *Lettres Persanes* [*ut* **K** § 91] and other liter. apologues of a kind so popular last cent. only pretended to be.

PANDIAN, Rev. T. B. England to an Indian Eye 1/ c 8° Stock

PILLAI, G. D. London and Paris through Indian Spectacles 8° Vaijayanti Press, *Madras* 98
A humorous view of London life, written originally for an Indian public.

*Japanese:* BERKELEY (C. H.) [ed.] Japanese Letters 6/ c 8° Murray 91
Said to be sel. fr. corresp. of two Japanese, TOKIWARA and YASHIRI. Deals in a very interesting and trenchantway w. some of princ. modern questions in theology, philosophy, morals and economics wh. are agitating the Western mind. A sort of new ed. GOLDSMITH's *Citizen of the World!* [*ut sup.*, *s.v.* Social Life]. *Vide also* **E** § 17, *s.v.* London (MARKINO).

*Persian:* NASIR AL-DIN, Shah Diary dur. Tour thro' Europe [tr.] [1874] *o.p.* [*pb.* 12/] c 8° Murray 74

" Diary during Journey to Europe [tr.] [1878] *o.p.* [*pb.* 12/] 8° Bentley 79

## 17: GREAT BRITAIN AND IRELAND (*b*): ENGLAND ACCORDING TO COUNTIES

**Bedfordshire**

FOSTER, Alb. J. Bunyan's Country—*ut* **K** § 50, *s.n.* Bunyan

*Victoria History of the County of Bedford, vols. i–ii—*ut* **E** § 16 [to occupy 3 vols.]

*Guides*—*v.* **E** § 16 *Place-names*—*v.* **K** § 120

*Dunstable:* SMITH (W. G.) Dunstable: its history and surroundings; ill. 6/ *n.* 8° Stock 04
Pre-Roman, Roman, Saxon, and Norman periods; also folklore, archit., nat. hist., etc.
*Elstow:* WIGRAM (S. R.) Chrons. of Abbey of Elstow 7/6 8° Parker 85
*Harrold:* STEWARD (Wm.) Glimpses of Hist. of a Beds. Village; ill. 16 c 8° Beds. Pub. Co., *Bedford* 98
*Luton:* COBBE (H.) Luton Church: historical and descriptive 12/6 *n.* 8° Bell 99
*Willey:* HARVEY (Wm.) Hist. & Antiqs. of Hundred of Willey, 9 Pts. [*w.* 150/] 4° *London* 72–8
*Woburn:* BEDFORD (D'ke of) A Great Agricultural Estate—*ut* **D** § 119

**Berkshire**

ASHMOLE, Elias Antiquities of Berks, 3 vols. [3rd ed. 1 v., f°, *Readg.* 1736] 8° *London* [1719] 1723
COOPER-KING, Lt.-Col. C. C. History of Berkshire [Popular County Histories] 7/6 8° Stock 87
DITCHFIELD, Rev. P. H. [ed.] Bygone Berkshire 7/6 8° Brown, *Hull* 96
Conts. good acc. of story of Amy ROBSART (by H. J. REID), arts. on White Horse (E. H. GARDINER), *Berks. Words and Phrases* (M. J. BACON), etc.
,, The Parson's Pleasance 10/6 *n.* 8° Mills & Boon 10
Full of rambling remarks on archæol., folklore, gardening, and gossip, by a Berks. rector.
FOWLER, J. K. [' RUSTICUS '] —*in his* Echoes of Old Country Life, *ut* **E** § 16, *s.v.* Soc. Life [interesting] Berks reminiscs.
HAYDEN, Elean. G. Travels round our Village; ill. 3/6 *n.* c 8° Constable [01] 05
,, From a Thatched Cottage 6/ c 8° Constable 02
LYSONS, D. + S. Berkshire, its Topography and History *o.p.* r 4° *London* [06] 68
RIMMER, A. —*in his* Pleasant Spots around Oxford, *ut inf.*, *s.v.* Oxford
SALMON, Miss L. Untravelled Berkshire; ill. 7/6 c 8° Low 09
*Victoria History of Berkshire, vols. i–ii—*ut* **E** § 16 [to occupy 4 vols.]
*VINCENT, J. E. Highways and Byways in Berks; ill. 6/ ($2 *n.*) c 8° Macmillan 06
*Guides* —*v.* **E** § 16
*Abingdon:* CHALLENOR (B.) [ed.] Selns. fr. Munic. Chrons. of Ab.: 1555–1897 42/ 4° Hooke, *Abingdon* 98
TOWNSEND, J. A History of Abingdon; 4 ill. 7/6 *n.* s 4° Clar. Press 10
*Bray:* KERRY (C.) Hist. and Antiqs. of Hundred of Bray *o.p.* 8° Bickers 61
*Chipping Lambourn:* FOOTMAN (J.) Hist. of Ch. of St Michael; ill. 7/6 8° Stock 93
*Finchampstead:* LYM (W.) Chronicles of Finchampstead 15/ *n.* 4° Longman 95
*Newbury:* MONEY (W.) History of Town and Boro' of Newbury; 3 maps 21/ r 8° Parker 87
*Reading:* GUILDING (J. M.) [ed.] Readg. Records: diary of Corporn., v. i–iv [1431–1654] r 8° 92–6
*Abbey:* GASQUET (Dom F. A.) Abbot H. Cook—*in his* Last Abbot of Glastonbury, *ut* **A** § 49
HURRY, J. B. History of Reading Abbey; ill. & plans 15/ *n.* 4° Stock 01
A full history to the Dissolution of the Monasteries.
*Three-Mile Cross:* MITFORD (Mary Russell) Our Village [1824–32]; Introd. Mrs. A. T. Ritchie; ill. Hugh Thomson [Cranford Ser.] 3/6 ($1·50) c 8° Macmillan [93]
,, The same; ill. H. Thomson, w. 16 col. pl. A. Rawlings 10/6 *n.* 4° Macmillan [93] 11
,, The same; w. same Introd. & ill. [Pocket Classics] 2/ *n.* (80 c. *n.*) f 8° Macmillan 02
,, The same; 25 col. ill. C. E. Brock [$2 Dutton, *N.Y.*] 5/ *n.* c 8° Dent 04
A ser. of charmg. rustic sketches (the first portn. orig. contrib. to *The Lady's Mag.* 1819): the nooks and corners, the haunts and copses to be found in immed. neighbd. of Readg., more esp. rd. Three-Mile Cross, a cluster of cottages in one of wh. authoress lived. Many other edns. fr. 1/ upw.
*Speen:* MONEY (W.) Collections for Hist. of Parish of Speen 8° Blacket, *Newburgh* 93
*Swallowfield:* RUSSELL (L'y) Swallowfield and its Owners; ill. 42/ *n.* 4° Longman 01
A somewhat rambling, but accurate, acc. of the families who have held the manor since the Conquest.
*Swindon:* JEFFERIES (Rich.) Jefferies Land: hist. of Swindon and environs; ill. 7/6 *n.* c 8° Simpkin 96
*Thatcham:* BARFIELD (S.) Thatcham and its Manors, 2 vols.; maps and ill. 42/ *n.* 4° Parker, *Oxon.* 01
Ed. by J. PARKER. Vol. i: hist. (chiefly manorial) fr. earliest times to 19 cent.; ii: illustrative documts.
*Ufton:* SHARP (A. Mary) History of Ufton Court and of the Perkins Family—*ut* **G** § 22
*Vale (The); The White Horse:* HAYDEN (Elean. G.) Islands of the Vale; ill. 7/6 *n.* c 8° Smith & Elder 08
*Wallingford:* HEDGES (J. K.) History of Wallingford, 2 vols. 30/ 8° Bradford, *Wallingford* 81
,, Short Hist. of Wallingford; pl. [quite popular] 2/6 8° Bradford, *Wallingford* 95
*Windsor:* DIXON (W. Hepworth) Royal Windsor, 4 vols. 60/ 8° Bickers [79–80] 80
The standard popular account of the chief events centering round Windsor.
HENTON, G. M. [art.] Windsor: 20 col. pl., w. l'rpr. Sir R. R. Holmes [$2·50 *n.* Macm., *N.Y.*] 7/6 *n.* sq 8° Black 08
LOFTIE, Rev. W. J. Windsor Castle, w. descrn. of Park, Town, Neighb.; ill. 6/ c 8° Seeley [87] 87
TIGHE (R. T.) + DAVIS (J. E.) Annals of Windsor, 2 vols.; ill. [castle & town] *o.p.* [*pb.* 25/] r 8° J. R. Smith [58] 64

WOODWARD, B. B. Windsor Castle, Picturesque and Descriptive; ill. 105/ f° Ward & Lock [70] 75
*Forest:* HUGHES (G. M.) Hist. of Windsor Forest, and Park 4° *priv. prin.* 90
MENZIES, W. Hist. of Windsor Great Park & Forest; photos. *o.p.* [*pb.* 168/] f° Longman 64
This hist. originated in the surveys and researches which were required for the valuation of the Royal Forests in 1854.

**Buckinghamshire**

BUCKS ARCHIT. & ARCHÆOL. SOC.: Records of Bucks: Annual vol. [only pb. of Soc.] 8° Bucks Arch. Soc. 54 *sqq., in prg.*
DITCHFIELD, Rev. P. H. [ed.] Memls. of Old Bucks; ill. [Memls. of Cos. of Eng.] 15/ *n.* 8° G. Allen 01
EELES, F. C. [ed.] Edwardian Inventories for Bucks [Alcuin Club] 21/ 4° Longman 08
FOWLER, J. K. ['RUSTICUS'] Records of Old Times—*ut* **E** § 16, *s.v.* Social Life: Bucks gossip, old & new
LIPSCOMB, Dr G. Hist. & Antiqs. of Co. of Bucks, 4 v.; 270 ill. *o.p.* [*pb.* £12 12/] 4° Sotheran 31–47
ROSCOE, E. S. Buckinghamshire Sketches; ill. [repr. fr. *St James' Gaz.*] 3/6 8° Cassell 91
,, Penn's Country; and other Bucks sketches; 13 ill. 4/6 c 8° Stock 07
SHEAHAN, J. J. History and Topography of Buckinghamshire *o.p.* [*pb.* 21/] 8° Longman 62
*SHORTER, Clement K. Highways and Byways in Bucks; ill. 6/ ($1·50) c 8° Macmillan 10
*Victoria History of the County of Buckingham, vols. i–ii—*ut* **E** § 16 [to occupy 4 vols.]
***Guides*** —*v.* **E** § 16
***Worthies:*** GIBBS (Rob.) Worthies of Buckinghamshire 10/6 8° *Aylesbury* 88
*Aylesbury:* GIBBS (Rob.) History of Aylesbury; photos. 17/6 r 8° *Aylesbury* 88
*Burnham:* HEATH (F. G.) Burnham Beeches; map and ill. *o.p.* [*pb.* 1/6] p 8° Ryder [79] 85
*Chiltern:* FOSTER (Rev. A. J.) The Chiltern Hundreds; ill. 5/ c 8° Virtue 97
SUMMERS, W. H. Lollards of Chiltern Hills—*ut* **A** § 62, *s.v.* Medieval Church
*Colnbrook:* GYLL (G. W. J.) History of Colnbrook *o.p.* 8° Bohn 62
*Eton* —*v. also* **E** § 157, *s.v.* Eton College
BRINTON, H. E. Eton: 24 col. pl.; w. l'rpr. C. Stone 7/6 *n.* sq 8° Black
LUXMORE, H. E. [art.] Eton from a Backwater 7/6 *n.* sq 8° Black
RIMMER, Alf. Rambles Round Eton and Harrow; 52 ill. 3/6 r 16° Chatto [82] 98
*Horton:* GYLL (G. W. J.) History of Horton *o.p.* 8° 62
*Newport Pagnell:* BULL (F. W.) History of Newport Pagnell 21/ 8° Ross, *Kettering* 01
*Olney:* WRIGHT (Thos.) The Town of Cowper 3/6 c 8° Low [86] 93
A pleasant medley of antiquities, history, and associations of Olney.
*Wraysbury, etc.:* GYLL (G. W. J.) History of the Parish of Wraysbury, Ankerwycke Priory, and Magna Charta Island *o.p.* [*pb.* 15/] 4° Bohn 62
*Wycombe:* PARKER (Jno.) Early Hist. and Antiqs. of Wycombe; pl. 4° *Wycombe* 78

**Cambridgeshire:** *Bibliography:* BOWES (Rob.) Cat. of Bks. pr. at or rel. to Univ., Town, & Co. of Camb. 10/6 *n.*; Index [by E. Worman] 7/6 *n.* 8° Bowes, *Camb.* 94; 94
A useful and trustworthy wk., contg. numerous bibliogr. and biogr. notes and 98 ill.: arrangemt. chronolog.: 1521–1893. Auth. and subj. Index.
CAMBRIDGE ANTIQUARIAN SOC.: Proceedings; ill. 4° Deighton, *Cambridge, in prg.*
,, Octavo Publications; ill. 8° Deighton, *Cambridge, in prg.*
CONYBEARE, Rev. Edw. Hist. of Cambridgeshire [Pop. County Hists.] 7/6; Ch. Ed. 3/6 *n.* 8° Stock 97; 06
One of the best volumes of the series.
Domesday Book: Cambridgeshire, ed. C. H. + H. G. Evelyn-White 5/ *n.* 8° Eliot Stock 11
RYE, Walt. [ed.] Pedes Finium of Cambridge: Rich. i to Rich. iii 8° *priv. prin.* 91
*History: Civil War:* KINGSTON (A.)—*in his* East Anglia, *ut inf., s.v.* Norfolk, etc.
*Churches:* HILL (A. G.) Archit. and Hist. Notes on Chs. of Cambs. *o.p.* 8° *priv. prin.* 80
Remarks on and descrns. of old brasses and tombs, inscrns., hists. of manors, pedigrees of anc. families (w. arms), etc.
*Guides*—*v.* **E** § 16 *Place-names*—*v.* **K** § 120
*Barnwell:* CLARK (J. W.) [ed.] Observances in Use at the Augustinian Priory of S. Giles & S. Andrew; w. tr. & gloss. 21/ *n.* 8° Bowes, *Cambridge* 97
,, [ed.] Liber Memorandorum Ecclesie De Bernewell; w. Introd. F. W. Maitland [$5 *n.* Putnam, *N.Y.*] 15/ *n.* 8° Camb. Press 07
*Bedford Level* —*v. inf., s.v.* Lincolnshire
*Cambridge* —*v. also* **D** § 157, *s.v.* Cambridge University
CLARK, J. W. Cambridge Etchings & Vignettes: 12 etchgs. & numer. vigns. 21/ f° Seeley 80
,, Cambridge [above text, w. reduced illns.] 6/ c 8° Seeley [90] 07
*CONYBEARE, Rev. E. Highways and Byways in Cambridge and Ely 6/ ($1·50) c 8° Macmillan 10

JEBB, Eglantyne Cambridge: brief study in social questions 4/6 *n.* c 8° Bowes, *Camb.* 06
LE KEUX, J. L. Memorials of Cambridge, 3 vols.; 154 steel pl. & 90 ill. 63/ 8° Macmillan [41] 81
LOGGAN, Dav. Cantabrigia Illustrata, ed. J. W. Clark—*ut* **D** § 157, *s.v.* Cambridge University
*MAITLAND, Prf. F. W. Township and Borough [$2·50 *n.* Putnam, *N.Y.*] 10/ r 8° Camb. Press 98
[Ford Lects.] A clear and thoro' exposn. of growth and govt. [13–19 cents.] of a community: a vivid pict. of medieval town-life.
,, + BATESON (Mary) [eds.] Charters of Boro' of Cambr. [$3 *n.* Putnam, *N.Y.*] 7/6 8° Camb. Press 01
Transcriptn., tr., and ed. of a valuable ser. of writs, showg. the successive steps whereby Engl. boros' fought their way to self-govt. and independence.
MATTHISON, W. [art.] Cambridge: 77 col. pl.,; w. l'rpr. M. A. R. Tuker
[$6 *n.* Macmillan, *N.Y.*] 20/ *n.* sq 8° Black
STUBBS, [Bp] C. W. Cambridge; ill. [Mediæv. Towns; $1·75 *n.* Dutton, *N.Y.*] 4/6 *n.* f 8° Dent 05
Previously (1903) pubd. in an *edition-de-luxe*, w. lithographic reprodns. of 24 of the ill., 21/ *n.*
*Ely*: GIBBONS (A.) [ed.] Calendar and Concise View of Ely Episc. Records 42/ 8° 91
*Cathedral and Abbey* —*for* Architecture *v.* **I** § 119
CHAPMAN [ed.] Sacrist Rolls of Ely Cathedral, 2 vols. 07
HAMILTON, N. E. S. A. Inquisitio Comitatus Cantab.: Inquisitio Eliensis 4° R. Soc. of Liter. 76
JAMES, Dr M. R. Sculptures in Lady Chapel at Ely; 55 collotype pl. 21/ *n.* 4° Nutt 95
STEWART, D. J. [ed.] Liber Eliensis, vol. i all [pubd.] [Anglia Christiana] *o.p.* 8° *London* 48
STUBBS, [Bp] C. W. Historical Memorials of Ely Cathedral; ill. 4/6 *n.* i 16° Dent 97
*Landbeach*: CLAY (W. K.) History of Landbeach *o.p.* [*pb.* 4/6] 8° Camb. Antiq. Soc. 61
*Newmarket*: HARPER, (C. G.) Newm., Bury, etc., Road—*ut* **E** § 16, *s.v.* Roads
HORE, J. P. History of Newmarket; 3 vols. [chiefly turf history] *o.p.* [*pb.* 37/6] 8° Baily 86
*Royston* —*v. inf.*, *s.v.* Hertfordshire
*Thorney* —*for* French Church *v.* **A** § 63 (Huguenot Soc.—PEET)
BEDFORD, D'ess of —*in* A Great Agricultural Estate, *ut* **D** § 119
WARNER, R. H. History of Thorney Abbey, from its foundation to its dissolution 7/6 8° *Wisbech* 79
*Waterbeach*: CLAY (W. K.) History of Waterbeach *o.p.* [*pb.* 5/] 8° Camb. Antiq. Soc. 59
*Wisbech*: GARDINER (F. J.) Hist. of Wisbech & Neighb.; ill. [1848–98] 26/ *n.* r 8° Gardiner, *Wisbech* 99
WALKER (N.) + CRADDOCK (T.) History of Wisbech and the Fens *o.p.* r 8° *Wisbech* 49

**Channel Islands**

ANSTED (D. T.) + LATHAM (R. G.) The Channel Islands, revised E. Toulmin Neville; ill.
7/6 c 8° W. H. Allen [62] 93
GALLIENNE-RÔBIN (E.) + CHILD (Har.) The Channel Islands; 14 maps & plans 2/ *n.* f 8° Richards 02
*Guides* —*v.* **E** § 16
*Scenery*: WIMBUSH (H. B.) [art.] Channel Islands: 76 col. pl., w. l'rpr. Edith F. Carey
[$6 *n.* Macm., *N.Y.*] 20/ *n.* sq 8° Black 04

**Guernsey**: DUNCAN (J.) Hist. of Guernsey [w. notices of Jersey] *o.p.* [*pb.* 15/] 8° Longman 41
Guernsey Scenery Pictured and Described by a Wayfarer; ill. 3/6 *n.* 8° Fairbairns 07
TUPPER, F. B. History of Guernsey; w. notices of Jersey 12/6 8° Simpkin [54] 76

**Sark**: BOWLES (Mrs) Sark: gem of Channel Islands; ill. 3/6 *n.* r 8° Fairbairns 07
TOPLIS, W. A. [artist] Book of Sark: 21 col. pl.; w. l'rpr. J. Oxenham 105/ *n.* 4° Hodder 08
In addn. to the notes on pictures, incls. Dr T. G. BONNEY on the Geology and E. D. MARQUAND on Flora.

**Cheshire** —*v. also inf.*, *s.v.* Lancashire

ANDREWS, Wm. [ed.] Bygone Cheshire [Bygone Series] 7/6 8° Brown, *Hull* 95
AXON, W. E. A. Cheshire Gleanings [worthies, assocns., folklore, etc.] 6/ c 8° J. Heywood, *Mancs.* 84
BARBER (Ven. E.) + DITCHFIELD (Rev. P. H.) [eds.] Memls. of Old Cheshire; ill.
[Memls. of Cos. of Eng.] 15/ *n.* 8° G. Allen 10
CHETHAM SOCIETY: Publications—*ut inf.*, *s.v.* Lancashire
COWARD, T. A. Picturesque Cheshire; ill. [a bicycle tour] 5/ *n.* c 8° Sherratt, *Mancs.* 01
Domesday Book of Cheshire and Lancashire, ed. Beaumont *priv. prin.* 82
HISTORICAL SOC. OF LANCS & CHESHIRE Transactions—*ut inf.*, *s.v.* Lancashire
Moss, Fletcher Pilgrimages in Cheshire and Shropshire; ill. 10/6 8° *priv. prin.* 01
Over 100 fine illns. of the old timbered houses for which these counties are famous. Text of small value.
*ORMEROD, Dr Geo. Hist. of Co. Pal. & City of Chester, ed. Thos. Helsby, 3 vols.; ports. & pl.
*o.p.* [*pb.* £20] f° Routledge [19] 82
The largest and one of the best modelled of our County Histories. For contin. by Thos. BAINES *v. inf.*, *s.v.* Lancs.
*Churches*: GLYNNE (Sir S. R.) Notes on the Churches of Cheshire s 4° Chetham Soc. 94
Ed. by Can. J. A. ATKINSON. Materl. coll during visits fr. 1832 to 1869: chiefly ecclesiological; supplemented by editor.

*Guides* —*v.* **E** § 16
*Halls* —*v. inf., s.v.* Lancashire (Halls-PHILIPS)
*History : Civil War :* ATKINSON (Can. J. A.) [ed.] Tracts rel. to Civil War in Cheshire [1641–9] s 4° Chetham Soc. 09
HALL, Jas. The Civil War in Cheshire, etc. 8° Wm. Salt Arch. Soc. 89
MALBON, T. Memls. of Civil War in Chesh. & Adj. Cties., ed. J. Hall 8° Lancs & Chesh. Rec. Soc. 91
An interestg. contemp. documt. by a Parliamentarian. In same vol. is *Providence Improved* by E. BURGHALL (Vicar of Acton, nr. Nantwich), whose Puritanism was much stronger than MALBON'S. Together they give a good idea of the feeling at the time of the great struggle.
*Birkenhead :* MOTT (C. Grey) Reminiscences of Birkenhead ; plans 4/6 *n.* 8° Young, *L'pool* 00
The story of the rise of town during the 19th century, municipal progress, etc.
ASPINALL, H. K. Birkenhead and its Surroundings ; ill. 5/ *n.* 8° L'pl. Bkslrs' Co., *L'pl.* 03
*Cheadle :* Moss (Fletcher) Hist. of Old Parish of Cheadle ; photos. [gossip] 8° Author, *Didsbury* 95
*Chester :* COMPTON (E. H.) [art.] Chester ; w. l'rpr. F. Duckworth [$3 *n.* Macm., *N.Y.*] 7/6 *n.* sq 8° Black
CRICKMORE, H. H. Old Chester ; 11 etchgs. & 20 ill. 7/6 *n.* s 4° Dent 95
FENWICK, G. L. History of the Ancient City of Chester ; ill. 31/6 4° Phillipson, *Chester* 96
A good popular acc. of the bldgs. and institns. and history of the city ; but weak in archæology.
GASTRELL, Bp F. [1662–1725] Notitia Cestriensis, ed. Rev. F. R. Raines, 2 v. in 4 s 4° Chetham Soc. 45–50
Historical notices of the diocese of Chester.
HOWSON (Dn J. S.) + RIMMER (A.) Chester as it Was ; ill. *o.p.* [*pb.* 14/] 4° Longman 72
MORRIS, Can. R. H. Chester in Plantagenet & Tudor Rgns. ; 77 ill. 31/6 i 8° *priv. prin.* (Griffith, *Chester*) 95
A valuable bk. on social, commerc., and civic life of the capital of the curious *imperium in imperio*, the Palatinate of its earls ; based largely on almost unwkd. archives of the Corpn., extrs. fr. wh. are incl. in text and footnotes.
WINDLE, B. C. A. Chester, Historical & Topographical ; ill. [Ancient Cities] 4/6 *n.* c 8° Methuen [03] 10
*Church of St John the Baptist :* SCOTT (Rev. S. C.) Lects. on Hist. of St John the Baptist Church and Parish in the City of Chester 10/6 *n.* 8° Phillipson, *Chester* 92
*Church of St Mary :* *EARWAKER (J. P.) Hist. of Ch. & Par. of St M., Ch. 21/ r 4° Love & Wyman 98
*Congleton :* HEAD (Rob.) Congleton, Past and Present r 8° *Congleton* 87
*Dee (River)* —*v.* **E** § 16, *s.v.* Rivers
*Knutsford :* PAYNE (Rev. G. A.) Knutsford ; ill. E. H. New [Temple Topogrs.] 1/6 *n.* c 8° Dent 04
,, Mrs. Gaskell and Knutsford—*ut* **K** § 24
*Macclesfield :* EARWAKER (J. P.) East Cheshire : hundred of Maccl., 2 v. ; ill. *subscr.* 90/ r 4° *priv. prin.* 77–80
*Nantwich :* HALL (Jas.) History of Town and Parish of Nantwich 4° *Nantwich* 83
*Prestbury :* RENAUD (F.) Contribns. tow. Hist. of Parish of Prestbury s 4° Chetham Soc. 76
*Sandbach :* EARWAKER (J. P.) History of Sandbach ; ill. [*w.* 21/] 4° *priv. prin.* 90
*Wirral :* IRVINE (W. F.) Notes on Old Halls of Wirral 3/6 *n.* 8° Young, *L'pool* 02
MORTIMER, W. W. History of Wirral Hundred *o.p.* [*pb.* 31/6] 4° Whittaker 47
SANDERS (F.) + IRVINE (W. F.) Wirral Notes & Queries : local gleanings, 2 vols. ; pl. 4° 93–4
STEWART-BROWN, R. The Wapentake of Wirral—*ut* **D** § 124
YOUNG, Har. E. Perambulation of Hundred of Wirral ; map & 59 pl. 6/ *n.* 8° Young, *L'pool* 10

**Cornwall :** *Bibliography :* BOASE (G. C.) + COURTNEY (W. P.) Bibliotheca Cornubiensis, 2 v. & Suppl. ea. 21/ r 8° Longman 74–8 ; 82
COURTNEY, W. P. Parliamentary Representation of Cornwall [earliest per. to 1832] 8° *priv. prin.* 89
CRAIK, [Mrs] D. M. Unsentimental Journey thro' Cornwall ; ill. *o.p.* [*pb.* 12/6] 4° Macmillan 84
DANIELL, J. J. Compendium of History & Geography of Cornwall 7/6 c 8° Netherton, *Truro* [ ] 94
GOULD, Rev. S. Baring- —*in his* A Book of the West, vol. ii, *ut inf., s.v.* Devonshire
,, Cornish Characters & Strange Events ; 62 pl. 21/ *n.* ($5 *n.*) 8° Lane 09
HARPER, C. G. The Cornish Coast (North)—*ut* **E** § 16, *s.v.* Coasts
,, —*in his* From Paddington to Penzance, *ut* **E** § 16, *s.v.* Roads
HIND, C. Lewis Days in Cornwall ; 16 col. pl. W. Pascoe, and 20 ill. 6/ c 8° Methuen 07
*NORWAY, A. H. Highways and Byways in Devon and Cornwall—*ut inf., s.v.* Devonshire
PAGE, J. L. W. The North Coast of Cornwall ; ill. 6/ c 8° Hemmons, *Bristol* 98
Description of a tour fr. Morwenstow to Land's End : scenery, people, legends, etc.
POLWHELE, R. Hist. of Cornwall : civil, milit., relig., archit., etc., 7 v. [*w.* £12 12/] 4° *London* [03–16] 16–36
SALMON, A. L. The Cornwall Coast ; maps & 32 ill. [County Coast Ser.] 6/ *n.* c 8° Unwin 10
*Victoria History of the County of Cornwall, vol. i—*ut* **E** § 16 [to occupy 4 vols.]
*Church Hist. :* LACH-SZYRMA (W. S.) Church Hist. of Cornwall and Truro 8° *priv. prin.* 87
*Early Christianity in Cornwall*—*v.* **A** § 62, *s.v.* Early Churches (BORLASE)
*Guides* —*v.* **E** § 16

*Smuggling in Cornwall* —*v.* **D** § 117 (CARTER)
*Wells (Holy)* —*v.* **B** § 3 (QUILLER-COUCH)
*Worthies*

HAWKER, Rev. R. S. Footprints of Former Men in Far Cornwall 5/ *n.* ($1·25 *n.*) c 8° Lane [70] 03
Ed. by C. E. BYLES, w. Introduction; ill. by J. Ley PETHYBRIDGE.

TREGELLAS, W. H. Cornish Worthies, 2 vols. 18/ 8° Stock 84

*Falmouth:* GAY (Susan E.) Old Falmouth; Introd. Sir J. Fayrer 7/6 *n.* 8° Headley 03

*Land's End; Penzance; Scilly Isles*

*HUDSON, W. H. Land's End: naturalist's impressns. in W. Cornwall; 49 ill. 6/ *n.* 8° Hutchinson [08] 11

LACH-SZYRMA, W. S. Short Hist. of Penzance, St Michael's Mt., etc. 7/6 4° *Truro* 78

MOTHERSOLE, Jessie Isles of Scilly; 24 col. pl. [story, people, flowrs.] 10/6 *n.* s 4° R.T.S. 10

TREGARTHEN, J. C. Wild Life at the Land's End—*ut* **I** § 147

UREN, J. G. Scilly and the Scillonians 6/ *n.* 8° *W. Mg. News* Off., *Plymouth* 07

WHITE, Walt. Walk to Land's End and Trip to Scilly; 4 maps 4/ p 8° Chapman [55] 79

*Launceston:* ROBBINS (A. F.) Launceston, Past and Present 88

*Lizard Head:* JOHNS (Rev. C. A.) A Week at the Lizard 2/6 f 8° S.P.C.K. [48] 74

*Mullyion:* HARVEY (E. G.) Mullyion: hist., antiqs., shipwks., etc. 7/6 4° Simpkin 75

*Pendennis; St Mawes:* OLIVER (S. P.) Pendennis and St Mawes [hist. sketch] 7/6 16° Simpkin 76

*St Austell:* HAMMOND (Rev. Jos.) A Cornish Parish; ill. [St Austell] 10/6 8° Skeffington 97

*St Ives, etc.:* MATTHEWS (J. H.) Hist. of Parishes of St Ives, Lelant, Towednack, and Zennor; ill. 31/6 8° Stock 92
An elaborate wk., carefully compiled and triply indexed, full of folklore, local custs., boro' accs., stories of worthies, electns., etc.

*Stratton:* GOULDING (R. W.) [ed.] Blanchminster's Charity Records 7/6 r 8° Goulding, *Louth* 99
A valuable colln. of extracts fr. the records of the charity, 1421–1832; w. a full history of the charity.

*Trigg:* MACLEAN (Sir J.) Paroch. & Fam. Hist. of Trigg Minor, 3 v.; ill. 4° *priv. prin.* 73–9

*Truro: Church History*—*v.* LACH-SZYRMA, *sup.*, *s.v.* Church History

## Cumberland; Westmoreland; Lake District

*BRADLEY, A. G. Highways and Byways in Lake District; ill. 6/ ($2 *n.*) c 8° Macmillan 01
Excellently ill. J. PINNELL. A cycle tour thro' the district, describg. all better-known localities.

CUMB. & WESTM. ANTIQ. & ARCH. SOC.: Transns., 16 v.; N.S., i–x 8° Thurnam, *Carl.* 74–00; 01–10 *in prg.*
EXTRA SERIES—
i: NICOLSON (Bp. W.), *Miscellany Accs. of Diocese of Carl.* [*ut inf.*] ed. R. S. FERGUSON, 12/6 '77
ii: GILPIN (Rev. W.), *Memrs. of Gilpin Family* [*ut* **G** § 22] ed. W. JACKSON 10/6 '79
iii: FERGUSON, *Old Ch. Plate of Carl.* [*ut* **I** § 114] 15/6 ['82] 08
iv: „ + NANSON, W. [eds.], *Munic. Recds. of Carl.* [*ut inf.*] 15/ 87
v–vi: *Papers and Pedigrees* JACKSON
vii: *Bk. of Records of Kirkbie Kendall* [*ut inf.*] FERGUSON 15/ '92
viii: *Old Manorial Halls of Westm. and Cumb.* M. W. TAYLOR [*ut inf.*] 21/ '92
ix: *Testamenta Karlcolensia* [*ut* **G** § 22] ed. FERGUSON 10/6 '93
x: *Royal Charters of Carlisle* [*ut inf.*] FERGUSON 21/ '94
xi: *Sculpt. Crosses, etc., of Carl.* [*ut* **G** § 14] W. S. CALVERLEY 15/ '99
xii: *Pipe Rolls of Cumbl. and Westm.* [*ut inf.*] ed. F. H. M. PARKER 25/ '05

„ Tract Series, Nos. i–ix [edited reprs., etc.] ea. 1/ to 3/6 Thurnam, *Carlisle, in prg.*

DICKINSON, W. Cumbriana: fragments of Cumbrian life 5/ f 8° Whittaker [75] 76

FERGUSON, R. Northmen in Cumberland and Westmoreland *o.p.* [*pb.* 5/] c 8° Longman 56

FERGUSON, R. S. History of Cumberland [Popular County Histories] 7/6 8° Stock 90

„ History of Westmoreland [Popular County Hists.] 7/6; Ch. Edn. 3/6 *n.* 8° Stock 94

HUTCHINSON, W. Hist. and Antiqs. of Cumberl., 2 v.; maps and pl. 4° *Carlisle* 1794

JACKSON, Wm. Papers & Pedigrees mainly rel. to Cumb. & Westm., 2 v. 15/ 8° Wilson, *Kendal* 92
Forming vols. iv–v of the *Transactions of Cumberld. and Westmoreld. Antiq. and Archæol. Soc.*

JEFFERSON, S. History and Antiquities of Carlisle, Leath Ward and Allerdale, 3 vols.; pl. & ill. *o.p.* 8° *Carlisle* 38–42

KNIGHT, Prf. Wm. Through the Wordsworth Country; 56 pl. H. Goodwin 4/6 f f° Sonnenschein [87] 92

„ Engl. Lake Distr. as interpr. in Poems of Wordsworth 4/6 c 8° Douglas, *Edin.* [78] 91

LINTON, [Mrs] Lynn The Lake Country; map and ill. *o.p.* [*pb.* 21/] 4° Smith & Elder 64

MARTINEAU, Harriet The English Lakes; pl., ill., & geol. map *o.p.* [*pb.* 21/] 4° *Windermere* [45] *n.d.* (58)

MILL, Dr H. R. The English Lakes; ill. and contoured maps 2/6 *n.* 8° Philip 95
Repr. fr. *Jl. R.G.S.* on bathymetr. surv. of Lakes, selectg. 10 as types. A useful contribn. to limnology.

NICOLSON (Jos.) + BURN (R.) Hist. & Antiqs. of Westm. & Cumb., 2 v. 4° *London* 1777

PARKER, F. H. M. [ed.] Pipe Rolls of Cumb. and Westmoreland 25/ 8° Cumb. Antiq. Soc. 05

PALMER, Wm. T. Lake Country Rambles 6/ c 8° Chatto 02
A full account of the various aspects of outdoor life in Lake Country: climbg. fishg., huntg., etc.

„ In Lakeland Dells and Fells; front. 6/ c 8° Chatto 03
Deals w. shepherd-life in Lake Country: fishg., walkg., rock-climbg., shootg., fox-huntg.

RAWNSLEY, Can. H. D. Life and Nature at the English Lakes 5/ *n.* c 8° MacLehose, *Glasgow* [99] 02
,, Rambler's Note-Bk. at English Lakes; ill. 5/ *n.* c 8° MacLehose, *Glasgow* 02
,, Lake Country Sketches; 100 ill. 5/ *n.* c 8° MacLehose, *Glasgow* 03
,, Months at the Lakes; ill. 5/ *n.* c 8° MacLehose, *Glasgow* 06
,, Round the Lake Country; ill. 5/ *n.* c 8° MacLehose, *Glasgow* 09
1, 2, $2; 3, 4, $1·75; 5, $1·50 *n.* Macm., *N.Y.* Papers on scenery, archæol., hist., rustic life, worthies of Lake Country.
,, Literary Associations of the English Lakes, 2 v. 10/ *n.* c 8° MacLehose, *Glasgow* [94] 06
$3·50 *n.* Macmillan, *N.Y.* i: Cumb., Keswick, and SOUTHEY'S Country; ii: Westm., Windermere, and haunts of WORDSWORTH. More on the lives of the men than on scenes and their historic interest.

ROBERTSON, Rev. Eric Wordsworthshire: introd. to a poet's country 7/6 *n.* 8° Chatto 11
SALT, H. S. On Cambrian and Cumbrian Hills—*ut* **E** § 18
*Victoria History of the County of Cumberland, vols. i–ii—*ut* **E** § 16 [to occupy 4 vols.]
WATSON, Jno. Annals of Quiet Valley in Wordsworth Country; 30 ill. 4/6 *n.* c 8° Dent 94
Sketches of peasant-life am. the 'statesmen' of Westm. valleys, and record of old customs.
WHELLAN, Wm. Hist. & Topogr. of Cos. of Cumb. & Westm. *o.p.* [*pb.* 40/] 4° *Pontefract* 60
WORDSWORTH, Wm. [1770–1850] Guide to Lakes, ed. Ern. de Sélincourt 2/6 *n.* (90 c.) c 8° Clar. Pr. [ ] 06
[Lib. of Prose & Poetry.] Exact repr. of 5th (1835) edn. of the famous *Guide*—a bk. wh. every visitor and every lover of the poet shd. read. Ed. w. meticulous care, w. Pref., bibliogr. notes, and the letters to Sir G. BEAUMONT, and on Kendal and Windermere Ry.; 8 ill.

*Churches:* BELLASIS (E.) Westmoreland Church Notes, 2 vols. 21/ r 8° Wilson, *Kendal* 88–9
Heraldry, epitaphs, inscripp. of 32 anc. parish churches and churchyards.

*Climbing—v.* **I** § 165 *Guides—v.* **E** § 16 *Place-names—v.* **K** § 120

*Halls:* TAYLOR (M. W.) Old Manorial Halls of Westm. and Cumb.; ill. 21/ 8° Cumb. Ant. Soc. 92
Cumberld. and Westmoreld. Archæol. Soc.: extra ser. A valuable and accurate work.

*Scenery:* COOPER (A. H.) [art.] Engl. Lakes: 75 col. pl., w. l'rpr. W. T. Palmer [$6 *n.* Macm., *N.Y.*] 20/ *n.* sq 8° Black 05
GOODWIN, Harry [artist] —*in* Knight's Through the Wordsworth Country, *ut sup.*
LYDON, A. F. [artist] English Lake Scenery; 24 col. pl. *o.p.* [*pb.* 12/] 4° Walker 82
[OGLE, T. (photogr.)] Our Engl. Lakes as Seen by Wordsworth: photos. *o.p.* [*pb.* 12/] 4° Provost [64] 70
PYNE, J. B. [artist] The English Lake Scenery: 25 litho. pl. 52/6 f° Sotheran [53] 69
The 1st edn. (pub. by Agnew; *w.* 63/) is vastly superior to this repr., in wh., moreover, the plates are reduced.

*Worthies:* ATKINSON (Geo.) Worthies of Westmoreland, 2 vols. *o.p.* [*pb.* 16/] 8° J. R. Smith 49–50
LONSDALE, H. Worthies of Cumb., 6 v. [vol. iv conts. Wordsworth] *o.p.* [*pb.* 7/6 ea.] c 8° Routledge 67–75
*Carlisle:* CREIGHTON ([Bp] M.) Carlisle [Historic Towns] 3/6 ($1·25) c 8° Longman 89
FERGUSON, R. S. Carlisle [Diocesan Histories] 2/6 f 8° S.P.C.K. 89
,, [ed.] Royal Charters of City of Carlisle [1221–1685] 8° Cumb. Antiq. Soc. 94
,, + NANSON (W.) [eds.] Some Municipal Records of City of Carl.; pl. 15/ 8° Cumb. Antiq. Soc. 87
MOUNSEY, G. G. [ed.] Occupn. of Carl. in 1745 by Pr'ce Stuart *o.p.* [*pb.* 9/] 8° Longman 46
NICOLSON, Bp W. [1655–1727] Miscellany Accs. of Dioc. of Carl., ed. R. S. Ferguson 12/6 8° Cumb. Ant. Soc. 77

*Derwentwater:* SYMONS (G. J.) Floating Isld. on Derw.: hist. and mystery 5/ s 4° Stanford 89
*Helvellyn:* HUSON (T.) [art.] Round about Helvellyn: 24 pl. 21/ r 8° Seeley 94
*Holm Oultram Abbey:* GILBANKS (Rev. G. E.) Records of a Cistertian Abbey 5/ *n.* 8° W. Scott 00
The abbey at one time had a high rank am. rel. foundns. of North. It is one of few Cist. abbeys still used f. worship.
*Kendal:* FERGUSON (R. S.) [ed.] Boke of Recorde of Kirkbie Kendall 15/ 8° Cumb. Ant. Soc. 92
'The Acts and Doings in Corporation of Kirkbie Kendal'. Of considerable interest for ancient manners and customs.
NICHOLSON, C. Annals of Kendal *o.p.* [*pb.* 10/] 8° Whittaker [40] 61
*Naworth Castle:* HOWARD (L'd W.) [ed.] Selns. fr. Househ. Bks. of, ed. Rev. G. Ornsby 15/ 8° Surtees Soc. 78

*Patterdale:* MORRIS (Rev. W. P.) Records of Patterdale: hist. & descr.; ill. 5/ 8° Wilson, *Kendal* 03
*Penrith:* FURNESS (W.) History of Penrith 8° 94
*Shappe:* WHITESIDE (Rev. J.) Shappe in Bygone Days 10/6 8° Wilson, *Kendal* [04] 04
*Solway:* NEILSON (G.) Annals of the Solway until A.D. 1307 MacLehose, *Glasgow* 99
A sound and hardy account, explaining the place of the Solway estuary in history.
*Troutbeck:* SCOTT (S. H.) A Westmoreland Village; ill. [Troutbeck] 3/6 *n.* c 8° Constable 04

**Derbyshire**

ANDREWS, Wm. [ed.] Bygone Derbyshire [by var. wrs.] 7/6 8° Brown, *Hull* 92
BRADBURY, E. ['STREPHON'] All about Derbyshire, 3/6; Ed. d. Luxe, 7/6 c 8° Simpkin 84
COX, Dr J. C. Three Centuries of Derbyshire Annals, 2 vols.; facs. 84/ r 8° Bemrose 90
The annals are gath. fr. recds. of Q'r Sessns. and comprise lists of lords lieut., high sheriffs, J.P.'s, dep. lieuts., coroners, clerks of peace, and other country dignitaries, gt. and small, an eccles. section, w. list of incumbts. 1602–3, interestg. partics. of persecution—as well as much other val. informn.

COX, Dr, J. C. [ed.] Calendar of Records of County of Derby 21/ *n.* 4° Bemrose 99
Full lists of all documents of the county, arranged in classes; only the deeds are calendered.
„ [ed.] Memls. of Old Derbyshire; ill. [Memls. of Cos. of Eng.] 15/ *n.* 8° G. Allen 07
DERBY, Henry, Earl of [afterw. HENRY IV] Derby Accounts, ed. Lucy Toulmin Smith + Prf. Prutz s 4° Camden Soc. 94
The accs. kept by treasr. of HY., EARL OF DERBY, dur. his expedns. to Prussia and Holy Ld. 1390–1 and 1392–3; w. val. *Introd.*
DERBYSHIRE ARCHÆOL. AND NATURAL HIST. SOC.: Journal, vols. i–xxxiii; ill. 8° Bemrose, *Derby, in prg.*
Domesday Book: Derbyshire, ed. Ll. Jewitt: facs., 10/6; Tr., 10/6 i 4° Bemrose
*FIRTH, J. B. Highways and Byways in Derbysh.; ill. 6/ ($2 *n.*) c 8° Macmillan 05
JEAYES, I. H. [ed.] Descriptive Catal. of Derbyshire Charters [pub. & priv. libs.] 42/ *n.* r 8° Bemrose 06
JENNINGS, L. J. Derby & South Downs: rambles am. the hills; ill. *o.p.* [*pb.* 12/] p 8° Murray 80
LEYLAND, J. Peak of Derbyshire: its scenery and antiqs.; ill. 7/6 c 8° Seeley 91
PENDLETON, Jno. History of County of Derby [Popular County Hists.] 7/6 8° Stock 86
ROBINSON, J. B. Derbyshire Gleanings; ports. and pl. 25/ r 8° *Derby* 66
*Victoria History of the County of Derby, vols. i– —*ut* **E** § 16 [to occupy 4 vols.]
YEATMAN, J. P. Feudal Hist. of County of Derby, 2 v. in 4; pl. *o.p.* 4° Bemrose 86–90
*Churches:* COX, Dr J. C. Notes on Churches of Derbyshire, 4 vols.; ill. 75/ r 8° Bemrose 75–9
An admirable and handsome wk., w. a modest title. i: *Scarsdale*, 15/; ii: *High Peak, Wirksworth*, 21/; iii: *Appletree*, etc., 21/; iv: *Morleston*, etc., 25/.
„ Chronicles of Colleg. Ch. of All Saints, Derby; ill. 42/ r 4° Bemrose 81
*Guides* —*v.* **E** § 16
*Halls; Manors:* T. (J.) Old Halls of Derbyshire, 2 vols. ea. 21/ 4° Wardley, *Buxton* 92–3
*Scenery:* CHANTREY (Sir F.) [art.] Peak Scenery, ed. J. Croston: 29 copper pl. 31/6 r 4° Murray, *Derby* 86
GARDNER, W. B. [art.] The Peak Country: 24 col. pl., w. l'rpr. A. R. H. Moncrieff 6/ *n.* sq 8° Black
*Beauchief Abbey:* ADDY (S. O.) Hist. Memls. of Beauchief Abbey 8° 78
*Chesterfield:* FOSTER (A. J.) Round about the Crooked Spire; ill. 5/ c 8° Chapman 94
YEATMAN, J. P. [ed.] Records of Borough of Chesterfield r 8° *Chesterfield* 84
*Croxall:* USSHER (Rev. R.) Histor. Sketch of Parish of Croxall; ill. 42/ r 4° Bemrose 81
*Dale:* WARD (Jno.) Dale and its Abbey; ill. 12/6 *n.* 4° Murray, *Derby* 91
*Derby:* DAVISON (A. W.) Derby, its Rise and Progress; 2 maps and 12 pl. 5/ c 8° Bemrose 05
*Haddon Hall:* CATTERMOLE (G.) [art.] Evenings at Haddon Hall; 24 pl. 5/ c 8° Bohn's Lib. [46]
„ History and Antiquities of Haddon Hall; lithos. 5/ 4° Bemrose 67
SMITH, G. Le Blanc Haddon, the Manor, the Hall, its Lords and Traditions; profusely ill. by author [text of small value] 10/6 *n.* 8° Stock 06
*Ilkeston, Dale Abbey, Kirk Hallam, W. Hallam, Shipley, Cossal*
TRUEMAN (E.) + MARSTON (R. W.) History of Ilkeston, w. Dale Abbey, etc.; pl. 42/ r 4° Pioneer Prtg. Co., *Ilkeston* 99
*Matlock:* BRYAN (Benj.) Matlock Manor and Parish; ill. [a compiln.] 12/6 *n.* c 8° Bemrose 03
*Melandra Castle:* CONWAY (R. S.) [ed.] Melandra Castle; 30 pl. 5/ *n.* 8° Sherratt, *Mancs.* 06
*Norton:* ARMITAGE (Har.) Chantrey Land; ill. [village of Norton] 10/6 *n.* 8° Low 10
*Peak (The):* CROSTON (Jas.) On Foot thro' the Peak 3/6 c 8° J. Heywood, *Mancs.* 89
DALE, Eliz. Scenery and Geology of Peak of Derbyshire; ill. 6/ m 8° Low 01
GARDNER, W. B. [art.] Peak Country: 24 col. pl., w. l'rpr. A. R. H. Moncrieff [$2·50 *n.* Macm., *N.Y.*] 6/ *n.* c 8° Black 08
JENNINGS, L. J. Rambles in the Peak and South Downs *o.p.* [*pb.* 12/] c 8° Murray 80
LEYLAND, Jno. Peak of Derbyshire: scenery and antiqs.; ill. 7/6 c 8° Seeley 91
*Repton:* HIPKINS (F. C.) Repton and its Neighbourhood—*ut* **D** § 157, *s.v.* Repton School

**Devonshire** —*v. also* Cornwall

*Bibliography:* BRUSHFIELD (Dr T. N.) Literature of Devonshire to Year 1640 *o.p.* 8° *Torquay* 93
Enums. and gives lives of 121 native authors prior to Long Parliament. A presidential address.
DAVIDSON, J. Bibliotheca Devoniensis; *and* Supplement *o.p.* 4° *Exeter* 52–61
DREDGE, Rev. J. I. Few Sheaves of Devon Bibliography, Pts. i–iii f° *pr. pr.* (Brendon, *Plymouth*) 89–92
50 copies of ea. Pt. repr. fr. *Transns.* of Devonsh. Assoc. for Ad. of Sci., etc. Careful bibliogrs. of wrgs. of Devonsh. authors.
WORTH, R. N. Three Towns Bibliotheca [Plym., Devonpt., Stonehouse] 8° *Plymouth n.d.* (73)
Devonshire Domesday and Geld Inquest: extensions, trs., indices, 2 vols. [*w.* 25/] 8° *priv. prin.* 84–92
GOULD, Rev. S. Baring- Book of the West: Devon & Cornwall, 2 v.; ill. ea. 6/ c 8° Methuen 99–02
i: *Devon*; ii: *Cornwall*. Chapters on local subjs., especially Saints and folklore.
„ A Book of Devon; 35 ill. 6/ c 8° Methuen [99] 02
„ Devonsh. Characters & Strange Events; 55 pl. aft. old prints 21/ *n.* ($7 *n.*) 8° Lane 08

HARPER, C. G. North Devon Coast; *and* South Devon Coast—*ut* **E** § 16, *s.v.* Coasts
HARRIS, J. H. My Devonshire Book [scenery, legends, etc.] 3/6 *n.* 8° *W. Mg. News, Plymouth* 07
HEATH, Sid. S. Devon. & Dorset Coast; maps & 33 ill. [County Coast Ser.] 6/ *n.* c 8° Unwin 10
MOORE, I. History of Devonshire, 2 vols. 4° *London* 29–31
NORTHCOTE, L'y Rosalind Devon: its moorlands, streams, and coasts; col. pl. 20/ *n.* s 4° Chatto 09
*NORWAY, A. H. Highways & Byways in Devon & Cornwall; ill. 6/ $2 *n.* c 8° Macmillan 97
A good description, based on a cycle-tour. Ill. Jos. PENNELL + Hugh THOMSON.
PHILLPOTTS, Eden My Devon Year; 38 ill. 6/ s 4° Methuen [03] 04
Studies of nature in Devonshire all the year round.
POLWHELE, R. History of Devonshire, 3 vols.; maps & pl. [*w.* £14 14/] f° *Exeter* 1793–1806
RISDON, Tristram Note Book: 1608–28, ed. J. Dallas + H. G. Porter 21/ *n.* 8° 97
ROGERS, W. H. H. —*in his* Memorials of the West, *ut inf.*, *s.v.* Somersetshire
ROWE, J. B. The Topography of Devon *o.p.* r 8° *Plymouth* 82
SHELL, F. J. [ed.] North Devon; col. pl. [$2 *n.* Macmillan, *N.Y.*] 6/ *n.* c 8° Black 06
" Memls. of Old Devonsh.; ill. [Memls. of Cos. of Eng.] 15/ *n.* 8° G. Allen 05
*Victoria History of the County of Devon, vol. i—*ut* **E** § 16 [to occupy 4 vols.]
WORTH, R. N. Hist. of County of Devon; ill. [Pop. County Hists.] 7/6; Ch. Ed. 3/6 *n.* 8° Stock 86; 89

*Blackmore Country:* SNELL (F. J.) Blackmore Country; 50 ill. [$2 *n.* Macm., *N.Y.*] 6/ sq 8° Black 06
*Churches:* STABB (J.) Some Old Devon Churches, v. i; 126 ill. 7/6 *n.* 8° Simpkin 08
" Devon Church Antiqs., v. i; 138 ill. [complem. to above] 6/ *n.* 8° Simpkin 09
*Coasts:* ARBER (E. A. N.) Coast Scenery of North Devon; ill. 5/ *n.* 8° Dent 11
PAGE, J. Ll. W. Coasts of Devon and Lundy Island; ill. 7/6 c 8° H. Cox 96
*Guides* —*v.* **E** § 16
*Rivers:* BRAY (Mrs A. E.) Borders of the Tamar and Tavy, 2 vols.—*ut* **B** § 23
PAGE, J. Ll. W. Rivers of Devon: fr. source to sea; ill. 7/6 c 8° Seeley 93
With acc. of towns and villages on their banks. A good companion for a tour. Map, 4 etchgs., and 16 ill.
*Scenery:* CLAYDEN (A. W.) History of Devonshire Scenery; ill. 10/6 *n.* 8° Commin, *Exeter* 06
Written in untechnical language, and well suited to readers who have no geology.
*Axe, River* —*v.* **E** § 16, *s.v.* Rivers
*Barnstaple:* COTTON (R. W.) Barnstaple & N. Dev. dur. Civ. War [1642–6] 10/6 8° *priv. pr.* (Unwin Bros.) 89
*Buckfastleigh:* HAMILTON (A.) Hist. of St Mary's Abbey, Buckfastleigh 8° 07
*Dartmoor:* GOULD (Rev. S. Baring-) Book of Dartmoor; 60 ill. 6/ c 8° Methuen 00
KING, R. J. Dartmoor Forest and its Borders *o.p.* [*pb.* 3/] 12° J. R. Smith 56
PAGE, J. Ll. W. Exploration of Dartmoor and its Antiqs.; ill. 3/6 c 8° Seeley [89] 95
ROWE, Rev. Sam. Perambulation of Dartmoor, ed. J. B. Rowe 15/ *n.* 8° Commin, *Exeter* [48] 96
New edn. of the standard acc. of the Forest, w. reprs. of hist. documts., notes, bibliogr., 24 pl. and num. vign. by F. J. WIDGERY. Chs. on *Geology* by W. A. E. USSHER, on *Botany* by Fcs. BRENT, on *Zoology* by J. D. PRICKMAN and W. P. STARK.
*Devonport* —*v. inf.*, *s.v.* Plymouth (WHITFIELD)
*Exeter:* CROCKER (J.) [artist] Sketches of Old Exeter: 60 pl. 42/ f° 86
FREEMAN, Prf. E. A. Exeter; 4 maps [Historic Towns Series] 3/6 ($1·25) c 8° Longman [87] 92
OLIVER, Dr Geo. History of the City of Exeter *o.p.* [*pb.* 12/6] 8° Longman 61
WORTHY, Chas. History of Suburbs of Exeter [mainly genealogical] 8/ *n.* c 8° Gray 92
*Exmoor* —*for* Stag-hunting *v.* **I** § 155
McDERMOT, E. T. Hist. of Forest of Exmoor *subscr.* 21/ *n.* r 8° Barnicott, *Taunton* 11
PAGE, J. Ll. W. Explorn. of Exmoor and Hill Country; ill. 3/6 c 8° Seeley [90] 95
RAWLE, E. J. Annals of Ancient Forest of Exmoor 20/ 4° Barnicott, *Taunton* (Truslove) 93
The material is derived largely fr. documts. in H.M. Public Record Office and Harleian MSS. in Brit. Mus.
SNELL, F. J. A Book of Exmoor; ill. 6/ c 8° Methuen 03
*Lundy Island* —*v. also* **E** § 16 *s.v.* Coasts (PAGE)
CHANTER, J. R. Lundy Island: descriptive and historical; ill. 3/6 12° Cassell 77
*Ottery St Mary:* COLERIDGE (L'd) Story of a Devonshire House 15/ *n.* 8° Unwin 05
*Plymouth:* WHITFIELD (H. F.) Plymouth & Devonpt. in War & Peace; ill. *o.p.* 8° Chapple, *Plymouth* 00
WORTH, R. N. History of Plymouth [full of research] 12/6 8° Brendon, *Plymouth* [71] 90
*Plympton:* ROWE (J. B.) History of Boro' of Plympton Erle 12/6 *n.* 8° Commin, *Exeter* 07
*Teignmouth:* CRESSWELL (Beat. F.) Teignmouth: history & surrdgs. 5/ *n.* c 8° Homeland Assoc. 00
*Tiverton:* SNELL (F. J.) Chronicles of Twyford 7/6 *n.* 8° Gregory, *Tiverton* 92
A history of Tiverton, w. account of Blundell's School [*v.* **D** § 157].
*Torquay:* WHITE (J. T.) History of Torquay; ill. 10/6 8° Iredale, *Torquay* 78

**Dorsetshire**

*Bibliography:* MAYO (Rev. C. H.) Bibliotheca Dorsetiensis s 4° *pr. pr.* (Chiswick Press) 85
EYTON, Rev. R. W. Key to Domesday [anal. and digest] 30/ 4° Taylor & Francis 78
HARPER, C. G. The Dorset Coast—*ut* **E** § 16, *s.v.* Coasts
HEATH, Sid. The South Devon and Dorset Coast—*ut sup.*, *s.v.* Devonshire
HUTCHINS, Rev. J. Hist. & Antiqs. of Co. of Dorset, ed. Shipp + Hodson, 4 v.; pl. [*w.* £15] r f° *Westmr.* [1774] 61–75
MAYO, Can. C. H. [ed.] Minute Bks. of Dorset Standing Co.: 1646–50 25/ 8° Pollard, *Exeter* 02
Well edited; valuable for the history of the county during the Puritan ascendancy.
MOULE, H. J. Old Dorset: chapters in history of county 10/6 8° Cassell 93
PERKINS (T.) + PENTIN (H.) [eds.] Memls. of Old D.; ill. [Memls. of Cos. of Eng.] 15/ *n.* 8° G. Allen 08
ROGERS, W. H. H. —*in his* Memorials of the West, *ut inf.*, *s.v.* Somerset
*TREVES, Sir Fredk. Highways and Byways in Dorset; ill. 6/ ($2 *n.*) c 8° Macmillan 06
*Victoria History of the County of Dorset, vol. ii.—*ut* **E** § 16 [to occupy 4 vols.]
*Guides* —*v.* **E** § 16
*History:* BAYLEY (A. R.) The Civil War in Dorset 10/6 *n.* 8° Barnicott, *Taunton* 10
*Houses:* HEATH (S.) + PRIDEAUX (W. De C.) Some Dorset Manor Houses; 40 ill. 30/ *n.* r 4° Bemrose 07
*Corfe Castle:* BANKES (G.) Story of Corfe Castle *o.p.* [*pb.* 10/6] 8° Murray 53
BOND, Thos. Hist. and Descrn. of Corfe Castle; ill. 7/6 8° Stanford 83
*Dorchester:* MAYO (Rev. C. H.) [ed.] Municipal Records of Dorchester *subscr.* 25/ 8° Pollard, *Exeter* 08
*Purbeck, Isle of* [S-E corner of Dorset]
ROBINSON, C. E. Royal Warren: rambles in I. of P. *o.p.* [*pb.* 35/] 4° Typogr. Etchg. Co. 82
WOODWARD, Ida In and Around I. of P., 36 col. pl. J. W. G. Bond 21/ *n.* 4° Lane 07
*Shaftesbury Abbey* —*v. inf.*, *s.v.* Somersetshire (Athelney–WALL)
*Wessex* —*v. also* **K** § 24, *s.n.* HARDY (Thos.)
TYNDALE, W. [art.] Wessex: 75 col. pl., w. l'rpr. C. Holland [$6 *n.* Macm., *N.Y.*] 20/ *n.* sq 8° Black
*Weymouth:* MOULE (H. J.) Descr. Catal. of Charters, Minute Books, and other Documts. of Boro' of Weymouth and Melcombe Regis [1252–1800] 4° *Weymouth* 83
*Wootton Glanville:* DALE (C. W.) Hist. of Glanville's Wootton [incl. zoo. & bot.] *o.p.* c 8° 78

**Durham**

ANDREWS, Wm. [ed.] Bygone Durham [pprs. by var. wrs.] 7/6 8° Brown, *Hull* 98
Archæologia Æliana: miscell. tracts rel. to antiq., Ser. iii, vols. i–vi *ann.* 21/ 8° Soc. of Antiq. (Reid, *Newc.*) 56–10 *in prg.*
The best local archæol. jl., contg. (esp. dur. last few yrs.) very good papers indeed. Ser. i is in 4 vols. 4° '22–'55; ii in 4 v., 8°.
Boldon Book: survey of Durham [1183], ed. Rev. W. Greenwell *not sep.* 8° Surtees Soc. 52
BOYLE, J. R. The County of Durham 7/6 sq 8° W. Scott 92
Castles, churches, and houses: more than a guide book. c. 800 pp.
FORDYCE, W. Hist. & Antiqs. of Co. of Durham, 2 v.; ill. *o.p.* [*pb.* 73/] r 8° Fullarton 57
HUTCHINSON, W. History of Durham, 3 vols. 4° *Newcastle* 1785–94
LAPSLEY, Dr G. T. The County Palatine of Durham $2 (10/6) 8° Longman 00
[Harvard Hist. Studs.] An exhaustive constit. hist. of the separate administration of the county fr. Norman times.
LEIGHTON, H. R. Memls. of Old Durham [Memls. of Cos. of Engl.] 8° G. Allen, *in prep.*
PERRY (J. T.) + HENMAN (C.) Illns. of Mediæval Antiqs. in Co. of Durham *o.p.* f° *Oxford* 67
RAINE, Jas., sen. [1791–1858] Hist. and Antiqs. of N. Durh.—*ut inf.*, *s.v.* Northumberld. [complemt. to SURTEES]
,, [ed.] Historiae Dunelmensis Scriptores Tres 10/ 8° Surtees Soc. 39
Gaufridus de Coldingham; Robertus de Greystanes; Willelmus de Chambre; w. App. of 665 orig. documts.
RICHARDSON, M. A. Local Historian's Table Book—*ut inf.*, *s.v.* Northumberland
SURTEES, Rob. Hist. & Antiqs. of Co. of Durham, vols. i–iii ea. 15/ *n.* r 4° Hills, *Sunderld.* [16–52] 08–10
i: *Sunderld. and Distr.*; ii: *Gateshd. and S. Tyne Sectn.*; iii: *Hartlepool and Distr.* A handsome repr. of the magnificent f° edn. (but without the ill.); reprodg. the orig. text and pedigrees (latter ed. H. M. WOOD), spellg., punctn., and capitalizn. Full indexes added.
SURTEES SOCIETY: Publications, vols. i–cxiii *v.pp.* 8° Surtees Soc. 35–10, *in prg.*
The more important vols. are entered separately throughout this work.
*Victoria History of the County of Durham, vols. i–ii—*ut* **E** § 16 [to occupy 4 vols.]
*Bishop Auckland:* RAINE (Can. J.) Account of Auckland Castle *o.p.* [*pb.* 21/] 4° Nichols 52
*Coldingham:* RAINE (J., sen.) [ed.] Corresp., Inventories, etc., of Cold. Priory 7/6 8° Surtees Soc. 41
*Darlington:* LONGSTAFFE (W. H. D.) Hist. of Antiqs. of Parish of Darl.; ill. 15/ *n.* r 8° Paul [54] 09
*Durham* [city, cathedral, churches]—*for* Architecture *v.* **I** § 119

BARMBY, Rev. J. [ed.] Durham Churchwardens' Accompts 15/ 8° Surtees Soc. 88
„ [ed.] Memls. of St Giles: the grassmen's accounts, etc. 15/ 8° Surtees Soc. 96
COSIN, Bp Jno. [1594–1672] Correspondence, ed. Rev. G. Ornsby, 2 vols. 17/6 8° Surtees Soc. 69–72
FOWLER, Can. [ed.] Extracts fr. Acct. Rolls of Abbey of Durh., v. i–iii [1278–1597] ea. 15/ 8° Surtees Soc. 98–01
„ [ed.] Rites of Durh. Monastery [1593] [too late for incl. in **A** § 117] 20/ 8° Surtees Soc. 03
GREENWELL, Rev. W. [ed.] Surv. of Durh. dur. Episc. of T. Hatfield [1345–82] 10/ 8° Surtees Soc. 57
„ [ed.] Foedarium Prioratus Dunelmensis 10/ 8° Surtees Soc. 72
A survey of the estates of Prior and Convent of Durh. in 15 cent.; ill. by grants and other evidces.
LONGSTAFFE (W. H. D.) + BOOTH (J.) [eds.] Halmota Prioratus Dunelm. 15/ 8° Surtees Soc. 89
A survey of the estates of the Priory and Convent of Durham fr. 1296 to 1384.
LOW, Rev. J. L. Durham [Diocesan Histories Series] 2/6 12° S.P.C.K. 81
RAINE, Dr Jas., sen. [ed.] Declarn. of Monumts., Rites, etc., of Durh. [1553] *not sep.* 8° Surtees Soc.
„ [ed.] Injunctions, etc., of R. Barnes, Bp of Durh. [1577–87] *not sep.* 8° Surtees Soc. 50
„ [ed.] Durham Househd. Bk. [Bursar's accs. 1530–4] 7/6 8° Surtees Soc. 44
„ [ed.] Sanctuarium Dunelmense et Sanctuarium Beverlacense 7/6 8° Surtees Soc. 37
Registers of persons who sought sanctuary at Durham and Beverley. Pref. T. CHEVALIER.
„ [ed.] Bede Roll of Jno. Burnaby, Prior of Durh. [1456–64] 7/6 8° Surtees Soc.
RAINE, Can. J., jun. [ed.] Deposns. in Criminal Cases bef. Northern Magistrs. [17 cent.] *not sep.* 8° Surtees Soc. 61
STEVENSON, Rev. J. [ed.] Liber Vitae Ecclesiae Dunelmensis 7/6 8° Surtees Soc. 41
„ Rituale Ecclesiae Dunelmensis—*ut* **A** § 117
*Finchale:* RAINE (Can. J., jun.) [ed.] Charters, Inventories, etc., of Finch. Priory 10/ 8° Surtees Soc. 37
REGINALDUS [monk of Durh.] Libellus de Vita S. Godrici, ed. Rev. J. Stevenson 7/6 8° Surtees Soc. 47
*Gateshead-on-Tyne* —*v.* Newcastle-on-Tyne, *inf.*
*Hartlepool:* SHARPE (Sir C.) History of Hartlepool *o.p.* [*pb.* 21/] 8° *Hartlepool* [16] 51
*Hexham:* RAINE (Can. J., jun.) [ed.] Priory of Hexham: chrons., endowmts., annals, 2 vols.; ill. 52/ 8° Surtees Soc. 64–5
*Jarrow* —*v.* Wearmouth, *inf.*
*Newcastle-on-Tyne* —*v. inf., s.v.* Northumberland
*Norham:* JERNINGHAM ([Sir] H. E. H.) Hist. of Norham Castle & Surroundgs. 10/6 8° Paterson, *Edin.* 83
*Sherburn:* WHEATER (W.) Hist. of Sherburn and Cawood *o.p.* 8° [ ] 82
*Shields (South):* HODGSON (G. B.) Borough of S. Shields [to 1900] 21/ 4° Reid, *Newcastle-o.-T.* 03
*Stockton-on-Tees:* HEAVISIDES (H.) Annals of Stockton-on-Tees *o.p.* 8° *Stockton* 65
RICHMOND, T. Local Records of Stockton & Neighbourhood *o.p.* [*pb.* 10/6] r 8° Marlborough 68
*Wearmouth; Jarrow:* BEDE [673–735] Lives of 1st 5 Abbots of W. & J. [tr.] 5/ *n.* 8° Hills, *Sunderld.* 10
BENEDICT, CEOLFRID, EOSTERWINE, SIGFRID, HUETBERT. Tr. Rev. P. WILCOCK, repr. fr. Garbutt's edn.; w. Apps., Life of BEDE, and 3 ill.
RAINE, J., sen. [ed.] Inventories & Acc. Rolls of Mons. of Jar. & Monkw. 1303–1537] 10/ 8° Surtees Soc. 54

**Essex**

ANDREWS, Wm. [ed.] Bygone Essex; ill. [by var. wrs.] 7/6 8° Brown, *Hull* 92
BARRETT, C. R. B. Essex: high-ways, by-ways & water-ways, 2 Ser. ea. 12/6 *n.* 4° Lawrence & Bullen 92–3
A good and orig. bk. Ser. i deals mainly w. boro's and small towns, ii w. villages and manor-houses. Ill. (by authr.) mostly architectural.
BECKETT, Reg. A. Romantic Essex: pedestrian impressions 3/6 *n.* c 8° Dent 01
ESSEX ARCHÆOLOG. Soc.: Transactions, 5 v.; New Sers., v. i–xi; ill. 8° Wiles, *Colchester* 58–10 *in prg.*
KELWAY, A. C. [ed.] Memorials of Old Essex [Memls. of Cos. of Engl.] 15/ *n.* 8° G. Allen 08
MORANT, P. Hist. & Antiqs. of Co. of Essex, 2 vols. [*w.* 60/] f° *Chelmsford* [1768] 16
PAGE, J. T. [ed.] Essex in the Days of Old 7/6 8° Andrews, *Colchester* 98
12 papers by different wrs. on hist. subjs.: witchcraft in Essex, Hadleigh Castle, Waltham Cross, etc.
SUCKLING, A. History & Antiqs. of Co. of Essex; pl. (some col.) *o.p.* [*pb.* 28/] 4° Weale 45
TINDAL, Rev. Nich. History of Essex, Pts. i–ii [all pubd.] 4° *London* 1720
TOMPKINS, H. W. Marsh-Country Rambles [a gd. wander-bk.] 6/ c 8° Chatto 04
*Victoria History of the County of Essex, vols. i–ii—*ut* **E** § 16 [to occupy 4 vols.]
*Churches:* BUCKLER (G.) 22 Churches of Essex Archit. Described *o.p.* [*pb.* 21/] r 8° Bell 56
*Scenery:* BRUHL (B.) [art.] Essex; w. l'rpr. A. R. H. Moncrieff; 75 col. pl. 20/ *n.* 8° Black 09
$6 *n.* Macmillan, *N.Y.* An excellent example of the literary guide-bk., pleasant in style and useful in matter.
MOUL, Duncan [artist] Picturesque Essex; w. l'rpr. R. H. E. Hill 6/ *n.* 4° Robinson 05
*Braintree; Bocking:* CUNNINGTON (May) + WARNER (S. A.) Braintree & Bocking; 69 pl. (13 col.) 3/6 *n.* 4° Fairbairns 06

*Chipping:* SMITH (Tom C.) History of Chipping 4° *priv. prin.* 92
*Coggeshall:* BEAUMONT (G. F.) History of Coggeshall 7/6 c 8° Marshall 90
*Colchester:* BENHAM (C. E.) Colchester Worthies: biogr. index of Colchester 2/ 8° Forster, *Colchester* 92
BENHAM, M. G. [ed.] Red Paper Bk. of Colchester [1350 onwards] 25/ *n.* 4° Benham, *Colchester* 03
" [ed.] The Oath Book of Colchester 30/ *n.* 4° Benham, *Colchester* 07
An excellent edn. of 'The Red Parchment Bk.', providg. a tolerably compl. ser. of picts. of local govt. fr. time of RICHARD ii to that of HENRY viii, w. some light on earlier and later centuries.
CUTTS, Rev. E. L. Colchester; 4 maps [Historic Towns Series] 3/6 ($1·25) c 8° Longman 88
*Dutch Church* —*v.* **E** § 63 (Hugenot Soc.—MOENS)
*Dagenham:* SHAWCROSS (J. P.) History of Dagenham 10/6 8° Skeffington 04
*Dunmow:* SCOTT (W. T.) Antiqs. of an Essex Parish [Dunmow] *o.p.* [*pb.* 5/] s 8° H. S. King 73
*Epping Forest:* BUXTON (E. N.) Epping Forest; maps & ill. [gd. & v. cheap bk.] 1/ obl 8° Stanford [85] 98
FISHER, W. R. Forest of Essex [hist., laws, admin., anc. customs] 35/ 4° Butterworth 87
PERCEVAL, P. J. S. London's Forest; ill. [hist., tradns., romance] 3/6 *n.* c 8° Dent 09
WALLACE, A. Russel —*in his* Studies, Scientific and Social, vol. ii, *ut* **H** § 43
*Lawford Hill:* [NICHOLS, F. M.] The Hall of Lawford Hall 42/ 4° Ellis & Elvey 91
Record of an Essex house and of its props., fr. Saxon times to HY. VIII. Of real histor., as well as topograph., value. By the present owner.
*Leyton:* KENNEDY (Rev. J.) History of Parish of Leyton; maps & ill. *o.p.* 4° Phelp, *Leyton* 95
*Southend:* BURROWS (J. W.) Southend & District; ill. [histor. notes] 5/ *n.* c 8° Burrows, *Southend* 09
*Stifford:* PALIN (Rev. W.) Stifford and Neighbourhood *o.p.* 8° *priv. prin.* 71
" More about Stifford *o.p.* 8° *priv. prin.* 72
*Theydon Mount:* HOWARD (J. J.) + BURKE (H. F.) Theydon Mt., its Lords & Rectors 4° *priv. prin.* 94

**Gloucestershire**

*Bibliography:* HYETT (Rev. F. A.) + BAZELEY (Rev. W.) Bibliographer's Manl. of Gloucs. Liter., 3 vols. ea. 10/6 8° Bellows, *Gloucs.* 95–7
List, w. descr. notices, of over 7,000 bks. or pts. of bks., pamphs., etc., rel. to Gloucs.
ATKYNS, Sir Rob. [1647–1711] Anc. and Pres. State of Gloucs.; pl. f° *Cambridge* [1712] 1768
BRISTOL & GLOUCS. ARCHÆOL. SOC.: Transactions, vols. i–xxiv; ill. (some col.) 8° B. & G. Archæol. Soc. 76–01 *in prg.*
Gloucestershire Notes & Queries; Ser. i, 4 vols.; N. S., vols. i–vi; ill. ea. 5/ 8° Davies, *Gloucs.* 81–96
MAITLAND, F. W. [ed.] Pleas of the Crown for County of Gloucester—*ut* **D** § 5
RUDDER, S. New History of Gloucestershire; pl. f° *Cirencester* 1779
*Victoria History of the County of Gloucester, vol. ii—*ut* **E** § 16 [to occupy 4 vols.]
WILLIAMS, W. R. Parliamentary History of the Co. of Gloucester *o.p.* 8° *Hereford* 98
*Churches:* GLYNNE (Sir S.) Gloucestershire Church Notes [169 churches] 5/6 8° Phillimore
*Guides*—*v.* **E** § 16 *Homes*—*v.* **E** § 16, *s.v.* Homes (HODGES)
*Berkeley:* SMYTH (Jno.) The Berkeley MSS., ed. Sir J. Maclean, 3 vols. 4° Br. & G. Arch. Soc. 83–5
i–ii: *Lives of Berkeleys, L'ds of the Honour, Castle and Manor of Berkeley* [1066–1618]; iii: *Descrn. of Hundred of Berkeley.*
*Bitton:* ELLACOMBE (Can. H. T.) History of Parish of Bitton, 2 vols. 4° *priv. prin.* 83–5
*Bristol:* BARKER (W. R.) St Mark's: the Mayor's Chapel, Bristol 12/6 8° Hemmons, *Bristol* 92
An archit. and ecclesiol. treat. on Hosp. of St Mark (form. called 'Ch. of the Gaunts') found. 1220 by Maur. de GAUNT (Berkeley family).
Customs Roll of Port of Bristol, tr. Edw. Scott [A.D. 1496–9] *subscr.* 10/6 *n.* 8° George, *Bristol* 97
HARVEY, Alf. Bristol; maps & 57 ill. E. H. New [Ancient Cities] 4/6 *n.* c 8° Methuen 06
HUNT, Rev. Wm. Bristol; 4 maps [Historic Towns Series] 3/6 ($1·25) c 8° Longman 87
HUTTON, Stanley Bristol & its Famous Associations; ports. & ill. 5/ *n.* 8° Arrowsmith, *Bristol* 07
LATIMER, Jno. Sixteenth-Century Bristol 7/6 8° Arrowsmith, *Bristol* 08
Orig. pubd. *sub tit. The Corporation of Bristol in the Olden Times*, repr. fr. *Bristol Mercury* '02–3.
" Annals of Bristol in the Seventeenth Century 13/6 8° George, *Bristol* 00
" Annals of Bristol in the Eighteenth Century 13/6 8° George, *Bristol* 93
" Annals of Bristol in the Nineteenth Century 16/ 8° Morgan, *Bristol* 87
" Annals of Bristol in Nineteenth Cent. (concluded) [1887–1900] 2/6 *n.* 8° George, *Bristol* 02
Excellent trustworthy accounts, compiled from the Corporation archives and other documents.
" History of Society of Merchant Adventurers of Bristol—*ut* **D** § 120
" [ed.] Calendar of the Charters of Bristol 7/6 *n.* 8° Hemmons, *Bristol* 10
'LESSER COLUMBUS' [=Laur. COWEN] Greater Bristol: a history; port. 6/ c 8° Greening 02
NICHOLLS (J. F.) + TAYLOR (J.) Bristol, Past and Present, 3 vols. 4° *priv. prin.* (*Bristol*) 81–2
PRYCE, G. Popular History of Bristol *o.p.* [*pb.* 12/] 8° Mack, *Bristol* 61

Red Book of Bristol (The Little): ed. F. B. Bickley, 2 vols.; 13 pl. 30/ 4° George, *Bristol* 00
A valuable contribn. to munic., commerc., and social hist., showg. growth of a large mediev. tradg. town: 1344–1574.

RICART, Rob. [15 cent.] Maire [Mayor] of Bristowe is Kalendar, ed. Lucy. T. Smith 5/ s 4° Camden Soc. 72
By the Town Clerk of Bristol, *temp.* Edward iv; illustrative of municipal antiquities.

SEYER, Saml. Memoirs, Hist. & Topogr., of Bristol & Neighbrhd., 2 v. *o.p.* 4° *Bristol* 21–3

*Clifton College* —*v.* **E** § 157

*Chipping Campden:* RUSHEN (P. C.) Hist. and antiqs. of Chipping Campden 8/6 8° Stock 98

*Cotswolds:* BADDELEY (W. St C.) A Cotteswold Manor [Painswick] 10/6 *n.* 4° Paul 07

" A Cotteswold Shrine [Hailes] 15/ *n.* 4° Paul 08

DAVIE, W. G. [photogr.] Old Cottages, Farm-houses, etc., in Cotsw. Distr. 21/ *n.* r 8° Batsford 05
Examples of Gloucs. architecture, w. an introductory account by E. G. DAWBER.

GIBBS, J. A. A Cotswold Village: ctry. sketches in Gloucs. 6/ c 8° Murray [98] 99
Light, well-wr. matter on manor-houses, villages, churches, trees, local customs, etc.

HUTTON, W. H. By Thames and Cotswold: sketches of country—*ut* **E** § 16, *s.v.* Rivers

NICHOLLS, G. F. [art.] The Cotswolds: 24 col. pl., w. l'rpr. F. Duckworth [$1·50 *n.* Macm., *N.Y.*] 6/ *n.* sq 8° Black 08

*Dean, Forest of:* NICHOLLS (H. G.) History of Forest of Dean *o.p.* [*pb.* 10/6] 8° Murray 58

*Dursley:* BLUNT (J. H.) Dursley and Nbrhd.: hist. memls. *o.p.* [*pb.* 5/] c 8° Simpkin 77

*Flaxley Abbey:* CRAWLEY-BOEVEY (A. W.) [ed.] Chartulary, etc., of Flaxley Abbey 4° *Exeter* 87

*Gloucester:* HYETT (F. A.) Gloucester in National History 4/ *n.* c 8° Bellows, *Gloucs.* [06] 07

STEVENSON, W. H. [ed.] Calendar of Records of Corpn. of Gloucs. 8° *Gloucester* 93

*Gloucester Cathedral (Abbey)* —*for* Architecture *v.* **I** § 119

HART, W. H. [ed.] Hist. et Cartularium Monast. S. Petri Gl., 3 v. ea. 10/ r 8° Rolls Ser. 63–7

SPENCE, Dn H. D. M. Dreamland in History—*ut* **A** § 57 [note to his 'Cloister Life' here]

" The White Robe of Churches of the 11th cent.; ill. 7/6 c 8° Dent 00
Popular elementary studies in architectural history and ecclesiology, mainly dealing with Gloucester Cathedral.

*Hailes; Painswick:* BADDELEY (W. St C.) A Cotteswold Shrine; ill. 15/ *n.* 4° Paul 08

*Kingswood Forest:* BRAINE (E.) History of Kingsw. Forest; map 3/6 8° Mack, *Bristol* [91] 93

*Tetbury:* LEE (Rev. A. T.) Hist. of Town and Parish of Tetbury *o.p.* [*pb.* 12/] 8° Parker 57

*Tewkesbury:* BLUNT (J. H.) Tewkesbury Abbey and its Associations 3/6 c 8° Simpkin [77] 98

*Winchcombe; Sudeley:* DENT (E.) Annals of Winchcombe & Sudeley 42/ 4° Murray 77

**Hampshire; incl. Isle of Wight**

*Bibliography:* GILBERT (H. M.) + GODWIN (G. N.) Bibliotheca Hantoniensis 3/6 *n.* 8° Gilbert, *S'hptn.* [72] 91

CLUTTERBUCK, R. H. Notes on Parishes . . . of Hants, ed. E. D. Webb; ill. 10/6 8° Bennett, *Salisb.* 98
Fyfield, Kimpton, Penton Mewsey, Weyhill, and Wherwell.

DEWAR, G. A. B. Wild Life in Hampshire Highlands [Haddon Hall Lib.] 7/6 *n.* 8° Dent 99

HAMPSHIRE RECORD SOC.: Publications—*ut* **G** § 22

HUDSON, W. H. Hampshire Days; 11 pl. & 36 ill. [wild life] 5/ *n.* ($2) 8° Longman [03] 06

JEANS, Rev. G. E. Memls. of Old Hampshire; ill. [Memls. of Cos. of Eng.] 15/ *n.* 8° G. Allen 06

MERRITT, Anna L. A Hamlet in Old Hampshire; 22 ill. 6/ c 8° Paul 01
An excellent book, descriptive of human and animal life in and about a Hampshire village.

MUDIE, Rob. Hampshire: past and present condition, 3 v. [*w.* 20/] 8° *Winchester* 38

*READ, [Miss] D. H. M. Highways and Byways in Hants; ill. 6/ ($2 *n.*) c 8° Macmillan 08

SHORE, T. W. Hist. of County of Hants, incl. Isle of Wight 7/6 8° Stock 92
[Popular County Histories.] An excellent *aperçu* of the subject. Good index.

*Victoria History of Hampshire and the Isle of Wight, vols. i–iii—*ut* **E** § 16 [to occupy 4 vols.]

WOODWARD (B. B.) + WILKS (T. C.) + LOCKHART (C.) General Hist. of Hampshire, incl. Isle of Wight, 3 vols.; ill. *o.p.* [*pb.* 105/] 4° Virtue *n.d.* (61–9)

YONGE, Charl. M. An Old Woman's Outlook in a Hampshire Village 3/6 ($1) c 8° Macmillan 92
Reminiscs. of social life and improvemt. wh. have in past 50 yrs. overtaken village-life, word-picts., and discursive notes.

*Guides* —*v.* **E** § 16

*Scenery:* BALL (W.) [art.] Hampshire: 75 col. pl., w. l'rpr. Rev. T. Varley [$6 *n.* Macm., *N.Y.*] 20/ *n.* 4° Black 09

*Basingstoke:* BAIGENT (F. J.) + MILLARD (J. E.) Ancient Town and Manor of Basingstoke; ill. 31/6 8° Jacob, *Basingstoke* 89

*Bournemouth:* MATE (C. H.) + RIDDLE (C.) Bournemouth: 1810–1910; ill. 6/ *n.* 8° Mate, *B'mouth* 10

*Bramshott:* CAPES (W. W.) Scenes of Rural Life in Hants; ill. 8/6 *n.* c 8° Macmillan 01
Papers illustrative of various histor. aspects of country life, arrgd. in chronol. order; w. Appendices of documts.

*Crondal :* Baigent (F. J.) [ed.] Crondal Recds. : histor. & manorial, Pt. i 20/ *n.* 8° Wells, *Winchester* 91
Records, etc., rel. to Hund. and Manor of Crondal—valuable 'strands of history': land-charters, Compotus Roll, a 13-cent. acc. givg. glimpses of old country-life, prices of farm-produce and wages, records of manorial customs, Court Roll, acc. of tenants' holdings, etc.

*Gorley :* Sumner (Heywood) The Book of Gorley ; 50 ill. by author 15/ *n.* 4° Gilbert, *S'hampton* 10
*Hursley :* Yonge (Charl. M.) John Keble's Parishes 8/6 *n.* c 8° Macmillan 98
*Hursley ; Otterbourne* —*v.* **A** § 76*, *s.v.* Keble (Warren ; Yonge)
*Hurstbourne* —*v.* St Mary Bourne, *inf.*
*Hyde Abbey* —*v. inf.*, *s.v.* Winchester (Birch), *and* Somersetshire (Athelney—Wall)
*Manydown Manor :* Kitchin (Dn G. W.) Manor of Manydown 15/ *n.* 8° Hants Record Soc. 95
*New Forest :* Cornish (C. J.) The New Forest ; ill. [Portfolio Monographs] 8° 2/6 *n.* 8° Seeley 94
de Crespigny (Rose C.) + Hutchinson (Hor.) The New Forest ; map & ill. 2/6 *n.* c 8° Murray [95] 03
Hist., tradns., folklore, sports, law of forest, local names, charcoal-burners, smugglers, gypsies, *etc.* ; also fauna, flora, and geol. formn. : attractive and well wr., formg. an admirable suppl. to Wise.

Gilpin, Rev. W. [1724–1804] Forest Scenery, ed. F. G. Heath—*ut* **E** § 16, *s.v.* Forests
*Hutchinson, Hor. G. The New Forest ; 54 col. pl. 6/ c 8° Methuen [04] 06
Deals w. everything of interest (incl. history) in this delightful 100,000 acres of varied scenery—woodland, moor, and heath, attractively ill. by 50 col. drwgs. by W. Tyndale and 4 by Lucy Kemp-Welch.

Rawnsley, Mrs W. [art.] New Forest ; 20 col. pl., w. l'rpr. by artist
[$2·50 *n.* Macm., *N.Y.*] 7/6 *n.* sq 8° Black 04
Turner, G. J. [ed.] —*in his* Select Pleas of the Forest, *ut* **D** § 5
Wise, J. R. The New Forest ; w. 63 ill. Walt. Crane 7/6 8° Sotheran [63] 95
Standard. Deals mainly w. roads, soil, histor. assocns., and places wh. forest-trees may be found : *v.* de Crespigny, *sup.*

*Pilgrim's Way*—*v. inf.*, *s.v.* Kent *Portsmouth Road*—*v.* **E** § 16 (Harper)
*Romsey Abbey :* Liveing (H. G. D.) [ed.] Records of Romsey Abbey 8° 06
*Saint Mary Bourne :* Stevens (Jos.) Parochial Hist. of St Mary Bourne ; 16 pl. 15/ i 8° C. J. Clark 88
*Selborne :* Macray (W. D.) [ed.] Calendar of Charters & Documts. rel. to Selborne & Priory in Magdalen College, Oxford 10/6 *n.* 8° Warren, *Wincs.* 91
White, Gilb. [1720–93] Natural History and Antiquities of Selborne—*ut* **H** § 76
*Silchester* —*v.* **G** § 1*
*Southampton :* Davies (Rev. J. S.) Hist. of S'hptn. [ed. partly fr. Speed's MS.] 15/ r 8° *Southampton* 83
McFadden, F. [art.] Vestiges of Old S'hptn. : 12 etchgs., w. l'rpr. T. W. Shore 63/ f° Gilbert, *S'hptn.* 91
Southampton Record Soc. : Publications *v.pp.* 8° S'hptn. Rec. Soc., *S'hptn.* 05 *sqq.*, *in prg.*

*Black Bk. of S'hampton* ed. Miss M. G. Sims *in prep.*
*Books of Examinations and Reposns.*, vol. i ed. F. Clarke + Miss G. H. Hamilton *in prep.*
*Books of Examinations and Reposns.*, vol. ii ed. F. J. C. Hearnshaw + Miss E. R. Aubrey
*Charters of Borough of S'hampton.* Pt. i ed. H. W. Gidden, 15/9 *n.*
*History of S'hampton* [*ut inf.*] J. Speed, 15/9 *n.*
*Leet Jurisdictn. in Engl. as ill. by Leet Records of S'hptn.* [*ut* **D** § 124] Hearnshaw 21/ *n.*
'*Oak Book*' *of S'hampton* P. Studer *in prep.*
*Southampton Atlas* [old maps and plans] ed. W. H. Rogers 15/9 *n.*
*S'hampton Leet Records* : 1550–77 ; 1578–1602 ; ed. Hearnshaw + Mrs Hearnshaw, ea. 15/9 *n.*
*S'hampton Leet Records : Index* to above, w. *Gloss., Notes on Dialect*, etc. 10/6 *n*

Speed, Dr Jno. [1703–81] Hist. and Antiq. of S'hptn., ed. Elinor R. Aubrey
15/9 *n.* 8° *S'hampton Record Soc.* [c. 1770] 10
*Walloon Church* —*v.* **A** § 63 (Huguenot Soc.—Godfray)
*Strathfieldsaye :* Griffith (Rev. C. H.) History of Strathfield Saye ; photos. 10/6 *n.* 4° Murray 92
A pleasant acc. of the village, fr. mediev. to recent times, incl. Strathfieldsaye House, home of 1st Duke of Wellington.

*Vyne (The) :* Chute (C. W.) History of the Vyne [house and antiqs.] 21/ 4° Jacob, *Winchester* 88
'*Wessex*' —*v.* **K** § 24, *s.n.* Hardy (Thos.)
*Winchester* (city and cathedral)
Baigent, F. J. [ed.] Regrs. of Bps. J. de Sandale & R. de Asserio [1316–23] 21/ *n.* 8° Wells, *Wincs.* 97
Ball, W. [art.] Winchester ; w. l'rpr. Rev. T. Varley [$3 *n.* Macm., *N.Y.*] 7/6 *n.* sq 8° Black
Benham, Rev. W. Winchester [Diocesan Histories] 3/ c 8° S.P.C.K. 84
Birch, W. De G. [ed.] Liber Vitae 15/ *n.* Hants Rec. Soc. (Simpkin) 91
The Register and Martyrol. of New Minster and Hyde Abbey, Wincs. The MS.—better kn. as *Hyde Register*—is pt. of Stowe coll., wh. recently passed into Brit. Mus.

Bramston (Rev. A. R.) + Leroy (A. C.) Historic Winchester, England's First Capital
6/ c 8° Longman [82] 84
„ „ A City of Memories ; ill. 5/ c 8° Warren, *Winchester* 93
Fearon (Archd. W. A.) + Williams (J. F.) [eds.] Par. Regrs. & Paroch. Docums. of Archd. of Wincs. 5/ *n.* 8° Warren, *Winchester* 09
Kitchin, Dn. G. W. Winchester [Historic Town Series] 3/6 ($1·25) c 8° Longman 90
„ [ed.] Compotus Rolls of Obedientaries of S. Swithun's Priory, Wincs 21/ *n.* 8° Hants Rec. Soc. 92
Conts. an Introduction on the organization of a convent. 2 maps.

„ + Madge (F. T.) [eds.] Documts. rel. to Foundn. of Chapt. of Wincs. 10/6 *n.* 8° Hants Rec. Soc. 89
Cover the period 1541–7. By the Dean and the Librarian of Wincs. Cathedral. Very fully edited, w. glossary, etc.

Le Strange, Rev. A. G. Royal Wincs. : wanderings ab. the anc. capital ; ill. 3/6 c 8° Longman [89] 91

**Isle of Wight** —*v. also sup., s.v.* Hampshire (Generally)

BOURGET, Paul Days in Isle of Wight [tr.] [orig. ed. 1880] 1/6 c 8° H. W. Bell 02

CORNISH, C. J. The Isle of Wight; ill. [Portfolio Monographs] 3/6 *n.* 8° Seeley 75

JAMES, Rev. E. B. Letters, Archæol & Histor., rel. to I. o. W., 2 v. *o.p.* [*pb.* 24/ *n.*] Frowde 96
**Contribns. to *I. o. W. County Press.* Much matter wh. does not concern I. o. W. and very little orig. matl.**

OGLANDER, Sir J. The Oglander Memoirs, ed. W. H. Long [1626–32] 10/6 4° Reeves & Turner 88
**OGLANDER was Dep.-Gov. of P'mouth and Dep.-Lt. of I. of W. 1595–1648. This vol. is a seln. of all most import. passages of local and histor. interest. The MSS. have been largely ref. to and quoted in most bks. ab. the Island.**

STONE, P. G. [art.] Archit. Antiqs. of I. o. W: 11–17 cents, 4 v.
ea. 63/ s f° Artist, 16, *Gt. Marlb. St., Lond.* 91–2

WHITEHEAD, Dr J. L. Undercliff of I. o. W.: past and present 10/6 *n.* 8° Knight, *Ventnor* 11

*Scenery:* COOPER (A. H.) [art.] Isle of Wight: 24 col. pl., w. l'rpr. A. R. H. Moncrieff
[$2·50 *n.* Macmillan, *N.Y.*] 7/6 *n.* 4° Black 08

**Herefordshire**

BEVAN (Rev. J. O.) + DAVIES (Jas.) + HAVERFIELD (F.) An Archæological Survey of Herefordshire of the Mediæval Period [pamphlet] *o.p.* 8° Jakeman, *Hereford* 96

BRADLEY, A. G. Shropshire, Hereford, and Monmouthshire—*ut inf., s.v.* Shropshire

CANTILUPE Soc.: Publications r 8° *Hereford* 05 *sqq., in prg.*
**CANTILUPE (Bp), *Register*, 2 Pts. ed. Can. CAPES**
**CHARLTON (Bp), *Register* ed. CAPES, *in prep.***
***Charters and Records of Heref. Cathedral* ed. CAPES**
**ORLETON (Bp A.), *Register*, 2 Pts. ed. Can. BANNISTER**
**SWINFIELD (Bp), *Register*, 2 Pts. ed. BANNISTER**
**TREVENANT (Bp), *Register* [1389–1404] ed. CAPES, *in prep.***
**TRILLECK (Bp), *Register* [1344–60] ed. CAPES**

DUNCUMB, Jno. [1765–1839] Collns. tow. Hist. & Antiqs of Co. of Heref., v. i–ii (1) [*w.* £6] 4° *Heref.* 04–12
***Continuation* (Murray '82–92) addns. to vol. ii (pp. 319–58, 151; pp. 359–404), ed. W. H. COOKE, 15/; iii: *Greytree Hundred*, ed. COOKE; pl., 52/6; iv: *Hund. of Grimsworth*, ed. COOKE, 2 Pts., 47/6; *Hund. of Huntington*, ed. Rev. M. G. WATKINS, 25/; *Hund of Radlow*, ed. WATKINS, 35/.**

READE, Rev. C. [ed.] Memls. of Old Heref.; ill. [Memls. of Cos. of Eng.] 15/ *n.* 8° G. Allen 05

TIMMINS, H. T. Nooks and Corners of Herefordshire; c. 150 ill. 21/ 4° Stock 92
**A descriptive wk., arrgd. in narrative form. Mainly architectural and picturesque.**

*Victoria History of the County of Hereford, vol. i—*ut* **E** § 16 [to occupy 4 vols.]

*Castles; Mansions; Manors*

ROBINSON, C. J. Hist. of Castles of Heref. & their Lords; ill. *o.p.* [*pb.* 25/] 4° Longman 69

" Hist. of Mansions & Manors of Heref.; ill. *o.p.* [*pb.* 52/6] 4° Longman 73

*History: Civil War:* WEBB (J.) Memls. of Civil War in Heref., 2 v. 42/ 8° Longman 79

WILLIAMS, W. R. Parliamentary Hist. of Herefordshire [1213–1896] *o.p.* 8° 96

*Worthies:* HUTCHINSON (Jno.) Herefordshire Biographies 21/ *n.* 4° Jakeman, *Hereford* 95
**Uniform in size w. DUNCUMB [*ut sup.*], to wh. it is intended to form a Biographical Suppl.**

*Ewyas Harold:* BANNISTER (A. T.) Hist. of Ewias Harold 21/ *n.* r 8° Jakeman, *Hereford* 02
**A history of the Castle, Priory and Church; w. trs. of the MSS. on wh. the history is based.**

*Hereford:* JOHNSON (Rich.) Ancient Customs of Hereford; w. trs. of charters, etc.; ill 4° [45] 82

PHILLOTT, Rev. H. W. Hereford [Diocesan Histories] 2/6 f 8° S.P.C.K. 88

SWINFIELD, Bp R. Registrum, ed. Can. W. W. Capes [1783–1807] 4° Canterb. & York Soc. 09

**Hertfordshire**

CLUTTERBUCK, R. Hist. and Antiqs. of Co. of Hertford, 3 vols.; ill. [*w.* £15] f° *London* 15–27

CUSSANS, J. E. Hist. of Hertfordshire, 16 Pts.=3 v.; col. pl. & ill. *subscr.* £16 16/ i 4° Sotheran 70–81

GEAREY, Carol. Rural Life, its Humour and Pathos [chfly. Herts] 6/ c 8° Long 99

HARDY, W. J. [ed.] Hertfordsh. County Records, vols. i–iii
[Sessn. Rolls; 1581–1894] ea. 5/ r 8° Longmore, *Hertfd.* 05–11

STANDING, Percy C. [ed.] Memls. of Old Herts; ill. [Memls. of Cos. of Eng.] 15/ *n.* 8° G. Allen 05

*TOMPKINS, H. W. Highways and Byways in Herts; ill. 6/ ($2 *n.*) c 8° Macmillan 02

*Victoria History of the County of Hertford, vols. i–ii—*ut* **E** § 16 [to occupy 4 vols.]

*Guides*—*v.* **E** § 16 *Place-names*—*v.* **K** § 120

*History:* KINGSTON (A.) Herts dur. Civil War and Long Parlt. [1640–60] 8/ *n.* 16° Stock 94

*Scenery:* MOUL (Dunc.) [art.] Picturesque Hertfordshire; w. l'rpr. F. G. Kitton 6/ *n.* 4° Robinson 03

*Barnet:* CASS (F. C.) East Barnet 4° Lond. & Mid. Arch. Soc. 85–92

*Beckhamsted:* COBB (J. W.) Hist. and Antiqs. of Berk. [2 lects.] r 8° 83

*Flamstead:* BULLARD (J. V.) Flamstead: its church and history; ill. 5/ *n.* 4° Cobb, *Rochester* 02

*Hatfield House:* BREWER (J. S.)—*in his* English Studies, *ut* **F** § 16

*Hitchin:* HUYSHE (Wentworth) The Royal Mànor of Hitchin; ill. 10/6 *n.* r 8° Macmillan 06

*Hoddesdon:* TREGELLES (J. A.) History of Hoddesdon 8° 08

*Monken Hadley:* CASS (F. C.) Monken Hadley 4° Lond. & Mid. Arch. Soc. 80

*Royston :* KINGSTON (A.) History of Royston ; ill. 10/ 8° Stock 06
His. *Fragms. of Two Cents.* [2/ c 8° Warren, *Royston* '93] relate mostly to Royston and neighbourhood.

*St Albans :* ASHDEN (C. H.) St Albans : historical and picturesque ; 100 ill. 42/ *n.* r 4° Stock 94
A compreh. acc. of Verulamium, its monastic records, lives of Abbots, battles of St Albans, Peasant Revolt, its historns., churches of SS. Michael, Peter, Stephen, *etc.* Il. F. G. KITTON.

CARR, J. Comyns Abbey Church of St Albans ; ill. & 5 etchgs. *o.p.* [*pb.* 18/] r 4° Seeley 76

GIBBS, A. E. [ed.] The Corporation Records of St Albans 5/ *n.* c 8° Gibbs, *St Albans* 90

JESSOPP, Dr A. St Albans and her Historian—*in* Studies, *ut* **F** § 19

*South Mimms :* CASS (F. C.) South Mimms 4° Lond. & Mid. Arch. Soc. 77

**Huntingdonshire** —*v. also* Cambridge, *sup.*

*Guides* —*v.* **E** § 16

*History :* NOBLE (Rev. W. M.) Huntingdonshire and the Spanish Armada 3/6 8° Stock 96
Account of preparns. made in the county to resist invasion of 1558 ; fr MS. and local sources.

*Aillington :* WHISTLER (Rev. R. F.) Hist. of Aillington, Aylton, or Elton ; 4 ill. 21/ r 8° Mitchell & Hughes 92

*Bedford Level* —*v. inf.*, *s.v.* Lincolnshire

*Hinchingbrooke :* SANDWICH (Earl of) Hinchingbrooke [hist. of his house] 5/ *n.* 8° Humphreys 10

*Little Gidding* —*v.* **A** § 62, *s.v.* FERRAR

*Peterborough* —*v. inf.*, *s.v.* Northamptonshire

*Ramsey :* HART (W. H.) + LYONS (P. A.) [eds.] Cartularium Mon. de Rameseia, 3 v. ea. 10/ r 8° Rolls Ser. 84–93

NEILSON, Nellie Econ. Condns. on Manors of Ramsey Abbey 8° *Philadelphia* 99

*Whittlesea Mere :* HEATHCOTE (J. M.)—*in his* Reminiscences, *ut inf.*, *s.v.* Lincolnshire

**Isle of Man**

*Bibliography :* HARRISON (W.) Bibliotheca Monensis 8° Manx Soc. [61] 76

„ [ed.] The Old Historians of Isle of Man 8° Manx Soc. 71
CAMDEN, SPEED, DUGDALE, COX, WILSON, WILLIS, GROSE.

BLUNDELL, Wm. History of Isle of Man, ed. W. Harrison, 2 vols. 8° Manx Soc. [1648–56] 76

CAINE, Hall The Little Manx Nation [3 lectures] 3/6 c 8° Heinemann 91
Very light talks about scenery, history, celebrities, superstitns. of his 'tight little island', by the Manxman novelist.

CALLOW, Edw. From King Orry to Qu. Victoria ; ill. [popular] 7/6 8° Stock 00

CHALONER, Jas. Short Treat. on Isle of Man, ed. Rev. J. G. Cumming 8° Manx Soc. [1656] 64

Chronicon : 1066–1313 —*in* John of Pian de Carpine, Texts and Versns. [1598], ed. C. R. Beazley *o.p.* 8° Hakluyt Soc. 03

CUMMING, Rev. J. G. History of the Isle of Man ; maps *o.p.* [*pb.* 12/6] c 8° Van Voorst 48
The physical, ecclesiastical, civil, and legendary history of the island.

FELTHAM, Jno. Tour thro' I. o. M., ed. Rev. R. Airy [1797–8] 8° Manx Soc. [1798] 61

„ + WRIGHT (E.) Memorials of 'God's Acre,' ed. Wm. Harrison—*ut* **G** § 17

HALLIWELL, [-PHILLIPPS] J. O. Roundabout Notes [chiefly on anc. stone-circles] *o.p.* [*pb.* 3/6] 8° J. R. Smith 63

HARRISON, Wm. [ed.] Mona Miscellany, 2 Ser. [provbs., etc.] 8° Manx Soc. 69–73

„ Records of Tynwald and St John's Chapels 8° Manx Soc. 71

HERBERT, Agnes Isle of Man ; 32 col. pl. Don. Maxwell 10/6 *n.* ($3·50 *n.*) 8° Lane 09

Illiam Dhone and the Manx Rebellion, ed. Wm. Harrison [1643–63] 8° Manx Soc. [1651] 77

MACKENZIE, Rev. W. [ed.] Legisln. by 3 of the 13 Stanleys, Kgs. of Man 8° Manx Soc. 60

MOORE, A. W. History of the Isle of Man, 2 vols. 32/ 8° Unwin 00
The best book (not takg. acc. of WALPOLE, *inf.*). Full history and acc. of pres. condn.

„ Manx Names—*ut* **K** § 120 [surnames and place-names]

MUNCH, P. A. [ed.] Chronica Regum Manniæ et Insularum, 2 vols. 8° Manx Soc. 74
Orig. pub. in Christiania, '60. Here revised by GOSS. The Chron. of Man and the Sudreys fr. MS. codex in Brit. Mus. ; w. notes.

OLIVER, J. R. [ed. & tr.] Monumenta de Insula Manniæ, 3 Pts. 8° Manx Soc. 60–2
A collection of national documents, B.C. 54 to A.D. 1770.

OSWALD, H. R. [ed.] Vestigia Insulæ Manniæ Antiquiora ; 11 pl. (2 col.) 8° Manx Soc. 60
A dissertn. on armorial bearings, regalities and prerogatives of the anc. kings, etc.

PARR, Deemster Abstract of Laws, Custs. & Ordins. of I. o. M., ed. J. Gell 8° Manx Soc. 62

SACHEVERELL, Wm. Account of Isle of Man, ed. Rev. J. G. Cumming 8° Manx Soc. [1702] 59
By a Govr. of I. o. Man. Contains also a dissertn. on the Mona of CÆSAR and TACITUS, by Thos. BROWN [repr. of 1703].

TRAIN, J. Account of the Isle of Man, 2 vols. *o.p.* [*pb.* 14/] 8° *Douglas* 45

WALDRON, G. Descrn. of I. o. M., ed. W. Harrison [laws, custs., manners, etc.] 8° Manx Soc. [1731] 65

WALPOLE [Sir] Spencer The Land of Home-Rule 6/ c 8° Longman 93
Sketch of hist. and constitn. of the isld. fr. pre-histor. to pres. times, by its Lt.-Gov. A ch. is devoted to 'Manx Magna Carta', the Act (1703) wh. converted a whole natn. of leasehrs. into perp. tenants at low quit-rent. 'Whatever may be the result of autonomy in other places, it has made of the Manx a loyal, orderly, easily-governed community'.

*Scenery:* COOPER (A. H.) [art.] Isle of Man: 20 col. pl.; w. l'rpr. W. R. Hall Caine [$2 *n.* Macmillan, *N.Y.*] 7/6 *n.* sq 8° Black

*Rushen:* CUMMING (J. G.) Story of Rushen Castle and Abbey *o.p.* [*pb.* 6/] c 8° Bell 57

**Isle of Wight** —*v.* Hampshire, *sup.*

**Kent**

*Bibliography:* SMITH (J. R.) Bibliotheca Cantiana *o.p.* [*w.* 3/6] 8° J. R. Smith 37

DITCHFIELD (Rev. P. H.) + CLINCH (G.) [eds.] Memorials of Old Kent 15/ *n.* 8° G. Allen 07
[Memls. of Counties of Eng.] 14 papers by var. wrs. One of the best vols. of this varying Series.

FURLEY, R. History of Weald of Kent, 2 vols. in 3 *o.p.* [*pb.* 12/ ea.] 8° J. R. Smith 71–4

HASTED, Edw. Hist. of Kent, ed. Dr H. H. Drake, Pt. i: Blackheath; ill. 100/ f° Mitchell & Hughes [1778–99] 86
Not continued. 1st edn., 4 vols., pl., f°, *w.* £20, *Canterbury* 1778–99; 2nd edn., 12 vols. and Atlas, 8° *ib.* 1797–1801.

IRELAND, W. H. New History of Kent, 4 vols. *o.p.* 8° 28–30

*JERROLD, Walt. Highways & Byways in Kent; 150 ill. Hugh Thomson 6/ ($2 *n.*) c 8° Macmillan 07

KENT ARCHAEOL. Soc.: Archæologia Cantiana. vols. i–xxiii; ill. 10/ 8° Kent Arch. Soc. 58–98

LAMBARD, W. [1536–1601] A Perambulation of Kent *o.p.* 8° *Chatham* [1576] 26
The first Engl. county-hist.: collected and wr. in 1570. The 1st edn. (1576) conts. acc. of the nobility, subseq. omitted.

ROBERTSON, W. A. S. Kentish Archæology, Pts. i–vi 8° 76–84

STEAD, Rich. [ed.] Bygone Kent [by var. wrs.] 7/6 8° Brown, *Hull* 92

*Victoria County History of Kent, vol. i—*ut* **E** § 16 [to occupy 5 vols.]

*Churches:* GLYNNE (Sir S.) Notes on the Churches of Kent; ill. 12/ 8° Murray 77

HUSSEY, Arth. Notes on Churches in Kent, Sussex, & Surrey *o.p.* [*pb.* 18/] 8° J. R. Smith 52

*Guides* —*v.* **E** § 16

*Scenery:* DAVIE (W. G.) [photogr.] Old Cottages and Farm-houses in Kent and Sussex; w. l'rpr. E. G. Dawber 21/ *n.* ($7·50) 4° Longman 01

GARDNER, W. B. [art.] Kent; w. l'rpr. W. T. Shore [$6 *n.* Macm., *N.Y.*] 20/ *n.* sq 8° Black 07

MOUL, Duncan [art.] Picturesque Kent; w. l'rpr. Gibson Thomson 6/ *n.* s 4° Robinson 01

*Worthies:* HUTCHINSON (J.) Men of Kent and Kentish Men [240 brief biogrs.] 5/ c 8° Cross, *Canterb.* 93

*Beckenham:* BORROWMAN (R.) Beckenham, Past and Present; ill. 21/ *n.* 4° Thornton, *Beckenham* 10

*Benenden:* HARDY (C. F.) Benenden Letters, London, Country, and Abroad 15/ 8° Dent 01
Correspondence between a land-agent at Benenden, and a friend in London: 1758–1821: of no value for public affairs.

*Blackheath* —*v. sup.*, *s.n.* HASTED (note: DRAKE)

*Boxley:* CAVE-BROWNE (J.) History of Boxley Parish 10/ 8° Author, *Maidstone* 92

*Canterbury* —*for* Architecture *v.* **I** § 119

BOGGIS, Rev. R. J. E. Hist. of St Monastery, Canterbury [careful compiln.] 3/ c 8° Cross, *Canterbury* 01

BRENT, J. Canterbury in Olden Time 12/6 8° Simpkin [60] 79

COX, Rev. J. C. Canterbury; ill. [Ancient Cities] 4/6 *n.* c 8° Methuen 05
$1·75 *n.* Dutton, *N.Y.* A good historical and topographical account.

GARDNER, W. B. [artist] Canterbury; 20 col. pl., w. l'rpr. W. T. Shore [$3 *n.* Macm., *N.Y.*] 7/6 *n.* sq 8° Black 07

HOPE, W. H. St John Excavations at St Austin's Abbey 3/6 8° Kent Arch. Soc. 02

JAMES, M. R. [ed.] Ancient Libraries of Canterbury and Dover—*ut* **K** § 4

JENKINS, Rev. R. C. Canterbury [Diocesan Histories] 3/ 12° S.P.C.K. 80

LEGG (J. W.) + HOPE (W. J. St J.) [eds.] Inventories of Christ Ch.; w. tr. & Introd. 21/ *n.* 8° Constable 02

OYLER (T. H.) Parish Churches of Dioc. of Canterb.; phots. & text 10/6 *n.* 8° Hunter & Longhurst 10

ROUTLEDGE, Rev. F. C. Hist. of St Martin's Church, Canterbury; front. 5/ c 8° Paul 91
A pleasantly written acc. of the oldest church in England, containg. many interesting ancient objects.

SEARLE, W. G. [ed.] Christ Church, Canterbury: chron. & lists 02

SHEPPARD, J. B. [ed.] Christ Church Letters [medieval colln.] s 4° Camden Soc. 77

" Literae Cantuarienses, 3 v. [L'r-bks. of Ch. Ch. 1296–1333] ea. 10/ m 8° Rolls Ser. 87–9

STANLEY, Dn A. P. Historical Memorials of Canterbury Cathedral; ill. 2/6 *n.* 8° Murray [55] 04
$1 *n.* Dutton, *N.Y.* *Landg. of Augustine; Murder of Becket; Edw. the Black Pr'ce; Becket's Shrine.*

STONE, J. [ed.] Christ Church, Canterbury: chronology [1415–71] 02

STUBBS, Bp W. [ed.] Epistolae Cantuarienses =vol. ii *of his* Chrons. & Memls. of Rich i—*ut* **F** § 19

THOMPSON, Sir E. M. [ed.] Customary of Bened. Mon. of St Aug., Canterb., v. i–ii Hy. Bradsh. Soc. 02–4

*Episcopal Palaces*

CAVE-BROWN, J. Mediaeval Life amg. Old Palaces—*in his* Lambeth Pal., *ut inf.*, *s.v.* Middlesex (London)

RAIT, R. S. [ed.] Engl. Episcopal Palaces: Prov. of Cant.; ill. 7/6 *n.* 8° Constable 10
Overflow material fr. the *Victoria County Hist.*, formg. a sort of Suppl. Vol. Pprs. by 6 ladies.

*Walloon Church* —*v.* **A** § 63 (Huguenot Soc.—CROSS; HOVENDEN)

*Chislehurst:* WEBB (E. A.) + MILLER (W. G.) + BECKWITH (J.) Hist. of Chisleh.; ill. 30/ *n.* 4° G. Allen 00
A full hist., w. account of topogr., nat. hist., and place names. Apps. cont. illustr. documts. Good ill.

*Dartford:* DUNKIN (J.) Hist. and Antiqs. of Dartford *o.p.* [*pb.* 21/] 8° J. R. Smith 44

*Deal:* CHAPMAN (H. S.) Deal, Past and Present [interesting] 3/6 s 4° Reeves & Turner 91

ROGET, J. Lewis Sketches of Deal, Walmer, Sandwich; 42 ill. (32 col.) 12/6 8° Longman 11

*Deptford* —*v. inf.*, *s.v.* London

*Dover* —*v. also* **E** § 16, *s.v.* Cinque Ports

PUCKLE, Jno. Church and Fortress of Dover Castle *o.p.* [*pb.* 7/6] 8° Parker 64

*STATHAM, Rev. S. P. H. Hist. of Castle, Town, and Port of Dover; ill. 10/6 ($3·50) c 8° Longman 99
A very full acc. fr. the records, w. lists of Constables of the town, etc. The standard work.

„ [ed. & tr.] Dover Charters and other Documents; ill. [1227–1569] 14/ *n.* 8° Dent 02

*St Martin's Priory* —*for* Catalogue of Library, *v.* **K** § 4 (JAMES)

*Dover Road* —*v.* **E** § 16, *s.v.* Roads (HARPER; HISSEY)

*Downs* (*The*) —*for* Goodwin Sands *v.* **D** § 128, *s.v.* Life-Boats

RUSSELL, W. C. Betwixt the Forelands *o.p.* [*pb.* 6/] c 8° Low 89

*Eastry:* SHAW (W. F.) Liber Estriae: memls. of Eastry *o.p.* [*pb.* 28/] 4° J. R. Smith 71

*Fordwich:* WOODRUFF (C. E.) History of Town and Port of Fordwich 8° Cross, *Canterbury* 95
A good local hist. of a curious relic of past, once port of Canterb., setting-up of Stour hg. proved its ruin.

*Gravesend:* CRUDEN (R. P.) Hist. of Gravesend and Port of London *o.p.* [*pb.* 28/] r 8° Pickering 43

*Greenwich:* FRASER (E.) Green. Hospital and U. Serv. Museum 2/6 *n.* c 8° Wells Gardner 11

L'ESTRANGE, A. G. Greenwich Palace and Hospital, 2 vols. *o.p.* [*pb.* 21/] 8° Hurst 86

*Hawkhurst:* JENNINGS (L'y) A Kentish Country House Billing, *Guildford* 94
Selns. fr. records of Hall House, Hawkh.: 1665–1887. The corresp. of Dr N. LARDNER (who was born there in 1684; d. 1768), w. 'my lady', describg. tour he made w. her son thro' Frce. and Holl. just aft. MARLBOROUGH's wars, is interestg. gossip.

*Hythe* —*v.* **E** § 16, *s.v.* Cinque Ports

*Ightham:* BENNETT (F. J.) Ightham: story of Kentish village 7/6 *n.* 8° Homeld. Assoc. 07

*Leeds Castle* (Kent): MARTIN (C. W.) Hist. & Descrn. of Leeds Castle *o.p.* f° 69

*London-Canterbury Road:* LITTLEHALES (H.) Notes on Road from London to Canterbury in Middle Ages = CHAUCER Soc. pubns., ii, 30

*Lydd* (*Romney Marsh*): HUSSEY (A.) + HARDY (M. M.) [eds.] Records of Lydd 8° *Kentish Expr.* Off. 11

*Maidstone:* RUSSELL (J. M.) History of Maidstone 7/6 8° Bunyard, *Maidstone* 81

*All Saint's Church:* CAVE-BROWN (J.) Hist. of All Sts, Maidstone 10/6 8° Bunyard, *Maidstone* 90

*Malling:* FIELDING (Rev. C. H.) Memories of Malling and its Valley 7/6 8° Oliver, *W. Malling* 93
Arrgd. chron. fr. Sax. era to 1892, w. gd. flora and fauna of Kent, provbs., custs., and 104 pp. of Par. and Fam. Regrs. Map and ill.

*Pilgrims' Way:* *BELLOC (Hilaire) The Old Road; photogravs. & ill. W. Hyde 7/6 *n.* 8° Methuen [04] 10
A careful study of the extremely anc. road fr. Wincs along the Surrey hills and flank of Kentish Weald to Canterb.

CARTWRIGHT, Julia [Mrs Hy. ADY] The Pilgrim's Way; ill. A. Quinton & 2 maps 10/6 4° Virtue [93] 01

PARR, Hy. New Wheels in Old Ruts; 50 ill. [$1·50 L'cott, *Phila.*] 3/6 c 8° Unwin 96

WARD, H. Snowden The Canterbury Pilgrimages; ill. 6/ 8° Black 04
THOMAS, of London, his murder, cult, and miracles; CHAUCER and his Pilgrims; Pilgrims' Way.

*Rochester:* FIELDING (Rev. C. H.; ed.) Registrum Roffense: records of Rochester 8° Snowden, *Dartf.* 11

*Romney* —*v. also* **E** § 16, *s.v.* Cinque Ports

CHAMPNEYS, B. A Quiet Corner of Engld.—*ut inf.*, *s.v.* Sussex (Winchelsea, etc.)

HOLLOWAY, W. History of Romney Marsh *o.p.* [*pb.* 12/] 8° J. R. Smith 49

*Sandwich* —*v.* Deal, *sup.*, and **E** § 16, *s.v.* Cinque Ports

*Strood:* SMETHAM (Hy.) History of Strood 8° Sweet, *Strood* 00

*Thanet:* COTTON (C.) Hist. & Antiqs. of Ch. & Par. of St Lawrence, 32 maps 30/ *n.* 4° Wilson, *Ramsgate* 95

SIMSON, Jas. Historic Thanet 5/ c 8° Stock 91

*Tritton:* TRITTON (J. H.) Tritton, the Place and Family 21/ *n.* 4° Humphreys 07

*Tunbridge:* HARPER (C. G.) —*in his* The Hastings Road, *ut* **E** § 16, *s.v.* Roads

*Walmer:* ELVIN (Rev. C. R. S.) Records of Walmer, and the 3 Castles; ill. 30/ *n.* r 4° H. Gray 90

„ History of Walmer and Walmer Castle [*v. also* Deal, *sup.*] 1/ 8° Cross, *Canterbury* 94

**Lancashire**

*Bibliography :* Bibliotheca Lancastriensis [w. App. of Chesh. bks.] 1/ s 4° Sutton, *Mancs.* 93
CHRISTIE, R. C. Old Church and Schl. Libraries of Lancs s 4° Chetham Soc. 85
FISHWICK, Lt.-Col. H. Lancs Library : bibl. acc. of bks. on Lancs *o.p.* [*pb.* 25/] 4° Routledge 75
HISTORIC SOC. OF LANCS & CHESHIRE : Catal. of Library and Museum 8° *Liverpool* 76
MANCS. LITERARY CLUB : List of Lancashire Authors, ed. C. W. Sutton 8° *Manchester* 76
SUTTON, C. W. [ed.] List of Lancs Authors : w. biogr. & bibl. notes [Mancs. Lit. Club] 10/ 8° A. Heywood, *Mancs.* 76

AXON, W. E. A. Lancashire Gleanings [worthies, assocs., hist., etc.] 6/ c 8° J. Heywood, *Mancs.* 83
„ Bygone Lancashire 7/6 8° Brown, *Hull* 92
„ Echoes of Old Lancashire 8° Brown, *Hull* 00
Pprs. on hist. of co.—the Popish plot, Jacobite rising, Reform agitn., old newspprs., families, etc.

BAINES, Edw. Hist. of Co. Pal. & Duchy of Lancaster, ed. J. Croston ; maps, ports. & ill., 5 vols. ea. 16/ 4° Heywood, *Mancs.* [36] 88–93
BAINES, Thos. Lancs & Cheshire, Past & Present, 2 v. ; ill. *o.p.* [*pb.* 73/6] 4° Routledge 68–9
Forms a continuation to Edw. BAINES' work, and to ORMEROD'S *Cheshire* [*ut sup.*].

Chetham Miscellanies : Ser. i, 6 vols. ; Ser. ii, vol. i–ii s 4° Chetham Soc. 51–78 ; 02–9
CHETHAM SOCIETY : Publications, 115 vols. ; N.S., vols. i *sqq.* *ann. subscr.* 20/ s 4° Chetham Soc. 40–82 ; 83 *sqq.*, *in prg.*
The chief vols. entd. separ. *inf.* and elsewhere. A useful *General Index to vols. i–cxiv* is pubd. in 2 vols.

CORRY, J. Hist. of Lancs, 2 vols. ; pl., coats-of-arms, etc. *o.p.* [*w.* 50/] 4° *London* 25
Domesday Book of Cheshire and Lancashire, ed. Beaumont—*ut sup.*, *s.v.* Cheshire
EARWAKER, J. P. [ed.] Constables' Accts. of Manor of Manchester, 3 v. ea. 12/6 r 8° Blacklock, *Mancs.* 92
Pubd. for Corporn. of City of Mancs., wh. recently recovered possessn. of the 2 MSS. here reprinted.

FISHWICK, Lt.-Col. H. History of Lancashire [Pop. County Hists.] 7/6 ; Ch. Edn. 3/6 *n.* 8° Stock 94 ; 02
A sound bk., simple and unpretentious, dealg. w. the co. as a whole, and not entering into personal or local details. Leaves the 19 cent. comparatively out of account and thus rids itself of what DICKENS called the 'cotton and cant' element.

„ + DITCHFIELD (Rev. P. H.) [eds.] Memls. of Old Lancs, 2 v. [Memls. of Cos. of Eng.] 25/ *n.* 8° Geo. Allen 09
GREGSON, M. Portfolio of Lancashire Fragments, ed. J. Harland ; ill. *o.p.* [*pb.* 73/6] f° Routledge [17] 69
GRINDON, Leo Lancashire : descriptive notes ; 40 ill. [pleasant papers] 7/6 c 8° Seeley [81] 92
HARLAND, J. [ed.] Lancs Lieutenancy under Tudors & Stuarts, 2 Pts. s 4° Chetham Soc. 59
Illustrated by Royal and other letters, Orders of Privy Council, etc. : chfy. fr. Shuttleworth MSS.

„ [ed.] Three Lancashire Documents of 14th & 15th Centuries s 4° Chetham Soc. 68
*De Lacy Inquisitn.* (1311) ; *Survey* (1320–46) ; *Custom Roll and Rental of Manor of Ashton. u. Lyne* (1422).

LANCS AND CHESHIRE ANTIQUARIAN SOC. : Transactions, vols. i– *ann. subscr.* 10/6 8° L. & C. Antiq. Soc. 83 *sqq.*, *in prg.*
LANCS AND CHESHIRE HISTORIC SOC. : Transactions, Ser. i–iii ; New Ser., 5 v. 8° *Liverpool* 49–90
LANCS AND CHESHIRE RECORD SOC. : Publications, ed. Col. H. Fishwick + Rylands + Earwaker, etc., vols. i– 8° 79 *sqq.*, *in prg.*
LANGTON, W. [ed.] Abstrs. of Inquisitns. Post Mortem, 2 v. [fr. Towneley MSS.] s 4° Chetham Soc. 75–6
LINCOLN, [2nd] EARL OF [1250–1311] Two Compoti of Lancs & Chesh. Manors, ed. Rev. P. A. Lyons ; w. Introd. J. E. Bailey [1294–6 ; 1304–5] s 4° Chetham Soc. 84
ORMEROD, Fk. Lancashire Life and Character 3/6 J. Heywood, *Mancs.* 10
PORTER, Jno. History of the Fylde of Lancashire 12/6 8° *Fleetwood* 76
POTTER, Louisa Lancashire Memories *o.p.* [*pb.* 6/] c 8° Macmillan 79
RAINES, Can. F. R. [ed.] Hist. of the Chantries in Co. of Lanc., 2 v. s 4° Chetham Soc. 59–60
ROPER, W. O. Materials for History of Lancaster, Pts. i–ii s 4° Chetham Soc. 08
SELBY, W. D. [ed] Lancs & Chesh. Records in Pub. Rec. Off., Lond., 2 Pts. 8° L. & C. Record Soc. 82–3
TAIT, J. Mediaeval Manchester and Beginnings of Lancashire—*ut inf.*, *s.v.* Manchester
*Victoria History of Lancashire, vols. i–iii—*ut* **E** § 16 [to occupy 5 vols.]
WILLIAMS, W. R. [ed.] Offic. Lists of Duchy & Co. Pal. of Lancs fr. Earliest Times 8° 01

*Battle-Fields, Historic Sites*

CROSTON, James Historic Sites of Lancashire and Cheshire, ill. 21/ 8° Heywood, *Mancs.* 83
HARDWICK, Chas. On Some Ancient Battle-Fields in Lancashire ; maps 6/ r 8° Simpkin 82
Their histor., legend., and æsthetic assocns.

*Churches :* GLYNNE (Sir S. R.) Notes on Chs. of Lancs, ed. Can. J. A. Atkinson s 4° Chetham Soc. 93
Inventories of Goods in Chs. and Chapels of Lancs, Pts. i–iii [1552] s 4° Chetham Soc. 79–02
[Chetham Miscellanies.] i : *Salford Hundred* (ed. J. E. BAILEY) ; ii : *W. Derby, Blackburn, and Leyland Hunds.* (BAILEY) ; iii : *Amounderness and Lonsdale Hunds.* (H. FISHWICK).

*Guides* —*v.* **E** § 16

*Halls :* PHILIPS (N. G.) [art.] Views of Old Halls of Lancs and Cheshire 42/ *n.* s f° Gray 93
These 28 pl., drawn c. 1822–4 and mostly engr. by artist himself, are prtd. fr. the orig. coppers, some for first time. L'rpr. by 24 wrs.

*History :* BEAMONT (W.) [ed.] Discourse of the Warr in Lancs s 4° Chetham Soc. 64

HIBBERT-WARE, S. Lancashire Memorials of the Rebellion [1715] s 4° Chetham Soc. 45

ORMEROD, G. [ed.] Tracts rel. to Milit. Pgs. dur. Civil War in Lancs s 4° Chetham Soc. 44

*Danes in Lancs :* PARTINGTON (S. W.) The Danes in Lancs ; ill. 5/ *n.* 8° Sherratt, *Mancs.* 09

*Worthies :* CHETHAM (H.) [1580–1653] Life of. By Can. F. R. Raines + C. W. Sutton, 2 v. s 4° Chetham Soc. 03

COLERIDGE, Hartley Lives of Worthies of Yorks and Lancs—*ut inf., s.v.* Yorkshire

ESPINASSE, Fcs. Lancashire Worthies, 2 Series ea. 7/6 c 8° *Manchester* 74–7

HEYWOOD, Rev. Oliver [1630–1702] Autobiography, Diaries, etc.—*v. inf., s.v.* Yorkshire

PICTON, Sir J. A. [1805–89] : PICTON (J. A.) [son] Sir J. A. Picton : a biog. *o.p.* [*pb.* 12/] 8° Isbister 91

*Bispham :* FISHWICK (Lt.-Col. H.) Hist. of Parish of Bispham s 4° Chetham Soc. 87

*Blackburn :* ABRAM (W. A.) History of Blackburn *o.p.* 8° *Blackburn* 77

,, Blackburn Characters of a Past Generation *o.p.* 8° *Blackburn* 94

HULL, G. The Poets of Blackburn [1793–1902] 8° *Blackburn* 02

*Cartmel* —*v.* also Furness, *inf.* (BARBER)

KIRBY, R. H., etc. [eds.] Rural D'ery of C. : (chs. & endmts. [12 parishes] 2/ 8° Atkinson, *Ulverston* 92

STOCKDALE, Jas. Annales Caermoelenses : annals of Cartmel *o.p.* [*pb.* 10/6] 8° *Ulverston* 72

*Cockersand Abbey :* FARRER (W.) [ed.] Chartul. of Cock. Abbey, 3 v., ea. in 2 Pts. s 4° Chetham Soc. 98–05

*Crosby :* GIBSON (Rev. T. E.) + GOSS (Bp) [eds.] Crosby Records s 4° Chetham Soc. 86

*Furness :* ATKINSON (Rev. J. C.) [ed.] Coucher Book of Furness Abbey, 3 Pts. s 4° Chetham Soc. 86–7

BARBER, Dr H. Furness & Cartmel Notes ; ill. [topogr., eccl., pop. antiqs.] 10/ 8° Atkinson, *Ulverston* 92

RICHARDSON, J. Furness Past and Present ; col. pl. & ill. 42/ 4° *Barrow in Furness* 80

*Garstang :* FISHWICK (Lt.-Col. H.) History of Garstang, 2 Pts. s 4° Chetham Soc. 78–9

*Gawthorpe Hall :* HARLAND (J.) [ed.] House & Farm Accts. of Shuttleworths, 4 v. s 4° Chetham Soc. 56–8

*Hawkshead :* COWPER (H. S.) Hawkshead : hist., archæol., folklore, etc. 30/ *n.* m 8° Bemrose 99
One of the completest and best parish-histories in existence. Maps and ill.

,, [ed.] Oldest Register Bk. of Parish of Hawkshead ; 4 ill. [1568–1704] 31/6 *n.* m 8° Bemrose 97

*Heywood :* GREEN (J. A.) Bibliography of the Town of Heywood 3/6 c 8° *Advertiser* Off., *Heywood* 02

*Kirkham :* FISHWICK (Lt.-Col. H.) Hist. of Parish of Kirkham s 4° Chetham Soc. 74

*Lancaster :* ROPER (W. O.) [ed.] Matls. for Hist. of Lancaster, 2 Pts. s 4° Chetham Soc. 07

,, [ed.] Matls. for Hist. of Ch. of Lancaster, 4 v. [texts & trs.] s 4° Chetham Soc. 92–06

*Liverpool*

*Bibliography :* JAGGARD (W.) L'pool Literature [deeds, codices, etc.] 2/6 *n.* 8° Shakesp. Press, *L'pool* 05

,, Liverpool Prints and Documents [382 pp.] 4° Reference Lib., *L'pool* 08

*Directory :* SHAW (G. T.) [ed.] Liverpool's First Directory : reprt. 3/6 *n.* 8° Young, *L'pool* [1766] 07

BAINES, Thos. History of Commerce and Town of Liverpool *o.p.* [*pb.* 26/] r 8° Longman 52

,, History of the Port and Town of Liverpool *o.p.* [*pb.* 5/] c 8° Longman 59

HAY, J. Hamilton [art.] L'pool ; 25 col. pl., w. l'rpr. D. Scott [$2·50 *n.* Macm., *N.Y.*] 6/ *n.* sq 8° Black 07

HERDMAN, W. H. [ed.] Pictures of Ancient Liverpool : 72 pl. ; 2 vols. 126/ f° Howell, *L'pool* 78

MOORE, Sir Edw. Liverpool in King Charles the Second's Time ; 5 pl. 21/ *n.* 4° Young, *L'pool* 99
Edited by M. F. IRVINE fr. a MS. wr. 1667–8, and known as *The Moore Rental*, prev. ed. for Chetham Soc. '47.

MUIR, Prf. Ramsay History of Liverpool ; maps & ill. 6/ *n.* c 8° Williams 07

,, + PLATT (Edith M.) History of Municipal Government in Liverpool—*ut* **D** § 24 [to 1835]

PICTON, [Sir] J. A. Memls. of Liverpool, Histor. & Topographical 2 v. 9/ *n.* c 8° Howell, *L'pool* [73] 75

,, [ed.] City of L'pl. Munic. Archives & Records, 2 Ser. [13 cent.–1835] 4° *L'pool* 83–6

WILLIAMS, Gomer Hist. of the L'pool Privateers & L'pool Slave Trade 12/ 8° Howell, *L'pl.* [97] 00
Mainly concerned w. the commercial causes of growth of L'pl. in 17th and 18th cents. Ill.

*Place-names* —*v.* **K** § 120

*Longridge :* SMITH (Tom C.) Hist. of Longridge & District ; map & 12 pl. 15/ f 4° Whitehead, *Preston* 88

*Lytham :* FISHWICK (Lt.-Col. H.) Hist. of the Parish of Lytham s 4° Chetham Soc. 07

*Manchester :* AXON (W. E. A.) Annals of Manchester [chronol. rec. to 1885] 7/6 8° J. Heywood, *Mancs.* 86

BAILEY, J. E. Rectors of Mancs. and Wardens of Coll. Ch., 2 Pts. s 4° Chetham Soc. 83–4

BEAMONT, W. [ed.] Jacobite Trials at Mancs. in 1694 [fr. unpub. MS.] s 4° Chetham Soc. 53
BROXAP, E. Siege of Manchester [1642]—*in* TOUT + TAIT [eds.] Histor. Essays, *ut* **F** § 16
CROSTON, Jas. Old Manchester and its Worthies
CROWTHER, J. S. Arch. Hist. of Cath. Ch. of St Mary, St Geo. & St Denys; ill. 42/ 4° Cornish, *Mcs.* 93
EARWAKER, J. P. [ed.] Court Leet Recs. of Manor of Mcs., 12 v. [1552–1846] ea. 10/6 r 8° Blacklock, *Mcs.* 84–90
GOSS, Bp A. [ed.] Abbott's Jl.; *and* Acct. of Tryalls in Mancs. 1694 s 4° Chetham Soc. 64
HARLAND, Jno. [ed.] Collectanea rel. to Mancs. and Neighbourhood, 2 vols, 4° Chetham Soc. 66–7
„ [ed.] Court Leet Records of Manor of Mancs., 2 v. [16 cent.] s 4° Chetham Soc. 64–5
* „ [ed.] Mamecestre, 3 vols. s 4° Chetham Soc. 61–2
**An important wk. on the early hist. of the Barony, L'dship or Manor, Vill. Boro' or Town, of Mancs.**

HIBBERT-WARE, S. History of the Foundations in Mancs., 3 vols. *o.p.* 4° *Mcs., London* 34–4
**i–ii: *Hist. of College and Collegiate Church*; iii: *Hist. of School*; *Hist. of Chetham Hospital* [last by W. R. WHATTON).**
PROCTER, R. W. Memls. of Bygone Manchester; ill. [incl. environs] 30/ r 8° J. Heywd., *Mancs.* 80
„ Memorials of Manchester Streets; ill. *o.p.* [*pb.* 15/] r 8° Chatto 74
RAINES, Can. F. R. Fellows of Colleg. Ch. of Mancs., ed. Dr F. Renaud, 2 Pts. s 4° Chetham Soc. 91
REILLY, Jno. Hist. of Mancs. fr. Earliest Period to 1860 *o.p.* [*pb.* 20/] r 8° J. R. Smith 65
RIMMER, Alf. Summer Rambles round Manchester; ill. 7/6 8° Heywood, *Mancs.* 90
SAINTSBURY, [Prf.] G. E. B. Manchester: a short history; w. 2 maps 3/6 c 8° Longman 87
**This bk. was wr. for *Historic Towns* Ser.; but, diffces. of opin. hg. arisen betw. author and edr., pubd. separ.**
SHAW, W. A. Manchester, Old and New; 3 vols.; ill. 31/6 4° Cassell 96
**Incl. a profuse account of leading men of the city, past and present, with ports.; also maps and plans.**
SWINDELLS, T. Manchester Streets & Manchester Men, Ser. i–iii ea. 3/ *n.* 8° Cornish, *Mancs.* 06–7
TAIT, J. Mediaeval Manchester and the Beginnings of Lancashire
[Mancs. Univ. Pubs.] 7/6 *n.* r 8° Sherratt, *Mancs.* 04
*Birch*: BOOKER (Rev. J.) Hist. of Anc. Chapel of Birch s 4° Chetham Soc. 59
*Didsbury; Chorlton*: BOOKER (Rev. J.) Hist. of Anc. Chapels of D. & Ch. s 4° Chetham Soc. 57
MOSS, Fletcher History of Didsbury 8° ***priv. prin.***
*Newton Chapelry*: CROFTON (H. T.) Hist. of Newton Chapelry, 4 vols. s 4° Chetham Soc. 04–6
*Stretford*: CROFTON (Rev. H. T.) Hist. of Anc. Chapel of Stretfd., 3 v. s 4° Chetham Soc. 99–03
**A large amt. of documentary matter (but poorly arrgd.): useful for genealogy, etc. Good index in vol. iii.**

*Moss Side*: CROFTON (H. T.) Old Moss Side 8° *Manchester* 03
*North Meols*: FARRER (Wm.) History of Parish of North Meols 21/ *n.* 4° Young, *L'pool* 03
*Oldham*: SHAW (Giles) [ed.] Oldham & Neighbd. in Bygone Times, 3 vols. 25/ 8° H. Gray 86–9
*Penwortham*: HULTON (W. A.) [ed.] Docs. rel. to Priory of Penwortham, etc. s 4° Chetham Soc. 53
*Poulton-le-Fylde*: FISHWICK (Lt.-Col. H.) History of Parish of Poulton-le-Fylde s 4° Chetham Soc. 84
*Preston*: FISHWICK (Lt.-Col. H.) History of Parish of Preston; ill. 27/6 4° Stock 00
*Ribchester*: SMITH (T. C.) + SHORTT (Rev. J.) Hist. of Parish of Ribchester
20/ 8°; Ch. Edn., 7/6 c 8° Bemrose 90
**First pt. (SHORTT) deals w. Roman Ribchester. A scholarly and satisfactory wk. Map and 18 pl.; Ch. Edn. map and 1 pl.**

*Rochdale*: FISHWICK (Lt.-Col. H.) History of Parish of Rochdale; ill. *o.p.* 4° *Rochdale* 89
RAINES, Can. F. R. Vicars of Rochdale, [posth.] ed. H. H. Howorth, 2 Pts. s 4° Chetham Soc. 82–3
*St Mary in Furness Abbey*: HOPE (W. St J.) Abbey of St Mary in Furness 30/ *n.* 4° Wilson, *Kendal* 02
**82 pp.; 4 plans and 30 ill. (200 copies). An account of the abbey founded on the recent excavations.**
*St-Michael's-on-Wyre*: FISHWICK (Lt.-Col. H.) Hist. of Parish of St-Mich.-on-Wyre s 4° Chetham Soc. 91
*Salford*: MANDLEY (J. G. de T.) [ed.] Portmote Records of S., 2 v. [1597–1669] s 4° Chetham Soc. 02
*Sefton*: CARÖE (W. D.) + GORDON (E. J. A.) Sefton; 17 pl. and 32 ill. 31/6 ($10) r 8° Longman 93
**A scholarly wk., based on notes and researches of late Rev. E. HORLEY (Rector 1871–83). Conts. also recs. of the Mock Corporn. (pract. a dining club).**

*Stockport*: HEGINBOTHAM (H.) Stockport, Ancient and Modern, 2 vols. ea. 10/6 4° Low 77–92
*Wardley Hall*: HART-DAVIS (H. V.) + HOLME (S.) History of Wardley Hall 8° 08
*Warrington*: BEAMONT (W.) Annals of Lords of Warrgn., 2 Pts. [11–16 cent.] s 4° Chetham Soc. 72
„ Warrington in 1465 s 4° Chetham Soc. 49
*Whalley; Clitheroe*: COOKE, Alice M. [ed.] Act Bk. of Eccl. Court of Wh.: 1510–38 s 4° Chetham Soc. 01
HULTON, W. A. [ed.] Coucher Bk. or Chartulary of Wh. Abbey, 4 v. s 4° Chetham Soc. 47–9
WHITAKER, Dr T. D. Hist. of Parish of Whalley & Honour of Clitheroe, 2 v.; pl.
*o.p.* [*pb.* 94/6] 4° Routledge [01] 72–6
*Wigan*: BRIDGEMAN (Can.) Hist. of Church and Manor of Wigan, 4 Pts. s 4° Chetham Soc. 86–8
SINCLAIR, D. History of Town and Suburbs of Wigan, 2 vols. 4° *Wigan* 82

**Leicestershire**

ANDREWS, Wm. [ed.] Bygone Leicestershire; ill. [by var. wrs.] 7/6 8° Brown, *Hull* 92
BURTON, Wm. Description of Leicester f° *Lynn* [1622] 1777
DRYDEN, Alice [ed.] Memls. of Old Leics. [Memls. of Cos. of Engl.] 15/ *n.* 8° G. Allen *in prep.*
LEICESTERSHIRE ARCHIT. & ARCHÆOL. SOC.: Transactions, vols. i–vi r 8° Clarke & Hodgson, *Leics.* 66–88
NICHOLS, Jno. Hist. and Antiqs. of Co. of Leics, 4 v. *scarce* [*w.* £60] f° *London* 1795–1815
*Victoria History of the County of Leicester, vol. i—*ut* **E** § 16 [to occupy 4 vols.]
*Guides* —*v.* **E** § 16
*Ashby-de-la-Zouch:* POYNTON (C. H.) Romance of Ashby-de-la-Zouch Castle 6/ *n.* c 8° Cornish, *Birm.* 02
Gives the story of the EARLS OF HUNTINGDON, and of HENRY HASTINGS.
*Charnwood Forest:* POTTER (T. R.) Hist. and Antiqs. of Charnwood Forest *o.p.* [*pb.* 21/] 4° Hamilton 42
*Leicester:* BATESON, Mary [ed.] Records of Boro' of Leic, vs. i–iii; 3 pl. ea. 25/ *n.* r 8° Camb. Press 99–05
Ea. $7·50 *n.* Putnam, *N.Y.* Vol. i: A.D. 1103–1327; ii: 1327–1509; iii: Extrs. fr. documts. in Corpn. archives, w. trs. and Introds. A valuable surv. of municipal hist., furnishg. a general idea of relns. betw. the Town and its lord, its domestic govt., trade, commerc. arrangemts., and, to some extent, social life.
JOHNSON, Mrs T. F. Glimpses of Anc. Leicester in 6 Periods; ill. 5/ *n.* 8° Spencer, *Leics.* 92
*Market Harborough:* STOCKS (J. E.) [ed.] Mark. Harb. Parish Records [to 1530] *o.p.* 8° 90

**Lincolnshire** —*v. also* Cambridgeshire. *sup.*

ALLEN, Thos. Hist. of the County of Lincoln, 2 vols.; ill. [*w.* 50/] 4° Hamilton [30] 34
ANDREWS, Wm. [ed.] Bygone Lincolnshire, 2 Ser. [by var. wrs.] ea. 7/6 8° Andrews, *Hull* 91–2
HISSEY, J. J. Over Fen and Wold—*ut* **E** § 16, *s.v.* Roads
LINCOLNSHIRE RECORD SOC.: Publications
MARRAT, Wm. Hist. of Lincs: topogr., hist., descrn., 3 v. 12° *Boston, Eng.* 14–6
MEDCALF, J. Lincolnshire in History and Lincolnshire Worthies; ill. 3/6 c 8° Ward & Lock 03
STUKELEY, Dr W. —*his* Life and Corresp. [*ut* **G** § 30] conts. a good deal ab. Lincs antiquities
SYMPSON, Dr E. M. Memls. of Old Lincs [Memls. of Cos. of Engl.] 8° G. Allen *in prep.*
*Victoria History of the County of Lincoln, vol. ii—*ut* **E** § 16 [to occupy 4 vols.]
*Churches:* LEWIN (S.) Lincolnshire Churches: Divisn. of Holland; 69 ill. *o.p.* 8° *Boston, Eng.* 43
*Guides* —*v.* **E** § 16
*History: Civil War:* KINGSTON, Alf. —*in his* East Anglia and the Great Civil War, *ut* **F** § 23
*Danes:* STREATFEILD (Rev. G. S.) Lincs and the Danes [largely philological] 7/6 c 8° Paul [83] 84
*Worthies* —*v. also sup.* (MEDCALF)
WATKINS, Rev. M. G. Worthies of Lincolnshire [pamphlet] 8° *London* 85
*Barton-on-Humber:* BROWN (Rob.) Notes on Earlier Hist. of B.-o.-H., 2 v.; ill. [to 1377] ea. 15/ *n.* 4° Stock 06–8
*Bedford Level; the Fenland* [tract of flat land extendg. rd. Wash into N'hptn., H'tgdn., Cambs, Lincs, Norf., Suff.: 750,000 acres]
HEATHCOTE, J. M. Reminiscences of Fen and Mere; ill. *o.p.* [*pb.* 28/] r 8° Longman 76
MILLER (S. H.) + SKERTCHLY (S. B.) Fenland, Past & Pres.; maps & ill. 31/6 r 8° *Wisbech* (Longman) 78
Geolog. sketch; prehist. inhabts.; history; drainage; botany, flora, fauna; geology; antiquities, etc.
Narrative of Draining the Great Level of Fens [1661]—*in* Arber [ed.] English Garner, vol. i, *ut* **K** § 89
SMILES, Dr S. J. Brindley—*in his* Lives of the Engineers, *ut* **I** § 2
WALKER (N.) + CRADDOCK (T.) History of Wisbech and the Fens—*ut sup., s.v.* Cambridgeshire
WELLS, Saml. History of Drainage of Gt Level of the Fens, 2 vols. *o.p.* r 8° *London* 30
WHEELER, W. H. History of the Fens of S. Lincolnshire 21/ *n.* r 8° Newcomb, *Boston* [68] *n.d.* (97)
2nd edn., rewr. Acc. of methods of drainage employed and hist. of drainage undertakings. 14 maps and 2 diagrs.
*Boston:* THOMPSON (P.) Hist. of Boston and Pts. of Lincs *o.p.* [*pb.* 31/6] r 8° Longman [ ] 56
*Croyland Abbey* —*v.* **F** § 19, *s.n.* INGULPH
*Gainsborough:* MOOR (C.) History of Gainsborough 8° *Gainsborough* 04
STARK, A. History and Antiquities of Gainsborough *o.p.* [*pb.* 21/] 8° Longman [41] 43
*Grantham:* TURNOR (E.) Colln s. for Hist. of Town and Soke of Grantham; pl. 4° *London* 06
*Horncastle:* WALTER (J. C.) History of Horncastle; ill. 5/ 4° Morton, *Horncastle* 08
*Ingoldmells:* MASSINGBERD (Rev. W. O.) [ed.] Ingoldmells Ct. Rolls 15/ *n.* 8° Author, *Ormsby, Alford* 04
*Lincoln:* BRADSHAW (Hy.) [ed.] Statutes of Linc. Cath., 2 Pts. in 3 [fully ed.] 12/6, 30/ 8° Camb. Pr. 92–7
i, $3·50 *n.*; ii, $7·50 *n.* Putnam, *N.Y.* Ed. Chr. Wordsworth. i: Text of *Liber Niger*; ii (2 Pts.): Early Customs of Lincoln, Awards, *Novum Registrum*, etc.
GIBBONS, A. [ed.] Liber Antiquus de Ordinationibus Vicarium temp. Hugonis Wells 8° *priv. prin.* 88
1209–1235. Conts. an acc. of the orig. endowmts. of vicarages in old diocese of Linc., extending fr. Humber to Thames.

GROSSETESTE, Bp R. Rotuli Canterb. & York Soc. 11

SALTER, Rev. H. [ed.] A Subsidy coll. in Dioc. of Linc. in 1526 12/6 *n.* 8° Blackwell, *Oxon.* 09
Gives approx. incumbts. and curates in diocese at beg. of 1527, and throws light on WOLSEY's admin.

STARK, A. History of the Bishopric of Lincoln *o.p.* [*pb.* 8/6] 8° Simpkin 52

SYMPSON, E. M. Lincoln: hist. & topogr. account; ill. E. H. New [Anc. Cities] 4/6 *n.* c 8° Methuen 06

*Lindsey:* WATERS (R. E. C.) [tr.] Roll of Owners of Land in Lindsey in rn. of Henry I: tr., w. comm. and comparison w. Domesday *o.p.* 8° *Lincoln* 83

*Louth:* GOULDING (R. W.) [ed.] Louth Records 7/6 r 8° Goulding, *Louth* 92
Reprints of ancient documts. rel. to town and Free Schl. of EDWARD VI.

VENABLES, Rev. E. [ed.] Chronicon Abbatie de Parco Lude Lincs Rec. Soc. 92
The Chronicle of Louth Park Abbey [fd. 1139]; w. Pref. (60 pp.). W. tr. Rev. A. R. MADDISON *en regard*, fol. by notes on archit. hist. and arrangemts. of Abbey by W. H. St John HOPE, and App. of documts. (mostly in abstr.).

*Scrivelsby:* LODGE (Can. S.) Scrivelsby, Home of the Champions; front. 10/6 *n.* c 8° Stock 93
Conts. sketch of hist. of 'the hereditary championship', its chief purport bg. to controvert common belief of its hered. character: shows that it descends w. the possession of the estate of Scrivelsby, of the parish of wh. author is Rector.

*Tennyson Land* —*v.* **K** § 24, *s.v.* Tennyson

**Middlesex; London**

ANDREWS, Wm. [ed.] Bygone Middlesex [by var. wrs.] 7/6 8° Brown, *Hull* 99

HARDY (W. J.) + PAGE (W.) [eds.] Calendar of Feet of Fines, 2 vols. [1189–1570] 8° 92–3

*JERROLD, Walt. Highways and Byways in Middlesex; ill. 6/ ($2 *n.*) c 8° Macmillan 09

LOND. AND MIDDLESEX ARCHAEOL. SOC.: Procgs., 1870–4; Transns.; pl. (some col.) & ill. 8° Lond. & Mid. Arch. Soc. 60–90
One of their useful pubns. was a facs. (1895) of OGILBY + MORGAN's *Map of Lond.*, 1677 (1 in. to 1 m.), w. Introd. and Index C. WELSH.

Middlesex Co. Records, ed. J. C. Jeaffreson, vols. i–iv: 1550–1688 8° Mid. Co. Rec. Soc. 88–92

„ Calendar of Sessions Bks., ed. W. J. Hardy: 1689–1709 13/ *n.* m 8° Nicholson, *Guildh., Westmr.* 05

PHILLIMORE, W. P. W. [ed.] London and Middlesex Note Book—*ut inf. s.v.* London

TAVENOR-PERRY, J. [ed.] Memls. of Old Middl.; ill. [Memls. of Cos. of Eng.] 15/ *n.* 8° G. Allen 09

*Scenery:* FULLEYLOVE (J.) [art.] Middlesex: 20 col. pl., w. l'rpr. A. R. H. Moncrieff [$3 *n.* Macm., *N.Y.*] 7/6 *n.* sq 8° Black

*Brentford; Ealing; Chiswick*

FAULKNER, T. Hist. and Antiqs. of Brentf., Ealg., Chisw. *o.p.* 8° 45

JACKSON, E. Annals of Ealing fr. Twelfth Century 8° 98

SHARPE, Montagu —*in his* Antiquities of Middlesex, *ut* **G** § 1*

TURNER, F. Brentford: literary and historical studies 1/6 *n.* c 8° Stock 98

*Edmonton:* ROBINSON (W.) History of Edmonton; ill. *o.p.* [*pb.* 25/] 8° Nichols 39

*Enfield:* HODSON (G. H.) + FORD (E.) History of Enfield *o.p.* [*pb.* 21/] r 8° Enfield Press 73

WHITTAKER, Cpt. C. W. Ill. Hist.; Statist., & Topogr. Acc. of Enfield; ill. 15/ *n.* r 8° Bell 11

*Hampton; Hampton Court*

CARTWRIGHT, Julia [=Mrs ADY] Hampton Court [past and present] 2/6 *n.* c 8° Wells Gardner 10

HUTTON, Rev. W. H. Hampton Court; 43 ill. Herb. Railton 10/6 s 4° Nimmo (Routledge) 97

*LAW, Ern. History of Hampton Court Palace, 3 vols. ea. 21/ 4° Bell 85–91
i: *Tudor Times*; ii: *Stuart Times*; iii: *Orange and Guelph Times*. Full of interestg. matter; well ill. by autotypes, coppers, etchgs, and maps.

„ Short History of Hampton Court; ill. 5/ c 8° Bell 00
$1·75 *n.* Macmillan, *N.Y.* A condensation of the above book.

RIPLEY, H. History and Topography of Hampton *o.p.* [*pb.* 5/] c 8° J. R. Smith 85

*Harrow:* RIMMER (A.) Rambles round Eton and Harrow—*ut* **D** § 157

THORNTON, P. M. Harrow School and its Surroundings—*ut* **D** § 157

*Hounslow; Isleworth:* AUNGIER (G. J.) Hist of Syon Monastery, Parish of Isleworth, and Chapelry of Hounslow *o.p.* [*pb.* 21/] 8° Nichols 40

*Monken Hadley:* CASS (F. C.) Monken Hadley 4° Lond. & Mid. Arch. Soc. 80

*Perivale:* BROWN (J. A.) Chrons. of Greenford Parva; ill. 10/6 f 4° Virtue 90

*South Mimms:* CASS (F. C.) South Mimms 4° Lond. & Mid. Arch. Soc. 77

*Tottenham:* ROBINSON (W.) Hist. & Antiqs. of Tottenham, 2 v.; ill. *o.p.* [*pb.* 42/] 8° Nichols 40

*Twickenham:* COBBETT (R. S.) Memorials of Twickenham *o.p.* [*pb.* 14/] 8° Smith & Elder 72

*Uxbridge:* SPRINGALL (S.) Country Rambles round Uxbridge 6/ *n.* c 8° Lucy, *Uxbridge* 07

**London** —*v. also* **D** § 124

*Bibliography:* SIMPSON (Dn W. Sparrow) St Paul's Cathedral Library 20/ 8° Stock 93
Catal. of Bibles, Rituals, bks. rel. to Lond. (esp. to St Paul's Cath.), incl. large colln. of Paul's Cross Sermons, maps, and views.

WELCH, C. Notes on London Municipal Literature *o.p.* s 4° Blades 95
Classif. bibliogr. of liter. dealg. w. City, not lim. to munic. liter. A ppr. read bef. Bibliogr. Soc.

Ackerman, R. [pub.] Microcosm of London: Lond. in miniature, 3 vols.; 104 col. ill. 63/ *n.* s 4° Methuen [1808] 1904
A descrn. of Lond. 100 yrs. ago. Reduced fr. the orig. edn. The col. ill. by Pugin + Rowlandson.

Apperson, C. L. Bygone London Life; ill. 6/ *n.* 8° Stock 04
Old restaurants, coffee-houses, 'swells', museums, linkboys, watermen, etc. Elizab. to Georgian era.

Arnold-Forster, H. D. Our Great City: Lond. the heart of Empire 1/9 c 8° Cassell 00

Arundell, Thos. Hist. Reminiscs. of City of Lond. & its Livery Cos.—*ut* **D** § 120, *s.v.* Gilds

Beavan, A. H. Imperial London; 60 ill. 12/6 *n.* r 8° Dent 02
Chapters on such subjects as *Legal London, Official London, Mercantile London,* etc.

Benham (Can. W.) + Welch (C.) Mediaeval London; 33 ill. [good resumé] 3/6 *n.* c 8° Seeley [01] 11

Besant, [Sir] Walt. London; 125 ill. [good] [$3 Harper, *N.Y.*] 7/6 8° Chatto [92] 94
A continuous pict. of Lond. and its people fr. age to age: 'instantaneous photographs', showg. streets, bldgs., people at wk. and at play at var. periods. Early post-Rom. times to rn. of Geo. ii incl. School Edn. *sub tit. The History of London*; ill., 1/9 c 8° *id.* '93; not merely abgmt. but adaptn. Ch. Edn. [St Martin's Lib.] 2/ *n.* 12° '04.

,, South London; 119 ill. [$3 Stokes, *N.Y.*] 7/6 8° Chatto [99] 01
A picturesque account; but inadequate for the history of the last century.

,, East London; 57 ill. 7/6 8° Chatto 01
$3·50 Century Co., *N.Y.* East End life only.

,, [ed.] Survey of London, 7 vols.; ill. ea. 30/ *n.* 4° Black 03–11
Ea. $7·50 *n.* Macmillan, *N.Y.* Freely ill., chiefly from old prints, etc.

*Early London*; 180 ill. '08. [The prehistoric period, Roman rule and Rom. remains, coming of the Saxons, success of the Danes, and dominance of the Normans. Much readable informn. and a consid. amt. of conjecture, insuff. revised by scholars. Ill. particularly good in this vol.]
*Mediaeval London*, vol. i: *Social and Historical*, 108 ill. '06; vol. ii: *Ecclesiastical*, 108 ill. '06 [Many notable omissions.]
*London in Time of Tudors*, 146 ill. and map, '04
*London in Time of Stuarts*, 115 ill. and map, '03
*London in Eighteenth Century*, 104 ill. and map, '02 [One of the best vols. of the series.]
*London in Nineteenth Century*, 124 ill. and map, '10
Division II: Topographical.
*London City*, 103 ill. and map '11
*London North*, 128 ill. and map, '11; *London South*, ill. and maps, '11

The last edn. of Stowe + Strype's *Survey* was issued in 1754, Maitland's survey appeared in 1750, Entick's in 1766, and Lambert's in 1806, since wh. time no actual Survey of Lond. has appeared. This wk., tho' announced to do so, by no means satisfies the requiremts. It is a very industrious and compreh. compiln., fr. a vast no. of sources of varying degrees of authority, and is full of interest, but conts. far too little original research. Covers the whole area (some 17 × 12 miles) within the jurisdictn. of the L.C.C.

,, + Mitton (G. E.) Fascination of London Series—*v. in f. s.v.* Fascination of London

Birch, G. H. London on Thames in Bygone Days; ill. [to end 18 cent.] 7/ *n.* i 8° Seeley 03

Brayley, E. W. Londiniana, 4 vols. *o.p.* 4° *London* 28–9

Brewer, J. S. Ancient London—*in his* English Studies, *ut* **F** § 16

Clode, C. M. London in Time of Great Rebellion 3/6 8° Harrison 93
Conts. some interestg. facts rel. to financial affairs of the City dur. rn. of Chas. i and the stormy yrs. wh. followed.

Compton-Rickett, A. London Life of Yesterday 7/6 *n.* 8° Constable 09

*Cook, Mrs E. T. Highways and Byways in London; ill. [Highways and Byways Ser.] 6/ ($2 *n.*) c 8° Macmillan 02

Creighton, Bp M. Elizabethan London—*in his* Historical Lectures, *ut* **F** § 1

Cunningham, Pet. London, Past and Present, ed. H. B. Wheatley, 3 v. 63/ 8° Murray [49] 91
$20 Scribner, *N.Y.* Hist., assocns., trades. Based on Cunningham's *Hdbk. f. Lond.* [49] 50, but so enlarged and improved as to be pract. a new wk.

Davey, R. P. B. The Pageant of London, 2 vols.—*ut inf.*, *s.v.* 'Scenery of London' (Fulleylove)

Davidson, Jno. [the poet] A Random Itinerary 5/ f 8° Mathews & Lane 94
A fresh and pleasant record of walks dur. marvellous spring and summer of 1893 in Lond. and environs.

Ditchfield, Rev. P. H. [ed.] Memls. of Old Lond., 2 v.; ill. [Memls. of Cos. of Eng.] 30/ *n.* 8° G. Allen 08

Doran, Dr J. London in the Jacobite Times, 2 v. [18th cent.] *o.p.* [*pb.* 36/] 8° Bentley 77

Entick, Jno. Hist. & Surv. of Lond. & Places Adjac., 4 vols. *o.p.* 8° *London* 1766

Fascination of London Series: by Sir W. Besant + G. E. Mitton ea. 1/6 *n.* c 8° Black *v.y.*
*Chelsea* | *Clerkenwell and St Luke's* | *Hackney and Stoke Newington* | *Hammersmith, Fulham, Putney* | *Hampstead and Marylebone* | *Holborn and Bloomsbury* | *Kensington* | *Mayfair and Bayswater* | *Shoreditch and East End* | *Strand* | *Thames* | *Westminster*
Ea. 90 c. *n.* Macm, *N.Y.* Topogr. matter coll. for Besant's *Survey* [*ut sup.*]. Often ill-digested and ill-arranged.

Fitzgerald, Percy Picturesque London: c. 100 ill. *o.p.* [*pb.* 25/] r 8° Ward & Downey 90

Francis, C. de la R. London, Historic and Social, 2 vols.; ill. $5 c 8° Coates, *Phila.* 02
A history from Roman times to King Alfred.

Fry, G. S. [ed.] Inquisitiones post Mortem rel. to City of Lond., Pt i [Tudor] r 8° Brit. Rec. Soc. 88–90

Gentleman's Mag. Library: London, ed. G. Laur. Gomme, 3 vols. ea. 7/6 8° Stock 04–5

Gomme, G. Laur. London in the Reign of Victoria: 1837–97 2/6 c 8° Blackie 98
[Victorian Era Ser.] A survey of progress in directors of Trade, Industry, Street Archit., Open Spaces, Educn., etc.

Hardy (W. J.) + Page (W.) [eds.] Calendar of the Feet of Fines—*ut sup.*, *s.v.* Middlesex

Hare, A. J. C. Walks in London, 2 v.; ill. [$3 Macm., *N.Y.*] 2/ c 8° G. Allen [78] 01

Harrison, Fredc. Historic London—*in his* The Choice of Books, *ut* **K** § 83

Heckethorn, C. W. London Souvenirs 6/ c 8° Chatto 99
$2 Wessels, *N.Y.* Mag. arts. on such subjs. as old Lond. coffee-houses, tea-gardens, etc.

,, London Memories 6/ c 8° Chatto 00
$2 Lippincott, *Phil.* Papers similar to above on old Lond. trades, windmills, earthquakes, fires.

HEMSTREET, Chas. + Marie Nooks and Corners of Old London; ill. 3/6 *n.* c 8° Laurie 10
HENSLOW, Pp [d. 1616] Diary; *and* Papers—*ut* **I** § 135
HOWELLS, W. D. London Films; ill. [little sketches] $2·25 *n.* (10/6) 8° Harper 05
HUEFFER, Ford Madox Soul of London: survey of a mod. city 5/ *n.* i 16° Rivers 05
5 chs. of discursive impressionistic writing: *From a Distance, Roads into Lond., Lond. at Leisure,* etc.
HUNT, Leigh The Town: its memorable characters & events; 45 ill. 2/6 f 8° Smith & Elder [48]
„ The same; w. the 45 ill. of the orig. edn., & 13 engr. ports. 12/6 8° Gibbings [48] 93
„ A Saunter through the West End *o.p.* [*pb.* 10/6] c 8° Hurst 61
HUTCHINGS, W. W. London Town, Past & Present, 2 v.; fully ill. ea. 10/ *n.* ($3 *n.*) 4° Cassell 09
KINGSFORD, C. L. [ed.] Chronicles of London; w. Introd., notes, & gloss. 10/ *n.* ($3·40) 8° Clar. Press 05
3 Chrons.: (1) Cotton. MS. Julius B ii.; (2) Cotton. MS. Cleopatra C iv.; (3) Cotton MS. Vitellius A xvj. Roughly continuous, coverg. per. 1189–1509.
KNIGHT, Chas. [ed.] London, Described & Illustrated, 4 vols.; 36 pl. & many ill. 90/ r 8° Virtue [41–4] *n.d.*
To this new edition was added J. TIMB's *Curiosities of London.* The whole ed. E. WALFORD.
LANG, Elsie Literary London; Introd. by G. K. Chesterton; 42 photos. 6/ c 8° Laurie 00
LETHABY, W. R. London before the Conquest; ill. 7/6 *n.* ($2·50 *n.*) c 8° Macmillan 02
Notes on a large number of prints connected with London history and ancient topography.
LOFTIE, Rev. W. J. A History of London, 2 vols.; maps and ill. 32/ 8° Stanford [83] 84
„ London; w. 3 maps [Historic Towns Series] 3/6 ($1·25) p 8° Longman 87
„ London City: hist., streets, bldgs., etc.; ill. 50/ 4° Leadenhall Press 91
$15 Scribner, *N.Y.* A scholarly text, w. about 300 good illns., largely architectural.
„ London Afternoons; ill. 10/6 *n.* c 8° Cassell 01
Pleasant historical papers: *Newgate; Old St Paul's; Ancient Rivers; City Churches;* etc.
LOND. & MIDDLESEX ARCHÆOL. SOC.: Proceedings, *and* Transactions, *ut sup., s.v.* Middlesex
LONDON TOPOGR. SOC.: London Topogr. Record, vols. i–v; ill. ea. 10/6 4° Stanford 97–10
The obj. of the Soc. is the pubn. of matl. illg. hist. of Lond. fr. earliest times: *v.* Maps, *inf.*
LUCAS, E. V. A Wanderer in London; 16 col. pl. & 36 ill. 6/ c 8° Methuen [06]
MCCARTHY, Justin Charing Cross to St Paul's; ill. J. Pennell 6/ c 8° Seeley [90] 93
MACHYN, H. [1498?–1563?] Diary—*ut* **F** § 22 [1550–63]
MAITLAND, W., etc. Hist. and Surv. of Lond, cont. J. Entick, 2 v. *o.p.* f° *London* [1756] 1772
MALCOLM, J. P. Londonium Redivivum: anc. hist. & mod. descrn., 4 v. *o.p.* 4° *London* 02–7
MASSON, Prf. Dav. Memories of London in the 'Forties 3/6 *n.* c 8° Blackwood 08
4 papers, repr. fr. *Blackwood's Mag.*, on CARLYLE; MAZZINI; Down St., Piccadilly; Museum Club.
MILNE, Jas. My Summer in London [lively anecdotal pprs.] 6/ *n.* c 8° Laurie 10
NORMAN, Pp. London Vanished and Vanishing—*ut inf. s.v.* Scenery
OGILVY, J. S. Relics and Memorials, 2 vols.—*ut inf., s.v.* Scenery
Old London: By R. Green & others [pprs. rd. at Archæol. Inst.] *o.p.* [*pb.* 12/] 8° Murray 67
ORDISH, T. Fairman Shakespeare's London—*ut* **K** § 24, *s.v.* Shakespeare
PHILLIMORE, W. P. W. [ed.] London and Middlesex Notebook; ill. 10/ 8° Stock 92
Deals w. local archæol., paroch. ch.-hist., archit., ch.-bells, parish-recs., family-hist., heraldry, folklore, custs., anc. manufs., tradesmen's signs and tokens, etc.
RILEY, Hy. T. [ed.] Mems. of London & London Life [13–15 cents.] *o.p.* [*pb.* 21/] i 8° Longman 68
Local, social, and polit. extrs. fr. early archives of City of London, A.D. 1276–1419; w. trs. *V. also inf., s.v.* Guildhall.
ROOK, Clarence London Side-Lights [by a journalist] 6/ c 8° Arnold 08
ROSS, Fredk. Bygone London 7/6 8° Andrews, *Hull* 92
ROUND, J. Horace The Commune of London and other Studies [12 cent.] 12/ *n.* 8° Constable 99
The title-essay and another on *London under Stephen* are valuable here.
SALA, G. A. Twice Round the Clock *o.p.* [*pb.* 2/6] c 8° Maxwell [59] 79
„ London up to Date 3/6 c 8° Black [94] 94
A sequel, adapted to later times and less Bohemian manners than the above.
SHARPE, Dr R. R. London and the Kingdom, 3 vols. ea. 10/6 ($3·50) 8° Longman 94–5
A history of London in rel. to the Kingdom, mainly fr. archives at Guildhall, w. valuable Appendices.
SIMS, G. R. In London's Heart [$1·25 Buckles, *N.Y.*] 3/6 c 8° Chatto 00
„ Biographs of Babylon: London's moving scenes 2/6 c 8° Chatto 02
„ [ed.] Living London, 3 vols.; profusely ill. ea. 12/ 4° Cassell 02–3
A popular work, encyclopædic in character, on all subjs. conn. w. modern London and its life.
SMITH, F. Berkeley In London Town $1·50 *n.* (6/) c 8° Funk & Wagnalls 06
Spirited gossip on restaurants, music-halls, Piccadilly, and other similar topics, by a Parisian American.
SMITH, J. T. [1766–1833; ed.] Ancient Topography of London *o.p.* 4° *London* [15] 92
Views of bldgs. and acc. of places and customs 'overlooked by Lond. historians', by Keeper of Prints in Br. Mus.
SMITH, Mrs Machell Our Rambles in Old London, arranged in six walks Low 95
160 pp. An account of things seen during unsystematic journeys to interesting places in London.
STEEVENS, G. W. —*in his* Glimpses of Three Nations, *ut* **E** § 11

*STOW, Jno. [1525–1605] Survey of London, ed. C. L. Kingsford; map and 4 ill., 2 vols. 30/ *n.* ($9·25) 8° Clar. Press [1598] 08
A definitive edn. of this immortal wk., repr. fr. text of 1603; w. valuable Introd. (100 pp., incl. a Life of STOW) and notes. The map (by Ralph AGAS) is c. 1600, reprod. 20 × 15 in. Glossary (by C. E. DOBLE), and Indexes of Persons, Places, and Subjs.

STREET, G. S. A Book of Essays 6/ c 8° Constable 02
$1·50 *n.* Dutton, *N.Y.* Nine papers on London life; descriptive and critical.

SURVEY OF MEMLS. OF GREATER LOND. (COMM. FOR): Publications; ill. 4° Batsford *in prg.*
*Bromley-by-Bow* [*ut inf.*] 21/ *n.* | *Chelsea, Parish of*, vol. i [*ut inf.*] 25/ *n.* | *Crosby Place, Bishopsgate* [*ut inf.*] 25/ *n.* | *Fulham, Sandford Manor* [*ut inf.*] | *Hackney, Brooke House* [*ut inf.*] 15/ *n.* | *Leyton, The Great House* [*ut inf.*] 21/ *n.* | *Mile End, Trinity Hospital* [*ut inf.*] 21/ *n.* | *Stepney, Ch. of St Dunstan* [*ut inf.*] 15/ *n.*

THORNBURY, Walt. Haunted London; ill. [*v. also* Walford, *inf.*] 7/6 c 8° Chatto [65] 80
Legendary houses, great men's birthplaces and tombs, haunts of poets, battle-fields of old factions, etc.

TIMBS, Jno. Curiosities of London—*ut sup., s.v.* KNIGHT

*Victoria History of London, vol. i—*ut* **E** § 16 [to occupy 3 vols.]

VILLARS, P. London & Environs: picturesque survey [tr.]; 200 ill. *o.p.* [*pb.* 7/6] r 8° Routledge 87

WALFORD, E. Londoniana: persons, places and things, 2 vols. *o.p.* [*pb.* 21/] c 8° Hurst 79

„ + THORNBURY, W. Old & New London; 6 vols.; 1,200 ill. [popular] ea. 9/ 4° Cassell [73–8] 87
Vols. i and ii [city, anc. and mod.] (THORNBURY); iii–vi [Westmr., etc.] (WALFORD). Contin. *inf., s.v.* Suburbs (WALFORD).

WELCH, Chas. Modern Hist. of City of London; ill. P. Norman 42/ *n.* 4° Blades 97
A pict. and descr. recd. of munic. and social progr. since 1761. Plan strictly chronol.

WHEATLEY, H. B. London, Past and Present—*ut supra, s.v.* Cunningham

„ Story of London; ill. [Mediæv. Town Ser.; $1·75 *n.* Dutton, *N.Y.*] 4/6 *n.* c 8° Dent [04] 06

„ Hogarth's London; ill. after Hogarth, etc. 21/ *n.* 8° Constable 09
$4·80 *n.* Dutton, *N.Y.* Pictures of the manners of London of the 18th cent.; w. ch. on literature of HOGARTH.

WILKINSON, Rob. [pub.] Londina Illustrata, 2 vols. *o.p.* 4° Wilkinson 19–25

### Amusements

BOULTON, W. B. The Amusements of Old London, 2 vols. 30/ *n.* s 4° Nimmo (Routledge) 01
12 hand-coloured ill. Well-informed essays on London amusements from the Restoration to 1837.

MACHRAY, Rob. The Night Side of London; ill. 6/ c 8° Macqueen 02
21 chapters on present-day London amusements: music-halls, clubs, ball-rooms, etc.

#### *Pleasure Gardens (Old)*

ROGERS, H. A. [pub.] Views of some of most celebrated Bygone Pleasure Gardens of London, 15 facs. pl.; w. contemp. l'rpr. 12/ 4° H. A. Rogers, *Hanley Rd., Lond.* 96

WROTH, W. Cremorne & the Later London Gardens [appendix to below] 6/ *n.* 8° Stock 07

„ + A. E. Lond. Pleasure Gardens of 18th Cent.; 62 ill. *o.p.* [*pb.* 15/ *n.*] 8° Macmillan 96
A scholarly bk., givg. incidentally a vivid idea of how Londoners amused themselves 100 yrs. ago. In 6 Groups (1) *Clerkenwell and Central Group*, (2) *Marylebone Group*, (3) *North London Group*, (4) *Hampstead Group*, (5) *Chelsea Group*, (6) *South London Group*.

### Anthology

HYATT, A. H. [ed.] The Charm of London 2/ *n.* 18° Chatto 08

MELVILLE, Hel. + Lewis [eds.] London's Lure [prose & verse; $1·25 *n.* Macm., *N.Y.*] 3/6 *n.* f 8° Bell 09

WHITTEN, Wilf. [ed.] London in Song; w. good notes 6/ c 8° Richards 98

**Atlas: STANFORD (E.; pb.) Indexed Atlas of Co. of Lond. [87 maps; 4 in. to 1 m.] 7/6 *n.* Stanford 11**

### Bridges

DREDGE, J. Thames Bridges from Tower to Source, 7 Pts. ea. 5/ 4° *Engineering* Off. 96 *sqq.*

TUIT, J. E. The Tower Bridge: hist. and construction 5/ 4° *Engineering* Off., 94

WELCH, Chas. Hist. of Tower Br. & other Bridges over Thames; ill. 25/ *n.* 4° Smith & Elder 94
Introd. by Can. W. BENHAM and a descrn. of the Tower Bridge by J. Wolfe BARRY, its engineer; also account of Bridge Ho. fr. 14th cent. Cf. also his *Numismata Londiniensia* [*ut* **G** § 20].

### Cemeteries

HOLMES, Mrs Basil The London Burial Grounds; ill. 10/6 *n.* i 16° Unwin 96
A cpl. histor. acc. of the bur.-grds. in Co. of Lond., espec. the unused grounds, of wh. full list given.

### Churches: *Collectively* —*for* Architecture *v.* **I** § 119

BENHAM, Can. W. Old London Churches; 25 col. pl. A. Garratt 42/ *n.* 4° Hodder 08

BIRCH, G. H. Lond. Churches of 17 and 18 Centuries 84/ *n.* f° Batsford 96
A fine folio, contg. 64 excel. photogr. pl., w. plans, details, and descr. text. Nearly all are wks. of WREN, owing their existence to the Fire of 1666.

BUMPUS, T. F. London Churches, Ancient and Modern, 2 Ser.; ill. ea. 6/ *n.* 8° Laurie 08
$4 *n.* Pott, *N.Y.* An excellent bk., displayg. wide archit. knowl. and careful observn.

CAMPBELL, W. S. The Passer-by in London [$1·75 *n.* Scrib., *N.Y.*] 6/ Chapman 08

DANIELL, A. E. London City Churches; ill. 3/6 *n.* c 8° Constable [96] 07

„ London Riverside Churches; ill. 3/6 *n.* c 8° Constable [97] 07

FISHER, Payne Cat. of Tombs in Chs. of City [1666], ed. G. B. Morgan [Genealogica Curiosa] 4° [1668] 85

GODWIN (G.) + BRITTON (J.) History of the Churches of London, 2 vols. *o.p.* [*pb.* 32/] m 8° Bogue 38–6

HENNESSY, Rev. G. [ed.] Novum Repertorium Parochiale Londinense 63/ *n.* 4° Sonnenschein 98
The London diocesan clergy-succession fr. the earliest times to 1898; w. notes. Based on Rich. NEWCOURT'S *Repert. Eccles. Paroch. Lond.*, 2 vols. f° *Lond.* 1708–10.

WOOD, A. Eccles. Antiquities of London and Suburbs 5/ f 8° Burns & Oates 74

**Corporation of City of London :** LORD MAYORS, ALDERMEN, SHERIFFS, etc.—*v. also inf.*, *s.v.* Guildhall, & **D** § 124

BADDELEY, J. J. The Aldermen of Cripplegate Ward : 1276–1900 5/ 8° Baddeley 01
Hist. of the City Aldermen generally and of the Common Council; with lives of the Aldermen of the ward.

BEAVEN, Rev. A. B. Aldermen of the City of London [13 cent. to 1908] 21/ *n.* 8° Eden Fisher 08

BIRCH, W. De Gray [ed.] Hist. Charters & Const. Documts. of C. of L. [11–18 c.] 5/ r 8° Whiting [84] 87

Calendar of Letter-bks. of City of London, ed. Dr R. R. Sharpe; vols. i–viii [1275–1399] ea. 5/ 8° J. E. Francis 99–7 *in prg.*
The L'r-bks. (50 vols.) are pres. at Guildh., and cont. the City records fr. EDW. I to JAS. I: ea. bk. disting. by l'r of alphab.

Calendar of Letters fr. Mayor & Corpn. of C. o. L., ed. R. R. Sharpe [1350–70] r 8° 85

COKAYNE, G. E. Some Acc. of L'd Mayors & Sheriffs of Lond. [1601–25] 12/6 r 8° Phillimore 97
Traces the parentage, marriages, children, and armorial bearings of the parties concerned.

GILBERT, W. The City : corpn., cos., chars., endowmts. *o.p.* [*pb.* 7/6] c 8° Daldy 77

GRAFTON, Rich. [d. 1572?] Chronicle, or History of England, 2 vols. *o.p.* 4° *London* [1562] 09
Appended is a *Table of Bailiffs, Sheriffs, and Mayors of London*, fr. 1189 to 1558.

London's Roll of Fame *o.p.* [*pb.* 12/6] 4° Cassell 84
Complimentary notes and addresses from the City on presentn. of hon. freedom of the City : 1757–1884; w. Introd.

NORTON, Geo. Comments. on Hist. & Constit. of C. o. L. *o.p.* [*pb.* 14/] 8° Longman [29] 69

RILEY, H. T. [ed.] Chronicles of Mayors and Sheriffs of Lond. *o.p.* 4° *London* 63
Tr. fr. *Liber de Antiquis Legibus*, attrib. to A. FITZ-THEDMAR [1188–1274]; *French Chron. of Lond.*, tr. fr. *Croniques de London* [1259–1343].

WOODCOCK, W. + R. Lives of Illustr. Lords Mayors and Aldermen *o.p.* 8° *London* 46

*Freemen :* WELCH (C.) [ed.] Register of Freemen of City of L. : rns. Hy. viii & Edw. vi 10/6 4° Lond. & Mid. Arch. Soc. 10

*London Government* —*v.* **D** § 124, *s.v.* London

**Foreign, American, etc., Impressions of London**—*v.* **E** § 16

**Inns ; Taverns** —*v. also inf.*, *s.v.* Southwark (RENDLE + NORMAN)

CALLOW, Edw. Old London Taverns; ill. *o.p.* [*pb.* 6/] c 8° Downey 00

SHELLEY, Hy. Inns and Taverns of Old London; 48 ill. 7/6 *n.* c 8° Pitman 10

**Inns of Court and of Chancery**

HOME, Gordon [art.] Inns of Ct.: 20 col. pl., w. l'rpr. C. Headlam [$2 *n.* Macm., *N.Y.*] 7/6 *n.* sq 8° Black 09

LOFTIE, Rev. W. J. Inns of Court and Chancery; ill. H. Railton 6/ c 8° Seeley [93] 94

PEARCE, R. R. History of Inns of Court and Chancery *o.p.* [*pb.* 15/] 8° Bentley 48

*Gray's Inn :* DOUTHWAITE (W. R.) Gray's Inn : history & assocns. 7/6 8° Reeves & Turner 86

FLETCHER, Rev. Reg. J. [ed.] Pension Bk. of Gray's Inn, 2 v.; ill. ea. 21/ *n.* 4° Stevens & Haynes 02–10
Vol. i: 1569–1669; ii: 1669–1800. Conts. the records of the benchers' proceedings: well edited and indexed.

FOSTER, J. [ed.] Register of Admissions to Gray's Inn : 1521–1889 r 8° *priv. prin.* 89

HOPE, Andrée Chronicles of an Old Inn [Gray's Inn] 5/ c 8° Chapman 87

*Lincoln's Inn :* BAILDON (W. P.) [ed.] Records of Linc's Inn : Black Books, 4 v.; facss. 8° *priv. prin.*
Prints everything of value in the recds., w. sep. arts. on pts. of interest. Covers period 1422–1845. Good indexes.

SPILSBURY, W. H. Account of Lincoln's Inn and its Library *o.p.* [*pb.* 6/] f 8° Pickering 50

*Staple Inn :* WILLIAMS (E.) Staple Inn : cust.-ho., wool-ct., inn of chanc. 6/ *n.* 8° Constable 06

WORSFOLD, T. C. Staple Inn and its Story *o.p.* [*pb.* 12/6 *n.*] 8° H. Bumpus 03
An excellent acc. of 'the fayrest Inne of Chancerie', the continued existence of wh. we owe to the Prudential Assur. Co., who bought it for £68,000, to save it from the house-breaker.

*Temple :* BELLOT (H. H. L.) The Inner and Middle Temple; ill. 6/ *n.* c 8° Methuen 02
A handy popular account, historical, descriptive, and biographical: fully indexed.

HOPWOOD, C. H. [ed.] Calendar of Middle Temple Records prior to 1800 10/ *n.* r 8° Butterworth 03
Affords some interesting glimpses of Temple life between 1501 and 1703.

HUTCHINSON, Jno. Catalogue of Notable Middle Templars 10/ *n.* r 8° Butterworth 02

INDERWICK, F. A. [ed.] Calendar of Inner Temple Records, vols. i–iii [1505–1714] ea. 20/ *n.* i 8° Stevens & Haynes 96–01 *in prg.*
Prints everything of importance for the history of the Temple. Period 1501 to 1703.

MARTIN, C. Trice [tr. & ed.] Minutes of Parliament of Middle Temple, 4 v. 40/ *n.* i 8° Butterworth 04–5
The recorded Memoranda or Repts. of business proceedgs. of the Govg. Body 1502–1703, earlier entries (in Lat.) tr. The entries cont. names of all members admitted. *Inquiry into Orig. and Early Hist. of the Inn*, by J. HUTCHINSON (the librn.) prefixed. Vol. iv. is *Index*.

Masters of the Bench of Inner Temple : 1450–1883; & Masters of the Temple : 1540–1883; Suppl. : 1883–1900 [w. Treasurers : 1505–1901] 8° *priv. prin.* 83; 01

Students Admitted to the Inner Temple : 1571–1625 8° *priv. prin. n.d.* (68)
THOMAS, P. [art.] Temple, London : 12 etchings, w. text Can. Ainger, 6 Pts. ea. 21/ 4° Frost, *Bristol* 98–9
THORPE, W. G. Still Life of Mid. Temp. ; w. its table-talk *o.p.* [*pb.* 15/] 8° Bentley 92
" Middle Temple Table-Talk [both reminiscs. ; poor] 6/ 8° Hutchinson [94] 95
*Temple Church :* BAYLIS (T. H.) Temple Church & Chapel of St Ann ; ill. 7/6 *n.* c 8° Philip [93] 10
WORLEY, G. Church of Knights Templars [Cath. Ser.] 1/6 *n.* c 8° Bell 07
WORSLEY, Chas. [1670–1739] Bk. of Middle Temple, ed. A. R. Ingpen ; w. Introd. 30/ r 8° Chiswick Press [1733] 10

**Literary and other Associations**—*v. also inf., s.v.* Adelphi (BRERETON)
HARRISON, Wilmot Memorable London Houses ; 100 ill. [w. anecdotes] 2/6 f 8° Low [89] 90
HEMSTREET, C. + Marie Nooks and Corners of Old London [chfly. assocns.] 3/6 *n.* c 8° Laurie 10
HUTTON, Laur. Literary Landmarks of London [7/6 Unwin] $1·75 c 8° Harper, *N.Y.* [85] 92
JESSE, J. H. Liter. & Histor. Memls. of London, 2 vols. ; ill. *o.p.* [*pb.* 28/] 8° Bentley 47
" London : its celeb. characters & remark. places, 3 v. *o.p.* [*pb.* 31/6] c 8° Bentley 71
L. C. C. : Histor. Houses : indicn. of houses of hist. int., 2 v. [*v.* Streets, *inf.*] ea. 2/ 8° P. S. King 07–9
RIDEING, W. H. Thackeray's London : scenes and haunts of his novels—*ut* **K** § 24
RYAN, W. P. Literary London : its lights and comedies *o.p.* [*pb.* 3/6] 8° Smithers 98
STEPHENSON, Prf. H. Thew Shakespeare's London—*ut* **K** § 24, *s.v.* Shakespeare

**Livery Companies** —*v.* **D** § 120

**Mansions ; Private Palaces**
CHANCELLOR, E. B. The Private Palaces of London ; c. 40 ill. 21/ *n.* 4° Paul 08
Apsley Ho., Chesterfield Ho., Crewe Ho., Devonshire Ho., Dorchester Ho., Grosvenor Ho., Lansdowne Ho., Montagu Ho., Norfolk Ho., Portman Ho., Spencer Ho., Stafford Ho., Bridgwater Ho., etc., incl. many that are no more.

**Maps (Early)** : LOND. TOPOGR. Soc. : Reprs. of early Maps of Lond. [nearly 20 to 1911] Stanford *in prg.*

**Medals** —*v.* **G** § 20

**Pageants**
FAIRHOLT, F. W. [ed.] Lord Mayors' Pageants ; w. Introd. and notes, 2 Pts. c 8° Percy Soc. 43–4
" [ed.] Civic Garland : songs fr. Lond. pagts. ; w. Introd. & notes Percy Soc. 45
[ " ] Catalogue of a Collection of Works on Pageantry bequeathed to Soc. of Antiquaries by Fairholt [*w.* 2/6] f° Soc. of Antiquaries 69
GREG, W. W. [ed.] List of Masques, Pageants, etc.—*ut* **K** § 22
HONE, Wm. —*in his* Ancient Mysteries Described ; ill. *o.p.* 8° Tegg [23]
NICHOLS, J. [ed.] Progresses and Public Processns. of Qu. Eliz., 3 v. *o.p.* 4° *London* [ ] 23
" [ed.] Progresses and Publ. Processions of James i, 4 vols. *o.p.* 4° *London* 28

**Palaces (Royal)** —*v. inf., s.v.* 'Scenery' (WAY), *and passim*, under names of Palaces

**Parks ; Gardens** —*for* Pleasure-Gardens *v.* Amusements, *sup.*
CECIL, Hon. Mrs Evelyn London Parks and Gardens ; col. ill. L'y V. Manners 21/ *n.* i 8° Constable 08
LARWOOD, J. Story of the London Parks ; ill. 7/6 c 8° Chatto [*n.d.* (72)] 73
SAXBY, Col. J. J. Municipal Parks, Gardens, etc., of London ; 184 ill. 21/ 4° Stock 99
*Hyde Park*
ASHTON, Jno. Hyde Park fr. Domesday Bk. to Date ; 22 ill. *o.p.* [*pb.* 12/6] 8° Downey 96
Illustrative extrs. and illustrations, givg. glimpse of what Londoners have been dur. past 800 yrs.
TWEEDIE, Mrs Alec Hyde Park, its Hist. and Romance ; ill. 15/ *n.* 8° Nash 08

**Prisons** —*v.* **D** § 123, *s.v.* Prisons

**Roman London** —*v.* **G** § 1*, **F** § 18

**'Scenery' ; Buildings**
BARTON, Rose [art.] Familiar London : 61 col. pl., w. l'rpr. [$6 *n.* Macm., *N.Y.*] 20/ *n.* sq 8° Black
CASSELL & Co. [pubs.] The Queen's London ; 400 photogr. ill. 9/ Cassell [ ] 97
COBURN, A. L. London : portfo. of 20 photogravures ; Introd. Hilaire Belloc 25/ *n.* f° Duckworth 09
FLETCHER, Hanslip London, Passed and Passing ; 70 ill. 21/ *n.* 4° Pitman 08
A pictorial record of destroyed and of threatened buildings.
FULLEYLOVE, Jno. [art.] The Pageant of London : 40 col. pl. ; 2 vols. 15/ *n.* 8° Methuen 06
Vol. i : to A.D. 1500 ; ii : 1500–1900. Text by Rich. DAVEY. Bibliogr. to ea. chapter.
HYDE, Wm. [art.] London Impressions : photogravs., w. text by Mrs Meynell 168/ *n.* r 8° Constable
LOVETT, Rev. R. [ed.] London Pictures [Pen and Pencil Ser. ; $3·20 Revell, *N.Y.*] 8/ i 8° R.T.S. 90

McNay, W. L. [ed.] Old London : 50 reprodns. of old engravgs. 3/6 *n.* 8° De La More Press [09] 09

Markino, Yoshio [art.] The Colour of London ; w. text W. J. Loftie 20/ *n.* 4° Chatto 07
A series of coloured plates by a Japanese artist, w. Introd. (chfly. on the picts.) by M. H. Spielmann.

" A Japanese Artist in London ; 12 pl. (8 col.) 6/ *n.* c 8° Chatto [10] 10
A very interestg. wk. on the metropolis fr. an observant Japanese's pt.-of-view. Charmingly wr.

Marshall, H. M. [art.] Scenery of London ; col. pl., w. text G. E. Mitton [$6 *n.* Macm., *N.Y.*] 20/ *n.* 4° Black 05

Moncrieff, A. R. Hope London ; w. col. pl. by var. arts. [$6 *n.* Macm., *N.Y.*] 20/ *n.* sq 8° Black 10

*Norman, Pp. [art.] London Vanished & Vanishing : 75 col. pl., w. text by author 20/ *n.* 4° Black 05
$6 *n.* Macmillan, *N.Y.* Good reprodns. of excellent water-colr. records of Old Lond., w. antiquarian text of consid. value.

*Ogilvy, J. S. [art.] Relics & Memorials of London City ; w. 64 col. pl. 25/ *n.* 4° Routledge 09

* " Relics & Memorials of London Town ; w. 52 col. pl. 25/ *n.* 4° Routledge 10
Ea. $7 *n.* Dutton, *N.Y.* Two series of beautiful and finished watercol. dwgs., well reprod. and admirably catching the spirit of the town in most of its moods. The text is based on a diligent study of unusual sources of informn. The whole easily forms the best ill. wk. of a general character on London.

Paul, R. W. [art.] Vanishing London : c. 40 pl. ; w. notes 15/ *n.* 4° Auth., 3, *Arundel St., Lond.* 96

Queen's London (The) [c. 400 good photos. of London and environs] 9/ obl 4° Cassell 96

Roberts, W. J. [photogr.] Some Old London Memorials ; phots. by author 2/6 *n.* 32° Laurie 07

Thorpe Six Photogravs. of Old Lond. before Fire [reprod. fr. his models] Lond. Drawing Off. 10

Way, T. R. [art.] Reliques of Old London ; w. text H. B. Wheatley 21/ *n.* s 4° Bell 96

" [art.] Later Reliques of Old London ; w. text H. B. Wheatley 21/ *n.* s 4° Bell 97

" [art.] Thames-side & Suburb. Reliques : lithos., w. l'rpr. H. B. Wheatley 21/ *n.* 4° Bell 99

" [art.] Suburban Reliques North of Thames : lithos., w. l'rpr. H. B. Wheatley 21/ *n.* 4° Bell 98

" [art.] Ancient Royal Palaces in and near London 21/ *n.* ($6 *n.*) f° Lane 02
Excellent lithographs of St James's, Kennington, Hampton Court, Windows, etc. : w. l'rpr. F. Chapman.

* " [art.] Ancient Halls of the City Guilds : 45 ill. 31/6 *n.* s 4° Bell 03
$10 *n.* Lane, *N.Y.* Text by Dr Pp. Norman.

**Signs and Signboards** —*v.* **G** § 29

**Squares**

Chancellor, E. B. The Squares of London ; ill. fr. old prints [hist. & topogr.] 21/ *n.* 4° Paul 07

**Streams ; Springs ; Spas** —*v. also* Fleet (The), *inf.*

Foord, A. S. Springs, Streams, and Spas of London ; 27 ill. 10/6 *n.* 8° Unwin 10
Descrs. the various streams wh. have given their names to London streets ; w. their hist. and assocns.

**Streets ; Street-names**

Baker, H. Barton Stories of the Streets of London ; ill. 7/6 c 8° Chapman 99

Edwards, P. J. Hist. of Lond. Street Imprvmts. : 1855–97 ; maps & plans 17/6 8° P. S. King & Son 98

Foord, A. S. —*in his* Springs, Streams, etc., *ut sup.*

Habben, F. H. London Street Names 6/ c 8° Unwin 96
$2 Lippincott, *Phila.* Orig., signific., and historic value. Interestg., but of no philological value.

L.C.C. : hist. of Streets and Places within Co. of Lond., 10/6 Suppl. 1/ P. S. King & Son 01 ; 09

**Street Cries** —*v.* **B** § 23, *s.v. Cries*

**Suburbs ; Environs**

Bell, Mrs A. G. The Skirts of the Great City ; 16 col. pl. & 17 ill. 6/ c 8° Methuen 07
Facts and assocns. conn. w. Hampst., Highg., Harrow to Eppg., Greenw., Croyd., Wimbl., and riverside places.

Fitzgerald, Percy London City Suburbs as They are To-day ; c. 300 ill. 42/ 4° Leadenhall Press 93
A compan. vol. to Rev. W. J. Loftie's *London City* [*ut sup.*], but unmethodical, discursive, and otherwise not nearly so good.

Harper, C. G. [Am.] Cycle Rides round London ; ill. 6/ c 8° Chapman 02

" Rural Nooks round London ; ill. 6/ *n.* c 8° Chapman 07
$2 *n.* Scribner, *N.Y.* Middlesex and Surrey.

Lysons, Dan. Environs of London within 12 Miles, 2 vols. *o.p.* 4° *London* [1792–6] 11

Suburban Homes of London ; map [by W. S. Clarke] *o.p.* [*pb.* 7/6] c 8° Chatto 81

Thorne, J. Hdbk. to Environs of Lond., 2 v. [arrgd. alphab.] *o.p.* [*pb.* 21/] c 8° Murray 76

Walford, Edw. Greater London, 2 vols. ; 400 ill. ea. 9/ 4° Cassell 83–4

**Banks**—*v.* **D** § 116 **Clubs**—*v.* **D** § 129 **Coins and Tokens**—*v.* **G** § 20 **Fairs**—*v.* **B** § 23

**Guides**—*v.* **E** § 16 **Guilds**—*v.* **D** § 120 **Theatres**—*v.* **I** § 135

---

**Adelphi :** Brereton (Austin) Liter. Hist. of Adelphi & Neighbrhd. ; ill. 10/6 *n.* 8° Unwin [07] 10

**Aldgate :** Atkinson (A. G. B.) St Botolph, Aldgate : story of a City parish 5/ *n.* c 8° Richards 98

Kemp, R. Some Notes on Ward of Aldgate 3/ *n.* s 4° Eden Fisher [04] 04

**Aldwych, Kingsway, etc.**

GORDON, Chas. Old Time Aldwych, Kingsway, & Neighbourhood; 60 ill. 7/6 *n.* 8° Unwin [04] 05
Acc. of the old bldgs. recently destroyed to make room for the handsome new thoroughfare.

**All Hallows, Barking:** BIGGS (Rev. C. R. D.) All Hallows, Barking 1/6 8° Waterlow 00

**Bermondsey:** CLARKE (E. T.) Bermondsey: its historic memories and associations 6/ *n.* 8° Stock 01

**Bloomsbury; St Giles:** BLOTT (W.) Chronicle of Blemundsbury; maps and facss. 21/ 4° Author, *S. Norwood* 92

CLINCH, Geo. Bloomsbury & St Giles, Past & Present; maps & ill. 12/ *n.* 4° Truslove 90

*St Giles's of the Lepers:* GREY (E. C. W.) St Giles's of the Lepers 3/6 *n.* ($1·50) c 8° Longman 05

**Bridewell:** COPELAND (A. J.) Bridewell Royal Hosp. [pal., hosp., prison, schl.] 3/6 c 8° Wells Gardner 88

**Bromley-by-Bow:** Bromley-by-Bow: register of historic and beautiful landmarks of parish; 36 pl. 21/ *n.* 4° Surv. of Memls. of Lond. 00

**Camberwell:** BLANCH (W. H.) Ye Parish of Camberwell *o.p.* [*pb.* 21/] 8° E. W. Allen 75

**Charing Cross:** MACMICHAEL (J. H.) Story of Char. Cross and Neighbhd. 7/6 *n.* 8° Chatto 06

**Charterhouse:** HENDRIKS (Dom. L.) London Charterhouse: monks and martyrs; ill. 15/ 8° Paul 89

ELWYN, Rich. [Master 1885–97] Life of. By P. Patterson 3/6 c 8° Wells Gardner 00

**Chelsea:** BEAVER (A.) Memorials of Old Chelsea; ill. and maps 42/ 4° Stock 92
An excellent and detailed hist. of the 'Village of Palaces,' well ill. by the author. Orig. pub. in 2/ pts. '91–2.

BLUNT, Reg. Illustr. Histor. Hdbk. to Parish of Chelsea; maps & ill. 2/6 *n.* c 8° Lamley 00
An excellently planned handbook and guidebook; with bibliography.

" Paradise Row: a broken piece of Old Chelsea 10/6 *n.* 8° Macmillan 06
The literary and personal assocns. of this famous 'village street', recently demolished.

BURGESS, Walt. W. [art.] Bits of Old Chelsea; w. descr. l'rpr. £10 10/ f° Paul 94
Forty-one etchings of historic houses and picturesque views in Chelsea.

FAULKNER, T. Histor. and Topograph. Descrn. of Chelsea and Environs, 2 vols.; map and ill. 8° *priv. prin., Chelsea* [10] 92
Standard. The best book for the older part of Chelsea.

GODFREY, W. H. The Parish of Chelsea, vol. i; 94 pl. 25/ *n.* 4° Surv. of Memls. of Gr. Lond. 09

L'ESTRANGE, Rev. A. G. Chelsea: the village of palaces, 2 vols. *o.p.* [*pb.* 21/] c 8° Hurst 80
A very readable and entertaining compilation.

MARTIN, Benj. E. Old Chelsea; ill. Jos. Pennell 3/6 c 8° Unwin [89] 91

MITTON, Geraldine E. Chelsea [Fascination of Lond.; 90 c. *n.* Macm., *N.Y.*] 1/6 *n.* f 8° Black 02

*Church:* DAVIES (Randall) Chelsea Old Church; 13 ill. [fr. orig. docs.] 52/6 *n.* i 8° Duckworth 03

**Clerkenwell:** PINKS (J. W.) Hist. of Clerkenwell, ed. E. J. Wood; ill. *o.p.* 4° *London* [63–5] 81

*St John's Church:* UNDERHILL (J.) St John's, Clerkenwell; pl. W. Monk f° Cadbury, Jones & Co. 95
Conts. a gen. sketch by Sir E. LECHMERE of hist. of Engl. branch of Knights of St John, and acc. of wrecking of their once magnif. house, its church and rare adornmts. by mobs of Jack STRAW, Wat TYLER and Dr SACHEVERELL; of the Spoliatn. of Order by HENRY VIII, and revival of Hospitallers. The pl. are highly pictorial etchgs. of the existg. remains of house of Hospitallers.

**Cripplegate**

*St Giles':* BADDELEY (J. J.) Acc. of Ch. and Parish of St Giles', Cr.; ill. 10/ r 8° Baddeley 88

DENTON, W. Records of St Giles', Cripplegate 4/ 8° Bell 83

*Crosby Hall; Crosby Place*

GOSS, C. W. F. Crosby Hall: chap. in hist. of Lond.; ill. 5/ *n.* r 8° Crowther 08

NORMAN (P.) + CARÖE (W. D.) Crosby Place; 39 pl. 25/ *n.* 4° Surv. of Memls. of Gr. Lond. 08
W. architect. descrn. by W. D. CARÖE. Pub. for Comm. f. Surv. of Memls. of Greater London.

**Deptford:** DEWS (N.) History of Deptford 2/6 c 8° Simpkin [ ] 84

**Downing St.:** PASCOE (C. E.) No. 10 Downing Street, Whitehall; ill. 21/ *n.* 4° Duckworth 08
The assocns. since days of WOLSEY of this famous ho., the offic. resid. of 1st L'd of Treasury since Sir Rob. WALPOLE.

**Dulwich** —*v. inf., s.v.* Norwood (GALER)

**Exchequer Houses, Old** —*v.* **D** § 117*, *s.v.* Exchequer

**Fleet (The); Fleet Street:** ASHTON (J.) The Fleet: rivers, prison, marriages—*ut* **D** § 123

ARCHER, Thos. Highway of Letters; ill. [Fl. St. in rel. to growth of liter.] 10/6 c 8° Cassell 93

PRICE, F. G. Hilton The Marygold by Temple Bar—*ut* **D** § 116, *s.v.* Child & Co.

**Fulham; Hammersmith**

CROKER, T. Crofton Walk fr. London to Fulh., ed. Beat. Horne; 120 ill. 7/6 *n.* c 8° Paul [60] 96

FAULKNER, T. Hist. and Topogr. Account of Fulham [incl. Hammersmith] *o.p.* 8° *London* 13

" History and Antiquities of Hammersmith *o.p.* 8° *London* 39

FÈRET, C. J. Fulham, Old and New, 3 vols.; ill. 63/ *n.* 4° Leadenhall Press 00
A minute historical and topographical account: quite the best book on the subject.

WEBB, W. A. Sandford Manor, Fulham; ill. 4° Surv. of Memls. of Gr. Lond. 07

**Gerrard St.:** WHEATLEY (H. B.) Gerrard St. and Neighbourhood c 8° *n.d.* (04)

**Guildhall:** PRICE (J. E.) Descr. Acc. of Guildhall; maps & ill. (some col.) f° Corporn. of London 86

RILEY, Hy. T. [ed.] Munimenta Gildhallæ Londoniensis, 3 v.; facss. ea. 10/ r 8° Rolls Series 59–62
: *Liber Albus* [compiled 1419 by Jno. CARPENTER, Common Clerk in WHITTINGTON'S mayoralty], givg. acc. of laws, regulns., and institns. of City fr. 12th to early 15th cent.; ii (2 Pts.): *Liber Custumarum* [comp. early 14th cent. dur. rn. of EDW. I] and *Liber Horn*, givg. acc. of same fr. 12th to early 14th cent.; iii: Tr. of the Ang.-Norm. passages in *Lib. Alb.*, glossaries, apps., index.

,, [tr.] Liber Albus: translated *o.p.* [*pb.* 9/] 4° J. R. Smith 42

**Hackney:** MANN (E. A.) Brooke House, Hackney; 10 ill. 15/ *n.* 4° Surv. of Memls. of Gr. Lond. 04

ROBINSON, W. Hist. and Antiqs. of Hackney, 2 v.; ill. *o.p.* [*pb.* 45/] 8° Nichols 42–3

*St John's Ch.:* SIMPSON (R.) Memls. of St John's, Hackney, 3 Pts. s 4° *priv. prin.* (*Guildford*) 81–4

*Hammersmith:* FAULKNER (T.) History and Antiquities of Hammersmith; ill. *o.p.* 8° *London* 39

**Hampstead:** BAINES (F. E.) [ed.] Recds. of Manor, Par. and Boro' of H.; ill. 24/ c 8° Whittaker 90

BARRATT, Thos. J. The Annals of Hampstead, 2 vols.; fully ill. (some col.) Black *in prep.*

HAMPSTEAD ANTIQ. AND HISTOR. SOC.: Transactions: 1898–1905, 2/6 to 5/ 8° Mayle, *Hampstead*, 98–05, *not cont.*

HOWITT, Wm. The Northern Heights of London; ill. *o.p.* [*pb.* 21/] 8° Longman 69
Hampstead, Highgate, Hornsey, Islington, *etc.*, with their historical associations.

PARK, J. J. Topography of the Village of Hampstead *o.p.* [*scarce*; *w.* 50/] 8° *London* [14] 18
Standard. A remarkable production for a young man who had not attained his majority when it was published.

WHITE, Carol. A. Sweet Hampstead and its Associations; ill. 7/6 *n.* c 8° Stock [00] 03

**Ham (East and West):** FRY (K.) E. and W. Ham Parishes, ed. Pagenstiche; ill. 21/ 8° Siegle 88

**Hanover Square** —*v.* **D** § 129, *s.v.* Oriental Club (BAILLIE)

**Hendon:** EVANS (E. T.) Hist. and Topogr. of Parish of Hendon; ill. 7/6 c 8° Courier Co., *Hendon* 91

**Highgate:** LLOYD (J. H.) History of Highgate *o.p.* 4° *Highgate* 88

PRICKETT, F. History and Antiquities of Highgate; ill. *o.p.* [*pb.* 6/] 8° Broadbent 42

**Holland House:** HOLLAND (L'y)—*in her* Journal, 2 vols., *ut* **F** § 27 [1791–1811]

LIECHTENSTEIN, P'cess. Marie Holland House, 2 vols.; ill. *o.p.* [*pb.* 16/] 8° Macmillan [73] 74

SANDERS, Lloyd The Holland House Circle; ill. 12/6 *n.* 8° Methuen 08

[WHISHAW, Jno.] The 'Pope' of Holland House; ill. [1813–40] 10/6 *n.* 8° Unwin 06
Selns. fr. correspce. of WHISHAW and his friends, ed. by L'y SEYMOUR; w. memr. of W. and acc. of 'The King of Clubs' by W. P. COURTNEY.

**Islington:** LEWIS (S.) Hist. of Parish of St Mary, Islington *o.p.* [*pb.* 42/] 4° Jackson 42

**Kennington:** MONTGOMERY (Bp) Hist. of Kennington and Neighbourhood *o.p.* [*pb.* 3/6] c 8° Gold 90

**Kensington; Kensington Palace**

DOBSON, Austin Old Kensington Palace, and other Papers—*ut* **K** § 83

FAULKNER, T. History and Antiquities of Kensington *o.p.* 8° *London* 20

HUNT, Leigh Old Court Suburb, ed. Austin Dobson, 2 v.; ill. & 60 photogravs. 21/ sq 8° Constable [55] 02

LAW, Ern. Kensington Palace [hist. hdbk.] 2/ *n.* c 8° Bell 99

LOFTIE, Rev. W. J. Kensington, Picturesque and Hist.; 300 ill. (some col.) *o.p.* [*pb.* 45/] 4° Field & Tuer 88

**Kew:** MARTIN (T. M.) [art.] Kew Gardens; 24 col. pl., w. l'rpr. A. R. Hope Moncrieff 6/ *n.* c 8° Black 08
$2·50 *n.* Macmillan *N.Y.* Hist. of Kew as royal residence, its popularity w. old-world society, and as public gardens.

*SANDERS, Lloyd Old Kew, Chiswick, and Kensington; 16 pl. 12/6 *n.* 8° Methuen 10

**Lambeth:** CAVE-BROWN (Rev. J.) Lambeth Palace and Assocns.; ill. 21/ 8° Blackwood [83] 83

**Leicester Sq.:** HOLLINGSHEAD (J.) Story of Leicester Square; ill. 1/ 4° Geo. Kenning 92

TAYLOR, Tom Leicester Square: its assocns. & worthies; ill. *o.p.* [*pb.* 10/6] c 8° Bickers 74

**Leyton:** The Great House, Leyton; 25 ill. 21/ *n.* 4° Surv. of Memls. of Gr. Lond. 03

**Lincoln's Inn Fields:** HECKETHORN (C. W.) Linc's I. Fds. & Localities Adjct. [compiln.] 21/ *n.* 4° Stock 96

**Marlborough House:** BEAVEN (A. H.) Marlborough House and its Occupants; ill. *o.p.* [*pb.* 6/] 8° White 96

**Marylebone; St Pancras:** CLINCH (G.) Marylebone and St Pancras; ill. 12/ *n.* 4° Truslove 90

SAUNDERS, Mrs Baillie The Great Folk of Old Marylebone; ill. 2/6 *n.* c 8° Glaisher 03
A social history of the district, its connexion of DICKENS, BROWNING and WESLEY, etc.

**Mayfair; Belgravia:** CLINCH (G.) Mayfair and Belgravia; maps and ill. 12/ *n.* 4° Truslove 91
Histor. acc. of parish of St George's, Hanover Sq. Mayfair dates back to early yrs. of CHAS. II; Belgravia came into existence after 1825, before wh. it was a swamp, known as The Five Fields: Thos. Cubitt was the creator of the district.

CHANCELLOR, E. B. Knightsbridge and Belgravia; ill. 20/ *n.* 4° Pitman 09

**Mile End:** *Trinity Hosp.:* Trinity Hospital; 13 pl. 21/ *n.* 4° Surv. of Memls. of Gr. Lond. 96

**Minories:** KINNS (Dr S.) Six Hundred Years; 80 ill. 15/ 8° Cassell 99
Disconnected sketches of men and women who have had contact w. Holy Trinity, Minories, fr. 1292 to 1893.

TOMLINSON, Rev. E. M. History of the Minories; 16 ill. [1300–1900] 18/ *n.* 8° Smith & Elder 07

**Monument:** WELCH (C.) Hist. of the Monument; maps and ports. 1/6 s 4° *sold at Monument* 93
Contains a history of the Fire of London of 1565.

**Norwood; Dulwich;** GALER (A. M.) Norwood and Dulwich, Past and Present 6/ *n.* 4° Truslove 90

**Old Bailey; Newgate** —*v.* **D** § 123, *s.v.* Prisons (Newgate)

**Paddington:** ROBINS (W.) History of Paddington *o.p.* [*pb.* 5/] p 8° Lemare 53

**Piccadilly; Mayfair; Pall Mall**—*v. also* **D** § 129, *s.v.* Clubs

CHANCELLOR, E. B. Wanderings in Piccadilly, Mayfair, & Pall Mall; ill. 2/6 *n.* c 8° Rivers 08

NEVILLE (Ralph) + JERNINGHAM (C. E.) Piccadilly to Pall Mall; 2 pl. 12/6 *n.* 8° Duckworth 08
A good bk. of anecdotes of Soc., turf, politics, clubs, restaurants, amusements, etc., of last 25 yrs.

STREET, G. E. The Ghosts of Piccadilly; ports. 10/6 *n.* 8° Constable 07
The crowded assocns. of this famous street excellently presented by one who knows its every aspect and every incident of its hist.

WHEATLEY, H. B. Piccadilly to Pall Mall *o.p.* [*pb.* 16/] 8° Smith & Elder 70

**Rotherhithe:** BECK (Rev. E. J.) Memorials to Serve for a History of the Parish of Rotherhithe; ill. 10/ *n.* 8° Camb. Press 07
$2 *n.* Putnam, *N.Y.* Incl. a ch. on Geology of Thames Valley and Rotherhithe by Dr T. G. BONNEY.

**St Bartholomew the Great, Smithfield** (fd. A.D. 1123 by RAHERE; oldest Lond. ch. exc. Norman Chapel in Tower)

BIRD, Chas. [art.] St Bartholomew the Great, Smithfield; 6 etchgs., w. l'rpr. Frost & Reed, *Bristol* 96

MOORE, N. St Bartholomew, West Smithfield *o.p.* 8° 97

**St Clement, Danes:** DIPROSE (J.) Acc. of St Clement Danes 12/6 4° Diprose 68

**St James' Palace:** SHEPPARD (Dn. J. E.) Meml. of St James' Palace, 2 vols.; 41 pl. and 32 ill. 36/ *n.* 8° Longman 94
An interestg. compiln., givg. full acc. of lives of chief residts. (one of best bg. that of CHARLES I, both in prosperity and in adversity), and of the events, ceremonies, and art-treas. The ports. of great interest.

**St James' Square:** DASENT (A. I.) History of St James' Square and the Foundation of the West-End of London; ports. & ill. 12/ *n.* 8° Macmillan 95
A learned, yet not dull, monogr., crammed w. facts. Conts. interestg. glimpse of Whitehall in rn. of CHARLES II.

**St Martin-in-the-Fields:** KITTS (J. V.) [ed.] Accs. of Churchwardens of St M.-i.-t.-F. [1525–1603] 42/ *n.* f° Simpkin 01

**St Mary at Hill:** Records of St Mary at Hill, 2 Pts. [1420–1559] 8° 04–5

**St Mary Overie** (*now* Southwark Cathedral, *q.v.*, *inf.*)

**St Olive's, Hart St.; All Hallows, Staining**

POVAH, Dr Alf. Annals of St Olive's and All Hallows, Staining; ill. 21/ *n.* 4° Blades 94
The two parishes were united 1870. A valuable wk., spec. interestg. in conn. w. the Plague and w. PEPYS, and contg. full accs. of Par. Recds., Regrs. of Bapts., Marrs., Burls., Ch.-wrdns.' Accs., etc.

**St Pancras** —*v.* Marylebone, *sup.*

**St Paul's Cathedral** —*for* Bibliogr. *v. sup.*, *s.v.* London; *for* Archit. *v.* **I** § 119

BENHAM, Can. W. Old St Paul's 5/ *n.* i 8° Seeley 02

MILMAN, Dn H. H. Annals of St Paul's Cathedral [standard] *o.p.* [*pb.* 18/] 8° Murray [68] 69

PAYNE, J. Orlebar St Paul's Cathedral in Time of Edward vi 2/6 8° Burns & Oates 93
An account of its treasures fr. a document in H.M. Public Record Office.

SIMPSON, Dn W. Sparrow Gleanings from Old St Paul's 7/6 8° Stock 89

" St Paul's Cath. and Old City Life [13–16 cents.] 7/6 8° Stock 94
Scholarly pprs. on the cath., its structure and possessns., its personal, eccles., and munic. assocns.

" [ed.] Documts. rel. to St Paul's Cath. [13 to beg. 18 cent.] 7/6 s 4° Camden Soc. 80

SINCLAIR, Archd. W. M. Memorials of St Paul's Cathedral; ill. 16/ *n.* 8° Chapman 09
An authoritative popular hist. of the cath. fr. earliest times, w. short lives of Bps and Dns and full acc. of WREN and his wk. Chap. on St Paul's Cross. Good illns. Louis WEIRTER.

*St Paul's Cross:* MARSH (J. B.) St Paul's Cross 3/6 4° Raithby 92
Sets forth all incids. ment. in annals, diaries, hists. and State-Pprs. as hg. occurred at Paul's Cross, an open-air pulpit nr. the Cathedral wh. stood on the meeting-place of the city folkmote, the antiq. of wh. is descr. as going bey. wr. recds. (first appearg. in 1191, when Wm. FITZ-OSBERT, otherwise 'Longbeard', deliv. his harangue from it agst. the divine right of kings (to govern wrong).

**Savoy:** LOFTIE (Rev. W. J.) Meml. of Savoy [Pal., Hospl., Chapel] *o.p.* [*pb.* 7/6] c 8° Macmillan 79

**Soho:** CARDWELL, Rev. J. H., etc. Two Centuries of Soho; 130 ill. 6/ *n.* 8° Truslove 98

" Men and Women of Soho 6/ *n.* 8° Truslove 03

RIMBAULT, Dr E. F. Soho and its Assocns., ed. G. Clinch 12/6 *n.* sq 8° Dulau 96

**Somerset House:** NEEDHAM (R.) + WEBSTER (A.) Somerset Ho., Past & Pres.; 57 ill. 21/ 4° Unwin 05
Its history fr. its foundn. (c. 1550); w. acc. of the present edifice erected by Sir Wm. CHAMBERS in 1776.

**Southwark:** BOGER (Mrs E.) Bygone Southwark; maps and ill. 7/6 8° Andrews, *Hull* 95
Eccles., liter., dramatic and antiq. assocns., local celebrs. and industries, famous fair, *etc.*

BOWERS, R. W. Sketches of Southwark, Old and New; 183 ill. 10/6 *n.* 8° Wesley 02

RENDLE, Wm. Old Southwark and its People *o.p.* 4° *London* 78

" + NORMAN (Pp.) Inns of Old Southwark and Assocns.; ill. *o.p.* [*pb.* 28/] r 8° Longman 88

*Southwark Cathedral:* THOMPSON (Can. W.) Hist. of St Saviour's, Southwark 5/ *n.* 8° Stock [94] 04

**Stepney:** HILL (G. W.) + FRERE (W. H.) [eds.] Memls. of Stepney [1579–1662] 8° 90–1
*Church of St Dunstan:* PEPYS (W. C.) + GOODMAN (E.) Ch. of St Dunstan; ill. 15/ *n.* 4° Surv. of Memls. of Gr. Lond. 05
**Stoke Newington:** ROBINSON (W.) History of Stoke Newington; ill. *o.p.* [*pb.* 21/] 8° Nichols 42
**Tower of London:** BARRETT (C. R. B.) [art.] The Tower: 13 etchgs. & 13 vigns.; w. l'rpr. 21/ i 4° Catty 89
BELL, D. C. Notices of Historic Persons buried in Chapel of St Peter ad Vincula; ill. 14/ 8° Murray 77
'In truth, there is no sadder spot on earth than this little cemetery'—MACAULAY.
BENHAM, Can. Wm. Tower of London; ill. [Portfolio Monogrs.] 7/ *n.* 8° Seeley 06
BROOKE-HUNT, Violet Prisoners of the Tower; ill. 5/ *n.* c 8° Dent 99
$2 Dutton, *N.Y.* A good popular account of the illustrious prisoners of the Tower from the beginning.
BRAYLEY, J. History and Antiquities of the Tower, 2 Pts. *o.p.* 8° *London* [21–5] 30
BRITTON (J.) + BRAYLEY (J.) Memoirs of the Tower of London *o.p.* s 8° *London* 30
DAVEY, Rich. The Tower of London; col. front. and 12 ill. 10/6 *n.* 8° Methuen 10
DE ROS, [20th] Bar. Memorials of the Tower of London *o.p.* [*pb.* 6/] c 8° Murray [66] 67
DIXON, W. Hepworth Her Majesty's Tower; Introd. W. J. Loftie, 2 vols.; 16 col. pl. 12/ r 8° Cassell [69–71] 02
FULLEYLOVE, J. [art.] Tower of London: 20 col. pl., w. l'rpr. A. Poyser [$2·50 *n.* Macm., *N.Y.*] 7/6 *n.* sq 8° Black 08
GOWER, Lord Ronald S. The Tower of London, 2 vols.; ill. 42/ *n.* 8° Bell 01–2
A popular acc. of chief episodes in its history. Vol. i: to ELIZ.; ii: JAS. I to pres. day. Excellent ill. w. col. front., 80 photogravs., and 28 blocks.
HARPER, C. E. Tower of London: fortress, prison, palace; ill. 6/ *n.* c 8° Chapman 09
PRESTON, T. Yeomen of Guard; ill. hist. [hist. 1485–1885] 5/ c 8° Harrison *n.d.* (85)
**Trinity House:** BARRETT (C. R. B.) Trin. Ho. of Deptford Strond; ill. 12/6 *n.* 4° Lawrence & Bullen 93
WHORMBY, J. Corpn. of Trinity House [orig., hist., functns.] r 8° *priv. prin.* [1746] 68
MAYO, W. H. Trinity House, Past and Present; ill. 5/ *n.* c 8° Smith & Elder 05

**Westminster** —*v. also sup., s.v.* London (STOW)
BESANT, Sir Walt. Westminster; 130 ill. and 1 etchg. 7/6 8° Chatto 95
$3 Stokes, *N.Y.* Not a connected history, but a series of sketches of the life of the place at different periods. Good ill.
„ + MITTON (G. E.) Westminster [Fascin. of Lond.; 90 c. *n.* Macm., *N.Y.*] 1/6 *n.* f 8° Black 02
EMDERY, Walt. [art.] Picturesque Westminster: 64 pl., w. l'rpr. [chfly. old bldgs.] f° Hentschel 02
SMITH, J. T. [1766–1833] Antiquities of City of Westminster; ill. *o.p.* [*pb.* 35/] 4° Bohn [07] 37
*St John the Evangelist, Westmr.:* SMITH (J. E.) St John the Ev., Westm.; ill. [anecdotic] 10/6 8° Wightman 93
*St Margaret:* SMITH (J. E.) Cat. of Westmr. Recds. in St Marg. and St John's Wightman 06
*Westminster Abbey* —*for* Architecture *v.* **I** § 119
BOND, Fcs. Visitor's Guide to Westm. Abbey; pl. 1/ *n.* (40 c.) f 8° Frowde 09
An admirable guide, contg. a good deal of fresh and valuable comment.
BRADLEY, E. T. [Mrs A. Murray SMITH] Annals of Westminster Abbey; 150 ill. 63/ 4° Cassell 95
Preface by Dn G. G. BRADLEY: chapter on building by J. T. MICKLETHWAITE. A good historical account.
„ Westminster Abbey: story & assocns.; ill. [repr. of above] 6/ c 8° Cassell 06
„ Roll-Call of Westminster Abbey; 5 plans & 25 ill. 6/ c 8° Smith & Elder [02] 02
The best account of the 'mighty dead' who lie buried in the Abbey; very full and accurate.
BROOKE-HUNT, Violet Story of Westminster Abbey; ill. 6/ c 8° Nisbet 02
Wr. for the young: a simple history of the buildings and accs. of those who lie buried there.
FLETE, Jno. [monk] Hist. of Westmr. Abbey, ed. Dr J. A. Robinson; w. Introd. and comm. 5/ *n.* r 8° Camb. Press 09
$2 *n.* Putnam, *N.Y.* The Latin hist. of the Abbey: by a monk of the house fr. 1420 to 1465. WIDMORE's excellent wk. (*Hist. of Ch. of St Peter, Westmr.*, 4°, 1751) makes free use of it.
FULLEYLOVE, J. [art.] Westm. Abbey: 21 col. pl.; w. l'rpr. Mrs A. Murray Smith 7/6 *n.* sq 8° Black
LOFTIE, Rev. W. J. Westminster Abbey; ill. Herb. Railton 7/6 8° Seeley [89] 93
$2·25 Macmillan, *N.Y.* A good popular book.
MORRIS, Wm. Architecture and History of Westminster Abbey—*ut* **I** § 119
NEALE (J. P.) + BRAYLEY (E. W.) Hist. & Antiqs. of Abbey Ch. of Westmr., 2 v.; ill. *o.p.* 4° *London* 18
Notes and Documents rel. to Westm. Abbey, ed. Dr J. A. Robinson, Nos. i–ii ea. 5/ *n.* r 8° Camb. Press 09 *in prg.*
Ea. $2 *n.* Putnam, *N.Y.* i: *The MSS. of Westm. Ab.* by EDR. + Dr M. R. JAMES; ii: FLETE (Jno.) *Hist. of Westm. Ab., ed.* EDR. [*ut sup*] iii: *Gilb. Crispin* [the Abb. und. Norman rule].
SMITH, Mrs A. Murray —*v.* Bradley, E. T., *sup.*
STANLEY, Dn A. P. Historical Memorials of Westminster Abbey; ill. 15/ 8° Murray [67]
TROUTBECK, Hy. The Founders of Westminster Abbey; 7 col. pl. 21/ *n.* c 8° Mowbray 11
LUCIUS; SEBERT; EDWARD, the Confessor; HENRY iii; HENRY vii.

**Whitehall :** LOFTIE (Rev. W. J.) Whitehall ; pl. and ill. [Portfolio monographs] 2/6 *n.* 8° Seeley 95
75 c. *n.* Macmillan, *N.Y.* A popular sketch of hist., topogr. and archit. of Whitehall, fr. earliest times to closing of Chapel Royal.

SHEPPARD, Rev. J. E. The Old Royal Palace of Whitehall ; 39 ill. 21/ *n.* m 8° Longman 02
A full historical account—the only one in existence.

**Monmouthshire**

BRADLEY, A. G. Shropshire, Hereford, and Monmouth—*ut inf.*, *s.v.* Shropshire

BRADNEY, J. A. History of Monmouthshire, Pts. i–ii ; ill. [in 6 vols.] ea. 42/ f° Mitchell & Hughes 04–7
Treats the descents of estates and pedigrees of families elaborately.

COXE, Archd. Wm. Historical Tour in Monmouthshire 30/ 4° Davies, *Brecon* [1801]

MORRIS, A. Hdbk. of Geogr. & Hist. of Monmouthshire 1/6 *n.* c 8° Dawson, *Newport, Mon.* 02

WILLIAMS, Dav. History of Monmouthshire ; ill. 4° *London* 1796

*Chepstow :* MARSH (J. F.) Annals of Chepstow Castle *o.p.* 8° 83

*Llanthony Abbey :* POVEY (J. M.) Nunnery Life in Ch. of Eng. By Sister Mary 3/6 c 8° Hodder 90

IGNATIUS, F'r [O.S.B. ; monk of L.A.] Life of. By B'ess de Bertouch ; ill. 10/6 *n.* 8° Methuen 04

**Norfolk ; East Anglia Generally**

*East Anglia :* DEFOE (Dan.) Tour thro' Eastern Counties [Natl. Lib.] 6*d.* (25 c. *n.*) 18° Cassell [1769] 88

*DUTT, W. A. Highways & Byways in E. Anglia ; ill. J. Pennell 6/ ($2 *n.*) c 8° Macmillan 01

,, Wild Life in East Anglia ; 16 col. pl. 7/6 *n.* 8° Methuen [06]

,, Norfolk and Suffolk Coast ; c. 40 ill. [County Coast Ser.] 6/ *n.* c 8° Unwin 09

HISSEY, J. J. Tour in Phaeton thro' Eastern Counties—*ut* **E** § 16, *s.v.* Roads

KINGSTON, Alf. East Anglia and the Great Civil War ; ill. 5/ *n.* 8° Stock [97] 02
A full history of the 'Eastern Association' and its achievements ; appendices give statistics. A full acc. of the rising of CROMWELL'S Ironsides in the Assoc. Cos. of Camb., Huntingdon, Lincoln, Norf., Suffolk, Essex, Hertfd.

POWELL, Edg. The Rising in East Anglia in 1381 [$1·90 *n.* Putn., *N.Y.*] 6/ 8° Camb. Press 96

RITCHIE, J. E. East Anglia : personal and historical assocns. 7/6 c 8° Jarrold [83] 93

SCOTT, Clement W. Poppy-land : scenery on the East Coast 1/ c 8° Carson [85] 97

VINCENT, J. E. Through East Anglia in a Motor-Car—*ut* **I** § 148*

WHITE, W. Eastern England, fr. Thames to Humber, 2 v. *o.p.* [*pb.* 18/] c 8° Chapman 65

*Literary Assocns. :* DUTT (W. A.) Some Literary Assocns. of E. Anglia ; ill. 10/6 *n.* 8° Methuen 07
BORROW, FITZGERALD, Sir T. BROWNE, Bp HALL, COWPER, Hannah MORE, CRABBE, EARL OF SURREY, TAYLORS of Norwich, MARTINEAUS, F. D. MAURICE, SKELTON, Sir J. SUCKLING, etc. 32 ill. (16 col.).

*Norfolk*

*Bibliography :* RYE (Walt.) Index to Norfolk Topography 18/ s 4° Index Soc. (*now* Brit. Rec. Soc.) 83

WOODWARD, S. Norfolk Topographer's Manl., ed. W. C. Ewing *o.p.* [*pb.* 21/] 8° Nichols 42
A catalogue of bks. and engravings rel. to the county.

ANDREWS, Wm. [ed.] Bygone Norfolk 7/6 8° Brown, *Hull* 98

ASTLEY, Dr H. J. Dunkinfeld [ed.] Memls. of Old Norf. ; ill. [Memls. of Cos. of Engl.] 15/ *n.* 8° G. Allen 08

BLOMEFIELD, Fcs. Topog. Hist. of Norf., 11 v. ; ill. 8° *Lond.* [1739–75] 05–10
The standard wk., contin. Rev. C. PARKIN. *Index Nominum*, by J. N. CHADWICK, was pubd. 8vo *King's Lynn* 62.

JESSOPP, Dr A. Arcady for Better for Worse 3/6 c 8° Unwin [87] 92

,, —*in his* Trials of a Country Parson 3/6 c 8° Unwin [90] 94

,, Village Life—*in his* Coming of the Friars, *ut* **F** § 14

,, —*in his* Random Roaming ; and other Papers 3/6 c 8° Unwin [94] 96

*MASON, R. H. History of Norfolk ; Pts. i–v ; ill. (some illum.) *o.p.* 4° Wertheim 82–5
The hist. of the County is cpl. (w. index) in first 4 Pts., commencg. the var. Townships and Parishes in alphab. order. No more of this valuable and elab. wk. will be pubd., author hg. died. The var. scient. portns. were wk. of specialists.

NORFOLK & NORWICH ARCHÆOL. Soc. : Norf. Archæology : miscell. tracts rel. to Norf. 8° *Norwich* 47 *sqq.*

Norfolk Antiquarian Miscellany : ed. Walt. Rye, Ser. i, 3 v. ; Ser. ii, v. i (3 Pts.) 8° Goose, *Norwich* 73–06

RYE, Walt. History of Co. of Norfolk [Popular County Hist.] 7/6 p 8° Stock 85

,, Norfolk Topography 81

,, Index Rerum to Norfolk Antiquities [pp. 104] *priv. prin.* 99

,, [ed.] Short Calendar of Feet of Fines for Norf., Pts. i–ii [1158–1484] 8° *Norwich* 85–6

,, [ed.] State Papers rel. to Musters, Beacons, Ship-money, etc., in Norfolk, fr. 1626 to beg. of Civil War Norf. & Norw. Arch. Soc. 07

*Victoria History of the County of Norfolk, vols. i–ii—*ut* **E** § 16 [to occupy 6 vols.]

WINTERS, Wm. Selection of Norfolk Antiquities : 36 pl. in 6 Pts. 4° 85–6

*Churches :* BRYANT (T. H.) Norfolk Churches, vols. i–iii ; ill. ea. 3/6 obl. 4° *Mercury* Off., *Norwich* 98–9

COX, Dr J. C. Norfolk, North and South, 2 vols. ea. 3/ *n.* c 8° G. Allen 10

*Guides* —*v.* **E** § 16

*Scenery* —*v. also sup., s.v.* Broads (DAVIES; EMERSON)
COTMAN, J. S. [art.] Etchgs. of Arch. & Pict. Remains, 2 v.; 240 pl. [chfly. Norf.] f° Grant, *Edin.* [18] *n.d.*
EMERSON, P. H. [ed.] Picts. of Anglian Life: 32 photogravs. & 15 ill. *o.p.* [*pb.* 105/] i 4° Low 88
„ [ed.] Pictures fr. Life in Field and Fen: photogravs. 63/ i 4° Bell 87
*Worthies:* JONES (Mrs Herb.) Some Norfolk Worthies; ports. 3/6 *n.* c 8° Jarrold 99

*Bedford Level* —*v. sup., s.v.* Lincolnshire
*Broads and Rivers* —*v. also* **H** § 102, **I** § 153
BICKERDYKE, Jno. Best Cruise on the Broads; ill. *o.p.* [*pb.* 2/6] c 8° Bliss 95
DAVIES, G. C. The Norfolk Broads and Rivers; ill. 6/ c 8° Blackwood [83] 84
„ The 'Swan' and her Crew in Rivers of Norfolk 3/6 16° Warne [76] 89
„ Etchings of Rivers and Broads; 24 photogrs. 21/ f° Jarrold, *Norwich* 89
DODD, Anna B. On the Broads; ill. Jos. Pennell $3 (10/6) s 4° Macmillan 96
DUTT, W. A., etc. Norfolk Broads; 77 ill. (48 col.) F. Southgate 6/ c 8° Methuen [03]
Descriptive; with arts. on fishing, fowling, botany, and natural history, by other contributors.
EMERSON, P. H. Idyls of the Norfolk Broads; 12 autogravs. 21/ f° Autotype Co. 87
„ Wild Life on a Tidal Water; ill. [Breydon Water] 25/ *n.* 4° Low 90
„ Marsh Leaves; w. photo. etchgs. 12/6 *n.* i 8° Nutt 95
„ On English Lagoons; ill. 7/6 8° Nutt 93
„ + GOODALL (T. F.) Life and Landscape on Norfolk Broads; 40 photogravs. 126/ f° Low 86
EVERITT, Nich. Broadland Sport 12/6 *n.* 8° Everett 01
Includes excellent account of the wild life of the Broads.
PATTERSON, A. H. Notes of an East Coast Naturalist; col. pl. 6/ c 8° Methuen [04]
„ Nature in Eastern Norfolk; 12 col. pl. 6/ c 8° Methuen [05]
„ Wild Life on a Norfolk Estuary; 40 ill. [Breydon Water] 10/6 *n.* 8° Methuen 07
„ Man and Nature on Tidal Waters; ill. 6/ c 8° Methuen 09
READY, O. G. Life and Sport on the Norfolk Broads; ill. 7/6 *n.* 8° Laurie 10
RYE, Walt. A Month in Norfolk Broads; maps & 22 ill. 1/6 c 8° Simpkin 87
STARK, Jas. [art.; 1794–1859] Scenery of Rivers of Norfolk: ser. of pl. f° *Norwich* 34
SUFFLING, E. R. The Land of the Broads; ill. 5/ c 8° Upcott Gill [85] 95
„ Innocents on the Broads; ill. 3/6 c 8° Jarrold, *Norwich* 01
*Cawston:* RYE (Walt.) Hist. of Church and Parish of Cawston, Pt. i 8° *priv. prin.* 98
*Cromer:* RYE (Walt.) Cromer, Past and Present; 40 ill. 21/ 4° Jarrold, *Norwich* 89
*Erpingham:* RYE (W.) Rough Matrls. of Hist. of N. Erpingham, 3 Pts. 8° *Norwich* 83–9
*Forncett:* DAVENPORT (Dr F. G.) [Am.] Econ. Developmt. of a Norf. Manor 10/ *n.* r 8° Camb. Press 06
$2·50 *n.* Putnam, *N.Y.* Skilfully grouped facts, interpretg. agric. and domest. hist. of period, 1086–1565. Map and 2 pl.
*Holkham:* COKE (T. W.) 1st Earl of Leicester, of Holkham, etc. [1752–1842]
Stirling, A. M. W. Coke of Norfolk and his Friends, 2 vols.; ill. 32/ *n.* ($10 *n.*) 8° Lane 07
*Lowestoft* —*v. inf., s.v.* Yarmouth
*Methwold:* GEDGE (J. D.) Hist. of a Village Community in E. Cos.; ill. 10/ 4° Goose, *Norwich* 93
*Norwich:* BAYNE (A. D.) History of Norwich 4/6 c 8° Jarrold, *Norwich* 89
**HAWKINS, C. B.** Norwich: a social study—*ut* **D** § 124
HUDSON, Rev. W. How the City of Norwich grew into Shape; maps 5/ 4° Goose, *Norwich* 97
An account of the topography and history of the city from primitive times to 13th century.
„ [ed.] Leet Jurisdiction in Norwich in 13–14 Cents. 4° Selden Soc. 92
„ +TINGEY (J.C.) [eds.] Recds. of City of N. vol. i-ii; w. Introd. ea. 25/ *n.* r 8° Jarrold, *Norwich* 06–10
JESSOPP, Dr A. Norwich [Diocesan Histories] 2/6 12° S.P.C.K. 84
„ [ed.] Monastic Visitations in Diocese of Norwich 15/ s 4° Camden Soc. 88
Shows the state of monastic life in diocese of Norwich on the eve of the Reformation.
KNIGHTS, Mark Highways and Byeways of Old Norwich; 50 pl. 21/ 4° Jarrold, *Norwich* 87
„ Peeps at the Past: rambles am. Norfolk antiqs.; ill. 21/ *n.* 4° Jarrold, *Norwich* 91
RYE, Walt. [ed.] Calendar of Norw. Freemen: 1317–1603 [8000; w. trades, etc.] 10/6 4° Stock 88
„ [ed.] The Norwich Rate Book: 1633–4 [pp. 94] *o.p.* 8° Jarrold, *Norwich* 03
„ [ed.] Calendar of Norwich Deeds Enrolled 8° *priv. prin.* 10
„ + HUDSON (W. H.) [eds.] Short Calendar of Deeds rel. to Norwich 8° *priv. prin.* 03
*Little Bethel Hospital:* BATEMAN (Sir F.) + RYE (W.) Hist. of Bethel Hosp. 4° *priv. prin.* 06

*Walloon Church* —*v.* **A** § 63 (Huguenot Soc.—MOENS)
*Sandringham :* JONES (Mrs Herb.) Sandringham, Past and Present 2/6 c 8° Jarrold, *Norwich* [83] 87
*Thompson :* CRABBE (Rev. G.) History of Parish of Thompson ; ill. 15/ 4° Goose, *Norwich* 92
*Yarmouth :* EMERSON (P. H.)—*in his* Wild Life on Tidal Water, *ut sup.*, *s.v.* Broads
MANSHIP, H. Hist. of Gt. Yarmouth ; cont. Palmer *o.p.* [*pb.* 21/] 4° J. R. Smith [54] 56
NALL, J. G. Great Yarmouth & Lowestoft, 2 vols. [w. glossary] *o.p.* [*pb.* 7/] f 8° Longman 66

**Northamptonshire**

ANDREWS, Wm. [ed.] Bygone Northamptonshire ; ill. [by var. wrs.] 7/6 8° Brown, *Hull* 91
BAKER, Geo. Hist. & Antiqs. of Northampton, vols. i–ii *o.p.* [*w.* 150/] f° *London* 22–41
BRIDGES, Jno. Hist. and Antiqs. of Northants, ed. P. Whalley, 2 v. [*w.* £5] f° *Oxford* 1791
DRYDEN, Alice [ed.] Memls. of Old Northants ; ill. [Memls. of Cos. of Eng.] 15/ *n.* 8° G. Allen 03
*Victoria History of the County of Northampton, vols. i–ii—*ut* **E** § 16 [to occupy 4 vols.]
*Guides* —*v.* **E** § 16
*Worthies :* ADKINS (W. R. D.) Our County : repres. men of Northants ; ill. 6/ *n.* 4° Stock 93
*Bedford Level* —*v. sup.*, *s.v.* Lincolnshire
*Doddridge :* ARNOLD (Rev. T.) + COOPER (Rev. J. J.) Hist. of Ch. of Doddridge ; ill. *o.p.* 8° Northants Pb. Co., *Kettering* 95
*Kettering :* BULL (F. W.) Sketch of History of Kettering *o.p.* r 8° *Kettering* 91
*Nene Valley :* SHARPE (Edm.) etc. Churches of Nene Valley ; 112 plans 44/ 4° Batsford 80
*Northampton*
COX (Dr J. C.) + MARKHAM (C. A.) [eds.] Records of Boro' of Northampton, 2 v. ; ill. 42/ *n.* r 8° Birdsall, *N'hampton* 98
Vol. i: *Liber Custumarum, Bk. of Anc. Usages and Customes of Town of Northampton* [to 1448]; 2 facss. ed. MARKAM. Trs. of the Latin and Norman-French extracts are added. | *Orders of Assembly* [1547–1835], mod. records, lists of officls., etc. ed. COX
*All Saints' Ch. :* SERJEANTSON (Rev. R. M.) Hist. of Ch. of All Sts', N. ; ill. 7/6 *n.* 8° Mark, *N'hampton* 04
*Ch. of Holy Sepulchre :* COX (J. C.) + SERJEANTSON (R. M.) Hist. of Ch. of H. Sep., N. ; ill. 6/ *n.* c 8° Mark, *N'hampton* 98
A good hist. of one of the four round churches still extant in Engl. (out of 8 known to have existed).
*Peterborough :* POOLE (Rev. G. A.) Peterborough [Diocesan Histories] 2/6 12° S.P.C.K. 81
STAPLETON, T. Chronicon Petroburgense [A.D. 1122 onwards] s 4° Camden Soc. 49
*Crowland (Croyland) Abbey*—*v.* **F** § 19, *s.n.* INGULPH
*Rockingham Castle :* WISE (Chas.) Rockingham Castle and the Watsons ; ill. 21/ 4° Goss, *Kettering* 91

**Northumberland** —*v. also* Durham, *sup.*

ANDREWS, Wm. [ed.] Bygone Northumberland [by var. wrs.] 7/6 8° Brown, *Hull* 99
BATES, C. J. Border Holds of Northumberland, vol. i *o.p.* 8° *Newcastle-o.-T.* 91
* ,, History of Northumberland [Pop. County Hists.] 7/6 8° Stock 95
BRADLEY, A. G. Romance of Northumberland ; 16 col. pl. & 12 photos. 7/6 *n.* 8° Methuen 08
CHRISTIE, Rev. Jas. Northumberland : hist., feats., people [popular] 2/6 *n.* c 8° Thurnam, *Carlisle* 95
HODGKIN, Dr T., etc. Northumbria 8° Reid, *Newcastle-o.-T.* 98
Lects. on Roman Occupn., Northumbrian Story and Song, Mark AKENSIDE, Dialect Speech, etc.
HODGSON, Rev. Jno. History of Northumberland, 7 vols. ; pl. and ill. [*w.* £35] 4° *Newcastle* 20–58
NORTHUMB. CO. HIST. COMMITTEE : History of Northumberld., cont. by others, vols. i–ix *subscr.* ea. 26/ 4° Reid, *Newcastle* 93–09 *in prg.*
An excellent example of mod. topogr. research, partly based on matls. left by late Jno. HODGSON, ed. E. BATESON, A. B. HINDS, J. C. HODGSON, and H. A. E. CRASTER. Whole will occ. 12 vols. Profusely ill. by old dwgs., plans of pre-hist. camps, photogravs. and unique ser. of anc. memol. maps (fr. origs. in Alnwick Castle).
PAGE, W. [ed.] Three Early Assize Rolls for Northumberld. [13 cent.] 15/ 8° Surtees Soc. 91
RAINE, Jas., sen. [1791–1858] History and Antiquities of North Durham, now united to Northumberland ; pl. [*w.* 70/] r f° Nichols 30–52
RICHARDSON, M. A. Local Historn's. Table Bk. of Remark. Occurs. conn. w. Newc., Northumb., Durh., 8 vols. *o.p.* r 8° *Newc.-o.-T.* 41–6
SURTEES SOCIETY —*ut sup.*, *s.v.* Durham
SYKES, J. Local Records, 4 vols. [A.D. 80–1875] *o.p.* 8° 66–76
TOMLINSON, W. W. Life in Northumberland during Sixteenth Century 4/ *n.* c 8° W. Scott 97
Deals chiefly with the domestic and social conditions of the county.
WHITE, Rob. Worksop, 'The Dukery', and Sherwood Forest *o.p.* [*pb.* 7/6] c 8° Simpkin 75
WILDRIDGE, T. T. [ed.] Northumbria : repository of antiquities ; ill. 10/ 4° Peck, *Hull* 91
Colln. of papers on antiqus. of Northumberld., Cumb., Westm., Durh., Yorks, Lancs, and Borders.

*Castles, etc.:* GIBSON (W. S.) Notices of N'ld. Castles, Chs., etc., 3 Ser. *o.p.* [*pb.* 22/6] 8° Longman 48–54
*Alnwick:* TATE (G.) Boro', Castle, and Barony of Alnwick, 2 v., ill. *o.p.* 8° *Alnwick* 66–9
*Berwick-on-Tweed:* SCOTT (J.) Hist. of Town & Guild of B.-o.-T.; ill. 36/ 4° Stock 88
*Brinkbury Priory:* PAGE (W.) [ed.] Chartulary of Brink Priory 10/ 8° Surtees Soc. 93
*Ford Castle:* NEVILLE (Rev. H. M.) [ed.] Under a Border Tower; ill. 10/ *n.* c 8° Mawson, *Newc.* 96
First half devoted to the charitable and artistic wk. of the 'late noble Châtelaine', LOUISA, MARCHIONESS OF WATERFORD [better in Hare's *Two Noble Lives, ut* F § 27], whose cartoons for the Ford Schl. are well reprod. here; rest topographical, on fox-htg., etc.
*Hexham:* HODGES (C. C.) Abbey of St Andrew; facss. and 63 pl. 63/ *n.* i f° W. Scott 88
RAINE, Can. J. [ed.] Priory of Hexham: chrons., endowmts., annals, 2 v. 52/ 8° Surtees Soc. 64–5
*Newcastle; Gateshead:* BARNES (Ambr.) Life of, ed. W. H. D. Longstaffe 10/ 8° Surtees Soc. 67
BOYLE, Rev. J. R. Vestiges of Old Newcastle and Gateshead; ill. 50/ *n.* 4° Stock 91
CHARLETON, R. J. Newcastle Town; ill. 5/ c 8° W. Scott 85
DENDY, F. Wm. [ed.] Recds. of Company of Hostmen of Newcle. [1600 to pres. day] 15/ 8° Surtees Soc. 01
Records of Merchant Adventurers, ed. J. W. Boyle + F. W. Dendy; 2 vols. [16–19 cents.] ea. 15/ 8° Surtees Soc. 95–9
RENDEL, Daphne Newcastle-on-Tyne: munic. origin and growth [popular] 3/6 c 8° Arnold 98
WELFORD, Rich. Chron. Hist. of Newc. & Gatesh., 3 v. [1301–1640] ea. 12/6 r 8° W. Scott 85–7
*Literary and Philosophical Society*
WATSON, Dr R. Spence Hist. of Lit. & Philos. Soc., Newc.-on-Tyne [1793–1896] 21/ *n.* 4° W. Scott 97
*Newminster Abbey:* FOWLER (Rev. J. T.) [ed.] Cartularium Abbatiæ de Novo Mon. 7/6 8° Surtees Soc. 78
*Norham Castle:* JERNINGHAM (H. E. H.) Hist. of Norham Castle and Surrgs. 7/6 8° Paterson, *Edin.* 83
*Shields (South):* HODGSON (G. B.) The Borough of S. Shields; ill. 10/6 4° Reid, *Newc.-o.-T.*
*Tyne (River)* —*v.* **E** § 16, *s.v.* Rivers
*Tynemouth Abbey:* GIBSON (W. S.) Hist. of Tynemouth Abbey, 2 vols. *o.p.* [*pb.* 126/] 4° Pickering 46–7

**Nottinghamshire**

BAILEY, Thos. Annals of Nottinghamshire, 4 v.; maps & ill. *o.p.* [*w.* 30/] 8° *Nottingham n.d.* (52–5)
BRISCOE, J. Potter Chapters in Nottinghamshire History; 40 ill. 4/ 8° Author, *Nottingham* 08
„ [ed.] Old Nottinghamshire, 2 vols.; ill. *o.p.* c 8° Author, *N'ham* 81–4
Papers on the history and topography of the county, by various writers.
BROWN, Cornelius Hist. of Nottinghamshire [Pop. County Hists.] 7/6; Ch. Edn. 3/6 *n.* 8° Stock 91; 96
GODFREY, J. T. [ed.] MSS. rel. to Co. of Nghm. in poss. of J. Ward *subscr.* 21/ *n.* r 8° Bell, *Nottingham* 00
MARSHALL, G. [ed.] Nottinghamshire Subsidies: 1689 8° *Worksop* 95
STEVENSON, Wm. Bygone Nottinghamshire [by var. wrs.] 7/6 8° Brown, *Hull* 93
THOROTON, R. Hist. of Nottinghamshire, ed. F. Throsby, 3 vols.; pl. 4° *London* [1677] 1797
*Victoria History of the County of Nottingham, vols. i–ii—*ut* **E** § 16 [to occupy 4 vols.]
*Churches:* GODFREY (J. T.) Notes on Chs. of Notts: Hund. of Rushcliffe 88
„ Notes on Churches of Notts: Hund. of Bingham Phillimore 08
*Guides* —*v.* **E** § 16
*Worthies:* BROWN (Corn.) Lives of Nottinghamshire Worthies 4° *Nottingham* 82
*Blyth:* RAINE (Jno.) Hist. and Antiqs. of Parish of Blyth *o.p.* 4° J. R. Smith 60
*Clayworth:* GILL (H.) + GUILFORD (E. L.) [eds.] The Rector's Bk., Clayw.; w. notes 10/6 *n.* 8° Saxton, *Nottingham* 10
Transcn. and edn. of a bk. of local memoranda made by Wm. SAMPSON, rector 1676–1701.
*'Dukery (The)'* The Dukery Records; 40 ill. 32/6 *n.* 4° White, *Worksop* 04
Principally trs. of anc. documts. rel. to the neighbrhd. in Brit. Mus., Record Off., and Bodl. Lib. Oxford.
*East Leake:* POTTER (Rev. S. P.) History of East Leake; map and ill. 8° Clarke, *Nottingham* 03
An excellent history: includes everything of importance except natural history.
*Newark:* BROWN (Corn.) Annals of Newark-upon-Trent; ill. 30/ 4° Sotheran 79
*Nottingham:* DEERING (Dr) Nottinghamia Vetus et Nova
Chicken, R. C. Index to Deering's 'Nottinghamia' [84 pp.] 10/6 *n.* 4° Murray, *Nottingham* 00
Records of Borough of Nottingham: extrs. fr. archives of Corpn., v. i–v 54/6 *n.* r 8° Quaritch 82–00 *in prg.*
Vols. i–iv ed. W. H. STEVENSON, 42/ *n.*; vol. v ed. W. T. BARKER, 12/6 *n.* 1155–1702. Facss.
*Castle:* HINE (T. C.) Nottingham: its Castle, etc.; Suppl. *o.p.* [*pb.* 30/] 4° Allen 76–9
*Guild Hall; Prison:* BRISCOE (J. P.) Old Guild Hall and Prison, N'm 3/6 4° Murray, *N'ham* 95
*Sherwood Forest:* RODGERS (Jos.) Scenery of Sherwood Forest; ill. 21/ *n.* r 8° Unwin [99] 08
*Southwell Minster:* LEACH (A. F.) [ed.] Visitns. and Mems. of S'well Minster 10/ s 4° Camden Soc. 91
An interestg. and learned wk., contg. results of much research and throwg. light on early Church life and discipline. 12–13 cents.

**Oxfordshire**

DITCHFIELD, Rev. P. H. [ed.] Memls. of Old Oxfordshire ; ill. [Memls. of Cos. of Eng.] 15/ *n.* 8° G. Allen 03
*EVANS, H. A. Highways & Byways in Oxford & Cotswolds ; ill. 6/ ($2 *n.*) c 8° Macmillan 05
FALKNER, J. Meade History of Oxfordshire [Pop. County Hists.] 7/6 ; Ch. Ed. 3/6 *n.* 8° Stock 99 ; 06
HENDERSON, Mrs Sturge Three Cents. in N. Oxfordshire ; 11 ill. 5/ *n.* 8° Blackwell, *Oxford Oxon.* [02] 08
Especially good for 18th century history of the district : a series of essays.
OXFORD HISTORICAL Soc. : Publications—*v.* **D** § 157, Oxford Univ.
PLOT, Rob. Natural History of Oxfordshire ; map and pl. f° *Oxford* [1677] 1705
STAPLETON, Mrs Bryan Three Oxfordshire Parishes [histories of Kidlington, Yarnton & Begbroke] 17/ *n.* 8° Oxf. Hist. Soc. 93
*Victoria History of the County of Oxford, vol. ii—*ut* **E** § 16 [to occupy 4 vols.]
WILLIAMS, W. R. Parliamentary History of County of Oxford 8° *priv. prin.* (*Brecknock*) 99
*Guides* —*v.* **E** § 16
*Bensington :* PEARMAN (Rev. M. T.) Hist. of Manor of Bensington 7/6 8° Stock 96
*Bicester :* BLOMFIELD (Rev. J. C.) Hist. of Deanery of Bicester, Pts. i–viii [full and accurate] ca. 9/ 8° Stock 82–94
*Burford :* HUTTON (Rev. W. H.) Burford Papers, and other Studies ; ill. 7/6 *n.* 8° Constable 05
The letters of Saml. CRISP to his sister at Burford. 1745–1845.
*Enstone :* JORDAN (J.) Parochial Hist. of Enstone *o.p.* [*pb.* 7/] 8° J. R. Smith 57
MARSHALL, E. R. Account of the Church of Enstone *o.p.* [*pb.* 3/] c 8° Parker, *Oxon* 68
*Eynsham Abbey :* SALTER (Rev. H. E.) [ed.] Cartulary of Eynsham Abbey, 2 vols. ea. 31/6 *n.* 8° Oxf. Hist. Soc. 07–8
*Godstow :* CLARK (Dr A. ; ed.) Engl. Register of Godstow Nunnery, 2 Pts. 25/ 8° E. Engl. Text Soc. 05–6
*Oseney Abbey :* CLARK (Dr A.) Engl. Register of Oseney Abbey, Pt. I 15/ 8° Early Engl. Text Soc. 07
*Oxford* —*v. also* **D** § 157, *s.v.* Gt. Britain (Oxford Univ.)
*Bibliography :* MADAN (F.) Rough List of MS. Matls. rel. to Hist. of Oxf. 7/6 ($1·90) 8° Clar. Press 87
Archæologia Oxoniensis : Pts. i–v in 1 vol. ; pl. *o.p.* [*pb.* 10/6 *n.*] 8° Frowde 92–5
BOASE, Rev. C. W. Oxford ; 2 maps [Historic Towns Ser.] 3/6 ($1·25) c 8° Longman [87] 87
FULLEYLOVE, Jno. [artist] Oxford ; w. l'rpr. T. Humphry Ward 42/ f° Fine Art Soc. 89
,, Oxford : 60 col. pl., w. l'rpr. Edw. Thomas 20/ *n.* sq 8° Black 02
$6 *n.* Macmillan, *N.Y.* Pictures of Oxford buildings and scenes, with excellent letterpress.
HEADLAM, Cecil Oxford and its Story ; 21 lithogr. Herb. Railton 21/ *n* 4° Dent 04
,, Story of Oxf. ; ill. H. Railton [Mediæv. Towns ; $1·75 *n.* Dutton, *N.Y.*] 4/6 *n.* c 8° Dent 07
HURST, Herb. Oxford Topography : an essay 21/ 8° Oxf. Hist. Soc. 00
The detailed topogr. of the anc. streets and streams and houses of Oxford, in form of a commentary on HUTTON'S *Antiquities of Oxford* [1625–30], text of wh. is repr. here Accompanies the *Old Plans, inf.*
HUTTON, Leon. Antiquities of Oxford [1625–30]—*v.* Hurst, *sup.*
LITTLE, A. G. The Grey Friars in Oxford—*ut* **A** § 57, *s.v.* Franciscan Order
MARSHALL, Rev. E. Oxford [Diocesan Histories] 2/6 12° S.P.C.K. 82
MINCHIN (H. C.) + PEEL (Rob.) Oxford ; 100 col. ill. 6/ c 8° Methuen 05
M[OWAT], J. L. G. Notes on the Oxfordshire Domesday *o.p.* [*pb.* 3/6 *n.*] 8° Frowde 92
OGLE, Octavius [ed.] Royal Letters to Oxford—*ut* **D** § 157, *s.v.* Oxford
Old Plans of Oxford : 15 pl. [*v.* Hurst, *sup.*] 21/ *n.* in portf° Oxf. Hist. Soc. 99
AGAS' *Plan* [1578–88], WHITTLESEY'S *Engr. of same* and BEREBLOCK'S *Elizab. Views* [1728], HOLLAR'S *Plan* [1643], LOGGAN'S *Plan* [1675].
PLUMMER, Rev. C. [ed.] Elizabethan Oxford [reprs. of rare tracts]—*ut* **D** § 157, *s.v.* Oxford
RIMMER, A. Pleasant Spots Round Oxford ; c. 70 ill. *o.p.* [*pb.* 21/] 8° Cassell *n.d.* (78)
ROGERS, Prf. J. E. Thorold [ed.] Oxford City Documents [1268–1665] 12/ *n.* 8° Oxf. Hist. Soc. 91
Financial and judicial docts. ; throwg. a good deal of light on lawlessness of Univ. men, and incid. on customs of time.
[ROWLANDSON, Thos. (art.)] Rowlandson's Oxford : 16 col. pl., w. l'rpr. A. H. Gibb 10/6 *n.* 4° Paul 11
A colln. of 16 of ROWLANDSON'S humorous drwgs., w. text on Varsity men of the Georgian era.
*WOOD, Ant. à [1632–95] Survey of Antiqs. of City of Oxfd., ed. Rev. A. Clark ; 3 vols. 66/ *n.* 8° Oxf. Hist. Soc. [1786–90] 89–99
i : *City and Suburbs*, 25/ *n.* ; ii : *Chs. and Relig. Houses*, 20/ *n.* ; iii : *Addenda and Indexes*, 21/ *n.* [Corresps. substantially to a pt. of WOOD'S wk. wh. he never wrote out, ed. with much new matter, notes, etc.]. The whole forms the most cpl. and elab. hist. of any Engl. town in 17 cent. Sir Jno. PESHALL'S *Antiqs. of Oxfd.* [4° *Oxon.* 1773], wh. contd. a garbled and inaccur. edn. of pt. of WOOD'S MSS., is wholly worthless.
,, Life & Times, ed. Clark [*ut* **G** § 30 : *v.* note thereto] : forms sort of suppl. to above
*Oxford Museum :* ACLAND (Sir H.) Oxford Museum 4/ *n.* G. Allen [59] 93
*St Frideswide's :* WIGRAM (Rev. S. R.) [ed.] Cartulary of St F., 2 vols. ea. 21/ *n.* 8° Oxf. Hist. Soc. 95–6
*St Martin's Ch. :* FLETCHER (Rev. C. J. H.) Hist. of Ch. & Par. of St M. 5/ *n.* c 8° Blackwell, *Oxon.* 97
A full account of the old church (demolished 1820) and the new building, pulled down 1896.

*St Mary the Virgin:* FFOULKES (Rev. E. S. F.) Hist. of Ch. of S. M. 10/6 ($3·50) c 8° Longman 92
JACKSON, T. G. The Church of St Mary the Virgin, Oxford; 24 pl. 36/ *n.* 4° Clar. Press 97
THOMPSON, Rev. H. L. Ch. of St Mary the Virgin in rel. to Engl. Hist. 3/6 *n.* c 8° Constable 04
*Shiplake:* CLIMENSON (Emily J.) History of Shiplake; pl. [500 pp.] *o.p.* 4° Eyre & Spottiswoode 94
An exhaustive wk. coverg. all departmts. of local hist., inclg. flora, fauna, Geology.
*Whitchurch:* SLATTER (Rev. J.) Notes on History of Parish of Whitchurch; ill. 5/ 8° Stock 95
*Woodstock:* MARSHALL (E.) Early Hist. of Woodstock and Environs, 2 v.; ill. *o.p.* [*pb.* 12/] c 8° Parker, *London* 73–4

**Rutland**

BLORE, Thos. Hist. and Antiqs. of County of Rutl., vol. i, Pt. 2 [E. Hund.; the only pt. pb.] [*w.* £3] f° *Stamford n.d.* (11)
*Victoria History of the County of Rutland, vol. i—*ut* **E** § 16 [to occupy 2 vols.]
WRIGHT, Jas. Hist. and Antiquities of County of Rutland f° *London* 1684
*Guides* —*v.* **E** § 16
*Burley-on-the-Hill:* FINCH (Pearl) Hist. of Burley-on-the-Hill, 2 vols.; ill. 42/ r 8° Bale 01
Vol. i: history of the house and the families who have owned it; ii: Catalogue of its contents.

**Shropshire**

*Bibliography:* WALCOTT (Rev. M. E. C.) Introd. to Sources of Salopian Topogr. 8° *Shrewsbury n.d.* (79)
ANDERSON, J. C. Shropshire; its early hist. and antiquities; ill. *o.p.* r 8° J. R. Smith 64
AUDEN, T. [ed.] Memls. of Old Shropsh.; ill. [Memls. of Cos. of Eng.] 15/ *n.* 8° G. Allen 08
BRADLEY, A. G. Shropshire, Hereford, and Monmouth; ill. 5/ *n.* c 8° Constable 08
[DUKE, T. F.] Antiqs. of Shropshire, ed. E. Lloyd [fr. MS.]; ill. *o.p* [*pb.* 63/] r 4° *Shrewsbury* 44
EYTON, Rev. R. W. Hist. & Antiqs. of Shrops., 12 v.; c. 150 pl. *o.p.* [*pb.* £12] i 8° J. R. Smith 53–61
A scholarly wk., treatg. chfly. of periods of Domesday and of the Anglo-Norman kings.
GASKELL, L'y Cath. M. Old Shropshire Life [folk-stories retold] 6/ c 8° Lane 04
,, Spring in a Shropshire Abbey; 18 ill. 9/ *n.* 8° Smith & Elder 05
GOMME, G. Laurence [ed.] Shropshire and Somersetshire [Gentlemen's Magazine Lib.] 7/6 8° Stock 98
HARE, A. J. C. Shropshire; 50 ill. 7/6 c 8° Geo. Allen 98
An interesting historical and descriptive book, including most of the important places and features.
HARTSHORNE, C. H. Salopia Antiqua: remains in Shropshire *o.p.* [*pb.* 24/] 8° Parker 41
Moss, Fletcher Pilgrimages in Cheshire and Shropshire—*ut sup, s.v.* Cheshire
TIMMINS, H. T. Nooks and Corners of Shropshire; 130 ill. [chfly. S. Salop] 21/ *n.* 4° Stock 00
*Victoria History of Shropshire, vol. i—*ut* **E** § 16 [to occupy 4 vols.]
WARTER, J. Wood An Old Shropshire Oak, ed. R. Garnett, 4 vols. 49/ 8° Paul 86–91
A ramblg. acc. of hist. of Salop, in wh. an old oak relates its reminiscs. of 600 yrs. Abounding in quotns., mostly poetical.
WASEY, G. L. Our Ancient Parishes [Quatfd., Morville, Aston Eyre] *o.p.* 8° *Bridgnorth* 59
*Churches:* CRANAGE (Rev. D. H. S.) Archit. Acc. of Churches of Salop, 10 Pts.; ill. ea. 10/ 4° Hobson, *Wellgtn., Salop* 94–11
*Guides* —*v.* **E** § 16
*Houses:* LEIGHTON (Stanley) [art.] Shropshire Houses, Past and Present 21/ *n.* 4° Bell 02
50 drawings of country seats, with notes on the families connected with them, etc.
*Ludlow:* BAKER (Oliver) Ludlow Town and Neighbourhood; 70 ill. 6/ 8° Woolley, *Ludlow* [89] 93
CLIVE, R. H. [ed.] Documts. conn. w. Hist. of Ludl. & L'd Marchers *o.p.* [*pb.* 31/6] i 8° Van Voorst 41
WRIGHT, T. [ed.] Churchwarden's Accs. of Ludlow [1540–1603] s 4° Camden Soc. 69
Parish Church of St Lawrence, Ludlow; 10 pl. 10/6 4° Woolley, *Ludlow* 93
A monograph of the Tower Restoration [1889–91].
*Oswestry:* CATHRALL (Wm.) History of Oswestry *o.p.* 8° *Oswestry n.d.* (55)
*Selattyn:* BULKELEY-OWEN (Mrs) History of Selattyn Parish 21/ *n.* r 8° Woodfall, *Oswestry* 98
*Shrewsbury:* AUDEN (Rev. Thos.) Shrewsbury; ill. [Anc. Cities; $1·75 *n.* Dutton, *N.Y.*] 4/6 *n.* c 8° Methuen 05
OWEN (H.) + BLAKEWAY (J. B.) Hist. of Shrewsbury, 2 vols. [*w.* £6] 4° *London* 25
*Tong:* GRIFFITHS (G.) Hist. of Tong; w. notes on Boscobel 5/ 8° Horne, *Newport* [ ] 94
*Wrekin (The):* BOORE (Emma) Wrekin Sketches; ill. [topogr. and loc. records] 3/6 c 8° Stock [97] 01

**Somersetshire**

*Bibliography:* BAKER (A. E.) Somerset Bibliography: 1896–1910 12/6 *n.* 4° Barnicott, *Taunton* 11
GREEN, Eman. Bibliotheca Somersetensis, 3 vols. 63/ *n.* 4° Barnicott, *Taunton* 02
Catal. of bks., pamphs., broadsides, etc. Vol. i: Introd. and bks. rel. to Bath; ii and iii: rest of county.
BARRETT, C. R. B. Somersetsh. Highways, Byways, & Waterways; ill. *o.p.* [*pb.* 21/] 8° Bliss & Sands 94

BATTEN, J. Historical and Topographical Collections rel. to Early History of Parts of Somerset 6/6 *n.* 8° Whitby, *Yeovil* 94
BOGER, Mrs E. Myths, Scenes, and Worthies of Somerset *o.p.* [*pb.* 10/6] c 8° Redway 87
COLLINSON, Rev. Jno. Hist. & Antiqs. of Co. of Somerset, 3 v.; ill. r 4° *Bath* 1791
Weaver (F. W.) + Bates (E. H.) Index to Collinson's 'Hist. of Somt.' 20/6 4° Barnicott, *Taunton* 98
EYTON, Rev. R. W. Domesday Studies, 2 vols. 52/6 4° Reeves & Turner 80
Anal. and digest of Somers. surv. and of Somers. Gheld Inquest of 1084 as collated w. Domesd. Bk.
GERARD, Thos. [of Trent; d. 1634] Partic. Descrn. of Somt. [1633], ed. E. H. Bates 4° Som. Rec. Soc. 00
GREEN, Eman. [ed.] Pedes Finium, vols. i–iv [1196–1485] 4° Som. Rec. Soc. 92–02
HEALEY, C. E. H. C. History of Part of West Somerset; map and ill. 42/ *n.* i 8° Sotheran 01
Parishes of Luccombe, Selworthy, Stoke Pero, Porlock, Culbone, Oare. Manorial hist., geneal., biography.
HUMPHREYS, A. L. [ed.] The Somerset Roll 10/6 *n.* r 8° Strangeways 97
,, Somersetshire Parishes, 8 Pts. ea. 5/6 4° Humphreys 06
JEBOULT, E. General Account of West Somerset [incl. Taunton] *o.p.* 4° *Taunton* 73
PHELPS, Rev. Wm. Hist. and Antiqs. of Som., 4 v. in 2; ill. 4° *London* 35–9
RAYMOND, Walt. The Idler out of Doors; ill. 6/ c 8° Richards 01
Essays on Somerset doings and customs.
ROGERS, W. H. H. Memorials of the West 16/ p 8° Iredale, *Torquay* 88
Somerset, Dorset, Devon. With 120 illns. of sepulch. monumts., ports., coats-of-arms, etc.
SNELL, F. J. [ed.] Memls. of Old Somerset; ill. [Memls. of Cos. of Eng.] 15/ *n.* 8° G. Allen 06
SOMERSET RECORD SOC.: Publications, vols. i–xxvii [Several entd. sep.] 8° Somerset Rec. Soc. 87–11 *in prg.*
*Victoria County History of Somerset, vol. i—*ut* **E** § 16 [to occupy 4 vols.]
WEAVER, Rev. F. W. [ed.] Somerset Incumbents [fr. Hugo MSS. in Brit. Mus.] 4° *priv. prin.* (*Bristol*) 89
*Carthusians* (*Somerset*) —*v.* **C** § 57 (THOMPSON)
*Church Towers*: PIPER (E.) [art.] Ch. Towers of Somt., 25 Pts. ea. 12/6 *n.* i 4° Frost, *Bristol n.dd.* (99–01)
A colln. of 51 etchgs., with letterpress by J. Ll. W. PAGE.
*Forests*: GRESWELL (Rev. W. H. P.) Forests & Deer Parks of Somerset 10/6 *n.* 8° Barnicott, *Taunton* 06
Selwood Forest, Mendip Forest, Petherton Forest, Neroche Forest, Exmoor Forest; w. chs. on huntg., etc. 2 maps.
*Guides* —*v.* **E** § 16
*Worthies* —*v. also sup.*, *s.n.* BOGER
KINGLAKE, R. A. Somersetshire Worthies *o.p.* 8° *London* 67
*Athelney*: BATES (E. H.) Two Cartularies of Muchelney Abbey & Athelney s 4° Som. Rec. Soc. 99
WALL, J. C. Alfred the Great: Abbeys of Hyde [Hants], Athelney, and Shaftesbury [Dorset] 5/ c 8° Stock 01
Contains a full history of the religious foundations from its foundation to the dissolution of the monasteries.
*Bath*: BARBEAU, Prf. A. Life and Letters at Bath in 18th Cent. [tr.]; ill. 12/6 *n.* r 8° Heinemann 04
Hist. of the town, w. stories of Beau NASH, PITT, PETERBOROUGH, WESLEY, POPE, SHERIDAN, and other celebrities. As THACKERAY says, 'All History went and bathed and drank there'.
HARPER, C. G. Bath Road—*ut* **E** § 16, *s.v.* Roads; *and* Somerset Coast, *ut ib.*, *s.v.* Coasts
KING (A. J.) + WATTS (B. H.) [eds.] The Municipal Records of Bath [1189–1604] 10/6 4° Stock 85
MELVILLE, Lewis Bath under Beau Nash; ports. and views 15/ *n.* 8° Nash 07
PEACH, R. E. M. Bath, Old and New: guide and hist.; ill. 3/ c 8° *Bath* 92
,, Street Lore of Bath [street-changes] 5/ c 8° *Bath* 93
TUNSTALL, Jas. Rambles about Bath and its Neighbourhood 6/6 12° Simpkin [47] 89
TYTE, Wm. Bath in the Eighteenth Century [gossip] Pickering, *Bath* 04
*History*: GREEN (Em.) Preparns. of Som. agst. Span. Arm. [1558–88] 9/ *n.* s 4° Gregory, *Bath* 02
,, March of Wm. of Orange thro' Somerset 9/ *n.* s 4° Gregory, *Bath* 92
HOPTON Narr. of Civil War; 1642–4, ed. C. E. H. Chadwyck-Healey 4° Som. Rec. Soc. [ ] 02
*Houses*
MEEHAN, J. F. Famous Houses of Bath and District; ill. 21/ *n.* 8° Meehan, *Bath* [01] 05
,, More Famous Houses of Bath; ill. 12/6 *n.* r 8° Meehan, *Bath* 06
PEACH, R. E. M. Historic Houses in Bath, and their Assocns., 2 vols. 4/ 4° Hallett, *Bath* 83–4
*Worthies*
ALLEN, Ralph [1694?–1764]
Peach, R. E. M. Life and Times of Ralph Allen; facs. ill. 7/6 *n.* s 4° Nutt 95
ALLEN (the orig. of FIELDING'S Squire Allworthy in *Tom Jones*) spent his self-earned wealth in unostentatious charity and benefactns. to Bath and in maintaing. a splendid hospitality at Prior Pk., built by himself. Incls. acc. of PITT'S conn. w. Bath and short memr. of BEAU NASH.
BRUMMELL, Geo. Bryan ['BEAU BRUMMELL'; 1778–1840]
Jesse, Cpt. W. Life of Beau Brummell 4/6 8° Sonnenschein [44] 93

MURCH, Jerom — Biogr. Sketches of Bath Celebrities, Anc. and Mod. 10/ 8° Lewis, *Bath* 93

NASH, Rich. ['BEAU NASH'; 1674–1762]

Deane (Mary B). — Mr Zinzan of Bath; ill. *o.p.* [*pb.* 6/] 4° Innes 91
**Pleasant pictures of Bath in the palmy days of Beau NASH and GEORGE II.**

Gosse, Prf. Edm. Beau Nash—*in his* Gossip in a Library, *ut* **K** § 18 [on Goldsmith's *Life of Nash*, 1762]
**AINSWORTH's novel *Beau Nash* [1880; *ut* K § 50] deals w. the Bath of NASH's day.**

*Bath Abbey:* BRITTON (J.) Hist. and Antiqs. of Bath Abbey Ch., ed. R. E. M. Peach 6/ c 8° Hallett, *Bath* [25] 87

HUNT, W. [ed.] — Two Chartularies of the Priory of St Peter s 4° Som. Rec. Scc. 93

*Hospital of St John Bapt.:* PEACH (R. E. M.) Hist. of Hosp. of S. J. Bapt. *o.p.* 4° *Bath* 86

*Bath and Wells* (*Diocese of*)

de DROKENSFORD, Bp Jno. Calendar of Register of, ed. Bp Hobhouse [1309–29] s 4° Som. Rec. Soc. 87

FOX, Bp Rich. — Register of, ed. E. C. Batten [1492–4; w. Life of Fox] r 8° 89

GIFFARD, Bp Walt. — Registers of, and of Bp H. Bowett, ed. T. S. Holmes [1265–6; 1401–7] s 4° Som. Rec. Soc. 99

HUNT, Rev. W. — Bath and Wells [to 19th cent.] [Diocesan Histories] 2/6 12° S.P.C.K. 85

SHREWSBURY, Ralph of [Bp] Register of, ed. T. S. Holmes, 2 vols. [1329–63] s 4° Som. Rec. Soc. 96

*Bridgwater:* JARMAN (S. G.) History of Bridgwater 7/6 8° Jarman, *St. Ives* 89

POWELL, Dr A. H. — The Ancient Borough of Bridgwater; ill. 10/6 8° Page, *Bridgwater* 07

" — Bridgwater in the Later Days; ill. [cont. of above] 10/6 8° Page, *Bridgwater* 08

*Bruton:* Cartularies of B. and Montacute, ed. Sir H.C. Maxwell-Lyte + Can. T.S. Holmes s 4° Som.Rec.Soc. 94

*Downside:* SNOW (Abbot T. B.) [O.S.B.] Sketches of Old Downside c 8° 03

*Dunster:* HANCOCK (Rev. F.) Dunster Church and Priory; ill. 10/ *n.* 8° Barnicott, *Taunton* 06

MAXWELL-LYTE, Sir H. C. Dunster and its Lords [1066–1881] r 8° *priv. prin.* 82

" — Hist. of Dunster & Families of Mohun & Luttrell, 2 v.; ill. 30/ *n.* 8° St Catherine's Pr. 09

*Glastonbury* —*v. also* Wells, *inf.* (HOLMES)

ELTON, C. I. [ed.] — Custumaria of Glastonbury Abbey, xiii Century 4° Som. Rec. Soc. 91

GASQUET, Dom F. A. — The Last Abbot of Glastonbury—*ut* **A** § 49

GRESWELL, Rev. W. H. P. Chapters on Early Hist. of Glastonbury Abb. 6/6 *n.* 8° Barnicott, *Taunton* 09
**A useful account of the hist. of the Abbey before the coming of St AUGUSTINE (A.D. 596).**

HENRICUS DE SOLIACO — Liber: inquisitn. of manors of Gl., ed. J. E. Jackson [1189] 4° Roxb. Club 82

WEAVER, Rev. F. W. [ed.] Foedary of Glastonbury Abbey: 1185–1345 4° Som. Rec. Soc. 10

WILLIAM OF MALMESBURY [d. 1143?] Antiqs. of Glastonb., tr. F. Lomax [A.D. 63–1126] 2/ *n.* 8° Talbot 08

*Ilchester:* BUCKLER (Rev. W.) [ed.] Ilchester Almshouse Deeds; w. notes [1200–1625] *o.p.* 8° *Yeovil* 66

*Kilmersdon:* HYLTON (L'd) Notes on Hist. of Parish of Kilmersdon 10/6 *n.* 8° Barnicott, *Taunton* 10

*Mendip:* BAKER (E. A.) + BALCH (H. E.) The Netherwold of Mendip—*ut* **G** § 12

COMPTON, Th. — A Mendip Valley; 50 ill. 10/6 8° Stanford 92
**Enlarged edn. of *Winscombe* [2nd ed. 1889]. Attempts to do for Winscombe what Gilb. WHITE did for Selborne.**

KNIGHT, Fcs. A. — Seaboard of Mendip; ill. [hist. archæol., nat. hist.] 7/6 *n.* 8° Dent 02

*Minehead:* HANCOCK (Rev. F.) Minehead: parish, manor, port 15/ *n.* 8° Barnicott, *Taunton* 03

*Montacute* —*v.* Bruton, *sup.*

*Muchelney Abbey* —*v.* Athelney, *sup.*

*Mynchin Buckland:* HUGO (Rev. T.) Hist. of M. B. Priory and Preceptory *o.p.* 4° J. R. Smith 61

WEAVER, Rev. F. W. [ed.] Chartulary of Mynchin Buckland Priory 4° Som. Rec. Soc. 09

*Norton-sub-Hamdon:* TRASK (C.) Norton-sub-Hamdon: notes on parish and manor 10/ 8° Barnicott, *Taunton* 99
**Papers; most interesting on the ancient agricultural conditions on the manor.**

*Quantock Hills:* CRESSWELL (B. F.) The Quantock Hills; ill. 2/6 *n.* c 8° Homeland Assoc. 04

GRESWELL, W. H. P. — The Land of Quantock; 3 maps and 15 ill. 15/ *n.* 8° Barnicott, *Taunton* 03

*Selworthy:* HANCOCK (Rev. F.) Parish of Selworthy in Somerset 10/6 *n.* 8° Barnicott, *Taunton* 01

*Swainswick:* PEACH (R. E. M.) Annals of Parish of Swainswick 10/6 4° Hallett, *Bath* 80

*Taunton:* HUGO (Rev. T.) History of Taunton Priory *o.p.* [*pb.* 9/] i 8° J. R. Smith 50

JEBOULT, E. —*in his* General Account of West Somerset, *ut sup.*

*Wellington:* ELWORTHY (F. T.) Notes on Wellington (Somerset) 10/6 *n.* 8° Barnicott, *Taunton* 93

HUMPHREYS, A. L. — Materials for Hist. of Town of Wellington *o.p.* [*pb.* 7/6] 8° H. Gray 89

" — The same, Pt. i: Wills, 1372–1811 [suppl. to above] 5/ *n.* 8° Humphreys 08

*Wells :* HOLMES (T. S.) Wells and Glastonbury ; ill. [Anc. Cities ; $1·75 *n.* Dutton, *N.Y.*] 4/6 *n.* c 8° Methuen 08

*Cathedral :* CHURCH (Can. C. M.) Chaps. in Early Hist. of Ch. of Wells ; ill. [1136–1333] 15/ 8° Barnicott, *Taunton* 94

FREEMAN, Prf. E. A. Hist. of Cathedral Church of Wells *o.p.* [*pb.* 3/6] c 8° Macmillan 70

JEWERS, A. J. Wells Cathedral : inscriptions & heraldry ; ill. 21/ r 8° Mitchell & Hughes 92
Gives every inscription line for line, w. genealog. annotations, extrs. fr. wills, registers, etc.

REYNOLDS, H. E. [ed.] Wells Cathedral : foundn., const. hist., statutes *o.p.* f° 82

*Winscombe* —*v. sup. s.v.* Mendip (COMPTON)

*Wiveliscombe :* HANCOCK (Rev. F.) Wifela's Combe *subscr.* 10/6 *n.* 8° Barnicott, *Taunton, in prep.*

*Wookey :* HOLMES (T. S.) History of Wookey *o.p.* 8° *Bristol n.d.* (86)

*Yarlington :* ROGERS (T. E.) Records of Yarlington *o.p.* s 4° 90

**Staffordshire**

*Bibliography :* SIMMS (Rup.) Bibliotheca Staffordiensis 21/ 4 Lomas, *Lichfield* 94
Bks. rel. to, prtd. in the county, or by native resident authors ; w. collatns. and biogr. notices. Incl. prints and ports.

BERESFORD, Rev. W. [ed.] Memls. of Old Staffs ; ill. [Memls. of Cos. of Eng.] 15/ *n.* 8° G. Allen 09

ERDESWICK, S. Survey of Staffordshire, ed. Rev. T. Harwood ; map *o.p.* [*pb.* 25/] 8° Nichols [1717] 44

EYTON, Rev. R. W. Domesday Studies : anal. & digest of Staffs survey *o.p.* [*pb.* 21/] 4° Trübner 81

HILL (Jos.) + DENT (R. K.) Historic Staffordshire 10/ *n.* 4° Midl. Ed. Trdg. Co., *Birm.* 96

LANGFORD, Dr J. A. Hist. of Cos. of Staff. & Warwick, 4 v. ; pl. 84/ 4° *London* 76

PLOT, Rob. The Natural History of Staffordshire [*w.* £10] f° *Oxford* 1686

SHAW, S. Hist. & Antiqs. of Staffs, vols. i–ii, Pt. i ; map & c. 100 pl. [*w.* £25] f° *London* 1798–1801

*Victoria History of the County of Stafford, vol. i—*ut* **E** § 16 [to occupy 4 vols.]

WM. SALT ARCHÆOL. SOC. : Collns. for a Hist. of Staffs, 18 v. in 20 ; New Ser., vols. i–xii 8° Halden, *Stafford* 80–1910 *in prg.*

*Guides*—*v.* **E** § 16 *Place-names*—*v.* **K** § 120

*Cheadle :* PLANT (R.) History of Cheadle *o.p.* 8° 81

*Hanley :* CRAPPER (J. S.) Ancient Corporation of Hanley, ed. Spairton [1783–1900] 8° 01

*Leek :* MILLER (W. H.) Olde Leeke *o.p.* 8° *Leek Times* Off. 91
Good gossip, w. some useful material ; repr. fr. *Leek Times.* Almost exclusively modern : not old, still less 'olde'.

SLEIGH, J. Hist. of Parishes of Leek, Horton, Cheddleton, Ipstones ; ill. *subscr.* r 4° *priv. prin.* [62] 83

*Lichfield :* BERESFORD (Rev. W.) Lichfield [Diocesan Histories] 2/6 12° S.P.C.K. 83

*Cathedral :* STONE (J. B.) Hist. of Lichfield Cath. fr. Foundn. *o.p.* [*pb.* 10/] 4° Longman 70

*Stafford :* GILLOW (J.) St Thomas' Priory : story of St Austin's, Staff., ill. 5/ c 8° Burns & Oates 94
Not a hist. of the Augustinian canonry of St Thomas the Martyr, but a laborious wk., based on prtd. bks. and archives of R.-C. community, on the fortunes of R.-C.'s of Staffd. since mid. 16th cent.

*Stoke-on-Trent :* HUTCHINSON (Rev. S. W.) The Archdeaconry of Stoke-on-Trent 10/6 8° Bemrose 93
Historical notes on North Staffordshire Abbeys, Churches, Chapels, and Parishes.

*Tettenhall :* JONES (J. P.) Hist. of Parish of Tettenhall [based on recds.] 21/ *n.* 8° Steen, *Wolverh.* 94

*Walsall :* WILLMORE (F. W.) History of Walsall and Neighbourhood 15/ 8° Robinson, *Walsall* 87

**Suffolk** —*v. also* Norfolk, *sup.*

*COPINGER, Dr W. A. The County of Suffolk, 6 vols. ea. 21/ *n.* 8° Sotheran 04–7
Gives substance of everythg. rel. to the Co. of a histor. or offic. character (some 100,000 documts.). Vol. vi is Index.

* ,, History of the Manors of Suffolk, vols. i–vii ea. 21/ *n.* r 4° Sotheran 06–11
Notes on the history and devolution of the Manors of Suffolk.

Domesday (Suffolk) : Latin text [extended], w. tr. Jno. Hervey, Marq. of Bristol, 2 v. [23 pp. only] c 8° *priv. prin.* (*Bury St Edm.*) 88–91

EMERSON, Dr P. H. Pictures of East Anglian Life—*ut sup., s.v.* Norfolk

GAGE, J. History and Antiquities of Thingoe Hundred [*w.* 35/] 4° *London* 38

GLYDE, Jno., jun. Hist. of Suffolk in 19th Cent. *o.p.* [*pb.* 12/] 8° *Ipswich n.d.* (56)

RAVEN, Dr J. J. History of Suffolk [Pop. County Hists.] 7/6 ; Ch. Ed. 3/6 *n.* 8° Stock 95 ; 07
Good for the more recent history ; also on dialect and topography.

REYCE, Rob. Suffolk in the Seventeenth Cent., ed. L'd Fcs. Hervey 10/6 *n.* s 4° Murray 02
Now pubd. for first time : ed. fr. MS. of 1618 in Brit. Mus., w. notes. Descriptive, and genealogical.

RYE, Walt. [ed.] Calendar of Feet of Fines of Suffolk [1189–1485] 8° Suff. Inst. of Archæol. 00

SUCKLING, Rev. A. Hist. and Antiqs. of Co. of Suffolk, 2 v. ; pl. *o.p.* [*pb.* 84/] 4° Weale 46–8

SUFFOLK INSTIT. OF ARCHÆOL. : Proceedings, vol. i *sqq.* 8° *Ipswich* 53 *sqq.*

*Victoria History of the County of Suffolk, vol. ii—*ut* **E** § 16 [to occupy 4 vols.]

WALTERS, J. C. Bygone Suffolk: hist., legend, folklore, etc. 7/6 8° Brown, *Hull* 01
*Aldeburgh:* HELE (W. F.) Notes or Jottings about Aldeburgh *o.p.* [*pb.* 7/6] c 8° J. R. Smith 70
*Bedford Level* —*v. sup., s.v.* Lincolnshire
*Blackbourne:* POWELL (Edg.) [ed.] A Suffolk Hundred in yr. 1283 10/6 8° Camb. Press 10
Putnam, *N.Y.* The assessmt. of Hundred of Blackbourne, consistg. of 28 parishes, analysed and annotated.
*Broads; Rivers* —*v. sup., s.v.* Norfolk
*Bury-St-Edmunds: St Edmund's Abbey*
*de BRAKELOND, Jocelin Chronica—*in* Memorials of St Edmund's Abbey, vol. i, *ut inf.*
" Monastic and Social Life in Twelfth Century in the Chronicles of Joc. de Brakelond, tr. T. E. Tomlins; w. notes [1173–1202] *o.p.* r 8° 44
JAMES, Dr M. R. On the Abbey of St Edmund at Bury 8° Cambr. Antiq. Soc. 95
Memorials of St Edmund's Abbey, ed. Thos. Arnold, 3 vols. [1020–1477] ea. 10/ r 8° Rolls Series 90–6
Comprises eventful hist. of one of oldest and richest of our monastic bodies dur. per. of nearly 500 yrs.; w. dissertns. on MSS. and gloss. notes to metrical life of St EDMUND. Cf. also CARLYLE, *Past and Present* [*ut* K § 89], and Dr A. JESSOPP in his *Studies* [*ut* F § 16].
*Buxhall:* COPINGER (Dr W. A.) Hist. of Parish of Buxhall; map & 44 ill. 25/ *n.* r 4° Sotheran 01
An exhaustive account, by the late l'd of the manor: prints many documts., incl. Parish Registers fr. 1500 to 1700.
*Cratfield:* HOLLAND (Rev. W.) Cratfield, ed. Dr Jno. Jas. Raven Jarrold, *Norwich* 96
*Hengrave:* GAGE (J.) Hist. and Antiqs. of Hengrave; pl. *o.p.* [*w.* 40/] f° *London* 22
*Ipswich:* BACON Annals of Ipswyche, ed. Richardson r 4° 84
GLYDE, Jno. Moral and Social Condition of Ipswich *o.p.* [*pb.* 12/] 8° Simpkin 50
TAYLOR, Dr J. E. In and about Ancient Ipswich; 50 pl. 21/ 4° Jarrold, *Norwich* 89
*Landguard Fort:* LESLIE (Maj. J. H.) Hist. of Landguard Fort; ill. 12/ 4° Eyre & Spottiswoode 98
A history of the Fort fr. its foundation under HENRY VIII to its demolition in 1898.
*Stowmarket:* HOLLINGSWORTH (A. G.) History of Stow-Market *o.p.* [*pb.* 15/] 4° Longman 44
*Stutton:* CRISP (F. A.) Account of the Parish of Stutton f° *priv. prin.* 81
*Theberton:* DOUGHTY (H. M.) Chronicles of Theberton; ill. [Domesd. Bk. to 1850] 7/6 *n.* Macmillan 10
*Wenhaston; Bulcamp:* CLARE (Rev. J. B.) Wenhaston and Bulcamp 2/6 8° Stock 06
*Wherstead:* ZINCKE (F. B.) Wherstead: matls. for hist., territorial and memorl. 10/6 8° Simpkin [87] 93

**Surrey**

AUBREY, J. Natural History and Antiquities of Surrey, 5 v. [*w.* £6] 8° *London* 1718–9
BARRETT, C. R. B. Surrey Highways, Byways, & Waterways; ill. *o.p.* [*pb.* 21/ *n.*] r 8° Bliss 95
Acc. of old houses and bldgs. of Surrey, somewhat rambling and cumbrous, but w. a good deal of curious informn.
*BRAYLEY, E. W. Topogr. Hist. of Surrey, ed. Edw. Walford, 4 v.; ill. *subscr.* 110/ r 4° [41–8] *n.d.* (78)
CAMDEN, Wm. [1551–1623] Britannia: Surrey and Sussex [repr. of Holland's tr., 1610]—*ut* **E** § 16, *s.v.* Early Topography
CHANCELLOR, E. B. Hist. & Antiqs. of Richmd., Kew, Petersham, Ham, *etc.* 25/ *n.* 8° Hiscoke, *Richm.* 94
CLINCH (G.) + KERSHAW (S. W.) Bygone Surrey [by var. wrs.] 7/6 8° Brown, *Hull* 94
COX, Dr J. C. Rambles in Surrey; map and 24 ill. 6/ c 8° Methuen 10
" [ed.] Memls. of Old Surrey; ill. [Memls. of Cos. of Engl.] 8° G. Allen *in prep.*
HISSEY, J. J. Holiday on the Road—*ut* **E** § 16, *s.v.* Roads [Kent, Sussex, Surrey]
JEKYLL, Gertr. Old West Surrey; 330 ill. 13/ *n.* ($4·50 *n.*) m 8° Longman 04
Old fashions, ways, and modes of life current in country S. of Hog's Back and W. of Dorking.
JENNINGS, Louis J. Field Paths & Green Lanes; ill. [Surrey & Sussex] 2/6 *n.* c 8° Murray [77] 07
JUDGES, E. A. Some West Surrey Villages; ill. 10/6 *n.* 8° *Surrey Times* Off., *Guildfd.* 01
MALDEN, H. E. Popular Hist. of Surrey [Pop. County Hists.] 7/6; Ch. Edn. 3/6 *n.* 8° Stock 00; 05
MANNING (O.) + BRAY (W.) **Hist. & Antiqs. of Surrey**, 3 vols.; maps & pl. [*w.* £20] f° *London* 04–14
*PARKER, Eric **Highways and Byways in Surrey**; ill. 6/ ($2 *n.*) c 8° Macmillan 08
'SON OF THE MARSHES (A)' On Surrey Hills; *etc.*—*ut* **H** § 51
SURREY ARCHÆOL. SOC.: Archæol. Collections rel. to Surrey, v. i–xvii 8° Surrey Arch. Soc. 58–02 *in prg.*
*Victoria History of the County of Surrey, vols. i–ii—*ut* **E** § 16 [to occupy 4 vols.]
*Churches:* HUSSEY (A.) Notes on Churches of Kent, Sussex, and Surrey—*ut sup., s.v.* Kent
WARE (Rev. H. R.) + PALMER (P. G.) Three Surrey Churches 12/ *n.* 4° Lasham, *Guildford* 02
St Nicolas, Compton; St Mary, Guildford; St Martha, Chilworth.
*Cottages:* NEVILL (Ralph) Old Cottage and Domestic Archit. of S.W. Surrey—*ut* **I** § 119
*Guides* —*v.* **E** § 16
*Scenery:* MOUL (D.) [art.] Picturesque Surrey; w. l'rpr. W. J. Hardy *o.p.* [*pb.* 6/ *n.*] 4° Robinson [02] 02
PALMER, Sutton [art.] Surrey: 75 col. pl., w. l'rpr. A. R. H. Moncrieff [$6 *n.* Macm., *N.Y.*] 20/ *n.* sq 8° Black 06

WAY, T. R. [art.] Architectural Remains of Richmond, Twickenham, Kew, Mortlake, Petersham *o.p.* 4° Lane 00

*Croydon:* ANDERSON (J. C.) Chronicles of Croydon 4° *priv. prin.* 74–9

„ Short Chron. conc. Parish of Croydon; ill. 8° *priv. prin.* 82

*Church:* ANDERSON (J. C.) Antiqs. of Croydon Church *o.p.* [*pb.* 7/6[ r 8° J. R. Smith 67

*Dorking:* BRIGHT (J. S.) Hist. of Dorking and Neighbrg. Parishes 12/6 8° Clark, *Dorking* 84

*Dover Road* —*v.* **E** § 16, *s.v.* Roads (HARPER, HISSEY)

*Epsom:* HORNE (G. C.) Epsom, its History and Surroundings; ill. 6/ *n.* 8° St Bride's Press 01

*Godalming:* WELMAN (S.) Parish and Church of Godalming; ill. 10/6 i 8° Stock 00

*Guildford:* WILLIAMSON (G. C.) Guildford in the Olden Time; ill. 5/ *n.* c 8° Bell 04

*Ham House:* ROUNDELL (Mrs C.) Ham House: hist. and art-treasures, 2 v. 105/ *n.* 4° Bell 05

*Kew* —*v. sup., s.v.* Middlesex and London

*Merton:* HEALES (A.) [ed.] Records of Merton Priory *o.p.* [*pb.* 12/6] r 8° Frowde 98

*Ockham:* BASHALL (H. St J. H.) The Oak Hamlet; pl. 5/ *n.* 8° Stock 01

*Pilgrims' Way* —*v. sup., s.v.* Kent

*Richmond:* *BELL (Mrs A. G.) Royal Manor of Richmond; 10 col. pl. 7/6 *n.* 8° Bell 08

CHANCELLOR, E. B. Historical Richmond 12/ 8° Bell 85

GARNETT, Dr R. Richmond: its assocns.; ill. [Portfol. Monogrs.; $1·25 *n.* Macm., *N.Y.*] 3/6 *n.* 8° Seeley 96

*Streatham:* ARNOLD (F., jun.) History of Streatham 10/6 8° Stock 86

*Sutton Place:* HARRISON (F.) Annals of an Old Manor House; ill. 42/ *n.* ($14 *n.*) 8° Macmillan 93
W. etchgs., plans, pedigrs. and arms, givg. hist. of one of few domestic bldgs. earlier than Reformn. wh. remain to a large extent unaltered. Its date is 1525.

*Tooting:* MORDEN (W. S.) History of Tooting-Graveney; ill. [fr. orig. docs.] 21/ *n.* 8° Seale 97

*Wimbledon:* BARTLETT (W. A.) Hist. and Antiqs. of Wimbledon *o.p.* [*pb.* 6/6] c 8° Simpkin 65

**Sussex**

*Bibliography:* BUTLER (G. S.) Topographica Sussexiana 8° *Lewes n.d.* (66)

AXON, W. E. A. [ed.] Bygone Sussex; ill. [by var. wrs.] 7/6 8° Brown, *Hull* 97

BECKETT, Arth. The Wonderful Weald; ill. 10/6 *n.* 8° Mills & Boon 11

BRABANT, F. G. Rambles in Sussex; ill. 6/ c 8° Methuen 09

Calendar of Post Mortem Inquisitions [1558–1802] 04

CAMDEN, Wm. [1551–1623] Britannia: Surrey and Sussex [repr. of Holland's tr., 1610]—*ut* **E** § 16, *s.v.* Early Topography

DALLAWAY (Rev. J.) + CARTWRIGHT (E.) Hist. of Western Divisn. of S., 2 v. in 3; ill. *o.p.* 4° Bensley 15–32

Domesday Book in rel. to Sussex, ed. W. D. Parish; map and facss. 21/ f° Sussex Arch. Soc. 86

EGERTON, Rev. J. C. Sussex Folk and Ways, ed. Dr H. Wace; ill. 5/ c 8° Chatto [84] 92

FLEET, Chas. Glimpses of our Ancestors in Sussex, 2 Ser. ea. 5/ 8° Farncombe, *Lewes* [82] 82; 83

HARE, Aug. J. C. Sussex; maps and 40 wood cuts 6/ c 8° G. Allen 94

HISSEY, J. J. Holiday on the Road—*ut* **E** § 16, *s.v.* Roads [Kent, Sussex, Surrey]

HORSFIELD, T. W. Hist., Antiqs., and Topogr. of Sussex, 2 vols.; pl. r 4° *Lewes* 35

JENNINGS, Louis J. —*in his* Derby & S. Downs, *sup., s.v.* Derbyshire; & Field Paths, *sup., s.v.* Surrey

LOWER, M. A. Compendious Hist. of Sussex, 2 vols.; map *o.p.* [*pb.* 25/] 8° J. R. Smith 70

*LUCAS, E. V. Highways and Byways in Sussex; ill. 6/ ($2 *n.*) c 8° Macmillan 04

MOUL, Duncan [artist] Picturesque Sussex; w. l'rpr. W. J. Hardy *o.p.* [*pb.* 6/ *n.*] f 4° Robinson 03

MUNDY, P. D. [ed.] Memls. of Old Sussex; ill. [Memls. of Cos. of Eng.] 15/ *n.* 8° G. Allen 09

SALZMANN, L. F. [ed.] Abstract of Feet of Fines, vols. i–ii [1190–1306] 03–8

SUSSEX ARCHÆOL. Soc.: Sussex Arch. Collns., vols. i–xlvi, and Index to i–xxv ea. 10/ 8° Suss. Arch. Soc., *Lewes* 48–03 *in prg.*
An invaluable coll. of material rel. to hist. and antiquities of the county. With good ill. (some col.).

*Victoria History of the County of Sussex, vols. i–ii—*ut* **E** § 16 [to occupy 4 vols.]

*Castles; Mansions; Manors:* ELWES (D. G. C.) + ROBINSON (Rev. C. J.) Hist. of Castles, Mansions, & Manors of W. Sussex, 3 vols.; pl. ea. 21/ 4° Longman 76–9

*Churches:* HUSSEY (A.) Notes on Churches of Kent, Surrey, and Sussex—*ut sup., s.v.* Kent

LOWER, M. A. The Churches of Sussex *o.p.* 4° *Brighton* 72

*Cottages, Farm-house* —*ut sup., s.v.* Kent (DAVIE)

*Dover Road* —*v.* **E** § 16, *s.v.* Roads (HARPER, HISSEY)

*History : Civil War :* THOMAS-STANFORD (C.) Sussex in the Great Civil War and the Interregnum : 1642–60 10/6 *n.* 8° Chiswick Press 10

*Parks and Forests :* ELLIS (W. S.) Parks & Forests of Sussex : anc. & mod. *o.p.* [*pb.* 12/] 8° 85

*Scenery :* BALL (Wilf.) [art.] Sussex : 75 col. pl. [$6 *n.* Macm., *N.Y.*] 20/ *n.* sq 8° Black 06

*Worthies :* LOWER (M. A.) Worthies of Sussex ; ill. [fr. earliest per.] *o.p.* [*pb.* 36/] r 4° *Lewes* 65

*Arundel :* TIERNEY (M. A.) Hist. and Antiqs. of Arundel, 2 v. [1066–1834] *o.p.* [*pb.* 32/] r 8° Dolman 34

*Battle Abbey* —*v.* **F** § 19

*Brickwall :* FREWEN (A. L.) Hist. of Brickwall, Northiam, Brede ; ill. 7/6 *n.* 8° G. Allen 10

*Brighton :* BISHOP (J. G.) Brighton in the Olden Time ; ill. 7/6 *n.* 8° *Brighton Herald* Off. [80] 93

KING, Maude E. Round about a Brighton Coach Office ; ill. 5/ *n.* c 8° Lane 95
Interesting and pleasant reminiscs. of Brighton in days of GEORGE IV, when it was still a small fishing-town.

MELVILLE, Lewis Brighton : hist., follies, fashions ; ill. 10/6 *n.* 8° Chapman 09

SALA, Geo. Aug. Brighton as I have known it *o.p.* [*pb.* 1/] f 8° Black 95

*Chichester :* STEPHENS (Rev. W. R. W.) Chichester [Diocesan Histories] 2/6 12° S.P.C.K. 81

" Memls. of S. Saxon See & Cath. of Chichester 8° 76

WALCOTT, M. E. C. Memorials of Chichester ; pl. *o.p.* 8° *Chichester* 64

*Cowdray :* ROUNDELL (Mrs C.) Cowdray : hist. of a gt. Eng. house 10/6 4° Bickers 84

*Eastbourne :* WRIGHT (J. G.) Bygone Eastbourne ; ill. [bldgs., etc.] 8° Spottiswoode 02

*Hailsham :* SALZMANN (L. F.) History of the Parish of Hailsham, Abbey of Otham, and Priory of Michelham 15/ 8° Farncombe, *Lewes* 01

*Hastings* —*v. also* **E** § 16, *s.v.* Cinque Ports

DAWSON, C. History of Hastings Castle, 2 vols. 42/ *n.* r 8° Constable 10
Based on the ser. of records [here tr.] 'unrivalled in local hist.'. A compreh. acc. of the gt. Castle and barony and viciss. of its lords. Deals also w. anc. mint and coinage of Hastings. Vol. ii, Pt. vi devoted to Battle of Hastings [*v.* **F** § 19].

MOSS, W. G. History and Antiquities of Hastings *o.p.* 8° 24

*Heathfield :* LUCAS (Perceval) Heathfield Memorials 21/ *n.* 8° Humphreys 10

*Hurstmonceaux :* VENABLES (E.) Castle of Hurstm. & its Lords *o.p.* [*pb.* 4/] 8° J. R. Smith [51] 56

*Lewes :* HORSFIELD (T. W.) Hist. and Antiqs. of Lewes and Vicinity, 2 v. ; pl. [*w.* 50/] 4° *Lewes* 24–7

*South Downs :* BECKETT (Arth.) The Spirit of the Downs ; ill. 10/6 *n.* 8° Methuen 09
A descrn. of the natl. features in their moods and aspects, w. stories of the people.

HUDSON, W. H. Nature in Downland ; 26 ill. 5/ *n.* ($2) 8° Longman [00] 06
Chiefly a naturalist's book, but full of impressions of the scenery and life of the Downs.

JENNINGS, Louis J. Rambles in Peak of Derbysh. and South Downs—*ut sup.*, *s.v.* Derbyshire

*Winchelsea ; Rye* —*v. also* **E** § 16, *s.v.* Cinque Ports

CHAMPNEYS, B. A Quiet Corner of England ; ill. 12/ r 8° Seeley 75
Winchelsea, Rye, Romney (Kent). Ill. by A. DAWSON.

COOPER, W. D. History of Winchelsea, Sussex *o.p.* [*pb.* 7/6] 8° J. R. Smith 50

HOLLOWAY, W. History of the Town and Port of Rye *o.p.* [*pb.* 21/] 8° J. R. Smith 47

INDERWICK, F. A. Story of King Edw. i. and New Winchelsea ; ill. 10/6 sq 8° Low 92
Story of the old town, its loss by encroachmt. of sea, bldg. of new town as port, arsenal, and fortr. (cpl. 1288), and final relapse, after gradual withdrawal of sea and French raid of 1418, into old-world village. A striking and unique subject, well treated.

" Acc. of Rye under the Commonwealth—*in* Suss. Arch. Collns., v. xxxix

## Warwickshire

ANDREWS, Wm. [ed.] Bygone Warwickshire 7/6 8° Brown, *Hull* 93
A many-authored miscellany, dealing w. stirring events, social life, anc. sports, customs, and folklore.

BURGESS, J. T. Historic Warwickshire, ed. Jos. Hill 10/ *n.* s 4° Midland Ed. Trdg. Co., *Birm.* [76] 93

DRYDEN, Alice [ed.] Memls. of Old Warwickshire ; ill. [Memls. of Cos. of Eng.] 15/ *n.* 8° G. Allen 08

DUGDALE, Sir W. Antiquities of Warwickshire ; pl. f° *Coventry* [1656] 1765
1st edn. 1656 [the only one admitted as evidence in a ct. of law] *w.* £20 ; 2nd edn. [1730], *w.* £30 ; above *w.* £5.

LANGFORD, Dr J. A. Hist. of Counties of Stafford and Warwick, 4 vols.—*ut sup.*, *s.v.* Staffordshire

MILLER, Rev. Geo. Rambles Round the Edge Hills 6/ c 8° Stock [ ] 01

TIMMINS, Sam. History of Warwickshire [Pop. County Hists.] 7/6 8° Stock 89

*Victoria History of the County of Warwick, vols. i–ii—*ut* **E** § 16 [to occupy 4 vols.]

*Guides* —*v.* **E** § 16

*Scenery :* WHITEHEAD (F.) [art.] Warwickshire : 75 col. pl., w. l'rpr. C. Holland [$6 *n.* Macmillan, *N.Y.*] 20/ *n.* sq 8° Black 06

*Worthies :* COLVILE (F. L.) Worthies of Warwickshire *o.p.* 4° *Warwick* 69

*Arden (Forest) :* HANNETT (J.) Forest of Arden : towns, vills., hamlets ; ill. 10/6 8° Lowe, *Birm.* [63] 92

*Avon: River and Valley*

BRADLEY, A. G. The Avon and Shakespeare's Country; 30 col. ill. 10/6 *n.* 8° Methuen 10
A desultory bk., contg. little informn. (and none of it new or v. well put). Charmg. illns. by A. R. QUINTON.

COUCH, A. T. Quiller ['Q'] The Warwickshire Avon; ill. Alf. Parsons 12/6 c 8° Osgood 91

SHOWELL Avon Valley: Leamington to Tewkesbury [66 pp.] *o.p.* 4° Cornish, *Birmingham* 02

*Baddesley Clinton:* NORRIS (Rev. H.) Baddesley Clinton Art & Book Co. 97
The manor, the Church, and the Hall; w. an account of the FERRERS family, owners of the manor.

*Birmingham:* Birmingham Institutions; 60 ill. [14 lects. by 14 lecturers] 5/ *n.* 8° Cornish, *Birm.* 11

DENT, R. K. Old and New Birmingham *o.p.* 4° *Birmingham* 79–80

„ The Making of Birmingham; 214 ill. 15/ *n.* 4° Allday, *Birm.* 94
Hist. of rise and growth of the Midland metropolis to pres. day: its Nonconformity, local manufs., educ. institns., philanth. activities, pulpit, press. A good bk., w. good Index.

HUTTON, Wm. History of Birmingham; ill. *o.p.* [*w.* 15/] 8° *Birmingham* [1781] 35

LANGFORD, Dr J. A. A Century of Birmingham Life, 2 v. [1741–1841] *o.p.* [*pb.* 42/] 8° *Birmingham* 68

„ Modern Birmingham & its Institns., 2 v. [1841–71] *o.p.* [*pb.* 42/] 8° *Birmingham* 73–7

„ Hist. of Counties of Stafford and Warwick—*ut sup.*, *s.v.* Staffordshire

SMITH, J. Toulmin Memorials of Old Birmingham *o.p.* r 8° *Birmingham* 64

*Corporation:* BUNCE (J. T.) + VINCE (C. A.) Hist. of Corpn. of Birm. 2 v. 42/ *n.* 8° Cornish, *Birm.* 78–02

*Coventry:* BLYTH (T. A.) History of Stoke *o.p.* 8° 97

HARRIS, Mary Dormer Life in an Old English Town; ill. 4/6 c 8° Sonnenschein 98
$1·50 Macmillan, *N.Y.* [Social England Ser.] An excellent hist. of Coventry fr. earliest times; compiled fr. offic. records.

„ Story of Coventry; ill. [Mediaev. Towns; Dutton, *N.Y.*] 4/6 *n.* s 8° Dent 11

„ [ed.] Coventry Leet Book, Pts. i–iii [Pt. iv to be *Introd.*] ea. 15/ 8° Early Engl. Text Soc. 07–9 *in prg.*

WHITLEY, T. W. Parliamentary Representn. of Coventry; ill. [1298–19 cent.] 8° Curtis, *Coventry* 95

*Lapworth:* HUDSON (R.) Memorials of a Warwicksh. Parish 15/ *n.* 8° Methuen 04
Papers mainly descr. of the local muniments (fr. 12th cent. onwards) of parish of Lapworth.

*Rowington:* RYLAND (J. W.) Records of Rowington; ill. Cooper, *Birmingham* 96

*Rugby:* BLOXAM (M. H.) Rugby: school and neighbourhood—*ut* **D** § 157, *s.v.* Rugby School

RIMMER, Alf. Rambles round Rugby; 73 ill. by author 21/ *n.* r 8° Percival 92
A cross betw. a county-history and a guide-bk., w. introd. ch. on the schl. Sumptuously produced.

*'Shakespeare's Country'* —*v. also sup.* (BRADLEY) *and inf.*, *s.v.* Stratford

BRASSINGTON, W. Salt Shakespeare's Homeland; 70 ill. 7/6 *n.* 8° Dent 03
$2·50 *n.* Dutton, *N.Y.* Sketches of Stratford-on-Avon, Forest of Arden, and Avon valley.

LEYLAND, J. Shakespeare Country Illustrated 10/6 *n.* i 8° Newnes 00

MORLEY, Geo. Shakespeare's Greenwood; ill. 5/ c 8° Nutt 00
Somewhat ill-arranged essays on Warwickshire dialect, folk-lore, customs, etc.

RIBTON-TURNER, C. J. Shakespeare's Land; 13 maps & pl. [guide-bk.] 7/6 f 8° Glover, *Leamgtn.* 93

WILLIAMS, J. L. Home and Haunts of Shakespeare; photogravs. $37·50 f° Scribner, *N.Y.* 93
A luxurious American folio, outvenerating English venerators of the Immortal Bard.

*Southam:* SMITH (Rev. W. L.) Historical Notices of Parish of Southam, 8 Pts. *subscr.* 30/ 4° Stock 94

*Stratford-on-Avon:* HALLIWELL [-PHILLIPPS] (J. O.) Acc. of New Place *o.p.* [*pb.* 63/] f° J. R. Smith 64

LEE, Sid. Stratford-on-Avon, fr. Earliest times to Shakespeare; pl. 6/ c 8° Seeley [85] 07

WARD, H. S. + Cath. W. Shakespeare's Town and Times; 100 ill. 7/6 *n.* 4° Dawbarn & Ward 97

WHEELER, R. B. Hist. and Antiqs. of Stratford-on-Avon s 8° *Stratford-on-Avon* 1806

*Church:* BAKER (Har.) Colleg. Church of Stratford-on-Avon 1/6 *n.* c 8° Bell 03

BLOOM, J. Harvey Shakespeare's Church; ill. [architectural] 7/6 *n.* c 8° Unwin 03

*Warwick:* KEMP, Thos. History of Warwick and its People 10/6 s 4° Cooke, *Warwick* 05

„ [ed.] Bk. of John Fisher, Town-Clerk: 1580–8 6/ *n.* 4° Cooke, *Warwick n.d.* (00)
A sort of offic. diary of author's acts as magistrate of Warwick; ed. fr. original MS.

„ [ed.] The Black Book of Warwick 10/6 s 4° Cooke, *Warwick* 98
Contains minutes of corporation meetings, records of elections and ceremonies, etc.

*Warwick Castle:* WARWICK (C'ess of) Warwick Castle and its Earls, 2 vols. 32/ *n.* r 8° Hutchinson 03
A full descrn. of the Castle, and histories of the families which have held it: appendices of documents. 2 pl. and 172 il.

*Wroxall:* RYLAND (J. W.) Records of Wroxall Abbey and Manor; ill. *priv. prin.* (Spottiswoode) 04
A very important contribution to Warwickshire history. Only 100 copies printed.

**Westmoreland** —*v.* Cumberland, *sup.*

**Wiltshire**

AUBREY, J. Topograph. Collns. rel. to Wilts, ed. J. E. Jackson; ill. [1659–70] *o.p.* [*pb.* 50/] 4° *Devizes* [21] 62

*BRADLEY, A. G. Round about Wilts; map & 30 ill. (14 col.) T. C. Gotch 6/ c 8° Methuen [07]

BRITISH RECORD SOC.: Abstract of Wilts Inquisitions: 1242–1326 r 8° Brit. Rec. Soc. 08
Domesday Book for Wiltshire, ed. H. Jones *o.p.* [*pb.* 31/6] 4° *Bath* 65
DOWDING, M. K. Old Wiltshire Market Towns and Villages 5/ *n.* 8° Houlston 96
DRYDEN, Alice [ed.] Memls. of Old Wilts; ill. [Memls. of Cos. of Eng.] 15/ *n.* 8° G. Allen 06
FRY, G. S. + E. A. [eds.] Abstract of Wilts Inquisitiones Post Mortem: rn. Chas. i r 8° Brit. Rec. Soc. 01
*HOARE, Sir R. C. Ancient Hist. of S. [and N.] Wilts, 2 vols. *o.p.* [*w.* £15] f° *London* 12–19
* „ [ed.] History of Modern Wiltshire, 6 vols. [*w.* £50] f° *London* 22–44
JEFFERIES, Rich. Life in a Southern County [Wiltshire] 6/ c 8° Smith & Elder [79] 97
WILTSHIRE RECORD SOC.: Publications 8° *Salisbury in prg.*
*Guides* —*v.* **E** § 16
*Scenery:* TYNDALE (T.) [art.] Worcestershire: 24 col. pl., w. l'rpr. A. G. Bradley [$3 *n.* Macm., *N.Y.*] 7/6 *n.* sq 8° Black 09
*Worthies:* STRATFORD (J.) Wiltshire and its Worthies 6/ 4° Brown, *Salisbury* 82
*Calne:* MARSH (A. E. W.) History of Calne, Wiltshire 8° 03
*Devizes:* WAYLEN (J.) Chronicles of Borough of Devizes *o.p.* [*pb.* 14/] 8° Longman 59
*Grittleton:* JACKSON (J. E.) Hist. of Parish of Grittleton 4° Wilts Topogr. Soc. 43
*Lydiard:* MCKNIGHT (Rev. W. H. E.) Lydiard Manor: its history 7/6 c 8° Mitchell & Hughes 93
A history of the place, first as a Manor House, and then as a school for young noblemen.
*Marlborough:* HULME (F. E.) Town, Coll., and Neighbrhd. of Marlb.—*ut* **D** § 157
WAYLEN, J. History of the City of Marlborough *o.p* [*pb.* 14/] 8° J. R. Smith 54
*Salisbury; Salisbury Cathedral*—*for* Architecture *v.* **I** § 119
JONES, Rev. W. H. R. Salisbury [Diocesan Histories] 2/6 12° S.P.C.K. 80
„ [ed.] Fasti Eccles. Sarisb., 2 Pts. [bps, archdeacons, etc.] 4° *Salisbury* 79–81
MACRAY, Rev. W. D. [ed.] Sarum Charters and Documents [12–13 cents.] 10/ r 8° Rolls Series 91
SWAYNE, H. J. F. [ed.] Churchwardens' Accs. of St Edm. & St Thomas: 1443–1702 8° Wilts Rec. Soc.
*Salisbury Plain* —*for* Stonehenge *v.* **G** § 14
HUDSON, W. H. A Shepherd's Life; ill. 7/6 *n.* c 8° Methuen 10
A series of studies of Salisbury Plain, w. hist. of family of a downland shepherd as connectg. link.

**Worcestershire**

BRASSINGTON, W. S. Historic Worcestershire; ill. 10/ *n.* 8° Midl. Educ. Co., *Birm.* [95]
Index Pedum Finium pro Com. Wigorn. [1 Ed. iii to Hen. vi] *o.p.* f° *Cheltenham* 65
NASH, T. R. Collections for Hist. of Worcs, 2 vols. & Suppl. [*w.* £20] f° *London* 1781–99
Amphlett, J. Index to above, Pt. i: Names of Persons f°; *also* i 8° Worcs Hist. Soc. 94
NOAKE, J. Worcestershire in the Olden Times *o.p.* [*pb.* 5/] 12° Longman 49
„ Notes and Queries for Worcestershire *o.p.* [*pb.* 5/] 12° Longman 56
„ Worcestershire Relics *o.p.* [*pb.* 5/] 12° Longman 77
*Victoria History of Worcestershire, vols. i–ii—*ut* **E** § 16 [to occupy 4 vols.]
WILLIAMS, W. R. Parliamentary History of Worcestershire *o.p.* 8° 97
WORCESTERSHIRE HISTORICAL SOC.: Publications i 8° Worcs Histor. Soc. *in prg.*
*Churches:* NOAKE (J.) Rambles to Churches in Worcs. *o.p.* [*pb.* 5/] 12° Longman 54
STANTON, G. K. Rambles & Researches amongst Worcestershire Churches 5/ 8° Simpkin [85] 87
*Place-names* —*v.* **K** § 120
*Scenery:* TOMPKINS (H. W.) In Constable's County; 15 col. pl. after Constable 12/6 *n.* 8° Dent 06
TYNDALE, Thos. [artist] Worcestershire: 24 col. pl., w. l'rpr. A. G. Bradley 7/6 *n.* sq 8° Black 09
*Bewdley:* BURTON (J. R.) Hist. of Bewdley and Neighbg. Parishes; ill. 8° *priv. prin.* 83
*Bromsgrove:* COTTON (W. A.) Bromsgrove Church: hist. and antiquities 7/6 r 8° Simpkin 81
*Clent:* AMPHLETT (J.) Short History of Clent [a good book] 5/ 8° Parker 90
*Hales Owen:* ROTH (H. L.) Bibliogr. and Chronol. of Hales Owen 8° Index Soc. 87
*Kidderminster:* BURTON (J. R.) Hist. of Kidderminster and Neighbg. Parishes; pl. 1 8° *priv. prin.* 90
*Pershore:* ANDREWS (F. B.) The Abbey of Pershore 8° Fearnside, *Pershore* 01
*Rous Lench:* CHAFY (Dr W. K. W.) History of Rous Lench; 11 ill. 8° Smith, *Evesham* 01
*Wike Burnell, etc.:* HUDSON (C. E. M.) Manors of Wike Burnell & Wyke Waryn 30/ *n.* 4° 03
*Worcester:* MILLER (Rev. Geo.) Parishes of Diocese of Worcester, vol. i 10/6 c 8° Griffith & Farren 89
SMITH (Rev. J. G.) + ONSLOW (Rev. P.) Worcester [Diocesan Histories] 3/6 12° S.P.C.K. 85

*St Wulstan's Hospital:* MARSH (F. T.) Annals of Hosp. of St Wulstan 21/ *n.* 4° Stock 90

**Yorkshire**

*Bibliography:* BOYNE (W.) The Yorkshire Library 4° *priv. prin.* (*Lond.*) 69

TURNER, J. Horsfall [ed.] Yorksh. Genealogist & Bibliographer, 2 v.; ill. ea. 7/6 8° Edr., *Bradfd.* 88–90

ANDREWS, Wm. Picturesque Yorks: York and N. Riding; 40 ill. 2/6 c 8° Valentine 05

,, [ed.] Yorkshire in Olden Times 4/ c 8° Simpkin 90

,, [ed.] Bygone Yorkshire [by var. wrs.] 7/6 8° Brown, *Hull* 92

BAILDON, W. P. Notes on Relig. & Secular Houses of Yorks, v. i [fr. Plea Rolls] 8° Yorks Archæol. Soc. 95

BAINES, Thos. Yorkshire Past and Present, 4 vols.; ill. ea. 25/ 4° Mackenzie *n.d.* (71–7)

BROWN, Wm. [ed.] Yorkshire Inquisitions, vols. i–iv [1241 *sqq.*] 8° Yorks Archæol. Soc. 92–06

,, [ed.] Yorkshire Lay Subsidy: 1297; Ditto 1301 8° Yorks Archæol. Soc. 94–7

,, [ed.] Pedes Finium Ebor. regnante Johanne [1199–1214] 10/ 8° Surtees Soc. 97

,, [ed.] Yorkshire Deeds 8° Yorks Archæol. Soc. 09

,, [ed.] Yorkshire Star Chamber Proceedings, vol. i 8° Yorks Archæol. Soc. 09

CLAY, J. W. [ed.] Yorkshire Royalist Composition Papers, 3 v. 8° Yorks Archæol. Soc. 93–6
Proceedings of the Committee for the compounding w. delinquents dur. the Commonwealth.

COLLINS, F. [ed.] Catal. of Inquisns. post Mortem f. Co. of York: rns. Jas. i and Chas. i 8° Yorks Arch. Soc. 85

COOPER, Rev. A. N. Round the Home of a Yorkshire Parson 3/6 *n.* c 8° Brown, *Hull* 03

DAVIS (J. W.) + LEES (F. A.) West Yorkshire: phys. geogr., geol., botany; ill. 21/ 8° Lovell Reeve 78

Domesday Book for Yorkshire: ed. R. H. Skaife 7/6 8° Yorks Archaeol. Soc.

FALLOW, T. M. [ed.] Memls. of Old Yorks; ill. [Memls. of Cos. of Eng.] 15/ *n.* 8° G. Allen 09

Feet of Fines [for Yorks] of the Tudor Period, ed. Dr F. Collins, 4 Pts. 8° Yorks Archæol. Soc. 87–90

,, for the County of York: 1327–47, ed. W. P. Baildon 8° Yorks Archæol. Soc. 10

FLETCHER, J. S. Picturesque History of Yorkshire, 3 vols.; ill. ea. 7/6 r 8° Dent 99–03

,, A Book about Yorkshire; ill. (some col.) 7/6 *n.* 8° Methuen 08
A popular bk., dealg. w. the co. topically: minsters, castles, the folk, dialect, liter. assocns., etc.

,, Recollections of a Yorkshire Village 6/ c 8° Digby 10

GOULD, Rev. S. Baring- Yorkshire Oddities, Incidents and Strange Events—*ut* **B** § 23

JACKSON (C.) + MARGERISON [eds.] Yorks Diaries and Autobiogrs. in 17 and 18 cents., 2 v. 28/6 8° Surtees Soc. 77–84

de KIRKBY, John Survey of Co. of York, ed. R. H. Skaife 15/ 8° Surtees Soc. 67
A good edn. of '*Kirkby's Inquest*'; w. inquisns. of Knights' fees, *nomina villarum* for Yorks, etc.

LAMPLOUGH, Edw. Mediæval Yorkshire 3/6 12° Hamilton 85

LELAND, Jno. [1506?–52] Itinerary of [pub. by T. Hearne], 9 vols. 8° *Oxford* [1710–12] 1769–70

LEYLAND, Jno. Yorks Coast and Cleveland Hills and Dales; ill. 7/6 c 8° Seeley 92

LISTER, J. [ed.] West Riding Sessions Rolls [1597/8–1602] 8° Yorks Archæol. Soc. 88

LOCKWOOD, P. H. Storm and Sunshine in the Dales; ill. [descrns. of scenery] 3/ c 8° Stock 98

MACQUOID, Kath. About Yorkshire; w. 67 ill. by T. Macquoid *o.p.* [*pb.* 10/6] 8° Chatto 83

MAYHALL, J. The Annals of Yorkshire, 3 vols. ea. 6/ c 8° Simpkin [66] 78

North Riding Record Pubns.: Ser. i, ed. Can. Atkinson, qv.; ii, ed. R. B. Turton, vols. i–iv 8° Yorks Archæol. Soc. *in prg.*

*NORWAY, A. H. Highways and Byways in Yorks; ill. [Highways & Byways Ser.] 6/ ($2 *n.*) c 8° Macmillan 99

PAGE, W. [ed.] The Yorkshire Chantry Surveys, 2 vols. ea. 15/ 8° Surtees Soc. 94–5

PLANTAGENET-HARRISON, Maj.-Gen. Hist. of Yorks, Pt. i: Wapentake of Gilling West; ill. 315/ f° Hazell 79

RADFORD, G. Yorkshire by the Sea; 12 etchgs. & 26 ill. [notes] 21/ i 8° Jackson, *Leeds* 91

SCHROEDER, Hy. The Annals of Yorkshire, 2 vols. *o.p.* 8° *Leeds* 51–2

SMITH, Wm. [ed.] Old Yorkshire, 5 v.; N. S., vol. i–iii; 3 ill. ea. 7/6 8° Longman 89–91

SURTEES SOCIETY: Publications—*ut. sup., s.v.* Durham

SUTCLIFFE, Halliwell By Moor and Fell; ill. 6/ c 8° Unwin 99
Contains a good deal about the BRONTË family and Haworth.

TURNER, J. [Horsfall [ed.] Yorkshire Notes and Queries, Folk Lore Journal, Genealogist, Bibliographer; 550 ill. [1700 pp.] 30/ 8° Author, *Bradfd.* 85–90

,, [ed.] Yorkshire County Magazine; 488 ill. [1140 pp.] 20/ 8° Author, *Bradfd.*

*Victoria History of Yorkshire, vol. i.—*ut* **E** § 16 [to occupy 8 vols.]

WHELLAN, Wm. History and Topography of Yorkshire, 3 vols. *o.p.* 8° Whittaker 57–71
WHITE, Walt. A Month in Yorkshire ; map *o.p.* [*pb.* 4/] c 8° Chapman [58] 79
WILDRIDGE, T. Tindall Northumbria 10/ 4° H. Gray 88
Antiquities of Yorks, Lancs, Westmoreland, Cumberland, Durham, Northumberland, and the Border.
YORKS ARCHÆOLOG. Soc. : Record Series, vols. i.–xxxvii ; Journal, vols i-xx *Leeds* 85–06 ; 69 *sqq., in prg.*
*Abbeys :* LEFROY (W. C.) Ruined Abbeys of Yorkshire ; ill. 2/ *n.* c 8° Seeley [82] 07
*Battles :* LAMPLOUGH, Edw. Yorkshire Battles 6/ 8° Andrews, *Hull* 91
LEADMAN, A. D. H. Proelia Eboracensia : battles fought in Yorkshire *priv. prin.* 91
Painstaking descriptions of the battles, repr. from the *Journal* of the Yorks Archæological Soc.
*Churches :* CLAY (J. W.) Yorkshire Church Notes [1619–31] 8° Yorks Archæol. Soc. 04
*Costume* —*ut* **G** § 25 (WALKER)
*Houses ; Mansions :* WHEATER (W.) Some Historic Mansions of Yorks, 2 v. ; etchgs. i 8° *priv. prin.* (*Leeds*) 88–9
*Literary Associations :* STUART (J. A. E.) Literary Shrines of Yorks ; 50 ports. and ill. 7/6 ($2·50) 8° Longman 92
Valleys of Aire and Calder treated fully, remainder of dales (12) in skeleton. Not very good.
*Rivers :* RADFORD (G.) Rambles by Rivers of Yorkshire ; 12 etchgs. 10/6 s 4° Jackson, *Leeds* 86
*Scenery :* HOME (G. C.) [art.] Yorkshire Painted and Described : 71 col. pl. 20/ *n.* sq 8° Black 08
,, [art.] Yorkshire Coast and Moorland Scenes ; 31 col. pl. 7/6 *n.* sq 8° Black 04
,, [art.] Yorkshire Dales and Fells ; 20 col. pl. 7/6 *n.* sq 8° Black 06
,, [art.] Yorkshire Vales and Wolds ; 20 col. pl. 7/6 *n.* sq 8° Black 08
(1) $6 *n.* ; (2) and (3) ea. $2·50 *n.* ; (4) $3 *n.* Macmillan, *N.Y.*
*Worthies :* COLERIDGE (Hartley) Worthies of Yorks and Lancs, 3 vols. *o.p.* [*pb.* 15/] s 8° Moxon [36] 52
DE LA PRYME, Abraham [1672–1704] Diary—*ut* **G** § 30
HAILSTONE, E. Portraits of Yorkshire Worthies, 2 vols. [w. biogr. notices] 4° *London* 69
HEYWOOD, Rev. Oliver [1630–1702] Autobiography, Diaries, Anecdote, and Event Books, ed. J. Horsfall Turner, 4 vols. ; ill. 24/ c 8° Edr., *Idel, Bradford* 82–5
PATTINSON, J. S. Celebrated Yorkshire Folk [69 biogs., anc. & mod.] 6/ *n.* 8° Spark & Son, *Leeds* 99
ROSS, Fredk. Celebrities of the Yorkshire Wolds *o.p.* [*pb.* 4/] c 8° Trübner 78
STUKELEY, Dr Wm. Life and Correspondence—*ut* **G** § 30
THORNTON, [Mrs] Alice [1626 or 7–1707] Autobiogr., ed. Chas. Jackson [ends 1669] 10/ 8° Surtees Soc. 75
TURNER, J. Horsfall Yorkshire Poets Ancient and Modern ; ill. 5/ 8° Author, *Bradfd.*
WILKINSON, Jos. Worthies, Families, & Celebrities of Barnsley & District 7/6 c 8° Bemrose 83
*Almondbury :* HULBERT (C. A.) Annals of Ch. & Parish of Almondb. ; ill. 15/ 8° Longman 82
*Askrigg :* WHALEY (Rev. C.) Parish of Askrigg 1/6 c 8° Skeffington 91
*Batley :* SHEARD (M.) Records of Parish of Batley 25/ 4° White, *Worksop* 94
*Bedale :* MCCALL (H. B.) Early History of Bedale 7/6 *n.* 4° Stock 07
*Beverley :* LEACH (A. F.) [ed.] Beverley Town Documents—*ut* **D** § 5 [14–15 cents.]
,, [ed.] Chapter Act Bk. of Ch. of St John, 2 vols. 55/ 8° Surtees Soc. 98–03
OLIVER, G. History of Antiquities of Beverley ; pl. [*w.* 30/] 4° *Beverley* 29
POULSON, G. Beverlac : hist. and antiqs. of Beverley, 2 vols. ; pl. [*w.* 30/] 4° *Beverley* 29
*Bingley :* SPEIGHT (H.) Chronicles and Stories of Old Bingley ; ill. 4/ *n.* c 8° Stock 97
TURNER, J. Horsfall Ancient Bingley : hist. and scenery ; 180 ill. 8/ 8° Author, *Bradfd.* 97
*Blyth* —*v.* Nottinghamshire, *sup.*
*Bradford :* JAMES (Jno.) Hist. and Topogr. of Bradford ; 2 vols. ; ill. *o.p.* 8° Longman 41–66
TURNER, J. Horsfall Bradford Sieges and History : 1644 2/ c 8° Author, *Bradfd.* 92
*Brighouse ; Rastrick ; Hipperholme :* TURNER (J. H.) Hist. of B., R. & H. ; ill. 10/ 8° Author, *Bradfd.* [96] 98
*Cawood* —*v.* Sherburn, *inf.* (WHEATER)
*Chapeltown :* HABERSHON (M. H.) Chapeltown Researches *o.p.* 8° 93
*Cleveland* —*v. also sup., s.n.* LEYLAND
ATKINSON, Rev. J. C. Forty Years in a Moorland Parish 5/ *n.* c 8° Macmillan [91] 07
Presents a charmg. and in pts. painful pict. of an old-time corner of Engl., Danby in Cleveland ; full of antiq., histor., geolog., dialectical, and folklore informn. Prob. Mr ATKINSON is the last Eng. parson who will be seriously called on, as he was by old Dinah, to lay the spirits who were makg. her house uncomfortable. 'I told her at last I could not, did not profess to, lay spirits, and her reply was : "Ah, but if I had sent for a priest o' t' au'd Church he wad 'a' done it. They wur a vast mair powerful conjurers than you Church-priests." '
ORD, J. W. History and Antiquities of Cleveland ; ill. *o.p.* [*pb.* 42/] 4° Simpkin 47
*Conisborough Castle :* SMITH (H. E.) History of Conisborough Castle 8° 87

*Craven :* DICKINSON (I. W.) Yorks Life & Character : a Craven vill. 60 yrs. ago 7/6 8° Andrews, *Hull* 94
SHUFFREY, Rev. W. A. Some Craven Worthies *o.p.* c 8° Robinson 03
SPEIGHT, H. Craven and N.-W. Yorks Highlands ; ill. 10/ *n.* 8° Stock 92
A good bk. on the history, scenery, and antiquities of the romantic district.
" Tramps & Drives in Craven Highls. ; ill. [bas. on above] 2/6 *n.* c 8° Stock [95] 97
" Craven and West Yorks Highlands 10/ 8° Stock 97
WHITAKER, Dr T. D. Hist. & Antiqs. of Deanery of Craven, ed. A. W. Morant, pl. 94/6 r 4° Dodgson, *Leeds* [05] 78
*Danby* —*v.* Cleveland, *sup.* (ATKINSON)
*Doncaster :* Calendar of Records of Borough of Doncaster, vols. i–iv 8° 99–03 *in prg.*
HUNTER, Jos. South Yorkshire, 2 vols. [*w.* £7 10/] f° *London* 28–32
The history and topography of the deanery of Doncaster.
MILLER, Edw. Hist. and Antiqs. of Doncaster and its Vicinity 4° *Doncaster, n.d.* (04)
TOMLINSON, J. Doncaster fr. Roman Occupn. to Pres. Time ; 12 pl. 42/ r 4° Tomlinson, *Doncaster* 87
*Ecclesfield :* EASTWOOD (J.) Hist. of the Parish of Ecclesfield *o.p.* [*pb.* 16/] 8° Bell 62
*Elland :* TURNER (J. H.) Elland Tragedies : 1330–50 2/ c 8° Author, *Bradfd.* 92
*Fountains Abbey :* HODGES (Dr G.) Fountains Abbey ; pl. [historical] 10/6 *n.* 8° Murray 04
HOPE, W. H. St J. Fountain's Abbey ; col. plan 10/6 8° Yorks Archæol. Soc.
OXFORD, A. W. The Ruins of Fountains Abbey ; 103 ill. 3/6 *n.* pott 8° Clar. Press 10
Gives in pop. lang. results of investigns. of the ruins made by W. H. St John HOPE and J. A. REEVE.
WALBRAN, J. R. [ed.] Memls. of Fountains Abbey, vol. i [*not sep.*], ii (1) 10/ 8° Surtees Soc. 63–78
*Guisborough :* BROWN (W.) [ed.] Cartularium Prioratus de Gyseburne, mcxix., 2 vols. ea. 15/ 8° Surtees Soc. 89–94
*Haddesley :* WORSFOLD (Rev. J. N.) History of Haddesley, Past and Present ; ill. 10/6 8° Stock 94
*Halifax :* MIDGLEY (S.) Halifax and its Gibbet-Law *o.p.* c 8° *Bingley* [1708] 86
ROTH, H. Ling The Yorks Coiners, *and* Old and Prehist. Halifax 21/ *n.* 8° King, *Halifax* 06
Former throws a good deal of fresh light on the Coiners [A.D. 1769–83], derived fr. orig. research ; w. facs. ill.
TURNER, J. Horsfall Halifax Gibbet Law 2/ c 8° Author, *Bradfd.* 91
WATSON, Jno. History and Antiqs. of Halifax, ed. F. A. Leyland f° *priv. prin.* [1775] 69
" Halifax Families and Worthies ; ill. 6/ 8° J. H. Turner, *Bradfd.* [ ]
WRIGHT, Rev. Thos. Antiqs. of Halifax, ed. J. H. Turner 1/6 c 8° Edr., *Bradfd.* [ ] 91
*Hallamshire :* ADDY (S. O.) The Hall of Waltheof : early condn. and settlemt. of Hallamsh. ; ill. 30/ *n.* 4° Townsend, *Sheffd.* 93
Devoted to archæol. and local hist. of distr. rd. Sheffd., w. some good folklore in it. . Title taken fr. statemt. in Domesd. in its brief acc. of Hallamsh. : *ibi habuit Wallef comes aulam.*
HUNTER, Jos. Hallamshire : hist. & topogr. of parish of Sheffield ; pl. *o.p.* [*pb.* 73/6] f° Virtue [19] 69
*Harewood :* JONES (Jno.) History and Antiqs. of Harewood ; ill. *o.p.* [*pb.* 10/6] 8° Simpkin 59
*Harrogate ; Knaresborough :* GRAINGE (W.) Hist. of Harr. & Forest of K. *o.p.* [*pb.* 10/6] 8° J. R. Smith 71
*Haworth :* TURNER (J. H.) Haworth, Past and Present 3/ c 8° Author, *Bradfd.* 79
*Hedon :* BOYLE (J. R.) Early Hist. of Town and Port of Hedon 21/ 8° Brown, *Hull* 95
PARK, G. R. History of Hedon 8° 95
*Hemingborough :* BURTON (T.) Hist. of Hemingborough, ed. Can. J. Raine ; ill. 21/ 4° Sampson, *York* 88
*Holderness ; Hullshire :* POULSON (G.) Hist. of Holderness, 2 vols. ; pl. 8° *Hull* 40–1
WILDRIDGE, T. T. [ed.] Holderness and Hullshire 10/ 4° Peck, *Hull* 9–
*Huddersfield :* HOBKIRK (C. P.) Huddersfield : history and natural history 5/ p 8° Simpkin [ ] 68
*Hull :* GENT (Thos.) History of Hull ; pl. [facs. repr.] *o.p.* 4° *Hull* [1735] 69
LAMBERT, J. M. Two Thousand Years of Gild Life—*ut* **D** § 120, *s.v.* Kingston-upon-Hull
SHEAHAN, J. J. History and Descrn. of Kingston-upon-Hull *o.p.* r 8° *Beverley* [64] 66
*Ilkley :* TURNER (J. H.) + COLLYER (R.) Ilkley, Anc. & Mod. ; 80 ill. 14/ 8° J. H. Turner, *Bradfd.* 85
*Ingleton :* BALDERSTON (R. R. + Marg.) Ingleton, Bygone and Present 4/6 c 8° Simpkin 88
*Kirkby Overblow :* SPEIGHT (H.) Kirkby Overblow and District 8° Stock 03
*Knaresborough* —*v. sup., s.v.* Harrogate (GRAINGE), and *inf., s.v.* Nidderdale (SPEIGHT)
WHEATER, W. Knaresborough and its Rulers 21/ *n.* 4° Paul 07
*Leeds :* PRICE (A. C.) Leeds and Neighbourhood : illn. of Eng. host. 3/6 (90 c.) s 8° Clar. Press 09
ROBINSON, Percy Relics of Old Leeds ; ill. by author 15/ *n.* 4° Batsford 97
TAYLOR, R. V. Biographia Leodiensis ; *and* Supplmt. [Leeds worthies, 1066–1865] 6/6 ; 3/6 c 8° *Leeds* 65–7

THORESBY, Ralph [1658–1725] Ducatus Leodiensis: topogr. of Leedes, ed. T. D. Whitaker [w. £3] r f° *Leeds* [1715] 16

Atkinson, D. H. Ralph Thoresby, his Town and Times—*ut* **G** § 30

WHITAKER, Dr T. D. Loidis and Elmete [w. £2] f° *Leeds* 16

An attempt to illustrate the districts descr. in these words by BEDE, and supposed to embrace the lower portions of Airedale and Wharfdale.

***Meaux Abbey*:** BOND (E. A.) [ed.] Chronica Monast. de Melsa, 3 vols. ea. 10/ i 8° Rolls Ser. 66–8

To 1396 by THOMAS DE BURTON, with contin. to 1406 'a monacho quodam ipsius domus'.

***Meltham*:** HUGHES (J.) Hist. of Township of Meltham *o.p.* [*pb.* 7/6] c 8° J. R. Smith 67

***Middleham*:** ATTHILL (W.) [ed.] Docs. rel. to Colleg. Ch. of Middleham s 4° Camden Soc. 47

***Morley*:** SMITH (W.) Morley, Ancient and Modern *o.p.* [*pb.* 8/] 8° Longman 86

***Mowbray*** —*v. inf.*, *s.v.* Richmondshire (BOGG)

***Nidderdale*:** LUCAS (J.) Studies in Nidderdale *o.p.* 8° *n.d.* (82)

SPEIGHT, Harry Nidderdale and the Garden of the Nidd; ill. 10/ *n.* 8° Stock 94

A good *popular* account, historical, scientific and descriptive, of the beautiful valley of the Nidd—largely based on local archives and unpubd. documents as well as on the sources in H.M. Public Record Office and the British Museum.

" Nidderdale fr. Nun Monkton to Whernside; ill. 8/6 *n.* c 8° Stock 06

" Upper Nidderdale, w. Forest of Knaresboro'; ill. 5/ *n.* c 8° Stock 06

***Northallerton*:** INGLEDEW (C. J. D.) Hist. and Antiqs. of Northallerton *o.p.* [*pb.* 15/] 8° Bell 58

***Nunburnholme*:** MORRIS (Rev. M. C. F.) Nunb.: hist. & antiqs.; ill. 12/6 *n.* ($5) 8° Clar. Press 07

A valuable hist. of the small parish, based on the records; w. chs. on birds, flowers, agric., dialect, etc.

***Pickering*:** HOME (Gordon) Evolution of an English Town (Pickering) 10/6 *n.* 8° Dent 05

***Pontefract*:** HOLMES (Rich.) [ed.] Pontefract: name, lords, castle; ill. 3/6 c 8° R. Holmes, *Pontefract* 78

" [ed.] Bk. of Entries of Pontefract Corporn. [1648–1726] 12/6 8° R. Holmes, *Pontefract* 82

" [ed.] The Sieges of Pontefract Castle: 1644–8; 18 ill. 18/ 8° R. Holmes, *Pontefract* 87

A repr. of Nathan DRAKE's Diary and other docs. conn. w. the sieges. The Jl. of 1st two sieges also cont. in *Miscellanea* of Surtees Soc., 1861 (not sold apart fr. series).

" The Black Friars of Pontefract—*ut* **A** § 57

***St John of Pontefract*:** HOLMES (R.) [ed.] Chartulary of St J. of P., 2 v. 8° Yorks Arch. Soc. 99–02

***Pudsey*:** RAYNER (S.) Hist. and Antiqs. of Pudsey, ed. W. Smith 8° 87

***Richmondshire*:** BOGG (E.) Richmondshire & Vale of Mowbray, 5 v. ea. 1/ *n.* c 8° Miles, *Leeds* [06–8] 09

" From Edendale to the Plains of York 4° *Leeds n.d.*

1,000 miles in the valleys of the Nidd and Yore.

SPEIGHT, Harry Romantic Richmondshire; ill. 10/ *n.* 8° Stock 97

TURNER, J. M. W. [artist] Richmondshire: 20 steel pl., w. l'rpr. Mrs A. Hunt 63/ r f° Virtue [23] 90

WHITAKER, Dr. T. D. History of Richmondshire, 2 vols.; pl. *o.p.* [w. £25] f° *London* 23

***Churches*:** McCALL (H. B.) Richmondshire Churches [gd. acc. of 10 churches] 7/6 *n.* 8° Stock 10

***Ri(e)vaux Abbey*:** ATKINSON (J. C.) [ed.] Cartularium de Rievalle 15/ 8° Surtees Soc. 89

***Ripon*:** FOWLER (Can. J. T.) [ed.] Memls. of Church of Ripon, 4 vols. ea. 5/ 8° Surtees Soc. 83–08

" [ed.] Acts of Chapter of Coll. Ch. of Peter & Wilfrid [1452–1506] 10/ 8° Surtees Soc. 75

Ripon Millenary: record of the festival; maps & ill. 25/ *n.* i 8° Harrison, *Ripon* 92

A sumptuous vol., a record of 'Millenary' fest. (1886), w. valuable hist. of City arrgd. und. its Wakemen (chief of police) and Mayors fr. 1400.

***Rotherham*:** GUEST (Jno.) Hist. Notices of Rotherham; ill. 63/ r 4° White, *Worksop* 79

***Ryedale*:** FRANK (G.) Rydale and North Yorks Antiqs.—*ut sup.*

***Scarborough*:** BAKER (J. B.) History of Scarborough 25/ 8° Longman 82

***Sedbergh; Garsdale; Dent*:** THOMPSON (Rev. W.) Sedbergh, Garsdale, and Dent; ill. 15/ s 4° Jackson, *Leeds* 91

***Selby*:** FOWLER, Rev. J. T. [ed.] Coucher Book of Selby, 2 vols.; ill. Yorks Arch. Soc. 91–3

A colln. of charters rel. to landed possns. of the gt. Yorks monastery, one of few larger Bened. Houses fd. after Norm. Conq. (? by WILLIAM himself). *Introd.* gives careful archit. hist. of Church. Ed. w. minute accuracy and good index, fr. unique (14 cent.) MS.

SCOTT, W. H. The Story of Selby Abbey; ill. Spencer, *Selby* 94

***Sheffield*:** HUNTER (Jos.) —*in his* Hallamshire, *ut sup.*, *s.v.* Hallamshire

LEADER, R. E. Sheffield in the Eighteenth Century 8° *Dy. Telegraph* Off. 01

" [ed.] Records of Burgery of Sheffield; w. Introd. 10/6 *n.* 8° Stock 97

Papers on and account of the ancient governing body of Sheffield, fr. 13th century.

***Sherburn; Cawood*:** WHEATER (W.) Hist. of Sherburn and Cawood *o.p.* 8° [66] 82

***Skipton*:** DAWSON (W. H.) History of Skipton; ill. 7/6 8° *Skipton* 82

***Slingsby*:** BROOKE (A. St C.) Slingsby and Slingsby Castle [a good bk.] 7/6 c 8° Methuen 04

***Snaith*:** ROBINSON (C. B.) Hist. of Priory and Peculiar of Snaith *o.p.* [*pb.* 6/] 8° Simpkin 61

***Sutton-in-Holderness*:** BLASHILL (T.) Sutton-in-Holderness: the manor, Berewic, and the village-community; ill. [bas. on orig. documts. & investign.] 6/ 8° Andrews. *Hull* [97] 00

*Wakefield:* BAILDON, W. P. [ed.] Court Rolls of Manor of W., v. i–ii [1274–1309] 8° Yorks Arch. Soc. 01–6
CAMERON, Jno. Notabilities of Wakefield and its Neighbourhood *o.p.* 8° *London* 43
LUPTON, J. H. Wakefield Worthies: biogr. sketches of Wakefield Men *o.p.* [*pb.* 5/] 8° Hamilton 64
TAYLOR, T. History of Wakefield 8° *Wakefield* 86
*Wharfedale:* BOGG (E.) Two Thousand Miles in Wharfedale; ill. 7/6 8° J. Heywood, *Mancs.* 04
SPEIGHT, Harry Upper Wharfedale; Lower Wharfedale ea. 6/ *n.* 8° Stock 00–2
Unsystematic archæological and historical information, local gossip, etc.
WHITAKER, T. D. —*in his* Loidis and Elmete, *ut sup.*
*Whitby:* ATKINSON (Can. J. C.) Memorials of Old Whitby; map & 11 pl. 3/6 *n.* c 8° Macmillan 94
Hist. gleangs. fr. anc. Whitby recds., throwg. a gd. deal of light on early hist. of town and of Abbey. Puts forward a new view as to character and nationality of CÆDMON.
,, [ed.] Cartularium Abbatiae de Whiteby, 2 vols. ea. 7/6 8° Surtees Soc. 79–81
HOLT, Rob. B. Whitby Past and Present *o.p.* 8° Horne, *Whitby* 97
*Whitby Abbey:* ATKINSON (Can. J. C.) [ed.] Cartularium of Whitby, 2 v. ea. 15/ 8° Surtees Soc. 79–81
*York:* CAINE (Rev. Cæsar) Martial Annals of City of York; 60 ill. 15/ r 8° Sampson, *York* 93
A readable epitome, fr. days of presence in York of 9th and 6th legions to that of Yorks Hussars and 1st Vol. Batt. W. Yorks Regt.
'CITIZEN OF YORK, A' [=Sir Thos. WIDDRINGTON] Analecta Eboracensia: some Remaynes of the Anc. City of York; facss. & ill. *subscr.* 42/ *n.* C. J. Clark 95
Ed. Rev. Caesar CAINE. Author was Speaker of Ho. of Commons: his wk. (the first attempt to compile a hist. of the city) was wr. c. 1650, but has never been hitherto prtd., tho' DRAKE in his *Eboracum* made use of the MS.
COLLINS, Dr F. [ed.] Register of Freemen of City of Y., vols. i–ii [1272–1759] ea. 15/ 8° Surtees Soc. 97–00
COOPER, T. P. City of York: walls, bars, castles 10/6 *n.* 8° Stock 04
A study of documents bearing on the history of the city, w. a view to its defences.
DRAKE, F. Eboracum: hist. and antiq. of York, 2 vols. 8° *London* [1736] 1788
ORNSBY, Can. G. York [Diocesan Histories] 3/6 12° S.P.C.K. 82
PAGE, W. [ed.] Inventories of Church Goods for Counties of York, Durham, and Northumberland 15/ 8° Surtees Soc. 97
RAINE, Can. Jas. York; map [Historic Towns Series] 3/6 ($1·25) c 8° Longman 93
SKAIFE, R. H. [ed.] Register of Guild of Corpus Christi, York 10/ 8° Surtees Soc. 72
WELLBELOVED, Chas. Eburacum: York under the Romans *o.p.* [*pb.* 12/] r 8° Longman 47
*Castle:* COOPER (T. P.) History of Castle of York; ill. *subscr.* 10/6 *n.* 8° Stock 11
Criminal Chronology of York Castle *o.p.* [*pb.* 3/] f 8° Simpkin [67] 69
TWYFORD (W.) + GRIFFITHS (W. A.) Records of York Castle *o.p.* [*pb.* 7/6] c 8° Griffith & Farren 80
*Cathedral (Minster):* BROWNE (Jno.) Hist. & Ants. of Yk. Cath., 2 v. *o.p.* [*pb.* 178/6] r 4° Longman 47
EGBERT, Abp [732–66] Pontifical of, ed. Rev. W. Greenwell *not sep.* 8° Surtees Soc. 53
GIFFARD, Abp W. [d. 1279] Register of, ed. Wm. Brown [1266–79] 15/ 8° Surtees Soc. 04
GRAY, Abp W. Register of, ed. Can. J. Raine, jun. [1215–55] 8° Surtees Soc. 72
HALFPENNY, Jos. Gothic Ornamts. in Cathedral Ch. of York, ed. Can. J. Raine; 105 pl. Jackson, *Leeds* [1795] 93
PUREY-CUST, Dn A. P. Heraldry of York Minster; 11 col. pl. & 130 ill. 84/ 4° Jackson, *Leeds* 96
Heraldry of the builders and benefactors of the Minster.
RAINE, Can. Jas., jun. [ed.] Fabric Rolls of York Minster *not sep.* 8° Surtees Soc. 59
,, [ed.] Historians of Ch. of York & Archbps., 3 v. [to 1522] ea. 10/ r 8° Rolls Ser. 79–94
de WICKWANE, Abp W. Register of York Minster [1279–85] 8° Surtees Soc. 07
*Inns:* COOPER (T. P.) Old Inns and Inn Signs of York; ill. 2/6 8° Delittle, *York* 98
*Pageant,* 1909: Book of the York Pageant; ill. [7 episodes, 800–1644] 25/ *n.* 4° Ben Johnson, *York* 09
*St Mary's Convent:* St Mary's Convent [hist.; Quart. Ser.] 7/6 8° Burns & Oates 87

## 18: GREAT BRITAIN AND IRELAND (*c*): WALES

*Bibliography:* Bibliotheca Celtica, ed. J. Ballinger: 1909 [bks. rel. to Wales] 8° Nat. Lib., Aberystwith (11) *ann.*
OWEN, E. Cat. of MSS. rel. to Wales in Br. Mus., Pt. i 8° Cymmrodorion Soc. (Nutt) 00
*BRADLEY, A. G. Highways and Byways in N. Wales; ill. 6/ ($2 *n.*) c 8° Macmillan [98] 05
* ,, Highways and Byways in S. Wales; ill. 6/ ($2 *n.*) c 8° Macmillan 03
BORROW, Geo. Wild Wales: its people, lang., scenery; 13 ill. 6/; 2/6 c 8° Murray [62] 01
$2 Putnam, *N.Y.* Ch. Edn. [New Univ. Lib.] 1/ *n.* pott 8° Routledge (50 c. Dutton, *N.Y.*).
BREESE, Edw. [ed.] Kalendars of Gwynedd; w. notes W. W. E. Wynne *o.p.* 4° 73
Lists of lords-lt., custodes rotulorum, sheriffs, Kts.-of-shire of Anglesey, Carnarvon, Merioneth.

CAMBRIAN ARCHÆOL. ASSOC. : Archæologia Cambrensis, vols. i *sqq.* ; ill. *ann.* 21/ 8° Cambr. Arch. Assoc. 46 *sqq. in prg.*

CYMMRODORION OF LOND., HON. SOC. OF : Y Cymmrodor [=Transactns. of the Soc.] r 8° Cymmrod. Soc. 80 *sqq., in prg.*

,, Record Series, vols. i–iv r 8° Cymmrod. Soc. (Nutt) 96–00 *in prg.*

*Black Book of St David's* [*ut inf.*] ed. Prf. J. W. WILLIS-BUND | *Catal. of MSS. rel. to Wales in Br. Mus.* Pt. i [*ut sup.*] Edw. OWEN | *Court Rolls of L'dsh. of Ruthin* [*ut inf.*] R. A. ROBERTS | GILDAS, *De Excidio*, etc. [*ut* F § 18] ed. H. WILLIAMS | For other pubns. of Soc. *v.* K § 282.

GIRALDUS CAMBRENSIS [1146?–1220?]—*ut* **F** § 41

GOULD, Rev. S. Baring- A Book of North Wales ; 49 ill. 6/ c 8° Methuen 03

,, A Book of South Wales ; 57 ill. 6/ c 8° Methuen 05

Popular sketches of the history and antiquities, customs, folklore, etc.

HALL, S. C. + Mrs S. C. Book of South Wales ; ill. *o.p.* [*pb.* 21/] s 4° Virtue 61

HISSEY, J. J. An Old-fashioned Journey—*ut* **E** § 16

HUDSON, A. E. L. A Geography of Wales [for Welsh studts.] 1/6 c 8° Macmillan 01

JONES, E. A. [ed.] Memls. of Old Wales ; ill. [Memls. of Cos. of Engl.] 15/ *n.* 8° G. Allen *in prep.*

KILNER, [Miss] E. A. Four Welsh Counties ; ill. 5/ c 8° Low 91

Account of a holiday tour in and about Brecknock, Carnarvon, Merioneth, Pembroke.

LELAND, Jno. [1506?–52] Itinerary in Wales : 1536–9, ed. Lucy Toulmin Smith 10/6 *n.* 8° Bell 06

Scattered portns. of the *Itinerary* [*ut* E § 16, *s.v.* Early Topogr.] rel. to Wales, brought together. Map and indexes.

PENNANT, Thos. Tour in Wales, ed. Prf. J. Rhys, 3 v. ; ill. [standard] *o.p.* 8° *Carnarvon* [1778–84] 83

ROSS, Martin Beggars on Horseback ; ill. E. Œ. Somerville 3/6 c 8° Blackwood 95

An amusing account of a riding-tour in North Wales.

SYKES, Wirt [Am.] Rambles and Studies in Old S. Wales ; ill. *o.p.* [*pb.* 18/] 8° Low 82

By the then American consul in Cardiff.

**Celtic Remains**—*v.* **G** § 2 **Climbing**—*v.* **I** § 165 **Ethnology**—*v.* **E** § 16 **Guides**—*v.* **E** § 16

**Life ; People**

BORROW, Geo. Wild Wales : its people, language, and scenery—*ut sup.*

'GLAS, DRAIG' ['BLUE DRAGON'] The Perfidious Welshman [an abusive satire] 2/6 *n.* 8° Stanley Paul 10

'Englishman, An' The Welshman's Reputation [reply to above] 2/6 *n.* c 8° Stanley Paul 11

PHILLIPS, Sir Thos. Wales : language, social condn., character, & religion *o.p.* [*pb.* 14/] 8° Parker 49

RHYS (Prf. J.) + JONES (D. B.) The Welsh People : orig., lang., history 16/ 8° Unwin [00] 06

STEPHENS, T. [ed.] Wales, To-day, and To-morrow 6/ *n.* 8° *Western Mail* Off., *Cardiff* 07

80 short pprs., by var. wrs. of differ. schools of thought, reflecting 'the fair fresh countenance' of Wales' rising Nationalism and the expandg. life of her people. An edn. in Welsh is also pubd.

TREVELYAN, Marie Glimpses of Welsh Life and Character 6/ c 8° Hogg 93

Stories of poets, musicns. and other 'worthies', superstns., customs, festivals, gentry, farmers, Eisteddfod, etc.

,, The Land of Arthur : heroes and heroines 6/ c 8° Hogg 95

**Scenery**

LOVETT, Rich. [ed.] Welsh Pictures : drawn w. pen and pencil ; 72 ill. 8/ i 8° R.T.S. 92

WALTON, Elijah [art.] Welsh Sceny. : 26 col. pl. w. l'rpr. [chfly. Snowdonia] *o.p.* [*pb.* 70/] 4° Thompson 75

---

**Brecknockshire**

JONES, Theoph. Hist. of Brecknockshire, 4 v. in 2 ; maps & ill. 42/ r 4° Blissett, *Brecon* [05–9] 08

Life and Letters of Theophilus Jones 7/6 8° Blissett, *Brecon*

LLOYD, Jno. The Great Forest of Brecknock Bedford Press 06

Mainly informn. pert. to questn. of legal positn. of allotmt.-owners who replaced old commoners und. Incl. Act of 1815.

*Aberhonddu :* MORGAN (G. E. F.) Aberhonddu ; ill. fr. old prints 7/6 8° Blissett, *Brecon*

**Cardiganshire**

MEYRICK, Sir S. R. History and Antiqs. of Co. of Cardigan ; ill. 30/ r 4° Blissett, *Brecon* [08]

*Aberystwith :* EVANS (Rev. G. E.) Aberystwith and its Court Leet ; 33 pl. 4° *Welsh Gaz.* Off., *Aberyst.* 03

*Cardigan Priory :* PRITCHARD (Emily M.) Cardigan Priory in Olden Days ; 7 ill. 10/ *n.* 8° Heinemann 05

*Lampeter :* EVANS (Rev. G. E.) Lampeter 05

*Strata Florida :* WILLIAMS (S. W.) Cistercian Abbey of Strata Florida ; 20 pl. 10/6 8° Whiting 89

**Carnarvonshire**

Record of Carnarvon (The) : ed. [fr. Harl. MS. 696] Sir Hy. Ellis 31/6 f° Rolls Series 38

An important coll. of documents (chfly. 14 and 15 cents.), bg. survey of counties of Anglesey, Carnarvon, Merioneth.

*Conway :* The Registers of Conway, vol. i [1541–1793] 25/ *n.* C. J. Clark

*Snowdon District:* HUGHES (H.) + NORTH (H. L.) Old Cottages of Snowdonia; ill. [architl.] 7/6 *n.* c 8° Jarvis, *Bangor* 09
HUSON, Thos. [art.] Round ab. Snowdon: 30 etchgs. & aquats., w. notes J. J. Hissey 21/ *n.* f° Seeley 93
SALT, H. S. On Cambrian and Cumbrian Hills [Snowdon; Scawfell] 3/6 *n.* c 8° Fifield 08
8 papers, by an enthusiastic mountain-lover, descriptive and observational.
TREVELYAN, Marie From Snowdon to the Sea 6/ c 8° Hogg 94

**Denbighshire**

*Ruthin:* ROBERTS (R. A.) [ed.] Court Rolls. of L'dsh. of Ruthin [Rec. Ser.] 21/ *n.* r 8° Cymmrod. Soc. 93
Cover period 1294–5. Well edited, with tr., notes, preface, and 1 facs. of orig. membrane.
*Wrexham:* PALMER (A. N.) Towns, Fields, and Folk of Wr. in time Jas. i 2/ 8° Woodhall, *Wrexham* 83
,, Hist. of Anc. Tenures of Land in Marches of N. Wales 6/ 8° Woodhall, *Wrexham* 85
,, History of Parish Church of Wrexham; ill. 6/ 8° Woodhall, *Wrexham* 87
,, Hist. of Older Nonconformity in Wr. and Nbrhd.; ill. 6/ 8° Woodhall, *Wrexham* 89
,, Hist. of Town of Wrexham; maps & ill. 9/ 8° Woodhall, *Wrexham* 93
,, Hist. of Country Townships of Old Parish of Wrexham 8° Woodhall, *Wrexham*
The last five together form an exhaustive and minute history of the town.

**Flintshire**

*Worthenbury:* PULESTON, Rev. Sir T. H. G. Story of Quiet Country Parish *o.p.* [*pb.* 4/] c 8° Roxburghe Pr. 95

**Glamorganshire**

BRADLEY, A. G. Glamorgan and Gower; ill. W. M. Meredith 3/6 *n.* 8° Constable 08
CLARK, G. T. Land of Morgan: contribs. to hist. of l'dsh. of Gl. 8° Camb. Arch. Soc. 83
,, [ed.] Cartae et alia Munimenta quae ad Dominium de Glamorgan pertinent, 4 vols. s 4° [1102–1689] *Cardiff* 85–93
GRIFFITH, J. Edward ii in Glamorgan 04
MERRICK, Rice Booke of Glam. Antiqs., ed. J. A. Corbett *o.p.* 4° [1578] 87
NICHOLAS, T. History and Antiquities of Glamorganshire *o.p.* [*pb.* 12/6] r 8° Longman 74
*Cardiff:* MATTHEWS (J. H.) [ed.] Cardiff Records, vols. i–v; ill. & facss. 105/ r 8° Cardiff 98–05
*Ewenny:* TURBERVILLE (Col. J. P.) Ewenny Priory, Monastery & Fortress; ill. 7/6 8° Stock 01
*Llandaff:* Liber Landavensis: ed. W. J. Rees; w. tr. and notes Welsh MSS. Soc., *Llandovery* 40
*Llyfr Teilo*, the ancient register of the Cath.-Church of Llandaff: to A.D. 1132.
,, Text of Bk. of Llan Dâv: facs., ed. J. G. Evans + J. Rhys *o.p.* 8° *Oxford* 93
Llandaff Records: vols. i–ii 05–8 *in prg.*
NEWELL, E. J. Llandaff—*ut* **A** § 75 [Diocesan Histories]
*Llantwit Major:* TREVELYAN (Marie) Ll. Maj.: hist., trads., archæol. 2/6 c 8° Southall, *Newpt., Mon.*
*Margam Abbey:* BIRCH (W. de Gray) A History of Margam Abbey; ill. r 8° C. J. Clark 97
*Neath Abbey:* BIRCH (W. de Gray) History of Neath Abbey 21/ *n.* 4° Richards, *Neath* 02

**Marches**

BRADLEY, A. G. Shropshire, Herefordshire, and Monmouth—*ut* **E** § 17, *s.v.* Shropshire
A new edn. of *In the March and Borderland of Wales.* Of consid. importce. on histor., geogr., and legendary, sides.
HARPER, C. G. Marches of Wales: notes on Welsh borders; 114 ill. 16/ 8° Chapman 94
'Fr. Severn to Sands of Dee', inclg. Ludlow, Raglan, Chepstow, and line of smaller fortresses on Heref. borders.

**Montgomeryshire**

EDWARDS, Griffith [GUTYN PADARN]—*in his* Works, ed. E. Owen, *ut* **A** § 75
The parochial history of Garthbeibio, Llanerfyl, Llangadfan.
LLOYD, J. Y. W. Hist. of the Princes, Lords Marcher, and Anc. Nobility of Powys Fadog, etc., 6 vols. *o.p.* 8° 81–7
LLOYD, W. V. [ed.] Sheriffs of Montgomeryshire: 1540–1639 *o.p.* 8° 76
*POWYS-LAND CLUB: Collns. rel. to Montgomeryshire, vols. i–xxvi; ill. *ann. subscr.* 21/ 8° Powys-Land Club 68–92 *sqq., in prg.*

DWNN, Lewys, *Pedigrees of Montgom Families* 10/6, 88
*Old Herbert Papers of Powis Castle and in Brit. Mus.* 86
WILLIAMS, Rich., *Hist. of Parish of Llanbrynmair* 89
,, *Montgomeryshire Worthies*

*Welshpool:* OWEN (R. E. M.) Wesh Pool and Powysland *o.p.* [*pb.* 3/6] r 8° Owen, *Welshpool* 97
A history of Powysland to 14th cent.; and a short account of Welshpool from that date.

**Monmouthshire** —*v.* **E** § 17

**Pembrokeshire**

*Bibliography:* Bibliographical Index of Pembrokeshire Literature Williams, *Solva* 97
CLARK, G. T. The Earls, Earldom, and Castle of Pembroke *o.p.* 8° *Tenby* 80
FENTON, Rich. Historical Tour through Pembrokeshire 30/ r 4° Blissett, *Brecon* [11]
Owen, H. Index to above *o.p.* 4° 94

LAWS, Edw. Hist. of Little England beyond Wales and the Non-Kymric Colony in Pembrokeshire *o.p.* 4° 88

OWEN OF HENLLYS, Geo., L'd of KEMES [1552–1613] Descrn. of Pembrokeshire, ed. H. Owen, Pts. i–iii 33/6 *n.* r 8° C. J. Clark 97–06
To occupy 5 Pts. [Cymmrodorion Rec. Ser.]. Notes and App. A colln. of misc. documts., of value for topogr. of Wales in Elizab. era.

PEMBROKE, 1st Earl of [1502–70] Survey of Lands of, ed. C. R. Straton, 2 v.; ill. 4° Roxburghe Club 09

Pembrokeshire Antiquities [' notes and queries ' fr. a local jl.] Williams, *Solva* 97

PHILLIPS, Rev. Jas. The History of Pembrokeshire 12/6 *n.* 8° Stock 09
Ends w. the days of the Commonwealth. Posthumously pubd.

TIMMINS, H. T. Nooks and Corners of Pembrokeshire; ill. 21/ c 4° Stock 95

*Worthies:* OWEN OF HENLLYS (Geo.) The Taylors Cussion: facs. edn., 2 vols. 50/ *n.* 4° Blades 08
A curious and interestg. commonplace bk., w. short but very good biogr. of the author by Emily M. PRITCHARD.

OWEN, Hy. Old Pembroke Families 4° *priv. prin.* (C. J. Clark) 02

*Manorbier Castle:* DUCKETT (Sir G. F.) Manorbier Castle and Early Owners 8° *priv. prin.* 98

*St David's:* BEVAN (Rev. W. L.) St David's [Diocesan Histories] 2/6 f 8° S.P.C.K. 88

Black Book of St David's, ed. Prf. J. W. Wills-Bund + Hy. Owen + Archd. Bevan Cymmrodorion Soc. 95
[Record Ser.] A detailed survey of possessns. of the see of St David's in A.D. 1326.

JONES (W. B. T.) + FREEMAN (E. A.) Hist. and Antiquities of St David's *o.p.* [*pb.* 40/] 4° J. R. Smith 56

*St Dogmael's Abbey:* PRITCHARD (Emily M.) Hist. of St Dogmael's Abbey; ill. 18/ *n.* 4° Blades 08

*Tenby:* GOSSE (P. H.) Tenby: a seaside holiday; ill. *o.p.* [*pb.* 21/] c 8° Van Voorst 56

HALL, S. C. + Mrs S. C. Tenby *o.p.* [*pb.* 4/] c 8° *Tenby* 60

LAWS (E.) + EDWARDS (Emily H.) [ed.] Church Book of St Mary the Virgin, Tenby 10/6 *n.* 8° Leach, *Tenby* 07

**Radnorshire:** WILLIAMS (Jon.) History of Radnorshire 30/ r 4° Blissett, *Brecon* [59]

## 19: GREAT BRITAIN AND IRELAND (*d*): SCOTLAND AND ISLANDS

**Bibliography:** TERRY (Prf. C. S.) Catal. of Pubns. of Scottish Historical and Kindred Clubs and Socs. 10/ *n.* r 8° MacLehose, *Glasgow* 09
A very useful bibliography, inclg. pubns. of H.M. Stationery Off. 1780–1908: w. Subject Index.

### Atlas

BARTHOLOMEW, J. G. [ed.] Atlas of Scotland: 62 maps and plans f° Bartholomew, *Edin.* 95
A sumptuous wk., one of the best specs. of mod. cartography.

### Early Travels and Accounts

BOSWELL, Jas. [1740–95] Journal of a Tour in the Hebrides—*ut* **K** § 24

*BROWN, P. Hume [ed.] Early Travellers in Scotland: 1295–1689; introd. & notes; 3 curious maps 14/ 8° Douglas, *Edin.* 91
Selns. fr. wks. of early Eng. and for. travrs. in Scotl. prior to close of 17 cent., deriv. fr. Brit. Mus. MSS., pubns. of learned socs. and little-kn. bks. Forms a considerable contrib. to study of Scottish civilizn., full of val. informn. on custs., insts., posn. of women, state of law and justice, archit., dress, foods, tournamts., chase, climate, scenery, *etc.*

" [ed.] Tours in Scotland: 1677 and 1681 5/ 8° Douglas, *Edin.* 92
Thos. KIRK in 1677 (much the longer and more interest. jl. of the two), Ralph THORESBY in 1681. For his *Scotl. before* 1700 *v.* **F** § 38.

CHALMERS, Geo. [1742–1825] Caledonia: hist. & topogr. acc. of N. Britain, 8 vols. ea. 25/ 4° Gardner, *Paisley* [07–24] 87–94
One of the monumts. of Scottish history and topography, correspg. to CAMDEN'S *Britannia.* Vol. iii: Index.

JUSSERAND, J. J. A Journey to Scotland in 1435—*in his* English Essays fr. a French Pen [tr.], *ut* **F** § 16

LEYDEN, Jno. [1775–1811] Journal of Tour in Highlds. and Western Islands—*ut inf., s.v.* Highlands

LOWTHER (C.) + FALLOW (R.) + MAUSON (P.) Tour in Scotland in 1629 5/ *n.* 8° Douglas, *Edin.* 94
Descrn. of tour fr. Carlisle to Perth *via* Selkirk, Galashiels and Edin., w. quaint remarks on people and places.

MACFARLANE, Walt. Geogr. Collns. rel. to Scotl., ed. Sir A. Mitchell, 3 v. 8° Scot. Hist. Soc. [1748–9] 06–8

POCOCKE, Bp Rich. Tours in Scotland, ed. D. W. Kemp [1747, 1750, 1760] Scot. Hist. Soc., *Edin.* 87

TAYLOR, Jos. Journey to Edenborough [1705], ed. Wm. Cowan—*ut* **E** § 16, *s.v.* Early Topography

WORDSWORTH, Dorothy [1771–1855] Recollections of a Tour made in Scotland in 1803—*ut* **K** § 24

### Topography, etc.

County Histories of Scotland; maps ea. 7/6 *n.* 8° Blackwood 96–00
*Aberdeen and Banff* [*ut inf.*] W. WATT | *Dumfries and Galloway*, 2 maps [*ut inf.*] Sir Herb. MAXWELL | *Fife and Kinross* [*ut inf.*] Dr Æneas J. G. MACKAY | *Inverness* Dr J. Cameron LEES | *Moray and Nairn*, 3 maps and plan [*ut inf.*] Dr Chas. RAMPINI | *Roxb., Selkirk, and Peebles* [*ut inf.*] Sir G. DOUGLAS

GRAMPIAN CLUB: Publications—*ut* **G** § 22

' HALIBURTON, Hugh ' [J. Logie ROBERTSON] Furth in the Field 5/ c 8° Unwin 94
Valuable essays in bypaths of Scot. life, lang., and liter. Pts. iv and v devoted to THOMSON and BURNS resp., both good, esp. latter.

" In Scottish Fields—*ut* **K** § 24, *s.v.* Burns

INNES, Cosmo [ed.] Origines Parochiales Scotiae, vols. i–iii; maps o.p. 4° Lizars, *Edin.* 51–5
An important wk. on eccles. and territorial antiqs. of parishes of Scotld. Copies were presented to members of Bannatyne Club on their Club-paper. The wk. was never completed, its cost hg. largely exceeded orig. intentions.

IRVING, Jos. West of Scotland in History [events, family trads., topogr., etc.] *o.p.* [*pb.* 15/] 4° *Glasgow* 85

LANSDALE, Maria H. Scotland, Historic & Romantic; 13 maps & 23 ports. 7/6 *n.* 8° Oliphant [03] 05

MASSON, Prf. Dav. Recollections of Two Cities [Aberd., Edinb.], 7/6 *n.* c 8° Oliphant, *Edin.* [92] 11
Originally pubd. *sub tit. Recollections of Three Cities*, including London also.

NEW SPALDING CLUB: Publications—*ut* **G** § 22

Statistical Account of Scotland: 15 vols. *o.p.* [*pb.* 336/] 8° Blackwood 45
A valuable, but no longer up-to-date, repertory of stat. informn., dealg. w. topogr., geol., landowners, paroch. regrs., local celebrs., antiquities, population and industries, prepared by ministers of respective parishes, etc.

SOC. OF ANTIQUARIES OF SCOTLAND *ann.* 21/ 4° Soc. of. Antiqs. of Sc. 1792 *sqq.*, *in prg.*
**Archæologia Scotica: Transns. of Soc.*; ill. 1792 *sqq.*, *in prg.*
*Proceedings*, Ser. i: 1852–78, £10 10*s.*; Ser. ii, vols. i *sqq.* ea. 10/6
DRUMMOND (J.), *Sculptured Monumts. in Iona, etc.* [*ut* **G** § 16] 63/

VILLARS, P. Scotland & Ireland [tr.]; ill. [picturesque survey] *o.p.* [*pb.* 7/6] r 8° Routledge 87

**Gazetteer**

*GROOME, F. H. [ed.] Ordnance Gazetteer of Scotland, 3 v.; ill. ea. 7/6 *n.* r 8° Caxton Press [85] 03

**Guides** —*v.* **E** § 16

**Abbeys; Castles; Houses** —*for* Architecture, *v.* **I** § 120

ADDIS, M. E. L. Scottish Cathedrals and Abbeys: hist. & assocns.; ill. 8/6 *n.* m 8° Blackwood 01
Iona, Glasgow, Brechin, Aberdeen, Dunblane, Edinburgh, Dunkeld, Kirkwall, Dunfermline, Paisley.

BILLINGS, R. W. Baronial & Eccles. Antiqs. of Scotl., ed. A. W. Wiston-Glynn, 4 v.; ill. ea. 7/6 *n.* 4° Foulis [45–52] 08–9
Descrs. and ill. in its 240 pl. and 60 text-illns. pract. every old bldg. in Scotld., w. legends and hist. assocns.

BLUNDELL, Otto Ancient Catholic Homes of Scotland 3/6 *n.* 8° Burns & Oates 07

BUTLER, Rev. D. Scottish Cathedrals and Abbeys 1/6 *n.* c 8° Black 01
The architecture of the buildings and the influences which produced them.

BUTTER, H. C. Scotland's Ruined Abbeys 12/ *n.* ($2·50) r 16° Macmillan 99
Illustrations by the author, and plans. The traditional and romantic lore of 18 Scottish Abbeys. Popular.

Castles of Aberdeenshire (The): histor. and descr. notices; 42 ill. Wm. Taylor *o.p.* 4° *priv. prin.* 87
Partly repr. fr. Sir A. Leith HAY's *Castellated Architecture of Aberdeenshire, f° Aberdeen, n.d.* (49).

FLEMING, J. S. Ancient Castles & Mansions of Stirling Nobility 21/ *n.* 4° Gardner, *Paisley* 02

FRAPRIE, F. R. Castles and Keeps of Scotland; ill. [7/6 *n.* Bell] $3 8° Page, *Boston* 07

MACGIBBON (D.) + ROSS (T.) Castellated and Domestic Architecture of Scotland—*ut* **I** § 120

MILLAR, A. H. Historical Castles and Mansions of Scotland; ill. 15/ 4° Gardner, *Paisley* 90

**Churches**

MUIR, T. S. Ecclesiological Notes on some of the Islands; ill. 21/ 8° Douglas, *Edin.* 85

**Highlands and Islands** —*v. also* Scenery, *inf.*

BURT, Cpt. Letters fr. North of Scotl. [1754], w. Introd. R. Jamieson, 2 v.; pl. 21/ 8° Paterson, *Edin.* 76
Conts. an account of the Highlands, Highland manners and customs, etc.

COLQUHOUN, J. The Moor and the Loch—*ut* **I** § 147 [Highland sports]

GRANT, Anne (of Laggan) Letters fr. the Mountains [1773–1803], ed. J. P. Grant [son] 2 vols. *o.p.* [*pb.* 21/] c 8° Longman [06] 45
Her *Memoirs and Correspondence* were also ed. by J. P. GRANT in 3 vols. *o.p.* c 8° Longman 45.

GREGORY, Don. Hist. of Western Highlands & Isles of Scotl. 12/6 8° Morison, *Glasgow* [36] 81
From 1493 to 1625; w. a short introd. sketch by Don. GREGORY, coverg. the yrs. A.D. 80–1493.

HAMERTON, P. G. A Painter's Camp in the Highlands *o.p.* [*pb.* 6/] c 8° Macmillan [62] 73

HIGHLAND SOC.: Transactions 1908 *sqq.*, *in prg.*

HOLMES, D. T. Literary Tours in Highlands & Islands of Scotland 4/6 *n.* c 8° Gardner, *Paisley* 09

IONA CLUB: Collectanea de Rebus Albanicis, ed. Don. Gregory + W. F. Skene *o.p.* [*pb.* 105/] 8° Stevenson, *Edin.* 47
A varied colln. of orig. pprs. and docums. rel. to hist. of Highls. and Isls. of Sc.: conts. also *Trsns.* of the Club.

KELTIE, J. S. [ed.] Hist. of Scot. Highlds., Clans, & Regimts., 2 v.; col. ill. 70/ i 8° Fullarton, *Ed.* [75] 85

LANG, Andr. [ed.] The Highlands of Scotl. in 1750 [fr. a Br. Mus. MS.] 5/ *n.* c 8° Blackwood 98

LEYDEN, Jno. [1775–1811] Journal of Tour in the Highlds. & W. Islands: 1800 6/ *n.* c 8° Blackwood 03
Ed. by Jas. SINTON; w. bibliography. Chiefly concerned with the geology of the Highlds. and w. OSSIAN's poems.

LORNE, Marq. of Adventures in Legend; ill. 6/ c 8° Constable 98
The last historic legends of the Western Highlands.

MCIAN, R. R. [art.] Highlanders at Home: Gaelic Gatherings; illns. 6/ *n.* c 8° Bryce, *Glasgow* [48] 00
Text by J. LOGAN. Interesting as recalling a state of things extant in the 'forties. Quaint illns.

MACLAUGHLIN, Rev. T. History of the Scottish Highlands, 8 Divisions; pl., etc. 60/ i 8° *n.d.*
In 3 Pts., i: *General History of Highlanders*; ii: *History of Clans*; iii: *History of Regiments*.

MACLEOD, Rev. Norm. Reminiscences of a Highland Parish—*ut inf.*, *s.v.* Skye

MACNAUGHTAN, [Miss] S. Us Four [descrn. of her childhd. in W. Highls.] 6/ c 8° Murray 09
MACPHERSON, Alex. Glimpses of Church and Soc. Life in H'lds in Olden Time—*ut* **A** § 71
REID, J. T. Art Rambles in Highlds. & Islds. of Scotl.; ill. *o.p.* [*pb.* 21/] r 8° Routledge 78
ST JOHN, C. Wild Sports & Natural Hist. of Highlands—*ut* **I** § 147
SCOTT, Sir Walt. Manners and Customs of Highlanders; and Histor. Acc. of Clan MacGregor 4/6 8° Morison, *Glasgow* 94
Two sketches orig. contrib. to *Quart. Rev.* The second, opening w. acc. of outlawed Clan MacGregor, is mainly taken up w. hist. of ROB ROY, and conts. the authentic materls. on which SCOTT founded his novel *Rob Roy.*
SKENE, W. F. The Highlanders of Scotland 10/6 *n.* 8° Mackay, *Stirling* [36] 02
Edited by Dr Alex. MACBAIN, with life of Skene, and valuable notes and corrections.
STEWART, Rev. Alex. 'Twixt Ben Nevis and Glencoe 7/6 p 8° Paterson, *Edin.* 85
,, Nether Lochaber 10/6 c 8° Paterson, *Edin.* 83
Both above cont. observatns. on quaint customs and legends, w. descrns. and odd bits of nat. hist. and folklore of Highlands.
STEWART, Gen. Dav. Sketches of Character, Institns., & Customs of Highlanders 5/ c 8° *Inverness*
*Clans; Tartans* —*v.* **G** § 22

**Life and People** —*v. also* **F** §§ 35–9
ALEXANDER, Wm. Notes, etc., of Northern Rural Life in 18th Century c 8° 77
CARMENT, Sam. [ed.] Glimpses of the Olden Times [life and manners] 3/ *n.* c 8° Macleod, *Edin.* 93
COCKBURN, H. T., L'd Circuit Journeys—*ut* **D** § 7
CROSLAND, T. W. H. The Unspeakable Scot [scurrilous invective] 1/ *n.* c 8° Richards [02] 03
GEIKIE, Sir Arch. Scottish Reminiscences [$2 Macmillan, *N.Y.*] 6/*n.* 8° MacLehose, *Glasgow* 04
GUTHRIE, Ellen J. Old Scottish Customs 3/6 c 8° Hamilton 85
HENDERSON, T. F. Old-World Scotland: glimpses of its modes and manners 6/ 8° Unwin 93
22 interesting papers repr. fr. *Natl. Observer* on wine and ale, usquebaugh, kale and beef, inns, vagabonds and minstrels, kirk discipline, the Cateran, the Highld. chief—and a new essay on the inevitable Darnley Murder.
,, + WATT (F.) Scotland of To-day; ill. (20 col.) F. Laing 6/ c 8° Methuen [07] 08
A good picture of Scotld. and the Scot of the present in their relations to the past.
HOOD, Rev. E. Paxton Scottish Characteristics 7/6 c 8° Hodder 83
JOHNSON, Clifton The Land of Heather; ill. [Scottish life] 8/6 *n.* ($2) r 16° Macmillan [03] 07
LOCKHART, J. G. [1794–1854] Peter's Letters to his Kinsfolk, 3 vols. *o.p.* 8° *Edinburgh* [ ] 19
LOGAN, Jas. Scottish Gael: Celtic Manners, ed. Rev. A. Stewart, 2 v. 28/ 8° *Inverness* [31] 76
A historical and descr. acc. of the inhabs., antiqs., and national peculiarities of Scotland.
MAXWELL, Dav. [ed.] Bygone Scotland [social and domestic life] 7/6 8° Andrews, *Hull* 94
MILLER, Hugh [1802–56] Scenes and Legends of North of Scotland 5/ c 8° Black [50] 69
,, My Schools and Schoolmasters—*ut* **D** § 157
MURRAY, Jas. Life in Scotland 100 Years Ago 3/6 c 8° Gardner, *Paisley* [00] 05
RAMSAY, Dn E. B. [1793–1872] Reminiscences of Scottish Life and Character 1/ *n.* pott 8° Routledge [*n.d.* (59)] 07
50 c. Dutton, *N.Y.* [New Univ. Lib.] The orig. edn. of this was entitled *Lect. on Changes in the Manners and Habits of Scotld. dur. Last Fifty Yrs.*, 8° *Edin.*, *n.d.*
SANDERSON, W. Scottish Life and Character; w. 20 col. pl. H. J. Dobson [$3 *n.* Macm., *N.Y.*] 7/6 *n.* sq 8° Black
SCOTTISH HISTORICAL SOC.: Publications—*ut* **F** § 35
SHARP, C. K. Letters from and to Sharp, ed. A. Allardyce, 2 vols. 52/6 8° Blackwood 88
SINCLAIR, Wm. Scottish Life and Humour 2/6 c 8° Sinclair *Haddington* 98
A collection of humorous stories of Scottish life, arranged under subjects; some are new.
STIRLING, Amel. H. Sketch of Scottish Industr. & Social Hist. in 18 & 19 Cents.—*ut* **D** § 117*
WALLACE, Wm. Scotland Yesterday: some old friends 6/ c 8° Hodder 93
Sketches of the life of 'yesterday' in a typical village of E. of Scotl. and in a typical country-town in West.

**Lochs**
MURRAY (Sir J.) + PULLAR (L.) Bathymetrical Survey of Freshw. Lochs of Sc. 21/ *n.* s 8° R.G.S. (Stanford) 09

**Place-names** —*v.* **K** § 120

**Rivers**
LAUDER, Sir T. Dick Scottish Rivers; ill. by author 6/ c 8° Morison, *Glasg.* [74] 90
*Clyde (The)*: CAMERON, D. [art.] The Clyde: 20 etchgs. of river and banks f° *priv. prin.* 90
DEAS, Jas. History of the Clyde to the Present Time 10/6 8° MacLehose, *Glasgow* 76
HUNTER, Mary Y. + J. Y. [arts.] Clyde: 67 col. pl., w. l'rpr. N. Munro [$6 *n.* Macm., *N.Y.*] 20/ *n.* sq 8° Black 07
MARWICK, Sir J. D. The River Clyde and Clyde Burghs 21/ *n.* 4° MacLehose, *Glasgow* 08

MILLAR, W. J. — The Clyde, from Source to Sea; ill. — 7/6 8° Blackie 88
WALKER, Rob. — The Clyde and the Western Highlands; ill. — 2/6 obl. Virtue 92
*Tweed:* MAXWELL (Sir H. E.) Story of the Tweed; ill. — 6/ *n.* c 8° Nisbet [05] 09
The first edn. (1905) was an *édition de luxe*, pubd. at 105/ *n.*, f°, Nisbet.

**Scenery:** CASSELL & Co. [pubs.] Pictorial Scotland; 220 ill. — 7/6 obl f° Cassell 02
EYRE-TODD, Geo. — Scotland, Picturesque & Traditional; 176 ill. 3/6 *n.* c 8° Gowans & Gray [95] 06
A book of travel in the central counties from Melrose to Inverness. Popular.
*GEIKIE, Prf. Arch. — The Scenery of Scotland; ill. — 10/ *n.* ($3·25 *n.*) c 8° Macmillan [65] 01
Viewed in connexion with its physical geology.
,, — Landscape in History, and other Essays—*ut* **E** § 2
GEIKIE, Walt. [art.] — Etchings illustrative of Scottish Character and Scenery: 92 pl. — 63/ 4° Paterson, *Edin.* [46] 85
GREEN, Rev. S. G. — Scottish Pictures, drawn with Pen and Pencil; ill. — 8/ i 4° R.T.S. [83] 86
LAWSON, J. P. [ed.] Scotld. Delineated by Gt. Painters: 72 tinted pl.; 2 v. *o.p.* [*pb.* 70/] f° Day & Son 47
LYDON, A. F. [artist] — Scottish Loch Scenery: a series of col. pl. — 12/ 4° Walker 82
PALMER, Sutton [art.] — Bonnie Scotland: 75 col. pl., w. l'rpr. A. R. H. Moncrieff — [$6 *n.* Macm., *N.Y.*] 20/ *n.* sq 8° Black 04
,, — Heart of Scotland—*v. inf.*, *s.v.* Perthshire
Scotland Sixty Years Ago: a series of 32 copper pl. — 105/ f° Gardner, *Paisley*

*Coast Scenery*
COWPER, Fk. — Sailing Tours, Pt. v.: West Coast of Scotland, etc. *ut* **I** § 150
LYNAM, C. C. — Log of the 'Blue Dragon'; ill. — [1892–1904] 6/ *n.* r 8° Bullen 07
YOUNG, Archib. — Summer Sailings, by an Old Yachtsman; ill. — 10/6 *n.* 8° Douglas, *Edin.* 99
Voyages round the coast of Scotland and to the Islands; Orkneys and Shetlands, etc. Well illustrated.
*Highlands:* SMITH (W.) [art.] Highlands and Islands of Scotland: 40 col. pl., w. l'rpr. A. R. Hope Moncrieff — [$3·50 *n.* Macmillan, *N.Y.*] 7/6 *n.* sq 8° Black 06

**Scotsmen Abroad** —*v. also* **E** § 20, *s.v.* Irish Abroad (Scotch-Irish Soc. of America)
BASKERVILLE, Beatr. [ed.] — Papers rel. to the Scots in Poland — 8° Scot. Hist. Soc. *in prep.*
BURTON, Dr J. Hill — The Scot Abroad—*ut* **F** § 35
CAMPBELL, Dr Wilf. — The Scotsman in Canada, 2 vols.; ill. — 8° Musson, *Toronto* 11
FISCHER, Th. A. — The Scots in Germany; ports. — 12/6 *n.* r 8° Schulze, *Edin.* 02
,, — Scots in Eastern and Western Prussia; ports. — 15/ *n.* 8° Schulze, *Edin.* 03
,, — The Scots in Sweden, ed. Dr J. Kirkpatrick — 15/ 8° Schulze, *Edin.* 08
GIBBON, J. M. — Scots in Canada: fr. earliest days to pres. times; ill. — 1/ *n.* c 8° Paul 11
HANNA, C. A. — The Scotch-Irish, or the Scot in N. Britain, 2 v. $10 *n.* (42/ *n.*) 8° Putnam 02
**Taverns:** KEMPT (Rob.) Convivial Caledonia: inns and taverns of Scotland — 2/6 c 8° Chapman 93

---

**Aberdeenshire** —*for* Place-names *v.* **K** § 120
*Bibliography:* JOHNSTONE (K.) Bibliogr. of Shires of Aberd., Banff, Kincardine 4° N. Spaldg. Club, *in prep.*
ROBERTSON, A. W. — Hand-List of Bibliogr. of Shires of Aberd., Banff, and Kincardine — 2/6 8° New Spald. Club 93
ALLARDYCE, Dr Jas. [ed.] —*in his* Hist. Papers rel. to Jacobite Period [1699–1750], 2 v.—*ut* **F** § 39
LITTLEJOHN, D. [ed.] Records of Sheriff Ct. of Aberdeenshire, v. i–iii [to 1660] 4° New Spalding Club 04–7
ROBERTSON, Jos. — Collns. for a Hist. of Aberdeensh. & Banff, 3 vols. — 4° Spalding Club 43–57
,, + GRUBB (Dr G.) Illns. of Topogr. & Antiqs. of Aberd. & Banff, 4 v. — 4° Spalding Club 47–69
SMITH, Alex. — New History of Aberdeenshire, 2 vols. — 21/ 8° *Aberdeen* 75
SPALDING CLUB: Miscellany, ed. Dr Jno. Stuart, 5 vols. — 4° Spalding Club 41–52
WATT, Wm. — History of Aberdeen and Banff — 7/6 c 8° Blackwood 00
[County Histories of Scotland.] One of the best volumes in the series.

*Aberdeen:* ANDERSON (P. J.) [ed.] Charters & Writs ill. Hist. of Burgh of Ab. 21/ 4° Univ. Pr., *Aberd.* 90
COOPER, Jas. [ed.] Cartularium Eccl. S. Nicholai Aberd., 2 v. [1340–1574] ea. 10/6 4° N. Spald. Cl. 88–92
GEDDES (W. D.) + DUGUID (P.) [eds.] Lacunar Basilicæ S. Macarii Aberd. *o.p.* [*pb.* 21/] 4° N. Spald. Cl. 88
GORDON, J. — Abredoniæ Utriusque Descriptio, ed. Cosmo Innes [17th cent.] 4° Spalding Club 42
MASSON, Prf. Dav. —*in his* Recollections of Three Cities, *ut sup.*, *s.v.* Topography, etc.
MUNRO, Alex. M. — Old Landmarks of Aberdeen [w. 28 sks. of old bldgs.] 15/ s 4° Wyllie, *Aberdeen* 86
,, — Records of Old Aberdeen, 2 v.; 10 pl. [1157–1891] ea. 10/6 4° N. Spalding Club 99–09

NEW SPALDING CLUB : Miscellany, vol. i, *o.p.* ; vol. ii 10/6 *n.* 4° New Spalding Club 90–08
Vol. i : *Register of Burgesses of Guild and Trade of Burgh. of Aberd.* 1399–1631, ed. A. M. MUNRO : *Inventories of Eccl. Records of N.E Scotl.*, ed. P. J. ANDERSON. ii : *Fiars Prices in Ab'shire fr.* 1603, by D. LITTLEJOHN ; Baptismal Regs. of St Paul's Ep. Chapel, 1720–93, ed. A. E. SMITH ; *Reg. of Burgesses* (cont. fr. vol. i), 1631–1700.

Registrum Episcopatus Aberdonensis, 2 vols. [1062–1560] 4° Spalding Club 45

ROBBIE, Wm. Aberdeen : its trad. & history ; 12 ill. & map of 1746 7/6 *n.* 8° Wyllie, *Aberdeen* 93

Selections fr. Records of Kirk Sessn., Presbytery, & Synod of Aberdeen [1562–1681] 4° Spalding Club 46

STUART, Dr Jno. [ed.] Records of Aberdeen 4° Spalding Club

,, [ed.] Extrs. fr. Council Register of Aberd., 2 v. [1398–1625] 4° Spalding Club 44–8

*Guilds* —*v.* **D** § 120 (BAIN ; BULLOCH)

*Street-names :* FRASER (G. M.) Aberd. Street Names : hist., meangs., assocns. 3/6 *n.* cr 8° Smith, *Aberdeen* 11

*Aberdour ; Inchcombe :* ROSS (Dr Wm.) Aberdour and Inchcombe : parish and monastery 6/ c 8° Douglas, *Edin.* 85
Contains a vivid descrn. of the past life of the Scottish people, ecclesiastical and social.

*Aboyne :* HUNTLY (C., Marq. of) [ed.] Records of Aboyne ; 11 pl. [1230–1681] 21/ 4° New Spaldg. Club 94

*Alford :* BELL (T.) [ed.] Records of Meetg. of the Exercise of Alford [1662–88] 4° N. Spalding Club 97

*Balmoral :* LINDSAY (Patricia) Recollections of a Royal Parish 7/6 *n.* 8° Murray 02
Pleasant notes on Queen VICTORIA's life at Balmoral, and the associations of the place.

VICTORIA, Qu. Leaves fr. Journal of our Life in Highlands [1848–61] *o.p.* c 8° Smith & Elder [68]

,, More Leaves fr. Jl. of Life in Highlands [1862–82] *o.p.* c 8° Smith & Elder [84]

*Banchory-Devenick :* ANDERSON (J. A.) Hist. of Parish of Banchory-Devenick ; pl. 10/6 p 4° Grant, *Edin.* 90

*Dee Valley :* MACKINTOSH (Jno.) Hist. of Valley of the Dee c 8° *Aberdeen* 95

*Deer :* Book of Deer, ed. Dr Jno. Stuart 4° Spalding Club 69

*Invercauld :* MICHIE (Rev. J. G.) [ed.] Records of Invercauld ; 9 pl. [1547–1828] 10/6 4° N. Spaldg. Cl. 01

*Inverurie ; Garioch :* DAVIDSON (J.) Inverurie and Earldom of Garioch 78

MORISON, A. [ed.] Blackhalls, Coroners, etc., of the Garioch 05

*Kintore :* WATT (A.) Early History of Kintore *o.p.* 8° 65

*Peterhead :* TAYLOR (W. L.) Peterhead Literature [a good compilation] 8° Scrogie, *Peterhead*

*Strathbogie :* Extracts fr. Presbytery Bk. of Strathbogie [1631–54] 4° Spalding Club 43

**Argyllshire** —*for* Place-names, *v.* **K** § 120

CAMPBELL, L'd Arch. Records of Argyll : legends, etc. 63/ 4° Blackwood 85

CRAVEN, Dr J. B. [ed.] Recds. of Diocese of Argyll & Isles [1560–1860] 10/6 l 8° Peace, *Kirkwall* 07

GILLIES, P. H. Netherlorn : Argyllshire & its neighbourhood ; 72 ill. 12/6 *n.* 4° Virtue 09

*Loch Etive :* SMITH (R. A.) Loch Etive, and the Sons of Uisnach ; ill., *o.p.* 8° Gardner, *Paisley* [79] 85

*Lorne :* BUCHANAN (R. W.) The Land of Lorne—*v.* Hebrides, *inf.*

**Ayrshire**

AYR & GALLOWAY ARCHÆOL. ASSOC. : Archæol. & Histor. Collns., v. i–x 4° Ayr & Gall. Arch. Ass. 78–99

BRYDEN, Rob. [art.] 22 Etchings of Ayrshire Castles ; w. descrns. f° *priv. prin.* 95

DOUGALL, C. S. The Burns Country ; ill. [$2 Macmillan, *N.Y.*] 6/ 8° Black 04

HEWAT, Rev. Kirkwood In the Olden Times [Ayrsh. places & worthies] 4/ *n.* c 8° Gardner, *Paisley* 98

PATERSON, Jas. Hist. of Counties of Ayr and Wigton, 5 v. ; ill. 28/ c 8° Morison, *Glas.* [47] 63

ROBERTSON, Wm. Ayrshire : its history & historic families, 2 v. 10/ 8° Dunlop, *Kilmarnock* 09

*Ayr :* Charters of Roy. Burgh of Ayr 4° Ayrsh. & Gall. Arch. Ass. 83

Charters of the Friar Preachers of Ayr 4° Ayrsh. & Gall. Arch. Ass. 81

*Ch. of St John Bapt. :* PATERSON (J.) [ed.] Obit Bk. of Ch. of St J. Bapt. *o.p.* 4° *Edinburgh* 48

*Crosraguel Abbey :* Charters of Abb. of Crosraguel, 2 v. [1225–1656] 4° Ayrsh. & G. Arch. Ass. 86

*Irvine :* Muniments of Roy. Burgh of Irvine, 2 vols. 4° Ayrsh. & G. Arch. Ass. 90–1

*Kilmarnock :* MACKAY (Arch.) Hist. of Kilmarnock ; w. biographical notices *o.p.* 8° *Kilmarnock* [48] 64

*Old Cumnock :* WARRICK (Rev. J.) Hist. of Old Cumnock ; 17 ill. [good, but too long] 7/6 *n.* 4° Gardner, *Paisley* 99

**Banffshire** —*v. also sup., s.v.* Aberdeenshire, *and inf., s.v.* Moray

*Banff :* CRAMOND (Dr Wm.) Annals of Banff, 2 vols. ; 20 pl. *o.p.* 4° New Spalding Club 91–3

*Cairngorm Mtns. ; Grampians :* BURTON (J. Hill) Cairngorm Mountains *o.p.* [*pb.* 3/6] c 8° Blackwood 64

MACNAIR, P. Geology & Scenery of the Grampians and Valley of Strathmore, 2 vols. ; ill. 21/ *n.* 8° MacLehose, *Glasgow* 08

**Berwickshire:** *Coldstream:* Chartulary of Priory of Coldstream 8° 79

*Eyemouth:* McIVER (D.) An Old-Time Fishing Town; ill. 5/ *n.* 8° McKelvie, *Greenock* 07

*Lauderdale:* THOMSON (A.) Lauder and Lauderdale; ill. 12/6 8° Craighead, *Galashiels* 03

**Border**

EYRE-TODD, Geo. By-ways on the Scottish Border; 12 ill. 4/6 *n.* s 4° Lewis, *Selkirk* [93] 94
An attractive acc. of pedestr. tour: St Mary's Loch, Yarrow, Yetholm, and Flodden.

GRAHAM, Jno. Condition of the Border at the Union 2/6 *n.* c 8° Routledge [ ] 09

SCOTT, Sir Walt. Border Antiquities, 2 vols. *o.p.* 4° 14–7

„ Essay on Border Antiquities—*in* Prose Works, vol. ii, ed. 1878 [*ut* **K** § 89]

*'Peel':* NEILSON (G.) Peel, its Meaning and Derivation 4/ *n.* s 4° Johnston, *Edin.* 96
An inquiry into the early hist. of this term now appl. to many border-towns.

*Repentance Tower:* NEILSON (G.) Repentance Tower and its Tradition 2/6 *n.* s 4° Johnston, *Edin.* 96
Furnishes a new and well-supported explan. of this Border mystery, givg. good acc. of romantic story of 'John the Reif'.

**Buteshire**

*Arran* [island]

*BALFOUR, J. A. [ed.] The Book of Arran: Archæology; ill. 21/ *n.* 4° Hopkins, *Glasgow* 10
*Buildg. up of the Isld.* (Sir A. GEIKIE); *Sepulchr. Remains* (Prf. T. H. BRYCE), and other papers by specialists.

LANDSBOROUGH, Rev. D. Arran: topogr., nat. hist., & antiquities; ill. *o.p.* [*pb.* 7/6] c 8° Houlston 75

*Bute (Isle of):* HEWISON (Rev. J. K.) Isle of Bute in Olden Time, 2 v.; ill. 30/ *n.* 4° Blackwood 93–7
Desultory, and not well wr. Incls. a cert. amt. of folklore, place-etymol., etc. Vol. i deals w. Celtic Saints and Heroes.

**Caithness:** HORNE (Jno.) County of Caithness; ill. [comprehensive] 7/6 *n.* 8° Rae, *Wick* 07

**Dumbartonshire:** IRVING (Jos.) Hist. of Dumbartonshire: civil, eccles., territ. *o.p.* 4° *Dumbarton* [57] 60

„ Book of Dumbartonshire: survey of country, 3 v.; ill. 126/ 4° Johnston, *Ed.* 79–80

*Dumbarton:* MACLEOD, Don. [ed.] Dumbarton, Ancient and Modern; ill. 21/ i 4° Bennett, *Dumbarton* 93

*Garelochside:* MAUGHAN (W. C.) Annals of Garelochside; ill. 7/6 4° Gardner, *Paisley* 97
Parishes of Row, Rosneath, and Cairdross: expansn. of his *Rosneath, Past and Pres.* [1893]. Excellent example of parish hist.

*Kilpatrick:* BROWN (Jno.) Parish of West K. and of Ch. in East In. 10/6 *n.* 8° Smith, *Glasg.* 93

**Dumfriesshire:** GRAY (Pet.) Dumfriesshire Illustrated, Pt. i: Nithsdale 7/6 4° Maxwell, *Dumfries* 94

MAXWELL, Sir H. E. Hist. of Dumfries and Galloway [Co. Hists. of Sc.] 7/6 *n.* 8° Blackwood 96

*Dumfries:* MACDOWALL (W.) Hist. of Burgh of Dumfries; col. ill. *o.p.* [*pb.* 14/] 8° *Edinburgh* [67] 73

*Nithsdale:* PATERSON (Jas.) [art.] Nithsdale: photogravs. of wr-clr. dwgs. 42/ *n.* f° MacLehose, *Glasgow* 94

*Sanquhar:* BROWN (Jas.) History of Sanquhar *o.p.* 4° Anderson, *Dumfries* 91
Tells much that is curious of old-world life, w. Covenanting memories of town, and brief acc. of 'Admirable Crichton'.

**East Lothian (Haddingtonshire):** GREEN (C. E.) East Lothian; 186 ill. 10/ *n.* r 8° Green, *Edin.* 07

*Auldhame Tyninghame & Whitekirk:* WADDELL (P. H.) An Old Kirk Chronicle 20/ *n.* r 8° Blackwood 94

**Edinburghshire:** *Edinburgh*

BONE, Jas. Edinburgh Revisited; ill. and 16 collotypes 21/ *n.* r 8° Sidgwick 11

CHAMBERS, Dr Rob. Traditions of Edinburgh 2/6 c 8° Chambers [25] 89

FOTHERGILL, G. A. Stones & Curiosities of Edinb. & Nbrhd., Pts. i–ii; ill. Orr, *Edin.* –11 *in prg.*

FYFE, W. T. Edinburgh under Sir Walter Scott; ill. 10/6 *n.* 8° Constable 06

GEDDIE, J. Romantic Edinburgh; ill. [$2·50 Dutton, *N.Y.*] 3/6 c 8° Sands 00

GILLIES, J. B. Edinburgh Past & Present; w. notes Dr Geikie; ill. 10/6 4° Oliphant, *Edin.* 86

GRANT, Jas. Old and New Edinburgh, 2 vols.; 600 ill. *o.p.* [*pb.* 18/] 4° Cassell 80–3

MASSON, Prf. Dav. Edinburgh Sketches and Memories [$1·75 Macmillan, *N.Y.*] 10/6 8° Black 92

„ —*in his* Recollections of Two Cities, *ut sup.*

OLIPHANT, Mrs. Royal Edinburgh: saints, kgs., prophs., poets; ill. 10/6 ($3) c 8° Macmillan [90] 91
A good popular bk.—in 4 Pts. (1) *Margaret of Scotl.*, (2) *Stewards of Scotl.* [Jas. i–v], (3) *Time of Prophets*, (4) *Modern City.*

REID, Jno. New Lights on Old Edinburgh 3/6 c 8° Douglas, *Edin.* 95
Conts. a good deal of curious matter, based on Town Co. munimts., title-deeds, etc. Mainly 18th cent.

SMEATON, Oliphant Story of Edinburgh; ill.
[Mediæv. Towns; $1·75 *n.* Dutton, *N.Y.*] 4/6 *n.* c 8° Dent [04] 05

STEVENSON, R. L. Edinburgh: etchgs. by S. Bough & W. E. Lockhart 18/ r 4° Seeley 79

„ Edinburgh: picturesque notes 6/ c 8°; 2/ *n.* 12° Seeley [79] 05
$1·40 *n.* Scribner, *N.Y.* The same text as 1879 edn., with reduced illustrations.

„ The same; 16 pl. T. H. Hamilton Crawford, etc. 6/ c 8° Seeley [79] 08; 04

WILLIAMSON, M. G. Edinburgh: hist. & topogr.; ill. [Ancient Cities] 4/6 *n.* c 8° Methuen 06

WILSON, Prf. D. Memorials of Edinb. in Olden Time, 2 v.; pl. & ill. *o.p.* [*pb.* 25/] 4° Black [48] 91

„ Reminiscences of Old Edinburgh, 2 vols. *o.p.* [*pb.* 15/] p 8° Douglas, *Edin.* 78

*Anthology:* HYATT (A. H.) [ed.] The Charm of Edinburgh 2/ *n.* 12° Chatto 08
*Buildings; Scenery:* FULLEYLOVE (J.) [art.] Edinburgh: 21 col. pl., w. l'rpr. Rosaline Masson [$3 *n.* Macmillan, *N.Y.*] 7/6 *n.* sq 8° Black 05
HOME, Bruce T. [artist] Old Houses in Edinburgh, 2 Ser. in portf° 25/ *n.* f° W. J. Hay, *Edin.* 07
Architectural drawings of a fine quality, drawn w. great pains and affection.
Municipal Buildings of Edinburgh; ill. [historical: 1145–1895] *Edinburgh* 95
STEVENSON, T. G. [ed.] Edinburgh in Olden Time: 63 pl., w. text 94/6 l f° T. G. Stevenson, *Edin.*
Facs. reprodns. of a ser. of orig. dwgs. coll. by Rev. Jno. SIME and bequeathed to Jas. Gillespie's Hospital by his widow. Old streets, bldgs., suburbs, Leith, etc., betw. yrs. 1717–1828.
*Literary Associations:* COCHRANE (R.) Pentland Walks: their assocns. 1/6 *n.* c 8° Elliot, *Edin.* 08
HARRISON, W. Memorable Edinburgh Houses; 38 ill. 3/6 c 8° Oliphant, *Edin.* 93
HUTTON, Laur. Literary Landmarks of Edinburgh; ill. $1 c 8° Harper, *N.Y.* 91
*Worthies:* CROMBIE (B. W.) [art.] Modern Athenians; w. notes W. S. Douglas *o.p.* 4° *Edinburgh* 82
97 col. ports. of Edinb. citizens: 1837–47. Forms good suppl. to KAY's *Port. and Caric. Etchgs.*, 2 v. 4° *Edin.* 37–8, repr. 2 v. 12/ c 8° *Edin.* 86.
***Fountainhall:*** LAUDER (Sir J.) Jl. of Foreign Tour [1665–6]; and other jls., ed. D. Crawford 8° Scot. Hist. Soc. 00
*Inveresk; Musselburgh:* LANGHORNE (Rev. W. H.) Remins. conn. w. Inveresk and Musselburgh 7/6 8° Douglas, *Edin.* 93
*Leith:* IRONS (J. C.) Leith and its Antiquities, 2 vols.; ill. 21/ 4° Morrison & Gibb, *Ed.* 98
*Newbattle Abbey:* INNES (C.) [ed.] Registrum S. Marie de Neubotle 4° Bannatyne Club 49
***Penicuik:*** CLERK (Sir Jno.) Memoirs, ed. J. M. Gray [fr. his jls. 1676–1755] 8° Scot. Hist. Soc. 91
***Ravelston:*** FOULIS (Sir Jno.) Account Book, ed. Rev. A. W. C. Hallen [1671–1707] 8° Scot. Hist. Soc. 93

**Elginshire** —*v. infra, s.v.* Moray

**Fifeshire:** GEDDIE (J.) The Fringes of Fife; ill. Louis Wéierter 5/ c 8° Douglas, *Edin.* 94
A description of a walking-tour fr. Kincardine to St Andrews, indicg. more attractive feats. and hist. assocns. of ea. town and village.
MACKAY, Dr Æneas J. G. Sketch of History of Fife and Kinross [a good bk.] 6/ c 8° Blackwood 90
* ,, A History of Fife and Kinross; 2 maps [Co. Hists. of Scotld.] 7/6 *n.* 8° Blackwood 96
An excellent popular work on hist., biogr., agric., industrs., custs., ballads, etc., incorporatg. his Scottish *Proverbs chiefly of Fife Origin.*
MILLAR, A. H. Fife, Pictorial & Historical, 2 v.; ill. [poor] 42/ *n.* l 8° Westwood, *Cupar-Fife* 95
An industrious and exhaustive acc., hist., topogr., and industrial, inclg. every parish (64 in all). With excursuses.
TAYLOR, J. W. Historical Antiquities of Fife, 2 v. [chfly. ecclesiastical] 8° *Edinburgh* [ ] 75
WOOD, Rev. Walt. East Neuk of Fife: hist. & antiq., Rev. J. Wood Brown 6/ c 8° Douglas, *Ed.* [62] 87
*Churches:* WALKER (J. R.) [art.] Pre-Reformn. Churches of Fife: 127 pl. 42/ f° *Edinburgh* 95
Ser. of photo-lithogr. dwgs. to scale of chs., porches, windows, slabs, plate, carvgs., etc.: text by Dr J. Anderson.
*Balmerino:* AITKEN (G. S.) Abbeys of Ardbroath, Balm., Lindores *o.p.* 4° *Dundee* 84
CAMPBELL, Dr Jas. Balmerino and its Abbey; map and 41 ill. 25/ *n.* 8° Blackwood [68] 00
*Crail:* BEVERIDGE (Erskine) The Churchyard Memorial of Crail; ill. 4° *pr. pr.* (Constable, *Ed.*) 93
Taking the tombstones of the old churchyd. as its text, gives full acc. of families and antiqs. of district.
*Dunfermline:* CHALMERS (Pet.) Histor. & Statist. Acc. of Dumf., 2 v. *o.p.* [*pb.* 26/] 8° Blackwood 44–59
GEDDES, Prf. Patr. City Development—*ut* **D** § 124
HENDERSON, E. Annals of Dunfermline and Vicinity: 1069–1878; ill. 21/ 4° *Glasgow* 79
INNES, Cosmo [ed.] Registrum de Dunfermelyn 4° Bannatyne Club 42
STEWART, Alex. Reminiscences of Dunfermline 60 Yrs. Ago 5/ c 8° *Edinburgh* 86
*Lindores Abbey* —*v. also* Balmerino, *sup.*, *s.n.* AITKEN
DOWDEN, Bp [ed.] Chartulary of Abbey of Lindores, 1195–1479; ill. 8° Scot. Hist. Soc. 03
Quite distinct from the *Chartulary of Lindores*, Abbotsford Club, 1841, which is not a chartulary at all.
LAING, Alex. Lindores Abbey and its Burgh of Newburgh; 23 ill. 21/ sq 8° *Edinburgh* 76
*St Andrews* —*v. also* **A** § 62 (BOYD, Dr A. K. H.)
FLEMING, D. H. [ed.] Register of the Kirk-Session, 2 Pts [1559–1600] 8° Scot. Hist. Soc. 88–9
KERR, D. R. St Andrews in 1645–46 [Prize Essay] 2/6 c 8° Blackwood 95
Period is that of struggle betw. Presb. rebels and Royalists, who had flocked to standard of CHAS. I, when MONTROSE's career of victory was brot. to close at Philiphaugh.
LANG, Andr. St Andrews; 32 ill. [hist. of town] 15/ *n.* 8° Longman 93
LYON, C. J. History of St Andrews, 2 vols. *o.p.* [*pb.* 28/] 8° *Edinburgh* 43

**Forfarshire**

INGLIS, J. Oor Ain Folk: Manse life in Mearns 6/ c 8° Douglas, *Edin.* 94
JERVISE, A. History and Traditions of the Land of Lindsays in Angus and Mearns, ed. Rev. J. Gammack 14/ 8° Douglas, *Edin.* [53] 82
,, Memls. of Angus and the Mearns, ed. Rev. J. Gammack, 2 v.; etchgs. 28/ 8° Douglas, *Edin.* [61] 85
Acc. of castles and towns of Angus (anc. name of Forfarsh.) and the Mearns (anc. name of Kincardineshire) visited by EDW. I, and of Barons, Clergy, etc., who swore fealty to England in 1291–6.

WARDEN, A. J. History of Angus: land and people, 5 v.; ill. 57/6 s 4° *Dundee* 81

*Arbroath:* HAY (Geo.) History of Arbroath 10/6 4° Buncle, *Arbroath* [76] 99

*Dundee:* Charters, etc., of Dundee: hosp. & Johnston's bequest [1292–1880] 4° *Dundee* 80

KIDD (Wm.) + MILLER (T. Y.) Dundee, Past and Present; 170 pl. 12/6 *n.* 4° Kidd, *Dundee* 10

LAMB, A. C. Dundee: quaint & historic buildings; maps & 60 pl. 126/ atl 4° Petrie, *Dundee* 95
One of the most sumptuous of mod. topogr. pubns., with magnificent reprodns. of Mat. PARIS' Map of Britain [*c.* 1250] and another 13 cent. map (both of wh. place Dundee on Firth of Forth). V. numer. ill. fr. paintgs., dwgs., photos, etc., reprod. by Wm. GIBB. Only 357 printed. Pb. for Ed. Bibliogr. Soc.

MAXWELL, A. History of Old Dundee [fr. contemp. annals] 21/ 4° Douglas, *Edin.* 84

" Old Dundee: ecclesiastical, burghal and social 12/6 4° Kidd, *Dundee* 91
A kind of belated predecessor of above, dealg. w. the 40 yrs. prior, as that did with the century subseq. to the Reformn. Based throughout on contemp. and unpub. documts., throwg. much light on pre-Reformn. Scotld., and formg. a very important contribn. to hist. of anc. Scottish burghs.

THOMSON, Jas. History of Dundee, ed. J. Maclaren; map & ill. *o.p.* 8° *Dundee* [47] 74

WEDDERBURNE, D. Compt Buik of: 1587–1630, ed. A. H. Millar—*ut* **D** § 117*

*Glamis Castle:* STRATHMORE (Earl of) [ed.] Book of Record, etc. ed. A. H. Millar [1684–9] 8° Scot.Hist.Soc. 90

*Monifieth:* MALCOLM (J.) Parish of Monifieth in Anc. and Mod. Times; ill. 7/6 *n.* 8° Green, *Edin.* 10

*Strathmore:* GUTHRIE (J. C.) The Vale of Strathmore *o.p.* [*pb.* 7/6] c 8° *Edinburgh* 75

MACNAIR, P. Geol. & Scenery of Grampns. & Vall. of Strathm., 2 v.—*ut sup.*, *s.v.* Banffshire

**Haddingtonshire** —*v.* East Lothian, *sup.*

**Hebrides and Western Islands**

ADAMNAN, Bp [624–704] —*in his* Life of St Columba, *ut* **A** § 71
Affords a wonderful picture of life in Hebrides in 9 cent. Edited w. minute knowledge and care.

BOSWELL, Jas. [1740–95] Journal of a Tour [1773] in the Hebrides w. Dr Johnson—*v.* **K** § 24

BUCHANAN, Rob. W. The Hebrid Isles 6/ c 8° Chatto [71] 83
Wandergs. in land of Lorne and Outer Hebrides. 1st edn. (1871) pubd. *sub tit. The Land of Lorne.*

GOODRICH-FREER, [Miss] A. The Outer Isles; ill. 5/ *n.* 8° Constable [02]
Travels in the Hebrides, contg. much informn. on their inhabs., flora, fauna, folk-lore, and ceilidhs.

GREGORY, Donald History of Western Highlds. and Isles of Scotl.—*ut sup.*, *s.v.* Highlands

HILL, Dr G. Birkbeck Footsteps of Dr Johnston 63/ 4° Low 90

JOHNSON, Dr Sam. [1709–84] Journey to the Western Islands [in 1773] 3/ c 8° Morison, *Glasg.* [1776] 76
A different work from BOSWELL's account, *ut sup.*

MACKENZIE, W. C. History of the Outer Hebrides 12/6 *n.* 8° Gardner, *Paisley* 03

MARTIN, Martin Description of Western Islands of Scotld. [facs. repr.] 12/6 8° Morison, *Glasg.* [1695] 84

MONRO, Sir Don. Descrn. of Western Islands of Scotland [facs. repr.] 5/ 8° Morison, *Glasgow* [1549] 82

PENNELL, Jos. + Eliz. R. Our Journey to the Hebrides; 43 ill. 7/6 c 8° Unwin 90

*Crofters* —*v. also* **D** § 119

CAMPBELL, L'd Arch. ['DALRIAD'] The Crofter in History 2/ c 8°

MACKENZIE, Alex. History of the Highland Clearances 7/6 c 8° Mackenzie, *Inverness* 83
Conts. reprs. of D. MACLEOD's *Gloomy Memories of Highlds., Isle of Skye in* 1882, a Rept. of trial of Braes and Glendale crofters.

*St Kilda:* CONNELL (R.) St Kilda and the St Kildians 2/6 c 8° Morison, *Glasgow* 87

HEATHCOTE, Norman St Kilda; 80 ill. 10/6 *n.* ($3·50) 8° Longman 00
A good and full account of the island's history, flora, fauna, etc.

KEARTON, R. With Nature and a Camera—*ut* **H** § 76

SANDS, J. Out of the World: life in St Kilda 3/6 c 8° *Edinburgh* [76] 77

SETON, Geo. St Kilda, Past and Present; 12 ill. 15/ 4° Blackwood 78

*Skye, Island of* —*for* Climbing *v.* **I** § 165

MACCULLOCH, Can. J. A Misty Isle of Skye [scenery, people, hist.] 2/6 *n.* c 8° Oliphant, *Edin.* [05] 10

MACLEOD, Norman Reminiscences of a Highland Parish *o.p.* [*pb.* 6/] c 8° Strahan [67] 68

SMITH, Alex. A Summer in Skye [New Univ. Lib.; 50 c. Dutton, *N.Y.*] 1/ *n.* pott 8° Routledge [65] 07

*Staffa; Iona; Fingal's Cave:* FERGUSON (Malc.) Trip. fr. Callander to Staffa & Iona *o.p.* c 8° *Dundee* [ ] 94

MACLEAN, J. P. Hist., Archæol. & Geogr. Exam. of Fingal's Cave; ill. 75 c. 8° Clarke, *Cincinnati* 91
Rewritten and enlarged fr. the original *Report* made to Smithsonian Institution in 1887.

MACMILLAN, A. Iona: hist., antiqs., carved houses 2/6 8° Houlston 90

TRENHOLME, Rev. E. C. The Story of Iona; 40 pl. 8/6 *n.* c 8° Douglas, *Edin.* 09

**Inverness-shire**

ANDERSON, L. H. Inverness before Railways *o.p.* c 8° 85

LEES, Dr J. Cameron History of Inverness; maps [Co. Hists. of Scotl.] 7/6 *n.* 8° Blackwood 97

MACPHERSON, A. Glimpses of Church & Social Life in H'lds. in Olden Times 25/ 1 8° Blackwood 93
An *omnium gatherum* of folklore and other odds and ends, gleaned fr. trustworthy sources, conn. chfly. w. lordship of Badenoch.

NOBLE, Jno. [ed.] Miscellanea Invernessiana, ed. Jno. Whyte [misc. pprs.] 6/ 8° Mackay, *Stirling* 03

*Beauly Priory:* BATTEN (E. C.) [ed.] Charters of Priory of Beauly, etc. [1231–1570] 8° Grampian Club 77

*Inverness:* MACKAY (W.) [eds.] Records of Presbyteries of Inv. and Dingwall 8° Scot. Hist. Soc. 96

MACKAY (W.) + BOYD (H. C.) [eds.] Selns. fr. Records of Inver., v. i N. Spalding Club, *Aberdeen in prep.*

*Lochaber:* DRUMMOND (N. W.) Loyal Lochaber 21/ 8° Morison, *Glasgow* 98

A very mixed production: informn. about the district, the clans assoc. w. it, its hist., etc.

KILGOUR, W. T. Lochaber in War and Peace 7/6 *n.* 8° Gardner, *Paisley* 08

Histor. incidents, legends, tradns., folklore, topography, and scenic beauties.

*Urquhart & Glenmoriston:* MACKAY (Wm.) Urquhart & Glenmoriston 21/ 8° N. Cos. Prtg. Co., *Inverness* 94

History, tradns., folklore, industr., social, the anc. royal Castle, Culloden, etc.

**Kincardineshire** —*v. sup., s.v.* Forfarshire (JERVISE)

*Urie:* BARRON (D. G.) [ed.] Court Book of Urie [1604–1747] 8° Scot. Hist. Soc. 92

**Kinross-shire:** MACKAY (Dr Œ. J. G.) Fife and Kinross—*ut sup., s.v.* Fifeshire

**Kirkcudbrightshire**

*Galloway* —*v. also Ayrshire, sup.*

AGNEW, Sir Andr. Hereditary Sheriffs of Galloway, 2 v.; ill. [to 1792] 25/ 8° Douglas, *Edin.* [64] 93

Their forbears and friends, courts and customs of their times, w. notes on early hist., eccl. legends, place-names, etc.

HARPER, M. McL. Rambles in Galloway; map and 70 ill. 6/ *n.* 8° Fraser, *Dalbeattie* [76] 96

MACKENZIE, W. History of Galloway, 2 vols. *o.p.* [*pb.* 12/] c 8° Nicholson 41

MCKERLIE, P. H. History of Lands & Owners in Galloway, 5 v.; ill. 75/ c 8° Paterson, *Edin.* 70–9

„ Galloway in Ancient and Modern Times 7/6 c 8° Blackwood 91

Contains some valuable genealogical and other material, but it is very badly sifted and arranged.

MAXWELL, Sir Herb. E. History of Dumfries and Galloway—*ut sup., s.v.* Dumfriesshire

„ Studies in the Topography of Galloway 14/ 8° *Edinburgh* 87

*Churches:* MACGIBBON (D.) + ROSS (T.) Five Great Churches of Galloway 99

*Gypsies* —*v.* **F** § 76

*Scenery:* FAED (J., jun.) [art.] Galloway; 24 col. pl.; w. l'rpr. J. M. Sloan [$2 *n.* Macmillan, *N.Y.*] 6/ *n.* sq 8° Black

*Lincluden:* MCDOWALL (W.) Chronicles of Lincluden as Abbey and College; pl. *o.p.* 4° Black 86

**Lanarkshire**

IRVING (G. V.) + MURRAY (A.) The Upper Ward of Lanarkshire, 3 vols. *o.p.* [*pb.* 63/] 8° J. R. Smith 64

*Clyde (The)* —*v. sup., s.v.* Rivers

*Glasgow* —*for* Cathedral *v.* **I** § 120

BELL, Dugald Among the Rocks round Glasgow; col. map 4/ c 8° MacLehose *Glasgow* [81] 85

BELL (Sir J.) + PATON (J.) Glasgow; its Municipal Organization and Administration—*ut* **D** § 124

MACGEORGE, A. Old Glasgow, fr. Roman Occupn. to 18th Cent.; ill. 10/6 r 8° Blackie [80] 88

MACGEORGE, Geo. Hist. of Glasgow fr. Earliest Period to Pres. Time; 36 ill. 12/6 8° Morison, *Glasgow* 81

Memoirs and Portraits of One Hundred Glasgow Men, 2 vols. 147/ 4° MacLehose, *Glasg.* 86

MILLAR, A. H. Quaint Bits of Old Glasgow; 70 ill. D. Small 63/ i 4° Bryce, *Glasgow* 87

MUIR, J. H. Glasgow in 1901; ill. 3/6 *n.* c 8° Hodge, *Glasgow* 01

An excellent description and history, social and industrial.

Old County Houses of Old Glasgow Gentry: 100 photos. *o.p.* [*pb.* 105/] 4° MacLehose, *Gl.* [70] 78

RENWICK, Rob. [ed.] Abstrs. of Protocols of Town-Clerks of Glasgow, 11 v. 58/6 4° Carson, *Glasgow* 98 *sqq.*

YOUNG, W. [ed.] Municipal Buildings of Glasgow: 20 collotype pl. 25/ f° Bryce, *Glasgow* 91

*Cathedral:* EYRE-TODD, G. [ed.] Book of Glasgow Cathedral; 118 pl. 21/ 4° Morison, *Glasgow* 98

An excellent wk., full of varied knowl. and sound histor. research. Contribns. by Abp EYRE, Dr J. F. S. GORDON, Dr P. McAdam MUIR, Jas. PATON, A H. MILLAR, J. HONEYMAN, and others.

*Literary Landmarks:* KILPATRICK (J. A.) Literary Landmarks of Glasgow; ill. 7/6 c 8° St Mungo Pr., *Glasgow* 98

*Lanark:* RENWICK, R. [ed.] Extrs. fr. Records of Royal Burgh of Lanark; 3 maps, 2 facss. and 1 pl. r 4° Carson & Nicol, *Glasgow* 94

A large body of first-rate hist. raw-matrl.: extrs. fr. Council minutes 1488–1722, town's royal charters 1227–1646, a *précis* of relative documts. 1150–1719, w. Introd. and gloss. Edr. is Town-Clerk of Glasgow.

*Corstorphine:* SELWAY (G. U.) A Mid-Lothian Village; 70 ill. [village and parish of Corstorphine] *o.p.* s 4° 90

*Craignethan:* HAY (Andr.) Diary, ed. A. G. Reid [1659–60] 8° Scot. Hist. Soc. 01

**Moray** [old geograph. division, incl. Elgin and Nairn, pts. of Invern. and Banff.].

ARCHIBALD, Rev. J. Hist. Episcopate in Columb. Ch. & in Dioc. of Moray 6/ 8° St Giles Prtg. Co., *Ed.* 93

**Bain**, Geo. History of Nairnshire 12/6 8° *Telegraph* Off., *Nairn* 93

**Dunbar**, E. Dunbar [ed.] Social Life in Former Days, chfly. in the Province of Moray, 2 Ser. [letters and family papers] *o.p.* [*pb.* 19/6] 8° Douglas, *Edin.* 65–6

,, [ed.] Documents rel. to Province of Moray [suppl. to above] *o.p.* 8° Douglas, *Edin.* 95

**Harvie-Brown** (J. A.) + **Buckley** (T. E.)—*in their* Fauna of Moray Basin, *ut* **H** § 102
Begins w. an elab. topogr. survey of the district and a descrn. of its phys. features.

**Rampini**, Dr C. Hist. of Moray and Nairn [Co. Hists. of Scotl.] 7/6 *n.* 8° Blackwood 97

**St John**, C. W. G. Notes on Natural History & Sport of Moray; ill. 50/ r 8° Douglas, *Edin.* [63] 85

,, Note-Books: 1846–53, ed. Adm. H. C. St John; ill. 7/6 *n.* r 8° Douglas, *Edin.* 02
A jl. kept by author 60 yrs. ago, dur. stay at Inverenne, Nairn, and Elgin. Descrn. and nat. hist.

**Shaw**, Lachlan Hist. of Prov. of Moray, ed. Rev. J. F. S. Gordon, 3 v. 30/ 8° Morison, *Glasgow* [1775] 82

***Elgin*:** **Cramond** (W.) [ed.] Records of Elgin, 2 v.; 23 pl. [1234–1800] ea. 10/6 4° N. Spalding Club 03–8

**Young**, Rob. Annals of Parish and Burgh of Elgin; ill. [12 cent. to 1876] i 8° *priv. prin.* 79

*Pluscardyn Priory:* Liber Pluscardensis—*in* Historians of Scotland, vols. vii, x, *ut* **F** § 35

**Macphail**, S. R. History of the Religious House of Pluscardyn *o.p.* 4° *Edinburgh* 81

**Orkneys; Shetland**

*Bibliography:* **Cursiter** (J. W.) List of Books & Pamphs. rel. to Ork. & Shetl.; w. notes *o.p.* 8° 95

*Early Accounts:* **Campbell** (Dr Jno.) Acc. of Greatest White-herrg. Fishery in Sc. [Zetld., etc.] 4/6 c 8° Brown, *Edin.* [1750] 85

Faereyinga Saga —*ut* **K** § 234 [*also* Magnus Saga; Orkneyinga Saga, *ut ib.*]

**Gifford**, Thos. Hist. Descrn. of Zetld. Islds. in 1733, ed. T. G. Stevenson 10/6 8° Stevenson, *Edin.* [1786] 79

**Hepburn**, Rev. Thos. Letter fr. Orkney in 1757 [on poverty of Ork. people] 4/6 c 8° Brown, *Ed.* [1757] 85

**Johnstone**, Rev. J. [tr.] Haco's Expedn. agst. Scotld. [1263] [tr. fr. Norweg. acc.] 6/ c 8° Brown, *Ed.* 82

**Low**, Geo. Tour thro' Islds. of Orkn. & Shetld. [1774], ed. J. Anderson; ill. 21/ 8° Peace, *Kirkwall* 79

**Mill**, Rev. Jno. Diary 8° Scot. Hist. Soc. 88
Gives a vivid idea of life in Shetland in 18th cent. Mill was a famous exorcist and a 'character'.

Willcock, Rev. J. A Shetland Minister of 18th Century 2/6 c 8° Oliphant, *Edin.* [97] 00
Copious extrs. fr. the *Diary*, w. informn. fr. other sources filling some gaps in it.

**Ployen** Reminiscences of Shetland, Orkney, & Scotl. [tr.] 3/6 8° Manson, *Lerwick* 96
Record of a visit paid to Scotl. in summer of 1839 by a former Amtmand and Commandant in Faroe Isles.

**Wallace**, Rev. Jas. Descrn. of Isles of Orkney, ed. J. Small; maps, pl., & notes 14/ 8° Brown, *Edin.* [1693] 83

*Recent Accounts; History*

**Burnard**, Fk. [artist] Picturesque Life in Shetld.: 27 pl., w. descr. notes 25/ *n.* r 4° Waterston, *Ed.* 90

**Fea**, Jas. Present State of Orkneys [w. acc. of fishg. at Shetld.] 7/6 c 8° Brown, *Edin.* [1775] 84

**Fergusson**, R. M. Rambles in the Far North 3/ c 8° Gardner, *Paisley* [ ] 84
Contains some interesting information concerning Orkney and its folklore.

**Gorrie**, Dan. Summers and Winters in the Orkneys; ill. 5/ c 8° Peace, *Kirkwall* 76

**Hibbert**, Dr S. Itinerary thro' I. of Shetl.; pl. & geol. map [of value] *o.p.* [*w.* 20/] 8° Constable, *Ed.* 22

**Lynam**, C. C. [ed.] Log of *Blue Dragon II* in Ork. & Sh.: 1909–10; ill. (some col.) 5/ *n.* 4° Sidgwick 11

**Reid**, J. T. Pictures from the Orkney Islands; ill. *o.p.* [*pb.* 25/] 4° Douglas, *Edin.* 81

,, Art Rambles in Shetland; ill. *o.p.* [*pb.* 25/] r 8° Douglas, *Edin.* 69

**Russell**, Rev. Jno. Three Years in Shetland [a gd. general acc.] 3/6 c 8° Gardner, *Paisley* 87

**Spence**, Cath. S. Earl Rögnuald and his Forebears 3/6 *n.* c 8° Unwin 96
A picturesque acc. (fr. the sagas), orig. wr. for children, of doings of Norsemen in Orkney and Shetland.

**Tudor**, J. R. ['Old Wick' of *Field*] Orkneys & Shetland: past & present state; ill. 21/ p 8° Stanford 83

*Place-names* —*v.* **K** § 120

***Kirkwall*:** **Brown** (Thos.; 1657–93) Diary, ed. A. F. Steuart [1675–93] 3/6 *n.* p 8° Peace, *Kirkwall* 98

**Dryden**, Sir H. Descrn. of Ch. of St Magnus, & Bp's Palace; ill. 1/6 *Kirkwall* 9–

,, [ed.] Illns. of some Pts. of Cathedral Ch. of St Magnus; 24 pl. 31/6 f° Stevenson, *Edin.* 93

**Hossack**, B. H. Kirkwall in the Orkneys; ill. and 4 maps 21/ 8° Peace, *Kirkwall* 00
A full and valuable history and minute description of the town.

**Mackintosh**, W. R. Glimpses of Kirkwall and People in Olden Time 3/6 c 8° Mackintosh, *Kirkwall* 87

,, Curious Incidents fr. Anc. Recds. of Kirkwall 3/6 c 8° Mackintosh, *Kirkwall* 92

**Peeblesshire**

**Buchan**, Jno. Scholar Gipsies 5/ *n.* c 8° Lane 96
18 descriptive essays dealing with the region of Upper Tweedale.

CHAMBERS, Wm. History of Peeblesshire ; maps and pl. *o.p.* [*pb.* 31/6] r 8° Chambers 64
DOUGLAS, Sir Geo. Roxburgh, Selkirk, and Peebles ; 3 maps 7/6 *n.* 8° Blackwood 99
[County Hists. of Scotl.] One of the best volumes of the series : full and accurate. Excellent bibliography (40 pp.).
RENWICK, Rob. Historical Notes on Peeblesshire Localities 7/6 *n.* 8° Watson, *Peebles* 92
*Broughton :* MURRAY (Jno.) Memorials of, ed. R. F. Bell [1740–7] 8° Scot. Hist. Soc. 96
*Peebles :* RENWICK (R.) Peebles : gleangs. fr. Burgh recds. [1604–52] 3/6 *n.* 8° Watson, *Peebles* 96
,, A Peebles Aisle and Monastery 8° Carson, *Glasgow* 98
WILLIAMSON, Rev. A. Glimpses of Peebles : forgotten chs. in its hist. ; ill. 4/6 c 8° Lewis, *Selkirk* 95

**Perthshire** —*v. also sup., s.v.* Highlands
BEVERIDGE, D. Culross and Tulliallan : Perthshire on Forth, 2 v. ; ill. 42/ 8° Blackwood 85
DRUMMOND, P. R. Perthshire in Bygone Days [100 biographies] *o.p.* [*pb.* 14/] 8° Whittingham 79
HUNTER, Thos. Woods, Forests, & Estates of Perthsh. [w. families] ; 30 ill. 12/ c 8° *Perth* 83
MACMILLAN, Dr Hugh The Highland Tay ; ill. 15/ 4° Virtue 01
7 descriptive articles on Strathfillan, Killin, Loch Tay, Kenmore, Aberfeldy, Strathtay, Dunkeld.
PALMER, Sutton [art.] Heart of Scotland : 24 col. pl. ; w. l'rpr. A. R. H. Moncrieff [$3 *n.* Macm., *N.Y.*] 7/6 *n.* sq 8° Black 09
*Military History* —*v.* **F** § 28
*Abernethy :* BROWN (Rev. D.) Ancient Church and Parish of Abernethy *o.p.* 8° Blackwood 98
*Auchterarder :* REID (A. G.) Annals of Aucht. and Memls. of Strathearn Philips, *Crieff*
22 interesting pprs. dealg. largely w. witchcraft and the 2 Jacobite rebellns., as these touched the locality.
*Methven :* MORRIS (T.) The Provosts of Methven [biogr. notices] 4°
*Ochtertyre :* COLVILLE (Dr Jas. ; ed.) House Booke of Ochtertyre [1737–9] 8° Scot. Hist. Soc. 07
*Perth :* COWAN (Sam.) The Ancient Capital of Scotland, 2 vols. 30/ *n.* r 8° Simpkin 04
An exhaustive hist. of Perth fr. invasion of AGRICOLA to passing of the Reform Bill.
FITTIS, Rob. Scott Ecclesiastical Annals of Perth [to Reformation] 8° *priv. prin.* (*Edin.*) 85
LAWSON, J. P. [ed.] The Book of Perth [charters and documts.] *o.p.* [*pb.* 12/] 8° Dolman 37
PEACOCK, Dav. Perth, its Annals and its Archives *o.p.* [*pb.* 7/6] c 8° Partridge 49

**Renfrewshire**
Collections tow. an Archæolog. & Histor. Survey of Co. of Renfrew, 2 v. ; pl. ea. 25/ 4° Gardner, *Paisley* 90
CRAWFORD, G. History of Renfrewshire, 2 Pts. [standard] *o.p.* 1782
HECTOR, W. [ed.] Selns. fr. Judicial Recds. of Renfrewsh., 2 v. ; facss. ea. 7/6 8° Gardner, *Paisley* 76–8
Illg. the admin. of laws of the County, and manners and condn. of the people in 17th and 18th cents.
METCALFE, Dr W. M. History of the County of Renfrew ; map 25/ *n.* 4° Gardner, *Paisley* 06
*Craigends :* CUNNINGHAM (Wm.) Diary & Account Bk., ed. Dr J. Dodds [1673–80] 8° Scot. Hist. Soc. 87
*Greenock :* AULD (W.) Greenock and Early Environmt. ; ill. 3/6 *n.* s 4° McKelvie, *Greenock* 07
BLAIR, Gardner Greenock Street Names : their hist. & romance ; ill. 3/ *n.* c 8° *Herald* Off., *Greenock* 07
WILLIAMSON, GEO. Old Greenock 25/ *n.* 4° Gardner, *Paisley* 86
,, Old Cartsburn 25/ *n.* 4° Gardner, *Paisley* 94
History of the estate from 1669 downwards : mainly family history.
*Paisley :* GILMOUR (D.) Reminiscences of the 'Penn Folk' Paisley Weavers of other Days 4/ c 8° Gardner, *Paisley* [73] 89
METCALFE, Dr W. M. History of Paisley : 600–1908 ; ill. 7/6 *n.* 8° Gardner, *Paisley* 09
,, [ed.] Charters & Documts. of Paisley : 1163–1665 ; w. Introd. 21/ *n.* 4° Gardner, *Paisley* 02

**Ross and Cromarty** —*for* Place-names *v.* **K** § 120
BAIN, Rob. History of Ancient Province of Ross Pefferside Press, *Dingwall* 99
As a history quite inaccurate and almost valueless ; but good acc. of Jacobite risings.
DIXON, J. H. Gairloch in N.-W. Ross-shire ; ill. [w. chs. by 3 others] 6/ 8° Co-op. Pub. Co., *Ed.* 88
MACGILL, W. [ed.] Old Ross-shire and Scotland 20/ 4° N. Counties Prtg. Co., *Inverness* 09
Repr. of the Tain and Balnagown documts., w. explan. matter under subj.-headings.
MILLER, Hugh [1802–56] Scenes and Legends of North of Scotland : the traditional hist. of Cromarty 3/6 c 8° Nimmo, *Edin.* [35]
*Dingwall* —*v.* Inverness-shire, *sup.* (MACKAY)

**Roxburghshire**
DOUGLAS, Sir Geo. Roxburgh, Selkirk, and Peebles—*ut sup., s.v.* Peeblesshire
,, Diversions of a Country Gentleman 6/ *n.* c 8° Hodder 02
Reprinted articles on the people, places, traditions, and sports of the Borders.
JEFFREY, Alex. Hist. & Antiqs. of Roxburghshire, 4 v. ; pl. *o.p.* [*pb.* 30/] 12° Whittaker 57–64

*Abbotsford, and Scott Country :* CROCKETT (W. S.) The Scott Country ; ill. 6/ 8° Black 02
$2 *n.* Macmillan, *N.Y.* Excellent descrn. of the Borders, held together by a thin thread of SCOTT biography.

„ Abbotsford ; w. 20 col. pl. W. Smith [$3 *n.* Macm., *N.Y.*] 7/6 *n.* sq 8° Black 05
A good companion to above bk., full and interestg., w. excellent picts. of Tweedside and surrdgs.

HUNNEWELL, J. F. Lands of Scott $2·50 8° Houghton, *Boston* 99

MAXWELL-SCOTT, Hon. Mrs. The Making of Abbotsford 7/6 *n.* c 8° Black 97

NAPIER, G. G. Homes and Haunts of Sir W. Scott ; ill. 21/ *n.* r 8° MacLehose, *Glasgow* 97

*Kelso Abbey :* Liber S. Marie de Calchou, 2 vols. [1113–1567] *o.p.* 46

*Melrose :* *CURLE (Jas.) A Roman Frontier Post & its People ; ill. 42/ *n.* 4° MacLehose, *Glasgow* 10
History of the Fort of Newstead in parish of Melrose ; w. c. 1350 ill. (some col., some photogravs.).

PINCHES, F. The Abbey Church of Melrose 21/ 4° *priv. prin.* 79
A series of views and architect. details ; with a history of the abbey, and remarks.

WATSON, Jas. Jedburgh Abbey ; w. Abbeys of Teviotdale 10/ *n.* r 8° Douglas, *Ed.* [77] 94

*Stitchill :* GUNN (Rev. G.) Recds. of Baron Court of Stitchill [1655–1807] 8° Scot. Hist. Soc. 05

**Selkirkshire**

ANGUS (W.) Ettrick and Yarrow 2/6 c 8° Lewis, *Selkirk* 99

*BROWN, T. Craig History of Selkirkshire, 2 vols. 90/ 4° Douglas, *Edin.* 86
One of the best of the Scottish County Histories, with col. maps, ports., pl., and cuts.

DOUGLAS, Sir Geo. Roxburgh, Selkirk, and Peebles—*ut sup.*, *s.v.* Peeblesshire

RUSSELL, Dr Jas. Reminiscences of Yarrow ; ill. 5/ c 8° Lewis, *Selkirk* [ ] 94

**Shetland**—*v.* Orkneys and Shetland, *sup.* **Skye**—*v.* Inverness-shire, *sup.*

**Stirlingshire**

FLEMING, J. S. [art.] Anc. Castles and Mansns. of Stirl. Nobility 21/ *n.* 4° Gardner, *Paisley* 02

NIMMO, W. History of Stirlingshire, ed. R. Gillespie, 2 v. *o.p.* [*pb.* 25/] 8° Morison, *Gl.* [1777] 80

STEWART, Kath. By Allan Water : true story of an old house 5/ *n.* c 8° Elliot, *Edin.* 01
Acc. (fr. parish-records, etc.) of Bridgend House and of the fortunes of the family wh. occup. it : 1632–1783.

*Kilsyth :* ANTON (Rev. P.) Kilsyth : a parish history *o.p.* c 8° Smith & Son, *Glasgow* 93

*Stirling :* FLEMING (J. S.) [art.] The Old Ludgings of Stirling : 40 ill. 7/6 *n.* s 4° Mackay, *Stirling* 97
Illustrated descrns. of old houses in Stirling once occup. by notable people.

RONALD, Jas. Landmarks of Old Stirling ; ill. 10/6 *n.* 8° Mackay, *Stirling* 99
Reprs. his *Parish Ch. of Stirlg.* ['89], *Old Crofts* ['90], *Old Bridge* [91], *Town Wall* ['93], *Seals* ['96], etc.

SMALL, J. W. Old Stirling ; ill. 21/ f° Mackay, *Stirling* 98

*Strathblane :* SMITH (J. G.) Parish of Strathblane & Inhabts. *o.p.* [*pb.* 21/] s 4° MacLehose, *Glasgow* 86

*Strathendrick :* SMITH (J. G.) Strathendrick and its Inhabitants ; ill. 31/6 *n.* 4° MacLehose, *Glasgow* 96

**Sutherlandshire**

EDWARDS-MOSS, J. E. A Season in Sutherland *o.p.* [*pb.* 4/6] c 8° Macmillan 88

GUNN (A.) + MACKAY (J.) [eds.] Sutherland and the Reay County *o.p.* c 8° *Glasgow* 97

SAINT JOHN, C. W. G. Tour in Sutherlandshire, 2 vols. ; ill. 21/ 8° Douglas, *Edin.* [49] 84

**Wigtonshire** —*v.* Ayrshire, *sup.* ; *for* Galloway *v.* Kirkcudbrightshire, *sup.*

## 20 : GREAT BRITAIN AND IRELAND (*e*) : IRELAND

**Early Accounts and Travel**

CUELLAR, Cpt. Adventures in Connacht and Ulster [1588] : tr.—*ut* **F** § 22

GIRALDUS CAMBRENSIS [=Gerald du BARRY ; 12 cent.]—*ut* **F** § 41

HOGAN, E. Description of Ireland and State thereof in 1598 10/6 4° Burns & Oates 78
From a MS. of Clongoweswood College, nr. Clane, Kildare. List of chieftains and their territories, etc.

POCOCKE, Archd. [1704–65] Tour in Ireland in 1752, ed. G. T. Stokes 5/ c 8° Hodges, *Dublin* 91
With Introd. and notes. Pococke was one of boldest and most indefatigable travellers of 18th cent. He had prev. explored Syria, Asia Min., and Egypt, and 'discovered' Switz. for Englishmen. His Irish jy., on horseback, extended rd. whole seaboard, and his acc. has a gd. deal of interest on geol., industrs., archit., antiqs., and scenery. Unlike YOUNG [*ut inf.*] he rarely noted social or moral condn. of people, and has nothing to say on politics.

*YOUNG, Arth. [1741–1820] Tour in Ireland, ed. A. W. Hutton, 2 vols. ea. 3/6 c 8° Bell [1780] 92
Ea. $1 *n.* Macmillan, *N.Y.* [Bohn's Lib.] Apart fr. repr. in PINKERTON'S *Coll. of Voys.* [*ut* E § 5], the first cpl. repr. of 1780 edn., inclg. also all author's subseq. wrgs. on Ireld. With bibl. of YOUNG by J. P. ANDERSON. Index, and map illg. YOUNG'S route. A most interesting and import. wk., unsurpassed in fulness and vividness of its descrn. of state of Irel. in 1776–9. Unfortunately, badly ed. : negligently, and in partizan (Home-Rule) spirit.

**General Topography**

AUSTIN, Alf. Spring and Autumn in Ireland 3/6 c 8° Blackwood 00
Two articles on Irish travel repr. from *Blackwood*, 1894–5 ; w. a poem (*To Ireland*) of same date.

DE BOVET, Mme. Three Months' Tour in Ireland, tr. [abgd.] ; 75 ill. 6/ c 8° Chapman 91

BULLIN, WM. Rambles in Eirinn ; maps and ill. 6/ 8° Gill, *Dublin* 07

CRAIK, [Mrs] D. M. — An Unknown Country ; ill. — 7/6 r 8° Macmillan 87
$2·50 Harper, *N.Y.* Chiefly Antrim and Down.

FALKINER, C. Litton — Essays relating to Ireland — 9/ *n.* ($3·50) 8° Longman 09
(1) *Studs. in Ir. Biogr.* (SPENSER, DAVIS, STONE, EMMET, etc.); (2) *Illns. of Ir. Topogr.*, (3) *Studs. in Ir. Hist.* (*Ir. Parly. Antiqs.*).

GWYNN, Steph. — The Fair Hills of Ireland ; 40 ill. Hugh Thomson (4 col.) — 6/ ($2) c 8° Macmillan 06
Suggestive and picturesque acc. of rambles, mostly of beaten tracks ; somewhat *couleur de rose.*

HALL, S. C. + Mrs S. C. — Ireland : its scenery, character, etc., 3 vols. ; ill. — r 8° Virtue [41–3] *n.d.* (83)

HISTORICAL AND ARCHÆOL. ASSOC. OF IRELAND—*ut inf.*, *s.v.* Kilkenny Archæol. Soc.

HOLE, Dn S. R. — Little Tour in Ireland ; c. 40 ill. J. Leech — 6/ i 16° Arnold [59] 96
First edn. pub. *sub nom.* 'AN OXONIAN'. Dublin, Galway, Connemara, Athlone, Limerick, Killarney, Glengarriff, Cork, etc.

HULL, Dr Edw. — Physical Geography and Geology of Ireland — 7/ 8° Stanford [78] 91

IRISH ARCHÆOLOG. AND CELTIC SOC. : Publications—*ut* **F** § 41

JOHNSON, Clifford — Isle of the Shamrock ; ill. — 8/6 *n.* ($2 *n.*) c 8° Macmillan 01

KILKENNY AND S.-E. OF IREL. ARCHÆOL. SOC. : Transactns., vols. i–ii ; Proceedings & Transactns., vol. iii — 8° Kilk. Arch. Soc. 49–55 ; 56

,, Journal [=*contin. of* Transactions], New Series, 6 v. — 8° Kilk. Arch. Soc. 56–67

,, Journal of Historical and Archæol. Assoc. of Irel. [=*contin.*] ; Ser. iii vol. i, & Ser. iv, vols. i–x — 8° Kilk. Arch. Soc. 68 *sqq.*
The name of the Society was later changed to the Royal Soc. of Antiquaries of Ireland [*v. inf.*].

LANE, T. O. — Round Erin : highways and byways in Ireland — c 8° *Abbeyfeale n.d.* (00)

POOLE, Stanley Lane- — North-West and by North : Ir. hills and Engl. dates — 3/6 c 8° Simpkin 03

ROY. SOC. OF ANTIQUARIES OF IREL. : Procgs. and Papers ; Journal ; Qtrly. Vols., ea. 2/6 ; Ann. Vols. — 8° R. S. of Ant. of I. (Hodges, *Dubl.*) 51 *sqq.*, *in prg.*

,, Publications — r 8° R. S. of Ant. of I. (Hodges, *Dublin*) *v.y.*
BERRY (H. F. ; ed.), *Register of Wills* [*ut* **G** § 22] 10/ *n.*
*Index to Journal of R.S.A.I.*, vols. i-xix [1849–89], 3 pts. ea. 3/6 *n.*
JOYCE (P. W.) [ed.] *Old Irish Folk-Music and Song* [*ut* **B** § 15] 10/6 *n.*
MACALISTER (R. A. S.) *Inscribed Slabs, Clonmacnoise* [*ut* **G** § 14] 10/ *n.*
MILLS (Jas. ; ed.) *Acc. Roll of Priory of H.Trin., Dubl.* [*ut inf.*] 10/ *n.*
MURPHY (Rev. Dennis ; ed.) *Annals of Clonmacnoise* [*ut inf.*] 10/ *n.*
STOKES (Marg.; ed.) *Chrn. Inscriptns. of Irish Lang.*, 2 v. [*ut* **G** § 16] 60/ *n.*
WAKEMAN (W. F.) *Inis Muiredach* (*Inismurray*) *and its Antiqs.* 7/6
WOOD-MARTIN (Col.), *Rude Stone Monumts. of Sligo, etc.* [*ut* **G** § 14] *o.p.*

,, Antiquarian Handbook Series, nos. i–v ; ill. — 8° R.S. of Ant. of I. 95–00 *in prg.*
i : *Dunsany, Tara, Glendalough*
ii : *Western Islds., Galway, etc.*
iii : *Western Islds., Clare, Kerry, etc.*
iv : *W. Islds. of Scotl., Orkney, etc.*
v : *Antiqs. of N. Portns. of Clare*

RUSSELL, T. O. — Beauties and Antiquities of Ireland ; ill. — 7/6 c 8° Paul 97

SHOEMAKER, M. M. — Wanderings in Ireland ; ill. — $2·50 *n.* (10/6 *n.*) 8° Putnam 08

**Castles :** ADAMS (C. L.) — Castles of Ireland : fortress hists. and legs. ; ill. — 10/6 *n.* r 8° Stock 05

**Ethnology**

BORLASE, W. C. — Origin of the Irish People — [five essays] *o.p.* r 8° Eglington 89

ELLIS, G. — Irish Ethnology, Socially & Politically Considered *o.p.* [*pb.* 3/6] 12° *Dublin* 52
General outline of Celtic and Saxon races : of some antiquarian value.

GREEN, Mrs. J. R. — Irish Nationality — [Home Univ. Lib.] 1/ *n.* s 8° Williams 11

PRICHARD (J. C.) + LATHAM (R. G.) Eastern Origin of the Celtic Nations — *o.p.* [*pb.* 6/] 8° Quaritch 57

**Guides** —*v.* **E** § 16

**Irish Abroad**

BAGENAL, P. H. D. — American Irish and their Influence on Irish Politics — 3/6 12° *London* 82

DAVIN, N. F. [Canad.] — The Irishmen in Canada — *o.p.* [*pb.* 16/] 8° Low 77

HOGAN, J. F. [Austral.] — The Irish in Australia — *o.p.* [*pb.* 2/6] c 8° Ward & Downey [87] 88

LUCY, E. W. — The Molly Maguires of Pennsylvania — 8° (*U.S.A.*) 82

MCGEE, T. Darcy — The Irish Settler in America — 8° (*U.S.A.*)

MAGUIRE, J. F. — The Irish in America — 12/6 p 8° Longman 68

O'CALLAGHAN, J. C. — History of Irish Brigades in Service of France — 2/ c 8° Cameron, *Glasgow* 70

SCOTCH-IRISH SOC. OF AMER. : Scotch-Irish in America : procgs. & addresses — ea. $1·50 8° var. pubrs., *ann.*

**Life ; People ; Economic and Political Condition** —*v. also* **D** § 142, **F** § 45

BECKER, B. H. — Disturbed Ireland — [l'rs wr. 1880–1] *o.p.* [*pb.* 6/] c 8° Macmillan 81

COLLES, Ramsay — In Castle and Court House — [reminiscences] 12/6 *n.* 8° Laurie 11

CONDER, A. — Discontent in Ireland : origin and cause — 6/ c 8° W. H. Allen 86

COYNE, W. P. — Ireland, Industrial & Agricultural ; maps & ill. — 5/ *n.* r 8° Browne, *Dublin* [01] 02
Enlarged collection of articles on Irish resources, products and industries, written at first for the Glasgow Exhibn.

CRAIG, J. D. — Real Pictures of Clerical Life in Ireland — *o.p.* [*pb.* 7/6] c 8° Nisbet 75

CUSACK, M. F. — The Case of Ireland Stated — 7/6 c 8° *Dublin* [80] 81

DARYL, Philippe — Ireland's Disease : notes & impressions [tr.] — *o.p.* [*pb.* 3/6] p 8° Routledge 88

DUBOIS, L. Paul — Contemporary Ireland [tr.], ed. T. M. Kettle 7/6 *n.* 8° Maunsel, *Dublin* 08

Guardian of Poor in Irel.' [ed.] Irish Peasant: sociol. study [$1 Scrib., *N.Y.*; Soc. Sci. Ser.] 2/6 c 8° Sonnenschein 92

GWYNN, Steph. — To-day & To-morrow in Ireland: essays on Ir. subjs. 5/ *n.* c 8° Hodges, *Dublin* 03

HALL, S. C. — —*in his* Retrospect of a Long Life [1815–83], *ut* **K** § 24

HALL, Mrs S. C. — Tales of Irish Life and Character; 16 col. pl. 5/ *n.* c 8° Foulis, *Edin.* [44] 09

HAMILTON, Jno. — 60 Years' Expernce. as an Irish Landlord 6/ c 8° Digby 94
Ed. Rev. H. C. WHITE. Record of efforts of a generous landld. to improve condn. of his tenantry at St Ernan's.

HITCHCOCK, F. R. M. — Types of Celtic Life and Art 3/6 c 8° Sealy, *Dublin* 06
A consideration of the whole Celtic social system.

HUSSEY, S. M. — Reminiscs. of an Irish Land Agent, ed. H. Gordon 12/6 *n.* r 8° Duckworth 04
Reminiscences: superficial, but lively, and sometimes instructive.

JOHNSON, Clifton — The Isle of the Shamrock; ill. $2 *n.* (8/6 *n.*) c 8° Macmillan [01] 07
Acc. of travels thro' and observns. on Ireld., mainly among peasants of the hill-country.

LLOYD, Clifford — Ireland under the Land League—*ut* **F** § 45

LOCKER-LAMPSON, G. — Consideration of State in Ireld. in 19 Cent. 18/ *n.* 8° Constable 07

LYND, Rob. — Home Life in Ireland; ill. 8/ *n.* 8° Mills & Boon 09

MCCARTHY, M. F. — Five Years in Ireland [1895–1900] 3/6 *n.* c 8° Simpkin [01] 03

,, — Priests and People in Ireland 7/6 c 8° Simpkin [02] 03

,, — Rome in Ireland 6/ c 8° Hodder 04

MACDONAGH, Mich. — Irish Life and Character [$1·75 Whittaker, *N.Y.*] 6/ c 8° Hodder 98

MACGRATH, T. — Pictures from Ireland *o.p.* [*pb.* 5/] c 8° Paul 80

de MANDAT-GRANCEY, E. — Paddy at Home: Irel. & Irish as seen by Frchman. 1/ c 8° Chapman [87] 89

MERRY, Andrew — The Green Country Richards 02

MOORE, Geo. [the novelist] — Parnell and his Ireland 2/6 c 8° Sonnenschein 87

O'DONNELL, F. H. — Paraguay on the Shannon 6/ *n.* 8° P. S. King & Son 08

O'HAGAN, L'd — —*in his* Occasional Papers and Addresses 7/6 c 8° Paul 84

PLUNKETT, Sir Hor. — Ireland in the New Century 1/ *n.* c 8° Murray [04] 05

REAL PADDY (A.) — Real Life in Ireland; ill. 3/6 *n.* 12° Methuen [21] 04

SCOTT-JAMES, R. A. — An Englishman in Ireland; 8 ill. 5/ *n.* c 8° Dent 10
Impressns. of Irish civilizn. and condns., made on a canoe-jy. along rivers, loughs, canals.

SENIOR, W. Nassau — —*in his* Journals, 2 vols., *ut* **F** § 45

SHAND, A. J. — Letters fr. West of Ireland [repr. fr. *Times*] 5/ 12° Blackwood 85

SULLIVAN, A. M. — New Ireland 1/ c 8° Cameron, *Glasgow* [77] 82

SYNGE, J. M. — In Wicklow, in West Kerry, in the Congested Districts, and under Ether = Coll. Wks., vol. iv—*ut* **K** § 89

THACKERAY, W. M. — The Irish Sketch-Book—*ut* **K** § 89

TRENCH, W. S. — Realities of Irish Life; pl. by J. S. Trench *o.p.* [*pb.* 5/] c 8° Longman [68] 69

YOUNG, Filson — Ireland at the Cross Roads 3/6 *n.* 8° Richards 03
Results of a tour thro' the country: observations on its condition, with proposals for remedying evils.

**Mountaineering**—*v.* **I** § 165 **Place-names**—*v.* **K** § 120

**Rivers**: *Shannon*: HARVEY (J. R.) The Shannon and its Lakes 3/6 c 8° Simpkin 96

**Scenery**

CASSELL & Co. [pubs.] — Pictorial Ireland; 100 ill. 5/ obl f° Cassell 02

LOVETT, Rich. — Irish Pictures Drawn w. Pen and Pencil; 113 ill. 8/ i 8° R.T.S. 88

VILLARS, P. — Scotland & Ireland: picturesque survey [tr.]; 200 ill. *o.p.* [*pb.* 7/6] r 8° Routledge 87

WALKER, Fcs. S. [art.] — Ireland: 77 col. pl.; w. l'rpr. F. Mathew 20/ *n.* sq 8° Black 05

,, — Ireland: 32 col. pl.; w. l'rpr. F. Mathew 6/ *n.* sq 8° Black 07
Former $6 *n.*, latter $2·50 *n.* Macmillan, *N.Y.*

**Antrim**: *GWYNN (Steph.) Highways and Byways in Donegal and Antrim—*ut inf.*, *s.v.* Donegal

*Belfast*: BENN (G.) Hist. of Town of Belfast; ill. [to 1800] *o.p.* [*pb.* 28/] 8° Marcus Ward [23] 77–80

YOUNG, R. M. [ed.] Town Bk. of Corpn. of Belfast: 1613–1816; ill. *o.p.* [*pb.* 28/ *n.*] r 8° Marcus Ward 92

,, [ed.] Historical Notices of Old Belfast & Vicinity; ill. *o.p.* [*pb.* 21/ *n.*] r 8° Marcus Ward 96
Incls. princ. portn. of hitherto unpubd. materl. coll. by W. PINKERTON, several narrs. rel. to times of C'wealth and Revoln., ser. of letters and petitions, etc.

**Aran**: BURKE (O. J.) The South Isles of Aran *o.p.* [*pb.* 2/6] c 8° Paul 87

SYNGE, J. M. — The Aran Islands; ill. J. B. Yeats 5/ *n.* c 8° Maunsel, *Dublin* 07
Also vol. iv of *Coll. Wks.* [*ut* **K** § 89]. Acc. of his life on these primitive isls., and of ways of people, and his talks w. them.

**Armagh** *(town)*: STUART (J.) Histor. Memls. of Armagh [to 1814] 10/6 *n.* 4° Tempest, *Dundalk* [19] 00
**Clare**: FROST (J.) History and Topogr. of Co. Clare [to 18 cent.] 11/ 8° Williams 93
MACNAMARA, N. C. Story of an Irish Sept; ill. [$4 L'cott, *Phila.*] 10/6 *n.* 8° Dent 96
WHITE, Vy. Rev. Patr. Hist. of Clare and Dalcassian Clans of Tipperary 10/6 8° *Dublin* 93
**Connaught**: CUELLAR (Cpt.) Adventures in Connacht and Ulster [1588] [tr.]—*ut* **F** § 22
HOUSTOUN, Mrs M. C. Twenty Years in Wild West [Connaught] 9/ c 8° Murray 79
**Connemara**: GWYNN, Steph. Holiday in Connemara [$2 *n.* Macmillan, *N.Y.*] 10/6 *n.* 8° Methuen 09
Through Connemara in a Governess Cart; ill. [by two ladies] 3/6 c 8° W. H. Allen 93

**Cork**: *County and City*
BRADY, W. M. [ed.] Records of Cork, Cloyne and Ross, 3 vols. *o.p.* [*pb.* 42/] 8° Longman 64
CORK HISTOR. & ARCHÆOL. Soc.: Journal 8° *Cork* 92–04
CUSACK, Mary F. History of City and County of Cork; ill. *o.p.* 8° *Dublin* 75
GIBSON, C. B. History of County and City of Cork, 2 vols. *o.p.* [*pb.* 21/] c 8° Newby 61
SMITH, C. [1715?–62] Antient & Present State of Co. & City of Cork, 2 v. [1750] 93–4
*Bandon*: BENNETT (Geo.) Hist. of Bandon and Town in W. Ridg., Cork *o.p.* 8° *Cork* [ ] 69
*Kinsale*: CAULFIELD (R.) [ed.] Council Bk. of Corpn. of Kinsale [1652–1800] s 4° *Guildford* 79
*Youghal*: CAULFIELD (R.) [ed.] Council Bk. of Corpn. of Youghal [1610–1800] s 4° *Guildford* 78
**Derry**: REEVES (Bp W.) [ed.] Acts of Abp Cotton in his Visitns. of Derry: 1397 50
**Donegal**: *GWYNN (Steph.) Highways & Byways in Donegal & Antrim; ill. 6/ ($2) c 8° Macmillan 99
**Down**: KNOX (Alex.) Hist. of County of Down, to Present Day; ill. *o.p.* 8° *Dublin* 75

**Dublin** *County and City*
ADAMS, Rev. B. W. Hist. & Descr. of Santry & Cloghran Parishes; ill. 10/6 r 8° Mitchell & Hughes 83
BALL, Fcs. E. History of the County of Dublin, Pts. i–iv; ill. r 8° Thom, *Dublin* 02–6
The best bk.; based on publ. and priv. records. Deals w. ea. parish separately.
CHART, D. A. Story of Dublin; ill. [Mediæv. Towns; $1·75 *n.* Dutton, *N.Y.*] 3/6 *n.* c 8° Dent 07
A not very felicitous combination of history and guide-bk. By Keeper of Record Tower in Dubl. Castle.
COSGRAVE (E. M.) + STRANGWAYS (L. R.) Dictionary of Dublin 2/6 *n.* c 8° Sealy, *Dublin* 08
FITZPATRICK, S. A. O. Dublin: hist. and topogr.; ill. [Ancient Cities] 4/6 *n.* c 8° Methuen 07
GERARD, Fces. A. Picturesque Dublin, Old and New; 100 ill. 12/ 8° Hutchinson 98
GILBERT, Dr [Sir] J. T. History of City of Dublin, 2 vols. *o.p.* [*pb.* 21/] 8° J. R. Smith 54–9
,, [ed.] Calendar of Anc. Recds. of Dubl., v. i–xiii [1171–1786] 8° Dollard, *Dublin* 89–07 *in prg.*
HALIDAY, Chas. Scandinavian Kingdom of Dublin, ed. J. P. Prendergast *o.p.* 8° *Dublin* [ ] 84
PETERS, A. Sketches of Old Dublin 2/6 *n.* c 8° Sealy, *Dublin* 07
*Cemeteries*: FITZPATRICK (W. J.) Hist. of Dublin Catholic Cemeteries c 8° *Dublin* 00
*All Saints Priory*: BUTLER (R.) [ed.] Registr. Prioratus Omn. SS. [12–15 cent.] 4° Ir. Arch. Soc. 45
*Dublin Castle*: GILBERT (J. T.) History of the Viceroys of Ireland *o.p.* [*pb.* 16/] 8° Duffy, *Dublin* 65
MORRIS, M. O'C. Dublin Castle 12/ 8° Harrison 89
Recollections of Dublin Castle and of Dublin Society [mid. 19 cent.] 6/ c 8° Chatto 02
*French Conformed Church* —*v.* **A** § 63 (HUGUENOT SOC.—LA TOUCHE; LE FANU)
*Holy Trinity Priory*: MILLS (Jas.) [ed.] Account Roll of H. Tr., Dubl. 10/ *n.* 8° R. Soc. of Ant. of Irel. 91
Accs. of a medieval Dubl. convt., w. prices of househd. wares, farm-produce, etc., *temp.* EDW. III; preceded by essay on house-keepg. in Dubl. in 13th cent. Conts. also *The Pride of Life*, a morality [*ut* **K** § 82].
*Hosp. & Free Schl. of Chs. ii*: FALKINER (Sir F. A.) Foundn. of Hosp., etc. 7/6 8° Sealy, *Dublin* 06
*Parliament Ho.*: GILBERT (J. T.) Acc. of Parliament House, Dubl. [1661–1800] 10/6 4° Hodges, *Dublin* 96
*St Mary's Abbey*: GILBERT (J. T.) [ed.] Chartularies, etc., of St Mary's Abbey, 2 v. D.
[1171–1540] ea. 10/ r 8° Rolls Series 84
*St. Thomas' Abbey*: GILBERT (J. T.) [ed.] Register of St. Thomas' Ab. [1172–1524] 10/ r 8° Rolls Series 89

**Fermanagh** —*v. also inf.*, *s.v.* Tyrone (BELMORE)
*Enniskillen* —*v. inf.*, *s.v.* Sligo (WOOD-MARTIN)
*Erne (Lough)*: HENRY (Rev. W.) [*d.* 1768] Upper Lough Erne in 1739: ed. Sir C. King
3/6 f 8° McGee, *Dublin* 92
An interestg. wk. of class similar to POCOCKE, *ut sup.*, now first pubd. Its chief value is conn. w. the wars of the Revoln.
**Galway**: FAHEY (J.) Hist. and Antiqs. of Diocese of Kilmacduagh; ill. 8/ 8° Gill, *Dublin* 93
*Tuam*: KNOX (H. T.) Notes on Early Hist. of Tuam, Killula, Achonry 10/6 *n.* 8° Hodges, *Dubl.* 04
**Kerry**: CUSACK (Mary F.) History of the Kingdom of Kerry; ill. *o.p.* [*pb.* 20/] 8° Longman 71
HICKSON, Mary A. [ed.] Selectns. fr. Old Kerry Records: hist. & geneal., 2 Ser. *o.p.* c 8° Longman 72–4

**King's County:** HITCHCOCK (F. R. M.) The Midland Septs and the Pale 3/6 c 8° Sealy, *Dublin* 08
An acc. of the early Septs and the later settlers of the King's Co. and of life in the Engl. Pale.

*Clonmacnoise:* MURPHY (Rev. D.; ed.) Annals of Clonmacnoise 10/ *n.* r 8° Roy. Soc. of Ants. of Irel.

**Limerick:** *County and Town*

Black Book of Limerick: ed. Rev. J. MacCaffrey; w. Introd. and notes 10/ *n.* r 8° Gill, *Dublin* 07

DOWD, Rev. Jas. Round about the County of Limerick; ill. *o.p.* 8° McKem, *Limerick* 99

LENIHAN, Maur. Limerick: history and antiquities; w. notes; ill. *o.p.* [*pb.* 12/] 8° *Dublin* 66

**Louth:** D'ALTON (J.) Hist. of Drogheda and Environs, 2 vols. *o.p.* 8° *Dublin* 44

*Kilsaran:* LESLIE (Rev. J. B.) Hist. of Kilsaran; maps and ill. 7/6 *n.* 8° Tempest, *Dundalk* 08

**Mayo:** KNOX (H. T.) Hist. of Co. of Mayo; maps [to 1600] 12/6 8° Hodges, *Dublin* 08

**Meath:** HEALY (Rev. J.) History of Diocese of Meath, 2 v. 8° 08

**Monaghan:** SHIRLEY (E. P.) History of County of Monaghan 84/ f° Pickering 77-80

SHIRLEY, Evelyn Pp. Hist. of County of Monaghan; ill. 84/ f° Pickering 80

*Corrib (Lough):* WILDE (Sir W. R. W.) Lough Corrib; w. notes on Lough Mask *o.p.* c 8° *Dublin* [ ] 72

*Farley:* SHIRLEY (E. P.) Account of Territory of Farley *o.p.* [*pb.* 21/] 4° Pickering 45

**Queen's County:** O'HANLON (Can. J.) + O'LEARY (Rev. E.) Hist. of Queen's Co., vol. 1 [to 1556] 20/ *n.* 8° Sealy, *Dubl.* 07

*Portarlington:* LEFANU [ed.] Regrs. of Fch. Ch. of Portarlington r 8° 08

**Roscommon:** *Loch Ce:* BURKE (Dn Fcs.) Loch Ce and its Annals *o.p.* 8° *Dublin* 95

**Sligo:** O'RORKE (Ter.) History of Sligo, 2 vols. *o.p.* 8° *Dublin n.d.* (90)

WOOD-MARTIN, Col. W. G. Hist. of Sligo, Co. & Town, v. i-ii, ea. 7/6 *n.*, iii, 15/ *n.* 8° Hodges, *Dubl.* 82-92
Compreh.: brings hist. down to pres. time, and conts. much of interest to historn., naturalist, and folklorist.

,, Sligo and the Enniskilleners: 1688-91 *o.p.* c 8° *Dublin* [ ] 82

*Achonry:* KNOX (H. T.) Notes on Early Hist.—*v. sup., s.v.* Galway (Tuam)

*Ballysadare; Kilvarnet:* O'RORKE (T.) Antiqs. and Pres. State of B. & K. 6/ 8° Duffy, *Dublin* 78

**Tyrone**

BELMORE, Earl of Hist. of the Two Ulster Manors of Finagh (Tyrone & Coole, Fermanagh) 5/ *n.* 8° Longman [81] 03
For author's *Hist. of Corry Family*, of Castlecoole, a sort of sequel to above, *v.* **G** § 22.

,, Parliamentary Memoirs of Fermanagh & Tyrone [1613-1885] 10/6 8° *Dublin* 87

O'GARA, Dr A. P. A. The Green Republic: visit to South Tyrone 6/ c 8° Unwin 02
Sketches written to promote agricultural enterprise in the district.

**Ulster:** Annals of Ulster —*ut* **F** § 41

ATKINSON, Rev. E. D. An Ulster Parish: history of Donaghdoney 2/6 *n.* c 8° Hodges, *Dublin* 99

HARRISON, Jno. The Scot in Ulster [hist. of the settlemt.] 2/6 c 8° Blackwood 88

HILL, Geo. Historical Account of Planting of Ulster [1608-20] *o.p.* 4° *Belfast* 77

LATIMER, W. T. Ulster Biographies: 1798 *o.p.* 8° *Belfast* 97

MACKNIGHT, Thos. Ulster as it is: experces. of Irish editor, 2 vols. 21/ *n.* 8° Macmillan 96
Acc. of the Ulster 'of the plains', British, industrious, prosperous, and loyal, as opposed to the Ulster 'of the settlements', Celtic. Author, an Englishman, followed Fk. H. HILL as edr. of *Northern Whig*, then and now a powerful Belfast newsppr. Gives interestg. acc. of growth, progr. and polit. hist. of Belfast, the valuation of wh. now surpasses that of Dublin. He adopted Home Rule w. GLADSTONE.

**Waterford:** RYLAND (R. H.) Hist., Topogr. and Antiqs. of Co. & City of Waterford *o.p.* 8° *London* 24

*Clonmel:* BURKE (W. P.) History of Clonmel 8° 07

**Westmeath:** WOODS (Jas.) Anc. and Mod. Sketches of Westmeath, 2 vols. 90

,, Annals of Westmeath, Anc. and Mod.; ill. 5/ *n.* 8° Sealy, *Dublin* 07

**Wexford:** HORE (P. H.) Hist. of Town & Co. of Wexford, 6 vols.; ill. ea. 20/ *n.* 4° Stock 00-7

WHEELER (H. F. B.) + BROADLEY (A. M.) The War in Wexford; ill. 12/6 *n.* 8° Lane 10
Account of the Rebellion in S. of Ireld. in 1798 told fr. orig. documts.; w. contemp. prints, etc.

**Wicklow:** *Bray:* One Hundred Years of Bray [1770-1870] 07

*Powerscourt:* POWERSCOURT (Visc.) Descrn. & Hist. of Powerscourt; ill. 42/ *n.* r 4° Hodges, *Dublin* 03

## 21: BRITISH EMPIRE (AND BRITISH COLONIES): COLLECTIVELY—*v. also* D § 136

*Vide also* **D** §§ 136, 143; **F** § 33

**Bibliography**

COLONIAL INSTITUTE (ROYAL): Catalogue: 1886-1901 [ed. J. R. Boosé] 21/ r 8° Roy. Colon. Inst. 01

PETHERICK, E. A. Index to the Literature of Geography—*ut* **E** § 1

**Atlases**

BISIKER, W. [ed.] British Empire (and Japan); ill. [213 maps] 21/ *n.* f° Geogr. Pb. Co. 09
16/ *n.* 4°. A useful and graphic atlas, shewg. phys. feats. in photo-relief. Statist. notes.

JOHNSTON, W. + A. K. [pubs.] The M.P. Atlas [41 col. pl.] r f° 25/ Johnston 07
Selected fr. *The Royal Atlas* [*ut* **E** § 4], w. extra commercial and physical maps.

LUCAS, C. P. [ed.] Our Empire Atlas [59 col. maps] 6/ r 4° Johnston 97

POOLE, R. Lane [ed.] Brit. Empire sectn. *of his* Hist. Atl. of Mod. Eur. [*ut* **F** § 16] [27 maps] 35/ *n.* ($10) f° Clar. Press 02

ROBERTSON (C. G.) + BARTHOLOMEW (J. G.) [eds.] Student's Modern Atlas of Brit. Empire 4/6 *n.* 4° Methuen 05
64 maps, w. numerous insets, histor. tables and notes, Introd., histor. Gazetteer, and index.

**Generally**

BONWICK, Jos. The British Colonies and their Resources *o.p.* [*pb.* 5/] c 8° Low 86

CALDECOTT, A. English Colonisation and Empire—*ut* **D** § 136

CASSELL & Co. [pubs.] The Queen's Empire, 2 vols.; fully ill. ea. 9/ 4° Cassell *n.d.*

DAWSON (G. M.) + SUTHERLAND (A.) Elem. Geogr. of Brit. Colonies; ill. [excellent little bk.] 2/ (80 c. *n.*) gl 8° Macmillan 92

DILKE, [Sir] C. W. Greater Britain [travs. in Am., Austral., Ind., 1866–7] 3/6 *n.* ($2 *n.*) c 8° Macmillan [68]

,, Problems of Greater Britain—*ut* **D** § 136

,, The British Empire 3/6 c 8° Chatto 99
Reprs. of newsppr. arts. (1898), givg. a good summary of chief facts, in rel. to position of var. members of the Imper. family.

FAUNTHORPE, Rev. J. P. Geography of British Colonies and Possessions 2/6 12° Philip [73] 81

FROUDE, J. A. Oceana: England and her colonies; ill. 3/6 c 8° Longman [86] 98
Acc. of his visit to C. Col. and Australasia in 1885, w. reflectns. on relns. betw. Mother-Country and her Colonies. *Vide* also *Engl. and her Cols.* and *Colonies Once More* in Ser. ii and iii resp. of his *Short Studies* [*ut* **F** § 1].

GRESWELL, Rev. W. P. The British Colonies and their Industries 1/6 f 8° Philip [93] 05

,, Outlines of British Colonization—*ut* **D** § 136

Harmony of the Empire (The): sketches in pictorial geography 5/ c 8° A. Heywood, *Mancs.* 01

v. HOCHBERG, C't F. An Eastern Voyage: travels thro' Brit. Emp., 2 v.; 25 col. pl. and 48 ill. [$10 *n.* Dutton, *N.Y.*] 31/6 *n.* 8° Dent 11

HOOPER, W. E. [ed.] British Empire in First Yr. of 20th Cent. and Last of Victorian Era, 2 vols.; ill. 4° Heywood, *Mancs.* 02
Mainly an album of illns. (some 400 photogravures), w. statistics and biographies.

v. HÜBNER, Bar. J. A. Through the British Empire [tr.], 2 vols. [1883–4] 24/ c 8° Murray 86
S. Afr., Australia, N. Zeal., Str. Settlements, India, S. Sea Isls., Calif. Oregon, Canada, i.e. same ground as FROUDE's *Oceana*, w. Canada added. Interestg. impressions of an observant and impartial foreigner.

de HUMIÈRES, Vic'te R. Through Isle and Empire [tr.] 6/ c 8° Heinemann 05

KNIGHT, E. F. Over-sea Britain: The Nearer Empire 6/ *n.* 8° Murray 07
Inform. on geogr., hist., ethnogr., polit. devel., and resources of Brit. possessns. in Mediterr, Brit. Afr., Brit. Amer. Another vol. will deal w. Asia and Oceania.

LANG, Jno. Outposts of Empire; 12 col. pl. [Romance of Empire] 6/ *n.* sq 8° Jack

LECKY, W. E. H. The Empire: value and growth [inaug. addr.] 1/6 c 8° Macmillan 93

MEAKIN, Walt. The Life of an Empire 6/ *n.* c 8° Unwin 08
An attempt to write of the Brit. Empire as if it were one vast country inhab. by different races. Fair and patriotic: a good educ. bk.

MEATH, Earl of, etc. Our Empire, Past and Present, 2 vols. ea. 7/6 8° Harrison 01–5

MURRAY, Col. A. M. Imperial Outposts fr. Strateg. and Commerc. Aspect—*ut* **D** § 138

*Ophir* (The): Voyage—*v.* **E** § 7

'O'RELL, Max' [Paul BLOUET] John Bull & Co.: Great Colonial Branches of Firm; ill. 3/6 c 8° Warne 94
A lively, epigrammatic, prejudiced and inaccurate, yet always amusing, acc. of a 2-yrs. lecturg. tour in Can., U.S., some Pacific Isls., Australia, Tasm., N. Z. and S. Afr. Chief blemish in book is a persistent attack on Protestantism.

POLLARD, A. F. [ed.] The British Empire: past, pres., and future 5/ c 8° League of Empire 09
By 15 various contributors. A useful book on the whole Empire.

*SEELEY, Sir J. R. The Expansion of England—*ut* **F** § 33

TEMPLE, Sir Rich. Cosmopolitan Essays; maps 16/ 8° Chapman 86
*Position of British Empire; Imperial Federation; Prospects of Canada, Burmah, India, Congo, America,* etc.

TILBY, A. Wyatt The English People Overseas, 6 vols.—*ut* **E** § 16, *s.v.* Ethnology; People

TRENDELL, A. J. R. [ed.] Her Majesty's Colonies 10/ 8° Clowes 86
The offic. hdbk. to Ind. and Col. Exhib. 1886. Papers by Roy. Commissrs., w. pref. J. R. SEELEY. A useful, permanent book.

WHITE, A. Silva [ed.] The Britannic Confederation [by var. wrs.] 3/6 c 8° Philip 92

WILLIAMS, E. E. The Imperial Heritage; ill. 2/6 c 8° Ward & Lock 98

**Series**

British Empire Series: 5 vols.; 12 maps ea. 6/ p 8° Paul 00–1
Vol. i: *India*; ii: *Brit. Africa*; iii: *Brit. America*; iv: *Australasia, Polynesia*; v: *General* [= smaller possessns.]. Reprs. of over 100 Sunday afternoon lects., by var. hands, at Finsbury Institute, dealg. w. life, resources, and prospects of the Empire. Of very unequal values.

Our Empire [series]: ill. ea. 3/6 *n.* c 8° Newnes 05 *sqq.*
*Australian Life; Canadian Life; Indian Life.*

Romance of Empire: ed. Jno. Lang; ea. w. 12 col. pl. ea. 6/ *n.* sq 8° Jack *in prg.*
*Australia* [*ut* **E** § 65] Dr W. H. Lang | *India* [*ut* **E** § 35] V. Surridge | *Outposts of Empire* [*ut sup.*] Jno. Lang
*Canada* [*ut* **E** § 55] B. Willson | *New Zealand* [*ut* **E** § 67] R. Horsley | *South Africa* [*ut* **E** § 50] I. D. Colvin

**Ethnography**

Fraser, J. F. Quaint Subjects of the King; ill. 6/ ($1·25 *n.*) c 8° Cassell 09

Native Races of the British Empire: ed. N. W. Thomas; ill. ea. 6/ *n.* 8° Constable 06 *sqq.*, *in prg.*
*Natives of Australia* [*ut* **E** § 65] Edr. | *Natives of Brit. N. Amer.* [*ut* **E** § 53] C. Hill-Tout | *Natives of Northern India* [*ut* **E** § 35] W. Crooke
*Natives of Brit. Centr. Africa* [*ut* **E** § 48] A. Werner
A very valuable and well ill. ser., w. descrns. of the countries as well as the natives.

**Historical Geography and History of British Empire**—*v.* **F** § 33

**Lost Possessions**

Lord, Walt. Frewen The Lost Possessions of England *o.p.* [*pb.* 6/] c 8° Bentley 96
Dunkirk, Tangier, Minorca, Cuba, Manila, Corsica, Buenos Ayres, Montevideo, Java, and Ionian Islds. United States omitted!

" Lost Empires of Modern World: essays in imperial history *o.p.* [*pb.* 6/] c 8° Bentley 97
A compan.-vol. to above. Portugal, Spain, Frce., and Holland. A novel feature of the book is author's avowed partiality for Portuguese.

**Resources, Trade, Statistics** —*v.* **D** § 148

## 22: GREECE (MODERN) AND ARCHIPELAGO

Allinson, Fcs. G. + Anne C. E. Greek Lands and Letters 7/6 *n.* 8° Unwin 10
A not very successful attempt to write a *Sentimental Journey* thro' Greece, bringing Gk. liter. to bear on ea. mtn. and river th. the travellers meet.

Armstrong, Isab. Two Roving Englishwomen in Greece; ill. *o.p.* [*pb.* 6/] c 8° Low 93
Amusing and full of high spirits, w. a vivid account of the monasteries of Meteora (Thessaly).

Baedeker, Karl Greece; ill. [$2·40 *n.* Scribner, *N.Y.*] 8/ s 8° Unwin [89] 09

Barrows, Sam. J. Isles and Shrines of Greece; ill. [popular] $2 c 8° Little & Brown, *Boston* 98

Farrer, R. R. Tour in Greece; 27 pl. [tour in 1880] 21/ r 8° Blackwood 82

Freeman, Prf. E. A. Studies of Travel: Greece $1 (2/6) 16° Putnam 93
Archæol. and hist. studies, of spec. interest to cultured travr's., bg. notes of travels in 1877, '81, '83.

Hanson, C. H. The Land of Greece; maps and ill. 8/ r 8° Nelson 86

Janeway, Cath. Glimpses at Greece 3/6 c 8° Paul 97

Leake, Lt.-Col. W. M. Travels in the Morea, 3 vols.; map and pl. *o.p.* 8° Murray 30

" Peloponnesiaca [suppl. to above] *o.p.* [*pb.* 15/] 8° Murray 46

" Travels in Northern Greece, 4 v.; maps & pl. *o.p.* [*pb.* 60/] 8° Murray 35
Standard wks. of refer. First is record of 2 tours (1805, '06), last of 4 tours (1804–10).

Linton, W. Greece and its Islands; ill. *o.p.* [*pb.* 42/] 4° Cassell 69

Macmillan & Co. [pubs.] Greece, incl. Archipel., Constant., Coasts of Asia Min., Crete, Cyprus; 36 maps & plans [Macmillan's Guides] 9/ *n.* ($2·75 *n.*) gl 8° Macmillan [06] 11

Mahaffy, Prf. J. P. [ed.] Greek Pictures: drawn w. pen and pencil 8/ i 8° R.T.S. 90
$3·20 Revell, *N.Y.* A delightful bk. on acc. of both text, wr. by one who knows Greece as few other Englishmen, and of its ill.

" Rambles and Studies in Greece 5/ *n.* ($1·50 *n.*) c 8° Macmillan [76] 07
Should be taken with them by all visitors to Greece. Scholarly—and handy in size. Seeks to bring the livg. feats. of Grce. home to student by connectg. them w. facts of older history. Much also about mod. Gk. politics and character.

Marden, P. S. Greece & the Ægean Islands; ill. [12/6 *n.* Constable] $3 *n.* 8° Houghton, *Boston* 07
A light-hearted acc. of travel, inaccurate and sentimental, but amusing and observant.

Moore, Mabel Days in Hellas; ill. and col. front. 6/ *n.* c 8° Heinemann 09

Murray, Jno. [pub.] Handbook for Travellers in Greece; maps & plans 20/ p 8° Murray [34] 00
Incl. Ionian Isl., Continental Greece, Peloponnese, Isls. of Ægean, Crete, Albania, Thessaly, Macedonia.

Richardson, Rufus B. Vacation Days in Greece; 2 maps and 16 ill. $2 *n.* 8° Scribner, *N.Y.* 03
7/6 Smith & Elder. Revised reprs. of mag. arts. of previous eleven years.

Rodd, [Sir] Rennell Customs and Lore of Modern Greece; 7 pl. *o.p.* [*pb.* 8/6] 8° Stott 91
An excellent study of mod. Gk. people by one who spent over 2 yrs. am. them, partly in most remote districts. Ch. i on Ethnology.

Sandys, Dr J. E. An Easter Vacation in Greece 3/6 12° Macmillan 87
With a bibliogr. of Gk. travel and topography, and map and plan of Olympia.

Sergeant, Lewis New Greece; maps 21/ 8° Cassell 79

" Greece [For. Countries and Brit. Colonies] 3/6 12° Low [80] 82

Symonds, J. A. Sketches and Studies in Italy and Greece, Ser. i—*ut* **E** § 24

Talbot, T. Greece and the Greeks *o.p.* [*pb.* 12/] 8° Low 80

Taylor, Bayard Greece & Russia; w. Excursn. to Crete; 2 pl. $1·50 12° Putnam, *N.Y.* [89] 82

TILLEY, H. A. Eastern Greece & Western Asia [Russia, Greece, Syria] *o.p.* [*pb.* 10/6] c 8° Longman 64

TOZER, Rev. H. F. Lectures on the Geography of Greece *o.p.* [*pb.* 9/] c 8° Murray 73
Brings out excellently the relations of the geography of Greece to its history.

,, Researches in Highlands of Turkey, 2 v.; ill. *o.p.* [*pb.* 24/] c 8° Murray 69
Includes visits to Mounts Ida, Athos, Olympos, Pelion, etc.

WALKER, Mary A. Old Tracks and New Landmarks; ill. *o.p.* [*pb.* 14/] 8° Bentley 98
Papers of travel in Crete, Macedonia, Mitylene, etc.

WORDSWORTH, Bp Chr. Greece, Pictor., Descr., & Histor., ed. H. F. Tozer; 400 ill. 31/6 r 8° Murray [39] 82

*Ancient Greece:* History of Geogr. *v.* **E** § 9; *Ancient Writers v.* **K** § 192

*Anthology:* Milford (H. S.) [ed.] Englishman in Greece; Introd. Sir R. Rodd 5/ *n.* ($1·75) f 8° Clar. Press 11

*Antiquities* —*v.* **G** § 5

**Life; People; Economic Condition, etc.**—*v. also* **E** § 30; *for* Ancient Life *v.* **F** § 11

BICKFORD-SMITH, R. A. H. Greece under King George; map *o.p.* [*pb.* 12/] 8° Bentley 93
An unbiassed acc. of Grce. of 1893, contg. a solid mass of well-digested facts and figs. rel. to populn., agric., industrs., commerce, and (its best pt.) culture, relig., constitn., politics, society.

'CONSUL'S WIFE (A)' [=Mrs J. E. BLUNT]—*in her* People of Turkey, *ut* **E** § 29

FERRIMAN, Z. D. Home Life in Hellas 8/ *n.* c 8° Mills & Boon 10

JEBB, Prf. R. C. Modern Greece 4/ *n.* ($1·75) c 8° Macmillan [80] 01
Genl. view (in 4 essays) of Gk. kgdm. and the Gk. questn., historically, politically and socially.

MILLER, W. Greek Life in Town and Country 3/6 *n.* c 8° Newnes 05

SAMUELSON, Jas. Greece: pres. condn. and recent progr.; ill. 3/6 c 8° Low 94
Wr. in Athens dur. financial troubles of the early Nineties, throws light on financ. and industr. condn.

SMITH, Agnes Glimpses of Greek Life and Scenery 15/ 8° Hurst 84
Account of a visit by three ladies in the Spring of 1883.

*SYMONDS, J. A. Sketches and Studies in Italy and Greece—*ut* **E** § 24

TUCKERMAN, C. K. The Greeks of To-day 50 c. 12° Putnam, *N.Y.* [72] 86

**Scenery**

FULLEYLOVE, Jno. [art.] Picts. of Class. Gk. Landsc. & Archit.: w. l'rpr. H. W. Nevinson 31/6 *n.* r 4° Dent 97

,, [art.] Greece: 75 col. pl., w. l'rpr. Dr J. A. McClymont [$6 *n.* Macm., *N.Y.*] 20/ sp 8° Black 06

**Seas; Islands**

COLBECK, Alf. A Summer's Cruise in Waters of Grce., Turk., Russia 10/6 8° Unwin 88

FIELD, Dr H. M. Greek Islands & Turkey after the War; maps & ill. $1·50 c 8° Scribner, *N.Y.* 85

HARRISON, J. A. Greek Vignettes: sail on Gk. seas $1·25 c 8° Houghton, *Boston* 78

STILLMAN, W. J. On the Track of Ulysses [archæol. of Gk. islds.] $4 4° Houghton, *Boston* 88

SCOTT-STEVENSON, Mrs On Summer Seas [Med., Æg., Ionian, Euxine] 16/ 8° Chapman 83

*Ægean Sea*

FITZ-PATRICK, T. An Autumn Cruise in the Ægean; ill. *o.p.* [*pb.* 10/6] c 8° Low 87

MARDEN, P. S. Greece and the Ægean Islands—*ut sup., s.v.* Greece

TOZER, Rev. H. F. Islands of the Ægean; maps 8/6 ($2·25) c 8° Clar. Press 90
Accs. of 2 jys. in Cyclades and Crete, and in Asiatic Gk. isls. (1875, '86); and of visits to Lemnos, Thasos, and Samothrace ('89).

*Asia Minor (Islands of)* —*v.* **E** § 30

*Cyclades*

BENT, J. Theod. The Cyclades: life amg. the insular Gks. 12/6 8° Longman 85
Deals w. the present people and the anc. monumts. of the Greek islands.

*Patmos:* GEIL (Rev. W. E.) The Isle that is called Patmos $1·50 c 8° Rowland, *Phila.* 97
A missionary account; but with special chapters on customs and life.

*Ionian Islands*

ANSTED, D. T. Ionian Islands in 1863; result of a visit *o.p.* [*pb.* 16/] 8° W. H. Allen 63

GISSING, Geo. By the Ionian Sea—*v.* **E** § 24, *s.v.* Calabria

JERVIS-WHITE-JERVIS, Hy. History of Ionian Islands [during 19th cent.] *o.p.* [*pb.* 3/6] c 8° Chapman 63

KIRKWALL, Visc. [ed.] Four Years in the Ionian Islands, 2 vols. *o.p.* [*pb.* 21/] c 8° Chapman 64

XENOS, S. East and West *o.p.* [*pb.* 12/] r 8° Trübner (Paul) 65
A history of the British annexation of the Ionian Islands.

*Corfu:* ATKINSON (Sophie; art.) An Artist in Corfu: col. pl., w. l'rpr. 18/ *n.* 4° Herbert & Daniel 11

**Aetolia:** WOODHOUSE (W. J.) Aetolia: geogr., topogr., and antiqs. 21/ *n.* ($6·75) r 8° Clar. Press 97
With maps and ill. A full treatmt. of anc. and mod. Aetolia, tho' not complete on hist. of district.

**Argolis:** HORTON (G.) In Argolis; ill. $1·75 *n.* c 8° McClurg, *Chicago* 03
A pleasant acc. of a summer holiday in Argolis: valuable for its details of Mod.-Gk. folklore.

**Attica ; Athens** —*for* Ancient Athens *v.* **G** § 5

CARNARVON, L'd. Reminiscences of Athens and the Morea *o.p.* [*pb.* 7/6] c 8° Murray 69

FREEMAN, Prf. E. A. First Impressns. of Athens—*in his* Hist. Essays, Ser. iii, pp. 278-302 [*ut* **F** § 1] : visit in May, '77

HORTON, Geo. Modern Athens ; ill. $1·25 *n.* c 8° Scribner, *N.Y.* 01
Entertaining, picturesque descrn. of streets and shops, cafés and parks, people and theatres.

SYMONDS, J. A. Athens—*in his* Sketches in Italy and Greece, pp. 207-233, *ut* **E** § 24

WORDSWORTH, Bp Chr. Athens and Attica [notes of a tour] *o.p.* [*pb.* 5/] c 8° Murray [36] 69

**Athos (Mt.)** : RILEY (Athelstan) Athos, Mountain of the Monks ; ill. 21/ 8° Longman 87

**Epirus ; Thessaly** : CHIROL (V.) Twixt Greek and Turk : thro' Thessaly, etc. 10/6 c 8° Blackwood 81

## HOLLAND—*v.* E § 13 : BELGIUM AND HOLLAND

## 23 : ICELAND, AND THE FAROE ISLANDS

ANNANDALE, Nelson Faroes and Iceland ; 24 ill. 4/6 *n.* c 8° Clar. Press 05
Studies in island-life ; w. Appendix on the Celtic pony by Dr F. H. A. MARSHALL.

ARI FRODI Bk. of Settlemt. of Iceld. : 874-934 [tr.] 5/ 8° Wilson, *Kendal* 97

BISIKER, W. Across Iceland ; 50 ill. and Maps 12/6 8° Arnold 02
$4 Longman, *N.Y.* Acc. of a seven-wks.' tour in the isl. : a good descrn. of chief points in geogrs., geol., flora. By far the best wk. on geogr. and geol. of Icel. is Th. THORODDSEN'S *Island*, formg. *Ergänzunshefte* 152-3 of PETERMANN'S *Mittheilungen*, 22 m. 4° Justus Perthes, *Gotha* 05-6. His *Gesch. d. isländ. Geogr.*, 2 vols. [to 18th cent.] was pubd. 1897-8.

BURTON, Cpt. R. F. Ultima Thule : a summer in Iceland, 2 vols. 32/ 8° Nimmo, *Edin.* 75

COLES, J. Summer Travelling in Iceland ; ill. [w. ch. on Askja] 18/ 8° Murray 82

CONYBEARE, C. A. V. Place of Iceland in History of European Institns. 4/6 p 8° Parker 77

DASENT, [Sir] C. W. Life in Iceland in the Tenth century, 2 vols. *o.p.* [*pb.* 28/] 8° Douglas, *Edin.* 61

DUFFERIN, Earl of Letters from High Latitudes ; w. Introd. Dr R. W. Macan 1/ *n.* (35 c.) pott 8° Frowde [57] 10
[World's Classics.] A delightful acc. of visit in *Foam* in 1856 to Icel., Jan Mayen, and Spitzbergen.

de FONBLANQUE, C. A. Five Weeks in Iceland *o.p.* [*pb.* 3/6] c 8° Bentley 80

FORBES, Comr. C. S. Iceland : volcanoes, geysers, glaciers ; ill. *o.p.* [*pb.* 14/] c 8° Murray 60

GOULD, Rev. S. Baring- Iceland : its scenes and sagas ; ill. *o.p.* [*pb.* 10/6] r 8° Smith & Elder [63] 64

HOWELL, F. W. W. Icelandic Pictures drawn w. Pen and Pencil ; ill. 8/ i 8° R.T.S. 93

HUTCHINSON, Hor. G. A Saga of the *Sunbeam* [Icel. ; Newfdld., etc.] 6/6 *n.* c 8° Longman 11

LEITH, Mrs Disney Three Visits to Iceland ; ill. 5/6 c 8° Masters 97
An unpretentious account of visits to Skalholt, Geysir, and Njala district.

LOCK, C. G. W. The Home of the Eddas [1875-6] *o.p.* [*pb.* 16/] 8° Low 79

McCORMICK, Rev. W. T. A Ride across Iceland *o.p.* [*pb.* 2/6] c 8° Digby 92

METCALFE, Rev. F. The Oxonian in Iceland *o.p.* [*pb.* 2/6] 12° Chatto [61] 67

OSWALD, E. J. By Fell and Fjord : scenes and studs. in Iceld. ; ill. 7/6 p 8° Blackwood 82

OTTÉ, [Miss] E. C. Denmark and Iceland [For. Countries and Brit. Cols.] 3/6 c 8° Low 82

PAIGKULL, C. W. A Summer in Iceland *o.p.* [*pb.* 14/] 8° Chapman 68

TAYLOR, Bayard Egypt and Iceland in the Year 1874 ; ill. $1·50 12° Putnam, *N.Y.* 75

TWEEDIE, Mrs Alec A Girl's Ride in Iceland ; ill. 1/ *n.* c 8° H. Cox [94] 95

WATTS, W. Lord Snioland : Iceland, its jökulls and fjalls *o.p.* [*pb.* 7/6] p 8° Longman 75

" Across the Vatner Jökull : scenes in Iceland *o.p.* [*pb.* 6/] p 8° Longman 77

**Faroe Islands**

RUSSELL-JEAFFRESON, J. The Faroe Islands ; map and ill. 7/6 c 8° Low 97

**Arctic Geography** —*v.* **E** §§ 68, 69

## 24 : ITALY AND ISLANDS

**Bibliography** : BLANC (J). Bibliogr. Italico-Franç. Universelle, 2 v. [Fch. bks. only, 1475-1885] 8° *Milan* 86

**Anthology** : SHEPARD-PHELPS (Ruth) [ed.] Skies Italian [poet. selns.] 5/ *n.* f 8° Methuen 10

WOLLASTON, G. H. [ed.] The Englishman in Italy [poet. selns.] 5/ *n.* ($1·75) f 8° Clar. Press 09

**Early Travel** : de BROSSES, Ch. [1709-77] Seln. fr. Letters, tr. L'd Ronald Gower 10/6 s 4° Paul 97
Very interesting memrs., excell. tr. DE BROSSES, a Fchman., in 1738, at age of 30, visited Italy and wrote his impressns. in a ser. of epistles to friends at Rome, Genoa, Flor., Ven., Nap., Vesuv., Rome.

de MONTAIGNE, M. E. [1533-92] Journal of Travels in Italy by way of Switz. & Germy. in 1580 & 1581, tr. W. G. Waters, 3 vols. ; w. Introd. 15/ *n.* 16° Murray 03

SMOLLETT, Tobias G. [1721–71] Travels through France and Italy—*ut* **E** § 14 [in 1763–5]

**Recent Travel and Description ; Guides**

de AMICIS, Edm. Travels in Italy [tr. (fr. Ital.)] ; ill. *o.p.* [*pb.* $1·50] c 8° Putnam, *N.Y.* [81] 83

BAEDEKER, Karl [pub.] Italy : hdbk. f. trav'rs., 3 v. ; maps & plans [Scrib., *N.Y.*] s 8° Unwin [ ] 06–9
i : *N. Italy*, 8/ ($2·40 *n.*) ; ii : *Centr. It. and Rome*, 7/6 ($2·25 *n.*) ; iii : *S. It. and Sicily*, 6/ ($1·80 *n.*).

,, Italy from the Alps to Naples [$2·40 n. Scribner, *N.Y.*] 8/ s 8° Unwin [ ] 09

BEAUCLERK, Dr W. N. Rural Italy [agricultural condn.] *o.p.* [*pb.* 9/] 8° Bentley 89

BELLOC, Hilaire The Path to Rome—*ut* **E** § 11

CRAWFORD, Marion Southern Italy and Sicily and Rulers of South ; 100 ill. 8/6 *n.* ($2·50 *n.*) c 8° Macmillan [00] 05

DEECKE, Prf. W. Italy [tr.] ; ill. 15/ r 8° Sonnenschein 04
$5 *n.* Macmillan, *N.Y.* Full of geographical and historical detail. Incls. Malta and Sardinia.

FREEMAN, Prf. E. A. —*in his* Historical Sketches—*ut* **F** § 53 [chiefly Italian]

,, Studies of Travel : Italy $1 (2/6) 16° Putnam 93
Veii, Ostia, Norba, Segni, and other places rarely visited by tourists.

GAUTIER, Théoph. Journeys in Italy, tr. B. B. Vermilye $3 *n.* 8° Brentano, *N.Y.* 02

GREGOROVIUS, Ferd. Latian Summers & an Excursion in Umbria [tr.] 6/ c 8° Junr. Army Stores 02
A tr. of the 2nd volume of his *Wanderjahre in Italien* [travels 1850–60].

HAGGARD, H. Rider A Winter Pilgrimage ; 21 ill. 12/6 *n.* ($1·50) c 8° Longman 01
Partly occupied with Italian travel on well-known routes in 1900.

HAWTHORNE, Nat. —*in his* French and Italian Note-Books—*ut* **E** § 14 [in 1858–9]

HEINE, Heinr. [1799–1856] Italian Travel Sketches, etc. [tr.] [Scott Lib.] 1/6 c 8° Walter Scott 92
Conts. only first pt. of Ital. sketches. HEINE's letters on French stage and short pref. by Th. GAUTIER make up the vol. *Vide* also **K** § 91.

HOWE, Maud Two in Italy [7/6 *n.* Paul] $2 *n* 8° Little & Brown, *Boston* 05

HOWELLS, W. D. Italian Journeys ; 83 ill. J. Pennell $3 ; Ch. Edn. $1·50 c 8° Houghton, *Boston* [67] 01
10/ *n.* Heinemann. Ch. Edn., 2 v., 18° 2/ Douglas, *Edin.* Travels whilst author was U.S. Consul at Venice.

JAMES, Hy. [Am.] Italian Hours ; ill. Jos. Pennell 25/ *n.* 4° Heinemann 09
$7·50 *n.* Houghton, *Boston.* Repr. essays dealg. w. Italy, travel there, impressns. of cities, etc.

,, Portraits of Places—*ut* **E** § 11

KING, Mrs R. M. Italian Highways *o.p.* [*pb.* 7/6] c 8° Bentley 96
An observant account, coverg. pretty well the whole of the tourist's Italy.

LATHROP, Elise Sunny Days in Italy ; 30 pl. & col. front. 10/6 *n.* 8° 11

LEYKEN, N. A. 'Where the Oranges Grow' [tr.] 6/ c 8° Greening 01
A humorous account of adventures of Russian travellers in Italy. Tr. fr. Russian.

LORIMER, Norma By the Waters of Italy ; 17 ill. (1 col.) 12/6 *n.* 8° Hutchinson 10
A pot-pourri of love, philosophy, and descrn. of scenery—including an apology for the inartistic in man and woman.

McCURDY, Edw. Roses of Paestum 3/6 *n.* c 8° G. Allen 00
Essays on Italy and various mediaeval themes.

MACMILLAN & Co. [pubs.] Italy & Sicily ; ill. [Macm.'s Guides] 10/ *n.* ($3·25 *n.*) gl 8° Macmillan [01] 11

MURRAY, Jno. [pub.] North Italy and Venice ; maps *o.p.* [*pb.* 10/] s 8° Stanford [60] 03

,, Central Italy and Florence 9/ c 8° Stanford [ ]

,, South Italy, 2 Pts. ea. 6/ c 8° Stanford [ ]

NORTON, C. E. Notes of Travel and Study in Italy $1·25 c 8° Houghton, *Boston* [60] 87
Valuable for its delicate apprecn. of value of art. Incl. acc. of bldg. Orvieto Cath. in 14 cent.

PLATT, D. F. Through Italy with Car and Camera ; 200 ill. $5 *n.* (21/ *n.*) 8° Putnam 08

RIDDELL, Charl. E. [Mrs J. H.] A Mad Tour [Centr. Italy on foot] *o.p.* [*pb.* 10/6] c 8° Bentley 92

RUSKIN, Jno. —*for his works on Italian Art, Monuments, etc., v.* **I** §§ 88, 97, 121

SLADEN, Douglas How to see Italy by Rail ; 130 ill. 7/6 *n.* s 8° Paul 11

SULLIVAN, T. R. Lands of Summer ; ill. $1·50 *n.* c 8° Houghton, *Boston* 08
6/ *n.* Constable. A personal record of journeys in Italy, Sicily, and Greece, by a cultured American.

SYMONDS, J. A. Sketches and Studies in Italy and Greece, ed. H. F. Brown, 3 Ser. ea. 7/6 c 8° Smith & Elder [74–83] 00
Ea. $2 *n.* Scribner, *N.Y.* Vol. i : *Sks. in It. and Greece* (1874) ; ii : *Sks. and Studs. in It.* (1879) ; iii : *Ital. Byways* (1883).

VILLARI, Linda Here and There in Italy and over the Border 5/ c 8° W. H. Allen 93

WHARTON, Edith N. J. Italian Backgrounds ; ill. [10/6 *n.* Macm.] $2·50 *n.* r 8° Scribner, *N.Y.* 03

ZANGWILL, Israel Italian Fantasies 8/6 *n.* 8° Heinemann 11

**Life and People**

*Eighteenth Century*

PIOZZI, Mrs [*form.* Mrs THRALE ; 1739–1821] Glimpses of Ital. Society ; ill. 6/ c 8° Seeley 92
$2 Scribner, *N.Y.* Selns. fr. once well-known *Journey of Mrs Piozzi* (friend of Dr JOHNSON) [1789] ; w. Introd. by C'ess Martinengo CESARESCO.

de STAEL, Mme. [1766–1817] Corinne ; or Italy [tr.] 3/6 c 8° Bohn's Lib. 88

de STAEL, Mme. The same [tr.], w. Introd. Prf. G. Saintsbury 5/ *n.* f 8° Dent 94
A poetical portrayal of Italy and the Italians; full of passion and beauty. Orig. appeared 1807.

*Modern:* de AMICIS (Edm.) Military Life in Italy [tr. (fr. Italian)]; 8 pl. *o.p.* [*pb.* $2] c 8° Putnam, *N.Y.* 82
BAGOT, Rich. My Italian Year; ill. 10/6 *n.* 8° Mills & Boon 11
BAZIN, René The Italians of To-day [tr.] $1·25 c 8° Holt, *N.Y.* 97
CARR, Mrs Comyns North Italian Folk; ill. *o.p.* [*pb.* 7/6] 8° Chatto [78] 82
DICKENS, Chas. Pictures from Italy—*ut* **K** § 50 [Italy in 1844]
GARLANDA, F. The New Italy [tr.] [pres. polit. and soc. condns.] c 8° Putnam *in prep.*
GISSING, Geo. By the Ionian Sea: ramble in Southern Italy 5/ c 8° Chapman [01] 05
GORDON, Lina Duff Home Life in Italy; ill. [$1·75 *n.* Macm., *N.Y.*] 10/6 *n.* 8° Methuen 09
HUTTON, Edw. Italy & the Italians; ill. [$1·50 *n.* Dutton, *N.Y.*] 6/ c 8° Blackwood [02] 03
KING (Bolton) + OKEY (T.) Italy To-day 6/ *n.* 8° Nisbet [01] 09
An excellent account of Italian politics and institutions; with much as to trade, social condns., etc.
de LAVELEYE, E. Letters from Italy [tr.] 3/6 c 8° Unwin [86] 92
Letters on art, scenery, antiquities, and political and economical questions.
MARTEL, C. Military Italy; map *o.p.* [*pb.* 12/6] 8° Macmillan 84
MYRES, J. L. —*in his* History of Rome, *ut* **F** § 12
Ch. i conts. one of best outls. of geogr. of It. as far as it has affected its hist.
VILLARI, Prf. L. Italian Life in Town & Country; ill. [Our Eur. Nbrs.] 3/6 *n.* c 8° Newnes 02
$1·20 *n.* Putnam, *N.Y.* Polit. and social life, econ. condns., home-life, relig., educ., etc.: a gd. suppl. to KING + OKEY, *sup.*
WADDINGTON, Mary A. K. Ital. Letters of a Diplomat's Wife [1880–1904] 10/6 *n.* 8° Smith & Elder 05
WHARTON, Anne H. Italian Days and Ways; ill. $1·50 *n.* c 8° Lippincott, *Phila.* 06
Travels of 3 Amer. ladies, wr. in form of letters.
WHITING, Lilian Italy, the Magic Land; 32 pl. 7/6 *n.* c 8° Cassell 11
ZIMMERN, Helen The Italy of the Italians 6/ *n.* c 8° Pitman 06

**Castles; Palaces; Villas**

CHAMPNEY, Eliz. W. Romance of Italian Villas: N. Italy; pl. & ill. $3 *n.* (15/ *n.*) 8° Putnam 06
D'AUVERGNE, E. B. Famous Castles and Palaces of Italy; pl. (some col.) 15/ *n.* 8° Laurie 11
WHARTON, Edith N. J. Italian Villas and their Gardens; ill. $5 (21/ *n.*) 8° Lane 04

**Cathedrals: Churches** —*v.* **I** § 121

**Cities; Towns:** *Collectively*

BLASHFIELD, E. H. + Evang. W. Italian Cities, 2 vols. 12/ c 8° Bullen 01
COLLINS, W. W. Cathedral Cities of Italy; 56 col. pl. 16/ *n.* 8° Heinemann 11
FROTHINGHAM, Prf. A. L. Roman Cities of N. It. & Dalmatia; ill. $2·25 *n.* (10/6 *n.*) 8° Macmillan 10
HARE, A. J. C. Cities of Northern Italy, 2 vols.; ill. *o.p.* c 8° G. Allen [76] 04
$3·50 Macmillan, *N.Y.* Vol. i: Florence, Siena and towns of Tusc. and Umbr.; ii: In the Emilia and Marche, and towns in Umbr. and Campagna.
,, Cities of S. Italy; ill. 5/ *n.* 8° Heinemann [83] 10
,, Cities of Central Italy, 2 vols.; ill. *o.p.* c 8° G. Allen [76]
MAUREL, André Little Cities of Italy [tr.]; 32 ill. $2·50 *n.* (9/ *n.*) 8° Putnam 11
Flor., San Gimignano, Monte Oliveto, Pisa, Lucca, Prato, Pistoia, Arezzo, Lecco, Bergamo, Verona, Vicenza, Padua, Mantua, Argua.
SYMONS, Arth. Cities of Italy [$2 Dutton, *N.Y.*] 4/6 *n.* c 8° Dent 08
A colln. of essays, remarkable for their delicate observation and fine criticism, dealing with Rome, Venice, Naples, Ravenna, Pisa, Siena, Verona, Bologna, Bergamo, Lorenzo Lotto, Brescia, Roumanino.
WILLIAMS, Egerton R. Hill-Towns of Italy $3 *n.* 8° Houghton, *Boston* 04
10/6 *n.* Smith & Elder. Interestg. and instructive descrns. of towns and Central Apennines, w. bits of medieval lore interspersed.
WILLIAMSON, G. C. Cities of Northern Italy [$1·25 *n.* Wessels, *N.Y.*] 3/6 *n.* c 8° Richards 01

**Islands:** *Collectively*

FORESTER, Thos. Rambles in Corsica and Sardinia—*ut* **E** § 14
VUILLIER, Gaston The Forgotten Isles [tr.]—*ut* **E** § 14
Corsica, Sardinia, Majorca, Minorca. 162 illns. by author.

*Capri*: GREGOROVIUS (F.) Island of Capri [tr.] [$1 Lee, *Boston*] 5/ sq 8° Unwin [79] 96
Scenery, historical assocns. (early Roman emperors, notably AUGUSTUS and TIBERIUS), ruins, legends, etc. Based on travel in 1853 *sqq.*
DOUGLAS, Norman Siren Land [Capri and Sorrento] 6/. *n.* c 8° Dent 11
WALTERS, Dr Alan A Lotos-Eater in Capri; map and ill. *o.p.* [*pb.* 10/6] c 8° Bentley 92

*Corsica* —*v.* **E** § 14

*Sardinia* —*for* History, *v.* **F** § 53
EDWARDES, Chas. Sardinia and the Sardes *o.p.* [*pb.* 14/] 8° Bentley 89
GRETTON, Mrs G. Englishwoman in Italy [Roman States and Sardinia] 6/ p 8° Hurst [60] 61
TENNANT, Rob. Sardinia and its Resources 12/6 l 8° Stanford 85

*Sicily* —*for* History of Sicily *v.* **F** §§ 12, 53

CAICO, Louise Sicilian Ways and Days ; 128 ill. 12/6 *n.* 8° Long 10

ELLIOT, Mrs F. Diary of an Idle Woman in Sicily, 2 vols. 2/ 18° Arrowsmith [81] 85

HARE, A. J. C. + BADDELEY (St C.) Sicily ; maps and ill. 3/ 12° Heinemann [83] 05

HOWE, Maud Sicily in Shadow and in Sun ; ill. [12/6 *n.* Stanley Paul] $3 *n.* 8° Little & B., *Bost.* 11
Incls. full acc. of relief wk. of Amer. citizens at Rome in conn. w. Messina earthquake.

JONES, H. F. Diversions in Sicily 5/ *n.* c 8° Rivers 09
A desultory—yet exact—bk., avoiding all such matter as is to be found in guides and handbks.

LORIMER, Norma By the Waters of Sicily ; ill. 10/6 *n.* 8° Hutchinson 01
Love story in epistolary form, giving much information about the island.

MONROE, Prf. W. S. Sicily, the Garden of the Mediterr. ; ill. [7/6 *n.* Bell] $3 8° Page, *Boston* 09

PATON, W. A. Picturesque Sicily ; ill. [scen., antiqs., life] $2·50 (10/6) c 8° Harper 98
A journalistic account of modern Sicily, with some particulars of antiquarian remains.

PERRY, W. Copland Sicily in Fable, History, Art, & Song ; maps 5/ *n.* ($1·50 *n.*) c 8° Macmillan 08

RIVELA (A.) + v. PERNULL (H.) Dead Cities of Sicily ; ill. [a guide-bk.] 4/ fr. 8° Virzi, *Palermo*

SLADEN, Douglas In Sicily, 2 vols. ; 300 ill. (13 col.) and maps 25/ *n.* r 8° Sands 02
1896, 1898, 1900. Attempts to give an exhaustive account of the island and its remains.

,, Segesta, Selinunte, and West of Sicily 10/6 *n.* 4° Sands 03

,, Sicily ; 334 ill. [an encyclopædia] 5/ *n.* c 8° Methuen 05

,, + LORIMER (N.) Queer Things about Sicily ; ill. 7/6 *n.* 8° Treherne 05

TWEEDIE, Mrs Alec Sunny Sicily ; 130 ill. 18/ *n.* 8° Hutchinson 04

WAERN, Cecilia Mediæval Sicily ; ill. [$4 *n.* Dutton, *N.Y.*] 12/6 *n.* r 8° Duckworth 10

WHITAKER, Tina [*née* SCALIA] Sicily and England 10/6 *n.* 8° Constable 07
Social and political reminiscences by the daughter of a Sicilian patriot, 1848–70.

**Lakes**

DU LANE, Ella [art.] Ital. Lakes : 69 col. pl. ; w. l'rpr. R. Bagot [$6 *n.* Macm., *N.Y.*] 20/ *n.* sq 8° Black 05

MCCRACKAN, W. D. Italian Lakes : quaint towns and villa-grdns. ; ill. $2 12° Page, *Boston* 07

*Como :* JOHNSTON (Virg. W.) Lake Como : a world's shrine ; ill. 03

LUND, Rev. T. W. M. Lake of Como : hist., art, archæol. ; ill. 5/ *n.* 16° Paul [87] 10

**Mountains** —*for* Etna *and* Vesuvius, *v.* **H** § 28

*Alps*

BUTLER, Sam. Alps & Sanctuaries of Piedmont & Canton Ticino ; well ill. 10/6 f 4° Fifield [81] *n.d.*

FRESHFIELD, D. W. The Italian Alps ; ill. *o.p.* [*pb.* 15/] p 8° Longman 75
Description of the mountains of Ticino, Lomb., the Trentino, Venetia.

*Apennines*

ALEXANDER, Fcsca. Christ's Folk in Apennine, ed. J. Ruskin 3/6 s 8° G. Allen, *Orpgtn.* [87] 89

'SCOTT, Leader' [Mrs BAXTER] A Nook in the Apennines 7/6 c 8° Paul 76

STOKES, Marg. Six Months in the Apennines—*ut* **I** § 86

**River** : *Tiber*

DAVIES, W. Pilgrimage of the Tiber [and its tributaries] 18/ 8° Low [73] 75

SMITH, S. A. The Tiber and its Tributaries *o.p.* [*pb.* 10/6] 8° Longman 77

**Scenery**

MANNING, S. Italian Pictures, drawn with Pen and Pencil ; ill. 8/ i 8° R.T.S. [76] 85

MURRAY, A. H. H. [art.] On the Old Road thro' Frce. to Florence—*ut* **E** § 14, *s.v.* Scenery

TROLLOPE, T. A. [ed.] Italy from Alps to Mt. Etna : tr. fr. Germ. ; 164 ill. 15/ s 4° Virtue [76] 88

**Seas**

PEIXOTTO, E. C. By Italian Seas ; ill. by auth. [12/ *n.* Hodder] $2·50 *n.* 8° Scribner, *N.Y.* 06
Ab. hf. the bk. is devoted to Dalmatia, Malta, Tunis. Of value for its delicate drwgs.

*Adriatic Sea* —*for* Austrian Side *v.* **E** § 12

*JACKSON, F. Berkeley Shores of the Adriatic, 2 Parts ; ill. ea. 21/ *n.* m 8° Murray 06–8
i : *Italian Side* ; ii : *Austrian Side.* A valuable architectural and archæological (incl. customs and folklore) 'tour'. The Second Pt. is less architectural than the First. Valuable ill.

PATON, A. A. Highlands and Islands of the Adriatic, 2 vols.—*ut* **E** § 12

**Shrines :** WATERS (W. G.) Five Italian Shrines ; ill. 12/ *n.* m 8° Murray 07
Tombs of S. Augustine, Pavia ; S. Dominic, Bologna ; S. Peter Martyr, Milan ; Tabernacle of Orcagna, Florence ; S. Donatus, Arezzo.

**Provinces ; Districts**

*Abruzzi :* MACDONELL (Anne) In the Abruzzi : country and people ; ill. 6/ *n.* c 8° Chatto 08

*Aosta :* FERRERO (F.) Valley of Aosta ; ill. [descr. and historical] $1·75 (7/6 *n.*) 8° Putnam 10

*Apulia:* Ross (Janet) The Land of Manfred; ill. 10/6 c 8° Murray 89
*Calabria:* GISSING, Geo. By the Ionian Sea; map and ill. 5/ *n.* c 8° Chapman [01] 05
Travels in Calabria. An interesting, well-written book, by the deceased novelist.
*Casentino:* ECKENSTEIN (Lina) Through the Casentino; col. pl. 2/6 *n.* f 8° Dent 02
NOYES, Ella The Casentino; col. pl. [$3·50 *n.* Dutton, *N.Y.*] 10/6 *n.* 8° Dent 06
*Etruria* —*v. also* G § 6, *s.v.* Etruria
GRAY, Mrs E. C. History of Etruria, 3 Pts. *o.p.* [*pb.* 36/] p 8° Hatchard 43–68
SEYMOUR, Fredk. Up Hill and Down Dale in Anc. Etruria; 12 ill. 10/6 *n.* 8° Unwin 10
*Lombardy:* CESARESCO (C'ess E. M.) Lombard Studies; ill. [descr. and hist.] 16/ 8° Unwin 02
*Piedmont:* BUTLER (Sam.) Alps & Sanctuaries of Piedmont & Canton Ticino; ill. 10/6 s 4° Fifield [82]
ROSSI, L. M. The Santuario of Madonna di Vico; ill. 21/ *n.* ($6·50 *n.*) 8° Macmillan 07
*Riviera* —*v.* E § 14
*Tuscany:* CAMERON (Mary L.) Old Etruria and Modern Tuscany; 32 ill. 7/6 *n.* 8° Methuen 09
CARMICHAEL, M. In Tuscany: towns, types, tongue, etc.; ill. 6/ *n.* c 8° Burns & Oates [01] 02
$2 *n.* Dutton, *N.Y.* Deals with places and things off the beaten track of the tourist; interesting and curious.
GOFF, Col. R. C. [art.] Florence & Some Tuscan Cities: 75 col. pl.; w. l'rpr. Clarissa Goff [$6 *n.* Macmillan. *N.Y.*] 20/ *n.* sq 8° Black 05
HEWLETT, Maur. Earthwork out of Tuscany—*v. inf., s.v.* Florence
" The Road in Tuscany: a commentary; 200 ill. 8/6 *n.* c 8° Macmillan [04] 06
HOWELLS, W. D. Tuscan Cities, ill. J. Pennell, etc. $3·50 4° Houghton, *Boston* [85] 86
Florence, Siena, Pisa, Lucca, Pistoja, Prato, Fiesole.
HUTTON, Edw. In Unknown Tuscany; 20 ill. 7/6 *n.* 8° Methuen 09
" Siena and Southern Tuscany; ill. c 8° Methuen 10
In a Tuscan Garden 5/ *n.* ($1·50 *n.*) c 8° Lane 02
" Author of Under Petraia; w. some saunterings 5/ *n.* ($1·50 *n.*) c 8° Lane 09
Pleasant chat on Tusc. life, gardens, etc., w. visits to Bologna, Padua, Venice, Verona, etc.
LEES, Dorothy N. Scenes and Shrines in Tuscany [$1·25 *n.* Dutton, *N.Y.*] 3/6 *n.* c 8° Dent 07
" Tuscan Feasts and Tuscan Friends 5/ *n.* c 8° Chatto 07
Acc. of author's life in an old Tuscan villa, descrg. life, customs, etc., of her poor neighbrs.
ROSS, Janet Italian Sketches [of the People, Scenery, etc., of Tuscany]; 14 ill. 7/6 c 8° Paul 87
'SCOTT, Leader' [Mrs BAXTER] Tuscan Studies & Sketches; ill. [topogr., antiqs., social] 10/6 i 16° Unwin 88
SEYMOUR, F. Up Hill and Down Dale in Ancient Etruria; ill. 10/6 *n.* 8° Unwin 10
Deals chfly. w. abandoned sites, and their antiqs.—inclg., however, Orvieto and Viterbo. Chs. on Etruscans and theories held ab. them.
VANE, Sir Fcs. Walks and People in Tuscany; ill. [walkg. tour] 5/ *n.* ($1·50 *n.*) c 8° Lane 10
VILLARI, Linda On Tuscan Hills and Venetian Waters; ill. 7/6 16° Unwin 84
*Games:* HEYWOOD (W.) Palio and Ponte; ill. 21/ *n.* r 8° Methuen 04
Deals w. the athletic sports of medieval Italy, espec. of that latest survival of the old chivalric games, the Palio of Siena.
*Umbria*
CRUIKSHANK, J. W. + A. M. The Umbrian Towns [histor. guide] 3/6 *n.* c 8° Richards 01
GREGOROVIUS, Ferd. Latian Summers and an Excursion in Umbra [tr.]—*ut sup.*
HUTTON, Edw. Cities of Umbria; ill. (20 col.) [$2 *n.* Dutton, *N.Y.*] 6/ c 8° Methuen 05
de SÉLINCOURT, Beryl D. Homes of First Franciscans in Umbria, Borders of Tuscany, and Northern Marches; 13 ill. [$1·50 *n.* Dutton, *N.Y.*] 4/6 *n.* c 8° Dent 05
*Assisi:* GOFF (Mrs. Rob.) Assisi of St Francis; ill. Col. R. Goff 20/ *n.* 4° Chatto 08
GORDON, Lina D. Assisi; ill. [Mediæv. Towns; $1·50 *n.* Dutton, *N.Y.*] 3/6 *n.* s 8° Dent 00
*Basso Padovano:* SYMONDS (Marg.) Days Spent on a Doge's Farm; 50 ill. 10/6 *n.* 8° Unwin [93] 08
Genial sketches of rural life and *villeggiatura* in Basso Padovano, a little-known corner of Italy (nr. Padua).
*Bologna:* JAMES (Edith E. C.) Bologna: history, antiqs., art 12/ *n.* ($4·15) 8° Clar. Press 10
*Ferrara:* NOYES (Ella) Ferrara; ill. [Mediæv. Towns; $1·75 *n.* Dutton, *N.Y.*] 4/6 *n.* s 8° Dent 04

**Florence** —*v. also* Tuscany, *sup.*; *for* History *v.* F § 53
ALLEN, Grant Florence [$1·25 *n.* Wessels, *N.Y.*] 3/6 *n.* f 8° Richards [97] 00
BIAGI, Dr Guido Men and Manners of Old Florence; 49 ill. 15/ *n.* 8° Unwin 09
Vivid sketches of social life in Flor. fr. 13th to beginning of 19th century.
BROWN, Rev. J. Wood The Builders of Florence; 74 ill. 18/ *n.* 4° Methuen 07
" Florence, Past and Present; maps and ill. 6/ c 8° Rivington 11
HARE, A. J. C. Florence, ed. St Clair Baddeley 3/6 12° G. Allen [84] 04–7
With *Venice* [*ut inf.*], in 1 vol., $2 *n.* Macmillan, *N.Y.*
*GARDNER, E. G. Florence; ill. [Mediæv. Towns; $1·75 *n.* Dutton, *N.Y.*] 4/6 *n.* s 8° Dent [00] 03

GRIFI, E. Saunterings in Florence; maps & ill. [useful informn.] 3/6 c 8° Unwin [98] 98

HEWLETT, Maur. Earthwork out of Tuscany: impressions & translations 4/ n. gl 8° Macmillan [95] 01
2·50 *n.* Putnam, *N.Y.* Aims, not very successfully, at givg. literary form to ideas collected fr. art and life dur. many visits to Italy, mainly Florence.

HORNER, [Misses] S. + J. Walks in Florence & its Environs, 2 v.; ill. 5/ c 8° Smith & Alder [73] 84

HUTTON, Edw. Florence & Cities of Northern Tuscany; 32 ill. (16 col.) 6/ c 8° Methuen 07

,, Country Walks about Florence; 52 ill. 5/ *n.* f 8° Methuen 08

JOHNSON, Virginia W. The Lilly of the Arno; 25 photogravs. $3 8° Estes, *Boston* 91
12/6 Gay & Hancock. A pleasant, discursive and informal hist. and descrn. of Florence and its modern life.

OLIPHANT, [Mrs] Marg. Makers of Florence; ill.
[Dante, Giotto, Savonarola] 10/6 ($2·50 *n.*) c 8° Macmillan [76]

ROSS, Janet Florentine Villas; ill. [$25 *n.* Dutton, *N.Y.*] 63/ *n.* f° Dent 01

,, Old Florence & Modern Tuscany; ill. [$1·50 *n.* Dutton, *N.Y.*] 3/6 *n.* c 8° Dent 04

,, Florentine Palaces & their Stories; ill. [$2 *n.* Dutton, *N.Y.*] 6/ *n.* 8° Dent 05

RUSKIN, Jno. Mornings in Florence—*ut* **K** § 89

'SCOTT, Leader' [Mrs BAXTER] Echoes of Old Florence, her Palaces and who have lived in them
5/ s 8° Unwin 94
Interesting and often curious notices of social and political life—ranging from Popes to woolcarders.

TAINE, H. A. Italy: Florence and Venice [tr.] $2·50 12° Holt, *N.Y.* [69] 75

VAUGHAN, Herb. M. Florence and her Treasures; ill. [incl. topogr. and hist.] 5/ *n.* f 8° Methuen

WHITING, Lilian Florence of Landor; ill. [10/6 *n.* Gay & H.] $2·50 *n.* 8° Little & Brown, *Boston* 05

YRIARTE, C. Florence [tr.]; 500 ill. 63/ i 4° Low 82

*Ch. of Sa. Maria Novella:* BROWN (Rev. J. W.) Dominican Ch. of S. Maria Novella; ill.
21/ *n.* 4° Schulze, *Edin.* 02

*Literary Associations:* HUTTON (Laur.) Literary Landmarks of Florence; ill. $1 p 8° Harper, *N.Y.* 97
Dante, Savonarola, Galileo, Landor, and the Brownings are the principal figures.

*Pitti Palace:* ADDISON (Julia de W.) Art of Pitti Palace $2 *n.* 12° Page, *Boston* 04
6/ *n.* Bell. Includes a short history of the building and its various owners.

**Genoa** —*for* History *v.* **F** § 53

CARDEN, R. W. The City of Genoa; 12 col. pl. and 20 ill. 10/6 *n.* 8° Methuen 08

JOHNSON, Virginia W. Genoa, the Superb: City of Columbus; photogravs. $3 c 8° Estes, *Boston* 92

**Gubbio:** McCRACKEN (Laura) Gubbio: hist., legend, archæol.; maps and ill. 5/ *n.* c 8° Nutt 05

**Lecce:** BRIGGS (M. S.) In the Heel of Italy 8/6 *n* c 8° Melrose 10

**Lucca:** Ross (Janet) Lucca [Mediæv. Towns; $1·75 *n.* Dutton, *N.Y.*] 4/6 *n.* s 8° Dent

**Milan:** NOYES (Ella) Story of Milan; ill. [Mediæv. Towns; $1·75 *n.* Dutton, *N.Y.*] 4/6 *n.* s 8° Dent 08

**Naples** —*for* History *v.* **F** § 53

*Bibliograph:* GÜNTHER (R. T.) Bibliogr. of Topogr. and Geol. Wks. on Phlegraean Fields—*ut* **H** § 28

FITZGERALD, A. [art.] Naples: 80 col. pl., w. l'rpr. Sybil Fitzgerald
[$6 *n.* Macm., *N.Y.* 20/ *n.* sq 8° Black 04

MUNTHE, Axel Letters from a Mourning City [tr.] 6/ c 8° Murray [87] 99
A new translation by the author of his account of the plague at Naples, 1884.

Naples Riviera (The); w. 25 col. ill. M. Greiffenhagen 6/ c 8° Methuen 07
Descrs. and illustrates many places of beauty lying betw. Bays of Naples and Salerno, incl. islds. of Ischia and Capri.

NORWAY, A. H. Naples, Past and Present; 40 ill. 6/ c 8° Methuen 01
Antiquities, folklore, life and scenery; a charming account.

ROLFE, E. Neville Naples in 1888; ill. [by Brit. Consul at Naples] *o.p.* [*pb.* 6/] c 8° Trübner (Paul) 89

,, Naples in the Nineties; ill. [sequel to above] 7/6 c 8° Black 97

**Padua**

FOLIGNO, Cesare Padua; ill. [Mediæv. Towns; $1·75 *n.* Dutton, *N.Y.*] 4/6 *n.* c 8° Dent 10

**Perugia**

SYMONDS, (Miss M.) + GORDON (Miss L. Duff) Story of Perugia
[Mediæv. Towns; $1·50 *n.* Dutton, *N.Y.*] 3/6 *n.* s 8° Dent 98
Charmingly-written—the best guide-book; but full of historical inaccuracies.

**Pisa**: Ross (Janet) Story of Pisa; ill. [Mediæv. Towns; $1·75 *n.* Dutton, *N.Y.*] 4/6 *n.* s 8° Dent 09

**Pompeii** —*v.* **G** § 6

**Varallo-Sesia:** BUTLER (Sam.) Ex Voto: acc. of Sacro Monte 5/ *n.* c 8° Fifield [88] *n.d.*

*Vincigliata:* 'SCOTT (Leader)' [Mrs BAXTER] Vincigliata and Maiano 25/ i 8° Unwin 91
Descr. of model of a medieval Tusc. stronghold erected by Mr TEMPLE-LEADER in the fifties on ruins of old castle of Vincigliata, its fabric, archit., and contents, w. summaries of histor. documts. rel. to it, and incidental criticisms on Etruscan remains, etc.

**Rome** —*for* History *v.* **F** § 53; *for* Archæology *v.* **G** § 6

BELLOC, Hilaire The Path to Rome—*ut* **E** § 11

CAPGRAVE, Jno. [15 cent.] Ye Solace of Pilgrimes, ed. C. A. Mills 7/6 *n.* ($3) 4° Frowde 11

CHAMPNEY, Eliz. W. Romance of Rom. Villas; Romance of Imp. Rome; ill. ea. (15/ *n.*) 8° Putnam 08–10

CHANDLERY, F'r P. J. Pilgrim Walks in Rome; a Guide to its Holy Places 7/ *n.* r 8° Manresa Pr.
87 ill. and map. Description of and information about all the chief R.C. sites and buildings in Rome.

CLEMENT, [Mrs] C. E. Rome, the Eternal City, 2 v.; 20 photogravs. $6 8° Estes & Lauriat, *Boston* 02
25/ *n.* Gay & Hancock. Contains a very large account of information useful and interesting to the traveller.

CRAWFORD, F. Marion Ave Roma Immortalis; studies 8/6 *n.* ($2·50 *n.*) c 8° Macmillan [98] 03
A very full and well-wr. acc. of histor. assocns. of city, arrgd. under the 14 wards into wh. Rome is divided.

DENNIE, Jno. Rome of To-day & Yesterday; maps & 58 ill. $3·50 (21/ *n.*) 8° Putnam [93] 98
Deals with Rome of the Republic and Empire.

ELLIOT, Fces. [Mrs MINTO] Roman Gossip 6/ c 8° Murray [94] 96
$1 Harper, *N.Y.* PIO NONO; C'ESS SPAUR; Card. ANTONELLI; 'Il Re Galantuomo'; GARIBALDI; The Roman BUONAPARTES; 'Madame Mère'; Qu. HORTENSE; P'cess PAULINE, etc.

FORBES, S. R. Rambles in Rome 3/6 p 8° Nelson 82

de la GOURNERIE, E. Christian Rome: Histor. View of its Monuments, etc.; 2 v. 15/ c 8° Rolandi 98
Translated by Lady Macdonald; preface by Cardinal Vaughan. A.D. 41–1867.

GREGOROVIUS, Ferd. Roman Journals of [tr.], ed. F. Althaus [Bohn's Lib.] 3/6 *n.* 8° Bell [07] 11
$1 *n.* Macm., *N.Y.* An interestg. picture of the period of mod. transformn. of Rome and Italy, of wh. he was eye-witness fr. 1852 to 1874.

" History of the City of Rome in Middle Ages [tr.]—*ut* **F** § 53

HARE, A. J. C. Walks in Rome, 2 v.; maps & ill. [$2·50 *n.* Macm., *N.Y.*] 10/6 *n.* c 8° Paul [71] 05

" Days nr. Rome, ed. St Clair Baddeley; map and 32 ill. [$2·50 *n.* Macm., *N.Y.*] 6/ *n.* f 8° Paul [74] 06

HOWE, Maud Roma Beata; ill. [letters] $1·50 *n.* 8° Little & Brown, *Boston* [04] 09

HOWELLS, W. D. Roman Holidays and Others; ill. $3 *n.* (10/6) 8° Harper 08
Madeira, Spain, Genoa, Naples, Pompeii, Rome, Leghorn, Pisa, Monte Carlo.

HUTTON, Edw. Rome; 16 col. pl. 6/ c 8° Methuen 09

'LEE, Vernon' [=Viol. PAGET] The Spirit of Rome: leaves fr. a diary 3/6 *n.* ($1·50 *n.*) c 8° Lane 05

MACMILLAN, Rev. Hugh Roman Mosaics [chfly. antiquities] 6/ gl 8° Macmillan 88

MARKINO, Yoshio [art.] The Colour of Rome: 60 col. pl., w. l'rpr. Olave M. Potter [$5 *n.* Jacobs, *Phila.*] 20/ *n.* 4° Chatto 09

MURRAY, J. [pub.] Rome and its Environs; 96 maps 10/ p 8° Stanford [62] 08

OLIPHANT, Mrs [Marg.] The Makers of Modern Rome; ill. 10/6 ($3 *n.*) c 8° Macmillan [95] 97
Bk. i: *Honourable Women not a Few*; ii: *The Popes who made the Papacy*; iii: *Lo Popolo, and the Tribune of the People*; iv: *The Popes who made the City*. Graceful and sympathetic sketches.

ORBAAN, Dr J. A. F. Sixtine Rome; 32 ill. [Rome of Sixtus V.] 7/6 *n.* 8° Constable 11

PISA, A. [artist] Rome: 70 col. pl., w. l'rpr. M. A. R. Tuker + Hope Malleson [$6 *n.* Macmillan, *N.Y.*] 20/ *n.* sq 8° Black 05

ROBERTS, R. Ellis A Roman Pilgrimage; 6 col. pl. and 8 ill. 10/6 *n.* 8° Methuen 11

SCHOENER, Dr Reinhold Rome [tr.]; 290 ill. [good] 42/ *n.* i 8° Low 99
A good account of the art treasures, scenery, life, etc., of the city.

STORY, W. W. Roba di Roma 10/6 c 8° Chapman [63] 77
$2·50 Houghton, *Boston*. Street-music, beggars, Lent, campagna, field-sports and races, Colosseum, Ghetto, etc.

TAINE, H. A. Italy: Rome and Naples [tr.] $2·50 12° Holt, *N.Y.* [67] 89

TUKER (M. A. R.) + MALLESON (Hope) Hdbk. to Chr. &. Eccles. Rome; ill. & col. pl. c 8° Black 97–00
Macmillan, *N.Y.* Pt. i: *Chr. Monumts.*, 7/6 ($2·50 *n.*); ii: *Liturgy in Rome* 5/ ($1·75 *n.*); iii–iv: (in 1 vol.) *Monasticism in Rome, and Eccles. Rome*, 10/6 ($2·75 *n.*).

WEY, Fcs. Rome; monumts., arts, antiqs., tr. W. W. Story; ill. 15/ s 4° Virtue [72] 87

YOUNG, Norwood Story of Rome; ill. [Mediæval Towns] 4/6 *n.* s 8° Dent 01
$1·75 *n.* Dutton, *N.Y.* Acc. of the history of the city, chiefly from the historical and political side.

*Campagna:* LANCIANI (R.) Wanderings in Roman Campagna [tr.]; ill. 21/ *n.* r 8° Constable 09
$5 *n.* Houghton, *Boston*. A very valuable work—chiefly archæological.

*Literary Landmarks:* HUTTON (Laur.) Literary Landmarks of Rome $1 c 8° Harper, *N.Y.* 97

*Museums:* AMELUNG (W.) + HOLTZINGER (H.) Museums & Ruins of Rome; ill. 10/ *n.* c 8° Duckworth 06
Ed. Mrs Arth. STRONG. A compreh. view of the bldgs. and art-collections.

*Vatican:* POTTER (Mary K.) The Art of the Vatican; 41 ill. 6/ *n.* c 8° Bell 03

SLADEN, Douglas Secrets of the Vatican—*ut* **A** § 97
Pt. ii deals w. the less known and less accessible parts, inclg. acc. of the crypt of St Peter.

**Siena** —*v. also* Hutton, *sup.*; *for* History, *v.* **F** § 53

CUST, R. H. H. Pavement Masters of Siena; ill. [Gt. Craftsmen] 5/ *n.* c 8° Bell 06
A detailed descriptive and histor. acc. of the wonderful Cathedral pavemt. and other pavement work, w. notices of each of the artists who took part in the work. 26 pl. and bibliography.

*GARDNER, Edm. G. Siena; ill. [Mediæv. Towns; $1·75 *n.* Dutton, *N.Y.*] 4/6 *n.* f 8° Dent [02] 04

HASTINGS, G. Siena, its Architecture & Art; 60 pl. photo. ill. 3/6 *n.* 4° De La More Press 02

HEYWOOD (W.) + OLCOTT (Lucy) Guide to Siena s 8° Torrini, *Siena* 04
A really useful and trustworthy guide to hist. of the town (HEYWOOD), and its art (OLCOTT).

SCHEVILL, F. Siena: story of a mediæval commune; maps & ill. 12/6 *n.* 8° Chapman 09

**Venice** —*for* History *v.* **F** § 53

ALLEN, Grant — Venice [$1·25 *n.* Wessels, *N.Y.*] 3/6 *n.* c 8° Richards [01] 09

BROOKE, Rev. Stopford A. — The Sea Charm of Venice 2/6 *n.* f 8° Duckworth 07
Essay on debt wh. Venice, the 'Rome at sea', owes to her sea-positn. for her beauty and hold on imagination.

BROWN, Horatio F. — Life in the Lagoons ; ill. 6/ c 8° Rivington [84] 97

,, — Venetian Studies 7/6 c 8° Paul 87

,, — In and around Venice ; maps and 15 ill. 6/ c 8° Rivington 05

CRAWFORD, F. Marion — Gleanings from Venetian History, 2 vols. ; ill. 21/ *n.* c 8° Macmillan 05

DOUGLAS, H. A. — Venice on Foot ; 75 ill. [an itinerary] 5/ *n.* f 8° Methuen 07

,, — Venice and her Treasures 5/ *n.* Methuen 10

DÜRER, Albrecht [1471–1528] Journeys to Venice and to the Low Countries [tr.], ed. Claude Phillips [Humanists' Lib. ; *v.* **K** § 1] $6 r 8° Merrymount Press, *Boston* 10

FREEMAN, Prf. E. A. — Sketches fr. Subject & Nghbr. Lands of Venice ; ill. *o.p.* [*pb.* 10/6] c 8° Macm. 81

GEORGE, Ern. [artist] — Etchings of Venice ; 12 etchgs. 63/ f° Fine Art Soc. 88

HARE, A. J. C. — Venice, ed. St Clair Baddeley ; maps and ill. 3/6 f 8° G. Allen [84] 04

HEADLAM, Cecil — Venetia and Northern Italy 7/6 *n.* 8° Dent 08

HODGSON, F. C. — The Early History of Venice 7/6 *n.* c 8° G. Allen 01
An exhaustive book ; from the foundation to the conquest of Constantinople (1204).

,, — Venice in the 13th & 14th Centuries ; map & 21 ill. [to 1400] 10/6 *n.* 8° G. Allen 10

HOWELLS, W. D. — Venetian Life ; 20 col. pl. E. H. Garrett $5 8° Houghton, *Boston* [66] 08
16/ *n.* Constable. A vivid and fairly compl. pict. of Venet. life, by late Am. Consul at Venice. Ch. Edn., 2 v., 18° 2/ Douglas, *Edin.*

MENPES, Mortimer [art.] Venice : 100 col. pl. ; w. l'rpr. Dor. Menpes [$6 *n.* Macm., *N.Y.*] 20/ *n.* sq 8° Black 04

MONNIER, Philippe — Venice in the 18th Century [tr.] ; front. 7/6 *n.* 8° Chatto 11

OKEY, Thos. — Venice ; ill. [Mediæval Towns ; $1·75 *n.* Dutton, *N.Y.*] f 8° Dent [03] 05
New edn., w. 40 col. pl. by O. F. M. WARD + W. K. HINCHLIFF, and other ill. by Nelly ERICHSEN and after ptgs., etc., 10/6 *n.* s 4° *id.* 10.

,, — Old Venetian Palaces ; ill. & 56 col. pl. T. Haddon 21/ *n.* 4° Dent 08

OLIPHANT, Marg. — The Makers of Venice ; ill. [Doges, conquerors, etc.] 10/6 ($2·50 *n.*) c 8° Macm. [87] 91

PERL, Hy. — Venice depicted by Pen and Pencil [tr.] ; 180 ill. 28/ 4° Low 94
The illns., by modern Venetian artists, are not very successful ; text is a 'combination of gush, twaddle, and Baedeker'.

RUSKIN, Jno. — St Mark's Rest : the history of Venice 3/6 12° G. Allen [79] 94

de SÉLINCOURT (Beryl) + HENDERSON (May Sturge) Venice ; ill. R. Barratt 10/6 *n.* r 8° Chatto 07
A sketch of the main lines along wh. the hist. of Venice moved.

SMITH, F. Hopkinson — Gondola Days ; 12 ill. [sentimental] $1·50 12° Houghton, *Boston* 97

TAINE, H. A. — Italy : Florence and Venice [tr.]—*ut sup.*, *s.v.* Florence

YRIARTE, Chas. — Venice : hist., art, industrs., life [tr.] ; ill. 52/6 i 4° Bell 80
One of the most attractive and instructive works on Venice.

*Literary Landmarks :* HUTTON (Laur.) Literary Landmarks of Venice $1 c 8° Harper 96

*St Mark's :* ROBERTSON (Dr Alex.) The Bible of St Mark ; 80 pl. 7/6 *n.* c 8° G. Allen 98
A history of St Mark's ; with a particular account of its carvings and mosaics : fr. the devotional side.

**Verona** —*for* History of Verona *v.* **F** § 53

RUSKIN, Jno. — Verona ; and other Lectures ; ill. 15/ m 8° G. Allen 94

WIEL, Alethea — Story of Verona ; ill. [Mediæval Towns Ser.] 4/6 *n.* f 8° Dent 02
$1·75 *n.* Dutton, *N.Y.* Four chs. on hist. of town ; 14 descriptions of its buildings, art, and liter. assocns.

**LAPLAND**—*v.* **E** § 26 **NETHERLANDS**—*v.* **E** § 13 **NORWAY**—*v.* **E** § 26

**POLAND**—*v.* **E** § 55

## 24* : LUXEMBURG

BAEDEKER, Karl [pub.] — *his* Belgium and Holland [*ut* **E** § 13] incls. Luxemburg

PASSMORE, Rev. T. H. — In Further Ardenne ; map and ill. 7/6 *n.* 4° Dent 05
An exhaustive study of the Grand Duchy from pts.-of-view, inclg. its history to 1890.

**Ardennes** —*for* Belgian Ardennes *v.* **E** § 13

## 24† : POLAND

ANDERSON, F. L. M. — Residence in Russian Poland [1863] *o.p.* [*pb.* 6/] c 8 Macmillan 64

BRANDES, Dr Geo. — Poland 12/ *n.* 8° Heinemann 03
$3 *n.* Macmillan, *N.Y.* Incls. acc. of present-day condns. of Poland, and a survey of its literature : eloquent *apologia* for this unfortunate people.

NORMAN, Marie Muriel — *in her* A Girl in the Carpathians, *ut* **E** § 12 [E. Galicia]

## 25 : RUSSIA-IN-EUROPE

**Bibliography**

Bibliotheque Imp. de St Petersb. : Catalogue de la Section des Russica, 2 v. 8° Bibl. Imp., *Petersb.* 73

STUCKENBERG, J. Ch. Versuch eines Quellen-Anzeigers f. d. Studium d. Geogr. d. russ. Reichs, 2 vols. 8° *Petersburg* 49–52

**Early Travels and Accounts**

v. HERBERTSTEIN, Bar. S. Notes upon Russia [tr.], ed. R. H. Major, 2 vols. 8° Hakluyt Soc. 51–2
Tr. of *Rerum Moscoviticarum Commentarii*, earliest acc. of Russia, by Ambass. fr. Ct. of Germ. to Grand Prince Vasiley IVANOVITCH in yrs. 1517–26.

JENKINSON, Anth., etc. Early Voyages and Travels to Russia and Persia, ed. E. Delmar Morgan + C. H. Coote 8° Hakluyt Soc. 86
In rn. of Eliz. (1553–83). Conts. acc. of first intercourse of Engl. w. Russia and Cent. Asia by way of Caspian Sea.

Russia at the Close of the Sixteenth Century, ed. E. A. Bond 8° Hakluyt Soc. 56
Conts. Giles FLETCHER'S *The Russe Common Wealth*, and Sir Jerome HORSEY'S *Travels* [printed fr. his MS.].

**Modern Travel :** BODDY (Alex. A.) With Russian Pilgrims ; maps and ill. 7/6 c 8° Wells Gardner 92
A pleasant acc. of a jy. thro' Holy Isles and by Old Trade Route up Dwina and Suchona to Ustyúg and Vólogda—an unusual route.

JEFFERSON, R. L. Awheel to Moscow and Back ; ill. 2/ c 8° Low 95

KNOX, T. W. Boy Travellers in Russian Empire ; ill. $2 c 8° Harper 87
Advents. of 2 youths in Europ. and Asiatic Russia, w. acc. of tour acr. Siberia.

MICHELL, Thos. Russian Pictures, drawn w. Pen & Pencil ; 124 ill. [picture-bk.] 8/ i 8° R.T.S. 89

MORFIL, W. R. Russia [Foreign Countries and Brit. Cols.] 3/6 12° Low 80

STEVENS, Thos. Through Russia on a Mustang ; ill. $2 (7/6) 8° Cassell 91
Story of ride in '90 fr. Moscow thro' Tula, Orel, Kursk, Karkov, to Crimea ; thence up Don and Volga to Nijni Novgorod.

STODDARD, Dr C. A. Across Russia ; ill. $1·50 c 8° Scribner, *N.Y.* 92
From Paris to Petersb., thence to Warsaw by Moscow, w. excursns. *en route.* Well-worn ground, w. no spec. novelty of treatmt.

TILLEY, H. A. Eastern Europe & Western Asia [Russia, Greece, Syria] *o.p.* [*pb.* 10/6] c 8° Longman 64

**Life ; People ; Politics ; Institutions, etc.**

BARING, Hon. Maur. A Year in Russia [$3·50 *n.* Dutton, *N.Y.*] 10/6 *n.* 8° Methuen [07] 08
Founded on l'rs contrib. to *Morning Post* in 1905–6. Political ; w. good view of life of people : *v.* also **E** § 34 and **F** § 56.

,, Russian Essays and Stories [non-political] 5/ *n.* c 8° Methuen 08

,, The Russian People—*ut* **F** § 56

BAZAN, Emilia P. Russia : people and literature [tr. fr. Span.] $1·25 12° McClurg, *Chicago* 90

BÉRARD, V. The Russian Empire and Czarism [tr.] 10/6 8° Nutt 06

BEVERIDGE, A. J. The Russian Advance ; maps $2·50 *n.* (10/6) 8° Harper 03
A picture of the Russian Empire and its people. Strongly pro-Russian.

BIGELOW, Poulteney Borderld. of Czar & Kaiser, *and* Germ. Emperor & his E. Neighbrs.—*ut* **E** § 15

BRANDES, Dr Geo. Impressions of Russia [tr. fr. Danish] $1·25 12° Crowell, *N.Y.* 89
2/6 Walter Scott. A calm, broadminded view of the Russian Empire.

v. der BRÜGGEN, Bar. E. Russia of To-day 6/ c 8° Digby 04

DECLE, Lionel The New Russia [journalistic] 7/6 8° Nash 06

DE WINDT, Harry —*in his* Through Savage Europe, *ut* **E** § 29

DIXON, W. Hepworth Free Russia, 2 vols. ; ill. *o.p.* [*pb.* 30/] 8° Hurst 70

DRAGE, Geoffrey Russian Affairs 21/ *n.* r 8° Murray 04

v. ECKHARDT, J. W. A. Modern Russia [tr.] *o.p.* [*pb.* 10/6] c 8° Smith & Elder 70
Deals with the 'physiology, as opposed to the anatomy, of society'.

[ ,, ] Russia before and after the War [tr.] *o.p.* [*pb.* 24/] 8° Longman 80

EDWARDS, H. Sutherland The Russians at Home and Russians Abroad, 2 v. 21/ c 8° W. H. Allen [61] 79

EYRE, Selwyn Sketches of Russian Life and Customs [1876–7] *o.p.* [*pb.* 7/6] p 8° Remington 78

FRASER, J. Foster Red Russia ; ill. 6/ c 8° Cassell 07
A dramatic and highly-coloured account, by a journalist, w. many photos. of interest.

GANZ, H. Downfall of Russia : behind the scenes—*ut* **D** § 126

GASIAROWSKI, Waclaw Tragic Russia, tr. Visc. de Buscancy ; 8 pl. 7/6 *n.* c 8° Cassell 08
A graphic acc. of Russian absolutism. Descrn. of Nihilist movemt. not wholly trustworthy.

GEDDIE, J. Russian Empire : historical and descriptive ; 2 maps 4/ c 8° Nelson [81] 85

GERRARE, Wirt Greater Russia $3 *n.* c 8° Macmillan 03
Siberia, Manchuria, and position of Russia on the Pacific.

GREENE, F. V. Sketches of Army Life in Russia *o.p.* [*pb.* $1·50] 12° Scribner, *N.Y.* 80

[GRENVILLE-MURRAY, E. C.] The Russians of To-day *o.p.* [*pb.* 6/] c 8° Smith & Elder 78

HAPGOOD, Isab. F. Russian Rambles $1·50 c 8° Houghton, *Boston* 95
6/ Longman. Picts. of manners, characters and daily life of the diverse peoples of Russia : intelligent and just.

HARE, A. J. C. Studies in Russia ; ill. [$2·50 *n.* Macm., *N.Y.*] 10/6 c 8° Smith & Elder 85

v. HAXTHAUSEN, Bar. A. Russian Empire: people, instits., resources [tr.], 2 v. *o.p.* [*pb.* 28/] 8° Chapman 56
The first bk. wh. revealed the real social condition of the country to the outer world.

HAYES, Cpt. Hor. Among Horses in Russia; 53 ill. 10/6 *n.* 8° Everett 00
A gossipy book on Russian horses, the Russian army, and the author's experiences in Russia.

HODGETTS, E. A. Brayley In the Track of the Russian Famine 2/6 c 8° Unwin 92
Pers. narr. of jy. thro' famine districts of Russia, giving melancholy descrn. of the distress of winter of 1891.

,, The Court of Russia, 2 vols.; ill. 24/ *n.* 8° Methuen 08

JOUBERT, Carl —*v.* **D** § 126, *s.v.* Nihilism

KENNARD, Dr H. P. The Russian Peasant—*ut* **D** § 119

'LANIN, E. B.' [=Valentine DILLON] Russian Characteristics *o.p.* [*pb.* 14/] 8° Chapman 92
A strong picture, by a dispassionate and disinterested witness, of vices of a semi-barbarous autocracy, corruptns. of a depraved society, and miseries of a starved and stunted populace. Repr. fr. *Fortnightly Review.* Incl. chs. on Prisons, Armenia, Finance, Jews, Finland, Famine, Sexual Morality, Thriftlessness, etc.

v. LANKENAU (H.) + OELSNITZ (L.) Russia, Past & Present [tr.]; ill. [gd. pop. bk.] 5/ c 8° S.P.C.K. 82

LATHAM, R. G. Russian and Turk: fr. geogr. & ethnogr. pt. of view 18/ 8° W. H. Allen 78

LATIMER, Eliz. W. Russia and Turkey in 19th Century; ill. $2·50 8° McClurg, *Chicago* 94

*LEROY-BEAULIEU, A. Empire of the Tsars & the Russians [tr.], 3 v. ea. $3 (12/6) 8° Putnam 93–6
The best general bk. in English on Russia, full of informn. imparted w. thoro' impartiality and in an interestg. manner. Vol. i: *Country and its Inhabts.*; ii: *Institns.*; iii: *Religion.*

LOGAN, J. A., jun. In Joyful Russia; 50 ill. (4 col.) $3·50 c 8° Appleton, *N.Y.* 97
10/6 Pearson. Travel in Russia, w. descrn. of the splendid ceremonies at coron. of Tsar, soc. life in Moscow, etc.

MARTIN, Rud. The Future of Russia (tr. (fr. Germ.)] 7/6 *n.* p 8° Smith & Elder 06

MEAKIN, Annette M. B. Russia: travels and studies; ill. 16/ *n.* 8° Hurst 06
A light, anecdotal, and picturesque account of normal Russia, not the Russia of war and revoln.

v. MOLTKE, F'ldm. Letters from Russia [tr.] 2/6 c 8° Paul [78] 81

NEVINSON, H. W. Dawn in Russia—*ut* **D** § 126, *s.v.* Nihilism

NOBLE, Edm. The Russian Revolt—*ut* **D** § 126, *s.v.* Nihilism

NORMAN, Hy. All the Russias; 4 maps and 137 ill. 18/ *n.* 8° Heinemann 02
$4 *n.* Scribner, *N.Y.* Acc. of a tour thro' Russian Emp., and a valuable study of its econ. and industr. condn.

PALMER, Fcs. H. E. Russian Life in Town and Country; 15 ill. 3/6 *n.* c 8° Newnes 01
$1·20 *n.* Putnam, *N.Y.* Perhaps the best compact account of the mode of life of the various Russian classes.

PARES, Bern. Russia and Reform [$3 *n.* Dutton, *N.Y.*] 10/6 *n.* 8° Constable 07
A competent and dispassionate survey of the polit., econ., constit., and social condn. of Russia.

PERRIS, G. H. Russia in Revolution—*ut* **D** § 126, *s.v.* Nihilism

PRELOOKER, Jaakoff Russian Flashlights; ill. [Nihilistic] 10/6 *n.* 8° Chapman 11

RADIZWILL, Pr'ess Cath. My Recollections 16/ 8° Isbister 04

RALSTON, W. R. S. —*his* Songs of Russn. People [*ut* **B** § 19] conts. excel. acc. of Russ. social life

RAPPOPORT, Dr A. Home Life in Russia; 12 ill. 10/6 *n.* 8° Methuen 11

ROTH, H. L. Agriculture and Peasantry of Russia *o.p.* [*pb.* 3/6] 12° Low 79

Russian Year-Book: ed. Dr H. P. Kennard 10/6 *n.* 8° Eyre & Spottiswoode 11 *ann.*

v. SCHIERBRAND, W. Russia: her strength and her weakness; maps $1·60 (7/6 *n.*) 8° Putnam 04

SEMENOFF, L. The Russian Government and the Massacres [tr.] 2/6 *n.* c 8° Murray 07
'A page of the Russian Counter-Revolution'. Introd. by Lucien WOLF.

STADLING (J. J.) + REASON (Will) In the Land of Tolstoi; 43 ill. 7/6 8° J. Clarke 97
$2 Whittaker, *N.Y.* By a Swede, tr. and arrgd. REASON. Pres. condn. of Russia, w. spec. ref. to var. classes of relig. dissenters (translating the Russn. into English, the Antichrists [Tartars], Sufferers, Wanderers, Fugitives, Dumb, Flagellants, Dancers, Mutilators, Suicides, Agnostics), and the philanthropic wk. of TOLSTOI dur. famine of 1892.

'STEPNIAK' [S. M. KRAVTCHINSKY] Underground Russia—*ut* **D** § 126, *s.v.* Nihilism

,, Russia under the Tsars [social] 2/6 c 8° Ward & Down [85] 94

,, The Russian Storm Cloud 7/6 8° Sonnenschein 86
Russia in her relations to neighbouring states.

,, The Russian Peasantry 3/6 *n.* c 8° Routledge [88] 05
$1·25 *n.* Dutton *N.Y.* The most trustworthy bk. on their agrar. condn., soc. life, and religion.

,, At Dawn of a New Reign 6/ c 8° Chatto [95–6] 05
1st edn. pb. *sub tit. King Stork and King Log.* A terrible pict. of Russia of the day, full of stories of outrage, persecution, and wrong.

STEVENI, W. Barnes Through Famine-stricken Russia 3/6 c 8° Low 92
States that there are 14 to 16 mills. of people in absol. want and dependent on charit. relief. Some graphic picts. of peasant-life.

TIKHOMIROV, L. Russia, Political and Social [tr.]; 2 vols. 9/ *n.* 8° Sonnenschein [88] 92
Deals w. social classes, industr. classes, intellectual movemt. and pres. polit. situatn. By a well-known Nihilist.

TISSOT, Victor Russians and Germans [tr. fr. French] *o.p.* [*pb.* 12/6] 8° Remington 82

Tsar and his People (The): social life in Russia; ill. [by var. Amer. writers] $3 8° Harper, *N.Y.* 90

ULAR, Alex. Russia from Within [tr.]—*ut* **D** § 126, *s.v.* Nihilism

VILLARI, Linda Russia under the Great Shadow; 84 ill. 10/6 *n.* 8° Unwin 05

WADDINGTON, Mary A. K.—*in her* Letters of a Diplomat's Wife; [1883–90] 10/6 *n.* 8° Smith & Elder 03

*WALLACE, Sir Don. M. Russia, 2 vols.; maps 24/ *n.* c 8° Cassell [77] 05
$5 Holt, *N.Y.* The standard wk., here thoroughly revised and brought down to date. Comprehensive and trustworthy.

WELLESLEY, F. A. With the Russians in Peace and War 12/6 8° Nash 05
Recollections of a military attaché, 1871–8.

WHISHAW, F. J. Out of Doors in Tsarland 7/6 ($2) c 8° Longman 93
A record of wanderings in Russia, w. sketches of Russ. peasant life, and adventures w. rod and gun.

,, The Romance of the Woods 6/ c 8° Longman 95
Repr. art. of Russn. and Finnish outdoor life and sport; w. good ess. on *Folklore of the Moujik.*

**Industries; Trade:** CRAWFORD (J. M.) [tr.] The Industries of Russia, 5 vols.; maps 8° *St Petersburg* 93–4
$6 Putnam, *N.Y.* P. S. King & Son. A complete summary of Russian industries, manufs., and trade, incl. Siberian: by U.S. Consul to Russia; prep. officially for Chicago's World's Fair.

**Jews in Russia**—*v.* **A** § 12 **Nihilism**—*v. also* **D** § 126 **Prisons**—*v.* **D** § 123

**Archangel**

ENGELHARDT, A. P. A Russian Province of the North [tr.]; maps and ill. 18/ 8° Constable 99
$6 Lippincott, *Phila.* A very full account of the resources of the province.

HARVEY-BROWN, Dr J. A. —*in his* Travels of a Naturalist in Northern Europe, *ut* **H** § 102

**Finland** —*v.* **E** § 26

**Kieff:** MORRIS (Isab.) Summer in Kieff: sunny days in S. Russia; ill. *o.p.* [*pb.* 10/6] 8° Ward & D. 91

**Kolguev:** TREVOR-BATTYE (A.) Icebound on Kolguev; ill. and maps 21/ *n.* 8° Constable 95
Acc. of a 3-months' visit by the author (who was intent on ornith.) and Merwyn POWYS, whose object was sport.

,, A Northern Highway of the Tsar; map and ill. 6/ c 8° Constable 98
Descrn. of the jy. home, *via* Archangel, up Pechora River and acr. the Tundra.

**Moscow:** GERRARE (Wirt) Story of Moscow; ill. [Mediæval Towns Ser.] 3/6 *n.* f 8° Dent 00
$1·50 *n.* Dutton, *N.Y.* An interesting popular histor. and topogr. account; w. good illns.

DE HAENEN, F. [art.] Moscow: 32 pl. (16 col.). w. l'pr. H. M. Grove [$2·50 *n.* Macm., *N.Y.*] 7/6 *n.* sq 8° Black

**Petchora:** HARVIE-BROWN (Dr J. A.)—*in his* Travels of a Naturalist in Northern Europe, *ut* **H** § 102

PEARSON, H. J. Beyond Petsora Eastward 22/6 *n.* r 8° Porter 99
Two ornithol. summer excursns. to Novoya Zemla, and the islands of Barents.

SEEBOHM, H. Siberia in Europe; ill. [valley of Petchora] 14/ 8° Murray 80

*Petschenga Monastery:* FRIIS (Prf. J. A.) The Monastery of Petschenga [tr.] 3/6 c 8° Stock 96
A delightful acc. of rise and fall of the Monastery, wh. arose from a hut built in 1524 by TRIFON, the runaway son of a Russ. priest (to-day celebrated throughout Gk. Ch. as one of her greatest Sts.), became a very import. centre of trade, and was destroyed by Swedes in 1589.

**St Petersburg:** DE HAENEN (F.) [art.] St Petersburgh: ill. (some col.), w. l'rpr. S. Dobson [$2·50 *n.* Macm., *N.Y.*] 7/6 *n.* sq 8° Black 10

**Russia-in-Asia**—*v.* **E** § 39 **Russian Turkestan**—*v.* **E** § 33 **Arctic Russia**—*v. also* **E** § 69

## 26: SCANDINAVIA: DENMARK; NORWAY; SWEDEN; LAPLAND; FINLAND

*For* Cathedrals, etc., *v.* **I** § 121; *for* Sporting Adventures *v.* **I** § 147

BAEDEKER, K. [pub.] Norw., Swed., Denm.; maps [$2·40 Scrib., *N.Y.*] 8/ s 8° Unwin [ ] 09

BALLOU, M. M. Due North: recent journey thro' Norway, etc. $1·50 Houghton, *Boston* 87

BRACE, C. L. Norse Folk: visit to homes of Norw., & Sw.; ill. $1·75 12° Scribner, *N.Y.* 57

CHAPMAN, Abel Wild Norway; ill. 16/ 8° Arnold 97
Hunting experiences in Norway, Sweden, Denmark, and on Spitzbergen.

DU CHAILLU, P. B. Land of the Midnight Sun, 2 v.; ill. 10/6 8° Newnes [81] 99
$5 Harper, *N.Y.* A detailed and vivid descrn. of scenes and life in Swed., Norw., Lapland, and Finland.

,, Land of the Long Night; ill. 7/6 8° Murray 00
$2 Scribner, *N.Y.* Acc. of a winter jy. fr. southern Swed. thro' Lappmark, Finld., and Finmark, to Nordkyn.

HARE, A. J. C. Sketches in Holland and Scandinavia—*ut* **E** § 13

KENNEDY, E. B. Thirty Seasons in Scandinavia [$3·80 *n.* Longm., *N.Y.*] 10/6 *n.* r 8° Arnold 03

TAYLOR, Bayard Northern Travel; 2 pl. [Sweden, Denmark, Lapland] $1·50 12° Putnam, *N.Y.* [57]

VINCENT, F., jun. Norsk, Lapp, and Finn; maps $1·50 c 8° Putnam, *N.Y.* 81
Account of travels in the Far East of Europe.

WOOD, C. W. Sweden and Norway [For. Countries and Brit. Cols.] 3/6 c 8° Low 82

**Denmark:** BRÖCHNER (Jessie) Danish Life in Town and Country; ill. 3/6 *n.* c 8° Newnes 03
$1·20 *n.* Putnam, *N.Y.* A general account of the country and people: life, customs, literature, etc.

BUTLIN, F. M. Among the Danes; col. pl. Ellen Wilkinson 7/6 *n.* 8° Methuen 09
Scenery, life, customs, and institutions.

EDWARDES, Chas. In Jutland with a Cycle 6/ c 8° Chapman 97

GOSSE, Dr Edm. Two Visits to Denmark [Denm. c. 1870] 7/6 *n.* p 8° Smith & Elder 11

OTTÉ, [Miss] E. C. Denmark and Iceland [For. Countries and Brit. Cols.] 3/6 c 8° Low 82

THOMAS, A. Marg. Denmark, Past and Present; ill. 6/ *n.* c 8° Treherne 02
A full, tho' commonplace, acc. of the cities and the country, w. chs. on institns. and literature.

WEITMEYER, H. Denmark: its hist., topogr., lang., liter., fine arts, soc. life & finance; map 12/6 8° Heinemann 91

*Copenhagen:* HARGROVE (Ethel C.) The Charm of Copenhagen; ill. 6/ c 8° Methuen 11

**Finland:** *Atlas:* GEBHARD (H.) [ed.] Atlas de Statist. Sociale d. Finlande 8° Soc. de Géogr., *Helsingfors* 08

ABERCROMBY, Hon. Jno. The Pre- and Proto-Historic Finns, 2 vols.—*ut* **B** § 33

CLIVE-BAYLEY, [Miss] A. M. C. Vignettes from Finland; map and ill. 7/6 c 8° Low 95
A bright account of the town- and country-life of Finland.

DE WINDT, Harry Finland as It Is; map and ill. 9/ *n.* c 8° Murray 01
$3 *n.* Dutton, *N.Y.* Account of a journalistic tour in 1900: useful information on Finnish industries.

Finland in Nineteenth Century. By Finnish Authors [tr.]; ill. 35/ *n.* 4° Stanford 94
Series of chs. by eminent Finnish writers illustr. of polit., social, scient., liter., artistic and industr. life of country.

FISHER, Jos. R. Finland and the Tsars 12/6 8° Arnold 99
A clear and succinct histor. sketch of relns. betw. Russ. and Finl. fr. 1809 to 1899.

FREDERIKSEN, Prf. N. C. Finland: its public and private economy; maps 6/ c 8° Arnold 01
$2 Longman, *N.Y.* A solid acc. of public and commerc. life and condns. of the country.

NORMAN, Sir Hy. —*his* All the Russians [*ut* **E** § 25] conts. acc. of Finland

RENWICK, Geo. Finland To-day [political and literary] 10/6 *n.* 8° Unwin 11

TRAVERS, Rosalind Letters from Finland; 32 ill. 7/6 *n.* 8° Paul 11
An excellent travel bk., w. careful acc. of institns., polit. parties, educn., industr. and soc. condns., art, literature.

TWEEDIE, Mrs Alec Through Finland in Carts; 18 pl. [$3 Macm., *N.Y.*] 6/ c 8° Black [97] 98

'WAINEMAN, Paul' [a lady] Summer Tour in Finland; 32 ill. (16 col.) 10/6 *n.* Methuen 08
Penetrates to Tornea, at N. of Gulf of Bothnia, and provides a fairly good descrn. of 'the lost daughter of the sea' and her honest, simple, and clean inhabitants.

*History:* BROWN (Dr J. C.) People of Finland in Archaic Times [for note *v.* **B** § 33] 5/ c 8° Paul 92

**Iceland** —*v.* **E** § 23

**Lapland**

HYNE, C. J. Cutcliffe Through Arctic Lapland; map and 16 ill. 10/6 p 8° Black 98
Account of a journey from Vardö Island to Haparanda.

JACKSON, F. G. The Great Frozen Land; ill. *o.p.* [*pb.* 15/ *n.*] 8° Macmillan 95

MACKINNON, D. D. Lapland: summer advents. in Arctic regns. 5/ c 8° Kerby [78] 78

RAE, Edw. Land of North Wind [Laplanders and Samoyedes] 10/6 c 8° Murray 75

,, White Sea Peninsula; map and ill. 15/ 8° Murray 81
A graphic account of travel in Russian Lapland and Karelia.

REED, Sir Edw. Letters from Russia [1875] [Russian Lapld. & Karelia] *o.p.* [*pb.* 5/] c 8° Murray 76

TROMHOLT, Dr Sophus Under Rays of Aurora Borealis [tr.], 2 v.; map & 150 ill. 30/ 8° Low 85
Gives the most minute acc. yet pub. of the home life and habits of one of the few remaining savage peoples of Europe—Lapps and Kreans.

**Norway** —*for* Mountaineering *v.* § **I** 165

BRADSHAW, J. Norway: fjords, fjelds, and fosses [a cruise; S. Norw.] 3/6 c 8° Digby 86

CHAPMAN, Abel Wild Norway; ill. by author and C. Whymper 16/ 8° Arnold 97
With chaps. on the Swedish Highlands, Spitzbergen, and Denmark.

FORBES, J. D. Norway and its Glaciers; pl. [visit of 1851] *o.p.* [*pb.* 21/] r 8° Simpkin 53

FROUDE, J. A. Norway Fjords, *and* Norway Once More—*in his* Spanish Armada & other Ess., *ut* **K** § 83
Two rambling and somewhat garrulous discourses. Repr. mag. articles, well written but of small value.

GOODMAN, E. J. The Best Tour in Norway [*v. also* Lange *inf.*] 7/6 c 8° Low [92] 97
Descrs. a circular tour thro' South-West of Norway, w. route-map and 34 pl.

,, New Ground in Norway; 60 ill. 10/6 8° Newnes 96
Acc. of travel in district of Ringerike, Telemarken, and Sœtersdalen and along S. Coast—not really 'new', as it was descr. by Rev. F. METCALFE [*ut inf.*] in 1856.

HARVIE-BROWN, Dr J. A. —*in his* Travels of a Naturalist in Northern Europe, *ut* **H** § 102
Norway, Archangel, Petchora.

KEARY, C. F. Norway and the Norwegians; maps and ill. 5/ c 8° Rivington 92
$1·50 Scribner, *N.Y.* A very interesting and trustworthy account of the people and of the country.

LEES, J. A. Peaks and Pines [shootg. and fishg.] 6/ c 8° Longman 00

,, + CLUTTERBUCK (W. J.) Three in Norway: by Two of Them 2/6 c 8° Longman [82] 88

METCALFE, Rev. F. The Oxonian in Thelemarken, 2 vols. [*v.* Goodman, *sup.*] *o.p.* [*pb.* 21/] 8° Hurst 56

MOCKLER-FERRYMAN, Maj. A. F. In the Northman's Land; ill. 7/6 c 8° Low 96
A modest and fresh acc. of experces. in Norw. travel and sport in fjords and fjelds of Hardanger; w. gossip on folklore.

MONROE, Prf. W. S. Norway: peoples, fjords, and fjelds; ill. $3 8° Page, *Boston* 08
7/6 *n.* Bell, *sub tit.* '*The Viking Land*'. Social, econ., and polit. condns., sport, etc.: the result of two vacation-visits.

**NANSEN, F.** Norway and the Union with Sweden 2/6 *n.* c 8° Macmillan [05] 05

Norway: Offic. pubn. f. Paris Exhibn., 1900; maps & ill. [standard] 8/6 8° Aktie-Bogtryk., *Christiania* 00

**Pritchett**, R. T. Gamle Norge: rambles and scrambles in Norway; ill. 21/ r 8° Virtue 79

**Smith**, Hubert Tent Life in Norway [with English gypsies] *o.p.* [*pb.* 21/] 8° H. S. King 73

**Spender**, A. E. Two Winters in Norway; 40 ill. 10/6 *n.* ($4) 8° Longman 02
Account of winter-sports of Norway; with notes of an expedn. to the Lapps.

**Tanner**, G. F. An Unconventional Tour in Norway; ill. 5/ c 8° Century Press 07

**Tweedie**, Mrs Alec A Winter Jaunt to Norway 7/6 8° Sands [94] 94

**Williams**, W. M. Through Norway with a Knapsack; map 6/ c 8° Stanford [59] 76

" Through Norway with Ladies; map and ill. 12/ c 8° Stanford 77

**Willson**, T. B. Norway at Home; ill. [Our Neighbours at Home] 5/ *n.* c 8° Newnes 08
A popular acc. of institns., customs, industries, etc.

**Woods**, Chas. W. Round about Norway; 63 ill. *o.p.* [*pb.* 12/] 8° Bentley 80

" Under Northern Skies *o.p.* [*pb.* 14/] 8° Bentley 86

" Norwegian Byways; 9 ill. 6/ ($2) 8° Macmillan 03
Acc. of a three-wks.' jy., largely along beaten tracks, in spite of the title.

**Wyllie**, M. A. Norway and its Fjords; 16 col. pl. W. L. Wyllie 6/ c 8° Methuen 07

*Guide:* **Willson (T. B.)** Handy Guide to Norway; maps and ill. 3/6 *n.* p 8° Stanford [ ] 11

*Mountaineering* —*v.* **I** § 165

*Scenery:* **Cooper** (A. H.) [art.] Norwegian Fjords: 24 col. pl., w. l'rpr.
[$2·50 *n.* Macm., *N.Y.*] 6/ *n.* sq 8° Black 07

**Jungman**, Nico [artist] Norway: 75 col. pl.; w. text Beatrix [=Mrs N.] Jungman
[$6 *n.* Macm., *N.Y.*] 20/ *n.* sq 8° Black 05

**Lange**, Paul Pictures of Norway: 50 photogravs., w. l'rpr. E. J. Goodman 52/6 *n.* f° Low 93
A ser. of finely-exec. photographic illns., by late Pres. of L'pool Amateur Photogr. Soc.; w. a running commentary.

**Lovett**, Rich. Norwegian Pictures, drawn w. Pen and Pencil; 127 ill. 8/ i 8° R.T.S. [85] 90

**Sweden**

**Andersen**, Hans Chrn. Pictures of Sweden [tr.] *o.p.* [*pb.* 5/] c 8° Bentley 51
A charming little bk., which should, if possible, be read in the original Danish, *I Sverrig.*

**Baker**, Mrs Woods Pictures of Swedish Life; ill. $2·50 8° Lentilhon, *N.Y.* 95
10/6 *n.* Hodder. First 3 sects., on soc. and domestic life in all its grades, are v. good; rest of bk., on liter. and hist., perfunctory.

v. **Heidenstam**, O. G. Swed. Life in Town & Country; ill. [$1·20 *n.* Putn., *N.Y.*] 3/6 *n.* c 8° Newnes 05

**Lloyd**, L. Scandinavian Adventures, 2 v.; ill. [sport; nat. hist.] *o.p.* [*pb.* 42/] r 8° Bentley 54

" Peasant Life in Sweden; ill. [custs., folklore, etc.—*cf.* **B** § 20] *o.p.* [*pb.* 18/] 8° Tinsley 70

'**Old Bushman**' [=H. W. **Wheelwright**] Ten Years in Sweden *o.p.* [*pb.* 16/] 8° Groombridge 65

***Sundbärg**, J. [ed.] Sweden, its People & Industry; c. 400 ill. & 50 maps 25/ 8° *Stockholm* 04
The offic. pubn. for the Paris Exhibn. of 1900. The Fch. edn. appeared 1900, the Swed. 1901: the Engl. (1904) is the most thoroughly up-to-date.

**Swedish Touring Club**: Guide to Sweden; 21 maps 5/ c 8° Stanford 98

**Thomas**, W. W., jun. Sweden and the Swedes; ill. $3·75 8° Rand & McNally, *Chic.* 93
A very eulogistic account of a holiday visit, including some sport (fishing and shooting). Of no permanent value.

**Wood**, Chas. W. Under Northern Skies—*ut sup., s.v.* Norway

## 27: SPAIN AND PORTUGAL (INCL. MALTA AND ISLANDS)

**Baedeker**, Karl Spain and Portugal; maps [$4·80 *n.* Scribner, *N.Y.*] 16/ s 8° Unwin [ ] 08
Includes excursions to Tangier and the Balearic Isles.

**O'Shea** + **Lomas** (J.) Guide to Spain and Portugal; maps and plans
[$2·60 *n.* Macm., *N.Y.*] 15/ c 8° Black [68] 95

**Portugal**

**Carnarvon**, [3rd] Earl of Portugal and Galicia: Basque Provs.
[travels in 1827] *o.p.* [*pb.* 3/6] c 8° Murray [36] 61

**Crawfurd**, Oswald Portugal, Old and New; ill. [*v. also* Latouche, *inf.*] 6/ 8° Paul [82] 82
By late H.M. Consul at Oporto. History, literature, and social life.

" Round the Calendar in Portugal; ill. 18/ r 8° Chapman 90
Habits and customs in town and country, folklore, arts, games, music, aspects of the country, nat. hist., etc.—arrgd. acc. to the months.

**Hume**, Maj. Martin Through Portugal; ill. 5/ *n.* c 8° Richards 07
Vivid picts. of the country, scenery, cultivation, and historical aspect.

**Jackson**, L'y Fair Lusitania; etchings [not wholly trustworthy] *o.p.* [*pb.* 21/] r 8° Bentley 74

**Koebel**, W. H. Portugal: land and people; 21 col. pl. and 59 ill. 16/ r 8° Constable 09
An interestg. descrn. of landscape, rural life, popular customs, etc.

'**Latouche**, J.' [=Oswald **Crawfurd**] Travels in Portugal; map and ill. 2/ c 8° Ward & Lock [75] 84

**Lock**, Jane Iberian Sketches: travels in Portugal and N.-W. Spain 6/ 8° Simpkin 84

**Loring**, Dr G. B. A Year in Portugal: 1889–1890; front. $1·50 (6/) 8° Putnam 91
Loring was U.S. Minister at Lisbon in 1889-90, and gives his impressns., mixed up w. guide-bk. informn.

SHORE, H. N. Three Pleasant Springs in Portugal; 15 pl. 12/6 8° Low 99

STREET, Eug. E. A Philosopher in Portugal [of small value] 5/ *n.* c 8° Unwin 03

WATSON, Gilb. Sunshine and Sentiment in Portugal; ill. Gilb. James 12/6 *n.* 8° Arnold 04
Explorn. of limestone caverns for prehist. remains forms foundn. of bk., and serves as excuse for discoursg. on men, things, and country of Portugal.

WORDSWORTH, Dorothea [Mrs QUILLINAN; 1804–47] Journal of Residence in Portugal *o.p.* [*pb.* 6/] c 8° Longman [47] 95
Ed. E. LEE. Incl. is *Glimpses of S. of Spain* (about one-third of bk.). Abounds in minute descrns. of Port. in 1845–6.

*Lisbon:* FIELDING (Hy.) Journal of a Voyage to Lisbon 7/6 *n.* c 8° Chiswick Press [17– ] 92
Ed. Austin DOBSON; w. Introd. and notes. Limited to 475 copies, and 25 on Japanese paper 15/ *n.*

INCHBOLD, A. C. Lisbon and Cintra; ill. 10/6 *n.* 8° Chatto 07
Incls. also accs. of other cities and historical sites in Portugal. A pleasant guide.

**Spain, and Islands** —*for* Motor Tours *v.* **I** § 148*

de AMICIS, Edm. Spain and the Spaniards [tr.]; 11 pl. $2 (7/6) c 8° Putnam, *N.Y.* [81] 95
'Guadalquiver Edn.'; ill. $15. Word-pictures describg. tour thro' Spain 1871–3.

ANDERSEN, Hans Chrn. Spain, tr. Mrs Bushby *o.p.* [*pb.* 10/6] c 8° Bentley 64

d'AULNOY, C'esse M. C. Lady ——'s Travels in Spain, ed. A. M. Huntington; pl. $1·50 (5/ *n.*) 12° Putnam [99] 00

*BATES, Kath. L. Spanish Highways and Byways $2 *n.* (6/) c 8° Macmillan 00

BERNARD, Hy. In Pursuit of Dulcinea; 15 ill. 6/ *n.* c 8° G. Allen 05
'A quixotic journey in Spain.'

BORROW, Geo. The Bible in Spain, 2 vols., ed. U. R. Burke; ill., 12/; in 1 vol., 6/; Ch. Ed. 2/6 *n.* [1835–42] c 8° Murray [43] 96
$1 *n.* Scribner, *N.Y.* Jys. whilst attemptg. to circulate. the Scripts. in Sp., but more a bk. of tourist-travels, contg. graphic picts. of life—high, middle, and low—in the byways and highways than a recd. of missionary labour. Introd.; good notes and glossary. Ch. Edn. [New Univ. Lib.] 1/ *n.* pott 8° Routledge (50 c. Dutton, *N.Y.*) For his wks. on Span. Gypsies *v.* **F** § 76.

CALVERT, A. F. Impressions of Spain; ill. 10/6 8° Philip 03
Somewhat conventional impressns. of cathedrals, cafés, mines, bull-fights, handsome women, etc.

" Moorish Remains in Spain, 2 v.; col. pl. & ill. ea. 42/ *n.* ($15 *n.*) r 8° Lane [04] 07; 06
i: *Cordova, Seville, Toledo,* w. 80 col. pl., 200 ill. and 200 diagrs.; ii: *Alhambra,* w. 80 col. pl. and 300 ill.

" Spain, 2 vols.; c. 1700 ill. [$15 *n.* Dutton, *N.Y.*] 42/ *n.* 4° Dent 11

CAMPION, J. S. On Foot in Spain; ill. [1876–7] *o.p.* [*pb.* 16/] 8° Chapman [78] 79

CAYLEY, G. T. Bridle Roads of Spain; or Las Alforjas 7/6 *n.* c 8° Unwin [53] 08
A quaint, fanciful bk.; w. *Introd.* by Maj. M. HUME, and *Recollns. of Author* by Mrs Cobden SICKERT.

CHAPMAN (Abel) + BUCK (W. J.) Unexplored Spain; c. 200 ill. 21/ *n.* 8° Arnold 11
A compan. wk. to their *Wild Spain, ut* **I** § 147. The outcome of 40 yrs.' wandgs. in less-kn. pts., describg. fauna of the desolate steppes and prairies, etc.

COLLINS, W. W. [R.I.] The Cathedral Cities of Spain; 60 col. ill. 16/ *n.* 8° Heinemann 09
One chap. to ea. city, its cathedral, and neighbouring places of interest.

DEVERELL, F. H. All Round Spain *o.p.* [*pb.* 10/6] 8° Low 84

ELLIOT, Frances Diary of an Idle Woman in Spain; ill. *o.p.* [*pb.* 6/] c 8° White [82] 84

FIELD, Kate Ten Days in Spain; ill. $1·25 18° Houghton, *Boston* 98

FINCK, Hy. T. Spain and Morocco [trivial but bright] $1·25 c 8° Scribner, *N.Y.* 91

FORD, Rich. Handbk. f. Travrs. in Spain & Readers at Home, 2 v.; maps & plans 20/ 8° Murray [45] 98

" Gatherings fr. Spain [extrs. fr. above; w. addns.] 1/ *n.* f 8° Dent [46] 06
35 c. *n.* Dutton, *N.Y.* [Everyman's Lib.] FORD's detailed study of the nation is the standard authority, quite classical in value: most modern writers have borrowed from it.

GADOW, Dr Hans In Northern Spain; map and 89 ill. 21/ 8° Black 97
One of the better recent books of travel in Spain; full of information and description.

GALLENGA, Ant. Iberian Reminiscences: 15 years' travelling, 2 vols. 32/ 8° Chapman 83

HALE, Rev. E. E. Seven Spanish Cities, and the Way to Them $1·25 16° Little & Brown, *Boston* [83] 99
Describes places made famous by the *Chanson de Roland*: Madrid, Cordova, Toledo, etc.

HARE, A. J. C. Wanderings in Spain; 17 pl. 7/6 c 8° G. Allen [73] 83
$2 *n.* Macmillan, *N.Y.* A pleasant, chatty little bk.: quite sketchy.

HARTLEY, C. G. Things Seen in Spain; 50 ill. [Things Seen Ser.] 2/ *n.* 12° Seeley 10

HOPE-EDWARDES, E.C. Azahar: a tour in Spain *o.p.* [*pb.* 7/6] c 8° Bentley 83

HOWE, Maud Sun & Shadow in Spain; ill. (4 col.) [12/6 *n.* Gay] $3 *n.* 8° Little & B., *Bost.* 09

HUNTINGTON, A. M. A Note-Book in Northern Spain *o.p.* [*pb.* $3·50] 8° Putnam 98
Account of short visits to various places in Galicia and Aragon.

HUTTON, Edw. The Cities of Spain; ill. (24 col.) 6/ ($2 *n.*) c 8° Methuen [06] 07

ISRAËLS, Jozef Spain: the Story of a Journey [tr.]; ill. *o.p.* [*pb.* 12/6 *n.*] r 8° Nimmo (Routledge) 00
40 illustrations by the well-known Dutch painter, with accompanying letterpress.

JACCACI, A. F. On the Trail of Don Quixote $2·50 8° Scribner, *N.Y.* 97
Fresh and vivid sketches of La Mancha, the region fr. wh. D.Q. came. Fine illns. by Dan. VIERGE.

KENNEDY, Bart A Tramp in Spain 10/6 *n.* 8° Newnes 03
An account of a walking-tour through the country, from Gibraltar to Andorra.

LAWSON, W. R. Spain of To-day [descr., industr., financial 3/6 c 8° Blackwood 90
LE BLOND, Mrs A. Cities and Lights of Spain; 56 ill. [guide-bk.] 5/ *n.* c 8° Bell [04] 09
LENT, W. B. Across the Country of the Little King $1·25 c 8° Bonnell, *N.Y.* 97
LOMAS, J. In Spain; map and 50 ill. 6/ *n.* c 8° Black 08
$2 *n.* Macmillan, *N.Y.* A rewritten edn. of his *Sketches in Spain from Nature, Art, and Life* [1884].
LOWELL, J. Russell Impressions of Spain $1·50 (5/) c 8° Putnam 99
Selections (by J. B. GILDER) fr. Lowell's official dispatches from Spain, 1877–80: somewhat dull.
LUFFMANN, C. B. A Vagabond in Spain 6/ c 8° Murray 95
Acc. of a walking-tour in the capacity of a tramp, by an ex-actor: 1,500 miles from Biarritz to Mediterranean.
,, Quiet Days in Spain 8/ *n.* 8° Murray 10
McCLINTOCK, F. R. Holidays in Spain: two tours [1880–1] 6/ c 8° Stanford 82
MARDEN, P. S. Travels in Spain; ill. [10/6 *n.* Constable] 8° *U.S.A.* 10
MARRIOTT, C. A Spanish Holiday; ill. 7/6 *n.* 8° Methuen 08
MOULTON, Louise C. Lazy Tours in Spain and Elsewhere $1·10 c 8° Roberts, *Boston* 06
NIXON, Mary F. With a Pessimist in Spain; ill. $1·50 12° McClurg, *Chicago* 98
OBER, F. A. The Knock-about Club in Spain; ill. $1·50 8° Estes & Lauriat, *Boston* 89
PATCH, Olive Sunny Spain: its people and places; ill. 5/ r 8° Cassell [84] 88
ST BARBE, Reginald In Modern Spain; ill. [country and people] 3/6 c 8° Stock 99
SCOTT, S. P. Through Spain: travel and adventure; ill. *o.p.* [*pb.* 16/] r 8° Bentley 78
SEYMOUR, F. H. A. Saunterings in Spain; ill. 10/6 *n.* 8° Unwin 06
Barcelona, Madrid, Toledo, Cordova, Seville, Granada.
SHAW, Rafael Spain from Within 7/6 *n.* 8° Unwin 10
Chiefly repts. of conversns. w. members of Span. wkg.-classes. Attribs. nearly all troubles of Spain to Ultramontanism.
STODDARD, Dr C. A. Spanish Cities, w. glimpses of Gibraltar & Tangiers; ill. $1·50 c 8° Scribner, *N.Y.* 92
7/ Chapman. By a N.Y. newsppr.-edr., who took his family along usual route. Commonplace.
THIRLMERE, Rowl. Idylls of Spain: varnished pictures of travel; ill. 4/6 *n.* c 8° E. Mathews 97
,, Letters fr. Catalonia & other Pts. of Spain, 2 vols. 24/ *n.* 8° Hutchinson 05
THOMAS, Marg. [Austral.] Scamper through Spain and Tangier; ill. 12/ 8° Hutchinson 92
Fresh sketches of visits to Luz, Burgos, Madrid, Toledo, Cordova, Seville, Granada, Malaga, Gibraltar, Tangier. It may be recommd. to those who wish to make a tour in Spain cheaply.
WEBSTER, Rev. W. Spain [For. Countries and Brit. Cols.] 3/6 c 8° Low 81
WHITWELL, Mrs E. R. Spain as we Found it in 1891 *o.p.* [*pb.* 5/] c 8° Remington 92
WILLIAMS, Leon. The Land of the Dons; ill. 15/ *n.* i 8° Cassell 02
WOOD, Chas. W. The Romance of Spain; ill. 10/ *n.* 8° Macmillan 98
,, Glories of Spain; ill. [popular; discursive] 10/6 *n.* 8° Macmillan 01
WORKMAN, Fanny B. + W. H. Sketches Awheel in Fin de Siècle Iberia; 30 ill. $2 c 8° Putnam, *N.Y.* 97
6/ Unwin. Interesting account of an extended cycle-tour in Spain, w. graphic sketches of scenery.
ZIMMERMANN, Jerem. Spain and her People; ill. [8/6 *n.* Unwin] $2 *n.* 8° Jacobs, *Phila.* 06
*Life and People:* BENSUSAN (S. L.) Home Life in Spain; 12 ill. 10/6 *n.* 8° Methuen 10
BYRNE, Mrs W. P. Spain and the Spaniards as they are, 2 vols. *o.p.* [*pb.* 21/] c 8° Strahan 66
ELLIS, Havelock The Soul of Spain; front. 7/6 *n.* 8° Constable 08
One of the best recent bks. on Spain: cities, people, art, literature, contemp. events, etc.
FIELD, Dr Hy. M. Old Spain and New Spain; map $1·50 c 8° Scribner, *N.Y.* 88
HARVEY, Mrs Cositas Españolas: everyday life in Spain 15/ 8° Hurst 75
HAY, Col. Jno. Castilian Days; 111 ill. J. Pennell $3 c 8° Houghton, *Boston* [70] 03
10/ *n.* Heinemann. Spanish manners, character, politics, etc., wr. dur. residence at Madrid.
HIGGIN, Louis Spanish Life in Town and Country; ill. 3/6 *n.* c 8° Newnes 02
$1·20 *n.* Putnam, *N.Y.* [Our Neighbours] A careful account of condns. of mod. Spain; w. 2 ch. on Portuguese life by Eug. E. STREET.
HOLLAND, Eliz., L'y Spanish Journal, ed. Earl of Ilchester—*ut* **F** § 26
PLUMMER, Mary W. [ed.] Contemporary Spain $1·25 12° Lane, *N.Y.* 99
A series of tr. extrs. fr. modern Span. novels, illg. Span. life. Introd. by E. E. HALE.
ROSE, H. J. Untrodden Spain & the Black Country, 2 v. *o.p.* [*pb.* 30/] 8° Tinsley [75] 75
,, Among the Spanish People, 2 vols. *o.p.* [*pb.* 24/] c 8° Bentley 77
TYLER, Royall Spain: study of her life and arts; ill. 12/6 *n.* 8° Richards 09
A useful, industriously compiled guide to architecture and art of Spain for tourists.
WARD, G. H. B. The Truth about Spain; 12 pl. 7/6 *n.* c 8° Cassell 11
*Bull-Fighting:* PRICE (Lake) [art.] Tauromachia; 26 lithos.; w. descrns. *o.p.* [*pb.* 84/] i f° Hogarth 52
A splendid work, very difficult to meet with. The letterpress is by Rich. FORD. An important Span. wk. is that of L. CARMENAY MITLÁN, *Bibliografia de la Tauromaquia*, 8vo Madrid '88, w. its Appendix *Tauromaquia: apuntes bibliograficas*, 8vo *ib.* '88.
*Palaces:* CALVERT (A. F.) [ed.] Royal Palaces of Spain; ill. [Spanish Ser.] 3/6 *n.* ($1·50 *n.*) c 8° Lane 09
*Scenery:* d'AVILLIER (Bar. C.) Spain [tr.]; 420 ill. Gustav Doré 42/ i 4° Low [75] 76

HADDON, Trevor [art.] Southern Spain : 75 col. pl. ; w. l'rpr. A. F. Calvert [$6 *n.* Macmillan, *N.Y.*] 20/ *n.* sq 8° Black 08

ROBERTS, Dav. [artist] Picturesque Views in Spain and Morocco : lithos. *o.p.* [*pb.* 126/] f° Moon 37

Spanish Pictures, drawn in Pen and Pencil 8/ i 8° R.T.S. 82

WIGRAM, E. T. A. Northern Spain : 75 col. pl. ; w. l'rpr. by artist [$6 *n.* Macmillan, *N.Y.*] 20/ *n.* sq 8° Black 06

**Gypsies of Spain** —*v.* **F** § 76

**Islands**

*Azores :* BOYD (Mary Stuart) The Fortunate Isles ; ill. 12/6 *n.* 8° Methuen 11
Chronicle of a holiday in Majorca, Minorca, and Iviza.

ROUNDELL, Mrs C. Visit to Azores ; w. ch. on Madeira ; 25 ill. 7/6 c 8° Bickers 89

WALKER, W. F. The Azores, or Western Islands 10/6 8° Trübner (Paul) 86
A political, commercial, and geographical account.

*Balearic Islands :* BIDWELL (C. T.) The Balearic Islands ; map and ill. *o.p.* [*pb.* 10/6] p 8° Low 76

FLITCH, J. E. Crawford Mediterranean Moods [Balearic Isl., Sardinia] 12/6 *n.* 8° Richards 11

VUILLIER, Gaston —*in his* The Forgotten Islands [tr.], *ut* **E** § 14

*Madeira :* BIDDLE (A. J. D.) The Land of the Wine, 2 vols. ; ill. $7·50 *n.* 8° Biddle, *Phila.* [96] 01
History and condn. of the Madeira islds. Previous edns. *s.t.* '*The Madeira Islands*'.

BROWN, A. S. Madeira and Canary Islands, w. Azores ; maps 2/6 c 8° Low [89] 01

GORDON, Surg.-Gen. C. A. Flower of the Ocean : Madeira f. invalid & naturalist 2/6 8° Baillière 94

JOHNSON, Jas. Y. Madeira : its climate and scenery ; maps 10/ c 8° Dulan [51] 85

KOEBEL, W. H. Madeira, Old and New ; ill. 10/6 *n.* 8° Griffiths 09
A full acc. of the life, scenery, and history, w. trs. fr. Chronicles of Gaspar FRUCTUOSO [16 cent.], etc.

MARSH, A. E. W. Holiday Wanderings in Madeira ; pl. and ill. 5/ c 8° Low 92

TAYLOR, Ellen M. Madeira : its scenery and how to see it ; map 7/6 c 8° Stanford [82] 88

THOMAS-STANFORD, C. Leaves fr. a Madeira Garden ; 16 pl. 5/ *n.* ($1·50) c 8° Lane 09

*Majorca ; Minorca :* MARKHAM (Sir Clemens R.) Story of Majorca and Minorca ; maps 7/6 *n.* 8° Smith & Elder 08

VUILLIER, Gaston —*in his* The Forgotten Islands [tr.], *ut* **E** § 14

WOOD, Chas. W. Letters from Majorca ; 100 ill. [gossipy letters to his sister] *o.p.* [*pb.* 14/] 8° Bentley 88

*Malta* —*for* Knights of Malta *v.* **F** § 14

BALLOU, Maturin M. The Story of Malta $1·50 c 8° Houghton, *Boston* 93

BORON, V. [art.] Malta : 20 col. pl., w. l'rpr. F. W. Ryan [$2·50 *n.* Macm., *N.Y.*] 7/6 *n.* sq 8° Black

HARDMAN, Wm. Hist. of Malta : 1798–1815, ed. Dr J. Holland Rose 21/ *n.* ($6·50 *n.*) r 8° Longman 09
A valuable hist. of the island dur. period of Fch. and Brit. occupns. 1798–1815, based on documts.

SEDDALL, Rev. H. Malta Past and Present [tr. Phœnicians to pres. time] 12/ 8° Chapman 70

---

**Alhambra ; Granada**

CALVERT, A. F. The Alhambra of Granada—*ut sup.*

" Granada and the Alhambra ; ill. [Spanish Ser.] 3/6 *n.* ($1·50 *n.*) c 8° Lane 07

" Granada, Present and Bygone ; ill. and 20 col. pl. 7/6 *n.* c 8° Dent 08

IRVING, Washington The Alhambra : "Darro Edn.', 2 v. ; 30 photogravs. $6 (25/ *n*) 8° Putnam [32] 91
Acc. of a residence in the Moorish palace, w. the historical and romantic legends conn. w. its history. Semi-fictitious, aboundg. in delightful legends, and full of romantic interest. Other edns. by Putnam : 'Hudson Edn.', $1·50 ; 'People's Edn.', 75 c. ; 'Student's Edn.', w. Introd. and notes 60 c. Also ill. Jos. PENNELL, 3/6 ($1·50) c 8° Macmillan [96] 08 ; ill. G. W. Hood, (7/6 *n.*) 4° Lippincott 10.

" Granada—*ut* **F** § 58

JONES, Owen [artist] The Alhambra, 2 vols. ; 102 pl. *o.p.* [*pb.* £24] i f° Longman [42–5] 48
Plans, elevations, and sections. 67 of the plates in gold and colours.

WILLIAMS, Leon. Granada 7/6 *n.* 8° Heinemann 06
'Memories, adventures, studies, and impressions'.

**Andalusia**

MAUGHAM, W. S. Land of Blessed Virgin 6/ *n.* 8° Heinemann 04
A picturesque record of travel in Andalusia, by the well-known novelist.

**Basque Mountains**

LIBERTY, Arthur L. Springtime in the Basque Mountains ; ill. [diary] 12/ 8° Richards 01

**Cantabria**

ROSS (M.) + COOPER (H. S.) Highlands of Cantabria ; 25 ill. [Biscayan provs. of Spain] 21/ 8° Low 86

**Catalonia**

CALVERT, A. F. [ed.] Catalonia & Balearic Islds. ; 250 ill. [Spanish Ser.] 3/6 *n.* ($1·50 *n.*) c 8° Lane 10

**Cordova**

CALVERT (A. F.) + GALLICHAN (W. M.) Cordova; 160 ill. [Spanish Ser.] 3/6 *n.* ($1·50 *n.*) c 8° Lane 07

**Galicia**

CALVERT, A. F. [ed.] Galicia; ill. [Spanish Ser.] 3/6 *n.* ($1·50 *n.*) c 8° Lane 10

CARNARVON, Earl of Portugal and Galicia—*ut sup.*

MEAKIN, Annette M. B. Galicia, the Switzerld. of Spain; map and ill. 12/6 *n.* 8° Methuen 09
A comprehensive, interestg., and trustworthy account of this N.-Western corner of Spain.

WOOD, Walt. A Corner of Spain 5/ *n.* c 8° Nash 10

**Gibraltar**

FIELD, Dr H. M. [Am.] Gibraltar; ill. 7/6 8° Chapman 89

Gibraltar and its Sieges [popular] 1/6 c 8° Nelson [79] 92

SAYER, Cpt. F. History of Gibraltar; map and pl. *o.p.* [*pb.* 14/] 8° Chapman [62] 65
The hist. in its political reln. to events in Europe; w. account of its 14 sieges.

**Leon; Burgos; Salamanca**

CALVERT, A. F. Leon, Burgos, and Salam.; 462 ill. [Span. Ser.] 3/6 *n.* ($1·50 *n.*) c 8° Lane 08

**Madrid**

CALVERT, A. F. Madrid; 450 ill. [Spanish Series] 3/6 *n.* ($1·50 *n.*) c 8° Lane 09

WILLIAMS, Leon. Toledo and Madrid—*ut inf.*, *s.v.* Toledo

*Escorial:* CALVERT (A. F.) The Escorial; ill. [Spanish Ser.] 3/6 *n.* ($1·50 *n.*) c 8° Lane 07

**Malaga**

HARRIS, Miriam C. A Corner of Spain $1·25 c 8° Houghton, *Boston* 98
A descrn. of life in Malaga, the Seville fairs, bull-fights, etc.

**Pyrenees** —*v.* **E** § 14

**Seville**

CALVERT, A. F. Seville; 300 ill. [Spanish Series] 3/6 *n.* ($1·50 *n.*) c 8° Lane 07

GALLICHAN, W. M. Story of Seville; ill. [Mediæval Towns] 4/6 *n.* f 8° Dent 03
$1·75 *n.* Dutton, *N.Y.* Includes 3 chapters on the artists of Seville, by C. G. HARTLEY.

SIDNEY, F. E. Anglican Movements in Spain; ill. 7/6 *n.* r 8° Simpkin 03
Mainly a description of a visit to Seville during Holy Week.

**Toledo**

CALVERT, A. F. Toledo; 300 ill. 3/6 *n.* ($1·50 *n.*) c 8° Lane 07

DICK, Stewart The Heart of Spain: an artist's impressn. of Toledo; 36 ill. (6 col.) 3/6 *n.* 8° Foulis 06

LYNCH, Hannah Toledo; ill. [Mediæval Towns; $1·50 *n.* Dutton, *N.Y.*] 3/6 *n.* f 8° Dent 98

WILLIAMS, Leon. Toledo and Madrid: records and romances; 35 ill. 12/6 *n.* 8° Cassell 03

**Valencia; Murcia**

CALVERT, A. F. [ed.] Valencia and Murcia; 345 ill. [Spanish Ser.] 3/6 *n.* ($1·50 *n.*) c 8° Lane 10

**Valladolid, etc.**

CALVERT, A. F. [ed.] Valladolid, Oviedo, Segovia, Zamora, Avila, and Zarazoza; 390 ill. [Spanish Ser.] 3/6 *n.* ($1·50 *n.*) c 8° Lane 08

**Vizcaya; Santander**

CALVERT, A. F. [ed.] Vizcaya and Santander; ill. [Spanish Ser.] 3/6 *n.* ($1·50 *n.*) c 8° Lane 10

## 28: SWITZERLAND; THE ALPS

*Vide also* **I** § 165: Mountaineering, where many of best bks. on Alps appear, *and* **I** § 148*: Motoring.

**Bibliography:** AVEBURY (L'd) [=Sir J. LUBBOCK]—*in his* The Scenery of Switzerland, *ut inf.*

CONWAY (Sir W. M.) + COOLIDGE (W. A. B.)—*their* Climbers' Guides [*ut inf.* **I** § 165] *cont. ample refs. to past and pres. Alpine literature*

COOLIDGE, W. A. B. Swiss Travel and Swiss Guide Books 10/6 c 8° Longman 89
A sort of hist. of Swiss travel, tracing the growth of guide-books and means of travel. With bibliography.

POLLOCK, Sir Fredk. Library of the Alpine Club—*his* Oxford Lectures, *ut* **D** § 1

**Anthology**

EBERLI, H. [ed.] Switzerland, Poetical and Picturesque; 87 ill. 12*m.* 8° Orell Füssli, *Zürich* 93

JAMES, N. G. B. [ed.] The Charm of Switzerland [prose and verse] 5/ *n.* c 8° Methuen 10

**Travel; Description**

BAEDEKER, Karl [pub.] Switzerland and Adjacent Portions of Italy, Savoy, and Tyrol; maps [$2·40 *n.* Scribner, *N.Y.*] 8/ s 8° Unwin [ ] 09

BAEDEKER, Karl [pub.] Eastern Alps, incl. Bavar. Highlds., Tyrol, Salzkammergut, Styria, Carinthia ; maps [$4·80 *n.* Scrib., *N.Y.*] 10/ s 8° Unwin [ ] 97

BELLOC, Hilaire The Path to Rome—*ut* **E** § 11

BONNEY, Rev. T. G. Alpine Regions of Switz. and Neighbg. Countries *o.p.* [*pb.* 12/6] 8° Bell 68

BURNABY, Mrs F. [=Mrs MAIN] The High Alps in Winter ; ill. *o.p.* [*pb.* 14/] c 8° Low 83

,, High Life and Towers of Silence 10/6 8° Longman 86

*CONWAY, Sir Martin The Alps from End to End ; 52 ill. 6/ 8° Constable [95] 00
Account of a tour through the entire Alpine system.

COOLIDGE, W. A. B. Switzerland [For. Countries and Brit. Cols.] 3/6 c 8° Low 81

* ,, The Alps in Nature and History ; ill. 7/6 *n.* c 8° Methuen 08

DAUDET, Alphonse Tartarin on the Alps [tr.]—*ut* **K** § 53 [fiction]

FORBES, Prc. J. D. Travels thro' Alps of Savoy, etc., ed. W. A. B. Coolidge 20/ *n.* r 8° Black [43] 00
$9 Macmillan, *N.Y.* With biogr. sketch and 4 wrgs. on Alp. subjs. : *Travel thro' Alps of Savoy* [1843], *High Alps of Dauphiné, Berne, and Savoy* [1853], *Pedestrianism in Switzerld.* [1857], *Topogr. of Chain of Mt Blanc* [1865].

HUGO, Victor The Alps and Pyrenees [tr.] 7/6 c 8° Bliss 98
$2 Dutton, *N.Y.* Letters of travel, written in 1839.

KUHNS, Oscar Switzerland ; map & 32 pl. [scenery, hist., assocns.] $2 *n.* c 8° Crowell, *N.Y.* 11

MAIN, Mrs My Home in the Alps *o.p.* [*pb.* 3/6] c 8° Low 92
Conts. a good acc. of mtn. snow and ice, w. numerous avalanche stories and anecdotes, remarks on guides, etc.

MARSH, Dr Herb. Two Seasons in Switzerland [Alpine Small-talk] 10/6 *n.* c 8° Unwin 95

MONTAIGNE, M. de Journal of Travels in Italy by way of Switzerland—*ut* **E** § 24

MOORE, A. W. The Alps in 1864 ; a private jl. ; ill. 36/ *n.* r 8° Douglas, *Edin.* [64] 02
Ed. Prf. A. W. B. KENNEDY ; w. 479 facss. of the orig. sketch-maps and views, and many excellent photographic illns.

PARTSCH, J. —*in his* Central Europe, *ut* **E** § 11

SOWERBY, J. The Forest Cantons of Switzerland ; map 3/6 c 8° Rivington 92
A sort of 'higher Guide-bk.' : much informn. on hist., commerce, lang., geol., flora, fauna, legendary lore of Luzern, Schwyz, Uri, Unterwalden.

TISSOT, Victor Unknown Switzerland [tr.] 6/ c 8° Hodder 89

UMLAUFT, Prf. F. The Alps [tr.] : ill., 2 maps and 31 pl. 25/ r 8° Paul 89

WEBB, F. Switzerland of the Swiss 6/ *n.* c 8° Pitman 09

WHITE, S. E. The Mountains ; ill. 7/6 8° Hodder 05
Descrns. of scenery and rough trails, denizens of high places, pursuit of game, etc.

ZINCKE, F. B. Month in Switzerland, 5/ ; Swiss Allemands, 7/6 c 8° Smith & Elder 73–4

**Life ; People :** CRAWFORD (Virginia M.) Switzerland of To-day [soc. progress] c 8° Sands 11

DAWSON, W. H. Social Switzerland 6/ c 8° Chapman 97
Progress in labour organizns. and legisln., factory-laws, liquor-laws, and other social matters.

DIXON, W. Hepworth The Switzers *o.p.* [*pb.* 15/] 8° Hurst 72

MOSSO, Prf. Angelo Life of Man on the High Alps [tr.] ; ill. 21/ r 8° Unwin 98
A physiological study in a popular style : made on Monte Rosa.

READ, Gen. Meredith Historic Studies in Vaud, Berne, & Savoy, 2 v. ; ill. $10·50 8° Scribner, *N.Y.* 97
28/ Chatto. A miscell. colln. of materls. rel. to these districts, fr. Roman times to 18 cent., throwg. light on lives of GIBBON, ROUSSEAU, VOLTAIRE, among others.

STORY, A. T. Swiss Life in Town and Country ; ill. 3/6 *n.* c 8° Newnes 02
$1·20 *n.* Putnam, *N.Y.* [Our Neighbrs.] An admirable popular account of customs and institutions.

SYMONDS, J. A. + Marg. [dau.] Our Life in the Swiss Highlands ; 20 col. pl. 7/6 *n.* sq 8° Black [92] 07
$2·50 Macmillan *N.Y.* A vol. of vivid descr. essays, givg. admir. and sympath. treatmt. of Swiss character in all its variety. SYMONDS may be said to have been the founder of colony of Davos, wh., as an invalid in search of relief, he 'discovered'.

**Scenery**

BARTLETT, W. H. [artist] Switzerld.: mountains, valleys, etc. ; 200 steel pl. ; w. l'rpr. 15/ 4° Virtue [55] 76

BROCKEDON, W. Illustrations of Passes of the Alps, 2 vols. ; ill. *o.p.* 8° *London* 28–9
In its best state, the most beautiful bk. ever pubd. on the Alps.

GSELL-FELS, Dr Switzerland : its scenery and people [tr.] ; 363 ill. 42/ r 4° Blackie 81

JARDINE, Effie [art.] Switzerland & People : 80 pl. (56 col.) ; w. l'rpr. C. Rook 20/ *n.* s 4° Chatto 07

KADEN, W. Switzerland : its mountains and valleys ; 200 ill. 15/ s 8° Virtue [78] 88
The author's name on the title-page of the English edn. of this bk. is misprinted 'RADEN'.

MCCORMICK, A. D. [art.] Alps : 70 col. pl. ; w. l'rpr. Sir W. M. Conway [$6 *n.* Macm., *N.Y.*] 20/ *n.* sq 8° Black 04

MANNING, Rev. S. [ed.] Swiss Pictures, drawn with Pen and Pencil ; ill. 8/ i 8° R.T.S. [66] 80

PYNE (C.) + MERCIER (J.) [arts.] Mountains & Lakes of Switzerld. : 64 col. pl. *o.p.* [*pb.* 42/] c 4° Bell 70

WALTON, Elijah [art.] Peaks and Valleys of the Alps : 21 col. views, w. l'rpr. Rev. T. C. Bonney *o.p.* [*pb.* 84/] f° Low [72] 78

,, [art.] Bernese Oberland : 12 scenes, w. l'rpr. Bonney *o.p.* [*pb.* 84/] f° Thompson 73

*Study of Scenery* —*v. also* **E** § 16

AVEBURY, L'd [Sir J. LUBBOCK] Scenery of Switzerld., & its Causes; ill. 6/ ($1·50 *n.*) c 8° Macm. [96] 06
A pleasant compan. for tourist, involvg. no extensive knowl. of geol. (Gloss. of tech. terms added.)

**Austrian Alps** —*v.* **E** § 12

**Constance (Lake of)**

CAPPER, S. J. Shores and Cities of the Boden See [1879–80] 8/ 8° De La Rue 81

**Château d'Oex**

LAMPDEN, E. D. Château d'Oex; 20 pl. (12 col.) 6/ *n.* c 8° Methuen 10
A popular handbk. to the scenery, excursions, and espec. the winter-sports.

**Dauphiné and French Alps** —*v.* **E** § 14

**Dolomites** —*v.* **E** § 12

**Engadin**

BROWNE, G. F. The Engadin—*in his* Off the Mill, *ut* **K** § 83

LEWIS, J. H. [art.] Upper Engadine: 24 col. pl.; w. l'rpr. S. C. Musson [$2·50 *n.* Macm., *N.Y.*] 6/ *n.* sq 8° Black

TISSOT, Victor Unknown Switzerland [tr. fr. French] [=the Upper Engadin] 6/ c 8° Hodder 89

**Geneva**

GRIBBLE, Fcs. Lake Geneva and its Literary Landmarks 18/ 8° Constable 01
Deals w. almost every name of revolutionary importance dur. the two great periods of European revoln.

LEWIS, J. H. [art.] Lake of Geneva: 60 col. pl.; w. l'rpr. F. Gribble [$6 *n.* Macm., *N.Y.*] 20/ *n.* sq 8° Black 07

„ + May H. [arts.] Geneva: 20 col. pl.; w. l'rpr. Gribble [$2 *n.* Macm., *N.Y.*] 7/6 *n.* sq 8° Black 08

READ, Gen. Meredith —*in his* Historical Stories in Vaud, Berne, and Savoy, *ut sup.*

SHARP, W. Literary Geography 5/ *n.* c 8° Pall Mall Press 07

**Grindelwald**

RHODES, D. P. A Pleasure-Book of Grindelwald; ill. [chatty] 6/ *n.* ($1·50 *n.*) c 8° Macmillan 03

**Grisons**

FRESHFIELD, Mrs H. Tour in Grisons and Ital. Valleys of Bernina *o.p.* [*pb.* 10/6] c 8° Longman 62

TOLLEMACHE, Beat. L. C. Grisons Incidents in Olden Times 2/6 s 8° Rivington 91
Chiefly made up, in a rather desultory manner, of historical stories connected w. the Grisons.

ZINCKE, F. B. Walk in the Grisons *o.p.* [*pb.* 6/] c 8° Smith & Elder 75

**Italian Alps** —*v.* **E** § 24

**Lausanne**

LEWIS, J. H. + May H. [arts.] Lausanne: 24 col. pl.; w. l'rpr. F. Gribble 7/6 *n.* sq 8° Black 09

**Montreux**

LEWIS, J. H. [art.] Montreux: 20 col. pl.; w. l'rpr. F. Gribble [$2·50 *n.* Macm., *N.Y.*] 7/6 *n.* sq 8° Black 08

**Mont Blanc**

MATHEWS, C. E. Annals of Mont Blanc *pb.* 21/ *n.* 8° Unwin 98
With a chapter on the geology of the mountain by T. G. BONNEY.

VIOLLET-LE-DUC, E. Mt. Blanc, tr. B. W. Bucknall; 120 ill.; [chfly. geodesical & geolog.] 14/ 8° Low 77

WHYMPER, Edw. Chamonix and Mont Blanc; maps and ill. 3/ *n.* c 8° Murray [06] 10

**Oberland**

GEORGE, H. B. The Oberland and Glaciers; ill. *o.p.* [*pb.* 42/] 4° Bennett 66

GRANDE, Julian The Bernese Oberland in Summer & Winter; maps & ill. 3/6 *n.* s 8° Nelson 11

RAWNSLEY, Canon H. D. Flowertime in the Oberland; 12 ill. 5/ *n.* c 8° MacLehose, *Glasg.* 03

**Piedmont** —*v.* **E** § 24

**Rhone-valley** —*v.* **E** § 14

**Tyrol** —*v.* **E** § 12

**Zermatt**

WHYMPER, Edw. Zermatt and the Matterhorn; maps and ill. 3/ *n.* c 8° Murray [97] 10

## 29: TURKEY-IN-EUROPE; AND ALL BALKAN PENINSULA (EXCEPT GREECE)

**Early Travel**

BENT, J. Th. [ed.] Early Voyages and Travels in Levant 8° Hakluyt Soc. 93
i: *Diary* of DALLAM [1599–1600]; Extrs. fr. *Diaries* of Dr J. COVEL [1670–9]; w. acc. of Levant Co. of Turkey Merchts.

COCKERELL, C. R. Travels in Southn. Europe & the Levant, ed. S. P. Cockerell [son] 10/6 8° Longman 03
Record of travel and studies in archit. and sculpture in Greece, As. Min., Italy, Sicily, and esp. Constant. and Athens, in 1810–7.

**Recent Travel ; Description** —*v. also* **E** § 30

BAKER, Lt.-Col. Jas. Turkey in Europe ; 2 maps [journeys 1874–7] 21/ 8° Cassell 77
CHISHOLM, G. G. [ed.] —*in his* Europe, vol. i, *ut* **E** § 11
CLARK, Edson L. Turkey $2 8° Dodd & Mead, *N.Y.* 83
CREAGH, Jas. Over Borders of Christendom & Eslamiah, 2 v. *o.p.* [*pb.* 25/] 8° Tinsley 76
CURZON, Rob. [=L'd ZOUCHE] Visits to Monasteries of Levant ; maps & ill. 2/6 c 8° Newnes [49] 97
A new edn. of a fascinating book of travel which has been out of print for many years.
DE WINDT, Harry Through Savage Europe ; 100 ill. 10/6 *n.* 8° Unwin 07
Narr. of a jy. as Special Correspondent of *Westmr. Gaz.* thro' Balk. States and Eur. Russia.
FARLEY, J. Lewis Modern Turkey [Syria, Turk.-in-Eur., Asia] *o.p.* [*pb.* 14/] 8° Hurst 72
FRASER, J. F. Pictures from the Balkans ; map and ill. 6/ ($2) c 8° Cassell 06
v. HERBERT, Cpt. F. W. By-Paths in the Balkans 10/6 *n.* 8° Chapman 06
GRENVILLE-MURRAY, E. C. Turkey : being Sketches from Life 7/6 c 8° Routledge [55] 77
**HENDERSON, Maj. P. E. A British Officer in the Balkans 16/ *n.* 8° Seeley 09**
An informative narr. of jy. thro' Dalmatia, Montenegro, Turkey in Austria, Magyarld., Bosnia, Herzegovina.
HOGARTH, D. G. The Nearer East ; ill. [Regions of World] 7/6 *n.* ($2) 8° Clar. Press 02
A scientific geogr. acc. of Balkan States. Incls. Asia Minor and Egypt.
,, A Wandering Scholar in the Levant—*ut* **E** § 30
HULME-BEAMAN, A. Twenty Years in the Near East 2/6 c 8° Methuen 98
$3·75 New Amst. Bk. Co., *N.Y.* A pleasant, gossipy acc. of scenery, soc. condns., and polit. sitn. of Balkan States, Egypt, Syr., Russia.
LEAKE, W. M. —*in his* Travels in Northern Greece, 4 vols., *ut* **E** § 22
LYDE (F. W.) + MOCKLER-FERRYMAN (Col. A. F.) Military Geogr. of Balk. Peninsula 5/ c 8° Black 05
Short and clear view of the historico-geograph. aspect of subj. ; w. good maps.
MACKENZIE (Georgina M.) + IRBY (Miss A. P.) Travels in Sclavonic Provs. of Turkey, 2 v. *o.p.* [*pb.* 21/] 8° Daldy [77] 77
MENZIES, Sutherland Turkey, Old and New ; 25 ill. [histor., geogr., statist.] *o.p.* [*pb.* 21/] 8° W. H. Allen [80] 83
MILNER, T. Turkish Empire : sultan, territory, people [popular] 3/ c 8° R.T.S. [76] 77
**MILTOUN (Fcs.) + MCMANUS (Blanche) In Land of Mosques and Minarets ; 75 ill. (some col.) 7/6 *n.* c 8° Pitman 08**
*PARTSCH, Dr Jos. Central Europe [Regions of World]—*ut* **E** § 11
The best book on the general geography of Roumania, Bulgaria, and Servia.
PATON, A. A. Historical Researches on Danube and Adriatic, 2 vols.—*ut* **A** § 12
RAMSAY, Prf. W. M. Impressns. of Turkey dur. 12 Yrs.' Wandergs. —*v.* **E** § 40
RUSSELL, R. H. The Edge of the Orient ; ill. [8/6 Paul] $2 c 8° Scribner, *N.Y.* 96
Acc. of trip along coast of Dalmatia and Montenegro thro' Constantinople to Cairo.
TOZER, Rev. H. F. Researches in the Highlands of Turkey, 2 vols.—*ut* **E** § 22
**TREVOR, Roy My Balkan Tour ; map and 100 ill. 21/ *n.* 8° Lane 11**
WOODS, H. C. Washed by Four Seas ; ill. 7/6 *n.* 8° Unwin 08
Acc. of an Engl. officer's travels : Adriatic, Ægean, Sea of Marmora, Black Sea.
*Guide :* MACMILLAN & Co. [pubs.] Guide to the Eastern Mediterranean—*ut* **E** § 11
*Motor Tours* —*v.* **I** § 148*

**Life ; People ; Ethnology ; Economic and Political Condition**

ABBOTT, G. F. Turkey in Transition ; ill. [$4·25 *n.* Longm., *N.Y.*] 12/6 *n.* 8° Arnold 09
AFLALO, F. G. Regilding the Crescent ; map and 24 ill. 10/6 8° Secker 11
Deals w. Turkey's recent effort at rehabilitn. and the reforms of the Young Turks.
BARRY, J. P. At the Gates of the East—*ut* **E** § 30
**de BUNSEN, Victoria The Soul of a Turk ; 8 pl. 10/6 *n.* 8° Lane 10**
**BUXTON, C. R. Turkey in Revolution 7/6 *n.* 8° Unwin 09**
CLARK, Edson L. Races of European Turkey [condn., prospects, etc.] 10/6 8° Oliphant, *Edin.* 78
'Consul's Wife' [=Mrs. J. E. BLUNT] People of Turkey, 2 vols. [20 years' residce.] 21/ c 8° Murray 78
CREAGH, Jas. Armenians, Koords, and Turks, 2 vols. *o.p.* [*pb.* 24/] 8° Tinsley 80
CURTIS, W. E. The Turk and his Lost Provinces $2 *n.* c 8° Revell, *N.Y.* 03
Journalistic sketches of the life of Turkey, Greece, Bulgaria, Servia, and Bosnia.
DAVEY, R. P. B. The Sultan and his Subjects 7/6 *n.* 8° Chatto [97] 07
A study of past hist. and pres. condn. of Turk. Empire, affordg. good insight into true meang. of East. Questn., and means of formg. intelligent opin. as to probable destiny of Turkish people.
DURHAM, M. Edith —*in her* The Burden of the Balkans, *ut* **F** § 60

ELIOT, Sir Chas. Turkey in Europe 7/6 *n.* c 8° Arnold [01] 08
$2·50 Longman, *N.Y.* One of best accs. of state of affairs, social, econ., polit.—in Balkan Pen. in past and pres. 1st edn. *s.n.* 'ODYSSEUS'.

FRASER, David Persia and Turkey in Revolt—*ut* **E** § 38

GARNETT, Lucy M. J. The Women of Turkey, 2 vols.—*ut* **B** § 31

" Turkish Life in Town and Country 3/6 *n.* c 8° Newnes 04
$1·20 *n.* Putnam, *N.Y.* [Our Neighbours]. Much interestg. historical informn., based on long residence in Turkey.

" The Turkish People ; ill. 10/6 *n.* 8° Methuen 09
A valuable descrn. of the life and customs of the modern Turks, wr. w. sympathy and knowledge.

" Turkey of the Ottomans [Countries and Peoples] 6/ *n.* c 8° Pitman 11

HAMLIN, C. Among the Turks [1837–72] *o.p.* [*pb.* 10/6] c 8° Low 77

HARVEY, Mrs Turkish Harems and Circassian Homes *o.p.* [*pb.* 15/] 8° Hurst 71

HOUTSMA (T.) + SELIGSOHN (M.) [eds.]—*in their* Encyclopaedia of Islam, *ut* **A** § 13

'KESNIN BEY' Evil of the East : truths ab. Turkey [tr. fr. Fch.] *o.p.* [*pb.* 2/] c 8° Vizetelly [88] 89

KINGLAKE, A. W. Eothen—*ut* **E** § 30

LATHAM, R. G. Russian and Turk, fr. geogr. and ethnogr. pt. of view 18/ 8° W. H. Allen 78

de LAVELEYE, E. The Balkan Peninsula [tr.] *o.p.* [*pb.* 16/] 8° Unwin 87
A lucid view of the situation in the East in 1887 : Turkey, Bulg. Roum., Servia, Bosnia.

LOTI, Pierre' [Julien VIAUD] Disenchanted, tr. Mrs Bell 6/ ($1·50) c 8° Macmillan 06
A good tr. of LOTI's latest of 3 attempts to describe the women of mod. Constantinople.

MILLER, Wm. Travels and Politics in Near East ; ill. 21/ 8° Unwin 98
A very interesting and impartial account of the Balkan states, etc., and political problems there.

MONROE, Prf. W. S. Turkey and the Turks ; 48 ill. [7/6 *n.* Bell] $3 8° Page, *Boston* 07
A brief picture of the incoherent Ottoman Empire and its complex civilizn. Bibliography.

MOORE, F. The Balkan Trail ; map and 62 ill. 10/6 *n.* 8° Smith & Elder 06

*PEARS, Sir Edwin Turkey and its People [competent authority] 12/6 *n.* 8° Methuen 11

RONALDSHAY, Earl of Sport & Politics und. an Eastern Sky—*ut* **E** § 31

SMITH, F. Hopkinson A Day at Laguerre's, and other Days $1·25 12° Houghton, *Boston* 92

THOMSON, H. C. The Outgoing Turk—*ut* **E** § 12

TOWNSHEND, Cpt. A. E. A Military Consul in Turkey ; ill. 16/ *n.* 8° Seeley 09
Chs. on travellg., inns, tents, food, officials, soldiers, and (incidentally) politics.

TUCKER, W. J. Life and Society in Eastern Europe *o.p.* [*pb.* 15/] 8° Low 86

UPWARD, Allen The East End of Europe 12/ *n.* 8° Murray 08
$4 *n.* Dutton, *N.Y.* An 'unofficial inquiry' into racial and relig. troubles of European Turkey.

VAKA, Demetra [Mrs Kenneth BROWN] Some Pages fr. the Life of Turkish Women 5/ *n.* c 8° Constable 09

VAMBERY, Arminius The Balkan Peninsula [tr.] ; map 16/ 8° Unwin 88

WOODS, H. C. Danger Zone of Europe ; ill. [problems of Near East] 8° Unwin 11

**Constantinople**

de AMICIS, Edm. Constantinople [tr. fr. Italian] ; ill. $2·25 (7/6) c 8° Putnam, *N.Y.* [78] 96

BAKER, Cpt. B. Granville The Walls of Constantinople ; ill. 16/ *n.* r 8° Milne 10
Gives a good idea of the majesty of the great Theodosian achievemt. in wall-building.

BRASSEY, L'y A. Sunshine and Storm in the East ; 103 ill. 1/ 4° Longman [80]

CLEMENT, Clara E. [Mrs WATERS] Constantinople, City of Sultans ; 20 photogrs. $3 8° Estes & Lauriat, *Boston* 95
12/6 *n.* Gay & Hancock. A popular bk. on scenery, bldgs., hist., antiqs., institns., and social life of Constantinople.

CRAWFORD, F. Marion Constantinople ; ill. Edw. L. Weeks 6/6 i 16° Macmillan, *N.Y.* 95
$1·50 Scribner, *N.Y.* A good descrn. of life and people, hist. assocns., and archit. and geogr. beauties of Constantinople.

DWIGHT, Dr H. O. Constantinople and its Problems ; ill. $1·25 c 8° Revell, *N.Y.* 01
6/ Oliphant. A study of social condn. and probls. of the city, by a broad-minded missionary.

ELLIOT, Mrs Minto Diary of an Idle Woman in Constantinople ; ill. 14/ c 8° Murray 93
A vivacious attempt to clothe famous sites of Constantinople w. their histor. assocns. : author's histor. knowledge incommensurate w. her enthusiasm.

GOBLE, Warwick [artist] Constantinople : 63 col. pl. ; w. l'rpr. Prf. A. van Millingen [$6 *n.* Macmillan, *N.Y.*] 20/ *n.* sq 8° Black 06

GROSVENOR, Prf. E. A. Constantinople ; Introd. Gen. Lew Wallace, 2 v. ; 200 ill. $10 r 8° Roberts, *Boston* 95
42/ Low. A handsome popular work, from the historical and archæological points of view.

HUTTON, W. H. Constantinople ; ill. [Mediæval Towns] 3/6 *n.* f 8° Dent [00] 04
$1·50 Dutton, *N.Y.* A very full and trustworthy acc. of both history and topography, treated separately.

MÜLLER, Georgina [Mrs F.] Max Letters from Constantinople ; 12 views 6/ ($1·75) c 8° Longman 97
Amusg. and interestg. letters, exhibg. a more favourable view of Turkey than is usually shown.

MURRAY, Jno. [pub.] Constantinople, Brûsa, and Troad ; maps 7/6 s 8° Stanford [93] 06

PASPATES, A. G. The Great Palace of Constantinople, tr. [fr. Gk.] Wm. Metcalfe—*ut* **F** § 13

SPRY, W. J. J. Life on the Bosphorus ; ill. Nichols 95
Pt. i is a descrn. of Constantinople and acc. of trial of MIDHAT PASHA ; Pt. ii is historical.

*Sancta Sophia, Church of* —*v.* **I** § 121

**Albania**

BROWN, H. A. A Winter in Albania ; ill. 10/6 c 8° Griffith 88

*DURHAM, M. Edith High Albania ; map and ill. 14/ *n.* 8° Arnold 09
$4 *n.* Longman, *N.Y.* An excellent and sympathetic acc. of the country, its inhabitants (the highest known, and the most attractive, type of savage), and their tribal affins. and customs, and the life of these wild mtn.-regions still untouched by mod. civilizn. Well and humorously wr.

KNIGHT, E. F. Albania & Montenegro : narr. of recent travels ; ill. *o.p.* [*pb.* 12/6] c 8° Low 80

WALKER, [Mrs] Mary A. Through Macedonia to the Albanian Lakes *o.p.* [*pb.* 20/] r 8° Chapman 64

WINGFIELD, W. F. Tour in Dalmatia, Albania, etc. *o.p.* [*pb.* 10/6] c 8° Bentley 59

**Asia Minor** —*v.* **E** § 30

**Bosnia and Herzegovina** —*v.* **E** § 12

**Bulgaria**

BARKLEY, H. C. Between the Danube and the Black Sea 10/6 p 8° Murray [76] 77

,, Bulgaria before the War [of 1878] *o.p.* [*pb.* 10/6] p 8° Murray 77

BOOTH, J. L. C. The Trouble in the Balkans ; ill. [1904] 10/6 *n.* 8° Hurst 05

Bulgaria of To-day [offic. pubn.] *gratis* Bulg. Ministry of Commerce 07

DICEY, Prf. Edw. The Peasant State : an account of Bulgaria in 1894 12/ 8° Murray [94] 94
Affords an accurate view of the present and a fair estimate of the future of Bulgaria.

FARLEY, J. Lewis New Bulgaria *o.p.* [*pb.* 2/6] 8° Newman 80

HUYSHE, Wentworth The Liberation of Bulgaria [1877] 6/ c 8° Sands 94

v. MACH, Rich. The Bulgarian Exarchate : its history, etc. [tr.] 3/6 *n.* 8° Unwin 07
The hist. and pres. positn. of the Bulg. Church in Turkey : of value in its bearg. on politics of Near East.

MINCHIN, J. G. Bulgaria since the War [of 1878] *o.p.* [*pb.* 3/6] 12° Paul 80

SAINT CLAIR (S. G. B.) + BROPHY Twelve Years' Residence in Bulgaria *o.p.* [*pb.* 9/] c 8° Chapman [69] 77

SAMUELSON, Jas. Bulgaria, Past & Present ; map & ill. [Pt. ii : Bulgaria to-day] 10/6 8° Trübner 88

**Crete**

BICKFORD-SMITH, R. A. H. Cretan Sketches ; ill. *o.p.* [*pb.* 6/] 8° Bentley 98
A good picture of Crete during the insurrection.

EDWARDES, C. Letters from Crete [pleasant, but not v. informg.] *o.p.* [*pb.* 15/] 8° Bentley 87

PASHLEY, Rob. Travels in Crete, 2 vols. *o.p.* [*pb.* 42/] 8° Murray 37

SKINNER, J. E. H. Roughing it in Crete *o.p.* [*pb.* 10/6] 8° Bentley 67

SPRATT, Cpt. T. A. B. Travels & Researches in Crete, 2 v. ; tinted pl. & ill. 40/ 8° Van Voorst 65

TAYLOR, Bayard Greece and Russia ; 2 pl. ; w. Excursion to Crete—*ut* **E** § 22

**Herzegovina**—*v.* **E** § 12 **Ionian Islands**—*v.* **E** § 22

**Macedonia** —*v. also* Servia *inf.*

ABBOTT, G. F. The Tale of a Tour in Macedonia 14/ *n.* 8° Arnold 03
$5 *n.* Longman, *N.Y.* Map and ill. An account of travel in the district around Serres only.

BOOTH, J. L. C. Trouble in the Balkans—*ut sup.*, *s.v.* Bulgaria [period 1904]

BRAILSFORD, H. N. Macedonia : its races and their future 12/6 *n.* 8° Methuen 06

CHIROL, Valentine 'Twixt Greek and Turk—*ut* **E** § 22

WALKER, [Mrs] Mary A. Through Macedonia to Albanian Lakes—*ut sup.*, *s.v.* Albania

**Montenegro**

CARR, W. Montenegro [Stanhope Prize Essay, 1884] 2/6 8° *Oxford* 84

DENTON, Rev. W. Montenegro : its people, history, etc. *o.p.* [*pb.* 6/] c 8° Daldy 77

STRANGFORD, L'y Montenegro and the Eastern Adriatic *o.p.* [*pb.* 18/] 8° Bentley 64

WILKINSON, Sir J. G. Dalmatia and Montenegro—*ut* **E** § 12

WYON (R.) + PRANCE (J.) In the Land of the Black Mountain ; 51 ill. 2/6 *n.* c 8° Methuen 03
An impressionist account of the whole of the Albanian frontier.

**Roumania**

BENGER, G. Rumania in 1900, tr. Prf. A. H. Keane ; ill. 10/ *n.* i 8° Asher 01
A very full, accurate, and valuable account of progress and present condition.

OZANNI, J. W. Three Years in Roumania *o.p.* [*pb.* 7/6] c 8° Chapman 82

SAMUELSON, Jas. Roumania, Past and Present ; maps and ill. *o.p.* [*pb.* 6/] c 8° Philip [82] 86

STRATILESCO, Tereza From Carpathian to Pindus ; maps and 63 ill. 15/ *n.* 8° Unwin 06

WALKER, Mrs Untrodden Paths in Roumania ; 78 ill. 10/6 8° Chapman 88

**Servia**

DENTON, Rev. W. Servia and the Servians *o.p.* [*pb.* 9/6] p 8° Bell 62

DURHAM, M. Edith — Through the Lands of the Serb — 14/ 8° Arnold 04
$5 *n.* Longman, *N.Y.* An extremely interestg. acc. of adventurous travel by an unprotected woman.

LAZAROVICH-HREBELIANOVICH, Pr'ce + Pr'ess — The Servian People, 2 vols.; ill — 24/ *n.* 8° Laurie 11
A hist. of the Servians and their 'past glory', w. speculns. as to their destiny. Incls. Montenegrins and Croats.

MIJATOVITCH, Chedo — Servia and the Servians — 16/ *n.* 8° Pitman 08
Vivid acc. of relig., soc. life, and tradns. of 'the Irish of the Balkans', by ex-Minister of Serv. at Ct. of St James.

STEAD, Alf. — Servia and the Servians — 12/6 *n.* 8° Heinemann 09

STRATILESCO, Tereza — From Carpathian to Pindus—*ut sup.*, *s.v.* Roumania

VIVIAN, Herb. — Servia, the Poor Man's Paradise; ill. — 15/ ($4) 8° Longman 97
Partly historical, but chiefly a popular description of present day Servian life.

,, — The Servian Tragedy: impressns. of Macedonia; ill. [1903] 10/6 *n.* 8° Richards 04

WRIGHT, Dr E. — Adventures in Servia, ed. Dr E. Bernard; pl. *o.p.* [*pb.* 10/6] 8° Sonnenschein 84

**Transylvania** —*v.* **E** § 12

---

# IV: Geography, etc., of Asia Minor

## 30: ASIA MINOR, incl. CRETE, CYPRUS, SYRIA—*v. also* A § 47 *and* E § 40

**Bibliography; Atlases; Maps**—*ut* **A** § 47

**Early Travel** —*v. also inf.*, *s.v.* Palestine

CASOLA, Pietro — Pilgrimage to Jerusalem in 1494, ed. Miss M. M. Newett; w. Introd; maps [Mancs. Univ. Pbs.] 7/6 *n.* 8° Sherratt, *Mancs.* 07

DERBY, HENRY, EARL OF [*afterw.* HENRY IV] Expeditions to Prussia and the Holy Land in 1390–91 and 1392–93, ed. Lucy Toulmin Smith—*ut* **F** § 13

IRBY (C. L.) + MANGLES (J.) Travels in the Holy Land [1817–8] *o.p.* [*pb.* 2/] c 8° Murray [23] 61

di VARTHEMA, Lud. — Travels in Egypt, Syria, Arabia, Persia, India, etc. [tr.], ed. Rev. G. P. Badger [1503–8] 8° Hakluyt Soc. 63

WHALEY, Thos. — Buck Whaley's Memrs., ed. Sir E. Sullivan—*ut* **F** § 25 [incl. his jy. to Jerus. 1797]

**Guides**

BAEDEKER (K.) + SOCIN (A.) Palestine and Syria—*ut* **A** § 47

HANAUER (Rev. J. E.) + MASTERMAN (Dr E. J.) Cook's Hdbk. for Pal. and Syria; maps 7/6 *n.* c 8° Cook & Son 06

MACMILLAN & Co. [pbs.] — Palestine and Syria; 18 maps — 5/ *n.* gl 8° Macmillan [01] 11

,, — Greece, Asia Minor, Crete, Cyprus, etc.—*ut* **E** § 11

MEISTERMANN, F'r B. — New Guide to Holy Land [tr.] [for R.-C. tourist] 7/6 *n.* c 8° Burns & Oates 07

REYNOLDS-BALL, E. A. — Guide to Jerusalem; maps and ill. [$1 Macm., *N.Y.*] 2/6 c 8° Black 01

**Historical Geography**

HENDERSON, Dr Arch. — Palestine: its historical geography—*ut* **A** § 47

HOGARTH (D. G.) + MUNRO (J. A. R.) Modern and Ancient Roads in Eastern Asia Minor = Suppl. Paper of R. G. S. 1893
Forms a valuable addn. to RAMSAY'S *Hist. Geogr.*, descr. jys. undertaken in 1890 and '91. Passes of E. Taurus and Anti-Taurus, milit. road fr. Cæsarea to Melitene on Euphrates, etc.

HUNTINGDON, Prf. E. — Palestine and its Transformation [8/6 *n.* Constable] 8° 11
A brilliant study of the geogr., fr. a histor. pt. of view, of a country as unique in its plys, feats, as in its influ. on world.

RAMSAY, Prf. W. M. — Historical Geography of Asia Minor; maps — 18/ r 8° Murray 90
Roy. Geogr. Soc. Suppl. Pprs., vol. v. 'Topography is the foundation of history', and this vol. is the massive foundn. for a Local Hist. of Asia Minor, but a little chaotic in form.

,, — Cities of St Paul, *ut* **A** § 51; Letters to Seven Churches of Asia, *ut* **A** § 43

,, — Pauline and other Studies, *ut* **A** § 51

,, — Luke the Physician, and other Studies in Hist. of Religion—*ut* **A** § 49

SKEEL, Carol. A. J. — Travel in the First Century after Christ—*ut* **A** § 47

SMITH, Prf. G. A. — Historical Geography of the Holy Land—*ut* **A** § 47

**Recent Travel and Description**—*v. also* **E** §§ 22, 29, *and* **A** § 47: Biblical Archæol.: Topogr.

BARKLEY, H. C. — Ride thro' Disturbed Districts of Asia Minor & Armenia 10/6 c 8° Murray 91
Sketch of manners and custs. of Turks, Armens., Kurds, Turcomans, etc. Ride was fr. Constant. thro' Anatolia, Cilicia, Mesopotamia, Taurus Mtns.

BARRY, Lt.-Col. J. P. — At the Gates of the East; ill. — 6/ *n.* 8° Longman 06
Travel impressns. dur. 2 jys. in E. Eur., Cairo, S. Greece. E. Adriatic, W. Balkans.

BARTLETT, Dr S. C. — Fr. Egypt to Palestine thro' Sinai, Wilderness, etc.; maps & ill. 18/ 8° Low 79

*BELL, Gertr. Lowthian — From Amurath to Amurath; ill. — 16/ *m.* 8° Heinemann 11
A brilliant bk. of travel and adventurous wandergs. in 1909 in Near East far fr. beaten tracks, w. descrns. of life and manners of people of As. Min. Startg. fr. Aleppo, author went along banks of Euphrates to Babylon, crossed Mesopot. to Bagdad, then followed line of Tigris to site of Nineveh.

* ,, — The Desert and the Sown—*ut inf.*, *s.v.* Syria

BIGHAM, Clive — A Ride through Western Asia; ill. 8/6 *n.* 8° Macmillan [97] 97
Asia Minor; Persia, North to South; Turkish Arabia; Persia, West to East; Central Asia. Maps and glossary.

BREEN, A. E. — Diary of My Life in the Holy Land; ill. $4·50 4° Smith, *Rochester, N.Y.* 06

BREWSTER, M. Augusta — Three Months' Travels in Egypt and Palestine; 12 ill. 5/ c 8° Nisbet 93

BURNABY, Cpt. F. — On Horseback through Asia Minor *o.p.* [*pb.* 10/6] c 8° Low [77] 78

B[UXTON], H. M. + C. E. + T. On Either Side of the Red Sea; 53 pl. & 21 ill. 10/6 *n.* s 4° Stanford 95
Extrs. fr. graphic letters wr. home by the Misses BUXTON, designed to serve as a thread to ser. of interestg. photos.

COCHRAN, W. — Pen and Pencil in Asia Minor: notes fr. Levant; 89 ill. 21/ 8° Low 87

DAVIS, E. J. — Anatolica: jl. of visit to anc. ruined cities 21/ 8° Grant 74

,, — Life in Asiatic Turkey; ill. 21/ 8° Stanford 79

DUNNING, Dr H. W. — To-day in Palestine; ill. 10/6 *n.* 8° Laurie 08

EWING, Wm. — Arab and Druz at Home; ill. [Damascus to Jericho] 5/ 8° Jack 07

FELLOWS, Sir Chas. — Travels and Researches in Asia Minor; pl. [1838; 1840] *o.p.* [*pb.* 9/] 8° Murray [39–43] 52

GOOCH-FREER, [Miss] A. — Inner Jerusalem; ill. [very readable] 12/6 *n.* 8° Constable 04

GRANT, Rev. Elihu — The Peasantry of Palestine $1·50 *n.* c 8° Pilgrim Press, *Chicago* 08

HAGGARD, H. Rider — A Winter Pilgrimage; 31 ill. [Silver Library] 3/6 ($1·50) c 8° Longman [01] 08
Acc. of travels thro' Palestine, Italy, and Cyprus, in the year 1900.

HAMILTON, W. J. — Researches in Asia Minor, Pontus, & Armenia, 2 v. *o.p.* [*pb.* 38/] 8° Murray 42
An important wk., to wh. RAMSAY bears full testimony, provg. th. more vestiges of antiquity really existed in Asia Min. than LEAKE or any of his predecessors dreamt of.

HEBER-PERCY, Maj. A. — A Visit to Bashan and Argob 7/6 s 4° R.T.S. 95

,, — Moab, Ammon, and Gilead 6/ 8° Simpkin 96

HICHENS, Rob. — The Holy Land; ill. [impressionist sketches] 25/ *n.* i 8° Hodder 10

HOGARTH, D. G. — The Nearer East—*ut* **E** § 29: incls. Asia Minor to Pers. frontier

,, — A Wandering Scholar in the Levant; map and ill. 7/6 c 8° Murray [96] 96
A lively and informg. acc. of travel in Near East, by a many-sided scholar and excellent writer, who accomp. Mr W. M. RAMSAY to Asia Minor and learned w. him the lesson of learned explorn.

HORNBY, Emily — Sinai and Petra; col. pl. F. M. Hornby [her jls. 1899, 1901] 6/ 8° Nisbet 07

HULME-BEAMAN, A. — Twenty Years in the Near East—*ut* **E** § 29

HUTTON, Laur. — Literary Landmarks of Jerusalem; ill. 75 c. p 8° Harper, *N.Y.* 95

JANEWAY, Cath. — Ten Weeks in Egypt and Palestine; ill. [chatty] 5/ c 8° Paul 94

**JEBB, Louisa [Mrs Roland WILKINS] By Desert Ways to Baghdad**—*ut* **E** § 40

KINGLAKE, A. W. — Eothen; w. biograph. sketch; port. 3/6 c 8° Blackwood [44] 96

,, The same: repr. of 1st edn.; w. Introd. Rev. W. Tuckwell; ill. 4/ *n.* s 8° Bell [44] 02

,, The same; w. Introd. D. G. Hogarth & notes H. V. Collins 2/6 (60 c.) s 8° Clar. Press [44] 11
[New Univ. Lib.] 1/ *n.* pott 8° Routledge (50 c. Dutton, *N.Y.*) Also Everyman's Lib., 1/ *n.* f 8° Dent (35 c. *n.* Dutton, *N.Y.*). A graphic and poetic description of jy. thro' Syria, across the desert to Egypt, and back to Syria, in 1834–5: cramful of acute observns.

LEAKE, W. M. — Journal of Tour in Asia Minor, etc. [*v. also* **E** § 22] *o.p.* 8° *London* 24
The wks. of LEAKE, who has been called 'the greatest of mod. topographers', form the foundn. of mod. research in Asia Minor.

LE STRANGE, Guy — Lands of the Eastern Caliphate; 10 maps 15/ c 8° Camb. Press 05
$4 *n.* Putnam, *N.Y.* [Camb. Geogr. Ser.] Mesopot., Pers., and Centr. Asia, fr. Moslem Conq. to time of TIMUR.

LIBBEY (Dr W.) + HOSKIN (Dr F. E.) Jordan Valley and Petra, 2 vols.; maps and 140 ill. [good] $6 (25/ *n.*) 8° Putnam 05

LOYSON, Mme Hyacinthe — To Jerusalem thro' Lands of Islam: among Jews, Christians and Moslems; ill. [10/6 *n.* Paul] $1·25 8° Open Ct. Pb. Co., *Chicago* 06

MCGREGOR, Jno. — *Rob Roy* [canoe] on Jordan, Nile, Red Sea, etc.; maps & ill. 2/6 c 8° Murray [70] 04
A racy descrn. of a canoe-jcy. down Jordan to Dead Sea in 1868–9

MACLEOD, Rev. N. — Eastward: travels in Egypt, Palestine, Syria; ill. *o.p.* [*pb.* 6/] c 8° Isbister [66] 72

MARGOLIOUTH, Dr D. S. — Cairo, Jerusalem and Damascus—*ut* **E** § 42

MURRAY, Jno. [pub.] — Hdbk. to Asia Minor. Ed. Sir C. Wilson; 23 maps 18/ s 8° Stanford 95

PERCY, Hy. A. G., Earl of — Highlds. of Asiatic Turkey; ill. [$5·50 Longm., *N.Y.*] 14/ *n.* r 8° Arnold 01

RAMSAY, Prf. W. M. — Impressions of Turkey—*ut* **E** § 40

,, + BELL (Gertr. Lowthian) The Thousand and One Churches—*ut* **G** § 8

ROSS, H. J. — Letters from East, 1837–57, ed. Janet Ross 12/6 *n.* 8° Dent 02

SCOTT-STEVENSON, Mrs — Our Ride through Asia Minor; map *o.p.* [*pb.* 18/] 8° Chapman 81

SELOUS, F. C. — —*in his* Sport and Travel East and West, *ut* **I** § 147

***SMITH, Prf. G. A.** — **Jerusalem, 2 vols.; maps and ill.** **24/ *n.* 8° Hodder 07**
$7·50 *n.* Armstrong, *N.Y.* An important study of the topogr., economics, and hist. of Jerusalem fr. earliest times to A.D. 70 by one who really knows his subj. fr. personal experience.

SPRATT (Lt. T. A. B.) + FORBES (Prf. E.) Travels in Lycia, Milyas, and Cibyratis, 2 v. ; ill. *o.p.* [*pb.* 36/] 8° Van Voorst 47

STODDARD, Chas. W. — A Cruise under the Crescent ; ill. $1·50 c 8° Rand & McNally, *Chicago* 99
A conventional tour : Jerusalem, Damascus, Baalbek, Beirut, Port Said, etc.

TAYLOR, Bayard — Land of Saracen [Pal., As. Min., Sic., Spain] $1·50 12° Putnam, *N.Y.* [55] 82

THOMAS, Marg. — Two Years in Palestine and Syria ; 16 col. pl. *o.p.* [*pb.* 12/6 *n.*] 8° Nimmo 99

,, [art.] — From Damascus to Palmyra : col. ill., w. l'rpr. J. Kelman [$6 *n.* Macm., *N.Y.*] 20/ *n.* sq 8° Black 08

VAN DYKE, Dr Hy. J. — Out of Doors in Holy Land [6/ *n.* Hodder] $1·50 *n.* c 8° Scribner, *N.Y.* 08

VAUX, W. S. W. — Greek Cities and Islands of Asia Minor 2/ 12° S.P.C.K. 77

WILSON, Rev. C. T. — Peasant Life in the Holy Land 12/ 8° Murray 06

**Armenia**—*v.* **E** § 40 **Asiatic Greek Islands**—*v.* **E** § 22 **Caucasus, Transcaucasia**—*v.* **E** § 39 **Crete**—*v.* **E** § 29

**Cyprus** —*v. also* **E** § 40

BAKER, Sir S. W. — Cyprus as I saw it in 1879 *o.p.* [*pb.* 12/6] 8° Macmillan 79

BRASSEY, L'y —*in her* Sunshine and Storm in the East, *ut* **E** § 29 : Cyprus and Constantinople

COBHAM, C. D. [ed. & tr.] — Excerpta Cypria 21/ *n.* 4° Camb. Press [95] 08
$6·30 *n.* Putnam, *N.Y.* A valuable colln. of texts and trs. of passages in anc., medieval, and mod. wrgs. rel. to the island. With Bibliogr.

DIXON, W. Hepworth — British Cyprus *o.p.* [*pb.* 15/] 8° Chapman 79

FYLER, Col. — Development of Cyprus, & Rambles in Isld. ; maps & col. ill. 7/6 8° Lund 99

HAGGARD, H. Rider —*in his* A Winter Pilgrimage, *ut sup.*

HUTCHINSON (Sir J. T.) + COBHAM (C. D.) Handbook of Cyprus ; 2 maps & front. 2/6 *n.* c 8° Stanford 05

LANG, A. H. — Cyprus ; ill. [hist., resources, prospects] *o.p.* [*pb.* 14/] 8° Macmillan 78

LEWIS, Agnes Smith — Through Cyprus ; map and ill. 15/ 8° Hurst 87

LEWIS, Mrs E. A. M. — A Lady's Impressions of Cyprus in 1893 *o.p.* [*pb.* 5/] c 8° Remington 94
Conts. a good deal of informn. on antiqs., hist., pres. condn. of Cyprus, w. remks. on effects of Brit. rule.

v. LÖHER, F. — Cyprus : historical & descriptive [tr.] ; 2 maps *o.p.* [*pb.* 10/6] c 8° W. H. Allen 78

MALLOCK, W. H. — In an Enchanted Island [visit to Cyprus in 1889] *o.p.* [*pb.* 6/] c 8° Bentley [89] 92

MARITI, Abbé Giov. — Travels in Island of Cyprus, tr. C. D. Cobham 4/ *n.* c 8° Camb. Press 09
$1·25 *n.* Putnam, *N.Y.* MARITI resided in Cyprus 1760–7 as an official of Impl. and Tuscan consulates.

SCOTT-STEVENSON, Mrs — Our Home in Cyprus 14/ 8° Chapman 79

STEWART, Basil — My Experiences in Cyprus ; 50 ill. [$2 *n.* Dutton, *N.Y.*] 6/ c 8° Routledge [06] 09
Presents good view of people, medieval cities, antiqs., and *résumé* of hist., w. ch. on econ. and polit. probls.

THOMSON, J. — Through Cyprus with the Camera, 2 vols. ; 60 photos. 105/ r 4° Low 79

VIZETELLY, E. — Cyprus to Zanzibar by Egyptn. Delta ; ill. 15/ 8° Pearson 01

*Levkosia :* SALVATOR (Archd. L.) Levkosia, the Capital of Cyprus *o.p.* [*pb.* 10/6] 4° Paul 81

VAN LENNEP, Dr H. J. — Travels in Little-kn. Pts. of Asia Minor ; 2 v. [1864] *o.p.* [*pb.* 24/] 8° Murray 70
With illns. of Biblical literature and archæological researches. Maps and illns.

WARNER, C. Dudley — In the Levant, 2 vols. ; 25 photograv. pl. $5 c 8° Houghton, *Boston* [77] 92
Palestine, Cyprus, Rhodes, Ægean Islands, Smyrna, Ephesus, Constantinople, Athens, Corinth.

*Mediterranean Sea* —*v.* **E** § 11

**Cyzicus** —*v.* **G** § 8

**Euphrates and Tigris ; Mesopotamia**

AINSWORTH, W. F. — Personal Narrative of Euphrates Expedition, 2 vols. 32/ f 8° Paul 88
By the Surgeon and Geologist to the Expedition. Map.

CHESNEY, [Gen.] Chas. — The Euphrates and Tigris Surv. Exped., 2 v. ; pl. ; & atlas [1835–37] *o.p.* [*pb.* 94/6] r 8° Longman 50

GEERE, H. Valentine — By Nile and Euphrates 8/6 *n.* 8° Clark, *Edin.* 04
Excellent and amusing descrn. of jy. by water and by land fr. Baghdad to Nippur and back. Describes also excavns. in Egypt.

JEBB, Louisa [Mrs Rol. WILKINS] By Desert Ways to Baghdad—*ut* **E** § 40
The main pt. of bk. is acc. of 3 weeks spent on a raft floatg. down the Tigris.

PETERS, J. P. — Nippur : explorns. and advents. on Euphr., 2 vols. $5 (25/) 8° Putnam, *N.Y.* 97

**Gaza** : MEYER (M. A.) Hist. of City of Gaza [Columb. Un. Studs.] $1·50 *n.* 8° Macmillan, *N.Y.* 07

**Phrygia**

*RAMSAY, Prf. W. M. Cities & Bishoprics of Phrygia, vol. i, Pts. 1–2 39/ *n.* ($12·50) r 8° Clar. Press 95–7
i (1) *Lycos Valley and S. Phryg.*, 18/ *n.* ($5·75) ; i (2) *West and W.-Centr. Phryg.*, 21/ *n.* ($6·75). Gathers up results of author's and others' research into a local history, treatg. ea. district and city separately, the anc. topogr. bg. restored largely by aid of inscriptns., the most import. of wh. are discussed in spec. Appendices. Hist. brought down to Turkish period. Suggests a solutn. to the 'Hittite Problem' [favourg. SAYCE's theory] ; other valuable digressns., e.g. essential idea of the Asiatic cult, constitn. of Rom. Imperl. Domain, religion of burial, prob. truth ab. the Neokorate, reason of CYRUS' route.

**Pontus** —*v. also* Hamilton, *sup.*

ANDERSON, J. G. C. Jy. of Explorn. in Pontus; maps and ill. [Studia Pontica, vol. i] 6/6 *n.* 8° Owen 03

**Rhodes**

TORR, Cecil Rhodes in Modern Times; 3 pl. 8/ 8° Camb. Press 87
For his *Rhodes in Ancient Times v.* **G** § 8.

**Syria** —*v. also* **A** § 47

APPLETON, T. G. Syrian Sunshine 6/ c 8° Macmillan 77

*BELL, Gertr. Lowthian The Desert & the Town: tales of Syrian travel; ill. 16/ *n.* 8° Heinemann 07
$5 *n.* Dutton, *N.Y.* A fascinatg. record of travel, mainly off beaten tracks, accomp. only by Arab attendants. Provides a more vivid portrait of the Arab than has hitherto existed. Fr. Jerus., thro' Damascus, Aleppo, and Antioch, to Alexandretta.

BURTON (Col. R. F.) + DRAKE (C. F. T.) Unexplored Syria, 2 v.; maps & ill. *o.p.* [*pb.* 32/] 8° Tinsley 72
Libanus, Tulúl el Safá, Anti-Libanus, etc.

CURTIS, G. W. Howadji in Syria 35 c. c 8° Hurst, *N.Y.* [52]

EWING, Wm. Arab and Druse at Home; map and 31 ill. 5/ c 8° Jack 07

GOODRICH-FREER, A. In a Syrian Saddle; ill. 7/6 *n.* 8° Methuen 05

INCHBOLD, A. C. Under the Syrian Sun, 2 vols.; 40 col. pl. and 8 ill. 24/ *n.* r 8° Hutchinson 06
A lady's acc. of her travels in Lebanon, Baalbek, Galilee, Judea. Pleasant text; col. pl. good.

JESSUP, H. H. Syrian Home Life $1·50 12° Dodd & Mead, *N.Y.* 74

PARRY, Oswald H. Six Months in a Syrian Monastery—*ut* **A** § 61

TERHUNE, A. P. Syria from the Saddle; ill. $1·50 c 8° Silver, *Boston* 97

THOMAS, Marg. Two Years in Palestine and Syria; 16 col. ill. 12/6 *n.* 8° Nimmo 99

VAN DER VELDE, C. W. M. Narrat. of a Journey thro' Syria & Palestine [tr.], 2 v.; maps & ill. [1851–52] 30/ 8° Blackwood 53

WORTABET, G. M. Syria and the Syrians, 2 vols. *o.p.* [*pb.* 21/] c 8° Madden 56

---

# V: Geography, etc., of Asia

## 31: ASIA: GENERALLY

**Early Travel and Accounts** —*v. also* **E** § 5

DE BENYOWSKY, M. A., C't [1741–86] Memoirs and Travels, tr. W. Nicholson [1790]; ill. 3/6 c 8° Unwin [93]
Ed. Cpt. S. P. OLIVER. [Adventure Ser.] Also 3/6 *n.* [Dryden Ho. Memrs.]. Paul '04. Siberia, Kamtchatka, Japan, Linkiu Islds., Formosa.

JORDANUS, Friar [14 cent.] Mirabilia Descripta: wonders of East, tr. Col. Hy. Yule [c. 1330] 8° Hakluyt Soc. 63
YULE's *Additional Notes and Corrections* to this bk. are cont. in his *Cathay*, pp. 193–6 [*ut* **E** § 34].

MANDEVILLE, [Sir] Jno. [14 cent.] Buke of: ed. G. F. Warner f° Roxburghe Club 89
The hitherto unpubd. Engl. versn. fr. Egerton MS. (Brit. Mus.), differg. widely fr. the versn. commonly known; w. the Fch. text, notes, and Introd.

„ Travels, fr. Cotton MS., w. 3 narrs. in ill. of it fr. Hakluyt 3/6 *n.* 8° Macmillan 00

„ Voiage and Travaile [edn. 1725], ed. J. O. Halliwell [-Phillipps]; facs. ill. 7/6 8° Reeves & Turner [39] 83

„ The same, ed. Jno. Ashton; facs. ill. 10/6 8° Pickering 88

„ The same, ed. w. 130 ill. by Arth. Layard 6/ c 8° Constable 95
A bk. of travels, ostensibly by Sir J. MANDEVILLE, composed ab. middle of 14 cent., purportg. to be an acc. of his travels in East, inclg. Turkey, Tartary, Persia, Egypt, India, and Holy Ld., but really a mere compiln. mainly fr. WILLIAM OF BOLDENSELE and Friar ODORIC OF BEAUVAIS.

Story of Marco Polo [extrs. interwoven w. narrative] $1·50 c 8° Century Co., *N.Y.* 99

Yule (Col. H.) + NICHOLSON—*Article* Mandeville, *in* Encyclo. Brit., 9th edn., vol. xv. [*ut* **K** § 1]

PINTO, Ferd. Mendez Voyages & Adventures, tr. by Hy. Cogan [Advent. Ser.] 3/6 c 8° Unwin [1663] 91

*POLO, Marco [13 cent.] Kingdoms and Marvels of the East, tr. and ed. Col. Sir H. Yule, w. notes, re-ed. H. Cordier; maps & ill., 2 vols. 63/ 8° Murray [71] 03
$16 *n.* Scribner, *N.Y.* YULE's edn. of this bk. is one of most learned and import. wks. ever pubd. in departmt. of histor. geogr. Memoir by Amy F. YULE [dau.].

„ Travels, tr. Marsden, ed. T. Wright [$1·50 *n.* Macm., *N.Y.*; Bohn's Lib.] 5/ c 8° Bell 83

„ Travels, tr. Marsden, ed. Wright [Thin-Paper Classics] 3/6 *n.* c 8° Newnes 04

„ „ [tr.] [35 c. *n.* Dutton, *N.Y.*; Everyman's Lib.] 1/ *n.* pott 8° Dent 08

„ Livre de, ed. Bar. A. E. Nordenskiöld [facs. of 14-cent. MS.] 55/ 4° *Stockholm* 82

di VARTHEMA, Lud. Travels in Egypt, Syria, Arabia, Persia, etc. [tr.]—*ut* **E** § 30 [1503–8]

VERTOMANNUS, Lewis Navigation and Voyages to Arabia, Egypt, Persia, Syria, Ethiopia and E. India in the year 1503 [tr.] *subscr.* 7/6 *n.* 8° Aungervyle Soc., *Edin.* [1576] 84
'Conteyning many notable and strange things, both Historicall and Naturall'. Tr. by Richarde EDEN, 1576. Only 300 privately reprinted.

YULE, Col. Hy. [tr. & ed.] Cathay and the Way Thither, 2 vols.—*ut* **E** § 34 [14–17 cent.]

**General Geography, Topography, and History**

HANNAH, Ian C. Eastern Asia : a history 7/6 *n.* 8° Unwin 11
A readable acc. of hist. of Asia east of Persia—China and Japan bg. made the chief centres of the story.

HOGARTH, D. G. The Nearer East [Regions of the World]—*ut* **E** § 29

JOHNSTON, A. Keith Short Geography of Asia 2/ c 8° Stanford 93

*KEANE, Prf. A. H. Asia ; 15 maps and 180 ill. [Compend. of Geogr.] ea. 15/ 8° Stanford [82] 06–9
Ea. $5·50 *n.* Lippincott, *Phila.* i : *Northern and Eastern Asia* ; ii : *Southern and Western Asia.* Largely rewritten from the former edition.

LITTLE, Arch. The Far East ; maps [Regions of the World] 7/6 *n.* ($2) 8° Clar. Press 05
A very useful bk. More descriptive and less scientific than the other vols. of the series.

RECLUS, Élisée Universal Geography : Asia [tr.], 4 vols.—*ut* **E** § 2

**Recent Travel, Description, etc.**—*v. also* **E** § 7, **I** § 147

ALLEN (T. G., jun.) + SACHTLEBEN (W. L.) Across Asia on a Bicycle ; ill. $1·50 c 8° Century Co., *N.Y.* 95
6/ Unwin. Record of an interestg. adventurous cycle-ride across Asia fr. Scutari to Pekin (15,000 miles).

ANGIER, A. G. Far East Revisited [$4·20 *n.* Scribner, *N.Y.*] 10/6 *n.* 8° Witherby 08
L'rs (by Edr. of *Lond. & China Express*) on polit., commerc., social, and general condns. of Malaya, China, Corea, Japan.

AUSTIN, Maj. H. H. Scamper thro' Far East ; maps & ill. [$5 Longman, *N.Y.*] 15/ *n.* 8° Arnold 09

BARZINI, Luigi Pekin to Paris ; [tr.] ; ill. [motor-tour ; $5 *n.* Kennerley, *N.Y.*] 16/ *n.* 8° Richards 07

BIGHAM, Clive A Ride through Western Asia—*ut* **E** § 30

BROWNE, G. W. New America and the Far East, 6 vols. $28 4° Marshall, *Boston* 07
With spec. arts. by specialists on Hawaii, Philippines, Jap., China, Cuba, Porto Rico. Maps, col. pl., and 1,200 ill.

BURNES, Sir Alex. Travels into Bokhara, etc., 3 vols. *o.p.* [*pb.* 18/] c 8° Murray [35] 39
Of value as an acc. of one of the earliest jys. beyond the North-West Frontier of India.

CANDLER, Edm. A Vagabond in Asia ; ill. 6/ c 8° Greening 00
A gossipy book of travels in Asia Minor, India, Siam, and Cochin China.

" The Mantle of the East 6/ c 8° Blackwood 10
First impressns., skilfully conveyed, of unfamiliar places, peoples, religions, customs, etc. Largely in India.

COLLIER, Price The West in the East : fr. an Amer. pt. of view 7/6 *n.* 8° Duckworth 11
A bright, fresh and clever bk. on the East—India, China, and Japan, incl. a defence of Brit. rule in India.

COLQUHOUN, A. R. Mastery of Pacific ; maps & 122 ill. [$4 *n.* Macm., *N.Y.*] 18/ *n.* r 8° Heinemann 02

COLQUHOUN, Ethel [=Mrs A. R.] Two on their Travels ; ill. (some col.) 10/ *n.* 8° Heinemann 02
$2·50 *n.* Barnes, *N.Y.* Philippines, Japan, Dutch East Indies, Siberia. A pleasant bk. of impressions.

ETHERTON, Lt. P. T. Across the Roof of the World ; maps & ill. 16/ *n.* 8° Constable 11
Acc. of remarkable pioneer jy. of 4,000 m. fr. India to Trans-Sib. ry.—on Pamirs, in Chin. Turk., Mong., Sib.

FORD, Jno. D. An American Cruiser in East ; maps & ill. $2·50 12° Barnes, *N.Y.* 00
Two and a hf. yrs.' cruising in a warship in Far East : Japan, China, Behring Sea, etc., w. acc. of battle of Manila (1898).

HART, Prf. A. B. The Obvious Orient [acc. of tour] (6/ *n.*) c 8° Appleton 11

HEDIN, Dr S. A. Through Asia [tr.], 2 vols. ; *and* Central Asia, 2 vols.—*ut* **E** § 33

" Overland to India [tr.], 2 vols.—*ut* **E** § 38

KRAUSSE, Alexis Far East : its hist. & its questions ; maps [$6 Dutton, *N.Y.*] 18/ 8° Richards 00

LANDOR, A. H. Savage Across Coveted Lands, 2 vols. ; maps and ill. 30/ *n.* 8° Macmillan 02
$7·50 *n.* Scribner, *N.Y.* From Flushing to Calcutta.

" The Gems of the East, 2 vols. ; map and ill. 30/ *n.* 8° Macmillan 04
'16,000 miles of research travel among wild and tame tribes of enchanting islands'.

LYNCH, Geo. The Path of Empire ; map and 90 ill.—*ut* **E** § 39
By the War-Correspondent of *The Daily Chronicle.* Of considerable value for the Far Eastern Question.

MCCARTHY, M. J. F. The Coming Power ; ill. 6/ c 8° Hodder 05
The history of the Far East from 1898 to 1905.

MILN, Louise J. When we were Strolling Players in East ; 28 ill. 16/ 8° Osgood 94
$4·50 Scribner, *N.Y.* A lively acc. of theatr. tour in China, Japan, India, Burma and Ceylon.

NORMAN, Sir Hy. Peoples and Politics of Far East ; 4 maps & 60 ill. 7/6 8° Unwin [95] 00
$4 Scribner, *N.Y.* Travels and studies in Brit., Fch., Span., and Port. colonies, Siberia, China, Japan, Corea, Siam, Malaya, 'the seed-bed of a multitude of new political issues'. Some adventurous jys. in untrodden ways in Corea, Siam, Japan, Malaya.

PENFIELD, F. C. Wanderings East of Suez ; ill. [10/6 *n.* Bell] $2 *n.* 8° Century Co., *N.Y.* 07

RONALDSHAY, Earl of Sport and Politics under an Eastern Sky ; ill. 21/ *n.* r 8° Blackwood 02
In 2 Pts. (1) acc. of jy. to Kashmir, valley of upper waters of Indus, and borders of Tibet after game, (2) acc. of route fr. Quetta thro' Baluchistan to Sistan, and thence *via* Persia. Feb. 1899–Mch. 1901. Six mos. spent at Simla as member of L'd CURZON's personal staff.

" On the Outskirts of Empire in Asia ; ill. 21/ *n.* 8° Blackwood 04
Of chief value on As. Min., Pers., Trans-Caspia, Turkestan. Also jy. along Trans-Sib. ry.

" A Wandering Student in the Far East, 2 vols.—*ut* **E** § 34

" An Eastern Miscellany 10/6 *n.* 8° Blackwood 11
A colln. of arts., speeches, and lects. on Asia, w. some purely political chs., e.g. *India and Impl. Reciprocity.*

S., D. W. European Settlements in Far East ; map and 38 ill. 7/6 c 8° Low 00
Informn. conc. Siberia, Japan, Corea, China, Hong-Kong, Macao, Indo-China, Siam, Philippines, etc.

STANLEY, H. M. My Early Travels and Advents. in Amer. and Asia, 2 v. 12/6 c 8° Low [95] 95
$3 Scribner, *N.Y.* Period fr. 1867 (Ind. wars as corresp.) to 1872 (search f. LIVINGSTONE). Egypt, As. Min., Centr. As., Pers.

STORY, Dougl. To-morrow in the East 6/ c 8° Chapman 07
Account of jy. thro' Egypt, Japan, China, Russia, Manchuria, etc.

TERRY, M. A. Six Months in the East; ill. [Far East] c 8° Dymock, *Sydney* 01

VAMBÉRY, A. Western Culture in Eastern Lands 12/ *n.* 8° Murray 06
$3·50 *n.* Dutton, *N.Y.* A comparison of methods adopted by England and Russia in the Middle East.

WEALE, B. L. Putnam [ = L. Lenox SIMPSON]—*v.* **E** § 37

WEEKS, E. L. From Black Sea thro' Persia & India; ill. by author $3·50 8° Harper, *N.Y.* 96
16/ Osgood. A lively narr. of jy. by author, an Amer. artist, in comp. w. Theod. CHILD (d. in Persia), fr. Trebizond thro' Tabriz to Ispahan, thence *via* Persian Gulf to Karachi, visitg. Lahore and the Punjab, Rajputana, Udaipur, etc. His ch. of *Notes on Indian Art* spec. fresh.

**Ethnology:** SPENCER (Herb.) Descriptive Sociology, No. 5: Asiatic Races, by Dr Duncan—*ut* **C** § 62

**Far Eastern Question** —*v. also* **E** §§ 34: China, 37: Japan, 38: Persia

## 32: ARABIA

**Bibliography** —*v.* **E** § 41

**Early Travel** —*v. also* **E** § 30

di VARTHEMA, Lud. Travels in Egypt, Syria, Arabia, etc. [tr.]—*ut* **E** § 30 [1503–8]

**Recent Travel and Descriptive**—*v. also* **E** §§ 30, 40

BENT, Theod. + Mrs Southern Arabia; maps and ill. 18/ 8° Smith & Elder 00
Travels, 1897–9: archæological details and description, partly of places formerly unknown.

BIGHAM, Clive —*in his* A Ride through Western Asia, *ut* **E** § 30

BURTON, Sir R. F. Pilgrimage to Al-Medinah and Meccah, 2 vols. 4/ *n.* f 8° Bell [55–6] 06
$1·60. Macm., *N.Y.* [York Lib.] Biogr. and crit. Introd. by S. Lane POOLE. 'Memorial Edn.' [2 v., *o.p.* [*pb.* 12/ *n.*] 8° Tylston] conts. ill. omitted here. Descrs. a jy. undertaken in disguise w. reckless courage to the holy cities of Arabia.

Burton, L'y [wife] Life of Sir Richard Burton, ill. 10/6 8° Duckworth [93] 99

Dodge, W. P. The Real Sir Richard Burton [6/ *n.* Unwin] $1·80 *n.* 8° Wessels, *N.Y.* 07

Hitchman, Fcs. Burton: his early, priv., and public life, 2 vols. *o.p.* [*pb.* 36/] 8° Low 87
Includes an abridgment of his travels and explorations.

Stisted, Georgiana M. True Life of Sir Richard Burton *o.p.* [*pb.* 5/ *n.*] c 8° Nichols 96

Wright, Thos. Life of Sir Richard Burton, 2 vols. 24/ *n.* 8° Everett 06

BUXTON, E. N. [ed.] On Either Side of the Red Sea—*ut* **E** § 30

COWPER, H. Swainson Through Turkish Arabia; 2 maps *o.p.* [*pb.* 18/] 8° W. H. Allen 94
Descrn. of jy. fr. Mediterr. to Bombay by Euphrates and Tigris valleys and Persian Gulf.

*DOUGHTY, C. M. Travels in Arabia Deserta, 2 vols.; ill. *o.p.* [*pb.* 63/] 8° Camb. Press 87–8
A detailed acc., in nearly 1,200 large 8° pp., of travels in Petræa in 1875, and in Arabia in 1876–8.

* ,, Wanderings in Arabia, 2 vols.; map 16/ *n.* r 8° Duckworth 08
Abgmt. of above, arrgd., w. Introd., by Edw. GARNETT. Personal narr. largely retained.

HAYNES, Alf. E. Man-Hunting in the Desert 21/ *n.* r 8° Cox 94
A circumstantial narr. of expedn. to Arabian Desert (1882–3) in search of late Prf. E. H. PALMER and his compans. Sir Chas. WARREN (who conducted) furnished much of materl., and Sir W. BESANT contribd. Memoir of PALMER.

HILL, Gray With the Bedouins; map and 68 ill. 15/ 8° Unwin 91
Acc. of 3 jys. by author and wife (1) to Mashita, Ammân, Es Salt, Jerash, El Husn, Galilee, Mt. Tabor; (2) Palmyra, Jaffa; (3) attempt to reach Petra, tho' they did not get bey. Kerak, where, taken by Bedouins, they were held for ransom.

HOGARTH, D. G. Penetration of Arabia; ill. [Story of Explorn.] 7/6 *n.* 8° Rivers [04] 05

,, —*in his* The Nearer East, *ut* **E** § 29

HUME-GRIFFITH, M. E. Behind the Veil in Persia and Turkish Arabia—*ut* **E** § 38

MAUGHAN, W. C. Alps of Arabia *o.p.* [*pb.* 6/] c 8° H. S. King [73] 76

PALGRAVE, W. G. Pers. Narr. of Jy. thro' Centr. & E. Arabia [1862–3] 3/6 8° Macmillan [65] 08

TAYLOR, Bayard Travels in Arabia [1872] $1·25 12° Scribner, *N.Y.* 81

ZWEMER, Rev. S. M. Arabia, the Cradle of Islam; 8 maps and 115 ill. $2 Revell, *N.Y.* 00
7/6 Oliphant, *Edin.* A good popular account of the geography, history, etc., w. some missionary informn.

,, + Amy E. Topsy-turvy Land; ill. [Arabia for children] 75 c. *n.* c 8° Revell, *N.Y.* [02]

**Life and People**

BLUNT, L'y Anne I. N. Bedouin Tribes of the Euphrates, 2 vols.; ill. [1877–8] 24/ 8° Murray 79

JESSUP, H. H. Women of the Arabs, ed. Robinson + Riley $2 c 8° Dodd & Mead, *N.Y.* 74

LANE, E. W. —*in his* Arabian Society in the Middle Ages, ed. S. Lane Poole, *ut* **F** § 60

POOLE, Stanley Lane Studies in a Mosque *o.p.* [*pb.* 12/] 8° W. H. Allen 83

SMITH, Prof. W. Robertson Kinship and Marriage in Early Arabia—*ut* **F** § 5

**Aden:** HUNTER (Cpt. F. M.) British Settlement of Aden in Arabia *o.p.* [*pb.* 7/6] p 8° Trübner 77

**Mecca; Medina:** BURTON (Sir R. F.) Narrative of Pilgrimage to Mecca and Medina, 2 vols.—*ut sup.*

HADJI KHAN + SPARROY (W.) With the Pilgrims to Mecca 12/6 *n.* ($3·50 *n.*) 8° Lane 05
Record of a somewhat hazardous jy. to Mecca in 1902, by HADJI KHAN, Spec. Corresp. of *Morning Post.*

KEANE, J. F. T. My Journey to Medinah [disguised as a Mohammedan] *o.p.* [*pb.* 10/6] 8° Tinsley 81

,, Six Months in Meccah *o.p.* [*pb.* 10/6] 8° Tinsley 81

**Midian :** BEKE (Dr C.) Discoveries of Sinai in Arabia, and of Midian *o.p.* [*pb.* 38/] r 8° Trübner 78
BURTON, Sir R. F. The Land of Midian Revisited, 2 vols. *o.p.* [*pb.* 32/] 8° Paul 79
,, Gold Mines of Midian & Ruined Cities of N.-W. Arabia *o.p.* [*pb.* 18/] 8 Paul [78] 78
**Neid :** BLUNT (L'y Anne I. N.) Pilgrimage to Nejd, Cradle of Arab Race, 2 v. ; ill. [1879] 24/ 8° Murray, 81
**Yemen :** HARRIS (W. B.) A Journey through Yemen ; ill. 16/ 8° Blackwood 93
Incls. descrn. of the 1892 revolt of the agric. tribes agst. their overtaxation by the Porte.

**Bagdad**—*v.* **E** § 40 **Sinai Peninsula**—*v.* **E** § 30

## 33 : CENTRAL ASIA

### Early Travel

BRETSCHNEIDER, Dr E. [ed. & tr.] Mediæval Researches fr. E. Asiatic Sources, 2 v. 21/ p 8° Paul 88
[Trübner's Oriental Ser.] Trs. of 4 Itineraries, i : of army of JENGHIZ KHAN [Cent. As. to Pers., in 1219]; ii : of envoy to JENGHIZ KHAN [thro' Cent. As.]; iii : chron. of jy. of CH'ANG CH'UN [Taoist monk ; China to Samarkand]; iv : of CH'ANG TE [Karakorum to Camp of Hulagu, in 1259]. Ea. foll. by bibl., ethnol. and geogr. notes. An epitome of all that is known of Cent. and W. Asiatic countries visited by Chin. travrs. dur. 13–17 cents. 2 maps.
POLO, Marco [13 cent.] Kingdoms and Marvels of the East [tr.]—*ut* **E** § 31
SCHUYLER, Eug. Mediaeval Travellers—*in his* Turkistan [tr.], *ut inf.*
SIDI ALI REÏS Travels and Adventures, tr. A. Vambéry ; w. notes [1553–6] 5/ c 8° Luzac 99

### Moghuls

MIRZA MUHAMMAD HAIDAR [d. 1551] The Tarikh-i-Rashidi, tr. E. D. Ross ; ed. N. Elias, w. comm. and notes ; map 30/ *n.* 8° Low 95
A hist. of the Moghuls of Cent. Asia—a highly important orig. documt. on Eastern hist. The bk. was used and several passages fr. it tr. by ERSKINE for his *Hist. of India under Moghuls*, vols. i–ii [all pubd. ; 1854]. Good Introd. and Index.

### Recent Travel and Description—*v. also* E § 39, *s.v.* Caucasus

BIGHAM, Clive —*in his* A Ride through Western Asia, *ut* **E** § 31
BONVALOT, G. Thro' Heart of Asia over Pamir to India [tr.], 2 v. ; 250 ill. 32/ r 8° Chapman 89
BOOKWALTER, J. W. Siberia and Central Asia—*ut* **E** § 39
BRUCE, Maj. C. D. In the Footsteps of Marco Polo ; ill. 21/ *n.* 8° Blackwood 07
CAMERON, Com. V. Lovett Our Future Highway to India, 2 vols. ; ill. *o.p.* [*pb.* 21/] c 8° Macmillan 80
COBBOLD, Ralph P. Innermost Asia ; maps and ill. 21/ 8° Heinemann 00
$5 Scribner, *N.Y.* Acc. of sporting journey thro' the Pamirs, and a short way into Russian territory.
FERRIER, J. P. Caravan Journeys in Persia, Afghanistan, Turkistan, and Beloochistan [tr.] *o.p.* [*pb.* 21/] 8° Murray 56
FRASER, Dav. The Marches of Hindustan ; maps and 150 ill. 21/ *n.* 8° Blackwood 07
Record of a jy. in Tibet, Trans-Himalayan India, Chinese and Russian Turkestan, and Persia.
GRODEKOFF, N. Ride from Samarcand to Herat, tr. C. Marvin *o.p.* [*pb.* 8/] 8° W. H. Allen [80] 85
*HEDIN, Dr Sven Through Asia, tr. J. T. Bealby, 2 vols. ; 6 maps & 300 ill. 36/ *n.* r 8° Methuen 98
$10 Harper, *N.Y.* 4 yrs.' travel, 1893–7 : 14,600 miles. Starting fr. Kashmir he travelled thro' Pamirs, desert of Takla-makan, Khotan River, Keriya River, Shah-yar, Tarim River, Lake Lop-nor, Tibet, Pekin, thro' Mongolia and Siberia, back to Stockholm. One of the great jys. of latter pt. of 19th cent. For *Geogr-wiss. Ergebnisse v.* **H** § 44.
,, Adventures in Tibet—*ut* **E** § 34, *s.v.* Tibet
* ,, Central Asia and Tibet towards Lassa [tr.], 2 vols. 42/ *n.* r 8° Hurst 03
$10·50 *n.* Scribner, *N.Y.* 5 maps, 8 col. pl., and 420 good illns. Further explorn. (1899–1902) over same area as above somewhat extended, inclg. attempt to reach Lhasa and descent by boat of Tarim river. For *Scientific Results v.* **H** § 44.
HOLDICH, Col. Sir T. H. The Indian Borderland ; map and 22 ill. 10/6 *n.* 8° Methuen 01
An interestg. descrn. of the Afghan and Baluch highlands and their economic conditions.
,, The Gates of India 10/ *n.* ($3·25 *n.*) 8° Macmillan 10
A history of exploration in Afghanistan and the neighbouring parts of Central Asia.
HUNTINGTON, Ellsworth The Pulse of Asia ; ill. 14/ *n.* 8° Constable 08
14/ *n.* Constable. Acc. of jy. in Centr. Asia, 'illustratg. the geogr. basis of history'. A good bk.
KNIGHT, E. F. Where Three Empires Meet ; map and ill. 3/6 ($1·25) c 8° Longman [93] 93
[Silver Lib.] A lively and graphic narr. of travel (1891–2) in Kashmir, Baltistan, Ladak, Gilgit, and adjacent countries, incl. visit to Lamaseries of W. Tibet, an explan. of our policy in Kashmir, etc., and of steps taken to safeguard our Indian interests. The acc. of Hunza-Nagar campaign of 1891 (in wh. author took pt. as volunteer) is spec. useful.
LANSDELL, Dr Hy. Russian Central Asia, 2 vols. ; ill. *o.p.* [*pb.* 42/] 8° Low 85
,, Thro' Central Asia ; ill. [extr. fr. above] 12/ 8° Low 87
,, Chinese Central Asia : ride to Little Tibet, 2 vols. ; maps & 100 ill. *o.p.* [*pb.* 36/] 8° Low 93
Treats of whole of China outside Gt. Wall fr. Manchuria to Pamirs, and descrs. Chinese Turkestan in its social, milit., and polit. condns. Apps. on Fauna and Bibliogr.
LE STRANGE, Guy —*in his* The hands of the Eastern Caliphate, *ut* **E** § 30 [to A.D. 1400]
MARVIN, Chas. Reconnoitring Central Asia ; pl. 7/6 8° Sonnenschein [84] 88
Advents. of Engl. and Russ. explorers, secret agents, and Spec. Correspts. in region betw. Caspian and India : 1863–84.
MOORCROFT (W.) + TREBECK (G.) Travels, ed. H. H. Wilson, 2 vols. [1819–25] *o.p.* [*pb.* 30/] 8° Murray 41
Himalayan Provinces, Ladakh and Kashmir, Peshawar, Cabul, Bokhara, etc.
PEROWNE, J. T. W. Russian Hosts & Engl. Guests in Central Asia ; ill. 7/6 8° Scientific Press 98
Account of the doings of a party of tourists in Central Asia in 1897.

PHIBBS, Isab. M. Visit to Russians in Central Asia; map and ill. 6/ *n.* c 8° Paul 99
$2·25 New Amsterd. Bk. Co., *N.Y.* Journey of an English party from Tiflis to Samarkand.

PREJEVALSKY, N. M. From Kulja across the Tian Shan to Lob Nor [tr.]—*ut* **E** § 39
Contains noti es of the Central Asian Lakes by Sir D. FORSYTH.

RONALDSHAY, Earl of On the Outskirts of Empire—*ut* **E** § 31

SHOEMAKER, M. M. The Heart of the Orient; 52 ill. $2·50 (10/6 *n.*) 8° Putnam 04
'Saunterings' thro' Georgia, Armenia, Persia, Turkomania, and Turkestan, to the Vale of Paradise, incl. descrns. of life fr. the high life of the Persian Court to low life in the tents of the Kirghiz.

STEIN, M. Aurel Explorations in Central Asia: 1906–8 [pp. 66] 8° R. G. S. Jl. (Stanford) 09

TAYLOR, Bayard Central Asia $1·25 12° Scribner, *N.Y.* [ ] 81

VÁMBÉRY, Arminius Travels in Central Asia [Caspian to Samarkand; 1863] *o.p.* [*pb.* 21/] 8° Murray 64

" Sketches in Central Asia [additl. chs. to above] *o.p.* [*pb.* 16/] 8° W. H. Allen 68

YOUNGHUSBAND, Cpt. F. E. The Heart of a Continent; maps, ports. and ill. 21/ m 8° Murray [96] 96
A very interestg. recd. of travel in Manchuria, Desert of Gobi, Turkestan, Himalayas, Hindu Kush, Pamirs, etc.: 1884–94.

**Biography:** BOULGER (D. C.) Central Asian Portraits *o.p.* [*pb.* 7/6] c 8° W. H. Allen 80
DOST MOHAMMED, SHERE ALI, Gen. KAUFMANN, YAKOOB BEG, ABDERRAHMAN, Gen. TCHERNAIEFF, SHUJA-UD-DOWLAH, YAKOOB KHAN, etc.

**England and Russia in Central Asia; Boundary Question** (1884–7)

BAKER, Col. Val. Clouds in East: travels on Perso-Turkoman frontier *o.p.* [*pb.* 18/] 8° Chatto 76

BOULGER, D. C. England & Russia in Central Asia, 2 vols.; maps *o.p.* [*pb.* 36/] 8° W. H. Allen 79

" Central Asian Questions: 3 maps 18/ 8° Unwin 85
24 mag. arts.: 1878–1884 on Afghanistan, China, and Central Asia.

CHIROL, V. —*in his* The Middle Eastern Question, *ut* **D** § 138

COLQUHOUN, A. R. Russia against India: struggle for Asia; maps 5/ ($1·50) c 8° Harper 00

*CURZON, G. N. [L'd] Russia in Central Asia in 1889; maps and ill. 21/ 8° Longman [89] 89
Acc. of jy. made in 1888 along the then newly completed Trans-Caspian Ry.; w. polit. essays; also bibliography.

EDWARDS, H. Sutherland Russian Projects agst. India: 1694–1877 *o.p.* [*pb.* 21/] 8° Remington 85

HANNA, Col. H. B. Indian Problems, 3 Series ea. 2/6 c 8° Constable 95–6
i: *Can Russia Invade India?*; ii: *India's Scient. Frontier*; iii: *Backwards or Forwards?*

v. HELLWALD, Bar. Fr. The Russians in Central Asia [tr.] *o.p.* [*pb.* 12/] 8° Paul 74

Indian Officer (An) ' Russia's March towards India, 2 vols.; map [unimportant]. *op.* [*pb.* 16/] 8° Low 94

KRAUSSE, Alexis Russia in Asia: 1558–1899—*ut* **E** § 39

LANSDELL, Dr H. —*in his* Through Central Asia, *ut sup.*

MARVIN, Chas. The Russian Advance towards India *o.p.* [*pb.* 16/] 8° Low 81

" Merv, the Queen of the World; ill. *o.p.* [*pb.* 18/] 8° W. H. Allen 81

" The Russians at Merv and Herat *o.p.* [*pb.* 24/] 8° W. H Allen 83

" The Russians at the Gates of Herat *o.p.* [*pb.* 2/6] c 8° Warne 85

POPOWSKI, Josef The Rival Powers in Central Asia [tr. (fr. Germ.)]; map 12/6 *n.* 8° Constable 93
Aims at showing th. Russia aspires to possesn. of India; examines polit. and strateg. rels. of Engl. and Russia, conclg. th. 'Engl. can neither arrest the advance of Russ. in Cent. Asia, nor go to war singlehanded—without allies—with Russia with any prospect of success'. An able book.

STEAD, W. T. The Truth about Russia 10/6 8° Cassell 89
Puts a favourable construction on Russia's movements. Partly repr. fr. *Pall Mall Gazette*.

STUMM, Hugo Russia in Central Asia [tr.]; maps [to 1873] 15/ 8° Harrison 85

TERENTYEF, M. A. Russia and England in Central Asia [tr.], 2 vols. *o.p.* 76

THORBURN, S. S. Asiatic Neighbours; 2 col. maps 10/6 *n.* 8° Blackwood 94
On relns. of India and Russia, future of Afghan., and means of maintaing. Ind. Emp. agst. dangers of internal troubles and for. invasn.

VALIKHANOF, Cpt. The Russians in Central Asia [tr.] *o.p.* [*pb.* 21/] 8° Stanford 65

VÁMBÉRY, Arminius Central Asia & Anglo-Russian Frontier [tr.] *o.p.* [*pb.* 7/4] p 8° Smith & Elder 74

" The Coming Struggle for India 5/ 8° Cassell 85

YATE, Lt. A. C. England and Russia face to face in Asia; maps & ill. 21/ 8° Blackwood 87

**Afghanistan; Cabul** —*v. also* **E** § 38

*Ethnology*

BELLEW, Surg.-Gen. H. W. The Races of Afghanistan *o.p.* [*pb.* 7/6] 8° W. H. Allen 80

" Inquiry into the Ethnography of Afghanistan 7/6 8° Oriental Inst., *Woking* 91

*History* —*v. also inf., s.n.* ELPHINSTONE

BELLEW, Surg.-Gen. H. W. Afghanistan and the Afghans *o.p.* [*pb.* 6/] c 8° Low 79

" Political Mission to Afghanistan [1857; under Lumsden] *o.p.* [*pb.* 16/] 8° Smith & Elder 62

FERRIER, J. P. History of Afghans, tr. Cpt. W. Jesse *o.p.* [*pb.* 21/] 8° Murray 58

MACCRINDLE, J. W. Invasion of India by Alexander the Great—*ut* **F** § 62

MALLESON, Col. G. B. History of Afghanistan; map [to 1878] *o.p.* [*pb.* 18/] 8° W. H Allen [78] 82

MUHAMMAD IBN 'ABD AL-JABBĀR Kitab-i-Yamini, tr. Reynolds
[c. 977–1010] *o.p.* [*pb.* 12/] 8° Orient. Tr. Fd. 58

NEAMET ULLAH History of the Afghans, tr. [fr. Pers.] B. Dorr, 2 Pts. 4° Oriental Tr. Fd. 29–36

NOYCE, Fk. England, India, and Afghanistan *o.p.* [*pb.* 3/ *n.*] c 8° Camb. Press 02
[Le Bas Prize Essay, 1902.] An accurate acc. of the history of our relations with Afghanistan.

THORBURN, S. S. Bannú, our Afghan Frontier *o.p.* [*pb.* 18/] 8° Trübner 76

*Abdur Rahman*, Amir [c. 1853–96]: Life of. Ed. Mir Munshi Mahomed Khar, 2 v.; maps & ill.
32/ 8° Murray 00

Gray, Jno. A. At the Court of the Amir; ill. [1889–93] 16/ 8° Macmillan [95] 01
Sketches by the Amir's late surgeon—also portrait-painter in ordinary and offic. taster of spirits produced in the capital.

Wheeler, Steph. Ameer Abdur Rahman [Publ. Men of To-day; $1·25 Warne, *N.Y.*] 3/6 c 8° Bliss 95

*Dost Mohammed Khan, Amir*: Life of. By Mohan Lal, 2 vols. *o.p.* [*pb.* 30/] 8° Longman 46

*Wars*: 1838–42; 1878–80 —*v.* **F** § 31

*Recent Travel and Description; etc.*

BELLEW, Surg.-Gen. H. W. From the Indus to the Tigris *o.p.* [*pb.* 14/] 8° Trübner [72] 74

BOUILLANE DE LACOSTE, Maj. Around Afghanistan [tr.]; 5 maps and 113 ill. 10/6 *n.* r 8° Pitman 09

BURNES, Sir A. Cabool: jy.to and resid. in [1836–8; standard] *o.p.* [*pb.* 18/] 8° Murray 42

ELPHINSTONE, Mountstuart Account of Kingdom of Caubul, 2 vols. *o.p.* [*pb.* 28/] 8° Bentley [15] 42

FISHER, F. H. Afghanistan and the Central Asian Question 3/6 p 8° J. Clarke 78

HAMILTON, Angus Afghanistan; map and ill. 25/ *n.* 8° Heinemann 06
$5 *n.* Scribner, *N.Y.* Mainly a gazetteer.

LANDOR, A. H. Savage —*in his* Across Coveted Lands, *ut* **E** § 31

MACGEORGE, F. St John —*in his* Lights and Shades of Indian Hill Life, *ut* **E** § 35

MACGREGOR, Maj.-Gen. Sir C. M. Jy. thro' Khorassan & N.-W. Frontier, 2 vols.
[1875] *o.p.* [*pb.* 30/] 8° W. H. Allen 79

MARSH, H. C. A Ride thro' Islam—*ut* **E** § 38 [Pers. and Afghan. to India]

MARTIN, F. A. Under the Absolute Amir; ill. 10/6 *n.* ($2·25) 8° Harper 07

OLIVER, E. E. Across the Border: Pathan [Afghan] & Biloch; map 14/ 8° Chapman 90

PENNELL, T. L. Among Wild Tribes of Afghan Frontier 16/ *n.* 8° Seeley 09
A very interesting account of 15 yrs.' work as a medical missionary.

RAVERTY, Maj. H. G. Notes on Afghanistan and Baluchistan, Pts. i *sqq.*
[India Off. Pub.] 10/ f° Trübner 80–92

RONALDSHAY, Earl of —*in his* Sport and Politics under an Eastern Sky, *ut* **E** § 31

WILLCOCKS, Sir J. From Kabul to Kumassi; ill. [soldierg. & sport] 21/ *n.* r 8° Murray 04

YATE, Maj. [Lt.-Col.] C. E. Northern Afghanistan: l'rs. fr. Afgh. Boundary Commissn. 18/ 8° Blackwood 88
Travels dur. delimitn. of the 'scientific frontier'. Of consid. value for the geography and ethnology of Bactria.

,, Khurasan and Sistan; ill. 21/ 8° Blackwood 01
Continuation of the above, describing Afghan Turkestan from Herat to Cabul.

*Gazetteer*: Imperial Gazetteer of Afghanistan and Nepal 8° 08

*Bannu* —*v.* **E** § 35

*Herat* —*v. also* Marvin, *sup.*

MALLESON, Col. G. B. Herat: granary and garden of Cent. Asia *o.p.* [*pb.* 8/] 8° W. H. Allen 80

*Khyber Pass*: TREVELYAN (R. L.) A Year in Peshawar and a Lady's Ride into the Khyber Pass
*o.p.* [*pb.* 9/] 8° Chapman 80

WARBURTON, Sir R. Eighteen Years in the Khyber; ill. [1879–98] 16/ 8° Murray 00

**Altai Mountains** —*v.* **E** § 39, *s.v.* Siberia and Mongolia

**Aral, Lake**: WOOD, (Maj. Herb.) The Shores of Lake Aral; maps *o.p.* [*pb.* 14/] 8° Smith & Elder 76

**Baluchistan**

DE WINDT, Harry Ride to India across Persia and Baluchistan—*ut* **E** § 38

FLOYER, E. A. Unexplored Baluchistan: journey thro' Western Baluchistan, etc.; ill. 28/ 8° Griffith 82

HUGHES, A. W. The Country Baloochistan: geogr. ethnogr., hist.; ill. 12/ c 8° Bell 77

Imperial Gazetteer of Baluchistan 8° 08

MACGREGOR, Maj.-Gen. Sir C. M. Wanderings in Baloochistan; maps and ill. 18/ 8° W. H. Allen 82

MASSON, C. Journeys in Baluchistan: w. mem. of E. Bal., Afghan., Punj., etc.,
4 vols.; maps and pl. *o.p.* [*w.* 15/] 8° Bentley 42–3

OLIVER, E. E. Across the Border—*ut sup.*, *s.v.* Afghanistan

RONALDSHAY, Earl of —*in his* Sport and Politics under an Eastern Sky, *ut* **E** § 31

TATE, G. P. The Frontiers of Baluchistan ; maps and 36 pl. 12/6 *n.* 8° Witherby 09
$5 *n.* Scribner, *N.Y.* Travels on the borders of India, Persia, and Afghanistan. Introd. by Col. Sir A. H. McMAHON.

*Ethnology :* DAMES (M. L.) The Baloch Race [R. A. S. Monogrs.] 5/ 8° Roy. Asiatic Soc. (Luzac)

**Bokhara :** *Recent Travel* —*v. also inf., s.v.* Turkestan (SCHUYLER)

BURNES, Sir Alex. Travels in Bokhara, etc., 3 vols.—*ut* **E** § 31

LE MESSURIER, Col. A. From London to Bokhara, and Ride thro' Persia *o.p.* [*pb.* 15/] 8° Bentley 89

*History :* VAMBÉRY (Arminius) History of Bokhara [fr. earliest per.] *o.p.* [*pb.* 18/] 8° H. S. King 73

**Caspian Region :** MARVIN (C.) Region of Eternal Fire ; ill. 6/ c 8° W. H. Allen [84] 91

**Kafiristan ; Dardistan ; Hindu Kush**

BIDDULPH, Maj. J. B. Tribes of the Hindoo Koosh *o.p.* [*pb.* 15/] 8° Trübner 80

LEITNER, Dr G. W. Languages and Races of Dardistan ; maps and pl.—*ut* **K** § 166*

,, The Hunza and Nagyr Handbook, Pt. i—*ut* **K** § 166* [largely ethnological]

,, Kafiristan 8° *Lahore* 81

ROBERTSON, Sir G. S. The Kafirs of the Hindu-Kush ; ill. *o.p.* [*pb.* 31/6] r 8° Lawrence & Bullen 96
An account of one of the most remarkable primitive communities extant in the world. The only previous European who has attempted to enter Kafiristan was Gen. (then Col.) LOCKHART, when in command of a mission to examine the Hindu Kush passes (1885–6).

**Khokand :** SINGH (S. H.) History of Kokand, ed. C. E. Bates 8° *Lahore* 78

**Oxus ; Indus**

BELL, Maj. E. The Oxus and the Indus ; map *o.p.* [*pb.* 3/] 8° Trübner [69] 74

MACGAHAN, J. A. Campaigning on Oxus, and Fall of Khiva ; ill. [1873] 7/6 c 8° Low [74] 76

WOOD, Cpt. Jno. Jy. to Source of Oxus by Indus, Kabul, etc. [1837] *o.p.* [*pb.* 12/] 8° Murray [41] 72
Ed. Col. H. YULE ; w. *Essay on the Geography of the Valley of the Oxus*, by YULE.

**Pamirs**

CUMBERLAND, Maj. C. S. —*in his* Sport on Pamirs and Turkistan Steppes, *ut* **I** § 147

CURZON, G. N. [L'd] The Pamirs and Source of the Oxus ; map 6/ *n.* r 8° R.G.S. (Stanford) 96
Revised repr. fr. *Jl.* of R.G.S., shewing 'what the Pamirs really are, as viewed fr. the double standpt. of hist. mention and pers. expce.' A thoro' treatmt. of subj., w. interestg. acc. of author's jy.

DUNMORE, Earl of The Pamirs, 2 vols. ; maps and ill. *o.p.* [*pb.* 24/] c 8° Murray [93] 93
On horsebk. and on ft. in 1892 thro' Kashmir, W. Tibet, Chin. Tartary, and Russn. Centr. Asia. Import. bk. on pract. side of Centr. Asian travel.

OLUFSEN, Lt. O. Through the Unknown Pamirs ; maps and ill. 15/ *n.* 8° Heinemann 04
Acc. of the 2nd Danish Pamir Expedn. 1898–9. The 1st was made in 1896–7, when he was said to have visited country till then untraversed by white men, and had discov. a race of cave-dwlg. dwarfs, owning dwarf breeds of domestic animals.

STEIN, M. Aurel Pamirs & Kwen Lun : photographed & annotated 20/ *n.* 4° R.G.S. (Stanford)

**Turkestan** —*v. also* **E** § 35 ; *for* Eastern (Chinese) Turkestan *v.* **E** § 34

*Early Travel :* DE CLAVIJO (Ruy Gonzalez) Embassy to Court of Timour, tr. & ed. [Sir] C. R. Markham [to Tamerlane ; 1403–6] 8° Hakluyt Soc. 59

*History :* SKRINE (F. H.) + Ross (Prf. E. D.) Heart of Asia ; ill. (after Verestchagin) 10/6 *n.* 8° Methuen 99
$3·50 Lippincott, *Phila.* Pt. i : Historical ; ii : Polit. condns. in Pamirs, and acc. of Russian territory.

*Biography :* Yakoob Beg [c. 1820–77] Yakoob Beg. By D. C. Boulger *o.p.* [*pb.* 16/] 8° W. H. Allen 78

*Recent Travel and Description*

ABBOTT, Col. Jas. Journey fr. Heraut to Khiva, Moscow, etc., 2 v. *o.p.* [*pb.* 24/] 8° W. H. Allen [43] 84
Narrative of journey during the Russian invasion of Khiva of 1840.

BURNABY, Col. F. Ride to Khiva ; 8 ill. [1875–6] 2/6 c 8° Cassell [76] 95

Wright, Thos. Life of Colonel Fred. Burnaby ; 60 pl. 12/ *n.* 8° Everett 08

CROSBY, O. T. Tibet and Turkestan—*ut* **E** § 34

CUMBERLAND, Maj. C. S.—*in his* Sport on the Pamirs & Turkistan Steppes, *ut* **I** § 147 [of some geogr. value]

CURTIS, W. E. Turkestan, the Heart of Asia ; map and ill. 10/6 *n.* 8° Hodder 11

JEFFERSON, R. L. A New Ride to Khiva ; ill. 6/ c 8° Methuen 99
A journey accomplished in great part on a cycle ; little new information.

KER, D. On the Road to Khiva ; ill. *o.p.* [*pb.* 12/] 8° H. S. King 74

MACGAHAN, J. A. Campaigning on the Oxus, and Fall of Khiva—*ut sup., s.v.* Oxus

MEAKIN, Annette M. B. In Russian Turkestan : a garden of Asia ; ill. 7/6 *n.* c 8° G. Allen 03
Journey to Tashkend, Samarkand, Kokand, etc. : much good matter on life of natives.

SCHUYLER, Eug. Journey in Turkistan, Khokand, Bukhara, etc., 2 v. [1873] *o.p.* [*pb.* 42/] 8° Low [76] 77

SHAW, R. Visit to High Tartary, Yarkand, & Kashgar ; ill. *o.p.* [*pb.* 16/] 8° Murray 71

VÁMBÉRY, Arminius —*in his* Travels in Central Asia, *ut sup.*

*Merv* —*v. also* MARVIN, *sup.*

O'DONOVAN, Edm. Merv Oasis : travels & adventures east of Caspian, 2 v. 36/ 8° Smith & Elder 82

,, Merv : a story of adventure [epitome of above] 6/ c 8° Smith & Elder [83] 85

## 34 : CHINA ; TIBET ; COREA

**Bibliography :** CORDIER (Prf. H.) Bibliotheca Sinica, 2 vols. and Suppts.—*ut* **K** § 152
**Atlas ; Map :** Atlas of Chinese Empire [22 maps] 10/6 *n.* 4° China Inland Missn. (Stanford) 08
BRETSCHNEIDER, Dr E. Map of China & Surrounding Regions Iliin, *St Petersburg* (Stanford) [96]
**Gazetteer :** PLAYFAIR (G. M.) Cities and Towns of China [a geogr. dict.] *o.p.* [*pb.* 25/] 8° Trübner 79

**Early Voyages and Description**

BRETSCHNEIDER, Dr E. Essays on intercourse of Chinese w. Western Countries in Mid. Ages—*ut* **D** § 117*
MARKHAM, [Sir] C. R. [ed.] Narratives of G. Bogle's Mission to Thibet [1774] ; *and* T. Manning's Journey to Lhasa [1810] [India Office pub.] *o.p.* [*pb.* 21/] 8° Trübner [76] 79
de MENDOZA, Juan Gonzalez Kingdom of China [tr.], ed. Sir G. T. Staunton, 2 v. 8° Hakluyt Soc. 53–4
PINTO, Ferd. Mendez Voyages and Adventures [travels 1537–58]—*ut* **E** § 31
POLO, Marco [13 cent.] Kingdoms and Marvels of the East [tr.]—*ut* **E** § 31
PURCHAS, Sam. [ed.] —*in his* Pilgrimes, *ut* **E** § 5
DE VEER, Gerrit Descrn. of Three Voyages by N.-East tow. Cathay & China [tr.]—*ut* **E** § 68 [1594–6]
YULE, Col. Sir Hy. [tr. & ed.] Cathay, and the Way Thither, 2 vols. 8° Hakluyt Soc. [66]
Ed. Prf. H. CORDIER. A valuable colln. of minor notices of China during the 14th to 17th centuries.

**General Geography :** LITTLE (Arch.) —*in his* The Far East, *ut* **E** § 31
RICHARD, L. Compreh. Geogr. of Chin. Emp. & Depends. [tr.] ; maps 17/6 *n.* r 8° *Shanghai* (Paul) 08

**Recent Travel and Description**

ANDERSON, Dr Jno. Mandalay to Momien ; ill. *o.p.* [*pb.* 21/] 8° Macmillan 76
Account of the 2 expedns. to Western China in 1868 and 1875 under Col. E. B. SLADEN and Col. H. BROWNE.
„ Report on Expedn. to West Yunan via Bhamo l 8° *Calcutta* 71
ARMSTRONG, Alex. In a Mule Litter to Tomb of Confucius 2/6 c 8° Nisbet 95
BARZINI, L. Pekin to Paris [tr.]—*ut* **E** § 31
BIGHAM, Clive A Year in China ; map and ill. 8/6 *n.* 8° Macmillan 01
Narrative of 10,000 miles travel in China, 1899–1900 ; w. acc. of siege of Pekin legations.
BIRCH, Jno. G. Travels in North and Central China ; ill. 10/6 *n.* 8° Hurst 02
Manchuria, Pekin, and the Yang-tse, by a railway projector ; a good descriptive book.
BISHOP, Mrs [*née* Isab. L. BIRD] Chinese Pictures 3/6 c 8° Cassell 01
Pictures of China, reproduced from photos taken by Mrs BISHOP in her travels ; with letterpress.
BLAKESLEE, Geo. H. [ed.] China and the Far East $2 *n.* 8° Crowell, *N.Y.* 10
COLQUHOUN, A. R. Across Chrysê, 2 vols. ; ill. [Canton to Mandalay] *o.p.* [*pb.* 42/] 8° Low 83
„ The 'Overland' to China ; map and ill. 16/ ($3) 8° Harper 00
To China fr. Europe overland : Pekin, Tientsin, Shanghai, and Yang-tse valley. Good on polit. matters.
CUMMING, [Miss] C. F. Gordon Wanderings in China ; ill. 6/ 8° Blackwood [86] 00
DE WINDT, Harry From Pekin to Calais by Land ; ill. 7/6 8° Chapman [89] 92
DUNMORE, Earl of —*in his* The Pamirs, *ut* **E** § 33
GEIL, W. E. A Yankee on the Yangtze ; ill. 8° 04
6/ Hodder. Narr. of a jy. fr. Shanghai thro' the Central Kingdom to Burma, describg. the same jy. and almost the identical route descr. in MORRISON'S *An Australian in China* [*ut inf.*].
„ The Great Wall of China ; ill. [21/ *n.* Murray] $5 8° Sturgis, *N.Y.* 09
GILL, Cpt. W. J. River of Golden Sand, 2 vols. ; ill. 7/6 p 8° Murray [80] 83
Account of journey thro' China and Eastern Tibet to Burmah, in 1876–7.
HART, Virgil C. Western China [journey to Mt Omei] $2 8° Houghton, *Boston* 88
HENRY, B. C. Ling Nam 12/6 c 8° *Shanghai* 86
Interior views of Southern China, with exploration of the Island of Hainan.
HOSIE, A. Three Years in Western China 6/ c 8° Philip [90] 97
HUC, Abbé E. R. + GABET Travels in Tartary, Thibet, and China [tr.]—*ut* **A** § 105
„ Christianity in China, Tartary, and Thibet [tr.]—*ut* **A** § 105
JACK, Dr R. Logan The Back Blocks of China ; maps and ill. 10/6 *n.* 8° Arnold 04
$4 Longman, *N.Y.* Narr. of experces. among Chinese, Sifans, Lolos, Tibetans, Shans, and Kachins betw. Shanghai and the Irrawaddi.
JAGAT-JIT SINGH, H. H. The Raja-i-Rajgan 12/6 *n.* 8° Hutchinson 05
An account of his travels and observations in China, Japan, and Java, in 1903.
JOHNSTON, R. F. Lion and Dragon in Northern China ; ill. 15/ *n.* 8° Murray
„ From Peking to Mandalay ; ill. 15/ *n.* 8° Murray 08
$5 *n.* Dutton, *N.Y.* Acc. of a jy. fr. N. China to Burma thro' Tibetan Ssuch'uan and Yunnan.
KEMP, Miss E. G. The Face of China ; 64 ill. by author (some col.) 20/ *n.* s 4° Chatto 09
$6 *n.* Duffield, *N.Y.* An interestg. acc. of travels in East, North, Central, and Western China.
LANSDELL, Dr Hy. Chinese Central Asia : a ride to Little Tibet—*ut* **E** § 33

de LESDAIN, Comte — From Pekin to Sikkim; ill. 12/ *n.* 8° Murray 08
$4 *n.* Dutton *NY.* Travels by the author and his wife thro' the Ordos, Gobi Desert, and Tibet, in 1904–5.

LIDDELL, T. H. — China, its Marvel and Mystery; 40 col. ill. by author 21/ *n.* 4° G. Allen 09

LOCH, L'd — Pers. Narr. of L'd Elgin's Embassy to China in 1860 2/6 *n.* c 8° Murray [69] 00

MACGOWAN, Rev. J. — Pictures of Southern China; ill. 10/6 8° R.T.S. 98
Mostly descriptions of the coast ports. Of small value.

MACMAHON, Maj.-Gen. A. R. Far Cathay and Farther India; ill. 12/ 8° Hurst 93
Deals princ. w. hist. (past and pres.) of Brit. relns. w. Burmah, later chs. w. var. peoples that surround that country on every side. Has little to say ab. China, exc. in ref. to her relns. w. Burma. Interesting but discursive. Author was Brit. Political Agent at Ct. of Ava.

MARGARY, A. R. — Journey fr. Shanghae to Bhamo & Back [1874–5] *o.p.* [*pb.* 10/6] p 8° Macmillan 76

MARTIN, W. A. P. — A Cycle of Cathay: China South and North 7/6 c 8° Oliphant, *Edin.* 96

MORRISON, Dr G. E. [Austral.] An Australian in China; map and ill. 6/ c 8° H. Cox [95] 02
Shanghai to Hankow and on to Ichang, thence by boat to Chungking, and on by land, dressed as a Chinese teacher, thro' W. China to Bhamo, whence to Mandalay, Rangoon, and by steamer to Calcutta. An uneventful journey, tho' without an interpreter, and cheerfully and humorously described.

MOULE, Archd. A. E. — New China and Old: notes on country and people; ill. 7/6 8° Seeley [91] 95

,, — Half a Century in China: recollns. & observns.; ill. 7/6 *n.* 8° Hodder 11

NICHOLS, F. H. — Through Hidden Shensi $3·50 *n.* 8° Scribner, *N.Y.* 02
Acc. of jy. 1901 fr. Pekin to Sian, thro' heart of the Boxers' country and acr. many roads rarely travelled by white men.

OLIPHANT, Laur. — Narr. of L'd Elgin's Missn. to China and Jap., 2 v.; pl. [1857–8] *o.p.* [*pb.* 42/] 8° Blackwood [59] 61

d'ORLÉANS, Henry, Pr'ce — From Tonkin to India [tr.]; 100 ill. [1895] 21/ r 8° Methuen 97
$5 *n.* Dodd & Mead, *N.Y.* Valuable acc. of 2,100 miles of travel in S. China, discov. of sources of Irrawaddy, etc.

PERCIVAL, W. S. — The Land of the Dragon 12/ 8° Hurst 89

PIASSETSKY, P. — —*in his* Russian Travellers in Mongolia and China [tr.], 2 vols.—*ut* **E** § 39

PRATT, A. E. — To the Snows of Tibet through China—*ut inf.*, *s.v.* Tibet

PRICE, Julius M. — From the Arctic Ocean to the Yellow Sea—*ut* **E** § 39

RALPH, Julian — Alone in China; 62 ill. 6/ c 8° Osgood 96

READY, Oliver — Life and Sport in China; map and 13 ill. 10/6 *n.* 8° Chapman 03

REID, Arnot — From Peking to Petersburg; maps 7/6 c 8° Arnold 99
Acc. of an ordinary 50 days' journey thro' Mongolia and the Desert of Gobi, etc., in 1898.

v. RICHTHOFEN, Bar. F. — Letters: 1870–72 [tr.] 18/ *n.* f° Paul [ ] 03

ROCKHILL, W. W. — —*in his* The Land of the Lamas, *ut inf.*, *s.v.* Tibet [China, Mongolia, Tibet]

RONALDSHAY, Earl of — A Wandering Student in the Far East, 2 v.; pl. 21/ *n.* 8° Blackwood 08
Vol. i mainly devoted to descrn. of jy. acr. interior of China; ii to polit. probls. of China and Japan.

STRAIGHT, J. O. P. — Houseboat Days in China; ill. 15/ *n.* m 8°

THOMSON, Jno. — Through China with a Camera; 114 ill. 7/6 8° Harper [98] 99
$5 Dodd & Mead, *N.Y.* Journeys in Hongkong, Canton, Macao, Shanghai, Formosa, Upper Yang-tse.

TREVES, Sir Fredk. — —*in his* The Other Side of the Lantern, *ut* **E** § 7

Twentieth-Century Impressions of Hong-Kong, Shanghai, etc. 4° Lloyd's Greater Brit. Pb. Co. 09

VAY DE VAYA & LUSKOD, C't — Empires and Emperors of Russia, China, Korea, and Japan: notes and recollections; ill. 15/ *n.* 8° Murray 06

WILLIAMS, Prf. S. W. — The Middle Kingdom, 2 vols.; map and ill. $9 8° Scribner, *N.Y.* [48] 99
The standard wk. on geogr., govt., liter., soc. life, arts, and hist. of the Chinese Empire and its inhabitants. 1,650 pp.

WILLIAMSON, A. — Jys. in N. China, Manchuria, and E. Mongolia, 2 v. *o.p.* [*pb.* 21/] c 8° Smith & Elder 70

WILSON, Gen. J. H. — China: travels and investigations $1·75 12° Appleton, *New York* 87

WINGFIELD, Hon. L. S. — Wanderings of Globe Trotter in Far East, 2 v. *o.p.* [*pb.* 21/] s 8° Bentley 89

### China Seas

ANDERSON, Cpt. Lindsay — Among Typhoons and Pirate Craft; ill. *o.p.* [*pb.* 5/] c 8° Chapman 92
$1·75 Scribner, *N.Y.* Conveys a very lively picture of a trader's life in the Chinese Seas.

BLAKENEY, Cpt. W. — On Coasts of Cathay and Cipango 40 Yrs. Ago; ill. 12/ *n.* 8° Stock 02
Notes on coast towns, and events there: by an officer dur. surveying cruise of the *Actæon* and *Dodge*. 1856–62.

BRODIE (J. B.) + RAY (A. F.) Log of H.M.S. *Goliath*. 1900–03 4/ c 8° Westminster Press 03
[The Log Series.] A diary kept by two petty officers while serving on the China station.

COLLINGWOOD, Cuthb. — Rambles of a Naturalist in China Seas *o.p.* [*pb.* 16/] 8° Murray 68

GUILLEMARD, Dr F. H. H. — —*in his* The Cruise of the 'Marchesa' to Kamschatka, etc., *ut* **E** § 7

PERRY, Commod. — Narr. of Exped. of Amer. Squad. to China Seas & Jap., 4 v. *o.p.* 4° *Washington* 56
With 100 tinted plates of views, portraits, manners, natural history (these coloured).

SAINT JOHN, Cpt. H. C. — —*in his* Notes and Sketches from Wild Coasts of Nipon, *ut* **E** § 37
Includes chapters on cruising after pirates in Chinese waters.

### Economic and Political Condition—*v. also* E § 138, *s.v.* Eastern Question, *and* F § 61

BERESFORD, L'd Chas. — The Break-Up of China; maps and ill. $3 (12/) 8° Harper 99
An epitome of the Chinese questn.: four-fifths of it a 'Blue-Bk.' on finance, politics, trade, etc.

BROOMHALL, Marshall [ed.] The Chinese Empire 7/6 *n.* 8° Morgan & Scott 07
A comprehensive, businesslike book of reference on things Chinese, inclg. missions.

" Islam in China 7/6 *n.* 8° Morgan & Scott 10

BROWN, Dr Arth. J. New Forces in Old China ; ill. (5/ *n.*) c 8° Revell 05

BROWN, C. Campbell China in Legend and Story ; ill. 3/6 *n.* c 8° Oliphant, *Edin.* 08
A vivid and sympathetic picture of modern China, by one who has resided there for 10 yrs.

CHANG CHIH-TUNG China's Only Hope : an appeal [tr.] 3/6 c 8° Oliphant, *Edin.* 00
$1·25. Revell, *N.Y.* An appeal for reform ; by a prominent Chinaman. Incl. an able diagnosis of China's positn.

CHIROL, Valentine —*in his* The Far Eastern Question, *ut* **E** § 37

COLQUHOUN, A. R. China in Transformation ; maps and ill. 16/ ($3) 8° Harper 98
Several valuable essays on geograph., econ., and social condns., with a considn. of the political positn.

ELIOT, Sir Chas. Letters from the Far East ; ill. 8/6 *n.* 8° Arnold 07
$2·40 *n.* Longman, *N.Y.* Deal w. the political, social, and literary characteristics of China and Japan.

GASCOYNE-CECIL, Rev. L'd Wm. Changing China ; map and 32 ill. 10/6 *n.* 8° Nisbet 10
A concise, clear, and impartial statemt. of the engrossing problems and movemts. now at issue in China, the main object of the bk., however, bg. to commend the scheme for the foundation of a Christian university in China.

GORST, Har. E. China ; map and 28 ill. [Imper. Interest Lib.] 6/ c 8° Sands 99

GUNDRY, R. S. China and her Neighbours ; maps 9/ 8° Chapman 93
France in Indo-China, Russia and China, India, and Tibet.

" China, Present and Past ; map 10/6 8° Chapman 95
Colln. of repr. arts. on China's foreign intercourse, progr., resources, educn., currency, trade, missionary questn., etc.

JOHNSTON, J. China and its Future ; ill. 3/6 c 8° Stock 00

KRAUSSE, Alexis China in Decay : a handbk. ; 6 maps and 21 ill. 5/ 8° Chapman [98] 00
A good compilation, giving full account of China and the history of its 'question' in small space.

LEAVENWORTH, C. S. The 'Arrow' [lorcha] War with China 3/6 *n.* c 8° Low 01

LEROY-BEAULIEU, P. Awakening of the East [tr.]—*ut* **D** § 138

LYNCH, Geo. The War of the Civilizations ; 22 ill. 6/ *n.* c 8° Longman 01
$2 Longman, *N.Y.* The experiences of the Special Correspondent of *The Sphere.* *Vide* also his *Path of Empire* [*ut* **E** § 39].

MARTIN, W. A. P. The Awakening of China ; ill. 16/ *n.* 8° Hodder 07

MORSE, Hosea B. Trade and Administration of the Chinese Empire—*ut* **D** § 148
7/6 *n.* Longman. Author, who went to China fr. Harvard in 1875, is Commr. of Customs and Statist. Secy. of China.

*PARKER, Prf. E. H. China : hist., diplomacy, and commerce ; 19 maps 8/ *n.* c 8° Murray 01
Short acc. of geogr. and hist. ; w. accurate informn. on commerc. relig., army, etc. An indispensable bk. *V.* also **F** § 61.

PARSONS, W. B. An American Engineer in China [1898–9] $1·50 c 8° McClure, *N.Y.* 00
Based on jy. acr. Hunan for ry. survey. Affords insight into factors of Chinese problem.

SARGENT, Prf. A. J. Anglo-Chinese Commerce and Diplomacy—*ut* **D** § 148
Mainly 19th century. Written to illustrate the interdependence of trade and politics.

WALTON, Jos. China and the Present Crisis 6/ c 8° Low 00
Notes, chiefly political ; the result of a 4-months' tour : with travel-jottings on Japan and Corea.

'WEALE, B. L. Putnam' [=L. L. SIMPSON]—*ut* **E** § 37

**Life and People**

BALFOUR, F. H. Waifs & Strays fr. Far East [essays rel. to China] *o.p.* [*pb.* 10/6] 8° Trübner 76

" Leaves from my Chinese Scrapbook *o.p.* [*pb.* 7/6] 8° Trübner 87

BALL, J. Dyer Things Chinese 10/ *n.* 8° Murray [92] 04
$5 *n.* Scribner, *N.Y.* A useful imitn. of CHAMBERLAIN's more successful *Things Japanese* (*ut* **E** § 37), contg. notes on var. subjects conn. w. China : the Hakkas, porc. and pottery, art, mutual and secret socs., Taouism, etc.

" The Chinese at Home ; ill. 5/ *n.* c 8° R.T.S. 11

BARD, E'mile The Chinese at Home [tr.] ; ill. 7/6 *n.* 8° Newnes 06

BELL, Mrs Arth. China and the Chinese 2/6 c 8° Hurst 99

BLAND, J. O. P. Houseboat Days in China ; ill. [$5 Longman, *N.Y.*] 15/ *n.* m 8° Arnold 09

*BRINKLEY, Cpt. F. Japan and China, 12 vols.—*ut* **E** § 37

CARL, Kath. A. With the Empress Dowager ; ill. 10/6 8° Nash 06

CARUS, Paul Chinese Life & Customs ; ill. [3/6 *n.* Paul] 75 c. *n.* 8° *Open Ct.* Pb. Co., *Chicago* 07

'CHINAMAN, John Coming' [=Arch. LAMONT] Bright Celestials : Chinaman at home and abroad 6/ c 8° Unwin 94
Chinese life in relation to missionary enterprize.

CHITTY, J. R. Things Seen in China ; 50 ill. 2/ *n.* 32° Seeley 08

COCKBURN, G. John Chinaman : his ways and notions 3/6 8° Marshall Bros. 96

COLTMAN, R. The Chinese : their present and future ; ill. $1·25 8° Davis, *Phila.* 91

CORNABY, W. A. —*in his* A String of Peach-stones, *ut* **B** § 36 [village-life and folklore]

" China under the Search-Light 6/ c 8° Unwin 01
A series of discursive essays on the leading features of Chinese life.

CURZON, G. N. [L'd] —*in his* Problems of the Far East : Japan, Korea, China, *ut* **E** § 37

DAVIDSON (R. J.) + MASON (Is.) Life in West China by Two Residents 3/6 *n.* c 8° Headley 05
DAVIS, J. F. The Chinese, 2 vols. [encyclopaedic ; standard] *o.p.* [*pb.* 9/] 8° Griffin [30] 57
DOOLITTLE, Rev. J. Social Life of Chinese ; 150 ill. [religs. custs., opins.] c 8° Bickers [66] 71
DOUGLAS, Prf. R. K. China ; map and ill. [concise ; popular] 5/ c 8° S.P.C.K. [82] 87
" Society in China ; 22 native and other ill. 2/ c 8° Ward & Lock [94] 01
A compreh. survey of the soc. and polit. condn., by a decidedly hostile critic, formerly in Consular Service.
FIELDE, Adèle M. A Corner of Cathay ; 12 native col. pl. $3 (8/6 *n.*) s 4° Macmillan 94
Graphic and intimate sketches of Chin. life and manners by an Amer. lady who had spent 15 yrs. in China, chiefly at Satow.
GILES, Prf. H. A. Chinese Sketches *o.p.* [*pb.* 10/6] 8° Trübner 76
" China and the Chinese $1·50 *n.* (8/ *n.*) c 8° Macmillan 02
[Columbia Univ. Ser.] Popular lects. on language, and (more important) on customs, constitn., and life of China.
GRAY, Archd. J. H. China, ed. W. G. Gregor, 2 vols. ; 150 facs. pl. *o.p.* [*pb.* 32/] 8° Macmillan 78
A standard wk., still indispensable, on history of the laws, manners, customs, etc., of the Chinese.
HALCOMBE, C. J. H. The Mystic Flowery Land ; ill. 7/6 8° Luzac [97] 99
Colln. of disjointed chs. illg. Chin. life ; a good deal conc. Shanghai. Author married a Chinese lady.
HARDY, Rev. E. J. John Chinaman at Home ; ill. 10/6 *n.* 8° Unwin 05
$2·50 *n.* Scribner, *N.Y.* A chatty and amusing bk. of travel and observation, by late Chaplain to the Forces at Hong Kong.
HENRY, B. C. The Cross and the Dragon : life in the Broad East 12/6 c 8° *Shanghai* 90
HOLCOMBE, Rev. Chester The Real Chinaman ; 77 illns. $2 c 8° Dodd & Mead, *N.Y.* 95
7/6 Hodder. Sketch of the Chinaman, his life, habits, relig., trade, educn., law, etc., by Sec. of Amer. Legation.
LEE, Yan Phou When I was a Boy in China [home-life] 60 c. c 8° Lothrop, *Boston* 03
Letters of John Chinaman [by G. L. Dickinson ; repr. fr. 'Sat. Rev.'] 1/ *n.* f 8° Dent [01] 03
LITTLE, Arch. Gleanings from Fifty Years in China ; ill. [mag. arts.] 7/6 *n.* 8° Low 10
LITTLE, Mrs Archib. In the Land of the Blue Gown ; 100 ill. 21/ *n.* l 8° Unwin 02
A view of the Chinese in their relns. w. foreigners ; partly repr. of *My Diary in a Chinese Town* (1898).
" Intimate China : Chinese as I have seen them 6/ 8° Hutchinson [99] 00
$2 Lippincott, *Phila.* A valuable, though discursive, detailed account of Chinese life. 120 illns.
" Round about my Peking Garden—*ut inf.*
" Out in China 2/6 c 8° Treherne 02
LYALL, Sir A. C. —*in his* Asiatic Studies, ser. i–ii, *ut* **A** § 9
MACGOWAN, Rev. J. Sidelights on Chinese Life ; 46 ill. (12 col.) 15/ *n.* r 8° Paul 08
MARTIN, Dr W. A. P. The Chinese : their education, philosophy, & letters $1·75 c 8° Harper, *N.Y.* 81
" A Cycle of Cathay : China South and North $2 c 8° Revell, *N.Y.* 96
7/6 Oliphant, *Edin.* Comments on diplom. history ; but of chief value for insight into manners, modes of thought, etc.
" The Lore of Cathay : the intellect of China ; ill. $2·50 *n.* r 8° Revell, *N.Y.* 01
10/6 Oliphant, *Edin.* Repr., w. addns. of *The Chinese* (N.Y. '81), itself a repr. of Ser. i of *The Hanlin Papers* (*Shanghai* '80).
MORSE, E. S. Glimpses of China & Chinese Homes ; ill. $1·50 *n.* c 8° Little & Brown, *Boston* 02
NORMAN, Sir Hy. —*in his* The Peoples and Politics of the Far East, *ut* **E** § 31
PARKER, Prf. E. H. John Chinaman, and a Few Others 8/ *n.* c 8° Murray 01
An attempt to make Chinese life real by numerous anecdotes of individual Chinamen, from writer's experience.
PLANCHUT, Edmund China and the Chinese [tr.] ; 58 ill. [pop. ; good] 2/6 c 8° Hurst 99
ROBERTSON-SCOTT, J. W. The People of China 3/6 c 8° Methuen 00
A condensed, encyclopædic account of the country, history, political outlook, customs, etc.
ROE, A. S. China as I Saw it ; 39 ill. [l'rs. of a lady] 12/6 *n.* 8° Hutchinson 10
SCIDMORE, E. R. China, the Long-Lived Empire $2·50 8° Century Co., *N.Y.* 00
8/6 *n.* Macmillan, *Lond.* Travel sketches, w. observns. on the people, their customs, polit. and econ. condns., etc.
SELBY, Rev. T. B. As the Chinese see us 6/ c 8° Unwin 01
" Chinamen at Home 3/6 *n.* c 8° Hodder 00
An account of his labours, by a missionary. Full of good stories.
SIMON, G. E. China : social, political, and religious life [tr.] *o.p.* [*pb.* 6/] c 8° Low 87
*SMITH, Dr Arth. H. Chinese Characteristics ; 16 ill. [10/6 Paul] $2 8° Revell, *N.Y.* [90] 00
An excellent and thoroughly impartial ser. of sketches, accur. describg. leadg. features of Chin. life, character, and habits.
* " Village Life in China ; ill. [7/6 Oliphant, *Edin.*] $2 8° Revell, *N.Y.* 00
TCHENG-KI-TONG, Gen. The Chinese Painted by Themselves [tr.] 6/ c 8° Field & Tuer *n.d.* (84)
" Chin-Chin : Chinaman at home, tr. [fr. Fch.] 3/6 *n.* c 8° Marsden 94
Sketches, by former member of Imp. Chin. Legn., of priv. amusemts., fetes, etc., of Chinese.
THOMSON, Jno. S. The Chinese ; ill. 12/6 *n.* 8° Laurie 10
TOWNLEY, L'y Susan My Chinese Note-Book ; 2 maps and 16 ill. 10/6 *n.* 8° Methuen 04
WILLIAMS, Prf. S. W. —*in his* The Middle Kingdom, 2 vols., *ut sup.*

**English Life in China**

FORTUNE, Rob. Residence among the Chinese ; ill. [1853–6] *o.p.* [*pb.* 16/] 8° Murray 57
GORDON, Maj.-Gen. C. G. —*for his* Life in China *v.* **F** § 29

GRAY, Mrs — Fourteen Months in Canton; ill. [1877–8] *o.p.* [*pb.* 9/] c 8° Macmillan 80
KNOLLYS, Maj. H. — English Life in China *o.p.* [*pb.* 7/6] c 8° Smith & Elder 85
LITTLE, Mrs Archib. — My Diary in a Chinese Farm; ill. 7/6 *n.* s 4° *Shanghai* 96

**Ethnology**

SPENCER, Herb. [ed.] — Descriptive Sociology: Chinese. Ed. E. J. C. Werner 63/ f° Williams 11
Appleton, *N.Y.* Vol. ix of the ser. [*v.* **C** § 62], by far the most extensive, w. over 10,000 classif. quotns. and extrs.

**Corea**

ALLEN, Dr Hor. N. — Things Korean: sketches & anecdotes; ill. $1·25 *n.* (3/6 *n.*) c 8° Revell 08
BISHOP, Mrs [*née* Isab. L. BIRD] Korea and her Neighbours; maps and ill. 5/ *n.* c 8° Murray [98] 05
1 vol., $2 Revell, *N.Y.* The best popular description; includes much history and polit. and industr. matter.
CARLES, W. R. — Life in Corea; ill. [by late H. M. Consul in Cor.] 12/6 8° Macmillan 88
CAVENDISH, Cpt. A. E. J. — Korea and Sacred White Mountain 15/ m 8° Philip [91] 94
An unpretentious narr. of travel, advent., and sport in 1891. 2 maps and 4 dwgs. (20 col.) illg. native manners by native artists.
CURZON, G. N. [L'd] — *—in his* Problems of the Far East [tr.], *ut* **E** § 37
GALE, Rev. Jas. S. — Korean Sketches; ill. [missionary] $1 c 8° Revell, *N.Y.* 98
GIFFORD, Rev. Dan. L. — Every-day Life in Korea; ill. $1·25 c 8° Revell, *N.Y.* 98
GILMORE, Rev. G. W. — Korea from its Capital $1·75 c 8° Presb. Bd. of Pb., *Phila.* 93
GOOLD-ADAMS, H. E. F. — Korea and White Mountain 94
GRIFFIS, Dr W. E. — Corea, the Hermit Nation; ill. [hist. & political] $2·50 8° Scribner, *N.Y.* [82] 07
,, — Corea, Without & Within [hist., manners, relig.] $1 16° Presb. Bd. of Pb., *Phila.* 85
HAMILTON, Angus — Korea; map and ill. 15/ *n.* 8° Heinemann [04] 04
A good, readable acc. of the then positn. and condn. of the Hermit Kingdom, w. informn. supplemg. Mrs BISHOP's bk.
HULBERT, Homer B. — History of Korea: B.C. 2257–A.D. 1904, 2 v.; ill. [30/ *n.* Paul] 8° 05
,, — The Passing of Korea; ill. $3·80 *n.* 8° Doubleday, *N.Y.* 06
16/ *n.* Heinemann. The country, its people, hist., life, folklore, archæol., and econ. and polit. positn.
LADD, Prf. G. T. — In Korea with Marquis Ito; ill. $2·50 *n.* 8° Scribner, *N.Y.* 08
In 2 Pts. (1) narr. of pers. expercces., (2) crit. and histor. inquiry: an apologia for Japan.
LANDOR, H. Savage — Corea, or Cho-sen, Land of Morning Calm 18/ 8° Heinemann 95
$4·50 Macmillan, *N.Y.* Almost wholly devoted to soc. life and manners. An amusg. and instructive bk. 38 ill. by author.
LONGFORD, Prf. J. H. — The Story of Korea; map and ill. 10/6 *n.* 8° Unwin 11
LOWELL, Percival — Chöson, Land of Morning Calm; maps and ill. $5 i 8° Houghton, *Boston* [85] 86
LYNCH, G. — *—in his* The Path of Empire, *ut* **E** § 39
MCKENZIE, F. A. — The Tragedy of Korea 6/ 8° Hodder 08
$2 *n.* Dutton, *N.Y.* A narr. of last 30 yrs., w. forecast of the future. Adverse criticism of Japan.
MILN, Louise J. — Quaint Korea $1·75 c 8° Scribner, *N.Y.* 95
5/ Osgood. Some bright sketches and descriptions; but full of cheap moralizing.
NORMAN, Hy. — *—in his* The Peoples and Politics of the Far East, *ut* **E** § 31
OPPERT, Ern. — A Forbidden Land: voyages to Corea; ill. *o.p.* [*pb.* 12/6] 8° Low 80
An account of Corean geography, history, products, commercial capabilities, etc.
ROCKHILL, W. W. — China's Intercourse with Korea [15 cent. to 1895] 3/6 *n.* 8° Luzac 05
ROSS, Rev. Jno. — History of the Corea, Ancient and Modern 12/6 8° Stock *n.d.* (80)
WHIGHAM, H. J. — Manchuria and Korea—*ut inf., s.v.* Manchuria

**Formosa**

de BENYOWSKI, C't M. A. — *—in his* Memoirs [tr.], *ut* **E** § 31 [1741–71]
CAMPBELL, Rev. Wm. [ed.] Account of Missionary Success in Formosa; w. appendices & notes, 2 v.; ill. 10/ c 8° Trübner [1650] 89
CAMPBELL, Rev. Wm. [missy.] Past and Future of Formosa; map 8° Kelly & Walsh, *Hong Kong* 96
,, [ed. & tr.] Formosa under the Dutch 12/ *n.* 8° Paul 03
A colln. of contemp. documts. tr. fr. Dutch bearg. on hist. of Formosa in 17 cent., w. spec. ref. to missionary labours.
*DAVIDSON, J. W. — The Island of Formosa, Past & Present; ill. $8·50 *n.* (25/ *n.*) 8° Macmillan 03
An admirable, full acc. of geogr., hist., and resources, trade, and products of the isld., by U.S. Consul for Formosa.
GUILLEMARD, F. H. — *—in his* Cruise of the 'Marchesa' to Kamschatka, etc., *ut* **E** § 7
HUGHES, Mrs T. F. — Among the Sons of Han [6 yrs. in China & Formosa] *o.p.* [*pb.* 12/] 8° Tinsley 81
de LACOUPERIE, Terrien — Formosa: notes on MSS., langs., & races [repr. fr. *Jl. R. A. S.*] 5/ 8° Nutt 87
MACKAY, Dr G. L. — From Far Formosa: isld., people, missions—*ut* **A** § 105
PICKERING, W. A. — Pioneering in Formosa: recollections; 25 ill. *o.p.* [*pb.* 16/] 8° Hurst 98
A valuable general description: the result of seven years' residence in the island.
YOSABURO, Takekoshi — Japanese Rule in Formosa [tr.]; map and 38 ill. 10/6 *n.* ($3 *n.*) 8° Longman 07
A more or less official presentmt. of the Japanese case, by a Member of the Japanese Diet.

**Hong-Kong**

BOWEN, Sir G. F. — *—in his* Thirty Years of Colonial Government, 2 vols., *ut* **E** § 65

CHAILLEY-BERT, J. —*in his* The Colonisation of Indo-China, *ut* **E** § 36
EITEL, Dr E. K. Europe in China [hist. of Hong-Kong to 1882] 15/ *n.* 8° Luzac 95

**Loochoo Islands**

de BENYOWSKY, C't M. A. —*in his* Memoirs [tr.]—*ut* **E** § 31 [1741–71]
GUILLEMARD, Dr F. H. H. —*in his* The Cruise of the 'Marchesa' to Kamschatka, etc.—*ut* **E** § 7
LEAVENWORTH, C. S. The Loochoo Islands; map and ill. 4/6 *n.* r 8° Paul 05

**Manchuria** —*v. also* **E** § 39; *for* Russo-Jap. War: 1904–5, *v.* **F** § 56

BARING, Maur. With the Russians in Manchuria 7/6 *n.* 8° Methuen 05
,, —*in his* A Year in Russia, *ut* **E** § 25
Begins w. acc. of jy. to Manchuria before peace was declared, descrs. how news of peace was recd. am. the Russn. troops, and then deals w. the return jy. and later events.
BEVERIDGE, A. J. The Russian Advance; maps $2·50 *n.* (10/6) 8° Harper 03
BROOKE, L. G. F. M. G., L'd An Eye-witness in Manchuria [1904–5] 7/6 8° Nash 05
FLEMING, G. Travels in Mantchu Tartary beyond Gt. Wall of China; map and ill. [on horseback] *o.p.* [*pb.* 42/] r 8° Hurst 63
FOX, Jno. Following the Sun-Flag 2/6 c 8° Constable 05
*HOSIE, Alex. Manchuria: people, resources, recent hist.; ill. 7/6 *n.* 8° Methuen [01] 05
First 4 chs. give hist. of Manch. since 1899; rest is best available descrn. of the country.
JAMES, H. E. M. The Long White Mountain 24/ 8° Longman 88
Natural history, people, administration, and religion of Manchuria. Map and ill., incl. 38 col. pl. of birds and plants.
KEMP, Miss E. G. The Face of Manchuria, Korea, and Russian Turkestan; 24 pl. (18 col.) by author 7/6 *n.* s 4° Chatto 10
PALMER, Fredk. With Kuroki in Manchuria; ill. 7/6 *n.* 8° Methuen [04] 04
'WEALE, B. L. Putnam' Manchu and Muscovite; ill. [l'rs wr. 1903] 10/ *n.* ($3 *n.*) 8° Macmillan [04] 07
,, The Re-Shaping of the Far East—*ut* **E** § 37 [a sort of sequel to above]
,, —*in his* The Coming Struggle in Eastern Asia, *ut* **E** § 37
WHIGHAM, H. J. Manchuria and Korea; map and ill. 7/6 r 8° Isbister (Pitman) 04
YOUNGHUSBAND, Col. F. E. The Heart of a Continent; map and ill. 6/ 8° Murray [96] 04
Narrative of travel in Manchuria, across the Gobi Desert, thro' the Himalayas, the Pamirs, and Hunza: 1884–94. By the British Commissioner for Tibet Frontier Matters. One of the best travel-bks. on China.
,, Among the Celestials; map and ill. [abgmt. of above] 7/6 c 8° Murray 98

**Marches** [a plateau W. of Ssu-ch'uan and E. of Tibet]

EDGAR, J. H. The Marches of the Mantze; ill. 1/6 c 8° Morgan & Scott 08

**Mongolia** —*v.* **E** § 39, *s.v.* Mongolia and Siberia

**Pekin**

FORTUNE, Rob. Yedo and Peking: a journey *o.p.* [*pb.* 16/] 8° Murray 63
HOOKER, Mary Behind the Scenes in Peking 7/6 *n.* c 8° Murray 10
A lively and picturesque account of the siege of 1901.
LITTLE, Mrs Archib. Round about my Peking Garden 15/ *n.* 8° Unwin 05
RENNIE, D. F. Peking and the Pekingese, 2 vols. *o.p.* [*pb.* 24/] c 8° Murray 65

**Shanghai:** MONTALTO DE JESUS (C. A.) Historic Shanghai; ill. 12/6 *n.* 8° *Shanghai* (Probsthain) 05

**Turkestan: Eastern (Chinese)**

CHURCH, Percy W. Chinese Turkestan with Caravan and Rifle—*ut* **I** § 147
DEASY, H. H. In Tibet and Chinese Turkestan—*ut inf.*, *s.v.* Tibet
HENDERSON (G.) + HUME (A. O.) Lahore to Yarkand *o.p.* [*pb.* 42/] r 8° Lovell Reeve 73
Account of the expedition under Sir Douglas FORSYTH.
HUNTINGTON, E. —*in his* The Pulse of Asia, *ut* **E** § 33
LANSDELL, Dr H. —*in his* Chinese Central Asia, *ut* **E** § 33
PREJEVALSKY, Gen. N. M. From Kulja acr. Tian Shan to Lob Nor [tr.]—*ut* **E** § 39, *s.v.* Mongolia & Siberia
*Kashgar:* BELLEW (Surg.-Maj. H. W.) Kashmir and Kashgar—*ut* **E** § 35 [1873–4]
KUROPATKIN, A. N. Kashgaria, tr. W. E. Gowen *o.p.* [*pb.* 10/6] r 8° Thacker, *Calcutta* 82

**Tian-Shan Mountains**

MERZBACHER, Dr Gottfr. The Central Tian-Shan Mountains; ill. 12/ *n.* 8° R.G.S. (Murray) 06
A valuable prelim. narr. (precedg. a full scient. Rept.) of the expedn. wh. started und. auspices of Imper.-Russn. Geogr. Soc. in 1902, embodying observns. on pres. and past glacier-condns. of the Tian-Shan, and on peculiarities in the phys. features of its valley-formatns. Good illns.
PREJEVALSKY, Gen. N. M. From Kulja across the Tian Shan to Lob Nor [tr.]—*ut* **E** § 39

**Tibet**

BISHOP, Mrs [Isab. BIRD] Among the Tibetans, ill. [pleasant bk. of travel] 1/6 c 8° R.T.S. [94] 04

BONVALOT, Gabr. Across Thibet [tr.]; 100 ill. & route-map, 2 vols. 32/ (1 v. $3·50) r 8° Cassell 91
Acc. of his 3rd gt. expedn. to High Asia. The route of the jy.—made in comp. of Pr'ce HENRY OF ORLEANS and F'r DEDEKEN (a Belg. missionary)—was fr. Russn. frontier to Lob Nor, thence to Tengri Nor, to Batang on 'River of Golden Sands', to Gulf of Tonkin, thence thro' Kuldja acr. Tian Shan. A vivacious acc., w. good descrns. of his bold advents. and explorns.

BOWER, Cpt. Hamilton Diary of Journey acr. Tibet; map and ill. 16/ 8° Rivington 94
By a Bengal cavalry officer, who crossed Tibet fr. E. to W., traversg. ab. 800 m. of unexplored country, and reachg. Tengri-Nor.

CANDLER, Edm. The Unveiling of Lhasa; map and ill. 15/ *n.* r 8° Arnold [05] 05
$5 Longman, *N.Y.* A graphic and impartial account of the British expedition to Tibet.

CAREY, Wm. Travel and Adventure in Thibet; ill. 6/ 8° Hodder 02
$1·50 *n.* Baker, *N.Y.* A readable acc. of Tibet. Incls. the Diary of Annie R. TAYLOR's missionary jy., 1892–3.

COOPER, T. T. Travels of a Pioneer of Commerce, in Pigtail and Petticoats *o.p.* [*pb.* 16/] 8° Murray 71

" Mishmee Hills [attempted jy. to Tibet fr. Assam] *o.p.* [*pb.* 10/6] 8° H. S. King 73

CROSBY, O. T. Tibet and Turkestan; ill. $2·50 *n.* (10/6 *n.*) 8° Putnam 05
'A journey through old lands and a study of new conditions'.

DEASY, Cpt. H. H. P. In Tibet and Chinese Turkestan; maps and ill. 6/ *n.* 8° Unwin [01] 01
$5 *n.* Longman, *N.Y.* A valuable account of surveying expeditions in Western Tibet.

DUNCAN, Jane E. Summer Ride thro' Western Tibet; map & 93 ill. 14/ *n.* 8° Smith & Elder 06

ETHERTON, Lt. P. T. Across the Roof of the World: sport and travel; ill. 16/ *n.* 8° Constable 11
Record of jy. of nearly 1,000 m. fr. Kashmir acr. the continent to Siberian ry. nr. Omsk.

FERGUSSON, W. N. Adventure, Sport & Travel on Tibetan Steppes; ill. 16/ *n.* 8° Constable 11
Mainly acc. of 2 jys. thro' China and Tibet by Lt. BROOKE (1906–8), who was murdered in Independent Lolo Land.

FRANCKE, Rev. A. H. History of Western Tibet; ill. [good pop. acc.] 2/6 *n.* c 8° Partridge 08

GILL, Cpt. W. J. —*in his* River of Golden Sand, 2 vols., *ut sup.*

GORDON, T. E. The Roof of the World [acr. Plateau of Tibet] *o.p.* [*pb.* 31/6] r 8° *Edinburgh* 76

GRENARD, F. Tibet and the Tibetans [tr.]; col. map 10/6 *n.* 8° Hutchinson 04

GUNDRY, R. S. —*in his* China and her Neighbours, *ut sup.*

*HEDIN, Dr Sven —*in his* Through Asia, 2 vols., *ut* **E** § 33
Pays spec. attention to geogr. of Gobi Desert and complicated Tarim river-system.

* " Adventures in Tibet 10/6 8° Hurst 04
Acc. of jy. acr. Central Asian desert and of 2 unsucessful attempts to enter Lhasa.

" Central Asia and Tibet tow. Holy City of Lassa, 2 vols.—*ut* **E** § 33

* " Trans-Himalaya: discovs. and advs. in Tibet, 2 v.; 10 maps and 388 ill. (some col.) 30/ *n.* ($7·50 *n.*) 8° Macmillan [09] 10
An admir. acc. of 26 months' genuine travel, adventure, and endurance, full of first-hand scientific informn.—perh. the greatest feat of Asiatic travel since that of PREJEVALSKY.

HOLDICH, Col. Sir Thos. Thibet the Mysterious; map and 50 ill. 4/6 *n.* 8° Rivers 06
[Story of Exploration.] Summarizes results of travellers and explorers fr. an early period to date.

HUC, Abbé + GABET Travels in Tartary, Thibet, and China—*ut sup.*

JOHNSTONE, D. L. Land of the Mountain Kingdom; ill. [mtns. of Tibet] *o.p.* [*pb.* 5/] c 8° Low 88

LANDON, Perceval Lhasa: the Tibet Expedition, 1903–4; ill. 10/6 m 8° Hurst [05] 06
Acc. of country and people of Central Tibet and of progress of the Engl. Govt.'s mission of 1903–4, by Spec. Corresp. of *Times*.

LANDOR, A. H. Savage In the Forbidden Land; 17 ill. 3/6 8° Heinemann [98] 04
$9 Harper, *N.Y.* Acc. of jy. in Tibet, capture by Tib. authorities, imprisonmt., torture, ultimate release.

" Tibet & Nepal Painted & Described; 75 pl. (50 col.) [$5 *n.* Macm., *N.Y.*] 20/ *n.* sq 8° Black 05

LE BLOND, Mrs Aubrey Adventures on the Roof of the World; ill. 10/6 *n.* 8° Unwin 04

LITTLE, Archibald Mount Omi and Beyond; map and ill. 10/ *n.* 8° Heinemann 01
$3·50 Stokes, *N.Y.* A pleasant acc. of a holiday-visit on the Tibetan border, inclg. Mt. Omi and other Buddhist shrines.

MARKHAM, [Sir] C. R. [ed.] Bogle's Missn. to Thibet [1774]; *and* Manning's Jy. to Lhasa [1810]—*v. sup.*

MARSTON, Annie W. The Great Closed Land; ill. [popular] 1/6 4° Partridge [*n.d.* (94)] 95

MILLINGTON, Powell To Lhassa at Last; front. 3/6 *n.* c 8° Smith & Elder [05] 05
A descrn. of personal impressns. dur. the Tibetan expedn.: a 'chronicle of the road'.

OTTLEY, Col. W. J. With Mounted Infantry in Tibet; ill. [1903–4] 10/6 *n.* 8° Smith & Elder 06

PRATT, A. E. To Snows of Thibet thro' China; ill.—*ut* **H** § 103
Mainly a scientific journey made 1887–9, 1890—*v.* **H** § 103. PRATT entered Tibet overland fr. Kia-Ting-Fu, reversg. routes usually taken.

*PREJEVALSKY, Gen. N. M. Mongolia, the Tangut Country, and N. Tibet [tr.]—*ut* **E** § 39, *s.v.* Mongolia
Author succeeded in getting as near the capital as Nya-ch'uk'a.

RAWLING, Cpt. C. G. The Great Plateau; map and ill. 15/ *n.* 8° Arnold 05
$5 Longman, *N.Y.* Acc. of the explorn. in Western Tibet of 1903, and of the Gartok expedn. of 1904–5.

REID, Wm. Jamieson Thro' Unexplored Asia; maps & ill. [W. China, & E. Tibet] $4·50 8° Estes, *Bost.* 99

RIJNHART, Susie C. With the Thibetans in Tent and Temple; ill. $1·50 c 8° Revell, *N.Y.* 01
6/ Oliphant, *Edin.* A good missionary acc. of 4 yrs. (1895–9) on the borders, and of a jy. into the interior.

ROCKHILL, W. W. Diary of a Journey [1891–2]; *and* Notes on Ethnology—*ut* **E** § 39
Conts. researches in some sectns. of Tibet hitherto unexplored by Europ. or Amer. travellers.

" Early History of Tibet—*in his* Life of Buddha, *ut* **A** § 14

" Land of the Llamas; 2 maps and 61 ill. $3·50 8° Century Co., *N.Y.* 91
15/ Longman. Like HUC + GABET (whose veracity, recently impeached by PREJEVALSKY, he vindicates) ROCKHILL entered Tibet fr. North, dressg. and livg. as a Chinaman. Failed to reach Lhasa; but his acc. of travels over many thousand m. in W. China and E. Tibet is valuable f. its copious hist., geogr., and ethnol. informn., deriv. chfly. fr. Chin. sources.

SANDBERG, Rev. Graham — Itinerary of the Route fr. Sikkin to Lhasa ; map — Bapt. Missn. Pr., *Calcutta* 02

" — The Exploration of Tibet, 1623–1904 ; map — Thacker 04
An excellent record, by a trustworthy authority, of progr. of explorn. fr. time of MARCO POLO to SARAT CHANDRA DAS.

" — Tibet and the Tibetans — [good popular acc.] 5/ c 8° S.P.C.K. 06

SARAT CHANDRA DAS — Indian Pandits in the Land of Snow — *o.p.* 8° 93

" — Journey to Lhasa & Central Thibet ; maps & ill. — 10/6 *n.* c 8° Murray [02] 04
$3·50 *n.* Dutton, *N.Y.* Ed. W. W. ROCKHILL. Repr. of Official Report of jy. made in 1881 by an Indian surveyor. The chief authority on S. Tibet and its capital.

SHERRING, Chas. A. — Western Tibet & British Borderland ; maps & 175 ill. — 21/ *n.* r 8° Arnold 06
An interestg. compiln., w. a good deal on legends and folklore (*v.* B § 30). G. T. LONGSTAFF contribs. a ch. descrg. attempt to climb Gurla Mandhata, the highest mtn. in W. Tibet.

WADDELL, Lt.-Col. L. A. — Lhasa and its Mysteries ; maps and 200 ill. — 25/ *n.* 8° Murray 05
$6 *n.* Dutton, *N.Y.* The best general record of the expedn. of 1903–4, by its chief medical officer.

WELBY, M. S. — Through Unknown Thibet ; maps and 60 ill. — 21/ 8° Unwin 98
Acccount of a journey of explorn. thro' new pts. of N. Tibet, fr. West to East.

YOUNGHUSBAND, Sir Fcs. — India and Tibet — 21/ *n.* 8° Murray 10
A hist. of the relns. betw. the 2 countries fr. time of Warren HASTINGS to 1910 ; w. acc. of mission to Lhasa of 1904.

*Irrawaddy River* : d'ORLEANS—*in his* Tonkin to India, *ut sup.*

*Karakoram Mtns.* — —*v.* **E** § 35, *s.v.* Himalayas (CONWAY ; ECKENSTEIN)

**Yang-tse ; Yunnan** — —*v. also sup.*, *s.nn.* GEIL, MORRISON, d'ORLÉANS

ANDERSON, Dr Jas. — Mandalay to Momien ; *and* Report—*ut sup.*, *s.v.* Recent Travel

ARNOLD-FORSTER, Mrs — In the Valley of the Yangtse ; 64 ill. — 2/6 16° Lond. Miss. Soc. 00

BISHOP, Mrs [*née* Isab. L. BIRD] — The Yangtze Valley & Beyond, 2 vols. ; maps & ill. — 21/ *n.* 8° Murray 99
$6 Putnam, *N.Y.* Travels in 1896–7. Shanghai, Hangchow, and upper Yangtse Valley to borders of Tibet. Full of informn., geogr., commerc., polit., and religious.

BLAKISTON, T. W. — Five Months on the Yang-Tsze — *o.p.* [*pb.* 18/] 8° Murray 62
Interestg. descrn. of the earliest voy. to Upper Yang-tse after it was opened to Europeans.

DAVIES, Maj. H. R. — Yün-nan : link betw. India and Yangtze — 16/ *n.* 8° Camb. Press 09
$5 *n.* Putnam, *N.Y.* Detailed geogr. acc. of his jys., coverg. 5,500 miles, ab. half of wh. prev. untrodden even by missionaries. Map and 73 pl.

GILL, Cpt. W. J. — —*in his* River of Golden Sand, 2 vols., *ut sup.*

HOSIE, Alex. — Three Years in Western China ; map and 8 pl. — 6/ 8° Philip [90] 97
Narr. of 3 jys. in Ssu-Ch'uan, Kuei-Chow, and Yün-nan. Introd. by Arch. LITTLE. Best bk. on these districts and the Yang-tse trade.

LITTLE, Archib. — Thro' Yang-tse Gorges : trade & travel in W. China ; ill. — c 8° Low [88] 98

" — Across Yunnan : a jy. of surprises ; ill. — 3/6 *n.* c 8° Low 10
Leavg. Yunnan, visited new Fch. railway fr. Hanoi to Yunnan-fu, and passed down Red R. to Hongkong.

## 35 : INDIA, AND CEYLON

**Bibliography :** CAMPBELL (Fk.) Index-Catal. of Bibliograph. Wks. of India — 3/6 *n.* r 8° Libr. Bureau 97
Deals chiefly w. English books, and includes many not properly bibliographical. 99 pp.

HUNTER, Sir W. W. — Bibliography of India—*in* Samuelson's India, *ut inf.*

**Atlases**

BARTHOLOMEW, J. G. — Hand Atlas of India — 14/ c 8° Constable 93
An excellent atlas of 60 maps and plans, very prettily produced, dealing w. physical and economic geography of India.

HUNTER, Sir W. W. [ed.] — Atlas of India : 16 maps and index — 7/6 4° Johnston 93
A rather commonplace atlas, of old-fashioned type, incl. only usual 'political' maps ; w. Histor-Introd. Sir W. W. HUNTER.

" [ed.] — Statistical Atlas of India = vol. xxvi *of his* Imperial Gazetteer, *ut inf.*
The 64 maps, phys., climatic, demographic, and topogr., w. plans of cities, are accomp. by a useful text.

SAUNDERS, T. W. — Statistical Atlas of India [fr. office of Surv.-Gen. of Ind.] 5/ 4° Stanford [88] 95

" — Atlas of India — [12 maps] 63/ f° Stanford 89

**Cyclopædias ; Gazetteers ; Directory**

BALFOUR, Surg.-Gen. E. — Cyclo. of India & of E. & S. Asia, 3 vols. — 105/ r 8° Quaritch [*Madras* 57–8] 85
Cramful of commercial, industrial, and scientific information ; but now largely out-of-date.

BANESS, J. F. — Index Geographicus Indicus ; 8 maps — *o.p.* [*pb.* 21/] r 8° Stanford 81

BARTHOLOMEW, J. G. — Hand-Gazetteer of India, ed. Dr J. Burgess — 10/6 c 8° Constable 99

District Gazetteers : 33 vols. — [Govt. pubn.] r 8° *Lahore* 83–95

*HUNTER, Sir W. W. [ed.] — Imperial Gazetteer of India, ed. R. Burn + J. S. Cotton, 26 vols. — £5 *n.* ($30) 8° Clar. Press [85–7] 07–9
A monumental wk., embodyg. the offic. spelling. Vol. i : *Descriptive* ; ii : *Historical* ; iii : *Economic* ; iv : *Administrative* ; v–xxiv : *Gazetteer* ; xxv : *Index* ; xxvi : *Atlas*. Separ., i–iv ea. 6/ *n.* ($2) ; *Atlas*, 15/ *n.* ($5).

Southern India : Gazetteer of ; w. atlas of maps [4°] — *o.p.* [*pb.* 63/] r 8° W. H. Allen

Territories under Viceroy of Ind., Gazetteer of. By E. Thornton, ed. Lethbridge + Wollaston — 28/ 8° W. H. Allen [54] 86

THACKER & Co. [pubs.] — Indian Directory ; maps — [commerc., offic., social, etc.] 36/ r 8° Thacker, *Calcutta* [62] *ann.*

**Guides :** BALL (E. A. REYNOLDS) The Tourist's India ; 24 pl. 10/6 *n.* 8° Sonnenschein 07
MURRAY, Jno. [pub.] Handbk. for Trav's. in India, Burma, Ceylon ; ill. 20/ s 8° Stanford 01

**General Geography and Topography**

BLANFORD, H. F. Elem. Geogr. of India, Burma, Ceylon 2/6 gl 8° Macmillan [90] 95
*HOLDICH, Col. Sir Thos. India ; maps and ill. [Regions of the World] 7/6 *n.* ($2) 8° Clar. Press 04
HUNTER, Sir W. W. Schl. Hist. and Geogr. of Northern India 2/ c 8° Clar. Press 91
MORRISON, Cameron New Geography of the Indian Empire 1 rupee c 8° Nelson 06
SMITH, G. Student's Geogr. of Brit. India : pol. and phys. ; maps 7/6 c 8° Murray 83
SURRIDGE, Victor India ; 12 col. pl. [Romance of Empire] 6/ *n.* sq 8° Jack 09

**Administration ; Economics ; Political Problems**—*v. also* **D** § 136, **D** § 117, *s.v.* India, **E** § 33

BRYCE, Rt. Hon. Jas. The Roman Empire and the Brit. Empire in India—*in his* Studies, *ut* **D** § 1
CHIROL, Valentine Indian Unrest, ed. Sir A. C. Lyall 5/ *n.* c 8° Macmillan 10
A timely and trenchant book : repr. (w. revisions) from *The Times*.
COLLIER, Price The West in the East—*ut* **E** § 31 [incl. defence of Brit. rule]
COOMARASWAMY, Dr A. K. Essays in Indian Nationalism [3/6 Probsthain] 8° Apothecaries' Co., *Colombo* 10
COTTON, Sir H. J. S. New India ; or, India in Transition 3/6 *n.* c 8° Paul [85] 04
CRAWFORD, Arth. T. Our Troubles in Poona and the Deccan ; ill. 14/ 8° Constable 97
CURZON, L'd Speeches on India, Jy.–Aug., 1904 6*d.* *n.* 8° Murray 04
DIGBY, Wm. 'Prosperous' British India [indictmt. of Brit. rule] 12/6 8° Unwin 02
DUTT, Romesh C. England and India 2/ c 8° Chatto 97
An attempt to trace the influence of English home politics on India during the 19th century.
,, Economic History of British India 7/6 8° Paul 02
,, India in the Victorian Age 10/6 8° Paul 04
FRASER, Lovat India under Curzon and After ; map and 4 pl. 16/ *n.* 8° Heinemann 11
GOKHALE, C. K. Speeches [by a memb. of Vice-Roy's Legisl. Council] 5/ *n.* 8° Luzac 08
HARDY, J. Keir India : impressions & suggestions [Socialist Lib.] 1/ *n.* c 8° Nat. Lab. Pr., *Salford* [10] 10
HUNTER, Sir Wm. W. Bombay 1885 to 1890—*ut* **F** § 62
,, The India of the Queen ; and other Essays 9/ *n.* ($3 *n.*) 8° Longman 03
HYNDMAN, H. M. The Bankruptcy of India—*ut* **D** § 117
ILBERT, Sir Courtenay The Government of India—*ut* **D** § 3 [a digest of statute law]
LEE-WARNER, Sir W. The Citizen of India 2/ c 8° Macmillan [98] 03
A short trustworthy account of the administration and government, central, municipal, and state.
,, The Native States of India—*ut* **D** § 107 [legal and diplom. relns.]
LEWIN, Maj. T. H. Fly on the Wheel : how I helped to govern India 18/ 8° W. H. Allen 85
LILLY, W. S. India and its Problems ; map *o.p.* [*pb.* 7/6 *n.*] 8° Sands 02
Attempts to summarize information on the races, history, literature, religions, and present day life of India.
MODY, H. P. The Political Future of India [prize-essay] 3/6 *n.* c 8° Hodder 09
A study of the aspirations of educated Indians towards self-government.
MORISON, Sir Theod. Imperial Rule in India 3/6 c 8° Constable 99
Author's idea of ultimate obj. of our rule is th. we shd. so govern India th. she may one day be able to govern herself.
,, The Economic Transition of India [lectures] 5/ *n.* c 8° Murray 11
MORRISON, Rev. Jno. New Ideas in India during the Nineteenth Century—*ut* **A** § 14
MÜLLER, Prf. Max India : what can it teach us ? 5/ ($1·75) c 8° Longman [83]
A course of lectures deliv. before Univ. of Cambridge to candidates for Indian Civil Service.
NEVINSON, H. W. The New Spirit in India ; ill. 10/6 *n.* 8° Harper 08
Descrs. the polit. and social unrest, and the new spirit demandg. a larger share in polit. control.
RANADE, M. G. Essays on Indian Economics [essays and speeches] 6/ c 8° Thacker 00
REES, Sir J. D. The Real India 10/6 *n.* 8° Methuen 08
An impartial record of polit., econ., and soc. condn. of India to-day, described fr. experce. of 25 yrs. in I.C.S., by a present M.P. Considers th. India cannot be governed on democratic lines.
,, Modern India ; map [econcs., admin., etc.] 6/ *n.* c 8° G. Allen 10
RONALDSHAY, Earl of —*in his* Sport and Politics under an Eastern Sky, *ut* **E** § 31
SAMUELSON, Jas. India, Past and Present : hist., social, polit. ; ill. 21/ 8° Paul 90
STORY, Douglas Insurrectionary India 12/6 *n.* 8° Chapman 09
Adopts the official view w. regard to present dangers of a recurrence of the Mutiny.
*STRACHEY, Sir Jno. India, its Administration and Progress, ed. Sir T. W. Holderness—*ut* **D** § 136
TEMPLE, Sir Rich. India in 1880 ; maps *o.p.* [*pb.* 16/] 8° Murray 80
TOWNSEND, Meredith Asia and Europe [$1·50 *n.* Putnam, *N.Y.*] 5/ *n.* c 8° Constable [01] 03
A study of the diffces. wh. separate the Englishman and the native Indian.

WALLACE, Rob. India in 1887 ; ill. 21/ 8° Simpkin 88

*Famines*

DAS, Abhay Charan Indian Ryot, Land-tax, and the Famine *o.p.* [*pb.* 12/] 8° Trübner 81

DIGBY, Wm. Hist. of Famine Campaign in S. India, 2 vols. *o.p.* [*pb.* 32/] 8° Longman 78

DUTT, Romesh C. Open Letters to Lord Curzon on Famines, etc. 7/6 c 8° Paul 00

„ Indian Famines : causes and prevention 6*d.* 8° P. S. King & Son 01

FRERE, Sir H. Bartle The Bengal Famine [w. suggns. for preventn.] *o.p.* [*pb.* 3/6] c 8° Murray 74

HUNTER, [Sir] W. W. Famine Aspects of Bengal Districts [1873] *o.p.* [*pb.* 7/6] p 8° Trübner 74

„ —*in his* Annals of Rural Bengal, *ut inf.*, *s.v.* Bengal

McMINN, C. W. Famine Truths, Half-Truths, Untruths 8° Thacker 02

MEREWETHER, F. H. S. Tour thro' Famine Districts of India ; ill. *o.p.* [*pb.* 16/] 8° Innes 98
$4·50 Lippincott, *Phila.* Newspaper-articles dealing with the 1897 famine.

NASH, Vaughan The Great Famine and its Causes ; 8 ill. 6/ ($2) c 8° Longman 00
A serious study of the subject, somewhat unfavourable to the British Government and its officials.

WALLACE, Rob. Lecture on Famines in India 1/ *n.* 8° Oliver & Boyd, *Edin.* 00

**Ethnology**

BONARJEE, P. D. Handbook of the Fighting Races of India 7/6 c 8° Govt. Press, *Calc.* (Thacker) 99

BREEKS, J. W. Primitive Tribes and Monumts. of the Nilaghiris ; ill. r 4° India Museum 73

*CROOKE, Wm. Tribes and Castes of N.-W. Provinces and Oudh, 4 vols. 8° *Calcutta* 96

„ The N.-W. Provinces of India—*ut inf.* [hist., ethnol., admin.]

* „ Native Races of Northern India ; ill. 6/ c 8° Constable 07
[Native Races of Brit. Empire.] A handy and readable pop. account ; very comprehensive and condensed.

DALTON, Col. E. T. Descriptive Ethnology of Bengal ; ill. *o.p.* [*pb.* 126/] 4° *Calcutta* 72

ELLIOT, Sir H. M. Memoir on History and Distribution of Races, etc., of N.-W. Provinces, ed. J. Beames, 2 vols. ; maps and 2 pl. *o.p.* [*pb.* 36/] 8° Trübner 69

HEWITT, J. F. Ruling Races of Prehistoric Times, 2 vols. 30/ 8° Constable 94–5
Eleven essays on prehistoric races of India, South-Western Asia, and Europe.

HODGSON, B. H. On the Aborigines of India ; pl. *o.p.* [*w.* 12/] 8° *Calcutta* 47
On the Kooch, Bodo, and Dhimal tribes.

„ Himalayan Ethnology ; *and other papers—in his* Miscellaneous Essays, *ut* **K** § 128

KITTS, E. J. Compendium of Castes & Tribes in India [bas. on 1881 census] *o.p.* [*pb.* 5/] f° Trübner 85

LEWIN, Cpt. T. H. Wild Races of South-Eastern Frontier of India *o.p.* [*pb.* 10/] p 8° W. H. Allen 70

„ Hill Tracts of Chittagong and Dwellers Therein *o.p.* [*w.* 9/] r 8° *Calcutta* 69

MADRAS GOVT. MUSEUM : Bulletins [many papers] Govt. Press, *Madras*, *in prg.*

NEWALL, Maj.-Gen. J. T. The Highlands of India, 2 vols. ; ill. 42/, *red. to* 10/ 8°
Vol. i : Strategical and historic account of the tribes of Highlands ; ii : Personal and sporting adventures.

OPPERT, Prf. Gust. On the Original Inhabitants of India 20/ 8° Constable [88–9] 93
Seeks to show that (excg. for. immigrts.) orig. inhabs. of India belong to one race, branches of wh. are spread over Asia and Eur.—the Finnish-Ugrian race.

RICHTER, Rev. G. Compendium on Castes and Tribes in Coorg f° *Bangalore* 87

RISLEY, Sir Herb. H. Tribes & Castes of Bengal, 2 vols. [anthropometric data] 8° Govt. Press, *Calcutta* 91

„ Tribes & Castes of Bengal : Ethnographic Glossary, 2 vols. r 8° Govt. Press, *Calcutta* 91–2
An elab. wk., consistg. of a *General Introd.* and full crit. disquisns. on the several tribes and castes.

„ The People of India ; map and 25 ill. 21/ *n.* 8° Thacker 08
Consists largely of author's contribn. to *Rept. on Census of India.* Ch. on *Caste in Provbs. and Pop. Sayings.*

„ The Castes and Tribes of Eastern India Murray, *in prep.*
By the Director of Ethnography, describg., in pop. lang., the results of the survey made in 1901.

ROWNEY, H. B. The Wild Tribes of India *o.p.* [*pb.* 5/6] c 8° De La Rue 82

SHERRING, Rev. M. A. Hindu Tribes and Castes in Benares, 3 vols. 4° *Calcutta* 72–81

THURSTON, Edgar Ethnographic Notes in Southern India ; 40 pl. 7/6 r 8° Govt. Press, *Madras* [06] 08
Valuable notes on marriage-customs, death-ceremonies, evil eye, charms, torture, corporal punishmt., slavery, hook-swinging, infanticide, etc. The *Bulletin* of the Madras Govt. Museum conts. many valuable papers by him (and others).

„ + RANGACHARI (K.) Castes and Tribes of Southern India, 7 vols. 23/ the set r 8° Govt. Press, *Madras* (Unwin) 09

WATSON (J. F.) + KAYE ([Sir] J. W.) People of India, 8 Pts. ; ill. *o.p.* [*pb.* 45/ ea.] f° W. H. Allen 68–75

*Adaman Islanders* —*v. inf.*, *s.v.* Andaman Islands

*Chittagong Hill Tribes :* RIEBECK (E.) Chittagong Hill Tribes [tr.] ; 21 pl. i f°

*Garos :* PLAYFAIR (Maj. A.) The Garos ; Introd. Sir J. B. Fuller 7/6 *n.* 8° Nutt 10

*Kacháris :* ENDLE (Rev. Sid.) The Kacháris ; ill. (some col.) 8/6 *n.* 8° Macmillan 11

*Kafirs* —*v.* **E** § 33, *s.v.* Kafiristan

*Khasis:* GURDON (Maj. P. R. T.) The Khasis: Introd. Sir C. J. Lyall; ill. 7/6 *n.* 8° Nutt 07

*Lushais:* SOPPITT (A. C.) Account of Kuki-Lushai Tribes 8° 87

*Meitheis* —*v.* **E** § 36, *s.v.* Burma

*Mikirs:* STACK (Edw.) The Mikirs; Introd. Sir C. J. Lyall 7/6 *n.* c 8° Nutt 08

*Nāga Tribes:* HODSON (T. C.) Nāga Tribes of Manipur; ill. 8/6 *n.* 8° Macmillan 11

*Pathans:* Dictionary of Pathan Tribes on N.-W. Frontier of India c 8° *Calcutta* 99

*Thugs; Dacoits:* HUTTON (Jas.) Thugs and Dacoits [hered. garotters, & robbers] 5/ p 8° W. H. Allen 81

*Todas:* MARSHALL (Col. W. E.) A Phrenologist am. the Todas; photos *o.p.* [*pb.* 21/] 8° Longman 73

RIVERS, W. H. R. The Todas; ill. 21/ *n.* ($6·50 *n.*) 8° Macmillan 06
Valuable materl. on social organizn. (inclg. polyandry) of this peculiar tribe of Nilghiri Hills in S. India. Forms also a demonstrn. of anthropological method in collectg. and co-ordinatg. material.

*Veddas* [Ceylon]: SELIGMANN (Dr C. G. + Mrs) The Veddas; ill. and 71 pl. 15/ *n.* 8° Camb. Press 11
Putnam, *N.Y.* [Camb. Arch. & Ethnol. Ser.] Study of soc. and relig. ideas of this nearly extinct race, one of most primitive extant.

**Castes and Sects** —*v. also sup., s.v.* Ethnology (CROOKE, KITTS, RICHTER, RISLEY, SHERRING) *and* **A** § 14, *s.v.* Hinduism

BHATTACHARYA YOGENDRA NATH Hindu Castes and Sects 16/ 8° Thacker, *Calcutta* 96
An exposn. of orig. of caste-syst. of bearg. cf the sects. tow. ea. other. Valuable as view of a native (member of Brahman caste). Index and glossary.

BOWER, H. Essay on Hindu Caste *o.p.* [*pb.* 2/6] 8° *Calcutta* 51

DUBOIS, Abbé J. A. Hindu Manners, Customs and Ceremonies [tr.]—*ut* **A** § 14 [Pt. i: Caste System]

MUIR, Dr Jno. Account of Caste—*in his* Original Sankrit Texts, Pt. i, *ut* **K** § 123

MÜLLER, Prf. F. Max —*in his* Chips from a German Workshop, vol. ii, *ut* **K** § 94

NESFIELD, J. C. Brief View of Caste System of N.-W. Provinces and Oudh *o.p.* 8° 85

RODRIGUEZ, E. A. Hindoo Castes of Brit. Ind., vol. i [all pub.]; col. pl. *o.p.* [*pb.* 168/] i 4° Ackerman 46

WILSON, Jno. Indian Caste, 2 vols. in 1 *o.p.* [*pb.* 31/6] 8° Blackwood 77

*Law of Castes* —*v.* **D** § 111

**Early Voyages and Accounts; Early Geography**

ABUL-FAZL 'ALLÁMÍ [16 cent.] Aín i Akbari [' Institutes of Akbar '], tr. [fr. Pers.] Col. H. S. Jarrett, 3 vols. 8° 91–5
A painstakg. and learned tr. of an inval. and compreh. surv. of India, a unique and honest compiln. of the systs. of admin. and control, faithfully and minutely recorded, w. array of facts illustrative of India's extent, resources, condn., populn., industry, and wealth: comparable to CAMDEN'S *Britannia* [*ut* **E** § 16].

ALBERUNI [b. 973] India, tr. [fr. Arab.] E. C. Sachau, 2 vols. [Orient. Ser.] 25/ *n.* 8° Paul [89] 10
A repertory of informn. on Ind. subjs. (philos., relig., liter., geogr., chronol., astron., customs, law, wr. c. A.D. 1036): designed for use of those who lived in friendly intercourse w. the Indians, and wished to gain insight into their modes of life and thought. Notes and indexes.

ALEXANDER THE GREAT: NIZAMI, Sikandar Nama [tr.]—*ut* **K** § 134

ARRIAN [2 cent.] Indica—*ut* **K** § 192

BARBOSA, Duarte [16 cent.] Coasts of E. Africa and Malabar in 16th cent. [tr.]—*ut* **E** § 48

BERNIER, Dr Frç. Travels in Mogul Empire [1656–68], tr. Irving Brock [1826], ed. Arch. Constable; ill. and reprodns. of early maps 6/ *n.* c 8° Constable [91] 94
Conscientiously ed., w. full bibliogr., notes, and index. 'Honest' BERNIER was a French physician, schoolfellow of GASSENDI and MOLIÈRE: went out to India in 1659 and remained till 1667, witnessing how ALAMGIR [the 'Aurangzeb' of DRYDEN] obtd. his imperial throne, and the foundatn. of his elabor. system.

BOWREY, Thos. Countries rd. Bay of Bengal, ed. Sir R. C. Temple; ill. [1669–79] 8° Hakluyt Soc. 05

[CARERI, Gemelli]: MACMILLAN (Prf. M.) A Globe-Trotter in India 200 Years Ago; and other Indian studies 4/6 c 8° Sonnenschein 95

COMPTON, Herb. Particular Account of European Military Adventures in Hindustan: 1784–1803; ill. 3/6 c 8° Unwin [92] 96
[Adventure Ser.] Lives of Benoit de BOIGNE, PERRON, and Geo. THOMAS. Appendix (80 pp.) conts. notices of 66 others.

COSMAS INDICOPLEUSTES [6 cent.] Christian Topogr. of, tr. J. W. McCrindle; w. notes 8° Hakluyt Soc. 97

CUNNINGHAM, Gen. A. Ancient Geogr. of India, vol. i: Buddhist Period 28/ 8° Trübner (Paul) 71
No more pubd. Includes campaigns of ALEXANDER and travels of HWEN-TSIANG. A learned work. 13 maps.

DALBOQUERQUE, Afonso Commentaries, tr. [fr. 1774, Portug. ed.] W. De Gray Birch, 4 vols. 8° Hakluyt Soc. 75–84
DALBOQUERQUE was second Viceroy of India.

EASTWICK, Cpt. Rob. W. [1773–1866] A Master Mariner, ed. Herb. Compton; 6 ill. 3/6 c 8° Unwin [91]
$1·50 Macmillan, *N.Y.* Affords a good view of way fortunes were made and lost by adventurous Europ. sea-cptns. in palmy days of the old East India Co. and the Fch. wars [fr. 1784 to 1803], givg. lives of de BOIGNE, PERRON and Geo. THOMAS [*v. sup. s.v.* COMPTON].

FÂ-HIEN [4–5 cent.] Record of Buddhistic Kingdoms [tr.]—*ut* **A** § 14, *s.v.* Buddhism [A.D. 399–414]
*V.* also **A** § 10, *s.v.* Chin. Buddhism. Travels of a Chinese monk in Ind. and Ceyl. in search of Buddh. Bks. of Discipline.

FENTON, Mrs. Journal; pref. Sir Hy. Lawrence 8/6 *n.* c 8° Arnold 01
A well-written narrative of the author's life in India, Mauritius, and Tasmania, 1826–30.

FITCH, Ralph [*fl.* 1583–1606]

Ryley, J. Horton [ed.] Ralph Fitch: England's Pioneer to India and Burmah 10/6 *n.* 8° Unwin 99
Many ill. An excellent edition of Fitch's narr. in his own words of his travels in India in 1583–91, with much historical and explanatory matter.

FRYER, Dr Jno. New Account of East India & Persia, ed. Wm. Crooke, v. i 8° Hakluyt Soc. 09
In 8 Letters, covering 9 years' travels from 1672 to 1681. Introd. and notes by CROOKE.

DA GAMA, VASCO [1450–1525], *and Portuguese in India—v. also* **F** § 62

„ Journal of First Voyage: 1497–9, tr. E. G. Ravenstein 8° Hakluyt Soc. 98
Excellent maps and ports. Includes extracts fr. 3 other Portuguese narratives, abridgmt. of Portuguese notes, appendices, etc.

Camoens, Luiz [1524–79] The Lusiad [tr.]—*ut* **K** § 78
VASCO DA GAMA is the central figure, personifying the genius of a race of crusaders and seamen. The epic sings the achievemts. of the Portuguese down to the eve of the expedn. agst. ALCACER, called by JAYNE 'the last Crusade'.

Correa, Caspar Three Voyages of Vasco da Gama, and his Viceroyalty [of India, 1524], tr. Ld Stanley of Alderley [w. orig. documts.] 8° Hakluyt Soc. 69

Danvers, F. C. The Portuguese in India, 2 vols. 42/ 8° W. H. Allen 94

D'Orsey, Rev. A. J. D. Portuguese Discoveries, Annexations, and Missions in Asia and Africa; maps 7/6 c 8° W. H. Allen 92
General subj. of title is treated only in some 50 pp.; remainder consists of elab. survey of study of Port. missns. in India and relns. w. Syrian Church of S. India [*v.* **A** § 105].

Jayne, K. J. Vasco da Gama and his Successors; ill. 10/6 *n.* 8° Methuen 10
A more or less continuous narr. of Portug. discovery and empire-bldg. fr. 1460 to 1580 (d. of D. JOAO DE CASTRO), w. chs. grouped under heads of *Judaism, Humanism, Church and Art and Literature.* A sound, critical bk., in excellent style. Conts. a good summary of causes of decline of Portug. power.

Whiteway, R. S. Rise of Portuguese Power in India [1497–1550] [learned] 15/ *n.* r 8° Constable 99

HAKLUYT, Rich. [ed.] —*in his* Principal Navigations, *ut* **E** § 5

HEDGES, [Sir] Wm. Diary, ed. Col. Yule, 3 vols. [1681–7] 8° Hakluyt Soc. 87–9
During his agency in Bengal and on his voyage and return overland.

HENRY OF PORTUGAL, Pr'ce [1394–1460] Voyages and Travels, 2 vols. [Arber's Engl. Garner] ea. 4/ *n.* s 8° Constable 96–9

de Azurara, G. E. Discovery and Conq. of Guinea, ed. R. Beazley + E. Prestage, 2 v. 8° Hakl Soc. 96–9
The chief authority for the life of Prince HENRY.

Beazley, C. R. Pr'ce Henry the Navigator; ill. [Heroes of Nations] $1·50 (5/) c 8° Putnam 95
Acc. of HENRY, Duke of Viseu, 4th son of JOHN I of Portugal: 'the originator of continuous modern discovery', patron of the earliest voyages to India *via* the Cape.

Major, R. H. Discoveries of Pr'ce Henry & their Results; maps & ill. 15/ 8° Low [68] 77

„ Life of Pr'ce Henry, the Navigator; ill. *o.p.* [*pb.* 25/] i 8° Asher 68

HIUEN TSIANG (YUAN CHWANG) [7 cent.] Si-yu-ki: Buddh. records of Western World [tr.], 2 v.—*ut* **A** § 10

Hwui + Yen-Tsung Life of Hiuen Tsiang [tr.]—*ut* **A** § 10

Walters, Thos. On Yuan Chwang's Travels in India, ed. T. W. Rhys Davids + S. W. Bushell, 2 vols. [Oriental Tr. Fund] 8° Roy. Asiatic Soc. 04–5

JOURDAIN, Jno. Journal of Voy. to E. Indies: 1608–17, ed. W. Foster; 4 maps 8° Hakluyt Soc. 05

LANCASTER, Sir Jas. Voyages; *with* Voyage of Cpt. Jas. Knight, ed. C. R. Markham 8° Hakluyt Soc. 77

VAN LINSCHOTEN, J. H. Voy. to E. Indies, Bk. i, ed. A. C. Burnell + P. A. Tiele, 2 v. 8° Hakluyt Soc. 85
Ed. fr. Engl. tr. of 1598. This First Bk. conts. his *Descrn. of the East*, vol. i, ed. BURNELL; ii ed. TIELE. Also in ARBER'S *English Garner*, vol. iv [*ut* **K** § 89].

McCRINDLE, J. W. [tr.] Ancient India, as descr. by Megasthenes & Arrian [tr. selns.] 7/6 p 8° Paul 77

„ [tr.] Ancient India as descr. by Ktesias, the Knidian [tr. selns.] 7/6 p 8° Paul 82

„ [tr.] Ancient India as descr. by Ptolemy [tr. selns.] 7/6 p 8° Paul 85

„ [tr.] Invasion of India by Alexander the Great 18/ *n.* 8° Constable 93
Trs. of such portions of wrgs. of ARRIAN, Q. CURTIUS, DIODORUS, PLUTARCH, JUSTIN, and other classical authors as descr. ALEX.'s campaigns in Afghan., Punjab, Sind, Gedrosia, Karmania; w. Introd. (contg. life of ALEXANDER), appendices, and copious notes. Maps and ill. of coins.

„ Ancient India as descr. in Classical Literature 7/6 *n.* 8° Constable 01

MAJOR, R. H. [ed.] India in the Fifteenth Century 8° Hakluyt Soc. 57
Narrative of early voyages precedg. the Portug. discovery of C. of Gd. Hope: tr. fr. Latin, Pers., Russ., and Ital. sources.

MANUCCI, N. Storio do Mogor: Mogul India, 1653–1708, tr. Wm. Irvine; w. Introd. and notes, 3 vols. [Indian Texts Ser.] ea. 12/ *n.* 8° Murray 07

OATEN, E. F. European Travellers in India dur. 15–17 Cents. 3/6 *n.* c 8° Paul 09

POLO, Marco [13 cent.] —*v.* **E** § 31

PURCHAS, Sam. —*in his* Pilgrimes, 20 vols., *ut* **E** § 5

PYRARD, Frc. [17 cent.] Voyage to E. Indies, Maldives, etc. [tr.]—*ut* **E** § 36 [1601–11]

RENNELL, Maj. Jas. [1742–1830]

Markham, Clements R. Major Rennell and Rise of English Geography 3/6 c 8° Cassell 95
RENNELL served at siege of Pondicherry [1761], and 5 years later left the navy, entering service of East India Co. as engineer; author of *The Geograph. System of Herodotus* [1800], *Compar. Geogr. of Western Asia* [1831; w. atlas]; *Illns. of Hist. of Expedn. of Cyrus and Retreat of Ten Thousand* [1816], *Investign. of Currents of Atlantic Ocean*, etc.

ROE, Sir Thos. [17 cent.] Embassy of, to Ct. of Gt. Mogul, ed. Wm. Foster, 2 v. [1615–9] 8° Hakluyt Soc. 99
A revised text of ROE'S *Journal*, contg. his narr. of his jy., w. extrs. fr. his letters, etc. Maps and ill.

ROSE (Sir Thos.) + FRYER (Dr Jno). Travels in India in the 17th Century *o.p.* [*pb.* 7/6] 8° Trübner 73

SIDI ALI REÏS [16 cent.] Travels and Adventures, tr. A. Vambéry; w. notes—*ut* **E** § 33 [1553–6]

*TAVERNIER, Bar J. B. Travels in India, tr. Prf. V. Ball, 2 v.; maps & ill. 42/ ($12) m 8° Macmillan 89
Tr. fr. Fch. edn. of 1676. Prev. tr. in HARRIS' *Coll. of Voyages* [1744–8] 1764. TAVERNIER has long been known as one of most import. travellers of 17 cent., and this is a literal tr. of portn. of his *Travels*, wh. rel. to India w. identificns. of localities w. mod sites, and elucidns. of obscure points.

Joret, Prf. Chas. J. B. Tavernier d'après documts. nouveaux [exhaustive] 7 fr. 50 8° Plon, *Paris* 86

TWINING, Thos. Travels in India 100 Years Ago; maps and port. 16/ 8° Osgood 93
Ed. Rev. Wm. H. G. TWINING. TWINING was a Civil Servt. of H.E.I. Co. Incl. also a visit to United States.

DELLA VALLE, Pietro [17 cent.] Travels to India, ed. E. Grey, 2 vols. 8° Hakluyt Soc. 92
Della VALLE visited India in earlier pt. of 17 cent., ab. 100 yrs. after Portuguese had been there. With Life of VALLE.

di VARTHEMA, Lud. Travels in Egypt, Syria, Arab., Pers., India, etc. [tr.]—*ut* **E** § 30 [1503–8]

VESPUCCI, Amerigo [1451–1521] Voyage fr. Lisbon to Ind., tr. C. H. Coote; notes 15/ *n.* 8° B. F. Stevens 94
Voy. of 1505–6. Facs. of a rare tract, w. tr. and notes. The *Prologue* is learned, but not very lucid.

YOUAN CHWANG —*v.* Hiuen Tsang, *sup.*

**Recent Travel and Description**

ABBOTT, G. F. Through India with the Prince 12/6 *n.* 8° Arnold 06

ABERIGH-MACKAY, Geo. Twenty-one Days in India; ill. 6/ W. H. Allen [81] 95

ARNOLD, Sir Edwin India Revisited; 32 pl. [visit of 1885] 6/ c 8° Trübner (Paul) [86] 91

BALL, Prf. V. Jungle Life in India: jys. and jls.; ill. 25/ r 8° De La Rue 80

BLAVATSKY, Mme. H. P. From the Caves and Jungles of Hindostan [tr.]—*ut* **A** § 94

BRADLEY, Shelland An American Girl in India [6/ Bell] $1·75 c 8° Macmillan, *N.Y.* 07

BREMNER, [Mrs] Christina S. A Month in a Dandi 6/ 8° Simpkin 91
A fresh, discursive descrn. of a jy. fr. Delhi to Simla, w. last 2 chs. on Natl. Indn. Congress and on 'the growing poverty of India'.

BROWNING, Oscar Impressions of Indian Travel 3/6 *n.* c 8° Hodder 03
Travel chiefly in North-West Provinces and Calcutta, Delhi, Benares, Agra, Baroda, Bombay.

BURTON, E. F. An Indian Olio *o.p.* [*pb.* 7/6] 8° Blackett 88

CAINE, W. S. Picturesque India; ill. [descrn. of tour] 10/6 c 8° Routledge [90] *n.d.*

CAIRD, Sir J. India: the Land and the People; map 7/6 8° Cassell [83] 84

CARPENTER, Edw. From Adam's Peak to Elephanta; ill. [Ceyl. & India] 4/6 c 8° Sonnenschein [92] 03

CHEVRILLON, André Romantic India [tr.] 7/6 *n.* 8° Heinemann 97
The scenery and incidents of a winter trip, by a Frenchman thoroughly fair to Brit. rule.

CONWAY, Moncure D. My Pilgrimage to Wise Men of East; ill. $3 *n.* 8° Houghton, *Boston* 06
12/6 *n.* Constable. Chiefly memories of and conversns. w. Buddhists, Brahmins, Parsees, Moslems in India, w. observns. on country.

COTTON, [Sir] H. J. S. —*in his* Colonies & Dependencies, Pt. i [Engl. Citizen Ser.] 3/6 c 8° Macmillan 82

CRAIK, Sir Hy. Impressions of India 3/ *n.* (90 c. *n.*) c 8° Macmillan 08

CRANE, Walt. India Impressions; w. notes on Ceylon; ill. 7/6 *n.* 8° Methuen 07
$2·50 *n.* Macmillan, *N.Y.* Of interest for its 300 clever black-and-white illns. Text is of no value whatever.

CUTHELL (Edith) + BURRELL (Cpt. W. S.) Indian Memories *o.p.* [*pb.* 6/] c 8° Bentley 93
The plains, hills, temples, zenanas, camp life, the mutiny, 'Black Hole' of Calcutta, etc.

DEL MAR, Walt. India of To-day: a bk. of travel; 32 pl. [$2·75 *n.* Macm., *N.Y.*] 6/ *n.* 8° Black 05

" The Romantic East; 64 pl. 10/6 8° Black 06
$2·75 *n.* Macmillan, *N.Y.* Burma, Assam, Kashmir.

DILKE, Sir C. W. —*in his* Greater Britain: record of travel [1866–7], *ut* **E** § 21

DUFF, Sir M. E. Grant —*in his* Notes from a Diary, *ut* **F** § 27 [Author was Gov. of Madras]

FORREST, G. W. [ed.] Selns. fr. Travels & Jls. in Bomb. Secretariat [1826–43] 8° Gov. Centr. Pr., *Bomb.* 06

FORSYTH, J. The Highlands of Central India *o.p.* [*pb.* 18/] 8° Chapman 71

FRASER, Dav. The Short Cut to India; 83 ill. 12/6 *n.* 8° Blackwood 09
Conts. careful notes and sound views on the Baghdad Railway.

HEADLAM, Cecil 10,000 miles through India and Burma—*ut* **I** § 161

'HOBBES, John Oliver' [Mrs P. M. T. CRAIGIE] Imperial India 1/ c 8° Unwin [03] 03
Notes and impressions of the great Durbar, 1902, and of the guests there.

HOBBES, R. G. Reminiscences of Seventy Years' Life, Travel, & Adventures, 2 v. ea. 15/ 8° Stock 93–5
Vol. i: *Soldiering in India* was pubd. *sub nom.* 'A Retired Officer of H.M. Civil Service'.

HOLDITCH, Col. Sir Thos. The Gates of India: histor. narr.; maps 10/ *n.* ($3·25 *n.*) 8° Macmillan 10
A valuable contribn. to frontier hist., by one who has had 20 yrs.' experce. in delimitn. of frontiers, esp. Indian Borderland.

HUNTER, Sir W. W. The Indian Empire: people, history and products—*ut* **F** § 62

JERVIS, Lt.-Col. W. P. [1797–1857] Thomas Bert Jervis 7/6 c 8° Stock 98
A good account of Jervis' geographical (and other) work in India.

KARAGEORGEVITCH, Pr'ce B. Enchanted India [tr.] 5/ c 8° Harper 99

KERR, S. Parnell From Charing Cross to Delhi; ill. 10/6 *n.* 8° Unwin 06
Discursive acc. of visits to Bombay, Ahmedabad, Agra, and Delhi.

KIPLING, Rudyard Letters of Marque—*ut* **K** § 89

KLEIN, Augusta Among the Gods: scenes of India; ill. 15/ 8° Blackwood 95

KNOX, T. W. Boy Travellers in the Far East, Pt. iii; ill. $2 c 8° Harper 02
Advents. of 2 youths in jy. to Ceylon and India, w. descrns. of Borneo, Philippine Isls., Burmah.

LANDON, P. Under the Sun; ill. 12/6 *n.* 8° Hurst 06

'LOTI Pierre' [=Julien VIAUD] India [tr.], ed. R. H. Sherard; front. 10/6 *n.* 8° Laurie 06

LOW, Sid. A Vision of India 10/6 *n.* 8° Smith & Elder 06
A newsppr.-correspondent's acc. of tour of Prince and Princess of Wales; w. shrewd observns. on condn. of India.

MALCOLM, Ian Indian Pictures and Problems; ill. 10/6 *n.* 8° Richards 07
Travel-sketches and reflections in India and in Burma. Partly repr. fr. English periodicals.

MURDOCH, W. G. Burn From Edinburgh to India and Burma 10/6 *n.* 8° Routledge 08
$3·50 *n.* Dutton, *N.Y.* A lively and familiar narr., by the artist-author, w. excellent col. and other illns.

MURRAY, Jno. [pb.] Habk. for India, Burma, and Ceylon; maps 20/ s 8° Murray [ ] 11

POLLOK, Lt.-Col. F. T. Fifty Years' Reminiscences of India 16/ 8° Arnold 96

POWER, Maud Wayside India; ill. by author 21/ r 8° Simpkin 06

PRINSEP, Val. C. Imperial India; maps and ill. *o.p.* [*pb.* 21/] 8° Bentley [79] 79

REED, Stanley The Royal Tour in India; ill.
The offic. recd. of tour of Pr'ce and Pr'ess of Wales in India and Burma. Good descriptive journalism.

REES, J. D. Duke of Clarence and Avondale in Southern India; ill. 31/6 r 8° Paul 91

" Lord Connemara's Tours in India: 1886–1890; maps 15/ m 8° Paul 92

ROBINSON, Phil. Under the Punkah 5/ c 8° Low 81

" In my Indian Garden 3/6 c 8° Low [78] 78

RONALDSHAY, Earl of —*in his* Sport and Politics Under an Eastern Sky, *ut* **E** § 31

RUSSELL, Dr [Sir] W. H. Prince of Wales' Tour in India; richly ill. 52/6 r 4° Low [77] 77

SCIDMORE, Eliza R. Winter India; 43 ill. $2 8° Century Co., *N.Y.* 03
10/6 *n.* Unwin. An intelligent and well-ill. acc. of an Amer. lady's expernces. dur. a jy. fr. Ceylon to the Khâibar.

SLEEMAN, Maj.-Gen. Sir W. H. Rambles & Recollns. of an Indian Official, 2 v. 12/ *n.* c 8° Constable [44] 93
Ed. V. A. SMITH. The former edn. has col. pl. In its day a very popular bk.; remains still fresh and of value.

STEEVENS, G. W. In India 6/ c 8° Blackwood 99
$1·50 Dodd & Mead, *N.Y.* Vivid impressionist sketches of India, political, social, and industrial. Cheap edn. 1/ *n.* f 8° Nelson.

STRATTON, A. W. [Canad.] Letters from India [N.-W. India and Kashmir] 10/6 *n.* 8° Constable 08

TEMPLE, Sir Rich. Jls. in Hyderabad, Kashmir, Sikkhim, Nepal, 2 v.; ill. 32/ 8° W. H. Allen 87

" Bird's-Eye View of Picturesque India; 32 ill. 6/ c 8° Chatto 98

WALLACE, Sir D. M. Web of Empire 21/ *n.* r 8° Macmillan 02
Diary of the imperial tour of Duke and Duchess of Cornwall and York in 1901.

WEEKES, Edwin Lord —*in his* From the Black Sea thro' Persia and India, *ut* **E** § 38

WHEELER, G. India in 1875–6 [visit of Pr'ce of Wales] 12/ p 8° Chapman 76

WHITNEY, Caspar Jungle Trails and Jungle People; ill. $3 *n.* 8° Scribner, *N.Y.* 06
12/ *n.* Laurie. Good illns., w. interestg. acc. of jungle-life in India, Sumatra, Malay, Siam.

WILLIAMS, Sir Monier Modern India and the Indians [Trübner's Orient. Ser.] 14/ 8° Paul [78] 87

WORKMAN, Dr W. H. + Mrs Thro' Town and Jungle; 200 ill. [2,000-m. cycle-tour] 21/ *n.* r 8° Unwin 04

**Indian Government Surveys** —*v. also* **I** § 3

BLACK, Chas. E. D. Memoir of Indian Surveys: 1875–1890; map [Ind. Off. pub.] 7/6 i 8° Stanford 91
Marine, trigon., topogr., revenue, geogr. survs.; Afgh. Boundary Commn.; Tidal and Levellg. obsns.; geodetic obsns.; geol. survs.; met., statist. survs., archæol. survs., etc.

MARKHAM, Clements R. Memoir of Indian Surveys, maps [Ind. Off. pub.] 10/6 i 8° Paul [71] 78

**Cities:** FORREST (G. W.) Cities of India, Past and Present; ill. 5/ *n.* 8° Constable [03] 05

LANDON, Perceval Under the Sun: impressns. of Indian cities; 19 pl. (7 col.) 12/6 *n.* 8° Hurst 06

**Scenery, etc.**

ADAMS, W. H. D. India, Pictorial and Descriptive [popular] 10/6 f° Nelson 87

MENPES, Mortimer [artist] India: 75 col. pl., w. l'rpr. F. A. Steel [$6 *n.* Macm., *N.Y.*] 20/ *n.* sq 8° Black 05

MURRAY, A. H. Hallam [art.] The Highroad of Empire; ill. (some col.) 21/ *n.* s 4° Murray 05

RAVEN-HILL, L. [artist] Indian Sketch-Bk.: impressns. of East and Durbar; ill. 2/6 *n.* 4° *Punch* Off. [03] 05

ROUSSELET, Louis India and its Native Princes [tr.]; richly ill. 42/ 4° Bickers [73] 77

SIMPSON [artist] India, Ancient and Modern: 50 col. pl.; w. text [Sir] J. W. Kaye, 2 vols. *o.p.* [*pb.* £24 3/] i f° *London* 70

URWICK, Rev. W. Indian Pictures drawn w. Pen and Pencil; ill. [picture-bk.] 8/ i 8° R.T.S. 81

**East India Company** —*v. also* **F** § 62 (esp. Hunter, Hist. of Br. Ind.)

*Bibliography* —*in* East India Co.'s Catalogue of Lib., 2 vols. 8° East India Co. 45–51

*BIRDWOOD, Sir Geo. [ed.] —*in his* Report on the Old Records of the India Office, *ut* **F** § 62
Conts. many papers dealing w. hist. of the Company, and entries ill. of hist. of articles of trade, etc.

*BIRDWOOD, Sir Geo. + FOSTER (W.) [eds.] Register of Letters, etc., of Govr. and Co. of Merchts. of Lond. tradg. into E. Indies
1600–1619. With valuable and full introd. by BIRDWOOD dealg. w. whole hist. of Europe's trade w. East fr. earliest to pres. day.

,, + ,, [eds.] Relics of the Hon. East India Company 52/6 *n.* 4° Quaritch 09
50 facss. repr. fr. *Jl. of Indian Art* (GRIGGS) of documts., old prints, etc., w. descr. l'rpr. to each.

Calendar of State Papers : Colonial Series, vol. viii : East Indies and Persia ; 1630–1634—*ut* **F** § 33
The 5th vol. of the series [*ut* **F** § 33] wh. deals w. the fluctuating fortunes of E.I. Co. dur. earlier stages of its career.

CAREY, W. H. The Hon. John Company, 2 vols. [1600–1858] 8° 06–7

DANVERS, F. C. [ed.] List of Marine Records of late East India Co. 8° 96

East India Company's First Letter Book : 1600–1619, ed. Sir Geo. Birdwood 42/ *n.* 8° Quaritch 93
A seln. of l'rs addressed to Lond. East India Co. by their agents at Bombay, Surat, and elsewhere in East.

*FORREST, G. W. —*ut* **F** § 62

FOSTER, Wm. [ed.] The Engl. Factories in India, vols. i–v ea. 12/6 *n.* ($4·15) 8° Clar. Press 06–11, *in prg.*
A calendar of documts. in India Off., Brit. Mus., and Publ. Record Off., fr. 1618 to 1636. Import. docs. prtd. in full.

GARDINER, S. R. [ed.] Documents ill. the Impeachmt. of Buckingham [1626] s 4° Camden Soc. 89

HEDGES, [Sir] W. Diary, ed. Yule, 3 vols.—*ut sup.* [1681–7]

JOURDAIN, Jno. —*in his* Journal, *ut sup.* [1608–17]

KAYE, [Sir] J. W. Administration of the East India Company *o.p.* [*pb.* 21/] c 8° Bentley 53

KEENE, H. G. A Servant of John Company 12/ 8° Thacker 97
Reminiscs. of 35 years in India (10 in E.I. Co.'s service), throwing much light on society before and after the Mutiny.

,, Here and There ; memories Indian & other 10/6 *n.* r 8° Brown & Langham 06

LANCASTER, Sir Jas. —*in his* Voyages to East Indies, ed. C. R. Markham, *ut sup.* [1591–1613]

Letters Received by the East India Co. from its Servants in the East, 6 vols.
[1602–17] ea. 21/ *n.* ($3·75) 8° Clar. Press 96–02
Vol. i, ed. F. C. DANVERS ; ii–vi, ed. W. FOSTER. Of consid. value f. study of hist. of explorn. of India

MUN, Thos. [1571–1641] England's Treasure by Forraign Trade—*ut* **D** § 117*

MURAKAMI (N.) + MURAKAWA (K.) [eds.] —*in their* Letters wr. by Engl. Residts. in Japan, *ut* **E** § 37 [1611–23]

PENNY, Rev. F. K. The Church in Madras—*ut* **A** § 105
Acc. of the East India Co.'s missionary action in 17–18 cents. Cf. also the *Serampore Letters, ut ibid.*

PRINSEP, C. C. Record of Services of Hon. E. India Co.'s Civil Servants in Madras Presid. 1741–1858 8° 85
Incls. chronol. lists of Governors, Commanders-in-Chief, Justices, and Judges, Directors, Chairmen, Presidents.

SAINSBURY, Ethel B. [ed.] Calendar of Court Minutes of East India Co., 2 v.
[1635–43] ea. 12/6 *n.* ($4·15) 8° Clar. Press 08–9
With an Introduction (32 pp.) by W. FOSTER and notes by him. The *Ct. Minutes* of the Co. prev. to 1635 are calendared in the *Calendars of State Papers*, vol. viii, *ut sup.*

SARIS, Cpt. Jno. —*in his* Voyage to Japan, *ut* **E** § 37 [1613]

STEVENS, Hy. [Am. ; ed.] Dawn of British Trade in East Indies 25/ 8° Stevens & Son 87
Printed fr. MS. *Court Minutes* of East India Company : 1599–1603. Conts. account of formation of the Company.

*Biographies* of BENTINCK *and* CANNING—*v.* **F** § 62

**Life and People :** *Native* —*v. also* **A** § 105 : Missions

AITKEN, E. H. Behind the Bungalow c 8° *Calcutta* [89] 90

' ARTIST, AN ' [Colesworthy GRANT] Rural Life in Bengal ; 166 ill. *o.p.* [*pb.* 18/] 8° Thacker 60

BOSE, Shib Chundar Hindoos as They are [manners, customs, domestic life] 12/6 8° *Calcutta* [ ] 83

BROUGHTON, Maj. T. D. Letters from a Mahratta Camp ; ill. 6/ *n.* c 8° Constable [13] 93
[Oriental Miscellany.] Affords a striking picture of native life in India in 1809. Introd. by Sir M. E. Grant DUFF.

BUTLER, Dr W. The Land of the Veda ; ill. $2 8° Eaton & Mains, *N.Y.* [71] 06
Reminiscs. of the people, castes, thugs, fakirs, religions, mythology, monumts., palaces, etc.

CAIRD, Sir J. —*in his* India, *ut sup.*

CARSTAIRS, R. Human Nature in Rural India [Lower Bengal] 6/ c 8° Blackwood 95
Incls. a thoro' *exposé* of ' venality of our native police ', favourg. syst. of village govt. thro' elective headmen.

COMPTON, Herb. Indian Life in Town and County ; ill. [Our Empire ser.] 3/6 *n.* c 8° Newnes 04

CROOKE, Wm. Things Indian : discursive notes on various subjects 12/ *n.* 8° Murray 06
Quaint and curious matters conn. w. India not specifically considered in ordin. bks. of referce.

CUST, R. N. Pictures of Indian Life [1852–81] *o.p.* [*pb.* 7/6] c 8° Trübner 81

DAS, Devendra N. Sketches of Hindoo Life *o.p.* [*pb.* 5/] 8° Chapman 87

DASS, Rev. Ishuree Domestic Manners and Customs of Hindus
[N.-W. Prov.] *o.p.* [*pb.* 7/6] 12° *Benares* [ ] 66

DAY, Rev. Lal Behári Bengal Peasant Life *o.p.* [*pb.* 6/] c 8° Macmillan [74] 80
1st edn. pub. *sub tit. Govinda Sámanta, or History of a Bengal Ráiyat*, 2 vols., 1874.

DUBOIS, Abbé J. A. Hindu Manners, Customs, and Ceremonies [tr.]—*ut* **A** § 14

**Dutt**, Ramesh Chunder — The Peasantry of Bengal — *o.p.* 8° *Calcutta* 64

'**Eha**' [E. H. **Aitken**] — Behind the Bungalow; 47 ill. [character-sketches of servants] 6/ c 8° Thacker, *Calcutta* 89

„ — Tribes on my Frontier; ill. 6/ c 8° Thacker, *Calcutta* 83

**Fraser**, Sir Andr. H. L. — Among Indian Rajahs and Ryots; 34 ill. 18/ *n.* m 8° Seeley [11] 11

**Frere**, Sir H. Bartle — Pandurang Hari, 2 vols. [memoir of a Hindoo] *o.p.* [*pb.* 21/] c 8° H. S. King [73] 73

**Fuller**, Sir Bamfylde — Studies of Indian Life and Sentiment; map 6/ *n.* c 8° Murray 10

**Gomes**, L. Luiz — The Brahmans, tr. J. de Silva 3/6 8° *Bombay* 89
Tr. from the Portuguese. A delineation of Anglo-Indian society previous to the Mutiny of 1857.

**Gore**, F. St J. — Lights and Shades of Indian Hill Life; maps and ill. 31/6 m 8° Murray 96

**Grierson**, G. A. — Bihar Peasant Life; ill. fr photos. *o.p.* [*pb.* 15/] r 8° *Calcutta* 85
A 'Discursive Catal. of the Surroundings of the People', prep. und. orders of Bengal Govt. A valuable wk., the 'remainder' of wh. was carelessly 'wasted' by Bengal Govt. in 1893.

**Hodgson**, B. H. — —*in his* Miscellaneous Essays rel. to Indian Subjects, 2 vols., *ut* **K** § 128

**Hurst**, Dr J. F. — Indika: country & people of India & Ceylon; ill. $5 4° Harper, *N.Y.* 91

**Jones**, Dr Jno. P. — India: its life and thought; ill. $2·50 *n.* (10/6 *n.*) 8° Macmillan 08

**Kipling**, J. L. — Beast and Man in India; ill. 7/6 ($2·25) c 8° Macmillan [91] 92

**Lyall**, Sir A. C. — —*in his* Asiatic Studies, Religious and Social, 2 vols., *ut* **A** § 9

**Monier-Williams**, Sir Monier—*in his* Modern India, *ut sup.*

**Morrison**, Rev. Jno. — —*in his* New Ideals in India during the Nineteenth Century, *ut* **A** § 14

**Nagesh Wishwanath Pai** — Stray Sketches in Chakmakpore 8° Kane, *Bombay* 95
A series of sketches of native life fr. native pt.-of-view. Of some interest to Western readers.

**Nevinson**, H. W. — —*in his* The New Spirit in India, *ut sup.*

**Newcombe**, A. C. — Village, Town, and Jungle Life in India; 30 pl. 12/6 *n.* 8° Blackwood 05
Expereces. of 28 yrs.' wk. as engineer am. canals and rys. of India fr. Bolan Pass to Trichinopoli.

**Nivedita**, Sister [Marg. E. **Noble**] The Web of Indian Life 7/6 8° Heinemann 04

**Oman**, Dr J. C. — —*in his* Cults and Customs, *his* Mystics, *his* Brahmans, *ut* **A** § 14

**Padfield**, Rev. J. E. — The Hindu at Home: sketches of daily life 3/6 *n.* 8° Simpkin 96
An interesting little bk., by a member of Church Missy. Soc.'s estab. at Masulipatam, S. India, dealg. w. superstns. and customs of Hindus.

**Pandian**, Rev. T. B. — Indian Village Folk: their works and ways 4/6 c 8° Stock 98

**Prichard**, Iltudus T. — Chronicles of Budgepore: sketches of life in Up. India 6/ c 8° W. H. Allen [80] 93

**Ramakrishna**, T. — Life in an Indian Village 6/ c 8° Unwin 91
A sketch of Indian village society from the inside; w. Introd. by Sir M. E. Grant **Duff**.

**Rice**, Rev. Hy. — Native Life in Southern India; ill. fr. native sources 2/6 c 8° R.T.S. 89

**Rice**, Stanley P. — Occasional Essays on Native S. Indian Life 10/6 ($3·50) 8° Longman 01
Slight essays describing the customs and folk-lore of the Urijas of Ganjam.

**Sorabji**, Cornelia — Love and Life behind the Purdah 3/6 c 8° Constable 01
Stories illustrating the life of Indian women, by an Indian woman. Introd. by Lord **Hobhouse**.

„ — Sun-Babies: studies in child-life in India 6/ *n.* 8° Murray 04

„ — Between the Twilights [studies of Indian women] 5/ *n.* c 8° Harper 08

**Thomas**, F. W. — Mutual Influence of Mohammedans & Hindus in India 2/6 8° Deighton, *Camb.* 92

**Wilkins**, W. J. — Daily Life and Work in India; 59 ill. 3/6 c 8° Unwin [87] 90

„ — —*in his* Modern Hinduism, *ut* **A** § 14

**Yusuf-Ali**, Abdullah — Life and Labour of People of India; ill. 12/ *n.* 8° Murray 07

***Women; Zenana Life*** — —*for* Missions *v.* **A** § 105

**Billington**, Mary Fces. — Woman in India; ill. 14/ 8° Chapman 95
On Hindu, Mussulman, and Parsee women; only incidentally with Native Christians and Eurasians. Deep sympathy w. the natives.

**Lloyd**, Helen — Hindu Women: w. glimpses into life and zenanas 2/6 c 8° Nisbet 81

'***Peerage*' *of India*:** **Lethbridge** (Sir R.) Golden Book of India *o.p.* [*pb.* 40/] r 8° Macmillan 93
A geneal. and biograph. dict. of the ruling princes, chiefs, nobles, and other persons, titled or decorated, of Ind. Emp.

***European Life in India***

**Arbuthnot**, Sir A. J. — Memories of Rugby and India—*ut* **D** § 157

**Bell**, J. H. — British Folks and British India Fifty Years Ago 6/ 8° Heywood, *Mancs.* 91

**Buckland**, C. T. — Sketches of Social Life in England 5/ c 8° W. H. Allen 84

**Curstairs**, R. — British Work in India 6/ c 8° Blackwood 91
A clear descrn. of the fabric of Indian social and political life, and of British responsibilities in India.

'**Cheem**, Aliph' [=Walt. **Yeldham**] Lays of Ind; 70 ill. [comic poems descrg. Ang.-Ind. soc. life] 10/6 o 8° Thacker, *Calc.* [ ] 89

**Cox**, Sir Edm. — My Thirty Years in India 8/ *n.* 8° Mills & Boon 09

CURRIE, Maj.-Gen. F. Below the Surface 6/ c 8° Constable 00
A study of the life of the English official and Indian native, and their mutual relations.

DIVER, Maud The Englishwoman in India 5/ *n.* c 8° Blackwood 09
Devoted partly to work, etc., of Englishwomen in India, partly to that of pioneer native women.

DUFFERIN, Marchioness of Our Viceregal Life in India [selns. fr. her Jl.; 1884–8] 7/6 c 8° Murray [89] 90

DUNN, Sarah H. Sunny Memories of an Indian Winter; 14 ill. 6/ 8° Walt. Scott 98

EDEN, Hon. Emily Up the Country *o.p.* [*pb.* 6/] c 8° Bentley [66] 66
Letters from the Upper Provinces of India. A more or less standard bk.

,, Letters from India, ed. by her Niece, 2 vols. *o.p.* [*pb.* 21/] c 8° Bentley 72

KING, Mrs R. Moss Diary of Civilian's Wife in India, 2 vols. [1877–82] *o.p.* [*pb.* 24/] c 8° Bentley 85

'RETIRED CHAPLAIN (A)' Episodes in Life of an Indian Chaplain 12/6 c 8° Low 82

RIVETT-CARNAC, Col. J. H. Many Memories of Life in India, etc. 10/6 *n.* 8° Blackwood [10] 10

THORNHILL, Mark Haunts and Hobbies of an Indian Official 6/ c 8° Murray 99

WILSON, Anne C. After Five Years in India; ill. 6/ c 8° Blackie 95
A pleasant sketch of daily life and wk. in outlying station in Punjaub, w. addit. chs. on Engl. systs. of admin. and educn.

WILSON, L'y Letters from India 7/6 *n.* 8° Blackwood 11
A series of fascinatg. letters, paintg. Indian scenes, Anglo Indian life, etc.

## SEPARATE PRESIDENCIES, PROVINCES, AND DISTRICTS

**Assam:** HUNTER (Sir W. W.) Statistical Account of Assam, 2 vols.; maps 15/ 8° Trübner 79

KINNEY, T. Old Times in Assam 5/ 8° *Calcutta* 96
Humorous sketches and stories, depicting life in the tea-gardens of Assam.

*Manipur:* GRIMWOOD (Ethel St C.) My Three Years in Manipur *o.p.* [*pb.* 15/] 8° Bentley 91

JOHNSTONE, Maj.-Gen. Sir Jas. My Experiences in Manipur and Naga Hills 16/ 8° Low 96
Furnishes a vivid picture of daily life and occupns. of an Indian official in an outlying district.

*Mishmi Country:* COOPER (T. T.) The Mishmee Hills—*ut* **E** § 34, *s.v.* Tibet

**Bengal** —*v. also sup., s.nn.* DAY, GRANT

BHOLANAUTH, CHUNDER Travels of a Hindu, 2 vols. *o.p.* [*pb.* 21/] 8° Trübner 69

CUNNINGHAM, Lt.-Col. D. D. Plagues and Pleasures of Life in Bengal; ill.—*ut* **I** § 46

GUTHRIE, Kath. B. My Year in an Indian Fort, 2 vols. [Belgaum] 21/ c 8° Hurst 77

,, Life in Western India, 2 vols. 21/ c 8° Hurst 81

HEDGES, [Sir] Wm. Diary, ed. Col. H. Yule, 3 vols.—*ut sup.* [1681–87]

HILL, S. C. [ed.] Bengal in 1756–57, 3 vols.; w. Introd. and notes 12/ *n.* 8° Murray 05
Pub. for Indian Govt. Seln. of publ. & priv. pprs. dealg. w. Brit. affairs in Bengal dur. rn. of SIRAJ-UDDAULA, inclg. Black Hole of Calcutta episode.

HUNTER, Sir W. W. Annals of Rural Bengal 7/6 c 8° Smith & Elder [68–72] 97
A description, by an eye-witness, of Bengal during the great famine of 1865–6.

,, Statistical Account of Bengal, 20 vols. [Ind. Off. pubn.] £5 8° *Poona* 77

,, Bombay: 1885–90 [study in administrn.] 15/ 8° Clar. Press 92

,, [ed.] Bengal MS. Records; w. hist. dissn. & index, 4 vols. 30/ 8° W. H. Allen 94
14,136 letters in Bd. of Revenue, Calc., 1782–1807, under Govr.-Generalships of HASTINGS, CORNWALLIS, and WELLESLEY, illg. status of Bengal landholders and condn. of landed prop. in Beng. at the time when British admin. was beginning to take shape. Compiled after manner of *Calendars of State Papers* pubd. by Master of Rolls.

,, The Old Missionary—*ut* **A** § 105

HUTCHISSON, W. H. F. Pen and Pencil Sketches: 18 yrs. in Bengal; ill. 18/ 8° Low 83

'EX-CIVILIAN' Life in the Mofussil, 2 vols. *o.p.* [*pb.* 14/] c 8° Paul 78

S., C. Leaves fr. a Diary in Lower Bengal; maps & ill. [1862–70] 21/ *n.* 4° Macmillan 96

SAMBHUCHANDRA Travels, etc., between Calcutta and Tipperah *o.p.* 8° 87

*Behar:* GRIERSON (G. A.) Bihar Peasant Life—*ut sup., s.v.* Life and People

*Calcutta:* BLECHYNDEN (Kath.) Calcutta, Past and Present 7/ f 8° Thacker, *Calc.* 05

BUSTEED, H. E. Echoes fr. Old Calcutta; ill. [1753–1835] 7/6 c 8° Thacker, *Calc.* [82] 97

COTTON, H. E. A. Calcutta, Old and New; ill. [1011 pp.] 8° Newman, *Calc.* 07

*Chin Lushai Land:* REID (Surg.-Lt.-Col. A. S.) Chin-Lushai Land; ill. 18/ 8° Thacker, *Calcutta* 94

*Chittagong:* LEWIN (Maj. T. H.) A Fly on the Wheel—*ut sup.* [*v. also* Ethnol., *sup.*]

*Chota Nagpore:* BRADLEY-BIRT (F. B.) Chota Nagpore; Introd. L'd Northbrook; ill. 12/6 *n.* 8° Smith & Elder [03] 10

*Dacca:* BRADLEY-BIRT (F. B.) Romance of an Eastern Capital 12/6 *n.* 8° Smith & Elder 06

*Dwars:* LOUIS (J. H.) —*in his* At the Gates of Tibet, *ut* **E** § 34

*Kistna:* MACKENZIE (Gordon) Manual of Kistna District; maps r 8° *Madras* 83

*Lushai:* WOODTHORPE (R. D.) The Lushai Expedition [1871–2] *o.p.* [*pb.* 15/] 8° Hurst 73

*Orissa:* HUNTER (Sir W. W.) Orissa, 2 vols. *o.p.* 8° 72

MACPHERSON, S. C. —*in his* Memls. of Service in India, ed. W. Macpherson *o.p.* [*pb.* 12/] 8° Murray 65

*Santal Parganas :* BRADLEY-BIRT (F. B.) Story of an Indian Upland ; ill. 12/6 *n.* 8° Smith & Elder 05

**Bombay and Western India**

DOUGLAS, Jas. Bombay and Western India ; maps and ill., 2 vols. 42/ *n.* r 8° Low 93
A good deal of informn. and gossip ab. men and places and social and commerc. life of Bombay in old days. Illns. good and some very interesting.

,, Glimpses of Old Bombay and Western India [19th cent.] 20/ r 8° Low 00

Gazetteer of Bombay Presidency : vols. i–xxvii ; maps
[India Office pub.] [several *o.p.*] ea. ab. 8/ r 8° *Poona* (Paul) 76 07, *in prg.*

MALABARI, P. B. M. Bombay in the Making [1661–1726] 12/6 *n.* 8° Unwin 10

Materials towards a Statistical Account of Town and Island of Bombay, vol. i 7/6 8° Bombay (Luzac) 94

WEST, Sir Edw.
Drewitt, Dr F. D. Bombay in the Days of George IV ; ill. 9/6 *n.* ($3·50) m 8° Longman 08
Memoirs of WEST, the Chief Justice of the King's Court dur. its conflict w. the East India Co., 1818–28.

*Baroda :* Imperial Gazetteer of Baroda [Govt. pub.] 1 8° 08

*Bijápur :* COUSENS (H.) Bijápur : old cap'l of Adil Sháki kings [guide to ruins] 6/ 8° *Poona* 89

*Gujurat*

BEHRAMJI M. MALABARI Gujarat & the Gujaratis : picts. of men & manners 3/6 c 8° W. H. Allen [82] 84

FORBES, A. K. Râs Malâ : Hindoo annals 12/ c 8° Richardson [ ] 78

*Canara :* FORBES (Gordon S.) Wild Life in Canara and Ganjam ; col. pl. 6/ c 8° Sonnenschein 85

STURROCK (J.) + STUART (Har. A.) South Canara, 2 vols. [Madras Distr. Manls.] r 8° *Madras* 94–5

*Poona :* CRAWFORD (A.) Our Troubles in Poona and Deccan ; ill. 14/ 8° Constable 97

ELWIN, E. F. Indian Jottings from 10 Years' Expce. ; ill. 10/6 *n.* 8° Murray 07

**Central India :** FORSYTH (Cpt. J.) Highlands of Central India ; col. pl. 12/ 8° Chapman [72] 89

MALCOLM, J. Memoir of Central India and Malwa, 2 vols. [standard] *o.p.* 8° [23] 32

*Rajputana :* ADAMS (Arch.) Western Rajputana States 21/ 8° Jun. Army & Navy St. 99

TOD, Lt.-Col. J. Annals and Antiquities of Rajast'han, 2 vols. 1 8° [29–32] 94–5

*Satpura Mtns.* ; STERNDALE (R. A.) Seonee : camp-life on the Satpura Range 21/ 8° Low [77] 77

**Central Provinces :** GRANT (Chas.) Gazetteer of Cent. Provs. of India *o.p.* [*pb.* 24/] 8° (Paul) 70

Imperial Gazetteer of Central Provinces of India 1 8° 08

**Coorg** —*v.* Mysore and Coorg, *inf.*

**Deccan :** GRIBBLE (J. D.B.) History of the Deccan, vol. i ; ill. [1294–1723] 8° Luzac 96
A continuous narr., constructed fr. orig. matls., of a v. confused period, the Mohamm. invasion and settlement.

HAIG, T. W. Historic Landmarks of the Deccan 5/ r 8° *Calcutta* 07

KING, J. S. History of the Bahmani Dynasty [1347–1518] 8° 00

*Hyderabad :* FRASER (Cpt. H.) Our Ally the Nizam *o.p.* [*pb.* 20/] 8° Smith & Elder 65

TEMPLE, Sir Rich. —*in his* Journals, 2 vols., *ut sup.*

*Vijayanagar :* SEWELL (R.) A Forgotten Empire : Vijayanagar 15/ r 8° Sonnenschein 00

**Gwalior :** COOPLAND (R. M.) Lady's Escape fr. Gwalior and Agra *o.p.* [*pb.* 10/6] c 8° Smith & Elder 59

**Kashmir :** ADAMS (A. L.) Wanderings of a Naturalist in India *o.p.* [*pb.* 10/6] 8° *Edinburgh* 67

BELLEW, Surg.-Maj. H. W. Kashmir and Kashghar [journey 1873–4] 10/6 8° Trübner 75

DOUGHTY, Marion Afoot through the Kashmir Valleys ; ill. 7/6 *n.* r 8° Sands 02

DREW, F. Jummoo & Kashmir Territories ; maps & pl. [geogr. acc.] 42/ 8° Stanford 75

,, Northern Barrier of India ; ill. [pop. abridgmt. of above] 12/ 8° Stanford 77

v. HÜGEL, Freih. C. A. A. Travels in Kashmir and the Punjab [tr.] *o.p.* [*pb.* 18/] r 8° Petheram 45

KNIGHT, E. F. —*in his* When Three Empires Meet, *ut* **E** § 33

LAMBERT, C. Trip to Cashmere and Ladak ; ill. *o.p.* [*pb.* 7/6] c 8° H. S. King 77

LAWRENCE, Walt. R. Valley of Kashmir ; maps and 17 pl. *o.p.* [*pb.* 12/ *n.*] 4° Clar. Press 95
A wk. of lasting value, formg. record of an attempt to attack corruption and cleanse an admin. notorious for dishonesty to ruler and cruel to ruled. Author was Settlement Commissioner of Kashmir and Jammu State. Chs. on geol. and archaeol., hist., flora and fauna, trade and agric.

MOLYNEUX, Maj. E. [art.] Kashmir ; w. I'rpr. Sir F. Younghusband
[$6 *n.* Macm., *N.Y.*] 20/ *n.* sq 8° Black 09

MORISON, Marg. Cotter A Lonely Summer in Kashmir ; 50 ill. 7/6 *n.* sq 8° Duckworth 04

MURRAY-AYNSLEY, Mrs Our Visit to Kashmir, Hindostan and Ladakb 14/ 8° W. H. Allen 79

NEVE, Dr Arth. Picturesque Kashmir ; ill. G. W. Millais 12/6 *n.* r 8° Sands 00

PIRIE, P. Kashmir, Land of Streams & Solitudes ; pl. (some col.) 21/ *n.* 8° Lane 08

RONALDSHAY, Earl of —*in his* Sport and Politics under Eastern Sky, *ut* **E** § 31 [1902]

v. SCHÖNBERG, Bar. E. Travels in India and Kashmir [tr.], 2 vols. o.p. 8° 53
SWINBURNE, Maj. T. R. A Holiday in the Happy Valley ; 24 col. pl. 16/ n. 8° Smith & Elder 07
TEMPLE, Sir Rich. —*in his* Journals, 2 vols., *ut sup.* [1887]
TORRENS, Lt.-Col. H. D'O. Travels in Ladak, Tartary and Kashmir o.p. [pb. 28/] 8° Saunders 62
WAKEFIELD, Dr W. Kashmir, the Happy Valley ; ill. o.p. [pb. 15/] 8° Low 79
*Karakoram Himalayas* —v. Himalayas, *inf.* (CONWAY ; ECKENSTEIN]

**Madras** (Presidency)
Imperial Gazetteer of the Madras Presidency, 2 vols. 1 8° 08
Manual of Administration of Madras Presidency, 3 vols. [vol. iii is Glossary] f° *Madras* 85–93
SRINIVASA RAGHAVAIYANGAR Memr. on Progr. of Madr. dur. last 40 Yrs. 8° 93
*Arcot:* COX (A. F.) North Arcot, ed. H. A. Stuart, 2 v. [Madr. Distr. Manls.] r 8° *Madras* 94–5
*Coromandel Coast:* PENNY (Mrs F. E.) On the Coromandel Coast 10/6 n. 8° Smith & Elder 08
*Cuddapah:* GRIBBLE (J. D. B.) Manual of Distr. of Cuddapah r 8° *Madras* 75
*Ganjam:* FORBES (G. S.) Wild Life in Canara and Ganjam—*ut sup.*, *s.v.* Bombay (Canara)
*Godavari:* MORRIS (Hy.) Descr. and Histor. Acc. of Godavery District o.p. [pb. 12/] 8° Trübner 78
*Madras* (City): LAWSON (Sir A. Chas.) Memories of Madras ; ill. 10/6 n. 8° Sonnenschein 05
Sketches of men and events in old Madras, fr. archives of Brit. Museum and India Office.
*Fort St George:* PENNY (Mrs Fk.) Fort St George, Madras ; ill. [a history] 10/6 n. 8° Sonnenschein 00
Pringle, Arth. [ed.] Diary and Consultation-Bk. of Agent Governor and Council of Fort St George: 95
Some useful matl., fr. wh. some idea of Madras 200 yrs. ago may be gleaned, and fr. what origins Hon. E.I. Co. sprang.
Records of Fort St George [1748] 8° 08
*Nellore:* BOSWELL (J. A. C.) Manual of the Nellore District ; maps r 8° *Madras* 73
*Nilgiri Hills:* BURTON (Sir R. F.) Goa and the Blue Mountains o.p. [pb. 10/6] c 8° Bentley 51
FLETCHER, F. W. F. Sport on the Nilgiris and in Wynaad—*ut* **I** § 147
GRIGG, H. B. Manl. of Nilgiri District ; maps and ill. [Distr. Manls.] 30/ 8° *Madras* 80
*Tinnevelly:* CALDWELL (R.) History of Tinnevelly [to 1801] o.p. 8° 81

**Malabar:** BIDDULPH (Col. J.) The Pirates of Malabar, and An Englishwoman in India 200 Years Ago ; map 6/ n. c 8° Smith & Elder 07
BRUCE, Hy. Letters from Malabar and on the Way ; pl. 6/ n. 8° Routledge 09
Articles on Malabar, Cochin, and Travancore, repr. fr. *Times of India* and *Madras Mail.*

**Mysore and Coorg:** ELLIOTT (R. H.) Expercs. of a Planter in Mysore, 2 v. o.p. [pb. 24/] 8° Chapman 71
,, Gold, Sport, and Coffee Planting in Mysore ; col. map 7/6 c 8° Constable 94
Imperial Gazetteer of Mysore and Coorg 1 8° 08
RICE, B. Lewis Gazetteer of Mysore and Coorg, 3 vols. ; maps o.p. 8° Constable [76–8] 99
A very full and trustworthy work. India Office pubn.

**Nepal:** EGERTON (F.) Winter's Tour in India & Visit to Nepaul, 2 v. o.p. [pb. 18/] c 8° Murray 52
FRESHFIELD, D. W. —*in his* Round Kangchenjunga, *ut inf.*, *s.v.* Himalayas
HODGSON, B. H. Essays and Lang., Liter., and Religion of Nepal—*ut* **K** § 155
,, —*in his* Papers on Colonizn., etc., *inf.* ; *and* Misc. Essays, 2 v., *ut* **K** § 128
Imperial Gazetteer of Afghanistan and Nepal—*ut* **E** § 33, *s.v.* Afghanistan
INGLIS, Jas. Sport and Work on Nepaul Frontier [by an indigo-planter] o.p. 8° 78
LANDOR, A. H. Savage —*in his* Tibet and Nepal Painted and Described, *ut* **E** § 34, *s.v.* Tibet
OLIPHANT, Laur. A Journey to Katmandu o.p. [pb. 2/6] c 8° Murray 52
Parbatiya: tr. Munshi Shew Shunker Singh + Shri Gunanand 10/6 r 8° Camb. Press 77
Ed. Dr Daniel WRIGHT. A history of Nepal; w. facs. illns.
SMITH, Cpt. T. Five Years' Residence at Nepaul, 2 vols. [1841–5] o.p. c 8° 52
TEMPLE, Sir Rich. —*in his* Journals, 2 vols., *ut sup.*

**North-West Provinces** —v. United Provinces of Agra and Oudh, *inf.*

**Punjab:** ELSMIE (G. R.) Thirty-five Years in the Punjab ; ports. 9/ n. 8° Douglas, *Edin.* 08
Gives a fairly good idea of the life and progress of a Civil officer in the Punjab, 1858–93.
GORE, F. St J. Lights and Shades of Hill Life—*ut inf.*, *s.v.* Himalayas
v. HÜGEL, Freih. C. A. A. Travels in Kashmir and the Punjab [tr.]—*ut sup.*, *s.v.* Kashmir
Imperial Gazetteer of the Punjab, 2 vols. 1 8° 08
MASSY, C. F. Chiefs and Families of Note in Punjab r 8° *Allahabad* 90
MUHAMMAD LATIF, Syad History of the Punjab [written in English] 18/ 8° Low 96
From remotest antiq. to pres. times, w. a full acc. of Punjab dur. eventful yrs. of 18th cent., when Afghans and the Sikhs, maddened by relig. fanaticism, fell upon ea. other and fought w. varied success for over 100 yrs. A laborious wk., based on native tradn. and English works.

THORBURN, S. S. The Punjab in Peace and War [19 cent.] 12/6 *n.* 8° Blackwood 04
*Ambala:* Gazetteer of the Ambala District [District Gazetteers] l 8° *Lahore* 92–3
*Amritsar:* Gazetteer of the Amritsar District [Distr. Gazetteers] l 8° *Lahore* 92–3
*Bannu:* Gazetteer of the Bannu District [Distr. Gazetteers] l 8° *Lahore* 83–4
THORBURN, S. S. Bannu; or, Our Afghan Frontier *o.p.* [*pb.* 18/] 8° Trübner 76
*Delhi:* FANSHAWE (H. C.) Delhi, Past and Present; ill. 15/ *n.* 8° Murray 02
Gazetteer of the Delhi District l 8° 83–4
HEARN, G. R. The Seven Cities of Delhi 10/6 *n.* c 8° Thacker 07
*Khyber Pass* —*v.* **E** § 33
*Lahore:* MUHAMMAD LATIF Lahore—*ut* **G** § 10
*Peshawar* —*v.* **E** § 33, *s.v.* Afghanistan, Khyber Pass (TREVELYAN)
*Sikhim:* DONALDSON (Flor.) Lepcha Land; ill. 10/6 *n.* 8° Low 00
A commonplace account of six weeks spent in the Sikhim Himalayas.
FRESHFIELD, D. W. Round Kangchenjunga—*ut inf.*, *s.v.* Himalayas
LOUIS, J. A. H. At the Gates of Thibet—*ut* **E** § 34
O'CONNOR, W. F. Routes in Sikkim 00
TEMPLE, Sir Rich. C. —*in his* Journals, 2 vols., *ut sup.*
*WADDELL, Maj. L. A. Among the Himalayas—*ut inf.*, *s.v.* Himalayas
WHITE, J. C. Sikhim and Bhutan: expercs. of 20 yrs.; map and ill.
[$6 *n.* Longman, *N.Y.*] 21/ *n.* r 8° Arnold 09

**Sind (Scind)** —*for* History *v.* **F** § 62
ALLEN, I. N. Diary of March thro Scinde & Afghan. [1842] *o.p.* [*pb.* 12/] p 8° Hatchard 43
BURTON, [Sir] R. F. Scinde; or the Unhappy Valley, 2 vols. *o.p.* [*pb.* 21/] c 8° Bentley 51
" Sind Revisited, 2 vols. *o.p.* [*pb.* 24/] 8° Bentley 77
HUGHES, A. W. Gazetteer of Province of Scinde *o.p.* [*pb.* 42/] 8° Bell [ ] 76
LANGLEY, E. A. Narr. of Resid. at Ct. of Ali Moorad, 2 v. *o.p.* [*pb.* 30/] 8° Hurst 60
v. ORLICH, L. Travels in 1842–1843 [tr.], 2 vols. *o.p.* [*pb.* 25/] 8° Longman 45
ROSS, D. Land of Five Rivers [Sind sketches] *o.p.* [*pb.* 12/] 8° Chapman 83
*Indus-Delta Country:* HAIG (Maj.-Gen. M. R.) The Indus Delta Country 5/ *n.* r 8° Paul 94
WOOD, Cpt. Jno. Journey to Source of Oxus—*ut* **E** § 33
*Karáchi:* BAILLIE (A. F.) Kurrachee, Past, Present, and Future; ill. 21/ r 8° Thacker, *Calcutta* 90
**Travancore:** HACKER (I. H.) 100 Years in Travancore; ill. [1806–1906] 2/6 *n.* r 8° Allenson 08
**United Provinces of Agra and Oudh:** BHOLANAUTH CHUNDER—*in his* Travels, 2 vols., *ut sup.*
CROOKE, Wm. The North-West Provinces of India; map and 16 pl. 10/6 8° Methuen 07
The best bk. on the history, ethnography, and administration of the region.
" —*in his* Tribes and Castes, *ut sup.*, *s.v.* Ethnology
Imperial Gazetteer of the United Provinces, 2 vols. l 8° 08
INGLIS, J. Tent Life in Tiger Land; col. pl. 18/ r 8° Low 88
*Benares:* HAVELL (E. B.) Benares, the Sacred City; ill. 12/6 *n.* 8° Blackie 05
Interestg. sketches of Hindu life and religion, by the Principal of the Govt. School of Art, Calcutta.
KENNEDY, Jas. Life and Work in Benares and Kumaon [1839–77] 6/ c 8° Unwin 84
SHERRING, Rev. M. A. The Sacred City of the Hindus [=Benares]; ill. *o.p.* [*pb.* 21/] 8° Trübner 68
*Bulandshahr:* GROWSE (F. S.) Bulandshahr: sketches of an Ind. district 4° *Benares* 84
*Cawnpore* —*v.* **F** § 62
*Dehra Doon:* WILLIAMS (G. R. C.) Hist. and Statist. Memoir of Dehra Doon r 8° *Roorkee* 74
*Kumaon* —*v. sup.*, *s.v.* Benares (KENNEDY); *inf.*, *s.v.* Himalayas (OAKLEY); **E** § 34 (SHERRING)
*Muttra:* GROWSE (F. S.) Muttra: a district memoir 4° *Benares* [ ] 83
*Oude:* Gazetteer of, vols. i–iii [India Office pub.] ea. 10/ 8° Paul 77–8
SLEEMAN, Sir W. H. Journey through Oude, 2 vols. [1849–50] *o.p.* [*pb.* 24/] c 8° Bentley 58

**Himalayas** —*v. also* Wilson, *sup.*, and **I** § 165
ADAIR, Cpt. F. E. S. A Summer in High Asia; map and 70 ill. 12/6 *n.* m 8° Thacker 99
A good record of travel and sport in Baltistan and Ladakh.
BRUCE, Maj. C. G. Twenty Years in the Himalaya; ill. 16/ *n.* 8° Arnold 10
Longman, *N.Y.* Mainly mountaineering in the chain fr. Bhutan and Sikkim to Chilas and Kerakoram. Conts. much also ab. natives of Nepal, Sikkim, and Chitral.
BURRARD, Col. S. G. Sketch of Geogr. & Geol. of Him. Mtns. & Tibet, 3 Pts.
ea. 2 rs. 8° Govt. Prtg. Off., *Calc.* 08

COLLIE, Dr J. Norman Climbing on the Himalaya & Other Mountain Ranges 16/ *n.* 8° Douglas, *Edin.* 02
Good account of recent climbing in Himalayas; also notes on climbs in Rockies and in Lofoden Isles.

CUMMING, [Miss] C. F. Gordon From the Hebrides to Himalayas, 2 vols.; ill. *o.p.* [*pb.* 42/] 8° Low 76

,, In the Himalayas and on Indian Plains; ill. 8/6 p 8° Chatto 84

DUNMORE, Earl of —*in his* The Pamirs, *ut* **E** § 33

ECKENSTEIN, Oscar The Karkorams and Kashmir: acc. of journey 6/ c 8° Unwin 96
Author was for a time attached to Sir W. M. CONWAY'S exped. His bk. consists of string of extrs. fr. l'rs and diaries: of next to no value.

FRESHFIELD, Dougl. W. Round Kangchenjunga—*ut* **I** § 165
Conts. a summary of the frontier problems and the Tibetan question.

GORE, F. St John Lights and Shades of Indian Hill Life in the Afghan and Hindu Highlands; maps and 72 ill. 31/6 m 8° Murray 95
Acc. and contrast of peaceful villagers of Kulu Valley am. Himalayas, and of warlike Afghan claps of Kurum on skirts of Suleiman Mtns. The narrative of travel is vivid, and series of photos in India very interestg. Throws considerable light on the methods of British admin.

HODGSON, B. H. Papers on Coloniz., Commerce, Geogr., etc., of Himalayas & Nepal *o.p.* 8° Trübner 57

HOOKER, Sir Jos. D. Himalayan Journals—*ut* **H** § 65
A fascinatg. acc. of a botanist's travels in Bengal, Sikkim and Nepal Himalayas, Khasia Mtns., etc.

KENYON, Maj. R. L. Sport and Life in the Further Himalaya—*ut* **I** § 147

'LADY PIONEER (A)' Indian Alps, & How we Crossed them; ill. & col. pl. *o.p.* [*pb.* 42/] i 8° Longman 76

MCCORMICK, A. D. An Artist in Himalayas; ill. 16/ 8° Unwin 95
A breezy narrative by one who accompanied Sir Wm. CONWAY. 100 sketches by the author.

MACINTYRE, Maj.-Gen. D. Hindu-Koh: wandgs. and sport in and bey. Himalayas; ill. 3/6 p 8° Blackwood [89] 94

MOORCROFT (W.) + TREBECK (G.) Travels in Himalayan Provinces, 2 vols.; map and ill. [1819–25] *o.p.* [*pb.* 30/] 8° Murray 41
Ladakh, Kashmir, Peshawar, Kabul, Bokhara, etc. Ed. H. H. WILSON.

MUMM, A. L. Five Months in the Himalayas—*ut* **I** § 165

OAKLEY, E. S. Holy Himalaya: rel., tradns., & scenery of Kumaon & Garhwal 5/ c 8° Oliphant, *Ed.* 05

RONALDSHAY, Earl of —*in his* Sport and Politics under Eastern Sky, *ut* **E** § 31

STONE, S. J. In and Beyond the Himalayas—*ut* **I** § 147

THOMSON, Dr Thos. Jy. in W. Himalaya and Tibet; col. pl. [1847–8] *o.p.* [*pb.* 15/] 8° Lovell Reeve 52
THOMSON was the first Englishman to reach the Karakoram Pass.

TYACKE, Mrs R. H. How I Shot my Bears; maps and ill. 7/6 c 8° Low 93
Record of Mrs TYACKE'S 2 yrs.' camp-life in Kullu and among the lamas in Lahoul, w. a certain amt. of sport. Ed. Mrs E. E. CUTHELL.

WADDELL, Maj. L. A. Among the Himalayas; 4 maps and 100 ill. 6/ 8° Constable [99] 00
A good account of Sikkim and its mountains. The best book since HOOKER: the result of several journeys there.

WILSON, Andr. The Abode of Snow *o.p.* [*pb.* 10/6] c 8° Blackwood [74] 75
Acc. of jy. fr. Chinese Tibet to Indian Caucasus thro' the valleys of the Himalayas.

WORKMAN, Fanny B. + Dr W. H.—*v.* **I** § 165

YOUNGHUSBAND. Cpt. F. K. —*in his* The Heart of a Continent, *ut* **E** § 34

**Andaman Islands:** Imperial Gazetteer of Andaman Islands 1 8° 09

KLOSS, C. Boden In Andamans and Nicobars; maps and ill. 21/ *n.* m 8° Murray 03
Observations on the inhabitants, fauna, etc., made during a scientific tour, 1900–1.

MAN, E. Horace Aborigines of Andaman Islands; map & 8 pl. *o.p.* [*pb.* 10/6] 8° Trübner *n.d.* (84)
With researches into the language by A. J. ELLIS.

MOUATT, Dr F. J. The Andaman Islanders: adventures & researches *o.p.* [*pb.* 16/] 8° Hurst 63

PORTMAN, M. V. History of our Relations with the Adamanese, 2 vols. 4° *Calcutta* 99

TURNER, C. H. Note on the Andaman Islands f° *Rangoon* 97

**CEYLON**

BAKER, Sir S. W. Eight Years' Wanderings in Ceylon; ill. [1845–53] 3/6 ($1·25) c 8° Longman [55] 90

,, Rifle and Hound in Ceylon; ill. 3/6 ($1·25) c 8° Longman [54] 90

CARPENTER, Edw. From Adam's Peak [Ceylon] to Elephanta [India]—*ut sup.*

CAVE, Hy. W. Picturesque Ceylon, 3 vols.; fully and well ill. 4° Low 93–5
i: *Columbo and Kelani Valley*, 21/ *n.*; ii: *Kandy and Peradeniya*, 23/ *n.*; iii: *Nuwara Eliya and Adam's Peak*, 28/ *n.* A series of beautiful photogr. illns. of scenery and life in Ceylon.

,, The Ruined Cities of Ceylon; 58 pl. 38/ *n.* 4° Low 97

,, Golden Tips: a description of Ceylon; 250 ill. 10/6 *n.* 8° Low 01
An excellent description of the island, with a very readable account of the tea-industry.

,, The Book of Ceylon; ill. and 6 maps 12/ *n.* 8° Cassell 08
A guide to the railway-system and account of its varied attractions for the tourist.

CLUTTERBUCK, Walt. J. About Ceylon and Borneo; maps and ill. 10/6 ($2) c 8° Longman 91
Descrs. Ceyl. as in 1877 (when author was tea-planter there), and as in 1891; w. some descr. of N. Borneo. Rather feeble.

CORNER, Caroline Ceylon, the Paradise of Adam; ill. 10/6 *n.* ($4 *n.*) 8° Lane 08

CUMMING, [Miss] C. F. Gordon Two Happy Years in Ceylon; 28 ill. 7/6 c 8° Blackwood [91] 92
Pleasant and vivid picts. of the isl. and of occupns. and industrs. of people, copiously interspersed w. notices of their hist., relig., folklore (a favourite subject) and the like. Authoritative and exhaustive, all parts of the island hg. been visited.

FARRER, Reg. In Old Ceylon; ill. 12/6 *n.* 8° Arnold 08

FERGUSON, Jno. Ceylon in 1893; map & c. 100 ill. 7/6 c 8° Ferguson, *Colombo* (Haddon) [83] 93
A useful bk. of refer., contg. notices of island's hist. bef. arrival of Port. and Dutch, and of condn. at time of Brit. occupn., changes since, etc. Appendices.

,, Ceylon in the Jubilee Year; maps & ill. 7/6 c 8° Ferguson, *Colombo* (Haddon) [87] 88

,, + A. M. Ceylon Handbook & Directory *ann. vol.* 25/ 8° Ferguson, *Colombo* (Paul) 88 *sqq.*, *ann.*

FORBES, Jon. Eleven Years in Ceylon, 2 vols. *o.p.* [*pb.* 21/] 8° Bentley 41

HAECKEL, Prf. Ernst A Visit to Ceylon [tr.] 7/6 p 8° Paul 83
Picturesque and sympathetic descrns. of tropical nature by a well-known scientist.

HORNADAY, W. T. Two Years in the Jungle; ill. $2·50 8° Scribner, *N.Y.* [85] 87

KNIGHTON, W. Forest Life in Ceylon, 2 vols. *o.p.* [*pb.* 21/] c 8° Hurst 54

KNOX, Cpt. Rob. Histor. Reln. of Isld. of Ceylon—*in* Fellowes (R.) Hist. of Ceylon 8° *London* [1681] 1817
Still esteemed the best acc. of the original inhabitants. New edn. McLehose, *Glasgow*, v. Life of Knox, 12/6 *n.* 11.

'OFFICER OF CEYLON RIFLES' [=Cpt. SUCKLING] Ceylon, Historical, Physical, Statistical, 2 vols. 28/ 8° Chapman 76

PARKER, H. Ancient Ceylon: acc. of aborigines and early civilizn.; ill. 25/ *n.* 8° Luzac 10
In 3 Pts. (1) *The Aborigines*, (2) *Structural Works*, (3) *Arts, Implements, and Games*. A masterly wk.

PRIDHAM, Chas. Historical and Polit. Account of Ceylon, 2 vols. *o.p.* [*pb.* 28/] 8° Boone 49

Rajavaliya: narr. of Sinhalese kings [to 17 cent.] 8° 00

SIRR, H. C. Ceylon and the Cingalese, 2 vols. *o.p.* [*pb.* 24/] c 8° Shoberl 50

SKINNER, Maj. Thos. Fifty Years in Ceylon [an autobiography] 15/ 8° W. H. Allen 91

STEUART, Mary E. Everyday Life on a Ceylon Cocoa-Estate; ill. 6/ f 8° Drane 05

*TENNENT, Sir J. E. Ceylon, Physical, Historical, Topographical, etc., 2 vols.; ill. *o.p.* [*pb.* 50/] 8° Longman [59] 60

,, The Natural History of Ceylon *o.p.* [*pb.* 12/6] 8° Longman 61

O'Brien, Cpt. C. Views in Ceylon [15 views illg. Tennent's wk.] *o.p.* [*pb.* 63/] f° Day 64

WALTERS, Dr Alan Palms and Pearls: scenes in Ceylon; front. *o.p.* [*pb.* 12/6] 8° Bentley 92
Incl. a visit to Anuradhapoora, the ancient royal city, and an account of an ascent of Adam's Peak.

WILLIS, Dr J. C. Ceylon: hdbk. for resident and traveller; ill. 5/ c 8° Dulau 08

WRIGHT, Arn. [ed.] Twentieth Century Impressions of Ceylon; ill. 63/ 4° Lloyd's Greater Brit. Pb. Co.
An encyclopædic acc. of the progress of the island from the earliest times. By various contributors.

*Biography:* GREGORY (Sir Wm.) [Gov.; 1817–92] Autobiography, ed. L'y Gregory 16/ 8° Murray 94

MAITLAND, Sir Thos. [1759–1824] Life of. By W. F. Lord 5/ c 8° Unwin 97

**Maldive Islands:** BELL (H. C. P.) The Maldive Islands; maps [statistical & descriptive] 10/6 8° *Colombo* 83

GARDINER, J. S. [ed.] Fauna and Geogr. of Maldives and Laccadives; ill. 4° Camb. Press 03
Putnam, *N.Y.* Results of expedn. of 1899–1900. Vol. i, Pts. i–iv, ea. 15/ *n.* ($4 *n.*); ii, Pts. i–iv, ea. 15/ *n.* ($4 *n.*); Suppl. i, 15/ *n.* ($4 *n.*); ii, 3/6 *n.* ($1 *n.*).

PYRARD, Frç., —*his* Voyage [tr.; 1601–11], *ut* **E** § 36 is still the standard authority on Maldives

## 36: INDO-CHINA AND EAST INDIES

### Early Voyages and Travel

LEGUAT, Frç. [*b.* ? 1637] Voyage to Rodriguez, Mauritius, Java and Cape of Gd. Hope—*ut* **E** § 41
LEGUAT was a Huguenot exile fr. France, and his bk. gives detailed descrn., long believed to be unique, of extinct Solitaire of Rodriguez Island, the veracity of wh. has in recent years been confirmed. *Vide also* note in **E** § 41.

MIDDLETON, Sir Hy. [d. 1613] Voy. to Bantam and Maluco Islands, ed. Bolton Corney [1606] 8° Hakluyt Soc. [55] 0–
The 2nd voy., 'set forth by the Governor and Company of Merchants of London trading in East Indies'.

de MORGA, Ant. [16 cent.] Philippine Isls., Moluccas, Siam, Cambodia, Japan, China, at Close of 16th Cent., tr. L'd Stanley of Alderley 8° Hakluyt Soc. 68

PINTO, Ferd. Mendez [16 cent.] Voyages and Adventures, ed. A. Vambéry 3/6 c 8° Unwin [91]
$1·50 Macmillan, *N.Y.* [Adventure Ser.] A much curtailed repr. of COGAN'S tr. [1st ed. 1663] of this quite untrustworthy acc. of travels in Abyss., Ormuz, Goa, China, Further India, Japan, etc., the veracity of wh., however, the Editor seeks to defend.

PYRARD, Frç., of Laval Voy. to E. Indies, Maldives, Moluccas and Brazil [tr.], 2 v. (in 3 Pts.) 8° Hakluyt Soc. 87–91
Has a spec. interest f. Englishmen, on acc. of its notice of sailors belongg. to *Hector* (Wm. HAWKINS), of Lond. E. I. Co.'s 3rd separ. voy. [1606–9]

SIMON, Pedro Expedn. of Ursua & Aguirre [1560–61], tr. W. Bollaert 8° Hakluyt Soc. 61
A tr. of the *Sexta Noticia Historiale* 1626. Introd. by [Sir] C. R. Markham.

VAN SPILBERGEN, Joris East and West Indian Mirror [tr.]—*ut* **E** § 7 [1614–7]

*History of Exploration and Colonization*

CHAILLEY-BERT, J. The Colonisation of Indo-China; maps 7/6 c 8° Constable 94
Tr. of a ser. of arts. in *Rev. des Deux Mondes*, bas. on Engl. Blue Bks. A good summary. Introd. and notes.

CLIFFORD, Hugh Further India; ill. [Story of Exploration Ser.] 7/6 *n.* 8° Rivers [04] 05

**General Geography** —*v. also* **E** § 31

DEL MAR, Walt. The Romantic East—*ut* **E** § 35 [Burma, Assam, Kashmir]

GUILLEMARD, F. H. H. Malaysia and the Pacific Archipelagoes = Australia, vol. ii, *ut* **E** § 2
[Stanford's Compend. of Geogr.] The best systematic acc. of the geogr. of Malay Archipelago in English.

KEANE, A. H. Eastern Geography: Malay Peninsular, Indo-China, E. Archipel., Philip., New Guinea 5/ c 8° Stanford [87] 92

NORMAN, Hy. —*in his* The Peoples and Politics of the Far East, *ut* **E** § 37

**Recent Travel, Accounts, etc.**

BICKMORE, A. S. Travels in East Indian Archipelago; ill. *o.p.* [*pb.* 21/] 8° Murray 68

BRADLEY, Jno. Travel and Sport in Burm., Siam, Malay *o.p.* [*pb.* 12/] 8° Tinsley 76

CABATON, A. Java, Sumatra, & other Isds. of Dutch E. Indies [tr.]; ill. 10/6 *n.* 8° Unwin 11

CADDY, Mrs Florence To Siam & Malaya in D'ke of Sutherld's Yacht [*Sans Peur*] 12/ 8° Hurst 89

COLQUHOUN, A. R. Across Chryse, 2 v. [S. China borderlds., Canton to Mandalay] 42/ 8° Low 83

COLQUHOUN, Ethel —*in her* Two of Their Travels, *ut* **E** § 7 [Dutch E. Indies, Philippines]

FORBES, H. O. Naturalist's Wanderings in Eastern Archipelago; ill. [1878–83] 21/ 8° Low 85
Cocos-Keeling Islands, Java, Sumatra, Moluccas, Timor-Laut, Buru, Timor. Forms a sort of suppl. to WALLACE'S *Malay Archip.*

,, Anna [wife of above] Insulinde: experiences in the E. Archip.; map 8/6 p 8° Blackwood 87

IRELAND, Alleyne [ed.] Report on Colonial Administration in Far East, 12 vols.—*ut* **D** § 136

MACGREGOR, Surg.-Maj. Jno. Through the Buffer State—*ut inf., s.v.* Siam [Borneo, Siam, Cambodia]

MACMAHON, Maj.-Gen. A. R. Far Cathay and Farther India—*ut* **E** § 34

MOUHOT, Henri Travels in Indo-China, Siam, Cambodia, & Laos, 2 v. [1858–60] *o.p.* [*pb.* 32/] 8° Murray 64

ROSS, J. Dill Sixty Years Life & Advent. in Far East, 2 vols.; map & ill. 24/ *n.* 8° Hutchinson 11
Life hists. of author and his father, one of old schl. of mercht. capts. who sailed their own ships on tradg. voys. betw. islds. of Far East: Singapore, Celebes, Spice Islds., Dutch N. Guin., Indo-China.

ROST, Dr R. [ed.] Misc. Papers rel. to Indo-China & Ind. Archipel., 5 vols. 56/6 8° Paul 86–9
[Trübner's Oriental Ser.] Repr. fr. *Jl. R. As. Soc.*, DALRYMPLE'S *Oriental Repertory* and *Asiatick Researches*, and *Jl. As. Soc. Beng.*

THOMSON, Jno. Straits of Malacca, Indo-China, etc.; ill. [10 yrs' travel] *o.p.* [*pb.* 21/] 8° Low 75

VINCENT, F., jun. The Land of the White Elephant; ill. *o.p.* [*pb.* 18/] 8° Low 73
Burma, Siam, Cambodia, Cochin China; 1871–2.

WHITNEY, Caspar —*in his* Jungle Trails and Jungle People, *ut* **E** § 35 [Sumatra, Malay, Siam]

**Ethnology:** CAMBR. ANTHROPOLOGICAL EXPEDN. TO TORRES STRAITS: Reports, ed. A. C. Haddon, 6 vols. 4° Camb. Press 01–10, *in prg.*
Putnam, *N.Y.* Vol. ii: *Physiol. and Psychol.*, Pt. i: *Introd. and Vision*, 9/ *n.* ($3 *n.*); Pt. ii: *Hearg., Smell, Taste, etc.*, 7/ *n.* ($2·25 *n.*); iii: *Linguistics* [*ut* **K** § 158], 30/ *n.* ($9 *n.*); v: *Sociology, Magic and Relign. of Western Islanders*, 22 pl., 25/ *n.* ($7·50 *n.*); vi: *Ditto of Eastern Islanders*, 30 pl., 21/ *n.*

FEATHERMAN, A. Social History of Races of Mankind: Papuo & Malayo Melanesians—*ut* **F** § 5

**Annam; Tonkin;** DAMPIER (W.) —*in his* Voyages, vol. ii, *ut* **E** § 7 [1688–9]

MANINGTON, G. A Soldier of the Legion; ill. 10/6 *n.* 8° Murray 07

D'ORLEANS, Pr'ce Henry Around Tonkin and Siam [tr.]; 28 ill. [mainly political] 14/ 8° Low 93

,, From Tonkin to India [tr.]—*ut* **E** § 35

SCOTT, J. G. France and Tongking [campaign of 1884, etc.] 16/ 8° Unwin 85

VASSAL, Gabrielle M. On and Off Duty in Annam; ill. 10/ *n.* 8° Heinemann 10
Acc. of life in Annan by an Englishwoman, married to a French army doctor.

**Borneo:** BECCARI (Dr O.) Wandgs. in Gt. Forests of Borneo [tr.]—*ut inf., s.v.* Sarawak

BEECH, Mervyn W. H. —*in his* The Tidong Dialects of Borneo, *ut* **K** § 158
Incls. a concise and vivid acc. of the almost unknown tribes who speak these dialects.

BOCK, Carl Head Hunters of Borneo; 30 col. pl. *o.p.* [*pb.* 36/] i 8° Low 82

BOYLE, Fred. Adventures among the Dyaks of Borneo *o.p.* [*pb.* 15/] 8° Hurst 65

BURBIDGE, F. W. The Gardens of the Sun *o.p.* [*pb.* 14/] c 8° Murray 80
Account of a naturalist's travels in Borneo and Sulu Islands in 1878.

CATOR, Dorothy Everyday Life among the Head-Hunters, etc.; ill. 5/ *n.* ($1·75) f 8° Longman 05

CLUTTERBUCK, Walt. J. About Ceylon and Borneo—*ut* **E** § 35

DENISON, Noel Tour amongst Land Dyaks of Upper Sarawak [1874] 8° *Singapore* 79

FURNESS, Dr H. H. Home Life of Borneo Head-Hunters; ill. $7·50 *n.* (42/ *n.*) r 8° Lippincott 02
An excellent description of the customs of the Borneo tribes; more complete than HADDEN'S book, *inf.*

GOMES, Rev. Edw. H. Seventeen Yrs. among the Sea-Dyaks of Borneo; ill. 16/ *n.* 8° Seeley 11
A careful acc. of life and culture of Sea Dyaks (quite distinct fr. the Land Dyaks), by a missionary who lived 17 yrs. at Sarawak.

HADDON, A. C. Head-Hunters, Black, White, and Brown—*v.* **E** § 65

HATTON, Fk. New Ceylon: British North Borneo *o.p.* [*pb.* 5/] c 8° Low 81

,, North Borneo; explorations & adventures; ill. *o.p.* [*pb.* 18/] 8° Low 86

KEPPEL, Cpt. H. Expedition to Borneo, 2 vols. *o.p.* [*pb.* 32/] 8° Chapman [46] 47
Acc. of expedn. for suppression of piracy, with extracts from BROOKE'S *Journal* (*inf.*).

POSEWITZ, Dr Theod. —*in his* Borneo: its geology and mineral resources [tr.], *ut* **H** § 38
In 4 Pts., 1st of wh. gives histor. acc. of early travellers fr. 1600 (when Dutch first landed) to 1888: w. a crit. discussn. of their discoveries.

ST JOHN, Sir Spenser Life in Forests of Far East, 2 v.; pl. [Borneo] *o.p.* [*pb.* 32/] 8° Smith & Elder [62] 63

WHITEHEAD, Jno. —*in his* Exploration of Mt Kina Balu, N. Borneo, *ut* **H** § 97 [mainly ornithological]

*Ethnology:* ROTH (H. L.) Natives of Sarawak and Br. N. Borneo, 2 v. 50/ *n.* r 8° Truslove 96
Map and 550 ill. Based on MS. matls. of late H. Brooke Low, who spent 18 yrs. in Borneo Govt. service.

*Sarawak:* BECCARI (Dr O.) Wanderings in Gt. Forests of Borneo [tr.] 16/ *n.* 8° Constable 04
Botanical and other nat. hist. notes, made some 40 yrs. ago, and still of consid. value. Ed. F. H. H. GUILLEMARD. Maps and ill.

BROOKE, Chas. Ten Years in Sarawak, 2 vols. *o.p.* [*pb.* 25/] 8° Tinsley 66

BROOKE, Sir Jas. [1803–68; Rajah of Sarawak]

,, Jl. of Events in Borneo & Celebes, ed. Cpt. R. Mundy, 2 v. *o.p.* [*pb.* 32/] 8° Murray 48

,, Private Letters, ed. J. C. Templer, 3 vols. *o.p.* [*pb.* 31/6] p 8° Bentley 53

Jacob, Gertrude L. Account of Sir James Brooke, 2 vols. *o.p.* [*pb.* 25/] 8° Macmillan 76

St John, Sir Spenser Life of Brooke, fr. his Papers and Corresp. 12/6 c 8° Blackwood 79

,, Rajah Brooke [Bldrs. of Greater Brit.; $1·50 Longm., *N.Y.*] 5/ c 8° Unwin 99

GOULD (Rev. S. B.) + BAMPFYLDE (C. A.) Hist. of Sarawak und. its Two White Rajahs [1839–1908] 15/ *n.* 8° Sotheran 08

McDOUGALL, [Mrs] H. Sketches of our Life in Sarawak 2/6 c 8° S.P.C.K. 82

**Burma:** ANDERSON (Dr J.) Mandalay to Momien—*ut* **E** § 34 [two expedns.: 1868, '75]

BIRD, Geo. W. Wanderings in Burma; maps and ill. 21/ *n.* r 8° Educ. Dept., *Burma* (Simpkin) 97
Gives the most complete details of natural and artificial features of country: a sort of guide-book.

BISHOP, Mrs [Isab. L. BIRD] The Golden Chersonese and Way Thither; ill. 14/ p 8° Murray 83

CHAILLEY-BERT, J. —*in his* The Colonisation of Indo-China [tr.], *ut sup.*

ELLIS, Beth An English Girl's First Impressions of Burma 3/6 *n.* c 8° Platt, *Wigan* [99] 99

FERRARS, Max B. Burma 30/ *n.* 4° Low 00

FORBES, Cpt. C. J. F. S. British Burmah and its People [1878] *o.p.* [*pb.* 10/6] c 8° Macmillan 78

FYTCHE, Lt.-Gen. A. Burmah, Past and Present, 2 v.; ill. [w. pers. remins.] 30/ 8° Paul 78

GASCOIGNE, Gwend. T. Among Pagodas and Fair Ladies *o.p.* [*pb.* 12/] m 8° Innes 96
Lively sketches of Burmese scenery and cities, men and women, customs and industries.

GEARY, Grattan Burmah after the Conquest *o.p.* [*pb.* 7/6] c 8° Low 86

GILL, Cpt. W. The River of Golden Sand; map and ill. *o.p.* [*pb.* 7/6] p 8° Murray [83] 83
Account of journey through China and Eastern Tibet to Burma.

GORDON, C. A. Our Trip to Burmah *o.p.* [*pb.* 21/] 8° Baillière 77

HART, Mrs Ernest Picturesque Burma, maps and 90 ill. 21/ *n.* r 8° Dent 97
$7·50 Lippincott, *Phila.* Deals w. past hist. and social life of Burmese, resources, and prob. future, w. travel-sketches.

INNES, E. Chersonese w. Gilding Off, 2 v. [reply to Bird, *sup.*] *o.p.* [*pb.* 21/] c 8° Bentley 85

*IRELAND, Alleyne Province of Burma, vols. i–ii—*ut* **D** § 136

KELLY, R. T. [artist] Burma: 75 col. pl., w. l'rpr. [$6 *n.* Macmillan, *N.Y.*] 20/ *n.* sq 8° Black 06

LAURIE, Col. W. F. Ashee Pyee, the Superior Country *o.p.* [*pb.* 5/] 8° W. H. Allen 82
On the attractions of Burma for British enterprise.

MACMAHON, Maj.-Gen. A. R. —*in his* Far Cathay and Farther India, *ut* **E** § 34

MITTON, Geraldine E. Bachelor Girl in Burma; ill. [6/ *n.* Black] $3 8° Macmillan, *N.Y.* 07

NISBET, Jno. Burma under British Rule and Before, 2 vols. 32/ *n.* 8° Constable 01
Valuable for reference on details of Burmese government, law, custom, superstition, trade, handicraft, etc. Map and ill.

O'CONNOR, V. C. Scott The Silken East, 2 v.; map & 200 ill. (20 col.) 42/ *n.* 8° Hutchinson 04
A compreh. work, of a standard character: finely ill. by Engl. and Burmese artists.

,, Mandalay and other Cities of Past in Burma; ill. 21/ *n.* 8° Hutchinson 07
An attempt to resuscitate the past of Burma as it finds expressn. in its cities. Well ill. w. 235 ill., 8 col. pl., and 7 maps and plans.

PASKE, Surg.-Gen. C. T. Myamma: life and travel in Lr. Burma 6/ c 8° W. H. Allen 92
Author voyaged out in the fifties. Reminiscences, moralizings, impressions, speculations and narrative. Ed. F. G. AFLALO.

PHAYRE, Lt.-Col. Sir A. P. Hist. of Burma [earliest times to 1830; Trübner's Or. Ser.] 14/ 8° Paul 83

SANGERMANO, F'r V. Burmese Empire 100 Yrs. Ago [tr.], w. introd. and notes Jno. Jardine 10/6 8° Constable [33] 93
SANGERMANO, an Ital. missionary, arrived in Burma 1783, and returned to Italy 1808 [*d.* 1819]. His descrn. of country is generally trustworthy and affords interestg. pict. of pre-annexn. days.

SCOTT, Sir Jas. G. Burma: hdbk. of pract., comm., & polit. informn.; ill. 10/6 *n.* c 8° De La More Pr. 06

SPEARMAN, H. R. British Burma Gazetteer, 2 vols. [India Off. pub.] 50/ 8° Paul 80

STUART Jno. Burma through the Centuries; ill. 2/6 *n.* c 8° Paul 09

TURNER, M. N. Report on the Sana Kachin Expedition [1895–6] f° *Rangoon* 96

WILLIAMS, C. Through Burmah to Western China [in 1863] 6/ c 8° Blackwood 68

WINSTON, W. R. Four Years in Upper Burma 3/6 c 8° Kelly 92

YOUNGHUSBAND, G. J. 1,800 miles on a Burmese Tat: Siam and Shan State 5/ c 8° W. H. Allen 88

*Life and People: Ethnology:* COCHRANE (H. P.) Among the Burmans; 20 ill. [missionary] Revell 04

CUMING, E. D. In Shadow of Pagoda; ill. [Burm. life and character] 6/ c 8° W. H. Allen 93

" With the Jungle Folk; w. native ill. 10/6 8° Osgood 97
Excellent descrns. of village types of characters in neighbourhood of Rangoon and banks of lower portions of the Tarawardy.

FERRARS, Max + Bertha Burma 30/ *n.* 4° 00
300 pp., 455 photo ill. Simple pictorial account of the country and life; appendices on chronology, commerce, money, music, etc.

HALL, H. Fielding A People at School 10/ *n.* ($3 *n.*) 8° Macmillan 06

" The Soul of a People, *and* The Inward Light—*ut* **A** § 14, *s.v.* Buddhism
The former is a singularly successful attempt to express the charm and beauty wh. the author saw in the life of the Burmese. In *A People at Schl.* he shows the effect of mod. civilizn. on them in 1880 (when Burma became a Brit. province). In latter he examines the whole structure of Buddhist teachg. (full of sympathy w. Buddhist thought).

HODSON, T. C. The Metheis; w. Introd. Sir A. C. Lyall; map & 16 pl. (some col.) 7/6 *n.* 8° Nutt 08

LINTON, Jas. H. The Burman as he is [favourable acc.] 3/ 8° *Calcutta* 88

MACMAHON, Lt.-Col. The Karens of the Golden Chersonese *o.p.* [*pb.* 16/] 8° Harrison 76

MASON, Rev. F. Burmah, its People and Products, 2 vols.—*ut* **H** § 38 [chfly. geol., flora, fauna]

SHWAY YOE [=Sir J. G. SCOTT] The Burman, his Life and Notions [1871–2] 19/ *n.* 8° Macmillan [82] 10

SMEATON, D. M. The Loyal Karens of Burma 4/6 c 8° Paul 87

YULE, Col. Hy. Narrative of Mission to Court of Ava [1855] *o.p.* [*pb.* 52/6] 4° Smith & Elder 58

*Gazetteer:* SCOTT (J. G.) + HARDIMAN (J. P.) Gaz. of Up. Burm. & Shan States, 5 v. 8° 00–1

*Sports* —*v.* **I** § 147

*Arakan:* HAY (J. O.) Arakan, Past, Present, and Future 4/6 8° Blackwood 92
Repr. fr. nwsprs., l'rs to officials, etc., wr. over 20 yrs. (a good deal therefore before annexn. of Burma) by a mercht. who lived many yrs. at Akyah.

*British Campaigns* —*v.* **F** § 51

**Cambodia** —*v. sup., s.nn.* MACGREGOR, MOHUT, VINCENT

**Celebes:** HICKSON (S. J.) —*in his* Naturalist in North Celebes; ill., *ut* **H** § 103
A narrative of travel in Minahassa, the Sangir and Talaut Islands; w. notices of fauna, flora, and ethnology.

**Cochin:** BROWN (Edw.) A Seaman's Captivity am. Chinese Pirates on Coast of Cochin China and dur. jy. on ft. acr. that country [1857–8] *o.p.* [*pb.* 8/6] c 8° Westerton 61

DAVY, Fr. Land of the Permauls: its past and present [*w.* 7/6] 8° *Madras* 63

VINCENT, Mrs Howard Newfoundland to Cochin China *o.p.* [*pb.* 7/6] c 8° Low 92
*Via* 'The Golden Wave', New Nippon, and the 'Forbidden City'.

**Java:** d'ALMEIDA (W. B.) Life in Java, 2 vols. *o.p.* [*pb.* 21/] c 8° Hurst 64

BOYS, H. S. Notes on Java and its Admin. by Dutch c 8° *Allahabad* 92

DAY, C. Policy & Administration of the Dutch in Java $2 *n.* (8/6 *n.*) 8° Macmillan, *N.Y.* 04

DE WIT, Augusta Java: fact and fancies 14/ *n.* 8° Chapman 05

JAGAT-JIT SINGH, H. H. —*in his* Travels, *ut* **E** § 34 [1905]

Letters Received by East India Co. fr. its Servants, vols. i–vi—*ut* **E** § 35, *s.v.* East India Co. [1602–17]

MIDDLETON, Sir Hy. [d. 1613] Voyage to Bantam and Maluco Islands [1606]—*ut sup.*

MONEY, J. W. B. Java, or How to Manage a Colony, 2 vols. *o.p.* [*pb.* 21/] c 8° Hurst 61

RAFFLES, Sir Stamford Hist. of Java, 2 v. and 4° Atlas of 90 pl. *o.p.* [*w.* 35/] 8° *London* [17] 30–4
A good piece of literary workmanship, and still the best acc. of the island. Author was govr. dur. temporary occupn. of Java by English.

SCIDMORE, Eliza R. Java, the Garden of the East; ill. $1·50 c 8° Century Co., *N.Y.* 98
7/6 Unwin. A good readable account of the island. The most accessible English book.

WORSFOLD, W. Basil A Visit to Java; ill. *o.p.* [*pb.* 14/] 8° Bentley 93
Conts. much informn. of use to travellers. Author's visit was confined to Batavia, Buitenzorg, and a neighbg. coffee-plantn. Give accs. of peculiar methods of admin. adopted by Dutch, and of foundg. of Singapore.

*Biography*

RAFFLES, Sir Stamford [1781–1826] BOULGER (D. C.) Life of Sir Stamford Raffles; ill. 21/ *n.* r 8° H. Marshall 97
A good and thorough acc. fr. original sources.

Egerton, Hugh E. Sir Stamford Raffles; maps and port. 5/ c 8° Unwin 00
$1·50 Longman, *N.Y.* [Builders of Greater Britain.]

**Kelantan:** GRAHAM (W. A.) Kelantan, a State of Malay Peninsula 5/ *n.* 8° MacLehose, *Glasgow* 08

**Malay Archipelago and Peninsula**

'ABD ALLAH IBN 'ABD AL KÁDIR Tr. fr. Hakayit Abdulla; w. notes J. T. Thomson c 8° 74

ANNANDALE (Nelson) + ROBINSON (H. C.) Fasciculi Malayenses: Anthropology, Pt. i; 18 pl. 15/ *n.*, Suppl. (map) 5/ *n.* 4° Longman 03
The anthropol. and zool. results of expedn. to Perak and Siamese Malay States, 1901–2. This Pt. gives ethnol. of Semang and Sakai tribes, of coast-people of Trang, and of Malays of Perak.

BADEN-POWELL, B. F. S. In Savage Isles and Settled Lands [Malaysia, Australasia, Polynesia, 1888–91] *o.p.* 8° 92

BELCHER, E. —*in his* The Voyage of *The Samarang*, 2 vols., *ut* **E** § 7 [1843–6]

BELFIELD, H. C. Handbk. of Federated Malay States 2/6 8° Stanford [ ] 06
BISHOP, Mrs [Isab. L. BIRD] —*in her* The Golden Chersonese, *ut sup.* [1883]
BOWREY, T. Countries round the Bay of Bengal [1669–79] 8° 05
CLIFFORD, Hugh In Court & Kampong : native life in Malay peninsula 6/ c 8° Richards [97] 03
A ser. of life-like picts. drawn fr. nature in illn. of social relns. wh., under Europ. influences, are rapidly disappearg. The stories deal w. natives of all classes, dwellers in Courts and peasants in their *Kampongs* (villages). Cf. also his tales and sketches *Studies in Brown Humanity*, 6/ Richards '98, *In a Corner of Asia*, 1/6 Unwin '99, *Bush-Whacking and other Sketches*, 6/ Blackwood, 01.
DAMPIER, W. [1652–1715] —*in his* Voyages [tr.], vols. i–ii, *ut* **E** § 7 [1681–91]
DENNYS, Dr N. B. Descriptive Dictionary of British Malaya 28/ 4° *London & China Telegr.* Off. 94
Based on Jno. CRAWFURD'S *Descr. Dict. of Indian Archipelago*, 8° *Lond.* 1856 and J. R. LOGAN'S bk. Conts. some 3,000 headgs., but badly arranged —often not arranged at all. Full, but not compl., Bibliogr.
GUILLEMARD, Dr F. H. H. Cruise of *Marchesa* to Kamschatska & N. Guinea ; ill. 21/ 8° Murray [86] 89
HORNADAY, W. T. —*in his* Two Years in the Jungle, *ut* **E** § 35
INNES, E. Chersonese with the Gilding Off, 2 vols.—*ut sup.*, *s.v.* Burma
I-TSING [7 cent.] Record of Buddhist Religion [tr.]—*ut* **A** § 14 [671–95]
JOURDAIN, Jno. —*in his* Journal, ed. W. Foster, *ut* **E** § 35 [1608–17]
MCNAIR, Maj. F. Perak and the Malays ; ill. *o.p.* [*pb.* 10/6] c 8° Cassell 78
MAXWELL, Geo. In Malay Forests 6/ *n.* c 8° Blackwood [06] 11
RATHBORNE, A. B. Camping and Tramping in Malaya $3·50 8° Macmillan, *N.Y.* 98
RICHINGS, Emily Through the Malay Archipelago 6/ c 8° Drane 09
St JOHN, H. S. R. The Indian Archipelago : hist. and pres. state, 2 vols. *o.p.* c 8° 53
SKEAT, W. W. Wild Tribes of the Malay Peninsula *o.p.* 8° Macmillan 03
,, + BLAGDEN (C. O.) Pagan Races of Malay Peninsula, 2 v. ; ill. 42/ *n.* ($13 *n.*) 8° Macmillan 06
SWETTENHAM, Sir Fk. A. Malay Sketches [Malay life and character] 6/ c 8° Lane [95] 03
,, The Real Malay : pen pictures 6/ ($1·50 *n.*) c 8° Lane 00
,, Unaddressed Letters 6/ ($1·50 *n.*) c 8° Lane 98
Letters on Eastern life in its various moods and phases.
,, British Malaya : orig. & progr. of Brit. influence ; ill. 7/6 *n.* ($2·50 *n.*) 8° Lane 07
THOMSON, J. T. Some Glimpses into Life in Far East *o.p.* [*pb.* 10/6] 8° Richardson [64] 65
,, Sequel to Glimpses into Life in Far East *o.p.* [*pb.* 10/6] 8° Richardson 65
*WALLACE, Dr Alf. Russel The Malay Archipelago ; ill. 7/6 *n.* ($2) c 8° Macmillan [69]
A model narr. of travel in 1854–62 ; w. studies by a leading evolutionist of man and nature.
WHITNEY, C. —*in his* Jungle Trails and Jungle People 12/ *n.* 8° Laurie 05
WRIGHT, Arnold [ed.] 20th Century Impressns. of Brit. Malaya ; ill. 63/ 4° Lloyd's Greater Brit. Pb. Co. 08
By var. Govt. officials. Full of informn. on hist., people, commerce, industries, resources of Malaya. Abgd. Edn., 12/6 *n.* '09.
YOUNGHUSBAND, G. J. —*in his* The Philippines and Round About, *ut inf.*, *s.v.* Philippines

**New Guinea** —*v.* **E** § 64

**Philippine Islands :** *Bibliography :* LECLERC (C.) Bibliotheca Americana [*ut* **E** § 52] : incls. Philippine Islds.
*ROBERTSON, J. G. Bibliography of the Philippine Islands $10 *n.* 8° A. H. Clark Co., *Cleveld.*, *O.* 08
*Discovery :* BUTTERWORTH (H.) Story of Magellan and Discov. of Philippines ; ill. $1·50 c 8° Appleton, *N.Y.* 99
*Early Voyages and Accounts :* BLAIR (Emma H.) + ROBERTSON (J. G.) [eds.] The Philippine Islands, 55 vols. [ea. 16/ *n.* Low] 8° A. H. Clark Co., *Cleveld.*, *O.* 03–8
A colln. of explorns. of early navigators, of descrns. of the islds. and their peoples, hist. and records of R.-C. missns. : tr. fr. origs. (Spanish, Fch., Ital., Latin, etc.), many here first pubd. Maps, ill., ports., facss., etc. 1,000 printed.
CROZET —*in his* Voyage to Tasmania, *etc.*, *ut* **E** § 62
DAMPIER, W. [1652–1715] Acc. of Philippines and New Holland—*in his* Voyages, *ut* **E** § 7
JAGOR, F. Travels in Philippines ; ill. [fr. tr. Spanish] *o.p.* [*pb.* 16/] 8° Chapman 75
de MORGA, Ant. [16 cent.] Philippine Islands, etc., at Close of 16 Cent. [tr.]—*ut sup.*
*Ethnology :* JENKS (A. E.) Bontoc Igorot 05
MEYER, A. B. Distribn. of Negritos in Phil. Isl. and Elsewhere 8° *Dresden* 99
MILLER, E. Bataks of Palawan 05
READ, W. A. Negritos of Zambales 04
SALEEBY, N. M. Studies in Moro Hist., Law, and Rel. r 8° *Manila* 05
SAWYER, F. H. The Inhabitants of the Philippines 14/ *n.* 8° Low 00
*Recent Travels and Accounts ; Life and People*
ATKINSON, F. W. The Philippine Islands ; ill. $3 *n.* (10/6 *n.*) 8° Ginn 05
BARROWS, D. P. History of the Philippines 80 c. *n.* c 8° Amer. Bk. Co., *N.Y.* 05

BOWRING, Sir Jno. Visit to the Philippine Isles *o.p.* [*pb.* 18/] 8° Smith & Elder 59

DAUNCEY, Mrs Campbell An Englishwoman in Philippines; map and ill. 12/ *n.* 8° Murray 06

FOREMAN, Jno. The Philippine Islands; map and front. 21/ 8° Low [91] 99
A study of hist., geogr., ethnol., and social and commerc. condns. of Archip. and its dependencies, based on several yrs'. resid. and study. Standard.

FREER, W. B. Philippine Experience of an American Teacher $1·50 c 8° Scribner, *N.Y.* 06

LANDOR, H. Savage The Gems of the East, 2 vols.; ill. 42/ 8° Macmillan 04
Gives a vivid account of the Philippine Islands and of the economy of life there.

LE ROY, J. A. Philippine Life in Town and Country; ill.
[Our Asiatic Neighbrs.] $1·20 *n.* (5/ *n.*) c 8° Putnam 05

LINDSAY, C. H. A. F. The Philippines under Spanish & American Rules; ill. $3 8° Winston, *Phila.* 07

LOLA, Raymond R. The Philippine Islands c 8° Continental Pub. Co., *N.Y.*
A historical account down to the American occupation.

MORGA History of Philippine Islands, 2 v.; ill. [1521–1600] $7·50 *n.* 8° Clark, *Cleveld., O.* 07

RUSSEL, Mrs Flor. K. A Woman's Journey thro' the Philippines; ill. $2·50 c 8° Page, *Boston* 07
Acc. of trip dur. winter of 1900–1 of ss. *Burnside* while laying Amer. cable betw. the Phil. islds.

STEVENS, J. E. Yesterdays in Philippines; 32 ill. [7/6 Low] $1·50 c 8° Scribner, *N.Y.* 98

WORCESTER, Prf. D. C. The Philippine Islands and their People $2·50 (15/ *n.*) 8° Macmillan 98
Narrative of the personal experiences of a party of naturalists in the islands, 1889 and 1890. No scientific matter.

WRIGHT, Hamilton M. Handbook of the Philippines; maps & 150 ill. $1·40 *n.* 12° McClurg, *Chicago* 07

YOUNGHUSBAND, Maj. G. J. Philippines and Round About; map and ill. 8/6 *n.* ($2·50) 8° Macmillan 99
A good account of Manila, the American occupation, politics in the islands: and a visit of Java and Saigon.

**Shan States:** COLQUHOUN (A. R.) Among the Shans *o.p.* [*pb.* 21/] 8° Field & Tuer 85
With histor. sketch by HALLETT, and an essay on *The Cradle of the Shan Race*, by Terrien de LACOUPERIE.

HALLETT, H. S. A Thousand Miles on Elephant in Shan States 21/ 8° Blackwood 90

MILNE, Mrs Leslie Shans at Home 15/ *n.* 8° Murray 10
A very sympathetic descrn. of an interestg., contented, and lovable race.

RIGBY, G. C. Report on Tour thro' Northern Shan States: 1894–5 f° *Rangoon* 95

YOUNGHUSBAND, Maj. G. J. —*in his* 1,800 Miles on a Burmese Tat, *ut sup.*, *s.v.* Burma

*Gazetteer:* SCOTT (J. G.) + HARDIMAN (J. P.) Gazetteer of Up. Burmah and Shan States, 5 vols.—*ut sup.*

*Laos:* BOCK (Carl) —*in his* Temples and Elephants, *ut inf.*, *s.v.* Siam

**Siam:** ANDERSON (Dr J.) English Intercourse with Siam in Seventeenth Century—*ut* **D** § 117*

BOCK, Carl Temples & Elephants: explorn. of Upper Siam & Laos; col. pl. *o.p.* [*pb.* 21/] 8° Low 84

BOWRING, Sir Jno. Kingdom & People of Siam, 2 v.; col. pl.
[w. narr. of 1855 missn.] *o.p.* [*pb.* 32/] 8° Parker 57

CAMPBELL, J. G. D. Siam in the Twentieth Century; ill. 16/ 8° Arnold 02
$5 *n.* Longman, *N.Y.* A valuable study of prospects of the country and possibility of internal development.

CARTER, A. Cecil [ed.] The Kingdom of Siam; ill. $2 (9/ *n.*) 8° Putnam 04
By various officials in different depts. of the Govt. service. Full of facts and statistics.

CORT, Mary L. Siam: heart of F'r India [habits, man'rs., beliefs, missns., etc.] $1 12° Lentilhon, *N.Y.* 86

GRINDROD, Mrs Siam: a Geographical Summary 5/ *n.* 8° Stanford 95
A useful and orderly compilation; incls. an incomplete Bibliography.

KÄMPFER, E. —*in his* History of Japan, w. descrn. of Siam [tr.], 2 v., *ut* **E** § 37 [1690–2]

LEONOWENS, Mrs Anna H. English Governess at Siamese Court *o.p.* 8° Trübner 70

,, Romance of Siamese Harem Life; ill. *o.p.* [*pb.* 14/] 8° Trübner 73

D'ORLEANS, Price Henry Around Tonkin and Siam [tr.]—*ut sup.*, *s.v.* Annam

MCCARTHY, Jas. Surveying and Exploring in Siam; maps and ill. 10/6 *n.* 8° Murray 00
Account of journeys undertaken from 1881–93 for map-making purposes.

MACGREGOR, Surg.-Maj. Jno. Through the Buffer State *o.p.* [*pb.* 6/] c 8° White 96
Wandgs. thro' Siam, w. suppl. accs. of Borneo and Cambodia, last 7 chs. contg. notices of Singapore, Malacca, Mandalay, Darjeeling.

*SMYTH, H. Warington Five Years in Siam, 2 vols.; maps and ill. [1891–6] 24/ c 8° Murray 98
$5 Scribner, *N.Y.* The best existing account of the country, and of travel there.

SOMMERVILLE, Prf. Maxwell On the Meinam, fr. the Gulf to Ayuthia $3 8° Lippincott, *Phila.* 97
14/ Low. Account of a steamer-trip up river and down again. Map and 50 ill.

TAYLOR, Bayard Siam $1·25 12° Harper, *N.Y.* 81

THOMPSON, P. A. Lotus Land; ill. 16/ *n.* 8° Laurie 06
A full acc. of the people, country, religion, art, and life of Siam; w. historical sketch.

VINCENT, F., jun. The Land of the White Elephant, *ut sup.*

WHITNEY, C. —*in his* Jungle Trails and Jungle People, *ut sup.*, *s.v.* Malay Archipelago

WRIGHT, Arnold [ed.] Twentieth Century Impressions of Siam; ill. 4° Lloyd's Greater Brit. Pb. Co. 09

YOUNG, Ern. The Kingdom of the Yellow Robe; ill. 5/ *n.* 8° Constable [98] 07
An excellent acc. of the domestic life and religious rites and ceremonies of Siam: chiefly Bangkok.

YOUNGHUSBAND, G. J. —*in his* 1,800 Miles on a Burmese Tat, *ut sup., s.v.* Burma
" —*in his* The Philippines and Round About, *ut sup.*

*Mekong River:* SMYTH (H. W.) Notes of Jy. on Upper Mekong 8° R. G. S. (Murray) 95
The jy. (1891–6) was undertaken to exam. the ruby and sapphire cy. for Siam. Govt. Vivid acc. of boat-, raft-, camp-, and jungle-life.

**Straits Settlements:** CAVENAGH (O.) Reminiscences of an Indian Official *o.p.* [*pb.* 10/6] c 8° W. H. Allen 84
McLARTY, F. M. Affairs of the Colony: hist. of Str. Settlem. and Brit. Protected States of Malay 8° *Penang* 94
VAUGHAN, J. D. Manners & Customs of Chinese of Str. Settlemts.; ill. 6/ p 8° *Singapore* 79
*Singapore* —*v. sup., s.v.* Java (RAFFLES; WORSFOLD)

**Sumatra:** BOCK (Carl) —*in his* Head-Hunters of Borneo, *ut sup., s.v.* Borneo

**Sulu Islands** —*v. sup., s.v.* Borneo (BURBIDGE)

**Sunda Islands:** *Lombok Island*
COOL, Cpt. W. With the Dutch in the East, tr. [fr. Dutch] E. J. Taylor; ill. 21/ r 8° Luzac 97
Acc. of the milit. operns. of Dutch Indian Army dur. 1894 in Lombok, w. acc. of native life, etc.

## 37: JAPAN

**Bibliography:** PAGÈS (Léon) Bibliographie Japonaise *o.p.* 4° *Paris* 59
670 titles fr. 15 cent. to 1858. Valuable f. its full recd. of early Cath. missns. Repr. in WENCKSTERN [*inf.*].
SERRURIER, L. Bibliographie Japonaise [bks. in Leyden Univ.] 15/ 8° Brill, *Leyden* 97
v. WENCKSTERN, F. Bibliography of Japanese Empire: 1859–1906, 2 v. ea. 25/ *n.* r 8° Paul 95–07
Contin. of PAGÈS [*sup.*], of wh. facs. repr. is incl. Classif. list (24 main hgs.) of bks., essays, and maps in all langs.

**Ethnology: Ainus** [Japan and Saghalien]—*for* Folklore *v.* **B** § 37
ASIATIC SOCIETY OF JAPAN: —*in* Transactions, *passim, ut inf.*
BATCHELOR, Rev. Jno. —*in his* The Ainu of Japan, *ut* **B** § 37
HOWARD, B. Douglas Life with the Trans-Siberian Savages 6/ c 8° Longman 93
An unvarnished acc. of manners, customs, and daily life of Saghalien Ainus, wr. fr. pers. observn. by a guest of Govr. of Russn. penal colony on isld.
LANDOR, A. H. Savage Alone with the Hairy Ainu; map & ill. 18/ m 8° Murray 93
Acc. of an advent. jy. (3,800 m.) on pack-saddle in Yezo, in wh. many places prev. unvisited by European were penetrated—also of a cruise to the Kurile Islands. A consid. contribn. to ethnogr. of N. Japan.
MACRITCHIE, D. The Aïnos = Suppl. *to* v. iv *of* Intern. Archiv für Ethnographie r 8° Vieweg, *Brnswk.* 92
Wr. in English; ill. w. 19 col. pl. fr. Jap. dwgs. Author thinks that, am. existg. races, none more nearly approaches condn. of 'primitive folk' than Ainus.
STARR, Fredc. The Ainu Group of St. Louis Exposition s 8° 04
3/6 *n.* Paul. A simple narr. of author's jy. in Yezo, and descrn. of the group of Ainu he brot. to America.

**Early Travel and Accounts** —*v. also* **E** § 5 (HAKLUYT, PURCHAS), **E** § 31 (PINTO, POLO)
ADAMS, Will [17 cent.] Letters [1611–17]—*v. inf., s.nn.* RUNDALL, *and* SLADEN + LORIMER
de BENYOWSKI, Ct M. A. [1741–86]—*in his* Memoirs and Travels [tr.]—*ut* **E** § 31
COCKS, Rich. Diary, ed. E. Maunde Thompson, 2 vols. 8° Hakluyt Soc. 83
Diary of a Cape merchant in an English factory in Japan, 1615–1622; w. correspondence.
KAEMPFER, Engelbert Hist. of Japan, 3 v.; facs. maps & ill. ea. 12/6 *n.* 8° MacLehose, *Glasgow* [1727] 06
[Libr. of Travels.] Acc. of K.'s travels in Japan, w. descrn. of manners and customs and of Shinto religion. Incls. a descrn. of Siam, 1690–2.
de MORGA, Ant. [16 cent.] Philippine Islands, Moluccas, Siam, Japan and China—*ut* **E** § 36
MURAKAMI (N.) + MURAKAWA (K.) [eds.] Letters wr. by Egl. Residts. in Jap, 1611–23 c 8° *Tokio* 00
RUNDALL, T. [ed.] Colln. of Early Documts. on Emp. of Japan in 16 & 17 Cents. 8° Hakluyt Soc. 50
Includes Will ADAMS' *Letters* [1611–1617].
SARIS, Cpt. Jno. Voyage to Japan in 1613, ed. Sir E. M. Satow; ill. 8° Hakluyt Soc. 00

**Recent Travel and Accounts; Life, People; Polit. Condn., etc.**—*v. also* **D** § 138, *s.v.* Eastern Question
ADAM, Evelyn Behind the Shoji: impressions of Japan 6/ c 8° Methuen 10
ALCOCK, Sir Rutherford The Capital of the Tycoon, 2 vols. *o.p.* [*pb.* 42/] 8° Longman 63
Account of 2 years' residence: still of considerable value. Map, col. pl., and ill.
ARNOLD, Sir Edwin Japonica; ill. [15/ Osgood] $3 r 8° Scribner, *N.Y.* 92
" Chs. xii to end of his 'Seas & Lands' [*ut* **E** § 7] descr. a yr's. visit to Japan
ASIATIC SOCIETY OF JAPAN: Transactions, vols. i–xxx 8° *Tokio* 02, *in prg.*
AYRTON, Mrs M. C. Child Life in Japan; ill. [w. child-stories; 20 c. *n.* Heath, *Bost.*] 6/ r 8° Griffith & Farran [79] 88
BACON, Alice M. Japanese Girls and Women; 62 ill. $1·25 c 8° Houghton, *Boston* [91] 05
5/ *n.* Gay & Bird. Childhd., educn., marr., divorce, wives, old-age, court-life, life in castle and *yashiki*, *Samurai* women, etc. Edn. ill. by KEISHU TAKENOUCHI, $4.
" A Japanese Interior [contin. of above; letters] $1·25 c 8° Houghton, *Boston* 93
5/ Gay & Bird. The daily experces. of an openminded Amer. girl who taught in the Tokio school for peeresses.
" In Land of the Gods: stories of Japan [5/ Constable] $1·50 c 8° Houghton, *Boston* 05
BAXTER, Kath. S. In Bamboo Lands; maps and 118 ill. $2·50 8° Merriam, *N.Y.* 97

BICKERSTETH, [Miss] M. Japan as we saw it; ill. 21/ 8° Low 93
$5 Scribner, *N.Y.* In great measure an account of Church of Engl. mission in Japan.

BISHOP, Mrs [*née* Isab. L. BIRD] Unbeaten Tracks in Japan; map and ill. 2/6 *n.* c 8° Murray [80] 05
$2·50 Putnam, *N.Y.* Interestg. acc. of travel on horseback in little-kn. pts. of interior and North, w. visits to Ainu of Yezo and shrines of Nikko and Ise.

Life of Isab. Bird [1821–1904] By Anna M. Stoddart; ill. 6/ *n.* c 8° Murray [06] 08
$5 *n.* Dutton, *N.Y.* Rocky Mtns., Japan, Tibet, Korea, Kurdistan, China, Morocco, etc.

BLACK, J. R. [Am.] Young Japan: Yokohama & Yedo, 2 vols. [1858–79] 42/ 8° *Yokohama* 80–1

*BRINKLEY, Cpt. F. Japan and China, 12 vols.; 226 pl. (100 col.) ea. 14/ *n.* r 8° Jack 03–5
Millet, *Boston.* The standard general wk. on hist., arts, sciences, manners, laws, religs., and liter. of these countries.

„ [ed.] Japan Described and Illustrated by the Japanese, 15 Pts. f° *Boston* 97

BROWNELL, C. L. The Heart of Japan; ill. 6/ c 8° Methuen 02
$1·50 *n.* McClure, *N.Y.* One of the better recent bks.; by a writer who has lived 5 yrs. in the interior. Not a travel-book: a descrn. of life.

BRYSON, Mrs M. J. Child Life in Japanese Homes 5/ 4° R.T.S. 85

*CHIROL, Valentine The Far Eastern Question 8/6 *n.* c 8° Macmillan 96
L'rs contrib. to *Times* 1895 by its foreign-correspt.: offers strong evid. for belief th. decadence of China is not superficial or temporary but th. it is in a condn. of moral bankruptcy. Gives valuable descrns. of Japan after the war, and seeks to shew th. Japan was victorious because she deserved to win, both morally and physically. Cf. also **D** § 138, *s.v.* Eastern Question.

CLEMENT, E. W. Handbook of Modern Japan; 2 maps & ill. $1·40 *n.* c 8° McClurg, *Chicago* [03] 04
6/ *n.* Paul. Well-digested informn. on the country and people, inclg. govt., lang., liter., manners, trade, agric., etc.

„ The Japanese Floral Calendar; ill. [2/6 *n.* Paul] 50 c. *n.* 12° *Open Ct.* Pb. Co., *Chicago* 05
On the part played by trees and flowers in the æsthetic life of Japan. Charmingly illustrated.

COLVILLE, Maj.-Gen. Sir Hy. The Allies 16/ *n.* 8° Hutchinson 07
A study of Japan designed to help England and Japan to understand one another.

CURTIS, Wm. E. The Yankees of the East [Japanese], 2 vols.; ill. $4 16° Stone, *Chicago* 96

CURZON OF KEDLESTON, L'd Problems of the Far East; maps and ill. 7/6 *n.* c 8° Constable [94] 96
Inquiry into polit., social, and economic condns. of China, Japan, and Corea, and their international relationships.

D'AUTREMER, J. The Japanese Empire & its Economic Conditions; 16 ill. 10/6 *n.* 8° Unwin 10

DAVIDSON, Augusta M. C. Present-day Japan; 74 ill. 5/ c 8° Unwin [04] 07

DEL MAR, Walt. Around the World through Japan; 50 ill.—*ut* **E** § 7
Includes one of the best existing accounts of Japan, the result of three-months stay in 1899.

DIÓSY, Arth. The New Far East; map and 12 Jap. ill. 6/ 8° Cassell [98] 00
$3·50 Putman, *N.Y.* A useful acc. of Japan and study of polit. condns. by a Jap. w. strong Brit. proclivities.

DIXSON, Prf. W. G. Land of Morning Sun: Japan & its people; ill.
*o.p.* [*pb.* 7/6] c 8° Gemmell, *Edin.* [69] 82

„ Gleanings from Japan 16/ 8° Blackwood 89

DYER, Prf. Hy. Dai Nippon, the Britain of the East 12/6 *n.* 8° Blackie 04
A very thoughtful 'study in national evolution', full of statistics and facts.

„ Japan in World Politics 12/6 *n.* 8° Blackie 10

EDWARDS, A. H. Kakemono: Japanese sketches 7/6 *n.* 8° Heinemann 06

EDWARDS, Osman Japanese Plays and Playfellows; 12 col. ill. 10/ *n.* 8° Heinemann 01
Plays, religious and secular, and acting, in Japan: popular songs, etc. Illns. are by Jap. artists.

FARRER, Reg. J. The Garden of Asia 6/ c 8° Methuen [04] 09
Rhapsodical 'impressions' of the country and its people.

FINCK, H. T. Lotus-Time in Japan, ill. fr. photos. [good] $1·75 c 8° Scribner, *N.Y.* 95
Written primarily for Americans: bright and vivacious, but not at all profound. Conts. a good deal about the women.

FINNEMORE, Jno. Peeps at Japan; 12 col. pl. [elementary] 1/6 *n.* c 8° Black 07

FORTUNE, Rob. Yedo and Peking *o.p.* [*pb.* 16/] 8° Murray 63

FRASER, Mrs Hugh A Diplomatist's Wife in Japan, 2 vols.; 250 ill. 32/ r 8° Hutchinson 99
$7·50 Macm., *N.Y.* Ch. Edn. 1/ *n.* Informative acc. of people and espec. women, characterized by great insight. Am. edn. *sub tit. Letters fr. Japan.*

GARDINER, R. S. Japan as we saw it; map and ill. $1·50 8° Rand, *Boston* 93

GRIFFIS, Dr W. E. The Mikado's Empire, 2 vols.; ill. $4 8° Harper, *N.Y.* [76]
20/ Paul. i: *History* B.C. 660–A.D. 1872; ii: *Personal Experiences, Observns., and Studies,* 1870–4.

„ The Japanese Nation in Evolution [6/ Harrap] $1·25 c 8° Crowell, *N.Y.* 07

„ Townsend Harris, First American Envoy in Japan $2 c 8° Houghton, *Boston* 95
Largely a jl. kept by HARRIS. A contribn. to the study of beginning of New Japan.

„ Verbeck of Japan; ill. $1·50 (6/) c 8° Revell [00] 02

GULICK, S. L. Evolution of the Japanese, Social and Psychic $2 *n.* (7/6 *n.*) c 8° Revell 03
A study of Jap. race characteristics, social, mental and moral, and of possibilities of western influence.

HARTSHORNE, Anna C. Japan and her People, 2 vols.; 50 photogravs. 21/ *n.* c 8° Paul 04

HATCH, E. F. G. Far Eastern Impressions; 3 maps and 80 ill. 6/ *n.* c 8° Hutchinson 04
Impressns. of travel in Japan, Corea, and China, w. observns. on commerc. and polit. problems.

*HEARN, Lafcadio Glimpses of Unfamiliar Japan, 2 vols. $4 c 8° Houghton, *Boston* [94] 05
15/ *n.* Paul. Descrns. of travel, of famous temples and neighbrhds., charmg. stories of personal experce.

„ 'Out of the East': reveries and studs. in New Japan $1·25 c 8° Houghton, *Bost.* 95
5/ *n.* Paul. On various phases of Japanese social thought.

* HEARN, Lafcadio — Kokoro : hints & echoes of Jap. inner life $1·25 16° Houghton, *Boston* [95] 06
3/6 *n.* Gay & Hancock. Sympath. and artistic pourtrayal of emotional life as seen in Jap. patriotism, relig., romantic love, etc.

* ,, — Gleanings in Buddha Fields—*ut* **B** § 37

,, — Exotics & Retrospectives [travel & descrn. ; 5/ *n.* Paul] $1·25 c 8° Little & Brown, *Boston* 98

,, — In Ghostly Japan $1·25 c 8° Little & Brown, *Boston* 99
5/ *n.* Paul. Miscellaneous papers on Japanese religion, games, amusemts., etc., and some short stories.

,, — Shadowings $1·25 c 8° Little & Brown, *Boston* 00
5/ *n.* Paul. 6 ghost-stories, pprs. on the cicada, Jap. female names, and old Jap. songs, and 7 short stories.

,, — A Japanese Miscellany [5/ *n.* Paul] $1·25 *n.* c 8° Little & Brown, *Boston* [01] 05

,, — Kottō : Jap. curios w. sundry cobwebs ; ill. $1·50 *n.* (6/ *n.*) c 8° Macmillan 02

,, — Japan : an attempt at interpretation $2 *n.* (8/6 *n.*) c 8° Macmillan 04

,, — Kwaidan : stories & studies of strange things ; ill. $1·50 c 8° Houghton, *Boston* 04
5/ *n.* Paul. A colln. of old Jap. *Mährchen* and insect studies (butterflies, mosquitoes, ants).

Bisland, Eliz. — Life & Letters of Lafcadio Hearn, 2 vols. ; ill. $6 *n.* 8° Houghton, *Boston* 06
24/ *n.* Constable. The Life, a model of discreet biogr., occupies first 160 pp. Born on an island in Ionian Sea. HEARN passed early years in Wales. Emigratg. to Amer. after yrs. of bitter struggle he got a post on a New Orleans paper. In 1890 he went to Japan, where he adopted Buddhism, married a Jap. wife, and spent last 14 yrs. of his life. 'I have pledged me' (he writes) 'to the worship of the Odd, the Queer, the Strange, the Exotic, the Monstrous. It quite suits my temperament.'

,, [ed.] — The Japanese Letters of Lafcadio Hearn ; ill. 12/ *n.* 8° Constable 11
A final coll. of HEARN's corresp., embodying his frankest views of Japan and the Japanese.

Bronner, Milton [ed.] — Letters from the Raven ; ill. $1.50 c 8° Brentano, *N.Y.* 08
5/ *n.* Constable. Letters to Hy. WATKIN, a printer who befriended him in his youth.

Gould, G. M. — Concerning Lafcadio Hearn $1·50 *n.* c 8° Jacobs, *Phila.* 08

Noguchi, Yoné — Lafcadio Hearn in Japan 6/ *n.* c 8° Kelly & Walsh, *Yokohama* (E. Mathews) 11
HEARN's books are indispensable for the study of the Japanese people, their ways of thought, and the 'hidden springs by which they move'. Good examples of the Japanolatry of these latter years.

HILDRETH, R. — Japan as it was & is, 2 vols. ; maps & ill. $3 c 8° McClurg, *Chicago* [4–] 06
12/6 *n.* Paul. Ed. E. W. CLEMENT, w. Introd. W. E. GRIFFIS. A standard bk. Ills. fr. Jap. prints.

HOLLAND, Clive — Japan, Old and New ; ill. 15/ *n.* 8° Dent 08

HOLTHAM, E. J. — Eight Years' Walk and Travel in Japan [1873–81] 9/ c 8° Paul 83

HUISH, Marcus B. — Japan and its Arts—*ut* **I** § 85

HUMBERT, Aimé — Japan and the Japanese [tr.] ; 207 ill. *o.p.* [*pb.* 21/] r 4° Bentley [74] 76
A good bk., well ill. by Fch. and Ital. artists. Author was Minister Plenipotentiary of Swiss Republic.

INAGAKI, M. — Japan and the Pacific ; maps 2/6 c 8° Unwin 90

INOUYE, Jukichi — Home Life in Tokio ; ill. by Jap. artist c 8° *Tokio* (Times Bk-Club) 11

JAGAT-JIT-SINGH, H. H. — *in his* The Raja-i-Rajgan, *ut* **E** § 34 [travels]

Japan in Beginning of Twentieth Century 25/ *n.* 8° Murray 04
Compiled by Dept. of Agric. and Commerce. A mine of informn. on geogr. and econ. of Japan.

JERNINGHAM, Sir Hubert — From East to West—*ut* **E** § 7
An agreeable acc. of a jy., with his nephew and the Earl of Leitrim, to Japan, etc.

KNAPP, Arth. M. — Feudal and Modern Japan, 2 vols. [laudatory] 8/ *n.* s 8° Duckworth 98

KNOLLYS, Maj. H. — Sketches of Life in Japan ; 7 ill. 12/ 8° Chapman 87

KNOX, G. W. — Imperial Japan : the country and its people 7/6 *n.* 8° Newnes 05

KNOX, T. W. — Boy Travellers in the East : Japan and China $2 c 8° Harper, *N.Y.* 80

LADD, Prf. G. T. — Rare Days in Japan ; 24 ill. 10/6 *n.* 8° Longman 10

LA FARGE, Jno. [art.] — An Artist's Letters fr. Japan ; ill. by author $4 8° Century Co., *N.Y.* 97
16/ Unwin. Primarily acc. of brief residence in Tokio and in holy mtn. of Nikko, w. excell. descrns., tho' rather out of date.

LAWSON, L'y — Highways and Homes of Japan ; 60 ill. (1 col.) 12/6 *n.* 8° Unwin 10

LEROY-BEAULIEU, P. — Awakening of the East [tr.]—*ut* **D** § 138 [Sib., Jap., China]

LLOYD, Arth. — Every-day Japan ; Introd. C't Hayashi 6/ *n.* 8° Cassell [09] 11
Based on first hand knowledge, after 20 yrs. residence and work in Japan.

LOWELL, Percival — The Soul of the Far East $1·25 c 8° Houghton, *Boston* 88

,, — Occult Japan $1·75 c 8° Houghton, *Boston* 95

MCKENZIE, F. A. — The Unveild East ; 3 maps and 29 ill. 12/ *n.* 8° Hutchinson 07
A careful bk. on polit., colon., and commerc. policy of Japan, on China, her army and trade, etc.

MENPES, Mortimer — Japan : a record in colour 20/ *n.* sq 8° Black 01
$6 *n.* Macmillan *N.Y.* 100 coloured ill. fr. the artist's dwgs., w. text transcribed by his daughter, Dorothy MENPES.

MITFORD, C. B. — A New Geography of Japan [schl.-bk.] 8° *Japan Gaz.* Press, *Yokohama* 06

MONTGOMERY, H. B. — The Empire of the East ; 17 pl. (1 col.) [Japan] 7/6 *n.* 8° Methuen 08

MOORE, Rev. Herb. — Half-Hours in Japan ; 90 ill. 6/ c 8° Unwin 00

MORRIS, J. — What will Japan do ? : a forecast *o.p.* [*pb.* 3/6] c 8° Lawrence & Bullen 98

MORRIS, J. M. — Advance Japan ! a nation thoroughly in earnest—*ut* **F** § 63
A good summary of the general hist. and progress and then (1895) condn., social and military.

MORSE, E. S. — Japanese Homes and their Surroundings ; ill. [10/6 Low] s 4° [86] 88

MOSSMAN, Sam. New Japan: land of rising sun [1853–73] 15/ 8° Murray 73
,, Japan [Foreign Countries and British Colonies] 3/6 12° Low 80
NITOBÉ, Prf. I. O. Bushido: the Soul of Japan $1·25 (5/ *n.*) c 8° Putnam [ ] 05
NORMAN, Sir Hy. The Real Japan: manners, morals, admin., politics; ill. 5/ *n.* c 8° Unwin [92] 08
$3 Scribner, *N.Y.* Conveys a fairly accurate idea of contemp. Japanese manners. The political chs. the best.
,, —*in his* The Peoples and Politics of the Far East, *ut* **E** § 31
OKAKURA-KAKUZO The Ideals of the East 5/ *n.* c 8° Murray 03
An attempt to present to the Western mind the true inwardness of Japanese national life. Spec. ref. to art.
,, The Awakening of Japan 5/ *n.* c 8° Murray 05
OKAKURA-YOSHISABURO, Prf. The Japanese Spirit; Introd. Geo. Meredith 3/6 *n.* c 8° Constable 05
OLIPHANT, Laur. Lord Elgin's Mission to China and Japan, 2 vols.—*ut* **E** § 34 [1857–9]
PAGE, Jesse Japan: people and missions—*ut* **A** § 105 [a good and cheap pop. compiln.]
PARSONS, Alf. [art.] Notes in Japan; ill. by author $3 c 8° Harper, *N.Y.* 96
12/6 Osgood. Acc. of an artist's sketching-tour. Fairly good reprodns. of the pictures: pleasant text.
PERRY, Commod. M. C. Narr. of Expedn. to China Seas—*ut* **E** § 34: one of best bks. since SIEBOLD
PERRY, R. B. The Gist of Japan; 8 pl.—*ut* **A** § 105 [missionary pt.-of-view]
PONTING, H. G. In Lotus-Land Japan; 104 ill. (8 col.) 21/ *n.* 4° Macmillan 10
Descrs. the most famous sights, most beautiful scenic districts and most famous mtn.-peaks.
PORTER, Rob. P. The Full Recognition of Japan [econ. progr. to 1911] 10/6 *n.* 8° Clar. Press 11
RANSOME, Stafford Japan in Transition $3 (16/) 8° Harper 99
A sound and useful compar. study of progress of the country since the war with China.
REDESDALE, L'd The Garter Mission to Japan 6/ c 8° Macmillan 06
Story of the mission of Pr'ce ARTHUR OF CONNAUGHT on visit to invest Mikado w. Order of Garter.
REED, Sir E. J. —*in his* Japan, vol. ii [*ut* **F** § 63]
REGAMEY, F. Japan in Art & Industry; w. glance at manners & customs [tr.]—*ut* **I** § 85
*REIN, Prf. J. J. Japan: travels & researches [tr.]; 2 maps & 20 ill. 25/ r 8° Hodder [84] 89
By far the best bk. on the physiography, natural history, and topography of the country.
* ,, Industries of Japan [tr.]; 3 maps and 44 ill. 30/ r 8° Hodder 89
W. agric., forestry, mining, arts, trade and commerce. Above 2 vols. are result of travels undertaken at cost of Prussian govt., and are extremely valuable.
RITTNER, G. H. Impressions of Japan; ill. 10/6 *n.* sq 8° Murray 04
RONALDSHAY, Earl —*in his* A Wandering Student in the East, 2 vols., *ut* **E** § 34
SAINT JOHN, Cpt. H. C. Notes and Sketches from Wild Coasts of Nipon; ill. 12/ 8° Douglas, *Edin.* 80
SCHERER, Prf. J. A. B. Japan To-day; 28 ill. $1·50 *n.* c 8° Lippincott, *Phila.* 04
,, Young Japan: story of Jap. people; ill. $1·50 *n.* c 8° Lippincott, *Phila.* 05
Ea. 6/ *n.* Paul. Latter deals considerably with educational development.
SCIDMORE, Eliza R. Jinrikisha Days in Japan; ill. $2 12° Harper, *N.Y.* 91
A descrn. of the most interesting localities in Japan as seen fr. a *Jinrikisha* (2-wheeled carriage).
SHIGENOBU OKUMA, C't, etc. Fifty Yrs. of New Japan, ed. M. B. Huish, 2 v. 25/ *n.* 8° Smith & Elder [10]
The most authoritative bk. in English on progress of mod. Japan. By var. moderate yet optimistic wrs.
SLADEN, Douglas The Japs at Home; *c.* 40 ill. 6/ 8° Hutchinson [92] 95
$3·50 Lippincott, *Phila.* A readable and light acc. of the people. The 5th (1895) edn. conts. addn. entitled *Bits of China.*
,, Queer Things about Japan 7/6 *n.* 8° Treherne [03] 04
Depicts the lighter and more humorous side of Japanese life and manners as they were some yrs. ago. Ill. by BOKUSAI.
,, + LORIMER (N.) More Queer Things; ill. 21/ *n.* 8° Treherne 04
Incl. a reprint of the *Letters of Will Adams*, wr. fr. Japan, 1611–17.
STEAD, Alf. Japan, our New Ally; ill. 6/ *n.* c 8° Unwin 02
Introduction by Marquis ITO. Includes valuable statistics of trade, population, etc.
,, Great Japan 10/6 *n.* ($2·50 *n.*) 8° Lane 06
,, [ed.] Japan by the Japanese [by var. Jap. authorities] 20/ *n.* 8° Heinemann 04
STOPES, Dr Marie C. A Journal from Japan; ill. 7/6 *n.* 8° Blackie 10
A racy picture of Japan as it presents itself to an English observer from day to day.
SUYEMATSU, Bar. A Fantasy of Far Japan 10/6 *n.* 8° Constable 05
A sort of *apologia* to England for Japan, in form of imaginary or remembered conversations.
,, The Risen Sun 12/6 *n.* 8° Constable 05
THOMAS, Rev. J. Ll. Journeys among the Gentle Japs; map 7/6 c 8° Low 97
A pleasant travel-book; with a special chapter on Japanese religions.
TODD, Mabel L. Corona and Coronet; ill. $2·50 c 8° Houghton, *Boston* 98
Describes the Amherst Eclipse expedition from 'Frisco to Japan, in 1896.
TRACY, Alb. Rambles through Japan without a Guide; ill. 6/ c 8° Low 92
A truthful and vivid picture of the wayside folk and peasantry of Japan.
TREVES, Sir Fredk. —*in his* The Other Side of the Lantern, *ut* **E** § 7
TRISTRAM, Can. H. B. Rambles in Japan; 45 ill. by E. Whymper 8° 10/6 R.T.S. 95
$2 Revell, *N.Y.* Lively travel-impressns. by an experienced traveller, field-naturalist, and collector. Much attention to missionary-wk.

TYNDALE, Walt. Japan and the Japanese; 32 col. pl. by author 18/ *n.* 8° Methuen 10
VAY DE VAYA AND LUSKOD, C't Empires and Emperors of Russia, China, Korea, and Japan—*ut* **E** § 34
WATSON, Gilb. Three Rolling Stones in Japan; ill. [entertaining] 12/6 *n.* 8° Arnold 04
WATSON, W. Petrie Japan: aspects and destinies; maps and ill. 12/6 *n.* 8° Richards [04] 04
A lively acc. of the 'congruous incongruities' of Japan: sensible but somewhat 'slapdash'.
" The Future of Japan 10/6 *n.* 8° Duckworth 07
Exam. of her status; acc. of her advance as it affects Europe; and explan. of polit. and social problems.
WEALE, B. L. Putnam [= L. Lenox SIMPSON] Re-Shaping of Far East, 2 vols.; map and ill. 25/ *n.* ($6 *n.*) 8° Macmillan 05
A useful summary of the political history since 1895 of China, Manchuria, Korea, Japan.
" Truce in East & its Aftermath; map & ill. [sequel] 12/6 *n.* 8° Macmillan 07
" The Coming Struggle in Eastern Asia; ill. 12/6 *n.* ($3·50 *n.*) 8° Macmillan [08] 10
Pt. i deals w. Russn. Emp. in Asia, w. study of milit. condns. dur. and after Russ. War.; ii (the New Problem of E. Asia) w. Japan; iii w. China and aspects of the posn. in Pacific, esp. attitude of U.S.A. Forecasts, with much certainty, a renewal of the w. between Russia and Japan.
WEBSTER, R. Grant Japan: from the Old to the New; ill. 6/ c 8° Partridge 05
WESTON, Rev. Walt. Japanese Alps: climbg. and explorg. in Centr. Japan—*ut* **I** § 165
YOUNGHUSBAND, F. E. On Short Leave to Japan 6/ c 8° Low 94

**Guides**

CHAMBERLAIN, Prf. B. H. Things Japanese: notes on subj. conn. w. Japan 7/6 8° Murray [90] 02
$4 *n.* Scribner, *N.Y.* A very useful and compreh. cyclo. of Things Japanese; in alphab. order. An 'essential' bk., to be used as a complement to *Murray.*
" + MASON (W. B.) Handbk. for Travellers in Japan 20/ p 8° Stanford [84]
*Topography:* WHITNEY (W. N.) Concise Dictionary of Roads, Town, and Villages of Japan; map, 8/; Supplement 3/ 8° *Tokyo* 89; 89
With populations, post offices and railways. *Suppl.* conts. Constit. of Japan, Laws and Statistics.

**Trade** —*v.* **D** § 148, *s.v.* Japan

**Kurile Islands:** LANDOR (A. H. Savage) Alone with Hairy Ainu—*ut sup.*, *s.v.* Ethnology
SNOW, Cpt. H. J. Notes on the Kuril Islands [R.G.S. Extra Vol.] 4/ 8° Murray 97
Much informn. on the geogr., people, and products of the isles., by the chief authority on them.
" In Forbidden Seas; ill. 12/6 *n.* 8° Arnold 10
Recollections of otter-hunting in the Kurils.

**Loochoo Islands** —*v.* **E** § 34
**Noto:** LOWELL (Percival) Noto, Unexplored Corner of Japan $1·25 16° Houghton, *Boston* 91
**Corea** —*v.* **E** § 54 **Eastern Question**—*v.* **D** § 138 **Formosa**—*v.* **E** § 34

## 38: PERSIA

**Early Travels**

BARBARO (J.) & CONTARINI (A.) Travels to Tana and Persia [tr.] 8° Hakluyt Soc. 73
Ed. L'd STANLEY OF ALDERLEY, w. narrs. of other Ital. travels in Persia, tr. and ed. Chas. GREY.
FRYER, Dr Jno. New Account of East India and Persia—*ut* **E** § 35 [travels 1672–81]
JENKINSON, Ant. [d. 1611], etc. Early Voyages and Travels to Russia and Persia, 2 vols.—*ut* **E** § 25
TEIXEIRA, Pedro Travels, tr. W. F. Sinclair; w. notes D. Ferguson 8° Hakluyt Soc. 02
Acc. of voy. 1604–5 fr. India to Italy, and of prev. voy. fr. It. to Spain by Philippines. Incls. also his *Kings of Harmuz* and extrs. fr. *Kings of Persia.*
de la VALLE, Pietro [17 cent.] Letters from Persia, etc., tr. and ed. Sir M. Nathan 8° Hakluyt Soc. *in prep.*
di VARTHEMA, Lud. Travels in Egypt, Syria, Arabia, Persia, etc. [tr.]—*ut* **E** § 30 [1503–8]

**Recent Travel and Accounts; Political Condition** —*v. also* **E** § 33; **E** § 39, *s.v.* Caucasus

ANDERSON, T. S. My Wanderings in Persia *o.p.* [*pb.* 10/6] 8° Blackwood 79
ANET, Claude Through Persia in a Motor-Car [tr.]; ill. 16/ *n.* 8° Hodder 07
Acc. of jy. of Pr'ce Emman. BIBESCO, author, 3 other men, and 2 ladies thro' Persia by Russia and Caucasus in 3 cars: penetrated Ispahan.
ARNOLD, Arth. Through Persia by Caravan, 2 vols. [1875] *o.p.* [*pb.* 28/] 8° Tinsey 77
BAKER, Col. Valentine Clouds in the East [Persia, Turkoman Empire] *o.p.* [*pb.* 18/] 8° Chatto [76] 78
BASSETT, Rev. Jas. Persia, Land of Imams [travel and resid. 1871–85] 7/6 c 8° Blackie 87
BELLEW, H. W. From the Indus to the Tigris *o.p.* [*pb.* 14/] 8° Trübner 74
BENJAMIN, S. G. W. Persia and the Persians; ill. [24/ Murray] $3 8° Houghton, *Boston* [87] 91
BIDDULPH, C. E. Four Months in Persia, and Visit to Trans-Caspia 3/6 r 8° Paul 93
BIGHAM, Clive —*in his* A Ride thro' Western Asia, *ut* **E** § 30
Incls. a journey in Persia, fr. Teheran to Shiraz and Baghdad, and back to Teheran.
BINNING, R. B. Travels in Persia, Ceylon, etc., 2 vols. *o.p.* [*pb.* 28/] 8° W. H. Allen 57
BISHOP, Mrs [= Isab. L. BIRD] Journeys in Persia and Kurdistan, 2 vols.; 36 ill. 24/ c 8° Murray 91
$6·50 Putnam, *N.Y.* A vivid acc. of people and life dur. caravan-jy. thro' least-kn. pt. of Cent. Persia and acr. Kurdistan to Black Sea. Incl. visit to the Rayab Nestorians.
BLUNT, L'y Anne I. N. —*in her* A Pilgrimage to Nejd, *ut* **E** § 32

**Browne**, Edw. G. A Year among the Persians; map [1887–8] 21/ 8° Black 93
$6 Macmillan, *N.Y.* A fascinatg. descrn. of the country, people, and relig. thought in 1887–8. *V. also* his wks. on Bâbi-ism in A § 13.

" Narrative of Recent Events in Persia; port. 1/ *n.* 8° Luzac 09
Includes a translation of the 'Persian Constitution'

**Chirol**, Valentine —*in his* The Middle Eastern Question, *ut* **D** § 138

**Collins**, E. Treacher In the Kingdom of the Shah; ill. 12/ 8° Unwin 96
Observations on Persian life and character, by an oculist, who went to Ispahan to examine the eyes of Prince Zille Sultan, eldest son of the Shah.

**Cresson**, W. P. The Awakening East; ill. 12/6 *n.* 8° Heinemann 08
A description of present day Persia, and the events of 1908.

***Curzon**, Geo. N. Persia & the Persian Question, 2 vols.; maps & ill. 42/ ($12) 8° Longman 92
Half wk. consists of pop., trustworthy, instructive descrn. of travels in all pts. of Persia in 1889–90; other and more learned half treats, in histor., polit., commerc., archæol. and geogr. sense, of Pers. provinces or territ. divns. (Transcaspia included), of army, navy, revenue, resources manufs., means of travellg., etc. Whole forms the most authoritative wk. we have on Persia as a nation and as a factor in politics of East.

**De Lorey** (E.) + **Sladen** (D.) Queer Things about Persia; 52 pl. 21/ *n.* 8° Nash 07

" The Moon of the Fourteenth Night; ill. 16/ *n.* 8° Hurst 10
Diary of a yg. Frenchman of the Legation at Teheran, incl. details of the Revolution.

**de Windt**, Harry Ride to India across Persia and Baluchistan 16/ 8° Chapman 91

**Durand**, L'y Autumn Tour in Western Persia; map and ill. 7/6 *n.* 8° Constable 02
Journey to Ispahan, Ahwaz, Luristan, etc.: a good descriptive book.

**Eastwick**, E. B. Jl. of Diplomate's Three Yrs.' Resid. in Persia, 2 v. *o.p.* [*pb.* 18/] c 8° Smith & Elder 64

**Fogg**, W. P. Arabistan, Land of the Arabian Nights *o.p.* [*pb.* 10/6] c 8° Low [75] 80

**Forrest**, G. W. [ed.] —*in his* Selection from Travels and Journals, *ut* **E** § 35 [1826–43]

**Fraser**, David Persia and Turkey in Revolt; ill. 12/6 *n.* 8° Blackwood 10
A trustworthy acc. of pres. condns., by the official correspondent to *The Times*, a close observer.

**Goldsmid**, Maj.-Gen. Sir F. Telegraph and Travel [in Persia] *o.p.* [*pb.* 21/] 8° Macmillan 74

" Persia [For Countries and Brit. Colonies] 3/6 12° Low 82

**Gordon**, Gen. Sir T. E. Persia Revisited, 1895; ill. 10/6 8° Arnold 96
Last 2 chs. cont. the best discussn. we have of situatn. of country in 1896. Author was for many yrs. milit. attaché and Oriental sec. to Brit. Legn. at Teheran.

**Hamilton**, A. —*in his* Problems of the Middle East, *ut* **D** § 138

**Harris**, Walt. B. From Batoum to Baghdad, 2 maps and ill. 12/ 8° Blackwood 96
Batoum, Tiflis, southw. by Lake Gokcha and Erivan to Lake Urumia (saltest lake in world), southw. thro' Pers. Kurdistan by Tabriz and Kermanshah, thence backwards by Baghdad.

**Hedin**, Dr Sven Overland to India [tr.], 2 vols.; 2 maps & 308 ill. (some col.) 30/ *n.* 8° Macmillan 10
The bulk of the bk. is occup. by a day-to-day narr. of the expedn. for the investign. of some of the great waste areas of Persia. The most import. sectn. of the jy. was thro' the Kevir (S.-E. of Caspian): thence fr. Tebbes, to Naibend, acr. the Dasht-i-Lut to Neh, acr. Hamun Lake, thro' Beluchistan to Quetta and to Simla.

**Hone** (J. M.) + **Dickinson** (P. L.) Persia in Revolution 5/ *n.* c 8° Unwin 10

**Houtum-Schindler**, Gen. A Eastern Persian Irak; map 5/ 8° Royal Geogr. Soc. (Murray) 96
An extremely complete account of the geography of the reign.

**Hume-Griffith**, M. E. Behind the Veil in Persia and Turkish Arabia; ill. 16/ *n.* 8° Seeley [09] 09
A readable bk., by wife of a medical missionary: result of 8 yrs.' residence.

**Jackson**, Prf. A. V. Williams Persia, Past & Present; map & 200 ill. $4 *n.* (17/ *n.*) 8° Macmillan 06
A valuable wk. of research and travel in the country known to Zoroaster, incl. Transcaspia and Turkistan. Mostly on horseback. Excellent illns. fr. author's camera. A second vol. to follow comprising acc. of Susa and E. Persia, w. descrn. of jy. fr. Baku to Samarkand.

**Landor**, A. H. Savage —*in his* Across Coveted Lands, *ut* **E** § 31

**Layard**, Sir A. H. Early Adventures in Persia, Susiana and Babylonia 7/6 c 8° Murray [87] 94
The travels described took place in 1839–42, and form an exciting narr. A large pt. of this bk. is devoted to the tragic story of the great Baktiyari chieftain, Mehemet Taki Than.

" —*in his* Autobiography and Letters, ed. W. N. Bruce, 2 vols.; ill. 25/ *n.* 8° Murray 03

**Le Messurier**, Col. A. —*in his* From London to Bokhara, and Ride thro' Persia, *ut* **E** § 33

**Le Strange**, Guy Lands of Eastern Caliphate, Mesopot., Pers., etc.—*ut* **E** § 30

**Malcolm**, Sir Jno. Sketches of Persia, 2 v. [manners & customs; Nat. Lib.] ea. 6*d.* 18° Cassell [28] 88

**Marsh**, H. C. A Ride thro' Islam [Pers. and Afghan. to India] *o.p.* [*pb.* 14/] 8° Tinsley 77

**Mounsey**, A. H. Through Caucasus and Interior of Persia—*ut* **E** § 39

**Persia Boundary Commission**: Eastern Persia, 2 vols.; col. pl. [1870–2] 42/ 8° Macmillan 76
i: *Geography*, by Majors St John Lovett and Euan Smith; ii: *Geology and Zoology*, by W. T. Blanford.

**Rees**, J. D. From Kasveen to Hamadan acr. Karaghan Country 8° *Madras* 85

'**Resident at Teheran** (A)' Persian Pictures: Safar Nameh *o.p.* [*pb.* 6/] c 8° Bentley 94
Amusing, rather than instructive, sketches of Persian life and manners, very pleasantly written (? by a lady).

**Ronaldshay**, Earl of —*in his* Sport and Politics under an Eastern Sky, *ut* **E** § 31

**Sparroy**, Wilf. Persian Children of the Royal Family 12/6 *n.* ($3·50 *n.*) 8° Lane 02
By the tutor to the sons of the Tillu's Sultan: a familiar account of present-day Persian life.

**Stack**, Edw. Six Months in Persia, 2 vols.; 7 good maps 24/ c 8° Low 82
Conts. good chs.: 'Geograph. Land Revenue Syst.', Present Condn. of Persia', 'Travelling in Persia'

**Stewart**, Col. C. E. Thro' Persia in Disguise; maps and ill. (2 col.) 15/ *n.* 8° Routledge 11
Dutton, *N.Y.* Author, dressed in garb of Armen. merclt., accomp. by only 2 followers, made his way thro' Ziganeh Pass, visited Erzeroum and Tabriz, and crossed the desert of Afghan frontier. Incl. also *Reminiscs. of Indian Mutiny.*

STUART, Donald — The Struggle for Persia; map — 6/ c 8° Methuen 02
A number of travel-notes, with an account of Russian aggression in Persia. Strongly anti Russian.

SYKES, Ella C. — Thro' Persia on a Side-saddle; map and ill. — 7/6 *n.* 8° Macqueen [97] 01
$2 *n.* Lippincott, *Phila.* Journeys from Tehran to Kerman, Kerman to Kelat, Kelat to Karachi; a pleasant description.

,, — Persia and its People; map and 20 ill. — 10/6 *n.* 8° Methuen 10

*SYKES, Maj. Percy M. — Ten Thousand Miles in Persia; maps and ill. — 25/ *n.* m 8° Murray 02
$6 *n.* Scribner, *N.Y.* 8 yrs.' travel (1893 onw.) in E. and S. Persia: a very valuable geogr. acc. Previous accs. of his jys. (crossg. Pers. in every directn.) appeared in *Jl.* of R.G.S., Dec. 1897 and Feb. 1902.

,, — The Glory of the Shia World; ill. and 4 col. pl. — 10/ *n.* 8° Macmillan 10
A wk. of imagination—not of travel, any more than is MORIER'S *Haji Baba*, but based on intimate knowl. of country and people, and contg. admirable, sympathetic picts. of Pers. life, customs, and character, aboundg. in anecdotes.

v. THIELMANN, Frhr. M. G. F. Journey in Caucasus, Persia, Turkey in Asia [tr.]—*ut* **E** § 39

'VIATOR' — Overland to Persia; ill. — 5/ *n.* c 8° Bumpus 06

WEEKS, Edwin Lord — From Black Sea thro' Persia and India; ill. — $2·50 8° Harper, *N.Y.* 95
Affords an excellent panorama of lively descrn. of everyday life, advents., and manners; w. many sound observns. and criticisms on art.

WHIGHAM, H. J. — The Persian Problem; maps and ill. — *o.p.* [*pb.* 12/6] 8° Isbister 03
Travel-letters contrib. to *The Morning Post;* w. study of Russian positn. in Persia and Baghdad Ry.

WILLIAMS, E. Crawshay — Across Persia; maps and ill. — 12/6 *n.* 8° Arnold 07
$3·50 *n.* Longman, *N.Y.* Acc. of jy. w. viceregal party in 1903 up Pers. Gulf and fr. Bushire to Caspian coast.

WILLS, C. J. [ed.] — Behind an Eastern Veil — 7/ 8° Blackwood 94
A blend of the romance and the bk. of travel, very much like MORIER'S *Haji Baba* [*ut* **K** § 50], dealg. w. 'the Inner Life of Ladies of the Upper Class in Persia', supplying some romantic incident and a graphic pict. of Pers. manners and customs in and ab. Teheran and Shiraz.

WILLS, Dr C. J. — In Land of Lion and Sun [resid. 1866–81] 2/ c 8° Ward & Lock [83] 91

,, — Persia as it is [mod. Pers. life and character] 8/6 c 8° Low [86] 87

WILSON, Rev. S. G. — Persian Life and Customs; map and ill. — $1·75 8° Revell, *N.Y.* [95] 96
7/6 Oliphant, *Edin.* Expercs. of Amer. Presb. missionary for 15 yrs. resid. in Tabriz.

WISHARD, Dr J. G. — Twenty Years in Persia — $1·50 n. (5/ *n.*) c 8° Revell 09
By the Director of the American Presbyterian Hospital, Teheran.

**Karún River:** AINSWORTH (W. F.) River Karún: openg. to Brit. comrce. *o.p.* [*pb.* 6/] c 8° W. H. Allen 90

**Persia, Gulf of**

BOEHM, E. C. — Persian Gulf and South Sea Isles — 6/ 8° H. Cox 04

REES, J. D. — Russia, India, and the Persian Gulf — 1/ 8° Harrison 03

**Yezd:** MALCOLM (Napier) Five Years in a Persian Town; ill. — 10/6 *n.* 8° Murray 05
$2 *n.* Dutton, *N.Y.* Account of author's work in Yezd as a missionary.

## 39: RUSSIA-IN-ASIA: CAUCASUS, MONGOLIA, SIBERIA

KRAUSSE, Alexis — Russia in Asia: a record and a study *o.p.* [*pb.* 10/ *n.*] 8° Richards [99] 00
Hist. of growth of Russn. power in Asia [1588–1899]; acc. of princs. and causes wh. have led to it; and exam. into relative interests of Russia and Gt. Brit. in Asia, w. glance at future developmts.

WEALE, B. L. Putnam [= F. Lenox SIMPSON]—*in his* The Coming Struggle in Eastern Asia, *ut* **E** § 37

WRIGHT, Prf. G. F. — Asiatic Russia, 2 vols.; ill. — $7·50 *n.* r 8° McClure, *N.Y.* 03
32/ Nash. Detailed acc. of phys. geogr., concise narr. of Russn. conq., descrn. of types of colonists, and discussn. of social, econ., and polit. condns.

**Caucasus and Transcaucasia** —*v. also* **E** §§ 25, 33

*Bibliography:* MEZHOV (V. I.) Recueil de Turkestan [system. and alphab. list of bks.] 8° *St Petersburg* 78

MIANSAROV, M. — Bibliographia Caucasica et Transcaucasica, vol. i — 8° *St Petersburg* 74–6
Most of the works are either Russn. or Armenian; v. incomplete in European.

WRIGHT, Dr G. F. —*in his* Asiatic Russia, 2 vols., *ut inf.*

*Ethnology:* v. HAXTHAUSEN (Bar.) Tribes of Caucasus — *o.p.* [*pb.* 5/] c 8° Chapman [55] 55

*Early Travel* —*v. also* **E** § 25

WILLIAM OF RUBRUCK *and* JOHN OF PIAN DE CARPINE Journeys to Tartary in 13th Century, tr. and ed. W. W. Rockhill [w. bibliogr.] *o.p.* 8° Hakluyt Soc. 00
The *Texts and Versns.* of above as first prtd. by HAKLUYT (1598) were ed., w. some shorter pieces, by C. R. BEAZLEY in 1903 [*ut* **E** § 5]: issued as vol. xiii of Extra Ser. of Hakluyt Soc.

*Recent Travel and Accounts:* ABERCROMBY (Jno.) Trip thro' Eastern Caucasus; ill. — 14/ 8° Stanford 90

BADDELEY, J. F. — Russian Conquest of Caucasus; maps and ill. — 21/ *n.* ($5 *n.*) 8° Longman 08
An admirable hist. of war betw. 1829 and 1859, when SHAMIL and his wild tribesmen resisted the Russn. advance in Caucasus—an early step tow. her projects in conn. w. mastery of Asia.

BRYCE, Jas. — Transcaucasia & Ararat: notes of tour [1876]; ill. 8/6 ($3·50) c 8° Macmillan [77] 96
Fourth edn., w. a Supplementary Chapter on the recent history of the Armenian Question.

CUNYNGHAME, Sir A. T. — Travels in the Eastern Caucasus, Daghestan, and the Frontiers of Turkey and Persia — *o.p.* [*pb.* 18/] 8° Murray 72

FRESHFIELD, D. W. — Travels in Central Caucasus and Bashan [1868] *o.p.* [*pb.* 18/] 8° Longman 69
Contains an account of the famous ascent of Mkhinvari (Mt. Kazbek).

* ,, — Exploration of the Caucasus, 2 vols.; maps & ill. — 21/ *n.* r 8° Arnold [96] 02
Record of explorn. of Caucasus since 1868 by members of Alpine Club, by President of the Club; and a narr. of his own recent jys. in that region. Incls. contribs. by H. W. HOLDER, J. G. COCKIN, H. WOOLLEY, M. de DÉCHY, and Prf. BONNEY. Of consid. importce., contg. digested study and experce. of nearly 30 yrs. Admirable illus.

GROVE, F. C. The Frosty Caucasus ; ill. o.p. [pb. 15/] 8° Longman 76
Account of a walk thro' Cauc. and ascent of Elbruz, in 1874.

HARRIS, Walt. B. —*in his* From Batum to Baghdad, *ut* **E** § 38

MOUNSEY, A. H. Journey thro' Caucasus & Interior of Persia [1866] o.p. [pb. 14/] 8° Smith & Elder 72

MUMMERY, A. F. My Climbs in the Alps and Caucasus—*ut* **I** § 165

NORMAN, Sir Hy. All the Russias : travels and studies ; ill. 18/ n. 8° Heinemann 02
A full account of the railway, the Caucasus region, etc. Trustworthy.

TELFER, Com. J. B. The Crimea and Transcaucasia, 2 vols. ; maps & pl. 36/ r 8° Paul [76] 77

v. THIELMANN, Bar. M. Journey in Caucasus, Persia & Turkey [tr.], 2 v. o.p. [pb. 18/] p 8° Murray 75

VILLARI, Luigi Fire and Sword in the Caucasus ; ill. 10/6 n. 8° Unwin 06

'WANDERER' [an English officer] Notes on the Caucasus 9/ 8° Macmillan 83

**Georgia :** WARDROP (Oliver) Kingdom of Georgia ; maps and ill. [w. bibliogr.] 14/ 8° Low 88

**Manchuria** —*v.* **E** § 34

**Mongolia and Siberia :** *Bibliography*

MEJOW (V. J.) + SIBERIAKOW (J. M.) Bibl. of Bks. and Arts. fr. Jls. conc. Siberia, 3 v. *St Petersburg* 96
Incl. historical documts., corresp., memoirs and biographies, some of great importance extending over a period of 3 cents. endg. w. 1892.

*Travel and Life :* ATKINSON (T. W.) Oriental and Western Siberia o.p. [pb. 21/] i 8° Hurst 58
A narr. of 7 yrs.' explorns. and advents. in Mongolia, Chinese Tartary, etc. ; w. illns. of scenery.

BARZINI, L. —*in his* Pekin to Paris [tr.], *ut* **E** § 31

BATES, Lindon, jun. The Russian Road to China ; ill. 8° 10
10/6 n. Constable. A well-wr. and instructive American travel-bk., w. histor. matter included.

BOOKWALTER, J. W. Siberia and Central Asia ; ill. $4 8° Stokes, *N.Y.* [99]
21/ n. Pearson. Incl. good acc. of Trans-Casp. Ry. The numerous photogr. illns. very good.

COLQUHOUN, Arch. R. The 'Overland' to China $3 (16/) 8° Harper 00
A Siberian railway-journey, describg. the new conditions of Siberia.

CURTIN, Jeremiah The Mongols : a history [12/6 n. Low] $3 n. 8° Little & Brown, *Boston* 08
To the early 15th cent., when the Mongols were finally expelled fr. China by the Ming dynasty.

" The Mongols in Russia [12/6 n. Low] $3 n. 8° Little & Brown, *Boston* 08

" A Journey in Southern Siberia ; ill. $3 n. 8° Little & Brown, *Boston* 09
12/6 n. Low. Acc. of the neighbourhd. of Lake Baikal and of the Buriats, their religion and myths.

DEUTSCH, Leo Sixteen Years in Siberia : 1884–1900 [tr.] ; 25 pl. 15/ n. 8° Murray 03
$4 n. Dutton, *N.Y.* A simple, fascinatg. acc. of the jy. to Siberia, prison-life there, etc., by a leader of the Revoluty. movemt.

DE WINDT, Harry From Pekin to Calais by Land ; ill. o.p. [pb. 20/] 8° Chapman 89

" Siberia as it is [tr.] o.p. [pb. 18/] 8° Chapman 92
Jy. fr. Perm to Tomsk in 1890, dealg. spec. w. social life of Russns. in Siberia and state of prisons (favourable).

" The New Siberia ; w. Appendix ; map and 57 ill. 14/ 8° Chapman 96
A graphic and impartial acc. of visit to penal Island of Sakhalien and polit. prisons and mines of Trans-Baikal District (E. Siberia). Finds the penal system, at least in these latter days, in most respects less rigorous than is generally supposed.

" From Paris to New York by Land—*ut* **E** § 7

EDEN, C. H. Frozen Asia : sk. of mod. Siberia ; ill. [juvenile] 5/ c 8° S.P.C.K. 79

FRASER, Jno. Foster The Real Siberia : dash thro' Manchuria ; ill. 3/6 c 8° Cassell [02] 04
An ordinary travel-bk., chfly. occup. w. the railway journey thro' Siberia. Very favourable view of the prison-system.

GERRARE, Wirt Greater Russia, the Continental Empire ; ill. 18/ n. 8° Heinemann 03
$3 n. Macmillan, *N.Y.* A valuable and fresh acc. of travel in Siberia, and the political situation there at the time.

GILDER, W. H. Ice-pack and Tundra—*ut* **E** § 69, *s.v. Jeannette*

GILMOUR, Rev. Jas. Among the Mongols ; *and* More about Mongols—*ut* **A** § 105 [missionary travels]

" —*for his* Diaries, Letters and Reports, *v.* **A** § 105

GOWING, L. F. Five Thousand Miles in a Sledge ; ill. [acr. Siberia] 8/ c 8° Chatto 89

GUILLEMARD, Dr F. H. H. —*in his* Cruise of *Marchesa* to Kamschatska, etc., *ut* **E** § 7

HAWES, Chas. In the Uttermost East ; 3 maps and 70 ill. 16/ 8° Harper 03
Acc. of natives and convict-settlemt. in Sakhalien, w. notes of travel in Korea, Sib., and Manchuria.

HEDLEY, Jno. Tramps in Dark Mongolia ; map & 52 ill. [missionary] 12/6 n. 8° Unwin 10

*HOWORTH, H. H. History of Mongols, Pt. i, 28/ ; ii, 42/ ($14·50) ; iii, 28/ ($9·50) [to 19 cent.] 8° Longman 76–88

" Roughing it in Siberia ; map and ill. 5/ c 8° Low 97
Acc. of trans-Siberian railway journey, and of the Russian gold-mining industry.

KENNAN, Geo. Siberia and the Exile System—*ut* **D** § 123

" Tent Life in Siberia & Adventures am. the Koraks $1·25 (10/6 n.) 8° Putnam [70] 10
Story of effort of Western Union to build a line of telegr. up the W. coast of Amer. and down the E. coast of Asia. The first bk. to give an accu. acc. of condns. in mod. Siberia.

LANSDELL, Rev. H. Through Siberia ; ill. [in 1879] o.p. [pb. 10/6] r 8° Low [82] 83

LEROY-BEAULIEU, P. —*in his* Awakening of the East [tr.], *ut* **E** § 37 [Sib., Jap., China]

LYNCH, Geo. The Path of Empire 10/ *n.* i 8° Duckworth 03
A journey over the ry. to Dalny and Port Arthur and backwards fr. Japan to Moscow, by a newsppr.-corresp.

MARSDEN, Kate On Sledge & Horseback to Outcast Sib. Lepers; ill. 2/6 8° *Record* Press [92] 93
Acc. of a remarkable enterprise, full of interest apart fr. its philanthropic purpose.

MEAKIN, Annette M. B. A Ribbon of Iron; ill. [thro' Sib.] 6/ c 8° Constable 01

MEIGNAN, Victor From Paris to Pekin over Siberian Snows [tr.]; 16 pl. 16/ 8° Sonnenschein 85

MELVILLE, G. W. In the Lena Delta—*ut* **E** § 69

NIEMOJOWSKI, L. Siberian Pictures, 2 vols.; 16 pl. [tr. fr. Polish] 21/ 8° Hurst 83

PRICE, Julius M. From Arctic Ocean to Yellow Sea; ill. 7/6 8° Low [92] 93
Jy. 1890–1 acr. Sib., Mong., Gobi Desert, and N. China—Sib. bg. reached id. N. Cape and thro' Kara Sea to Yenesei estuary, and thence to Yeniseisk all the way by steamer fr. Blackwall to heart of Siberia.

PIASSETSKY, P. Russian Travellers in Mongolia & China [tr.], 2 v.; ill. 24/ c 8° Chapman 84

PREJEVALSKY, Gen. N. M. Mongolia, Tangut Country, N. Tibet, etc. [tr.], 2 v. 42/ 8° Low 76

,, From Kulja across Tian Shan to Lob Nor [tr.] *o.p.* [*pb.* 15/] 8° Low 79

ROCKHILL, W. W. —*in his* The Land of the Llamas, *ut* **E** § 34

,, Diary of Jy. thro' Mong. & Tibet 1891–2; ill. Smithson. Inst., *Washgtn.* 94
A valuable contribn. to knowl. of Tibet [*ut* E § 34] and espec. of Mongolia. The outward route was fr. Pekin thro' Kalgan, Kuei-Hua, and Ho-Kóu, along Yellow River to territory s. of the Koko-Nor, and thence to the Tengri-Nor, at wh. point author was stopped and compelled to turn homeward thro' Chamdo, Batang, Chunging and Shanghai. The explorn. was undertaken partly und. auspices of Smithsonian Institn.

,, Notes on Ethnology of Tibet—*in* Ann. Rept. of U.S. Nat. Mus. 1894 Smithson. Inst., *Washgtn.* 95
A running commentary on colln. of hundreds of examples of ethnogr. objects fr. Tibet preserved in U.S. Nat. Mus., Washington.

SEEBOHM, H. Siberia in Asia; ill. [Yenesay valley in E. Siberia] *o.p.* [*pb.* 14/] c° 8° Murray 82

,, Siberia in Europe—*v.* **E** § 25 [valley of Petchora]

SHOEMAKER, M. M. The Great Siberian Railway; map and 30 ill. $2 *n.* (9/ *n.*) c 8° Putnam 03
An ordinary account of an ordinary journey across the railway and in Korea.

SIMPSON, Jas. Y. Side-Lights on Siberia; map and ill. 16/ 8° Blackwood 98
Acc. of the Sib. Ry. (as in 1893) and of the great rivers and river life in Sib. Also prison-syst. (on whole favourable).

STADLING, J. Through Siberia, ed. F. H. H. Guillemard; ill. 18/ 8° Constable 01
A well-wr. acc. of jy. across Sib. by ry. and N. to Arctic Ocean in search of traces of ANDRÉE.

SWAYNE, H. G. C. Through the Highlands of Siberia; map & ill. 12/6 *n.* r 8° Rowland Ward 04

TREVOR-BATTYE, Aubyn A Northern Highway of the Czar; ill. 6/ c 8° Constable 98
Description of a journey from Kolguev Island thro' Northern Russia to Vologda.

TURNER, Sam. Siberia: recd. of travel, climbg., explorn.; ill. 21/ *n.* 8° Unwin 05
$6 *n.* Jacobs, *Phila.* Straightforward acc. of visit to Sib. and climbg. in the Altai (inclg. some first ascents).

'VLADIMIR' Russia on Pacific and Siberian Railway 14/ 8° Low 99
Partly historical, partly descriptive and political. Maps and ill.

WIGGINS, Cpt. Jos.
Johnson, Hy. Life & Voyages of Joseph Wiggins, F.R.G.S.; maps & ill. 15/ *n.* 8° Murray 07
Based on WIGGINS' journals and corresp. Story of his discovery of the Kara Sea route to Siberia.

WILLIAMSON, A. Jys. in N. China, Manchuria & E. Mongolia, 2 vols. *o.p.* [*pb.* 21/] c 8° Smith & Elder 70

**Amur:** ATKINSON (T. W.) Travels in Upper and Lower Amoor; ill. *o.p.* [*pb.* 42/] i 8° Hurst 60

BAX, Cpt. Cruise in Eastern Seas [Corea to River Amur] *o.p.* [*pb.* 12/] c 8° Murray 75

RAVENSTEIN, E. G. The Russians on the Amur; 4 pl. and 3 maps *o.p.* [*pb.* 15/] 8° Trübner 61

**Baku:** HENRY (J. D.) Baku, an Eventful History; ill. 12/6 *n.* 8° Constable 05

**Khotan:** ROCKHILL (W. W.) Early Hist. of Khotan—*in his* Life of Buddha, *ut* **A** § 14

STEIN, Dr M. Aurel Sand-buried Ruins of Khotan; map & 120 ill. 21/ *n.* m 8° Unwin 03

,, Ancient Khotan, 2 vols.; 72 ill. 105/ *n.* ($33·75) 4° Clar. Press 07
Former is a popular acc., latter the Detailed Rept. of the archæol. explorns. in Chinese Turk. carried out und. auspices of Indian Govt. Vol. i: Text, w. descr. list of antiqs. by F. H. ANDREWS, and Appendices by var. archæologists; ii conts. the collotype pl. and illns.

**Petchora**—*v.* **E** § 25 **Russia-in-Europe**—*v.* **E** § 25 **Saghalien:** *Ainus*—*v.* **E** § 37 **Turkestan**—*v.* **E** § 33

## 40: TURKEY-IN-ASIA

BARKLEY, H. C. Ride thro' Disturbed Districts of Asia Minor and Armenia—*ut* **E** § 30

BIGHAM, Clive A Ride through Western Asia; ill.—*ut* **E** § 31

,, With the Turkish Army in Thessaly; maps & ill. *o.p.* [*pb.* 6/6 *n.*] 8° Macmillan 97

COWPER, H. Swainson Through Turkish Arabia—*ut* **E** § 32

CURTIS, W. E. Turkestan, the Heart of Asia; ill. 8° Hodder, *in prep.*
Narrative of a visit to Khiva, Samarkand, Askabad, Bokhara, and other places.

DAVIS, E. J. Anatolica; *and* Life in Asiatic Turkey—*ut* **E** § 30

FARLEY, J. Lewis Egypt, Cyprus, and Asiatic Turkey *o.p.* [*pb.* 14/] 8° Trübner 78

,, Modern Turkey *o.p.* [*pb.* 14/] 8° Hurst 72

SMALL CAPS FARLEY, J. Lewis — Turks & Christians: solutn. of Eastern Questn. *o.p.* [*pb.* 10/6] 8° Simpkin [76] 76
GEARY, Grattan — Thro' Asiatic Turkey, 2 vols. [Bombay to Bosphorus] *o.p.* [*pb.* 28/] p 8° Low 78
HALIL HALID — Diary of a Turk; ill. [$1·75 Macm., *N.Y.*] 5/ c 8° Black 03
From the standpoint of an enlightened Turk. Instructive.
HARRIS, Walt. B. — From Batum to Baghdad—*ut* **E** § 38
HOGARTH, D. G. — —*in his* The Nearer East [Regions of the World], *ut* **E** § 29
KINGLAKE, A. W. — Eothen—*ut* **E** § 30
LAYARD, Sir A. H. — Nineveh and its Remains; *and* Fresh Discoveries—*ut* **G** § 8
Interestg. records of travel in 1845–51 over a large part of Asiatic Turkey.
LE STRANGE, Guy — Baghdad during the Abbasid Caliphate 16/ *n.* ($2·25) 8° Clar. Press 01
A most valuable study of the topography of the city, w. 8 plans of it at various periods.
MCCOAN, J. C. — Our New Protectorate: geogr., races, resources, govt., 2 v. 24/ c 8° Chapman 79
MEAKIN, Annette M. B. — In Russian Turkestan; 16 ill. 7/6 *n.* c 8° G. Allen 03
PERCY, Hy. A. G., Earl of [*then* L'd WARKWORTH] Notes from a Diary in Asiatic Turkey; ill. 21/ *n.* r 8° Arnold 98
A good acc. of jy. w. a polit. object thru' As. Turkey, fr. Scutari, thro' Angora *via* Samstin to Trebizond, thence thro' Turk. and Russn. Armenia to Nineveh, whence *via* Aleppo to the sea.
,, — The Highlands of Asiatic Turkey—*ut* **E** § 30
Acc. of jy. fr. Kaisariyeh, by Lake Van, and Tigris to Baghdad and Bassorah; excellent descrn. of condn. of country.
PETERS, Dr Jno. P. — Nippur: explorations & adventures, 2 vols. ea. $2·50 (12/6) 8° Putnam 97
Narr. of Univ. of Pennsylvania Expedn., 1889–1900. Travels in search of archæological remains. Maps and illns.
PUMPELLY, R. — Explorns. in Turkestan [expedn. 1903] [pp. 336] 4° Carnegie Institn., *Washington* 05
RAMSAY, Prf. W. M. — Impressions of Turkey during 12 Years' Wanderings 6/ c 8° Hodder 97
SYKES, Mark — Through Five Turkish Provinces; map and ill. 7/6 8° Bickers 00
From Damascus thro' Aleppo, Deir, Baghdad, Mosul, Bitlis, and Van to Chengil.
TOZER, H. F. — Researches in the Highlands of Turkey, 2 vols.—*ut* **E** § 22
,, — Turkish Armenia and Eastern Asia Minor [jy. 1879] *o.p.* [*pb.* 16/] 8° Longman 81
WARKWORTH, L'd — —*v.* Percy, H. A. G., Earl, *sup.*

**Arabia**—*v.* **E** § 32 **Asia Minor**—*v.* **E** § 30

**Armenia**: ARGYLL, (D'ke of) Our Responsibilities for Turkey 3/6 c 8° Murray 96
AZHDERIAN, Antranig — Turk and Land of Haig $1·50 12° 98
BARKLEY, H. C. — Ride thro' Disturbed Districts of Asia Minor and Armenia—*ut* **E** § 30
BLISS, Rev. E. M. — Turkey and the Armenian Atrocities; ill. 10/6 8° Unwin 96
BRYCE, Jas. — —*in his* Transcaucasia and Ararat, *ut sup.*
HAMILTON, W. J. — Researches in Asia Min., Pontus, and Armenia, 2 vols.—*ut* **E** § 30
HARRIS, Dr J. R. + Mrs Rendel L'rs. fr. Scenes of Recent Massacres in Arm. [moderate] 6/ c 8° Nisbit 97
HARRIS, Walter B. — —*in his* From Batoum to Baghdad, *ut* **E** § 38
HEPWORTH, Rev. Geo. H. — Through Armenia on Horseback; ill. $2 8° Dutton, *N.Y.* 98
By the special correspondent of the *New York Herald*. An important account.
HODGETTS, E. A. Brayley — Round about Armenia; map 6/ c 8° Low 96
Record of a jy. thro' Turkey, Caucasus, and Persa, by *Dy. Graphic* corresp. Gossipy.
LEPSIUS, Dr J. — Armenia and Europe [tr.] [indictmt. of Sultan] 5/ c 8° Hodder 97
LYNCH, H. F. B. — Armenia: travels and studies, 2 vols. 42/ *n.* m 8° Longman 01
A compreh. wk., full of research and firsthd. observn. on geogr., races, politics, etc. Maps and illns.
NORMAN, C. B. — Armenia and Campaign of 1877 [by *Times* corresp.] 21/ 8° Cassell 78
'OLD INDIAN (AN)' — Historical Sketch of Armenia of the Armenians 5/ c 8° Stock 96
SETH, Mesrovb J. — History of the Armenians in India 7/6 *n.* c 8° Luzac [*Calc.* 94] 97
'SPECIAL CORRESPONDENT (A)' [=A. Fraser MACDONALD] The Land of Ararat 6/ c 8° Remington 93
Jy. made in winter 1891–2 by sea fr. Constant. to Trebizond, thence by Zigana Pass to Erzeroum, and return jy. thro' Russia by Tiflis to Batûm.
SYKES, M. — Dar-ul-Islam; maps and ill. 15/ r 8° Bickers 04
Record of a journey through ten of the Asiatic provinces of Turkey.
TOZER, Rev. H. F. — Turkish Armenia and Eastern Asia Minor—*ut sup.*
WOOD, Cpt. J. N. Price — Travel and Sport in Turkestan; 100 ill. 15/ *n.* 8° Chapman 10

**Mesopotamia**: de BUNSEN (Victoria) The Soul of a Turk; 8 pl. 10/6 *n.* ($3·50 *n.*) 8° Lane 09
By the companion of Mrs. WILKINS (*inf.*). A colln. of highly varied sketches; much of interest fr. pt.-of-view of comparative religion.
JEBB (Louisa) (Mrs Roland WILKINS) By Desert Ways to Baghdad; map & ill. 5/ *n.* 8° Unwin [08] 10
An excellent travel-book, conveyg. essential facts of East as seen by sympath. eyes: an admir. expoen. of the 'psychology of travel': Constant. to Brusa, caravan to Nicæa, rail to Konia, caravan to Adana; thence thro' S. Kurdistan to Diarbekr, down the Tigris to Baghdad, and on to Babylon, Palmyra, Damascus.
IBN SERAPEION — Descrn. of Mesopotamia and Bagdād [*c.* A.D. 900] 8° 96
Ed. and tr. Guy LE STRANGE; w. notes. An important contribn. to hist. of Mesopot. geogr. in 'Abbāsid times, excellently and learnedly edited fr. unique MS. in Brit. Mus., w. admirable map. The most valuable contribn. to knowl. of Mesopot. geogr. since *Chesney's* [*ut* **E** § 30].

**Asia Minor**—*v.* **E** § 30 **Egypt**—*v.* **E** § 42 **Russia-in-Asia**—*v.* **E** § 39 **Turkey-in-Europe**—*v.* **E** § 29

# VI : Geography, etc., of Africa

## 41 : AFRICA : GENERALLY

**Bibliography**

GAY, Jean — Bibliogr. des Ouvrages rel. à l'Afrique et à l'Arabie 20 fr. 8° Gay, *San Remo* 75

KAYSER, Gabr. — Bibliographie de l'Afrique 8 fr. 8° *pr. pr.*, *Brussels* (Challamel, *Paris*) 87

PAULITSCHKE, Philipp — Afrika-Literatur : 1500–1750 4m 8° Brockhausen, *Vienna* 82

**Development ; Partition**

BROWN, Dr Rob. — *in his* Story of Africa and its Explorers, vol. iv, *ut inf.*
This 4th (last) vol. has for sub-title *Europe in Africa*, and deals mainly w. the Europ. settlemt. of the continent.

HERTSLET, Sir Edw. — Map of Africa by Treaty, 3 vols. ; maps 31/6 Eyre & Spottiswoode [95] 97
Vol. i : *Abyssinia to Gt. Brit. (Colonies)* ; ii : *Gt. Brit. and France to Zanzibar* ; iii : *Appendix, Index, Chronol. List.*

JOHNSTON, Sir Harry H. — Hist. of Colonizn. of Afr. by Alien Races 6/ c 8° Camb. Press 99
$1·50 *n.* Putnam, *N.Y.* [Cambr. Hist. Ser.] A clear and interestg. hist., w. short acc. of indig. peoples and 8 good maps.

,, — The Opening-up of Africa [Home University Ser.] 1/ *n.* f 8° Williams 11

KELTIE, J. Scott — The Partition of Africa ; 24 maps 16/ p 8° Stanford [93] 95
Excell. succinct statemt. of all import. facts conn. w. distribn. of territory am. the rival States, a sketch of relns. of outer world to the 'distressful continent' fr. earliest times, and a general summary of results and digest of econ. condns. ; accomp. by admirable ser. of histor. col. maps ill. continent at var. perds. up to partition of 1893.

KINSKY, C't C. — The Diplomatist's Handbook for Africa ; map 10/6 8° Paul 97
Somewhat on the same lines as HERTSLET'S *Map of Africa by Treaty, ut sup.*

STANLEY, Dr H. M., etc. — Africa, its Partition and Future ; map $1·25 c 8° Dodd & Mead, *N.Y.* 98
Presents the actual standing in Africa of the various Europ. nations in 1898, and their chief ambitions.

WHITE, Arth. Silva — The Development of Africa ; 14 col. phys. maps 7/6 c 8° Philip [90] 92
Summarizes the physical conditions of the continent and its economic value.

WILMOT, Hon. A. — The Expansion of South Africa ; maps 5/ 8° Unwin 94
Contains nothing which is not to be found in other, and better, publications on South Africa.

*Great Britain in Modern Africa*

JOHNSTON, Sir Harry H. — Britain across the Seas : Africa ; maps and ill. 10/6 *n.* 8° National Soc. 10
A clear, popular, impartial, and comprehensive narrative, w. about 250 good illns. fr. photos. and drwgs.

SANDERSON, Edg. — Great Britain in Modern Africa ; map and ill. 5/ *n.* c 8° Seeley 07
Partly repr. (in revised form) fr. his *Africa in Nineteenth Century, ut inf.*

**Early Voyages and Travel**

LEGUAT, Frç [*b.* ?1637] — Voyage to Rodriguez, Mauritius, Java and Cape of Good Hope, ed. Cpt. S. P. Oliver, 2 vols. 8° Hakluyt Soc. [1708] 93
Affords much informn. reg. Dutch admin. and colonizn. in E. I. and Cape tow. end 17 cent. ; w. graphic sketch of Fch. Huguenot emigrn. fr. Eur. to S. Afr. at that epoch.

LEO AFRICANUS [AL-HASSAN IBN-MOHAMMED AL-WEZAZ AL-FASI ; 15–6 cent.] History & Description of Africa, ed. Dr Rob. Brown, 3 vols. 8° Hakluyt Soc. 96
A valuable edn. of what was until compar. recent times chief authority for a consid. pt. of Afr. LEO, a Span. Moor, early in 16 cent. crossed the desert by usual caravan route as far as Timbuctu and the Niger, visitg. several of the 'kingdoms' in basin of that river. This edn. is that of Jno. PORY (1600) (revised), w. a long Introd. on LEO, his life, w. predecessors and edns., copious notes, and maps of Afr. acc. to LEO's descrns.

**General Geography ; Travel over Large Areas**

BUXTON, Edw. North — Two African Trips ; map and 80 ill. 15/ *n.* 8° Stanford 02
Two trips : to Brit. East Africa by Mombasa, and to the White Nile south of Omdurman.

COLVILE, Mrs Zélie — Round the Black Man's Garden ; maps and ill. 16/ 8° Blackwood 93
Descrns. of travel of Col. and Mrs. COLVILE dur. 6 mos. of 1888–9 : Red Sea, Arab. littoral, Madag., Quillimane and home by Durban, Transvaal and Cape.

GIBBONS, Maj. A. St H. — Africa fr. S. to N. thro' Martotseld., 2 v. ; ill. 32/ *n.* ($7·50 *n.*) 8° Lane 04
Contains a very full description of the Zambesi. Good maps.

GROGAN (E. S.) + SHARP (A. S.) From the Cape to Cairo ; map and ill. 21/ *n.* c 4° Hurst 00
An interesting narrative of travel ; of some geographical value.

HALL, Mary — A Woman's Trek from the Cape to Cairo ; maps & ill. 16/ *n.* 8° Methuen 08

HEAWOOD, E. — Elementary Geography of Africa ; map & ill. 2/6 gl 8° Macmillan [97] 03
A school-bk. : physical, ethnographic, geograph., political. Careful and trustworthy.

KASSNER, Theo. — From Rhodesia to Egypt ; maps and 107 ill. 12/6 *n.* 8° Hutchinson 11
Acc. of jy. on foot fr. Cape Town to N. of Afr., thro' E. Congo and Germ. and Brit. E. Afr., w. an ascent of Ruwenzorie.

*KEANE, Prf. A. H. — Africa, 2 vols. =Stanford's Compendium of Geography, *ut* **E** § 2
An excellent repertory of geogr. informn., w. so much of hist., ethnogr., and polit. vicissitudes as are required to ill. and explain the geogr.

LANDOR, A. H. S. — Across widest Africa, 2 vols. ; maps and ill. 42/ *n.* r 8° Hurst 07
Acc. of longest trans-Afr. jy. yet made fr. E. to W. (8,500 m.), w. descrns. of country and people of E., Central, and W. Africa.

PEASE, Alf. E. — Travel and Sport in Africa, 1892–1901, 3 vols. 210/ *n.* 4° Humphreys 02
Algeria, Tunisia, the Sahara, Somaliland, Abyssinia. 900 ill. (60 coloured).

READE, W. Winwood — Savage Afr. ; ill. [Equatorial ; S.W. ; N.W.] *o.p.* [*pb.* 21/] 8° Smith & Elder [63] 64

,, — African Sketch Book, 2 vols. ; ill. [Equatorial ; W.] *o.p.* [*pb.* 24/] c 8° Smith & Elder 73

RECLUS, Elisée — Africa, 4 vols. ; maps and 700 ill. =Universal Geography [tr.], *ut* **E** § 2

SANDERSON, Edg. Africa in the Nineteenth Century [1 summary] 5/ c 8° Seeley 98

VINCENT, F. R. Actual Africa; or, The Coming Continent $5 8° Appleton, *N.Y.* 95
24/ Heinemann. Tour of Coast States, w. extensive trips into the interior. Map and 100 illns.

VIZETELLY, Edw. Cyprus to Zanzibar; ill. 15/ 8° Pearson 01

**History of Exploration**

BROWN, Dr Rob. Story of Africa and its Explorers, 4 vols. ea. 4/ 4° Cassell [92–5] 98
A very good popular bk., dealg. w. the whole continent. Profusely ill. For note on vol. iv *v. sup.*

JONES, C. H. African Exploration from Herodotus to Livingstone $5 8° Holt, *N.Y.* 75

KELTIE, Dr J. Scott Africa and Explorn. as told by its Explorers, 2 v. 42/ r 8° Low
A hist. of Afr. explorn. fr. time of Phœnicians to pres. day. Maps and about 600 illns.

WEBB, E. J. Africa as seen by its Explorers [schl.-bk.] 2/ c 8° Arnold 99
A short acc. of the explorn. told by extrs. fr. the wrgs. of explorers of all ages.

**Lives of Explorers:** *Collectively*: BOMPIANI (S.) Italian Explorers in Africa; ill. 2/ c 8° R.T.S. 91

BOURNE, C. E. Heroes of African Discovery, 2 Ser.; ill. [popular] ea. 3/6 c 8° Sonnenschein [83] 89

BUEL, J. W. Heroes of the Dark Continent; maps & ill. $3 8° Histor. Pb. Co., *St Louis* 90

EDEN, C. H. Africa Seen thro' its Explorers; ill. [popular] 5/ c 8° S.P.C.K. 80

Great Explorers of Africa, 2 vols.; ill. 25/ r 8° Low 94

KINGSTON (W. H. G.) + Low (C. R.) Great African Travellers; 100 ill.
[$2 Dutton, *N.Y.*] 7/6 8° Routledge [73] 03

LATIMER, Eliz. W. Europe in Africa in Nineteenth Century; ill. $2·50 12° McClurg, *Chicago* 95
A readable acc. of discovs. since those of MEHEMET ALI in 2nd decade of 19 cent., and of forces wh. have influenced Eur. colonizn.

*Individually* —*v. also* **A** § 105

BAKER, Sir Saml. W. [1821–93]

Murray (T. D.) + White (A. Silva) Sir Samuel Baker: a memoir; maps & ill. 21/ 8° Macmillan 95
A vivid acc. of BAKER in his personal and offic. relns. and in conn. w. his wk. and wrgs. on discovery of Nile Sources, opening-up of Soudan, promotn. of Brit. interests and suppressn. of Slave Trade in Africa. Incls. an interestg. correspce. w. Gen. GORDON.

BRUCE, Jas. [1730–94] —*v.* **E** § 44

BURTON, Isabel, Lady

Burton (L'y) + Wilkins (W. H.) Romance of Isabel, Lady Burton 10/6 8° Hutchinson 97
In part a vindication of Lady BURTON from the charges brought by her husband's relatives.

BURTON, Sir Rich. [1821–90]—*v.* **E** § 32

EMIN PACHA [=Dr SCHNITZLER; 1840–92]—*v.* **E** § 48

GRENFELL, Geo. [1849–06] —*v.* **E** § 48

LIVINGSTONE, Dr Dav. [1813–73]—for his works (largely autobiographical) *v.* **E** §§ 47, 48

Blaikie, Dr W. G. Personal Life of David Livingstone 6/ p 8° Murray [80] 82

Hughes, Thos. David Livingstone [Men of Action Ser.] 2/6 (75 c. *n.*) c 8° Macmillan 89

Johnston, [Sir] Harry H. Livingstone and Explorn. of Central Africa 3/6 c 8° Philip 91
$1·25. Dodd & Mead, *N.Y.* [World's Great Explorers.] One of the best volumes of the series.

MOFFATT, Rob. [1795–1883] & Mary [wife] Lives of. By J. S. Moffatt [son]; ill. 3/6 c 8° Unwin [85] 88

OSWELL, Wm. Cotton [1818–93] W. C. Oswell, Hunter and Explorer, 2 vols. By W. E. Oswell; ill. 25/ *n.* 8° Heinemann 00
Introduction by Fcs. GALTON. Contains some formerly unpublished Livingstone matter.

PARK, Mungo [1771–1805] —*v.* **E** § 46

STANLEY, H. M. [1841–1904] Autobiography, ed. L'y Stanley; 16 ill. 21/ *n.* m 8° Low 10

George, Thos. Birth, Boyhood, & Younger Days of Stanley *o.p.* [*pb.* 2/6 c 8° Roxburghe Press 95
An attempt to prove that STANLEY was born in Wales.

THOMSON, Jos. [1858–95]

Thomson, Rev. J. B. [bro'] Joseph Thomson, African Explorer; maps and ill. 7/6 c 8° Low [96] 97

**Ethnology** —*for special tribes and districts v.* **E** §§ 42–51 *passim*; *for* Folklore *v.* **B** § 34

SPENCER, Herb. [ed.] Descriptive Sociology, No. 4: African Races. By Dr Duncan—*ut* **C** § 62

*Negroes* —*v. also* **D** § 130

DOWD, J. The Negro Races: a sociological study, vol. i $2·50 *n.* (10/6 *n.*) 8° Macmillan 07
A useful discussn. of the reln. betw. geogr. and social condns. This vol. deals w. Negritos (Pygmies, Bushmans, Hottentots: Centr. and S. Afr.); Nigritians (Jolots, Mandingos, Hausas, Ashantis, Dahomans, etc.: Sudan); Tibbus (Sahara), Fellatahs (Centr. Sudan).

*Pigmies* —*v.* **E** § 3, *s.v.* Pigmies

## 42: EGYPT AND NUBIA

*Bibliography*: IBRAHIM-HILMY (Pr'ce) Liter. of Egypt & Soudan, 2 v. ea. 31/6 8° Trübner (Paul) 86–7

BONOMI, Jos. Egypt, Nubia, & Ethiopia; w. notes S. Sharpe; ill. *o.p.* [*pb.* 63/] 4° Smith & Elder 62

BUTCHER, E. L. Things Seen in Egypt [popular] 2/ *n.* f 8° Seeley 09

EBERS, Prf. Geo. Egypt: descriptive, histor., picturesque [tr.], 2 v.; 800 ill. 42/i 4° Cassell [81–2] 88

GORDON, L'y Duff Letters from Egypt 7/6 c 8° Brimley Johnson [65] 02
$2·50 *n.* McClure. Introduction by Geo. MEREDITH; memoir by her dau., Mrs Janet Ross. Remarkable travel-letters, wr. 1863–5.

" Last Letters from Egypt *o.p.* [*pb.* 9/] c 8° Macmillan 75

de GUERVILLE, A. B. New Egypt; 200 ill. 10/ *n.* 8° Heinemann [05] 06
$5 *n.* Dutton. An excellent bk. for the tourist to take with him.

HICHENS, Rob. The Spell of Egypt, col. pl. J. Guérin 6/ c 8° Hodder [08] 10
The first edn. [1908] was pubd. *sub tit. Egypt and its Monuments*, 20/ *n.* sq. 8°.

HOGARTH, D. G. —*in his* Nearer East, *ut* **E** § 29
Includes an account of Egypt from the modern geographical standpoint.

HULME-BEAMAN, A. Twenty Years in the Near East—*ut* **E** § 29

KELLY, R. T. [art.] Egypt Painted & Described: 75 col. pl., w. l'rpr. [$6 *n.* Macm., *N.Y.*] 20/ *n.* sq 8° Black 03

LOFTIE, Rev. W. J. Ride in Egypt fr. Sioot to Luxor; ill. [1879] *o.p.* [*pb.* 10/6] c 8° Macmillan 79

LORIMER, Norma By the Waters of Egypt 16/ *n.* 8° Methuen 09

'LOTI, Pierre' [Jules VIAUD] Egypt, tr. W. P. Baines; 8 col. pl. A. O. Lamplough 15/ *n.* 8° Laurie 10

MANNING, Rev. S. Land of Pharaohs; w. pen & pencil [pict.-bk.] 8/ i 8° R.T.S. [75] 87

MARDON, H. W. Geography of Egypt and the Sudan [schl.-bk.] 2/ c 8° Blackie 02

MASPERO, Prf. Sir Gaston New Light on Anc. Egypt; *and* Egypt: anc. sites & mod. scenes tr.]—*ut* **G** § 9

MAY, Dr W. P., etc. Helwân, and Egyptian Desert; ill. [guide-bk.] 3/ c 8° G. Allen 01

'MONTBARD, Georges' [C. A. LOYES] Land of the Sphinx; 186 ill. by author 16/ r 8° Hutchinson 94
The ill. are the wk. of a true artist and thoroughly interestg.; the text, tho. contg. bright apprecns. of life and manners, is next to worthless.

PEEL, W. A Ride thro' the Nubian Desert *o.p.* [*pb.* 5/] c 8° Longman 52

POLLARD, Jos. Land of Monuments: notes of Egyptn. travel; ill. 7/6 c 8° Hodder [96] 98

POOLE, Reg. Stuart The Cities of Egypt 5/ c 8° Smith & Elder 82

POOLE, Stanley Lane Egypt [Foreign Countries & Brit. Colonies] 3/6 c 8° Low 81

SLADEN, Douglas Queer Things about Egypt; 65 ill. 21/ *n.* 8° Hurst [10] 10

STEEVENS, G. W. Egypt in 1898; ill. 6/ c 8° Blackwood 98
$1·50 Dodd & Mead, *N.Y.* Engl. rule and influence, descrn. of a Nile trip and visit to Coptic monastery of St Mark, etc.

STUART, H. W. Villiers Egypt after the War: notes of tour; col. pl. *o.p.* [*pb.* 31/6] r 8° Murray 83

THACKERAY, Lance [art.] The Light Side of Egypt: 36 col. pl. 10/ *n.* sq 8° Black 08
$2·50 *n.* Macmillan, *N.Y.* The impressns. of a well-known humorous artist, w. a little descriptive text.

THURSTON, Maj. A. B. Egypt and Unyoro—*ut* **E** § 48, *s.v.* Uganda

TRAILL, H. D. From Cairo to the Soudan Frontier 5/ *n.* ($1·50) c 8° Lane 96
Detached sketches of scenes and incidents of two visits; repr. fr. *The Daily Telegraph.*

TYNDALE, Walt. [artist] Below the Cataracts: 60 col. pl., w. l'rpress 16/ *n.* 8° Heinemann 07

WARD, Jno. Egypt, its Pyramids and Progress; 720 ill. 7/6 *n.* r 8° Eyre & Spottiswoode [00] 05
Young, *N.Y.* A popular acc. of the country, anc. and mod. bldgs., etc.: useful as a guide, esp. to Upper Nile.

WEIGALL, A. E. P. Travels in the Upper Egyptian Deserts; ill. 7/6 *n.* 8° Blackwood 09
By Chief Inspector of Upper Egypt, Dept. of Antiqs. Tho' inclg. results of archæol. research, is pre-eminently a bk. of the desert (wh. he loves), representg. the private side of some of his official jys. Glossary.

WHITE (Arnold) + CARTWRIGHT (H. A.) [eds.] Twentieth-Century Impressions of Egypt; fully ill. f° Lloyds' Greater Brit. Pb. Co. 09

ZINCKE, F. B. Egypt of the Pharaohs & the Khedive *o.p.* [*pb.* 16/] 8° Smith & Elder [71] 73

### Guides

BAEDEKER, K. [pb.] Lower & Upper Egypt; 24 maps, 76 plans, 59 vigs. 15/ s 8° Unwin [78–92] 08

BUDGE, Dr E. A. Wallis Cook's Handbook for Egypt and the Sûdân 10/ c 8° Simpkin [04] 07
An indispensable adjunct to the tourist's baggage. Incl. sketch of history, skeleton Arabic grammar, etc. 9 maps and plans and 150 ill.

MACMILLAN & Co. [pbs.] Egypt & the Sudan; 35 maps & plans 5/ *n.* ($1·60 *n.*) gl 8° Macmillan [06] 11

MURRAY, Jno. [pb.] Hdbk. for Egypt & Soudan. By H. R. Hall; 58 maps & ill. 14/ c 8° Stanford [4–] 07

### Life and People; Economic and Political Condition

ADAMS, Fcs. The New Egypt: a social sketch 5/ c 8° Unwin 93
A picture of Khedive and his 2 chief ministers, interviews w. L'd CROMER, RIAZ, and TIGRANE, etc., and good ch. on Eg. peasant.

ALEXANDER, J. The Truth about Egypt 7/6 8° Cassell 11
A hist. of the yrs. 1906–10. Regards spread of Egyptn. nationalism w. serious apprehension.

BAKER, A. J. Court Life in Egypt; 8 ill. *o.p.* [*pb.* 12/] 8° Chapman 88

BELL, C. F. Moberly From Pharaoh to Fellah; well ill. 7/6 4° Wells Gardner [74] 88

BLUNT, Wilf. Scawen Secret Hist. of Engl. Occupn. of Egypt 15/ *n.* 8° Unwin [07] 07
An acc., based on personal knowl. and 'confidential native sources' of the Natl. Egyptn. movemt. of 1881–2, and of the polit. and financ. intrigues wh. led to the Brit. occupn. Mainly irrelevant gossip—much in shape of a diary.

BROWNE, Hadji A. Bonaparte in Egypt and Egyptians of To-day 10/6 *n.* 8° Unwin 07
A histor. study of the developmt. of the Egyptn., by an Anglo-Irish convert to El Islâm.

BUTLER, Sir Wm. —*in his* Autobiography 16/ *n.* 8° Constable 11

CAMERON, D. A. Egypt in the Nineteenth Century [to 1882] 6/ c 8° Smith & Elder 98
A historical retrospect, chfly. early half of the century, based on intimate knowledge.

CHENNELLS, [Miss] E. Recollections of an Egyptian Princess; 3 ports. 7/6 p 8° Blackwood [93] 93
Acc. of 5 yrs.' resid. at Ct. of ISMAEL PASHA, Khedive, by late governess to his daughter. Vivid pict. of Eg. soc. and harem-life.

COLVIN, Sir Auckland Making of Modern Egypt; maps and ports. 18/ *n.* 8° Seeley 06
Masterly summary of benefits conferred on Egypt by Brit. enterprise and influences. Fr. arrival of L'd DUFFERIN (1882) to 1904.

*CROMER, Earl Modern Egypt, 2 vols.; map & port. [1863–1907] 7/6 *n.* 8° Macmillan [08] 11
A comprehensive and excellent treatment of the whole subject.

DE LEON, Edwin The Khedive's Egypt *o.p.* [*pb.* 8/6] c 8° Low [77] 79

" —*in his* Thirty Years on Three Continents, 2 vols. *o.p.* 8° 90

DICEY, Edw. England and Egypt [1877–81] *o.p.* [*pb.* 6/] c 8° Chapman 81

" Story of the Khedivate [1805–99] 16/ 8° Rivington 02

" The Egypt of the Future 3/6 *n.* c 8° Heinemann 07
Highly controversial. Advocates England's assumption of an avowed and permanent Protectorate over Egypt.

EDWARDS, Amelia B. Pharaohs, Fellahs, and Explorers; ill. 18/ 8° Osgood [91] 92
$2·50 Harper, *N.Y.* Substance of a ser. of lects. deliv. in U.S. in 1889. *Explorer in Egypt, Buried Cities, Portrait Ptg. in Egypt* (and its origin: the most interestg. pt. of bk.), *Egypt as Birthplace of Gk. Decor. Art*, and other chs. on liter. and relig. of anc. Egptns. By an Egyptolog. enthusiast, who was soul of Eg. Explorn. Fd. (d. 1893).

FARMAN, E. E. Egypt and its Betrayal $2·50 *n.* 8° Grafton Press, *N.Y.* 08
Acc. of country dur. periods of ISMAIL and TEWFIK PASHAS, and of 'how England acquired a new empire'.

FULLER, Fredk. W. Egypt and the Hinterland; map 10/6 *n.* ($3·50) 8° Longman 01
A valuable summary of the history of the British occupation and of recent progress of the country.

FYFE, H. Hamilton The New Spirit in Egypt 5/ *n.* c 8° Blackwood 11
A vivacious 'journalistic' bk., affordg. large views ab. serious problems in a nutshell.

KEAY, J. S. Spoiling the Egyptians: a tale of shame [1862–82] *o.p.* [*pb.* 1/] 8° Paul 82

KLUNZINGER, C. B. Upper Egypt, its People and Products [tr.]; ill. *o.p.* [*pb.* 14/] 8° Blackie 78

LANE, Edw. W. Manners & Customs of Mod. Egyptns. [Minerva Lib.] 2/ (75 c.) c 8° Ward & Lock [36] 02

" The same [Everyman's Lib.; 35 c. *n.* Dutton, *N.Y.*] 1/ *n.* f 8° Dent [36] 08

Poole, S. Lane Life of E. W. Lane *o.p.* [*pb.* 7/6] 8° Williams 77

Letters fr. an Egyptian upon Affairs of Egypt, ed. J. M. Robertson 2/6 *n.* c 8° Routledge 08

MACCOAN, J. C. Egypt as it is *o.p.* [*pb.* 21/] 8° Cassell 76

" Egypt under Ismael [1863–79] 7/6 c 8° Chapman 89

MIÉVILLE, Sir Walt. Under Queen and Khedive 6/ c 8° Heinemann 99
A personal narrative, describing the author's work in Egypt.

MILNER, Alf. [L'd] England in Egypt 6/ c 8° Arnold [92] 99
$2 Longman, *N.Y.* One of most lucid and statesmanlike records of admin. reforms ever wr., showg. by irrefragable argumt. why Eng. influ. (under wh. the country has been raised fr. bankruptcy to wealth, a syst. of educn. has been estab., and by irrign. wks. producg. power of land in the Delta has been nearly doubled) shd. still remain paramount.

'MONTBARD, Georges' [C. A. LOYES] Case of John Bull in Egypt, Transvaal, Venezuela, and Elsewhere [persiflage rather than criticism] 2/6 c 8° Hutchinson 96

MYERS, A. B. R. Life w. Hamran Arabs [Upper Nubia; chfly. sportg.] *o.p.* [*pb.* 12/] p 8° Smith & Elder 76

ORPEN, Adela E. Chronicles of the Sid: life and travs. of A. Gates; ill. 7/6 c 8° R.T.S. 93
Jys. in 1887 to Alger. Sahara, Egypt as far S. as Wady Halfa, Palest., N. Cape, and Iceld. *Sid* [= 'lady' or 'mistress'] is title by wh. Miss Adela GATES, first schl.-tchr., then factory-girl in E. States of Am., then member of a settler's house in Kansas, the artist, was known in Sahara.

PENFIELD, F. C. Present-day Egypt; ill. $2·50 8° Century Pb. Co., *N.Y.* [99] 03
By U.S. Consul-Gen. 1893–7. Life in Cairo and Alex., story of Suez Canal, of Engld.'s positn., etc.

POOLE, Stanley Lane Social Life in Egypt; pl. *o.p.* [*pb.* 21/] 4° Virtue 84

RAE, W. Fraser Egypt of To-day: from first to third Khedive *o.p.* [*pb.* 16/] 8° Bentley 92
Finances, public wks., cts. of justice, newsp.-press, etc., wh. have been estab. or reformed in Egypt since Brit. occupn.

ROTHSTEIN, Theod. Egypt's Ruin: financial and admin. record 6/ *n.* c 8° Fifield 10

SLADEN, Douglas Egypt and the English; map and 40 ill. 21/ *n.* r 8° Hurst 08
Vivid descrns. of Egypt, of a jy. up the Nile, etc.; w. much polit. and social information.

TRAILL, H. D. England, Egypt, and the Sudan 12/ 8° Constable 00
A valuable account of Britain's doings in Egypt from the time of Napoleon to 1900.

WALLACE, D. M. Egypt and the Egyptian Question [1881–2] *o.p.* [*pb.* 14/] 8° Macmillan 83

WHITE, A. Silva Expansion of Eg. und. Anglo-Eg. Condominium; maps 15/ 8° Methuen 99
Outline of the history and survey of industrial and commercial conditions and results.

" From Sphinx to Oracle; 2 maps and 57 ill. 16/ 8° Hurst 98
A narrative of a journey to the oasis of Siwa (formerly Jupiter Ammon).

*WILKINSON, Sir J. G. Manners & Customs of Ancient Egyptians, 3 vols. 84/ 8° Murray [37–41] 78
Ed. S. BIRCH; w. ill. and col. pl. The modern view of ancient Egypt.

" Manners and Customs of Modern Egyptians; ill. *o.p.* [*pb.* 42/] 8° Murray 44

" Popular Account of Ancient Egyptians, 2 vols.; 500 ill. 12/ p 8° Murray [54]

WOOD, H. F. Egypt under the British 4/ c 8° Chapman 96
Mainly the personal aspect of the situatn. Restates 'Engl. case' much better stated by MILNER, *sup.*

WORSFOLD, W. Basil The Redemption of Egypt; 94 ill. 25/ *n.* s 4° G. Allen 99
$7·50 Longman, *N.Y.* Chiefly an acc. of the accomplishmts. of English in Egypt; w. chs. on art and history.

**Cairo**

LANE, Edw. W. Cairo Fifty Years Ago, ed. Stanley Lane-Poole 6/ c 8° Murray 96
$2·40 *n.* Scribner, *N.Y.* Wr. *c.* 1835. Traces hist. fr. A.D. 641 to his own time, and descrs. older capitals of Egypt, their streets, etc.

MARGOLIOUTH, Prf. D. S. Cairo, Jerusalem, and Damascus 20/ *n.* 8° Chatto 07
Interesting accounts of three chief cities of the Egyptian Sultans. Col. pl. by W. S. S. TYRWHITT and Reg. BARRATT.

POOLE, Stanley Lane Cairo; profusely ill. 6/ r 8° Virtue [92] 97
Sketches of its history, monumts., and social life. Final ch. treats of good results of Brit. occupn.

,, The Story of Cairo; ill. 4/6 *n.* s 8° Dent 02
$1·75 *n.* Dutton, *N.Y.* [Mediaeval Towns.] An excellent short summary; indispensable to visitors to Cairo.

REYNOLDS-BALL, E. A. The City of the Caliphs; 20 ill. 10/6 c 8° Unwin 97
$3 Estes, *Boston.* Wholly a compiln.: city, environs, Nile, etc.: not above guide-bk. level.

,, Cairo of To-day [$1 *n.* Macm., *N.Y.*; gde. to C. & Nile] 2/6 f 8° Black [9–] 04

SLADEN, Douglas Oriental Cairo, City of 'Arab. Nights'; 64 ill. 21/ *n.* sq 8° Hurst 11

TRAILL, H. D. From Cairo to the Soudan Frontier—*ut sup.* [good descrns. of Cairo streets, etc.]

**Libyan Desert** —*v.* **E** § 43

**Nile north of Omdurman** —*for* White Nile and Sources of Nile *v.* **E** §§ 43, 48; *for* Blue Nile, **E** § 44

APPLETON, T. G. A Nile Journal; ill. *o.p.* [*pb.* 6/] p 8° Macmillan 76

BACON, Mrs Lee Our Houseboat on the Nile; 12 col. pl. $1·75 *n.* 8° Houghton, *Boston* 01
7/6 *n.* Constable. Acc. of a leisurely pilgrimage in a dahabiyeh fr. 1st to 2nd Cataract.

BELL, Can. C. D. Winter on Nile at Egypt, and in Nubia 6/ c 8° Hodder [88] 89

BOWLES, C. + S. M. A Nile Voyage of Recovery 7/6 16° Low 97

BUDGE, Dr E. A. Wallis The Nile: notes for travellers 10/ *n.* s 8° Thos. Cook & Son 00

DUNNING, Dr H. W. To-day on the Nile; 17 photogravs. $5 *n.* 8° Pott, *N.Y.* 05
10/6 *n.* Gay & Hancock. Combined acc. of 6 trips. Much useful informn. for travellers.

EDWARDS, Amelia B. A Thousand Miles up the Nile; 70 ill. 7/6 8° Routledge [77]
$2·50 Dutton, *N.Y.* An excellent companion and guide-bk., w. authoritative informn. on anc. hist. and monumts.

GEERE, H. Valentine By Nile and Euphrates—*ut* **E** § 30

GIBSON, Chas. Dana Sketches in Egypt $3 *n.* 8° Doubleday, *N.Y.* 99
Cairo and the Nile to the first Cataract. Sketches good; text of no value.

GRANT, Col. J. A. Walk acr. Africa: domestic scenes fr. my Nile Jl.; ill. *o.p.* [*pb.* 15/] 8° Blackwood 64

JOHNSTON, Sir Harry H. The Nile Quest; maps and ill. [Story of Exploration] 4/6 *n.* 8° Rivers 03
$1·35 *n.* Stokes, *N.Y.* A fascinatg. acc. of the whole history of Nile explorn. fr. prehist. times to discoveries in the Sobat and Bahr-el-Ghazel regions, conclg. w. a geography of whole Nile basin. Bibliography.

LYONS, Cpt. H. Physiography of the Nile Basin *Cairo* 96
The best scientific account of the Nile basin and of the Nile flood.

STUART, H. W. Villiers Nile Gleanings concerning Ancient Egypt *o.p.* [*pb.* 31/6] r 8° Murray 80

WARNER, C. D. My Winter on Nile am. Mummies & Moslems $2 8° Houghton, *Boston* [76] 99
A new edition of his *Mummies and Moslems*, 8° *Hartford* '76.

WILKIN, Arth. On the Nile with a Camera; 111 ill. 21/ 8° Unwin 97
An interestg. narr. of a six-weeks' trip fr. Cairo to the Second Cataract.

**Pyramids** —*v. also* **G** § 9

**Suez:** CHAPMAN (Cpt. Chas.) The Suez Canal [acc. of opening] *o.p.* 8° *London* 70

FITZGERALD, Percy H. Great Canal at Suez, 2 v. [polit., engin., & financ. hist.] *o.p.* [*pb.* 30/] 8° Tinsley 67

de LESSEPS, F. Suez Canal: documts. descript. of rise & progr. [tr.] [1854–76] *o.p.* [*pb.* 10/6] 8° Paul 76

,, History of Suez Canal: personal narrative *o.p.* [*pb.* 2/6] 12° Blackwood 76

Smith, G. Barnett Life and Enterprises of De Lesseps 7/6 c 8° W. H. Allen [93] 93

## 43: EGYPTIAN SOUDAN AND WHITE NILE BASIN

ALEXANDER, Lt. Boyd —*in his* Niger to Nile, 2 vols., *ut* **E** § 46, *s.v.* Nigeria

ALFORD (Lt. H. S. L.) + SWORD (Lt. W. D.) Egyptian Soudan, its Loss and Recovery; maps and ill. 10/ *n.* 8° Macmillan 98
Incls. sketch of its hist., pers. narr. of Dongola Expedn. (1896), and full acc. of Nile Expedn. (1897–8).

BUDGE, Dr E. A. Wallis The Egyptian Soudan; its hist. and monumts., 2 vols.—*ut* **G** § 9

BUXTON, Edw. N. —*in his* Two African Trips, *ut* **E** § 41

CHURCHILL, Winston L. S. The River War 10/6 *n.* ($4) 8° Longman [99] 02
A historical acc. of the reconquest of the Soudan, w. lists of contemp. narrs. and Govt. pubns.

COMYN, Lt. D. C. E. ff. Service in Sport and the Sudan 12/6 *n.* 8° Lane 10
Acc. of journeys to and surveys of River Pibor (triby. of Sobat), upper reaches of Sobat, Nile-Congo watershed, borders of Fch. Equat. Afr., oases of Selima, Teklis, and Eyn Aga, etc.—largely *terra incognita*, with a good deal of sport. Map and ill.

FOTHERGILL, Edw. Five Years in the Sudan; 32 pl. 16/n. 8° Hurst 10
Experces. of an official and sportsman dur. earlier period of Brit. occupn.: people, fauna, life, sport.

GESSI, Romolo Seven Years in the Soudan; ill. 18/8° Low 92
Explorations, adventures and campaigns against Arab slave-hunters. Ed. Felix Gessi [son].

GLEICHEN, C't A. E. W. Handbook of the Soudan; *also* Supplement c 8° War Office 98; 99

" The Anglo-Egyptian Soudan, 2 vols. 17/6 4° Wyman 05
A compendium prepared by officers of the Soudan government.

GORDON, Gen. C. J. [1833–85]—*for his* Life *v.* **F** § 29

JAMES, F. L. Wild Tribes of the Soudan; map and 20 ill. *o.p.* [*pb.* 7/6] c 8° Murray [83] 87
Travel and sport, chiefly in the Basé country.

JUNKER, Dr W. J. —*in his* Travels [tr.], 3 vols., *ut* **E** § 48 [1875–86]

KNIGHT, E. F. Letters from the Sudan; ill. [repr. fr. 'Times'] 8/6 *n.* r 8° Macmillan 97

KUMM, Dr Karl From Hausaland to Egypt; maps & 90 ill. (some col.) 16/*n.* r 8° Constable 11
A ponderous narr. of missionary travel; w. record of adventure, sport, scientific and anthrop. observn.

LEPSIUS, Dr R. Letters fr. Egypt, Ethiopia, and Sinai [tr.]; maps 5/c 8° Bohn's Lib. 53

LLOYD, Alb. B. Uganda to Khartoum: life and adventure; 81 ill. 10/6 *n.* 8° Unwin [06] 06
A fascinating bk. of travel over unhackneyed ground, spec. good on Acholi country (non-Bantu).

NEUFELD, Chas. A Prisoner of the Khaleefa; maps and ill. 12/8° Chapman 99
$4 Putnam, *N.Y.* Acc. of prison-experces. (in Omdurman, 1887–98) of author, who was captured by dervishes while on tradg. expedn. to Soudan.

OHRWALDER, F'r Jos. Ten Years' Captivity [1882–92] in Mahdi's Camp; maps & ill. 21/8° Low [92] 93
Ed. Maj. F. R. WINGATE fr. orig. MSS. of OHRWALDER, who in 1892 escaped w. 2 sisters-of-mercy on camels fr. Mahdi's camp. A personal acc. of events in Sudan since rise of Mahdiism, throwg. light on Mahdi's unprincipled and despotic successor. Abgd. Edn. 2/6 c 8° [93] 94.

OLIPHANT, Laur. The Land of Khemi [Middle Nile] 10/6 c 8° Blackwood 82

PEEL, Hon. Sid. Binding of Nile and New Soudan; map 12/6 *n.* 8° Arnold 04
$5 Longman, *N.Y.* Deals solely w. the new irrign. wks. in Egypt and the occupn. of the Soudan.

ROBINSON, C. H. Hausaland: 15,000 miles thro' Central Soudan; ill. 14/8° Low 96
A remarkably interestg. descrn. of jy. up Niger to Lokoja, thence up Benue to Loko, northward by land to Kano, thence back to Lokoja, and home. Full of informn. on country and people, esp. slavery and slave-raiding.

RUSSELL, Hy. Ruin of the Soudan: cause, effect, remedy; maps and ill. 21/8° Low 92
$4·50 Scribner, *N.Y.* Historical more than geograph., aboundg. in quotns. fr. Blue-Bks. and other offic. docums.

SARTORIUS, [Mrs] E. Three Months in the Soudan *o.p.* [*pb.* 14/] 8° Paul 85

SCHWEINFURTH, G. —*in his* The Heart of Africa, *ut* **E** § 48 [1868–71]

SLATIN PASHA, R. C. Fire and Sword in the Sudan [tr.] 6/8° Arnold [96]
$2 Longman, *N.Y.* Descrs. escape of SLATIN PASHA in 1895, and gives vivd acc. of Upper Nile Provinces under rule of Khalifa.

SPEEDY, Cornelia M. My Wanderings in the Soudan, 2 vols. *o.p.* [*pb.* 21/] c 8° Bentley 84

TANGYE, H. Lincoln In the Torrid Sudan; ill. 12/6 *n.* 8° Murray 10
Sport, travel, geogr., history, internal condns., admin., and development.

TAYLOR, Bayard Central Africa; 2 pl. & ill. [Cairo to White Nile] $1·25 12° Putnam, *N.Y.* [54] 81

TRAILL, H. D. From Cairo to the Sudan Frontier—*ut* **E** § 42

WARD, Jno. Our Sudan: its pyramids and progress; 720 ill. 21/*n.* c 8° Murray [05] 05
An excellent acc. of the Anglo-Egyptn. Soudan. New edn. conts. orograph. map of whole Nile valley.

WERNE, F. Expedn. to Discover Sources of White Nile [tr.], 2 v. [1840–1] *o.p.* [*pb.* 21/] c 8° Bentley 49

" African Wanderings [tr.], 2 Pts. *o.p.* [*pb.* 5/] c 8° Longman 52
Sennaar to Taka, Basa, Beni-Amer, etc.

WILSON (Rev. C. T.) + FELKIN (R. W.) Uganda & Egyptian Soudan, 2 v.; ill. *o.p.* [*pb.* 28/] 8° Low 82

WINGATE, Maj. [Sir] F. R. Mahdiism & the Egyptian Sudan; maps *o.p.* [*pb.* 30/ ($10)] 8° Macmillan 91
Hist. of events in Soudan dur. 1882–91 w. fullest possible details as to fall of Khartoum.

YACOUB PASHA ARTIN England in the Soudan [tr.]; map and ill. 10/*n.* 8° Macmillan 11
L'rs wr. by author (formerly Under-Sec. in Eg. Educ. Dept.) to his wife whilst journeying up Blue Nile and White Nile, in company w. Prf. SAYCE in 1908–9. An honest (and favourable) acc. of Brit. rule in the Soudan. Tr. fr. Fch.

**Egyptian Campaign, Soudan Wars, etc.**—*v.* **F** § 31

**Ethnology:** FEATHERMAN (A.) Social History of the Races of Mankind: Nigritians—*ut* **F** § 5

THOMSON (Arth.) + RANDALL-MACIVER (D.) The Ancient Races of the Thebaid; ill. 42/*n.* ($12·75) 4° Clar. Press 05
An anthropomet. study of inhabts. of Upper Egypt fr. prehist times to Mohammedan Conquest, based on exam. of 1,500 crania.

**Guides** —*v.* **E** § 42

**Libyan Desert:** BEADNELL (H. J. Ll.) An Egyptian Oasis; ill. 10/6 *n.* 8° Murray 09
A thoro' study of oasis of Kharga in Libyan Desert, by head of land reclamn. operations.

RANDALL-MACIVER (D.) + WILKIN (A.) Libyan Notes; 25 pl. 20/*n.* 8° Macmillan 01
An attempt to settle the question of the connexion between the ancient Libyan and the modern Berber.

ST JOHN, Bayle The Libyan Desert 2/c 8° Murray [46]
Tho' pubd. over hf. a cent. ago, still of value, as not much more is known of the desert now than then.

**Nile Sources and Tropical Nile**—*v.* **E** § 48, *s.v.* Uganda

## 44: ABYSSINIA AND BLUE NILE BASIN; SOMALILAND

### Early Travels

ALVARES, Père Fr. [16 cent.] Narrative of Portuguese Embassy to Abyssinia, tr. and ed. L'd Stanley of Alderley [1520–27] 8° Hakluyt Soc. 81

BRUCE, Jas. [1730–94] Travels to Discover Source of [Blue] Nile [1768–73] 3/6 c 8° Black [1790] 78

„ The same 2/c 8° Chambers [1790]
Describes the first modern travels in Africa, dating from 1768 to 1770.

LOBO, Jeron. Voyage into Abyssinia [1624] [National Lib.] 6*d.* 18° Cassell [1735]

WHITEWAY, R. S. [tr. & ed.] Portuguese Expedition to Abyssinia [1541–3] 8° Hakluyt Soc. 03

### Recent Travel and Accounts

BAKER, Sir S. W. Nile Tributaries of Abyssinia & Hamran Arabs; ill. 6/c 8° Macmillan [67] 80
Narrative of jy. in 1861–2 preliminary to author's expedn. to the Nile sources.

BENT, J. Theod. The Sacred City of the Ethiopians; map and 73 ill. 10/6 8° Longman [93] 96
Acc. of jy. by Mr and Mrs BENT into Abyss. in spring of 1893, chief object of wh. was to examine archæol. remains at Aksum, the sacred city of Ethiopns. since bef. Xtn. era. Incidentally the places passed thro', the people and their ways, are descrd. Prf. H. D. MÜLLER (Vienna) adds a ch. on Inscripn. fr. Yeha and Aksum [9 cent. B.C. to 5 cent. A.D.; w. trs.] and Dr J. G. GARSON. App. on morpholog. character of the Abyssns. Whole bk. is of consid. archæol. interest.

BLANC, Dr H. Narrative of Captivity in Abyssinia; ill. *o.p.* [*pb.* 12/] c 8° Smith & Elder 68

BLAND-SUTTON, J. Man and Beast in Eastern Ethiopia; 204 ill. 12/ *n.* 8° Macmillan 11
Observns., by an eminent surgeon, on a jy. fr. Mombasa to Vict. Nyanza and back thro' Soudan and Nile valley.

BULPETT, C. W. L. A Picnic Party in Wildest Africa; ill. $3·50 *n.* 8° Longman 07
12/6 *n.* Arnold. Acc. of expedn. to survey Musha and Boma plateaux betw. Lake Rudolf and River Akobo.

de COSSON, E. A. Cradle of Blue Nile, 2 vols.; ill. *o.p.* [*pb.* 21/] p 8° Murray 77
Account of the author's visit to King John of Ethiopia.

GLEICHEN, C't A. E. W. With the Mission to Menelik; ill. 16/ 8° Arnold [97] 98
A popular, but not very informing, account of the mission of 1897.

HARRIS, Sir Wm. Cornwallis The Highlands of Æthiopia, 3 vols. *o.p.* [*pb.* 42/] 8° Longman 44

HAYES, Dr A. J. The Source of the Blue Nile 10/6 *n.* 8° Smith & Elder 05
Record of jy. thro' Soudan to Lake Tsana in W. Abyssinia, and of return to Egypt by valley of Atbara.

HINDLIP, L'd Sport & Travel: Abyssinia & Br. East Africa; maps & ill. 21/ *n.* 8° Unwin 06

KRAPF, Rev. J. Lewis Travels & Missionary Labours in Afr. and Abyss. [tr.]; ill. [1837–55] 21/ 8° Trübner [60] 67

KUMM, H. K. W. Khont-Hon-Noffer: the lands of Ethiopia 6/ 8° Marshall Bros. 11

PARKYNS, Mansfield Life in Abyssinia; 30 ill. [3 yrs.' residence] *o.p.* [*pb.* 7/6] r 8° Murray [53] 68

PEARSE, Alf. E. —*in his* Travel & Sport in Africa, 3 vols., *ut* **E** § 41 [Abyssinia, Somaliland, etc.]

PLOWDEN, W. C. Travels in Abyssinia, ed. by his Brother *o.p.* [*pb.* 18/] 8° Longman 68

PORTAL, Sir Gerald H. My Mission to Abyssinia; map and ill. 15/ 8° Arnold 92
Acc. of Engl. missn. to Abyss. in '87–8, wh. had its orig. in intrusn. of Italns. into the country on shore of Red Sea abandoned by Egyptns. in '84, to wh. the Abyssns. had set up a claim. The narrative is personal and descriptive rather than political.

POWELL-COTTON, Maj. P. H. G. A Sporting Trip through Abyssinia—*ut* **I** § 147

RASSAM, H. British Mission to Abyssinia, 2 vols. *o.p.* [*pb.* 28/] 8° Murray 69
Contains notices of the countries traversed.

SKINNER, Rob. P. Abyssinia of To-day; map and ill. 12/6 *n.* 8° Arnold 06
$3 *n.* Longman, *N.Y.* Acc. of first missn. sent by the Amer. Govt. to the 'King of Kings', by the Amer. Consul-General.

SMITH, Dr A. Donaldson Through Unknown African Countries; ill. 21/ *n.* r 8° Arnold 97
$5 *n.* Lane, *N.Y.* Author, an American doctor, accomp. by 2 Englishmen, startg. fr. Berbera, crossed Somaliland to Milmil, thenceto Bari, Shebeli, crossed the Juba and over Borakna Galla country to Lake Stephanie, wh. was explored: thence to Lake Rudolf, and back to coast *via* Rendile country and the Nyiro. Of much geograph., nat. hist., and astron. importance. Also much sport. Valuable Appendices.

SMITH, F. Harrison Thro' Abyssinia: envoy's ride to King of Zion 7/6 8° Unwin 90
$2 Armstrong, *N.Y.* Author, a naval man, accomp. Sir W. Hewett on missn. to Abyss. wh. led to a treaty in wh. Engl. guaranteed to late kg. JOHN possessn. of Bogos country and free trade thro' Massawa, in considn. of his help in releasg. Egyp. garrisons at that time still in Sudan.

STERN, Hy. A. The Captive Missionary [cy. & people of Abyss.] *o.p.* [*pb.* 21/] 8° Cassell [60] 68

„ Wanderings am. Falashas in Abyssinia *o.p.* [*pb.* 15/] 8° Wertheim 62

STIGAND, Cpt. C. H. To Abyssinia through an Unknown Land; ill. 16/ *n.* 8° Seeley 10
Largely thro' cy. prev. unexplored by a European; struck due N. fr. L. Rudolf, followed Omo River, and crossed into Abyss., describg. pass in Loregai Mtns., the difficult tract fr. Naisichu to Koroloi, and wild Rendile country, and their 20 tribes. Valuable informn. on ethnol., langs., and customs of these non-Bantu tribes.

VIVIAN, Herb. Abyssinia: through the Lion-Land; ill. 15/ 8° Pearson 01
$4 Longman, *N.Y.* A popular account of a visit to a part of Abyssinia, thro' Somaliland.

WELLBY, Cpt. M. S. 'Twixt Sirdar and Menelik; map and ill. $2·50 *n.* (16/) 8° Harper 01
Acc. of jy. thro' unknown pts. of the country to Lake Rudolf, along the Ruzi and Sobat, and to Cairo.

WINSTANLEY, H. Visit to Abyssinia: acc. of mod. Ethiopia, 2 vols. *o.p.* [*pb.* 21/] c 8° Hurst 81

WYLDE, A. B. '83 to '87 in the Soudan, 2 vols. *o.p.* [*pb.* 30/] 8° Remington 88
Account of Sir Wm. HEWETT's mission to KING JOHN of Abyssinia.

„ Modern Abyssinia; map and port. 15/ *n.* 8° Methuen 01
A very valuable and comprehensive account, geographical and political, of the country.

**Expedition to Abyssinia** —*v.* **F** § 31

**Somaliland** —*v. also* **I** § 147

HAMILTON, Angus Somaliland ; map and 23 ill. 12/6 *n.* 8° Hutchinson 11
By Reuter's Special War-Corresp. in Somaliland for 2 yrs., telling the whole story of the 4 expedns. fr. start to finish.

HERBERT, Agnes Two Dianas in Somaliland ; 24 ill. [shootg.-trip] 12/6 *n.* ($4 *n.*) 8° Lane 07

JAMES, F. L. The Unknown Horn of Africa ; map and 28 ill. 7/6 c 8° Philip [88] 91
Narrative of a sporting tour. Berbera to the Leopard River.

PEARCE, Cpt. Fcs. B. Rambles in Lion Land ; ill. 10/6 8° Chapman 98
An account of three months' travel and sport.

PEEL, C. V. A. Somaliland ; map and ill. *o.p.* [*pb.* 7/6 *n.*] r 8° Robinson [99] 03
A commonplace descrn. of travel and sport ; w. lists of every known animal and bird there, and of reptiles coll. by author.

SMITH, Dr A. Donaldson Thro' Unknown African Countries—*ut sup.*

SWAYNE, Fces. A Woman's Pleasure Trip in Somaliland ; ill. 4/*n.* 8° Wright, *Bristol* 07
The first descrn. of Somaliland as a holiday-resort. By a sister of the late Administrator.

SWAYNE, Cpt. H. G. C. Seventeen Trips to Somaliland ; ill. [1885–93] 18/ 8° Rowland Ward 95
An authoritative wk., descrg. author's explorns. and reconnaissances dur. 1885–93, his advents. and investigns. am. the curious and little-known nomadic tribes of interior, wild fauna of country and (not least) the sport he had. Apps. deal w. fitting-out of Somali expedns., phys. geogr., and trade.

WILLES-JENNINGS (Maj. J.) + ADDISON (Dr C.) With Abyssinians in Somaliland ; ill. 10/6 *n.* 8° Hodder 05
WILLES-JENNINGS was principal Medical Officer of the Force, Abyss. and English, wh. made the Somaliland expedn. of 1903–4, and, w. Cpt. H. N. DUNN, was attached to Emp. MENELIK's troops.

## 45: THE BARBARY STATES

*Bibliography :* ASHBEE (H. S.)—*his* Bibl. of Tunis [*inf.*] *incls. bks. on Barb. States wh. deal also w. Tunis*

FIELD, Dr Hy. M. The Barbary Coast ; map and ill. $2 c 8° Scribner, *N.Y.* 93
Travel sketches of Gib., Morocco, Algiers, Tunis, Sahara, w. notes on hist. and social and relig. life.

FOSTER, Jno. Fraser The Land of Veiled Women ; ill. and 4 col. pl. 6/ c 8° Cassell 11
Graphic sketches of wanderings in Algeria, Tunisia, and Morocco.

GREVILLE-NUGENT, Mrs Land of Mosques & Marabouts [tour in Algeria & Tunis] 14/ 8° Chapman 94

NESBITT, Fces. E. [art.] Algeria & Tunis : 70 col. pl., w. l'rpr. [$6 *n.* Macm., *N.Y.*] 20/*n.* sq 8° Black 06

PEARSE, Alf. E. —*in his* Travel and Sport in Africa, 3 vols., *ut* **E** § 41 [Algeria, Tunisia, etc.]

PHILLIPPS, L. Mard In the Desert 12/6 *n.* 8° Arnold 05
$2 Longman, *N.Y.* A descrn. of the conquest and occupation of N. Africa by the French.

SHOEMAKER, M. M. Islam Lands ; ill. (12/6 *n.*) 8° Putnam 11
Nubia, Soudan, Algeria, Tunisia, inclg. delightful sketch of Kairwan.

*Barbary Corsairs* —*v.* **F** § 15

**Algeria ; Algiers**

*Bibliography :* PLAYFAIR (Col. Sir R. L.) Bibliogr. of Algeria [1541–1887] 4/ 8° R.G.S. (Murray) 88

" Supplement to Bibliography of Algeria [to 1895] 5/m 8° R.G.S. (Murray) 98

BARCLAY, E. Mountain Life in Algeria ; ill. *o.p.* [*pb.* 16/] 4° Paul 82

BELLOC, Hilaire Esto Perpetua : Algerian studies & impressns. ; 45 ill. 3/6 *n.* sq c 8° Duckworth 06

BOISSIER, Gaston Roman Africa [tr.] [archæol. walks in Alg. & Tunis] $1·75 (6/) c 8° Putnam 99

BRIDGMAN, F. A. Winters in Algeria ; ill. $2·50 sq 8° Harper, *N.Y.* 90

de CASTELLAINE, C'te Souvenirs of Milit. Life in Algeria [tr.], 2 v. *o.p.* [*pb.* 24/] 8° Remington 82

CROUSE, M. Eliz. Algiers ; 24 pl. $4 *n.* 8° Pott, *N.Y.* 07
10/6 *n.* Gay & Hancock. An enthusiastic attempt to express a first impressn. of the Orient obtd. dur. 5 months in Algiers.

DUDGEON, Mat. [17 cent.] True Relations of Travels and Perilous Adventures 5/ c 8° Longman 94
Autobiogr. acc. of a lengthy captivity in Algiers of a London merchant ab. mid. 17 cent. Now first pub.

EDWARDS, Matilda Betham- A Winter with the Swallows *o.p.* [*pb.* 15/] 8° Hurst 67

GASKELL, G. Algeria as it is *o.p.* [*pb.* 7/6] p 8° Smith & Elder 75

GORDON, L'y Duff [tr.] The French in Algiers [trs. fr. Germ. & Fch.] 2/ p 8° Murray [45] 61

HERBERT OF LEA, L'y A Search after Sunshine ; ill. [Algiers in 1871] *o.p.* [*pb.* 16/] 8° Bentley 72

HILTON-SIMPSON, M. W. Algiers and Beyond ; ill. [incls. interior] 12/*n.* 8°

KNOX, A. A. The New Playground *o.p.* [*pb.* 6/] c 8° Paul [81] 83

LEEDER, S. H. The Desert Gateway ; 10 ill. 6/*n.* c 8° Cassell 11
A description of Biskra (as gateway to the Sahara) and neighbourhood.

MANINGTON, Geo. A Soldier of the Legion ; maps and ill. 10/6 *n.* 8° Murray 07
An Englishman's advents. under the Fch. flag in Algeria and Tonquin. Ed. W. B. SLATER + A. J. SARL.

PEASE, Alf. E. Biskra and Oases of Desert of the Zibans 4/6 c 8° Stanford 93

PLAYFAIR, Col. Sir R. L. Travels in Footsteps of Bruce [Algeria and Nubia] 63/ 4° Stanford 77

The Scourge of Christendom 14/ 8° Smith & Elder 84
Annals of British relations with Algeria, 1540–1830.

SEGUIN, L. G. [=Mrs STRAHAN] Walks in Algiers and its Surroundings ; ill. 6/ c 8° Chatto [78] 88

WATSON, Gilb. The Voice of the South 10/6 *n.* 8° Hurst 05
Acc. of jy. across the Algerian Sahara with an interesting Arab guide.

WILKIN, Anth. Among the Berbers of Algeria; ill. 16/ 8° Unwin 00
A good popular descriptive book brings up to date and supplements BARCLAY's bk., *sup.*

WORKMAN, Fanny B. + W. H. Algerian Memories: bicycle tour over Atlas to Sahara; 23 ill. $2 c 8° Randolph, *N.Y.* 96
6/ Unwin. Lively acc., by an Am. and his wife, of cycle-tour: many pleasant picts. and curious details of land and inhabs., esp. of Kabyles.

WRIGLEY, M. Algiers Illustrated; 100 ill. [residence 1887–88] 45/ r 4° Low 89

*Biskra:* LEEDER (S. H.) The Desert Gateway; ill. [acc. of a winter at Biskra] 6/ *n.* c 8° Cassell 11

**Barca (Cyrenaica)**

BEECHY, F. + H. Proogs. of Expedn. to N. Coast of Africa [1821–2] *o.p.* [*pb.* 63/] 4° Murray
Comprehends an account of the Greater Syrtis and the Cyrenaica. 9 maps and illns.

HAMILTON, Jas. Wanderings in North Africa *o.p.* [*pb.* 12/] p 8° Murray 56

SMITH + PORCHER Recent Discoveries at Cyrene *o.p.* [*pb.* 126/] f° Day
Acc. of expedn. to the Cyrenaica in 1860–1. 12 maps and pl., tinted lithos., and woodcuts.

**Morocco**

*Bibliography:* de la MARTINIÈRE (H. M. P.)—*his* Morocco [*ut inf.*] *conts. bibliogr.* 1844 *to* 1877

PLAYFAIR (Col. Sir R. L.) + BROWN (Dr Rob.) Bibliogr. of Morocco fr. Earliest Times to end of 1891 = Suppl. Ppr. R. G. S. 1893 (Murray)
Titles of over 2,000 bks. and papers on hist., geogr., and politics of Morocco, preceded by essay on the country and its people.

*Early Account:* PELLOW (T.) Adventures, ed. Dr Rob. Brown; ill. [Advent. Ser.] 3/6 c 8° Unwin [*n.d.*] 90
$1·50 Macmillan, *N.Y.* Acc. [questionably quite genuine] of his 23 years' captivity [1715–38] am. Moors, giving frightful pict. of state of Morocco, cruelty of rulers, and furious civil wars. Introd. (by BROWN) gives a readable acc. of the Barbary pirates.

*Recent Travel and Accounts*

AFLALO, F. G. The Truth about Morocco 7/6 *n.* ($2 *n.*) c 8° Lane 04
Indictmt. of Brit. policy in Anglo-Fch. agreemt., urging that she shd. be associated in any important foreign control.

de AMICIS, E. Morocco, People & Places tr.], 2 v.; [50 ill. [$5 Coates, *Phila.*] 21/ *n.* c 8° Cassell [78] 97

ASHMEAD-BARTLETT, Ellis Passing of the Shereefian Empire; ill. 15/ *n.* 8° Blackwood 10
An interestg. and sympathetic study of last days of an anc. semi-barbarous Empire.

AUBIN, Eug. Morocco of To-day; 2 maps [$2 *n.* Dutton, *N.Y.*] 6/ *n.* c 8° Dent 06

BONSALL, Steph., jun. Morocco as it is; map and ill. *o.p.* [*pb.* 7/6] c 8° W. H. Allen [92] 93
By a Special Corresp. of the *Central News*. With an account of Sir Chas. EUAN-SMITH's mission to Fez.

COLVILLE, H. E. Ride fr. Fez to Algerian Frontier ['in petticoat & slippers'] *o.p.* [*pb.* 12/] 8° Low 80

DAWSON, A. J. Things Seen in Morocco; ill. 10/6 *n.* 8° Methuen 04
Cf. also his *Hidden Manna*, a novel giving an extremely good picture of Moorish life (6/ c 8° Heinemann '02).

FITZGERALD, Sybil In the Track of the Moors 21/ *n.* r 8° Dent 05
$6 *n.* Dutton, *N.Y.* Sketches in Northern Africa and in Spain; w. ill. and 50 col. pl. by Augustine FITZGERALD.

FORREST, A. S. [art.] Morocco: 74 col. pl., w. l'pr. S. L. Bensusan [$6 *n.* Macm., *N.Y.*] 20/ *n.* sq 8° Black 04

GRAHAM, R. B. Cunningham Mogreb-el-Acksa: jy. in Morocco; map 9/ 8° Heinemann 98
An unsuccessful journey to Tarudant in Sus: valuable only as a series of well-expressed impressions.

GREY, Hy. M. In Moorish Captivity: the Tourmaline Expedition 16/ 8° Arnold 99
An account of the commercial expedition to Sus, 1897–8, and of the author's captivity which resulted from it.

GROVE, L'y A. G. Seventy-one Days' Camping in Morocco; 33 ill. 7/6 *n.* 8° Longman 02
A pleasantly written book, but of no value as an account of Moorish life.

HALIBURTON, R. G. The Dwarfs of Mount Atlas 1/ 8° Nutt 91
Statemts. of natives of Morocco and of Europ. residents; w. notes on dwarfs and dwarf-worship. 41 pp.

HARRIS, Lawr. With Mulai Hafid at Fez 7/6 *n.* 8° Smith & Elder 09

HARRIS, Walt. B. The Land of an African Sultan; ill. [1887–9] 2/6 c 8° Low [89] 96
Narr. of tour fr. Tangier along coast to Arzila and El-Araish, then inland to Mequinez and Fez, returng. by El-K'sar el-Kebir and Wazzan.

,, Tafilet: narr. of jy. of explorn. to Atlas Mtns. and Oases of N.-W. Sahara; 2 maps and ill. *o.p.* [*pb.* 12/] 8° Blackwood 95
A lively record of an adventurous and perilous jy., w. acc. of Tafilet itself, its people, their manners and customs.

HAY, Sir Jno. Drummond [1816–93] Morocco and the Moors *o.p.* [*pb.* 2/] c 8° Murray [3–] 61
By a British Representative at the capital of Morocco before 1844. *Vide* also Memoir of him in F § 27.

HOOKER (Sir J. D.) + BALL (J.) Tour in Morocco and Great Atlas; ill. *o.p.* [*pb.* 21/] 8° Macmillan 78
Full descrn. of the country, tho' the expedn. was made w. a botanical object.

LEARED, A. Morocco and the Moors, ed. Sir Rich. Burton; ill. 16/ 8° Low [76] 90

'LOTI, Pierre' [=Jules VIAUD] Into Morocco [tr.]; ill. $1 12° Rand, *Chicago* [89] 92
Description of the embassy fr. France to Fez in 1889. Full of action and colour.

MACKENZIE, Donald The Khalifate of the West; ill. 10/6 8° Simpkin 11

MACNAB, Fces. Ride in Morocco [$5 Longman, *N.Y.*] 15/ 8° Arnold 02

de la MARTINIÈRE, H. M. P. Morocco [tr.]; maps, charts, etc. [jys. to Fez; w. bibliogr.] 14/ 8° Whittaker 89

*MEAKIN, Budgett The Moorish Empire; ill. 15/ 8° Sonnenschein 99

* ,, The Land of the Moors; ill. 15/ 8° Sonnenschein 01
$5 *n.* Macmillan, *N.Y.* The standard authority. Based on personal residence and travel and a study of all the literature of the subject.

*MEAKIN, Budgett — The Moors: a comprehensive description; ill. 15/ 8° Sonnenschein 02
$5 n. Macmillan, *N.Y.* Detailed and trustworthy descrn. of social and religious condns. and customs.

" — Life in Morocco and Glimpses Beyond; ill. 12/6 n. 8° Chatto 05
Disconnected pen-pictures of Berber life and history; partly repr. fr. magazines

'MONTBARD, Georges' [C. A. LOYES] Among the Moors; fully ill. by author 21/ 8° Low 94
Descrs. same tour as HARRIS (*Ld. of Afr. Sultan, sup.*), whom author accomp. HARRIS' acc. is superior.

MOORE, F. — The Passing of Morocco; map and 12 pl. 5/ n. c 8° Smith & Elder 08

RANKIN, Reg. — In Morocco with General d'Amade; ill. 9/ n. ($2·50 n.) 8° Longman 08

ROHLFS, G. — Journeys thro' Oases of Draa and Tafilet [tr.]; ill. *o.p.* [*pb.* 12/] 8° Low 74

SAVORY, Isabel — In the Tail of the Peacock; 49 ill. 16/ n. 8° Hutchinson 03
Ordinary experiences of two English ladies in Morocco.

STERNBERG, C't A. — The Barbarians of Morocco [tr.]; ill. 6/ n. 8° Chatto 08

STUTFIELD, H. E. M. — El Maghreb: 1,200 miles' ride thro' Morocco 8/6 c 8° Low 86

THOMSON, Jos. — Travels in Atlas and Southern Morocco; 68 ill. and 2 maps 9/ c 8° Philip 89
Gives a good account of Morocco city and of the Atlas range.

TROTTER, Cpt. C. P. — Our Mission to Coast of Morocco; 41 photos. *o.p.* [*pb.* 24/] 8° Douglas, *Edin.* 81
Account of the mission under Sir J. Drummond HAY in 1880.

WARD, H. J. B. — Mysterious Morocco and How to Appreciate it; ill. 2/6 c 8° Simpkin 10

WATSON, R. S. — A Visit to the Sacred City of Wazan *o.p.* [*pb.* 30/6] 8° Macmillan 80

WEIR, T. H. — The Shaikhs of Morocco; map 6/ n. c 8° Morton, *Edin.* 04
Colln. of lore of Moorish saints in 16 cent., chfly. tr. fr. contemp. wrgs. of IBN ASKAR.

*Moors in Spain* — —*v.* **F** § 58

**Tripoli:** *Bibliography:* PLAYFAIR (Sir R. L.) Bibliogr. of Tripoli—*in* Suppl. Pprs. of R. G. S. (Murray

BARTH, Hy. — —*in his* Travels and Discoveries, *ut* **E** § 46 [journeys 1849–55]

BODDY, A. A. — —*in his* To Kairwân, *ut inf., s.v.* Tunis

DENHAM (D.) + CLAPPERTON (Cpt.) + OUDNEY (Dr)—*in their* Travels, *ut* **E** § 46

FURLONG, C. W. — The Gateway to Sahara; ill. (some col.) [Tripoli] 12/6 n. 8° Chapman 09

RAE, Edw. — —*in his* The Country of the Moors, *ut inf., s.v.* Tunisia [Tripoli to Kairwân]

THOMPSON, G. E. — Life in Tripoli: with peep at anc. Carthage; 30 ill. 6/ c 8° Howell, *Liverpool* 93

**Tunisia; Tunis:** *Bibliography:* ASHBEE (H. S.) Bibliogr. of Tunis 5/ n. r 8° Dulau 89
Enlarged fr. Graham + Ashbee's *Tunisia, ut inf.* Ends w. 1888. A very compreh. and excellent piece of special bibliogr. Index.

*History:* BROADLEY (A. M.) Last Punic War: Tunis past & present, 2 vols. 25/ p 8° Blackwood 82
With a narrative of the French conquest. Maps and ill.

ROUSSEAU, Bar. A. — Hist. of Conquest of Tunis by Ottomans 8° *Algiers* 83

*Travel:* BODDY (A. A.) To Kairwân, the Holy *o.p.* [*pb.* 6/] c 8° Paul 85

BRUUN, Cpt. D. — The Cave-Dwellers of Southern Tunisia [tr.]; ill. 12/ 8° Thacker 99
An account of the cave-dwellers of the Matmata Mtns.; w. notes on other races.

DUMERGUE, E. — The Chotts of Tunis *o.p.* [*pb.* 2/6] c 8° W. H. Allen 83

GRAHAM (Alex.) + ASHBEE (H. S.) Travels in Tunisia; 50 ill. [w. bibliogr.] 25/ r 8° Dulau 87

GREVILLE-NUGENT, P. — The Land of Mosques and Marabouts; ill. 14/ 8° Chapman 94

v. HESSE-WARTEGG, E. — Tunis, the Land and the People; ill. *o.p.* [*pb.* 3/6] c 8° Chatto 82

LORIMER, Norma — By the Waters of Carthage 12/ n. 8° Hutchinson 06

PETRIE, Graham [artist] — Tunis, Kairouan, and Carthage: 48 col. pl. 16/ n. r 8° Heinemann 08
Illns. of mosques, streets, cafés, markets, and bazaars of these ancient Moslem towns, w. histor. and topogr. notes.

RAE, Edw. — Country of the Moors; ill. [Tripoli to Kairwân] *o.p.* [*pb.* 12/] c 8° Murray 77

REID, T. Wemyss — Land of the Bey [impressns. of Tunis under Fch.] *o.p.* [*pb.* 10/6] c 8° Low 81

SLADEN, Douglas — Carthage and Tunis, 2 vols.; 6 maps and 68 pl. 24/ n. 8° Hutchinson 06

VIVIAN, Herb. — Tunisia and Modern Barbary Pirates; maps and ill. 15/ 8° Pearson 99
$4 Longman, *N.Y.* Some history and a good deal of descrn. of manners, trade, agric., educ., folklore, etc.

## 46: WEST AFRICA, including NIGERIA AND SAHARA

**Ethnology**

DENNETT, R. E. — At Back of Black Man's Mind; ill. 10/ n. ($3·25 n.) 8° Macmillan 06
Notes on the Kingly Office in West Africa.

ELLIS, Lt.-Col. A. B. — West African Sketches *o.p.* Chapman 81

" — The Land of Fetish *o.p.* [*pb.* 12/] 8° Chapman 83

" — Tshi-speaking Peoples of the Gold Coast 10/6 8° Chapman 87

" — Ewe-speaking People of Slave Coast of W. Africa 10/6 8° Chapman 90

" — Yoruba-speaking Peoples of Slave Coast of W. Africa 10/6 8° Chapman 94
On the religion, manners, customs, laws, langs., etc., of these peoples. Three important bks. for ethnol. and philology.

NASSAU, Rev. R. H. Fetishism in West Africa; 12 ill.—*ut* **B** § 34

THOMAS, N. W. Anthrop. Report on Edo-speaking Peoples of Nigeria, Pts. i–ii ea. 4/ *n.* c 8° Harrison 11
Full of facts gleaned dur. 14 mos. tour. Incls. many folk-tales and a dictionary (w. transliterations).

**Early Travel:** di CADAMOSTO (Luigi) Voyages, tr. H. Y. Oldham [1455, 1456] 8° Hakluyt Soc.

PARK, Mungo [1771–1805] Travels in Interior of Afr. [Everym. Lib.; 35 c. *n.* Dutton *N.Y.*] 1/ *n.* 12° Dent

„ Travels to Discover Source of Niger; 8 col. pl. 3/6 c 8° Black [ ]

Life and Travels of Mungo Park in Africa; ill. [a good popular bk.] 2/ c 8° Chambers 96

Maclachlan, T. B. Mungo Park [Famous Scots; 75 c. Scribner, *N.Y.*] 1/6 c 8° Oliphant 98

Thomson, Jos. Mungo Park and the Niger; maps and ill. 3/6 c 8° Philip 90
$1·25 Dodd & Mead, *N.Y.* [Great Explorers.] Combines with PARK's life a hist. of discovery of the regions he opened up.

**Modern Travel and Description**

BARTH, Hy. Travs. & Discovs. in N. & Cent. Afr.; ill. 2/ (75 c.) c 8° Ward & Lock [57–8] 90
[Minerva Lib.] 1849–55. Incls. accs. of Tripoli, Sahara, Kgdm. of Bornu, and countries rd. L. Chad. *V.* also Timbuctoo, *inf.*

BURTON, Sir Rich. F. Wanderings in West Africa, 2 vols. *o.p.* [*pb.* 12/] 8° Tylston [63] 9–
Liverpool to Fernando Po. Full of interesting descrns. of West Africa in 1862.

DENHAM (D.) + CLAPPERTON (Cpt.) + OUDNEY (Dr) Travels in N. & Centr. Afr., 2 v.
[1822–4] *o.p.* 8° *London* [ ] 28

*KINGSLEY, Mary H. Travels in West Africa, Congo Français, Corisco, and Cameroons; ill.
21/ *n.* ($6·50 *n.*) 8° Macmillan 96
A bright, breezy narr. of travel, often in places hitherto unvisited by whites, by a good observer and fascinatg. writer, w. excellent descrns. of native customs, tradns., characteristics, and sectn. on *Fetish*. App. by Dr GÜNTHER on zool. results of jy. Abgd. Edn. 7/6 ($2) '97.

* „ West African Studies; maps and ill. 7/6 ($2·25) c 8° Macmillan [99] 01
Essays of great value on people, scenery, state of commerce, trade, fetich-worship, etc.

LUCAS [Sir] C. P. West Africa, ed. H. E. Egerton; 5 maps = Hist. Geogr. vol. iii
7/6 ($2) c 8° Clar. Press [94] 00

READE, Winwood —*in his* African Sketch Book, 2 vols., *ut* **E** § 41

**History**

de AZURARA, G. E. Chron. of Discov. and Conq. of Guinea, 2 vols. 8° Hakluyt Soc. 96–9
Ed. by C. R. BEAZLEY + Edg. PRESTAGE. The 1st tr. of this import. chronicle. Incls. life of AZURARA.

GEORGE, Claude Rise of British West Africa, 2 Pts. ea. 2/ 8° Houlston 04
Notes ab. progress of events down to yr. 1827: of small value.

KINGSLEY, Mary H. Story of W. Africa [Story of Empire Ser.] 1/6 c 8° H. Marshall 99

MOCKLER-FERRYMAN, Maj. A. F. Imperial Africa, vol. i: British West Africa; maps
*o.p.* [*pb.* 2/6] 8° Imperial Press 98
Not a history, though including some history; a miscellaneous account and compilation; a useful book.

MOREL, E. D. Affairs of West Africa; maps and ill. 12/ *n.* r 8° Heinemann 02

WALLIS, Cpt. C. Braithwaite Advance of our West Africa Empire; 64 ill. 21/ m 8° Unwin 03
Acc. of his experces. as Acting District Commr. in Sierra Leone Protectorate dur. and after the hut-tax rebellion of 1898.

**Angola:** BATTELL (Andr.) Strange Adventures, ed. E. G. Lavenstein—*ut* **E** § 48, *s.v.* Congo [1589–1610]

CAPELLO (H.) + IVENS (R.) From Benguella to the Yacca Territory [tr.], 2 vols.—*ut* **E** § 48

LOOMIS, Prf. E. J. An Eclipse Party in Africa; ill. $4·50 8° Roberts, *Boston* 96
Acc. of expedn. to St Paul de Loanda, led by Prf. D. P. TODD, to make observns. on total eclipse of Dec. 22, '89.

MONTEIRO, J. J. Angola and River Congo, 2 vols.; ill. *o.p.* [*pb.* 21/] c 8° Macmillan 75

NEVINSON, H. W. A Modern Slavery; ill. and port. $2 *n.* (6/) 8° Harper 06
Descrn. of jy. in Angola, West Central Africa, and Portug. islands of San Thomé and Principe.

**Ashanti and the Gold Coast**

BURTON (Sir R. F.) + CAMERON (Com. V. L.) To Gold Coast f. Gold, 2 v.; maps *o.p.* [*pb.* 21/] c 8° Chatto 83

CRUICKSHANK, Brodie Eighteen Years on the Gold Coast, 2 vols. *o.p.* [*pb.* 21/] c 8° Hurst 53

*ELLIS, Lt.-Col. A. B. History of the Gold Coast 10/6 8° Chapman 93
Commencg. w. HERODOTUS' story ab. circumnavign. of Afr. and the Periplus of HANNO, traces the long fortunes of Gold Coast und. Portug., Dutch, Fch., and English. A good contrib. to our Colonial history.

„ The Tshi-speaking Peoples of the Gold Coast—*ut sup.*

FREEMAN, Rich. A. Travels and Life in Ashanti and Jáman 21/ 8° Constable 98
The best account of the countries; result of a mission there in 1897. 2 maps and 100 illns.

HAYFORD, C. Gold Coast Native Institutions—*ut* **D** § 3 [partly crit. of Brit. policy]

KEMP, Rev. Dennis Nine Years on the Gold Coast; ill. [missionary-wk.] 12/6 *n.* ($5) Macmillan 98

MACDONALD, Geo. The Gold Coast, Past and Present; ill. 7/6 ($2·50) c 8° Longman 98
A storehouse of general information.

MOORE (Decima) + GUGGISBERG (Maj. F. G.) We Two in West Africa; ill. 12/6 *n.* 8° Heinemann [09] 09
Descrn. by Dec. MOORE (Mrs GUGGISBERG) of their expedns. in conn. w. his wk. as Director of Surveys on Gold Coast.

RAMSEYER (F. A.) + KÜHNE (J.) Four Years in Ashantee; w. Introd. Dr Gundert; ill.
[missy.; 1869–72] 5/ c 8° Nisbet [65] 75

REINDORF, Rev. C. C. History of the Gold Coast and Asante 9/ *n.* 8° Author, *Basle* 95
Based on traditions and historical facts, comprising a period of more than three centuries [1500–1860].

SARBAH, Jno. Mensah — Asanti and other Akan Tribes of West Africa — 15/ *n.* 8° Clowes 07
Incls. a short acc. of discovery of Gold Coast by Portuguese navigators, and another of early Engl. voyagers.

STUART, J. M. — Ancient Goldfields of Africa; maps and ill. — 7/6 s 4° Wilson 91
In spite of its title deals almost exclus. w. goldfields recently brot. bef. the public. Chiefly quotns. fr. wrgs. of travellers.

*Ashanti Expedition—v.* **F** § 31 *Gold Fields—v.* **I** § 79

**Congo State and River** —*v.* **E** § 48

**Dahomey:** BURTON (Sir R. F.) Mission to Gelele, King of Dahome, 2 v. *o.p.* [*pb.* 25/] c 8° Tylston [64] 93

FORBES, Com. F. E. — Dahomey & Dahomans, 2 v. [2 missns. 1849–50] *o.p.* [*pb.* 21/] c 8° Longman 51

**Gambia:** ARCHER (F. Bisset) Gambia Colony and Protectorate — 10/ *n.* 8° St Bride's Press 05

**Hausaland** —*v.* **E** § 43 (KUMM, ROBINSON)

**Liberia:** DURHAM (F. A.) — The Lone Star of Liberia—*ut* **D** § 130

JOHNSTON, Sir Harry H. — Liberia, 2 vols.; maps and ill. — 42/ r 8° Hutchinson 06
The standard wk. on this negro republic. Full of information.

MCPHERSON, Dr J. H. T. — Afr. Colonizn.: hist. of Liberia
[Johns Hopk. Univ. Studs.] 50 c. 8° Johns Hopk. Pr., *Baltim.* 91

**Nigeria (Northern and Southern); River Niger**

*ALEXANDER, Lt. Boyd — From the Niger to the Nile, 2 vols.; maps and ill. — 36/ *n.* 8° Arnold 07
$10 *n.* Longman, *N.Y.* Hist. of a great jy. (1904–7) by routes hitherto ill-explored—some never before visited—w. Lake Chad as middle objective Of consid. geograph., nat.-hist., and ethnogr. value, with much sport on the way. He was accomp. by Cpt. Claud ALEXANDER, Cpt. G. B. GOSLING, P. A. TALBOT, and José Lopez (interpreter).

ALLEN (Cpt. W.) + THOMSON (T. R. H.) Narr. of Expedn. to Niger, 2 v. [1841] *o.p.* [*pb.* 32/] 8° Bentley 48

BINDLOSS, Har. — In the Niger Country; 2 maps — 12/6 8° Blackwood 99
A popular book, dealing mainly with the country and life of the people about the delta.

DENHAM (D.) + CLAPPERTON (Cpt.) + OUDNEY (Dr)—*in their* Travels, 2 vols., *ut sup.*

FALCONER, J. D. — On Horseback through Nigeria; map and 32 ill. — 12/6 *n.* 8° Unwin 11

GLOSSOP, B. R. M. — Sporting Trips of a Subaltern; ill. — 10/6 8° Harper 06

HAZZLEDINE, G. D. — The White Man in Nigeria; map and ill. — 10/6 *n.* 8° Arnold 04

HOURST, Lt. — Exploration of the Niger [tr.]; maps and 190. ill. — 24/ 8° Chapman 98
Account of the first voyage down the whole length of the Niger.

HUTCHINSON, T. J. — Narr. of Explorn. of Niger, Tshadda, & Binuë *o.p.* [*pb.* 2/6] c 8° Longman 55

KISCH, Martin S. — Letters and Sketches fr. Northern Nigeria; ill. — 6/ *n.* c 8° Chatto 10
Posth. pubd. wrgs. by a keen recruit in the Political Staff of W. Nigeria. Map and bibliography.

LAIRD (M.) + OLDFIELD (R. A. K.) Expedn. into Interior of Afr. by Niger, 2 v.
[1832–4] *o.p.* [*pb.* 28/] 8° Bentley 37

LANDER, R. L. — Record of Clapperton's Expedition, 2 vols. — *o.p.* 8° *London* 30

„ + Jno. — Adventures on the Niger, 2 vols. — *o.p.* [*pb.* 7/] c 8° Tegg [32] 56

LARYMORE, Constance — A Resident's Wife in Nigeria; ill. — 4/6 *n.* c 8° Routledge [08] 11
A bright narr. of everyday life and experces. dur. 5 yrs., w. informn. of practical value to intending colonists.

LEONARD, Maj. A. G. — The Lower Niger and its Tribes; map — 12/6 *n.* ($4 *n.*) 8° Macmillan 06

LUGARD, L'y [Flora L. SHAW] A Tropical Dependency — 18/ *n.* 8° Nisbet 05
An outl. of the hist. and civilizn. extant bef. those of Egypt—Ghana, Songhay, Sokoto; w. accs. of Melle and Timbuctu as noted seats of learng. while Eur. was still in Dark Ages. Then descrs. fully Northern Nigeria.

MACWILLIAM, Dr J. O. — Medical Hist. of Expedn. to Niger, 1841–2 *o.p.* [*pb.* 10/] 8° Macmillan 43

MOCKLER-FERRYMAN, Cpt. [Col.] A. F. Up the Niger; map and ill. — 16/ 8° Philip 92
Narr. of Maj. Claude MACDONALD's missn. to Niger and Benin rivers, obj. of wh. was to report to Brit. govt. on condn. and admin. of Niger region by Roy. Niger Co. App. on native musical Instruments by Cpt. C. A. DAY.

„ — British Nigeria; 16 ill. — 12/6 *n.* 8° Cassell 02
An account of the exploration, history, and present condition of the district.

MOREL, E. D. — Nigeria: peoples and problems; 2 maps and 32 pl. 10/6 *n.* r 8° Smith & Elder 11

ORR, Cpt. C. W. J. — The Making of Northern Nigeria; maps — 8° Macmillan, *in prep.*

PARK, Mungo [1771–1805] Travels to Discover Source of Niger—*ut sup.*

PARTRIDGE, C. — Cross River Natives; maps and ill. — 12/6 *n.* 8° Hutchinson 05
Notes on primitive pagans of Obubura Hill District, Southern Nigeria, stone-circles of Aweyong River.

RICHARDSON, Rob. — Story of the Niger: record of travel and advent.; 31 ill. — 2/6 c 8° Nelson 93
Story of the discoveries of Mungo PARK, CLAPPERTON, the LANDERS, Adolphe BURDO, Cpt. GALLIENI, THOMSON, etc. A boy's bk.

ROBINSON, Rev. Chas. H. — Nigeria, our Latest Protectorate; ill. — 5/ *n.* c 8° H. Marshall 00
Much information concerning the Hausa people, language, and customs. Of some ethnographical value.

SHAW, Flora L. — —*v.* LUGARD, L'y, *sup.*

TREMEARNE, Cpt. A. J. N. — The Niger and the West Sudan — 6/ *n.* 8° Hodder 10
A vade-mecum for Britons in W. Afr.: condns. of life, kit, provisions., language, etc.

TROTTER, Lt.-Col. J. K. — Niger Sources and Borders of Sierra Leone — 5/ c 8° Methuen 98
Descrs. the wk. of the Anglo-French Boundary Commission, 1895–6. Good map and ill.

VANDELEUR, Lt.-Col. Seymour Campaigning on Upper Nile and Niger; maps and ill. [1894–7] 10/6 c 8° Methuen 98
Narr. of his services (1) in Equatorial Lakes and Upper Nile (1895–6); (2) under Sir Ew. GOLDIE in Niger campaign (1897), describg. capture of Bida and Ilorin and Fch. occupn. of Boussa.

Maxse, Col. F. I. Seymour Vandeleur [b. 1869; d. 1901]: story of a Brit. officer 12/6 8° *Natl. Rev.* Office 05

*Abeokuta:* BURTON (Sir R. F.) Abeokuta and Camaroons Mtns., 2 vols. *o.p.* [*pb.* 25/] c 8° Tinsley 63

*Benin:* BACON (R. H.) Benin, the City of Blood; ill. 7/6 8° Arnold 97

BOISRAGON, Cpt. Alan The Benin Massacre; maps 3/6 c 8° Methuen 98
A graphic account of the massacre, by one of the two survivors.

ROTH, H. Ling Great Benin: customs, art, and horrors—*ut* **B** § 34

*Yoruba:* DENNETT (R. E.) Nigerian Studies: relig. & pol. syst. of Yoruba; ill. 8/6 *n.* 8° Macmillan 10

ELLIS, Lt.-Col. A. B. Yoruba-speaking Peoples—*ut sup.*

STONE, Rev. R. H. In Afric's Forest and Jungle [missionary] $1 c 8° Pacific Pr., *Oakld., Cal.* 99

**Sahara (The):** BARTH (H.) —*in his* Travels in N. and Centr. Afr. [tr.], *ut* **E** § 46

DENHAM (D.) + CLAPPERTON (Cpt.) + OUDNEY (Dr)—*in their* Travels, 2 vols., *ut sup.*

DUMERGUE, E. The Chotts of Tunis—*ut* **E** § 45, *s.v.* Tunis

KING, W. J. Harding In Search of the Masked Tawareks; ill. 12/6 8° Smith & Elder 03
Acc. of travel and adventure in N. Sahara. Author succeeded in running down these dangerous nomads and obtaing. ports. of them unmasked, tho' the custom of wearg. a black mask is as essential a pt. of their soc. decency as is the veil to Mohamm. women.

MACKENZIE, D. Flooding the Sahara *o.p.* [*pb.* 10/6] 8° Low 77
Description of a plan for opening up Central Africa to commerce.

PEARSE, Alf. E. —*in his* Travel and Sport in Africa, 1892–1901, 3 vols., *ut* **E** § 41

PHILLIPPS, L. March In the Desert—*ut* **E** § 45

POMMEROL, Mme J. Among the Women of Sahara [tr.]; 90 ill. 12/ *n.* 8° Hunt 00

RICHARDSON, Jas. [1806–51] Travels in Desert of Sahara, 2 vols. [1845–6, etc.] *o.p.* [*pb.* 30/] 8° Bentley 48

TRISTRAM, Can. H. B. Great Sahara: wandgs. S. of Atlas Mtns.; ill. *o.p.* [*pb.* 15/] 8° Murray 60

VISCHER, Hanns Across the Sahara; map and ill. 12/6 *n.* 8° Arnold 09
$3·50 *n.* Longman, *N.Y.* A very interestg. and valuable acc. of a caravan-jy. fr. Tripoli to Bornu: of considerable scientific value.

WORKMAN, Fanny B. + W. H.—*in their* Algerian Memories, *ut* **E** § 45

*Libyan Desert* —*v.* **E** § 43

**Senegambia:** MITCHINSON (A. W.) The Expiring Continent [travs. in Seneg.] 18/ 8° W. H. Allen 81

**Sierra Leone:** *Bibliography:* LUKACH (H. C.) Bibliogr. of Sierra Leone 8/6 *n.* 8° Clar. Press 11
A scholarly classified bibliography, inclg. in its 826 items over 100 dealing w. African languages. 2 maps.

ALLDRIDGE, T. J. The Sherbro and its Hinterland 15/ *n.* 8° Macmillan 01
An excellent account of the geography, products, commerce and native life, based on 10 yrs.' residence.

,, A Transformed Colony; 66 ill. 16/ *n.* 8° Seeley 10
Sierra Leone as it was and is, its progr., peoples, customs, and undevel. wealth.

BANBURY, G. A. Lethbridge Sierra Leone, the White Man's Grave; ill. *o.p.* [*pb.* 3/6] c 8° Sonnenschein [88] 89

INGHAM, Bp C. E. Sierra Leone after a Hundred Years; 16 ill. 6/ c 8° Seeley 94
Brief surv. of hist. of colony (wh. in '87 celebr. its 1st centenary); w. descrn. of pres. relig. and soc. state: mainly fr. missy. pt.-of-view.

RANKIN, F. H. Visit to the White Man's Grave, 2 vols. *o.p.* [*pb.* 21/] c 8° Bentley 36

TROTTER, Lt.-Col. J. K. Niger Sources, and Borders of Sierra Leone—*ut sup.*, *s.v.* Nigeria

*Timbuctoo:* BARTH (H.) Timbuktu and the Niger 2/ c 8° Ward & Lock [6–]
Still of considerable value, and of surpassing interest. Not very full on Timbuctoo.

DUBOIS, Félix Timbuctoo the Mysterious [tr.]; 11 maps and 153 ill. 12/6 8° Heinemann 96
$3·50 Longman, *N.Y.* Descrs. an import. jy. fr. Paris to the Niger, givg. accs. of Niger valley and towns, the Longhoi empire, and Timbuctoo and its hist. to the Fch. conquest. Exc. PARK in 1805, Maj. LAING in 1825, Réné CAILLIÉ c. 1825 (who wrote a bk. ab. it), and BARTH, no one succeeded in reachg. and leaving Timb. alive before DUBOIS.

**Islands:** ELLIS (Lt.-Col. A. B.) The West African Islands *o.p.* [*pb.* 14/] 8° Chapman 85

**Ascension:** GILL (Mrs D.) Six Months in Ascension: acc. of scient. expedn. 9/ c 8° Murray 78

**Canary Islands; Teneriffe:** BONTIER (P.) + LE VERRIER (J.) Conquest & Conversion of the Canarians [1402], by Jean de Bethencourt, tr. & ed. R. H. Major 8° Hakluyt Soc. 72

BROWN, A. S. Madeira and the Canary Islands; 8 maps—*ut* **E** § 27

D'ESTE, Marg. In the Canaries with a Camera; ill. 7/6 *n.* c 8° Methuen 09

EDWARDES, C. Rides and Studies in the Canary Islands; ill. 10/6 c 8° Unwin 88

de ESPINOSA, A. Guanches of Tenerife, tr. Sir C. R. Markham [1594] 8° Hakluyt Soc. 07
Descrn. of the island, its former inhabts. the Guanches (contractn of, Guanchinerfe, 'son of Tenerife'), their customs, etc.

LATIMER, S. F. The English in the Canary Isles; 8 ill. [statistical, etc.] 4/ 8° *Plymouth* 88

PÉGOT-OGIER, E. The Fortunate Islands [tr.], 2 vols. *o.p.* [*pb.* 21/] c 8° Bentley 71

STONE, Olivia M. Tenerife and its Six Satellites, 2 v.; maps and ill. [v. complete] *o.p.* [*pb.* 15/] 8° Marcus Ward [87] 89

TAYLOR, J. C. Health Resorts of the Canary Islands—*ut* **H*** § 57

WHITFORD, Jno. Canary Islands as a Winter Resort; 7 maps and 25 ill. 7/6 c 8° Stanford 90

**St Helena:** BROOKE (T. H.) History of Isl. of St Helena *o.p.* 8° *London* 1808

JACKSON, E. L. St Helena, the Historic Island; ill. Ward & Lock 03
A loosely-put-together compiln., yet contg. a good deal of valuable historical and geogr. material.

MELLISS, J. C. St Helena; col. pl. 42/ r 8° Lovell Reeve 75
A physical, historical and topographical description. Continues the history of BROOKE fr. 1823 to 1875.

## 47: EASTERN EQUATORIAL AFRICA

**Early Account:** BARBOSA (D.) Coasts of E. Afr. & Malabar in beg. of 16 Cent., [tr.] 8° Hakluyt Soc. 66

**Ethnology** —*v. also inf., s.v.* ROUTLEDGE

HOBLEY, C. W. Ethnol. of A-Kamba and other E. Afr. Tribes; ill. 7/6 *n.* 8° Camb. Press 10
Putnam, *N.Y.* [Cambr. Archæol Soc.] A good presentatn. of all that appertains to the life (and death) of the A-Kamba.

HOLLIS, A. C. The Nandi: language and folklore; ill. 16/ ($5·25) 8° Clar Press 09

**Historical Geography:** LUCAS (Sir C. P.) South and East Africa [=Hist. Geog., vol. iv] 9/6 ($2·40) c 8° Clar. Press 98–03

**Travel and Description:** BADEN-POWELL (Maj.-Gen. R. S. S.) Sketches in Mafeking and E. Africa; ill. 21/ *n.* obl 4° Smith & Elder 07

DECLE, Lionel Three Years in Savage Africa; ill. 21/ 8° Methuen 98
Descrn. of jy. fr. Cape to Bechuanald., the Zambesi, Matabeleld., Mashonald., Portug. settlemt. on Zambesi, Nyassald., Ujiji, Germ. E. Afr., Uganda, and Brit. E. Afr. (7,000 miles in all); w. observns. on customs, etc. 5 maps and 100 ill.

ELTON (J. F.) + COTTERILL (H. B.) Travels in Eastern and Central Africa; ill. 21/ 8° Murray 79
ELTON's journals, edited by COTTERILL.

FRENCH-SHELDON, Mrs Sultan to Sultan; ill. *o.p.* [*pb.* 21/] 8° Saxon 93
Travels am. Masai and other tribes of E. Afr., by the only woman of Europ. orig. who had then penetrated to the Equatorial region and the neighbourhd. of Kilima-Njaro—the only notable thing ab. the bk.

KRAPF, Rev. J. L. —*in his* Travels dur. Residence in E. Africa [tr.], *ut* **E** § 44

MACLEOD, Lyons Travels in East Africa, etc., 2 vols. *o.p.* [*pb.* 21/] c 8° Hurst 60

MACQUEEN, Peter In Wildest Africa; 64 pl. 7/6 *n.* 8° Bell 10
Record of hunting and explorn. thro' Uganda, Victoria Nyanza, Vict. Nyanza regn., Brit. E. Africa, w. acc. of ascent of snowfields of Mt. Kibo and descrn. of var. native tribes.

PATTERSON, Lt.-Col. J. H. The Man-Eaters of Tsavo and other East African Adventures; ill. 7/6 *n.* ($2 *n.*) 8° Macmillan 07
A record of adventure, hairbreadth escapes, and travel. Foreword by F. C. SELOUS.

SCHILLINGS, C. G. With Flashlight & Rifle in Equat. E. Afr. [tr.] 12/6 *n.* 8° Hutchinson [06] 07
An interesting record of hunting advents. and studies of wild life in Equat. East Africa. 302 illns.

WASON, J. Cathcart East Africa and Uganda 3/6 *n.* c 8° Griffiths 05

YOUNGHUSBAND, Ethel Glimpses of E. Afr. and Zanzibar; 58 ill. 12/6 *n.* 8° Long 10
Affords a good picture of life of a Brit. officer's wife who accomps. her husband on tropical service.

**British East Africa:** ARKELL-HARDWICK (A.) Ivory Trader in N. Kenia; ill. 12/6 *n.* 8° Longman 03
Straightforward chron. of huntg. and advent. fr. Mombasa thro' Kikuyu to Gallald.; w. acc. of little-known Rendile and Burkenji tribes.

BRODE, Dr H. British and German E. Afr.: econ. and commerc. relns. 7/6 *n.* c 8° Arnold 11

BUXTON, Edw. N. —*in his* Two African Trips, *ut* **E** § 41

CHANLER, W. A. Thro' Jungle and Desert; 2 maps and ill. $5 (21/ *n.*) l 8° Macmillan 96
Acc. of an important expedn. to cy. betw. Mt. Kenia and Lake Rudolf region (1892–3), wh., after makg. valuable researches (descrn. of Rendile tribe most import. pt. of bk.) ended in a ser. of disasters, inclg. a mutiny of Zanzibaris. Good accs. of sport.

CHAPMAN, Abel On Safari; fully and well ill. 16/ *n.* 8° Arnold 08
$4·50 *n.* Longman, *N.Y.* An excellent jungle-bk. of Equat. Afr., w. App. on Bird-life. In Swahili (the *lingua franca* of Central Africa) *safari* is a term wh. means an expedn. or caravan mobilized for any jy., whether sportg. or otherwise, not made by rail.

ELIOT, Sir Chas. The East Africa Protectorate; maps and ill. 15/ *n.* 8° Arnold 05
$5 Longman, *N.Y.* An excellent acc. of the Protectorate and a valuable contribn. to probl. of admin. of Equat. Africa.

FITZGERALD, W. W. A. Travels in Coastlands of Brit. East Africa 28/ 8° Chapman 98
Investigations carried out, 1891–3: agriculture and products; incls. Zanzibar and Pemba. 15 maps and 117 illns.

GREGORY, Dr J. W. The Foundation of British East Africa 6/ *n.* c 8° H. Marshall 01
A masterly acc. of phys. feats. of E. Afr., its races, explorn., and developmt. to 1899; incls. Uganda and Unyoro.

* ,, Great Rift Valley: jy. to M. Kenya and L. Baringo 21/ 8° Murray 96
A compreh. and import. wk., contg. in addn. to unassumg. record of adventurous travel, carrd. out agst. serious disadvants. w. grt. success, an excellen acc. of geogr., geol., races, fauna, and flora. Maps and ill.

HINDLIP, L'd C. A. British East Africa: past, pres., & future [controversial] 3/6 *n.* c 8° Unwin 05

,, Sport and Travel: Abyssinia and British East Africa—*ut* **E** § 44

v. HÖHNEL, Lt. L. —*in his* Discov. of Lakes Rudolf and Stefanie [tr.], 2 vols., *ut* **E** § 48

JOHNSTON, H. H. —*in his* Kilima Njaro Expedition, *ut inf., s.v.* Masai

KASSNER, Theo. —*in his* From Rhodesia to Egypt, *ut* **E** § 41

LUGARD, Cpt. [Gen.] F. D. Rise of our East African Empire, 2 vols. 42/ l 8° Blackwood 93
An import. wk, dealg. w. our early efforts in Uganda and Nyassald. fr. beg. of Brit. influ.: w. suggestns. for future admin. and exam. of Afr. probls. Conts. also acc. of his pers. wk., sport, and travel in E. Afr. The series of 14 maps is very valuable, and the 128 illns. are fine.

MCDERMOTT, P. L. British East Africa; or Ibea; maps and ill. 6/ c 8° Chapman [93] 95
Hist. of formn. and wk. of Br. E. A. Co., fr. offic. documts. and records of the Co. Pt.-of-view that of the Co. Appendices.

MACDONALD, Maj. J. R. L. Soldiering and Surveying in British East Africa ; ill. 16 / 8° Arnold 97
Author, w. Cpt. PRINGLE as second in command, was engaged by now defunct Imp. Brit. E. Afr. Co. to make surv. for proposed ry. fr. Mombasa to Victoria Nyanza. Covers 1891–4.

MACQUEEN, Peter —*in his* In Wildest Africa, *ut sup.*

NEUMANN, A. H. Elephant-Hunting in East Equat. Africa ; col. pl. 21 / *n.* 8° Rowland Ward 98
Three yrs. ivory-htg. under Mt. Kenia and am. Ndorobo savages of Lorogi Mtns. Also Lake Rudolf.

PATTERSON, Lt.-Col. J. H. In the Grip of the Nyika ; ill. 7/6 *n.* ($2 *n.*) 8° Macmillan 09

PLAYNE, Somerset East Africa (British), ed. F. H. Gale ; ill. 25 / r 8° For. & Col. Compilg. Co. 09
A very comprehensive popular wk. on hist., people, commerce, industries, resources of the country.

POWELL-COTTON, Maj. P. H. G.—*in his* In Unknown Africa, *ut* **E** § 48, *s.v.* Uganda

PURVIS, J. B. Hdbk. to Brit. East Afr. & Uganda ; ill. [guide-bk.] 2 /6 c 8° Sonnenschein 00

*ROUTLEDGE, W. S. + Kath. With a Prehistoric People, 136 pl. 21 / *n.* m 8° Arnold 10
A very important and interesting ethnological wk. on the A-ki-kú-yu ; of unusual authority and detail : *v.* also note in **F** § 5.

THOMSON, Jos. —*in his* Through Masai Land, *ut inf.*

*Suk (The) :* BEECH (Mervyn W. H.) The Suk : lang. and folklore ; 3 maps and 24 pl. 12/6 *n.* ($4·15) 8° Clar. Press 11
Investigns. made by Acting Distr. Commr. of Baringo. Suk belong to same group as Masai, Nandi and Turkana.

**Galla Country :** ARKELL-HARDWICK (A.)—*in his* Ivory Trades in N. Kenia, *ut sup., s.v.* Brit. East Africa

PLOWDEN, W. C. —*in his* Travels in Abyssinia, *ut* **E** § 44

SMITH, Dr G. D. —*in his* Unknown Africa, *ut* **E** § 44

WAKEFIELD, E. S. Thos. Wakefield, Missionary and Geographical Pioneer in East Equatorial Africa ; 9 ill. 3/6 c 8° R.T.S. 04

**German East Africa :** WEULE (Prf. K.) Native Life in East Africa [tr.] 12 /6 *n.* 8° Pitman 09
A record of travel and observn. in German E. Afr. 1906–7, a mine of anthropol. and topograph. informn. on life and habits of the Makonde, Makua, Matambive, and other tribes. Maps and ill.

**Kilima Njaro, Mount :** MEYER (Hans) Across East African Glaciers [tr.] 32 / r 8° Philip 91
$10·50 Longman, *N.Y.* Incls. acc. of first ascent of Mt. Kilima Njaro. 3 col. maps and 40 ill. App. of scient. notes, and bibliogr.

*JOHNSTON, Sir Harry H. Kilima Njaro Expedition : scientific explor. in East Equat. Africa ; 6 maps and 80 ill. 21 / 8° Paul 86

**Masai Land**

FRENCH-SHELDON, Mrs Sultan to Sultan—*ut* **E** § 47

HINDE, S. L. + Hildegarde The Last of the Masai ; ill. 15 / *n.* 4° Heinemann 01

HOLLIS, A. C. The Masai : language and folklore ; ill. 14 / ($4·75) 8° Clar. Press 05

*THOMSON, Jos. Through Masai Land 2 /6 c 8° Low [85] 95
Record of exciting advents. am. the Masai on jy. thro' East Equatorial Africa in 1883–4.

**Nyassa ; Nyassaland :** BUCHANAN (J.) Shirè Highlands as Colony and Mission 5 / c 8° Blackwood 85

CADDICK, Helen —*in her* A White Woman in Central Africa, *ut* **E** § 48

DRUMMOND, Hy. Tropical Africa ; 6 maps and ill. 3 /6 c 8° Hodder [88] 91
$1 *n.* Scribner, *N.Y.* Picturesque and trustworthy descrns. of the Lake Nyassa region, pleasantly written.

DUFF, H. L. Nyasaland under the Foreign Office, map & ill. 7 /6 *n.* c 8° Bell [03] 06

FOTHERINGHAM, L. M. Adventures in Nyassaland ; ill. 7 /6 c 8° Low 91
Account of two years' struggle with Arabian slave-dealers.

JOHNSTON, Sir Harry H. —*in his* British Central Africa, *ut* **E** §§ 49–50, *s.v.* Rhodesia
Includes a history of the opening up of Nyassaland.

LIVINGSTONE, Dr D. [1813–73] Missy. Travels & Researches in S. Africa [1840–56] *o.p.* 8° Murray 57

„ Narr. of Expedn. to Zambesi and Tributaries [1858–64] *o.p.* 8° Murray 65

„ Popular Acc. of Travels & Advents. ; maps & ill. [1840–56] 7 /6 p 8° Murray [73] 75

„ Popular Acc. of Expedn. to Zambesi ; maps & ill. [1858–64] 7 /6 p 8° Murray 75
For his *Last Journals v.* **E** § 48 ; for his *Life v.* **E** § 41 *s.v.* Lives of Explorers.

LUGARD, Cpt. [Gen.] F. D. —*in his* Rise of the East African Empire, 2 vols., *ut* **E** § 47

PRINGLE, M. A. Towards the Mountains of the Moon ; ill. 12 /6 8° Blackwood 84

RANKIN, D. J. Zambesi Basin and Nyassaland—*ut inf., s.v.* Zambesi

ROWLEY, Rev. H. Twenty Yrs. in Centr. Afr. [story of Univ. missn.] 3 /6 c 8° Wells Gardner [66] 85

WERNER, A. —*in his* Natives of British Central Africa, *ut* **E** § 48

WORSFOLD, W. B. Portuguese Nyassaland ; ill. 7 /6 *n.* 8° Low 99
Not much more than a glorified prospectus of the Nyassa Company.

YOUNG, E. D. Nyassa 7 /6 c 8° Murray 77

**Portuguese East Africa ; Mozambique :** MACKAY (W.) A Prisoner of Chiloane ; ill. 7 /6 8° Trischler 90

MACLEOD, Lyons —*in his* Travels in East Africa, 2 vols., *ut* **E** § 47 [1860]

MAUGHAM, R. C. F. Portuguese East Africa : Manica and Sofala 15 / *n.* 8° Murray 06
History, scenery, flora, fauna, big game and advents. in pursuit thereof, customs, characteristics, dialects.

PRINGLE, M. A. —*in his* Towards the Mountains of the Moon, *ut sup., s.v.* Nyassa

THEAL, Dr G. McCall —*v.* **E** § 41

WEALE, J. P. M. Truth ab. the Portuguese in Africa 2/6 c 8° Sonnenschein 91

*Delagoa Bay:* JESSETT (M. G.) Key to South Africa: Delagoa Bay 6/ c 8° Unwin 99
A brief and clear account of the Bay, its importance, and the politics conn. w. it. Now out-of-date.

MONTEIRO, [Mrs] Rose Delagoa Bay: natives and natural history; 20 ill. 9/ c 8° Philip 91
Edn. w. col. front. (new Afr. butterflies) 12/. An interesting and well-written account of life in tropics.

*Gaza Land:* GILLMORE (Col. Parker) Through Gaza Land; map 7/6 8° Harrison 90
Account of a journey of a hunter in search of gold and ivory.

**Somaliland**—*v.* **E** § 44 **Uganda**—*v.* **E** § 48

**Zambesi River and Basin; Zambesia**

GIBBONS, Maj. A. St H. —*in his* Africa from South to North, 2 v., *ut* **E** § 42 [full descrn. of Zambesi]

LIVINGSTONE, Dr Dav. [1813–73]—*in his* Expedition, 1858–64, *ut sup.*

MATHERS, E. P. Zambesia, England's El-Dorado in Africa; ill. 7/ 8° King & Sell 91
Acc. of fdg. of Zambesia, w. descrn. of Matabeleld., Mashonald., and less-known adjacent territories, and Gold Fields in Brit. S. A.

MAUGHAM, R. C. F. Zambesia; map and ill. 15/ *n.* 8° Murray 10
A general descrn. of the valley of the Z., w. its hist., agric., flora, fauna, and ethnography.

PINTO, Maj. A. de Serpa —*in his* How I Crossed Africa, 2 vols. [tr.], *ut* **E** § 48

RANKIN, D. J. Zambesi Basin and Nyassaland; maps and ill. 10/6 c 8° Blackwood 93
A personal record of experce.—for most pt. rather trivial, and an estimate of colonial and commerc. value, pres. and future, of regns. traversed.

SCHULZ (Dr A.) + HAMMAR (A.) The New Africa; map and 70 ill. 28/ 8° Heinemann 97
Jy. up the Chobé and down the Okovanga rivers: exploration and sport.

SELOUS, F. C. —*in his* Travel and Adventure in S.-E. Africa, *ut* **E** §§ 49–50, *s.v.* Mashonaland

YOUNG, E. D. Livingstonia: advents. in explorg. L. Nyassa 7/6 p 8° Murray 78

**Zanzibar:** BURTON (Sir R. F.) Zanzibar: city, island, Coast, 2 vols. *o.p.* [*pb.* 30/] 8° Tinsley 72

FITZGERALD, W. W. A. Travels in Coast Lands of British East Africa and the Islands of Zanzibar and Pemba; ill. 28/ 8° Chapman 98

LYNE, R. N. Zanzibar in Contemporary Times; ill. 10/6 *n.* 8° Hurst 05

**Indian Ocean:** COLOMB (Cpt. P. H.) Slave Catching in Indian Ocean—*ut* **D** § 130

SULIVAN, G. L. Dhow Chasing in Zanzibar Waters, and on Afr. Coast—*ut* **D** § 130

## 48: CENTRAL AFRICA

ALEXANDER, Lt. Boyd —*in his* From the Niger to the Nile, 2 vols., *ut* **E** § 46, *s.v.* Nigeria

BAKER, Sir Sam. W. Ismailïa; ill. 6/ c 8° Macmillan [74] 78
Narrative of an expedn. to Central Africa to suppress the slave trade; 1870–2.

BARTH, Hy. Travels in North and Central Africa—*ut* **E** § 46

BROWNE, J. Penman Travel and Adventure in the Pygmy Country 8° Laurie 07
Author stayed and hunted w. the pygmies thro' the depths of the Ituri Forest for some time.

BURTON, Sir R. F. Lake Region of Central Africa, 2 vols.; ill. [1857–59] *o.p.* [*pb.* 31/6] 8° Longman 60
Includes account of the discovery of Lake Tanganyika.

CADDICK, Helen A White Woman in Central Africa; 16 ill. 6/ c 8° Unwin 00
$1·25. Descrn. of a lady's journey to Lake Tanganyika from the mouth of the Zambesi.

CAMERON, Com. V. L. Across Africa; 200 ill. [1873–6] *o.p.* [*pb.* 7/6] 8° Philip [77] 88

CAPELLO (H.) + IVENS (R.) From Benguella to Yacca Territory [tr.], 2 vols.; ill. *o.p.* [*pb.* 42/] 8° Low 82

CASATI, Maj. Gaetano Ten Years in Equatoria and Return w. Emin Pasha [tr.], 2 vols.; 4 maps, 80 col. pl., and 100 ill. 12/6 *n.* ($5 *n.*) m 8° Warne [91] 98
Of no very great interest, and badly put together. Confirms STANLEY's criticism of EMIN. Maps sketchy, and some of illns. execrable.

COILLARD, Frç. On the Threshold of Central Africa [tr.]; ill. 15/ i 8° Hodder 97
A valuable acc. of 20 yrs.' missionary pioneering among the Barotse of Upper Zambesi. Much ab. Kg. LEWANIKA.

DU CHAILLU, Paul Advents. in Great Forest of Equatorial Africa; ill. 7/6 c 8° Murray [61] 90
Jy. 1855–60. Conts. the accs. of the dwarfs and the gorilla; both much discredited at the time.

„ Jy. to Ashango-land & Further Penetration into Equat. Afr.; ill. *o.p.* [*pb.* 21/] 8° Murray 67

DU PLESSIS, J. A Thousand Miles in Heart of Africa—*ut* **E** § 105

ELLIOTT, G. F. Scott A Naturalist in Mid Africa; ill. and 3 maps *o.p.* [*pb.* 16/] 8° Innes 96
Mtns. of Moon and Tanganyika. A very interestg. acc. of a brilliant piece of pioneer-explorn., w. well-wr. sketches of wild life and of nature, and discussn. of transport, meteorol., outfit, botany [*v.* **H** § 66], and geol.

ELTON (J. F.) + COTTERILL (H. B.) Travels in Eastern and Central Africa—*ut* **E** § 47

FAULKNER, H. Elephant Haunts: search for Livingstone *o.p.* [*pb.* 15/] 8° Hurst 68

FOÀ, Edouard After Big Game in Central Africa [tr.]—*ut* **I** § 147 [wholly conc. w. sport]

GEIL, W. E. A Yankee in Pigmy Land; ill. $1·50 8° Dodd & Mead, *N.Y.* 05
6/ Hodder. Narr. of jy. acr. Africa fr. Mombasa thro' the Pigmy Forest to Banana.

GIBBONS, Maj. A. St H. Exploration and Hunting in Central Africa; ill. 15/ 8° Methuen 98
Acc. of travel and adventure amg. the Marotse and contiguous tribes, w. big-game hunting. Covers the hitherto unexplored region betw. the Zambezi and Kafukwi rivers and fr. 18° to 15° S. lat.

GORDON, Maj.-Gen. C. G. Gordon in Central Africa, ed. G. B. Hill 7/6 c 8° De La Rue [81] 84

GROGAN (E. S.) + SHARP (A. S.)—*in their* From the Cape to Cairo, *ut* **E** § 41

JOHNSTON, Dr Jas. [*M.D.*] Reality *v.* Romance in S. Centr. Afr.; maps & 51 pl. $4 8° Revell, *Chic.* 93
21/ Hodder. Fr. Benguella on West, thro' Bihe, Barotse, Kalahari Desert, Mashonald., Nyassa, Shiré Highlds., to mouth of Zambesi on E. A good deal of keen observn.

JUNKER, Dr W. J. Travels in Afr. dur. yrs. 1875–86 [tr.], 3 vols. 63/ 8° Chapman 90–2
i: Years 1875–8, 21/; ii: 1879–83 [really ends '81], 21/; iii: 1882–6, 21/. i: Suakin to Berber, Khartoum, Meshra er-Req, etc.; iii: Up White Nile, Meshra er-Req, Dem Soliman Province, river Makua-Welle, etc.; iii: Makua-Welle regn., Lado (on banks of Nile, stay w. EMIN PACHA), Dufileh (on the Bahr-el-Jebel), Zanzibar, etc. An exhaustive acc. of an extensive ser. of travels, aboundg. in observns. on nat. hist., char. and habits of natives, and geogr. Maps, pl. and ill.

KERR, W. M. The Far Interior, 2 vols.; ill. *o.p.* [*pb.* 32/] 8° Low 86
Account of a journey from the Cape of Good Hope to the Lake Regions.

de LACERDA E ALMEIDA, F. J. M. Journey to Cazembe [tr.] [1798] *o.p.* 8° R.G.S. (Murray) 73

LIVINGSTONE, Dr D. [1813–73] Last Jls. in Centr. Afr., ed. Rev. H. Waller, 2 v.; ill. [1865–73] 15/ 8° Murray [74] 80

LLOYD, A. B. In Dwarf-Land & Cannibal Country; maps & 146 ill. 21/ *n.* r 8° Unwin 99
Record of jy. fr. Uganda to West Coast. Incls. also account of the Uganda rebellion.

LONG, Col. Chaillé Central Africa: naked truths of naked people *o.p.* [*pb.* 18/] 8° Low 76

MACDONALD, D. Africana: the heart of heathen Africa, 2 vols. 21/ 8° Simpkin 82

MECKLENBURG, A. F., D'ke of In Heart of Africa [tr.]; 2 maps & 151 pl. (4 col.) 15/ *n.* l 8° Cassell 11
Acc. of a one yr's. scient. explorn. by a geologist, a topographer, a botanist, a zoologist, a doctor, an ethnologist, and an artist, workg. on blank space on the map betw. the Kagera and the Kakitumbe, N. of Mpororo.

PARK, Mungo [1771–1805] Travels—*ut* **E** § 46

PINTO, Maj. Serpa How I Crossed Africa, 2 vols.; ill. *o.p.* [*pb.* 15/] 8° Low 81
From the Atlantic to the Indian Ocean: 1877–9.

PORTMAN, Lionel Station Studies 5/ *n.* ($1·50 *n.*) c 8° Longman 02
Sketches of native life in story form; by a British official in Central Africa.

PRUEN, S. T. Arab and African: experiences 6/ c 8° Seeley 91

SCHWEINFURTH, G. The Heart of Africa: 3 yrs.' travels [tr.], 2 vols.; ill. ea. 3/6 c 8° Low [73] 90
Account of a typical scientific exploration in the Eastern and Central Soudan. 1868–71.

" Artes Africanæ, 21 pl. [industr. arts of Cent. Afr. tribes] *o.p.* [*pb.* 28/] f° Low 75

SPEKE, Cpt. J. H. Journal of Discovery of Source of Nile 1/ *n.* f 8° Dent [63] 06
35 c. *n.* Dutton, *N.Y.* [Everyman's Lib.] Acc. of a fine piece of pioneer-exploration, 1856.

STANLEY, Dr H. M. How I found Livingstone; ill. [$3·50 Scrib., *N.Y.*] [1871–2] 6/ c 8° Low [72] 04

" Thro' the Dark Continent; ill. 12/6 c 8° Low [78] 04
$7·50. Harper, *N.Y.* One of the most stirring bks. of Afr. travel ever pubd. Details the discov. and first navign. of the Congo River system in 1878. Incls. Nile sources and Lake regions. Also 2 vols., ill., l 8° ea. 7/6 Newnes '99.

" In Darkest Africa; maps and 150 ill. 6/ c 8° Low [90] 04
$7·50 Scribner, *N.Y.* The 'official' pubn. recordg. STANLEY's last jy. in Afr. (1889), for the quest and rescue of Emin, Govr. of Equatoria. An exciting narr. of advents., privatns., dangers, and discovs. in Congo State and thence to East coast.

SWANN, A. J. Fighting the Slave-Hunters in Central Africa—*ut* **D** § 130 [Tangan. and great lakes]

*THOMSON, Jos. To the Central African Lakes and Back; ill. 7/6 c 8° Low [81] 88
An important record of explorn. in 1878–80, the first jy. of this successful traveller. For his Life *v.* **E** § 41.

WERNER, [Miss] A. Natives of British Central Africa 6/ c 8° Constable 06
Mainly races of the Shire valley and country round Lake Nyassa. A valuable colln. of facts.

v. WISSMANN, Maj. H. My Second Journey thro' Equatorial Africa [tr.] 16/ 8° Chatto 91
From the Congo to the Zambesi in the years 1886 and 1887. Map and 92 ill.

YOUNG, E. D. Search for Livingstone: a diary 6/ f 8° Letts 68

**Emin Expedns.:** BARTTELOT (Maj. E. M.) L'rs & Diaries, ed. W. G. Barttelot *o.p.* [*pb.* 16/] 8° Bentley 90
A record of his services in Afgh., Egypt, Nile Relief Expedn., and on Congo w. STANLEY. Maps.

BOURNE, H. R. Fox The Other Side of Emin Pasha Expedition 6/ c 8° Chatto 91
A sort of judicial inq. into whole of the circs. attendg. the expedn., arrivg. at decision decidedly unfavourable to STANLEY.

CASATI, Maj. Gaetano —*in his* Ten Years in Equatoria, *ut sup.*

EMIN PACHA [=Dr SCHNITZLER] Letters & Jls., ed. Schweinfurth + Ratzel [tr.] 16/ r 8° Philip 88
Chiefly his correspondence. Contains graphic descriptions of his journeys in Central Africa.

Little, Rev. H. W. Life and Work of Emin Pasha in Equat. Africa 12/6 c 8° Chapman 89

Schweitzer, Geo. Pasha: life and work, 2 vols. 32/ 8° Constable 98
A badly-arranged, yet complete biography; from diaries, letters, etc.

JAMESON, J. S. Story of Rear Column of Em. Pasha Relief Expn.; ill. 16/ 8° Porter 91
$3·50 U.S. Bk. Co., *N.Y.* Posth. ed. by his wife, partly in vindicn. of him agst. STANLEY's charge of his hg. provoked a horrible scene of cannibalism.

MOUNTENEY-JEPHSON, A. J. Emin Pasha and Rebellion at Equator; ill. 21/ 8° Low [90] 90
$3·75 Scribner, *N.Y.* By one of STANLEY's officers. Told w. excellent temper and taste, self-forgetfulness and modesty.

PARKE, Dr T. H. My Personal Experiences in Equatorial Africa; ill. 21/ 8° Low [91] 91
$6 Scribner, *N.Y.* By Med. Officer to Expedn. Best supplemt. to STANLEY's own bk., fillg. up gap in narr. (the many-months stay at Fort Bodo.)

PETERS, Dr Carl New Light upon Dark Africa [tr.] 10/6 r 8° Ward & Lock [91] 96
The story of the German Emin Pacha Expedition by its Commander. Map and ill.

STANLEY, H. M. —*in his* In Darkest Africa, 2 vols., *ut sup.*

TROUP, J. Rose With Stanley's Rear Column; ill. 16/ 8° Chapman [90] 90
$5 Lippincott, *Phila.* A narr. of the expedn., by the Transport Officer.

WARD, Herb. My Life w. Stanley's Rear Guard 1/6 c 8° Chatto 91

WAUTERS, A. J. Stanley's Emin Pasha Expedition [tr.]; maps & ill. *o.p.* [*pb.* 6/] c 8° Nimmo 90

WERNER, J. R. Visit to Stanley's Rear-guard 16/ 8° Blackwood 89
Describes the visit to Barttelot's Camp on the Aruhwimi, w. acc. of Red River life. Maps and ill.

**Congo River and State:** *Bibliography:* WAUTERS (A. J.) Bibliographie du Congo: 1880–95 8° *Brussels* 95

*Early Travel and Accounts:* BATTELL (Andr.) Strange Advents., ed. E. G. Lavenstein 8° Hakluyt Soc. 02
The earliest record of travels in Congoland and Angola. Repr. fr. PURCHAS [*ut* E § 5], w. Bibliogr. and Glossary.

LOPEZ, D. [ed.] Kingdom of Congo, fr. Wrtgs. of Lopez [1591] [tr.] *o.p.* 8° *London* 81

*Generally:* BENTLEY (W. H.) Pioneering on Congo, 2 v.; map & 206 ill. [$5 Revell, *N.Y.*] 16/ *n.* 8° R.T.S. 00

BOULGER, Demetrius C. The Congo State; 60 ill. 16/ 8° Thacker 98
A well-written and elaborate defence of the State against the charges made against it.

BOURNE, H. R. Fox Civilisation in Congoland; map 10/6 *n.* 8° P. S. King & Son 03
A full history of the State, w. the 'story of international wrong-doing'.

BULA N'ZAU Travel & Advent. in Congo Free State, & its Big Game Shooting—*ut* **I** § 147

BURROWS, Cpt. Guy The Land of the Pigmies; 200 ill. 21/ 8° Pearson 98
Information on the dwarf-race of the Aruwimi district among whom the author lived for some time.

" The Curse of Central Africa; map and ill. 21/ *n.* r 8° Everett 03
Incls. *A Campaign among Cannibals*, by E. CANISIUS. Brings a number of serious charges agst. Congo govt.

BURTON, Sir R. F. Gorilla Land, and Cataracts of Congo, 2 vols.; ill. *o.p.* [*pb.* 28/] 8° Low 76

CASTELEIN, Prf. A. [S.-J.] The Congo State: origin, rights, duties 3/ *n.* c 8° Nutt 07
Reply to the accusers of the Belgium and her King, by late chairman of Belg. Soc. of Social Economy.

DAVIS, R. Harding The Congo and Coasts of Africa; ill. $1·50 *n.* c 8° Scribner, *N.Y.* 07
6/ Unwin. Repr. of l'rs to Amer. press. Incls. a vigorous indictmt. of the Congo State.

DENNETT, R. E. Seven Years among the Fjort: trader on Congo *o.p.* [*pb.* 7/6] c 8° Low 87

DESCAMPS, Prf. E. E. F. J. New Africa [tr.] [weak defence of Congo State] 5/ c 8° Low 03

DORMAN, M. R. P. Journal of a Tour in Congo Free State 6/ *n.* c 8° Paul 05

DU CHAILLU, Paul —*in his* Journey to Ashango Land, *ut sup.*

" My Apingi Kingdom *o.p.* [*pb.* 6/] c 8° Low 71

GLAVE, E. J. Six Years of Adventure in Congoland; 75 ill. $2 8° Russell, *N.Y.* 92
7/6 Low. By one of STANLEY'S pioneer officers, descrg. his life, and contg. careful study of manners and customs.

GRENFELL, Geo.

Hawker, Rev. Geo. Life of George Grenfell; map and 33 pl. [missy. side] 6/ *n.* 8° R.T.S. 09

*Johnston, Sir Harry H. George Grenfell and Congo, 2 vols.; maps and ill. 30/ *n.* r 8° Hutchinson 08
Hist. and descrn. of Congo Indep. State and adjoining distrs. of Congoland, their natives, langs., fauna and flora; w. notes on Cameroons and isl. of Fernando Po—founded on GRENFELL'S diaries and researches and on the records of Bapt. Missionary Soc. 14 maps and 498 illns. The most import. histor. and geogr. acc. of Congo basin and of one of its most distinguished pioneers. For GRENFELL'S missionary achievemts. *v.* **A** § 105. *s.v.* Africa.

HINDE, Cpt. S. L. Fall of the Congo Arabs; ill. [1892–4] 12/6 8° Methuen 97
Acc. of Belg. expedn. to Upper Congo under Bar. DHANIS, and of the war w. the Arab slave-raiders, of whom 70,000 are said to have perished. Discusses fully questn. of cannibalism, most of author's time hg. been spent amidst cannibal races, w. horrible revelns conc. the subject.

HOBLEY, C. W. East Uganda: ethnography 02

*JOHNSTON, [Sir] Harry H. River Congo: fr. its mouth to Bólóbó; ill. 2/6 c 8° Low [84] 95
Valuable descrns. of the scenery, nat. hist., and people of Western Congo, as observed in 1882–3.

KASSNER, Theo. —*in his* From Rhodesia to Egypt, *ut* **E** § 41 [Eastern Congo]

KINGSLEY, Mary H. —*in her* Travels in West Africa, etc., *ut* **E** § 47 [French Congo]

MONTEIRO, J. J. Angola and the River Congo—*ut* **E** § 46, *s.v.* Angola

MOREL, E. D. The British Case in French Congo; map 6/ c 8° Heinemann 03

" King Leopold's Rule in Africa; ill. 15/ *n.* 8° Heinemann 04
A severe indictmt. of Congo State misrule—'a revival, under new and worse forms, of the Afr. slave-trade'.

MOUNTMORRES, Visc. The Congo Independent State; ill. [a private Report] 6/ *n.* r 8° Williams 06

READING, J. H. Ogowe Band: narr. of Afr. travel; ill. $3 8° Reading, *Phila.* 90

ROBY, Marguerite My Adventures in the Congo; map and ill. 12/6 *n.* 8° Arnold 11

STANLEY, H. M. The Congo, and the Founding of the Free State; 2 v.; ill.
[$7·50 Harper, *N.Y.*] 21/ 8° Low [85] 9–

TIPPOO TIB: BRODE (Dr H.) Tippoo Tib: story of his care [tr.] 10/6 *n.* 8° Arnold 07
$3 *n.* Longman, *N.Y.* TIPPOO TIB was an Arab explorer who started in 1867 fr. Zanzibar, and spent some 15 yrs. for most part in Congo, where he ruled over a vast territory, tradg. in slaves, and bearg. for a time title of Sultan of Utetera.

WARD, Herb. Five Years with Congo Cannibals; 92 ill. 14/ r 8° Chatto 90
$3 Bonner, *N.Y.* By one of survivors of STANLEY'S ill-fated Rear-gd., the disasters attendg. wh. he attribs. chfly. to STANLEY. Good descrn. of domestic and daily life, habits and customs of Congo savages.

" A Voice from the Congo; ill. 12/6 *n.* 8° Heinemann 10
Stories, anecdotes, and notes, giving a graphic acc. of Congo native, his customs and life.

WOLLASTON, A. F. R. Ruwenzori to Congo—*ut sup.*

*Cazembe:* de LACERDA E ALMEIDA (F. J. M.)—*in his* Journey to Cazembe [tr.], *ut sup.*

*Kasaï River:* BATEMAN (C. S. L.) First Ascent of Kasaï; col. pl. and ill. 21/m 8° Philip 89

SIMPSON, M. W. Hilton Land and Peoples of the Kasai; 83 ill. (8 col.) 16/*n.* 8° Constable 11
The experces. of author and Emil TORDAY, the Hungarian traveller, dur. 2 yrs. am. the cannibals of Equat. forest and am. tribes of S.W. Congo. Valuable scientific and ethnolog. contribns.

*Katanga:* MOLONEY (Dr J. A.) With Captain Stairs to Katanga; ill. 8/6 c 8° Low 93
Descrn., by its medl. officer, of successful expedn. (1891) of Katanga Co. under Cpt. STAIRS to secure Katanga for Congo Free State.

*Stanley Falls:* SMITH (Rev. H. S.) Yakasu, the very Heart of Africa 6/*n.* 8° Marshall Bros. 11
An interestg. missionary acc. of wk. and life among the Lokele.

**Rudolf and Stefanie Lakes:** v. HÖHNEL (Lt. L.) Discov. of Lakes Rudolf and Stefanie [tr.], 2 vols.; 6 col. maps and 179 ill. 42/8° Longman 94
Descrn. of C't. TELEKI's explorg. and huntg. expedn. in E. Eq. Afr. in 1887–8, by his companion.

**Tanganyika Lake:** ELLIOTT (G. F. Scott)—*in his* Naturalist in Mid Afr., *ut sup. v. also* BURTON, **E** § 48

HORE, Annie B. Lake Tanganyika in a Bath Chair; ill. *o.p.* [*pb.* 7/6] c 8° Low 86

HORE, E. C. Tanganyika: 11 yrs. in Central Africa; maps & ill. 7/6 p 8° Stanford [92] 93
Story of Lond. Missy. Soc.'s Cent. Afr. Missn. fr. commencemt. (1877) to 1888, incl. pioneer jy. to Tanganyika, and acc. of geogr. and ethnol. Affords a vivid picture of actual life in Cent. Afr.

MOORE, J. E. S. The Tanganyika Problem; maps and ill. 25/*n.* r 8° Hurst 03
Acc. of researches conc. existence of marine animals in Central Africa.

SPEKE, Cpt. J. H. What Led to Discovery of Source of Nile *o.p.* [*pb.* 14/] 8° Blackwood 69

**Uganda**—*v.* **E** § 48 **Zambesi River and Basin**—*v.* **E** § 47

**Uganda:** ANSORGE (Dr W. J.) Under the African Sun; 136 ill. 21/*n.* r 8° Heinemann 99
$5 Longman, *N.Y.* A somewhat ill-arranged collection of information on native life, customs, sport, etc.

ASHE, Rev. R. P. Chronicles of Uganda; 26 ill. [1854–93] 7/6 c 8° Hodder 94
Fr. pt.-of-view of Ch. Missionary Soc. Reviews whole story of events wh. led to acquisn. of region as a Brit. protectorate.

AUSTIN, Maj. H. H. With Macdonald in Uganda; maps and ill. 15/*n.* 8° Arnold 03
$6 Longman, *N.Y.* Acc. of the explorn. and surveying done by MACDONALD's expedn. 1897–9.

,, Among Swamps & Giants in Equat. Africa; maps & 32 pl. 15/*n.* 8° Pearson 02
Acc. of 2 survey-expedns. into unexplored regns. betw. Egyptn. and Abyss. boundaries (Sobat, jy. fr. Sacchi river along W. shores of Lake Rudolf to Baringo).

COLVILLE, Col. Sir Hy. The Land of the Nile Springs; ill. 16/8° Arnold 95
Record of experces. of author as sen. officer and Acting Commr. of Uganda: climate, politics, people, peoples, etc.

COOK, Dr A. R. A Doctor and his Dog in Uganda; ill. 2/c 8° R.T.S. 03

CUNNINGHAM, J. F. Uganda and its Peoples; 200 ill. 24/*n.* s 4° Hutchinson 04
Valuable notes on the Protectorate, esp. on the anthrop. and ethnol. of its indigenous races.

FISHER, Ruth B. On the Borders of Pigmy Land 3/6 c 8° Marshall Bros. 05
Acc. of jy. thro' the provinces of Uganda, Toro, etc., and to Lake Albert Edward.

HATTERSLEY, Rev. C. W. [missy.] Uganda by Pen and Camera; ill. 2/c 8° R.T.S. 06

,, The Baganda at Home; 80 pl. 5/*n.* 8° R.T.S. 09

*JOHNSTON, Sir Harry H. The Uganda Protectorate, 2 vols.; ill. 42/*n.* r 8° Hutchinson [02] 05
The standard wk. Geogr., races, langs., flora, fauna, zool., minerals, meteorol., hist., all fully treated. 506 ill., 48 col. pl., and 9 maps.

KIRKLAND, Carol. Some African Highways; map and ill. 6/*n.* c 8° Duckworth 08
$1·50 Estes, *Boston.* Acc. of tour of two American ladies to Uganda and the Transvaal. Introd. by Gen. BADEN-POWELL.

LLOYD, Alb. B. —*in his* Uganda to Khartoum, *ut* **E** § 43

LUGARD, Gen. F. D. Story of Uganda Protectorate [Story of Emp. Ser.] 1/6 c 8° H. Marshall 00

PATTERSON, J. H. —*in his* Man-eaters of Tsaro, *ut* **E** § 47

PORTAL, Sir Gerald The British Mission to Uganda in 1893, ed. Rennell Rodd; w. Introd. L'd Cromer; 40 ill. [posthum.] 21/8° Arnold 94

POWELL-COTTON, Maj. P. H. G. In Unknown Africa; ill. 21/*n.* m 8° Hurst 04
A narrative of twenty months' travel and sport among hitherto unknown tribes.

PURVIS, Rev. J. B. [missy.] Thro' Uganda to Mount Elgon; 242 ill. 6/c 8° Unwin 09

SYKES, Cpt. C. A. Service and Sport on the Tropical Nile 12/*n.* c 8° Murray 03
A simply-written account of a soldier's experiences.

THURSTON, Maj. A. B. African Incidents: Egypt and Unyoro 14/8° Murray 00

TREVES, Sir Fredk. Uganda for a Holiday; map and 72 ill. 9/*n.* l 8° Smith & Elder [10] 10

TUCKER, Bp A. R. Eighteen Years in Uganda and E. Afr., 2 v.; 60 pl. 30/*n.* 8° Arnold 08
Mainly an acc. on an extensive scale of episcopal missionary life and work.

VANDELEUR, C. F. S. Campaigning on Upper Nile and Niger—*ut* **E** § 46, *s.v.* Nigeria

WASON, J. Cathcart East Africa and Uganda—*ut* **E** § 47

WILSON (C. T.) + FELKIN (R. W.) Uganda and the Egyptian Soudan, 2 vols.—*ut* **E** § 43

WOLLASTON, A. F. R. From Ruwenzori to the Congo; maps and 59 ill. 15/*n.* 8° Murray 08
$5 *n.* Dutton, *N.Y.* By the medical officer, botanist, and entomologist to expedn. to Ruwenzori (1906) for collectn. of specs. of local flora and fauna for Brit. Mus. After conclusn. of labours author (w. another member of party) visited great lakes to south, and completed traverse of Afr. by canoe-voy. down Congo.

*Baganda:* ROSCOE, Rev. Jno. The Baganda: native customs and beliefs; ill. 15/*n.* 8° Macmillan 11

*Albert Nyanza:* BAKER (Sir S. W.) Albert N'yanza, and Explorn. of Nile Sources; ill. [1861-5] 3/6 *n.* ($1·75) c 8° Macmillan [66] 98
Describes the discovery of the Albert Nyanza in 1864.

BEKE, C. T. Sources of Nile [gen. surv. and hist. of discov.] *o.p.* [*pb.* 6/] 8° Madden 60

*Mountains of the Moon; Mt. Ruwenzori:* de FILIPPI (Filippo) Ruwenzori: acc. of expedn. of D'ke of Abruzzi to Snow Ranges betw. Equat. Lakes of Centr. Afr.; maps & ill. 31/6 *n.* r 8° Constable 08
$8 *n.* Dutton, *N.Y.* Narr. of the jy. and the actual explorn. wk, w. meteorol. and astron. notes. A second vol., contg. geolog. and mineralog. report (by Dr A. ROCCATI). w. repts. on zool. and botan. specs. brot. back, is pubd. in Ital. only. Finely illd.

JOHNSON, T. Broadwood Tramps round Mountains of the Moon and thro' the Back Gate of Congo State; 30 ill. 6/ c 8° Unwin 08
Experces. amg. natives (in and beyond Brit. territory) by a Cambr. man workg. w. missionaries.

KASSNER, Theo. —*in his* From Rhodesia to Egypt, *ut* **E** § 41

MOORE, J. E. S. To the Mountains of the Moon; maps and ill. 21/ *n.* 4° Hurst 01
A vivid, popular account of some districts traversed by the Tanganyika expedn. 1899-1900.

STANLEY, Dr H. M. —*in his* In Darkest Africa, *ut* **E** § 48

WOLLASTON, A. F. R. —*in his* Ruwenzori to the Congo, *ut sup.*

*Victoria Nyanza:* ASHE (R. P.) Two Kings of Uganda; ill. 6/ c 8° Low 89
Life by the shores of the Victoria Nyanza.

DICKINSON, Cpt. F. A. Lake Victoria to Khartoum w. Rifle and Camera; ill. 12/6 *n.* 8° Lane 09

GRANT, J. A. —*in his* A Walk across Africa, *ut* **E** § 42, *s.v.* Nile

KOLLMANN, Lt. P. Victoria Nyanza: land, races, customs [tr.]; ill. 7/6 l 8° Sonnenschein 99

SPEKE, J. H. —*in his* Journal of Discovery of Source of Nile, *ut sup.*

STANLEY, Dr H. M. —*in his* Through the Dark Continent, *ut* **E** § 48

*Zambesi River and Basin* —*v.* **E** § 47

## 49-50: SOUTH AFRICA; RHODESIA

*Bibliography:* MENDELSSOHN (S.) S. Afr: Bibliography, 2 vols.; w. notes; ill. 42/ *n.* i 8° Paul 10

ANDERSON, A. A. Twenty-five Years in a Waggon; ill. *o.p.* [*pb.* 12/] 8° Chapman [87] 88

BARNARD, L'y Anne South Africa a Century Ago 7/6 8° Smith & Elder 01
Letters written from the Cape, 1797-1802; valuable as a light on the social side of life there.

BLELOCH, W. The New South Africa; ill. 9/ 8° Heinemann 01
A useful collection of facts and figures upon trade, industry, revenue, etc.

BRAND, Hon. H. R. The Union of South Africa—*ut* **D** § 143

BROWNE, J. H. Balfour South Africa—*ut* **D** § 143

BRYCE, Rt. Hon. Jas. Impressions of South Africa 6/ c 8° Macmillan [97] 00
$3·50 Century Co., *N.Y.* The most authoritative acc. of phys. feats., condns. of cy., its econ. resources and race-probls.; w. outl. of history.

BRYDEN, H. A. Nature and Sport in South Africa 6/ c 8° Chapman 97
An admirable naturalist's guide and handbk. Half the bk. is a lament of disappce. or extermn. of big game fr. what were once the grandest huntg. grds. of world.

" From Veldt Camp Fires: stories of S. Africa 3/6 c 8° Hurst 00

BUCHAN, Jno. The African Colony: studies in the reconstruction 15/ *n.* 8° Blackwood 03
Pt. i deals w. the past, ii writes of S. Afr. as a place to live in, iii is a summary of probls. of Transvaal.

BUTLER, Lt.-Gen. Sir Wm. From Naboth's Vineyard—*ut* **D** § 143

COLQUHOUN, Arch. R. The Renascence of South Africa; map 6/ c 8° Hurst 00
A surv. of geogr., hist., etc.; w. sensible chs. on trade and agric. *V.* also his *Africander Land, ut* **D** § 143.

COLVIN, Ian D. South Africa; 12 col. pl. [Romance of Empire] 6/ *n.* sq 8° Jack

CRESWICKE, Louis [ed.] South Africa and its Future 7/6 *n.* 4° Jack 02
Papers by a number of eminent contributors on the trading, agricultural, mining, and other possibilities.

CUMBERLAND, Stuart What I think of S. Afr., its People and Politics 5/ c 8° Chapman 96
Sketches of leading men in Cape Colony, the Orange Free State, Natal, and the South African Republic. Ill.

DECLE, Lionel —*in his* Three Years in Savage Africa, *ut* **E** § 47

DEVEREUX, Mrs Roy Sidelights on South Africa; map *o.p.* [*pb.* 6/] c 8° Low 99
$1·75 Scribner, *N.Y.* Impressns. of the chief places—Cape Town, Kimberley, Mafeking, Pretoria, Johannesburg, etc.

DURAND, Sir H. Mortimer A Holiday in South Africa 6/ c 8° Blackwood 11
Cape Town, scenes of Boer War, Kimberley and diamond-mines, etc.

ELLIS, Lt.-Col. A. B. South African Sketches *o.p.* [*pb.* 6/] c 8° Chapman 87

FINDLAY, F. R. N. Big Game Shooting and Travel in South Africa—*ut* **I** § 147

FROUDE, J. A. South Africa [two lectures] *o.p.* [*pb.* 5/] c 8° Longman 80

FULLER, Rob. H. South Africa at Home; ill. [Our Neighbours at Home] 5/ *n.* c 8° Newnes 08
A good popular account of the country and the life of its inhabitants.

GALTON, Fcs. Travels in Tropical South Africa; ill. [Minerva Lib.] 2/ c 8° Ward & Lock [53] 89
Pioneer jys. to the N. of Cape Colony; with vacation tours by F. GALTON, SIR GEO. GROVE, and W. G. CLARK.

GILLMORE, Col. Parker — The Great Thirst Land [Natal, Or. Fr. St., Transv., etc.] 7/6 8° Cassell [78] 78
" — The Hunter's Arcadia; ill. [S. Africa] *o.p.* [*pb.* 10/6] c 8° Chapman 87
GRESWELL, Rev. W. P. — Our South African Empire, 2 vols. *o.p.* [*pb.* 21/] 8° Chapman 85
" — Geography of Africa South of Zambesi; maps 7/6 ($2) c 8° Clar. Press [92] 97
With notes on industries, wealth, and social progress. Pub. under auspices of Roy. Colonial Instit. Princ. devoted to Cape Colony.
HARMSWORTH, Cecil — Pleasure & Problem in South Africa [journalistic] 5/ *n.* ($1·50 *n.*) c 8° Lane 08
HILLIER, A. P. — South African Studies 6/ c 8° Macmillan 00
HOLUB, Dr Emil — Seven Years in South Africa, 2 vols.; ill. [1872-9] *o.p.* [*pb.* 42/] 8° Low 81
HUTCHINSON, G. T. — From the Cape to the Zambesi; ill. 9/ *n.* 8° Murray 05
IWAN-MÜLLER, E. B. — Lord Milner and South Africa; 2 ports. 15/ *n.* r 8° Heinemann 02
JUTA, René — The Cape Peninsula; col. ill. W. Westhofen 8° Juta, *Cape Town* 10
Good descrns. of some newer and older aspects; w. good illns.
KEANE, Prf. A. H. — The Boer States, Land, and People 6/ c 8° Methuen 00
A good summary of the geography, ethnology, and history.
KERR, W. Montague — The Far Interior, 2 v.; ill. *o.p.* [*pb.* 32/] 8° Low 86
Account of a jy. fr. Cape of Good Hope across the Zambesi to the Lake Regions.
KIRKUP, Thos. — South Africa, Old and New 3/6 c 8° Black [ ] 06
KNIGHT, E. F. — South Africa after the War; 17 ill. 10/6 *n.* 8° Longman 03
L'rs repr. fr. *Morning Post*, contg. an excel. acc. of the country, esp. good on Victoria Falls and Zambesi River, w. sound treatmt. of S. Afr. problems.
LACY, Geo. ['The Old Pioneer'] Pictures of Travel, Sport, and Adventure 15/ 8° Pearson 00
Chiefly hunting adventures, mainly in South Africa. Ill.
LAURENCE, Dr Percival — On Circuit in Kaffirland 7/6 c 8° Macmillan 03
Unconnected papers, mostly on South African affairs; by the well-known South African judge.
LITTLE, J. Stanley — South Africa: sketch-bk. of men and manners *o.p.* [*pb.* 10/6] 8° Sonnenschein [84] 88
LITTLE, Can. W. J. Knox — Sketches & Studies in South Africa [C. T. to Pretoria] 10/6 8° Pitman [99] 00
LIVINGSTONE, Dr Dav. [1813-73] Missionary Travels—*ut* **E** § 47 [1857]
MACKINNON, Jas. — South African Traits [hist., politics, character] 7/6 c 8° Hunter, *Edin.* 87
MCNAB, Fces. — On Farm and Veldt 3/6 c 8° Arnold [97] 97
A pleasant bk. on Cape Colony, Bechuanald., Natal, Transvaal: much informn., inclg. the drawbacks of the country.
MARKHAM, Violet R. — South Africa, Past and Present; ill. 10/6 c 8° Smith & Elder 00
In three Parts, i: Historical; 2: Native questions; 3: Diary of travel. A good book.
MATTHEWS, Dr J. W. — Incwadi Yami: twenty years in South Africa; ill. *o.p.* [*pb.* 14/] r 8° Low 87
Narr. of personal expercs. in S. Afr., w. full acc. of diamond mining at Kimberley.
METHUEN, A. M. — Tragedy of S. Africa =*new edn. of* Peace or War in S. Afr., *ut* **D** § 143
MILLAIS, J. G. — A Breath from the Veldt; 150 ill. 42/ *n.* 4° Sotheran 99
Chiefly an account of hunting expeditions: beautifully illustrated.
MOFFAT, Dr Rob. [1795-1883] Missionary Labours—*ut* **A** § 105 [1842]
NICHOLSON, G. — Fifty Years in South Africa; ill. 6/ c 8° Greener 98
NOBLE, Jno. — South Africa, Past and Present *o.p.* [*pb.* 7/6] p 8° Longman 77
A history of the European settlements at the Cape.
ORPEN, J. M. — Reminiscences of Life in S. Africa, vol. i. 2/6 *n* 8° Davis, *Durban* 08
An interesting and spirited record of a full and adventurous life, from 1846 to date. Author (b. 1828) was assoc. w. Gordon CUMMING in early days of Orange Free State, fought in several Kafir wars, was ambassador to Moshesh, sat in many Parliaments, etc.
RANSOME, Stafford — The Engineer in South Africa; ill. 7/6 *n.* 8° Constable 03
A review of industr. sitn. in S. Afr. after the Boer War and a forecast of possibilities, by an engineer, for engineers.
" — Sport and Travel East and West; ill. 12/6 *n.* r 8° Longman 00
SOUTHEY, Rosamund — Storm and Sunshine in S. Afr.; ill. 1893-1904] 12/ *n.* 8° Murray 10
STATHAM, F. Reg. — Boers, Blacks, and British *o.p.* [*pb.* 6/] c 8° Macmillan 81
" — South Africa as it is 5/ c 8° Unwin [94] 97
THEAL, G. McCall — South Africa [Story of the Nations] 5/ c 8° Unwin 94] 10
$1·50 Putnam, *N.Y.* On the Union of South Africa, Rhodesia, and all other territories south of the Zambesi.
THOMAS, Owen — Agricultural and Pastoral Prospects of South Africa 6/ 8° Constable 04
TROLLOPE, Anth. — South Africa *o.p.* [*pb.* 6/] c 8° Chapman [78] 80
Cape Colony, Natal, Transvaal, Griqualand West, Orange Free State, Native Territories, in 1877.
WARNER, G. T. — Geography of British South Africa [schl.-bk.] 1/6 c 8° Blackie 04
WILSON, L'y Sarah — South African Memories 15/ *n.* 8° Arnold 09
$4·20 *n.* Longman, *N.Y.* 'Social, warlike, sporting'.
WORSFOLD, W. Basil — South Africa: its history and future; map 6/ c 8° Methuen 95
A compiled survey of past hist. and pres. condns., w. a good deal of informn. fr. offic. documts., etc., and fr. pers. observn.
" — Lord Milner's Work in South Africa 15/ *n.* 8° Murray 06
Begins w. short sketch of S. Afr. hist. up to MILNER's arrival at Cape, and conts. story in detail to surrender at Vereeniging.
YOUNG, Sir F. — A Winter Tour in S. Africa; ill. [1889] *o.p.* [*pb.* 7/6] 8° Petherick 90
YOUNGHUSBAND, Cpt. F. — South Africa of To-Day; ill. 8/6 ($2) 8° Macmillan 98
Next to BRYCE (*ut sup.*) the best bk. at time it was written. Repr. of l'rs to *Times* dur. period of Jameson Raid.

**Atlas:** Bartholomew (J. G.) Advanced Atlas for S. Afr. Schools 4 / 4° Nelson
A series of maps, showing physical, historical, political, and economic conditions in South Africa.
Stanford, E. [pub.] Atlas of British Africa; 17 maps 2/6 *n.* Stanford

**Biography:** Gray (Bp Rob.) [1847–75] Life of. Ed. by his Son, 2 vols. *o.p.* [*pb.* 32/] 8° Rivington 76
Anderson-Morshead, A. E. M. A Pioneer and Founder [remins. of Gray] 5/ *n.* c 8° Skeffington 05
Hervey, Hubert J. A. [4th Earl Grey; 1859–96] Hubert Hervey, a Memoir *o.p.* 8° *London* 99
Kruger, S. J. Paul [1825–1904] Rise and Fall of Krugerism. By J. Scoble + H. R. Abercrombie 2/6 *n.* c 8° Heinemann [00] 00
Molteno, Sir J. C. [1814–86] Life of. By P. A. Molteno, 2 vols. 28/ 8° Smith & Elder 00
Montagu, Jno. [Col. Sec. 1843–53] Memoir of. By W. A. Newman *o.p.* [*pb.* 15/] 8° Harrison 55
Rhodes, C. J. [1853–1902]
'Imperialist' Cecil Rhodes: a biography and appreciation 7/6 c 8° Chapman 97
Wholly eulogistic of Rhodes and his policy and admin. With *Personal Reminiscences* by Dr Jameson as Appendix.
Jourdan, Pp. [his sec.] Cecil Rhodes: his private life 7/6 *n.* c 8° Lane 10
Michell, Sir Lewis Life of C. J. Rhodes, 2 vols.; ill. [$7·50 *n.* Kennerly, *N.Y.*] 30/ *n.* 8° Arnold 10
'Vindex' Cecil Rhodes, his Political Life and Speeches: 1881–1900 12/ *n.* 8° Chapman 00
Southey, Sir Rich. [1810–1901; Col. Sec. Cape Colony and Lt.-Gov. of Griqualand West]
Wilmot, Alex. Life and Times of Sir Richard Southey; 2 pl. 15/ *n.* 8° Low 04

**Ethnology:** South Afr. Native Races Comm. Native Races of S. Afr.; maps 12/ *n.* 8° Murray 02
,, [ed.] South African Natives: condn. and progr. 6/ *n.* 8° Murray 09
Stow, Geo. W. Native Races of South Africa, ed. G. M. Theal; ill. 21/ *n.* 8° Sonnenschein 05
$6·50 *n.* Macmillan, *N.Y.* A hist. of intrusion of Hottentots and Bantu into huntg.-grds. of Bushmen (the aborigines).
Theal, G. McCall Hist. and Ethnogr. of Africa South of Zambesi, 3 vols.—*ut* **F** § 65
,, Yellow and Dark-skinned People of Afr. S. of Zambesi; 15 pl. 10/6 8° Sonnenschein 10
Descrn. of the Bushmen and the Hottentots (particularly the Bantu); w. folk-tales.
,, The Portuguese in South Africa—*v.* **F** § 65
*Kaffirs:* Angas (G. F.) The Kaffirs Illustrated: 30 litho. pl. [Natal] *o.p.* [*pb.* £9] r f° Hogarth 49
Kidd, Dudley Essential Kafir; 100 pl. [$6 *n.* Macmillan, *N.Y.*] 18/ *n.* 8° Black 04
,, Savage Childhood: study of Kafir children—*ut* **B** § 34
,, Kafir Socialism and the Dawn of Individualism 7/6 *n.* c 8° Black 08
$2·75 *n.* Macm., *N.Y.* Considers th. conflict betw. Eur. individualism and Kafir socialism constits. heart of native problem.

**Colonials in S.A.:** Stirling (Jno.) The Colonials in S. Africa: 1899–1902 12/6 *n.* 8° Blackwood 00

**Gold and Diamond Fields and Mines**—*v.* **I** § 79

**Guides:** Brown (A. S. + G. G.) Guide to S. Africa; maps & plans 2/6 c 8° Juta, *Cape Town* [93] *ann.*
2/6 Low. Deals w. the history, topography, commercial conditions, etc., of South Africa.

**Historical Geography:** Lucas (C. P.) Hist. Geogr. of Brit. Colonies, v. iv: South & East Afr.—*ut* **E** § 21

**History** —*v.* **F** § 65

**Basutoland:** Barkly (Mrs) Among Boers and Basutos *o.p.* [*pb.* 2/6] c 8° Roxburghe Press [93] 96
Vivid pictures of life among the Basutos, by widow of Arth. Barkly, of Barkly's Horse.
Lagden, Sir Godf. The Basutos, 2 vols.; 9 maps and 70 ill. 24/ *n.* 8° Hutchinson 09
An excellent account of this mountaineering race and their country.
MacGregor, J. C. Basuto Traditions; 8 ill. [traditional hist. of B's.] 3/6 *n.* s 8° Paul 05
Martin, [Mrs] Minnie Basutoland—*ut* **B** § 34

**Bechuanaland; British Bechuanaland**

Baden-Powell, Maj.-Gen. R. S. S. Sketches in Mafeking and East Afr.; ill. (some col.) 21/ *n.* obl 4° Smith & Elder 07
Bryden, H. A. Gun and Camera in Southern Africa; map and ill. 15/ 8° Stanford 93
An interestg. and instructive descrn. of a yr.'s wandgs. in Bech., Kalahari Desert, and Lake-River cy.: w. notes on mode of travel, colonizn., natives, nat. hist., sport.
Gillmore, Col. Parker Days and Nights in the Desert; pl. 10/6 8° Paul 88
Knight-Bruce, Mrs Wyndham Khama, the African Chief [chief of Bechuana] 2/ f 8° Paul [93] 95
Lloyd, Rev. E. Three Great African Chiefs 3/6 c 8° Unwin 95
Acc. of Khama, Sebele, and Bathoen, their countries and people. Author (a missy. of Lond. Missy. Soc.) was long resid. in Bechuanaland.
Mackenzie, J. Austral Africa: losing it or ruling it?, 2 vols. 32/ 8° Low 87
Willoughby, W. C. Native Life on the Transvaal Border 3/6 c 8° Simpkin 00
*Kalahari Desert:* Farini (G. A.) Thro' Kalahari Desert to Lake Ngami; ill. 21/ 8° Low 86
Hodson, Lt. A. W. Trekking the Great Thirst: sport and trav. in Kal. Desert; ill. 12/6 *n.* 8° Unwin 11
*Khama's Country:* Hepburn (Rev. J. D.) Twenty Years in Khama's Country; ill. 6/ c 8° Hodder [95] 96

**Cape Colony:** *Early Voyage* —*v.* **E** § 4, *s.n.* LEGUAT [17 cent.]

AUBERTIN, J. J. Six Months in Cape Colony and Natal *o.p.* [*pb.* 6/] c 8° Paul 86

BARNARD, L'y Anne South Africa a Century Ago, ed. W. H. Wilkins 7/6 c 8° Smith & Elder 01
$2·50 *n.* Dodd & Mead, *N.Y.* L'rs wr. fr. C. of G. H. 1797–1801, by wife of Sec. of colony, when Br. flag was first hoisted over Cape Town.

BRYDEN, H. A. Kloof and Karoo: sport, legend, etc., in C. Colony 10/6 8° Longman 89

BURTON, A. R. E. Cape Colony of To-day 2/ 8° Townshend, *Cape Town* 07

,, Cape Colony for the Settler; map and pl. 2/6 *n.* 8° P. S. King & Son 03

HALL, A. Vine Table Mountain: pictures with pen, brush, etc. 6/ *n.* f 4° Miller, *Cape Town* [ ] 02

JUTA, René The Cape Peninsula: ill. W. Westhofen 7/6 *n.* sq 8° Black 11

MARTIN, [Mrs] Annie Home Life on an Ostrich Farm; 11 ill. 3/6 c 8° Philip [90] 91
$1·25 Appleton, *N.Y.* A short, bright descrn. of life on a farm in the Karroo, nr. Port Elizabeth; w. a good deal of informn. ab. S. Afr. in general and the ostrich in particular. Belongs to that agreeable category of bks. wh. Macaulay called 'breakfast books'.

TROTTER, Mrs A. P. Old Cape Colony: chron. of her men & houses; ill. 10/6 *n.* 8° Constable 03
1652–1806. A short epitome of history: valuable as light on the social life and architecture of the colony.

WALLACE, R. Farming Industries of Cape Colony 10/6 8° P. S. King & Son 95
Studies of agric. wealth of S. Afr. of the greatest importce. in formg. a judgmt. of real character of the colony.

**German West Africa:** BAINES (Thos.) Explorations in South-West Africa *o.p.* [*pb.* 21/] 8° Longman 64
From Walvisch Bay to Lake Ngami.

**Griqualand West:** WARREN (Gen. Sir C.) On the Veldt in the Seventies 16/ 8° Isbister 02
Observations made c. 1877, when the author was acting as an engineer in the country. Maps and ill.

**Natal; Zululand:** AUBERTIN (J. J.) Six Months in Cape Colony and Natal, *ut sup.*, *s.v.* Cape Colony

BIRD, Jno. Annals of Natal, 2 vols. [1495–1845] 20/ r 8° *Pietermaritzbg.* 88–9

BROOKS (H.) + MANN (Dr) History, Description, & Resources of Natal; ill. 21/ 8° Lovell Reeve 76

COLENSO, Bp J. W. [1814–83] Life of—*v.* **A** § 62

DIXIE, L'y Flor. In the Land of Misfortune; ill. *o.p.* [*pb.* 18/] 8° Bentley 82

FIELDEN, Mrs J. L. My African Farm [Natal in 1852–7] 7/6 c 8° Low

GIBSON, J. Y. The Story of the Zulus c 8° Davis, *Pietermaritzbg.* 03

GILLMORE, Col. Parker On Duty: ride thro' hostile Africa *o.p.* [*pb.* 16/] 8° Chapman 80

HAGGARD, H. Rider Cetywayo and his White Neighbours 3/6 c 8° Paul [82] 96
[Paternoster Lib.] Remarks on events in Zululand, Natal, and the Transvaal.

JENKINSON, T. B. Amazulu: Zulus, their hist., customs, lang., etc. 6/ c 8° W. H. Allen [82] 84

LUCAS, T. J. The Zulus and the British Frontiers *o.p.* [*pb.* 16/] 8° Chapman 79

RUSSELL, Rob. Natal, the Land and its Story; map [schl.-bk.] 2/6 c 8° Dent [94] 99

Twentieth Century Impressions of Natal; ill. Lloyd's Greater Br. Pb. Co., *Durban* 05

VIJN, Cornelius Cetshwayo's Dutchmen, tr. and ed. Bp J. W. Colenso *o.p.* [*pb.* 5/] c 8° Longman 80

*Zulu Campaign* —*v.* **F** § 31

**Rhodesia:** BROWN (Wm. Harvey) On the South African Frontier $3 8° Scribner, *N.Y.* 99
12/6 *n.* Low. A record of seven years' pioneering in Mashonald. and Matabeleld. 2 maps and 32 pl.

CHAMBERS, Strachey The Rhodesians: sketches of English S. Afr. life 3/6 ($1·25) c 8° Lane 00
A powerfully written account, giving a very low idea of life in Rhodesia.

DU TOIT, S. J. Rhodesia, Past and Present; 16 pl. 7/6 c 8° Heinemann 97
By the founder and presid. of the Afrikander Bond: a view (extremely favourable) of the territory as it presented itself to Dutch eyes.

FERGUSON, F. W. Southern Rhodesia; ill. 25/ *n.* r 8° Collingridge 07
Up-to-date informn. on econ. condns., etc.; geography and geology dealt with briefly.

GOULDSBURY (C.) + SHEANE (H.) The Great Plateau of N. Rhodesia; 40 pl. 16/ *n.* 8° Arnold 11

HENSMAN, H. History of Rhodesia; map [to 1900; not very complete] 6/ c 8° Blackwood 00

HONE, Percy F. Southern Rhodesia; ill. 10/6 *n.* 8° Bell 09
A clear and exhaustive acc. of country, people, govt., industries, commerce; w. forecast.

HYATT, S. P. The Northward Trek 10/6 *n.* 8° Melrose 09
Traces the genesis of the northward movemt. and follows up the pioneers engaged in it.

,, Off the Main Track 12/6 *n.* 8° Laurie 11
Detached papers, inclg. an attack on Chartered Co., previously vigorously dealt w. in his *Land of Promises*.

*JOHNSTON, Sir Henry H. British Central Africa 18/ *n.* i 8° Methuen [97] 99
$10 Lane, *N.Y.* 6 maps and 223 ill. A comprehensive general acc. of pres. condn. and resources of Brit. Central Africa Protectorate, on lines of author's *Uganda*, *ut* **E** § 48.

KEANE, Prf. A. H. Gold of Ophir: whence brought and by whom? 5/ *n.* 8° Stanford 02
Argues that Rhodesia is the source of the gold brought to Canaan in SOLOMON's time.

KNIGHT, E. F. Rhodesia of To-day 2/6 c 8° Longman 95
A lucid and comprehensive account by *Times* corresp. in Br. S. Afr. Co.'s territory.

LEONARD, Maj. A. G. How we Made Rhodesia 6/ p 8° Paul [96] 96
Of value for hist. of origin of Rhodesia and of the personalities concerned in the 'making'.

MANSFIELD, Charlotte Via Rhodesia; ill. 16/ *n.* 8° Stanley Paul 11

PETERS, Dr Carl The Eldorado of the Ancients; ill. 21/ *n.* l 8° Pearson 02
Account of archæological remains in Makembe's country on the Zambesi, and theory regarding them.

RANDALL-MACIVER, D. Mediaeval Rhodesia 20/ *n.* ($6·50 *n.*) s 4° Macmillan 06
Deals w. the less famous sites in S.-E. Rhodesia as well as those wh. have been described before.

RHODES, Cecil [1853-1902] Life of—*v. sup., s.v.* Biography

SELOUS, F. C. A Hunter's Wanderings in Africa; ill. 7/6 *n.* ($2·50 *n.*) c 8° Macmillan [81] 07
An excellent acc. of nine years' sport and travel in the interior.

" Sunshine and Storm in Rhodesia—*v.* **F** § 31, *s.v.* Matabele Campaign, 1896

TANGYE, H. L. In New South Africa; map & 26 ill. [Transv.; Rhodesia] 10/6 8° H. Cox 96

THOMSON, H. C. Rhodesia and its Government; ill. 10/6 c 8° Smith & Elder 98
A somewhat unfavourable criticism of the South African Chartered Company and its methods.

WILMOT, Hon. A. Monomotapa (Rhodesia): its monumts. & history; ill. 6/ c 8° Unwin 96

*Barotseland:* ARNOT (Rev. F. S.) Bihé and Garenganze 2/6 c 8° Hawkins 95

" Garenganze: missn.-wk. in Centr. Africa 2/6 c 8° Hawkins [89] 89

BERTRAND, Alf. The Kingdom of the Barotse [tr.]; maps and ill. 16/ Unwin 99

COILLARD, F. —*in his* On the Threshold of Central Africa [tr.], *ut* **E** § 48

GIBBONS, A. St H. —*in his* Africa fr. S. to N. thro' Marotseland, 2 vols., *ut* **E** § 41

HARDING, Col. Colin In Remotest Barotseland; ill. 10/6 *n.* 8° Hurst 05
Acc. of jy. of over 8,000 m. thro' wildest pts. of Lewamka's empire, by Commandant of Barotse native police.

*Mashonaland:* ALDERSON (Lt.-Col.) With the Mashonald. Field Force; ill. [1896] 12/6 8° Methuen 98

BALFOUR, Alice B. —*in her* Twelve Hundred Miles in a Waggon [1895] 16/ 8° Arnold 95

BENT, J. Theod. The Ruined Cities of Mashonaland; ill. 3/6 ($1·25) c 8° ($5) 8° Longman [92] 95
[Silver Lib.] Has ch. on Orientation and mensurn. of the Temples by R. M. W. SWAN. Descr. of the remarkable ruins existg. in Mashonald., and results of excavns. by author in 1891 at Zimbabwe (once capital of country), wh. had several temples devoted to sun and primitive nature-worship, all oriented to rising or setting sun. The further journeyings thro' Mash. of auth. and his wife are also descr., detailg. manners, custs., religs., etc.

BLENNERHASSETT (Rose) + SLEEMAN (Lucy) Adventures in Mashonaland 3/6 c 8° Macmillan [93] 94
A bright acc. of the journey of two brave hospital-nurses to the pioneer camp at Umtali.

CHURCHILL, Lord Randolph S. Men, Mines and Animals in S. Africa; ill. 2/6 c 8° Low *N.Y.* [92] 95
$5 Appleton, *N.Y.* Repr. of l's to *Dy. Graphic*, descrg. investigns. of gold-ming. prosps., incids. of travel and sport.

HALL (R. N.) + NEAL (W. G.) The Ancient Ruins of Rhodesia; maps & 70 ill. 10/6 *n.* 8° Methuen [02] 40
A very full acc. and accurate descrn. of the 'Zimbabwes' so common in Rhodesia.

" (*alone*) Great Zimbabwe; ill. and plans 21/ *n.* r 8° Methuen 05
A contin. (1902-4) of the wk. of explorn. descr. in above, to wh. it forms a sequel. Introd. A. H. KEANE.

" Pre-historic Rhodesia: 915-1760; ill. 12/6 *n.* 8° Unwin 09
Histor., ethnol. and evidences as to orig. and age of rock-mines and stone-bldgs. Incls. a Gazetteer of Medieval S.-E. Africa.

KEANE, Prf. A. H. —*in his* Gold of Ophir, *ut sup., s.v.* Rhodesia

KNIGHT, E. F. Rhodesia—*ut sup., s.v.* Rhodesia

KNIGHT-BRUCE, Bp G. W. H. Memories of Mahonaland [1895] 10/6 8° Arnold 95

ROMILLY, Hugh Letters from the Western Pacific and Mashonaland—*ut* **E** § 63 [1893]

SELOUS, F. C. Travel & Adventure in S.-E. Africa; map, port. & ill. 25/ *n.* 8° Rowland Ward 93
An admirable, straightforwd., and absol. trustworthy narr. of 11 yrs. spent in pioneering and sport by an intrepid yet modest Englishman (primarily a huntsman) on the Zambesi and its tribs.; w. ser. of chs. descr. settlemt. by Chartered S. A. Co., progr. of gold-industry there, acc. of Matabele people, etc. An important contribn. to contemp. colon. hist. as well as an excellent record of sport [*v.* **I** § 147].

de WAAL, D. C. With Rhodes in Mashonaland, tr. [fr. Dutch] *o.p.* 8° Juta, *Cape Town* 96

WILLOUGHBY, Sir J. C. Narr. of Further Excavations at Zimbabye 3/6 c 8° Philip 93
A continuatn. of BENT's investigns. concerning the mysterious ruins. Ill. and col. plans.

**Matabeleland** —*v. also* Mashonaland, *sup.*

CARNEGIE, Rev. D. Among the Matabele [missionary] 1/6 c 8° R.T.S. 94

COOPER-CHADWICK, J. Three Years with Lobengula & Experiences in S. Afr. 2/6 c 8° Cassell [94] 96
Story of pioneer-life in S. Africa, supplying a vivid picture of LOBENGULA and his life at Bululwayo before the war.

NORRIS-NEWMAN, Cpt. C. L. Matabeleland & How we got it [fairly impartial] *o.p.* [*pb.* 7/6] c 8° Unwin 95

WOOD, J. G. Through Matabeleland *o.p.* [*pb.* 3/6] c 8° Richards 93
Account of a journey of 10 months in an ox-wagon thro' Matabeleland and Mashonaland.

*Matabele Campaign:* 1896 —*v.* **F** § 31

*Victoria Falls:* MOHR (Ed.) To Victoria Falls of Zambesi [tr.] *o.p.* [*pb.* 24/] r 8° Low 76

OATES, Fk. Matabele Land and Victoria Falls; ill. 21/ 8° Paul [81] 90
Ed. C. G. OATES. A naturalist's wanderings. Col. pl., maps, and ill.

**Orange Free State; Orange River Colony:** BOON (M. J.) Hist. of Orange Fr. St. *o.p.* [*pb.* 5/] c 8° 85

MATURIN, Mrs Fred Petticoat Pilgrims on Trek—*ut inf., s.v.* Transvaal

WARREN, Gen. Sir Chas. On the Veldt in the Seventies, *ut sup., s.v.* Griqualand West

**Transvaal:** BIGELOW (Poultney) White Man's Africa; ill. 2/6 p 8° Harper [98] 00

BLACKBURN (D.) + CADDELL (Cpt. W. W.) Secret Service in South Africa 10/6 *n.* 8° Cassell 11

BOVILE, Rev. J. H. Natives under the Transvaal Flag 3/6 c 8° Simpkin 00

DISTANT, W. L. A Naturalist in the Transvaal—*ut* **H** § 104

DIXIE, L'y Florence —*in her* The Land of Misfortune, *ut sup., s.v.* Natal

EDWARD, Neville — The Transvaal in War and Peace; ill. — 7/6 *n.* 8° Virtue 99

FISHER, W. E. Garrett — The Transvaal and the Boers — 10/6 8° Chapman [96] 00
A lucid and just acc. of the Boer, genesis and growth and his State, and his characteristics.

HILLEGAS, H. C. — Oom Paul's People — $1·50 c 8° Appleton, *N.Y.* 99
An American's pers. impressns. Sketches history, polit. sitn., govt., people, leaders. Strongly favours Boers.

HOBSON, Mrs Carey — At Home in the Transvaal — 3/6 c 8° Sonnenschein [86] 99

" — The Farm in the Karoo; ill. — 2/6 c 8° Sonnenschein [83] 96

JEPPE, Carl — The Kaleidoscopic Transvaal — 7/6 *n.* 8° Chapman 06
Represents a moderate and sane view, by one who accepted Brit. rule under L'd CARNARVON, and thus reverted to progressive republicanism in opposition to KRUGER.

KEANE, Prf. A. H. — —*in his* Boer States, Land, and People, *ut sup.*

LACY, Geo. — Picts. of Travel, Sport, and Adventure; ill. — 15/ 8° Pearson 00
Includes a valuable account of Boer life.

Letters from an Uitlander, 1899–1902: with intro. by Sir Bartle Frere — 5/ *n.* c 8° Murray 03
On the political situation.

LEYDS, Dr W. J. — First Annexation of the Transvaal — 21/ *n.* 8°
Pt. i treats of earlier relns. of Boers w. Brit. govt.; ii in greater detail w. the annexn. in 1877.

MCCORMICK, Rev. W. T. — 2,000 Miles thro' S. Africa — [Transvaal] 2/6 *n.* c 8° Thynne 00

MATURIN, Mrs Fred — Petticoat Pilgrims on Trek — 7/6 *n.* 8° Nash 09
A chatty diary of 2 yrs. spent in Transvaal and Orange River Colony just after the Boer War.

OSBORNE, Oliver — In the Land of the Boers — 2/ c 8° Everett 00
Ill. An account based on a visit to the country before 1890.

PHILLIPS, Flor. [Mrs Lionel] — South African Recollections; 37 ill. — 7/6 ($2·50) 8° Longman 97
Record of her expeces. in Johannesburg and her recollns. of events conn. w. the Jameson Raid.

" Lionel — Transvaal Problems: some notes on current politics — 12/ *n.* 8° Murray 05

RANKIN, Reg. — —*in his* A Subaltern's Letters to his Wife, *ut* **F** § 31, *s.v.* Boer War
Largely descriptive of natural and social conditions.

ROCHE, [Mrs] H. A. — On Trek in the Transvaal — *o.p.* [*pb.* 10/6] c 8° Low [78] 78

TANGYE, H. L. — —*in his* New South Africa, *ut sup.*, *s.v.* Rhodesia

WARREN, Gen. Sir Chas. — —*in his* On the Veldt in the Seventies, *ut sup.*, *s.v.* Griqualand West

WITHERS, Hartley — English & Dutch in S. Africa: a historical retrospect — 3/6 c 8° Clement Wilson 96

*Boer War: Jameson Raid* — —*v.* **F** § 31, *s.v.* Boer War

*Cecil Rhodes* — —*v.* **F** § 27

**Tristan d'Acunha:** BARROW (K. M.) Three Years in Tristan Da Cunha — 7/6 *n.* 8° Skeffington 10
Occupied by Gt. Brit. in 1816: occupn. ceased next yr., 3 of garrison bg. allowed to remain. Fr. these and occas. immigrants and shipwrecked sailors the pres. populace has come—a mixed race, no white woman hg. come to the island. By wife of the missionary there.

TAYLOR, W. F. — Account of Tristan d'Acunha — *o.p.* 8°

## 51: MADAGASCAR AND NEIGHBOURING ISLANDS

**Bibliography:** GRANDIDIER (G.) Bibliographie de Madagascar, Pt. i — 8° *Paris* 05

SIBREE, Rev. J. — Madagascar Bibliography [92 pp.; i. alphab., ii. chronolog.] — 5/ 8° *Antananarivo* 85

### Early Voyages and Accounts

DRURY, Rob. [18 cent.] — Jl. dur. 15 Yrs' Captiv. in Madag.; 13 ill. — 3/6 c 8° Unwin [1722] 97
$1·50. Macmillan, *N.Y.* [Adventure Ser.] Ed. Cpt. S. P. OLIVER. A famous bk. in its day, orig. ed. by DEFOE, or under his influ., w. high reputn. for trustworthiness until M. E. BLANCHARD, in *Revue des Deux Mondes*, first doubted its authenticity—doubts confirmed by pres. edr. It is v. interestg., but little more than a romance.

D[U] B[OIS], Sieur [17 cent.] — Voyages to Islds. of Madagascar and Bourbon, tr. Cpt. P. Oliver; maps and ill. — [1669–72] 10/6 8° Nutt 97
Supplements the Edr.'s edn. of LEGUAT'S *Voy. to Rodriguez, Mauritius, Java, and C. of Gd. Hope*, 2 vols. [*ut* **E** § 41].

### Modern Travel and Accounts

BURLEIGH, Bennett — Madagascar and Ashantee — 2/ f 8° R.T.S. 96
A war-correspondent's experces. dur. Fch. advance on Antananarivo, and in Ashanti dur. expedn. of Sir Fcs. SCOTT to Kumassi.

COLVILLE, [Mrs] Zélie — Round the Black Man's Garden—*ut* **E** § 41
The best pt. of bk. is the march across Madagascar thro' Antananarivo to Majanga.

COUSINS, Rev. W. E. [missy.] — Madagascar of To-day; ill. — 2/ c 8° R.T.S. 95

DAWSON, E. W. — Madagascar: its capabilities and resources — 2/ 8° Philip 95

ELLIS, Rev. Wm. [missy.] — History of Madagascar, 2 vols. — *o.p.* [*pb.* 25/] 8° Tallis 38

" — Three Visits to Madagascar — [1853, 54, 56] *o.p.* [*pb.* 16/] 8° Murray [58] 60

" — Madagascar Revisited; ill. — [1862–5] *o.p.* [*pb.* 16/] 8° Murray 67

KELLER, Prf. C. — Madagascar, Mauritius & other East Afr. Islds. [tr.] — 7/6 8° Sonnenschein 01
The most complete acc. in compact form of the islands, their geol., geogr., flora, fauna, peoples.

KNIGHT, E. F. — Madagascar in War Time; map and 16 ill. — *o.p.* [*pb.* 12/6] 8° Longman 96
An excellent acc. of the isl. as seen by *The Times* Spec. Corresp. w. the Hovas dur. Fch. invasion in 1895.

LITTLE, Rev. H. W. [missy.] — Madagascar: its history and people — 10/6 8° Blackwood 84

McLeod, Lyons Madagascar & its People [by Br. Consul at Mozambique] *o.p.* [*pb.* 10/6] 8° Longman 65
Matthews, Rev. T. T. Thirty Years in Madagascar ; 60 ill. 6/ 8° R.T.S. 04
Descrns. of the country and of the people, their customs, religion, lang., and social life, by a missionary.
Maude, Col. Fcs. C. Five Years in Madagascar 5/ c 8° Chapman 95
Mullens, Rev. Jos. [missy.] Twelve Months in Madagascar 7/6 p 8° Nisbet [75] 75
Oliver, Cpt. S. P. Madagascar and the Malagasy *o.p.* [*pb.* 42/] r 8° Day 66
" Madagascar and its Former Dependencies, 2 vols. 52/6 8° Macmillan 86
" True Story of the French Dispute in Madagascar 9/ 8° Unwin 85
Shaw, Rev. G. A. Madagascar & France ; ill. [people, resources, developmt.] 6/ c 8° R.T.S. 85
Sibree, Rev. Jas. Madagascar & its People ; ill. [chfly. missy. prospects] 6/6 16° R.T.S. [70] 81
" The Great African Island *o.p.* [*pb.* 12/] 8° Trübner 80
Accs. of the more import. researches in phys. geogr., geol., explorn., nat. hist., customs, lang., beliefs, folklore, etc., of diff. tribes.
" Madagascar before the Conquest ; map and ill. 16/ 8° Unwin 96
Smith, Rev. G. Herb. Among the Menabe ; ill. 1/6 f 8° S.P.C.K. 96
Account of a missionary's experiences among a branch of the Sakalora tribe.

**Mauritius :** Bowen, (Sir G. F.) —*in his* Thirty Years of Colonial Government, 2 vols. 32/ 8° Longman 89
Boyle, C. J. Far Away : scenery and society in Mauritius *o.p.* [*pb.* 9/] c 8° Chapman 67
Malleson, Col. G. B. Final French Struggles in India and Indian Seas 10/6 c 8° W. H. Allen 78
Pike, Nich. Sub-tropical Rambles in Land of Aphanapteryx *o.p.* [*pb.* 18/] 8° Low 73

**Réunion Island :** Oliver (W. D.) Crags and Craters : rambles in Réunion ; ill. 6/ c 8° Longman 96
Acc. of a six-months' visit, with much information on geogr., hist., statistics, scenery, manners and customs.

**Seychelles :** Estridge (H. W.) Six Years in Seychelles ; 30 photos. 21/ s 4° *priv. prin., London* 85
Fauve, A. A. [ed.] Unpub. Documents rel. to the Seychelles Islands 8° Mahé *Seychelles* 09
37 old maps (earliest 1501), in portfolio, accompany the book.

---

# VII : Geography, etc., of America

## 52 : NORTH AMERICA : GENERALLY

**Bibliography** —*v. also* **E** § 54
Clarke & Co., R. [bkslrs.] Bibliotheca Americana 50 c. *n.* 8° Clarke, *Cincinnati* 93
A useful classified list (under 72 heads) of 7,488 titles of bks. and pamphs., w. prices. No Author's Index.
Leclerc, Ch. Bibliotheca Americana : hist., géogr., archéol., linguistique 15 fr. 8° *Paris* 78
Rich, O. Bibliotheca Americana Nova, 2 v. & Suppl. [bks. 1701 to 1841] *o.p.* [*pb.* 32/] 8° Rich 35–41 ; 46
Sabin, Jos. Bibliotheca Americana, Pts. i–cxv
Pts. i–xliv, ea. $2 *n.* ; xlv *sqq.* ea. $5 *n.* 8° Sabin, *N.Y.* 68–91
An almost exhaustive dictionary of bks. relating to America fr. discovery to present time.
Stevens, H. Historical Nuggets, 3 vols. *o.p.* 12° Stevens 62–85
3,000 alphab. arrgd. titles of *rare bks.* rel. to Amer., in his own colln. ; w. collatns. and values.
*Maps :* Philips (P. L.) List of Maps rel. to Am. in Lib. of Congress 8° Govt. Prtg. Off., *Washgtn.* 02
Winsor, Justin The Kohl Colln. of Maps rel. to America $1 8° Govt. Prtg. Off., *Washgtn.* 05

**Geographical Textbooks :** Hayden (F. V.) + Selwyn (A. R.) North America ; ill. —*v. inf., s.v.* Stanford's Compendium of Mod. Geogr. (note)
Herbertson, Mrs F. L. D. North America [Descr. Geogr. ; 2/ Black] 75 c. *n.* c 8° Macmillan 01
Reynolds, J. B. The Americas ; maps & ill. [2/ Black ; Regional Geogr.] 70 c. *n.* c 8° Macmillan, *N.Y.* 07
Russell, Prf. Isr. C. North America ; maps [Regions of the World] 7/6 *n.* ($2) 8° Clar. Press 04
Descrs. some of the more prominent and attractive aspects of the natural condns. pertaing. to N. Am. (esp. U.S.).
Shaler, Prf. N. S. Story of our Continent [geogr. and geol. reader] $1 12° Ginn, *Boston* 92
Stanford, E. [pub.] Compendium of Geography : N. America, 2 v. ; maps and ill. ea. 15/ 8° Stanford 97
Vol. i : *Canada and Newfdld.* [*ut* **E** § 55], 18 maps and 90 ill., Dr S. E. Dawson ; ii : *United States* [*ut* **E** § 56], 16 maps and 72 ill., Hy. Gannett. Carefully prepared and full of interesting matter : readable as well as instructive. Replaces Hayden + Selwyn's wk. (1883) in same series.
Terry (R. S.) + McMurry (F. M.) North America [largely U.S. dependcies.] 75 c. *n.* c 8° Macmillan 00

**Modern Travel and Description**—*for* Early Travel, *v.* **E** § 54
Audubon, J. J. Journals, ed. M. R. Audubon, 2 vols. ; ill. $7·50 8° Scribner, *N.Y.* 98
Baillie-Grohman, W. A. Sport and Life in Western America 15/ r 8° H. Cox 99
416 pp., ill. Mostly concerned with sport ; appendix on Chinese servants by Mrs Baillie-Grohman.
Boyd, Alec. J. [Austral.] The Shellbock ; or At Sea in the Sixties 6/ c 8° Cassell 99
A diffuse descrn. of a voyage to Callao, the Guano Islands, and round the Horn to England.
Browne, G. W. [ed.] New America and the Far East, 6 vols. ; maps and ill. $28 4° Jones, *Boston* 07

COOK, Joel — America, Picturesque and Descriptive 3 vols.; ill. $7·50 8° Coates *Phila.* 00
,, — Pen Pictures of America, 6 vols.; ill. $7·50 c 8° Syndicate Pb. Co., *Phila.* 03
FOUNTAIN, Paul — Great North-West & Great Lake Region of N. America $4 (10/6 *n.*) 8° Longman 04
Primarily intended for the naturalist and sportsman. Accurate and careful.
HOWARD OF GLOSSOP, L'y — Journal of Tour in U.S., Canada and Mexico 7/6 c 8° Low 97
A good tourist book: some rather little known parts are described. 32 ill.
JAMES, Hy. — Portraits of Places—*ut* **E** § 11
LUBBOCK, A. Basil — Round the Horn Before the Mast 8/ c 8° Murray 02
Diary of a voyage on a merchant-vessel fr. San Francisco to Engl.: a true picture of a sailor's life.
MADDEN, Jno. — The Wilderness and its Tenants, 3 v. [travs. in N. Am.] 42/ 8° Simpkin 97
MURPHY, J. M. — Rambles in North-West America *o.p.* [*pb.* 16/] 8° Chapman 79
MURRAY, D. Christie — A Cockney Columbus [U.S., Can., Austral.] *o.p.* [*pb.* 6/] c 8° Downey 97
ROBERTS, Morley — Western Avernus: toil & travel in further N. America 7/6 *n.* c 8° Constable [87] 96
$2 Little & Brown, *Boston.* A very interestg. autobiogr. acc. of hand-to-mouth struggles and wandergs. in Far West.
ST MAUR, Mrs Alg. — Impressns. of a Tenderfoot in Search of Sport 12/ c 8° Murray 90
Descrn. of jy., chfly. in search of sport, in Brit. Col., Manitoba, and W. North Amer., inclg. visits to Banff, Cowichan Lake, Vancouver, Selkirk Mtns., Findlay Creek, etc. A pleasant literary *olla podrida.* A 'tenderfoot' in Western slang is the equivalent of what is known in Australia as a 'new chum'. Map and ill.
SCAIFE, W. B. — America, its Geographical Hist.: 1492–1892; map $1·50 8° J. Hopkins Pr., *Baltimore* 92
[Johns Hopk. Univ. Studies.] 6 lects. to graduate studts. *Developmt. of Atlantic Coast in Consciousness of Eur., Developmt. of Pacific Coast Geogr. Geogr. of Interior and Polar Regions, Histor. Notes on Geogr. Names* (Am., Brazil, Canada), *Developmt. of Am. Natl. and State Boundaries,* etc.

**Coasts:** AGASSIZ (A.) — Three Cruises of the *Blake*—*v.* **E** § 7
ENOCK (C. R.) — The Great Pacific Coast; 32 pls. 16/ *n.* 8° Richards 09
Acc. of life and travel in W. States of N. and S. Amer., fr. Calif., Brit. Columbia, and Alaska to Mex., Panama, Peru, Chile.
FINCK, H. T. — The Pacific Coast Scenic Tour; 24 pl. $2·50 c 8° Scribner, *N.Y.* 90
10/6 Low. Fr. Southern California to Alaska. The Yosemite, Canadian Pacific Ry., Yellowstone Park, and the Grand Cañon.
JOHNSON, Clifton — Highways and Byways of Pacific Coast; ill.; $2 *n.* (8/6 *n.*) c 8° Macmillan 08
VACHELL, Hor. A. — Sport and Life on the Pacific Coast 7/6 *n.* 8° Nash 08
15 chaps. on 'life', 5 on 'sport'.

**Deserts:** FOUNTAIN (P.) — Great Deserts and Forests of N. America $3·75 (9/6 *n.*) c 8° Longman 01
A very well wr. series of studies of nature, fr observns. of 30 yrs. ago: not a scientific account.

**Insular Possessions:** FORBES-LINDSAY (C. H. A.) America's Insular Possessions, 2 v.; maps and ill. $5 8° Winston, *Phila.* 07

**Rivers:** RUSSELL, Prf. Isr. C. — River Developmt. as ill. by Rivers of N. Am.; ill. 6/ c 8° Murray 99
[Progressive Science Ser.] Amer. edn. *sub tit. The Rivers of America,* $2 Putnam, *N.Y.* A full study of river-action.

**Rocky Mountains** —*v.* **E** § 55: Dominion of Canada

**Scenery:** BRYANT (W. C.) [ed.] Picturesque America, 4 vols.; 14 steel pl. & 200 ill. ea. 42/ r 4° Cassell [74] 82–8
MANNING, Rev. S. — American Pictures, drawn w. Pen and Pencil; ill. 8/ i 8° R. T. S. 76

**Greater America:** COLQUHOUN (A. R.) Greater America; maps and ill. 16/ ($2 *n.*) 8° Harper 04
Presents America as a world-power, dealg. largely w. the Pacific Coast and the transformn. of Asia.

## 53: AMERICAN INDIANS: HISTORY, SOCIAL LIFE, ETHNOLOGY

**Bibliography** —*v. also* **K** §§ 162–4
BRINTON, Prf. D. G. — Aboriginal American Authors and their Productions—*ut* **B** § 35
BROOKS, E. S. — —*his* Story, *ut inf.*: conts. bibliogr. of best 100 bks. on Am. Indns.
FIELD, T. W. — Essay tow. an Indian Bibliography [cat. of bks. in his lib.] $5 8° Scribner, *N.Y.* 73
PILLING, J. C. Bibl. of Eskimauan Lang.; Bibl. of Siouan Langs. 1 8° Smithsonian Inst., *Washn.* 87; 87
,, Bibliogr. of Iroquoian Langs.; Bibl. of Muskhogean Langs. 1 8° Smithson. Inst., *Washn.* 88; 89
,, Bibliogr. of Algonquian Langs.; Bibl. of Athapascan Lang. 1 8° Smithson. Inst., *Washn.* 91; 93
Excellent examples of exhaustive bibliogs. of prtd. bks., MSS., mag.-arts., tracts, reviews, and announcemts. The 'Dictionary Plan' is followed to its extreme limits, subject and tribal indexes, refs. to libraries, etc., bg. incl. in one alphab. Facss. of title-pp. of rare bks. liberally added (e.g. 82 in vol. v.).

**Collectively:** BANCROFT (H. H.) Native Races of Pacific States of N. Am., 5 v. ea. $5·50 8° Appleton, *N.Y.* 75–6
i: *Wild Tribes*; ii: *Civilized Nations*; iii: *Mythology and Langs.*; iv: *Antiquities*; v: *Primitive History.* A mine of facts.
BEACH, W. W. — Indian Miscellany; ill. $4 8° Munsell, *Albany* 77
BETTANY, G. T. — Red, Brown, and Black Men of America and Australia, and their White Supplanters [popular] 2/6 ($1) f 8° Ward & Lock 90
BOURKE, Cpt J. G. — On the Border with Crook [1872–3] $2·50 8° Scribner, *N.Y.* [91] 96
Lively descrns. of skirmishes w. Am. Indns. (Apaches in Arizona 1871, Sioux and Cheyennes in Montana 1876), commencing w. sketch of state of affairs bef. arrival of Gen. CROOK. Author, who served for over 20 yrs. w. CROOK, strongly condemns U.S. policy and treatmt. of Indians.
BRINE, Adm. Lindesay — Travels amongst Amer. Indians; maps and ill. 21/ 8° Low 94
W. descrns. of anc. earthwks. and temples. Incl. jy. to Guatemala, Mexico, and Yucatan, and visit to ruins of Patinamit, Utatlan, Palenque, and Uxmal.

BRINTON, Prf. D. G. Essays of an Americanist—*ut* **B** § 35

,, The American Race—*ut* **K** § 162

A linguistic classification and ethnographic descrn. of the native races of America.

,, [ed.] Library of Aboriginal American Literature, 8 vols.—*ut* **B** § 35

BROOKS, E. S. Story of the American Indian ; ill. [w. bibliogr.] $1·50 c 8° Lothrop, *Boston* 87

CATLIN, Geo. Illns. of Manners & Customs of N. Am. Indns., 2 v. ; col. pl. 63/ r 8° Chatto [42] 76

,, Portfolio of Illustrations to same *o.p.* [*pb.* 105/ ; col. 210/] f° Bohn 42

The result of his 8 yrs.' sojourn am. N.-Am. Indns. He brot. many of them and their curiosities over to Eur., and attracted a good deal of attention by his publ. exhibns. of them.

,, Life among the Indians [8 years] 2/6 12° Gall [61] 89

Donaldson, T. The George Catlin Indian Gallery ; col. maps & 142 pl. 8° *Washington* 85

The Catlin Gallery is in U.S. Natl. Mus. (Smithson. Instit., Washgtn.). This bk. (900 pp.) conts. full acc. of N.-Am. Inds., am. whom CATLIN lived for 8 yrs.

COLDEN, C. Hist. of the Five Indian Nations of Canada dependent on the Province of New York, 2 vols. $2 *n.* c 8° New Amsterd. Bk. Co., *N.Y.* [ ] 02

DELLENBAUGH, F. S. The North Americans of Yesterday ; 350 ill. $4 *n.* (21/) 8° Putnam 01

A learned argument for unity of race among the different tribes of Indians.

DENISON, T. S. The Primitive Aryans of America 8° T. S. Denison, *Chicago* 09

Seeks to show that the Aztecs and other Mexican tribes were orig. Aryans fr. Western Asia !

DODGE, Col. R. I. Plains of the Great West, and their Inhabitants $4 8° Putnam, *N.Y.* [63] 76

,, Our Wild Indians $2·75 12° Worthington, *Hartford* 82

DOMENECH, Abbé Seven Years in the Desert of N. America, 2 vols. *o.p.* [*pb.* 36/] 8° Bohn 60

DRAKE, F. S. Indian Tribes of U.S., 2 vols. ; 100 pl., some col. *o.p.* r 4° Lippincott, *Phila.* 84

An abridgmt. of SCHOOLCRAFT's 6-vol. bk. [*inf.*], w. addtl. matter, and in some parts re-written.

DRAKE, S. G. Books of the Indians, ed. J. W. O'Neill *o.p.* [*pb.* $4] r 8° *Boston* [33] 52

EGGLESTONE, E., etc. Famous American Indians, 5 vols. ea. $1·25 12° Dodd & Mead, *N.Y.* 78–80

TECUMSEH and the Shawnee Prophet ; RED EAGLE ; POCAHONTAS ; BRANT and RED JACKET ; MONTEZUMA.

ELLIS, G. E. Red Man & White Man in N. Am. [fr. earliest times] $3·50 8° Little & Brown, *Boston* 82

FEATHERMAN, A. Social Hist. of Races of Mankind : Aoneo-Maranonians [N. Amer. & Esquimaux]—*ut* **F** § 5

FOSTER, J. W. Prehistoric Races of U. S. Am. ; ill. [chfly. archæol.] $3 c 8° Scott, *Chicago* [73] 74

GRINNELL, G. B. Story of the Indian ; 16 pl. [Story of West ser.] $1·50 c 8° Appleton, *N.Y.* 95

6/ Chapman. A pict. of actual Indian, his home-life, relig. observces., amusemts., warlike and sportg. instincts. and effects of civilizn. upon him. Author is an adopted chief of Pawnees and also of Blackfeet.

,, The North American Indians of To-day ; ill. $5 4° Stone, *Chicago* 00

21/ Pearson. An excellent description of the United States tribes of Indians.

HAINES, E. M. The American Indian ; ill. $5 8° Mas-sin-ná-gan Co., *Chicago*, 89

HILL-TOUT, C. Native Races of Brit. Emp. : Brit. North America, i : The Far West, the Home of the Salish & Déné ; ill. [Alaska, etc.] 6/ *n.* 8° Constable 07

HODGE, F. W. [ed.] Hdbk. of Am. Inds. N. of Mexico, Pts. i–ii. ; ill. 4° Smithson. Inst., *Washgn.* 07–11

INTERNATL. CONGRESS OF ANTHROPOLOGY, Chicago, 1883 : Memoirs ed. C. Stainland Wake 8° *Chicago* 83

A ser. of pprs. by leadg. Am. (and a few Engl.) wrs., affordg. a compreh. view of pres. condn. of main questns. wh. are interesting Am. ethnologists.

JACKSON, Mrs H. H. Century of Dishonour [U.S. gov.'s dealgs. w Indns.] $1·50 8° Roberts, *Boston* [81] 85

Jesuit Relations, ed. R. G. Thwaites—*ut* **A** § 105, *s.v.* America

Of considerable importance for native manners, customs, rites, mode of life, etc.

JONES, C. C., jun. Antiquities of Southern Indians [esp. Georgia tribes] $6 8° Appleton, *N.Y.* 73

KANE, Paul Wandgs. of an Artist am. Inds. of N. Am. ; ill. *o.p.* [*pb.* 21/] 8° Longman 59

KRAUSE (E.) + GRÜNWEDEL (Dr) North-West Coast of America [tr.] ; 13 pl. *o.p.* [*pb.* $10] f° *New York* 82

Results of ethnological researches ; fr. collections at Berlin Museum.

LUMMIS, C. F. Strange Corners of our Country ; ill. $1·50 12° Century Co., *N.Y.* 92

A bk. for young people, w. chaps on the Indian 'snake' dances, Indian customs, etc.

MCKENNY (T. L.) + HALL (J.) Hist. of Indian Tribes of N. Am., 2 vols. ; 50 col. ports. *o.p.* [*pb.* $33] i 8° Rice, *Phila.* [38–44] 68

MCLAUGHLIN, Jas. My Friend the Indian ; ill. [10/6 *n.* Constable] 8° Houghton, *Boston* 10

On past and pres. of the Indian, by ex-agent to Sioux in N. Dakota, now Indian Inspr. to U.S. govt.

MANYPENNY, G. W. Our Indian Wards $3 8° Clarke, *Cincinnati* 80

MESSITER, C. A. Sport and Adventure among N. Amer. Indians ; ill. 12/6 8° Porter 90

PARKMAN, F. The Oregon Trail—*ut* **F** § 67 ; conts. a good picture of Indian life

,, The Conspiracy of Pontiac—*ut* **F** § 67

REMINGTON, Fredc. Pony Tracks—*ut* **E** § 55 ; Crooked Trails ; both ill. by author $2 8° Harper, *N.Y.* 95–8

SCHOOLCRAFT, H. R. Thirty Years with the Indian Tribes [1812–42] $3 8° Lippincott, *Phila.* [51] 54

,, Hist., Cond. & Prosps. of Ind. Tribes of U.S., 6 v. ; ill. $90 i 8° Lippincott, *Phila.* 53–7

Pprs. ld. bef. Congress on hist., antiqs., langs., ethnol., rites, superstitns., and mythol. of Indians ; illd. by Cpt. S. EASTMAN w. over 300 pl. (some col.). *Vide* DRAKE, *sup.* Picturesque rather th. scientific, contg. much useless matter.

SCHULTZ, J. W. My Life as an Indian ; ill. [6/ *n.* Murray] $1·50 c 8° Doubleday, *N.Y.* 07
An intimate reveln. of domestic life of Indian, by one who had long resid. w. Blackfeet at period when tribe lived in primitive way.

SHORT, J. T. The North Americans of Antiquity $3 8° Harper, *N.Y.* 80

SMITHSONIAN INSTITUTION, Bureau of Ethnology : Annual Reports ; col. pl., ill. and maps 4° Govt. Prg. Off., *Washgtn.* 79 *sqq., ann.*

,, Contribns. to N. Amer. Ethnology ; pl. (some col.), v. i and foll. 4° Govt. Prg. Off., *Washgtn.* 77 *sqq.*

SPENCER, Herb. [ed.] Descriptive Sociology, No. 2 : Anc. Amer. Races ; No. 6 : Amer. Races [N. & S.]—*ut* **C** § 62

STARR, Fredk. [Am.] The Redskin at Home ; ill. [schl. bk.] (2/6) 12° Harrap 07
A compendious acc. of the var. tribes in their distribn. over the States, their dress, houses, habits, pastimes, religions, and customs.

THATCHER, B. B. Indian Biography, 2 vols. $1·50 18° Harper, *N.Y.* [32] 43

U.S. GEOLOG. AND GEOGRAPHICAL SURVEY OF ROCKY MOUNTAIN REGION—*ut* **H** § 39

WINSOR, Justin —*in his* Narr. & Crit. Hist. of America, vol. i : Pre-Columbian America—*ut* **F** § 66

YAWGER, Rose N. The Indian & the Pioneer : hist. study, 2 v. in 1 ; ill. $3 8° Clarke, *Cincinnati* 93

*Missions to Amer. Indians*—*v.* **A** § 105 *Indian Wars w. U.S.*—*v.* **F** § 70 *Mythology & Folklore*—*v.* **B** § 35

*Place-names :* RUTTENBER (E. M.) Footprints of the Red Men ; maps $3 8° N.Y. State Hist. Soc. 07
Indian geogr. names in valley of Hudson's River, valley of Mohawk, and on the Delaware.

**Algonquins :** POLLARD (J. G.) Pamunkey Indians of Virginia 8° 94

SCHULTZ, J. W. —*in his* My Life, *ut sup.*

TOOKER, W. W. Algonquian Series : researches, 10 vols. $15 *n.* 8° F. P. Harper, *N.Y.* 01–2

**Apaches** —*v.* **E** § 57, *s.v.* New Mexico (COZZENS, LUMMIS)

**Aztecs** —*v.* Mexicans, *inf.*

**Blackfeet :** McCLINTOCK (W.) The Old North Trail ; ill. (8 col.) $4 *n.* (15/ *n.*) 8° Macmillan 10
Life, legends, institns., religion. By adopted son of one of the high chiefs. An admirable bk.

**Cakchiquels :** BRINTON (D. G.) Annals of the Cakchiquels—*ut* **B** § 35

**Cherokees :** PARKER (T. V.) Cherokee Indians [w. ref. to U.S. govt.] $1 *n.* 12° Grafton Press, *N.Y.* 07

THOMAS, Cyrus The Cherokees in Pre-Columbian Times ; ill. $1 12° Hodges, *N.Y.* 90
An attempt to trace back the history of a single tribe into the pre-historic, or mound-building, age.

**Cheyennes :** DORSEY (G. A.) The Cheyenne—*ut* **B** § 35

**Chippeways** —*v.* Ottaways, *inf.*

**Crees :** YOUNG (Rev. E. R.) By Canoe and Dog-Train ; ill. [am. Crees and Sioux] $1·25 16° Hunt & Eaton, *N.Y.* 90

**Crows :** BECKWOURTH (J. P.) Life and Adventures, ed. Chas. G. Leland 3/6 c 8° Unwin 93
$1·50 Macmillan, *N.Y.* [Advent. Ser.] BECKWOURTH was mountaineer, scout, pioneer, and Chief of Crow Indians. Orig. wr. fr. his dictation.

**Flatheads :** CROSBY (Rev. Thos.) Among the An-ko-memums ; ill. [Pacific Coast] 12° Briggs, *Toronto* 07

RONAN, Rev. P. Hist. Sketch of Flathead Ind. Nation ; ill. [1813–90] $2 8° 90

**Gaspesians** —*v.* Micmacs, *inf.*

**Guiana Tribes :** BRETT (Rev. W. H.) Indian Tribes of Guiana 18/ 8° Bell [52] 68

,, Legends and Myths of Indians of British Guiana 12/6 8° Wells Gardner 80

IM THURN, E. F. Among Indians of Guiana ; ill. [chfly. anthropological] 18/ 8° Paul 83

**Haidas :** SWAN (J. G.) Haida Indns. of Qu. Charlotte's Islds. *o.p.* 8° 76

**Hidatsas :** MATTHEWS (Washn.) Ethnogr. and Philology of Hitatsa Indians $6 8° Govt. Prg. Off., *Washington* 77

**Hudson River Tribes :** RUTTENBER (E. M.) Indian Tribes of Hudson's River *o.p.* [*pb.* $3·50] 8° Munsell, *N.Y.* 72

**Iroquois** —*v. also* **B** § 35 (HALES, MORGAN)

BEAUCHAMP, W. M. Hist. of New York Iroquois (' the Six Nations ') 75 c. 8° N.Y. State Educ., *N.Y.* 05

SCHOOLCRAFT, H. R. —*in his* Notes, *ut sup.* [1846]

**Klamaths :** GATSCHET (D. S.) Klamath Indians of S. W. Oregon 90

MILLER, J. Life among the Modocs *o.p.* [*pb.* 14/] 8° Bentley 73

**Lenguas :**

GRUBB (W. B.) An Unknown People in an Unkn. Ld. ; ill. 16/ *n.* 8° Seeley [11] 11
A valuable and interestg. acc. of the Lengua Indian of the Paraguayan Chaco.

**Mayas :** BRINTON (D. G. ; ed.) Chronicles of the Mayas—*ut* **B** § 35

LE PLONGEON, Alice D. Sacred Mysteries of Mayas and Quiches $2·50 8° *New York* 81

PARRY, F. Sacred Maya Stone 8° 93

SALISBURY, S. The Mayas 8° 77

TOZZER, A. M. Compar. Study of Mayas and Lacandones ; ill. $1·25 *n.* 8° Macmillan, *N.Y.* 07

**Mexicans :** STARR (Prf. Fredk.) The Indians of Southern Mexico obl 4° Author, *Chicago* 99
An album of 141 pl. illustrating the people of 13 tribes; w. 32 pages of explanatory text. Results of 9 journeys.

,, Physical Characters of Indns. of S. Mexico; 31 ill. 75 c. *n.* 4° Univ. Press, *Chicago* 02

,, In Indian Mexico; ill. $5 8° Forbes, *Chicago* 08
Narr. of 'travel and labour' in conn. w. expedns. 1896–1901 made to investigate the types of Mexican Indians.

TYLOR, Dr E. B. Anahuac: Mexico & Mexicans, anc. & mod.; ill. *o.p.* [*pb.* 12/] 8° Longman 61

*Aztecs :* BIART (L.) The Aztecs: history, manners, customs [tr.] $2 8° McClurg, *Chicago* [87]

HONEYMAN, A. Van D. The Aztecs *subscr.* $35 *n.* 4° Honeyman, Plainfield, *N.J.*

*Yncas (Incas) :* de GAMBOA (Cpt. P. S.) Hist. of Incas, tr. & ed. Sir C. R. Markham; w. Suppl. 8° Hakluyt Soc. [1572] 08
The text was first ed. Dr R. PEITSCHMANN, w. Introd. and notes (Wissensch. Gesellsch., *Göttingen*, 1906): here tr. 'Without doubt the most authentic hist. of the Incas wh. has yet appeared' (*Markham*). 2 maps and 10 ill. The *Suppl.* conts. tr. of *Narrative of Vice-Regal Embassy to Vilcabambal* [1571] *and of Executn. of the Inca Tupac Amaru* [Dec. 1571], by Friar Gabr. de OVIEDO, 1573.

MARKHAM, C. R. The Incas of Peru; 2 maps and 12 pl. 10/6 *n.* s 8° Smith & Elder 10

,, [ed.] Narratives of Rites and Laws of Yncas—*ut* **B** § 35

de la VEGA, G. [ed.] Royal Commentaries of Yncas, tr. C. R. Markham, 2 vols.—*ut* **B** § 35

**Micmacs :** LECLERCQ, Chr. [17 cent.] New Relatn. of Gaspesia, ed. w. tr. Prf. W. F. Ganong—*ut* **F** § 67

MILLAIS, J. G. —*in his* Newfoundland, *ut* **E** § 55, *s.v.* Newfoundland

**Modocs** —*v.* Klamaths, *sup.*

**Mohawks :** REID (W. Max) The Mohawk Valley—*ut* **B** § 35

WALWORTH, Ellen H. Life & Times of Kateri Tekakwitha [1656–80] $1·25 8° Paul, *Buffalo, N.Y.* 91

**Moquis :** BOURKE (Cpt. J. C.) Snake Dance of the Moquis of Arizona; ill.—*ut* **B** § 35
Important for native Indian institutions.

**Mosquitos :** BELL (C. N.) Tangweera: life and advs. am. gentle savages; ill. 16/ 8° Arnold 99

**Ojibways :** COPWAY (G.) Hist. of Ojibway Nation; ill. [by Chief of Ojibways] $1 12° *Boston* 51

**Omahas :** DORSEY (J. O.) Omaha and Ponka Letters c 8° 91

**Oneidas :** BLOOMFIELD (J. K.) The Oneidas; ill. [historical] $2·25 *n.* 8° Alden Bros., *N.Y.* 08

**Ottaways :** 'BLACKBIRD (Andr. J.)' Hist. of Ottawa & Chippewa Indians $1 16° Prtg. Ho., *Ypsilanti* 87
Author's native name is MACK-E-TE-BE-NESSY; he is son of Ottaway Chief, MACK-A-DE-PE-NESSY.

**Pennsylvanian Tribes :** HECKEWELDER (J.) The Indns. of Pennsylv. $3·50 8° Lippincott, *Phila.* [22] 76

**Poncas :** DORSEY (J. O.) Omaha and Ponka Letters—*ut sup.*, *s.v.* Omaha

ZYLYFF Ponca Chiefs 50 c. 16° *Boston*

**Pueblos :** EICKEMEYER (C. + Lilian W.) Among the Pueblo Indians; ill. $1·75 8° Merriam, *N.Y.* 95

FYNN, A. J. The American Indian as a Product of Environment; ill. [w. spec. ref. to Pueblos] $1·50 *n.* 12° Little & Brown, *Boston* 07

PEET, S. D. —*in his* Prehistoric America, vol. iii., *ut* **G** § 11

**Sioux** —*v. also* Crees, *sup.*

CATLIN, Geo. O-Kee-pa *o.p.* [*pb.* 14/] 8° Trübner 67

COLLIER, Price Mr Picket Pin and his Friends; ill. 3/6 c 8° Sonnenschein 94
$1 Dutton, *N.Y.* A lively acc. of a hunting-trip am. Sioux, w. descrn. of life, habits, customs, etc.

DORSEY, J. O. —*in his* Omaha and Ponka Letters, *ut sup.*, *s.v.* Omahas

FINERTY, J. F. War-Path and Bivouac: conquest of Sioux; ill. $2 8° Finerty, *Chicago* 90

MOONEY, J. Siouan Tribes of the East *o.p.* 8° 94

POOLE, D. C. Among the Sioux of Dakota $1·25 12° Van Nostrand, *N.Y.* 81

**Wampanoags :** MILLER (W.) Notes concerning Wampanoag Indians $1 12° *Providence*

**Yncas** —*v.* Mexicans, *sup.*

## 54 : AMERICA : DISCOVERY, CONQUEST, EARLY VOYAGES

**Bibliography** —*v. also* **E** § 52

COLE, G. W. Catalogue of Bks. rel. to Discov. and Early Hist. of N. & S. Amer., vol. i–v: 1482–1884 $35 4° Dodd & Mead, *N.Y.*, *in prg.*
A catalogue of a portion of the library of E. Dwight CHURCH.

Facsimiles of MSS. in European Archives relating to America: 1773–83 Stevens & Brown

HARRISSE, H. Bibliotheca Americana Vetustissima *o.p.* i 8° *New York* 66
An accurate chronol. descrn. of wks. rel. to Amer. pub. 1492–1551; w. collatn. of ea. and alph. index at end. A *Supplement* was pub. at *Paris* in 1872 [w. 35/]: it contains ab. 200 addtl. wks.

,, Excerpta Columbina: bibliogr. de 400 pièces du 16e siècle non décrites jusq'ici 35 fr. r 8° *Paris* 87

WATSON, P. B. Bibliogr. of Pre-Columbian Discoveries of America—*app. to* Anderson, *inf.*

**Early Voyages and Accounts ; Lives, etc., of Discoverers :** *Collectively ; Series*

ARBER, E. [ed.] First Three English Books on America 21/ 4° Arber's Rep. 85
Chfly. trs., compilns., etc., made 1553–5 by Rich. EDEN fr. wks. of PIETRO MARTIRE [PETER MARTYR, 1455–1526], Seb. MÜNSTER [1489–1552], and Seb. CABOT [1474–1557].

GEORGES SOCIETY : Publications Gorges Soc., *in prg.*
BANKS, (Dr C. E.) [ed.] *New England's Vindication* $2
BAXTER (J. P.) *George Cleeve of Casco Bay* $5
LEVITT (Cpt. Chr.) *Voyage into New England in* 1623, ed. J. P. BAXTER
ROSIER, *Reln. of Waymouth's Voyage*, ed. Dr H. S. BURRAGE $3·50
THAYER (H. O.) *The Sagadhoc Colony* [Lambeth MS.] $4

HAKLUYT, Rich. [ed.] —*in his* Principal Navigations, 12 vols., *ut* **E** § 5

Original Narratives of East American History ; maps, etc. ea. $3 *n.* c 8° Scribner, *N.Y.* 07 *sqq.*, *in prg.*
BURRAGE (Dr H. S.) [ed.] *Early Engl. and Fch. Voys.* [1534–1608] [chfly. fr. HAKLUYT]
de CHAMPLAIN (S.) *Voyages* : 1604–18, ed. W. L. GRANT [*ut* **E** § 55]
HODGE (F. W.) + LEWIS (T. H.) [eds.] *Spanish Explorers in Southern U.S.* : 1528–43
OLSON (J. E.) + BOURNE (E. G.) [eds.] *Voys. of Northmen, Columbus Cabot* [985–1503] [*ut* **E** § 54]
TYLER (L. G.) [ed.] *Narrs. of Early Virginia* [*ut* **E** § 57]

*Individually*

BENZONI, Girolamo Travels in America, tr. & ed. Adm. W. H. Smyth [1542–56] 8° Hakluyt Soc. 57

BOONE, Dan. [1734–1820]
Bruce, H. A. Daniel Boone & the Wilderness Road ; ill. $1·50 *n.* (6/6 *n.*) i 8° Macmillan 10
Story of the pathfinder of the Wilderness Road, wh. led fr. the Virginian valleys over the Cumberland highlands to the rich pastures of Kentucky ; graphically and simply told.

BRERETON, J. Discoverie of North Part of Virginia—*ut* **E** § 57, *s.v.* Virginia

CABOT, Jno. [15 cent.] and Sebastian [son ; 1474–1557]
Beazley, C. R. John and Sebastian Cabot [Builders of Greater Britain] 5/ c 8° Unwin 98
$1·50 Longman, *N.Y.* A good matter-of-fact summary of what is known. Bibliography.
Harrisse, Hy. John Cabot & Sebastian, his Son ; maps & ill. 30/ *n.* 8° Stevens & Brown 96
A maritime hist. of Engl. und. Tudors, 1496–1537—researchful and accurate ; based wholly on orig. documts.
„ Discovery of North America by John Cabot 1/ *n.* c 8° Stevens & Brown [ ] 97
„ Did Cabot Return fr. his Second Voyage ? [affirm. reply] Stevens & Brown 98
Nicholls, J. F. Life of Sebastian Cabot ; map and port. *o.p.* [*pb.* 7/6] c 8° Low 69
Ober, Fredk. A. John and Sebastian Cabot ; ill. $1 *n.* 12° Harper, *N.Y.* 08
Thatcher, J. B. The Cabotian Discovery
Weare, G. E. Cabot's Discovery of America ; maps and ill. $3·50 8° Lippincott, *Phila.* 97
The facts of CABOT's discovery, preceded by the reln. of the legends and folklore conc. the Atlantic islands. The 12 ill. incl. TOSCANELLI's map of 1474, BEHAIM's globe of 1492, the *Mappa Mundi*, and other early maps.
Winship, G. P. Cabot Bibliography 18/ 8° H. Stevens 00
With an introductory essay on the careers of the CABOTS.

COLUMBUS, Christopher [c. 1445–1506]
*Bibliography :* Brit. Mus. : Excerpts fr. Gen. Catalogue : Columbus *o.p.* [*pb.* 6*d.*] 4° British Museum
„ Letter to Luis de Sant Angel, 15 Feb.–14 Mar., 1493 21/ s 4° Ellis & Elvey 91
Facs. reprodn. of the l'r announcg. discovery of the New World. In Spanish ; w. Engl. tr. and Introd.
„ First Letter on Discovery of America 50 c. s 4° Lennox Lib., *N.Y.* [1493] 93
1/8 *n.* Quaritch. Reduced facs. of Span. edn. of *Barcelona* 1493 ; w. Engl. tr. The unique original is now in the Lennox Lib., New York.
„ Latin Letter announcing Discovery of America 1/3 *n.* s 4° Quaritch [1493] 93
Facsimile of the Latin edn. of *Rome* 1493 ; w. Engl. tr. and Introduction.
„ Jl. dur. his First Voyage, tr. C. R. Markham 8° Hakluyt Soc. 93
Excellently ed., w. valuable Introd. and notes. Conts. also documts. rel. to voys. of the CABOTS and CORTE-REAL.
„ Select Letters, ed. and tr. R. H. Major 8° Hakluyt Society [47] 70
Includes other original documts. rel. to COLUMBUS's four voyages.
„ Columbus' Own Book of Privileges, ed. B. F. Stevens 105/ *n.* f° B. F. Stevens [1502] 93
Photogr. facs. of MS. in For. Off. in Paris (now first pubd.). Conts. C's own bk. of patents, privileges, concessions, granted him by FERD. and ISAB., w. expanded tr. G. F. BARWICK and hist. Introd. H. HARRISSE. App. of 48 documts.
Adams, Prf. C. K. Christopher Columbus : his life and work $1 c 8° Dodd & Mead, *N.Y.* 92
[Makers of America.] A careful estimate of character and wk. of COLUMBUS, derived fr. latest research.
de Belloy, Marq. Chr. Columbus & Disc. of New World ; 8 pl. & 51 ill. $3 8° Gebbie, *Phila.* [77] 89
Elton, Chas. The Career of Columbus ; map 10/6 ($1·25) 8° Cassell 92
Scholarly, interesting, and very readable, founded on most recent Am. and Ital. liter. on subj. Deals mainly with explorer's character.
Harrisse, Hy. Christophe Colomb, 2 vols. ; ill. 100 fr. 8° Leroux, *Paris*
From unpublished documents in the archives of Genoa, Madrid, etc.
Helps, Sir Arth. Life of Columbus [Bohn's Lib. ; $1 *n.* Macm., *N.Y.*] 3/6 c 8° Bell [69] 96
Irving, Washington Life & Voyages of Christopher Columbus, 3 v. ea. $1·25 (6/) c 8° Putnam [28]
„ The same, 2 vols. [Bohn's Lib. ; ea. $1 *n.* Macm., *N.Y.*] ea. 3/6 c 8° Bell [28] 82
„ The Companions of Columbus, 2 vols. ea. $1·25 (6/) c 8° Putnam [31]
„ Christopher Columbus and his Companions ; ill. $1·50 (5/) c 8° Putnam 98
[Heroes of the Nations Ser.] Condensed fr. the larger wk., ed. Evelyn ABBOTT.
Kayserling, Dr M. Christopher Columbus and the Participation of the Jews in the Spanish and Portuguese Discoveries [tr.] 5/ ($1·25) c 8° Longman 94
Very little ab. COLUMBUS, and not much ab. Luis de SANTANGEL, who advanced the money for fitting out the ships wh. sailed fr. Palos. The bk. is mainly devoted to acc. of suffergs. of Jews und. Inquisitn.—a story a good deal better told by MOCATTA [*ut* **F** § 7].

Knight, Rev. A. G. [S.-J.] Life of Christopher Columbus 6/ c 8° Burns & Oates 77
75 c. Cath. Pub. Co., *N.Y.* A scholarly book showing his personal character and lofty piety.

Markham, [Sir] C. R. Christopher Columbus ; maps and ill. [Great Explorers] 3/6 c 8° Philip 92
$1·25 Dodd & Mead, *N.Y.* A clear and judicious narr., by a Columbus enthusiast, hg. all elements of lasting popularity in it.

Monteiro, Mariana [R.-C.] Christopher Columbus : life, labours, discovs. [Heroes of Cross] 3/6 *n.* c 8° Hodges 93

Saunders, Fredk. Story of Discovery of New World by Columbus $1 c 8° Whittaker, *N.Y.* 92
3/6 Stock. A pleasant account, by the then Librarian of the Astor Library, *N.Y.* Maps, facss., and ill.

Tarducci, Prf. Fr. Life of Columbus, aft. latest documts. [tr.], 2 vols. ; pl. $2 8° Brownson, *Detroit* 90

Thatcher, J. B. Chr. Columbus : life, wk., remains, 3 vols. ; ill. ea. $9 *n.* (36/ *n.*) r 8° Putnam 03–4
A sumptuous bk., formg. a libr. of Columbian literature, and incl. 41 ports. of COLUMBUS, facss. of his handwrg., etc. W. ab. 300 pl. No single wk. of equal importance has been pubd. on the subject, save the unconnected pprs. in the *Raccolta* issued by Ital. Govt. in 14 vols., magnificently ill. (1893 *sqq.*, c. 500 fr.).

Vignaud, H. Toscanelli and Columbus 10/6 *n.* 8° Sands 02
A controversial book, attempting to overthrow received opinions as to the object of COLUMBUS' voyage.

Winsor, Justin Columbus : examination of condns. under wh. Western Continent was discovered to Europe $4 8° Houghton, *Boston* 92
21/ Low. The personal life, tellg. truth for first time ab. the gt. discoverer's weakness of character and temper, whilst doing full justice to his strength and enthusiasm.

Young, Filson Chr. Columbus and New World of his Discovery, 2 v. 25/ *n.* 8° Richards 06
Presents in picturesque form the mass of new material recently unearthed.

DOMINIGUEZ, Luis L. [ed.] The Conquest of La Plata : 1535–55 8° Hakluyt Soc. 91
Conts. SCHMIDT'S *Voyage to Rivers La Plata and Paraguai* and Alvar Nunez Cabeza de VACA'S *Commentaries.*

DRAKE, Sir Fcs. [1545–96]

Barrow, Sir Jno. Life, Voyages, & Exploits of Sir Francis Drake *o.p.* [*pb.* 2/] 12° Murray [43] 61

Christy, Miller The Silver Map of the World 12/6 *n.* Stevens & Styles 00
A monograph arguing th. the medallion so named was struck in commem. of DRAKE'S voyage.

Corbett, Julian Sir Francis Drake [English Men of Action] 2/6 (60 c.) c 8° Macmillan 91

Froude, J. A. Drake's Voyage round the World—*in his* English Seamen of xvi Century, *ut* **F** § 30

HARRIOT, Thos. [1560–1621] Narrative of First Plantation of Virginia ; ill. s 4° Quaritch [1588–90] 93
Repr. of orig. edn., w. ill. fr. DE BRY. HARRIOT accomp. RALEIGH to Virginia in 1584.

HENNEPIN, F'r L. New Discovery of a Vast Country in America, ed. Dr R. G. Thwaites, 2 vols. $6 *n.* sq 8° McClurg, *Chicago* [1698] 03
[Libr. Reprs. of Americana.] Exact repr. of 2nd edn. (1698), w. facss. of title-pp., maps, and ill., Introd. and notes.

HUDSON, Hy. [d. 1611] —*v.* **E** § 55, *s.v.* Hudson Bay Territory

de LAHONTAN, Bar. New Voyages to America, ed. Dr R. G. Thwaites, 2 vols. $7·50 *n.* sq 8° McClurg, *Chicago* [1703] 05
[Libr. Reprs. of Americana.] Exact repr. of Engl. edn. of 1703, w. facss. of orig. title-pp., maps, and ill., Introd. and notes.

LEWIS (Cpt. Meriwether ; 1774–1809) *and* CLARK (Cpt. Wm. ; 1770–1838) Original Jls. of the Lewis and Clark Expedn., ed. R. G. Thwaites, 7 vols. and Atl. ; maps & ports. $60 *n.* 8° Dodd & Mead 05
Printed fr. the orig. MS. in Lib. of Amer. Philosoph. Soc., and other orig. MSS. Introd., notes, and index.

" Hist. of Expedn. of Lewis and Clark, ed. Prf. E. P. Coues, 4 vols. $12·50 *n.* 8° Clarke, *Cincinnati* [14]
50/ *n.* H. Stevens & Son. The offic. narr. of first white men who crossed continent of N.-Am. fr. Mississippi, thence acr. Rockies and down Columbia river to Pacific Ocean ; performed in 1804–5–6. A standard and authoritative wk. of endurg. value and gt. accuracy. W. copious notes, bibliogr. and biogr. prefaces, index, route-map, ports., and ill.

" The same, ed. Dr J. K. Hosmer, 2 vols. $5 *n.* sq 8° McClurg, *Chicago* [14] 02
[Libr. Reprs. of Americana.] Repr. of 1814 edn., w. facs. maps, ports., Introd., and index.

Brooks, Noah First Across the Continent [Lewis & Clark] $1·50 *n.* c 8° Scribner, *N.Y.* 01

Dye, Eva E. The Conquest ; ill. $1·50 c 8° McClurg, *Chicago* 02
Biographies of LEWIS and CLARK and an account of their expedition.

Gass, Journal of Lewis & Clark Expedn., ed. Dr J. K. Hosmer $3·50 *n.* sq 8° McClurg, *Chicago* [11]
[Libr. Reprs. of Americana.] Repr. of 1811 edn., w. facss. of orig. ill., and an Introd.

McMaster, Prf. J. B. Hist. of Expedn. of Lewis and Clark, 3 vols. 10/6 *n.* c 8° Nutt 05

PIKE, Z. M. [1779–1813] Expedn. to the Mississippi Headwaters, etc., ed. Prf. E. P. Coues, 3 vols. [expedn. of 1805–6–7] $10 *n.* 8° F. P. Harper, *N.Y.* 99

SMITH, Cpt. Jno. [1579–1631]—*v.* **E** § 57, *s.v.* Virginia

DE SOTO, Hernando

Daly, D. [ed. and tr.] The Adventures of Roger L'Estrange 2/6 c 8° Sonnenschein [96] 98
An autobiographical account of the adventures of one of DE SOTO'S followers. Introd. by H. M. STANLEY.

Graham, R. B. Cunningham Hernando de Soto 6/ c 8° Heinemann
A plain, well-written life, fr. contemp. sources ; w. an acc. of Gonçalo SILVESTRE.

King, Grace De Soto and his Men in Land of Florida 50 c. *n.* (6/) c 8° Macmillan 98

VESPUCCI, Amerigo [1451–1512] Letters and other Documts. illg. his Career, tr. Sir C. R. Markham ; w. Introd. and notes 8° Hakluyt Soc. 91
Edr. says : ' The evidence agst. VESPUCCI is cumulative and quite conclusive. His first voyage is a fabrication. He committed a fraud w. a dishonest purpose ' (Introd.).

VESPUCCI, Amerigo [1451–1512] Lettere delle Isole novamente trovate : fasc. repr. 105/ s 4° Quaritch [ ] 84

,, The same, tr. ; w. pref. notes 52/6 s 4° Quaritch 84

,, Account of First Four Voyages : facs. ; w. tr. 3/ *n.* s 4° Quaritch [1505] 93

Harrisse, Hy. Americus Vespuccius 0 4° Stevens & Brown 95
The bibliogr. and hist. surv. shows the part taken by merchant princes of Augsburg and Nuremburg in celebrated expedn. of Francesco d'ALMEIDA to India in 1505, and traces orig. of alleged Vespuccian *Reyse van Lissabone* of 1508 to its real source.

Thatcher, Jno. Boyd —*in his* The Continent of America, *ut inf.*
Incls. a new and elaborate attempt to whitewash VESPUCCI. Does not deal w. MARKHAM'S *Introd.* (*sup.*).

WAFER, Lionel New Voyage and Descrn. of Isthmus of Amer., ed. G. P. Winship ; ill. $3 8° Burrows, *Cleveld.* 02

**Buccaneers :** BURNEY (Cpt. Jas.) Hist. of Buccaneers of Amer. ; maps 4/6 *n.* 8° Sonnenschein [16] 91
$2 Macmillan, *N.Y.* An unvarnished hist. of doings of Engl., Dutch and Fch. buccaneers in W. Indies, Span. Main and Pacific.

*ESQUEMELING, Jno. Hist. of Buccaneers of Amer., ed. H. Powell ; maps & pl. 15/ r 8° Sonnenschein [1684–5] 93
$5 Scribner, *N.Y.* Repr. of whole wk., incls. scarce *Fourth Pt.*, wh. conts. Basil RINGROSE'S acc. [1685]. A most graphic hist. of the 'most remarkable assaults committed of late yrs. upon Coast of W. Indies by Buccaneers of Jamaica and Tortuga, both Engl. and Fch.', by one of buccaneers himself, eye-witness of and sharer in the exploits.

Lang, Andr. —*essay on* Esquemeling's 'Hist. of Bucc'rs', *in his* Essays in Little, *ut* **E** § 17

HARING, C. H. The Buccaneers in West Indies in Sixteenth Century 10/6 *n.* 8° Methuen 10

MASEFIELD, Jno. On the Spanish Main ; ill. [$3·50 Macm., *N.Y.*] 10/6 *n.* 8° Methuen 06
English forays on Isthmus of Darien, w. descrn. of the buccaneers and old-time ships and sailors.

PYLE, Howard [ed.] The Buccaneers and Marooners of America ; ill. 3/6 c 8° Unwin 91
$1·50 Macmillan, *N.Y.* [Advent. Ser.] Conts. selns. fr. ESQUEMELING [tr.], and fr. JOHNSON'S *Hist. of Pyrates of New Providence* ; w. Introd.

STOCKTON, F. R. Buccaneers and Pirates of Our Coasts $1·50 (6/) c 8° Macmillan 98
A good popular account, down to Captain KIDD.

**English Colonization of America**—*v.* **F** § 67

**Modern Writers :** BIGGAR (H. P.) Early Trading Companies of New France—*ut* **D** § 117* [1497–1632]

BROWN, Alex. Genesis of the United States, 2 vols. ; map $15 *n.* 8° Houghton, *Boston* 90
73/6 Heinemann. Narr. of movemt. in Engl. 1605–1616 wh. resulted in plantation of N. America by Englishmen.

DELLENBAUGH, F. S. Breaking the Wilderness ; maps $3·50 (15/ *n.*) 8° Putnam 05
A very readable, compreh. survey of the hist. of the conquest of the Far West (w. details of the careers of pioneers) fr. the day when de VEGA planted his foot on the virgin soil to the day when Rev. Dr TODD 'asked a blessing' on the last-driven spike of the completed railroad.

EGGLESTON, Edw. The Beginnings of a Nation $1·50 12° Appleton, *N.Y.* 96
Hist. of source and rise of earliest Engl. settlemts. in Amer., w. spec. ref. to life and char. of people.

FISKE, Jno. Discovery of America, 2 vols. ; maps and ill. $4 c 8° Houghton, *Boston* 92
18/ Macmillan. A compreh. surv. of aborig. Amer. in light of researches of POWELL, BANDELIER and others, its spec. service consistg. in rendg. clear by what slow degrees and by the unconscious help of how many persons existce. of a New World was brot. to knowl. of those who inhabd. the Old.

,, Discovery & Colonization of North America ; map & ill. $1·25 12° Ginn, *Boston* 05

,, —*in* J. H. Wright [ed.] History of All Nations, vols. xxi.–xxii, *ut* **F** § 1

FOWLER, Maj. Jac. Journal of Adventure from Arkansas, etc. $3 *n.* 8° F. P. Harper, *N.Y.* 99
First printed edn. of a journey in 1821–2 : Kansas, Colorado, New Mexico, etc.

HANNA, Chas. A. The Wilderness Trail, 2 vols. ; maps and ill. 8° Putnam 11
A monumental wk. on the ventures and adventures of the old Pennsylv. traders on the Allegheny Path.

HARRISSE, Hy. Discovery of North America, 2 vols. ; 23 maps & pl. 105/ r 4° H. Stevens & Sons 92
A v. import. contribn. to compar. cartography, of immense industry and scope, but not always wholly trustworthy, and rather dogmatic. Forms a sort of cartograph. complemt. to his *Bibl. Amer. Vetust.* and its Supplemts. [*ut sup.*].

,, Diplomatic History of America ; its 1st Chapter [1452–94] $2·50 *n.* c 8° Dodd & Mead, *N.Y.* 97

HELPS, Sir Arth. Spanish Conquest in Amer., ed. M. Oppenheim, 4 v. ea. ($1·50) c 8° Lane [55–61] 00–3

MARCEL, G. [ed.] Réprodn. de Cartes et de Globes rel. à l'Am. d. 16–18 Siècle 100 fr. f° Leroux, *Paris* 93

MILTON (Visc.) + CHEADLE (Dr) The North-West Passage by Land ; 12 ill. 2/ c 8° Cassell 01

MULHALL, Marion McM. Explorers in New World bef. and aft. Columbus 6/6 *n.* ($2·25 *n.*) c 8° Longman 09

NORDENSKIÖLD, Bar. A. E. [ed.] Facs. Atlas to Early Hist. of Cartography [tr.] 150/ *n.* atl. f° *priv. prin.* 89
A systematic colln. of reprodns. of import. maps of 15 and 16 cents. : of consid. value for hist. of discov. of Amer. and Australia.

PARKMAN, F. Works—*ut* **F** § 67

PARRISH, Randall The Great Plains ; ill. $1·75 *n.* c 8° McClurg, *Chicago* 07
'The romance of Western American explorn., warfare, and settlement.'

*PAYNE, E. J. History of New World called America, 2 vols., i–ii, Pt. i. 32/ ($6·50) 8° Clar. Press 92–9
i : *Discovery*, 18/ ($3·50) ; ii, Pt. i : *Aboriginal America*, Pt. i, 14/ ($3). Based on Span. authorities.

SCAIFE, W. B. America, its Geographical History—*ut* **E** § 52

STEVENS, Hy. Hist. & Geogr. Notes on Earliest Discovs. of Amer. *o.p.* 8° *Newhaven, U.S.* 69
Period 1453–1530. Conts. photo.-lith. facsimiles of 16 of earliest known maps of America.

THATCHER, Jno. Boyd The Continent of America : discovery and baptism $25 *n.* 4° Benjamin, *N.Y.* 96
(*V. sup., s.v.* Vespucci.) Naming of the Continent, landings of COLUMBUS and VESPUCCI, etc. : not much th. is new. Maps and ill.

WEISE, A. J. Hist. of Discoveries of Amer., to 1525 ; facss. of 12 rare maps $4·50 8° Putnam, *N.Y.* 84

WINSOR, Justin [ed.] —*in his* Histor. and Critical Hist. of America, vols. ii–iv, *ut* **F** § 66
ii : *Span. Discovs. and Conq. of Am.* ; iii : *Engl. Discovs. and Settlemts. in Am.* ; iv : *Fch. Discovs. and Settlemts. in Am.*

WINSOR, Justin [ed.] Cartier to Frontenac; contemp. cartograph. ill. $4 8° Houghton, *Boston* 94
Study of geogr. discov. in interior of N. Am. in its histor. relns.: 1534-1700, w. ch. *Fr. Columbus to Cartier*. Substantially an abridgmt. of the matter cont. in bk. above.

,, The Mississippi Basin $4 8° Houghton, *Boston* 95
The struggle for Amer. betw. Engl. and France. Continues the story where the above bk. left it.

**Discovery by Chinese:** LELAND (C. G.) Fu-Sang: discovery of America by Chinese Buddhist Priests in Fifth Cent. $1·75 c 8° Bouton, *N.Y.* 75

**Discovery by Norsemen:** ANDERSON (R. B.) Amer. not Discov. by Columbus $1 12° Griggs, *Chicago* [74] 83
Claims discovery for the Norsemen in 10th cent. Full bibliography by P. B. WATSON.

BEAMISH, N. L. Discovery of America by Northmen in Tenth Century *o.p.* [*pb.* 10/] 8° Boone 41

BROWN, Marie E. Icelandic Discoveries of America [*v.* Shipley, *inf.*, note] *o.p.* [*pb.* 7/6] c 8° Trübner 87

DE COSTA, Dr B. F. [tr.] Pre-Columbian Discovery of America $3 8° Munsell, *Albany, N.Y.* [68] 89
Reputed discovery by Norsemen. Tr. fr. Icelandic sagas; with notes and General Introduction.

FISCHER, Jos. [S.-J.] Discoveries of the Norsemen in Am. [tr.] [favourable] $2 *n.* 8° Herder, *St Louis* 03

NEUKOMM, E. The Rulers of the Sea; ill. $1·50 c 8° Estes, *Boston* 96
6/ Low. The Norsemen in America from the 10th until the 15th century.

OLSON (J. E.) + BOURNE (E. G.) [eds.] Voyages of Northmen, Columbus, and Cabot [A.D. 985-1503] [Orig. Narrs. of Early Am. Hist.] $3 *n.* 8° Scribner, *N.Y.* 10

RAFN, C. C. Antiquitates Americanæ; maps & pl. *o.p.* [*w.* 40/] i 4° R. Soc. of North. Ant. 45
The authentic documents: to prove the pre-Columbian discovery of America by Northmen.

REEVES, Arth. M. [ed.] The Finding of Wineland the Good 50/ ($11) 4° Clar. Press 96
Hist. of Icelandic discov. of Amer. Ed. and tr. fr. earliest records, w. phototype pl. of the vellum MSS. of the sagas.

SHIPLEY, J. B. + Marie E. The English Re-discovery and Colonisation of America 4/ f 8° Stock 91
Contends th. the orig. discoverer was Leif ERICKSON, a bold Icelander, and the date A.D. 1000, i.e. nearly 500 yrs. bef. Columbus' voyage. Mrs SHIPLEY wrote on this vexed question previously, und. her maiden name BROWN.

SMITH, J. Toulmin Discovery of America by Northmen in Tenth Century *o.p.* [*pb.* 6/] 12° Orr [39] 42

**Discovery by Welsh:** BOWEN (B. F.) America Discovered by Welsh in 1170 $1·25 16° *Philadelphia* 76

DANE, Joan Prince Madog, Welshman who disc. Amer., 1170; 3 col. pl. 6/ *n.* p 8° Stock 09
Claims discov. for MADOG on basis of records in Abbeys of Strata Florida and Conway.

STEPHENS, Thos. Madoc: essay on discov. of Amer. *o.p.* [*pb.* 7/6] 8° Longman 93
A learned and laborious essay sent in for Eisteddfod competn. of 1858. Rejecting the evid. as wholly insuffic. to estab. th. MADOC ever reached shores of Mexico, the essay was itself rejected; and is here pubd. for first time, ed. Llywarch REYNOLDS.

**Canada** —*v.* **E** § 55

## 55: DOMINION OF CANADA; NEWFOUNDLAND

**Bibliography:** HARRISSE (Hy.) Notes pour Servir à l'Hist., la Bibliogr. et la Cartogr. d. l. Nouvelle France 30 fr. 8° Welter, *Paris* 72

Review of Historic Pubns. rel. to Canada, vols. i-xv [1910] ea. $1·50 8° Morang, *Toronto* 96-11 *in prg.*

**Atlases:** *WHITE (Jas.) Atlas of Canada 22/6 Dept. of Interior, *Ottawa* 06
Maps, isothermal charts, town-plans, diagrs. of populn., agric., commerce, rys., fisheries, etc.

HURLBERT, J. B. Physical Atlas of Canada f° *Ottawa*

**Geographical Textbooks**

DAWSON, Dr S. E. Canada and Newfoundland; 18 maps & 90 ill. 15/ c 8° Stanford [ ] 97
[Stanford's Compendium of Geogr.] A well-proportioned, trustworthy, and useful general handbook.

GRESWELL, Rev. Wm. P. Geography of Dominion of Canada and Newfoundland; 10 maps 6/ ($1·50) c 8° Clar. Press 91
Geography in its wider sense—incl. populn., trade, industries, etc. Issd. under auspices of Roy. Colon. Institute.

SELWYN (A. R. C.) + DAWSON (S. E.) Physical Geography and Geology of Canada [pubn. of Can. Survey] 8° *Montreal*

**Discovery; Colonization; Early Travel**—*v. also* **F** § 67 (esp. PARKMAN)

BIGGAR, H. P. Early Trading Companies of New France—*ut* **D** § 117*

BURY, Visc. Exodus of Western Nations, 2 vols. *o.p.* [*pb.* 32/] 8° Bentley 65
A standard history of the English colonization of Virginia and of Canada.

'CANUCK' (A) Pen-Picts. of Early Pioneer Life in Upper Canada 8° Briggs, *Toronto*

CHAMPLAIN SOC. Pubns.—*ut* **F** § 67

de CHAMPLAIN, S. Voyages, ed. W. L. Grant [1604-18] [Orig. Narrs.] $3 *n.* 8° Scribner, *N.Y.* 07

de CHARLEVOIX, P. F. X. Hist. and Gen. Descrn. of New Frce. [tr.], 6 vols.; ill. ea. $3 *n.* 8° F. P. Harper, *N.Y.* [1744] 02
Ed. and tr. by Dr J. G. SHEA. Gives the early annals of Maine, Vermont, New Hampshire, N.Y., etc.

COUES, Prf. Elliot P. New Light on Early Hist. of Greater Northwest, 3 v. $18 8° F. P. Harper, *N.Y.* 99
Hitherto unpubd. jls. of Alex. HENRY, fur-trader, and Dav. THOMSON, explorer, 1799-1814. The Red, Saskatchewan, and Columbia rivers. Maps.

FOXE (Cpt. Luke) *and* JAMES (Cpt. Thos.) Voyage to Hudson's Bay, ed. Miller Christy, 2 vols. [1631-2] 8° Hakluyt Soc. 94

HENRY, Alex. Travels and Adventures in Canada and the Indian Territories between 1760 & 1776, ed. J. Bain, w. notes; ill. $4 *n.* 8° Little & Brown, *Boston* [ ] 02

,, *and* THOMPSON (D.) MS. Journals, ed. Prf. E. P. Coues, 3 v. [1799–1814] 8° F. P. Harper, *N.Y.* 97

LUCAS, Fred. W. Appendiculæ Historicæ, *ut* **F** § 67
Of considerable value for the early geography and cartography of Canada.

WINSOR, Justin —*in his* Geographical Discovery in the Interior of America: 1534–1700, *ut* **E** § 54

,, [ed.] —*in his* Narrative and Critical History of America, *ut* **F** § 66

**Emigration:** COPPING (A. E.) The Golden Land; col. pl. 6/ 8° Hodder 11
A pourtrayal of modern emigrn.-condns.: wages, farming, labour, etc.

RITCHIE, J. Ewing To Canada with Emigrants: record of experience; ill. 7/6 c 8° Unwin 85

**Gazetteer:** LOVELL (J.) Gazetteer & Hist. of the Dominions, 9 v.; ill. £16 8° *Montreal* 88–94
Each vol. of vols. i.–viii. is devoted to one of the 8 Provinces; the ninth contains maps.

**Guide:** BAEDEKER (K.) [pb.] Dominion of Canada; maps, etc. [$1·50 *n.* Scribner, *N.Y.*] 6/ c 8° Unwin [94] 07

**Historical Geography:** LUCAS (Sir C. P.) Histor. Geogr. of Br. Cols., vol. v.: Canada, 4 Pts. c 8° Clar. Press 01–11
Pt. i (LUCAS), 6/ ($1·50); ii: *Hist. Geogr.* (Prf. H. E. EGERTON), 4/6 ($1·10); iii: *Geographical* (J. D. ROGERS), 4/6 ($1·10); iv: *Newfdld.* (ROGERS), 4/6 ($1·10).

**Recent Travel and Accounts** —*for* Sport in Canada, *v.* **I** § 147

ABERDEEN, C'ess. of Through Canada with a Kodak; ill. 3/6 8° W. H. White, *Edin.* 93

ARNOLD, Sir Edwin —*in his* Seas and Lands, *ut* **E** § 7

BINDLOSS, Harold A Wide Dominion 2/ c 8° Unwin 00
[Over-Seas Library.] Experiences of present-day settlers in Canada.

BRADLEY, A. G. Canada in the Twentieth Century 16/ *n.* 8° Constable 03
A good book, descriptive of the country and its life.

CLARK, Georgina B. Summer on the Canadian Prairie; ill. 6/ c 8° Arnold [10] 10
Acc. of 2 Engl. girls' visit to their bro' who, w. another Englishman, had taken up a grant of land in N.-W. and was trying to convert it into a farm. An excellent realistic descrn. of daily life.

DUFFERIN and AVA, March'ess My Canadian Journal; map and ill. 12/ c 8° Murray 91
Extrs. fr. letters wr. home 1872–8 when Earl of D. was Gov.-Gen. Picturesque, witty, and sincere, full of apprecn. of Can. people amd climate. Has a good deal to say ab. politicians, but nothing about politics.

GARRY, Nich. Diary (Quaritch) 02
Record of jy. 1821 fr. L'pl. to York Fort on Hudson Bay and back. Repr. fr. *Trns. R. Soc. of Canada.*

GORDON, D. M. Journey from Victoria to Winnipeg; ill. *o.p.* [*pb.* 8/6] p 8° Low 80

GRIFFITH, W. L. The Dominion of Canada [All Red Series] 7/6 *n.* 8° Pitman 11

HOGAN, J. F. The Sister Dominions [trav. in Canada & Australia] *o.p.* [*pb.* 3/6] c 8° Ward & Downey 95

KOHL, J. G. Travels in Canada & thro' N.Y. and Penn. [tr.], 2 v. *o.p.* [*pb.* 21/] p 8° Trübner 67

LUMSDEN, Jas. Thro' Canada in Harvest Time; maps and ill. 6/ c 8° Unwin 03
The travels, during 6 weeks, of a party of British journalists, chiefly in North-West.

McDOUGALL, Rev. Jno. Twenty Years of Frontier Life in Western Canada; 27 pl. [1842–62] $1 c 8° Briggs, *Toronto*

MARSHALL, C. The Canadian Dominion *o.p.* [*pb.* 12/6] 8° Longman 71

MONCK, Fces. E. O. [Hon. Mrs RICH] My Canadian Leaves [visit 1864–5] *o.p.* [*pb.* 15/] 8° Bentley 91

NICHOLSON, Byron The French-Canadian; ill. [sk. of character] c 8° Bryant Press, *Toronto* 02

'O'RELL, Max' [= Paul BLOUET]—*in his* A Frenchman in America, *ut* **E** § 56 [4 chs. on Canada]

OSBORNE, E. B. Greater Canada; map 3/6 c 8° Chatto 00
A short book on the past and future, the history and resources, of the North-West.

PARKIN, Dr G. R. [Canad.] The Great Dominion: studies of Canada—*ut* **D** § 143
A striking picture of Canada, especially of the Western Provinces, in 1895.

PAULI, F. G. Record of a Trip thro' Canada's Wilderness to L. Chibogamoo and L. Mistassini; maps and ill. [in 1906] $1 8° Pauli & Co., *N.Y.* 07

RAE, W. F. Columbia and Canada *o.p.* [*pb.* 14/] 8° Daldy 77

,, Newfoundland to Manitoba *o.p.* [*pb.* 6/] s 8° Low 81

,, Canada [For. Countries and Brit. Colonies] 3/6 12° Low 82

RALPH, Julian On Canada's Frontier; ill. $2·50 8° Harper, *N.Y.* 92
10/6 Osgood. Sketches of hist., sport and advent. of Indians, missionaries, fur-traders, and settlers.

ROPER, Edw. By Track and Trail: jy. thro' Canada; ill. *o.p.* [*pb.* 18/] 8° W. H. Allen 91
Unassuming, cheerful and readable; with a sprinkling of sport.

RUSSELL, W. H. Canada: its defences, condition, & resources *o.p.* [*pb.* 10/6] p 8° Bradbury 65

SILVER, A. P. Farm-cottage, Camp, & Canoe in Maritime Canada; 97 ill. 6/ l 8° Routledge 08
$2 *n.* Dutton, *N.Y.* Sportg. expedns., full of breath of mtn., forest, and plain. Introd. by L'd STRATHCONA.

SLADEN, Douglas [Canad.] On the Cars and Off; pl. and 80 ill. 7/6 m 8° Ward & Lock [95] 97
A picturesque, lively and well-informed acc. of jy. acr. Continent fr. Halifax (Nova Scotia) to Victoria (Vanc. Isld.).

STEWART, Basil — The Land of the Maple Leaf; pl. — 6/ c 8° Routledge 08
Devoted largely to politics and to criticism of Can. and Impl. policy, one obj. bg. to give acc. of actual condns. of life to expl. the disillusionmt. of immigrants.

VERNEDE, R. E. — A Fair Dominion; 12 col. pl. C. Cuneo — 7/6 *n.* 8° Paul 11

WHITE, S. E. — The Forest [cy. N. of L. Superior] $1·50 *n.* c 8° Outlook Co., *N.Y.* 03

WITHROW, W. H. — Our Own Country — $3 r 8° Briggs, *Toronto* 86

WRIGHT (Prf. R.) + MAVOR (Prf. J.) The Handbook of Canada; map — *o.p.* 8° 97
In its day a very accurate and full acc. of geography, history, industry, and trade.

YEIGH, Fk. [Canad.] — Thro' the Heart of Canada; 34 ill. — 10/6 *n.* 8° Unwin 10

YOUNG, Sir F. — A Pioneer of Imperial Federation in Canada — 7/6 c 8° G. Allen 02
A descrn. of author's tour in Canada in 1901; w. Appendix on Imper. Federation.

**North-West Canada; West Canada**

BEGG, Alex. — History of the North-West, 3 vols. — 50/ 8° Hunter, *Toronto* 94–5

BUTLER, Lt.-Gen. Sir Wm. — The Great Lone Land; map and 15 ill. — 5/ c 8° Burns & Oates [72] 73
Acc. of Red River Expedns. 1869–70, and subseq. travels and advents. in Manitoba country; and a winter-jy. acr. Saskatchewan Valley to Rockies.

„ — The Wild North Land — 5/ c 8° Burns & Oates 73
Story of a winter's jy. with dogs across Northern North America.

DRAKE, S. A. — Making of Great West; ill. [1512–1853] $1·50 c 8° Scribner, *N.Y.* 94

FERGUSON, Emily — Janey Canuck in the West — 6/ c 8° Cassell 10
Expercs. in Manitoba, Saskatchewan, and espec. among the curious alien settlers, the Dukhobors.

HAMILTON, J. C. — Prairie Province; ill. [L. Ontario to Winnipeg] 6/ c 8° *Toronto* 76

HANBURY, D. T. — Sport and Travel in Northland of Canada — 16/ *n.* m 8° Arnold 04
$4·50 *n.* Macmillan, *N.Y.* Appendix on geol., flora, commerce, and Esquimaux of N. Canada. Maps, ill., and col. pl.

JOHNSON, R. Byron — Very Far West — 2/ c 8° Low [72] 73

MACBETH, R. G. — Making of Canadian West; ill. — [pp. 230] c 8° Briggs, *Toronto* 98

MOORE, Chas. — The Northwest under Three Flags; ill. — $2·50 c 8° Harper, *N.Y.* 00
A full narrative from 1635 (when European exploration began) to 1796.

PIKE, Warburton — The Barren Ground of Northern Canada — 10/6 ($2) 8° Macmillan 92
Acc. of an expedn. (1891), full of peril and advent., in purs. of game thro' pt. of N. Can. hitherto unreached by Europeans.

„ — Through the Subarctic Forest; maps and ill. — 16/ 8° Arnold 96
Acc. of jy. of 4,000 m. fr. Fort Wrangel to Pelly Lakes and down Yukon river.

REMINGTON, Fredc. — Pony Tracks; ill. — $1·75 c 8° Harper, *N.Y.* 95
Advents. w. Gen. MILES in N.-W.: scoutg. expedns., ranch-life, bear-huntg., police-duty.

ROBERTS, Morley — *—in his* Western Avernus: toil and travel in further N. Amer., *ut* **E** § 52

SOMERSET, H. Somers — The Land of the Muskeg; ill.—*ut* **I** § 147

TYRRELL, J. W. — Across Sub-Arctics of Canada; map and ill. — $1·50 8° Briggs, *Toronto* 98
Acc. of jy. of 3,200 miles by canoe and snow-shoe thro' the barren lands, w. list of plants.

WHITNEY, Caspar — On Snow Shoes to the Barren Grounds; ill. — $3·50 8° Harper, *N.Y.* 96
16/ Osgood. Acc. of an expedn. of 2,800 m. after musk-oxen and wood-bison, not so successful as that descr. in PIKE's *Barren Grd.* (*sup.*). Chief value of bk. lies in insight it gives into lives of scattered mongrel Indian populn. more or less attached to Hudson Bay Co.

**History of Canada**—*v.* **F** § 67 **Irish in Canada**—*v.* **E** § 20

**Life and People; English Visits to and Impressions of Canada**—*v. also* **E** § 56

British America; 2 maps — [British Empire Ser.] 6/ 8° Paul 00
Lectures by distinguished men on various aspects of Canadian life and conditions.

COLBY, Prf. C. W. — Canadian Types of the Old Régime — [1608–98] 10/6 *n.* 8° Bell 09
A clear and authoritative view of period of French influence in Canada, wr. by a Canadian.

FRECHETTE, Louis — Christmas in French Canada; ill. — 6/ c 8° Murray 00

GREENOUGH, W. P. — Canadian Folk-life and Folk-lore — $1·50 c 8° Taylor, *N.Y.* 97
A pict. of the Fch.-Canadian as he lives and occupies himself in modern days.

HAYDON, A. L. — Canada, at Work and at Play; col. pl. — 2/6 ($1) 8° Cassell 05

MORGAN, H. J. — Types of Canad. Men and Women conn. w. Can. — 8° Briggs, *Toronto* [03] 04

„ + BURPEE (L. J.) Canad. Life in Town & Country; ill. [Our Empire] 3/6 *n.* c 8° Newnes 05

**Economic Condition, Resources, etc.**—*v. also* **D** §§ 148, 136

ARGYLL, D'ke of — Yesterday and To-day in Canada; map — 6/ *n.* c 8° G. Allen 10
[British Empire Ser.] Imp. Conference, trade, history, game, natural beauty, life, etc.

BIGGAR, E. B. — Canada: statistical and descr. hdbk.; ill. — $2·50 8° *Montreal* 89

BRADLEY, A. G. — Canada in the Twentieth Century; 50 pl. — 5/ *n.* 8° Constable [03] 05
An impartial, trustworthy compendium of modern Canada and Canadian life, politics, econcs., sport, etc.

DURHAM, Earl of — A Report on Brit. N. America; w. introd. note — 4/6 *n.* 8° Methuen [39] 05
Literal repr. of famous *Rept. on N. Amer.* pubd. in 1839, one of most import. documts. in Brit. hist.

FRASER, Jno. Foster — Canada as it is; ill. — 6/ ($2) c 8° Cassell [05] 11
A fairly accurate picture of the dominion and its policy; w. descrns. of the Far West.

HOBSON, J. A. — Canada of To-day — 3/6 *n.* c 8° Unwin 06
$1 Wessels, *N.Y.* An excellent bk.; deals largely with the tariff controversy.

KENNEDY, H. A. New Canada and the New Canadians; ill. 3/6 c 8° H. Marshall 07
A commonsense, unbiassed acc. of the Canadian West. Partly repr. fr. l'rs to *Times*.

SIEGFRIED, A. The Race Question in Canada 7/6 8° Nash 07
A valuable study of the French Canadians and the future of Canada, by a French visitor.

WHATES, H. R. Canada, the New Nation 3/6 f 8° Dent 06

**Rivers:** American Waterways Series—*ut* **E** § 56
- Incls. Columbia R., Hudson R., Niagara R.

*Hudson R.:* JOHNSON (Clifton) The Picturesque Hudson; ill. $1·25 *n.* (5/ *n.*) c 8° Macmillan, *N.Y.* 09

*Mackenzie R.:* MAIR (C.) Through the Mackenzie Basin; ill. 8/ *n.* c 8° Simpkin 08
Narrative of the Athabasca and Peace River Treaty Expedition of 1899.

RUSSELL, Fk. Explorations in the Far North; ill. 8° Univ. of Iowa 99
Acc. of a nat.-hist. collector's jy. in Mackenzie R. region and on the Barren Grounds.

*St. Lawrence R.:* COMEAU (N. A.) Life and Sport on Lower St. Lawrence; ill. 12/6 *n.* 8° Laurie 10

DAWSON, Dr S. E. St. Lawr. Basin & Border Land; ill. [Story of Explorn.] 4/6 *n.* 8° Rivers 05
A detailed account of the gradual unfolding of the country.

JOHNSON, Clifton The Picturesque St. Lawrence; ill. $1·25 *n.* (5/ *n.*) c 8° Macmillan, *N.Y.* 10

*Saskatchewan R.:* NEWTON (Can. Wm.) Twenty Yrs. in the Saskatchewan 5/ c 8° Stock 97

**Scenery:** GRANT (G. M.) Picturesque Canada, as it Was and Is, 2 v.; 500 ill. ea. 63/ 4° Cassell 87

LORNE, Marq. of Canadian Pictures, drawn w. Pen and Pencil; ill. 8/ i 8° R.T.S. 85

MARTIN, T. M. [art.] Canada: 76 col. pl., w. l'rpr. W. Campbell [$6 *n.* Macm., *N.Y.*] 20/ *n.* sq 8° Black 07

**Alaska**—*v.* **E** § 56 **Baffin Bay** and **Land**—*v.* **E** § 68 **Behring Sea** and **Str.**—*v.* **E** § 68

**Bermuda (Somers' Islands):** *Bibliography:* BUTLER (N.) Hist. of Bermudas, ed. Sir J. H. Lefroy 8° Hakluyt Soc. 82

COLE, G. W. Bermuda in Periodical Liter.; ill. $3 *n.* 8° Boston Bk. Co., *Bost.* 07

GODET, T. L. Bermuda *o.p.* [*pb.* 9/] 8° Smith & Elder 60
An account of the history, geology, climate, commerce, government, etc.

HEILPRIN, Prf. Angelo Bermuda Islands; 19 pl. [scenery, phys. hist., zool.] $3·50 r 8° Author, *Phila.* 89

HURDIS, Jno. H. Rough Notes rel. to Nat. Hist. of Bermudas—*ut* **H** § 67

JONES, J. M. A Naturalist in Bermuda—*ut* **H** § 67

LEFROY, J. H. Discovery and Settlement of Bermudas, 2 vols. *o.p.* [*pb.* 90/] r 8° Longman 77–9
Vol. i: 1511–1652; ii: 1650–1687. A polit., commercial, and geogr. account, compiled fr. Colonial Recds. and other orig. sources.

NEWTON, Marg. Glimpses of Life in Bermuda [incl. Windward Isls.] 6/ c 8° Digby 97

VERRILL, A. E. Bermuda Islands; ill. $4 8° A. E. Verrill, *New Haven* 03

*Guide-bk.:* STARK (J. H.) Bermuda [Stark's Illd. Guide-bks.] 6/ c 8° Low 98

**British Columbia; Vancouver's Island**

BAILLIE-GROHMAN, W. A. Fifteen Years' Sport and Life in Hunting Grounds of Western America and British Columbia; maps and 77 ill. 15/ *n.* i 8° H. Cox 00

BANCROFT, H. H. British Columbia [Pacific States of N. Am.] $4·50 8° History Co., *San Francisco* 87

BARRETT-LENNARD, Cpt. C. E. Travels in B. Columbia w. Yacht rd. B. Col. *o.p.* [*pb.* 14/] 8° Hurst 62

BEGG, Alex. History of British Columbia; map $3 8° Briggs, *Toronto* 94
12/6 Low. Full of facts, but without liter. pretensns. In 3 Periods: 'The Fur-trading', 'The Colonial', 'The Confederation'.

BROWN, Dr Rob. The Adventures of John Jewitt 5/ c 8° C. Wilson 96
A narrative of three years captivity among the Indians of Nootka Sound, 1805–8.

BURPEE, L. J. The Search for the Western Sea; 60 ill. 16/ *n.* 8° Rivers 08
Deals w. that portn. of explorn. of B. C. which closed w. MACKENZIE's overld. expedn. to Pacific, FRASER's descent of the Fraser, and THOMPSON's explorn. of the Columbia in early 19th cent. Based on orig. documts. Bibliogr. (16 pp.).

GRAINGER, M. Allerdale Woodsmen of the West 7/6 *n.* Arnold 08
A graphic narrative of 'logging', in the language of 'loggers', by one who went to Vancouver and became a 'logger'.

HERRING, Fces. E. Among the People of British Columbia 6/ *n.* c 8° Unwin 03
A somewhat trite and ill-wr. bk., partly in form of fiction, dealg. w. life of the various races.

" In the Pathless West; ill. [B. C. in the '50's] 6/ *n.* c 8° Unwin 04

LEES (J. A.) + CLUTTERBUCK (W. J.) B. C., 1887: ramble in Br. Columbia; 75 ill. [Silver Lib.] 3/6 ($1·25) c 8° Longman [88]

LORD, J. K. Naturalist in Vanc. Isl. and B. C., 2 vols. *o.p.* [*pb.* 24/] c 8° Bentley 66

MACDONALD, D. G. F. British Columbia and Vancouver's Island *o.p.* [*pb.* 16/] 8° Longman 62
Hist., character, climate, populn., nat. hist., manners and customs of native Indians, etc.

MACFIE, Mat. Vancouver's Island and British Columbia *o.p.* [*pb.* 18/] 8° Longman 65

MACNAB, Fces. British Columbia for Settlers; 3 maps 6/ c 8° Chapman 98
A collection of facts rel. to mines, trade, and agriculture.

MEANY, E. S. Vancouver's Discovery of Puget Sound; ill. $2·50 *n.* (10/6 *n.*) 8° Macmillan 07

MORICE, Rev. A. G. Hist. of N. Interior of Br. Col.; ill. [1660–1880] 16/ *n.* 8° Lane 04

PEMBERTON, J. D. Facts & Figures ab. Vanc. Island & Brit. Columbia *o.p.* [*pb.* 10/6] c 8° Longman 60

RATTRAY, A. Vancouver's Island and British Columbia *o.p.* [*pb.* 5/] c 8° Smith & Elder 62
ST JOHN, M. Sea of Mountains, 2 vols. [acc. of L'd Dufferin's tour] 21/ p 8° Hurst 77
TALBOT, F. A. The New Garden of Canada; 48 ill. 7/6 *n.* c 8° Cassell 11
VAN DYKE, Jno. C. The Desert; ill. $1·25 *n.* c 8° Scribner, *N.Y.* 01
7/6 Low. A well-wr. ser. of descrns. and reflectns., with the great desert of Pacific coast acr. Arizona and Sonora as subject.

**Cape Breton:** BOURINOT (J. G.) Histor. & Descr. Acc. of Isl. of Cape Breton 8° Forster, *Montreal* 92
By a native of the island. A good monograph, giving the French history in great detail.
,, Cape Breton and its Memorials; ill. 10/6 4° Forster, *Montreal* 92
BROWN, Rich. Cape Breton: a history of the island *o.p.* [*pb.* 15/] 8° Low 69
GOW, Jno. M. Cape Breton Illustrated: historic, pict., descr.; fully ill. $3 4° Briggs, *Toronto* 96
MORLEY, Marg. W. —*in her* Down North and Up Along, *ut inf.*, *s.v.* Nova Scotia
WARNER, C. D. Baddeck, and that Sort of Thing [excursn. to C. Breton] $1 c 8° Houghton, *Boston* 74

**Hudson Bay Territory** —*v. also* **E** §§ 68–9; *for* Hudson Bay Co. *v.* **D** § 117*, Hudson River, *sup.*
CAMPBELL, Roderick The Father of St Kilda 6/ c 8° Russell 01
A well-wr. acc. of the experces. of a servant of the Hudson Bay Co., fr. 1859 onwards.
FOXE (Cpt. Luke) *and* JAMES (Cpt. Thos.) Voyages to Hudson's Bay, ed. Miller Christy—*ut sup.*
HUDSON, Hy., the Navigator [16–17 cent.]
Asher, G. [ed.] Collection of Original Documts. rel. to H. Hudson 8° Hakluyt Society 60
Murphy, H. C. [ed.] Henry Hudson in Holland 10 fl. 4° Nijhoff, *The Hague* [59] 09
Inquiry into orig. and objects of voy. wh. led to discovery of Hudson River. With trs., notes, and bibliogr. (22 pp.).
Read, J. M., jun. Historical Inquiry concerning Henry Hudson $5 8° Munsell, *Albany* 66
LAUT, Agnes C. Conquest of the Great North West, 2 vols.; maps and ill. $5 8° Moffat, *N.Y.* 09
21/ *n.* Hodder. Practically a history of the Hudson Bay Co., based on the copious archives in London.
MACLEAN, J. M. 25 Years' Service in Hudson Bay Territory, 2 vols. *o.p.* [*pb.* 21/] 8° Bentley 49
MARTIN, Arth. Hudson Bay Company's Land Tenures; ill. 15/ r 8° Butterworth 98
A book of legal and historical interest: treats the occupn. of Assiniboia by L'd Selkirk's settlers fully.
Report of the Expedition to Hudson Bay and Cumberland Gulf: 1897 Marine Dept. of Canada 98
An account of investigations into the and conclusions on navigability of Hudson Bay.
ROBINSON, H. M. The Great Fur Land; ill. 50 c. 16° Putnam, *N.Y.* [80] 82
12/6 8° Low. Travel in the Hudson Bay Territory.
TYRELL, J. W. Across the Sub-Arctics of Canada; 65 ill. $2 8° Dodd & Mead, *N.Y.* 98
7/6 Unwin. A journey (1893) of 3,200 m. fr. Edmonton to Chippewyan, down Telzoa river to Hudson Bay.
WHITNEY, Caspar On Snow-Shoes to the Barren Grounds—*ut sup.*, *s.v.* North-West Canada

**Labrador** —*v. also* **E** §§ 68–9
GOSLING, Dr W. G. Labrador: discovery, explorn., developmt. 21/ *n.* 8° Rivers 10
GRENFELL, Dr W. T. Vikings of To-day; ill. [amg. L'dor fishermen] 3/6 c 8° Marshall Bros. 95
,, Down to the Sea; ill. [$1 *n.* Revell, *N.Y.*] 3/6 *n.* c 8° Melrose 10
,, etc. Labrador, the Country and the People; ill. 10/ *n.* ($2·25 *n.*) 4° Macmillan 10
HIND, H. Y. Explorns. in Interior of Labrator, 2 v., maps & col. pl. *o.p.* [*pb.* 32/] 8° Longman 63
HUBBARD, Mrs Leonidas Woman's Way thro' Unknown Labrador 10/6 *n.* 8° Murray 08
Acc. of explorns. of Nascaupee and George Rivers. Incls. diary of expedn. on wh. her husband lost his life.
PRICHARD, H. Hesketh Through Trackless Labrador; ill. 15/ *n.* 8° Heinemann 11
STEARNS, W. A. Labrador: peoples, industries, natural history $1·75 12° *Boston* [85] 87
PACKARD, Dr A. The Labrador Coast; maps and ill. $3·50 8° Harper, *N.Y.* 91
Jl. of 2 summer-cruises in 1860 and '64, w. notes on early discov., on its phys. geogr., geol. (spec. full) and nat. hist., on the Eskimo, and bibl. of bks., arts. and charts (poor). Full of val. informn., some of wh. is out of date, bk. bg. made up largely of old pprs. and memoirs wr. at time of or shortly after the cruises.
TOWNSEND, Dr C. W. Along the Labrador Coast; ill. $1·50 8° Dana Estes, *Boston* 07
5/ *n.* Unwin. Desultory record of summer jy. along Lab. coast, hg. for chief obj. study of birds of S. and E. shores.
WALLACE, Dillon Lure of the Labrador Wild; maps and ill. $1·50 c 8° Revell, *N.Y.* 05
Story of explorg. expedn. of 1903 conducted by Leonidas HUBBARD, jr., whom author accompanied.
,, The Long Labrador Trail; map and ill. $1·50 *n.* 8° *Outing* Pb. Co., *N.Y.* 07
Story of the more recent trip into the same unexplored regions.

**Manitoba:** BELL (C. N.) The Selkirk Settlement and the Settlers; ill. 8° *Winnipeg* 87
,, Some Red River Settlement History 8° *Winnipeg* 87
BRYCE, Dr G. [Canad.] Manitoba: infancy, growth, pres. condn. 7/6 c 8° Low 82
Acc. of the development of the great grain-growing district of Canada in 1882.
,, Lord Selkirk's Colonists; ill. [settlemt. in Manitoba] 7/6 *n.* c 8° Low 10
BUTLER, Lt.-Gen. Sir Wm. —*in his* The Great Lone Land, *ut sup.*
FITZGIBBON, Mary Trip to Manitoba *o.p.* [*pb.* 10/6] c 8° Bentley 80
HALL, M. G. C. Lady's Life on Farm in Manitoba *o.p.* [*pb.* 2/6] c 8° W. H. Allen 84

HIND, H. Y. Red River Expedition: 1857, 2 vols. *o.p.* [*pb.* 42/] 8° Longman 60
HUYSHE, G. L. The Red River Expedition: 1870 *o.p.* [*pb.* 10/6] 8° Macmillan 71
LEGGE, A. O. Sunny Manitoba: people & industries; ill. [$2·50 Putnam, *N.Y.*] 7/6 c 8° Unwin 93
MACOUN, Jno. Manitoba and the Great North-West; maps 12/ 8° Jack 83

**Newfoundland**

GILBERT, Sir Humphrey [1539 (?)–83; discoverer of Newfoundland]
Gosling, Dr W. G. Sir Humphrey Gilbert; ill 12/6 *n.* 8° Constable 11
HARVEY, Dr Moses Short History of Newfoundland; map [2/6 Collins] $1 8° Doyle, *Boston* [85] 90
,, Newfoundland as it is in 1897; map & ill. $1·50 8° New Amst. Bk. Co., *N.Y.* 97
5/ Low. A good short account, pubd. on 400th anniversary of discovery of the island.
HATTON (J.) + HARVEY (M.) Newfoundland, Oldest British Colony; ill. 18/ 8° Cassell 83
MILLAIS, J. G. Newfoundland & its Untrodden Ways; maps & ill. 21/ *n.* ($6 *n.*) r 8° Longman 07
A hunter's bk., dealg. mainly w. nat. hist. and chase of animals and birds; incid. w. life of Micmac Indians. Profusely and finely illus.
PEDLEY, Rev. C. History of Newfoundland [discovery to 1860] *o.p.* [*pb.* 10/] 8° Longman 63
*PROWSE, Judge D. W. History of Newfoundland, fr. the Records; map and 35 ill. 6/ Eyre & Spottiswoode [95] 97
A valuable hist. of the most ancient and most unfortunate of our colonies. Divided into 4 gt. epochs: (1) *Early or Chaotic Era* [1497–1610]; (2) *Fishing Admiral Era* [1610–1711], a dismal time of struggle betw. the colonists and the Western adventurers or ship-fishermen fr. England—practically the Colonization Period; (3) *Colony und. Naval Governors* [1711–1825, the advent of first Resid. Gov., Sir T. COCHRANE]; (4) *Modern Era* = the struggle for autonomy.
ROGERS, J. D. Newfoundland = Vol. V., Pt. iv. of Lucas, Hist. Geogr. of Br. Cols.—*ut sup.*
TOCQUE, P. Newfoundland as it Was and as it Is [in 1877] *o.p.* [*pb.* 10/6] c 8° Low 78
WILLSON, Beckles Truth ab. Newfoundland; or The Tenth Island 3/6 gl 8° Richards [97] 01
A good summary of informn. on the cy., people, politics, and peculiarities.

**Nova Scotia:** BOURINOT (Sir Jno.) Builders of Nova Scotia; ill. 8° Copp, Clark & Co., *Toronto* 96
Partly historical, partly personal recollections. Appendix contains. valuable documents.
CALNEK, W. A. Hist. of County of Annapolis, ed. Judge Savary; ill. *o.p.* 8° 97
HARDY, Campbell Forest Life in Acadie; ill. [sport and nat. hist.] *o.p.* [*pb.* 18/] 8° Chapman 69
HUTCHINSON, J. R. 'Way Down East *o.p.* [*pb.* 3/6] c 8° Ward & Downey 96
MORLEY, Marg. W. Down North and Up Along $1·50 c 8° Dodd & Mead, *N.Y.* 00
A fresh and exhilarating acc. of a summer jaunt in Nova Scotia and Cape Breton Island.
RICHARD, E. Acadia: missing links of a lost chapter in America $2 8° Home Bk. Co., *N.Y.* 95
WILLSON, Beckles Nova Scotia, the Province that has passed by 10/6 *n.* 8° Constable 11

**Ontario:** KINGSFORD (Dr W.) Early Bibliography of Province of Ontario c 8° *Toronto* 92

**Ottawa:** EDGAR (Hon. J. D.) Canada and its Capital; ill. [city & its life] 10/6 c 8° Morang, *Toronto* 98

**Prince Edward Island:** CAMPBELL (Duncan) Hist. of Pr. Ed. Island *o.p.* [*pb.* $1·50] 12° *Charlotte-town* 75

**Quebec:** COFFIN (Dr V.) Province of Quebec and Early Amer. Revoln. 8° Univ. Pr., *Madison* 97
An original view of the action of Great Britain towards the French-Canadians.
DIONNE N. E. Inventaire Chronol. d. Livres, etc., en Lang. Franç. en la Prov. de Québec [1764–1905] 20 fr. 8° Renault, *Quebec* 05
DOUGHTY, A. G. The Cradle of New France; map and ill. 6/ *n.* c 8° Longman 08
,, Siege of Quebec & Battle of the Plains of Abraham, 6 vols.; ill. 8° Dussaulx, *Quebec* 01
DOUGLAS, J. Old France in New World; ill. [Q. in 17 cent.] $2·50 *n.* 8° Burrows, *Cleveld., O.* [05] 06
GRANT, G. M. [ed.] Picturesque Quebec; fully ill. $5 4° Belford Co., *N.Y.* 90
King's Book of Quebec, The: 2 vols.; ill. 4° Mortimer Co., *Ottawa* 11
PARKER, Sir Gilbert Quebec, the Place and the People, 2 vols. $4 8° Macmillan 02
,, + BYRAN (C. J.) Old Quebec; the Fortress of New France; ill. 15/ *n.* ($3·75 *n.*) 8° Macmillan 03
A full history of the town from its foundation: valuable and accurate. Ill., 25 ports., 97 pl. and 5 maps.

**Queen Charlotte Islands:** POOLE (F.) Queen Charlotte Islands *o.p.* 8° 72

**Red River Settlement and Expeditions**—*v.* Manitoba, *sup.*

**Rocky Mountains** (CANADIAN and AMERICAN)

BAILLIE-GROHMANN, W. A. Camps in the Rockies *o.p.* [*pb.* 12/6] c 8° Low 82
A hunter's wandergs., affordg. a vivid picture of the country, w. acc. of cattle-ranches.
BISHOP, Mrs [*née* Isab. BIRD] Lady's Life in Rocky Mtns.; 8 ill. 7/6 p 8° Murray [79] 80
COLEMAN, Dr A. P. The Canadian Rockies: new and old trails 12/6 *n.* 8° Unwin 11
A full acc. by the President of Alpine Club of Canada. 3 maps and 41 illns.
GREEN, Wm. Spotswood Among the Selkirk Glaciers; map and ill. 7/6 ($2·25) c 8° Macmillan 90
An excellent account of a mountaineering trip.
'HECLAVA' In the Heart of the Bitter Root Mtns.; ill. $1·50 (6/) c 8° Putnam 95
HORNADAY, W. T. Camp-fires in the Canadian Rockies; ill. $3 *n.* 8° Scribner, *N.Y.* 06
16/ Laurie. An Amer. zoologist's descrn. of his advents. in the home of the mountain-goat.
,, Camp-fires on Desert & Lava; maps, ill. & 8 col. pl. $3 *n.* 8° Scribner, *N.Y.* 08
16/ *n.* Laurie. Story of expedn. fr. Tucson, Arizona, acr. desert to hitherto unkn. regn. surroundg. Pinacate in N.-W. Mexico.

INGERSOLL, Ern. Knocking round the Rockies; ill. $2 c 8° Harper, *N.Y.* 83
Account of the daily life and incidents of the Hayden survey.

IRVING, Washington Astoria, 2 vols. ea. $1·25 (6/) c 8° Putnam, *N.Y.* [36]
An excellent bk. on huntg. and explorn. in the West—not less interestg. because the condns. are now so widely different. Cheap edn., *s.t. The Fur Traders of Columbia River, and the Rocky Mtns.* [Knickerbocker Liter. Ser.] 90 c. *id.* '03.

" Adventures of Captain Bonneville $1·25 (6/) c 8° Putnam, *N.Y.* [37]
The Journal of BONNEVILLE, shaped and abgd., describg. his wanderings in the Rockies in 1831–5.

JAMES, Edwin Expedition to Rocky Mtns., 3 vols. [1819–20; und. Long] *o.p.* 8° 23

JOHNSON, Clifton Highways & Byways of Rocky Mtns.; ill. $2 *n.* (8/6 *n.*) c 8° Macmillan 10

McCLURE, A. K. Three Thousand Miles thro' Rocky Mountains; ill. $2 c 8° Lippincott, *Phila.*

MILLS, Enos. A. Wild Life on the Rockies; ill. [6/ *n.* Constable] $1·75 *n.* 4° Houghton, *Boston* 09

OUTRAM, Jas. In the Heart of the Canadian Rockies $2·50 *n.* (10/6 *n.*) 8° Macmillan 05
Record of experces. gained in explorn. of hitherto untrodden peaks and passes, and descrs. the grand scenery along the chain of the Divide, fr. Mt Assiniboine to Mt Columbia. Incls. also accs. of the more notable 'first ascents.'.

PARKMAN, F. The Oregon Trail—*ut* **F** § 67
The authors' first bk.: descrs. his wandgs. in 1846, w. a company of Sioux Indns., acr. regions of Platte River, buffalo-htg. in Black Hills, and return thro' Rockies.

POCOCK, Roger A Frontiersman 6/ c 8° Methuen 03
Incls. acc. of a record-breaking ride from Canada to city of Mexico, along the Rockies.

PRICE, Maj. Sir Rose L. A Summer on the Rockies; map and ill. 6/ c 8° Low 98

SCHAFFER, Marg. I. S. Old Indian Trails; 100 ill. $2 *n.* 8° Putnam, *N.Y.* 11
Incidents of camp and trail life dur. 2 yrs.' explorn. of Rockies of Canada.

STUTFIELD (H. E. M.) + COLLIE (Prf. J. N.) Climbs and Explorns. in Canadian Rockies; ill. 12/6 *n.* ($5) 8° Longman 03
A narr. of the authors' several ascents, mostly in diary-form, w. a mass of geogr. informn., rectifying and supplementg. previous informn.: they traced Athabasca, Saskatchewan and Columbia rivers to an almost common source, discov., localized and named many new mtns., etc. Excellent illns.

WHEELER, A. O. The Selkirk Range 8° Govt. Press, *Ottawa* 0–
A record of exploration, previous surveys, and mountain-climbing in the Selkirk Range.

WILCOX, W. D. The Rockies of Canada; finely ill. $5 *n.* 4° Putnam, *N.Y.* [96] 09
A revised edn. of his *Camping in the Canad. Rockies* [1896]. Mostly in regn. rd. L. Louise, Vermilion Pass, Kicking Horse Pass, Mt Assiniboine, and Waputeh Range. Camp-life, geol., flora, fauna, etc.

## 56: UNITED STATES OF AMERICA (*a*): COLLECTIVELY

**Bibliography** —*v. also* **F** § 68

Boston Public Lib.: Index of Articles on Amer. Local Hist. in Historical Collns. of Bost. Pub. Lib.; *and* Suppl. 83–
225 pp. in double columns. Edited by A. P. Clark GRIFFIN. Incl. titles of arts. in over 300 sets or series of histor. pubns.

PERKINS, F. B. Check List for American Local History 8° *Boston* 76

**Series:** American Commonwealths: ed. H. E. Scudder; maps [ea. 4/6 *n.* Constable] ea. $1·25 *n.* 16° Houghton, *Boston* 79–08 *in prg.*

*California* Prf. J. ROYCE | *Connecticut* Prf. Alex. JOHNSTON | *Georgia* U. B. PHILLIPS | *Illinois* J. H. FINLEY | *Indiana* J. P. DUNN, jun. | *Iowa* Alb. SHAW | *Kansas* L. W. SPRING | *Kentucky* Prf. N. S. SHALER | *Louisiana* A. PHELPS | *Maryland* W. H. BROWNE | *Massachusetts* E. CHANNING | *Michigan* T. M. COOLEY | *Missouri* Lucien CARR | *New Hampshire* F. B. SANBORN | *New Jersey* Prf. Austin SCOTT | *New York*, 2 vols. E. H. ROBERTS | *Ohio* Rufus KING | *Oregon* F. H. HODDER | *Pennsylvania* Talcott WILLIAMS | *Rhode Island* I. B. RICHMAN | *Texas* G. P. GARRISON | *Vermont* R. E. ROBINSON | *Virginia* J. E. COOKE | *Wisconsin* R. G. THWAITES

BANCROFT, H. H. Hist. of Pacific States of N. America; maps and ill. ea. vol. $4·50 8° History Co., *San Francisco* 82–90

i–iii: *Central America*, 3 v.
iv–ix: *Mexico*, 6 v.
x–xi: *N. Mexican States; Texas*, 2 v.
xii: *Arizona and New Mexico*
xiii–xix: *California*, 7 v.
xx: *Nevada, Color., Wyoming*
xxi: *Utah*
xxii–xxiii: *North-West Coast*
xxiv–xxv: *Oregon*, 2 v.
xxvi: *Washington, Idaho, Montana*
xxvii: *British Columbia*
xxviii: *Alaska*
xxix: *California Pastoral*
xxx: *California inter Pocula*
xxxi–xxxii: *Popular Tribunals*, 2 v.
xxxiii: *Essays and Miscellany*
xxxiv: *Literary Industries* [*ut* **K** § 29]

Perhaps the most colossal liter. achievemt. of any individual of 19th cent. BANCROFT [d. 1893] commenced collectg. matl. in 1858; and his lib. (for wh. he erected a fire-proof brick bldg. and wh. has constantly grown) was more thoroughly laid under tribute th. any lib. bef. it. Territory covered by the wk. is equiv. to one-twelfth of earth's surface, and comprises western half of N. Am., incl. whole of Mexico and Cent. Amer.

Story of the States: ed. E. S. Brooks; maps, ports., and ill. ea. $1·50 12° Lothrop, *Boston* 88–92

*Kentucky* [*ut* **E** § 57] Emma M. CONNELLY | *Louisiana* [*ut* **E** § 57] M. THOMPSON | *Massachusetts* [*ut* **E** § 57] E. E. HALE | *New Mexico* [*ut* **E** § 57] H. O. LADD | *New York* [*ut* **E** § 57] E. S. BROOK | *Ohio* [*ut* **E** § 57] A. BLACK | *Vermont* [*ut* **E** § 57] J. L. HEATON | *Wisconsin* [*ut* **E** § 57] R. G. THWAITES

**Atlases:** SCRIBNER'S SONS [pbs.] Statist. Atl. of U.S., ed. F. W. Hughes + H. Gannett 168/ r f° Scribner, *N.Y.* 86

WALKER, F. A. Statistical Atlas of United States, 3 Parts $18 4° Bien, *Washington* 75

**Gazetteers:** DE COLANGE United States Gazetteer $7·50 8° *Cincinnati* 84

**Geographical Text-books; Physical Geography**—*v. also* **E** § 52

BRIGHAM, Prf. A. P. Geographic Influences in Amer. Hist. $1·25 (6/) 12° Ginn, *Boston* 03
Also in Chautauqua Home-Rg. Ser. Admirably defines physiogr. feats. wh. have influenced industr. and natl. life of U.S.

" From Trail to Railway acr. the Appalachians (2/6) c 8° Ginn, *Boston* 07
An excellent schl.-bk., givg. acc. of geogr and hist. of U.S. (roads and Western movemt. the main theme).

GANNETT, Hy. United States; 16 maps & 72 ill. [Compendium of Geogr.] 15/ 8° Stanford 98
$5·50 *n.* Lippincott, *Phila.* [Compendium of Geogr.] Topogr., geol., climate, hist., populn. thoro'ly, yet concisely, treated.

RECLUS, E. Universal Geography, vol. xvi: U.S. [tr.]—*ut* **E** § 2

SEMPLE, E. C. American History & its Geographical Conditions $3 *n.* 8° Houghton, *Boston* 03
Forms a useful complement to BRIGHAM *Geogr. Influences* [*ut sup.*].

SHALER, Prf. N. S. Nature and Man in Amer. $1·50 *n.* c 8° Scribner, *N.Y.* 92
6/ Smith & Elder. Touches on the changes induced by American environment in European races.

„ [ed.] The United States of America, 2 vols. [3/6 Low] 8° 94
A ser. of essays by 20 specialists on all aspects of U.S.; geogr. portion by SHALER.

WHITNEY, J. D. United States: facts & figs. ill. physical geography $3 8° Little & Brown, *Bost.* 89

**Guides:** APPLETON [pb.] General Guide to U.S. and Canada $2·50 c 8° Appleton, *N.Y.*

BAEDEKER, K. [pb.] United States; 33 maps & 48 plans [$3·60 *n.* Scribner, *N.Y.*] 15/ s 8° Unwin [93] 09
Incls. excursions to Mexico, Cuba, Porto Rico, and Alaska.

**Scenery:** BRYCE (J.) Picturesque America, 4 vols.—*ut* **E** § 52 [almost exclusively U.S.]

LOVETT, Rich. United States Pictures; 155 ill. [$3·20 Revell, *N.Y.*] 8/ i 8° R.T.S. 91

**Coasts** —*v.* **E** § 54, *s.v.* Coasts

**Colonies:** JEFFERY (R. W.) The Thirteen Colonies of N. America; map & 8 ill. 7/6 *n.* 8° Methuen 08
A compact but detailed narr. of those colonies wh., tho' no longer Brit. possessns., may be regarded as foundn. of Brit. Empire.

**Highways:** HULBERT (A. B.) Historic Highways of America, 16 vols. ea. $2 *n.* c 8° Clark, *Cleveland* 02
Gives the history of America as pourtrayed in its highways.

**Islands:** FORBES-LINDSAY (C. H. A.) America's Insular Possessions, 2 vols. $5 8° Winston, *Phila.* 06
Vol. i treats of Gt. Antilles, Porto Rico, Guam, Hawaii, Panama; ii is devoted to Philippines. Maps and illns.

**Rivers; Valleys:** American Waterways; ill.
[prev. entitled Hist. Rivers Ser.] ea. $3·50 *n.* (15/ *n.*) 8° Putnam 03–10 *in prg.*

*American Inland Waterways* H. QUICK | *Colorado River* F. S. DELLENBAUGH | *Columbia River* W. D. LYMAN | *Connecticut River* Edwin Munroe BACON | *Hudson River* Edgar Mayhew BACON | *Mississippi River and Valley* J. CHAMBERS | *Narragansett Bay* E. M. BACON | *Niagara River* A. B. HULBERT | *Ohio River* A. B. HULBERT | *Romance of the Gt. Lakes* J. O. CURWOOD | *St Lawrence River* G. W. BROWNE

SMITH, Rich. Tour of Four Great Rivers in 1769; maps & ill. $5 *n.* 8° Scribner, *N.Y.* 06
Hudson, Mohawk, Susquehanna, Delaware—the jl. of R. SMITH, of Burlington, N.J., ed. F. W. HALSEY, w. a short hist. of the pioneer settlemts.

WINTHROP, Theod. The Canoe & Saddle [N.-W. rivers & forests] 75 c. c 8° Dodd & Mead, *N.Y.*

*Colorado R.:* DELLENBAUGH (F. S.) Romance of the Colorado River—*ut sup.*, *s.v.* American Waterways
The story of its discovery in 1540, w. later explorns. (esp. voys. of POWELL thro' the great canyons).

Glimpses of the Grand Cañon of the Colorado; ill. $2·50 4° Thayer, *Denver* 00

JAMES, G. W. In & Around Grand Canyon of Colorado; ill. $2·50 8° Little & Brown, *Boston* 01
Descrn. of the canyons and var. trails by wh. they are approached; w. structure, geol., etc. Pasedena Edn. $10 *n.*

POWELL, J. W. Canyons of the Colorado; ill. [good pop. acc.] 8° Flood, *Meadville* 95

*Hudson R.*—*v.* **E** § 57, *s.v.* N.Y. State; *Mississippi* and *Missouri Rs.*—*ib.*, *s.vv.* Mississippi, Missouri

*Ohio R.* —*v.* **E** § 57, *s.v.* Ohio

**Towns:** Great Cities of the Republic ea. $1·75 *n.* (6/) c 8° Putnam 89
*Boston* [*ut* **E** § 57] A. GILMAN | *New York* [*ut* **E** § 57] C. B. TODD | *Washington* [*ut* **E** § 57] C. B. TODD

Historic Towns: ed. Dr Lyman P. Powell; ill. ea. $3 (15/) 8° Putnam 99–01 *in prg.*
*Hist. Towns of Middle States* | *Hist. Towns of New England* | *Hist. Towns of Southern States* | *Hist. Towns of Western States*
Full descrns., by different wrs., of the more important towns of U.S., their hist. and assocns.

**Recent Travel and Accounts** —*v. also* **E** § 52

CAMPBELL, Sir Geo. White and Black [travels in United States] 14/ 8° Chatto 79

DAVIS, Jno. Travels of Four Years and a Half in U.S.A.: 1798–1802: facs. reprod.,
w. Introd. and notes A. J. Morrison 10/6 *n.* 8° Bell [1803] 10

ENOCK, C. R. Farthest West: life and travel in U.S.; 32 pl. [$4 *n.* Appleton, *N.Y.*] 15/ *n.* 8° Long 10

HARDY, L'y Duffus Through Cities and Prairie Lands *o.p.* [*pb.* 14/] 8° Chapman 81

„ Down South *o.p.* [*pb.* 14/] 8° Chapman 83

KING, E. The Southern States of North America; ill. *o.p.* [*pb.* 31/6] r 8° Blackie 75
Records of travel in Louisiana, Texas, Indian territory, Missouri, Arkansas, Mississippi, Florida, Virginia, etc.

LUMMIS, C. F. A Tramp across the Continent; ill. $1·25 c 8° Scribner, *N.Y.* 92
6/ Low. An excellent acc. for boys of a tramp fr. Cincinnati to California (3,507 miles) in 1884.

RALPH, Julian Our Great West $2·50 8° Harper, *N.Y.* 93
A study of present condns. and future possibilities of Chicago, the Dakotas, Montana, Washington, Colorado, Wyoming, Utah, San Francisco.

ROBERTS, Cecil Adrift in America: work and adventure in States *o.p.* [*pb.* 5/] 8° Lawrence & Bullen 91
Moneyless and friendless, he wandered fr. N.Y. to Dakotah, southward to Texas and back to N.Y., working his way as farm labourer, cook, dish-washer, ry. 'section hand', firewood chopper, and pedlar, bar-keeper in gambling ho., shepherd, mule-driver, etc., and tramp between-whiles: w. expercs. more varied than agreeable.

STODDARD, C. A. Beyond the Rockies; ill. [good] $1·50 c 8° Scribner, *N.Y.* 94
Expercs. in a winter-jy. fr. N.Y. by Southern Route to California.

WHITING, Lilian The Land of Enchantment; ill. 7/6 *n.* p 8° Siegle 10
Travel fr. Pike's Peak to the Pacific: Denver, Colorado, New Mexico, Arizona, Los Angeles, the Grand Cañon.

**Life and People ; Economic Conditions ; Foreigners' Impressions**

America and the Americans from a French Point of View 3/6 c 8° Heinemann 97
$1·25 Scribner, *N.Y.* A bright and sketchy comparison of American w. Continental customs. Somewhat hostile.

ARCHER, Wm. America To-day 6/ c 8° Heinemann 00
Scribner, *N.Y.* ' Observations ' of American places, customs, institutions : ' Reflections ' on American questions.

ARNOLD, Sir Edwin —*in his* Seas and Lands, *ut* **E** § 7

ARNOLD, Mat. Discourses in America [Eversley Ser.] 5/ ($1·50) g 8° Macmillan [85] 96

BASCOM, J. Growth of Nationality in the United States $1·25 (6/) c 8° Putnam 00

*BOURGET, Paul Outre-Mer : impressns. of America [tr.] $1·75 8° Scribner, *N.Y.* 97
16/ Unwin. A sober study of Am. society fr. pt.-of-view of a critic of liter. and psychol. novelist.

BOWDEN-SMITH, [Miss] A. G. A English Student's Wander-Year in America—*ut* **D** § 157

BRADFORD, Gamaliel, jun. Types of American Character 75 c. (3/) 32° Macmillan 95
7 essays on types of New Engl. character: *The Pessimist, The Epicurean, The Idealist, The Man of Letters,* etc.

BREMER, Frederika The Homes of the New World [tr.], 3 vols. [1849–51] *o.p.* s 8° 53

BROOKS, J. G. As Others see us : study of progress in U.S. $1·75 *n.* (7/6 *n.*) c 8° Macmillan 09
Collects and classifs. the opins. of Europ. travellers during last 100 yrs. as basis f. reflections on Am. society.

BRYCE, Prf. Jas. —*in his* The American Commonwealth, 2 vols., *ut* **D** § 145
The standard bk. on the political and social organization of U.S.A.

BUSBEY, Kath. G. Home Life in America ; 12 ill. 10/6 *n.* 8° Methuen 10

BUTLER, Dr N. M. The American as he is $1 *n.* (4/ *n.*) c 8° Macmillan 09

DAVIS, Rebecca H. Silhouettes of American Life $1 12° Scribner, *N.Y.* 93
Conts. some admirable sketches of ' back ' country life, and other humorous and characteristic traits of Eastern America.

DE BARY, Rich. The Land of Promise 6/ *n.* ($1·50 *n.*) 8° Longman 08
Shows the inner spiritual forces wh. unite Americans and the promise of a ' mightier, holier, brotherlier, comradeship wh. it seems Amer. has been called into being to bring to pass for the world '

DICKENS, Chas. American Notes—*ut* **K** § 56 [1842]

FAITHFULL, Emily Three Visits to America 9/ 8° Douglas, *Edin.* 84

FIRTH, J. C. Our Kin across the Sea [by a N. Zeal. colonist] 6/ c 8° Longman 88

FITZ-PATRICK, Dr T. A Transatlantic Holiday ; ill. 10/6 c 8° Low 91
Acc. of visit to N.Y., the New Engl. States, Niagara and Washington ; pleasant and scholarly.

FRANCIS, Alex. Americans : an impression 6/ *n.* 8° Melrose 09
A scholarly and penetrating investigation of Amer. temperamt. and national character.

FRASER, J. Foster America at Work 6/ c 8° Cassell 03
An account of modern business America, its methods, etc.

FREEMAN, Prf. E. A. Some Impressions of the United States [in 1883] 6/ c 8° Longman 83

GLYN, Elinor S. Elizabeth Visits America [$1·50 Duffield, *N.Y.*] 6/ c 8° Duckworth 09

GORDON, H. Panmure Land of the Almighty Dollar ; 60 ill. 3/6 ($2·50) c 8° Warne [92] 93
By a member of the London Stock Exchange. Independent and ' commonsensible '

GREY, Grattan + Mrs [Australs.] With Uncle Sam and his Family 6/ *n.* c 8° Griffiths 11

HARDY, Iza Duffus Between Two Oceans : sketches of Am. travel 15/ 8° Hurst 84

HATTON, Jos. To-day in America : studies of Old World & New, 2 v. 18/ c 8° Chapman 81

,, [ed.] Henry Irving's Impressions of America, 2 vols. 6/ c 8° Low [84] 84
Sketches, conversations with IRVING, etc.

HAWTHORNE, Nath. Passage from American Note Books—*ut* **K** § 90 [his Diary, 1835–53]

HOLE, Dn S. R. More Memories : thoughts upon England spoken in Amer. 16/ 8° Arnold 94

,, Little Tour in America ; ill. 16/ 8° Arnold 95
Acc. of 4 mos. spent in States, as lecturer : bright, witty, full of good stories.

IRVING, Sir Hy. —*v.* Hatton, *sup.*

JAMES, Hy. The American Scene $3 *n.* (12/6 *n.*) 8° Harper 07
Impressions of America after an absence of nearly a quarter of a century. By the well-known novelist.

KING (M.) + SWEETSER (M. F.) Handbook of the United States (10/) 8° Osgood 91
Statistics, illustrations, and maps of each State. A useful reference bk.

KLEIN, Abbé Félix In the Land of the Strenuous Life [tr.] ; ill. $2 *n.* 8° McClurg, *Chicago*

LOW, A. Maurice The American People : study in natl. psychology $2·25 *n.* c 8° Houghton, *Boston* 09
8/6 *n.* Unwin. On orig., growth, and developmt. of the Am. people, tracg. causes wh. have produced ' a new race '.

,, America at Home ; ill. [Our Neighbours at Home] 5/ *n.* c 8° Newnes 08

MARRYAT, Florence Tom Tiddler's Ground [visit 1885] *o.p.* [*pb.* 7/6] 8° Sonnenschein 86

MEAKIN, Annette M. B. What America is Doing 10/6 *n.* 8° Blackwood 11
L'rs wr. fr. place to place, full of the fresh and orig. observn. of a trained traveller.

MORRIS, Hon. Martin Transatlantic Traits [3 essays] 5/ c 8° Stock 97

MUIRHEAD, J. F. America, the Land of Contrasts 6/ *n.* ($1·20 *n.*) c 8° Lane [00] 02
A excellent account by a keen and well-trained observer, author of BAEDEKER'S *United States*.

MÜNSTERBERG, Prf. H. American Traits fr. pt.-of-view of a German $1·60 *n.* c 8° Houghton, *Boston* 01
" The Americans [tr.] [12/6 *n.* Williams] r 8° 05
The philosophy of Americanism—a study of the American man and his inner tendencies.
" American Problems $1·60 *n.* 12° Moffat, *N.Y.* 10
Nerves, prohibition, women, vocations, scholarships, books, lang., markets, and ghosts.
'O'RELL, Max' [= Paul BLOUET] Jonathan and his Continent [tr.] 2/6 c 8° Arrowsmith, *Bristol* 89
" + 'ALLYN (J.)' A Frenchman in America [tr.]; 130 ill. 3/6 f 8° Arrowsmith 91
A humorous view of Amer. people, w. some good stories and shrewd observns. 4 chaps. devoted to Canada.
PORTER, T. C. Impressions of America; ill. 10/6 8° Pearson 99
An instructive acc. of a trip acr. America; w. interesting scientific details and discussions.
'RITA' [Mrs Desmond HUMPHREYS] America—through English Eyes 2/6 *n.* c 8° Stanley Paul 11
ROBINSON, H. Perry The Twentieth Century American; map 7/6 ($1·75 *n.*) c 8° Putnam 08
A temperate and fair comparative study of the Amer. and Engl. nations, by a thoughtful Englishman.
DE ROUSIERS, Paul American Life [tr.] 12/6 8° Cassell 92
Systematic exposn. and pers. experces. over a long stay. A v. interestg. bk. contg. perhaps clearest general acc. of America in Engl.
SALA, G. A. America Revisited; ill. *o.p.* [*pb.* 12/] 8° Vizetelly [82] 83
SHALER, Prf. N. S. [ed.] The United States: study of Amer. C'wealth, 2 v. ea. $5 Appleton, *N.Y.* 94
36/ Low. By var. wrs. Nat. resources, people, industries, manufs., commerce, educn., etc.
SINCLAIR, Upton The Industrial Republic: study of Amer. 10 yrs. hence—*ut* **D** § 126
SMALLEY, Geo. W. Anglo-American Memories, 2 Ser. ea. 12/6 *n.* 8° Duckworth 11
Much suggestive matter conc. leadg. events and persons of last 50 yrs.
STEEVENS, G. W. Land of the Dollar: scamper thro' the States 6/ c 8° Blackwood 97
75 c. Dodd & Mead, *N.Y.* A bright, sketchy view of the Americans, espec. political men, in a light, critical vein. Repr. fr. *Dy. Mail.*
STEVENSON, R. Louis Across the Plains—*ut* **K** § 83 [descr. his jy. as emigrant amg. emigrants acr. Amer. continent]
TWINING, Thos. —*his* Travels in India 100 Yrs. Ago [*ut* **E** § 35] *includes a visit to U.S.*
VAN DYKE, Prf. Hy. The Spirit of America [7 lectures] $1·50 *n.* (6/6 *n.*) c 8° Macmillan 10
VAY DE VAYA AND LUSKOD, C't Inner Life of the United States 12/ *n.* 8° Murray 08
VIVIAN, H. H. Notes of a Tour in America 9/ 8° Stanford [77] 78
WARNER, C. Dudley [Am.] Studies in South & West: w. comments on Canada $1·75 12° Harper, *N.Y.* 89
Describes certain representative developments, tendencies, and dispositions.
WELLS, H. G. The Future in America—*ut* **D** § 126
WHIBLEY, C. American Sketches 6/ c 8° Blackwood 08
WILLSON, Beckles The New America: a study of the Imperial Republic 10/6 *n.* 8° Chapman 02
A study of American politics, business, army and navy, and literature since the Spanish war.
*Foreigners' Impressions of American Women*—*v.* **D** § 132

**Houses and Homesteads; Literary Haunts**

BROWN, Abram E. Beside Old Hearthstones; ill. $1·50 c 8° Lee & Shepard, *Boston* 97
DRAKE, S. A. Our Colonial Homes; 20 ill. $2·50 c 8° Lee & Shepard, *Boston* 93
GLENN, T. A. Some Colonial Mansions, 2 Ser.; 320 ill. $5 s 4° Coates, *Phila.* 00
HARLAND, Marion Some Colonial Homesteads; 28 ill. $3 8° Putnam 97
" More Colonial Homesteads; 80 ill. $3 8° Putnam 99
Excellent accounts of some of the older houses of the U.S. and their associations.
WOLFE, Dr T. F. Literary Shrines: haunts of Amer. authors $1·25 12° Lippincott, *Phila.* 95
" Literary Haunts & Homes of Amer. Authors $1·25 12° Lippincott, *Phila.* 98

## 57: UNITED STATES OF AMERICA: (*b*) INDIVIDUALLY

**Alabama:** BROWN (W. G.) History of Alabama f. Schools $1 12° University Pb. Co., *N.Y.* 01
PICKET, A. J. History of Alabama, Georgia, & Mississippi, 2 vols. $7·50 12° *Charleston* [51] 51
SAUNDERS (J. E.) + STUBBS (Mrs E. S.) Early Settlers of Alabama; ill. $3·25 8° Stubbs, *New Orleans* 00
**Alaska; Klondyke** —*v. also* California, *inf.* (WEBB, FINCK)
ADNEY, T. The Klondyke Stampede; ill. $3 8° Harper, *N.Y.* 00
BALLOU, M. M. The New Eldorado; maps [a summer jy. to Alaska] $1·50 16° Houghton, *Boston* [89] 91
*BANCROFT, H. H. Alaska: 1730–1885 [Pacif. St. of N. Am.] $4·50 8° History Co., *San Francisco* 86
BROKE, G. With Sack & Stock in Alaska; 2 maps [by memb. of Alpine Club] 5/ ($1·75) c 8° Longman 91
BRUCE, Miner Alaska, its History and Resources; maps and ill. $2·50 c 8° Putnam, *N.Y.* [97] 99
Instructive chaps. on hist., animals, inhabs., and minerals, w. spec. directns. for prospectors.
BURROUGHS, Jno. Far and Near 5/ *n.* c 8° Constable 05
Nearly hf. the bk. occup. w. acc. of Harriman Expedn.; rest on birds and wild nature.
COLLIS, Septima M. A Woman's Trip to Alaska; ill. $2·50 c 8° Cassell, *N.Y.* 90

COOK, Dr Fredk. A. To the Top of the Continent—*ut* **I** § 165

DALL, W. H. Alaska and its Resources *o.p.* [*pb.* $5] 8° Lee & Shepard, *Boston* 70

De WINDT, Harry Thro' Gold-Fds. of Alaska to Bering Straits; ill. 16/ 8° Chatto 98
$2·50 Harper, *N.Y.* Account of journey in 1897 thro' some little-known parts of the country.

EDWARDS, Wm. S. Into the Yukon $1·50 12° Clarke, *Cincinnati* 05
A narrative of a tour thro' the Klondyke region to California and the Western States.

ELLIOTT, Hy. W. Our Arctic Province, Alaska & Seal Islands; ill. $2·50 8° Scribner, *N.Y.* 86

FILIPPI, Dr Filippo de Ascent of Mount St Elias [tr.]; 2 maps and 150 ill. 31/6 *n.* 8° Constable 00
An account of the Duke of ABRUZZI's expedition.

GARLAND, Hamlin The Trail of the Gold-Seekers $1·50 (6/) c 8° Macmillan [99] 06
An excellent descrn. of a journey to Klondyke: 'a record of travel in prose and verse'.

Harriman Expedition: Results of, 2 vols.; 5 maps and 350 ill. $14 4° Doubleday, *N.Y.* 01
63/ *n.* Murray. Also 14 vols., ea. $7·50 *n.* 8° '03. A popular acc., by 9 wrs., of results of the Harriman Expedn. Vol. i: Narr., glaciers, natives; ii: Hist., geogr., resources.

HAYNE, M. H. E. The Pioneers of Klondyke; ill. 3/6 c 8° Low 97
A good narrative of the opening up of the district, by a mounted policeman. Ed. H. W. TAYLOR.

HEILPRIN, Angelo Alaska and the Klondyke; ill. $1·75 c 8° Appleton, *N.Y.* 99
7/6 Pearson. A full account of the district and its geology; incls. informn. on mining laws.

HEISTAND, Col. H. O. S. Alaska: hist., climate, resources, etc.
[5/ *n.* Paul] $1 c 8° Hudson-Kimberly Pb. Co., *Kansas*

HENDERSON, Alice P. The Rainbow's End: Alaska; ill. $1·50 12° Stone, *Chicago* 98
Acc. of a journey in 1897 from Chicago to Dawson by the Yukon River.

HERBERT (Agn.) + SHIKÁRI (A.) Two Dianas in Alaska; ill. 12/6 *n.* ($4 *n.*) 8° Lane 08

HIGGINSON, Ella R. Alaska, the Gt. Country; map & 48 ill. [7/6 *n.* Bell] $2·50 c 8° Macmillan, *N.Y.* 08

HITCHCOCK, Mary E. Two Women in the Klondyke; ill. $3 8° Putnam 99
A somewhat trite diary of a tour to Dawson by way of Yukon and out by White Pass.

INGERSOLL, Ern. Golden Alaska: acc. of Yukon Valley; maps 25 c. c 8° Rand & McNally, *Chicago* 97

KARR, H. W. Seton Shores and Alps of Alaska [a good bk.] 16/ 8° Low 87

KEIM, De B. Randolph Our Alaskan Wonderland and Klondyke Neighbour
75 c. 8° Harrisbg. Pb. Co., *Harrisbg.* 99

KIRK, R. C. Twelve Months in Klondyke [Dawson city] 6/ *n.* c 8° Heinemann 99

KNAPP (Fces.) + CHILDE (R. L.) The Thlinkets of Southeastern Alaska; ill. $1·50 16° Stone, *Chicago* 96

LEONARD, Jno. W. The Gold Fields of Klondyke 2/6 c 8° Unwin 97

LYNCH, Jerem. Three Years in the Klondyke; ill. [$3 Longm., *N.Y.*] 12/6 *n.* 8° Arnold 04

MACDONALD, A. In Search of El Dorado [Yukon, and Australia] 10/6 *n.* 8° Unwin 06

McLAIN, J. S. Alaska and the Klondyke; ill. $2 *n.* 8° McClure, *N.Y.* 05

PALMER, Frederick In the Klondyke; ill. $1·50 c 8° Scribner, *N.Y.* 99
Over Chilkoot pass to Dawson, w. dogs and sledges, March–May 1898. A graphic and truthful picture.

PIKE, Warburton —*in his* Through the Subarctic Forest, *ut* **E** § 55, *s.v.* N.-W. Canada

POWELL, Addison M. Trailing and Camping in Alaska; ill. 7/6 *n.* c 8° Hurst 10
Acc. of 10 yrs.' experces. as scout and trail-maker while prospecting for the copper deposits of Copper River district.

Report of Internatl. Polar Expedn. to Point Barrow; maps and pl. (some col.)
$4 4° Govt. Prg. Off., *Washgtn.* 85

SECRETAN, J. H. E. To Klondyke and Back [1897] 6/ 8° Hurst 98

SETON-KARR, Lt. H. W. Shores and Alps of Alaska; ill. *o.p.* [*pb.* 16/] 8° Low 87

" Bear Hunting in White Mountains; ill. [Alaska] 4/6 8° Chapman 91
A graphic acc. of a little-kn. section of country. The 'White Mtns.' are in portion of Alaska drained by Chilcat R. and its tribs.

SHELDON, Chas. The Wilderness of the Upper Yukon; ill. 8° 11
Unwin. Diary record of field experces. after wild sheep, as hunter and naturalist, studying their colour-variations (other big game included). Incls. acc. of trip up MacMillan River in company w. F. C. SELOUS.

SWINEFORD, Hon. A. P. Alaska; its history, climate, and resources; ill. $1 12° Rand, *Chicago* 98

WHYMPER, F. Travels in Alaska and on the Yukon; ill. *o.p.* [*pb.* 16/] 8° Murray 68

WILEY, W. H. + Sara K. The Yosemite, Alaska, and the Yellowstone; ill. $3 *n.* 4° Wiley, *N.Y.* 93

WOODMAN, Mrs J. A. Picturesque Alaska; ill. [mountains, glaciers, seas] $1 c 8° Houghton, *Boston* 89

**Arizona**: BANCROFT (H. H.) Arizona and New Mexico: 1530–1888
[Pacif. St. of N. Am.] $4·50 8° History Co., *San Francisco* 88

BISHOP, W. H. —*in his* Old Mexico, *ut* **E** § 57

COZZENS, S. W. The Ancient Cibola: Arizona & New Mexico $2 s 8° Lee & Shepard, *Boston* [76] 90
2/6 Low. First pub. (1874) *s. t. The Marvellous Country.* Acc. of 3 yrs.' visit, w. a hist. of the Apaches.

JAMES, G. W. In and Around Grand Canyon of the Colorado—*ut* **E** § 56, *s.v.* Rivers

PEABODY, H. G. Glimpses of Grand Canyon of Arizona; ill. 50 c. obl 8° Harvey, *Kansas* [00] 03

**California**: *History, etc.* BANCROFT (H. H.) California, vols. i–vii [to 1890] [Pac. St. of N. A.] $4·50 8° History Co., *San Franc.* 84–90
„ California Pastoral [Pacif. States of N. Am.] $4·50 8° History Co., *San Franc.* 88
„ California inter Pocula [Pacif. States of N. Amer.] $4·50 8° History Co., *San Franc.* 88
Former on social life, etc., of California; latter deals w. the Calif. Inferno of 1884, etc.
BLACKMAR, F. W. Span. Institns. of South West; ill. [Univ. Studs.] $2 8° J. H. Univ. Pr., *Baltim.* 91
FARNHAM, T. J. Early Days of California $2 12° Potter, *N.Y.*
HITTELL, J. S. History of San Francisco and of California $4 8° *San Francisco* 79
HITTELL (T. H.) + FAULKNER (R. D.) History of California 50 c. *n.* c 8° Whitaker, *N.Y.* [86] 98
ROYCE, J. California: fr. the Conquest [Am. C'wlths.; 6/ Putn., Lond.] $1·25 16° Houghton, *Boston* 88
SOULÉ Annals of San Francisco $5 8° *New York* 56
TAYLOR, Bayard, El Dorado: advents. in path of empire [Mexico & Calif.] $1·50 12° Putnam, *N.Y.* [50] 81
VAN DYKE, T. S. Southern California $1·50 12° Fords, *N.Y.* 86
WILLEY, S. H. Transition Period of California $1 12° Whitaker, *San Francisco* 01
Acc. of Calif. from a province of Mexico in 1846 to a State of the Amer. Union in 1850.
*Resources*: CRONISE (T. F.) The Natural Wealth of California r 8° *San Francisco* 68
HITTELL, J. S. The Resources of California $1·25 12° Roman, *San Francisco* [63] 74
LINDLEY (W.) + WIDNEY (J. P.) California of the South; ill. [phys. geog., climate, resources, etc.] $2 12° Appleton, *N.Y.* [88] 90
NORDHOFF, C. California, for Health, Pleasure, and Residence 12/6 r 8° Low [73] 87
*Travel and Description*: ALFALO (F. G.) Sunset Playgrounds [Calif. and Canada] 7/6 *n.* 8° Witherby 09
CARTER, C. F. Some Byways of California $1·25 *n.* 12° Grafton Press, *N.Y.* 03
CUMMING, C. F. Gordon Granite Crags; ill. [Yō-semité Regions] 16/ 8° *Blackwood* 84
FINCK, H. T. The Pacific Coast Scenic Tour [S. Calif. to Alaska]—*ut* **E** § 56
HOLDER, C. F. Channel Islands of Calif.; maps and 150 ill. [7/6 *n.* Hodder] $2 *n.* c 8° McClurg, *Chicago* 10
KING, Clarence Mountaineering in the Sierra Nevada $1·50 c 8° Scribner, *N.Y.* [71] 03
7/6, Unwin. A popular account of adventure in the heights of California.
MUIR, Jno. The Mountains of California $1·50 c 8° Century Co., *N.Y.* 94
7/6 Unwin. A pleasant bk., but written with irritating luxuriousness of language, on California under its physical aspects.
„ etc. Picturesque California & Regns. W. of Rocky Mtns., 30 Pts. ea. $1 r 8° Barrie, *Phila.*
NORDHOFF, C. Peninsular California [Lower California] $1 r 8° Harper, *N.Y.* 88
PEIXOTTO, Ern. Romantic California; ill. 10/6 *n.* 8° Unwin 10
STEVENSON, R. Louis Silverado Squatters 2/ *n.* f 8° Chatto [83] 86
$1 Scribner, *N.Y.* Descrs. a picknicking episode, undertaken for health, on a mtn.-top in California; w. many humorous touches.
STODDARD, C. W. In the Footprints of the Padres $1·50 *n.* c 8° Robertson, *San Francisco* 02
VACHELL, Hor. A. Life and Sport on the Pacific Slope $1·50 c 8° Dodd & Mead, *N.Y.* 00
6/ Hodder. A sketch of life in California: well-written.
WARNER, C. D. The American Italy; ill. $2·50 8° Harper, *N.Y.* 91
Amer. edn. *sub tit.* '*Our Italy*'. The prevailing condns., climatic, social, and econ., of S. California.
WEBB, Dr W. S. California & Alaska, & over Canad. Pac. Ry.; ill. $2·25 (10/6) 8° Putnam, *N.Y.* [90] 91
Descrn. of expedn. in 1889 fr. N.Y. to Calif., *via* Omaha, and thro' Montana, Minnesota, and Manitoba, to Vancouver by C.P.R.

**Carolina, N. and S.**: FAUST (J. O.) + ALLEN (M.) Geogr. of N. Carolina 30 c. *n.* c 8° Macmillan, *N.Y.*
HAWKS, F. L. History of N. Carolina, 2 vols.; maps and ill. $5 8° Hale, *N.Y.* [57–58] 63
HAYWOOD, M. De L. Govr. Wm. Tryon and his Administrn.; facss. [1765–71] $2 4° Williams, *Raleigh, N.C.* 03
HOLDER, C. F. Southern California: life in the open; 92 ill. $3·50 (15/ *n.*) m 8° Putnam 06
HOUSTON, Prf. D. F. Critical Study of Nullification in South Carolina $1·25 (6/) 8° Longman 96
[Harvard Historical Studies.] Covers the period 1789 to 1844.
MACCRADY, Edw. History of South Carolina, vols. i–iv ea. $3·50 *n.* (14/ *n.*; iv, 15/ *n.*) 8° Macmillan 97–02
i: *Under the Proprietary Govt.* [1670–1709]; ii: *Dur. the Roy. Govt.* [1719–76]; iii–iv: *Dur. the Revoln.* [1775–83].
MOORE, J. W. Hist. of N. Carol., 2 v., $5; Schl. Hist. of N. Carol. 85 c. 8° Amer. Bk. Co., *N.Y.* 80
NORTH, A. W. The Mother of California; ill. $2 *n.* 8° Paul Elder, *N.Y.* 08
An histor. sketch of land of Baja California fr. days of CORTEZ to present time. Bibliogr.
RAMSAY, D. History of South Carolina, 2 vols. [to 1808] $4 12° Duffie, *Columbia* 67
RAPER, Dr C. L. North Carolina: study in Engl. Colon. govt. $2 *n.* (8/6 *n.*) 8° Macmillan 04
SIMMS, W. G. History of South Carolina [brief] $2·25 12° *New York* [40] 60
SMITH, Dr W. Roy S. Carolina as Royal Province [1719–76] $2·50 *n.* (10/6 *n.*) 8° Macmillan 03
*Blue Ridge*: TORREY (B.) A World of Green Hills [the Blue Ridge] $1·25 c 8° Houghton, *Boston* 98
*Charleston*: RAVENEL (Mrs H. H. R.) Charleston: place & people; ill. $2 *n.* (10/6 *n.*) c 8° Macmillan 06

**Colorado** —*v. also* **E** § 56 (BANCROFT); *for* Colorado River *v.* **E** § 56, *s.v.* Rivers

CHAPIN, F. H. Mountaineering in Colorado; ill. [peaks ab. Estes Pk.] $2 c 8° Appalachian Mtn. Club., *Bost.* 89

GAGE, Emma A. Western Wanderings thro' Picturesque Colorado $2 8° Friedenwald, *Baltimore* 00

NORDENSKIÖLD, G. Cliff-Dwellers of the Mesa Verde $20 *n.* f° Stechert, *N.Y.* 01
Incl. also RETZIUS (G.) *Human Remains from the Cliff Dwellings of the Mesa Verde.*

**Connecticut** —*v. also* New England, *inf.*

*History*

ATWATER, Rev. E. E. History of the Colony of New Haven $4 8° Clarke, *New Haven* 81

" History of the Town of Plymouth; ill. $3 *n.* 8° Darrow, *Rochester* 96

HOLLISTER, G. H. History of Connecticut, 2 vols. *o.p.* [*pb.* $5] 8° Brown, *New Haven* 57

JOHNSTON, Prf. Alex. Connecticut [Am. C'wlths.; 4/6 *n.* Constable] $1·25 12° Houghton, *Boston* [87] 03

PERKINS, [Miss] My. E. Old Houses of Antient Town of Norwich: 1660–1800; ill. $10 8° Noyes, *Norwich, Ct.* 96

PETERS, S. General History of Connecticut $1·50 8° Appleton, *N.Y.* 77

TRUMBULL, B. History of Connecticut, 2 vols. [diffuse] $7·50 8° Utley, *New London* [18] 00

**Florida**: *History; Discovery and Early Voyages*

de BRY, Theod. French Expedition to Florida, ed. Le Mayne *o.p.* [*pb.* $10] 4° *Boston* 75

CHAMBERS, H. E. West Florida and its rel. to Histor. Cartography of U.S. 8° Johns Hopkins Univ. Press, *Baltimore* 98
Clears up the confusion regarding the historical boundaries of West Florida.

FAIRBANKS, G. R. History of Florida: 1512–1842 *o.p.* [*pb.* $2·50] 12° Lippincott, *Phila.* 71

" The Spaniards in Florida *o.p.* [*pb.* $1·50] 12° Drew, *N.Y.* [55] 68

LOWERY, W. Spanish Settlements within present Limits of U.S., i.: 1513–61; ii: Florida, 1562–74; maps ea. $2·50 *n.* (10/6 *n.*) 8° Putnam, *N.Y.* 01–5

de SOTO, F. [1500–42] Disc. and Conq. of Florida [1611], ed. W. B. Rye, tr. R. Hakluyt 8° Hakluyt Soc. 51

Abbott, J. S. C. Ferdinand de Soto [Amer. Pioneers] $1·50 c 8° Dodd & Mead, *N.Y.* 74

Graham, R. B. Cunningham Hernando de Soto 6/ c 8° Heinemann 03
With an account of Gonçalo SILVESTRE, one of his captains.

Irving, Theod. History of De Soto's Conquest of Florida *o.p.* [*pb.* $2·25] 12° Putnam, *N.Y.*

Shipp, B. History of De Soto and Florida: 1512–68 $6 8° Lindsay, *Phila.* 81

***Description***: AFLALO (F. G.) Sunshine and Sport in Florida and W. Indies [$4 *n.* Jacobs, *Phila.*] 16/ *n.* 8° Lane 07

BILL, Ledyard A Winter in Florida; ill. *o.p.* [*pb.* $1·25] 12° Wood, *N.Y.* [69] 71

DELAND, Marg. Florida Days; ill. [by auth. of *John Ward, Preacher*] $4 8° Little & Brown, *Boston* 89

DIMOCK, A. W. + J. A. Florida Enchantments; ill. [12/ *n.* Hodder] $3 *n.* 8° Outing Pb. Co., *N.Y.* 08

HARDY, Iza Duffus Oranges & Alligators: sketches of S. Flor. life *o.p.* [*pb.* 5/] c 8° Ward & Downey 86

HEILPRIN, Angelo —*in his* Exploration on West Coast, *ut* **E** § 54

HENSHALL, J. A. Camping and Cruising in Florida; ill. $1·50 12° Clarke, *Cincinnati* 84

LANIER, Sid. Florida: scenery, climate, & history; ill. $1·50 c 8° Lippincott, *Phila.* [76]
The most valuable pt. is its descrn. of climate and localities.

NORTON, C. L. Handbook of Florida; 49 maps and pl. $1·25 (5/) c 8° Longman 91

TORREY, Bradford Florida Sketch-Book $1·25 c 8° Houghton, *Boston* 94

TOWNSHEND, F. T. Wild Life in Florida; w. visit to Canada *o.p.* [*pb.* 15/] 8° Hurst 75

VILLIERS-STUART, W. H. —*in his* Adventures amidst the Equatorial Forest of South America, *ut* **E** § 61

WILLOUGHBY, H. L. Across the Everglades; map and ill. $1·50 c 8° Lippincott, *Phila.* 98
6/ *n.* Dent. A good descrn. of a canoe-jy. thro' pt. of S. Florida where the Seminole Indians found refuge.

***Oke-cho-bee Lake***: OBER (F. A.) Knock-About Club in Everglades; ill. $1·50 8° Estes, *Boston* 87

**Georgia**: HARLEY (Rev. Tim.) Southward Ho!: tour to and thro' State of Georgia; ill. 5/ c 8° Low 87

JONES, C. C. History of Georgia; maps & ill. [chfly. social hist.] $10 r 8° Houghton, *Boston* 83

'NATIVE GEORGIAN (A)' Georgia Scenes; ill. [1st hf. 19th cent.] $1·25 p 8° Harper, *N.Y.* [ ] 97

SMITH, G. Gillman Story of the Georgia People; ill. $2 8° G. G. Smith, *Macon, Ga.* 01

STEVENS, W. B. History of Georgia to 1798, 2 vols.; map & ill. *o.p.* [*pb.* $5] 8° Claxton, *Phila.* 47

WOOLLEY, Dr H. E. C. Reconstrn. of Georgia [1865–70] [Col. Univ. Studs.] $1 *n.* 8° Macmillan, *N.Y.* 01

***Savannah***: WILSON (Adelaide) Histor. & Picturesque Savannah; ill. $5 8° Bost. Photograv. Co., *Boston* 89

**Illinois**: BATEMAN (N.) + SELBY (P.) Histor. Encyclopædia of Illinois $12·50 4° Munsell, *Chicago* 00

Collections of Illinois State Historical Lib., v. i–ii *not for sale* 8° Ill. St. Hist. Lib., *Springfd.* 06–7 *in prg.*
MASON, E. G. Illinois [Am. C'wlths.; 4/6 *n.* Constable] $1·25 12° Houghton, *Boston* 89
" Chapters from Illinois History $2·50 c 8° Stone, *Chicago* 00
MOSES, J. Illinois, Historical & Statistical, 2 vols.; ill. ea. $3·50 8° Fergus, *Chicago* 89–93
REYNOLDS, J. Pioneer History of Illinois [1673–1818] $5 8° Fergus, *Chicago* [86] 87
SPARKS, E. E. [ed.] English Settlement in the Illinois $2·50 8° Torch Press, *Cedar Rapids* 07
Reprs. of 3 rare tracts on the Illinois country, w. map of a Brit. colony house at Albion.
WALLACE, Jos. Hist. of Illinois & Louisiana und. Fch. Rule $2·50 12° Clarke, *Cincinnati* [93] 99
A condensed hist. of Mississippi valley fr. earliest settlemt. by French till final surrender of Ill. to English in 1765 and of Louisiana to Spaniards in 1769, to wh. is added sketch of Engl. sway in Ill. till 1778.
*Chicago:* GALE (E. O.) Reminiscences of Early Chicago; ill. $2 *n.* 8° Revell, *Chicago* 02
JAMES, Edm. J. [ed.] The Charters of City of Chicago, Pts. i–ii [1833–51] ea. 50 c. *n.* r 8° Univ. Press, *Chicago*
KIRKLAND, Jos. Story of Chicago: history to 1894, 2 vols.; ill. ea. $3·50 12° Dibble, *Chicago* [92] 95
" The Chicago Massacre of 1812 $1 c 8° Dibble, *Chicago* [93] 95
MOSES + KIRKLAND History of Chicago
*Exhibition of* 1893: BANCROFT (H. H.) The Book of the Fair, 2 vols.; profusely ill. [well] $25 f° Bancroft, *Chicago* 94

**Indiana:** BALL (T. H.) North-Western Indiana fr. 1800 to 1900 $2 12° Dakin, *La Porte, Ind.* 00
DILLON, J. B. History of Indiana $3 12° *Indianapolis*
DRYER, C. R. Studies in Indiana Geography [a good bk.] 8° Terre Haute Pb. Co. 97
DUNN, J. P., jun. Indiana: a redemptn. fr. slavery [Am. C'wlths.; 6/ Putn., *Lond.*] $1·25 12° Houghton, *Boston* 88
LEVERING, Julia H. Historic Indiana; map and ill. $2·50 *n.* (12/6 *n.*) 8° Putnam 09
NICHOLSON, Meredith The Hoosiers $1·25 (5/) c 8° Macmillan 00
An account of the State and some of its famous citizens.
SMITH, W. H. History of the State of Indiana, 2 vols. $5 8° Western Pb. Co., *Milwaukee* 03

**Kansas:** CORDLEY (R.) Pioneer Days in Kansas $1 *n.* 12° Pilgrim Press, *Boston* 03
CUSTER, Eliz. B. Tenting on the Plains; ill. [in Kansas and Texas] $1·50 c 8° Harper, *N.Y.* 88
EBBUTT, P. G. Emigrant Life in Kansas; pl. *o.p.* [*pb.* 10/6] 8° Sonnenschein 86
Conts. a good descr. of everyday existence in the West, w. accs. of farming, herding, animals, Indians, *etc.*
ROBINSON, Sara T. D. Kansas: its interior and exterior life 8° Lawrence Journal Co. [59] 00
Valuable as an account of important events, by an eyewitness.
SPRING, L. W. Kansas [Am. C'wlths.; 6/ Putn., *Lond.*] $1·25 12° Houghton, *Boston* [85] 87
*Biography:* BROWN (Jno.) Life of. By H. von Holst, ed. F. P. Stearns $1·50 12° Cupples, *Boston* 88

**Kentucky:** ALLEN (J. L.) Blue-Grass Region of Kentucky; *etc.* $2·50 8° Harper, *N.Y.* 92
Entertaining sketches of life and manners in the famous 'Blue-Grass Region' and other Kentucky localities.
COLLINS, Lew Historical Sketches of Kentucky; ill. $10 8° R. H. Collins, *Maysville* [48] 74
CONNELLY, Emma M. Story of Kentucky; ill. [Story of the States] $1·50 12° Lothrop, *Boston* 91
FILSON CLUB: The Centenary of Kentucky [1892] $2 c 8° Clarke, *Cincinnati* 92
FOX, Jno., jun. Blue-grass & Rhododendron: outdoors in old Kentucky $1·75 *n.* c 8° Scribner, *N.Y.* 01
HOVEY (Dr H. C.) + CALL (Dr R. E.) Mammoth Cave of Kentucky; a manl. 50 c. 8° Mortin, *Louisville* 97
KINKEAD, Eliz. S. History of Kentucky 75 c. 12° Amer. Bk. Co., *N.Y.* 97
MARSHALL, H. History of Kentucky, 2 vols. $14·50 8° *Frankfort* [24]
SHALER, N. S. Kentucky [Am. C'wlths.; 6/ Putnam, *Lond.*] $1·25 12° Houghton, *Boston* [79] 85
WATTS, Wm. Courtney Chronicles of a Kentucky Settlement $2 (9/) c 8° Putnam 97
Story of the early days of Kentucky, w. some stirring adventures.

**Louisiana:** FRENCH (B. F.) [ed.] Historical Collections of Louisiana $4 8° Mason, *N.Y.* [46–53] 75
GAYARRÉ, Chas. History of Louisiana, 4 vols. $10 *n.* 8° Hansell, *New Orleans* [51–4] 03
Standard. Covers the whole hist. of Louisiana dur. dominion of Spanish and Fch.
HENNEPIN, L. [tr.] Description of Louisiana, tr. fr. La Salle [1683] $6 8° Shea, *New Jersey* 80
HOWARD, J. Q. History of the Louisiana Purchase $1·50 *n.* c 8° Callaghan, *Chicago* 02
MARTIN, Judge F. X. Hist. of Louisiana [to 1815], con. by J. F. Condon [to 1861] $6 8° *New Orleans* [27] 83
PIKE, Z. M. —*in his* Expeditions to Head Waters of Mississippi, 3 vols., *ut inf.*, *s.v.* Mississippi
THOMPSON, M. Story of Louisiana; ill. [Story of the States] $1·50 8° Lothrop, *Boston* 89
*New Orleans:* HOWE (W. W.) Municipal Hist. of New Orleans 25 c. 8° J. Hopk. Univ. Pr., *Baltim.* 89
KING, Grace New Orleans: the place & the people; ill. $2 *n.* c 8° Macmillan, *N.Y.* [95] 07

*Creoles:* CABLE (G. W.) The Creoles of Louisiana; ill. Jos. Pennell $1·50 12° Scribner, *N.Y.* 85
,, Old Creole Days $1·50 12° Scribner, *N.Y.* [83]
Also Cameo Edn. $1 *n.*; Ill. A. HERTER, $3·50. Practically a history, and a very good one too, of the State.
FORTIER, Alcée Louisiana Studies $1·50 c 8° Hansell, *New Orleans* 94
A colln. of papers on literature, customs, dialects, folklore and hist. of Creoles; mostly repr. fr. magazines.

**Maine** —*v. also* New England, *inf.*
DRAKE, S. A. Pine Tree Coast; ill. [country along Coast of Maine] $3 8° Estes, *Boston* 91
HUBBARD, L. L. Woods and Lakes of Maine [a canoe voyage] $3 8° Houghton, *Boston* 83
STEELE, T. S. Canoe and Camera: 200 m. tour thro' Maine $1 Estes, *Boston* [80] 82
,, Paddle & Portage fr Moosehead Lake to Aroostook River $1 Estes, *Boston* 82
THOREAU, H. D. Maine Woods [Riverside Edn.] $1·50 12° Houghton, *Boston* [64] 93
'His power of observn. seemed to indicate additl. senses. He saw as w. a microscope, heard as w. an ear trumpet'—R. W. Emerson.
VARNEY, G. J. A Brief History of Maine $1·25 12° McLellan, *Portland* [88] 90
WILLIAMS + DEAN [eds.] Documentary History of State of Maine, 2 vols. 8° *Portland* 69–77
WILLIAMSON, W. D. History of Maine, 2 vols. [1602–1820] *o.p.* 8° *Boston* [32] 39

**Maryland:** ALSOP (G.) Character of Province of Maryland, ed. M. D. Mereness
$2 8° Burrows, *Cleveland, O.* [1666] 02
BOZMAN, J. L. Hist. of Maryland: 1633–60, w. prelim. sketch, 2 v. $5 r 8° Murphy, *Baltimore* [37] 61
The *Preliminary Sketch* was first published separately in 1811.
BROWNE, W. H. Maryland [Am. C'wlths.; 6/ Putnam, *Lond.*] $1·25 12° Houghton, *Boston* [78] 84
HARRY, Jas. W. The Maryland Constitution of 1851 8° Johns Hopkins Univ. Press, *Baltimore* 02
McSHERRY, J. History of Maryland: 1634–1848 $3·50 8° Baltimore Bk. Co., *Baltimore* 04
MERENESS, N. D. Maryland as a Proprietary Province $3 *n.* (12/6 *n.*) c 8° Macmillan 01
NEILL, E. D. Terra Mariæ: colonial history of Maryland $2 12° Lippincott, *Phila.* 6–
SCHARF, J. T. History of Maryland, 3 vols. *o.p.* 8° Turnbull, *Baltimore* 79
SCHMECKEBIER, L. F. Hist. of the Know Nothing Party in Maryland 8° J. Hopk. Univ. Pr. *Baltimore* 99
The story of a powerful, though now a dead, political organization, 1849–1860.
THOMAS, J. W. Chronicles of Colonial Maryland; ill. $5 *n.* 8° Cushing, *Baltimore* 00

**Massachusetts:** —*v. also* New England, *inf.*
*Bibliography:* COLBURN (J.) Bibliography of the Local History of Massachusetts $6 8° *Lunt, Boston* 71
*History:* ADAMS (Brooks) Emancipation of Massachusetts [hostile to Puritans] $1·50 12° Houghton, *Boston* 87
ADAMS, C. F. Massachusetts: its historians and its history $1 c 8° Houghton, *Boston* 93
,, Three Episodes of Massachusetts History, 2 vols. $4 8° Houghton, *Boston* 92
*The Settlement of Boston Bay; The Antinomian Controversy; A Study of Church and Town Government.*
BARRY, J. S. History of Massachusetts, 3 vols. $8·50 8° Burnham, *Boston* 55–7
Standard. i: *Colonial Period*; ii: *Provincial Period*; iii: *Commonwealth.*
BOLLES, Fk. The Land of the Lingering Snow $1·25 c 8° Houghton, *Boston* 91
Short essays descrg. tramps nr. Boston or in eastern Mass.: much informn. on birds.
BOWEN, J. L. Massachusetts in the War of 1861–5 $4 4° Bowen, *Springfield* 90
BRIDGMAN, A. M. [ed.] Souvenir of Massachusetts Legislators; ill. $4 8° Bridgman, *Stoughton, Mass.* 00
CUSHING, H. A. Hist. of Transitn. fr. Provincial to C'w. Govt. in Mass. 8° Columbia Coll. 96
ELLIS, G. E. Puritan Age & Rule in Colony of Mass. Bay [1629–85] $3·50 8° Houghton, *Boston* 88
GARRETT, E. H. Pilgrim Shore $2 12° Little & Brown, *Boston* 00
HALE, E. E. Story of Massachusetts; ill. [Story of the States] $1·50 12° Lothrop, *Boston* 92
HARDING, S. B. Contest over Ratification of the Federal Constitn. in State of Mass.
[Harv. Hist. Studies] $1·25 8° Longman 96
HUTCHINSON, T. [Govr. of Mass.] Hist. of Prov. of Mass. Bay: 1628–1774, 4 v. [stand.] 8° *Boston* 1764–74
,, Diary & Letters, ed. P. O. Hutchinson, 2 v. [1774–80] ea. $5 *n.* 8° Houghton, *Boston* 83–6
Throws very important light on the period just before the Revolution.
POPE, C. H. Pioneers of Massachusetts $12 4° C. H. Pope, *Boston* 00
SCHOULER, J. Massachusetts in the Civil War, 2 vols. *o.p.* [*pb.* $10] 8° *Boston* 68
SEWALL, Sam. [1652–1729–30] Diary, ed. Jos. Sewall
The most important contemporary authority on Colonial Massachusetts, covering about forty years.
SMITH, Sarah S. Founders of the Massachusetts Bay Colony; ill. $5 *n.* c 8° Woodward, *Washington* 02
*Biography:* ADAMS (Sam.) [1722–1803] Samuel Adams. By J. K. Hosmer
[Amer. Statesmen] $1·25 c 8° Houghton, *Boston* [66] 85
GREENHALGE, F. T. Life and Work of. By J. E. Nesmith $3 8° Roberts, *Boston* 97
HUTCHINSON, Thos. [1711–80] Life of. By Prf. J. K. Hosmer $4 8° Houghton, *Boston* 96

VANE, Sir Harry [1613–62] Life of Young Sir H. V. By Prf. J. K. Hosmer $4 8° Houghton, *Boston* 88
18/ Low. VANE was Governor of Massachusetts Bay and leader of the Long Parliament.

WINTHROP, Jno. [1588–1649] J. Winthrop the Younger. By T. F. Waters 8° Hist. Soc., *Ipswich, U.S.* 99

WINTHROP, Mary [*née* TYNDAL; d. 1647]

Earle, Alice Morse [Am.] Margaret Winthrop; facs. [Women of Colon. and Revol. Times] $1·25 c 8° Scribner, *N.Y.* 96
5/ Murray. A pleasant pict. of the wife of the Govr. and of Puritan Engl. und. JAMES i and Boston in 17 cent.

*Berkshire*: ADAMS (Jno. C.) Nature Studies in Berkshire; ill. $2·50 8° Putnam 99

*Boston*; *Concord* [now a suburb of Boston]

BUSHEE, F. A. Ethnic Factors in Populn. of Bost. [Am. Econ. Ass.] $1 c 8° Macmillan, *N.Y.* 03

DRAKE, S. A. Historic Mansions & Highways ard. Boston; ill. $2·50 8° Little & Brown, *Bost.* [73] 99

GILMAN, Arth. Story of Boston; ill. [Great Cities of Republic] $1·75 p 8° Putnam, *N.Y.* 89

GREEN, S. A. [ed.] Ten Facs. Reprodns. rel. to Old Boston & Nbrhd. $10 *n.* f° Littlefield, *Boston* 01

HALE, E. E. Historic Boston & its Neighbourhood [schl.-bk.] 50 c. *n.* Appleton, *N.Y.* 98

HOWE, M. A. De W. Boston: the place & the people; 80 ill. $2·50 *n.* (10/6 *n.*) c 8° Macmillan 03

LODGE, H. Cabot Boston; 2 maps [Historic Towns Ser.] 3/6 ($1·25) c 8° Longman 91

PELHAM, Hy. Greater Boston in 1777: facs. of Pelham's Map $1 27 × 38 in. Butterfield, *Boston* [1777] 07

PORTER, Rev. E. G. Rambles in Old Boston, New England; ill. $6 *n.* 4° Cupples, *Boston* 87

STARK, J. H. [ed.] Antique Views of ye Towne of Boston $5 4° Clarke, *Boston* 02

STEARNS, F. P. Sketches from Concord and Appledore—*ut* **K** § 28

THOREAU, H. D. A Week on Concord & Merrimack Rivers—*ut inf.*, *s.v.* New England

WHITING, Lilian Boston Days $1·50 *n.* c 8° Little & Brown, *Boston* 03
10/6 *n.* Low. Deals chiefly with the intellectual life and worthies of Concord and Boston: exaggerated style.

WINSOR, J. [ed.] Memorial Hist. of Boston, 4 v.; ill. [by several wrs.] $25 8° Osgood, *Boston* 80–2

*Literary Landmarks*: SWIFT (L.) Literary Landmarks of Boston; ill. 35 c. *n.* c 8° Houghton, *Boston* 03

*Cambridge*: HIGGINSON (T. W.) Old Cambridge $1·25 (5/) c 8° Macmillan 99
The intellectual history of the town; and critical memoirs of HOLMES, LONGFELLOW, and LOWELL.

PAGE, L. R. Cambridge, its History, etc. $7·50 8° *Boston* 77

*Cape Cod*: THOREAU (H. D.) Cape Cod $1·50 c 8° Houghton, *Boston* [93] 96
Ill. Edn., 100 col. pl., 2 v., c 8° $5·'97. The wk. of a keen lover and student of nature and observer of men. A fine contribn. to histor. materls. for analysis of Amer. character.

*Charlestown*: HUNNEWELL (J. F.) Century of Town Life; pl. [hist. 1775–1887] $3·50 8° Little & Brown, *Bost.* 88

*Milton*: TEALE (A. K.) [ed.] History of Milton, Mass.: 1640–1887; ill. $3 8° Clarke, *Boston* 88

*Oxford*: DANIELS (G. F.) History of Town of Oxford, Mass.; ill. $4 8° Author, *Oxford, Mass.* 92

*Plymouth*: Records of Town of Plymouth, vol. i: 1636–1705 $1·50 *n.* 8° Clarke, *Boston* 89

*Quabbin*: UNDERWOOD (F. H.) Quabbin: story of a small town $1·50 c 8° Lee & Shepard, *Boston* 93
Account of the town about 1831, and the old-fashioned Puritan life there.

**Michigan**: CAMPBELL (Judge J. V.) Outline of Polit. Hist. of Michigan $4·50 8° Schober, *Detroit* 76

COOLEY, T. M. Michigan [Am. C'wlths.; 4/6 *n.* Constable] $1·25 12° Houghton, *Boston* [79] 86

FARMER, Silas History of Detroit and Michigan; ill. $10 4° Farmer, *Detroit* 84

LANMAN, J. H. History of Michigan 75 c. 18° Harper, *N.Y.* [39]

SHELDON, Electra M. Early History of Michigan [to 1815] $2·50 c 8° Barnes, *N.Y.* 56

**Minnesota**: HALL (C. W.) Geogr. & Geol. of Minnesota, vol. i; ill. $1·20 16° Wilson, *Minneapolis* 03

NEILL, E. D. History of Minnesota to the Present Time $2·50 8° Lippincott, *Phila.* 58

OLIPHANT, Laur. Minnesota and the Far West *o.p.* [*pb.* 12/6] 8° Blackwood 55

**Mississippi**: State, River, and Valley—*v. also* Alabama, *sup.*

CLAIBORNE, J. F. H. History of Mississippi, 2 vols. $7 8°

CLEMENS, S. L. [' Mark TWAIN '] Life on the Mississippi $1·75 c 8° Harper, *N.Y.* [83]

DE SOTO, F. [1500–42] Discovery and Conquest of Florida [tr.]—*ut sup.*, *s.v.* Florida

FISKE, J. Mississippi Valley in the Civil War; maps $2 c 8° Houghton, *Boston* 00

FOSTER, J. W. The Mississippi Valley: its physical geography, etc. *o.p.* [*pb.* $3·50] 8° *Chicago* 69

FOUNTAIN, Paul —*in his* Great Deserts and Forests of North America, *ut* **E** § 52

GALE The Upper Mississippi $2·25 12° *Chicago*

GARNER, J. W. Reconstruction in Mississippi [1849–75] $3 *n.* 8° Macmillan, *N.Y.* 01

HOSMER Short History of the Mississippi Valley $1·20 *n.* c 8° Houghton, *Boston* 01

HUMPHREYS (A. A.) + ABBOTT Report on the Mississippi River $15 4° *Philadelphia*

JOHNSTON, Clifton Highways and Byways of the Mississippi Valley; ill. by author [Highways and Byways Ser.] $2 *n.* (8/6 *n.*) c 8° Macmillan 06

de LA SALLE, R. C. Jl. of Last Voyage [1684–7], ed. Joutel [tr.] $5 *n.* 8° McDonough, *Albany, N.Y.* [1714] 06

LOWRY (R.) + McCARDLE (W. H.) History of the Mississippi $3·50 8° *Jackson, Mississippi* 91
From the discovery of river by DE SOTO, incl. early settlemt. by Fch. under IBERVILLE, to death of Jefferson DAVIS [1889].

" + " History of Mississippi; ill. [State Hist. Series] $1 12° University Pb. Co., *N.Y.* [93] 00

MERRICK, G. B. Old Times on the Upper Mississippi $3·50 *n.* 8° Clark, *Cleveld., O.* 09

MONETTE, J. W. Hist. of Discovery and Settlemt. of Miss. Valley, 2 vols. *o.p.* 8° *New York* 46

OGG, Fredc. The Opening of the Mississippi $2 *n.* (8/6 *n.*) c 8° Macmillan 04
A thorough hist. surv. of the gt. arterial river of N. Am. fr. its discovery to 1814.

PIKE, Z. M. Expeditions to Headwaters of Mississippi, 3 vols. [1805–7] $10 *n.* 8° F. P. Harper, *N.Y.* 95

ROZIER, F. A. Hist. of Early Settlemt. of Miss. Valley; ill. $1·50 *n.* c 8° St Louis News Co., *St Louis* 90

SCHOOLCRAFT, H. R. Narr. of Explor. Expedn. to Sources of Missi. [1820] $3 8° Lippincott, *Phila.* [21] 54

*SHEA, J. G. Hist. & Explorn. of Missi. Valley; facss. & map $5 *n.* 4° McDonough, *Albany* [52] 03
Incls. the orig. narrs. of MARQUETTA, ALLOUEZ, MEMBRE, HENNEPIN, and Anastase DOUAY.

* " Early Voyages up and down the Mississippi $4 *n.* 4° McDonough, *Albany* [61] 02
Voyages of CAVELIER, St COSME, Lo SUEUR, GRAVIER, and GUIGNAS.

SPEARS (J. R.) + CLARK (A. H.) History of Mississippi Valley; ill. & maps $5 *n.* 8° A. S. Clark, *N.Y.* 03

**Missouri:** CARR (Lucien) Missouri [Am. C'wlths.; 4/6 *n.* Constable] $1·25 12° Houghton, *Boston* 88

DIXON, A. True History of the Missouri Compromise [1787–1854] $4 8° Clarke, *Cincinnati* 99

LARPENTEUR, Chas. Forty Yrs. a Fur-Trader on Upper Missouri, 2 v.; ill. $6 8° F. P. Harper, *N.Y.* 98

MARBUT, C. F. Evolution N. Part of South-East Missouri $1·25 8° Univ. of Missouri 02

SWITZLER, W. F. Illustrated History of Missouri: 1541–1877; ill. $2·50 8° Barns, *St Louis* 79

*St. Louis:* BILLON (F. L.) [ed.] Annals of St Louis in its Early Days; ill. $5 8° Nixon, *St Louis* [86] 89
Deals w. Fch. and Span. dominatns., and based on orig. offic. Fch. and Span. documts., most of wh. here tr.

**Nebraska:** CURLEY (E. A.) Nebraska: resources, etc.; ill. $4 8° Am. News Co., *N.Y.* 75

**New England** [=Conn., Maine, Mass., New Hampshire, Rhode Is., Vermt.]—*v. also* **A** § 88

ABBOTT, Kath. M. Old Paths and Legends of New England; ill. $3·50 *n.* (15/ *n.*) 8° Putnam 03

BACON, E. M. Historic Pilgrimages in New England [a good bk.] $1·50 c 8° Silver, *N.Y.* 98

" Literary Pilgrimages in New England [chfly. E. Mass.] $2 c 8° Silver, *N.Y.* 02

BOLLES, Fk. Chronicles of a Stroller in New England, 2 Pts. ea. $1·25 16° Houghton, *Boston* 91–3
Pt. i: Jan. to June, *s. t. Land of the Lingering Snow* [*ut sup. s.v.* Massachusetts]; ii: July to Dec., *s. t. At the North of Beauchamp Water.*

DRAKE, S. A. Nooks & Corners of New England Coast; ill. $2·50 4° Harper, *N.Y.* [75] 97
Descriptive and historical sketch of the coast from Mt. Desert to Long Island Sound.

" Book of New England Legends and Folklore $2·50 8° Little & Brown, *Boston* [84] 01

EARLE, Alice M. Customs and Fashions in Old New England $1·25 c 8° Scribner, *N.Y.* 93
7/6 Nutt. Child Life, Courtship, Homes, Foods, Drinks, Holidays and Festivals, Sports, Books, Raiment, Funerals, *etc.*

" Colonial Dames and Good Wives $1·50 c 8° Houghton, *Boston* 95

" Home Life in Colonial Days; ill. $2·50 c 8° Macmillan, *N.Y.* 98
Homes, Utensils, Occupations (and, to some extent, recreations) minutely described.

" Child-Life in Colonial Days; ill. $2·50 (8/6 *n.*) c 8° Macmillan 99
Old-time babyhd., schl.-life, manners, relig. traing., bks., games, costume, etc.

" Stage-Coach and Tavern Days; ill. $2·50 (10/6) c 8° Macmillan 00

FISKE, Jno. The Beginnings of New England $2 8° Houghton, *Boston* 89

" New France and New England—*ut* **F** § 67

GARRETT, Edm. H. Romance & Reality of Puritan Coast; ill. $2 12° Little & Brown, *Boston* 97

GORGES SOCIETY —*ut* **E** § 54

GREEN, S. A. [ed.] Ten Facsimile Reprodns. rel. to New England $10 f° Littlefield, *Boston* 02

HALE, Dr E. E. Tarry at Home Travels; ill. $2·50 *n.* (10/6 *n.*) 8° Macmillan 07
Sketches of 6 of the N.-Engl. States (and N.Y. State); w. their assocns., reminiscences, etc.

JOHNSON, Clifton The Farmer's Boy; ill. by author [good] $2·50 8° Appleton, *N.Y.* 94
Work, play, and yearly routine of the New-Engld. country-boy.

" New England Country: 100 4-views; w. text $2·50 4° Lee & Shepard, *Boston* 93

" Book of Country, Clouds, & Sunshine; ill. $2·50 8° Lee & Shepard, *Boston* [96] 97

" New England and its Neighbors; 335 ill. $2 *n.* (8/6 *n.*) c 8° Macmillan 02
A record of travel, with full descriptions of places passed through.

MacLEAR, Anne B. Early New England Towns; Massachusetts [Columbia Univ. Studies] $1·50 *n.* 8° Macmillan, *N.Y.* 08

POWELL, Lyman P. Historic Towns of N. Eng.; ill. [Am. Hist. Towns] $3·50 (15/ *n.*) 8° Putnam 98

ROBINSON, Rowl. E. In New Engl. Fields and Woods [Thoreau-esque] $1·25 16° Houghton, *Boston* 96
THOREAU, H. D. A Week on Concord & Merrimack Rivers; ill. 50 c. 16° Crowell, *N.Y.* [67] 00
WHARTON, A. H. Through Colonial Doorways $1·25 c 8° Lippincott, *Phila.* 93
Historical gossip ab. social, intellectual, and home life of prominent people of revol. period: mainly Philadelphia.
" Colonial Days and Dames $1·25 c 8° Lippincott, *Phila.* 95
Extrs. fr. old letters and papers, connected by comments, conjectures, and deductions.
WHITING, Chas. G. Walks in New England $1·50 *n.* (5/ *n.*) c 8° Lane 03
WINTHROP, J. History of New England, ed. J. Savage, 2 vols. *o.p.* [*pb.* $5] 8° *Boston* [25–6] 53
Covers the period 1630–49. WINTHROP was the first Governor of Massachusetts. A standard authority.
*Inns:* CRAWFORD (Mary C.) Little Pilgrimages am. old N. E. Inns; ill. $2 8° Page, *Boston* 07

**New Hampshire** —*v. also* New England, *sup.*
BELKNAP, J. New Hampshire, 3 vols. *o.p.* [*rare; w.* $12] 8° *Boston* 13
M'CLINTOCK, J. N. History of New Hampshire; maps and ill. $3 8° Russell, *Boston* 89
RIDLON, G. T. Saco Valley Settlements and Families $5 *n.* 4° Ridlon, *Portland* 96
1,250 pp. A monumental work, being a full history of the district and the families settled there to the present day.
TORREY, B. Footing it in Franconia $1·10 *n.* c 8° Houghton, *Boston* 01
*Isles of Shoals:* THAXTER (Celia) Among the Isles of Shoals $1·25 c 8° Houghton, *Boston* 01
*Portsmouth:* ALDRICH (T. B.) An Old Town by the Sea $1 c 8° Houghton, *Boston* 93
*White Mountains:* APPALACHIAN MTN. CLUB Guide to White Mtns., Pt. i; maps $1 *n.* 24° Ap. Mtn. Club, *Bost.* 07
DRAKE, S. A. Heart of the White Mountains; ill. $3 4° Harper, *N.Y.* [82] 82
OLMSTEAD, F. L. Jy. in Back Country in Winter 1853–4, 2 vols. $5 *n.* (25/ *n.*) 8° Putnam [60] 07
WARD, Julius H. White Mountains: guide to interpretation $1·25 12° Houghton, *Boston* [90] 96

**New Jersey:** NELSON (W.) + WHITEHEAD (W. A.) etc. [eds.] Documts. rel. to Colonial Hist. of State of New Jersey, vols. i–xxvi ea. $3 8° N. J. Hist. Soc., *Newark* 08
i–vi, xi, xii, xix–xxvi cont. newsppr. extrs. 1704–39; xiii–xviii the jl. of the Govr. and C'cil 1682–1775.
RAUM, J. O. History of New Jersey, 2 vols. $5 8° McVey, *Phila.* 80
SCOTT, Austin New Jersey [Am. C'wlths.; 4/6 *n.* Constable] $1·25 12° Houghton, *Boston* 89
SYPHER (J. R.) + APGAR (E. H.) Hist. of New Jersey; ill. *o.p.* [*pb.* $1·25] 12° Lippincott, *Phila.* 70
TANNER, E. P. Province of New Jersey: 1664–1738 [Columb. Un. Sts.] $4·50 8° Longman 08
*Houses:* MILLS (W. J.) Historic Houses of New Jersey; ill. $5 *n.* 8° Lippincott, *Phila.* 02

**New Mexico** —*v. also* Arizona (BANCROFT; COZZENS)
HAYES, A. A. New Colorado and the Santa Fé Trail; ill. $2·50 8° Harper, *N.Y.* 80
INMAN, Col. Hy. The Old Santa Fé Trail; map and ill. $3·50 8° Macmillan, *N.Y.* 98
JOHNSON, Pioneer Spaniards in North America; ill. $1·20 *n.* 8° Little & Brown, *Boston* 03
LADD, H. O. Story of New Mexico [Story of the States] $1·50 12° Lothrop, *Boston* 92
LUMMIS, C. F. The Land of Poco Tiempo; ill. $2 8° Scribner, *N.Y.* 93
10/6 Low. An interestg. and graphic acc. of inhabs., aborig. and Europ., of N. Mexico., Ariz., S.-W. Texas, and Mex. proper: country, manners, folklore.
" Some Strange Corners of our Country $1·50 c 8° Century Co., *N.Y.* 92
Descrns. of Amer. Sahara and great canyon of the Colorado; w. vivid characterizations of the Indian.
NICHOLL, Edith M. Observations of a Ranchwoman in New Mexico $1·75 (6/) 8° Macmillan 98

**New York State** —*v. also* New England, *sup.*
ANDERSON (J. J.) + FLICK (A. C.) Short History of State of New York; ill. $1 12° Maynard, *N.Y.* 01
BRODHEAD, J. R. Hist. of State of N.Y., 2 v. [1609–91: valuable but dry] $6 8° Harper, *N.Y.* 53–71
BROOKS, E. S. Story of New York; ill. [Story of States] $1·50 8° Lothrop, *Boston* 88
FERNOW, B. [ed.] Documents rel. to Hist. of Towns on Hudson Bay & Mohawk River [exc. Albany; 1630–84] $3 8° Welch, *Albany* 81
FLICK, Prf. A. C. Loyalism in New York dur. Amer. Revoln. $2 *n.* 8° Macmillan, *N.Y.* 01
[Columb. Univ. Studs.] A valuable study of period 1770–84; chfly. fr. MS. sources.
JONES, Judge T. Hist. of New York dur. Revolutionary War, 2 vols. [1752–92] $15 r 8° *New York* 79
O'CALLAGHAN, E. B. [ed.] Documts. rel. to Hist. of N.Y., 10 v. [1609–1800] *o.p.* 4° *Albany, N.Y.* 49–54
PRENTICE, W. R. History of New York State; ill. $1·50 12° Bardeen, *Syracuse, N.Y.* 00
ROBERTS, Ellis H. New York, 2 v. [Am. C'wlths.; 4/6 *n.* Constable] ea. $1·25 12° Houghton, *Boston* 87
TARR, Prf. R. S. Physical Geography of New York State; ill. $3·50 *n.* 8° Macmillan, *N.Y.* 02
*Adirondacks:* MURRAY (W. H. H.) Adventures in the Wilderness $1·25 12° Osgood, *Boston* [ ] 77
NORTHRUP, A. J. Camps & Tramps in the Adirondacks $1·25 c 8° Bardeen, *Syracuse, N.Y.* 80
WARNER, C. D. In the Wilderness [summer-life in Adirondacks] $1 c 8° Houghton, *Boston*

*Hudson River:* BACON (E. M.) Hudson River fr. Ocean to Source; 100 ill. $4·50 *n.* (18/ *n.*) 8° Putnam 02
BRUCE, W. The Hudson; ill. $1·50 12° Houghton, *Boston* 81
*Long Island:* FLINT (Martha B.) Early Long Island; map $3·50 *n.* 8° Putnam, *N.Y.* 96
An excellent piece of local history.
WILSON, Rufus R. Historic Long Island; ill. $2 8° Berkeley Press, *N.Y.* 02
*Mohawk Valley:* REID (W. Max) Mohawk Valley: legends and hist.; ill. $3 *n.* 8° Putnam, *N.Y.* 01
A history of the valley and European settlements there from its discovery to 1780.

*New York City*

ANDREWS, W. Loring The James Lyne's Survey; or Bradford Map $4 *n.* 8° Dodd & Mead, *N.Y.* [93] 00
Accomps. the facs. of an actual surv. of N.Y. at time of grantg. of Montgomerie Charter: made by LYNE and prtd. by BRADFORD (1731).
BACON, E. M. Chrons. of Tarrytown & Sleepy Hollow [antiquarian] $1·25 c 8° Putnam, *N.Y.* 98
BOOTH, M. L. History of the City of New York; ill. *o.p.* [*pb.* $4] 8° Dutton, *N.Y.* [ ] 80
COBURN, A. L. New York: p'fo. of 20 photogravs. 25/ *n.* f° Duckworth 10
DISTURNELL, J. [ed.] New York as it Is and as it Was; ill. $3 8° Disturnell, *N.Y.* 76
EARLE, Alice M. Colonial Days in Old New York $1·25 c 8° Scribner, *N.Y.* 96
4/ *n.* Nutt. Town and country life, chls., Sunday dress, manners, etc., under Dutch and early Engl. rule.
FERNOW, B. [ed.] Records of the City of New Amsterdam, 7 v. ea. $1·50 8° Putnam, *N.Y.* 97
Vols. i–vi give records during the whole period of Dutch control: 1653–54 and 1673–74; vol. vii is Index.
GOODWIN, Maud W., etc. Historic New York, 2 vols.; ill. ea. $2·50 8° Putnam, *N.Y.* 97–8
HASWELL, C. H. Old New York: remins. of an octogenarian; ill. [1816–60] $3 c 8° Harper, *N.Y.* 96
HEMSTREET, Chas. Nooks and Corners of Old New York; ill. $2 12° Scribner, *N.Y.* 99
" Story of Manhattan; ill. $1 *n.* 16° Scribner, *N.Y.* 01
" When Old New York was Young; ill. $1·50 *n.* 8° Scribner, *N.Y.* 02
HUGHES, R. Real New York; ill. 7/6 *n.* c 8° Hutchinson 05
INNES, J. H. New Amsterdam and its People; ill. $2 *n.* 8° Scribner, *N.Y.* 02
IRVING, Washington Knickerbocker's Hist. of N.Y., 2 v.; ill. ea. $1·25 (6/) c 8° Putnam, *N.Y.* [1809]
JANVIER, T. A. In Old New York; maps and ill. $1·75 c 8° Harper, *N.Y.* 94
Traces the evolution of topography, business, and social aspects of the city.
" The Dutch Founding of New York; maps & ports. $2·50 *n.* 8° Harper, *N.Y.* 03
LAMB, Mrs M. J. History of the City of New York, 2 vols.; ill. $20 4° Barnes, *N.Y.* 81
" Wall Street in History; ill. $2 8° Funk & Wagnalls, *N.Y.* 83
LOSSING, B. J. New History of New York City, 2 vols. $1·25 f° Barnes, *N.Y.* [85] 86
MACCRACKEN, H. M. Hall of Fame: offic. bk. of N.Y. Univ. Senate; ill. $1·75 12° Putnam, *N.Y.* 01
MAURICE, A. B. New York in Fiction; ill. of houses, etc. $1·35 *n.* c 8° Dodd & Mead, *N.Y.* 00
O'CALLAGHAN, E. B. Hist. of New Netherlands, 2 vols.; ill.
[N.Y. under Dutch] *o.p.* [*pb.* $6] 8° Appleton, *N.Y.* [46] 55
PHISTERER, F. N.Y. in War of Rebelln. [1861–5; histor. & statist.] $5 8° Phisterer, *Albany, N.Y.* 90
van RENSSELAER, Mrs. Schuyler The Goede Vrouw of Mana-ha-ta [1609–1760] $2 8° Scribner, *N.Y.* 98
An account of the life of the female section of the community in Dutch New York.
" History of the City of New York, 2 vols. $5 *n.* 8° Macmillan, *N.Y.* 09
Covers the hist. fr. settlemt. planted by Dutch on isl. of Manhattan to accessn. of WM. and MARY. Based on orig. research.
ROOSEVELT, Theod. New York; 3 maps [Historic Towns Series] $1·25 (3/6) c 8° Longman 91
Readable, but not very novel. Recent events well treated.
SINGLETON, Esther Social New York under the Georges; ill. [1714–76] $5 *n.* 8° Appleton, *N.Y.* 02
TODD, C. B. Story of City of New York; ill. [Gt. Cities of Repub.] $1·75 p 8° Putnam, *N.Y.* 88
VAN DYKE, J. C. The New New York; ill. Jos. Pennell $3·50 *n.* (17 / *n.*) m 8° Macmillan 09
WILLIAMS, Jessie L. New York Sketches; ill. [6/ *n.* Newnes] $2 *n.* 8° Scribner, *N.Y.* 03
WILSON, Jas. Grant [ed.] Memorial Hist. of City of N.Y., 4 v.; ill. ea. $7·50 8° History Co., *N.Y.* 92–3
Contrib. to by var. Am. historians and antiqs., and based chiefly on orig. docum. matter. Profusely ill.; inclg. facs. documts., etc.
WILSON, Rufus R. New York, Old and New, 2 vols.; ill. $3·50 *n.* c 8° Lippincott, *Phila.* 02
*Families:* HAMM (Margherita A.) Famous Families of N.Y., 2 v.; ill. $15 *n.* 4° Putnam, *N.Y.* 02
*Houses:* PELLETREAU (W. S.) Early New York Houses; ill. $10 *n.* 4° F. P. Harper, *N.Y.* 01
*Literary New York:* HEMSTREET (C.) Literary New York: landmks. and assocns.; ill.
$1·75 *n.* (7/6 *n.*) 8° Putnam, *N.Y.* 03
*Streets:* JENKINS (S.) The Greatest Street in World; map & ill. [Broadway] $3·50 *n.* 8° Putnam, *N.Y.* 11

*Niagara:* HOLLEY (G. W.) History of Falls of Niagara; 30 ill. $3 8° Armstrong, *N.Y.* 82
HULBERT, Prf. A. B. The Niagara River; ill. and maps $3·50 *n.* (15 / *n.*) 8° Putnam 08
PRITCHARD, M. T. [ed.] The Poetry of Niagara; ill. $1 12° Lothrop, *Boston* 01

SEVERANCE, F. H. Old Trails on the Niagara Frontier $2·50 *n.* 8° Burrows, *Cleveld., O.* [ ] 03
*Troy:* WEISE (A. J.) Troy's One Hundred Years; ill. [1789–1889] $3 sq 8° Young, *Troy, N.Y.* 92
**Ohio:** *Bibliography:* THOMSON (P. G.) Bibliography of Ohio $8 4° Thomson, *Cincinnati* 80
ABBOTT, J. S. C. History of Ohio $4 8° *Detroit*
BLACK, A. Ohio; ill. [Story of the States] $1·50 12° Lothrop, *Boston* 88
DRAKE, S. A. Making of Ohio Valley States: 1660–1837; ill. [popular] $1·50 12° Scribner, *N.Y.* 94
FERNOW, B. The Ohio Valley in Colonial Days $5 8° Munsell, *Albany, N.Y.* 91
FOWKE, G. Archaeol. Hist. of Ohio; ill. [mound-bldrs. & Indns.] $5 8° Ohio Arch. Soc., *Columbus* 02
HOWE, Hy. Hist. Collns. of Ohio, 3 v.; 500 ill. [sort of Ohio cyclo.] $13·35 8° *Columbus* 89–91
HOWELLS, W. C. Recollections of Life in Ohio from 1813 to 1840 $2 c 8° Clarke, *Cincinnati* 94
KING, Rufus Ohio [Am. C'wlths.; 4/6 *n.* Constable] $1·25 12° Houghton, *Boston* [89] 03
REID, Whitelaw Ohio in the War, 2 vols. $5 r 8° Clarke, *Cincinnati* 96
Vol. i: Hist. of the State dur. the war, and lives of its Generals; ii: hist. of Ohio regiments.
TAYLOR, J. W. History of State of Ohio, Period i: 1650–1787 *o.p.* [*pb.* $6] 12° *Cincinnati* 54
THWAITES, Dr R. G. On the Storied Ohio; ill. $1·20 *n.* c 8° McClurg, *Chicago* [97] 03
Acc. of 1,000 m. in a skiff, explaing. histor. interest of every point along the route.
„ + KELLOGG (Louise P.) [eds.] The Revoln. on Upper Ohio: 1775–7; ill. $1·50 8° Wisconsin Hist. Soc., *Madison* 08
VENABLE, Dr W. H. Beginnings of Literary Culture in Ohio Valley $3 8° Clarke, *Cincinnati* 91
**Oregon:** *Bibliography:* HORNER (J. B.) Oregon Literature; ill. $1 *n.* 12° Gill, *Portland* [ ] 02
BANCROFT, H. H. Oregon: 1834–88, 2 vols. [Pacif. States of N. Am.] ea. $4·50 8° Bancroft Hist. Co., *San Francisco* 86–86
BARROWS, W. Oregon [Am. C'wlths.; 4/6 *n.* Constable] $1·25 12° Houghton, *Boston* [84] 86
BULFINCH, T. Oregon and Eldorado: romance of the rivers $2·50 12° Tilton, *Boston* 66
GRAY, W. H. History of Oregon [1792–1849] *o.p.* [*pb.* $5] 8° *Portland* 70
IRVING, Washington Astoria—*ut* **E** § 55, *s.v.* Rocky Mountains
NASH, W. Oregon: there and back in 1877 *o.p.* [*pb.* $2] p 8° Macmillan 78
„ Two Years in Oregon; ill. $1·50 c 8° Appleton, *N.Y.* 82
PARKMAN, Fcs. The Oregon Trail—*ut* **F** § 67
*Biography:* MCLOUGHLIN (J.) J. McL., F'r of Oregon. By F. V. Holman $2·50 8° Clark, *Cleveld.* 07

**Pennsylvania:** AGNEW (D.) Hist. of Region of Penn. N. of the Ohio $2 c 8° Kay, *Phila.* 87
BOLLES, A. S. Pennsylvania Province & State, 2 vols. [1609–1790] $5 8° Wanamaker, *Phila.* 99
CORNELL, W. M. History of Pennsylvania; ill. $3·50 8° Quaker City Pb. Co., *Phila.* 76
DICKINSON, J. Letters fr. a Farmer in Penn. to the Inhabitants of the Brit. Colonies; w. Introd. R. T. H. Halsey; port. $7·50 8° Longman, *N.Y.* 03
EAGLE, W. H. History of Pennsylvania $5·50 8° *Harrisburg* [76] 82
FISHER, Sid. G. The Making of Pennsylvania $1·50 12° Lippincott, *Phila.* 96
Acc. of the numerous nationalities and religions wh. made up the populn. of Penn. whilst still a State in embryo.
„ Pennsylvania, Colony & Commonwealth; map $1·50 12° Coates, *Phila.* 97
Takes up narr. of former vol. fr. social and polit. aspect, dealg. mainly w. PENN, the proprietary govts., the Indians, and the Revoln.
HAZARD, W. P. Annals of Phila. and Penn. in the Olden Time $3·75 8° Porter, *Phila.* 79
MCVEAGH, W. Pennsylvania [Am. C'wlths.; 4/6 *n.* Constable] $1·25 12° Houghton, *Boston* 89
PROUD, Rob. History of Pennsylvania, 2 vols. [1681–1742] $12 8° *Philadelphia* [1797]
SHARPLESS, Prf. Is. Two Centuries of Pennsylvanian Hist. [schl.-bk.] $1·25 *n.* 12° Lippincott, *Phila.* 00
SHEPHERD, W. R. History of Proprietary Government in Pennsylvania $4·50 *n.* 8° Macmillan, *N.Y.* 96
TORREY, Bradford A World of Green Hills $1·25 12° c 8° Houghton, *Boston* 98
A pleasant account of rambles in the Southern Alleghanies after ravens.
*Biography:* ARMOR Lives of the Governors of Penn.: 1609–1703; ill. $3·50 8° Davis, *Phila.* 74
Biographical Encyclopædia of Pennsylvania of Nineteenth Century $25 4° Robson, *Phila.* 75
*Germans and Swiss in Pennsylvania*
DIFFENDERFFER, F. R. [ed.] German Immigrn. into Pa. thro' Port of Phila., 2 Pts. ea. $3 8° Edr. *Lancaster, Pa.* –00
KUHNS, L. O. German and Swiss Settlemts. of Colonial Pa. $1·50 12° Holt, *N.Y.* 00
SACHSE, J. F. Fatherland: 1450–1700; ill. $3·50 *n.* 8° Author, *Phila.* 97
„ German Pietists of Provincial Penn.: 1694–1708; ill. $5 8° Author, *Phila.* 95
„ German Sectarian Pennsylvania: 1708–42; ill. $5 8° Author, *Phila.* 99

*Irish in Pennsylvania*—*v.* **F** § 35 *Quakers in Pennsylvania*—*v.* **A** § 89

*Philadelphia:* COOK (Joel) Brief Summer Rambles nr. Philadelphia $1 12° Lippincott, *Phila.* 82
KING, Moses Philadelphia and Notable Philadelphians; ill. $5 4° Moses King, *Phila.* 02
REPPLIER, Agnesr Philadelphia, the Place and the People; ill. $2·50 (8/6 *n.*) c 8° Macmillan 98
RHOADES, Lillian I. The Story of Philadelphia; ill. 85 c. 12° Amer. Bk. Co., *N.Y.* 00
SCHARF (J. T.) + THOMPSON (W.) Hist. of Philadelphia, 3 vols.; ill. [1609–1884] $25 4° Everts, *Phila.* 84
**Sylvan City, The**: or Quaint Corners in Philadelphia; ill. $2 12° Fords, *N.Y.* 83
WESTCOTT, T. Historic Mansions and Buildings of Philadelphia $5 *Philadelphia* 77
WOOLSEY, S. C. [= 'Susan COOLIDGE'] Short Hist. of City of Philadelphia $1·25 12° Roberts, *Boston* 87
*Pittsburgh:* CHURCH (S. H.) Short History of Pittsburgh [1758–1908] $1·25 8° De Vinne Press, *N.Y.* 08

**Rhode Island** —*v. also* New England, *sup.*

*Bibliography:* BARTLETT (J. R.) Bibliography of Rhode Island 8° Rider, *Providence* 64
ARNOLD, S. G. Hist. of State of R. I. and Providence Plantns., 2 v. $7·50 *n.* 8° Preston, *Providence* [59–60] 94
BATES, Prf. F. G. Rhode Island and the Formation of the Union $2 *n.* 8° Macmillan, *N.Y.* 01
[Columbia Univ. Studies.] Study of hist. of State up to the Union, and of struggle over the constitn.
GREENE, G. W. Short History of Rhode Island $2 12° Reid, *Providence* 77
KIMBALL, Gertr. S. [ed.] Correspce. of Col. Govrs. of Rh. Isl.: 1723–75, 2 v. ea. $5 *n.* 8° Houghton, *Bost.* 03
„ [ed.] Pictures of Rhode Island: 1642–1833 $2 *n.* 8° Preston, *Providence, R.I.* 00
MOWRY, A. M. The Dorr War: constitl. struggle in R.I.; ill. $7·50 *n.* sq 8° Preston, *Providence* 01
POTTER, E. R. Memr. conc. Fch. Settlemts. in Rhode Island $1·25 s 4° Rider, *Providence* 80
RICHMAN, I. B. Rhode Island: its making & meaning, 2 vols $4·50 *n.* (21/ *n.*) 8° Putnam 03
SMITH, J. J. [ed.] Civil & Mil. List of R.I.: 1647–1800; 1800–50 ea. $7·50 *n.* 8° Preston, *Providence* 00–1
*Biography:* HOPKINS (Stephen) A Rhode Isle Statesman. By W. E. Foster $5 8° Rider, *Providence* 84

**Tennessee**: CARPENTER History of Tennessee 12° *Philadelphia* 63
CRADDOCK, C. E. The Story of Old Fort London $1·50 12° Macmillan 99
HAYWOOD, Judge Jno. Civil and Pol. Hist. of State of Tenn. [to 1796] $3·50 8° Meth. Ep. Pb. Ho., *Nashville* [23] 91
HUGHES, Thos. Rugby, Tennessee [account of English settlement in Tenn.] 4/6 c 8° Macmillan 81
PHELAN, J. History of Tennessee: making of a State $2 12° Houghton, *Boston* 88
RAMSEY, J. G. M. Annals of Tennessee to end of 18th Century $2·50 8° Lippincott, *Phila.* 60
TEMPLE, O. P. Union Leaders of East Tennessee [Civil War] $3·50 *n.* 8° Clarke, *Cincinnati* 99
THRUSTON, G. P. Antiquities of Tennessee & Adjacent States; ill. $4 *n.* 8° Clarke, *Cincinnati* 90
A series of historical and ethnological studies on the state of aborig. society in scale of civilizn.
TORREY, Bradford Spring Notes from Tennessee [bird-studies] $1·25 16° Houghton, *Boston* 96

**Texas**: *History:* BAKER (De W. C.) Brief History of Texas $1·25 12° Barnes, *N.Y.* 73
„ Texas Scrap Book $5 8° Barnes, *N.Y.* 75
BANCROFT, H. H. Mexican States and Texas, 2 vols. [1531–1889] [Pacific States of N. Am.] $4·50 8° History Co., *San Francisco* 83–9
GARRISON, G. P. Texas [Am. C'wlths.; 4/6 *n.* Constable] $1·10 *n.* c 8° Houghton, *Boston* 03
LUBBOCK, Fcs. R. Six Decades in Texas, ed. C. W. Raines; ill. $2·50 8° Gammel, *Austin, Tex.* 00
THRALL, H. S. Pictorial Hist. of Texas, $4·75; Schl. Hist. of Texas $1 8° Cushing, *St Louis* 79; 76
WILLIAMS, A. M. Sam Houston and War of Indep. in Texas $2 8° Houghton, *Boston* 93
YOAKUM, H. History of Texas, 2 vols. [1685–1846] *o.p.* [*pb.* $8] 8° *New York* 56
*Travel, etc.:* ADAMS (Andy) Reed Anthony, Cowman [autobiogr.] $1·50 c 8° Houghton, *Boston* 07
BARTLETT, J. R. Exploration in Mexico and Texas, 2 vols. *o.p.* 8° *New York* 54
CUSTER, E. B. Tenting on the Plains $1·50 c 8° Harper, *N.Y.* 88
Account of General CUSTER in Kansas and Texas.
HUGHES, Thos. Gone to Texas: Letters from Our Boys 4/6 c 8° Macmillan 84
MACDANIELD (H. F.) + TAYLOR (N. A.) 2,000 Miles on Horseback thro' Texas $1·50 12° *New York* 78
POLLOCK, Cpt. J. M. The Unvarnished West: ranching as I found it; ill. 2/6 *n.* c 8° Gregory, *Tiverton* 07
SWEET (A. E.) + KNOX (J. A.) On a Mexican Mustang thro' Texas; 265 ill. 3/6 8° Chatto [84] 05

**Utah** —*for* Mormonism *v.* **A** § 85

INMAN (Col. H.) + CODY (Col. W. F.) The Great Salt Lake Trail; maps & ill. (14/ *n.*) 8° Macmillan 99
A lengthy account, giving experiences of trappers and explorers and much historical matter.
RAE, W. Westward by Rail: a journey to Francisco *o.p.* [*pb.* 10/6] c 8° Longman [70] 71

STANSBURY, Maj. H. Expedition Valley of Gt. Salt Lake; maps and ill. [1850–1] $4 r 8° Lippincott, *Phila.* [52] 55

**Vermont** —*v. also* New England, *sup.*

COLLINS, E. D. History of Vermont; maps and ill. [school-bk.] 75 c. 12° Ginn, *Boston* 03

HALL, Benj. H. History of Vermont from its Discovery [to 1791] *o.p.* [*pb.* $4] 8° *Albany* 69

" History of Eastern Vermont; ill. [to 1800] *o.p.* [*pb.* $5] 8° Appleton, *N.Y.* 58

HEATON, J. L. Vermont; ill. [Story of the States] $1·50 12° Lothrop, *Boston* 89

ROBINSON, Rowland E. Vermont [Am. C'wlths.; 4/6 *n.* Constable] $1·25 16° Houghton, *Boston* 92

THOMPSON, Prf. Z. History of Vermont $4·50 8° *Burlington* 41

WILBUR, La Fayette Early History of Vermont, vols. i–ii ea. $1·50 8° Roscoe, *Jericho, Vt.* 00

*Newbury:* WELLS (F. P.) Hist. of Newbury; ill. [w. geneals.] $2·25 8° Caledonian Co., *St Johnsbury, Vt.* 02

*Woodstock:* DANA (H. S.) History of Woodstock $4 *n.* 8° Houghton, *Boston* 89

**Virginia:** ALLAN-OLNEY (M.) New Virginians, 2 vols. *o.p.* 8° 80

BOYD, C. R. Resources of South-western Virginia $3 8° Wiley, *N.Y.* 81

BRADLEY, A. G. Sketches from Old Virginia 6/ ($1·50) c 8° Macmillan 97
Sketches of Virginia as it was left after the Civil War: with some account of present day life there.

BRERETON, J. Briefe and True Relation of Discoverie of North Part of Virginia: reprodn. of 1st edn. $2·50 *n.* sq 8° Dodd & Mead, *N.Y.* [1602] 03

BRUCE, Dr Pp. A. Econ. Hist. of Virginia in 17 Cent.—*ut* **D** § 117*
A well-written account, bringing much new matter to light.

" Social Life of Virginia in the 17th Century $1·50 *n.* c 8° Bell, *Richmond* 07

" Institutional Hist. of Virginia in 17th Cent., 2 vols. $6 *n.* (25/ *n.*) 8° Putnam 10

BURWELL, Letitia M. A Girl's Life in Virginia before the War $1·50 c 8° Stokes, *N.Y.* [95]

CAMPBELL, C. History of Colony & Anc. Dominion of Virginia *o.p.* [*pb.* $2·50] 8° Lippincott, *Phila.* 60

COOKE, J. E. Stories of the Old Dominion; ill. 60 c. 12° Am. Bk. Co., *N.Y.* [79] 00

" Virginia [Am. C'wlths.; 4/6 *n.* Constable] $1·25 12° Houghton, *Boston* [84] 03

DRAKE, S. A. Making of Virginia & the Middle Colonies; ill. [1578–1701] $1·50 12° Scribner, *N.Y.* 94

EGGLESTON, Dr Edw. The Beginners of a Nation; 8 maps [7/6 Longman] $1·50 c 8° Appleton, *N.Y.* 97

FISKE, Prf. Jno. Old Virginia and her Neighbours, 2 vols. $4 8° Houghton, *Boston* [97] 00
A fully detailed hist. of settlemt. of Va.; w. much of value on Maryland and the Carolines.

GOODWIN (*née* WILDER), Maud The Colonial Cavalier $2 c 8° Little & Brown, *Boston* 95
Entertaing. inform. ab. Southern home-life, educn., churches, social customs, etc., before the Revolution.

HARIOT, Thos. [1560–1621] Narrative of First Plantation of Virginia [1590]—*ut* **E** § 54

" Brief & True Report of New Found Land of Virginia $2·50 *n.* sq 8° Dodd & Mead, *N.Y.* [1588] 03

HOWISON, R. R. Hist. of Virginia, fr. Discovery to Present Time, 2 v. *o.p.* [*pb.* $6] 8° *Philadelphia* 46–8

JAMES, C. F. Docum. Hist. of Struggle f. Rel. Liberty in V. $1·25 12° Bell, *Lynchburg, V.* 01

MUNFORD, B. B. Virginia's Attitude tow. Slavery & Secession $2 *n.* (9/ *n.*) 8° Longman 10

O'NEILL, E. D. [ed.] Virginia Vetusta dur. rn. of James i [letters & documts.] 12° *Albany* 85

PRYOR, Mrs R. A. The Mother of Washington & her Times; ill. $2·50 *n.* (12/6 *n.*) 8° Macmillan 03

SMITH, Cpt. Jno. [1579–1631] Generall Historie of Virginia and Summer Isles, 2 vols. 25/ *n.* 8° MacLehose, *Glasgow* [1626] 07
$6 Macmillan, *N.Y.* [Elizab. Travels Series.] A handsome reprint, w. reprodns. of all the maps and illns.

" Works, ed. Edw. Arber 12/6 8° Arber's Reprts. [1608–31] 84
Conts. early informn. resp. first Engl. settlemts. in Virginia, Bermuda, New Engld., Guiana, Barbadoes, Newfdld., etc.

" True Travels and Adventures [50 c. Dutton, *N.Y.*; New Univ. Lib.] 1/ *n.* pott 8° Routledge 07

Bradley (A. G.) Captain John Smith [Engl. Men of Action] 2/6 (75 c.) c 8° Macmillan 05

Woods (Kath. P.) True Story of Capt. John Smith [2/ *Times* Bk. Club] c 8°

SMITH, M. V. The Governors of Virginia; ill. [1492–1892] $2·50 8° Lowdermilk, *Washington* 94
A brief review of discovery of N. Amer., w. a hist. of executives of Colony and Commonwealth of Virginia.

STEVENS, B. F. Campaign in Virginia: 1781, 2 vols. 88

STITH, W. First Discovery & Settlemt. of Virginia, ed. J. Sabin $7·50 8° Sabin, *N.Y.* [1747] 60

STRACHEY, Wm. [ed.] Historie of Travaile into Virginia, ed. R. H. Major *o.p.* 8° Hakluyt Soc. 49

TYLER, Dr L. G. [ed.] Narratives of Early Virginia: 1606–25; maps $3 *n.* c 8° Scribner, *N.Y.* 07

WARNER, C. D. On Horseback [tour in Va., N. Car., Tenn.] $1·25 c 8° Houghton, *Boston* 88

WISE, Jno. S. The End of an Era $2 c 8° Houghton, *Boston* 99
Reminiscences of the State during the author's boyhood, at the time of the Civil War.

WITHERS, A. S. Chrons. of Border Warfare [1831], ed. R. G. Thwaites $2·50 8° Clarke, *Cincinnati* [ ] 95
Hist. of the settlemt. by the whites of N.-W. Va. and of the Indian Wars and massacres there. Memr. and notes by Dr L. C. DRAPER.

*Biography :* WISE (Hy. A. ; former Govr.) Life of. By B. H. Wise $3 8° Macmillan, *N.Y.* 99

**Washington State and City** : BANCROFT (H. H.) Washington, etc.
[Pac. States of N. Amer.] $4·50 8° History Co., *San Francisco*

EVANS, G. G. Washington Illustrated ; ill. [a sort of guide-bk.] $2 12° Evans, *Phila.* 92

MEANY, Prf. E. S. History of the State of Washington ; ill. $2·25 *n.* (10/ *n.*) 8° Macmillan 09

SEELYE, Eliz. E. Story of Washington, ed. Dr E. Eggleston ; ill. $1·75 12° Appleton, *N.Y.* 93

TODD, C. B. Story of Washington [Great Cities of Republic] $1·75 8° Putnam, *N.Y.* 89

WILSON, Rufus R. Washington, the Capital City, 2 vols. ; ill. $3·50 *n.* c 8° Lippincott, *Phila.* 01

*Puget Sound :* MEANY (Prf. E. S.) Vancouver's Discovery of Puget Sound ; ill.
$2·50 *n.* (10 /6 *n.*) 8° Macmillan 07

Mainly a repr. of some 8 chs. of VANCOUVER's *Journal of the Voyage of the 'Discovery'* (1792).

*Rainier, Mt.* (*Tacoma*) : WILLIAMS (J. H.) The Mtn. that was 'God' ; ill. $1·50 *n.* 8° Putnam, *N.Y.* [ ] 11

**Wisconsin :** SMITH History of Wisconsin, 2 vols. 8° *Madison*

THOMSON, A. M. Political History of Wisconsin ; ill. $5 *n.* 8° Caspar, *Milwaukee* [00] 02

THWAITES, Dr R. G. Story of Wisconsin ; ill. [Story of the States] $1·50 12° Lothrop, *Boston* 90

,, Stories of the Badger State 60 c. 12° Am. Bk. Co., *N.Y.* 00

*Yellowstone Valley and Park*

*CHITTENDEN, Cpt. H. M. Yellowstone Natnl. Pk. [histor. & descr.] $1·50 *n.* c 8° Clarke, *Cincinnati* [ ] 03

DUNRAVEN, Earl of The Great Divide ; ill. [the Upper Yellowstone] *o.p.* [*pb.* 18/] 8° Chatto [74] 76

MUIR, Jno. —*in his* Our National Parks $1·75 *n.* c 8° Houghton, *Boston* 01

SYNGE, Georgina M. A Ride through Wonderland 3/6 c 8° Low 92

## 57* : MEXICO

**Early Voyages**

CORTES, Hern. [1485–1547] Five Letters to Chas. V, tr. F. A. MacNutt, w. notes, 2 v. ; ports.
10 *n.* (42/ *n.*) 8° Putnam 08

MacNutt, F. A. Fernando Cortes ; ill. [Heroes of Nations] $1·35 (5/) c 8° Putnam 09

Helps, [Sir] Arth. Life of Cortes, and Conqu. of Mexico, 2 vols. *o.p.* [*pb.* 15/] c 8° Bell 71

Prescott, W. H. —*in his* History of the Conquest of Mexico, *ut inf.*

DIAZ DEL CASTILLO, B. True History of the Conquest of New Spain, tr. Prf. A. P. Maudslay ;
w. Introd. and notes, vols. i–iii. 8° Hakluyt Soc. 98–10

**History :** BANCROFT (H. H.) Resources & Devel. of Mexico ; ill. $4·50 8° History Co., *San Francisco* 93

,, Mexico, 8 v. : 1516–1889 [Pac. States of N. Am.] ea. $4·50 8° History Co., *San Francisco* 83–9

,, Popular History of Mexican People ; ill. 15/ 8° Trübner 88

BISHOP, W. H. Old Mexico and her Lost Provinces $2 12° Harper, *N.Y.* [83] 87

BUTLER, Dr W. Mexico in Transition fr. Power of Polit. Romanism to Civil
& Religious Liberty ; ill. $2 8° Hunt & Eaton, *N.Y.* 92

ENOCK, C. R. Mexico : its ancient and mod. civilizn. ; 64 pl. 10/6 *n.* 8° Unwin 09

$3 Scribner, *N.Y.* [South Amer. Series.] Incls. hist., polit. condns., topogr., and natural resources.

FROST, J. History of Mexico and its Wars ; ill. $4 8° Hawkins, *New Orleans* 82

HALE, Susan Mexico ; ill. [Story of Nations ; 5/ Unwin] $1·50 c 8° Putnam, *N.Y.* 91

NOLL, A. H. Short Story of Mexico $1 16° McClurg, *Chicago* 90

*PRESCOTT, W. H. Hist. of Conquest of Mexico, ed. J. Foster Kirk, 3 v. $3 8° Lippincott, *Phila.* [43]

Cheap Edn., ed. same, 3 vols., *id.* $1·50. Ed. same, Lib. Edns., 2 vols., 10/ 8° Routledge ; 4/6 *n.* 8° Sonnenschein ; 3/6 c 8° Routledge.

SIERRA, J. [ed.] Mexico, its Social Evolution [tr.], 3 vols. f° Ballesa, *Mexico* 05

WELLS, Dav. A. A Study of Mexico $1 12° Appleton, *N.Y.* [86] 90

**Biography**

DIAZ, Porfirio

Godoy, J. F. Porfirio Diaz, Master-builder of a Gt. C'wealth ; ill. $2 *n.* (10/6 *n.*) 8° Putnam 10

Tweedie, Mrs Alec Porfirio Diaz, 7 times Pres. of Mexico ; ill. 21/ *n.* 8° Hurst 06

JUAREZ, Benito [Constit. President of Mexico]

Burke, Ulick R. Life of Benito Juarez 5/ c 8° Remington 94

An account of the reign of MAXIMILIAN from the point of view of a Mexican Liberal.

MAXIMILIAN and CARLOTTA

de Keratry, C't E. Maximilian, his Rise and Fall [tr.] *o.p.* [*pb.* 10/6] 8° Low 67

de Malortie, Bar. Empress Carlotta's Ride to Calvary—*in his* Here, There, & Everywhere, *ut* **F** § 1

Taylor, Jno. M. Maximilian and Carlotta; ill. $1·50 (6/ *n.*) 8° Putnam 94
Account of NAPOLEON's attempt to set MAXIMILIAN on throne of Mexico; fr. pt.-of-view of a Mexican Liberal.

**War with U.S.** —*v.* **F** § 70, *s.v.* Mexican War

**Travel and Description:** ANDERSON (A. D.) The Silver Country $1·75 8° Putnam, *N.Y.* 77

AUBERTIN, J. J. A Flight to Mexico; ill. *o.p.* [*pb.* 7/6] c 8° Paul 82

BANDELIER, A. F. Mexico; ill. $5 4° Cupples, *Boston* 85

BARTLETT, J. R. Exploration in Mexico and Texas, 2 vols. *o.p.* 8° *New York* 54

BARTON, Mary Impressions of Mexico w. Brush and Pen; col. ill. 10/6 *n.* 8° Methuen 11

BEEBE, C. W. Two Bird-Lovers in Mexico; ill. [6/6 *n.* Constable] $3 *n.* c 8° Houghton, *Boston* 05

BROCKLEHURST, T. U. Mexico To-day; ill. [w. acc. of prehist. remains] 21/ m 8° Murray 83

CARSON, W. E. Mexico, the Wonderland of the South $2·25 *n.* (10/ *n.*) 8° Macmillan 09

CHARNAY, Désiré Ancient Cities of the New World [tr.]; 100 ill. 31/6 r 8° Chapman 87
Account of travels in Mexico and Central America from 1857 to 1882.

EDWARDS, Wm. S. On the Mexican Highlands; map & ill. $1·50 *n.* c 8° Jennings, *Cincinnati* 07

GADOW, Hans F. Through Southern Mexico; maps and ill. 18/ *n.* 8° Witherby 08
$6 *n.* Scribner. *N.Y.* A valuable account of a naturalist's travels and mod. condns. in S. Mexico.

GOOCH, Fanny C. Face to Face with the Mexicans; 200 ill. $4·25 r 8° Fords, *N.Y.* 90
16/ Low. Details ab. people, domestic life, educn., literature, etc. Mrs GOOCH, a native of Texas State, lived 17 yrs. in Mexico.

'GRINGO, Harry' [= A. WISE] Through the Land of the Aztecs; ill. 6/ c 8° Low 92
A 'Gringo' is a slang term used fr. Mexico to Chili for an Englishman or American. This is an American's acc. of 7 yrs.' life and travel in Mexico.

HAMILTON, L. C. Mexican Handbook [resources, trade, laws, etc.] 8/6 c 8° Low 84

HORNADAY, W. T. Camp Fires on Desert and Lava; maps and ill. $3 *n.* 8° Scribner, *N.Y.* 06
16/ *n.* Laurie. Story of expedn. fr. Tucson, Arizona, acr. desert to region surroundg. N.-W. Mexico.

KIRKHAM, S. D. Mexican Trails [3 yrs.' wanderings] $1·75 *n.* (7/6 *n.*) 8° Putnam 09

KNOX, T. W. Boy Travellers in Mexico [good pop. bk.] $2 8° Harper, *N.Y.* 90

LUMHOLTZ, Carl Unknown Mexico, 2 vols.; ill. [good] $12 *n.* 4° Scribner, *N.Y.* 02
50/ *n.* Macmillan. A valuable record of 5 yrs.' explorn. am. tribes of Western Sierra Madre district. Bibliogr.

LUMMIS, C. F. Awakening of a Nation: Mexico of to-day $2·50 c 8° Harper, *N.Y.* 98
Repr. newsppr arts., givg. enthusiastic acc. of the country and its future. Map and illns.

" —*in his* The Land of Poco Tiempo, *ut* **E** § 57, *s.v.* New Mexico

MARTIN, P. F. Mexico in the Twentieth Century, 2 vols. $8·50 *n.* 8° Dodd & Mead, *N.Y.* 07
30/ *n.* Arnold. Valuable for mod. condns. Vol. ii deals w. nature of country and industries.

Mexican Year Book; 23 maps and pl. [c. 1,000 pp.] ea. 21/ 8° McCorquodale *ann.*
Comprehensive statistics, commercial, econ., industr., etc. Issued und. ausp. of Dept. of Finance.

OBER, F. A. Travels in Mexico and Life among Mexicans; 190 ill. 7/6 8° Warne [84] 88

OSWALD, F. L. Summerland Sketches: rambles in Mex. & Cent. Am.; ill. $3 8° Lippincott, *Phila.* 80

PERCIVAL, Olive Mexico City; ill. $1·25 16° Stone, *Chicago* 01

PIKE, Z. M. —*in his* Expeditions, 3 vols., *ut* **E** § 54 [1805–7]

ROMERO, Matias Mexico and the United States $4·50 8° Putnam 98
A cyclopædic colln. of useful informn. on relations of the two nations. A reference-work.

" Geographical and Statistical Notes on Mexico $2 8° Putnam 98
Physical features, geology, climate, flora, populn., condn., etc.

SHERRATT, Mrs H. W. Mexican Vistas; ill. [a tourist's-bk.] $1·50 12° Rand, *Chicago* 99

SMITH, F. Hopkinson A White Umbrella in Mexico; ill. $1·50 16° Houghton, *Boston* [89] 92

SMITH, L. Eaton Flying Visits to City of Mexico and California; ill. 6/ c 8° Young, *L'pool* 03

STARR, Fredk. In Indian Mexico; ill. $5 *n.* 8° Forbes, *Chicago* 08

TURNER, Jno. K. Barbarous Mexico 7/6 *n.* c 8° Cassell 11

TWEEDIE, Mrs Alec Mexico as I saw it; map and 100 ill. 21/ *n.* c 4° Hurst 01
$5 *n.* Macmillan, *N.Y.* Cheap Edn. 1/ *n.* Nelson. A well-wr. acc. of a tour thro' all more important parts of the country.

WALLACE, D. Beyond the Mexican Sierras; ill. [7/6 *n.* Hodder] $2 *n.* 8° McClurg, *Chicago* 10
Informn. ab. the area betw. the tableland and Pacific: State of Sinaloa, Western Durango, and Tepic Territory.

WRIGHT, Marie Picturesque Mexico; 330 ill. $10 4° Barrie, *Phila.* [98]

## 58: CENTRAL AMERICA

**Bibliography** —*in* HERBERTSON, *and in* PIM + SEEMAN, *ut inf.*

**Early Voyages and Travel** —*v. inf., passim, and* **E** §§ 54, 61 *passim*

**General Geography**

HERBERTSON, F. D. + A. J. Central and South America, with the West Indies 2/6 c 8° Black [02] 03
70 c. *n.* Macmillan, *N.Y.* [Descriptive Geographies.] 128 extrs. fr. wks. of travellers, going in detail over the various countries. Bibliogr.

STANFORD, E. [pb.] Central and South America, 2 vols.; maps and ill. [Compendium of Geogr.] ea. 15/ 8° Stanford [78] 01
Ea. $5·50. Lippincott, *Phila.* Vol. i: *South America*: ii: *Central America and W. Indies.* By Prf. A. H. KEANE, ed. Sir C. R. MARKHAM.

**Recent Travel and Accounts:** AGASSIZ (A.) Three Cruises of the *Blake*, 2 vols.—*ut* **E** § 7
BANCROFT, H. H. Central America: 1501–1887, 3 vols.
[Pacific States of N. Am.] ea. $4·50 8° History Co., *San Francisco* 82–7
BODDAM-WHETHAM, J. W. Across Central America; pl. *o.p.* [*pb.* 15/] 8° Hurst 77
BYAM, Geo. Wild Life in the Interior of Central America *o.p.* [*pb.* 5/] f 8° Parker 49
By a thorough sportsman and accurate observer.
CHARNAY, Désiré Ancient Cities of the New World [tr.] —*ut* **E** § 57
CHILD, Theod. —*in his* Spanish American Republics—*ut* **E** § 60
CURTIS, W. E. Capitals of Spanish America; map and 360 ill. $3·50 r 8° Harper, *N.Y.* 88
18/ Low. Mexico, Central America, South America.
DAVIS, R. H. Three Gringos in Venezuela and Central America—*ut* **E** § 61, *s.v.* Venezuela
PALMER, F. Central America and its Problems [10/6 *n.* Laurie] $2·50 *n.* 8° Moffat, *N.Y.* 10
Acc., by an Amer. journalist, of jy. fr. Rio Grande to Panama, w. chs. on Mexico, etc. Bibliogr.
PIM (Cpt. B.) + SEEMAN (Dr B.) Dottings on Roadside in Panama, Nicaragua, and Mosquito
*o.p.* [*pb.* 18/] 8° Chapman 69
SANBORN, Helen J. Winter in Centr. America and Mexico $1·50 12° Lee & Shepard, *Boston* 86
SQUIER, E. G. Travels in States of Cent. Amer., 2 v.; ill. [esp. Nicar.] *o.p.* [*pb.* $4] r 8° Harper, *N.Y.* 53
„ Notes on Central Amer.; ill. [Honduras, San Salvador] *o.p.* [*pb.* $2·50] 8° Harper, *N.Y.* 55
STEPHENS, J. L. Incidts. of Travel in Cent. Am., Chiapas, & Yucatan; 82 pl.
*o.p.* [*pb.* 12/] 8° Hall [41–2] 54
Ed. F. CATHERWOOD. This tour (1839–40) was undertaken w. a view to exam. of remains of anc. art extant in the dense forests.
VINCENT, A. In and Out of Central America; ill. $2 12° Appleton, *N.Y.* 90

**Costa Rica:** CALVO (J. R.) Repub. of Costa Rica [tr.]; w. Introd.; ill. $2 12° Rand & McNally, *Chicago* 90
CHURCH, Col. G. E. Costa Rica—*in* Jl. R. G. Soc., July, 1897 8° Murray 97
A very valuable and comprehensive acc. of the republic and its people; w. a good map.

**Guatemala:** BRIGHAM (W. T.) Guatemala, Land of the Quetzal; maps & 105 ill. $5 8° Scribner, *N.Y.* 87
MAUDSLAY, Anne C. + A. P. Glimpse at Guatemala; maps and ill. [good] 84/ *n.* 4° Murray 99
Excellent acc. of travel in 1894 interspersed w. archæological informn. on anc. monumts. of Centr. Amer.

**Honduras:** CHARLES (Cecil) Honduras, the Land of Great Depths $1·50 c 8° Rand & McNally, *Chicago* 90
CORTES, Hernan Fifth Letter to Emperor Charles v [tr.] 8° Hakluyt Soc. 88
Tr. fr. the Spanish. Contains an account of his expedition to Honduras in 1525–6. *Vide* also **E** § 57*, *s.n.* CORTES.
GIBBS, A. R. British Honduras, Historical and Descriptive 7/6 c 8° Low 83
LOMBARD, T. R. The New Honduras $2 8° Brentano, *Chicago* 87
MORRIS, D. Colony of British Honduras: resources & prospects; map 2/ *n.* i 16° Stanford 84
'SOLTERA, Maria' [= Mary LESTER] Lady's Ride acr. Spanish Honduras; ill. 12/6 p 8° Blackwood 84
SQUIER, E. G. Honduras: descriptive, historical, etc. *o.p.* [*pb.* 3/6] c 8° Hamilton 70

**Nicaragua; Panama,** incl. **Panama Canal**
ABBOT, H. P. L. Problems of the Panama Canal $2 *n.* (8/6 *n.*) 8° Macmillan [05] 11
BELL, C. N. Tangweera 99
BELT, Thos. Naturalist in Nicaragua; map and ill. 7/6 p 8° J. Bumpus [74] 88
At the gold-mines of Chontales. A standard work on tropical nature, describg. jys. in 1868–72.
BIDWELL, C. T. The Isthmus of Panama *o.p.* [*pb.* 16/] 8° Chapman 65
BRANSFORD, J. F. Archaeological Researches in Nicaragua 8° 81
COLQUHOUN, A. R. Key of the Pacific: the Nicaragua Canal; ill. 21/ *n.* 8° Constable 96
$7 *n.* Longman, *N.Y.* A full discussn. of the nature and commerc. possibilities of the proposed canal thro' Lake Nicaragua.
CORNISH, Dr Vaughan The Panama Canal and its Makers $1·50 *n.* c 8° Little & Brown, *Boston* 09
5/ Unwin. An interestg. acc. of the magnificent struggle and ultimate victory over the natural difficulties of the extraord. isthmus.
DELEVANTE, M. Panama Pictures: nature and life of the canal; ill. $1 8° Alden, *N.Y.* 07
FORBES-LINDSAY, C. H. A. Panama: the isthmus and the canal $1 *n.* 8° Winston, *Phila.* 06
„ —*in his* America's Insular Possessions, 2 vols., *ut* **E** § 52
JAMES (E. J.) + HAUPT (L. M. A.) Two Papers on Canal Questn. [Am. Ec. Ass.] $1 *n.* 8° Macm., *N.Y.* 07
JOHNSON, Willis F. Four Centuries of Panama Canal [12/ *n.* Cassell] $3 *n.* 8° Holt, *N.Y.* 07
NELSON, Dr W. Five Years at Panama 7/6 c 8° Low 89
PEPPER, C. M. From Panama to Patagonia: Isthmian canal and W. coast countries
$2·50 *n.* 8° McClurg *Chicago* 06
10/6 *n.* Hodder. Discusses effect that Panama Canal will have on developmt. of the Pacific Ports of S. Amer.
PIM, Cpt. B. The Gate of the Pacific *o.p.* [*pb.* 18/] 8° Lovell Reeve 63
„ Panama, Nicaragua, and Mosquito *o.p.* [*pb.* 18/] 8° Chapman 69
„ + SEEMAN (Dr B.) —*in their* Dottings, *ut sup.*

SHELDON, Hy. I. Notes on the Nicaragua Canal; maps & ill. $1·25 8° McClurg, *Chicago* [97] 02
A plea for the route of the proposed canal; w. much informn. ab. the country.

SIMMONS, W. E. The Nicaragua Canal; ill. $1·25 12° Harper, *N.Y.* 00

SQUIER, E. G. Nicaragua: people, scenery, monumts., resources; ill. $4 8° Harper, *N.Y.* [52] 71

WALKER, J. W. G. Ocean to Ocean; ill. $1·25 *n.* 8° McClurg, *Chicago* 02
Some account of travel, and clear descriptions of the various schemes for the canal.

WICKHAM, H. A. Rough Notes of Journey fr. Trinidad *o.p.* [*pb.* 15/] 8° Carter 72

**Salvador:** MARTIN (P. F.) Salvador in Twentieth Century; ill. 15/ *n.* 8° Arnold 11

**Yucatan:** ARNOLD (C.) + FROST (F. J.) The American Egypt; ill. 16/ *n.* 8° Hutchinson 09
$3·80 *n.* Doubleday, *N.Y.* A graphic and picturesque acc. of a tour by Englishmen in Yucatan.

FANCOURT, C. St J. History of Yucatan [to end 17 cent.] *o.p.* [*pb.* 12/] 8° Murray 54

Le PLONGEON, Alice D. Here and There in Yucatan 50 c. c 8° Lovell, *N.Y.* [86] 89

MERCER, Hy. C. The Hill-Caves of Yucatan $2 8° Lippincott, *Phila.* 96

STEPHENS, J. L. —*in his* Incidents of Travel, *ut sup.*

## 59: WEST INDIES

**Early Voyages and Travel** —*for* Buccaneers *v.* **E** § 54

d'ACOSTA, F'r Jos. Natural and Moral History of the Indies, tr. E. Grimston, ed. C. R. Markham, 2 vols. 8° Hakluyt Soc. [1604] 80

CHAMPLAIN, Sam. Voyage to West Indies, tr. & ed. Alice Wilmere [1599–1602] 8° Hakluyt Soc. 59

DAMPIER, Wm. [1652–1715] —*in his* Voyages, ed. Jno. Masefield, 2 vols., *ut* **E** § 7
Vol. i conts. narr. of his life in W. Indies w. the buccaneers between 1679 and 1688.

DUDLEY, Rob. Voyage to West Indies & Guiana, ed. Dr G. F. Warner 8° Hakluyt Soc. 99
Three narrs. of voy. 1594–5, one by DUDLEY, other two by KENDALL, the pilot, and by Cpt. WYATT.

FROUDE, J. A. —*in his* English Seamen of the Sixteenth Century, *ut* **F** § 30

HOOD, L'd Letters fr. West Indies in 1781–3, ed. Dav. Hannay—*ut* **F** § 28 (Navy Records Ser.)

de LAS CASAS, Bartol. [1474–1566]

Helps, [Sir] Arth. Life of Las Casas, Apostle of the Indies *o.p.* [*pb.* 6/] c 8° Bell [68] 68

MacNutt, F. A. Barth. de Las Casas: life, apost., wrgs.; ill. $3·50 *n.* (15/ *n.*) 8° Putnam 09

VENABLES, Gen. R. Narrative of 1655, ed. C. H. Firth [Roy. Hist. Soc. pubns.] 10/ 4° Longman 00
Appendix conts. pprs. rel. to expedn. to W. Indies and conquest of Jamaica, 1654–5.

**General Geography** —*v.* **E** § 58 (HERBERTSON, STANFORD)

**Guides:** ASPINALL (A. E.) Pocket Guide to West Indies; 10 maps & 26 ill. 5/ *n.* f 8° Duckworth [07] 10

OBER, F. A. Guide to West Indies & Bermudas; maps & ill. $2 *n.* 8° Dodd & Mead, *N.Y.* 08

**Historical Geography:** LUCAS (Sir C. P.) West Indian Colonies = Hist. Geogr. of Br. Cols., vol. ii 7/6 ($2) c 8° Clar. Press [01] 05

**Recent Travel and Accounts:** AFLALO (F. G.) Sunshine and Sport in Florida and West Indies—*ut* **E** § 57

ARTHUR, R. Ten Thousand Miles in a Yacht round West Indies and up the Amazon; maps and ill. $2 *n.* Dutton, *N.Y.* 06

BULLEN, F. T. Back to Sunny Seas [West Indies] 6/ c 8° Smith & Elder 05

DODSWORTH, F. Book of the West Indies; ill. [kind of guide-bk.] 6/ 8° Routledge 04

EDEN, C. H. The West Indies [For. Countries and Brit. Colonies] 3/6 c 8° Low 80

EVES, C. W. The West Indies; maps & ill. [Roy. Colon. Inst. pubn.] 7/6 c 8° Low [89] 97

FORREST, A. S. [art.] W. Indies: col. pl., w. l'rpr. J. Henderson [$6 *n.* Macm., *N.Y.*] 20/ *n.* sq 8° Black 05

FROUDE, J. A. English in West Indies; 9 ill. [visit of 1887] 3/6 c 8° Longman [88] 09
$1·50 Scribner, *N.Y.* [Silver Lib.] Picturesque descrns. of Barbadoes, Dominica, Hayti, Jamaica, St Vincent, Tobago, Trinidad; w. comment on govt., condns., prospects.

Thomas, J. J. [a negro] Froudacity [reply to above] 6/ c 8° Unwin 89

HEARN, Lafcadio Two Years in the French West Indies $2 12° Harper, *N.Y.* 90

*HILL, Rob. T. Cuba & Porto Rico; w. other islds. of W. I.; ill. $3 8° Century Co., *N.Y.* 98
16/ Unwin. The best general geogr. acc. of topogr., climate, flora, products, industries, people, and polit. condns. of the islds.

JAY, E. A. Hastings Glimpse of Tropics; ill. [4-mos.' cruise] 6/ c 8° Low 00

KINGSLEY, Can. C. At Last!: a Christmas in the West Indies [1869] 3/6 ($1·25) c 8° Macmillan [70] 10
Enthusiastic apprecn. of beauty of W. Ind. scenery, among the finest descrn. of tropical countries to be found. Ch. Edn. 1/.

LEWIS, M. G. Jl. of Residence am. Negroes in W. Indies *o.p.* [*pb.* 2/] c 8° Murray [34] 45

MORRIS, I. N. With the Trade Winds [sketches of Venez. & W. I.] $1·25 c 8° Putnam, *N.Y.* 97

OBER, F. A. Knock-About Club in Antilles & Thereabouts; ill. $1·50 8° Estes, *Boston* 88

PHILLPOTTS, Eden In Sugar-Cane Land [ordinary tourist's descrn.] 3/6 f 8° McClure 93

RODWAY, Jas. West Indies and the Spanish Main; ill. $1·75 c 8° Putnam, *N.Y.* [96] 02
5/ Unwin. An accurate but discursive short hist. of the Europ. settlemts. in W. Indies.

STOKES, A. P. Cruising in the West Indies $1·25 *n.* 8° Dodd & Mead, *N.Y.* 02

TREVES, Sir Fredk. The Cradle of the Deep; 40 pl. and 4 maps 12/ *n.* 8° Smith & Elder 08
$4 *n.* Dutton, *N.Y.* A fresh and attractive bk. in the West Indies and the Spanish Main.

TROLLOPE, Anth. The West Indies and the Spanish Main *o.p.* [*pb.* 5/] c 8° Chapman [59] 69

VILLIERS-STUART, H. —*in his* Adventures amidst Equatorial Forests & Rivers of S. America, *ut* **E** § 61
Incls. acc. of advs. in Jamaica [*s.v. Jamaica Revisited*, comparg. it w. what it was in 1859] and W. Inds. generally.

WALKER, H. de R. The West Indies and the Empire 7/6 *n.* 8° Unwin 01
A discussion of economic and administrative questions relating to the British West Indies.

*History:* Calendar of State Papers: Colonial Series, ed. W. Noel Sainsbury, vol. ix: America and West Indies: 1675–6—*ut* **F** § 33
Incls. some interesting correspce. rel. to massacre of Indians in Dominica and negro risings in Jamaica and Barbadoes.

FISKE, A. K. Story of the West Indies $1·50 (6/) c 8° Putnam 99
An admirable brief history of the islands, w. acc. of their natural resources and condition.

KENNEDY, Arnold Story of the West Indies; maps [elementary] 1/6 c 8° H. Marshall 99

**Antigua:** OLIVER (V. L.) History of Island of Antigua, 3 vols.; ill. 8° Mitchell & Hughes 95–9
An elab. and exhaustive colln. of hist. documts., genealogies and other materl. ill. of hist. of the island, 1635–1899.

**Bahamas:** POWLES (L. D.) Land of the Pink Pearl [life in Bahamas] 10/6 8° Low 88

SHATTUCK, Dr G. B. [ed.] The Bahama Islands; ill. $10 *n.* (42/) i 8° Macmillan 05
Results of labours of a scientific expedn. to Bahamas sent by Geogr. Soc. of Baltimore.

STARK, J. H. [pb.] Bahama Islands; ill. [Stark's Ill. Guidebks.] 6/ *n.* c 8° Low 98

**Barbadoes:** DAVIS (N. D.) Cavaliers and Roundheads in Barbadoes [1650–2] $1·25 c 8° *New York* 83

SCHOMBURGH, Sir R. H. History of Barbadoes; ill. [geogr. & statist.] *o.p.* [*pb.* 31/6] r 8° Longman 48

STARK, J. H. [pb.] Barbados and the Caribbee Island [Stark's Ill. Guidebks.] 6/ *n.* c 8° Low 98

**Bermuda** —*v.* **E** § 55

**Caribbees (Windward Islands):** NICHOLAS (F. C.) Around the Caribbean & Across the Panama; maps and ill. $2 8° Caldwell, *Boston* 03

OBER, F. A. Camps in the Caribbees $1·50 8° Lee & Shepard, *Boston* 80
Record of nat. hist. researches for Smithsonian Institn. in the Lesser Antilles, 1876–8.

PATON, W. A. A Cruise to the Caribbees; ill. $2·50 8° Scribner, *N.Y.* 88

STARR, Ida M. H. Gardens of the Caribbees, 2 vols.; ill. $2·40 *n.* 16° Page, *Boston* 03

STODDARD, Rev. C. A. Cruising among the Caribbees; 16 ill. $1·50 12° Scribner, *N.Y.* [95] 07
9/ Paul. Acc. of winter-trip, w. notes on discov., people, customs, folklore, etc. 1903 edn. incls. Jamaica and Porto Rico.

STOKES, A. P. Cruising in Caribbean w. a Camera; ill. $1·25 *n.* 8° Dodd & Mead, *N.Y.* 03

TROWBRIDGE, W. H. R. Gossip of the Caribees: sketches of W. Ind. life; ill. $1·50 12° Tait, *N.Y.* 93

**Cuba:** BALLOU (M. M.) Due South: Cuba past and present $1·50 12° Houghton, *Boston* [85] 98

BLOOMFIELD, J. H. A Cuban Expedition $2·25 i 16° Scribner, *N.Y.* 99
A vivid narr. of pers. service in one of earlier of its numerous filibusterg. expedns. [1868–78] fitted out in U.S. for aidg. Cuban insurrectionists agst. Span. Govt. The expedn. was a failure; and author was one of the 7 who (out of 285) escaped w. their lives.

BONSAL, S., jun. The Real Condition of Cuba To-day 60 c. c 8° Harper, *N.Y.* 97

BROWNE, G. W. [ed.] —*in* New America and the Far East, vol. vi, *ut* **E** § 52

CABRERA, R. Cuba and the Cubans; map and ill. $1·50 c 8° Levytype Co., *Phila.* 96

CALLAHAN, Dr Cuba and International Relations 8° Johns Hopkins Univ. Pr., *Baltimore* 99
An international hist. of Cuba and of questns. (Span., Brit., American) wh. have clustered round it.

CLARK, Wm. J. Commercial Cuba: a bk. for business-men $4 8° Scribner, *N.Y.* 99
A storehouse of commercial facts and statistics. Maps, plans, and ill.

DANA, R. H., jun. A Trip to Cuba and Back [1859] $1·25 12° Houghton, *Boston* [59] 98

DAVEY, Rich. Cuba Past and Present; map and ill. $3 8° Scribner, *N.Y.* 98
12/ Chapman. A fairly full history and description of the island.

DAVIS, R. H. Cuba in War Time; ill. 50 c. 12° Russell, *N.Y.* [97] 98
A picture of the military situatn. and the desolation prevalent in 1896 in the once beautiful island.

,, The Cuban & Porto Rican Campaigns; maps & ill. $1·50 c 8° Scribner, *N.Y.* 99

HALSTEAD, M. Story of Cuba: her struggles for liberty $2 8° Werner Co., *Akron, O.* [ ] 98

*HILL, Rob. T. Cuba and Porto Rico—*ut sup.*

v. HUMBOLDT, Alex. The Island of Cuba [tr.] *o.p.* [*pb.* 7/6] c 8° Low 56

MATTHEWS, F. New-born Cuba $2·50 8° Harper, *N.Y.* 99

NOA, F. M. The Pearl of the Antilles 75 c. 16° F. M. Noa, *Geneva, N.Y.* 98
A small book giving some account of the actions of the Spanish authorities which led to the final insurrection.

PEPPER, C. M. To-morrow in Cuba $2 8° Harper, *N.Y.* 99

PORTER, Hon. Rob. P. Industrial Cuba; maps and 62 ill. $3·50 (15/) 8° Putnam 99
An excellent acc. of the commerc. and industrial condns. of Cuba after the Spanish-American War.

QUISENBERRY, A. C. Lopez's Expedns. to Cuba: 1850-1; ill. [Filson Club pb.] $4 4° Morton, *Louisville* 06
ROBINSON, A. G. Cuba and the Intervention $1·80 *n.* (7/6 *n.*) 8° Longman 05
ROWAN (A. S.) + RAMSEY (M. M.) Island of Cuba [descriptive and historic] $1·25 c 8° Holt, *N.Y.* [97] 98
STEELE, J. W. Cuban Sketches, $1·50; Popular Edn. 50 c. $1·50 12° Putnam, *N.Y.* 81; 85
TOWNSHEND, Cpt. F T. Wild Life in Florida: a visit to Cuba 15/ 8° Hurst 75
WRIGHT, Irene A. Cuba; ill. $2·50 *n.* (10/6 *n.*) c 8° Macmillan 10

**Haiti; San Domingo:** HAZARD (S.) Santo Domingo, Past and Present; ill. $3·50 8° Harper, *N.Y.* 73
KIMBALL, R. B. Life in San Domingo $1·50 12° Carleton, *N.Y.*
LÉGER, J. N. Haiti, her History and her Detractors $3 8° Neale Pb. Co., *Washington* 07
PRITCHARD, Hesketh Where Black rules White; ill. 12/ 8° Constable 00
Agst. Haitian govt., w. acc. of jy. acr. the republic. Cf. his *Thro' Haiti*, in *R.G.S. Jl.*, Sept. '00.
ST JOHN, Sir Spencer Hayti; or, The Black Republic; map 8/6 p 8° Smith & Elder [84] 89

**Jamaica:** *History, Economical Condition, etc.—for* Slave-trade *v.* **D** § 130
GARDNER, Rev. W. J. History of Jamaica [discovery to 1872] 7/6 *n.* 8° Unwin [73] 09
Handbook of Jamaica: pubd. by authority 6/ *n.* 8° Govt. Prtg. Off., *Jamaica* (Stanford) *ann.*
An excellent spec. of a Colonial Yr.-Bk. Contents very various and complete, ranging fr. meteor repts. to last yr's. cricket.
NUGENT, L'y [Maria SKINNER] Journal: Jam. 100 yrs. ago, ed. F. Cundall; ill. 5/ *n.* c 8° Black [39] 07
$2 *n.* Macmillan, *N.Y.* Repr. fr. a jl. Rept. fr. 1801 to 1815, and issued f. priv. circn. in 1839.
*Recent Travel and Description:* CAINE (W. R. Hall) Cruise of *Port Kingston;* ill. 10/6 *n.* 8° Collier 08
FORREST, A. S. [art.] Jamaica: 24 col. pl., w. l'rpr J. Henderson [$2 *n.* Macm., *N.Y.*] 6/ *n.* sq 8° Black 07
HILL, Rob. T. Geology & Physical Geography of Jamaica; ill. 8° Harvard Univ., *Camb.*, *U.S.* 99
LEADER, A. Thro' Jamaica with a Kodak; ill. [letters] 6/ *n.* 8° Simpkin 07
PULLEN-BURRY, B. Jamaica as it is; map and ill. 6/ *n.* c 8° Unwin 03
,, Ethiopia in Exile: Jamaica revisited 6/ c 8° Unwin 05
First 13 chs. descr. latest phases of Jam. hist.; last 8 devoted to study of Amer. negro.
SCOTT, Sir J. S. D. To Jamaica and Back *o.p.* [*pb.* 10/] p 8° Chapman 76
VENABLES, Gen. R. —*in his* Narrative, ed. C. H. Firth, *ut sup.*, *s.v.* Early Voyages, etc.
VILLIERS-STUART, H. Jamaica Revisited—*in his* Adventures amidst Equat. Forests, *ut* **E** § 61
*Guide:* STARK (J. H.; pb.) Jamaica [Stark's Ill. Guidebks.] 6/ *n.* c 8° Low 98

**Martinique:** HEARN (Lafcadio) Two Years in French W. Indies $2 c 8° Harper, *N.Y.* 90
Mainly on Martinique. Descriptive portn. largely interwoven w. legends, poems, music, folklore.
HEILPRIN, Prf. Angelo Mount Pelée & Tragedy of Martinique; ill. $3 *n.* (15/ *n.*) r 8° Lippincott 03
,, Tower of Pelée: new studies of gt. volcano; ill. $3 *n.* (15/ *n.*) r 8° Lippincott 04

**Porto Rico:** BONSAL (S.) —*in his* Golden Horseshoe, *ut* **E** § 36, *s.v.* Philippines
BROWNE, G. W. [ed.] —*in* New America and the Far East, vol. vi, *ut* **E** § 52
DINWIDDIE, W. Puerto Rico: its conditions and possibilities $2·50 8° Harper, *N.Y.* 99
DRAKE (Sir Fcs.) Voyage [1595]. By T. Maynarde, ed. W. D. Cooley 8° Hakluyt Soc. 49
Ed. fr. the orig. MS. Con'ts. also the Spanish account of DRAKE's attack on Puerto Rico. For Life, etc., of DRAKE, *v.* **E** § 54.
FEWKES, J. W. Aborigines of P. R. & Neighbg. Islds.; ill. [21/ *n.* Wesley] 4° Bur. of Am. Ethnol. 07
FORBES-LINDSAY, C. H. A. —*in his* America's Insular Possessions, 2 vols., *ut* **E** § 52
FOWLES, G. M. Down in Porto Rico; ill. 75 c. *n.* c 8° Eaton, *N.Y.* 06
HAMM, M. A. Porto Rico and the West Indies $1·25 c 8° Neely, *N.Y.* 99
OBER, F. A. Puerto Rico and its Resources $1·50 c 8° Appleton, *N.Y.* 99
RECTOR, C. H. Story of Beautiful Porto Rico; maps & 60 ill. $1·25 c 8° Laird, *Chicago* 98
ROBINSON, Alb. G. Porto Rico of To-day; maps and 24 ill. $1·50 12° Scribner, *N.Y.* 99
VAN MYDDELDYK, R. A. Hist. of Puerto Rico, ed. M. G. Brumbaugh; ill. $1·25 *n.* 12° Appleton, *N.Y.* 03

**Trinidad:** FRASER (L. M.) Hist. of Trinidad, v. i-ii [1781-1839] ea. 12/ *n.* 8° *Trinidad* (Simpkin) 91-6
HORT, Daniel Trinidad: historical and statistical view of island *o.p.* 8° Saunders 65
de VERTEUIL, L. A. A. Trinidad: geography, resources, condition, etc. 21/ 8° Cassell [58] 84
WICKHAM, H. A. Rough Notes on Trinidad, Brazil, etc. *o.p.* [*pb.* 15/] 8° Carter 72
*Guide:* STARK (J. H.; pb.) Trinidad [Stark's Ill. Guidebks.] 6/ *n.* c 8° Low 98

## 60: SOUTH AMERICA (*a*): COLLECTIVELY

**Bibliography** —*v.* **E** § 54 (COLE)
*Maps:* URICOECHEA (E.) Mapoteca Colombiana *o.p.* [*pb.* 6/] 8° Trübner 60
All the maps indicated in this esteemed bibliography of S. Am. maps are in the Brit. Museum.

**Early Travels: Buccaneers** —*v.* **E** § 54

**Ethnology** —*v. also* **E** § 53

UHLE, Max — Culture and Industries of S. Am. Peoples, 2 v.; 55 pl. ea. 80/ f° Asher 89
Illustrated by the collections in the Leipzig Ethnographical Museum.

**General Geography** —*v.* **E** § 58 (HERBERTSON, STANFORD)

**Series:** South American Series: ed. W. A. Hirst; maps and ill.
[ea. $3 *n.* Scribner, *N.Y.*] ea. 10/6 *n.* 8° Unwin 07 *sqq., in prg.*
*Argentine [ut inf.]* W. A. HIRST | *Mexico [ut* **E** *§ 57*]* C. R. ENOCK | *Uruguay [ut* **E** *§ 61]* W. H. KOEBEL
*Chile [ut inf.]* C. F. Scott ELLIOTT | *Peru [ut* **E** *§ 61]* C. F. Scott ELLIOTT |

**History; Economic Conditions;** etc.

AKERS, Chas. E. — History of South America: 1854–1904; maps and ill. 21/ *n.* 8° Murray 04
A concise hist. of the var. S. Am. States since they attained independence of Spanish control.

ALCOCK, Fredk. — Trade and Travel in South America 12/6 *n.* 8° Philip 03
Of great value to the merchant, the ordinary traveller, and interesting to the general reader.

'AMERICAN (AN)' — Hist. of S. America fr. its Discovery [tr.] 10/6 8° Sonnenschein 99
$3 *n.* Macmillan, *N.Y.* A fairly good general sketch, tr. from the Spanish.

BLACKMAR, Fk. W. — Spanish Colonization in the South West 50 c. 8° Johns Hopk. Univ Press, *Baltim.* 90
" — Spanish Institutions of the South West; ill. $2 8° Johns Hopk. Univ. Press, *Baltim.* 91

BOLIVAR, Simon [leader in revolt agst. Spain in Venez., N. Gran., Peru]
Petre, F. L. — Simon Bolivar: 'El Libertador 12/6 *n.* ($4 *n.*) 8° Lane 10

BOURNE, E. G. — Spain in America: 1450–1580 8° 04

CLEMENCEAU, Georges — South America To-day; 8 ill. 12/6 *n.* 8° Unwin 11

DAWSON, T. C. — South American Republics, 2 vols.; maps and ill.
[ea. 5/ Unwin; Story of Nations] ea. $1·35 *n.* c 8° Putnam 03–4

Handbk. of Amer. Republics, Bulletins 1 *sqq.*; maps & ill. *n.pp.* 8° Govt. Ptg. Off., *Washgn.* 91 *sqq., in prg.*
Issued by Bureau of Amer. Repubs., givg. infcrmn. f. producers, merchts., and others, w. refer. to independent nations of America.

HELPS, [Sir] Arth. — The Spanish Conquest in America, 4 vols.—*ut* **E** § 54

MITRE, Gen. Don B. — Emancipation of South America [tr.]; maps [1778–1830] 12/ 8° Chapman 93
A condensed tr. of *Hist. of San Martin* (the revol. leader who in co-oper. w. DUNDONALD and Simon BOLIVAR liberated Chili and Peru) by the First Constit. Pres. of Argentine Repub. A straightforward soldier's account, on the whole impartial, but a poor history.

MOSES, B. — Establishment of Spanish Rule in America $1·25 c 8° Putnam, *N.Y.* 98

MULHALL, M. G. — The English in S. Amer.; ill. [16 cent. to 1877] *o.p.* [*pb.* 16/] 8° Stanford 78

WATSON, R. G. — Spanish & Portuguese S. Amer., 2 v. [Colonial period] *o.p.* [*pb.* 21/] p 8° Trübner 84

**Indians** —*v.* **E** § 53

**Recent Travel and Description**

*Adventure & Beagle:* By King, Fitzroy & Darwin [1826–36]; *also* Darwin's Voy. of Naturalist—*ut* **H** § 44

AKERS, Chas. E. — Argentine, Patagonian, and Chilian Sketches 5/ c 8° Harrison 93

ALCOCK, F. — Trade and Travel in South America; maps and ill. 6/ *n.* 8° Philip [03] 07

BALL, J. — Notes of a Naturalist in South America 8/6 8° Paul 87

BALLOU, Maturin M. — Equatorial America $1·50 c 8° Houghton, *Boston* 92

CARPENTER, F. G. — South America: social, industrial, political; ill. $3 8° Saalfield, *Akron, O.* 00
Much informn. on ways of living in Southern hemisphere. Profusely illd., furnishg. a panorama of S. Am. life.

CHILD, Theod. — Spanish-American Republics; ill. $3·50 4° Harper, *N.Y.* 92
Travel 1890–1, describg. life, people, industries, progress of Chili, Peru, Argentine, Paraguay, Uruguay.

CRAWFORD, Rob. — Across the Pampas and the Andes; ill. *o.p.* [*pb.* 7/6] c 8° Longman 84
" — South American Sketches 6/ ($2) c 8° Longman 98

CRICHFIELD, G. W. — American Supremacy, 2 vols. [25/ *n.* Unwin] $6 *n.* 8° Brentano, *N.Y.* 07
An exhaustive arraignmt. of the Latin-Am. repubs., their hist., and personal, social, polit., and commerc. condns. Bk. iii (131 pp.) devoted to Monroe Doctrine, Bk. iv (149 pp.) to 'Civilizn. *v.* Barbarism'. 'I see the U.S. of the future . . . ploughing up the anarchy and barbarism of Latin Amer., as tho' they were poisonous weeds in a garden'.

CROMMELIN, May — Over Andes fr. Argentine to Chili & Peru; ill. *o.p.* [*pb.* 12/6] 8° Bentley 96

CURTIS, W. E. — Capitals of Spanish America; ill. $3·50 8° Harper, *N.Y.* 88
" — Between the Andes and the Ocean; ill. $2·50 8° Stone, *Chicago* 00

DOMVILLE-FIFE, C. W. — The Great States of South America; maps and ill. 12/6 *n.* 8° Bell 10
A concise descrn. of ea. cy., its products, econ. developmt., commerc. interests, Govt. concessns., etc.

FORD, Is. N. — Tropical America; map and 16 ill. $2 c 8° Scribner, *N.Y.* 93
10/6 Stanford. A brightly-wr. acc. of visits to Rio, Brazil, Argent., Chile, Lima, Guayaquil, Cartagena, Jamaica, Bahamas, Mexico, San Juan, etc. Largely political and throughout impartial (tho' strongly imbued w. Pan-American ideas).

FOUNTAIN, Paul — Great Mountains & Forests of S. America; ill. $4 (10/6 *n.*) 8° Longman 02
Word-pictures of natural scenes and bird and animal life in the Andes and the great forest of Brazil.

GALLENGA, A. — South America [repr. fr. *Times*] *o.p.* [*pb.* 14/] 8° Chapman 80

HALE, Dr A. — The South Americans: story of S. A. republics; ill.
$2·50 *n.* 8° Bobbs-Merrill Co., *Indianapolis* 07

HOLDICH, Sir Thos. H. The Countries of the King's Award—*ut* **E** § 61, *s.v.* Argentine Republic
Includes a short general view of South American geography.

v. HUMBOLDT, Alex. Personal Narrative of Travels to Equinoctial Regns. of New Continent, 3 v. ea. 5/ c 8° Bell [19–29] 77
Ea. $1·50 *n.* Macmillan, *N.Y.* [Bohn's Lib.] One of the first jys. [1799–1804] of scientific explorn. Of great historical interest.

KNIGHT, E. F. The Cruise of the *Falcon*—*ut* **E** § 61, *s.v.* Paraguay

KNOX, T. W. Boy Travellers in South America; ill. [popular] $2 c 8° Harper, *N.Y.* 86

MANN, Alex. Yachting on the Pacific 6/ c 8° Duckworth 09
Gives a good deal of informn. ab. islands and other places visited, startg. fr. Guayaquil and proceedg. to Galapagos Isld.

MARCOY, Paul Jy. acr. S. Amer. fr. Pacific to Atlantic, 2 v.; ill. [1848–60] 42/ i 8° Blackie 74

MARKWICK (W. F.) + SMITH (W. A.) S. Amer. Republic [World & its People] 60 c. *n.* c 8° Silver, *N.Y.* 01

MARTIN, Percy F. Thro' Five Republics of South America; maps & ill. $5 *n.* 8° Dodd & Mead, *N.Y.* 05
21/ Heinemann. A formalistic descrn. of Argentina, Brazil, Chile, Uruguay, Venezuela. Chiefly concerned w. the econ. developmt.

'MOZANS, H. J.' Along the Andes and Down the Amazon; ill. $3 *n.* (12/6 *n.*) r 8° Appleton 11
Startg. fr. Panama, auth. journeyed to Ecuador, thence to Peru, crossed the Andes to the Amazon, and down it to coast.

MULHALL, [Mrs] Marion Between the Amazon and the Andes; ill. *o.p.* [*pb.* 10/6] 8° Stanford 81
Account of ten years' travels in Buenos Ayres, Argentine Republic, Uruguay, Paraguay.

,, Explorers in the New World before & after Columbus 6/6 *n.* ($2·25 *n.*) 8° Longman 09
Incls. repts. of several chs. fr. above. Mainly on S. Am. in 18 and 19 cents. Added is *Story of Jesuit Missions of Paraguay.*

NICOLL, J. —*in his* Three Voyages of a Naturalist, *ut* **H** § 105
Voys. am. S. Pacific islds. (Trinidad, Martin Vas, Tristan d'Acuna, Str. of Magellan, etc.) in search of birds.

PEPPER, C. M. From Panama to Patagonia—*v.* **E** § 58

PETROCOKINO, A. Along the Andes, in Bolivia, Peru, and Ecuador 7/6 r 8° Gay & Bird 03
A very honest (but dull) record of hard day-to-day journeying in little-kn. repubs. of S.-W. South Amer.

PORTER, Hon. Rob. P. The Ten Republics [Dutton, *N.Y.*] 2/6 *n.* c 8° Routledge 11

RUHL, Arth. The Other Americans 8/6 *n.* 8° Laurie 08
Accs. of the cities and country, people and customs, of the countries of S. Amer. to-day.

SPRUCE, Dr R. Notes of a Botanist, 2 vols.—*ut inf.*, *s.v.* Brazil: Amazon

VILLIERS-STUART, H. Advents. amidst Equatorial Forests and Rivers of S. Amer.: also in the W. Indies and Wilds of Florida; to wh. is added 'Jamaica Revisited'; maps and ill. 21/ r 8° Murray 95
A graphic descr. of pers. advents. on trip to Surinam in 1858, a jy. up the Orinoco (as far only as Angostura), a visit to some of Antilles, and a second visit to Jamaica. His descrns. of equator. forests are very good, tho' otherwise there is more of sportsman than naturalist in cast of his observns., wh. comprise notes on topogr., geol., nat. hist., climatol., etc.

VINCENT, Fk. Around and about South America; ill. $5 8° Appleton, *N.Y.* [90] 95
21/ Paul. Author made entire circuit of S. Am. in 20 mos., visitg. every capital, chief city, and important seaport.

VINCENT, Mrs Howard —*in her* China to Peru over the Andes, *ut* **E** § 7

WATERTON, C. Wandergs. in S. Amer., N.-W. of U. S. & Antilles; 100 ill. 3/6 *n.* ($1·50) c 8° Macmillan [25] 07
A naturalist's travels in 1812, 16, 20, 24. Pop. Edn., 6*d*. Also in Cassell's Nat. Lib., 6*d*. 18° '89.

*Amazon River* —*v.* **E** § 61, *s.v.* Brazil: Amazon

**River Plate Republics [Argentina, Paraguay, Uruguay]**

DOMINGUEZ, L. L. Conquest of River Plate [tr.] [1535–55] 8° Hakluyt Soc. 91

LATHAM, Wilfrid States of the River Plate [industries & commerce] *o.p.* [*pb.* 12/] 8° Longman [66] 68

MORANT, G. C. Chili and River Plate in 1891—*ut* **E** § 61, *s.v.* Chile

MULHALL, M. G. + E. T. Handbook of River Plate; ry. map *o.p.* [*pb.* 6/] c 8° Paul [69] 93

## 61 : SOUTH AMERICA (*b*) : INDIVIDUAL STATES

**Argentina** —*v. also* **E** § 60, *s.v.* River Plate Republics

Argentine Year-Book [10/6 *n.* Wyman] 8° Grant, *Buenos Ayres, ann.*

DOMINGUEZ, L. L. History of Argentine Republic [tr.], vol. i [1492–1807] *o.p.* 4° *Buenos Ayres* 65

'ESTANCIERO (AN)' Ponce de Leon: rise of Argentine Republic 12/6 *n.* 8° Laurie [78] 10

*HIRST, W. A. Argentina; Introd. Martin Hume; ill. [S. Amer. Ser.] 10/6 *n.* 8° Unwin 10
$3 *n.* Scribner, *N.Y.* The best account of the country in English. Historical, polit., industr., social condns.

HOLDICH, Sir Thos. H. The Countries of the King's Award; ill. 16/ *n.* 8° Hurst 04
Deals in detail with the Andes of Argentina and Chile, espec. the boundary dispute.

KOEBEL, W. H. Modern Argentina, the El Dorado of To-day; 123 ill. 12/6 *n.* 8° Griffiths 07

,, Argentina Past and Present; ill. 12/6 *n.* 8° Paul 10
Both useful bks.; latter givg. the more compreh. picture of the Republic.

MARTINEZ, A. B. The Argentine in Twentieth Century [economical] 12/6 *n.* 8° Unwin 10

MILL, H. R. —*in his* New Lands: resources & prospective advantages 5/ c 8° Griffin 00
Contains a valuable chapter on Argentina.

PARISH, Sir Woodbine Life of. By Nina L. Kay Shuttleworth 15/ *n.* 8° Smith & Elder 10
Incls. acc. of foundn. and early hist. of Arg., to wh. PARISH was sent by CANNING as Minister Plenipotentiary.

PELLESCHI, Giov. Eight Months on Gran Chaco of Argentine Republic 8/6 8° Low 86

PENNINGTON, A. S. The Argentine Republic 10/6 *n.* 8° Stanley Paul 10
A thorough piece of work, spec. strong on nat. hist. of country. Little on trade.

TARMIENTO, D. F. Life in the Argentine Republic 8/6 c 8° *London* 68

TURNER, Thos. A. Argentina and the Argentines; ill. 15/ 8° Sonnenschein 92
83 Scribner, *N.Y.* Lively, uncomplim. sketches of Argentine society and finance, throwg. a strong light on country. Author spent 1885-90 there.

WHITE, E. W. Cameos from the Silver Land, 2 vols. 30/ 8° Van Voorst 81-2

*Buenos Ayres:* HUTCHINSON (T. J.) Buenos Ayres and Argentine Gleanings *o.p.* [*pb.* 16/] 8° Stanford 65

RUMBOLD, Sir Hor. The Great Silver River 12/ 8° Murray [87] 90
Notes of residence in Buenos Ayres, 1880-1.

*Cape Horn:* LUBBOCK (A. B.) Round the Horn before the Mast; ill. 1/ *n.* c 8° Murray [02] 11

SPEARS, Jno. R. The Gold Diggings of Cape Horn $1·75 c 8° Putnam 96
A well-written account of life in Tierra del Fuego.

*La Plata:* *HUDSON (W. H.) —*in his* The Naturalist in La Plata, *ut* **H** § 105

*Magellan Strait:* Voyage of the *Adventure* and *Beagle*—*ut* **H** § 44

MARKHAM, Sir C. R. [ed. & tr.] Early Spanish Voyages to Magellan Strait 8° Hakluyt Soc. 11

SARMIENTO DE GAMBÓA, P. [b. 1532] Nars. of Voys., ed. & tr. Sir C. R. Markham [1579-87] 8° Hakluyt Soc. 95

*Life of Ferd. Magellan* [1480-1521] —*v.* **E** § 7

*Patagonia:* *Alert, H.M.S.:* Cruise of. By Dr R. W. Coppinger—*ut* **H** § 44

BEERBOHM, J. Wanderings in Patagonia; map and ill. $1 16° Holt, *N.Y.* [79] 81
3/6 Chatto. Descrn. of life among the ostrich-hunters in 1877.

DIXIE, L'y Florence Across Patagonia; ill. [1878-9] *o.p.* [*pb.* 15/] 8° Bentley 80

GUINNARD, A. Three Years' Slavery among the Patagonians [tr.] *o.p.* [*pb.* 10/6] c 8° Bentley 71

HOLDICH, Sir Thos. H. —*in his* The Countries of the King's Award, *ut* **E** § 60

*HUDSON, W. H. Idle Days in Patagonia—*ut* **H** § 105
Full of keen observn. on plants and animals, amd their habits in the Pampas of Argentina. By no means so valuable as his *La Plata, ut sup.*

MUSTERS, Cpt. G. C. At Home w. the Patagonians; map & 10 ill. *o.p.* [*pb.* 7/6] p 8° Murray [71] 73
Descrn. of a yr's. wandergs. fr. Strait of Magellan to the Rio Negro.

PEPPER, C. M. —*in his* From Panama to Patagonia, *ut* **E** § 58

PRITCHARD, H. Hesketh Through the Heart of Patagonia; ill. 21/ *n.* 8° Heinemann 02
Acc. of explorn. acr. Patag. plain and up into foothills of Andes; big game, nat. hist., geogr., tribes, etc. Cheap edn. 1/ *n.* Nelson '11.

SKOTTSBERG, Dr Carl The Wilds of Patagonia; maps and ill. 15/ *n.* 8° Arnold 11
A narrative of the Swedish expedition of 1907-9 to Patagonia Tierra del Fuego, and Falkland Islands.

**Bolivia:** CONWAY (Sir Martin) Climbg. & Explorn. in Bolivian Andes; ill. 12/6 ($3 *n.*) 8° Harper [01] 02
A record of climbg. and explorn. in Cordillera Real in 1898-1900. Authoritative.

DAWSON, T. C. —*in his* South American Republics, 2 Pts., *ut* **E** § 60

MATHEWS, E. D. Up the Amazon and Madeira Rivers—*ut inf., s.v.* Amazon

WRIGHT, Marie R. Bolivia, Central Highway of S. America; 350 ill. $10 *n.* f° Barrie, *Phila.* 07

**Brazil:** *Bibliography:* RODRIQUES (J. C.) Cat. annot. d. Livros sobre o Brasil, Pt. i 8° Rodriques, *Rio d. J.* 07

*Early Accounts:* STADE (Hans) Captivity of, in Brazil [tr.], ed. R. F. Burton [1547-55] 8° Hakluyt Soc. 74

FRITZ, F'r S. Diary of Jy. to Gran Para, tr. Rev. G. Edmundson [1689] 8° Hakluyt Soc.

*History:* SALDANHA, D'ke of [1791-1876] Memrs. By Conde da Carnota [tr.], 2 v.; maps 32/ 8° Murray 80
SALDANHA, who began his career by fightg. agst. NAPOLEON, afterw. fought in S. Am., and was Gov. of Rio Grande: ultimately offered an independent kingdom.

*Statistics:* Brazilian Year-Book: ed. J. P. Wileman [21/ McCorquodale] r 8° *ann.*

*Travel and Description:* AGASSIZ (Prf. L. + Mrs A.) Journey in Brazil $2·50 8° Houghton, *Boston* [68] 95
A fascinating acc. of nature and man in South Brazil and on the Amazon in 1865-6.

ANDREWS, C. C. Brazil: its condition and prospects $1·25 12° Appleton, *N.Y.* [87] 91

BURTON, Cpt. [Sir] R. F. The Highlands of the Brazils, 2 vols. *o.p.* [*pb.* 30/] 8° Tinsley 69
Record of a visit in 1868; w. account of the gold and diamond mines.

COOK, Rev. W. A. Thro' the Wildernesses of Brazil; ill. [missionary] 7/6 *n.* 8° Unwin 11

CRAWFORD, R. —*in his* Across the Pampas and the Andes, *ut* **E** § 60

DENIS, Pierre Brazil, tr. Bernard Miall; ill. [econ. and commercial; S. Amer. Ser.] 10/6 *n.* 8° Unwin 11

DENT, H. C. A Year in Brazil; maps and ill. 18/ 8° Paul 86

HADFIELD, W. Brazil, River Plate, and Falkland Islands; pl. 10/ 8° Stanford 77

HARTT, C. F. Geology and Physical Geography of Brazil; ill. $5 8° Osgood, *Boston* 70

HUMPHREY, Alice R. A Summer Journey to Brazil; ill. $1·25 12° Bonnell, *N.Y.* 00

KIDDER (D. P.) + FLETCHER (J. C.) Brazil & the Brazilians; 150 ill. $4 8° Little & Brown, *Boston* [57] 80

MULHALL, M. G. + E. T. Handbook of Brazil *o.p.* 8° *Buenos Ayres* 73

NERY, Baronne Santa Anna Land of Amazons [tr.]; ill. [$4 *n.* Dutton, *N.Y.*] 16/ *n.* 8° Sands 01
ROLLINS, Mrs A. W. From Palm to Glacier; ill. [Brazi, Bermuda, Alaska] $1·75 8° Putnam, *N.Y.* 92
SMITH, H. H. Hist. of Brazils, Amazons, & the Coast; map & ill. $5 8° Scribner, *N.Y.* 79
TOUSSAINT-SAMSON, Emma A Parisian Brazil, tr.; ill. $1 c 8° Earle, *Boston* 91
WELLS, J. W. Exploring and Travelling 3,000 miles through Brazil, 2 vols.; ill. [$8 Lippincott, *Phila.*] 32/ 8° Low [86] 87
WRIGHT, Marie R. New Brazil: its resources & attractions: 350 ill. $10 *n.* 4° Barrie, *Phila.* [01] 06

*Amazon, Madeira, and Rio Negro Rivers and Valleys*

*BATES, H. W. —*in his* Records of a Naturalist on the River Amazon, *ut* **H** § 105
BROWN (C. B.) + LIDSTONE (W.) 15,000 Miles on Amazon & Tributaries; ill. *o.p.* [*pb.* 21/] 8° Stanford 78
CRAIG, N. B. Recollections of an Ill-fated Expedition; ill. $4 *n.* (18/ *n.*) 8° Lippincott 07
Account of the Collins Expedition to Madeira River.
ENOCK, R. R. The Andes and the Amazon—*ut inf.*, *s.v.* Peru
KELLER, F. Amazon & Madeira Rivers: sketches & descrns. *o.p.* [*pb.* 9/] 8° Chapman [74] 76
MARKHAM, [Sir] C. R. [ed.] Expeditions into Valley of Amazon [1539, 1540, 1639] 8° Hakluyt Soc. 59
MATHEWS, E. D. Up the Amazon and Madeira Rivers [Bolivia and Peru] 18/ 8° Low 79
MOZANS, H. J. —*in his* Along the Coast and down the Amazon, *ut* **E** § 60
ORTON, J. The Andes and the Amazon *o.p.* [*pb.* $3] 8° Harper, *N.Y.* [70] 76
*Pelorus, H.M.S.*: HIGHAMS (E. E.) Acr. the Continent in a Man of War 5/ *n.* c 8° Westminster Press 09
[Log Ser.] Log of commission of H.M.S. *Pelorus*, 1906–9; w. acc. of her cruise of 2,000 m. up Amazon.
SPRUCE, Dr R. Notes of a Botanist on Amazon & Andes, 2 vols.; ill. 21/ *n.* ($6·50 *n.*) 8° Macmillan 08
Ed. Dr A. R. WALLACE. Recds. of travel (1849–64) in pts. of Peru, Ecuador, Columbia, Venezuela, Brazil. *V. also* H § 67.
*WALLACE, Dr A. Russel Travels on the Amazon and Rio Negro [1848–52] 2/ 8° Ward & Lock [53] 89
[Minerva Lib.] It was by his observns. on this jy. (when he was companion of BATES), confirmed by those he later made in Malay Archipel., that WALLACE arrived independently of DARWIN at the theory of Natl. Selection.

*Parana*

BIGG-WITHER, T. F. Pioneering in South Brazil, 2 vols.; maps & pl. *o.p.* [*pb.* 24/] p 8° Murray 78
An account of two years spent in Parana.
HUTCHINSON, T. J. Parana [w. acc. of Paraguay War (1681–8]) *o.p.* [*pb.* 21/] 8° Stanford 68
*Trinidad*: KNIGHT (E. F.) Cruise of the *Alerte*; ill. 3/6 ($1·25) c 8° Longman [91] 92
[Silver Lib.] Narrative of an (unsuccessful) search for reported treasure in the desert island of Trinidad.

**Buenos Ayres** —*v.* Argentine Republic, *sup.*

**Chile, Republic of** —*v. also inf.*, *s.v.* Peru (DRAKE; MARKHAM)
AUBERTIN, J. J. By Order of the Sun to Chile; ill. 5/ c 8° Paul 94
Account of a jy. by author at age of 75 to waterless deserts of Chile, to observe total eclipse of sun on 16 Apl. 1893. A chatty narr. of travel; w. interestg. partics. of doings of the professional astronomers.
BOYD, R. N. Sketches of Chili & Chilians dur. War [1879–80]; ill. 10/6 c 8° W. H. Allen 81
*ELLIOTT, G. F. Scott Chile; ill. [South American Series] 10/6 *n.* 8° Unwin 07
$3 *n.* Scribner, *N.Y.* History of Chile fr. earliest times to the earthquake of 1906, its natl. feats., products, commerce, and pres. condns.
HANCOCK, A. U. History of Chile; maps & pl. [moderately good] $2·50 8° Sergel, *Chicago* 93
HERVEY, Maurice H. Dark Days in Chile; 15 pl. 15/ 8° Arnold 91
A vivid account of the Revolution of 1891 by an eye-witness, a Balmacedist and the *Times* correspondent there.
HOLDICH, Sir Thos. H. —*in his* The Countries of the King's Award, *ut sup.*, *s.v.* Argentine Republic
MORANT, G. C. Chili and River Plate in 1891 [travel-remins.] *o.p.* [*pb.* 3/6] c 8° Waterlow 92
ORTUZAR, A. Chile of To-day: commerce, production, resources; ill. $5 4° Lomas, *N.Y.* 07
SMITH, W. Anderson Temperate Chile, a Progressive Spain; map 10/6 8° Black 99
$3·50 Macmillan, *N.Y.* An informing book, tho' wr. in an obscure style, and over-critical.
WRIGHT, Marie R. Chile: growth, resources, industrs.; 350 ill. $10 *n.* 4° Barrie, *Phila.* 05

*Aconcagua, Mt. and Valleys*

CONWAY, Sir Martin Aconcagua and Tierra del Fuego; 27 ill. 12/6 *n.* 8° Cassell 02
Climbg., travel, explorn., inclg. acc. of a sporting ascent of Aconcagua.
FITZGERALD, Edw. A. The Highest Andes; 40 pl. $6 *n.* r 8° Scribner, *N.Y.* 99
30/ *n.* Methuen. Incls. acc. of the 'conquest' of Aconcagua and Tupungato by the wr. and Mr VINES.
GOSSE, P. H. Natural History of the Aconcagua Valleys—*ut* **H** § 105

**Colombia, U.S. of**: BINGHAM (H.) Jl. of Expedn. acr. Venezuela and Colombia—*ut inf.*, *s.v.* Venezuela
MILLICAN, Alb. Travels and Adventures of an Orchid Hunter; ill. *o.p.* [*pb.* 12/6] 8° Cassell 91
Acc. of canoe and camp life in Colombia and northern Andes, whilst collecting orchids. Poorly narrated.
PETRE, F. L. The Republic of Colombia; map and 36 ill. 8/6 *n.* 8° Stanford 06
SCRUGGS, Wm. L. Colombian & Venezuelan Republics; maps & ill. $1·75 8° Little & Brown, *Bost.* [00] 05
Accs. of the cy., climate, positns. of towns, politics; w. notes on other pts. of Cent. and S. Amer. Ch. on Panama Canal.

*Orinoco River* —*v. inf.*, *s.v.* Venezuela

*Panama* —*v.* **E** § 58

**Ecuador, Republic of**

SIMSON, Alf. Travels in Wilds of Ecuador & Explorn. of Putumayo R.; map 8/6 c 8° Low 86

*WHYMPER, Edw. Travels am. Great Andes of Equator; 4 maps & 140 ill. 21/ *n.* 8° Murray [92] 92

* ,, Supplementary Appendix *to same;* 61 figs. 21/ *n.* 8° Murray 92

Former $2·50 Scribner, *N.Y.* An import. acc. of first ascent of Chimborazo and other Andean mtns., made dur. 1880–2: a record of indomitable perseverance. Several experts have since worked on his zool. and miner. collns., details of wh. appear in *Suppl.*, adding materially to scient. value of this elab. wk. A feature of expedn. was the care taken in comparison of rgs. of mercurial and Aneroid barometers—results of wh. appear in a separate pamph. [*ut* **H** § 29]. Admirably ill. Cheap Edn. 1/ *n.* Nelson '11.

**Falkland Islands:** ROUTLEDGE (R. M.) Falkland Islands—*in* Scottish Geogr. Mag., May, 1896

Describes the country, its administration and social order.

SNOW, W. P. Cruise of Tierra del Fuega, Falkld. Islds., 2 v. *o.p.* [*pb.* 24/] p 8° Longman 57

WHITINGTON, G. F. The Falkland Islands *o.p.* 8° Smith & Elder 40

**Guianas:** *Early Voyages:* RALEIGH (Sir W.) Discoverie of Guiana, ed. Sir R. H. Schomburgk, re-ed. Sir E. F. im Thurn *o.p.* 8° Hakluyt Soc. [48]

Jl. of 1595. A fine example of historical adventure [1595–6]. Also 6*d.* Blackie '05, and in Cassell's Natl. Lib., 6*d.* For Life of RALEIGH *v.* **F** § 22.

STORM VAN'S GRAVESANDE Rise of British Guiana, ed. C. A. Harris, 2 vols. 8° Hakluyt Soc. 11

*Ethnology:* BRETT (W. H.) The Indian Tribes of Guiana 18/ 8° Bell 68

im THURN, [Sir] E. F. Among the Indians of Guiana; 53 ill. 18/ 8° Paul 83

An excellent acc., chfly. anthropological; w. fine ill. of the Indians and their mode of life.

*Recent Travel and Description*

ANDRÉ, E. A Naturalist in the Guianas; ill. 14/ *n.* 8° Smith & Elder 04

An excellent contribn. to the literature of the S. Amer. forest; dealg. w. a portion of the Orinoco forest, watered by its affluent, the Caura, whose sources lie in the almost untrodden Guiana highlands.

BAYLEY, G. D. [ed.] Handbook of British Guiana [general and statistical] 5/ 8° Dulau 09

BODDAM-WHETHAM, J. W. Roraima and British Guiana [1878] 15/ 8° Hurst 79

British Guiana and its Resources. By Auth. of 'Sardinia and its Resources' 2/6 c 8° Philip 95

BRONKHURST, H. V. P. Colony of Brit. Guiana & Labouring Population *o.p.* [*pb.* 10/6] p 8° Woolmer 83

BROWN, C. B. Canoe & Camp Life in British Guiana; col. pl. [1868–72] 21/ 8° Stanford 76

CROOKALL, Rev. L. British Guiana; 26 ill. [missionary] 6/ c 8° Unwin 98

KEMY, Cpt. Lawrence Voyage to British Guiana, ed. Jas. Rodway [voy. 1596] 8° Hakluyt Soc., *in prep.*

KIRKE, Hy. Twenty-five Years in British Guiana; ill. 10/6 8° Low 98

Deals chiefly with negro-life: an amusing book.

RODWAY, Jas. Hist. of Brit. Guiana, 3 v.; ill. [1668 to date; a good bk.] 8° Argosy Pr., *George Town, Demarara* 91–4

,, In the Guiana Forest; 16 pl. $2 c 8° Scribner, *N.Y.* [94] 11

7/6 *n.* Unwin. 'Studies of nature in rel. to the struggle for life'. A ser. of essays on Survival of Fittest as illd. by tropical forests of S. Am. By an evolutionary naturalist, contg. a good deal of first-hand observn.

,, In the Guiana Wilds $1·25 c 8° Page, *Boston*

,, Story of Forest & Stream; ill. [Usef. Knowl. Lib.] 40 c. 12° Wessels, *N.Y.* 97

Sketches forest-growths, drawg. a parallel between the tropical and temperate zones.

*Guide:* STARK (J. H.; pb.) British Guiana; ill. [Stark's Ill. Guidebks.] 6/ *n.* c 8° Low 98

*Dutch Guiana:* PALGRAVE (W. G.) Dutch Guiana; map *o.p.* [*pb.* 9/] 8° Macmillan 76

**Paraguay, Republic of** —*v. also* **E** § 60, *s.v.* River Plate Republics

DE BOURGADE LA DARDYE, E. Paraguay: land and people [tr.]; map and pl. 7/6 c 8° Philip 92

A valuable and authentic monogr. on social, polit. and industr. condns., based on personal observn.

BURTON, Cpt. [Sir] R. F. Letters fr. Battle Fields of Paraguay; ill. *o.p.* [*pb.* 18/] 8° Tinsley 76

CARLYLE, Thos. Dr Francia—*in his* Essays, *ut* **K** § 89

CRAWFORD, Rob. —*in his* South American Sketches, *ut* **E** § 60

GRAHAM, R. B. Cunninghame A Vanished Arcadia 9/ r 8° Heinemann 01

An account of the Jesuit settlements and missions in Paraguay, 1607–1767; and of the remains of their era still seen.

GRUBB, W. B. An Unknown People in an Unknown Land—*ut* **E** § 53

HEAD, Cpt. [Sir] F. B. Pampas Journeys 2/ c 8° Murray [28] 61

Acc. of jy. acr. Pampas and along Andes in 1828: first descrn. of these great stretches of cy.

KNIGHT, E. F. Cruise of the *Falcon*; map and ill. 3/6 ($1·25) c 8° Longman [83] 91

[Silver Lib.] A fascinatg. acc. of an adventurous voy. in 30-ton yacht acr. Atlantic and up rivers Parana and Paraguay.

MASTERMAN, G. F. Seven Eventful Years in Paraguay 5/ c 8° Low [69] 70

MULHALL, [Mrs] Marion From Europe to Paraguay & Matto Grosso; ill. *o.p.* [*pb.* 5/] 8° Stanford 77

,, Story of Jesuit Missions of Paraguay—*in her* Explorers of New World, *ut* **E** § 60

WASHBURN, C. A. Hist. of Paraguay, 2 vols.; map & ill. [1526–1868] $7·50 8° Lee & Shepard, *Bost.* 71

**Patagonia** —*v.* Argentine Republic, *sup.*

**Peru, Republic of** —*v. also sup., s.v.* Brazil

*Early Voyages and Accounts:* d'ACOSTA (J.) Hist. of Peru—*in his* Hist. of Indies [tr.], vol. ii, *ut* **E** § 59

de ANDAGOYA, P. Narrative, ed. [Sir] C. R. Markham 8° Hakluyt Soc. 65
Contains the earliest notice of Peru.

DRAKE, Sir Fcs. The World Encompassed; Introd. W. S. W. Vaux 8° Hakluyt Soc. 54
Account of his voyage to Chili and Peru in 1577.

de CIEZA DE LEON, P. Chrons. of Peru, Pt. i, incl. Travels, tr. & ed. [Sir] C. R. Markham 8° Hakluyt Soc. 64

,, Chronicles of Peru, Pt. ii, tr. & ed. [Sir] C. R. Markham 8° Hakluyt Soc. 83

PIZARRO, Franc. [d. 1541]

Helps, Sir Arth. Life of Pizarro 6/ c 8° Bell [69] 82

Towle, G. M. Life of Pizarro [maps, pl., facs., and ill.] $1 c 8° Lee & Shepard, *Boston* 78

Reports on Discovery of Peru: tr. & ed. [Sir] C. R. Markham; w. notes [1525–34] 8° Hakluyt Soc. 72

SARMIENTO DE GAMBOA, P. History of Incas, tr. and ed. Sir C. R. Markham 8° Hakluyt Soc. 07
Orig. edn. 1572. Added is *The Execution of the Inca Tupac Amaru*, by Cpt. BALTHASAR DE OCAMPO.

de la VEGA, Y. G. Royal Commentaries of the Incas, tr. & ed. [Sir] C. R. Markham, 2 vols.—*ut* **B** § 35

*History:* DALTON (Wm.) Stories of Conquests of Mexico & Peru [popular] 3/6 c 8° Paterson, *Ed.* [72] 87

MARKHAM, [Sir] Clements R. Memr. of C'ess of Chincon & Vice-Queen of Peru [1629–39] *o.p.* s 4° 74

,, War between Peru and Chili [1879–82] 10/6 c 8° Low [83] 83

* ,, Latin-American Republics: hist. of Peru; 5 maps & 25 pl. 10/6 8° Gay & Bird 92
$2·50 Sergel, *Chicago.* An authentic summary of hist. of Peru in anc. and mod. times, esp. valuable since War of Indep. [1824] and for its pict. of Peru in 1890. Author holds a brief for Peru and is slightly biassed; but the bk. is nevertheless an excellent general hist. of Peru, and forms a useful supplemt. to PRESCOTT'S classical *Conquest.* Bibliogr.

* ,, The Incas of Peru; map and 12 pl. 10/6 *n.* s 8° Smith & Elder 10
A series of essays embodying results of much material since days of PRESCOTT. Tr. of a drama of time of Incas occupies 85 pp. at end.

*PRESCOTT, W. H. Hist. of Conquest of Peru, ed. J. Foster Kirk, 2 v. $2 c 8° Lippincott, *Phila.* [43]
The standard work. Also in 3 vols. $1·50 *id.* Ed. KIRK, Lib. Edn., 2 vols., 8° Routledge; 1 vol. 4/6 *n.* Sonnenschein. Ch. Edn. 3/6 Routledge.

*Recent Travel and Description:* CLARK (E. B.) Twelve Months in Peru; ill. 5/ c 8° Unwin 91
Some interestg. informn., unassumingly given. Miss CLARK'S Xmas was spent amg. Cholo Indns. of Peruv. Cordilleras.

COLE, G. R. The Peruvians at Home 6/ c 8° Paul 84

DUFFIELD, A. J. Peru in the Guano Age *o.p.* [*pb.* 4/] c 8° Bentley 77

,, Prospects of Peru [w. acc. of guano-deposits] *o.p.* [*pb.* 2/6] c 8° Bentley 81

ENOCK, C. Reg. The Andes and the Amazon; ill. 21/ 8° Unwin 08
Mainly accounts of life and travel in Peru. Well illustrated.

* ,, Peru; ill. [South American Series] 10/6 *n.* 8° Unwin 08
$3 *n.* Scribner, *N.Y.* The best account of the country in English hist., civilizn., topogr., resources, commerce.

GARLAND, A. Peru in 1906 [tr.]; ill. 4° La Industria Prg. Off., *Lima* 07
A comprehensive work compiled by order of the President of the Republic.

GUINNESS, Geraldine Peru: its story, people, and religion 7/6 8° Morgan & Scott 08

HUTCHINSON, T. J. Two Years in Peru, 2 vols.; ill. [w. antiquities] *o.p.* [*pb.* 28/] 8° Low 73

MARKHAM, [Sir] C. R. Travels in Peru and India *o.p.* [*pb.* 16/] 8° Murray 62
Descrs. the cinchona forests of Peru, and the introdn. of the tree into India.

,, Peru; ill. [Foreign Countries and British Colonies] 3/6 c 8° Low 80

MARTIN, Percy F. Peru of the Twentieth Century; ill. 15/ *n.* 8° Arnold 11

MATHEWS, E. D. Up the Amazon and Madeira Rivers—*ut sup., s.v.* Amazon

SEEBEE, Felix Travelling Impressions in and Notes on Peru 3/6 c 8° Stock 01

SQUIER, E. G. Peru: travels & exploration in land of Incas; 300 ill. $5 8° Harper, *N.Y.*

v. TSCHUDE, J. J. Travels in Peru [tr.] [1838–42; still of value] *o.p.* [*pb.* 12/] 8° Bogue 47

WRIGHT, Marie R. The Old & the New Peru: the land & its people; 350 ill. $10 4° Barrie, *Phila.*

*Lima; Cuzco:* FUENTES (M. A.) Lima, the Capital of Peru; 40 pl. *o.p.* [*pb.* 21/] i 8° *Paris* 66

MARKHAM, [Sir] C. R. Cuzco & Lima: the anc. & mod. capitals of Peru *o.p.* [*pb.* 14/] c 8° Chapman 56

**Plate, River** —*v.* **E** § 60

**Uruguay, Republic of** —*v. also* **E** § 60, *s.v.* River Plate Republics

CRAWFORD, Rob. South American Sketches $2 (6/) c 8° Longman 98
By a railway-engineer: experiences during three and a half years in the country.

HUDSON, W. H. The Purple Land that England Lost 6/ c 8° Low [85] 07
$1·50 *n.* Dutton, *N.Y.* An excellent descrn. of travel and adventures in the Banda Oriental in 1884.

*KOEBEL, W. H. Uruguay; ill. [$3 *n.* Scrib., *N.Y.*; S. Amer. Ser.] 10/6 *n.* 8° Unwin 11

MURRAY, J. H. Travels in Uruguay [w. acc. of sheep-farming] *o.p.* [*pb.* 8/6] c 8° Longman 71

Republic of Uruguay: geography, history, industries, commerce, etc. *o.p.* [*pb.* 6/] c 8° Stanford [83] 83

**Venezuela, Republic of**

ANDRÉ, E. —*in his* Naturalist in the Guianas, *ut sup., s.v.* Guianas

BINGHAM, H. Jl. of Expedn. acr. Venezuela and Colombia ; ill. [1906–7] $2·25 *n.* 8° Yale Pb. Ass., *New Haven* 09

CURTIS, W. E. Venezuela, a Land where it's always Summer $1·25 p. 8° Harper, *N.Y.* 96

DANCE, C. D. Recollections of Four Years in Venezuela *o.p.* [*pb.* 7/6] p 8° Paul 76

DAVIS, R. H. Three Gringos in Venezuela & Central America ; ill. $1·50 c 8° Harper, *N.Y.* 96
7/6 Gay & Hancock. Entertaing. and fresh sketches. One of the 'Gringos' (foreigners) is son of L'y Hy. SOMERSET.

EASTWICK, E. B. Venezuela : life in a South American republic *o.p.* [*pb.* 16/] 8° Chapman 68

MORRIS, Ira N. With the Trade Winds ; ill.—*ut* **E** § 59 [Venezuela and W. Indies]

PAEZ, Ramon Travels & Advents. in S. & Centr. America *o.p.* [*pb.* $2] c 8° Belknap, *Hartford, Conn.* 73
Incls. acc. of his life in the llanos of Venezuela, pb. 1863 *sub tit. Wild Scenes in S. America.*

SCRUGGS, W. L. Columbian and Venezuelan Republics—*ut sup., s.v.* Columbia

SPENCE, J. M. Land of Bolivar, 2 vols. [advents. in Venezuela ; 1871–2] 31/6 8° Low 78

*Boundary :* STRICKLAND (J. ; ed.) Documents and maps on Boundary Question betw. Venez. and Brit. Guiana $4 f° Scribner, *N.Y.* 97

*Orinoco R. :* MOZANS (H. J.) Up the Orinoco and down the Magdalena ; ill. $3 *n.* (12/6 *n.*) r 8° Appleton 10
Travel on foot thro' islds. and lands of S. Am. borderg. Caribbean and to ports. of Venez. and Colombia.

TRIANA, Perez Down the Orinoco in a Canoe $1·25 c 8° Crowell, *N.Y.* 02
6/ Heinemann. Acc. of jy. on mule-back down Andine plateau to Bogotá, thence to upper watershed of Orinoco, and thence by canoe fr. one river to another, striking the Orinoco above its rapids, and down it to Atlantic.

# VIII : Geography of Australasia

## 62 : AUSTRALASIA : GENERALLY

**Bibliography**

Free Public Lib., Sydney : Catal. of Bks. rel. to, or pub. in, Australasia 12/ 4° Potter, *Sydney* 93
By R. C. WALKER, late Chf.-librn. Some 8,000 bks. and pamphs., catald. und. Authors, then und. Colonies ; w. classif. catals. of subjs. and titles, and Gen. Index of Subjs.

**Atlas**

BARTHOLOMEW, J. G. Royal Atlas and Gazetteer of Australasia [28 maps, etc.] 12/ i 8° Nelson 91

**Cyclopædias :** BLAIR (D.) Cyclopædia of Australasia : dict. of facts, events, etc. 42/ 4° *Melbourne* 81

LEVEY, G. C. Australasian Encyclopædia, incl. New Zealand ; map 7/6 *n.* c 8° Hutchinson 91
A gazetteer, account of events, nat. hist., scenery, resources, laws, statistics, biogrs. of discovrs., officials, colonists to 1885.

**Early Voyages ; Early Cartography**—*v. also* **E** § 65

Cartography of Australia : as understood by Dutch cartographers F. Muller & Co., *Amsterdam* 95
About 15 large maps of 17 cent., showg. the var. epochs in cartography of Australia. 100 printed.

CROZET Voyage to Tasmania, New Zealand, Ladrone Islands, and Philippines, tr. H. L. Roth ; 31 ill. [1771–2] 10/6 *n.* 8° Truslove 91
The first English translation of this important *Voyage.*

HAWKINS, Sir Rich. Observns. in his Voy. into S. Sea, ed. Cpt. C. R. D. Bethune *o.p.* 8° Hakluyt Soc. 48

" The same, ed. [Sir] Clements R. Markham [1593] 8° Hakluyt Soc. 78

NORDENSKIÖLD, Bar. A. E. —*in his* Facsimile-Atlas to Early History of Cartography [tr.], *ut* **E** § 54

**Ethnology** —*v. also* **B** § 29, **E** §§ 65, 67

FEATHERMAN, A. Social History of the Races of Mankind : Oceano-Melanesians—*ut* **F** § 5

MUSEUM GODDEFROY [Hambg.] : Ethnographical Department of. By J. D. E. Schmelz + R. Krause 25/ 4° *Hamburg* 81
Forms a handbook of ethnology of the South Sea Tribes, incl. Australians ; w. map, 46 fine plates, and 28 photos.

**General Geography :** CHISHOLM (G. G.) School Geogr. for Australasia ; maps 3/6 (60 c.) c 8° Longman 88

HERBERTSON, Mrs F. L. D. Australia and Oceania [Descr. Geogr. ; 80 c. Macm., *N.Y.*] 2/6 c 8° Black 03

LYDE, Lionel Geography of Australasia and East Indies 1/4 c 8° Black 03

RANKEN, G. The Federal Geography of British Australasia 6/ c 8° Turner, *Sydney* 91
An excellent textbook, wr. by an Australian fr. Australian schools.

*STANFORD, E. [pb.] Australasia, 2 vols. [Compendium of Geogr.] ea. 15/ 8° Stanford [79–94] 07–8
Ea. $5·50 Lippincott, *Phila.* Vol. i : *Australia and N. Zeal.* (Prf. J. W. GREGORY), 33 maps and 80 ill. ; ii : *Malaysia and Pacific Archipelagoes* (Dr F. H. H. GUILLEMARD, ed. Prf. A. H. KEANE). An excellent systematic treatise. Former edn. of vol. i by Dr A. R. WALLACE.

WILKINS, W. Australasia, Descriptive & Pictorial ; ill. [Australia & N.Z.] 2/6 c 8° Blackie 87

**Historical Geography :** ROGERS (J. D.) Australasia = Lucas, Hist. Geogr. of Br. Cols., vol. vi 7/6 ($1·90) c 8° Clar. Press 07
With 22 maps. Separately, Pt. i : *Historical,* 4/6 ($1·10) ; Pt. ii : *Geographical,* 3/6 (90 c.).

**History ; Biography**

BLAIR, Dav. History of Australasia, to Establishment of Self-govt. 42/ 4° *Glasgow* 78

HEATON, H. Australian Dictionary of Dates and Men [1542–1879] 10/6 r 8° *Sydney* 79

JENKS, Prf. E. Hist. of the Australasian Colonies [Camb. Hist. Ser.] 6/ c 8° Camb. Press [95] 97
$1·50 *n.* Putnam, *N.Y.* An adequate pop. bk., by wr. whose knowl. is first-hand, statemts. impartial, views moderate. Ends at 1893.

LAURIE, J. S. Story of Australasia : discov., colonizn., developmt. 10/6 8° Osgood 96

MENNELL, Pp. [ed.] Dictionary of Australasian Biography [incl. N. Z. and Fiji] 7/6 *n.* c 8° Hutchinson 92
Notices of leadg. colonists (and Britons holdg. temp. offic. positns.) fr. inaug. of respons. govt. (1855) to 1892. Some 2,000 in all.

WESTGARTH, W. Half a Century of Australasian Progress 12/ 8° Low 89

**Resources ; Statistics ; Economic Condition**

Australasian Handbook and Dictionary [incls. N.Z., Fiji, N. Guinea] Gordon & Gotch 93 *ann.*

BONWICK, Jas. British Colonies in Australasia : resources, prospects, etc. 1/ c 8° Low [81] 86

COGHLAN, T. A. [Austral.] Statistical Account of the Seven Colonies of Australasia
3/ 8° Govt. Press, *Sydney* [92] 00

DAVITT, Michael Life and Progress in Australasia 6/ c 8° Methuen 98
A good, though unconnected, account of political and economic advance in Australasia.

REEVES, W. P. State Experiments in Australia and New Zealand, 2 vols.—*ut* **D** § 126

SCHMEISSER (K.) + VOGELSANG (K.) The Gold Fields of Australasia, 2 v. [tr.] 30/ *n.* r 8° Macmillan 98
With p'fo of 13 maps and plans. The most trustworthy summary of knowledge on the subject.

WALLACE, R. Agriculture and Rural Econ. of Australia and N. Zeal. 21/ *n.* 8° Low 91
Account of a critical study of the Australasian colonies in 1890.

**Recent Travel and Description**

ARTHUR, J. K. Kangaroo and Kauri : sketches and anecdotes ; ill. 7/6 8° Low 94

BADEN-POWELL, Lt. B. F. S. In Savage Isles and Settled Lands *o.p.* [*pb.* 21/] 8° Bentley 92
A pleasant and unpretentious acc. of 3 years' travel in Malaysia, Australasia, and Polynesia : 50,000 miles in all.

British Empire Series : Australasia ; 2 maps [*v.* **E** § 21] 6/ 8° Paul 00

BULLEN, Fk. T. [Austral.] Advance Australasia 6/ c 8° Hodder 07
A day-to-day record of a visit to Australasia. Repr. fr. *The Standard.*

COOTE, Walt. Wanderings South and East ; ill. *o.p.* [*pb.* 10/6] c 8° Low [81] 83

FERGUSON, Dugald —*in his* Vicissitudes of Bush Life in Australia and New Zeal., *ut* **E** § 67

GREY, J. Grattan Australasia, Old and New 7/6 c 8° Hodder 01
Valuable for its views on society and government in the British colonies.

MOORE, F. F. From the Bush to the Breakers [Australia & Pacif. Isls.] 3/6 c 8° S.P.C.K. 93

VERSCHUUR, G. At the Antipodes : travels in many lands [tr.] ; ill. 7/6 c 8° Low 91
A lively acc. of travels in Australia, N. Zeal., Fiji, New Hebrides, New Caledonia, S. Amer., in 1888–89.

WILDEY, W. B. Australasia, & the Oceanic Regions, inclg. New Guinea 10/6 12° *Melbourne* 76

**Scenery :** GARRON (Dr A. ; ed.) Picturesque Atlas of Australasia, 3 v. ; 1000 ill. £15 f° *Sydney*

,, [ed.] Australasia Illustrated : discov., settlemt., progr., 3 v. ; ill. ea. 63/ Australasia Pb. Co. 93

## 63 : POLYNESIA (*a*) : GENERALLY

**Ethnology** —*v. also* **B** § 29, **E** § 65

BROWN, Dr Geo. Melanesians & Polynesians : their life-histories ; ill. 12/ *n.* 8° Macmillan 10
A mass of informn. on ethnol., relig., customs, etc. Author, a missionary, spent 50 yrs. in E. and W. Pacific.

BROWN, J. Macmillan Maori and Polynesian—*ut* **E** § 67

*CODRINGTON, Dr R. H. The Melanesians : studies in anthrop. and folklore—*ut* **B** § 29

FORNANDER, A. Acc. of Polynesian Race, 3 v. [iii is vocab.] *o.p.* [*pb.* 27/] p 8° Trübner [78] 90 ; 80 ; 85

PARTINGTON (J. E.) + HEAKE (C.) [eds.] Ethnograph. Album of Pacific Islds., 3 Ser.
42/ *n.*, 42/ *n.*, 45/ *n.* obl 4° *priv. prin.* (Palmer, *Mancs.*) 91–8
Weapons, tools, ornaments, dress, etc., fr. public and private collns. in England. Only 150 copies printed. Ser. i. *o.p.* (very scarce).

SPENCER, Herb. [ed.] Descriptive Sociology, No. 3 : Types of Lowest Races. By Prf. D. Duncan—*ut* **C** § 62

WALLACE, Dr A. Russel —*in his* Studies, Scientific and Social, vol. i, *ut* **H** § 43

**Early Voyage :** de QUIROS (P. F.) Voys., tr. & ed. Sir C. R. Markham, 2 v. [1595–1606] 8° Hakluyt Soc. 04

**General Geography** —*v. also* **E** § 62

*GUILLEMARD, Dr F. H. H. Malaysia & Pacific Archipelagoes = Stanford's Compend. of Geogr.—*ut* **E** § 62

**History ; Biography :** GILL (Rev. W. W.) Historical Sketches of Savage Life in Polyn. 8° *Wellington* 80

LANG, Rev. J. D. View of Origin and Migrations of Polynesian Nation 10/6 12° *Sydney* [34] 77
Demonstrates the settlement of America.

PATTESON, J. C. [Bp of Melanesia] Life—*ut* **A** § 105

ROMILLY, Hugh L'rs fr. West. Pacific & Mashonald., ed. S. H. Romilly [bro.]; 17 ill. 7/6 8° Nutt 93

**Recent Travel and Description**

*Adventure & Beagle*: Narrative of Surveying Voyages, 4 vols.—*ut* **H** § 44

*Alert, H.M.S.* Cruise of. By Dr R. W. Coppinger; pl.—*ut* **H** § 44 [four years' cruise]

AWDRY, Fces. In the Isles of the Sea [50 yrs. in Melanesia] 5/ i 8° Bemrose 02

BEEKE, Louis Wild Life in the Southern Seas 5/ c 8° Unwin 97

„ Notes from my South Sea Log 6/ *n.* c 8° Laurie *n.d.* (05)

Former $1·50 New Amst. Bk. Co., *N.Y.* Two well-written volumes of descriptive travel-sketches.

BODDHAM-WHETHAM, J. W. Pearls of the Pacific; ill. *o.p.* [*pb.* 15/] 8° Hurst 76

CHURCHWARD, W. B. 'Blackbirding' [= slave-catchg.] in S. Pacific—*ut* **D** § 130, *s.v.* Slave Trading

COOK, Cpt. Jas. [1728–79] —*v.* **E** § 7

COOMBE, Florence Islands of Enchantment; 100 ill. [Melanesia] 12/ *n.* 8° Macmillan 11

COOPER, H. S. The Islands of the Pacific *o.p.* [*pb.* 6/] c 8° Bentley [80] 83

Fiji, Tongan, Samoan, and Society Islands as fields for colonization.

COOTE, W. Islands North-East of Australia: the Western Pacific 2/6 c 8° Low 83

CUMMING, [Miss] C. F. Gordon Lady's Cruise in a French Man of War; ill. 12/6 8° Blackwood [82] 87

DARWIN, Chas. —*in his* Voyage of a Naturalist Round the World, *ut* **H** § 44

ELLIS, Rev. Wm. Polynesian Researches, 4 vols. *o.p.* [*pb.* 14/] c 8° Bohn [29] 59

Researches on natural history, mythology, arts, etc.

GAGGIN, Jno. Among the Man-Eaters [Overseas Lib.] 2/ c 8° Unwin 00

An interesting record of a trader's adventures in South Seas; with much accurate observation.

GILL, Rev. W. W. Life in Southern Seas; *and* Jottings from the Pacific—*ut* **A** § 105

GRIMSHAW, Beatr. From Fiji to the Cannibal Islands; ill. 12/6 *n.* 8° Nash 07

A pleasant, chatty bk., givg. her experces. dur. horseback rides in some unbeaten tracks in Fiji.

„ In the Strange South Seas; 56 ill. 16/ *n.* 8° Hutchinson 07

Descrns. of people and products of Society Islds., Cook Archip., Friendly Islds., Samoa. Ch. Edn. 1/ *n.*

GUPPY, Dr H. B. Observns. of a Naturalist in Pacific, 2 vols. [1896–9] 36/ r 8° Macmillan 03–6

Vol. i: *Vanua Levu, Fiji*, 15/ *n.*; ii: *Plant Dispersal*, 21/ *n.*

HALL (D. B.) + OSBORNE (L'd A. E. G.) Sunshine & Surf: yr's wandg. in S. Seas; ill. 12/6 8° Black 01

$4 Macmillan, *N.Y.* An ordinary tour to various Pacific Islands, in coasting steamers.

KNOX, T. W. Boy Travellers in Australasia; ill. [popular] $2 8° Harper, *N.Y.* 89

Advents. of 2 youths in Sandwich, Marquesas, Society, Samoan, and Fiji islands.

LAMBERT, C. + S. Voy. of *Wanderer* to S. Pac., Sand. Isl., & rd. World; pl. 21/ r 8° Macmillan 83

MORESBY, Cpt. J. Discoveries and Surveys in N. Guinea and Polynesia 15/ 8° Murray 76

A cruise in Polynesia, D'Entrecasteaux Islds., and N. G., w. pearl-fishing stations in Torres Straits. Maps and pl.

NICOLL, M. J. Three Voyages of a Naturalist; 56 pl. 7/6 *n.* 8° Witherby [08] 09

An interestg. acc. of little-known ocean-islands and the life upon them.

PALLANDER, Edw. Log of an Island Wanderer; 32 ill. 6/ c 8° Pearson 01

An over-humorous account of a tour: conts. nothing original.

PENNY, Rev. Alf. Ten Years in Melanesia—*ut* **A** § 105

A missionary account, but full of popular information.

'Peripatetic Parson (A)' Parts of the Pacific; ill. 10/6 8° Sonnenschein 96

A really entertaing. travel-bk., descrg. author's travels in N. Queensland, Fiji, New Zeal., and Hawaii, and contg. much informn. rel. to colonial life, missy. methods, and church wk. at Antipodes.

PRITCHARD, W. T. Polynesian Reminis. [by Brit. Consul at Samoa & Fiji] *o.p.* [*pb.* 16/] 8° Chapman 66

REEVES, Edw. Brown Men and Women; 60 ill. 10/6 8° Sonnenschein 98

A series of traveller's glimpses of life in chief Pacific groups in 1895–6.

ROMILLY, H. H. Western Pacific and New Guinea; map [natives, etc.] 7/6 8° Murray [86] 87

„ Letters from the Western Pacific; ill. [1878–91] 7/6 c 8° Nutt 93

SHOEMAKER, M. M. Islands of the Southern Seas; ill. $2·25 8° Putnam 98

Notes by a sympathetic and observant traveller of a jy. in Hawaii, Australasia, and Java.

South Sea Bubbles By the Earl [of Pembroke] & The Doctor [G. H. Kingsley] 1/ *n.* f 8° Macmillan [72] 11

The 1st edn. is worth ab. 10/6, on acc. of freedom of language used by 'the Earl' (then an 'infant'): subsequently omitted.

STEVENSON, Rob. Louis In the South Seas 2/ *n.* f 8° Chatto [96] 08

$1·50 Scribner, *N.Y.* Acc. of 2 cruises on yacht *Casco* (1888) and cruise in schooner *Equator* (1889). Marquesas, Paumatus, and Gilbert Islds.

„ Essays of Travel 6/ c 8° Chatto 05

Early papers fr. periodicals, prev. reprinted in his *Works* [*ut* **K** § 89]. For other works on his life in the Pacific *v.* **K** § 24.

STODDARD, C. W. Summer Cruising in South Seas: South Sea Idyls $1·50 c 8° Scribner, *N.Y.* [73] 05

6/ *n.* Chatto. 'The lightest, sweetest, wildest, freshest things that have ever been written about the life of that summer ocean'.—W. D. Howells.

„ Isld. of Tranquil Delights: a S. Sea idyl and others; ill. [6/ *n.* Chatto] $1·50 c 8° Scribner, *N.Y.* [74] 05

TURNER, Rev. G. Nineteen Years in Polynesia: missy. life & travels *o.p.* [*pb.* 6/] 8° Snow 61

WALKER, H. W. Wanderings among South Sea Savages; 48 pl. 7/6 *n.* 8° Witherby 09

Experces. amongst the wildest tribes in New Guinea, Borneo, Fiji, Philippines, etc.

WAWN, Cpt. W. T. S. Sea Islanders & Queensld. Labour Trade; maps & ill. 18/ r 8° Sonnenschein 93
$4 Macmillan, *N.Y.* Record of voys. and expercs. in W. Pacific 1875–1891, aboundg. in accs. of little-kn. places and peoples, told in a straight-forward sailorly manner, and affording a vivid insight into Labour Recruiting in the Pacific. Maps and ill.

WILKES, Chas. Nar. of U.S. Exploring Ex., 5 v.; ill. $25 r 8°; Abmt. 1 v. 8° $3·50 8° Govt. Pr., *Washgtn.* 45; 45
The American Expedition to Polynesia and the Antarctic Regions, 1838–42.

WRAGGE, Clement L. Romance of the South Seas; 84 ill. 7/6 *n.* c 8° Chatto 06
Pt. i is on 'The Prison of the Pacific' [= New Caledonia]; ii descrs. trip to Tahiti *via* Barotonga and Raiatea.

**Missions** —*v.* **A** § 105

**Scenery:** HARDY (N. H.; art.) The Savage South Sea: 68 col. pl., w. l'rpr. E. W. Elkington
[$6 *n.* Macmillan, *N.Y.*] 20/ *n.* sq 8° Black 07

## 64: POLYNESIA (*b*): INDIVIDUAL ISLANDS

**Borneo** —*v.* **E** § 36

**Caroline Islands:** CHRISTIAN (F. W.) The Caroline Islands; maps and ill. 12/6 *n.* 8° Methuen 99
$4 Scribner, *N.Y.* A full and scholarly acc. of the islds. and their inhabts., w. much on languages of the islands.

FURNESS, Wm. H. The Island of Stone Money; 30 ill. $3·50 *n.* (15/ *n.*) 8° Lippincott 09
A lively account of a visit in 1903 to Uap, the westernmost island of the group.

**Christmas Island:** ANDREW (C. W.) Monograph of Christmas Island; map and ill. British Museum 00
A full account of the phys. features and geol., w. descrns. of flora and fauna by other wrs.

**Easter Island:** GONZALEZ (Cpt. Don F.) Voyage to Easter Island, ed. B. G. Corney; ill.
[1700–1] 8° Hakluyt Soc. 08

**Ellice Islands:** *Funafuti:* DAVID (Mrs E.) Funafuti; map and ill. 12/ 8° Murray 99
Well-written account of the island and experiences of the Coral-boring expedition there, '98.

**Fiji Islands:** ANDERSON (J. W.) Travels in Fiji and New Caledonia, 2 vols. *o.p.* [*pb.* 10/6] 8° Ellisen 80

BURTON, Rev. J. W. The Fiji of To-day; ill. [missionary] 7/6 *n.* c 8° Kelly 10

CUMMING, [Miss] C. F. Gordon At Home in Fiji; ill [$1·25 Armstrong, *N.Y.*] 7/6 p 8° Blackwood [81] 86

DE RICCI, J. H. Fiji, our New Province in South Seas; ill. *o.p.* [*pb.* 9/] 8° Stanford 75

FORBES, Dr Litton Two Years in Fiji; ill. 8/6 p 8° Longman 75

GRIMSHAW, Beatr. From Fiji to the Cannibal Islands—*ut* **E** § 63

HORNE, J. A Year in Fiji [botany, agric., resources] 5/ 8° Stanford 81

ROWE, Rev. G. S. [ed.] Fiji and the Fijians, 2 vols. *o.p.* c 8° 58
Vol. i: *Islands and Inhabitants*, by T. WILLIAMS; ii: *Mission History*, by J. CALVERT.

SEEMANN, Dr B. Viti: acc. of Govt. mission to Fiji Isls. [1860–1] *o.p.* [*pb.* 14/] 8° Macmillan 62

SMYTHE, Mrs Ten Months in Fiji Islands; 4 col. pl. and 3 maps *o.p.* [*pb.* 15/] 8° Parker 64

THOMSON, Basil South Sea Yarns; ill. 3/6 c 8° Blackwood [94] 95
'Yarns' ab. Fijians, by one thoroughly conversant w. their country and themselves, yet not 'South-Sea-islandized' (to use L'd PEMBROKE's expression), givg. excellent idea of their moral and intellectual characters.

" The Fijians: study of Decay of Custom; ill. 10/6 *n.* 8° Heinemann 08
A storehouse of matls., yet very readable, formg. an object-lesson on decay of a primitive society in contact w. civilizn. Important chap. on cousin-marriage.

WILLIAMS (Rev. T.) + CALVERT (J.) Fiji and the Fijians, 2 vols. *o.p.* [*pb.* 12/] c 8° Heylin 58
The island and the natives by WILLIAMS; with a mission history by CALVERT.

**Friendly Islands [Tonga Islands]**

THOMSON, Basil Diversions of a Prime Minister; map and ill. 15/ 8° Blackwood 94
Acc. of author's admin. of Tonga as nominee and representative of Brit. High Commissr.: very lively reading, wr. w. quiet humour and a keen eye to ludicrous incident and amusg. traits of character.

*Savage Island:* KING (Jos.) W. G. Lawes of Savage Isl. & New Guinea; ill. [missy.] 5/ *n.* 8° R.T.S. 09

THOMSON, Basil Savage Island; map and ill. 7/6 *n.* c 8° Murray 02
An interesting account of a mission to Niué and Tonga.

**Hawaii (Sandwich Islands):** *Bibliography:* HUNNEWELL (J. F., etc.) Bibliogr. of Hawaiian Islands
*o.p. Boston* 69

*History:* ALEXANDER (W. D.) Brief History of the Hawaiian People $1·50 12° Amer. Bk. Co., *N.Y.* 97

BLACKMAN, Prf. W. F. The Making of Hawaii 10/6 *n.* ($2·50 *n.*) 8° Macmillan [99] 06
An elab. and exhaustive hist. of developmt. of Hawaii, fr. Cpt. COOK's discovery.

CARPENTER, Edw. J. America in Hawaiian Islands $1·50 12° Small, *Boston* 99
5/ Low. Hist. of the archipel. fr. discov. by COOK (1778) to raisg. of Amer. flag at Honolulu (1898).

CHAMBERS, Hy. L. Constitutional History of Hawaii
[J. Hopk. Un. Studs.] 25 c. 8° Johns Hopk. Univ. Pr., *Baltim.* 96

FORNANDER, A. —*in his* Account of the Polynesian Race, 3 vols., *ut* **E** § 63

HOPKINS, Manley Hawaii, Past, Present, and Future *o.p.* [*pb.* 10/6] c 8° Longman [66] 68

JARVES, J. J. Hawaiian or Sandwich Islands, ed. H. W. Whitney *o.p.* 8° *Honolulu* [43] 72

KROUT, Mary H. Hawaii and a Revolution $2 c 8° Dodd & Mead, *N.Y.* 98
10/6 Murray. Experiences of a newspaper correspondent after the 1893 revolution.

LILINOKALANI [deposed Qu. of the islands] Hawaii's Story ; ill. $2 8° Lee & Shepard, *Boston* 98
Really an account of the author's own life and defence of her government.

'OWEN, J. A.' [+ Mrs VISGER] The Story of Hawaii 5/ c 8° Harper 98
Quite incomplete, but an interesting, short and gossipy account.

*Recent Travel and Description*

BISHOP, Mrs Isab. [*née* BIRD] Hawaiian Archipelago ; ill. [6 mos.' visit ; 1874] 2/6 *n.* p 8° Murray [75] 05

BODDHAM-WHETHAM, J. W. —*in his* Pearls of the Pacific, *ut* **E** § 63

CUMMING, [Miss] C. F. Gordon Fire Fountains : kgdm. of Hawaii, volcs., missns., 2 v. ; ill. 25/ 8° Blackwood 83

GOWEN, Rev. H. H. [missy.] The Paradise of the Pacific (Hawaii)—*ut* **A** § 105

NORDHOFF, C. Northern California, Oregon, & Sandwich Islands ; ill. $2·50 8° Harper, *N.Y.* 74

TWOMBLY, A. S. Hawaii and its People ; ill. [5/ Gay & Hancock] $1 12° Silver, *N.Y.* 99

WHITNEY, Caspar Hawaiian America $2·50 8° Harper, *N.Y.* 97
A good general account of the islands, w. some matter on hist., resources, prospects.

YOUNG, Lucien The Real Hawaii $1·50 12° Doubleday, *N.Y.* [98] 99
1st edn. *sub tit. The 'Boston' at Hawaii.* Mainly a narr. of Revoln. of 1893, defending officers of U.S.

**Marianne (Ladrone) Islands** —*v.* **E** § 62 (CROZET)

**Marquesas Islands :** CHRISTIAN (F. W.)—*in his* Eastern Pacific Lands, *ut inf., s.v.* Society Islands

MELVILLE, Hermann Typee ; *and* Omoo—*ut* **K** § 51
The first acc. pubd. of residence am. Polynes. natives by a white man who lived w. them in their own fashion and on terms of social equality. Thoroughly interesting, realistic, and curious ; but w. a strong admixture of fiction.

de QUIROS, P. F. —*in his* Voyages [tr.], 2 vols., *ut* **E** § 62

STEVENSON, M. I. From Saranac to Marquesas $2 *n.* c 8° Scribner, *N.Y.* 03

STEVENSON, R. L. —*in his* In the South Seas, *ut* **E** § 63

**New Britain (Neu-Pommern)**

POWELL, Wilfrid Wanderings in a Wild Country : 3 yrs. amongst cannibals ; ill. 5/ 8° Low [83] 84

PULLEN-BURRY, [Miss] B. In a German Colony [4 wks. visit] 5/ *n.* c 8° Methuen 09

**New Caledonia :** ANDERSON (J. W.) —*in his* Travels in Fiji and New Caledonia, 2 vols., *ut sup., s.v.* Fiji

GRIFFITH, Geo. C. In an Unknown Prison Land—*ut* **D** § 123

WRAGGE, Clement L. —*in his* Romance of the South Seas, *ut* **E** § 62

**New Guinea :** *Bibliography :* RYE (E. C.) Bibliogr. of N. Guinea—*in* Suppl. Pprs. of R.G.S. 1884 (Murray)

d'ALBERTIS, L. M. New Guinea : what I did & what I saw, 2 vols. ; ill. [1871–7] 42/ 8° Low [80] 81

BEVAN, Theod. F. Toil, Travel and Discov. in Brit. N. Guinea ; maps 7/6 c 8° Paul 90

CAYLEY-WEBSTER, Cpt. H. Through New Guinea & Cannibal Countries ; 350 ill. $5 8° Stokes, *N.Y.* 98
Travels for scient. purposes in N. Guin., Solomon and Admiralty Isls. Valuable, but overcoloured.

CHALMERS, Rev. Jas. Work and Advent. in N. Guinea ; *and other bks.*—*ut* **A** § 105

GILL, Rev. W. W. Life in the Southern Seas—*ut* **A** § 105

" Gems fr. Coral Islands [missy. wk. in N. Guinea] 2/6 c 8° Stock [55–6] 71

GRIMSHAW, Beatrice The New New Guinea ; map and 49 ill. 12/6 *n.* 8° Hutchinson 10
A light and unconventional acc. of the scenery, people, customs, etc.

GUILLEMARD, Dr F. H. H. Cruise of *Marchesa* to Kamschatka & N. Guinea ; ill. 21/ 8° Murray [86] 89

KEANE, A. H. —*his* Eastern Geography [*ut* **E** § 36] *incls. New Guinea*

LINDT, J. W. Picturesque New Guinea ; w. histor. Introd. ; 50 autotypes 42/ 4° Longman 87

LYNE, Chas. New Guinea ; ill. [acc. of establ. of Brit. protectorate] 10/6 c 8° Low 85

MACGILLIVRAY, Jno. Voyage of H.M.S. *Rattlesnake*, 2 vols. ; ill. *o.p.* [*pb.* 36/] 8° Boone 52
Account of the E. B. Kennedy Expedition, 1846–50.

MACGREGOR, Sir Wm. British New Guinea : country and people 4/ 8° R.G.S. (Murray) 97
[Extra Vol. of R.G.S.] The most authoritative account. Map and ill.

MORESBY, Cpt. J. Discoveries and Surveys in N. Guinea and Polynesia—*ut* **E** § 63

PITCAIRNE, W. D. Two Years amgst. Savages of N. Guinea ; map *o.p.* [*pb.* 5/] c 8° Ward & Downey 91

PRATT, A. E. Two Years among New Guinea Cannibals ; map & 54 ill. 16/ *n.* 8° Seeley 06
Acc. of a naturalist's sojourn am. aborigines of unexplored parts of New Guinea.

ROMILLY, H. H. The Western Pacific and New Guinea—*ut* **E** § 63

" From my Verandah in New Guinea—*ut* **B** § 29

SCRATCHLEY (Sir P.) + KINLOCK-COOKE (C.) Austral. Defences & N. Guinea ; maps 14/ 8° Macmillan 87
SCRATCHLEY bore an import. pt. in planning defences wh. have been carried out, and COOKE had access to all his papers. The bk. conts. an *Introd. Memoir* and acc. of SCRATCHLEY'S work as High Commr. of N. Guinea.

STRACHAN, Cpt. J. Explorations and Adventures in New Guinea ; ill. 12/ c 8° Low 88

SELIGMANN, Dr C. G. The Melanesians of British New Guinea ; 131 ill. 21/ *n.* r 8° Camb. Press 10
$7 *n.* Putnam. *N.Y.* Descrs. soc. organizn., customs, etc., of princ. tribes and ethnic groups as distinct fr. Papuans (the orig. inhabs.).

THOMSON, J. P. [Austral.] British New Guinea ; map and 50 ill. 21/ m 8° Philip 92
A good, compreh. bk., largely based on Sir W. MACGREGOR'S explorns. ; w. contribns. by Bar. F. v. MÜLLER, Sir W. MACGREGOR, and other Australians. The orig. MS. and ill. went down w. the *Quetta*, so th. the MS. had to be hastily rewr., of wh. it shows traces.

TREGANCE, Louis Adventures, ed. Rev. H. Crocker [9 yrs. captive in N.G.] 6/ c 8° Low 76

WALLACE, Dr A. Russel —*in his* Studies, Scientific and Social, vol. i, *ut* **H** § 43

*Missions* —*v.* **A** § 105

**Papua :** CHIGNELL (Rev. A. K.) An Outpost in Papua ; 32 pl. 10/6 *n.* 8° Smith & Elder 11
An unpretentious narrative of a primitive and hitherto quite unknown village.

MACKAY, Col. Kenneth Across Papua ; map and 40 pl. 7/6 *n.* 8° Witherby 09
Recounts his experces, as chief of Roy. Commissn. to Papua ; w. descrns. of the country and natives.

**New Hebrides :** BRENCHLEY (J. L.) Cruise of *Curaçoa* am. S. S. Islds. ; ill. [1865] 42/ 8° Longman 73

GRIMSHAW, Beatr. —*in her* From Fiji to the Cannibal Islands, *ut* **E** § 63

LAMB, Rob. Saints and Savages : 5 yrs. in N. Hebrides ; ill. 6/ 8° Blackwood 05

MARKHAM, Cpt. A. H. Cruise of *Rosario* am. New Hebrides & Santa Cruz Isls. *o.p.* [*pb.* 16/] 8° Low 73

PATON, Maggie W. [Mrs Dr Jno. PATON] Letters fr. the New Hebrides 6/ c 8° Hodder 94

de QUIROS, P. F. Voyages, tr. and ed. Sir C. R. Markham *ut* **E** § 63 [1595-1606]

*Missions* —*v.* **A** § 105

**Papua** —*v.* New Guinea, *sup.*

**Pitcairn Island :** BARROW (Sir Jno.) Mutiny of the *Bounty* 6/ c 8° Ward & Lock [31] 83

BECKE (Louis) + JEFFERY (W.) The Mutineer 6/ c 8° Unwin 98
A story founded on hist. of mutiny of H.M.S. *Bounty* in 1790 and subseq. settlemt. of mutineers on desert island.

BELCHER, L'y Mutineers of the *Bounty* and their Descendants *o.p.* [*pb.* 12/] c 8° Murray 70

MURRAY, Rev. T. B. Pitcairn : island, people, and the pastor 3/ c 8° S.P.C.K. [54] 85

YOUNG, Rosalind A. Mutiny of the *Bounty*, etc. *o.p.* c 8° Paul [ ] 90

**Samoa (Navigators' Islands) :** CHURCHWARD (W. B.) My Consulate in Samoa *o.p.* [*pb.* 15/] 8° Bentley 87

CHURCHILL, [Mrs] Llewella P. Samoa 'Uma : where life is different ; 20 ill. $1 c 8° Forest, *N.Y.* 02
7/6 *n.* Low. Account of a residence in and travels through the Samoan group of islands.

STAIR, J. B. Old Samoa : flotsam and jetsam fr. Pac. Ocean 5/ c 8° R.T.S. 97
Researches of an amateur into the customs and myths of Samoa.

STEVENSON, R. L. A Foot-note to History [1883-92] 6/ c 8° Cassell [92] 93
$1·50 Scribner, *N.Y.* Hist. of the troubles in Samoa fr. time when Gt. Brit., U.S., and Germy. stepped in to preserve the peace, insistg. on recogn. of MALIETOA as King of all Samoa, to gt. hurricane [adm'rably descrd.], wh. Brit. ship *Calliope* alone escaped, and wh. suddenly changed current of affairs.

" Letters from Samoa—*in* Works, vol. xvii, *ut* **K** § 89

" Vailima Letters [1890-4 ; 2 v. $2·25 *n.*, Stone, *Chic.*] 7/6 c 8° Methuen 95

Stubbs, Laura Stevenson's Shrine : recd. of a pilgrimage ; 20 ill. 5/ *n.* s 4° Moring 03
For other books on STEVENSON'S life in Samoa *v.* K § 24, *s.v.* Stevenson.

TURNER, Dr Geo. Samoa a Hundred Years Ago and Long Before—*ut* **B** § 29
Contains also notes on the cults and customs of 23 other Pacific Islands.

**Sandwich Islands** —*v.* Hawaii, *sup.*

**Society Islands ; Tahiti :** BRASSEY (L'y) Tahiti ; 31 photos. *o.p.* [*pb.* 21/] 4° Low 82

CHRISTIAN, F. W. Eastern Pac. Lands ; maps & ill. [Tahiti ; Marquesas Isls.] 7/6 *n.* sq 8° Rob. Scott 10

**Solomon Islands :** de MENDANA DE NEYRA (A.) Discovery of Solomon Islands, ed. & tr. L'd Amherst + Basil Thomson, 2 vols. ; 5 maps & 33 ill. [1568] 8° Hakluyt Soc. 01

*GUPPY, Dr H. B. Solomon Islands & their Natives ; map & ill. *o.p.* [*pb.* 25/] r 8° Sonnenschein 87
A careful scientific descrn., contg. a tr. of Hernando GALLEGO'S important *Descubrimento de las Islas Salomon* [1566], hitherto untr.

" Solomon Islands : geol., gen. feats., etc. ; maps *o.p.* [*pb.* 10/6] r 8° Sonnenschein 87

de QUIROS, P. F. —*in his* Voyages [tr.], 2 vols., *ut* **E** § 63 [1595-1606]

WOODFORD, C. M. A Naturalist am. the Head-Hunters ; 3 maps & 16 pl. 8/6 c 8° Philip [90] 90
$2·75 Longman, *N.Y.* A good acc. of advants. and scient. observns. dur. 3 visits in 1886, '87, '88.

**Tonga Islands** —*v.* Friendly Islands, *sup.*

**Torres Straits :** CAMBRIDGE ANTHROPOL. EXPEDN. TO TORRES STRAITS—*ut* **E** § 36

HADDON, Dr A. C. Head Hunters, Black, White, and Brown 15/ 8° Methuen 02
An interesting acc. of the islands and islanders of the Torres Straits—a preliminary general acc. of the Cambr. Univ. Expedn. to Torres Straits, 1898.

## 65 : AUSTRALIA (*a*) : GENERALLY

**Bibliography** —*v.* **E** § 62

**History of Discovery and Exploration**

CALVERT, A. F. The Discovery of Australia ; maps and 28 pl. 10/6 s 4° Dean [93] 02
A record of early voyages down to COOK, w, appendix contg. 10 letters fr. COOK.

" The Explorn. of Australia, 2 Pts. [to 1896] ea. 10/6 i 8° Philip 95-6
Retells the well-worn story of navigators and inland explorers painstakingly, but dully.

COLLINGRIDGE, G. The Discovery of Australia ; ill. and 12 maps 25/ r 4° *Sydney* 95
' A crit., documentary, and hist. investign. conc. the priority of discov. in Australasia by Europeans before 1770 '

FAVENC, Ern. History of Australian Exploration ; maps *o.p.* [*pb.* 21/] 8° Griffith 88
From 1783 to STOCKDALE's expedn. fr. Cambr. Gulf to overland telegr. line [1885]. Moderately good.

,, Explorers of East, Centre, & West-of-Australia ; ill. 12/6 8° Whitcombe, *Melbourne* 08

GILES, Ern. Geographic Travels in Central Australia [1852–74] 7/6 8° *Melbourne* 75

,, Australia Twice Traversed, 2 vols. ; 6 maps and ill. 30/ 8° Low 89
Narr. compiled fr. Jls. of 5 expedns. into and thro' Cent., S. and W. A. ; 1872–6. Introd. summarizes previous jys.

HOWITT, Wm. History of Discovery of Australia, etc., 2 vols. *o.p.* [*pb.* 28/] 8° Longman 65

LEE, Ida [Mrs C. B. MARRIOTT] Coming of British to Aust. : 1788–1829 ; ill. 7/6 *n.* ($2·50 *n.*) 8° Longm. 06

SCOTT, Ern. Terre Napoleon 10/6 *n.* 8° Methuen 10
A hist. of Fch. explorns. and projects in Australia, claimg. to show that NAPOLEON expedn. despatched in 1804 under BAUDIN (wh. is fully narrated) was purely a scientific one, and th. NAPOLEON had no intention of foundg. a second fatherland in Australia.

THYNNE, R. Story of Austr. Explorn. ; maps & ill. [popular ; interestg.] 5/ c 8° Unwin 94

WOODS, Rev. J. E. T. Hist. of Discov. and Explorn. of Australia, 2 vols. *o.p.* [*pb.* 28/] 8° Low 65

**Biography and Works of Discoverers : Collectively**

BECKE (Louis) + JEFFERY (W.) Naval Pioneers of Australia ; ill. 7/6 *n.* c 8° Murray 99
$3 Scribner, *N.Y.* A popular account of DAMPIER, COOK, PHILLIP, BASS, FLINDERS, BLIGH, etc.

EDEN, C. H. Australian Heroes ; ill. [popular ; good] 5/ 12° S.P.C.K. 75

FAVENC, Ern. The Explorers of Australia & their Life-work 12/6 *n.* 8° Whitcombe & Tombs 08

MAJOR, R. H. [ed.] Early Indications of Terra Australis 8° Hakluyt Soc. 59
A colln. of documents on or by ARIAS, TORRES [1607], TASMAN [1644], POOL [1629], DAMPIER [1687–8, 99], and others.

SCOTT, G. Firth Romance of Australian Exploring ; maps and ill. 6/ c 8° Low 99
A popular account of all the chief explorers and their journeys.

*Individually (w. their Writings)*—*v. also* **E** § 7 (COOK, DAMPIER, MAGELLAN)

COMMERSON, Philibert [d. 1773] Life of. By Cpt. S. P. Oliver, ed. G. F. Scott Elliot ; ill. 10/6 *n.* 8° Murray 09
COMMERSON was ' Naturaliste du Roi ' ; his travels are here descr. ; last ch. on his scient. wk. (botany).

FLINDERS, Mat. [1774–1814] Life of. By Rob. Thynne ; ill. [popular] 3/6 c 8° Hogg 97

STURT, Cpt. Chas. [1795–1869] Life of. By Mrs N. G. Stuart [dau.-in-law] 16/ 8° Smith & Elder 99

TASMAN, Abel J. [1602–59] MS. Jl. of Discovery of Australia—*ut* **E** § 66, *s.v.* Tasmania

**Atlas :** New Atlas of Australia : 100 col. maps, 5 v. [ea. sep. 30/] 108/ i f° *Sydney* 86
i : *New South Wales* ; ii : *Victoria* ; iii : *Queensland* ; iv : *South Australia* ; v : *Western Australia*.

HUGHES, W. [ed.] Atlas of the Australian Colonies 31/6 f° Philip *n.d.*

**Ethnology :** *Collectively* —*v. also* **B** § 29, **E** §§ 62–3—*for* special ethnol. *v.* **E** §§ 66–7

BETTANY, G. T. The Red, Brown and Black Men of America and Australia—*ut* **E** § 53

CURR, E. M. Australian Race : orig., langs., custs., etc., 3 v. & atlas (4°) 42/ 8° *Melbourne* 86–7
His theory is th. Austrns. are Afric. negroes, or rather of same stock, crossed by an unkn. element bef. they reached mainld.

FISON (L.) + HOWITT (Dr A. W.) Kamilaroi and Kurnai—*ut* **F** § 5
On group-marriage and relationship, and marriage by elopement—drawn fr. usage of Australian aborigines.

HADDON, A. C. —*in his* Decorative Art of British New Guinea 14/ *n.* 4° Williams 95

Horn Scientific Expedition to Central Australia, Pt. iv—*ut* **H** § 106

LANG, Andr. Australian Problems 07

MATHEW, Rev. Jno. Eaglehawk & Crow : study of Austral. Aborigines 18/ *n.* 8° Melville, *Melb.* (Nutt) 99
A study of problem of peopling of Austr. and Tasmania : w. surv. of Austr. langs. [illegible]

RIDLEY, W. —*in his* Kámìlarói and other Australian Languages, *ut* **K** § 160

SPENCER (B.) + GILLEN (F. J.) Northern Tribes of Central Australia 21/ *n.* 8° Macmillan [99] 04

THOMAS, N. W. Natives of Australia ; 32 pl. [Nat. Races of Br. Emp.] 6/ *n.* 8° Constable 06
An excellent ' popular ' bk., preceded by a lucid sketch of phys. condns. of Austr. continent, incl. flora and fauna.

,, Kinship Organization and Group Marriage 8° 06

WHEELER, G. C. Tribe and Intertribal Relations in Australia ; Pref. Prf. E. A. Westermarck 3/6 *n.* 8° Murray 10

*Central Australia :* Horn Scientific Expedn. to Centr. Australia, vol. iv.—*ut* **H** § 106

*SPENCER (Prf. B.) + GILLEN (F. J.) Native Tribes of Cent. Aust. ; ill. 21/ *n.* ($6·50 *n.*) 8° Macmillan 99
Deals chiefly with the Arunta tribe ; the most authoritative collection of facts.

*North Australia :* *SPENCER (Prf. B.) + GILLEN (F. J.) Native Tribes of Northern Territory of Australia ; ill. 21/ *n.* ($6·50 *n.*) 8° Macmillan 04

**General Geography ; Commercial Geography**—*v. also* **E** § 62

BARTON, C. H. Outlines of Australian Physiography [schl.-bk.] 2/ c 8° *Maryboro'* 95

GREGORY, Prf. J. W. Australia and New Zealand—*ut* **E** § 61, *s.v.* Stanford

TAYLOR, Griffith Australia in its Physiogr. & Economic Aspects ; 60 ill. 3/6 (90 c.) c 8° Clar. Press 11
[Oxford Geographies.] An introduction to the study of the commercial geogr. of Australia.

**History**

**Bonwick**, Jas. — First Twenty Years of Australia — [1788–1808] *o.p.* [*pb.* 5/] 12° Low 82
**Lang**, Dr W. H. — Australia; 12 col. pl. — [Romance of Empire Ser.] 6/ *n.* sq 8° Jack 08
**Ralph**, Edith — Empire Builders in Australia — 5/ *n.* c 8° Unwin 11
*__Rusden__, G. W. — History of Australia, 3 vols. — 50/ 8° Chapman 83
**Sutherland**, A. + G. Hist. of Austr. & N.Z.: 1606–1890; 52 ill. [school-bk.] 2/6 (90 c.) c 8° Longman [78] 94
**Tregarthen**, G. — Australian Commonwealth; maps & ill. [Story of Nations] 5/ c 8° Unwin 93
$1·50 Putnam, *N.Y.* Incl. Tasmania and N.Z. Readable. Forms first of a sub-series of *Story of Nations* on Engl. colonies.
**Turner**, Hy. G. — First Decade of Australian Commonwealth — [1901–10] 9/ 8° Longman 11
**Wise**, Hon. B. R. — Commonwealth of Australia; maps & ill. [All-Red Series] 7/6 *n.* 8° Pitman 09
A good popular bk. on the laws, institns., politics, etc., by one who has played a pt. in its publ. life.

**Life and People; Australia as seen by others**

**Adams**, Fcs. — The Australians: a social sketch — *o.p.* [*pb.* 10/6] 8° Unwin 93
Economic, social, and polit., fr. a democratic and vaguely Socialistic stdpt. Suggestive, penetrative, and 'smart'.
**Baden-Powell**, [Sir] G. — New Homes for the Old Country; ill. — *o.p.* [*pb.* 21/] 8° Bentley 72
On the political and domestic life, industries, etc.
**Buchanan**, Alf. — The Real Australia — [present-day life] 6/ c 8° Unwin 07
**Buley**, E. C. — Australian Life in Town and Country; ill. — 3/6 *n.* c 8° Newnes 05
**Cambridge**, Ada — Thirty Years in Australia — [1870–1902] 7/6 8° Methuen 03
**Dale**, Dr R. W. — Impressions of Australia — [educ., relig., life, etc.] 5/ c 8° Hodder [89] 89
**Fraser**, J. Foster — Australia; the making of a nation — 6/ c 8° Cassell 10
**Hogan**, J. F. — The Australian in London and America — *o.p.* [*pb.* 6/] c 8° Ward & Downey 89
**Inglis**, J. ['Maori'] — Our Australian Cousins [chs. on N.S.W. and Queensld.] 14/ 8° Macmillan 80
**Parker**, [Sir] Gilb. — Round the Compass in Australia; ill. — 3/6 8° Hutchinson [92] 97
General review of Austrn. affairs, descrn. of life in towns and in country, discussns. of industries, resources, etc.
**Pioneer** (A) ' [Jno. **Phillips**] Reminiscences of Australian Early Life; ill. — 5/ c 8° Marsden 93
An unaffected descrn. of state of things long since passed away. Life as servant, owner of a run, and at goldfields. 1840–53.
**Praed**, Mrs Campbell — Australian Life, Black and White; ill. — *o.p.* [*pb.* 8/] p 8° Chapman 85

*Bush Life* — —*for* Bushrangers *v.* **D** § 123

**Boothby**, Guy — On the Wallaby; 8 pl. and 85 ill. — 18/ 8° Longman 94
'On the Wallaby' [= On the March] is usually appl. to persons trampg. the Bush in search of employmt. This narr. is full of strange wanderings., and is wr. (and ill.) w. vigour and good humour.
**Dunderdale**, Geo. — The Book of the Bush — 3/6 c 8° Ward & Lock 96
Sketches of early Colonial life of squatters, whalers, convicts, diggers, etc.
**Haygarth**, H. W. — Bush Life in Australia — *o.p.* [*pb.* 2/] c 8° Murray [48] 61
Records experiences for eight years in the Bush, before 1848.
**Matthews**, Rev. C. H. S. — A Parson in the Australian Bush; ill. — 6/ *n.* c 8° Arnold 08
$2 Longman. *N.Y.* Provides a vivid pict. of life and manners, and of clerical work, in the Bush.
**Nichols**, A. — Wild Life & Advent. in Austr. Bush, 2 v.; 8 pl. *o.p.* [*pb.* 21/] c 8° Bentley 87
**Praed**, Mrs Campbell — My Australian Girlhood — 6/ *n.* c 8° Unwin [02] 04
Sketches and impressions of bush life in Queensland. Well-written.
**Semen**, Prf. Rich. — In the Australian Bush, etc.; maps and ill. — 21/ *n.* r 8° Macmillan 9
Account of a zoologist's travels, etc. Australia, New Guinea, the Moluccas.

*Irish in Australia:* **Hogan** (J. F.) The Irish in Australia—*ut* **E** § 20

**Resources; Statistics; Economic Condition**—*v. also* **D** §§ 126, 136

Australian Year-Book — 10/6 8° *Melbourne* [81] *ann.*
**Fitzgerald**, J. F. — Australia; maps and ill. [For. Countries & Brit. Colonies] 3/6 12° Low 81
**Galloway**, W. J. — Advanced Australia: on the eve of federation — 3/6 c 8° Methuen 99
**Gordon & Gotch** [pubs.] — Australian Handbk.; maps [incl. N. Zeal., Fiji, N. Guinea] 10/6 *n.* 8° Gordon & Gotch *ann.*
Official Year-Book of the Commonwealth of Australia — 8° McCarron, *Melb.* (P. S. King & Son) *ann.*
**Reeves**, W. P. — State Experiments in Australia and New Zealand, 2 vols.—*ut* **D** § 126
**Rowland**, Percy — The New Nation — 7/6 c 8° Smith & Elder 03
Reprinted articles on Australian history, politics, literature, and the economic and political future.
**Wallace**, R. Rural Econ. and Agric. in Australia & N. Z.—*ut* **E** § 62
Year Book of Australia — 10/6 8° Brit. Austral. Pb. Co. *ann.*

**Recent Travel and Description**

**Brady**, E. J. — The King's Caravan: acr. Australia in a Wagon; ill. — 12/6 *n.* 8° Arnold 11
**Brereton**, J. Le Gay — Landlopers — [trampg. in Australia] 3/6 c 8° Unwin 00

CAMERON, Agnes D. The New North $3 *n.* (10/6 *n.*) 8° Appleton 09
Account of a jy. fr. Edmonton to the mouth of the Mackenzie.

CRAIG, W. My Adventures on Australian Goldfields 6/ c 8° Cassell 03
A graphic acc. of his perils and advents. as a pioneer to the Goldfds. in the early 'fifties.

DEMARR, Jas. Advents. in Australia 50 Yrs. Ago; maps & pl. [1839–44] 6/ 8° Sonnenschein 93

DILKE, [Sir] C. W. Greater Britain: a record of travel—*ut* **E** § 21
Nearly half the work treats of the Australian Colonies.

EDEN, C. H. The Fifth Continent; ill. [popular; good] 5/ 12° S.P.C.K. 76

FERGUSON, Dugald Vicissitudes of Bush Life in Australia and New Zealand—*ut* **E** § 67

FROUDE, J. A. Oceana: England and her colonies—*ut* **E** § 21 [the Australian colonies]

FURNISS, Harry Australian Sketches, Made on Tour; ill. [feeble] 2/6 c 8° Ward & Lock 99

FINCH-HATTON, Hon. H. Advance Australia [8 yrs. in Qusld., N.S.W., Vict.] 7/6 c 8° W. H. Allen [85] 86

HILL, J. G. The Calvert Scientific Exploring Expedition [1896] 2/ 8° Philip

HOGAN, J. F. The Sister Dominions: thro' Canada to Austr. *o.p.* [*pb.* 3/6] c 8° Ward & Downey 96

Horn Scientific Expedition to Central Australia, ed. Prf. B. Spencer, vol. i—*ut* **H** § 106

JOSE, Arth. W. Two Awheel and Some Others Afoot; ill. 3/6 c 8° Dent 03
One of the very few good bks. written by a cyclist.

LE SOUËF, W. H. Dudley Wild Life in Australia; 170 ill. 7/6 c 8° Whitcombe, *Melbourne*

MACDONALD, Alex. In the Land of Pearl and Gold 10/6 *n.* 8° Blackie 07
A pioneer's wanderings in the back blocks and pearling of Australia and N. Guinea.

MARSHALL, Archib. Australian Impressions; ill. [enl. fr. *Dy. Mail*] 6/ c 8° Hodder 11

MURRAY, A. S. 1,200 Miles on the River Murray 42/ obl 4° Robertson, *Melbourne* 98
Letterpress of small value; good ill., some coloured.

NISBET, Hume A Colonial Tramp; ill. [Australia, N. Guin.] *o.p.* [*pb.* 6/] c 8° Ward & Downey 91

SEARCEY, Alf. In Australian Tropics; map and 52 ill. 10/6 *n.* 8° Paul 08
Narr. of cruises after smugglers, fights w. Malays and Blacks, etc., by sub-collr. of customs, Port Darwin.

SPENCE (B.) + GILLEN (F.) Across Australia; ill. (some col.) 8° Macmillan, *in prep.*
A popular account of their travels in the interior: *v. sup. s.v.* Ethnology.

TAYLOR, Dr J. E. Our Island Continent 2/6 c 8° S.P.C.K. 86
A delightful little bk., describing a naturalist's holiday in Australia.

TROLLOPE, Anth. Australia & N. Zealand, 2 vols., 30/, 8°; Abrgmt. 1/ c 8° Ward & Lock 73; 84

WARBURTON, Col. E. Journey across Western Interior of Australia; ill. *o.p.* [*pb.* 16/] 8° Low 75
An interestg. narrative of an important overland expedition.

WISE, Hon. B. R. The Commonwealth of Australia [All-Red Ser.] 7/6 *n.* c 8° Pitman 09

**Scenery** —*v. also* **E** § 62, *s.v.* Scenery

GARRAN, Dr A. [ed.] Picturesque Atlas of Australia; in 40 Pts. [1606–1888] ea. 5/ f° *Sydney* 86–9

MORRIS, Prf. E. E. [ed.] Picturesque Australasia, 4 vols.; 1,000 ill. ea. 7/6 r 8° Cassell [87–9]

SPENCE, P. F. S. [art.] Australia: 75 col. pl., w. l'rpr. F. Fox [$6 *n.* Macm., *N.Y.*] 20/ *n.* sq 8° Black 10

WILLOUGHBY, Howard Australian Pictures: drawn with pen and pencil 8/ i 8° R.T.S. 87

## 66: AUSTRALIA (*b*): INDIVIDUAL COLONIES

**New South Wales:** *History; Biography*

BARTON, G. B. Hist. of N.S. Wales: fr. offic. recds., vol. i: Gov. Phillip, 1783–9; maps and ill. 15/ 8° Govt. of N.S.W. 89

BEAN, C. E. W. On the Wool Track 5/ *n.* c 8° Rivers 10
Provides a vivid pict. of the vast pastoral areas, village homesteads, life, sheep, etc., 'out back'.

BLADEN, F. M. [ed.] Historical Records of New South Wales, vols. i–vii [to 1811] 8° Govt. Press, *Sydney* –02 *sqq. in prg.*

COGHLAN, T. A. Picturesque New South Wales 01

COLLINS, Lt.-Col. Dav. [1756–1810] English Colony in N.S.W., ed. J. Collier; 18 pl. 7/6 *n.* 8° Whitcombe & Tombs [1798–1802] 10
A valuable contemp. narr. of foundn. of Brit. Emp. in Austr.; w. Life of COLLINS, who sailed w. earliest batch of Gov. PHILIP's conscript colonists for Botany Bay in 1787.

FLANAGAN, Rod. Hist. of N.S.W., 2 v. [and other Austr. settlemts.] *o.p.* [*pb.* 24/] 8° Low 62

HUTCHINSON, F. [ed.] N.S.W., Mother Colony of the Australias 5/ c 8° Potter, *Sydney* 96
37 arts. by var. authorities on all aspects of N.S.W., historical, geogr., econ., and social.

LANG, Rev. J. D. Hist. and Statist. Account of N.S.W., 2 vols. 21/ p 8° Low [34] 75
There have been 4 edns. of this valuable bk.: 1834, '37, '52, '75: ea. re-wr., and the older ones of consid. intrinsic value still.

PARKES, Sir Hy. [1815–96] An Emigrant's Home Letters 6/ c 8° Angus, *Sydney* 97
L'rs. wr. betw. 1838 and 1844 to his family, pathetically descrg. his early struggles.

„ Fifty Yrs. in Making of Austr. Hist., 2 v. 32/ ($5) 8° Longman 92
PARKES, an entirely self-made man, who landed at Pt. Jackson (without 1/ in pocket and a Chartist) without introdns., was Prime-Minister of N.S.W. 1872–5, '77, '78–9, and his autobiogr. is of consid. general interest.

Lyne, C. E. Life of Sir Henry Parkes 16/ 8° Unwin 97
A careful life of 'the Grand Old Man of Australia'. Deals exclusively w. his public career.

PHILLIP, Adm. Arth. [1738–1814]—*v. also* BARTON, *sup.*
Becke (L.) + Jeffrey (W.) Adm. Phillip: foundg. of N.S.W. [Bldrs. of Gt. Br.] 5/ c 8° Unwin 99

PHILLIPS, Marion N.S.W. under Governor Macquarie [1810–21] 10/6 *n.* 8° P. S. King & Son 08
Of main interest as showg. how MACQUARIE's 'military' autocracy led to beginning of constitutional govt. in 1823.

RICHARDS (T.) + BOURNE (A.) Epitome of Official History of N.S.W. 8° *Sydney* 83

*Resources; Statistics*

COGHLAN, T. A. Wealth & Progr. of N.S.W. [by Govt. statistician] 5/ 8° Govt. Press, *Sydney* [92] *ann.*

JAMES, Jas. L. Shall I try Australia [health, business, pleasure] 3/6 8° Upcott Gill 92

Year Book of New South Wales 8° Agent Gen. N.S.W., *Lond. ann.*

*Ethnology:* PARKER (Mrs K. Langloh) The Euahlali Tribe; ill. 7/6 *n.* 8° Constable 06
A substantial contribn. of first-hand evidence on the usages, language, and ideals of the Euahlalis. Introd. by Andr. LANG.

**Queensland:** *History; Biography*

BOWEN, Sir G. F. [1821–99] Thirty Years of Colonial Govt., ed. S. Lane Poole [chfly. Australia] 32/ ($10·50) 8° Longman 89
BOWEN was successively Governor of Queensland, New Zealand, Victoria, Mauritius and Hong Kong.

RUSSELL, H. S. The Genesis of Queensland; facs. maps, etc. *o.p.* [*pb.* 21/] 8° Petherick 88

*Travel and Description:* ALLEN (C. H.) Visit to Qnsld. and her Goldfields *o.p.* [*pb.* 8/] c 8° Chapman 70

BANFIELD, E. J. The Confessions of a Beachcomber; 53 ill. $4 *n.* 8° Appleton, *N.Y.* 08
15/ *n.* Unwin. [Pubns. of Univ. of Pennsylvania.] Advents. in Queensld. dur. the Colony's early days.

BICKNELL, A. C. Travel and Advent. in N. Queensland; ill. 15/ ($5) 8° Longman 95

EDEN, C. H. My Wife & I in Queensland: 8 yrs.' experce. *o.p.* [*pb.* 9/] p 8° Longman 72

HOGAN, Jas. F. The Gladstone Colony 7/6 8° Unwin 98
Account of the settlement of the Port Curtis district; w. notes on GLADSTONE's colonial policy.

KENNEDY, Edw. B. The Black Police of Queensland—*ut* **D** § 123, *s.v.* Police

KNIGHT, J. J. In the Early Days: hist. & incids. of pioneer Qnsld. Sapsford, *Brisbane* 96

Letters from Queensland repr. fr. *The Times* [Dec. '92, Jan.–Feb. '93] 2/6 c 8° Macmillan 93
Six chs. containing much information on the actual state and future prospects of the colony.

LUMHOLTZ, Dr Carl Among Cannibals: 4 years' travels amg. Aborigines 24/ m 8° Murray 89
A graphic account of the life of the 'Black Fellows' in Queensland. Maps and 120 ill.

Missing Friends: advents. of a Danish emigrant in Queensland; ill. [Adventure Ser.] 3/6 c 8° Unwin 92
$1·50 Macmillan, *N.Y.* Purports to give the advents. over 14 yrs. of a Danish carpenter; but prob. by an Englishman.

NICOLS, A. —*in his* Wild Life in the Australian Bush, 2 vols., *ut* **E** § 65, *s.v.* Bush Life

Our First Half Century: review of Queensland progress; ill. [pp. 257] 4° Cumming, *Brisbane* 10

PITCAIRN, W. D. —*in his* Two Years in New Guinea, *ut* **E** § 64: conts. a ch. on N. Queensland

ROWAN, Mrs. A Flower Hunter in Queensland; map and ill. 14/ 8° Murray 98

De SATGE, Oscar Pages from Jl. of a Queensland Squatter 10/6 *n.* 8° Hurst 01
Account of pioneering in Queensland from 1853 onwards. Illns.

STIRLING, A. W. The Never, Never Land [ride in N. Queensland] 8/6 c 8° Low 84

WAWN, Cpt. W. T. South Sea Islanders and Queensland Labour Trade—*ut* **E** § 63

*Bush Life:* [CARRINGTON (G.)] Colonial Adventure [bush life in Qusld.] *o.p.* [*pb.* 7/6] c 8° Bell [71] 82

GRANT, A. C. Bush Life in Queensland *o.p.* [*pb.* 6/] c 8° Blackwood [81] 82

*Ethnology:* MATHEW (Jno.) Two Representative Tribes of Queensld. 5/ *n.* c 8° Unwin 10
A firsthand study. Incls. *Enquiry conc. orig. of Austral. Race.* Map and 6 ill.

ROTH, Walter E. Ethnolog. Studies am. N.-W. Centr. Qnsld., Aborigines; ill. 8° Gregory, *Brisbane* 97
A valuable study of language, customs, and ceremonies.

*Great Barrier Reef* —*v.* **H** § 79 (KENT)

*Port Mackay:* ROTH (H. L.) Discov. and Settlemt. of Port Mackay; maps and ill. 10/6 *n.* s 4° King, *Halifax* 08

**South Australia:** *Bibliography:* GILL (Thos.) Bibliography of South Australia 3/6 8° *Adelaide* 88

*History; Biography*

ANGAS, George Fife [1789–1879]: HODDER (E.) George Fife Angas 12/ 8° Hodder 91
ANGAS, if not precisely the 'Father and Founder of S. A.', was an admirable projector and pioneer, early shareholder and director in S. A. Land Co., and full of hopes of rivalling PENN as a pioneer of civilizn. and Xtianity.

BULL, J. W. Early Experiences of Life in S. Australia *o.p.* [*pb.* 7/6] c 8° Low 83

FINNISS, B. T. Constitutional History of S. Australia [last 21 yrs.] 9/ c 8° *Melbourne* 89

GOUGER, Rob. Founding of South Australia, ed. E. Hodder 6/ c 8° Low 98
As recorded in the Journals of the first Colonial Secretary.

GREY, Sir Geo. [1812–98]
Collier, Jas. Sir George Grey: an historical biography 12/6 *n.* 8° Whitcombe & Tombs 09

Henderson, Prf. Sir Geo. Grey, Pioneer of Empire; maps and ill. 12/6 n. 8° Dent 08
Rees, W. L. + L. Life and Times of Sir George Grey 6/ 8° Hutchinson [92] 98
GREY was successively Governor of S. Australia, New Zealand, Cape Colony, and Premier of New Zealand.

HARCUS, W. [ed.] South Australia [by various writers] *o.p.* [*pb.* 7/6] 8° Low 76
Hist., phys. geogr., govt., laws, rys., mines, agric., industries, educn., relig., explorns., flora, fauna, meteorol., statistics.

HAY, Alex.: Hay (Mrs A.) Footprints: memr. of Alex. Hay 3/6 c 8° Stock 99
A short biography of one of the Fathers and early colonists of South Australia.

HODDER, Edwin History of South Australia, 2 vols.; maps 24/ c 8° Low 93
A useful reference-bk. as a recd. of events fr. foundn. of colony (1802) to yr. of Jubilee (1892); but dry as narrative.

WAKEFIELD, E. J. [1796–1862] Life of. By Dr R. Garnett 5/ c 8° Unwin 98
$1·50 Longman, *N.Y.* [Builders of Greater Brit.] The colonization of S. Australia and New Zealand.

*Resources; Statistics:* BOOTHBY (J.) Statist. Sketch of S. Aust. [repr. fr. Harcus, *sup.*] 3/6 12° Low 76
STOW, J. P. South Australia: hist., prodns., natural resources 8° *Adelaide* 83
WOODS, J. D. The Province of South Australia [official] 5/ 8° *Adelaide* 94
*Ethnology:* HOWITT (Dr A. W.) Native Races of South-East Australia 21/ *n.* 8° Macmillan 04
WOODS, J. D. [ed.] Manners & Custs. of Native Tribes of S. Aust. [by 6 wrs.] 16/ 8° *Adelaide* 79
*Recent Travel and Description:* HORN SCIENTIFIC EXPEDN. TO CENTRAL AUSTRALIA, 4 Pts.—*ut* **H** § 106
SEARCY, R. —*in his* In Australian Tropics, *ut* **E** § 65
*Scenery:* ANGAS (G. F.) S. Australia Illustrated: 60 col. pl., w. l'rpr. *o.p.* [*pb.* £10 10*s.*] f° McLean 47
*Adelaide:* WORSNOP (T.) Hist. of City of Adelaide [fr. foundn. to 1836] 8° *Adelaide* 78
*Eyre, Lake:* GREGORY (Dr J. W.) The Dead Heart of Australia; maps and ill. 16/ *n.* 8° Murray 06
Acc. of expedn. in conn. w. geolog. schl. of Melb. Univ. Around Lake Eyre in 1901–2.

**Tasmania:** *History*

BONWICK, Jas. The Last of the Tasmanians; col. pl. and ill. 16/ 8° Low 70
" The Lost Tasmanian Race [abgmt. of above] 4/ c 8° Low 84
" The Daily Life and Origin of the Tasmanians 12/6 8° Low 70
CALDER, J. E. Acc. of Wars, Extirpn., Habits, etc., of Tasmanians 12° *Hobart* 75
FENTON, Jas. Hist. of Tasmania; maps & col. ports. [discov. (1642) to 1884] 16/ 8° Macmillan [84] 85
LLOYD, G. T. Thirty-three Years in Tasmania and Victoria *o.p.* [*pb.* 8/6] c 8° Houlston 62
NOWELL, E. C. Hist. of Relatns. betw. 2 Houses of Parl. in Tasm. & S.A. 5/ 8° (*Tasmania*) 90
WEST, Rev. Jno. History of Tasmania, 2 vols. *o.p.* 8° *Launceston* 52
*Ethnology:* ROTH (H. L.) Aborigines of Tasmania; ill. 21/ *n.* 8° King, *Halifax* [90] 99
BULTON, Hy. Flotsam & Jetsam: floatg. fragmts. of life in Engl. & Tasm. 7/6 *n.* 8° Birchall, *Launceston* 11
*Recent Travel and Description:* CROZET Voy. to Tasmania, N.Z., etc. [tr.]—*ut* **E** § 62 [1771–2]
MURRAY, A. S. Tasmanian Rivers, Lakes, & Flowers; ill., w. l'rpr. 42/ obl 4° Robertson, *Melbourne* 00
SMITH, Geoff. A Naturalist in Tasmania; map and 33 pl. 7/6 *n.* ($2·50) 8° Clar. Press 09
TASMAN, Abel J. [1602–59] MS. Jl. of Discov. of Austr.; & other docs.; w. tr. Muller, *Amsterdam* 95
A photolith. full-sized reprodn. of documts. in Hague archives, etc.; annotated by var. scholars. MS. incls. 53 maps.

**Victoria**

*History; Biography:* BONWICK (J.) Port Phillip Settlements; ill. [1803–40] 21/ 8° Low 83
Acc. of settlemts. of Port Phillip [1803], Western Port [1826], Portland [1834], Yarra Yarra and Geelong Distrs. [1835], Discov. of Gipp's Land by Angus MCMILLAN, Narratives of Batman [founder of Victoria], MACKILLOP and others. With orig. documts., etc.

BOWEN, Sir. G. F. [1821–99] —*in his* Thirty Years of Colonial Government, 2 v., *ut sup.*, *s.v.* Queensland
HIGINBOTHAM, Geo. [1826–82]
Morris, Prf. E. E. [son-in-law] Memoir of G. Higinbotham; pl. 9/ c 8° Macmillan 95
The biography of a leading Colonial statesman and lawyer, late L'd Chf.-Justice of Victoria (1856).

DE LABILLIÈRE, F. P. Early History of Victoria, 2 vols. 21/ c 8° Low 78–9
From its discovery (1797) to its establishment as a province of British empire (1856).

PEARSON, C. H. C. H. Pearson: memrs. by Himself, his Wife, & Friends 14/ ($4 *n.*) r 8° Longman 00
Ed. Wm. STEBBING. An interestg. life of authr. of *Natl. Life and Character*, Educ. Minr., scholar, and thinker.

SHILLINGLAW, J. J. Historical Records of Port Phillip [Grimes' Jl. 1802–3, etc.] r 8° *Melbourne* 79
TURNER, H. G. History of Colony of Victoria, 2 vols. 21/ ($7) 8° Longman 04
From its discovery to its absorption into Commonwealth of Australia (1900).

WESTGARTH, Wm. Australia Felix [account of Port Phillip] *o.p.* [*pb.* 16/] 8° Low [48] 64
*Ethnology:* DAWSON (Jas.) Australian Aborigines *o.p.* [*pb.* 10/6] 4° *Melbourne* 81
On the languages and customs of aborigines of Western Victoria.

SMYTH, R. B. Aborigines of Victoria; w. notes on other natives, 2 vols.; ill. 63/ i 8° *Melbourne* 78
*Resources; Statistics*
Government Handbook of Victoria 8° Govt. Press, *Melbourne*, *ann.*

HAYTER, Hy. H. Notes on Victoria: hist., geogr., meteor. statist. 8° *Melbourne* 76
Statistical Register of Colony of Victoria: compiled fr. offic. recds. of Govt. statist. 8° Brain, *Melbourne* 89
Victorian Year Book: 2 vols. 8° *Melbourne* [92] *ann.*
Vol. i: record of progress, populn., etc., w. summary of history, recd. of ministries, compar. tables, etc.; ii deals w. finance and vital statistics. A model of its kind.

*Bush Life; Gold-digging*

CRAIG, Wm. My Adventures on the Australian Goldfields 6/ c 8° Cassell 03
Chiefly a narrative of gold-digging experiences in Victoria, from 1850 onwards.
KIRBY, Jas. Old Times in Bush of Australia 3/6 c 8° Robertson, *Melb.* 97
Trials and experiences of bush life in Victoria in the 'forties.
THOMSON, Jas. [ed.] Illustrated Hdbk. of Victoria; 74 ill. [by 7 wrs.] 5/ r 8° *Melbourne n.d.* (86)
Victoria and its Metropolis, Past and Present, 2 vols.; over 500 ill. 126/ 4° *Melbourne* 88
WALCH, Garnet Victoria in 1880; 100 ill. 21/ r 4° Robertson, *Melbourne* 81
One of the finest productions of the Australian Press: a worthy memorial of the Exhibition Year.
*Melbourne:* 'BOLDREWOOD, Rolf' [T. A. BROWNE] Old Melbourne Memories [local gossip] 3/6 c 8° Macmillan [96] 99

**Western Australia:** *History*

KNIGHT, W. H. Western Australia: history, progr., condn., prospects *o.p.* c 8° *Perth, W.A.* 70
NICOLAY, Rev. C. G. Handbook of Western Australia *o.p.* 8° *Perth, W.A.* 80
*Ethnology:* CALVERT (A. F.) Aborigines of Western Australia 1/ c 8° Simpkin 94

*Recent Travel; Resources, etc.*

BARKER, L'y [*now* L'y Napier BROOME] Letters to Guy [fr. W. A.] 5/ c 8° Macmillan 85
" Colonial Memories 6/ *n.* 8° Smith & Elder 04
Chiefly N.Z., Natal, and W. A., of wh. her husb. became Govr. in 1882, and Trinidad, to wh. he was apprd. Govr. in 1891.
BOND, Cath. Goldfields and Chrysanthemums; 12 ill. 7/6 *n.* 8° Simpkin 98
Travel in Western Australia and in Japan.
CALVERT, A. F. Western Australia and its Goldfields 1/ c 8° Philip 93
" Mineral Resources of Western Australia 2/ c 8° Philip 94
" My Fourth Tour in Western Australia; ill. [Gold-fields] 7/6 *n.* 4° Dean [97] 01
CARNEGIE, Hon. D. W. Spinifex and Sand: five years' pioneering 21/ 8° Pearson 98
Travel in search of gold thro' unexplored regions of northern West Australia. Ill. and 4 maps.
FAVENC, Ern. Western Australia *o.p.* 8° *Sydney*
FORREST, Sir Jas. Explorations in Australia [condn., etc., of W. A.; 1869–74] 16/ 8° Low 75
HART, Fcs. Western Australia in 1893; maps and ill. 2/ 8° Bruton 93
Offic. pubn., by Registrar-Gen. of W. A. Full of informn. on mineral resources and W. A. as field for investmt. or immigrn.
MENNELL, Pp. The Coming Colony: pract. notes on W. A. 1/6 8° Hutchinson 92
PRICE, Julius M. The Land of Gold; map and ill. 7/6 *n.* c 8° Low 96
A lively narr. of visit to W. A. Gold Fields in 1895 as Artist Corresp. of *Illustr. London News.*
TAUNTON, Hy. Australind: wandgs. in W. A. and Malay East 10/6 *n.* 8° Arnold 03
$4 Longman, *N.Y.* Varied advents. in the seventies and eighties in W. A., and subseq. pearl-fishg. on coast and shippg. horses over to Java.
WARBURTON, Col. P. E. Journey across Western Interior of Australia *o.p.* [*pb.* 16/] 8° Low 75
Western Australian Year Book 8° Govt. Press, *Perth, W.A. ann.*

## 67: NEW ZEALAND

**Bibliography:** DAVIS (J. D.) Contribn. towards a Bibliography of N.Z. 3/ c 8° *Wellington* 87
Literature relating to New Zealand: a bibliography 10/6 r 8° *Wellington* 89
Earliest time to 1889; w. notes. Classif. chronol., acc. to subjects and acc. to authors. Preface signed J. C.
THOMSON, Dr A. S. —*ut inf.* (ends at 1858)
**Cyclopædia:** BLAIR's Cyclopædia of Australasia 42/ 4° *Melbourne* 81
**Early Voyages:** COOK (Cpt.)—*in his* Three Voyages rd. World, *ut* **E** § 7
CROZET Voyage to Tasmania, N.Z., etc. [tr.]—*ut* **E** § 62 [1771–2]
Contains a specially valuable account of the Maories of the 18th century.

**Ethnology; History and Life of the Maories**—*v. also* **B** § 29, **E** § 65

ANDERSEN, Joh. C. Maori Life in Ao-Tea; ill. 15/ 8° Whitcombe & Tombs 08
A trustworthy encyclopædic wk., givg. in form of a loosely-knit narr. (after the manner of BECKER'S *Charicles* and *Gallus* [*v.* **F** §§ 10, 12]), a complete conspectus of manners, customs, and beliefs of Ao-Tea, the North Isld. Indexes, and glossaries of words.
ANGAS, G. F. New Zealanders Illustrated: 60 col. pl., w. l'rpr. *o.p.* [*pb.* £10 10/] f° McLean 46
BROWN, J. Macmillan Maori and Polynesian 6/ c 8° Hutchinson 07
A concise summarized study of the orig., hist., and culture of the Maori and Polynesian.
COWAN, Jas. The Maories of New Zealand; 60 ill. 15/ *n.* 8° Whitcombe & Tombs 10
[Makers of Australasia.] Based on firsthand observation and intimate knowl. of the people.

[CRAIK, G. L. ; 1798–1866] John Rutherford, the White Chief, ed. Jas. Drummond ; ill. 3/6 *n.* c 8° Whitcombe & Tombs [2–] 08
Memrs. of a sailor who lived ten yrs. amg. Maoris. Abgd. fr. orig. edn. in Lib. of Entertg. Knowl.

FENTON, F. D. Suggestns. for Hist. of Orig. and Migrns. of Maori People 8° *Auckland* 85

GUDGEON, T. W. History and Traditions of Maoris : 1820–40 5/ *n.* 8° Brett, *Auckland* 85

HAMILTON, A. Illustrations of Maori Art, 5 Pts. N.Z. Institute, *Wellington* 98–02
Highly valuable illns. of an ethnogr. colln. Prob. the finest bk. yet produced in N.Z. Pt. i : *Canoes*, 7/6 ; ii : *Dwellgs.*, 15/ ; iii : *Weapons and Tools* ; iv : *Dress and Pers. Decorn.* ; v : *Social Life* (games, toys, war-dances, sports, etc.). Gloss. of words.

JOHNSTONE, Cpt. J. C. Maoria : sketch of aborigines of New Zealand *o.p.* [*pb.* 7/6] p 8° Chapman 74

' PAKEHA MAORI (A) ' [= F. E. MANING] Old New Zealand ; & Hist. of War in North agst. the Chief Heke in 1845 ; *also* Maori Traditions ; ed. Introd. Earl of Pembroke 6/ c 8° Macmillan [63 *etc.*] 00

,, The same bks., ed. Dr Hocken 3/6 *n.* c 8° Whitcombe & Tombs [63 *etc.*] 07

SMITH, S. Percy Hawaii, the Original Home of the Maoris 5/ *n.* 8° Whitcombe & Tombs 07

,, Maori Wars of the Nineteenth Century 5/ *n.* 8° Whitcombe & Tombs 07

TAYLOR, Rev. R. Te Ika a Maui—*ut* **B** § 29

WHITE, Jno. [Austral.] Ancient History of the Maori, 4 vols.—*ut* **B** § 29

*Mythology and Folklore* —*v.* **B** § 29

*Tattooing :* ROBLEY (Maj.-Gen.) Moko ; or, Maori Tattooing ; 180 ill. 42/ r 4° Chapman 96
$16·80 Scribner, *N.Y.* An elab. monogr. on the 'moko' (more akin to carving th. tattooing w. a needle). Several chs. devoted to 'Mokomokai, (dried heads adorned w. 'moko'), in wh. a brisk traffic was carried on w. trading schooners early in 19 cent.

**Geography**

GREGORY, Dr J. W. Australia and New Zealand—*ut* **E** § 62, *s.v.* Stanford

HOCHSTETTER, Dr F. N. Zeal. : phys. geogr., geol., nat. hist. [tr.] ; ill. 25/ i 8° *Stuttgart* (Williams) 67
Orig. edn. 1863. The standard wk., but, on acc. of explorns. of subseq. yrs., largely out of date.

MARSHALL, P. Geography of New Zealand ; maps and ill. 4/6 *n.* c 8° 04

**History ; Biography** —*v. also* **E** § 65, *s.v.* History

BLAKE, A. Hope Sixty Years in New Zealand 6 / c 8° Hodder 09

BOWEN, Sir G. F. [1821–99] —*in his* Thirty Yrs. of Colonial Govt., 2 vols., *ut sup.*, *s.v.* Queensland

[CAMPBELL, J. L.] Poenamo : sketches of early days of New Zealand 6/ c 8° Williams 81

COX, Alf. Men of Mark in New Zealand, vol. i 12/6 c 8° *Christchurch* 86

GISBORNE, Wm. Colony of New Zealand : hist. & descr. ; 3 maps *o.p.* [*pb.* 6/] c 8° Petherick [88] 91

,, [ed.] New Zealand Rulers and Statesmen ; 50 ports. [1840–97] 5/ c 8° Low [86] 97

GODLEY, J. R. Letters to C. B. Adderley [L'd Norton] [1839–61] *o.p.* 8° *London* 63

,, Writings & Speeches, ed. J. E. Fitzgerald *o.p.* [*pb.* 16/] 8° *Christchurch, N.Z.* 63

GORST, Sir Jno. E. New Zealand Revisited : recollns. of days of youth 12/6 *n.* 8° Pitman 08
Author began public life in N. Z. betw. local Taranaki war of 1860 and outbreak of war of races in 1863. Revisited 1906.

GUDGEON, T. W. The Defenders of New Zealand ; maps & ill. 30/ *n.* 4° Brett, *Auckland* 87
Biogrs. of ab. 130 colonists : also a native acc. of Pakeha-Maori wars by Lt.-Col. McDONNELL.

,, Reminiscences of War in New Zealand 10/6 c 8° Low 79

HAMILTON-BROWNE, Col. G. With the Lost Legion in New Zealand ; ill. 12 /6 *n.* 8° Laurie 11
Gives a good idea of the sort of life men of the Lost Legion led during wars from 1866 to 1871.

HOCKEN, T. M. Contribns. to Early Hist. of N.Z., vol. i : Settlemt. of Otago ; ill. 14/ 8° Low 98

HORSLEY, Reg. New Zealand ; 12 col. pl. [Romance of Empire] 6/ *n.* sq 8° Jack 08

IRVINE (R. F.) + ALPERS (O. T. J.) Progress of New Zealand in the Century 5/ *n.* c 8° Chambers 02

MCNAB, Rob. Murihiku : hist. of South Isld. of N.Z. [1642–1835] 15 / *n.* 8° Whitcombe & Tombs 09

REEVES, Hon. Wm. P. The Long White Cloud, Ao-tea-roa 6/ *n.* 8° H. Marshall 98
A full popular history with some description. Maps and ill.

,, New Zealand [Story of the Empire] 1/6 c 8° H. Marshall 98

*RUSDEN, G. W. History of New Zealand, 3 vols. ; maps 45/ 8° Melville, *Melbourne* [83] 95
A learned and compreh. wk., the leadg. authority. 1st edn. led to libel-suit, in wh. author lost heavy damages.

SAUNDERS, A. History of New Zealand, 2 vols. *Christchurch, N.Y.* [96–9]

SELWYN, G. A. [Bp of N.Z. 1841–69, of Lichfield 1867–78] Life of, by Rev. H. W. Tucker, 2 v. 24/ 8° Wells Gardner 79

SHERRIN (R. A. A.) + WALLACE (J. H.) Early Hist. of N.Z., ed. T. W. Leys ; 200 ill. 45/ *n.* 4° Brett, *Auckland* 90
From the earliest times to 1840 by SHERRIN, 1840–5 by WALLACE. A good bk., well illustrated.

Te Manuwiri : sketches of early colonization in New Zealand 3/6 c 8° Whitcombe & Tombs 07

THOMSON, Dr A. S. The Story of New Zealand, 2 vols. ; 20 ill. *o.p.* [*pb.* 24/] c 8° Murray 59
An interesting, valuable, and comprehensive work, which is unfortunately out of print.

WAKEFIELD, E. J. [1796–1862] Life of. By Dr Rich. Garnett—*ut* **E** § 66, *s.v.* S. Australia
,, [ed.] The Founders of Canterbury *o.p.* 8° *Christchurch* 68
Letters of GIBBON, WAKEFIELD, GODLEY, and others: 1847–1850.

**Life and Manners**

BARKER, L'y [L'y Napier BROOME] Station Life in New Zealand 3/6 c 8° Macmillan [70] 83
,, Station Amusements in New Zealand 3/6 c 8° Hunt [73] 75
,, Colonial Memories—*ut* **E** § 66, *s.v.* Western Australia
BRADSHAW, Jno. [Austral.] New Zealand as it is 12/6 8° Low 83
,, New Zealand of To-day 14/ 8° Low 88
BULLER, Rev. Jas. Forty Years in New Zealand: personal narr. [missionary] 10/ 8° Hodder 78
,, New Zealand, Past and Present 3/6 p 8° Hodder 80
BUTLER, Annie R. Glimpses of Maori Land; ill. [life, missions, etc.] 5/ 16° R.T.S. 86
ELKINGTON, E. Way Adrift in New Zealand 10/6 *n.* 8° Murray 06
An enthusiastic acc. of aimless ramblings, w. observns., of a shrewd easy-going man.
HAY, W. De Lisle Brighter Britain: settler & Maori in Northern N.Z., 2 v. *o.p.* [*pb.* 24/] p 8° Bentley 82
HERZ, Dr Max New Zealand; 81 ill. [life and people] 12/6 *n.* 8° Laurie 12
INGLIS, J. ['MAORI'] Our New Zealand Cousins 6/ s 8° Low 87
LOUGHNAN, Hon. R. A. New Zealand at Home; ill. 5/ *n.* c 8° Newnes 08
**Scenery:** BARRAUD (C. D.) New Zealand, Graphic and Descr.; col. pl. and ill. 168/ f° Low 77
GULLY, J. N.Z. Scenery: 15 col. pl., w. l'rpr. Sir J. v. Haast *o.p.* [*pb.* 105/] i f° Marcus Ward 77
PERCEVAL, Sir W. B. [ed.] Picturesque New Zealand; ill. 6/ 8° Cassell 95
WRIGHT, F. + W. [arts.] New Zealand: 75 col. pl., w. l'rpr. W. P. Reeves
[$6 *n.* Macm., *N.Y.*] 20/ *n.* sq 8° Black 98

**Resources; Statistics; Economic Condition**—*v. also* **D** §§ 126, 136

DOUGLAS, Sir A. P. The Dominion of New Zealand [All-Red Series]—*ut* **D** § 136
LLOYD, H. D. Newest England: notes of democratic traveller $2·50 8° Doubleday, *N.Y.* 03
5/*n.* Gay & Hancock. Descrn. of N. Z. experimts. in social, polit., and economic improvemt. Optimistic and suggestive.
New Zealand Official Handbook 1/6 8° Eyre & Spottiswoode [ ] 93 *ann.*
REEVES, Hon. W. P. State Experiments in Australia and New Zealand, 2 vols.—*ut* **D** § 126
SCHOLEFIELD, Guy H. New Zealand in Evolution—*ut* **D** § 136 [industr., econ., political]
Statistics of the Colony of New Zealand 8° Govt. Press, *Wellington, ann.*
A Govt. pubn., similar in size and character to our own Blue-Books, and dealing w. populn., trade, and commerce.

**Recent Travel and Description**

CRAWFORD, J. C. Recollns. of Travel in N.Z., Australia, etc. [1839–80] *o.p.* [*pb.* 18/] 8° Trübner 80
DIEFFENBACH, E. Travels in New Zealand, 2 vols. *o.p.* [*pb.* 24/] 8° Murray 43
Mainly on geography, geology, botany, and natural history of New Zealand.
DILKE, [Sir] C. W. —*in his* Greater Britain [*ut* **E** § 21]: conts. a good descrn. of N.Z. [1866–7]
FERGUSON, Dugald Vicissitudes of Bush Life in Australia & N.Z. 3/6 c 8° Sonnenschein [91] 93
A medley of advents., farming, fighting, courtship, self-help. By an old colonist, who knows his world well.
HEMPELMAN, Cpt. The Piraki Log or Diary of Cpt. Hempelman 6/*n.* ($2·40) 8° Frowde 11
HEMPELMAN [d. 1880] was first European to start shore whaling station in S. Isl. of N.Z. His chron. of events extends 1835–1844 and throws light on relns. of Maoris and Europs. and on events of 1840, when N.Z. became Brit. possessn. Glossary-index.
KERRY-NICHOLLS, J. H. The King Country; ill. 21/ 8° Low [84] 86
An account of 600 miles of travel and exploration in New Zealand.
LOWTH, Alys Emerald Hours in New Zealand; ill. 5/ *n.* 4° Whitcombe & Tombs 07
MORELAND, A. Maud Through South Westland; ill. 7/6 *n.* 8° Witherby 11
Enthusiastic acc. of a jy. to the Haast and Mt. Aspiring, w. descrn. of the forest-mountain glories.
PAYTON, E. W. Round about New Zealand: 3 years' wandgs.; 20 pl. 12/ c 8° Chapman 88
Philosopher Dick: adventures and contemplations of a New Zealand shepherd 6/ c 8° Unwin [90] 91
Believed to be by a Mr CHAMIER. Gives a good idea of early-day society of New Zealand.
WAKEFIELD, E. J. [d. 1879] Adventure in N.Z., ed. Sir Rob. Scott 7/6 *n.* 8° Whitcombe & Tombs [65] 08
WAKEFIELD was only son of E. G. WAKEFIELD, who played a lge. pt. in settlent. of N. Z. and South Austral. Covers period 1839–44.
WILSON, Mrs Rob. In the Land of the Tui; ill. [jl. in N.Z.] 7/6 c 8° Low 94
*Alps of New Zealand* —*v.* **I** § 165 (GREEN, FITZGERALD, HARPER, MANNERING)
*Rotomahana:* MUNDY (D. L.) Rotomahana, and Boiling Springs of N.Z.: 16 photos., w. l'rpr.
42/ f° Low [75] 75
*Taranaki:* WELLS (B.) The History of Taranaki 8° *New Plymouth* 78

# IX: North-Polar Regions

## 68: N.-POLAR REGIONS (*a*): HISTORY OF DISCOVERY AND EXPLORATION

*Bibliography:* CHAVANNE (J.; etc.) Literature of Polar Regions 6 m 8° Hölzel, *Vienna* 78

BRUCE, Dr W. S. Polar Exploration; maps [Home University Lib.] 1/ *n.* f 8° Williams 11

BRYCE, Geo. Siege and Conquest of the North Pole 7/6 8° Gibbings 10
A fairly accurate, yet eclectic, acc. of some expedns.: three-fifths devoted to American.

CHISHOLM, Mrs Perils of the Polar Seas; ill. [popular] 6/ p 8° Murray 73

DOUGLAS, [Miss] M. Across Greenld's. Ice-Flds. [accs. of Nansen; Peary] 80 c. (2/) c 8° Nelson 96

„ Breaking the Record: North Polar Expeditions; ill. 80 c. (2/) c 8° Nelson 97

„ The White North [Nordenskiöld; Nansen] 80 c. (2/) c 8° Nelson 98

GORDON, W. J. Round about the North Pole; ill. E. Whymper 15/ *n.* m 8° Murray 07
$5 *n.* Dutton, *N.Y.* Story of the successive voyages to Arctic regns., explaing. spec. importance of each.

GREELY, Gen. A. W. Handbook of Polar Discoveries; maps $1·50 *n.* c 8° Little & Brown, *Boston* [96] 09
6/ *n.* Unwin. A compreh. and compact record of whole course of Arctic discov., 1497–1895; w. bibliography.

HARTWIG, Dr G. The Polar World; ill. [popular] 7/6 *n.* ($3) 8° Longman [69] 92

„ Heroes of Arctic Regions; ill. [repr. fr. above] 2/ c 8° Longman 88

HOARE, J. D. History of Arctic Exploration; 4 maps and 16 ill. 7/6 *n.* 8° Methuen 06
$3 *n.* Dutton, *N.Y.* A usef. summary of N. and S. Polar explorn., w. interestg. details of voys. fr. times of Norsemen to Bar. TOLL's expedn. (1900).

MCCORMICK, R. Voyages in Search of Franklin and in Antarctic, 2 vols.—*ut* **E** § 69

MARKHAM, Cpt. A. H. Northward Ho! [voys., inclg. Phipps' explns. 1773] 10/6 c 8° Macmillan 76

MARKHAM, [Sir] C. R. [ed.] Arctic Navy List [Arctic & Antarct. Officers 1773–1873] 3/6 8° Griffin 75

„ The Threshold of the Unknown Region; maps 10/6 c 8° Low [73] 75
An account of our knowledge of the Arctic Regions down to the yr. 1875.

*NANSEN, Dr F. In Northern Mists [tr.], 2 vols.; maps, etc. 30/ *n.* 4° Heinemann 12
An enthrallg. hist. of the earliest and early Arctic explorn., based on wide research. Ends w. CABOT and CORTE-REAL.

NOURSE, Prf. C. F. American Explorations in Ice Zones; map & ill. $3·50 8° Lothrop, *Boston* 84

RUNDALL, T. [ed.] Early Voys. tow. N.W. Cathay and India *o.p.* 8° Hakluyt Soc. 49

SCOTT, G. Firth From Franklin to Nansen *o.p.* [*pb.* 3/6] c 8° Bowden 99
Stories of arctic adventure based on the original documents: a book for boys.

„ The Romance of Polar Exploration; maps & 24 ill. 5/ 8° Pearson 06
Interesting descrns. of Arctic and Antarctic adventure fr. earliest time to voyage of *Discovery*.

SHILLINGLAW, J. F. Narrative of Arctic Discovery [a good little bk.] *o.p.* [*pb.* 10/6] 12° Shoberl [50] 51

WRIGHT, Helen S. The Great White North; ill. $2·50 *n.* (10/6 *n.*) 8° Macmillan 10
A good compiln., givg. the story of POLAR explorn. from earliest times to discovery of the Pole.

## 69: N.-POLAR REGIONS (*b*): VOYAGES AND TRAVEL; BIOGRAPHY

**Collectively**

CONWAY, Sir W. M. [ed.] Early Dutch & Engl. Voys. to Spitzb. in 17 Cent. 8° Hakluyt Soc. 02
Incls. H. GERRITSZ's *Hist. du Spitsberghe* (1613), tr. B. H. SOULSBY, and Jac. SEGERSZ VAN DER BRUGGE's *Journael of Dagh Register* (1634), tr. J. A. J. DE VILLIERS. Maps and ill.

Documents on Spitzbergen and Greenld., ed. Ad. White [1630–71] 8° Hakluyt Soc. 55
F. MARTIN's *Voy.* [1671]; DE LA PEYRÈRE's *Hist. of Greenld.* [1663; tr.]; PELHAM's *Voy.* [1630].

*Alert:* MARKHAM (Cpt. A. H.) The Great Frozen Sea; ill. [1875–6] 6/ c 8° Paul [78] 80
Descrs. the last great Brit. Arctic expedn., in wh. he came nearer to the N. Pole than any predecessor.

MOSS, Dr E. L. Shores of Polar Sea; col. pl. [*Alert*, 1875–6] *o.p.* [*pb.* 105/] f° Marcus Ward 78

NARES, Sir G. S. Voyage to Polar Sea, 2 v.; ill. [*Alert* & *Discovery*, 1875–6] 42/ 8° Low [78] 78

*Aurora:* LINDSAY (D. M.) Voyage to the Arctic in *Aurora*; ill. $2 8° Dana Estes, *Boston* 11
7/6 *n.* Routledge. A graphic account of adventure in a whaler.

BAFFIN, Wm. [d. 1622] Voyages, ed. [Sir] C. R. Markham; Introd. & notes [1612–22] 8° Hakluyt Soc. 81

BARENTS, Wm. [d. 1597]: de VEER (G.) Three Voys. of Barentz tow. Cathay & China by N.E., ed. C. T. Beke [1594–5–6] 8° Hakluyt Soc. 76

BERING, Vitus [1680 (?)–1741]: LAURIDSEN (P.) Vitus Bering [tr.] $1·25 12° Griggs, *Chicago* 89

CARSTENSEN, A. R. Two Summers in Greenland: artist's adventure; ill. 14/ 8° Chapman 90

COATS, Cpt. Wm. Geogr. of Hudson's Bay, ed. [Sir] Jno. Barrow [1727 and 51] 8° Hakluyt Soc. 52

CONWAY, Sir W. M. First Crossing of Spitzbergen; maps & ill. (some col.) 30/ *n.* m 8° Dent 97
$10 Scribner, *N.Y.* With contribus. by Dr J. W. GREGORY, A. TREVOR-BATTYE, and E. J. GARWOOD.

„ With Ski and Sledge over Arctic Glaciers; ill. 6/ *n.* c 8° Dent 98
$2 Wessels, *N.Y.* A supplement to *First Crossing*. Chief value is in its observns. on the glaciers.

*Danish Expedns.:* GOSCH (C. C. A.; ed.) Danish Arctic Expedns., 2 v.; maps & ill. 8° Hakluyt Soc. 97
Accs. of 3 Dan. voys. to Huds. Bay and Greenld., 1605-7; w. that of Jens HALL, and tr. of Cpt. Jens MUNK's voy. to H. B. 1619—20.

DAVIS, Jno. [1550–1605] Voyages and Works, ed. Cpt. A. H. Markham 8° Hakluyt Soc. 80

Markham, [Sir] C. R. John Davis; 4 maps and 24 ill. [World's Gt. Explrs.] 4/6 c 8° Philip 89
Incls. account of the work of DAVIS' successors in Arctic exploration.

*Discovery* —*v. Alert, sup., s.n.* Nares

DU CHAILLU, Paul The Land of the Long Night; ill. 7/6 c 8° Murray 00

DUFFERIN, Earl of Letters from High Latitudes—*ut* **E** § 23 [Iceland, Spitzbergen, etc.]

*Dutch Expedn.:* van CAMPEN (S. R.) Dutch in Arctic Seas, vol. i: Dutch Arctic Expedn. *o.p.* [*pb.* 10/6] 8° Trübner [76] 77
Appendix conts. chronolog. table of Arctic voyages from A.D. 860 to 1876; w. results.

*Entreprise:* COLLINSON (Cpt. R.) Jl. of Voy. of *Entreprise;* 6 maps *o.p.* [*pb.* 14/] 8° Low 89
A painfully interestg. narr. of search (1850–5) for and discov. of sole extant record of cruise of *Erebus* and *Terror.*

FIALA, Com. Anth. Fighting the Polar Ice; ill. and 9 col. pl. 16/ *n.* r 8° Hodder 07
$3·80 *n.* Doubleday, *N.Y.* Recd. of 2 yrs. (1903–5) in Arctic spent by 2nd Ziegler Polar Expedn. (organized by Wm. ZIEGLER, an Amer. capitalist) w. FIALA, of Brooklyn, as leader. The 1st expedn., wh. retd. unsuccessful, was in 1901.

*Fox:* McCLINTOCK (Sir F. L.) Voy. of *Fox* in Arctic Seas in Search of Franklin and his Companions; maps and ill. [75 c. Coates, *Phila.*] 2/6 *n.* c 8° Murray [59] 08
Acc. of one of the most brilliant and successful adventures (1859–60) ever carried out in Arctic sea.

FRANKLIN, Sir Jno. [1786–1847] Jy. to Shores of Polar Sea; maps & pl., 2 v. [1819–22] 4° *London* [23] 24

" Second Expedition to Polar Sea; maps and pl. [1825–7] 4° *London* 28

Beesley, A. H. Sir John Franklin [Makers of History] *o.p.* c 8° Marcus Ward [81] 94
75 c. Caldwell, *Boston.* Originally (1881) pubd. in the New Plutarch Series.

Markham, Cpt. A. H. Franklin and N.-W. Passage [World's Gt. Explrs.] 4/6 c 8° Philip 91
$1·25 Dodd & Mead, *N.Y.* A happy combination of biogr. and hist. of search for N.-W. Passage fr. earliest times to voy. of MACHURE. Maps and ill.

Traill, H. D. Life of Sir John Franklin; maps & ill. 16/ 8° Murray 96
Based on materls. coll. by Miss Sophie CRACROFT [niece]. The standard biography.

FROBISHER, Martin [1535–94] Three Voyages, ed. Adm. Collinson; w. seln. of l'rs. 8° Hakluyt Soc. 67

Jones, F. Life of Martin Frobisher *o.p.* [*pb.* 6/] c 8° Longman 78

GILDER, W. H. Schwatka's Search; ill. [for recds. of Franklin] $3 8° Scribner, *N.Y.* 82

" Ice-pack and Tundra; 50 ill. $4 8° Scribner, *N.Y.* 83
18/ Low. Acc. of the search for the *Jeannette* and of sledge-jy. thro' Siberia.

*Gjöa:* AMUNDSEN (R.) The North-West Passage, 2 vols.; maps & ill. 31/6 *n.* 8° Constable 08
Record of the remarkable first navign. of the entire passage to the West, 1903–7, in a sloop of 47 tons, w. a crew of six; w. Suppl. by Lt. HANSEN, vice-Commr.; 2 chs. on the Eskimos.

*Grinnell:* KANE (Dr E. K.) [1820–57] U.S. *Grinnell* Expedn. in Pursuit of Franklin *o.p.* r 8° *New York* 53

" Arctic Explorations: second *Grinnell* expedn., 2 vols. [1853–5] *o.p.* [*pb.* $4·50] 8° Colomb. Bk. Co., *Hartfd.* [56]

" Arctic Explorns. in Search of Franklin *o.p.* [*pb.* $4·50] 8° *Hartford n.d.* (67)
The story of a remarkable expedn. in 1853–5, when KANE believed he had discovered an open Polar sea.

" Physical Observations in Arctic Seas, 4 Pts. $4 4° Smithsonian Inst., *Washgtn.* 58–60

Elder, Wm. Biography of Elisha Kent Kane *o.p.* 8° *Phila.* 58

*Hansa:* KOLDEWEY (Cpt. K.) N. Germ. Polar Expedn. [tr.]; col. pl. & maps [1869–70] 35/ r 8° Low 74

*Harmsworth Expedn.:* JACKSON (F. G.) 1,000 Miles in Arctic, 2 vols. 32/ ($6) 8° Harper 99
A full acc. of Jackson-Harmsworth Expedn. to Franz Josef Land, 1895–8. Ill. and 5 maps. *V. also* JACKSON, *inf.*

HARRISON, Alf. H. In Search of a Polar Continent; map and ill. [1905–7] 12/6 *n.* 8° Arnold 08
$3·50 *n.* Longman, *N.Y.* Acc. of travel (1905–6) 1,800 m. by waterway thro' N. Canada to delta of Mackenzie R.; thence to Arctic Ocean; and by steamer to Banks Land. Much time w. Eskimos.

HAYES, I. I. An Arctic Boat Journey, ed. Norton Shaw; ill. [1854] $1·50 12° Houghton, *Boston* [60] 83

" Open Polar Seas; ill. [in *United States*; 1860–1] 75 c. McKay, *Phila.* [66] 67

" Land of Desolation; ill. [adventure in Greenld.] 14/ ($1·75) 8° Harper, *N.Y.* 71

" Physical Observations in Arctic Seas $5 4° Smithsonian Inst., *Washington* 67

*Investigator:* McCLURE (Sir Rob. J. Le M.; 1807–3)

OSBORN, Adm. Sherard Discovery of a North-West Passage [1850–2] 3/6 c 8° Blackwood [56] 73
McCLURE all but completed North-West Passage, but fr. E. to W., not W. to E. This bk. gives acc. of the voyage.

*Isbjörn:* MARKHAM (Cpt. A. H.) A Polar Reconnaissance; ill. [to Nova-Zembla, 1879] 16/ 8° Paul 81

JACKSON, F. G. The Great Frozen Land; maps & ill. [1893–4] 15/ *n.* ($4·50) 8° Macmillan 95
Ed. fr. his jls. by Arth. MONTEFIORE. A straightforward record of jy. thro' unkn. regns. at extreme N. of Eur. Russia, w. informn. on Samoyads and Lapps, and 4 Appendices (*a*) rare birds (J. R. JEAFFRESON, *ut* **H** § 97), (*b*) meteorol. (JACKSON), (*c*) topogr., (*d*) descrn. of Jackson-Harmsworth Expedn., of wh. this jy. was a precursor.

*Jeannette:* DE LONG (Com. G. W.) Voyage of *Jeannette*: jls., ed. his Wife, 2 v.; ill. [U.S. Expedn. 1873–81] $7·50 8° Houghton, *Boston* 83

NEWCOMB, R. L. Our Lost Explorers *o.p.* 8° 82

LACHAMBRE (H.) + MACHURON (A.) Andrée and his Balloon; 45 pl. 6/ c 8° Constable 98
$1·50 Stokes, *N.Y.* Pt. i describes the balloon and its appliances; Pt. ii the beginning of the journey.

LAMONT, E. H. Yachting in the Arctic Seas 18/ 8° Chatto 76
Account of five voyages to Spitzbergen and Nova Zembla.

LE BLOND, Mrs Aubrey — Mountaineering in the Land of the Midnight Sun—*v.* I § 165

MARKHAM, Cpt. A. H. — A Whaling Cruise to Baffin's Bay & Gulf of Boothia [1874] 7/6 p 8° Low 74

MELVILLE, G. W. — In the Lena Delta, ed. Melville Philips; maps $2·50 8° Houghton, *Boston* 85
Narr. of search for DE LONG of the *Jeannette* and of the BREELY relief-expedn.

MIKKELSEN, Ejnar — Conquering the Arctic Ice 20/ *n.* 8° Heinemann 09
Record of Anglo-Amer. Polar Expedn., 1906–7—an interestg. narr. of adventure and hardship, and a graphic acc. of Alaskan Eskimos.

*Miranda:* WALSH (H. C.) — The Last Cruise of the *Miranda*; ill. $1·50 c 8° Transatlantic Pb. Co., *N.Y.* 96
Story of remarkable ser. of advents. th. befell Dr COOK's Arctic expedn. of 1894, and wreck of *Miranda*. Papers on *Atmosph. Dust in Arctic Regions* (Prf. BREWER), descrn. of Greenlanders (Dr F. A. COOK), *Flora of Greenld.* (S. P. ORTH).

MURPHY, G. R. [ed.] — Beyond the Ice: region rd. N. Pole 3/6 c 8° Low 94
Edited from Dr Fk. FAIRLEIGH's Diary.

NANSEN, Dr Fridtjof — The First Crossing of Greenld. [tr.]; ill. & maps 3/6 ($1·25) c 8° Longman [90] 95
[Silver Lib.] Narr. of passage acr. S. Greenld., commencg. w. survey of prev. explorn. A well-wr. and exciting narr. of a notable feat wh. inaugurated a new princ. of Arctic travel, that of hg. no line of retreat, success thus dependg. on pushg. onward. Orig. edn., 2 vols., 36/ ($10·50).

„ Eskimo Life [tr.]; 16 pl. and 15 ill. 16/ ($4) 8° Longman 93
A sort of Suppl. to above, descrs. his life w. Eskimos dur. a whole winter, in wh. he lived in their huts, took pt. in their huntg. expedns., and lived their life.

„ Farthest North: voyage of *Fram* [tr.]; 2 maps & 20 ill. 6/ c 8° Constable [97] 00
$3 Harper, *N.Y.* Record of a 15-mos.' sleigh-jy.: an unrivalled expedn., unlike all others both in plan and in success. The orig. edn. [42/ ($10)] conts. 4 maps, 16 col. pl., and c. 100 ill.

„ Scient. Results of Norweg. North Polar Expedn.: 1893–6, 6 vols.; pl. 179/ *n.* ($44·75) 4° Longman 00–6
A full account of the scientific results of the expedition.

Bain, J. A. — Life of Nansen, Scientist & Explorer; ill. [75 c. Revell, *N.Y.*] 6/ c 8° Simpkin 97

Brogger (W. C.) + Rolfsen (N.) Fridtjof Nansen: 1861–93 [tr.]; maps & ill. 12/6 ($4) 8° Longman 96
A life of the explorer and national hero; very full of detail. His biological wk. descr. by Prf. G. RETZIUS, hist. of Arctic explorn. condensed by A. ARSTAL, and other monographs added.

Johansen, Lt. F. H. — With Nansen in the North; 70 ill. 6/ c 8° Ward & Lock 99

v. NORDENSKIÖLD, Bar. A. E. [1832–1901] Voyage of the *Vega* rd. Asia & Europe, 2 v.; ill. 45/ 8° Macmillan 81
With a review of all previous voyages along North coast of Old World. Popular Edn., 1 vol., 6/ c 8° '82.

Hovgaard, Lt. A. — Popular Account of Voyage of *Vega* [tr.]; ill. *o.p.* [*pb.* 21/] 8° Low 81

Leslie, A. — Arctic Voys. of Nordenskiöld: 1858–79; ill. 16/ 8° Macmillan 79

*Novara:* PAYER (J.) — New Lands within Arctic Circle [tr.], 2 vols.; ill. *o.p.* [*pb.* 32/] 8° Macmillan 76
Account of the discovery of Franz Josef Land in 1872–4.

*Pandora:* MACGAHAN (J. A.) Under the Northern Lights; ill. *o.p.* [*pb.* 18/] 8° Low 76

YOUNG, Sir Allen — The Two Voyages of the *Pandora* [1875–6] 10/6 r 8° Stanford 79

PARRY, Sir W. E. [1790–1855] Voy. of Discov. of N.-W. Passage; charts & pl. [*Hecla & Gripper*, 1819–20] *o.p.* 4° *London* [21] 31

„ Second Voyage; maps & pl. [*Fury & Hecla*, 1821–3]; Appendix *o.p.* 4° *London* 24; 25

„ Third Voyage [*Hecla & Fury*, 1824–5] 1/4 c 8° Blackie [26] 94

„ Attempt to Reach North Pole; charts and pl. [1827] *o.p.* 4° *London* 28

„ Three Voyages f. Discov. of N.-W. Passage, 2 vols. $1·50 18° Harper, *N.Y. n.d.*

Parry, E. [son] — Memoir of Rear-Admiral Sir W. E. Parry *o.p.* [*pb.* 5/] f 8° Longman [57] 57

*Peary Expeditions, and Relief Expedition*

PEARY, Com. R. E. — Northward over the Great Ice, 2 vols. $5 *n.* r 8° Stokes, *N.Y.* 98
32/ *n.* Methuen. Full acc. of his life and work in Greenld. in 1886 and 1891–7. Incls. acc. of the little tribe of Smith Sound Eskimos (most northerly beings in the world), and of discov. and bringing home the 'Saviksue' (Cape York meteorites). Maps and 800 ill.

„ Nearest the Pole; 2 maps, 98 ill., & col. front. $4·80 *n.* r 8° Doubleday, *N.Y.* 07
21/ *n.* Hutchinson. Narr. of expedn. 1905–6 of Peary Arctic Club in s.s. *Roosevelt*, 1905–6, contg. first full acc. of plantg. Amer. flag nearest the Pole (174 m. off).

„ The North Pole; map and 116 ill. [Geograph. Lib.] 42/ *n.* 4° Hodder 10
Record of 8th expedn. by PEARY in little over 20 yrs. In main features this expedn. was like th. of 1905–6: success marks the one difference. Ill. excellent, and valuable circumpolar map added.

ASTRUP, Eivind — With Peary near the Pole; ill. 10/6 8° Pearson 98
An interesting book, especially in its account of the inhabitants of Greenland.

HEILPRIN, Prf. A. Arctic Problem & Narr. of Peary Rel. Exp. $1·25 12° Contemp. Pb. Co., *Phila.* 93
About half bk. given to acc. of Relief Exp.: other (and more inport.) hf. to clear and logical re-statemt. of 'Arctic problem'.

KEELY (Dr R. N.) + DAVIS (Dr G. G.) In Arctic Seas; maps, ports. & ill. $3·50 8° Hartranft, *Phila.* 92
Narr. of voyage of the *Kite* (w. a transcript of log), and of Relief Expedn. KEELY was surgeon to expedn. sent to accompany PEARY.

PEARY, Mrs Josephine (DIEBITSCK) My Arctic Journal; maps & ill. $2 c 8° Contemp. Pb. Co., *Phila.* 93
12/ Longman. Descrn. of a yr. amg. ice-fields and Eskimos, w. acc. of the great white jy. acr. Greenland.

PEEL, Helen. Polar Gleams; pl. [$2·50 *n.* McClurg, *Chicago*] 15/ 8° Arnold 94
An unaffected and bright acc. of voy. in yacht *Blencathra* thro' Kara Sea to Yenesei River.

*Polar Star:* ABRUZZI (D'ke of) On *Polar Star* in Arctic Sea [tr.], 2 vols. 42/ *n.* 8° Hutchinson 03
$12·50 *n.* Dodd & Mead, *N.Y.* Acc. of first Italian expedn. to North Polia, *via* Franz Josef Land: 1899–1900. Maps and 200 ill.

„ Farther North than Nansen; ill. ['1st acc.' of above] 3/ r 8° H. W. Bell 02

*Polaris:* BLAKE (E. V.) — Arctic Experiences [*Polaris; Tigress*] 25/ r 8° Low 74

NOURSE, J. E. Narr. of Second Arctic Expedn. of C. F. Hall; ill. *o.p.* [*pb.* 28/] 4° Trübner [79] 81
Narrative of the voyage of the *Polaris* in 1864-9.

*Proteus*: GREELY (Gen. A. W.) Three Years of Arctic Service; charts and 120 ill. [1881-4] $5 r 8° Scribner, *N.Y.* [86] 94
Offic. narr. of L'y Franklin Bay expedn. (1881-4), wh. gained the farthest N. pt. on W. of Greenld.

LANMAN, C. Farthest North: expln. of Lt. Lockwood [Greely Exp.] $1·25 c 8° Appleton, *N.Y.* 85

SCHLEY (W. S.) + SOLEY (J. R.) The Rescue of Greely; maps and ill. $2 8° Scribner, *N.Y.* [85] 86

RICHARDSON, Sir Jno. [1787-1865] Voy. thro' Rupert's Ld. for Franklin, 2 v.; ill. *o.p.* [*pb.* 31/6] 8° Longman 51

" The Polar Regions; ill. *o.p.* [*pb.* 14/] 8° Longman 61

McIlraith, J. Life of Sir John Richardson *o.p.* [*pb.* 5/] c 8° Longman 68

ROSS, Sir Jno. [1777-1856]

Mackinder, H. J. Ross and Antarctic [World's Gt. Explrs.] 4/6 c 8° Philip 91

SVENDRUP, Cpt. O. New Land: four yrs. in Arctic regns. [tr.], 2 vols.; map and ill. 36/ *n.* ($10·50 *n.*) 8° Longman 94
Acc. of 2nd voy. of *Fram*, to lands N-W. of Baffin Bay Vol. ii conts. Appendices on scient. results.

*Swedish Expedn.*: NATHORST (A. G.) Swedish Arctic Expedn. of 1898—*in* Jl. R.G.S. (Murray), July, 1899
Exploration of Spitzbergen and the smaller islands round about it.

*Tigress* —*v. Polaris, sup., s.n.* Blake

*Traveller*: CLUTTERBUCK (W. J.) Skipper in Arctic Seas; 39 ill. [advent. & sport] 10/6 ($2·25) c 8° Longman 90

TREVOR-BATTYE, A. Icebound on Kolguev; *and* Northern Highway—*ut* **E** § 25

*Vega*: NORDENSKIÖLD (Bar. A. E.) Voy. of *Vega* rd. Coasts of Asia & Eur. 6/ ($1·75) c 8° Macmillan [81] 82
Conts. hist. of all prev. N.-E. voys.; and descrs. first and only circumnavign. (1878-80) of Eur. and Asia. Maps and ill.

Hovgaard, Lt. A. Pop. Account of Voy. of *Vega* [tr.]; ill. [1879] 21/ 8° Low 82

Leslie, A. The Arctic Voyages of Baron Nordenskiöld; maps & ill. [1858-79] 16/ 8° Macmillan 79

WELLS, Cpt. J. C. Gateway to the Polynia [voy. to Spitzbergen] 6/ c 8° Paul [73] 76

WRIGHT (Prf. F. G.) + UPHAM (W.) Greenld. Icefields & Life in N. Atlantic $2 c 8° Appleton, *N.Y.* 96
Good acc. of scenery, glacial phenomena, nat. hist., people, and explorns. of Greenld.: outcome of visit by WRIGHT in summer of 1894.

ZENO, N. & A. [14 cent.] Voyages to North Seas, tr. and ed. R. H. Major 8° Hakluyt Soc. 73

Lucas, F. W. The Voyages of the Brothers Zeno 42/ *n.* r 4° Stevens & Brown 98
Overthrows, fairly completely, the account of the voyage of the 'Brothers Zeni' to Greenland.

**Eskimos**: *Ethnology, Life, etc.*

HALL, Cpt. C. F. Life w. Esquimaux and Discov. of Frobisher's Remains [1860-2] *o.p.* [*pb.* 6/] i 8° Bickers [64] 71

PEARY, Mrs Josephine The Snow Baby; ill. $1·30 *n.* c 8° Stokes, *N.Y.* 01
The true story of the little American, Marie PEARY, born in Greenland.

" Children of the Arctic; ill. $1·20 *n.* c 8° Stokes, *N.Y.* 03
Story of a year spent am. icebergs and great ice-fields, glaciers, polar bears, and Eskimo children.

RASMUSSEN, Knud The People of the Polar North; 150 ill. (some col.) 21/ *n.* r 8° Paul 08
$5 *n.* Lippincott, *Phila.* Compiled fr. Danish originals of RASMUSSEN and ed. G. HERRING. Deals w. the 3 Eskimo branches wh. make up the populn. of Greenld., esp. the group of nomads here called 'the Polar Eskimos', whose customs and legends are treated as well as the travellers' expercees.

RINK, Dr H. Eskimo Tribes [distribn., characteristics, lang., etc.] 4/6 8° Williams 87

SCHWATKA, Fredk. Children of the Cold; ill. $1·25 c 8° Educ. Pb. Co., *Boston* [88] 02
Descrn. of habits, homes, and plays of Eskimo children by one who lived among them for 2 yrs.

WHITNEY, Harry Hunting with the Eskimos; 64 ill. 12/6 *n.* 8° Unwin 09
Narr. of 14 months among the Eskimos, w. accs. of huntg. narwhal, seal, walrus, etc.

**History, etc., of Greenland** and **Spitzbergen**

CONWAY, Sir W. M. No Man's Land; 13 maps and 11 pl. 10/6 *n.* r 8° Camb. Press 06
$3 *n.* Putnam, *N.Y.* A hist. of Spitzbergen fr. its discovery in 1596 to beginning of scientific explorn.

CRANTZ, D. History of Greenland, 2 vols.; maps and ill. *o.p.* 8° Longman 20

EGEDE, Hans Description of Greenland [tr. fr. Danish] *o.p.* [*pb.* 12/] 8° *London* [1745] 45

JONES, Prf. T. R. Natural History, Geology, and Physics of Greenld. 13/6 8° Stanford 75

NANSEN, Dr Fridtjof Eskimo Life—*ut sup.*

RINK, Dr H. Danish Greenland [tr.]; ill. [people & products] *o.p.* [*pb.* 10/6] c 8° King 77

**Alaska**—*v.* **E** § 57 **Hudson's Bay & Str.**—*v.* **E** § 55 **Iceland; Faroe Isls.**—*v.* **E** § 23 **Labrador**—*v.* **E** § 55

## 70: ANTARCTIC REGIONS

**History of Discovery** —*v. also* **E** § 68, *passim*

MILL, Dr H. R. Siege of the South Pole; ill. [Story of Explorn.] 4/6 *n.* 8° Rivers 05
$1·60 *n.* Stokes, *N.Y.* A fascinating account of Antarctic discovery; w. good bibliography.

SMITH, G. Barnett — Romance of the South Pole — [popular] 2/ (80 c.) c 8° Nelson 00

**Voyages**

ARMITAGE, Lt. A. B. — Two Years in the Antarctic — 15/ *n.* 8° Arnold 05
$5 Longman, *N.Y.* Narr. of Brit. Natl. Antarctic Expedn. ARMITAGE was 2nd in command and navigator of *Discovery*, 1901–1904, and 2nd in command of Jackson-Harmsworth N. Polar Expedn. 1894–7.

BERNACCHI, Louis — To the South Polar Regions; ill. — 12/ *n.* 8° Hurst 01
Account of the Newnes Expedn. (1899–1900), w. much scientific matter.

BORCHGREVINK, C. E. — First on the Antarctic Continent; maps and 186 ill. — 10/6 *n.* 8° Newnes 01
$3 *n.* Scribner, *N.Y.* Another account of the Newnes Expedition. 1898–1900.

BULL, H. J. — Cruise of the *Antarctic* to South Polar Regions — 15/ 8° Arnold 96
$4 Lane, *N.Y.* Describes the first landing on the Antarctic continent.

CHARCOT, Dr — The Voyage of the *Why-Not?* [*Pourquoi Pas?*] [tr.]; ill. — 20/ *n.* r 8° Hodder 11
Voy. 1908–10, wh. did not get far beyond Antarctic Circle, but wh. obtained some import. scient. results.

COOK, Dr F. A. — Through the First Antarctic Night; 100 ill. — $2 *n.* 8° Doubleday, *N.Y.* [00] 00
20/ *n.* Heinemann. Narr. of de Gerlache's Belgian expedn., in the *Belgica*, to Palmer archipelago, etc., 1898–9. A good *résumé* of the *Belgica* expedn. (by H. ARCTOWSKI) is cont. in *Jl. R.G.S.*, Feb., 1901.

FRICKER, Dr Karl — The Antarctic: its geogr., explorn., etc. — 7/6 8° Sonnenschein 00
$3 Macmillan, *N.Y.* An excellent general account. Maps, ill., and bibliography.

HAMMOND, Thos. W. — On Board a Whaler; ill. — $1·35 *n.* (6/) c 8° Putnam 02

McCORMICK, R. — Voys. in search of Franklin & in Antarctic, 2 v.; ill. — [1827, '52–3] 52/6 r 8° Low 84
Author was surgeon on one of vessels of Ross' Antarctic Expedn., of which he here gives an independent narr.

MURDOCH, W. C. Burn — From Edinburgh to the Antarctic — 18/ 8° Longman 94
Diary of the artist who accompanied a whaling expedn. fr. Dundee to Southern Seas in 1892–3.

NORDENSKJÖLD (O. G.) + ANDERSON (Dr J. G.) Antarctica; 200 ill. — 18/ *n.* 8° Hurst 05
$5 *n.* Macmillan, *N.Y.* Account of two years among the ice of the South Pole.

ROSS, Sir Jas. C. — Voy. of Discov. in Antarctic Regions, 2 vols. — [1839–43] *o.p.* [*pb.* 36/] 8° Murray 47

ROYAL GEOGRAPH. SOCIETY — Antarctic Manual, ed. Geo. Murray—*ut* **E** § 8

*Scotia*: Voy. of. By Three of Staff [R. N. R. Brown, R. C. Mossman, J. H. H. Pirie] — 21/ *n.* 8° Blackwood 06
Acc. of expedn. (1902) of Scottish Natl. Antarct. Expedn. (led by W. S. BRUCE), wh. did excellent oceanograph. and meteorol. wk. in Atlantic divn. of Antarctic waters and islds. 3 maps and 105 ill.

Report on Scientific Results of Voy. of *Scotia*—*ut* **H** § 44
Vol. i.: *Narrative of the Voyage*, by Dr. W. S. BRUCE, is in preparation.

SCOTT, Cpt. R. F. — Voyage of *The Discovery*, 2 vols.; maps & ill. — 10/ *n.* p 8° Smith & Elder [05] 07
$3 *n.* Scribner, *N.Y.* Acc. of British South Polar expedn. 1901–4. Appendices by FERRAR (geol.) and WILSON (zool.).

Mulock, Lt. G. F. A. Antarctica: charts of *The Discovery* [folded in case] 12/6 *n.* 4° R.G.S. (Murray) 08

Royal Society: National Antarctic Expedn.: 1901–4—*ut* **H** § 44

South Polar Times; w. Pref. by Cpt. Scott, 2 vols.; ill. (some col.) — 126/ *n.* 4° Smith & Elder 07
The periodical issued on board of *The Discovery* dur. winters of 1902 and 1903. Instruction combined w. amusemt.

*SHACKELTON, Sir Ern. — The Heart of the Antarctic, 2 vols.; maps & ill. — 36/ *n.* c 4° Heinemann 09
$10 *n.* Lippincott, *Phila.* Story of the Brit. Antarctic Expedn. 1907–9, wh. reached the farthest S. yet attained. Introd. by Dr H. R. MILL, and acc. of first jy. to the south magnetic pole by Prf. T. W. E. DAIRD. Ch. Edn. 6/ *n.* '10.

*Southern Cross* (*The*): Report of Collns. of Nat. Hist. [Newnes Expedn.]—*ut* **H** § 44

WILKES, Chas. — Narr. of U.S. Exploring Expedn.—*ut* **E** § 63 [Polynesia and Antarctic]